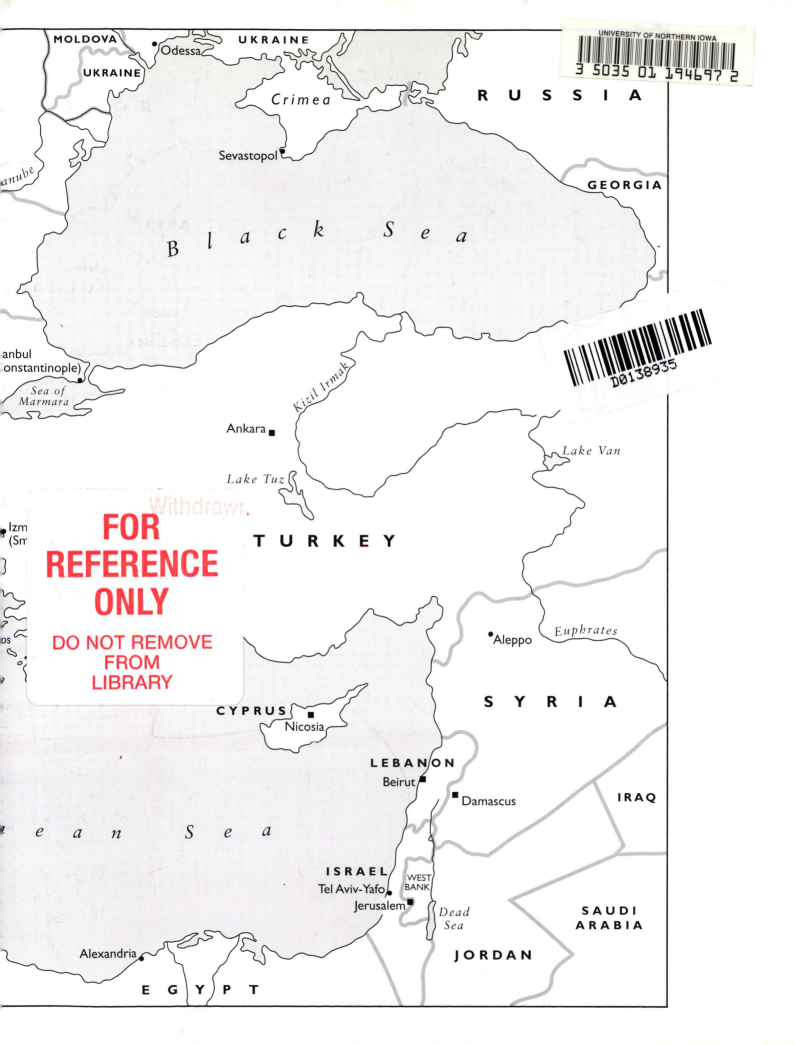

MOLDOVA

UKRAINE

Odessa

UKRAINE

Crimea

RUSSIA

Sevastopol

GEORGIA

B l a c k   S e a

anbul
onstantinople)

*Sea of
Marmara*

Kizil Irmak

Lake Van

Ankara ■

Lake Tuz

Izm
(Sm

T U R K E Y

•Aleppo

Euphrates

os

S Y R I A

CYPRUS

Nicosia ■

LEBANON

Beirut ■

■ Damascus

IRAQ

ean   Sea

ISRAEL

Tel Aviv-Yafo

WEST
BANK

SAUDI
ARABIA

Jerusalem ■

*Dead
Sea*

Alexandria ■

J O R D A N

E G Y P T

ENCYCLOPEDIA OF
GREECE
AND THE
HELLENIC
TRADITION

Volume 2

ENCYCLOPEDIA OF
GREECE
AND THE
HELLENIC
TRADITION

Volume 2
L–Z

Editor
GRAHAM SPEAKE

FITZROY DEARBORN PUBLISHERS
LONDON · CHICAGO

Copyright © 2000 by
FITZROY DEARBORN PUBLISHERS

All rights reserved including the right of reproduction in whole or
in part in any form. For information write to:

FITZROY DEARBORN PUBLISHERS
919 North Michigan Avenue, Suite 760
Chicago, Illinois 60611
USA

or

310 Regent Street
London W1B 3AX
England

British Library and Library of Congress Cataloguing in Publication Data are available

ISBN 1-57958-141-2

First published in the USA and UK 2000

Typeset by Lorraine Hodghton, Radlett, Herts, UK
Printed and bound by Butler and Tanner Ltd, Frome and London

Cover design by Philip Lewis

Cover illustrations:
vol. 1: Alexander the Great: portrait bust in marble, sculptor unknown,
   Graeco–Roman Museum, Alexandria.
vol. 2: Alexander the Great: mural by Theophilos (1868–1934),
   Museum of Greek Folk Art, Athens, reproduced by permission of
   the Greek Ministry of Culture Archaeological Receipts Fund.

CONTENTS

MAPS AND SITE PLANS

ALPHABETICAL LIST OF ENTRIES

THEMATIC
LIST OF ENTRIES

Entries by Category

Patmos
Patras
Pella
Pergamum
Petra
Phaestus
Piraeus
Plataea
Prespa, Lake
Priene
Pylos
Ravenna
Rhodes
Rome

St Catherine's Monastery, Sinai
Salamis (city)
Salamis (island)
Samos
Samothrace
Santorini
Serres
Sicily
Sinope
Skopje
Smyrna
Sparta
Sporades
Symi

Syracuse
Tarentum
Thasos
Thebes
Thessalonica
Tinos
Tiryns
Trebizond
Trikkala
Tripolis
Venice
Verroia
Volos
Xanthus

Regions

Acarnania
Achaea
Aetolia
Africa, North
Albania
Anatolia
Apulia
Arabia
Arcadia
Argolid
Armenia
Athos, Mount
Attica
Australia
Bactria
Bithynia
Black Sea
Boeotia
Bosnia
Britain
Bulgaria
Byzantium
Calabria

Canada
Cappadocia
Caucasus
Chalcidice
Chersonese, Thracian
Cilicia
Crimea
Croatia
Cyrenaica
Dalmatia
Egypt
Epirus
France
Georgia
Italy
Laconia
Lycia
Macedonia
Magna Graecia
Mani
Messenia
Moldavia
Montenegro

Palestine
Pamphylia
Pelion, Mount
Peloponnese
Persia
Pindus
Pontus
Romania
Rumeli
Russia
Serbia
South Africa
Spain
Souli
Syria
Thessaly
Thrace
Turkey
Ukraine
USA
Wallachia
Zagori

Ethnic Groups

Aeolians
Arabs
Bulgars
Byzantines
Catalans
Copts
Dorians
Etruscans
Genoese
Goths
Gypsies
Hellenes
Illyrians

Ionians
Jews
Karamanlides
Laz
Mardaïtes
Minoans
Muslims
Mycenaeans
Normans
Ottomans
Parthians
Paulicians
Persians

Phoenicians
Pomaks
Romans
Sarakatsans
Sassanians
Seljuks
Serbs
Slavs
Tsakonians
Venetians
Vlachs

THEMES

Social History

Abortion
Adoption
Adultery
Ancestor Worship
Anthropology
Antiquity, Reception of
Antisemitism
Aristocracy
Baptism
Birth
Burial Practices
Celibacy
Children
Cities
City State
Contraception
Corruption
Death
Demography
Diaspora
Divorce

Dowry
Dreams
Dress
Emigration
Eunuchs
Fairs and Markets
Family
Food and Drink
Foreigners
Freedom
Games and Sports
Gender
Guilds
Health
Hippodrome
Homosexuality
Honour and Shame
Hospitality
Imperialism
Inheritance
Kafeneion

Karamanlides
Kinship
Land Tenure
Literacy
Marriage
Men
Metics
Minorities
Onomastics
Patronage
Prostitution
Refugees
Slavery
Symposium
Town Planning
Transhumance
Travel
Urbanization
Village Society
Women

Cultural History

Acropolis of Athens
Aesthetics
Agora of Athens
Alphabet
Anthology, Greek
Archaeological Service
Anti-westernism
Archaic Period
Architecture
Archives
Biography and
    Autobiography
Books and Readers
Byzantine Period, Early
Byzantine Period, Middle
Byzantine Period, Late
Censorship
Ceremony, Byzantine
Chronicles
Cinema
Classical Period
Comedy
Commonwealth, Byzantine
Coronation
Dance
Dark Age
Dialects
Dithyramb
Dress
Education

Enamel
Enlightenment
Epigram
Epistolography
Fable
Folklore
Furniture
Gardens
Gems and Seals
Geometric Period
Glass
Gold
Grammar
Great Idea
Great Palace
Hellenism and Neohellenism
    in the Greek tradition
Hellenism as viewed by
    visiting artists
Hellenistic Period
Hellenization
Hippodrome
Historiography
Humanism
Identity
Instruments, Musical
Ivory
Jewellery
Kafeneion
Karaghiozis

Language
Latin Empire
Libraries
Linear B
Literacy
Manuscripts
Marble and other decorative
    stones
Media
Metalwork
Minoans
Modern Period
Monasticism
Mosaic
Museum of Alexandria
Museums
Music
Mycenaeans
Neoclassicism
Novel
Olympic Games
Opera and Operetta
Oral Tradition
Orthodoxy and Hellenism
Orthodoxy and Nationalism
Ottoman Period (Tourkokratia)
Painting
Papyrus, parchment, and paper
Patronage
Photography

Poetry, Epic
Poetry, Lyric
Portraiture
Pottery
Prehistory
Printing
Purple
Renaissance, Palaiologan
Renaissance, Veneto-Cretan
Rhetoric

Roman Period
Romance, Byzantine
Romanticism
Satyr Play
Scholarship, History of
Schools and Universities
Sculpture
Second Sophistic
Shrines, Wayside
Silk

Silver and Lead
Song
Syllabary, Cypriot
Symposium
Theatres
Tragedy
Translation from Greek
Translation into Greek
Venetokratia
Woodworking

Political and Military History

Armatoloi
Army
Asia Minor Campaign and
    Disaster
Balkan Wars
Berlin, Treaty of
Brigandage
Bureaucracy
Candia, Fall of
Chaeronea, Battle of
City State
Civil War
Colonization
Communist Party
Constantinople, Fall of
Constantinople, Sack of
Constitution
Corinth, Sack of
Corruption
Crusades
Delian League
Democracy
Diplomacy
Eagle, Double-Headed
EAM and ELAS
Enosis
European Community and
    European Union

Exile and Detention
Fascism
Federal States
Fire, Greek
Graeco-Turkish War
Great Idea
Hetairists
Hospitaller Knights of St
    John
Imperialism
Independence, War of
Inscriptions
Janissaries
Judicial Procedure
Junta
Kodjabashis
Lausanne, Treaty of
Law
Magistrates
Manzikert, Battle of
Marathon, Battle of
Military League
Monarchy
Nationalism
NATO
Navy
Oligarchy
Ostracism

Pelagonia, Battle of
Peloponnesian War
Persian Wars
Phanariots
Philhellenes
Political History to 490 BC
Political History 490–323 BC
Political History 323–31 BC
Political History 31 BC–AD 330
Political History 330–802
Political History 802–1204
Political History 1204–1261
Political History 1261–1453
Political History 1453–1832
Political History since 1832
Pydna
Republic
Sèvres, Treaty of
Siegecraft
Sublime Porte
Theme System
Trojan War
Tyranny
Warfare
World War I
World War II
Yarmuk, Battle of

Religious History

Afterlife
Altars
Ancestor Worship
Antisemitism
Apophthegmata Patrum
Apostasy
Atheism
Baptism
Bishops
Burial Practices
Canonization
Canon Law
Celibacy

Christianity
Church-State Relations
Conversion to Islam
Councils, Ecumenical
Cult
Dead, cult of the
Demons and Spirits
Diocese
Divination
Ecumenism
Evil Eye
Fasts
Fate

Festivals
Fundamentalism, Orthodox
Games and Sports
Gnostics
Gods and Goddesses
Hades
Hagia Sophia
Hagiography
Healing Cults
Heresy
Heroes and Heroines
Hesychasm
Hymnography

Science, Medicine, Philosophy

Economic History

Geography

INDIVIDUALS AND FAMILIES

Antiquity

Orators
Aeschines
Demosthenes
Isocrates
Lysias

Poets, Scholars, Prose Writers
Achilles Tatius
Aeschylus
Aesop
Apollonius Rhodius
Aratus
Archilochus
Aristarchus of Samothrace
Aristides, Aelius
Aristophanes
Aristoxenus
Athenaeus
Babrius
Bacchylides
Callimachus
Crates of Mallus
Dio Cocceianus
Dionysius of Halicarnassus
Euripides
Hecataeus of Miletus
Heliodorus
Herodas
Herodes Atticus
Hesiod
Homer
Longus
Lucian
Lycophron
Menander
Nicander
Pausanias
Philodemus
Pindar
Sappho
Simonides
Sophocles
Strabo
Theocritus

Rulers, Politicians, Warriors, Lawgivers
Agesilaus II
Alcibiades
Alexander III the Great
Antigonids
Antiochus III the Great
Attalids
Cimon
Cleisthenes
Cleomenes III

Cleopatra
Dionysius I
Epaminondas
Evagoras
Hadrian
Hieron I
Julian the Apostate
Leonidas
Lysander
Mausolus
Nero
Pericles
Philip II
Philip V
Philopoemen
Pisistratus
Ptolemies
Pyrrhus
Seleucids
Solon
Themistocles
Zenobiao

Philosophers, Scientists, Mathematicians
Anaxagoras
Anaximander
Apollonius of Perge
Aratus
Archimedes
Aristides, Aelius
Aristotle
Aristoxenus
Carneades
Dio Cocceianus
Diogenes of Sinope
Dioscurides
Empedocles
Epicurus
Erasistratus
Eratosthenes
Euclid
Eudoxus
Galen
Heraclitus
Herodes Atticus
Heron
Herophilus
Hipparchus
Hippocrates
Hypatia
Parmenides
Philo
Philodemus
Plato
Plotinus

Plutarch
Porphyry
Ptolemy
Pyrrho
Pythagoras
Socrates
Theophrastus
Zeno of Citium

Historians and Biographers
Appian
Arrian
Cassius Dio
Diodorus Siculus
Diogenes Laertius
Dionysius of Halicarnassus
Ephorus
Hecataeus of Miletus
Herodotus
Hieronymus of Cardia
Josephus, Flavius
Plutarch
Polybius
Posidonius
Strabo
Theopompus
Thucydides
Timaeus
Xenophon

Religious
Apologists, Greek
Clement of Alexandria, St
Ephraim the Syrian, St
Evagrius of Pontus
Ignatius, St
Irenaeus
Isaac the Syrian, St
Justin Martyr, St
Macarius (pseudo-)
Mary, Blessed Virgin
Nemesius
Origen
Paul, St
Philo

Artists
Amasis
Apelles
Execias
Lysippus
Phidias
Polygnotus
Praxiteles
Scopas

Byzantium

Scholars and Teachers
Arethas of Caesarea
Argyropoulos, John
Blemmydes, Nikephoros
Choricius of Gaza
Chrysoloras, Manuel
Eusebius
Eustathios
Gaza, Theodore
George of Trebizond
Gregoras, Nikephoros
Kabasilas, Nicholas
Leo the Mathematician
Libanius
Metochites, Theodore
Michael of Ephesus
Philoponus, John
Photios
Planudes, Maximos
Plethon, George Gemistos
Proclus
Procopius of Gaza
Simplicius
Synesius
Themistius
Triklinios, Dimitrios
Tzetzes, John

Rulers and Politicians
Alexios I Komnenos
Andronikos I Komnenos
Andronikos II Palaiologos
Basil I
Basil II
Constantine I the Great
Constantine V
Constantine VII
Constantine IX Monomachos
Constantine XI Palaiologos
Doukas family
Herakleios
Irene
John I Tzimiskes
John II Komnenos
John III Vatatzes
John VI Kantakouzenos
John VIII Palaiologos

Justinian I
Kantakouzenos family
Komnenos family
Laskaris family
Leo III
Leo V
Leo VI
Manuel I Komnenos
Manuel II Palaiologos
Metochites, Theodore
Michael VIII Palaiologos
Palaiologos family
Romanos I Lekapenos
Stephan IV Dushan
Theodora (497–548)
Theodora (d. 867)
Theophilos
Zoe

Historians and Prose Writers
Akropolites, George
Doukas family
Eusebius
Gregoras, Nikephoros
Komnene, Anna
Kritoboulos, Michael
Procopius of Caesarea
Psellos, Michael
Simokattes, Theophylaktos
Sphrantzes, George
Symeon the Logothete
Theophanes the Confessor, St
Zonaras, John

Religious and Theologians
Akindynos, Gregory
Anastasios of Sinai, St
Andrew of Crete, St
Arethas of Caesarea
Athanasios of Athos, St
Athanasius of Alexandria, St
Barlaam of Calabria
Basil the Great, St
Bessarion
Cyril, St
Cyril of Alexandria, St
Demetrius, St

Dionysius the Areopagite,
    pseudo-
Epiphanius of Salamis, St
Eusebius
Eustathios
Germanos I
Gregory of Nazianzus, St
Gregory of Nyssa, St
Gregory Palamas, St
Helena, St
Italos, John
John Chrysostom, St
John Klimakos, St
John of Damascus, St
Kabasilas, Nicholas
Maximos the Confessor, St
Methodios, St
Neophytos Enkleistos
Nestorius
Philoponus, John
Photios
Procopius of Gaza
Symeon of Thessalonica, St
Symeon the New Theologian,
    St
Synesius
Theodore of Stoudios, St
Theodoret
Theophanes the Confessor, St
Tzetzes, John
Zonaras, John

Poets, Musicians, Artists
Andrew of Crete, St
Apseudes, Theodore
Chrysaphes, Manuel
Digenis Akritis
Geometres, John
George of Pisidia
Joseph the Hymnographer, St
Kassia
Koukouzeles, St John
Nonnus
Panselinos, Manuel
Prodromos, Theodore
Romanos the Melodist, St

Tourkokratia/Frangokratia

Scholars and Teachers
Corydalleus, Theophilos
Dionysios of Phourna
Korais, Adamantios
Maximos the Greek, St
Moisiodax, Josephos
Theotokis, Nikiphoros

Voulgaris, Evgenios

Writers
Byron, George Gordon, Lord
Chortatsis, Georgios
Kalvos, Andreas
Kornaros, Vitsentzos

Makriyannis, Yannis
Velestinlis, Rigas

Rulers, Warriors, Politicians
Ali Pasha of Ioannina
Botsaris, Markos
Bouboulina, Laskarina

Kapodistria, Count Ioannis
Karaiskakis, Georgios
Kolokotronis, Theodore
Makriyannis, Yannis
Mavrokordatos family
Mavromichalis family
Mehmet II
Miaoulis, Andreas
Soutsos, Mikhail
Velestinlis, Rigas

Ypsilantis family

Religious and Theologians
Argenti, Eustratios
Cyril I Lukaris
Gennadios II Scholarios
Gregory V
Jeremias II Tranos
Kosmas the Aetolian, St
Maximos the Greek, St

Paisy Velichkovsky, St

Artists
Damaskinos, Michael
Dionysios of Phourna
Klontzas, Georgios
Theophanes of Crete
Theotokopoulos, Domenikos
  (El Greco)
Tzanes, Emmanuel

Modern

Writers, Artists, Musicians, Film Directors
Andronikos, Manolis
Angelopoulos, Thodoros
Cacoyannis, Michalis
Callas, Maria
Cavafy, Constantine
Chatzidakis, Georgios N.
Chatzimichail, Theophilos
Dimaras, K.T.
Doxiadis, Constantinos
  Apostolou
Elytis, Odysseus
Gatsos, Nikos
Ghika
Gyzis, Nikolaos
Hadjidakis, Manos
Kaftantzoglou, Lysandros
Kazantzakis, Nikos
Kontoglou, Photis
Lytras, Nikephoros
Myrivilis, Stratis
Palamas, Kostis
Pallis, Alexandros
Papadiamantis, Alexandros
Paparrigopoulos, Konstantinos

Parren, Callirrhoe
Pikionis, Dimitris
Politis, Nikolaos
Prevelakis, Pantelis
Psycharis, Yannis
Ritsos, Yiannis
Roidis, Emmanouil
Sakellarides, John Theophrastos
Seferis, George
Sikelianos, Angelos
Skalkotttas, Nikolaos
Solomos, Dionysios
Theodorakis, Mikis
Tsarouchis, Ioannis
Varnalis, Kostas
Vizyinos, Georgios
Xenakis, Iannis

Rulers, Warriors, Politicians
Constantine I
Deliyannis, Theodoros
George I
George II
Kanaris, Constantine
Karamanlis, Constantine
Kolettis, John

Makarios III, Archbishop
Melas, Pavlos
Metaxas, Ioannis
Otho
Papadopoulos, George
Papagos, Alexandros
Papanastasiou, Alexandros
Papandreou family
Plastiras, Nikolaos
Theotokis, George
Trikoupis, Charilaos
Velouchiotis, Ares
Venizelos, Eleftherios
Zervas, Napoleon

Industrialists
Chandris, Antony
Livanos, George P.
Niarchos, Stavros
Onassis, Aristotle

Religious
Athenagoras
Nektarios of Aegina, St
Makarios III, Archbishop

CHRONOLOGICAL LIST OF INDIVIDUALS

*fl.*8th or 7th century BC	Hesiod	*c.*390–*c.*340 BC	Eudoxus
*fl.*8th or 7th century BC	Homer	d. *c.*386 BC	Aristophanes
*fl.*7th century BC	Archilochus	384–322 BC	Aristotle
*c.*640–*c.*560 BC	Solon	384–322 BC	Demosthenes
b. *c.*630 BC	Sappho	383/82–336 BC	Philip II
*fl.*6th century BC	Aesop	378/77–*c.*320 BC	Theopompus
*fl.*6th century BC	Amasis	*c.*371–*c.*287 BC	Theophrastus
*fl.*6th century BC	Execias	b. *c.*370 BC	Apelles
*fl.*6th century BC	Pythagoras	b. *c.*370 BC	Aristoxenus
b. *c.*557/56 BC	Simonides	*c.*365–275 BC	Pyrrho
d. *c.*547 BC	Anaximander	*c.*364–?260 BC	Hieronymus of Cardia
*c.*530–480 BC	Leonidas	d.362 BC	Epaminondas
d. *c.*528 BC	Pisistratus	*fl.*360–335 BC	Scopas
*fl.*525–505 BC	Cleisthenes	356–323 BC	Alexander III the Great
*c.*525–456 BC	Aeschylus	d.353 BC	Mausolus
*c.*525–459 BC	Themistocles	342–292 BC	Menander
*c.*518–*c.*438 BC	Pindar	341–270 BC	Epicurus
*c.*515–*c.*440 BC	Parmenides	335–263 BC	Zeno of Citium
b. *c.*510 BC	Bacchylides	*c.*330–*c.*260 BC	Herophilus
*c.*510–*c.*450 BC	Cimon	d. 320s BC	Diogenes of Sinope
*fl.*6th–5th centuries BC	Hecataeus of Miletus	*c.*320–*c.*240 BC	Callimachus
*fl. c.*500 BC	Heraclitus	319–272 BC	Pyrrhus
*fl.*5th century BC	Polygnotus	*c.*315–*c.*240 BC	Erasistratus
*c.*500–428 BC	Anaxagoras	*fl.*4th–3rd centuries BC	Euclid
*c.*496–406 BC	Sophocles	*fl.*3rd century BC	Apollonius of Perge
*c.*492–429 BC	Pericles	*fl.*3rd century BC	Herodas
*c.*492–432 BC	Empedocles	*fl.*3rd century BC	Theocritus
*c.*490–420s BC	Phidias	*c.*295–215 BC	Apollonius Rhodius
484–*c.*425 BC	Herodotus	*c.*287–212/11 BC	Archimedes
*c.*480–*c.*407/06 BC	Euripides	d. *c.*260 BC	Timaeus
*fl.*478–466 BC	Hieron I	260–219 BC	Cleomenes III
470–399 BC	Socrates	*c.*252–182 BC	Philopoemen
*c.*460–*c.*370 BC	Hippocrates	*c.*242–187 BC	Antiochus III the Great
*c.*459/58–*c.*375 BC	Lysias	d. *c.*240 BC	Aratus
451/50–404/03 BC	Alcibiades	238–179 BC	Philip V
*c.*445–374/73 BC	Evagoras	b. *c.*215 BC	Crates of Mallus
*c.*444–359 BC	Agesilaus II	*c.*215–*c.*143 BC	Aristarchus of Samothrace
*c.*436–338 BC	Isocrates	214/13–129/28 BC	Carneades
*c.*430–367 BC	Dionysius I	d. *c.*200 BC	Eratosthenes
*c.*430–*c.*353 BC	Xenophon	*fl.*3rd or 2nd century BC	Lycophron
429–347 BC	Plato	*fl. c.*2nd century BC	Nicander
*fl.*4th century BC	Praxiteles	*fl.*2nd century BC	Hipparchus
*c.*400–*c.*320s BC	Ephorus	*c.*200–*c.*118 BC	Polybius
d. *c.*395 BC	Thucydides	*c.*135–*c.*51 BC	Posidonius
d.395 BC	Lysander	*c.*110–40 BC	Philodemus
b. *c.*390 BC	Lysippus	*fl.*1st century BC	Dionysius of Halicarnassus

*fl.*1st century BC	Diodorus Siculus
69–30 BC	Cleopatra
*c.*64 BC–*c.*AD 19	Strabo
*c.*20 BC–*c.*AD 50	Mary, Blessed Virgin
*fl.*1st century AD	Philo
*c.*AD 30–107	Ignatius, St
37–68	Nero
37–after 93	Josephus, Flavius
*c.*40–112	Dio Cocceianus
*fl. c.*45–75	Dioscurides
*c.*50–120	Plutarch
d. *c.*64	Paul, St
76–138	Hadrian
*c.*90–160	Arrian
*c.*95–160s	Appian
*fl.*1st or 2nd century	Babrius
*fl.*1st or 2nd century	Heron
*fl.*2nd century	Achilles Tatius
*fl.*2nd century	Ptolemy
*c.*100–*c.*165	Justin Martyr, St
*c.*101/03–177	Herodes Atticus
*c.*115–180	Pausanias
117–*c.*180	Aristides, Aelius
*c.*120–180	Lucian
129–?208/16	Galen
*c.*130–*c.*202	Irenaeus
b. *c.*150	Athenaeus
*c.*150–*c.*215	Clement of Alexandria, St
*c.*164–after 229	Cassius Dio
184/85–254/55	Origen
*fl.*2nd or 3rd century	Diogenes Laertius
*fl.*2nd or 3rd century	Longus
*fl.*3rd century	Zenobia
205–269/70	Plotinus
234–*c.*305	Porphyry
*c.*255–*c.*330	Helena, St
*c.*260–339	Eusebius
273/74–337	Constantine I the Great
d. *c.*300	Demetrius, St
*fl.*4th century	Heliodorus
*fl.*4th century	Macarius (pseudo-)
*fl.*4th century	Nemesius
*c.*300–373	Athanasius of Alexandria, St
*c.*306–373	Ephraim the Syrian, St
314–*c.*393	Libanius
*c.*317–*c.*388	Themistius
*c.*329–*c.*390	Gregory of Nazianzus, St
*c.*330–379	Basil the Great, St
*c.*330–*c.*395	Gregory of Nyssa, St
331/32–363	Julian the Apostate
*c.*345–399	Evagrius of Pontus
*c.*347–407	John Chrysostom, St
370–413	Synesius
*c.*370–415	Hypatia
*c.*378–444	Cyril of Alexandria, St
*c.*381–*c.*451	Nestorius
*c.*393–*c.*466	Theodoret
d.403	Epiphanius of Salamis, St
*fl.*5th century	Nonnus
410/11–485	Proclus
*c.*475–*c.*538	Procopius of Gaza
*c.*482–565	Justinian I
*c.*490–570s	Philoponus, John
*c.*497–548	Theodora

*fl. c.*500	Dionysius the Areopagite, pseudo-
*fl.*6th century	Choricius of Gaza
*fl.*6th century	Simplicius
d. after 555	Romanos the Melodist, St
d. *c.*560	Procopius of Caesarea
*c.*575–641	Herakleios
*c.*575–*c.*649	John Klimakos, St
580–662	Maximos the Confessor, St
*fl.*7th century	Anastasios of Sinai, St
*fl.*7th century	George of Pisidia
*fl.*7th century	Isaac the Syrian, St
*fl.*7th century	Simokattes, Theophylaktos
*c.*660–740	Andrew of Crete, St
*c.*685–741	Leo III
*fl.*7th–8th century	Germanos I
718–775	Constantine V
d. *c.*750	John of Damascus, St
*c.*752–803	Irene
759–826	Theodore of Stoudios, St
*c.*760–818	Theophanes the Confessor, St
*c.*780–820	Leo V
*c.*790–after 869	Leo the Mathematician
*fl.*9th century	Kassia
*c.*810–*c.*893	Photios
812/13–842	Theophilos
812/18–*c.*886	Joseph the Hymnographer, St
*c.*815–885	Methodios, St
826/27–869	Cyril, St
*c.*830–886	Basil I
866–912	Leo VI
d.867	Theodora
*c.*870–948	Romanos I Lekapenos
*fl.*10th century	Geometres, John
*fl.*10th century	Symeon the Logothete
905–959	Constantine VII
*c.*925–976	John I Tzimiskes
*c.*927/30–*c.*997	Athanasios of Athos, St
d. after 932	Arethas of Caesarea
949–1022	Symeon the New Theologian, St
958–1025	Basil II
*c.*978–1050	Zoe
*c.*1000–1055	Constantine IX Monomachos
1018–after 1081	Psellos, Michael
b. *c.*1025	Italos, John
*c.*1057–1118	Alexios I Komnenos
1083–*c.*1153/54	Komnene, Anna
1087–1143	John II Komnenos
*fl.*12th century	Apseudes, Theodore
*fl.*12th century	Michael of Ephesus
*fl.*12th century	Prodromos, Theodore
*fl.*12th century	Zonaras, John
*c.*1110–after 1165	Tzetzes, John
*c.*1115–*c.*1195	Eustathios
1118–1180	Manuel I Komnenos
*c.*1118/20–1185	Andronikos I Komnenos
1134–1219	Neophytos Enkleistos
*c.*1192–1254	John III Vatatzes
1197–1272	Blemmydes, Nikephoros
1217–1282	Akropolites, George
*c.*1225–1282	Michael VIII Palaiologos
*c.*1255–*c.*1305	Planudes, Maximos
1259/60–1328	Andronikos II Palaiologos
1270–1332	Metochites, Theodore
*c.*1280–*c.*1340	Triklinios, Dimitrios

*c.*1290–1348	Barlaam of Calabria
1290/94–1358/61	Gregoras, Nikephoros
*c.*1295–1383	John VI Kantakouzenos
1296–1359	Gregory Palamas, St
*fl. c.*1300	Panselinos, Manuel
*fl.*13th–14th centuries	Koukouzeles, St John
*c.*1300–*c.*1348	Akindynos, Gregory
*c.*1319–*c.*1391	Kabasilas, Nicholas
*c.*1350–1415	Chrysoloras, Manuel
1350–1425	Manuel II Palaiologos
d. 1355	Stephan IV Dushan
*c.*1360–1452	Plethon, George Gemistos
1392–1448	John VIII Palaiologos
1395–1472/73 or *c.*1484	George of Trebizond
*fl.*15th century	Chrysaphes, Manuel
*fl.*15th century	Kritoboulos, Michael
*c.*1400–1472	Bessarion
*c.*1400–1475/76	Gaza, Theodore
1401–1477/78	Sphrantzes, George
1405–1453	Constantine XI Palaiologos
*c.*1405–*c.*1472	Gennadios II Scholarios
*c.*1415–1487	Argyropoulos, John
d.1429	Symeon of Thessalonica, St
1432–1481	Mehmet II
*c.*1470–1556	Maximos the Greek, St
*c.*1490–1559	Theophanes of Crete
*fl.*16th century	Chortatsis, Georgios
*c.*1530–*c.*1592	Damaskinos, Michael
*c.*1530–1595	Jeremias II Tranos
*c.*1535–1608	Klontzas, Georgios
*c.*1541–1614	Theotokopoulos, Domenikos (El Greco)
1553–*c.*1614	Kornaros, Vitsentzos
1570–1638	Cyril I Lukaris
*c.*1574–1646	Corydalleus, Theophilos
*c.*1610–1690	Tzanes, Emmanuel
*c.*1670–after 1744	Dionysios of Phourna
*c.*1687–*c.*1757	Argenti, Eustratios
1714–1779	Kosmas the Aetolian, St
1716–1806	Voulgaris, Evgenios
1722–1794	Paisy Velichkovsky, St
*c.*1725–1800	Moisiodax, Josephos
1731–1800	Theotokis, Nikiphoros
1745–1821	Gregory V
1748–1833	Korais, Adamantios
1750–1822	Ali Pasha of Ioannina
*c.*1757–1798	Velestinlis, Rigas
1769–1835	Miaoulis, Andreas
*c.*1770–1825	Bouboulina, Laskarina
1770–1843	Kolokotronis, Theodore
1774–1847	Kolettis, John
1776–1831	Kapodistria, Count Ioannis
1778–1864	Soutsos, Mikhail
1782–1827	Karaiskakis, Georgios
1788–1824	Byron, George Gordon, Lord
1790–1823	Botsaris, Markos
1792–1869	Kalvos, Andreas
1795–1877	Kanaris, Constantine
1797–1864	Makriyannis, Yannis
1798–1857	Solomos, Dionysios
1811–1885	Kaftantzoglou, Lysandros
1815–1867	Otho
1815–1891	Paparrigopoulos, Konstantinos
1826–1905	Deliyannis, Theodoros
1832–1896	Trikoupis, Charilaos
1832–1904	Lytras, Nikephoros
1836–1904	Roidis, Emmanouil
1842–1901	Gyzis, Nikolaos
1844–1916	Theotokis, George
1845–1913	George I
1846–1920	Nektarios of Aegina, St
1848–1941	Chatzidakis, Georgios N.
1849–1896	Vizyinos, Georgios
1851–1911	Papadiamantis, Alexandros
1851–1935	Pallis, Alexandros
1852–1921	Politis, Nikolaos
*c.*1853–1938	Sakellarides, John Theophrastos
1854–1929	Psycharis, Yannis
1859–1940	Parren, Callirrhoe
1859–1943	Palamas, Kostis
1863–1933	Cavafy, Constantine
1864–1936	Venizelos, Eleftherios
1868–1922	Constantine I
1870–1904	Melas, Pavlos
1871–1941	Metaxas, Ioannis
1873–1934	Chatzimichail, Theophilos
1876/79–1936	Papanastasiou, Alexandros
1883–1953	Plastiras, Nikolaos
1883–1955	Papagos, Alexandros
1883–1957	Kazantzakis, Nikos
1884–1951	Sikelianos, Angelos
1884–1974	Varnalis, Kostas
1886–1972	Athenagoras
1887–1968	Pikionis, Dimitris
1890–1947	George II
1891–1957	Zervas, Napoleon
1892–1969	Myrivilis, Stratis
*c.*1895–1965	Kontoglou, Photis
1900–1971	Seferis, George
1900 (or 1906)–1975	Onassis, Aristotle
1904–1949	Skalkottas, Nikolaos
1904–1992	Dimaras, K.T.
1905–1945	Velouchiotis, Ares
1906–1994	Ghika
1907–1998	Karamanlis, Constantine
1909–1986	Prevelakis, Pantelis
1909–1990	Ritsos, Yiannis
1909–1996	Niarchos, Stavros
1910–1989	Tsarouchis, Ioannis
1911–1996	Elytis, Odysseus
1913–1975	Doxiadis, Constantinos Apostolou
1913–1977	Makarios III, Archbishop
1916–1995	Gatsos, Nikos
1919–1992	Andronikos, Manolis
1919–1999	Papadopoulos, George
1922–	Xenakis, Iannis
1922–	Cacoyannis, Michalis
1923–1977	Callas, Maria
1924–1984	Chandris, Antony
1925–	Theodorakis, Mikis
1925–1994	Hadjidakis, Manos
1926–1997	Livanos, George P.
1935–	Angelopoulos, Thodoros

NOTE ON TRANSLITERATION

Transliteration is always a problem when dealing with a non-Roman alphabet across such a vast span of time and space, and it is as impossible to please everybody as it is to be consistent within the rules one has set. But, on the principle that good transliteration like good writing is by definition inconspicuous, the aim throughout has been to present the reader with the form of any word which is likely to be the most familiar and least jarring. In general, ancient names have been presented in their "Latin" form (e.g. Thucydides), but medieval and modern names in their "Greek" form (e.g. Alexios I Komnenos). Since a point in time had to be chosen for the switch from "Latin" to "Greek" forms, that (entirely arbitrary) moment is taken to be the death of Justinian I (14 November, 565) who was probably the last Byzantine emperor to speak Latin. Greek is always transliterated into the Roman alphabet. Here again the more usual "ancient" system (e.g. *basileus*) is employed until (simply because a date had to be chosen) 1453 when the switch is made to the "modern" system (e.g. *vasilefs*). Places that have a standard ancient (or English) form (such as Thessalonica or Athens) retain that form throughout. Nevertheless inconsistencies and infelicities are inevitable and we can only crave the reader's indulgence where they occur.

GRAHAM SPEAKE

The Greek Alphabet

Capital	Lower Case	Name		Transliteration (pre-1453/post-1453)
A	α	Alpha	=	*a*
B	β	Beta	=	*b/v*
Γ	γ	Gamma	=	*g* (hard, as in "good")
Δ	δ	Delta	=	*d*
E	ε	Epsilon	=	*e* (as e in "net")
Z	ζ	Zeta	=	*z*
H	η	Eta	=	*e* (as ee in "meet")
Θ	θ	Theta	=	*th*
I	ι	Iota	=	*i*
K	κ	Kappa	=	*k*
Λ	λ	Lambda	=	*l*
M	μ	Mu	=	*m*
N	ν	Nu	=	*n*
Ξ	ξ	Xi	=	*x*
O	o	Omicron	=	*o* (as o in "spot")
Π	π	Pi	=	*p*
P	ρ	Rho	=	*rh, r*
Σ	σ ς	Sigma	=	*s* (ς when final letter)
T	τ	Tau	=	*t*
Y	υ	Upsilon	=	*u/f* after *a* and *e*
Φ	φ	Phi	=	*ph*
X	χ	Chi	=	*ch* (hard, as in "chord")
Ψ	ψ	Psi	=	*ps*
Ω	ω	Omega	=	*o* (as o in "lone")

BYZANTINE EMPERORS

Constantine I the Great	324–337	Romanos I Lekapenos	920–944
Constantine II	337–340	Stephen and Constantine Lekapenos	944–945
Constans I	337–350	Constantine VII	945–959
Constantius II	337–361	Romanos II	959–963
Julian	361–363	Nikephoros II Phokas	963–969
Jovian	363–364	John I Tzimiskes	969–976
Valens	364–378	Basil II	976–1025
Theodosius I	379–395	Constantine VIII	1025–1028
Arcadius	395–408	Romanos III Argyros	1028–1034
Theodosius II	408–450	Michael IV Paphlagon	1034–1041
Marcian	450–457	Michael V Kalaphates	1041–1042
Leo I	457–474	Zoe and Theodora	1042
Leo II	473–474	Constantine IX Monomachos	1042–1055
Zeno	474–491	Theodora	1055–1056
Basiliscus	475–476	Michael VI Stratiotikos	1056–1057
Anastasius I	491–518	Isaac I Komnenos	1057–1059
Justin I	518–527	Constantine X Doukas	1059–1067
Justinian I	527–565	Romanos IV Diogenes	1068–1071
Justin II	565–578	Michael VII Doukas	1071–1078
Tiberios I	578–582	Nikephoros III Botaneiates	1078–1081
Maurice	582–602	Alexios I Komnenos	1081–1118
Phokas	602–610	John II Komnenos	1118–1143
Herakleios	610–641	Manuel I Komnenos	1143–1180
Herakleios Constantine and Heraklonas	641	Alexios II Komnenos	1180–1183
Constans II	641–668	Andronikos I Komnenos	1183–1185
Constantine IV*	668–685	Isaac II Angelos	1185–1195
Justinian II	685–695	Alexios III Angelos	1195–1203
Leontios	695–698	Isaac II and Alexios IV Angelos	1203–1204
Tiberios II	698–705	Alexios V Doukas	1204
Justinian II (second reign)	705–711	Theodore I Laskaris	1205–1222
Philippikos	711–713	John III Vatatzes	1222–1254
Anastasios II	713–715	Theodore II Laskaris	1254–1258
Theodosios III	715–717	John IV Laskaris	1259–1261
Leo III	717–741	Michael VIII Palaiologos	1259–1282
Constantine V	741–775	Andronikos II Palaiologos	1282–1328
Leo IV	775–780	Michael IX Palaiologos	1294–1320
Constantine VI	780–797	Andronikos III Palaiologos	1328–1341
Irene	797–802	John V Palaiologos	1341–1391
Nikephoros I	802–811	John VI Kantakouzenos	1347–1354
Staurakios	811	Andronikos IV Palaiologos	1376–1379
Michael I Rangabe	811–813	John VII Palaiologos	1390
Leo V	813–820	Manuel II Palaiologos	1391–1425
Michael II	820–829	John VIII Palaiologos	1425–1448
Theophilos	829–842	Constantine XI Palaiologos	1449–1453
Michael III	842–867		
Basil I	867–886		
Leo VI	886–912		
Alexander	912–913		
Regency for Constantine VII	913–920		

Constantine III was a usurper emperor in the western empire, 407–411

L

Laconia

Region of the southeastern Peloponnese

The district of Laconia – Homer's "hollow Lacedaemon" – occupies the southeastern part of the Peloponnese, around the valley of the river Eurotas. To the west is the mountain range of Taygetus, the highest in the Peloponnese, whose summit is usually snow-covered at least into May. To the east is the Parnon range, which runs southwards to the peninsula of Malea. In the Homeric poems this is the homeland of Menelaus, brother of Agamemnon and husband of Helen whose abduction by the Trojans was the whole cause of the siege of Troy. Menelaus is the second-rating, after his brother, of the Argive kings, which would lead one to expect in Laconia a Bronze Age palace and citadel comparable with that at Mycenae, and at least the equal of the "Palace of Nestor" in neighbouring Messenia. If such a palace existed, it has not been found, though, adjacent to a natural mound on which in Classical times the shrine of the deified Menelaus and Helen was situated, there is a sequence of Late Bronze Age structures of some quality, not, however, palatial in scale. This, like other Mycenaean sites in Laconia, was destroyed about 1200 BC, at which point Laconia relapsed into total obscurity and, it would seem, was largely denuded of its population.

At least two centuries later, and probably not before the middle of the 10th century BC, Dorian newcomers settled in the upper reaches of the Eurotas, about 50 km from the sea, opposite the site of the Mycenaean buildings, but on lower ground. Here they formed a group of villages which collectively became the Classical city state of Sparta though, as Thucydides famously pointed out in the introductory chapters of his *History*, even at the end of the 5th century BC physically the city remained nothing more than a collection of villages. Four of them formed the city itself, while a fifth was politically part of the same city state structure, at Amyclae, a short distance to the south. The institutions of the Spartans, similar to those of the Dorian settlers in Crete, remained notoriously distinctive and primitive through the Classical period. They retained, almost to the end of their independence, a curious dual kingship, the reasons for which can only be guessed at. The purpose of these institutions was to create and sustain a military elite, the Spartiates, who alone had full citizenship rights, and with this to establish and maintain a supremacy which was extended, probably by the end of the 8th century BC, over the whole of Laconia, and in the following century crossed the mountain boundary of Taygetus to incorporate Messenia. Outside Sparta the population of Laconia comprised two categories: the Helots (a term which probably denotes that they were "prisoners"), who worked the land – to which they were tied – on behalf of Spartiate landlords, who were thus freed from labour to pursue their military functions; and the *perioikoi*, the "dwellers round" who were free, living in their own communities, but subject to Spartan control and under an obligation to render military support when called on to do so (the same distinctions were extended into conquered Messenia).

The land round Sparta is extremely rich agriculturally; fertile alluvium, well watered by streams fed by the melting snow on the mountain, running into the Eurotas and making it a river which continues to flow throughout the summer. For this reason, at the present day the district has suffered less than most parts of Greece from rural depopulation – with virtually all basic commodities produced locally there is less incentive to migrate to Athens. Conversely, the promontory at the southern end of Taygetus, the Mani, is desperately poor land, with much consequent migration, particularly to Australia. It was undoubtedly the wealth of the land round Sparta that led to it becoming a major city of Classical Greece, though situated at such a distance from the sea.

The communities of *perioikoi* were more varied. Some, like Geronthai (modern Geraki) southeast of Sparta, had long antecedents, but being in areas with poorer agricultural resources could never achieve the power of Sparta, and were satisfied to be part of the Spartan system (conversely, the reason they were not reduced to Helot status was probably that their land was less desirable to the Spartans). Other such communities served more specialized functions, the most important of these being Gytheum, which was the chief harbour town.

Despite being so far inland, Sparta experienced the same artistic development as the other leading areas of Greece in the 8th and 7th centuries BC, resulting from the renewal of overseas trade. Goods imported from the Near East are found there, while Laconian pottery evolved into a distinctive style, after the dull wares of the Dark Age, and was exported to north Africa (Cyrene) and south Italy, where Taras (Tarentum, modern Taranto) was a Spartan colony. There is good evidence for the development of Spartan poetry, and the creation of the shrine to Menelaus and Helen, the Menelaion, on the mound which looks as though it were their tomb (though in reality it is a natural outcrop of rock) shows that the Spartans of the 8th and 7th centuries were well aware of the Homeric poems and the story of the siege of Troy. It was probably the difficulties of maintaining control over rebellious Messenia – another source of wealth – which in the later 7th and 6th centuries caused the Spartans to turn their back on this development, and reinstate with great rigidity (to the curiosity of progressive Greeks, such as the Athenians) the primitive militaristic training and regime for which they became notorious.

After the defeat of the Spartans by the Boeotian League in 371 BC, and the consequent loss of Messenia, Sparta dwindled in political importance; but the potential strength of Laconia was realized once more, after 150 dormant years, when king Cleomenes III carried out a redistribution of the land, and so recreated a substantial citizen army, only to be defeated by the Macedonian army of Antigonus Doson.

In Roman times Laconia became a quiet backwater, enjoying some imperial and other external patronage. Substantial theatres were built at Sparta and Gytheum, and the mosaic pavements of Spartan houses attest to a comfortable standard of living. In the troubled later Roman period fortifications, incorporating the theatre, defended only a reduced area. The city was sacked by Alaric in AD 396, but survived, though the later habitations built over the theatre are wretchedly squalid. Laconia, however, remained a vitally important area, though in the Middle Ages the centre of interest shifted to Mistra, the stronghold city on the foothills of Taygetus. Originally a Frankish foundation, Mistra was recovered by the Byzantines, and blossomed as a centre of late Hellenic culture, where George Gemistos Plethon's teachings took Platonism as the means to emphasize an intellectual continuity from the Classical world. Mistra, in turn, dwindled under Turkish occupation, though still equipped with a splendid series of late Byzantine churches. With the freeing of Greece after the War of Independence, the attempt to recreate the Classical cities led to the redevelopment of a modern city on the approximate site of Sparta. With its inevitable grid plan of streets, and an imposing Neoclassical town hall, splendidly restored in recent years, Sparta remains a relatively small but very prosperous market town for Laconia, whose good land now grows citrus fruit in abundance (the small town of Hagios Stephanos has an annual Festival of the Oranges): the perioikic land of Geraki is devoted largely to olive groves.

R.A. TOMLINSON

See also Mistra, Sparta

Summary

A district in the southeastern part of the Peloponnese, Laconia was prominent in the Bronze Age as the traditional homeland of Menelaus. In the 10th century BC Dorians settled a group of villages that later became the Classical city state of Sparta. Defeated by the Boeotian League in 371 BC, Sparta lost power; but Laconia rose again briefly under Cleomenes III. In the late Byzantine period Mistra blossomed as a centre of Hellenic culture.

Further Reading

Cartledge, Paul, *Sparta and Lakonia: a Regional History, 1300–362 BC*, London and Boston: Routledge and Kegan Paul, 1979

Cartledge, Paul and Antony Spawforth, *Hellenistic and Roman Sparta: A Tale of Two Cities*, London and New York: Routledge, 1989

Catling, H.W., *Excavations at the Menelaion 1973–76*, Archaeological Reports for 1976–77, London: British School at Athens, 1977

Cavanagh, William *et al.*, *The Laconia Survey: Continuity and Change in a Greek Rural Landscape*, London: British School at Athens, 1996

Coulson, W.D., "The Dark Age Pottery from Sparta", *Annual of the British School at Athens*, 83 (1988): pp. 21ff

Dawkins, R.M. (editor), *The Sanctuary of Artemis Orthia at Sparta, Excavated and Described by Members of the British School at Athens, 1906–1910*, London: Macmillan, 1929

Forrest, W.G., *A History of Sparta, 950–192 BC*, 2nd edition, London: Duckworth, 1980

Hope-Simpson, R. and H. Waterhouse, "Prehistoric Laconia", *Annual of the British School at Athens*, 55 (1960) and 56 (1961)

Lazenby, J.F., *The Spartan Army*, Warminster, Wiltshire: Aris and Phillips, and Chicago: Bolchazy Carducci, 1985

Powell, Anton (editor), *Classical Sparta: Techniques Behind Her Success*, London: Routledge, and Norman: University of Oklahoma Press, 1989

Sanders, Jan Motyka (editor), *Philolakon: Lakonian Studies in Honour of Hector Catling*, London: British School at Athens, 1992

Land tenure

Throughout the history of the Greek people access to use and ownership of arable land has been a central concern. The classical polis restricted land ownership to those who were citizens and, more often than not, refused full political rights to those who were too poor to own land. In the countryside the transition from ancient civilization to Byzantium was marked by the gradual disappearance of the small freeholder who worked his plot with the assistance of chattel slaves, and the spread of a class of technically free persons who were only conditional cultivators of the property of large landholders. Increasingly exploitative practices under the Ottoman rulers resulted in the virtual depopulation of many areas of rural Greece, and it was not a simple matter for the first post-independence governments to create the conditions under which land could be distributed and made productive again.

In exploring the question of land tenure from the 8th century BC to modern times certain issues keep recurring. Could one alienate land? What laws of inheritance applied to land? Does the payment of taxes or rent imply a less than full ownership of the land? In addition to exploring these rather legalistic issues, one must also keep in mind a recurring theme in Greek beliefs about landholding: the most desirable state of affairs is for all citizens to have roughly the same amount of land. Social and legal mechanisms which tend to work against the formation of large estates are a stated goal of lawgivers and political theorists at least until the 4th century BC.

The earliest Greek writer to deal specifically with these questions is Hesiod. At the very end of the 8th century BC he composed *Works and Days*, a didactic poem addressed to his brother Perses. Hesiod covers a wide variety of subjects as he lectures Perses, but his central complaint involves land ownership: his brother has snatched most of their joint inheritance with the connivance of "bribe-eating lords", in spite of their private, apparently more equitable, agreement. In view of this, and his advice later in the poem to have only one son (in order that the family's wealth should grow), it is clear that in Boeotia of Hesiod's day it was the practice for all sons to inherit a part of their fathers' land. He also makes it clear that land could be alienated when he promises that, if Perses follows his advice, he will be able to buy the land of other people, instead of seeing his own land bought up by others. Finally, the complaints against the corrupt officials indicate that by the 8th century such disputes could be taken to an authority outside the family.

Evidence for Archaic and Classical Greece is far more abundant, but often confusing and contradictory. Both the 7th and 6th centuries BC and the 4th to the 2nd centuries BC were eras of widespread civil strife in many poleis, where conflict centred around disparities in wealth. Therefore, later writers tend to reconstruct earlier conflicts in terms of contemporary conditions. In the case of early 6th-century Athens, for example, Solon was appointed archon to deal with the crisis of debt bondage. Although this much is certain, the genesis of the crisis, its exact nature, and the content of Solon's legislation remain the subject of considerable dispute. Solon's own words about his aims and how he viewed his accomplishments in his legislative programme have survived, but as poems, not official documents. Adding to the confusion are various 4th-century sources which tried to coopt Solon's legacy in support of their own oligarchic or democratic philosophies. Any modern attempt to reconstruct the situation which Solon faced and how he dealt with it must take into account his own statement that, while he did cancel debts, he did not redistribute land, though some apparently expected him to do so. Current opinion holds that the land which the poor worked as sharecroppers was either their own land which they had been forced to mortgage (Burford, 1993, p. 51) or public land which had been commandeered by the wealthy (Rihll, 1991, pp. 123–24). Solon in effect gave this public land back to the community, allowing the cultivators to become the owners. He is also credited by ancient writers with making it illegal to alienate one's inherited plot. The alienability of land in Classical Athens continues to be a controversial topic among scholars. On the one hand, there are specific cases of land being sold by at least the late 5th century, and on the other hand, there was obviously great social pressure against sales of this kind. The law of Athens went to great lengths at times to ensure that land would stay in the family, as is attested by the rules concerning the marriage of an *epikleros*, an heiress. When a man died leaving behind a daughter, but no son, this daughter was to be married to her nearest male relative. Ideally, she would bear two sons; one of whom would inherit from his father, and one from his maternal grandfather. This would also reconcile two conflicting desiderata: to give each son an inheritance and to keep the family holding undivided.

Other poleis had other strategies for preserving a rough equality among the citizens, ensuring each family a minimum livelihood. The Spartans called themselves *homoioi* ("equals"). Each male Spartiate was entitled to a portion of land which was worked by helots, and from this he contributed to the communal mess. Inability to make this contribution resulted in the loss of citizen rights. Again, Spartans were theoretically unable to alienate their ancestral plots. But by the 4th century BC the number of Spartans who were financially eligible to serve as hoplites had fallen disastrously. Wealth had accumulated in the hands of a relatively small portion of the population due to the transfer of property through dowry and inheritance by women: the wealthy were able to absorb more and more of the community's land through advantageous marriages.

The situation which allowed the Greeks to approach most nearly the ideal of equality among the citizens was the founding of a new colony. Beginning in the 8th century BC and continuing into the 5th century poleis would often solve their demographic problems by sending a portion of their citizens out to non-Greek territories to found a new city. Prospective settlers went on the understanding that the territory of the new polis would be allocated on an equitable basis. This did not mean that everyone would get exactly the same amount of land, but that, with no preexisting claims to the territory, and taking into account the variable quality of the lots, each would get a reasonable portion of the total land resources. When the division was done, the colonists would often swear an oath to abide by the distribution, and there might be actual legal penalties brought against anyone who in the future sought to have land redistributed.

In the 4th century the orator Isocrates described Greece as a land rent with civil strife and filled with destitute fugitives who posed a continuing threat to social order. His proposed solution, eventually made a reality by Alexander the Great, was a war of conquest against the barbarians, which would provide new lands on which to settle this horde. Whether or not conditions were quite so desperate in reality as in the speeches of Isocrates, it is certain that many Greeks left their homeland to settle in Egypt and the Near East as a result of Alexander's conquests. Those who went as soldiers were often rewarded for their services with grants of land. Since these grants were generally conditional upon continued military service, they frequently found it more profitable to lease the land to native cultivators. Furthermore, while the Greek poleis had avoided imposing direct taxes on land, seeing it as a sign of tyranny, those who received their plots from the Hellenistic kings usually found that they came with a whole host of taxes in kind and in cash. Individuals or colonies might be granted immunity from these taxes, but even this immunity served to underscore the fact that all the land was ultimately the possession of the king and not of the citizen body.

In the Greek homeland this emigration did not lead to a more stable situation with regard to agricultural conditions. Instead, there was a continuing tendency for the few to accumulate larger properties, or a larger number of scattered properties, which would be leased to the increasing numbers of those without land or without enough land to live on. In recent years archaeological surface surveys have confirmed, independent of literary testimony, that the number of rural sites decreases from the beginning of the 2nd century BC, particularly at the time of the Roman conquest of Greece. These sites are generally associated with small independent proprietors. Sites that continue to appear in the archaeological record tend to be larger and show signs of affluence. On the basis of this evidence it has been suggested that the rural landscape came increasingly under the control of a few wealthy landlords. Their large estates would have been devoted to the production of cash crops and worked with large numbers of slaves. Alternatively, income could have been produced by leasing out plots to produce rents (Alcock, 1993, p. 72).

The late Roman landscape of Greece, however, shows a significant increase in the number of rural sites and there is a general sense of modest prosperity in the countryside. This is not really surprising, given that the peasants of the eastern Roman empire were not nearly as vulnerable to the pressures of large landowners as those in the western provinces, where the medieval institution of serfdom was already evolving. In the 4th and 5th centuries AD village communities of Asia Minor, Syria, and Egypt were still benefiting from the Hellenistic legacy of widespread urbanism. With towns and cities in which to market their products the peasants were able to pay their rents and taxes and maintain at least a measure of independence. This is not to say that conditions were not felt to be oppressive. Taxes were collected on both the land and its cultivators, peasants were always subject to extra assessments of produce and to demands for corvée labour. They had neither unrestricted freedom of movement nor an unlimited right to alienate their land. Reactions to these oppressive conditions often took the form of brigandage (Haldon, 1990, pp. 31–32), a phenomenon which also characterized the late Ottoman period.

The chaotic conditions of the 7th century AD may have led to a lessening of central control and a growth in the number of villages composed of small holders whose only responsibilities were the taxes which they paid directly to the Byzantine state. A tantalizing text called *The Farmer's Law*, which may date back to the 7th or even 6th century AD, paints a picture of a countryside dominated by this type of settlement. But the history of land tenure under the Byzantine empire is one increasingly dominated by peasants dependent on private landlords, the Church, or the state itself. In the 10th century the Byzantine state proclaimed itself the ultimate owner of all the lands of the empire. In effect, all private property was at risk from imperial confiscation (Kazhdan and Wharton, 1985, p. 17). An increase in the proportion of dependent peasants is also seen at this time. By the 13th century virtually all the peasants are referred to as *paroikoi* ("tenants"). *Paroikoi* had definite legal rights in that they could dispose of their property either by bequest or by sale. However, they were dependent in that they paid state taxes and rent to their landlord, owed him labour, and were not allowed to leave his service (Laiou-Thomadakis, 1977, pp. 144–45).

With the Ottoman conquest the lands of the Byzantine empire came under a regime whose ideology with regard to property was fundamentally different from that found in Romano-Byzantine law. Under a strict interpretation of Muslim holy law, private land ownership was not permitted. The sultan functioned as the custodian of the land on behalf of its true proprietor, God. In practice, individuals enjoyed the use and possession of land under various conditions – ranging from a form of feudalism to true private ownership. Ottoman law tended to identify cottage sites, their gardens, orchards, and vineyards as private property, while unimproved arable

was retained as state land. Many aspects of Ottoman land tenure tended to undermine the ability of the actual cultivator to gain even a subsistence return from the land, but the fundamental source of corruption was the practice of granting individuals the right to take profits from land while having no responsibility for its cultivation (McGrew, 1985, pp. 21–31).

When Greece won its independence, the new government found itself the proprietor of a vast amount of land, and very few other sources of wealth. Initial attempts to redistribute land through public auction failed because the government was attempting to use the sales to raise money as well as put the land back into productive use. The Greek population, impoverished, suspicious of all governing authority, and well aware that much of the land would need a significant input of labour in order to provide a return, refused to participate. It was only some 40 years later, in 1871, that a plan was developed which met some success. This was principally because it was largely an offer to squatters to legitimize their holdings, provided they accepted a mortgage in favour of the state (McGrew, 1985, pp. 207–14).

In some ways modern Greek patterns of landholding tend to resemble those of antiquity. The countryside is typified by nuclear villages from which farmers go out to work their fields. Families tend to own only a small amount of land, with 6 hectares making for a large farm. One of the most striking features, to outsiders, of Greek patterns of landholding is how highly fragmented they tend to be. A farmer may spend hours travelling between parcels. There is no pragmatic reason for this fragmentation, since given the chance farmers will attempt through sale and trade to consolidate their holdings near their home village. Dowry and inheritance rules have been seen as the root cause of this phenomenon, and in at least one important respect they are different from those which prevailed in the ancient world. As in ancient Athens, all sons must inherit and daughters must receive a dowry. This does not necessarily have to be land, but traditionally it has been a component of both. Even sons who have left the land are frequently awarded a token piece of property "so they will not forget their father". One important difference however, is that the strict rules against marrying close kin which are enforced by the Orthodox Church all but ensure that young people will marry outside their own village. Combined with a strong tradition of patrilocal residence after marriage this inevitably leads to a family's holdings being scattered in several locations (Friedl, 1962, pp. 48–68).

BARBARA FIEDLER

See also Inheritance

Further Reading

Alcock, Susan E., *Graecia Capta: The Landscapes of Roman Greece*, Cambridge and New York: Cambridge University Press, 1993

Asheri, D., "Laws of Inheritance, Distribution of Land and Political Constitutions in Ancient Greece", *Historia*, 12 (1963): pp. 1–21

Burford, Alison, *Land and Labor in the Greek World*, Baltimore: Johns Hopkins University Press, 1993

Fine, John V.A., *Horoi: Studies in Mortgage, Real Security and Land Tenure in Ancient Athens*, Baltimore: American School of Classical Studies at Athens, 1951

Finley, M.I. (editor), *Problèmes de la terre en Grèce ancienne*, Paris: Mouton, 1973

Finley, M.I., *The Ancient Economy*, 2nd edition, London: Hogarth Press, and Berkeley: University of California Press, 1985

Friedl, Ernestine, *Vasilika: A Village in Modern Greece*, New York: Holt Rinehart, 1962

Fuks, Alexander, *Social Conflict in Ancient Greece*, Jerusalem: Magnes Press, and Leiden: Brill, 1984

Haldon, J.F., *Byzantium in the Seventh Century: The Transformation of a Culture*, Cambridge and New York: Cambridge University Press, 1990

Hanson, Victor Davis, *The Other Greeks: The Family Farm and the Agrarian Roots of Western Civilization*, New York: Free Press, 1995

Harrison, A.R.W., *The Law of Athens*, 2 vols, Oxford: Clarendon Press, 1968–71

Hodkinson, Stephen, "Land Tenure and Inheritance in Classical Sparta", *Classical Quarterly*, 36 (1986): pp. 378–406

Kazhdan, A.P. and Ann Wharton Epstein, *Change in Byzantine Culture in the Eleventh and Twelfth Centuries*, Berkeley: University of California Press, 1985

Laiou-Thomadakis, Angeliki E., *Peasant Society in the Late Byzantine Empire*, Princeton, New Jersey: Princeton University Press, 1977

Lane Fox, Robin, "Aspects of Inheritance in the Greek World" in *Crux: Essays Presented to G.E.M. de Ste. Croix on His 75th Birthday*, edited by Paul Cartledge and F.D. Harvey, Exeter: Imprint Academic, 1985

McGrew, William W., *Land and Revolution in Modern Greece, 1800–1881: The Transition in the Tenure and Exploitation of Land from Ottoman Rule to Independence*, Kent, Ohio: Kent State University Press, 1985

Rihll, T.E., "Hektemoroi: Partners in Crime?", *Journal of Hellenic Studies*, 111 (1991): pp. 101–27

Walbank, F.W., *The Hellenistic World*, revised edition, London: Fontana, and Cambridge, Massachusetts: Harvard University Press, 1992

Landscape

The great beauty and diversity of the Greek landscape were seldom fully appreciated by ancient Greeks, to whom these wonders were commonplace, or by modern tourists, who miss the glamorous parts. The best description of what the ancient Greek landscape looked like is the vision of the 12 mountains of Arcadia in the early Christian prophecy of Hermas, an Arcadian shepherd.

Greek landscapes are dominated by tectonics. Greece lies near the junction of two of the world's great tectonic plates, where Africa is burrowing under Europe. Over millions of years the forces of collision have generated the dramatic mountain landscapes of Greece, with their cliffs, gorges, and fault-scarps, especially around the gulf of Corinth and in Crete. Secondary effects include erosion and deposition, and the re-erosion of materials deposited during earlier periods of mountain building. Erosion has created the surrealistic gullied badlands of Macedonia and the northern Peloponnese, and the corresponding deposition has created many of the cultivable soils of Greece. Mountain building is, of course, still continuing today. At least three volcanoes – Santorini, Methana, and Nisyros – have erupted in historic times.

Most of modern Greece is rocky, with cultivation limited to plains or to places where soil has washed off the hillsides and accumulated in basins. Areas of land for cultivation were extended by the construction of terraces, bands of soil held up by retaining walls. Terraces created a level surface, got rid of boulders by building them into walls, accumulated and held soil, broke up the bedrock so that roots (especially of vines) could penetrate it, and increased absorption of water in times of heavy rain.

Wild vegetation in Greece ranges from forest to desert, depending mainly on rainfall and how much moisture is stored in the soil and bedrock (see the article on Climate). Forests occur mainly in mountains, especially in western Greece; often they occur on fissured limestone with no soil. In drier or more heavily used terrain forest gives way to maquis, land dominated by shrubs, most of which are in fact trees stunted into a shrubby form by browsing, burning, or woodcutting. Alternatively trees may form part of savanna, where large trees grow scattered in grassland or heath. Where moisture is more limited, the vegetation consists of *phrygano* ("scrub"), dominated by heathlike, spiny, or aromatic undershrubs which are not potential trees. Steppe is herbaceous vegetation with grasses, bulbous and tuberous plants. Patches of maquis, *phrygano*, and steppe typically occur intermingled, rather than in separate areas.

In Ancient, Byzantine, and Early Modern Greece wild vegetation was not underused land. It provided pasturage, fuel, materials for crafts, honey, edible plants, and medicinal herbs. The plants, except for those limited to cliffs, have the ability to resist, or recover from, browsing, burning, and woodcutting.

In pre-Neolithic times Greece was more wooded than it is now; in the drier east the trees probably formed savanna. There is some evidence for steppe, but *phrygano* was probably limited to particular, mainly coastal, areas. Crete and other islands may have differed from the mainland, owing to their peculiar faunas (nearly all extinct by the Bronze Age), including tiny elephants and mini-hippopotamuses. Lacking predators, these animals would have flourished sufficiently to bring about an ecological condition that would today be regarded as excessive browsing.

During the Neolithic and the Bronze Age the Greek landscape was affected both by increasing human activity and by the advent of a drier climate. Forests on good soils were uprooted to create farmland; on the remaining land native animals were replaced by domesticated – goats, sheep, and cattle. Forests retreated to places with moisture or good root penetration, being replaced by maquis or savanna. Undershrubs profited from the changes to establish areas of *phrygano*. The date, nature, and consequences of deforestation are controversial, but there is no firm evidence that Greece in Classical times was more wooded than it is today.

By Classical times ecological changes were largely completed. The landscape looked not very different from Greece today, aside from urbanization, road making, and bulldozing. An important difference is the disappearance of fens, most of which were destroyed in the 19th century. Classical Greece had much more grain and legume cultivation than today, and much less olive-growing; they kept cattle and pigs, as well as sheep and goats. At least half the land was natural vegetation (forest, savanna, maquis, *phrygano*, steppe, and fen). There was already the infrastructure of a cultural landscape in the form of roads, field walls, pollarded trees, and some terraces. Terracing, begun in the Bronze Age, was probably more limited than in Early Modern times; no ancient author definitely mentions it.

The coast of Greece has also changed. After the last ice age the world's sea level rose some 100 m to about its present level. This created bays, which have since become river deltas or have been filled with material eroded from the hills. At the same time the land has been jerked up or down by tectonic movements. A famous example of coastal changes in historic times is at Thermopylae, where the site of the ancient sea-cliff battles is now well inland and deeply buried.

Ancient city states varied hugely in the territory and resources that they controlled. Athens and Sparta were giants, with access to all ecological zones, from mountains to the sea. But even Athens was not self-sufficient in timber and not always so in grain. Some of the smallest cities had recourse to only one or two ecological zones, like the three states on the barren mountain isle of Amorgos, or the city of Tarrha at the mouth of the gorge of Samaria in Crete, which apparently had no ecological resources at all except cypress timber.

In antiquity Greece was not, as today, a land of cities and large villages set in otherwise uninhabited countryside. Instead there were small towns, small villages, hamlets, and single farms, grading into field houses that were inhabited only seasonally. Such a dispersed pattern of settlement still survives in western Crete, the Mani, and the island of Cythera; elsewhere, especially in the Middle Ages and the 16th century, houses have clustered into villages.

The use of the land would also have fluctuated over the centuries, as the human population rose and fell and as opportunities for trade changed. At times of prosperity, cultivation and pasturage would have increased so that the land would have been fully used or overused. In leaner times trees and other vegetation would have been left to invade fields and pastures.

Good and bad land have not always been the same as now. Some rugged, water-retaining, fertile mountain areas, such as northern Parnon, have a history of dense population. Some apparently promising plains, as at Nemea, have had periods of use only as pasture. Undrained fens, now despised, were precious as summer pasture for cattle. Coastal plains, though offering good land, and small islands have not always been favoured for cultivation or settlement because of the danger of raids by pirates.

The 19th century was a time of unusual population growth, leading to an exceptionally high rural population in the 20th century. New settlements were founded, especially on previously uninhabited coastal plains and in drained marshes. Around existing settlements terraces were extended to the limits of cultivable soil. American plants became important crops. Crete, especially, had an overcrowded appearance: most wild trees, even on cliffs, bear the marks of having been cut down for wood many times.

After 1950 rural populations declined, as people migrated to cities and coastal towns or to overseas colonies. The remaining rural life has become more specialized. Cultivation has retreated from terraces on to level ground where tractors can be used. Olive growing, market gardening, greenhouses, and irrigated orchards have greatly increased; cereals have disappeared from many areas. Cattle, horses, and donkeys are relatively rare. Woodcutting has almost disappeared, partly because of the advent of fossil fuels, but also because pruning olive and fruit trees produces firewood without the labour of felling trees. In many mountain villages the economy has been reduced to olives, goats, and sheep, sometimes not even these. This is not because traditional land-uses have proved unsustainable, but because tourism, bureaucracy, industry, and commerce have created easier ways of making a living.

This has resulted in extensive areas of abandoned terraces, and often also of abandoned pasture. Natural vegetation has greatly increased. Substantial forests have replaced terraces or savanna. Often these are of pines, which are extremely susceptible to, but have a natural ability to survive, fire. Where cultivation persists it has been intensified, bulldozers often being used to dig new fields out of hillsides. Further havoc is wrought by works to provide water for irrigation. What was once a complex, stable landscape has been reduced to large tracts of uniform vegetation, periodically burnt in conflagrations, and liable to erosion wherever the bulldozer has been deployed.

OLIVER RACKHAM

See also Animals, Climate, Demography, Ecology, Geology, Plants

Further Reading

McNeill, J.R., *The Mountains of the Mediterranean World: An Environmental History*, Cambridge and New York: Cambridge University Press, 1992 (puts the traditional view, contrary to this article, that irreversible degradation of environment and vegetation is a critical influence)

Osborne, Robin, *Classical Landscape with Figures: The Ancient Greek City and Its Countryside*, London: George Philip, and Dobbs Ferry, New York: Sheridan House, 1987

Rackham, Oliver, "Ancient Landscapes" in *The Greek City from Homer to Alexander*, edited by Oswyn Murray and Simon Price, Oxford: Clarendon Press, 1990

Rackham, Oliver and Jennifer Moody, *The Making of the Cretan Landscape*, Manchester: Manchester University Press, 1996

Rackham, Oliver and A.T. Grove, *The Nature of the European Mediterranean*, Yale University Press, 2000

Snodgrass, Anthony M., *An Archaeology of Greece: The Present State and Future Scope of a Discipline*, Berkeley: University of California Press, 1987

Wells, Berit (editor), *Agriculture in Ancient Greece*, Stockholm: Swedish Institute in Athens, 1992

Language

The term "Greek" refers to the language spoken by the Indo-European inhabitants of Greece from their first arrival in that land to the present day. Greece was already populated when they arrived (probably not long after 2000 BC), but the original inhabitants spoke another language of which little trace remains; since there is no consensus even as to which language family it belonged, it is simply referred to as "pre-Greek". Greek itself belongs to the Indo-European family of languages and is thus related not only to Latin (and hence French, Spanish, and all the other Romance languages), but also to Sanskrit (and hence Hindi, Bengali, etc.), Hittite, Armenian, Albanian, Tocharian, Persian (and Kurdish, Afghan, etc.), the

Celtic languages (Irish, Welsh, etc.), the Germanic languages (English, German, etc.), the Baltic languages (Lithuanian, etc.), and the Slavic languages (Russian, Bulgarian, etc.). Since all languages change over time, however, these relationships were much closer in ancient times than they are today.

The original Proto-Indo-European language from which Greek and all of these other languages evolved was highly inflected; it had eight cases for nouns and divided number not into singular and plural but into singular, dual (used for two objects or people), and plural (used for three or more). It also had a number of sounds that have since disappeared from many of its descendants, such as vocalic (vowel-like) forms of L, R, M, and N, aspirated consonants such as DH, BH, and GH, and mysterious "laryngeal consonants", the exact pronunciation of which remains uncertain. On the other hand the parent language lacked many sounds with which we are familiar, such as F, V, J, CH, Z, and TH.

Greek is one of the oldest attested Indo-European languages; its earliest known form is Mycenaean, the language of the Linear B tablets. Since these tablets date from the 13th century BC or earlier, the history of Greek can now be traced over a period of 33 centuries. Because Linear B was written in a syllabary that did not indicate all the sounds of a word, however, and because it was used for writing lists rather than literature, much remains unknown about Mycenaean Greek. Nevertheless, we can see that it had already evolved to be recognizably Greek rather than Proto-Indo-European. The dual and some consonants that Greek would later lose (Q, W, Y, H) were retained, but the old case system was somewhat simplified and a number of consonants and vowels had disappeared. Mycenaean Greek, as we have it, does not appear to be divided into dialects; tablets from Thebes, Pylos, and Crete show only minor variations in language. Nevertheless it is likely that speakers of other Greek dialects were present somewhere in Greece during the Mycenaean period: not all classical Greek dialects can be descended from Mycenaean, but all show evidence of contact with the pre-Greek population and thus of having existed in Greece for a similar length of time.

The Mycenaean period ended around 1200 BC and was followed by a time known as the Dark Ages, when writing was unknown throughout most of Greece. (A relative of the Linear B script seems, however, to have survived in Cyprus, where it later reemerged as the Cypriot syllabary.) There is thus a gap during which one cannot trace the evolution of the Greek language; after the Mycenaean period, it next appears with our earliest evidence of the Greek alphabet, in the 8th century BC. By this time the number of cases had been reduced to five, the dual was in the process of disappearing, Q and Y had been entirely lost, and W was on its way out. Moreover, the Greek language was divided into a vast number of local dialects. Of these, only those spoken in Arcadia and in Cyprus appear to be direct descendants of the Mycenaean dialect; the other dialect groups, including Attic (the dialect of Athens), Ionic (the dialects of Greeks in Asia Minor), Aeolic (the dialects of the Lesbians, Thessalians, and Boeotians), and Doric (the dialects of Crete and most of the Peloponnese) seem to be descended from something slightly different. All the dialects, however, are clearly part of the same language and were mutually comprehensible.

The language normally described by the term "Classical Greek" is Attic, the dialect of Athens in the 5th century BC. At the beginning of the 5th century BC this dialect had no special status, but Athens' rise to political prominence during the Persian Wars and the extraordinary quantity of first-class literature produced by Athenians in the 5th and 4th centuries BC rapidly made Attic the most important Greek dialect. This is not to say that all ancient Greek literature was written in Attic; far from it. The earliest surviving literature, the Homeric poems, is written in a mixed dialect based on Ionic and containing almost no trace of Attic, and the poets who first followed Homer used a variety of dialects, none of them Attic. The Attic dialect first came into prominence with the development of tragedy, which was a distinctively Athenian genre. Even tragedies, however, were not simply written in the native dialects of their authors. The dialogue portions were composed in an artificial and elevated literary Attic with many features from other dialects, while the sections sung by the chorus were written in what was nominally Doric, though in some ways it would be more accurate to describe it as a Doricized Attic.

Comedy, however, made much more use of ordinary Attic, as did many prose genres. A peculiarity of Greek literature of the Archaic and Classical periods was that literary genre rather than the author's origin normally determined the dialect used. Thus although two of the greatest early Greek poets, Hesiod and Pindar, both came from Boeotia and would naturally have spoken an Aeolic dialect, Hesiod wrote in the Ionic-based epic dialect and Pindar wrote in Doric, because these were the dialects appropriate to their chosen genres (respectively epic poetry and choral lyric). Tragic choruses had to be composed in Doric because of the tradition of Doric choral song out of which the tragic genre evolved. Scientific and historical prose was originally written in Ionic, but as time went on Athenian prose authors began to write in an Ionicized version of their own dialect. Many of these literary dialects, however, were rather different from the same dialects as used for non-literary purposes by native speakers and attested in local inscriptions; they contained features of other dialects and were usually meant to be separated from and elevated above the usages of ordinary speech.

In the 4th century BC the political power of Greece was gradually eclipsed by that of its northern neighbour Macedonia. The issue of whether the Macedonians could be considered Greeks was debated in ancient times much as it is today. Little remains of their original language (which is unconnected to the modern Slavic language known as "Macedonian"), and from that little it is possible to argue either that Macedonian was a bizarre Greek dialect or that it was a different but related language. The Greeks themselves seem not to have understood it as easily as they understood each other's Greek dialects. Culturally, however, it seems that the Greeks looked down on the Macedonians as uncivilized barbarians, and the Macedonian monarchs reacted to their own feelings of inferiority by a programme of linguistic and cultural Hellenization. Greek was adopted as the official language of the Macedonian court, where from the time of Philip II Greek literature and education were highly valued. Because of the political and literary importance of Athens, the form of Greek adopted by the Macedonians was an Ionicized Attic.

The Macedonians soon became far more powerful than the Greeks from a political point of view, but even after conquering Greece they retained their respect for its language and culture. The conquests of Alexander the Great in the late 4th century BC thus had the effect of spreading the use of the Greek language and the appreciation of Greek literature and culture over a huge section of the ancient world. In the Hellenistic kingdoms that resulted from Alexander's conquests, Greek became the language not only of the court, but also of business, administration, and most upper-class interaction. Education normally consisted of training in the Greek language and literature, and knowledge of Greek was required for entry into the civil service and the army. Greek rapidly became the mother tongue of the elite as well as being widely spoken as a second language by much of the population. The less educated lower classes went on speaking their own languages most of the time, but these languages were less likely to be used in written communication.

The Greek used in the Hellenistic kingdoms was based on the Ionicized Attic adopted by the Macedonians, but it was sufficiently distinct from the dialect of Athens that it acquired a new name, the *koine* or "common dialect". The Koine was in some senses a uniform dialect; the differences between Koine documents from different parts of the Hellenistic world are minimal compared to, say, the differences between Attic and Doric. In other respects, however, it was far from uniform; there was some local variation, and a good deal more variation based on the level of education of the writer and his intended audience. The most highly educated Hellenistic scholars, however, could and did produce not only Koine but also the various literary dialects of the earlier periods.

In Greece itself the loss of the individual city states' political autonomy in the Hellenistic period led to the decline of the local dialects. Although most of the ancient dialects survived into the Roman period as spoken languages, the use of Koine came to be seen as a mark of education, in Greece as in the rest of the Hellenistic world. The result was that Koine supplanted the local dialects as the language of the elite and gradually became the official written language of cities that had once proudly displayed their own dialects in inscriptions.

Eventually Greece and the various states that had been part of Alexander's empire fell under Roman rule. This meant the introduction of Latin into Greece, but since the Romans had no cultural heritage to compare with that of Greece, the status of their language suffered greatly. The use of Latin never became widespread in Greece, but Greek grew more and more popular in educated circles in Rome. Meanwhile, in the other states that had been part of Alexander's empire, a tripartite linguistic situation arose: Latin became the language of some administrative and military circles, but Greek remained the language of education and culture, while much of the native population went on speaking the language that they had spoken before Alexander's arrival. The most important and prestigious of these three languages was normally Greek; in Egypt, for example, where large quantities of public and private documents have been preserved on papyrus fragments buried in sand, it is clear that most writing was done in Greek. In fact, the eastern half of the Mediterranean in the Roman period was often called the "Greek east". The degree to which Greek actually replaced local languages, however, depended on the region; in Egypt, despite the vast numbers of Greek papyri, most of the peasants spoke Coptic, but in Asia Minor the native languages tended to die out completely during the Roman period.

The dialect of Greek involved, of course, was still the Koine, but after centuries of evolution and of being used as a second language it showed some significant differences from the Ionicized Attic with which it had begun. These differences are perhaps greatest in phonology, for the pronunciation of Greek changed dramatically during the Hellenistic and Roman periods. At the time when the Greeks began to use the alphabet (the 8th century BC), their language contained ten simple vowels (A, E, I, O, U, each of which had separate long and short forms) and a wide variety of diphthongs (AI, EI, OI, UI, AU, EU, and OU, many of which could have either a long or a short vowel as their first element). By the Classical period, however, the short diphthongs EI and OU had already been monophthongized, and shortly afterward those diphthongs that consisted of a long vowel followed by I lost the I. (As a result, this I was not normally written in ancient documents, but it now appears in Classical texts as the iota subscript.) Then the short diphthong AI merged with short E, UI and short OI both merged with U, and the already monophthongized short EI merged with I. Eventually the distinction between long and short vowels was lost altogether.

The consonants phi, theta, and chi, which had originally been aspirated stops (P followed by H for phi, T followed by H for theta, K followed by H for chi), turned into the fricatives F, TH (as in English "thing"), and CH (as in German "ich", not English "change"), while in most contexts the voiced stops B, D, and G became the voiced fricatives V, TH (as in English "the"), and the voiced equivalent of CH (which does not exist in English). In the Classical period Greek did not have a stress accent as in English, where one syllable of each word is perceived as pronounced more emphatically than the others, but rather a pitch accent as in modern Norwegian, where an accented vowel is perceived as pronounced on a higher pitch (one Greek grammarian speaks of the voice being raised by a musical fifth). In Koine, however, the Greek pitch accent changed to the stress accent that is still used in Modern Greek.

It is sometimes difficult to pinpoint the date of these changes in pronunciation, not only because they occurred gradually and probably took effect in some regions before others, but also because the Classical spelling remained in use for most written documentation. Spelling mistakes, however, are very useful in tracing linguistic evolution: when papyri regularly show AI for E and E for AI, this is evidence that the two were pronounced the same, and the date when this mistake becomes common (the 2nd century BC) can be taken as one by which the change was complete, at least in Egypt. Borrowings into and from other languages also give us clues: when the Romans first began to borrow Greek words containing the letter phi, they represented it with PH, showing that the sound in question was an aspirated P. But later on the sound of phi changed to F, and at that point (the 1st century AD) the Romans used F to represent it.

The complex grammar and syntax of Classical Attic were also simplified in Koine. Two past tenses, the perfect ("I have done") and aorist ("I did") became interchangeable so that either could be used in either sense; eventually the perfect died out and only the aorist was used. The optative, a verbal mood used to express wishes and potentiality and which replaced the subjunctive after verbs in a past tense, disappeared from Koine almost entirely. The middle voice, which in Classical Greek was distinct from both the active and the passive in meaning, if not always in form, was also lost. At the same time many irregularities of declension and conjugation were eliminated; thus, for example, the verbs that had originally ended in -MI began to lose their distinctive conjugation, although this change was completed only in the Byzantine period. During the Roman period many words of Latin origin also found their way into Greek.

The changes in grammar, syntax, and vocabulary were more often reflected in writing than those in pronunciation, but they too could be avoided by more educated authors. The New Testament, for example, is a document of the early Roman period written in a fairly basic form of Koine; it displays a grammar and syntax that are much simpler than those of Classical Attic. But it is not a uniform text written by a single author, and in some portions, for example the Gospel of Luke, even the optative appears. Other writers of the early Roman period, such as Polybius and Plutarch, wrote in a very different type of Koine far closer to Classical Attic. Since Greek education stressed the reading and memorization of Classical texts, there was a certain status attached to an ability to write Greek in a manner closer to that of those texts. Writers with a good education normally came from a fairly high-status background and naturally wanted their works to show this education and background, although if they were writing for a popular audience they might simplify their language in the interests of comprehensibility. People with little education did not normally become writers – the New Testament is something of an exception in this regard – but they often composed private letters which have survived on papyrus and tell us much about the evolution of non-literary Koine.

One of the most significant linguistic events of the Roman period was the revival of literary Attic in the 2nd century AD. Whereas earlier well-educated writers had been able to win respect using a form of Koine relatively close to Attic, it was now necessary for them to use "pure" Attic, a language as close as possible to that of Plato and the Classical orators. In the 2nd century AD Attic came to be seen as "Greek"; everything else was simply evidence of lack of education. The great writers of the period, such as Lucian, managed to achieve Atticism to a remarkable degree. Purity of language was required not only in writing but also in speech, and the opprobrium heaped on men of letters who accidentally delivered themselves of a non-Attic word or phrase is well documented. This does not of course mean that everyone in the Greek-speaking world began to speak Attic in the 2nd century; far from it. But everyone with literary pretensions tried. The reason for this revival seems to have been a desire for closer association with the glorious Greek past, since continuity of culture, the one thing that the Greeks had in a world dominated by the Romans, appeared to be assured by linguistic closeness to the past.

After the 2nd century AD the extremes of the Atticizing movement were modified, but the achievements of the period had a lasting effect on literary Greek; Attic always remained as an ideal, even if fewer writers pursued it. Written Greek came to consist of a range of styles combining Attic and Koine; at the top end of the spectrum were compositions in almost pure Attic, but these were the exception rather than the rule, and most writing showed some or many Koine features. Virtually all writing, however, was conducted in a language distinct from that used in normal speech. Learning to write involved learning the use of written Greek, rather than learning how to transcribe one's own speech. This situation is not so different from that which exists today for English, where learning to write involves learning the difference between "too" and "to", and at a higher level between "its" and "it's".

Starting in the 3rd century AD military imperatives forced a gradual administrative division of the Roman empire into eastern and western halves, with a resulting decline in linguistic interaction. In the 4th century the capital of the empire was moved from Rome to Byzantium (refounded as Constantinople), a move that bolstered the status of Greek as an imperial language and led in time to its official recognition as such. The use of Greek in the West and that of Latin in the East was sharply reduced, particularly after the early 5th-century collapse of the western Roman empire. The eventual result was a government in Constantinople that used Greek and ruled a largely Greek-speaking (whether as first or second language) populace, but which still regarded itself as being the Roman empire. From this situation arose the use of the term Romaic ("Roman") as a name for the Greek language; this term remained in use as late as the 19th century as a means of referring to spoken, as distinct from written, Greek. Even today, some Greeks use *Romios* to mean "a Greek person".

The Middle Ages in Greece are known as the Byzantine period; they begin in the 4th or 5th century AD and end with the capture of Greece by the Turks in the 15th century. During this period the language continued to change, although in many cases the changes were merely completions of processes that had begun much earlier. In pronunciation, long E merged with I, as did U; this meant that original long E, EI, I, U, UI, and OI now all had the same pronunciation (like the "ee" in "queen"). The U in the diphthongs AU and EU came to be pronounced as F or V (depending on the letter following). The sound H, which had been losing ground since the Hellenistic period, was lost altogether. Unstressed initial vowels were generally lost, meaning that verbal augments often disappeared. Nouns of the first and third declensions converged and became more and more similar, and there was a further suppression of irregular paradigms. Many pronouns were replaced; among the most striking such replacements is that of the relative pronoun, which in classical Greek had been fully inflected for gender, number, and case, and which in the Byzantine period was replaced by an uninflected word originally meaning "where" (*pou* or *hopou*). The dative case, which had also been gradually eroded, disappeared from colloquial usage. The wide variety of prepositions used in classical Greek was greatly reduced. The use of the infinitive declined dramatically, as did that of the participle, and the old future tense began to be replaced by a periphrasis formed with the verb "want" (*thelo hina*); later this periphrasis would be simplified into the uninflected particle *tha* used to form the future in Modern Greek. Following the loss of the perfect tense, a new periphrastic pluperfect was formed using the past tense of the verb "have"; later a new perfect would also be formed on this model.

This period also marks the beginning of a famous linguistic phenomenon known as the "Balkan *Sprachbund*", in which languages that are fundamentally distinct (Greek, Albanian, Romanian, Serbian, and Bulgarian) have certain grammatical features in common as a result of the prolonged interaction of their populations. These features include the replacement of infinitive phrases with subjunctive clauses and the formation of the future with a particle derived from the verb "want".

Spoken Greek of the Byzantine period is called the vernacular, rather than Koine; the Koine of the Roman period remained in use as a literary language, but, as we have seen, the uneducated spoken language became more and more distant from it. Literary Greek still had many different levels: there was a high register which at its purest was not greatly different from Classical Attic, though generally more ornate, and below this register came a variety of less and less Atticizing ones, which generally carried less prestige the less archaizing they were. "Atticizing", however, did not refer to an exclusive use of Classical models as it had in the 2nd century AD; the Byzantines saw writers of the Roman period, and even later, as equally suitable for imitation. The tradition of writing "good" Greek was seen as a continuous one, and what counted was a writer's style, not his date. A number of Byzantine scholars were extremely well educated in Classical literature and could write in a variety of different forms of Greek; they used highly Atticized language or more basic Koine depending on their intended audience. Some earlier literature was rewritten to conform to the linguistic demands of its new audience; in some cases this meant recasting in a less archaizing style, but in other cases works were rewritten in higher rather than lower registers.

There was a tradition of oral poetry during the Byzantine period, and in the 14th and 15th centuries a number of written poems appeared that seem to derive from this tradition; at the same time romances, chronicles of recent history, and some other types of popular literature started to be written in a language closer to the vernacular than that of most Byzantine writing. It is likely, however, that the language of these works is still somewhat archaizing compared to that in use in uneducated speech. The rise of this vernacular literature is probably related to the fact that from the 13th century much of the Byzantine world was ruled by western Europeans, particularly French and Italians. The Byzantine state with its centralized bureaucracy, education system, and Church had exerted a standardizing and unifying influence on the written language, and much of that influence was lost with the decline of the central authority.

Other linguistic developments in the late Byzantine period have the same cause. Many French and Italian words entered the Greek language as a result of contact with the new rulers, and a new system of dialects became apparent. These dialects had grown up gradually over the centuries (they are not descendants of the Classical dialects, but of Hellenistic Koine), but the centralization of the empire had prevented their developing radical differences or breaking up the language in the way that Latin was dissolved into the Romance languages during the same period.

After the Turkish conquest in the 15th century, literary production and the general level of education both fell dramatically. The bastion of learning that remained in Greece proper was the Church, and thus the Greek used by the Church became the written standard of the period. This was not the vernacular, but a form of Koine that could be more or less Atticizing as necessary, as the language of the Byzantine court had been. Despite this restoration of a form of central control, the language did not remain unchanged by Turkish occupation, for many Turkish words were absorbed into Greek. A large number of these have since been expunged by patriotic reforms, but some still remain. The local dialects became rapidly more distinct from one another, as communication and mobility within the Greek world were reduced.

In the early 19th century Greece became independent from Turkey, and the modern Greek state was established. The existence of a state immediately led to what is known as the "Language Question": which of the innumerable spoken and written varieties of Greek would become the official language of the new country? Some advocated a return to Attic, others a written form of the vernacular, and many some form of compromise. It is important to note that the Language Question is a modern phenomenon; different forms of Greek had existed since ancient times, but previously they had coexisted fairly happily, and there had been a general consensus that different forms of language were appropriate to different linguistic situations.

In the end, a standard spoken language established itself. The dialect of the Peloponnese, which was more prosperous and had closer ties with the influential expatriate Greek community than the rest of Greece, was closer to Koine than many of the dialects of other regions. In addition, it was the dialect of the first part of Greece to be liberated from Turkey. This dialect began to be used more and more widely in the new Greek state, even ousting the Old Athenian dialect from the new capital at Athens. In the 20th century, with the advent of mass media and increased mobility, the Peloponnesian dialect has almost entirely replaced the others, resulting in the virtually complete standardization of spoken Greek.

The written standard posed a different sort of problem. Initially, official preference was given to what later came to be called *katharevousa*, a form of Greek based on the spoken language but extensively "cleansed" of modern features. Virtually all prose in the new state, literary and non-literary, used this medium, and most poetry composed in Greece did as well, though some expatriate poetry (which later became extremely influential) did not. The problem with *katharevousa* in the 19th century, however, was that any standard deciding how much cleansing should take place was artificial and easily perceived as such; this resulted in an escalating competition of archaization, with writers trying to outdo each other in their revival of long-vanished linguistic features. Meanwhile some of the proponents of what came to be called demotic, a language closer to the spoken standard, went to the other extreme and produced neologisms that did not actually exist in the spoken language. At the same time, however, literary figures were increasingly won over to demotic, and by the end of the 19th century it had become the language of most creative literature.

The linguistic debate became increasingly polarized and vicious, leading to riots at the beginning of the 20th century when demotic translations of ancient works were produced. The issue was then politicized, with advocates of *katharevousa* being seen as politically conservative and supporters of demotic as left-wing. This politicization meant that in the 20th century there was some change in the language of school instruction virtually every time there was a change of government, as well as that the linguistic choices of individuals were constrained by politics. Eventually in 1974 a military government that had mandated *katharevousa* was ousted, and the enormous unpopularity of that government guaranteed that demotic would become and remain the official language. Today *katharevousa* is rarely used in Greece, although the fact that it was the official language until only a few decades ago means that most Greeks retain at least a passive knowledge of it. Demotic, however, has now absorbed many of the features of *katharevousa*, including some elements that had been lost for centuries from the spoken language, and is markedly distinct from the language advocated by early radicals. It is now known as Standard Modern Greek to acknowledge that fact.

Although the phonology of Standard Modern Greek is greatly different from that of the Classical language, the traditional spelling of most words has been retained. This can cause some confusion for learners; it means that the sound "ee" can be spelt E, I, EI, OI, or U, for example. On the other hand, the rough or smooth breathing indicating whether or not H used to be present on an initial vowel has been abolished, and it is no longer necessary to make the distinction (meaningful only with a pitch accent) among acute, grave, and circumflex accents. Modern texts of works in ancient Greek, however, do have both accents and breathings in addition to a fully ancient orthography.

ELEANOR DICKEY

See also Alphabet, Dialects, Grammar, Linear B, Syllabary

Further Reading

Allen, W. Sidney, *Vox Graeca: A Guide to the Pronunciation of Classical Greek*, 3rd edition, Cambridge and New York: Cambridge University Press, 1987

Browning, Robert, *Medieval and Modern Greek*, 2nd edition, Cambridge and New York: Cambridge University Press, 1983

Buck, Carl Darling, *Comparative Grammar of Greek and Latin*, Chicago: University of Chicago Press, 1933, reprinted 1959

Holton, David, Peter Mackridge and I. Philippaki-Warburton, *Greek: A Comprehensive Grammar of the Modern Language*, London and New York: Routledge, 1997

Horrocks, Geoffrey, *Greek: A History of the Language and Its Speakers*, London and New York: Longman, 1997

Lejeune, Michel, *Phonétique historique du mycénien et du grec ancien*, Paris: Klincksieck, 1972

Mackridge, Peter, *The Modern Greek Language: A Descriptive Analysis of Standard Modern Greek*, Oxford and New York: Oxford University Press, 1985

Palmer, Leonard R., *The Greek Language*, London: Faber, and Atlantic Highlands, New Jersey: Humanities Press, 1980, reprinted Norman: University of Oklahoma Press, 1996

Smyth, Herbert Weir, *A Greek Grammar for Schools and Colleges*, New York: American Book Co., 1920, revised by Gordon M. Messing as *Greek Grammar*, Cambridge, Massachusetts: Harvard University Press, 1963, reprinted 1972

Larissa

City in Thessaly

Larissa is located in the middle of the Thessalian plain on the right bank of the river Peneus. It is about 32 km from the sea, and bestrides the major north–south routes between Athens and Macedonia. Among the few remains of the early city are a late Hellenistic theatre excavated near the modern main square, a low hill to the south of the square marking the site of the ancient acropolis, and the remains of the Byzantine *phrourion* (fortress) to the east of the square.

The name Larissa is pre-Greek, and means "citadel". (Indeed, settlement on the site goes back to palaeolithic times, as is attested by archaeological remains.) According to Greek mythology, however, the city was founded by Acrisius, the father of Danae and the grandfather of Perseus, and was named after a nymph (whose likeness appears on coins of the 4th century BC). Unlike other places in the area, such as Phthia, Larissa is not named in the catalogue of ships in book 2 of the *Iliad*, or indeed in the rest of the *Iliad* or *Odyssey*, though some scholars have wanted to associate Larissa with the city Argyssa, which is mentioned in the catalogue of ships.

When Larissa first became important in Greek history, it was dominated by the powerful family of the Aleuadae. Their influence in Larissa, and, to a lesser extent, in Thessaly as whole, lasted from the early 6th to the end of the 4th century BC. The founder of the family was Aleuas, who claimed descent from Heracles. Although tradition more strongly associates Heracles with the rival (and related) Scopadae of nearby Crannon, the late 6th- and early 5th-century BC poet Simonides is cited by Theocritus (in *Idyll*, 16. 34–46) as praising Aleuas among other Thessalian grandees, such as the Scopadae and the Creondae, for his wealth: "Many slaves drew their monthly rations / in the palaces of Antiochos / and King Aleuas" (tr. Barriss Mills).

The Aleuadae were renowned as patrons of literature; writers of different generations and genres such as the poet Pindar, the Presocratic philosopher and rhetorician Gorgias, and the physician Hippocrates are all said to have spent time in Larissa as their guests. The fact that both Gorgias and Hippocrates are said to have died there may be a less than ringing endorsement of Aleuad hospitality.

Politically speaking, the legacy of the Aleuadae was more mixed. They were strongly associated with the political and military organization of Thessaly along federal lines. Thorax, the leader of the Aleuadae at the time, and his brothers sided with the Persians, during Xerxes' invasion of Greece in 480 BC, as did the neighbouring Macedonians. This realpolitik led to a loss of influence by the Aleuadae after the Greeks defeated Xerxes and drove his army out of Greece. Furthermore, by the end of the 5th century BC, a democratic revolt in Larissa and the rise of tyrants at Pherae had weakened the power of the Aleuadae. In the 4th century BC they made the fatal mistake of calling upon their fellow Heraclid, Philip II of Macedon, as an ally against the tyrant of Pherae. Philip annexed all of Thessaly and held it, despite an unsuccessful revolt of the Aleuadae in a belated attempt to undo their mistake. The Aleuadae faded from history thereafter.

Larissa was ceded to the Romans after the second battle of

Cynoscephalae in 197 BC, and became the capital of a new Thessalian confederation (which lasted until Diocletian's reorganization of the provinces at the start of the 4th century AD). Achilleius, the city's patron saint, was its first bishop, and attended the Council of Nicaea in 325. The city's fortunes were varied in late antiquity and under the Byzantine empire. It was attacked by such foes as the Ostrogoths, the Bulgarians (who carried off relics of St Achilleius in 985), the Normans, and Boniface of Montferrat of the Fourth Crusade. In the 8th and 9th centuries it served as the metropolis of Hellas, but in the 13th and 14th centuries it was ruled at different times by the Lombards, the despotate of Epirus, the Serbs, and the Byzantines, before passing under Turkish rule in 1393. During the Tourkokratia, which lasted for Larissa until 1881, it was eclipsed by Trikkala, from where the Turks ruled Thessaly, as had the Serbs before them, until 1870. A strong Turkish garrison kept Larissa from participating in the War of Independence, and some Turks continued to live there until the 1920s. The city suffered severe damage in 1941, when it was defended by a combined Graeco-British force against the invading Germans, and also suffered under German occupation. Today, it is the capital of the province of Thessaly, and the chief city of its nome. The Greek First Army has its headquarters in Larissa, and it is the seat of the Metropolitan Bishop of the Second Thessaly and Exarch of All Hellas.

ERIC KYLLO

See also Thessaly

Summary

Larissa, the chief city of Thessaly, lies on the right bank of the river Peneus in the middle of the Thessalian plain. In mythology founded by Acrisius and named after a nymph, the city was ruled by the Aleuadae in the Classical period. Having made an alliance with the invading Persians the city lost influence in the 5th century BC following their defeat. Under the Romans it was the capital of the Thessalian confederacy, but under the Turks it was eclipsed by Trikkala.

Further Reading

Abramea, Anna P., *He Byzantine Thessalia mechri tou 1204: symbole eis ten historiken geographian* [Byzantine Thessaly until 1204: A Contribution to Historical Geography], Athens, 1974

Helly, Bruno, *L'État thessalien: Aleuas le Roux, les théâtres et les "Tagoi"*, Lyons: Orient Méditerranéen, 1995

Stählin, Friedrich, *Das hellenische Thessalien: landeskundliche und geschichtliche Beschreibung Thessaliens in der Hellenischen und Romischen Zeit*, Stuttgart: Engelhorns, 1924, reprinted Amsterdam: Hakkert, 1967

Theocritus, *Idylls*, translated by Barriss Mills, West Lafayette, Indiana: Purdue University Studies, 1963

Westlake, H.D., *Thessaly in the Fourth Century BC*, London: Methuen, 1935, reprinted Groningen: Bouma, 1969

Laskaris family

Rulers of the empire of Nicaea (1204–1261)

The Laskaris family, or the Laskarids, ruled the Byzantine empire in exile in Nicaea (1204–61). Although the family name Laskaris is known from the middle of the 11th century, no prominent members of it are known to have entered the upper tier of the Byzantine aristocracy during the rule of the Komnenoi (1081–1185) and the Angeloi (1185–1204). The founder of the Nicaean empire was Theodore I Laskaris (1204–22). Having distinguished himself in battle in the Balkans, Laskaris had been awarded the title of despot and had married the daughter of the emperor Alexios III Angelos (1195–1203). After the Latin conquest of Constantinople on 12 April 1204 and the establishment of the Latin empire, he organized the resistance of the Greeks in western Asia Minor. One of Theodore Laskaris's five brothers, Constantine Laskaris, might have been the unknown Laskaris to whom an assembly in Hagia Sophia had offered the imperial crown the night before the Latin conquest, but afterwards he disappears from the sources as a holder of the imperial office.

In 1205 the people of Nicaea acclaimed Theodore I Laskaris as emperor of the *Romaioi* in the aftermath of the Latin defeat at the battle of Adrianople by the Bulgarians. In order to bolster his imperial claims, Theodore chose Michael IV Autoreianos (1208–14) as ecumenical patriarch in 1208. In the same year the newly appointed patriarch crowned and anointed Theodore I Laskaris as a divinely chosen emperor. Yet the legitimacy of the Laskarids was questioned by Alexios III Angelos, Theodore's father-in-law, who had found refuge at the Seljuk court in Konya. The Seljuks invaded Nicaea in the spring of 1211, but Theodore I Laskaris defeated them in a pitched battle in 1211 near Antioch-on-the-Menander, killed the Seljuk sultan Kay-Khusraw I (1195–97 and 1205–11), and captured Alexios III who was then imprisoned for the rest of his life in a monastery. The rulers of Epirus, the other important Greek successor state that had emerged after 1204, were also rivals of the Laskarids. The imperial claims of the Epirote ruler Theodore Komnenos Doukas (*c.*1215–30), crowned as emperor in Thessalonica in 1227, came to an end when the latter was captured by the Bulgarians in 1230.

The chief source of strength of the Laskarid dynasty was the conviction that the Nicaean empire was the Byzantine empire recreated in exile and that they were destined to restore Constantinople as the seat of rule. Theodore I Laskaris followed the Byzantine imperial model in the organization of court life and administration. In comparison with the Byzantine empire of the 11th and 12th centuries, however, the empire of Nicaea was better administered and a more vigorous state. The aristocracy enjoyed fewer privileges and tax immunities, while the small landholders could meet their obligations to the state fisc. The Laskarids protected local commerce and manufacturing, cloth production in particular. Only one commercial privilege, given to Venice in 1219, is known for the whole period of Laskarid rule. Administrative posts and other positions of power were systematically entrusted to people of low social origin and to members of the emperor's inner circle. The anti-aristocratic policy of the Laskarids culminated in the reign of the Theodore II Laskaris (1254–58). The powerful landed aristocracy felt excluded from power, abandoned the Laskarids, and supported the claims of Michael Palaiologos, first as regent (1258) of the young John IV Laskaris (1258–61), then as a coemperor (1259), and finally as a sole ruler (1261).

Imperial succession under the Laskarids was by and large hereditary. It is true, however, that they took pains to hand the imperial office to an able successor. Theodore I Laskaris passed over his son by a second marriage to an Armenian princess in favour of his son-in-law, John III Doukas Vatatzes (1221–54), most likely on the grounds that his son was still a child. John III was succeeded by his son Theodore II (1254–58), who in turn was followed by his son John IV (1258–61). The chief aim of the foreign policy of the Laskarids was the recovery of Constantinople, whether by diplomatic or military means. Theodore I suffered a big defeat by the Latins in October 1211. Subsequently, he attempted to forge a dynastic alliance by marrying a Latin princess as his third wife and by arranging a marriage for his daughter to the Latin emperor Robert de Courtenay (1221–28), but in the second case he met with ecclesiastical opposition. John III Vatatzes was more successful in his foreign policy. He drove the Latins out of northwestern Asia Minor in 1224, repudiated the claims of the rulers of Epirus, and recovered Thrace in 1235 and Macedonia in 1246 from the Bulgarians. By the end of his reign, John III Vatatzes had reduced the territory of the Latin empire solely to Constantinople and its environs.

The Laskarids of Nicaea were not only good statesmen, but also generous patrons of arts and letters. Nicaea became known in this period as "the new Athens" and a centre of Hellenic education. The court in Nicaea and Nymphaion included such scholars as the polymath Nikephoros Blemmydes (1197–1272) and the emperor Theodore II Laskaris. Theodore II Laskaris saw himself as a Platonic philosopher-king, and wrote numerous theological and rhetorical works as well as a political treatise based on Isocrates and Aristotle. A new sense of Hellenic identity developed in Nicaea at the expense of the traditional Roman one. Still, this shift was far from complete, and was suppressed to a large extent by the recovery of Constantinople in 1261 and the revival of old ideological constructs.

The Greek population of Asia Minor cherished the memory of the Laskarids after the demise of their dynasty. After Michael VIII Palaiologos usurped the throne in 1261, the people of Nicaea rebelled in support of the child emperor John IV Laskaris who was to spend the rest of his life imprisoned in a castle in Dakibyze on the Sea of Marmara. The patriarch Arsenios (1254–60 and 1261–65) excommunicated Michael VIII for blinding John IV Laskaris, but paid for this daring behaviour with his deposition. His followers, the Arsenites, were not reconciled with the Palaiologan dynasty until 1310. Supporters of the Laskarids in Asia Minor backed the rebellion of the general Alexios Philanthropenos during the reign of Andronikos II (1282–1328) in 1295. A conspirator against Andronikos II in 1305–06 sought popular support by pretending to be the legitimate emperor John IV Laskaris. In a similar way to the posthumous fame of John III Vatatzes, John IV was honoured as a saint in the 14th century. While the cult of John III Vatatzes was centred in the region of Magnesia in Asia Minor, however, the relics of the last Laskarid ruler were venerated in the monastery of St Demetrios in Constantinople itself.

DIMITER G. ANGELOV

See also Nicaea, Political History 1204–1261

Further Reading

Andreeva, M.A., *Ocherki po kul'ture vizantijskogo dvora v XIII veke*, Prague, 1927

Angold, Michael, *A Byzantine Government in Exile: Government and Society under the Laskarids of Nicaea, 1204–1261*, London: Oxford University Press, 1975

Gardner, Alice, *The Lascarids of Nicaea: The Story of an Empire in Exile*, London: Methuen, 1912

Trapp, E., "Downfall and Survival of the Laskaris Family", *Macedonian Studies*, 1/2 (1983): pp. 45–49

Latin Empire 1204–1261

The Latin empire had its formal beginning with the election of Baldwin of Flanders as the first Latin emperor on 9 May 1204 and his subsequent coronation on 16 May, just over one month after the capture of Constantinople by the army of the Fourth Crusade on 12 April. Its end as a political and military entity came 57 years later on 25 July 1261, when Baldwin II fled the city in the face of the entry of a Greek force from Nicaea led by Alexios Strategopoulos in the name of Michael VIII Palaiologos. For the period of its existence, the empire had been governed by a succession of five emperors: Henry (1206–16); Peter de Courtenay (1217); Robert (1221–28); John de Brienne (1229–37); and Baldwin II (1237–73). Paradoxically, the line of titular Latin emperors, which came to an end only in 1382 with the death of Jacques des Baux, may be said to have exerted far more political influence than their predecessors who actually ruled in Constantinople. It was an indicator that the Latin empire depended on material support and patronage from the Latin west.

Judgements on the empire and its rulers have been harsh: a barren and bankrupt experiment that in no way matched the great days of Byzantium. Certainly the new empire had tremendous military and financial problems which it was never to solve; yet it did mark a watershed in the place of Constantinople and its rulers in East–West relations. Conceived from the start as a territorial empire, the Latin empire never controlled very much land outside Constantinople itself, but it did incorporate that city very much into Western Christendom and to some extent established a Western ownership of the city which was to continue after the expulsion of the last Latin emperor by the forces of Michael VIII Palaiologos in 1261. Its brief existence was also to mark a substantive change in Western perceptions of subsequent Byzantine emperors and brought the latter much more into a reactive relationship with the West—initially in fending off Western attempts to recapture the city, and to unite the Roman and Orthodox Churches and latterly to work with the West in resisting Ottoman expansion. Constantinople had not endured to the Second Coming as many had foretold, and after 1261 the economic, political, and even cultural organization of the West was outstripping that of Byzantium.

The Latin emperors used Byzantine ceremonial and titles, but their administration and council were based on Western lines. The new Latin emperorship, no matter what Byzantine traditions it might seek to echo to reconcile its Greek subjects, was never fitted by either the pope or other Western rulers into the imperial model worked out in the West since AD 800.

Baldwin I was never regarded as one of the universal authorities in the medieval world who could create kingdoms and principalities; yet in the world of the Aegean he was to do just that with regard to lands in western Turkey, Thessalonica, and Achaea. Unlike his Byzantine predecessors he had his imperial title confirmed by pope Innocent III. This was necessary for papal support; but it also signalled that the new empire marked the union of the Greek and Latin communions, admittedly more in desire than in fact. Baldwin's title was the same as that used by his Byzantine predecessors. In its Latin version it ran *Balduinus, Dei Gratia Fidelissimus in Christo Imperator, a Deo Coronatus, Romanie Moderator et Semper Augustus*. Baldwin wore Byzantine imperial regalia and followed Byzantine imperial protocols, possibly to some effect among his Greek subjects; but despite all this the Latin emperors never gained imperial recognition in the West. Baldwin and his successors were always deferential to the pope, whose support they needed, and in no way did they exhibit any caesaropapal behaviour. Papal support was worth having. Pope Honorius III coined the epithet *Nova Francia* in 1224 to bolster Western and particularly French support for the new Crusader states in the Aegean. In times of military setback the pope would preach crusades to bolster the Latin empire as in 1223, 1262, and 1264, but these calls lacked appeal to would-be Western crusaders. The negative side of all this was the presence of a succession of papal legates in Constantinople which prevented the Latin emperors from working out any religious modus vivendi with their Greek subjects similar to that agreed by the Western rulers of Achaea.

From the start the emperors were advised by a council of their own choosing made up of their household officials and men who had their trust. This had led to difficulties with those excluded from these councils, particularly the Venetian interest in the city. In October 1205, on taking over the regency after the capture of his brother Baldwin I by the Bulgarians, the future emperor Henry of Hainault (1206–16) agreed to be advised by an "official" council made up of the Venetian *podestà*, the *podestà*'s council, and, somewhat vaguely, the principal Frankish vassals of the empire. This might answer an emergency situation when it was unclear whether Baldwin was alive or dead, but no ruler could be bound in this way for long. In practice two councils, the personal and the official, worked in parallel and sometimes in opposition. The Latin emperors seemed keen to use Greek advisers in their inner council, which provoked complaints to Western rulers from those in Constantinople who felt that this was inappropriate. This in turn led to interference from Western backers like the pope and the French royal family. The circumstances of the creation of the Latin empire by the contracting parties to the Fourth Crusade also meant that its sacramental basis was weakened and led to an attempt to define and thus limit imperial powers. This conformed with contemporary western-European constitutional developments and it is certainly not improbable that the barons of the Fourth Crusade had ideas of their own about the limitation of monarchical power.

The pact of March 1204, which had been primarily concerned with unity in the Crusader ranks at a time of crisis, had made provision for the election of an emperor and a Latin patriarch, for the division of spoils, and the carving out of fiefs. After the conquest it received surprising significance in the Latin empire. Each new emperor confirmed the pact on his accession and as such it acquired the status of law. It has been called the constitution of the Latin empire, yet it had nothing to contribute to the organization of the Latin state, but was concerned with protecting sectional interests and limiting the executive functions in all but name.

The partition of the former Byzantine empire which followed in October 1204 created spheres of influence rather than defining territorial grants. This was inevitable in that all lands of the former Byzantine empire had to be conquered and held by would-be Western rulers. The emperor received one quarter of the notionally available land; the remainder was divided between the other Crusaders, including the Venetians. The emperor's sphere was limited to parts of Constantinople, to eastern Thrace, and to Bithynia and the Troad in Asia Minor, an area roughly conceived as west of a line from Nicomedia to Philadelphia. Certainly in these areas the first Latin emperors sought to secure support by generous land grants and the creation of dukedoms. In all three areas the new empire confronted formidable enemies that did not permit the establishment of these lordships. Not only did the empire fail to expand, but after 1205, with a brief interlude between 1208 and 1211, it was on the defensive on all its borders.

The emperor was the suzerain of the Frankish states of the Aegean, yet this suzerainty had to be enforced and exercised to be effective. The defensive stance of the empire itself meant that only on occasion could this in fact be done. The Western conquest of Greece was carried out under the direction of Boniface of Thessalonica (d. 1207), a rival, rather than by Baldwin or Henry. The Latin emperors were clearly aware of this problem and, as soon as circumstances permitted, in March–May 1209 Henry visited central Greece and imposed his authority over the Western rulers there; but soon the emperors became preoccupied with defending their own frontiers against the Greeks of Nicaea and Epirus and against the Bulgarians. Conflict on three fronts left little time for exercising overlordship over Greek lands, establishing settled revenue streams, or reconciling Greeks to Latin rule.

In 1204 the Crusaders had rudely rejected the overtures of Kalojan and his Vlacho-Bulgar confederacy. In April 1205 he routed a Latin army near Adrianople, capturing the emperor Baldwin and killing some leading barons. In the next two years Thrace was ravaged and Kalojan began a campaign of extermination designed to win over Greek supporters of the Latin regime. The loyalty of the Greeks was critical to the Latin position, which now quickly deteriorated to the north and west of Constantinople. In April 1205 over 7000 Latins lost confidence in the future of the new empire and returned home. The Latin position in Thrace was saved only by the death of Kalojan in October 1207. The Latins had failed to capitalize on the advantage they had gained with the capture of Constantinople. They had not gained the dominant position in the Aegean and instead had become merely an additional element in the regional mosaic made up of the Byzantine successor states in Nicaea, Epirus, and Trebizond, and the Bulgarian power bloc to the north. None of these elements was powerful enough on its own to knock out the others. The Crusaders were quickly to develop a policy of negotiating to preserve their position. The odds were tipped against them.

Attrition and the backflow of Western settlers would eventually favour natives over incomers.

Immigration and reinforcements from the west were fitful and disappointing. Direct appeals for reinforcements were made in 1204, 1205, 1206, and 1212. A crusade, mounted mainly from northern Italy in 1223 to relieve Thessalonica, was poorly coordinated and broke up. Papal taxation of the clergy in support of the empire roused resentment in the west. The 30th request in 1239 went uncollected, a subsidy proposed in 1245 was still being collected in the 1260s, and another subsidy proposed by pope Urban IV in 1262 to restore the emperor Baldwin II seems never to have been collected.

The Latin empire was both a symptom and a casualty of changing western-European interests and perceptions. Founded as a staging point for the liberation of the Holy Land, it became just one of a number of worthy options as the variety of crusading experience widened in the 13th century. The anonymous annalist of the abbey of Santa Justina at Padua penned the epitaph of the empire in 1262 as but "a shadow of a great name". However, in a purely Aegean context, it did shield the developing states of Frankish Greece from the principal aggressors of the region in the early 13th century and allowed them some space to develop structures which enabled them to survive until the 15th century.

PETER LOCK

See also Political History 1204–1261

Summary

Dating from 1204 to 1261, the Latin empire began with the capture of Constantinople by the Fourth Crusade. Dependent for material support and patronage from the Latin west, it incorporated the city of Constantinople into western Christendom. It included parts of the city, eastern Thrace, Bithynia, and the Troad. Never vigorous, the empire eventually succumbed to Western apathy and Eastern aggression.

Further Reading

Carile, Antonio, *Per una storia dell'imperio latino di Constantinopoli*, Bologna: Patron, 1972, 2nd edition, 1978

Lock, Peter, *The Franks in the Aegean, 1204–1500*, London and New York: Longman, 1995

Longnon, Jean, *L'Empire latin de Constantinople et le principauté de Morée*, Paris: Payot, 1949

Nicol, Donald M., "The Fourth Crusade and the Greek and Latin Empires, 1204–1261" in *The Byzantine Empire*, edited by J.M. Hussey, Cambridge: Cambridge University Press, 1966 (*The Cambridge Medieval History*, vol. 4, part 1, 2nd edition)

Wolff, R., "The Latin Empire of Constantinople" in *The History of the Crusades*, edited by Kenneth M. Setton, 2nd edition, vol. 2, Madison: University of Wisconsin Press, 1969

Laurium

District in Attica

The district of Laurium played a pivotal role in the history of ancient Athens. It covered an area of about 200 square km, extending from Anaphlystus south to Sunium and then north to Thoricus. Hilly with only a few plains and subject to scarce

Laurium: washery used in processing lead ore

rainfall, Laurium's importance in antiquity lay in its argentiferous lead, mined by slaves for centuries. Mining may have occurred as early as the Middle Bronze Age (at least at the site of Thoricus), when open-cast mining was used to extract silver and lead. As excavations have shown, mining in Laurium continued down through the Archaic period. Shafts or adits were sunk to reach the highly argentiferous ore deep under the surface; while some shafts were simple passages cut into the ground, other shafts reached a depth of over 130 m and were fitted with wooden ladders, huge galleries, and ventilation shafts. The extracted ore was sent to workshops (*ergasteria*), which included grinders, washeries, cisterns, furnaces, and cupellation work-areas. Athens considered the mines state property, but leased them at annual fixed rates (typically 4 per cent) to private individuals or companies (*poletai*), which employed slaves and condemned criminals. (Many of these lease arrangements have been published; see the bibliography below.) The mines proved especially important in the 5th century BC. In 483 a particularly rich vein was struck at Maronea, immediately yielding 100 talents of silver. With the Persians advancing on Greece, the Athenians, on the advice of Themistocles, elected to use the silver to finance an additional 100 triremes; the augmented Athenian fleet defeated the

Persian navy at the decisive battle of Salamis in 480, preventing a barbarian conquest of Greece. The mines continued to produce large amounts of silver during the century as Athens built its maritime empire. In the later stages of the Peloponnesian War, production ceased when the Spartan army, on the advice of the renegade Athenian general Alcibiades, occupied the nearby mountain pass of Deceleia, thereby blocking the land route from Euboea to Athens. In 413 over 20,000 slaves at Laurium reportedly defected to the Spartans. The mines were reopened after Athens had established in 377 the Second Athenian Confederacy; extensive mining was conducted for the rest of the 4th century. However, mining ceased in the 3rd century (the last dated lease is from 306 BC) due to a precipitous decline in the price of silver caused by the flooding of Macedonian gold coinage. Limited and sporadic mining occurred down to the end of the 2nd century, but slave uprisings in the 130s and 100s helped bring about the closing of deep mining. During the Roman empire slag heaps on the surface were resmelted, but otherwise the area was abandoned. It is estimated that altogether 2,000,000 tons of ore were smelted, with a yield of 1200 tons of silver and 400,000 tons of lead. The mining and processing of cadmium, magnesium, and lead continues in the area to the present day.

The administrative and economic centre of ancient Laurium was the city of Thoricus, located in the very northeast corner of the district. The ancient site is spread over on the side and top of the mountain Velatouri; its harbour, a refuge fortress built during the Peloponnesian War on the St Nikolaos peninsula, also served as a naval base. The lower slopes of the mountain were ringed by a fortification wall. Inside the wall are remains of numerous houses, workshops, ore washeries, an extensive industrial quarter, three sanctuaries, and a theatre. The theatre, with a unique design and shape, was first built in the 6th century BC and later expanded in the mid-4th to a seating capacity of 5000–6000; a temple of Dionysus formed part of the west entrance. Nearby necropolises have yielded nearly 200 tombs from the Protogeometric to the Hellenistic periods; some of the Geometric houses found among the graves show signs of silver working. Higher up, on the Velatouri, are prehistoric remains. Three Mycenaean tholoi or beehive tombs and a Mycenaean chamber tomb have been excavated; signs of cult worship in the Archaic period are evident. Trial trenches have demonstrated that the acropolis was inhabited as early as the beginning of the Early Bronze Age (c.2900 BC) down through the Geometric period, when houses were built over the remains of prehistoric dwellings. The site was abandoned during the early Roman empire. Neighbouring silver-mining sites in the Agrileza district, Pountazeze Bay, Mekala Perka, and Gaïdhouromandra Bay have recently been uncovered.

STEVEN M. OBERHELMAN

See also Silver and Lead

Summary

A district of southern Attica, Laurium was of particular importance for its silver and lead mines. Mining may have started as early as the Middle Bronze Age, but it became especially significant in the 5th century BC. The discovery of a very rich vein in 483 enabled the Athenians to build a fleet of 100 extra triremes with which they defeated the Persians at Salamis. Mining on a large scale ceased in the 3rd century BC. Mining of other metals continues today.

Further Reading

Boeckh, Augustus, *The Public Economy of Athens*, 4 vols, London: John Murray, 1828, vol. 2, pp. 415–96 (discusses the silver mines of Laurium)

Conophagos, Constantin E., *Le Laurium antique et la technique grecque de la production de l'argent*, Athens: Ekdotike Hellados, 1980

Crosby, M., "The Leases of the Laureion Mines", *Hesperia*, 19 (1950): pp. 189–312

Cunningham, C.J.R., "The Silver of Laurion", *Greece and Rome*, 14 (1967): pp. 145–56

Healy, John F., *Mining and Metallurgy in the Greek and Roman World*, London: Thames and Hudson, 1978

Hopper, R.J., "The Attic Silver Mines in the Fourth Century BC", *Annual of the British School of Athens*, 48 (1953): pp. 200–54

Hopper, R.J., "The Laurion Mines: A Reconsideration", *Annual of the British School of Athens*, 63 (1968): pp. 293–326

Hopper, R.J., *Trade and Industry in Classical Greece*, London: Thames and Hudson, 1979

Jones, J.E., "The Laurion Silver Mines: A Review of Recent Researches and Results", *Greece and Rome*, 29 (1982): pp. 169–83

Langdon, M.K., "Poletai Records" in *Inscriptions: The Athenian Agora*, vol. 19, edited by Gerald V. Lalonde, Princeton, New Jersey: American School of Classical Studies in Athens, 1991

Mussche, H.F. *et al.* (editors), *Thorikos*, 9 vols, Brussels: Comité des Fouilles Belges en Grèce, 1968–82

Mussche, H.F., *Thorikos: A Guide to the Excavations*, Brussels: Comité des Fouilles Belges en Grèce, 1974

Mussche, H., Paule Spitaels and F. Goemaere-De Poerck, *Thorikos and the Laurion in Archaic and Classical Times*, Ghent: Belgian Archaeological Mission in Greece, 1975

Lausanne, Treaty of 1923

The Treaty of Lausanne, an international agreement signed by, among others, Britain, France, Greece, and Turkey, in July 1923, was a remarkable Turkish achievement and a heavy blow for Greece and its visions of a greater Greece. Alone among the countries defeated in World War I, Turkey was able to reject, by force of arms, the terms imposed on it by the victorious allies at the conclusion of the war. The treaty signed at Lausanne rendered null and void the Treaty of Sèvres (1920), which had carved up the Ottoman empire and distributed the various pieces to the victors, and gave to Turkey the territorial integrity and full independence that the Ottomans had lost as a result of their defeat in 1918. For the Greeks, the most consequential sections of the treaty were those that settled the territorial and population issues remaining between the two countries as a result of war and the upending of international agreements. Greece had formally to surrender eastern Thrace, several Aegean islands, and the city of Smyrna and its hinterland in western Anatolia. All of these territories had been awarded to it in the Treaty of Sèvres of 1920. In addition, the long and vibrant history of Hellenism in Asia Minor was brought to a close. All "Turkish nationals of the Greek Orthodox religion established in Turkish territory" (with the exception of those living in Istanbul) were to be forcibly sent to Greece, in exchange for "Greek nationals of the Muslim religion established in Greek territory" (with the exception of the Muslims of Thrace), who had to depart for Turkey. It is estimated that about one and half million Greek Orthodox and half a million Muslims were affected by this population exchange.

The reason that the settlement so favoured Turkey was simple: between 1920 and 1923 the Turkish nationalists had realized an amazing string of military victories. Accustomed to dealing with an obsequious Ottoman sultan, the Allies were astonished to learn, in February 1920, that an army of 20,000 Turkish troops operating deep inside Anatolia under the command of Mustafa Kemal (later Atatürk) had defeated a small French contingent at Marash in southern Anatolia. But this was just the beginning. By an odd coincidence, the very month, May 1919, that Mustafa Kemal began his journey into Anatolia, the Greek government received permission from the Allied powers to land Greek troops in Smyrna on the coast of western Anatolia. The understanding was that the Greek government would administer Smyrna and its hinterland, with a Greek population of more than one million, for five years. At that point a plebiscite on union with Greece would be held. Finally, it seemed, the Greeks were going to be able to build the Greece of "Two Continents and Five Seas" that they had dreamed of for so long. Greek troops quickly landed and occupied not only the territories assigned to them, but began to advance into the interior of Anatolia as well. Thus it was only a matter of time before they would run into Kemal's army. Kemal and his forces were determined to reverse the dismemberment of Anatolia that the Allies (including Greece), in collusion with the Ottoman sultan, had begun to implement. It was at the Sakarya river, deep inside Anatolia, that Kemal, in August 1921, managed to stop the Greek advance, although he had to sustain severe casualties in order to do so. The Greek army, stranded in the interior of Anatolia and deserted by its allies, began to retreat. The final blow came one year later, when Kemal launched his final offensive and drove the remaining soldiers, along with civilian refugees, into Smyrna and, famously, even into the sea itself.

The expulsion of the Greek community of Asia Minor was a singular event in modern Greek history and came to be known as the Great Catastrophe. The Treaty of Lausanne was as bitterly resented in Greece as the Treaty of Sèvres had been in Turkey. It brought to an end the pursuit of the Great Idea, which had dominated Greek politics since the middle of the 19th century. The Great Idea envisioned the expansion of the Greek state to include all the Greek communities (however defined) of the Balkans and the Near East. Now that dream had to be abandoned and Greece had to come to terms with the disaster that had befallen it.

The population exchange enforced by Convention VI of the Treaty of Lausanne continued and actually reinforced the demographic upheaval that had been ongoing in the Balkans and the Near East since 1912. As war engulfed the region, first the Balkan Wars, then World War I, then the Graeco-Turkish War, and the War of Turkish Independence, many people found themselves on the wrong side of the border and began to flee. In 1912, for example, 100,000 Balkan Muslims fled before the successful armies of the Balkan League. The result of this massive flight over the course of a decade was a radical restructuring of the area's population in the direction of what was considered to be greater ethnic homogeneity. Against the backdrop of such extreme violence, the European diplomats who worked out the idea of a formal population exchange felt that it was the best way to ensure stability in Europe. Others, however, were uneasy with this method of dealing with the problem of minorities. A Red Cross officer writing at the time pointed out that neither the Greeks of Asia Minor nor the Muslims of Macedonia had any desire to leave their homeland. Greek refugees marched by the thousand in Athens, carrying black banners of mourning at the Lausanne decision that they must never return to their homes. Despite the general feeling of a catastrophe, the Greek government was able to derive at least one significant benefit from the massive influx of refugees. By settling large numbers in Greek Macedonia, they effectively Hellenized an area where non-Greek populations had historically been strong.

MOLLY GREENE

See also Asia Minor Campaign, Great Idea, Refugees

Further Reading

Alexandres, Alexis, *The Greek Minority of Istanbul and Greek–Turkish Relations, 1918–1974*, Athens: Center for Asia Minor Studies, 1983

Fromkin, David, *A Peace to End All Peace: Creating the Modern Middle East, 1914–1922*, New York: Holt, and London: Deutsch, 1990

Housepian, Marjorie, *Smyrna 1922: The Destruction of a City*, Kent, Ohio: Kent State University Press, 1988

Llewellyn Smith, Michael, *Ionian Vision: Greece in Asia Minor, 1919–1922*, London: Allen Lane, and New York: St Martin's Press, 1973, reprinted with a new introduction, London: Hurst, and Ann Arbor: University of Michigan Press, 1998

Pentzopoulos, Dimitri, *The Balkan Exchange of Minorities and Its Impact upon Greece*, Paris: Mouton, 1962

Psomiades, Harry J., *The Eastern Question: The Last Phase: A Study in Greek–Turkish Diplomacy*, Thessalonica: Institute for Balkan Studies, 1968

Law

Evidence for the legal history of Greece is patchy. For some periods there are only the legislative texts, for others only contracts or court decisions. In these cases, the extent of the gap between the law and its application remains unknown. This article will attempt to provide a brief overview of the available sources of law in different historical periods. For reasons of convenience the discussion is divided into four chronological sections: (1) antiquity (late-7th century BC to AD 212), (2) the Romano-Byzantine period (AD 212–1453), (3) the Tourkokratia (1453–1821), (4) modern Greece (1821–present).

Antiquity

The sources of law in ancient Greece include inscriptions preserving laws and decrees of the assemblies of the city states, private transactions (sales, manumissions, wills, leases, loans), interstate agreements, lawcourt speeches pertaining to political and legal disputes in 4th-century BC Athens, philosophical and sociological treatises, and, to a lesser degree, literature (comedy and drama). A particular case in the ancient Greek world is Egypt under the Ptolemies. The legal system, developed over almost ten centuries, is preserved in numerous papyri written in Greek, including all kinds of documents from receipts for deliveries and censuses to marriage and divorce agreements, inheritance settlements, loans, etc.

The several hundred tablets of Linear B, the earliest deciphered form of writing in Greece, from 13th-century BC Pylos, Knossos, and Thebes reveal very little, if anything at all, about the legal aspect of Mycenaean society. They relate mainly to the administrative structure of these kingdoms and the status of the land.

The earliest information on law concerns procedural affairs or what is sometimes called dispute settlement. In the 8th-century society of the Homeric poems and especially in the famous scene on Achilles' shield (*Iliad*, 18. 497–508), the disputants over the payment for homicide present their case to the assembled elders. Hesiod, the next earliest source, refers to gift-devouring kings when it comes to adjudicating disputes. In the late 7th century BC there was a wave of legislators, especially in the colonies of southern Italy (Zaleucus Epizephyrii at Locri, Charondas at Catana) and only subsequently in Athens (Draco), Sparta (Lycurgus), and Mytilene (Pittacus). The content of their legislation is preserved in a piecemeal way by later authors, who underline the moral and pedagogical aspect of their legislation (laws about revenge, about amending laws, banning the sale of land, regulating family life, etc). The first firmly attested laws come from late-7th-century Crete. They mainly concern procedural matters, such as the ban on magistrates serving a second term in office in the small town of Driros (*M-L*, 2). However, the most famous example of legislation from Crete is the early-5th-century inscription known as the "law-code of Gortyn" (*IC*, 4. 72). The Gortyn laws regulated property affairs between spouses in case of divorce or death, inheritance, adoption, sexual offences, personal status, and procedural matters associated with them. Recent research suggests that these laws did not form part of a codification programme but were the outcome of successive stages of codification and amendment.

The best-known legal system of the ancient Greek world is that of Athens. The first major legislative effort was made by Solon in 594 BC. It comprised constitutional reforms (establishment of a council), the abolition of debts, and innovations in the inheritance laws. Further reforms in the constitutional framework were introduced by Cleisthenes in 509 BC (new administrative units and a reformed council) and in 462 BC by Ephialtes (reduction of the political powers of Areopagus). The text of the Draconian law on homicide survives from the late 5th century. The main characteristics of law in Athens in the 5th and 4th centuries BC were: (1) law thought of as a piece of evidence, (2) the lack of autonomy of the legal sphere, (3) the interaction of politics and law in the domain of public law, (4) the multiplicity of procedures available to the prosecutor, (5) popular courts appointed by lot, (6) lack of definitions of offences, and (7) absence of a professional class of jurists and lawyers.

For the remaining city states and kingdoms, with the exception of the literary (and for some questionable) tradition on the Lycurgan legislation in Sparta, there are only fragmentary and isolated pieces of evidence about their legal systems. These are mainly decrees of the assembly honouring individuals, registers of acts of manumission, of leases, sales of land or other transactions, which do not provide a coherent picture of legal life.

The rise of the kingdom of Macedonia followed by the foundation of numerous Greek colonies in the Middle East, Egypt and Anatolia resulted in the interaction of the laws of the city states among themselves and with the laws of the colonized lands. Egypt is the best-documented example of this interaction between the laws of the Greek settlers, soldiers, and officials and the local population. In Greece proper the Macedonian domination did not affect the legal life of the cities to the point of obliterating their autonomy. Certainly, the kings of Macedonia and their successors granted conquered land and privileges to their friends and friendly cities. But they did not interfere directly with the legal institutions. In the same way, the Roman conquest of Macedonia in 168 BC and of the remaining Greek cities in 146 BC did not mean the abolition of their legal autonomy. Most cities kept their legal institutions and rules except in the area of public law, which had to accommodate Roman wishes. The Romans applied Roman law only to Roman citizens while the affairs of the conquered people and the allies were regulated by the *jus gentium*. That period ended with the grant of Roman citizenship by Caracalla in AD 212 to every free inhabitant of the empire. From that moment, Roman law superseded the laws of the remaining city states. The extent to which local laws and customs disappeared or influenced the application of the rules of Roman law is still debated.

The Romano-Byzantine period

The sources of law in Greece in the Romano-Byzantine period are preserved in the major codifying efforts of Byzantine emperors, such as Theodosius I (379–95), Justinian I (527–65), Leo III (717–41), Leo VI the Wise (886–912), their compilations, and commentaries as well as monographs and the sporadic collections of court decisions. From the 11th century onwards, the archives of the monastic communities of Mount Athos, pertaining to the landed property of the monasteries in Macedonia, provide interesting insights into the sociolegal conditions of the era.

The history of law in Greece in this period joins the development of Roman law. In the late 3rd century AD the need for a collection of the imperial constitutions had become evident. Three attempts were made: *Codex Gregorianus* (AD 291) and *Codex Hermogenianus* (AD 295) were probably private collections containing imperial constitutions from Hadrian to Diocletian, while the *Codex Theodosianus* (AD 438) included constitutions from the reign of Constantine the Great onwards. But the compilation by Justinian known as *Corpus Juris Civilis* (AD 533/4) was more ambitious. It included not only opinions of the most famous Roman jurists (*Digest*), but provisions from previous codes and those approved in the meantime (*Codex*), an introductory course for students of law (*Institutiones*), and laws issued by the emperor (*Novellae*). No commentaries were allowed but only the teaching of law. However, after the death of Justinian two major commentaries on the legislation appeared in the late 6th century AD by Theodoros Hermopolitis and Athanasios Emesinos. In parallel there were several works addressing the needs of the practitioners of law – *Ropai* (About Deadlines), *Peri Bathmon Syggeneias* (About Kinship), *Peri Enantiophaneion* (About Contradictions). The structure of the administration of justice was reformed by Justinian. Until his reign justice was part of the remit of civic and military officials. Justinian appointed 13 judges to resolve disputes in Constantinople, while appeals were addressed to the emperor's *consilium*. Another aspect was the extension of the *episcopalis audentia*, that is the jurisdiction of bishops to resolve private disputes when the litigants so wished, recognized by Constantine. From this early Byzantine period also date the first collections of ecclesiastical rules, later known with the inclusion of civil rules as *nomokanones*.

In AD 741 the Isaurian emperors Leo III and Constantine V introduced the *Ekloge* (Ecloga), an epitomization of *Corpus Juris Civilis* in a more accessible structure and language. Major novelties were introduced in marriage (recognition of a civil and religious wedding), inheritance, and above all in penal law (limiting the application of the death penalty and the discretion of the judge in imposing penalties). Among other laws issued were the *Georgikos Nomos* (mainly concerning property law) in the late 7th or early 8th century, the *Nomos Rodion Nautikos* (codification of maritime custom of the eastern Mediterranean) in the 7th or 8th century, and the *Stratiotikos Nomos* (pertaining to military penal law) between the late-6th and mid-8th centuries.

The emperors of the Macedonian dynasty (867–1081) reintroduced the legislation of Justinian with *Procheiros Nomos* (879) and *Eisagogi ton Nomon* (c.885) in which the dual power of emperor and patriarch in the Byzantine state was recognized as ultimate. Then, in about 900, Leo VI the Wise produced a compilation of the *Digest* in 60 books, called the *Basilika*. The *Eparchike Biblos* (c.911 or 963) addressed to the city prefect responsible for the supervision of guilds, contained rules concerning their organization and duties. A significant number of compilations and commentaries were subsequently drawn up, among them the *Epitome ton Nomon* (c.913), *Epitome ad Prochiron Mutata*, *Ecloga Privata Aucta* (a collection from the 9th century including rules from the Isaurian *Ekloge*), *Ecloga ad Prochiron Mutata*, *Eisagoge Aucta* (a collection of the 10th or 11th century from the legislation of the Macedonian dynasty), *Synopsis Basilicorum Maior* (a collection of the main provisions of *Basilika* of the mid-10th century), *Tipoukeitos* (an index to *Basilika* by judge Patzes at the end of the 11th century), and the *Ecloga Basilicorum Librorum I–X* (a selection with comments from the first 10 books of *Basilika* composed in the 12th century). In the following centuries three major compilations appeared: the *Synopsis Minor* of *Basilika* in the end of 13th century, the *Prochiron Auctum* (c.1300) including regulations from several compilatory works and codes, and the *Hexabiblos* by K. Armenopoulos in 1345, which was a compilation from the *Procheiros Nomos* and other earlier collections in six books, that tried to answer the problems of applying the law. Two teaching handbooks of law appeared, *Synopsis ton Nomon* (11th century) by Michael Psellos, politician and philologist, and *Ponima Nomikon* (c.1073) a synopsis of *Basilika* by Michael Attaleiatis.

There were also three major collections of judicial decisions: *Peira, Igoun Didaskalia ek ton Praxeon tou Megalou Kyrou Eustathiou tou Romaiou*, (Know-How, or Teachings from the Acts of the Great Cyrus Eustathios the Roman, c.1040–1050), and at the end of the 12th century the decisions of bishops Dimitrios Chomatianos and Ioannis Apokaukos on ecclesiastical and civil law matters. Several monographs were published: among them the most important were *Peri Hypobolou, Hypomnema peri Duo Exadelphon Labonton Duo Exadelphas* (Note on the Marriage of Cousins) by Eustathios Romaios, *Peri Diaireseos Phonon kai ton Prospheugonton ti tou Theou Megali Ekklisia* (On the Distinction of Terms and those who Take Refuge in the Great Church of Christ) by Konstantinos Garidas (11th century).

In the 12th century (and probably earlier), the judicial system was divided into courts of higher status with jurisdiction and courts of lower status without jurisdiction. The former could delegate cases to the latter, decide on criminal cases, and authorize certain actions by the litigants. As a rule, the prosecutor/plaintiff had to go to the court of the defendant's place of residence; there was exceptional jurisdiction for the clergy, military, senators, and guild members as well as for fiscal matters.

A new *Nomokanon* appeared c.883 including resolutions of synods convened in the meantime. Major works on ecclesiastical law were written by Balsamon and Zonaras, who prepared commentaries on the *Nomokanon*. An encyclopedia of ecclesiastical law with some provisions of civil law, known as the *Syntagma kata Stoicheion* (Elements of the Law) by Matthaios Blastaris, appeared in 1335.

In the 12th and 13th centuries there was a marked decline in legal studies and an increasing involvement of clerics in dispensing justice and theorizing about it. One reason for this may lie in the gradual weakening of the central authority and the Latin conquest of Constantinople in 1204, which led to the fragmentation of political and judicial authority. Crete remained under the influence of Venetian law until 1669; the Ionian islands until 1797. The laws of the Venetian republic and the regulations issued by the governor were applied in the areas where the Venetians were dominant while there is some evidence for the application of customary law. A collection of laws used in the Latin kingdoms of the east (mainly of mainland Greece), known as the *Assizes of Romania*, survives from the early 14th century.

The Tourkokratia

The Ottoman conquest of mainland Greece, which lasted for four and in some areas for five centuries, passed the responsibility for administering justice among Christians to the Orthodox Patriarchate. The legal sources for the period from the 15th to the 19th century include the compilations of earlier Byzantine (civil) law (especially of *Basilika*) and rules of ecclesiastical law, which were made mainly for the use of bishops, and the archives of notaries preserved in the Cyclades and Ionian islands.

Three layers of jurisdiction were created: the Islamic law pertaining to property affairs, the Romano-Byzantine law administered by the Patriarchate and applied in disputes among Christians, and, finally, the locally operating customary law. The main instruments for administering justice by the ecclesiastical authorities were compilations of Byzantine law (especially Harmenopoulos' *Hexabiblos*) with rules of ecclesiastical law, known as *nomokanones* or *nomika*.

Modern Greece

Law in the modern Greek state closely follows the models established in post-revolution France and Germany. The judiciary is independent from the executive, although the head of the Supreme Court (*Areios Pagos*) is appointed by the Minister of Justice. Judges are professionals, while there is a limited role for juries. Most often codes provide the rules of substance and procedure in criminal, civil, and administrative courts.

During the War of Independence and under the influence of the French Revolution, three constitutional texts were produced (1822, 1825, 1827). Subsequent constitutional law has followed the political history of the country from the demand for a constitution in 1843 (establishing a constitutional monarchy), to the enactment of a new constitution in 1864 (as amended in 1911), to the establishment of the republic in 1924 after the defeat in the Graeco-Turkish war of 1920–22, to the restoration of a constitutional monarchy after the civil war of 1944–49 (1952), and finally to the restoration of democracy following the collapse of the 1967–1974 dictatorship (1975, amended 1986).

In the area of civil law the Bavarian administration ordered the collection of local customs but discouraged the idea of drawing up a civil code. Provisionally, the decree of 23 February/7 March 1835 sanctioned that the compilation of Harmenopoulos (*Hexabiblos*) be used as civil law until the elaboration of a civil code. A civil code was finally introduced in 1946 (amended in 1982) and with it came the abolition of local codes, such as the Ionian Civil Code, the Civil Code of Crete, and the Civil Code of Samos. A penal code was introduced in 1951, and has been amended several times since, as well as a Code of Penal Procedure (1952). A Code of Civil Procedure was introduced in 1968, replacing the one elaborated by Maurer in the 1830s, and has already undergone several amendments. Finally, the entry of Greece into the European Union in 1981 meant the adoption of the legal order of the European Union, since in most cases European legislation and courts prevail over national ones.

I. N. ARNAOUTOGLOU

See also Canon Law, Constitution, Judicial Procedure, Nomokanon

Collections of Sources

Actes de l'Athos, 6 vols, St. Peterburg: Akademika Nauk, 1903–13, reprinted Amsterdam: Hakkert, 1964–75

Arnaoutoglou, Ilias (editor), *Ancient Greek Laws: A Sourcebook*, London and New York: Routledge, 1998

Ashburner, Walter (editor), *Nomos Rhodon Nautikos: The Rhodian Sea Law*, Oxford: Clarendon Press, 1909

Behrends, Okko, *et al.* (editors), *Corpus Iuris Civilis: Text und Übersetzung*, Heidelberg: Müller, 1990–

Burgmann, Ludwig (editor), *Ecloga: das Gesetzbuch Leons III und Konstantinos' V*, Frankfurt: Löwenklau, 1983

Burgmann, Ludwig (editor), *Ecloga Basilicorum*, Frankfurt: Löwenklau, 1988

Carey, Christopher (editor), *Trials from Classical Athens*, London and New York: Routledge, 1997

Dareste, Rodolphe, Bernard Haussoullier and Théodore Reinach (editors), *Recueil des inscriptions juridiques grecques: texte, traduction, commentaire*, 2 vols, Paris: Leroux, 1895–1904

Dujčev, Ivan (editor), *To Eparchikon Biblion: The Book of the Eparch: Le Livre du Prefet*, London: Variorum, 1970

Effenterre, Henri van and Françoise Ruzé (editors), *Nomima: recueil d'inscriptions politiques et juridiques de l'archaisme grec*, 2 vols, Rome: École Française de Rome, 1994–95

Gines, D.S. (editor), *Nomikon poiithen kai suntachthen eis aplin phrasin ypo tou panierotatou ellogimotatou episkopou Kampanias kuriou kuriou Theophilou tou ex Ioanninon (1788)* [A Collection of Laws: Drafted and Assembled in Simple Terms by Theophilus, Bishop of Kampania from Ioannina (1788)], Thessalonica, 1960

Gines, D.S. (editor), *Perigramma istorias metabyzantinou dikaiou* [An Outline of the History of Post-Byzantine Law], Athens, 1966; addenda in *Epetiris Etaireias Byzantinon Spoudon* [Yearbook of the Society for Byzantine Studies], 39–40 (1974): pp. 201–46 and 43 (1977–78): pp. 152–87

Gines, D.S. and N.I. Pantazopoulos (editors), *Nomokanon Manouel Notariou tou Malaxou tou ek Naupliou tis Peloponnesou metenechtheis eis lexin aplin dia tin ton pollon opheleian* [The Nomocanon of Manuel the Notary, Son of Malaxos of Nauplia in the Peloponnese, Cast into Simple Terms for General Use], Thessalonica, 1985

Harmenopoulos, Konstantinos, *Procheiron nomon, Hexabiblos*, edited by K. Armenopoulos and Konstantinos Pitsakes, Athens, 1971

Karatzas, Theodoros B. and Nigel P. Ready (editors), *The Greek Code of Private Maritime Law*, The Hague: Nijhoff, 1982

Konidaris, I.M. and G.E. Rodolakis, "Oi praxeis tou notariou Kerkyras Ioanni Chontromati (1472–1473)" [Acts of the Corcyra Notary John Chontromatis (1472–1473)], *Epetiris Kentrou Ereunis Istorias Ellinikou Dikaiou* [Yearbook of the Centre for the Study of Greek Law], 32 (1996): pp. 139–206

Körner, Reinhard (editor), *Inschriftliche Gesetzestexte den frühen griechischen Polis*, Cologne: Böhlau, 1993

Lollis, Nicholas B. (translator), *The Greek Penal Code*, South Hackensack, New Jersey: Rothman, 1973

Meyer, Paul M., *Juristische Papyri: Erklärung von Urkunden zur Einführung in die juristische Papyruskunde*, Berlin: Weidmann, 1920

Mitteis, Ludwig and Ulrich Wilcken, *Grundzüge und Chrestomathie der Papyruskunde*, 2 vols, Leipzig: Teubner, 1912

Rodolakis, G.E. and L. Paparriga-Artemiadi, "Oi praxeis tou notariou Agiou Matthaiou Kerkyras Petrou Varagka (1541–1545)" [Acts of the Corcyra Notary Petrou Varagka (1541–1545)], *Epetiris Kentrou Ereunis Istorias Ellinikou Dikaiou* [Yearbook of the Centre for the Study of Greek Law], 32 (1996): pp. 207–340

Scheltema, H.J., N. van der Waal and D. Holwerda (editors), *Basilicorum libri LX*, Groningen: Wolters, 1955–88

Sitzia, Francesco, *Le Rhopai*, Naples: Jovene, 1984

Thür, Gerhard and Hans Taeuber (editors), *Prozessrechtliche Inschriften der griechischen Poleis: Arkadien*, Vienna: Akademie der Wissenschaften, 1994

Tourtoglou, M., "I nomologia ton kriterion tis Mykonou (170s–190s ai.)" [Case Law of the Mykonos Courts], *Epetiris Kentrou Ereunis Istorias Ellinikou Dikaiou* [Yearbook of the Centre for the Study of Greek Law], 27–28 (1980–81): pp. 1–257

Waal, N. van der and B.H. Stolte, *Collectio Tripartita: Justinian on Religious and Ecclesiastical Affairs*, Groningen: Forsten, 1994

Watson, Alan, Theodor Mommsen and Paul Krueger (editors and translators), *The Digest of Justinian*, 4 vols, Philadelphia: University of Pennsylvania Press, 1985, revised 1998

Willetts, Ronald F. (editor), *The Law-Code of Gortyn*, Berlin: de Gruyter, 1967

Zepos, I.D. and P.I. Zepos (editors), *Jus Graecoromanum*, 8 vols, Athens 1930–31, reprinted Aalen: Scientia, 1962

Thematic Bibliographies

In issues of *Byzantinische Zeitschrift* (on Byzantine law)

Calhoun, George M. and Catherine Delamere, *A Working Bibliography of Greek Law*, Cambridge, Massachusetts: Harvard University Press, 1927

Centre de Documentation des Droits antiques, *Bibliographie*, annually 1990–

In *Epetiris Etairias Byzantinon Spoudon* [Yearbook of the Society for Byzantine Studies] (mainly Greek bibliography)

Gilissen, John (editor), *Introduction bibliographique à l'histoire du droit et à l'ethnologie juridique*, vol. 7: *Grèce*, Brussels: Institut de Sociologie, 1963

Gilissen, John (editor), *Introduction bibliographique à l'histoire du droit et à l'ethnologie juridique*, vol. 8: *Monde hellénistique*, Brussels: Institut de Sociologie, 1963

In *Revue d'Histoire du Droit Français et Etranger* (under Monde byzantin, Monde grec, and Monde greco–romain)

Further Reading

Ashburner, Walter (editor), *Nomos Rhodion Nautikos: The Rhodian Sea Law*, Oxford: Clarendon Press, 1909

Berneker, Erich (editor), *Zur griechischen Rechtsgeschichte*, Darmstadt: Wissenschaftliche Buchgesellschaft, 1968

Biscardi, Arnaldo, *Diritto greco antico*, Milan: Giuffrè, 1982

Cartledge, Paul, Paul Millett and Stephen Todd (editors), *Nomos: Essays in Athenian Law, Politics, and Society*, Cambridge and New York: Cambridge University Press, 1990

Foxhall, L. and A.D.E. Lewis (editors), *Greek Law in its Political Setting: Justifications not Justice*, Oxford: Clarendon Press, and New York: Oxford University Press, 1996

Gagarin, Michael, *Early Greek Law*, Berkeley: University of California Press, 1986

Harrison, A.R.W., *The Law of Athens*, 2 vols, Oxford: Clarendon Press, 1968–71

Havelock, Eric A., *The Greek Concept of Justice from Its Shadow in Homer to Its Substance in Plato*, Cambridge, Massachusetts: Harvard University Press, 1978

Jones, John Walter, *The Law and Legal Theory of the Greeks: An Introduction*, Oxford: Clarendon Press, 1956

Kazhdan, A.P. "Do we Need a New History of Byzantine Law?", *Jahrbuch der Österreichische Byzantinistik*, 39 (1989): pp. 1–28

Kerameus, Konstantinos D. and Phaedon J. Kozyris, *Introduction to Greek Law*, 2nd edition, Deventer: Kluwer, 1993

Laiou, Angeliki E. and Dieter Simon (editors), *Law and Society in Byzantium, 9th–12th Centuries*, Washington D.C.: Dumbarton Oaks, 1994

MacDowell, Douglas M., *The Law in Classical Athens*, London: Thames and Hudson, and Ithaca, New York: Cornell University Press, 1978

MacDowell, Douglas M., *Spartan Law*, Edinburgh: Scottish Academic Press, 1986

Saradi, H., "The Byzantine Tribunals: Problems in the Application of Justice and State Policy, 9th–12th Century", *Revue des Études Byzantines*, 53 (1995): pp. 165–204

Scheltema, H.J., "Byzantine Law" in *The Byzantine Empire*, edited by J.M. Hussey, Cambridge: Cambridge University Press, 1967 (*The Cambridge Medieval History*, vol. 4, part 2), pp. 55–77

"Symposion: Vortrage zur griechischen und hellenistischen Rechtsgeschichte", 1971–95 (annual symposia; various publishers)

Taubenschlag, Rafal, *The Law of Greco-Roman Egypt in the Light of the Papyri, 332 BC–640 AD*, 2nd edition, Warsaw: Państwowe Wydawnictwo Naukowe, 1955

Todd, S.C., *The Shape of Athenian Law*, Oxford: Clarendon Press, 1993

Triantaphyllopoulos, Johannes, *Das Rechtsdenken der Griechen*, Munich: Beck, 1985

Troianos, Spiros, *Oi piges tou Byzantinou Dikaiou: Eisagogiko boithima* [Sources for Byzantine Law: An Introductory Companion], Athens: Komotini, 1986

Troianos, Spiros and I. Velissarapoulou–Karakosta, *Istoria Dikaiou: Apo tin archaiotita sti neoteri Ellada* [History of Law: From Ancient Times to Modern Greece], 2nd edition, Athens, 1997

Wal, N. van der and J.H.A. Lokin, *Historiae iuris graeco-romani delineatio: Les sources du droit byzantin de 300 à 1453*, Groningen: Forsten, 1985

Wolff, Hans Julius, *Beiträge zur Rechtsgeschichte Altgriechenlands und des hellenistisch-römischen Ägypten*, Weimar: Böhlaus Nachfolger, 1961

Wolff, Hans Julius, *Das Justizwesen der Ptolemäer*, Munich: Beck, 1962

Wolff, Hans Julius, *Das Recht der griechischen Papyri Ägyptens in der Zeit der Ptolemäer und der Prinzipats*, Munich: Beck, 1978

Laz

Ethnic group from the Caucasus region

The Laz are a mysterious people to be found in the southeastern corner of the Black Sea, speaking a Caucasian language akin to Georgian. Until the collapse of the Soviet Union about 50,000 Laz-speakers could be found in that country and about the same number in Turkey. Georgian independence, followed by civil war and the secession of Abkhazia, and the dubious status of the district near the Turkish border have confused the issue, with the Laz now scattered among a number of territories and joining a growing band of refugees in the Caucasus. Prior to 1923 the Laz population of this area on the Black Sea was interspersed with the large Greek community around Trebizond. Because the exchange of populations following the Greek defeat in Asia Minor was conducted on religious rather than linguistic grounds, Christian Laz may have been evacuated to Greece. There are references to Laz in Greek statistics, although such immigrants would seem to have been assimilated fairly quickly, and there may be confusion between Pontic Greeks in general, and Laz in particular. Both in ancient and in modern times, Lazica as a geographical term for the Caucasian corner of the Black Sea coast clearly encompassed a great many races other than the Laz. Ancient sources are hardly likely to be specific about the mosaic of different languages in the Caucasus, and since until very recently Laz was not a written language, modern authorities have found it hard to take it seriously.

Lazica appears in Greek legend as Colchis, the land of Medea and the Golden Fleece. A Greek colony on the river Phasis was founded by Miletus. Xenophon in his *Anabasis* encountered tribes hostile to him and to each other. Pliny and Strabo both mention the multiplicity of different languages in the area. Lazica had been part of the empire of Mithradates of Pontus until Rome under Pompey entered the region. For the next 700 years the southern Caucasus was hotly disputed between Persia on the one hand, and the Roman or Byzantine empire on the other, sometimes acting as an independent ally to both sides. Western Lazica generally fell in the Roman sphere. The gold of the Golden Fleece made it valuable, and it was an important staging post on the silk road from China. The coming of Christianity in the 4th century should have strengthened the links with the Roman empire, but the decline of this empire meant that in the time of Justinian I (527–65) an independent Lazica owed allegiance to the Persians. Procopius describes in long and tedious detail how Justinian reversed this state of affairs. The Arab invasions drove back the Byzantines temporarily, but they never really lost control over the central district near Trebizond in spite of the presence of the Arabs and the Turks and the independent and powerful kingdom of Georgia under the Bagrationi dynasty. The Georgians were Christians and usually allied to the Greeks. Indeed it was the famous queen Tamara of Georgia who was able to help her nephews David and Andronikos Komnenos carve out a domain in Trebizond which survived until 1461.

Laz and Greeks appear to have survived in harmony both in Trebizond and in the multi-ethnic kingdom of the Bagrationis. But the arrival of the Ottoman Turks changed this. Georgia survived with some difficulty until the Russians annexed it at the begining of the 19th century, but it lost control of Lazica. Under the Ottomans in both the Georgian and the Byzantine parts of Lazica, most of the Laz converted to Islam. Some may have already become Muslims at the time of the Arab invasions. As in Albania, in addition to financial benefits for conversion there were linguistic reasons as well. Services in Greek or Georgian are unlikely to have been comprehensible or congenial to the average Laz; Islam is less demanding.

Russian and Turkish troops fought different campaigns in the Caucasus during World War I; as a result the Laz were divided between the hardly sympathetic regimes of Kemal Atatürk in Turkey and the Bolsheviks in Russia. Their language would have been ripe for extinction, but recent interest in minorities and the efforts of the German scholar W. Feurstein to give the Laz a language and an identity may preserve this improbable fossil.

T.J. WINNIFRITH

See also Georgia

Summary

An ethnic group from the Caucasus region, the Laz inhabit the area known to Greek legend as Colchis. Taken for the Romans by Pompey, the region was disputed by Romans and Persians for 700 years but remained largely Christian until the coming of the Ottomans, when most Laz converted to Islam.

Further Reading

Allen, W.E.D., *A History of the Georgian People: From the Beginning down to the Russian Conquest in the Nineteenth Century*, London: Routledge and Kegan Paul, and New York: Barnes and Noble, 1971

Ascherson, Neal, *Black Sea*, London: Cape, and New York: Hill and Wang, 1995

Bryer, Anthony A.M., *The Empire of Trebizond and the Pontos*, London: Variorum, 1980

Feurstein, W., "Volker der Kolchis" in *Caucasologie et mythologie comparée*, edited by Catherine Paris, Paris: Peeters, 1992

Honigmann, Ernst, *Die Ostgrenze des Byzantinischen Reiches von 363 bis 1017, nach Griechischen, Arabischen, Syrischen und Armenischen Quellen*, vol. 3 of *Byzance et les arabes*, edited by A.A. Vasiliev, Brussels: Institut de Philologie et d'Histoire Orientales, 1968

Lebadea

City in Boeotia

In antiquity Lebadea was best known as the site of the oracle of Trophonius. Today, it is the largest city in Boeotia.

The town spreads out on both sides of the river Hercyna, which issues from an impressive gorge, dominated at one end by a Frankish castle and at the other by a graceful Turkish bridge. Lebadea lies south of Chaeronea, southwest of Orchomenus, and west of Coronea, from which it is separated by Mount Laphystion. Like Mount Laphystion, the later polis of Lebadea originally belonged to Orchomenus. Legendary connections linking Lebadea and Laphystion to Orchomenus (Trophonius and Agamedes were sons of Erginus of Orchomenus, and Athamas king of Orchomenus attempted to sacrifice his children to Zeus Laphystius) support the impression that Lebadea was originally a dependency of Orchomenus (Lebadea's absence from the Homeric Catalogue of Ships – strongly felt by later inhabitants, who identified their polis with Homeric Mideia – is another indication).

The earliest contemporary references to Lebadea by name occur in the 5th century BC. Lebadea and the oracle of Trophonius seem to have come to the notice of the outside world, that is to say, Athens, at the time of the battle of Coronea in 446 BC, after which the oracle began to become famous. Lebadea was independent by the end of the 5th century BC. Under the federal constitution described by the Oxyrhynchus Historian, Lebadea at this period took turns with Haliartus and Coronea in contributing one of the 11 Boeotarchs (Hell. Oxy. 16 [11]. 2–4). Although attacked and plundered by Lysander in 395, the polis recovered sufficiently to issue its own independent coinage after the King's Peace (the absence of any coins attributable to Lebadea in the late 6th century is another indication that it had not yet become independent at that time).

Lebadea was one of few towns in Boeotia to survive and prosper throughout antiquity. By AD 100 it was one of the most important towns on the mainland, and an almost obligatory stop on any visitor's "grand tour", no doubt because of the oracle of Trophonius, its best-known sanctuary. This was just outside the town, on the banks of the river Hercyna. The oracle functioned as early as the 6th century BC and perhaps even earlier. It shares the characteristics of two distinct types of oracle. The first, exemplified elsewhere in Boeotia at the Amphiareion near Oropus (and also possibly at the Thesprotian Nekromanteion), is one where the god lives underground and is approached directly at night by the consultant. Trophonius' oracle was also one of a number clustered around Lake Copais, each situated more or less at the limits of its polis. Here the predominant features were a hill or mountain represented by a young god, and a spring issuing from it, represented by a nymph who was usually the god's *trophos* (nurse). Divination came through inspiration caused by drinking the water of the spring, which was the real medium.

The traveller Pausanias (second half of the 2nd century AD) gives a vivid description of his own consultation of Trophonius. First, he spent several days in a house sacred to the Good Daemon and Good Fortune, bathing only in the water of the Hercyna, and sacrificing to the divinities of the sanctuary. The entrails of each victim were scrutinized to see if the omens were favourable. On the night of the actual descent he put on special clothes. The procedure began with the sacrifice of a ram over a pit and invocation of Agamedes: only if the omens from this sacrifice were favourable could the consultation proceed. He was taken to the Hercyna, anointed and washed, and then to two adjacent fountains of Forgetfulness and Memory, from which he drank. Then, after worshipping the early cult image of Trophonius, he proceeded to the oracle, where he was let down into the chasm by means of a ladder. At the bottom he lay on his back, holding honey-cakes in his hands, and thrust his feet and legs into a narrow gap between the wall and floor of the pit, whereupon he was pulled through the hole. Inside he was confronted by the god (Pausanias says that prophecy could come by sight or sound, but does not say what his own experience was), and then thrust out again feet first through the same hole. Back on ground level, he was seated by the priests on the throne of Memory, and asked to describe his experience.

The other important cult at Lebadea was that of Zeus Basileus (the King), probably the same as the god worshipped on neighbouring Mount Laphystion. He is best known in connection with the games called *Basileia*, which the Boeotians, under the leadership of the Thebans, founded to commemorate their victory over Sparta at the battle of Leuctra (371 BC). The Thebans chose the site carefully, to emphasize their own domination of Boeotia and the consequent humiliation of Orchomenus.

The intertwined development of the two cults – of Trophonius and Zeus Basileus – reveals how religion, politics, and commerce interacted in the life of a polis. In the latter part of the 3rd century BC the polis of Lebadea undertook a major building project, which would affect its two outstanding attractions, the sanctuaries of Trophonius and Zeus Basileus. The plan was to build a temple of Zeus – huge by the standards of mainland Greece – on the top of a hill which dominated the route leading past Lebadea to Delphi, as it still does. They also planned to move the site of the oracular chasm from inside the sanctuary of Trophonius to the mountain top. The plan to build the temple failed due to shortage of funds. The project was eventually taken over by the Boeotian Confederacy, but too late, for very soon afterwards the confederacy was dissolved by the Romans and all that was left of the undertaking were the foundations of the building – on the hill called Profitis Ilias – and a pan-Boeotian college of *naopoioi* (temple fabric officers) who, since their work was never finished, were never disbanded.

The other part of the project was completed. It is quite clear from Pausanias that the oracle was not in the sanctuary of Trophonius itself, but beyond and above it, on the hill which also bore the temple of Zeus Basileus. In fact, the remains of this man-made hole were discovered between the foundations of the temple of Zeus Basileus and the chapel of Profitis Ilias (although it has since vanished with the complete rebuilding of the chapel).

Aside from these two important sanctuaries, relatively little is known about public religious activity at Lebadea. There has been no systematic excavation in the ancient town site: accidental finds late in the 1930s revealed evidence for the worship of the mother of the gods, of Artemis Eileithyia, and Zeus Meilichius. Their find spot, although it was clearly not at their original sites, suggests that the sanctuaries of these deities were at or near the outskirts of the urban area of the polis. Pausanias says only that Lebadea had all the amenities of a normal Greek polis, but he does not describe them. To him they were banal, and not as interesting as the oracle of Trophonius.

The oracle operated at least into the 3rd century AD, and possibly even later. The town itself, probably because the hilltop above the gorge of the Hercyna was ideally suited for the siting of a castle, flourished throughout the Middle Ages, being held successively by Franks, Catalans, and Turks. The castle itself may have been built early in the 13th century, during which Lebadea belonged to the dukes of Athens (who were based at Esteves, that is, Thebes). After the defeat of the knights of the Morea by members of the Catalan Company in 1311, Lebadea became for a time the third city of the Catalan duchy of Athens and Neopatros.

In the 15th century, after further vicissitudes, it was ceded to Mehmet II, and remained a major site throughout the Tourkokratia (even today, the elegant bridge over the Hercyna and a small number of buildings – among them, a bathhouse – bear testimony to this period). Greek again since 1829, Lebadea is the capital of the nomos of Boeotia, and the seat of the bishop of Thebes and Lebadea.

ALBERT SCHACHTER

See also Oracles

Summary

This city in Boeotia was best known in antiquity for its oracle of Trophonius, where the consultant approached the deity directly by descending underground. Lebadea was an important fortified site during the Frankish and Catalan periods, and later flourished under the Tourkokratia. Today it is the capital of the nomos of Boeotia and seat of the bishop of Thebes and Lebadea.

Further Reading

Hansen, M.H., "An Inventory of Boiotian Poleis in the Archaic and Classical Periods" in *Introduction to an Inventory of Poleis*, edited by Mogens Herman Hansen, Copenhagen: Munksgaard, 1996

Lauffer, Siegfried (editor), *Griechenland: Lexikon der historischen Stätten von den Anfängen bis zur Gegenwart*, Munich: Beck, 1989

Rossiter, Stuart, *Greece*, London: Benn, and Chicago: Rand McNally, 1981 (*Blue Guide* series)

Schachter, Albert, *Cults of Boiotia*, London: University of London Institute of Classical Studies, 1981

Lemnos

Island in the northern Aegean

The position of Lemnos in the northern Aegean, where it lies midway between the tip of the Mount Athos promontory and the coast of Asia Minor, meant that control over it was always sought after. Any ships entering or leaving the Hellespont (the Passage of Romania, now the Dardanelles) could do so only with the knowledge (and often the permission) of the current rulers of Lemnos. The frequency with which their identity might change is a symptom of its strategic importance to the Hellenic world throughout its history. The island is now administered under the nomos of Lesbos.

Lemnos has an area of 476 sq km and, like a number of the Aegean islands, its shape indicates its volcanic origins, two bays to north and south almost dividing the island in two; the smaller, eastern, sector was where the capital of the island in antiquity, Hephaestus, was situated, while on the coast of the western sector, larger and much more mountainous with the highest peak of Mount Skopia reaching 430 m, the medieval and modern capital of Myrina is located. The low-lying and flatter areas of the island are quite fertile, and produce a variety of crops. A tradition, already current in antiquity and still existing in the 20th century, credited Lemnian earth, excavated on one day each year, with the power of healing many kinds of wounds; it was exported all over the Hellenic world.

In antiquity Lemnos figured both in Homeric legend and in Hellenic history. Herodotus (4. 145) related how the Argonauts, who according to legend had arrived on the island and left progeny there, were driven out of Lemnos three generations later by the Pelasgi. Later (5. 26) he described how Lemnos, with Imbros, was taken from the Pelasgi by Otanes, who had already occupied Byzantium and Chalcedon. The stronghold of Myrina figured early in the history of the island, as when Miltiades, having called on the Pelasgi to leave the island – a call which the townspeople of Hephaestus obeyed – was defied by the inhabitants of Myrina, whom he besieged (no doubt secure in their rock-perched fortress) before eventually ejecting them by force.

An indication of the importance in the Greek world that Lemnos must already have attained by the early 4th century AD is suggested by the fact that the island's bishop was one of only three from all the Aegean islands to attend the First Church Council at Nicaea in 325. The site of an early Christian basilica is still preserved at Livadochori, close to the narrowest part of the island. The island's ecclesiastical importance was further increased when, under Leo VI (885–912), it was raised to a metropolitan see; this was probably in part due to an attempt to counter the rise of Saracen maritime power in the northern Aegean, and in 924 a Byzantine fleet decisively defeated the Saracens off the coast of Lemnos. By 1136 Venice, already always anxious to establish and extend its trading opportunities, reached an agreement with the island's metropolitan to grant the use of a chapel at the port of Kotsinas (modern Kokkino) in the bay on the north coast; this foothold in Byzantine territory is a further indication of the island's continuing strategic and economic significance.

In the Deed of Partition that followed the Fourth Crusade in 1204 Lemnos was awarded to the new Latin emperor in Constantinople, but he was unable to maintain control of the island and from 1207 it became a domain of the Venetian family of the Navigaiosa, who were styled grand dukes. When the first duke, Philocole, died in 1214, Lemnos remained in the family's control, being divided in half, his son ruling one half and his two daughters the other. This arrangement continued until 1276, when Michael VIII Palaiologos was able to reestablish Byzantine possession. It was inevitable that with the rise of Genoese power in the northern Aegean, and the corresponding weakness of Byzantium, control of Lemnos should pass to the Gattilusi family, with Jacopo Gattilusi (lord of Mytilene) ruling there 1414–19.

It was by chance that in 1442, while travelling back to Constantinople from Lesbos with his young bride Caterina Gattilusi, Constantine Palaiologos, later to become the last Byzantine emperor, stopped at Lemnos; they stayed at the castle beside the port of Kotsinas, first built by the Venetians in 1397, but the Turks had been informed of their presence and blockaded the port. While there Caterina, who probably by then was pregnant, became ill and in August, her condition aggravated by the stress of their situation, she died; she was buried at Palaiokastro, the site of the ancient Hephaestus, but her grave has disappeared. Had she lived for just another seven years, she could have become the last Byzantine empress.

With the fall of Constantinople in 1453 the Gattilusi again controlled Lemnos, but their rule was so oppressive that a secret plea was sent by the people of Lemnos to the Turkish sultan Mehmet II to take over the island. This development was forestalled when, in 1456, the island became involved in a papal crusade carried out in the name of pope Callixtus III to recover Constantinople from Islam. In that year a papal force under a Venetian cardinal, Lodovico Trevisan, occupied Lemnos, Samothrace, and Thasos, installing garrisons and governors in the name of the pope. His successor, Pius II, even founded a completely new religious military order, the Order of Our Lady of Bethlehem, which had its headquarters on Lemnos. These interventions by western powers all came to an end in 1470 with full Turkish occupation.

From then until 1912, when it again became part of Greece and passed to official Greek control, Lemnos was occupied either by the Turks or, briefly, the Russians. It was always to be its strategic significance that gave the island its importance; this was the reason why it figured in numerous 20th-century treaties and agreements. In 1915 the harbour at Myrina became the assembly point for the British fleet that was to make the famous and disastrous assault on the Gallipoli peninsula, and it was only in 1936 that Greece regained the right to fortify Lemnos and Samothrace; as late as 1983 the previous illegal fortification of Lemnos by Greece became the issue which caused the Greeks to withdraw (at Turkish insistence) from a combined exercise of NATO forces.

PAUL HETHERINGTON

Summary

An island located in the northern Aegean, Lemnos is strategically placed to control the passage of the Dardanelles. In the late Middle Ages Lemnos was disputed between the Venetians, Genoese, and Byzantines. It was under Turkish rule from 1470 to 1912, when it reverted to Greece.

Further Reading

Haldon, J.F., "Limnos, Monastic Holdings and the Byzantine State ca. 1261–1453" in Continuity and Change in Late Byzantine Society, edited by Anthony Bryer and Heath Lowry, Birmingham: University of Birmingham Centre for Byzantine Studies, and Washington, D.C.: Dumbarton Oaks, 1986

Miller, William, The Latins in the Levant: A History of Frankish Greece, London: John Murray, and New York: Dutton, 1908, reprinted Cambridge: Speculum Historiale, and New York: Barnes and Noble, 1964

Miller, William, *Essays on the Latin Orient*, Cambridge: Cambridge University Press, 1921, reprinted New York: AMS Press, 1983

Setton, Kenneth M., *The Papacy and the Levant, 1204–1571*, 4 vols, Philadelphia: American Philosophical Society, 1976–84

Hussey, J.M. (editor), *The Byzantine Empire*, Cambridge: Cambridge University Press, 1966 (*The Cambridge Medieval History*, vol. 4, part 1, 2nd edition)

Woodhouse, C.M., *Modern Greece: A Short History*, 5th edition, London and Boston: Faber, 1991

Leo III *c.*685–741

Emperor

When the Arabs entered the Byzantine empire in 716, proposing to take Constantinople, they were aware that the general responsible for defending the eastern frontier, Leo, had refused to recognize the de facto emperor, Theodosios III (recently set on the throne by the rebellious army of the Opsikion); they therefore assumed that if they recognized Leo as emperor they would find in him an ally. Leo, realizing that he had inadequate forces to resist them, reached some kind of agreement. The Arab generals had their men proclaim him emperor and, to avoid pillaging the territory under his jurisdiction, led their army into southern Anatolia to winter. As soon as the way was clear, Leo, with his few forces, headed for Constantinople. Theodosios promptly abdicated and entered a monastery. For the seventh time in 22 years the throne had been seized by force. The Isaurian dynasty, which Leo founded, ruled until 802.

When the Arab general Masalmas realized that Leo had tricked him he crossed to Thrace, took a number of minor strongholds, and laid the country waste before moving on Constantinople. In August 717 he set his army in position around the city and had a deep ditch dug around the walls with a drystone wall above it. On 1 September an Arab fleet of 1,800 vessels, comprising large warships and lighter, fast craft, anchored along the sea wall of the city. But because this position was unsuited to a long siege, as soon as a favourable wind arose the fleet started to move to sites where camps could be established; Leo took advantage of their difficulties in the unfamiliar currents, and sent ships equipped to spray them with Greek fire. According to Theophanes, as the fire took hold, some of the vessels were thrown in flames against the sea walls, some went down with all hands, and some were carried, burning furiously, as far as Oxeia and the island of Plateia.

The winter was bitterly cold, and the Arabs' provisions ran out. In the spring supplies were brought by another Arab fleet which, warned of the Greek fire, approached by night, unseen, and went into hiding. It came, however, from Egypt, from the shipyards recently conquered by the Arabs, and the Egyptian crew escaped under cover of darkness and joined the Byzantines, revealing the presence of the fleet and the location of their anchorage. So they too had to face Greek fire; their arms and supplies were seized; and furthermore the warm weather brought disease to the Arab camp. Leo also persuaded the Bulgars to attack them. Finally in August or September 718 the Arab fleet sailed away. This siege of Constantinople is also related in the form of an Apocalypse, with Leo as saviour king.

The Arab siege, which had provoked two attempts at usurpation, convinced Leo that God was displeased. He tried to counteract this by forcing all Jews and Montanists in the empire to be baptized. This did not prevent the fleet sent to quell disorders in Italy from foundering in the Adriatic; and Arab expeditions into Asia Minor resumed, regularly wintering in Byzantine territory.

Then on 26 October 726 the volcano of Thera (Santorini) erupted. Both the historians of the reign, Theophanes the Confessor and the patriarch Nikephoros, agree that this was what moved Leo to take action against icons – wrong action, according to them; but the next uprising (originating in the naval forces and the Cyclades) was successfully suppressed. In the summer a combined raiding party, of 15,000 light-armed Arabs under Omar and 8,500 under Moawiya, appeared before Nicaea. Sources hostile to Leo say that Omar and Moawiya left with a great number of captives and much booty, demonstrating to the impious man (Leo) that he had not overcome them because of his piety, as he boasted; but it was at least to some extent a Byzantine success, certainly claimed by Leo as such, and attributed to correct worship.

Though he is often represented as primarily the initiator of iconoclasm, Leo's two great contributions to history are having interrupted 22 years of successive usurpations and intermittent civil strife, and having taken the first steps towards halting the Arab advance. He also took measures to reorganize an empire fallen into anarchy. Data on this, except for his law code, the *Ekloge*, are minimal. Taxation was a priority: with war permanent and many sources of revenue lost, those that remained had to be exploited with all possible efficiency. Three measures are documented (two because of the opposition with which they met): new fiscal measures were introduced (against which pope Gregory led Roman resistance in 724); registration of male babies was instituted (Theophanes, 410. 9–17); and (a measure mentioned without condemnation) a tax was raised to cover the rebuilding of the walls of Constantinople after the earthquake of 740. Reorganization of the army and of provincial administration were major priorities.

When Leo III instituted iconoclasm, in either 726 or 730, he held mass meetings to explain his policy and win popular support, and repeated this tactic in 740 for the tax to rebuild the walls. The iconoclast emperors were without exception extremely popular with the Constantinople masses (hostile sources underline this as the ultimate proof of their vileness). This understanding of themselves as the ones to whom the people have entrusted power, to whom they are, at least formally, accountable, goes back to Augustus' formulation rather than to Hellenistic concepts of empire, but there are Hellenistic elements present.

PATRICIA KARLIN-HAYTER

See also Iconoclasm, Law

Biography

Born *c.*685 at Germanikeia, Leo was probably brought up in Mesembria. He came to notice as the defender of the eastern frontier. Having forced Theodosios III to abdicate he entered Constantinople by force in 717 and reigned as emperor until 741. His main concerns were with the defence of the empire and of the city against the Arabs.

He revised the laws of Justinian with his *Ekloge* and in 726 he instituted iconoclasm. He died at Constantinople in 741.

Further Reading

Alexander, Paul Julius, *The Patriarch Nicephorus of Constantinople: Ecclesiastical Policy and Image Worship in the Byzantine Empire*, Oxford: Clarendon Press, 1958

Brown, Peter, "A Dark-Age Crisis: Aspects of the Iconoclastic Controversy", *English Historical Review*, 88 (1973): pp. 1–34

Bury, J.B., *A History of the Later Roman Empire from Arcadius to Irene, 395 AD to 800 AD*, vol. 2, London and New York: Macmillan, 1889, reprinted Amsterdam: Hakkert, 1966

Bury, J.B., *A History of the Eastern Roman Empire from the Fall of Irene to the Accession of Basil I, AD 802–867*, London and New York: Macmillan, 1912, reprinted New York: Russell, 1965

Charanis, Peter, *Church and State in the Later Roman Empire: The Religious Policy of Anastasius the First, 491–518*, 2nd edition, Thessalonica: Kentron Vyzantinon Ereunon [Centre of Byzantine Research], 1974

Galavaris, George, *The Icon in the Life of the Church: Doctrine, Liturgy, Devotion*, Leiden: Brill, 1981

Gero, Stephen, *Byzantine Iconoclasm during the Reign of Leo III*, Louvain: Corpus SCO, 1973

Gero, Stephen, *Byzantine Iconoclasm during the Reign of Constantine V*, Louvain: Corpus SCO, 1977

Mango, Cyril, *The Brazen House: A Study of the Vestibule of the Imperial Palace of Constantinople*, Copenhagen: Munksgaard, 1959

Millingen, Alexander van, *Byzantine Constantinople: The Walls of the City and the Adjoining Historical Sites*, London: John Murray, 1899

Theophanes the Confessor, *The Chronicle of Theophanes the Confessor: Byzantine and Near Eastern History, AD 284–813*, translated by Cyril Mango and Roger Scott, Oxford, Clarendon Press, and New York: Oxford University Press, 1997

Leo V *c.780–820*

Emperor

Leo V (813–20) is most famous for starting the second period of official iconoclasm in the Byzantine empire, in 815. He was born around 780 in the Anatolikon theme (or province) to prominent Armenian parents. His father, Bardas the patrician, may have been the ex-*strategos* (or general) of the Armeniakon theme who was exiled by the empress Irene around 780. Leo may also have been related to the general Bardanes Tourkas, in whose retinue he served during the latter's abortive coup against the emperor Nikephoros I in 802/03. For reasons unknown, Leo deserted Bardanes and joined Nikephoros, being richly rewarded with a military post (commander, or *tourmarch*, of the Federates, a garrison unit in Constantinople) and property in the city. He was joined in his actions by his companions Michael Travlos ("the Stutterer", later Michael II, 820–29) and Thomas the Slav (later to lead a famous rebellion against Michael II that led to Thomas's execution in 823). Leo fell out of favour with Nikephoros I around 808 due to the revolt of Arsaber the quaestor, to whom Leo was related, but returned to imperial favour under his friend Michael I Rhangabe (811–13) in the capacity of *strategos* of the Anatolikon theme. Leo served Michael until the latter's abdication in 813 during a disastrous war with the Bulgarians. At

that point he was offered the crown by the senate and the army and entered the capital on 11 July 813. He was immediately acclaimed and crowned, and ruled until Christmas 820, when he was murdered in Hagia Sophia by followers of Michael Travlos. At Christmas 813 he crowned his son Smbat co-emperor, with the new name of Constantine.

The Byzantine sources present a mostly hostile view of Leo because of his decision to restore iconoclasm, which had been officially abandoned at the Council of Nicaea II in 787. Thus the chroniclers speak of duplicity surrounding his accession, including the betrayal of Michael I, but these accounts seem to represent a later blackening of his image. Leo's Armenian stock and the increased presence of Armenians in positions of power during the 8th and 9th centuries also appear to have disturbed some Byzantine contemporaries.

In 813/14 Leo began moves to restore iconoclasm, later arguing that the iconophile ("icon-venerating") emperors before him had all lost their thrones, if not their lives, in disastrous reigns and that this indicated God's displeasure with icons. In this policy he found great favour with sections of the military who still venerated the memory of the great iconoclast emperor Constantine V (741–75). By 815 Leo had summoned the council of Hagia Sophia to revoke Nicaea II, and embarked on a period of persecution of the more stalwart iconophiles, mostly monks and especially those of the Stoudios monastery. He also exiled the iconophile patriarch and theologian Nikephoros (806–15). Leo's motives, however, were less involved with theology than with discipline. Leo, who saw himself as a warrior emperor in the image of the early Isaurians, was concerned that any disobedience to him or his religious policies would undermine his power to control the affairs of state. His iconoclasm does not seem to have involved the destruction of icons, but only their removal from places where they might receive undue veneration.

Even Leo's enemies agree that he was a good ruler and soldier. He managed to reverse the tide against the Bulgars (whose dangerous khan, Krum, died – almost miraculously – shortly after Leo's accession) with great skill and managed to establish a 30-year truce with Krum's successor Omurtag, probably in 816 after the battle of "Leo's Hill" where the Bulgars were crushed.

Relationships with the West during Leo's reign were built on the settlement reached by the Byzantine embassy to Aachen in 812, but by 817 they had stalled on agreement over borders in Dalmatia. In the same year, however, Leo funded the building of the church of San Zaccaria in Venice and sent the saint's relics to the city as a gesture of goodwill. Civil turbulence in the Caliphate also meant that Leo could stabilize the border in the east, and he even managed to rebuild some of the border fortresses lost under Irene (780–802).

Leo's capability was shown not only on the battlefield but also in his attempts to regulate economic and administrative life. Plausible accusations of corruption, depravity, and misrule are curiously quite mild, almost non-existent, in some of the works that nevertheless harshly criticize the emperor's iconoclasm. He was against corruption and appears to have chosen capable administrators, ignoring the fact that many were crypto-iconophiles in favour of their skills and personal qualities. One extant edict attributed to Leo III and Constantine V

Leo V: illustration from the 11th-century chronicle of Skylitzes showing Leo being crowned by his predecessor Michael I Rhangabe in 813, Biblioteca Nacional, Madrid

on divorce and inheritance has been attributed by one scholar (Kresten, 1980) to Leo V and his son Constantine-Smbat.

One of the emperor's proclivities mentioned more than once in the sources is his penchant for prophecies and "holy men" who could predict the length and course of his reign. An important source, now lost and preserved fragmentarily in other sources, appears to have been a long poem by the iconophile monk and saint Theophanes Graptos (d. c.843,) based on the curious fates of Leo, Michael, and Thomas, from their days with Bardanes Tourkas to the civil war between Thomas and Michael following Leo's murder. The revolt has been interpreted as a revenge for Michael's actions and as a possible iconophile backlash against Leo's policies, but iconophile sources are almost universally critical of Thomas and the strife he caused.

Leo may have had a great interest in cultural life. He was a close friend of the learned John the Grammarian, the iconoclast intellectual who was to become patriarch in 836/37, and appears to have been interested in music and singing. He was by no means a bigoted sovereign, and members of his immediate family and court were iconophiles, a fact to which he seems to have turned a blind eye as long as they were personally loyal to him and kept their convictions to themselves. His persecution of the iconoclasts was actually light, even by 20th-century standards, and today one senses the strain of iconophile apologists in trying to fit Leo into the mould of tyrant.

The murder of Leo V by Michael II was, curiously, avenged by Michael's son, Theophilos, when he ascended the throne in 829 and arrested those who had hewn Leo down while singing vigorously near the altar in Hagia Sophia on Christmas Day 815.

Many modern Greek accounts of the Byzantine empire ignore the rejection of Leo's qualities by Byzantine sources and stress his forceful actions to save the state and his keen sense of justice and administrative propriety. As such, they reflect the western Enlightenment verdict on Byzantium, which tended to see all supporters of the traditional ecclesiastical and theological order as enemies of progress and champions of superstition.

DAVID R. TURNER

See also Iconoclasm

Biography

Born *c.*780 to Armenian parents, Leo "the Armenian" grew up in Anatolia. For service to Nikephoros I he was rewarded with a military post and property in Constantinople. He served Michael I as general and became emperor after the latter's abdication in 813. Leo was a good soldier and an effective administrator but is best known for restoring iconoclasm in 815. He was murdered in Hagia Sophia in 820.

Further Reading

Anastos, M., "Iconoclasm and Imperial Rule 717–843" (chapter 3) in *The Byzantine Empire*, edited by J.M. Hussey, Cambridge: Cambridge University Press, 1966 (*The Cambridge Medieval History*, vol. 4, part 1, 2nd edition)

Bury, J.B., *A History of the Eastern Roman Empire from the Fall of Irene to the Accession of Basil I*, AD 802–867, London and New York: Macmillan, 1912, reprinted New York: Russell, 1965

Kresten, O., "Datierungprobleme 'isaurischer' Eherechtsnovellen", *Forschungen zur Byzantinischen Rechtgeschichte: Fontes Minores*, 4 (1980): pp.37–106

Treadgold, Warren, *The Byzantine Revival, 780–842*, Stanford: Stanford University Press, 1988

Turner, D., "The Origins and Accession of Leo V (813–820)", *Jahrbuch der Österreichischen Byzantinistik*, 40 (1990): pp. 171–203 (with bibliography)

Leo VI 866–912

Emperor

The emperor Leo VI (886–912) earned the epithet "the wise" in his own lifetime, and part of the explanation for this is his extensive literary activity. He spent most of his life in the city of Constantinople, and has the image of a sedentary scholar emperor. An episode in the *Life* of St Blasios of Amorion describes how Blasios, when in the palace for an audience with the emperor, stumbled by accident upon Leo; as the emperor was occupied with calligraphy, as was his custom, Blasios did not initially recognize him. A number of poems and speeches dedicated to Leo by contemporary authors also celebrate his wisdom and erudition. It is known that he received an appropriate education for a child of the imperial family, and at one time was taught by the famed Photios. As such Leo's work appears to owe a debt both to this master and to the cultural trends of the day, when Byzantium was reclaiming the knowledge of the past under the impetus of the iconoclastic debate. Leo was active in many literary fields, including poetry, homilies, military manuals, and legislation.

Leo seems to have had a particular enthusiasm for hymns, and produced texts of his own. Eustratiades has even described him as one of the most important Byzantine ecclesiastical poets; the emperor's most familiar piece is the anacreontic ode on the Second Coming. But Leo did not just write ecclesiastical poetry; it is known that he wrote poems on the fall of Thessalonica, the desertion of Andronikos Doukas, and his brother Alexander, though none of these texts has survived. He also composed and recited a poem in order to persuade bishops to support ecclesiastical toleration for his fourth marriage. Leo composed his verse in anacreontics, a form fashionable among the 9th- and 10th-century literati.

Leo is perhaps best known as a speech writer, homilist, and orator, due to the survival of a collection of his work. This collection contains 40 texts, and was probably produced during his own lifetime for his spiritual father the monk Euthymios. It incorporates speeches on feast days, saints' days, dedication days of churches, and other unique occasions –

most famously Leo's *Epitaphios* on his parents; it seems that the last text was written not at the time of Basil's death in 886 (Eudokia had died first, *c*.882/83) but two years later. Antonopoulou (p. 259) opines that Leo's homiletic work marks a stage in the genre at which the rhetorical execution of the speeches was more significant than the dogmatic message, and that his homilies are "the first to display so consistently the preferences of the following generation".

Leo's overtly religious bent (scholars have noted his infrequent use of the Classics over traditional ecclesiastical texts; for instance the *Epitaphios* owes much to Gregory of Nazianzus' funeral orations on his brother Caesarius and on Basil the Great) is again reflected in a work of spiritual advice on the monastic life, organized in 190 chapters. It seems likely that this text was composed for Euthymios and his monastic community, whose monastery Leo had built and patronized.

While Leo's literary work seems to be dominated by religious and ecclesiastical concerns, his most famous single text is probably the *Taktika*, a military manual. Dating from around 900, and addressed to a generic general, it consists of an introduction, an epilogue, and 20 constitutions. The value of the text for the study of the late 9th-/early 10th-century Byzantine army is called into question by historians, for it is in fact based extensively on pre-existing military handbooks, notably the 6th-century *Strategikon*, the *Strategikos* of Onesander, and the *Tactica Theoria* of Aelian. However to Leo's mind this clearly enhanced the importance of his work, not the opposite. Despite its literary debts, Leo did add some new material as well, most notably a section on the Arabs, and a constitution on naval warfare. It is worth noting also that the *Taktika* is not the only military text connected with Leo VI. In his youth he produced the *Problemata* (again exploiting the 6th-century *Strategikon*), and the *Taktika* itself refers to another work of Leo's, a compilation of excerpts on warfare. The emperor also commissioned a text dealing with imperial military expeditions, produced by Leo Katakalon.

The *Taktika* is marked by the didactic, legislative character of 9th- and 10th-century literature which is taken to exemplify the revival of knowledge in this period, the so-called Macedonian renaissance. But Leo was also active in the field of pure legislation (again redolent of the Macedonian renaissance). Not only does it seem that it was under Leo that the *Basilika* project of Basil I was completed, but Leo issued his own collection of new laws (*Novels*) – again inspired by the work of Justinian I (527–65), and in some cases a direct response to that emperor's own *Novels*. (Schminck [1986], also argues that the *Procheiron*, a legal handbook issued in the names of Basil, Constantine, and Leo, was in fact a revision of the *Epanagoge*, to remove the taint of Photios.) But the legislative work of Leo forms a bridge to his other writings, for it is characterized by its rhetorical and advisory style.

The rhetoric-loving Byzantines also valued highly the art of letter writing, and we have references to letters that Leo wrote, but unfortunately no examples of his literary activity in this area have survived.

As noted, much of Leo's work epitomizes the style and type of literature produced during the so-called Macedonian renaissance of the 9th and 10th centuries. Leo's unique contribution was perhaps the fact that he was an *imperial* author. In this sense his greatest impact seems to have been upon his son

Constantine VII Porphyrogennetos (913–59), who stands as the epitome of the encyclopedic movement, but who owes much in reality to the example of his father. Indeed it was under Constantine VII that the *Taktika* was copied and incorporated into a corpus of strategic writings, and it was Constantine who found and exploited Leo Katakalon's text dealing with imperial military expeditions. In the wider field Leo's *Taktika* appears to have spawned a host of 10th-century tactical writing; he is acknowledged, and used, by subsequent texts linked with Nikephoros II Phokas and Nikephoros Ouranos.

Beyond his legislative work Leo's reign was marked by the scandal over his fourth marriage (the tetragamy), the military threat of both Bulgaria and the Arab navy, and notable relationships with his military and civil officials. Leo married for a fourth time in 906, following the birth of a son to his lover Zoe Karbonopsina. However, fourth marriages were illegal and Leo found himself excommunicated, though he planned to have his marriage sanctioned by the church. This was granted in 907, though Leo had had to depose the patriarch of Constantinople for his opposition prior to the meeting of the synod. During Leo's reign the recently Christianized Bulgaria emerged as a military threat in under its khan Symeon (893–927); several conflicts marked the 890s, but a peace was finally concluded in 896. At sea the Arabs proved devastating, striking key sites such as Samos, Demetrias, Lemnos and Thessalonica, approaching Constantinople itself in 904. Leo responded to this situation by making Himerios admiral; he led the Byzantine navy to some success though a campaign to Crete in 911 failed. Internally Leo fostered close relations with his military and civil officials (notably his eunuchs). This seems to have resulted in some tensions; the eunuch Samonas's machinations seem to have caused the general Andronikos Doukas to flee to the Arabs in 906.

But one of the most enduring legacies of Leo VI is his peculiar connection with the prophet Leo the Wise and his oracles, as studied by Cyril Mango in his classic "The Legend of Leo The Wise" (1960). Mango argues that Leo VI became linked with the figure of the prophet through a confusion with Leo the Philosopher especially but also with Leo Choirosphaktes, though it could be argued that Leo VI had as much a stake in the creation of the prophet as these two men (see, for instance, Magdalino, 1988). A set of oracles, with illustrations, was known by the 12th century, and a second set emerged probably in the 13th century. After the fall of Constantinople the oracle collection attained mass popularity in East and West, and remained salient for the East due to the Turkish occupation.

SHAUN TOUGHER

Biography

Born in 866 probably in Constantinople, the second son of Basil I, Leo was a pupil of Photios and received a good education. He had a bookish reputation and was known as "the wise" during his lifetime. A collection of his homilies and a military manual survive; he also wrote poetry and hymns and issued legislation. His fourth marriage caused controversy. He died in Constantinople in 912.

Further Reading

Antonopoulou, Theodora, *The Homilies of the Emperor Leo VI*, Leiden: Brill, 1997

Brubaker, Leslie (editor), *Byzantium in the Ninth Century: Dead or Alive?*, Aldershot, Hampshire: Ashgate, 1998

Cicollela, F., "Il carme anacreontico di Leone VI", *Bolletino dei Classici*, series 3, 10 (1989): pp. 17–37

Dain, A. and J.-A. Foucault, "Les Stratégistes byzantins", *Travaux et Mémoires*, 2 (1967): pp. 317–92

Eustratiades, S., "Leon o Sophos kai ta poiitika autou erga" [Leo the Wise and his Poetic Works], *Romanos o Melodos*, 1 (1932–33): pp. 69–81

Fögen, M.T., "Legislation und Kodifikation des Kaisers Leons VI", *Subseciva Groningana*, 3 (1989) pp. 23–35

Jenkins, Romilly, *Byzantium: The Imperial Centuries, AD 610–1071*, London: Weidenfeld and Nicolson, 1966

Jenkins, Romilly, *Studies on Byzantine History of the 9th and 10th Centuries*, London: Variorum, 1970

Karlin-Hayter, Patricia, *Vita Euthymii Patriarchae CP*, Brussels: Editions de Byzantion, 1970 (text, translation, introduction, and commentary)

Karlin-Hayter, Patricia, *Studies in Byzantine Political History*, London: Variorum, 1981

Lemeule, Paul, *Byzantine Humanism, The First Phase: Notes and Remarks on Education and Culture in Byzantium from Its Origins to the 10th Century*, Canberra: Australian Association for Byzantine Studies, 1986

Magdalino, P., "The Bath of Leo the Wise and the 'Macedonian Renaissance' Revisited: Topography, Iconography, Ceremonial, Ideology", *Dumbarton Oaks Papers*, 42 (1988): pp. 97–118

Magdalino, P., "The Non-Juridical Legislation of Leo VI", *Fontes Minores (Athener Reihe)*, 1 (1996): pp. 73–86

Mango, C., "The Legend of Leo the Wise", *Zbornik Radova-Vizsantološkog Instituta*, 6 (1960): pp. 59–93

Markopoulos, A., "Epigramma pros time tou Leontos ST´ tou Sophou" [An Epigram in Honour of Leo VI the Wise], *Symmeikta*, 9 (1994): pp. 33–40

Matons, José Grosdidier de, "Trois Etudes sur Léon VI", *Travaux et Mémoires*, 5 (1973): pp. 181–242

Schminck, Andreas, *Studien zu mittelbyzantinischen Rechtsbüchern*, Frankfurt: Löwenklau, 1986

Schminck, Andreas, "'Frömmigkeit ziere das Werk': Zur Datierung der 60 Bücher Leons VI", *Subseciva Groningana*, 3 (1989): pp. 79–114

Tougher, Shaun, *The Reign of Leo VI, 886–912: Politics and People*, Leiden: Brill, 1997

Vogt, A. and I. Hausherr, "Oraison funèbre de Basile I par son fils Léon VI le sage", *Orientalia Christiana*, 26 (1932): pp. 5–79

Leo the Mathematician *c.*790–after 869

Scholar

Born around 790, Leo studied "grammar and poetics" in Constantinople, and "rhetoric, philosophy, and arithmetic" on the island of Andros, where he "happened on a learned man". (It has been suggested that he went to Andros because no one who taught these subjects could be found in Constantinople, but there is no evidence for this; education was at a low ebb, but the degree has been much exaggerated.) Having mastered the elements of these disciplines, Leo "headed for some mountains" where he found monasteries with manuscripts that enabled him to pursue his studies. He returned to Constantinople "master of philosophy and her sisters, arithmetic, geometry, astronomy, and music". (The Pythagoraean relationship between philosophy, mathematics, and music was still dominant.)

Back in Constantinople, Leo earned his living by giving lessons privately for several years before coming to the attention of the emperor Theophilos (829–42). This occurred, say the chroniclers, when a mathematician pupil of his was taken prisoner and brought before the caliph Mamun (813–33), who was known for his interest in Greek science. When Leo's pupil informed Mamun that his mathematics were as nothing compared to his master's, Mamun, already impressed, wrote to Leo, offering him great wealth if he would come to his court. Leo turned the letter in to the palace, where it was submitted to the emperor; he promptly sent for Leo and, recognizing his gifts, set him up to "teach publicly".

To this period must be dated a great technical achievement of Leo's: news of frontier violation reached Constantinople, through a chain of beacon-lights, within the hour, it is estimated, from the fortress at Loulon, just north of Tarsus. The message had been simply that there was frontier trouble; but Leo made it possible to choose between 12 different messages, identified by the hour of arrival. Only three of these have come down to us: hour one meant a small raid; hour two, full-scale war; hour three, enemy incendiarism. Achieved through the synchronization of clocks in Constantinople and at Loulon, and by introducing the division of the day, at all seasons, into twice 12 standardized hours, the importance of this system for defence is obvious.

In 840 Leo was made metropolitan of Thessalonica. Finding the city in the grip of famine due to repeated crop failure,

> He told them not to despair ... And when he recognized through astrology, thanks to the rising and phases of certain stars, that an emanation and sympathy with things earthly were present, he [told them to] place the seed in earth's bosom, resulting in such fertility and fruitfulness that, when spring came and the harvest season arrived, they had enough for several years.

Leo presumably found in his manuscript of Ptolemy what signs in the heavens should precede sowing. No clear distinction was made between astronomy and astrology. Leo's astrology, unlike that of John the Grammarian, has the enthusiastic approval of the chroniclers.

Although probably not an iconoclast, Leo was inevitably removed from the see of Thessalonica in the purge that accompanied the Restoration of Orthodoxy. He reappeared at the time of the foundation of the "University" of the Magnaura by the empress-regent Theodora's brother, Bardas, well after Theophilos's death, perhaps in 855/56. Bardas made Leo head of the philosophy school and possibly of the whole institution. There were three other "faculties" – geometry, astronomy, and "grammar" (in fact language and literature; the incumbent, Cometas, was a great Homer specialist).

Leo produced a "corrected" edition (diorthosis) of some of the works of Plato; even though it has not survived, it served Arethas for his "edition", as emerges from a marginal note to Laws, 5 (743b): "End of the corrections due to Leo the Philosopher". He quotes Gregory of Nazianzus, and he knew Porphyry as well as Achilles Tatius' romance Cleitophon and Leucippe (on which Photios and Leo express differing views).

Our limited knowledge of Leo's reading is gleaned from references such as the scholion quoted above to Plato's Laws or brief poems by him in the 10th-century Palatine Anthology. There are more general references in a curious poem addressed by one Constantine the Sicilian to a "former teacher" of his, called Leo, "who taught profane learning ..., losing his soul in that sea of godlessness"; this is probably our Leo, whom Constantine proceeds to send to "Tartarus and Pyriphlegethon" where he will find all the authors his "heart desires", listing Chrysippus, Socrates, Proclus, Plato, Aristotle, Epicurus, Euclid, Ptolemy, Homer, Hesiod, and Aratus.

A little more is known of Leo's scientific reading. Only one manuscript that belonged to him seems to have come down to us, of Ptolemy's Almagest (Biblioteca Apostolica Vaticana gr. 1594, one of the oldest extant minuscule manuscripts), but his verses show that he had Euclid, Apollonius of Perge's Conic Sections, treatises on mechanics (now lost) by Kyrinos and Markellos (apparently Latin: Quirinus and Marcellus), on astronomy by Theon of Alexandria, and on geometry by Proclus of Xanthus. The greater part of our text of Archimedes is thought to be due to him.

One sermon that Leo is said to have preached in Thessalonica is preserved; it is decidedly individual. The occasion was, in theory, the Annunciation; the sermon begins, however, with considerations on the names of Easter ("Phasek to the Hebrews ... escape from Egypt, that is darkness – so should 'Egypt' be interpreted") and Pentecost, at considerable length. After various digressions on the properties of numbers and a brief if gushing paragraph on the Virgin, he finally passes to the miraculous healing and conversion of a young Jewess that had taken place in the same church about the year 500; to this he devotes more than half the sermon, giving quite an important role to two icons.

PATRICIA KARLIN-HAYTER

Biography

Born c.790, Leo was educated in Constantinople and on Andros. The emperor Theophilos appointed him to a teaching position. From 840 to 843 he was metropolitan of Thessalonica. In 855/56 he became head of the philosophy school at the "University" of the Magnaura. He made important contributions to the textual transmission of Ptolemy, Plato, and Archimedes. He died in Constantinople after 869.

Further Reading

Lemerle, Paul, Byzantine Humanism, the First Phase: Notes and Remarks on Education and Culture in Byzantium from its Origins to the 10th century, Canberra: Australian Association for Byzantine Studies, 1986, especially chapters 6 and 9

Wilson, Nigel G., Scholars of Byzantium, 2d edition, London: Duckworth, and Cambridge, Massachusetts: Medieval Academy of America, 1996

Leonidas c.530–480 BC

King of Sparta

Leonidas was famous for his heroic attempt to hold the pass of Thermopylae in central Greece against the advance of the Persians under king Xerxes in 480 BC. His father,

Leonidas: remains of marble statue of Leonidas, hero of Thermopylae, in the Sparta museum. It provided the inspiration for a modern memorial to Leonides and the 300 set up in 1955 at the battle site

Anaxandrides of the Agiad royal house (Sparta had a dual kingship with two royal houses, the Agiads and the Eurypontids), had married his niece but had no children, whereupon the ephors and the council of elders (Gerousia) forced him to take a second wife, who produced a son and successor, Cleomenes I. But shortly after Cleomenes' birth, the first wife, who was hitherto childless, produced three sons: Dorieus, who died in a failed attempt to plant a colony in Sicily, Leonidas, and Cleombrotus. After Cleomenes lost his throne around 490 BC, probably shortly before the battle of Marathon in that year, Leonidas succeeded, having married Cleomenes' only child, Gorgo.

In 480 BC the Persians, whose expeditionary force had been defeated at Marathon ten years earlier, launched a massive invasion: their army, led by Xerxes himself, crossed the Hellespont by pontoon bridges and advanced through northern Greece while the navy, carrying supplies, cruised along the coast. The Greek states that were willing to resist allied themselves under Spartan leadership, and first attempted to make a stand at the vale of Tempe in Thessaly, but the commanders of the joint land and naval force that was dispatched there withdrew once they realized the position was indefensible. A second attempt was made at the pass of Thermopylae, where the road between the Malian Gulf and Mount Kallidromos was much narrower than today. Leonidas was sent there with an allied force totalling perhaps 7,000 foot-soldiers, including 300 elite "Spartiates" of the royal bodyguard, and a comparatively large naval contingent was sent to Artemisium at the northern tip of the island of Euboea to prevent any joint operation between the Persian fleet and the army on land.

However, Leonidas' force was unaware that there was another path bypassing Thermopylae along the ridge of Kallidromos, known locally as the Anopaea. When they learned about it on their arrival, many, particularly those from the region south of the isthmus of Corinth, where the allies from the Peloponnese were building a defensive wall, wanted to withdraw. But Leonidas quelled the panic and assigned the 1,000-strong contingent from Phocis, who knew the terrain, to guard the Anopaea.

For two days the Greeks warded off all Persian efforts to force the pass. But then a traitor, whom the Greeks identified as Ephialtes from neighbouring Malis, offered to lead the Persians along the Anopaea, and Xerxes assigned his elite corps of 10,000 "Immortals" to the manoeuvre. At dawn on the third day Leonidas learned from his scouts that the Persians were circling at his rear by the Anopaea. He sent home the allied contingents from the states to the south of the isthmus of Corinth, while he himself, with his 300 Spartiates, and 700 Thespians and 400 Thebans from north of the isthmus, secured their retreat by remaining behind in the pass and fighting to the death. The Greek fleet at Artemisium, which had engaged the Persian navy timidly while the battle at Thermopylae was taking place, retreated to Salamis off the coast of Attica as soon as it learned of the disaster.

Leonidas' decision to stay and fight was a rational choice made to save the bulk of his army, but he and his brave "Three Hundred" entered mythology almost immediately. Herodotus, who published his *Histories* around 425 BC, reports that Sparta had received an oracle from Delphi that said that either Sparta itself would be destroyed or a Spartan king would perish, and Leonidas, knowing the oracle, chose to save his state by his death. Thermopylae became the chief building block of the Spartan mystique of utter devotion to duty, which was epitomized by the couplet that Sparta engraved on the monument erected where Leonidas' Spartiates made their last stand: "Go, stranger, to the Spartans tell / That here, obeying their commands, we fell." More than half a century later, in 425 BC, when a force that included some 120 elite Spartiates surrendered to the Athenians at the bay of Navarino during the Peloponnesian War, Greece was amazed that they did not die fighting. Leonidas himself became the paradigm of the soldier who obeys orders without question. For the Renaissance, he represented the virtue of Fortitude: at the Collegio del Cambio in Perugia, Perugino depicted the *Four Cardinal Virtues*, each with three examples from history; for Fortitude the examples are Leonidas, Lucius Sicinnius, and Horatius Cocles. For the neoclassicists of the French Revolution, Leonidas represented courageous resistance to tyranny, and a painting of Thermopylae was, among contemporaries at least, one of the most famous works of the "official artist" of the revolution, Jacques Louis David. The Greek War of Independence of the 1820s evoked Leonidas again, along with other heroes of the Classical past; the Souliot leader, Markos Botsaris (died 1823), the defender of Missolonghi who died at the battle of Karpenisi shortly before Lord Byron's arrival in Greece, was called the "modern Leonidas", though the claim to be the modern Spartans belonged to the Maniotes from the southern tip of the Taygetus range. More than a century later, during the German invasion of 1941, his memory was evoked again when the British made an unsuccessful attempt to hold Thermopylae against the German tank divisions. In 1955 a white marble monument surmounted by a heroic bronze sculpture of Leonidas in full hoplite armour was unveiled at Thermopylae by King Paul of Greece. However, the ideal of unquestioning obedience is no longer as attractive to the military mind, and Crane Brinton's judgement on Leonidas' heroism (*A History of Western Morals*, New York, 1959, p. 84) represents a general feeling in the post-World-War-II era: "[it is Thermopylae] much better than the charge of the Light Brigade on which we now surely accept French Marshal Bosquet's verdict, 'C'est magnifique, mais ce n'est pas la guerre'". Brinton goes on to quote a stanza from Tennyson's poem *The Charge of the Light Brigade* as an example of an earlier generation's silliness.

JAMES ALLAN EVANS

See also Persian Wars

Biography

Born *c*.530 BC, Leonidas became king of Sparta after the death of his half-brother Cleomenes in 490. In 480 he attempted to hold the pass of Thermopylae against the Persian army with a hand-picked force of 300 Spartiates and 1100 Boeotians. Their fight to the death immediately entered mythology. His memory has regularly been invoked ever since as the model of resistance to tyranny.

Further Reading

Brookner, Anita, *Jacques-Louis David*, London: Chatto and Windus, and New York, Harper and Row, 1980

Burn, A.R., *Persia and the Greeks: The Defence of the West, c. 546–478 BC*, 2nd edition, London: Duckworth, and Stanford, California: Stanford University Press, 1984

Evans, J.A.S., "The 'Final Problem' at Thermopylae", *Greek, Roman and Byzantine Studies*, 5 (1964): pp. 231–37

Evans, J.A.S., "Notes on Thermopylae and Artemisium", *Historia*, 18 (1969): pp. 189–221

Hignett, Charles, *Xerxes' Invasion of Greece*, Oxford: Clarendon Press, 1963

Lazenby, J.F., *The Defence of Greece, 490–479 BC*, Warminster: Aris and Phillips, 1993

Lesbos

Aegean island

Physical remains and the Homeric poems associate Bronze Age Lesbos with Anatolia and the Troad; despite a tradition of Greek migration two generations after the Trojan War, Greek artifacts are rare before the 10th century BC. After 900 BC Anatolian connections continued in personal names (Myrsilos), cult (Cybele), and material culture, but Lesbos' cities (Antissa, Arisba, Eressos, Methymna, Mytilene, Pyrrha) were inhabited by speakers of a Greek dialect (Aeolic) and no allophone ("Pelasgian") population remained. In the 8th century Aeolian Greeks established settlements on the coasts opposite Lesbos and in the Troad; by 700, except for Assos, they were controlled by Mytilene, and Methymna had enslaved Arisba. Inter-city hostility became a constant of Lesbian history.

Mytilene's dependencies in Asia Minor, outposts in Pontus, Thrace (Aenus), and Egypt (Naucratis), good relations with the Lydian monarchy, and flourishing trade in oil and wine, made Lesbos a major cultural force from 700 to 500 BC. Among their accomplishments were close-fitting polygonal masonry (*Lesbia oikodome*), "Aeolic" capitals with vertical volutes (linking Phoenician models with later Greek orders), and lyric poetry, associated with the cult of Orpheus at Antissa, the home of Terpander (676 BC); Mytilenean hegemony may explain why Terpander and Arion of Methymna worked in mainland Greece. Around 600, Sappho and Alcaeus wrote for and about Mytilene in Lesbian dialect, which was used in inscriptions as late as the 3rd century AD; Lesbian accentuation is maintained in modern place-names (Yéra for Hierá). Besides their poetic influence, Sappho and Alcaeus illustrate much about archaic Lesbian society. Sappho shows how much less restricted women's roles were on Lesbos than in democratic Athens, more like Lydia, where women chose their own husbands; the pejorative use of terms derived from "Lesbos" for sexual behaviours reflects male hostility to such freedom as much as to Sappho's sexuality. Mytilenean politics, as presented by Alcaeus, provided a paradigm of the relationship between aristocracy and tyranny. Mytileneans, with ties to Sardis, may have been the first Greeks to use the Lydian term *tyrannos* for their rulers; it was applied also to the constitutional rule of Pittacus around 590 BC.

After Persian domination the Lesbian cities joined the Delian League in 479, to which Mytilene and Methymna provided ships rather than tribute. In 428 Methymna and Tenedos denounced to Athens Mytilenean plans to unify Lesbos by force; the punishment of Mytilene's subsequent revolt became an eloquent symbol of Athenian imperialism.

In the 4th century Aristotle conducted primary research on Lesbos. In the Hellenistic period Methymna and Eressos were Ptolemaic but Mytilene remained independent. Methymna was an early ally of Rome, but Antissa was destroyed by Rome in 169 BC for supporting Macedonia, and Mytilene, the most persistent supporter of Mithradates of Pontus, was conquered by Rome in 80.

In 62 BC Pompey gave Mytilene back its independence as a favour to his friend, the historian Theophanes. Mytilene developed a special relationship with Rome; several Mytileneans, including the descendants of Theophanes, the sophist Potamon, and the poet Crinagoras, had significant careers in the capital, while important Romans, notably Agrippa and his family, resided in, and were honoured by, Mytilene.

The pastoral novel *Daphnis and Chloe* is part of this relationship. Set on Lesbos by an author with a Roman name, its account of the island's cults had special resonance for descendants of Theophanes, who led a Dionysiac cult near Rome. Longus' assimilation of the pastoral form to that of the love romance and his choice of fertile Lesbos as its setting affected all subsequent pastorals.

Lesbos prospered in late antiquity. Mosaics from the 4th or 5th century AD portraying scenes from Menander show the continuance of pagan culture, and several Christian basilicas were built in the 5th to 7th centuries.

When the Fourth Crusade took Constantinople in 1204, Lesbos was assigned to the emperor Baldwin, but was recovered in 1229 by the empire of Nicaea. In 1355, Genoese Francesco Gattilusio received it as the dowry of his wife Maria, sister of John V Palaiologos, whom Francesco helped regain the imperial throne. The Gattilusi came to control much of the northeast Aegean, and were more popular with their Greek subjects than other Frankish regimes: their authority came from the emperor, they spoke Greek, brought Greek notables into their council, and maintained the Orthodox hierarchy. Their imperial connections gave Lesbian products (especially wine) preferred access to markets in the capital. Most medieval remains on Lesbos were built by the Gattilusi; their castle in Mytilene reused much ancient material.

When Lesbos was taken by the Turks in 1462, the urban population was transported to Constantinople, and much of the city of Mytilene, in which remains of antiquity were still visible, was destroyed. Many rural communities were abandoned under Turkish rule, and there was substantial migration to the adjoining mainland, where Kydonia (modern Aivali), granted self-government in 1770, became a centre of Greek learning.

In the 18th and 19th centuries the Greek community on Lesbos flourished as they, rather than the Turkish landowners, profited from liberalized trading regulations; wealthy Lesbians built traditional *pyrgoi* (tower houses) in the villages, and fine villas in the southern suburbs of Mytilene. Lesbians participated in the War of Independence, including the destruction of a Turkish warship at Eressos, but remained under Turkish rule until 1912.

Along with Kydonia, Mytilene saw a great advance in learned culture in the 19th century, typified by the philologists Dimitrios and Grigorios Bernardakis. Towards the end of the century Argyris Eftaliotis (1849–1923) became a leading figure in the creation of literary demotic. His portrayal of 19th-

Lesbos: Aeolic capital, late 7th or early 6th century BC, predecessor of the Ionic order

century island life draws on Lesbos' particularly rich folklore tradition, which preserves memories of the Gattilusi, if not of antiquity.

Liberation from Turkey in 1912 and the military catastrophe in Anatolia in 1922 presented Lesbos with a severe challenge to integrate a large refugee population. The response included a movement of political and literary reform with which were associated both Lesbians and refugees. They included the most moving witnesses of Greece's experience of the war years and the Asia Minor catastrophe, Elias Venezis and Stratis Myrivilis, whose idyllic portrait of the island recalls Sappho and Longus. Lesbos' revived culture also supported visual artists, of whom the best known is the folk painter Theophilos Chatzimichail (1873–1934), whose paintings on the walls of buildings on Lesbos are especially fortunate in recalling traditional Greek society, and are symbolic of the role of folk culture in Greek society, to which Lesbos bears particularly eloquent witness.

HUGH J. MASON

Summary

A large island in the northeast Aegean, Lesbos was inhabited by Aeolian Greeks in ancient times. The island was prosperous and an early centre of culture from 700 to 500 BC, making important contributions to music, lyric poetry, and architecture. It prospered again in late antiquity; but under the Turks many communities were abandoned. Prosperity returned in the 18th and 19th centuries and cultural creativity in the 20th.

Further Reading

Andrewes, Antony, *The Greek Tyrants*, London: Hutchinson, 1956

Betancourt, Philip P., *The Aeolic Style in Architecture: A Survey of Its Development in Palestine, the Halikarnassos Peninsula, and Greece, 1000–500 BC*, Princeton, New Jersey: Princeton University Press, 1977

Gold, Barbara K., "Pompey and Theophanes of Mytilene", *American Journal of Philology*, 106 (1985): pp. 312–27

Holton, D.W., " 'The Leprous Queen': A Ballad from Lesbos", *Byzantine and Modern Greek Studies*, 1 (1975): pp. 98–109

Mason, Hugh J., "The Literature of Classical Lesbos and the Fiction of Stratis Myrivilis", *Classical and Modern Literature*, 9 (1989): pp. 347–57

Mason, Hugh J., "Mytilene and Methymna: Quarrels, Borders and Topography", *Echos du Monde Classique*, 37 (1993): pp. 225–50

Miller, William, "The Gattilusj of Lesbos" in his *Essays on the Latin Orient*, Cambridge: Cambridge University Press, 1921, reprinted New York: AMS Press, 1983, pp. 313–53

Morgan, John R., "*Daphnis and Chloe*: Love's Own Sweet Story" in *Greek Fiction: The Greek Novel in Context*, edited by J.R. Morgan and Richard Stoneman, London and New York: Routledge, 1994

Page, D.L., *Sappho and Alcaeus: An Introduction to the Study of Ancient Lesbian Poetry*, Oxford: Clarendon Press, 1955, reprinted 1979

Spencer, Nigel, *A Gazetteer of Archaeological Sites in Lesbos*, Oxford: Tempus Reparatum, 1995

Spencer, Nigel, "Lesbos between East and West: A 'Grey Area' of Aegean Archaeology", *Annual of the British School at Athens*, 90 (1995): pp. 269–306

Libanius AD 314–c.393

Teacher of rhetoric

Libanius was born at Antioch, where he belonged to one of the leading curial families. He was the most highly esteemed teacher of rhetoric of his time, and attracted pupils from all over the Near East. Yet he spent most of his life teaching in his native city and died there. Libanius wrote in an elaborate Atticizing Greek that was admired and imitated for most of the Byzantine period. In consequence a large part of his literary output survives: almost 1600 letters, 64 orations on topical questions, 51 declamations, and numerous rhetorical exercises. We therefore know Libanius better than all but a very few individuals of antiquity, and his writings are an almost inexhaustible source of information about social life, politics, administration, entertainments, and education in the 4th century AD; thanks to Libanius, Antioch is by far the best-known provincial city of late antiquity.

Libanius was above all a traditionalist. He was an Atticist in the tradition of the Second Sophistic. His vocabulary, syntax, and sentence structure are based on those of Classical Athenian authors. He was an admirer of Aelius Aristides (AD 117–c.189), but he was thoroughly familiar with the Classical authors themselves, above all Homer, Demosthenes, and Thucydides. References and allusions to Plato also occur frequently in his writings. He pays respect to the wisdom of Plato the philosopher, but what he adopted for his own use was Plato's mastery of language. Above all he used him as a source of rhetorical comparisons and analogies. Socrates was a great hero, a kind of pagan Christ. He does not appear to have used Aristotle at all. Unlike his contemporary and admirer the emperor Julian the Apostate, Libanius seems to have had very little use for the philosophy either of the Classical thinkers, or of contemporary Neoplatonists. Declamations with an Athenian setting show that Libanius had a very detailed knowledge of the history, institutions, and customs of classical Athens.

Libanius' writings contain very few allusions to historical events later than the reign of Alexander the Great. Though he

– like most free inhabitants of the empire by the 4th century – was a Roman citizen, and though his life was shaped by decisions of Roman emperors and officials, he showed no interest whatsoever in things Roman, seeing Roman and Latin law as the dangerous rivals of the Greek rhetorical education, based as it was on close familiarity with Classical Greek authors, which it was his life's work to maintain and propagate. In the realms of politics he appreciated the need for an emperor and empire to keep off barbarians and to uphold law and order within the borders, but his personal allegiance was to his birthplace rather than to the empire. More particularly he mistrusted Constantinople as an upstart that was draining human and material resources from cities such as his own Antioch. Libanius was a pagan and made no attempt to hide his paganism. But his Hellenic educational ideal had a strong moral component not very different from the moral teaching of Christianity, and his correspondents included Christians as well as pagans. Libanius was honoured by the Christian emperor Theodosius I. Christian and pagan parents alike sent him their sons to educate. John Chrysostom and Theodore of Mopsuestia were almost certainly his pupils; Basil and Gregory of Nazianzus are likely to have been.

The life and career of Libanius thus illustrate the peaceful coexistence of Christians and pagans in an age better known for religious conflict; and his work as a teacher actively contributed to the assimilation of Hellenic traditions into a Greek Christian civilization.

J.H.W.G. LIEBESCHUETZ

See also Rhetoric

Biography

Born at Antioch in 314, Libanius was educated in Athens and taught rhetoric at Constantinople and Nicomedia. He declined the offer of a chair of rhetoric at Athens but accepted one at Antioch where he remained for most of his life. His pupils included many famous men. His surviving works includes letters, orations, declamations, and rhetorical exercises. His prose style was much admired by the Byzantines. He died at Antioch *c.*393.

Writings

Opera, edited by Richard Foerster, 12 vols, Leipzig: Teubner, 1903–27 (Greek text)
Autobiography (Oration I): The Greek Text, edited and translated by A.F. Norman, London and New York: Oxford University Press, 1965
Selected Works, translated by A.F. Norman, 4 vols, Cambridge, Massachusetts: Harvard University Press, and London: Heinemann, 1969–92 (Loeb edition)
Imaginary Speeches: A Selection of Declamations, edited and translated by D.A. Russell, London: Duckworth, 1996 (includes "Defence of Socrates" and "The Silence of Socrates")

Further Reading

Petit, Paul, *Libanius et la vie municipale à Antioche au IVe siècle après J.-C.*, Paris: Geuthner, 1955
Petit, Paul, *Les Etudiants de Libanius*, Paris: Nouvelles Editions Latines, 1957
Schouler, Bernard, *La Tradition hellénique chez Libanios*, 2 vols, Paris: Belles Lettres, 1984
Wiemer, Hans-Ulrich, *Libanios und Julian: Studien zum Verhältnis von Rhetorik und Politik im vierten Jahrhundert n. Chr*, Munich: Beck, 1995

Libraries

Libraries in the ancient Greek world were an important medium for the preservation and storage of literature. Since books had to be copied individually and by hand, many less popular books were fated to survive in the long term only in the collections of one or two libraries or of the occasional enthusiastic bibliophile.

Private book collections began to exist as soon as written literature multiplied, certainly by the 6th century BC. A book trade must have emerged soon after, dealing in second-hand copies. Booksellers may also have provided – speculatively, or to order – new copies of the latest writings: certainly they did this in later periods. At Athens, already in the 5th century BC, a distinct part of the city market was occupied by booksellers. Quite soon two types of libraries emerged to meet the needs that private collections and the book trade were unable to satisfy.

Schools, mainly philosophical and medical, needed to have permanent access to works that were relevant to the teaching and research they conducted, especially texts compiled by their own teachers. By the 4th century BC we know of two such school libraries. The books now known as the Hippocratic Corpus (anonymous medical texts by many authors, traditionally ascribed to Hippocrates himself) were evidently the nucleus of the working library of the Hippocratic school at Cos – broad-mindedly including several works that adopt the theories of the rival school at Cnidus. The contents of the library of the Peripatetic school led by Aristotle, and after him by Theophrastus, also partly survive, in the form of research texts attributed to these two philosophers themselves, though in several cases they are evidently not the actual authors. This library was bequeathed outside the school by Theophrastus, was not available to later Peripatetics, and was nearly lost for good; its history is outlined by Strabo (*Geography*, 13. 1. 54).

True public libraries were needed as soon as the range of texts that people wanted to read grew to the point at which a book dealer could not find or supply them all. If it is true that Pisistratus, tyrant of Athens, established a public library, this need must have been felt as early as the mid-6th century BC. The Latin author Aulus Gellius (*Attic Nights*, 7. 17. 3), the only source of information on Pisistratus' library, adds that it was seized and taken to Persia when Xerxes invaded Greece.

But little is known for certain of libraries before Alexander's time. It was under the Hellenistic kings, with their need to establish and assert Greek culture across the Near East, that major public libraries appeared. The Library at Alexandria (closely associated with the Museum), founded by Ptolemy I Soter (reigned 305–283/82 BC), was one of the great libraries of all time, classified in accordance with a system developed by Aristotle and eventually with a stock of 700,000 papyrus rolls, according to Gellius. Ptolemy persuaded the Athenian state to lend the archive copies of Classic Athenian drama for copying. Having received them, the Alexandrian library kept the old manuscripts and sent new copies back to Athens. The 3rd-century BC poet Callimachus worked at the library and was credited with the authorship of the *Pinakes*, "Tables", which were a thematic listing of Greek writings up to his time and a subject catalogue of the Alexandrian library: sadly, only a few fragments survive.

A second great library of the Hellenistic period was founded under the patronage of the Attalid kings of Pergamum. It had grown to 200,000 volumes when Mark Antony seized it and presented it to Cleopatra. From the excavations of Pergamum some details of the floor plan of this library can be reconstructed: three large rooms, with wooden bookcases, held the manuscripts; a fourth room was apparently for readers' use; and there were colonnades that provided an additional location for reading and discussion. Bookcases for papyrus rolls took the form of sets of pigeon holes: rolls had labels hanging from one end, which could be read without removing the roll from its place.

The Seleucid kings also had an important library at Antioch. Two further Hellenistic libraries, that of the kings of Macedon at Pella and that of Mithradates, king of Pontus, were both taken to Rome as booty by victorious generals. The great library at Alexandria was burned (though not completely destroyed, it is thought) by Julius Caesar's troops in 47 BC. Rome's own public libraries – the first was founded in 39 BC – were probably better stocked with Greek than with Latin literature.

In general, Greek libraries continued to flourish under the Roman empire, and inscriptions and excavations give us occasional clues regarding their operation. They were naturally to be found at centres of Greek learning. The emperor Hadrian founded a magnificent library near the Agora in Athens in AD 131.

Constantinople, the new capital of the Roman empire, eventually became the focus of Greek cultural life. Here it was that Greek literature survived, in libraries and private collections, through medieval times. The emperor Constantius II founded a public library there. Julian added his own book collection to it in AD 362, and it survived until 726.

Byzantine institutional and private libraries suffered in the sack of Constantinople in 1204 and the long period of instability and decline that followed. It is probable that many Classical texts that had survived in Byzantine collections until 1204 were lost for ever in that year. By 1453, when the city fell to the Turks, some of the most important remaining manuscripts had travelled, with fleeing Byzantine scholars, to Italy, and they now enrich the libraries of western Europe.

The chequered history of the libraries of the capital was not shared by the monastic libraries of the Byzantine provinces. Some of these were never destroyed or looted, and, where monasteries have remained active, libraries continue to retain their valuable medieval collections. This is notably the case with several of the monastery libraries of Mount Athos, which date back to the 10th century, and those of Meteora. Also rich is the library of the monastery of St John at Patmos, founded in 1088.

The intellectual climate in Greece in the 16th to 18th centuries, under Turkish rule, did not favour the maintenance or foundation of libraries. In the late 18th century, however, an important landmark was the establishment of schools, several of which were soon equipped with libraries. With very limited funds and absolutely no official support, these naturally collected their stock in a haphazard way, yet the early collections of several of the school libraries (Ioannina, Chios, Dimitsana, Andritsaina, Zagora, and Melies are examples) are

now of great importance in the history of the Greek intellectual and political revival.

As Greece became independent and Athens asserted its role as the national capital, the city became the base for scientific and literary societies and for higher education. Thus, in the 19th century, some larger and modern libraries were developed in Athens (occasionally rivalled by Thessalonica).

By the early 20th century the National Library and the Library of Parliament had emerged as the major research libraries in Greece. The National Library, founded at Aegina in 1829, had moved to Athens in 1834 and merged with the Athens University Library in 1842. It did not gain the privilege of legal deposit until 1943. Its collection of early manuscripts and printed books is fairly small, but it is rich in documentation of the struggle for Greek independence. The Library of Parliament was established in 1845, with the privilege of legal deposit and with reliable funding for foreign purchases. It has the best collection of early Greek newspapers and periodicals, and also contains some important collections bequeathed by politicians and scholars.

Other collections of current importance include those of the Academy of Athens, the British, German, and American Schools at Athens, and, more notable than any of these, the privately founded Gennadios Library, which is outstanding in its collections on modern Greek history. It opened in 1921.

ANDREW DALBY

See also Archives, Books and Readers

Further Reading
Kenyon, F.G., *Books and Readers in Ancient Greece and Rome*, 2nd edition, Oxford: Clarendon Press, 1951; Norwood, Pennsylvania: Norwood Editions, 1975
Pfeiffer, Rudolf, *History of Classical Scholarship: From the Beginnings to the End of the Hellenistic Age*, Oxford: Clarendon Press, 1968
Platthy, Jenö, *Sources on the Earliest Greek Libraries with the Testimonia*, Amsterdam: Hakkert, 1968
Thompson, Lawrence S., "Roman and Greek Libraries" in *Encyclopedia of Library and Information Science*, vol. 26, edited by Allen Kent and Harold Lancour, New York: Dekker, 1979, pp. 3–40
Wilson, Nigel G., "The Libraries of the Byzantine World", *Greek, Roman and Byzantine Studies*, 8 (1967): pp. 53–80
Wilson, Nigel G., *From Byzantium to Italy: Greek Studies in the Italian Renaissance*, London: Duckworth, and Baltimore: Johns Hopkins University Press, 1992

Linear B

The oldest surviving written record of the Greek language

Linear B is the name given to the script that records the oldest known form of Greek (dated to the 15th to 13th centuries BC) and therefore is most probably the earliest evidence of the Hellenic people. It was used in the royal palaces of Bronze Age Crete and mainland Greece as a means of recording the transactions of the palace economy and administration until the destruction of the Mycenaean palaces. The first Linear B script,

producers of the content, most probably wine or olive oil. Most Linear B inscriptions come from Knossos (*c.*5600), Pylos (*c.*1200), Thebes (*c.*420), Mycenae (*c.*90), and Tiryns (*c.*80), but a small number of inscriptions have been found also at Chania (tablets and jars), Midea (a sealing), Orchomenus, Gla, Vlicha, Kreusis, Eleusis, Mameloukos Cave, Armenoi, and Mallia (jars).

The clay tablets show the last stage of the script in use, since they were preserved by being baked in the fire that destroyed the palaces which housed them. The dating of the inscriptions is a controversial matter. Those from Knossos are dated to Late Minoan IIIA2 period (*c.*1375 BC), while those from mainland sites are dated to Late Helladic IIIB (*c.*1200 BC). The tablets from Chania in west Crete, however, are dated to Late Minoan IIIB1 (*c.*1275–1250 BC), which brings the Cretan and mainland scribal traditions closer together. The inscribed pottery on the other hand dates from the 15th to 14th centuries BC, which shows that Linear B was invented in the 15th century BC or possibly earlier.

The Linear B script consists of syllabic signs (87), ideograms (*c.*160), and numerals (1 to 10,000). It was derived from Linear A, a script probably devised for a non-Greek language, and is not well suited to the writing of Greek. All the syllabic signs stand for open syllables, i.e. single vowels standing on their own or syllables ending in a vowel, most of which consist of one consonant followed by one vowel. This is not a convenient feature for writing Greek which contains many words with consonant clusters and final consonants. When a syllable comprises v(owel) + c(onsonant) or c + v + c, the consonant which closes the syllable is usually omitted (e.g. *te-me-no* for *temenos*; *ka-ko* for *khalkos*), whereas when a syllable consists of c + c + v, it is usually written out as two syllables, the first containing the vowel of the succeeding syllable as a "dead" vowel (e.g. *ko-no-so* for Knossos). Apart from a small number of special signs such as *ha*, *au*, *dwe*, and *pte*, the script can represent only 5 vowels and 12 consonants (transcribed as *d, j, k, m, n, p, q, r, s, t, w, z*). This increases the difficulty in representing Greek. For example, the transcriptions *a, e, i, o, u* can stand for short, long, aspirated (h-), and unaspirated vowels; the transcriptions *ka, ke, ki, ko, ku* can stand for k-, kh-, or g-; *pa, pe, pi, po, pu* can stand for p-, ph-, or b-; and l- and r- have the same set of signs in common. The resulting writing is not always clear. What provided the most decisive evidence for the successful decipherment was its occasional practice of adding ideograms, which are often visually recognizable, to the words spelt in syllabic signs, such as "horse" and "tripod". Despite the incomplete nature of the writing, there is sufficient evidence for identifying many dialectal features which show it to be most closely related to the Classical Arcadian and Cypriot dialects.

The contents of the Linear B tablets are mostly lists of people, animals, and goods with short statements, but they do reveal many aspects of palace economy and administration. We can gather from them, for example, the administrative division of the territory, movement of people and livestock, land tenure, offerings to the gods, food rations for workers, production of wool and textiles, production of scented oil, and storage of vessels, utensils, weapons, armour, and chariots. It also appears that the man called *wanax* ("lord"; *anax* in later Greek) was the most powerful person at each palace, and in

Linear B: clay tablet showing fragment of writing in Linear B from Knossos, *c.*1450 BC, Ashmolean Museum, Oxford

written on a clay tablet, was found at Knossos in 1878, and this discovery among other things motivated Arthur Evans, a British archaeologist, to carry out a systematic excavation of the site. Evans's excavations at Knossos from 1900 revealed a palace complex older than the palace at Mycenae excavated by Heinrich Schliemann, and it no longer seemed appropriate to label the civilization of Bronze Age Crete "Mycenaean". Evans named the newly found civilization of Crete "Minoan" after the legendary king Minos. He found three distinctive writing systems at the palace which he named Hieroglyphic (or Pictographic), Linear A, and Linear B, according to their physical appearance. Soon Linear B inscriptions were found also at Pylos and other Mycenaean palaces on the mainland, but because they were assumed to be Minoan they were taken to be evidence of Minoan domination of mainland Greece. However, in 1952 Linear B was deciphered by Michael Ventris, a British amateur, and the language was found to be an old form of Greek. The older hieroglyphic and Linear A inscriptions are still undeciphered, but are thought to represent non-Greek languages.

The Linear B inscriptions were either scratched on clay tablets, labels, and sealings, which were subsequently sun-dried, or painted on large clay vessels. Of the clay tablets, some are called "page" type and others "palm-leaf" type, after their respective shapes. The page type can measure up to *c.*24 × 11 cm, whereas the palm-leaf type measures only up to *c.*18 × 4 cm. There is a sort of hierarchical system among the different classes of clay documents. At least some clay sealings appear to have functioned as delivery notes of goods to various administrative centres. Palm-leaf-type tablets recorded shorter entries and page-type longer ones, and some entries on palm-leaf-type tablets were found to be collected and duplicated on page-type tablets. Clay labels were attached to the containers of sets of tablets to function as indexes. In addition, since the surviving tablets refer only to "this year" and "last year" with no reference to earlier years, it is likely that they were only temporary records for the particular year and that longer-term records were kept on some more perishable material. The inscriptions painted on pottery appear to indicate the places of origin or the

the Mycenaean pantheon the most prominent divinity was a goddess (or a group of goddesses) called *Potnia* ("Lady"), surrounded by some familiar names such as Zeus, Hera, Poseidon, and Dionysus as well as others totally unknown. Some tablets from Pylos seem to refer to preparations for an attack expected from the sea, offering an interesting glimpse of the last days of the Mycenaean palaces.

Literacy disappears from most of the Greek world after the demise of Linear B until the introduction of the alphabet in the early part of the first millennium BC. However, a sister script known as Cypro-Minoan, also derived from Linear A, survived in Cyprus, and eventually evolved into the Cypriot Syllabary which remained in use into the Classical period.

NAOKO YAMAGATA

See also Language, Literacy, Mycenaeans

Further Reading

Chadwick, John, *The Decipherment of Linear B*, 2nd edition, Cambridge: Cambridge University Press, 1967, reprinted with a new postscript, 1992

Chadwick, John, *The Mycenaean World*, Cambridge: Cambridge University Press, 1976

Chadwick, John, *Linear B and Related Scripts*, London: British Museum Publications, 1987

Dickinson, Oliver, *The Aegean Bronze Age*, Cambridge and New York: Cambridge University Press, 1994

Hooker, James Thomas, *Mycenaean Greece*, London and Boston: Routledge and Kegan Paul, 1976

Hooker, James Thomas, *Linear B: An Introduction*, Bristol: Bristol Classical Press, 1980

Palmer, Leonard Robert, *The Interpretation of Mycenaean Greek Texts*, Oxford: Clarendon Press, 1963

Taylour, William, *The Mycenaeans*, 2nd edition, London and New York: Thames and Hudson, 1983

Ventris, Michael and John Chadwick, *Documents in Mycenaean Greek*, 2nd edition, Cambridge: Cambridge University Press, 1973

Vilborg, Ebbe, *A Tentative Grammar of Mycenaean Greek*, Göteborg: Elanders, 1960

Literacy

The earliest known Greek script is Linear B, an adaptation of the Cretan Linear A to accommodate the sounds of Greek, which was devised, perhaps by Minoans rather than by Mycenaeans, at some unknown date (the oldest surviving examples are probably from the late 14th century BC). Although a few Linear B symbols are found on pottery, it seems to have been primarily a secretarial tool for recording palatial inventories of personnel and property on unbaked clay tablets. (There is no scholarly consensus as to whether the "baleful signs" in a folded tablet mentioned in the *Iliad* (6. 168–69) refer to a Greek lexigraphic script, just possibly Linear B, or semasiographic writing or whether they are simply a Near Eastern element imported into the tale of Bellerophon.) Mycenaean society was, therefore, almost exclusively illiterate, a fact which makes more intelligible the Greeks' complete loss of the skill of writing after the collapse of Mycenaean institutions in the 12th century. Knowledge of their past was preserved during the Dark Age (*c.*1200–700 BC) by oral means, most notably in the material that lies behind the Homeric poems.

An alphabet based upon the Phoenicians', but with the adaptation of certain signs to symbolize vowels, was created probably through mercantile contacts and possibly as early as the late 9th century (the earliest known inscription dates from *c.*740 BC). Despite the optimism of many modern scholars, this cannot be proved to have led to widespread literacy throughout the Greek world, even at the most elementary level.

Erection in public places of marble columns inscribed with law codes, first known from the 7th century, did indeed make them available to all, but citizens could rely on intermediaries to read them. Ostracism similarly need not have depended upon common literacy, as the illiterate could have names written for them (a cache has been found of 191 *ostraka* all bearing the name of Themistocles and written in only 14 separate hands). Poetic texts were written down at least as early as the 7th century, but books were always expensive and even in the second half of the 5th century BC Euripides was considered strange for possessing a few papyrus rolls. Schools, though not the only means of transmitting literacy, seem to have arisen first only in the second half of the 6th century (the earliest specifically attested belong to the early years of the 5th) and were never universal. Society remained largely oral, even reading being performed aloud. Although written records of Olympic victors were reputedly made from 776 BC and in the late 6th century Attic demes began to keep records of their members, until at least the 4th century BC legal proceedings were carried out almost exclusively orally, and commercial deals were made by verbal agreements of the parties concerned, the attestation of witnesses, when necessary, being unwritten. There was, moreover, even a distrust of the written word as being more dishonest than the spoken (Isocrates, *Epistles*, 1. 2–3), and Plato, whose inspirational hero Socrates wrote nothing, argues (if *Epistles*, 7 is accepted as genuine) against writing down truly serious things for fear of misuse (344c), and in the *Phaedrus* rightly points out (274e–275b) that literacy militates against memorization.

Although illiteracy seems to have involved no social stigma and created no economic disadvantages even to members of the elite during the Archaic age (*c.*700–479 BC), writing and reading (presumably the more common, especially of lapidary texts) became less unusual accomplishments particularly in the last few decades of the period. They were not confined to the upper classes: inscriptions on vases began as early as the second half of the 8th century and became ubiquitous in the 6th; from 593/92 there survive at Abu Simbel graffiti made by Greek mercenaries; curse tablets first appeared in the 6th century; and even though the earliest known exchange of historical letters in Greek (those of Polycrates of Samos and king Amasis of Egypt) dates only from the 520s, there has been discovered on the island of Berezan, in the estuary of the Bug near Olbia, from only some 20 years later a letter in Milesian Ionic from a private individual (admittedly poorly written, on lead, and probably not even by the sender). Sappho and her circle in late 7th-century Lesbos, though probably exceptional, show that literacy was not exclusively a male preserve. Nevertheless, W.V. Harris concludes that in the Archaic Age "it would be astonishing if as much as 10 per cent of the population as a whole was literate" in any way.

In the Classical period (479–323 BC) there was clearly a great disparity in literacy between city and country, but not necessarily between large and small cities (the minor city of Mycalessus in Boeotia possessed at least three schools in 413, although their type is not mentioned). Most of the known evidence is from Athens, Pericles' "School of Hellas", and thus may be misleading for Greece as a whole. Nevertheless, although Sparta with its need for permanent military preparedness placed little emphasis upon reading and writing, there is evidence that Athens was not atypical (except in its fondness for monumental public inscriptions which need not, however, reflect either a high rate of literacy or democratic policies). Accepting the leadership of the Delian League in 478/77, Athens needed to keep written records (partially surviving) of members' contributions; from 425 are attested both the earliest written manumission and the earliest written litigant's pleading and from about that time, or possibly a little earlier, the first political pamphlet ("The Old Oligarch"); in the last quarter of the century booksellers began to appear; in the last decade a law was passed prohibiting the use of unwritten laws and a state archive was established; by c.360 written service and apprenticeship contracts and large loan agreements had appeared and written testimony was required in court; c.330 standard texts of the tragedians were placed in the state archives.

During this period literacy for the whole population, including slaves (some of whom were literate), probably reached little more than 10 per cent, but few urban, adult, free males could be expected to be entirely ignorant of letters. The very word *agrammatos* came into existence and signified both "illiterate" and "uncultivated"; Euripides' lost *Theseus* contained a scene whose appreciation was possible only through a knowledge of the shapes of letters of the alphabet; Xenophon in his *Oeconomicus* takes it for granted that not only the landowner Ischomachus but also his wife are literate; Aristotle claims (*Politics*, 1338a15–17) that literacy is useful for "business, running the household, learning and many civic activities".

In the Hellenistic period (323–31 BC) literacy among urban freeborn men reached perhaps 40 per cent. From one area, Egypt, there survive for the first time written ephemera in the form of documents and letters of minor officials and common people, although it is somewhat hazardous to extrapolate from here to the rest of the Greek world. Clearly paperwork (on papyrus) was increasing greatly and was being used for even fairly trivial purposes. However, the many hundreds of documents (at least 1500 from the Hellenistic, Roman and early Byzantine periods) that explicitly mention the illiteracy of one or more of the parties suggest that the majority of male farmers and artisans were unable to write, and that only a very tiny proportion of their wives could. For the elite, however, literacy was now a sine qua non, and institutional libraries, initially probably modelled on Aristotle's at the Lyceum, were established, most notably at Alexandria and Pergamum.

Despite growing bureaucratization and interest in buying books, evident from papyrus finds in Egypt, the percentage of literate Greeks perhaps declined slightly under Roman rule (Harris believes that the peak had been passed by the mid-2nd century BC), as certainly did that of all inhabitants of the Roman empire after c.AD 200. It is notable that a village clerk in Egypt was still ineptly practising his signature formula while in office at some point between AD 184 and 187; and that in AD 263 a rich woman considered her literacy sufficiently exceptional to be ground for requesting privileges from the prefect of Egypt.

Although no thorough study has been made of literacy at any period in Byzantine history, it is clear that, even at its lowest ebb in the 8th century, it was always far more common than in the contemporary Latin west. The complex administrative system of the empire necessitated in both the capital and the provinces numerous officials, who depended upon vast numbers of scribes and copyists and whose own literacy is emphasized by the deliberate noting of exceptions (there were reportedly two illiterate emperors, Justin I and Basil I). Many shorthand scribes too were required for taking legal testimony and minutes of church councils and even for recording sermons. Although in the mid-6th century Justinian I found it necessary to legislate that all bishops should be literate, the importance of the Bible and liturgical texts ensured that most ordinary monks (and many nuns) could read (in one document from Athos dated to 991 only three out of 18 monks were unable to sign their names, and it has been estimated that approximately one half of all scribes in the 10th to 11th centuries were monks, although the percentage declined later). Army commanders too were expected to be able to read military manuals. Although the rate of literacy was clearly higher in the cities, and especially in Constantinople, saints' Lives give evidence that many children were able to pick up some knowledge of letters even in remote communities. In the late 9th century Leo VI permitted oral testimony to authorize wills in country areas, but throughout Byzantine history most documents required the signature of witnesses, and Leo's father Basil I decreed that fractions in all tax documents should be written in full so that they should be interpretable by peasants. The cultural elite, which included some women, prided itself on fluency in the "High Language", an approximation of Classical Greek, and scorned as illiterate those familiar only with demotic, the commonly spoken language, or even *koine*, in which the Bible was written.

Evidence for Byzantine libraries is very incomplete and of little aid in assessing general literacy. The huge number of book reviews written by Photios in the 9th century must have required a substantial library or libraries, while letters that mention borrowing as well as inscriptions in surviving manuscripts attest to numerous personal collections after the Iconoclastic period. Monasteries too had libraries ranging from a handful of volumes to a few hundred. In Constantinople itself there were an imperial and a patriarchal library and, at the times when these institutions were in existence, libraries attached to the patriarchal academy and the secular university; but to determine to what extent these collections were accessible to the public is problematic. In the 13th century the emperor Theodore Doukas Laskaris gathered books which were distributed to various cities with the specific instruction that they were to be available to everyone; but this was noted as an innovation. Public access to libraries was not as great during the Byzantine period as it had been during the Hellenistic and particularly Roman eras.

Except among the Phanariots, who often sent their children to be educated in Italy, literacy during the Tourkokratia was for many years minimal (it was higher among the Greeks in areas ruled by western states). The most educated person in a village was usually the priest who, although he had probably been taught his letters at a nearby monastery, still struggled with his liturgical texts and relied largely on memory. However, growing opposition to the Ottomans and a sense of nationalism promoted the creation of so many unofficial schools that at the time of Greek independence (c.1821) at an elementary level Greeks could claim to be one of the more literate nations of Europe; although within a few decades they had been largely overtaken.

The last half of the 20th century saw a great diminution in illiteracy in Greece, and the promise of its almost complete eradication, through more regular attendance and more years of schooling. One minor obstacle to illiteracy, albeit an aid to comprehension, was also eliminated in the last two decades of the 20th century by the gradual abolition of breathings (originally indicating whether or not an initial vowel was aspirated) and the compression into one of the three accents (originally indicating pitch but by the 4th century AD only stress). The abolition of these Alexandrian diacritical signs had been frequently mooted in modern times, but opposition had been such that in the 1940s the University of Athens publicly censured one of its professors for publishing a book without accents.

The first serious attempt to eradicate illiteracy in modern Greece was the establishment by the government of Eleftherios Venizelos in 1929 of night schools to provide elementary education for those above the legal age for primary school. During World War II various resistance organizations attempted to educate especially farmers, and in 1943 an Adult Education Service was developed at the Ministry of Education. Nevertheless, in 1951, after the end of the Civil War, 25.9 per cent of the population aged 15 and over was deemed illiterate (including 49.9 per cent of rural females). Three years later a Central Committee to Combat Illiteracy (KEKA) began to establish night schools at which attendance was compulsory for illiterates and semiliterates up to the age of 20 and voluntary for those older. By 1981 the illiteracy rate had dropped to 9.5 per cent and by 1991 to 4.8 per cent, while of the 389,067 classified in the latter year as illiterate 51.1 per cent were women over the age of 65 (the percentages for Cyprus were higher, but showed a more rapid diminution).

Literacy may be measured also by publication of books, library holdings, and newspaper circulation. In 1995, 4134 new titles were published in Greece, "literature" accounting for the extraordinarily high percentage of 38.6. However, apart from the National Library in Athens and the libraries of higher education, the 669 public libraries housed in 1994 only 9,558,000 books, slightly fewer than one for each inhabitant. This was, to some extent, offset by the fact that 168 daily newspapers had in 1995 a circulation of 153 per thousand of the population, continuing a growing literate trend which had been reversed in most other European countries by dependence on the orality of radio and television.

A.R. LITTLEWOOD

See also Archives, Books and Readers, Education, Libraries

Further Reading

Boring, Terrence A., *Literacy in Ancient Sparta*, Leiden: Brill, 1979

Bowman, Alan K. and Greg Woolf, *Literacy and Power in the Ancient World*, Cambridge and New York: Cambridge University Press, 1994

Browning, Robert, "Literacy in the Byzantine World", *Byzantine and Modern Greek Studies*, 4 (1978): pp. 39–54

Browning, Robert, *History, Language and Literacy in the Byzantine World*, Northampton: Variorum, 1989

Cole, S.G., "Could Greek Women Read and Write?" in *Reflections of Women in Antiquity*, edited by Helene P. Foley, New York: Gordon and Breach, 1981

Harris, William V., *Ancient Literacy*, Cambridge, Massachusetts: Harvard University Press, 1989

Havelock, Eric A., *The Literate Revolution in Greece and its Cultural Consequences*, Princeton, New Jersey: Princeton University Press, 1982

Hedrick, C.W. Jr, "Writing, Reading, and Democracy" in *Ritual, Finance, Politics: Athenian Democratic Accounts Presented to David Lewis*, edited by Robin Osborne and Simon Hornblower, Oxford: Clarendon Press, and New York: Oxford University Press, 1994

Thomas, Rosalind, *Oral Tradition and Written Record in Classical Athens*, Cambridge and New York: Cambridge University Press, 1989

Thomas, Rosalind, *Literacy and Orality in Ancient Greece*, Cambridge and New York: Cambridge University Press, 1992

Wilson, Nigel G., "The Libraries of the Byzantine World", *Greek, Roman and Byzantine Studies*, 8 (1967): pp. 53–80

UNESCO *Unesco Statistical Yearbook* (annual publication), Paris: Unesco

Liturgy

In Classical Greek the word liturgy (*leitourgia*) referred to any kind of public service. In Christian usage it came to mean the service offered to God by the Christian community, gathered for common prayer. Central to that service is the Eucharist; and in Orthodox tradition the Eucharist is called the (Divine) Liturgy. But liturgical worship includes more than the Eucharist, and here liturgy is used in its wider sense, to include all aspects of corporate Christian worship in the Greek-speaking world.

In common with other Christian traditions, the fully developed pattern of Greek Orthodox worship includes the daily services of the Church – Vespers, Orthros, and the lesser Hours – as well as the sacramental rites of baptism, chrismation (confirmation), the Eucharist, confession, unction, marriage, and ordination. These are called "mysteries" in the Orthodox tradition. In addition there are various rites less often used, such as monastic profession and the consecration of a church, and blessings of various kinds. These services are contained in a number of books. The Euchologion includes the prayers and litanies used by the priest and deacon. The fixed parts of the daily services are in the Horologion. Variable texts for Sundays and weekdays are found in the Oktoechos, those for Lent in the Triodion, for Eastertide in the Pentecostarion, and for the fixed feasts in the 12 Menaia, one for each month of the year. Scriptural readings are set out in two lectionaries, the Apostle and the Gospel. The Typikon gives instructions for celebrating the services throughout the year within the framework of the liturgical calendar, and combining the texts supplied by these various books. Together, these services and the books that contain them make up what is called the Byzantine rite.

In Orthodox worship the architectural and iconographic setting of services is hardly less important than their liturgical texts. The church building itself is understood to be sacramental. It is heaven on earth, an image of the cosmos. Its interior iconography makes its sacramental significance explicit, and presents in pictorial images the saving events celebrated in the liturgy itself. Traditional interpretation of the symbolism of the church building and its services enables worshippers to enter into the inner meaning of Orthodox worship. In no other rite has there emerged the synthesis of art, architecture, text, ceremonial, and music characteristic of the Byzantine rite, which was essentially complete in its present form by the 15th century.

The origins of this developed pattern of worship are to be sought in the worship of the Jewish community, within which Jesus Christ himself and Christianity were born. Relatively little is known about the development of Christian liturgical worship in the first three centuries. Its setting was domestic: Christians met in private houses, sometimes adapted for the community's use. Only towards the end of the 3rd century were special church buildings occasionally erected. New Christians were admitted by baptism, and then shared regularly in the Sunday Eucharist. There were gatherings for common prayer, reading scripture, and exhortation; and Christians were encouraged to pray at various hours during the day. Easter was the annual celebration of salvation through the death and resurrection of Jesus Christ, Sunday its weekly celebration. The only other elements in the Christian year were commemorations of martyrs. Within a broadly common tradition there was considerable variety of local custom. Some evidence indicates that the Eucharistic prayer was extempore, precluding any standardization.

Significant developments in liturgical worship began in the 4th century. Constantine's recognition of Christianity enabled worship to move into imposing basilicas. Ceremonial developed, as bishops acquired the status of civil magistrates. Liturgical rites came to be written out, and the texts of prayers fixed. Two cycles of festivals emerged: the lunar, centred on Easter, and the solar, centred on Christmas, so giving its basic form to the calendar. Church organization developed, based on the civil administration, and ecclesiastical centres emerged, of which the two oldest were Alexandria and Antioch. Jerusalem rose to rapid prominence after the discovery of the holy sepulchre; and the new capital, Constantinople, soon enjoyed the same prestige as Old Rome. The liturgy of these centres, later called patriarchates, began to acquire distinctive characteristics. Each had its rites of Christian initiation, including baptism, chrismation or confirmation, and participation in the Eucharist, which often took place at the Easter vigil. Each developed its own eucharistic rite, with its own eucharistic prayers, or anaphoras. By the end of the 7th century each of these centres had its own distinctive rite. That of Constantinople is usually known as the Byzantine rite, from the city's original name. These rites gradually spread to other local churches within their sphere of influence, and mutually influenced one another. For the future development of Greek

Orthodox worship Constantinople and Jerusalem were of particular importance.

The Church of Jerusalem enjoyed immense prestige. Cyril, bishop of the holy city c.349–87, is usually credited with devising the complete sequence of Holy Week observances, which other Churches in the East and West soon borrowed and adapted. The eucharistic theology of Cyril's *Mystagogical Catecheses*, with its emphasis on the transformation of the Eucharistic bread and wine into the body and blood of Christ by the invocation of the Holy Spirit, influenced all Eastern Eucharistic worship. The monasteries of Palestine, especially that of Mar Saba, were to have a profound influence on the development of Orthodox worship. The monks used the same Eucharistic rite as the rest of the Church, but developed their own forms of daily worship, the Hours that made up the divine office. Their content was distinct from that of the cathedral office, which they were destined ultimately to supplant. Much of the liturgical poetry characteristic of the later Byzantine rite was composed, from the 6th century onwards, in Palestine.

Constantinople derived its liturgical tradition from Antioch, but from the end of the 4th century its rite began to acquire distinctive characteristics. The reign of Justinian (527–65) was particularly significant for its development. His new church of Holy Wisdom (Hagia Sophia) completed in 537, was both cathedral and palace chapel. It was the first church building to be given an explicit symbolic meaning as the house of God. Its great dome symbolized heaven, and the church itself was both heaven on earth and an image of the cosmos. Its services were performed with imperial splendour. Its worship, especially the Eucharist, was believed to be a participation in the worship of heaven. This understanding was reflected in liturgical texts, and systematized in the 7th century by Maximos the Confessor, whose *Mystagogia* gives a full interpretation of the church building and of the Eucharist celebrated in it. By the end of the 7th century the rite of Constantinople had acquired its own consistency. This is reflected in the liturgical canons of the Council in Trullo (691–92), and in the first surviving liturgical text from the Great Church. The Codex Barberini 336, from the middle of the 8th century (now in the Biblioteca Apostolica Vaticana), is a Euchologion, containing the prayers of the two Eucharistic rites of St Basil and St John Chrysostom, with those of other services.

The 7th and 8th centuries were highly significant for Orthodox liturgical development. In the early 7th century Alexandria, Antioch, and Jerusalem came under Islamic rule. They had already been weakened by the loss of the majority of Christians in their regions to the non-Chalcedonian Churches. Their influence declined, and their rites came under increasing Byzantine influence. By the 12th century local Eucharistic rites had been almost entirely replaced by those of St Basil and St John Chrysostom. At the end of the century Theodore Balsamon, patriarch of Antioch, held that only the rite of the Great Church should be used by those who considered themselves Orthodox.

The iconoclast controversy (726–75, 814–43) ended with the Triumph of Orthodoxy and the restoration of the icons. It marked the beginning of the domination of the Orthodox Church by monks. The monastery of Stoudios in Constantinople, refounded by Theodore in 799, became an important liturgical centre. Theodore invited monks from Mar

Saba in Palestine to help in the defence of icons and the renewal of monastic life. They brought with them their own daily services, containing a wealth of liturgical poetry, fully orthodox in content. In the monasteries of Constantinople this Palestinian Horologion was combined with the cathedral office of the Great Church. The resulting synthesis was the basis of the final form of the Byzantine daily Hours. The cathedral office continued in use in Hagia Sophia until the Latin conquest (1204–61), when the monks took charge of the services, and in Thessalonica until the 15th century. But the Stoudite office became more and more widely used. At the same time the Holy Week rites of Constantinople and Jerusalem were also exerting a mutual influence on one another, and the final Byzantine Holy Week liturgy was a synthesis of the two rites.

Meanwhile the liturgy of Constantinople continued to develop, and with it the tradition of liturgical interpretation. A century after Maximos, Germanos I, patriarch of Constantinople (715–c.733), composed his *Ecclesiastical History*. This liturgical commentary, while not abandoning the understanding of the Eucharist as an image of the worship of heaven, gives greater emphasis to the more historical interpretation first found in Theodore of Mopsuestia in the 4th century. Germanos interprets the Eucharist chiefly as a symbolic representation of the life of Christ. The Little Entrance represents the first appearing of Christ; the Great Entrance represents his passion and burial. The dominance of this more literal interpretation of the Eucharist in the later Byzantine tradition coincided with post-iconoclastic developments in church decoration. From the 9th century the interiors of churches, now usually small, were increasingly covered with iconography in mosaic or fresco. The fully developed scheme depicted heaven and its worship, the saving events in the life of Christ, and the communion of saints. The iconography of the church matched the interpretation of the liturgy celebrated in it.

The liturgical poetry originating in Mar Saba was gradually brought together and arranged for use in liturgical books. From the 8th century the Oktoechos came into being, containing the daily services; from the 10th century the Triodion and Pentecostarion, containing the Lenten and Eastertide texts, and the Menaia, containing the fixed festivals. Rules for combining these texts were given by a series of typika, which begin to appear in the 9th or 10th century. The Stoudite typikon became the most influential, and by the 12th century it had spread throughout the Orthodox world. It was used by the first monasteries on Mount Athos.

The process of cross-fertilization continued. The Stoudite typikon was adopted in Palestine, but also adapted there. This neo-Sabaitic synthesis, as it is sometimes called, influenced the Stoudite rite in the capital. The typikon of Mar Saba gradually ousted the Stoudite typikon, and was adopted on Mount Athos, which, since the Latin occupation of Constantinople, had become the chief monastic centre of Orthodoxy. In the final stage of the development of the Byzantine rite the influence of Athonite usage was paramount. After the triumph of hesychasm in the 14th century, hesychast monks controlled the Byzantine Church. Philotheos, while abbot of the Great Lavra, composed two *Diataxeis*, or books of ceremonial instructions. One contained the rubrics for the divine office, the other those

for the Eucharist. When he became patriarch of Constantinople (1353–55, 1364–76), their use spread rapidly. They were incorporated into the first printed texts of the Byzantine liturgical books in the 16th century.

By the fall of Constantinople in 1453, Byzantine Orthodox liturgical worship had reached the form it largely still has today. The church building and its iconographic decoration had also reached their final form. In the 16th century the use of printing made possible the standardization of liturgical texts and usage, which up to then had varied. This fully developed Orthodox rite played an important part in preserving the identity of the Christian peoples of the Ottoman empire. Its wealth of liturgical texts, steeped in Christian doctrine and ascetic teaching, helped to preserve and transmit the Christian faith to succeeding generations when few other means existed.

HUGH WYBREW

See also Hymnography, Orthodox Church

Further Reading

Bornert, René, *Les Commentaires byzantins de la divine liturgie du VIIe au XVe siècle*, Paris: Institut Français d'Etudes Byzantines, 1966

The Festal Menaion, translated by Mother Mary and Kallistos Ware, London: Faber, 1969

The Lenten Triodion, translated by Mother Mary and Kallistos Ware, London: Faber, 1978

Mathews, Thomas F., *The Early Churches of Constantinople: Architecture and Liturgy*, University Park: Pennsylvania State University Press, 1971

Schmemann, Alexander, *Introduction to Liturgical Theology*, 3rd edition, Crestwood, New York: St Vladimir's Seminary Press, 1986

Schulz, Hans-Joachim, *The Byzantine Liturgy: Symbolic Structure and Faith Expression*, New York: Pueblo, 1986

Taft, Robert, *The Great Entrance: A History of the Transfer of Gifts and Other Preanaphoral Rites of the Liturgy of St John Chrysostom*, Rome: Pontificum Institutum Studiorum Orientalium, 1975

Taft, Robert, *The Liturgy of the Hours in East and West: The Origins of the Divine Office and Its Meaning for Today*, Collegeville, Minnesota: Liturgical Press, 1986

Taft, Robert, *The Byzantine Rite: A Short History*, Collegeville, Minnesota: Liturgical Press, 1992

Wellesz, Egon, *A History of Byzantine Music and Hymnography*, 2nd edition, Oxford: Clarendon Press, 1961

Wybrew, Hugh, *The Orthodox Liturgy: The Development of the Eucharistic Liturgy in the Byzantine Rite*, London: SPCK, 1989; Crestwood, New York, St Vladimir's Seminary Press, 1990

Wybrew, Hugh, *Orthodox Lent, Holy Week and Easter: Liturgical Texts with Commentary*, London: SPCK, 1995; Crestwood, New York: St Vladimir's Seminary Press, 1997

Wybrew, Hugh, *Orthodox Feasts of Christ and Mary: Liturgical Texts with Commentary*, London: SPCK, 1997

Livanos, George P. 1926–1997

Shipowner

George P. Livanos was born into a family originating from Kardamyla in Chios, the island that throughout the 20th century was foremost in Greek shipping. In addition to the willingness to take large risks that is common among Greek shipowners, Chiots are notable for their mastery of the technical aspects of the market and ships alike. Livanos shared all these qualities.

He was born in New Orleans, educated in Greece at Athens College, carried out US military service, and studied engineering at Hofstra University in New York. His professional career was marked by exceptional qualities of innovation. In 1968, against the general trend towards much larger vessels (so as to reduce the cost of transport per ton), he pioneered the "Mini Bulker", a 3000-ton deadweight shallow-draft vessel equally adapted to river and ocean navigation. More than 50 were built. The United Nations used them to move relief cargoes to Bangladesh following the war of 1970–71.

In 1976 Livanos introduced Russian high-speed hydrofoil vessels to the Aegean, thus providing rapid transportation between Piraeus and many Greek islands; by greatly reducing the travel time, this revolutionized the economy of several island regions. In 1985 he entered the specialized chemical transportation field, eventually becoming one of the three largest carriers of chemical products in the world. By the early 1990s he was one of the world's largest shipowners, operating VLCCs (Very Large Crude Carriers) and ULCCs (Ultra Large Crude Carriers) totalling about 3.5 million tons deadweight in a fleet of nearly 100 vessels and almost 5 million tons.

Many shipowners of Kardamyla (from where Livanos's wife, Fotini Carras, also came) were noted for their sense of public service. Both the Livanos and the Carras families had spent much of their first profits from shipping creating their towns' schools. Livanos continued the tradition, painting on a broader canvas. He was personally generous to employees and philanthropic causes alike. He was deeply involved in the interface between American and Greek politics during the 1970s and 1980s. He formed the Hellenic American Alliance in Washington and was himself continuously active in urging on US legislators the importance of a just solution to the Cyprus problem and of maintaining a proper balance in military aid to Greece and Turkey. It is unlikely that this balance would have been maintained during the 1980s without his efforts.

Livanos was committed to the environmental movement. He was a cofounder of *Elliniki Etairia* (the Greek Society), Greece's leading conservation organization, in 1972. Later in his life he was a member of the Council of the World Wildlife Fund (now the World Wide Fund for Nature) and its president in Greece. He was a member of the Club of Rome. His greatest contribution was his foundation in 1982 of HELMEPA (Hellenic Marine Environment Protection Association), a joint effort of the shipping community and the Greek Seamen's Federation to reduce ship-generated pollution. HELMEPA's educational efforts were successful and imitated by CYMEPA (Cyprus), TURMEPA (Turkey), and BRIMEPA (Britain), to all of which HELMEPA contributed valuable knowhow. A man of great ability, extraordinary (almost childlike) enthusiasm, broad generosity, and burning idealism, Livanos made a difference, both to Greece and to the world.

COSTA CARRAS

See also Ships and Shipping

Biography

Born in New Orleans in 1926, George Livanos was educated at Athens College and studied engineering at Hofstra University in New York. One of the world's largest shipowners, he introduced high-speed hydrofoil vessels to the Aegean and became one of the largest carriers of chemical products. He was active in the environmental movement. He died in 1997.

Further Reading

Batis, Stathis, *Portraita se Ble Fondo* [Portraits with a Blue Background], Athens: Finatec Multimedia, 1999

Harlaftis, Gelina, *Greek Shipowners and Greece, 1945–75: From Separate Development to Mutual Interdependence*, London: Athlone Press, 1993

Harlaftis, Gelina, *A History of Greek-Owned Shipping: The Making of an International Tramp Fleet, 1830 to the Present Day*, London and New York: Routledge, 1996

Lilly, Doris, *Those Fabulous Greeks: Onassis, Niarchos and Livanos*, London: W.H. Allen, and New York: Cowles, 1970

Logic

Logic, the study of valid inference, was developed by Greek philosophers as a result of their interest in arguments of every kind, not only those used in philosophy, but also those used in mathematics, in politics, or in the lawcourts. The first technical term for what we now call "logic" was used by Aristotle, and this was "dialectic"; the first occurrence of the ancient term "logic", meaning the discipline of correct reasoning, is to be found in Aristotle's commentator Alexander of Aphrodisias.

Aristotle is traditionally considered to be the founder of logic. At the end of his *Sophistical Refutations* he himself claimed with some pride to have been the first to conceive of a systematic treatment of correct inference as such and to formulate its rules. But Aristotle was certainly not the first to be concerned with valid reasoning. Before Aristotle philosophers knew how to argue and taught others how to argue; for they were mainly interested in producing arguments to defend their theses or to refute those of their opponents. What is more, already before Aristotle philosophers were aware, and availed themselves, of certain abstract patterns of inference which would ensure the conclusiveness of arguments constructed according to them. Thus it is clear from our sources that already Zeno of Elea in his paradoxes made use of argument patterns like that of the reduction to the impossible. Similarly Plato, in the second part of his dialogue *Parmenides*, obviously inspired by Zeno, constructed an elaborate argument, following a complex formal pattern which explicitly is said to be applicable to any other philosophical subject or discussion. Quite generally, even if Plato might have been averse to the study of reasoning for its own sake, his dialogues present argument systematically set forth in such a way as to make their validity apparent, but also to invite reflection on their validity, rather than simply on the truth of their premises and conclusions. For instance, given Plato's and his followers' concern with the method of division, one easily sees how one would come to formulate general principles of the kind "if A is a genus of B, and B is a genus of C, then A is a genus of C". But to develop such a body of general principles is not yet to provide a formal account of valid inference, an account which identifies what precisely it is about an inference which makes it valid.

Aristotle's logical writings were later known under the collective title *Organon*, i.e. an instrument of philosophy, for they were regarded as the works to be studied first, since it is by means of logic that we come to have the knowledge about reality and human behaviour which constitutes philosophy. But not all of the six treatises of the *Organon* deal with logic in the modern sense. The first of these works, namely the *Categories*, classifies the different types of predicates and is often interpreted as a metaphysical or dialectical treatise, rather than as a logical one. Those editors who placed it in the *Organon* thought that it dealt with the terms of propositions of the form "A is B". The *Topics* discusses dialectical arguments of the kind used in the dialectical exercises which formed an important part of the philosophical training in Plato's Academy. The *Sophistical Refutations* is an appendix to the *Topics* and considers logical fallacies. The *Posterior Analytics* investigates the special requirements that scientifically demonstrative arguments have to satisfy beyond being formally valid. Hence, Aristotle's main contributions to the discipline of logic in the modern sense are to be found, first, in his short treatise *On Interpretation,* which presents his theory of the structure of propositions, their truth conditions, and the logical relations between them, in particular their contradictoriness, and their contrariety; and second, in the *Prior Analytics*, in which Aristotle expounds his theory of the syllogism, by considering different kinds of arguments according to their forms.

It is important to note that in his logical writings Aristotle was the first to use letters ("A", "B", "C") to stand in place of the terms of propositions ("white", "animal", "man"). This Aristotelian innovation is regarded by modern logicians as one of the crucial steps in the history of logic, because it implies an awareness of the distinction between logical form and logical matter, and also marks a significant simplification in the representation of the form of arguments. More specifically, in Aristotle's *On Interpretation* four kinds of proposition are distinguished: universal affirmatives, of the form "A holds of every B" (e.g. "white holds of every man"); universal negatives, of the form "A holds of no B" (e.g. "white holds of no man"); particular affirmatives, of the form "A holds of some B" (e.g. "white holds of some man"); and particular negatives, of the form "A does not hold of some B" (e.g. "white does not hold of some man"). A convention going back to the Middle Ages marks each of the four kinds of proposition with a vowel, and thus they may be abbreviated as "AaB", "AeB", "AiB", "AoB", respectively. The universal affirmative is contrary to the universal negative and contradictory to the particular negative, whereas the particular affirmative is contrary to the particular negative and contradictory to the universal negative.

It is next in the *Prior Analytics* that Aristotle presents his theory of the syllogism, by any account one of the greatest achievements in the history of logic. He starts with his standard definition of a syllogism as an argument in which certain things being posited something different from the things posited comes about by necessity, in virtue of the fact that the things posited are so. Hence three distinct propositions are involved in every syllogism, two premises and a conclusion,

and they must be related in the appropriate way to be specified. To begin with, the two premisses must have a term in common, the so-called "middle term", and the two terms of the conclusion, i.e. "the extremes", must each appear in one of the premisses. Thus the three propositions of any syllogism exhibit altogether precisely three terms, and the premisses may, as a pair, show any one of the following structures: (1) A of B, B of C; (2) B of A, B of C; (3) A of B, C of B. These three structures determine the three figures of Aristotelian syllogistic; a syllogism belongs to the first figure if its premisses exhibit structure 1, to the second figure if they exhibit structure 2, and to the third figure if they exhibit structure 3. In later times the various forms in which syllogisms may be constructed within the figures came to be called "moods". Aristotle distinguishes 14 valid moods, which are commonly known by their medieval names. For instance, the first valid mood of the first figure is called Barbara and runs as follows: "A holds of every B; B holds of every C; therefore A holds of every C." A typical Aristotelian example in this mood would then be: "Mortal holds of every animal; animal holds of every man; therefore mortal holds of every man." All the valid moods of the first figure are said to be "perfect", because their validity is self-evident. The syllogisms in the other figures are "imperfect", but they can become perfect, inasmuch as they can be reduced to first-figure syllogisms whose validity is self-evident. Aristotle employs three methods of perfection or reduction, which means three ways of proving that a given syllogistic form is valid; namely, transformation by conversion, reduction to the impossible, and exposition. In this way Aristotle presents his syllogistic as a system of deductive inference in which the 14 valid moods of the first, second, and third syllogisms can be reduced to the four moods of the first figure; thus these four syllogistic moods constitute the axioms of the system. The axiomatic character of Aristotle's syllogistic bears clear signs of influence by the developments in the mathematical sciences of his time, and its ingenuity and elegance have often been praised even in our times. Aristotle also made a beginning in what we nowadays call modal logic, i.e. the study of propositions containing modal operators like "necessary" or "possible", but his treatment of modal logic in the *Prior Analytics* proves to be unsatisfactory and presumably in the end incoherent.

Some of the Peripatetics followed Aristotle's interest in logic and tried to elaborate further his logical doctrines. Theophrastus, in particular, is said to have been chiefly concerned with the development of certain aspects of Aristotelian logic, but unfortunately none of his logical works has survived. From later authors we learn that he spent some time on an area of logic that was only briefly mentioned by Aristotle, namely syllogisms "from a hypothesis". These are syllogisms whose first premise at least is a "hypothetical" proposition, i.e. a negated conjunction or a disjunction or a conditional. In the works of Aristotle's commentators the syllogisms with such premisses are called "hypothetical" syllogisms, and are contrasted with the standard Aristotelian syllogisms which are called "categorical" syllogisms. It seems, though, that Theophrastus' account of hypothetical syllogisms never acquired the character of a fully fledged systematic logical theory: that is, a theory of the kind which the Stoics were to produce later on.

In the Hellenistic period, largely independently of Aristotle's term "logic", the logic of propositions, mainly hypothetical syllogistic, as opposed to categorical, was advanced to its highest level. Its beginnings may be traced back to philosophers like Diodorus Cronus and Philo of Megara, who were not only concerned with the study of logical puzzles or paradoxes, like the Liar and the Sorites, but also put forward original theories about the logical modalities and the truth conditions of conditional propositions. But the logic of propositions was finally systematized by the Stoics, who in Chrysippus had a logician of the highest calibre. His numerous works unfortunately are almost entirely lost, and we need to reconstruct Stoic logic from relatively few and not always reliable fragments. Stoic propositional logic was based on the connectives "if ... then" for conditionals, "either ... or" for exclusive disjunctions, "both ... and" for conjunctions, and the prefixed negative "it is not the case that". The Stoics used ordinal numbers ("the first", "the second", "a", "b") to stand in place not of terms but of simple propositions. Their hypothetical syllogistic, like Aristotle's syllogistic, also was developed as an axiomatic system. It was grounded on five types of "indemonstrable" arguments, i.e. elementary syllogisms the validity of which is in no need of demonstration, since it is self-evident, and four rules, the so-called themata, by the use of which all other syllogisms were claimed to be reducible to the indemonstrables. Hence these rules allow one to establish the formal validity of non-indemonstrable arguments by "analysing" them in one or more steps into one or more indemonstrable arguments. The form of the standard five indemonstrables was expressed as follows: (1) "If the first, then the second; but the first; therefore the second." (2) claimed. "If the first, then the second; but not the second; therefore not the first." (3) "Not both the first and the second; but the first; therefore not the second." (4) "Either the first or the second; but the first; therefore not the second." (5) "Either the first or the second; but not the first; therefore the second." A typical Stoic example of the first indemonstrable is: "If it is day, it is light; but it is day; therefore it is light."

The two systems of logic – term logic and the logic of propositions – were considered by the Peripatetics and the Stoics as rivals, rather than as complementary, each supposed to cover all formally valid arguments. In late antiquity, however, we find the attempt to combine the two traditions of the categorical and the hypothetical syllogistic into one logical system. The commentators on Aristotle's logical works, such as Alexander of Aphrodisias, Ammonius, and Philoponus, integrated into their works many Stoic elements, including a doctrine of hypothetical syllogisms. Finally, Galen made a more successful attempt to synthesize the two systems in his *Introduction to Logic*, in which he also deals with relational arguments which are not satisfactorily accounted for either by Aristotle or by the Stoics; that is, arguments like "A is greater than B; B is greater than C; therefore A is greater than C." In general, however, logicians in this period made no substantial logical discoveries, though there are in the writings some terminological innovations. For the most part they stated expansively what Aristotle had stated briefly and elliptically. On the other hand, the logical works of this period preserve historical information, which is invaluable.

The syncretistic tradition of late antiquity was continued with an emphasis on didactic simplicity, first by Byzantine scholars such as Michael Psellos, John Italos, Theodore Prodromos, Leon Magentinos, Manuel Holobolos, Nikephoros Blemmydes, George Pachymeres, John Pediasimos, John Chortasmenos, and George Scholarios, and after the fall of Constantinople by philosophers such as Theophilos Corydaleus, George Koresios, Meletios Syrigos, Gerasimos Vlachos, George Sougdouris, Stephanos Tzigaras, Vikentios Damodos, and Neophytos Doukas. Unfortunately most of the logical writings of these authors have not yet appeared, at least in critical editions, and therefore their study has been seriously neglected.

KATERINA IERODIAKONOU

See also Dialectic, Philosophy

Further Reading

Barnes, Jonathan, *Logic and the Imperial Stoa*, Leiden and New York: Brill, 1997

Corcoran, John (editor), *Ancient Logic and Its Modern Interpretations*, Dordrecht: Reidel, 1974

Frede, Michael, *Die stoische Logik*, Göttingen: Vandenhoeck & Ruprecht, 1974

Kneale, William and Martha Kneale, *The Development of Logic*, Oxford: Clarendon Press, 1962

Lee, Tae-Soo, *Die griechische Tradition der aristotelischen Syllogistik in der Spatantike*, Göttingen: Vandenhoeck & Ruprecht, 1984

Łukasiewicz, Jan, *Aristotle's Syllogistic from the Standpoint of Modern Formal Logic*, Oxford: Clarendon Press, 1951; reprinted New York: Garland, 1987

Mates, Benson, *Stoic Logic*, Berkeley: University of California Press, 1953

Patzig, Gunther, *Aristotle's Theory of the Syllogism: A Logico-Philological Study of Book A of the Prior Analytics*, Dordrecht: Reidel, 1968

Longus

Novelist of the 2nd or 3rd century AD

Longus was the author of *Daphnis and Chloe*, a fine but untypical example of the ancient Greek novel, probably dating from the end of the 2nd or beginning of the 3rd century AD. In outline the story follows the romantic stereotype, narrating the love and adventures of its eponymous heroes, culminating in marriage, and even retains some of the common motifs of the genre, such as pirates, shipwreck, and unwanted rivals. *Daphnis and Chloe* is unique, however, in its pastoral setting: although they turn out to be the exposed children of urban aristocrats, its hero and heroine grow up as goatherd and shepherdess in the countryside of Lesbos, of which Longus was possibly a native. Despite its topographical plausibility, however, the setting is not realistic: Longus draws ostentatiously on the pastoral poetry of Theocritus (not least for Daphnis' name) and, probably, of Philetas of Cos, after whom one of the most important secondary characters is named. As befits the Lesbian setting, the poetry of Sappho also provides a number of plot elements, notably in an episode where Daphnis fetches Chloe an apple from the highest branches of a tree. The urban reader, in effect, is invited to take a holiday in a literary landscape of bucolic fantasy and turn a blind eye to the hardships of real agricultural life.

Elements of travel and adventure of the kind found in other ancient novels are miniaturized and parodied. Raiding pirates take Daphnis only a few hundred metres before their ship is capsized by performing cows; war nearly breaks out between Mytilene and Methymna after a goat gnaws through a makeshift mooring-rope. This lack of physical movement is related to Longus' most profound innovation: his treatment of love, which he presents as a developing and maturing condition. His lovers begin as completely ignorant of Eros, and only gradually become aware of their feelings for one another. They need to be educated in the "name and deeds of love", first by the old herdsman Philetas, who in lyrically elevated prose identifies Eros as the motive power of all creation, and then by a benevolently predatory sex-starved neighbour, Lycaenion, who gives Daphnis a practical tutorial in the woods. Childish fumblings give way to formal courtship and marriage in the city, after the two lovers discover their real identities. The lovers' journey is thus an inner one, from the innocence of rural childhood to the knowledge of socialized maturity. The paradigmatically natural quality of their love is stressed by the way it follows the rhythm of the seasons, awakening in spring, growing in summer, resting in winter, and finding its fulfilment in the second autumn; significantly the novel is in four books. Three myths of metamorphosis, narrated by characters in the story and forming a sequence of increasing violence and sexuality, counterpoint the main narrative in the first three books. Implicitly the fourth and final metamorphosis is Chloe's passage from virgin to wife, and the final myth the novel itself.

A preface presents the novel as an *ekphrasis* ("description") of a painting discovered by the narrator while hunting in Lesbos. It also claims – with a mischievous allusion to Thucydides – a universal applicability for its story. The experiences of Daphnis and Chloe are thus an educative allegory of human love and its place in nature, but the novel is also a self-referential meditation on the nature of literary fiction, which, like the love it depicts, and like a pair of symbolic gardens in the story, is a symbiosis of art and nature, artifice and reality.

Although there is no external evidence to date the novel, its lightly worn erudition and multiple layers of meaning, as well as the artful simplicity of its prose, mark it as a product of the period of the Second Sophistic. The story is set in a timeless Hellenic past, when the two chief cities of Lesbos were independent and war between them was a possibility; there is no attempt to recreate a more precise historical milieu. There is no trace of Rome, but, in its displaced fashion, *Daphnis and Chloe* reflects contemporary concerns with self and sexuality, and, in its ethical but not simplistic confrontation of town and country, echoes a prevalent urban nostalgia for a non-existent bucolic simplicity.

Surprisingly, Longus' exquisite novel does not appear to have enjoyed wide circulation. No papyrus fragments have yet come to light, and the work is not noticed by Byzantine critics, although it is alluded to in the 12th-century verse romance of Evgenianos. In the west *Daphnis and Chloe* has periodically enjoyed a certain vogue, both by virtue of its explicit sexual scenes, and for its literary merits, which were famously commended by Goethe. It is also the only ancient Greek novel

to have left a clear trace in modern Greek fiction: Myrivilis's novel *Daskala me ta Chrysa Matia* (*The Schoolmistress with the Golden Eyes*, 1933) features an erotically tinged description of the Lesbian countryside, which evokes *Daphnis and Chloe* for the hero.

J.R. MORGAN

See also Novel

Biography
Otherwise unknown, Longus was the author of the novel *Daphnis and Chloe* which may be dated to the late 2nd or early 3rd century AD. The setting suggests that he may have been a native of or visitor to Lesbos. The style places it in the period of the Second Sophistic. The treatment of love as a developing condition is innovative.

Writings
Daphnis et Chloe, edited by Michael D. Reeve, Leipzig: Teubner, 1982, 2nd edition 1985 (Greek text)
Daphnis and Chloe, translated by Christopher Gill, in *Collected Ancient Greek Novels*, edited by B.P. Reardon, Berkeley: University of California Press, 1989, pp. 285–348
Daphnis and Chloe, translated by Paul Turner, Harmondsworth: Penguin, 1989

Further Reading
Chalk, H.H.O., "Eros and the Lesbian Pastorals of Longos", *Journal of Hellenic Studies*, 80 (1960): pp. 32–51
Goldhill, Simon, *Foucault's Virginity: Ancient Erotic Fiction and the History of Sexuality*, Cambridge and New York: Cambridge University Press, 1995
Hunter, R.L., *A Study of Daphnis and Chloe*, Cambridge and New York: Cambridge University Press, 1983
McCulloh, William E., *Longus*, New York: Twayne, 1970
MacQueen, Bruce D., *Myth, Rhetoric and Fiction: A Reading of Longus's Daphnis and Chloe*, Lincoln: University of Nebraska Press, 1990
Morgan, J.R., "Daphnis and Chloe: Love's Own Sweet Story" in *Greek Fiction: The Greek Novel in Context*, edited by J.R. Morgan and Richard Stoneman, London and New York: Routledge, 1994
Teske, Dörte, *Der Roman des Longos als Werk der Kunst: Untersuchungen zum Verhältnis von Physis und Techne in Daphnis und Chloe*, Münster: Aschendorff, 1991
Turner, P., "Daphnis and Chloe: An Interpretation", *Greece and Rome*, 7 (1960): pp. 117–23
Winkler, John J., *The Constraints of Desire: The Anthropology of Sex and Gender in Ancient Greece*, New York and London: Routledge, 1990

Lucian c.AD 120–180

Prose writer

Lucian of Samosata was by birth a Syrian rather than a Greek but became one of the most important Greek literary figures of his time. He wrote in an exceptionally pure form of the literary language of the 2nd century AD, an Atticizing Greek almost indistinguishable from that of Plato and very different from the non-literary Greek of his day. This purity of style was essential to his success as an orator and travelling speaker in an age where enormous importance was attached to the use of correct Greek at all times. (Two of Lucian's works, *The Mistaken Critic* and *A Slip of the Tongue in Greeting*, are elaborate defences of the author after he had been accused of making, in the course of casual speech, linguistic errors that to us would seem utterly trivial.) The quality of Lucian's language was also one of the main reasons for the continued popularity of his works after his death and their influence on later literature.

Most of Lucian's writings are humorous; they were written to entertain rather than to instruct or defend. Perhaps most famous are the satiric dialogues, in which the author mocks insincere philosophers, the rich, and the major figures of classical mythology. Thus for example in *The Downward Journey*, which like many of his works is set in Hades, the author depicts the humiliation of a rich tyrant after his death while also making fun of awe-inspiring mythological figures such as Charon and Clotho. In *Zeus Catechized* he shows Zeus confounded by a human who asks how the power of the gods can be compatible with the existence of preordained destiny, and the same problem is discussed in worried tones among the gods themselves in *Zeus Rants*. In *Philosophers for Sale* various philosophical creeds are auctioned off as slaves, and in the *Fisherman* the founders of the major philosophical schools, returning to life in order to punish Lucian for his attacks on philosophy, discover the vices of their current followers and repudiate them.

These works show that Lucian had an extensive knowledge of Greek literature from Homer onwards and no scruples about parodying it, and they remain extremely funny to anyone with the background to appreciate them. Some parodies are also written in a narrative rather than a dialogue format, such as the *True Story*, the tale of an imaginary voyage with fantastic adventures. Less popular nowadays are the panegyrics and the rhetorical exercises in which Lucian shows his oratorical skill by defending an unlikely or indefensible point; his legal speeches were not intended for actual court proceedings, but for show. Many of the works are set in Classical times or contrast the present unfavourably with those times, and the works that most influenced Lucian (Old and New Comedy, Plato's dialogues, and the lost satires of the 3rd-century BC Cynic Menippus) were all written long before his own time. Thus both in his archaizing language and in his choice of subject matter Lucian reflects the preoccupation of his day with a distant and glorious Greek past, but at the same time he is conscious of rivalling the Classical authors both in language and in wit.

Lucian's works enjoyed immediate popularity that continued into the late antique period, when he was read by figures such as Libanius, Julian, and Alciphron. With the ascendancy of Christianity his status became problematic; his ridicule of the pagan gods and of moral decadence in general was attractive to the Christians, but his *The Passing of Peregrinus*, a biting satire against a charlatan philosopher who had been for a time a Christian, includes some unflattering comments about Christianity and the folly of its practitioners. Although mild compared to the opprobrium Lucian heaped on other groups, these comments drew the ire of many Byzantine Christian writers; thus for example in the influential 10th-century lexicon known as the *Suda* Lucian is identified as "Lucian of Samosata, also called the blasphemer or the slanderer, or rather

the atheist" and condemned in the strongest terms. It is significant, however, that Lucian merits a place in the lexicon despite its author's obvious dislike of him, and another large Byzantine manual, Photios's 9th-century *Library*, contains no mention of the anti-Christian material and simply praises Lucian's style and his attacks on immorality and paganism.

In the end, however, it was not Lucian's beliefs but the quality of his writing that ensured his popularity among Byzantine writers. They admired and imitated his language, judging it the equal of Classical Attic (it receives elaborate praise from authors as diverse as Photios and the 12th-century Gregory of Corinth), and they continued to read and laugh at his satires, which some later Byzantine writers (among them Theodoros Prodromos and Manuel Philes) also attempted to imitate. His influence contributed to the development of a genre of satirical dialogues and another of descriptions of imaginary voyages.

Like most Classical authors, Lucian declined in direct influence on the Greek world after the Turkish conquest. This does not however mean that he was forgotten, for the first translation of Lucian into modern Greek was done surprisingly early, *c*.1770, by Constantine Dapontes. In the 18th and 19th centuries Lucian's works enjoyed a renewed popularity, though they continued to cause controversy. At this period the debate about his religious and moral worth was resolved into a solid condemnation from the Church, who associated Lucian with the ideas of the Enlightenment. At the same time, however, his ideas were attractive to many outside the Church establishment, and his style and wit were greatly admired and imitated, even by some religious leaders. In 1806, for example, Michael Perdikaris relied heavily on Lucian in composing a long satiric poem that ridiculed both the leaders of the Enlightenment and those of the Church, and some Church leaders wrote serious defences of piety in Lucian's style. In the late 19th and 20th centuries Lucian's influence once again declined, but it is far from gone; ideas taken from Lucian can be found in a number of 20th-century Greek literary works. Although neither his religious convictions nor his Greek style are now considered major issues, Lucian's works continue to be read and enjoyed today for their sophisticated humour.

ELEANOR DICKEY

Biography

Born at Samosata in Syria around AD 120, Lucian was a prolific and influential writer of Atticizing Greek. Little is known of his life, but he seems to have travelled a good deal and to have spent time in Athens and later in Egypt. Among his writings the satiric dialogues are best known, and his prose style was much admired by the Byzantines. He died around 180.

Writings

Lucian, translated by A.M. Harmon, 8 vols, London: Heinemann, and New York: Macmillan, 1913–67 (Loeb edition)

Further Reading

Bompaire, J., *Lucien écrivain: imitation et création*, Paris: Boccard, 1958

Robinson, Christopher, *Lucian and His Influence in Europe*, Chapel Hill: University of North Carolina Press, 1979

Lyceum

Site of Aristotle's Peripatetic school in Athens

The Lyceum was one of the main public gymnasia in Athens, named after the sanctuary dedicated to Apollo (Lykeios). In the 5th and 4th centuries BC various Sophists lectured in the Lyceum and Socrates spent time there too. Here Aristotle founded his own school in 336/35 BC. For a long time the exact location of the Lyceum was a matter of speculation. In 1996 the foundations of a large building were discovered in Odos Regillis containing a palaestra which must have belonged to a great gymnasium, plausibly identified as that of the Lyceum. The identification is supported by the date, the use, and the construction of the gymnasium and it corresponds with written sources on the location of the Lyceum.

There is no direct evidence for the motives behind the foundation of Aristotle's school, but it is arguable that Aristotle wanted to influence philosophical education in a way that was not possible in the Academy. Aristotle's school was called "Peripatos" by the members of the school itself. It is more likely that the school was named after the site of the gymnasium than from the activity of walking. Aristotle, unlike Plato, was a metic and thus he could not own property. Theophrastus, Aristotle's successor, though a metic, acquired property with the help of Demetrius of Phaleron. Theophrastus' will (*Diogenes Laertius*, 5. 51–57) is very informative about the architecture and the outlook of the school. The scholarch was the legal owner of the school, which relied on his financial means. The core of the instruction was the scholarch's lectures, but Aristotle also trained his students in dialectic and rhetoric. Aristotle's esoteric works represent to a great extent the lecture material. The Peripatos, like the Academy, did not require adherence to a set of doctrines. Aristotle's views were modified or questioned by early and later Peripatetics alike.

The first generation of Peripatetics is characterized by extraordinary productivity and diversity. Theophrastus became head of the Lyceum when Aristotle left Athens on the death of Alexander the Great in 323 BC. His voluminous works show a clear concern to continue and develop Aristotelian philosophy. It is controversial whether Theophrastus consciously departed from Aristotle's views, but he certainly rejected Aristotle's god, the unmoved mover, although he retained a belief in the divinity of the heavens and the eternity of the world. Theophrastus was preoccupied primarily with natural science but he also showed a keen interest in ethics and rhetoric. He is well known for his *Characters*, and he presumably foreshadowed later developments in Stoic ethics. Important Peripatetics of Theophrastus' generation included Dicaearchus, Aristoxenus, Eudemus, Clearchus of Soli, Phaenias of Eresus, and Chamaeleon. These early Peripatetics showed a strong interest in cultural topics, such as literary criticism (Chamaeleon), rhetoric, and biography (Dicaearchus, Aristoxenus, Phaenias, Clearchus), and their writings were probably used by the Alexandrian scholars a century later. Following Aristotle, they also showed a strong interest in the history of philosophy, logic, and natural science.

The Hellenistic Peripatos was less prominent than its rival philosophical schools. Strato (scholarch 287–269 BC) became known as "the natural philosopher". He rejected Aristotle's theory of place and maintained the existence of the void in the world. Anticipating the Stoics, he made nature and not god the ultimate cause of all phenomena and like earlier Peripatetics (Dicaearchus, Aristoxenus) he maintained the materiality of the soul. Strato's successor Lyco (299–225 BC) is a rather insignificant figure. He tried to revive the school and to attract more students by focusing again on ethical issues, fashionable among the Hellenistic schools. After Lyco the Peripatos declined rapidly and there is no evidence of any serious philosophical activity until the 1st century BC. Hieronymus of Rhodes is better known than Lyco's successor Aristo of Cos for his theory that happiness consists in freedom from pain. Critolaus (2nd century BC) resumed metaphysics; he modified the Aristotelian doctrine of providence, extending it into the sublunary world, while he also claimed that soul and intelligence consist of ether.

In the 1st century BC the Peripatos enjoyed a revival with Andronicus of Rhodes, the acclaimed editor of Aristotle's works. Signs of a recovery were evident before Andronicus. Ariston and Cratippus, both pupils of the Academic Antiochus of Ascalon, abandoned the Academy for the Peripatos. Yet there is no evidence that any of them (including Andronicus) ever became head of the Peripatos. Like the Academy and the Stoa, the Peripatos presumably ceased to exist after the sack of Athens by Sulla in 87/86 BC. Yet the desertion of Aristo and Cratippus makes sense only if some form of Peripatetic school existed. The decline and the revival of the Peripatos are traditionally associated with the fortunes of Aristotle's writings. It has been argued that after Theophrastus the Peripatetics had only Aristotle's exoteric writings at their disposal, whereas his esoteric treatises came to light due to Andronicus' editorial activity. Andronicus received help from the grammarian Tyrranio who provided him with copies of Aristotle's works found in the library of Appelicon which were first moved to Athens and after the sack of the city by Sulla to Rome (*Strabo*, 13. 1. 54; Plutarch, *Sulla*, 4). There Andronicus prepared his edition which included the esoteric works in a certain arrangement and was furnished with commentaries on some treatises and a catalogue. Yet it is not safe to assume that Andronicus was the first to make Aristotle's works available after many centuries or that their present arrangement goes back to him. With Andronicus and his circle (Boethus, Xenarchus) a conscious attempt was made to present Aristotle's philosophy as a system, and to explain real or apparent discrepancies in his writings. From this time on Aristotle's works would be read and commented on by philosophers of all schools, but it was not Andronicus' new edition with triggered this.

There is meagre evidence for any philosophical activity of Peripatetics after Andronicus. Nicolaus of Damascus (64 BC–AD 4) wrote a compendium of Aristotle's teaching. To the 1st century AD presumably belongs the Peripatetic Aristocles of Messene who wrote a long work *On Philosophy* in which he recounts the development of philosophy and criticizes Sceptics, Epicureans, and Cyrenaics. A substantial revival of Aristotelian philosophy took place in the 2nd century AD with Adrastus, Aspasius, and especially with Alexander of Aphrodisias. Both Adrastus and Aspasius wrote a number of commentaries on Aristotle's works. Other Peripatetics of this period include Sosigenes, Herminus, and Alexander of

Mytilene, all of them teachers of Alexander of Aphrodisias. Marcus Aurelius set up chairs of philosophy in AD 176 and the first Peripatetic incumbent was Alexander of Damascus. His successor, Alexander of Aphrodisias, excelled as a commentator on Aristotle and he had a strong impact even among Platonists. Although Alexander's contribution is very significant, especially in logic and metaphysics, no pupils of his are mentioned. After him nothing more is heard of the Peripatetics. With the introduction of Aristotle into the Neoplatonic curriculum, Aristotle was appropriated by the Platonists who now undertook the writing of commentaries. Aristotle's works, especially the *Organon*, now served as an introduction to Platonist philosophy. This change of the Platonists' attitude to Aristotle is to be associated mainly with Porphyry and Iamblichus (3rd–4th centuries AD). Aristotle was seen through Platonist eyes and this version of Aristotle was the one that was inherited by the Middle Ages and the Renaissance.

GEORGE E. KARAMANOLIS

See also Aristotle, Theophrastus

Summary

The Lyceum was a sanctuary of Apollo in Athens, used as a place of teaching by the Sophists. Aristotle founded his school there in 336/35 BC which was known as the Peripatos. When Aristotle left Athens, Theophrastus became head of the school. Late in the 3rd century BC the school declined. In the 1st century BC there was a revival but the school presumably ceased to exist after 86 BC, when Athens was sacked.

Texts

Aristotle, *The Complete Works: The Revised Oxford Translation*, edited by Jonathan Barnes, Princeton, New Jersey: Princeton University Press, 1984

Commentaria in Aristotelem Graeca, Berlin: Reimer, 1882–1909, reprinted Berlin: de Gruyter, 1981 (contains the commentaries of Adrastus and Aspasius and the works of Alexander of Aphrodisias)

Heiland, Hermann (editor), *Aristoclis Messenii Reliquiae*, Giessen: Meyer, 1925

Wehrli, Fritz (editor), *Die Schule des Aristoteles: Texte und Kommentare*, 2nd edition, 10 vols, Basel: Schwabe, 1967–69 (fragments of Dicaearchus, Aristoxenus, Clearchus, Demetrius, Straton, Lyco, Ariston, Heraklides Ponticus, Eudemus, Phaenias, Chamaeleon, Praxiphanes, Hieronymus, and Critolaus)

Further Reading

Barnes, Jonathan, "Roman Aristotle" in *Philosophia Togata 2: Plato and Aristotle at Rome*, edited by Jonathan Barnes and Miriam Griffin, Oxford: Clarendon Press, and New York: Oxford University Press, 1997

Brink, K.O., Peripatos entry in *Real-Encyclopädie der klassischen Altertumswissenschaft*, edited by August Pauly *et al.*, supplement 7, 1940, 899–949

Düring, Ingemar, *Aristotle in the Ancient Biographical Tradition*, Gothenburg: Göteborg Universitets Arsskrift, 1957, reprinted New York: Garland, 1987

Gottschalk, H.B., "Aristotelian Philosophy in the Roman World from the Time of Cicero to the End of the Second Century AD" in *Aufstieg und Niedergang der römischen Welt*, edited by Hildegard Temporini *et al.*, 2.36.2, 1079–1174

Jaeger, Werner, *Aristotle: Fundamentals of the History of his Development*, 2nd edition, Oxford: Clarendon Press, 1948

Lynch, John Patrick, *Aristotle's School: A Study of a Greek Educational Institution*, Berkeley: University of California Press, 1972

Moraux, Paul, *Der Aristotelismus bei den Griechen: von Andronikos bis Alexander von Aphrodisias*, 2 vols, Berlin: de Gruyter, 1973–84

Moraux, Paul, "Diogène Laërce et le 'Peripatos'", *Elenchus*, 7 (1986): pp. 147–294

Sharples, R.W., "The School of Alexander" in *Aristotle Transformed: The Ancient Commentators and Their Influence*, edited by Richard Sorabji, London: Duckworth, and Ithaca, New York: Cornell University Press, 1990

Wehrli, F., "Der Peripatos bis zum Beginn der römischen Kaiserzeit" in *Ältere Akademie, Aristoteles, Peripatos*, edited by Hellmut Flashar, Basle: Schwabe, 1983

Lycia

Region of southwest Asia Minor

The Lycians may have had contact with the Greek world in the Bronze Age, to judge from scattered archaeological remains. Contact had been re-established by the 8th century BC, when the Lycians borrowed their alphabet from the Rhodian Greeks. In the east of Lycia in the 7th century BC there was a strong Rhodian presence, including the cities of Rhodiapolis, Corydalla, Gagae, and Phaselis, though only Phaselis maintained a distinct Greek character through the Classical period.

In mythology and cult Lycia was early associated with Apollo, who had an epithet Lykeios, and was sometimes said to have been born there; an oracular site is known as early as Herodotus (1. 182). Lycia also formed the setting for Bellerophon's encounter with the Chimaera. The Lycian heroes Sarpedon and Glaucus are highly prominent in the *Iliad*, with Sarpedon second only to Hector himself on the Trojan side; one of the classic expositions of the code of the Homeric hero is placed into Sarpedon's mouth, in discussion with Glaucus (*Iliad*, 12. 307–30).

Because of Lycia's important position on the naval route from the eastern Mediterranean to the Aegean, it was strategically of great value, and was often disputed in the struggles between Greek hegemonies and Persia, and then those between the Hellenistic states (and eventually Rome). Alexander the Great invaded Lycia to deny naval bases to Persia, and Ptolemaic Egypt felt it important to maintain control over the area in the 3rd century BC.

Lycia was ruled by a semifeudal aristocratic monarchy, with a number of quasi-independent dynasts being attested (claims that it had a "federal" constitution before the Hellenistic period are unfounded). This system, under Hellenic influence, culminated in individuals such as Pericles of Limyra (c.380–370 BC), who displayed some of the aspects of personal rule later seen in Mausolus of Caria and the successors to Alexander.

From the 6th century BC the Lycians were commissioning Greek (or Greek-trained) artists to produce sculpture for them, though often applying Greek styles to native or oriental themes (note the frequency of the oriental audience scene, e.g. on the "Harpy Tomb" at Xanthus); such commissions may have contributed to the further spread of Greek artistic traditions.

By the end of the 5th century the Lycians had begun to use the Greek language in inscriptions; in the 4th century some Lycians adopted Greek names. The process of Hellenization continued through the following centuries (including some Greek settlement, but to a degree which is difficult to judge), until it reached the point where Cicero could speak of them as "a Greek people" (*In Verrem*, 4. 10. 21). Nevertheless, aspects of Lycian society can be seen feeding into the main Hellenic tradition. The Lycians were pioneers in the use of portraits of living individuals on coinage (in the late 5th century BC), and their blend of Hellenic and oriental influences in their art and architecture can be seen as a microcosm of the Hellenistic world that followed. In particular, early 4th-century Lycian podium tombs with facades imitating Greek temples, such as the "Nereid Monument" at Xanthus and the Heroön of Pericles at Limyra, influenced the Mausoleum of Halicarnassus and ultimately funerary architecture throughout the Hellenistic world.

Several Greek writers are known to have been native Lycians. Leaving aside the semimythical poet Olen, sometimes supposed to be from Xanthus, there was the 4th-century BC historian/mythographer Menecrates of Xanthus, the 3rd-century BC writer Mnaseas, and the 5th/6th-century AD geographer/historian Capiton of Lycia. Theodectus, a 5th-century BC tragic poet, came from Phaselis, and the late Epicurean philosopher Diogenes (2nd century AD?) was from Oenoanda in north Lycia, where he left a massive inscription detailing his philosophy. Only fragments survive of most of these authors' works, and the same is true of the numerous *Lykiaka* (works on Lycia) written by non-Lycian writers.

After c.200 BC a federal league appeared in Lycia, which was a significant force in eastern Mediterranean politics until Lycia became a Roman province in AD 43, and even after that continued to provide an administrative framework for the region. With the coming of the *pax Romana* Lycia became a quiet backwater, occasionally visited by Roman emperors and high officials (Augustus' heir Gaius Caesar died there in AD 2), which was slipping into economic decline by the 3rd century AD. Lycia did, however, make one contribution to the development of Christianity and the Greek Orthodox Church: St Nicholas was born in the Lycian city of Patara, and was bishop of the neighbouring city of Myra. After the Arab invasions of the 7th century AD and the abandonment of the cities Lycia largely ceased to be part of the Greek world, though the island of Megiste, off the Lycian coast, continues to be a Greek settlement and part of Greece.

In 1838 the English dilettante Charles Fellows arrived in Lycia, in search of Greek antiquities. In the course of a number of subsequent visits up to 1844, he explored most of the cities of Lycia, and supervised the removal of a number of antiquities to the British Museum in London, where they remain the responsibility of the Department of Greek and Roman Antiquities. The popular success of Fellows's expeditions contributed to further exploration of the Greek heritage of Anatolia.

ANTONY G. KEEN

Summary

The people of Lycia in southwest Asia Minor were using the Greek alphabet by the 8th century BC. The region was of strategic importance for its position on the sea route to the eastern Mediterranean.

Greek artists were employed from the 6th century. Lycians were among the first to use portraits on coinage. Lycia became a Roman province in AD 43 and reverted to obscurity, before falling under Arab influence in the 7th century.

Further Reading

Bean, George E., *Lycian Turkey: An Archaeological Guide*, London: Benn, and New York: Norton, 1978, reprinted London: John Murray, 1989

Borchhardt, Jürgen, *et al.*, *Götter, Heroen, Herrscher in Lykien*, Schallaburg: Schloss Schallaburg, 1990

Bryce, Trevor R., *The Lycians*, vol. 1: *The Lycians in Literary and Epigraphic Sources*, Copenhagen: Museum Tusculanum Press, 1986

Fellows, Charles, *Travels and Researches in Asia Minor, more Particularly in the Province of Lycia*, London: John Murray, 1852, reprinted Hildesheim and New York: Olms, 1975

Jones, A.H.M., revised by Michael Avi-Yonah *et al.*, *The Cities of the Eastern Roman Provinces*, 2nd edition, Oxford: Clarendon Press, 1971

Keen, Antony G., *Dynastic Lycia: A Political History of the Lycians and Their Relations with Foreign Powers, c.545–362 BC*, Leiden: Brill, 1998

Kolb, Frank and Barbara Kupke, *Lykien: Geschichte Lykiens im Altertum*, Mainz: Zabern, 1992

Larsen, J.A.O., *Greek Federal States: Their Institutions and History*, Oxford: Clarendon Press, 1968

Magie, David, *Roman Rule in Asia Minor, to the End of the Third Century after Christ*, Princeton, New Jersey: Princeton University Press, 1950

Slatter, Enid, *Xanthus: Travels of Discovery in Turkey*, London: Rubicon Press, 1994

Troxell, Hyla A., *The Coinage of the Lycian League*, New York: American Numismatic Society, 1982

Lycophron

Hellenistic poet

Lycophron's claim on our attention rests on a single text, the *Alexandra*, formally a hypertrophic messenger's speech, a dramatic monologue of over 1400 lines reporting the prophecy of the Trojan War and its aftermath delivered by Cassandra (here Alexandra) when Paris set out for Sparta. Its erudite and lively-minded author is usually identified as Lycophron of Chalcis, the contemporary of Callimachus who organized the texts of comedy for the Alexandrian library under Ptolemy II (282–246 BC) and composed not only numerous tragedies (of which merely one fragment and 20 titles survive), but also a satyr play with a contemporary subject, his teacher Menedemus of Eretria (see Snell, *Tragicorum Graecorum Fragmenta*, vol. 1, no. 100). The traditional attribution has been questioned because the poem's references to a widely acknowledged Roman supremacy (1226–80 and, probably, 1446–50) appear incompatible with a date in the first half of the 3rd century BC, and some have therefore argued for composition in the early 2nd century BC, whether pseudepigraphically or by a younger poet of the same name; but it is more likely that these passages are later interpolations (see below).

The poem presents the matter of Troy from the Trojan standpoint; Cassandra's peculiar perspective is crucially important. Greek achievement is persistently denigrated, Greek misfortune stressed. Relatively little space (31–386) is devoted to the war itself and to Troy's downfall; here Cassandra concentrates on what concerns her family and herself, culminating with the horror of Ajax' assault when she had taken sanctuary in Athena's temple. In expiation for his act of sacrilege the Greek host undergoes manifold suffering both on the journey home (387–1089) and thereafter (1090–1282); in Locris, Ajax' homeland, his people will pay the penalty for 1000 years (the Locrian maiden tribute). Cassandra's vision then extends to further conflict between Asia and Europe, the Persian Wars, and the victories of Alexander the Great, concluding with the triumphs by land and sea of her (not easily identifiable) kinsman (1283–1450). With immense ingenuity Lycophron works into this framework episodes from other cycles of legend (such as the Argonautica), basic to the Greek cultural identity of his day. Interwoven with relatively familiar narratives, often given a new slant by the narrator's non-Hellenic standpoint, is material relating to the western Mediterranean, the foundation legends of Greek colonies, and strange tales inspired by the attempt to accommodate various native peoples within the Greek ethnographic framework. Wide reading and a magpie mind have resulted in a masterpiece of intertextual virtuosity, rich in colourful and curious detail. A narrative covering more than 1000 years is unified by the Aeschylean and Herodotean theme of the rivalry between Asia and Europe, an immensely grand conception matched by Lycophron's elevated, somewhat Aeschylean style.

The obscurity of Lycophron's manner of expression is often exaggerated, but certainly he must have envisaged erudite readers prepared to spend time in working out oracular conundrums; the modern reader is seriously handicapped by the loss of much literature which Lycophron could assume to be generally familiar to the educated. In any case, long-standing Indo-European tradition favoured a degree of inaccessibility in prophecy, where the presence of obstacles between the message and its recipient required the latter to exert himself, so that he would be the more likely to value the guidance offered at its proper worth.

Virgil evidently read the *Alexandra* with appreciation; it provided the most obvious model for the extensive use of prophecy to bridge the gap between the heroic age and the poet's own day, and for a narrative of Troy's fall presented from the standpoint of the defeated (though Aeneas' perspective is somewhat different from Cassandra's). To the same period belongs the commentary by Theon of Alexandria from which our scholia derive; without this guidance very much would be unintelligible to us. Though Lycophron does not figure among the authors recommended by Quintilian to aspirant orators, Statius' schoolmaster father apparently included him along with Callimachus in his syllabus (*Silvae*, 5. 3. 156f.); he is similarly mentioned as a school author, along with Callimachus and Euphorion, by Clement of Alexandria (*Stromateis*, 5. 50. 3). This difficult, allusive poetry did not lack readers in provincial towns; from Roman Egypt we have papyri representing three separate copies (P.Oxy. 2094+3445, 2nd century AD; P.Oxy. 3446, 2nd century AD; P.Mon. 156, 1st–2nd century AD).

The poem's popularity in the Byzantine period, no doubt at least as much due to its wealth of mythological learning as to its literary qualities, is indicated by the proliferation of manuscripts; the Pontifical Institute of Mediaeval Studies in Toronto has produced a list of nearly 150 (see Robert E. Sinkewicz, *Manuscript Listings for the Authors of Classical and Late Antiquity*, microfiche 4, Toronto: Pontifical Institute of Medieval Studies, 1990). It was regular reading in Byzantine schools; Gregory of Corinth recommended the clearer passages of Lycophron (along with Sophocles) as models in the composition of iambics. Eustathios refers to him more than to any other poet apart from Homer, on occasion quoting him without name, his habit only with works that he knew very well (see further M. van der Valk, *Eustathii Archiepiscopi Thessalonicensis Commentarii ad Homeri Iliadem Pertinentes*, vol. 1, Leiden: Brill, 1971, p. LXXXV); it is highly probable that he contemplated composing a commentary on the *Alexandra*.

Lycophron's stock stood very high in the 16th century; nine editions of the *Alexandra* had been published by 1600, and the poem was esteemed by the Pléiade, the erudite circle to which Ronsard belonged. A steep decline in its standing set in at the beginning of the 19th century, with the invention of the Lycophron Question, which turns on the poem's references to Rome's supremacy. Cassandra's prediction of the manifold tribulations in store for the Greeks concludes with a lengthy passage on the future fame of Aeneas' line settled in Italy (1226–80), an unqualified encomium of the rising power of Rome which in the first half of the 3rd century BC might be thought to indicate authentic prescience. Little attention was paid to this problem until it attracted notice from B.G. Niebuhr and, independently, the Whig politician Charles James Fox. Niebuhr postulated a later Lycophron, writing in the early 2nd century BC after the Roman conquest of Greece; Fox diagnosed interpolation. A further passage is affected; Cassandra's prophecy culminates (1446–50) in the victories of a kinsman of hers, some time after Alexander the Great, "a unique wrestler" who will triumph by land and sea. There is too much detail for this to be taken as an unspecific hope for the future; but the identity of the conquering hero is highly controversial, though there seems currently to be general agreement that he must be a Roman, and probably Titus Quinctius Flamininus, the victor of Cynoscephalae (197 BC), enjoys the strongest support. The surprisingly brief treatment of Alexander's achievements (1439–45) rather suggests that a process of updating led to some curtailment of the original culmination of Cassandra's prophecy; we should expect her to display more interest in the decisive role to be played by a second Alexander in the intercontinental feud initiated by her brother. Thus, though the *Alexandra* is permeated by a sense of historical development over a millennium and creates the expectation of a political or ideological message, we are frustrated by the problem of identifying the figure on whom Cassandra has set her hopes.

STEPHANIE WEST

Biography

Traditionally identified with Lycophron of Chalcis, tragedian and contemporary of Callimachus (early 3rd century BC, but some prefer a 2nd-century date). He was the author of one surviving poem, entitled *Alexandra*. It reports the prophecy of Cassandra relating to the Trojan War and its aftermath.

Writings

Alexandra, edited by Eduard Scheer, 2 vols, Berlin: Weidmann, 1881–1908

Alexandra, edited by Carl von Holzinger, Leipzig: Teubner, 1895

The Alexandra, translated by George W. Mooney, London: Bell, 1921, reprinted New York: Arno Press, 1979

In *Callimachus, Lycophron, Aratus*, translated by A.W. Mair, London: Heinemann, and New York: Putnam, 1921 (Loeb edition)

In *Tragicorum Graecorum Fragmenta*, 4 vols, edited by Bruno Snell et al., Göttingen: Vandenhoeck & Ruprecht, 1971–85

Alessandra, edited by Massimo Fusillo, André Hurst and Guido Paduano, Milan, 1991

Further Reading

Fraser, P.M., *Ptolemaic Alexandria*, Oxford: Clarendon Press, 1972

Fraser, P.M., "Lycophron on Cyprus" in *Report of Department of Antiquities, Cyprus*, 1979

Fusillo, Massimo, "L'Alessandra di Licofrone: racconto epico e discorso 'drammatico'", *Annali della Scuola Normale Superiore di Pisa, Classe di Lettere e Filosofia*, series 3, 14/2 (1984): pp. 495–525

Geffcken, J., "Zur Kenntnis Lykophrons", *Hermes*, 26 (1891): pp. 567–79

Graf, F., "Die lokrischen Mädchen", *Studi e Materiali di Storia delle Religioni*, 2 (1978): pp. 61–79

Hensel, Ludwig, *Weissagungen in der alexandrinischen Poesie*, Giessen: Lange, 1908

Josifović, S., Lykophron entry in *Real-Encyclopädie der klassischen Altertumswissenschaft*, edited by August Pauly et al., supplement 11, 1968, 888–930

Rengakos, A., "Lykophron als Homererklärer", *Zeitschrift für Papyrologie und Epigraphik*, 102 (1994): pp. 111–130

Strecker, C., *De Lycophrone, Euphorione, Eratosthene comicorum interpretibus*, Greifswald, 1884

Trencsényi-Waldapfel, L., "Das Bild der Zukunft in der Aeneis", *Studii Classice*, 3 (1961): pp. 281–304

West, S., "Notes on the Text of Lycophron", *Classical Quarterly*, 33/9 (1983): pp. 114–35

West, S., "Lycophron Italicised", *Journal of Hellenic Studies*, 104 (1984): pp. 127–51

Ziegler, K. Lykophron (8) entry in *Real-Encyclopädie der klassischen Altertumswissenschaft*, edited by August Pauly et al., vol. 13, 1927, 2316–82

Lysander

Spartan general of the 5th century BC

A member of a noble family that claimed descent from the founding heroes, the sons of Heracles, Lysander first appears in the sources when appointed to command the Spartan fleet in the east Aegean in 407 BC. The Spartans' prospects had declined since the renewal of the naval war in 412 BC after the disastrous failure of the Athenians' expedition to Sicily. Then, with the Athenians' allies beginning to secede and the Persians contemplating intervention against Athens, the Spartans reacted vigorously by sending a fleet to the west coast of Asia Minor. The Athenians, however, had proved resilient, despite internal dissension, while Spartan admirals were ineffective and failed to establish good relations with the Persian satraps, who supplied some money but failed to commit themselves. In late 411 and 410 BC the Athenians, inspired by Alcibiades, who had returned from exile to join their fleet, had won two victo-

ries, the second off Cyzicus leading to the destruction of a Spartan fleet of 60 ships. They had gone on recovering lost allies and by June 407 BC, when Alicibiades made a triumphant return to Athens, were looking to complete the restoration of their old naval dominance.

On taking up his command, Lysander was fortunate in that a Spartan embassy had just returned from Susa, having secured the Persian king's agreement to renew support for Sparta and his appointment of his younger son, Cyrus, to take charge of the three western satrapies and of the implementation of the agreement. Lysander at once established good relations with Cyrus, whose support enabled him to refit and strengthen the fleet he took over at Ephesus. By late August it numbered 90 ships. With these he was able to take advantage of Alcibiades' temporary absence at Phocaea and of the inexperience of his deputy to destroy 22 of his 100 ships, a victory that led to the removal from his command of Alcibiades, who never returned to Athens.

At the end of the year, under the Spartan system, Lysander was replaced. His successor, Callicratidas, obstructed by Lysander's supporters, fell out with Cyrus and was defeated off the Arginusae islands. In consequence both Cyrus and their Greek allies urged the Spartans to restore Lysander to the command and they responded by giving him effective control for the year 405 BC as the nominal second-in-command to Aracus. Cyrus, whose original funds had long been exhausted, somehow found the money to enable him to rebuild his fleet; in the late summer, after some clever manoeuvring in the central Aegean, he reached the Hellespont (the Dardanelles) ahead of the Athenian fleet, taking Lampsacus by assault and from there threatening to intercept the ships bringing Athens' corn supplies from the Black Sea. The Athenians followed him into the straits and, to avoid having to battle continually with the powerful southwest-flowing current, based themselves on an unsuitable beach at Aegospotami. On four successive days they rowed out to offer battle, but without response, and on the fifth Lysander, who had observed how the Athenians, after beaching their ships in the evenings, had scattered in search of food or rest, waited for them to retire and then ordered his ships to attack. All but 10 of the Athenians' 180 ships were taken with little resistance in what was truly a decisive victory. It was the last fleet that the Athenians could muster, but until that evening they could still have avoided defeat and even won the war.

Lysander then toured the Aegean, driving Athenian settlers back to increase the hungry mouths at home and removing their friends from power in the various cities, and then brought his fleet, now of 150 ships, to Aegina to join the land armies in the final siege of Athens. When surrender terms were agreed in the spring of 404 BC, he sailed into the Piraeus to supervise the demolition of the walls. Soon after he assisted in the establishment of an oligarchic regime, the "Thirty Tyrants", which soon proved cruel and oppressive.

While the Athenians could hardly have expected anything better (and many, no doubt, feared worse), the Spartans' new allies in and around the Aegean must have hoped for more generous treatment than they now received at the end of a war that the victorious Spartans at the start had declared was undertaken to "free the Greeks" (Thucydides, 1. 129 and 2. 8). Lysander, however, favoured close control, in this very probably looking to secure the allies' loyalty to himself as much as to Sparta. According to Plutarch (*Lysander*, 5), he was already in 407 BC plotting with local aristocrats to set up decarchies (councils of ten) to rule liberated cities, and after Aegospotami in 405 BC he carried out this policy, installing Spartan officers (harmosts) in the cities to support the new regimes; Plutarch adds (13) that he assisted in a number of massacres, a generalization illustrated by his later account (19), supported by that of Diodorus (13. 104), of events at Miletus. Lysander's recall to Sparta and the modification of his policies, probably in 403 BC, failed to convince most of the new allies, who broke away when the Spartan fleet was defeated by the Persians off Cnidus in 394 BC.

Meanwhile in mainland Greece Lysander maintained a hard line. In 403 BC he would have suppressed the resurgent Athenian democrats, had he not been superseded by king Pausanias, who brought an end to civil war with an amnesty and restored the democracy. He remained influential, helping to secure the kingship for Agesilaus II in a disputed succession in 400 BC, but being rejected by him when he accompanied the king on his expedition to protect the Asiatic Greeks against the Persians (396 BC) and the allies assumed that he, not the king, was really in charge. In 395 BC, irked by the independent line taken by the Thebans since Athens' surrender, he was very probably one of those who persuaded the Spartan leadership to declare war on Thebes on behalf of the Phocians (Plutarch, *Lysander*, 28). This was the Corinthian War, during which the Athenians recovered real independence and the Spartans, under pressure, were restored to their leading position in 387 BC only after regaining Persian support. Lysander was at once sent with an army to collect a Phocian contingent, invade Boeotia, and link up with Pausanias at Haliartus, but on arriving there early he rashly became engaged in a battle and was killed. His personal ambition had done much to damage the Spartan position, but whether he planned to have the rules of the Spartan kingship altered to open it up to leading men outside the two royal houses, such as himself, as was alleged after his death (Plutarch, 30), is doubtful.

Lysander has not had a great impact on the modern world. A type of aircraft that gave good service to the British Royal Air Force in World War II in many regions including Greece was named after him, but this could well have been due to his being included among the "great men" in the marching song *The British Grenadiers*; he probably owed his presence there to the fact that his name rhymes with Alexander.

T.T.B. RYDER

See also Peloponnesian War

Biography

Lysander was appointed admiral of the Spartan fleet in 407 BC and won a great victory over the Athenians at Aegospotami in 405, during the Peloponnesian War. Having secured the surrender of Athens in 404 he assisted in the establishment of the "Thirty Tyrants". At Sparta he secured the kingship for his lover Agesilaus II in 400. In 395 he helped persuade the Spartans to declare war on the Thebans and was himself killed in battle.

Further Reading

Cartledge, Paul, *Sparta and Lakonia: A Regional History, 1300–362 BC*, London and Boston: Routledge and Kegan Paul, 1979

Kagan, Donald, *The Fall of the Athenian Empire*, Ithaca, New York: Cornell University Press, 1987

Lewis, D.M. *et al.* (editors), *The Fifth Century BC*, Cambridge: Cambridge University Press, 1992 (*The Cambridge Ancient History*, vol. 5, 2nd edition)

Lewis, D.M. *et al.* (editors), *The Fourth Century BC*, Cambridge: Cambridge University Press, 1994 (*The Cambridge Ancient History*, vol. 6, 2nd edition)

Plutarch, *Plutarch's Lives*, translated by Bernadotte Perrin, 11 vols, London: Heinemann, and New York: Macmillan, 1914–26 (Loeb edition; vol. 4)

Plutarch, "Life of Lysander" in *The Rise and Fall of Athens: Nine Greek Lives*, translated by Ian Scott-Kilvert, Harmondsworth: Penguin, 1960, reprinted 1975

Xenophon, *Hellenica*, translated by Carleton L. Brownson, London: Heinemann, and New York: Putnam, 1918 (Loeb edition; many reprints)

Xenophon, *A History of My Times*, translated by Rex Warner, revised edition, Harmondsworth and New York: Penguin, 1978

Lysias *c.459/58–c.375* BC

Athenian orator

Lysias' father was a Syracusan who, in the mid-5th century BC and on the invitation of Pericles, settled in Athens as a resident alien. He became extremely wealthy, since he was a manufacturer of arms and armour at a time when Athens was almost continuously at war. Lysias himself, with his brother Polemarchus, spent some time at Thurii in southern Italy, but returned to Athens well before the end of the 5th century BC. After being decisively defeated by Sparta, Athens was ruled in 404–403 BC by a group of men who (with Spartan backing) operated as a collective dictatorship and earned the name "the Thirty Tyrants". They killed Polemarchus, arrested Lysias, and seized all the property held by the family in Athens. Lysias managed to escape, and through his property abroad and rich foreign friends he was able to give significant financial help to the Athenian exiles who eventually expelled the Thirty and restored democracy. He died *c.*375 BC.

As a resident alien Lysias could not participate directly in Athenian political life, but he was greatly in demand as a speech writer for people involved in litigation, who were required to speak in person, for there were no professional "solicitors" or "barristers" in Athens, and prosecutions for criminal offences were normally conducted by individual citizens motivated by patriotism, officiousness, political ambition, or enmity towards the defendant. Oratory had always been regarded in the Greek world as a major art form, a key to success not only in the courts, but also in councils and assemblies, and from the mid-5th century BC, at least in a democratic city such as Athens, there were rhetoricians who professed to teach oratory to politically ambitious young men.

A generation before Lysias the Athenian Antiphon inaugurated the practice of circulating speeches composed for clients, and Lysias followed this practice. So did other speech writers, and the formal structure of a speech was extended to what are sometimes called political pamphlets but correspond most closely to modern articles in periodicals of general interest. So far as concerns forensic speeches, it is of course impossible to find out the relation between the written text and what was actually said in court. We very rarely know the outcome of a case, but an ancient tradition, originating perhaps in a boast by a friend or a relative of Lysias after his death, alleged that he lost only two cases in his life.

At the end of the 4th century BC there existed no fewer than 425 speeches attributed to Lysias. A high proportion of those attributions is likely to have been false, because in an age where there were no publishers' contracts, no law of copyright, no royalties, and indeed rather little documentation in general, booksellers (like music sellers in the early 18th century AD) had the profitable habit of ascribing to famous names works actually composed by very obscure authors. In the late 1st century BC literary critics ruled out as spurious – mainly on stylistic, sometimes highly subjective, grounds – practically half the total of speeches sold under the name of Lysias. This was a time of reaction against the over-elaborate, formalized style which had come to dominate Greek oratory, and Lysias came to be admired not only for his spare, lively, and natural style but also for the way in which he seemed to invest a speaker with a character that was consonant with that speaker's status and likely to make a favourable impression on a jury (which had no presiding judge to sum up or guide it on points of law). In any country nowadays where ancient Greek is taught, selections from Lysias often constitute the learner's first introduction to Classical Attic prose texts.

In late antiquity Lysias, together with others who have come to be labelled the minor Attic orators, was overshadowed by Demosthenes (born about the time of Lysias' death), and only 27 speeches attributed to Lysias, plus seven truncated or mutilated, survived into the Middle Ages. They include a funeral speech for the Athenian war dead of a year in the late 390s BC and a portion of a ceremonial speech at the Olympic Games. Plato inserts in his *Phaedrus* a sophistic exercise in paradox which he presents as a composition by Lysias, but whether it is genuine or a clever parody by Plato remains disputed. It is difficult for us to form opinions of our own on the authenticity of any of the surviving speeches except no. 12, which was delivered by Lysias himself, prosecuting a member of the Thirty for the murder of his brother Polemarchus. Some of them, however, exhibit distinctive features of language which cannot all be explained by difference of genre or characterization.

KENNETH DOVER

Biography

Born c.459/58 BC the son of Cephalus, a resident alien (metic) in Athens from Syracuse, Lysias and his brother Polemarchus went to Thurii in southern Italy. They left Thurii after the Athenian military disaster in Sicily and returned to Athens as metics. In 403 both brothers were arrested by the "Thirty Tyrants" and Polemarchus was killed. Lysias escaped and achieved distinction as a speech writer. He died c.375 BC.

Writings

Lysias, translated by W.R.M. Lamb, London: Heinemann, and Cambridge, Massachusetts: Harvard University Press, 1930 (Loeb edition)

Further Reading

Anonymous (but transmitted with the manuscripts of Plutarch), "Lysias", in *Lives of the Ten Orators*, part of *Moralia*, by Plutarch, vol. 10, translated by H.N. Fowler, London: Heinemann, and Cambridge, Massachusetts: Harvard University Press, 1930 (Loeb edition)

Blass, Friedrich, *Die attische Beredsamkeit*, vol. 1, Leipzig: Teubner, 1887

Dionysius of Halicarnassus, "Lysias" in *The Critical Essays*, vol. 1, translated by Stephen Usher, London: Heinemann, and Cambridge, Massachusetts: Harvard University Press, 1974 (Loeb edition)

Dover, Kenneth J., *Lysias and the Corpus Lysiacum*, Berkeley: University of California Press, 1968

Kennedy, George, *The Art of Persuasion in Greece*, London: Routledge and Kegan Paul, and Princeton, New Jersey: Princeton University Press, 1963

Lavency, M., *Aspects de la logographie judiciaire attique*, Louvain: Bibliothèque de l'Université, 1964

Voegelin, Walter, *Die Diabole bei Lysias*, New York: Arno Press, 1979 (first published 1943)

Lysippus

Sculptor of the 4th century BC

Lysippus was a sculptor from Sicyon in the Peloponnese. Although Pliny (*Naturalis Historia*, 34. 51) places him in the 113th Olympiad (i.e. 328–325 BC), Lysippus was active long before. For example, his statue of Troilus of Elis, victor in the chariot race at Olympia, is likely to date from soon after 372–368 BC (Pausanias 6.1.4), and his portrait of Pelopidas, a Theban general, was dedicated by the Thessalians at Delphi c.363/62 BC. Lysippus may have been active as late as 316 BC when he was apparently commissioned to make an amphora for Cassander on the occasion of the foundation of the town of Cassandreia (Athenaeus, 2. 784). This suggests that he was probably born around 390 BC.

Lysippus, like the Athenian Praxiteles, was celebrated in antiquity for his achievement in representing realism (Quintilian, *Institutio Oratoria*, 12. 10. 1–10). Pliny (*Naturalis Historia*, 34. 65) specifically commented on the way that Lysippus represented hair, and noted the way in which he made the heads of his statues smaller than his predecessors. His statues were also said to be slender, which apparently had the effect of making them seem taller. The overall effect, in ancient eyes, was that Lysippus represented men "as they appeared". His genius is reflected in the fact that ancient art historians considered that he had no teacher; Pliny (*Naturalis Historia*, 34. 61) records the tradition that he was inspired to become a sculptor by the painter Eupompus.

Pliny noted that Lysippus was a prolific sculptor, and some 50 statues have been attributed to his hand. His popularity is reflected in the story that on his death he had 1500 gold coins stored away, one for each of the statues he had created. Such numbers are unlikely and probably represent his influence on his "school"; Pliny (*Naturalis Historia*, 34. 66) accepts that it was hard to distinguish between the works of Lysippus and those of his pupils. Lysippus seems to have made largely bronze statues.

One of his famous statues was a colossal bronze *Heracles* which once stood on the acropolis of the Greek colony of Tarentum in southern Italy. This was carried away to Rome by Fabius Maximus in 209 BC and was displayed on the Capitoline. It was apparently taken to Constantinople, where the Byzantine historian Niketas Choniates described it in the 13th century. This statue has been associated with the marble statue of a muscular *Heracles* leaning on his club that was found in the baths of Caracalla in Rome (it is now in Naples), but this Roman copy was in fact the creation of an Athenian sculptor, Glycon. A second colossal bronze statue, 18.3 m (40 cubits) high, also from Tarentum, could still be seen in the agora of the city in the 1st century AD, and is recorded there by Strabo (6. 3. 1).

As with other Greek sculptors, Lysippus' works were collected and copied in the Roman period. Pliny records the tradition that Lysippus' *Apoxyomenos* was removed from in front of the baths of Marcus Agrippa and placed in the bedroom of the admiring emperor Tiberius. One of Lysippus' smaller statues was the *Heracles Epitrapezios*, which by the late 1st century AD was in the private collection of one Novius Vindex and celebrated by both Martial (9. 44) and Statius (*Silvae*, 4. 6. 32–47). The statue, which shows the seated hero holding out a drinking cup, had apparently been made for Alexander. Although small-scale Roman copies are known, a large-scale copy was discovered at Alba Fucens in Italy, which might suggest that Lysippus himself produced the same statue type at different scales. Lysippus followed Praxiteles in making a bronze (rather than marble) statue of *Eros* for the Boeotian city of Thespiae; possible Roman copies have been identified.

There is a tradition, undoubtedly erroneous, that Lysippus alone was allowed to create portraits of Alexander. However what is clear is that Lysippus was engaged in making royal portraits and images of members of Alexander's court. This association between Lysippus' home polis of Sicyon and Macedonia can perhaps be explained by the friendship between Aristratus, tyrant of Sicyon and the Macedonian royal family. Lysippus' portraits of Alexander apparently showed the subject with his face turned upwards towards the sky; Plutarch (*Alexander*, 4) noted that Lysippus recorded the main characteristics of Alexander: "the poise of the neck turned slightly to the left and the melting glance of the eyes". Such a pose can be recognized in Hellenistic portraits of Alexander, such as those found at Pella and Pergamum.

One of the monuments that Lysippus created was to commemorate the 25 companions who died in Alexander's victory over the Persians at the river Granicus (in northwest Turkey) in 334 BC. This group, which included a portrait of Alexander, was erected at Dion in Macedonia and is probably to be identified with "Alexander's Squadron", a group mentioned by Pliny. It was carried off to Rome by Quintus Metellus in 148 BC. Another of Lysippus' Macedonian groups was the *Alexander's Hunt* which was dedicated at Delphi. The inscription from the base of this bronze group shows that it was erected by the son of Craterus, one of Alexander's generals.

DAVID W.J. GILL

See also Sculpture

Biography

Born at Sicyon in the Peloponnese perhaps *c*.390 BC, Lysippus was active as a sculptor from about 370 to 316 BC. He was prolific: some 50 statues are attributed to him. In antiquity he was celebrated for representing realism. His subjects included Alexander the Great. His works were popular at Rome.

Further Reading

Boardman, John, *Greek Sculpture: The Late Classical Period and Sculpture in Colonies and Overseas*, London and New York: Thames and Hudson, 1995

Edwards, C.M., "Lysippos" in *Personal Styles in Greek Sculpture*, edited by Olga Palagia and J.J. Pollitt, Cambridge and New York: Cambridge University Press, 1996

Johnson, Franklin P., *Lysippos*, Durham, North Carolina: Duke University Press, 1927

Loewy, E.M., *Inschriften Griechischer Bildhauer: Greek Inscriptions Recording Names and Works of Ancient Sculptors*, Leipzig: Teubner, 1885, reprinted Chicago: Ares, 1976

Pollitt, J.J., *Art in the Hellenistic Age*, Cambridge and New York: Cambridge University Press, 1986

Pollitt, J.J., *The Art of Ancient Greece: Sources and Documents*, Cambridge and New York: Cambridge University Press, 1990

Ridgway, Brunilde Sismondo, *Hellenistic Sculpture*, vol. 1: *The Styles of c.331–200 BC*, Bristol: Bristol Classical Press, and Madison: University of Wisconsin Press, 1990

Sjöqvist, Erik, *Lysippus*, Cincinnati: University of Cincinnati, 1966

Stewart, Andrew, *Greek Sculpture: An Exploration*, New Haven, Connecticut and London: Yale University Press, 1990

Lytras, Nikephoros 1832–1904

Painter

Nikephoros Lytras was one of the principal members of the so-called Munich School which included Greek artists trained at the Bavarian capital, such as, among others, Nikolaos Gyzis (1842–1901), Polychronis Lembessis (1849–1913), Konstantinos Volanakis (1837–1907), and Georgios Iakovides (1853–1932). Lytras was the first major Greek painter, moreover, who, after completing his training abroad, returned to his homeland to undertake the artistic formation of a younger generation of Greek artists at the School of Fine Arts in Athens. He therefore deserves his epithet as "father of the modern Greek school of painting".

Lytras's own training began in the fledgling art school of the Athens Polytechnic of the mid-1850s under the guidance of mostly foreign teachers who lived and worked in Athens, primarily the Bavarian painter Ludwig Thiersch (1825–1909). Thiersch was a graduate of the Munich Academy and a follower of the Nazarenes who had revived interest for Italian Renaissance religious painting in the manner of early Raphael using the technique of fresco. Accordingly, Lytras' earliest works, murals in small local churches in Athens and its vicinity, combine his teacher's interest in religious art with an effort to evoke Greek traditional forms of sacred art inspired from his study of Byzantine mosaics in the nearby churches of Daphni and Hosios Loukas. He sent an early example of his work to the Paris International Exposition of 1855 – a *Madonna and Child* (Monastery of the Virgin, Tinos), in which the figures of the Virgin and infant Christ followed Byzantine models and were depicted against the traditional gold-leafed background of Byzantine icons.

His interests shifted dramatically, however, during his years of study at the Munich Academy, between 1860 and roughly 1865. There he came under the influence of the academic history painter Karl Theodor von Piloty (1826–86), who became his teacher, as well as that of the old masters, especially Rubens and Rembrandt, whose works he studied in the Alte Pinakothek. Even during those years of complete immersion into a western European art tradition, however, he pursued his attempts to merge his Greek heritage with the example of his teacher's academic historicism. A case in point is Lytras's painting *Antigone Discovers the Body of Polynices* (1865, National Picture Gallery, Athens), with its subject inspired from Sophocles cast in the compositional and stylistic terms of Munich-style academic history painting, particularly Piloty's celebrated painting *Seni before the Body of the Dead Wallenstein* (1855, Bayerische Staadtsgemaldesammlungen, Munich). At the same time, however, he frequented the circle of younger artists in Munich, including Wilhelm Leibl, Wilhelm Trübner, Hans von Drefregger, and Franz von Lenbach, who explored portraiture and everyday-life themes ("genre painting") with an ethnographic character depicted in a realistic manner. Two artists from Dusseldorf, Benjamin Vautier and Ludwig Knauss, whose works exemplified picturesque ethnographic genre painting, also served as his models.

It was portraiture and genre painting that constituted the majority of Lytras's output after his return to Greece in 1865–66 and his appointment to a professorship at the School of Fine Arts in Athens. Apart from his teaching, he received commissions from public institutions, but also from wealthy, educated, cosmopolitan bourgeois patrons who formed the new Athenian upper class of the post-Ottonian years. His portraits reflect German academic models, and also his awareness of the French avant-garde. For example, his portrait of *Lysandros Kaftantzoglou* (1885–86, National Picture Gallery, Athens), the Director of the Athens Polytechnic, represents him seated at his desk in the manner of Manet's famous portrait of Emile Zola (1868, Musée d'Orsay, Paris) which Lytras could have seen during his visit to Paris in September 1876, the year of the second Impressionist exhibition. Later portraits include the two life-size portraits of king Otho and his wife Amalia commissioned by the Philekpaideutiki Etairia, an educational society, for their headquarters. These show Greece's first Bavarian king and his queen dressed in Greek national dress posing against the ruins of the Acropolis in the background (1893, Philekpaideutiki Etairia, Athens).

At the same time, his interest in history and genre painting, developed during his years in Munich, was applied to themes inspired from modern Greek history and customs. The large history painting *Kanaris Blowing up the Turkish Flagship* (c.1873, Athens, private collection) shows an episode from the Greek War of Independence, a feat of sabotage performed by Constantine Kanaris and his companions in 1822, which was followed by brutal Turkish reprisals on the population of the island of Chios. From the same period, 1870–90, date some of his best-known scenes of ethnographic genre, with an emphasis on local traditions and customs, local costumes, and sentimental, anecdotal plots. *The Carol Singers* (c.1873, private collection, Athens,) and the unfinished *Mourning the Dead in Psara* (c.1880, National Picture Gallery, Athens) illustrate customary rites and rituals of Greek rural life in a style imbued by the sentimental realism of Dusseldorf and Munich genre painters. These and similar works reflect the contemporary literary trend towards rustic, ethnographic narratives as represented by the novels of Dimitrios Vikelas (for which Lytras intended to supply illustrations), Alexandros Papadiamantis, and Georgios Vizyinos. Lytras's use of a familiar, realistic formal treatment in his paintings parallels the contemporary struggle of the popular demotic dialect to prevail over its better-established rival, the sophisticated *katharevousa*, or "pure one". (Ironically when it came to linguistic preferences, Lytras supported the latter.) A trip to Asia Minor in 1873 in the company of his friend and fellow painter Nikolaos Gyzis prompted several paintings with orientalist subject matter – chieftains, pirates, Arabs – similar in spirit to those highly popular works of his contemporary, the French painter Jean-Léon Gérôme.

Lytras' influence was felt on his numerous pupils at the Athens School of Fine Arts. They included Lembessis, Iakovides, Spyros Vikatos (1878–1944), and his own son Nikolaos Lytras (1882–1927). They carried on the tradition of rural, ethnographic themes while incorporating some of the advances of Impressionism in their use of *plein-air*, a more luminous palette, and a lighter brushstroke.

NINA ATHANASSOGLOU-KALLMYER

See also Painting

Biography

Born in Tinos in 1832, Lytras began his training at the Athens Polytechnic under the Bavarian painter Ludwig Thiersch. In the early 1860s he moved to the Munich Academy where he was a pupil of Karl Theodor von Piloty. Returning to Greece in the mid-1860s, he became a professor at the School of Fine Arts in Athens. He concentrated on portraiture and genre painting, receiving commissions from public institutions and wealthy individuals. He died in 1904.

Further Reading

Athanassoglou, N., "O Zographos Nikephoros Lytras 1832–1904" [The Painter Nikephoros Lytras, 1832–1904] (dissertation), University of Thessalonica, 1976

Christou, Chrysanthos, *Greek Painting, 1832–1922*, Athens: National Bank of Greece, 1981

Giofyllis, F., *Istoria tis Neoellinikis Technis* [A History of Modern Greek Art], 2 vols, Athens, 1962

Lydakis, Stylianos (editor), *Oi ellenes Zographoi* [Greek Painters], 4 vols, Athens, 1976 (see vol. 3, pp. 137–54)

Papanikolaou, Miltiades, *He Ellenike Ethnographike Zographike tou Dekatou Enatou Aiona* [Greek Genre Painting of the 19th Century], Thessalonica, 1978

M

Macarius (pseudo-)

Monastic writer of the 4th century

From at least the early 6th century a substantial body of works has been ascribed to St Macarius the Great, founder of the monastic community at Scetis. A 13th-century manuscript carries a marginal note that casts doubt on this ascription, a suspicion that was developed by the 18th-century Athonite scholar Neophytos Kavsokalivites. It has in the 20th century become the scholarly orthodoxy that the works, with the exception of one letter, are not the work of Macarius the Great.

The material is voluminous, containing homilies, treatises, letters, answers to questions, and other occasional pieces. It has come down to us in the original Greek in four main collections. Collection I is the largest collection, with 64 *Logoi*. Collection II, the 50 *Spiritual Homilies*, is the best-known recension. Collection III has 43 *Logoi*, Collection IV, 26. There is some overlap between the collections, Collection IV, for example, being contained wholly in Collection I.

The Macarian writings are the collected teachings of the anonymous director of a monastic community of the semi-eremitic type, probably located in eastern Asia Minor or northern Mesopotamia. They may roughly be dated to the 370s and 380s. They are connected with the amorphous ascetic tendency known as Messalianism. The dearth of evidence surrounding the real nature of the Messalian tendency does not allow any crude identification of the writings with that movement. Furthermore, it is clear from the writings themselves that the author was an opponent and reformer of the kind of monasticism later condemned as Messalianism.

The writings may initially have circulated anonymously, ascribed to one Macarius or "blessed one". The addition "of Egypt" may have crept in later. Some material circulated under the name of St Symeon the Stylite, other pieces under that of St Ephrem or, in one instance, of St Basil. Whatever their origins, the writings are a testimony of a spirituality of the highest order.

The master theme of the writings is the vision of the mutual indwelling of man and God. By virtue of his incarnation, God comes to dwell in man and raises man up to dwell in God. The writings are centred upon the heart, the physical and spiritual centre of the human person. With the intellect as governor, the heart reigns over the whole body. It is the vehicle by which grace is experienced by the whole person. The centrality of the heart gives the writings a strongly affective and experiential tone. To illustrate his teaching, ranging from the sheer effort required to acquire the virtues to the highest states of divine contemplation and participation, Macarius uses a host of images and metaphors that give his work an intensely visual and colourful character. The writings are deeply Christocentric, focusing especially on the imitation of Christ. They are also profoundly Trinitarian, and provide the clearest possible picture of man's encounter with God in the Holy Spirit.

Much has recently been made of the Syrian background of the texts. That there is a significant element drawn from the traditions of Syrian asceticism is incontestable. There is also, however, an equally important element drawn from the Hellenic tradition. In fact, much of the interest of the writings stems from their integration of these two very different thought-worlds. Macarius was indebted to the Alexandrine tradition of Clement and Origen. He may have come to know this tradition through the Cappadocian Fathers, with whom he was connected. Macarius develops the concept of *apatheia* (freedom from the passions) inherited from Clement. While he clearly perceives the ontological gulf between creature and Creator, Macarius also works with intuition of the complementarity of the sensible and intelligible worlds that derives ultimately from Plato. The locating of the intellect in the heart does not imply any material restriction upon its activity. Indeed Macarius speaks of the intellect as "rising out of materiality", overcoming the blindness and forgetfulness occasioned by the Fall. Through the gathering of the dispersed and multiple thoughts of the soul into one divine thought by the wings of the Spirit, one comes to "commingle with unoriginate intellect". Macarius' Hellenic culture is a diffused one, mediated by the Alexandrine tradition. It is, however, an aspect that must be taken into account when considering his work as a whole.

Macarius has exercised a profound influence on the development of the Christian spiritual tradition, comparable to that of Evagrius. Echoes of his work are found in the mid-5th-century *Life of Hypatius*. He was certainly known by St Diadochus of Photice, writing in the latter half of the 5th century, and by Mark the Monk (5th century). The *Asceticon* of Abba Isaiah (5th/6th century) shows many affinities with the Macarian writings. St Maximos the Confessor drew upon the Macarian tradition to balance the traditions of Evagrius of Pontus and Dionysius the Areopagite within his own synthesis. St Symeon the New Theologian is also very much in the Macarian line. By his time the manuscript tradition had settled into the four main recensions mentioned above. The fact that four distinct collections evolved is an indication of an abundant manuscript tradition during the Byzantine period. The 11th-century compilation attributed to St Symeon Metaphrastes is reproduced in the *Philokalia*. It was made on the basis of Collection IV, the oldest of the main Greek collections. The Macarian writings provided an important source for the 13th- and 14th-century hesychasts. St Gregory Palamas cites the "great Macarius" as one of the principal sources for his understanding of the place of the body in the spiritual life and for his teaching on the nature of the light witnessed in prayer. The Macarian writings continued to be popular among both monastic and secular audiences. Their predominantly encouraging tone has led to their being thought especially useful for novices.

MARCUS PLESTED

See also Philokalia

Biography
The unknown author of a corpus of monastic writings formerly ascribed to St Macarius the Great. The texts, dating from the 370s and 380s, divide into four collections and probably originate from a monastic community in eastern Asia Minor or northern Mesopotamia. They have been very influential on the development of the Eastern Christian spiritual tradition.

Writings
Fifty Spiritual Homilies, translated by A.J. Mason, London: SPCK, and New York: Macmillan, 1921
Oeuvres spirituelles, vol. 1: *Homélies propres à la Collection III*, edited and translated by Vincent Desprez, Paris: Sources Chrétiennes, 1980
The Philokalia: The Complete Text, translated by G.E.H. Palmer, Philip Sherrard and Kallistos Ware, vol. 3, London and Boston: Faber, 1984 (selections from Collection IV)
The Fifty Spiritual Homilies, and The Great Letter, translated by George A. Maloney, New York: Paulist Press, 1992

Further Reading
Jaeger, Werner, *Two Rediscovered Works of Ancient Christian Literature: Gregory of Nyssa and Macarius*, Leiden: Brill, 1954
Louth, Andrew, *The Origins of the Christian Mystical Tradition from Plato to Denys*, Oxford: Clarendon Press, and New York: Oxford University Press, 1981, chapter 6
Stewart, Columba, *'Working the Earth of the Heart': The Messalian Controversy in History, Texts, and Language to AD 431*, Oxford: Clarendon Press, and New York: Oxford University Press, 1991

Macedonia

The latest archaeological findings have confirmed that Macedonia took its name from a tribe of tall, Greek-speaking people, the Makednoi (*ma(e)kos* = length). They shared the same religious beliefs as the rest of the Hellenic world but up until the Classical period remained outside the cultural and political development of the southern city states. From the 7th century BC onwards Makednoi, under the leadership of the Temenid dynasty, started to move from the highlands of present Greek western Macedonia to the southeast, initially in the winter pastures of Pieria, expelling, subduing, or assimilating a number of Thracian and Phrygian tribes. By the 5th century the Macedonian kingdom was strong enough to occupy all the lands to the east of the Pindus and to the west of the Strymon river and stretched more or less as far north as the present northern border of Greece. This was achieved through agricultural and military reforms which created an upper class of noble landlords as well as an army of landowning soldiers.

Reform and expansion overlapped with the peak of Athenian domination, resulting in a lengthy period of tension which took many forms. Anxious to exploit rich Macedonian resources, Athens tried to colonize eastern Macedonia, destabilize the ruling dynasty, encourage barbarian invasions, and facilitate disintegration. But it was during the same period of Athenian hegemony that the Macedonian kingdom started to come into closer contact with the southern civilization, Classical art, literature, philosophy, and the Attic dialect. The Macedonian court and nobility, rough and tough pastoralist highlanders, were overwhelmed and easily assimilated into Athenian culture. Even their local dialect, northwestern Greek, was replaced by Attic and left only a handful of written monuments in the form of inscriptions. The presence and work of Zeuxis the painter, Timotheos and Agathon the poets, and, most of all, Euripides secured for Athens what strategy had failed to accomplish: complete and perpetual cultural integration.

Yet "vulgar" Macedonians were not unanimously accepted by "refined" southern Greeks, especially by Athenians, as brethren; occasionally they were classified as "barbarians". This was not due to some latent but still distinguishable Thracian and Paeonian cultural influences or to local linguistic peculiarities. To a certain extent Athenian reluctance could be attributed to the Macedonians' rough manners, their monarchic government, and their delayed appearance on the scene. But the main source of antipathy was more than a century of conflict over eastern Macedonia, Thrace, the Chalcidice colonies, and, of course, the final victorious military involvement of Macedonia in southern affairs from 350 BC onwards, which signalled the end of the Classical period.

Philip II of Macedon was anxious to pacify and unify Greece at any cost – except his own – in order to attack the Persian empire. His dream was fulfilled by his son Alexander III the Great, who in no more than 12 years at the head of a Greek army occupied a major part of the then known world from the Aegean Sea to the frontiers of India. The scientific knowledge derived from his campaigns and explorations was significant. Moreover, the dissemination of Greek culture and language over this vast territory had a tremendous longterm impact on the shaping of the Roman empire, Christendom, and Byzantium. But Alexander's own dazzling personality, his adventures among strange peoples, and his unmatched strategic abilities outlived and overshadowed all his cultural achievements. These achievements became the stuff of popular myths, folklore, literature, ideals, and art among eastern and western

23. The expansion of Macedonia in the 4th century BC

people, and, above all, they nourished the Greek national imagination.

In the short term the kingdom of Macedonia did not survive as long as Macedonian pride. Although Macedonians gained a sense of superiority and abundant wealth from the east, they simultaneously experienced a dramatic demographic haemorrhage of manpower due to the Asian campaign and later on due to emigration to Syria and Egypt. During the wars of Alexander's successors and the Celtic invasion (279 BC) the country also suffered from relentless plundering and war indemnities. Moreover these endless and bloody wars alienated Alexander's generals individually from each other and collectively from the southern Greeks. In less than two centuries (323–148 BC) Macedonia was steadily reduced from a glorious world empire to a Roman province.

In 168 BC the Roman legions dealt a fatal and lasting blow to Macedonian autonomy. Macedonia was stripped of its possessions and was divided into four administrative districts. In 148, after an ill-prepared revolt, it was reunited and officially integrated within the Roman empire. The presence of legions however did not discourage barbarian invasions. It was only between the end of the Roman Civil Wars (31 BC) and the early Gothic raids (later 3rd century AD) that Macedonia enjoyed the benefits of the *Pax Augusta*, and especially the advantages of the Via Egnatia. It was during the same period that its numerous old and new gods made way for the rapid Christianization of the region.

From the early Middle Ages onwards the country suffered numerous barbarian invasions, most of them targeting Thessalonica, which was evolving into a major emporium as the second city of the Christian Byzantine empire. Goths, Alans, Huns, Avars, Slavs, and Bulgars raided, plundered, and occasionally settled in Macedonia. The question of whether the Slav tribes in Macedonia were absorbed or not by the Bulgarians (already Slavicized Huns) will probably never be resolved. Nor will it ever be agreed whether and to what extent these settlers were "Hellenized". There is evidence that some of their warlords were culturally assimilated, but the indisputable fact is that all settlers were Christianized and lived next to various colonists evacuated from the Asiatic provinces of the empire.

Although in the 9th century some Slav settlers were already being employed in the Byzantine army, the 10th century was marked by continuous warfare between Byzantium and Bulgaria, with Macedonia usually being the battlefield. Symeon, Samuel, Peter Deljan, Alousianos, Michael Ivatzi, and the Asen brothers all challenged Byzantine authority and occasionally managed to occupy extensive territories until the mid-13th century. Their defeats by the Byzantine emperors Leo VI, Basil II (the Bulgar-slayer), Michael IV, and Alexios III resulted in the eclipse of the Bulgarian threat and political authority, the archbishopric of Achris (modern Ohrid) – a Bulgarian ecclesiastical institution at the time – being the only remnant.

While the Macedonian hinterland was being devastated, in the urban centres, especially in Thessalonica, Byzantine culture flourished. Various metropolitans of this city are known for their contribution to theology, literature, and law, the best-known being Eustathios (12th century), who commented on Homer, and St Gregory Palamas and Neilos Kabasilas (14th century), both of whom strongly influenced Orthodox theology. Important teachers of Classics and law are also known to have worked in Thessalonica, especially after 1204: John Apokaphkos, Thomas Magistros, Matthew Vlastaris, Constantine Armenopoulos, Dimitrios Triklinios, etc. Even better known are the Byzantine architectural and artistic masterpieces of the so-called "Macedonian school", not only in Thessalonica but also in Kastoria, Serres, Achris, Prespa, Stromnitsa, Melenikon, and especially within the monastic community of Mount Athos, established officially in the 10th century. The presence of Slavs in Macedonia is related in particular to two important cultural developments: the "Miracles of St Dimitrios", the patron saint of Thessalonica, i.e. rhetorical ecclesiastical accounts recalling the 7th-century sieges of Thessalonica and the early Slav–Byzantine contacts; and the work of two Byzantine brothers from Thessalonica, Constantine (Cyril) and Methodios, who in the 9th century became the apostles to the Slavs and inventors of the Cyrillic alphabet, initially used for the translation of religious texts.

The threat from the north was not the only problem for medieval Macedonia. The Arabs (Saracen pirates) looted Thessalonica in 902 and the Normans, who invaded from the west, in 1185. Macedonia was also invaded by the crusaders in the early 13th century, the Albanians, and Catalan mercenaries, and it became part of the short-lived Serbian empire of Stephan Dushan (1334–55), amid Latin and Byzantine dynastic clashes which lasted into the 14th century and paved the way for the Turks. By the early 15th century Ottoman rule had been imposed over all Macedonian territories including Thessalonica. It was not to be interrupted for more than five centuries.

Throughout the Byzantine period Macedonia was never a separate administrative region. In fact the name Macedonia was assigned to a Byzantine administrative unit (theme) in Thrace and the imperial Macedonian dynasty originated from Adrianople. The term had lost its former geographical and other implications. The same is true for the Ottoman era. After the Ottoman settlement and the sporadic Islamization of Christians and Jews, Macedonia was not only an ill-defined region but also a linguistic mixture of Greek-, Slav-, Turkish-, Albanian-, and Vlach-speaking Christians and Muslims, as well as Spanish-, Greek-, and Turkish-speaking Jews. In such a multilingual milieu and under the Islamic law linguistic differences were entirely meaningless. In fact, these differences were related more to the cultural division of labour than to the actual origin of the people. As a rule, for example, Christian peasants were Slav-speakers, shepherds Vlach-speakers, traders Greek- and Vlach-speakers. All Christians shared a post-Byzantine culture which was determined by Orthodox dogma and nourished by Byzantine legends. They were mainly loyal to their family, clan, and community and had little sense of ethnic distinction. Alexander the Great, whose adventures were the topic of a well-known Greek folk song (rimada) and a booklet (fyllada) – a version of Pseudo–Callisthenes popular

in Byzantium – was probably the only figure from antiquity to have survived medieval illiteracy and Christian anathema. He and his royal family were to be recalled from the past to participate in yet one more Hellenic expedition in the 18th and 19th centuries AD.

A Christian merchant class was shaped in the context of the unbalanced European-Ottoman commercial relations. In southern Greece they were Greek- and Albanian-speaking shipowners. In Macedonia they were Greek- and Vlach-speaking merchants. The Vlach-speakers, from the 18th century onwards, slowly descended from the highlands into Macedonian towns. They had secured the necessary capital, family network, and connections among the armatoloi (border guards) and brigands to pursue trade between the Ottoman Balkans, the Habsburg domains, and western Europe. Merchants replaced what was left of the Byzantine aristocracy in Macedonia and became the urban class, flattered by the romantic revival of Hellenic culture, strongly attracted by Greek education, and proud to choose for their offspring the names of Alexander's generals.

Such merchants and chieftains at the head of various pastoralists and peasants, who had hoped that liberation from the Turks would also bring economic emancipation, participated eagerly in the Greek War of Independence (1821–32) as well as in various Greek revolts throughout the 19th century after Greek independence. It was all to no avail in spite of a heavy toll paid in blood. After 1870 the Greeks did not possess the monopoly of irredentism in Macedonia. The establishment of the Bulgarian Church (exarchate) and the creation of an independent Bulgarian principality (1878) provided a second option. As the Eastern Question entered its final stage, it was evident that the Macedonian heritage would belong to that state which could argue most convincingly in front of the Great Powers for its demographic and historical rights in that region.

Vigorous educational campaigns were launched from Athens and Sofia and to a lesser extent from Belgrade to enlighten their brethren in Macedonia and bring them up to date with their respective nationalisms; but not surprisingly such ideologies were not easily absorbed by the agrarian societies which were so badly needed to affirm demographic supremacy. Greeks had the copyright of Macedonia's ancient history which they exploited as best as they could. After the schism of the Bulgarian Church from the Ecumenical Patriarchate (1872) they also had the advantage of shared religion with the target population. But linguistic arguments were in favour of the Bulgarians, who were also helped by Samuel's medieval legacies and, most of all, by various social and economic cleavages which fed back to Bulgarian nationalism: the word "Bulgars" had become synonymous with illiterate peasants, heavily taxed by the Church and the state, scorned and exploited by the mercantile class. It was only natural that some of them opted for the exarchate.

The peak of Bulgarian intervention in Macedonia was the Ilinden Uprising (1903) which failed to bring a Bulgarian-sponsored autonomy but did bring the Greeks into the game anew. Educational and ecclesiastical antagonism soon resulted in an undeclared and bloody Graeco–Bulgarian war of bandits (1903–08) in what was still Ottoman–held Macedonia, fought to win or to reverse national allegiances. European involvement, aiming to secure temporary tranquillity through finan-

Macedonia: rally in Thessalonica on 14 February 1992 protesting at the use of the name "Macedonia" by the former Yugoslav republic

cial reform, failed to produce any permanent result. It helped, however, to standardize the term "Macedonia" as identical to the three Ottoman prefectures under reform, thus stretching the region's northern limits further than Philip and Alexander had done, as far north as Tetovo and Kumanovo. It was that expanded Macedonia which was divided in 1913 at the end of the Balkan Wars between Greeks (51 per cent), Bulgarians (10 per cent), and Serbs who, though latecomers, took 38 per cent, taking full advantage of Stephan Dushan's titles and their own war efforts.

In the following years voluntary and compulsory population exchanges between Greece, Bulgaria, and Turkey were intended to pacify the region by achieving ethnic homogeneity. This was not always an easy task in Greek and Bulgarian (Pirin) Macedonia; nor was it the same as the acculturation policy implemented by Belgrade in Serbian (Vardar) Macedonia. The integration of the three parts into their respective nation states, occasionally under absolutist regimes, sometimes revived previous loyalties or even created new ones. Slav Macedonian ethnic identity in particular is the interwar product of an interaction between Bulgarian revisionism, Balkan Communism, Serbian and Greek centralization, and colonization policies. During World War II, the Greek Civil War, and the postwar period, Macedonian identity and nationalism became an important lever to neutralize Bulgarian aspirations in the Yugoslav Socialist Republic of Macedonia, to avoid Serbian colonization, to maintain some grip on the Greek part of Macedonia, and also to gain influence in the large and multiethnic Macedonian diaspora.

The shaping of this latest of all Balkan nationalisms followed the same recipe: ancient ethnic roots and ethnic continuity are indispensable for the survival of a nation state. It was too difficult a task for historians in Skopje to achieve but not an entirely unsuccessful venture. They continue to lack the consent of their Greek and Bulgarian colleagues, who safeguard the respective traditions of ancient Macedonia, the medieval Slav kingdoms, and anti-Turkish revolts as their own precious heritage. In Greece the Greek Macedonian heritage has been enriched by two generations of national heroes who fought against the Turks in the 19th century and the Bulgarians in the early 20th, in the so-called "Struggle for Macedonia". The establishment in 1991 of an independent replublic (the Former Yugoslav Republic of Macedonia) in place of the Yugoslav Socialist Republic of Macedonia intensified antagonism for the past and strengthened the importance of symbols. Even though the diplomatic aspects of the modern Macedonian Question are not beyond solution, a compromise over the legacy of Alexander for the Greeks and Tsar Samuel for the Bulgarians is highly improbable as long as Macedonian history and Balkan politics are analysed in ethnic terms.

BASIL C. GOUNARIS

Summary

Ancient Macedonians shared the same religious beliefs and language as the rest of the Hellenic world but had remained politically distinct. Expansion and reform in the 5th century BC coincided with Athenian hegemony and resulted in conflict and Macedonian domination of southern Greece in the 4th century BC. By 148 BC Macedonia was a Roman province. Throughout the Middle Ages it suffered numerous invasions but also evolved into a centre of Byzantine culture. In the 19th century, after five centuries of Ottoman rule and considerable demographic change, Macedonia became a focus for the Greek nationalist cause, and its borders were redefined by various conflicts. Its position in the central Balkans has made it an apple of discord between Greece, Bulgaria, and Yugoslavia since the late 1940s.

Further Reading

Apostolski, M. et al., A History of the Macedonian People, Skopje: Macedonian Review Editions, 1979

Gounaris, B. et al., Tautotites sti Makedonia [Identities in Macedonia], Athens: Papazisis, 1997

Hornblower, Simon and Antony Spawforth (editors), The Oxford Classical Dictionary, 3rd edition, Oxford and New York: Oxford University Press, 1996, entries on Macedonia, Macedonia: cults, and Macedonian language

Kofos, Evangelos, Nationalism and Communism in Macedonia: Civil Conflict, Politics of Mutation, National Identity, New Rochelle, New York: Caratzas, 1993

Koliopoulos, I. and I. Chassiotis (editors), Neoteri kai Synchroni Makedonia: Istoria, Oikonomia, Koinonia, Politismos [Modern and Contemporary Macedonia: History, Economy, Society, Culture], Athens and Thessalonica: Papazisis and Paratiritis, n.d.

Pribichevich, Stoyan, Macedonia: Its People and History, University Park: Pennsylvania State University Press, 1982

Sakellariou, M.B. (editor), Macedonia: 4,000 Years of Greek History and Civilization, Athens: Ekdotike Athenon, 1983

Vakalopoulos, Apostolos E., History of Macedonia, 1354–1833, translated by Peter Megann, Thessalonica: Institute for Balkan Studies, 1973; 2nd edition in Greek, Thessalonica: Vanias, 1988

Magic

In one form or another, magical beliefs and rituals have always found a place in the Greek tradition, although it must be said that magic, as a distinct and easily recognizable category, is one no longer readily accepted by modern scholarship. For the sake of the present discussion, however, and while acknowledging the considerable debate on the topic, it may be understood in the present context to indicate that end of a continuous and largely undifferentiated spectrum of religious thought and behaviour deemed unacceptable to the dominant culture at any given period because of the purposes for which it is employed, because of the methods and the powers it is believed to use, and because of the assumptions it makes about the nature of the cosmos.

The ancient Greek religious tradition included a vast array of magical techniques through which it was believed that people could attain material enrichment and success; could protect themselves against misfortune, ill health, and malice; could discover normally hidden information; or could cause those they wanted to love them and those they hated to suffer or die. Indeed, it seems likely that most people's religious beliefs and practices contained much that may be categorized at the magical end of the spectrum. In an atmosphere of general uncertainty, insecurity, and helplessness, magic claimed to provide a method that worked directly and relatively dependably to solve all the problems, difficulties, and unfulfilled aspirations of everyday life.

Firm evidence of belief in magical power and practice goes back to the earliest Greek literature, although this undoubtedly represents a far older tradition in prehistory: Circe, in Homer's Odyssey, for example, knows how to summon spirits of the dead and uses magic rituals to transform humans into animals, while in myth Medea possesses the power of the evil eye and can cause all manner of harm by magical means. Important references to magical practices and beliefs are found in literature from the entire span of ancient Greek culture, for example in Hesiod, Plato, Aristotle, Theocritus, Apollonius of Rhodes, Plutarch, Lucian, Plotinus, and Iamblichus. Knowledge derived from this material is supplemented by archaeological artefacts, in particular curse tablets, figurines, and amuletic gemstones. The most detailed information concerning magic in the older Hellenic tradition comes, however, from the Greek magical papyri that originate in Egypt and date between the 2nd century BC and the 5th century AD. This very rich collection of material demonstrates clearly that the Greek tradition of magic cannot be taken in isolation from the Egyptian, Jewish, and other near Eastern traditions, and confirms that magic was practised at many different levels, from villages to courts, and by practitioners ranging from itinerant to highly institutionalized individuals.

The magic revealed by these sources is primarily concerned with using the supernatural forces believed to control and influence the world in which humans exist, whether these are gods and goddesses, intermediary powers such as angels, demons, and decans, or spirits of the dead. Those associated with nature, such as solar and astral powers, feature prominently, while in the papyri, with their particular cultural context, the Jewish god Iao is most frequently named; but in general the forces of the underworld (notably Hecate) were undoubtedly those thought most helpful and potent. Magical practice, ranging from the crude and casual to the elaborate and formal, was thought to be empowered in almost all cases by a combination of speech and ritual action. Although sometimes no more than vestigial at a low level, these words and actions, which often involved overt symbolic linkage to the desired outcome, were underpinned at the most complex end of the scale by a vast system of knowledge of numerous levels of often highly individualized supernatural powers, and of the names, words, and practices to make them responsive or submissive. It was vital to know all the natural materials (animal, vegetable, or mineral) thought to be particularly favourable or potent in relation to the purposes of the magic in hand and either sympathetic or antipathetic to the powers being used; important too was knowledge of correct timing (generally determined by complicated astrological lore) and location (e.g. a crossroad or a place of violent death). Just as most people today, however, use modern technology with almost no knowledge of the underlying scientific theory, so most who employed magical techniques in the ancient world had no real understanding of their formal and complex intellectual basis.

For the purposes of analysis, magical practice in the Greek tradition may be said to fall into one of three general categories: protection, manipulation, and the discovery of normally hidden knowledge. For protection, amulets were most commonly used. These operated at all levels from individual to communal and were either worn on the body or placed strategically, on the doorpost of a house, for example, or on a city gate. All manner of materials were used, but all were thought to have some special apotropaic efficacy, whether physical or symbolic; this might be increased by combining elements, by adding written formulae, and by preparing them at the proper time and place.

Best known among the enormous range of popular techniques of magical manipulation, particularly for ill, is the use of curse tablets and "voodoo dolls". In the former case imprecatory and magical formulae were most often inscribed on a lead tablet that was then associated with the enforcing powers by, for example, being inserted in a tomb or buried at a crossroads. The tablet was also frequently "bound" or "fixed" symbolically during the ritual, perhaps being tied with elaborately knotted thread, or pierced with a nail. Practices involving magical figurines were generally similar, although wax or clay might be used and rituals of piercing and binding were often more complicated; symbolic melting or severing of the image might occur and it might be associated with the victim by using personal materials (hair, nail clippings, etc.) and by inscribing personal names on specific body parts. In both cases ritual action was carefully timed and located and was accompanied by equally elaborate verbal elements. Such practices were believed to cause general loss of performance (e.g. in oratorical skill or reproductive capacity), illness (physical or mental), overwhelming lust, or even death; these effects might extend not only to humans but to livestock and crops as well. Other manipulatory techniques involved summoning and then compelling supernatural powers or spirits; in their more elaborate forms complex rituals of invocation took place and interaction with the powers might be thought to occur in a trance state or by means of visions seen, perhaps, in the shining surface of a vessel of water or a mirror. The latter practices relate closely to some used for determining hidden knowledge (see the article on Divination). Also related to these manipulatory techniques are the late antique rites of theurgy.

The emergence of Christianity and its rise to a position of cultural dominance in the Greek world certainly had a major effect on the concept and practice of magic, but it by no means eliminated it. Due to the monotheistic and supplicatory nature of the Christian religion, almost all pagan practices that survived tended to be condemned as magical by the Church authorities because their attitude was implicitly coercive and because they were seen as employing evil powers. Many very common elements of religious practice in the ancient Greek tradition, such as sacrifice, divination, and the use of amulets, were thus now shifted to the magical end of the religious spectrum by Christian doctrinalists, but, although some of these dwindled significantly in the public sphere, there is abundant evidence that they still continued to play an important part in popular and private belief and practice at all social levels. Many of the ancient magical practices, considered above, continued, while many outwardly Christian practices that were employed for culturally unacceptable ends or in ways that conflicted technically with Orthodox principles might also now be viewed as magical: making offerings to images of holy figures, for example, in the belief that they might be coerced into providing a guaranteed response, wearing Christian symbols as amulets in the belief that automatic protection would result, or believing that evil spirits could be controlled for personal ends by the use of Christian words of power and sacred materials. Defined in these terms, then, religious activity deemed to be magical may actually be said to have increased during Christian times; indeed, the new religion itself brought to the centre of the Greek tradition some Middle Eastern notions of magic that had previously been recognized only on its fringes (e.g. techniques of exorcism), and some passages in both the Old and New Testaments did nothing to undermine belief in the efficacy of magic. It remains true, however, that the notion of magic in the Byzantine and modern Greek world is an essentially artificial one imposed both by contemporary Christian doctrinalists and by modern scholarship. It is clear that most ordinary people, untrained in theology or uncommitted to its finer points, have seen magic simply as an alternative way of attaining results when the recourse to the normal routes offered by standard Christian practice has appeared to be inappropriate or to have failed.

Ancient magical techniques were still employed throughout the Byzantine period and down to the beginning of the 20th century in almost exactly the same forms and contexts as they had been in antiquity. There was something of a decline in the use of curse tablets and undoubtedly there was an increase in the Christian content of many of the rituals and verbal formulae, but most practices remained substantially unchanged: take, for example, amuletic inscriptions against the female spirit believed to cause sudden infant death (Gylou or Yello in the later tradition); the consultation or conjuration of spirits in vessels of water; the concept of "binding" or "fixing" enemies and rivals; or belief in the evil eye (see the article on Evil Eye).

In the Christian period the notion of "witchcraft", where the human operator of magic is believed to possess inherent supernatural power, is almost totally absent from the Greek tradition, with the notable exception of the evil eye; instead, almost all Greek magic is, technically, "sorcery", consisting of learned techniques passed on in a verbal or literary tradition. Detailed evidence of this tradition occurs first in the magical papyri and other works, such as the *Testament of Solomon* and the *Kyranides*, dating from the early Christian era, but it reappears, in a clearly recognizable form, in manuscripts of magic dating from the 15th to 19th centuries. Versions of these works, known popularly in the modern tradition as *solomon-aiki*, continued to be published to the present day.

During the 20th century there was certainly a significant decline in recourse to magic in the Greek world but it persists to an extent. Practices associated with belief in the evil eye are still widely attested, as are some forms of divination, although neither appears to be taken as seriously by many people as they once were. The use of amulets in one form or another is also still widespread and some of the old apotropaic symbols may occasionally be found displayed in public places (on the dashboard of a bus, for example, or over the window of a house). Some people still apparently believe that sorcerers exist and they attribute to them many of the old techniques derived from the written tradition – binding, cursing, causing uncontrollable love, divining by means of evil spirits, and so on – but recent anthropologists have been unable to find either such people themselves or individuals who have personally visited them, and have thus expressed doubts over their continued existence. What does unquestionably continue, however, is an attitude to religious practice that falls at the magical end of the scale in the sense that "automatic" results are believed to be attainable through otherwise standard Orthodox Christian practices.

RICHARD P.H. GREENFIELD

See also Divination, Evil Eye, Necromancy

Further Reading

Aune, D.E., "Magic in Early Christianity" in *Aufstieg und Niedergang der römischen Welt*, edited by Hildegard Temporini et al., 2.23.2, Berlin: de Gruyter, 1980, 1507–57

Betz, Hans Dieter (editor), *The Greek Magical Papyri in Translation, including the Demotic Spells*, Chicago: University of Chicago Press, 1986; 2nd edition, 1992

Blum, Richard and Eva Blum, *The Dangerous Hour: The Lore of Crisis and Mystery in Rural Greece*, London: Chatto and Windus, and New York: Scribner, 1970

Dodds, E.R., *The Ancient Concept of Progress and Other Essays on Greek Literature and Belief*, Oxford: Clarendon Press, 1973

Faraone, Christopher A. and Dirk Obbink (editors), *Magika Hiera: Ancient Greek Magic and Religion*, Oxford and New York: Oxford University Press, 1991

Faraone, Christopher, "Binding and Burying the Forces of Evil: The Defensive Use of 'Voodoo Dolls' in Ancient Greece", *Classical Antiquity*, 10 (1991): pp. 165–205

Gager, John G. (editor), *Curse Tablets and Binding Spells from Antiquity and the Ancient World*, Oxford and New York: Oxford University Press, 1992

Graf, Fritz, *Magic in the Ancient World*, translated by Franklin Philip, Cambridge, Massachusetts: Harvard University Press, 1997

Greenfield, Richard P.H., *Traditions of Belief in Late Byzantine Demonology*, Amsterdam: Hakkert, 1988

Johnston, Sarah, *Hekate Soteira: A Study of Hekate's Role in the Chaldean Oracles and Related Literature*, Atlanta: Scholars Press, 1990

Luck, Georg (translator), *Arcana Mundi: Magic and the Occult in the Greek and Roman Worlds: A Collection of Ancient Texts*, Baltimore: Johns Hopkins University Press, 1985

Maguire, Henry (editor), *Byzantine Magic*, Washington, DC: Dumbarton Oaks, 1995

Meyer, Marvin, Richard Smith and Neal Kelsey (editors), *Ancient Christian Magic: Coptic Texts of Ritual Power*, San Francisco: HarperCollins, 1994

Meyer, Marvin and Paul Mirecki (editor), *Ancient Magic and Ritual Power*, Leiden and New York: Brill, 1995

Stewart, Charles, *Demons and the Devil: Moral Imagination in Modern Greek Culture*, Princeton, New Jersey: Princeton University Press, 1991

Waegeman, Maryse (translator and editor), *Amulet and Alphabet: Magical Amulets in the First Book of Cyranides*, Amsterdam: Gieben, 1987

Magistrates

The monarchic political system of Mycenaean Greece was largely superseded during the Dark Age, the powers of the kings being redistributed among various magistrates (*archai*). As so often, our main evidence comes from Classical Athens, though the sheer size of the city makes it wholly exceptional in its great range of offices. A figure of 700 internal offices (*endemoi archai*) and a corrupt figure of 700 external ones (*hyperorioi archai*) are given for the 5th century BC by the *Constitution of Athens* (24.3), the second half of which (chapters 43–62) comprises a summary of the 46 main magistrates and boards of magistrates (adding up to a total of about 320 officials). These include financial officials, various sortitive annual officials, the archons, the quadrennial *athlothetai* (officials responsible for the Panathenaea festival), elective and military officials. As many as 71 different magistracies and boards are attested in the sources, adding up to some 450 magistrates (excluding the council, or *Boule*, of 500).

Various laws defined the basic criteria for magistrates at Athens: they were chosen by election or lot; they underwent a preliminary examination (*dokimasia*) before entering office; they served for at least 30 days; and they rendered accounts (*euthynai*) at the end of their term. In addition there was a minimum age-limit of 30; and all *archai* swore an oath that they would carry out their duties properly and in accordance with the laws. Magistrates regularly served for a period of one year only and in many cases were not eligible for a second term. Those in oligarchic states were chosen from the wealthiest citizens, but at Athens, after a long process of development, eligibility was extended to all four of the Solonian property classes, though formally only members of the first three classes were eligible for office even in the 4th century. Another contrast between oligarchic and democratic states was that magistrates in the former exercised real power, whereas many of those in the latter were essentially administrators, and all were subject to the will of the popular assembly. Magistrates summoned and presided over meetings, prepared the agendas and put motions to the vote, and most importantly executed the decisions of the assembly. To this end they had legal protection and the power to impose small fines on those who resisted them.

The administration of Athens was not hierarchical in structure (though some posts carried far greater prestige than others), and the great majority of magistrates were selected by lot from candidates who volunteered themselves. Sortition was a mark of the radical democracy; in moderate democracies and oligarchies election was the norm. At Athens, going by the figure in the *Constitution of Athens*, some 1100 magistrates were chosen by lot every year (including the 500 members of the council), and about another 100 were elected, from a pool of about 20,000 citizens over 30. This involved a heavy commitment on the part of Athens' citizens, especially since it was forbidden to hold the same sortitive office twice, except in the case of the council (where a man could serve twice but not in successive years). They could, however, be selected for different offices, and in theory, at least, they might therefore serve every other year (since they had to pass their *euthynai* after office before holding another position). The literary sources indeed suggest there was plenty of competition for office, though inscriptional evidence indicates that not all boards of magistrates were always filled, again with the exception of the council. The ten generals (*strategoi*), the most important financial officials and other officials such as the superintendent of the water supply (*epimeletes ton krenon*) were among the 100 or so magistrates who were directly elected, regularly after being proposed by another and with or without their consent. A check on individual power in democracy existed in the form of collegiality – all members of a board of magistrates were equal.

With this mixture of selection by lot and election it was inevitable that the elected officials tended to wield the most power. Down to the 5th century the leading Athenian magistrates were the nine archons. Three archons had taken over the powers of the kings: the *basileus* (who performed religious duties), the eponymous *archon* (the civilian head of state), and the *polemarchos* (who commanded the army); and alongside these were the six *thesmothetae* (judicial officials). At some point a secretary of the *thesmothetae* was added, so that the archons formed a board of ten (ten or a multiple of ten being the regular figure for boards after Cleisthenes reorganized the citizens into ten tribes). But the power of the archons waned after 487/86, when the method of sortition from an elected short list was introduced, and as the 5th century progressed their place at the head of Athenian politics was taken over by the ten generals. The archons' position declined still further when sortition replaced election at the first stage of selection as well, and in the late 5th and 4th centuries the archons performed mainly religious and judicial functions. However, the power of the generals also declined in the 4th century, as civil magistrates took over the leading role.

Magistrates at Athens were paid in the 5th century, but payment was abolished in 411, except for the archons and members of the council. Overseas officials, who included *archontes*, *episkopoi* ("overseers"), and garrison commanders, were also paid.

The civil magistrates at Sparta, and in several Dorian states, were called the ephors ("overseers"). The annually elected board of five ephors wielded considerable executive, judicial, and disciplinary powers, among them the right to control the conduct of the two kings. Evidence exists for the survival of the ephorate until at least the 3rd century AD.

In the Hellenistic period, although democracy was espoused and new cities were established with a council, assembly, and magistrates, as also was the revamped Achaean League of the early 3rd century BC, the balance of power very definitely shifted towards the wealthy. The kings paid professional magistrates, and there were numerous high- and low-ranking officials. The former tended to be Macedonians and Greeks, the latter natives, though by the 2nd century BC natives were beginning to rise to higher office.

Despite the advent of Roman rule, much responsibility was left to local communities. The power of the wealthy was consolidated by the institution of wealth qualifications for office, and to the end of antiquity the cities of the Roman empire tended to be ruled by local magistrates. Under the empire the main provincial officials were called "generals" (*strategoi*), as military titles frequently lost their military connotations. Police and judiciary officials were called "praetors", a title given from the end of the 10th century AD to the civil administrator of a province. From the 9th century various officials were called the *katepano*, who might be the commander of a military unit, and by the end of the 10th century this term was used of the governors of major provinces, who were also called *doux*. The "quaestor of the sacred palace" (*quaestor sacri palatii*), a post created by Constantine I, drafted imperial laws and heard petitions addressed to the emperor, and as the emperor's adviser in legal matters wielded considerable influence until the 9th century. Constantine also created the post of "master of the offices" (*magister officiorum*), as a

check on the power of the Praetorian Prefect, the commander of the emperor's bodyguard who from the 4th to 7th century would be an important regional civil official. The *magister officiorum* was the head of the civil administration in the late empire and a powerful figure at court, but again the importance of this official waned from the 7th century. One other important group of officials was the college of twelve *kritai tou belou*, who operated from the 10th to the beginning of the 13th century in Constantinople. These judges were so named because they met behind a curtain (*belon*; Lat. *velum*) at the Hippodrome.

MICHAEL J. EDWARDS

See also Law

Further Reading

Develin, Robert, *Athenian Officials, 684–321 BC*, Cambridge and New York: Cambridge University Press, 1989

Ehrenberg, Victor, *The Greek State*, 2nd edition, London: Methuen, 1969

Hansen, Mogens Herman, *The Athenian Democracy in the Age of Demosthenes: Structure, Principles, and Ideology*, Oxford and Cambridge, Massachusetts: Blackwell, 1991

Headlam, James Wycliffe, *Election by Lot at Athens*, 2nd edition, revised by D.C. Macgregor, Cambridge: Cambridge University Press, 1933

Michell, H., *Sparta*, Cambridge: Cambridge University Press, 1952

Staveley, E.S., *Greek and Roman Voting and Elections*, London: Thames and Hudson, and Ithaca, New York: Cornell University Press, 1972

Magna Graecia

"Magna Graecia", the Latin translation of the Greek *Megale Hellas*, was the conventional name for the Greek colonies in southern Italy, which were to provide Rome with its first contacts with Greek culture. The term first appears in 5th-century BC writings and is used to refer to the Greek world as a whole. The earliest instance of its use to indicate the Greeks of Italy is in Polybius (2. 39. 1), writing in the 2nd century BC but referring to the banishment of the Pythagoreans and subsequent formation of the Italiote League by Greek cities in the region of Italy which was known as *Megale Hellas*. By the 1st century BC the name was in common usage among Greek and Latin authors and referred to the territory stretching from Cumae near Naples in the north to Tarentum (Greek Taras) in the south, but excluding Sicily.

The first western Greeks came from Euboea where the chief cities were Chalcis and Eretria, and their first colonial foundation was Pithecusae on Ischia in the bay of Naples. The site of Pithecusae is at the northwest extremity of the island, the acropolis being Monte di Vico, with the cemetery in the adjacent Valle San Montano and beyond it on the Mezzavia hill, a suburban area. Excavations began in 1952, under the direction of Giorgio Buchner. The best-known find is the so-called "Nestor Cup", a drinking cup of Rhodian manufacture placed around 720 BC in the cremation grave of a boy about ten years old. The cup bears a three-line retrograde inscription in the Greek alphabet of Chalcis, the second and third lines of which are hexameters, and it reads, "Nestor had a fine drinking cup, but anyone who drinks from this cup will soon be struck with desire for fair-crowned Aphrodite." This is one of the earliest examples of the Greek alphabet, and the only surviving excerpt of Greek verse from the period when the Homeric epics made the transition from oral to written poetry. Scraps of Phoenician inscriptions have also been found, indicating that Pithecusae's population included Phoenicians; indeed David Ridgway has suggested that the boy whose grave yielded the "Nestor Cup" may have been of Levantine extraction. Buchner thought that these Levantine residents were not merchants, but rather artists and craftsmen commissioned by the Greeks to work in the orientalizing style.

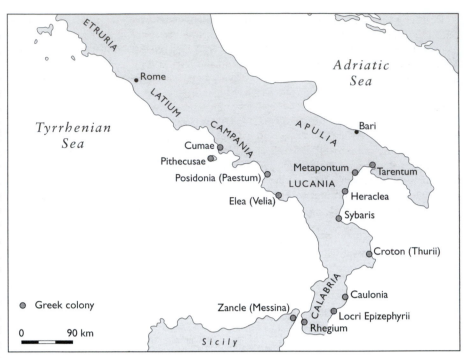

24. Greek colonies in southern Italy

According to Strabo, the Eretrians and Chalcidians at Pithecusae quarrelled, which may be a reflection of the hostilities between their mother cities, and the Eretrians left. In any case, the first foundation on the mainland was Chalcidian, at Cumae, opposite Ischia, some 20 km west of Naples. The site has a steep acropolis and good farmland nearby, but no harbour, though it has been suggested that an ancient harbour may have silted up. The pottery from the earliest Greek tombs at Cumae dates to shortly before 725 BC and the colony's foundation date is probably slightly earlier. The site's chief attraction was its proximity to the markets of central Italy which bought not only Greek manufactures but objects from Syria and Phoenicia. Parthenope, on the site of Naples, and Dicearchia, Roman Puteoli (modern Pozzuoli), founded between Naples and Cumae (c.530 BC) by Samians fleeing the tyranny of Polycrates at home, were both within the Cumaean orbit. Chalcidians from Zancle (modern Messina) along with emigrants driven by famine from Chalcis and Messenians from the Peloponnese also founded Rhegium (modern Reggio Calabria), thereby consolidating the Euboean grip on the trade route up Italy's west coast.

The instep of Italy first attracted the Achaeans from the northwest Peloponnese, who founded Sybaris c.720 BC, which commanded a fertile plain as well as a good commercial location, for it was the southern terminus for an overland route to the Tyrrhenian Sea, and was well placed to profit from the east–west trade route along the south coast of Italy. The city's wealth was famous; so also was its utter destruction by its neighbour Croton (modern Crotone) in 510 BC which diverted the river Crathis over the site. The city was refounded in 443 BC as Thurii by Athens, although the colonists were a Panhellenic group which included the historian Herodotus. Croton, founded about 710 BC, commanded a fertile but smaller agricultural area as well as a small double harbour. The philosopher Pythagoras migrated there when his homeland, Samos, fell under the tyranny of Polycrates, and founded a brotherhood which supported oligarchic government and was driven out by a popular uprising in the mid-5th century BC. Croton in turn founded Caulonia (modern Monasterace

Marina) on the south shore of the toe of Italy. The earliest pottery found there dates to the early 7th century BC, but nothing indicates extensive settlement before the mid-6th century. Some 9.5 km southwest of Caulonia, at Capo Colonna, is the temple of Hera Lacinia of which a single column and some foundation blocks remain. It was the meeting-place of the Italiote League until it was dissolved by the tyrant of Syracuse, Dionysius I, when he invaded Italy in the 390s.

Another Achaean foundation was Metapontum (modern Metaponto), some 48 km west of Taranto. Its sanctuary area, marked off by a circuit wall, contains ruins of temples (A, B, C, D, and E), the largest of which (temple A), dedicated to Lycian Apollo (580 BC, reconstructed 530 BC), yielded the first examples of polychrome terracotta revetments which are a feature of Archaic temple rooftops in Magna Graecia. North 3.2 km from Metaponto is the so-called "Tavole Palatine", a temple of Hera (6 × 12 columns) built about 500 BC on a low hill where there had been a native settlement. Five Doric columns on the south side and ten on the north remain standing. The last major Achaean site was Posidonia (later Paestum, modern Pesto), which was founded by Sybaris on the coast of the Tyrrhennian Sea some 80 km southeast of Cumae. The site has three well-preserved temples, the mid-6th-century "Basilica" (actually a temple of Hera), the so-called "Temple of Neptune" a century later, which was also a Heraion, and the "Temple of Ceres" (late 6th century) which was probably dedicated to Athena. The area was a centre for the worship of Argive Hera, as is suggested by the discovery of a sanctuary at the mouth of the river Sele, 13 km distant, with several temples and treasuries, the largest of which was a Heraion, a Doric building of 500 BC or slightly earlier. The sanctuary must date before the late 7th century BC, for Corinthian pottery of that period has been found there.

In the 670s Locris in central Greece founded Locri Epizephyrii on the east coast of Calabria. The earliest remains have not been found, but in the Classical and Hellenistic periods Locri, sited between the coastline and the hills of the interior, grew into a city covering 230 hectares, protected by a wall 7.5 km long. But the city which maintained its independence from Rome longest was Taras, or Tarentum, to give it its Latin name, remains of which lie beneath modern Taranto on a fine peninsular site with an superb harbour. Tradition told that it was founded in 706 BC by *parthenioi* from Sparta who were the bastard offspring of helots and Spartan women begotten while the Spartan army was away suppressing the revolt of Messenia. It suffered a calamitous defeat *c.*473 BC at the hands of the native Messapians, the worst defeat ever suffered by a Greek army, according to Herodotus (7. 170), but it recovered to become physically the largest city in Italy a century later, and leader of a revived Italiot League. Taras in turn, together with Thurii, founded Heraclea (433/32 BC) west of Metapontum, which marked the rebirth of the only Ionian settlement in the area, Siris, which had been destroyed in the mid-6th century by its Dorian neighbours Metapontum, Croton, and Sybaris. Siris had been founded about 650 BC by refugees from Colophon in Ionia, fleeing from the Lydians. A steep hill with a flat top at modern Policoro, the site of Heraclea, has yielded evidence of a great mudbrick wall of shortly after 700 BC, and this may mark the location of Siris. The last south Italian colony was Elea, Roman Velia, founded *c.*535 BC on Posidonian territory by Phoceans from Asia Minor after they had lost their city to the Persians. Elea was to produce one of the most rigorous Presocratic philosophers, Parmenides, the founder of the Eleatic school.

By the 4th century Oscan-speaking Sabellian people were filtering south into Apulia, Lucania (modern Basilicata), and Bruttium (modern Calabria). They captured Cumae in 421 BC, expelling or killing most of the Greek inhabitants, and 11 years later they took Posidonia, renaming it Paestum. Naples admitted its Oscan inhabitants to the citizenship and perforce allowed them a share of political control, but it remained substantially a Greek city. Elsewhere, the foray of Dionysius I in the 390s meant that Croton, Caulonia, Rhegium, and Locri fell under the rule of Syracuse and were garrisoned by Syracusan troops for 12 years before they could eject them. Taras escaped Dionysius' aggression, however, and in the 4th century ranked as the chief city of Magna Graecia, a distinction owed in part to its leading statesman, Archytas, a Pythagorean philosopher who was a friend of Plato and intervened to deliver him from house arrest when he made his second visit to Syracuse with the vain hope of making Dionysius II an ideal statesman.

The threat from its Italic neighbours spurred Taras to bring in a series of *condottieri* from Greece. A Spartan king Archidamas campaigned with some success in 343–338 BC. Alexander the Great's brother-in-law, Alexander I the Molossian from Epirus who arrived in 334 BC, achieved more, and even made a treaty with Rome, but his personal ambitions made him suspect and the Greeks were relieved when he was killed in battle in 330 BC. His territorial gains were lost after his death. The most famous of these generals was Pyrrhus, also from Epirus, who arrived with 22,500 infantry, 3000 cavalry, and a corps of 20 Indian war elephants. He won two victories at Heraclea and Ausculum over the Romans, which cost him heavy casualties and made the term "Pyrrhic victory" a byword. Then, failing to make a peace treaty with Rome, he abandoned Italy at the invitation of Syracuse to campaign in Sicily against Carthage. He returned with a reduced force in 275 BC for a last battle against Rome at Malventum (later Beneventum) where he was outnumbered and suffered a decisive defeat, after which he left Italy for good. Tarentum, as it was henceforth, held out three more years before Rome conquered it. By then the other city states of Magna Graecia were already allies of the Roman people, and, since most were ports and commanded forests in their hinterlands, they formed the nucleus of Rome's naval allies.

Rome had early connections with Magna Graecia. It learned the Chalcidian Greek alphabet from Cumae, and developed the Latin alphabet from it. It may also have learned the name "Graeci" (i.e. "Greek") there as well, for among Cumae's original settlers was a contingent of *Graioi* from a small state in eastern Boeotia. Tradition also connects early Rome with the Cumaean Sibyl whose cave was discovered in 1932, for Rome preserved a collection of oracles called the "Sibylline Books" in the temple of Capitoline Jupiter until it was burned in 83 BC; these had been sold by the Sibyl to Tarquinius Priscus, an Etruscan king of Rome. Livius Andronicus (*c.*284–204 BC), whose translation of the *Odyssey* into Latin marks the beginning of Roman literature, was probably a Tarentine Greek who was taken to Rome after the capture of Tarentum in 272 BC. But Magna Graecia did not enter the Roman imperial orbit until the Second Samnite War when a Roman army besieged Naples (327/26 BC) which was surrendered by a pro-Roman group in the city, and signed a treaty of alliance on very favourable terms. By the 290s Rome's web of alliances stretched into Lucania and Apulia and cities which had supported the Samnites were conquered. Velia was taken in 293 BC. At Paestum a Latin colony was installed in 273 BC, and a forum, complete with a temple of Jupiter Capitolinus, was cut into the middle of the city plan. The fall of Tarentum and the peace treaty that followed probably mark the end of the Italiote League. However, when Hannibal invaded Italy and defeated Rome disastrously at Cannae (216 BC), Tarentum, Thurii, Croton, Locri, and Metapontum, all leading members of the old Italiote League, went over to the Carthaginians, while further north the alliances remained firm. Cumae, which had held the status of Roman "citizenship without the vote" since its capture by Rome in 334 BC, resisted all pressure to defect, and the alliance with Naples remained firm. In the south, however, only Rhegium remained a loyal ally.

Details of Rome's settlement of Magna Graecia after Hannibal's defeat are scant, but Tarentum, which had been sacked in 209 BC, was put under military government for a couple of decades after the war. Croton and Thurii received colonies. A good deal of land was confiscated, and became *ager publicus*, land owned by the Roman people, much of which was to be allotted to Roman settlers by the Gracchi brothers, and later by Pompey and the emperor Nero. The Social War between Rome and its allies in the early 1st century BC marked the end of the Greek cities as nominally free states: after 89 BC they formed part of the Roman state either as colonies (*coloniae*) or municipalities (*municipia*). The final act came with the emperor Augustus who divided Italy into 11 regions. Magna Graecia was broken up among three regions and lumped together with its ancient enemies, the Sabellian peoples.

But that was not quite the end. In the years after Hannibal's defeat, the interest of Rome's elite in Greek culture increased rapidly along with its wealth, and villas sprouted around the bay of Naples. Greek culture, however, now flowed for the most part directly from Greece and not through the medium of Magna Graecia. In the Byzantine period there was one last flowering of Greek culture, centred particularly in Calabria. Under Justinian (AD 527–65) the Roman empire, as it still considered itself to be, recovered Italy from the Ostrogoths, but lost most of it to Lombard invaders shortly after Justinian's death. Constans II (641–68), despairing of Constantinople, decided to move his capital west, and in 663 landed at Tarentum and pushed the Lombards back to Beneventum, which, however, he failed to take. After his assassination, the Lombards retook most of Apulia. Arab raids on Sicily and Italy also intensified; Palermo fell in 831, and following that, the Arabs took Bari and Tarentum, and left Byzantium with little more than Calabria. Under Basil I (867–86) and Leo VI the Wise, (886–912) of the Macedonian dynasty, the Byzantines riposted: Apulia was retaken, and Leo VI established two themes in Byzantine Italy, Longobardia ruled by a military governor at Bari, and Calabria ruled generally from Reggio (Rhegium). By the end of the millennium, Byzantine power in what used to be Magna Graecia was paramount and was not seriously challenged until the advent of the Normans. Robert Guiscard's capture of Bari in 1071 extinguished Byzantine rule.

This last flowering saw Greek replace the Latin language in Calabria and, less throughly, in Apulia. The Greek Church replaced the Roman Church in the south, though in Naples there was a lively contest between the Greek and Latin hierarchies. The Basilian monasteries of Calabria offered shelter to Greek monks migrating from Arab Sicily and became centres of Byzantine culture. St Neilos of Rossano (c.910–1004) in particular was a talented hymnist and brought fame to his monastery in the Merkourion district. The Norman conquest did not terminate Greek influence immediately, but with the capture of Bari a chapter was ended.

JAMES ALLAN EVANS

See also Italy

Summary

Magna Graecia (*Megale Hellas* in Greek) was the conventional term for the Greek colonies of southern Italy but excluding Sicily. Colonization began in the 8th century BC. The settlements provided the Romans with their first taste of Greek culture. By the 1st century BC all the cities were absorbed into the Roman state, but Greek culture persisted. Magna Graecia was recovered by the Byzantines and not finally lost until 1071.

Further Reading

Barker, Graeme and John Lloyd (editors), *Roman Landscapes: Archaeological Survey in the Mediterranean Region*, London: British School at Rome, 1991

Bérard, Jean, *La Colonisation grecque de l'Italie méridionale et de la Sicile dans l'Antiquité: l'histoire et la légende*, Paris: Boccard, 1941

Berger, Shlomo, *Revolution and Society in Greek Sicily and Southern Italy*, Stuttgart: Steiner, 1992

Boardman, John, *The Greeks Overseas: Their Early Colonies and Trade*, 4th edition, London and New York: Thames and Hudson, 1999

Ciaceri, E., *Storia della Magna Grecia*, 2nd edition, 3 vols, Milan: Albrighi Segati, 1927–32

Greco, Emanuele, *Magna Grecia*, 2nd edition, Bari: Laterza, 1981

Lomas, Kathryn, *Rome and the Western Greeks, 350 BC–AD 200: Conquest and Acculturation in Southern Italy*, London and New York: Routledge, 1993

Pugliese Carratelli, Giovanni (editor), *Magna Grecia*, vol. 2: *Lo sviluppo politico, sociale ed economico*, Milan: Electa, 1987

Ridgway, David, *The First Western Greeks*, Cambridge and New York: Cambridge University Press, 1992

Makarios III, Archbishop 1913–1977

President of Cyprus

Archbishop Makarios III, president of the newly independent Republic of Cyprus from 16 August 1960 until his death on 3 August 1977, was a central figure in the history of Cyprus. He was born Michael Mouskos in August 1913 to a peasant family in the Greek-Cypriot village of Pano Panagia on the high western slopes of Mount Troodos.

It had been a strength of the Church under Ottoman rule that its hierarchy was largely drawn from the ablest sons of the poor. It was to prove one of Makarios's strengths, first as elected archbishop and ethnarch and then as president, that he combined the traditional legitimacy stemming from an autocephaly that dated to the 5th century and from eight centuries' experience of a subject community gathered around its archbishop, with the modern democratic legitimacy of popular election. His sense of empathy with his community was unparalleled: it is doubtful whether he ever misinterpreted the majority will on any important issue. This ability to read and express his community's mind (to a degree unmatched by professional politicians like Constantine Karamanlis and the Papandreous) was simultaneously his greatest disadvantage in governing an island containing another community, namely the Turkish-Cypriot.

He entered Kykko Monastery in 1926 as a novice aged 13. In 1933 he was sent to the Pan-Cyprian Gymnasium in Nicosia. He returned to Kykko as a teacher in 1936. After being ordained Deacon Makarios at the age of 25, he studied theology at Athens University from 1938 to 1942, experiencing war, occupation, and the civil strife of 1944, when he entered law school. Ordained priest in 1946, he served in a working-class parish of Piraeus until a World Council of Churches scholarship enabled him to continue theological studies in Boston between 1946 and 1948, when he received the unsought honour of election as bishop of Kitium (Larnaca and Limassol).

The postwar campaign for union with Greece (*enosis*), which expressed both the genuine aspirations of Greek Cypriots and the hierarchy's determination to recover the initiative from the communist AKEL (*Anorthotikon Komma Ergazomenou Laou*, the Progressive Party of the Working People) while civil war raged in Greece, had already begun. In

December 1949 the ethnarchy announced that if the British governor did not hold a plebiscite the Church would. Makarios organized this in January 1950. Of those eligible (all Greek Cypriots over the age of 18) 95.7 per cent signed their names for *enosis*. In June 1950 archbishop Makarios II died, and in October Makarios III, aged 37, was elected archbishop and ethnarch by indirect popular vote.

Makarios's political life can be divided into four periods: the unsuccessful struggle for self-determination and *enosis* in the 1950s; his term as president of a united but diarchic republic from 1960 to the end of 1963; his attempts as president to achieve a new constitution while increasingly beleaguered by enemies outside and within; and his overthrow and restoration as president after the Greek junta's coup and the Turkish invasions of 1974.

The first period, when Makarios was politically inexperienced, partly determined the other three. Ecclesiastical and national tradition dictated Makarios's original aim: the union of a united island with Greece. Since, until autumn 1955, London rejected both self-determination and independence, Makarios pressed the Greek government to take Cyprus's cause to the UN. Eden's harsh private treatment of Alexandros Papagos and the public "never" in the House of Commons achieved this in 1954, but Greek recourse to the UN over five years proved fruitless, partly because anti-colonialist countries supported struggles for independence, not irredentism.

More immediately successful, but disastrous in the long term, was the decision to extend the liberation struggle for *enosis* by the use of violent means through the EOKA campaign, intended by Makarios to be limited to sabotage, under George Grivas. EOKA (*Ethniki Organosi Kyprion Agoniston*, the National Organization of Cypriot Fighters) began operations in April 1955, making the British position most uncomfortable, but the tradition thus created of the national legitimacy of secret and violent conspiracy was ultimately to lead Cyprus and Makarios to disaster. Worse, London now ensured that Ankara brought itself into the equation, demanding partition. The Greek community of Istanbul paid a heavy price in September 1955; Greek Cypriots have been paying ever since.

One chance to escape from the impending impasse may have been the constitutional negotiations – nearly successful – of 1955/56 with the then governor, Sir John Harding. Failure was followed by Makarios's exile to the Seychelles from March 1956 until March 1957, when he went to Athens. The situation in Cyprus deteriorated quickly during his exile. Intercommunal violence broke out in June 1958 with Greek-Cypriots the initial victims, and separate Turkish-Cypriot municipalities were set up.

In June 1958 the Macmillan plan offered seven years of self-government followed by shared sovereignty between Britain, Greece, and Turkey. Makarios reacted in September by proposing the alternative of independence. In December the Turkish and Greek foreign ministers, Fatin Zorlu and Evangelos Averof, started the contacts which led to the Zurich–London agreements guaranteed by Britain, Greece, and Turkey. From the Greek-Cypriot point of view the agreements were necessary to avoid partition; but they involved commitments to abandon the century-old aspiration for *enosis* and to implement a complex diarchic constitution entrenching extensive

Archbishop Makarios III, president of Cyprus 1960–77

Turkish-Cypriot veto powers. Greek-Cypriot opinion accepted independence but was unhappy with one or both of the restrictions. Even before independence pro-*enosis* statements on the one side and the importation of arms on the other (the "Deniz" incident in which a Turkish ship was intercepted by the British) had begun to create a vicious circle of mistrust.

Elected president in December 1959 with two-thirds of the votes against the more rigid Enotists and AKEL, Makarios demonstrated his qualities of leadership. He did not suppress AKEL, as Karamanlis and Adnan Menderes had planned, but brought it into the political system. He showed his capacity for administration and economic management to the benefit of state, Church, and people alike. He cut an impressive figure on the world stage, joining the Third World countries but sometimes differentiating his position, as when he became one of the first declared supporters of a united Germany.

No one will ever determine whether Makarios's public pro-*enosis* statements represented actual policy, sincere lip-service to an impracticable but still popular ideal, or a necessary concession to his most dangerous opponents. The second possibility would have permitted him to use his statements for the first and third as events demanded, and is therefore the most likely hypothesis.

It seems he finally decided to propose constitutional change after the Turkish-Cypriot representatives refused to pass an income-tax bill in December 1961. The constitutional proposals of November 1963 were the ultimate consequence.

Considered an acceptable opening position by the then British High Commissioner in Nicosia, they were rejected out of hand first by Ankara and then by the Turkish Cypriots.

Earlier there had also been tensions over the composition of the public service and separate municipalities. The Turkish-Cypriot vice-president's veto of an integrated army in a 60/40 ratio resulted in the creation of official/unofficial armies on both sides with contingency plans or instructions to their armed groups. In December 1963 tension between them exploded into widespread violence.

The official Turkish-Cypriot response was withdrawal from state institutions and self-enclosure in enclaves, thus giving Makarios de facto majority control of the government, but at the cost of territorial division and serious bloodletting in many parts of the island. Although about half of the Turkish-Cypriot population continued to live peaceably in areas under Greek-Cypriot control, the destruction of Turkish-Cypriot neighbourhoods, the intercommunal strife, and Ankara's threats of intervention led the Security Council to create UNFICYP (United Nations Force in Cyprus) in March 1964 to keep the peace wherever possible. Makarios could be satisfied that the relevant resolution recognized the Cyprus government's legitimacy, but there was lasting damage to the Greek Cypriots' international image as a result of incidents in which Greek-Cypriot irregulars attacked Turkish-Cypriot individuals and villages.

From 1964 to 1967, with Grivas in command of a large Greek force illegally infiltrated, pressure on the Turkish-Cypriot community was maintained in a variety of ways. Consistent with his fundamental adherence to the unity of Cyprus, Makarios in 1964 rejected the American "Acheson plan" as essentially partitionist.

The Greek junta's coup in 1967 and the autumn attack on Hagios Theodoros precipitated a major crisis resulting in the withdrawal of Grivas and the Greek army, a declared shift of policy by Makarios to the feasible strategy of majority-rule independence (as opposed to the desirable dream of *enosis*), and the abolition of barriers to free movement for Turkish Cypriots. During 1968 serious intercommunal talks began and Makarios was reelected president against an Enotist with 95 per cent of the vote.

Perhaps Makarios's greatest single error was in not pressing for an agreement with the Turkish Cypriots in 1968 when they seemed to accept local autonomy and majority rule. From 1969 the security situation swung against him as the junta organized pro-Enotist clandestine opposition to his policy. In 1970 he escaped assassination by a miracle. In 1971 Grivas returned illegally to the island. In 1972 the three other bishops tried to defrock him and the junta's supporters almost mounted a coup, which was foiled by a temporary alliance between Makarios and Grivas (an Enotist but not a junta supporter). In 1973 Makarios was re-elected president unopposed, but violence continued and there was another assassination attempt. In January 1974 Grivas died and his clandestine movement was taken over by the junta.

Despite Makarios's able manoeuvring, the hatred of the Athens junta increasingly hemmed him in. Officially Athens favoured the intercommunal talks: behind the scenes it supported *enosis*, even if this implied territorial concessions to Ankara. Threatened again by a coup, Makarios counterattacked with his letter of 2 July to the Greek president demand-

ing the withdrawal of officers plotting against him. His optimism that he had thus overcome the danger was misplaced: on 15 July the Greek-officered National Guard overthrew the legitimate government. Again almost miraculously, he escaped first to Paphos and then abroad.

Greek involvement gave Turkey an opportunity to intervene. While London washed its hands, Ankara carried out two military interventions, in July and August, that led to loss of life on Cyprus unparalleled since 1571. This open attempt to impose partition through the expulsion of Greek Cypriots from the occupied areas, and to ensure that any settlement would rest not on democratic principle but on Ankara's absolute control of part of Cyprus and veto rights over the remainder, was effectively opposed during Makarios's lifetime only by the US Congress.

Makarios was never more admirable than with his life's work in ruins. He rallied his community to the need for a long struggle rather than surrender, correctly judged that economic recovery was a priority and quickly set it in train, and before he died made the crucial concession to the Turkish Cypriots of accepting a federal solution (still within the boundaries of acceptable democratic theory) which was agreed by both communities in February 1977 and has been confirmed by numerous Security Council Resolutions since.

It is easy to judge Makarios as a leader who failed either to achieve *enosis* or to preserve a united island, his two original aims. Weaker in strategic vision than Karamanlis, and less successful tactically than Andreas Papandreou, he proved better at administration and economic management than either. Effectively he created a state he originally had had no intention of creating. His legacy, a democratic, prosperous, and consensual society, may ultimately prove attractive to all its citizens, and not only the Greek-Cypriot community which he so faithfully represented and served.

It is also easy to judge Makarios as a churchman, committed indeed to charitable and missionary work in Africa, but irremediably compromised by involvement in politics, resort to violence, and repeated disingenuousness. This is a common western view, which displays a lack of human understanding. Cypriot archbishops had been required to represent their people in a potentially self-sacrificial manner since 1571: the pursuit of any subjected people's best interests is likely to involve the exercise of guile. The lessons of centuries of subservience were not to be unlearnt in a few years even had the situation been ideal, and it was never that.

It was in human qualities that Makarios shone. A close collaborator, Stella Soulioti, has said: "He remained to the end a shepherd boy – a shepherd with the manners of a king." Beneath the surface of a shrewd diplomat lay an almost childlike innocence, unassuming, gentle, and self-critical. A deep calm underpinned the courage displayed in the lack of precautions taken for his personal safety when his life was in constant danger. He was immediately available to ordinary Greek Cypriots: his humour and consideration for others were notable, while his simplicity and directness in human contact were the opposite of that fundamental deviousness so confidently ascribed to him in the western press.

His integrity may be seen in his having personally lodged Turkish-Cypriot hospital staff at the Archbishopric for a night in December 1963 before sending them to the safety of their own community; and by the experience of an unexpected caller who, when told he was officiating in the cathedral, entered to find the Archbishop conducting the funeral of a beggar, for whom he was the only mourner.

Makarios therefore was a living example of the differing qualities admired by those in the Anglo-Saxon and Hellenic traditions. An admiration for humour, courage, and dignity combined with simplicity is shared. The traditions then part, one putting overriding emphasis on adherence to ethical norms and the overall consequences of actions; the other on existential commitment and humanity. In his commitment to and his sense of communion with his people, Makarios expressed a quintessentially Orthodox Christian view of the scale of priorities in human life.

COSTA CARRAS

See also Enosis

Biography

Born Michael Mouskos in 1913 to a peasant family in the Greek-Cypriot village of Pano Panagia, he entered Kykko monastery as a novice in 1926. After three years at the Gymnasium in Nicosia, he returned to Kykko as a teacher in 1936 and was ordained a deacon in 1938. He studied theology at Athens University in 1938–42 and was ordained a priest in 1946. He studied in Boston in 1946–48 and was then elected bishop of Kitium. In 1950 he was elected archbishop and ethnarch and in 1959 president of an independent Cyprus, which he remained until his death in 1977.

Further Reading

Attalides, Michael A., *Cyprus, Nationalism and International Politics*, Edinburgh: Q Press, and New York: St Martin's Press, 1979

Clerides, Glafkos, *Cyprus: My Deposition*, 4 vols, Nicosia: Alithia, 1989–92

Durrell, Lawrence, *Bitter Lemons*, London: Faber, and New York: Dutton, 1957

Foley, Charles, *Island in Revolt*, London: Longman, 1962

Hitchens, Christopher, *Hostage to History: Cyprus from the Ottomans to Kissinger*, 3rd edition, London: Verso, 1997

Holland, Robert, *Britain and the Revolt in Cyprus, 1954–1959*, Oxford: Clarendon Press, and New York: Oxford University Press, 1998

Kyle, Keith, *Cyprus: In Search of Peace*, London: MRG, 1997

Mayes, Stanley, *Makarios: A Biography*, London: Macmillan, and New York: St Martin's Press, 1981

Stephens, Robert, *Cyprus, A Place of Arms: Power Politics and Ethnic Conflict in the Eastern Mediterranean*, London: Pall Mall Press, and New York: Praeger, 1966

Stern, Laurence, *The Wrong Horse: The Politics of Intervention and the Failure of American Diplomacy*, New York: Times Books, 1977

Vanezis, P.N., *Makarios: Life and Leadership*, London: Abelard Schuman, 1979

Makriyannis, Yannis 1797–1864

A leading figure of the Greek War of Independence and Othonian Greece

Yannis (Ioannis) Makriyannis was a distinguished figure in Greece's political history in the 19th century. He was born in 1797 and, after spending several years working, he joined the *Philiki Hetaireia* and participated in the War of Independence. He took part in various memorable battles and was repeatedly injured, a fact that was to affect decisively his life afterwards. He also held several strategic posts (e.g. as military head of Athens in 1825), tried to bring order among Greek irregulars, and associated himself with well-known war personalities. After the end of the war Makriyannis, being liberal by nature, disagreed with Ioannis Kapodistria's policies and lost his position as head of the Executive Committee. Although he believed that king Otho's arrival would ameliorate Greece's situation, Makriyannis was disappointed by later developments including the unfair treatment of veterans by the government and he had conflicts with the regency member count Armansperg. After that Makriyannis avoided any involvement in public affairs until 1840. Between 1836 and 1839 he occupied himself with the creation – together with the painter Panayotis Zographos – of aquarelles (five series of 25 uniform paintings) devoted to the War of Independence and based on his own battle experiences and memories. One series of aquarelles survives today at the Gennadion Library in Athens and another at Windsor Castle.

Yet, Makriyannis's sense of justice, integrity, and patriotism could not keep him away from politics. He realized the need for a constitutional charter and after 1840 he worked in clandestine meetings for such a plan. This materialized on 3 September 1843 through the intervention of the army under Dimitrios Kallergis and the participation of the people, fortunately without bloodshed. In 1844 Makriyannis was elected representative of Athens in the National Assembly where he distinguished himself for his resolutions concerning the Church, the Greek citizens, and the rights of the veterans. He was also appointed major-general. In 1852 Makriyannis was accused of a conspiracy against Otho's life, imprisoned, brought to trial, and sentenced to death. But his conviction caused heated reactions from the public and the press, which forced the conversion of his death penalty initially into life and later into a ten-year sentence. On 2 September 1854, however, Makriyannis was set free, but his health had seriously deteriorated due to previous injuries. In the anti-Othonian movement of 10 October 1862 the Greek public remembered Makriyannis's contributions and honoured him as a folk and national hero. He was reinstated in his previous office, but his already poor health weakened further, and he died on 27 April 1864.

Although Makriyannis had received no education at all and barely knew how to write, he still left two works behind that were published posthumously and were considered seminal contributions to modern Greek culture. The first is his *Memoirs*, which Makriyannis started writing in February 1829 and completed in 1850. They constitute a first-hand description of the War of Independence and Othonian Greece. This work was discovered, transcribed, and published for the first time in 1907 by Yannis Vlachoyannis. Makriyannis's second prose work, entitled *Visions and Miracles*, was written in 1851–52, left unfinished, and published for the first time in 1983. Both works are important for their historical content, for their use of the demotic language, as it was spoken in Greece then, and for their literary merit. Thus, it is no wonder that Makriyannis's personality attracted the attention, the

Yannis Makriyannis: statue of general Makriyannis at the old entrance to Athens, below the Acropolis

positive appreciation, and the admiration of numerous renowned Greek thinkers (e.g. George Seferis, Yorgos Theotokas, Odysseus Elytis, Zisimos Lorentzatos).

The importance of Makriyannis's thought lies in his holistic view of Greek history. He professed the fundamental unity between Hellenism and Orthodoxy, and he considered the latter as the decisive factor for the preservation of the former. He was convinced that God was behind the just war of the Greeks against the Ottomans and had granted them their liberation against all adversities (e.g. in the period of anarchy, 1831–33). His fervent patriotism was religiously legitimized. Makriyannis had a simple but deep faith in God and never vacillated between the Scylla of rationalism and the Charybdis of unbelief. The fear of God for him was a prerequisite for maintaining order, piety, and ethics in human societies.

Makriyannis's social criticism was mainly directed against Greece's multiple dependence on the West and its impact upon the Orthodox popular ethos. Greece's religious estrangement signified political and social subordination too. He was alarmed by the policies of the Bavarian regime, such as the closing of numerous monasteries and the confiscation of their property, and by the increased proselytism of foreign missionaries. Makriyannis was very critical of the "Westernized" Greeks (e.g. Theophilos Kairis), who, he believed, were transformed into slaves of Western interests. Despite his defence of Orthodoxy against Western designs, Makriyannis simultaneously supported religious tolerance. Human freedom was for him inviolable and any form of proselytism unacceptable. The view of human destiny as a dynamic struggle between life and death was instrumental in forging his self-understanding and in motivating his activities. Makriyannis was thus influenced by the fundamental Orthodox orientation that regards this transient earthly life as a preamble for the eternal life to come.

Later interpretations and assessments of Makriyannis's thought and legacy vary considerably. For some, the illiterate Makriyannis is the most authentic embodiment of the uncontaminated Orthodox ethos, whose presuppositions and criteria are quite different from those of the West. His simple and apparently naive, but also realistic and effective solutions to various problems are considered useful from a contemporary perspective too. Makriyannis is seen as expressing the authentic voice of the Greek people. Others, however, emphasize the traumatic experiences in Makriyannis's life and the serious effects they might have had not only on his physical but also on his mental health. They argue that Makriyannis might have suffered from illusions, aberrations, and epileptic crises combined with superstitions and a morbid religiosity. In other words, he was some kind of a "madman". The objectivity of his judgements is also questioned, because Makriyannis seems to have been an obstinate, quarrelsome, intransigent, and embittered person. As a result, without discarding his views entirely, some scholars suggest that they should be treated carefully and with reservations. The same applies to the historical information contained in his works.

Despite these differences in evaluating Makriyannis, it is undeniable that his works include much useful material relating to Greek culture, its past, and its relationship to the West. As such, they constitute weighty documents of modern Greek history. Makriyannis pointed out with honesty, clarity, and simplicity the sources of Greece's many problems and offered several viable solutions. He did not present an idealistic version of Greece's situation, but was very sincere, had a sense of self-respect, showed no self-interest in his dealings, and viewed himself as on a mission to safeguard his country. He outspokenly castigated his compatriots for their multiple transgressions and deficiencies. Therefore, it is understandable why his ideas and proposals have been so much discussed and why they will certainly become the focus of varying approaches and interpretations in the future too.

VASILIOS MAKRIDES

See also Independence (War of)

Biography

Born in 1797, Makriyannis received no education but joined the *Philiki Hetaireia* (Friendly Society) and played a distinguished part in the War of Independence, becoming military head of Athens in 1825. After the war he withdrew from politics until 1840 when he began to work for the creation of a constitution. In 1844 he was elected to the National Assembly. He died in 1864. Two works were published posthumously: his *Memoirs* and *Visions and Miracles*.

Writings

The Memoirs of General Makriyannis, 1797–1864, edited and translated by H.A. Lidderdale, London and New York: Oxford University Press, 1966

Apomnimonevmata Makriyanni [Makriyannis's Memoirs], Athens, 1979

Mémoires, translated into French and edited with preface by Pierre Vidal-Naquet, Paris: Michel, 1986

Oramata kai Thamata [Visions and Miracles], edited by A.N. Papakostas, 3rd edition, Athens, 1989

Further Reading

Asdrachas, Spyros I., *Ellenike Koinonia kai Oikonomia: 18 kai 19 ai.: Ypotheseis kai Prosengiseis* [Greek Society and Economy: 18th and 19th Centuries: Situation and Approaches], Athens, 1982, pp. 315–49, 407–20

Diavazo, 101 (5 September 1984), Makriyannis special issue

Gourgouris, Stathis, *Dream Nation: Enlightenment, Colonization, and the Institution of Modern Greece*, Stanford, California: Stanford University Press, 1996, pp. 175–200

Holton, David, "Ethnic Identity and Patriotic Idealism in the Writings of General Makriyannis", *Byzantine and Modern Greek Studies*, 9 (1984/85): pp. 133–60

Kyriazidis, N.I. (editor), *A Tagged Concordance of and Other Indices to the Opera Omnia of Makriyannis*, 7 vols, Athens, 1992

Lorentzatos, Zisimos, *To tetradio tou Makrygianni, MS 262* [Makriyannis's Copy Book, MS 262], Athens, 1984

Makriyannis invenit Zographos fecit: Pictures from the War of Greek Independence, 1821/ Images de la guerre de l'Indépendance hellénique, 1821, Athens: National Bank of Greece, 1976

Metallinos, Georgios, *Orthodoxia kai Ellinikotita: Prosengiseis sti Neoelliniki Tavtotita* [Orthodoxy and Greekness: Approaches to Modern Greek Identity], Athens, 1987, pp. 87–163

Panagopoulos, S.P. *et al*, *Keimena gia ta Oramata kai Thamata tou Makrygianni* [Texts for the "Visions and Miracles" of Makriyannis], Athens, 1984

Pentzopoulou-Valala, Tereza, *O Stratigos Makriyannis opos philosophise pano ston agona tou '21* [How General Makriyannis Philosophized on the Struggle of 1821], Thessalonica, 1987

Petropulos, John Anthony, *Politics and Statecraft in the Kingdom of Greece, 1833–1843*, Princeton, New Jersey: Princeton University Press, 1968

"Pragmata kai Oramata tou Stratigou Makriyanni" [Deeds and Visions of General Makriyannis] in *Tetradia Efthynis*, vol. 30, Athens, 1990

Protopsaltis, E.G. (editor), *I diki tou stratigou Makriyanni* [The Trial of General Makriyannis], Athens, 1963

Puchner, Walter, "Die Memoiren des griechischen Revolutionsgenerals Makryjannis aus kulturanthropologischer Sicht", *Südost-Forschungen*, 34 (1975): pp. 166–94

Seferis, George, *Dokimes* [Experiments], vol. 1: *1936–1947*, 5th edition, Athens, 1984, pp. 228–63

Sherrard, Philip, *The Wound of Greece: Studies in Neo-Hellenism*, London: Collings, 1978; New York: St Martin's Press, 1979

Simopoulos, Kyriakos, *Ideologia kai Axiopistia tou Makriyanni* [Makriyannis's Ideology and Reliability], Athens, 1986

Stroungari, Magda, "O Logiotatismos kai i Epidrasi tou sta Graphta tou Makriyanni" [Logicality and Influence in the Writings of Makriyannis], *Dodoni*, 8 (1979): pp. 111–215

Valais, Dionysios D., "I Thriskevtiki Diastasi sti Zoi kai to Ergo tou Yanni Makriyanni" [The Religious Dimension in the Life and Works of Yannis Makriyannis] (dissertation), Katerini, 1994

Zographos, Demetrios, *The War of Independence in Pictures: Copies by Demetrius Zographos from originals by his father Panayotis Zographos commissioned by General Makriyannis and presented to Her Majesty Queen Victoria through her Minister at Athens, Sir Edmund Lyons, 1839*, catalogue by H.A. Lidderdale, Birmingham: University of Birmingham Centre for Byzantine Studies, 1976

Mallia

Town in Crete

The archaeological site and modern town of Mallia is located on the island of Crete, less than 40 km east of Herakleion. It lies within a narrow plain on the northern coast that is bounded to the south by the Dikte mountain range dominated by Mount Selena (1559 m), the site of the Bronze Age peak sanctuary, which rises steeply behind the little church of Prophitis Ilias. From ancient times to the present day the area surrounding Mallia, including the plain, the mountains, and the valleys leading to them, has been characterized by its rich agriculture. Today, the produce includes potatoes, olives, and other fruits, as well as cereals. The herding of sheep and goats as well as traditional cheese making continues to be practised in the mountains to the south. Fishing is also an important activity along the coastal plain and there is evidence of two ancient harbours in the vicinity that would have served both fishing and sea trade in Minoan times.

Mallia is famous today as the site of the third greatest Minoan palace after those at Knossos and Phaestus. The presence of antiquities at the site was first discovered in the late 19th century after a shepherd found some gold leaf by the sea and the local inhabitants began digging for Minoan treasure. In 1915 Joseph Hazzidakis, then ephor of Cretan antiquities, began a more formal exploration of the site. Since 1922, however, systematic excavations have been undertaken by a team from the École Archéologique Française d'Athènes, led by Fernand Chapouthier, Jean Charbonneaux, and others. By 1932 the excavation of the palace was completed. The French archaeologists continue their excavations in the Minoan town and ancient cemeteries by the sea, publishing the results of their investigations in the series *Études Crétoises*.

While the palace at Mallia lacks the mythological fame of Knossos and is less sumptuously decorated and smaller in size (nearly 8900 sq m or about the size of the palace of Phaestus), it is beautifully sited with a view of the sea. It is also remarkable for having its ground plan preserved virtually intact and, unlike Knossos, it remains unreconstructed. Concrete and iron supports as well as protective roofs have been used only where necessary to preserve the Minoan buildings, providing visitors with a unique opportunity to experience the ancient architecture without controversial modern interventions.

The earliest traces of habitation at the site of Mallia are prepalatial, dating to the Early Minoan III–Middle Minoan IA period (c.2300–1900 BC). The first phase of the palace, known as the Old Palace, dates from the Middle Minoan IB–II period (1900–1700 BC) and is contemporary with the Old Palaces at Knossos and Phaestus – all of which were destroyed by a large earthquake at the end of the Middle Minoan II period. The Old Palace at Mallia is known mainly from some large plastered rooms in the northwestern corner that were richly appointed. It was from these rooms that the famous sword with the pommel covered by gold and decorated with an arched acrobat in low relief, now in the Herakleion Museum, was found. Also dating from the time of the Old Palace is the unique double row of four circular structures, each built around a central pillar that probably supported a roof, which is located in the southwestern corner of the palace. These structures were most likely used as silos or granaries.

Most of what is visible today, however, belongs to the New Palace, which dates from the Middle Minoan III–Late Minoan IB period (c.1700–1425 BC). Except for the fact that there is no monumental theatral area, this structure has all the characteristics of a typical Minoan palace, including a central court with an unusual open pit for burnt offerings, storage magazines with large pithoi and channels to collect drippings of oil, and a number of ritual chambers including a pillar crypt in the west wing. In one of these chambers, on a floor dating to the Old Palace, were found the ceremonial leopard's-head axe and the large sword with a gilded blade and pommel of crystal and amethyst, both outstanding examples of Minoan craftsmanship now on display in the Herakleion Museum. Some of the more unusual features of the palace include the pillared hall to the north, probably used for banquets, and the great circular *kernos* (offering-stand) stone, located in the southwestern corner of the central court, which has a large hollow at the centre and 34 smaller ones around the circumference that may have been used for the offering of first fruits to a deity. The New Palace was destroyed in the Late Minoan IB period and subsequent pillaging left few objects of value from this phase for modern excavators. One exception is a remarkable triton shell, carved from chlorite with relief decoration, that was found in the northeastern corner of the palace and now resides in the Archaeological Museum in Agios Nikolaos.

To the north of the palace, French excavators have also brought to light a large open area with a plaster floor, called the Agora, as well as a series of plastered basement rooms with benches, known as the Hypostyle Crypt. The lack of significant finds from these unique structures, which belong to the period of the Old Palace, has led to the suggestion that they served as a kind of council chamber. The Minoan town surrounding these structures and the palace itself is composed of quarters (*quartiers*) belonging to different periods of use. Most of the houses within these quarters are modest but include a number of well-preserved examples of Minoan domestic architecture. An exception, however, is Quartier Mu, whose special significance is indicated by rich finds and buildings from the period of the Old Palace that include a heiroglyphic archive, a small sanctuary with its furnishing still in situ, and the oldest roofed lustral basin in Crete.

The cemeteries of ancient Mallia are located to the north of the settlement along the seashore. They include a number of early ossuaries as well as some tombs of the Late Minoan III period (c.1390–1070 BC). Most significant, however, is the cemetery of Chrysolakkos (pit of gold), a large rectangular burial enclosure dating to the Middle Minoan IB–II period (1900–1700 BC). The facade of this building is constructed of partly dressed limestone blocks which are among the earliest examples of ashlar masonry on Crete. Although the Chrysolakkos cemetery was plundered by local tomb robbers in the 1880s, it is famous as the source of the well-known gold pendant of two conjoined bees or wasps with a honeycomb (dated c.1700 BC), now in the Herakleion Museum, that was found by Pierre Demargne in 1945. Based on comparisons with this piece, Reynold Higgins once suggested that the hoard of Minoan gold jewellery known as the Aegina Treasure, acquired by the British Museum in 1892, also came from the Chrysolakkos. New finds from Aegina, however, make this theory unlikely. On the beach to the west of the Chrysolakkos, there is also evidence for a sizeable Roman settlement including houses and tombs as well as an early Byzantine basilica.

The modern town of Mallia, about 2 km to the west of the archaeological site, is split by the highway that is always congested due to the large number of tourist shops, hotels, tavernas, bars, and nightclubs that line it and continue down to the sea. There is a long sandy beach here that today attracts crowds of tourists who rarely visit the archaeological site or cross the highway into the older part of the town with its charming narrow streets and whitewashed walls.

ANN M. NICGORSKI

See also Crete, Minoans

Summary

Mallia is the site of the third-greatest Minoan palace on Crete after those of Knossos and Phaestus. Formal exploration of the site began in 1915. The earliest traces are prepalatial. The Old Palace remains date from 1900 to 1700 BC. Most of what is visible today belongs to the New Palace which dates from c.1700 to 1425 BC. The cemeteries have yielded significant finds.

Further Reading

Cameron, Pat, *Crete*, 6th edition, New York: Norton, 1998 (*Blue Guide* series)
Davaras, Costis, *Guide to Cretan Antiquities*, Park Ridge, New Jersey: Noyes Press, 1976
de Grummond, Nancy Thomson, Malia (Mallia) entry in *An Encyclopedia of the History of Classical Archaeology*, edited by de Grummond, Westport, Connecticut: Greenwood Press, and London: Fitzroy Dearborn, 1996, vol. 2, pp. 712–13
Graham, J. Walter, *The Palaces of Crete*, revised edition, Princeton, New Jersey: Princeton University Press, 1987
Higgins, Reynold, *The Aegina Treasure: An Archaeological Mystery*, London: British Museum Publications, 1979

Hood, Sinclair, *The Arts in Prehistoric Greece*, Harmondsworth and New York: Penguin, 1978

Matt, Leonard von *et al.*, *Ancient Crete*, London: Thames and Hudson, and New York: Praeger, 1968

Myers, J. Wilson, Eleanor Emlen Myers and Gerald Cadogan (editors), *The Aerial Atlas of Ancient Crete*, Berkeley: University of California Press, and London: Thames and Hudson, 1992

Pelon, Olivier, *Le Palais de Malia*, vol. 5, Paris: Geuthner, 1980

Tiré, Claire and Henri van Effenterre, *Guide des fouilles françaises en Crète*, 3rd edition, Paris: Ecole Française d'Athènes, 1983

Vandenabeele, Frieda, *Malia: The Palace of Malia and Chersonissos*, Athens, 1992

Mani

Region in the southern Peloponnese

For the past 1100 years the names Maïni, Braccio di Maina, Vrachion tis Manis, and Mani have demarcated the land which occupies the middle of the three peninsulas in the southern Peloponnese. The peninsula, 75 km in length and 10–20 km in width, consists of the Taygetus massif, the Mediterranean end of the Alpine branch of the Pindus chain. Its southernmost point is the promontory of Tainaro or Cape Matapan, at the same latitude (36 degrees) as southern Italy and the straits of Gibraltar. The ancient name of the Mani was Lakoniki (Laconia).

During centuries of historical upheaval the geography of this isolated and mountainous area, deprived of important natural resources, made it a safe refuge and hideout, the home of a large population with a unique way of life with primitive features. Thus it came to stand out as a separate geographical, historical, and cultural entity.

The Taygetos mountain range divides the Mani into the "sunny" (east) and "shady" (west) parts. The region is also divided traditionally into several large sections with distinctive characteristics. The northwestern section or Outer Mani has a rich landscape and consists of the lower slopes and highest summits of Taygetus (Profitis Ilias, at 2407 m, is the highest peak in the Peloponnese). The northeastern section or Lower Mani has a varied landscape and fine bays, including both the main port of Gytheion and the rocky gorge with the Passava fortress. The southern part or Inner Mani is occupied by the limestone crystalline range of Kato Taygetos, with an arid rocky coastal plateau to the west. It slides down to the Mediterranean at the tiny promontory of Tainaro, which in antiquity was considered to be the gate into Hades.

Archaeological finds (from several coastal caves) indicate that the area was inhabited in the Palaeolithic era, in the Neolithic period (4500–2800 BC, Diros caves, etc.), in the Helladic period (2800–2000 BC, a number of settlements on low hills and plains), and the Middle and Late Helladic periods, when the Achaeans held power. Homer's *Iliad* I refers to eight towns in the Mani at the time of the Trojan War. At the same time Cape Tainaron was already an important place of worship dedicated to Helios-Apollo.

The Dorians invaded Lakonike in the 12th century BC, originally settling in Sparta and expanding gradually along the coast. They hemmed in the local populations, incorporating them as *perioikoi* ("dwellers around") into the military and political system of the Spartan city state. It appears that the *komes*, that is, the small towns and agricultural communities of the peninsula, retained some autonomy and numerous religious practices. Gytheion became the main Spartan port, while at Cape Tainaron, dedicated to the chthonic god Poseidon, there was a sanctuary with a sacred precinct for the conducting of the dead and an oracle of the dead.

When Sparta's power declined, the coastal towns of Lakonike increased their autonomy and from the beginning of the 2nd century BC, with the support of the Romans, formed the League of the Lacedaemonians, with ten towns in the Mani itself. During the Roman period this federation was renamed the League of the Free Laconians and prospered thanks to trade (in marble, porphyry, etc.). Violent earthquakes (AD 375) and Gothic raids (AD 395) signalled the end of the ancient period.

In the centuries that followed, many of the coastal sites became insecure. The population withdrew into the hinterland, as evidenced by the ruins of "megalithic" settlements of various sizes. The houses of these settlements, with their masonry of large stones and the massive stone beams which served to cover their spaces, were, with the war towers and cisterns, the starting point from which the Maniot buildings and settlements of more modern times slowly evolved. However, some of the coastal centres were still active in the 6th and 7th centuries. In the Dark Ages of the 7th and 8th centuries, the Mani suffered pirate raids and the Slav incursions. Starting in the 9th century, some Slavic tribes settled on Ano Taygetos. At this time the peninsula first appears under the name Maïni or Mani. It became a part of the theme of the Peloponnese and was caught up in the process of reorganization of the Byzantine provinces. In the Middle Byzantine period (late 9th–12th centuries) the Christianization of the Slavic and Maniot communities was actively promoted and was accompanied by the construction of a series of elaborate churches with distinctive architecture, sculpture, and painting which is thought to have influenced the later churches of Mistra.

After the Frankish period (1204–1432 in the Peloponnese, 1249–1261 in the Mani), the peninsula became a dependency of the despotate of Mistra and in 1415 the Palaiologan army pulled down the medieval fortifications there in order to weaken local centres of resistance. The scholars of Mistra and other centres described in dark colours the insubordinate, savage, and warlike Maniots, while medieval sources mention the primitive indigenous customs and the megalithic buildings. The castles of Maïna (Tigani), Passava, and Gisternes (Beaufort) date from the medieval period.

After the subjugation of the mainland by the Turks, the Mani put up stiff resistance and to them and was incorporated into a special privileged system which included internal autonomy, permission for the inhabitants to bear arms, and the obligation to pay an annual tribute. Under these conditions, the population of the Mani increased significantly. The self-ruling patriarchal system, organized in armed consanguineous groups (clans, lineages, etc.) with patrilocal installations, was retained as a basic way of life. Agricultural activities, commerce, and piracy were based on the power of weapons and the land was strengthened with effective fortifications against invaders from land or sea.

After the Turkish–Venetian war in Crete (1645–65), the Turks achieved greater control of the Mani, appointing as governor ("Giaour pasha") the local pirate Limberakis Gerakaris and constructing castles at Zarnata, Port-Kayio, and Kelefa. During the final decades of the 17th century, the dire conditions arising from the Turkish oppression and the deadly Maniot civil wars led many inhabitants to move to the Ionian islands and to Spanish and Genoese possessions (Taranto, Tuscany, Corsica). Under Venetian rule (1685–1715), Venetian administrators and garrisons were installed in the forts of the Mani, to which the area of Vardounia was also added. The Venetians officially recognized the chiefs of the various small districts, who were given the title of *kapetanioi* (captains). The *kapetanies* established in the north of the peninsula made progress, but in the south the new system did not take root. In 1715 the Turks prevailed over the Venetians again and imposed a yearly tribute; their control was loose, but they instigated local civil strife. After 1740 the northern Mani enjoyed a relative degree of socioeconomic development, while in the south increasing demographic pressure led to intensified disturbances, piracy, feuds, and the destruction of entire villages.

After the Russian-inspired Orloff rising of 1770 the Turks endeavoured to increase their influence, proclaiming the Mani a *Bas Beiliki* and appointing a powerful local *kapetanios* as "Maniatbey", with responsibility for the actions of the Maniots and for the collection of the annual tribute. There were eight Maniatbeys during the last 45 years of Ottoman rule.

On the eve of 1821 the intervention of the *Philiki Hetaireia* brought the hostilities among the leading families to a halt and the Mani became the "military centre of the Morea". The population reached 35,000 at this time. During the War of Independence, the Maniots fought courageously and decisively both inside and outside the Morea.

The unusual man-made environment of the Mani reflects faithfully the varied local social system, which was based on blood kinship. In the northern parts the clans were hierarchically ordered and stratified; endogamy was practised, and there were hereditary chieftains. The chieftains owned considerable tracts of land and had fortified strongholds which stood out in the villages themselves, at crucial points along the coast, and in the hinterland. The tower houses of the powerful families had between three and five storeys and were used both as residences and as refuges or fortresses. In the more official buildings (towers, churches, bell towers, fountains), features betraying Western or Ottoman influence can be identified, while the beys possessed remarkable walled enclosures – some simple, some more complex.

In the south the clans were internally equal, strictly exogamous, and their classification was based primarily on the number of their members (*douphekia*, rifles). The chieftains were elected and their authority could be revoked. Control over vital areas was exercised collectively by decision of the council of elderly men (the *yerondiki*). The war tower, the cannon, the cemetery, and the church were unconditionally the collective property of the clan or the specific lineage. The powerful clans (*megaloyennites*, the well-born) recognized one another, and kept under their protection and control the weaker clans (the *achamnomeri*, the thin ones) and the lowest inhabitants of all (the *phameyi*, or dependants).

The clans were localized in villages which were generally small and arranged in wards or neighbourhoods of one or more lineages. The houses of the families huddled in a carefully arranged pattern around the collective war tower. These houses were oblong rectangular nuclei, usually with two storeys, with people on the upper level and animals on the lower. This fixed prototype was augmented by outbuildings in the courtyards and combined with other familial nuclei so as to shape the composite defensive installation of the patrilineal group. The *achamnomeri* lived in separate neighbourhoods, and if they managed to gain strength (by amalgamation or by an increase in the number of their members) they could acquire towers of their own. Until the mid-18th century technical limitations made it difficult to build tall towers, but after the 19th century the introduction of mortar and dressed masonry enabled the construction of war towers and tower houses 18–20 m in height with between four and seven storeys.

In addition to wars against external foes and the threat of piracy, the distinctive and endemic features of the Maniot system were the internal hostilities (*echthres*, feuds), armed conflicts (*polemoi*, wars), and killings of vengeance (*dikiomoi*), which were the permanent expression of the contradictions inside Maniot society. The dialogue with "Charon" was expressed also in the tragic dirges called *moirologia* typical of the Mani and in the cult of dead ancestors and family members. Many of the traditions and legends of the Mani dwell on relationships between mortals and the chthonic powers and souls in the depths of the Underworld.

The Maniots, who had actively contributed to the struggle for independence, were incorporated into the new Greek state with great difficulty. The period down to 1836 was characterized by conflicts, revolutionary movements, the assassination of Count Ioannis Kapodistria by the Mavromichalis clan, and clashes with the Bavarian regency. Turmoil and civil strife continued down to 1870, especially in the south. Later, with the gradual establishment of state justice, of the money economy, and of education, the closed local system, with its numerous medieval characteristics, had to adapt in many significant respects. The emigration of a significant proportion of the work force and the reduction of local autonomy transformed the traditional social hierarchy. By the late 19th century the population had reached its zenith, 50,000, distributed among 200–250 settlements.

New settlements were established along lines of communication and in some coastal situations. The port of Gytheion flourished once more. In the villages the houses began to spread away from the traditional focuses of the clans, and houses were also built in the fields. The appearance of many villages changed with the construction of workshops, olive presses, shops, cafés, communally owned churches in the larger settlements, and many new tower houses.

Between the early 20th century and 1940 the economy, based on the cultivation of the olive tree, reached its highest level of productivity. But urbanization and the upheavals of World War II and the Greek Civil War (1940–49) caused the population to shrink and drastically limited local activities. The construction of the main motor road made the exodus easier and contributed to the decline of the ports. Many of the

Mani: the village of Kita "of the many towers" in southern Mani, *c*.1930. Many of the towers are now in ruins.

smaller villages were completely deserted and the local phrase "a house with a kitchen and a husband in Athens" shows the mentality of the times. In 1990 the population was approximately 25,000.

In recent decades some utilities and infrastructure networks have been installed. The requirements of new constructions, holiday housing, and tourist accommodation have often created problems of despoliation of the environment. Regional planning and development studies have emphasized the need to protect and develop a unique historical and cultural heritage, recognizing it as a basic local resource of national importance.

Certain public-sector programmes and projects have functioned in this direction since 1974: numerous buildings and sites were classed as monuments, and 78 per cent of the Maniot villages have been declared traditional settlements. In 1978, 71 villages – 31 per cent of the total – were scheduled for protection (as against a scheduling level of 0.6 per cent in the Peloponnese as a whole). Special building regulations have been introduced for the villages and the landscape of the southern Mani. The caves of Diros and a small museum with Neolithic finds have been opened to the public, restoration work has been done on many Byzantine and post-Byzantine churches, a number of guest houses have been established in traditional tower houses, and some important historical buildings have been converted into museums. Urban design projects for some villages and projects to document the history, society, and habitat of the peninsula are also under way.

YANIS SAITAS

See also Peloponnese

Summary

The region of Mani occupies the middle of the three peninsulas of the southern Peloponnese. Throughout history its geographical isolation has made it a safe refuge. It was invaded by Dorians in the 12th century BC and the population was incorporated in the Spartan city state. Autonomy increased under the Romans but Slavs invaded in the 7th and 8th centuries. From 1261 until the arrival of the Ottomans it was a dependency of the despotate of Mistra. Special privileges granted by the Turks brought increased autonomy. Maniots played a full part in the War of Independence. More recently it has suffered from depopulation. The unusual man-made environment of the Mani represents a historical and cultural heritage of national importance.

Further Reading

Alexakis, Eleutherios, *Ta Geni kai i Oikogenia stin Paradosiaki Koinonia tis Manis* [Clans and Families in Mani Traditional Society], Athens, 1980

Avraméa, Anna, "La Magne Byzantin: Problèmes d'histoire et de topographie" in *Evpsychia: Mélanges offerts à Hélène Ahrweiler*, Paris: Publications de la Sorbonne, 1998

Daskalakis, A., *I Mani kai e Othomaniki Avtokratoria, 1453–1821* [Mani and the Ottoman Empire, 1453–1821], Athens, 1923

Dimitrakos-Mesisklis, D., *Oi Niklianoi* [The Nikliani], vol. 1, Athens, 1949

Eliopoulou-Rogan, Dora, *Mani: History and Monuments*, Athens: Lycabettus, 1973

Fermor, Patrick Leigh, *Mani: Travels in the Southern Peloponnese*, London: John Murray, and New York: Harper, 1958

Greenhalgh, Peter and Edward Eliopoulos, *Deep into Mani: Journey to the Southern Tip of Greece*, London and Boston: Faber, 1985

Kassis, K., *Laographia tis Mesa Manis* [Folklore of Mid Mani], Athens, 1980

Komis, K., *Plythismos kai Oikismoi tis Manis, 15os–19os aionas* [Population and Settlements of Mani, 15th–19th Centuries], Ioannina, 1993

Koutsilieris, A., *Maniatika meletimata* [Mani Studies], Athens, 1978

Koutsilieris, A., *Historia tis Manis* [History of Mani], Athens, 1993

Mexis, Demos, *Mani kai oi Maniates* [Mani and the Maniots], Athens, 1977

Panayotopoulos, V., *Plythismos kai oikismoi tis Peloponnisou, 130s–180s aionas* [Population and Settlements of the Peloponnese, 13th–18th Centuries], Athens, 1985

Papachatzis, N., *Pausaniou Ellados Periigisis: Korinthiaka-Lakonika* [Pausanias' Description of Greece: Corinth and Lakonia], Athens, 1976

Saitas, Yannis, *Mani: Greek Traditional Architecture*, Athens: Melissa, 1987

Saitas, Yannis (editor), *Temoignages sur l'éspace et la société de Mani*, Athens: NHRF, 1996

Seremetakis, C. Nadia, *The Last Word: Women, Death, and Divination in Inner Mani*, Chicago: University of Chicago Press, 1991

Vayakakos, D., *Mani (Mesa Mani): o Topos, oi Vyzantinoi naoi, oi Pyrgoi, to Moirologi* [Mani (Mid Mani): the Place, the Byzantine Churches, the Towers, the Tragic Dirge], Athens, 1968

Manuel I Komnenos 1118–1180

Emperor

Manuel I (1143–80), the fourth and youngest son of John II Komnenos and his Hungarian wife Piroska-Irene, was born on 28 November 1118. He succeeded to the throne in 1143, aged 25, despite having one surviving elder brother, Isaac. He died on 24 September 1180. The latest research, by Paul Magdalino, has demonstrated that Manuel's reign is best treated in two parts: 1143–60 and 1160–80.

In his early years Manuel did little more than continue his father's policies, and seek to consolidate his tenuous hold on power. He chose to make political capital from his youthful accession, placing an image of Christ Emmanuel on his coins, and enjoyed the praise of encomiasts for his vigour and energy. These he expressed in the field, since he was committed to his father's policy of aggressive campaigning in the east. This required stability in the west, which was guaranteed by cooperation with Germany. His marriage in January 1146 to Bertha of Sulzbach, the sister-in-law of the German emperor Conrad III, sealed a Byzantine alliance with the Germans that lasted until c.1156. The professed common ambition of both imper-

ial powers was to eliminate the Norman presence in southern Italy.

After 1160 Manuel was increasingly preoccupied with the pretensions of the German emperor Frederick I Barbarossa (1152–90). In the aftermath of the Second Crusade (1147–48), western and eastern concerns were more intimately linked, and the rhetoric produced at Barbarossa's court promoted the notion of a unified Christendom under the suzerainty of the German "Holy Roman" emperor. Manuel responded with his own ecumenical rhetoric, which he backed up with grand gestures and actions. This had significant ramifications in the east, where to further his own claims and interests Manuel was willing to forge alliances with both the Latins of the crusader principalities (for example by his second marriage to Maria of Antioch at Christmas 1161) and the Turks (a treaty with the Seljuk sultan Kilij Arslan in 1162). Manuel's grandest gestures were the aborted assault on Egypt in 1167 and the march to Iconium in 1176, both undertaken in support of the crusading princes and intended to bind them more closely to him. Both were unmitigated failures, and the latter resulted in a devastating defeat at Myriokephalon. If we no longer believe that either Barbarossa or Manuel fully intended to fulfil the claims of their panegyrists, we must still concede that they believed each other's propaganda, fuelling the "cold war" that prevailed for most of the period 1160–80.

Manuel has been considered a "Latinophile", and a survey of his foreign-policy ambitions reveals a clear Latin (if not always western) bias. While we cannot countenance the notion that his actions precipitated the crisis of 1204 – a proposal first articulated by the 13th-century historian Niketas Choniates, and revived in the 20th century by Ferdinand Chalandon – Manuel's achievements in the west were certainly ambiguous. His preoccupation with Germany led him to advance the empire's frontier across the Danube, and to make inroads into Italy and Hungary through strategic use of force and aggressive diplomacy. Meanwhile, however, smaller powers gained ground in the Adriatic and Mediterranean. Hungary made much progress in the northern Balkans, and the Venetians were able more freely to switch allegiance between Byzantium and Germany, while advancing their own interests in Dalmatia and the Holy Land. The Normans never suffered a joint Byzantine–German assault on southern Italy, and the shift of attention after 1160 allowed William I and William II further to consolidate their authority in Sicily and Apulia. Within the northern Balkans regional and municipal potentates benefited from Manuel's "chequebook diplomacy", without committing themselves fully to his cause. Soon after 1180 the semiautonomous regions of Bulgaria and Serbia became independent kingdoms.

We have two full narrative accounts of Manuel's reign, by John Kinnamos and Niketas Choniates, which are in turns complementary and contradictory (so much so that it is likely that Choniates had read and determined to refute many of Kinnamos's claims). However, the fullest account of Manuel's activities is contained in the panegyrical orations delivered by Manuel's encomiasts. The so-called "Manganeios" Prodromos provides the largest dossier on events before 1160, presenting a rhetorical image that far outstrips even Kinnamos's eulogisitic biography. Manuel's image as a conquering warrior owes much to the ideals developed by his father's image makers, and he emulated and developed John II's triumphal processions through Constantinople. According to encomia produced for these occasions, Manuel surpassed John, indeed all his predecessors, and his victories are greater than his father's, greater even than his Roman or mythical forebears. His deeds are compared favourably to those of great leaders and warriors of myth and history.

Manuel's martial prowess, and his victories across the frontiers of his empire gave him much-needed kudos in his early years, demonstrating the importance of foreign policy for domestic consumption. Much of this show was directed at impressing his own magnates, and most of all the increasingly divisive ranks of his closest kin, the *sebastoi*. Manuel made full use of his palaces, particularly the development at Blachernae where building work continued apace, and the walls were decorated with frescos of his vanquished foes and prostrate subjects. The walls of his subordinates' houses were similarly decorated, and one, Alexios Axouch, was notoriously condemned for choosing instead to decorate his residence with pictures detailing the exploits of the Seljuk sultan.

After 1160 Manuel sought also to project his image beyond Constantinople, to confront the wider world with his imperial vision in their own courts: the papal curia in Rome, the Hungarian royal court at Esztergom, in the streets of Antioch and Jerusalem, or even improvised tribunals in the Serbian highlands. The ideological foundation for his foreign policy in the second part of his reign was his claim to be "king of kings", the sole Roman emperor recognized by the papacy and by subordinate rulers within and beyond his borders. He backed his claims with actions, and demonstrated his suitability to preside over a hierarchy of Christian rulers by his tolerance and philanthropy in Dalmatia and Italy, and by a moderate policy towards Hungary and the crusader states. Manuel's ecumenical claims, and antique pretensions, are expressed clearly in his conciliar edict of 1166, preserved in an inscription (a plaster copy of which is displayed today in the outer narthex of Hagia Sophia in Istanbul).

It is of great significance that Manuel was remembered fondly in the peripheral lands of the empire as a fine Christian emperor, a powerful general, and a liberal distributor of largesse. The citizens of the Dalmatian cities spent his money gratefully, as no doubt did the Russian princeling Vasilko who was granted authority over four major trading cities on the lower Danube. And his reputation for generosity spread further afield: Robert of Clari, a participant in the Fourth Crusade, heard it told that Manuel was "a most worthy man and the richest of all Christians who have ever lived, and the most generous. Never did anyone ask him for anything of his ... but that he would give him a hundred." Manuel's fine reputation lived on as a contrast to those of his successors, and the wealth that he had been able to amass from his extensive empire, larger than at any time since the reign of Basil II, was soon to pass into other hands even before the advent of the Fourth Crusade.

Shortly before his death Manuel took the monastic name Matthew. He was buried in his father's foundation, the Pantokrator monastery in Constantinople. Cyril Mango has identified the lid of his sarcophagus, carved in the shape of a church with seven domes, in a drawing of 1750 (reproduced in Mango, 1993). A poetic epitaph for the emperor has been preserved in the *Geography* of Meletios of Ioannina (died 1714), which records the features of the monastery.

PAUL STEPHENSON

Biography

Born in Constantinople in 1118 the son of John II Komnenos, Manuel came to the throne in 1143 despite having an elder brother living. He spent the first part of his reign campaigning in the east and the second part dealing with the German emperor Barbarossa. Manuel enjoyed great success in the field but was defeated by the Seljuks at Myriokephalon in 1176. He died at Constantinople in 1180.

Further Reading

Angold, Michael, *The Byzantine Empire, 1025–1204: A Political History*, 2nd edition, London and New York: Longman, 1997

Chalandon, Ferdinand, *Les Comnène: études sur l'empire byzantin au XIe et XIIe siècles*, vol. 2: *Jean II Comnène (1118–1143) et Manuel I Comnène (1143–1180)*, Paris: Picard, 1912

Lilie, Ralph-Johannes, *Byzantium and the Crusader States, 1096–1204*, Oxford: Clarendon Press, and New York: Oxford University Press, 1993

Magdalino, Paul, *The Empire of Manuel I Komnenos, 1143–1180*, Cambridge and New York: Cambridge University Press, 1993

Mango, Cyril, "The Imperial Sarcophagi Discovered in 1750", "Notes on Byzantine Monuments", and "The Conciliar Edict of 1166", all in his *Studies on Constantinople*, Aldershot, Hampshire: Variorum 1993

Stephenson, Paul, *Byzantium's Balkan Frontier: A Political Study of the Northern Balkans, 900–1204*, Cambridge: Cambridge University Press, 2000

Manuel II Palaiologos 1350–1425

Emperor

Manuel II (1391–1425) was the second son of the emperor John V and Helena Kantakouzene. Not destined for the throne, he received an exceptionally fine education. By the age of 20, with the title of despot, he was given responsibility for governing Thessalonica, and it was from there that he went to Venice to assist his father after his elder brother, Andronikos, as regent in Constantinople, had denied help with John's foreign debts (1370). Andronikos's further treachery prompted John to replace him in the succession with Manuel (1373) but, in a settlement following an abortive coup by Andronikos (1382), Manuel was displaced again. He then established himself independently in Thessalonica, taking a vigorous stance against the aggressive Turks until they drove him out of the city (1387). After a brief disgrace, he recovered favour by aiding his father against the attack of Andronikos's son, John VII (1390). When his discredited father died (16 February 1391) Manuel secured the throne. The following year he took as his wife the Serbian princess Helena Dragaš.

By the end of the 14th century the Byzantine empire was reduced to the city of Constantinople and small, scattered subject territories. It survived only through humiliating vassalage to the Ottoman Turks, as they extended their conquests in the Balkans. Manuel maintained his father's policy of subservience as long as he could, until the arrogance of sultan Bayazid I drove him into a break (1393). As the Turks

Manuel II: portrait of the emperor on a silver hyperper, early 15th century, Barber Institute, Birmingham

began a debilitating siege of Constantinople (1394), and when the so-called Crusade of Nicopolis (1396) failed in its attempt to end Turkish power in the Balkans, it seemed only a matter of time before Bayazid would take the great capital city and end the Byzantine state.

Hoping that the Latin powers of western Europe could be persuaded to send military aid to save Byzantium, Manuel undertook a virtually unprecedented journey of appeal to the west (1399–1403), during which he visited parts of Italy, Paris, and London. But western Europe's own problems (the Hundred Years' War, the Great Schism) and internal distractions forestalled any actual help. It was only the unexpected defeat and capture of Bayazid by Timur at the Battle of Ancyra (28 July 1402) that gave Byzantium a reprieve. Manuel returned home to involve himself in the 11-year struggle for the Turkish succession, fortunately backing the winner, Mehmet I, with whom he established amicable relations that sustained an outward truce.

But Manuel had no illusions about the longterm threat of the Turks, and he laboured to shore up his depleted realm. Ending his family feud with his nephew John VII, he devoted particular attention to safeguarding the Byzantine position in the Peloponnesian Morea, ruled by his brother and then his own son. Manuel himself spent a year there (1415–16), restoring the famous Hexamillion fortifying the isthmus of Corinth and putting down internal rebellion. Following that, he had his eldest son, the future John VIII, spend a military apprenticeship in the Peloponnese, winning territory from the neighbouring Latin powers there.

At the same time, and despite outward peace with the sultan, Manuel renewed appeals to western powers to send aid against the Turkish threat before it was too late. The possibilities of ecclesiastical reunion with Rome were dangled as bait, but the western Church leadership was too preoccupied with other matters at the landmark Council of Constance (1414–17) to deal with the issue. Subsequent contacts between

Manuel and the new pope Martin V revealed that Church union would be far more complicated than a mere submission of suppliant Constantinople to domineering Rome and would require the formal mechanism. Though such a pursuit would subsequently be taken up by Manuel's successor John VIII, he himself regarded union as but a diplomatic bargaining point, something too unacceptable to the Orthodox community to be pursued to actual conclusion. Manuel did, however, open other doors to the west by arranging Latin marriages for his sons John and Theodore.

Manuel's cautious outward policy of accommodating the Turks was challenged by his son John, crowned co-emperor in 1421. Manuel wearily allowed John the initiative. His misguided overreaching brought down the wrath of the new sultan, Murad II, on Byzantine territories. A fierce but short-lived siege of Constantinople itself (summer 1422) was beaten off, partly because Manuel – who resumed control of the government – created diplomatic distractions for the sultan. But Manuel soon suffered a stroke (1 October) that left him effectively paralysed for the rest of his life. John took over full control of the government, not always with the full confidence of Manuel, who found his son more ambitious and pretentious than the pathetic state of their realm justified. As his health declined further, Manuel adopted the monastic garb on his deathbed (taking the name of Matthew), and died on or around 21 July 1425, aged 75. His funeral was the occasion of an unprecedented outpouring of grief by his apprehensive subjects.

Manuel was a remarkable personality by any measure. His political and diplomatic skills were worthy of the empire's earlier, greater days, when he would have been a magnificent sovereign; given his circumstances, his steering of his ravaged realm through its declining perils still ranks him as Byzantium's last truly great ruler. A superlative politician, he was also one of the leading cultural figures of his age, an outstanding example of the Byzantine type of the intellectual emperor. From early youth he acquired a hunger for learning and a facility in letters, thanks to his teacher, the leading Byzantine intellectual of the 14th century, Demetrios Kydones, who remained his friend to the end of the latter's life. Manuel himself has left us a large and significant literary legacy, including a collection of fascinating letters, writings for and about his family, theological efforts, occasional pieces, and a range of rhetorical exercises, all composed in the loftily complex and obscure style beloved of Byzantine savants.

From all accounts, Manuel was an individual of warm personality and noble character. A handsome man of great physical presence, even into his later years, he impressed all who encountered him. During his long stay in Paris, French artists became fascinated with his appearance and used his image as a model for representations, in painting and medallions, of the Magi, of the earlier emperors Constantine and Herakleios, and of the German emperor Charles IV. He was also the last emperor to receive first-class portrayal in Byzantine art: two manuscripts now in Paris preserve splendid images of him in imperial glory, in a solo portrait in a copy of his funeral oration for his brother Theodore (in the Bibliothèque Nationale), and in a family portrait (with his wife and their three eldest sons) in a manuscript of Dionysius the Areopagite (in the Louvre).

He was equally proud of his "Roman" imperial dignity and of his pure Orthodox faith. His personality and achievements represent perhaps the last great flourishing of the Byzantine embodiment of medieval Hellenism.

JOHN W. BARKER

Biography

Born in Constantinople in 1350, the second son of John V, Manuel received a good education. He ruled Thessalonica as despot from 1382 until 1387. He succeeded as emperor in 1391 and in 1392 married Helena Dragaš of Serbia. He toured western capitals in the hope of gaining military support for Byzantium and he established good relations with the sultan Mehmet I. He also left a significant body of writings. He died in Constantinople in 1425.

Writings

The Letters, edited and translated by George T. Dennis, Washington, D.C.: Dumbarton Oaks, 1977

Further Reading

Barker, John W., "On the Chronology of the Activities of Manuel II Palaeologus in the Morea in 1415", *Byzantinische Zeitschrift*, 55 (1962): pp. 39–55

Barker, John W., *Manuel II Palaeologus, 1391–1425: A Study in Late Byzantine Statesmanship*, New Brunswick, New Jersey: Rutgers University Press, 1969

Charanis, Peter, "The Strife among the Palaeologi and the Ottoman Turks" in his *Social, Economic, and Political Life in the Byzantine Empire*, London: Variorum, 1973

Dennis, George T., *The Reign of Manuel II Palaeologus in Thessalonica, 1382–1387*, Rome: Pontificum Institutum Orienatalium Studiorum, 1960

Dennis, George T., "Official Documents of Manuel II Palaeologus", *Byzantion*, 41 (1971): pp. 45–58

Dölger, Franz, "Johannes VII, Kaiser der Rhomäer, 1390–1408", *Byzantinische Zeitschrift*, 31 (1931): pp. 21–36

Marinesco, Constantin, "Deux Empereurs byzantins: Manuel II et Jean VIII Paléologue vus par des artistes occidentaux", *Le Flambeau*, 40 (November–December 1957): pp. 758–62

Nicol, Donald M., "A Byzantine Emperor in England: Manuel II's Visit to London in 1400–1401", *University of Birmingham Historical Journal*, 12 (1971): pp. 204–25

Nicol, Donald M., *The Last Centuries of Byzantium, 1261–1453*, 2nd edition, Cambridge and New York: Cambridge University Press, 1993

Ostrogorsky, George, *History of the Byzantine State*, 2nd edition, Oxford: Blackwell, 1968; New Brunswick, New Jersey: Rutgers University Press, 1969

Schlumberger, Gustave, *Un Empereur de Byzance à Paris et à Londres*, Paris: Plon, 1916

Manuscripts

Manuscripts in the technical sense of hand-written documents on a variety of supports have been produced in the Hellenic world since writing was first used in earliest times, and have continued in production up to the present day. Included under this heading, therefore, could be pottery fragments (*ostraka*) from Hellenistic Egypt containing short notes or messages, a luxury copy of the Psalter made for a Byzantine emperor around the year 1000, and an annotated draft of Kazantzakis's *Odysseia* (first printed in 1938). Such a range of material is so vast and heterogeneous that some narrowing of focus is generally considered helpful if it is to be surveyed. Yet even the term "Greek manuscript" as usually understood – that is, to refer to primarily literary material of, roughly speaking, the last two millennia – still embraces a huge field. The interest and importance of the manuscript in the Hellenic world, however, is not due merely to the size and scope of the theme, but to the fact that it provides most of our knowledge of that world before modern times. If we set aside, for purposes of discussion, the visual, topographical, and archaeological evidence of the past, it can be asserted that Greek manuscripts are not merely the prime source of literature in Greek, they are in a crucial sense the prime source of the history of things Greek.

Most surviving Greek manuscripts are written on parchment, sheets of animal skin prepared according to a formula reputedly invented in Hellenistic Pergamum (from which the word parchment, *pergamene*, is derived). Parchment gradually supplanted papyrus as the writing support of choice in the early centuries AD, and was on occasions replaced by paper of Near Eastern manufacture from around the 9th century, and more generally by western (primarily north Italian) paper from around 1300. Together with the replacement of papyrus by parchment came the replacement of the (horizontal) scroll by the folded, gathered, sewn, and bound book (or codex) that still remains today an indispensable aspect of our culture. This development also took place in the Hellenized world of the eastern Mediterranean and its hinterland, and is often linked, albeit loosely, with the growth and spread of Christianity. Taken together, the invention of parchment – with its extraordinary durability – and its use in the convenient and commensurately durable codex must rank among the most far-reaching contributions of Hellenic culture. It is no exaggeration to say that not only would our knowledge of the history and literature of the past be very scant without the contribution of parchment codices, but without such books that history and that literature would themselves have been altogether different.

The vast preponderance of manuscripts written in Greek that have survived (more than 60,000) date from the Byzantine period (*c.*324–1453), although we have many earlier fragments of papyrus (generally very small in scale), and the production of significant numbers of manuscript books, notably in the monasteries of Mount Athos, continued into modern times. Undoubtedly vast numbers of manuscripts have been lost over the centuries, but it is important to bear in mind that this loss has not affected all types of manuscripts equally. In particular we can assert that the more important a book was perceived to be at any time, the greater were the chances that it would be preserved.

The manuscript book is eminently portable, and while this may on occasions ensure its preservation (snatched from a fire that destroyed the building in which it was housed, for example), it is always a complicating factor in seeking to understand what such manuscripts can tell us. The turbulent political history of the lands that once formed part of the Byzantine empire is a further complication. The largest numbers of Greek manuscripts are now to be found in the Vatican Library in Rome and the Bibliothèque Nationale de France in Paris, with major holdings in libraries in many other countries, including Greece; but there are only a small number of such manuscripts still in Istanbul, even though for a thou-

Manuscripts: gospel illumination of St Luke writing at his desk, 12th century, National Library, Athens

sand years (as Constantinople) the city must have been the most important centre for the production and consumption of such books. Whereas the medieval holdings of monasteries and other religious houses in Britain, for example, can be extensively reconstructed, nothing comparable can be done in the former Byzantine lands (except perhaps in part for the library at Patmos). It is well known that the famous Codex Sinaiticus in the British Library was taken from St Catherine's Monastery by von Tischendorf in 1859, presented by him to tsar Alexander II, and in 1933 purchased by the British Museum from the Soviet government for £100,000, raised by public subscription. Yet exactly where, when, and under what circumstances this great bible was made in the decades around 400, and how and when it came to Sinai, are matters on which we are uninformed. There are very few surviving Greek manuscripts of any period about whose precise origins in the Hellenic world we can speak with confidence.

Manuscripts preserve and transmit information. Some are by intention linked to a specific historical moment without the expectation that they will subsequently be copied, and hence transmitted, whether horizontally (so to speak) in order to reach a wider audience of contemporaries, or vertically, to ensure preservation and use by future generations. Charters and documents of all sorts (even if produced in duplicate or triplicate) are a good example of this time-bound category.

Various monasteries on Mount Athos, for example, preserve imperial charters originally authenticated with a gold seal (hence *chrysobull*), along with other documents relating in particular to the management and ownership of land and other resources. Some idea of the losses in this area can be gauged, paradoxically, by the survival (and rediscovery through archaeological or chance excavation) of tens of thousands of detached lead sealings, most dating from the 6th to the end of the 12th century. The Byzantine world was a bureaucracy par excellence, in which the production of documents of all sorts, testifying to the power of the written word, was highly developed.

The largest subcategory of Greek manuscripts includes all those more self-consciously "literary" forms of writing, such as history, drama, philosophy, poetry, mathematics, theology, astrology, exegesis, geography, geometry, hagiography, homily, liturgy, politics, rhetoric, myth (all of these categories still defined, it may be noted, by Greek words), medicine (for which a Latin term came to be preferred), together with the New Testament (composed in Greek) and the Old Testament (already translated into Greek for the use of Hellenized Jews in the last centuries BC). The single most important point to note in this context is that, with a few striking exceptions from the Byzantine era, even the earliest surviving manuscripts of these texts do not preserve versions produced under authorial supervision, but are later copies at a number of removes from a postulated "original", a position that causes particular problems, and prompts the adoption of specific approaches. Some of these removes might be termed technological. It is apparent, for example, that a text preserved during antiquity on one or more papyrus rolls will have survived to modern times (unless in a favoured archaeological context, such as the recently discovered Derveni papyrus, for example) only if copied into a parchment codex. A further crucial sorting occurred as a result of the increasing use in manuscripts of a formal minuscule bookhand, from around 800, in place of the stately majuscule scripts of earlier centuries (cursive scripts had long been used informally). Any text not transcribed in minuscule in, for the most part, the 9th or 10th century, stood little chance of being transmitted into modern times. We thus owe to a relatively small number of intellectuals of the Byzantine world, some known to us by name such as patriarch Photios of Constantinople (d. 891) and archbishop Arethas of Caesarea (d. c.935), most of what we know of the writings of the pre-Christian Greek world. The only surviving manuscript to contain all 11 known plays of Aristophanes, for example, was produced in the mid-10th century (it has been in Ravenna since the 16th century). Along with this activity went works of lexicography and anthology in which were preserved (generally as excerpts) many texts of which no more complete version now exists.

The act of copying a text in a parchment manuscript, because of the high cost of the materials (not to mention any costs associated with the scribe's lengthy work), implies certain prerequisites. In particular it presupposes a demand: such books were always made in response to a specific commission, not "on spec". Once made – and this point is too easily overlooked by those familiar with printed books and the modern situation – such manuscripts enjoyed very little "circulation", and hence were not in any broad sense "published" or even "public". A liturgical book, it is true, would be read from to a congregation, and its text thus transmitted to a large audience, but the book itself, somewhat paradoxically, remained a private object to be consulted by one or perhaps two people at a time, although its covers could generally be seen if the book was displayed or carried processionally. The point is important when we consider the physical appearance of such books: their exteriors could make a public statement, but any interior elaboration of their content with images or decoration remained hidden from the view of all but a few specially privileged individuals. With numerous caveats it can be said that the number of copies of a text that have been preserved can thus be a very approximate indicator of the extent of knowledge of (and interest in) that text (or its images) in the society for which it was made.

The use of images in Greek manuscripts is one of their most intriguing and justly celebrated aspects. Christianity, in the period of its first triumphal development in and beyond the Greek-speaking world in the 4th to 6th centuries, became, to an extraordinary extent, a religion not merely of the word (i.e. the Gospel), but of the image (i.e. the icon in its broadest sense). Gradually, from the 5th century onward, this came to be reflected in religious books, where within a hundred years or so craftsmen had experimented with virtually every conceptual link between word and image that the bound book would permit (the frontispiece cycle, the marginal image, the literal illustration, and so forth), approaches that were then repeated throughout the Middle Ages in both East and West.

Because of the long and bitter iconoclast controversy in Byzantium (c.730–843) the use of images in religious books in later centuries was always carefully considered. Images in Byzantine manuscripts were never merely alternatives to words, but made their own points and required viewing according to their own conventions. The evangelists, for example, were traditionally represented in copies of the gospels as saintly craftsmen, engaged in the production of manuscript books, sometimes transcribing the text from a scroll, or surrounded by the paraphernalia of the workshop: pens, inks, knives, etc. An image of an event from Christ's life was not primarily an aide-memoire, or merely a focus for prayer, but a statement of theological truth: it affirmed the historical reality of the Incarnation, demonstrated that the Godhead could be represented and circumscribed, and was held to be a traditional aspect of Christian activity that had originated in apostolic times. The vast repertory of images found in such manuscripts has sometimes been regarded as providing insights into a lost world of images of earlier centuries, but the situation is problematic, and the approach questionable.

Greek manuscripts have been systematically collected in the west since the 15th century, notably under the influence of various enthusiasms: humanist, biblical, scholarly, museological, acquisitive. Their current dispersal is as great as (perhaps greater than) the Greek diaspora. At any one time, however, only a tiny proportion of the surviving material is on temporary or permanent exhibition. Some of the contents of these manuscripts has been absorbed over the centuries into the very foundations of western consciousness. But a surprising amount, especially of the religious literature of Byzantium, is unpublished, and much of it is still untranslated. Although scholars and collectors no longer scour the monasteries of the Levant in the hope of finding some hitherto unknown masterwork of Classical Greek literature, Greek manuscripts still have many secrets to yield to new research.

JOHN LOWDEN

Further Reading

Barbour, Ruth, *Greek Literary Hands AD 400–1600*, Oxford: Clarendon Press, and New York: Oxford University Press, 1981

Buckton, David (editor), *Byzantium: Treasures of Byzantine Art and Culture from British Collections*, London: British Museum Press, 1994

Byzantine Books and Bookmen, Washington D.C.: Dumbarton Oaks, 1975

Evans, Helen C. and William D. Wixom (editors), *The Glory of Byzantium: Art and Culture of the Middle Byzantine Era, AD 843–1261*, New York: Metropolitan Museum of Art, 1997

Gamillscheg, Ernst and Dieter Harflinger (editors), *Repertorium der griechischen Kopisten, 800–1600*, Vienna, 1981–

Glénisson, Jean *et al.*, *La Paléographie grecque et byzantine*, Paris: Centre National de la Recherche Scientifique, 1977

Hutter, Irmgard, *Corpus der byzantinischen Miniaturenhandschriften*, vols 1–3: *Oxford, Bodleian Library*; vol. 4: *Oxford, Christ Church*, Stuttgart: Hiersemann, 1977–93

Lowden, John, *The Octateuchs: A Study in Byzantine Manuscript Illustration*, University Park: Pennsylvania State University Press, 1992

Lowden, John, *Early Christian and Byzantine Art*, London: Phaidon, 1997

Marava-Chatzinicolaou, Anna and Christina Toufexi-Paschou, *Catalogue of the Illuminated Byzantine Manuscripts of the National Library of Greece*, 2 vols, Athens: Publications Bureau of the Academy of Athens, 1978–85

Mioni, Elpidio, *Introduzione alla paleografia greca*, Padua: Liviana, 1973

Pelekonidis, S.M. *et al.*, *The Treasures of Mount Athos / Oi Thesauroi tou Agiou Orous*, 4 vols, Athens: Ekdotike Athenon, 1973–91 (only vols 1–2 in English)

Reynolds, L.D. and N.G. Wilson, *Scribes and Scholars: A Guide to the Transmission of Greek and Latin Literature*, 3rd edition, Oxford: Clarendon Press, and New York: Oxford University Press, 1991

Treasures of Mount Athos, exhibition catalogue, Thessalonica: Organization for the Cultural Capital of Europe, 1997

Turner, Eric G., *The Typology of the Early Codex*, Philadelphia: University of Pennsylvania Press, 1977

Turner, Eric G., *Greek Manuscripts of the Ancient World*, 2nd edition, revised by P.J. Parsons, London: University of London, Institute of Classical Studies, 1987

Weitzmann, Kurt, *Ancient Book Illumination*, Cambridge, Massachusetts: Harvard University Press, 1959

Weitzmann, Kurt *et al.*, *The Place of Book Illumination in Byzantine Art*, Princeton, New Jersey: Art Museum, Princeton University, 1975

Weitzmann, Kurt and George Galavaris, *The Monastery of Saint Catherine at Mount Sinai: The Illuminated Greek Manuscripts*, vol. 1, Princeton, New Jersey: Princeton University Press, 1990

Williams, John (editor), *Imaging the Early Medieval Bible*, University Park: Pennsylvania State University Press, 1999

Wilson, Nigel, *Mediaeval Greek Bookhands: Examples Selected from Greek Manuscripts in Oxford Libraries*, Cambridge, Massachusetts: Mediaeval Academy of America, 1973

Manzikert, Battle of

Battle fought between Seljuk Turks and Byzantines in 1071

Manzikert (ancient Arzashkun, then Menuaskert; Armenian Manazkert) is a village in the ancient Armenian homeland, some 30 km to the north of Lake Van in the region of Taraun (or Taron). Never a major centre in classical Armenian times, it is nowadays only a small town in eastern Turkey, known as Malazkirt. Its name is remembered today (in Graeco-Armenian form) almost exclusively as the locale of one of the most significant battles in the history of the Byzantine empire.

A recurrently strategic point in the centre of Armenian territories, Manzikert was located in the areas of ancient Perse-Armenia that, since the 5th century AD, had been in dispute as spheres of interest between the eastern Roman empire and first the Sassanian Persians, then the Arabs. In the 9th century it was the seat of an Arab emirate. By the late 10th century it was passing back and forth between the Armenian and Georgian Bagratid dynasts, and in 1000 it was part of the territories annexed by the emperor Basil II in an early phase of the Byzantine dismantling of the Armenian realms (completed in 1045).

This Byzantine territorial expansion eliminated an important buffer zone by extending the empire's frontiers eastward and exposing them almost immediately to the first raids by Turkish and other forces under the leadership of the house of Seljuk. Such raids turned into more systematic campaigns of conquest, reaching a climax in the Turkish capture of the Armeno-Byzantine capital of Ani in 1064 and the final destruction of the old Armenian world. This mounting menace to the empire's eastern Anatolian lands came, moreover, at a time when the Byzantine government was allowing its military resources to fall into decay, leaving it perilously vulnerable.

A crisis in the Doukas regime in Constantinople prompted in 1068 the elevation to the throne of the military emperor Romanos IV Diogenes. An experienced soldier, Romanos attempted to revitalize Byzantine forces and mount a counter-offensive, despite the court intrigues against him. Organizing a major effort to clear Anatolia in the summer of 1071, he moved to confront the Seljuk sultan Alp Arslan in a show-down. The Byzantine army was deceptively large – at least four times the size of the Turkish forces, according to some estimates – but in fact an unstable assemblage in which limited and insecurely loyal native forces were joined by a motley array of foreign units (Frankish, Russian, Turkish, etc.). Unwisely dividing these forces, Romanos led his reduced army into battle near Manzikert on either 19 or 21 August 1071. Using clever and mobile tactics, the Seljuks were aided by the desertion of the emperor's Turkish auxiliaries and the insubordination of Andronikos Doukas, whose withdrawal from battle at a crucial point on the second day caused the collapse of the Byzantine army. Though fighting valiantly, the emperor was captured: treated courteously, he was obliged to sign a relatively moderate treaty of peace on Turkish terms. On his way back to Constantinople, however, Romanos was betrayed by his rivals there, deposed, and blinded.

Usually represented as a catastrophic landmark in Byzantine history – leading to the loss of Asia Minor, part of the empire's heartland – the Battle of Manzikert was not in itself a military disaster of great magnitude, either in manpower losses or immediate territorial transfers. But, with hindsight, its aftermath proved crucial. For the next ten years the Byzantine government was hopelessly ineffectual, so that there was no opposition to the Turks' penetration of Anatolian territories, with their Turkmen and other allies. The invasions of earlier centuries, by Persians and Arabs, had always taken the main highroads to strike directly at major cities and, eventually, Constantinople itself, while the isolation of the geographically and topographically fragmented hinterlands had escaped systematic occupation. Now, however, broad areas of the whole region could be overrun with impunity, and the process of destroying its Hellenic and Christian culture was initiated. Occupying perhaps two-thirds of Asia Minor, the Seljuks created a regional sultanate whose first capital was Nicaea, perilously close to Constantinople; after its recapture in 1096 by Alexios I and the forces of the First Crusade, the sultanate relocated in Ikonion, where it was to endure as late as the 14th century. The definitive loss of most of Asia Minor by Byzantium as a result of Manzikert was not truly confirmed until 1176, when the emperor Manuel I was disastrously defeated by the Seljuk sultan at Myriokephalon, and any serious hope for Byzantine recovery of the Anatolian heartland was thereby lost for good (though the northern and western territories were retained for some time thereafter).

Accordingly, the Battle of Manzikert assumes its ultimate significance only in retrospect, as the death sentence for Hellenic Asia Minor – a verdict whose reversal was sought as late as the Anatolian campaign mounted in 1922 by the modern government of Greece. Moreover, the date of Manzikert, 1071, is also the date of the loss of Bari, the last Byzantine stronghold in Italy, as the climax of the Norman conquests there. Taken together, these two events symbolize the definitive turn of Byzantium into its long centuries of decline and collapse thereafter.

JOHN W. BARKER

See also Seljuks

Summary

The Battle of Manzikert was fought in 1071 between the emperor Romanos IV Diogenes and the Seljuk sultan Alp Arslan to secure the Byzantine empire's eastern Anatolian borders. Though superior in numbers, the Byzantine army collapsed and the emperor was captured; though later released, he had to accept Turkish terms for peace. The battle paved the way for the Turkish capture of Byzantine Asia Minor.

Further Reading

Angold, Michael, "The Byzantine State on the Eve of the Battle of Manzikert", *Byzantinische Forschungen*, 16 (1990): pp. 9–34

Angold, Michael, *The Byzantine Empire, 1025–1204: A Political History*, 2nd edition, London and New York: Longman, 1997

Cheynet, J.C., "Mantzikert: un désastre militaire?" *Byzantion*, 50 (1980): pp. 410–38

Der Nersessian, Sirarpie, *Armenia and the Byzantine Empire: A Brief Study of Armenian Art and Civilization*, Cambridge, Massachusetts: Harvard University Press, 1945

Friendly, Alfred, *The Dreadful Day: The Battle of Manzikert, 1071*, London: Hutchinson, 1981

Lang, David Marshall, *Armenia: Cradle of Civilization*, 3rd edition (corrected), London and Boston: Allen and Unwin, 1980

Vryonis, Speros Jr., *The Decline of Medieval Hellenism in Asia Minor and the Process of Islamization from the Eleventh through the Fifteenth Century*, Berkeley: University of California Press, 1971

Mar Saba

Greek monastery in Palestine

The monastery of Mar Saba, on the east bank of Nahal Kidron, southeast of Jerusalem, is the earliest and best known of the Sabaite Greek Orthodox monasteries of Palestine. In AD 478 Sabas, the founder of the Sabaite monastic order in Palestine, established his residence in a cave on the mountain on which the monastery was later built. This monastery was to have huge influence on the subsequent development of Orthodox monasticism within Palestine. Its history is intimately connected to the history of its charismatic founder, Sabas, whose dedication and commitment to monasticism effected dramatic results on Palestinian monastic life.

Sabas was born in Cappadocia in 439, to a family of distinguished Christian descent. From the age of 8, he grew up in the Flaviana monastery, near his birthplace, and received the formal education and training of a monk. Already by an early stage of his education he had learned the regulations of the communal life of monks, and was fully accustomed to the monastic life. In 456, at the age of 18, he left for Jerusalem with the intention of spending his life as an eremetic monk in the Judaean desert. While in Jerusalem, he rejected offers to join one of the city's monasteries, and, determined to live as a hermit in the desert, he sought the counsel of St Euthymius, whose life he wished to emulate. Having joined Euthymius' order in 457, Sabas was sent to the coenobium of Theoctistus, where he spent the next 12 years as a monk. In 469, at the age of 30, he was granted permission to live outside the coenobium in a cave as a hermit. Five days of each week were spent in solitary prayer and contemplation; for two days he rejoined his fellow monks in the coenobium. Following the death five years later of Euthymius, and, one week after that, of his successor Domitian, Sabas, now 35, departed from the order. This set him off on the path by which he would ultimately become the founder of his own order and the spiritual leader of all Orthodox Christians in Palestine.

In 478 Sabas arrived in the region of Jebel Muntar, the highest peak in the Judaean desert, the area in which most later Sabaite monasteries would be built. According to tradition, an angel directed Sabas to the east bank of a tributary of the Nahal Kidron, where he discovered the cave that was to become the core of the Mar Saba monastery. Sabas spent five years in the cave (478–83), after which the area grew to become the physical centre (the Great Lavra) of his order. Over the next two decades a complex of buildings grew up around the site that came to be the Mar Saba monastery. This small cave on the Nahal Kidron was thus both the physical and spiritual centre for Sabas's monastery and his followers. Of Saba's earliest disciples, five went on to become founders and leaders of other Sabaite monasteries: James, who founded the Lavra of the Towers by the Jordan river; John, who ultimately became the head of the New Lavra; Firmius, who founded the lavra near Mikhmas; Severianus, founder of the monastery near Kaparbaricha; and Julian, who founded the lavra of Neelkeraba near the River Jordan. Sabas and his followers together established 13 monasteries, thus dramatically changing the nature of both the Judaean desert and early Orthodox monastic development.

The Great Lavra, the Mar Saba monastery built around Sabas's cave, came to hold a position of leadership within the see of Jerusalem. First and foremost, it was significant as the anchor and foundation for what was to become a widespread and growing monastic tradition within Palestine. Moreover, the influence of Sabas himself and the Mar Saba monastery was such that the monastic tradition as a whole came to be well respected and regarded throughout the region. Over time, the Sabaite monasteries grew to be thriving centres for literary and theological activity, and to enjoy a superior reputation not just in the region, but in the west, particularly the Balkans, as well. Sava of Serbia (1175–1235), who founded the autocephalous Church of Serbia, received his training at Mount Athos, and upon becoming a monk took Sabas's name as a token of his reverence and admiration. Sava himself visited Jerusalem and the area's Sabaite monasteries on two occasions, and the reverence in the Balkans for Sabaite Palestinian monasticism endures to this day. So too does Mar Saba itself, which remains an active monastic centre, a living relic of 5th-century eastern monasticism.

K.E. FLEMING

See also Monasticism

Summary

The earliest and best known of the surviving Greek Orthodox monasteries of Palestine, Mar Saba was founded by the monk Sabas in a cave southeast of Jerusalem in AD 478. By the end of the century a complex of buildings had sprung up on the site. In time it became a thriving centre for theological and literary activity.

Further Reading

Avigad, Nahman, *Discovering Jerusalem*, Nashville: Nelson, 1983; Oxford: Blackwell, 1984

Avi-Yonah, M., *The Holy Land: From the Persian to the Arab Conquests, 536 BC to AD 640: A Historical Geography*, Grand Rapids, Michigan: Baker, 1966

Cameron, Averil, *Continuity and Change in Sixth-Century Byzantium*, London: Variorum, 1981

Hunt, E.D., *Holy Land Pilgrimage in the Later Roman Empire, AD 312–460*, Oxford: Clarendon Press, 1982

Patrich, Joseph, *Sabas, Leader of Palestinian Monasticism: A Comparative Study in Eastern Monasticism, Fourth to Seventh Centuries*, Washington, D.C.: Dumbarton Oaks, 1995

Marathon, Battle of

Battle fought between Greeks and Persians in 490 BC

In 490 BC a large Persian expeditionary force under the experienced commander Datis landed at Marathon in Attica not far from Athens. The Athenians and their Plataean allies under Miltiades repulsed the invasion, and so won one of the most famous battles in history. Not all agreed. The renowned historian Theopompus wrote that "the battle at Marathon was not what everyone keeps repeating it was, and all the other things that the city of the Athenians brags about and uses to dupe the Greeks" (in Jacoby, 1962, fr. 153, pp. 569–70; translation by the author). Hence the very nature and significance of the battle is worth reconsidering. In 490 BC an Athenian army some 10,000 strong confronted a much stronger force of Persian infantry and cavalry. The Athenians sent the runner Pheidippides to Sparta requesting help, but in the event they and their Plataean neighbours faced the enemy alone. At Marathon the Athenian and Plataean armies, under the command of Miltiades, waited drawn up in a strong position against which the Persians could not attack even with their superior numbers. Rapidly running out of time, Datis decided to sail direct against Athens. He chose the first night after the full moon to reembark his cavalry, a time-consuming process, and then the majority of his infantry. To cover his movements he stationed the rest of his troops where they could serve as a substantial rearguard. Datis' bold move was revealed by some Ionian deserters who approached the Athenian camp and said only "the cavalry is away". Fully realizing that Datis was withdrawing, Miltiades ordered his men to their places, ready to attack at first light. Dawn caught the Persians in the middle of their operations, without the time needed to embark their rearguard.

Miltiades promptly ordered the assault, the Athenians on the right and centre and the Plataeans on the left. Their centre was thin, but the wings deeper and stronger. Their line was equal in length to the Persian one, which strongly suggests that the numbers actually engaged were roughly equal, with the Persians probably enjoying some numerical superiority. Little is known of the Persian dispositions except that the Persians and Sacae, a warlike people from Central Asia, formed the very strong centre of the line, which was about 1600 m distant from the Greeks.

After a favourable sacrifice, the Athenians began their advance. Once within bowshot of the Persians, they charged on the run, the boldness of their attack taking the Persians by surprise and reducing the effectivenenss of their archers and slingers. Once engaged, the Persians broke the Athenian centre after hard fighting and then pursued the survivors. At the same time the Greek wings routed their opponents, whom they allowed to flee. The Athenians and Plataeans next swung their victorious wings against the Persians and Sacae, converging on the centre in a pincer movement. The Persian centre was already in some disarray owing to the absence of those still pursuing the defeated Athenians opposite them. The Athenians and Plataeans crushed both of the exposed flanks of the Persian centre, whereupon the entire Persian army broke and ran. Some fled towards the great marsh trying to reach the safety of their camp. In their confusion and terror they lost their way and became mired in the marsh, where they suffered their greatest losses. Meanwhile the Athenians pursued the remnant of the centre, cutting them down in their flight until some of them reached the sea. A fierce struggle swirled around the ships, which took on board as many fugitives as possible before shoving off the beach. Although the Athenians failed to stop them, they nevertheless captured seven ships. The casualties were stunningly uneven. The Persians lost some 6400 men,

a high proportion of those engaged. Of the Athenians, 192 fell, primarily those holding the centre of the line. Plataean losses are unnoted. After cremation, the Athenian dead were buried in the Soros and the Plataeans in a tumulus nearby.

Miltiades forestalled Datis' dash to Athens by a forced march. Thus thwarted, the Persian fleet returned to Asia Minor. The campaign of Marathon was over. Nonetheless, controversy still surrounds the Persian cavalry. Herodotus repeatedly emphasizes the importance of cavalry in Persian planning, but no ancient source, literary or epigraphical, mentions horsemen in combat at Marathon, hence they could not have been a factor in it. Their absence is further proof that the battle was a rearguard action.

The Athenians celebrated their victory in an outpouring of literature and art that still inspires today. The glory was not solely Athenian, but Greek. In literature they crafted the famous Marathonian epigrams, brilliant gems of poetry that commemorated the day when Athenian soldiers "saved Greece from seeing the day of slavery". Even the great tragedian Aeschylus adorned his tombstone not with allusions to his plays but with the notice that he had fought at Marathon. In art the Athenians honoured their patron goddess and themselves by minting exquisite silver tetradrachms portraying Athena crowned with an olive wreath, a sign of simplicity that contrasts with oriental pomp. Prominently displayed in the Stoa Poikile in the Athenian Agora was a dramatic painting of the battle depicting its progress from the outset through the clash of the two armies to the destruction of the Persian force. The most splendid monuments of the victory were architectural. The Athenian treasury at Delphi, which still stands in quiet beauty and dignity, was built from the spoils of the battle. On the Acropolis of Athens stands the Ionic temple of Athena the Victorious, small, elegant, a graceful memorial to a fateful day. Even the modern marathon races of 26 miles have their inspiration in the run of the Athenian messenger who brought news of the victory from Marathon to Athens.

In one sense, Theopompus was right. The battle about which Athens so boasted was not quite the supreme victory that it claimed. It was instead a splendid rearguard engagement of grand proportions. The significance of Marathon was indeed military, but it was also a symbol of the pride of the Greeks in their way of life and a justification of their love of freedom. That is also the legacy of Marathon to the world today, and the years have not dimmed it.

JOHN BUCKLER

See also Persian Wars

Summary

The Battle of Marathon was fought in 490 BC between a Persian invading force under Datis and the Athenians and their Plataean allies under Miltiades. The Greeks caught the Persians unawares as they were trying to withdraw and routed them. Persian losses were heavy (6400), Athenian losses very few (192). By a forced march Miltiades reached Athens before the Persian fleet, which promptly sailed away. Marathon symbolizes the pride of the Greeks in their way of life and their freedom.

Further Reading

Burn, A.R., *Persia and the Greeks: The Defence of the West, c.546–478 BC*, 2nd edition, London: Duckworth, and Stanford, California: Stanford University Press, 1984

Gomme, A.W., "Herodotos and Marathon", *Phoenix*, 6 (1952): pp. 77–83

Jacoby, Felix (editor), *Die Fragmente der griechischen Historiker*, 2.b., Leiden: Brill, 1962

Lazenby, J.F., *The Defence of Greece, 490–479 BC*, Warminster: Aris and Phillips, 1993, pp. 45–80

Pritchett, W. Kendrick, *Marathon*, Berkeley: University of California Press, 1960

Whatley, N., "On the Possibility of Reconstructing Marathon and Other Ancient Battles", *Journal of Hellenic Studies*, 84 (1964): pp. 119–39

Marble and other decorative stones

Many different decorative stones were used by the ancient Greeks and Romans for construction, sculpture, and small items. The sedimentary rocks, limestone and gypsum, were most important in construction, but the most significant and evocative material was the metamorphic rock marble. Igneous rocks, such as granite and lavas, were used in construction and for small items. We start first with the sedimentary rocks.

Limestone generally forms in the sea, from the accumulation of shells, some microscopic, or by direct chemical precipitation. Greece is particularly rich in limestone because 250 to 145 million years ago it was a region of shallow tropical seas, far from mountains, and limestone production is favoured in this environment. Most limestones are fine-grained and grey, but white, black, red, and even green varieties are known. Limestone is generally layered with beds a few centimetres to a few metres in thickness. The only important mineral in limestone is calcite (calcium carbonate), but the crystals are commonly too small to be seen. The calcite in some limestones is replaced by the related mineral dolomite. This produces a rock that is slightly harder than limestone, but otherwise very similar.

Although much limestone is uniform, breccias are common in many areas. They consist of angular blocks of limestone, set in fine-grained red mudstone. These are formed in limestone caves that are produced by the solution of rock in percolating rainwater. Blocks of limestone fall from the roof and accumulate on the floor of the cave, together with a fine red mud that is the insoluble residue of the limestone. The mixture is later cemented by calcite to form a solid breccia.

Travertine was another type of limestone exploited as a decorative stone and for construction. This commonly porous rock was deposited around many springs in ancient Greece, but has often been completely removed. It is fine-grained and grey when initially deposited, but may develop large crystals later. The fossilized remains of plants that grew around the springs are often preserved in the rock. It forms by the loss of carbon dioxide gas from the spring waters and the consequent precipitation of calcite. Stalagmites, stalactites, and dripstone form in caves in the same way and were also used sparingly as decorative stones.

Gypsum (alabaster) is a soft, pale brown, yellow, or pink rock that may be layered. It was used in Minoan times as a decorative stone in the palace at Knossos, at Akrotiri on Thera, and elsewhere, but soon lost favour. The rock is soluble in water and hence was used only inside buildings: gypsum blocks left open to the weather after the excavations have lost more than 1 cm of material in 30 years. Gypsum was obtained from quarries on the hill of Gypsadhes near Knossos and in the underground mines of Gortyn. It was formed by the evaporation of seawater when the Mediterranean dried up about 6 million years ago. Bands in the rock formed during deposition and were folded later by tectonic forces. The presence of calcite or dolomite impurities in some samples increases their strength and resistance to erosion. The finer-grained varieties of gypsum were used for facing stones and for floor slabs, whereas the coarse-grained varieties were used in columns. So-called "Egyptian alabaster" is actually a form of limestone.

Marble is limestone or, more rarely, dolomite whose structure and mineralogical composition have been changed by the action of heat and pressure (metamorphism). Quarry workers and some archaeologists often refer to a number of other softer rocks as marble as well, such as limestone, lavas, and serpentinite, but to a geologist only metamorphosed limestone or dolomite is marble. Marble was an important material for sculpture and building materials in antiquity because it was relatively easy to work, produced a fine edge, and was abundant in many parts of the Aegean region. The ancient Greeks were more interested in white or grey marble, but the Romans also exploited coloured marbles extensively.

Marble is produced in the earth at depths of several kilometres. The source of the heat is the natural increase in temperature with depth in the earth. As the limestones are buried under other rocks, the temperature increases at a rate of about 1°C for each 30 metres. The metamorphism induces the recrystallization of the calcite so that the crystals are visible to the unaided eye and can also lead to the formation of new minerals, and hence change the colour of the rock. The hot rock is much weaker than cold limestone, hence it is commonly deformed without cracking by natural stresses in the earth.

The textures of marble are a combination of those originally present in the limestone and those produced during metamorphism. Layering and breccias in the original limestone are inherited by marble, but metamorphism may deform or smear them. However, deformation can produce new layering and new breccias can form in caves in the marble, giving a myriad of varieties of textures, and textures within textures. Metamorphism can also produce another texture, veining. In the rock there is often a thin film of water between the crystals that is saturated with calcite in solution. If there is a sudden loss of pressure, or increase in stress, then a crack can open up that may soon be filled with relatively pure, white calcite. These veins are a good way to distinguish marble from limestone.

The colour of marble reflects the amounts of minor minerals present because pure calcite and dolomite are white. Red is produced by the mineral haematite, from iron oxide impurities. Grey and black are commonly due to graphite, produced during metamorphism from organic matter, such as plant or animal remains. These colours can also be produced by

Marble: fresh blocks cut for use in the current programme of restoration of the Parthenon

magnetite or manganese oxides. The presence of the minerals chlorite, muscovite mica, or serpentine gives green marbles.

White and pale grey marble occurs throughout the Aegean region, but was exploited extensively at only a few locations, for historical and geological reasons. The quarries of Attica supplied the white and grey marble used in Athens. Mount Penteli produced the best white marble, whereas the grey came from Hymettus, but both mountains contain white and grey. The best-known white marble of the Cyclades was that of Paros, known as *lychnites*, because it was mined underground by the light of a lamp. This marble is very pure so that quite thick pieces are translucent. Naxos also produced large quantities of a coarse-grained white marble. The quarries of white, dolomitic marble on Thasos were some of the largest in antiquity. Their exploitation reached a maximum during Roman times, when the marble was widely exported. Pale grey streaky marble from the island of Marmora was very popular since it could be extracted in large blocks.

The best-known green marble was known to the Romans as Marmor Carystium and more recently by the Italian name of Cipollino, because it resembles an onion in section. It was produced from a number of quarries in southern Euboea, around Carystus. It was used for monolithic columns, public fountains, and wall-facings in Roman and Byzantine buildings from the 1st century BC to the 7th century AD. It was widely exported all around the Mediterranean and as far as Britain. Cipollino is made of layers rich in calcite separated by layers rich in the green minerals muscovite and chlorite. Quartz and feldspar are also present and stand out from the other softer minerals after erosion.

Rosso Antico is a fine-grained, red to purplish red marble, with some varieties streaked with white veins and patches. It was first extracted from quarries on the Mani peninsula in Minoan and Mycenaean times, between 1700 and 1300 BC, for use in architecture and for stone vases. It was not in regular use again until about AD 50, when as Lapis Taenarius it is found in Roman and later in early Christian buildings, decorating walls and floors. Reused pieces were popular in the Middle Ages and later for floor decorations, and were frequently mistaken for imperial porphyry, an igneous rock from Egypt. The Rosso Antico quarries also yielded white, grey, and green marble, and were also exploited very early, for example in the treasury of Atreus at Mycenae.

Other variegated marbles were exploited at many locations, but in small quantities and mostly during Roman times. The best known were on Skyros, the Fior di Pesca of Euboea, the Africano of Teos, and the Portasanta of Chios. Yellow marble was imported from the imperial quarries in Tunisia.

Verde Antico is the name given by Italian masons, from the Renaissance onwards, to a green decorative stone that was first used in the 1st century AD, but was most popular in the 5th–6th centuries, after the imperial porphyry quarries in Egypt closed (about AD 450). Its ancient name was Marmor Thessalicum or Marble of Atrax. The quarries lie on a small hill beneath the western slopes of Mount Ossa, just north of Chasambali. Verde Antico is a conglomerate composed of rounded serpentinite and marble blocks set in a fine-grained matrix of similar composition (the geological term for this rock is ophicalcite). The rock is layered, with contrasting sizes and compositions of blocks in the different beds. The blocks were transported by rivers, but could not have travelled far because serpentinite is a very soft rock and hence erodes readily. Therefore, this rock probably formed very rapidly in a broad river valley surrounded by high mountains of serpentinite. This rock was not formed recently, but probably during the Tertiary period and is a variant of the conglomerates seen in the Meteora.

Of the igneous rocks both lava and granite were exploited in antiquity. A widely used green porphyritic rock was known to the Romans as Lapis Lacedaemonius, to Italian masons as Porphido Verde Antico, and to us as Spartan Basalt or Andesite. It was popular in Minoan and Mycenaean times for stone vases and sealstones and under the Roman and Byzantine empires for the decoration of walls and floors. According to Pausanias,"These stones were used for decorating temples, swimming pools, and fountains." Later, Roman and Byzantine stones were reused extensively, for example in St Mark's, Venice, and Westminster Abbey, London, until the late 18th century. Spartan Porphyry is a porphyritic andesite and comes from a lava dome 2000 metres long of mid-Triassic age (about 230 million years ago) near Krokeai, Laconia. Such domes form when viscous lava erupts quiescently on to the surface. The prominent crystals in the lava are plagioclase, now metamorphosed to a fine-grained mixture of albite and green epidote. Sometimes several plagioclase crystals started to crystallize from the same point, to give rosettes of crystals. In parts of the dome the fine-grained matrix of the rock has been reddened by the oxidation of iron minerals to haematite. This rock is generally highly fractured, with most blocks less than 50 cm in diameter. Similar porphyritic lavas were also exploited locally on Samothrace.

Granite was an important decorative material for the Romans and was traded widely throughout the Mediterranean. There were two major sources of granite in the Aegean: Marmo Misio (or Granito Bigio) from near Kozac, 15 km northwest of Pergamum, and Marmo Troadense (or Granito Violetto) from Mount Cigri, 10 km southwest of Ezine. Both rocks are grey, fine-grained, and principally composed of quartz, feldspar, and biotite. Both intrusions are about the same age as the volcanic rocks in the region. Plutonic rocks such as granite and lavas such as imperial porphyry from other Roman imperial quarries were imported into Greece in small quantities, especially from Egypt.

It is only recently that the susceptibility of marble and limestone to erosion by pollution has become a problem. The most direct problem is the solution of the mineral calcite in the marble by strong acids (for example sulphuric and nitric acids) present in polluted rain. Some acid gases in the atmosphere also directly attack marble. The most common end product is gypsum, which is more soluble in water than calcite. The transformation of calcite to gypsum also involves an increase in volume, hence the surface of the marble flakes off. Another problem relates to algae that live just below the surface of the marble. They feed off petroleum products deposited from the air and produce acid waste products, with the same results. Sandstones cemented with calcite are also attacked in the same way.

MICHAEL D. HIGGINS

See also Geology

Further Reading
Borghini, Gabriele *et al.*, *Marmi Antichi*, Rome: De Luca, 1989
Dworakowska, Angelina, *Quarries in Ancient Greece*, Wrocław: Ossolińskich, 1975
Fant, J.C. (editor), *Ancient Marble Quarrying and Trade*, Oxford: BAR, 1988
Gnoli, Raniero, *Marmora Romana*, Rome, Italy: Elefante, 1971
Lepsius, G.R., *Griechische Marmorstudier*. Berlin: Königlichen Akademie der Wissenschaften, 1890
Monna, Dario and Patrizio Pensabene, *Marmi dell'Asia Minore*, Rome: Consiglio Nazionale delle Ricerche, 1977
Waelkens, Marc, Norman Herz, and Luc Moens (editors), *Ancient Stones: Quarrying, Trade and Provenance: Interdisciplinary Studies on Stones and Stone Technology in Europe and Near East from the Prehistoric to the Early Christian Period*, Leuven: Leuven University Press, 1992

Mardaïtes

The Mardaïtes appear in the 7th century as inhabitants of the Amanus and Taurus ranges on the borders of Syria and Cilicia. Their origin is uncertain, though possibly Armenian or Persian, and they were undoubtedly Christian (but whether monophysite or monothelite is unclear). They were known to the Arabs as al-Jarajima after their stronghold al-Jurjuma. Most information on them comes from al-Baladhuri's and other Arab histories and Theophanes the Confessor's *Chronographia*, which last was used for and supplemented by Constantine VII Porphyrogennetos's *De Administrando Imperio*. Considerable uncertainty, however, still shrouds many of their activities.

The Mardaïtes are first heard of after the seizure of Antioch in 636–37 by the Arabs, who coerced them into agreeing to act both as irregular troops and as scouts to guard the defiles of the Amanus, with exemption from the poll tax and the right to battle spoils; but their loyalty was very precarious and they indiscriminately plundered both Arab Syria and Byzantine Cilicia. A major raid as far south as Jerusalem, in which they were probably aided by Constantine IV, was so successful that it not only encouraged fugitive slaves (probably Greek) and other malcontents to join them but also played a part, according to Theophanes, in forcing the Umayyad caliph Muawiya in 678 to abandon his siege of Constantinople and agree to a humiliating peace treaty to effect the withdrawal of Byzantine financial and military support from the Mardaïtes. Justinian II, however, subsidized a similar raid in the late 680s and thereby induced Caliph Abd-al-Malik, embattled by internal rebellions, to follow Muawiya's precedent. This time, despite having to make substantial payments, the Arabs obtained a far more advantageous agreement through the stipulation that the Mardaïtes were to be resettled in Byzantine territory. Substantial numbers nonetheless remained to raid Arab lands, and Theophanes' "bronze wall" between the two powers was not effectively eliminated until al-Jurjuma was destroyed *c.*707 by Abd-al-Malik's son Maslama. Some survivors fled westwards into Byzantine Anatolia but many were transplanted to Syria, some being drafted without the demand for religious conversion into the caliphal army, in which they helped suppress rebellions in Iraq in the 720s. In Syria they gradually lost their individual identity and were absorbed, perhaps becoming components of the Maronite communities.

In accordance with the treaty, Justinian II removed, with their families, at least 12,000 and possibly eventually as many as 18,000 Maradaïtes, whom he enrolled as oarsmen in the *Karabisianoi* (the regular fleet established probably by Constantine IV a decade earlier and which had presumably hitherto depended on local levies). Whether or not their arrival prompted the immediate establishment of the themes of Kibyrrhaiotai and Hellas, in the early 8th century they certainly formed the major element of the former (a naval theme stretching from Cilicia to Miletus). One of the principal officials of Kibyrrhaiotai, appointed directly by the emperor, was known as the *catepan* (governor) of the Mardaïtes and resided at Attaleia in Pamphylia. Others were employed as oarsmen in Hellas, and when in the early 9th century the new themes of Peloponnesos and Kephalenia were created, their garrisons, presumably drawn from the Mardaïtes of the old theme of Hellas, were known as the Mardaïtes of the West. By the 10th century some were stationed in the theme of Nicopolis in Epirus, earlier probably a part of Peloponnesos. Most of the Mardaïtes' battle honours were won in wars against the Arabs in both the eastern and western Mediterranean.

A.R. LITTLEWOOD

Summary

Christian freebooters on the borders of the Umayyad Caliphate and Byzantine empire, Mardaïtes were used by both as guerrillas in the 7th century. After an invasion of Syria in the 680s many were resettled in Byzantine territory and served the empire as oarsmen. Others remained in Syria.

Further Reading

Ahrweiler, Hélène, *Byzance et la mer: la marine de guerre, la politique, et les institutions maritimes de Byzance aux VIIe–XVe siècles*, Paris: Presses Universitaires de France, 1966

Bartikian, C.M., "I Lysi tou Ainigmatos tou Mardaitou", in *Byzantium: Tribute to Andreas N. Stratos*, edited by Nia A. Stratos, vol. 1, Athens, 1986, pp. 17–39

Canard, M., "Djarādjima" in *The Encyclopedia of Islam*, new edition, vol. 2, Leiden: Brill, 1965, pp. 456–8

Cheira, M.A., *La Lutte entre Arabes et Byzantins: la conquête et l'organisation des frontiers au VIIe et VIIIe siècles*, Alexandria: Société de Publications Égyptiennes, 1947, pp. 150–76

Moosa, M., "The Relation of the Maronites of Lebanon to the Mardaites and al-Jarājima", *Speculum*, 44 (1969) pp. 597–608

Stratos, Andreas N., *Byzantium in the Seventh Century*, translated by H.T. Ionidis, vols 4–5, Amsterdam: Hakkert, 1978–80

Treadgold, Warren T., "The Army in the Works of Constantine Porphyrogenitus", *Rivista di Studi Byzantini e Neohellenici*, new series, 29 (1992) pp. 115–21

Treadgold, Warren T., *Byzantium and its Army, 284–1081*, Stanford, California: Stanford University Press, 1995

Treadgold, Warren T., *A History of the Byzantine State and Society*, Stanford, California: Stanford University Press, 1997

Marriage

Marriage has been a central cultural and economic institution of Hellenic society since antiquity and, while both the practicalities and the perceived function of marriage have undergone various changes, it has demonstrated a remarkable continuity through time. Indeed it has been claimed that the pivotal role of marriage and the family, together with religion, has been a crucial factor in sustaining Greek identity and culture, particularly through the Tourkokratia (see McNeill, 1978; Sanders, 1967).

For antiquity, and for Classical Athens in particular, marriage was informed by two dominant and purposive imperatives: first, the production of legitimate children (*gnesioi*, contrasted with bastards, *nothoi*) for the husband's *oikos* (household, family) and of legitimate citizens for the state; second, the formation and maintenance of social and interfamilial alliances.

The first point finds its mythical illustration in the Athenian legend of Cecrops who, long ago, "found men and women having sexual intercourse at random, so no son could identify his father, and no father his son" (scholion on Aristophanes, *Plutus*, 773). Cecrops rectified this promiscuity by inventing the institution of marriage. Here the critical concern was to clarify lines of patrilineal descent and inheritance, a concern important especially for democratic Athens where legitimacy of birth was a prerequisite of citizenship. The flowering of the Athenian empire in the 5th century BC and the concomitant importance of being Athenian were reflected in the state's unusually narrow marriage regulations; before Pericles' law of 450/51 BC Athenian birth was a requirement of the father only, but after this both parents of legitimate children had to be Athenian. Thus citizen marriage at Athens was endogamous, and exogamy could have legal consequences (Demosthenes 59, a prosecution from the 4th century BC which deals with an Athenian citizen allegedly living as if married with an alien woman, is a good example of the practical consequences of this law against mixed marriages). One product of the importance of legitimacy was the emphasis on female chastity. Brides were expected to be virgins (the Greek word *parthenos* denotes both the unmarried girl and the virgin, social and physical categories that, preferably, coincided) and wives were expected to be chaste.

Also important and perhaps a particular concern for the rich elite was the notion that marriage could forge ties, concentrating power and wealth within social groups. Despite anxieties about incest, endogamy extended to "keeping it within the family"; marriages between first cousins, niece and uncle, and even half-siblings were common and, in Sparta at least, marriage between uterine siblings was sanctioned (Philo, *On*

Special Laws, 3. 4. 22). Indeed kinship was a positive factor for marriage: one legal speech brings as proof of a family quarrel the fact that an uncle has not married his daughter to his nephew (Isaeus, 7. 11–12), while another describes the reciprocal giving in marriage of female relatives within a family (Demosthenes, 59. 2). Friendship obligations were important too: another speaker in court describes how his sister was given in marriage to a friend of his dead father as a favour (Isaeus, 2. 3–5). These cases highlight the fact that an Athenian girl was given in a marriage over which her male natal guardian (*kyrios*, normally the girl's father or, if he was dead, her brother) exercised a formal control; indeed a wife's natal *kyrios* had the power to revoke her marriage, demanding the return of both woman and dowry, and divorce and remarriage were frequent. It was possible too for women to be the objects of bequests in wills (Demosthenes, 27. 5; 45. 28; Diogenes Laertius, 5. 11–16).

Marriage then at Athens can be seen as a form of exchange between households in which women were given out, conditionally, to bear children for their husbands and citizens for Athens, and was crucial for the creation of new households, for the continuation of descent groups, for the city's stock of citizens, and for citizens themselves for whom only marriage provided legitimate heirs.

For women too marriage was crucial and was seen as the fulfilment of a culturally prescribed role, indeed as the only proper role available to women, a notion that has gone largely unchallenged until the very recent past. While temporary celibacy was required of priestesses during the period of religious office, no respectable alternative to marriage and motherhood was available to women, either social or biological – the Greek medical writers envisage a horrendous fate for girls deprived of sex and babies (see in particular the *Peri Partheneion*, part of the Hippocratic corpus which remained influential throughout the medieval period). So strong was the notion that marriage was the only fitting career for a woman that girls who died unmarried were commemorated as brides of Hades.

In ancient Greece the state played no formal role in marriage which was essentially a private arrangement between families. As a result, identifying the definitive moment of the marriage ceremony (*gamos*) becomes somewhat problematic; no state or religious official pronounced the couple married and there was no marriage certificate. The basic signifier of marriage may simply have been for a couple to live together as if married (*synoikein*), and lawcourt speeches of the 4th century BC concerned with legitimacy and inheritance attest to the potential difficulty of deciding whether or not a marriage had taken place. The act of bethrothal (*engue*), however, in which the bride was bestowed for the ploughing of legitimate issue, marked the first step of marriage for an Athenian, and only children born of a woman so betrothed, apart from those of an *epikleros* (heiress), were legitimate (Demosthenes, 46. 18; Isaeus, 8. 19). *Engue* was not an irreversible contract (there was no notion of "breach of promise"), but normally was followed by the *ekdosis*, the handing over of the bride by her natal *kyrios* to her new *kyrios*, her husband. *Ekdosis* could happen some time after *engue*; Demosthenes reports that his sister's marriage was delayed by ten years since she was an infant when betrothed, a reminder that girls were married young, ideally shortly after puberty, perhaps to ensure as far as possible the bride's virginity.

The bride dedicated her childhood toys and a lock of hair to Artemis, was bathed and veiled. Then followed the sacrificial wedding feast during which libations were made to the gods, particularly Hera, the goddess of weddings and marriage and whose own divine union with Zeus was celebrated throughout Greece. The bride was unveiled before her husband who accepted her with his right hand and led her to his house.

Marriage in militaristic Sparta differed markedly from that in democratic Athens. Spartan men were expected to marry in their twenties but lived apart from their families in all-male barracks until the age of 30, encouraged to visit their wives only occasionally, at night and by stealth. The Spartan marriage ceremony was characterized by the real or symbolic rape of the bride who, hair cropped and dressed as a boy, waited in the dark to receive her new husband. Spartan attitudes to female chastity also differed from those of the Athenians. Many texts suggest a more flexible marriage bond and a more relaxed approach to extramarital sex and, while the production of Spartiate soldiers was of vital importance to the state, Spartan custom held that all sons belonged in common to fathers and vice versa. This unconcern with legitimacy was related perhaps to Sparta's inheritance and landowning patterns; until the late 5th century BC the state controlled the allocation of land and thus the male line was not important, a good indication of the way in which marriage and marital behaviour reflect upon other political and social institutions.

Hellenistic Egypt reveals new emphases on marriage as a union of two individuals and on the sexual fidelity of both partners; an Alexandrian marriage contract from 92 BC insists that the husband may have neither concubines nor catamites (Tebtunis papyrus 104). Furthermore, the image of the married couple became a significant feature of Hellenistic rule. Marital alliances among the elite were a traditional feature of Greek society, not only of the royal houses of Sparta and Macedonia but also of aristocratic Athenians, but Hellenistic queens acting as their husbands' consorts, such as Arsinoë the wife of Ptolemy II Philadelphus, took the principle a stage further. Arsinoë was also Ptolemy's sister, and such unions were a strategy for consolidating power within one family, following the Egyptian model. In Byzantium several imperial brides, although not born royal, exercised considerable political and religious influence through marriage and motherhood, often wielding most power as widows. Irene in the 8th century was regent for 5 years, while in the following century Theodora II was regent for 14 years, both women achieving and maintaining power by manipulating their positions as wives and mothers.

Marriage remained the central role for women throughout the Christian era in a Church that esteemed motherhood highly, assigning to Mary the epithet *Theotokos* (Mother of God) at the Council of Ephesus in AD 431. Christian teaching introduced several changes to the ancient concept of marriage and, while the husband retained his superiority as head of the household, Christian men and women were subject to a greater mutuality of rights and obligations. Ecclesiastical marriage services became the norm throughout the empire and by the

9th century civil ceremonies were no longer recognized as valid.

The Church, however, offered a radical new role for both men and women, that of religious celibacy. In his First Epistle to the Corinthians Paul declared that celibacy was the highest good (although for those who could not aspire to such goodness marriage was necessary to contain sexual desire). Before this innovation lifelong virginity and celibacy were not considered feasible options for either sex; now for the first time Hellenic society was presented with an alternative to marriage. Yet such a role had a narrow application. While some early Christian writers urged men not to marry (for example Jerome, *Against Jovinianus*, 47), unmarried girls in particular who wished to opt for celibacy met frequently with family opposition and in the 4th century John Chrysostom in a denunciation of enkratic (enforced) virgins insisted that "marriage is honoured by all and the marriage bed is free from stain" (*De Virginitate*, 8. 2). The situation was easier for widows, such as St Theodora of Thessalonica, whose decision not to remarry the Church supported since it viewed marriage as a life commitment. For those who could not avoid marriage there was always the compromise of a "spiritual marriage" (that is, a celibate marriage, sometimes entered into only after the birth of a child).

The later Church supported convents for unmarried girls, perhaps due to the growing influence of the cult of the Virgin which was strengthened by the decision of the Fifth Ecumenical Council of Constantinople in 553 to accord Mary the title *Aeiparthenos* (Ever-Virgin) and by the Marian devotion of influential women, for example the empress Sophia in the late 6th century. Yet this religious commitment was itself characterized as a form of marriage; just as the virgins of early Greece who met an early death wed Hades, so Christian virgins who chose celibacy over marriage wed Christ (Jerome, *Letter*, 22. 25).

While religious celibacy provided an alternative to marriage for a few, the Church continued to consider marriage and children the proper role for most men and women. Greek Orthodoxy maintains this tradition of honouring marriage (to the extent of allowing married clergy), regarding it as a state of grace conferred in the sacrament of Holy Matrimony. There are two steps in the Orthodox marriage service, once held separately but now successively. The Office of Betrothal, which recalls the *engue* of classical Athens, comprises the blessing and an exchange of rings signifying the mutual consent of bride and groom, a notable change from the ancient past when the consent of the bride was irrelevant. In the Office of Crowning the couple are crowned with leaves and flowers after which they drink wine from the same chalice in homage to the wedding feast at Cana, symbolizing their shared future life. While marriage is regarded by the Church as a life commitment, Orthodox canon law allows second and third marriages (although not a fourth).

Marriage and the family have retained their central role in Hellenic society and several continuities bridge past and present. Arranged marriages (*proxenia*) together with premarital dowry negotiations were common until very recently, especially in rural Greece, while the proportion of children born within marriage is the highest within the European Union. Yet there have been changes: according to the Athenian

Constitution (article 4, para. 2, 1975), Greek men and women now have the same obligations in life, while the Family Law Act (1983) not only abolished dowry and insisted that family matters should be decided jointly by husband and wife, but also declared that a woman no longer has to change her surname when she marries.

EUGÉNIE FERNANDES

See also Adultery, Celibacy, Children, Divorce, Dowry, Kinship, Men, Women

Further Reading

Brown, Peter, *The Body and Society: Men, Women, and Sexual Renunciation in Early Christianity*, New York: Columbia University Press, 1988; London: Faber, 1990

Burkert, Walter, *Greek Religion*, Oxford: Blackwell, and Cambridge, Massachusetts: Harvard University Press, 1985

Cameron, A., "The Cult of the Theotokos in Sixth-Century Constantinople", *Journal of Theological Studies*, 29 (1978): pp. 79–108

Campbell, J.K., "Traditional Values and Continuities in Greek Society" in *Greece in the 1980s*, edited by Richard Clogg, London: Macmillan, and New York: St Martin's Press, 1983

Carson, A., "Putting Her in Her Place: Woman, Dirt and Desire" in *Before Sexuality: The Construction of Erotic Experience in the Ancient World*, edited by David M. Halperin, John J. Winkler and Froma I. Zeitlin, Princeton, New Jersey: Princeton University Press, 1990

Erler, Mary and Maryanne Kowaleski (editors), *Women and Power in the Middle Ages*, Athens: University of Georgia Press, 1988

Goody, Jack, *The Development of the Family and Marriage in Europe*, Cambridge and New York: Cambridge University Press, 1983

Herlihy, David, *Medieval Households*, Cambridge, Massachusetts: Harvard University Press, 1985

Herrin, J., "In Search of Byzantine Women: Three Avenues of Approach" in *Images of Women in Antiquity*, edited by Averil Cameron and Amélie Kuhrt, London: Routledge, and Detroit: Wayne State University Press, 1993

McNeill, William H., *The Metamorphosis of Greece since World War II*, Chicago: University of Chicago Press, 1978

Meyendorff, John, *Marriage: An Orthodox Perspective*, Crestwood, New York: St Vladimir's Seminary Press, 1975; revised edition, 1984

Patterson C., "Marriage and the Married Woman in Athenian Law" in *Women's History and Ancient History*, edited by Sarah B. Pomeroy, Chapel Hill: University of North Carolina Press, 1991

Peristiany, J.G. (editor), *Mediterranean Family Structures*, Cambridge and New York: Cambridge University Press, 1976

Pomeroy, Sarah B., *Goddesses, Whores, Wives, and Slaves: Women in Classical Antiquity*, New York: Schocken, 1975; London: Hale, 1976

Pomeroy, Sarah B., *Women in Hellenistic Egypt: From Alexander to Cleopatra*, New York: Schocken, 1984; revised edition, Detroit: Wayne State University Press, 1990

Ranke-Heinemann, Uta, *Eunuchs for the Kingdom of Heaven: Women, Sexuality, and the Catholic Church*, New York: Doubleday, and London: Penguin, 1990

Redfield, J., "Notes on the Greek Wedding", *Arethusa*, 15/2 (1982): pp. 181–201

Reilly, J., "Many Brides: Mistress and Maid on Athenian Lekythoi", *Hesperia*, 58 (1989): pp. 411–44

Sanders, T., "Greek Society in Transition", *Balkan Studies*, 8 (1967): pp. 317–32

Sissa, Giulia, *Greek Virginity*, Cambridge, Massachusetts: Harvard University Press, 1990

Todd, S.C., *The Shape of Athenian Law*, Oxford: Clarendon Press, 1993

Ware, Timothy, *The Orthodox Church*, 2nd edition, London and New York: Penguin, 1993

Martyrdom

The Christian concept of martyrdom is derived from two sources: first, as witness to Christ's death and resurrection and thence to the truth of the Christian faith even to death; and secondly, from a belief in the honour of dying for a noble cause, which Christians shared with pagans and Jews in the Greek east.

Neither pagans nor Jews use the term "martyr" (which means "witness"). Both, however, record heroic deaths in causes which they believed to be righteous. Pagan heroism is represented best in the *Acta Alexandrinorum*. There was glory to be won in dying for one's native city, Alexandria (Heliodorus to the gymnasiarch Appian in *Acta Appiani*), as well as in the example of Socrates as he faced death, and other philosophers like him, such as those executed in the reign of Domitian (81–96). In Judaism from the 2nd century BC onwards Jews looked back on the history of their people as one of righteous suffering from the time of Abel to their own day (cf. 4 Maccabees 18. 1l–18). As Josephus wrote *c.*AD 95 (*Contra Apionem*, 1. 8), "For it becomes natural to all Jews immediately and from their very birth to esteem those books [of the Law] above all else to contain divine precepts, and to persist in them and if necessary die for them." Such thinking influenced Christians of the first three centuries profoundly. Blandina, the heroine of the martyrs of Lyons in 177, is compared directly to the heroic mother of the Maccabean martyrs from 2 Maccabees, and on the eve of the Great Persecution major churches in north Africa, such as Tigisis, included the books of the Maccabees in their libraries, and these were read and quoted (Secundus of Tigisis in 303 citing Eleazer as an example of courage from 2 Maccabees 6. 21–28, recorded by Augustine, *Brevis Collocatio cum Donatistis*, 3. 13. 25). The effect of the example of the Maccabees on the Christian concept of martyrdom cannot be overestimated.

The first occurrence of the term "martyr", however, is strictly as a witness to Christ's resurrection, and regarded as an essential qualification for admittance to the Twelve (Acts 1: 21–22). It was not long before witness involved danger of death, as Peter experienced when he was brought before the Sanhedrin (Acts 5: 32–33). A little later, Stephen, who had a vision of the Son of Man standing at the right hand of God before he was stoned (Acts 7: 56) was regarded by the martyrs of Lyons in 177 as "the perfect martyr" (Eusebius, *Historiae Ecclesiastica*, 5. 2. 5). By the time the Book of Revelation was compiled (*c.*AD 90), death on account of witness to the faith was being identified with "martyrdom" (Revelation 6:9–10). The souls "of them that were slain for the word of God and for the witness that they gave, lay beneath the altar". This provided the biblical justification for placing bones of martyrs or relics beneath church altars, particularly in Donatist north Africa.

The violent but sporadic persecutions of Christians during the 2nd century produced martyrs and also refined the concept of martyrdom. To be a Christian was now a crime for which punishment was death, though more often than not the authorities were more anxious to secure recantation and due acknowledgement of the Roman gods than to execute the recalcitrant. Though Ignatius of Antioch does not use the word "martyr" in 107, by 160 death during a persecution was regarded as martyrdom (Eusebius, 4. 23. 2). The account of the martyrdom of Polycarp of Smyrna (either in 156 or 166/67) combines refusal to give the slightest credence to the Genius of Caesar or other pagan deities (following the tradition of the Maccabees) with witness to the death on behalf of the teaching of Christianity and loyalty to its founder (Eusebius, 4. 15. 18–24). At the time of the persecution of the Christians of Lyons in 177, the accolade of martyrdom was being accorded to those who on arrest simply confessed their faith. This annoyed the confessors who survived. They reminded their hearers that martyrs "were those who had already passed away", and that only Christ was the "faithful and true martyr and first-born of the dead and author of the life with God". Despite their bravery and willing sacrifice they remained "humble confessors" (Eusebius, 5. 2. 2–3.).

For many Christians, however, at this period desire for martyrdom and its reward of heavenly salvation in glory was irresistible. Writing *c.*178 Celsus, the anti-Christian Platonist, described how some Christians "deliberately rush forward to arouse the wrath of an emperor or governor which brings upon us [i.e. the Christians] blows and tortures and even death" (Origen, *Contra Celsum*, 8. 65). Shortly afterwards, Christians in the province of Asia appeared before the proconsul and demanded to be put to death. They were told they had halters or precipices if that was what they wanted (Tertullian, *Ad Scapulam*, 5). Orthodox churchmen would refuse the title of martyr to such, whom they deemed exhibitionists (Polycarp, in *Martyrium Polycarpi*, 4. 1 and Clement of Alexandria, *Stromata*, 4. 17. 1, and for the early 4th century, Canon 60 of the Council of Elvira). Meanwhile, the Montanists of Phrygia continued the tradition of prophetic religion, leading to a climax in martyrdom (Eusebius, 5. 18. 5, 11).

The first officially sponsored and universal persecution under Decius in 250 resulted in both types of martyrdom. While the great majority of Christians appear to have obeyed the emperor's call to perform sacrifice for the safety of the empire in face of the Gothic invasions, some refused and went to their deaths. The account of the martyrdom of the presbyter Pionius from near Smyrna gives a graphic contemporary account of a Christian for whom arrest and death were everything. He was accompanied to martyrdom by a Marcionite dissident whose church also accepted martyrdom as in accord with Christ's teaching (*Martyrium Pionii*, 21. 5).

The persecution under Valerian in 257–59 explicitly condemned Christian clergy who persisted in their faith, first to exile, and then to death. Dionysius, bishop of Alexandria, was exiled to the oasis of Kephro in 257, but escaped death (Eusebius, 7. 11. 5). He was more fortunate than some of the Christian leaders, especially in the west, notably Cyprian of Carthage (martyred 14 September 258) and Pope Xystus and his four deacons, who were arrested in the catacomb of

Callistus and executed on the spot on 6 August 258 (Cyprian, *Letters*, 80. 1).

Valerian was captured by the Persians near Edessa in June 260. Persecution ended, and for the next 43 years the Church was practically unmolested. It flourished, and when in February 303 Diocletian and Maximian launched a final effort to destroy Christianity, the Church was strong in town and countryside alike in some major Mediterranean provinces. "No martyrs" had been Diocletian's intention (Lactantius, *De Mortibus Persecutorum*, 12) and during that year martyrdoms, except for those who provoked it, were few. "I am a Christian and I want to die for the name of Christ", Euplus was reported to have shouted at the surprised *corrector* (governor) of Sicily when he interrupted the progress of a meeting held in the latter's office at Catania. He had his wish, but he was exceptional at this stage.

The Fourth Edict of Persecution initiated by Diocletian's Caesar Galerius in the spring of 304 brought about a change of tempo. Now all were commanded to sacrifice. Christians such as Euplus, who were regarded as "enemies of the emperor", were joined by many others. Resistance was strongest among the Copts of Egypt and the north Africans. Eusebius' account of the martyrs of Palestine shows how the Egyptian Christians were the most prominent among those encouraging Christians to witness to their faith regardless of the risk of being sent for hard labour in the mines or of execution. In the last final spasm of persecution under the emperor Maximian (308[-13) in 311–12 Eusebius himself witnessed how Coptic Christians in Upper Egypt volunteered one after another for martyrdom, encouraging each other to face the headsman's axe or condemnation to the flames (8. 9. 4–5).

The triumph of Constantine ended martyrdom and persecution, except for brief flurries under Licinius in 319–24 and under Julian in 362–63. Undoubtedly in the Great Persecution the constancy of the martyrs drew many in the east towards Christianity (see Lactantius, *Divine Institutes*, 5. 23). Previously the effect had been less powerful; the Gallic provincials who had witnessed the deaths of the martyrs of Lyons could only wonder that they could forfeit their lives for the sake of a god that did not rescue them (Eusebius, 5. 1. 60), and Pionius was openly mocked as desperate attempts were made to save him from what the great majority of the provincials thought sheer folly (e.g. *Martyrium Pionii*, 20, 21).

Among the Donatist majority Church in north Africa the theology of martyrdom as the goal of a Christian life persisted through the 4th century (Augustine, *Contra Litteras Petiliani*, 2. 89, 196, written *c*.401). Elsewhere, actuality gave way to epic and commemoration. In the 4th and later centuries Christians looked back to the age of the martyrs as a golden age of Christian heroism that ultimately triumphed and secured the victory of the faith in east and west alike.

WILLIAM H.C. FREND

See also Neomartyrs

Further Reading

Barnes, T.D., "The Pre-Decian Acta Martyrum", *Journal of Theological Studies*, new series 19 (1968): pp.509–31

Bisbee, Gary A., *Pre-Decian Acts of Martyrs and Commentarii*, Philadelphia: Fortress Press, 1988

Bowersock, G.W., *Martyrdom and Rome*, Cambridge and New York: Cambridge University Press, 1995

Campenhausen, Hans von, *Die Idee des Martyriums in der alten Kirche*, 2nd edition, Gottingen: Vandenhoeck & Ruprecht, 1964

Delehaye, Hippolyte, *Les Passions des Martyrs et les genres littéraires*, Brussels: Bureau de la Société des Bollandistes, 1921

Delehaye, Hippolyte, *Les Légendes hagiographiques*, 4th edition, Brussels: Société des Bollandistes, 1955

Eusebius of Caesarea, *The Ecclesiastical History and The Martyrs of Palestine*, translated by H.J. Lawlor and J.E.L. Oulton, 2 vols, London: SPCK, 1954

Frend, W.H.C., *Martyrdom and Persecution in the Early Church: A Study of a Conflict from the Maccabees to Donatus*, Oxford, Blackwell, 1965; New York: New York University Press, 1967

Knopf, Rudolf, *Ausgewählte Märtyreracten*, Tübingen and Leipzig: Mohr, 1901, 4th edition edited by Gerhard Ruhbach, Tübingen, 1965

Lane Fox, Robin, *Pagans and Christians*, London: Viking, 1986; New York: Knopf, 1987

Lazzati, Giuseppe, *Gli sviluppi della litteratura sui martiri nei primi quattro secoli*, Turin: Società Editrice Internazionale, 1956

Musurillo, Herbert A., *The Acts of the Pagan Martyrs*, Oxford: Clarendon Press, 1954; reprinted New York: Arno Press, 1979

Musurillo, Herbert A., *The Acts of the Christian Martyrs*, Oxford: Clarendon Press, 1972

Rougé, Jean *et al.*, *Les Martyrs de Lyon (177)*, Paris: Centre National des Recherches Scientifiques, 1978

Wood, Diana (issue editor), "Martyrs and Martyrologies", *Studies in Church History*, 30 (1993)

Mary, Blessed Virgin

According to the gospels, the Jewish girl Mary, while still a virgin, conceived the child Jesus, whom Christians believe to be the Incarnation of the Son of God. Apart from the infancy narratives of the gospels of Matthew and Luke, Mary makes very few appearances in the gospel narrative, but she is present at the foot of the cross, and after the Resurrection she is mentioned together with the disciples in the upper room, and presumably present with them at the descent of the Holy Spirit at Pentecost. The apocryphal gospels show much less reticence: the so-called *Protevangelium of James* of the late 2nd century, in particular, gives an account of Mary's miraculous birth to her barren parents, Anna and Joachim; her presentation in the Temple, where she was brought up; and her betrothal to Joseph. Ancient legend associates Mary's later years with Ephesus, but according to the later (post 4th-century) accounts of her death (dormition, *koimesis*) she returned to Jerusalem to die, after which her body was assumed into heaven. These legends are important for the later liturgical celebrations of the Mother of God (*Theotokos*, as she is generally known in the Orthodox Church): the Nativity (8 September), the Presentation (25 November), the Meeting of the Lord (2 February; called in the West the Purification), the Annunciation (25 March), and the Dormition (15 August) are all counted among the Twelve Great Feasts of the Orthodox Church.

The dogmatic beliefs of the Byzantine Church about the Blessed Virgin are, however, largely independent of this legendary tradition. They can be summed up in three titles: Mother of God (*Theotokos*, literally: "one who gave birth to

Mary: icon of the Virgin and Child, 14th century, Byzantine Museum, Athens

God"), Ever-Virgin (*Aeiparthenos*), All-Holy (*Panagia*). The conciliar authority for these titles is indirect: they were all ascribed to Mary to safeguard Orthodox doctrine about her Son. The title *Theotokos*, formally defined at the Third Ecumenical Council (Ephesus, 431), is primarily intended to safeguard the doctrine of the true divinity of Christ. The titles *aeiparthenos* (used, and thus endorsed, by the Fifth Ecumenical Council of 553) and *panagia* (implicitly endorsed by the use of the epithet *achrantos*, "without stain", at the Seventh Ecumenical Council of 787) are corollaries of Mary's being *Theotokos*: her continuing virginity and her personal holiness are evidence of the worthiness of her from whom God assumed human nature.

The fact that beliefs about the Mother of God are summed up in titles ascribed to her corresponds closely to the fact that Orthodox Christians express their faith in the Mother of God primarily through devotion to her. Such devotion is very ancient, the earliest prayer to the Mother of God being found on a papyrus dating from the late 3rd or early 4th century: the prayer "Beneath your compassion", in which Mary is addressed by the title *Theotokos*. In succeeding centuries such devotion became all-pervading, taking both private and public forms, and expressed in particular through the veneration of

her icons. In an Orthodox church the icon in the iconostasis to the left of the Holy Doors is always an icon of the Mother of God. No Orthodox liturgical service takes place without invocation of the Mother of God: at the end of every litany Mary is invoked as "our all-holy, pure, most blessed and glorious Lady, Mother of God and Ever-Virgin Mary", and most sequences of *troparia* (short hymns) close with a *theotokion*, a brief *troparion* in honour of the Mother of God. The most famous liturgical poem in honour of the Mother of God is the *Akathist* hymn, probably from the 6th century, a kontakion which celebrates the Mother of God under her many titles, with the refrain "Hail [or Rejoice], Bride unwedded!" The imagery in which devotion to the Mother of God finds expression is drawn predominantly from the natural order and from the Old Testament: she is the perfect creature, she is everything that Israel in its expectation of the coming redeemer was meant to be; she is the "joy of all creation" and the "beauty of Jacob". As the one who made possible the Saviour's advent into the world, Mary is closely associated with her son's continuing work of salvation. She is hailed as the "New Eve", whose obedience counteracted the disobedience of the first Eve, and great faith is placed in her intercession and her care or protection (*episkepsis*). Early Byzantine sermons dwell on the power of her intercession and her protection of Christians, especially the people of Constantinople, who ascribed their successful resistance to sieges, especially the series of sieges from 626 to 718, to her care for the city. Invocation of her protection during sieges took the form of processions with her icon round the city walls, accompanied by the singing of litanies and hymns in her honour, especially the *Akathist*. The composition of one of the *prooimia* (introductory hymns) of the *Akathist*, "To thee, Champion and Commander" (*Tei Hypermachoi*), is credibly ascribed to the patriarch Sergios, under whose leadership the city resisted a siege in 626. Many other places in the Byzantine world claimed the protection of the Mother of God, notably the monastic communities located on the Holy Mountain of Athos.

Icons of the Mother of God take many forms. Apart from her appearance in icons of the various liturgical feasts associated with her, the different forms of her icons either celebrate one of her many titles, *Eleousa* ("compassionate"), *Nikopoios* ("victory-maker"), *Platytera* ("wider [than the heavens]"), or are named after the place where the icon was kept, such as Blachernitissa or Zoodochos Pege ("life-giving spring", after the miracle-working spring in Constantinople). Many such icons became the focus of pilgrimage, one of the most famous in the present-day Greek world being that on the island of Tinos.

ANDREW LOUTH

Summary

The gospels tell us little about the life of Mary, the mother of Jesus: she was a virgin at the time of her son's conception (and, in Orthodox and Catholic tradition, ever afterwards), she was present at the Crucifixion, and she was with the disciples after the Resurrection and at Pentecost. The apocryphal gospels provide more information and there are many legends. Her significance for Orthodox Christians may be summarized in her three titles: Mother of God, Ever-Virgin, All-Holy.

Further Reading

Du Manoir de Juaye, Hubert, *Maria: études sur la Sainte Vierge*, vol.
   1, Paris: Beauchesne, 1949
Graef, Hilda, *Mary: A History of Doctrine and Devotion*, vol. 1,
   London and New York: Sheed and Ward, 1963
Heiser, Lothar, *Maria in der Christus-verkündigung des orthodoxen
   Kirchenjahres*, Trier: Paulinus, 1981
Ledit, Joseph, *Marie dans la liturgie de Byzance*, Paris: Beauchesne,
   1976
O'Carroll, Michael, *Theotokos: A Theological Encyclopedia of the
   Blessed Virgin Mary*, revised edition, Wilmington, Delaware:
   Glazier, 1983

Massilia

City in southern France

The city of Massilia (modern Marseilles) was located to the east of the Rhône delta, at the end of a long inlet with its entrance facing the Mediterranean sea, in the territory of a Ligurian tribe, the Segobriges. Its position enabled it to participate in, and control, the trade in precious metals from the eastern coast of Spain and the tin route from Britain. The colony was founded by Phocaeans from Asia Minor *c*.600 BC after they were forced out of their homeland by the Persians. According to Pompeius Trogus, a Gaul of the Vocontii, the foundation legend for the city current in the 1st century BC related that the Greeks sailed up the inlet and there met a tribe of Ligurians led by their king, Nannus. After some negotiation it was agreed that Phocis (or Protis) would marry Gyptis, the daughter of the king, and that the couple would settle down in Ligurian territory.

The site was known to the Greeks before the establishment of a settlement there, since it had previously served as a trading post for both the Rhodians and the Etruscans on their journeys to and from Spain. At first the inhabitants of the new city were oriented towards the sea, engaging in fishing, trading along the Mediterranean coast, and piracy. Their new settlement served as a base for the trade in metals and as a staging post for Greek traders making the journey from their homeland, with stops at the Sicilian cities to the east, or Massilia, before reaching their final destination. Perhaps it was part of a strategy developed in conjunction with the Phocaeans of Rhegium, who controlled the Straits of Messina, to funnel trade along the northern routes in the Mediterranean in the heyday of Ionian commerce in the late 6th and early 5th centuries BC.

Massilia became very prosperous as a result of this trade. A variety of pottery from the early period has been found at the site, indicating far-reaching contacts with the Greek homeland. Massilia itself soon established colonies in Spain and on the Ligurian coast, including Emporium (Ampurias) and Nicaea (Nice). It also founded Alalia on Corsica *c*.565 BC, perhaps to allow the Phocaeans to avoid the trade route along the coast of north Africa controlled by the Phoenicians. As a result, Massilia soon became involved in struggles with Carthage and its Etruscan allies in the western Mediterranean, which continued throughout the 6th and 5th centuries; its new colony on Corsica was abandoned in 540 as a result.

Archaeological evidence from recent excavations presents an interesting sequence of pottery at Massilia. Initially, Ionian,

East Greek, and Corinthian ceramics were found on the site. This changes quite suddenly in the second quarter of the 6th century BC when Etruscan wares predominate. Soon after that they decline, and in the middle of the 6th century Attic imports take over, especially flourishing after 530. Earlier prestige gifts present at native inland sites consist of Rhodian bronzes, perhaps carried by an overland route through the Alps from Italy; Athenian pottery is not present. Suddenly in the second half of the 6th century wares from Attica appear in the interior. It seems that Athenian ceramics were passing through Massilia, then being transported upriver to sites in the hinterland. The city had begun to broaden its focus of trade, expanding its interests inland rather than concentrating all its commercial efforts on the sea.

In the second half of the 6th century BC Massilia itself developed a strong pottery industry, producing amphorae to transport local wine. In return for this local beverage and luxury goods from Greece, it received grain, amber, and tin. The growing trade up the Rhône valley influenced both the Hallstatt and La Tène cultures of the Celts. Ligurian and Iberian sites have produced much imported pottery from the late 6th century as well as providing evidence of Greek influence in other areas, such as fortifications, architecture and art, cultivation of the vine and olives, and perhaps even a law code.

Massilia was well known in antiquity for the stability of its oligarchic form of government with its council of 600 (*timouchi*), an additional minor council of 15 members, and three top magistrates, as well as a body of strict Ionian laws transplanted from its homeland (Strabo, 4. 1. 5). Aristotle wrote a work, the *Constitution of Massilia*, now lost, which outlined the structure of its government. Massilia retained the cults of its mother city, such as Artemis of Ephesus, Delphinian Apollo, Cybele, and Leucothea. In addition, it maintained a strong connection with its Greek homeland, as well as advertising the city's prosperity and success, by construction of the Treasury of the Massilians at Delphi. Its wealth is also evident from the attractive series of coins minted in the city.

Prosperity appears to have lessened in the 5th century BC as the result of the expansion of Carthaginian power in the Mediterranean (although this view may be altered by finds from recent excavations in the city), but it continued to develop its own products for export, such as wine and olives. The Hellenization of the hinterland was completed by the second third of the century, but the Phocaean role as a civilizing force lasted until at least the late 5th century.

By the 4th century BC trade once again flourished, particularly after the voyage of Pytheas, a Massilian astronomer and geographer, who sailed through the straits of Gibraltar, exploring the west coast of Africa and circumnavigating Great Britain, drawing on the nautical knowledge and geographical information contained in the 6th-century work, the *Periplous*.

In the Hellenistic period the Massilians sided with Rome against Carthage, increasing their territory with the Romans' help. Massilia and Rome had an early agreement, which later developed into an official alliance. Massilia was a loyal ally, providing information and ships to Rome in the Second Punic War (218–201 BC), and Rome in return allowed the city to maintain its control over the trade route to Spain. In 125, after aggressive action by local tribes, Massilia appealed to Rome for help, which led to the absorption of the area into the Roman sphere of influence and the formation of the first Gallic province of the Roman empire – Gallia Narbonensis. Little remains of the Greek settlement, the site of which is occupied by the modern city of Marseilles, but there is evidence of a theatre, port facilities, a Hellenistic aqueduct, fortification towers, and a Greek cemetery.

Massilia retained its independence until 49 BC, when it sided with Pompey against Julius Caesar. After Pompey's defeat, Caesar stripped the city of its fleet, and reduced its treasury and territory, but it retained a certain degree of autonomy due to its status as a *civitas foederata*. Its constitution remained in effect until the 1st century AD when it finally lost its independence to the expanding Roman empire. At that time Massilia's commercial and political power also declined, but it remained a centre of Greek culture and learning until the 6th century AD, ending only with the domination of the Franks.

KATHLEEN DONAHUE SHERWOOD

See also France

Summary

Massilia (modern Marseilles) was an important commercial power as a result of its role as an intermediary in the trade between the Iberians to the west, the Ligurians and other tribes on the coast, the Celts of the hinterland, and the Greeks of its homeland, not only monopolizing the trade in precious metals but also providing Greek products such as pottery and wine in return for grain and amber. Founded *c.*600 BC, it also played an important role in the Hellenization of Gaul and Spain. It remained a centre of Greek culture in the area until the end of the Roman empire.

Further Reading

Bats, M. *et al.* (editors), *Marseille grecque et la Gaule*, Lattes: ADAM, and Aix-en-Provence: Université de Provence, 1992

Boardman, John, *The Greeks Overseas: Their Early Colonies and Trade*, 4th edition, London and New York: Thames and Hudson, 1999

Clavel-Lévêque, Monique, *Marseille grecque: la dynamique d'un impérialism marchand*, Marseilles: Lafitte, 1977

Clerc, Michel, *Massalia: l'histoire de Marseille dans l'antiquité*, vols 1–2, Marseilles: Tacussel, 1927–29; reprinted Marseilles: Lafitte, 1971

Dunbabin, T.J., *The Western Greeks: The History of Sicily and South Italy from the Foundation of the Greek Colonies to 480 BC*, Oxford: Clarendon Press, 1968

Euzennat, M., "Ancient Marseille in the Light of Recent Excavations", *American Journal of Archaeology*, 84 (1980): pp. 133–40

Graham, A.J., "The Expansion of the Greek World" in *The Expansion of the Greek World: Eighth to Sixth Centuries BC*, edited by John Boardman and N.G.L. Hammond, Cambridge: Cambridge University Press, 1982 (*The Cambridge Ancient History*, vol. 3, part 3, 2nd edition)

Shefton, B.B., "Massalia and Colonization in the North-Western Mediterranean" in *The Archaeology of Greek Colonisation*, edited by Gocha R. Tsetskhladze and Franco De Angelis, Oxford: Oxford University Committee for Archaeology, 1994

Stillwell, Richard (editor), *The Princeton Encyclopedia of Classical Sites*, Princeton, New Jersey: Princeton University Press, 1976, pp. 557–88

Mathematics

Though mathematics is in some way the most typical, and is arguably the most enduring, of the achievements of the ancient Greeks, it was not originally their invention. The Greeks themselves believed that geometry had come to them from Egypt (e.g. Herodotus, 2. 109), and Aristotle (*Metaphysics*, 1. 1. 981b23) explained the origins of mathematics in Egypt by the fact that the Egyptian priests were a leisured class, who had time to spend on intellectual pursuits. It is also now known that the Babylonians had an impressive and ancient system of mathematics (though this is noticed hardly at all by ancient Greek sources). The fact, however, that mathematics (if mathematics is taken to mean techniques for manipulating figures and numbers, and expressing relationships between them) was not original to the Greeks does not detract from their achievement of devising the concept of mathematical proof and developing the idea of the mathematical system which takes as its starting point the simplest axioms possible and proceeds from there by a process of rigorous proof to the demonstration of quite complex propositions. The result was to transform mathematics from a subject which was practically useful (and which also might be quite interesting, but only as a by-product) to a discipline which provided a new (and more demanding) paradigm of knowledge, and could be regarded as culturally and intellectually, rather than practically, important. Indeed, there is a rich tradition of anecdotes decrying those who hoped to get practical advantage from the study of mathematics, exemplified by the story told of Euclid by Proclus, that when one of his pupils asked him what was the use of learning mathematics, he told a slave to give the pupil a small coin "since he must profit by what he learns".

Unfortunately, since the works of Euclid are the earliest complete mathematical treatises which survive, and since extant accounts of the work of earlier mathematicians have probably been restated in Euclidean form, the process by which the distinctive features of Greek mathematics developed remains speculative. Though there is some evidence of early work on arithmetic (or more properly number theory), it is only in geometry that the distinctively Greek axiomatization and systematization of mathematics can be seen to its fullest extent. Though there is a persistent tradition that the Pythagoreans were prominent in the early stages of Greek mathematics (the importance given to mathematics in Pythagorean philosophical system certainly seems to have influenced the direction Greek mathematics took) and despite the prominence of individual Pythagorean mathematicians such as Archytas, in general those to whom the earliest discoveries were credited (Thales of Miletus for example) were not Pythagoreans. The earliest mathematicians did not give proofs as rigorous as those demanded later; at any rate, some of the propositions credited to them can be proved only by means of techniques developed much later. Greek mathematicians often made a distinction between the discoverer of a proposition and the person who produced the proof. Hippocrates of Chios (working in the 2nd half of the 5th century BC) was said to have been the first to produce an *Elements*, a systematic arrangement of geometrical theorems in logical order.

In the 5th and 4th centuries BC geometry developed to the point where it became the kind of mathematics recognizable today. The tradition as reported in the sources is that at this period geometry was concerned largely with problems about constructing certain figures, three of which became especially famous.

The first, the duplication of the cube, is sometimes referred to as the Delian problem, from the story that it originated when an oracle told the people of Delos that they could avert a plague by doubling the size of Apollo's altar, which was cubical; when the mathematics of this proved beyond them, they consulted Plato, who set it as a problem to his students (the story is certainly apocryphal, since Hippocrates of Chios, well before the date of Plato's activity, had reduced the problem to one of finding two mean proportionals in continued proportion between two lines, one twice the length of the other). A number of attempted solutions of this problem have been preserved, including a remarkable one by the Pythagorean Archytas of Tarentum (early 4th century BC), perhaps the first attempt at three-dimensional geometry, involving the intersection of a cylinder, a right cone, and a torus.

The second problem was the squaring of the circle, that is to say the construction of a square having the same area as a given circle. Since a circle (like other curves) can coincide with a straight line only at certain points, and not over any finite distance, the problem of relating areas bounded by straight lines with those bounded by curves inevitably made it necessary for mathematicians to confront the difficulties of handling infinite divisibility and infinitesimal magnitudes (though Hippocrates of Chios' work on the quadrature of lunes – areas cut off by the intersection of two arcs of circles – which contains the oldest geometrical proof to have survived, may have been an attempt, ultimately unsuccessful, to solve it without involving infinitesimals). An allusion to this problem in Aristophanes' *Birds* (line 1005) suggests that it attracted the interest of a wider public. Antiphon, the Athenian Sophist (5th century BC), is said to have tried to find a solution by inscribing within a circle polygons with more and more sides in the hope that they would eventually coincide with the circle; Aristotle treated this approach with open contempt. In the 4th century Bryson used both inscribed and circumscribed polygons which, if it was not simply a more complex application of Antiphon's fallacious approach, may have been an attempt to arrive at a ratio between the two polygons which would represent the area of the circle; if so, it was an important step towards the solution eventually found by Eudoxus. Later mathematicians approached the problem through the use of higher curves.

The third problem, the trisection of any angle (which probably arose from attempts to construct polygons), was approached by the Sophist Hippias of Elis (5th century BC) through the use of the *quadratrix*, one of the first higher curves, the locus of the intersection of the radius of a circle moving through 90 degrees and a straight line at right angles to the original position of the radius moving from the circumference to the centre of the circle uniformly in the same time; it was also used in a solution to the problem of the squaring of the circle.

Theodorus of Cyrene (late 5th century) did important work on irrational numbers (a problem which was raised initially following the discovery that the relationship between the side and diagonal of a square was the ratio of 1 to the square root of 2, which cannot be expressed by a ratio between any combi-

nation of whole numbers), which was developed by his pupil Theaetetus (d. 369 BC) into a general theory of irrationals. At about the same time Eudoxus of Cnidus (first half of the 4th century BC) not only put forward a theory of proportion which would deal with both commensurable and incommensurable magnitudes, but also devised a strategy of proof (usually misleadingly referred to as the "method of exhaustion") which evaded the problem of indivisible magnitudes, and so opened the way to serious work on figures and solids bounded by curves.

The Hellenistic period, building on the work of the 4th century, was the most creative period of Greek mathematics. The geometry of the previous period was summarized and systematized in the first surviving Greek mathematical work, Euclid's *Elements*. Archimedes (d. 212/11 BC), perhaps the greatest of Greek mathematicians, did impressively innovative work on planes and solids bounded by curves, and extended mathematical methods to mechanics and hydrostatics, and Apollonius of Perge (late 3rd or early 2nd century BC) wrote a definitive work on the geometry of the parabola, the hyperbola, and the ellipse (referred to at this period as conic sections).

Though it was only in geometry that the distinctive Greek concept of formal proof was fully developed, other branches of mathematics were not neglected. Diophantus' *Arithmetica* dealt with problems in algebra, through worked examples and without proof, and Hero of Alexandria demonstrated that he could perform various complicated mathematical operations, including solving quadratic equations by a method quite close to the formula still used. Greek astronomers were familiar with some of the most important trigonometrical functions, and Ptolemy produced a table of chords which expresses the same relationships as a modern sine table.

Although there were no significant new developments in Greek mathematics, or in mathematics in general, until the development of algebra by the Arabs, the work of Italians in the later Middle Ages and the Renaissance (building on the achievement of Diophantus), and the invention of calculus in the 17th century, serious mathematical work continued. Pappus, in the 3rd or 4th century AD, composed a series of works, most of which still survive in a compilation called the *Synagoge* or *Collection*, which consists largely of commentary on and expansion of earlier work, with some new material (which may or may not be Pappus' own). It is not only an invaluable source for the history of Greek mathematics, but is also good evidence for the continuing vigour of the subject. From the 3rd to the 5th century AD the Neoplatonic school of philosophy (which stressed the metaphysical significance of mathematics, and the spiritual benefits to be gained from studying it) produced a number of commentaries on mathematical works which, though not original in themselves, preserve a great deal which might otherwise have been lost. In particular, Proclus (AD 412–85) wrote a commentary on the first book of Euclid's *Elements*, whose historical sections draw in part on a lost history of mathematics written by Eudemus in the 4th century BC; further information is contained in Proclus' commentaries on various dialogues of Plato. Later, in the 6th century AD, Eutocius produced a series of commentaries on the major works of Archimedes, revealing evidence of vigorous mathematical activity which would otherwise be lost. At about the same time, Anthemius of Tralles, one of the architects of

Justinian's Hagia Sophia, was a mathematician of some importance. A surviving fragment of one of his works, *On Burning-Mirrors*, reveals that it was not simply a discussion of an optical device, but a serious contribution to the study of conic sections. The importance of mathematics in the educational system in the Byzantine period is evident from a work attributed to Michael Psellos in the 11th century on arithmetic, music, geometry, and astronomy (though the degree of mathematical competence it shows is unimpressive), and a work by George Pachymeres (1242–1310) on the educational syllabus, which draws heavily on Euclid and Diophantus. A curious confirmation of the continuing fascination of the educated classes in the Byzantine period with mathematics is given by Anna Komnene (*Alexiad*, 9. 10) who records that Nikephoros Diogenes, imprisoned and blinded for plotting against the emperor Alexios (1081–1118), consoled himself by taking up the study of geometry, which he achieved by the use of diagrams whose lines were in relief, so that he could feel them with his fingers. During the Byzantine period many Greek mathematical works were translated into Arabic (and some indeed survive only in Arabic) and became the basis of the mathematics of the Islamic world. That the movement of ideas was not simply one way is shown by Planudes's exposition of the system of Arabic (or, as he more properly refers to them, Indian) numerals in the 13th century, and Isaac Argyros' use of Persian material in the 14th century.

RICHARD WALLACE

Further Reading

Fowler, D.H., *The Mathematics of Plato's Academy: A New Reconstruction*, Oxford: Clarendon Press, and New York: Oxford University Press, 1987

Heath, Sir Thomas Little, *Greek Mathematics and Science*, Cambridge: Cambridge University Press, 1921

Klein, Jacob, *Greek Mathematical Thought and the Origin of Algebra*, Cambridge, Massachusetts: MIT Press, 1968

Knorr, Wilbur Richard, *The Evolution of the Euclidean Elements: A Study of the Theory of Incommensurable Magnitudes and its Significance for Early Greek Geometry*, Dordrecht and Boston: Reidel, 1975

Lasserre, François, *The Birth of Mathematics in the Age of Plato*, Larchmont, New York: American Research Council, and London: Hutchinson, 1964

Szabó, Árpád, *The Beginnings of Greek Mathematics*, Dordrecht and Boston: Reidel, 1978

Mausolus

Ruler of Caria in the 4th century BC

In 392 BC Hecatomnus, father of Mausolus, was appointed one of several native satraps who ruled Asia Minor (Anatolia) for the Persian king in the early 4th century BC. Hecatomnus' initial assignments for the Great King were to crush Evagoras, rebel ruler of Cyprus, and to secure Caria against an expansionist Sparta, leader of the Greek states after the Peloponnesian War.

Mausolus became satrap *c*.377 BC amid a tangled confusion of Athenian, Spartan, Egyptian, Cyprian, Anatolian, and Persian politics, intrigues, rebellions, and wars. He played an important role in Graeco-Persian politics of his day. In the miscarried revolt of the western satraps (366–359 BC), though himself a rebel, he somehow retained his position and served Persia until his death in 353 BC. In 357–355 BC he supported the Greek rebels in the Social War that ended Athens' Second Confederacy. He at first ruled with his sister (who was also his wife) Artemisia; ruled alone from 353 to 351 BC. The couple had no children. The ancient sources for the career of Mausolus are his contemporaries Isocrates and Demosthenes, as well as Diodorus Siculus, Dionysius of Halicarnassus, and Arrian.

The King's Peace of 387/86 BC, imposed on the Greeks by King Artaxerxes II (404–358 BC), had placed Anatolia officially under the rule of Persia, a status that endured until the conquests of Alexander the Great in 334 BC. But Athens, temporarily disarmed, still sought to thwart Spartan expansion. Hence the Second Athenian League of 377, formed ostensibly for that purpose.

Mausolus' transfer of his capital from inland Mylasa to Halicarnassus soon after his accession was probably a response to this Athenian confederacy. The new capital gave Caria a prominent maritime base, accessible to Greek commercial and cultural influences. Mausolus now built a navy and constructed on the offshore islet of Zephyrion what has been called the first Hellenistic palace.

The revolt of the western satraps had no single cause. Even after Cyrus was defeated in 401 BC, Egypt still defied the Persian power successfully. In 372 BC Datames, satrap of Cappadocia, asserted his independence. Persia's failure immediately to crush him or the Egyptians raised the hopes of other satraps; some hoped to achieve success by forming alliances with Athens or with Sparta.

In 366 BC Mausolus and Autophradates, satrap of Sardis, were sent against Ariobarzanes, another rebellious satrap. Instead, they joined Agesilaus of Sparta (campaigning to undermine the King's Peace) in supporting Ariobarzanes, and Mausolus paid Agesilaus to supply him with mercenaries of his own. It was money that Mausolus had, in fact, collected as tribute on behalf of the king.

More disaffections from Persian rule occurred, peaking in 362 BC. Phrygia, Armenia, Lycia, Ionia, Lydia, Phoenicia, and Syria joined the revolt. Inexorably, by 359 BC, the Persians had reduced this alliance, but Mausolus was among the satraps who retained their status in defeat.

Athens' aggressiveness in an effort to regain old cleruchies created distrust among the members of its alliance and led to the Social War. Mausolus was aware of the resistant mood of Athens' island confederates in the face of what seemed to be Athens' quest for another empire. Indeed, according to Demosthenes in 351 BC, it was Mausolus who had incited Chios, Cos, and Rhodes to rebel and Athens' other allies to full revolt. Though Mausolus' intrigues and participation played a part, Athens had brought it on itself. In 355 BC Isocrates had delivered his speech *On the Peace*, urging the Athenians to dissolve their maritime league, and Athens conceded the independence of Cos, Chios, Rhodes, and Byzantium. Mausolus moved in with Carian garrisons and replaced their democratic governments with oligarchies.

To touch Athens was to be Hellenized. As Athens had long ago attached all of Attica to itself by *synoikismos* (political amalgamation of settlements), so Mausolus synoecized Halicarnassus, gathering the native communities into a single coastal city. This was his most significant legacy, as his tomb was his most lasting. During his own lifetime Mausolus supervised a design for his Mausoleum, possibly as a monument to the entire Hecatomnid dynasty. (Oddly, the word for it was originally *mnema* or *taphos* – "monument" or "tomb".) It was completed by his wife Artemisia, who was also buried there. The Mausoleum was a triumph of Hellenic architecture and sculpture, or more correctly of the Hellenic spirit. Its decoration was the achievement of the four greatest Greek sculptors of the time: Scopas, Leochares, Bryaxis, and Timotheus. It was designed by the architect Pytheus, who had already designed the Ionic temple of Athena at Priene; he was a revolutionary artist with a new vision of sculptural and architectural harmony.

Even with detailed descriptions of the tomb by Pliny the Elder and Vitruvius, much confusion exists. The Mausoleum, about 50 m tall and with a circumference of 150 m, occupied only a small section on an artificial terrace of 105 by 242 m, surrounded by a wall of white marble. On this podium (really the tomb chamber), whose 160,000 building blocks each weighed about 70 tons, were constructed three columned tiers surmounted by a pyramid of 24 steps, on top of which was Pytheus' colossal four-horse chariot of marble. Great stone lions "protected" the pyramid at its base. Each tier had a sculptural frieze and a group of intercolumnar statues in the round, all manifesting a different theme. The friezes depicted Amazons in battle, centaurs, and chariot races. The themes are common, but the chariot frieze might have depicted the actual games held by Artemisia at Mausolus' funeral. On the lowest tier the statues were life size; above, they were one-and-a-third times life size; and at the top they were one-and-two-thirds life size. The splendid portrait statues of Mausolus and Artemisia still survive. These statues, of the largest size, stood within the great sepulchre and not, as generally believed, in the apex chariot. They are now in the British Museum among the numerous sculptures found by excavators in 1857.

With its new conception of size and space and its colonnades with heroes walking among them, the Mausoleum had great influence over the grandest buildings of the Hellenistic age. Alexander the Great had buried his father in the customary modest Macedonian manner, but after seeing Halicarnassus and the gleaming white tomb of Mausolus in its centre, he built an immense tomb for his friend Hephaestion.

The Mausoleum was still standing in the 12th century. In 1495 the Hospitaller Knights of St John used its stones for their castle (still to be seen in the harbour of modern Bodrum). Today only Mausolus' theatre may be seen; nothing is left of the tomb or palace.

Mausolus' influence is remarkable. He promoted Greek culture – institutions, arts, and language – in southwestern Anatolia. The synoecism of Halicarnassus and the mingling of native Carians and Greek culture were precursors of the Persian–Greek integration credited to Alexander. With his Mausoleum, agora, temples, and theatre, Mausolus bridged the Classical and Hellenistic worlds, as the "last of the satraps and the first of the diadochs".

DANIEL C. SCAVONE

Biography

The son of Hecatomnus, Mausolus was ruler of Caria from 377 to 353 BC together with his sister (also his wife) Artemisia. With the title satrap, he ruled under Persian auspices. But by moving his capital from Mylasa to Halicarnassus he opened it to Greek cultural influences. Having incited Athens' allies to rebel, he annexed Cos, Chios, Rhodes, and Byzantium. He and Artemisia were buried in the monumental Mausoleum, one of the seven wonders of the ancient world.

Further Reading

Hornblower, Simon, *Mausolus*, Oxford: Clarendon Press, and New York: Oxford University Press, 1982 (best single work on Mausolus)

Jeppesen, Kristian, *The Maussolleion at Halicarnassus*, 2 vols, Copenhagen: Jutland Archaeological Society, 1981–86

Olmstead, A.T., *History of the Persian Empire: Achaemenid Period*, Chicago: University of Chicago Press, 1948

Romer, John and Elizabeth Romer, *The Seven Wonders of the World: A History of the Modern Imagination*, London: Michael O'Mara, and New York: Holt, 1995, chapter 4

Mavrokordatos family

The progress of the Mavrokordatos family in public office is inextricably linked with memorable events which had a lasting effect on the state of affairs of the Ottoman empire, of Romania, and of modern Greece. The origins of the family can be traced to the beginning of the 15th century, when members of the Mavro and Cordato families were united by marriage; they had fled Constantinople a few years before its fall and sought refuge in Chios, where they pursued commercial activities.

Alexander, the founder of the dynasty, was born in Constantinople of a Chiot father, Nicholas, whose fortunes were considerably improved by his marriage to Roxandra Scarlatou; she belonged to the Phanariot circle of the capital, composed of surviving members of the Byzantine aristocracy. Towards the middle of the 17th century Alexander was sent to Rome, where he graduated from the Collegio Greco of St Athanasius; subsequently he followed courses in medicine and philosophy at the universities of Bologna and Padua, from which he graduated by submitting a thesis on the circulation of the blood. Upon his return to Constantinople he became director of the patriarchal academy, where he taught medicine and Classical philosophy while taking lessons in oriental languages. In 1673 he was appointed to the post of the Grand Dragoman (chief interpreter) in the Sultan's Divan (council). In this capacity he was instrumental in drawing up the Treaty of Karlowitz in 1699, through which he did not neglect to safeguard the sultan's suzerainty over the Holy Land, thus securing the administration of the holy sites to the Orthodox Christians. The sultan had conferred on him the title of *muharrir esrar*, that is, keeper of secrets, from which is derived his appellation *Ex Aporreton* (Exaporite). He translated into Turkish his treatise on the circulation of the blood, Mercator's *Atlas*, and Blaeu's *Theatrum Mundi*, a cartographic work in 12 volumes. Among his works written in Greek, the *Phrontismata* stand out as an original collection of dicta and moral reflections on the art of governing and good living.

Alexander's son Nicholas (1680–1730), although he was appointed dragoman (interpreter) in 1698, and was the first in the long dynasty of Phanariots to occupy the thrones of Moldavia and Wallachia by becoming *hospodar* (prince) of Moldavia in 1709, was happier in his scholarly activities than in his political functions. He reopened the Academy of Jassy in 1714 and he attracted a number of literati to his court in Bucharest, among whom we may distinguish Antoine Epis, Nicholas Wolff, Stefan Bergler, George Chrysogonos, and Demetrios Prokopiou Pamperis. He corresponded with Chrysanthos Notaras, Jean Le Clerc, the archbishop William Wake, and Johannes Fabricius. He was an accomplished polyglot, with a firm command of several oriental, European, and classical languages. He was the author of *Philotheou Parerga*, now viewed as the first modern Greek novel staged in Constantinople at the time of the Enlightenment, and of a philosophical work, *Peri Kathikonton*, which blends the old Stoic teaching on duties with the sophiological genre of the mirror of princes, the whole recast in the Orthodox patristic tradition.

It seems that this exhortative work found a responsive recipient in the person of Nicholas's son Constantine who, following his studies in Italy, succeeded his father in 1730, and ruled wisely by applying realistic policies in the government of the principalities. Although he occupied the throne intermittently until 1769, his reign was marked by significant reforms which improved the living conditions of the peasants. Serfdom was abolished in his domains a century earlier than in Russia; he founded schools and helped poor children to complete their studies; he alleviated the burden of taxation; and he bestowed on the principalities a minor constitution which he named *Reforma*.

Alexander, the last influential representative of the family, was born in 1791 in Constantinople. After studies in Italy he was employed as secretary by his uncle Ioannis Karadjas, *hospodar* of Wallachia. Soon he was promoted to the presidency of the ministerial cabinet. When his uncle fell from the sultan's favour, he followed him in his escape to Russia and Italy. The English philhellenes met him in Pisa and were at once inspired by the idealistic love of freedom which emanated from his forceful personality. In 1821 Shelley dedicated his drama *Hellas* "to His Excellency Prince Alexander Mavrocordato, late Secretary for foreign affairs to the Hospodar of Wallachia", and two years later Byron, in a letter to John Cam Hobhouse written from Cephalonia, referred to him as "the only civilised person amongst the liberators". In another letter he likened him to Washington and Kosciusko. By that time Alexander had assumed a position of leadership in the War of Independence. He was president of the first Greek national assembly at Epidaurus. Although he was defeated in the battle of Peta, the common-sense diplomacy that he displayed later in Missolonghi and his call to unity to the divided parties of the Greeks earned him the respect of the various warring factions. Nevertheless, his Anglophile stand and his being perceived as a newcomer from abroad did not help in healing the persisting divisions among the army, accentuated by the Russophile party headed by the popular warlord Kolokotronis and the rival Phanariot Dimitrios Ypsilantis. When Greece gained its independence, Alexander was given a minor post in the government of Ioannis Kapodistria, from which he resigned in 1828.

He played a more prominent role under King Otho when he was appointed successively minister of finance, and in 1833 premier; in 1834 he was sent as Greek envoy to Munich, Berlin, and London. He became premier again in 1841, and strongly advised Otho on the necessity of constitutional liberties; shortly thereafter he was dispatched to Constantinople as ambassador. He returned to Athens in 1844 and participated in the deliberations for the establishment of the constitution. He was elected the first constitutional prime minister of Greece, but he was toppled by his old rival Kolettis in 1850, and took up the post of ambassador to Paris. Upon his return to Greece in 1853 he withdrew to his magnificent estate in Aegina, where he died in 1865.

This remarkable family exerted lasting influence in the political, legal, and cultural spheres of the countries in which they operated. With their translations of books and the introduction of new ideas from Europe into the Ottoman empire, they precipitated the flowering of the Ottoman renaissance known as the Tulip Era, which spread in a different fashion to Romania and Greece.

LAMBROS KAMPERIDIS

See also Phanariots

Further Reading

Bouchard, J., "Les Relations épistolaires de Nicolas Mavrocordatos avec Jean Le Clerc et William Wake", *O Eranistis*, 11 (1974): pp. 62–92

Camariano, Nestor, *Alexandre Mavrocordato, Le Grand Drogman: son activité diplomatique (1673–1709)*, Thessalonica: Institute for Balkan Studies, 1970

Camariano-Cioran, Ariadna, *Les Académies princières de Bucarest et de Jassy et leurs professeurs*, Thessalonica: Institute for Balkan Studies, 1974

Henderson, G.P., *The Revival of Greek Thought, 1620–1830*, Albany: State University of New York Press, 1970; Edinburgh: Scottish Academic Press, 1971

Kamperidis, Lambros, "The Notion of Millet in Mavrokordatos' *Philotheou Parerga* and his Perception of the Enlightened Ottoman Despot", *Journal of the Hellenic Diaspora*, 18 (1992): pp. 67–78

Kamperidis, Lambros, "I Sophiologiki Paradosi kai to Peri Kathikonton tou Nikolaou Mavrokordatou" [The Scholarly Tradition and Nicholas Mavrokordatos's "On Duties"], *Palimpsiston*, 14/15 (1995): pp. 37–52

Legrand, E., *Généalogie des Mavrocordato de Constantinople rédigée d'après les documents inédits*, Paris: Maisonneuve, 1900

Mavrocordatos, Nicolas, *Les Loisirs de Philothée*, translated and edited by J. Bouchard, Athens and Montreal, 1989

Runciman, Steven, *The Great Church in Captivity: A Study of the Patriarchate of Constantinople from the Eve of the Turkish Conquest to the Greek War of Independence*, London: Cambridge University Press, 1968

Mavromichalis family

Prominent Maniot family

In the last century of Ottoman rule in Greece the strongest, most numerous, and wealthiest of the clans in the Mani (or "Maina") was the Mavromichalis family. Their hereditary stronghold was the fortress of Tsimova (modern Areopolis), which commanded the only pass through the Taygetus mountains from the Eurotas valley to the port of Gytheion. Theodore Kolokotronis, who had fought alongside the head of the clan, Petrobey Mavromichalis, in the capture of Kalamata in 1821, the first military success against the Ottomans, wrote in his *Memoirs* that the Mavromichali "had poured out much of its blood in the cause of our independence, but it was a family that always had a propensity to commit assassinations".

The Mani, where the Mavromichali established dominance in the course of the 18th century, comprises the last 50 km of the Taygetus range, stretching south to Cape Matapan and, until modern roads were built, outsiders found it virtually inaccessible, which made it a secure refuge against a succession of invaders, whether they were barbarians, the Frankish Villehardouin princes of Achaea, or the Turks. It contained more than a hundred villages with numerous fortified towers of refuge, many of which still survive as mute evidence of feuds among the various leading families, or Nyklians, as they were called locally. The Mavromichali, who according to one tradition had been a Thracian family named Gregorianos that fled from their homeland shortly after the Turks crossed into Europe in 1340, were settled in the Mani certainly by the 16th century and had become the leading Nyklian family before the War of Independence. The Maniots were noted fighters, who claimed descent from the ancient Spartans; their little pirate ships preyed on Turkish and Venetian vessels in the waters south of the Peloponnese, and their interfamily feuds were notorious, though sometimes groups of them would export their skills as warriors by serving as mercenaries in the army of the doge of Venice. But they would unite to repel attacks by the Turks, who in the end left them alone under a Maniot prince designated a "Bey". The first of these, Liberakis Yerakaris, appointed in the middle of the 17th century, proved too enterprising for Ottoman taste and the office lapsed until after the Orloff revolt (1770–74), which the Mani supported. After the revolt collapsed, the Turks revived the office, and the eighth and last of the Beys of the Mani was Petros Mavromichalis, better known as Petrobey.

Petrobey joined the *Philiki Hetaireia* (Friendly Society) in August 1818, evidently under the impression that its leader was Ioannis Kapodistria, who was a secretary of state to the Russian Tsar, Alexander I, and in 1820 he sent an emissary, Kyriakos Kamarinos, to St Petersburg with letters for Kapodistria. The letters have not survived, but we can guess their content from Kapodistria's cautious reply, which granted Petrobey funding for an elementary school in Sparta, but was at pains to deny support for a revolt or any personal connection with the *Philiki Hetaireia*. However, even though Kapodistria distanced himself from the *Philiki Hetaireia*, he did not betray its plans, and on 6 March 1821 the society launched an abortive invasion under Alexander Ypsilantis into Moldavia. Revolt in the Peloponnese began a month later. Petrobey with a following of 2000 Maniots as well as a number of klephts, including two famous ones whom Petrobey was protecting from the Ottoman authorities, Kolokotronis and Anagnostaras, took the field and attacked Kalamata which held a Turkish garrison. It surrendered on 4 April; on the next day 24 priests held a service of thanksgiving for the victory beside the stream that flowed through Kalamata, with 5000 armed men attending, and a few days after this historic celebration Petrobey addressed a declaration to all Christian nations, signed "Petrobey Mavromichalis, Prince and Commander in Chief", in which he proclaimed the determination of the Greeks to free themselves from Ottoman rule and asked all Christendom to aid their fellow Christians.

Petrobey became the nominal commander-in-chief in the Peloponnese, but could exercise little real authority. But he did fight in battle after battle, and, as Kolokotronis noted, the Mavromichali suffered heavy losses: 49 members of the family lost their lives. Petrobey's eldest son, Elias, died in Euboea in 1822: he and his uncle Kyriakules had taken a force of 600 Maniots to lay siege to Carystus, but the Turkish troops were under the command of an energetic officer, Omer Bey, and Elias lost his life in a skirmish. Kyriakules was to die later the same year in a defeat at Splanga in Epirus, and his body was taken to Missolonghi for burial.

When Lord Byron arrived at Cephalonia on his way to Greece in 1823, among the communications from various Greek commanders soliciting his aid was a blunt letter from Petrobey. He wrote that the true way to free Greece was for Byron to lend him £1000 with which he would raise a force of 3000 Spartans and overthrow the Ottomans. In the summer of 1826 Ibrahim Pasha, whose campaign of that year laid waste great areas of the Peloponnese, attempted twice to penetrate the Mani, but on both occasions he was repelled, and Ibrahim lacked the resources to push home an attack. Nonetheless the Mani suffered substantial losses, and Petrobey felt he had a legitimate case for recompense from the Greek government. His demands, however, were rejected by Kapodistria.

Kapodistria, who was elected president for seven years by the National Assembly which met at Troezen on 14 April 1827, aimed at a centralized administration that rode roughshod over Maniot traditions of independence. The Mavromichali had two grievances: one was inadequate compensation for losses in the war, and the other was Kapodistria's claim to collect taxes in the Mani, which the Maniots had never conceded to the Turks. In December 1830 they rebelled. Petrobey was residing in Nauplia, for he was a senator and *proboulos* (chairman) of one of the three sections of the senate (*Panhellenion*), and Kapodistria insisted that he write a firm letter to his people denouncing the uprising. However Petrobey slipped away from Nauplia secretly, hoping to return to the Mani, but in Katakolo he was arrested, brought back to Nauplia, and incarcerated. His son George and his brother Constantine were also brought to Nauplia and put under surveillance. Kapodistria refused any reconciliation; a meeting between himself and Petrobey was arranged for 8 October, but Kapodistria cancelled it, which Petrobey took as a slight to his honour. On Sunday 9 October, as Kapodistria was about to enter the church of St Spyridon in Nauplia for the Liturgy, he was assassinated by George and Constantine. Constantine was mortally wounded by one of Kapodistria's companions whom Kolokotronis identified as a one-armed Cretan, and George was caught, tried, and put to death. In the general anarchy following Kapodistria's death, the Mavromichali tried to make good their claim to collect the taxes in Messenia but their attempts to gain control of the rich Messenian plain were unsuccessful.

The government of the young king Otho scored no military successes in the Mani, but the Maniots made peace with the royal government, for which the Mavromichali can take some credit. Schools were built, family feuding was suppressed, and local elected government was introduced. The Mani itself was divided between the nomes of Kalamata and Laconia. Petrobey became an honoured member of the government of King Otho, though he was overshadowed by other politicians, and he died a respected statesman in 1848. The Mavromichalis family have remained prominent in Greek politics and, as befits the descendants of the Spartans, royalist sentiment has remained strong in the Mani.

JAMES ALLAN EVANS

See also Independence (War of), Mani

Further Reading

Fermor, Patrick Leigh, *Mani: Travels in the Southern Peloponnese*, London: John Murray, and New York: Harper and Row, 1958, reprinted London: John Murray, 1984

Finlay, George, *History of the Greek Revolution and the Reign of King Otho*, London: Zeno, 1971 (reprint of vols 6 and 7 of Finlay's *A History of Greece from its Conquest by the Romans to the Present Time, BC 146 to AD 1864*, Oxford, Clarendon Press, 1877, reprinted New York: AMS Press, 1970)

Kaldis, William Peter, *John Capodistrias and the Modern Greek State*, Madison: State Historical Society of Wisconsin, 1963

Kokkinakis, Dimitrios N., *Poio skotosan ton Kapodistria?* [Who Killed Kapodistria?], Athens, 1998 (suggests that Kapodistria was not shot by members of the Mavromichalis family)

Kolokotronis, T., *Memoirs from the Greek War of Independence, 1821–1833*, translated by G. Tertzetis, Chicago: Argonaut, 1969

Woodhouse, C. M., *Capodistria: The Founder of Greek Independence*, London and New York: Oxford University Press, 1973

Maximos the Confessor, St 580–662

Monk and theologian

Maximos was probably born in Constantinople, where he was educated. With the accession of Herakleios in 608 he became his *protasecretis* (head of the imperial chancellery), but he resigned after only a few years in this position, and became a monk, first at Chrysopolis, later at Cyzicus. He fled from there in 626, before the advancing Persian army, and by 630 had settled in a Greek-speaking monastery in north Africa, where he was to remain for the next 15 years. In 633 his spiritual mentor Sophronios, soon to become patriarch of Jerusalem, protested vigorously against the imperial policy of Monenergism, the doctrine that in Christ the two divine and human natures were united in a single person and single theandric activity, by which the emperor Herakleios hoped to reconcile the Christians in the eastern part of the empire. Maximos, however, did not come out publicly against such Christological compromise until the promulgation of the *Ekthesis* in 638, which endorsed Monothelitism (the doctrine that Christ had a single will) as imperial orthodoxy. His opposition to this policy led him to Rome, where he seems to have been the inspiration behind the Lateran Council of 649, which condemned both Monenergism and Monothelitism. Pope Martin I and Maximos were both eventually arrested for their opposition to

imperial policy. Maximos was tried in Constantinople in 655, condemned, and exiled to Thrace, where attempts were made to break his will. Tried again in 662, he was found guilty of heresy, had his tongue and right hand cut off, and exiled to Lazica, in present-day Georgia, where he died on 13 August. His relics were preserved there, and a local cult developed, but although in the empire the orthodox doctrine of Christ, for which he had given up his life, was vindicated at the Sixth Ecumenical Council in 680–81, no mention was made of either Maximos or Martin I. By the 9th century many of his writings were known and read in Constantinople; Photios, who found him "unclear and difficult to interpret", discusses many of them. In the 11th century Maximos's writings were the favourite reading of Irene, Anna Komnene's mother, to the amazement of her daughter. Maximos was valued by the hesychasts, and more space is devoted to his writings (mostly in select excerpts) than to any other writer in the 18th-century hesychast anthology, the *Philokalia*. He is perhaps the most highly revered of the Fathers among modern Orthodox theologians.

In his writings there is to be found a profound synthesis of the spiritual, dogmatic, and philosophical strands that are interwoven in Byzantine theology. There is, however, nothing systematic about the way that Maximos presents his theology, which is nearly all occasional in form, or put together for the purpose of monastic catechesis. Several works take the monastic form of the century, a collection of 100 paragraphs concerned with ascetical or theological matters, arranged for meditation. The form was popularized (or even invented) by Evagrius, the Origenist theorist of the wisdom of the Desert Fathers, and Maximos's two sets of centuries, *Four Centuries on Love* and *Two Centuries on Theology and the Incarnate Dispensation*, both seem to be conceived as Maximian reworkings and corrections of themes drawn from Evagrius and Origen respectively. Origenism, despite its condemnation at the Fifth Ecumenical Council (553), was still, as is evident from Maximos's writings, a serious problem in Byzantine monasticism, and much of his writing is concerned with countering it. His most famous work, the so-called *Ambigua* ("Difficulties", since they are all concerned with difficult passages in the writings of, almost exclusively, St Gregory of Nazianzus, "the Theologian"), has been called "a refutation of Origenism ... with a full understanding and will to retain what is good in the Alexandrian's doctrine, a refutation perhaps unique in Greek patristic literature" (Sherwood, 1952, p. 3). The *Ambigua*, and his other great work, his *Questions to Thalassius*, both take the form of questions and answers (*erotapokriseis*), the former in reply to questions from a certain Thomas and John, bishop of Cyzicus (the *Ambigua* is really two separate works), and the latter to questions from Thalassius, an abbot in Libya. In the early 640s Maximos was engaged in the Monothelite controversy, and composed many brief works (opuscula) in defence of orthodox doctrine. Despite the informal character of his writings, they express a coherent vision of the created order, ordained for union with God, which was to be articulated and achieved by the human person, created in the image of God, who constitutes the focus and bond of the cosmos. This has been thwarted by human refusal to fulfil the designated role, which entailed cosmic catastrophe and which can be restored only by the Incarnation of the person of God himself. The

Incarnation, revelation, the sacraments, and ascetic struggle are all interlocking parts of the restoration of the original harmony of the cosmos. Maximos's defence of Christological orthodoxy was inspired by his conviction, grounded in this cosmic vision, that in redeeming humanity God would not disregard the integrity of the natural order, something entailed by his assumption of an imperfect human nature, as Monothelitism proposed.

The case of Maximos poses in an acute form the question as to whether Byzantine Orthodoxy is Hellenic or Christian. At his trial he was asked: "Why do you love the Romans and hate the Greeks?" To which Maximos replied, "We have a precept, not to hate anyone: I love the Romans as sharing the same faith, and the Greeks as sharing the same language." Maximos valued his Greek cultural heritage, but it was his faith, which he at that time shared with the pope, for which he was willing to sacrifice his life. One who was perhaps the greatest of Byzantine theologians was bitterly opposed by the theologians of Byzantium, and found his Byzantine identity in faithfulness to the Christian tradition.

Maximos's popularity in modern Orthodox (not least Greek Orthodox) theology is based on his cosmic vision, which is seen to undergird modern ecological concerns, but perhaps even more on the profundity of his metaphysical reflection, especially on the notion of the person.

ANDREW LOUTH

Biography

Born in 580, probably in Constantinople, Maximos was educated there and became *protasecretis* (head of the chancellery) to the emperor Herakleios in 610. But he soon became a monk and by 630 was a member of a monastery in north Africa under the spiritual guidance of Sophronios. He attacked Monothelitism and went to Rome to support Pope Martin I. Accused of treason, he was exiled first in 655 to Thrace and then in 662 to Georgia, where he died the same year.

Writings

Patrologia Graeca, edited by J.-P. Migne, vols 90–91

In *Corpus Christianorum: Series Graeca*, Turnhout: Brepols, 1980–, vols 7, 10, 22, 23

Selected Writings, translated by George C. Berthold, London: SPCK, and New York: Paulist Press, 1985

Further Reading

Balthasar, Hans Urs von, *Kosmische Liturgie: Das Weltbild Maximus' des Bekenners*, 2nd revised edition, Einsiedeln: Johannes, 1961

Blowers, Paul M., *Exegesis and Spiritual Pedagogy in Maximus the Confessor: An Investigation of the Quaestiones ad Thalassium*, Notre Dame, Indiana: University of Notre Dame Press, 1991

Larchet, Jean-Claude, *La Divinisation de l'homme selon Saint Maxime le Confesseur*, Paris: Cerf, 1996

Loudovikos, Nikolaos, *I Evcharistiaki Ontologia* [Eucharistic Ontology], Athens, 1992

Louth, Andrew, *Maximus the Confessor*, London and New York: Routledge, 1996 (includes translations)

Matsoukas, Nikos, *Kosmos, Anthropos, Koinonia kata ton Maximo Omologiti* [Cosmos, Man, and Communion in the Works of Maximos the Confessor], Athens, 1980

Sherwood, Polycarp, *An Annotated Date-List of the Works of Maximus the Confessor*, Rome: Orbis Catholicus, 1952

Sherwood, Polycarp, *The Earlier Ambigua of Saint Maximus the Confessor and his Refutation of Origenism*, Rome: Orbis Catholicus, 1955

Thunberg, Lars, *Microcosm and Mediator: The Theological Anthropology of Maximus the Confessor*, 2nd edition, Chicago: Open Court, 1995

Maximos the Greek, St *c.*1470–1556

Scholar known as the Enlightener of the Russians

Maximos the Greek, also known as Maximos Vatopedinos and in Russian as Maksim Grek, was an eminent patristic scholar of the 16th century and a highly learned educator and enlightener of Russia. He was born in Arta (Epirus) *c.*1470 into a wealthy family of Laconian origin. His father was Manuel Trivolis, his mother was called Irene, and Maximos' secular name was Michael.

The young Maximos left Arta to complete his studies, initially in Corfu and later in Italy. In the main Renaissance educational centres – Padua, Venice, and Florence (*c.*1492–95) – Maximos made connections with the leading representatives of Italian humanism, Angelo Poliziano, Marsilio Ficino, Aldus Manutius, and Gianfrancesco Pico della Mirandola. A very decisive influence on his thought was the Dominican preacher Girolamo Savonarola (1452–98), so much so that Maximos entered the Dominican order in 1502. Maximos also studied under the distinguished Greeks Janus Laskaris, Laonikos Chalkokondylis, and Constantine Laskaris and was employed as a copyist and corrector in the publishing house of Aldus Manutius.

After leaving Italy and the Dominican order, Maximos returned to Greece around 1506 and went to the monastery of Vatopedi on Mount Athos, which perhaps he chose for its opulent library, to take monastic vows. Because of his intellectual abilities, the monastery of Vatopedi sent him on missions to Macedonia and the Aegean islands. His philological knowledge was complemented on Mount Athos by his intensive occupation with the Church Fathers. In 1516, after ten years as a monk, at the request of the ruler of Russia, Vasiliy III, Maximos was sent to Russia to translate biblical and patristic texts into the Old Church Slavonic language. On his way there, Maximos met the patriarch in Constantinople and heard of the latter's plans for Russia.

Russian sources do not explain clearly why Maximos was sent to Russia, though they state that he went there to seek contributions for his monastery. This is endorsed by his subsequent adversary, Bishop Daniil, who said that Maximos went "to beg for alms", because he asked Vasiliy not to forget the penury of the Holy Monastery of Vatopedi. Moreover, the abbot of Vatopedi, Anthimos, writing to bishop Varlaam, expressed the hope that because of the services offered by Maximos the subsidies of the Great Ruler would increase. Notwithstanding the confusion caused by the accusations of Bishop Daniil, it is certain that Maximos's move to and stay in Russia were at the written request of Vasiliy, who asked for a translator of books.

Maximos departed from Athos, accompanied by the Greek monk Neophytos and the Bulgarian monk Lavrentii. He arrived in Moscow in 1518 and was received with honour by Vasiliy and bishop Varlaam. He immediately started translating the Psalter with the help of the Russians Dmitri Gerasimov and Vlasii. The whole project was complex, since Maximos had to translate from Greek into Latin and then his colleagues translated into Old Church Slavonic. This procedure, which was followed for other books too, understandably led to some mistakes in translation, for which Maximos later paid a high price. After all, the translation of the Psalter was directed against the special interpretation of the book by the sect of the Judaizers and was deemed very important.

Illiteracy was prevalent in Russia at the time. As prince Andreas Rourbski, a student of Maximos and a first-rate scholar of the 16th century, wrote, Russians languished from spiritual hunger. Ritualism, Pharisaism in religious worship, combined with occultism and astrology, also flourished. Against this backdrop Maximos with great devotion continued to translate various biblical and patristic books as well as to correct the liturgical books, which were full of errors. Thus he strove to educate the Russians by writing and preaching. In a publication of Maximos's works in Old Church Slavonic by the Academy of Razan in 1859, it is written that "in a difficult period, this eminent scholar came from Greece. Orthodox Greece through him offered help in time of need for our Church ... He followed carefully everything that happened at the time and gave his opinion on every special event in his sagacious speeches. He protected the Russian Church from the claims of the Church of Rome. He wrote against the rationalistic teachings of the Reformation, against the Jews, the pagans and the Muslims."

Yet several of his contemporaries could not appreciate his merits, despite the fact that Maximos now commanded great authority in Russia and had obtained imperial patronage. Aside from the difficulties with the translation work, Maximos attempted a new interpretation of the *Nomokanon* and praised the cenobitic style of Athonite monasticism, while criticizing Russian monasteries for their landholdings and the Church for the accumulation of wealth. This criticism of the lifestyle of the Russian clergy caused rancour among a group of clerics and monks, under the leadership of bishop Daniil of Moscow, a student of the influential monk Joseph of Volokolamsk. Maximos had also openly supported the group of "non-possessor" monks under Vassian Patrikeev. Bishop Daniil then deliberately asked Maximos to translate Theodoret's *Religious History*, which favoured Daniil's convictions about monastic property. Since this book also contained epistles by various heretic leaders, Maximos did not accept the assignment, a fact which increased Daniil's antipathy. Furthermore, Maximos objected to the divorce and second marriage of the ruler, for which he was accused of collaborating with the ruler's enemies, the boyars. All these things earned him considerable enmity in princely and ecclesiastical circles alike.

It is no wonder then that Maximos was denounced as a heretic (for changes to the liturgical books) and a danger to the security of the country (for alleged secret contacts with the Turks). A synod in 1525 voted to excommunicate Maximos and to confine him for life in the monastery of Volokolamsk. His protests at this unjust punishment led Daniil to call a second synod in 1531. A further charge was added, that of the reproof of the Russian Church for the unlawful cessation of relations with the patriarchal see of Constantinople. The charges also included the practice of sorcery, the criticism of the Great Ruler, and the attacks on ecclesiastical and monastic property. Maximos was once more condemned to life imprisonment, this time in Tver', and to life privation of Holy Communion. Some of these accusations (including that of sorcery) were certainly unfounded, but others (such as citing the illegal status of the Russian Church) were valid, at least from a Russian perspective. In the 1530s Maximos' imprisonment became more relaxed and he was given the right to read and write. In 1545 the patriarchs of Constantinople and Alexandria asked tsar Ivan IV for his release, but without success. In 1548 his excommunication and imprisonment were annulled, and Maximos moved to the Zagorsk monastery, where he wrote and taught until his death in 1556.

Only posthumously were Maximos's personality and contributions acknowledged officially. About 100 years after his death patriarch Nikon agreed to his canonization, which was authorized by the patriarchates of both Moscow and Constantinople in 1988. Maximos's legacy of literary and theological works was considerable and significant. He wrote about 365 books, of which 163 remain unpublished. Though controversial in his time, he was the most famous and influential scholar in Russia through his work on Byzantine patristic literature, his polemics against western Scholasticism and Lutheranism, and his contributions on dogmatic, liturgical, and canonical issues. Finally, Maximos lived in an important transitional period in which the ecclesiastico-political division between Constantinople and Moscow had started to become evident and was to grow more so in the centuries to come.

FR. NEKTARIOS DROSOS

Biography

Born in Arta *c.*1470 to a wealthy family, Maximos (whose secular name was Michael Trivolis) studied in Corfu and then in the main Humanist centres of Renaissance Italy. In 1502 he joined the Dominican order. In 1506 he returned to Greece and became a monk on Mount Athos. At the request of the Russian ruler Vasiliy III he was sent in 1516 to Moscow to translate books into Old Church Slavonic. Denounced as a heretic, Maximos was imprisoned in 1525. He died at the Zagorsk monastery in 1556.

Further Reading

Denissoff, Elie, *Maxime le Grec et l'Occident: contribution à l'histoire de la pensée religieuse et philosophique de Michel Trivolis*, Paris: Brouwer, 1943

Denissoff, Elie, "Une Biographie de Maxime le Grec par Kourbski", *Orientalia Christiana Periodica*, 20 (1954) pp. 44–84

Geanakoplos, Deno J., "Maximos the Greek: His Mission and Aspects of his Reform of Orthodoxy in Muscovite Russia" in *The Legacy of Saints Cyril and Methodius to Kiev and Moscow*, edited by Anthony-Emil N. Tachiaos, Thessalonica: Hellenic Association for Slavic Studies, 1992

Gromov, M.N., *Maksim Grek*, Moscow: Mysi, 1983

Haney, Jack V., *From Italy to Muscovy: The Life and Works of Maxim the Greek*, Munich: Fink, 1973

Iera Moni Osiou Gregoriou Agiou Orous [Athonite Monastery of Gregoriou], *Agios Maximos o Graikos, o photistis ton Rosson* [St Maximos the Greek, Enlightener of the Russians], Athens, 1991

Ikonnikova, V.S., *Maksim Grek i ego vremia*, Kiev, 1915

Langeler, Arno, *Maksim Grek: byzantijn en humanist in Rusland*, Amsterdam: Mets, 1986

Laskaridis, Christos P., *Maximos o Graikos kai oi ekklistiastikes epidioxeis tis Moschas* [Maximos the Greek and the Ecclesiastical Aspirations of Moscow], Thessalonica, 1991

Obolensky, Dimitri, *Six Byzantine Portraits*, Oxford: Clarendon Press, and New York: Oxford University Press, 1988, pp. 201–19

Olmsted, H.M., "A Learned Greek Monk in Muscovite Exile: Maksim Grek and the Old Testament Prophets", *Modern Greek Studies Yearbook*, 3 (1987) pp. 1–73

Papamichail, Gregorios, *Maximos o Graikos o protos photistis ton Rosson* [Maximos the Greek, the First Enlightener of the Russians], Athens, 1951

Pheidas, Vlasios, *Maximos o Graikos, photistis ton Rosson* [Maximos the Greek, Enlightener of the Russians], Athens, 1988

Podskalsky, Gerhard, *Griechische Theologie in der Zeit der Türkenherrschaft, 1453–1821*, Munich: Beck, 1988, pp. 89–97

Praktika Diethnous Synedriou gia ton Agio Maximo ton Graiko [Proceedings of the International Conference on St Maximos the Greek], Arta, 28–30 October 1988

Schultze, Bernhard, *Maksim Grek als Theologe*, Rome: Institutum Orientalium Studiorum, 1963

Sinitsyna, N.V., *Maksim Grek v Rossii*, Moscow: Nauka, 1977

Tsiliyannis, Konstantinos, *O Agios Maximos o Graikos o Vatopaidinos Monachos* [St Maximos the Greek, the Monk of Vatopedi], Thessalonica 1991

Media

The Greek media have developed in an insecure political environment, which was characterized by a polarization of opinion and the dominance of factionalism. As part of the Greek democratic system, they have never enjoyed a long period of continuous stability in which to develop a free and independent communication culture. According to Nicos Mouzelis's views on the Greek political system and its uncertain ability to guarantee sufficient civil and political rights for its citizens, and Nikiforos Dimandouros's view on traditional and "underdog" culture in Greece, the political institutions and in particular the Greek media have difficulties in identifying and focusing attention on the main problems in order to serve the public interest in Greece.

The Greek media have developed under continuous threat from hostile forces both externally and internally. When democracy and civil society are weak, the military will have a much greater involvement in politics and government than in a more stable political environment. Therefore it was extremely difficult for the Greek media to serve the public interest and to protect such principles as freedom of expression, impartiality, and professionalism (Gantzias and Kamaras, forthcoming).

The Greek media system has changed since the 1980s primarily on account of changes in communication technology, most recently with the emergence of the new digital television channels and the Internet, but also because of pressures from the European Union. As a result the press and broadcasting channels now face new competition from a variety of regional and global media conglomerates (Gantzias and Kamaras, 2000).

The Press

The origins of the Greek press can be traced back to the end of the 18th century in Vienna. The first Greek newspaper, *Ephimeris* (Gazette), was published in Vienna in 1790 and contained foreign news, trade news, classified advertisements, and poetry. In the early years of the 19th century, before the Greek War of Independence of 1821, a number of Greek scholars aimed to establish a channel of communication with the expatriate communities abroad, as well as with the occupied Greek territories. *Ermis o Logios* (Hermes the Scholar) was published by several Greek intellectuals and educators in order to raise the morale of mainland Greeks and to educate them (Mayer, 1957; Karikopoulos, 1984).

On 1 August 1821 in Kalamata *Salpinx Elliniki* (Greek Trumpet) appeared, the first newspaper ever to be published in free Greece; but the first handwritten mainland newspaper was *Pseftofyllada tou Galaxidiou* (Galaxidi Liar), published a few months earlier at Galaxidi in central Greece. The *Ephimeris ton Athinon* (Athens Gazette) was published in 1824, and the *Ephimeris tis Kyverniseos* (Government Gazette) was founded in Nauplia in February 1833 and moved to Athens in 1834. The first opposition newspaper was *Apollon* (Apollo), founded on the island of Hydra in 1831. A few years later, a donation of three printing presses from a philhellene organization in London boosted printing activity on the mainland.

After four centuries of Turkish occupation there was no democratic tradition or government machinery to provide a framework in which political and civil life could develop along with a market economy. In this chaotic and disorganized sociopolitical environment, patron–client relationships flourished as a means of introducing some degree of order and security into the precarious life of the people (Mouzelis 1986, 1995). The press played an important role in the intense competition between the various factions struggling for power and its partisan identification with one group or another was the natural result of political clientelism. The government institutions supported their clients, gaining political power in return for favours; and by protecting particular sections of the press, they maintained their power base.

A series of printing efforts followed the early revolutionary press. By the end of the 19th century 9 more daily newspapers had appeared on the Greek market, and during the first quarter of the 20th century 17 more daily titles were launched; but out of the total of 26 newspapers that were published before 1925, only 5 titles remain in existence today. These are *Estia* (Hearth), first published in 1894, *Rizospastis* (Radical, 1908), *Ethnos* (Nation, 1913), *To Vima* (Tribune, 1922), and *Kathimerini* (Daily, 1922) (Leandros, 1992; Zaharopoulos and Paraschos, 1993).

By the end of the 20th century the publisher-typographer of the revolutionary years had gradually been replaced by the publisher-journalist who was also an entrepreneur. Especially after World War II, new forms of financing emerged, as well as direct and indirect lines of dependence between the press, the state, and entrepreneurial capital (Karikopoulos, 1984). After 1909 the press reflected changes created by the political dominance of the progressive wing associated mainly with Eleftherios Venizelos and the Liberal Party. Newspaper titles such as the *Hronos* (Time, 1903–39), the *Patris* (Homeland, 1905–35), *Esperini* (Afternoon, 1903–35), *Ethnos* (Nation, 1913–70; relaunched 1981), *Kathimerini* (Daily, 1919), *Vradini* (Evening, 1923), and *Eleftheron Vima* (Free Tribune, 1922) played an important role in recording, and occasionally participating in, the political developments in Greece during the first half of the 20th century. In the early decades of the century, press circulation increased. In 1915 the total circulation of the Athens daily press was estimated to be around 150,000 copies and in the period 1930–36 circulation reached an average of 350,000–360,000.

A constitution drafted by R. Fereos in the revolutionary years called for "unlimited freedom of publishing" (Article 122). The Epidaurus Constitution (1822) and the Declaration of Independence, as well as in the Astros Constitution (Epidaurus Law, 1823), state that all Greeks have the right to publish their views via the press providing that they do not attack Christianity or established ethical principles, and they abstain from personal insults.

In the Trizina Constitution (1827) freedom of the press was reinforced with the declaration that the right to publicize opinions in writing and to publish in the press would not be subject to censorship. Later, in the Constitution of 1832, more details were included, such as the right of all citizens to become publishers if properly educated and to be held responsible for any material they published. In the Constitution of 1844 censorship was clearly prohibited as well as any other preventative measures against publishing. In the Constitution of 1911 confiscation of newspapers or any other printed intellectual material was forbidden, except in extreme cases of insults against Christianity, common decency, and the king.

Freedom of expression and of the press was included in various constitutional acts: 1823 (Epidaurus Law), 1827 (Trizina Political Constitution), 1844 Constitution, 1848, and 1864; in 1911 press freedom was specifically stated as an individual right (article 14). Later, the freedom of the press was heavily tested during the Balkan Wars, World War I, the Asia Minor campaign, and the disaster that followed. Article 14 (declaring freedom of the press) was stressed in the Constitution of 1927 and a new law on the press (Law 5060/1931) was put into effect. The Constitution of 1925 introduced the prosecution of press offences (although they were not characterized as a serious crime), a clause that was reversed in the Constitution of 1952.

The restoration of democracy and a series of measures aimed at the protection of the new polity in the mid-1930s led to the cancellation of press freedom in August 1936. During the Metaxas dictatorship the press was fostered and guided by the regime. A series of laws ruled against press freedom, referring to such issues as trade unionism, newspaper finances, etc. The most important law was the Obligatory Law 1092/1938, a serious blow to press freedom. A "secret" press emerged that became an outlaw press during the Nazi occupation.

In the period 1941–44, when Greece was under Nazi occupation, the newspapers that initially maintained their circulation remained, until their final closure, passively critical of the German-Italian military, refusing to print propaganda articles, and contributing to the general resistance movement against the occupying forces. More than 100 papers were published during the occupation, such as *Krypho Scholeio* (Secret School, 1943–44), *Elliniki Foni* (Greek Voice, 1943–44), *Machomeni Hellas* (Fighting Greece, 1942–44), *Machi* (Battle, 1942–44), *Hellinon Aima* (Greek Blood, 1942–45), and many others (Mayer, 1957, Paraschos, 1995).

The press was also targeted by the Papagos government which passed Law 2493/1953 referring to offences committed through publications in the press, creating havoc in journalistic circles, and forcing the Athens press to protest by stopping its presses in July 1953. By the end of the 1950s the daily political newspaper market consisted of 13 titles: 6 morning and 7 afternoon.

During the years of the military junta (1967–74) a substantial number of newspapers ceased operations, either because they were severely censored and finally closed down by the regime, or of their own accord as a response to the coup d'état. Out of 14 daily newspapers in circulation on 21 April 1967, only 9 remained open in 1974. *Kathimerini* and *Mesimvrini*, with a daily average of 130,000 copies between them, stopped their presses in protest against the colonels (Vlachou, 1992). Also *Eleftheria* (Freedom) as well as the left *Avgi* (Dawn) and *Dimokratiki Allagi* (Democratic Change) were banned by the regime in the early days of the junta. Over a two-month period (April–May), the total average daily circulation decreased by 36.2 per cent.

During the dictatorship press censorship ranged from the full subordination of newspapers in the early months of military rule to relative relaxation in the years 1969–71. The regime had seen the role of the press as an essential state mechanism, whose primary job was to disseminate established views, support the administration, and contribute to the formation of public opinion (Stratos, 1995; Zaharopoulos and Paraschos, 1993).

In the Constitution of 1968 freedom of the press was included in principle, although certain inserted clauses reflected the dictatorship's views on the issue. Article 14 was encumbered with so many provisions that it appeared almost impossible for the press to publish any opposition views. These restrictions remained in the Constitution of 1973, and were eventually abolished in the Constitution of 1975 with the restoration of democracy.

After the restoration of democracy on 26 July 1974, the circulation of the daily press increased by 61.3 per cent between June and August, reaching the peak of the decade with an average of 1,128,000 copies, recorded in August 1974. The abolition of all restrictions on the press, which led to the relaunch of newspapers previously banned by the regime, as well as the public's thirst for freedom of information and unrestricted expression of personal and political beliefs, were the main reasons for the increase in circulation. However, this rapid increase in circulation did not last long. One year later, in 1975, circulation started to decline. Five years later, in 1980, the total circulation had descended to the level almost of the junta period, with the morning press suffering the greater losses. Government laws and regulations had captured the "market" by placing a number of heavy constraints on its future development. The Greek newspapers have not developed in a media market such as that which operates in Western European countries. Many forces, both external (Turks and Balkans) and internal (civil war and dictatorship), have combined in various ways to constrain the "free" spirit of the press.

Some of the factors that have influenced the media system in Greece, such as technological change and new style of ownership during the 1980s, have transformed the Greek press into a commercial enterprise. In 1989 the new private broad-casting channels, which introduced a competitive element into the monopolistic broadcasting market, indirectly affected the existing newspaper market. Businessmen from all sectors of the economy, such as construction, manufacturing, oil, and ship-ping, were entering the broadcasting channels and the press market, replacing many of the traditional newspaper propri-etors (Gantzias and Kamaras, 2000).

The new commercial publishers were willing to invest heavily in the media market to gain access to publicity. Although the dominant publishers tried hard to launch new newspaper titles during the 1980s, 17 out of 23 new national newspaper titles were forced to close down within two years because of the constraint of the established press market. Moreover, the press in Greece suffers from low circulation and too many medium-size publications. In the 1980s technologi-cal developments changed the traditional newspaper produc-tion process. The replacement of linotype printing machines with the modern practice of phototypesetting was a major breakthrough for Greek newspapers, and desktop publishing and the use of computers in general have contributed to the emergence of a new era for the printing industry. Generally, technological improvements have allowed most newspapers to modernize their appearance and to become more efficient in news gathering and processing. The results of technology and the use of computing in printed media were evident in the areas of printing techniques, layout, and the extensive use of colour.

The nine-year period 1981–89, during which the country was ruled by successive PASOK governments, was a golden age for the Athens daily political press. Daily circulation remained constantly at a level of 900,000 to 1 million copies, with even higher figures being achieved in pre-election periods. In 1994 new press legislation (Law 2243/1994), put forward by a PASOK administration, abolished the Metaxas law and contributed to the modernization and systematic codification of press legislation. In the 1990s a series of initiatives to launch new titles materialized, some of which were unsuccessful. On the other hand, the periodical press, such as life-style maga-zines and specialized journals, was strengthened. The increased demand for specialized titles relating to the economy, business, and financial activity was a result of the further evolution and maturity of the Greek economy, which was associated with the growth of the stock market, the development of modern financial services, and the emergence of a new generation of businessmen who invested heavily in public relations and publicity.

Moreover, the decline in circulation during the 1990s created a high level of insecurity in the press marketplace. For example, the total average circulation of 840,800 copies in 1990 fell to 470,000 in 1998, and the evening press fell from 767,200 copies sold in 1990 to 407,700 copies in 1998. Before 1980 the Greek press had been supported financially by differ-ent political parties and the government, and this was the main reason for the problems it experienced when floated in a competitive media market in the 1990s. The broadcasting monopoly and the diversity of interests in the publishing sector had created a very "cosy" environment in the Greek media market. In the late 1990s the press was challenged by the Internet and by the emergence of a variety of private and digital television channels.

Broadcasting

Both radio and television grew up in non-democratic periods of Greek history: radio under the Metaxas dictatorship (1935–40) and the German occupation during World War II, and television under the junta of 1967–74. The Metaxas dicta-torship and later the Nazis during their occupation of Greece used radio as a propaganda tool to disseminate their ideas and to influence public opinion.

The radio and television channels were used by the junta to disseminate its anti-communist propaganda and to influence public opinion. Moreover, the democratic administrations that were formed after 1974 followed the same practice, using state-owned broadcast media for propaganda purposes. The fact that broadcasting emerged in periods when democracy and freedom of speech were suppressed had numerous side-effects on its future development. The radio and television channels were the main avenues for the government of the day to publish its policies during the main news programmes. The broadcasting channels were controlled heavily by the state and by a group of interested parties – the advertisers, the advertising agencies, and the private production sector who were the main programme providers (Paraschos, 1995; Pathanassopoulos, 1989; Dimitras and Doulkeri, 1986; Zaharopoulos and Paraschos, 1993).

In 1981 PASOK gained power and promised the democrati-zation of television, as well as freedom of speech in state broadcasting. Despite this initial aim, the party did not wish to lose control of television, which was seen as an important means of state propaganda and of promoting government policy. Consequently, the Greek broadcasting media remained heavily underdeveloped and state-controlled until 1989, the year when private television was launched. The transition from the stage of underdevelopment to liberalization was very prob-lematic. The rapid and uncontrolled development of private television in the 1990s was characterized by extreme commer-cialization and a market-driven attitude, not to mention the lack of a coherent policy in frequency allocation, advertising breaks, and broadcasting programmes.

The late introduction of new legislative frameworks (Laws 1866/89 and 2325/95) and the institution of independent authorities (e.g. National Broadcasting Council), which might be expected to act as a regulating mechanism to monitor the broadcasting system and control the private sector, in fact achieved the opposite results. Neither the legislation nor the regulatory body has been very effective in regulating the chaotic broadcasting market (Gantzias and Kamaras, forth-coming; Kiki, 1989; Paraschos, 1995; Venizelos, 1989).

Broadcasting in Greece is in a transitional stage. Analogue television will soon have to control the developments of digital technology. The new law on digital television channels (2644/98) is another piece of legislation that is likely to be very soon out of date when the new digital television channels broadcast their programmes in Greece (Gantzias and Kamaras, 2000). The broadcasting market is seeking its identity, while the government tries to tune the market with digital technol-ogy. Insecurity in the broadcasting market together with competition from numerous legal and technically illegal broad-casting stations have created an unsuitable environment for the development of healthy competition in the analogue media market.

GEORGE K. GANTZIAS AND DEMETRIS I. KAMARAS

See also Censorship

Further Reading

Datoglou, P.D, *Radiotileorasi and Syntagma* [Broadcasting and Constitution], Athens: Sakoulas Komotini, 1989

Diamandouros, P. Nikiforos, "Politics and Culture in Greece, 1974–91: An Interpretation" in *Greece 1981–89: the Populist Decade*, edited by Richard Clogg, Basingstoke: Macmillan, and New York: St Martin's Press, 1993

Dimitras, P. and T. Doulkeri, "Greece" in *Electronic Media and Politics in Western Europe*, edited by Hans J. Klensteuber, Denis McQuail and Karen Sione, Frankfurt: Campus, 1986

Gantzias, G., *The Info-Communication Industry: Digital Services, Global Markets*, London: Loizou, 1998

Gantzias, George K. and Demetris Kamaras, *Psifiaki Epikinonia, Nea Mesa kai Koinonia ton Pliroforion stin Ellada: Siglisi, Ilektroniko Emporio kai Portals* [Digital Communication, New Media and the Information Society in Greece: Convergences, Electronic Commerce and Portals], London: Loizou, 2000

Gantzias, George K. and Demetris Kamaras, *Media Power, Digital Communication and Digital Markets in Greece*, London: Loizou (forthcoming)

Karikopoulos, Panos, *200 Chronia apo ton Elliniko Typo* [200 years of the Greek Press], Athens: Gregory, 1984

Katsoudas, D.K, "Greece: A Politically Controlled State Monopoly Broadcasting System", *West European Politics*, 8/2 (2 April 1995): special issue on broadcasting and politics in western Europe

Kiki, Joanna, "Greek Broadcasting Law: Past and Present", *Journal of Media Law and Practice* (1989): pp. 24ff.

Leandros, N, *Entypa MME stin Ellada* (Journals in Greek Media), Athens: Dolphin, 1992

Lyrintzis, C., "Political Parties in Post-Junta Greece: A Case of Bureaucratic Clientism?", *West European Politics*, 7/2 (1984)

McDonald, Robert, *Pillar and Tinderbox: The Greek Press and the Dictatorship*, London: Marion Boyars, 1983

Mayer, Kostas, *I Istoria tou Ellinikou Typou* [The History of the Greek Press], Athens: Dimopoulos, 1957

Mouselis, N.P., "Greece in the Twenty-First Century: Institutions and Political Systems" in *Greece Prepares for the Twenty-first Century*, edited by Dimitri Constas and Theofanis G. Stavrou, Washington D.C.: Woodrow Wilson Center Press, and Baltimore: Johns Hopkins University Press, 1995

Papathanassopoulos, Stylianos, "Greece: Nothing is More Permanent than the Provisional", *Intermedia*, 17 (June-July 1989)

Paraschos, M.E., 1995, "The Greek Media Face the Twenty-First Century: Will the Adam Smith Complex Replace the Oedipus Complex?" in *Greece Prepares for the Twenty-First Century*, edited by Dimitri Constas and Theofanis G. Stavrou, Washington D.C.: Woodrow Wilson Center Press, and Baltimore: Johns Hopkins University Press, 1995

Stratos, Konstantinos, *Antithesi kai Diafonia* [Opposition and Disagreement], Athens: Kastaniotis, 1995

Venizelos, Evangelos, *I Radiotileoptiki Ekrizi* [The Broadcasting Eruption], Thessalonica: Paratiritis, 1989

Vlachou, Eleni, *Dimosiographika Chronia: Peninta kai Kati* [Journalistic Years: Fifty and Beyond], Athens: Zedros, 1992

Zacharopoulos, Thimios and Manny E. Paraschos, *Mass Media in Greece: Power, Politics, and Privatization*, Westport, Connecticut: Praeger, 1993

Medicine

The earliest sources of detailed Greek medical knowledge are Homer's *Iliad* and *Odyssey*, both written in the 8th century BC. In the *Iliad* Homer mentions 147 different wounds, for most of which he gives detailed and accurate descriptions. Homer also recorded the medical care given to injured warriors, which focused on providing comfort to the wounded soldier rather than treating the wound itself. Among the warriors some were considered specialists in the art of healing through bandaging and herbal medicine. Two of these specialists were Machaon and Podalirius, who are both described as sons of Asclepius. After Machaon was wounded himself, he was treated by being given a cup of hot wine sprinkled with grated goat cheese and barley. Homer did not discuss any diseases, except for the case of Thersites which contains a typical description of rickets.

An influential development in Greek medicine was the Asclepius cult, which originated in Epidaurus and spread rapidly throughout the 4th century BC. Asclepius, who in the *Iliad* is described only as a skilful physician, was here worshipped as a god of medicine, truth, and prophecy. He was a son of Apollo who had learned the art of healing from the centaur Chiron. The god figure may have been derived from a human Asclepius who is credited with many miracles in healing and lived around 1200 BC.

By the end of the 4th century BC Asclepius was worshipped in about 200 temples, of which those at Epidaurus, Cnidus, Cos, and Pergamum were the most important. The sick would visit the temples for a ritual healing incubation. After purifying themselves through baths, fastings, and sacrifices they slept in a dormitory, or *abaton*, where they were visited in a dream by Asclepius or one of his priests. In the morning the priests would interpret the dream and give advice. Since the priests wanted to ensure that the sick had a chance of recovery, they became skilful in diagnosis. The extent and variety of the temple cures can be seen from the tokens the cured left behind. At the Asclepieion at Epidaurus about 10 cubic m of terracotta replicas of afflicted limbs and organs have been found, illustrating successful case studies. Inscriptions on the temples show that the treatment of diseases consisted of rest, exercise, diet, and magic.

It was not the priests, however, but the Presocratic philosophers, starting with Thales of Miletus (6th century BC), who led the way towards a naturalistic medicine. In the cosmologies of the Presocratics the inner workings of the human body became subject to the very same principles as the outward phenomena. Of special significance is Empedocles of Acragas (*c*.490–*c*.435 BC), founder of the medical school in Sicily, whose four-element cosmology (fire, earth, water, air) anticipated the doctrine of the four bodily fluids or humours: blood, phlegm, choler (or yellow bile), and melancholy (or black bile). Just as the order of the universe depended on a harmony of the four elements, so was one healthy when the four humours were in balance.

The views of Empedocles influenced Hippocrates of Cos (*c*.460–377 BC), who is generally considered the father of medicine. A contemporary of Plato, Hippocrates lived in the golden age of Greek thought and culture. As with many early Greek figures little is known of his life, and the name may refer to several different people. About 70 medical treatises, generally called the Hippocratic corpus, are traditionally attributed to him, but it is not clear whether he wrote even one of them. The treatises vary greatly in length and style, and it is generally believed that they used to make up the library of a medical school, probably at Cos, which became the most important centre of medical thought and practice in the 4th century BC – a role that was later taken over by Alexandria. Today Hippocrates is best known for the Hippocratic oath, an ethical code that is still upheld, albeit in radically revised versions. According to the original oath, the physician should use medicine solely for the benefit of the patient, abstain from surgery, keep information about the patient confidential, and refrain from asking a fee for teaching others his trade.

The Hippocratic theory built upon the idea of the Presocratic philosophers that man and nature are subject to the same rules and on Empedocles' theory of the four elements. Reliance on the speculative cosmologies of the Presocratic philosophers was crucial to the Hippocratic theory, since physicians could not engage in dissection to familiarize themselves with the inner workings of the human body. Following Empedocles' theory of the four elements, Hippocratic medical practice consisted of restoring the balance of the four humours. To cure a patient one had to make the offending humour escape or balance itself out. The Hippocratic physicians sought to do this primarily through diets, purgation, bloodletting, and draining abscesses.

One interesting element of the Hippocratic corpus, and a clear mark of its scientific character, is that besides successful treatments medical mistakes were also included. This is especially clear in book 5 of the *Epidemics*, which contains case studies of ill-timed purgatives, badly done cauterizations, irritating wound dressings, and others. Some of the Hippocratic methods, such as treating a dislocation of the hip, remained unsurpassed until the 19th century. Part of the corpus, most prominently the *Aphorismi*, was used as a textbook up to the 19th century.

The other two major centres of Greek medicine during this period were Cnidus and Sicily. Two important figures of the school at Cnidus were Euryhon and Ctesias, both contemporaries of Hippocrates. Euryhon made anatomical studies, explained pleurisy as a lung affection, and discovered that haemorrhage can occur from the arteries as well as the veins. He also believed that disease was caused by insufficient evacuation of the faeces. In Sicily Philistion of Locri, who met Plato at Syracuse, did much to diffuse the medical knowledge of the island and to ensure its synthesis with the views at Cnidus and Cos.

Although Aristotle was not a physician himself, his impact on the development of Greek medicine can hardly be overestimated. Born in 384 BC, he was a son of Nicomachus, who was the court physician to Amyntas II, king of Macedon. Aristotle's main contributions concern his development of the scientific method, to which his formal logic added an element of precision, and his work in comparative anatomy and embryology.

After Aristotle the centre of Greek culture shifted to Alexandria, where a famous medical school was established around 330 BC. Important figures of this period were Herophilus and Erasistratus. Both lived during the single brief period in which the ban on human dissection was lifted. This change in attitude towards dissection was due largely to the teachings of Plato and Aristotle on the soul. According to

Galen, Herophilus of Chalcedon (*c*.335–*c*.280 BC) was the first to perform public dissections on human cadavers. He distinguished nerves, tendons, and blood vessels, and gave precise accounts of the retina, liver, pancreas, and the genital organs of both sexes. Herophilus followed the Hippocratic method of balancing the four humours through drugs, diet, and exercise, and is believed to have been the first to measure the pulse, and use it to diagnose a fever.

Herophilus' rival at Alexandria, Erasistratus of Chios (*c*.304–*c*.250 BC), is known especially for his studies of the circulatory systems, including the nervous system, since he thought the nerves were hollow tubes filled with fluid. Erasistratus proposed mechanical explanations for many bodily processes, including digestion, and is often considered the founder of physiology. In the 1st century AD Celsus accused both Herophilus and Erasistratus of performing human vivisection, an accusation that was empathically repeated by Tertullian and St Augustine, but for which there is no evidence.

During the first centuries of the Christian era, many Greek physicians moved to Rome. Among them was Pedanius Dioscurides (*fl.* AD 20), a Greek pharmacist and author of *De Materia Medica*, which contained descriptions of about 600 plants with an explanation of their medical uses, and included many scientific illustrations to help identify them. Dioscurides greatly simplified the pharmacopoeia, and his work is the basis of modern pharmacology.

The first eminent Greek physician in Rome was Asclepiades of Bithynia (*fl.*150 BC), who opposed the humoral theory of medicine. Asclepiades drew upon the atomism of Democritus of Abdera (*fl.*420 BC), attributing disease to the contracted or relaxed condition of tiny solid particles he believed made up the body. This explanation became the basis of a school of medicine that extended until well into the 7th century. It largely disregarded the findings of anatomy and physiology and concentrated on therapeutic massages, fresh air, and corrective diet. Soranus of Ephesus (2nd century AD), who followed Asclepiades' atomist approach, also came to Rome. Soranus wrote on childbirth, including the podalic (feet-first) delivery, infant care, women's diseases, and nervous disorders. An opponent of abortion, he devised several methods of contraception.

The most illustrious Greek physician in Rome was no doubt Galen of Pergamum (*c*.AD 130–201). Galen began his career at the Asclepius temple in Pergamum and came to Rome around AD 163. He was a brilliant and prolific writer with great rhetorical skills. About 300 titles are attributed to him, of which about half survive. They cover close on every aspect of the medical theory and practice in his day. For his own views he combined ideas from Plato and Aristotle with the Hippocratic tradition. Like the Hippocratic physicians, Galen believed that health required an equilibrium of the four humours, but unlike the holistic Hippocratics he argued that imbalances can also be confined to particular organs.

For Galen anatomy formed the basis of medical knowledge and he frequently dissected and experimented on animals. Notable are his vivisection experiments, such as tying off the ureters to show the functions of kidney and bladder. Because of a ban on human dissections, his anatomy was based largely on the dissection of mammals, which often led to errors. His description of the uterus, for instance, is largely that of a dog.

Galen saw the body as three connected systems: the brain and nerves are responsible for sensation and thought; the heart and arteries are responsible for life-giving energy; and the liver and veins are responsible for nutrition and growth.

Although observation does play a role in Galen's system, his general tenet was to explain everything in pure theory, to which his rhetorical skills gave the air of being infallible. This led to a strong tendency to dogmatism among his followers. Galen's approach is in this respect almost the opposite of the Hippocratic method, which tried to remain close to the facts and proceeded through a careful description of case studies.

The Byzantine period is often depicted as a time of stagnation and plagiarism, generating little more than compilations of earlier works. Byzantine medicine, however, is a lively mixture of Greek medical theory, magic, and folk medicine, in which old theories were combined with new observations and adapted for a predominantly rural society. Although the dominant Church was on the whole favourable to medicine, it favoured not the secular healing of physicians, but that of praying, fasting, and the laying on of hands. Consequently, it was the priests that were first consulted in cases of illness. Secular medicine was tolerated as an alternative medicine on which true Christians could also rely. A central feature of Byzantine medicine is the emergence of the hospital, in which respect it was far ahead of developments in the West. Between the 4th and the 12th century Christian houses for the poor, or *xenones*, became well-organized and fully staffed hospitals. Often these *xenones*, like John Chrysostom's *nosokomeia* (places to care for the sick), were associated with cities. Initially, the *xenones* were governed by priests, but by the 12th century physicians had obtained full control over the therapeutic and often also the management side of the hospitals.

Several figures deserve special attention. Alexander of Tralles (525–605) wrote on intestinal worms and developed a complex system of drug prescriptions involving no fewer than 495 different pharmaceuticals. He also sanctioned magic, especially when the patient's belief in it aided the cure. Theophilos Protospatharios (*fl.* AD 630) wrote an influential work on uroscopy and a book on excrements, which indicates the continued use of dungs in pharmaceuticals. Paul of Aegina (7th century) wrote extensively on surgery, providing detailed descriptions of more than 120 different operations, including mastectomy and operations for hernia, tumours, and bladder stone.

CORNELIS DE WAAL

See also Anatomy, Disease, Healing Cults, Health

Further Reading

Edelstein, Emma J., *Asclepius: Collection and Interpretation of the Testimonies*, Baltimore: Johns Hopkins University Press, 1998

Lang, Mabel L., *Cure and Cult in Ancient Corinth: A Guide to the Asklepieion*, Princeton, New Jersey: American School of Classical Studies at Athens, 1977

Livingstone, R.W. (editor), *The Legacy of Greece*, Oxford and New York: Oxford University Press, 1969

Longrigg James (editor), *Greek Medicine: From the Heroic to the Hellenistic Age: A Source Book*, London: Duckworth, and New York: Routledge, 1998

Phillips, E.D., *Aspects of Greek Medicine*, Philadelphia: Charles Press, and London: Croom Helm, 1987

Scarborough, John (editor), *Symposium on Byzantine Medicine*, Washington: Dumbarton Oaks, 1985

Taylor, Henry Osborn, *Greek Biology and Medicine*, New York: Cooper Square, 1963

von Staden, Heinrich, *Herophilus: The Art of Medicine in Early Alexandria*, Cambridge: Cambridge University Press, 1989

von Staden, Heinrich, "In a Pure and Holy Way: Personal and Professional Conduct in the Hippocratic Oath", *Journal of the History of Medicine and Allied Sciences*, 51 (1996): pp. 404–37

Megalopolis

City in Arcadia

Megalopolis – the ironically named "Great City" – was founded at the instigation of Epaminondas and the Boeotian federation after their shattering victory over the Spartans at the Battle of Leuctra in 371 BC and their subsequent incursion into the Peloponnese during the winter of 370/69, at the invitation of the Arcadian League.

During this incursion Epaminondas had stopped short of attacking the city of Sparta itself, even though it was unwalled, but he successfully removed one of the main supports of Spartan power, their possession of Messenia, reconstituting it as an independent state with a vastly fortified city at Messene. In the next year, 368, he followed this up with a second invasion of the Peloponnese. He used his successes this time to strengthen the Arcadian League. It was at some point during this that he organized the creation of Megalopolis (Pausanias says a few months after Leuctra, when Phrasicleides was archon at Athens, that is in 371/70 BC, but this is too early).

The new city served several purposes. It was situated in southern Arcadia, in an area of upland plain drained by the headwaters of the river Alpheus (which then flows westwards, past Olympia). This area also has access to the Eurotas valley to the southeast, and to Messenia and Mount Ithome to the southwest. It was thus strategically vital if the Spartans were to be restricted to their homeland of Laconia, and an anti-Spartan stronghold here was a crucial part of Epaminondas' new order for the Peloponnese. It was designed also to strengthen the unity of the Arcadian League, to create a formidable single power in the central Peloponnese which would in turn prevent any Spartan resurgence. Arcadia had come rather late to the formation of city-states, and this had made possible the formation of the federal league. Of the existing cities, Mantinea had been formed out of constituent villages, and broken up into villages by the Spartans in 385 BC. Tegea had existed as a recognizable city for centuries, but there was rivalry with the neighbouring Mantineans, who were unlikely to recognize it as the leading state in the Arcadian League. Megalopolis therefore served as a new, artificial, neutral city which all the other Arcadians could recognize as their capital without loss of face. According to Pausanias (2nd century AD), it became the youngest city, not just in Arcadia, but in all Greece, excluding colonies founded by the Romans. He names the founders, probably on the basis of a record kept at Megalopolis itself, as Lycomedes and Hopleas from Mantinea, Timon and Proxenos from Tegea, Creolaos and Acriphios from Cleitor, Eucampidas and Hieronymus from Maenalos, and Possicrates and

Megalopolis: the 4th-century BC theatre seated 21,000, making it one of the largest in Greece

Theoxenos of Parrasia, that is, two from each of the main cities of Arcadia, thus emphasizing its position as a centre for all Arcadians. The actual population came from the existing villages in the vicinity. Pausanias gives a list of their names; he adds that some had to be coerced.

The remains of ancient Megalopolis are not well preserved, and virtually nothing of its surrounding city walls can be seen, though their line has been traced. They enclosed a large area, as at Messene, but from the start the city seems to have been designed for a substantial population, moved in from the villages, unlike Messene whose walls were intended to provide a place of refuge in emergency for Messenians living outside the city. The architectural importance of Megalopolis rests with the buildings constructed to enable it to function as the capital of the Arcadian League: a roofed hall for the council of the league, called the Thersilion after its founder, and the adjacent theatre which, quite apart from any use for the performance of drama, would also have been the seat of the 10,000-strong representative assembly of the league. The porticoed entrance to the Thersilion served as the stage building (*scaenae frons*) of the theatre. Both were excavated by the newly founded British School at Athens as its first major excavation in 1891. The theatre, one of the largest in Greece, was fairly well preserved (though earth tremors have caused subsequent damage). The Thersilion, however, had been reduced to its foundations, perhaps indicating a structure of mud brick; it was already in this state when Pausanias saw it. It was a rectangular building, 66 m wide, 52 m from front (the portico) to back; as with all ancient Greek enclosed buildings of this size its roof had to be supported on a forest of columns, but these were arranged as a series of lines radiating from an area between the centre and the main entrance of the building which was obviously the place from which speakers addressed the council, thus giving direct lines of vision to the speaker from the assembled councillors. Another important building originally excavated by the British School in 1891 (it is now being re-examined by a German archaeological team) was the principal portico building of the agora, the stoa of Philip, a huge Doric building, measuring 155 m in length, with projecting wings at either end. The facade has no fewer than 86 Doric columns; the interior was divided into three aisles by double rows of Ionic columns, with two extra columns in each wing. Such a colossal building could only be the gift of a king; in this case Philip of Macedon, seeking to confirm the support of the Arcadians, and almost certainly Philip II, in the aftermath of Chaeronea and the refusal of the Spartans to join the Peace, rather than Philip V, reviving Megalopolis after it had been sacked by the Spartans under Cleomenes III in 223 BC.

In the Hellenistic period Megalopolis was a firm supporter of Macedon, notably in the 240s when it was ruled by a tyrant,

Lydiades, probably installed with Macedonian assistance. Nevertheless, finding himself increasingly isolated he had joined the Achaean League; it was this that provoked Cleomenes' attack, the effect of which was reversed by the unexpected alliance of the Achaean League with Macedon and the defeat of Cleomenes at the battle of Sellasia in 222 BC. Thereafter Megalopolis continued as a member of the Achaean League, and so became embroiled against Rome in the Third Macedonian War, resulting in the son of its leading politician Lycortas being taken to Rome as a hostage. This was the historian Polybius, whose writings make him not only the greatest historian of the Hellenistic period, and of the involvement of Greece and Rome, but also by far the most eminent citizen of Megalopolis.

After the Roman incorporation of Greece as its province of Achaea, Megalopolis continued without any political importance (and hence the ruin of the Thersilion) as a small provincial city. It faded away in later antiquity, the population dispersing once more into villages. After the War of Independence it was selected, like Sparta and Thebes, as one of the places where a city of Classical Greece was artificially revived, but it was the least successful. Today it remains a small place serving the local lignite mines and the smoke-producing power station.

R.A. TOMLINSON

Summary

Founded after the Battle of Leuctra (371 BC) at the instigation of Epaminondas and the Boeotian Confederacy, Megalopolis was created as the capital of the Arcadian League. The population was drawn from neighbouring villages. It supported Macedon in the Hellenistic period and was a member of the Achaean League. It was the birthplace of Polybius. It declined in the Roman period.

Further Reading

Gardner, Ernest Arthur et al., Excavations at Megalopolis, 1890–91, London: Macmillan, 1892

Hornblower, Simon, "When was Megalopolis Founded?", Annual of the British School at Athens, 85 (1990): pp. 71 ff.

Lauter, H., "Am der Philippos-Halle in Megalopolis", Archäologisches Anzeiger (1987): pp. 389 ff.

Recent German excavations are reported in Archaeological Reports for 1995 and 1996, London: Hellenic Society and the British School at Athens

Megara

City in central Greece

Situated between Eleusis (19 km distant) and the isthmus of Corinth (33 km away), close to the north shore of the Saronic Gulf, the ancient city of Megara was topographically focused on the twin acropolises of Alcathous and Caria: the same is true of the modern town.

The ancient harbour, now silted up, was about 1.5 km away at Nisaea, opposite Salamis and to the west of modern Pachi, which is of no importance. On the west side of the site of the Nisaea harbour area is the hill of Palaikastro (later the site of a Frankish fort), which was probably ancient Minoa. Minoa is

mentioned in ancient sources as either an island or a cape. To the east, the hill of Hagios Georgios has ancient fortifications and was probably the acropolis of Nisaea.

Although the small plain in which Megara itself lies is fertile and produces vines and olives, the hinterland is mostly mountainous and barren, dominated by the Yerani and Pateras ranges to the west and east respectively.

At its greatest extent the territory of Megara covered the whole of the peninsula between Eleusis and the isthmus, and included Aegosthena and Pagae to the north and east, and Perachora to the west. Pagae, near modern Alepochori, is close to the shore of the easternmost arm of the Corinthian Gulf (the so-called Halcyonic Gulf). Megara's ports thus gave access to two seas. Through its territory passed important land routes between Attica and the isthmus and between central Greece and the isthmus. The position of Megara on these strategic routes, although advantageous to trade and communications, was also the cause of misfortunes since armies ravaged the city in passing or brought it into conflicts through use as a base.

The settlements of Rous (to the north) and Tripodiskos (to the northwest, on Mount Yerani), and the sanctuary of Zeus Aphesios (above Kakia Skala) were also Megarian.

Only limited traces of Neolithic settlement have so far been found (at Lake Vouliagmeni, near Perachora). Finds of potsherds show that the acropolis area of Megara town (where there is also "Cyclopean" walling which may be prehistoric), as well as the probable sites of ancient Nisaea and Minoa, were inhabited in the Bronze Age. Myths suggest that in very early times Megara may have been subject to Athens.

But as a Dorian state it became important only from the 8th century BC. Its situation was favourable for trade and it was active in the colonial movement. Its foundations included Megara Hyblaea and Selinus in Sicily, and Chalcedon and Byzantium on the Bosporus.

Megara was ruled by tyrants for much of the Archaic period. The best known of them is Theagenes (mid-7th century), whose son-in-law Cylon attempted a coup at Athens.

Its territory was diminished in the 6th century when the Athenians, under Solon, took Salamis, and the Corinthians the western part of the peninsula. Megara took part in the Persian Wars.

In 461 the Athenians built the long walls connecting the city with Nisaea and garrisoned both this harbour and that at Pagae. In 456 the Athenians withdrew when the Megarians rejoined the Peloponnesian side. This caused enormous resentment at Athens and resulted in the "Megarian decree" of 432 by which the city was banned from Athenian markets. The Athenians continued to harass the city, building the fort at Boudoron on Salamis to check Nisaea.

After the start of the Peloponnesian War, in which Megara suffered badly, partly because of its changing allegiance, its territory was invaded twice annually. For a time in 424 the Athenians took control of Nisaea and Minoa, but did not succeed in capturing Megara itself.

Recovering in the 4th century, the inhabitants rebuilt the long walls, again with Athenian help, as a defence against Philip of Macedon. In 315 the city was used by Cassander as a base against the Peloponnese. In 307 it was besieged by Demetrius Poliorcetes who took away all the slaves, thus devastating the economic infrastructure. In the 3rd-century

"Chremonid" War (between Athens-Sparta and Macedon) Megara was controlled by the Macedonians, and later (243 BC) the city joined the Achaean League. Pagae and Aegosthena then became independent.

With its territory and power circumscribed, Megara was less important in the Hellenistic and Roman periods. The city suffered at the hands of Roman armies but remained rich in the buildings and works of art described by Pausanias.

In AD 395 Megara suffered a catastrophic destruction at the hands of Alaric's Goths after which its significance was minimal. Nevertheless, although little is known about the history of Megara in the Early Christian and Byzantine periods, it is clear from several surviving churches and monasteries, such as the 12th-century Panagia Kiparissiotissa in the monastery of Hagios Ierotheos, 6 km northwest, and the 12th-century church of Hagia Sotira in the plain to the northeast, that there was considerable activity in the area.

Franks and Ottomans used Megara as a base, the latter for operations in the Peloponnese. The remains of a Frankish fort survive on "Minoa". In the 14th and 15th centuries Albanian settlers arrived in the area, encouraged by the Franks. Various small post-Byzantine churches tell a story of smallscale but continuous occupation up to the 19th century. In 1771 the Megarians supported the commander Mitromaras in the rebellion of Orloff and suffered accordingly. In the early 19th century Ypsilantis used the town as a base for campaigns in Boeotia. In more recent times the Megarian economy has been based on chicken farming and smallscale industry. Today the town is a busy but pleasant backwater.

Study of the town's antiquities began in the 19th century with the work of H. Reinganum and has continued since. Megara's most impressive surviving ancient monument is the so-called Fountain of Theagenes, ascribed to the tyrant. In fact this is a large reservoir, its roof supported by pillars, originally fed by an acqueduct.

Pausanias saw numerous public buildings and works of art. The sites of several of these have been identified by excavations or the discovery of inscriptions. Most of the public buildings either are no longer to be seen (a stoa of the agora, beneath the modern Plateia Metaxa) or have been incorporated in later buildings (inscriptions and a temple of Athena in churches, especially that of the Ypapandi, and houses on Alcathous). Numerous fragments of the fortifications (4th century BC) have been found, allowing the line of the circuit – and some of its gates – to be clearly defined. Megara was known for the quality of its houses, with capacious basements, many examples of which have been excavated.

Famous Megarians included the elegiac poet Theognis (7th or 6th century BC) and Eucleides, founder of the 4th-century BC post-Socratic Megarian school of philosophy.

ROBIN L.N. BARBER

Summary

Megara lies between Athens and Corinth and was often overshadowed by its powerful neighbours. In the 8th century BC it founded colonies in Sicily and on the Bosporus. In the 5th century it suffered as a result of changing allegiances. Refortified in the 4th century, the city was besieged by Demetrius Poliorcetes. In 243 BC it joined the Achaean League. Under the Romans its importance dwindled but it was rich in fine buildings and works of art.

Further Reading

Bouras, Charalampos *et al.*, *Ekklesies tis Attikis* [Churches of Attica], Athens, 1969

Hammond, N.G.L., "The Main Road from Boeotia to the Peloponnese through the Northern Megarid", *Annual of the British School at Athens*, 49 (1954): pp. 103–22

Highbarger, E.L., *The History and Civilisation of Ancient Megara*, Baltimore: Johns Hopkins University Press, 1927

Legon, Ronald P., *Megara: The Political History of a Greek City-State to 336 BC*, Ithaca, New York: Cornell University Press, 1981

Pauly, August *et al* (editors), *Real-Encyclopädie der klassischen Altertumswissenschaft*, vol. 2, 1931, 152–205; and supplement 12, 1970, 842–851

Pausanias, *Description of Greece*, translated by W.H.S. Jones, 5 vols, London: Heinemann, and New York: Putnam, 1918–35 (Loeb edition; several reprints), book 1, chapters 39–44

Simpson, R. Hope and O.T.P.K. Dickinson, *A Gazetteer of Aegean Civilisation in the Bronze Age*, vol. 1, Gothenburg: Åström, 1979 (sites A 93, Megara; A 94, Palaiokastro; A 94a, Ag. Georgios)

Skawran, Karin M., *The Development of Middle Byzantine Fresco Painting in Greece*, Pretoria: University of South Africa, 1982, pp. 169, 175–76

Society for the Promotion of Hellenic Studies and British School at Athens, *Archaeological Reports*, annually: summaries of recent archaeological work in Megara and references to the Greek sources for the reports.

Travlos, John (editor), *Bildlexikon zur Topographie des antiken Attika*, Tübingen: Wasmuth, 1988, Megaris entry, pp. 258–87

Mehmet II 1432–1481

Ottoman Turkish sultan

Mehmet was born in Edirne (Adrianople) on 30 March 1432, the third son of Sultan Murad II (1421–1451) and his slave concubine Hatun bint Abdullah, whose ethnic origins are obscure and much debated. Entrusted from childhood with token positions of responsibility, he developed early a stubborn, precocious, and contentious personality. The murder of Murad's favourite second son Alaeddin Ali in 1443 prompted the sultan to prepare Mehmet for succession, even though there was little warmth between the arrogant young prince and his moderate, affable father. Amid a mixture of military dangers Murad appointed the 12-year-old Mehmet, if not as full sovereign, then as regent in the European territories while he retired to attend to matters in the Asian regions. The crisis of the resurgent crusade launched in the Balkans by Latin Christian powers was more than young Mehmet and his advisers could manage, and Murad returned to Europe to lead the Turkish forces in their total victory over the crusaders at Varna (10 November 1444).

Murad had devoted his life to mastering what had once been the core territories of old Byzantium, combining much of Asia Minor with the southern Balkans. That control, and the seemingly inevitable conquest of the old Byzantine capital, Constantinople, had been unexpectedly derailed, decades before, by the defeat and capture of Murad's grandfather, Bayazid I (1389–1405), by Tamerlane in 1402. Following a succession struggle, his surviving son, Mehmet I (1413–1421), had reconstituted the Ottoman regime, and Murad had continued that task of restoring and consolidating power. Long years of war had wearied a man of his mild and introspective character and so, after the victory at Varna, Murad formally abdicated in favour of his son. Young Mehmet's yet undisciplined personality, plus court intrigues, bred opposition and a revolt of the elite Janissary corps in the spring of 1446, which forced Murad to end his retirement and resume control once again. His remaining five years were devoted to renewed warfare against hostile or rebellious elements in the Balkans, in the Byzantine Morea, and in Asia Minor, but leaving to his successor to go beyond preserving the status quo.

Aged 19 at his succession, Mehmet made no dramatic changes at first. He did initiate the practice of the new sultan murdering his surviving brothers as potential rivals. But he retained his father's cautious and conservative advisers. He was, however, clearly in sympathy with more activist counsellors and had identified himself since 1444 with the goal of taking Constantinople, the last barrier to the confirmation of the Ottoman regime's imperial status, and its necessary capital.

Devoting initial efforts to neutralizing all possible distractions from internal or neighbouring forces, Mehmet began steadily marshalling his resources for the stroke on which he staked his power and reputation. He supervised the rapid six-month building of Rumeli Hisari, the mighty fortress on the European side of the Bosporus, as a direct threat to Constantinople. He launched the actual siege on 6 April 1453, and conducted it personally with relentless energy. He had hoped to force the city's surrender, but he pressed recurrent assaults, using siege cannon of unprecedented size. After more than 50 days, when the outcome remained in doubt, he insisted on one final, massive assault on 29 May 1453. Upon its success, Mehmet entered the city in triumphal procession. He deplored the pillaging of the city that he was obliged to allow to his troops, but he endeavoured to control it, claiming public buildings and dedicating Hagia Sophia as a mosque.

His landmark victory had earned him the title of *Fatih* or "the Conqueror" usually fused to his name. Valuing his new prize, he made every effort to repair and restore Constantinople, repopulating it (including Greek elements) and initiating its architectural identity as an Islamic capital. Mehmet was anxious to salvage and incorporate elements of the previous Byzantine order, and he was particularly aware of the value of the Orthodox Church as an agency through which the subject Christian population might be coordinated and ruled. Accordingly, he had the Byzantine patriarchate reconstituted under the able Gennadios II Scholarios, former opponent of Byzantine Church union with the Latin west, with whom he developed a relationship of mutual respect. On the other hand, determined to complete his replacement of the old Byzantine state with the new Ottoman imperial regime, he stamped out the remaining centres of Greek independence. After a preliminary reduction of the Morea (1458) he annexed it fully in 1460, ending the Byzantine principality (despotate) there and renewing its conquest four years later after a brief Venetian seizure. In 1461 he formally ended the feeble regime of the Greek emperors of Trebizond.

Mehmet's three decades of rule continued his and his generals' recurrent campaigns against other Christian powers in the Balkans and against Muslim rivals in the east, as well as intermittent hostilities with Venice. In 1456 he unsuccessfully besieged Belgrade but in 1459 he seized the fortress of Semendria (Smederevo), completing the subjection of Serbia;

by 1478 he had reduced Albania. In 1475 he annexed Genoese holdings in the Black Sea regions and established lordship over the Mongol Khanate of the Crimea. In 1480 his forces launched an unsuccessful attack on the Hospitaller Knights of St John in Rhodes, while a daring expeditionary force seized Otranto in a brief attempt to establish a Turkish beachhead in Italy. Only his death brought some respite to Ottoman momentum.

Mehmet's character was complex and sometimes contradictory, a mix of impassioned autocracy and acts of depraved violence combined with open-minded tolerance and enlightened benevolence. With his own diverse ethnic background, he was sensitive to the diverse traditions that constituted his realms and his world – indeed, he was respectful of them and even curious about them. He could display treacherous meanness, as in his brutal murder of Byzantine survivor Loukas Notaras. But he had a lifelong respect for Mara, the Serbian Branković princess who was his stepmother and who, in honoured retirement (outliving him by six years), was always able to intercede with Mehmet. Fascinated by the past, he collected Christian and Byzantine antiquities, assembling them in his new palace complex that we know as Topkapi. He patronized Greek scholarship as well as Islamic, and was inspired by such ancient Greek figures as Achilles and Alexander. Fascinated likewise by new extra-Islamic culture, he cultivated western artists and scholars. To help train artists of his court, he arranged the visit of the great Venetian painter Gentile Bellini, the most notable of several western artists who produced portraits of the conqueror.

Among contemporary Byzantine historians who chronicled the cataclysm of 1453, one of them – the collaborationist official Kritoboulos of Imbros, who won the sultan's favour by negotiating the subjection of Imbros and Lemnos – actually cast his account as a flattering tribute to Mehmet, portraying him as the new Alexander and a true heir to past Byzantine glories.

JOHN W. BARKER

Biography

Born at Edirne in 1432, Mehmet was the third son of Sultan Murad II. After the murder of his second son, Murad began to prepare Mehmet to succeed him, which he duly did in 1451. Successfully taking Constantinople on 29 May 1453, Mehmet assumed the title *Fatih* ("the Conqueror"). He repopulated the city, making it his capital, and established a working relationship with the patriarch Gennadios. He died near Gebze in 1481.

Further Reading

Babinger, Franz, *Mehmed the Conqueror and his Time*, edited by William C. Hickman, Princeton, New Jersey: Princeton University Press, 1978
Imber, Colin, *The Ottoman Empire, 1300–1481*, Istanbul: Isis, 1990
Inalcik, Halil, "The Policy of Mehmed II toward the Greek Population of Istanbul and the Byzantine Buildings of the City", *Dumbarton Oaks Papers*, 23–24 (1969–70): pp. 231–49
Inalcik, Halil, *The Ottoman Empire: The Classical Age, 1300–1600*, London: Weidenfeld and Nicolson, and New York: Praeger, 1973
Karpat, Kemal H., "Ottoman Views and Policies towards the Orthodox Christian Church", *Greek Orthodox Theological Review*, 31 (1986): pp. 131–55
Kritoboulos, M., *History of Mehmed the Conqueror*, Princeton, New Jersey: Princeton University Press, 1954

Runciman, Steven, *The Fall of Constantinople, 1453*, Cambridge: Cambridge University Press, 1965

Melas, Pavlos 1870–1904

Officer, guerrilla leader, and Greek national hero

Pavlos Melas was born in 1870 in Marseilles to a wealthy merchant family. In 1876 they moved to Athens, where Michael, Pavlos's father, entered politics and became actively engaged in irredentist societies, such as the *Ethniki Amina* (National Defence) and, later on, the *Ethniki Hetaireia* (National Society), supporting nationalist movements among the unredeemed Greeks of Crete, Epirus, and Macedonia. A multi-ethnic province of the Ottoman empire, Macedonia caused increasing concern, for at that time the Bulgarian national movement was starting to make its presence felt. The Bulgarians had managed in 1870 to break away from the Ecumenical Patriarchate of Constantinople, which was increasingly perceived as a bastion of Greek nationalism, and to establish their own national Church, the Exarchate. The Slav-speaking peasants, the largest ethnic group in Macedonia, were then prompted (with increasingly violent means) to abandon the patriarchate and opt for the Exarchate instead.

Melas, a receptive and accommodating boy, was growing up at a time of successive national upheavals, when the *Megali Idea* (Great Idea), a chimerical dream of uniting all Greeks (or more precisely, all Christians who had some association with "Hellenism" by language, persuasion, or history) within the confines of a Greek state, was the order of the day. The electrifying atmosphere, combined with his upbringing in a family where the intensity of its patriotism was matched only by the volume of its wealth, ensured that Melas was immersed into a romantic brand of nationalism that became the driving force of his short life. In his vivid boyish imagination the klephts of the 1821 revolution were fused with contemporary realities, and blended into a heroic "klephtic" ideal which he perceived at an early stage to be his destiny. This powerful blend profoundly shaped his adult life and ultimately took it.

At the age of 16 he entered the *Stratiotiki Scholi Evelpidon*, the Greek Military Academy, a prestigious (and expensive) school, and therefore a fitting career move for well-bred Athenians. He graduated in 1891 as a second lieutenant in the Artillery, an elite corps. His personal life was to remain virtually inseparable from the nationalist fever that engulfed Greece in the 1890s. In 1892 he married Natalia, daughter of Stephanos Dragoumis, a prominent politician from Macedonia. In Dragoumis's house, a hotbed of irredentist activity, the couple spent much time: Natalia sipping tea with the other women of the house, and Melas, animated and enthusiastic, talking with Dragoumis and his guests about how the Greeks could counter the Bulgarians in Macedonia.

In 1897, the year of the Graeco-Turkish War, the Greeks were plunged into their most humiliating defeat. Melas fervently believed that the time had come for the liberation of Macedonia to become a reality, rather than a debate in smoke-filled drawing rooms. But the battlefield, with which he did not have the direct contact he hoped for despite his emotional plea to join the front line, soon shattered his dreams. After a few days of restlessness, during which he wrote to Natalia that he would see her soon, for "unfortunately" there would be "no opportunity for us to be killed here", Melas joined the pitiful remnants of the Greek army in a "dishonourable, dishonourable, dishonourable" retreat. For him, the shame of 1897 was particularly painful. As the humiliated nation looked for scapegoats and started accusing the *Ethniki Hetaireia*, his father did not find the strength to face the defeat (and its consequences), and died soon afterwards.

A period of depression followed. Back in Athens, Melas continued to be preoccupied (or, rather, possessed) by the future of Macedonia. His only hope was that one day he himself would cross the border with a band, as a true klepht. In early 1904 his wish came true, as four officers (including Melas) were sent on a fact-finding mission in Macedonia. "Today my desire is at last fulfilled", he wrote in February, heading towards the border. Unwavering dedication to his mission, and sheer enjoyment at having at last the opportunity to be (and look like) a klepht sustained him through a difficult and at times disheartening undertaking. By 1904 the Bulgarian movement in Macedonia was already firmly established. Many Christian Slav-speakers, who just called themselves "Christians" whenever they were given the opportunity to do so, started declaring themselves "Bulgarians" under duress from Bulgarian guerrillas, the *comitadjis*. Others, who continued to call themselves "Greeks", meaning in most cases followers of the "Greek" Ecumenical Patriarchate, faced devastating reprisals. In the course of their journey Melas and the other officers visited a number of villages, talked to the peasants, and tried to restore faith in the Greek cause. Soon, however, he was ordered to leave, for the Turks had been informed of his activity. Devastated by the "idiocy by which they separate me from the idea I now work for", he returned heartbroken to Athens. In July 1904, after securing 20 days' leave, he secretly set out on his second journey, which proved even more frustrating and difficult. "I had neither men, nor money, nor contacts", he wrote in moments of despair. But he continued his efforts to form bands from fearful peasants, or from old brigands, and to set up some sort of Greek defence.

However, Melas was temperamentally unsuited for that job. He was at his best in giving enthusiastic speeches to the peasants (of their impact, we shall never know), but he felt unable to participate in the game of terror that the nature of the struggle required. In Macedonia, nationalism (whatever that meant) rested on the barrel of a gun, but he could not pull the trigger. He realized that he had "to kill, to commit murders", but when the opportunity arose, he was left tearful and shaken and the job was delegated to his companions; they showed less remorse. Melas looked like a klepht, but a true one he never was.

In August he returned to Athens, but soon he was back for his third, and last, journey. He just left a note: the "quiet, family life" really suited him best, but a "superior power" pushed him to Macedonia. As it happened, it pushed him to his fate too. With his band he visited many villages in western Macedonia, organizing the Greek defence and talking passionately to local peasants and students of Greek schools. But the Turks were informed of his whereabouts. On 13 October 1904 their detachments reached the village of Statista (now Mela), into which he had moved, and in the ensuing battle he was shot. He died shortly afterwards in the arms of one of his men. The news shocked the country. The death of a prominent young Athenian under such circumstances, his passionate devotion to his mission, and his remarkable conduct in a field where violence prevailed, ensured that he quickly became the first (and only) national hero of the "Macedonian Struggle" (*Makedonikos Agonas*), the struggle of Greek bands (which started in 1904 and ended four years later) against the *comitadjis*. It is in that that his most important contribution to the Greek cause in Macedonia actually lies.

DIMITRIOS LIVANIOS

See also Macedonia

Biography

Born in Marseilles in 1870 to a wealthy merchant family, Melas moved to Athens and was educated at the Greek Military Academy, graduating in 1891 as a second lieutenant in the Artillery. In 1892 he married Natalia, the daughter of Stephanos Dragoumis, a prominent Macedonian politician. In 1904 he was sent on a fact-finding mission to Macedonia and returned there twice more that year to organize the Greek defence against Bulgarian guerrillas. In October he was shot dead by the Turks and became a Greek national hero of the "struggle for Macedonia".

Further Reading

Dakin, Douglas, *The Greek Struggle in Macedonia, 1897–1913*, Thessalonica: Institute for Balkan Studies, 1966
Melas, Natalia P., *Pavlos Melas*, Athens and Ioannina, 1992 (in Greek)

Melos

Island in the Cyclades

The geographical location of Melos, the most southwesterly of the Cyclades, gave it a position of considerable importance from earliest times, since it was the first of the Aegean islands that mariners would encounter after rounding the southern Peloponnese at Cape Malea on their way to the many ports of the Aegean. The island has an area of 147 sq km and, like a number of other Aegean islands, has volcanic origins, and it is consequently rich in a variety of minerals; the export of these, which include alum, sulphur, keolin, and many others, provided a continuing source of wealth for its inhabitants. The use of millstones produced in Melos was also widespread throughout the Hellenic world. The crater of the volcano that formed the island provides one of the deepest and best-protected harbours in the Aegean. The terrain of Melos is abundant in crops, although its hilly interior has been much mined for its mineral wealth; the highest of its mountains, Prophetis Elias towards the southwest of the island, rises to 751 m.

During the 2nd millennium BC the island formed part of the Cretan and Mycenaean kingdoms, and was later settled by Dorians from Laconia. The Melians provided two penteconters for the Athenians at Salamis (Herodotus, 8. 48), but during the Peloponnesian War they antagonized the Athenians, who mounted a successful siege of the main city, later killing or enslaving the entire population. Thucydides (8. 85–110)

provided a record of the dialogue that preceded, and was the ultimate cause of, this event.

From early in the Christian era the prosperity of Melos allowed the island to contribute in several ways to the Hellenic world. Unique in the whole Aegean area is an extensive catacomb at Trypiti where up to 12 galleries were excavated in the soft sandstone. It was probably used from the 3rd to the late 4th centuries AD, and had between 1500 and 2000 Christian burials. Sadly, already by 1843, when the first published account appeared, there had been wholesale robbing of the sarcophagi it contained, and when Theodore Bent visited it in 1884, not a single grave was left untouched. It was close to this site that the famous statue of Venus, now in the Louvre, was discovered in 1820; it is scarcely an exaggeration to claim that although the statue was mutilated its qualities of idealized perfection of the human figure have since come to represent the Hellenic spirit and its aesthetic message more completely than any other single work of art.

Further evidence of continuing prosperity is the fact that Melos was among the few Aegean islands to send its own bishops to the Sixth and Seventh Church Councils in Constantinople and Nicaea. Attacks by Arab raiders in the later 8th–9th centuries were the probable cause for the abandonment of the island between the later 9th and 12th centuries. The fortunes of Melos after the Fourth Crusade of 1204 and the Deed of Partition followed those of many of the Cyclades, when it came under the control of the Duchy of Naxos from 1206. The proximity of Melos to the Peloponnese, and particularly to Monemvasia, however, meant that with the return of Byzantine rule in Constantinople after 1261 it rejected Latin occupation more readily and actively than any of the other islands. A Greek monk from Monemvasia headed a revolt and drove out the Latins from their castle stronghold. This was to be the last moment until Greek independence that Melos experienced Hellenic rule.

Although the Venetian duke Marco II Sanudo reimposed his rule by force and installed another member of his family, in 1316 the island was raided by the Catalan Company, then establishing themselves in Attica, who carried off some 700 of the inhabitants. In the treaty of 1418 between Venice and the sultan Melos was acknowledged as belonging to Venice, but by 1557 the island had followed the rest of the archipelago into Turkish occupation. Unlike Tinos or Santorini, no outpost of Venetian presence was retained into later centuries. The island was to remain under the Muslim yoke until the coming of Greek independence, developing its own economic and religious life, even for a time supporting a consul who was appointed to assist British interests. There were many changes in the life of the island over these centuries, with Western powers and the Roman Catholic Church always ready to increase their foothold in the Aegean; but Melos was not to play a part that would cause it to stand out from the rest of the islands of the Cyclades.

PAUL HETHERINGTON

See also Obsidian

Summary

A volcanic island in the southwest Cyclades, Melos was the main source of obsidian in the Bronze Age. Its crater provides one of the best harbours in the Aegean. The island's inhabitants were massacred or enslaved by the Athenians in 416/15 BC. There are remains of extensive catacombs from the early Christian period.

Further Reading

Miller, William, *The Latins in the Levant: A History of Frankish Greece, 1204–1566*, London, John Murray, and New York: Dutton, 1908; reprinted Cambridge: Speculum Historiale, 1964

Miller, William, *Essays on the Latin Orient*, Cambridge: Cambridge University Press, 1921; reprinted New York: AMS Press, 1983

Slot, B.J., *Archipelagus Turbatus: les Cyclades entre colonisation latine et occupation ottomane, c.1500–1718*, 2 vols, Istanbul: Nederlands Historisch Archaeologisch Instituut de Istanbul, 1982

Tournefort, Joseph Pitton de, *Relation d'un voyage au Levant*, Lyon, 1717; as *A Voyage into the Levant*, London, 1718

Men

Hellenic woman is as ubiquitous as Hellenic man, yet across the centuries it is man who has held centre stage in the public domain, and he has consequently more often than his counterpart given rise to civilizations and genealogies, eternal ideas, innovative art, has waged wars, and has been the celebrated object and subject of intimate love and fraternity. While woman is the pillar of domestic life, muse, backstage conspirator, it is man who wears the laurels, wields the sword, runs the races, and heralds the dawn of every great triumph. If Zeus and patrilinealism are to the Greek imagination what Isis and matrilinealism are to the Egyptian, it is the gods who have made it so. Yet human agency has perpetuated the myth.

The patrimony of three thousand years of Hellenic culture is threaded together by a clear distinction between private and public life. With notable exceptions, women determine the former, and men are left with the latter. Family farms and homesteads during the Ottoman empire encouraged these distinctions, as does modern agricultural life, where men are associated with labour and tilling the fields and women with kneading the bread and keeping house, with equal feats of endurance. In some communities, women till as much as they knead. But when women do take centre stage, their dignity is unsurpassable and memorable, for such public presence is culturally unseemly, yet the odds against these occurrences, once great, lessen with each passing decade. In recent years women have gained ever greater entrée into politics, the arts, and higher-degree professions. By and large, men and women are proceeding into the new millennium arm-in-arm. But it is the men in the drama of the Greek experience, ever at the proscenium, we now recollect.

The task of making generalizations about men in the Hellenic world is a formidable one. To circumscribe them in a homogeneous mould would do more damage that it would offer insights, and stereotypes are inevitable. Like any other citizen of the world, the Hellene is complex, enigmatic, and multifarious, yet artistic representation, history, and social constructions do offer some clues. Though the main ports and remote outposts of manhood may be miles apart, we shall try to survey the topography none the less. If there are overarching themes of manhood, manliness, or masculinity within Hellenism, for the most part they are culturally determined.

Yet, reinvent themselves they do, as the romantic hero, the premodern entrepreneur, modern stay-at-home husband, or postmodern poet. One commonality rings true across class, station, and political ideology – most Greek men value their masculinity, which embodies a sextet of attributes: endurance, duty, freedom, love of beauty, passion for knowledge, and love of life. Some value schooling more than others, yet even those with an elementary education will quote Marx, will tell you whence the wind blows in December, will discourse knowledgeably on world politics. Classicism, with or without its nuances, indubitably makes itself known somewhere in the Greek man's mind and sticks. And because of this renowned heritage, real or imagined, a certain amount of braggadocio enters the picture, and for this an audience must be found. Conversation, thus, is the sine qua non of his existence. Without community, comrades, or friends, life's purpose would evade him. An Epicurean fragment: "Remove sight, association, and contact, and the passion of love is at an end."

Men of the Hellenic world communicate not only through speech, but with the eyes and hands. The eyes, possessing inner or outer vision, are the proverbial windows to the soul, and they matter. With radial lines at the outer fringes, knowing much laughter, weathered with experience, they speak volumes. The hands – dirtied by work, the pristine hands of the politician, hands stained by cigarettes, veined, long-nailed, delicate, or strong – greet in kindred manner: firmly. In countenance and comportment variety is the norm. All types factor into the mix – bearded like Dionysus, fresh as Adonis, spectacled, stout, towering, cologned, flat-nosed, cultured, blond, blue-eyed, coffee-skinned, dark, fair, the curly-headed ones, rogue, family man, marauder, pious one, tempestuous, tender. Yet, what matters is truth, not oblivion, and this is conveyed through a steady gaze, universally.

With the birth of Archaic Greek sculptural arts, one witnesses the most lasting memorial to the Hellenic male figure, inherited from the civilization across the sea in Egypt, in the form of the free-standing *kouros*. Strong-limbed and planar in construction, the *kouros* gazes straight ahead and smirks, while one foot steps forward into what will be a continuous unshakeable history, a testimony to his fortitude. Lacking the ease of hip and *contrapposto* fluidity of his later metamorphosis, the static *kouros*-as-museum-piece is very much alive in spirit in contemporary Greece and its diasporas. What it represents is more than an idea. It is an ideal, a perpetual reminder of proportional harmony and stability, against which man measures all things.

What of the world of the homoerotic, the stereotypical love figure adorning those vases one sees in museums in western capitals? Not just a question of sexuality, but a question of beauty. The Alexandrian poet Constantine Cavafy captured the cultural convergences as well as the lure of the sensual in "Of the Jews (AD 50)":

> Painter and poet, runner, discus-thrower,
> beautiful as Endymion: Ianthis, son of Antony.
> From a family on close terms with the Synagogue.
>
> "My most valuable days are those
> when I give up the pursuit of sensuous beauty,
> when I desert the elegant and severe cult of Hellenism,
> with its over-riding devotion
> to perfectly shaped, corruptible white limbs,

and become the man I would want to remain forever:
son of the Jews, the holy Jews."

A most fervent declaration on his part: "...to remain
forever
a son of the Jews, the holy Jews."

But he didn't remain anything of the kind.
The Hedonism and Art of Alexandria
kept him as their dedicated son.

Where social relations in ancient Greece delineated sharply between men's work and leisure in the social realm and women's work or play in the private (despite the heady and sporadic appearances of an Aspasia or a Sappho), fraternal and erotic love objects were legendarily men. As much as wives bore the children and stood by their men, the rules governing apprenticeships in philosophy or the arts or the nascent sciences occasionally transcended into elite homoerotic patronages. The elder courting the younger, the younger of perfect body and shapable mind, the elder of knowledge and experience. Plato's idealized Republic made some things clear: the guardians of the city were to be honed and shaped internally and externally. Mathematics, astronomy, musical training, sporting activity, made for the consummate citizen. An advocate of some kind of communism, inclusive of women, sharing the labour and expenditures of a variety of energies in the service of the city, with a wink and a nod in retrospect, one understands none the less the privileged place of men in that structured, hierarchical city.

The Epicureans, however, advanced Plato's invention, acknowledging for the fraternal brotherhood nature's – not god's – roll of the dice. Perambulating through the ether of the planned cosmos are the primordia, first beginnings, random chaotic particles, sensed but not apprehended. How beautiful an idea, random collisions of primordia, just like men, suddenly finding themselves together in commune, eating, drinking, and discussing. In this randomized cosmos, without divine intervention or teleology, how should man live his life? Epicurus' answer: seek pleasure and avoid pain, with temperance. A higher regression from the model city, these Epicurean communards disposed of Aristotle's legendary dictum and lived their lives not solely as political animals but as friends, eschewing public obligations though recognizing the mutual exercise of justice.

The honour-bound heroes of the Trojan War, of conflicts with Sparta, of Alexander's armies, of wars for independence, or wars against fascists, one part reluctant, one part fate-tempting, are long-lasting images of the Hellenic and Hellenic worlds and the Greek nation state. "Dearest, your own great strength will be your death", admonished Homer's Andromache, the loving, white-armed wife of Hector, tragic hero of the Trojan camp, breaker of horses. "Hector, you are father to me, and my honoured mother, you are my brother, and you it is who are my young husband", continued the pre-death eulogy of Andromache, whose name means, "she who fights like a man". To which the adoring husband replied, in Pope's verse:

"Andromache! my soul's far better part,
Why with untimely sorrows heaves thy heart?
No hostile hand can antedate my doom,
Till fate condemns me to the silent tomb."

No man is immortal, not even the hero Achilles, who was dipped into the river Styx for protection against fate, though it was his heel, where he was held, that was to be his downfall. With heroism comes human frailty, not decadent protection. For Homer, man was man, as was the great Alexander of Macedon. Plutarch's character study of him recalls his precocious and determined childhood, his competence, like Hector, to tame a wild horse with gentleness, "a confident voice, and a touch of the heel". Philip, noting his prodigal son's aptitudes, advised, "my son, look for a kingdom equal to yourself, for Macedonia has not space for you." The discontented pioneer, his soldiers haggard, traversed the continents establishing his own outposts of Hellenism, hybridizing his own tribes with those of the east, erstwhile barbarians. Both benevolent and vindictive, Alexander met his death not far from his bath, exhausted. Of these magnificent exploits "the end is always small", wrote the poet Yiorgos Chouliaras.

Homer's high heroic verse resounds archetypically, but from the lyric poets of the 7th and 6th centuries BC to the modern idiomatic poets, poetic subjects remind one of the timelessness of which we are a part. Bawdy like the rest of us, they are cynical, reverent, awesome. This gem from the Byzantine period, a caveat against a careless appearance: "Tall and wavy are the crops/on your hairy face./Scissors?/Never./Throw them away and bring out a plough." Michael Herzfeld's assessment of 20th-century Glendiots is fitting, where he writes "there is less focus of 'being a good man' than on 'being *good* at being a man' – a stance that stresses *performative excellence.*" Socially, men do this best in the *kafeneia*, or coffee shops, of the modern day, gesticulating and talking their way to bravadoes.

Ever reveried, again enduring, still politicking, leaving home to find it elsewhere among their own kind, driving taxis, serving tasty morsels, crafting memorials of words and steel, airborne and stubborn, naughtily and forgivingly they persevere and clamour at the gates of hell and paradise. "Try to enjoy the great festival of life with other men", said the Greek Epictetus, enslaved to a Roman master.

BARBARA SYRRAKOS

See also Homosexuality, Kafeneion, Women

Further Reading

Barnstone, Willis (translator), *Greek Lyric Poetry*, New York: Bantam, 1962

Boardman, John, *Greek Sculpture: The Classical Period*, London: Thames and Hudson, 1991

Boardman, John, Jasper Griffin, and Oswyn Murray (editors), *The Oxford History of Greece and the Hellenistic World*, Oxford and New York: Oxford University Press, 1991

Cavafy, Constantine, *The Complete Poems*, translated by Rae Dalven, with an introduction by W.H. Auden, London: Hogarth Press, and New York: Harcourt Brace, 1961; expanded edition, 1976

Dubisch, Jill (editor), *Gender and Power in Rural Greece*, Princeton, New Jersey: Princeton University Press, 1986

Friar, Kimon (translator and with introduction), *Modern Greek Poetry*, New York: Simon and Schuster, 1973

Gaskin, John (editor), *The Epicurean Philosophers*, London: Everyman, 1995

Glotz, Gustave, *The Greek City and its Institutions*, New York: Barnes and Noble, and London: Routledge and Kegan Paul, 1965

Hadas, Moses, *A History of Greek Literature*, New York: Columbia
    University Press, 1950

Herzfeld, Michael, *The Poetics of Manhood: Contest and Identity in
    a Cretan Mountain Village*, Princeton, New Jersey: Princeton
    University Press, 1985

Homer, *The Iliad*, translated by Alexander Pope, London and New
    York: Penguin, 1996 (Pope's translation first published 1715–20)

Homer, *The Iliad*, translated by Richmond Lattimore, Chicago:
    University of Chicago Press, 1951

Kazantzakis, Nikos, *Zorba the Greek*, translated by Carl Wildman,
    New York: Simon and Schuster, and London: Lehmann, 1952

Laiou, Angeliki E. and Henry Maguire (editors), *Byzantium: A World
    Civilization*, Washington, D.C.: Dumbarton Oaks, 1992

Panourgiá, Neni, *Fragments of Death, Fables of Identity: An
    Athenian Anthropography*, Madison: University of Wisconsin
    Press, 1995

Plato, *The Republic*, translated by Allan Bloom, New York: Basic
    Books, 1991

Plutarch, *Selected Lives and Essays*, Roslyn, New York: J. Black,
    1951

Siotis, Dinos and John Chioles (editors), *Twenty Contemporary
    Greek Poets*, San Francisco: Wire Press, 1979

Veis, George, review of *O Thisavros ton Balkanion* [The Treasure of
    the Balkans] by Yiorgos Chouliaras, in *Modern Greek Studies
    Yearbook*, edited by Theofanis G. Stavrou, Minneapolis:
    University of Minnesota, 1989

Menander 342–292 BC

Comic playwright

Not only was Menander, in the opinion of his Hellenistic
followers as well as of modern critics, the greatest playwright
of New Comedy, but he is also among the most influential
authors in the history of literature. In him the modern attitudes
to quotidian existence, human character, life's vicissitudes, and
society's conventions were first crystallized. Unconcerned in his
works with Sophocles' tragic confrontations with time and the
cosmos (though his subtle diction refers often to tragedy), he
shows us as we are, with tolerance, affection, and a wisely critical eye. Subsequent writers of drama, when not tragic, usually
took his approach for a model, from Shakespeare to Molière
to Oscar Wilde.

Menander (or Menandros) was born in Athens of a good
family at the end of the Classical period. Among his teachers
was Theophrastus, whose *Characters* was surely an influence;
Theophrastus' teacher was another realist, Aristotle, and
Aristotle, of course, was Plato's student. In 338 BC Philip of
Macedon made the Greeks his subjects, and Athens, after a last
burst of heroic resistance under Demosthenes, began its slide
from Hellas's most energetic city to a provincial town living on
its reputation.

Menander's first play, *Orge* (Rage), was produced in 321
BC, and he died, supposedly drowned in the harbour of Piraeus,
in 292 BC, a generation after the immense changes in Athenian
society wrought by the conquests of Philip's son, Alexander the
Great. His work anticipates and then reflects that later world,
when men had lost belief in heroism and trust in public religion, and found fulfilment more as private individuals than as
active members of the polis. That explains why Menander's
plays do not resemble those of the 5th-century BC master of
Old Comedy, Aristophanes, but rather the strange late

romances of Euripides (who in old age forsook Athens for
Macedonia); in plays such as *Alcestis* and *Ion* that disillusioned
master abandoned ideals of high morality and noble citizenship and the tragic conception with them. In the satirical
fantasies of Aristophanes the main character is the chorus,
which represents the polis, i.e. us, the *demos*, while in
Menander the chorus, left to the care of producers, merely
provides entr'acte entertainment. Because Menander's plays do
not comment directly on political life, they were equally at
home in any Greek theatre, i.e. they were international. The
inheritor of the whole Classical age, Menander helped to
define the lesser but still brilliant Hellenistic age for his viewers
and for us. Our notion of comedy is his.

Meaning, Menander thought, now that freedom and glory
are gone, must needs be sought in the paradoxes of private life,
at home and on the street. His characters are types – the
curmudgeonly father, the wronged wife, the clever slave, the
sweet-souled courtesan – and his plots, with their coincidences,
mistaken identities, belated recognition of foundling children,
and acceptance of young lovers by parents, became so.
Elements of them can be found hundreds of years later in the
Greek romance "novels". His time is contemporary and his
location often Athens or Attica. But these provide a framework
for the lifelike and sympathetic exploration of the problems of
everyday happenstance. Although there is always a love interest, his themes are various and lead to reconciliation in the
family and with neighbours. Stylized romantic plots expose
society's humdrum insecurities. The long modulated speeches
so attractive to skilled actors in masks, the theatrical effects of
surprise, the rapid dialogue in which one easy phrase may
contain several meanings, the aphoristic wit, the moving direct
appeals to the audience – the more we recover of him, the more
diverse and profound he seems. His characters are rich, poor;
old, young; male, female; free, slave; sophisticated, rustic; his
range, so far as we can judge from the 5 per cent of his work
that we know, is Shakespearean. (Hamlet's remark,
"Conscience doth make cowards of us all", is taken from fragment 632.) His people quarrel, love, go to court, lend and
borrow, yearn for riches and romance, get drunk, try to be
good. His sympathy with slaves, for example, is almost
unprecedented; in *The Farmer* he even shows a slave in love.
His convincing understanding of human character, his colloquial and graceful language (mostly in iambic trimeter), and
his sheer skill as a constructor of entertaining plays keep his
work fresh and illuminating. He never moralizes, but he
quietly puts forward ideals of tolerance, generosity, kindliness,
and understanding. In other words, he is typically Greek in
that he seeks *dike*, or justice – but in ordinary life, with forgiveness always the resolution.

Menander's immense skill is clearly evident in the early
Dyscolus (The Curmudgeon), in the character of the gruff
grouch Knemon, while the subtle clash and contrast of character and ethical principle in such plays as *Perikeiromene* (The
Rape of the Lock), and *Adelphoe II* (Second Brothers), constitute his greatest achievement.

The works of most ancient writers have come down to us in
tatters, and Menander, the last great poet of Athens, is no
exception. Although he wrote more than one hundred comedies, only the *Dyscolus* (it won the prize in 317 BC) survives
nearly intact; half a dozen plays are tantalizingly incomplete

but sufficient for literary judgement, and a sheaf of fragments completes our knowledge. The longer pieces were discovered on Egyptian papyrus strips only in the 20th century. The comedies of Plautus and Terence, who flourished a century after Menander, are often either a close adaptation or even translation of Menander or other New Comedy playwrights, so that Roman drama could hardly have existed without his example. Before the recent discoveries, most of his immense influence derived from them; now at least we have originals.

Menander's reputation, like that of Euripides, grew steadily after his death. Although he won only eight first prizes during his life, his plays became the basis of the comic repertoire. Because of this international popularity, he contributed to the fixing of the koine, or standard Attic Greek, that was the east's language of culture for hundreds of years. Byzantine students down to at least AD 600 and probably much later learned many of his sententious aphorisms, although in context (which was vanishing) these gnomes are always dramatic and often ironic. Now that Aristophanes, without his polis, was incomprehensible, comedy for a Greek, and indeed for us, meant Menander.

A few fragments have yet to be translated, and it is not unlikely that more will come to light. In our age of fragile relationships and moral confusion, we need them.

JEFFREY CARSON

See also Comedy

Biography

Born in Athens in 342 BC, Menander was a pupil of Theophrastus and a friend of Epicurus and Demetrius of Phalerum. As the author of over a hundred plays, he was and still is held to be the greatest playwright of New Comedy. His plays were popular in antiquity (he won eight first prizes) and were translated into Latin by Plautus and Terence. He died in 292, apparently by drowning in the sea off Piraeus.

Writings

Plays and Fragments, translated by Philip Vellacott, Harmondsworth and Baltimore: Penguin, 1967

The Plays, translated by Lionel Casson, New York: New York University Press, 1971

Menander, translated by W.G. Arnott, 2 vols, London: Heinemann, and Cambridge, Massachusetts: Harvard University Press, 1979–96

Plays and Fragments, translated by Norma Miller, London and New York: Penguin, 1987

Menander: The Grouch, Desperately Seeking Justice, Closely Cropped Locks, The Girl from Samos, The Shield, translated by David R. Slavitt and Palmer Bovie, Philadelphia: University of Pennsylvania Press, 1998

Further Reading

Bieber, Margarete, *The History of the Greek and Roman Theater*, 2nd edition, Princeton, New Jersey: Princeton University Press,1961

Frost, K.B., *Exits and Entrances in Menander*, Oxford: Clarendon Press, and New York: Oxford University Press, 1988

Goldberg, Sander M., *The Making of Menander's Comedy*, Berkeley: University of California Press, and London: Athlone Press, 1980

Gomme, A.W. and F.H. Sandbach, *Menander: A Commentary*, London: Oxford University Press, 1973

Henry, Madeleine Mary, *Menander's Courtesans and the Greek Comic Tradition*, Frankfurt and New York: Peter Lang, 1985

Ireland, Stanley, *Menander: Dyskolos, Samia and Other Plays: A Companion to the Penguin Translation of the Plays of Menander by Norma Miller*, London: Bristol Classical Press, 1992

Sutton, Dana F., *Ancient Comedy: The War of the Generations*, New York: Twayne, 1993

Walton, J. Michael and Peter D. Arnott, *Menander and the Making of Comedy*, Westport, Connecticut: Greenwood Press, 1996

Webster, T.B.L., *Greek Theatre Production*, 2nd edition, London: Methuen, 1970

Webster, T.B.L., *An Introduction to Menander*, Manchester: Manchester University Press, and New York: Barnes and Noble, 1974

Wiles, David, *The Masks of Menander: Sign and Meaning in Greek and Roman Performance*, Cambridge and New York: Cambridge University Press, 1991

Zagagi, Netta, *The Comedy of Menander: Convention, Variation and Originality*, London: Duckworth, 1994

Messene

City in the southern Peloponnese

Ancient Messene, located in the very centre of the modern province of Messenia, was one of the best-fortified cities of ancient Greece. Situated at the foot of Mount Ithome, it was protected by an acropolis. The city was named after Messene, the mythological first queen of Messenia, but it is not clear when it was founded. It is generally thought that the Theban leader Epaminondas founded Messene in 369 BC, after the battle of Leuktra. But Plato (*Laws*, 683d) and Isocrates (*Arch.*, 22), among other 4th-century BC authors, allude to the existence of the polis of Messene long before that date. Only later sources, such as Strabo (8. 58) and Pausanias (4. 1. 3–4), attribute the foundation of Messene to Epaminondas. Pausanias does however mention an earlier city on that spot, but refers to it as Ithome (4. 9. 2).

From 371 BC the Thebans diminished Sparta's power by uniting the Peloponnesian people in strong cities. Argos and Mantinea were fortified. The Arcadian League was formed with its newly built capital at Megalopolis. The independence of Messenia was to be guaranteed by constructing the walled city of Messene. In 369 Epaminondas sent envoys to southern Italy and Libya to invite the Messenians of the diaspora to return to their homeland. Many of them did so and thus they populated the city.

Messene was built in a short time, by the joint efforts of Thebans, Arcadians, Argives, and Messenians, who together laid out streets and built houses, temples and circuit walls. At the same time Epaminondas built a harbour for the Messenians, at Kyparissia on the west coast. Pherae (Kalamata) would have been more suitable as a harbour, but there the Spartan threat would always have been near. Epaminondas' master plan succeeded, and Sparta's power was restricted between the Taygetus and Parnon mountains.

When Philip II of Macedon led his troops against the Greek city states, the Messenians formed an alliance with him. They did not take part in the Battle of Chaeronea (338 BC), because they refused to bear arms against fellow Greeks. After Alexander the Great's death (323 BC), however, the Messenians joined the Greek revolt and thus lost their friendship with the

Macedonians. In 213 BC Philip V visited the citadel of Messene with his counsellors Aratus of Sicyon and Demetrius of Pharos, under the pretext of making an offering to Zeus. He was in fact planning to capture this attractive bastion and after making the offering he asked his counsellors for advice. Demetrius warned him that if he did not take the citadel, he perhaps would be sorry afterwards. "Remember that it is only by holding both his horns that you can keep the ox down" (Polybius, 7. 12). The horns referred to the bastions of Mount Ithome and the Acrocorinth, and the ox to the Peloponnese. Aratus advised Philip to withdraw, and thus avoid arousing the hostility of the other Greek states. Philip took Aratus' advice, but soon afterwards regretted it. The same year Aratus died, presumably poisoned by Philip. A year later Demetrius of Pharos tried to capture Messene by a surprise attack, but the inhabitants resisted fiercely and defeated the Macedonian troops. Demetrius was killed in battle.

Messene was finally captured by Nabis, the tyrant of Sparta, in 195 BC. He abandoned the city after a short time, due to the threat of an attack by the Achaean League. In 191 BC Messene was forced by the Romans to join the Achaean League and in 146 BC, like all Greek cities, it became part of the Roman empire. Hostility with Sparta continued to play an important role in foreign policy. As the Spartans favoured Octavian (later Augustus) in his struggle for power, Messene was forced to choose Mark Antony's side. After the battle of Actium in 31 BC Messene lost control of the cities in the Mani.

The city of Messene flourished until the end of Roman control over Greece. It remained the capital of the free Messenian state until the 4th century AD. In AD 395 the Goths destroyed and depopulated the city, which was never to be inhabited again. The village of Mavromati, between the ancient city and Mount Ithome, is a recent settlement.

On top of Mount Ithome stand the remains of the sanctuary of Zeus Ithomatas. It was there that Philip V of Macedon was tempted to seize the city. On the way down one crosses the remains of a temple. This might be the temple of Artemis Laphria, mentioned by Pausanias (4. 31. 7). However, an inscription found at the spot refers to Artemis Limnatis. Other public buildings revealed by archaeologists are a theatre and a stadium. The most striking feature of the city is the vast Asclepieum. The temple of Asclepius and his daughter Hygieia is surrounded by smaller temples of unknown use, a bouleuterion, an odeum, and, of course, baths. The Sebasteum to the north of the temple proves that the city flourished in Roman imperial times. The worship of Asclepius in Messene is also evidenced by the fountain in the centre of the city, assigned to Arsinoe, in Messenian mythology the mother of Asclepius.

The walls of Messene are as imposing to the modern visitor as they were to the ancients. Pausanias (4. 31. 5) was impressed by their construction and considered them stronger than those of Byzantium and Rhodes. The 10-km circuit connects the city with the acropolis on Mount Ithome. Two city gates are well preserved: the Laconian Gate on the saddle between Mount Ithome and Mount Eva and the impressive Arcadian Gate on the western side of the city. The wall is best preserved in this western section with its round and square

two-storey towers occuring at intervals; it makes the site one of the most interesting examples of 4th-century BC architecture.

MAARTEN J. GROND

Summary

The chief city of ancient Messenia, Messene was traditionally founded by Epaminondas in 369 BC, following up his victory at the Battle of Leuctra. It was fortified with a particularly fine circuit of walls, much of which remains standing. Messene flourished during the Roman period but was sacked by the Goths in AD 395 and never inhabited again.

Further Reading

Kaltsas, Nikos, *Ancient Messene*, Athens, 1989 (in Greek)
Kiechle, Franz, *Messenische Studien: Untersuchungen zur Geschichte der Messenischen Kriege und der Auswanderung der Messenier*, Kallmünz: Lassleben, 1959
Pausanias, *Description of Greece*, translated by W.H.S. Jones, 5 vols, London: Heinemann, and New York: Putnam, 1918–35 (Loeb edition; several reprints), book 4
Stamatopoulos, Dimitris, *Messinia*, Kalamata, 1987 (in Greek)

Messenia

Region of the Peloponnese

Messenia is one of the seven provinces of the Peloponnese. It covers the southwestern part of the peninsula. Like most Greek provinces its boundaries are formed by sea and mountains. The eastern approach is blocked by the inhospitable Taygetus ridge, which offers passage only far down in the Mani or through the Langada pass. To the north, Messenia ends halfway across the Tetrazion mountains. Here also access is only possible through narrow passes from the plain of Megalopolis and along the coast.

The province includes the fertile Messenian plain, which leads to the Messenian Gulf, and a narrow, more or less flat, coastal area to the west. These plains are divided from the north to the southernmost point by the Aigalion ridge, of which St Barbara is the most conspicuous peak (1112 m). Kalamata is the provincial capital and with its 44,000 inhabitants by far the largest city. Other local centres are Pylos (2000 inhabitants) and Kyparissia (4500 inhabitants).

According to Pausanias (4. 1. 1–2), Messenia owes its name to its first queen, Messene. She was married to Polycaon, the younger brother of the Laconian king. She was also the daughter of the king of Argos, and therefore too proud to be satisfied with her husband's minor role in Laconia. She took Polycaon and his retinue from Argos and Sparta and crossed the Taygetus mountains. This land from then on was called Messene. Many generations later, Messenia passed to the Neleid dynasty. Neleus and his son Nestor lived in prosperity in their palace at Pylos. Nestor took 90 ships to the Trojan War, which suggests he was the second most powerful ruler, surpassed only by Agamemnon. Nestor's wealth must have been based on the agricultural resources of the Messenian plain. The Linear B tablets, found in the Mycenaean "Palace of Nestor" near the modern village of Pylos, confirm this picture. The ruler of the palace subjected the population of Messenia to a strict taxation system. The range and quantity of products were vast: wine, honey, wheat, barley, olives, figs, spices, pigs, horses, sheep, goats, etc.

After the Dorian invasion of the Peloponnese Messenia was assigned to Cresphontes. Much more violent were the Spartan invasions of the country, better known as the Messenian Wars. During the Archaic period, when other city states solved their overpopulation problems by setting up colonies, Sparta conquered Messenia and subdued its population. Much is written, but little is known about these wars. Pausanias gives a detailed report, but he undertook his travels in Roman imperial times. Therefore our knowledge of dates and facts is far from accurate. In the second half of the 8th century BC the Spartans for the first time crossed Mount Taygetus and attacked the Messenian plain. For 20 years the Messenians fought back, first under the inspiring leadership of their king Euphaes, a descendant of Cresphontes, and after his death under Aristodemus. Finally, however, the Spartan hoplites conquered the last Messenian stronghold on Mount Ithome. The Messenians kept their autonomy by paying the Spartans half of the produce of their land. After a rebellion in the second half of the 7th century many Messenians emigrated to Rhegium in southern Italy, where, in 493 BC, their descendants captured Zancle and renamed it Messana (now Messina). The remaining inhabitants were reduced to serfdom. The Third Messenian War (500–489 BC) may have kept the Spartans away from the battlefield of Marathon in 490 BC. The Fourth Messenian War (464–459 BC) was a Pyrrhic victory for the Spartans. Although Messenia was once again brought under Spartan dominion, exiled Messenians were settled by Athens in Naupactus. It was these Messenians who in 425 BC supported the Athenians at the siege of Sphacteria and thus put an end to Sparta's reputation for invincibility. After the Peloponnesian War the Messenians were driven from Naupactus by the Spartans and again went in exile to southern Italy and to Euhesperides in Libya (later Berenice). Finally, after the Battle of Leuctra (371 BC), where the Spartan army was defeated by Theban forces, Epaminondas repatriated the Messenians from the diaspora and built (or refortified) for them the strong city of Messene at the foot of Mount Ithome. He also rebuilt Kyparissia, to be used as the port and harbour of Messene. Sparta never regained control of this area and Messenia remained independent until the Roman conquest of Greece in 146 BC.

Information about Messenia under Roman rule is very scarce. The country seems to have had a certain kind of autonomy, but being a part first of the province of Macedonia, and after 31 BC of Achaea, Roman authority was never far away. Emperor Augustus gave the cities of the Mani to Sparta; Tiberius assigned the cities on the western flank of the Taygetus mountains to Messenia.

The barbarian raids of the 4th century AD mark the end of antiquity. Alaric and his Visigoths invaded Greece and sacked the major cities and sanctuaries. In AD 395 the city of Messene was destroyed and depopulated. It does not appear to have been reinhabited in the medieval period. During the 7th and 8th centuries AD Slavs settled in Messenia. Medieval city names such as Sitsova, Tsernitsa, and Gialova are proof of this immigration. Byzantine families built fortresses over ancient foundations in Kyparissia and Kalamata.

From the 12th century on, Frankish crusaders started building strongholds in the Peloponnese. Counts from Belgium and France occupied parts of the country and built impressive fortresses mostly at inaccessible places. Geoffrey I de Villehardouin erected the *kastro* at Kalamata; Nicholas II de Saint Omer built the fortress of Palaiokastro, on the site of ancient Pylos. At this time, too, Venetians appeared in the area. In order to defend their trade routes to the Levant they erected seaside strongholds, such as Methone and Corone. For 300 years the Venetians controlled the country.

From 1460 on, the Turks started to play a role in Messenia. Sultan Mehmet II conquered the country, leaving only Methone, Corone, and Palaiokastro to the Venetians. In 1500 Sultan Bayezid II captured Methone after a month's bombardment, thus bringing all Messenia under Turkish rule. Strategic points such as Methone, Corone, Palaiokastro, Neokastro, and Kalamata were reinforced. Apart from the brief second Venetian period following Morosini's conquest in 1685–1715, Messenia remained in Turkish hands until the War of Independence.

Kalamata is said to have been the first city to have revolted against the Turks in 1821. Ibrahim Pasha's counterattack in 1825 once again destroyed the Greek hope for freedom. However, they did not have to wait long for the decisive move in this war. In July 1827 France, Great Britain, and Russia signed the "Triple Alliance" in London: Turkey should stop its war in Greece within a month. After the one month had expired, the Turks had not only ignored the Treaty of London, but had reinforced their fleet at Navarino. On 20 October 1827 an allied fleet, numbering 26 warships, entered the bay of Navarino, as a warning to Ibrahim Pasha to withdraw his Turko-Egyptian fleet from the Peloponnese. After some unsuccessful negotiations a few shots fired by the Turks brought about general action. In four hours the Turkish fleet had lost 55 ships and 6000 men. The allies lost 174 men, but not a single ship. The victory at Navarino weakened Turkish power in the Morea. In 1828 the French general Maison landed 14,000 troops in Petalidi, thus causing the hasty departure of the Turkish occupying force. The French soldiers immediately started to restore the country's infrastructure, by founding and building the new village of Pylos and by constructing a road from Pylos to Methone.

Nowadays Messenia is still an agricultural area, where the cultivation of olives and grapes provides the people with a certain degree of wealth. Tourism on the other hand has not yet fully developed, mainly because the road system is not adapted to modern traffic. Therefore visitors are welcomed heartily and the hospitality that Telemachus enjoyed at Nestor's court in *Odyssey* book 3 is still available.

MAARTEN J. GROND

Summary

This province in the southwest Peloponnese was named after Messene, daughter of the king of Argos. It was ruled by Nestor in the Bronze Age. It was occupied by Sparta in the Archaic period in a series of Messenian Wars, though the Messenians retained their autonomy for much of the Classical period. Kalamata claims to be the first city to have revolted against the Turks in 1821. The area relies on agriculture for its wealth.

Further Reading

Chadwick, John and Michael Ventris, *Documents in Mycenaean Greek*, 2nd edition, Cambridge: Cambridge University Press, 1973

Chadwick, John, *The Mycenaean World*, Cambridge and New York: Cambridge University Press, 1976

McDonald, William A. and George R. Rapp Jr, *The Minnesota Messenia Expedition: Reconstructing a Bronze Age Regional Environment*, Minneapolis: University of Minnesota Press, 1972

Stamatopoulos, Dimitris, *Messinia*, Kalamata, 1987 (in Greek)

Valmin, Mattias Natan, *Etudes topographiques sur la Messénie ancienne*, Lund: Blom, 1930

Metalwork

A knowledge of the processing of metals came to the Greek world in the Early Bronze Age (3000–2000 BC), in all probability from the east. The finding and working of copper and iron are attributed by such authors as Dioscurides, Strabo, Pliny, and Diodorus Siculus to the mythical demons, the Cabiri (Phrygian) and Curetes (Cretan).

In Homer we have the earliest description of the way in which a coppersmith's shop operated; the coppersmith is Hephaestus, god of fire, himself a deity who came from the island of Lemnos in the Aegean. The first examples of the coppersmith's art were found in the Cyclades – the Zia cave on Naxos, Kefala on Kea – at Knossos in Crete, at Yali in the Dodecanese, and in Cyprus. The on-the-spot processing of the metal copper and its alloy bronze required collective action, the pre-existence of deposits, and organized trade. We possess no more than 100 metal objects from Neolithic Greece.

In the Early and Middle Bronze Age (3000–1450 BC) metal vessels imported from the Near East seem to have affected the shapes of ceramics in Thessaly (Dimini, phase 1), although there is early evidence for the morphological independence of metal objects in the Greek world. There is a silver *skyphos* (cup, can) from Amorgos in the Cyclades, another *skyphos*, and two gold vessels of primitive shape in the Benaki Museum in Athens. Gold *kymbes* (cups) and elliptical *skyphoi* with a spout seem to have served as drinking cups – such as the one found at the Heraea of Arcadia (in the Louvre), which has been shaped by hammering from a single leaf of gold, apart from the handle. These show that the inhabitants of mainland Greece also made vessels from precious metals.

In Crete silver objects from the early Minoan period have been discovered on the islet of Mochlos. One cup, with a handle, was full of gold jewellery. In the Minoan palace period (Knossos, Mallia, Phaestus) a brilliant civilization, considered to be Europe's first, developed; it dominated the whole of the Aegean and had constant contacts with the east and with Egypt. At the beginning of the 2nd millennium BC metalwork and metal vessels developed to the point where they became models; their shapes were copied and their grooved and chased naturalistic decoration appeared in paint on ceramic vessels. The horde discovered at Tôd in Egypt (tomb of Amenemhet, 1940–1938 BC), consisting of 153 silver cups and only one in gold, is in all probability from Crete. There were deposits of silver on certain of the Cyclades, at Akrotiri on Thera, and in the Laurium region in Attica, all workable before 1600 BC.

The commonest type of vessel made of gold or silver in Crete seems to have been the drinking cup. The gold cup with relief decoration consisting of spirals and rosettes from the so-called Aegina Treasure in the British Museum must also be Cretan. Objects made by the "Kaptaru" (Cretans) were, according to texts from Mari in the mid-Euphrates, much sought after. Small scale carving (seal carving) and the art of metalwork reached their highest point during the "New Palace" period, which produced superb chased ritual swords with inlaid gold, decorative gold double axes – symbols of the Minoan religion (votive offerings from the sacred cave of Arkalochori, of 1600 BC, in the Herakleion Museum), figurines, chased or cast, relief or engraved vessels, inlaid with sacred bulls' heads, and bronze *lebetes* (cauldrons) to hold a whole sheep for boiling. The handles of cups and the upper part of closed vessels such as *prochoi* (jugs) and *hydriai* (water jugs) were made from separate pieces of metal; although it seems that the craftsmen of the Aegean area knew the art of soldering, they nevertheless preferred to join the parts by riveting.

The eruption of the volcano of Thera (Santorini) around 1500 BC swept away the peaceful matriarchal and refined Minoan civilization which was succeeded by the equally brilliant Mycenaean civilization of mainland Greece. Large centres of Mycenaean culture have been identified at Mycenae, Tiryns, Pylos, Athens, Thebes, Orchomenus, and Iolcus. The best-known branch of art in the early part of the Mycenaean period, influenced by the Minoans, is metalwork, as is illustrated by the wealth of vessels, tools, and jewellery found in the royal tombs, reminiscent of the high standard of living; figurines are comparatively few. Purely Mycenaean metalwork makes its appearance in the many bronze household utensils – in all their different forms with engraved or relief ornamentation – that were handed down from generation to generation as heirlooms or dowries (the Dentra tombs, the hearth with the tripod at Knossos, Perati in Attica, Curium in Cyprus). The fine gold cups from a tomb at Vapheio (Sparta), for example, show the capture of wild bulls (Athens Archaeological Museum). Also striking are the huge bronze figure-of-eight shields and gold engraved seals, the swords decorated with inlaid gold and niello (a blue-black alloy of copper and silver with sulphur), and the gold masks made to adorn the faces of dead kings and notables, with their imposing features, such as that once thought to be Agamemnon's with its engraved moustache and beard.

The Panhellenic campaign of the Achaeans against Troy is an indisputable historical event. A dramatic scene from a siege is shown on the famous "siege *rhyton*" (drinking horn) from the acropolis of Mycenae, grave IV (Athens Archaeological Museum). At the time of the campaign against Troy and in the early 12th century BC that followed, there was a distinct decline in the arts throughout the Aegean, coinciding with the destruction of the centres of Mycenaean civilization for reasons that are unknown to us. Nevertheless, there was a significant change in the technology of metals, bronze being replaced by iron for tools and weapons, though metal objects were rare. In the 11th century BC the early Geometric style marked the beginning of a long process leading in the end to the achievements of Archaic and Classical Greece.

The establishment of Greek colonies, from the Pillars of Hercules, Italy, Sicily, the Crimea, and Asia Minor to Phoenicia, brought a lively trade with the Near East, which gave a new boost to the demand for and working in metals. The development of metalworking from the early 8th century BC onwards was impressive. All the metal figurines (of copper or bronze), male and female, are shown nude. The females convey a sense of immobility, with their arms held down the sides of the body, while the male figurines, which form the overwhelming majority down to the 8th century BC, are shown with their hands raised in an attitude of worship, as in the case of the male figurines from Gazi and from Karfi in Crete. In the Geometric period the stylized depiction in figurines of animals such as the lion and a great number of bronze colts from workshops at Argos, Olympia, Corinth, and Laconia made its appearance.

Around 725 BC bronze figurines from Attica take a more naturalistic and less stylized form. The beginnings of the depiction of organic details (clavicles, chest muscles, indication of the locks of hair) can be seen in the figure of a warrior wearing a helmet, from the Acropolis.

Before the end of the Archaic period, scenes from everyday life made their appearance in metalworking, together with figures such as a drinker or flute-player from Sparta or Olympia, a lyre player from Herakleion in Crete, an archer from Delphi, and a number of compositions in bronze, such as charioteers on their chariots, the most important example being the well-known *Charioteer of Delphi*. In historical times iron, and a knowledge of how to work in it, prevailed over bronze throughout the Greek world, without the use of bronze going completely into abeyance. Nevertheless, since iron rusts and breaks up, only a very few examples have survived, such as a gilded iron ring in the Athens Archaeological Museum. One of the regions richest in copper ores was Cyprus – hence the Latin *cuprum*. Homer knew of the copper of Tamassos in Cyprus, which he mentions in the *Odyssey*.

It was from Cyprus, from around the middle of the 2nd millennium BC, that a standardized mass of pure copper in the shape of a pillow, weighing one talent, went to many parts of the ancient world as raw material. Sardinia and southern Spain (Tartessus) were also important sources of copper. The origins of the tin that was necessary for the hardening of the prehistoric alloys remain obscure – perhaps it came from Afghanistan – but in historical times we know that the tin used was derived from the Tin Islands (Cassiterides) – Britain – and that it reached the Mediterranean via the Iberian peninsula and Gaul. Lead may also have been used for the hardening of the alloy. This was to be found in large quantities in Greece, for example, in the mines of Laurium, as a by-product of the production of silver (tin was totally absent).

The two principal methods of making bronze objects (figurines of animals or human beings, tripods, jewellery) in early antiquity, and throughout the centuries down to the present, were the casting of the molten alloy in a suitably prepared mould (such as, for example, the plaster moulds of the late 10th century BC from Lefkandi on Euboea for the making of tripod feet), and beating it out with a hammer. The best bronze sheeting had a 5–10 per cent admixture of tin. An increase of the tin content rendered it fragile, but gave it a superb yellowish colour like gold, as is demonstrated by the

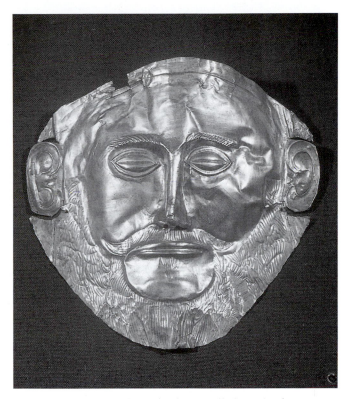

Metalwork: gold death mask, the so-called Mask of Agammemnon, Mycenae, late 16th century BC, National Archaeological Museum, Athens

famous Derveni *krater* (mixing bowl) of Hellenistic times, whose metal has a 15 per cent tin content. The chasing technique was used extensively in the 8th and 7th centuries BC for the production of statues of medium size. Famous works of chasing are the *Divine Triad* of the 8th century BC from Dreros, Crete, of a height of 0.80 m, nailed to a wooden core (Herakleion Archaeological Museum), and the silver bull from Delphi of the 5th century BC. In the case of larger cast statues, for reasons of economy of the metal, from the mid-seventh century BC the technique known as the "lost wax" method was devised.

From the 5th century, meanwhile, a new technique of "indirect" casting came to be used whereby a clay model was made and a mould ("negative") was produced from this, making it possible to have a large number of identical cast objects. The details, such as the hair, the eyes, and the nails, were incised with a sharp instrument. Often the pupils of the eyes were of inlaid ivory, and the nipples and lips of plain inlaid bronze.

The success of the Athenians and their allies against the Persians (490–479 BC) led to the splendours of the age of Pericles and of Classical Greece with its humanistic philosophical systems and its universally admired art. The Chalkotheke, the building next to the Parthenon on the Acropolis of Athens, housed the metal votive offerings to the goddess Athena – some of bronze, but chiefly of precious metals.

The Spartan Telestas, of the 6th century BC, and the great Myron, of the 5th century BC, belong to the same category of craftsmen: they were at one and the same time workers in bronze and silversmiths. Myron is credited with the making of silver drinking cups, while the great sculptor Phidias himself

Metalwork: silver plate, probably for holding the Eucharistic bread, Cyprus, c.580, British Museum, London

produced the parts in silver of the chryselephantine Zeus, as can be seen from the earthenware moulds found in his workshop at Olympia.

Herodotus tells us that Corinth was an important centre of working in bronze. In Classical times, gold and silver vessels, chiefly *hydriai*, were made in southern Greece, as can be seen from the catalogues of the Chalkotheke on the Acropolis, but not a single one has survived. In the 4th century BC, bronze figurines and *hydriai* for funerary purposes ceased to be made at Athens, while *hydriai* and receptacles for ashes continued to be produced in gold and silver. In Magna Graecia, Tarentum was an important centre for repoussé metalwork. Silver folding mirrors with scenes in relief and silver vessels with gilt details, now in the Metropolitan Museum of Art in New York, have been found in tombs.

Modern archaeological research has demonstrated that the inhabitants of central Macedonia (Sindos) in the 6th century BC, and those of Acanthus in Chalcidice (a colony of the island of Andros), were silversmiths of exceptional skill, producing silver cups, kraters, etc. (Herodotus, 7. 119). The silver mines of Siphnos and Lesbos, and later those of Laurium in Attica, have provided us with valuable information on the advanced technology in this field.

The biggest centre for such work in Hellenistic times was Alexandria, and a striking description of the city of Ptolemy II Philadelphus (271 BC) is given by Athenaeus in his *Deipnosophistai* (5. 196a–203b). The city's luxury and wealth were fabulous. In its processions 1600 children each carried a gold and a silver vessel, and Athenaeus describes a vast silver *krater* with relief decoration of the Samian type and four equally enormous gold *kraters* of the Laconian type with vine wreaths, etc. These descriptions should not be regarded as exaggerations, since they correspond to the vast quantities of gold and silver vessels that were paraded in the streets of Rome as spoil from Greek cities conquered in Magna Graecia and Sicily in the late 3rd century, and from Greece itself in the first half of the 2nd century BC. Greek metal workers settled in Rome and brought their art with them (witness the masterpieces from Pompeii). A find of exceptional rarity came to light at Dion in 1992. This is a bronze *hydraulis* (water organ) of the 1st century BC. The first *hydraulis* was made in Alexandria by the engineer Ctesibius. In the Middle Ages this instrument developed into the church organ of the Western Church.

Until Classical times the products of metalworking were not made for interior decoration or to serve as collectors' items. But from the moment that Lysippus made a small-scale "tabletop" Heracles for the symposia of Alexander the Great in the 4th century BC, a new relationship grew up between humans and works of art. From then on, statuettes were used for the decoration of rooms or for collection and consequently forgeries started. After the Battle of Pydna (146 BC) the Roman soldiers prised open Greek graves at Corinth, for instance, in order to collect, for sale in Rome, the *nekrocorinthia*, bronze vessels that were grave offerings, the *signa Corinthiae* statuettes, and much sought-after bronze vessels, the *aeria Corinthiae*.

In Byzantine times the art of cast bronze flourished in many centres of the empire: Italy, Egypt, Asia Minor, Syria. Later, when the Byzantines lost their provinces, working in bronze was confined to Constantinople itself and mainland Greece. An equestrian statue of the emperor Theodosius I survived until the city fell to the Turks in 1453; it was, however, subsequently destroyed. Another colossal statue was taken by the crusaders in 1204 to Bari in Italy. The statue consists of cast plates, made separately and then assembled, exactly like the Greek statues of the Geometric and Classical periods.

With the triumph of Christianity, craftsmen turned to the production of objects for liturgical and domestic use: cast crosses, large ones for churches and smaller ones to be worn, candlesticks, lamps in various designs, censers, some with scenes from the life of Christ (the most sumptuous of these are today in Vienna), and items of every kind for the household with figures in relief and vegetal decoration. Designs differed as they followed varying trends, but these objects continued to be produced throughout the Byzantine period. The craftsmen who cast them had their own quarter in the city of Constantinople.

The most noteworthy works to have survived are the large monumental bronze doors with lions' heads from which the knockers hang and rich foliate decoration with crosses (Hagia Sophia in Constantinople; St Mark's in Venice; and a double door, said to come from Hagia Sophia, preserved in the Vatopedi monastery on Mount Athos). Many bronze weights with busts of emperors have survived, while a bronze plaque with inlaid silver of the 4th century AD is today in the Louvre and another in the Florence Archaeological Museum. A superb portable triptych of gilt bronze has survived intact, now in the Victoria and Albert Museum in London.

The Helsinki treasure (4th century AD), today in London, was produced in Rome but, like the silver objects in the Mildenhall treasure in London and the Traporain treasure in Edinburgh, already shows eastern features. Byzantine style manifests itself more clearly in a large disc portraying the emperor Theodosius I (AD 388), in Madrid, a work produced in Thessalonica.

In the time of Justinian (527–65), imperial stamps appear on the reverse of many of the works of silversmithing; these are a great help for historical and stylistic classification. At this period we find a clear preference for ancient Greek mythological subjects, as on a silver disc with a Silenus at Dumbarton Oaks. In the 6th century, as Corippus and Paul the Silentiary inform us, the churches and palaces of Constantinople were packed with works of art in gold and silver, votive crowns, altar revetments, and the great "automata" of the palace, covered in enamel. Of these, nothing has survived.

The period of iconoclasm (726–843) was a setback in the field of metalwork, but the workshops continued to operate. Under Basil I (867–86), metalworking flourished afresh, with many works in gold and silver for sacred and secular use. The sanctuary of churches now tended to be enclosed by the iconostasis, which was often adorned with enamelled plates, as in the Pala d'Oro of Venice. The Byzantine silver- and gold-smith matched the vivid colours of the enamel and of precious stones to the precious metals, and to the bronze, and this new technique was the triumph of Byzantine craftsmanship. The few examples that have survived are on Athos or in St Mark's in Venice. Small portable icons were also adorned with plates of silver and enamel which left visible only the unclothed parts of the figures' bodies.

With recent memories of Byzantine civilization as a model, modern Greek gold- and silversmithing, continuing an even older, "atavistic" tradition, absorbed and reshaped an aesthetic based not only on indigenous features but also on those borrowed from the West and the East. These arts during the difficult centuries of Ottoman rule are marked by a spontaneous inspiration and originality. There is no evidence for the trading in and export of the products of metalwork at this time. There were, however, blacksmiths' and coppersmiths' shops in many villages in Greece, particularly in Chalcidice, Pelion, and the Peloponnese, and here occupational and household tools and utensils were made and repaired. Tools made of iron have Greek names: *amoni*, *physero*, *sphyri*, *sidero*, *molyvi*, *kleidaria*, *syrtis*, etc. These items were worked by hammering from a single sheet of metal as they had been in antiquity; now, however, they were often engraved and decorated with niello – a technique very widely used in the modern Greek period, as it had been in the Mycenaean.

In the 19th century, with the Industrial Revolution and the liberation of the Greeks from the Ottoman occupation from 1821 onwards, the first halting steps were taken towards industrialization. The year 1864 saw the revival of smelting at Laurium of the ancient plumbiferous scoria by the French–Greek–Italian Roux company. From 1935 onwards there was an increase in mining production, and exports were made. Metallurgical manufacturing developed, producing items for household use, for building work, and engineering purposes: electric motors, farming implements, items for aircraft repairs, etc. There are still a very few workshops in the principal urban centres where silver objects, intended for gifts, are worked by hand with the repoussé technique. However, efforts are being made by various bodies, with the Benaki Museum in the lead, to teach lost techniques by means of seminars, and there are now more than 200 people who have learnt the ancient craft of chasing with handmade tools such as those used in antiquity.

LILA DE CHAVES-CHRONOPOULOS

See also Coinage, Copper and Tin, Enamel, Gold, Iron, Jewellery, Sculpture, Silver and Lead

Further Reading

Boardman, John *et al.* (editors), *The Prehistory of the Balkans, The Middle East and the Aegean World, Tenth to Eighth Centuries* BC, Cambridge: Cambridge University Press, 1982 (*The Cambridge Ancient History*, vol. 3, part 1, 2nd edition)

Catling, H.W., *Cypriot Bronzework in the Mycenaean World*, Oxford: Clarendon Press, 1964

Evans, Helen and William Wixom, *The Glory of Byzantium: Art and Culture of the Middle Byzantine Era*, AD 843–1261, New York: Metropolitan Museum of Art, 1997 (exhibition catalogue)

Frazer, E.M., *Byzantine Enamels and Goldsmith Work: The Treasury of San Marco, Venice*, Milan, 1984 (exhibition catalogue)

Hood, Sinclair, *The Arts in Prehistoric Greece*, Harmondsworth and New York: Penguin, 1987

Lafontaine-Dosogne, Jacqueline (editor), *Splendeur de Byzance*, Brussels: Musées Royaux d'Art et de Histoire, 1982

Makres, Kitsos A., *He laïke techne tou Peliou* [Popular Art of Pelion], Athens, 1976

Ministry of Culture, *Byzantine and Post-Byzantine Art*, Athens: Byzantine Museum, 1986 (exhibition catalogue)

Pleiner, Radomír, *Iron Working in Ancient Greece*, Prague: National Technical Museum, 1969

Simantoni-Bournia, Eva, *Archaiologia ton Proimon Ellinikon Chronon (1050–600 pC)* [Archaeology of the Early Period in Greece (1050–600 BC)], Athens 1997

Snodgrass, A., *The Dark Age of Greece: An Archaeological Survey of the Eleventh to the Eighth Centuries* BC, Edinburgh: Edinburgh University Press, 1971

Spirey, Nigel, *Understanding Greek Sculpture: Ancient Meanings, Modern Readings*, London and New York: Thames and Hudson, 1996

Vermeule, Cornelius, *Greek Art: Socrates to Sulla*, Boston: Museum of Fine Arts, 1980

Metaphysics

Metaphysics is the study of the ultimate nature of everything. The topics investigated include being, body and mind, souls and God, space and time, matter and motion, causality, identity and change, possibility and necessity, particulars and universals. Basic questions include: what is everything made of? Is it one "stuff" or many "stuffs"? What is the nature of the ultimate? What is appearance and what is reality?

Metaphysics literally means "after (*meta*) physics (*ta physika*)". Tradition says the name was first used by the librarian Andronicus of Rhodes (1st century BC) who was cataloguing the collected works of Aristotle. Faced with an untitled work, he labelled it *Metaphysics,* because it was the next book placed on the shelf after the books Aristotle wrote on physics.

The study of metaphysics began with the speculations of the pre-Socratic philosophers. For about 200 years prior to the time in which Socrates flourished this rather varied group of thinkers sought answers about the nature of ultimate reality. The first of them was Thales (c.625–547 BC) of Miletus in

Ionia. Seeking to understand nature, in terms of nature itself, Thales speculated that the source of all things in the visible world was water.

Thales' protégé at Miletus, Anaximander (c.610–540 BC), was the second member of the Milesian school. He speculated that the ultimate was the "boundless" or "unlimited" (*apeiron*) which was a sort of odourless, tasteless, colourless, weightless, "stuff" out of which everything comes. The "boundless" also moved in a sort of vortex motion to produce the visible things of the world.

Anaximenes (*fl. c.*546 BC) was the third and last of the Milesian school. He speculated that the first principle of all things was air. His great achievement seems to have been the suggestion that there was continuity and serial development in the pattern of the condensation of air "downwards" into denser materials and the corresponding rarefaction of dense material "upwards".

Xenophanes (c.570–478 BC) of Colophon objected to the theology of the poets. His problem with Homer and Hesiod, as well as many other poets, was that they told stories of the gods and goddesses engaging in shameful behaviour. They could be hateful, violent, capricious, selfish, adulterous, lying, and scheming. He speculated that there must be one ultimate god who was the source of all.

Heraclitus (*fl. c.*500 BC) of Ephesus is famous for the saying, "I step into a river once, but I cannot step into the same river twice." By this he speculated that the only thing that does not change is change. He identified the ultimate stuff of the universe with fire, but also found it to have order inherent in it. The ordering principle he identified as reason (*logos*). The Ionians (discussed above) were materialistic in their cosmological explanations. They were also monists (claiming that there is only one kind of basic reality) The Italian school (Pythagoras, Parmenides, Zeno, Melissus, Empedocles), on the other hand, claimed that ultimate reality was of more than one kind.

Pythagoras (*fl. c.*530 BC) of Samos moved to Croton on the south Italian coast. According to tradition, one day he passed by the blacksmith's shop and heard different pitches from hammers ringing on anvils. From this experience he developed a theory of music and a theory of the origin of the universe. For Pythagoras the discovery of quantity in everything led to the speculative belief that everything is made of numbers. This view replaces a material cause of the universe with a non-material one, namely numbers. So the origin of the universe can be viewed as coming from an intellectual source.

Parmenides (b. c.515 BC) of Elea learned of the views of Heraclitus and completely rejected the argument that the world is constantly changing. Instead he argued that change is an illusion. For Parmenides everything that exists has being, and being is the basic stuff of the universe. To say that something has being means that it is. But, if it is, then it cannot both be and not be. Change, or becoming, means that something both "is" and simultaneously "is-not". For Parmenides something either "is" or it "is-not". For something to exist and not exist at the same time would violate the laws of logic. What is can neither be created nor be destroyed, so change he concluded is an illusion.

Zeno (c.490–454 BC) of Elea was a younger follower of Parmenides. He developed a number of paradoxes to defend the view that change is an illusion. Most of these paradoxes argued that motion is an illusion. The paradoxes include the Stadium, the Arrow, Achilles and the Tortoise, and the Grain of Millet.

Melissus (*fl.* mid-5th century BC) of Samos, famous as an admiral, became a follower of Parmenides and produced a book entitled *On Nature and Being*. Among his contributions is the view that there exists a plenitude of being in the cosmos.

Empedocles (c.492–432 BC) of Acragas in Sicily was a member of the pluralist school. He accepted Parmenides' principle of being as a starting point and then postulated four basic "stuffs" – earth, air, fire, and water. These were the roots of things. They combined and separated through love and strife. Yet these are merely appearances.

Anaxagoras (c.500–428 BC) of Clazomenae was also a member of the pluralist school. His great contribution is the idea that there is a mind that organizes the clumped stuff of the universe into an ordered whole. Unlike the Creator of Genesis who issues divine commands, Anaxagoras' creator-god is pure mind which distinguishes and separates qualities to produce an ordered cosmos.

The Atomist school comprised the last of the pre-Socratics. Leucippus is considered to be the father of the school. Little is known for certain about his views; however, it is generally believed that his younger follower, Democritus (b. c.460 BC) of Abdera, preserved and developed his speculations. Democritus is reported to have said, "I take this material and I cut it until it can be cut no further and I have the basic stuff of the universe, 'the uncuttable' (*atome*)." An *atomos* of Democritus is different from modern atoms. It is like a tiny rock, the centre of which cannot be split. Democritus taught that there are a myriad different atoms which combine by physically hooking together rather like burrs on clothing, or run freely in liquid fashion like marbles. The resulting view is that there is a plurality of atoms. Furthermore, Democritus taught that everything is made of atoms moving in the void. Even the gods are made of atoms. This meant that only atoms moving in the void were eternal. The gods, goddesses, the world, and all people were simply the product of a chance combination of atoms. Even souls were the product of atoms. In addition the forces of movement in the void would eventually produce a new rearrangement of the atoms and therefore even the gods were not immortal.

When pre-Socratic speculation failed to reach a single unified answer about the nature and origin of the cosmos, intellectual attention turned to other concerns. The Sophists focused on rhetoric, and Socrates on social philosophy and ethics.

Plato (c.429–347 BC) gave metaphysical speculation new life. Plato was deeply influenced by the teaching of the Pythagoreans. Seeking to explain both change and permanence, he combined the ideas of Heraclitus and Parmenides. Plato used the Socratic method of dialogue to seek for knowledge of the ultimate. He found the ultimate nature of the universe to be derived from ideas. Just as everything in the universe has quantity, so it also has a shape or a form (*ideos*). In the forms of things he found the ultimate stuff of the universe. The visible world is ever a world of Becoming, composed of copies of the eternal forms. These reside in the invisible world of Being. In the *Timaeus* he describes how a creator-god mixes the forms with matter to make the visible world.

Aristotle (384–322 BC), the most famous of Plato's students, wrote about the topic of metaphysics calling it "first philosophy" because it dealt with the first things of the cosmos. Among his metaphysical ideas are the four causes: material, formal, efficient, and final. He rejected Plato's forms for being as substance. Aristotle's great achievement was to summarize in an orderly fashion and extend the speculations of the Classical period.

After the death of Aristotle the changed political conditions brought about by the conquests of Alexander the Great reoriented the focus of philosophical speculations to "philosophies of withdrawal". Cyrenaics, Epicureans, Sceptics, Cynics, and Stoics all advocated philosophies of life which sought to find meaning in life apart from the state. Epistemology, ethics, and social philosophies were the main concern.

Neoplatonism developed a rich literature of metaphysical speculation that posited God as the source of the forms. From the 3rd to the 6th century AD this philosophy developed the idea of the chief form being the One. The One emanates or overflows in being to create the visible world. The most important members of this school were Plotinus and Proclus.

Christians encountered a dynamic mix of philosophical schools in the Greek-speaking world. In particular they found three competing cosmologies widely discussed: pantheism, materialism, and Platonism. Of these three Platonism was closest to the Christian view on the origin and nature of the world. As people of philosophical training became Christians they applied their philosophies to theological interpretation for both apologetic and dogmatic purposes.

The emperor Constantine I the Great, seeking to unify his empire on a religiously uniform basis, called for an ecumenical council of the Church to meet at Nicaea in AD 325. The debates and resulting creed were fraught with philosophical metaphysical ideas. These were used to describe the nature of the Trinity. Later councils would also deal with the *Logos* Christology of the Gospel of John in order to describe the two natures of Christ. For its theological needs Christianity utilized Greek metaphysical ideas.

Byzantine history continued the story of the development of the association of philosophy and Christian faith. Philosophy was a frequent topic for study, but little original work was done until the 11th century when there was a great revival of Platonism led by Psellos. John Mavropos, bishop of Euchaita, was a devoted Platonist. John Italos developed some heretical ideas from Pythagoreanism. The most original of the Byzantine philosophers seems to have been George Gemistos Plethon (c.1360–1452), who was the last great Neoplatonist.

A.J.L. WASKEY, JR

See also Philosophy

Further Reading

Aristotle, *Metaphysics*, translated by Hippocrates G. Apostle, Bloomington: Indiana University Press, 1966

Armstrong, A.H. (editor), *The Cambridge History of Later Greek and Early Medieval Philosophy*, Cambridge: Cambridge University Press, 1970

Copleston, Frederick Charles, *A History of Philosophy*, revised edition, New York: Doubleday, 1962

Cornford, Francis MacDonald (translator), *Plato and Parmenides: Parmenides' Way of Truth and Plato's Parmenides*, London: Kegan Paul, Trench, Trubner, and New York: Harcourt Brace, 1939

Diogenes Laertius, *Lives of Eminent Philosophers*, translated by R.D. Hicks, 2 vols, London: Heinemann, and New York: Putnam, 1925 (Loeb edition)

Guthrie, W.K.C., *The Greek Philosophers from Thales to Aristotle*, New York: Harper and Row, 1975

Hussey, Edward, *The Presocratics*, New York: Scribner, 1972. pp. 127–48

Hyland, Drew A., *The Origins of Philosophy: Its Rise in Myth and the Pre-Socratics*, New York: Putnam, 1973

Nahm, Milton C., *Selections from Early Greek Philosophy*, 4th edition, New York: Appleton Century Crofts, 1964

O'Meara, Dominic J. (editor), *Neoplatonism and Christian Thought*, Norfolk, Virginia: International Society for Neoplatonic Studies, 1982

Plato, *The Republic*, translated by F.M. Cornford, Oxford: Clarendon Press, 1941; New York: Oxford University Press, 1972

Raven, J.E. and G.S. Kirk, *The Presocratic Philosophers: A Critical History with a Selection of Texts*, Cambridge: Cambridge University Press, 1957

Russell, Bertrand, *A History of Western Philosophy*, New York: Simon and Schuster, 1945; London: Allen and Unwin, 1946

Stead, Christopher, *Philosophy in Christian Antiquity*, Cambridge and New York: Cambridge University Press, 1995

Stumpf, Samuel Enoch, *Philosophy: History and Problems*, 5th edition, New York: McGraw Hill, 1994

Taylor, Richard, *Metaphysics*, 4th edition, Englewood Cliffs, New Jersey: Prentice Hall, 1992

Wheelwright, Philip (editor), *The Presocratics*, New York: Odyssey Press, 1966

Zeller, Eduard, *Outlines of the History of Greek Philosophy*, 13th edition, revised by Wilhelm Nestle, New York: Meridian, 1967

Metaxas, Ioannis 1871–1941

Army officer and dictator

Metaxas's dictatorship of 1936–41 saw the imposition of a regime similar in many ways to other European dictatorships of the period, during which the state became increasingly important. His firm leadership at the start of World War II at first defended Greece from an Italian invasion.

Metaxas was born on the island of Ithaca on 12 April 1871. Choosing a military career, he attended the Greek Military Academy, graduating in 1890. He saw active service in the 1897 Graeco-Turkish War, after which he was sent to Germany to attend the War Academy at Berlin, returning in 1903. In 1912 Venizelos, the prime minister, embarked on a modernization of the army which he entrusted to crown prince Constantine, who in turn appointed Metaxas to the General Staff. Metaxas became a loyal supporter of Constantine and a lifelong monarchist. In 1913 he was promoted to colonel and became Chief of the General Staff. At the outbreak of World War I Constantine (by then king) and Metaxas agreed that it would be folly for Greece to become involved, a view not shared by Venizelos. Promoted to general in 1916, Metaxas left Greece when Constantine vacated the throne in 1917. He was tried for treason in absentia, but was pardoned in 1921 and returned at Constantine's restoration. He took no part, however, in the disastrous Asia Minor campaign, having consistently warned of the military folly of such a venture. When a republic was proclaimed in 1923, he participated in an abortive monarchist coup, after which he again left Greece. When he returned, he founded his own pro-monarchist Free Opinion Party. In 1928 he briefly held office as minister of communications, going again into opposition for a further seven years. In 1935, with the restoration of the monarchy, Metaxas accepted office as a minister of state without portfolio, and then as minister of war. Shortly afterwards the prime minister died, and king George II turned to Metaxas, who with only six followers in the parliament became prime minister in April 1936. His way was smoothed by the chance fact that many of Greece's senior statesmen died in 1936: Georgios Kondilis (in January), Eleftherios Venizelos (in March), Panayoti Tsaldaris (in May), Paul Kondouriotis (in August), and Alexandros Zaimis (in September).

Metaxas moved rapidly to consolidate power in what he saw as a dangerous period for Greece, both domestically with the problems caused by the world economic crisis and externally in a Europe drifting towards war. On 4 August he suspended parliament, which as events transpired would not meet again for a decade. Metaxas was now, in effect, dictator of Greece. Freedom of the press was abolished, censorship was introduced (even of some of the classics), and some opponents were sent into internal exile. Though he was not a fascist, Metaxas's regime rapidly began to adopt many of the attributes of other contemporary authoritarian regimes. He talked of creating a Third Hellenic Civilization, the first two being those of antiquity and Byzantium. As part of this ideal, and to lessen the linguistic schism, he promoted demotic Greek over katharevousa, commissioning the first demotic grammer. Underlying the concept of the Third Hellenic Civilization was the aim of rebuilding the country by returning it to its roots, removing the un-Hellenic accretions of recent centuries. A compulsory National Youth Organization (*Ethnikos Organismos Neoleas*, EON) was created to co-opt the young, whose members had to be deemed to be true Hellenes, not Jews or other minorities. EON was the first mass organization to be introduced in Greece. Metaxas used titles to describe himself such as "First Peasant", "National Father", and "Leader". He envisaged a much greater role for the state in national life, introducing social insurance, a minimum wage, maternity benefits, child welfare legislation, compulsory labour arbitration, and peasant debt relief, and he embarked on a ten-year programme of public works to improve the country's infrastructure.

As Europe entered World War II, Greece could not avoid becoming caught up in the vortex. In October 1940 Italy, having already occupied Albania, turned on Greece. Metaxas was awakened at 3 am on 28 October to receive an ultimatum from Italy's ambassador. With firmness and dignity he rebuffed the humiliating demands. Known as Ochi ("No") Day, 28 October has been a public holiday in Greece ever since. The Italian dictator had assumed on the basis of old reports that morale in the Greek army was low, but Metaxas had paid particular attention to rebuilding the army which now threw back the invaders and proceeded to occupy much of southern Albania. At the height of these successes Metaxas died unexpectedly at the end of January 1941. His resoluteness in defending Greece against the Italian fascist aggressors did much to redress his image as one of Europe's crop of interwar right-wing dictators.

ERIK GOLDSTEIN

Biography

Born in Ithaca in 1871, Metaxas was educated at the Greek Military Academy and saw active service in the Graeco–Turkish War of 1897. A staunch monarchist, he opposed Greece's involvement in World War I and in the Asia Minor campaign. He was appointed minister of war in 1936 and later that year became prime minister (effectively dictator) until his death in 1941. He rejected the Italian ultimatum of 28 October 1940 and drove back the Italian invaders.

Further Reading

Higham, Robin and Thanos Veremis (editors), *The Metaxas Dictatorship: Aspects of Greece, 1936–1940*, Athens: Hellenic Foundation for Defence and Foreign Policy (ELIAMEP), 1993

Kofas, Jon V., *Authoritarianism in Greece: The Metaxas Regime*, Boulder, Colorado: East European Monographs, 1983

Vatikiotis, P.J., *Popular Autocracy in Greece, 1936–41: A Political Biography of General Ioannis Metaxas*, London: Cass, 1998

Meteora

A group of monasteries in Thessaly

The monasteries collectively called the Meteora ("raised in the air") are directly north of Kalambaka ("Black Town"), the Classical Aiginion and Byzantine Stagoi, in northwestern Thessaly. From the plain created by the river Peneus there rises, over an area of approximately 2.5 sq km and enclosing a curving valley, a jungle of striated and pitted iron-grey monoliths, up to 275 m high, created by erosion and consisting of a polymictic conglomerate of plutonic and regional metamorphic rocks. Unmentioned in Classical literature (apart from a possible allusion in Homer, *Iliad*, 2. 729), this most spectacular geological feature of Greece has from the 18th century awed foreign visitors, including Edward Lear who sketched one of its monasteries (Barlaam).

Its monastic history cannot be traced before the 14th century, and is based largely upon documents most of which were discovered in its own libraries. Principal among these are the *Lives* and *Testaments* of the founders of three of the monasteries; the *Historical Discourse*, written perhaps in 1521 to contest the claim to supremacy of the Great Meteoron monastery; and the *Chronicle of Ioannina* (known also from elsewhere) of *c.*1440, which details the Serbian empire in Thessaly. It is not known how many monasteries there were at any one time or even in total: the *Historical Discourse* gives 14, a mid-17th-century list names 19, while oral tradition reports at least 24, but some of these were undoubtedly merely eremitic communities dependent upon a regular monastery.

The earliest known monks were anchorites forming what they called the "Thebaid of Stagoi" after the heartland of Egyptian monasticism. They lived in the shallow caves of a large rock known as Doupiani (from Serbian *dupljane* or Bulgarian *dupljak* meaning "cavity"), and were under the supervision of a *protos* ("first" monk) rather than an abbot.

Meteora: woodcut showing the monasteries of Meteora

They gathered for a communal liturgy every Sunday below the rock at a tiny basilical church which was rebuilt in 1861. By sometime before 1336, however, there was also a small monastery built in one of the bigger caves, for a *chrysobull* (imperial charter) issued in that year by the Byzantine emperor Andronikos III Palaiologos (the text is painted on a wall of the cathedral church at Stagoi) in quoting from an earlier *prak-tikon* (inventory) refers to a small dependent monastery of the bishopric called the Theotokos of Doupiani.

Protection in those tumultuous times was given to the fledgeling community by the pious "Emperor of the Serbs and Greeks of Thessaly", Symeon Uroš Nemanjić Palaiologos (1359–71?), whose spiritual adviser was the *protos* Neilos. Neilos expanded his skete and built four small churches, of which only one can be located today, the Hypapanti (Presentation) in a cave halfway up a cliff to the northeast of Doupiani. Sometime later, monastic cells were added in an adjoining cave linked to the first by a short tunnel. Neilos is himself depicted in a fresco in the church kneeling at the Virgin's feet.

The move at the Meteora from troglodytic eremiticism to cenobitic monasticism was largely due, despite his reluctance, to the hesychast Athanasios. Notwithstanding his occupation of caves high up on the precipitous sides of the massive rock known as the *Platys Lithos* (Broad Rock), his holiness enticed disciples to join him and this forced him to the top of the rock to accommodate them all. There he built a church and wrote a typikon (charter) for the community, which after his death in 1383 came into the care of the monastery's "second founder", Symeon's son and successor John Uroš, who a decade earlier had become the monk Joasaph (the church contains three portraits of both Athanasios and Joasaph).

The example of the Great Meteoron encouraged other foundations, first in 1390 the now vanished Hypselotera on an even higher monolith, and then about ten years later Hagiou Stephanou, founded by Antonios Kantakouzenos, nephew of Symeon and grandson of the Byzantine emperor John VI. Although the 15th century saw not only external threats from Turkish conquest and occupation but also internal corruption and fraternal power-struggles, a few monasteries continued to be founded, including the surviving Hagiou Nikolaou Anapavsa and Hagias Triados (though both on the sites of earlier eremitic occupation). Around 1490 the diocese of Stagoi came under the jurisdiction of the archbishopric of

Larissa, and the Great Meteoron, soon to be followed by other communities, became self-governing; while in 1540 it, again to be followed by others, was granted stavropegial rank and thus came directly under the authority of the patriarch. The golden age that the monasteries of the Meteora were now able to enjoy was, nevertheless, more due to the settled nature of the reign of the sultan Süleyman I the Magnificent (1520–66), who lifted the ban on ecclesiastical construction. In the absence of Byzantine and Serbian rulers to grant lands and privileges to the monasteries the semi-independent Wallachian and Moldavian *voievozi* filled the breach as the patrons of Orthodoxy, although no Meteoran foundation ever acquired the wealth of the poorest Athonite monastery.

The caves at the Meteora were occupied mainly by anchorites (although one of the largest served as the monastic prison). Most, and with the exception of Hypapanti all of the surviving, monasteries were, however, constructed on precipitous monoliths; but, whereas the Great Meteoron covers about an acre, the small 16th-century Rousanou seems on all sides to be a mere extension of its rock and at Hagiou Nikolaou a slight backward step by a monastic gardener would precipitate him directly to the base of its rock. Entry used to be achieved either by climbing precarious and vertiginous wooden ladders (up to 40 m long), the upper reaches of which the monks drew up at night and in time of peril, or by being hauled up in nets by a rope from a windlass in a projecting tower (in the 1920s to the dismay, and contempt, of many monks bridges were built and steps cut into the rocks on the instructions of Polykarpos, bishop of Trikkala).

The oldest surviving frescos are probably those in the nave of Hypapanti, painted in a lively and popular style of the late Palaiologan period. These contrast with the more formal and at times austere art of the richer monasteries such as the Great Meteoron and its 16th-century neighbour Barlaam. The most famous painter known to have been employed at any of these monasteries was the influential Cretan Theophanes, who worked at Hagiou Nikolaou Anapavsa in 1527.

The fortunes of the Meteora declined drastically during the 18th and early 19th centuries and were never to recover (in 1899, 18 years after the cession of Thessaly to Greece, even their independence was lost to the bishop at Trikkala). The Phanariot rulers of the Romanian principalities proved far less interested than their indigenous predecessors in giving support, and, more serious, the stirrings of Greek independence led to both unrest and retaliation from the Turks which was often directed against hapless monks, while the virtually independent Ali Pasha of Ioannina imposed crippling taxes. Moreover, the very inaccessibility of these monasteries, which had in part protected them from the depredations suffered by other foundations (some of which had even sent relics and other valuables to the Meteora for safe keeping), became itself the cause of serious damage during not only the Greek War of Independence, but also World War II and the ensuing Civil War, when bands of klephts, partisans, and communists respectively made them their headquarters. Hagiou Dimitriou was completely destroyed in 1809 by Turkish firepower, while Italian troops looted Barlaam in 1943 and German troops shelled and looted Hagiou Stephanou and Hagias Triados. Subsequently the Greek government embarked on a programme not only to repair the shattered buildings but also to restore the frescos and protect the libraries and treasures.

Nevertheless, the construction of a metalled road further weakened the precarious monastic hold on the Meteora by giving numerous tourists access by charabanc to all the surviving monasteries except Hypapanti. Many monks fled to the comparative quietude of Athos and elsewhere, while the determination of those few willing to test their ability to maintain an inward peace proof against external turbulence (Hagias Triados was even used for the James Bond film *For Your Eyes Only*) rarely lasted long. Although the Church has attempted with some success to maintain a presence, occupation of individual monasteries by small groups of both monks and nuns (and occasionally by a solitary monk) has been fitful: even Hypapanti, rarely found by a tourist, has been abandoned, although for a brief time in the early 1970s it was home to two monks from the Great Meteoron.

A.R. LITTLEWOOD

See also Monasteries, Monasticism

Summary

A group of monasteries in northwestern Thessaly, the Meteora ("raised in the air") occupy a spectacular geological setting. Their history dates from the 14th century when monks were fleeing Athonite monasteries which were under attack. The Meteora flourished in the 16th century but declined in the 18th and 19th. A metalled road in the 20th century facilitated access to the monasteries, since when most of the monks have departed to Athos.

Further Reading

Bees, N.A., "Symboli eis tin Istorion ton Monon ton Meteoron" [Contribution to the History of the Monasteries of the Meteora], *Byzantis*, 1 (1909): pp. 191–331

Bees, N.A., "Serbika kai Byzantiaka Grammata Meteorou" [Serbian and Greek Bibliography of the Meteora], *Byzantis*, 2 (1911): pp. 1–100

Bees, N.A., *Ta Cheirographa ton Meteoron Kodikon ton apokeimenon eis tas Monas ton Meteoron* [The Scripts of the Meteora Codices Kept in the Meteora Monasteries], Athens, 1967

Nicol, Donald M., *Meteora: The Rock Monasteries of Thessaly*, revised edition, London: Variorum, 1975

Methodios, St *c*.815–885

Missionary to the Slavs

St Methodios was, together with his younger brother St Cyril, the inventor of the Slavonic Glagolitic alphabet and a prominent Byzantine missionary. St Methodios cuts a less conspicuous profile than St Cyril, but his superb qualities as an administrator and organizer secured to a large extent the successful introduction of the Slavonic liturgy and writing.

Born in the city of Thessalonica, St Methodios must have been well educated with good connections at the court in Constantinople, since we first find him as an imperial governor of a Slav-inhabited territory in Macedonia. Later he renounced the world and became the abbot of a monastery on Mount Olympus in Asia Minor, which was, at that time, the most important centre of Byzantine monasticism. Methodios seems to have been constantly in contact with Cyril, who joined him in the monastery for a period after his Arab mission (851 or 855–56). He appears to have accompanied Cyril on his journey to the Khazar court (860–61). The learned patriarch Photios and the emperor Michael III (843–67) sent both brothers on the Moravian mission, where they worked together on the organization of a Slavonic Church.

The individual achievements of SS Cyril and Methodios in Moravia (862–69) are very hard to distinguish. Methodios was active not only in Moravia, but also in Pannonia in the Slavic principality of prince Kocel. In any case, Methodios emerged into the forefront as the leader of the mission after the death of Cyril in Rome in 869. After pope Hadrian II (867–72) had given his blessing for the Slavonic liturgy and writing, he appointed Methodios papal legate to the Slavs and ordained him archbishop of the revived diocese of Sirmium with jurisdiction over both Moravia and Pannonia. Methodios had to face, however, the renewed opposition of the Frankish clergy in Moravia, where prince Rastislav's nephew prince Svatopluk (870–96) had usurped power with the help of Louis the German (817–76). Captured by the Frankish bishops and accused of heresy at the court of Louis the German, Methodios was kept in prison for three years (870–73). Freed upon the insistence of pope John VIII (872–82), he worked during the next 12 years to build up the Slavonic Church in central Europe. He managed to educate around 200 disciples, and the Slavonic liturgical and literary tradition penetrated Bohemia, Croatia, and perhaps even southern Poland. Still Methodios continued to infringe on the interests of the Frankish clergy and nobility. A doctrinal point of conflict was added in the clash concerning the issue of the *filioque*, i.e. the procession of the Holy Spirit from both the Father and the Son, an innovation to the Nicene Creed supported by the Franks but not by the papacy at that time. During the second journey of Methodios to Rome in 880, pope John VIII confirmed his orthodoxy and declared his endorsement of the vernacular Slavic liturgy. In the next year Methodios went back to Constantinople, where patriarch Photios and the new emperor Basil I (867–86) gave their renewed support to the Moravian mission. In 885 Methodios died in Moravia; soon thereafter prince Svatopluk, influenced by his Frankish advisers, imprisoned his principal disciples and sold them into slavery. The Moravian mission failed in the country in which it was originally meant to succeed. The state of Moravia itself fell under the onslaught of the Hungarians in the early 10th century.

Still, the years 873–85 were the most productive period of the Moravian mission. St Methodios, who outlived his brother by 16 years, was responsible for a significant expansion in the number of translations from Greek into Old Church Slavonic. According to his Slavonic *Life*, composed most likely by his disciple Kliment of Ohrid, Methodios completed the translation of the entire Bible into Slavonic. This first Slavonic translation of the Bible has not been preserved. Other translations attributed to Methodios include the *nomokanon* (a Byzantine manual of canon law and imperial edicts concerning the Church), patristic books, and a service in honour of St Demetrius, the patron of his native city of Thessalonica. The *Life* credits him also with the conversion of the pagan Slavs from southern Poland.

St Methodios was a bridge between Byzantium and the West in a period when the unity between eastern and western Christendom was endangered by the Photian schism (863–70) and by missionary competition over the proselytization of the Slavs. In this difficult period Methodios won the approval of both Rome and Constantinople for the establishment of a Slavonic Church in Moravia. Doubtless the resolution of the Photian schism in the Constantinopolitan councils of 869–70 and 879–80 also played a role in acquiring the combined support of Rome and Constantinople for his work. A first-rate diplomat, organizer, and teacher, Methodios succeeded in preparing a number of disciples who were able to continue successfully the introduction of Slavonic vernacular liturgy and writing. After his death in 885, the Slavic Church of Moravia no longer enjoyed the favour of the papacy and of prince Svatopluk, but his disciples succeeded in carrying on the tradition of Methodios in Bulgaria, and hence in Serbia and Russia. The first Christian king of Bulgaria, Boris (852–93), received with honour in 885–86 three of his disciples – Kliment of Ohrid, Naum of Preslav, and Angelarios. They were entrusted with replacing the Greek liturgy with one written in Old Church Slavonic, but still based on Byzantine liturgical practices. Byzantium itself interfered to save the work of the "Apostles the Slavs". When Methodios visited Constantinople in 881, the patriarch Photios retained two of his students and Slavonic liturgical books for the purpose of future missionary activities. Thus, having initiated the Moravian mission, Byzantium also played a crucial role by saving its fruits and disseminating them among the Slavs.

DIMITER G. ANGELOV

Biography

Born in Thessalonica c.815, St Methodios was governor of a territory in Macedonia. Then he became a monk and later abbot of a monastery on Mount Olympus. With his brother St Cyril he was sent on a mission to Moravia to organize a Slavonic Church. They invented the Glagolitic alphabet and translated the Bible and other texts into Old Church Slavonic. He died in 885.

Further Reading

Bowlus, Charles R., *Franks, Moravians, and Magyars: The Struggle for the Middle Danube, 788–907*, Philadelphia: University of Pennsylvania Press, 1995

Duichev, Ivan (editor), *Kiril and Methodius, Founders of Slavonic Writing: A Collection of Sources and Critical Studies*, Boulder, Colorado: East European Monographs, 1985

Dvornik, Francis, *The Making of Central and Eastern Europe*, London: Polish Research Centre, 1949

Dvornik, Francis, *Byzantine Missions among the Slavs: SS. Constantine-Cyril and Methodius*, New Brunswick, New Jersey: Rutgers University Press, 1970

Methodiana: Beiträge zur Zeit und Persönalichkeit, sowie zum Schicksal und Werk des heiligen Methodios, Vienna: Böhlau, 1976

Obolensky, Dimitri, *The Byzantine Commonwealth: Eastern Europe, 500–1453*, London: Weidenfeld and Nicolson, and New York: Praeger, 1971

Vlasto, A.P., *The Entry of the Slavs into Christendom: An Introduction to the Medieval History of the Slavs*, Cambridge: Cambridge University Press, 1970

Metics

Resident aliens

The word *metoikoi* in ancient Greek literally means "co-inhabitants" and was used to define the foreigners resident in an ancient city state, who had a special status and special rights in contrast to the citizens (and also in contrast to the foreigners who were only travelling through and had no rights at all). Metics existed in every Greek town (under different names, e.g. *epoikoi* or *synoikoi*), but what is known about the term is mainly shaped by the evidence from ancient Athens. There especially (though not exclusively) the development of such a status of "resident aliens" seems to have been conditioned by two factors: on the one hand, the frequency of immigration (Athens was a magnet for foreign merchants and artisans in Classical times), and on the other, the pride of native Athenian citizens who refused easy access to full citizenship. This is already reflected in Solon's law about the exceptional admission of foreigners into the citizen body (Plutarch, *Solon*, 24. 4), thereby favouring the emergence of a class of "second-class citizens".

Metics were free people, but had lesser rights than citizens; their group was made up not only by foreigners migrating from other cities (or countries, non-Greek ones included) but also by former slaves who had been set free by their masters. In the former case, they had to be registered a certain time (probably a month) after their arrival and to pay the *metoikion*, a poll tax (which was not levied on citizens), as well as some other taxes imposed on foreigners and a special fee if they wanted to deal in the Agora. (If they failed to pay the *metoikion*, they could be sold into slavery.) Metics had to be enlisted in an Attic deme (local community or village) to acquire the right to dwell there (in inscriptions this is indicated by the expression "living in ... " behind the metic's name); in many cases this was Piraeus, the centre of Athenian commercial activity. Although metics enjoyed full control over their portable possessions, they were not allowed to acquire land or buy a house in Athens; therefore numerous metics put their skills into trade and crafts; the world of money transactions was largely dominated by them as well. Metics could attain *isoteleia*, i.e. citizen-like status with respect to financial duties to the polis; in court, however, a so-called *prostates* (a citizen acting as guardian) had to represent them. Metics had a clearly defined role in the city's great festivals: they had a fixed position in the procession of the Panathenaea, and they could even function as a choregus (i.e. a sponsor) at the Lenaea, but not at the Great Dionysia. Moreover, they had to do military service, usually in the infantry. On the whole, metics had no political rights and almost never a possibility to acquire full citizen status, because that status could only be conveyed by birth, and the rigid citizenship law of Pericles of 451/50 BC even required Athenian descent on both paternal and maternal sides. Exceptionally, though, the Athenian people's assembly (*ekklesia*) could bestow citizenship on foreigners for outstanding merits.

It is not clear how many metics lived in Athens (as also the exact number of the whole Athenian population is still a very controversial subject); a population count in the late 4th century – reported from the census of Demetrius of Phalerum probably in 317 BC – suggests that there were about 10,000 metics and 21,000 citizens. The Athenians were not always very well disposed towards the metics – they seem to have been made fun of in several comedies the titles of which are preserved – probably because there were many former slaves from "barbarian" countries among them; still, because of their commercial activities and their military service they were absolutely indispensable for the Athenian state, and in fact the barbarians among them were probably the best fitted for long-distance commerce (e. g. the grain trade with the Black Sea region), because they were acquainted with these areas. In the middle of the 4th century Xenophon (*De Vectigalibus*, 2. 6) even proposed to give more rights to the metics, arguing that their activities in Athens would enhance the prosperity of the city. Numerous metics seem to have become rich (especially famous are the wealthy bankers Pasion and Phormion), and they also used their means to cultivate their native religions: the cult of the Thracian goddess Bendis was officially established in Athens already in 429/28 BC, and there is evidence for about 15 foreign cults (e.g. of Egyptian, Carian, Phrygian, Syrian, and Phoenician gods and goddesses) in Piraeus; moreover there are sumptuous grave stelae with bilingual inscriptions of Phoenician metics. (An alleged common cult of "Metoikios Zeus", however, seems to be only a fancy of the late lexicographer Phrynichus.)

The status of the metics began to lose its distinctive features in the 4th century BC, when they were allowed to act in court on their own (without a *prostates*), and came to an end in Hellenistic times, when the purchase of citizenship became very frequent (probably because the law of Pericles lost much of its importance in the 3rd century, as also did the decisions of the *ekklesia*). In this period, even foreigners staying only a short time in Athens could occasionally get the status of metics, but without having to pay the concomitant taxes.

In Hellenistic and Roman times, free people living on the territory of a polis without being citizens were called *paroikoi*, in Asia Minor also *katoikoi*.

BALBINA BÄBLER

Further Reading

Baba, K., "On Kerameikos Inv. I 388 (SEG XXII 79)", *Annual of the British School at Athens*, 79 (1984): pp. 1–5 (a note on the formation of the Athenian metic status)

Boegehold, Alan L. and Adele C. Scafuro (editors), *Athenian Identity and Civic Ideology*, Baltimore: Johns Hopkins University Press, 1993

Davies, J.K., *Democracy and Classical Greece*, 2nd edition, Cambridge, Massachusetts: Harvard University Press, 1993

Duncan-Jones, R.P., "Metic Numbers in Periclean Athens", *Chiron*, 10 (1980): pp. 101–109

Fraser, P.M., "Citizens, Demesmen and Metics in Athens and Elsewhere" in *Sources for the Ancient Greek City-State*, edited by Mogens Herman Hansen, Copenhagen: Munksgaard, 1995

Gerhardt, Paul, "Die attische Metoikie im vierten Jahrhundert" (dissertation), Königsberg, 1935

Hansen, Mogens Herman, *The Athenian Democracy in the Age of Demosthenes: Structure, Principles and Ideology*, Oxford and Cambridge, Massachusetts: Blackwell, 1991

Harding, Phillip, "Metics: Foreigners or Slaves? The Recipients of Honours in IG II2 10", *Zeitschrift für Papyrologie und Epigraphik*, 67 (1987): pp. 176–82

Harrison, A.R.W., *The Law of Athens*, vol. 1: *The Family and Property*, Oxford: Clarendon Press, 1968

Hommel, Hildebrecht, Metoikoi entry in *Real-Encyclopädie der klassischen Altertumswissenschaft*, edited by August Pauly *et al.*, vol. 15. 2, 1932, 1413–1458

Lacey, W.K., *The Family in Classical Greece*, Ithaca, New York: Cornell University Press, and London: Thames and Hudson, 1968

Thür, Gerhard, "Wo wohnten die Metöken?" in *Demokratie und Architektur: Der hippodamische Städtebau und die Entstehung der Demokratie* edited by Wolfgang Schuller, Wolfram Hoepfner and Ernst Ludwig Schwandner, Munich: Deutscher Kunstverlag, 1989

Whitehead, David, *The Ideology of the Athenian Metic*, Cambridge: Cambridge Philological Society, 1977

Whitehead, David, "Xenocrates the Metic", *Rheinisches Museum*, 124 (1981): pp. 223–44

Metochites, Theodore 1270–1332

Statesman and scholar

Theodore Metochites distinguished himself both as a statesman and as a scholar. He was the son of George Metochites, the archdeacon of Constantinople, who supported the union of the Churches and, for that reason, in 1283 was sent with his family into exile in Asia Minor. Despite such hardship, Theodore acquired a formidable education and, when Andronikos II visited Nicaea in 1290, his extensive learning and skills impressed the emperor greatly. He became a member of the imperial court, was sent as an ambassador to Cyprus, Cilicia, and Serbia, and was appointed *logothetes ton angelon* (supervisor of the state herds of horses and mules), *logothetes ton oikeiakon* (supervisor of the household), *logothetes tou genikou* (supervisor of the fisc), *mesazon* (chief imperial minister), and finally *megas logothetes* (prime minister). But in 1328 Andronikos II was dethroned, and Metochites was imprisoned and sent into exile in Didymoteichon. In 1330 he was allowed to return to Constantinople, where he died as the monk Theoleptos in the monastery of Chora.

Theodore Metochites is representative of the humanism of the Palaiologan renaissance. Although burdened with administrative responsibilities, he devoted himself to the study of philosophy and literature. In addition, at an advanced age he studied astronomy with Manuel Bryennios, the author of an

Theodore Metochites: mosaic in the church of St Saviour in Chora, Constantinople, showing Metochites presenting the restored church to Christ, *c.*1330

extant treatise on musical theory. He was an avid collector of books and spent much time comparing manuscripts. He donated his library to the Chora monastery, and he was also responsible for the redecoration of its church with new mosaics and frescos, which are perhaps the greatest achievement of late Byzantine art. He had a group of pupils, of whom the most illustrious was the astronomer and historian Nikephoros Gregoras.

Metochites's main work is a collection of essays, notes, and annotations, the *Miscellanea Philosophica et Historica Graece*. Many of these essays discuss issues concerning Classical authors, for example, the obscurity of Aristotle's style, the development of ancient mathematics, Plutarch, Xenophon, and Philo. He also wrote paraphrases of Aristotle's works on natural philosophy, and an introduction to astronomy based in all essentials on Ptolemy. In his treatise *Ethikos* (On Education), as well as in his essay comparing Demosthenes with Aristides, he comments on the importance of education, the role of the scholars of his time, and the differences between the contemplative and the active life. More specifically, he stresses the importance of the active life, which in his view was devalued by the ancient philosophers as inferior to the contemplative life, and he attempts to dissociate the latter from any kind of mysticism that advocates the union of the human psyche to God. Finally, he wrote hexameter poems, rhetorical works, and enkomia.

The long debate between Metochites and his former friend and rival Nikephoros Choumnos marks most of his intellectual career. He was criticized by Choumnos for his obscure style, and he defended himself by arguing that Thucydides perhaps was stylistically the most unattractive of all the Classical authors, though he was at the same time one of the greatest. But the centre of the dispute concerned their different views on astronomy. Choumnos accused Metochites of abandoning Plato's theory about the seven revolutions and endorsing Ptolemy's views on the eight celestial spheres. Since there was a difference between Ptolemy and his predecessors concerning the number of the spheres, Metochites decided to remove the discrepancy and harmonize Ptolemy with Plato by altering the Platonic text in some places.

Yet whatever reservations one may have about Metochites as an astronomer, it is important to note that he regarded astronomy as a science, and he saw no conflict between science and religious belief. In fact, there is no doubt that he regarded astronomy, and the mathematical sciences in general, as the supreme sciences. He thus gave great importance to the study of mathematics, and was influenced by Plato's philosophy of mathematics, though it seems that his knowledge of Plato was most probably indirect, through the writings of Iamblichus and Nicomachus. He claimed that the mathematical sciences are superior to physics, because they constitute a source of tranquillity for the soul since their conclusions are indisputable, whereas physical sciences give rise to disputes in their attempt to understand physical phenomena. In his attitude towards Aristotle, Metochites, like many Byzantine scholars, was rather ambivalent. On the one hand, he was obviously an admirer of Aristotle's logic and physics, on the other he believed that Aristotle had included in his *Metaphysics* so many contradic-

tions and ambiguities that it would have been much better if this work had never been written.

KATERINA IERODIAKONOU

Biography

Born in 1270 the son of George Metochites, archdeacon of Constantinople, he followed his family into exile in Asia Minor in 1283. Still he got a good education and attracted the attention of Andronikos II. He had a distinguished career at the imperial court until Andronikos was dethroned in 1328. Metochites was exiled, but allowed to return in 1330. As a scholar he studied philosophy and literature. He died a monk in Constantinople in 1332.

Further Reading

Beck, Hans Georg, *Theodoros Metochites: Die Krise des byzantinischen Weltbildes im 14. Jahrhundert*, Munich: Beck, 1952

Ševčenko, Ihor, *Etudes sur la polémique entre Théodore Métochite et Nicéphore Choumnos*, Brussels: Byzanthion, 1962

Ševčenko, Ihor, "Theodore Metochites, the Chora, and the Intellectual Trends of his Time" in *The Kariye Djami*, vol. 4, edited by Paul A. Underwood, New York: Bollingen Foundation, 1975

Vries-van der Velden, Eva de, *Théodore Métochite: une réévaluation*, Amsterdam: Gieben, 1987

Miaoulis, Andreas 1769–1835

Naval hero of the Greek War of Independence

Andreas Miaoulis was born Andreas Vokos on the island of Hydra on 20 May 1769. He came from a wealthy family of merchants and ship masters. Following the family tradition, Andreas took to sea at a young age and quickly gained notoriety as a marauder, who sailed as far as Malta, southern France, and Syria in pursuit of booty. Legend has it that Andreas and his raiders once sailed up the Nile as far as Cairo. Later, a clash with Maltese buccaneers off the southern coast of the Peloponnese resulted in the sinking of Andreas's ship and his unceremonious return home. But, determined not to surrender to the whims of fortune, he soon embarked again, this time in command of his own ship, a Turkish brig named *Miaoul*, which had been purchased with the proceeds of his successful grain-trading ventures in the Aegean islands. In time, he became known as "Miaoulis", a name that was to become deeply feared by his Turkish enemies.

By the time of the outbreak of the Greek revolution in 1821, the 52-year-old Miaoulis was one of the most respected figures on Hydra. He had practically retired from the sea and was leading a comfortable life as a wealthy sea merchant. A man of conservative habits in his private life, Miaoulis remained nevertheless a fervent enemy of Ottoman rule. He was thus immediately seen as an obvious choice to assume command of the revolution's naval forces. By the end of 1821 Miaoulis was formally named admiral of Hydra by the leaders of the island and was quietly recognized as the revolution's chief of naval operations.

With ships from his own island as well as those of Spetsai and Psara, Miaoulis sought to keep the superior, but cumbersome, Turkish fleet off balance. However, the destruction of the island of Chios and the massacre of its population by the

Turks in mid-1822 brought Miaoulis into the eastern Aegean to seek a decisive engagement with the enemy. Recognizing that the Greek fleet could not sustain a head-on collision with the Turkish fleet, a war council in Psara decided to strike the Turks with fireships. The attack led to the sinking of the Turkish flagship by the Psara fireship commander, Constantine Kanaris, and registered the first major victory at sea for the revolution.

In the following years Miaoulis's naval strategy faced two imperatives. On the one hand, he needed to disrupt the enemy's transportation of troops and supplies to suppress the revolution on the mainland. On the other hand, the Greek naval forces had to engage in what would be recognized today as "limited sea denial" in an effort to protect the main Greek islands and cause as much damage to enemy naval forces as possible. When Psara was destroyed and its people put to the sword by a Turkish landing in 1824, Miaoulis returned to the island and surprised and sank 20 enemy gunboats. He then turned to defending the much bigger island of Samos, which the Turks wished to make into another example of the horrors awaiting those who revolted against the Porte. In a series of engagements against the numerically superior Turkish squadrons, culminating in the Battle of Gerondas, Miaoulis defeated the Turkish attempt to land on Samos and forced the enemy to retreat.

Beginning in 1825, Miaoulis concentrated his slim forces on battling a fearsome invasion of the Peloponnese by the Egyptian Ibrahim Pasha. Ibrahim's invasion was carried out with extreme brutality, causing the near extinction of the revolution. Miaoulis deployed his slim forces in an unequal battle to disrupt Ibrahim's sea lines of communication with Egypt and to sink as many troop ships as possible. In September 1825 he surprised an Egyptian squadron in the harbour of Methoni and burnt 28 of its ships. In January 1826 he joined the desperate effort to resupply with food and essentials the heroic city of Missolongi in western Greece, which was under siege by Ibrahim's army. During the Battle of Cavo Papa (28 January 1826) he engaged the Turkish fleet with an inferior force, but he did not hesitate to manoeuvre aggressively, facing the enemy ships of the line and then exchanging fierce cannon fire with them for more than three hours. As a result, the Turks hastily retreated to the safe haven of Patras harbour.

In 1827, with the Great Powers taking an increasing interest in the Greek struggle, Miaoulis, despite his undisputed position as naval leader of the revolution, immediately agreed to serve under a British admiral as a simple captain. The historic Battle of Navarino (October 1827), where Ibrahim's fleet was destroyed by a combined British, French, and Russian force, broke the Ottoman grip on Greece and led to the founding of the modern Greek state. The first governor of Greece, Ioannis Kapodistria, reappointed Miaoulis as chief of the Greek navy and ordered him to pursue the pirates plaguing Greek seas. However, Miaoulis sympathized with those war veterans who opposed Kapodistria's administration, which they found arbitrary and autocratic. With his home island of Hydra up in arms against the governor, Miaoulis himself staged a naval mutiny at the Poros naval station in the summer of 1831. The rising was quickly subdued by the cannons of a Russian squadron, but not before Miaoulis had scuttled two ships of the line and escaped to Hydra.

Kapodistria's assassination brought an end to plans of prosecuting Miaoulis for the Poros mutiny and, in 1832, the revolutionary hero was put in charge of the Greek delegation that went to Bavaria to offer the Hellenic crown to prince Otto. Upon the arrival of the new king in 1833, Miaoulis was appointed chief of the royal navy. In 1834 he was the first naval officer of the new Greek state to be promoted to the rank of rear-admiral and appointed inspector general of the fleet. The following year he was awarded the title of state councillor. He died in Athens in June 1835 from respiratory complications stemming from tuberculosis.

Andreas Miaoulis, a man of only the most rudimentary education, was recognized by his contemporaries as a master naval planner and strategist. His grasp of the broader tactical implications of naval action, his steady command under fire, and his ability to move his crews into action under the most dire adversities were legendary, among both his countrymen and the foreign officers who were sent to support the Greek cause. Miaoulis never blinked. Legend has it that once during the Napoleonic wars the young Miaoulis was captured by an English man-of-war while trying to run the British blockade in Spanish waters. He was then taken directly to admiral Horatio Nelson, who proceeded to interrogate the young captive in broken Spanish. "Why are you breaking the blockade?", Nelson asked. "Because it is to my profit", Miaoulis answered. And what would have happened, Nelson enquired, if he had commanded that smuggler's vessel, and Miaoulis had captured him? "I would have hanged you by your neck from the yard arm", Miaoulis coolly retorted. He was then ordered to be freed by Nelson, who congratulated him on both his bravery and his candour.

ANESTIS T. SYMEONIDES

Biography

Born in 1769 on the island of Hydra, the son of Andreas Vokos, he came from a wealthy merchant family but received only rudimentary education. Going early to sea, he became known as Miaoulis after taking command of a Turkish ship named *Miaoul*. From 1821 he became naval leader of the Greek revolution. Kapodistria appointed him chief of the navy, a position he retained until his death in 1835.

Further Reading

Alexandris, Konstandinos, *To Nautikon tou Yper anexartesias Agonos tou 1821–29 kai i Drasis ton Pyrpolikon* [The Navy of the War of Independence of 1821–29 and the Use of Fire Ships], Athens, 1968

Black, W.G. (editor), *Narrative of Cruises in the Mediterranean in HMS "Euryalus" and "Chanticleer" during the Greek War of Independence, 1822–1826*, Edinburgh: Oliver and Boyd, 1900

Clogg, Richard (editor), *The Struggle for Greek Independence: Essays to Mark the 150th Anniversary of the Greek War of Independence*, London: Macmillan, and Hamden, Connecticut: Archon, 1973

Henty, G.A., *In Greek Waters: A Story of the Grecian War of Independence, 1821–1827*, London: Blackie, 1892; New York: Scribner, 1902

Kokkinou, Dionysiou, *Historia tes Neoteras Hellados* [History of Modern Greece], 4 vols, Athens, 1970–72

Phillips, W. Alison, *The War of Greek Independence, 1821 to 1833*, London: Smith Elder, and New York: Scribner, 1897

Michael of Ephesus

Scholar of the 12th century

Michael of Ephesus was most probably a member of the circle of scholars around Anna Komnene that contributed greatly to the revival of Aristotelianism in the 12th century. When Anna Komnene retired from court in 1118 to a convent in Constantinople, and before she started writing her history in 1138/39, she charged a group of Byzantine scholars, among them Michael of Ephesus and Eustratios of Nicaea, with the task of writing commentaries on Aristotle. Michael of Ephesus composed detailed commentaries on many of Aristotle's works, and he later complained that his eyesight was spoiled because he had to work through the night to comply with Anna Komnene's wishes. However, most facts about his life are obscure and thus still disputed, for example the date of his birth, or whether he had been a student of Michael Psellos.

Several of his commentaries are still extant: on the *Sophistici Elenchi*, which was wrongly attributed to Alexander of Aphrodisias; on the *Ethica Nicomachea*; on the *Parva Naturalia*; on the *De Generatione Animalium*, which was wrongly attributed to Philoponus; on the *De Partibus Animalium*, the *De Animalium Motione*, and the *De Animalium Incessu*; on the *Metaphysica E–N*, which was also wrongly attributed to Alexander of Aphrodisias; and on the *Politica*. But there are also commentaries by him that are still unedited, for example his commentary on the pseudo-Aristotelian treatise *De Coloribus*. Others that are either completely lost or only fragmentarily extant in the mass of the surviving, often anonymous, scholia, include his commentaries on the *Topica*, the *Analytica Priora*, the *De Caelo*, the *Physica*, and the *Rhetorica*.

Michael of Ephesus's interpretations of Aristotelian passages are generally clear and sensible, never disputing Aristotle's authority. Among his comments, there are few genuinely new ones; most are taken from previous commentators, such as Alexander of Aphrodisias. But even if they are not always his own, his comments are sober and helpful especially in those cases in which no other commentary has survived. His commentaries not only shed light on Aristotle's thought and provide otherwise lost information concerning the history of philosophy, but they are also of interest from a historian's point of view, since they sometimes contain references to the contemporary political situation, for example criticism of the emperor and discussions about the contemporary educational system. As to his style, it often betrays the fact that such commentaries were actually used for oral teaching.

Though not particularly original, Michael of Ephesus was very influential. There is no doubt that all later Byzantine scholiasts looked to him when they wanted to write scholia, and even his very words appear quite frequently in the commentaries and paraphrases from the 13th to the 15th centuries.

KATERINA IERODIAKONOU

Biography

Next to nothing is known of the life of Michael of Ephesus. He was probably one of the group of scholars associated with Anna Komnene that contributed to the revival of Aristotelianism in the 12th century. He wrote commentaries on many of Aristotle's works, of which several survive.

Further Reading

Browning, R., "An Unpublished Funeral Oration of Anna Comnena", *Proceedings of the Cambridge Philological Society*, 188 (1962): pp. 1–12

Ebbesen, Sten, *Commentators and Commentaries on Aristotle's Sophistici Elenchi: A Study of post-Aristotelian Ancient and Medieval Writings on Fallacies*, vol. 1, Leiden: Brill, 1981, pp. 262–85

Prächter, K., "Michaelis Ephesii in libros de partibus animalium", *Göttingische Gelehrte Anzeigen*, 168 (1906): pp. 861–907

Prächter, K., "Michael of Ephesos und Psellos", *Byzantinische Zeitschrift*, 31 (1931): pp. 1–12

Michael VIII Palaiologos *c*.1225–1282

Emperor

Michael VIII (1259–82) was the eldest of three sons in a long-established family of Byzantium's military nobility. His father, Andronikos Palaiologos, held the office of Grand Domestic (*Megas Domestikos*), the highest military command, in the Laskarid government-in-exile of Nicaea during the Latin occupation of Constantinople.

Michael at first attracted the attention and favour of the second Nicene emperor, John III Vatatzes (1221–54). But in the autumn of 1253 he was accused of treasonous dealings and, despite his evasion of punishment, remained under suspicion thereafter. Married to John II's grandniece, and holding important military posts, he was again held in suspicion by the new emperor, Theodore II Laskaris (1254–58), who had a paranoid hatred of the nobility. In 1256 Michael actually fled to the Seljuk Turkish sultan, whom he served briefly in military command. Allowed back to the Byzantine court in early 1258, he faced wild alternations of disgrace and reconciliation until Theodore's premature death (August 1258). Theodore's son and successor was a boy only 8 years old, John IV Laskaris. Designated as regent and guardian was Theodore's close friend and adviser, George Mouzalon, who was of low birth and universally hated. Michael skilfully manipulated the situation and, within a few weeks, instigated the brutal murder of Mouzalon and his relatives. Choice of the new regent and guardian of the young emperor logically fell to Michael, who in rapid sequence took the titles first of grand duke (*Megas Doux*), then of despot (*despotes*, "Master"), which suggested rights of succession, and finally that of emperor. In early January 1259 he and his wife were crowned as sovereigns; the boy John Laskaris – whose succession rights had been guaranteed – was given only token recognition.

Through fortune and diligence Michael consolidated his grasp of power. At this time Michael Angelos, the independent Greek lord of Epirus, in northwestern Greece, had made an alliance with Manfred, the Hohenstaufen king of Sicily, and the Latin prince Guillaume II Villehardouin of Achaea, aimed against the Nicene state in general and Michael Palaiologos in particular. Resorting first to diplomacy, Michael contacted the papacy with an offer to reunite the Greek and Latin Churches in exchange for recognition and mediation. This failing, he sent troops under his brother John. After ravaging Epirus, the Nicene forces met the disorganized allied army and smashed it at the Battle of Pelagonia (summer/autumn 1259).

With the Epirote threat to Nicaea and the future of Latin power in the Byzantine sphere thus doomed, Michael's next goal was the recovery of Constantinople, which had long evaded the sovereigns of Nicaea. Michael made a small and abortive attack on a region of the city in 1260, without effect. The following year he sought to strengthen his naval capacities by negotiating a treaty of alliance with Genoa. By apparent chance, however, a Nicene reconnoitring party, under the general Alexios Strategopoulos, was able to seize Constantinople from its debilitated Latin regime on 25 July 1261. Michael carefully orchestrated the symbolism of this success, making an official entry into the old capital on 15 August, at which time he had himself crowned for a second time. One last, cruel step completed his spectacular vault to power: by the end of 1261 the unhappy John IV Laskaris was decisively removed from any competition by blinding.

As the self-proclaimed "New Constantine", Michael poured out his energies and resources to restore the battered capital and its monuments, repopulating it with Greek ethnic elements from the surrounding region and from the Morea. He repaired the fortifications of the city, and attempted to rebuild a fleet. For Michael, the repossession of Constantinople meant reasserting Byzantium's status as a world power, while it obliged him to continue the recovery of the European territories lost to the Latins after the Fourth Crusade – especially in the Morea, where he strove to expand a Byzantine beach-head he had opened. On both counts he faced the hostility of Latin powers, which eventually received militant focus from the ambitions of the new ruler of Sicily and southern Italy, Charles of Anjou. In May 1267, the year after his destruction of Manfred at Benevento, Charles created by the Treaty of Viterbo an alliance of Michael's enemies committed to his and Byzantium's destruction.

A diplomat of considerable skill, Michael pursued a range of negotiations aimed at forestalling Charles's scheme of conquest. He revived his strongest asset, the proposal to the papacy that the Byzantine Church might be reunited with the Latin Church of Rome. His predecessors, and he himself, had pursued this idea for diplomatic reasons. At length, he negotiated with pope Gregory X (1271–76) an official union (i.e. submission to Rome), accepted by Byzantine negotiators and proclaimed at the Council of Lyons in 1274. That ecclesiastical commitment, as well as Michael's promise to refrain from further attacks on Latin holdings in Greek lands, obliged the pope to restrain Charles, who was also distracted by other Byzantine diplomatic manoeuvrings.

The price of such progress was mounting clerical and popular hostility to Michael at home. He already faced one Church schism as a result of his deposition in 1265 of the patriarch Arsenios, an early supporter who felt betrayed by Michael's treatment of the young John IV. But Michael's union with Rome antagonized a yet larger sector of public opinion, and even members of Michael's own family joined in bitter and disruptive opposition to him.

Michael consequently delayed implementation of the union in his realm. That failure, as well as his relentless prosecution of war against the Latins in Greece, disillusioned the papacy.

The strongly pro-Angevin pope Martin IV (1281–85) turned his back on Michael and became party to Charles's new anti-Byzantine coalition, the Treaty of Orvieto (July 1281). Feeling betrayed after he had risked so much at home (and never officially renouncing the union himself), Michael joined a grand conspiracy with the king of Aragon and local dissidents to provoke and exploit the great popular rising known as the Sicilian Vespers (March 1282), which deprived Charles of the foundation of his power and definitively spared Byzantium the threat of his conquest.

While Michael's progress against the Latins in the Morea proved indecisive, he was able to assert ascendancy in the Balkans. In 1264 he reduced his rival, the Epirote despot Michael Angelos, and his descendants to a feeble dependency confirmed by further pressures. The same year witnessed a dangerous inroad into the Balkans by the Tatars of the Golden Horde of southern Russia. This and a second devastating attack in 1271 prompted Michael to negotiate the following year an important treaty with the Mongol khan Nogai, which facilitated an encirclement of Michael's restless Bulgarian neighbours, while Michael's matrimonial ties with the Hungarian crown brought pressure on another dangerous Byzantine neighbour, Serbia. Finally, in 1282, Michael obliged John II Komnenos, emperor of the separatist Greek state of Trebizond, to come to Constantinople and relinquish any remaining claims to the Byzantine imperial title.

By such means Michael gave an image of power and importance to the restored empire of Palaiologan Byzantium, while transferring to the recovered capital the burgeoning cultural revival he had inherited from Laskarid Nicaea. But much of his achievement was illusory. He was unable to drive the Latins out of all the Morea or eliminate other Angelan rivals in Thessaly. His heavy concentration of attention on his western territories and international diplomacy, combined with pro-Laskarid opposition to him in parts of Asia Minor, led him to neglect until virtually the last minute the important eastern lands on which the post-1204 Byzantine recovery had been founded. He left these lands in such weakness that, within a few years, they became easy prey to the nascent power of the Ottoman sultanate. Above all, his arbitrary use of Church union as a diplomatic tool had brought violent controversy to his people and hatred upon himself. When he died suddenly on 11 December 1282, he was denied burial rites by the Church. He left to his hapless son and successor, the mediocre but well-intentioned Andronikos II (1282–1328), the tasks of liquidating the detested union and of adjusting the restored Byzantine empire to its actual status of a minor local power amid the realities of an altered world.

JOHN W. BARKER

See also Palaiologos Family

Biography

Born *c.*1225 the eldest son of Andronikos Palaiologos, Michael chose a military career. Theodore II Laskaris died in 1258 leaving his young son John IV a minor. Michael had the boy's regent murdered and was himself crowned co-emperor in 1259. After victory at Pelagonia (1259) he entered Constantinople in triumph in 1261 and set about restoring the city. He agreed to the union of Churches at Lyons in 1274. He died in Thrace in 1282.

Writings

"Imperatoris Michaelis Palaeologi de vita sua", translated by Henri Grégoire, *Byzantion*, 29–30 (1959–60): pp. 447–76 (Michael's "autobiography", in Greek and French)

Further Reading

Angold, Michael, *A Byzantine Government in Exile: Government and Society under the Laskarids of Nicaea, 1204–1261*, Oxford: Oxford University Press, 1975

Bartusis, Mark C., *The Late Byzantine Army: Arms and Society, 1204–1453*, Philadelphia: University of Pennsylvania Press, 1992

Chapman, Conrad, *Michel Paléologue: restaurateur de l'empire byzantin, 1261–1282*, Paris: Figuière, 1926

Dölger, Franz, "Die dynastische Familienpolitik des Kaisers Michael VIII. Palaiologos" in his *Paraspora*, Ettal: Buch-Kunstverlag, 1961

Franchi, Antonino, *I vespri siciliani e le relazioni tra Roma e Bisanzio: studio critico sulle fonti*, Palermo: Facoltà Teologica di Sicilia, 1984

Gardner, Alice, *The Lascarids of Nicaea: The Story of an Empire in Exile*, London: Methuen, 1912

Geanakoplos, Deno John, "Greco-Latin Relations on the Eve of the Byzantine Restoration: The Battle of Pelagonia, 1259", *Dumbarton Oaks Papers*, 7 (1953): pp. 99–141

Geanakoplos, Deno John, "Michael VIII Palaeologus and the Union of Lyons (1274)", *Harvard Theological Review*, 46 (1953): pp. 19–89

Geanakoplos, Deno John, *Emperor Michael Palaeologus and the West, 1258–1282*, Cambridge, Massachusetts: Harvard University Press, 1959

Gill, Joseph, *Byzantium and the Papacy, 1198–1400*, New Brunswick, New Jersey: Rutgers University Press, 1979

Miller, William, *The Latins in the Levant: A History of Frankish Greece, 1204–1566*, London: John Murray, and New York: Dutton, 1908; reprinted Cambridge: Speculum Historiale, and New York: Barnes and Noble, 1964

Raybaud, Léon Pierre, *Le Gouvernement et l'administration centrale de l'empire byzantin sous les premiers Paléologues, 1258–1354*, Paris: Sirey, 1968

Runciman, Steven, *The Sicilian Vespers: A History of the Mediterranean World in the Later Thirteenth Century*, Cambridge: Cambridge University Press, 1958

Miletus

City in Ionia

Miletus, situated on the Aegean coast at the mouth of the Maeander river, was one of the great cites of Ionia. Archaeological evidence points to Minoan and Mycenaean settlements on the site. According to Homer, the Milesians were Carians and fought on the Trojan side. Neleus son of Codrus is said to have founded the Ionian settlement.

In the 7th and 6th centuries BC, when the Ionian cities were under pressure first from the Lydians then from the Persians, Miletus took a lead in colonization, founding settlements on the Bosporus and all round the Black Sea: notably at Abydus, Cyzicus, Sinope, Amisus, Trapezus, Phasis, Panticapaeum, Olbia, Istrus, and Tomis. Subsequently a remarkable art grew up in mixed Scythian and Greek communities of what is now southern Russia. Milesians also took a leading part in the establishment of the Greek trading settlement at Naucratis in Egypt. Familiarity with Egypt and Egyptians made possible by this Greek oasis in Egypt was to have very great influence on Greek architecture, sculpture, vase painting, and many other aspects of the developing Greek civilization. In the 6th century the Milesians Thales, Anaximander, and Anaximenes started Greek philosophy. Hecataeus was a pioneer in both geography and historiography. He was also one of the leaders of the unsuccessful Ionian revolt against Persian rule (499–494). Miletus was sacked and many of its inhabitants killed, enslaved, or exiled. Between 479 and 412 Miletus was part of the Delian League which became the Athenian empire. Subsequently it was under Persian rule until liberated by Alexander the Great.

Miletus flourished in the Hellenistic period, and the Seleucid kings funded some of the monumental buildings which have been excavated by German archaeologists. Others were built when the city was ruled by the Romans from 129 BC. In AD 51 St Paul preached at Miletus. The city never became a provincial capital. It nevertheless prospered under Roman rule, particularly in the 1st and 2nd centuries AD when some remarkable harbour and market buildings were constructed. However, constant effort was needed to prevent the harbour, that was the source of the city's wealth, from silting up. The site is now 14 km from the sea. Miletus went into decline in the 4th century. Under Justinian I (527–65) Miletus received a new cathedral, the baths were restored, and the harbour dredged. The bishop, who had been a suffragan of Aphrodisias, became an autocephalous archbishop. Latros to the northeast of Miletus became a centre of monasticism. In the late 6th or 7th century a new circuit of walls was built enclosing only part of the old city area, and within this the theatre was later transformed into a citadel. Eventually all occupation beyond the citadel seems to have ceased. Legend made the remains of the theatre into those of a palace, *palatia*, from which Balat, the modern name of the locality is derived.

The great oracular sanctuary of Apollo lies 16 km south of Miletus at Didyma. Founded and administered by the priestly clan of the Branchidae, it was very influential in the 6th century BC. It was refounded by Alexander the Great, and enjoyed another period of great influence in the 2nd and early 3rd centuries AD. It was sometimes consulted on the nature of god and responded in terms of a philosophical syncretism approaching monotheism. The oracle encouraged Diocletian to persecute the Christians. The ruins of the temple (118×16 m) are highly impressive.

Miletus seems to have been the setting of the *Milesian Tales* of Aristides, written around 100 BC, a collection of short, lewd, and erotic tales which were translated into Latin and appear to have influenced tales told in Lucian's *Onos (Ass)* and Apuleius' *Metamorphoses*, as well as the *Satyricon* of Petronius.

J.H.W.G. LIEBESCHUETZ

Summary

Miletus was an Ionian city at the mouth of the river Maeander on the west coast of Asia Minor. Traces of Minoan and Mycenaean settlements have been found. Miletus played a leading part in colonizing the Bosporus and Black Sea regions and Naucratis in Egypt. Milesians were pioneers in philosophy and geography. Miletus was sacked by Persia for its part in the Ionian revolt (499–494 BC). It prospered under Roman rule but declined in the 4th century AD.

Miletus: the Temple of Apollo at Didyma, which brought great wealth to nearby Miletus

Further Reading

Boardman, John, *The Greeks Overseas: Their Early Colonies and Trade*, 4th edition, London and New York: Thames and Hudson, 1999

Fontenrose, Joseph, *Didyma: Apollo's Oracle, Cult, and Companions*, Berkeley: University of California Press, 1988

Foss, Clive, "Archaeology and the 'Twenty Cities'" in his *History and Archaeology of Byzantine Asia Minor*, Aldershot, Hampshire: Variorum, 1990

Müller Wiener, Wolfgang, "Das Theaterkastell von Milet", *Istanbuler Mitteilungen*, 17 (1967): pp. 279–90

Müller Wiener, Wolfgang, "Die Bischofskirche von Milet", *Istanbuler Mitteilungen*, 23–24 (1973–74): pp. 131ff

Müller Wiener, Wolfgang, *Milet, 1899–1980: Ergebnisse, Probleme und Perspektiven einer Ausgrabung*, Tübingen: Wasmuth, 1986

Parke, H.W., *Oracles of Apollo in Asia Minor*, London: Croom Helm, 1985

Stillwell, Richard (editor), *The Princeton Encyclopedia of Classical Sites*, Princeton, New Jersey: Princeton University Press, 1976, Miletus entry

Walsh, P.G., *The Roman Novel: The 'Satyricon' of Petronius and the 'Metamorphoses' of Apuleius*, Cambridge: Cambridge University Press, 1970, pp. 10–18

Wiegand, Theodor (editor), *Milet: Ergebnisse der Ausgrabungen und Untersuchungen seit dem Jahre 1899*, 18 vols, Berlin: Reimer, 1906–73

Military League

Military leagues played an important role in Greek interstate relations from the late 6th century BC. The creation of a military league was based on the agreement of two (or more) states to fight together (*symmachein*), either for a limited period or for all times. The standard Greek term for such a league is therefore *symmachia*. Participating states were obliged to have "the same friends and enemies". To coordinate warfare, military leagues usually established some sort of political body, such as a *synedrion* (council) or a board of magistrates. The leadership was transferred to the most powerful state, the *hegemon*. Unlike a *symmachia*, an *epimachia* was defensive in character, i.e. it was limited to defensive fighting exclusively.

The earliest – and most lasting – military alliance was the Peloponnesian League. Its origins can be traced back to the mid-6th century BC, when Sparta entered into a series of alliances, starting with Tegea, in which its allies swore to accept Spartan superiority and to expel the Messenians from their respective country. Similar treaties seem to have been concluded with other poleis, most notably Corinth and Sicyon. These alliances were all with Sparta alone, so mutual obligations did not necessarily exist between the allies. This bilateral system, reflected in its designation "the Spartans and their allies", was the nucleus of the Peloponnesian League proper as inaugurated between 505 and 501 BC, when a league congress was first established. Its main concern was to debate and make decisions (*dogmata*) on confederate wars. All members had an equal vote and enjoyed internal autonomy. Sparta's decision, taken in its own assembly, was equal to that of the allies put together. *Dogmata* of the allies were passed with its approval exclusively. Only the Spartans could summon the congress and were privileged to supply all commanders of league forces. A treaty from the last decades of the 5th century attests the oaths taken at the reception of new members: each ally swore to have the same friends and enemies as the Spartans, to follow them wherever they led, and not to make peace without Sparta's permission. In return, the allies were granted protection against hostile encroachment. In the 5th century the league grew beyond the Peloponnese and adopted several new members, such as Megara, Aegina, and the Boeotian, Phocian, and Locrian Confederacies. Its attraction was increased by anti-Athenian and – as explicitly stated in the Peloponnesian War – anti-democratic resentment among oligarchic states. After Sparta's victory over Athens and its allies in 404, Athens itself was forced to join, though only for a brief period. In the 4th century two major changes in the organization of the league were introduced. By 382 it was agreed that a member state's stipulated contribution in troops might be commuted to a contribution in cash, and that fines were to be levied on the allies that defaulted. The second innovation, brought about after 379, was to divide the league into ten geographically grouped *mere* (districts), which were presumably meant to be roughly equal in number of troops. Despite these reforms, the alliance soon disintegrated after Sparta's defeat in the Battle of Leuctra in 371.

The Delian League (frequently called "Athenian empire", though the degree of Athenian "imperialistic" rule is disputed among scholars) was founded in 478/87 BC to continue warfare against the Persians after their retreat from Greece. Apparently at the request of the founding members, the leadership was transferred to Athens. All members, including Athens, had one vote in the confederate *synedrion*, to determine strategy. From the outset the Athenians provided all the league's officials, such as the ten *hellenotamiai* (treasurers) and the commanders of allied forces, and settled which members had to send ships and which to pay money into the treasury at Delos. The first assessment of tributes (*phoroi*), allegedly 460 talents, was made by Aristides. The league fought a series of successful battles against the Persians (at the Eurymedon c.466 BC) and quickly expanded to 200 member states, most of them in the Aegean, on the west and south coast of Asia Minor, in Thrace, and in the Hellespont and Propontis regions. There was soon dissaffection with Athenian leadership, however. Many states tried to secede (starting with Naxos c.470 and Thasos c.465), but were forced back in by Athens. After a defeat in Egypt in 454 BC, the treasury was moved from Delos to Athens. One-sixtieth of the allied tribute was thence claimed as an offering to Athena (see the Athenian Tribute Lists in Merritt *et al.*, 1939). Although the alliance had lost its original justification with the removal of its anti-Persian objectives – probably stipulated in the so-called Peace of Callias with Persia in c.449 – Athens

continued to levy annual *phoroi* and inflicted cleruchies on members who were suspected of revolt (first known at Andros, Lemnos, Naxos, and Carystus in c.450). Disloyal states received a harsh punishment (notably Samos c.439 and Mytilene c.427). The autonomy of the allies was infringed by Athenian decrees on the legislation, jurisdiction, and financial policies of the member states. Epigraphic evidence indicates a shift in the designation from "the Athenians and their allies" to "the cities the Athenians rule". In the early years of the Peloponnesian War, Pericles openly called the Athenian hegemony a tyranny over the allies. The core of the alliance, however, remained remarkably stable throughout the war (despite a massive increase of assessment of allied tributes), which indicates that the league to some degree served the interests of the allies. After its final defeat at Aegospotami, Athens was forced to surrender its fleet and to join the Peloponnesian League. The Athenian empire was dissolved.

A second Athenian Confederacy was established in spring 378 by Athens and the founding members Chios, Byzantium, Rhodes, Mytilene, Methymna, and perhaps Thebes. After an attempted Spartan raid on the Piraeus, the Athenians invited all states to enter the confederacy on the principles laid down in the King's Peace, so "that the Lacedaimonians shall leave the Greeks free and autonomous". Eventually up to 70 members joined. Each state had one vote in the common council at Athens (except the Athenians), who were entrusted with the hegemony, but were not represented in the *synedrion*. The allies were guaranteed autonomy and freedom from tribute. Athenian ownership of land or property in allied states was prohibited, i.e. the Athenians refrained from the system of cleruchies. In practice, the alliance soon deviated from these principles. By 373 BC tributes – called *syntaxeis*, to avoid the term *phoroi* – were collected to meet the costs of campaigning. Probably in 365 BC the practice of cleruchies was revived at Samos (though technically not a member of the league). The integrity of the league was severely threatened by revolts of Rhodes, Chios, Cos, and Byzantium in 357 BC (supported by Mausolus of Caria), which led to the Social War between Athens and its allies. In 355 BC Athens was forced to accept the secession of virtually all significant members, except Euboea and a few northern Aegean islands.

Unlike the partial alliances of Sparta and Athens, several attempts were made to establish a combined military league of – at least theoretically – all Greek states. The scope of a "Hellenic League" was to defend Greece proper against foreign invaders. In autumn 481 BC a Hellenic League was founded at Sparta, to meet the impending invasion by Persia. Its designation, promoted by its members and widespread among historians, is slightly misleading, since the league by no means included all Greeks. The allies agreed to end wars among themselves and to give mutual aid at all times. Each member state elected one *proboulos* (representative) and had an equal vote in the council. Meetings were held in the precinct of Poseidon at Corinth. Since the Spartans had the greatest military strength of land forces, it was agreed that they should exercise the *hegemonia*. Athens, contributing more than half of the fleet, had some claims on the maritime command, but the allies distrusted it. The symmachy fell apart when the Spartans withdrew from the alliance in 478 BC. A second Hellenic League was founded in 340 BC against Philip of Macedon, mainly on the initiative of Demosthenes. A *synhedrion* was established in March 340 at Athens. The hegemony rested with the Athenians, who were also responsible for the collection of allied *syntaxeis* (tributes). The league was defeated on the battlefield at Chaeronea in 338 BC. In return, Philip summoned the Greeks to Corinth the following summer and united all Greek states (except Sparta) in the so-called League of Corinth. Its constitution, set down by Philip, embodied traditional clauses both of earlier military leagues and of common peace treaties from the 4th century. Each member state had one vote in the *synedrion* and was obliged to send troops according to its population. Philip himself, the league's *hegemon*, presided over the *synedrion*. The allies swore not to change their constitutions and not to revolt against the king, which reveals that the league was designed to consolidate Philip's position after Chaeronea. Its military purpose, sponsored by Philip and propagandistically heralded at Corinth, was to make war against Persia. The concept of a Hellenic League was temporarily revived by Antigonus Monophtalmus and Demetrius Poliorcetes in 302 BC, and finally by Antigonus Doson in 224 BC, envisaged as a league of federal states.

HANS BECK

See also Federal States

Further Reading

Baltrusch, Ernst, *Symmachie und Spondai: Untersuchungen zum griechischen Völkerrecht der archaischen und klassischen Zeit (8.–5. Jahrhundert v. Chr.)*, Berlin: de Gruyter, 1994

Brunt, Peter A., "The Hellenic League against Persia", *Historia*, 2 (1953–54): pp. 135–63

Buraselis, Kostas (editor), *Enotita kai Enotetes tis Archaiotetas* [Unity and Units in Antiquity], Athens, 1994

Busolt, Georg, *Griechische Staatskunde*, 2 vols, Munich: Beck, 1920–26

Cargill, Jack L. Jr., *The Second Athenian League: Empire or Free Alliance?*, Berkeley: University of California Press, 1981

Cartledge, Paul A., "A New 5th Century Spartan Treaty", *Liverpool Classical Monthly*, 1 (1976): pp. 87–92

Cawkwell, George L., "The Foundation of the Second Athenian Confederacy", *Classical Quarterly*, 23 (1973): pp. 47–60

de Ste. Croix, G.E.M., *The Origins of the Peloponnesian War*, London: Duckworth, and Ithaca, New York: Cornell University Press, 1972

Finley, Moses I., "The Fifth-Century Athenian Empire: A Balance Sheet" in *Imperialism in the Ancient World*, edited by P.D.A. Garnsey and C.R. Whittaker, Cambridge and New York: Cambridge University Press, 1978

Gschnitzer, Fritz, *Ein neuer spartanischer Staatsvertrag und die Verfassung des Peloponnesischen Bundes*, Meisenheim: Hain, 1978

Hammond, N.G.L. and G.T. Griffith, *A History of Macedonia*, vol. 2: *550–336 BC*, Oxford: Clarendon Press, 1979

Jehne, Martin, *Koine Eirene: Untersuchungen zu den Befriedungs- und Stabilisierungsbemühungen in der griechischen Poliswelt des 4. Jahrhunderts v. Chr.*, Stuttgart: Steiner, 1994

Larsen, J.A.O., "The Constitution of the Peloponnesian League", parts 1 and 2, *Classical Philology*, 28–29 (1933–34): pp. 257–76, 1–19

Lewis, D.M. *et al.* (editors), *The Fifth Century BC*, Cambridge: Cambridge University Press, 1992 (*The Cambridge Ancient History*, vol. 5, 2nd edition)

Lewis, D.M. *et al.* (editors), *The Fourth Century BC*, Cambridge: Cambridge University Press, 1994 (*The Cambridge Ancient History*, vol. 6, 2nd edition)

Meiggs, Russell, *The Athenian Empire*, Oxford: Clarendon Press, 1972

Merritt, Benjamin Dean, H.T. Wade Gery, and Malcolm Francis McGregor (editors), *The Athenian Tribute Lists*, 4 vols, Princeton, New Jersey: American School of Classical Studies, 1939–53

Schuller, Wolfgang, *Die Herrschaft der Athener im Ersten Attischen Seebund*, Berlin: de Gruyter, 1974

Minerals and other natural resources

A large number of different minerals and other natural resources have been exploited in Greece over the centuries. Those used in antiquity tend to be rather different from those used more recently, which will be treated last. Major metallic ore minerals (gold, copper and tin, silver and lead, iron) exploited in antiquity are discussed elsewhere.

Clay was a very important resource in antiquity – most was used for pottery, but some special types had medicinal uses. To a geologist the term clay applies to both a group of platy minerals, and a rock dominated by these minerals. Clay minerals are commonly formed by a chemical process – weathering of older rocks on the surface, or the action of hot water (200–400°C) associated with volcanism or the emplacement of intrusions. Most deposits of the rock clay are formed by the physical process of erosion of clay-mineral-bearing rock. The liberated clay is then transported and sorted by rivers and finally deposited in a lake or the sea. Many of these clay-rock deposits were exploited directly. However, many clays are mineralogically unsuitable for making pottery as they are too stiff or they do not fire well. Suitable clays were commonly deposited in shallow continental lakes surrounded by vegetation. Eventually accumulation of sediments made the lake so shallow that plants grew abundantly. The plants died but did not decay in the stagnant water and their remains were transformed into lignite, a low-grade coal. Some red pottery clays were also obtained from the *Terra Rosa* soils developed on limestone by washing and settling of the liquid, a treatment that resembles the natural processes.

Alumen is the name given to a natural mineral that was used as a deodorant, as a salve when mixed with honey, and as an emetic when mixed with copper salts. It was also used in dyeing, soldering, and in cloth finishing. It was probably bentonite, a clay produced by the weathering and alteration of volcanic rock, that is common on Melos.

Ochre is a red powdery earth made dominantly of hydrated iron oxide. It was used for cult purposes and as a pigment, but not as a source of iron metal. It can be produced by alteration of iron deposits or by deposition directly from springs. Ochre comprises several different minerals – haematite gives a red colour whereas the iron hydroxides geothite and limonite give yellows and browns. In Palaeolithic times red ochre was extracted on Thasos for cult purposes from one of the largest underground mines in Europe. Another important source of ochre was Moschylos on Lemnos. Lemnian earth was used from antiquity down to the 19th century for its medicinal properties, and is still used locally. It was known to the Romans as Terra Sigillata, or "stamped earth", as it was made into little cakes, stamped with the head of Artemis. Lemnian earth was deposited from former springs. Rainwater falling on the nearby volcanic tuffs soaked into the rock and broke down the minerals. Iron was thus liberated and dissolved in the water. Where the springs debouched, the iron was oxidized by the air and precipitated as ochre.

Pigments used in frescos were derived from a variety of sources, both organic and inorganic, and artificial and natural. These pigments should not be confused with glazes on fired pottery, which have very different compositions. Black pigments were based either on carbon from charcoal, or on preparations of hydrated manganese oxides which occur in some sedimentary rocks. Two different blue pigments were used. The strongest blue was obtained from imported Egyptian blue. Although dominated by copper compounds, the presence of tin suggests that it may have been prepared from bronze. A much paler grey-blue or purple pigment was derived from the mineral glaucophane, which is found in metamorphic rocks from the Cyclades. A range of red, yellow, and brown pigments were all natural forms of ochre (see above). Haematite also gives a red colour.

The bright yellow mineral sulphur was used for many purposes: the pungent fumes given off when it is burnt were used as a disinfectant and for religious purification; it had many external medical uses and was applied as a poultice; it was also used in wool preparation to make it white and soft. Sulphur occurs as the native element in volcanically active areas. It can be gathered directly from the surface and purified by melting. Sulphur has been mined sporadically on Melos and Nisyros at least since Hellenistic times. Sulphur crystallizes directly from hot volcanic vapours where they leave the ground (fumaroles). These gases are usually dominated by steam and carbon dioxide, but commonly contain small amounts of sulphurous gases which crystallize to form the mineral sulphur on or just beneath the surface. The sulphur in these gases is probably derived largely from the molten rock itself, unlike the water which is generally recycled groundwater. Sulphur does not survive for a long time on the surface as it is easily oxidized to the gas sulphur dioxide or consumed by bacteria and turned into sulphate.

Emery was important as an abrasive to shape marble and other stone. It contains corundum, a hard oxide of aluminium, together with magnetite and other minerals. It is formed by the metamorphism of bauxite layers in limestone (see below). Although it occurs at several places in the Aegean, rarely does the quality match that found on Naxos. In antiquity emery was extracted form a large number of shallow quarries, principally in the eastern part of the island. More recently it was extracted from underground mines and transported by aerial tramways to the coast.

Asbestos was used for making fireproof cloth. That used in Greece is a fibrous form of the serpentine mineral antigorite that crystallizes in veins up to 5 cm wide in the rock serpentinite. The crystals are generally lined up at right angles to the direction of the vein, and form as the vein opens up. The ancient sources were on Mount Ochi northeast of Carystus in Euboea, but the mineral has been exploited recently elsewhere.

Very little metallic zinc was produced in antiquity, but brass, an alloy of copper and zinc, seems to have been known in Greece from about 700 BC. Zinc ore is quite common, often in association with lead and copper ores. The main ores are the sulphide sphalerite or calamine, a mineral produced by alteration of sphalerite on the surface. Metallic zinc was rarely produced because it is volatile at the temperatures necessary for smelting it. The resulting zinc vapour condenses on the sides of the furnace, where most of it is converted to zinc oxide. In some cases the oxide was the desired product as a salve, as recorded by Galen on a visit to Cyprus. Pliny mentions zinc oxide as *lauriotis*, probably after the mines at Laurium. In the 19th century zinc and antimony were produced on Siphnos and Thasos, partly from mines that produced lead and silver in antiquity.

Mercury was known in the Old World from around 1600 BC. It was used for silver and gold plating (gilding) and in the recycling of gold thread from cloth but not apparently for mining gold. Mercury is a volatile metal and it was recovered from the sulphide ore cinnabar by distillation. The main sources in the Aegean were around Smyrna (modern Izmir), where the ore is associated with young volcanic rocks. In Roman times much mercury was produced in Spain.

Obsidian was a rare and important resource in the prehistoric period as it could be readily formed into sharp blades. It is a natural volcanic glass. That used in the eastern Mediterranean for blades mostly came from Melos; further west, Lipari was the main source. Obsidian was used extensively in early times for the manufacture of tools and weapons and fulfilled the same functions as flint (which forms in sedimentary rocks) did in northern Europe. It was not completely displaced by copper or bronze as it was sharper and cheaper than both metals. Only the use of iron finally supplanted obsidian in weapons and tools. However, its use did continue in ornaments and mirrors.

Bitumen (pitch), a natural petroleum product, was used in antiquity for caulking ships and wine barrels, for protecting metals, and for magical and medicinal purposes. It is the residue left where petroleum has seeped up to the surface and the lighter, more volatile components (similar to paraffin/kerosene and petrol/gasoline) have been lost by evaporation. There are natural springs and pools of bitumen near Limni Keri, Zakynthos, that were mentioned by Herodotus. The bedrock here is Paleocene-Oligocene limestone, but the petroleum is probably derived from deeper rocks, perhaps the Cretaceous limestones seen elsewhere in the island. In such sedimentary rocks petroleum forms from plant remains by the action of heat in the absence of oxygen. It is lighter than water and hence tends to migrate upwards through permeable rocks or along faults, unless trapped. Despite the presence of bitumen, economic reserves of petroleum have not yet been found in the region.

Amber was used for jewellery and small items. There are no sources in the Aegean region – all must have been transported overland from the Baltic sea, where it occurs abundantly along the coast. Amber is light and few journeys would be necessary to furnish all the amber found so far.

Recently a number of minerals and rocks have been exploited in the Aegean region. Marble and gypsum continue, of course, to be very important commodities. The aluminium ore bauxite has been mined in the area around Mount Parnassus. It was formed by extreme weathering of limestone when a tropical climate prevailed in Greece 200 to 65 million years ago. The same climate acting on different rocks produced laterites, rocks rich in iron and nickel. These have been exploited in eastern Boeotia and the ore refined at Larimna. Magnesite is a mineral used in the manufacture of refractory bricks. It formed during metamorphism and has been mined on Lesbos, northern Euboea, and the Chalcidice peninsula. The ancient mining heritage of Melos continues today with the extraction of the clays bentonite and kaolinite, as well as perlite, a volcanic rock that can be expanded to make insulating material. Lignite is a form of low-grade coal that is extensively exploited for the generation of electricity in both Greece and Turkey. Its combustion commonly produces much pollution. Thera (modern Santorini) was formerly the main source of pumice, but now it is mined in Yiali and Melos for use as an abrasive.

MICHAEL D. HIGGINS

See also Copper and Tin, Gold, Iron, Marble, Obsidian, Silver and Lead

Further Reading

Brinkmann, Roland, *Geology of Turkey*, Stuttgart: Enke, 1976

Craddock, Paul T., *Early Metal Mining and Production*, Edinburgh: Edinburgh University Press, and Washington D.C.: Smithsonian Institution Press, 1995

Higgins, Michael Denis and Reynold Higgins, *A Geological Companion to Greece and the Aegean*, Ithaca, New York: Cornell University Press, and London: Duckworth, 1996

Jacobshagen, Volker (editor), *Geologie von Griechenland*, Berlin: Borntraeger, 1986

Mines and Quarries

The common use of the Greek word *metallon* to describe both a mine (e.g. Xenophon, *De Vectigalibus*, 4. 4) and a quarry (e.g. Strabo, 9. 1. 23) shows that little distinction was made between the two in antiquity. Both types of working were considered to provide resources which were of benefit to the community, either as building material or for financial profit.

Mines

Iron is found in several locations throughout Greece and the Aegean. Some of the more significant workings were in Boeotia and Laconia. It is perhaps no coincidence that the earliest Laconian currency consisted of iron "spits". Strabo (10. 1. 9) recorded the presence of copper and iron mines at Chalcis, on the island of Euboea, though there is little substantive evidence. Iron ore was extracted on Seriphos during the 14th century by the Venetians.

Precious metals were mined at several sites throughout Greece and the islands. Silver was mined on the island of Siphnos from the Bronze Age onwards and a number of workings have been investigated at Hagios Sostis in the northeastern part of the island; some of the ancient workings were identified as early as 1700 by P. de Tournefort. Further investigations in the 19th century and in more recent decades have revealed evidence of slag, litharge, and tuyères. Study of the workings themselves shows that metal chisels and picks were used in the galleries. Carbon samples suggest that some of this activity can be dated to the first half of the 3rd millennium BC. Further evidence of metalworking, though not of mine workings, has been found in the southeast of the island. The mines continued to be productive in the Archaic period; this is attested by the presence of Archaic pottery at Hagios Sostis, and the city felt able to dedicate as a tithe a treasury in the sanctuary of Apollo at Delphi. It was reputed to be the richest treasury at Delphi, on account perhaps of its contents rather than of the sculptural decoration on the outside (Herodotus, 3. 57). Coinage issued during the 5th century BC suggests that the mines continued to be worked after the Archaic period. It seems that the workings eventually went too deep, with the result that the mines were flooded at some point before the 2nd century AD (Pausanias, 10. 11. 2).

Some of the best-investigated silver mines in the Greek world are those located around Laurium in southern Attica. At Velatouri mining activity can be traced back at least to the Early Bronze Age. A particularly rich discovery at Maroneia probably in 483/82 BC provided funds that allowed the Athenians, under Themistocles' guidance, to construct a fleet which was to defend the Greek world in the Battle of Salamis. It seems from inscriptions and other historical records that mining concessions were leased out to individuals. Leases show that some individuals held concessions at more than one location. The system largely depended on slave labour for mining and processing of the ore. Nicias was reported to have had 1000 slaves hired to work in the mines during the late 5th century BC, and Xenophon reported than some 10,000 publicly owned slaves were employed in the mines.

Linked to the mines themselves were a number of processing installations for washing and processing the ore. One of these *ergasteria* (workshops) was the subject of a speech by Demosthenes (37). The *ergasterion* concerned had been acquired by Pantaenetus and employed around 30 slaves. As the money needed to acquire the *ergasterion* had had to be raised on credit, these 30 slaves had to work hard enough for the installation to make at least the 1260 drachmas necessary to pay off the interest on the loan. A series of *ergasteria* have recently been excavated at Agrileza; material suggests that they were in use in the 4th century BC. The level of output from the Laurium mines is hard to estimate and there are few firm figures. The Maroneia mine may have yielded between 50 and 100 talents (the equivalent of 1.3–2.6 tons of silver). The mines themselves were probably abandoned during the Hellenistic period, as by Strabo's day (9. 1. 23) the silver supplies were described as having failed, and indeed the slag heaps were being processed to extract ore.

The output of the Laurium mines may well have been small compared to that of mines in Macedonia and Thrace. Ancient sources hint at the wealth derived from these sources. For example, the gold mine at Dysoron in Macedonia had a daily output in the mid-5th century BC of one talent of silver (Herodotus, 5. 17). Mines controlled by Philip II of Macedon near the later site of Philippi apparently had an annual output in the region of 1000 talents (Diodorus, 16. 8. 6). The source of wealth of individual cities in the region is reflected in the depiction of metal ingots and picks on the coinage. The island of Thasos was also widely exploited by mining and Herodotus (6. 47) was able to observe a mountain which had been ransacked by such activity. Sometime in the 460s BC the

Mines and Quarries: Mons Porphyrites in Egypt, source of the highly prized stone, porphyry

Thasians came into conflict with the Athenians and as a result were forced to hand over control of their mine on the mainland opposite their island (Thucydides, 1. 100. 2). The historian Thucydides himself had control of gold mines in Thrace.

One of the more unusual materials mined in antiquity was miltos on the island of Ceos. It was used for a variety of purposes including medicine and fulling, as well as its more popular use as a wash on the surface of Attic pottery. A number of possible mine workings have been found on the island, including those at Trypospilies. There is a reference to this ore in an inscription from the Acropolis in Athens.

Quarries

Quarries, or *latomeia*, were widespread throughout the Greek world. Often such quarries are linked to building projects in nearby cities or sanctuaries. The extensive quarries of Syracuse were used as a prison for some 7000 Athenian prisoners after the disastrous Sicilian expedition. Some of the earliest examples of marble quarrying have been found at Apollona on Naxos. A number of unfinished male statues (*kouroi*) have been discovered there, including what appears to be a large statue of Dionysus which was never removed from the quarry face. Naxian expertise in working marble during the Archaic period is reflected in their major dedication of a colossal statue, along with a substantial marble base, on the island of Delos. Marble quarries have also been identified on Paros. In the Archaic period marble from the island was transported over long distances, for example for building on the island of Siphnos (Herodotus, 3. 57).

Some of the finest marble in the Greek world came from Attica itself, and in particular from the quarries on Mount Pentelikon and Mount Hymettus, which were celebrated by Strabo (9. 1. 23). Pentelic marble, in particular, was widely used for architecture, sculpture, and inscriptions. Indeed the *metalleis* mentioned among those involved with the Periclean building programme at Athens may have been quarrymen (rather than miners). Study of stones from the Periclean buildings shows that Pentelic marble was used in a wide range of temples including the Parthenon, the Erechtheum, the Hephaesteum, and temple of Athena Nike, as well as public buildings in the Agora such as the stoa of Zeus. In the 4th century BC Pentelic marble was used for part of the Telesterion at Eleusis. Pentelic marble continued to be exported in the Roman period; for example, it has been identified at Cyrene, where it was used in the Antonine period.

The Pentelic quarries seem to have been located on the western and northeastern sides of the mountain, where the existence of some 25 quarries has been located. These were certainly active in the Archaic period, as is suggested by the find of an unfinished *kouros*. It has been estimated that some 400,000 cubic m may have been extracted. Facilities for removing the stone included the paved road which has been found at the Spelia quarry. The quarries on Hymettus may be linked to activity in the Roman period. These seem to have been located on the northwestern slopes of the mountain and also to have been served by a quarry road. Hymettan marble, with its bluish tinge, was used for the roof tiles of the Hekatompedon on the Acropolis during the Archaic period.

In spite of the quality of the marble from Pentelikon and Hymettus, other buildings in Attica were constructed of locally quarried marble and stone. Indeed it is rare for buildings in Attica to feature stone from quarries more than 4 km distant. For example, the marble for the temple of Poseidon at Sunium was extracted from a quarry in the Agrileza valley just a few kilometres away. In the workings by the cliff tower, cuttings in the quarry suggest that one of the column drums had been extracted from there. The temple of Nemesis at Rhamnous features marble quarried locally at Hagia Marina.

Attic quarries are occasionally mentioned in inscriptions. For example, one dispute related to the rent on a quarry at the Piraeus in the late 340s BC. Rent from quarries could contribute to the maintenance of cult. For example, the sacrifices at the Asclepieum at the Piraeus were paid for by the rental of the quarry, and at Eleusis quarrymen in 332/31 BC made payments to the cult of Heracles in Akris.

Black limestone from near Eleusis was used on the Erechtheum and the Propylaea. Local limestones (poros) were used for public buildings in the Agora such as the Old Bouleuterion, as well as for building projects at Brauron and the Amphiareion. Imported stones in Attica include Aeginetan stone that was used on the Erechtheum and the Hephaesteum, and Parian marble for the Hephaesteum. At Eleusis stones were imported from the Piraeus, Steiria, and Aegina, suggesting the relative ease with which stone could be transported by sea.

Some of the major building projects in Greek sanctuaries required the movement of stone from quarries some distance from the place where it was to be used. For example, rebuilding of the temple of Apollo at Delphi in the 6th century BC involved marble from Paros (Herodotus, 5. 62), and in the 4th century BC the whole temple was rebuilt in limestone quarried from near Corinth. Marble imported from Paros was also used for the pediments and metopes of the temple of Zeus at Olympia. The blocks needed to carve the pair of centaurs with lapith women in the west pediment would originally have weighed some 15 to 20 tons. It has been estimated that the construction of the temple of Zeus would have required approximately 160 tons of marble.

More specialized marbles were also quarried in Greece. *Rosso antico*, also known as *marmor Taenarium*, was a red to purple fine-grained marble quarried on the east side of the Taenarus peninsula in Laconia. The quarries, noted by Strabo (8. 5. 7), may have been worked as early as the Bronze Age. Marble from here was used in the so-called Treasury of Atreus – a Mycenaean tholos tomb – at Mycenae; other examples of its use are known in Crete and Thera. The marble seems to have become popular for inscriptions during the Hellenistic period, and two honorary decrees from Delos, one for a Spartan and the other for a resident of Cythera, used the stone. It was even exported to Cyrene for a statue of Ptolemy II Soter. Sculpture in *rosso antico* also became popular in the late Hellenistic and early imperial periods. From the same area was quarried *nero antico*, a grey to black marble (Pliny, *Historia Naturalis*, 36. 135).

Other exotic stones from Laconia include *verde antico*, which Pliny the Elder (*Historia Naturalis*, 36. 55) described as "brighter than any other marble". These quarries were mentioned by Pausanias (3. 21. 4) as being near the village of Krokeai. The stone was apparently extracted like river pebbles. In the Roman period the mines may have been imperial property. Other Laconian quarries are known in Taygetus, which may have been Roman imperial property, as Strabo (8. 5. 7) recorded that they had been newly opened in his day. On the island of Euboea green cipollino was quarried in Carystus (Pliny, *Historia Naturalis*, 36. 48). Strabo (10. 1. 6) noted that in his day the quarry from which the columns came was located at Marmarium. Strabo (9. 5. 16) noted other exotic marbles from the Greek world, including "decorated" (*poikile*) marble from the island of Skyros.

Archaeological evidence for later quarrying in Greece has been hard to detect. Quarries on Mount Tisaion in Thessaly were probably worked in the Byzantine period, and perhaps also the white marble quarry at Aliki on the southeastern coast of Thasos. The latter appears to have continued being worked into the Middle Ages.

DAVID W.J.GILL

See also Gold, Iron, Marble, Silver and Lead, Slavery

Further Reading

Adam, Sheila, *The Technique of Greek Sculpture in the Archaic and Classical Periods*, London: Thames and Hudson, 1967

Anderson, Matwell L. and Leila Nitsa (editors), *Radiance in Stone: Sculptures in Colored Marble from the Museo Nazionale Romano*, Rome: De Luca, and Atlanta: Emory University, Museum of Art and Archaeology, 1989

Ashmole, Bernard, *Architect and Sculptor in Classical Greece*, New York: New York University Press, and London: Phaidon, 1972

Cherry, J.F., J.L. Davis, and E. Mantzourani, *Landscape Archaeology as Long-term History: Northern Keos in the Cycladic Islands from the Earliest Settlement until Modern Times*, Los Angeles: UCLA Institute of Archaeology, 1991

Conophagos, Constantin E., *Le Laurium antique et la technique grecque de la production de l'argent*, Athens, 1980

Dworakowska, Angelina, *Quarries in Ancient Greece*, Wroclaw: Ossolinskich, 1975

Dworakowska, Angelina, *Quarries in Roman Provinces*, Wroclaw: Ossolinskich, 1983

Ellis, S.E., R.A. Higgins, and R. Hope Simpson, "The Facade of the Treasury of Atreus at Mycenae", *Annual of the British School at Athens*, 63 (1968): pp. 331–6

Gale, N.H. and Z.A. Stos-Gale, "Cycladic Lead and Silver Metallurgy", *Annual of the British School at Athens*, 76 (1981): pp. 170–224

Healy, John F., *Mining and Metallurgy in the Greek and Roman World*, London: Thames and Hudson, 1978

Hopper, R.J., "The Attic Silver Mines in the Fourth Century BC", *Annual of the British School at Athens*, 48 (1953): pp. 200–54

Hopper, R.J., "The Laurion mines: A Reconsideration", *Annual of the British School at Athens*, 63 (1968) pp. 293–326

Hopper, R.J., *Trade and Industry in Classical Greece*, London: Thames and Hudson, 1979

Jones, J.E., "The Laurium Silver Mines: A Review", *Greece and Rome*, 29 (1982): pp. 169–84

Jones, J.E., "Laurion: Agrileza, 1977–83: Excavations at a Silvermine Site", *Archaeological Reports*, 31 (1984–85): pp. 106–23

Korres, Manolis, *From Pentelicon to the Parthenon: The Ancient Quarries and the Story of a Half-Worked Column Capital of the First Marble Parthenon*, Athens: Melissa, 1995

Osborne, Robin, *Demos: The Discovery of Classical Attika*, Cambridge and New York: Cambridge University Press, 1985

Osborne, Robin, "Island Towers: The Case of Thasos", *Annual of the British School at Athens*, 81 (1986): pp. 167–78

Osborne, Robin, *Classical Landscape with Figures: The Ancient Greek City and its Countryside*, London: George Philip, and Dobbs Ferry, New York: Sheridan House, 1987

Shepherd, Robert, *Ancient Mining*, London and New York: Elsevier Applied Science (for the Institution of Mining and Metallurgy), 1993

Waterhouse, H. and R. Hope Simpson, "Prehistoric Laconia: part 2", *Annual of the British School at Athens*, 56 (1961): pp. 114–75

Wycherley, R.E., "Pentelethen", *Annual of the British School at Athens*, 68 (1973): pp. 349–53

Minoans

Bronze Age inhabitants of Crete

This people, termed Minoans by archaeologists after the legendary king Minos, created between 3500 and 1000 BC a palace-based culture akin to those of the Near East and Egypt. Many of their trappings were adapted later by the Mycenaeans of the mainland (c.1600 BC).

The varied natural terrain and therefore resources (organic rather than mineral) of this strategically placed island permitted Neolithic peoples (from Anatolia and the mainland) to prosper by 4000 BC, after three millennia of slower development: their main achievement was the tell at Knossos. Though their material culture was unspectacular, these Neolithic farmers provided the solid base on which the Minoans flourished.

During the pre-palatial or Early Minoan (EM) period (3500–2000 BC) small farming communities were increasingly established in the most accessible and fertile areas – in the coastal plains and the Mesara – though the marginal zones were also exploited and transhumance was probably practised. Many arts and crafts were established, if at a relatively simple level: ceramics, textiles, woodworking, seals, and vases of stone were developed using local resources, but trade and exchange were required to import obsidian, all metals, ivory, faience, and so on. No doubt ideas and concepts accompanied them. Houses were fairly simple, but they had acquired considerable sophistication of plan and furniture by 2500 BC. Tomb architecture tended to be communal: round tholoi were common at the centre of the island, while square bone enclosures and caves were used elsewhere. The burial customs are somewhat obscure, but inhumations were the rule. The varied grave goods deposited point to a hierarchical society. Evidence for religion (and dress) is mostly procured from clay figurines; many were deposited at open-air sanctuaries set on high peaks within sight of the villages they served.

As the population increased and more land was occupied, regional centres emerged: some (e.g. Knossos, Phaestus, Mallia) were destined to last, others (e.g. Monastiraki) were eclipsed. Since weapons were fashioned, this process was probably not entirely a peaceful one. By 2000 BC (Middle Minoan I, or MM I) the first palaces had emerged – administrative and religious centres, controlling territories in the island. The physical expressions of this development had much in common: the palaces were ranges of rooms built around a central court and oriented to the compass points. The social complexities that created them also demanded a system of writing (hieroglyphic), as well as an ever-increasing range of material products, partly for the consumption of the elite, partly for exchange in markets abroad. Though hard to document, expertise in almost every craft was established: Kamares pottery, the exploitation of hard stones, and objects in metals are notable. New ideas continued to flow to Crete down these trading arteries, especially from the east.

Damage, perhaps from earthquakes, around 1700 BC (MM III) only served to spur on Minoan efforts: the Second Palaces arose. The next two centuries witnessed the culmination of power and material splendour – an intensification of all the existing themes. This is the likely time of Minos' thalassocracy:

certainly Minoan culture was enormously influential throughout the Aegean and into the Peloponnese; Minoan traders moved and settled from Asia Minor to Egypt, visiting north Greece and probably travelling west to Italy. Modern appreciation of Minoan culture is largely based on the range and quality of goods that poured from the artisans' work areas: elegant, flowing designs; a lively palette; a concentration on natural subjects, courtly themes, and the interplay of this and the other world. The apparent harmony and balance are to our tastes, but they were not achieved in a Utopia. In comparison with the Near Eastern civilizations, the Minoans were less overtly militaristic and grandiose in their portrayal of their world; but they were not pacifists. There is ample evidence for military activities from artefacts and portrayals of warfare; some sports were violent; human sacrifice was practised. Knossos may have achieved a dominance over other cities at this time – as much through economic and religious avenues as by sheer strength. The religious centres were more localized on the palaces; chamber tombs were for collective burials of ordinary people; a few graves, as with the town and country houses, were more splendid and destined for the elite. Indeed, the building campaigns throughout the island represented a profligate expenditure of energy that may have overstretched Minoan resources: there are indications of troubled times in the 1500s BC, perhaps partly prompted by the natural disasters accompanying the eruption of Santorini. Whatever the exact mix of causes, during the last decades of LM Ib (Late Minoan Ib, after 1500 BC) settlements both great and small were destroyed, often by force, and not immediately reoccupied.

Whatever the reasons, the ultimate benefactors were the Mycenaeans, those seemingly aggressive and expanding kingdoms of southern and central Greece who took over Crete around 1450 BC. This can be deduced from the appearance on Crete of material objects, details of dress, burial customs, and other cultural traits that have precursors on the mainland. The centre (Knossos to Phaestus) of Crete became the axis of the Mycenaean power base, their control of the island being loosest in the east. Essentially, the newcomers merely adopted existing Minoan customs: by means of a scribal bureaucracy the palaces maintained a firm grasp on the human and natural resources of the domains, assessing what was available and determining what produce was expected where and from whom. Labour forces in some intensive crafts (such as textiles) were maintained by rations and appear to have been of a subordinate status. Writing was essential to regulate this activity and the script employed is known as Linear B, a syllabary adopted from the earlier Minoan equivalent (Linear A), but now used to write Greek. The Mycenaean/Minoan elite was every bit as successful as its predecessor, the only real departure being the decline in some luxury goods.

By 1375 BC (LM IIIA1) Crete had recovered something of its former pattern of settlement and a prosperous level of material comfort (e.g. burials with bronzes): whatever the exact amalgam of Minoan and Mycenaean, society appeared to be settled. But evidently it was not: Knossos, both town and palace, went up in flames. The cause – disaffected Minoans, another jealous Mycenaean power, or some raid from further afield – is not known. The aftermath is not yet fully comprehended by modern scholarship: debate is divided between those who believe that Knossos and the Mycenaeans remained

Minoans: glazed figure of snake goddess with upraised arms, Crete, c.13th century BC, Ashmolean Museum, Oxford

in control for another two centuries, and those who think that palatial control was now mostly swept away.

Something of both factors may have been involved: the pattern of subsequent habitation and burial activities at Knossos and in the Phaestus region points to at least a decline in population and material prosperity, though at Chania something more traditional persisted for some generations. If the balance of control moved away from centralization, nonetheless a broad-based prosperity is much in evidence in the post-palatial period (LM IIIA2–IIIC). Trade networks, an integral factor in Mycenaean control of the Aegean, were still crucial to the acquisition of metals – at least one commodity can be recognized in the large-scale export of oil (perhaps perfumed) in jars manufactured in west Crete. This solid prosperity had a very practical base to it: gone are the luxurious aspects of life, gone indeed are the more rarefied crafts themselves. Gradually new religious icons (goddess with upraised arms) appear; new cultural traits gain favour (larnax, or coffin, burials); iconographies alter (increased stylization in patterns).

Though it is an island, Crete could not escape the disconcerting events that unfolded throughout the eastern Mediterranean after 1200 BC. Most of these had negative consequences for the established cultures: destruction and disturbance of peoples became common from Anatolia to Greece to Egypt. Such events are visible in Crete in the abandonment of settlements and cemeteries from 1200 BC (later LM

IIIB), in increasing material impoverishment and regionalization (e.g. small tholoi at the east). After 1100 BC (LM IIIC) people took to the hills in scattered refugee settlements (e.g. Karphi). This erosion was periodic, but relentlessly accumulative; all but the most immediate survival needs were jettisoned. The ebb and flow may have removed some Cretans east to Cyprus, and introduced other elements from the west and north into the island, including those that later became culturally definable as Dorian Greeks. (The east of the island preserved more of its Bronze Age characteristics.) By 1000 BC the Iron Age was evolving: the cemeteries north of Knossos show some continuity, retained by an energetic and emerging society with ties to Athens and further afield east and west.

What memories survived from the Bronze Age are largely centred around legends concerned with Minos; more tentative connections were kept alive by such factors as the recognition that the inhabitants of eastern Crete (the Eteo-Cretans) were in some way more "native". Symbols derived from the Bronze Age past were always used: local pride placed the labyrinth on Knossian coins; Minoan finds were portrayed on stamps of the new Cretan state at the start of the 20th century. To many Cretans today the Minoans are somehow their direct ancestors, whose achievements are to be lauded, protected, and kept unsullied.

DON EVELY

See also Architecture (Palaces), Crete

Summary

Minoan culture evolved on Crete around 3500 BC. It was based on agriculture and overseas trade. The first palaces emerged c.2000 BC as religious and administrative centres. The second phase of palaces arose c.1700 BC. The Mycenaeans took over c.1450 BC, and the palaces decayed in the following century or two. Crete became increasingly destabilized after 1200 and gave way to Dorian Greek institutions after 1000 BC.

Further Reading

Betancourt, Philip P., *The History of Minoan Pottery*, Princeton, New Jersey: Princeton University Press, 1985

Davaras, Costis, *Guide to Cretan Antiquities*, Park Ridge, New Jersey: Noyes Press, 1976

Hägg, Robin and Nanno Marinatos (editors), *The Minoan Thalassocracy: Myth and Reality*, Stockholm: Svenska Institutet i Athen, 1984

Hägg, Robin and Nanno Marinatos (editors), *The Function of the Minoan Palaces*, Stockholm: Svenska Institutet i Athen, 1987

Hägg, Robin (editor), *The Function of the 'Minoan Villa'*, Stockholm, 1997

Hallager, Erik, *The Mycenaean Palace at Knossos: Evidence for a Final Destruction in the IIIB Period*, Stockholm: Medalhavsmuseet, 1977

Hood, Sinclair, *The Minoans: Crete in the Bronze Age*, London: Thames and Hudson, 1971

Hood, Sinclair, *The Arts in Prehistoric Greece*, Harmondsworth and New York: Penguin, 1978

Krzyszkowska, Olga and Lucia Nixon (editors), *Minoan Society*, Bristol: Bristol Classical Press, 1983

Marinatos, Nanno, *Minoan Religion: Ritual, Image, and Symbol*, Columbia: University of South Carolina Press, 1993

Myers, J. Wilson (editor), *The Aerial Atlas of Ancient Crete*, Berkeley: University of California Press, and London: Thames and Hudson, 1992

Palaima, Thomas G. (editor), *Aegean Seals, Sealings and Administration*, Liège: Université de Liège, 1990

Popham, Mervyn R., *The Destruction of the Palace at Knossos: Pottery of the Late Minoan IIIa Period*, Gothenburg: Åström, 1970

Shaw, Joseph W., *Minoan Architecture: Materials and Techniques*, Annuario della Reale Scuola Archeologica di Atene, 33 (1971): Rome

Turner, Jane (editor), *The Dictionary of Art*, London: Macmillan and New York: Grove, 1996, vol. 21, Minoan entries

Warren, Peter and Vronwy Hankey, *Aegean Bronze Age Chronology*, Bristol: Bristol Classical Press, 1989

Minorities

Minorities are seen in relation to the majorities that define them. Minorities and majorities are two sides of the same coin, and to attempt to talk of a minority without reference to the majority that defines it obscures by omission or commission the fact that minorities are usually targets of discrimination by the elite of the majority against whom they are defined. A social minority is rarely purely a minority in purely numerical terms. The subordination of a numerically inferior social group is given substance by its exclusion from access to power and the resources available to the social majority. Each age produces its own minorities, but though they should not be thought of as the product of the Hellenic tradition, five categories of outsiders – by class, religion, race, gender, and sexual orientation – can be identified in the four broad periods of the tradition: Classical, Byzantine, Ottoman, and modern. These categories of social outsider are modern in origin; so is the concept of the social minority. In dealing with this subject it is important to remember that, although these categories would not have been familiar to the people of the time, there are indeed modern constructs that we apply to past societies in an honest (it is hoped) attempt to understand those societies better.

Most easily dealt with here are the minorities defined by their sexual orientation. For the Classical period there is considerable evidence for male homosexuality, but lesbianism is much less apparent from the sources. Scholars have now begun to argue in earnest about the nature and prevalence of homosexuality in the Byzantine period, and the nature of the evidence to be used. Evidence of homosexuality in the Ottoman period for the Hellenic tradition should really be seen as an appendix to the Byzantine period, drawing as it does on the same evidence. In the modern period the post-Stonewall "gay liberation" arrived late in Greece, and it remains to be seen how the Hellenic tradition will accommodate it. This material is dealt with in the article on "Homosexuality".

Most clearly a cause for anxiety is the idea of minorities by race. More exactly, this should be defined as minorities by ethnic origin. In the Classical period the most definite component of this group were the barbarians, those who could not speak Greek and whose language sounded to the proud educated Greeks, polished in their speech, like the mouthings of meaningless syllables: "Bar bar ...". The polarization between Greeks and barbarians points out two important facets of the concept of minorities: the barbarians were clearly more numerous than the Greeks, and the Greeks became "the Greeks" by distinguishing themselves from the barbarians and making language a significant marker of difference. Other subdivisions of "barbarians" existed in the Classical period, most notably the Persians and then later the Romans with whom the Greeks perforce came to some accommodation. While the barbarians were useful as a defining concept "out there", minorities by ethnic origin within the Classical city states were more difficult to deal with. Though foreign enemies could neatly be confined to the "opponent" role beyond the walls, the responses and social roles available for the foreign merchants, allies, or "resident aliens" who came to reside in cities such as Athens needed to be and indeed were many and varied. The Classical period is when we first see the social minority by ethnic origin not only as an aspect of the great mass of barbarians "out there", but also as placeholders on a spectrum of shaded proximity to the citizen. During the Byzantine period this "double standard" continued, compounded and confused as it was by the problematic nature of who the "Byzantines" were. The majority called themselves "Roman" if they gave themselves an ethnic identity at all, but spoke Greek; yet to them in their own tongue (Greek), "Hellenic" or "Hellene" meant "pagan" as opposed to Christian. At the same time, however, ethnic identifiers existed for minorities within the empire such as Armenians, Iberians, Cappadocians, and Isaurians. At one level it is clear that there was a shorthand in use, by which "Roman" meant "people like us" (or at least "like me"), but in addition, the Byzantine authors whose works survive show that they were capable of distinguishing between ethnic minorities within the empire if it suited their purpose.

In the Ottoman period the role of the ethnic minority within the Hellenic tradition was clearly reduced since it was of course the "Hellenes" – here conterminous with the Orthodox Christians – who were one of the ethnic minorities (though constituted by the state as a religious minority) in the Ottoman empire. In the modern period the nature of the ethnic minority in the Hellenic tradition is as convoluted as it is for most other societies. How Greek are third-generation Greeks in the United States or Australia? Does "being Greek" mean being able to speak the language? And is that enough, or does it require literacy as well? In addition to the diaspora, which is still scattered, how different are the descendants of those Greeks who returned in the 1920s from Anatolia, or indeed who were incorporated into the Greek state after the Balkan Wars at the beginning of the 20th century? And what is to be made of other ethnic groups that may have self-consciousness but whose existence may appear threatening to a nation state unconvinced that its borders are not subject to the envious glances of its neighbours? What is clear at least is that it is possible to create ethnic minorities when desired. How such minorities are treated – ignored, tolerated, repressed, exterminated, or celebrated – depends a great deal on the nature and self-confidence of the dominant social majority.

Women have always been a minority. Until recently, many observers opined that such a large grouping could not be considered a social minority, but the work of many different kinds of feminists (theoretical, empirical, applied) has shown that women as a social group can be viewed as a minority because of their differential access to power and their ability to participate in the general life of wider society. Excluded from the political and restricted to the "private sphere" of hearth and home, women form a minority by gender. In the Classical period the women were the citizens who were "not there". The women who appear in the Platonic dialogues or on vases were not the wives and daughters of citizens in an honourable occupation. Their closeted lives are now recovered to a degree, but we know much less about the lives of women than about male citizens. The advent of Christianity (especially in the Orthodox faith with its devotion to icons) is held to have improved the lot of women, who could now escape the fate of child-bride and brood-mare for the role of perpetual virgin and bride of Christ. Sources for the Byzantine period tell us about aristocratic women and nuns, but these escape routes were limited for the mass of those who found themselves in the social minority by gender. The fate of women in the early modern compared to the medieval period is hard to differentiate. The evidence is unclear, and it is often a vested question whether evidence is to be read back to a Byzantine origin or credited as being a development during the Ottoman period. Women as a social minority in modern Greece share all the trials and triumphs of their sisters in other societies who are making the transition from largely agrarian rural communities to modern urbanized industrial democracies.

The minority by religion is a category now firmly out of favour, provoking memories of the Inquisition. In the Classical period the lack of religious uniformity might be thought to preclude the formation of minorities by religion. However, leaving to one side the various schools or choices that arose among the philosophers, a certain basic level of "decency" was expected to prevail, a level below which Socrates was felt to have sunk, even though the charges had all the hallmarks of a stitch-up. The development of Christianity as a credal religion meant that there was much room for disagreement, arguments in which the Greeks appeared to revel. For all the polemics of the first five great ecumenical councils and the bitter acrimony of the iconoclast controversy, the Hellenic tradition in its Orthodox manifestation did not develop the means of dealing with minority viewpoints favoured by the Holy Office in western Catholicism. The minority by religion came into its own in the Ottoman period, when the *millet* (community) system meant that to be Greek was synonymous with being Orthodox Christian. In modern Greece the minorities by religion are the Muslims, Catholics, Protestants, and Jehovah's Witnesses, mixtures of incomers and converts that show the multiple origin of these social minorities.

The final category of minority is that created by class. In the Classical period, in addition to the poorer citizens, there was the numerous class of slaves, a source of labour without which the civilization of Athens would probably never have emerged. This differentiation based on wealth implies a further distinction based on education or rather the access to education. The speeches that have come down to us from the Athenian assemblies make it plain that it was important not to alienate the jurors by appearing to talk down at them. Perhaps even because of their awareness that they lacked the education of some of the leading citizens, it was all the more important not to be seen alluding to it. This concern with education as the pre-eminent marker of class continued in the Byzantine period.

Education gained in Constantinople meant that one had arrived; education could be obtained in the provinces, but it would always remain rustic in character. Though a hierarchical and stratified society, Byzantium was not closed to advancement by merit (usually by means of an education) and the criticisms levelled at these *nouveaux riches* indicate that the phenomenon was not unknown. But in general the accumulation of wealth as an end in itself was not common: Byzantium was a meritocracy, not a plutocracy. Though learning was also a feature of the elite of the Phanar in the Ottoman period, this was usually put to good use in the accumulation of capital, which was then expended in gaining one of the offices of the Ottoman state. The theme of education and how one spoke was one of the great fracture lines for the first 150 years of the modern Greek state. The question of the "two languages" (whether modern Greek was to be in the form commonly spoken by "the people" – i.e. demotic – or in a "purified" form that revived Attic forms or created Atticisms – i.e. katharevousa) should not be seen as a class question; but, as with the more overtly political struggles between parties in modern democratic Greece, there are aspects allied to class in the questions of how one should vote and how one should speak.

This article has imposed a strict order on the minorities that have existed in the Hellenic tradition since the Classical period. In doing so, I have done disservice to the many people who lived and died as part of those minorities. All human beings experience life as a cluster of different social roles; some are definitive and enduring, some are ephemeral. The roles, no matter how many or how few, are not static; nor are they exclusive. Even roles that to us appear impossible in combination, may be united in one individual for some period of time. Human experience comes in infinite diversity and infinite combination. The idea of minorities is one way of attempting to come to understand that diversity. We fail in our task however if we stress the analytical category of "minority" over the people who formed the minority and gave it life.

Dion C. Smythe

See also Foreigners, Homosexuality, Muslims, Slavery, Women

Further Reading

Alexander, Paul Julius, "Religious Persecution and Resistance in the Byzantine Empire of the Eighth and Ninth Centuries: Methods and Justifications", *Speculum*, 52 (1977): pp. 238–64

Beck, Hans-Georg, "Formes de non-conformisme à Byzance", *Academie Royale de Belgique: Bulletin de la Classe des Lettres et de Sciences Morales et Politiques*, series 5, 65/6–9 (1979): pp. 313–29

Browning, Robert, "The Class Struggle in Ancient Greece", *Past and Present*, 100 (1983): pp. 147–56

Charanis, Peter, *The Armenians in the Byzantine Empire*, Lisbon: Bertrand, 1963

Gerolymatos, André, *Espionage and Treason: A Study of the Proxenia in Political and Military Intelligence Gathering in Classical Greece*, Amsterdam: Gieben, 1986

Hall, Edith, *Inventing the Barbarian: Greek Self-Definition through Tragedy*, Oxford: Clarendon Press, and New York: Oxford University Press, 1989

McKechnie, Paul, *Outsiders in the Greek Cities in the Fourth Century BC*, London and New York: Routledge, 1989

Strauss, Johann, "Die nichtmuslimischen Minderheiten in Istanbul", *Südosteuropa-Jahrbuch*, 19 (1989): pp. 255–69

Missionaries

The Great Commission is the missionary duty given to Christians by Jesus Christ before his Ascension. The Gospel of Matthew reports that Jesus commanded his followers to "go out, and make disciples of all nations" (28: 19). Christianity is a universal religion that enjoins its followers to spread the good news of salvation to the ends of the earth. The universal character of the Christian faith contrasts starkly with the local or tribal and non-missionary character of most other religions.

The book of Acts records the beginning of the great apostolic missionary work, when the apostle Peter preached in Jerusalem at the Jewish Feast of Pentecost. Several thousand people became converts on that day (Acts 2: 1–41), and the new faith quickly spread to Greek-speaking Jews in Jerusalem. These were so numerous that a conflict developed between the Aramaic-speaking and Greek-speaking converts over the distribution of food to the widows in the community. To handle this a special ministry was created, the office of deacon. The first deacons all have Greek names (Acts 6: 5).

One of the original deacons, a Hellenistic Jew named Stephen, was the first martyr (*martyrion*, witness) of the Church. His death signalled open persecution, which caused the new community to disperse. This provided the opportunity for new fields of mission over the known world of the day. Acts describes how Philip, another Hellenistic deacon, converted an Ethiopian. The man is identified as a eunuch, and the treasurer of the queen of the Ethiopians (Acts 8: 26–39). The story illustrates the point that the universal message of the Gospel is no respecter of human conditions, but accepts all.

More than half of Acts is devoted to the missionary work of the apostle Paul who made three major missionary journeys. On the first he left Syrian Antioch, sailed to Cyprus, crossed the island, sailed to Pamphilia, and then travelled to other places including Iconium before returning to Antioch. The second journey again started in Asia Minor: Paul travelled to Macedonia after receiving a vision of a man there beckoning him to come over. Eventually he arrived in mainland Greece. Everywhere new churches were started. The third journey reinforced the work of the previous two.

The mission work of Paul was facilitated by the Greek language. As the lingua franca of the eastern part of the Roman empire it made communication with vast numbers of people possible. The translation of the Hebrew scriptures into Greek, the Septuagint, had occurred well before the Christian era. This meant that Paul and other missionaries could use the Old Testament in Greek. Also the widespread use of koine Greek offered a ready medium for writing the documents that eventually became the New Testament. All but five of the New Testament books are pastoral letters by Paul or others. Most of them were written to mission churches to deal with pastoral concerns.

There were many Greeks or Hellenistic Jews in Paul's circle of missionary associates. Yet from internal evidence in the Book of Acts and other New Testament sources, such as Paul's letters to Timothy who was ministering on Crete, it is evident that from the beginning much of the mission work was being done by nameless Greek-speaking individuals.

The works of the early Church Fathers, both before and after the Council of Nicaea, report conversions among different peoples and the establishment of new churches in India, Ethiopia, Armenia, Georgia, and elsewhere. The mission work of Greek-speaking Christians continued under the Byzantine Church. In the 9th century two brothers, Greeks from Thessalonica, Methodios and Cyril, became missionaries to the Slavs. In order to translate the Bible and other religious books into Slavic languages a new alphabet was developed: the Slavonic alphabet is based on the Greek alphabet, but it employs different characters to express Slavic sounds. The mission work of Cyril and Methodios converted the Moravians (who were later reconverted to Roman Catholicism, but with a remembrance that would eventually usher in the Hussite Wars and later still the mission work of the revived Moravian Church). Eventually the east Slavs, and most of the south Slavs, were converted to Christianity by Byzantine missionaries, whose work followed the pattern set by Cyril and Methodios. Byzantine converts included the Bulgarians, Serbians, Russians, Ukranians, and even the Latin Romanians.

The mission work of the Greek Orthodox Church was severely retarded by the Muslims after the fall of Constantinople in 1453. For more than 300 years only the Russian Orthodox Church among the churches of the East was free to continue missions. By the 1800s the Greek Orthodox Church began to regain its independence, and missionary work started to recover soon afterwards. Towards the end of the 19th century the mission tradition was revived.The modern Greek diaspora has generated new mission work by various Orthodox associations, much of it to emigrant Greeks around the world. Mission efforts in East Africa and among non-Greek peoples in North America and Australia is also bearing fruit.

A.J.L. WASKEY, JR

Further Reading

Barclay, William (translator), *The Acts of the Apostles*, revised edition, Philadelphia: Westminster Press, and Edinburgh: Saint Andrew Press, 1976

Bornkamm, Günther, *Paul/Paulus*, New York: Harper and Row, and London: Hodder and Stoughton, 1971

Bruce, F.F., *New Testament History*, 4th edition, London: Pickering Inglis, 1982

Bruce, F.F., *The Pauline Circle*, Grand Rapids, Michigan: Eerdmans, and Exeter: Paternoster, 1985

Chadwick, Henry, *The Early Church*, revised edition, London and New York: Penguin, 1993

Daniélou, Jean, *Gospel Message and Hellenistic Culture*, vol. 2, Philadelphia: Westminster Press, and London: Darton, Longman and Todd, 1973

Eusebius, *The Ecclesiastical History*, translated by C.F. Cruse, London: Bohn, 1851; reprinted Peabody, Massachusetts: Hendrickson, 1998

Goodspeed, Edgar Johnson, *Paul*, Nashville: Abingdon Press, 1947

Kee, Howard Clark, Franklin W. Young, and Karlfried Froehlich, *Understanding the New Testament*, 3rd edition, Englewood Cliffs, New Jersey: Prentice Hall, 1973

Lohse, Eduard, *The New Testament Environment*, translated by John Steely, Nashville: Abingdon Press, and London: SCM Press, 1976

Neill, Stephen, *A History of Christian Missions*, 2nd edition, Harmondsworth and New York: Penguin, 1986

Piepkorn, Arthur C., *Profiles in Belief: The Religious Bodies of the United States and Canada*, vol. 1: *Roman Catholic, Old Catholic, Eastern Orthodox*, New York: Harper and Row, 1977

Pollock, John, *The Man who Shook the World*, Wheaton, Illinois: Victor Books, 1976

Price, James L., *Interpreting the New Testament*, 2nd edition, New York: Holt Rinehart, 1961

Schaff, Philip and Henry Wace (editors), *Nicene and Post-Nicene Fathers*, 2nd series, 14 vols, reprinted Peabody, Massachusetts: Hendrickson, 1994

Ware, Timothy, *The Orthodox Church*, 2nd edition, London and New York: Penguin, 1993

Missolonghi

Town in Acarnania

Missolonghi, a fishing town on the shore of an extensive shallow lagoon, became one of the most famous names of the Greek War of Independence both because Lord Byron died there in April 1824 and because of the bravery and suffering of its defenders during the siege of 1825–26.

Missolonghi, with other parts of western Greece, joined the revolution in June 1821, massacring almost all its Muslim inhabitants. The town's strategic importance for communications between Roumeli and the Morea (the Peloponnese) helped to make it the headquarters of various groups over the next few years and particularly of Alexander Mavrokordatos and his supporters. Mavrokordatos was present during the first Turkish siege (November 1822–January 1823). Turkish and Albanian forces laid siege to the town following their victory at Peta. The defenders, including Markos Botsaris and his Suliots, were helped by bad weather, disease in the Turkish ranks, successful exaggeration of the number of foreign volunteers present, and Hydriot ships which broke through the Turkish blockade with supplies. By the time the besiegers risked a major assault on Christmas Day (6 January 1823) up to a thousand men from the Morea had managed to get through to reinforce the Missolonghiots. The assault failed and the siege collapsed; heavy losses were suffered on the Turkish side as the defenders became pursuers.

In December 1823 Mavrokordatos returned to Missolonghi with 14 Hydriot ships which broke the renewed blockade, and was re-established as director-general of western Greece. On 13 December he was joined by Colonel Leicester Stanhope, and in January 1824 by Byron, the representatives of the London Greek Committee. Among the measures they encouraged or undertook was a strengthening of the town's hitherto weak defences. (The blockade had been reimposed soon after Byron's arrival.) Stanhope engaged also in educational planning, set up a dispensary, and established a printing press which printed, among other works, an edition of Dionysios Solomos's *Hymn to Liberty* and two newspapers: the *Ellenika Chronika* (January 1824–February 1826), in Greek and edited by the Swiss philhellene and pharmacist Jean-Jacques Meyer, and the Italian *Telegrafo Greco* (March–December 1824). (On the whole the newspapers reflected the Benthamite utilitarian views of Stanhope and supported Mavrokordatos; probably they were read mostly by foreign sympathizers.)

Byron's death catapulted Missolonghi to European and American fame, preparing the way for its further association with heroism after its fall in 1826. Reshid Pasha commenced his siege in the spring of 1825. It long seemed likely to fail; Miaoulis's ships succeeded in delivering supplies in June and in August recaptured islands in the lagoon taken by Reshid. The defenders made successful sorties on 21 September and 13 October. But the situation changed radically once Ibrahim Pasha and his large force of Egyptians arrived on the scene in December. The blockade was tightened and supplies began to run low (a situation only partially and temporarily alleviated when Miaoulis again managed to get through with supplies in January 1826; his attempt to repeat this on 12 April failed). Even in early April Turkish and Egyptian attacks were beaten back by defenders by now, apparently, living mostly on seaweed and in a town shattered by heavy bombardment. They stoutly refused the Turkish offer to accept a conditional surrender. Finally, it was decided that the garrison and people of Missolonghi – except those too weak to try – would make a great sortie or *exodos* on the night of 22–23 April 1826, in the hope that as many as possible could escape to safety through enemy lines. This was to be facilitated by a simultaneous Greek attack from the besiegers' rear. But a deserter revealed the plan and the element of surprise was lost. An uncertain number succeeded in the sortie, in many cases only to fall prey to the Albanian cavalry who awaited them on the slopes of Mount Zigos. (About 1500 people survived and reached the safety of Amphissa.) Many more rushed back to the batteries amid general confusion. The Turks and Egyptians seized the walls. At dawn they moved in to sack the town. Some of the inhabitants blew up themselves and some of their assailants at the first and second powder magazines and at a windmill which held out until 24 April. The others were killed or enslaved. Estimates of numbers vary, but roughly 8000–10,000 of the 10,000–12,000 in Missolonghi before the *exodos* died or lost their freedom. (The town was regained by the Greeks when its Albanian garrison surrendered on 18 May 1829 after Sir Richard Church's successful campaign in western Greece.)

There was widespread shock at the fall of Missolonghi, tempered by admiration for the heroism of the defenders. The tone most often associated with the last months of Missolonghi is that of a letter from Jean-Jacques Meyer written a few days before he and so many others died in the final sortie: "It is an exhilarating spectacle to behold the ardour and devotion of the garrison amid so many privations. ... I declare to you, that we have sworn to defend Mesolonghi foot by foot, to listen to no capitulation, and to bury ourselves in its ruins. ... History will do us justice, and posterity weep over our misfortunes." Even George Finlay, one of the most sceptical of philhellenes and historians, felt that "A spirit of Greek heroism, rare in the Greek Revolution – rare even in the history of mankind – pervaded every breast" on this occasion; "the conduct of the defenders ... will awaken the sympathies of freemen in every country as long as Grecian history endures." The sort of great and inspiring events which western Europe generally sought in ancient contexts was found, importantly for the maintaining of philhellenic feeling, in the modern siege; it rivalled that of Plataea [in the Peloponnesian War], said Finlay, "in the energy and constancy of the besieged". To the already mighty surge of responses to Byron's death, which often included at least a mention of Missolonghi, were added, mostly in 1826–28 and mostly in French, German, or English, pamphlets, maps, cantatas, poems, plays, novels, all related to the siege and fall of the town. One of the best-known responses is Eugène Delacroix's painting *Greece on the Ruins of Missolonghi* (1826). And in Greece itself the siege was commemorated in poems including Solomos's *The Woman of Zakynthos* (*c.*1827) and *The Free Besieged*, the memoirs of survivors and their contemporaries such as Nikolaos Kasomoulis, and – with the other notable events of the 1820s – the Garden of Heroes in Missolonghi. This includes the tomb of Markos Botsaris, Byron's statue (1881), and the tumulus of the defenders killed in April 1826.

It would be difficult to maintain that the town's fall alone had any lasting effect on the course of the war, but it was clearly a major factor in encouraging European and American philhellenes to contribute an amount estimated by Douglas Dakin at £70,000 to the Greek cause during 1826, and helped to move foreign governments further in the direction of intervention.

MARTIN GARRETT

See also Independence (War of)

Summary

A fishing town on the coast of Acarnania, Missolonghi was the centre of resistance to the Turks in western Greece during the War of Independence. A Turkish siege in 1822–23 was beaten off. Byron died there of fever on 19 April 1824. The final siege took place in 1825–26 resulting in huge Greek losses. The town was regained by the Greeks in 1829.

Further Reading

Dakin, Douglas, *The Greek Struggle for Independence, 1821–1833*, London: Batsford, and Berkeley: University of California Press, 1973

Droulia, Loukia, *Philhellénisme: ouvrages inspirés par la guerre de l'indépendance grecque, 1821–1833*, Athens: Centre de Recherches Néo-Helléniques de la Fondation Nationale de la Recherche Scientifique, 1974

Finlay, George, *History of the Greek Revolution*, 2 vols, Edinburgh: Blackwood, 1861

Garrett, Martin, *Greece: A Literary Companion*, London: John Murray, 1994

Gordon, Thomas, *History of the Greek Revolution*, 2 vols, Edinburgh: Blackwood and London: Cadell, 1832

Makris, Nikolaos, *Istoria tou Mesolongiou* [History of Missolonghi], vol. 19 of *Apomnemoneumata agoniston tou '21* [Memoirs of the Contestants of '21], Athens, 1968

Mazarakis-Aenian, "The Missolonghi Printing Press" in *Lord Byron in Greece*, edited by Fani-Maria Tsigakou, Athens: Greek Ministry of Culture and British Council, 1987

St Clair, William, *That Greece Might Still Be Free: The Philhellenes in the War of Independence*, London and New York: Oxford University Press, 1972

Mistra

City in the Peloponnese

Mistra remains today as probably the best-preserved of all later Byzantine sites, and its relative completeness allows the visitor to experience in the most authentic way the qualities of a Byzantine town developed in the last two centuries before the coming of the Tourkokratia. Its assemblage of churches, palaces, and houses, which have not been significantly altered since the 15th century, represents the most complete reflection of the appearance, architecture, and art of a Byzantine town of that period that we have.

It consists of a fortified city, located some 5 km to the west of Sparta in the Peloponnese, occupying the steep slope of a spur of Mount Taygetus; its summit is crowned by a castle. Mistra has no Classical, early Christian, or earlier Byzantine history; the name first enters sources in the mid-13th century when Guillaume de Villehardouin, the fourth of the Frankish princes of Achaea, chose it as the site of one of the four castles that he built to contain the Slav tribes that then occupied the southern Peloponnese.

The ruins of his castle still dominate the hilltop, with sheer cliffs falling away to the south and southwest. The keep and enceinte indicate the scale of his installation here, but he was only to be in possession of it for little more than ten years; in 1262, two years after he was taken prisoner at the Battle of Pelagonia, he was forced to cede it to the Byzantines, with three other Frankish castles in the Peloponnese, as the price of his freedom. It was at this point that the history of Byzantine Mistra began, although it was the elevation of the city to being the seat of the despot of the Morea in 1348 that was to usher in the period of its greatest renown. This lasted for just over a century, until in 1460 the last despot, Dimitrios, was forced to hand over the city to the victorious sultan, Mehmet II.

The importance of Mistra for the Hellenic tradition lies in two separate fields: its physical survivals and the vigorous intellectual life that flourished there. Among its buildings pride of place must go the palace of the despots; this substantial L-shaped complex, built in several stages on the only major piece of level terrain, contains a large hall some 40 m long,

Mistra: view from the gate looking southwest to the castle

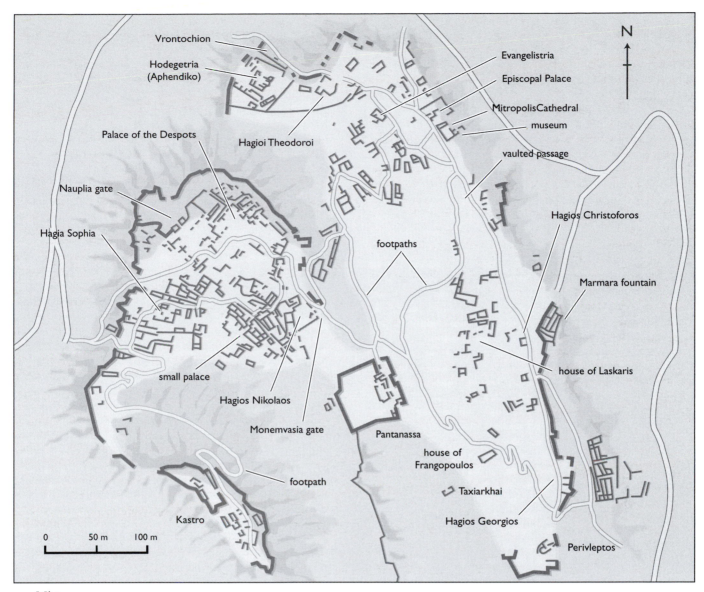

25. Mistra

which must have served as a throne room. This is in all probability the best reflection we have of that used in the Blachernae palace in Constantinople. Among other secular buildings, besides a number of smaller houses, there are two further large dwellings, one known as the Palataki ("Little Palace") and the other as the House of the Laskarids; these again provide some of the most authentic surviving evidence for the appearance of later Byzantine domestic architecture as used by a relatively affluent official or merchant.

The church of the Mitropolis, dedicated to St Dimitrios, was always intended to be the cathedral of Mistra, and has undergone major reconstruction; first built as a three-aisled basilica in 1291/92, it was the only church without a dome in the city until it was altered (probably in the 15th century) by having the barrel-vaulted roof removed and a dome erected. Both the foundation and the reconstruction are recorded in inscriptions as being by bishops of Lacedaemonia. Six other churches in Mistra have been preserved, all built between the later 13th and early 15th centuries, all domed, and most

displaying a knowledge of contemporary building practice in Constantinople. That of the S Theodore, begun just after 1290, has an octagonal design that may have been an emulation of the church of Hagia Sophia in Monemvasia but relates to other important church designs such as that of Dafni, near Athens. The plan that was most frequently adopted by builders in Mistra was first used early in the 14th century in building the church known as the Aphendiko, dedicated to the Virgin Hodegetria. Its main characteristic is that of a basilica with galleries on to which a domed cross-in-square has been imposed; an open colonnade occupies the exterior of the south side, which is a characteristic of several other churches of the city. The frequency with which this type was used may have been because it could accommodate larger numbers on a given ground area than a more conventional inscribed cross design.

Other foundations of the 14th century are those of the Virgin Peribleptos, its design accommodated to its being built against a cliff, and Hagia Sophia, which was founded by a despot, Manuel Kantakouzenos, and probably intended as a palace church. One of the last major churches to be built in Mistra, and that with the most Western characteristics, was that of the Pantanassa; founded by an important official of the despotate, John Phrangopoulos, and dedicated in 1428, it continues to be used as a convent, and is the only building still remaining in use.

Most of these churches retain much of their original decoration, and this again allows a glimpse of the brilliant final phase of Palaiologan art as it developed in the last two centuries of the Byzantine era. The high quality of the church architecture of Mistra was complemented by artists of equal accomplishment; the wall paintings that they have left indicate the increased interest in liturgical subject matter and extensive cycles of secondary themes, with series of the Twelve Great Feasts of the life of the Virgin, Passion cycles, and figures of individual saints.

The location of Mistra, relatively remote from Constantinople, meant that during its last century as a despotate a spirit of intellectual enquiry developed that would not have been tolerated in the capital. First under the Kantakouzene despots Michael, Matthew, and Dimitrios, and then increasingly under the Palaiologan despots, the two Theodores, Thomas, Dimitrios, and Constantine, the city became a prominent intellectual centre. The famous philosopher, George Gemistos, who later took the name of Plethon, taught here from c.1410 until his death in 1452, after his friend the emperor Manuel II Palaiologos had advised him that his radical approach was upsetting the conservative clerics in the capital. Among those who came to learn from him were George Scholarios and John Moschos, who was to be his successor as the leading philosopher of the city. But his most renowned pupil was John Bessarion, the native of Trebizond who, as a cardinal, was to become one of the most famous Greek converts to Roman Catholicism, and who studied for several years at Mistra under Plethon from 1431. It was to be the fame of Mistra as an intellectual centre that also brought Italian scholars to study the language and thought of the ancient Greeks that Byzantium had guarded for so long; it was through them that the Hellenic tradition was to be widely disseminated in western Europe.

Mistra began its history under Turkish occupation as the favoured residence of the Pasha who governed the Peloponnese, but it did not retain this distinction after the outbreak of the War of Independence. In September 1824, in the course of the appalling destruction wrought by Ibrahim Pasha right across the Morea, Mistra was left a smoking ruin. It was not until late in the 19th century that the French Byzantinist, Gabriel Millet, was to initiate the restoration of the city which is now so much admired as an embodiment of medieval Hellenic culture.

PAUL HETHERINGTON

See also Renaissance (Palaiologan)

Summary

First occupied as the site of a castle by Guillaume de Villehardouin in the mid-13th century, Mistra was ceded to the Byzantines in 1262 after the Battle of Pelagonia. In 1348 it became the seat of the despot of the Morea. It has important remains of a complete Byzantine town. It was also the centre of a vigorous intellectual culture. It fell to the Turks in 1460 and was destroyed in 1824.

Further Reading

Chatzidakis, Manolis, *Mystras: The Medieval City and the Castle: A Complete Guide to the Churches, Palaces, and the Castle*, Athens: Ekdotike Athenon, 1981

Hussey, J.M. (editor), *The Byzantine Empire*, Cambridge: Cambridge University Press, 1966 (*The Cambridge Medieval History*, vol. 4, part 1, 2nd edition)

Miller, William, *The Latins in the Levant: A History of Frankish Greece, 1204–1566*, London: John Murray, and New York: Dutton, 1908; reprinted Cambridge: Speculum Historiale, and New York: Barnes and Noble, 1964

Miller, William, *Essays on the Latin Orient*, Cambridge: Cambridge University Press, 1921; reprinted New York: AMS Press, 1983

Millet, Gabriel, *Monuments byzantins de Mistra*, Paris: Leroux, 1910

Runciman, Steven, *Mistra: Byzantine Capital of the Peloponnese*, London: Thames and Hudson, 1980

Modern Period

The study of Greece in the modern period has often been made in terms of failure. Why did Greece suffer so many political and economic crises? Why was its ability to create wealth substantially less than that of many other countries? Why could Greece not prevent the haemorrhaging of its population in migration? Why did so few of its cultural products achieve international circulation? These questions tended to measure performance in comparison with other states (sometimes unnamed) that have enjoyed much more favourable geographical and historical circumstances than Greece, leading automatically to negative conclusions. Now that Greece is increasingly successful even by such externally drawn measures, it is time to change the approach. Greece has a position towards the bottom of social and economic indicators for the European Union, but far above its neighbours in southeastern Europe. In cultural terms, it is extremely active in comparison with other developed states of its size, especially surprising in spheres where comprehension of Greek is essential for full enjoyment of the works produced. International cultural success for small countries is haphazard and frequently owed, as will be seen, to factors connected with their very political and economic marginality and weakness. The brief and schematic analysis that follows will begin by looking at Greece as far as possible in its own terms and sketching the development of a specific Greek identity in the modern world. It will then examine the relationship of that identity to modern Greek culture and its reception outside Greece.

Towards the end of the Tourkokratia the first traces of industry were beginning to appear in the Greek lands. Most Greeks, however, were subsistence farmers with little or no education. This group has, naturally, left little record of its thoughts and aspirations, except for those fighters in the War of Independence who found ways of leaving written memoirs. It is clear that most Greeks resented the Turks' oppressive and arbitrary behaviour towards their subject populations. It is less certain what was felt to be the alternative – Greek dreams of what their world might be like if Turkish rule were removed. Probably most were still thinking within the framework of the

Byzantine empire. Since the foundation of Constantinople a millennium and a half before, the whole area had been ruled as a multicultural empire centred on that city. The characteristics of the rulers had varied, particularly with the fundamental change to a Turkish sultan in 1453. But the overall politico-geographical structure had remained the same. Rigas Velestinlis, a democrat intellectual, promoted a multicultural democracy within a Byzantine envelope. Most of the fighters of 1821 probably had something similar in mind, perhaps thinking of a Greek emperor ruling a diverse population.

Greek urban structures during the period were idiosyncratic. Besides the few towns in the Greek lands there were large Greek populations in Constantinople and Smyrna and substantial Greek minorities in towns in the Romanian principalities beyond the periphery of regular Greek habitation. More important still, the arbitrariness of Ottoman rule had led to the establishment of significant Greek communities in western European commercial cities. These were groups of merchants, managing much of the trade of the Ottoman empire from a position beyond the reach of its officials. This external Greek bourgeoisie was in close contact with some of the most advanced entrepreneurial groups in Europe. It was also a major channel for the ideas of the Enlightenment into Greece. It financed, for example, a major redirection of the printing of books for the Greek market away from Orthodox service books and popular devotional literature towards other functions, especially connected with ancient Greece. This change reflects Enlightenment interest in Classical studies, secularism, and nationalism, which came together in the promotion of a modern Greece as a direct descendant of ancient Greece. It is clear that some merchants of the diaspora were beginning to link the removal of Turkish power with the establishment of a specifically Greek state. It is uncertain how many had made the imaginative leap required to redraw the political map of southeastern Europe from a single empire to a series of small nation states. One important factor is that the diaspora retained a Greek identity, though it might easily have been assimilated into local populations. The image of the Greek merchants was also cosmopolitan and attractive to the countries in which they were active, especially in eastern Europe.

The Greeks of Greek lands largely called themselves "Romioi", a name deriving from the multicultural identity of Byzantium as the eastern continuation of the Roman empire. Outside the Ottoman empire the name "Hellenes" was becoming more current. This had specific Greek connotations, looking back to the ancient name of the Greeks. It can be used to trace the rise of a specifically Greek nationalism based on connections with the ancients. The two world views met in the memoirs of the illiterate general Makriyannis at the moment of the revolution. Before the declaration of independence, the heroes of the story were the Romioi. After that time the same characters generally became Hellenes. In the areas of fighting the war caused an unprecedented movement of people and of ideas, particularly nationalist ideas. The revolutionaries were mainly Greek-speaking, though certainly not exclusively so. The project of a Greek national state provided some much-needed cohesion among the fighters. It soon became clear that the areas that might hope to be free as a result of the revolution would be the regions that had been central parts of ancient

Greece. What is more, the reception of the conflict in the capitals of western Europe was as a renaissance of ancient Greece. Greeks and philhellenes seeking money and support there – or at least abstention from intervention in favour of the status quo – found the Greek national identity and its links with antiquity were useful arguments for their cause. Ancient Greece had been in favour in Europe throughout the Renaissance and the Enlightenment and had dominated Romantic Neoclassicism, which was still an important cultural movement in 1821.

The nationalist intellectual revolution of the 18th century which led to the basically nationalist political revolution of 1821 was continued in the establishment of the modern Greek state. This had been born, largely coincidentally, at a moment when its ancient culture was the centre of world romantic interest. As a result, it was natural for Greece to give enduring prominence to that aspect of its traditions. Greece has presented itself to the world to a large extent as a country of descendants of the glorious ancients. This fact has had a major influence over its cultural development.

The spread of such ideas in Greece was only increased by a high-profile attempt to deny them. The Austrian historian Jakob Philipp Fallmerayer published his work *Geschichte der Halbinsel Morea* in 1830, when Greek independence had been achieved but its nature remained uncertain. He listed the evidence for major settlements of Slavs and Albanians in Greek lands during the Middle Ages. From these facts he drew the ridiculously overstated conclusion that there was no ancient Greek blood at all in the veins of the modern Greeks, thus dissolving the genealogical basis of current Greek nationalism. Reactions to Fallmerayer were intense. In fact, parts of 19th-century Greek scholarship appear to have been moulded by the need to prove him wrong, such as the prominence of *laographia* (folklore) as an academic discipline devoted to finding remnants of ancient Greek culture in the contemporary Greek countryside. At another level Fallmerayer also contributed to the rehabilitation of Byzantium in Greek history. It became obvious that extreme nationalist historical constructs that jumped from the Roman conquest of Greece in the 2nd century BC to the revolution of 1821, treating everything between as a foreign occupation, were dangerous because of the huge temporal gap between the designated Greek elements, whose genuineness could thus be undermined. Konstantinos Paparrigopoulos cemented his place as the founder of modern Greek historiography by establishing a tripartite view of Greek history, with ancient, Byzantine, and modern periods, which has been dominant ever since.

The 19th century saw the promotion in Greece of all things ancient Greek, but in ways that were often shallow and uncomprehending – the so-called *progonoplexia* or ancestor-obsession. The 20th century saw a less intense continuation of the same tendency, particularly during the right-wing regimes of Metaxas (1936–41) and the Colonels' Junta (1967–74). To this day activities celebrating ancient Greece are more likely to win Greek diplomatic support outside Greece than those related to later periods. But however indiscriminate this support of Classical culture may have been, it is difficult to avoid the assumption that it has performed a useful function, at least inside Greece and on its borders. The different areas of Greece, as they were successively freed from foreign control and added to the Greek state, contained numbers of ethnic and linguistic minorities. Many of these had the potential to cause intercommunity friction of types distressingly frequent to the north of Greece in the 1990s. With the help of the exchange of populations in 1922 and other historical circumstances that forced some of the disparate elements across the northern borders, Greece has been able to absorb and assimilate all but the Turks of Thrace. What was the reason for this success? The difference between the Greek identity and less effective equivalents to the north must surely have been its complexity, great historical depth, and sweeping claims to cultural importance on a world scale.

The success of the national connection to the ancient world has been spectacular, but not unchallenged. The privileged position it gave to ancient Greece has been seen by many (not without justification) as a western European concept imported into the Greek identity, and has been unwelcome to some defenders of Orthodoxy and nationalists with an anti-Western slant. The Romioi are still occasionally promoted as alternatives to the Hellenes. This is the first of several tensions to be mapped here: ancient Greece and Byzantium (with its extension into the Turkish period) are not only successive elements in Paparrigopoulos's tripartite division, but also, in some minds, competing focuses of national identification and of the authentication of Greek importance in world history.

This ambiguity had a major influence over the Greek language question. All levels of Greek in the Turkish period had developed features, especially lexical items, that showed Turkish influence. The written language, developed from that of Byzantium, included a varying degree of archaism. At the spoken level, Greek was a closely related set of dialects which had yet to go through the discipline of the creation of a national language. Besides these the nationalism of the 18th century grafted a preference for ancient Greek, which had also played a considerable role in the linguistic discussions of the American and French revolutions. Thus the first phase of the language question involved three linguistic levels: two written patterns linked to the ancient and Byzantine worlds respectively, and the developing spoken vernacular.

Adamantios Korais was a passionate believer in the civilizing, revolutionary force of Ancient Greek. Yet, as a democrat and linguist, he realized that a national language must be based on spoken Modern Greek. He therefore created his "middle way", katharevousa, claiming a vernacular basis but selectively using the fluidity of the spoken language to build as many bridges as he could to Ancient Greek, so that the young Greeks on whom he based his revolutionary hopes should have as much access as possible to the revolutionary power of the ancients. It was obvious soon after his death that this experiment was a failure in its own terms. But the language that resulted was not very different from the old Byzantine written language, purged of Turkish elements and brought up to date for the demands of national independence. When Korais's influence was removed, the two forms united. Katharevousa thus inherited the support both of the conservative and Byzantine tradition of the early Turkish period and of the radical new nationalism linked to Ancient Greek. The former tendency gradually subsumed the latter, but never obliterated it.

Katharevousa became on one level a mark of snobbery, the way in which the well-educated separated themselves off from those less privileged. But it was also supported by many who were disappointed by a perceived failure of the Greek state to live up to the traditions of Hellenism. It was admirably suited to abstract discussions of the destiny of the Greek nation – in support, for example, of the Great Idea. From the final decades of the 19th century it was opposed by an organized demoticist movement, whose first leader was Yannis Psycharis. The demoticists refused to take the sources of national identity from any past tradition, but based themselves on the living language and traditions of the Greek people. They made play with the fact, as mentioned above, that the prominent position of ancient Greek in the nationalist construct was essentially a Western idea. The most successful of the demoticists were the "Generation of the 1930s", as we shall see. They succeeded in establishing a demotic view of the national identity to provide a powerful counterbalance to the learned traditions used to support katharevousa. The language struggle has been the dimension of Greek life in which the issue of identity has been fought most openly. It was inevitable that the demotic side should win, though surprising that it took so long – till 1975. There is now some recognition that all the parties in this long struggle represented more or less valid Greek traditions which need to be integrated into a more inclusive Greek identity.

There was discussion above of one major tension in the Greek identity, that represented by the labels Romioi and Hellenes. A second, simpler, tension is between Eastern and Western elements in Greek culture. At one level Greece is a member of the European Union, proud that the ancient Greeks laid the groundwork for Western culture, and regarding the West as synonymous with all that is positive and democratic. Constant disagreements with their large neighbour Turkey tend to confirm Greeks in rejection of the East. But at another level, many Greeks fail to identify completely with the western European lifestyle and capitalist work ethic, and often suggest that they have more in common with the Middle East than food and popular music. This dichotomy is particularly strong in Cyprus, where Greeks feel closer to the Levant than to Athens, while simultaneously being more influenced by western European values as a result of their British colonial heritage. Orthodoxy also connects Greece to Slavic eastern Europe. Greek separation from western Europe is inscribed in the language: a Greek going to Brussels (or Paris or Berlin) for a European Union committee can describe him or herself as "going to Europe", implying that Athens is outside Europe at one level of his or her mental map.

Another tension in the Greek identity may also be illustrated linguistically. The word for "country" or "fatherland" used in patriotic discourse is *patrida*. But this is not the most common use of that word: it usually means a narrower area, probably the village or town from which a person originates, or perhaps a wider area such as Epirus, Macedonia, or Crete. Much of Greece is geographically divided into small areas, such as islands or valleys surrounded by high mountain walls. This led to fragmentation in the ancient world, and perhaps predisposes modern Greeks to narrow loyalties. The use of the word *patrida* shows that the nation and state are not so firmly established in Greek consciousness as in equivalent countries where nationhood was achieved earlier. The adjective *xenos* (strange, foreign) may be used to prove the same point from the opposite perspective. "Strangers" or "foreigners" for a Peloponnesian villager may be Turks or Epirots, but they could equally well be fellow-Peloponnesians, even from the next village. At its most extreme, the focus of loyalty can be reduced to the family, which remains the main Greek economic unit. Anthropologists have drawn the conclusion that a Greek has a variety of possible identities, spreading from his or her immediate surroundings out to the level of the Greek state. The meanings of *patrida* and *xenos* in each case need to be negotiated in and out according to context – surely an extremely flexible and functional system to provide individual satisfaction, but not one that makes the Greek government and economy easy to run.

A substantial proportion of the world population of Greeks and Cypriots is not normally resident in Greece or Cyprus. This new Greek diaspora, made up of migrants who left Greece for economic reasons (or Cyprus as a result of the Turkish invasion), is found on every continent in larger or smaller numbers, making up a total of perhaps a third or a half of the metropolitan populations. The Greek identity is a pervasive one, operating at the level of language, religion, and what is called "behaviour and customs" (*ithi kai ethima*). In most parts of the world, Greeks have resisted assimilation for longer than most other nationalities – though of course assimilation will happen eventually, especially if the country of settlement speaks a major world language. The diaspora Greek needs the metropolitan centre to preserve a Greek identity in the new country, but is often rather contemptuous of some factors in Greece, particularly the economic problems and lack of unity. On the other hand Greece's representatives in countries with many Greek migrants, seeking to preserve their compatriots' Greek identification and waning linguistic skills, need their support to send money home and to put pressure, at moments of crisis, on their new governments, especially that of the United States, on behalf of the Greek or Cypriot states. Greeks outside Greece are often economically very successful. Unfortunately they are rarely easy to coordinate into an organized lobby.

None of the tensions mentioned here is unique to Greeks. But the combined force of these arguments may indicate that Greekness is unusually complex, demanding, and interesting. The root of the complexity is that the Greek identity, especially if one includes elements usually placed under the heading "Romioi", has a much longer and more celebrated history than the Greek state. That state may be viewed as a Western imposition from the perspective of a defender of Eastern Orthodoxy, as an alternative focus of loyalty by a proud Cretan, as a cesspit of cynical politics by those who would prefer to speak in terms of ancient Greek idealism, or as a beloved country that nevertheless has to be left behind by the Greek migrants of Toronto or Melbourne. Thus the Greek state is usually seen in a comparative way, often at a disadvantage, rather than forming a more uncontested background to individual identities, as in many other countries.

On the other hand the Greek identity of which the state is the core has undoubtedly been very successful in maintaining Greekness among populations where it is challenged. We have noted its power at several historical stages: among the merchant diaspora in Europe before the Revolution, among minorities in the expanding Greek state, and among the wider diaspora of economic migrants in the 20th century.

It remains to examine briefly the development of Greek literature, music, and the visual arts. There are detailed treatments of the different cultural fields available elsewhere in this encyclopedia. This article will concentrate on the ways in which Greek culture and its reception outside Greece reflect and are influenced by the elements of identity already discussed.

The diachronic quality of the Greek identity, including ancient Greece and Byzantium along with modern Greece, is pervasive throughout Greek culture. The most obvious technique is simple juxtaposition, the inclusion of persons or objects from the past in a modern Greek urban scene or countryside, surprising the viewer or hearer with a kind of anachronism, as in the paintings of Konstantinos Parthenis, the cinema of Thodoros Angelopoulos, or the poems of Yiannis Ritsos. Elsewhere there is a juxtaposition of genres: the reference may place ancient or Byzantine phrases in a modern demotic framework, or use a musical structure combining Byzantine chant with modern rhythms inspired by folk songs and *rebetika* (low-life music). The poem *Axion Esti* of Odysseus Elytis and its musical setting as an oratorio by Mikis Theodorakis are sustained examples. The audience for Greek culture has learned to expect such references, which have become almost a defining characteristic of various genres, bringing their own idiosyncratic aesthetic charge. There has been at times some tendency to undervalue Greek works which concentrate on issues that Greece shares with the rest of Europe or the world, in favour of those that have an exclusively Greek dimension, and therefore offer wide scope for diachronic treatment. This tactic gives cohesion and unity to Greek culture, and can lead to striking artistic success, though it can easily be overdone.

Another characteristic of Greek culture which has become popular abroad derives from Greece's position on the borders of Europe and Asia, East and West, combined with the fact of its recent rapid urbanization and industrialization. Just beneath the surface of Athenian society one may find the rhythms of the Greek countryside, where most middle-aged Athenians were born. What is more, the popular culture of Greece has for many Europeans and Americans an oriental and exotic otherness, often discovered via tourism. An excellent example of the resulting cultural influences is Michalis Cacoyannis's film *Zorba the Greek* (1964). The folkloric picture of Greece provided is true neither to the Kazantzakis novel on which it is based nor to the real country life of Crete that both novel and film purport to portray: the film succeeded, in part, because it fulfilled a Western need for exoticism in setting and behaviour. An even more extreme example of this syndrome is the popularity of *rebetika* music, in some non-Greek circles as well as among the Greek middle class. The culture of drugs and crime reflected in *rebetika* lyrics brings a dangerous whiff of the Middle Eastern bazaar and hashish den which is clearly attractive to the many upright citizens who collect the recordings. Such concentration on the countryside and the underworld of Greece easily leads, of course, to a reductionist view of the country's culture.

Some of Greece's cultural development has been strongly influenced by the diaspora. The most obvious example is Constantine Cavafy, an Egyptian Greek and one of several prominent Greek poets who have been bilingual. Cavafy's English reading took him outside the traditional framework of Greek literature and encouraged him to speak of Greek tradition from an unconventional diaspora viewpoint. Cavafy adds to the aesthetic of diachronic reference discussed above an extra frisson of pleasure derived from cultural mixture and ambiguity, in which he finds an obvious affinity between the Egypt of his own day and the Hellenistic kingdoms and Eastern Roman world deriving from the empire of Alexander the Great. On other levels, recordings of *rebetika* from the US diaspora added considerably to the vogue for that music, while Maria Callas benefited from her status as an American immigrant, which gave her an easy choice of career paths inside and outside Greece.

Greece's political instability in the 20th century has also influenced its cultural development and the reception of that culture outside the country. In particular, for most of the 40-year period between the establishment of the Metaxas regime in 1936 and the fall of the Colonels' Junta in 1975 much of the intellectual and cultural establishment of the country found it hard to identify with the Greek (or, for a time, German) authorities in Athens. It was not only a question of political disagreement, but of a total rejection of those governments' legitimacy. Many cultural figures went through periods of silent protest or silence enforced by censorship: the publishing history of a poet such as Ritsos is, as a result, very disturbed and complex. Much cultural production was aimed at foreign markets, to be circulated abroad so as to put pressure on the Greek government via foreign public opinion, and often was to be published abroad for clandestine circulation in Greece. One prominent example, Vasilis Vasilikos's documentary novel *Z* about the murder of the left-wing politician Grigorios Lambrakis in May 1963, was successfully published in several European languages. The French film of the same name by Constantin Costa-Gavras was even more effective in raising consciousness abroad about the crude methods used on the Greek front of the Cold War. During the 40 years of political alienation and especially towards its end, during the Junta period, affirmations of Greekness and poems of protest by some of Greece's greatest poets were set to music by Mikis Theodorakis and (later) Manos Hadjidakis. This made their names widely known in anti-authoritarian circles throughout the world. The result was a genre of power and originality, combining incisive lyrics with popular music from many Greek sources written by composers of great conventional talent. It had some success in focusing anti-Junta sentiment, as was acknowledged by clumsy attempts to ban the circulation of the songs. Greek culture was achieving recognition, in part, as a result of Greece's political weakness.

However the major political role of Greek culture in the 20th century has been rewarded by many international honours, and is one of modern Greece's proudest achievements. When the Great Idea came to grief in military defeat in Asia Minor, the burning of Smyrna, and the exchange of populations, the country lost the expansionist ideology that had guided it for the first century of nationhood. Against the power of resurgent Turkey, further widening of the borders would be all but impossible, and the Greek populations were no longer in Asia Minor to provide the motive and justification for that expansion. Rather unexpectedly, the closest thing to a replacement ideology was provided by the cultural leaders of the Generation of the 1930s, especially the poets. The prime mover was George Seferis, who seems to have had a programme of regeneration in mind since the early 1930s. His ablest contemporaries proved to be Odysseus Elytis, who began with poetry of the Aegean sea and beaches strongly influenced by Surrealism, and Yannis Ritsos, whose early poetry in favour of a very Moscow-aligned Communism was written in socialist realist mode, but soon changed to include traditional Greek genres.

During the 1940s Greece lost control over its destiny. After rule from Berlin during the Nazi occupation, the country narrowly missed during the Civil War what might have been domination from Moscow, only to fall victim to what many called control from Washington. There was a natural reaction in the 1940s and 1950s towards the exploration of Greekness as an independent alternative to subjection to competing blocs, and a series of poems and critical essays were written that may be read as a struggle of different political and cultural forces to lay claim to the diachronic Hellenic ideal – Seferis, whose views were the most significant because first expressed, combined a demythologized version of the ancient world with some Byzantine symbols, some writers in katharevousa who may be constructed as popular, a limited number of demoticist poets, and some visual artists working in a naïve vein. The whole remains to this day the most influential construct of the national identity – though there is a persistent complaint that it has an anti-intellectual tendency. Elytis and Ritsos too wrote many poems providing Greekness with a definition largely compatible with that of Seferis. The popularity of their poems was greatly increased by their setting to music. The contributions of these three poets to filling the vacuum of Greek ideology made them giants in literary terms. Seferis and Elytis were awarded Nobel Prizes for literature; the communist Ritsos, whose nomination for the Nobel Prize could not be easy in Cold War Greece, received equivalent Moscow prizes. Subsequent Greek poets, whatever the quality of their work, have not been called upon to reconstruct the national psyche, and so seem pygmies by comparison.

But there is a danger in measuring success by international acclaim. Several areas of Greek cultural production have been extremely active and successful by any measure apart from the haphazard forces of foreign recognition. One example is the theatre, which has a pervasive presence in every corner of the Greek urban world. There are considerable numbers of serious, ground-breaking Greek works to set beside the ubiquitous translations of foreign plays at every level and high-profile traditional farces. Greek painting has filled the country's major galleries with works that cover in most creative ways every facet of the Greek identity sketched above, and others that are not so easily categorized. Greek architecture, often the butt of criticism because it has filled the cities with concrete blocks of flats, has many achievements to boast in cases where it is able to escape from such straightjackets. The Greek novel, whose international success pales before that of Greek poetry, has shown great inventiveness in the exploration of contemporary Greece and the Greek heritage. Greek novelists have, particularly more recently, shared in the same developments as their counterparts in other literary traditions and made similar experiments in areas conventionally labelled as postmodern.

Greece is a country with a small population, slightly increased by the addition of the diaspora. Its cultural production is much more diverse and vigorous than these numbers might be expected to support. Greek culture has often been recognized outside Greece, but sometimes for haphazard and even negative reasons, including geographical marginality, political instability, and its marking of forced and rapid ideological change. Within its natural Greek audience, that culture has been specially concerned with the exploration of different facets of the Greek identity and their imaginative combination and recombination into new and exciting constructs, which provide a variety of angles from which to view the Greek present. Some artists and poets have played significant roles in expressing the Greek view of themselves and their place in the world, at the most fundamental levels. It is this experimentation that is the major defining characteristic of the country's cultural production. In a global village where identity is constantly in question, and where different elements of the Greek past are used in this quest in many parts of the world, Greek culture has a strong claim on international attention.

MICHAEL JEFFREYS

See also Identity, Language

Summary

Dated from 1821 to the present, the cultural history of the modern period has been dominated by the struggle to find a recognizable Greek identity and an acceptable form of the Greek language. The events of 1922–23 resulted in a remarkable degree of national homogenization inside the newly established borders. In their wake there have been striking developments in Greek literature, music, and the visual arts.

Further Reading

Beaton, Roderick, *An Introduction to Modern Greek Literature*, 2nd edition, Oxford: Clarendon Press, 1999

Browning, Robert, *Medieval and Modern Greek*, 2nd edition, Cambridge and New York: Cambridge University Press, 1983

Clogg, Richard, *A Concise History of Modern Greece*, Cambridge and New York: Cambridge University Press, 1992

Herzfeld, Michael, *Ours Once More: Folklore, Ideology, and the Making of Modern Greece*, Austin: University of Texas Press, 1982, reprinted New York: Pella, 1986

Holst-Warhaft, Gail, *Theodorakis: Myth and Politics in Modern Greek Music*, Amsterdam: Hakkert, 1980

Holton, David, "Ethnic Identity and Patriotic Idealism in the Writing of General Makriyannis", *Byzantine and Modern Greek Studies*, 9: pp. 133–60

Philippides, Dia, *Census of Modern Greek Literature: Check-List of English-Language Sources Useful in the Study of Modern Greek Literature (1824–1987)*, New Haven: Modern Greek Studies Association, 1990

Seferis, George, *Dokimes* [Experiments], 2 vols., 4th edition, Athens, 1990

Vitti, Mario, *He Genia tou Trianta: Ideologia kai Morphi* [The Thirties Generation: Ideology and Actuality], 2nd edition, Athens, 1977

Moisiodax, Josephos *c.1725–1800*

Intellectual of the 18th century

Josephos Moisiodax was a towering cultural and social critic within the Greek Enlightenment, though his life, on the basis of surviving evidence, can only be partially reconstructed. He was born around 1725 at Czernawoda, a village today in southeastern Romania. Moisiodax was not ethnically Greek, but a Hellenized Vlach. Yet, his education in Thessalonica, in Smyrna, and at the Athonias Academy under Evgenios Voulgaris was entirely Greek. Moisiodox wrote and published solely in Greek. He is thus a typical example of the effect of the supra-national dissemination of Hellenic culture in the Balkans during the 18th century, which was not bound to a particular state and had a homogenizing impact upon the orientations, values, and perceptions of Balkan peoples.

Moisiodax continued his studies in physical sciences at the University of Padua, while he preached at the Greek church in Venice. There he published a Greek translation of Antonio Muratori's *Moral Philosophy* (1761) with his own prolegomena including his pleas for a Greek revival on the basis of the Enlightenment. Upon returning to the Danubian principalities, Moisiodax taught mathematics and physical sciences at the Princely Academy of Jassy in 1765–66 and later in 1776–77, where he also transmitted the ideas of the Enlightenment. His innovative teaching met with the unfavourable reaction of traditionalist teachers and circles, which forced him initially to resign and later to travel from 1777 to 1781 in various cities of central Europe (e.g. Budapest, Vienna, Venice). During this period he published four of his books. One of them, entitled *Pedagogy or Treatise on the Education of Children* (1779), was influenced by John Locke's pedagogical views and pointed out the interconnection between education and social practice and values while criticizing the backwardness of Greek education and its social background. In 1780 he published in Vienna his most important book, the *Apology*, which had a self-revelatory character and contained various texts and manifestos as responses to his ideological opponents and their accusations. In 1781 he also published a *Theory of Geography*, which comprised all major scientific discoveries including the heliocentric system. Scientific issues (e.g. the tides) were also discussed in his last book, *Physiological Notes* (1784), which was directed against the false perceptions of the ignorant masses concerning natural phenomena.

Moisiodax showed a particular predilection for discussing vital issues of his day including those concerning pedagogy, natural sciences, mathematics, and philosophy. One of the major contributions of his *Apology* to Greek thought was the undermining of traditional philosophy and its abstract, metaphysical concerns. Moisiodax supported wholeheartedly Cartesian rationalism and an empirically oriented scientific research as well as its achievements (e.g. Newtonian philosophy). Profoundly influenced by the Enlightenment's optimism, he stressed incessantly the social utility of science in terms of its technical applications. He also demonstrated that the preservation of the neo-Aristotelian status quo in Greek school curricula was motivated by socioeconomic reasons and personal interests. By supporting the outdated neo-Aristotelian system, conservative teachers tried to cover up their inabilities and ignorance of modern developments. As a result, they feared losing their privileges and influence within the educational system and society. Their reaction to the innovators like Moisiodax was not due to sincere scholarly interests and a quest for the truth, but to selfish and base motives. This constituted a major aspect of Moisiodax's fierce and uncompromising sociocultural criticism, which brought him many conflicts in the course of his life and eventually disappointment and frustration. His last years in Bucharest until his death in 1800 are generally marked by silence, despite his short teaching period in 1797 at the Princely Academy there.

Moisiodax applied the important intellectual conflict in 17th-century Europe between the Ancients and the Moderns to the Greek case. Due to his infatuation with modern science and progress, Moisiodax criticized the backwardness of Greek society in comparison to the West and tried to modernize it by suggesting far-reaching changes in many domains on the basis of modern European developments. In this context he also envisaged a political reform from arbitrary despotism to a liberal and law-abiding republican regime of civic rights, such as the Swiss Commonwealth, which would be in a position to carry out such radical reforms. In this way Moisiodax became a chief advocate of social and cultural reform as the most pressing need of the day. He was also very critical towards various authorities which might have hindered Greece's future development. He did not restrain himself from criticizing his eminent teacher Voulgaris on various issues including his teaching method, although he acknowledged Voulgaris's unusual intellectual capacities and his numerous contributions. Moisiodax was also a pioneer in using the vernacular instead of an archaic dialect in his lectures and writings, thus making them easily accessible and comprehensible to a wider audience.

Without being antireligious at all, Moisiodax, who early in his life had taken holy orders, tried systematically through his works to wrest ideological power from the Church and to undermine its authority in matters pertaining to science, culture, and history. He was convinced that humans through education and rational enquiry could master the world surrounding them. Religion had to be confined to things pertaining to the mystical, supernatural realm, the salvation of the soul, and moral conduct, issues lying beyond the grasp of science. Likewise, the Bible had to be considered solely as a religious text and never as a scientific treatise. The importance of Moisiodax's points can be captured by taking into account the vivid ideological conflicts concerning the Copernican world system around the end of the 18th century in Ottoman Greece. Moisiodax, with his social critique, tried to liberate Greek thought from superstition and prejudice, which were often connected with traditional religious notions. Finally, Moisiodax – unlike his teacher in Smyrna, Ierotheos Dendrinos, and several other Orthodox – did not think that studying in western Europe at that time could pose serious problems to the preservation of the Orthodox faith due to the potential espousal of western Christian or atheistic views. In his opinion the many-sided contacts of the Greek world with the West, its cultural evolution, and its scientific progress did not impinge necessarily upon its Orthodox identity. Westernization was thus not coterminous with an abandonment of Orthodoxy. Such and similar arguments were quite usual among many bearers of Enlightenment ideas. In this way

they intended, on the one hand, to legitimize their closer contacts with the West and, on the other hand, to neutralize the reactions of traditionalist Orthodox and other conservative circles.

In short, Moisiodax can be hailed as an architect of Greek ideological innovation during that important period of intellectual transition under the influence of the Enlightenment. His articulate socio-cultural criticism had a decisive influence upon other bearers of Enlightenment ideas, who continued his pioneering work.

VASILIOS MAKRIDES

See also Enlightenment

Biography
Born *c*.1725 in Czernawoda in modern southeast Romania, Moisiodax, a Hellenized Vlach, was educated in Thessalonica and Smyrna and at the academy on Mount Athos under Voulgaris. He went on to study physics at the University of Padua and took holy orders at an early age. Returning to the Danubian principalities, he taught mathematics and physics at the Princely Academy in Jassy and transmitted ideas about the Enlightenment. He died in Bucharest in 1800.

Writings
Apologia, Vienna, 1780; republished with an introduction by Alkis Angelou, Athens, 1976

Further Reading
Camariano-Cioran, Ariadna, "Un Directeur eclairé à l'Académie de Jassy il y a deux siècles: Iosip Moisiodax", *Balkan Studies*, 7 (1966): pp. 297–332

Camariano-Cioran, Ariadna, *Les Académies Princières de Bucarest et de Jassy et leurs professeurs*, Thessalonica: Institute for Balkan Studies, 1974, pp. 464, 569–98

Cicanci, Olga, "Une lettre inédite de Joseph Moesiodax", *Revue des Études Sud-Est Européennes*, 27 (1989): pp. 65–71

Kinini, Katerina, "Le discours à Nicoclès par Misiodax", *Ellinika*, 29 (1976): pp. 61–115

Kitromilides, Paschalis M., "The Last Battle of the Ancients and Moderns: Ancient Greece and Modern Europe in the Neohellenic Revival", *Modern Greek Studies Yearbook*, 1 (1985): pp. 79–91

Kitromilides, Paschalis M., *Iosipos Moisiodax: Oi Syntetagmenes tis Valkanikis Skepsis ton 18o aiona* [Josephos Moisiodax: The Coordinates of 18th-Century Balkan Thought], Athens, 1985

Kitromilides, Paschalis M., "Cultural Change and Social Criticism: The Case of Iossipos Moisiodax", *History of European Ideas*, 10 (1989): pp. 667–76

Kitromilides, Paschalis M., *The Enlightenment as Social Criticism: Iosipos Moisiodax and Greek Culture in the Eighteenth Century*, Princeton, New Jersey: Princeton University Press, 1992

Vukelić, Miroslav, "Ein Brief des Josepos Moesiodax aus dem Jahre 1760", *Balkan Studies*, 28 (1987): pp. 59–64

Moldavia

Moldavia was founded by Vlach immigrants from Hungary under the legendary Dragosh Bogdan in the first half of the 14th century. Until that time the Moldavian lowlands were still held by Tatar tribes. In 1372, in an agreement between emperor Charles IV and king Louis of Hungary, the *voievozi* of

Moldavia was recognized as a dependency of the crown of St Stephen (of Hungary). Rival claims by Poland and Hungary were a constant source of conflict between the two kingdoms. This rivalry was laid to rest in 1412 in an agreement between emperor Sigismund, acting as king of Hungary, and the Polish king Ladislas II, which provided for the joint Pologno-Hungarian defence of Moldavia against any Turkish invasion and its subsequent division between the two allies. While Polish influence was in the ascendant during the first half of the 15th century, during the long reign of Stephen the Great (1457–1504) Moldavia was consolidated as an independent principality. He defeated three Turkish invasions in 1476, 1478, and 1484, and the Polish invasion of 1487. In the following year he himself invaded Poland and annexed the Polish province of Prokutia. Under Stephen's reign Moldavia, excluding Prokutia, extended from the river Milcovu on the border with Wallachia to the river Dniestr; it included the Carpathian region of the Bukovina (Slavonic "the beech-wood"), the Budzak (Turkish "the corner", the later Bessarabia), Chilia (Russian Kiliya), and Moncastro (Russian Byelgorod; Turkish Akkerman; Romanian Cetatea Alba) as well as the left bank of the Danube from Galatz to the Sulian mouth. The country was predominantly Eastern Orthodox in religion, dependent on the patriarchate of Ohrid; the official language was Slavonic; the title of the ruler was *Nachalnik i Voievoda Moldavlasi* (prince and duke of the Moldavlachs), and the succession was strictly hereditary.

Stephen's successor, Bogdan III ("the One-Eyed"), sought to alleviate the country's position between Hungary and Poland through an alliance with the Ottoman empire, which was already surrounding Moldavia on the Wallachian and Crimean frontiers. In 1513 Moldavia became a tributary to the Turks. From now on Turkish influence grew steadily; so much so that in the mid-16th century *voievod* Elias (1546–51) converted to Islam in an effort to appease the sultan.

It was at this time that the curious interlude of Jacob Basilius took place. Basilius was Greek by birth. The adopted son of Jacob Heraklides, the despot of Paros, Samos, and other Aegean islands, he was a well-educated man, a student of astronomy, who corresponded with Philip Melanchthon, the divine and who wrote historical works dedicated to Philip II of Spain. Above all he was an ambitious man. His succession to his stepfather's title left him unsatisfied, and he produced the fabricated claim of kinship with the Moldavian *voivode*. Supported by emperor Ferdinand, and with Hungarian aid, he routed the superior Moldavian forces in 1561 and deposed the *voievod* Alexander Lepasheanu (1552–61 and 1563–68). He even purchased Turkish confirmation of his usurped title. Shortly afterwards he assumed the new title of *basileus moldavias*. Jacob Basilius was an energetic educational and religious reformer, but his orthodoxy remained suspect, and when he levied a new tax on the population the *boyars*, the indigenous nobility, rose against him and killed him in 1563.

The last uprising against continued Turkish encroachment upon Moldavia occurred during the brief voievodate of John the Terrible (1572–74). After his defeat Turkish influence became ever more dominant. The *voivode*, or *hospodars*, were appointed and then deposed in quick succession, although prince Vasilie Lupul (Basil the Wolf) tenaciously clung to power for some 20 years.

Moldavia was devastated in the successive wars of the Polish king Jan Sobieski against the Ottomans. After Sobieski's death in 1696, Moldavia turned to the rising Russian power for protection. In 1711 the *voievod* Demetrius Cantemir concluded a secret agreement with tsar Peter the Great by which both countries committed themselves to a war against Turkey, after which Moldavia was to become a vassal state under Russian protection. Cantemir's troops, however, deserted in the face of the advancing Turks and the Russian campaign failed. Ottoman influence was now supreme. The Sublime Porte farmed out the hospodarship to a succession of wealthy Greeks, mostly from the Phanar quarter of Constantinople. The chief families that held the office during the so-called Phanariot regime were the Mavrokordato, Ghica, Callimachi, Ypsilanti, and Murusi. The *hospodars* thus installed were mere puppets dangling from strings pulled at Constantinople; and having to expend a large tribute, or *bakshish* ("tip"), every three years, and a smaller one every year, to have their appointments confirmed, they regarded their tenure of office largely as an opportunity for exploitation. At the same time, however, the Phanariot regime also brought about a significant educational improvement in Moldavia, especially under Gregory Ghica (1774–77).

Since the mid-16th century Moldavia's independence had been steadily eroded. The Russo-Turkish War (1768–74) delivered a fatal blow to the country's integrity. The Treaty of Kutchuk-Kainardji, of 15 July 1774, which ended the hostilities, restored Moldavia and Wallachia to the Porte but reserved for Russia the right to interfere in the affairs of the Danubian principalities. It was the beginning of Russia's advance on the Balkan peninsula. Moldavia's integrity, however, was infringed by Austria, which annexed the Bukovina in 1775. In 1802 Russia forced the Porte to accept further restrictions on Turkish suzerainty over Moldavia which amounted to a de facto Russian protectorate. During the next Russo-Turkish War (1806–12) Moldavia and Wallachia were occupied by Russia. The Treaty of Bucharest of 1812 restored the two principalities to Turkey under the previous stipulations. Bessarabia, however, was ceded to Russia. The river Pruth was now Moldavia's new border.

During the period of the Russo-Turkish wars a new Greek movement was formed in Moldavia. Around 1780 Rigas Velestinlis, a Hellenized Vlach from Macedonia, also known under the Greek name Rigas Pheraios, founded in Bucharest the *Hetaireia ton Philon* (the "Friendly Society"), a Greek patriotic and revolutionary association. Gradually the Hetairist movement gained substantial influence in Moldavian affairs. In 1810 the metropolitan of Wallachia, Ignatius, founded a Greek literary society that soon turned into a political movement. Many similar bodies sprang up in Moldavia, finally to be merged into one secret society, the *Hetaireia*. The political aims of the movement were only vaguely defined, suffused however with the ideas propagated by the French Revolution. In its more extreme forms it aimed at the restoration of the Byzantine empire.

The year 1821 marked the apogee of the Hetairist movement. Alexander Ypsilantis, son of a Phanariot *voievod* and an aide-de-camp to tsar Alexander I, entered Moldavia at the head of the Hetairists. But both the movement and its leader had become too closely associated with the Phanariot past.

Opposed by the indigenous Slav majority, lacking support, and eventually even repudiated by Russia, Ypsilantis's adventure ended in failure. His forces were crushed by the Turks and Moldavia was occupied by a Turkish army until 1824. The Russo-Turkish convention of Akkerman of 1826 and the peace treaty of Adrianople of 1829 confirmed the privileges of the Wallachian and Moldavian principalities. Their internal constitution was governed by the "Organic Law" which largely maintained the feudal position of the *boyars*. Socially, financially, and politically Russia was now the predominant influence in the two Danubian principalities. Between 1834 and 1848 their secret but all-powerful ruler was the Russian consul-general at Bucharest.

The European revolution of 1848 also reached Moldavia where it aimed at the overthrow of Russian influence institutionalized in the "Organic Law". The revolution was squashed by a joint Russo-Turkish intervention; and the "Organic Law" was restored. At the Treaty of Paris, which marked the end of the Crimean War in 1856, both Wallachia and Moldavia were restored under the suzerainty of Turkey but now collectively guaranteed by the great powers of Europe; they were granted complete internal independence from the Sublime Porte; and Bessarabia was restored to Moldavia. In September 1857 a European commission, instituted by the Paris peace treaty, prepared the way for a union of Moldavia and Wallachia under the name of Romania, to be governed by a foreign European prince. The merger of the two principalities came into force in January 1859.

T.G. OTTE

See also Phanariots, Romania

Further Reading

Anderson, Matthew Smith, *The Eastern Question, 1774–1923: A Study in International Relations*, London: Macmillan, and New York: St Martin's Press, 1966

Bossy, Raoul V., "La diplomatic russe et l'union des principautés romaines, 1858–1859", *Revue d'Histoire Diplomatique*, 3 (1962)

Dima, Nicholas, *From Moldavia to Moldova: The Soviet–Romanian Territorial Dispute*, 2nd edition, Boulder, Colorado: East European Monographs, 1991

East, William David Gordon, *The Union of Moldavia and Wallachia, 1859: An Episode in Diplomatic History*, Cambridge: Cambridge University Press, 1929

Jelavich, Barbara, *History of the Balkans*, vol. 1: *Eighteenth and Nineteenth Centuries*, Cambridge and New York: Cambridge University Press, 1983

Jelavich, Barbara, *Russia and the Formation of the Romanian National State, 1821–1878*, Cambridge and New York: Cambridge University Press, 1984

Monarchy

The political landscape of the Mycenaean period consisted of independent powers of different size with a palace as their political and economic centre. The head of each palace and its surrounding territory was a king (*wanax* in Linear B) whose power was based on his control of the palace economy and his military leadership. It has also been assumed by scholars that the king was the high priest of his realm and thus also had a prominent cultic function. His power seems not to have been unrestricted, however, since he had to consider the demands of a strong aristocracy.

To a certain extent the societies of the Homeric epics resemble the Mycenaean world. Essentially an aristocratic world is depicted, though the terminology for the leading authorities is not absolutely consistent. Basically a single ruler and a council of noblemen have to be distinguished. The designation *basileus* for the noblemen obviously derives from the Linear B word *qasireu/pasireu*, which describes an official with certain limited powers. In contrast the *basileis* of the Homeric epics form the leading group of a community. The translation of the word *basileus* as "king" may be misleading at this stage; the terms "leader", "lord", or "chief" correspond better with the actual connotation. The *basileis* of the Homeric epics are distinguished from the other people by certain conditions. They are members of the leading families, which implies that they descend more or less directly from a god and that they had a profound material basis. Within this group of *basileis* there existed a code of virtues, the most prominent of which are courage, wisdom in council, and piety. Adherence to these virtues determined the actual status of a *basileus*.

Whereas the term *basileus* is often used in the plural, the denomination *anax*, which derives from the Linear B word *wanax*, is exclusively used in the singular form, thus implying some sort of monarchical power. The word may be translated as "master" or "prince". In each community, whether within the Greek army at Troy or in the smaller principalities, there exists just one *anax*. The *anax* himself is also a *basileus*, that is a nobleman. The *anax* fulfils a number of functions within the community: he is responsible for sacrifices; he is the commander-in-chief of the army; and he administers justice, thus combining sacral, civil, and military roles. His powers are not unlimited, however, since he has to consult the council of *basileis* on important questions. Although the actual status of the *anax* depends on his adherence to virtues, his position, being basically hereditary, is never seriously contested.

In the Archaic period the reality and the terminology of monarchy experience a considerable development. First, on the island of Cos, the term *monarchos* appears to become fixed quite early in the Archaic period to describe the phenomenon of a single magistrate ruling the polis. Second, and more important, the Greek world in the 7th and 6th centuries BC experienced the phenomenon of more or less unrestricted monarchs ruling a polis. The term *tyrannos* for these monarchs derives from the Anatolian languages of western Asia Minor. The prototype of a tyrant was the Lydian Gyges who in the early 7th century BC came to power by usurpation. The Phrygio-Lydian term can be translated as "chief" or "master".

While the word *tyrannos* was absent from Homer and Hesiod, archaic poets, especially Solon, Theognis, and Alcaeus, contrasted it to the denomination *basileus* as actually expressing the opposite of aristocracy: the monarchical power of a tyrant contradicted the claims of the aristocratic class for equality (*isonomia*) among themselves. The tyrant, as a member of the leading group which consisted of *basileis*, aimed at monarchical power, thus opposing the values of his class. This opposition to the values and virtues of aristocratic society was called *hybris* (presumption, insolence). In the Archaic age therefore to be a tyrant meant being in the possession of monarchical power, but not necessarily being a violent despot. That meaning of the term developed in the course of the experience of violent rule of tyrants and within the theoretical discussion of the Classical period.

Whereas tyrannies, especially in Ionian Greece, continued to proliferate under Persian rule, in mainland Greece they had mostly disappeared by the end of the 6th century BC. In the 5th century BC some monarchies existed at the fringes of the Greek world, in Macedonia, Epirus, and Aetolia. In central Greece with the growth of democracy and in the aftermath of the Persian Wars a negative view of monarchical power prevailed: it was regarded as a form of government fitting slavish barbarians, not the free citizens of a Greek polis. Sparta had had a double kingship since Archaic times, but for the limited power of these kings the term monarchy is not really appropriate.

The movement of the Sophists stimulated theoretical discussions about different forms of government. It was in this context that monarchy began to be regarded at least theoretically as a good form of government. The rise of new monarchies in the Greek world in the 4th century BC and especially the growing power of the Macedonian monarchy under Philip II stimulated a wide-ranging discussion on the basis of the terminology of the Sophists. The discussion is well reflected in Aristotle's *Politics* (3. 14-18, 4. 10). Theoretically monarchy could have a good form, *basileia*, and a bad one, *tyrannis*. The shift of meaning since the Archaic period is noticeable. The main criterion for *basileia*, to be translated here as "royalty" or "kingship", was to rule according to the law and for the benefit of the subjects. Against this, tyranny meant the usurpation of power to rule for one's own benefit.

In the 4th century BC several treatises on kingship were written, sometimes aimed at particular kings, e.g. the "Cyprian orations" of Isocrates to Nicocles. In those treatises the picture of an ideal king was developed. A common model of an ideal king was the Persian Cyrus about whom Xenophon's treatise *Cyropaedia* has survived. Plato developed the concept of the philosopher king possessing absolute knowledge and goodness. Treatises of the 4th century BC have some basic features in common. Essentially the ideal king is portrayed as ruling for the benefit of his subjects which requires him to be generous, to be a military figure, and to be very pious.

Monarchy became the predominant political feature in Greece after the conquests of Philip II and his son Alexander the Great. After his conquest of central Greece Philip became the leader (*hegemon*) of the Corinthian League. It has to be remembered that the constitutions of the Greek cities remained unchanged. With Alexander the character of Greek monarchy changed considerably. After his conquest of Babylon in 330 BC he assumed the Persian title "king of Asia" and tried to model his royalty on Persian kingship, but he met the resistance of his Macedonian companions. Eventually his monarchy turned out to combine Persian and Macedonian elements and some new characteristics. The most important new feature was the order to the Greek cities in 324 BC to grant him divine honours, which was inspired by his achievements as conqueror and his unlimited monarchical power.

After Alexander's death in 323 BC and the wars of the Successors the Macedonian rulers of his divided empire in 306-304 BC assumed the title *basileus* themselves. By this time, royalty had become primarily dependent on military conquest. The ability to lead an army decided the royal status. Like Alexander, the Hellenistic kings regarded their territory as spear-won land and thus as a personal possession. The other predominant prerequisite of royalty was wealth. The nuclei of the Hellenistic monarchies, as with the Macedonian and Persian monarchies, were the companions (*philoi*) of the king, a group of nobles who together with the army formed the royal establishment. "King, friends, and army" was a common phrase in Hellenistic times.

Apart from these common features the Hellenistic monarchies had considerable differences. These primarily depended on the traditions of their subject peoples and the structures of their empires. The Ptolemies in Egypt established themselves in the tradition of the pharaohs. The Seleucids, who reigned in Syria, but whose empire at its peak stretched as far as India, had many different traditions to cope with. In general they showed piety towards indigenous gods. Both the Ptolemies and the Seleucids received divine honours from the Greek cities. They were honoured as liberators of the cities, as founders, or as benefactors. The cults could be for the worship of the living ruler or of his dynasty. In contrast the Antigonids in Macedonia did not receive divine honours.

In the Hellenistic period a wide range of treatises on kingship were written. Like their predessessors of the 4th century BC, they were mostly aimed at particular rulers. Most of the treatises are lost, but a good insight is provided by the 3rd-century BC *Letter of Aristeas* and the Neopythagorean writers Ecphantus, Diotogenes, and Sthenidas. The virtues and achievements of a king according to these treatises are military leadership, generosity, philanthropy, wealth, justice, security, and peace.

With the battle of Actium in 31 BC the last Hellenistic monarchy fell, and for 360 years the Greek world was ruled from Rome. Many traces of Hellenistic monarchy may be observed in the Roman principate. With the establishment of Constantinople as capital of the eastern Roman empire and the final division of the empire in AD 395 the circumstances of monarchy in Greece changed considerably. The emperors regarded themselves as Romans and Christianity was the imperial religion. The official ideology of the emperor consisted of his being chosen by God as lord over the world, as his vicar on earth. The way to power was usually by usurpation: when the usurper was successful, this meant he was chosen by God. Thus, as in previous periods, military victory was one of the determinants of imperial status, both internal and external. The title *basileus* was introduced in 629 as the official style of the Byzantine emperor by Herakleios after his victory over Persia in memory of Alexander the Great's conquests. The 10th-century *Suda*, referring to Philip II and the Successors, makes the ability to lead an army the most important virtue of the *basileus*. Victories were celebrated very extensively and the Christian cross became a sign of victory.

In theory the emperor had unlimited power. He was the commander-in-chief, the supreme judge, the sole lawgiver, the protector of the Church, the guardian of the faith, and he made decisions over war and peace. In practice he had to take into consideration factions at court and in the Hippodrome of Constantinople, where the people expressed their consent or dissent through acclamation. Until the final capture of Constantinople by the Turks in 1453 the Byzantine court was the centre of the empire. The ceremonial at court was essential for the determination of the palace hierarchy.

An important feature of the Byzantine period is panegyric, the praise of an emperor. Through the criticism or the depiction of an exemplary king, often chosen from the Greek or Roman past, the emperor could be given to understand what was expected of him. There was a wide range of imperial virtues such as courage, justice, temperance, wisdom, and clemency. Such virtues could be categorized as physical, intellectual, and moral skills. Most of these features are derived more or less explicitly from 4th-century BC and Hellenistic treatises on kingship. The focus on individual virtues could vary. Although there was always criticism of particular rulers, the monarchical system itself was never questioned during the Byzantine period.

In the Greek War of Independence monarchy played a minor role. The independence movement was influenced by ideas of the Enlightenment and the French Revolution. To be considered in this context is the Great Idea (*Megali Idea*), which aimed at the reconstruction of the Byzantine empire, but here also the idea of monarchy was of minor importance. Contrary to Greek draft constitutions, Russia, France, and Britain in 1833 made Otho of Bavaria king of Greece. He wielded absolute power, regarding himself as being king by divine grace until 1843–44, when he was forced to accept a constitution that was upheld as a treaty between king and subjects. After the revolution of 1862 the principle of the sovereignty of the people was introduced. But prince George I of Denmark was appointed by the Great Powers as king of the Hellenes. The Asia Minor disaster of 1922 dealt a severe blow to the monarchy and was followed by a period of republican rule (1924–35). A rigged plebiscite enabled the king to return in 1935 and apart from wartime exile the monarchy survived until 1967, when a military junta assumed power. The monarchy was finally abolished by a referendum in 1974.

ULF SCHARRER

See also Government, Imperialism, Tyranny

Further Reading

Actes du colloque international sur l'idéologie monarchique dans l'antiquité, Warsaw and Krakow: Nakładem Uniwersytetu Jagielloúskiego, 1980

Austin, M.M., "Hellenistic Kings, War, and the Economy", *Classical Quarterly*, 36/2 (1986): pp. 450–66

Barceló, Pedro, *Basileia, Monarchia, Tyrannis: Untersuchungen zu Entwicklung und Beurteilung von Alleinherrschaft im vorhellenistischen Griechenland*, Stuttgart: Steiner, 1993

Bilde, Per et al. (editors), *Aspects of Hellenistic Kingship*, Aarhus: Aarhus University Press, 1996

Bulloch, Anthony et al. (editors), *Images and Ideologies: Self-Definition in the Hellenistic World*, Berkeley: University of California Press, 1993

Carlier, Pierre, *La Royauté en Grèce avant Alexandre*, Strasbourg: AECR, 1984

Clogg, Richard, *A Short History of Modern Greece*, 2nd edition, Cambridge and New York: Cambridge University Press, 1986

Devere-Summers, Anthony, *War and the Royal Houses of Europe in the Twentieth Century*, London: Arms and Armour Press, 1996

Drews, Robert, *Basileus: The Evidence for Kingship in Geometric Greece*, New Haven and London: Yale University Press, 1983

Finer, S.E., *The History of Government from the Earliest Times*, 3 vols, Oxford and New York: Oxford University Press, 1997

Goyon, Jean-Claude et al. (editors), *L'Idéologie du pouvoir monarchique dans l'Antiquité*, Paris: Boccard, 1991

Habicht, Christian, *Gottmenschentum und griechische Städte*, 2nd edition, Munich: Beck, 1970

Heurtley, W.A. et al., *A Short History of Greece from Early Times to 1964*, Cambridge: Cambridge University Press, 1965

McCormick, Michael, *Eternal Victory: Triumphal Rulership in Late Antiquity, Byzantium, and the Early Medieval West*, Cambridge and New York: Cambridge University Press, 1986

Magdalino, Paul (editor), *New Constantines: The Rhythm of Imperial Renewal in Byzantium, 4th-13th Centuries*, Aldershot, Hampshire: Variorum, 1994

Nicolson, Harold George, *Monarchy*, London: Weidenfeld and Nicolson, 1962

Price, S.R.F., *Rituals and Power: The Roman Imperial Cult in Asia Minor*, Cambridge and New York: Cambridge University Press, 1984

Walbank, F.W., "Monarchies and Monarchic Ideas" in *The Hellenistic World*, edited by Walbank et al., Cambridge: Cambridge University Press, 1984 (*The Cambridge Ancient History*, vol. 7, part 1, 2nd edition)

Whitby, Mary (editor), *The Propaganda of Power: The Role of Panegyric in Late Antiquity*, Leiden and Boston: Brill, 1998

Woodhouse, C.M., *Modern Greece: A Short History*, 5th edition, London and Boston: Faber, 1991

Monasteries

Monasteries consist of a building or group of buildings housing monks or nuns who live as a community, apart from the world, in prayer and work dedicated to God. They vary in size, accommodating a minimum of three monks to several hundred. The term monastery (*moni*) refers to various types of ascetic houses. The ancient Greek terms *lavra* (a group of dispersed hermits' cells, *kellia*), adapted from the Greek word meaning a lane or passageway, and *koinobion* (community of monks or nuns) denote both the monks' mode of life and the architectural layout of the building(s).

The Greek monastic tradition originated in certain 3rd- and 4th-century ascetic dwellings in Egypt. By AD 350 three coexisting modes of ascetic life had emerged. The hermits (*eremia*, "desert") led solitary lives in huts or caves, and even in tombs. Following the example of St Antony of Egypt (251–356), some went to extremes by living in the branches of trees, or on top of pillars. The monks dwelt in the same house and followed the general cenobitic routine (*koinobion*) suggested by St Pachomius of Egypt (285–346) and St Basil the Great (329–79). In between these two ascetic lifestyles were groups of between three and six monks who led semi-eremitic lives under an elder (*geron*, "old man") of discernment and wisdom, a guide in spiritual matters. These monks dwelt in their houses during the week, occupied with prayer and manual labour, and attended the services in the church built in the middle of the monastic village (*lavra*) at weekends. Well-known *lavras* in Egypt included Nitria and Scetis (the modern Wadi Natrun), which had produced many outstanding monks by the end of

Monasteries: monk tending the gardens at the monastery of Pantokratoros, Mount Athos; the aim is self-sufficiency in food

the 4th century. Most *lavras* were in remote rural locations, but a few were in suburban and urban areas.

Byzantine monastic architecture also originated in Egypt and Syria. Its development mirrors the change from the *lavra* layout to the *koinobion* fortress, St Catherine's on Mount Sinai being a prototype. The typical *koinobion* had strong, defensive walls more than ten metres high, housing the monks' or nuns' cells, together with stables, workshops, storage buildings, and a tower. The main church (the *katholikon*) was in the centre of the courtyard, and the canopied fountain, the reservoir for holy water (*phiale*), stood in front of it. The refectory (*trapeza*) was in the courtyard opposite the church. The tower was built to defend the only entrance to the monastery, and served as the final refuge in case of raids by pirates and robbers. It also functioned as a storehouse for food, and as a library for important monastic documents, manuscripts, and books. Some of the towers had a small chapel at the top.

In the course of time, more monasteries were built in towns, notably in Constantinople, making monasticism an urban phenomenon. The accumulation of agricultural land and other properties provided the monks with food and an income to maintain the buildings and operate the monastery, and gave them an important role in the city's economy. The general form, rule, and variety of monasteries were complete by the birth of Byzantium.

Two foundation deeds (*typikon* and *brevion*) and certain imperial laws were implemented to regulate the rapid growth of monasteries and to "tame" them to serve both Church and society. The foundation charter (*typikon*) specified the rights and duties of the monks and nuns, with the proviso that they should pray for their founder and, after his or her death, inter-

cede on behalf of his or her soul. The belief in the effect of prayer was often the main reason why benefactors founded new monasteries or supported existing ones. The *brevion* stated the founder's wishes regarding the litany, and listed all endowments. This effectively standardized the mode of life in the new communities.

The monasteries were classified as imperial, patriarchal (*stavropegion*), or episcopal, and as private or independent depending on the law that regulated them. The imperial houses were subject to the emperor or his representative, and the patriarchal ones were privileged to be under direct patriarchal control. Most were episcopal and under diocesan control. Some small houses were completely independent (*autodespotai*), albeit mostly connected and affiliated to farming lands (*metochia*). This network of ruling monasteries and dependencies was crystallized by the 9th century. Byzantine sources record more than 1000 monasteries, one third of which were located in Constantinople or its immediate surroundings.

Each monastery had a superior, *hegoumenos*, usually elected for life. His election was stipulated in the *typikon* and was normally confirmed by the diocesan bishop. The *hegoumenos* was responsible for the spiritual and temporal well-being of the monastery, and he commanded absolute obedience. Other officials included the steward (*oikonomos*), the sacristan (*ekklesiarches*), and a number of brethren responsible for the refectory, treasury, and archives.

This hierarchy emerged hand-in-hand with the development of monasticism from a lay movement to an organized cenobitic community. Initially there were only two classes of monks: the literate choir monks responsible for singing the daily offices, and the uneducated servant brethren (*diakonetai*) doing manual labour. This division was reflected in their food and dress, their seating in the refectory, and even in their place of burial. When members of the nobility donned the habit, they were accompanied by servants. Having made substantial donations to the monastery, they dwelt in suites rather than single cells. Despite their vows of poverty, they were allowed to retain some personal property.

The monastery as an institution soon became an essential part of the social and religious fabric of Byzantium. The daily routine consisted of eight hours of prayer, eight hours of work, and eight hours of rest, not in succession, but intermingled with the liturgical hours of day and night services. The *hegoumenos* appointed each monastic to specific duties, making use of everyone's individual gifts. Most monks and nuns were occupied in agricultural and manual work, although some studied the scriptures, copied manuscripts, or composed hymns and hagiographical works.

In the early and late centuries of Byzantium there were double monasteries housing two separate but adjacent communities of men and women, under the same superior. The self-evident difficulties posed by such close proximity of monks and nuns made Justinian I (546) prohibit these institutions. The inefficiency of the legislation allowed double monasteries to exist from time to time. Around 810 patriarch Nikephoros I closed all double monasteries. In the Palaiologan period these monasteries were re-established, principally so that the family of the founder could remain close even after renouncing the world, but by the end of the 14th century these institutions were again closed down.

With Palestine and Sinai in Arab hands, the monastery of Stoudios in Constantinople, the heart of Byzantium, became the leading monastery for the Eastern Orthodox Churches. As its *hegoumenos*, St Theodore (759–826) made it a strong cenobitic community, by both practical example and written regulation. He defended the use of icons in the iconoclast controversy, and defined the role of monastic discipline in his *Catecheses*, modelled after the rules of St Basil. Stoudios soon became progressive and led the way in providing food for the poor, lodging for foreign pilgrims and commercial travellers, as well as homes for orphans and old people. The monasteries in Constantinople were the first to establish hospitals with employed doctors and male nurses.

In the 10th century Mount Athos succeeded Constantinople as the spiritual centre of Orthodoxy, and 20 ruling monasteries were established on the Holy Mountain in the next 500 years. These still own the entire peninsula, which is divided into 20 areas. All other monastic properties located on any of the land of the ruling monasteries are known as dependencies (*exartemata*): 12 monastic villages (*sketai*), several hundred cottages (*kellia*), and farming land (*metochia*). There are also various kinds of retreat known as *hesychasteria*, hermitages (*kathismata*), eremitic huts (*kalyves*), and ascetic huts or caves (*spilia*), situated on high cliffs at the southern tip of the peninsula. Only Great Lavra, the first and oldest of the 20 ruling monasteries, founded in 963, uses the term *lavra* in its name, thereby denoting the origin of Athonite monasticism. Today all the ruling monasteries are impregnable fortresses.

With the fall of Constantinople in 1453, Mount Athos became the last bastion of Byzantium and a haven for refugees,

exiled bishops, and banished patriarchs. The Athonites played a significant role in the Christianization of the Slavs and Russians as far north as Karelia, the Kola peninsula, and the Petsamo monastery in Finland. During the Tourkokratia (1430–1912), the heavy ransoms and taxes imposed by the sultan forced many of the Athonite monasteries to adopt the idiorrhythmic system (*idios rhythmos*, "own way of life"). Each monk earned his own living through agriculture, icon-painting, or handicrafts. This individual lifestyle, which became common in the Palaiologan era (1261–1453), had a negative connotation throughout the Byzantine period, and this attitude has persisted until the present time. Since the 1980s, the idiorrhythmic monasteries have readopted the cenobitic system, one by one, Pantokratoros being the last in 1992.

Unlike western practice, education was never a function of Byzantine monasticism. Many *typika* specifically forbade the admission of children for educational purposes. Nevertheless, monasteries played an integral role in the intellectual and cultural life of the empire. Many of its most important literary figures were monks. The ability to read was essential from the very beginning of monasticism. Literate nuns, for example, were encouraged to teach their illiterate sisters enough to chant the office, maintain the monastery accounts, and work as librarians (*bibliophylax*). Monks and nuns formed the majority of the empire's literati in the early 9th century, and about 25 per cent in the 14th century.

The Stoudios and Hodegon monasteries in Constantinople housed scriptoria producing, copying, and illuminating manuscripts, as well as composing hymns, saints' lives, theological treatises, and historical chronicles for both internal and external use. Most monasteries had librarians who looked after the scriptures, liturgical books, and works on hagiography, patristics, and theology. The librarian was also responsible for the selection of texts to be read in the refectory during mealtimes. Only a few monasteries had any manuscripts or books by ancient Greek authors, although some did benefit from the personal book collections of their founders. The Chora library in 14th century Constantinople was the best in the capital, where the leading Classical philologists of the day prepared editions and commentaries on Classical authors.

When the Turks strengthened their hold on Asia Minor, monks and clergy fled to Patmos, which became an intellectual centre that was also culturally and artistically linked with Crete. The monks founded the celebrated Patmian School in 1713. It soon became the centre of Orthodox higher education in the Greek-speaking world, but fell into decline within 40 years. The curriculum included Latin, rhetoric, philology, and religious studies.

Efforts to keep learning and literacy alive were also made on Mount Athos. The librarians at the Vatopedi monastery in particular, notably Maximos the Hagiorite (b. 1480) who had travelled widely and studied in Paris and Italy, were conscious of the inestimable value of the library collections. The Athonites jointly bought the splendid library of Michael Kantakouzenos, one of the wealthiest men of the period, in 1578.

In the 18th century Nikodimos of the Holy Mountain, known as "the Hagiorite" and "the encyclopaedia of Athonite learning", contributed significally to the era of spiritual awakening by compiling and editing the *Philokalia*, the fundamental anthology of mystical and ascetic texts written between the

4th and 15th centuries. Despite the Athonites' anti-intellectualism and suspicion of western values, they founded the Athonite Academy near Vatopedi, the leading monastery on Athos at the time, in 1753. But its curriculum proved too liberal and it was soon closed, its buildings destroyed by fire.

The monasteries in the Byzantine and post-Byzantine periods have wielded immense power and, at times, caused serious problems for rulers. Since the birth of monasticism, the monks' supposed gifts of healing the sick, driving evil from people's souls, and foretelling the future have encouraged the laity to support the holy men and women devoted to the ascetic life. During the 4th and 5th centuries the monks played a major role in ecumenical councils. Since many monasteries were havens of refuge for people from all walks of life, from peasants to patricians, ex-teachers to emperors, many realized the significance of patronage. Eventually, many a ruler, more by force than choice, exchanged his purple robes for the black habit. Increasingly it became the custom to recruit bishops and patriarchs from the leading monasteries. Although the fortunes of the monasteries waxed and waned as the empire grew and contracted, even in difficult times there were always wealthy patrons, pious benefactors, and rulers who gave substantial gifts and landholdings. Justinian (527–65) granted monasteries special economic privileges that made them very wealthy. This became a serious problem for the empire in the late Byzantine period when nearly half of the land was controlled by monks. In the late 14th century, forced by the rapidly worsening state of the economy, the emperors attempted to redistribute the land in order to maintain the army. The monasteries resisted this strongly, which contributed to the fall of the empire, since Byzantium was threatened by enemies on all sides.

The Ottoman era and the many wars in the first half of the 20th century diminished the monasteries' influence over the religious life of Greece, resulting in a decline in the number of monks (from 150,000 in the 11th century to fewer than 3,000 today). This has left hundreds of monasteries deserted. Since the early 1970s, a modest but steady revival has been taking place, which is significant because it is not only pious peasants, but also educated young men and women who are entering monastic life in increasing numbers. Apart from Mount Athos, the most renowned are the monastery of St John the Theologian on Patmos, founded in 1088, and Meteora in Thessaly. The latter is a group of six monasteries – once 24 – established in the early 14th century, but today little more than museums. The Old Calendarist monastery of the Transfiguration at Kouvara and the monastery of the Paraclete at Oropos also house a healthy number of youngish monks.

Since the 1920s, the number of nuns has increased from a few hundred to 2,500. Nuns have taken over houses abandoned by men, including St Nicholas's nunnery on Euboea. The convent of the Annunciation at Ormylia in Chalcidice, a dependency of Simonospetras on Mount Athos, and the Kechrovouni convent on the island of Tinos, renowned as a pilgrimage centre, are attracting educated women in particular.

RENÉ GOTHÓNI

See also Athos, Mar Saba, Meteora, Monasticism, Patmos, Pilgrimage, St Catherine's Monastery

Further Reading

Brown, Peter, *The Body and Society: Men, Women, and Sexual Renunciation in Early Christianity*, New York: Columbia University Press, 1988; London: Faber, 1990
Bryer, Anthony, "The Late Byzantine Monastery in Town and Countryside" in *The Church in Town and Countryside*, edited by Derek Baker, Oxford: Blackwell, 1979
Bryer, Anthony and Mary Cunningham (editors), *Mount Athos and Byzantine Monasticism*, Aldershot, Hampshire: Variorum, 1996
Gothóni, René, *Paradise within Reach: Monasticism and Pilgrimage on Mt. Athos*, Helsinki: Helsinki University Press, 1993
Gothóni, René, *Tales and Truth: Pilgrimage on Mount Athos Past and Present*, Helsinki: Helsinki University Press, 1994
Hellier, Chris, *Monasteries of Greece*, London: Tauris Parke, 1996
Kazhdan, A.P. (editor), *The Oxford Dictionary of Byzantium*, 3 vols, New York and Oxford: Oxford University Press, 1991
Kitromilides, Paschalis M., "Athos and the Enlightenment" in *Mount Athos and Byzantine Monasticism*, edited by Anthony Bryer and Mary Cunningham, Aldershot, Hampshire: Variorum, 1996
Knowles, David, *Christian Monasticism*, London: Weidenfeld and Nicolson, and New York: McGraw Hill, 1969
Kokori, Dimitriou, *Orthodoxa Ellinika Monastiria* [Greek Orthodox Monasteries], Athens, 1997
Morris, Rosemary, *Monks and Laymen in Byzantium, 843–1118*, Cambridge and New York: Cambridge University Press, 1995
Rousseau, Philip, *Pachomius: The Making of a Community in Fourth-Century Egypt*, Berkeley: University of California Press, 1985
Savramis, Demosthenes, *Zur Soziologie des byzantinischen Mönchtums*, Leiden: Brill, 1962
Talbot, Alice-Mary, "A Comparison of the Monastic Experience of Byzantine Men and Women", *Greek Orthodox Theological Review*, 30/1 (1985): pp. 1–20
Talbot, Alice-Mary, "An Introduction to Byzantine Monasticism", *Illinois Classical Studies*, 12 (1987): pp. 229–41
Ware, Timothy, *The Orthodox Church*, 2nd edition, London and New York: Penguin, 1993

Monasticism

The rise of monasticism brought nothing essentially new into the early Church. It was a new expression of the same enthusiastic or eschatological dimension of Christianity that martyrdom had embodied in earlier centuries. Monastic life is, of course, not distinctively Christian, answering as it does to a deep, perhaps universal human instinct. Yet while Christian monasticism may have borrowed from, or may even present parallel practices to, other ascetic traditions – such as the notions of solitude and struggle, concentration and contemplation, passion and dispassion – these were not the reasons for its rise.

Rather, it was the dilution of commitment – when Christianity no longer constituted a question of life or death – that accounted for several factors in the early Church, one of which was monasticism. Following the Edict of Toleration (313), it was the monastics who assumed the responsibility of witnessing to the Kingdom, of reminding people that the Church is not "of the world" (John 17: 36). The "baptism of conscience" (asceticism) thus succeeded the "baptism of blood" (martyrdom), ideologically and chronologically.

We think of Antony and Pachomius in Egypt; Antony's disciple, Hilarion, in Syria and Palestine; Cassian (d. 432) and

Monasticism: a new monk is tonsured during the Vigil for the Nativity on Mount Athos

Benedict (d. 547) in the West; Basil and the Gregories in Asia Minor. Monasticism soon acquired a particular significance for all Christians. The *Life of Antony* (by Athanasius), the *Life of Paul of Thebes* (by Jerome), the *Lausiac History* (by Palladius) – these and similar texts rapidly became favourite reading in Byzantium.

In the 4th century Egypt, Syria, Palestine, and Asia were the forcing-ground where every kind of monastic life was experienced and experimented. The roots even of western religious life clearly lie in the Egyptian east, where monasticism began on a Sunday morning in the year 270 or 271. The Gospel of the day included the words: "If you want to be perfect, go and sell what you possess, give to the poor, and you will have treasure in heaven; and come, follow me" (Matthew 19: 21). In the congregation was a young man called Antony who, upon hearing these words, sought a life not merely of relative poverty but of radical solitude. Antony's step into the uninhabited desert was little noticed outside, or even inside, his village at the time. But when he died at the age of 106, as his friend and biographer Athanasius of Alexandria (d. 373) informs us, his name was known "all over the road". "The desert", he writes, "had become a city". Before retiring to the desert, Antony had placed his sister in a "home for virgins", a fact that perhaps reveals that women were organized into Christian communities earlier than men.

In Egypt there now appeared three main types of monasticism, roughly corresponding to three geographical locations: (1) the *eremitic* life, found in lower Egypt, where Antony was the model. Here monks lived an isolated and austere life of prayer and detachment in pursuit of evangelical perfection. This is the oldest and most rudimentary form of organization. (2) The *cenobitic* or communal form of monasticism, found in upper Egypt, where Pachomius (d. 346) was the prototype. Here monks prayed and worked together, in a lifestyle where the emphasis was now on the common life. And (3) the *middle way*, located in Nitria and Scetis where Amoun founded this monastic way around 311. Here a small and intimate family of monks looked to a common spiritual elder, or "abba". Since these "sketes" were also closer to the city, they became meeting places or crossroads between the world and the desert.

The focus of eastern monasticism moved from Egypt to Asia Minor in the late 4th century, to Palestine in the 5th, to Sinai in the 6th, and in the 10th century to Mount Athos, where these three types of monasticism are still in existence, bearing witness to a remarkable tradition of living continuity in the monastic life.

Other regions saw a variety of lifestyles: in Syria, for example, we find examples of "stylites", people who chose to live on pillars. Contemporary research reminds us that Syriac monasticism is at least as ancient as Egyptian, and developed quite independently; but in Syria there was no single model or founder like Antony. Elsewhere, in Cappadocia, a more learned, liturgical, and social monasticism appeared under the inspiration and influence of Basil the Great (d. 379). In Palestine the profound tradition of spiritual direction was established by Isaiah of Scetis (d. 489), Barsanuphius and John (both d. *c*.543), Dorotheus of Gaza (d. *c*.560), Euthymius (d. 473) and Sa[v]vas (d. 532). On Sinai a more silent, or "hesychast", spirituality was founded by John Klimakos (d. *c*.649) whose *Ladder of Divine Ascent* was so influential in the development of the Jesus prayer.

The remarkable growth of monasticism was also apparent in Churches outside the Byzantine empire: this is true of Ethiopia, where the *Life of Antony* and the *Life of Pachomius* were among the first books to be translated; it is also true of Mesopotamia, where the great organizer Abraham of Kashkar (d. 586) lived; it is furthermore true of Armenia, where monasteries such as Echmiadzin became active spiritual and cultural centres; it is true, finally, of Georgia, where monasticism was attributed to the "13 Fathers" from Syria.

Naturally, the flowering of monasticism was still more remarkable within the Roman empire. Egypt always remained an active centre, but already by 518 Constantinople numbered some 70 communities for men alone. Monks became increasingly influential in ecclesiastical and social life: they intervened in theological disputes; they informed liturgy and spirituality; they inspired the laity, who tended to follow the charismatic leaders of monasticism; gradually, even the order of the episcopate was restricted to monks.

The monks were always passionate in their defence of theological principles, and especially of the doctrine that in the person of Christ human and divine natures were reconciled. It was this doctrine that monastics pursued with such ferocious intellectual vigour and ascetic rigour in their own struggle to unite body and soul. In the mind of the monastics, mystical theory and ascetic practice had a common vision. Theology and spirituality shared the same language. Union with God or vision of God (*theoria*) was made possible only through a life of spiritual purification and total renunciation, a self-stripping not only of material possessions, but even of intellectual projections. This was the way of negation, or of "apophatic" knowledge, whereby the unknown God was venerated through a series of negations that revealed God as "ever beyond". The apophatic approach was applied on the moral level (as purification from wrongful desires) as well as on the intellectual level (as a laying aside of worldly concepts and images of God).

Yet eastern monasticism in fact always manifested a greater degree of flexibility and a lesser emphasis on uniformity than religious life in the West. The Christian East never had someone like Benedict who would provide monastic life with a strict set of regulations or an order of life. Basil's "rules" are very different from the *Rule* of Augustine (d. 430) or of Benedict. And they are not nearly as systematic in form: his *Longer Rules* are a series of sermons on the monastic life, while his *Shorter Rules* are answers to questions raised by monastics as Basil visited the monasteries of his diocese. Even Theodore of Stoudios (d. 826), perhaps the greatest monastic authority after Basil, who instituted a significant reform during the 9th century, sought primarily to return to the early tradition of the East. His *Monastic Testament* by no means resembles the clarity and completeness of Benedict's writings. The entire development of the monastic communities on Mount Athos from the mid-10th century was based on Theodore. So there was no generally accepted rule or order. One simply became attached to a specific monastery with a particular tradition. The emphasis lay less on "stability" and more on "sitting in one's cell". In the *Sayings of the Desert Fathers*, Abba Moses (d. 407) reveals that "the cell teaches us everything".

The spirituality of the cell was inevitably connected to the life of silent prayer. And it was such prayer that constituted the primary social service of the Byzantine monastic. This is why, although some monastics existed in larger cities – Theodore's monastery, Stoudios, was in the centre of Constantinople – the classical notion of the monastery in the East was that it was situated in desolate areas, remote from civilization. Such deserted places were areas chosen for prayer: Mar Saba monastery in the Holy Land, St Catherine's monastery on Mount Sinai, the monastic republic of Mount Athos, and the rocks of Meteora in central Greece.

Any other service to the world was considered secondary, extrinsic to the essential vocation of the monk and nun. Their main purpose was prayer. And visitors to their monasteries expected to find places of prayer, to discover persons of prayer, and to encounter holy people with the gift of spiritual direction. In the West, monasteries often became nurseries of scholarship; but in the East, they were always centres of spirituality. In the West, at least by the 9th century, most monks were ordained; but in the East, Byzantine monasticism remained largely a lay movement, with only just enough priests in a given monastery for its liturgical needs.

Among the secondary or outward services of eastern monasteries were: (1) education – not as a scholarly skill, but as a manual labour for the more educated monastics. The monk was primarily a healer, not a teacher. (2) Evangelism – while few monasteries prepared monks for preaching, there were certain cases of individual monks who assumed this ministry (St Nikon in the 10th century and St Kosmas in the 18th century). (3) Spiritual direction – confessions were heard and advice was sought from monastics. This service is closely related to prayer. (4) Charitable work – there were examples of monasteries and many cases of monastics who performed this function of social welfare.

The most precious service of eastern monasticism was its ever-burning flame of prayer and spirituality. There was a monastery in Constantinople called "Akoimetoi" (literally, the sleepless ones), where prayer was ongoing, 24 hours a day, with monks taking turns to recite prayers.

The ideal in eastern monasticism always remained the life of the Spirit. Monastic life was an experience of charismatic enthusiasm, a Pentecostal reality. The monk was a "*pneumatophoros*" (Spirit-bearer), bearing witness to the abiding presence of the Spirit in the Church. One might even suggest that Antony and the less conspicuous monks of the Egyptian desert were, in a way, a more significant and lasting ingredient of the Byzantine tradition than many other cultural aspects held in such esteem by historians. More than any monuments and manuscripts, the Byzantine monastics – known and unknown – betray a mystical force and become icons, windows through which one is initiated into an entire tradition.

JOHN CHRYSSAVGIS

Further Reading

Brown, Peter, *The Body and Society: Men, Women, and Sexual Renunciation in Early Christianity*, New York: Columbia University Press, 1988; London: Faber, 1990

Chadwick, Owen, *John Cassian: A Study in Primitive Monasticism*, 2nd edition, London: Cambridge University Press, 1968

Chitty, Derwas J., *The Desert a City: An Introduction to the Study of Egyptian and Palestinian Monasticism under the Christian Empire*, Oxford: Blackwell, and Crestwood, New York: St Vladimir's Seminary Press, 1966

Clarke, W. K. Lowther, *St. Basil the Great: A Study in Monasticism*, Cambridge: Cambridge University Press, 1913

Evelyn-White, Hugh G., *The Monasteries of the Wadi'n Natrûn*, 3 vols, New York: Metropolitan Museum of Art, 1926–33; reprinted New York: Arno Press, 1973

Gould, Graham, *The Desert Fathers on Monastic Community*, Oxford: Clarendon Press, and New York: Oxford University Press, 1993

Griggs, C. Wilfred, *Early Egyptian Christianity: From its Origins to 451 CE*, Leiden and New York: Brill, 1990

Hardy, Edward Rochie, *Christian Egypt, Church and People: Christianity and Nationalism in the Patriarchate of Alexandria*, New York: Oxford University Press, 1952

Harvey, Susan Ashbrook, *Asceticism and Society in Crisis: John of Ephesus and the Lives of the Eastern Saints*, Berkeley: University of California Press, 1990

Malone, Edward Eugene, *The Monk and the Martyr: The Monk as the Successor of the Martyr*, Washington D.C.: Catholic University of America Press, 1950

Nicol, Donald M., *Meteora: The Rock Monasteries of Thessaly*, revised edition, London: Variorum, 1975

Nikonanes, Nikos, *Meteora: A Complete Guide to the Monasteries and their History*, Athens: Ekdotike Athenon, 1987

Rousseau, Philip, *Pachomius: The Making of a Community in Fourth-Century Egypt*, Berkeley: University of California Press, 1985

Vööbus, Arthur, *A History of Asceticism in the Syrian Orient*, 3 vols,
    Louvain: Corpus Scriptorum Christianorum Orientalium,
    1958–88
Wimbush, Vincent L. and Richard Valantasis, *Asceticism*, Oxford
    and New York: Oxford University Press, 1995

Monemvasia

Town in the southeast Peloponnese

Monemvasia is a fortified town that occupies a towering and
massively rocky coastal site in the southeast of the
Peloponnese; it is joined to the mainland by a causeway which
explains its name, which means "single entry". Its exceptional
strength as a stronghold has dominated its history from its
foundation, and accounts for its sobriquet, the "Gibraltar of
Greece". Evidence of pre-Christian habitation here is minimal,
but its foundation as a new town seems to have taken place in
the later 6th century AD, and during the Slav invasions it
became a place of refuge for the Laconians. There was already
a bishop of Monemvasia by 787, probably a suffragan of
Corinth; in the 10th century its bishop, called Paul, referred to
the town as a *kastron*. The great natural strength of
Monemvasia meant that its citizens were able to sustain a more
individualistic stance in relation to external powers, and it was
always to be the last outpost to fall to successive invaders.

The Monemvasiotes successfully repulsed an attempted
Norman invasion in 1147, and it was not until 1248 that the
Franks under William II de Villehardouin were able to capture
the town, more than 40 years after they had subdued the rest
of the Peloponnese, and then only after a two-year siege.
Fourteen years later the Byzantines recovered it, when William,
who had been taken prisoner at the battle of Pelagonia in
1259, had to cede four of his castles in the Morea as the price
of his freedom. Thereafter Monemvasia remained in Byzantine
hands until 1460, enjoying special trading privileges, which
were renewed on several occasions, and with its metropolitan
elevated by Michael VIII from the 34th to the 10th in the hierarchy of the whole Byzantine empire. Even the victorious
sultan, Mehmet II, refrained from trying to take it while subduing the rest of the Peloponnese.

After a brief spell of four years' subjugation to the papacy,
during which Pius II confirmed and renewed the city's trading
privileges, Monemvasia became one of the many Aegean
outposts of the empire of the Venetians, with their control
lasting from 1463 to 1540, and again from 1690 to 1715.
During the intervening years the town was subject to Turkish
rule, which came to an end in 1821 with one of the earlier
episodes of the Greek War of Independence. The Turkish garrison had capitulated after a four-month siege on terms that
involved their being allowed to embark in vessels that would
take them back to Asia Minor; such was the impregnability of
Monemvasia that these favourable terms had been proposed
by them, and accepted by the Greeks. The Turks were,
however, attacked as they entered their boats to leave, and
some were killed.

Two texts are associated with Monemvasia. One is the so-
called *Chronicle of Monemvasia* written in the 10th century by
a bishop of the town called Paul (mentioned above); the first
publication of the work, which exists in four 16th-century
manuscripts, all somewhat different, was in 1749. It describes
events in the Peloponnese between the 6th and the 9th
centuries, and recounts the abandonment of the region of
Lacedaemonia and the foundation of a new town called
Monemvasia. An added section covers some events from the
11th to the 14th centuries. The other text is in effect a forgery
that was probably composed by a 15th-century metropolitan
of Monmevasia, Makarios Melissenos; it is known as the
Chronicon maius of Sphrantzes, since Melissenos used the
Chronicon minus of the diplomat and historian as the basis of
his work, expanding and elaborating it to include a range of
extra material. The same metropolitan also forged an imperial
decree of Andronikos II Palaiologos (1282–1328), which he
stamped with a counterfeit seal, to establish (falsely) his rights
in a territorial dispute in the Peloponnese.

The buildings of Monemvasia are divided between the
Lower Town, entered through a massive fortified gateway, and
the Upper Town or Kastro, reached up a steep path and itself
heavily defended and with a long entrance tunnel. Of the 25
churches still to be seen in the Lower Town, 17 were either
built or restored during the second period of Venetian occupation, of 1690–1715. Among them is the cathedral, which is the
largest church in the province of Laconia, and dates from the

Monemvasia: the Byzantine town has been restored to provide holiday homes for wealthy Athenians

period when Andronikos II raised the town to metropolitan rank in 1293; it has the rare dedication of the Elkomenos Christou (literally "The dragging of Christ" [to the Crucifixion]), and it was largely renewed in 1597. An important icon of this subject was in the possession of this church, and was greatly coveted by the emperor Isaac II Angelos (1185–95), who had to employ deceit to obtain it; the large icon of the Crucifixion that is now in the Byzantine Museum, Athens, and which also came from this church, was probably one of a group of icons of the Passion that included the icon taken by Isaac II.

The Upper Town is still circled by continuous fortifications, and the highest point was dominated by a fortress of which ruins survive; by 1154 Monemvasia was said to have "a castle very high above the sea, from which one may look across to Crete", and these remains are no doubt a relic of this 12th-century stronghold. It was used by the Venetians as a powder magazine, and it exploded during a Turkish attack in 1589. But the most impressive building in Monemvasia is the church now known as Hagia Sophia; traditionally founded by Andronikos II, its plan follows the domed design of churches such as the *katholikon* (principal church) at Dafni near Athens, with the large cupola carried on an octagon of vaults giving maximum light and space to the area beneath. Until the 19th century its dedication was to the Theotokos Hodegetria.

By a curious irony, the form in which Monemvasia became best known in western Europe was not as one of the great natural European strongholds, but through the wine that was exported from here; this dark, sweet wine was known to the British by the name of Malmsey, and for the French *vin de Malvoisie*. Shakespeare's public would have recognized this association when the murderers of the Duke of the Clarence threaten him with drowning in a "malmsey butt" (*Richard III*, 1. 4).

PAUL HETHERINGTON

Summary

Perched on a massive rock on the southeast coast of the Peloponnese, Monemvasia has earned the nickname of "the Gibraltar of Greece". Perhaps founded in the 6th century AD, Monemvasia was not taken by the Franks until 1248 and was Byzantine again from 1259 to 1460. Mehmet II did not attempt to take it. It was in Venetian hands 1463–1540 and 1690–1715 and reverted to Greece in 1821. It is now being elegantly restored.

Further Reading

Elliott, W.R., *Monemvasia: The Gibraltar of Greece*, London: Dobson, 1971

Finlay, George, *A History of Greece from its Conquest by the Romans to the Present Time*, BC 146 to AD 1864, revised by H.F. Tozer, 7 vols, Oxford: Clarendon Press, 1877; reprinted New York: AMS Press, 1970, vol. 6

Hussey, J.M. (editor), *The Byzantine Empire*, Cambridge: Cambridge University Press, 1966 (*The Cambridge Medieval History*, vol. 4, part 1, 2nd edition)

Kalligas, Haris, *Byzantine Monemvasia: The Sources*, Monemvasia: Akroneon, 1990

Miller, William, *The Latins in the Levant: A History of Frankish Greece, 1204–1566*, London: John Murray, and New York: Dutton, 1908; reprinted Cambridge: Speculum Historiale, and New York: Barnes and Noble, 1964

Miller, William, *Essays on the Latin Orient*, Cambridge: Cambridge University Press, 1921; reprinted New York: AMS Press, 1983

Monophysites

Monophysites believe that in the person of the incarnate Christ humanity and Godhead were united in a single nature, as opposed to the orthodox doctrine, which teaches that after the Incarnation Christ should be acknowledged in two natures, perfect humanity and divinity, each retaining its own characteristics but united in one being. The rift between orthodox and Monophysite emerged slowly after the Council of Chalcedon in 451, until by the middle of the 6th century the Coptic, Nubian, Armenian, Ethiopian, much of the Syrian and Persian Churches, and parts of the Church in Asia Minor were Monophysite. Their theology was inspired by Cyril of Alexandria (patriarch 412–44) and by the theologian and teacher Severus, patriarch of Antioch from 512 to 518. Monophysitism was to contribute to a sense of national identity among the Copts, Nubians, Ethiopians, and Armenians.

The distant origins of Monophysitism may be traced back to interpretations of John 1:14 ("The Word became flesh and dwelt among us"). No theological issue arose, however, until the Council of Nicaea (325) in whose creed it was asserted that Christ was to be acknowledged as "of one substance with the Father". This safeguarded Christ's divinity but left his relation to humanity open. This latter question did not come to the fore until the 370s, near the end of the Arian controversy, when Apollinaris of Laodicea, a lifelong friend of Athanasius of Alexandria who shared many of his views, set out in radical terms how "one substance with the Father" should be understood. He asserted in a letter to the bishops of Syria that "the supreme point of our salvation is the incarnation of the Word", but that involved the Word becoming flesh without having assumed a human mind, which was subject to change and evil thoughts, "but existing as a divine mind immutable and heavenly". This view was sharply opposed by the Cappadocian Fathers who argued that "what he did not assume [i.e. manhood] he could not redeem". Apollinaris and his teaching were condemned at the Second Ecumenical Council in 381.

The question of the relation of the divine and human in the person of Christ was allowed to sleep for the next 45 years until in 428 Nestorius became archbishop of Constantinople while Cyril was archbishop (later patriarch) of Alexandria (412–44). The two major sees of eastern Christendom found themselves representing diametrically opposed understandings of the person of Christ. The resulting Council of Ephesus in June 431 (Third Ecumenical Council) condemned Nestorius. Cyril, however, in refuting his enemy, had used language that brought him near to the Apollinarian position. In his 12 Anathemas sent for Nestorius' assent in November 430 he spoke of "the one hypostasis [person] of the incarnate Word". This statement was not condemned by the council.

Cyril died in 444. His successor Dioscorus I (444–51, d. 454) was less cautious. He aimed not only at asserting Cyril's doctrine as the orthodoxy of Christendom as a whole, but also at vindicating the ecclesiastical superiority of Alexandria over Constantinople. Alexandria was in his eyes "the city of the orthodox". He found an ally in Constantinople in the monk Eutyches who asserted that the flesh of Christ was "God-made", and so Christ could in no sense be "consubstantial with us". Eutyches was condemned by a council presided over by Flavian, archbishop of Constantinople, on 22

November 448, but not before he had produced as proof of the veracity of his views a number of tracts written under the name of orthodox churchmen, including Athanasius and pope Julius I, which in fact were forgeries compiled by disciples of Apollinaris. Eutyches appealed to what he called the councils of other archiepiscopal sees, and this brought Rome into the debate. Early in 449, however, the emperor Theodosius II (408–50) convoked a new council to meet at Ephesus under Dioscorus' presidency. This resulted in the acquittal of Eutyches, the condemnation of Flavian and his fellow archbishop Domnus of Antioch, and the discomfiture of pope Leo's legates. A tract written by Leo in defence of Flavian, setting out the views of the papacy, known as the *Tome* of Leo, in which the two natures of Christ, human and divine, were affirmed, was conveniently not read. Dioscorus appeared to be triumphant.

Theodosius died on 28 July 450 from a fall from his horse, and there was an immediate reaction at the imperial court at Constantinople. A new council was summoned, to meet at Chalcedon (on the east side of the Bosporus) at the end of October 451.

This time the decisions went against Alexandria. Dioscorus was deposed, though for "indiscipline" rather than doctrinal heresy, and the sentence against Eutyches confirmed. A Definition of Faith was drawn up that declared that Jesus Christ "was made known to us in two natures unconfusedly, unchangeably, indivisibly, and inseparably", the "properties of each being in no way removed because of the union, but each nature being preserved and concurring into one Prosopon [outward personality] and one Hypostasis". Christ in two natures after the Incarnation had been affirmed and unity between Rome and Constantinople restored. However, the 28th canon of the council confirmed a decision taken by the Second Ecumenical Council, that Constantinople as New Rome was the chief bishopric in Christendom, though yielding a primacy of honour to Rome itself. This was Constantinople's title deed, and the reason why Chalcedon could never be renounced in its entirety. It was, however, unacceptable to Rome, not least because no reference was made to Peter and the Petrine primacy.

The next two centuries were to be occupied by increasingly desperate but unsuccessful efforts to find compromises between the one-nature and two-nature Christologies, and the questions of ecclesiastical primacy raised in the Second Council of Ephesus and Chalcedon. The subsequent disputes fall into four phases: (1) from Chalcedon to the *Henotikon* of Zeno (451–82); (2) the Acacian schism (482–519); (3) the Chalcedonian reaction (519–36); and (4) the final parting, post 536.

The decisions of Chalcedon were well received in Constantinople, Antioch, and Rome, but were greeted with explosions of popular anger in Jerusalem and Alexandria. Imperial troops restored order in Jerusalem allowing the double-faced patriarch Juvenal to return to his see. In Alexandria, however, the anti-Chalcedonians found leaders in Timothy Aelurus ("the Cat") and Peter Mongus ("the hoarse one"), both supporters of Eutyches. In March 457 Proterius, the Council of Chalcedon's choice as patriarch, was lynched and Timothy consecrated in his stead. The imperial government, with Leo I (457–74) as emperor, stepped in, and between

459 and 475 Timothy was in exile in the south Russian town of Kherson. At length, events forced the government to compromise. An 18-month usurpation by Basiliscus (January 475–August 476) aimed against Leo's successor Zeno (474–91), and the victory of the anti-Chalcedonian party in Antioch, where opponents of Chalcedon found a leader in Peter "the Fuller", led to the publication by Zeno of the Instrument of Unity (*Henotikon*) on 28 July 482. In this the emperor asserted that the safety of the Roman world depended on a universal acceptance of the creed of Nicaea confirmed at Constantinople (in 381). Both Eutyches and Nestorius were condemned, but Cyril's "one-nature" statements contained in his 12 Anathemas were upheld, and Christ "incarnate of the Virgin" was to be acknowledged as "one and not two". Anyone who taught anything different, "either at Chalcedon or any other synod whatever, we anathematize". The emperor (not a Church council) had spoken.

The *Henotikon* remained the official doctrine of the empire for 37 years. It was accepted by Alexandria, Antioch, Jerusalem, and Constantinople, but not by Rome. Pope Felix III (484–92) condemned it. The opponents of Chalcedon had no intention, however, of seceding from the Church administered and guided by the emperor and his patriarch, Acacius. The schism between Rome and Constantinople over the latter was not concerned principally with doctrinal difference, but with the question whether Acacius had deceived pope Simplicius (468–83) by denouncing Peter Mongus as "a son of darkness" and then accepting him as patriarch of Alexandria in succession to Timothy "the Cat".

The schism lasted from 483 to 519. In the meantime, the empire, governed by Zeno and Anastasius (491–518), moved steadily in the direction of one-nature Christology. Only the Latin-speaking provinces in the western Balkans remained wholeheartedly in favour of the Chalcedonian definition. The decisive moment came in 508 when Severus, a monk from a monastery at Maiuma, near Gaza in Palestine, was appealing against the pro-Chalcedonian attitude of Elias, patriarch of Jerusalem. Severus was a thrusting character as well as a fluent representative of one-nature Christology. He quickly gained the ear of the emperor Anastasius.

Meanwhile, the scene moved to Antioch, where in 510 Severus' ally, Philoxenus of Mabboug (Hieropolis) in Syria, quarrelled with his superior, the patriarch Flavian II of Antioch. To prevent an outright schism Anastasius promulgated a Formula of Satisfaction in 511. This document was ostensibly based on the *Henotikon* but denounced the *Tome* of Leo, and reduced the council of Chalcedon to the level of a disciplinary synod, while retaining the validity of the all-important canon 28. Next year Severus persuaded Anastasius to get rid of the patriarch Macedosius of Constantinople, while in 512 Philoxenus secured the same fate for Flavian II. In November 512 Severus became patriarch of Antioch and the anti-Chalcedonian movement became explicitly Monophysite.

Severus was originally from Sozopolis in Pisidia (Asia Minor), but he became leader of the movement whose two centres were Alexandria and Antioch. His theology was based uncompromisingly on what he believed had been that of Cyril of Alexandria. Everything that Cyril wrote, he stated (*Select Letters*, l. 9), should be regarded as canonical. He was prepared to accept the *Henotikon* and disciplinary decisions against Dioscorus and Eutyches; his one-nature Christology had a place for Christ's consubstantiality with man: "In the last times He [the Divine Word]" took flesh of the Holy Spirit, and of the holy Theotokos and Ever-Virgin Mary, flesh consubstantial with us and animated by an intelligent and reasoning soul. "The same being was both God and man". Out of two natures there was now one. He was in consequence unsparing in his denunciation of pope Leo and his *Tome*, condeming it as self-contradictory and "Jewish", though he praised popes, supposedly forerunners of Monophysitism, such as Julius I, whose name the Apollinarians had appropriated.

The death of Anastasius on 9 July 518 brought about an immediate change. Justin I (518–27) was a Latin-speaker from Illyricum and he made his first aim that of restoring communion with the Roman see. The "two Romes" should work in harmony on the basis of mutual acceptance of the Council of Chalcedon and the removal of all traces of the Acacian schism. The latter was accomplished at the end of March 519, but Rome received no satisfaction regarding canon 28. Severus, however, found himself an exile in Alexandria, and 55 bishops, including Philoxenus, suspected of Monophysite leanings were similarly deposed between 519 and 522. Only in Egypt were the Monophysites left alone.

These arrests and depositions deprived numerous congregations, especially in Syria, of their pastors. The result was that by 530 pressure to ordain clergy not in communion with the see of Constantinople became overwhelming. John of Ephesus records how "every day 100 or sometimes 200 or 300 presented themselves for ordination … It was like a river that had burst its banks." Confronted with the prospect of a permanent Monophysite schism, the new emperor Justinian (527–65) summoned orthodox and Monophysite leaders to a conference. Discussions lasted from February 532 to March 533. Agreement was nearly reached on the Theopaschite formula put forward by the emperor himself. This confessed that both the miracles and the sufferings of Christ were to be attributed to the same being, so that on the cross "one of the Trinity suffered for us". While Leo's *Tome* could be rejected, Chalcedon could not, and hence the division persisted.

Justinian left the door open for reconciliation with Severus, now embarrassed by a dispute with fellow exile Julian of Halicarnassus and his followers, who asserted that since Adam had been created incorruptible and immortal, and his fall had been the consequence of sin, Christ must also have been free from sin, and hence his flesh was incorruptible. Severus disagreed, arguing that Christ's body only assumed those qualities after the Resurrection. Esoteric though this dispute may have seemed, Julian won sufficient support in Egypt to threaten Severus' authority.

This, however, was bolstered by the emergence of the empress Theodora as a champion of the Monophysite cause. In 535 she influenced her husband to bring Severus to Constantinople. Here he persuaded the new patriarch, Anthimus of Trebizond, to accept the Monophysite thesis. The triumph was short-lived. Next year pope Agapetus visited the capital on a mission from king Theodahad, the Ostrogoth ruler of Italy. He persuaded Justinian to depose Anthimus on the grounds that his transfer from Trebizond to Constantinople was an offence against canon 15 of the Council of Nicaea which forbade bishops to move from one see to another. A letter signed by Justinian and Agapetus re-emphasized the orthodoxy of two-nature Christology. In June 536 a synod held at Constantinople excommunicated Anthimus and Severus as heretics, and persecution was renewed against other Monophysite leaders. Next year a Chalcedonian patriarchate was established in Alexandria. Severus' colleague Theodosius, elected patriarch despite Julianist opposition in 535, was ordered to Constantinople. The schism was now complete.

Justinian's aim of uniting the Church ultimately under a Theopaschite formula was frustrated by two events. First, with the aid of Theodora, a Monophysite mission to the Nubian kingdom of Nobatia succeeded from 542 onwards in converting that kingdom and later its southern neighbours Makouria and Alwah to Monophysite Christianity. Secondly, Jacob Baradaeus, bishop of Edessa, fleeing as a fugitive from the emperor's police, travelled the length and breadth of Syria and Asia Minor ordaining bishops and other clergy in opposition to the Chalcedonians (hence the name Jacobites for the Syrian Monophysites). By his death in 578 a new, hierarchically constituted Monophysite Church had come into being.

At the Fifth Ecumenical Council in 553 the emperor again tried to conciliate the Monophysites by having Theodore of Mopsuestia, Ibas of Edessa, and Theodoret of Cyrrhus condemned as inspirers and supporters of Nestorius. This merely led to a crisis among the western Churches without winning over the Monophysites.

Justinian's successor, Justin II (565–78), influenced by his wife Sophia, published two versions of a *Henotikon* (567 and 571) conciliatory to the Monophysites, though without explicitly condemning Chalcedon as they demanded. When repression again failed, the Monophysite Churches were in general left in peace through the reigns of Maurice Tiberius (578–82) and his successor, Maurice (582–602). In these years, largely due to the development of monasteries as landowners and their consequent influence over their tenants, Monophysitism consolidated its hold in Syria and Egypt. A tradition preserved in the *History of the Patriarchs* tells of an area near Alexandria where "there were 600 flourishing monasteries all inhabited by the orthodox", and that "their cultivators all held the true faith [Monophysitism]".

The Persian occupation of Syria and Egypt between 614 and 630 favoured the Monophysites, as being Christians opposed to the creed of the emperor. Herakleios's victory over the invaders in 630 produced one final effort to end the schism. The attempt in 633–34, however, to win first the Syrian and then the Egyptian Monophysites to a formula based on acknowledging a single source of activity, *energeia*, in the incarnate Christ, failed largely due to the highhandedness of Herakleios's viceroy in Egypt, Cyrus "the Caucasian". In protest, from now on, Monophysitism in Egypt was associated with the Copts as opposed to the "imperial" Melchite Church. When ultimately Herakleios published the *Ekthesis* in 638 asserting the single will in Christ (Monothelitism), the loss of Syria and Egypt to the Arabs rendered this as well as all previous efforts to repair the schism futile.

The dispute over acknowledging the incarnate Christ as "out of two natures, one", or "out of two natures, two", proved insoluble. Through the 6th century it marked a division between Constantinople and its richest provinces, gradually fostering a spirit of independence in these. On the other hand, it contributed to the permanent rift between Constantinople and Rome, as the imperial capital strove to reconcile the views of the papacy and the majority of the eastern provincials. These reflected the ideas of the great monasteries which had come to own the land on which they worked. Though the debate was conducted throughout in terms of Hellenistic philosophy and theology, Monophysitism gradually provided a national identity for the Copts, Nubians, Armenians, and Ethiopians, preserving the national languages from absorption into a Greek lingua franca. From a dispute over wording, Monophysitism proved to be the major issue between Constantinople and the rest of Christendom from Chalcedon to the Arab invasions.

WILLIAM H.C. FREND

See also Councils, Schism

Summary

Monophysites believe a One-nature Christology, that the incarnate Christ is one person in which humanity and Godhead are united in a single nature. The movement began in the first half of the 5th century and found support in Alexandria. The Council of Chalcedon (451) condemned the Monophysites but the differences were not resolved. The movement has persisted and forms part of the cultural identity of Copts, Nubians, Armenians, and Ethiopians.

Texts

Severus of Antioch, *The Sixth Book of the Select Letters of Severus, Patriarch of Antioch*, edited and translated by E.W. Brooks, London: Williams and Norgate, 1902–04, reprinted Farnborough: Gregg, 1969

Severus of Antioch, *A Collection of Letters*, edited and translated by E.W. Brooks, Paris: Firmin Didot, 1919–20 (Patrologia Orientalis 12.2 and 14)

Severus of Antioch, *Le Philalethe*, edited and translated by Robert Hespel, 2 vols, Louvain: Durbecq, 1952 (Syriac text and French translation; Corpus Scriptorum Christianorum Orientalum, Scriptores Syri 68–69)

Further Reading

Draguet, René, *Julien d'Halicarnasse et sa controverse avec Sévère d'Antioche sur l'incorruptibilité du corps du Christ*, Louvain: Smeesters, 1924

Engberding, P.H., "Das chalkedonische Christusbild und die liturgien der monophysistischen Kirchen-Gemeinschaften" in *Das Konzil Chalkedon*, edited by Aloys Grillmeier and Heinrich Bacht, vol. 2, Würzberg: Echter, 1953

Frend, W.H.C., *The Rise of the Monophysite Movement: Chapters in the History of the Church in the Fifth and Sixth Centuries*, Cambridge: Cambridge University Press, 1972

Frend, W.H.C., Monophysitism entry in *The Coptic Encyclopedia*, edited by Aziz S. Atiya, New York: Macmillan, 1991, vol. 4, pp. 1669–78

Grillmeier, Aloys, *Christ in Christian Tradition*, 2nd edition, 2 vols, London: Mowbray, and Atlanta: John Knox Press, 1975–95

Lebon, J., "La Christologie du Monophysisme syrien" in *Das Konzil Chalkedon*, edited by Aloys Grillmeier and Heinrich Bacht, vol. 1, Würzberg: Echter, 1951

MacCoull, J.S.B., "A Monphysite Trishagion for the Nile Valley", *Journal of Theological Studies*, new series 40 (1989): pp. 29–35

Meyendorff, John, *Christ in Eastern Christian Thought*, Washington, DC: Corpus, 1969

Simonetti, M., Monophysitism-Monophysites entry in *Encyclopedia of the Early Church*, edited by Angelo Di Berardino, 2 vols,

Cambridge: James Clarke, and New York: Oxford University Press, 1992, vol. 1, pp. 569–70

Montenegro

In its early history Montenegro (Crna Gora in Serbian) was part of Illyricum and the Roman province of Dalmatia. After Diocletian's administrative reforms of 297, it was included in the newly created province of Praevalitania. The nature of its mountainous terrain in the hinterland of the Adriatic coast (a section which in modern times stretches from the gulf of Kotor to Ulcinj and the Albanian border) played a noticeable role in its history. In the pre-Roman period there was a strong influence of Greek culture, especially along the coast. Trade was lively between the nearby Greek colonies at Lissos (Lješ) and Epidaurus (Cavtat) on the one hand, and the Illyrian maritime settlements, especially Buthua (Budva) and Rhizon (Risan), on the other. It is believed that the region east of Rhizon was the land of the Encheleans, to whom the Greek myth of Cadmus and Harmonia is linked. Their rocks were situated on the gulf of Kotor, which to ancient authors was know as the mouth of the Rhizon river. Traces of an ancient serpent cult point to the tradition of the Cadmus-Harmonia myth; it is corroborated by archaeological finds and survives in some folkloric customs.

According to a legend preserved in *De Administrando Imperio* by Constantine VII Porphyrogennetos (945–59), the foundation of Dioclea, originally a *kastron* (fort) at the confluence of the rivers Morača and Zeta, is ascribed to Diocletian himself. Although this is historically incorrect, Dioclea's early prominence is confirmed not only by archaeological remains dating from the pre-Christian period onward, but also by the fact that its name (Duklja) was eventually applied to the whole region. In the Middle Ages it was also known as Zeta. The earliest recorded mention of the name Crna Gora is in a charter issued by the Serbian king Stephan Uroš II Milutin (1282–1321), but it became current only in modern times.

With the gradual spread of Christianity, Skutari (Skadar) became the seat of an archbishop in the 4th century. First under the jurisdiction of the exarch of Thessalonica, it came under that of Justiniana Prima after 535.

The political and economic structure of Praevalitania's Romanized cities, based on trade as well as on the resources provided by livestock rearing, agriculture, exploitation of mines, and handicraft, crumbled under the attacks of Avars and Slavs in the 7th century, but its cultural achievements left an imprint on later periods.

Constantine Porphyrogennetos reports that, after a first attempt at Christianization during the reign of Herakleios (610–41), Serbs who settled in the regions of Travunia, Konavli, Zahumlie, and Dioklea were converted in the 9th century, during the reign of Basil I. Similar data are gathered from the *Chronicle of Bar* by the anonymous 12th-century author known as the Priest of Dioclea. There is evidence that the beginnings of Slavonic literacy in these parts, resulting from the missionary work of the disciples of St Cyril and St Methodios, also occurred in the 9th century. In the same period there emerged the beginnings of the cult of some eastern saints, among them St Tryphon, patron saint of Kotor, and St

Sergius and St Bacchus, whose shrine was on the Bojana river, near Skadar. In memory of the Syrian city where St Sergius was martyred, Skadar was sometimes referred to as Rosafa.

The rise to power of prince Stephan Vojislav of Dioclea (Zeta) represented a serious challenge to Byzantine rule. In 1042, near Antivari (Bar), Vojislav defeated the Byzantine army sent from Dyrrachium and created an independent state. Further blows to Byzantium were dealt by his son Michael, who in 1077 received a royal crown from Pope Gregory VII and became his vassal. Michael's son Constantine Bodin enlarged the realm by joining to it Raška and Bosnia. Soon, however, the centre of power in Serbian lands moved to Raška. During the reign of the grand župan (satrap) Stephan Nemanja (1169–96) Zeta and Raška were united and remained one state until the death of tsar Stephan Uroš IV Dushan, in 1355. Like Nemanja himself, who established his court in Kotor, all rulers of his dynasty accorded Zeta a privileged position in the realm. Zeta provided a vital link for commerce with Italy, Dubrovnik, and other Adriatic cities. One of the inland routes, leading from the coast, north of Lake Skadar, through Peć, the field of Kosovo to Niš, and further to Bulgaria, was named Via de Zenta.

In the cultural sphere, an attractive symbiosis of western and Byzantine influences prevailed in the ever-increasing building activity in the region. As old ecclesiastical centres in Zeta's coastal towns were left outside the jurisdiction of the Byzantine archdiocese of Ohrid (created around 1019), their gravitation towards Rome was reinforced after the Great Schism of 1054. The situation remained unchanged during the Nemanjić period and members of the ruling family often made donations to Catholic establishments. However, Orthodoxy spread in the surrounding countryside and in the hinterland, especially after the creation of the autocephalous Serbian Church in 1219, with Nemanja's youngest son Sava at its head. As scores of Orthodox churches and monasteries were built in the newly founded bishoprics of Zeta, connections with the Greek-speaking world increased, thanks to the strong spiritual and material links with Thessalonica and Mount Athos. Wall paintings dating from 1252 preserved at Morača, in a church built by Nemanja's grandson Stephan, and smaller fragments in St Peter at Bogdašić, near Tivat, built by Neophyt, the Serbian bishop of Zeta, in 1268–69, rank among the highest achievements in the art of the Byzantine world.

When circumstances allowed it, church-building revived in the Ottoman period: a remarkable monument is the monastery of Piva, with wall paintings dating from 1605. Of great historical importance are clusters of churches, now mostly in ruins, in the Lake Skadar area: Starčeva Gorica, Beška, Prečista Krajinska, Moračnik, and others.

With the disintegration of central authority in the second half of the 14th century, Montenegro's feudal lords, former heads of clans, were involved in the turbulent events caused by the coming of the Turks. The families Balšić and Crnojević gained prominence in this early phase of a protracted period of conflict over the Adriatic, in which the Ottoman empire, Venice, and other European powers were chief protagonists. For a long time, deprived of its coast and under constant Turkish attacks, a tiny Montenegro, reduced to its most inaccessible parts with the centre at Cetinje, maintained a variable degree of autonomy. The land was governed by a council of clan leaders, headed by successive bishops, among whom was the celebrated poet Petar II Petrović-Njegoš (1830–51). In Njegoš's works, with the tragic position of his people as his main concern, elements of poetry inspired by Classical authors and those of Romanticism are brilliantly woven into his own Orthodox spirituality.

As the Ottoman empire weakened, the virtual independence of Montenegro spread over a wider territory. This was not always readily sanctioned by the Great Powers, but the Montenegrins' frequent rebellions against the Turks, their courage and perseverance, earned them renown and sympathy abroad.

A kingdom under Nicholas I from 1910, Montenegro was victorious in the Balkan Wars (1912–13) with its Greek, Serbian, Bulgarian, and Romanian allies, when much of its territory was regained, except for lands given to the newly created state of Albania. In 1918 Montenegro joined Serbia in "The Kingdom of Serbs, Croats, and Slovenes", soon to be called Yugoslavia.

ZAGA GAVRILOVIĆ

Further Reading

Bešić, Zarije et al., *Istorija Crne Gore*, vol. 1, Titograd, 1967

Blagojević, Miloš and Momčilo Spremić, "Slom Crnojevića" in *Istorija Srpskog Naroda*, vol. 2, edited by Jovanka Kalić, Belgrade, 1982

Božić, Ivan, "Potiskivanje pravoslavlja" in *Istorija Srpskog Naroda*, vol. 2, edited by Jovanka Kalić, Belgrade, 1982

Ćirković, Sima et al., *Istorija Crne Gore*, vol. 2 (parts 1 and 2), Titograd, 1970

Ćirković, Sima, "Osamostavljivanje i uspon dukljanske države" in *Istorija Srpskog Naroda*, vol. 1, edited by Sima Ćirković, Belgrade, 1981

Djurić, Vojislav, "Raško i primorsko graditeljstvo" in *Istorija Srpskog Naroda*, vol. 1, edited by Sima Ćirković, Belgrade, 1981

Djurić, Vojislav, "Crkva Sv. Petra u Bogdašiću i njene freske", *Zograf*, 16 (1985): pp. 26–40

Durham, Mary E., *Through the Lands of the Serb*, London: Arnold, 1904

Evans, Arthur, *Illyrian Letters: A Revised Selection of Correspondence from the Illyrian Provinces of Bosnia, Herzegovina, Montenegro, Albania, Dalmatia, Croatia, and Slavonia, Addressed to the Manchester Guardian during the Year 1877*, London: Longman, 1878

Foster, I.L. (editor), *Jugoslavia*, vol. 2: *History, Peoples and Administration*, London: Naval Intelligence Division, 1944

Goldsworthy, Vesna, *Inventing Ruritania: The Imperialism of the Imagination*, New Haven and London: Yale University Press, 1998

Goy, E.D. *The Sabre and the Song: Njegoš, The Mountain Wreath*, Belgrade: Serbian PEN Centre, 1995

Jelavich, Barbara, *History of the Balkans*, vol. 1: *Eighteenth and Nineteenth Centuries*, Cambridge and New York: Cambridge University Press, 1983

Korać, Vojislav, *Crkva Svetog Luke u Kotoru*, Kotor, 1997

Skovran, Anika, *Art Treasures of Piva Monastery*, Cetinje and Belgrade, 1980

Spremić, Momčilo, "Pripajanje Zete Despotovini i širenje mletačke vlasti u Primorju" in *Istorija Srpskog Naroda*, vol. 2, edited by Jovanka Kalić, Belgrade, 1982

Stanojević, Gligor and Milan Vasić, *Istorija Crne Gore*, vol. 3 (part 1), Titograd, 1975

West, Rebecca, *Black Lamb and Grey Falcon: A Journey through Yugoslavia*, 2 vols., New York: Viking, 1941; London: Macmillan, 1942

Mosaic

Mosaic is a surface decoration consisting of different particles, such as stone or glass, set in a foundation, usually a mortar bed. It is primarily a form of monumental decoration, but it may also be used on a small scale.

The earliest mosaics, dating from the 4th millennium BC, were found in Mesopotamia. Mosaics existed in ancient Egypt and Minoan Crete, ancient Greece, the Roman Empire, and its Christian successor states, as well as in the medieval Islamic world. There are extensive survivals of early Christian and medieval mosaics in Italy, but the importance of mosaic as an art form there diminished in the Renaissance; north of the Alps mosaic was used only sporadically during the Middle Ages. In Byzantium the medium was exploited on a vast scale, even though its use as the most expensive form of Orthodox Church decoration declined in the second half of the 14th century. Mosaic was revived as a monumental decoration in western Europe in the 19th century, and continued to be employed in the 20th.

Even though pebbles and other natural materials are used for mosaics, in its more developed form it is made from square or rectangular particles specially shaped for the purpose, known as *tesserae* (Latin: "dice"). The more regular shape of the tesserae makes for greater precision in laying the mosaics and allows for special visual effects. The size of the tesserae is often varied, small cubes being used for faces and hands and larger ones for drapery and backgrounds. Apart from different types of stone, tesserae are made of glass and terracotta, but mother-of-pearl, shells, and semi-precious stones have also been found among mosaics. At times, mosaics are touched up with paint.

Glass tesserae are found in Roman mosaics from the 1st century AD. They were employed primarily in wall mosaics, because their brittleness did not make them suitable for floor covers. The effects of glass mosaic on walls were exploited fully only in the medieval period. Ancient and medieval glass was made from sand, potash, and lime and coloured with metal oxides; tesserae were produced by breaking sheets of glass into small particles. Gold tesserae were made by placing gold leaf on a sheet of glass and then enclosing it within another layer of glass. In early gold tesserae the lower layer of glass was colourless, but from the 8th century onwards red glass came to be used, adding lustre to the metal. Silver tesserae are made by using either silver or tin leaf. Gold and silver tesserae were rarely used before the 4th century AD.

Wall mosaics were executed in situ on a scaffolding. The tesserae were placed in the last of several layers of mortar or plaster that coated the wall (on curved surfaces nails or clamps served to hold the plaster in position). The final layer of plaster was applied in patches corresponding in size to the amount of tesserae that could be laid by the mosaicists before the plaster dried up. Rough outline drawings or, at times, highly finished paintings (e.g. at the Kariye Camii in Istanbul) were applied directly to the plaster to guide the craftsmen. Very little is known about the working methods of mosaicists. The 12th-century mosaics in the church of the Nativity at Bethlehem are signed by a certain Ephraim who identifies himself as a painter and mosaicist, but usually there was probably a distinction between artists designing the imagery and those executing the

mosaics, not to mention artisans specializing in preparing the plaster bed. Mosaicists are likely to have worked in teams. Larger areas requiring a single colour may have been worked on by apprentices, leaving the faces and other details to more highly skilled craftsmen. In order to facilitate the laying of mosaics, the tesserae were probably sorted into trays according to colour and size. A technical examination of the 11th-century mosaics in St Sophia at Kiev, which appear to have been executed by Byzantine craftsmen, has given some idea of the speed at which mosaics were laid: the 640 square metres of mosaic were executed in 320 days.

Even though there are some examples of mosaics on the outside of churches, especially in the Italian peninsula, wall mosaics are essentially a medium for the interior of buildings. In dimly lit interiors and on curved surfaces they are a visually more effective medium than fresco. In Byzantine art, in particular, the properties of mosaic are exploited to full effect. Mosaicists used the curved surfaces of domes, squinches, and apses to catch the natural light in order to make the mosaics sparkle and glitter. The refraction of natural light on the tesserae is enhanced by the irregular surfaces; cubes tilted at different angles and irregularly spaced are essential to creating glitter. Mosaic is, however, an inflexible medium because it consists of blocks of pure colour. But because mosaics were designed to be seen from a distance, mosaicists were able to overcome this limitation and created, in the eyes of viewers, the optical illusion of colour gradation.

The earliest surviving mosaics from ancient Greece are the pebble mosaics from Gordium in Asia Minor (8th century BC). Pebbles were used to represent mythological scenes at Olynthus (c.400 BC) and Pella (4th century BC), both in northern Greece. Gradually, mosaic makers realized the advantages of using tesserae. At the temple of Zeus at Olympia pebbles are used in conjunction with cut stones. Mosaics made of tesserae from the 2nd century BC exist on the island of Delos. Pergamum was an important centre of mosaic production. Sosos, who, according to Pliny the Younger was the most famous mosaicist of the ancient world, is said to have been active there. He is credited with having invented the motif of the *asarotos oikos* ("unswept floor") and of doves perched on a vase, both motifs being widely used in Hellenistic mosaics. Greek mosaicists were active at Pompeii, as is suggested by the name Dioscurides of Samos, which is found in two Pompeian mosaics. The surviving mosaics at Herculaneum include not only floor but also wall mosaics, as well as mosaics embellishing garden furnishings, such as fountains and niches. There are extensive survivals of late Roman mosaic floors at Antioch (3rd century AD). The bucolic scenes in the floor mosaic of the imperial palace at Constantinople are a very late example of this tradition, dating from the 7th century AD. Floor mosaics also occur in some Christian churches (Aquileia, 4th century; Palestine, 6th and 7th centuries; 12th-century France and Italy), but the rarity of such floors indicates that Christian subject matter was generally considered unsuitable for floors.

The earliest surviving Christian wall mosaics are found in Rome (crypt of Old St Peter's, c.330, Santa Costanza, c.350, and Santa Maria Maggiore, 432–40) and in Ravenna (Mausoleum of Galla Placidia, c.430–50, and the Orthodox Baptistery, c.460). The earliest extant mosaic decoration in the Greek-speaking part of the Roman empire is in the church of

Mosaic: Apollo (right) and Daphne in a mosaic panel from the House of Dionysus, Nea Paphos, Cyprus, 3rd century AD

Hagios Georgios in Thessalonica, formerly the mausoleum of Galerius (died 311); they date from the 5th century, marking perhaps the conversion of the mausoleum into a church. The surviving sections of this mosaic show a series of over-life-size male saints against an elaborate architectural backdrop on a gold background. Other early Christian mosaics in Thessalonica are the fragments in the 5th-century church of the Theotokos Acheiropoietos and the apse decoration in the church of the Latomos monastery (now called Osios David), dating from the 5th or 6th century. This mosaic, which shows Christ enthroned on a rainbow in the presence of St John and an Old Testament prophet, is the earliest extant apse mosaic in the Greek world. The last of the major schemes of mosaic decoration in Thessalonica prior to the iconoclast controversy are the now largely destroyed mosaics in the church of St Demetrios, dating from the early 7th century, which present a visual hagiography of the saint.

When Ravenna was incorporated into the Byzantine empire by Justinian's army, the city had a rich tradition of mosaic decoration (San Apollinare Nuovo, c.500, and the Arian Baptistery, c.500–25, in addition to the buildings mentioned above). Justinian, the empress Theodora, and their court are shown on two large panels among the 6th-century mosaics in San Vitale. The imperial couple do not appear to have been involved in the embellishment of the church. Two 6th-century schemes of mosaic decoration are far more closely associated with Justinian, occurring in buildings commissioned by the emperor. These are the earliest mosaics at Hagia Sophia in Constantinople, depicting crosses as well as geometric and floral motifs on a gold background (532–37), and the apse decoration in the main church of St Catherine's monastery at Mount Sinai, showing the Transfiguration (c.565/67).

The aniconic nature of the early mosaics at Hagia Sophia undoubtedly contributed to their survival during the period of iconoclasm. A mosaic in a small room in the patriarchal palace next to the church demonstrates the fate of many religious figurative mosaics during the iconoclast period. These mosaics show two crosses, the main form of religious decoration during iconoclasm. Golden tessarae underneath the cross show signs of disturbance. There are remnants of inscriptions, indicating that the crosses replace pre-iconoclast depictions of saints. Most iconoclast mosaic decoration was replaced with figurative decoration after the end of iconoclasm. This process could be seen in the apse mosaic of the church of the Dormition at Nicaea (Iznik), now destroyed. The ghostly outlines of a cross appear behind a depiction on the mosaic of the Virgin and Child. The apse mosaic at Iznik consisted of three different phases: a pre-iconoclast Virgin and Child, an iconoclast cross, and a post-iconoclast figurative image. Documentary evidence suggests that the art of mosaic making flourished during the iconoclast period in secular contexts, decorating imperial palaces. Mosaic decorations in the Dome of the Rock in Jerusalem (680s) and the great mosques in Damascus (c.715) and Córdoba (961–68), which appear to have been executed by Byzantine craftsmen, testify to the vitality of Byzantine mosaic decoration during and immediately after iconoclasm.

Most of the mosaic decoration at Hagia Sophia dates from the post-iconoclast period. The apse mosaic of the Virgin and Child enthroned was dedicated in 867 and the series of patriarchs in the tympanum dates from the late 9th century. The Great Church contains a number of mosaics showing emperors and empresses. These include an emperor in *proskynesis* (veneration) before Christ above the royal doors opening into the nave of the church (late 9th to early 10th century), the

Virgin and Child with Constantine and Justinian (early 10th century), and the panels showing Constantine IX Monomachos (1042–55) and Zoe and John II Komnenos (1118–43) and Irene making pious donations to, respectively, Christ and the Virgin.

The emergence of a centralized church plan in the post-iconoclast period was accompanied by the development of an extensive programme of pictorial decoration. Mosaic is used at the church of Hosios Loukas (early 11th century) in central Greece, Nea Moni on the island of Chios (mid-11th century), and Daphni (c.1100) west of Athens, to depict a hierarchical scheme of decoration, with the image of the Christ Pantokrator in the dome surmounting New Testament scenes and images of saints and, often, the Theotokos and Christ in the apse.

There are no survivals of Byzantine mosaics from the 12th century, but there is evidence for mosaics in that period. The Pantokrator monastery in Constantinople, founded by John II Komnenos (1118–43), was decorated with mosaics. The mosaics of Norman Sicily (Cefalù, and the Cappella Palatina and the Martorana in Palermo), which were executed at least partially by Byzantine craftsmen, give a good idea of Byzantine mosaic decoration in the 1140s.

There are considerable survivals of Byzantine mosaics from the last two centuries of the Byzantine empire. These include the decoration of the Theotokos Paregoritissa at Arta (1294–96), the Fetiye Camii (c.1300) and Kariye Camii (c.1320) in Constantinople, and the church of the Holy Apostles in Thessalonica (1310–14).

A special feature of Byzantine art is mosaic icons, of which some 48 survive, dating in the main from after 1261. In these icons the tesserae are set in a hollowed wooden tablet and fixed in a bed of resin or wax. Although the size of mosaic varies, many are very small. Consequently, the tesserae, which consist of gold, gilded copper, silver, ivory, and semi-precious stones, are minute, often not exceeding one square millimetre. These precious icons were probably used in private devotion.

BARBARA ZEITLER

See also Painting

Further Reading

Bertelli, Carlo (editor), *Mosaics*, New York: Gallery, 1989
Furlan, Italo, *Le icone bizantine a mosaico*, Milan: Stendhal, 1979
Glasberg, V., *Repertoire de la mosaïque médiévale, pariétale and portative: Prolégomènes à un corpus*, Amsterdam: Hakkert: 1974
Harding, C., Mosaic entry in *The Dictionary of Art*, edited by Jane Turner, London: Macmillan, and New York: Grove, 1996, vol. 22, pp. 154–66
James, Liz, *Light and Colour in Byzantine Art*, Oxford: Clarendon Press, and New York: Oxford University Press, 1996
Lowden, John, *Early Christian and Byzantine Art*, London: Phaidon, 1997

Museum of Alexandria

The *Mouseion* (Museum) in Alexandria was the most famous of all in antiquity. The members of a *mouseion* were originally connected with the cult of the Muses, who were worshipped at an altar, often in open-air porticoes or courts rather than in a temple, and were dedicated to the arts inspired by them. They were significant centres of literature and education, and often the focus of a society dedicated to the creation of literary compositions.

The Museum was located at Alexandria in Egypt, a city founded by Alexander the Great in 331 BC. Although we cannot as yet identify its exact location within the ancient city, we do know that it was near, or in the grounds of, the royal palace, or *Basileia*, which lay close to the harbour on the northern side of the city. It was founded in 280 BC by Ptolemy I Soter, one of Alexander's generals and a historian himself, on the advice of Demetrius of Phalerum. The latter had been one of Aristotle's pupils at the Lyceum in Athens, but was expelled from the city for his pro-Macedonian sentiments. Demetrius was influenced by the so-called Peripatetic school's approach to the acquisition of knowledge, and upon his arrival in Alexandria he persuaded Ptolemy I to establish an institution dedicated to the pursuit of knowledge along the lines of the Athenian model. The Museum was greatly expanded by Ptolemy II Philadelphus (308–246 BC).

Since we do not have any extant remains, we must rely on Strabo's description of it (*Geography*, 17. 1. 6–10) during the period when he was resident in the city – the late 1st century BC. He states that the Museum was part of the royal palace, and served as a gathering place for scholars, artists, and literary figures who held property in common. The facilities consisted of an *exedra*, or crescent-shaped arcade with seats for lectures, a *peripatos*, or covered walkway planted with trees where discussions often took place, and a large house with a communal dining area.

We know that the Museum was separate from, but closely associated with, the Library, also established by Ptolemy I. It may have had its own collection of books housed in nearby storerooms, but this is only conjectural. The names of those associated with the institution are not known, except for its last member, Theon (c. AD 380), but a number of prominent scholars and scientists lived in Alexandria, some of whom were affiliated with the Library, and no doubt participated in some of the activities at the Museum. These scholars were drawn from a variety of disciplines – both literary and scientific – and are represented by individuals such as Euclid, Eratosthenes, Callimachus, Apollonius Rhodius, Herophilus, Aristarchus of Samothrace, Aristarchus of Samos, Aristonicus, and Apelles. They flourished in an environment of sophisticated literature at the court and the metropolitan atmosphere of the city.

Ptolemy I Soter followed in the tradition of enlightened cultural support practised by kings and tyrants from the 6th century BC (the Pisistratids in Athens and Hieron in Sicily) down to the Macedonian kings in the 4th century BC. There was also a tradition in Egypt, as in the Greek world, of the association of religion with learning, and temples served as centres of literacy and repositories for knowledge. A third factor was the competition between the successors of Alexander the Great for cultural supremacy in an empire divided into factions after his death. The forerunners of the Museum at Alexandria were Plato's Academy in Athens, where the emphasis was on science and philosophy, and Aristotle's Lyceum, also in Athens, which was concerned with the systematic collection, organization, and preservation of knowledge.

The Museum flourished under the rule of the Ptolemies (304–31 BC) and received continued support under the Roman emperors. Its members served as a group of resident scholars invited to Alexandria by the king, who then maintained them at his expense. They were provided with living quarters and food and given salaries; they were also exempt from taxation. The king appointed a president who served as an administrator, or *epistates*, and the priest in charge of the cult of the Muses (*hiereus*). The primary focus was on research, although there may have been lectures, but its members were not required to teach. Dinners and symposia were held, characterized by a search for solutions to a stated problem; the resolutions were later recorded on papyri. Scholars were drawn from all parts of the Greek world to participate in state-subsidized learning – the acquisition of knowledge for knowledge's sake, rather than as the means to a specific end.

Research at the Museum focused on science and literature, unlike its Athenian predecessors, which often emphasized philosophy. In the field of science, the emphasis was on experimentation and the collection of empirical data to support observations and theories, resulting in the development of a scientific methodology for the solution of problems. Textual criticism, and the collection and cataloguing of literary works in order to ensure the preservation of knowledge of Greek and other Near Eastern civilizations – an antiquarian approach to history – were the hallmarks of the institution's literary endeavours. In the course of textual criticism, critical judgements were made regarding the relative importance of different versions of a single text. Revision involved the weeding out of versions considered to be inferior. It is clear from the papyri that one of the great contributions of the Museum was the stability of the texts of ancient authors, especially Homer.

The environment created in the Museum was one of a "worldwide" intellectual tradition resulting from a fusion of oriental and Mediterranean knowledge with an international centre of culture at Alexandria, where the study of science and literature flourished. This in turn contributed to the formation of a fairly uniform metropolitan urban civilization in the Hellenistic period, of which Alexandria was one of the first examples. The Museum was instrumental in the development of the concept of an institution dedicated solely to the acquisition of knowledge, a forerunner to the universities and research institutes of the present day.

This changed somewhat in the 2nd century BC, when the native segment of the population at Alexandria reacted against the influence of Hellenism. It was reinforced by an economic crisis characterized by rising prices and social unrest, in addition to hostility among members of the royal family. Ptolemy VI Philometor expelled foreign scholars and immigrants (c.146 BC), and their places in the Museum were occupied by native Alexandrians. Now other centres of culture and learning competed with Alexandria for scholars and students – at Pergamum, Athens, Antioch, and Rome. At this point the city lost its position as the primary cultural centre of the Greek world.

The fate of the Museum is still disputed. It seems to have escaped destruction in 48 BC when Julius Caesar burned the ships in the nearby harbour, setting part of the royal quarter on fire. It enjoyed renewed prosperity under the *Pax Augusta*, and the Roman emperors visited and extended the buildings, especially the philhellene Hadrian. In the Roman period the acquisition of knowledge became more secularized, but Alexandria continued to be an important centre of Greek learning. Many renowned residents and visitors were still associated with its research institutions, such as Plutarch, Ptolemy of Alexandria, Lucian, and Plotinus.

Research in science and medicine flourished, as did the study of philosophy which was closely intertwined with religion, but there was a marked decline in literary endeavours. In the 2nd century AD it was famous for the New Rhetoric, and in the 3rd century for Neoplatonism. The Museum suffered under Caracalla, who expelled its foreign members and abolished sustenance payments for others in AD 216. It appears to have been destroyed by Aurelian after the city made an abortive attempt at independence after his defeat of Zenobia, queen of Palmyra, in AD 272, but it soon resumed its activities. In the 4th century Ammianus Marcellinus (22. 16) reports scientific activity, but admits that there was a decline in scholarship. In all probability the Museum did not survive long after Theodosius I's edict in 391 requiring the destruction of all pagan temples.

The collected and evaluated information and wisdom of antiquity, as well as new strides made in the acquisition of knowledge in a variety of scientific and literary fields by members of the Museum in Alexandria, have been transmitted to the present day through Islamic rulers, who were themselves very interested in Graeco-Roman civilization. In the Arab world of the 7th–11th centuries there was a period of cultural awakening characterized by an interest in learning, and translation of ancient texts by Arab scholars. Great libraries and research centres based on the Alexandrian model, such as the one at Baghdad, were established in the Islamic world. The knowledge acquired by scholars in Hellenistic Alexandria was essential to the scientific experiments of Arab scholars, also conducted according to scientific methods of research developed in that city's institutions.

The Museum at Alexandria, then, was the inheritor of the Classical Athenian tradition of the acquisition of knowledge in an environment dedicated solely to that purpose. It in turn passed that tradition on in a new form, developed as a result of its position as the centre of Greek culture in the 4th and 3rd centuries BC, and the institution continued to diffuse the heritage of Greek culture to the rest of the world in the Hellenistic and Roman periods. Its members contributed a new body of scientific information and methods, and procedures for textual revision and literary criticism in addition to their efforts at collection, collation, and preservation in an attempt to save the knowledge of the past. The Museum passed on a tradition of pure research in the context of an institutional setting to other Graeco-Roman centres as well as the Arab world. Medieval and Islamic scholars, and later Christian scholars and humanists of the European Renaissance interested in Greek and Roman civilization, built on the foundations developed at the Museum in Alexandria. They too established their own research centres dedicated to higher learning – the forerunners of modern-day universities and research institutes.

KATHLEEN DONAHUE SHERWOOD

See also Libraries, Scholarship

Summary

The Museum (*Mouseion*) of Alexandria was founded in 280 BC by Ptolemy I Soter. Modelled on Plato's Academy and Aristotle's Lyceum, it was a cultural centre for scholars, artists, and writers which provided facilities for teaching, discussing, and dining. It was separate from, but closely linked with, the Library. It survived until the 4th century AD.

Further Reading

Austin, M.M., *The Hellenistic World from Alexander to the Roman Conquest: A Selection of Ancient Sources in Translation*, Cambridge and New York: Cambridge University Press, 1981, pp. 388–92

Bowman, Alan K., *Egypt after the Pharoahs, 332 BC–AD 642: From Alexander to the Arab Conquest*, 2nd edition, Berkeley: University of California Press, 1996

El-Abbadi, Mostafa, *The Life and Fate of the Ancient Library of Alexandria*, 2nd edition, Paris: UNESCO/UNDP, 1992, pp. 73–102

Fraser, P.M., *Ptolemaic Alexandria*, vol. 1, Oxford: Clarendon Press, 1972, chapter 6

Green, Peter, *Alexander to Actium: An Essay on the Historical Evolution of the Hellenistic Age*, Berkeley: University of California Press, and London: Thames and Hudson, 1990

Hornblower, Simon and Antony Spawforth (editors), *The Oxford Classical Dictionary*, 3rd edition, Oxford and New York: Oxford University Press, 1996, Museum entry pp. 1002–03

Marlowe, John, *The Golden Age of Alexandria: From its Foundation by Alexander the Great in 331 BC to its Capture by the Arabs in 642 AD*, London: Gollancz, 1971

Pfeiffer, Rudolf, *History of Classical Scholarship from the Beginnings to the End of the Hellenistic Age*, Oxford: Clarendon Press, 1968

Stillwell, Richard (editor), *The Princeton Encyclopedia of Classical Sites*, Princeton, New Jersey: Princeton University Press, 1976, pp. 36–38

Museums

Because of the Turkish occupation, museums in Greece were slow to become established. During the 18th century some foreigners in Athens with antiquarian interests had assembled collections in their homes, which they showed to interested travellers. Prominent among them were the two rivals, Luisieri, the Italian painter who was Lord Elgin's agent in Greece, and the Frenchman Louis-François-Sebastien Fauvel, Choisseul-Gouffier's representative in Greece and consul of France in Athens from 1803.

By the early 19th century the idea of a Greek museum had become linked with the notion of the revival of the Greek nation. In 1807 the leading Greek intellectual Adamantios Korais, angered by the pillage of Greek relics, put forward a proposal for the foundation of a Greek museum in a safe building that would house manuscripts, coins, and other antiquities, donated and bought, and all to be inventoried, with details of their provenance. Korais's suggestions were not implemented and it was only in 1829, after independence, that a Greek National Museum came into existence. The island of Aegina, where some of the earliest and most impressive finds had been made, was chosen by Kapodistria's government to host the museum, in a disused orphanage. But it soon became evident that space was at a premium, and after the assassination of Kapodistria in 1831 and the establishment of the first Archaeological Service in 1833, attention was focused on Athens, and provisions for a museum there were made in the First Archaeological Law of 1834. In preparation, the dispersed antiquities of Athens were collected in various designated buildings, and after the closure of the Aegina museum in 1834, the antiquities from there were gradually transported to Athens and also housed in those buildings. In 1837 the *Archaiologiki Hetaireia* (Archaeological Society) was founded and undertook the systematic collection of antiquities, through purchase and donations. In 1858 a large room in the newly built Athens University was set aside for the university's own substantial collection. This was the first museum open to the public. It was later transferred to the Varvakeion school, and from there to the Polytechnic in 1881. From 1877 it housed Schliemann's finds from Mycenae and had to charge admission to provide for its upkeep.

Only in 1866 were the foundations laid for a National Archaeological Museum in Athens, and construction was not completed until 1889. In 1858 Demetrios Bernardakis, a Greek from Petroupolis in Russia, had contributed 200,000 drachmas towards the building, but disagreement over the site and architectural plans caused much delay. The problem of location was resolved through the donation by Eleni Tositsa in 1866 of land on Patision Street, next to a plot that she had previously donated for the construction of the Polytechnic. The plans adopted were those that the German painter and architect Ludwig Lange had proposed a few years earlier, with various alterations, supervised in the last stages of construction by the architect E. Ziller. The museum housed the most significant antiquities from the whole of Greece, as well as the numismatic collection (today in the Iliou Melathron, Schliemann's former home) and the epigraphic collection, both of which had previously been in the Aegina Museum; in 1983 the *Archaiologiki Hetaireia* handed over its own sizeable collection. During the middle decades of the 19th century the Acropolis Museum, close to the Parthenon, was also built.

Other Athenian museums were not established until the 20th century. These include the Keramaikos Museum (1936), the Byzantine Museum (1926), and the Museum of Popular Art (1918, in new premises since 1973). Today Athens is home to 30 museums and galleries. Some of these are private and semi-private museums open to the public (important private collections having existed in Athens since the early 19th century), notably the prestigious Benaki Museum, housed in the family home of the donor, Emanuel Benaki, since 1931, the Kanellopoulos Museum (1972), and the Goulandris Museum of Cycladic art (1982).

The archaeological law of 1834 which provided for the establishment of museums in Athens also provided for the foundation of provincial museums, to house local finds not destined for the capital. The first purpose-built provincial museums date from the second half of the 19th century (at Sparta, Olympia, and Epidaurus), but most were built in the 20th century. Even today many small museums continue to be housed, more or less successfully, in a variety of buildings, including private houses, churches, and mosques. Thessalonica, the second largest city in Greece, did not acquire a modern archaeological museum until 1962. Since then great developments have taken place, including a new Museum of Byzantine Culture inaugurated in 1994. As European City of

Museums: National Archaeological Museum, Athens, built in 1866–69

Culture in 1997, the city boasted nearly the same number of museums as Athens, some of which were refurbished or relocated for the occasion.

In the last decades of the 20th century the Ministry of Culture (which is responsible for museums) has had to deal with three main problems with regard to museums: the often critical lack of space for storing and displaying the ever-increasing number of excavated antiquities; the enormous overheads generated by the running of a large number of museums; and the safety of collections that are increasingly at risk, particularly in provincial museums (the theft of 276 antiquities from the Corinth Museum in 1986 highlighted these risks). A growing awareness of issues of conservation and environmental monitoring has left its mark on the larger museums, with more trained conservators now being employed, but the progress has yet to trickle down to the provincial museums, many of which are entirely deprived of funding for such services. Since the 1970s plans have been afoot for a new, larger Acropolis museum, with suitable space and environ-

mental conditions to display the Parthenon Marbles, if and when they are returned, but progress has been predictably slow.

Like all museums in the West, Greek museums today face the challenge of their greatly enhanced scope and function: the provision of designer displays, frequent temporary exhibitions, and high standards of cataloguing. The need to modernize is a concern for all Greek museums, but the results depend on the availability of resources, organizational skills, and expertise, and these vary greatly from museum to museum.

CHRISTINA SOUYOUDZOGLOU-HAYWOOD

See also Archaeological Service

Further Reading

Kokkou, Angelike, *I Merimna gia tis Archaiotetes sten Hellada kai ta Prota Mouseia* [The Care of Antiquities in Greece and the First Museums], Athens, 1977

Music

Music has featured prominently in Hellenic society since the dawn of Greek civilization. The dominant form of musical expression for all periods has been song, the sacred and secular genres of which have included cultivated, rural ("demotic"), and popular repertories. Despite the existence of Hellenic systems of musical notation since at least the 3rd century BC, the historical reliance of Greek performers on oral methods of transmission has resulted in the loss to posterity of most pre-modern melodies. All of the complete works and substantive fragments preserved from antiquity in vocal and instrumental notations based on the Greek alphabet, for example, fit comfortably on a single compact disc. This loss is offset to some degree by the survival of many ancient song texts, from which certain rhythmic details may be recovered, as well as by rich philosophical and theoretical traditions of writing about music. No secular melodies have been preserved from the Byzantine empire, but its liturgical chant is transmitted in neumatic notation by an impressive body of manuscripts dating from the 10th to the 20th century AD. However, the realization of these neumed sources presupposes knowledge of orally transmitted conventions of performance practice, the amount of which increases with the antiquity of the manuscripts.

These daunting gaps in the historical record have made it difficult for scholars either to trace the development of Hellenic music as a continuous tradition or to draw more than superficial conclusions about its diachronic character. Interpretation of the available evidence, particularly with regard to the musical effects of interaction with neighbouring peoples, has been further complicated by the cultural politics of the 19th and 20th centuries. While some Greek scholars have made exaggerated claims for continuity, Western musicologists have until recently tended to see mainly discontinuity between the musics of ancient Greece, Byzantium, and modern Greece. Reflecting such broader cultural phenomena as the struggle to define a modern Greek identity in the face of

Music: dancers and an *aulos* player among the figures depicted on a vase found in Boeotia, 5th century BC, National Archaeological Museum, Athens

Western expectations, these views have led to a priori rejections by various groups of a wide array of living and historical repertories as unacceptably tainted by foreign influence, usually identified as either "Arabo-Turkish" or "Western". These criticisms notwithstanding, only in the later decades of the 20th century has the study of problems for which enough sources survive to make comparative study meaningful – for example the relationship of post-Byzantine and Ottoman music – progressed sufficiently to yield reliable preliminary results.

The following brief historical survey will be limited to music created and performed by speakers of the Greek language. Further developments of Hellenic musical traditions by others – notably the medieval Latin, Arabic, and Turkish extensions of ancient Greek and Byzantine music theory, and the impact of Renaissance humanist study of Classical Greek music and drama on the development of opera – will therefore not be considered. For technical expositions of Greek and Byzantine music theory, readers are referred to the specialized studies in the appended bibliography.

Portrayals of musicians and musical instruments in Cycladic, Minoan, Mycenaean, and Cypriot art of the 2nd and 3rd millennia BC show that these societies employed music in public ritual and domestic entertainment. Echoes of these early traditions may be discerned in the narratives and poetic structures of the Homeric epics, works which mark the transition from an era of purely oral transmission to one in which the texts of certain cultivated genres of song were regularly committed to writing by their poet-composers. Witnesses to the subsequent development of Hellenic music include the texts of Greek lyric poetry, literary references to music, and depictions of musicians in pottery and other art. A formative era

reportedly marked by Phrygian and Lydian influence was followed in the 7th and 6th centuries BC by the emergence of regional schools of composition and the diffusion of their characteristic forms. Lesbos produced intimate monody in the form of Sappho's Aeolian lyric, while more public forms of art were encouraged by the city states of the Greek mainland through their sponsorship of music competitions held in conjunction with such civic and religious festivals as the Spartan Carneia and the Pythian Games of Delphi. At these events professional soloists demonstrated their skill on the *kithara* (lyre) and the *aulos* by performing set pieces (*nomoi*), while choirs of amateur singers and dancers were incorporated into presentations of choral lyrics, out of which eventually developed both the Dionysian dithyramb and tragedy.

As the traditional repertories of cultivated song reached their apogee in the 5th century BC with the works of Pindar and the Attic tragedians, the study and performance of *mousike* – music conceived as an indissoluble complex of poetry and melody – achieved an unprecedented (and since unequalled) level of significance in Greek society. The ideal Hellenic gentleman thus became a cultivated amateur musician trained by an educational curriculum in which poetry sung to lyre accompaniment held a place of honour. By the turn of the 4th century BC, however, the cultural consensus surrounding music began to dissolve in the face of internal and external pressures. Melodic and metrical innovations by such composers as Euripides and the virtuoso Timotheus (*c*.450–*c*.360 BC) transgressed the stylistic boundaries between traditional genres, provoking harsh criticism from Aristophanes and other musical conservatives. Symptomatic of these changes was the progressive replacement of an older modal system of melodically and rhythmically distinct modes (the Dorian, Phrygian, etc. *harmonia*) with a complex system of interlocking scales (also called *harmoniai*) designed to facilitate modulations. The bonds between music and poetry in Greek culture were thus left greatly weakened for the remainder of antiquity, as were the ties between amateur and professional music making. Although musical performances remained ubiquitous in the Hellenistic and Roman periods, vocal and instrumental music outside cult and state ceremony was largely reduced to entertainment. Professional musicians, whether male virtuoso kitharists or female *aulos* players offering sexual services to symposiasts, were accordingly relegated to a low place in the social order.

Perhaps the most enduring musical legacies of the Classical period are to be found in the critical, scientific, and speculative traditions of writing about music that emerged from it. The figure of Pythagoras (*fl. c.*530–497 BC) stands at the head of two complementary streams of Greek musical thought: the one emphasizing philosophical, social, and metaphysical concerns, and the other a theoretical tradition originally concerned not so much with the craft of composition (the subject of most Western "music theory" since the Renaissance) as with the physics of sound and the systematization of tonal systems. Fundamental to both approaches was a belief in the kinship of mathematics and music, a concept extrapolated from observing that a resonating string divided in length according to the ratios 2:1, 3:2, and 4:3 produced the intervals of, respectively, an octave, a fifth, and a fourth. The influence of Damon and other early authors whose writings are now lost may be discerned in the works of Plato, a musical conservative who eschewed the use of technical terminology while exalting an idealized version of the previous century's cultivated amateurism. In the *Laws* and the *Republic*, Plato assigned *mousike* a prominent but carefully regulated role in education by emphasizing the governance of texts over melodies, which should be set only in the Dorian and Phrygian *harmoniai*. He wished to ban the remaining modes from his perfect state because of their inherently unsuitable ethical qualities, thus reflecting his belief that each of the Greek modes possessed a distinct ethos which could be imparted through habituation. The means for achieving these effects are intimated in the *Timaeus*, in which Plato echoes Pythagorean doctrine by suggesting that both the human soul and the universe as a whole are constructed according to the mathematical proportions of the harmonic series. Aristotle, while sharing Plato's distaste for contemporary virtuosity, rejected such metaphysical speculations in favour of a more empirical approach. Believing that ethos could be mediated by abstract instrumental as well as by texted vocal works, Aristotle saw the ethical force of music arising from the embodiment of emotional states in sound and rhythm, a theory subsequently disseminated by his students and further developed by the Stoics. Although advocating in his *Politics* a total proscription of the *aulos*, Aristotle more closely reflected the societal standards of his time by admitting all the modes and accepting entertainment alongside education as a legitimate use of music.

Despite Aristotle's objections, philosophical writing about music well into the Byzantine period continued to be influenced by Pythagorean and Platonic thought, particularly as refracted through Plotinus. Neoplatonist views of music were also expressed by the Fathers of the Christian Church, whose fierce polemic against secular music rested not only on the pagan origin of its texts and the suspect morality of its performers (cf. the *Apostolic Constitutions*, which denied baptism to instrumentalists who had not renounced their profession), but also on a belief in its inherently deleterious ethos. As an antidote, St John Chrysostom and other patristic authors proposed the cultivation of biblical psalmody, whereby a believer's soul would profit from the felicitous combination of text and melody. The doubts cast on the spiritual utility of the latter by such ascetics as St Athanasius and St Gregory of Sinai notwithstanding, the tradition of extolling melodious psalmody for its ethical benefits may be traced through St John of Damascus to the hesychast saints Gregory Palamas and Theoleptos of Philadelphia.

Treatises of music theory also demonstrate a remarkable degree of continuity from antiquity through the Byzantine period, the significance of which is much debated because of uncertainties about the degree to which theory and practice diverged after the 4th century BC as the academic study of music became firmly entrenched among the sciences. Ancient theorists pursued two basic approaches to the definition of tonal space, both of which may be regarded as approximate theoretical rationalizations of actual practice: the accurate but cumbersome Pythagorean tradition of defining musical intervals arithmetically according to ratios of string lengths; and the linear method of Aristotle's student Aristoxenus, who believed intervals to be capable of infinite subdivision and proffered scales built on units of equal size. All ancient theorists after Aristoxenus, however, followed him in constructing larger tonal systems spanning two octaves (the Greater Perfect, Lesser Perfect, and Immutable Systems) from sets of conjunct or disjunct perfect fourths. Whereas the outer notes of these tetrachords were fixed, the relative positions of their inner pitches were determined by their genus (diatonic, chromatic, or enharmonic) and "colour" (*chroa*). In the surviving fragment of his *Harmonics*, Aristoxenus gives the following sequences of whole (=1) and fractional tones for the tetrachord E-F-G-A:

Genus	Sequence of Intervals (E - - - A)
Tense diatonic	½ – 1 – 1
Soft diatonic	½ – ¾ – 1¼
Tonic chromatic	½ – ½ – 1½
Hemiolic chromatic	⅜ – ⅜ – 1¾
Soft chromatic	⅓ – ⅓ – 1⅚
Enharmonic	¼ – ¼ – 2

The theories of Aristoxenus were rearticulated in a group of treatises from the first few centuries AD, some of which modify them with material drawn from the Pythagorean tradition. These works include the comprehensive expositions of Claudius Ptolemy and Aristides Quintilianus, as well as the practical handbooks by Cleonides, Gaudentius, and Alypius, the last of which contains the fullest surviving account of the vocal and instrumental systems of ancient Greek musical notation. Manuscripts of these and other theoretical treatises not only continued to be studied and copied throughout the Byzantine period, but some treatises previously identified as

Late Antique may have been compiled at the court of Constantine VII Porphyrogennetos (913–59). Western scholars have nevertheless customarily dismissed Byzantine interest in the theoretical tradition of antiquity as encyclopedism covering an ever-widening gap between musical theory and practice. This hypothesis is currently being reconsidered by researchers who see evidence for a dynamic application of ancient theory to liturgical music in an enigmatic compilation known as the *Hagiopolites* (a 14th-century manuscript some of whose contents may be several centuries earlier), as well as in the discussions of modal theory contained in the late-13th-century treatises of Manuel Bryennios and George Pachymeres.

A more detailed evaluation of the links between ancient Greek and Byzantine music is frustrated by the chasm of approximately six centuries separating the sole fragment of a Christian hymn in ancient notation – the famous late 3rd-century "Hymn to the Trinity" from the Oxyrhynchus Papyrus 1786 – from the first manuscripts of Byzantine chant. When the latter finally appear, they do so with a modal system (the Octoechos attributed to St John of Damascus) that had undergone considerable development and completely new systems of notation (the various families of Byzantine neumes). Greek scholars have tended either to ignore these differences, or to see them as the result of evolutionary processes comparable to those that brought about the replacement of quantitative metres with others based on stress or syllable-count during the first centuries of the Byzantine empire. Employing the same evidence, Egon Wellesz and other Western pioneers in the study of Byzantine chant perceived a radical break with antiquity followed by development on a new basis. Wellesz notably argued that Christian liturgical song was derived primarily from non-Hellenic and especially Semitic sources, in particular the psalmody of the synagogue and Syriac hymnody. Without minimizing either the crucial influence exercised by Jewish precedents on the formation of Christian liturgy or that of St Ephraim the Syrian on St Romanos the Melodist, later 20th-century scholarship has called into question central elements of Wellesz's "Oriental hypothesis". His stylistic assessment of the Oxyrrhynchus hymn as non-Hellenic has, for example, been challenged by West, while advances in the study of Jewish and early Christian liturgy have discredited theories postulating the total dependence of the Christian liturgy of the hours and its psalmody on the synagogue.

Escaping simplistic binary oppositions between tradition and discontinuity, scholars of early Christian and Byzantine music began in the later decades of the 20th century to draw on more sophisticated developmental models from the closely related discipline of liturgiology. The repertories of Byzantine chant are thus viewed within their native liturgical context as the products of interaction over many centuries between regional traditions of worship ("rites") that emerged in the cities and deserts of Egypt, Palestine, Syria, and Cappadocia soon after Constantine's legalization of Christianity in AD 313. Geographic differences were transcended during this formative period by distinct cathedral and monastic approaches to the chanting of biblical psalmody, which dominated Late Antique services after all but the most venerable of non-scriptural hymns (e.g. the "Phos Ilaron") were proscribed as a defence against heresy. While urban services employed melodically interesting settings of psalms with refrains designed to encour-age congregational participation, early ascetics cultivated musically austere practices of verse-by-verse performance (i.e. without refrains). These forms of worship were soon blended in hybrid "urban monastic" services, the existence of which is documented in Jerusalem at the turn of the 5th century AD by the Spanish pilgrim Egeria.

Following the Byzantine empire's loss of Egypt and Syria, the development of Byzantine worship and its music was governed by competition and borrowing between the liturgical families of Constantinople and Jerusalem. The former originally encompassed a monastic rite practised by so-called "sleepless monks" (*akoimetai*) and the cathedral rite of Justinian's Great Church of Hagia Sophia, a textually conservative system of cathedral worship notable for the splendour of its ceremonial entrances. Until its reform by Symeon of Thessalonica in the early 15th century, music in the Rite of the Great Church consisted mainly of antiphonal and responsorial psalmody performed by soloists (some of whom, prior to 1204, were eunuchs), choristers, and congregations. Non-scriptural hymnography played only a minor role in the "sung office" (*asmatiki akolouthia*) of the Constantinopolitan cathedral rite and was most frequently encountered in the form of refrains to psalmodic antiphons. The kontakia (verse homilies) composed by St Romanos and other melodists after Syrian precedents were originally composed for paraliturgical performance between the offices of a popular vigil (*pannychis*) and therefore constituted only a partial exception to the usual practice. In Palestine, on the other hand, the convergence between the local cathedral and monastic traditions of the church of the Holy Sepulchre and the monastery of Mar Saba that occurred after the destruction of Jerusalem by the Persians in 614 gave rise to a school of prolific hymnographers who composed works for interpolation among the psalms and canticles of the Palestinian liturgy of the hours. Sabaïtic hymnography became firmly established in Constantinople after St Theodore of Stoudios adopted the Palestinian divine office for use at his monastery in 799, thereby inaugurating four centuries of coexistence with the rite of the Great Church. The cathedral rite entered into steep decline after the Latin occupation of Constantinople (1204–61), leaving the rite of Mar Saba in its 14th-century Athonite recension to form the basis for all modern Orthodox worship.

The earliest Byzantine liturgical manuscripts with musical notation date from the 9th century. Initially, systems designed primarily to convey melodic or rhythmic nuances rather than precise pitch were employed: lectionary or "ecphonetic" notation for the recitation of scriptural pericopes, a system appearing in manuscripts from the 9th to the 14th century; and "Paleo-Byzantine" forms of melodic notation to convey the tunes of hymns and psalms from the 10th century. The latter included variants of the so-called Coislin and Chartres notational systems, thus named by modern scholars after the libraries in which they were first discovered, and respectively associated with, the traditions of Jerusalem and Constantinople. In the later 12th century the Coislin notation developed into a fully diastematic family of neumes ("Middle Byzantine" or "Round" notation) indicating a melody's precise succession of intervals with quantitative signs ("bodies") and its nuances with qualitative signs ("spirits"), the realizations of which continued to be transmitted orally and through cheironomy, the lost Byzantine art of choral conducting. Although the available evidence precludes definitive reconstructions of pre-modern musical performances, it is more than sufficient to chart the development of Byzantine musical style from the appearance of notated manuscripts. The earliest transcribable books of chant contain fully formed repertories in several styles based on standardized melodic formulae. The Asmatikon and Psaltikon transmit anonymous choral and solo settings of psalms and hymns from the urban tradition of Constantinople in a florid idiom characterized by the occasional intercalation of meaningless syllables. Office hymns in a simpler melodic style by St John of Damascus, Kassia, and other composers of the monastic rite are contained in the Sticherarion and the Heirmologion. According to recent studies by Van Biezen (1968) and Arvanitis (forthcoming), the *stichera* (for an explanation of this term see the article on Hymnography) and canons in these collections of hymnography appear to preserve a certain modified form of pitch accent from ancient Greek music.

After the establishment of Crusader states throughout the eastern Mediterranean, Greek musicians were exposed to Western music through such institutions as the Lusignan court of Cyprus, the source of a remarkable manuscript of Latin chant and *Ars Nova* polyphony. Meanwhile, Byzantine chant continued to develop along established lines in a shrunken Palaiologan empire dominated musically by Constantinople, Thessalonica, and Mount Athos. St John Koukouzeles and a host of other eponymous composers began to cultivate distinct personal styles through the composition of multiple settings of psalms and hymns, breaking thereby the one-to-one relationship that had generally obtained between text and music in Orthodox worship. Many of their works were written in a virtuosic new "beautified" or "kalophonic" idiom employing textual troping, melismatic passages, and vocalizations on nonsense syllables (teretisms). Teretisms are found both as interludes within texted works and as independent compositions known as *kratemata* (see Hymnography), some of which bear evocative titles (e.g. "Viola" or "Persian"). In the 15th century, evidence of Western influence on Byzantine music in the form of settings of the Nicene creed and simple two-part polyphony appears amongst the works of the theorist (and later Uniate bishop of Methone) John Plousiadenos, and the imperial court musicians Manuel Gazes and Manuel Chrysaphes.

The fall of Constantinople to the Turks in 1453 left the Hellenic peoples split politically and musically into areas dominated either by Latin Christians or the Ottomans. Renaissance Crete, the Ionian islands, and southern Italy evolved distinct Western dialects of Byzantine chant often supplemented in performance by "chanting on the book" ("*cantare super librum*"), a practice of improvising polyphony that survives to the present day in certain areas. Some musicians, including Frangiskos Leontaritis (1518–72), a Cretan composer of polyphonic masses and motets, and Hieronymos Tragodistes (*fl. c.*mid-16th century), a Cypriot student of the Renaissance theorist Gioseffo Zarlino, also became fully proficient in the idioms of their Latin rulers. Following the Turkish conquest of Cyprus and Crete, Western forms of art music blossomed in the Ionian islands. Italian opera was staged in Corfu from at least 1733, laying the foundation for an indigenous Ionian

school of opera composers led by Nikolaos Halkiopoulos-Manztaros (1795–1872) that flourished during the 19th century.

Analogous patterns of musical activity developed among the Romaic Greeks of the Ottoman empire after a 17th-century revival of Byzantine chanting centred on the Ecumenical Patriarchate. Working mostly within the stylistic categories bequeathed by their late-Byzantine predecessors, Panagiotes the "New Chrysaphes" (*c.*1623–*c.*1682), Germanos of New Patras (*c.*1625–*c.*1685), Balasios the Priest (*c.*1615–*c.*1700), and Petros Bereketes (*c.*1665–*c.*1725) enriched the received repertories with orally transmitted formulae (*theseis*) while creating the new genre of the kalophonic *eirmos* (model stanza). During this period it also became customary for Romaic cantors to acquire fluency in what was commonly referred to as "foreign music" (*exoteriki mousiki*), namely the Arabo-Persian art music of the Ottoman court. Zacharias Chanantes (also known as Mir Cemil, 1680–1750) and Petros Peloponnesios (Petraki-i Kebir?, d. 1778) distinguished themselves in both Byzantine and Ottoman music, a feat that was to be emulated by Romaic musicians well into the 20th century.

Musical life in Romaic communities during the 18th century was affected by the growing popularity of Western music among the Ottoman empire's bourgeoisie and an internal movement towards the systematization of the received repertory of Byzantine chant. The latter began with attempts to notate more fully the orally transmitted *theseis* through a process of transcription or "interpretation" (*exigisis*). This process was continued by Petros Peloponnesios and his student Petros Byzantios (d. 1808), who also offered their own revised versions of the Sticherarion and Heirmologion as alternatives to the embellished medieval and post-Byzantine repertories then in use, thereby laying the basis for all modern Greek chanting. Two attempts by Agapios Paliermos (d. 1815) to replace Byzantine neumes with forms of Western notation were defeated by conservative forces in the patriarchal chapel, but a third comprehensive reform proposed by Chrysanthos of Madytos (*c.*1770–1843) modifying the traditional system with borrowings from ancient Greek and Western music was accepted by the Ecumenical Patriarchate in 1814. Chrysanthos drastically reduced the number of qualitative signs in Byzantine notation, replaced the traditional intonations with a Western-style system of solmization, introduced precise means of notating chromaticism and subdivisions of the basic beat, and revived the Aristoxenian distinction between diatonic, chromatic, and enharmonic modes. Nearly the entire received repertory was transcribed into this "New Method" by Chrysanthos's associates Chourmouzios the Archivist (*c.*1770–1840) and Gregorios the Protopsaltis (*c.*1778–1821), whose works achieved widespread circulation in the first printed volumes of Byzantine chant. The "New Method" survived the challenge of a competing notational system introduced by George of Lesbos in 1840 and remains in use today with some modifications. In 1881 a Patriarchal Commission on Music corrected the scales of Chrysanthos, while more recently Simon Karas (d. 1999) revived certain qualitative signs from medieval Byzantine notation and, somewhat less successfully, proposed further minor revisions to the tunings of the Byzantine modes.

The history of music in the modern state of Greece has been marked by conflicting attempts to create popular and art repertories consonant with evolving conceptions of modern Greek identity that have alternately rejected elements of Italo-Greek and Romaic culture as unduly tainted by foreign influence. The task of creating a common musical idiom was initially complicated by the fact that none of the existing Hellenic centres of cultivated sacred or secular music fell within the borders of the small Greek kingdom that emerged from the revolution of 1821. While "folk" (demotic) song persisted among Greece's rural inhabitants, its new urban elite imported art and popular music from the Ionian islands and western Europe. Despite the grumbling of some traditionalists, king Otho's institution in 1834 of public performances by military bands and other similar efforts to broaden the audience for Western styles of music were generally well received. Two notable exceptions were attempts in 1836 and 1869 to introduce polyphony during Easter services at the cathedral of Athens, both of which were halted by rioting congregations. In 1870, however, at the instigation of queen Olga a polyphonic choir of men and boys was successfully founded in the royal chapel by Alexander Kantakouzenos (1824–92), formerly of Odessa. The following year Kantakouzenos became the first director of the Athens Conservatory, an influential institution that was one of many organizations founded in Greece during the last three decades of the 19th century to provide an expanding bourgeoisie with various styles of music, whether created abroad or, increasingly, locally. In addition to the introduction of French operetta, the 1870s witnessed the appearance of two competing styles of musical cafés, each of which attracted a highly partisan following: the *café chantant* as a venue for western European popular music and dancing, viewed as immoral by certain traditionalists; and the *café aman*, featuring an ethnically heterogeneous mix of popular musical repertories borrowed from the Romaic Greeks of Asia Minor and viewed by some westernizers as havens of debased Oriental culture. Parallel controversies over the relative merits of Western and Oriental musical styles occurred in the field of liturgical music, reaching their height in the first decade of the 20th century with the bitter disputes between the reformer John Sakellarides and the traditionalist Konstantinos Psachos.

Interest in the hitherto ignored tradition of demotic music was sparked among Greece's intellectual elite by Louis Bougault-Ducoudray's publication of a collection of 30 rural and Romaic popular songs harmonized according to his own classicizing theories of modality. The rather selective collections of his Greek imitators contributed to the institutionalization of a sanitized version of rural culture concordant with contemporary political ideology, while also providing some with a pretext to reject the Italo-Greek art music of the Ionian school in favour of central European ideas of musical nationalism. Advanced by George Nazos (1862–1934), a German-trained musician who drastically revised the curriculum of the Athens Conservatory upon his appointment as its director in 1891, this artistic reorientation climaxed with the emergence of a "national school" of composers led by Manolis Kalomiris (1883–1962) that claimed to draw its primary inspiration from demotic music. Kalomiris spent the second decade of the 20th century composing a notable series of works leading up to his Symphony no. 1, the *Levendia*, a paean to the "Great Idea"

written between 1918 and 1920, while Dimitri Mitropoulos (1896–1960) bypassed the nationalism of his colleagues completely with *Soeur Béatrice*, an opera in French based on a text by Maeterlinck. The complexity of these ambitious compositions heralded the arrival of an era in which "serious" and "popular" music in Western styles began to develop along rather different lines in Greece, as elsewhere. The phenomenally successful operettas of Theophrastos Sakellarides (1883–1950) and other composers setting Greek librettos in a contemporary Viennese style were thus succeeded by popular songs in such foreign idioms as the foxtrot and the tango.

The burning of Smyrna and the destruction of its cosmopolitan musical culture in 1922 were succeeded over the course of the 20th century by the dispersal of Romaic musical communities throughout Turkey and the Middle East. At first, the exchange of populations mandated by the Treaty of Lausanne appears to have had little impact on Greece's recent achievement of a preliminary musical synthesis on a mostly Western basis. This was particularly true of "serious" music, in which the conservative "national school" held sway within the country until well after World War II, effectively banishing the works of Schoenberg's pupil Nikos Skalkottas (1904–49). Popular music was affected somewhat sooner by the revival of the *café aman* by the Asia Minor refugees, whose music soon began to mix with that of the urban underclass. The result was a bouzouki-based genre of popular songs known as *rebetika* that came to exist in parallel with what Voliotis-Kapetanakis (1989) has called the music of the "official culture", exemplified in the popular sphere by the cabaret music of Attik (Kleon Triantaphyllou, 1895–1944) and Michalis Souyioul (1905–58). As *rebetika* achieved commercial success through recordings and nightclub performances, they gradually lost their taboo status and evolved into *laïka* ("popular music"), a musically syncretic genre that transformed the bouzouki into a virtuoso instrument.

Greece's deep political divisions as it emerged from the 1940s were mirrored in music by conflicts between advocates of the increasingly outmoded cultural synthesis of the 1920s and partisans of genres stigmatized by their opponents as relics of oriental domination, represented at opposite ends of the social spectrum by Byzantine chant and *rebetika*. The intellectual foundations for a rapprochement between the two factions were provided notably by Simon Karas, who defended the integrity of the received tradition of Byzantine chanting through teaching and scholarship, and Manos Hadjidakis (1925–94), who scandalized Athenian musical society with a lecture in 1949 exalting *rebetika* as quintessentially Greek music. Hadjidakis went on to employ melodic and rhythmic elements of *rebetika* in his own compositions as he repeatedly crossed and ultimately transcended the boundaries between art and popular music, revitalizing Greek popular song and musical theatre during the 1950s with his eclectic style. The breaking down of cultural barriers in Greek music was soon carried further by Mikis Theodorakis (b. 1925), a student of Olivier Messiaen. Convinced of the cultural bankruptcy of the "national school" and inspired by socialist ideology, Theodorakis forsook the international career in avant-garde music chosen by his fellow Messiaen pupil Iannis Xenakis (b. 1922) in order to devote himself to the creation of what he hoped would be a truly representative Greek musical idiom drawing stylistically on the bouzouki music of the lower classes. Theodorakis's penchant for setting the works of such highly regarded poets as Elytis and Ritsos in a popular style was imitated by others including Stavros Xarchakos (b. 1939) and Yannis Markopoulos (b. 1939), thus initiating the so-called "popular art song" (*entechni laïki mousiki*) movement. Composers who had similarly rejected the "national school" but refrained from immersing themselves in popular song included not only internationalists such as Theodore Antoniou (b. 1935), Yannis Chrestou (1926–70), and Anestis Logothetis (1921–94), but also Michael Adamis (b.1929) and Dimitris Terzakis (b. 1938), both of whom have applied avant-garde techniques to material of Byzantine and demotic origin. By the end of the 1970s, "popular art song" had largely run its course and Theodorakis returned to the creation of symphonies and other forms of art music as star performers eclipsed song writers in popular genres. Among the succeeding generation of composers, only Thanos Mikroutsikos (b. 1947) has achieved equal levels of success in popular and art music.

During the last two decades of the 20th century strife over Greece's musical orientation between East and West receded as large numbers of its people adopted an eclectic multi-cultural-ism embracing purist revivals of Byzantine chanting, demotic song, and Ottoman court music alongside Western rock, jazz, and early music. This process has been facilitated by growth of the Greek media and the long overdue construction of the Athens Concert Hall (Megaron), as well as by the founding of music departments at the universities of Thessalonica, Athens, and Corfu. Outside Greece itself, many musicians of Greek extraction have continued to distinguish themselves in a variety of genres. Christos Hatzis (b. 1953), Peter Michaelidis (b. 1930), George Tsontakis (b. 1951), and Tikey Zes (b. 1927) are among the composers of the diaspora who have created works drawing explicitly on Hellenic musical traditions.

ALEXANDER LINGAS

See also Dance, Hymnography, Instruments, Opera, Song

Further Reading

Alevizos, Susan and Ted, *Folk Songs of Greece*, New York: Oak, 1968

Alexiou, Margaret, "The Lament of the Virgin in Byzantine Literature and Modern Greek Folk-Song", *Byzantine and Modern Greek Studies*, 1 (1975): pp. 111–40

Anderson, Warren D., *Music and Musicians in Ancient Greece*, Ithaca, New York: Cornell University Press, 1994

Anogeianakis, Phoivos, "I Mousiki sti neoteri hellada" [Music in Modern Greece], in *Historia tis mousikis* [History of Music] by Karl Nef, translated by Phoivos Anogeianakis, 2nd edition, Athens, 1985 (original Swiss edition (in German), 1920)

Anoyanakis, Fivos [= Anogeianakis, Phoivos], *Greek Popular Musical Instruments*, Athens: National Bank of Greece, 1979

Arvanitis, Ioannis, "A Way to the Tranbscription of Byzantine Chant by Means of Written and Oral Tradition" in *Byzantine Chant: Tradition and Reform*, vol. 2, edited by Christian Troelsgård, Aarhus: Aarhus University Press, 1997

Arvanitis, Ioannis, "The Rhythmical and Metrical Structure of the Byzantine Heirmoi and Stichera as a Means to and as a Result of a New Rhythmical Interpretation of the Byzantine Chant" in *Le chant byzantin: état des recherches*, edited by Christian Hannick and Marcel Pérès, Grâne: Créaphis, forthcoming

Bachmann, Werner, "Das byzantinische Musikinstrumentarium" in *Anfänge der slavischen Musik*, edited by Ladislav Mokry, Bratislava: Slovenská Akadémia Vied, 1966

Barker, Andrew (editor), *Greek Musical Writings*, 2 vols, Cambridge and New York: Cambridge University Press, 1984–89

Baud-Bovy, Samuel, *Essai sur la chanson populaire grecque*, 2nd edition, Navplia, 1994

Beaton, Roderick, "Modes and Roads: Factors of Change and Continuity in Greek Musical Tradition", *Annual of the British School at Athens*, 75 (1980): pp. 1–11

Bourgault-Ducoudray, L.A., *Trente mélodies populaires de Grèce et d'Orient*, 4th edition, Paris: Lemoine, 1876, reprinted Katerini, 1993

Braun, Joachim, "Musical Instruments in Byzantine Illuminated Manuscripts", *Early Music*, 8 (1980): pp. 312–27

Conomos, Dimitri E., *Byzantine Trisagia and Cheroubika of the Fourteenth and Fifteenth Centuries: A Study of Late Byzantine Liturgical Chant*, Thessalonica: Patriarchal Institute for Patristic Studies, 1974

Conomos, Dimitri E., "The Iviron Folk-songs: A Re-examination" in *Studies in Eastern Chant*, vol. 4, edited by Miloš Velimirović, Crestwood, New York: St Vladimir's Seminary Press, 1979

Conomos, Dimitri E., "Experimental Polyphony 'According to the...Latins' in Late Byzantine Psalmody", in *Early Music History*, 2 (1982): pp. 1–16

Conomos, Dimitri E. *Byzantine Hymnography and Byzantine Chant*, Brookline, Massachusetts: Hellenic College Press, 1984

Conomos, Dimitri E., *The Late Byzantine and Slavonic Communion Cycle: Liturgy and Music*, Washington, D.C.: Dumbarton Oaks Research Library, 1985

Desby, Frank Harry, "The Modes and Tunings in Neo-Byzantine Chant" (dissertation), University of Southern California, 1974

Desby, Frank Harry, "Growth of Liturgical Music in the Iakovian Era" in *History of the Greek Orthodox Church in America*, edited by M.B. Ephthimiou and G.A. Christopoulos, New York: Greek Archdiocese of North and South America, 1984

Filopoulos, Giannes, *Eisagogi stin helliniki polyphoniki ekklesiastiki mousiki* [Introduction to Greek Polyphonic Ecclesiastical Music], Athens, 1990 (with a very brief summary in English)

Frye, Ellen (editor), *The Marble Threshing Floor: A Collection of Greek Folk Songs*, Austin: University of Texas Press, 1973

Gauntlett, Stathis, *Rebetika Carmina Greciae Recentioris: A Contribution to the Definition of the Term Rebetiko Tragoudi through a Detailed Analysis of its Verses and of the Evolution of its Performance*, Athens: Denise Harvey, 1985

Georgiades, Thrasybulos, *Greek Music, Verse and Dance*, translated by Erwin Benedict and Marie Louise Martinez, New York: Merlin, 1956, reprinted New York: Da Capo, 1973

Holst, Gail, *The Road to Rembetika: Music of a Greek Sub-Culture, Songs of Love, Sorrow and Hashish*, 3rd edition, Athens: Denise Harvey, 1983, reprinted 1994

Jeffery, Peter, "The Earliest Christian Chant Repertory Recovered: The Georgian Witnesses to Jerusalem Chant", *Journal of the American Musicological Society*, 47 (1994): pp. 1–39

Lampelet, Georgios, *I Helliniki Dimodis Mousiki: 60 Tragoudia kai Choroi* [Greek Popular Music: 60 Songs and Dances], [n.p.], 1933, reprinted Katerini, 1995

Lingas, Alexander, "Hesychasm and Psalmody" in *Mount Athos and Byzantine Monasticism*, edited by Anthony Bryer and Mary Cunningham, Aldershot, Hampshire: Variorum, 1996

Lingas, Alexander, "Performance Practice and the Politics of Transcribing Byzantine Chant" in *Le chant byzantin: état des recherches*, edited by Christian Hannick and Marcel Pérès, Grâne: Créaphis, forthcoming

Lingas, Alexander, *Sunday Matins in the Byzantine Cathedral Rite: Music and Liturgy*, Amsterdam: Harwood, forthcoming

Maas, Martha and Jane McIntosh Snyder, *Stringed Instruments of Ancient Greece*, New Haven and London: Yale University Press, 1989

McKinnon, James, *Music in Early Christian Literature*, Cambridge and New York: Cambridge University Press, 1987

McKinnon, James (editor), *Antiquity and the Middle Ages: From Ancient Greece to the 15th Century*, London: Macmillan, 1990; Englewood Cliffs, New Jersey: Prentice Hall, 1991

McKinnon, James, *The Temple, the Church Fathers, and Early Western Chant*, Aldershot, Hampshire: Ashgate, 1998

Maliaras, Nikos, *Die Orgel im byzantinischen Hofzeremoniell des 9. und des 10. Jahrhunderts: eine Quellenuntersuchung*, Munich: Institut für Byzantinistik und Neugriechische Philologie der Universität, 1991

Mathiesen, Thomas J., *Apollo's Lyre: Greek Music and Music Theory in Antiquity and the Middle Ages*, Lincoln: University of Nebraska Press, 1999

Mazarake, Despoina B., *Mousiki Ermeneia Demotikon Tragoudion apo Agioreitika Cheirographa* [The Musical Interpretation of Folk Songs from Athonite Manuscripts], 2nd edition, Athens, 1992

Michaelides, Solon, *The Music of Ancient Greece: An Encyclopedia*, London: Faber, 1978

Mitsakis, Kariofilis, "Byzantine Parahymnography" in *Studies in Eastern Chant*, vol. 5, edited by Dimitri Conomos, Crestwood, New York: St Vladimir's Seminary Press, 1990

Mitsakis, Kariofilis, *Modern Greek Music and Poetry: An Anthology*, Athens, 1979

Mylonas, Kostas, *Istoria tou Ellinikou Tragoudiou* [History of Greek Song], vols. 2–3, Athens, 1985–92

Patrinelis, Christos G., "Protopsaltae, Lampadarii and Domestikoi of the Great Church during the post-Byzantine Period (1453–1821)" in *Studies in Eastern Chant*, vol. 3, edited by Miloš Velimirović, Oxford: Oxford University Press, 1972

Pennanen, Risto Pekka, "The Development of Chordal Harmony in Greek Rebetika and Laika Music, 1930s to 1960s", *British Journal of Ethnomusicology*, 6 (1997): pp. 65–116

Perrot, Jean, *The Organ, from its Invention in the Hellenistic Period to the End of the Thirteenth Century*, translated by Norman Deane, London and New York: Oxford University Press, 1971

Quasten, Johannes, *Music and Worship in Pagan and Christian Antiquity*, translated by Boniface Ramsey, Washington, D.C.: National Association of Pastoral Musicians, 1983

Romanos, St, *On the Life of Christ: Kontakia*, translated by Ephrem Lash, San Francisco: HarperCollins, 1995

Stathis, Gregorios, "An Analysis of the *Sticheron Ton helion krypsanta* by Germanos, Bishop of New Patras (The Old 'Synoptic' and the New 'Analytical' Method of Byzantine Notation)" in *Studies in Eastern Chant*, vol. 4, edited by Miloš Velimirović, Crestwood, New York: St Vladimir's Seminary Press, 1979

Strunk, Oliver, *Essays on Music in the Byzantine World*, New York: Norton, 1977

Symeonidou, Aleka, *Lexiko Ellinon Syntheton* [Dictionary of Greek Composers], Athens, 1995

Taft, Robert F., *The Byzantine Rite: A Short History*, Collegeville, Minnesota: Liturgical Press, 1992

Tillyard, H.J.W., "The Rediscovery of Byzantine Music" in *Essays Presented to Egon Wellesz*, edited by Jack Westrup, Oxford: Clarendon Press, 1966

Topping, Eva Catafygiotu, *Sacred Songs: Studies in Byzantine Hymnography*, Minneapolis, Minnesota: Light and Life, 1997

Touliatos, Diane, "The Traditional Role of Greek Women in Music from Antiquity to the End of the Byzantine Empire" in *Rediscovering the Muses: Women's Musical Traditions*, edited by Kimberly Marshall, Boston: Northeastern University Press, 1993

Tripolitis, Antonia, *Kassia: The Legend, the Woman, and Her Work*, New York: Garland, 1992

Troelsgaard, Christian, "Ancient Musical Theory in Byzantine Environments", *Université de Copenhague Cahiers de l'Institut du Moyen-âge grec et latin*, 56 (1988): pp. 228–38

Troelsgård, Christian (editor), *Byzantine Chant: Tradition and Reform*, vol. 1, Athens: Danish Institute at Athens, 1997; vol. 2, Aarhus: Aarhus University Press, 1997

Trypanis, Constantine A. (editor), *The Penguin Book of Greek Verse*, Harmondsworth: Penguin, 1971, reprinted 1979

Van Biezen, J., *The Middle Byzantine Kanon-Notation of Manuscript H: A Palaeographic Study with a Transcription of the Melodies of 13 Kanons and a Triodion*, Bilthoven: Creyghton, 1968

Velimirović, Miloš, "Liturgical Drama in Byzantium and Russia", *Dumbarton Oaks Papers*, 16 (1962): pp. 351–85

Velimirović, Miloš, "The Byzantine Heirmos and Heirmologion" in *Gattungen der Musik in Einzeldarstellungen: Gedenkschrift Leo Schrade*, edited by W. Arlt, E. Lichtenhahn, and H. Oesch, Bern and Munich: Francke, 1973

Voliotes-Kapetankais, Elias, *Enas Aionas Laïko Tragoudi: Politismos, Aristera kai Hellinike Koinonia*, Athens, 1989

Watts, Niki, *The Greek Folk Songs*, Bristol: Bristol Classical Press, and New Rochelle, New York: Caratzas, 1988

Wellesz, Egon, *A History of Byzantine Music and Hymnography*, 2nd edition, Oxford: Clarendon Press, 1961

West, Martin Litchfield, *Ancient Greek Music*, Oxford: Clarendon Press, 1992

Williams, Edward V., "A Byzantine Ars Nova: The Fourteenth-century Reforms of John Koukouzeles in the Chanting of Great Vespers" in *Aspects of the Balkans: Continuity and Change*, edited by Henrik Birnbaum and Speros Vryonis, Jr, The Hague: Mouton, 1972

Williams, Edward V., *The Bells of Russia: History and Technology*, Princeton, New Jersey: Princeton University Press, 1985, pp. 3–25

Winnington-Ingram, R.P. *et al*, Greece entry in *The New Grove Dictionary of Music and Musicians*, edited by Stanley Sadie, London: Macmillan, and Washington, D.C.: Grove, 1980, vol.7, pp. 659–82

Wybrew, Hugh, *The Orthodox Liturgy: The Development of the Eucharistic Liturgy in the Byzantine Rite*, London: SPCK, 1989; Crestwood, New York: St Vladimir's Seminary Press, 1990

Zakythinos, Alexis D., *Discography of Greek Classical Music*, 2nd edition, Buenos Aires, 1988 (an updated Greek-language edition was published in Athens and Ioannina by Dodoni in 1993)

Muslims

The presence of Muslims on Greek national territory can be traced back to the time of the Ottoman empire. Originally most of the Muslims lived in western Thrace – where they constituted the majority of the population until the 1920s – as well as in Macedonia, Epirus, and Crete. Their community included groups speaking Turkish, Albanian, Slavonic, and Greek. The majority of Cretan Muslims spoke Greek.

In Greek historiography, and often in popular tradition, the relation of the Muslims to the Christian Orthodox population tends to be described in terms of enmity; all the different Muslim groups tend to be lumped together and considered as Turks. This approach has its origins in the Greek–Turkish conflicts over the legacy of the Ottoman empire, during which Islam and Christianity were the official religions of two rival nations.

However, numerous shared traditions show that the Orthodox Christian and Muslim populations influenced each other in both cultural and social terms during the Ottoman period. A similar interaction is also evident in the religious sphere, at least in terms of popular religion. Syncretic ritual acts point to the interpenetration of Orthodox Christian and Islamic approaches to faith: the worship of saints, the holy places, and the graves of holy men are typical of both the

Balkan region and northern Greece. Historians of religion tend to attribute this to the influence of actual representatives and bearers of such syncretic religious traditions in the Balkans – the Dervish brotherhoods and the Bektashi order in particular. These rituals survive to the present day in the popular beliefs of many west Thracian Muslims, although they have probably moved some distance from their original content. Perfect examples are the cult of saints and the spring festival called the "Hidrellez". The latter is celebrated today on 6 May, mainly in the Rhodope region; at its origin is the interweaving of three different saint figures: Elias from the Jewish tradition, al-Hadr from the Muslim tradition, and George from the Christian tradition.

The minority status of the Muslim community in Greece is connected with the foundation of the independent Greek state, whose predominant religion, according to the Greek constitution (article 3 §1 paragraph 1), is Eastern Orthodox Christianity. The rights of religious and linguistic minorities within the newly proclaimed Greek state were protected under the London Protocol of 22 January 1830. Following the annexation of Thessaly and a part of Epirus to Greece (Treaty of Constantinople, 1881), large numbers of Muslims living in these areas came to be resident on Greek national territory. The Epirus Muslims were Albanians, known as "Tsamides". The Treaty of Constantinople (1881) went into some detail on Greece's obligations towards its Muslim minorities.

The Lausanne Conference of 20 November 1922 was a landmark in terms of the Muslim presence in Greece: among other things it decreed an "obligatory exchange of population" between Greece and Turkey along religious lines. Greek Christians living in Istanbul and Muslims resident in western Thrace were exempted from this compulsory exchange and from this time onward constituted minority populations in their respective countries. The Lausanne Convention on the Protection of Minorities laid down the obligations of both states towards the minorities living on their territories.

According to the first census in Greece after the Lausanne Convention, carried out in 1928, there were 102,621 Muslims living in western Thrace, the majority of them in the department of Rhodope. However, these Muslims did not form a unified community – at least three separate groups can be identified (by their language and by their distinct lifestyles within mainly homogeneous communities): Turks (Turkish-speaking), Pomaks (Slavophone), and Muslim Gypsies (speaking both Turkish and Romany). In addition there were numerically less significant groups of Circassians, Kurds, and a Turkish-speaking group of African origin. The Pomaks lived mainly in the foothills of the Rhodope mountains, the Turks mainly in the southern lowland and in the towns, the Gypsies mainly on the outskirts of towns and the southern lowland.

The Muslim community in central Greece (the "Tsamides") was gradually eliminated through repression, but the Muslim communities of western Thrace still exist today. They are the only officially recognized minority in Greece, and have been granted Greek citizenship since the 1920s.

After World War II the Muslim population in Greece increased through the annexation of the Dodecanese islands (Paris Peace Treaty of 1947). On the Dodecanese (principally on the islands of Rhodes and Cos) there were around 4937 Muslims, accounting for some 4.1 per cent of the islands'

population. These Muslims have Greek citizenship but they are not recognized as a minority by the Greek state; nor are they protected by the Lausanne Treaty as this refers exclusively to the Muslims of western Thrace.

The highest religious and administrative body for the Muslim minority in western Thrace is the Mufti office. This institution is based on Articles 45 and 16 of the Lausanne Convention for the Protection of Minorities, itself based on the Treaty of Sèvres (1920). However, the introduction of the Mufti office ultimately derives from the Treaty of Constantinople (1881), which was subsequently extended by national legislation (for example, law ALI/1882 of 22 June 1882, law 2345/1920 of 24 June 1920, and most recently law 1920/1991 of 24 December 1990). In 1923 there were three Mufti offices in Greece; the number rose to ten in January 1928 and to 12 in April 1928. In the meantime the number of Muslims had risen significantly due to the annexation of Epirus after the Balkan Wars. In July 1953 and after the elimination of the Epirus Muslims, the number of offices was reduced to three: these are still based in the west Thracian towns of Xanthi, Komotini, and Didymoteichon. Today, there is an additional Mufti office on Rhodes.

The Lausanne Treaty also provided for a special educational system (at primary level) for the Muslims of western Thrace, although the mainstream educational system was also open to them as an alternative. In 1997 there were 232 minority primary schools in western Thrace, with a total of around 8500 pupils. The minority schools have private status and are administered by the Mufti office. The schools' principal sources of funding are religious establishments (the awqaf), contributions by pupils, and in some cases subsidies from the Greek state. There are also some secondary-level minority schools alongside the mainstream educational system, run on the basis of a bilateral agreement between Greece and Turkey in those regions inhabited exclusively by Muslims. In addition there are two religious institutes (medrese) for training holy men. The Pedagogical Academy was founded in Thessalonica in 1968 to train teachers for the minority education system: only members of the Muslim community are allowed to study here.

The identity of the Muslims of western Thrace has been a subject of dispute between Greece and Turkey since the 1920s: Turkey rejects the description "Muslim", maintaining that the minority in western Thrace is exclusively ethnically Turkish. Greece, by contrast, sees this minority as consisting of fundamentally heterogeneous groups of Muslims and denies that the community as a whole can be defined as Turkish. The Pomaks were also a subject of latent conflict between Greece and Bulgaria up to the 1970s: Bulgaria regarded the Pomaks as Bulgarians who had converted to Islam and thus maintained that there was a Bulgarian minority in northern Greece.

Participation in parliamentary elections provides an indicator of the standing of Muslims in the Greek political system. Until the 1980s Muslim candidates were put forward only in the electoral lists of the established parties. The one exception was the "Tsamourgia" party of Epirus, which offered its own list of candidates in the 1926 parliamentary elections. After this Greece did not see another Muslim political party until 1985, when a Muslim party from western Thrace, called "Eirini" (Peace), took part in parliamentary elections in the prefecture of Xanthi, albeit without success. In the years following this, two more parties were founded: "Empistosyni" (Trust) in Rhodope and "Pepromeno" (Fate) in Xanthi. However, members of the minority community still appear on the electoral lists of the established parties.

The exact number of west Thracian Muslims can only be estimated: the Greek official statistics office does not provide any data on the Greek minorities after the census of 1951. In terms of social standing, the Muslims living in western Thrace still belong mainly to the most underprivileged strata of Greek society, although some improvements have been apparent since the 1980s. Over the last 15 years the Muslim population has become far more mobile: large numbers of former farmers and tobacco producers (especially Pomaks) have been leaving the Rhodopes for the cities of the region. There has also been a significant increase in the migration of west Thracian Muslims to cities all over Greece, especially Athens and Thessalonica, and also to western Europe (mainly Germany).

SEVASTI TRUBETA

See also Minorities

Summary

There have been Muslims in Greece since the time of the Ottoman empire, mostly in western Thrace, Macedonia, Epirus, and Crete, and since 1947 in the Dodecanese. The Epirus Muslims have been eliminated by repression. The western Thrace Muslims are officially acknowledged in the Lausanne Treaty of 1923. They are not a homogeneous group, being made up of Turks, Pomaks, and Gypsies.

Further Reading

Alexandris, Alexis *et al.*, *Oi Ellinotourkikes Scheseis 1923–87* [Greek–Turkish Relations 1923–1987], Athens, 1991

Babinger, Franz, "Der Islam in Südosteuropa" in *Südosteuropa*, edited by Wilhelm Gülich, vol. 1: *Völker und Kulturen Südosteuropas*, Munich, 1959

Georgoulis, Stamatis, *O Thesmos tou Moufti stin Elliniki kai Allodapi Ennomi Taxi* [The Institution of Mufti in Greek and Foreign Legislation], Athens, 1993

Kissling, Hans-Joachim, "Zum islamischen Heiligenwesen auf dem Balkan vorab im thrakischen Raume", *Zeitschrift für Balkanologie*, 1 (1962): pp. 46–59

Ladas, Stephen P., *The Exchange of Minorities: Bulgaria, Greece, and Turkey*, New York: Macmillan, 1932

League of Nations Treaty series, *Protection of Minorities*, vol. 28, 1924

League of Nations Treaty series, *Convention Concerning the Exchange of Greek and Turkish Populations*, vol. 32, 1925

Meinardus, Roland, "Die griechisch–türkische Minderheitenfrage", *Orient*, 26 (1985): pp. 48–61

Nikolapoulos, Elias, "Politikes Dynameis kai Eklogiki Symperiphora tis Mousoulmanikis Meionotitas sti Dyti Thraki, 1923–55" [Political Powers and the Conduct of Elections among the Muslim Minorities in Western Thrace, 1923–55], *Deltio Kentrou Mikrasiatikon Spoudon* [Bulletin of the Centre for Asia Minor Studies], 7 (1990–91): pp. 23–25

Trubeta, Sevasti, *Konstitution von Minderheiten und die Ethnisierung sozialer und politischer Konflikte: eine Untersuchung am Beispiel der im griechischen Thrakien ansässigen "Moslemische Minderheit"*, Frankfurt: Peter Lang, 1999

Zeginis, Evstratios, *O Bektasismos sti Dytiki Thraki* [The Bektash System in Western Thrace], Thessalonica, 1988

Mycenae

Bronze Age type site

Mycenae stands on a rocky knoll tucked into the northeast corner of the Argolid. Today it appears as a walled citadel with an external circuit of about 1 km. On the slopes to the north and west lie areas of settlement and beyond that at least 250 family chamber tombs in 27 separate cemeteries. These lie along a network of well-built roads which link the site to the rest of the Argolid and to the Corinthia to the north. The overall area thus used has been estimated at 32 hectares.

The site is known from Homer as the home of Agamemnon, leader of the Achaean forces before Troy, and has been the scene of archaeological investigation since the middle of the 19th century when in 1841 Kyriakos Pittakis completed the clearance of the Lion Gate on behalf of the Archaeological Society of Athens. Heinrich Schliemann's excavations of 1874 and 1876, which followed his work at Troy, disclosed the rich tombs now known as Grave Circle A and brought international renown. These finds form the spectacular core of the Mycenaean Room in the National Museum at Athens. The site has given its name to the Late Bronze Age civilization of mainland Greece but its remains are too rich for the site to be considered typical of that period. Subsequent research has been by the Archaeological Society: Panaiotis Stamatakis, Christos Tsountas, Ioannis Papadimitriou, George Mylonas, and Spiros

Mycenae: vase in the shape of a bull's head, Mycenae, 16th century BC, Ashmolean Museum, Oxford

Mycenae: engraving from 1878 of Heinrich Schliemann's 1874 illustration of one of the grave circles at Mycenae

Iakovides, and (through the generosity of the Archaeological Society) by the British School at Athens (BSA): Alan Wace and Lord William Taylour. The site was mapped in 1887/88 by Bernard Steffen; an area survey by Iakovides and Elizabeth B. French (BSA) has recently been completed.

It is now known that the site was settled in the Neolithic period (6500 BC) but only became rich in the late Middle Bronze Age (c.1650 BC) when it seems to have taken over hegemony of the Argive plain from Argos. A series of warrior princes were buried in shaft graves (Grave Circles B and A) or, later, in built tholos tombs of which there are nine in total in three groups of three. There was a bureaucratic, centralized, possibly "palatial" society. Overseas links extended throughout the eastern Mediterranean and as far as Italy, Sardinia, and on occasion Spain to the west. It seems probable that it was the ruler of Mycenae to whom a letter from the Hittite king was addressed using the terms "Brother" and "Great King". At Mycenae itself, as elsewhere on the mainland of Greece and at Knossos, records were kept in the Linear B syllabic script, shown by the decipherment by Michael Ventris in 1952 to be an early form of Greek. This society collapsed around 1200 BC, probably as the result of earthquakes which disrupted the elaborate economic system. There was however no cultural break and the site continued to be inhabited, though by ever smaller numbers of people, until the Persian Wars when Herodotus says Mycenae, with Tiryns, sent a contingent of 400 to fight at Plataea. The name is inscribed on the serpent column which originally held the memorial tripod for this battle at Delphi but was later removed to the Hippodrome at Constantinople. The continued inhabitation of the site may have been linked to its control of Argive religious centres or to its position in Greek mythology. As well as an Archaic temple (of Hera or Athena) on the summit of the acropolis, there are Archaic dedications at the Treasury of Atreus and a shrine with dedications to Agamemnon of Hellenistic date, though the shrine itself originated in the late Geometric period. It has been suggested that this timing may reflect the circulation of the Homeric poems.

In 468 BC the town was attacked and captured by Argos and its fortifications disabled. The 5th-century BC tragedians, when dealing with the myths of the Oresteia cycle, mix Mycenae and Argos. Details in Aeschylus' *Agamemnon*, particularly the account of a series of beacon stations linking to Troy, seem to belong to Mycenae itself and the naming of Argos is thought to reflect political considerations at a date, 458 BC, soon after the downfall of the site. Schliemann thought that Euripides must have known the site in order to describe it so tellingly.

In the Hellenistic period Mycenae was revived as a *koma* or fortified settlement by Argos; the citadel walls were repaired, the lower town enclosed by a wall, the temple rebuilt, and a theatre and fountain house built. This town gradually declined

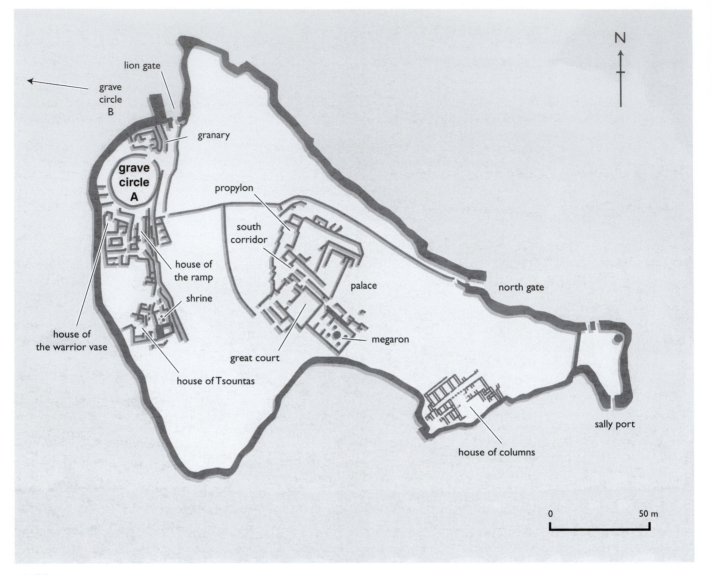

26. Mycenae

and by the 1st century BC to the poets of the *Greek Anthology* (notably Alphaeus of Mylitene) had become a byword for faded glory. However, in the 2nd century AD Pausanias saw monuments which can be related to the site as known today, particularly the Lion Gate itself and the tholos tomb which he called the "Treasury of Atreus".

Though well known by name, the site is not correctly positioned on maps until the late 18th century and the Lion Gate is not mentioned after Pausanias until a Venetian document of 1700. Some damage was done to two tholos tombs (those known as the Treasury of Atreus and the Tomb of Clytemnestra) by Veli Pasha in the early 19th century and both Lord Elgin and Lord Sligo brought back pieces of the facade of the Treasury of Atreus which are now in the British Museum. The lion sculpture over the main gate was luckily considered too heavy to move. During the 19th century the site was frequently visited and was illustrated mainly in watercolour by many travellers, but it has appeared in literature, either Greek or other European, less frequently. Sartre's terrifying *Les Mouches* is once again set in Argos. A notable exception is

Sacheverell Sitwell's *Agamemnon's Tomb*, reflecting an aspect little felt by the modern tourist.

ELIZABETH FRENCH

Summary

The citadel of Mycenae occupies a hilltop in the northeast corner of the Argolid. It flourished in the Middle to Late Bronze Age (1650–1200 BC) as the centre of a warrior society. Impressive grave goods and documents in Linear B have been found. The site continued to be occupied on a smaller scale until 458 BC and was reoccupied in the Hellenistic period.

Further Reading

Fitton, J. Lesley, *The Discovery of the Greek Bronze Age*, London: British Museum Press, and Cambridge, Massachusetts: Harvard University Press, 1996

Mylonas, George E., *Mycenae, Rich in Gold*, Athens: Ekdotike Athenon, 1983

Schliemann, Heinrich, *Mycenae: A Narrative of Researches and Discoveries at Mycenae and Tiryns*, London: John Murray, and New York: Scribner, 1878; reprinted New York: Arno Press, 1976

Tsountas, Chrestos and J. Irving Manatt, *The Mycenaean Age: A Study of the Monuments and Culture of Pre-Homeric Greece*, Boston: Houghton Mifflin, 1897; reprinted Chicago: Argonaut, 1969

Wace, Alan J.B., *Mycenae: An Archaeological History and Guide*, Princeton, New Jersey: Princeton University Press, 1949

Mycenaeans

"Mycenaeans" is the term applied both to the inhabitants of Mycenae itself and to the inhabitants of the whole of southern and central Greece (as far as Mount Olympus) in the Late Bronze Age (1600–1050 BC). The term was also originally used by Sir Arthur Evans for the inhabitants of Crete at a similar date before, in 1905, he put forward the new term "Minoan".

It is now known for certain, since the decipherment in 1952 by Michael Ventris of their written language in the Linear B script, that the Mycenaeans were Greeks. It is still a matter for debate when this Indo-European people entered Greece or if the language developed in situ from the original core. A common interpretation of the evidence postulates that they can be identified as immigrants from northwest Anatolia whose different, rather inhibited, culture can be widely seen in the closing years of the 3rd millennium BC.

By about 1600 BC a warrior elite had come to power at a number of centres, notably in Messenia and at Mycenae. The growth of wealth among this group can clearly be traced in the finds from Grave Circle B at Mycenae, followed by those of Grave Circle A. The presence in the 15th century BC of single tholos tombs at various sites suggests the model of Early State Modules which become linked through vassaldom, intermarriage, etc. This structure can still be seen in the Homeric poems, especially the Catalogue of Ships, which appear to reflect Bronze Age conditions with adjustments for later political factors.

The simple basic culture of the late Early Bronze Age and the Middle Bronze Age developed with the access of wealth and under Cretan artistic inspiration (and possibly actual craftsmen). However, it retained its separate identity and is notable for the stylization of natural motifs into symmetrical often heraldic patterns and for the portrayal of warfare with only the rarest representations of the actual rulers in any guise.

Between 1400 and 1200 BC the influence of the Mycenaeans grew throughout the Mediterranean. They had contact, presumably from trade, with an area stretching from Sardinia in the west to the Levant coast in the east and to the north into Albania and Macedonia. Sporadic Mycenaean imports are also found in Egypt. Current research is investigating the degree of acculturation which resulted in the various regions with which they had contact. The growth of power and influence caused the culture to become more centralized and an elaborate bureacracy is attested in the Linear B documents. Artefact production seems, from what has been preserved, to have changed from elite specialities to bulk manufacture.

The second half of the 14th century and the 13th century formed the acme of Mycenaean influence. The term *Ahhiyawa*, as used in Hittite texts, seems to refer to the Mycenaeans during this period; the ruler is on one occasion refered to as "Great King", a term usually employed for the ruler of Egypt and other major contemporary states.

At the end of the 13th century BC a series of disasters, possibly the result of earthquake or climatic instability, caused the collapse of the centralized bureacracy. Though the period called Mycenaean continued until the mid-11th century BC, the artistic and cultural activity of the various regions of Greece is more diverse and there is no further evidence of literacy. By the point at which the hallmark stirrup jar is no longer produced, the Mycenaeans can be considered to have given way to the more obviously direct ancestors of the Classical Greeks.

The later Greeks were well aware of their ancestors of the Mycenaean period, though the term "Mycenaeans" is never used to refer to them. In Homer the adjective applies only to the people of the city itself. It was once thought that this awareness was not the result of cultural continuum from the Bronze Age but resulted from the rediscovery of tombs of Bronze Age date, often assigned to heroes, and from an interest in the past revived by the epics of Homer. Archaeology has now shown this not to be the case; for instance the "heroic" burial at Lefkandi in Euboea dates to the 10th century BC but is of Homeric type. The influence of this legacy on the development of myth and of legends associated with local heroes is much discussed. Homer is now thought to reflect a mainland oral tradition. The cumulative result is seen in all the surviving works of ancient authors, from Hesiod to Pausanias. The respect accorded to heroic ancestors, whether genuine or invented, is epitomized by such events as the diversion of Alexander to make offerings at the supposed tomb of Achilles in the Troad.

ELIZABETH FRENCH

See also Linear B

Summary

Mycenaeans were not only the inhabitants of ancient Mycenae, but those of all southern and central Greece in the Late Bronze Age (1600–1050 BC). Their script, known as Linear B, is an early form of Greek. They were a wealthy warrior society with trading contacts throughout the Mediterranean. The Classical Greeks were aware of these ancestors but did not refer to them as Mycenaeans.

Further Reading

Antonaccio, Carla M., *An Archaeology of Ancestors: Tomb Cult and Hero Cult in Early Greece*, Lanham, Maryland: Rowman and Littlefield, 1995

Chadwick, John, *The Mycenaean World*, Cambridge and New York: Cambridge University Press, 1976

Christopoulos, George A. and John C. Bastias (editors), *History of the Hellenic World*, vol. 1: *Prehistory and Protohistory*, translated by Philip Sherrard, translation edited by George A. Phylactopoulos, University Park: Pennsylvania State University Press, 1974

Dickinson, Oliver, *The Aegean Bronze Age*, Cambridge and New York: Cambridge University Press, 1994

Iakovidis, Spyros E., *Late Helladic Citadels on Mainland Greece*, Leiden: Brill, 1983

Mountjoy, P.A., *Mycenaean Pottery: An Introduction*, Oxford: Oxford University Committee for Archaeology, 1993

Mylonas, George E., *Mycenae and the Mycenaean Age*, Princeton, New Jersey: Princeton University Press, 1966

Sherratt, E.S., "Reading the Texts: Archaeology and the Homeric Question", *Antiquity*, 64/245 (1990): pp. 807–24

Stubbings, Frank H., *Prehistoric Greece*, New York: Day, and London: Hart Davis, 1972

Wardle, K.A., "The Minoan and Mycenaean Palace Societies" in *The Oxford Illustrated Prehistory of Europe*, edited by Barry Cunliffe, Oxford and New York: Oxford University Press, 1994

Wardle, K.A. and Diana Wardle, *The Mycenaean World: Cities of Legend*, London: Bristol Classical Press, 1997

Warren, Peter, *The Aegean Civilizations: From Ancient Crete to Mycenae*, 2nd edition, London: Phaidon, 1989

Myrivilis, Stratis 1892–1969

Novelist

A sarcastic narrator, a nostalgic extoller of the Greek pastoral landscape, and a fervent exponent of the human condition, Myrivilis was the initiator of the war novel in Greek literature. He also made a tremendous contribution to the emergence and perfection of war literature as a particular literary genre while, at the same time, playing a substantial role in the development and emancipation of the so called anti-war, humanist movement in modern literature.

Myrivilis produced an amazing variety of work ranging from novels and short stories, to poems, essays, critical treatises, and reviews. His best-known works include *Kokkines Istories* (Red Stories, 1915) and *Oiigimata* (Narrations, 1928). The publication of these two collections of stories – in the aftermath of World War I and the Asia Minor disaster respectively – inaugurated the first phase of war literature in Greece. As Myrivilis's reputation grew, he proceeded to write some of his most lengthy, wide-ranging, mature novels including *I Zoi en Tapho* (Life in the Tomb, 1924), *I Daskala me ta Chrysa Matia* (The Schoolmistress with the Golden Eyes, 1933), *O Argonavtis* (The Argonaut, 1936), and *I Panagia i Gorgona* (The Mermaid Madonna, 1949). These works signified the second, most fertile phase of Greek war literature, which laid the foundations for the subsequent arrival of the anti-war dimension in literature.

Myrivilis's novels were marked by a density of personal style as well as an artfully elaborated, flawless expression. His novels are characterized by the use of well-structured phraseology and a stimulating imagery able to recreate and intensify the war experience. Although Myrivilis was mainly preoccupied with the overriding theme of his novels, he never underestimated the significance and primary role played by linguistic skill, style, expression, and idiom in a literary work.

Myrivilis participated in the Balkan Wars (1912–13) by joining the front line as a volunteer, in World War I, and in the military expedition in Asia Minor. Having experienced the brutality and bloodthirsty inhumane reality of war, he wrote about his own experiences and relayed his anti-war message to future generations. By persistently describing the barbarous reality of fighting and depicting the animal instincts of the people involved in it, he attempted to exalt the value of life itself as the most precious gift of human existence. Indeed, the context of his work acquired a special importance, its character magnified in his readers' minds to an extent that they would consider both his life and work as if they were crystals produced in reaction to the times.

The unique elements of Myrivilis's work have to do with the particular perspective he endorsed, as well as his distinct outlook. He experienced war and he succeeded in describing its drama in every possible detail from the position of a simple soldier of the front line or the trench, and not that of the senior officer or the politician. By adopting this point of view, he spelled out the individual man's experience of war, the central place occupied by his feelings, instincts, necessities, passions, and the need for survival. In this way, Myrivilis expressed his denunciation of war and set himself against those whom he held responsible for the outbreak and continuation of such a misery. By emphasizing the contrast between the condition of life in peace and death in war, he was able to dispatch his anti-war message. Such a treatment of his subject combined with the deployment of realistic imagery of the moment of war reminiscent of Homer or Thucydides made him a traditional writer. By selective use of the ideas and methods of earlier war writers, Myrivilis produced a synthesis of utterance with which he continued to deplore combat. At the same time, he recognized a change of circumstances (not of a deeper reality) from those experienced by previous writers. His great contribution to the Hellenic literary tradition lies in the fact that he prepared the way for an entire generation of war authors to follow, such as Ilias Venezis, Angelos Vlachos, Angelos Terzakis, Loukis Akritas, George Theotokis, Alexandros Kotzias, Thitho Sotiriou, and Nikos Kasdaglis.

Myrivilis's world of ideas is (as one might expect of a developed writer) not so much the expression of a simple idea, or even of different ideas joined together; it is much more the work of one idea developed in opposition to itself, and in this he expressed precisely his central dilemma as a humane, creative person occupied more or less efficiently in the activity of slaughter. As a fighting man dedicated to the arts of peace, his life, like that of most other soldiers, could not be other than contradictory; and in that paradox the expression of his position is founded on a dilemma.

Myrivilis preached extensively in his novels the value of life and peaceful human existence. Having experienced the destructive reality and madness of the most barbarous collective activity of humankind, he soon discovered the anti-heroic, corruptive, and humiliating boredom of the trench and recognized the imperishable nature of human life. In such awareness lies the innovative quality and didactic element of his writing. The traditional heroic spirit of the Greeks that characterized their never-ending struggle for peace seems to wane before the mystery of life and the grandeur of human nature. This does not mean that the writer separates himself from the tradition but, on the contrary, he declares his intention to go one step further. By raising his anti-war voice, he claimed that the continuation and preservation of tradition could be achieved only through life. Human existence for Myrivilis reflects God's goodness and is the evidence of His handiwork. Such a perspective resulted in influences from the biblical tradition in which God is identified with life and beauty. However, Myrivilis goes a little further in identifying life with the inner human soul. To discover the meaning of life is to discover your psyche. At this point, his work seems to elicit a deeper religious existential thinking. His work is a synthesis of Homeric ideas, Christian thought, and folklore morality. This is why he is regarded as a link between the philosophical polytheism of ancient Greece and the monotheism of Christianity.

Another frequently analysed idea in Myrivilis's work is that of the vital need for shared human contact. The writer opposes the condition of the solitary man. This shows how two principles of Aristotelian philosophy exerted a profound influence on Myrivilis: that man is by nature a social animal and that man cannot live alone, otherwise he becomes either God or beast. Myrivilis also draws attention to the idea of Rousseau's primitive human soul and proceeds to compose an encomium for the primeval unspoiled innocent soul.

By his ability to merge the lyric and epic elements in his novels without losing the balance between them, Myrvilis produced allegorical didactic novels which gave expression to his talents and his alert conscience. His work is consistent with War in a wider context than the war offers, so that for him the focus of his novels is an idea of the otherness and the confining totality of experience. His characters are strongly built just like the figures of the biblical or tragic tradition. In this manner, he especially influenced the construction of Venezis's characters.

For these reasons, Myrivilis's writing works both as a moral agent requiring an alteration in the reader's psyche and thus in the conduct of society, which is made up of these readers; but it also functions as a literary artefact.

MARIA ROUMBALOU

Biography

Stratis Myrivilis was the pen name of S. Stamatopoulos who was born on Lesbos in 1892. He took part in the Balkan Wars, the First World War, and the ill-fated expedition to Asia Minor. In his novels he wrote about the bitter experience of war. He also wrote short stories, poetry, essays, and reviews. He died in Athens in 1969.

Writings (in translation)

Life in the Tomb, translated by Peter Bien, Hanover, New Hampshire: University Press of New England, 1977; London: Quartet, 1987 (Greek edition 1924)

The Schoolmistress with the Golden Eyes, translated by Philip Sherrard, London: Hutchinson, 1964 (Greek edition 1933)

The Mermaid Madonna, translated by Abbott Rick, New York: Crowell, 1959 (Greek edition 1949)

Further Reading

Harris, P., *Ellines Pezographoi* [Greek Novelists], vol. 4, Athens, 1973

Karantonis, A., "Stratis Myrivilis" (in Greek) in his *Apo ton Solomo ston Myrivili* [From Solomos to Myrivilis], Athens, 1969

Kotzioulas, G., *O Stratis Myrivilis Ke i Polemiki Logotechnia* [Stratis Myrivilis and War Literature], Athens, 1931

Mirabel, A., "Stratis Myrivilis, romancier de la Grèce des legendes et de réalité" in *Mercure de France*, 1165 (1960): pp. 90–112

Vitti, M., *I Istoria tis Neoellinikis Logotechnias* [History of Greek Literature], Athens, 1978

Mysticism

The term "mysticism" is a neologism. It is, in fact, characteristic of the Greeks not to have invented a separate, abstract, term for the kind of experience they deemed inseparable from true philosophy and theology. What we do have in Greek are terms for "mystery", "mystic", and "mystical", deriving from the verb *muein*, to close the eye, to initiate into the mysteries. These terms denote that which is hidden, that which lies beyond the realm of ordinary existence. In this essay we shall take a broad definition of mysticism: the quest for, and experience of, unmediated contact with the divine.

Alongside the anthropomorphic polytheism of Greek religion there was an alternative form of religion represented by the mystery cults. These offered a direct apprehension of the divine unattainable within the civil religion. Of these cults the Eleusinian and Dionysian mysteries are of particular importance. The origins of the Eleusinian mysteries are pre-Hellenic. They consisted in the re-enactment of the myth of Demeter, the earth-mother, and her daughter Kore, or Persephone. They involved several stages of initiation, producing fellowship with the goddesses and culminating with the beholding (*epopteia*) of the revelation of these deities at the shrine of Eleusis. The Dionysian mysteries went beyond the Eleusian in seeking actual possession by and union with the deity. This was to be attained through rites of an orgiastic character in an outgoing of consciousness, or ecstasy. Both cults were associated with the triumph over death and the rebirth into immortality. The myth of the death and rebirth of Dionysus became a prominent feature of the Orphic movement, active from the 6th century BC. The Orphics sought deliverance from the cycle of transmigration and reincarnation through union with the divine, understood not merely as a transient ecstatic experience but as a permanent state of blessedness.

Plato's philosophy has a profound mystical element. His philosophy was pre-eminently a way, a means whereby man might reacquire true, participatory knowledge of the real, the eternal. The way's end is variously described: it is Being in the *Phaedo*, the Good in the *Republic*, Beauty in the *Symposium* and the *Phaedru*s, and the One in the *Philebus*. Unawakened to the real, eternal world, man perceives only the phenomenal world, the world of sense perception. In his famous cave simile Plato compares the situation of the unawakened to men shackled in a cave, able to see only the shadows of those who pass by behind them. Reawakening to the real world, the noumenal world of ideal Forms, is a painful but necessary experience. From that awakening one must strive for the apprehension of the transcendent reality that is the source of all that is. This way of contemplation and of intuitive, participatory, knowledge is a guiding principle in Plato's work. It is, for example, the way that the rulers of the city state must follow. It was to be an important influence in shaping the Christian mystical tradition.

The mystical way enunciated so clearly by Plato suffuses much of the Hellenic philosophical tradition. Aristotle, notwithstanding the many differences he had with his master, speaks of the contemplative life as a participation in the divine life in which the subject–object distinction between man and the divine disappears. The successors of Plato elaborated the mystical element in his work. The Stoicized form of Platonism known as Middle Platonism, which held sway roughly from the 1st century BC to the 3rd century AD, developed a much clearer idea of the transcendence of God, as opposed to the divine, than that found in Plato himself. It was against this intellectual background that many of the most outstanding examples of Hellenic mysticism emerged.

The work of Philo (late 1st century BC–mid-1st century AD) represents a form of Judaism profoundly shaped by the Middle Platonism of his day. Philo presents God as radically unknowable in himself but made known in his powers or operations. This distinction, not original to Philo, was to have a long and eventful history. For Philo, God reveals himself according to man's capacity to apprehend him. To describe this process of revelation, Philo does use the language of the mystery religions, although he was not directly influenced by them. He describes the soul's journey to God as beginning with conversion and the recognition of the createdness of the universe. Through moral purity the soul comes to know itself and to recognize its utter dependence upon God. Knowledge of God is a divine grace, not a natural capacity. It entails a going out of oneself, a form of ecstasy seen most clearly in the Hebrew prophets. The shining of the light of God within entails the suspension of the faculties, entails "ecstasy and divine possession and madness". In such a state the soul is "superior to man but less than God".

The Hermetic movement that developed in Egypt in the first three centuries of the Christian era made some use of the Egyptian religion, and certainly drew upon Judaism, but was profoundly Hellenic in inspiration. The Hermetic texts present a guide to mystical experience, viewed from a variety of standpoints. They speak of God as ineffable but knowable by man by virtue of man's divine nature. The great evil is ignorance; the mystical way consists therefore in the reacquisition of self-knowledge, which is knowledge of the divine, and the ascent to the ecstatic vision of God in which man is deified, or rather realizes his own divinity.

The extraordinarily complex and seductive set of traditions known as Gnosticism posed a grave threat to Christianity in the first three centuries of the Christian era. While teachings and practices varied greatly, Gnosticism was essentially an attempt to present Christianity as a mystery religion, analogous to the mysteries of Mithras, Cybele, and Isis that were flourishing at the time. Teaching a radical form of dualism between God and the world, the Gnostics offered an initiatory form of knowledge whereby those who had a divine spark within them might escape from the material world and find salvation. Gnostic dualism found a new expression in the 3rd century AD with the rise of the Manichaean religion.

The finest example of Hellenic mysticism is to be found in the teachings of Plotinus (AD 204–70), founder of the tradition known as Neoplatonism. Plotinus took up the perception of the transcendence of God found in Middle Platonism and developed it into a thoroughgoing statement of divine incomprehensibility. Plotinus' teaching is centred upon the soul's ascent to reunion with the One. We know from his biographer, Porphyry, that Plotinus himself experienced mystical union with the One on several occasions. Plotinus teaches a way whereby the obscurities and accretions of the material life might be removed and the return to God accomplished. Plotinus had a far more positive attitude to the material world than did the Gnostics, but is at the same time unequivocal in his understanding that the material is to be left behind on the soul's journey back to God. The return to the contemplation of God in Plotinus is also the return to oneself. It is a return to the vision of light in which the subject–object distinction between man and God disappears, in which the soul becomes that light, being "raised to Godhood or, better, knowing its Godhood". Centre coincides with centre: "This is the life of gods and of the godlike and blessed among men, liberation from the alien matter that besets us here, a life taking no pleasure of the things of the earth, the passing of the alone to the Alone."

The Christian mystical tradition took up and reshaped many features of the mysticism of the Hellenistic period, being principally indebted to Philo and Plotinus. Indeed, while Philo's influence on the Jewish tradition was initially minimal, and many of Plotinus' successors lapsed into theurgy, or magic, it was the Christians who preserved many of the insights of these two great teachers within the context of a living tradition.

Clement of Alexandria integrated much of Philo's mystical teaching within the Christian tradition, most notably the motif of the divine darkness of Mount Sinai used to express God's incomprehensibility. Clement went beyond Philo in speaking quite unambiguously of man's deification. Like Philo, Clement used the language of the pagan mysteries to describe the mysteries of his own faith: "O truly holy mysteries, O light undefiled. I am led by the torch-bearer to be initiated into heaven and God. Through initiation I become holy; the Lord is my hierophant and as one-who-leads-by-light [*photogogos*] seals the votary for himself." We should not forget how attractive this sort of language would have been to the 2nd-century Alexandrine ear.

Origen's work has a deeply mystical character, something that those familiar only with his *On First Principles* and *Contra Celsum* can be prone to overlook. For Origen the mystical life is a realization of the union with Christ effected at baptism. His *Commentary* and *Homilies* on the Song of Songs develop this theme. Origen takes Proverbs, Ecclesiastes, and the Song of Songs to refer to the three stages of the ascent to God, that is, to the acquisition of the virtues, to the proper understanding of the natural world, and, finally, to enoptic, or inspective, contemplation of God. In this understanding, the goal of the mystical life is union of the spiritual intellect, or *nous*, to God through contemplation. It does not entail ecstasy.

The Alexandrine mystical tradition formed a crucial component of the teaching of the Cappadocian Fathers. This is most evident in St Gregory of Nyssa's *Life of Moses*. It is also apparent in the works of Evagrius of Pontus and pseudo-Macarius. Evagrius made Origen's threefold distinction of the spiritual life classic. He also refrains from speaking about ecstasy. Macarius is less reserved, and speaks of the intellect as "utterly suspended and ravished", carried away by prayer and become one with it. He also follows Clement and Philo in using the phrase "sober drunkenness", a motif avoided by both Origen and Evagrius.

There was a danger in the Christian usage of the Hellenic mystical tradition that the mystical life would be seen as circular, as an escape from matter and a return to pre-cosmic unity. This element of circularity is palpable in the teachings of Origen and Evagrius. It was avoided by the Cappadocians and by Macarius in their emphasis on personhood and the integrity of the body. Union with God in these writers has no connotations of reabsorption into the divine. The teachings of pseudo-Dionysius the Areopagite, deeply influenced by the Neoplatonism of Plotinus and Proclus, do not adequately avoid the dangers of circularity. While their wonderful evocations of the suprarational and ecstatic apprehension of God in the state of perfect unknowing were to be enormously influential, they lacked the personalistic element so vital to true Christian mysticism.

St Maximos the Confessor produced in the 7th century an original and creative synthesis of the eastern Christian mystical tradition. Maximos built on the synthesis between Macarius and Evagrius made by Diadochus of Photice in the 5th century. Using the Cappadocian emphasis on the person, he was able to integrate the valuable insights of the Areopagite within his own synthesis. Maximos's theology is governed by mystical experience. His defence of the two wills – divine and human – in Christ was based not on abstract theological principles, but on the lived experience of the saints of the synergistic and personalistic character of union with God.

The vision of the divine light recounted so vividly by St Symeon the New Theologian is an illustration of the eastern Christian mystical tradition at its most vibrant and audacious. The nature of that light, which the hesychast monks also claimed to witness in prayer, became the subject of controversy in 14th-century Byzantium. The recognition by the Church of the divine nature of that light is a further example of mystical experience being taken as normative in the formulation of Christian doctrine.

It is examples such as these that led the Orthodox theologian Vladimir Lossky (1903–58) to declare that in the eastern Church there is no theology without mysticism and vice versa. The eastern Church has certainly been less susceptible than the West to the tendency to separate theology from mysticism. It has not, however, been immune. The *Philokalia*, for example, was produced to combat just such a separatist tendency that was very evident in 18th-century Greece. There has been a revival of interest in the theory and practice of the eastern Christian mystical tradition in the latter part of the 20th century. Against the prevailing academicism of the theological schools and the Protestant moralism of the Brotherhoods, a renewed interest in the well-springs of the Christian mystical tradition has become evident, for example among the circle of theologians influenced by the "Paris school" of Orthodox theology. This revival has also been very evident on Athos in recent years, somewhere where the mystical tradition has never died, but has often been very hard to find.

MARCUS PLESTED

See also Orgiastic cults

Further Reading

Clément, Olivier, *The Roots of Christian Mysticism: Text and Commentary*, 5th edition, London: New City, 1998

Louth, Andrew, *The Origins of the Christian Mystical Tradition from Plato to Denys*, Oxford: Clarendon Press, and New York: Oxford University Press, 1981

Spencer, Sidney, *Mysticism in World Religion*, Harmondsworth and Baltimore: Penguin, 1963

Zaehner, R.C., *Mysticism, Sacred and Profane: An Inquiry into Some Varieties of Praeternatural Experience*, Oxford: Clarendon Press, 1957

Mythology

The Greek word *mythologia*, which occurs for the first time in Plato, simply means "storytelling". But in modern usage "mythology" refers both to the corpus of myths and to its systematic study. Taken in the former sense, Greek mythology consists of a large number of stories about gods, heroes, the nature of the cosmos, and religious practices. According to one well-known classification associated with early 19th-century folklorists and students of non-classical legends, including the brothers Jacob and Wilhelm Grimm (cf. H.J. Rose, *Handbook of Greek Mythology*, (1964), ch. 1), these stories consist of three main types.

(1) Myths proper, i.e. pre-scientific and imaginative explanations of real or supposed phenomena which appeal to emotion rather than reason. As these phenomena are mostly natural, nature myths are preponderant. The stories are mainly concerned with gods, their birth, their relationship to one another, victories over monsters and rivals, love affairs, special powers, connections with shrines, or rituals. They are often aetiological in purpose, in that they attempt to provide explanations of phenomena which appear wonderful or puzzling. They are concerned with the causes of all manner of things from apparent movement of the heavenly bodies to the shape of a neighbouring hill or the origin of a local custom.

(2) Legends or sagas, i.e. accounts of heroes who were thought of as actually having lived in the distant past and as having taken part in quasi-historical events, such as battles and adventures, which were generally accepted as actually having happened. Thus the story of the Trojan War, whose origin tradition traced to Paris' abduction of Helen, is thought to reflect a concerted attempt by the Achaeans, a conquering feudal aristocracy, to seize the Black Sea trade at the beginning of the 12th century BC. It seems to have consisted in a blockade of the fort of Ilium, thus interrupting Trojan communication with neighbouring countries, and the issue seems to have been decided by the economic and military exhaustion of the Trojans which led to the subjugation of the cities allied with them and finally to the fall of Ilium itself. Thus the story is based on some kind of memory of the past and, with the exception of the part played by the gods (which really belongs to myth proper), the progress of the war is described in largely realistic terms. It is a human story unfolding in a human environment. With constant repetition through many generations such legends undergo all sorts of mutations – additions (mostly of imaginary and therefore picturesque material), omissions (mostly of real details), modifications, and rehandlings. Occasionally, the story may be completely fictional, but it will nevertheless be modelled upon real semi-historical narratives. On the other hand, there are instances of fragments of real history being preserved in legends of the peasantry over an extraordinary length of time.

(3) Folk tales told for popular entertainment, mostly stories of adventure dealing with natural or supernatural matters. Varieties include fairy tales, animal fables, and stories about witches, giants, ogres, and magical objects. Despite these supernatural elements, the main character is generally a human being, usually of humble origin, striving to achieve a human goal in spite of, or with the help of, such fantastic forces. The theme may also be a contest or trial, e.g. to defeat a monster

Mythology: marble statue group of the priest Laocoon and his sons being attacked by serpents, *c.*50 BC, Vatican Museums, Rome

or win a bride; or it may involve a more domestic challenge such as circumventing a malicious stepmother or jealous brothers or sisters. Many of these characteristically involve trickery or ingenuity or the use of magic. There may also be an element of wish fulfilment or the acquisition of a treasure or a great reward for apparently small but often highly moral actions, such as the solving of a riddle. A story, such as that of Cadmus, Perseus, Heracles, or the Argonauts, may contain elements from more than one of these types.

The ancient Greeks themselves had various attitudes to their myths. Some people no doubt accepted them as literally true and considered their narratives to be historical accounts. However, many thoughtful people must have found it difficult to accept them or their implications. Their reaction was broadly twofold: rationalization, which appears to have begun with Hecataeus of Miletus (550–480 BC); and allegorization, which probably began with Theagnes of Rhegium in the 6th century BC and, through its use by the Stoics, persisted until late antiquity and survives in the work of some early Christian writers and artists.

Myths performed a number of important functions in ancient Greek society in the various spheres in which they were employed. Turned into epic, they served to preserve and immortalize the famous deeds of men (*klea andron*). They provided education (often intertwined with entertainment) as examples or allegories. They gave pleasure and aroused feelings which, in some cases such as tragedy (if one follows the interpretation of *katharsis* as purgation) may have been considered therapeutic. Myths were also employed, especially in rhetoric, to explain the present in terms of the past, and to justify political or military decisions.

Greek mythology probably originated from the primitive forms of worship which existed in ancient Crete from about 3000 BC, and which were associated with animistic and magical beliefs. Over time such beliefs evolved into a body of legends involving natural objects, animals, and the anthropomorphic gods, and some of these legends found their way into the corpus of Greek myth. It may be observed that many of the principal Greek myths are connected with centres of Minoan and Mycenaean civilization. The legends of Perseus and Atreus are associated with Mycenae itself, while that of Oedipus is associated with Thebes, and that of Heracles with Thebes and Tiryns. It is therefore possible that these myths existed in some form in Mycenaean times.

Clay tablets from the time of the Mycenaean civilization (which reached its peak between 1400 BC and 1200 BC) provide earliest records of Greek mythology, and suggest that some of the main Greek gods and goddesses were known in the late Bronze Age. According to them, Poseidon was the principal god of the Mycenaeans, while Zeus held a less important place. The presence of the formulae "mother of the gods" and "Drimius, son of Zeus" suggests a divine genealogy. During the so-called Dark Age this mythology combined with that of the Dorians to form the mythology of Classical Greece.

The variety of factors that contributed to the formation of Greek myths and mythological personages resulted in the lack of unity, consistency, or coherence that pervades Greek mythology. The immense diversity stems partly from geographical considerations, since in widely differing regions there evolved different conceptions of the gods of the Greek world and varying rituals of propitiation. Moreover, the myths are often found in fragmentary form and in sources ranging in date from the 2nd millennium BC to the beginning of the Christian era, and it is important to realize that the older sources do not necessarily preserve earlier or more authentic traditions. In many cases the myths and fragments belong to large mythological cycles current in various communities and often not known to us in their entirety. Moreover, the myths contain elements originating in a varied historical and cultural background. In particular, the Mediterranean peoples, who worshipped an earth goddess, were conquered by successive waves of Hellenes bringing with them some form of tribal sky god. Thus, while gods like Zeus represent mainly the Indo-European cultural element, Demeter, Aphrodite, and Rhea probably represent Minoan-Mycenaean and Near Eastern elements. In fact, many deities, such as Demeter, Athene, and Zeus himself, combined in a single divinity both Mediterranean and Hellenic traits. Moreover, the myths have been subject to interpretation by poets and philosophers who have utilized many strands and varied traditions of the mythological cycles. The diversity of local legends may serve to explain the frequent sexual alliances of gods and heroes with their close relations, an idea repugnant to Greek custom. This may be the result of blending together of different legends representing a god and goddess (such as Zeus and Hera) either as husband and wife, or as brother and sister.

Greek myths are nevertheless relatively free of cloudy, grotesque, and horrible details such as are found in the legends of many other nations. Even their monsters are not particularly ugly or uncouth; nor is there much that is dreadful in their witches, ghosts, and demons.

Present knowledge of Greek myths rests principally on ancient Greek literature. The earliest surviving literary sources are the poems of Homer and Hesiod. The *Iliad* and the *Odyssey* focus on events surrounding the Trojan War, but involve the activities of the gods and refer to earlier legends such as the Theban cycle, the voyage of the Argo, and the exploits of Heracles. Hesiod narrates the birth of the cosmos, the succession of divine rulers, the ages of human existence, the origin of mankind's sufferings, and the source of sacrificial practices. Other sources of myths are the Homeric hymns, fragments of the cyclic poets, lyric poets (especially Pindar), the tragedians and comedians, Hellenistic poets and scholars, and writers under the Roman empire such as Plutarch and Pausanias. To these must be added various representations in the visual arts, among which temple friezes and vase paintings are of special importance.

Greek religion was not based on revelation and, with few exceptions (mostly associated with mysteries) did not involve spiritual teaching; and, although state officials in charge of religious matters are not unknown, there were no formal structures and no written codes embodied in a sacred book. There was, therefore, a great variety of beliefs and practices, and a resulting multitude of variations in the myths. The Greek myths embrace most of the themes commonly found in the mythologies of the world such as creation and origins (aetiological myths), birth of gods and other divine beings, death and the afterlife (eschatological myths), and the renewal and rebirth of the world.

Greek myths show certain characteristic features. They embody an anthropomorphic and non-fantastic view of the gods: the gods are depicted in human form and have human feelings. Strange and scandalous details, which have survived in locally established traditions, are usually suppressed in Homer and other archaic poets. The gods lived on Mount Olympus in Thessaly, in a society that ranked them in terms of authority and powers. They moved freely, however, and individual gods came to be associated with the three principal domains – the sky, the sea, and the underworld – while the earth was held in common. They were immortal, and controlled all aspects of nature. Human lives were totally dependent on their goodwill. Relations between men and gods were generally friendly; but the gods severely punished mortals whose behaviour was unacceptable to them. Excessive arrogance, ambition, or even extreme prosperity provoked divine wrath and punishment. Consequently, there emerged the idea of a dual motivation according to which human destiny came to be viewed as the outcome of joint action by men and gods. Hence the *Odyssey* attributes the destruction of both Odysseus' crew and Penelope's suitors to their own folly and the action of divine justice. Similarly, the Sophoclean Oedipus, while attributing his blinding to Apollo, nevertheless says that it was his own hand that did it (*Oedipus Tyrannus*, 1329–31]. Since the Greek gods were largely personifications of natural phenomena, Greek mythology emphasized human weakness in facing the awesome powers of nature.

Most, if not all, heroes of Greek legends were mortal. They were subject to birth, old age, and death. Nevertheless, they associated with the gods, and many of them claimed their descent from the gods. The majority of Greek heroes and heroines belong to one of two principal groups, namely, those who lived before the Trojan War (such as Jason, Theseus, and Oedipus) and those who fought in that war (such as Hector, Achilles, and Odysseus). Some of the heroic tales, such as those of Helen and Achilles, appear to go back to Indo-European times, while others, such as that of the cattle-raiding Heracles, may go back even further. Another distinctive feature of Greek mythology is the prominence of initiatory myths. It has been pointed out that early accounts of pan-Hellenic expeditions contain many elements of male initiation, while legends of heroines reflect the final transition into womanhood.

As scholars such as Peter Walcot (1966) and Martin West (1971) have demonstrated, Greek mythology is also heavily indebted to the rich mythologies of Anatolia and Mesopotamia, probably through contacts during the Early Iron Age. In his *Theogony* Hesiod has incorporated some violent myths of Hurrian origin concerning, among other things, the cannibalism of the gods which, at a later date, evinced the protests of Pindar: "It is not for me to call one of the blessed gods a cannibal: this I avoid." The castration of Uranus by his son Cronus derives ultimately from the Hurrians through Hittite and Phoenician intermediaries; the division of the universe by lot between Zeus, Poseidon, and Hades (*Iliad*, 15. 187–93) derives from the Akkadian epic *Atrahasis*; and the figures of Oceanus and Tethys (*Iliad*, 14. 201) derive from Apsu and Tiamat in the Babylonian creation epic *Enuma Elish*. The last great wave of mythological invention was the result of Greek colonization of the Mediterranean and the Black Sea during the 8th and 7th centuries BC. Not only the *nostoi* but also the much older voyage of the Argonauts enabled newly founded colonies to relate themselves to the pan-Hellenic past as reflected in these myths and legends. Dynasties and heroic feats were among the more favoured themes of Archaic legend; but with the evolution of a more organized society, family relations received greater attention. Stress within the family leads to lies, betrayal, counter-seduction, and other forms of inhuman revenge – situations which Aristotle advised the poet to seize upon – but occasionally the family acts together to repel stresses from outside. The implicit drama of family stress is not confined to semi-realistic legends such as those of the houses of Labdacus and Atreus, but is also exemplified in the myths of the gods. Moreover, Athenian tragedy, in particular, concentrated more on the role of the individual in relation to the city-state and the value of democratic institutions. A large number of the stories belong to the category of aetiological myths, i.e. they originated as explanations of the birth or function of natural phenomena or religious rituals. In the latter case, it often happens that the myth survives in a detached form even after the ritual has disappeared. Many such myths are recorded by Pausanias (2nd century AD). Closely related are the myths of metamorphoses which, though found as early as Homer (e.g. Niobe and Proteus), came into their own in the Hellenistic age. The Hellenistic versions are aetiological in that they explain a present creature or landmark, though they lack the moral symbolism and the correspondence of animal and human traits characteristic of Ovid's narrative.

The commonest themes of Greek myth emphasize such preoccupations as contests and quests, particularly involving monsters; the relations between men and gods, whether of love, protection, or oppression; and the already mentioned stresses within the family, leading to acts of vengeance and displacement. Other themes emphasize fertility (though it did not find in Greece many different forms of mythical, as distinct from ritual, expression) and the displacement of elders. Eschatological myths include narratives of the imaginary world of the dead: how gods or defunct mortals pass beneath the earth, what they see on their way, the geography of the underworld and the aspect of its rulers and their subjects, the sufferings caused to the dead by neglect of their funerary rituals on earth, and so on. The developed and detailed eschatology is reflected not only in Near Eastern-type stories of disappearing gods, but also in the theme of heroic *katabasis*, or descent into Hades, e.g. that experienced by Heracles, Theseus, Orpheus, and Odysseus. The so-called Orphic tablets of the late 4th century BC instruct the dead about the topography of Hades, the springs of remembering and forgetting, and what the soul must say to prove its purity. Similar Orphic beliefs are also attested by Plato. Herodotus, probably rightly, traces such eschatological myths and rites to Egypt, but Mesopotamian influence cannot be ruled out (cf. G.S. Kirk, 1970, pp. 260–61).

Although the collection and interpretation of myths as a serious discipline did not begin until the latter part of the 18th century, ancient Greeks were not without thinkers and writers who reflected critically on their myths and expounded them. The first Greek physicist, Thales of Miletus (6th century BC), is represented as adopting a critical attitude towards the myths. By maintaining that the earth floats on water and that things come from water and go back to water, he attempted to correct, with the help of foreign myths known to him, what he saw as defects in the mythical cosmology of the Greeks. Criticism of the myths thus constituted a search for a rational understanding and control of the world. Myths lend themselves to change and adaptation to altered historical circumstances, and in ancient Greece this process continued down to the time when the claims of truth had to satisfy the new requirements of an emerging rationalism. Xenophanes attacked the anthropomorphic depiction of the gods in the myths, and this attack took on a moral dimension with him as well as with Pindar, Euripides, and Plato, on the grounds that the gods were depicted as immoral, adulterous, vengeful, and generally inferior to human beings. Allegorical interpretations (both physical and moral/psychological) were basically reactions to these attacks.

Herodotus (2. 53) believed that many Greek rituals were inherited from the Egyptians, and that the systematization of the Greek pantheon was due to Homer and Hesiod, who gave the deities their titles and distinguished their several provinces and special powers. Before that, the Pelasgians, on all occasions of sacrifice, called upon "the gods", but gave neither title nor name to any of them. Thus, according to Herodotus, and in the words of J. Harrison the mythology (or theology) of the Greeks "was not in the main the simple outcome of popular faith; still less was it a compilation due to a priesthood; it was the work of the poets". Prodicus of Ceos taught that the gods were personifications of natural phenomena. Plato employed myths and mythical modes to provide an insight into the deeper truths of philosophy not accessible to dialectical reasoning (cf. especially the *Symposium*). Although Aristotle is known to have been critical of the myths as fanciful and failing to embody truth about human life and the world, he realized their value in producing the tragic effect and, in his *Poetics*, advised would-be poets to keep as far as possible to the traditional stories. In the 4th century BC the mythographer Euhemerus in his *Sacred History* gave expression to the widely accepted belief of his time that myths were nothing other than distorted history, and that the gods were in effect kings and heroes who had been glorified over time and were worshipped for their deeds. Thus Zeus was an ancient king of Crete who rebelled against his father Cronus, the former king, and overthrew him. Biographies of other gods were similarly provided. Against this it has been argued that, to make a dead man into a god, one must already believe in some sort of gods, so that this theory cannot serve as an explanation of the origin of either religion or mythology.

During the Hellenistic period Greek beliefs were gradually modified under the influence of new philosophies (such as Stoicism) and the influence of neighbouring civilizations, but the myths recorded and adapted by Callimachus and his contemporaries were not directed at the general public (as were those of the Classical Greek poets), but at a small circle of connoisseurs. The Hellenistic and early imperial period saw a number of collections of myths compiled by scholars in order to elucidate allusions in the Classical authors. Most significant in this respect was the collection of mythological scholia on Homer which circulated as a separate book at least during the first five centuries of the Christian era. There were also collections which concentrated on a single theme, such as the book of star myths compiled by Eratosthenes, and the famous *Bibliotheca* ascribed to Apollodorus which organized the myths according to families. It is chiefly to collections such as these that we owe our knowledge of the lesser-known Greek myths. With the coming of Christianity, the gods of antiquity came to be interpreted either euhemeristically or as inferior demons, while the myths themselves came to be rejected as untrue or were interpreted allegorically as moral or exemplary stories – an approach which persisted until the Renaissance. A striking example is the 3rd-century fresco from the Catacombs of Domitilla in which the risen Christ is represented as Orpheus returned from Hades. Appropriated thus by Rome, both pagan and Christian, Greek mythology has been repeatedly represented through the ages in the literature, painting, sculpture, drama, dance, and music of the west; and its impact on certain other cultures (e.g. Hindu and Buddhist legends) has now been established, even though the theory of Greece borrowing from India still has its adherents also.

The study of Greek myths in the modern age began in France during the 18th century, but soon shifted to Germany and England. The 19th century was dominated by the work of Heyne, who emphasized the historical, natural, and national aspects of myth. Friedrich Creuzer (1771–1858) was the principal modern exponent of the symbolic interpretation, and his best-known opponent was C.A. Lobeck (1781–1860), author of the *Aglaophamus* (1829), who emphasized the need to examine carefully the source of a tale and determine its date. K.O. Muller's main interest was the determination of the provenance of the myths. The most prominent in their application of the comparative method to the study of mythology were the German J.W.E. Mannhardt (1831–80) and the Briton Andrew Lang. The oriental philologist F. Max Muller revived the doctrine that mythology sprang from imaginative treatment of physical forces, while the school of psychological thought associated chiefly with the names of Sigmund Freud and Karl Jung has devoted considerable attention to myths and tried to explain their genesis. In the 20th century the classical attitude to myth has been dominated by the trends initiated by J.G. Frazer. The new knowledge of comparative anthropology was applied to the study of myth and religion by Jane Harrison, A.B. Cook, Gilbert Murray, and F.M. Cornford. The driving force behind their work is the idea that the motives of custom and myth in primitive societies can illuminate those of more developed cultures, including that of the ancient Greeks. They therefore used the findings of comparative social anthropology to elucidate enigmatic practices of ancient Greek religion. The centre of the group was Jane Harrison, author of *Prolegomena to the Study of Greek Religion* (Cambridge, 1903) and *Themis* (Cambridge, 1912), who had studied the works of Darwin, Freud, Marx, and Nietzsche. Other influences included Durkheim, Levy-Bruhl, and Bergson. Under these influences they furthered the concept of collective beliefs and emotions, inspired by E.B. Tylor's idea of a special kind of "primitive mentality", an idea which has since been drastically revised by Lévi-Strauss in his *La Pensée sauvage* (Paris, 1962). Comparatively little has been achieved since then, apart from

following their views or moving away from them. This is true of M.P. Nilsson, H.J. Rose, Karl Kerenyi and Mircea Eliade, Robert Graves, G.S. Kirk, R. Farnell, L. Deubner, and most recently W. Burkert. However, their attention has been drawn more to cults, festivals, and other aspects of Greek religion than to myths proper, whose study they have nevertheless influenced, and recent work has concentrated mainly on the relationship between myth and ritual and the explanatory and normative functions of myth. Meanwhile, widely differing views on the speculative function of myths have been expressed by Bronislaw Malinowski on the one hand and Claude Lévi-Strauss on the other. The recent interest of Classicists in gender studies has resulted in the production of several works on women in Greek mythology, and the need to study Greek heroines independently, rather than as mere counterparts to the heroes, has been duly emphasized.

D.P.M. WEERAKKODY

See also Gods and Goddesses, Heroes and Heroines

Further Reading

Ackerman, Robert, *The Myth and Ritual School: J.G. Frazer and the Cambridge Ritualists*, New York: Garland, 1991

Ahlberg-Cornell, Gudrun, *Myth and Epos in Early Greek Art: Representation and Interpretation*, Jonsered: Astroms, 1992

Bonnefoy, Yves (editor), *Greek and Egyptian Mythologies*, Chicago: University of Chicago Press, 1992

Bremmer, Jan (editor), *Interpretations of Greek Mythology*, Totowa, New Jersey: Barnes and Noble, 1986; London: Croom Helm, 1987

Burkert, Walter, *Structure and History in Greek Mythology and Ritual*, Berkeley: University of California Press, 1979

Buxton, Richard, *Imaginary Greece: The Contexts of Mythology*, Cambridge; New York: Cambridge University Press, 1994

Cahill, Jane, *Her Kind: Stories of Women from Greek Mythology*, Peterborough, Ontario: Broadview Press, 1995

Carpenter, Thomas H., *Art and Myth in Ancient Greece: A Handbook*, London: Thames and Hudson, 1991

Clinton, Kevin, *Myth and Cult: The Iconography of the Eleusinian Mysteries*, Stockholm: Svenska Institutet i Athen, 1992

Condos, Theony, *Star Myths of the Greeks and Romans: A Sourcebook*, Grand Rapids, Michigan: Phanes Press, 1997

Cook, Irwin F., *The Odyssey in Athens: Myths of Cultural Origins*, Ithaca, New York: Cornell University Press, 1995

Detienne, Marcel, *The Creation of Mythology*, Chicago: University of Chicago Press, 1986

Dodds, E.R., *The Greeks and the Irrational*, Berkeley: University of California Press, 1951

Dowden, Ken, *The Uses of Greek Mythology*, London and New York: Routledge, 1992

Edmunds, Lowell (editor), *Approaches to Greek Myth*, Baltimore: Johns Hopkins University Press, 1990

Edmunds, Lowell, *Myth in Homer: A Handbook*, 2nd edition, Highland Park, New Jersey: Mill Brook Press, 1993

Forbes Irving, P.M.C., *Metamorphosis in Greek Myths*, Oxford: Clarendon Press, and New York: Oxford University Press, 1990

Gantz, Timothy, *Early Greek Myth: A Guide to Literary and Artistic Sources*, Baltimore: Johns Hopkins University Press, 1993

Graf, Fritz, *Greek Mythology: An Introduction*, Baltimore: Johns Hopkins University Press, 1993

Graves, Robert, *The Greek Myths*, 2 vols., London and Baltimore: Penguin, 1955

Guthrie, W.K.C., *The Greeks and their Gods*, London: Methuen, 1950

Harris, Stephen L. and Gloria Platzner, *Classical Mythology: Images and Insights*, Mountain View: Mayfield, 1995

Harrison, Jane, *Myths of Greece and Rome*, London: Benn, 1927; Garden City, New York: Doubleday Doran, 1928

Hedreen, Guy Michael, *Silenus in Attic Black-figure Vase-Painting: Myth and Performance*, Ann Arbor: University of Michigan Press, 1992

Kirk, G.S., *Myth: Its Meaning and Functions in Ancient and Other Cultures*, Cambridge: Cambridge University Press, and Berkeley: University of California Press, 1970

Kirk, G.S., *The Nature of the Greek Myths*, Harmondsworth: Penguin, 1974; Woodstock, New York: Overlook Press, 1975

Malkin, Irad, *Myth and Territory in the Spartan Mediterranean*, Cambridge and New York: Cambridge University Press, 1994

Mylonas, George E., *Eleusis and the Eleusinian Mysteries*, Princeton, New Jersey: Princeton University Press, 1961

Nilsson, Martin P., *The Mycenaean Origin of Greek Mythology*, Berkeley: University of California Press, 1932

Nilsson, Martin P., *A History of Greek Religion*, 2nd edition, Oxford: Clarendon Press, 1949

Penglase, Charles, *Greek Myths and Mesopotamia: Parallels and Influence in the Homeric Hymns and Hesiod*, London and New York: Routledge, 1994

Powell, Barry B., *Classical Myth*, Englewood Cliffs, New Jersey: Prentice Hall, 1995

Pozzi, Dora C. and John M. Wickersham (editors), *Myth and the Polis*, Ithaca, New York: Cornell University Press, 1991

Reid, Jane Davidson (editor), *The Oxford Guide to Classical Mythology in the Arts, 1300–1990s*, 2 vols, New York and Oxford: Oxford University Press, 1993

Rose, H.J., *A Handbook of Greek Mythology*, 6th edition, London: Methuen and New York: Dutton, 1965

Ruck, Carl and Danny Staples, *The World of Classical Myth: Gods and Goddesses, Heroines and Heroes*, Durham, North Carolina: Carolina Academic Press, 1994

Saïd, Suzanne, *Approches de la mythologie grecque*, Paris: Nathan, 1993

Scheid, John, and Jesper Svenbro, *The Craft of Zeus: Myths of Weaving and Fabric*, Cambridge, Massachusetts: Harvard University Press, 1996

Shapiro, H.A., *Myth into Art: Poet and Painter in Classical Greece*, London and New York: Routledge, 1994

Tripp, Edward, *The Meridian Handbook of Classical Mythology*, New York: Meridian, 1974

Versnel, H.S., *Inconsistencies in Greek and Roman Religion*, vol. 2: *Transition and Reversal in Myth and Ritual*, Leiden and New York: Brill, 1993

Veyne, Paul, *Did the Greeks Believe in their Myths? An Essay on the Constitutive Imagination*, Chicago: University of Chicago Press, 1988

Walcot, Peter, *Hesiod and the Near East*, Cardiff: Wales University Press, 1966

West, Martin Litchfield, *Early Greek Philosophy and the Orient*, Oxford: Clarendon Press, 1971

West, Martin Litchfield, *The East Face of Helicon: West Asiatic Elements in Greek Poetry and Myth*, Oxford and New York: Clarendon Press, 1997

Whitman, Cedric H., *Euripides and the Full Circle of Myth*, Cambridge, Massachusetts: Harvard University Press, 1974

N

Nationalism

As a protean and resilient phenomenon, nationalism has stimulated scholars to attempt to trace its rudimentary manifestations far back in history: from the ancient Greeks' ethnocentric sentiment of cultural identification and arrogance towards the non-Greek world, to medieval movements of cultural separatism, usually linked to the emergence and consolidation of states. Nationalism both as a movement and an ideology, however, is principally a phenomenon of modern history, of explosive force and magnetism, whose energy has remained unabated over the last two centuries to the present day.

In the late 18th century and the two first decades of the 19th, and springing from the ramifications of the European Enlightenment and the cataclysmic impact of the French Revolution, Greek nationalism introduced a vanguard approach of social collectivity and attachment against the traditional background of the Ottoman-ruled lands. Imbued by liberal and secular European tenets, Greek intellectuals within and outside the Ottoman empire produced a matrix of a new Balkan ethnography which moulded and politicized Greeks' hitherto unformed sense of ethnic belonging, particularly among the Orthodox Greek-speaking subjects of the empire. They questioned the homogeneity of the enslaved and religiously self-identified society of the Balkans, articulated in the system of the *millets* (religious communities) and underpinned by the ecumenical values of the Orthodox Church, and they sought to reintegrate that society into fresh collectivities on the basis of distinction and differentiation, notably of language and the memory of their own perceived past. The Greek War of Independence (1821–27), leading eventually to a truncated Greek kingdom, was the successful outcome of this ideological ferment of the so-called Greek Enlightenment (1750–1821), which, out of an inextricable blend of nationalism and liberalism, cultivated and rallied collective beliefs around the idea of a nationally defined political entity: the nation state.

Once independence was attained, it was clear that within the confines of the newly established kingdom the Greek nation was lacking the cohesion, uniformity, loyalty, and enthusiasm with which the Greek intelligentsia had endowed it in the prerevolutionary stage. National allegiance and identity were objectives still to be pursued, rather than intrinsic, let alone primordial, attributes of the free nation. They were in serious competition with local attachments, social cleavages, and sectional political interests, already at work from the time of the struggle for independence. Even the Greek language, conceived of as an integrating factor, was in practice a pluralism of idioms to the point of confusion, aside from the fact that the nation embraced non-Graecophone groups which had actively participated in the Greek cause. Thus, in consolidating the national community, the Greek state was to play a decisive role; in this, it was largely in line with the major process unfolding in modern European history, in which nation states were indoctrinating their peoples with national and nationalist culture. Through national institutions, namely the army, the administration, the judiciary, and education, not only did the state extend and secure control over society, but it also imbued its citizens with national and nationalist values. To this process of statecraft-building with ideological implications subscribed the uncanonical proclamation in 1833 of the autocephalous status of the Greek Church and its independence from the ecumenical patriarchate, initiated by the Bavarian regency. Disregarding the Orthodox Church's deep-seated traditions, Greek nationalism made that highly influential and supranational authority comply with national prerequisites and, in time, develop as a component part of nationalist policies.

The early years of the Bavarian administration witnessed a readjustment of Greek nationalism in the formation of the political ideology of the new state. Stripped of its liberal and democratic origins, nationalism maintained its secular tradition and predilection for ancient Greece to sponsor the vision of a classicist state entertained by the new ruling elite. Classicism, as an ideological facade of the prospect of Europeanization, introduced an externally directed national ideology which, in its attempt to define Greek culture as "European" in the eyes of Europe, reproduced in cultural terms the subjugation of a rural, traditionally minded population to a governing elite. The gradual subsidence of the political legacy of the Greek Enlightenment, recorded *inter alia* in the revival of Orthodoxy as a backlash to the state-directed secular crackdown, reflected the response of the traditional culture and society to unfamiliar postulates claiming national originality. To mend this antithesis there would be an attempt in the course of time to mitigate Neoclassicism in favour of forms linked more deeply to Greek culture in the light of an organic concept of society.

This was put forward with the formulation of the so-called

Great Idea in its national sense – an overarching nationalist vision which became the Greek symbol of collective identity and destiny. Initiated in 1844 by John Kolettis in a speech in the National Assembly, the new doctrine visualized the unity of Hellenism far beyond the bounds of the Greek kingdom to comprise all the Greeks living under Ottoman administration, with the addition of the Greeks of the Ionian islands. By integrating state territorial ambitions with religious impulse and folk mythology, the doctrine of the Great Idea cemented the national identity and would enthral the nation to the point of furnishing its raison d' être for nearly the next 80 years. At home, the new doctrine acted as an exemplary diversion of social dissatisfaction, and strengthened national unity, which, from the very inception of the independent kingdom's life, had been undermined by significant centrifugal forces. It is symptomatic of its homogenizing intent that the Great Idea was inaugurated in the midst of a national rift generated at the time by the heated debate, crossing the confines of the National Assembly into everyday politics, over the eligibility of the heterochthonous Greeks to enjoy an equal status with their autochthonous fellow citizens in the Greek state. As to foreign policy, it set territorial enlargement as a national exigency, and related any course of external policy to the extent to which it would realize its maximalist goals; for the Great Idea, however ambiguous in representing a precise foreign-policy programme itself, was broadly construed as a restoration of the Byzantine empire with Constantinople resurrected as the Greek capital.

Greek nationalism found in the person of Jakob Philipp Fallmerayer, a German historian, both a virulent critic and an unintended source of vigour and dynamism. By denying modern Greeks their direct natural connection with their ancient ancestors, Fallmerayer launched by reaction in Greece a prolific literature aimed at elaborating and solidifying the injured Greek national identity. The result was that out of that national trauma, Greek nationalism re-emerged fully fledged, gaining momentum, flexibility, and self-confidence. Rectifying the selective and vulnerable dogma of the Greek Enlightenment, which had opted for Classical Greece alone as the field of reference of the Greek national consciousness, Greek nationalism, thanks to the historical works of Konstantinos Paparrigopoulos, a history professor at Athens university, aptly incorporated the repudiated medieval Byzantine past in the national ideology. His five-volume *History of the Greek Nation* (published between 1864 and 1875) furnished the printed embodiment of the new national self-perception. In this way Hellenism transmuted itself into a cultural entity which assumed a more convincingly uninterrupted continuum from Homeric times to the present. Furthermore, in quest for authoritative evidence for this reconstructed concept of national history, a nationalist-orientated academic discipline – folklore – attracted keen scholarly preoccupation with a typically Romantic approach.

Of all the attributes of the now culturally based Greek nationalism, its inviting nature was the most instrumental factor in advancing foreign-policy aspirations. Embracing the unredeemed Greeks in one united nation state implied the integration of all the Greek-inhabited territories, which ethnologically presented an uneven and, in some regions, hopeless ground for straightforward territorial reshufflings. After the nationally compact Ionian islands were incorporated into Greece (1864), the rest of the targeted territories, particularly those of the more northerly Balkan heartland and the vast provinces of Asia Minor, were inhabited by peoples not only of various ethnic origin, but usually of floating and unshaped ethnic feelings. These could roughly be described as a rural and linguistically assorted majority, mostly Orthodox in the Balkans and Muslim in Asia, although religious confessions were much intermingled as well, with large numbers of Orthodox Christians and Muslims living on either side, not to mention the Jews. Consequently, winning over all these populations to the Greek national idea was a challenge to Greek nationalism, which in its fresh and inviting cultural guise allowed the equal accession of the Albanian-speaking, the Vlach-speaking, or the Turkish-speaking Orthodox with that of the Greek-speaking, provided they could learn to recognize themselves as members of the envisaged national community, regardless of ethnic origin. In cultivating Greek national identification among these groups, the hegemonic rank of Greek culture and education in the Balkans gave Greek nationalism a valuable advantage over rival nationalist sentiments propagated in the relevant lands from the other Balkan national states. Through an expanded and expansive cultural network of primary schools and societies run by local communities and sponsored in the areas by Greek consular authorities, Greek nationalism sought to incorporate local populations psychologically and thus to strengthen its claim to the coveted territories they inhabited. Against the background of European imperialism in the Balkans, the collision of the Greek Great Idea with the contending ones of the other Balkan states over the ethnological mosaic of geographical Macedonia accounts for the emergence of the turbulent Macedonian question from the last third of the 19th century onwards. At the same time, the discreet antagonism between the Greek state and the patriarchate in Constantinople for influence over the Ottoman Greeks gradually died down in favour of Athens, which assumed the role of the undisputed "national centre" for the destinies of the unredeemed brethren. Early on, this claim had been postulated symbolically on the accession of George I to the throne as "king of the Hellenes" (1863) in contrast to the mere "king of Greece" with which his predecessor Otho assumed the Greek crown.

In parallel to its territorial dimension as a unifying vision, the Great Idea embodied the orientations of sociopolitical camps at home over the evolution of Greek society. More specifically, the translation of the Great Idea into politics gave rise to two divergent paradigms personified at this stage in the conflict between Trikoupis and Deliyannis, or Venizelos and his rivals in the 1910s–20s. The first view stood for the construction of an efficient and responsible infrastructure of a modern state as a precondition of pursuing the enlargement of the Greek boundaries. The second one, by contrast, gave the top priority to the territorial issue and the special role Greece could play, not so much within the western European framework, as in the Balkans and the east. In other words, the treatment of the Great Idea as national ideology related to the options before the question of modernization and Europeanization of the country.

The debacle of the 1897 Graeco-Turkish War came as a bitter affront to the assertions and aspirations of Greek nationalism. Launched in a climate of popular furore and conspicuous military unpreparedness, the war, the first involving the national army since the independent state was founded, brought the Greeks down to earth, confronting them with the discrepancy between the inflated national dreams and their actual potential. Nationalist intellectuals, however, by hurling every obloquy at the state, were anxious to qualify the demoralizing effect of the defeat so as not to taint the Great Idea as the ideology of national integration. What was defeated, they contended, was the state as an administrative mechanism, not the nation as a collective spiritual and indestructible unity destined to achieve distinction in history.

To this intellectual and psychological milieu belonged the eastern Greek vision of the scholar and diplomat Ion Dragoumis, arguably the foremost nationalist theoretician of his time. Out of an ambiguous blend of notions deriving from nationalism, socialism, and orientalism, Dragoumis propounded the idea that Hellenism was bound to thrive and rule over any other cultural and ethnic element in the Ottoman empire, provided it opted for the east as its privileged geocultural space. In place of the Greek state's aspirations for prompt enlargement and territorial conquest, Dragoumis reposed his firm belief in the assimilating potential of Hellenism, to which he attributed elemental cultural impact, to decide what he saw as an intrinsic and long-running process.

Such elaborations of Greek nationalism induced a rupture between the nation and the state, which, from the time the national state was achieved, had been perceived as aiming to be united. Only with the political ascendancy of Eleftherios Venizelos at the head of the Greek state, and the realization of the enlargement of Greece in the Balkan Wars (1912–13), did the ideological antithesis subside and the two entities become reconciled anew. Yet, at the apogee of Greek ambitions, with the Greek army marching into Asia Minor evoking the prospect of realizing the summit of nationalist yearnings, the Great Idea came to its shattering end in the wake of the Asia Minor disaster of 1922.

From the interwar period onwards, Greek nationalism shed its irredentist dimension, adhering to the state borders acknowledged by the Treaty of Lausanne (1923). Moreover, the eclipse of the Great Idea, from being the hegemonic culture of Greek society for nearly the whole of its independence period, induced an intellectual and cultural ferment in the light of the profound socio-economic crisis and political fluidity of the time. This gave rise to competing ideological trends revolving around the theme of national identity and nationalism. In a climate of reorientation and introspection, the discourse of the time sought to redefine the national identity and pin down "Greekness" in a way compatible with a sense of national sufficiency. Politics became interwoven with divergent nationalist approaches in the attempt of contending social forces to express themselves within a floating national framework. More specifically, it was at this stage that trends ranging from disciplinary nationalism and monarchic populism to lower-middle-class radicalism and Greek agrarianism elbowed one another in the wake of the retreat of the People's Party's (conservative) influence after the 1922 defeat. This ideological fragmentation, however, correlated to the stalemate of the modernizing endeavour of Greek society through republican forms, and led to the authoritarian and quasi-fascist nationalism of the late 1930s.

From the late interwar period onwards nationalism became manifestly associated with the right. This ideological appropriation deprived it of much of its hitherto unifying role as a cross-party point of reference and entangled it crudely in party politics and political conflicts. General Ioannis Metaxas, always obsessed with the idea of the organic state and of the disciplined undifferentiated society, had early pronounced in favour of self-sufficiency, including the territorial question, as a precondition of the creation of a "new Hellenic civilization". Once in office by virtue of usurped power, his "Regime of 4 August 1936" expounded the notion of the "Third Hellenic Civilization", an attempt to meld the ancient Greek and Byzantine cultures into a third quasi-fascist form deriving from imitation of contemporaneous fascist models.

In the 1940s, and throughout the anomalous constitutional period following the Greek civil war (1945–49), nationalism assumed a further populist complexion to operate in the terms of the "national schism" between nationalists and communists. It provided an ideological arm of the right against the rising popularity of the left-wing movement, with a view to compromising its opponents by hijacking the national sentiment for its exclusive use. Lastly, the 1967 colonels' junta attempted ephemerally, next in succession after the Metaxas dictatorship, but in a more ungainly manner, to produce a new grandiloquent version of Greek nationalism, now labelled "Helleno-Christian Civilization" – a term dating back to Greek Romanticism, coined in 1850 by the historian Spyridon Zampelios. As an ill-digested mixture of nationalist postulates and slogans, however, it only added to nationalism's discredit among the people, who perceived it as an abuse of sound patriotism. The dictators' abortive effort to enforce the union of Cyprus with Greece, leading ultimately to the Turkish occupation of the northern part of the island (1974) – the last area of substantial Greek population in the region remaining outside the borders of the Greek state and the last unredeemed land still pending in the minds of the Greeks after World War II – drove the last nail into the coffin of nationalism in its territorial aspect in contemporary Greece.

Whatever the ideological and political cleavages, Greek nationalism in the post-1922 state demonstrated a remarkably effective and, in retrospect, homogenizing role in the ethnological field. As an example of cultural and intellectual socialization it coalesced with state policies orientated to national compactness as a safeguard to territorial integrity. The massive influx of some 1.5 million refugees from Asia Minor, along with the parallel exodus of the Muslims (excluding western Thrace) as provided by the Population Exchange Convention of Lausanne (1923), cemented national homogeneity not only in overall numbers, but also specifically in regional ratios, for the bulk of the incoming refugees were channelled for settlement to Macedonia and Thrace, with their own ethnological peculiarities; the process was further advanced by the departure of the secessionist-inclined Slav-Macedonian element with the end of the Greek civil war. These population developments, particularly in the light of the traditionally centralized administrative and educational state system transmitting the values of Greek nationalism, allowed Greece to emerge as an overwhelmingly homogeneous society (95.6 per cent Greek-speaking and 97.9 per cent Orthodox according to the 1951 census), a picture consolidated to a maximum in time. Allowance should be made, however, for the unrecorded, mostly illegal, massive immigration from the Balkan and eastern European states in the 1990s, which today has added remarkable linguistic and ethnic diversity to contemporary Greece.

The disintegration of the former Yugoslavia (1991), engendering a variety of destabilizing effects in the Balkans, rekindled nationalist overtones in Greek political rhetoric as a side-effect of the nationalist-defined and, not infrequently, inflammatory discourse in and about southeastern Europe during the 1990s. Far from containing implicit territorial ambitions, arguably with the exception of marginal extremist groups, this was symptomatic of Greece's concern lest it should become unintentionally entangled in a broader Balkan crisis; in fact it spasmodically reflected insecurity for its own territorial integrity in the long run, especially in the light of Turkey's proclivity to aggrandizement. Once again, at any rate, nationalism was afforded the climate to reiterate its role at home for ideological manipulation and social cohesion.

Lastly, as a current sign of the tenacity and universality of nationalist stereotypes outside the country, it is perhaps worth remembering the vituperative criticism that appeared at times in the European press attributing rampant nationalism to Greece's Balkan policy. By disparaging the Greeks more or less as a racial medley, not only did it descend to a nationalist-defined controversy, which it allegedly repudiated, but, worse, it crystallized an anachronism in terms of Greek nationalism itself, in that it resuscitated the obsolete and long-abandoned racially based version of Greek nationalism.

Rennos Ehaliotis

See also Enlightenment, Enosis, Folklore, Great Idea, Identity, Macedonia

Further Reading

General

Anderson, Benedict, *Imagined Communities: Reflections on the Origin and Spread of Nationalism*, London: Verso, 1983, revised 1991

Deutsch, Karl Wolfgang, *Nationalism and Social Communication: An Inquiry into the Foundations of Nationality*, 2nd edition, Cambridge, Massachusetts: MIT Press, 1966

Gellner, Ernest, *Nations and Nationalism*, Oxford: Blackwell, and Ithaca, New York: Cornell University Press, 1983

Hobsbawm, Eric J., *Nations and Nationalism since 1780: Programme, Myth, Reality*, Cambridge and New York: Cambridge University Press, 1990

Ignatieff, Michael, *Blood and Belonging: Journeys into the New Nationalism*, London: Vintage, and New York: Farrar, Straus, and Giroux, 1994

Kedourie, Elie, *Nationalism*, 4th edition, Oxford and Cambridge, Massachusetts: Blackwell, 1993

Kohn, Hans, *The Idea of Nationalism: A Study in Its Origin and Background*, New York: Macmillan, 1944

Kohn, Hans, *Nationalism: Its Meaning and History*, Princeton: Van Nostrand, 1955

Smith, Anthony D., *Theories of Nationalism*, London: Duckworth, and New York: Harper and Row, 1971

Smith, Anthony D., *The Ethnic Origins of Nations*, Oxford and New York: Blackwell, 1986

Sugar, Peter F. and Ivo J. Lederer (editors), *Nationalism in Eastern Europe*, Seattle: University of Washington Press, 1969

Greek Nationalism

Arnakis, George G., "The Role of Religion in the Development of Balkan Nationalism" in *The Balkans in Transition*, edited by Barbara Jelavich and Charles Jelavich, Berkeley: University of California Press, 1963

Augustinos, Gerasimos, "The Dynamics of Modern Greek Nationalism: The Great Idea and the Macedonian Problem", *East European Quarterly*, 6/4 (1973): pp. 444–53

Augustinos, Gerasimos, *Consciousness and History: Nationalist Critics of Greek Society, 1897–1914*, Boulder, Colorado: East European Quarterly, and New York: Columbia University Press, 1977

Barker, Elisabeth, *Macedonia: Its Place in Balkan Power Politics*, London: Royal Institute for International Affairs, 1950, reprinted Westport, Connecticut: Greenwood Press, 1980

Blinkhorn, Martin and Thanos Veremis (editors), *Modern Greece: Nationalism and Nationality*, Athens: Sage / Eliamep, 1990

Clogg, Richard, "The Greek Millet in the Ottoman Empire" in *Christians and Jews in the Ottoman Empire: The Functioning of a Plural Society*, edited by Benjamin Braude and Bernard Lewis, vol. 1: *The Central Lands*, New York: Holmes and Meier, 1982

Dakin, Douglas, *The Greek Struggle in Macedonia, 1897–1913*, Thessalonica: Institute for Balkan Studies, 1966, reprinted, 1993

Driault, Edouard, *La Grande Idée: La Renaissance de l' Hellénisme*, Paris: Alcan, 1920

Frazee, Charles A., *The Orthodox Church and Independent Greece, 1821–1852*, London: Cambridge University Press, 1969

Geanakoplos, Deno J., "The Diaspora Greeks: The Genesis of Modern Greek National Consciousness" in *Hellenism and the First Greek War of Liberation, 1821–1830: Continuity and Change*, edited by Nikiforos P. Diamandouros et al., Thessalonica: Institute for Balkan Studies 1976

Herzfeld, Michael, *Ours Once More: Folklore, Ideology, and the Making of Modern Greece*, Austin: University of Texas Press, 1982

Kitromilides, Paschalis M., "Tradition, Enlightenment and Revolution: Ideological Change in 18th and 19th Century Greece" (dissertation), Cambridge, Massachusetts: Harvard University, 1978

Koliopoulos, John S., *Brigands with a Cause: Brigandage and Irredentism in Modern Greece, 1821–1912*, Oxford: Clarendon Press, and New York: Oxford University Press, 1987

Koumoulides, John T. A. (editor), *Greece in Transition: Essays in the History of Modern Greece*, London: Zeno, 1977

Mackridge, Peter and Eleni Yannakakis (editors), *Ourselves and Others: The Development of a Greek Macedonian Cultural Identity since 1912*, Oxford and New York: Berg, 1997

McNeill, William H., *The Metamorphosis of Greece since World War II*, Chicago: University of Chicago Press, 1978

Mouzelis, Nicos P., *Modern Greece: Facets of Underdevelopment*, London: Macmillan, and New York: Holmes and Meier, 1978

Petropulos, John Anthony, *Politics and Statecraft in the Kingdom of Greece, 1833–1843*, Princeton, New Jersey: Princeton University Press, 1968

Pollis, Adamantia, "Greek National Identity: Religious Minorities, Rights, and European Norms", *Journal of Modern Greek Studies*, 10 (1992): pp. 171–95

Poulton, Hugh, "Greece and Its Minorities" in his *The Balkans: Minorities and States in Conflict*, London: Minority Rights Publications, 1993

Stavrianos, L.S., *The Balkans since 1453*, New York: Holt Rinehart, 1958

Stokes, Gale, "Church and Class in Early Balkan Nationalism", *East European Quarterly*, 13/3 (1979): pp. 259–70

Tatsios, Theodore George, *The Megali Idea and the Greek–Turkish War of 1897: The Impact of the Cretan Problem on Greek Irredentism, 1866–1897*, Boulder, Colorado: East European Monographs, 1984

Vergopoulos, Costas, *Les Nationalismes grecs entre les deux guerres, 1922–1940*, Paris: Université de Paris I, 1971

Vryonis, Spiros, "The Greeks under Turkish Rule" in *Hellenism and the First Greek War of Liberation, 1821–1830: Continuity and Change*, edited by Nikiforos P. Diamandouros *et al.*, Thessalonica: Institute for Balkan Studies 1976

Vryonis, Spiros, "Some Ethnogenetic Theories of Greeks, Romanians, Bulgarians and Turks in the 19th–20th Centuries", *Septième Congrès International d' Etudes du Sud-Est Européen* Athens, 1994

Wilkinson, H.R., *Maps and Politics: A Review of the Ethnographic Cartography of Macedonia*, Liverpool: Liverpool University Press, 1951

NATO

Drawn up at the outset of the Cold War, the North Atlantic Treaty of 1949 brought into being the primary alliance of the Western states and united their determination "to preserve their security through mutual guarantees" (NATO, 1995, p. 17). Since 1949, the North Atlantic Treaty Organization (NATO) has provided the military and political structure which enables the goals of the alliance to be implemented. Greece acceded to the treaty and became a NATO member in February 1952.

Various considerations led Greece to join NATO. During the Civil War (1946–49), the official Greek government's primary concern had been to avoid defeat by the communist forces and other members of the left-wing resistance – an objective achieved in part by direct and extensive American military and economic backing. By 1952, NATO membership was perceived as the mechanism to consolidate and formalize these existing security links with the USA. Also instrumental was the "northern danger": Greece's perception of the security threat from neighbouring communist Albania, Yugoslavia, and Bulgaria, and its assumption that NATO membership would couple Greek defence to Western security priorities. The last factor was Greece's objective in maximizing political independence from the USA while simultaneously ensuring American security guarantees. Alliance membership appeared to offer not only protection against Balkan communism, but also "a door to a community of democratic European states and a partial emancipation from exclusive American control" (Veremis, 1988, p. 242). Despite earlier reservations on the part of Great Britain and the Scandinavian countries, by 1952 the existing NATO members considered Greek membership as essential because "as Cold War tensions heightened, Greece was increasingly viewed as a bulwark against communism" (ibid., p. 241). Within the alliance's containment strategy, inviting Greece and Turkey to join simultaneously also offered the prospect of formalized and extended pan-Mediterranean security arrangements to contain the Soviet fleet in the Black Sea.

Between 1952 and 1974 Greece was steadily integrated into NATO's military structure. In October 1953 agreements were concluded with the USA which authorized construction of military bases and supporting facilities in Greece. Expanded throughout the 1950s, these bases were essential instruments of containment vis-à-vis the Soviet Union (and its Balkan allies) and formed a credible NATO commitment to the defence of Greece. Against what was then perceived as the major threat to Greece – Warsaw Pact expansion – the facilities strengthened NATO's strategic capabilities in the area, guarded Aegean Sea approaches to the Mediterranean, and provided key surveillance facilities for monitoring Soviet forces in the eastern Mediterranean. During the military junta (1967–74), military cooperation was extended through the 1972 home-port agreement which allowed the stationing of US Navy carrier forces near Athens.

After 1974 Greece's political relations with NATO deteriorated. In domestic political terms the overthrow of the military junta in 1974 accentuated widespread public perceptions in Greece that the USA had openly and unequivocally supported the dictatorship. Moreover, NATO's inability to deter (or stop) the Turkish invasion of Cyprus throughout July and August of 1974 was interpreted as a tilt in favour of Turkey. The result was a cooling of relations with the USA but also a threat re-evaluation: Turkish, rather than Warsaw Pact, expansion was now considered the major threat to Greek sovereignty. These factors were instrumental in the Karamanlis government's decision to withdraw from the NATO military structure in August 1974.

Between 1974 and 1980, and outside the NATO military structure, the New Democracy administration's political relations with the alliance were constrained by two areas of dispute with Turkey. The first arose as Turkey contested, *inter alia*, Greek mineral rights in the Aegean and prerogatives in the Aegean Flight Information Region (FIR), and also Greece's long-standing policy of a 16-km airspace for its Aegean islands. The second stemmed from Turkish attempts to take advantage of Greece's withdrawal from NATO to promote Ankara's role and operational control in the alliance's southern region. Despite the fact that key disputes with Turkey remained unresolved, Greece began the process of reintegration into the NATO military command in October 1980.

After 1981, and the election of Papandreou's Panhellenic Socialist Movement (PASOK), the new administration's rhetoric emphasized the removal of American bases from Greek soil, non-alignment, and consolidation of the view that the major threat to Greece's security came from Turkey rather than the Soviet bloc. Despite the anti-NATO tone of his policy statements, however, and the internal strains on the alliance brought about by requests for NATO to extend a security guarantee for Greece's frontiers against Turkish aggression, "Papandreou's eight-year tenure brought no major shift in Greece's broader relations with NATO" (Papacosma, 1995, p. 252).

Since the end of the Cold War in 1989, Greece's military commitment to NATO has remained significant in terms of the allocation of its own land, maritime, and air assets. However, the demise of the Soviet Union and increased volatility in the Balkans have strained Greece's political relations with its NATO allies on important questions. During the Cold War, Greek and Turkish security interests were "accommodated within NATO, and where antagonisms flared, they were contained to the point of avoiding war" (RUSI, 1994, p. 60). Since 1989, however, increases in Greek and Turkish arms imports under NATO's "cascade" programme (whereby smaller alliance members qualify to receive free heavy weaponry from allies) and volatility in the Aegean caused by Turkey's challenges to Greek territorial waters have heightened regional tensions. In addition, the revival of Greece's traditional friendship with Serbia and its positions on the Former Yugoslav Republic of Macedonia and the Turkish Kurds have brought Greece's policies "into direct opposition with western powers" (ibid.) leading to criticism from its NATO allies.

Since joining NATO, Greece's political relations with the alliance have been volatile. This has reflected Greek perceptions since 1974 that the primary threat is intra-alliance in the form of potential Turkish aggression, and more recently from Greece's historical and cultural links with states and groupings in the Balkan region. However, Greece's military relations with NATO have been cordial and reflect successive administrations's realpolitik calculations about the overriding benefits that the alliance can provide. These benefits – that Greece can counterbalance Turkish influence within the alliance on the Aegean and Cyprus questions, maintain access to American military aid, and benefit from the "cascade" programme – are the fundamental factors that bind Greece's defence and security interests to NATO membership.

MATTHEW R.H. UTTLEY

See also Turkey

Further Reading

Haralambopoulos, "Turkey Should Abandon Her Expansionist Claims", *NATO's Sixteen Nations*, 32 (1987): pp. 14–19

North Atlantic Treaty Organization, *NATO Handbook*, Brussels: NATO Office of Information and Press, 1995

Papacosma, S.V., "NATO and the Balkans" in *NATO in the Post-Cold War Era: Does It Have a Future?*, edited by Papacosma and Mary Ann Heiss, Basingstoke: Macmillan, and New York: St Martin's Press, 1995

Royal United Services Institute, "Greece and Turkey: A Fragile Stability", *RUSI Newsbrief*, 14/8 (August 1994): pp. 59–60

Snyder, Jed C., *Defending the Fringe: NATO, the Mediterranean and the Persian Gulf*, Boulder, Colorado: Westview Press, 1987

Valinakis, Y.G., "The US Bases in Greece: The Political Context" in *US Bases in the Mediterranean: The Cases of Greece and Spain*, edited by Thanos Veremis and Yannis Valinakis, Athens: Hellenic Foundation for Defense and Foreign Policy, 1989

Varvitsiotis, I., "The Defence of Greece", *NATO's Sixteen Nations*, 37/5 (1992): pp. 11–14

Veremis, Thanos, "Greece and Nato: Continuity and Change" in *NATO's Southern Allies: Internal and External Challenges*, edited by John Chipman, London and New York: Routledge, 1988

Naucratis

City in Egypt

Naucratis, on the east bank of the Canopic branch of the Nile, 84 km southeast of Alexandria, was a Greek city in Egypt. It was the birthplace of Athenaeus, and Sappho's brother Charaxas visited the city on business.

Naucratis has been identified with the mounds of Kom Ga'if. Excavations of the site were first carried out in 1884–86 by W.M.F. Petrie and E.A. Gardner, followed by D.G. Hogarth in 1899 and 1903. Since 1977 an excavation and survey by an American team led by W.E. Coulson have been under way.

Half the site was destroyed by local people in the 19th century and a lake now covers the area of the old excavations. Modern excavations thus focus on the outskirts of the site and its surrounding territory.

Although both Herodotus (2. 178–9) and Strabo (17. 1. 18) provide lengthy information on Naucratis, many questions relating to the city remain unanswered and subject to dispute. It was initially established as a trading settlement (*emporion*) in about 650 BC, during the reign of the pharaoh Psammetichus I (664–610 BC) and under pharaonic control. Under Amasis (570–526 BC) the Hellenion was built by Ionians from Chios, Teos, Phocaea, and Clazomenae, and by Dorians from Rhodes, Cnidus, Halicarnassus, Phaselis, and Aeolian Mytilene. Aegina, Samos, and Miletus had erected their own temples dedicated to Zeus, Hera, and Apollo (Herodotus, 2. 178–9).

The earliest Greek pottery at the site, about 21 known examples, dates from the last quarter of the 7th century BC and belongs to the transitional and early Corinthian period. There are substantial quantities of middle Corinthian and early Attic black-figure ware, dating from the end of the 7th/early 6th century BC onwards, which probably reflect the extensive scale of Greek activity in Naucratis from the end of the 7th century BC. Nearly all archaic pottery found there accords with information given by Herodotus on the joint establishment of Naucratis by a number of Greek cities: there are ceramics of Rhodian type; Chian and Samian pottery; *fikellura* of Rhodian, Samian, or Milesian production; Clazomenian, Spartan, Corinthian, and Athenian vases; and Aeolian (Lesbian) plain pale grey *bucchero*.

Architectural remains are in very bad condition. Dedicatory inscriptions and offerings to temples help to identify to which gods or goddesses temples were erected. The temple of Aphrodite, not mentioned by Herodotus, lies in the southern part of the town. Temples to Hera and Apollo stand next to one another, and a small shrine to the Dioscuri (again not mentioned by Herodotus) was excavated in the northern part of the site. In this area of the city a large sanctuary was discovered. Inscriptions on vases unearthed there mention several deities, sometimes just "the gods of the Greeks", and these dedications give grounds for identifying this sanctuary as the Hellenion mentioned by Herodotus, the joint foundation of several eastern Greek states. Archaeological material from these temples shows that these cults date back to the early days of the settlement, and the temples were rebuilt or replaced several times in different periods.

East of the temple of Aphrodite was a small factory that produced faience scarab seals. It was active mainly in the first half of the 6th century BC. There were also local workshops producing Greek-style pottery (identified by style and technique) for local use as votives. Faience scarabs and figure vases were well known throughout the Greek world. In the 6th and 5th centuries BC there are isolated instances of Greek-manufactured objects directed to specific sites in Egypt. Thus, the inhabitants of Naucratis, not a large settlement, supported themselves by trade and craft work. In the literature, Naucratis is often compared with such commercial outposts of the British empire as Hong Kong or Shanghai.

The exact status of Naucratis is disputed. According to Herodotus and some modern scholars, the settlement was divided into two parts: a polis, inhabited by permanent settlers, and an *emporion* (trading settlement) peopled by Hellenion (visitors). It is possible that when Naucratis was under Persian rule in the 5th–4th centuries BC it was a polis. What little evidence exists (decrees and a tombstone with the ethnic of settlement as part of a personal name) is not very clear. By the Ptolemaic period, immediately after Alexander's conquest of Egypt, Naucratis did have the status of an autonomous polis. It had its own laws (including a ban on intermarriage), citizenship, and coinage. Graeco-Macedonian rulers recognized the site as a centre of Hellenic culture. With the Macedonian conquest the separate sanctuary area (the northern part of the settlement) lost its importance and was combined with the rest of the city (the southern part of the settlement). The settlement was reformed and adopted the Milesian calendar and laws.

In the Roman period Naucratis retained its Greek constitution; citizens had no right of intermarriage with Egyptians. It had a *boule* (council) and held annual public games. It remained a trade and craft centre throughout the Ptolemaic and Roman periods.

GOCHA R. TSETSKHLADZE

See also Egypt

Summary

A Greek city in Egypt, Naucratis began as a trading station established *c.*650 BC. Archaeology confirms the statement of Herodotus that it was a joint foundation by a number of Greek cities. The inhabitants lived by trade and craft work. By the Ptolemaic period it was an autonomous polis with its own laws and coinage.

Further Reading

Austin, M.M., *Greece and Egypt in the Archaic Age*, Cambridge: Cambridge Philological Society, 1970

Boardman, John and N.G.L. Hammond (editors), *The Expansion of the Greek World, Eighth to Sixth Centuries* BC, Cambridge: Cambridge University Press, 1982 (*The Cambridge Ancient History*, vol. 3, part 3, 2nd edition)

Boardman, John, *The Greeks Overseas: Their Early Colonies and Trade*, 4th edition, London and New York: Thames and Hudson, 1999

Bowden, H., "The Greek Settlements and Sanctuaries of Naukratis" in *More Studies in the Ancient Greek Polis*, edited by Mogens Herman Hansen and Kurt Raaflaub, Stuttgart: Steiner, 1996

Coulson, William D.E. and Albert Leonard (editors), *Ancient Naukratis*, vol. 2, part 1, Oxford: Oxbow, 1996

Gardner, E.A., *Naukratis*, vol. 2, London: Trübner, 1888

Lewis, D.M. *et al.* (editors), *The Fourth Century* BC, Cambridge: Cambridge University Press, 1994 (*The Cambridge Ancient History*, vol. 6, 2nd edition)

Petrie, W.M.F., *Naukratis*, vol. 1, London: Trübner, 1886

Naupactus

Port on the gulf of Corinth

Naupactus (modern Nafpaktos) is a strategically located port on the northern coast of the gulf of Corinth, just east of its narrowest part. Originally called Locris (Apollodorus, 2. 8. 2–3), it became known as Naupactus ("ship-construction" or "shipyards") after the Heraclid Temenus built a fleet there (see also Pausanias, 10. 38. 10; Polyaenus, *Stratagems*, 1. 9; Suda s.v. *Naupaktos*). According to Apollodorus, this fleet was later destroyed at Naupactus when one of the Heraclids, Hippotes, killed a prophet whom he mistook for a Peloponnesian. The killing of this prophet apparently angered the gods, who brought doom upon the Heraclid forces and their fleet.

Other myths or legends associated with Naupactus are not extensive. Aeschylus (*Suppliant Women*, 260–70) relates that Apollo's son Apis, a prophet and healer, came from Naupactus and rid the Argolid of monsters that threatened humans. One tradition also suggests that Ktimenos and Antiphos, Ganyktor's sons, murdered the poet Hesiod at Naupactus (Pausanias, 9. 31. 6; Plutarch, *De Sollertia Animalium*, 969e), and that Hesiod was buried there (Pausanias, 9. 38. 3). Numerous references exist to an epic poem called the *Naupaktia*, which according to Pausanias (2. 3. 9) described Jason's life on Corfu after his expulsion from Iolkos. The authorship of the poem was uncertain; though Pausanias (10. 38. 10) reports that by tradition the poem was usually attributed to a Milesian, he believed that the author was Carcinus of Naupactus.

The strategic importance of Naupactus emerges in the 5th century BC. In the early 450s BC the Athenians, under the command of Tolmides, captured Naupactus from the Ozolian Locrians, who had apparently colonized Naupactus during the first quarter of the 5th century BC. After capturing Naupactus (probably by the mid-450s BC), the Athenians colonized it with some Messenians, who had rebelled against the Spartans, were besieged by them on Mount Ithome, and eventually surrendered. The Spartans, however, at the behest of the Delphic oracle, allowed the Messenians to leave the Peloponnese, after which they were received by the Athenians, who colonized Naupactus with Messenians because of their mutual enmity towards the Spartans. Having an ally at Naupactus would allow the Athenians to put both military and economic pressure on the Spartans' ally, Corinth. With Athens' own port in the east and Naupactus in the west, the Athenians could dominate the Greek seas. (See Thucydides, 1. 103. 1–3, 2. 9. 4; Isocrates, 12. 94 (*Panathenaicus*); Diodorus, 11. 84.6–7, 12. 44.3, 12. 47. 1; Pausanias, 4. 24. 7, 31. 7, 10. 38. 10).

Messenian occupation of Naupactus continued for the next few decades, and when the Peloponnesian War broke out in 431 BC, Messenian hatred of the Spartans and their friendship with Athens allowed the Athenians to use Naupactus as a base of operations against the Spartans and their allies. With Naupactus at their disposal, the Athenian naval presence in the gulf of Corinth could counter the Spartans' allies Corinth to the east, as well as the Spartan-controlled port of Patras. Moreover, thanks to superior naval forces, the Athenians held sway in the gulf of Corinth during the Peloponnesian War. Phormio's victory over the Peloponnesians in 429 BC, despite being outnumbered in ships more than two to one, is still admired for its tactical brilliance (see Thucydides, 2. 69.1, 2. 83; Diodorus, 12. 47. 1–48. 1; Pausanias, 4. 26. 1; Polyaenus, *Stratagems*, 3. 4). By the century's end, though, the Spartans had crushed the Athenians, and between 403 BC and 397 BC they expelled the Messenians from Naupactus (see Xenophon, *Hellenica*, 3. 2. 21–3. 1; Diodorus, 14. 34. 2; Pausanias, 4. 26. 2; 10. 38. 10).

After the expulsion of the Messenians, Naupactus came under Locrian control. Between 395 BC and 389 BC the

Locrians were again supplanted by the Achaeans, who held Naupactus until 366 BC when Epaminondas drove them out. After this, Naupactus again became a Locrian possession. How long the Locrians retained Naupactus is not clear, but Demosthenes (9. 34) indicates that in 342 BC the Achaeans held the port and this continued until 338 BC when Philip II of Macedonia seized it and handed it over to the Aetolians.

Naupactus resurfaces in 217 BC as the site of a conference between Philip V of Macedonia and the Aetolians and Achaeans, a meeting that resulted in a peace accord between the two sides (Polybius, 5. 102–103). Livy reports that Roman commanders made use of the port in 211 BC and 208 BC, and that the Aetolians used it as a meeting place in 200 BC, 193 BC, and 191 BC. The Romans besieged Naupactus in 191 BC when the Aetolians revolted against the Roman cause. After two months, though, the siege was ended through negotiations (Livy, 36. 35), but the enmity between the Aetolians and Romans ultimately became irrelevant since Greece became a Roman province in 146 BC.

During the later Roman republic and empire, little mention of Naupactus exists other than the Caesarian Calvisius' expulsion of a Pompeian garrison there in 48 BC. In the 2nd century AD Pausanias (10. 38. 6–7) describes a few shrines and sanctuaries dedicated to Poseidon, Artemis, Aphrodite, and Asclepius, the last of which was in ruins in Pausanias' day and of which a few remains are extant.

After the division of the Roman empire in the 3rd century AD, the Byzantines controlled Naupactus. In 431 the bishop Callicrates represented Naupactus at the third Ecumenical Council at Ephesus. At the fourth Ecumenical Council (451) at Chalcedon the bishop Eirenaios represented Naupactus. In AD 551 Procopius (On the Wars, 8. 25. 17) reports that Naupactus and several other towns were levelled by an earthquake. Naupactus was rebuilt and in the mid-10th century it is listed in the theme of Hellas (Constantine VII Porphyrogenetos, On the Themes, 5. 12). After the sack of Constantinople in 1204 by the Venetians and the Crusaders, the Venetians claimed Naupactus. During the Venetian occupation the name Lepanto appears, although Naupactus remained in use. "Lepanto" appears to have evolved from "Nepantum", a corruption of "Naupactus", which seems to have been further corrupted to "Lepanto".

The Venetians controlled Naupactus until 1361, when it fell to the Catalans. By 1407, however, the Venetians recovered the city, but in 1499 lost it to Bayezid II and his Ottoman Turks. On 7 October 1571 Christian forces commanded by John of Austria crushed an Ottoman fleet, under Uluç Ali Pasha, in a conflict now known as the Battle of Lepanto, which was the first major Christian victory over an Ottoman navy that had previously been considered invincible. The Christian victory checked Ottoman efforts to control the Mediterranean. The Battle of Lepanto was the last major battle in which galleys were the primary naval vessel employed. It is also worth noting that the Spanish novelist Miguel de Cervantes lost the use of his left hand in this battle.

Though Christian forces were victorious at Lepanto, Naupactus remained an Ottoman possession until the Greeks finally cast off Turkish rule in 1830. Other than the German occupation of Greece during World War II, Naupactus has remained under Greek control. Today Naupactus has about 10,000 inhabitants, a pleasant beach, limited remains of Byzantine architecture, sculpture, and inscriptions, and a primarily Venetian castle whose ramparts embrace the town's harbour. Naupactus' importance, though, has greatly diminished since the 5th century BC, due to its relative isolation from the northern interior of Greece and its location in one of the least populated regions of Greece. From 1980 to 1986, for example, Naupactus was not listed by name among the principal ports of Greece (Statistical Yearbook of Greece: 1988, pp. 396, 399).

JOHN E. THORBURN

Summary

A port on the north shore of the gulf of Corinth, Naupactus was important during the Peloponnesian War. After 1204 it was in Venetian hands and was known as Lepanto. In 1571 it was the site of a major sea battle between Christians and Turks. Since then it has declined in importance.

Further Reading

Badian, E, From Plataea to Potidaea: Studies in the History and Historiography of the Pentecontaetia, Baltimore: Johns Hopkins University Press, 1993

Gregory, Timothy E., Naupaktos entry in The Oxford Dictionary of Byzantium, vol. 2, edited by A.P. Kazhdan, New York and Oxford: Oxford University Press, 1991

Hussey, J.M. (editor), The Byzantine Empire, Cambridge: Cambridge University Press, 1966–67 (The Cambridge Medieval History, vol. 4, parts 1–2, 2nd edition)

Kourvetaris, Yorgos A. and Betty A. Dobratz, A Profile of Modern Greece: In Search of Identity, Oxford: Clarendon Press, and New York: Oxford University Press, 1987

Lerat, Lucien, Les Locriens de l'ouest, Paris: Boccard, 1952

Lewis, D.M. et al. (editors), The Fifth Century BC, Cambridge: Cambridge University Press, 1992 (The Cambridge Ancient History, vol. 5, 2nd edition)

Merker, Irwin L., "The Achaians in Naupaktos and Kalydon in the 4th Century", Hesperia, 58 (1989): pp. 303–11

Nicol, Donald M., Byzantium and Venice: A Study in Diplomatic and Cultural Relations, Cambridge and New York: Cambridge University Press, 1988

Oldfather, William, Naupaktos entry in Real-Encyclopädie der klassischen Altertumswissenschaft, edited by August Pauly et al., vol. 16.2, 1935, 1979–2002

Statistical Yearbook of Greece: 1988, Athens: National Statistical Service of Greece, 1990

Woodhouse, William J., Aetolia: Its Geography, Topography, and Antiquities, Oxford: Clarendon Press, 1897, reprinted New York: Arno Press, 1973

Nauplia

City in the Peloponnese

Nauplia (modern Navplion, medieval Anapli or Napoli di Romania), an important and picturesque harbour town of about 12,000 people, is situated on the Argolic Gulf in the Argolid region of the northeast Peloponnese. It lies beside the sea at the base of two summits: Akronavplia (or the Its Kale), a relatively low but precipitous promontory of c.84m, and the Palamidi, a rocky peak of some 215m on which stands an imposing fortress. The town is now best known as a cultural and tourist centre, but it has had a long and illustrious, if sometimes very troubled, history.

Tradition associates Nauplia both with the mythical Nauplius, son of Poseidon, and with Nauplius the Argonaut who avenged himself on the Greek participants in the Trojan War after they betrayed and killed his son, Palamedes. Settlement at the site may be traced as far back as the palaeolithic period, with remains from that date and from neolithic times found on Akronavplia. During the Bronze Age the main centre of habitation seems to have been the Pronoia area to the east of the old town; Mycenaean chamber tombs have also been found nearby. The settlement continued to exist in the Dark Age and a cemetery of the Geometric period has been excavated. Traces of occupation continue until the Hellenistic period, but evidence is rather limited. Indeed, historical accounts mention that Nauplia was destroyed by its neighbours, the Argives, during the reign of king Damocratidas (no later than c.600 BC), after which the town became the harbour of Argos (as it may have been in Mycenaean times). By the Roman period the site was deserted since Pausanias, who visited it in the 2nd century AD, reports only a sanctuary of Poseidon there; even the fortress walls were in ruins by his day.

The period of desertion evidently lasted for several centuries, but Akronavplia may have been refortified as early as the 3rd–4th century AD and, by the 6th century, Nauplia was once again a thriving and developing centre, becoming the seat of a bishop by 879 and of an archbishop by 1189. During the Komnenian revival in the 12th century, a number of churches were built in the area and the town, which probably occupied the western (seaward) end of the fortified promontory of Akronavplia at this time, with only the harbour below, became a fairly important commercial centre enjoying trade relations with the Venetians. As the central authority of the Byzantine empire waned in the later part of the century, Nauplia briefly came under the semi-independent control of the local Greek magnate Theodore Sgouros and subsequently of his son Leo, who also ruled Argos and Corinth. The Franks arrived in 1204, however, following the sack of Constantinople by the forces of the Fourth Crusade and, after determined resistance, the town eventually fell in 1210 to Geoffrey de Villehardouin, although the Greeks continued to hold out at the seaward end of the promontory of Akronavplia in one of the two fortresses which had been constructed there.

Following the fall of Argos in 1212, control of Nauplia was given over to the Burgundian de la Roche family which had established itself at Athens, and it remained, directly or nominally, in their hands for more than a hundred years. In the 14th century the town came into the possession of the Enghien family and thence passed, in 1389, to the Venetians, despite an attempt by Theodore I Palaiologos, the Byzantine despot of the Morea, to bring it back under Greek control from Mistra. Nauplia became one of the most important Venetian holdings in Greece and retained its prominence into the 16th century, but its viability was gradually undermined by the growing Turkish presence in the Peloponnese and, after a long and bloody siege, the town surrendered to them in 1540. Another period of prominence as the Turkish capital of the Morea was followed by a renewed decline in the 17th century until, in 1686, Nauplia was retaken by the Venetians. The town's

fortunes revived once again, its population expanded, and, now the Venetian capital of the Morea, it was given the name 'Napoli di Romania'. It was at this time too that the Venetians, beginning with the general François Morosini, embarked on a campaign to strengthen the fortifications on both Akronavplia and the Palamidi (using designs provided by the French engineers LaSalle and Levasseur), as well as those on the island of the Bourtzi (Agioi Theodoroi) which guarded approaches to the harbour. In 1715, however, only a year after the work was completed, the Turks invaded again and, despite the magnificent fortifications, the inadequate garrison proved to be no match for the far superior Turkish force. After a siege of only eight days the Palamidi fell and the Venetians, who unsuccessfully attempted to take refuge in the fortress on Akronavplia, were either massacred or sold into slavery. This proved to be the end of Venetian control not only of Nauplia but of the whole Peloponnese.

The next phase in the town's history comes with the Greek War of Independence. In 1821 the Greeks besieged the Palamidi and, when it fell the following year, they finally recovered Nauplia from the Turks. This event did not bring immediate peace, however, for internal rivalries among the Greek leaders led to a struggle for control of the town. On 7 January 1828 Count Kapodistria moved his provisional capital to Nauplia, and it was there, in 1831, that he was assassinated; the bullet hole is still visible in the wall of the church of St Spiridon in the centre of the town. On 25 January 1833 Otho, the first king of Greece, arrived in Nauplia and, during that year and the next, the town enjoyed a brief but glorious phase as the capital of the country until it relinquished this role to Athens in September 1834. For the rest of the 19th and the early part of the 20th century Nauplia continued to be a prosperous provincial town and port, but memories of its troubled past were reawakened during the German invasion of Greece in April 1941 when it became one of three main sites in the Peloponnese used for the evacuation of Allied troops; the operation was a desperate one and some serious losses were incurred. Liberation did not come until the autumn of 1944.

Much of Nauplia's charming Neoclassical architecture dates to the period of revival in the first half of the 19th century, but there are many reminders of the Turkish occupation still evident in the town, most strikingly perhaps in the fountains and mosques, one of which (the Voulevtiko), at the southwest corner of the main square (Syntagma), was the site of the first Greek parliament between 1827 and 1834. Even more noticeable are the traces left by the long Venetian presence: in addition to the fortifications which still dominate Nauplia, a number of their churches and other buildings remain, including the former naval barracks which stand at the west end of the main square and now house the Archaeological Museum.

Today Nauplia has put its violent and troubled history behind it and prides itself as a cultural and artistic centre. Tourism, both international and Greek, has brought prosperity, but this has not been allowed to spoil its charm or its architectural heritage. A flourishing and beautiful town, Nauplia's older buildings, squares, and monuments have been carefully maintained and restored in recent years, while new development, including housing, some industry, and a sizeable army base, has been controlled and largely confined to areas outside the old town.

A. FOLEY

Summary

Situated on the gulf of Argos, Nauplia was the port for Argos in antiquity but was deserted by the 2nd century AD. Flourishing again by the 6th century, it became the seat of a bishop by 879 and of an archbishop by 1189. Taken by the Franks in 1210, Nauplia passed to the Venetians in 1389. Turkish after 1540 (but Venetian again from 1686 to 1715), Nauplia played a prominent role in the War of Independence. In 1833–34 it was the first capital of Greece.

Further Reading

Andrews, Kevin, *Castles of the Morea*, Princeton, New Jersey: American School of Classical Studies at Athens, 1953, reprinted Amsterdam: Hakkert, 1978

Barber, Robin, *Greece*, 6th edition, London: A. & C. Black, and New York: Norton, 1995 (*Blue Guide* series)

Foley, Anne, *The Argolid 800–600 BC: An Archaeological Survey Together with an Index of Sites from the Neolithic to the Roman Period*, Gothenburg: Åström, 1988

Lock, Peter, *The Franks in the Aegean, 1204–1500*, London and New York: Longman, 1995

Paradissis, Alexander, *Fortresses and Castles of Greece*, vol. 2, Athens: Efstathiadis, 1972

Themelis, Petros G., *Mycènes, Nauplie*, Athens: Delta, n.d.

Navy

Greece has a mainland coastline of about 16,600 km together with over 4000 islands, islets, and rocks. It occupies an important geostrategic position in the eastern Mediterranean and merchant shipping has become a significant element of the national economy. Not surprisingly, Greece has a long naval history and maritime tradition, and it is to its naval fighting abilities "that Greece owes its existence – an existence whose character was formulated and strengthened by the sea" (Alexandris, 1987, p. 92).

The development and employment of maritime power was a vital characteristic of Greece's ancient history. In the 2nd millennium BC the Minoan empire in Crete emerged as the first organized naval power in the world. Later, during the 5th century BC, the success of Athens and the "golden age" of Pericles depended on the systematic development of sea power. Though the first Persian invasion of Greece by Darius in 490 BC was defeated by the Athenian army at Marathon, the Athenian politician Themistocles was quick to recognize that, in any future attack, land forces alone would not be enough in the face of the vast numerical superiority of the Persian army. Using new-found revenues from the state silver mines at Laurium, the Athenians decided to build a large fleet. The principal fighting element of the new fleet, and a significant Athenian technological innovation, was the trireme – the fastest warship of its time, which could ram and sink enemy ships without exposing itself to the risk of grappling and boarding its opponents.

Themistocles' rationale for developing a naval capability was subsequently vindicated. During 480 BC the Persians,

under the generalship of Xerxes, attacked northern Greece with land forces and a fleet of over 500 ships. The invading army destroyed an outnumbered Spartan force at Thermopylae and then engaged in an indecisive naval battle with a Greek fleet off Artemisium. At the subsequent Battle of Salamis, the Persian and Greek fleets were evenly matched in numerical terms, but the edge provided, *inter alia*, by the triremes enabled the Greeks to win a decisive victory. The Battle of Salamis conclusively demonstrated the ability of Athens to wage war from the sea and it was an essential precursor to its wealth and dominion.

After the defeat of Athens by Sparta and its allies in 404 BC the role of seapower in Greece declined relative to the part played by land armies. Throughout the period of Macedonian rule, for example, despite major military victories and conquests, there were no remarkable naval feats. Because of his unfamiliarity with maritime affairs, Alexander the Great elected to develop a small navy and avoided engaging his enemies at sea. Instead, Alexander achieved sea control indirectly by attacking and capturing the naval forces of his enemies from land. Though Rhodes subsequently became an important maritime power and formulated the "Rhodian Sea Law", the oldest maritime code in the world, and though the Greeks struggled to control sea routes to the western Mediterranean against the sizeable navy of Ptolemy, in the Hellenistic and Roman periods the development and use of force at sea remained subservient to maintaining strength on land.

The Byzantine empire relied heavily on its navy at key moments to prevent foreign invasion. Byzantium's fleet played an important role in defeating attacks by the Arabs and during the Gothic wars. Other notable naval successes included the fleet's ability under the emperor Herakleios (610–41) to prevent the Persians, in alliance with the Avars, from attacking Constantinople, and beating off the Arab Muawiya's attempt to capture Constantinople in 674–78. The major naval victories of the Byzantines were dependent upon two factors: organization and technology that were superior to those of their adversaries. In organizational terms the fleet was arranged as part of the empire's system of themes during the 7th century. Functionally, it was divided into the imperial navy (*vassilikon ploimon*) of Constantinople, and the navy of the themes (*thematikon ploimon*), which covered the provinces of the empire, operating under a commander-in-chief of the navy. This structure was instrumental in defeating the empire's naval opponents. In technological terms the fleet also had a decisive edge. The principal battleships of the Byzantine fleet were "dromonds": boats with sails and two banks of oars crewed by up to 300 personnel. The combination of the ramming spur of the dromonds and the skill with which the Byzantines manoeuvred their vessels provided a formidable capability. However, the more significant technological factor, and a strictly guarded state secret, was "Greek fire". Invented by the Syrian Greek Kallinikos, Greek fire was an inextinguishable mixture of sulphur and other combustible materials that was hurled at enemy vessels either by catapult or rudimentary hand grenades, or was piped through a hose. This brilliant technical achievement of Byzantine naval science was a further precursor to maritime success.

Navy: illustration from an 11th-century manuscript of the *Cynegetica* of Pseudo-Oppian (3rd century AD) showing two warships about to meet in combat, Biblioteca Nazionale Marciana, Venice

It is important to note, however, that Byzantine naval policy was not without its limitations. The most serious was the tendency to neglect and underfund the fleet when there was no immediate naval threat to the empire. Notable here was the increasing weakness of the fleet after the invasion of the Seljuks in the 12th century, a weakness demonstrated by the fact that the empire was forced to enlist the help of the Venetians and grant major trade concessions in return. By this stage, Byzantium had made the fatal mistake of relying on the navy of Venice and thus lost its own control of the sea in the longer term.

Despite the absence of naval forces during the Tourkokratia, the years between 1453 and 1821 were important for Greek maritime development in a number of respects. The period of the Turkish occupation witnessed the emergence and growth of the Hellenic merchant marine, and an associated increase in seaborne trade. The environment in which Greek merchant shipping had to operate was hostile: merchantmen had to fight frequently against pirate vessels and the warships of the European powers that regularly blockaded the Mediterranean sea routes. A consequence was that Greek crews became trained in the art of sea warfare and acquired a knowledge of basic military organizational structures. This was to prove significant in the War of Independence after 1821 because Hellenic merchant shipping was easily converted into a rudimentary naval force which then harassed and skirmished with Turkish maritime assets.

The origins of the modern Greek navy can be traced to developments in the late 19th century. In 1884, at the request of the Greeks, a French Naval Training Mission was invited and the Naval Cadet School was established. During 1907 the General Naval Staff was created and, in 1909, a British Naval Training Mission was invited. By 1911, in response to the growth in Turkish naval capabilities, the Hellenic navy had acquired three battleships and the battlecruiser *G. Averoff*. The procurement of a submarine capability followed and during World War I the naval air force became an organic part of the Hellenic navy. Despite the occupation of Greece during World War II the navy continued operations from abroad in support of the Allied war effort. By 1953, following the adoption of the concept that a unified direction was required for the Greek armed forces, the Hellenic navy adopted what remains its present organizational structure.

Today the general staffs of the navy, army, and air force are directed by the Ministry of National Defence, through the National Defence General Staff. The Hellenic navy is headed by the Chief of the Hellenic Navy General Staff, who also acts as Commander Eastern Mediterranean (COMEDEAST) in the NATO command structure. It is organized under three major commands: Fleet Command (at Salamis), Naval Training Command (at Skaramanga), and Naval Logistic Command (at Athens). The operational concept of the Hellenic navy reflects "the combined requirements of national and NATO strategic concepts" (Drikos, 1992, p. 32). The major roles of the Hellenic navy are fourfold: to perform sea control missions in COMEDEAST's area; to protect the Greek coast and islands; to provide support to Greek and allied armed forces; and to safeguard Greek interests including the economic zone of the sea bed in the Aegean and Ionian seas. Since the end of the Cold War the ambit of Greek naval responsibility has included planning for operations aimed at preventing the development of regional crises and/or restoring international law and peace, and providing the allied naval forces with appropriate units to support the monitoring or enforcement of United Nations resolutions.

The composition of the Hellenic navy reflects these national and alliance priorities. In personnel terms the regular strength is approximately 19,500 (2600 officers) with a further 23,500 reservists. The Hellenic navy has four destroyers (*Charles F. Adams* class) and 11 frigates (six *Kortenaer*, three *Knox*, and two *Hydra* (Meko 200)) with anti-surface, anti-air, and anti-submarine capabilities for deployment in sea control missions. Sea denial roles are covered by eight Type 209 *Glavkos* submarines. The navy's ability to project power ashore with amphibious forces is provided by ten landing ships and 57 associated craft. Finally, it should be noted that the Greek merchant marine plays a vital role in NATO military planning: it provides some 20 per cent of all merchant ships assigned to NATO, and 21 per cent of ships assigned for the trans-Atlantic sea lift of external reinforcements.

Throughout the centuries the interests of Greece have been sustained by its long-standing maritime tradition. In the words of a recent Chief of the Hellenic Navy General Staff: "Greece preserves its long naval tradition by maintaining a dominant presence in the [Mediterranean] area by the acquisition and operation of a substantially powerful, flexible and efficient naval force" (Drikos, 1992, p. 32).

MATTHEW R.H. UTTLEY

See also Fire (Greek), Ships and Shipping

Further Reading
Alexandris, S., "The Importance of Greek Shipping Today", *NATO's Sixteen Nations*, 32 (1987): pp. 92–95
Baumgartner, Frederic J., *From Spear to Flintlock: A History of War in Europe and the Middle East to the French Revolution*, London and New York: Praeger, 1991
Baynes N.H. and H. St. L.B. Moss, *Byzantium: An Introduction to East Roman Civilization*, Oxford: Clarendon Press, 1961
Drikos, I., "Maritime Perspectives of Greece", *NATO's Sixteen Nations*, 37/5 (1992): pp. 31–36
Green, Peter, *Armada from Athens*, New York: Doubleday, 1970; London: Hodder and Stoughton, 1971
Hobkirk, Michael D., *Land, Sea or Air? Military Priorities, Historical Choices*, Basingstoke: Macmillan, and New York: St Martin's Press, 1992
International Institute for Strategic Studies, *The Military Balance*, Oxford: Oxford University Press (annual publication)
Lagaras, E., "Sea Control Operations in the Eastern Mediterranean: The Importance of the Aegean Sea and Its Islands for Success", *NATO's Sixteen Nations*, 34/5 (September 1989): pp. 102–04
Pappas, N., "Submarine Operations in the Eastern Mediterranean", *NATO's Sixteen Nations*, 31/1 (March 1986): pp. 62–71
Pavlides, A., "The Greek Mercantile Marine", *NATO's Sixteen Nations*, 37/5 (1992): pp. 44–46
Philpott, T.A., "NATO's New Maritime Strategy", *Army Quarterly* (January 1996): pp. 45–47
Rodgers, William Ledyard, *Greek and Roman Naval Warfare: A Study of Strategy, Tactics, and Ship Design from Salamis (480 BC) to Actium (31 BC)*, Annapolis, Maryland: United States Naval Institute, 1937, reprinted 1964, 1990
Shepard, Arthur MacCartney, *Sea Power in Ancient History: The Story of the Navies of Classic Greece and Rome*, Boston: Little Brown, 1924; London: Heinemann, 1925
Simpsas, M., "The Hellenic Navy: Past and Present", *Navy International*, 88/7 (July 1983): pp. 418–22

Naxos

Island in the Cyclades

At 428 sq km in area, Naxos is the largest island of the Cyclades. It is also the most fertile, being provided with a large coastal plain to the southwest. The interior of the island is mountainous, the highest peak being Mount Zas, which takes its name from the father of the gods; an inscription on the mountain reads "Mountain of Zeus Milesios". The cave of Zas on this mountain is said to be the place where Zeus and Dionysus were reared, and Naxos is said to have been called both "Zia" and "Dionysia" in ancient times. Dionysus is especially associated with Naxos, where he was said to have taken Ariadne from Theseus. Fittingly, Naxos was known for its viticulture in ancient times and continues to produce wine to the present day. Other produce, such as grain, figs, olives, and citrus, is also abundant and it is not surprising that Naxos has been renowned for its prosperity.

Naxos is also rich in marble, as well as the emery used to work it. It is the sole source of emery in the Cyclades, and its white marble is plentiful but coarser than Parian marble. Naxian sculptors are first in evidence in the early Cycladic period, when they produced fine vessels and the stylized figures with triangular heads that are unique to the Cycladic culture. Many have been found in the area of Grotta, near the site of modern Naxos city, which appears to have been inhabited almost continuously over the past 5000 years. The later Bronze Age was less productive, but at the beginning of the Archaic period in the late 7th century BC Naxos was at the forefront of Greek marble sculpture production. Indeed, it has as good a claim as anywhere in Greece to be the birthplace of the Archaic style of monumental statuary. The nearby island of Delos received many statues from Naxos, including the female figure dedicated by Nikandre, which is the earliest surviving complete marble statue of monumental size, the Naxian sphinx, and a colossal *kouros*, which was famous in ancient times but is now lost. *Kouroi* were youthful male figures, pictured naked with one foot advanced, and often associated with Apollo. They are the most abundant Naxian work, including several unfinished sculptures remaining in Naxian quarries. A 10m-long unfinished colossus is locally believed to represent Apollo, but has a wedge left by the chin that could represent a beard, in which case it would be disqualified as a *kouros*. The entire area of the quarry is, in fact, associated with Apollo, including the nearby village of Apollonia. A large marble temple, variously attributed to Apollo and Dionysus, was erected on a small island outside Naxos city. It is said to have been commissioned by the tyrant Lygdamis. Today only a pair of doorposts and a lintel remain as a landmark. By the time that sculpture passed into the severe Classical style in the late 6th century BC, Naxian marble had faded from prominence. The reasons for this decline, and for the unfinished statues, are unknown.

Lygdamis had risen to power in Naxos in the middle of the 6th century BC, and carved himself an empire in the surrounding islands with the help of Pisistratus, tyrant of Athens, to whom he had given aid at the time of his exile and restoration. By 528 BC the Naxian tyranny had weakened, and the deposed oligarchs were recalled. Interestingly, among the few records of these events, there is mention of unfinished statues to be returned to them. Twelve years later, according to Diodorus, the Naxians controlled a thalassocracy, which lasted a decade. Coinage was becoming widespread in the Aegean at this time, and Naxian influence on the silver trade may have led to the story that coinage was invented on Naxos. In 499 BC the island was conquered by the Persians. The Naxians helped to expel the Persians in the last stages of the war, but did not fully regain their former power. They joined the Delian League, then later resigned from it. Athenian influence was succeeded by Spartan after the Peloponnesian War, although Naxos was the site of a major Athenian victory in 376 BC.

Naxos: view of Naxos town: 360 years of Venetian rule have left their mark on the island, not least in the survival of a substantial Roman Catholic minority in the upper town

Along with the rest of Greece, Naxos passed through the control of the Macedonian, Roman, and Byzantine empires. After the Fourth Crusade in 1204 the Venetians gained title to the Cyclades. The produce and emery of Naxos were among the goods that made them eager to secure the islands for trade, but not so eager that the state was prepared to undertake their governance directly. Instead, a Venetian of prominent family, Marco Sanudo, was given official sanction to capture what he could. He besieged and conquered Naxos, then took the neighbouring islands without resistance, establishing Naxos as the capital of the Duchy of the Archipelago by 1207. The Sanudi built many towers and fortifications, the most notable being the fortified upper section of Naxos city, which remains predominantly Roman Catholic in contrast to the Greek Orthodoxy of the rest of the island. The Crispi dukes succeeded the Sanudi around the time of the Turkish conquest of mainland Greece. Although the Turks did not take control of the duchy until 1564, they twice ravaged Naxos and demanded tribute. Piracy was also taking a toll at this time, as it had frequently in the past, and the people of Naxos became impoverished and discontented. Finally, the last of the Crispi line so disgusted his subjects that they volunteered to accept another ruler from the Turks. Unlike the Franks, the Turks never settled on Naxos, only sending necessary officials. In 1821 the Naxians won their independence, and in 1830 they joined the new Greek state. At that time the people of Naxos, especially those living in remote mountain villages, retained many uniquely Hellenic traditions and practices, having felt little outside influence for many centuries, despite their foreign rulers.

JENNIFER Y.T. KENNEDY

See also Cyclades

Summary

The largest island of the Cyclades, Naxos is rich in marble and emery. Naxian sculptors were prominent in the Cycladic period and especially in the Archaic age. In the late 6th century Naxos dominated the Cyclades. After the Fourth Crusade in the early 13th century Naxos became the capital of the Duchy of the Archipelago. It fell to the Turks in 1564.

Further Reading

Barber, R.L.N., *The Cyclades in the Bronze Age*, Iowa City: University of Iowa Press, and London: Duckworth, 1987

Bent, J. Theodore, *The Cyclades; or, Life Among the Insular Greeks*, London: Longman, 1885, reprinted Chicago: Argonaut, 1965

Cheetham, Nicolas, *Mediaeval Greece*, New Haven and London: Yale University Press, 1981

Lock, Peter, *The Franks in the Aegean, 1204–1500*, London and New York: Longman, 1995

Miller, Molly, *The Thalassocracies*, Albany: State University of New York Press, 1971

Renfrew, Colin, *The Cycladic Spirit: Masterpieces from the Nicholas P. Goulandris Collection*, London: Thames and Hudson, and New York: Abrams, 1991

Richter, Gisela M.A., *Kouroi, Archaic Greek Youths: A Study of the Development of the Kouros Type in Greek Sculpture*, with Irma A. Richter, 3rd edition London: Phaidon, 1970, reprinted New York: Hacker, 1988

Ridgway, Brunilde Sismondo, *The Archaic Style in Greek Sculpture*, 2nd edition, Chicago: Ares, 1993

Necromancy

Belief in necromancy, the employment of the spirits of the dead in divinatory or magical techniques, is attested from almost all periods of the Greek tradition; while treated with disapproval or scepticism by some, and at times subject to harsh legal sanctions, its existence and validity appear, nevertheless, to have been widely accepted on a popular level. It forms only one part of a much wider range of belief and practice concerning the dead within this tradition, however, and also contains elements drawn over time from neighbouring cultures, such as Judaism.

Although the idea of necromancy almost certainly goes back to prehistoric times, the first evidence for it in the Greek literary tradition is found in the *Odyssey* of Homer (10. 501-11) where an elaborate sacrificial ritual for summoning the spirits of the dead is described by Circe and then carried out by Odysseus and his men. A number of references to it in writings of the Classical period suggest a general attitude of intellectual scepticism but popular belief (see, for example, Aeschylus' *Persae*, 609-842, Aristophanes' *Birds*, 1553ff., and Plato's *Laws*, 10. 909b; cf. 11. 933a-e). Herodotus (5. 92) recounts how the Corinthian tyrant Periander sought the help of the oracle of the dead on the river Acheron in Thesprotia and, much later, Plutarch (*Consolatio ad Apollonium*, 109b-d) also refers to such a cult (*psychomanteion*); in the latter case, at least, the ritual concluded in an incubation, with the spirits appearing and revealing in a dream vision the information being sought. Evidence that necromancy continued to find a place in the Greek tradition during the Roman imperial period may also be found, for example, in such works as Lucian's satirical *Menippus* (or *Nekyomanteia*), written in the 2nd century AD, and Heliodorus' *Aethiopica* (6. 14-15), written in the 3rd; both describe necromantic practices in some detail and at least provide evidence of popular views on the subject, if not necessarily of their own belief in its efficacy or acceptability. The information they give is paralleled by contemporary treatments of the subject in a number of Latin authors, while the Romans legislated severely against necromancy and various references show that the allegation of involvement with it could form a useful and dangerous weapon for attacking political or other opponents.

Apart from information to be obtained from literature, there is also a wealth of material evidence for belief in necromancy from the older Greek tradition, particularly in the form of inscribed curse tablets. These tablets, together with bound figurines and similar objects that belong to related practices, were being placed in graves and at other places where the spirits of the dead might be thought to lurk from at least the 5th century BC, but their use appears to have been most common in the Hellenistic era and does not fade away until the advent of Christianity. Material evidence of ancient necromantic practice also comes from archaeological excavations such as those near Ephyre in Epirus which have uncovered the remains of an elaborate oracle of the dead, evidently conducted in an underground chamber beneath a sanctuary complex; there are many indications (see, for example, the episode recounted by Herodotus) that this area around the river Acheron was that most widely associated in Greek antiquity with necromantic rituals, but it seems that similar oracles existed from time to time at other locations notorious as entrances to the underworld. The oracle of Ephyre, which evidently developed from the 4th century to peak in the 3rd and 2nd centuries BC, appears to demonstrate that necromancy was not confined to individual belief and practice but also played a role in highly organized and officially sanctioned oracular cults, although some have challenged this view.

Much of the information on necromancy provided by the various literary sources, as well as that derived from the curse tablets, tallies closely with technical material on the subject to be found in surviving manuals of magic. Thus many passages in the Greek magical papyri (2nd century BC to 5th century AD) reveal that the spirits, or perhaps "ghosts" of the dead (the usual term is *nekydaimon*), were believed to act as intermediaries between the magician and the chthonic powers; especially useful were those thought to be trapped in some way between the worlds of the living and the dead, those, for example, who had suffered an untimely or violent death (the *aoroi* or *biaiothanatoi*). Made vulnerable and weak by their marginal status, these souls still possessed the power to bridge the divide between the different levels of existence and so were ideal instruments of the magician in effectuating the aims of a particular procedure, whether this was a curse, a love spell, or a divination. Furthermore, because these spirits fell within the sphere of control normally ascribed to the major deities of the underworld and to others, such as Hecate or Hermes Psychopompus, these greater powers also came to be associated with and invoked in such magical procedures as attempts were made to ensure their compliance. At other times in these sources, however, the notion of the spirits of the dead as mere intermediaries (and often as more or less witless beings) is replaced by one that treats them as malevolent forces in their own right, quite capable of vindictively pursuing the victims of the magician who is manipulating them and, indeed, of turning on their employer if due precautions are not taken. In both cases, however, it is clear that the spirits of the dead were thought to be of crucial importance in empowering many techniques of ancient Greek magic and this undoubtedly explains why, at least in popular belief, magicians were associated with such things as the theft of corpses, ritual murder, and infanticide.

Although the Church always strongly condemned belief in magic and sought to discredit its intellectual foundations, the emergence of Christianity did not immediately destroy belief in necromancy. The story of the "witch" (*engastrimythos*) of Endor in the Old Testament (1 Samuel 28:3-25), in which Saul consulted the spirit of Samuel in an undeniably necromantic ritual that correctly predicted his imminent death, thus appeared to provide clear biblical validation for the concept, although a more doctrinally acceptable explanation was available. Indeed, even the central events of the Christian story, the death and resurrection of Jesus, might, to those unversed in the niceties of theology, appear to be the ultimate proof that the souls of those who had died an untimely and violent death could act as intermediaries between the worlds of the living and the dead, while certain elements in the cult of saints and their relics might also reflect necromantic tendencies.

Passing references to necromancy in the works of writers from all periods of the Byzantine era (e.g. from Iamblichus, John Chrysostom, and Synesius of Cyrene in the 4th and 5th centuries AD to Nikephoros Gregoras in the 14th) confirm that it continued to find at least some place in conceptions of divination and magic. Indeed, necromantic techniques are also generally implicit, if only occasionally explicit, in many of the procedures outlined in Byzantine and early modern magical manuals dating from the 15th–19th centuries; the most common summoning and divinatory rituals are thus clear survivals of ancient traditions that originally involved using the spirits of the dead as intermediaries. It is nonetheless clear that distinctions between various supernatural intermediaries apparent in the ancient tradition were largely lost in this period. Orthodox Byzantines, echoing the doctrinally acceptable explanation for necromancy that was developed by the early Christian Fathers, did not view the spirits employed in it as actually being those of the dead but rather as demons disguised as such. As the rich variety of ancient spiritual beings was reformulated into the simpler paradigm of the demons that Christian culture had created, explicit awareness of much of the old content of the magical tradition disappeared, including ideas of necromancy: it seems likely that even the practitioners of sorcery in later periods may have been unaware that many of the rituals prescribed in their manuals were originally necromantic techniques as opposed to methods of summoning and manipulating demons.

This process appears to have continued and, in common with a decline noticeable in many magical practices and beliefs, most explicit traces of necromancy disappeared from the Greek tradition in the 20th century. There is, however, evidence that, as late as the 1970s, villagers still believed that the old methods of divination and sorcery, implicitly underpinned by necromantic techniques, were being practised by professional magicians, and some divinatory practices (such as forms of lecanomancy) associated with necromancy in the ancient world survive to this day.

RICHARD P.H. GREENFIELD

See also Divination, Magic, Oracles

Further Reading

Betz, Hans Dieter (editor), *The Greek Magical Papyri in Translation, Including the Demotic Spells*, Chicago: University of Chicago Press, 1986, 2nd edition, 1992

Dodds, E.R., *The Ancient Concept of Progress and Other Essays on Greek Literature and Belief*, Oxford: Clarendon Press, 1973

Gager, John G. (editor), *Curse Tablets and Binding Spells from the Ancient World*, Oxford and New York: Oxford University Press, 1992

Garland, Robert, *The Greek Way of Death*, London: Duckworth, and Ithaca, New York: Cornell University Press, 1985

Greenfield, Richard P.H., *Traditions of Belief in Late Byzantine Demonology*, Amsterdam: Hakkert, 1988

Halliday, W.R., *Greek Divination: A Study of its Methods and Principles*, London: Macmillan, 1913, reprinted Chicago: Argonaut, 1967

Johnston, Sarah, *Hekate Soteira: A Study of Hekate's Role in the Chaldean Oracles and Related Literature*, Atlanta: Scholars Press, 1990

Kelsey, Neal, Marvin Meyer and Richard Smith (editors), *Ancient Christian Magic: Coptic Texts of Ritual Power*, San Francisco: HarperCollins, 1994, reprinted Princeton, New Jersey: Princeton University Press, 1999

Luck, Georg, *Arcana Mundi: Magic and the Occult in the Greek and Roman Worlds: A Collection of Ancient Texts*, Baltimore: Johns Hopkins University Press, 1985; Wellingborough: Crucible, 1987

Meyer, Marvin and Paul Mirecki (editors), *Ancient Magic and Ritual Power*, Leiden and New York: Brill, 1995

Nektarios of Aegina, St 1846–1920

Metropolitan of Pentapolis

St Nektarios of Aegina is probably the most widely revered modern saint in the Greek Orthodox world. Canonized by the ecumenical patriarchate in 1961, he was the object of local veneration from the time of his death, and reports of the miraculous cures effected by prayer at his tomb or use of oil from the lamp hanging above it rapidly spread his fame. More than 20 churches in Greece are dedicated to him, and others have been erected throughout the Greek diaspora.

Although consecrated metropolitan of Pentapolis (with effective control of the Alexandrian patriarchate churches in Egypt) at the age of 46, Nektarios was never a successful Church establishment figure. He was suspended from office a year later, and subsequently asked to leave Egypt, for "moral and ethical" reasons "known to the patriarchate"; and although retaining the title of metropolitan, he was never to serve as a hierarch again (the patriarchate of Alexandria was finally to rescind his suspension in 1998, expressing regret at his treatment and naming 1999 "the year of St Nektarios"). His irregular canonical status as a priest unattached to any jurisdiction was never resolved, and his subsequent posts (as preacher in Euboea and Phthiotis, and subsequently as director of the Rizarios school, a secondary school and seminary in Athens) were gained on the strength of his academic theological education at Athens university and the intercession of influential Egyptian friends. Similarly, the canonical status of the nunnery that he founded on Aegina in 1904 remained unresolved at the time of his death 16 years later, as did the status of two female subdeacons whom he had ordained there during the last years of his life.

Nektarios was a prolific writer throughout his life, a systematic and thorough expounder of dogmatics, ethics, and pastoral theology: many of his books were intended for class use in the Rizarios school or as handbooks for the clergy. He shows an extensive knowledge of the Fathers, especially the Three Hierarchs, the hesychasts, the Fathers of the *Philokalia* and St Nikodemos of the Holy Mountain, and the Kollyvades, but also does not hesitate to draw upon the philosophers of Classical Greece. Writing at a time when Athens was under the influence of a westernized court, he is careful to point up the differences between Orthodox, Protestant, and Roman

Catholic positions on such questions as papal supremacy and the *filioque*, and compiled a two-volume history of the Great Schism which asserted the impossibility of reunion. He also wrote several volumes of religious poetry for private devotional use, a *Catechism*, and a harmony of the Gospels based upon Tischendorf's *Synopsis Evangelica*. With the spread of his cult in recent years many of these volumes have been reprinted.

Nektarios was deeply concerned by the inability of the contemporary Church to respond to the challenges posed by westernization, scientism, and the scepticism of a newly educated laity: many of the upper clergy were in his view cynical careerists, while rural priests had little theological knowledge. Being denied active participation in the Church's ministry, he sought to remedy these needs by education, first by training seminarians who were both spiritually and dogmatically competent, and later by a project (unrealized) for a girls' school adjacent to his monastery on Aegina offering a syllabus of religion, ethics, handicrafts, and home economics. Nektarios realized that "in educating the mothers we educate their children", and often quoted St Kosmas the Aetolian's slogan "schools–letters–schools". His foundation of a nunnery dedicated to the Holy Trinity on Aegina, although primarily a response to a direct request from a group of his spiritual children, may also have been an active response to the low ebb of much contemporary monasticism: it may not be insignificant that one of the convent's founding members (and its first abbess) had home connections with the founder of the Zoe movement.

Throughout his life those that knew him were impressed by the saint's spiritual charisma (he was a constant practitioner of the Jesus Prayer), by his unfailing self-sacrificial generosity towards those in need, and by his spiritual power as a preacher, confessor, and exorcist. He gave his own clothes away to the poor, and rebuilt the ruined church and conventual buildings of the Aegina nunnery at his own expense. He raised the theological standards and the spiritual tone of the Rizarios school, where many key churchmen of the interwar years passed through his hands, but was frequently at odds with the school governors, whose accusations of organizational incompetence were given seeming weight by his customary refusal, following the example of Christ, to speak in his own defence or to spare financial thought for the morrow.

It is perhaps ironical that St Nektarios should gain widespread veneration as a posthumous wonderworker: his own writings on the miraculous (e.g. *God's Revelation to the World*, 1892) address with caution the radically divided attitudes of his contemporaries – suspicion and contempt among the educated (including many of the higher clergy), and uncritical adulation from the ignorant. Nektarios defends the reality of miracles as a means of divine self-revelation, and insists that their breach of natural laws must be viewed as evidence for the existence of a spiritual domain within the natural, where such laws do not obtain; but he also emphasizes that miracles were never intended as a basis for faith, and can never replace the believer's life of prayer and obedience to the gospels.

D.J. EDMONDS

Biography

Born Anastasios Kephalas in 1846, Nektarios studied theology at the University of Athens. He was consecrated Metropolitan of Pentapolis in 1892 but suspended in 1893 and later asked to leave Egypt. He became a preacher in Euboea and Director of the Rizarios school in Athens. In 1904 he founded the nunnery of Hagia Trias on Aegina. He died in 1920 and was canonized in 1961, the first modern saint of the Orthodox Church.

Further Reading

Cavarnos, Constantine, *Saint Nectarios of Aegina*, 2nd edition, Belmont, Massachusetts: Institute for Byzantine and Modern Greek Studies, 1988

Chondropoulos, S., *Saint Nektarios: A Saint for Our Times*, Brookline, Massachusetts: Holy Cross Orthodox Press, 1989

Gerasimos Mikragiannitis, *The Service of our Father among the Saints Nectarius*, Aegina: Monastery of the Holy Trinity, 1985

Matthaiakis, T., *O Osios Nektarios Kephalas* [The Venerable Nektarios Kephalas], Athens, 1955

Matthaiakis, T., *O Agios Nektarios Pentapoleos* [Saint Nektarios of Pentapolis], Athens: Apostoliki Diakonia, 1965

Theodoretos Athonitis, *O Agios Nektarios: O Agios, O Logios, O Askitis* [Saint Nektarios: The Saint, the Scholar, the Ascetic], Athens: Monastery of the Transfiguration, Kouvara, 1970

Nemesius

Bishop of Emesa in the late 4th century

More is known of Emesa than of this bishop of the see. Situated on the Orontes in Syria, it reached a level of modest prosperity. What may be said with certainty about Nemesius is to be derived from an analysis of his treatise *On Human Nature*. Attempts have been made to identify him with the Nemesius with whom Gregory of Nazianzus was acquainted. He was a pagan, a governor of Cappadocia, in whom Gregory detected signs of Christian sympathy, even the possibility of his being won over to the faith. Gregory addressed four letters to him, also dedicating a poem urging conversion. Such an identification is only conjecture, calling as it would for acceptance of the view that he had, in fact, been converted *c*.390, encompassing within a decade elevation to the episcopate, the composition of a treatise, and death. It seems wiser to remain content with ignorance of his life and concentrate on his writing.

Written by a bishop, emerging as significant in apologetic terms, and with relevance for specifically theological debates of its day, *On Human Nature* incorporates a wide conspectus of non-Christian thinking on the nature of the psyche, as Nemesius reviews a selection of opinions drawn from writers including Plato, Aristotle, Epicurus, Plotinus, Porphyry, Iamblichus, Posidonius, among other Stoics, and Galen. In a treatise that appears not to have been finished (there are references to discussions never written) there are inconsistencies and ambiguities. Yet it is worthy of study, containing a serious exploration of long-standing questions of the body–soul relationship.

In attempting to represent a human being as an identifiable psychophysical entity, Nemesius shows Neoplatonic influence. The psyche is immaterial, its highest part being *nous* ("intellect"), and the argument is developed on regular anti-Stoic lines. Yet he never plays down the essentially Christian doctrine that the soul, no less than the body, is part of the created order. He presents the human being as a microcosm, an image of the whole of creation, the bond (*syndesmos*) of creation, a being on the borderline of the intelligible and the sensible worlds, which, since both are part of divine creation, are not dualistically opposed but are capable of meeting in humanity, spirit, and matter harmoniously combined into a unity. The status of mankind is stressed in the view that the whole of the rest of creation exists for the benefit of man. He lives within the constraints of physical existence, while preserving an essential kinship with the intelligible through the rationality of the human mind. The soul, however, is not pure reason, in its embodied state being linked with passions. There is some ambiguity, coming from his Neoplatonic predilections, as to whether the soul may nevertheless remain in some recognizable sense impassible. Nemesius has his own borderline positions. It is still clear that, whatever his tensions, he contrives to maintain some firm views. He is committed to the reality of human free will, over against fatalism of any kind, whether it be Stoic or grounded in the Manichaean dualism to which his native Syria was prone. Again, his knowledge of the human body, derived from medical writers such as Galen, is extensively used in his writing and shows a deep interest in the whole human person. Physiology is no embarrassment. Rather it is the start of an exploration into the interaction of soul and body, of the modifications that can be traced within what is perceived as a psychophysical unity. Importantly, the senses are given a place of respect as a fascinating part of the whole human composition.

While this work aims at a survey of non-Christian sources, it still reflects interest in specific contemporary concerns of the Christian Church. In Christology Nemesius shows affinities with Antiochene thinkers such as Theodore of Mopsuestia in stressing the completeness of the human nature taken by Christ, being critical of what he saw as the deficiency of Apollinarius in this respect. Eunomius, representing a form of Arianism attacked by the Cappadocians, was from another angle subject to the censure of Nemesius.

Shadowy though he may have been, Nemesius cast certain shadows before him, aided perhaps by his very obscurity. The attribution of *On Human Nature* to Gregory of Nyssa, whose own writings on the soul were well known, and with whom Nemesius has affinities, must have furthered the promulgation and acceptance of the work. John of Damascus draws on it extensively, bestowing the authority of one who was widely seen as the culmination of Greek patristic theology, while its translation into Latin made it accessible to Albertus Magnus and Thomas Aquinas. Again, during the Renaissance, Nemesius emerged into publication, sometimes disguised as Gregory of Nyssa, but increasingly often recognized under his own name. As well as influencing the theory of Christian anthropology, this "Christian eclecticism" (Gilson) has been thought to affect later Byzantine aesthetic perceptions, as Nemesius' awareness of the value of the sense of touch led to a greater appreciation of the tactile in art.

D.A. SYKES

Biography

Nothing is known of the life of this 4th-century bishop of Emesa in Syria except that he was the author of a treatise on the nature of the psyche called *On Human Nature*. It is a survey of non-Christian sources but it reflects interest in contemporary concerns of the Christian Church.

Writings

In *Patrologia Graeca*, edited by J.-P. Migne, vol. 40, 508 ff.
Cyril of Jerusalem and Nemesius of Emesa, edited and translated by William Telfer, London: SCM Press, and Philadelphia: Westminster Press, 1955

Further Reading

Cross, F.L. (editor), *The Oxford Dictionary of the Christian Church*, 3rd edition, Oxford and New York: Oxford University Press, 1997 (contains bibliography, listing texts and editors)
Gilson, Etienne, *History of Christian Philosophy in the Middle Ages*, London: Sheed and Ward, and New York: Random House, 1955
Grillmeier, Aloys, *Christ in Christian Tradition*, vol. 1: *From the Apostolic Age to Chalcedon*, translated by John Bowden, 2nd edition, London: Mowbray, and Atlanta: John Knox Press, 1975
Mathew, Gervase, *Byzantine Aesthetics*, London: John Murray, and New York: Viking, 1963
Norris, Richard Alfred, Jr, *Manhood and Christ: A Study in the Christology of Theodore of Mopsuestia*, Oxford: Clarendon Press, 1963
Quasten, Johannes, *Patrology*, vol. 3: *The Golden Age of Patristic Literature, from the Council of Nicaea to the Council of Chalcedon*, Utrecht: Spectrum, and Westminster, Maryland: Newman Press, 1960
Wolfson, Harry Anstryn, *The Philosophy of the Church Fathers*, 3rd edition, vol. 1, Cambridge, Massachusetts: Harvard University Press, 1970

Neo-Orthodoxy

The term "Neo-Orthodoxy" has been widely used in Greece since the 1980s to designate an unorganized and multi-dimensional religious and intellectual current. The term was coined from the leftist journal *Scholiastis* in 1983 as a negative characterization of the religious quest of some left-wing intellectuals, men of letters, and artists (e.g. S. Ramphos, K. Zouraris, K. Moskof, D. Savvopoulos, N.-G. Pentzikis) who showed an unusual degree of interest in the Orthodox tradition and in the spiritual legacy of Athonite monasticism. These personalities from the left camp, which had never traditionally been on good terms with religion in general, were influenced by some progressive theologians and clerics (e.g. C. Yannaras, P. Nellas, abbot Vasileios Gontikakis). These had inititated a fresh quest for the rediscovery of a forgotten but authentic Orthodox tradition (e.g. the hesychast tradition of the 14th century), away from the conventionalism of the Church hierarchy, the pietistic precepts of Orthodox fundamentalists, and the superficial acquaintance of the general Greek public with Orthodoxy. This quest was thought to be a productive encounter with the genuine, uncontaminated sources of Greek Orthodox civilization, clearly differentiated from the West. Yet, the individuals involved in this movement never accepted the term of opprobrium "Neo-Orthodox", which they considered misleading. This term, nevertheless, has been generally established and used, in journalistic and scholarly circles alike.

Because Neo-Orthodoxy was in essence an unsystematic endeavour, no clear definition of the movement has yet been provided. Neo-Orthodoxy was not some sort of Orthodox revival, which has been a much wider phenomenon since the 1960s. It is therefore preferable to describe Neo-Orthodoxy with reference to some important events of the early 1980s: an unofficial dialogue between Orthodoxy (as differentiated from Western Christianity) and Marxism/communism; a tract from the Holy Community of Mount Athos concerning the education of the Greek nation; a widespread interest in Athonite monasticism and Orthodox spirituality; the debates concerning C. Yannaras's election to a chair of philosophy at the Panteion University of Athens, and heated discussions about the relationship between philosophy and theology as well as between Orthodoxy and rationality; the appearance of the new theological journal *Synaxi*, in which articles by Neo-Orthodox thinkers were published; the first publication in 1983 of *Oramata kai Thavmata* [Visions and Marvels] by the War of Independence general Yannis Makriyannis, which was considered to be an authentic document of the popular Orthodox ethos; and finally, the record *Ta Trapezakia Exo* [The Tables Outside] and various interviews by the popular singer D. Savvopoulos, who often and explicitly acknowledged his great debt to Orthodoxy. These examples reveal various enquiries in the religiocultural domain to locate the idiosyncrasy of the Greek Orthodox tradition.

Neo-Orthodoxy, however, was initially a marginal and remained basically an elitist movement. It had no mass appeal, except among some educated individuals and certain university students (e.g. the Greek Christian Orthodox Socialist Youth and its journal *Simadia*). An important reason for this was that Neo-Orthodoxy was supported neither by the official Church nor by the political parties. Another reason was that the movement lacked the organization necessary to ensure its longevity and wider impact. Additional reasons can be found in the radical sociopolitical changes and the collapse of Marxism-Leninism in Eastern Europe, which has meant that the aim of an Orthodox–Marxist rapprochement has in fact been unproductive. These events notwithstanding, there was a renewed interest in Orthodoxy in Greece in the 1990s in the wake of the revival of Orthodoxy in former Eastern bloc countries. This enabled several Neo-Orthodox thinkers to become involved in a wider attempt to locate the particular Greek Orthodox way of life and to construct a modern Greek identity with reference to its Hellenic and Orthodox past in order to face the challenges of the modern competitive world system. Some Neo-Orthodox thinkers were consequently called Hellenocentric as well and the influence of their ideas was manifest in overt and covert forms alike. Though there was never an official Neo-Orthodox programme, it is useful to outline some basic features that characterize this broad current of ideas, in addition to the positive appreciation of Orthodoxy.

First, the Neo-Orthodox opposed the Orthodox hardliners, the uninformed neutrals, and the enthusiastic westernizers. They considered both the past and the modern Greek intelligentsia as myopic because of its neglect of Greece's own incomparable cultural resources. The result was the modern disorientation of the country between the Scylla of traditionalism and the Charybdis of modernity, viz. westernization. The Neo-Orthodox thus intended to consider the history of Greece from an inward perspective and not according to western historiographical presuppositions. Second, the Neo-Orthodox put particular emphasis on a personal, experiential philosophy as well as on a communal way of life, as exemplified in the communalist tradition of the Orthodox east during Byzantium and the Tourkokratia. This perspective understood the human person as an erotic being in relation to other humans and the entire material world. The idea of personhood constituted for the Neo-Orthodox a clear difference between the Orthodox ethos and western individualism. In this context, they also distinguished between religion and ecclesiastical Orthodoxy. The former signified the satisfaction of fragmented individualistic needs, the latter the total fulfilment of human life. Third, the Neo-orthodox attempted to find the diachronic elements of Greek Orthodox culture and the underlying structure of Hellenicity from ancient times through Byzantium to the present, away from western adulterating influences and indigenous distortions. They did not support the uninterrupted continuity (ethnic/national) of Hellenism over a span of 3,000 years, but looked for features of Greek duration, patent and latent alike, throughout this long period. For them, Hellenism never represented a narrow geographical area (*topos*), but a specific way (*tropos*) of life. Finally, the Neo-Orthodox emphasized the exquisite value and superiority of the Greek Orthodox culture as well as the "aristocracy" of the Greek nation. This entails the abandonment of the inferiority complex of modern Greeks, especially vis-à-vis the West and its cultural imperialism. Greek Orthodox culture has an unsurpassed cosmopolitan universalism and can furnish viable solutions to the pressing problems of the contemporary international environment. The Neo-Orthodox criticism of the West, however, does not mean its wholesale rejection, but a fruitful interaction with it.

In short, the Neo-Orthodox movement should be understood in relation to the deep identity crisis and orientation problems that have tantalized modern Greece since its foundation. Despite its influence on contemporary Orthodox theology and Greek culture in general, Neo-Orthodoxy has drawn serious criticism from various perspectives, Orthodox, Marxist, and otherwise, as an elitist, nationalistic, isolationist, illusory, idealized, ahistorical, unfounded, biased, and even heretical current. This is indicative of deep cleavages within the modern Greek religious, intellectual, and socio-political scene with regard to all aspects of Greek identity, namely its past, its present, and its future.

VASILIOS MAKRIDES

Further Reading

Begzos, Marios, *Orthodoxia i misallodoxia?* [Right Belief or Hatred of Other Belief?], Athens, 1996, pp. 27–47

Clément, Olivier, "Orthodox Reflections on 'Liberation Theology'", *St. Vladimir's Theological Quarterly*, 29 (1985): pp. 63–72

Giephtits, Athanasios (editor), *Orthodoxia kai Marxismos* [Orthodoxy and Marxism], Athens, 1984 (contributions by S. Ramphos, K. Zouraris *et al.*)

Kasiouras, Dimitris, *Marxismos kai neoorthodoxoi* [Marxism and the Neo-Orthodox], Athens, 1986

Makrides, Vasilios N., "Neoorthodoxie: eine religiöse Intellektuellenströmung im heutigen Griechenland" in *Die Religion von Oberschichten: Religion, Profession,*

Intellektualismus, edited by Peter Antes and Donate Pahnke, Marburg: Diagonal, 1989

Makrides, Vasilios N., "Christian Orthodoxy Versus Religion: Negative Critiques of Religion in Contemporary Greece" in *The Notion of "Religion" in Comparative Research*, edited by U. Bianchi, Rome: Bretschneider, 1994

Makrides, Vasilios N., "Byzantium in Contemporary Greece: The Neo-orthodox Current of Ideas" in *Byzantium and the Modern Greek Identity*, edited by Paul Magdalino and David Ricks, Aldershot, Hampshire: Ashgate, 1998

Makris, Petros, *Marxistes kai Orthodoxia: Dialogos i diamachi?* [Marxists and Orthodoxy: Dialogue or Conflict?], Athens, 1983

Mésoniat, Claude, "Le Mouvement "néo-orthodoxe" en Grèce", *Contacts*, 36 (1984): pp. 331–40

Theoklitos Dionysiatis, *O Nikolaitikos Erotismos ton Neorthodoxon (me Theoritiko ton k. Yannara)* [The Nicolaitan Eroticism of the Neo-Orthodox (with Yannaras the Theoretician)], Athens, 1989

Wenturis, Nikolaus, *Griechenland und die Europaische Gemeinschaft: Die soziopolitischen Rahmenbedingungen griechischer Europapolitiken*, Tübingen: Francke, 1990, pp. 191–93

Xydias, Vasilis, "'New' or 'Old': Orthodoxy in the Limelight", *Journal of the Hellenic Diaspora*, 11 (1984): pp. 69–72

Yannaras, Christos, *Kritikes paremvaseis* [Critical Interventions], 2nd edition, Athens, 1987

Neoclassicism

The establishment of the modern Greek state in 1833 signalled a concerted national turn towards ancient Greek culture. The monuments of Classical Athens provided initial inspiration. Neoclassical architecture, introduced by the Bavarian government (1833–62), became the dominant architectural style throughout the 19th century. It offered concrete references to the ancient Greek past and provided a common vocabulary for the modern Greek nation. Furthermore, as a widespread European style, it created a visual link between Athens and other European cities that Athens aimed to emulate. By the late 19th century, the development of new internal and external influences redefined the cultural orientation of the Greek nation, signalling a turn away from Neoclassicism, and towards a closer examination of local vernacular architecture.

While Classical architecture originated in ancient Greece, Neoclassicism was a western European architectural movement. Developed in the second half of the 18th century, it was initially inspired by Roman antiquities, because they were more accessible to European architects and scholars. A desire for adventure, archaeological curiosity, and the search for architectural inspiration were the main reasons that brought young architects first to the Italian peninsula, and later to Greece. Travel had always been an important aspect of architectural education, allowing one to experience important buildings in situ, and to expand one's knowledge beyond the few published examples. By the 18th century travel came to be expected of professional architects, while the range of architectural sites on the itinerary continuously expanded.

Although today the Parthenon is one of the most revered ancient buildings, its artistic prominence was not always undisputed. Originally, the ruins of Roman antiquity were considered superior to those of Greece, in part because the Greek works were less familiar to western scholars. During the Ottoman period, visits to the Greek lands were less common, being both cumbersome and expensive. The art historian J.J. Winckelmann was the first to challenge the artistic superiority of the Romans over the Greeks in his *Geschichte der Kunst des Alterthums* (1764); for him Hellenistic art was superior to both the Classical Greek and the Roman periods. The publications of Le Roy, *Les Ruines des plus beaux monuments de la Grèce* (1758), and especially Stuart and Revett, *The Antiquities of Athens* (1762–1830), offered the first scientific descriptions of Classical Greek architecture. By the early 19th century, taste and aesthetic preferences had shifted towards Greece, and the artistic production of Athens in the 5th century came to represent the highest standard of artistic excellence. But while antiquity provided the inspiration, 18th- and 19th-century architects could not simply copy existing ancient buildings. First of all, most of them lay in ruins, or were partially underground and had to be reconstructed in the imagination. Secondly, the functions of the ancient monuments differed radically from the needs of modern society. The layout, design requirements, and building materials of Neoclassical museums, hotels, private clubs, or banks were uniquely modern. It was rather in the relationship and proportion of the parts and in the decorative vocabulary that architects sought inspiration in antiquity.

After the establishment of the Greek kingdom, several young, foreign, and foreign-trained architects travelled to Greece, full of dreams for grand projects and archaeological restorations. Most notable among them were the Danish brothers Christian Hansen (1803–83) and Theophilos Hansen (1813–91), and the Greeks Stamatios Kleanthes (1802–62), who was trained in Berlin under Karl Friedrich Schinkel, and Lysandros Kaftantzoglou (1811–85), who was educated in the Academy of San Luca in Rome. The first major Neoclassical structure was the royal palace (1836–43), designed by Friedrich von Gaertner (1792–1847), who worked in Munich for Otho's father, king Ludwig, and came to Athens only briefly to supervise the construction. The imposing palace, while uninspired in its design, sent a welcome signal of permanence to the war-torn country. Its construction encouraged other wealthy Greeks from abroad to move to Greece and contribute to the country's reconstruction. Yet, it was the buildings of the Athenian trilogy – the University, the Academy, and the Library, all on Panepistimiou Street – that stamped the elegant Neoclassical vocabulary on the Athenian landscape, and were emulated by other architects and builders throughout the 19th century. The University (1839–64) was designed by Christian Hansen, while the Academy (1859–87) and the Library (1884–1902) were the work of his brother Theophilos. Also noteworthy are the Polytechnic (1861–76) and the Arsakeion School (1846–52) by Kaftantzoglou, the Archaeological Museum (1866–89), designed by Ludwig Lange (1808–68) and Panagiotes Kalkos (1818–75), and the Zappeion Exhibition Hall (1874–88) by F. Boulanger and T. Hansen.

Many of the architects involved in the rebuilding of Athens also worked on archaeological excavations and restorations. The simplicity and austerity of the ancient examples were often reflected in their own creations, thus forging a Neoclassical idiom that was unique to Greece. By the end of the 19th century, however, this simplicity gave way to a much more decorated style that also borrowed from the rounded forms of Italian Renaissance architecture. The most prominent architect

Neoclassicism: Athens University, designed by the Danish architect Christian Hansen in 1839–42

in the late 19th and early 20th century was the prolific Ernst Ziller (1837–1923), who designed the house of Heinrich Schliemann (1879), the Royal Theatre (1895–1901), several hotels and civic buildings, and numerous houses. In his competent hands, this turn-of-the-century development of ornate Neoclassicism became synonymous with national Greek architecture.

The Neoclassical style of the capital was quickly exported to the rest of Greece. In fact, some of the best-preserved examples of Neoclassical architecture can be found in the Aegean islands, notably in the capital of Syros, Hermoupolis, and in many cities of the mainland, for example, Piraeus, Nauplia, Patras, etc. Local builders, having been apprenticed under trained foreigners, went on to apply what they had learned to more modest building commissions of their own. Even humble residences began to assume a regular, symmetrical façade, a scaled-down version of the major Athenian structures.

Some scholars have also used the term "Neoclassical" to describe the rational, orthogonal town plans of the 18th and 19th centuries that were inspired by Enlightenment theories and were initiated by the army of Napoleon I in France and Italy. Engineers from the French army also laid out some of the first cities designed under the regimes of Kapodistria (1828–31) and Otho. Characterized by regular geometry and symmetry, the plans consisted of rectangular building blocks,

arranged around a central civic and administrative square. These regularly planned cities provided the backdrop for the new civic buildings in the Neoclassical style that were erected after the liberation. In the period between 1828 and 1912, more than 175 settlements were planned on the Greek mainland. Among others, new plans were designed for the following cities and towns: Argos (1829), Corinth (1829), Patras (1829), Eretria (1834), Nauplia (1834), Sparta (1834), Kalamata (1860), Thebes (1879), Volos (1882), Larissa (1883), Amfissa (1896), etc. While these plans did not completely erase the existing street patterns, they imposed a high degree of regularity on them.

New plans signalled an era of independence from Ottoman rule, national unity, and westernization. Greece, of course, was not the only country to undergo such modernizing, urban transformations. In fact, the Ottoman empire also invited western-trained architects and planners to design new civic and government buildings and to make proposals for urban transformations. And many of the foreign architects who worked in Greece worked in other countries as well. Theophilos Hansen's design for the Vienna parliament (1874–83), for example, bears a marked resemblance to his design for the Athenian Academy. Nevertheless, while there are stylistic similarities among the various Neoclassical buildings in Europe, their symbolic meaning is closely tied to the specific history and culture of each location. As the poet George Seferis remarked, the Athenian Academy is so embedded in the Greek culture that, "most of the time, when we speak about the Greekness of a work of art, we are speaking about the Academy building" (G. Seferis, *Dokimes*, vol. 1, 1974).

Though prominent, Neoclassicism was not the only architectural style in 19th-century Greece. Byzantine architecture also provided inspiration for new buildings, as is evident in the work of Kaftantzoglou, Kleanthes, and several other architects known primarily for their Neoclassical buildings. In fact, when Otho announced an architectural competition in 1846 for the completion of Athens cathedral, he stipulated that the design be in the Greek-Byzantine order. Connection with the Byzantine epoch strengthened the Christian tradition of the modern Greek nation and helped to forge a continuous historical line from antiquity to the present.

By the turn of the 20th century, the Classically based, intellectual underpinnings of the modern Greek culture were challenged by a new wave of writings that focused on local people, customs, and traditions. The architect Dimitris Pikionis (1887–1968) was one of the first to study the vernacular landscape, exalting the "natural" and "true" elements of Greek popular (*laiki*) architecture. He urged his students to study the methods of traditional builders and adapt them to their own designs. His own work, however, like the work of most of his contemporaries, while it borrowed extensively from local vernacular architecture, was also influenced by the international modern movement. The sunset of Neoclassicism in Greece, however, was not only the result of ideological shifts in architectural theory and practice. Increasingly, technological and industrial advancement, rather than attachment to antiquity, was considered the true demonstration of progress. An unstable economy, combined with the continuous military undertakings that came to an end with the Asia Minor disaster of 1922, also forced the country to concentrate on the present and the future. The few Neoclassical buildings that survived the wholesale rebuilding of the 1960s and 1970s are once again revered and restored, often to house the offices of banks, international companies, art galleries, and small hotels.

ELENI BASTÉA

See also Architecture (Public)

Further Reading

Bastéa, Eleni, *The Creation of Modern Athens: Planning the Myth*, Cambridge and New York: Cambridge University Press, 2000

Bires, Kosta, *E Hai Athenai: Apo tou 19on eis ton 20on Aiona* [Athens From the 19th to the 20th Centuries], Athens, 1966, reprinted 1996

Eitner, Lorenz, *Neoclassicism and Romanticism, 1750–1850*, 2 vols, Englewood Cliffs, New Jersey: Prentice Hall, 1970

Hastaoglou-Martinidis, Vilma, "City Form and National Identity: Urban Designs in 19th-Century Greece", *Journal of Modern Greek Studies*, 13/1 (May 1995): pp. 99–123

Philippides, Dimitri, *Neoellenike Architektonike* [Modern Greek Architecture], Athens, 1984

Porphyrios, Dimitri, "Neoclassical Architecture in Copenhagen and Athens", *Architectural Design*, 57/3–4 (1987)

Tournikiotis, Panayotis (editor), *The Parthenon and Its Impact in Modern Times*, Athens: Melissa, 1994

Travlos, Ioannes, *Neoklassike Architektonike sten Hellada* [Neoclassical Architecture in Greece], Athens, 1967

Travlos, Ioannes and Angeliki Kokkou, *Hermoupolis: The Creation of a New City on Syros at the Beginning of the 19th Century*, Athens: Commercial Bank of Greece, 1984

Neomartyrs

The Orthodox Church considers as neomartyrs all those who have been persecuted for their faith by heterodox oppressors. Although most of the new witnesses to the faith suffered martyrdom at the hands of their Muslim masters, it is wrong to impute their persecution only to the latter. The term neomartyr was used for the first time in the 8th century by the iconodules to qualify those persecuted for their Orthodox beliefs regarding the veneration of icons. Several cases of martyrdom occurred also during the reign of Michael VIII Palaiologos (1259–82) resulting from his policy on the union of the Churches, and under Frankish and Venetian rule.

Had it been possible to account for all the neomartyrs, including the 20 monks of the Mar Saba monastery in Palestine who were killed by the Arabs in 797, the 42 defenders of Amorion who refused to embrace Islam and died a martyr's death in 838, or the 13 monks killed under the Lusignans in Cyprus in 1231, with all the anonymous witnesses to the faith whose memory was lost through the long centuries of persecution and foreign invasion, the official count of 162 neomartyrs who fell during the period of Tourkokratia proper would easily swell to a few hundred.

The traditional martyrs of the early Church were primarily bearing witness to the faith they were holding; in a sense they were witnesses to the events directly related to their salvation. The neomartyrs were living testimonies of a more complex set of truths and values. In most cases they were forced formally to renounce their faith and embrace Islam. Their conversion implied not only a change of religion but the total denial of their identity. When they "turned Turk" they had to assume a foreign lifestyle, name, attire, manners, and, above all, a fundamental change of attitude towards their fellow Christians including members of their own family.

Akylina's father had converted to Islam to avoid punishment for killing a Turk. The girl, who was raised as a Christian, objected vehemently to embracing Islam and was brought by her own father to the Turkish authorities. All along she was encouraged by her mother not to renounce her ancestral faith. She was badly whipped for several days and she expired in her mother's arms on 27 September 1764.

For many renegades their apostasy came at a high price and led to banishment from their former community, bringing upon them hatred and isolation; life in these conditions, although relieved of the burden of excessive taxation imposed upon the non-Muslim Ottoman subjects, became unbearable and led to the repudiation of their former abjuration. This was usually followed by a sincere *metanoia* (repentance), a quest for guidance from a spiritual father, usually at an Athonite monastery, and an ardent desire to make in public a formal declaration of their ancestral faith. Their spiritual guides were reluctant in granting them permission to suffer martyrdom. Nevertheless, at their unmitigated insistence, they complied with their wish to efface the stigma of apostasy by an ultimate act of sacrifice; indeed, martyrdom seemed to be the only honourable way to regain and reclaim their lost identity for all eternity.

The *Life* of St Polydoros of New Ephesus (first published in Venice in 1799) offers interesting details on the painful process undertaken by an apostate for his re-entrance into the Church. Having pronounced the *Shahada*, the Islamic confession of faith, in a bout of drunkenness while on a business trip to Egypt, he was unable to cope with the consequences of his conversion. He sought spiritual advice from a hierarch in Beirut, who advised him to retire to a monastery of Mount Lebanon. Desiring martyrdom, he went to Acre; from there he boarded a ship for Egypt and after several adventures he finally reached Smyrna with the intent of making a public confession of his faith; he was prevented from accomplishing this by the spiritual fathers of Smyrna, who were mindful of the consequences on the Christian population of a second martyrdom in the same city only a few weeks after the beheading of the neomartyr Alexander the Dervish. He left for Chios where he received approval for his martyrdom from "a foreign spiritual father". After an intense period of penance and preparation with fasting, prayers, genuflections, *parakliseis* to the Theotokos, and readings of martyrs' Lives, he came to such contrition, crying bitterly during many sleepless nights, sighing from the depths of his heart and calling on Theotokos to help him, so that those who saw and heard him were moved to profound mercy and sympathy. He went to New Ephesus (Kushadasi) where, following an illuminating interview with a Turkish judge, which includes a rare catechetical exposition of the faith to a non-Christian, and being offered the option of departing to live as a giaour, holding "whatever religion he may please, Frankish or Armenian", he persisted in his desire to die for Christ and he was hanged on 3 September 1794.

The Orthodox Church did not keep an official register of neomartyrs and never followed specific rules concerning the canonization of saints. St Nikodemos of the Holy Mountain put together a collection of *Lives* from hearsay and from *Lives* existing in manuscript form at the Athonite monasteries. Another source must have been the Akolouthiai, liturgical offices published for the local veneration of the neomartyrs. The ordering for the composition of such a service to commemorate the martyrdom of two Spezziots in Chios by "the Bishop of Scio" addressed in a letter to the Spezziots is quoted by Hasluck, who concludes that "the admonition of the bishop was duly attended to". The result of St Nikodemos's compilation is the *New Martyrologion*, published in 1799 in Venice. As is the case with other works of St Nikodemos, characterized by their popular tenor, the main purpose of this work was to stem the tide of apostasy and, as put forth in the Preface, to incite Christians "to burn from divine love, so that they also in turn may be ready to endure the martyrdom for Christ".

The inclusion of a neomartyr in the assembly of the saints was not necessarily dictated by ecclesiastical approval but rather by popular canonization and local veneration. A moving account of the local cult of an anonymous neomartyr of Skiathos (his name is rendered simply as the "Shepherd") is given by A. Papadiamantis in his short story "Poor Saint". St John the Russian was all but unknown in Greece until some Cappadocian refugees, following their exodus from Asia Minor, brought his miraculously preserved body from Prokopi to their new settlement of Neo Prokopi in Euboea in 1925.

It is important to note that in the assembly of neomartyrs several non-Greek Christians were venerated throughout the Orthodox world. Under the name of Ioannis alone one may count a Turkish dervish (?1814), Ioannis the Goldsmith from Sumna, Bulgaria (?1802), Ioannis the Wallachian (?1662), not to mention St John the Russian. One Ioannis from Trebizond, martyred in Akkerman (?1492), was buried in Suceava of Moldavia and his cult was popular throughout the Slavic world.

LAMBROS KAMPERIDIS

Summary

Neomartyrs are Christians who have been persecuted for their Orthodox faith. The term was first used in the 8th century to refer to those who defied iconoclasm. In the 13th century there were others who refused to accept the union of the Orthodox and Catholic Churches, but most suffered their martyrdom as a result of Muslim oppression during the Tourkokratia. For this period the official number stands at 162.

Further Reading

Clogg, R., "A Little-Known Orthodox Neo-Martyr, Athanasios of Smyrna (1819)", *Eastern Churches Review*, 5 (1973): pp. 28–36

Hasluck, F.W., *Christianity and Islam under the Sultans*, Oxford: Clarendon Press, 1929, reprinted New York: Octagon, 1973

Nikodemos the Hagiorite, *Neon Martyrologion*, Venice, 1799, reprinted Athens, 1961

Perantones, Ioannes M., *Lexicon ton Neomartyron*, 3 vols, Athens, 1972

Russell, N., "Neomartyrs of the Greek Calendar", *Sobornost*, 5/1 (1983): pp. 36–62

Salaville, S., "Pour un Répertoire des Néo-Saints de l'église orientale", *Byzantion*, 20 (1950): pp.223–37

Theocharides, I. and D. Loules, "The Neomartyrs in Greek History, 1453–1821", *Etudes Balkaniques*, 25/3 (1989): pp.78–86

Zachariadou, E.A., "The Neomartyr's Message", *Deltio Kentrou Mikrasiatikon Spoudon*, 8 (1990–91): pp. 51–63

Neophytos Enkleistos 1134–1219

Cypriot monk

Neophytos Enkleistos (the Enclosed, or Recluse) was a Cypriot monk and author, an unusual founder of a famous monastic institution from the base of his cliff hermitage above Paphos. The site, still active today, has important frescos that indicate much about the process and understanding of sanctification in later Byzantine practice.

His life is given in his own autobiographical accounts which survive in the Typikon (monastic constitution) he wrote for his community. He was born near Leukara in southern Cyprus in 1134. In 1152, when he was 18, he left his family, which was poor, and was tonsured at the monastery of St John Chrysostom on Mount Koutzoubendi. Working there for five years in the vineyards, he received a literary education and was promoted to the office of subsacristan (parekklesiarch). In 1159, when he was 25, he made a pilgrimage to the Holy Land, visiting Jerusalem and the renowned monasteries of

Palestine. After spending some time in the Mar Saba monastery he was confirmed in his vocation to be a hermit. He tells, however, how a vision instructed him that God awaited him in another place, and so he made his way back to Cyprus. He left the monastery of Koutzoubendi, trying to make for the monasteries of Mount Latros where he intended to become a hermit. Arriving as an unknown in Paphos, and waiting to take ship there, he narrates his providential adventure, as he was taken for a deserter and thrown into the local prison. There he was robbed of the money he had for his fare, and only just escaped from a long term of imprisonment. Completely penniless, and shaken by his experience, he left Paphos and went a short distance up into the surrounding hill country looking for a suitable place of retirement. On 24 June 1159, a day that he regarded as auspicious, for it was the birthday of John the Baptist, patron of monks, he found a soft escarpment with a cave, at the end of a ravine. He tells how he tested the tranquillity of the site, living only with the wild birds, until September of that year when, satisfied as to its suitability, he began to enlarge the cave for his permanent use, completing his work on the Feast of the Cross (14 September) the following year.

After five years, in 1165, he set out to find a relic of the True Cross, indicating his intention to make a permanent religious foundation, and, being successful in his quest, brought it back for the cave church that he had made adjoining his cell. In 1166 he was also instructed by the newly elected bishop of Paphos, Basil Kinnamos, to receive ordination as a priest and to accept monastic followers. On the arrival of the early disciples, he enlarged the primitive Enkleistra, and it became a series of cells stretching across the whole length of the escarpment. The small church, dedicated to the Holy Cross, served as the Katholikon for the foundation, still reached by a ladder, though today an arched walkway has been constructed. In 1183, the 24th year of his seclusion, the whole cell and church were painted, under the patronage of Basil Kinnamos, by the fine iconographer Theodore Apseudes. The wall-paintings are among the most interesting on Cyprus, not only because of their quality, but for what they reveal historically, for the series most unusually depicts the founder Neophytos being carried to heaven by two angels – and this was painted several years before his death. After the initial paintings, in the late 12th or early 13th century, the nave of the church was enlarged once again and decorated with additional saintly ascetics and Passion scenes.

The depredations of Richard the Lionheart had caused much disruption to rural life on Cyprus, and Neophytos castigates the king in his writings. Pilgrims and aid-seekers began to cluster round the monastery, and many attempted to join the community. Neophytos regulated this by stating categorically in his Typikon that the foundation was not to receive monks unless they were genuine penitents (*Typike Diatheke*, 13), and for good measure he had this text written in the narthex of the church, and ordered it to be read aloud each Sunday. In 1196 the influx of monks and visitors seeking guidance and help became too much for the recluse, who decided to abandon his original cell and carve out a place for himself higher up the escarpment, much more difficult of access. The story of his adventures excavating this "New Sion" are recounted in a small work called *Theosemeia* in which he narrates his miraculous deliverance from a rock fall. The seclusion was so effective here that he seems to have been forgotten on more than one occasion (for he complains about it) when his community, overwhelmed with the needs of visitors, neglected to send him any food for the day. The original monastery was also enlarged, and he tells in the Typikon of the later gardens, herds, and buildings that had sprung up (*Typike Diatheke*, 18–20).

In this later period of expansion Neophytos developed his work of writing, setting out instructions for the permanent regulation of a community. Bishop Basil and his own brother John, who had become the *hegoumenos* (abbot) at Mount Koutzoubendi, encouraged him in his literary work. In addition to his monastic instructions, he also wrote panegyrics, homilies, and a commentary on the Song of Songs. His work shows an intelligent awareness even of theological controversies taking place in Palestine and Constantinople, as well as offering sharp comment on contemporary political problems in Cyprus. For 23 years he lived in strict seclusion in New Sion, acting as founder and *higumen* of the community around him, until his death in 1219. In accordance with instructions he gave in advance in the Typikon, a new *higumen* was chosen to succeed him, who was to be installed in the seclusion of the founder's cave after the customary funeral rites had been observed, and after the founder's body had been buried in the original cell below, which was now set apart as a shrine adjacent to the cave church.

The life of Neophytos has recently been interpreted as an example of blatant self-glorification. The preparing of a tomb for his body, together with frescos in the church where that body would be received, and the supplying of texts indicating both his stature as a founder and how the Theotokos miraculously saved him from death, have been pointed to as all the necessary elements to comprise a Byzantine "canonization" – icon, relics, and hagiography – which in this case had all been made ready by the protagonist himself before his death. Another commentator has called this not self-glorification but rather "une transparence enfantine". In the Byzantine religious mindset, however, it was a commonplace that the faithful pursuit of the monastic life would almost inevitably lead the founder (one seen as specially inspired by God) to heavenly glory. What strikes the modern observer as peculiarly self-aggrandizing is more a reflection of the widespread belief in the Byzantine ascetical doctrine of *apatheia*: that years of dedication to God in the monastic life would stabilize the "Abba" in the very life of God himself – a deification even in this world. The fresco that has caused most controversy is that of the founder, over the site of his tomb, being lifted up by two angels. This should be properly interpreted not as a pre-death self-canonization, but as an iconic prayer of intercession that the monk Neophytos, having lived the angelic life on earth (the monastic state), would be admitted into the company of the other monastic saints who line the walls of the church. It is also clear that this expectation that the monastic complex would continue to be a place of pilgrimage after the founder's death (as it had been already in his lifetime) was a view shared widely, not least by the bishop who commissioned the wall paintings, and by the larger community itself.

The monastic complex has survived to the present day with its (later) church and community buildings around a fountain courtyard, opposite and below the surviving Byzantine troglodyte church and upper cell of the founder. The continuing popularity of the place testifies to the enduring warmth of the relationship between the Greeks and their local monastic settlements. There is a lively tradition of the later "invention" of the relics of the founder, and the saint's skull is today preserved in the lower church where it continues to act as a pilgrimage focus.

J.A. McGuckin

Biography

Born in 1134 in southern Cyprus, Neophytos "the Recluse" became a monk at the age of 18. In 1159 he visited the Holy Land and spent time at the Mar Saba monastery. Returning to Cyprus, he became a hermit above Paphos. He enlarged his cell to take disciples and it became a monastery. He died in 1219 and his relics remain a focus of pilgrimage.

Further Reading

Congourdeau, M.H., "L'Enkleistra dans les écrits de Néophytos le Reclus" in Les Saints et leur sanctuaire à Byzance: textes, images et monuments, edited by Catherine Jolivet-Lévy, Michel Kaplan and Jean-Pierre Sodini, Paris: Publications de la Sorbonne, 1993

Delehaye, H., "Saints de Chypre", Analecta Bollandiana, 26 (1907): pp. 274–97

Epstein, A.W., "Formulas for Salvation: A Comparison of Two Byzantine Monasteries and Their Founders", Church History, 50/4 (1981): pp. 385–400

Galatariotou, Catia, The Making of a Saint: The Life, Times and Sanctification of Neophytos the Recluse, Cambridge and New York: Cambridge University Press, 1991

Jugie, M., "Un Opuscule inédit de Néophyte le Reclus sur l'incorruptibilité du corps du Christ dans l'Eucharistie", Revue des Etudes Byzantines, 7 (1949): pp. 1–11

Kazhdan, A.P., Neophytos Enkleistos entry in The Oxford Dictionary of Byzantium, edited by Kazhdan, Oxford and New York: Oxford University Press, 1991, vol. 2

Mango, Cyril and E.J.W. Hawkins, "The Hermitage of St. Neophytos and Its Wall-Paintings", Dumbarton Oaks Papers, 20 (1966): pp.119–206

Petit, L., "Vie et ouvrages de Néophyte le Reclus", Echos d'Orient, 2 (1898–99): pp. 257–68

Stiernon, D., "Néophyte le Reclus" in Dictionnaire de spiritualité, edited by Marcel Viller et al., vol. 11, Paris: Beauchesne, 1982, columns 99–110

Tokekovic, S., "Ermitage de Paphos: Decors Peints pour Néophyte le Reclus" in Les Saints et leur sanctuaire à Byzance: textes, images et monuments, edited by Catherine Jolivet-Lévy, Michel Kaplan and Jean-Pierre Sodini, Paris: Publications de la Sorbonne, 1993

Tsiknopoullou, Ioannou P., "To Syngraphikon Ergon tou Hagiou Neophytou" [The Writings of Saint Neophytos], Kypriakai Spoudai, 22 (1958): pp. 67–214

Tsiknopoullou, Ioannou P., "I thaumaste Prosopikotes tou Neophytou Presbyteroumonachou kai Enkleistou" [The Remarkable Character of Neophytos, Priest-Monk and Recluse], Byzantion, 37 (1967): pp. 311–413

Tsiknopoullou, Ioannou P., Kypriaka Typika [Cypriot Typika], Nicosia, 1969

Tsiknopoullou, Ioannou P. (editor), "I Theosemeia tou Hagiou Neophytou" [The Divine Revelation of Saint Neophytos], Byzantion, 39 (1969): pp. 361–78

Neoplatonism

"Neoplatonism" is a modern label for the Greek philosophy of the late ancient, early Byzantine period (late 3rd to 7th century AD). The label is inadequate. First, "Neoplatonism" amounted to Greek philosophy in general: it incorporated Aristotelian, Stoic, and Pythagorean tenets (Epicureanism was rejected) and had no other philosophical competitors. Second, there were many diverse, often rival, brands. Third, "Neoplatonism" is very different from the standard Plato, yet shows close links with some renditions of the late Plato and the early Academy. The Neoplatonists fostered allegiance to the Classical past (Neoplatonists wrote most of the commentaries on Aristotle and Plato), but simultaneously promoted a fresh, dynamic philosophy.

Neoplatonism was consolidated and brought into mainstream academic teaching by the Athenian school, and especially Proclus. Its principal founders were Plotinus, Porphyry, and Iamblichus.

The Neoplatonists were primarily philosophers with their own ideas about truth and reality. They reasoned that these come in degrees or levels, each appropriate to the means of knowledge in use. Sense-perception addresses the physical mode of things, reason the conceptual, abstract, or mathematical mode of things, and direct intellectual apprehension the essences, principles, and Forms of true reality. However, all knowledge and being derive from an ultimate principle, the "One", which by definition is beyond the system.

In descending order, the main metaphysical levels were, the One, Being/Intellect (ousia/nous), and Psyche (as self-organizing life/soul/mind). Body and Matter in themselves were considered passive. More detailed orderings made explicit the functions of the One (transcendent – causal, determinative – unlimited), and the structure of Being/Intellect as essence, potency (dynamis), and overt actuality (energeia).

Neoplatonism is neither just idealism nor realism. Objects are contained in consciousness, and differ according to the mode of awareness and cognition. At the level of pure intellection, being and thought coincide. However, phenomena and reliable conceptions depend on transpersonal realities, which are self-sufficient.

Psyche in Greek philosophy meant the self-propelled (autokineton) life that defines living beings. Human psyche consists of a rational (mind) and a non-rational life (self-movement, senses, instincts). With the psyche man can compare sense-perceptions and thoughts, mentally weigh evidence, and arrive at conclusions and understanding (logos). Each psyche, however, has only a "particular" perspective. Because of this combination of self-motivation and limited vision, which is its individuality, it "dares" to leave its level, and invariably "fall" into body. Yet, psyche is an extension of atemporal, unlimited, objective principles. To these it yearns to "ascend" by the Neoplatonic routes of love, contemplation, and faith.

From their readings the late Greek philosophers concluded that Plato was nearest to a complete account, provided his writings were interpreted correctly. Aristotle, Plato's rival, was valid for the domain of sense-experience, ordinary language, and basic logic. Neoplatonic education, as taught at Athens and Alexandria, thus started with Aristotle and progressed to Plato; studying could last six years. Learning stimulates the soul to reflect on its self, and through it on the levels of reality that substantiate it. Salvation comes with the deepening of knowledge, for philosophy aids the soul to recover its full integrity. This is preserved by a unity, which is of divine origin.

Accordingly, Neoplatonists studied an encyclopaedic range of subjects and philosophies, including literary works and criticism, psychology, politics, Pythagoreanism, Stoicism, and Hedonism. First they trained in ethics and logic, i.e. the basics of good living and sound reasoning. Then they learnt physics and mathematics (geometry, arithmetic, astronomy, and harmonics) as the representations of reality. Thinking about being, existence, properties, and causes, and about concepts, knowledge, and truth brought the students nearer to the core concerns. In the final step of "analysis", they encountered the ultimate foundation of metaphysics, epistemology, and ethics: the unconditioned, ineffable unity, whose traditional appellation is God.

Plotinus (3rd century AD) was born in Hellenized Egypt, and first sought philosophy with the scholastic teachers of Alexandria. Having found them disappointing, he turned to an Ammonius Saccas, who propounded the agreement of Plato with Aristotle. Among his audience were Longinus and the Christian Origen. After 11 years, and a short adventure in the East, Plotinus settled in Rome, where he attracted a large circle of followers, including senators.

For Plotinus, inward contemplation of human nature takes the philosopher on a journey of discovery. Man's inner capacities reveal universal realities, and exemplify deep philosophical issues. The relation of body with psyche, for example, shows the difficulty of referencing immaterial existence by the normal material-bound standards. He regarded Plato correct, and Aristotle selectively wrong, especially on the categories of being. Yet, Plotinus' doctrines were not dogmas but the results of lengthy debates with his followers. He was conscious of his unorthodox Platonism: that the Forms are identical with the contents of divine Intellect (interpretation traceable to the 2nd-century Aristotelian professor Alexander of Aphrodisias), and that an aspect of human psyche remains undescended in body. Later Neoplatonists accepted a modified articulation of the former, but rejected the latter.

Plotinus' writings were edited and publicized by Porphyry. Although Porphyry records their chronological order, he arranged them in six thematic groups of nine, henceforth known as the *Enneads*. In this they conform to an ascending scale from ethics and physics, to psyche, *nous*, and finally on to the divine One. This is the hierarchy of virtue, being, and knowledge, which will typify later Neoplatonism and its curriculum.

Porphyry (3rd to early 4th century AD) was born in Hellenized Phoenicia of Syrian parents, and first studied at Athens with the prominent scholastic Longinus. From him he inherited breadth of learning and source material, organized, critical thinking, and clear, concise expression. However, he became more attracted to Plotinus' philosophy. After five years, he disagreed with Plotinus, left him, and pursued his "harmonization" of Aristotle's logic and metaphysics with Plato. Nevertheless, Plotinus entrusted him with the publication of his doctrines. Porphyry disseminated widely their new philosophy with his numerous writings (including a key work

on vegetarianism and ecological philosophy) and high scholarly reputation.

For Porphyry, Aristotle is true, within the limits of sense-experience, physical reference, logic, and semantics. Plato addresses the intelligible but intangible reality. In ethics and religion, Porphyry promoted the ideal of the simple living philosopher-priest. He was the first to write on the "Chaldaean Oracles", proverbs written in Greek but of uncertain origin, that later Neoplatonists used as revelatory support for their ideas; he was also the first to elevate faith, love, and truth alike to the divine virtues. Porphyry saw reason as the surest path to God, and rejected Christianity and Gnosticism as irrational or fraudulent. Indeed, the "harmonization" was motivated by his concern to defend Hellenic philosophy.

In the meantime, Plotinus' chief spokesman, Amelius, had also left him and settled in Apamea, Syria. Amelius bravely postulated that the Platonic Forms must be infinite (subsequent Neoplatonists rejected it), and, unlike Porphyry, believed that ritual practices enable contact with divinity. Further, he introduced a tripartite distinction in *nous*. His first doctrine influenced Theodore of Asine, a student of Iamblichus, but was rejected by other Neoplatonists. The last two show influence from Numenius, a Neopythagorean who flourished at Apamea in the 2nd century AD. He had introduced ideas later typical of Neoplatonism (Plotinus was once accused of plagiarizing Numenius): the Forms as contents of *nous*, threefold divisions, the Pythagorean reading of Plato, theurgy, and the value of revelatory oracles.

The Syrian Iamblichus (4th century) was at first an acolyte of Porphyry, but disagreed over the role of theurgy. After a short stay at Caesarea, he established a school at Apamea, which seems to have offered both philosophy and conventional rhetorical education. Iamblichus' school proved exceptionally popular, only to be surpassed by that of his student Aedesius the Cappadocian, at Pergamum. Their students spread and influenced the Byzantine empire from its very beginning. Iamblichus' student Sopater of Apamea advised the emperor Constantine the Great, and presided over the consecration of Constantinople's foundation in 330. Aedesius, through Maximus of Ephesus, converted the emperor Julian (361–3) from Christianity to a universalist "Hellenism".

Iamblichus took Porphyry's "harmonization" of Aristotle with Plato further into ontology and psychology, and added Neopythagorean number metaphysics. He sought to mathematize all areas of philosophy and religion, because mathematics made possible their scientific study. He analysed the Neoplatonic levels into transcendent and immanent aspects, and, for the first time, he saw time not as a by-product of psychological activity but as substantial reality. He concluded, against Porphyry, that divinity cannot be reached by reason but by an appropriate act of transcendence: supra-rational theurgy. Against Plotinus, he pointed out that embodied souls do not access higher planes, but are fully immanent in matter. Nevertheless, they contain a divine spark which is the source of salvation both of individual souls and of matter.

The Iamblichean version incorporated most of Porphyry and Plotinus, but rejected Theodore of Asine. In a modified form it was eventually accepted by the chief mainstream schools of Athens and Alexandria. Through them the

Neoplatonic educational philosophy became the curriculum of Byzantine higher education until the 15th century.

At Athens in the late 4th to 5th centuries AD, the self-styled "Academy" was the premier centre of higher learning, and the beneficiary of major endowments by aristocratic families. It was successively headed by Plutarch of Athens, Syrianus, and Proclus. They taught a curriculum mainly based on Aristotle and Plato, where the former is the necessary preparation for the latter. Against Iamblichus, they restored Plato's dialectic over Pythagorean number metaphysics, and a single One as both transcendent and causal. The Athenians' theoretical developments included the "ones" (henades) as the transcendent existents and essences of beings at all levels, matter as the direct emanation of the One and Good, space as body and light, etc.

Proclus was succeeded by Marinus and Isidore. The last scholarch of Athens was Damascius (taught by Ammonius Hermeiae at Alexandria). He highlighted the metaphysical, epistemological, and linguistic problems of transcendence, which led him to new expressions of scepticism (theology as scepticism relative to dogmatic rationalism and science resurfaced periodically, notably in the 13th-century Byzantine Metochites). With the emperor Justinian's ban on public teaching by pagans in 529, the Athenian school closed. After an unsuccessful journey to the Persian emperor, the Athenian scholars dispersed. But one of them, Simplicius, flourished after the closure, writing and teaching privately somewhere in the Byzantine empire. He wrote the most extensive commentaries on Aristotle. They are invaluable for both new and old ideas, particularly the reports of the first Greek philosophers, the Presocratics.

In this period, Alexandrian philosophy came from Athens. The first to be unambiguously a philosopher at Alexandria was Hierocles, a student of Plutarch of Athens. The next head, Hermeias, was taught by Syrianus (to whom he was related), and was succeeded by his son Ammonius, taught by Proclus. Ammonius of Hermeias, in turn, taught Damascius, Simplicius, and John Philoponus who edited several of Ammonius' lectures, which had originated in Proclus. Some evidence suggests that the Alexandrians were specially interested in the relation of Being to divine Intellect.

The Alexandrian school was not as rich or self-sufficient as the Athenian, which was the complaint of its next head, Olympiodorus. Yet, he continued to flourish even after Justinian's ban, still as a pagan public teacher. It is evident from Olympiodorus' lectures that he was the first to promote deliberately the conciliation of "Hellenic" philosophy (Neoplatonism) with Christianity, in the classroom. All subsequent heads at Alexandria were Christians but philosophically remained Neoplatonists. One of its later members, Stephanus, took the sole philosophy chair at the imperial university of Constantinople (610).

Greek Christians influenced by Neoplatonism included the Cappadocian Fathers of Orthodoxy, Basil, Gregory of Nazianzus, and Gregory of Nyssa (4th century). They were educated at Caesarea, Athens, and Alexandria. There they learnt the power of logical argument and the sophistication of Greek philosophy through Neoplatonism. Familiarity with Plotinus and Porphyry is evident, as well as exposure to Iamblichean ideas, which were prevalent at that time and place. For example, God's creation is expressed in "remaining, procession, and return", while God's wisdom emanates as light. In Christian theology, the Cappadocians were influenced by Origen (3rd century) who had been a fellow student of Plotinus under Ammonius Saccas at Alexandria.

In early to mid 6th-century Alexandria, a Christian student of the Neoplatonist Ammonius, the grammarian John Philoponus, composed vast commentaries on Aristotle. He employed his Neoplatonic education in defence of Monophysitism. He wrote against both other Christians and the pagan philosophers, particularly Proclus. Thus he provided the first philosophical arguments in favour of Christian cosmology, creation, and the perishability of the physical cosmos.

At Gaza the rhetorician Aeneas, a student of the Alexandrian Neoplatonist Hierocles, founded a Christian school. It promoted the philosophical value of Christianity through (Neo)Platonism. His friend Zacharias, later bishop of Mytilene, converted from Monophysite Christianity to Orthodoxy, and wrote against Ammonius of Hermeias.

The corpus attributed to Dionysius the Areopagite was written in the late 5th century, but gained Orthodox recognition after its defence by John Scythopolis (early 6th century), Maximos the Confessor (7th century), and the Patriarch Germanos (8th century). It is immersed in Proclus' Neoplatonism, at least in terminology, ranging from the tripartite distinctions of essence-power-activity and of participation, to the apophatic theology and theurgy. Nevertheless, it adhered to Christian doctrine, and contained novel formulations.

The so-called Aristotelian renaissance of 7th-century Byzantium was owed to the Neoplatonic integrated curriculum of Plato *and* Aristotle. Maximos the Confessor (saint in both the Greek and Latin Churches) introduced fresh philosophical rigour into Orthodox theology. For this he employed the typical Neoplatonic distinctions, such as intelligible versus sensible created being, essence–power–activity, and remaining–procession–return.

The Neoplatonic elements in Orthodox theology also surfaced in the major controversy over the role of icons. Proclus had written extensively on the modal existence as a principle, thing in itself, and as "image" (eikon), and on the relation of "archetype" to "image". Such philosophical concepts helped those who supported the veneration of icons (e.g. John Damascenus) to win the argument, and thus maintain the physical domain, and the means of understanding it, intellect, in divine grace.

Among the prominent Byzantines who wrote on Neoplatonism were Psellos (11th century), George Pachymeres, Nikephoros Blemmydes, and Nikephoros Choumnos (13th to 14th century), Plethon and his student Bessarion (15th century). At the invitation of the Medicis, Bessarion flourished in Italy. The Florentine Academy became the epicentre of western European Renaissance.

Through Neoplatonism, Greek universal learning informed the rise of Arab, Jewish, and European philosophy and theology. In the east, Neoplatonism influenced Islamic (Avicenna, Averroes) and Jewish thought (Gabirol). In the west, Neoplatonism influenced mystics and scholars (often through Porphyry and the commentaries on Aristotle): Boethius, king Alfred the Great, Duns Scotus, Richard St Victor, Anselm of

Canterbury, Abelard, Eriugena, Albertus Magnus, Grosseteste, Aquinas, and John Milton; the Renaissance figures Ficino and Pico, the humanists Sir Thomas More and Ralph Cudworth, and the astronomer Johannes Kepler. In modern literature Neoplatonism inspired William Blake, Samuel Coleridge, Percy Shelley, and W.B. Yeats. In modern philosophy, Neoplatonism influenced Benedict Spinoza, and the Idealists such as George Berkeley, Henri Bergson, Georg Hegel, Francis Bradley, John McTaggart and, in the 20th century, the London University professor F.C. Copleston.

LUCAS SIORVANES

See also Academy, Philosophy, Plato

Further Reading

Armstrong, A.H. (editor), *The Cambridge History of Later Greek and Early Medieval Philosophy*, 2nd edition, Cambridge: Cambridge University Press, 1970

Blumenthal, H.J., *Aristotle and Neoplatonism in Late Antiquity: Interpretations of the De Anima*, Ithaca, New York: Cornell University Press, and London: Duckworth, 1996

Bowersock, G.W., *Hellenism in Late Antiquity*, Cambridge: Cambridge University Press, and Ann Arbor: University of Michigan Press, 1990

Fowden, Garth, *The Egyptian Hermes: A Historical Approach to the Late Pagan Mind*, Cambridge: Cambridge University Press, 1986; Princeton, New Jersey: Princeton University Press, 1993

Gersh, Stephen, *From Iamblichus to Eriugena: An Investigation of the Prehistory and Evolution of the Pseudo-Dionysian Tradition*, Leiden: Brill, 1978

Hornus, J., L. Benakis and L. Couloubaritsis, "La Philosophie grecque de 415–750" in *Philosophy and Science in the Middle Ages*, edited by Guttorm Fløistad, Dordrecht and Boston: Kluwer, 1990

Lamberton, Robert, *Homer the Theologian: Neoplatonist Allegorical Reading and the Growth of the Epic Tradition*, Berkeley: University of California Press, 1986

Lloyd, A.C., *The Anatomy of Neoplatonism*, Oxford: Clarendon Press, and New York: Oxford University Press, 1990

O'Meara, Dominic J. (editor), *Neoplatonism and Christian Thought*, Albany: State University of New York Press, 1982

O'Meara, Dominic J., *Pythagoras Revived: Mathematics and Philosophy in Late Antiquity*, Oxford: Clarendon Press, and New York: Oxford University Press, 1989

Saffrey, H.D., *Recherches sur le néoplatonisme après Plotin*, Paris: Vrin, 1990

Schrenk, Lawrence P. (editor), *Aristotle in Late Antiquity*, Washington D.C.: Catholic University of America Press, 1994

Shaw, Gregory, *Theurgy and the Soul: The Neoplatonism of Iamblichus*, University Park: Pennsylvania State University Press, 1995

Siorvanes, Lucas, *Proclus: Neo-Platonic Philosophy and Science*, Edinburgh: Edinburgh University Press, and New Haven, Connecticut: Yale University Press, 1996

Sorabji, Richard (editor), *Aristotle Transformed: The Ancient Commentators and Their Influence*, Ithaca, New York: Cornell University Press, and London: Duckworth, 1990

Steel, Carlos G., *The Changing Self: A Study on the Soul in Later Neoplatonism: Iamblichus, Damascius, and Priscianus*, Brussels: Paleis der Acadamiën, 1978

Wallis, R.T., *Neoplatonism*, 2nd edition, London: Duckworth, and Indianapolis: Hackett, 1995

Nero AD 37–68

Roman emperor

Nero (54–68) had a more complex relationship with Greece than any Roman emperor before or after him. Although other men, such as the Egyptian Amasis (Herodotus, 2. 178) and the Roman general Antony (Plutarch, *Antony*, 23), had been called philhellenes, Nero as Roman emperor had unprecedented power to express his love for Greece on a vast scale. Nero's philhellenism can be divided into two categories: first, there is his own personal pursuit of Greek culture, music, and literature; secondly, there is his adoption of a foreign policy that was beneficial to Greece as a country.

Early signs of Nero's love of Hellenic culture are clear from his enthusiasm for the Greek language: under Claudius, he gave speeches in the senate in Greek on behalf of the Rhodians and the Trojans. Some critics have suggested that Nero did not write these speeches himself (cf. Tacitus, *Annals*, 13. 3. 3: Nero was "the first ruler to need borrowed eloquence"). That may be so, but his public demonstration of competence in the Greek language certainly contrasts with previous emperors, such as Tiberius, who could speak Greek fluently, but only ever did so in private. Another early sign of his philhellenism can be seen in his staging of Pyrrhic dances by young Greeks in AD 57 (Suetonius, *Nero*, 12. 2). Yet it was not until after the murder of his mother Agrippina that Nero was able to give full and free expression to his personality. In AD 59 Nero himself performed on the cithara at the Juvenalia, where he celebrated the first shaving of his beard (Suetonius, *Nero*, 11. 1; Tacitus, *Annals*, 14. 15. 1; Dio, 61. 19. 1). Not only Nero but certain Roman aristocrats also appeared on stage, acting dramatic roles. Yet the Juvenalia took place within the palace grounds in private: it was not until AD 64 that the 27-year-old Nero made his debut on the public stage, at Naples (Tacitus, *Annals*, 15. 33–34 and Suetonius, *Nero*, 20. 2–3). Conspicuously, he avoided Rome for this performance, perhaps anticipating a hostile reaction.

Yet his confidence quickly grew. In AD 60 he had instituted a quinquennial contest along Greek lines called the Neronia, in which participants competed for prizes in oratory, singing, playing the lyre, and poetry (Tacitus, *Annals*, 14. 20. 21; Suetonius, *Nero*, 12. 3; Dio, 61. 21. 2). According to the sources, at the second Neronia in AD 65, despite the senate's attempts to dissuade the emperor from performing, Nero recited a poem on stage and then accompanied his singing on the lyre (Tacitus, *Annals*, 16. 4. 5; Suetorius, *Nero*, 21; Dio, 62. 29. 1). If these festivals were designed to inspire fellow Romans with a passion for Greek culture, Nero was unsuccessful. Subsequent historical and literary accounts cast the emperor in a tyrannical light, partly because the spectators at his shows were increasingly obliged to become the focus of attention themselves: either they performed on the stage or their reactions to Nero's display were carefully monitored by imperial agents. Nero's manipulation of his fellow Romans was too overbearing and superficial, rather as when Peter the Great tried to make his fellow Russians more "western" by getting them to shave off their beards.

When Nero died, the pretence of philhellenism that had gripped Rome perished with him. The new Flavian dynasty bolstered their own power by reversing many of Nero's policies and ideologies. Thus, Vespasian rejected Nero's infamous Golden House as an imperial residence, rehabilitated the colossal golden statue of Nero to represent the sun, and refurbished the temple to the Divine Claudius, which Nero had deliberately neglected. The theatrical philhellene Nero had temporarily redefined the imperial identity, but this proved unpopular with the senate, so the more austere Vespasian wisely took as his role model Augustus rather than Nero. Yet there is evidence that Nero was missed by some. After his death, no fewer than three men appeared, each one falsely claiming to be the emperor. The first surfaced on the island of Cynthus in AD 69 (Tacitus, *Histories*, 2. 8–9), the second in Asia Minor in AD 80 (Dio, 66. 19), and the third among the Parthians in AD 88–89 (Suetonius, *Nero*, 57. 2). Whatever their personal motives, such impostors clearly hoped to win the public approval of those who, long after the emperor's death, "used to lay spring and summer flowers on Nero's grave" (Suetonius, *Nero*, 57). The fact that all three pretenders materialized in the east suggests that Nero's posthumous standing there was much stronger than in the west.

Nero's treatment of Greece itself can be seen as inconsistent. After the fire of Rome in AD 64, the emperor sent agents to Greece to remove treasures (including statues of the gods) from shrines at Athens, Delphi, Olympia, and Thespiae. Pausanias says that Nero "robbed Apollo of five hundred bronze statues, some of gods and some of men" (10. 7. 1). This move may have been necessitated by short-term financial expediency, but it should warn us not to over-romanticize Nero's relationship with Greece. He owes his reputation as a philhellene above all to his liberation of Greece from taxation and Roman administration. This flamboyant emancipation took place at a special celebration of the Isthmian games at Corinth on 28 November AD 67, while Nero was conducting an artistic tour of Greece. By this action he recalled the actions of Titus Flamininus in 196 BC, who had also liberated Greece (Polybius, 18. 46). On a damaged marble stele a version of Nero's speech from this occasion is preserved, together with a decree from Akraiphiai in Boeotia honouring the emperor (*Inscriptiones Latinae Selectae*, edited by Hermann Dessau, 1892, reprinted 1979, no. 8794). Although Nero told his Greek audience that he acted "not out of pity for you but out of goodwill", there are hints in the speech that his action was not entirely altruistic. Nero also boasted proudly that although other leaders had liberated cities, only he had liberated a province. The competitive emperor seems concerned here, not with promoting the well-being of Greece, but with bolstering his own reputation. At one point Nero even wishes paradoxically that Greece were still at its peak so that more people might enjoy his favour. This, surely, is a revealing formulation, which puts into perspective Nero's reputation as a philhellene, as did the fact that he called his Greek games the Neronia, after himself. The Akraiphiai decree shows that in AD 67 there was gratitude in Greece for the liberation, but this may not reflect universal opinion: as Tacitus says in a different context, "Services are welcome as long as it seems possible to repay them, but when they greatly exceed that point they produce not gratitude but hatred" (*Annals*, 4. 18). In any case, Nero died so soon afterwards that no consolidation of the grant was possible. After the civil wars of AD 68–69 the new emperor Vespasian complained that Greece had forgotten how to be free and Nero's gift was swiftly cancelled.

Nero's benefaction had an immediate impact in the short term, as the Akraiphiai decree shows, but did his treatment of Greece make any long-term difference? In some ways, it was a mixed blessing for Greece to have received such a conspicuous benefaction from this disgraced emperor. Even in the Akraiphiai decree Nero's name was deliberately erased from the stele after the senate had condemned the dead emperor to oblivion (*damnatio memoriae*). Nero himself was quickly cast in the literary tradition as a yardstick for monstrosity even by Greek writers, as when Philostratus makes Vespasian say that he would rather have Nero come back to life than surrender the empire to Vitellius (*Vita Apollonii*, 32). Even so, despite the backlash against Nero, there are signs that some Romans began to embrace Greek culture. Juvenal (2nd century AD) included in one satire a xenophobic tirade about Rome being infiltrated by Greek habits (*Satires*, 3. 58–125), and under Trajan (AD 98–117) new senators were recruited from Athens and Sparta, which resulted in significant cultural interaction. During the 2nd and 3rd centuries AD there was a period of cultural renaissance in Greece, which became known as the "Second Sophistic". Some scholars suggest that Nero's short-lived liberation of Greece even provided the spark that caused this intellectual revival. Nero's unsubtle attempts to inculcate philhellenism in his fellow Romans certainly failed, but the theatrical liberation of AD 67 still heralded a remarkable new era of literary creativity in Greece.

RHIANNON ASH

Biography

Born in AD 37, Nero succeeded Claudius as emperor in 54. After the death of his mother Agrippina he felt free to indulge in his love of Greece. He himself sang and performed on stage, and he introduced Greek-style games at Rome (called the Neronia). In 66–67 he toured Greece and liberated the province from Roman administration and taxation. The gift was cancelled soon after his death in 68 but it may have helped to pave the way for the Second Sophistic movement of the 2nd and 3rd centuries.

Further Reading

Alcock, S.E., "Nero at Play? The Emperor's Grecian Odyssey" in *Reflections of Nero: Culture, History, and Representation*, edited by Jas Elsner and Jamie Masters, London: Duckworth, and Chapel Hill: University of North Carolina Press, 1994

Bartsch, Shadi, *Actors in the Audience: Theatricality and Doublespeak from Nero to Hadrian*, Cambridge, Massachusetts: Harvard University Press, 1994

Bieber, M., "Roman Men in Greek Himation", *Proceedings of the American Philosophical Society*, 103 (1959) pp. 374–417

Boesche, R., "The Politics of Pretence: Tacitus and the Political Theory of Despotism", *History of Political Thought*, 8/2 (1987): pp. 189–210

Bradley, K.R., "The Chronology of Nero's Visit to Greece AD 66/7", *Latomus*, 37 (1978): pp. 61–72

Brenk, F.E., "From *Rex* to *Rana*: Plutarch's Treatment of Nero" in *Il Protagonismo nella Storiografia Classica*, Genoa: Università di Genova, 1987

Dunkle, J.R., "The Greek Tyrant and Roman Political Invective of the Late Republic", *Transactions of the American Philological Association*, 98 (1967): pp. 151–71

Edwards, C., "Beware of Imitations: Theatre and Subversion of Imperial Identity" in *Reflections of Nero: Culture, History, and*

Representation, edited by Jas Elsner and Jamie Masters, London: Duckworth, and Chapel Hill: University of North Carolina Press, 1994

Frazer R.M., Jr., "Nero, the Singing Animal", *Arethusa*, 4 (1971): pp. 215–18

Gallivan, P.A., "Nero's Liberation of Greece", *Hermes*, 101 (1973): pp. 230–34

Gallivan, P.A., "The False Neros: A Re-Examination", *Historia*, 22 (1973): pp. 364–65

Griffin, Miriam T., *Nero: The End of a Dynasty*, London: Batsford, 1984; New Haven, Connecticut: Yale University Press, 1985

Manning, C.E., "Acting and Nero's Conception of the Principate", *Greece and Rome*, 22 (1975): pp. 164–75

Price, S.R.F., "Gods and Emperors: The Greek Language of the Roman Imperial Cult", *Journal of Hellenic Studies*, 104 (1984): pp. 79–95

Ramage, E.S., "Denigration of Predecessor under Claudius, Galba and Vespasian", *Historia*, 32 (1983): pp. 201–14

Schumann, Gerhard von, *Hellenistische und griechische Elemente in der Regierung Neros*, Leipzig: Schwarzenberg & Schumann, 1930

Wallace-Hadrill, A., "Civilis Princeps: Between Citizen and King", *Journal of Roman Studies*, 72 (1982): pp. 32–48

Woodman, A.J., "Amateur Dramatics at the Court of Nero (*Annals* 15. 48–74)" in *Tacitus and the Tacitean Tradition*, edited by T.J. Luce and Woodman, Princeton, New Jersey: Princeton University Press, 1993

Nestorius *c.*381–*c.*451

Archbishop of Constantinople

Nestorius was born in Germaniceia in the province of Syria Euphratensis (east Syria) and at an early age entered the monastery of Euprepeia near Antioch. In Antioch he acquired, like John Chrysostom before him, a great reputation as a preacher, strongly influenced by the theological views of Theodore, bishop of Mopsuestia (died 428), and in general by the Antiochene school of theology. Theodore's biblical commentaries used scientific, literary, and historical methods of interpretation that contrasted with the allegorical method favoured by the Alexandrians. This involved an understanding of Christ as subsisting in two complete natures, Godhead and manhood united by will, or, as Theodore expressed it, by "good pleasure", into one intimately related but outward person (*prosopon*). As Nestorius himself was to write towards the end of his life, "The Maker is in every way other than that which is made" (*Bazaar of Heraclides*, p.27). The unity between the *Logos* (Divine Word) and the man, Jesus Christ, was achieved by the *Logos* uniting himself with the human Jesus, a view justified in scripture from Philippians 2: 6–7: Jesus Christ, "being in the form of God, thought it not robbery to be equal with God, but made himself of no reputation and took upon himself the form of a servant and was made in the likeness of men". This voluntary self-emptying of divinity enabled the *Logos* to form a union of wills with Jesus, to become a single personality, share in human experiences, including the cross and death, and so redeem mankind.

This Christology, however, differed fundamentally from that of Alexandria. The Alexandrians stressed the divinity of Jesus Christ as one divine person, as stated in John 1:14: "the Word became flesh and dwelt among us". Godhead and manhood were therefore fused in a unity of essence, a hypo-static union as Cyril of Alexandria would claim, not simply a conjunction (*synapheia*) of wills in one personality.

These contrasting concepts were long-standing and had existed side by side without open conflict through the first quarter of the 5th century. However, on the early death of archbishop Sisinius (426–27) the clergy of Constantinople failed to agree on a successor. The emperor Theodosius II thereupon broke the deadlock by sending for the presbyter Nestorius. The latter's character and lack of judgement created a crisis between the two Christologies.

The Constantinopolitan historian Socrates wrote of Nestorius (*c.*439) that he was "a man of extreme lack of tact, ignorance, and garrulity" (*Historia Ecclesiastica*, 7. 29), qualities he showed in the first days of his episcopate. The Arians, though finally condemned as heretics at the second Ecumenical Council at Constantinople in 381, were still respected in the capital, as were other dissenters, such as the Macedonians and Novatianists. Nestorius deprived the Arians of their chapel within the walls of the city and soon afterwards acted against the Macedonians, Montanists, and Novatians. "Give me, O emperor, the earth purged of heretics, and I will repay you with heaven. Assist me in destroying heretics and I will help you harry the Persians", he had said during his consecration sermon (Socrates, loc. cit.). He was as good as his word. Unfortunately a fire broke out in the city shortly afterwards, which earned Nestorius the title of "firebrand" and alienated the inhabitants from him.

Nestorius had brought a number of Antiochene priests with him. On 24 November one of these, the presbyter Anastasius, preached a sermon in which he attacked the term *Theotokos* ("one who gave birth to God") as applied to the Virgin Mary. Nestorius insisted that Mary was the bearer of Christ and that the proper term was *Christotokos*. Socrates (*Historia Ecclesiastica*, 7. 32) points out that *Theotokos* was not a novelty in the east and could be found in the writings of Eusebius of Caesarea and Origen. Nestorius in his view was simply ignorant. Nestorius' antipathy to *Theotokos* did not go unnoticed by Cyril, archbishop of Alexandria, who had official and unofficial agents in the capital. These kept him quickly, if inaccurately, informed of Nestorius' views and actions. Soon afterwards, early in 429, Pelagian exiles led by Julian, bishop of Eclanum, arrived in Constantinople. Though Nestorius informed pope Celestine (422–32) and requested, somewhat peremptorily, information about them, he did not receive them unfavourably, thus antagonizing the papacy and the powerful North African Church led by Augustine.

For the moment the issue between Nestorius and Cyril was the term *Theotokos*. However, the see of Alexandria had long coveted the primacy over the eastern Churches accorded to Constantinople at the council of 381. Cyril, annoyed by reports sent to him by his agents that Nestorius was making mischief for him with the emperor, wrote urging him to cease his opposition to *Theotokos* (June 429), and implying that Rome might be concerned about Nestorius' doctrine. In the spring of 430 he composed the five-book *Adversus Nestorium* (Against Nestorius) for his monastic and Alexandrian audience. Nestorius, though unpopular in the imperial city, retained the ear of the emperor.

He does not seem to have replied to Cyril's attacks, and early in 430 Cyril tried once more. Again there were complaints about Nestorius' alleged hostility, but this second Letter to Nestorius contained a full-dress statement of Alexandrian Christology. Cyril stressed the union (*henosis*) of the two natures of Godhead and manhood in the Incarnate Christ's one divine person. Reject this personal union, he argued, and the alternative was two Sons, one divine and the other human, while *Theotokos* followed naturally from the single divine person. For good measure Cyril sent a copy of his letter with a Latin translation to pope Celestine.

Nestorius replied to Cyril in June 430. He pointed out that in the Creed of Nicaea Christ was described as "Lord Jesus Christ", thus indicating his existence in two complete natures in the same person, Christ. Christ suffered and died in his bodily nature, while the divine Word remained as it was, not subject to change or suffering. The body served as "its temple" which God raised "in three days" (cf. John 2: 13). This clarification of doctrine, Nestorius added, coincided with the exceedingly prosperous state of the empire. A copy, but not translated, was sent to Celestine.

Not surprisingly, the pope took Cyril's side. Celestine remembered that Ambrose of Milan had spoken in terms suggesting that Mary was Theotokos. At a council held in Rome in August 430 he condemned Nestorius, ordering him to recant his views within ten days on pain of deposition. He empowered Cyril to see that the sentence was carried out. The emperor, however, still supported Nestorius. A third letter by Cyril in November 430 set out 12 statements regarding the doctrine of the Incarnation to which he demanded Nestorius' assent. "You must declare in writing and on oath that you anathematize your impious tenets and believe what we believe." Some of Cyril's statements verged on Apollinarian heresy, and now opinion in the bishoprics under the jurisdiction of Antioch began to rally to Nestorius. Before Cyril's letter with its 12 anathemas could be delivered to Nestorius, the emperor had decided to summon a General Council at his archbishop's request to meet at Ephesus at Whitsun the following year.

During the following months opinion hardened on each side. Nestorius gained the support of the Syrian bishops, but Cyril was assured of that of Rome and the majority of the bishops in Asia Minor who were jealous of Constantinople's exercise of metropolitan authority over them. He also had the backing of the powerful and ambitious Juvenal, bishop of Jerusalem. In the event, Cyril accompanied by 50 Egyptian bishops arrived at Ephesus early in June 431. His allies, apart from the papal delegates, arrived shortly afterwards. Without waiting for the arrival of John, bishop of Antioch, and the Syrians he opened the council on 22 June. The question at issue was whether his or Nestorius' doctrine accorded best with the Creed of Nicaea, regarded in East and West alike as the touchstone of orthodoxy. Since the crucial statement in the Creed was that Christ was "of one substance with the Father", the odds were stacked heavily in Cyril's favour. Nevertheless he made doubly sure. As Nestorius was to state, the council was Cyril's. "Cyril presided; Cyril was accuser; Cyril was bishop of Rome [i.e. behaved as if he were the pope]; Cyril was judge" (*Bazaar of Heraclides*, p.117). By the evening of the same day Nestorius had been condemned as "the new Judas", deposed from his see, and deprived of ecclesiastical orders. The crowd and Memnon, bishop of Ephesus, shouted in delight.

This was not quite the end. On 26 June John of Antioch arrived at Ephesus with 68 bishops. At once he excommunicated Cyril and Memnon and all the bishops who had accepted Cyril's 12 anathemas. Deadlock was not broken by the arrival of papal legates early in July and their support for Cyril. By August, however, the scene moved to Constantinople. In the complicated negotiations that followed, Nestorius was sacrificed in return for the healing of the breach between Alexandria and Antioch, which took place in 433 through the Formula of Reunion. He returned to his monastery at Antioch. Later (*c*.435) he was removed in exile to the Great Oasis in Upper Egypt where he died, believing that the papacy in the person of pope Leo and the *Tome* he wrote in 449 had vindicated his two-nature theology of the Incarnation. It was there that he composed his long apologia, known as the *Bazaar* [or *Book*] of Heraclides.

The "tragedy of Nestorius" will always be debated. On the then current interpretations of John 1: 14 and the Christology of the Council of Nicaea Cyril was in the right. The decision of the Council of Constantinople in 381 that declared Constantinople to be "the new Rome", reserving only the primacy of honour to Rome and the papacy, was unacceptable to him and also to the see of Alexandria. Moreover, Nestorius' lack of tact and statesmanship contributed to his fate. On the other hand, his defence of the full humanity of Christ and interpretaion of the Incarnation in that sense preserved the Church from a purely Platonic understanding of the life and work of the Master. Generations better equipped to consider that event in terms of history will be grateful to Nestorius and his Antiochene allies.

Nestorius' views survived to inspire the majority Church in Persia during the 5th and later centuries. Nestorian missionaries took their faith along the Silk Route to eastern China from the 7th century. In the 14th century the Nestorian Church suffered severely through persecutions by the Muslim Mongols. It survives as the Church of the Assyrian Christians, living in mountainous areas in Kurdistan.

WILLIAM H.C. FREND

See also Heresy

Biography

Born in Syria *c*.381, Nestorius entered the monastery of Euprepeia at Antioch and may have been a pupil of Theodore of Mopsuestia. He gained a reputation as a preacher and was summoned by the emperor Theodosius II. He became archbishop of Constantinople in 428. He incited controversy and was opposed by Cyril of Alexandria and Pope Celestine. Deposed by the Council of Ephesus in 431, he died in exile in Upper Egypt *c*.451.

Writings

In *Creeds, Councils and Controversies: Documents Illustrating the History of the Church, AD 337–461*, edited and translated by J. Stevenson and W.H.C. Frend, London: SPCK, 1989, pp.295–312 (translations of Cyril's Second and Third Letters to Nestorius, Nestorius' reply to the Second Letter, and extracts from the *Bazaar of Heraclides*)

Further Reading

Cross, F.L. (editor), *The Oxford Dictionary of the Christian Church*, 3rd edition, Oxford and New York: Oxford University Press, 1997 (includes bibliography of works relating to Nestorius)

Hall, Stuart G., *Doctrine and Practice in the Early Church*, London: SPCK, 1991; Grand Rapids, Michigan: Eerdmans, 1992 (see especially chapter 20)

McGuckin, John A., *St Cyril of Alexandria: The Christological Controversy*, Leiden: Brill, 1994 (see chapter 2)

Simonetti, M., Nestorius / Nestorianism entry in *Encyclopedia of the Early Church*, edited by Angelo Di Berardino, vol. 2, Cambridge: James Clarke, and New York: Oxford University Press, 1992, p. 594

New Testament

The Greek equivalent of our phrase "New Testament" is *kaine diatheke*, which signified initially the new covenant cemented in Jesus Christ. Since, however, Christians are sons and heirs to God, the *diatheke* is also represented in the apostolic writings as a testament whose provisions were made irrevocable by the death of the testator, God himself (Hebrews 8: 16; Galatians 3: 15). Hence the Latin *novum testamentum* became the title of the book in which the legacy was sealed. Though Clement of Alexandria writing around 200 would appear to have been the first to speak of a body of Christian writings as a *kaine diatheke*, and the description of its contents as a "canon" is even later, there can be little doubt that all the works comprising our New Testament were accepted as authoritative by the end of the 2nd century. By this time, the status of other works that had temporarily enjoyed the same authority was waning, and though the "apocryphal gospels" might continue to be cited, it was always as historical testimonies, not as arbiters in doctrinal controversy. The earliest Greek catalogues of the New Testament date only from the 4th century, but a Latin canon, the Muratorian Fragment, whose contents suggest a date before the end of the 2nd century, is sometimes thought to have been based on a Greek original. Although this text implies that date and provenance were criteria of admission, even ancient witnesses admit that they do not know the author of Hebrews or Revelation, yet accept them on the endorsement of the Church.

The first writings of our New Testament to be called "scripture" (2 Peter 3: 16) are the letters of St Paul, which, where authentic, must have been written before AD 65. The ones most commonly reckoned to be authentic (1 Thessalonians, Galatians, Romans, 1 and 2 Corinthians) are addressed to Gentile Churches that were not yet free from pagan ways of thinking or secure against the Judaizing tendencies that may be represented by the letter ascribed to James. Philippians and Philemon, which are probably genuine works of Paul's imprisonment, accord a new importance to the human Christ as a model of patient suffering and humility. The letters to the Colossians and Ephesians (only one of which is likely to be genuine) issue precepts that are suitable for all churches and supported by a doctrine of election in the pre-existent Christ. The letter to the Hebrews, much of which reads like a commentary on difficulties in other Pauline letters, reflects a time of widespread persecution and apostasy, and may well

have been written by a late follower of Paul. Few scholars now accept the Pauline authorship of the pastoral epistles (Titus, 1 and 2 Timothy) which, in extolling the ecclesiastical hierarchy as a bulwark against false teaching, savour more of the 2nd century than the 1st. Also 2 Thessalonians appears to be a spurious document, written for a time when persecution had aroused false expectations of the End. Affliction and apostasy also furnish the occasion for 1 and 2 Peter and the letter of Jude; the last two are all but identical in places, and few would now attribute any of the three to their titular authors.

The tendency to emphasize (perhaps even to exaggerate) the diversity of the New Testament is apparent in modern study of the four gospels. Tatian already presumed their canonicity when he compiled his *Diatessaron* around AD 170, and ten years later they were already a fourfold cord of truth to Irenaeus; it is common now, however, to maintain that each was intended for a different audience and originally current in different regions. If we may rely on the Ignatian correspondence, Matthew's gospel was used in the district of Antioch around AD 100. John's, though claimed by Ephesus, is first attested around AD 130 in Egypt; the Rylands papyrus, which tells us this, does not tell us whether the readership was orthodox or Gnostic (if indeed it makes sense to ask). Tradition attributes both texts to apostles, while revering Mark as a disciple of Peter and Luke as a companion of Paul. The evidence for the latter claim is furnished by the Acts of the Apostles, to which Luke's gospel is a preface. Most modern critics, however, doubt that any is the product of an eyewitness, and believe that all of them presuppose the events surrounding the fall of Jerusalem in AD 70. Mark's gospel, the least regarded in the early Church, is now often believed to be the source for the narratives of Luke and Matthew, though the "Griesbach hypothesis" argues that it is rather a digest of them. These "synoptic gospels" are the source of ecclesiology and ethics for the main Churches, while that of John has generally been accepted as a more "spiritual" record, furnishing materials for Christology and Trinitarian dogma. The three letters attributed to John denounce opponents of his teaching as the Antichrist; in Revelation, the only book that claims to be by a man named John, the Antichrist is a human tool of Satan, and his oppression of the saints is prophesied in vivid detail. The authority of this text was doubted even in the 3rd century, both because of its dubious authorship, and because of the unfruitful speculations to which it led.

Greek is the language of the whole New Testament, and probably the first language of all its authors, though in some cases (especially the words ascribed to Jesus in Matthew's gospel) it is tinged with Aramaic idioms. The one Greek book that can be said to have served the canonical authors as a model for style or content is the Septuagint, and although the resulting dialect is often described as the common Greek or koine of the period, it contains a large number of idioms not found in other literary works. Even Luke, who shows some knowledge of Classical conventions, would not have satisfied a contemporary purist. The oldest complete Greek manuscripts of the New Testament, the Codex Vaticanus and Codex Sinaiticus, are dated to the 4th century. Since the Reformation, the recovery and translation of the most primitive texts have preoccupied western scholars; the Greek Church, on the whole, has shown little interest in this enterprise. This is not because the New Testament plays no part in eastern Christendom; it supplied the only prooftexts for the ecumenical councils, and has always been regarded as a treasury of wisdom by the mystics. In the patristic era, distinguished commentaries on the gospels and the letters of Paul were produced by Origen, Didymus, Theodore, Chrysostom, Cyril, and Theodoret. Theodore, Theodoret, and Chrysostom, the "Antiochenes", even anticipate the modern interest in the historical circumstances of Paul's writing, and therefore tend to interpret him more literally than their western counterparts. Moreover the Greeks, no less than western Christians, rely upon the New Testament to establish the authority and clarify the meaning of the Old. Nevertheless, the New Testament is not, in Greek eyes, the source of Christianity, but a witness to the apostolic teaching that the Orthodox tradition both inherits and upholds.

Mark Edwards

See also Christianity

Further Reading

Brown, Schuyler, *The Origins of Christianity: A Historical Introduction to the New Testament*, Oxford and New York: Oxford University Press, 1993

Bultmann, Rudolf, *The Theology of the New Testament*, 2 vols, London: SCM Press, 1952–55

Caird, G.B., *New Testament Theology*, Oxford: Clarendon Press, and New York: Oxford University Press, 1994

Dodd, C.H., *The Apostolic Preaching and Its Developments*, London: Hodder and Stoughton, 1936, reprinted New York: Harper and Row, 1964

Dunn, James D., *Unity and Diversity in the New Testament: An Inquiry into the Character of Earliest Christianity*, 2nd edition London: SCM Press, and Philadelphia: Trinity Press, 1990

Filson, Floyd V., *A New Testament History: The Story of the Emerging Church*, Philadelphia: Westminster Press, 1964; London: SCM Press, 1965

Fitzmyer, Joseph A., *Essays on the Semitic Background of the New Testament*, London: Geoffrey Chapman, and Grand Rapids: Eerdmans, 1971, reprinted with *A Wandering Aramean: Collected Aramaic Essays*, 1997

Hahnemann, Geoffrey M., *The Muratorian Fragment and the Development of the Canon*, Oxford: Clarendon Press, and New York: Oxford University Press, 1992

Jeremias, Joachim, *New Testament Theology*, London: SCM Press, and New York: Scribner, 1971

Kittel, Gerhard (editor), *Theological Dictionary of the New Testament*, 10 vols, Grand Rapids: Eerdmans, 1964–76, abridged in 1 vol., 1985

Koester, Helmut, *Introduction to the New Testament*, 2nd edition, 2 vols, New York: de Gruyter, 1995

Kümmel, Werner Georg, *Introduction to the New Testament*, revised edition, London: SCM Press, and Nashville, Tennessee: Abingdon Press, 1975

Metzger, Bruce M., *The Canon of the New Testament: Its Origin, Development, and Significance*, Oxford: Clarendon Press, and New York: Oxford University Press, 1987

Metzger, Bruce M., *The Text of the New Testament: Its Transmission, Corruption, and Restoration*, 3rd edition, Oxford and New York: Oxford University Press, 1992

Moule, C.F.D., *The Birth of the New Testament*, 3rd edition, London: A. & C. Black, 1981; San Francisco: Harper and Row, 1982

Neill, Stephen and Tom Wright, *The Interpretation of the New Testament, 1860–1986*, 2nd edition, Oxford: Oxford University Press, 1988

Robinson, John A.T., *Redating the New Testament*, London: SCM Press, and Philadelphia: Westminster Press, 1976

Streeter, Burnett Hillman, *The Four Gospels: A Study of Origins*, London: Macmillan, 1924, reprinted 1964

Theissen, Gerd, *The Social Setting of Pauline Christianity: Essays on Corinth*, edited and translated by John H. Schütz, Edinburgh: Clark, and Philadelphia: Fortress Press, 1982

Wright, N.T., *The New Testament and the People of God*, London: SPCK, 1992

Niarchos, Stavros 1909–1996

Shipowner

Stavros Niarchos was one of the "Golden Greeks", a group of entrepreneurs (another was his long-standing business rival, Aristotle Onassis) who made vast fortunes for themselves and acquired fame and often notoriety in the international jet set of the post-war world. Niarchos was born in Piraeus in 1909; his parents, originally from the southern Peloponnese, had emigrated to the US, but returned to Greece before Stavros was born. He thus missed the chance to acquire US citizenship.

His family was comfortably off until 1923, when his father went bankrupt; the experience was probably traumatic and Stavros, 14 at the time, is said to have vowed never to be poor again. In 1928 he started work as an office assistant in the flour-milling firm owned by his maternal uncles, the Coumandaros brothers. He managed to persuade them to invest in ships to carry the grain to their mills, resulting in large savings on grain importation costs and bigger profits; he himself then invested in the ships. In the late 1930s he acquired a 60 per cent share and operational control of one of his uncles' ships and started building a shipping company.

At the outbreak of World War II, along with most of the Greek shipowners, he chartered his modest fleet to the Allies. He joined the Greek Navy and at the end of the war he was demobilized with the rank of lieutenant. For three years after the war (1945–47) he was the Greek honorary naval attaché in New York.

Most of his ships did not survive the war, but Niarchos collected considerable sums in insurance, having had the foresight to insure against war risks before the war, when the premiums were still low. With the insurance payments he started to buy and build ships on a large scale, starting with Liberty and Victory bulk carriers and T2 tankers. His business fortunes were helped at different times by sharp rises in freight rates; the Korean War, the Suez crisis, and the Six-Day War all worked in his favour.

Niarchos's success was at least partly based on his talent to analyse and forecast business trends. Both Niarchos and Onassis had foreseen that oil and its transportation were going to be crucial for the world economy. In the 1950s both men pioneered the supertankers: in 1954 Niarchos ordered the largest tanker in the world at the time, the 45,000-tonne *World Glory*. Supertankers proved to be immensely profitable, allowing for the investment to be recouped quickly, sometimes in as few as four voyages. In 1953 Niarchos (along with Onassis) was prosecuted by the US Department of Justice for acquiring ships not intended for US citizens. Though a compromise was worked out, he transferred his operations to Europe soon afterwards.

Niarchos's early fortune was based on ships. By 1956 he owned more than 50 ships with more than 2 million tonnes' capacity. Ten years later he had 72 ships and another 16 on order. By the late 1970s his fleet had shrunk to fewer than 30 ships. Nevertheless in the early 1980s he still reputedly had one of the largest private tanker fleets, between 4 and 5 million tonnes deadweight. By 1986 this had come down to around 3 million tonnes deadweight, and before his death it had shrunk further to around 1 million tonnes (18 ships), ranking him 15th among Greek shipowners.

However, even if he is known primarily as a shipping magnate, Niarchos diversified early on. In the 1950s he had fought his arch-rival, Onassis, for the franchise of Olympic Airways (and lost); in 1956 he founded the Hellenic Shipyards in Skaramangas, with more than 10,000 employees at one time; and in 1970 he acquired a lucrative oil refinery in Aspropyrgos (both enterprises are near Athens). He also owned stud farms in France and the US as well as racehorses, and real estate all over the world, including a private island, Spetsopoula, 100 km south of Piraeus (bought in 1957; Onassis retaliated by buying the island of Skorpios in the Ionian Sea soon afterwards), the 18th-century Hôtel des Chanalleines (originally a present of Louis XIV to his son, the Duc de Maine), and other real estate in Monte Carlo, St Moritz, Antibes, Normandy, and the Caribbean; he is also believed to have been the largest private investor in Citibank.

His art collections were fabulous. As early as 1958 he had bought the E.G. Robinson art collection, to which he continued adding: reputedly he owned ten Renoirs, six Gauguins, and seven Van Goghs, works by El Greco (including his magnificent *Pietà* of 1585), Rubens, and Goya. By the mid-1980s only 15 per cent of his wealth was in ships, the remaining 85 per cent believed to be invested in art, gems, and gold as well as property and racehorses. This diversification (along with sheer size) cushioned his fortune from the effects of the shipping slump of the 1980s. At the time of his death, *Fortune* magazine ranked Niarchos the 32nd-richest person in the world, with an estimated fortune of more than $5 billion.

Niarchos's lifestyle style was flamboyant – to the point of vulgarity, some said; and though he was more private than his arch-rival Onassis, he was nonetheless a legendary spender, lavishing hospitality to guests. In the 1950s it was said he was attending or giving five or more parties a week, some on his luxurious yachts or his private island.

His personal life was turbulent. Two marriages, in 1930 and 1939, lasted one and six years respectively. In 1947 Niarchos married Evgenia Livanou, daughter of Stavros Livanos, himself a Greek shipowner. A year earlier Onassis had married Tina Livanou, the younger of the two sisters, so the two men became brothers-in-law; this did nothing to diminish their business rivalry. Niarchos's marriage to Evgenia proved the longest-lasting of his five marriages: they had four children. They separated in 1964 when Niarchos married Charlotte Ford (daughter of Henry Ford II); they had a daughter, Elena (whom he never formally recognized) but the marriage was declared invalid since Niarchos's marriage to Evgenia had not been formally dissolved in Greece. In 1967 his marriage to

Charlotte Ford was dissolved and he returned to Evgenia. She died in Spetsopoula in 1970 in rather mysterious circumstances, from a sleeping-pill overdose (though the post-mortem also showed signs of physical abuse). Niarchos was charged with murder but the charges were later dropped. Nevertheless he left Greece soon after. In 1971 Niarchos married Tina Onassis, former wife of his business rival and formerly his own sister-in law; some said he did it to spite Onassis. Tina died in Paris in 1974. Niarchos never remarried, though he allegedly had a series of affairs, including, it is rumoured, one with Pamela Harriman, the former wife of Winston Churchill's son, Randolph.

In 1991 Niarchos underwent back surgery, which made it difficult for him to walk. His last years were spent in isolation, in a sterilized room in his villa in St Moritz, from which he communicated by microphone with his family and visitors. He died in Zurich on 15 April 1996. Throughout his life Niarchos would say: "I am Greek and I feel Greek." He proved his affection for his homeland in his will. His legendary fortune was split between the four children from his marriage with Evgenia and the Stavros Niarchos Foundation, a non-profit body financing charitable projects, many in Greece.

GEORGE KAZAMIAS

See also Ships and Shipping

Biography
Born in Piraeus in 1909 to a well-off family, Niarchos was 14 when his father was bankrupted. Joining the family flour-milling business in 1928, he persuaded his uncles to invest in ships and in the late 1930s he himself started a shipping company. His pioneering of oil tankers in the 1950s was particularly successful and his wealth became legendary. He died in Switzerland in 1996.

Further Reading
Franco, Victor, *Un Conquérant des mers*, Paris: Fayard, 1960
Harlaftis, Gelina, *Greek Shipowners and Greece, 1945–75: From Separate Development to Mutual Interdependence*, London: Athlone Press, 1993
Lilly, Doris, *Those Fabulous Greeks: Onassis, Niarchos and Livanos*, London: W. H. Allen, and New York: Cowles, 1970
Limperopoulos, Demetres, *Niarchos, o stolarchos: megalofyis, aplistos, maniakos* [Niarchos the Admiral: Genius, Grab-All, Lunatic], Athens, 1997

Nicaea

City in northwest Asia Minor

Nicaea (modern Iznik) is strategically located on main highways at the edge of a lake in northwest Asia Minor, a day's journey from Constantinople. A centre of Hellenism in the Hellenistic, Roman, and Byzantine periods, it played a major role in the history of the Christian Church.

Established originally by Antigonus I, Nicaea was refounded around 300 BC by Lysimachus who named it after his wife. From 281 to 74 BC it was one of the centres of the kingdom of Bithynia. Under the Romans, Nicaea controlled a vast territory, and struck an extensive and varied coinage. It was built on a rectangular plan and adorned with numerous

Nicaea: view of the Lefke Gate which according to an inscription was dedicated to Hadrian in AD 123

public buildings, some of them on an extravagant scale that attracted unfavourable comment from Pliny, who governed the region from AD 110 to 112. Few monuments have survived from these peaceful centuries. The troubles of the 3rd century, however, produced powerful surviving fortifications that allowed Nicaea to resist all attacks for a thousand years.

Nicaea was an early centre of Christianity (a late tradition has its church founded by St Andrew) and home of several saints and martyrs. In 325 the first Ecumenical Council met there. The emperor Constantine presided over the gathering of 318 bishops who defined orthodox doctrine against the Arians, producing the creed that is still recited. During late antiquity Nicaea flourished as an administrative centre, but suffered from devastating earthquakes and the growth of nearby Constantinople. Several of its buildings were restored by the emperor Justinian in the 6th century.

In the 8th and 9th centuries Nicaea was a major bastion against the Arabs, protecting the approaches to Constantinople and successfully resisting capture. It was head-quarters of the Opsikian theme, the military province closest to the capital, and thus seat of a general, garrison, and civil administration. In 787 the city gained further renown as the site of the seventh Ecumenical Council, at which Orthodoxy was restored after a long period of Iconoclasm. In the prosper-ous centuries that followed, Nicaea remained an important regional centre, home of churches and monasteries, and with-stood foreign and domestic enemies. Nevertheless, it fell into the hands of the Turks in 1081 and became the centre of their first state in Asia Minor. The First Crusade recaptured the city in 1097 after a memorable siege, and returned it to Byzantine rule.

The greatest age for Nicaea was the 13th century, when for a moment it was capital of the Byzantine empire. After the capture of Constantinople by the crusaders in 1204, the new emperor Theodore Laskaris (1205–22) took up residence in Nicaea, where he was joined by numerous refugees including leaders of the aristocracy and the Church. Its powerful walls and strategic site made it a suitable capital for the exiled empire, and a valuable base for repelling the attacks of the Latins of Constantinople, the Seljuk Turks, and breakaway Greek states. With the election of a new patriarch in 1208, Nicaea became the spiritual capital of the Orthodox Church. As such, it was the site of synods and negotiations with the Catholics. The Nicene empire reached its height under John Vatatzes (1222–54) who usually resided in the southern part of his domains, but still devoted much attention to Nicaea. The patriarchate was richly endowed as the state expanded and prospered. The city also became an important centre of learn-ing: leading scholars of the day studied and taught there, and an imperial school provided education in rhetoric and poetics.

The most noteworthy products of this revival are two elaborate speeches of the 13th century in praise of Nicaea.

The recapture of Constantinople in 1261 introduced a period of rapid decline as the patronage of Church and state was removed. As imperial attention shifted to the west, Asia Minor was rapidly lost. By the early 14th century Nicaea was one of a few walled cities holding out against the Turks. After a long blockade it finally succumbed in 1331. By then it was virtually deserted.

Although the first century of Ottoman rule brought considerable recovery, the Christian community dwindled away rapidly; by 1381 it no longer had the resources to support a bishop. During the next five centuries only a handful of Christians remained in the constantly declining town. By the end of the 19th century they were using Turkish in their liturgy. Hellenism finally came to an end in 1921, when the last standing church was despoiled.

The most impressive remains of Nicaea's glorious past are the fortifications. A product of the late 3rd century, they were extensively rebuilt by Leo III (716–41) after a major Arab attack, and by Michael III (842–68) who used Nicaea as a base for his advances to the east. An earthquake of 1065 provoked further repairs, but it remained for the Laskarids to execute the greatest rebuilding. Theodore I added several powerful towers, while John Vatatzes doubled the circuit by the addition of a low outer wall. Distinctive styles of construction reflect a thousand years of the city's history.

The only excavation has been in the Roman theatre, the remains of which reveal the state of Byzantine Nicaea: during the whole period the theatre was abandoned and used as a quarry for restoring the walls, and as a dump. Much of the area within the walls was in fact empty after the 6th century.

Although the palace where the first Council was held has long since disappeared, the site of the seventh still stands. The church of St Sophia, converted into a mosque soon after the Ottoman conquest, was built in the 5th or 6th century, rebuilt in the 9th and 11th, and expanded by Vatatzes. The church of the Dormition (originally the monastery of Hyacinth) had the longest continuous history. A product of the 6th or 7th century, it was richly decorated with mosaics (which show an iconoclastic period) and cut marble. It appears to have been the cathedral during the empire of Nicaea. Several other churches, mostly of the Laskarid period, are attested by texts and remains.

CLIVE FOSS

Summary

A city in northwestern Asia Minor, Nicaea was a major Greek centre in the Hellenistic, Roman, and Byzantine periods. It was also an early centre of Christianity, the seat of the First and Seventh Ecumenical Councils. It flourished in the 13th century as the capital of the Byzantine empire in exile. It preserves massive fortifications and the remains of churches.

Further Reading

Foss, Clive, *Nicaea: A Byzantine Capital and Its Praises*, Brookline, Massachusetts: Hellenic College Press, 1996

Merkelbach, Reinhold, *Nikaia in der römischen Kaiserzeit*, Opladen: Westdeutscher Verlag, 1987

Raby, Julian, "A Seventeenth Century Description of Iznik Nicaea", *Istanbuler Mitteilungen*, 26 (1976): pp. 149–88

Nicander

Poet of the (?)2nd century BC

Nicander of Colophon, a Hellenistic poet of disputed date (probably 2nd century BC), wrote at least 20 works, most in dactylic hexameters or elegiac couplets. Like other erudite Hellenistic poets, he also wrote works of a lexicographic and linguistic nature in prose. A "metaphrast", he converted the prose treatises of earlier writers into epic verse, even when he had no expert knowledge of the subject. Only his *Theriaca* (958 hexameters on poisonous creatures and on antidotes for their bites and stings) and *Alexipharmaca* (630 hexameters on antidotes to poisons) are extant. Among his more influential lost poems are *Georgics* and *Melissourgika* [Bee Keeping], both of which were used by Virgil in his *Georgics*, and *Heteroioumena* [Metamorphoses], which directly or indirectly provided Ovid and Antoninus Liberalis with material for their *Metamorphoses*. Fragments of other poems, for example on geography and local history, are extant, but of many attested works (such as Nicander's rendering in epic verse of the Hippocratic treatise *Prognostic*) there is almost no trace.

The poem *Theriaca* is probably an adaptation of the prose work *On Wild Animals* by an early 3rd-century BC expert on poisons, Apollodorus. Both *Theriaca* and *Alexipharmaca* also discuss the effects of plants on the human body, and for this Nicander likewise appears to have been indebted to Apollodorus, who in turn might have used Diocles of Carystus' work *Rhizotomikon* [Root-Cutting].

The ostensible aim of *Theriaca* is to help those suffering from the stings and bites of snakes, lizards, tortoises, turtles, frogs, toads, fish, scorpions, spiders, bees, wasps, beetles, moths, and flies. Like other Hellenistic scholar-poets, Nicander in fact strives to amaze his readers with a dazzling display of technical virtuosity in the poetic representation of a recalcitrant, unpoetic subject. Seemingly disparate, incompatible elements – archaic epic diction (including numerous Homeric hapax legomena), bold neologisms, technical zoological terminology, epic verse, botany, medical prescriptions ostensibly addressed to a physician, and learned allusions to earlier poetry (especially to Callimachus) – are skilfully woven into a recondite, affectively rich poem.

Exploiting the tensions between his science and his poetry, between his subject and his presentation thereof, Nicander in *Theriaca* describes the poisonous aggressors and their poisoned victims in such a way as to convey his predecessors' "objective" zoological, botanical, and medical expertise, while also using striking metaphors, similes, and aetiological myths to evoke the physical peril, the aesthetic revulsion, and the fright and terror to which the victims are exposed. The tension between science and poetry, which is also reflected in many lexical, semantic, metrical, and syntactic strains in Nicander's language, is thus cleverly translated into a suggestive tension between the victim as scientific object and as terrorized subject in need of the poet's aid.

Further evidence of the poet's aspiration to display technical virtuosity is the insertion of an "epic" catalogue of 82 plants (*Theriaca*, 837–914) in the concluding section on general remedies – plants whose "clinical" applications are not specified – and the covert integration of an acrostic signature of

Nicander's own name (*Theriaca*, 345–53) in a purple passage on the burning thirst caused by the bite of a smallish viper, the dipsas. *Theriaca* ends not only with another reminder of the poet's name and of his birthplace (Clarus, near Colophon), but also with a bold attempt to assimilate Nicander's didactic metaphrasis to Homeric epic: "And now you should hereafter preserve the memory of Homeric Nicander, too, whom the snow-white town of Clarus nurtured" (*Theriaca*, 957–58).

Nicander's hexametric poem *Alexipharmaca* exhibits many of the same characteristics as his *Theriaca*. After a proem addressed to Protagoras of Cyzicus, it presents 22 substances and entities – animal, vegetable, and mineral – that are fatal or harmful to human beings. Some of the more notorious toxic substances known to antiquity are included: hemlock, aconite, opium, henbane, and blister beetle. In each case, the poet first describes the symptoms produced by the poison, and then the antidotes. The poem ends with a *sphragis* (authorial "seal") very similar to the one in *Theriaca*: "And now you should hereafter preserve the memory of Nicander, composer of songs, and guard the law of Zeus, protector of guest-friendships" (*Alexipharmaca*, 629–30). In both extant "seals" Nicander therefore presents a poetic, not a scientific self-understanding ("Homeric Nicander", "composer of songs"), signalling that his poetic identity is a key to understanding his extant works.

Nicander's influence on later Greek and Latin literature was considerable. Not only did Virgil, Ovid, and Antoninus Liberalis draw on his works (see above), but Lucan, Pliny the Elder, Erotian, Aelian, and Athenaeus of Naucratis also bene-fited from direct or indirect familiarity with Nicander. In the 1st century BC the enormously learned scholar Didymus ("Chalcenterus") appears to have made extensive use of Nicander's lexicographic contributions. Although Dioscurides only twice cites Nicander's views in his *Materia Medica* (3. 29, 4. 99), Galen in his pharmacological works quotes a number of verse passages from Nicander. Papyrus fragments from the 1st to 3rd centuries AD further confirm Nicander's popularity in the Roman empire.

An invaluable corpus of ancient scholia became attached to Nicander's two extant poems. The extant scholia not only explain many of Nicander's words, expressions, and references but also report extensively on the views of Hellenistic authors whose works are lost, including three of the six attested ancient commentators on Nicander. Furthermore, the scholia offer rich data on folk traditions, including superstitions concerning spiders, snakes, toads, frogs, wasps, and salamanders.

Extant Greek paraphrases of *Theriaca* and *Alexipharmaca* were composed by Eutecnius some time after the 2nd century AD. They are included in one of the most famous Byzantine scientific manuscripts, the illuminated "Vienna Dioscurides" (Vienna, Österreichische Nationalbibliothek) produced in Constantinople in AD 512–13. Eutecnius' prose versions here are accompanied by magnificent illustrations of snakes, insects, spiders, scorpions, and other animals. These illustra-tions also appear in a 10th-century copy of the "Vienna Dioscurides" (now in the Pierpont Morgan Library, New York). In the 10th century a remarkable illuminated manu-script of Nicander's two poems was produced (Paris, Bibliothèque Nationale, Suppl. gr. 247). It contains images not only of the snakes, scorpions, plants, etc. mentioned by Nicander, but also of human figures displaying the effects of the poisonous substances or illustrating Nicander's mythologi-cal allusions. In the 13th century Maximos Planudes also showed a keen interest in Nicander, producing a manuscript (Florence, Biblioteca Medicea-Laurenziana) that contained both poems.

The scholia, paraphrases, and illustrations are further evidence not only of the interest that Nicander continued to stir among the later ancient and Byzantine cultural elite but also of their fascination with the amalgam of science, folklore, myth, poetry, and magic that is characteristic of much of the ancient Greek toxicological tradition. This fascination contin-ued to a striking degree in the 16th century, during which many printed editions, several translations into Latin, includ-ing one in epic verse, and a verse translation into French were published. A critical appreciation of Nicander's technical virtuosity was widely shared in the early modern period.

HEINRICH VON STADEN

Biography

Born at Clarus near Colophon probably in the 2nd century BC, Nicander wrote at least 20 works, of which two survive: *Theriaca* on poisonous creatures, with remedies against their stings and bites, and *Alexipharmaca* on antidotes to poisons. Both are indebted to Apollodorus. They mix superstition with botany and medicine. Lost works include poems on geography, local history, and medicine.

Writings

Nicandrea: Theriaca et Alexipharmaca, edited by Otto Schneider, Leipzig: Teubner, 1856

The Poems and Poetical Fragments, edited and translated by A.S.F. Gow and A.F. Scholfield, Cambridge: Cambridge University Press, 1953, reprinted London: Bristol Classical Press, 1997

Further Reading

Beavis, Ian C., *Insects and Other Invertebrates in Classical Antiquity*, Exeter: University of Exeter Press, 1988

Davies, Malcolm and Jeyaraney Kathirithamby, *Greek Insects*, London: Duckworth, and New York: Oxford University Press, 1986

Effe, Bernd, *Dichtung und Lehre: Untersuchungen zur Typologie der antiken Lehrgedichts*, vol. 69, Munich: Beck, 1977

Kádár, Zoltán, *Survivals of Greek Zoological Illuminations in Byzantine Manuscripts*, Budapest: Akadémiai Kiadó, 1978 (contains Byzantine illustrations of Nicander and Eutecnius)

Keller, Otto, *Die antike Tierwelt*, 2 vols, Leipzig: Engelmann, 1909–13, reprinted Hildesheim: Olms, 1963

Omont, Henri, *Miniatures des plus anciens manuscrits grecs de la Bibliothèque Nationale du VIe au XIVe siècle*, 2nd edition, Paris: Champion, 1929 (contains 10th-century illustrations of Nicander)

Weitzmann, Kurt, *Illustrations in Roll and Codex: a Study of the Origin and Method of Text Illustration*, Princeton, New Jersey: Princeton University Press, 1947, reprinted with addenda 1970

Weitzman, Kurt, *Studies in Classical and Byzantine Manuscript Illumination*, edited by Herbert L. Kessler, Chicago: University of Chicago Press, 1971

White, H., *Studies in the Poetry of Nicander*, Amsterdam: Hakkert, 1987

Nicopolis

City in Epirus

Situated on the isthmus of the Preveza peninsula 6 km north of Preveza, which is itself at the entrance to the Ambracian Gulf opposite Actium, Nicopolis was founded by Octavian on the site of his army encampment during his campaign against Mark Antony in 31 BC. From the outset it operated as an administrative centre serving the cities of northern Epirus. Self-consciously Greek, it never accepted (unlike Corinth) the status of a Roman *colonia*. Its pride in its status is instanced by Epictetus, who lived there at the end of the 1st century AD (*Dissertationes*, 4. 1. 14), and confirmed by its coinage that continued to be minted until the reign of Gallienus (AD 253–68). During its early years, in the reign of Augustus, it had been chosen as the site of the Actian Games, celebrated every four years and given equal status with the major Panhellenic games.

Christianity came early to Nicopolis. Paul asks Titus to come to him there for he "had determined there to winter" (Titus 3: 12) at an unknown date, depending on the chronology of Paul's last years. There was a well-organized community in the city in the early 3rd century AD, for Origen visited Nicopolis *c.*220 and found a copy of the scriptures there, which he used as an authority in compiling the *Hexapla* (Eusebius, *Historia Ecclesiastica*, 6. 16. 2). In the 4th century Nicopolis achieved metropolitan status and, as elsewhere in the Hellenic world, Christianity gradually became the predominant religion in the city. Two large basilicas dating from the early 6th century have been discovered and excavated. One, built by bishop Alkison (died *c.*515) within the city's walls, measured 68.90 by 31.60m; the other, built by bishop Dunetios, had excellently preserved mosaics. The site of the metropolitan's palace was found near Alkison's basilica.

Nicopolis's ecclesiastical pre-eminence was matched by its civil position as the capital city of Epirus under Diocletian's reconstruction of the imperial provinces. It remained an important city in the 4th and 5th centuries and survived seizure by Gaiseric's Vandal fleet and army in 475. It was at the height of its prosperity as a Christian metropolis during the early part of the 6th century, but it became involved in the wars between the Byzantines and Goths for the control of Italy, the Gothic leader Totila laying its surrounding territory waste in 551. Nicopolis seems to have survived the Slav invasions better than most Byzantine cities in the Balkans, for it was still worth contesting between the Byzantines and Bulgars in the 10th and 11th centuries. Final decline did not set in until control fell to the Bulgars in 1040. More recently Nicopolis was the site of a signal Greek victory over the Ottomans in 1912.

WILLIAM H.C. FREND

Summary

A city in Epirus, Nicopolis was founded by Octavian in 31 BC. As Augustus, he chose it as the site of the Actian Games. Under Diocletian it became the capital city of Epirus. It survived the Slav invasions but declined after falling to the Bulgars in 1040. It was the site of a major victory over the Ottomans in 1912.

Further Reading

Hammond, N.L.G., *Epirus: The Geography, the Ancient Remains, the History and Topography of Epirus and Adjacent Areas*, Oxford: Clarendon Press, 1967

Hornblower, Simon and Antony Spawforth (editors), *The Oxford Classical Dictionary*, 3rd edition, Oxford and New York: Oxford University Press, 1996, Nicopolis entry, pp. 1043–44

Oberhummer, E., Nicopolis entry in *Real-Encyclopädie der klassischen Altertumswissenschaft*, edited by August Pauly *et al.*, vol. 17. 1, 1936, 511–18

Nomokanon

Compilation of secular and sacred law

Nomokanon comes from the Greek words *nomos*, meaning "law", and *kanon*, meaning "rule" or "measure" (*kanon* is the Greek word for a measuring stick or ruler). The word, appearing first in the 11th century, referred to collections or compilations consisting of both sacred and secular laws relevant to Church government; hence, *nomos* – referring to secular law – and *kanon* – referring to sacred law. Justification for mixing civil and sacred law in a canonical list included the important role that civil leaders played in securing the physical protection, political well-being, and ecclesial practice of the Church. (It should be kept in mind that lists of secular laws included sacred law as well.)

Perhaps the most difficult obstacle facing the early Church was lack of cohesiveness. In the first three centuries at least, it lacked substantial political, doctrinal, legislative, and liturgical unity. Constantine established a political stability that made subsequent institutional ordering possible. That ordering, or at least the foundation of subsequent ordering, included theological and doctrinal development, the establishment of codes of conduct for Church officers, and the development of a juridical system to oversee and regulate the Church.

The numerous legislative and regulatory questions facing the early Church included proper liturgical practice, requirements for admission to the Church, relations among Churches and Church officers – Church organization – relations between Church law and secular law, the proper disposition of heretics, enforcement of Church regulations, etc. On many such questions the New Testament writers were silent, though clearly their writings put forward standards of moral action. In response to this need for guidelines there arose various declarations of Church law – canon law – giving directions on such problems. These declarations were gradually committed to writing. The sources for these written declarations included: (1) alleged writings of the apostles, e.g. *Apostolic Constitutions*; (2) common practice or custom; (3) formal councils, both parochial (e.g. Sardica) and ecumenical, foremost of which was Nicaea; (4) civil laws and collections of civil laws such as the *Codex Justinianus*; (5) doctrinal and regulatory declarations made by certain of the Church Fathers (the epistles of Basil were important in the East), the pope, and other high ecclesial officers – such decisions are called "decretals". A brief history of canonical collections will clarify the concept of *nomokanon*, which is, after all, a species of canonical collection.

The growth of Church government was gradual but steady. Given their relative circumstances, local Churches formulated unwritten rules of conduct and Church procedure based upon the limited directions available in scripture as well as certain other texts such as the *Apostolic Constitutions* (*c.*380), an eclectic book of instruction and directions allegedly written by the apostles. This text has appended to it 85 apostolic canons of which a substantial number deal, like many other early canonical material, with clerical behaviour.

A group of proximate local Churches would often hold formal regional councils in which to harmonize their practices and procedures as well as deal with regional issues, such as how to adjudicate disputes between bishops or how to deal with lapsed clerics. Such conciliar resolutions were called "canons" or rules of conduct and government. Important examples of such parochial councils include Ancyra (314), Neo-Caesarea (315), and Antioch (341). These councils issued lists of their resolutions and decrees. Canon 1 of Ancyra, for example, forbids presbyters and deacons who have observed pagan sacrifice from returning to their priestly functions. Canon 18 deals with rogue bishops who engage in sedition or disruptive behaviour in another Church's region.

Ecumenical councils, councils to which all or nearly all bishops were invited, met for similar reasons as regional councils and also issued canons. Their resolutions often incorporated all or part of the regional canons while adding to them depending on the nature and scope of issues before them. The Council of Chalcedon (451), for example, refers to the *corpus canonum* – a body of canons – which developed over previous years as more and more regional councils issued their canonical lists. Ecumenical councils would incorporate material from earlier lists and, like the regional councils, would incorporate decretals, instructions given by the Church Fathers. Of particular decretal importance were the 96 canons of Basil the Great. Also important were the canons of certain archbishops such as Dionysius, Peter, Athanasius, Timothy, Theophilus, all archbishops of Alexandria, and the Cappadocian theologians Gregory of Nyssa – brother to Basil the Great – and Gregory the Theologian.

The first seven ecumenical councils, Nicaea particularly, acquired an authority and standing such that their canons served as a kind of metacanon for all other councils. So St Augustine of Hippo, at the regional Council of Carthage (419), insisted that a particular resolution should not contradict the Nicaean canons. Ecumenical councils, while deciding doctrine, therefore, incorporated other lists of canons in their own resolutions.

As the number of canonical lists grew, there were efforts to compile and catalogue them. Thus, at Antioch, in the late 4th century, there arose a *syntagma canonum* containing the resolutions of the earliest regional councils, Ancyra, Neo-Caesarea, Gangra, Antioch, and Laodicea. This list is the *corpus canonum* referred to at Chalcedon. Subsequent compilers add to this list the ecumenical councils of Nicaea, Constantinople I, and Chalcedon (451). As Munier points out, the foundation of canon law consists of this *syntagma* along with 6th-century additions: the canon of Ephesus (431), the 133 canons of the Council of Carthage (419), and the Council of Sardica (343).

The number, growth, and intramural inconsistencies of canonical collections led to the Council *in Trullo* (Constantinople 692), which canonized the canonical collections, so to speak, by establishing one approved list of canonical collections (Canon 2). The list included the decretals of the Church Fathers, the 85 apostolic canons from the *Apostolic Constitutions*, the *syntagma* of Antioch, the canons of Constantinople (394), and the 102 canons of the council itself.

Roughly simultaneous to and paralleling the growth of canonical lists, the emperors Theodosius and later Justinian had compilers gathering secular law, largely in an effort to establish a single, harmonious set of laws to be observed by the entire empire. Theodosius and Justinian wished to replace early compilations such as the *Codex Gregorianus*, a collection of laws issued between 196 and 295. Early lists were inconsistent with each other and contained irrelevant and obsolete material. The *Codex Theodosianus* (438), named after Theodosius II who commissioned it, was a collection of all the imperial constitutions published since the time of Constantine I. The compilation included commentary and relevant material from other jurists and became the legal code for the entire Roman empire. It was superseded by another compilation: the important *Corpus Juris Civilis*, a compilation of secular laws arranged according to topic. The corpus included four other compilations, the *Codex Justinianus*, a collection of imperial constitutions from Hadrian to Justinian I, the *Digest*, *Institutes*, and *Novels*. This work, like the previous collections, included material relevant to ecclesiastical problems and controversies including numerous ecclesiastical regulations. Basil I began yet another collection (finished by Leo VI, 888) intended to incorporate but modernize previous collections. Named the *Basilika*, "imperial laws", it contained much edited material from the *Corpus Juris Civilis* and its compendia, and, like previous collections, the civil laws contained much material governing Church action. The concept of *nomokanon* refers, most precisely, to the practice of combining materials from lists of canon law as well as civil law. Such intermixing of kinds began as early as the 4th century as the emperors directly involved themselves in the conciliar resolutions. Of such nomokanonical lists there are two that are most noteworthy: *Nomokanon of Fourteen Titles* (630) and *Nomokanon of Fifty Titles* (*c.*570). The *Nomokanon of Fourteen Titles* was the most important source of canon law for the Eastern Church, much of which was incorporated into other collections of canons. It was compiled during the rule of the emperor Herakleios (7th century) as a chronological list of canons. Subsequent editions that incorporate additional canonical legislation appear in the late 9th (by Photios?), 11th (by Theodore Bestes), and 12th (by Theodore Balsamon) centuries. Theodore Balsamon includes a commentary. Among the sources of civil laws incorporated into the work is the *Corpus Juris Civilis*.

Another important canonist in the East was John III Scholastikos, patriarch of Constantinople (565–77), who composed the *Nomokanon of Fifty Titles*, which introduced a more efficient cataloguing system over previous lists; i.e. John arranged canons by topic rather than chronological sequence. This work included all 85 apostolic canons and 67 fragments from the epistles of Basil, and other conciliar resolutions.

Rome also had its *nomokanons* and nomokanonists. The most important compiler in Rome was a monk named Dionysius Exiguus who compiled, in the mid-6th century, a number of canonical lists remarkable for their breadth. His book of decretals, the *Liber Decretorum*, and his compilation of eastern, North African, and Roman lists, the *Liber Canonum*, which included 20 resolutions of Sardica (343), 138 canons of Carthage (419), 50 apostolic canons, and resolutions from 8 eastern councils (Nicaea, Ancyra, Neo-Caesarea, Gangra, Antioch, Laodicea, Constantinople, and Chalcedon) together formed the *Dionysiana* given by pope Hadrian I to Charlemagne in 774 as a basis for legislative and juridical conduct.

Efforts to harmonize and eliminate irrelevant canons were undertaken by Theodore Balsamon, patriarch of Antioch, who wrote a commentary on the *Nomokanon of Fourteen Titles* and by Matthew Blastera (died 1346), a monk living in Thessalonica.

JAMES L. SIEBACH

See also Canon Law, Councils

Further Reading

Canon Law Society of America, *Code of Canons of the Eastern Churches*, Washington D.C.: Canon Law Society of America, 1992

Meyendorff, John, *Byzantine Theology: Historical Trends and Doctrinal Themes*, 2nd edition, New York: Fordham University Press, 1983

Munier, C., Nomokanon entry in *Encyclopedia of the Early Church*, edited by Angelo Di Berardino, 2 vols, Cambridge: James Clarke, and New York: Oxford University Press, 1992

Nicolaides, J. (translator), *The Rudder of the Orthodox Catholic Church: The Compilation of the Holy Canons by Saints Nicodemus and Agapius*, Chicago, 1983

Owen, Dorothy M., *The Medieval Canon Law: Teaching, Literature, and Transmission*, Cambridge and New York: Cambridge University Press, 1990

Percival, H.R., *The Seven Ecumenical Councils of the Undivided Church*, vol. 14 of *Nicene and Post-Nicene Fathers*, 2nd series, edited by Philip Schaff and Henry Wace, reprinted Peabody, Massachusetts: Hendrickson, 1994

Nonnus

Epic poet of the 5th century AD

Although Nonnus was born in Panopolis, he most probably lived in Alexandria, and travelled extensively in the eastern part of the empire, particularly Asia Minor and Constantinople. He wrote an epic poem of approximately 25,000 lines with the title *Dionysiaca*. As the title suggests, it is about Dionysus, dealing particularly with the subject of Dionysus in India (books 13–40). There was a fascination with Dionysiac themes in both art and literature in late antiquity and Nonnus was not the first to deal with this topic: Euphorion and Dinarchus from Delos were his predecessors in the choice of Dionysiac themes in poetry.

His work stands on the borderline between the ancient and the Byzantine worlds. There is an apparent imitation of Homeric forms, although the metrical similarity is strictly technical. The decision to write an epic poem would almost inevitably put an author in competition with the Homeric poems. Nonnus uses Homeric vocabulary, although as a student of Hellenistic poetry he transforms it into more sophisticated usage. He is inspired by Homeric narrative techniques as well as the epic heroic atmosphere, which he tries to recreate in his own work. Passages such as the two proems, the weaving of Aphrodite in book 24, the shield of Dionysus in book 25, the theomachy in book 36, the various extensive catalogues (books 13, 14, and 26), as well as the presentation of the gods bear witness to both a structural and a more substantial inheritance from Homer. Nonnus was also influenced by Hellenistic poetry. There are many parallels with some love epigrams of the *Greek Anthology*. His use of *propemptika* (dirges) and erotic narrative, as well as his erudite concern with aetiological stories and pastoral motifs, place him in the literary tradition of the Alexandrian school. The pastoral mode is only too evident in the episodes of Actaeon and Ampelus, and Hymnus and Nicaea.

The context of the *Dionysiaca* is inspired by Alexander's expedition to India, the "new Dionysus". This gives Nonnus the opportunity to present an accumulation of various legends and fables on the Dionysiac tradition, with the defect of creating a heavily erudite style, as many scholars argue. Such condemnations, however, do not take into consideration the literary tradition that Nonnus had inherited and the transition in the literary tradition that took place at this very time, with the result that even recent scholarship lacks appreciation of late antique poetry. The historical element that is inserted in an epic context reshapes the poetic ideals of the epic. On the other hand, a rigorous rhetorical tradition has been established and plays an important role in contemporary literary products. There is also a significant debate as to whether there are intertextual allusions to Latin poetry, particularly Ovid and Virgil, which has not yet reached a conclusion. His choice of fusing Dionysian motifs with Alexandrian legends could be appropriated by the emperors who campaigned in the east, revealing also that literature is not alien to contemporary politics, and has a cultural, historical, and even political context.

A major innovation is Nonnus' choice to make Dionysus the central hero of an epic that clearly is indebted to the Homeric epics, even though Dionysus is almost absent in Homer. There was a rich literary and artistic tradition associated with the figure of Dionysus that Nonnus exploited. Dionysus, the wandering god, who transformed himself from youth to old man and vice versa, enjoyed an immense popularity and proved to be the other side of the coin to the Alexandrian theme. Dionysus had a particular appeal to contemporary ideological tensions, for both pagans and Christians. According to Eusebius, Dionysus played an important role in soteriological hagiography, since he appeared from antiquity as a god offering salvation. John Malalas, a historian of the 6th century AD, argued that Dionysus was a mortal, stating that his tomb could be found at Delphi. Glen Bowersock (in Hopkinson) writes that the parallel between Christ and Dionysus was responsible for producing the semi-theatrical work *Christos Paschon* [Christ Suffering], in which Christ replaces Dionysus in a verse borrowed from Euripides, an identification that lies, according to Eusebius and Malalas, at the heart of the Nonnian epic.

Nonnus is also believed to be the author of a paraphrase in epic hexameters of St John's gospel, with the title *Metabole of*

John's Holy Gospel. This is not a simple paraphrase of the gospel, and it renders the personality of Nonnus even more complicated. Some scholars have argued against Nonnian authorship of this work, adducing mostly stylistic arguments. Although the Christian religion had long been established in the Roman empire, the polarities of paganism and Christianity still existed. Some scholars have argued that it is due to Nonnus' conversion to Christianity that the *Dionysiaca* was left unfinished; others say that the domination of pagan motifs was not as unacceptable as we may think for a Christian poet, and place Nonnus' conversion much earlier, if it ever happened.

ANDROMACHE KARANIKA-DIMAROGONA

See also Poetry (Epic)

Biography

Born in Panopolis in Egypt in the first half of the 5th century AD, Nonnus probably lived in Alexandria and travelled widely in the eastern empire. He was the author of an epic poem entitled *Dionysiaca* in 48 books which deals particularly with Dionysus in India. He is also credited with a poetic paraphrase of St John's gospel.

Writings

Dionysiaca, translated by W.H.D. Rouse, 3 vols, London: Heinemann, and Cambridge, Massachusetts: Harvard University Press, 1940–42 (Loeb edition; several reprints)
Les Dionysiaques, edited by Joelle Gerbeau and Francis Vian, Paris: Belles Lettres, 1992 (Greek text and French translation)

Further Reading

Chuvin, P., *Mythologie et géographie dionysiaques: Recherches sur l'oeuvre de Nonnos de Panopolis*, Clermont-Ferrand: ADOSA, 1991
Fauth, Wolfgang, *Eidos poikilon* [Varied Form]: *Zur Thematik der Metamorphose und zum Prinzip der Wandlung aus dem Gegensatz in den Dionysiaca des Nonnos von Panopolis*, Göttingen: Vandenhoeck & Ruprecht, 1981
Hopkinson, Neil (editor), *Studies in the Dionysiaca of Nonnus*, Cambridge: Cambridge Philological Society, 1994

Normans

The Normans were former Vikings who had settled in Normandy under Rollo in 911 and had become Frenchified. It is said that they were great assimilators who, once established, aped the manners of their neighbours, perhaps as a form of self-improvement, doing so in Normandy, England, southern Italy, Sicily, Antioch, and Edessa. The Byzantines themselves employed the Normans as mercenaries, as did most of the other kingdoms of Europe.

It seems likely that it was its reputation as a land of milk and honey that first attracted the Normans to southern Italy. The Norman kingdom that was established in 1130 was regarded as one of the strongest and wealthiest monarchies in western Europe, yet there never was a Norman masterplan for its creation: it emerged as events took their course. At all times the Normans were a tiny minority in Italy, far fewer in number than their fellows who had invaded England in 1066.

The first definite reference to Normans being employed as mercenaries by the Lombard nobility of southern Italy is in 1017. The year 1030 was something of a landmark too when Rainulf le Tonnelier (Ralph the Cooper) was granted land at Aversa by Sergius IV, duke of Naples. Around 1035 Drogo, Humphrey, and William from the impoverished Norman family of Hauteville arrived and entered the service of Gaimar of Salerno. In the years 1038–40 Byzantine forces campaigned against the Muslims of Sicily assisted by Gaimar and Norman mercenaries. The Lombards, backed by the Normans, rose in revolt against the overbearing conduct of the Byzantine general George Maniakes. It was not until the last stages of the rebellion in 1042 that the Normans began to take advantage of the situation. Up to 1040 they had seemed content to remain mercenaries. During the next century they established their hold over southern Italy and Sicily, capturing Messina (1061), Bari, the last Byzantine base in Italy (1071), Palermo (1072), and Syracuse (1085).

In 1046 Robert de Hauteville (Guiscard) arrived to join his half-brothers Drogo and Humphrey. In 1057 he succeeded them as count of Aversa. The most famous of the Norman adventurers, he was in many ways an appalling man who had gained his by-name from his stratagems but one who became a national hero and was placed by Dante in Paradise. Just as Guiscard (d. 1085) was not interested in his lands *per se* but went on to ever further conquests, so his brother Roger (d. 1101), who joined him in 1058, seems to have been a man of genuine political ability who held Sicily as a fief from his brother.

The Normans were hated in Italy and not surprisingly neither the western nor the eastern emperors would recognize their conquests. Their initial reception by the popes had been hostile too; in 1053 Leo IX had led an army against them which they had defeated at Civitate. Yet in 1059 there was something of a reconciliation when the pope recognized Guiscard as duke of the yet unconquered Sicily, seeing in the Normans a strong power to the south of Rome that might be used to counterbalance a strong imperial presence in northern Italy. Friction between pope Gregory VII (1072–85) and Guiscard troubled relations between the monasteries of southern Italy and their would-be Norman patrons. Following the reconciliation of Gregory and Guiscard at Ceprano in June 1080, lavish grants were made by Guiscard and his second wife to Montecassino and other monasteries; their example was followed by lesser Normans in southern Italy. In 1084 it was the Normans who rescued Gregory VII from Rome and the clutches of the German king and Holy Roman emperor Henry IV (1050–1106) and his antipope Wibert (Clement III), but with appalling bloodshed and destruction. Gregory spent the last year of his life under Norman protection at Salerno.

There was little response among the Norman rulers of southern Italy to Urban II's call for a crusade in 1095. Only Bohemond, prince of Taranto, left in 1096. On Guiscard's death in 1085 he had been passed over as ruler of southern Italy in favour of his half-brother Roger Borsa (d. 1111) and he seemed to have no future in the south. In 1098 he became prince of Antioch.

It was Guiscard's nephew Roger II (died 1154) who became count of Sicily in 1105, and it was he who united the Norman territories in southern Italy. First he was recognized as heir to Guiscard's mainland territories by pope Honorius II in 1128 and one year later he secured recognition as suzerain by Robert II of Capua. In 1130 he took advantage of a papal schism between Innocent II and Anacletus II to secure a royal coronation from the latter who was desperate for support. The Norman counts of Sicily had become kings of Sicily and southern Italy. Once established, the Norman kings took part in the dynastic history of Europe.

In any Mediterranean-orientated society Sicily will be of immense commercial and strategic importance. Their possession of the island led its Norman rulers into military ambitions elsewhere in the Mediterranean, although interestingly when they turned from infiltration to outright conquest they met with middling success. In 1091 Malta was conquered, but attacks on the coast of North Africa (approximating to modern Algeria) in 1118 and 1123 did not result in a permanent settlement. Norman attempts to conquer the southern Balkan peninsula were similarly frustrated by Byzantine and Venetian opposition. First in the years 1081–85 Guiscard's attacks on Corfu and Dyrrachium (Durazzo) were checked by Alexios I; in 1107 Bohemond was defeated in a second attack on Dyrrachium and was forced to sign the Treaty of Devol acknowledging Byzantine suzerainty over his principality of Antioch; in 1147 Roger II raided Thebes and Corinth carrying off silk workers to Sicily; and finally in 1185 the Normans briefly occupied Thessalonica before being driven out by a Byzantine relieving force under Alexander Branas. The occupation and the Norman's behaviour towards the Greeks were described by Eustathios of Thessalonica. All in all, Norman attempts at conquests in the Byzantine empire were heavily defeated. Neither Byzantium nor Venice could tolerate one power controlling both shores of the southern Adriatic.

In southern Italy and Sicily there emerged a cosmopolitan and remarkable state – one that owed little to Norman institutions but relied upon Greeks, Muslims, and settlers brought in from mainland Italy where the official languages were French, Greek, Arabic, and Latin, and where four religions coexisted in apparent harmony. It is a state all too easy to eulogize. Through time Latin elements came to predominate in the administration, Muslims were largely confined to the fortress settlement of Lucera, and Greek priests came under considerable pressure to Latinize. Norman Sicily appears none the less remarkably tolerant for its age and the capture of Palermo in 1072 stands as a monument to wise concessions and compares favourably to the capture of Jerusalem in 1099.

PETER LOCK

See also Sicily

Summary

The Normans first appeared in Italy as mercenaries to the Lombards in 1017. After 1040 they began to make their own conquests, taking Messina (1061), Bari (1071), Palermo (1072), and Syracuse (1085). The Norman kingdom of Sicily was established in 1130. But the Normans had no success against the Byzantines in the Balkans.

Further Reading

Abulafia, David, *The Western Mediterranean Kingdoms, 1200–1500*, London and New York: Longman, 1997

Loud, G., " How Norman Was the Norman Conquest of Southern Italy?", *Nottingham Medieval Studies*, 25 (1981): pp. 13–34

McQueen, W., "Relations between the Normans and Byzantium, 1071–1112", *Byzantion*, 56 (1986): pp. 427–76

Matthew, Donald, *The Norman Kingdom of Sicily*, Cambridge and New York: Cambridge University Press, 1992

Nicol, D., "Symbiosis and Integration: Some Greco-Latin Families in Byzantium in the 11th to 13th Centuries", *Byzantinische Forschungen*, 7 (1979): pp. 113–35

Shepard, J., "When Greek Meets Greek: Alexius Comnenus and Bohemond in 1097–98", *Byzantine and Modern Greek Studies*, 12 (1988): pp. 185–277

Novel

Ancient

Five complete lengthy fictional prose narratives (conveniently called "novels" or "romances") survive from Classical antiquity: *Callirhoe* by Chariton of Aphrodisias (8 books; probably 1st century AD); *Ephesian Story* by Xenophon of Ephesus (5 books; probably pseudonymous; 1st–2nd century AD); *Leucippe and Cleitophon* by Achilles Tatius (8 books; late 2nd century AD); *Daphnis and Chloe* by Longus (4 books; 2nd–3rd century); and *Ethiopian Story* by Heliodorus of Emesa (10 books; 3rd–4th century AD). In addition Photios in the 9th century read and summarized at length two works now lost: *The Wonders beyond Thule* by Antonius Diogenes (24 books; late 2nd century AD) and *Babylonian Story* by Iamblichus (16 books; soon after AD 165). Since the 19th century, our knowledge has been supplemented by the discovery of papyrus fragments of several more lost novels, the most important of which is the so-called *Ninus Romance*, probably of the 1st century BC and thus the earliest known example of the genre.

The extant works form a tightly knit corpus of "ideal" romances, all sharing essentially the same plot: a beautiful and noble couple fall in love and, either before or just after marriage, pass through a number of adventures, generally including separation and extensive and perilous journeys during which they encounter pirates and suffer shipwreck, apparent death, and unwelcome amatory advances from rivals of both sexes, remaining faithful to one another until they are eventually reunited and return home, implicitly to live happily ever after in a state of wedded bliss. The patron gods of the romantic world are Tyche (Chance) and Eros; the role of the protagonists is generally to suffer nobly and lament tragically, rarely to act decisively. Despite the skill that some novelists show in characterization, the interests of the form as a whole are with plot rather than psychology. However, all the individual writers vary the basic formula to some extent, and some of the papyri are radically different in tone and content, indicating that the apparent uniformity of the genre is in fact largely due to the tastes of Christian Byzantium.

The novel was the last of the literary genres to appear in antiquity, and much scholarly labour has been devoted to the question of its origins. Particularly influential was Erwin Rohde's hypothesis that it arose from a combination of travel stories and Hellenistic erotic narrative poetry. Others have suggested that the novel evolved out of Hellenistic historiography, with its concern for emotional effect, or New Comedy, with which it shares plot elements of amatory intrigue, or obscure local legends, or have sought the roots of the Greek novel in the narrative traditions of Egypt and the Near East. More recently, however, a consensus has emerged that the undoubted similarities and references to earlier literature – particularly the central texts of Homeric epic, and Classical tragedy, rhetoric, and historiography – are less a sign of the genre's origins than of a deliberate self-positioning in the Classical tradition on the part of its exponents.

This bears on the important question of the readership of these early novels. There is very little direct evidence on this point. The novel was neglected by ancient critics, to the extent that there was not even an agreed term for this type of literature before the Byzantine period. The few references to novels and novel-reading are unanimously uncomplimentary. This silence played to the prejudices of 19th-century scholars against romantic fiction, and gave rise to a widely held view that the novel was intended for a mass readership created by the spread of literacy in Hellenistic times, and including such marginal groups as women, young people, and the half-educated. However, as physical objects the novel papyri are indistinguishable in quality from other texts, in no way suggesting a cheap and down-market product, and their numbers remain relatively modest, although we cannot be certain to what extent any given copy may have circulated from reader to reader. Even the simplest of the novels would require a high level of literacy on the part of its readers, and the intertextual play of most of them implies an audience intimately familiar with a wide range of literature. In other words, it looks as if the people who bought and read novels were more or less those who read the rest of Greek literature.

This conclusion in its turn implies that the novel as a genre emerged to supply a market demand for pleasurable reading among the educated urban elite of the Greek east in the Hellenistic and imperial periods. We must not, of course, assume that every reader at every period had the same motive for reading novels, but it seems likely that the novel, as a form, was intended for private reading and that the thematic centrality of love reflects a new concern with the individual self. Moreover, all the novels deal in some oblique form with the question of what it means to be Greek and stress a continuity with the Hellenic past that pointedly ignores the very existence of Rome. Interestingly, none of the surviving novelists was a native of the Greek mainland, and several of them were of non-Greek extraction, indicating that the national identity they assert was cultural rather than racial. The central feature of the romantic plot, the exclusive and passionate love of a heterosexual couple, is an important cultural innovation. The Classical model of disparity between sexual partners with an interior dialectic to master potentially disruptive emotions is replaced by a fully reciprocal passion, viewed positively as a valid basis for personal happiness and marital stability. It is difficult to know to what extent the sexual ethic of the novels reflects a movement towards romantic behaviour in real life, but the aspirations it embodies are as much civic as personal. The marriage that is consummated or resumed at the climax of the plot is not just a way of socializing passion, but is in itself a social function, a celebration of the ancestry and self-perpetuation of Hellenic aristocracy and its values and culture.

The earliest novels have a distinctly historical thrust, as if legitimizing their problematic fictionality by filling up the unwritten corners of history. The earliest known novel takes the legendary figures of Ninus and Semiramis – accepted as historical from Herodotus onwards – and transforms them into romantically attached adolescent cousins coyly seeking parental assent to an early marriage. Chariton sets his story in the years following the Peloponnesian War, with a heroine who is a historically attested daughter of the Syracusan statesman Hermocrates, and a Persian king Artaxerxes facing a revolt in Egypt apparently modelled on that of 360 BC. Among the fragmentary novels is one whose protagonists are the son of Miltiades and the daughter of Polycrates of Samos, and whose scenario plays out around events recorded by Herodotus. Later novels emancipated themselves from literal historicity, and in some cases moved their plots into more exotic locations, which none the less adhere to a geographical and historical verisimilitude defined by Greek literary tradition.

There is a marked division among the five extant novels between, on the one hand, Chariton and Xenophon, who are relatively simple in construction and expression, and, on the other, the three later authors, whose erudition and complexity are clearly linked with the rhetorical renaissance known as the Second Sophistic. Chariton tells his story with pace and skill, in a style modelled on that of Xenophon, maintaining the pose of a historian roughly contemporary with the events he narrates. Although his is probably the earliest European novel to have survived, it is already playing with the ethical simplicity of its generic stereotypes. Its heroine, for example, is apparently kicked to death by her beloved but jealous husband near the beginning of the book. Reviving in the tomb, she is stolen by tomb-robbers and taken to Miletus, where she discovers that she is pregnant and reluctantly agrees to a bigamous second marriage for the sake of her unborn child. The second husband, who fills the conventional role of rival, is no villain, but a cultivated and morally scrupulous gentleman, agonizing over his infatuation. Xenophon's novel is, in terms of literary quality, the weakest of the five: baldly narrated and luridly imagined adventures succeed one another rapidly and with little rational connection, prompting the theory that what we have is only an epitome of a more satisfactory original. Of the sophistic novelists, Achilles Tatius is the only idealistic novelist to employ a first-person narrator, and his story often comes close to parodying the genre: the heroine Leucippe, for instance, would be only too happy to lose her virginity prematurely to the hero and narrator, Cleitophon, and is saved only by a comically sexual dream that leads her mother to interrupt their illicit tryst. Later, the theme of apparent death takes a Grand Guignol twist when Leucippe is ritually disembowelled before her lover's eyes and her entrails cooked and eaten, only for him to learn a couple of pages later that her sacrifice was an elaborately staged trick with a retractable knife and a sheep's bladder. Cleitophon for his part, when Leucippe is apparently decapitated, obsessively maintains his chaste devotion despite being married to an amorous and increasingly frustrated widow from Ephesus; but when his beloved and his wife's husband return miraculously from the dead, he casually consummates the now void marriage on a jailhouse floor before escaping disguised as a woman. Achilles packs his pages with sophistic digressions and rhetorical debates, for example on the relative merits of heterosexual and homosexual intercourse or the effects of love in the natural world. Of the two novels summarized by Photios, that of Antonius Diogenes was untypical of the genre: immensely long and relegating the love interest to subordinate episodes, it dealt primarily with travel and geographical paradoxography, leavened by a dose of black magic and the supernatural, and was elaborately structured as a series of concentric narratives, including some plausibly serious Neopythagorean philosophy. Iamblichus' novel seems to have been full of sensational and melodramatic incident, and innovated by keeping its lovers together in body but separated by psychological forces such as the heroine's homicidal jealousy.

The ideal romance was not the only form of fiction written in ancient Greek, but the absence of critical discussion from antiquity makes it impossible to know precisely how fictional genres were conceptualized. The old distinction between the serious idealistic Greek romance and the comic-realistic novel represented by the Latin writers Petronius and Apuleius seems untenable in the light of the recent identification of fragments such as those of the *Phoenician Story* of a certain Lollianus, which combine blood-curdling horror and scatological comedy. It may be that other boundaries, such as that between full-length novels and *Milesian Tales*, short stories of scabrous content, are equally illusory.

With the probable exception of Heliodorus, the production of novels apparently ceased early in the 3rd century AD, although papyri indicate that they were still read, at least in Egypt, in the 7th. The disappearance of the genre may be partly due to its inherent limitations and progressive ossification, but the most important causes must be sought in the changing cultural circumstances of late antiquity which removed its market appeal. However, motifs from the romances find their way into Christian narratives such as hagiographies, martyrologies, and apocryphal acts, and at least one of them (*Metiochus and Parthenope*) was absorbed into Near Eastern traditions. In Byzantium, Heliodorus and Achilles Tatius were to some extent privileged by the fact that their authors were believed to be Christian; Achilles' protagonists even resurface as the parents of St Galaktion of Emesa! Despite spasmodic signs of interest, including Photios in the 9th century and a spate of learned imitations in the 12th, the survival of the rest was precarious, and they had little direct influence either on the later vernacular romances or on the birth of the modern Greek novel, both of which looked to models from western Europe.

J.R. MORGAN

See also Romance

Texts

Achilles Tatius, *Le Roman de Leucippé et Clitophon*, edited by Jean-Philippe Garnaud, Paris: Belles Lettres 1991 (Greek text and French translation); as *Leucippe and Clitophon*, translated by John J. Winkler, in Reardon 1989

Chariton, *Callirhoe*, translated by G.P. Goold, Cambridge, Massachusetts: Harvard University Press, 1995 (Loeb edition)

Reardon, B.P. (editor), *Collected Ancient Greek Novels*, Berkeley: University of California Press, 1989

Stephens, Susan A. and John J. Winkler (editors), *Ancient Greek Novels: The Fragments*, Princeton, New Jersey: Princeton University Press 1995

Xenophon of Ephesus, *Ephesiacorum libri V: De amoribus Anthiae et Abrocomae*, edited by A.D. Papanikolaou, Leipzig: Teubner 1973; as *An Ephesian Tale*, translated by Graham Anderson, in Reardon 1989

Further Reading

Doody, Margaret Anne, *The True Story of the Novel*, New Brunswick, New Jersey: Rutgers University Press, 1996; London: HarperCollins, 1997

Fusillo, Massimo, *Il romanzo greco: polifonia ed eros*, Venice: Marsilio, 1989

Hägg, Tomas, *The Novel in Antiquity*, Oxford: Blackwell, and Berkeley: University of California Press, 1983

Heiserman, Arthur, *The Novel before the Novel: Essays and Discussions about the Beginnings of Prose Fiction in the West*, Chicago: University of Chicago Press, 1977

Holzberg, Niklas, *The Ancient Novel: An Introduction*, London and New York: Routledge, 1995

Konstan, David, *Sexual Symmetry: Love in the Ancient Novel and Related Genres*, Princeton, New Jersey: Princeton University Press, 1994

Morgan, J.R. and Richard Stoneman (editors), *Greek Fiction: The Greek Novel in Context*, London and New York: Routledge, 1994

Perry, B.E., *The Ancient Romances: A Literary Historical Account of Their Origins*, Berkeley: University of California Press, 1967

Reardon, B.P., *The Form of Greek Romance*, Princeton, New Jersey: Princeton University Press, 1991

Rohde, Erwin, *Der griechische Roman und seine Vorläufer*, 4th edition, Hildesheim: Olms, 1960

Schmeling, Gareth (editor), *The Novel in the Ancient World*, Leiden: Brill, 1996

Swain, Simon (editor), *Oxford Readings in the Greek Novel*, Oxford and New York: Oxford University Press, 1999

Tatum, James (editor), *The Search for the Ancient Novel*, Baltimore: Johns Hopkins University Press, 1994

Modern

The rise of the novel in 18th-century England is not normally associated with ancient or medieval Greek novels such as those by Longus or Heliodorus as these were not part of the regular Classical curriculum. It was different in Greece where in the early 19th century a revival or interest in Classical culture led to claims that Greeks had invented the novel. Thus the first Greek novels published after Independence, with their strong emphasis on romantic love, undoubtedly have affinities with ancient and medieval models. This is true of the first modern Greek novel, *Leander*, published in 1834 by Panayotis Soutsos, although references to Johann Wolfgang Goethe and Ugo Foscolo in the preface show other influences. Soutsos's brother Alexandros in the next year published *The Exile of 1831* dealing with recent history in the fashion of Sir Walter Scott. With inspiration both from Greece and Western Europe, a rich Classical and Byzantine heritage, and a turbulent and sometimes tragic history to draw upon, Greek novelists have no shortage of material. Indeed, it could be argued both that individual Greek novelists became confused by the wealth of subject matter, and that the history of the Greek novel as a whole is confused by the variety of different influences.

Most 19th-century novelists were strongly realist, but Greece lacked professional novel writers like Charles Dickens and Honoré de Balzac, and until the end of the century did not really have a novel-reading public as in Western Europe. A few names stand out. Pavlos Kalligas's novel *Thanos Vlekas* (1855) owes something to the ancient Greek novel with its highflown style and simple allegory of the fight between good and evil, although there are nice touches of social realism. Emmanouil Roidis's *Pope Joan* (1866) is a bitter satire against the Orthodox Church. Both authors had been educated in the West; a more typically Greek product was Alexandros Rangavis's *Lord of the Morea* (1850), a historical novel owing a debt to *The Chronicle of the Morea* and to Scott. Towards the end of the century, although often fiction writers chose to write short stories rather than novels, there were moves forwards under the influence of Emile Zola towards total realism and to experimentation with novels challenging the realistic convention. Andreas Karkavitsas's *The Beggar* (1896) and Alexandros Papadiamantis's *The Murderess* (1903) display both these characteristics.

In the 20th century pressing political events such as the disaster in Asia Minor, World War II and the subsequent Civil War, and the ideological clashes between left and right played an important part in a great many novels. Simultaneously, novelists were affected by literary movements in the West, notably symbolism, and by a wish to bring in Greece's Classical and medieval past. Greece's most famous novelist is Nikos Kazantzakis (1883–1957). Like many other Greek writers of fiction, he was also active in poetry and drama, most of his novels being written towards the end of his life. *Zorba the Greek*, published in 1946, although written in the period of the Nazi occupation, deals with 20th-century Crete, but has references to Plato's dialogues, and like his earlier epic poem *The Odyssey* is full of links to the literature of the world. *Christ Recrucified*, written in 1949, but published in 1954, is set in Anatolia just before the disastrous war of 1919–22, but reflects on perceptions Kazantzakis had gained outside Greece, reaches outside the bounds of realism, and has echoes of the Civil War, a subject to which he returned in *The Fratricides*, posthumously published in 1963, but written much earlier. Kazantzakis is the Greek novelist most readily available in translation. He is hardly typically Greek, having spent most of his life as a novelist in the United States, but his novels do reflect Greece's explosive and encyclopedic heritage.

Less well-known novelists with a rather longer career are Stratis Myrivilis (1892–1969) and Ilias Venezis (1904–73). Both lived in Mytilini, and both were affected by the Anatolian campaign. Both gave a new edge to that type of Greek novel which had concentrated on life in a small community, adding a few romantic touches. Myrivilis's *Life in The Tomb* (1924) dealing with World War I and Venezis's *Number 31328* (1924) dealing with the aftermath of the Anatolian campaign are clearly based on first-hand experience but ask deep metaphysical questions. Later novels by both authors such as *The Mermaid Madonna* (1949) by Myrivilis and *Aeolian Earth* (1943) by Venezis ran into difficulty with censorship under the Metaxas dictatorship and the war years. Experimental novels such as Yorgos Theotokas's *Argo* (1933) show the weight of history with which the Greek novel has to contend. There are references to contemporary historical characters such as Venizelos and Mussolini as well as glances back to Byzantine history and Classical legend, and the novel is full of religious symbolism as well as including links with European fiction. And yet, in spite of the breathless speed of its second volume, *Argo* achieves a kind of detachment as well as preserving its essential Greekness. Both of these latter features are lacking in the work of M. Karagatsis (1909–60) whose tragic characters, all foreigners, are driven to their doom by a sexual passion too powerful for them to control.

Karagatsis and Theotokas were able to bring Greek fiction into line with the main stream of European literature, as represented by such authors as Gustave Flaubert and Fyodor Dostoevsky. Another group of writers based on Thessalonica were more interested in writers such as James Joyce and tried to break away from realism altogether. Yannis Skirimbos (1893–1984) anticipates Samuel Beckett. Nikos Pentzikizis (1909–92) has a hero in his first novel who turns himself into a pot plant before drowning himself in despair in a manner reminiscent of some of Franz Kafka's heroes.

These experiments came to a fairly abrupt end with the imposition of the Metaxas dictatorship in 1936, followed by three years of Axis occupation. None of the writers previously mentioned was particularly sympathetic to communism or subject to censorship and repression, but a number of the novelists who had seemed experimental in the 1920s and early 1930s now returned to more traditional themes, often reverting to the experiences of their early years, sometimes delving back into the remoter past. Myrivilis and Venezis wrote about rural villages before 1922, Theotokas about Constantinople at the turn of the century, Pentzikis in his second novel *The Dead Man and the Resurrection*, finished in 1938, published in 1944, described the history of Thessalonica. Kosmos Politis (1888–1974), who had previously written novels about smart Athenian society, in *Eroica* (1937) deftly blended memories of his native Smyrna with parallels from the *Iliad*. Both novels contain innovative touches and, as with Melpi Axioti in *Difficult Nights* (1938), perhaps try to do too much in linking modernist trends with the weight of oral tradition and in trying to be both European and Greek.

Two women novelists, writing at the very beginning of the Civil War, chose to retreat to the 1930s, although both *Straw Hats* (1946) by Margarita Lymberaki and *Contretemps* by Mimika Kranaki (1947) are full of ominous portents, and the latter novel touches upon the German invasion and the People's Army. Angelas Terzakis and Karagatsis wrote long novels, *Without a God* (1951) and *The Yellow File* (1956) respectively, which end on the brink of World War II, but contain implied criticisms of communism. *The Yellow File* is an elaborate construction about the life of a novelist who thought he could view the world with scientific objectivity and even reform it accordingly, but ignored human nature. There were realistic attempts to portray the war. Yannis Beratis, who also wrote experimental novels, produced in 1946 an account of the Albanian campaign and the struggle of the right-wing guerrillas in Epirus in *The Broad River* and *Itinerary of 1943*. Theotokas wrote *Sacred Way* (1950) and *Invalids and Travellers* (1964) about the war against the Germans and the Civil War in the same almost documentary fashion.

Experimental novels did not really become more popular until the more prosperous 1960s, although Lymberaki published *The Other Alexander* (1950), a curious allegorical novel about two branches of a family with an explicit reference to the Civil War. Tatiana Gritsi-Milliex in *Behold A Pale Horse* (1963) and Stratis Tzirkas in *Drifting Cities* (1960–65) wrote accounts of recent events from a left-wing viewpoint with a certain amount of experimentation. The best-selling novel of the 1960s, frequently reprinted thereafter, was *Farewell Anatolia* by Dido Sotiriou (1962). This dealt with the Anatolian disaster, but said that it was international capitalism which had brought it about. Other allegorical novels were *The Dam* (1967) by Spyros Plaskovitis, a surprising last novel by Theotokas, *The Bells* (1966), and Pentzikis's masterpiece, *The Novel of Mrs Ersi* (1966), a good combination of traditional Greek motifs and western postmodernism.

Novels by Lymberaki, *The Rite* (1976), by her daughter, Margarita Karapanou, *Cassandra and the Wolf* (1977), *Usurped Authority* (1979) by Alexander Kotzias, and *Fools' Gold* (1979) by Maro Douka reflect the conditions under the Colonels, and *The Box* (1974) by Aris Alexandrou is an allegorical tale of the Civil War made more bitter by recent experiences. All of these works deal with Greek history, but not as objective truth; the narrator's search for the exact truth in *The Box* is shown to be as empty as the box in which he supposedly carries the papers which record his mission. *Fool's Gold* admits that the heroine's reminscences of the 1967 coup may be inaccurate, and points out the inadequacy of language to describe reality.

Three novels of the 1980s, *History* (1982) by Yoryis Yatromanalakis, *The Seventh Garment* (1983) by Evyenia Fakinou, and *The Life of Ismail Ferik Pasha* (1989) by Rea Galanaki, all deal with the recent Greek past, all recall the ancient Greek past, and all try to come to terms with modern Western influences. Like other writers, notably Kazantzakis, they may be accused of taking on too much, of trying to do many things at once; at the same time they achieve a fair amount of success, and the way forward for the Greek novel looks as promising if as baffling as it does for the novel in general.

T.J. WINNIFRITH

Further Reading

Beaton, Roderick, *An Introduction to Modern Greek Literature*, 2nd edition, Oxford: Clarendon Press, 1999

Bien, Peter, *Nikos Kazantzakis: Novelist*, Bristol: Bristol Classical Press, and New Rochelle, New York: Caratzas, 1989

Politis, Linos, *A History of Modern Greek Literature*, Oxford: Clarendon Press, 1973

O

Obsidian

Obsidian is a kind of volcanic glass, normally dark blue to black in colour. It is exceptionally hard, fractures in the same way as flint, and, like flint, was employed to provide razor-sharp cutting edges for tools (including knives and sickles) and weapons (including arrowheads). Studies of the techniques of manufacture of marble figurines have suggested that obsidian implements were among the tools employed.

In use from the Palaeolithic period, obsidian seems to have been most commonly employed in the Aegean during the Neolithic and Early Bronze Age, before bronze had become widely available. In the Late Bronze Age, vessels were occasionally manufactured of this material, usually a variegated type.

Investigation of the extent to which obsidian continued to be used in later antiquity has proved somewhat inconclusive but it seems likely that, in addition to flint and chert, it was a regular alternative to metal in places where the latter was unavailable because of cost or inaccessibility. Today these materials are still sometimes used by primitive agricultural communities for the "teeth" of sickles and threshing sledges, and they have been employed for gun flints.

The only two ancient Aegean sources of obsidian are on the islands of Melos (in the southwestern Cyclades) and Yiali (by Nisiros in the Dodecanese). That on Melos was the earlier and by far the most important; Yiali obsidian was used for most of the Late Bronze Age vessels mentioned previously. Melian obsidian is widely distributed on prehistoric sites in the central and south Aegean and on the Greek mainland as far north as Thessaly. Sometimes it is found in the form of finished artifacts, sometimes as unworked cores. The finer blades were struck off larger "cores", or else detached by "pressure flaking" with a wooden tool.

Obsidian was probably an important item of trade in prehistoric times. One theory sees the commodity exploited by the Melians and exported by them, either worked or unworked; another holds that the raw material was removed by visitors to the island, without reference to the locals, and worked elsewhere.

The significant contributions of obsidian to the Greek tradition seem chronologically limited to the prehistoric phase. It certainly played an important part in technological developments which affected warfare and various "industries" and crafts. Just as important however was its role in stimulating trade and contact, and in giving the Aegean area in general and Melos in particular some economic and cultural sway over their neighbours. Apparently Melian features in the pottery of other islands, and Cycladic exports to and influence on sites on the Greek mainland in the Early and Middle Cycladic periods, may have been brought about in this way.

In Classical and later times the use of obsidian helps to demonstrate the natural dependence of poorer and more remote communities on cheap and accessible raw materials, and thus relatively primitive technology. In this way clearly documented uses of the material can often illuminate prehistoric finds where direct evidence for the function is lacking. Such links also suggest a long and continuous history of use.

ROBIN L.N. BARBER

Further Reading

Barber, R.L.N., *The Cyclades in the Bronze Age*, London: Duckworth, 1987, pp. 113–19

Bosanquet, R.C., "The Obsidian Trade" in *Excavations at Phylakopi in Melos*, edited by T.D. Atkinson *et al.*, London: Macmillan, 1904

Getz-Preziosi, Pat, *Sculptors of the Cyclades: Individual and Tradition in the Third Millennium BC*, Ann Arbor: University of Michigan Press, 1987, p. 35

Oustinoff, E., "The Manufacture of Cycladic Figurines: A Practical Approach" in *Cycladica*, edited by J. Lesley Fitton, London: British Museum Publications, 1984

Renfrew, C., J.R. Cann, and J.E. Dixon, "Obsidian in the Aegean", *Annual of the British School at Athens*, 60 (1965): pp. 225–47

Runnels, C.N., "Flaked-Stone Artifacts in Greece during the Historical Period", *Journal of Field Archaeology*, 9 (1982): pp. 363–73

Theocharis, Demetrios R., *Neolithic Greece*, Athens: National Bank of Greece, 1973, p. 151, figs. 120, 155, 281

Torrence, Robin, "The Obsidian Quarries and their Use" in *An Island Polity: The Archaeology of Exploitation in Melos*, edited by Colin Renfrew and Malcolm Wagstaff, Cambridge and New York: Cambridge University Press, 1982

Torrence, Robin, *Production and Exchange of Stone Tools: Prehistoric Obsidian in the Aegean*, Cambridge and New York: Cambridge University Press, 1986

Warren, Peter M., *Minoan Stone Vases*, London: Cambridge University Press, 1969, pp. 135–36

Odessa

City on the north Black Sea coast

Odessa, now a city of more than one million inhabitants, is in Ukraine between the estuaries of the Dnieper and Dniester. Though long sought by the tsars, it was only in the time of Catherine the Great (1762–96) that Russian rule over the north coast of the Black Sea became a reality. Under Catherine two cities were founded in this newly acquired territory. The first was Kherson, near the mouth of the Dnieper on a site wrongly identified with ancient Greek Cherson. In 1794, two years after the Treaty of Jassy had further extended Russian rule, Catherine decided on a second port on the recommendation of Joseph de Riba, a Naples-born Spanish adventurer of Irish extraction. The site selected was Khadzhibei. Again a Greek name was chosen: Odessa; and again the identification was erroneous, for the new port lay far from the ancient Greek colony of Odessos which is Varna in Bulgaria. Perhaps it was hoped that the name would attract Greek merchants. The feminine *Odessa* for *Odessos* is said to have been chosen by Catherine at a court ball.

Odessa was at once an enormous success: it was soon the fastest-growing city in Europe. It "had no infancy", as a contemporary said. It occupied a splendid position on cliffs rising 60 m above the sea, a contrast to the dreary steppe to the north. The climate was benign, but for the dust storms from the thin limestone soil which turned to mud in winter. The deep harbour had ice only in January. Already by 1805 Odessa was the busiest port in the Black Sea. Until the Crimean War (1853–56), the black earth lands of Ukraine supplied much of western Europe with wheat, and even later in the century Odessa continued to supply Italian needs, for the high gluten content of wheat from Ukraine made it especially suitable for pasta. Religious toleration, encouragement of foreign immigrants, and low tariffs led to a burgeoning population swollen by runaway serfs, a "European Australia". Visitors remarked on the easy atmosphere which tolerated smoking in the streets, a practice frowned on in St Petersburg.

From 1803 to 1814 the governor appointed by the tsar was Armand Emmanuel du Plessis, Duc de Richelieu, a great-nephew of the cardinal, a hero of Byron and Pushkin and later minister of Louis XVIII. Richelieu was an attractive figure – modest, industrious, affable, and a good linguist – who mixed freely with the inhabitants. To him Odessa owes its gridiron plan, its spacious streets, and characteristic acacia (actually, locust) trees. Under his governorship, the population rose from 7500 to 35,000. In 1838 the American traveller John Stephens found Odessa with its broad, straight streets just like an American city. In the 1860s Mark Twain shared the same feelings. A Swiss visitor heard 20 tongues spoken and claimed that ten religions were practised. Italian then Greek were the principal business languages. Half the wheat exported from the docks went to Italy and the street names were in Italian as well as Russian.

Within a year of its foundation, Greeks, whether transient merchants or settlers from the archipelago, made up about 10 per cent of the population. A Greek battalion fought with the Russians against the Turks, and the Greek community made a financial contribution to the Russian war effort against Napoleon. By 1817 there were three Greek insurance companies, who established what became known as the second-best school in Odessa. Many Greek merchants became rich and powerful. Among these were the Inglesi, one of whom, Dimitrios, became mayor in 1818–21. John Ralli, whose family originated on Chios and whose connections extended over three continents, served as United States consul from 1832 to 1859. Stephens describes meeting him. Ralli was president of a society for the welfare of animals, although the ferocity of his dogs was such that rumour claimed they attacked his own servants. Also from Chios was the Rodonachi family with members in Livorno and Marseilles. Greek churches were built (one remained open in the Soviet period) and a monastery of St Panteleimon on the model of the Russian monastery on Athos (it is now the planetarium). The Mavrokordatos family contributed to industrial and cultural life. In 1814 a house in Odessa, now a museum, was the birth place of the *Philiki Hetaireia*. Greek coffee houses flourished. Later in the century, the Greeks were eclipsed by the Jews who became the second-largest group in the city after the Russians. The Greeks tended to resist the policy of assimilation favoured by the Russian authorities. There was endemic hostility between the Greek and Jewish populations and the pogrom of 1871 arose from Jewish–Greek rivalry. By the time of the censuses of 1892 and 1897 less than 2 per cent of the population spoke Greek and Greek-speakers were only the sixth-largest group. Many were only temporary residents. By then about half the population spoke Russian or Ukrainian, while just over 30 per cent spoke Yiddish.

During the Crimean War an Anglo-French squadron bombarded Odessa. The base of the statue of Richelieu was damaged, but a frigate, the *Tiger*, was lost and one of its guns is displayed not far from the statue. The years before World War I saw a decline in the fortunes of the city: development was inhibited by shortages of coal, wood, and fresh water; the railway was slow to come; industrial discontent grew and political and nationalist dissent flourished, as did crime. In June 1905 the mutinous battleship *Potemkin* sailed into Odessa; in subsequent disturbances some 600 people were killed and the docks were destroyed. (The famous scene on the monumental steps in Eisenstein's film is largely invention.)

The modern visitor can still enjoy the spacious boulevards with planes and chestnuts, as well as the acacias. Many buildings have been restored in pleasing pastel colours. The vines which festoon many apartment blocks produce grapes for New Year parties. The archaeological museum houses important exhibits from the Greek colony of Olbia on the Bug; these include coins, figurines, vases, and an inscription in Latin and Greek confirming privileges granted by the emperor Antoninus Pius (138–61). Other finds displayed are from Berezan island and from Tyras, Panticapaeum, and other Greek colonies on the northern shore of the Pontus.

M.E. MARTIN

See also Black Sea, Crimea

Summary

A city on the coast of the Ukraine, Odessa was founded by Catherine the Great in 1794. It grew fast and by 1805 was the busiest port in the Black Sea with a cosmopolitan population. The principal export was wheat. The Greek community was rich and powerful for much of the 19th century. It was the birthplace of the Friendly Society (*Philiki Hetaireia*) in 1814.

Further Reading

Herlihy, Patricia, "Greek Merchants in Odessa in the Nineteenth Century", part 1, *Harvard Ukrainian Studies*, 3–4 (1979–80): pp. 399–420

Herlihy, Patricia, *Odessa: A History, 1794–1914*, Cambridge, Massachusetts: Harvard University Press, 1986

Stephens, John, *Incidents of Travel in Greece, Turkey, Russia and Poland*, 2 vols, New York: Harper, 1838

Twain, Mark, *The Innocents Abroad*, Hartford, Connecticut: American Publishing Company, 1869; reprinted Oxford and New York: Oxford University Press, 1996

Ohrid

City in western Macedonia

The history of medieval and modern Ohrid – which is located on the northeast shore of Lake Ohrid very close to the site of ancient Lychnidos on the Via Egnatia – is mainly distinguished by ecclesiastical developments. The local diocese, which played an important role in Balkan history, was under Greek control for centuries.

The earliest references to medieval Ohrid are linked to the spread of Christianity in the Slavic Balkan areas in the late 9th century. As a result of Boris I's decision to adopt the Christian faith and to opt for the Eastern Orthodox Church, the Christianization of the south Slavs was accelerated and the basis for the foundation of a Bulgarian Church was laid down, in a period when Bulgarian rule extended in the western Balkans as far as the Adriatic. Yet, the establishment of the Orthodox Church proceeded differently in the eastern and western parts of the Bulgarian dominions. In the eastern part, the task was undertaken by Greek-speaking Byzantine clergy sent directly from Constantinople. But the Christianization of the western Bulgarian dominions in Macedonia and Albania was initiated by a mission of Slavonic-speakers led by St Clement and St Naum, both of whom were disciples of St Constantine (Cyril) and St Methodios who had led the Moravian mission (863). St Clement arrived in the region in 886 and settled in Ohrid, which is first recorded with respect to those events. There he worked towards the training of a Slavic-speaking clergy and also organized the building of churches and monasteries, including the earliest (trefoil) phase of St Panteleimon in Ohrid (which later became a mosque and is known as the *imaret*).

More emphasis was given to Ohrid later, when Samuel (*c*.976–1015) chose to establish a Bulgarian patriarch there in the heyday of his shortlived empire. In fact, Samuel's ecclesiastical arrangements were followed by his great enemy, the Byzantine emperor Basil II (976–1025), who, after crushing the last remnants of Bulgarian resistance in 1018 and aiming at the integration of the west Balkan Slavic population into the Byzantine empire, took the decision to preserve a Bulgarian Church based in Ohrid. His plans materialized in the formation of the archbishopric of Bulgaria, an autonomous ecclesiastical body under the patriarchate of Constantinople, with authority over the lands of Macedonia, Serbia, and Albania which were incorporated into the Byzantine state in 1018. Apparently the archbishopric of Ohrid had no authority over the eastern areas of Bulgaria proper. Moreover, the area of its jurisdiction was reduced in periods when the Serbians had their own independent Church, i.e. between 1219 and the Ottoman conquest, and after 1537 with the establishment of the Serbian patriarchate at Peć.

Basil II's plan was to preserve the Slavic character of the archbishopric of Bulgaria, so the first archbishop he appointed, John, was a Slav. The decision to Hellenize the archbishopric was taken by his successors who, as a first step, replaced John with a Greek archbishop, Leon, who is especially renowned for building the cathedral church of St Sophia in Ohrid. So began the line of Greek archbishops that lasted until the archbishopric was abolished in 1767. Among them were some important scholars, such as Theophylact (late 11th–early 12th centuries), whose works include a *Life of St Clement*, and Demetrios Chomatenos (d. *c*.1234), who crowned Theodore Doukas of Epirus emperor of the Romans in 1224. Apart from the archbishops, the other senior clergy were Greeks too, and Greek was the official language. Nevertheless, Slavic was not completely excluded and was used by many of the lower clergy.

The Greek dominance of the archbishopric was not affected by Bulgarian (1205/07–15 and 1230–46), Serbian (1334–71), Albanian (from 1371), or Ottoman (from the 1390s onwards) rule in Ohrid. As a matter of fact, this Greek dominance of the archbishopric became a primary factor in the development of Greek cultural influence, not just in Ohrid itself, but in the rest of the archbishopric's jurisdiction as well. The Greek element of the town's population was not limited to the staff of the church, but included many among the local elite, both landowning and commercial, and probably others. A distinguished personality among the Greeks of Ohrid was Prodromos Sgouros, who patronized the building of the Peribleptos church in the 13th century. Three centuries later, this church was rededicated to St Clement (it still bears this name) and became the archbishop's seat, after the church of St Sophia was converted into a mosque. As with several towns in Macedonia that had a strong Greek element, the history of Ohrid in the 18th century is marked by the development of Greek education and the foundation of Greek schools. It is unquestionable, however, that the majority of the town's population were Slavic, as they are today. The Greek element of Ohrid declined and finally perished in the years after 1913, as a result of the town's annexation by Serbia and the subsequent abolition of Greek educational and ecclesiastical institutions.

KONSTANTINOS P. MOUSTAKAS

Summary

A city now in the Former Yugoslav Republic of Macedonia, Ohrid is first mentioned in the 9th century when St Clement arrived to establish Christianity. It was probably the capital of the empire of Samuel of Bulgaria. Basil II established a Bulgarian Church with an archbishopric at Ohrid. From later in the 11th century until 1767 (when the archbishopric was abolished) the archbishops and senior clergy were Greeks. Local elites were also Greek to a considerable extent until 1913, when the town was annexed by Serbia.

Further Reading

Castellan, Georges, *Histoire des Balkans: XIVe–XXe siècle*, Paris: Fayard, 1991

Fine, J.V.A. Jr, *The Late Medieval Balkans: A Critical Survey from the Late Twelfth Century to the Ottoman Conquest*, Ann Arbor: University of Michigan Press, 1987

Gelzer, Heinrich, *Der Patriarchat von Achrida: Geschichte und Urkunden*, Leipzig, 1902

Kravari, Vassiliki, *Villes et villages de Macédoine occidentale*, Paris: Lethielleux, 1989

Snegarov, Ivan, *Istoriia na Okhridskata Arkhieskopiia*, 2 vols, Sofia, 1924–32

Theophylact, Archbishop of Bulgaria, *Life of St Clement of Ohrid* (medieval Greek text), in *Patrologia Graeca*, edited by J.-P. Migne, vol. 126

Vacalopoulos, A.E., *History of Macedonia, 1354–1833*, Thessalonica: Institute for Balkan Studies, 1973

Olbia

City on the north Black Sea coast

Olbia, situated on the right bank of the river Hypanis (today Bug), near the mouth of the river Borysthenes (now Dnieper) in modern Ukraine, was founded by the Milesians, possibly as early as the end of the 7th century BC (according to the finds). It was one of the largest Greek colonies on the north coast of the Black Sea and was well known in the ancient world. Surrounded by native tribes (Scythians, later Sarmatians), Olbia had close, but sometimes tense, relations with its hinterland. Already in the first half of the 6th century numerous small settlements had developed on both banks of the Hypanis and Borysthenes, the most important of them on the island of Berezan.

Written sources about Olbia are rather scarce (and are for the most part inscriptions), but there are rich archaeological finds; as there was no later reoccupation of the site, it has consequently suffered only from being used as a quarry in the 18th and 19th centuries for the construction of the Turkish (and later Russian) fortress at Ochakov, and for building houses in the neighbouring village of Parutino. The area has been excavated in many campaigns since 1901.

The ancient city had a triangular shape with an upper town and a lower one which is now largely submerged beneath the waters of the Bug. The upper town began to be settled in the 6th century BC; some of the excavated streets go back to that time (it has now become clear that Olbia never had a unified rectangular street system, as was long assumed). About 550 BC the temenos of Apollo Iatros was constructed, some 20 years later that of Apollo Delphinios, and – to the south of it – the agora followed. About 500 BC the style of private housing changed from dug-out dwellings to surface buildings.

The city was most prosperous from the 5th to the 3rd centuries BC. Its harbour was one of the main emporia on the Black Sea for the export of cereals, fish, and slaves to Greece, and for the import of Attic goods to Scythia. Its silver and bronze coins (not minted but cast) circulated widely. In the 5th century Olbia may have been intermittently under the sway of a local tyrant or of Scythian princes; at the beginning of the 4th century the city acquired a democratic constitution (*demos* and *boule* appear regularly in inscriptions). Already in the middle of the 5th century it had undertaken intense building activity (around this time Herodotus visited the city to gather information about the surrounding regions). The territory of the city increased, with the lower town now being populated as well; a water supply system and probably also the first city wall were built. The construction of private houses reached a peak at this time; the houses (built with stone or brick walls and tiled roofs), of one or two storeys, often had a cellar, wall painting, and mosaics. In the necropoleis found to the north, west, and south of the city many graves had vaulted tombs in a form characteristic of the north Pontic area.

The central *temenos* (precinct), dominated by the Ionic temple of Apollo Delphinios, was enlarged and given its trapezoidal form; apart from the main altar (with a platform probably for the priest and three holes for wine offerings), there were several other buildings in the precinct (further altars, a treasury, a cistern, a workshop for bronze). In the agora area a gymnasium was built, probably with a bath (enlarged in Hellenistic times). The western *temenos*, with a columned hall at its entrance, contained sanctuaries for Apollo Iatros and later for Hermes, Aphrodite, and the mother of the gods, a building of unclear function with three round and six rectangular altars. Since the 6th century BC one of the most important cults in the lower Bug region had been that of Achilles, imported by the Milesian colonists and originally centred on the island of Leuce (thought to be the dwelling place of the great hero), where the inhabitants of Olbia erected several monuments with inscriptions; countless magical graffiti, including the name of Achilles, were found in Olbia itself and its surroundings. Moreover, in the central *temenos* little plates made from bone with graffiti on them testify to the existence of a thriving community devoted to Orphism (a mystery cult centred around Dionysus and Orpheus) at Olbia in the 5th century. Many works of art (sculpture in stone, clay, and bronze and reliefs), imported from Greece as well as of local origin, have been found, such as a late Archaic *kouros* (naked youth) of limestone from the gymnasium, the famous grave stele of Molpagores' son Leoxos (490/480 BC) showing a naked youth in Greek style on one side and a person in Scythian clothing on the other, and the votive relief of the *sitones* (see below). There was also extensive local production of vases.

Reports of further political events are scarce. At the beginning of the Hellenistic period (probably around 325 BC) Zopyrion, Alexander the Great's governor of Thrace, made an unsuccessful attempt to take Olbia by force. New building activity shows the ongoing importance of Olbia as well as the persistence of threats from outside: numerous fortified farmhouses were built in the vicinity; the agora was provided with an impressive portico, and other new public buildings were constructed, the town walls renewed, and several towers added; a new cult, that of the god Demos ("people"), was established. Since the middle of the 3rd century BC, however, the whole agricultural territory of Olbia was repeatedly pillaged by invading barbarians, which put the nutritional base of the city severely at risk. A board of five *sitones* (food commissioners) was then installed who had to procure cereals and distribute them among the inhabitants; later the city tried to check famine, social unrest, and external threats by courting the leaders of the semibarbarian "Mixellenes" as allies. This led to the loss of the city's independence. In the middle of the 2nd century BC Olbia was under the overlordship of the Scythian king Skiluros, and in the 1st century BC it became part of the Bosporanian kingdom of Mithridates Eupator. The biggest disaster, however, came with the sack of the city by the Getae under King Burebista in 55 BC: Olbia was burned down and lost two-thirds of its settled area. Still, it continued to exist, albeit on a much smaller scale; more and more native people were integrated among the citizens, and these Scythian elements began to play a major role in the political life of the city. Olbia was in this state when it was visited by Dio of Prusa during his wanderings (i.e. shortly before AD 96); Dio has left a vivid description of the city (which he calls Borysthenes, as others do, because of the proximity of the harbour of Borysthenes on the river of that name) in his *Borysthenitic Discourse*. In the 2nd century AD a new period of prosperous stability began: under Antoninus Pius a Roman garrison built the citadel in the southern part of the upper town; under Septimius Severus the region was incorporated into the province Lower Moesia. Two destruction levels show that Olbia was burned down twice in the 3rd century, probably during the so-called Scythian or Gothic wars. When exactly it ceased to exist is uncertain: Byzantine coins found at the site suggest that a settlement (though very much reduced) may have outlasted antiquity.

BALBINA BÄBLER

See also Black Sea

Summary

Olbia was a Milesian colony on the north shore of the Black Sea, founded in the late 7th century BC. It flourished especially from the 5th to the 3rd centuries BC. Its harbour was an important entrepot and fine buildings were constructed. Ruled by Scythians in the 2nd century BC and by Mithridates Eupator in the 1st, Olbia was sacked by the Getae in 55 BC. On a reduced scale it continued to exist, possibly into the Byzantine period.

Further Reading

Belin de Ballu, E., *Olbia: cité antique du littoral nord de la Mer Noire*, Leiden: Brill, 1972

Bylkova, V., "Excavations on the Eastern Boundary of the Chora of Olbia Pontica", *Echos du Monde Classique / Classical Views*, 40 (1996): pp. 99–118

Diehl, Erich, Olbia (4) entry in *Real-Encyclopädie der klassischen Altertumswissenschaft*, edited by August Pauly *et al.*, vol. 17.2, 1937, 2405–23

Krapivina, V.V., "The City of Olbia in the I–IV Centuries AD", *Echos du Monde Classique / Classical Views*, 39 (1995): pp. 355–75

Kryzhitskii, Sergei D. and V.V. Krapivina, "A Quarter-Century of Excavation at Olbia Pontica", *Echos du Monde Classique / Classical Views*, 38 (1994): pp. 181–205

Lebedev, Andrei, "The Devotio of Xanthippos: Magic and Mystery Cults in Olbia", *Zeitschrift für Papyrologie und Epigraphik*, 112 (1996): pp. 279–83

Lifshitz, Baruch, "Le Culte d'Apollon Delphinios a Olbia", *Hermes*, 94 (1966): pp. 236–38

Vinogradov, Jurij G. and Sergej D. Kryzickij, *Olbia: Eine altgriechische Stadt im nordwestlichen Schwarzmeerraum*, Leiden: Brill, 1995

Wasowicz, Aleksandra, *Olbia pontique et son territoire: l'aménagement de l'espace*, Paris: Belles Lettres, 1975

Zhmud', L., "Orphism and Grafitti from Olbia", *Hermes*, 120 (1992): pp. 159–68

Old Calendarists

Greek Orthodox traditionalist movement

Orthodox Christians who refuse the Gregorian calendar, introduced into the Greek Church in 1924, are called Old Calendarists. By the 6th century AD the calendar promulgated by Julius Caesar as Pontifex Maximus (46 BC) had displaced the Macedonian calendar, widely used in the Greek east since apostolic times. The Julian year is 11 minutes and 14 seconds longer than the solar year. Thus by 1324 the Byzantine astronomer Nikephoros Gregoras observed that the spring equinox was falling seven days earlier than at the time of the First Council of Nicaea (325), which had stipulated that Easter be celebrated on the first Sunday of the full moon following the spring equinox and after the Jewish Passover. Informed of the discrepancy, the emperor Andronikos II Palaiologos refused to alter the calendar. The discrepancy was ten days by the 15th century, when Pope Gregory XIII promulgated a new calendar which excepted from a leap day those century years that are not divisible by 400 (e.g. 1700, 1800, 1900, 2100) and renamed 5 October 1582 as 15 October. Thus the spring equinox was restored to 21 March, its date at the time of Nicaea. One consequence of the Gregorian reform was that Easter might be celebrated on or before Passover.

The pope dispatched Greek legates to Constantinople to win the approval of the patriarch, Jeremias II, for the calendar reform. Jeremias rejected the new calendar as an affront to tradition, a unilateral break with the paschal calendar of Nicaea, and potentially an instrument of Latin proselytism. Jeremias and the patriarchs of Jerusalem and Alexandria imposed anathemas on anyone who might accept the new calendar and *paschalion* (set of dates for Easter) of the pope (1583, 1593).

A change in the attitude of the Constantinople patriarchate is apparent from the encyclical of 1920, "To the Churches of Christ wheresoever they may be", which proposes the adoption of a common calendar as a first step towards uniting the various Christian denominations. The adoption of the Gregorian calendar was promoted by two churchmen with close ties to the Venizelist party, Meletios Metaxakis and Chrysostomos Papadopoulos. As ecumenical patriarch, Meletios convened a Pan-Orthodox congress (10 May–8 June 1923) which recommended a programme of liberal reforms including adoption of the Gregorian calendar and *paschalion*. In February 1923 the revolutionary dictatorship of Colonel Nicholas Plastiras installed Chrysostomos as archbishop of Athens and imposed the Gregorian civil calendar in Greece. With the help of the Plastiras regime Chrysostomos won the permission of the General Synod and the ecumenical patriarchate to proceed with the change of the ecclesiastical calendar on 10/23 March 1924. By retaining the traditional paschal calendar Chrysostomos could argue that he had not incurred the anathemas against the Gregorian calendar imposed by Jeremias and his successors.

The monks of Mount Athos rejected the calendar change and patriarch Photios of Alexandria was sharply critical. Nevertheless, the clergy of the Church of Greece by and large accepted the new calendar. Resistance to the Gregorian calendar within Greece was primarily a lay movement, with the support of zealot monks from Mount Athos including Arsenios Kotteas, Parthenios Skourlis, and Matthaios Karpathakis. In April 1926 the Church of Greece declared all who refused the calendar change schismatic and excommunicated, and attempted to close the chapels of the Old Calendarists. The apparition of a cross in the sky over the chapel of St John the Theologian on Mount Hymettus on the vigil of the Exaltation of the Cross (14/27 September 1925) afforded miraculous confirmation to hundreds of Old Calendarist worshippers. In 1926 Kotteas founded the "Holy League of the Zealot Monks of Mount Athos" for the purpose of organizing the Old Calendarists. In November 1927 the movement received its first martyr in the person of Catherine Routis, killed by police while seeking to prevent the arrest of an Old Calendarist priest. Traditionalist periodicals such as the *Voice of Orthodoxy* (1927) and the *Orthodox Herald* (1930) were founded. By 1930 there were about 800 chapters of Old Calendarists in Greece.

The movement remained without bishops until 1935, the same year that the monarchy was restored in Greece. At this time Chrysostomos Kavouridis of Florina and two other metropolitans of the state Church were emboldened to break with the new calendar and formed the Synod of True Orthodox Christians of the Church of Greece. They proceeded to consecrate four new bishops, including Matthew Karpathakis. The seven bishops were then put on trial by the Church of Greece; three recanted and returned to the state Church while the others were banished or confined to monasteries.

A split among the Old Calendarists developed after 1937, when metropolitan Chrysostomos of Florina declared that the state Church was to be considered only potentially and not definitively schismatic. Rejecting this position, bishop Matthew constituted his own synod and in 1948 proceeded uncanonically to consecrate four new bishops by himself. The Matthewite synod, currently under archbishop Andreas, continues to deny the validity of all sacraments in the state Church.

Chrysostomos died in 1955 without leaving any successor bishops. In 1962 archbishop Leonty of the Russian Church Abroad travelled to Greece where, together with Akakios Pappas who had been consecrated by other prelates of the Russian Church Abroad, he consecrated three more bishops for the Florinite group without the permission of his synod. On the death of archbishop Akakios in 1963, Auxentios Pastras was elected archbishop of the Florinite synod, a post he held until 1985 when he was deposed for simony in the unauthorized consecration of a defrocked New Calendarist churchman. Since then the Florinites have been led by archbishop Chrysostomos Kiousis. Another schism arose in 1995 when six bishops left the synod under threat of canonical judgement; two of these, Paisios and Vikentios, were attached to the ecumenical patriarchate in 1998. In 1986 bishop Kyprianos Koutsoumbas of the Florinite Synod was deposed for his close relations with New Calendarist clergy. His Synod in Resistance has since then established relations with the Russian Church Abroad. Kyprianos has consecrated numerous bishops, most of whom are not Greeks, and has undertaken an active apostolate against the ecumenical activities of the state Church. Unlike other Old Calendarist groups the Synod in Resistance

does not require chrismation before offering the Eucharist to those baptized in the state Church.

The number of Old Calendarists in Greece may be estimated at 150,000. About 60 per cent of these are associated with the Florinite synod of Chrysostomos Kiousis, 20 per cent with the Matthewites, and the remainder with other groupings. Most of the zealot monks on Mount Athos, including the monastery of Esphigmenou and several sketes, are associated with the Kiousis synod. Other important monasteries include those of Kerateas, Kozani, Examilia and Agion Taxiarchon in Corinth, and Koimisis tis Theotokou on Mount Parnes.

The diverse Old Calendarist synods regard the ecumenical activities of the state Church and the patriarchate of Constantinople as evidence that the calendar change was not merely an attack on the liturgical unity of the Church. They see adoption of the papal calendar as part of a programme to undermine Orthodox traditions and to reduce the Church to a position of equality with other religions.

C.G. BROWN

See also Calendar, Zealots

Summary

Old Calendarists are those Orthodox Christians who continue to follow the Julian calendar, denying the validity of the Gregorian calendar which was introduced by pope Gregory XIII in 1582. The Gregorian reform was rejected by patriarch Jeremias II at the time and was not adopted by the Greek Orthodox Church until 1924. Divided into several synods, Old Calendarists in Greece today number perhaps 150,000.

Further Reading

Barker, Patrick G., *A Study of the Ecclesiology of Resistance*, Etna, California: Center for Traditionalist Orthodox Studies, 1994

Chrysostomos Florinis, *Apanta proin Florinis Chrysostomou* [Works of Chrysostomos, Former Bishop of Florina], Gortyn, 1997

Chrysostomos, Bishop of Oreoi, *The Old Calendar Orthodox Church of Greece*, Etna, California: Center for Traditionalist Orthodox Studies, 1984, reprinted 1991

Delibasis, A.D., *Pascha Kyriou: Dimiourgia-Anakainisis kai Apostasia* [The Lord's Pascha: Creation, Reform, and Apostasy], Athens, 1985

Giannakoulopoulos, Ioil, *Palaion kai Neon Imerologion* [Old and New Calendar], 1997

Giannakoulopoulos, Kalliopios, *Ta Patria: Perigraphi gegonoton ap tous iroikous Agonas ton Gnision Orthodoxon Christianon* [Our Inheritance: An Account of the Heroic Struggle of True Orthodox Christians], Piraeus, 1987

Holy Orthodox Church in North America, *The Struggle Against Ecumenism: The History of the True Orthodox Church of Greece from 1924 to 1994*, Boston: Holy Transfiguration Monastery, 1998

Kokoris, Dimitrios T., *Imerologio Eortologio: Diorthosis, Lathos i Epibeblimeni?* [Festal Calendar: Its Correction, Essential or Mistaken?], Athens, 1998

Ktenas, Lampros, *Piso ap'o, ti phainetai sto imerologiako* [What's Behind the Calendar Question], Athens, 1994

Paraskeviadis, Christodoulos, *Istoriki kai Kanoniki Theorisis to Palaioimerologitikou Zitimatos kata te tin Genesin kai tin Exelixin autou en Elladi* [Historical and Canonical Basis of the Old Calendar Question According to its Origins and Development in Greece], Volos, 1981

Oligarchy

Rule by the "few"

Oligarchy ("rule by the few") was a fluid term that first emerged in 5th- and 4th-century BC Greek historical, political, and philosophical texts. In a precise context, oligarchy meant broad-based constitutional government by property owners of the Greek city states, who as exclusive citizens could both vote and hold office; but in a wider sense, oligarchs came to be identified as any group who, whether through legal means or by force, sought to check the power of democracy.

Government during the later Mycenaean period (1600–1200 BC) was dynastic, controlled by a king (*wanax*) who occupied a centralized fortified palace and its surrounding countryside. And while Linear B tablets reflect cadres of other high political officials, rule was clearly in the hands of a supreme chief who claimed power through inherited privileges.

Myths and stories found in later Greek literature give the impression that local chiefs (*basileis*) controlled tribal organizations during the Dark Ages (c.1200–700 BC). Power was probably in the hands of a single individual, and was passed on to male children. Whereas there were obviously a select few local princes who consulted the king, most government was not constitutional, but based largely on the ability of local potentates to muster subservient shepherds and farmers into successful military bands.

The emergence of more than 1000 Greek city states in the 8th century BC ushered in the first period of truly constitutional government in the Mediterranean – local communities were now often represented by independent landowners who sought political power commensurate with their hoplite infantry prowess and agricultural expertise. Yet, this transition from aristocratic government to rule by property owners was not automatic, but often characterized by periods of autocracy, as transitional tyrants for two or three generations – most often in the commercial, seafaring states near the isthmus or in the islands – might wrest control from noble families in the purported interest of the common people. In some areas of Greece – Thessaly and Sparta are good examples – vestiges of monarchy, coupled with consulting bodies of aristocratic families and supported by serfdom, continued for centuries.

By 700 BC many poleis were beginning to establish governments by property-owning citizens, which might constitute a third to half of the resident native-born male population. Aristotle later called such constitutions either "polities" ("polis governments") or "timocracies" – rule by those who enjoyed influence, prestige, and property. In fact, such timocratic governments were moderately oligarchic, allowing small landholders to vote on legislation proposed by elected senior officials.

By the 5th century BC the rights to participate in the assembly and hold office were extended to the landless poor at a few cities – most notably Athens – as part of a slow liberalizing Panhellenic trend that would be characterized by office-holding by lot, public works, navies, urban fortifications, and subsidized pay for jury service and assembly attendance. During the rise of democracy in the 5th century, the definition of oligarchy crystallized as a reactionary alternative to more egalitarian constitutions, and the two words democracy ("power of the people") and oligarchy ("power of the few") first appeared in the Greek language and in clear antithesis to each other.

In reality, it was often difficult to calibrate whether a city state was oligarchic or democratic, since most had councils and elective officials. Aristotle later attempted, without much success, in book 4 of his *Politics* to create a typology of constitutions, characterized by four variants of both oligarchic and democratic government. But "the few" and "the people" were relative terms – some "oligarchic" states might have very low property qualifications and a high percentage of citizen participation, while the offices of nominally "democratic" constitutions could de facto be staffed exclusively by more prosperous landholders.

By the late 5th and 4th centuries, and especially during the Peloponnesian War (431–404 BC), oligarchy took on a far more precise definition: rule of those with capital and in alliance with Sparta. Thus the great revolutions at Corfu and elsewhere during the war were not marked so much by disagreements over the voting franchise or the constitution per se, as by strife among larger landowners and businessmen against those without money. The former welcomed the intervention of Spartan infantry to protect their interests, the latter looked to the Athenian fleet to champion the cause of the poor, who saw democracy not so much as voting privileges but rather as entitlements and subsidies for the landless. Indeed, Aristotle concluded that oligarchy had come to mean simply "rule by the rich", democracy "rule by the poor".

The defeat of Athens (404 BC) did not result in a spread of oligarchies championed by the victorious Spartans. Rather, the increasing monetarization of the Greek economy and the corruption of census rubrics brought on by the demands of the war led to a rise in democratic government. States in Boeotia and in the northern Peloponnese increasingly liberalized their constitutions to include participation by most native-born residents, and often gathered neighbouring communities into federal leagues under democratic auspices that would survive into Roman times. Coups by both radical and moderate oligarchs at Athens, Argos, and Mantineia were often short-lived. The harsh nature of Spartan hegemony, and the insular nature of Spartan society, did little to encourage a return among the city states to oligarchic rule.

Most Greek thinkers, themselves aristocrats, preferred moderate oligarchies, as consistent with the traditional values of the old agrarian polis, and a bulwark against the financial and cultural liberalism spawned by imperial Athens. Thucydides felt the brief rule of 5000 property owners at Athens in 411 was the best constitution in the history of the state. Aristotle lamented the passing of the rule of a middling agrarian population that had avoided the extremes of both reactionary autocracy and radical democracy. The so-called "Old Oligarch" – author of an anonymous 5th-century BC political tract – described the reckless dynamism of Athens largely in terms of its abandonment of traditional oligarchic restraint. Plato's political ideas are confusing; he clearly did not favour democracy but instead looked to government based on either natural or enforced hierarchies.

In the later 4th century BC the wealthy of the polis continued to yearn for government by the few, and now looked not to traditional oligarchies, but rather to the growth of

Macedonian monarchy. Philip II and his son Alexander the Great sought to subsidize wealthy politicians in the Greek city states, promising local autonomy to oligarchic cadres who could maintain order, provide tribute, and furnish manpower for the Macedonian cause. The successors of Alexander in both Greece and Asia Minor continued to favour such oligarchies, which were increasingly narrow groups of wealthy urban elites, often absentee owners of estates in the countryside. Class strife in the ancient world is largely a Hellenistic phenomenon, and was waged by those dispossessed farmers who increasingly became the urban unemployed or rural serfs, and now lacked both the freedom and the rights that had existed under traditional oligarchy.

The nomenclature of Hellenistic government as it survives in the histories and on inscriptions is confused and often euphemistic. It can be assumed that reference to "the people" and "the council" usually meant a select few, who governed under the aegis of monarchy and on the basis of vast wealth. While there were still democratic councils among the federated leagues in Achaea and Aetolia, most city states were increasingly governed by elites owing allegiance to kings. Gone was any traditional idea of oligarchy as the rule by a substantial landowning minority of the town's residents, who were responsible entirely for a community's defence, foreign policy, and financial health. Popular rule in the Hellenistic age simply meant for most cities control by the indigenous rich in service to a foreign monarchy. No local oligarchies in the Hellenistic age enjoyed real autonomy.

After the Roman conquest of Greece (146 BC), most Hellenic provinces were run by local oligarchic councils who reported to a Roman executive proconsul. While deliberations were often by consensus vote, and while the language of constitutional government might suggest popular assemblies, in fact foreign executives, backed by the legions, retained the real power. In general, the Romans found that local elite oligarchies ensured that taxes were promptly paid and social unrest minimal.

After the breakup of the western empire (5th century AD) Greek oligarchic councils continued to enforce the law of the emperor at Byzantium. The Turkish occupation changed little, as Greek aristocrats now managed affairs under Ottoman auspices. The basis of Greek constitutions during the 19th and 20th centuries was in theory democratic, but in fact characterized more by extended periods of autocracy as local dynasts, dictators, and generals seized power from elected assemblies. Following a practice established since Classical times, Greek officials, who distrusted popular assemblies and sought to rule by the advice and consent of a few wealthy men, used the nomenclature of democracy, not oligarchy. After the 5th century BC the term oligarchy would for ever describe reactionary autocracy and plutocracy rather than the original, more liberal Greek notion of simple majority rule by moderate property owners.

VICTOR DAVIS HANSON

See also Government

Further Reading

Hanson, Victor Davis, *The Other Greeks: The Family Farm and the Agrarian Roots of Western Civilization*, New York and London: Free Press, 1995

Larsen, J.A.O., *Representative Government in Greek and Roman History*, Berkeley: University of California Press, 1955

Ostwald, Martin, *From Popular Sovereignty to the Sovereignty of Law: Law, Society and Politics in Fifth-Century Athens*, Berkeley: University of California Press, 1986

Rahe, Paul A., *Republics Ancient and Modern: Classical Republicanism and the American Revolution*, Chapel Hill: University of North Carolina Press, 1992

Whibley, Leonard, *Greek Oligarchies: Their Character and Organization*, New York: Putnam, and London: Methuen, 1896; reprinted Chicago: Ares, 1975

Olive

The olive is a fruit-bearing tree that is imbued with a symbolic meaning and a practical value that make it of pivotal importance to the understanding of everyday life in Greece, of the socioeconomic realities of the country, and of ritual practices, beliefs, and customs. The olive is the national tree of Greece, while olives and olive oil are its national products.

The olive is one of the oldest cultivated trees in the world. The Greeks were among the first to engage in its systematic cultivation, in the Early Bronze Age, that is in the 3rd millennium BC, though archaeological evidence reveals that olive-oil production started much later, in the Late Bronze Age. Its extraction was facilitated by the introduction of the lever press, which in various combinations remained in use up to the 20th century.

Olives constituted an important ingredient in the diet of the ancient Greeks. It has been suggested that a wealthy household would consume approximately 200–330 kg of olive oil per year. It had many uses, and in antiquity it was considered to be a "luxury product". It was first used as a perfume or as an essential substance in the production of perfumes and ointments for bodily care, probably because of its therapeutic and cleansing qualities. It was also often used as a means to heal maladies; Hippocrates, the father of medicine, suggested more than 60 uses of olive oil for healing purposes. From the 6th century BC onwards, olive oil was introduced to food and acquired great economic significance. At around the same time it was also increasingly used for lighting. Olive wood was employed for building and in the making of various artefacts. Occasionally olive kernels and wood were also used as fuel.

The olive tree is evergreen and is characterized by its longevity and durability. These three distinct characteristics earned it a central position in Greek religion. Moreover, its sacred symbolism was derived from the great economic importance of its fruits and their products. It is for this reason that the olive tree was considered to be the sacred tree of the goddess of wisdom, Athena, who was said to have created it on the Acropolis in her contest with the sea god Poseidon for the control of Attica. The olive branch was a symbol of peace and victory and at the Olympic Games olive wreaths adorned the heads of victors. Similarly, olive oil was given as a prize to the victorious athletes at the Panathenaic Games. Because of its

Olive: range of varieties for sale in an Athens market. The olive remains the most enduring material ingredient of Greek culture.

symbolic value olive oil was frequently also used for ritual purposes. It was used to smear bodies before burial, offered in the form of libation to the dead and the gods, and fed the lamps in the temples.

The uses of olive oil in the Orthodox Christian tradition were not new inventions, but they reflected these ancient and solidly consolidated practices. Its symbolism was enhanced by the similarity of the Greek word for oil – *elaion* – to *eleos*, meaning "mercy". It thus symbolized God's mercy and grace and was used in the sacrament of unction for the anointing of the sick and for the forgiveness of sins. In liturgical practice oil was used for various kinds of anointing. It is the basic substance of the "chrism" used in baptism, confirmation, and holy orders. From the 7th century onwards coronation ceremonies involved anointing with oil. Olive oil is also used for the oil lamps that burn in front of icons, and many Greek Orthodox today, seeking miraculous healing, use this sanctified oil to anoint themselves. Due to its association with the strengthening of the body, in strict periods of fasting the Greek Orthodox abstain from oil, but not from olives, which are probably one of the most widely consumed food substances during fasts. Finally, olive oil of the best quality is often offered by the faithful to the church as a gift to the saints and to God.

According to historians, in the 12th century more olives were produced in the southern Peloponnese than anywhere else in the world. In the late Middle Ages, however, there is evidence that the systematic cultivation of olive trees was restricted, particularly in the main olive-producing areas of Greece, such as Crete. This was probably due to the unstable political and socioeconomic conditions, and to the prevalence of cereal and vine cultivation. Moreover, the development of stock raising in this period resulted in the replacement of olive oil by pig fat in food and in lighting.

During the period of Ottoman rule, expropriation of land and high taxes prevented any increase in the production of olive oil. It still remained a luxury product because of its high price, and its consumption was governed by strict economic restrictions, reflecting the social divisions of the day. By contrast, raw olives with bread occupied a central place in the nutritional diet of peasants, farm labourers, and of the poorer and middle classes of the Greek urban population.

The olive fruit and olive oil became important factors for the economic development of the newly founded Greek state. Olive groves owned by Turks passed to state ownership and, eventually, to private ownership for a price. Thus in the 19th and 20th centuries there was a noticeable rise in olive plantings and increased production of olives and olive oil. From that time onwards, olive cultivation became one of the most significant sources of income from the agricultural sector of the Greek economy. Just before World War II modern oil-processing factories were installed, which not only resulted in increased production of oil for domestic consumption but also for exports.

Olive trees with vines and citrus trees provide the arboricultural character of Greece today. Olive groves exist in most parts of Greece, since the trees can be grown in poor soil and on rocky terrain with little irrigation. The warmer and drier areas favour the production of olive oil, while the cooler areas favour the production of raw olives. Olives cover 17 per cent of the Greek cultivated land. There are more than 120 million olive trees, of which 95 million are used for the production of oil. The average annual production of olive oil is 250,000 tons. Crete produces the greatest quantity of olive oil (30 per cent), followed by the Peloponnese (26 per cent), Lesbos (10 per cent), and the Ionian islands (8 per cent); 450,000 Greek families are engaged in olive cultivation and the average annual consumption of olive oil is 18.5 kg per head, the greatest in Europe.

ELENI SOTIRIU

See also Agriculture

Further Reading

Amouretti, Marie-Claire, *Le Pain et l'huile dans la Grèce antique: de l'araire au moulin*, Paris: Belles Lettres, 1986

Anagnostopoulos, P. T., *I Katagogi tis Elaias* [The Origins of the Olive], Athens, 1951

Blitzer, H., "Olive Cultivation and Oil Production in Minoan Crete" in *La Production du vin et de l'huile en Méditerranée / Oil and Wine Production in the Mediterranean Area*, edited by Marie-Claire Amouretti and Jean-Pierre Brun, Paris: Boccard, 1993

Elia kai Ladi, 40 Triimero Ergasias, Kalamata, 7–9 Maiou 1993 [Olive Tree and Oil: Proceedings of the 40th Three-Day Conference, Kalamata, 7–9 May 1993], Politistiko Technologiko Idrima ETBA, 1996

"Ellinika Elaiolada" [Greek Olive Oil], *Elliniki Georgia* [Greek Agriculture], 7 (June 1988)

Fooks, Richard, *To Biblio tis Elias* [The Book of the Olive], Athens, n.d.

Hamilakis, Y., "Wine, Oil and the Dialectics of Power in Bronze Age Crete: A Review of the Evidence", *Oxford Journal of Archaeology*, 15 (1996): pp. 1–32

Kiritsakis, A.K., and Paul Apostolos, *Olive Oil: From the Tree to the Table*, Trumbull, Connecticut: Food and Nutrition Press, 1998

Sordinas, Augustus, *Old Olive Mills and Presses on the Island of Corfu*, Memphis: Memphis State University, 1971

Vickery, Kenton Frank, *Food in Early Greece*, Urbana: University of Illinois, 1936

Olympia

Sanctuary in the Peloponnese

Olympia is situated in a valley at the confluence of the Alpheus and Cladeus rivers in Elis in the northwest of the Peloponnese. It attracted not only pilgrims and athletes to the sanctuary, but developed into a kind of fairground for traders, artists, and literary figures. Olympia at the time of the festival was said to be crowded, hot, noisy, and full of flies. There was a taboo against females, certainly married women, from participating in the festival. Girls, however, had their own festival there called the Heraia. The importance of Olympia, an otherwise insignificant place, may lie in its association with the cult of Zeus. Strabo also records that its reputation came from its oracle of the Earth Goddess.

The site was not identified during the Middle Ages, but was discovered by Chandler in 1766, albeit covered with some 4 m of alluvium from the changing courses of the rivers. French archaeologists under Maison started digging in 1829 and removed to the Louvre some of the metopes from the temple of Zeus. The later school of German archaeologists to work on

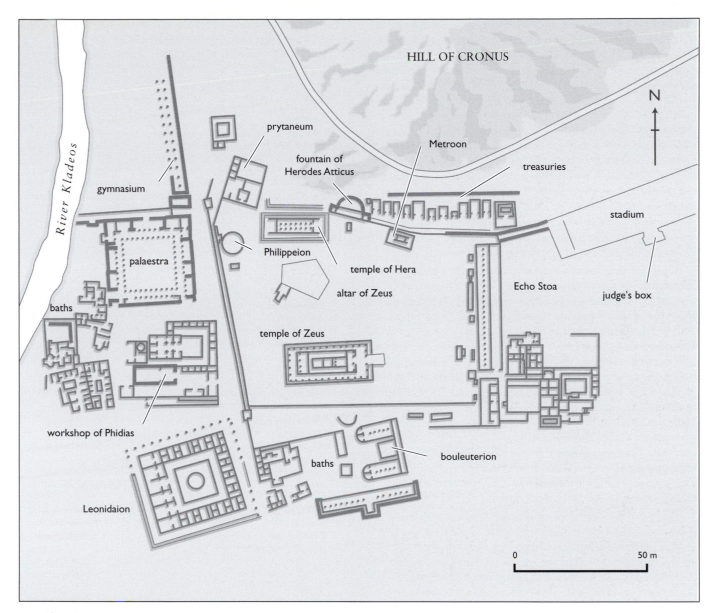

27. Olympia

this site include Curtius, Dörpfeld, Furtwängler, Kunze, Mallwitz, and Sinn. Many recent discoveries are changing traditional ideas about Olympia, especially dating.

The traditional belief is that there are Mycenaean remains as early as 1500 BC, that the first shrine to Zeus was built about 1000 BC, that athletics were first recorded in 776 BC, and that the games ended in AD 393 with the edict of the Christian emperor Theodosius I. Mallwitz, however, has argued that there is no convincing evidence for a Mycenaean sanctuary, but that Olympia became a sanctuary first in the 9th or 8th century BC and that athletics came later. The foundation date of 776 BC for the games is derived from the lost victory list of Hippias of Elis, but the archaeological evidence of the site, especially the appearance of wells in the eastern part near the stadium at the end of the 8th century BC, may point to a date closer to 700 BC. Recent inscriptions with the names of victors show that the games were still going strong in the 3rd and 4th centuries AD. Coins and other finds in the stadium seem to suggest that the

games extended for at least a century longer than the traditional closing of AD 393, and that Christianity, far from destroying pagan cults, existed side by side with them.

The Altis was the walled, sacred area, a grove consisting largely of plane and olive trees. The chief shrine there was the great altar of Zeus, said to be 7 m high, but Olympia was not dedicated to Zeus alone, for Pausanias (5. 14. 4–10) records more than 70 altars in the Altis, although most of them are not directly connected to Zeus and the games, and very few of them can be located with any accuracy. The oldest shrine was that of Pelops. The major buildings in the historical period included the temple of Zeus, the temple of Hera, the precinct of the Earth Goddess, the precinct of Pelops, and the 12 treasuries, which were used by the city states as "bank vaults" and for the display of wealth. Outside the Altis *inter alia* were the council chamber for the Hellanodikai (officials and judges), the workshop of Phidias, and primitive bathing places. In the 4th century BC were added the Metroon, the Echo portico separating the Altis from the stadium, the Phillipeion erected by Philip II of Macedon (showing the political importance of Olympia), and outside the Altis the Leonidaion (the guest house) and southern portico. In the Hellenistic period the triumphal archway into the stadium from the Altis was built. Several baths date from the Roman period, as the site became more developed. A good water system was made possible by Herodes Atticus in the 2nd century AD with the construction of the monumental fountain known as the nymphaeum. A Christian basilica was built on the foundations of the workshop of Phidias. Other buildings are being discovered including the clubhouse in the southwestern corner of the site. The Altis was also used as a "Hall of Fame", where victorious athletes were allowed to set up statues of themselves. Bases of statues of Zeus (Zanes) were erected at the foot of the Hill of Cronus at the expense of athletes who had cheated.

Traces of three stadia remain to the east of the Altis on approximately the same site, a flat area at the foot of the Hill of Cronus. Stadium I was partly within the Altis and dates from the Archaic period, though little is known about it. Stadium II, dating from the late 6th century BC, had artificial embankments for spectators on the north and south. Stadium III was more elaborate and was located about 75 m to the east with additional embankments on the east and west together with a judges' box. The altar of Demeter can still be seen in the stadium. The palaestra and gymnasium were added in the Hellenistic period, but it has recently been suggested that the gymnasium was used not for athletic training, but for cultural purposes. Nothing remains of the hippodrome, although its location between the stadium and the Alpheus river, the elaborate starting device in the shape of the prow of a ship, and other features are known from Pausanias (6. 20. 10–19).

The most famous work of art, the monumental statue of *Zeus* (more than 13 m high) was made of gold and ivory by Phidias, and was considered one of the seven wonders of the ancient world. It stood in the entrance to the Doric temple of Zeus built by Libon, but no longer survives, having been transported to Constantinople in the 4th century AD, where it was destroyed by fire. The museum sculptures include the pediments and metopes of the temple of Zeus, the colossal head of Hera, the *Nike* of Paeonius, the *Hermes* of Praxiteles, clay sculptures of the head of Athena and of Ganymede and Zeus, thousands of bronze statuettes, bronze sheets with reliefs, and various bronze weapons, architectural bronzes, and tripods (the most common votive offering at Olympia).

Olympia was partly destroyed by the invasion of the Heruli in the 3rd century AD and the later invasions of the Slavs. An earthquake in the 6th century destroyed the temple of Zeus and other buildings. The changing courses of the Alpheus and Cladeus have covered parts of the site, especially the hippodrome (still unexcavated). Today Olympia is a tourist attraction, with a museum area (originally founded in 1886, but now a modern building). The stadium, as we now see it, is based on the stadium as it was thought to be in the 2nd century AD, with start and finish lines visible about 200 m apart. It remains unimpressive to look at (by comparison with the stadium at Delphi) with grassy banks, dusty track, and no seats for spectators (as it probably was originally), and is totally unsuitable for modern sports. For every modern Olympiad the Olympic torch is ritually lit at the site of ancient Olympia.

NIGEL B. CROWTHER

See also Olympic Games

Summary
Located in the northwestern Peloponnese, Olympia is associated with the cult of Zeus. It probably first became a sanctuary in the 9th or 8th century BC. The festival of athletics (traditionally dated to 776 BC) may not have begun much before 700. Finds suggest that it continued well into the 5th century AD (beyond the traditional closing date of AD 393). Many buildings were destroyed by earthquake in the 6th century AD.

Further Reading
Andronicos, M., *Olympia*, Athens: G.A. Christopoulos, 1985 (useful for the museum collection)
Crowther, N.B., "Studies in Greek Athletics", part 1, *Classical World*, 78/5 (1985): pp. 497–524 (for works up to 1982; there is a bibliographical section in the journal *Nikephoros* listing later publications)
Drees, Ludwig, *Olympia: Gods, Artists, and Athletes*, New York: Praeger, and London: Pall Mall Press, 1968
Ebert, J., "Zur neuen Bronzeplatte mit Siegerinschriften aus Olympia (Inv. 1148)", *Nikephoros*, 10 (1997): pp. 217–33
Finley, M.I. and H.W. Pleket, *The Olympic Games: The First Thousand Years*, London: Chatto and Windus, and New York: Viking, 1976
Gardiner, Edward Norman, *Olympia: Its History and Remains*, Oxford: Clarendon Press, 1925
Golden, Mark, *Sport and Society in Ancient Greece*, Cambridge and New York: Cambridge University Press, 1998
Hönle, Augusta, *Olympia in der Politik der griechischen Staatenwelt, von 776 bis zum Ende des 5. Jahrhunderts*, Bebenhausen: Rotsch, 1972
Mallwitz, Alfred, *Olympia und seine Bauten*, Munich: Prestel, 1972
Morgan, Catherine, *Athletes and Oracles: The Transformation of Olympia and Delphi in the Eighth Century BC*, Cambridge and New York: Cambridge University Press, 1990
Mouratidis, J., "Heracles at Olympia and the Exclusion of Women from the Ancient Olympic Games", *Journal of Sport History*, 11/3 (1984): pp. 41–55
Raschke, Wendy J. (editor), *The Archaeology of the Olympics: The Olympics and other Festivals in Antiquity*, Madison: University of Wisconsin Press, 1988
Romano, David Gilman, *Athletics and Mathematics in Archaic Corinth: The Origins of the Greek Stadion*, Philadelphia: American Philosophical Society, 1993
Sinn, Ulrich, *Olympia: Kult, Sport und Feste in der Antike*, Munich: Beck, 1996
Ulf, C., "Die Mythen um Olympia: politischer Gehalt und politische Intention", *Nikephoros*, 10 (1997): pp. 9–51
Wacker, C., *Das Gymnasium von Olympia: Geschichte und Funktion*, Würzburg: Würzburger Forschungen zur Altertumskunde, 1996
Weiler, I., "Olympia – jenseits der Agonistik: Kultur und Spektakel", *Nikephoros*, 10 (1977): pp. 191–213 (on Olympia as a fairground)

Olympic Games

The Olympic Games were the principal athletic games in the ancient world. First recorded in 776 BC, they were banned in

AD 393, but survived in some form until the early 6th century, and were revived as a global event in 1896.

Greek myth attributes the establishment of the Olympic Games to the Idaean Dactyls, the iron-working attendants of the mother goddess Adrasteia who are identified with the guardians of the infant Zeus, to Heracles, and to Pelops in celebration of his conquest of Oenomaus in a chariot race. The traditional date for their establishment in 776 BC may, therefore, indicate merely a revival, but nothing is known of their possible earlier history. They were held at Olympia, a sanctuary named for the presiding deity Zeus Olympios (i.e. of Mount Olympus). Although there is evidence at Olympia, in the western Peloponnese, for habitation from the Early Helladic period, in the Archaic, Classical, Hellenistic, and Roman periods it was only a sacred site (the altis) with an associated stadium and an increasing number of buildings for administration, training, and lodging. It was first under local Pisatan and from c.470 BC under Elean control.

In 776 BC the games consisted of no more than the stade race with athletes drawn from the surrounding area, the inaugural winner being traditionally a local baker, Coroebus. Other athletic events were added in the late 8th century BC, equestrian and boys' events in the 7th century BC, and further additions followed, including competitions for trumpeters and heralds in 396 BC. Many of the early victors were Spartan, but by the 6th century BC the games were truly Panhellenic, competitors travelling from all the Greek-speaking areas of the world and especially from southern Italy and Sicily. The games grew also in duration, from one day to six days in the Classical period. During the Hellenistic period there was no lessening of popularity, as Hellenistic monarchs vied with each other to add new buildings. Although the Roman conquest initially involved a vast diminution in the games' prestige, they now become open to at least some non-Greeks (the last known victor, of boxing in AD 369, was Varazdates, the crown prince of Armenia). In the late 1st century BC, however, king Herod of Judaea became president of the games and by a huge endowment encouraged a revival that was continued by subsequent imperial patronage: Augustus' right-hand man Agrippa repaired the temple of Zeus and both Tiberius and Germanicus won chariot races, while at games postponed for his own convenience (held probably in AD 67) Nero competed in and fraudulently won various events (including chariot racing and some unique musical and literary competitions). Still very popular in the 2nd century AD, the games suffered during the uncertainty of the following century and the sanctuary had to be fortified c. AD 268 because of the threat of the marauding Heruli. Held every four years without intermission from 776 BC until AD 261, they may possibly have been held only sporadically thereafter. Despite St Paul's enthusiasm for athletics, the games' combination of nudity and paganism must have made the growing number of Christians agree with the words of St Cyprian: "True Christians must shun with eyes and ears those vapid, dangerous, tasteless performances." They certainly would have come under the ban of the edict of Theodosius I in AD 393 that closed pagan cults and sites, but archaeological evidence suggests use of the stadium at Olympia until the early 6th century, and in some form they continued at Daphne, near Antioch, until AD 521.

Through most of their history they were the premier athletic festival. Next in rank were the Pythian Games, held quadrennially at Delphi in honour of Apollo and including many musical competitions, and the other two "crown games", the Nemean and the Isthmian, both held biennially in honour of Zeus and Poseidon respectively. The Olympic Games furthermore served as a model for many other festivals, some of which proudly proclaimed themselves "isolympic".

In the Classical period the first day of the celebrations was probably devoted to sacrifices, prayers, oath taking, and the checking of qualifications. Competition began on the second day. The sacrifice of 100 oxen (hecatomb) was the religious highlight of the third day, and the sixth day ended with further sacrifices and a celebratory banquet for the victors. In addition to the athletic competitions the festival gave visitors a huge fair with a wide array of entertainers, hucksters, and pickpockets.

Before the games Elean heralds proclaimed the Olympic Truce: this demanded safe conduct for all competitors and spectators travelling to and from Olympia and forbade any state to make war against the Eleans. Politics did, however, still intrude into the games, as Pheidon, tyrant of Argos, temporarily took over their organization in the early 7th century BC, and the Spartans turned the celebration of 428 BC into an anti-Athenian demonstration, while being themselves debarred from participation in 420 BC for their refusal to pay the fine imposed by Olympic law for attacking an Elean fortress.

Women, but according to Pausanias not girls, were banned even as spectators since athletes competed nude (there were separate games for girls held at Olympia in honour of Hera, but documentation is sparse). Athletes were required to train at home for at least ten months prior to the games, and during the 30 days of practising at Elis the poorest were weeded out by the judges since only the best would not do dishonour to Zeus. Judges were all Pisatan and later Elean and famous for their impartiality. Infringements of the rules for events resulted in beatings on the spot, disqualifications, and fines, the last of which were spent on statues (Zanes) erected in the sanctuary to give warning to others. Although prizes were merely garlands of wild olive, victors were generally richly rewarded by their home states. Since they could also win valuable prizes in kind and, increasingly in the Hellenistic period, monetary prizes at minor festivals, many were undoubtedly professional. Paid trainers became common from the 5th century BC and by c.50 BC athletes had formed their own trade union.

With the publication by the historian Timaeus, c.300 BC, of a synchronic list of Olympic victors (Olympionikai) the practice arose of dating other events by the Olympic quadrennia, Eratosthenes adding the refinement of subdivision into individual years (e.g. summer 774 to summer 773 BC is the third year of the first Olympiad). Despite problems of equating this system with the bewildering variety of other dating systems known in the Classical world, it survived well into the Byzantine period.

The first modern figure interested in a revival of the ancient games seems to have been Gustav Schartau, who held the *Jeux Olympiques Scandinaves* in Sweden in 1834 and 1836, but these were for winter sports. More serious revivals began in England and Greece. William Penny Brookes, a physician of Much Wenlock in Shropshire, established in 1850 his Annual Wenlock Olympian Games, which have since been held most years up to the present. These emphasized athletic events, but included also other games such as cricket, association football,

Olympic Games: starting line of the 100 m sprint at the first modern Olympic Games, Athens, 1896

and quoits. Other Olympic Games sprang up in imitation elsewhere in England (four already by 1870). In Greece the poet Panagiotis Soutsos first suggested a revival in 1835, but it was not until 1859 that, with money from the millionaire Evangelis Zappas, his efforts reached fruition in Panhellenic games which were held in what is now Athens' Plateia Koumoundourou; and even then governmental interference resulted in athletics being overshadowed by displays of industry, agriculture, and animal husbandry. The Zappas Games were held sporadically until 1889.

International Olympic Games are due to the vision of the Frenchman, Pierre, Baron de Coubertin. His original impulse came from reading Thomas Hughes's *Tom Brown's School Days* in 1875 and Hippolyte Taine's *Notes sur l'Angleterre*, whose remarks on English education suggested to him that an introduction of ball-games into the French educational system might enable the youth of his country to compete with the Prussians, who had made *Turnen* (gymnastics) a vital part of their curriculum. Becoming less chauvinistic, being increasingly in touch with Brookes, and, ironically, being inspired by the German excavations of ancient Olympia between 1875 and 1881, he conceived the idea of Olympic Games with athletics at their centre being held every four years, as in antiquity, but open to nationals of every country and held at different sites to promote the idea of world peace. In June 1894 he convened an international congress in Paris, at which the body that came to be the International Olympic Committee (IOC) was formed, under the presidency of the Greek Demetrios Vikelas, and the decision taken (after, it seems, some clandestine negotiations) to hold the first modern Olympic Games in 1896 at Athens (instead of London, the choice of the majority of delegates).

The games were duly held in the ancient and now reconstructed Panathenaic Stadium, but, eschewing a mere antiquarian revival, they included such events as cycling, fencing, and lawn tennis and rewarded with medals the first three competitors rather than, with a vegetal crown, only the winner.

Summer games have been held quadrennially since 1896, but, unlike in antiquity, there have already been cancellations due to war (3 out of the first 13, which have, however, all been counted in the numbering of the Olympiads). Figure skating featured in the games of 1908 and various winter sports events were held in 1920, though not sanctioned by the IOC, but from 1924 to 1992 official winter games were held quadrennially (apart from the cancelled celebrations of 1940 and 1944) in the same year as the summer games: thereafter winter games were held in 1994 and 1998 and have been scheduled to take place in the future quadrennially between the summer games. Equestrian events have been part of the summer games in 1900 and since 1912, but in 1956 were held separately (at Stockholm rather than Melbourne). From 1912 to 1948 medals were awarded for different categories of architecture, literature, music, painting, sculpture, and even "Merit for Aeronautics" (one gold) and "Merit for Alpinism" (three gold). Although women first competed when a Greek unofficially joined the marathon for most of its course in 1896, they did not appear in appreciable numbers until the 1920s, partly because of de Coubertin who claimed, as late as 1935, that "their role should be chiefly, as in the ancient games, to crown the victors". About 245 representatives from 14 nations took part at Athens in 1896, since when numbers have grown, to more than 10,000 from 197 nations in 1996. Britain is the only country that has not failed to send representatives to all the modern Olympic Games, including the irregular ones, since 1896 (Greeks did not participate in the winter games until 1936). The exclusion of professional athletes began to break down in 1962. Its practice had been due to both the mores of the times and the misconception that all ancient Olympic athletes had been amateurs.

All events at the first celebration in Athens were individual except for tennis doubles and gymnastic "teams" (rowing was cancelled due to rough seas), but association football, cricket, croquet, polo, rugby union, water polo, and the tug-of-war were introduced in 1900. Thereafter many sports and events have been included, as part of the official programme and as "exhibition sports", and many have been discontinued. Achievements by Greek nationals have been modest. With the exclusion of the poorly attended intercalated games at Athens in 1906, Greeks had won up to 1998 a total of 21 gold (including one in sculpture) and 60 other medals. Of these only one, a gold, has been won by a woman and none at the winter games.

The only ceremonial features of the modern games to have any ancient forerunners are the Olympic oath and flame. The latter is a deliberate reminiscence of the flame on the altar of Zeus that burned during the ancient festival and of ancient torch-relays, which were in fact more cultic than sporting: it was introduced in 1928 and first kindled at Olympia and brought to the site of the games by a relay of runners in 1936. De Coubertin is responsible for establishing the Olympic motto, creed, flag, and oath. The motto, "citius, altius, fortius" ("faster, higher, and more strongly"), he adopted from a Parisian schoolmaster, Father Didon, in one of whose schools the words are inscribed over the main entrance. The creed, emphasizing, in complete contrast to the ancient Greeks, that participation is more important than victory, de Coubertin claimed came from a sermon by Ethelbert Talbot, bishop of Central Pennsylvania, that was delivered in St Paul's Cathedral at the time of the games in 1908, but its wording is more probably the baron's own remembrance of a passage in Ovid's *Metamorphoses* (9. 5–6), whose context is erotic. The flag with its five interlocking rings dates from 1914 and was probably inspired by the two rings that symbolized the union of two French athletic associations: de Coubertin intended the six colours to represent the flags of the nations that had competed in the five games so far held (this, rather than continents, probably explains also the number of rings). The oath was devised by de Coubertin for the games in 1920.

Among the incalculable influences of the Greeks in the modern world the Olympic Games are probably the one of which the general public is the most aware.

A.R. LITTLEWOOD

See also Olympia, Games and Sports

Further Reading

Findling, John E. and Kimberly D. Pelle (editors), *Historical Dictionary of the Modern Olympic Movement*, Westport, Connecticut: Greenwood Press, 1996

Finley, M.I. and H.W. Pleket, *The Olympic Games: The First Thousand Years*, London: Chatto and Windus, and New York: Viking, 1976

Guttmann, Allen, *The Olympics: A History of the Modern Games*, Urbana: University of Illinois Press, 1992

Kamper, Erich and Bill Mallon, *The Golden Book of the Olympic Games*, Milan: Vallardi, 1993 (records to 1992)

Raschke, Wendy J. (editor), *The Archaeology of the Olympics: The Olympic and Other Festivals in Antiquity*, Madison: University of Wisconsin Press, 1988

Young, David C., *The Modern Olympics: A Struggle for Revival*, Baltimore: Johns Hopkins University Press, 1996 (history of the modern Olympic movement to 1896)

Olympus, Mount

Mountain in Thessaly

Olympus is the highest mountain in Greece and the second highest in the Balkan peninsula. It bears the ancient name "Thessalian Olympus" and is the deified mountain bridging Thessaly and Macedonia. It occupies the northeastern part of Thessaly and the southwestern end of central Macedonia, and straddles the boundaries of the counties of Larissa (province of Elasson) and Pieria. The mountain is shaped like a vault, having at its peak a plateau, from which other peaks rise by more than 2500 m. Above a gorge, some 600 m deep, the peaks rise of Mytikas or Pantheon (2,917 m), Stefani or the Throne of Zeus (2,909 m), Skala (2,866 m), and Scholio (2,911 m), forming a semicircle.

Olympus is a large mountain covering a relatively small area. Its width from east to west is no more than 25 km, from north to south 28.5 km, its perimeter 150 km, and its area 500 sq km. It is distinguished by its pointed peaks, its lengthy ridges, and its steep slopes that are traversed by deep gorges. Its main body, known as High or Upper Olympus, is distinguished from Lower Olympus (of which some specialists consider it to be a part) by the stream of Ziliana, the plain of Carya, and the river Elassonitiko.

The rock consists mainly of limestones and dolomites. From the streams that run down the mountain slopes only one has water throughout the year, the river Enipeas that passes through Litochoro; the rest are seasonal. The vegetation is limited. Typically alpine at 2,000 m and above, the lower zone is covered by forests, which in the higher regions consist of fir trees and in the lower of pines. The eastern side has more forests than the western. More than 1,700 plants have been registered in the area, i.e. about 25 per cent of the entire Greek flora. The fauna does not present any particular features. Some 32 different species of mammals have been identified as well as 108 bird species, while the mountain is famous for its many kinds of butterflies. In antiquity Pausanias reported the existence of lions on Olympus.

The climatic conditions are highly variable. At the foot of the mountain the climate is typically Mediterranean, while the northern and eastern slopes have greater rainfall. Average temperatures range from 0° to 20° C in the summer, and in the winter from -20° to +10° C. The mountain is covered by snow for about seven months of the year, usually from November to May.

Historically Olympus has been the target of various expeditions and was known as an ideal place for hunting (e.g. by

Mount Olympus, with several peaks over 2900m, is the highest mountain in Greece, seen here from the east

Sultan Mehmet IV). The botanists Theodor von Heldreich and Theodoros Orphanidis carried out a great deal of research on Olympus in the 19th century, while one ambitious expedition was undertaken by the German geographer H. Barth. In 1937 the first National Greek Forest Area was established on Olympus in order to protect the geomorphology, the fauna, and the flora of the mountain. Since 1981 this protected area has been incorporated in the "Programme on Man and the Biosphere" of UNESCO.

In ancient Greek mythology Olympus was considered to be the sacred mountain of Greece. After the victory of Zeus over the Titans, it came under the control of Zeus and became the home of the Olympian gods. Zeus' throne was believed to be at the highest peak, while the other gods resided on the surrounding ones. The mountain was also connected with Orpheus, who taught the Orphic mysteries and died there. It was also dedicated to the Olympian or Pierian Muses.

The name "Olympus" appears for the first time in the Orphic texts and is subsequently mentioned as such by all ancient Greek writers. It is generally held to be derived from a name used by the Aeolians, who lived on the western and southern shores of Asia Minor, and dates back to 1800 BC. The etymology of the word is uncertain.

Olympus was of great symbolic importance to the ancient Greeks. As the home of the gods, it symbolized immortality, high honour, and ideals. The epithet "Olympian" was given primarily to Zeus and thus signified grandeur and godliness. It occupied a central position in ancient Greek religion and cosmology, was connected with a specific philosophical world-view and attitude towards the world. The Olympian gods were the symbols of a particular *Weltanschauung*, which permeated ancient Greek culture as a whole. It is no wonder that, according to one view, while Delphi represented the *omphalos* (navel) of the earth, Olympus constituted its head (= mind).

In historical times the regions around Olympus were populated by various Greek tribes. Its mountainous routes were of the utmost importance during military expeditions, ranging from the period of the Persian Wars to the Roman conquest of Greece. At the foot of the mountain several significant cities were founded, including Dion and Python. The first human settlement on Olympus must have been established around 1000 BC near Hagios Vasileios and Mesonisi, where several tombs have been uncovered dating from 1000 to 700 BC. Further archaeological excavations and topographical research have unearthed numerous inscriptions, coins, and artefacts from various historical periods that point to relations with both Thessaly and Macedonia.

The great mythical value of Olympus has left an indelible impact upon the popular consciousness of the Greeks, who still consider it a majestic place. Olympus is also considered the focal point at which ancient Greece meets modern Hellenism. Many legends have been created about the peak of Olympus touching the sky and therefore the divine. Numerous popular songs have been composed praising the mountain. Under Ottoman rule Olympus became the hiding place of many klephts and *armatoloi* and was extolled in demotic traditions. During the Greek War of Independence it was also a place where various military operations took place.

The location of Olympus almost at the centre of Greece has created an idiosyncratic system of socio-economic dependences. Up to the beginning of the 18th century its position in the economic life of the country was of no particular importance, but under later Ottoman rule it functioned as the guardian of Greek sociocultural traditions that remained untouched by foreign influences. While many villages have been depopulated due to the unfavourable conditions obtaining in the Greek countryside, the villages on or around Olympus retained their populations because of the various economic opportunities on the mountain. From the latter half of the 18th century onwards, there was a noticeable economic development in the area, due to the establishment of commercial ties between Thessaly and the greater Balkan area as well as Central Europe, which transformed the inhabitants of Olympus into the main bearers of commerce in central Greece. This financial prosperity went hand in hand with significant cultural developments, since many schools, libraries, wealthy mansions, churches, and monasteries were established around the mountain. Even today the greater Olympus area remains an important centre of various economic and cultural activities, and therefore a considerable tourist attraction.

NEKTARIOS DROSOS

Summary

The highest mountain in Greece (2917 m), Olympus lies on the borders of Thessaly and Macedonia. In mythology it was the home of the gods, and Zeus occupied the highest peak. It still has many legendary associations. During the Tourkokratia it preserved many Greek cultural traditions. In the War of Independence it was a focal point for banditry.

Further Reading

Barton, G., "Mount Olympus", *Journal of the Geological Society*, 131 (1975): pp. 389–96

Freshfield, Douglas, "The Summits of Olympus", *Geographical Journal*, 47 (April 1916): pp. 293–97

Heuzey, Leon Alexandre, *Le Mont Olympe et l' Acarnanie: exploration des ces deux régions*, Paris: Firmin Didot, 1860

Leake, William Martin, *Travels in Northern Greece*, London: Rodwell, 1835; reprinted Amsterdam: Hakkert, 1967

Meade, C.F., "Mount Olympus", *Alpine Journal*, 32/219 (1919)

Nezis, Nikos, *Olympus*, Athens, 1986

O Olympos stous aiones [Olympus Over the Centuries]: *Proceedings of a Conference Organized by the Cultural Committee of the Municipality of Elason*, vols 1–7, 1982–95

Phoutrides, A.E. and F.P. Farquhar, "With the Gods on Mount Olympus", *Scribner's* (November 1915)

Schultz, Joseph P. and Lois Spatz, *Sinai and Olympus: A Comparative Study*, Lanham, Maryland: University Press of America, 1995

Strid, Arne K., *Wild Flowers of Mount Olympus*, Kifissia: Goulandis Natural History Museum, 1980

Olynthus

City in Chalcidice

Olynthus was located at the head of the Cassandra gulf on the Chalcidice peninsula, approximately 4 km inland from the sea. It was built on two flat-topped hills rising about 30–40 m above the surrounding plain. According to mythology, the city was named after Olynthus, a son of Heracles and Volve. Another myth refers to Olynthus as a son of the king of Thrace, Strymonas, who was killed during a lion hunt. Thus, Vraggas built the city of Olynthus to honour his brother's memory. The ending of the word Olynthus implies a pre-Hellenic provenance for it. Although the location of the city has been known since the 19th century, it was in the 1920s and 1930s that extensive excavations were carried out by the American Archaeological Mission led by David M. Robinson. The destruction of Olynthus in the mid-4th century BC has preserved a full ground plan as well as individual details of housing, providing unique information for the Classical Greek city.

In the Neolithic period a small settlement was established on the south hill of Olynthus, but Bronze Age remains are lacking. Occupation begins in about the 7th century BC. Herodotus (8. 127) and Thucydides (2. 99) reported that around 650 BC the district was inhabited by the Bottiaeans, a Thracian tribe, under whose rule the city of Olynthus remained until 479 BC. Together with other towns in the area, Olynthus supplied troops and ships to Xerxes in 480 BC, while during the Persian retreat from Greece (479 BC) Artabazus besieged and captured the city, suspecting a revolt. He then slaughtered its inhabitants and handed Olynthus over to Critobulus of Torone. Around that time new settlers from nearby Chalcidian communities immigrated to Olynthus, which thus became a Chalcidian city.

By the mid-5th century BC Olynthus was a relatively small city. As a member of the Delian League, it paid on average 2 talents of tribute from 454 to 432 BC, much less than other neighbouring Chalcidian cities (e.g. Scione paid 9, Mende paid 8, Torone paid 6). The archaeological remains from this period down to the last third of the 5th century BC are exclusively concentrated on the south hill. Two streets ran roughly north–south along the east and west sides of the hill separated from the brow by one or two rows of rooms. Two cross-streets running east–west have also been excavated, while public buildings were located at the north end of the hill. Moreover, a section of the fortification wall was uncovered in this area.

In 432 BC, facing Athenian aggression, Perdiccas, king of Macedonia, persuaded the inhabitants of a number of coastal Chalcidian cities to move inland to Olynthus and to form a single fortified city (Thucydides, 1. 58). This moving up (*anoikismos*) is thought to have given the impetus for the expansion of the old city of Olynthus to the flat-topped hill to the north, and for the laying out of a new grid-planned section of the city there. Olynthus thus became the chief city west of the Strymon and revolted against Athens.

The north hill was not inhabited until the *anoikismos* of 432 BC. This area, measuring 600 × 350 m, was laid out on an orthogonal plan, according to the Hippodamian town-planning system, with a few irregularities. Seven parallel "avenues"

5–7 m wide, running from north to south, were traversed by streets 5 m wide. Each of the blocks thus formed was 35.40 ¥ 86.34 m and usually included ten houses, grouped in two rows of five separated by a narrow alley. On the east side of the hill, however, the blocks were shortened to allow the roads to follow the topography of the hill.

The population of Olynthus numbered 15,000 inhabitants at the end of the 5th century BC. The houses at Olynthus, sometimes two-storeyed, were grouped around an open courtyard, with rooms on two or more sides. As in most ancient Greek houses, the courtyard was located in the southern part of the house with the portico and the main rooms to the north. The rooms had earth floors, unplastered walls, and very few or no features specifying their function. The houses at Olynthus are modest, lacking large common areas; exceptional are a few "villas" with mosaic floors which stood on the southeast slope of the hill (e.g. the Villa of Good Fortune, the House of the Comedian). Public buildings have been excavated both on the south and the north hills. The agora (marketplace) of Olynthus was located on the west side of the north hill and consisted of an open plaza (85 × 130 m), a stoa with shops, a building with a central colonnade (*bouleuterion*), and a fountain house. The three cemeteries of Olynthus were situated outside the city walls.

The city was fortified by a brick wall against which the first row of houses rested. Originally the city wall followed the contour of the hill. However, during the course of the 4th century BC, the city expanded to the east, creating a new suburb down on the plain. The agora occupied a free space where the old and the new settlements met.

The establishment of the Chalcidian League – a political union of certain cities of Chalcidice under the leadership of Olynthus – in 423 BC contributed substantially to the further development of the city. Following the end of the Peloponnesian War the development of the league was rapid. Around 390 BC it concluded a treaty with Amyntas, king of Macedonia, and by 382 it had extended its domination over the majority of Greek cities west of the Strymon and had even taken possession of Pella (Xenophon, *Hellenica*, 5. 2. 12). The league also issued its own coinage. In 382 BC Sparta was persuaded by an embassy from Acanthus and Apollonia, which was threatened by the rapid growth of the league, to send an expedition against Olynthus. Three years later (379 BC) the Lacedaemonians invaded Olynthus and the confederacy was dissolved. After the demise of Sparta, however, Olynthus re-established a league with 32 cities and became very powerful.

When the war between Athens and Philip II broke out in 357 BC, both powers sued for alliance with the league. Olynthus was at first in alliance with Philip, who offered the fertile region of Mygdonia as well as Potidaea to the Chalcidian League (356 BC). Subsequently, alarmed at the growth of his power, the Olynthians dissolved their alliance with the Macedonians and concluded an alliance with Athens (352 BC). Philip used as a pretext the Olynthians' refusal to hand over his brothers Arrhidaeus and Menelaus, who had taken refuge in their city, and razed Olynthus to the ground and sold the people into slavery for having broken their oath as his allies (348 BC). Demosthenes, the Athenian orator, delivered three Olynthiac speeches, urging Athens to send forces to protect Chalcidice. By the time the Athenian fleet reached

Chalcidice, Olynthus and other cities of the Chalcidian League were being besieged. Olynthus was partially reoccupied after 348 BC, but a few years later most of the survivors were sent by Cassander to settle in Cassandreia in 315 BC.

ELENI ZIMI

Summary

A city in Chalcidice about 4 km from the sea, Olynthus was occupied from the 7th century BC and was ruled by the Bottiaeans until 479 BC. Its inhabitants were slain by the retreating Persians and the city was resettled as a Chalcidian colony and member of the Delian League. Perdiccas of Macedon in 432 BC persuaded the inhabitants of several neighbouring towns to move to Olynthus, thus increasing its size. From 423 it headed the Chalcidian League. In 348 BC it was destroyed by Philip II.

Further Reading

Boardman, John, "Social Life in Classical Greece" in *Plates to Volumes V and VI: The Fifth and Fourth Centuries BC*, edited by John Boardman, Cambridge: Cambridge University Press, 1994 (*The Cambridge Ancient History*)

Cahill, Nicholas Dunlap, "Olynthus: Social and Spatial Planning in a Greek City" (dissertation), Berkeley: University of California, 1991

Gude, Mabel, *A History of Olynthus: With a Prosopographia and Testimonia*, Baltimore: Johns Hopkins University Press, 1933

Robinson, David Moore, *Excavations at Olynthus*, vols 1–13, Baltimore: Johns Hopkins University Press, 1928–33

Zahrnt, Michael, *Olynth und die Chalkidier: Untersuchung zur Staatenbildung auf der Chalkidischen Halbinsel im 5. und 4. Jahrhundert v. Chr.*, Munich: Beck, 1971

Onassis, Aristotle 1900 (or 1906)–1975

Shipowner

Aristotle Onassis is the most famous Greek shipowner of the 20th century. His name is synonymous with fame, wealth, and success; he is the archetype of the cosmopolitan, self-made, and talented entrepreneur. During the years when he dominated world shipping, from the mid-1940s to the mid-1970s, Onassis was a focus of publicity, often extravagantly presented by the world's mass media. His exuberant personality rendered him highly popular, a popularity that stemmed not only from his successful entrepreneurial activity, but also from his intense and glamorous private life.

Onassis was born the son of a tobacco merchant in the prosperous and cosmopolitan Greek community of Smyrna either in 1900 or 1906. The destruction of the city in September 1922 after the unsuccessful campaign of Greek forces in Asia Minor brought him to Greece along with hundreds of thousands of Greek refugees from the Ottoman lands. He stayed only one year in Athens before he followed the immigrant wave from the eastern Mediterranean to South America. Arriving in Argentina in 1923, he initially worked there as a telephone operator. His first business activity was related to his family business, and very soon he was importing tobacco from Greece; at the same time, he expanded his business in Buenos Aires, and soon produced cigarettes for women. Within a decade he had accumulated enough capital to turn, in 1933, to shipping, an entrepreneurial interest that lasted until his death.

When Onassis bought his first two steamships from the London office of the Dracoulis brothers, world shipping (and consequently ship prices) were at rock-bottom levels. This was a time of negative growth rates in world shipping, with the exception of the Greeks, who took advantage of the crisis and bought ships when everybody else was selling. Consequently the Greek-owned fleet in the interwar period had become the second biggest tramp operator in the world after the British, carrying bulk cargoes between third countries. This was a fleet that had seen a continuous rise since the formation of the Greek state in the late 1820s. During this period traditional shipping families came mainly from five islands – Cephalonia, Ithaca, Andros, Chios, and Kassos – and kept chains of branch offices that stretched from the ports of the Black Sea to the main economic and shipping centre of the world, London. They formed an international and exclusive informal shipping "club". Up to World War I these shipping families carried grain from the Black Sea to western European ports, with coal as the main return cargo. The expansion to the Atlantic routes, on a more massive scale, took place during the war, when Greece was neutral and the closure of the Dardanelles meant the loss of the Black Sea grain cargoes. The sea route on which Greek shipping thrived, and in which it replaced the British fleet during the interwar period, was from Argentina to northern Europe; carrying cargoes of grain and returning cargoes from the UK with coal. Hundreds of Greek ships visited the river Plate during the 1920s and it was then that Onassis met Kostas Gratsos, an Ithacan from a traditional shipping family, and subsequently a close friend and collaborator. Following the tradition of Greek seafarers he named his first two ships after his parents: *Socrates Onassis* and *Penelope Onassis*. These were second-hand vessels, cargo steamships of Standard B type, built in 1919.

In Buenos Aires, however, Onassis learnt the practices not only of Greek shipowners but also of the Norwegians, the other big international tramp operators. Norwegian shipowners were involved in a new trade, oil, and the ships that carried it, tankers, and it was Onassis's insight that made him realize the potential of oil as the world's main energy source. In 1938 he ordered his first tanker in Gotnenburg and became the first Greek shipowner to enter this market. Various legal difficulties created by the Greek government of Metaxas in some European ports led him to hoist the Panamanian flag on this new tanker together with another ship of his fleet (the Panamanian flag was already used by other traditional shipowners such as Kulukundis). The advantages of this decision were evident within two years. The outbreak of World War II found Onassis's ships under flags of countries that remained neutral. Hoisting the flags of Panama and Sweden, his ships were free to travel anywhere and could earn high profits, since transportation needs were very great during the war.

The earnings that came from the operation of the fleet during the war formed the basis of his post-war development. If his ships had been under the Greek flag they would have been requisitioned by the Greek government and the responsibility for their operation would have been taken over by the Allied forces, as happened with the Greek-flag ships. Onassis was one of the few who could exploit the opportunities offered by neutrality during the war. His involvement in shipping convinced Onassis that Buenos Aires was no longer the best place to be, and during the war he transferred his business to New York. It was there that he was introduced to the circles of traditional Greek shipowners, many of whom had also just moved to New York from Greece and London because of the war.

Greek shipowners kept a very tight international business and social circle; through their business they had formed international maritime networks based on Greek identity and Greek culture. Kinship, island, and ethnic ties – all of which implied trust in business apart from contributions to the actual organization and function of the shipping firm – provided the same advantages as membership of an elitist private club: access to information about the market, chartering, sales, and purchases of second-hand ships; shipbuilding, ship-repairing, and scrapping; financing from credit institutions; Premium and Insurance (P&I) clubs; and links with all other aspects of the shipping industry through access to London, the world's main maritime market. The intrusion of Onassis, a "foreigner", into the shipping world brought a much-publicized conflict with the leading figure of the Greek shipping community, Manolis Kulukundis, particularly on the controversial subject of the American-built ships, the Liberties, that were made available after the war to shipowners of allied governments on state guarantee. But Onassis took care to become a member of the community by the traditional Greek method: in 1946 he married the younger daughter of Stavros Livanos, a prominent Greek shipowner from Chios, and was thus "officially" admitted to the international Greek shipping family. An important aspect of this exclusive shipping clique that has played a major role in the growth of the fleet has been the constant competition and imitation of each other's practices even within individual families. In 1947 the other big shipowner and "foreigner" in Greek shipping circles, Stavros Niarchos, married the elder daughter of Stavros Livanos.

It was in these immediate post-war years that Onassis, together with Niarchos, was the first shipowner seriously to enter the tanker market. At this time the destroyed shipyards of Germany and Britain were looking for contracts that could contribute to their reconstruction. Onassis became one of the pedestals of this reconstruction and in 1949 he placed an order for the building of 16 tankers in the West German shipyards of Howaldswerke on very favourable terms. The opportunity to enter the tanker market was given by the Norwegians: because of foreign currency shortages, from 1948 to 1951 a ban was placed on the import of ships in Norway. Norwegian shipowners, who had been heavily involved in tanker shipping during the interwar period, were thus unable to benefit from the trade boom created by the Korean war in 1951, leaving the door open to Onassis, Niarchos, and other Greek shipowners to enter the tanker business.

Traditional families had always saved the profits of existing operations to buy a new ship; in so far as they depended on credit, it was usually limited to the guarantees that the mortgage on the ship provided and was paid off as quickly as possible. The ships they operated were largely tramp ships involved in the dry-cargo market. By contrast, Onassis and Niarchos entered the tanker market by using credit rather than cash for the purchase of ships, and they guaranteed their loans with five- to ten-year charters from large American oil companies. This method of financing had first been used by the Norwegians in the interwar period. American banks could not refuse credit to previously unknown clients who made such compelling cases for loans.

By competing with each other, these two leading shipowners further developed ship-financing methods: rather than ordering one tanker at a time, they started ordering whole new series of tankers, backed by a single charter. Ordering a series of vessels at one shipyard reduced costs and also guaranteed employment in the yards for a number of years. The shipbuilders were able to exploit the economies that the increased scale of production provided and thus were able to offer reduced prices. Onassis was also the first to realize that costs could be reduced if the carrying capacity of a ship was increased. This realization encouraged him to become the first shipowner in the world to build a "supertanker": *Tina Onasis*, built in 1953, with a tonnage of 45,320 deadweight was considered a technological achievement. The tactic that Onassis used to enter the oil market was soon followed by many traditional Greek shipowners. Even more important for Greek-owned shipping, however, was the fact that Onassis and Niarchos succeeded in penetrating the US financial markets, by securing finance for their projects, and thus paving the way for other Greek shipowners.

In less than a decade Onassis became one of the biggest independent tanker owners. His entrepreneurial spirit, however, and international orientation brought him into direct contact with the oil-producing countries, and consequently into trouble with the oil-consuming countries and US multinational interests. By signing an agreement with Saudi Arabia, he provoked the wrath of the oil companies and created an international scandal. According to the agreement, Onassis was to transfer tankers of 500,000 GRT to the Saudi Arabian flag, and pay a certain amount per carried ton to the Saudi Arabian government. In return, the Saudi Arabian government agreed to give priority to Onassis's tankers in the loading and transportation of oil. It is not difficult to imagine what effect an independent Saudi Arabian tanker shipping company would have on the interests of oil companies and the countries they represented. The reactions were immediate: the US State Department protested to the Saudi Arabian government, and the British government brought the issue before the European Organization of Economic Co-operation (which claimed that the contract would cause discrimination against other maritime nations). Onassis was attacked on all fronts: US and European oil companies refused to charter his newly built tankers; his newly acquired whale-hunting fleet was attacked by Peruvian warships in the Pacific Ocean (partly motivated by Peruvian whaling interests); and the American government demanded taxes of 20 million dollars. Not surprisingly, the Onassis–Saudi Arabian agreement was never enforced; but luck turned this financial crisis to an extremely profitable outcome: the closure of the Suez Canal in 1956, which increased the world tanker demand and hence the freight rates, came at a time when Onassis was the only shipowner who had a large number of tankers free for charter. Thus, he not only avoided bankruptcy but also strengthened his financial status and further increased his fleet.

Despite the fact that Onassis's name was associated with tankers, his fleet also consisted of cargo ships and bulk carriers. This protected him from the risk of depending on a sole charter market. Besides, his interests were not restricted to bulk shipping: in 1950 he had already created one of the biggest whale-hunting fleets in the world. Moreover, among his investments that gave him weight and reputation was the acquisition in 1953 of the famous hotel and casino Hôtel de Paris in Monte Carlo. For a short period Onassis tried unsuccessfully to enter the shipbuilding industry, acquiring the Scottish shipbuilder Harland & Wolff. Banking was another sector in which Onassis was interested: he bought a small bank in Switzerland, the Banque de Dépôts, which was sold after his death.

During the 1950s he invested heavily in Greece. In 1957 he purchased the Greek national airline for the huge sum of 35 million dollars. The company was renamed Olympic Airways and within a short time it expanded its network of domestic and international destinations, contributing to the development not only of the tourist industry but of Greece as a whole. Onassis invested a great deal in the development of Olympic, although he never considered it his main business, unlike his son Alexander who was dedicated to it. In the late 1960s he proposed to the Greek government a 700-million-dollar project, which included the building of a refinery, investment in the aluminium industry in cooperation with the Aluminum Company of America, and the construction of an electricity-generating company. This project, which was partly in collaboration with Niarchos, was cancelled by Onassis in 1972, for reasons that were never made clear.

Factors that contributed much to the entrepreneurial success of Aristotle Onassis included his talent to recruit good advisers and loyal employees and his ability to communicate with them and take advantage of their ideas and proposals. Kostas Gratsos, who came from a traditional shipping family and was effectively his right-hand man, not only gave him the benefit of his valuable experience but also saw that his ships were manned by highly skilled seamen from Ithaca, one of Greece's traditional maritime islands. Onassis's talent for selecting and trusting able young men proved valuable even after his death, and many of his faithful executives and employees continue to stand up for his interests to the present day.

Onassis's private life was as colourful as his business career. In 1946 he married Tina Livanos, the younger daughter of Stavros Livanos, one of the biggest shipowners of the Greek-owned fleet in the 1950s. Tina, who was more than 20 years his junior, gave him two children, Christina and Alexandros; but their marriage lasted only until 1958. For the next decade Onassis's name was linked with the world-famous Greek soprano Maria Callas in what proved to be a long-lasting passionate affair that marked both their lives. But Aristotle Onassis again shook the international social circles by his marriage to Jackie Kennedy, widow of the assassinated American president, which took place in October 1968 on Skorpios, his private island in the Ionian Sea. Onassis's extraordinary raison d'être came to a halt five years later. The death of his son Alexander at the age of 25 in an aeroplane accident in 1973 was a tragedy from which he never recovered and he died in Paris two years later.

At his death, apart from his deposits in 217 banks around the world, his own bank in Switzerland, 25 per cent of Harland & Wolff, his island of Skorpios, his skyscraper in New York, and his fleet of 56 ships of 2.5 million tons deadweight, the rest of his wealth was estimated to be about one and a half billion US dollars. This consisted of investments in European, Latin American, and US companies in finance and banking, industry, real estate, shipping and transport, the construction industry, tourism, and other general enterprises. Onassis's entrepreneurial talent was still there, even after his death, and survives to the present day, as reflected in his will and in his choice of executors.

His daughter Christina inherited half of Onassis's assets while the other half went to the Alexander Onassis Foundation, set up in 1975 and named after her dead brother. Christina was in control of the business for a short period but she entrusted the running of her property to a group of Onassis's collaborators, who have continued since her death in 1988 to manage it for her daughter Athina. The Alexander Onassis Foundation remains one of the largest and most active foundations in Greece; under the management of a team of executives whom he chose, it continues to run successfully the fleet and other profit-making organizations as well as a wide range of charitable activities that he planned.

Aristotle Onassis, "Ari" as he was popularly known, personally created the myth of the Greek tycoon, and 25 years after his death his legend still makes headlines. Books, films, and documentaries on his life are still being produced. He epitomizes the Greek entrepreneur par excellence. It is certainly no coincidence that Anthony Quinn, the actor who impersonated Kazantzakis's hero Zorba the Greek, was also the one chosen to play Onassis on screen.

GELINA HARLAFTIS

See also Ships and Shipping

Biography

Born in either 1900 or 1906 in Smyrna, Onassis fled to Athens after the Asia Minor disaster and emigrated to Argentina in 1923. There he imported tobacco from Greece until he had enough capital in 1933 to turn to shipping. He took advantage of the slump, and later of the need for transport in World War II, and invested in supertankers for oil in the 1950s. In 1957 he bought the Greek national airline. His wealth was legendary. He was married first to Tina Livanos and secondly (after a long affair with Maria Callas) to Jacqueline Kennedy. He died in Paris in 1975.

Further Reading

Fraser, Nicholas *et al.*, *Aristotle Onassis*, London: Weidenfeld and Nicolson, and Philadelphia: Lippincott, 1977

Harlaftis, Gelina, *Greek Shipowners and Greece, 1945–1975: From Separate Development to Mutual Interdependence*, London: Athlone Press, 1993

Harlaftis, Gelina, *A History of Greek-owned Shipping: The Making of an International Tramp Fleet, 1830 to the Present Day*, London and New York: Routledge, 1996

Joesten, Joachim, *Onassis: A Biography*, New York: Abelard Schuman, 1963

Onomastics

Onomastics is the study of names and naming practices. In this article, names are defined as personal names (place names are a different, though related and interesting, study), and Greek personal names are names borne by Greeks, whether in Greece itself or elsewhere in the world where Greeks have settled. In antiquity, as today, that imposes a very wide geographical scope, for already by the 8th century BC Greek cities were sending colonies abroad, in a diaspora which would leave Greeks settled on the Black Sea, in Asia Minor, north Africa, Sicily, south Italy, and beyond. Names always reflect the concerns and values of society, and are responsive to political, cultural, and religious influences. Changes over time are to be expected, but it is important also to register that there have always been regional variations, at any one time, within the Greek-speaking world.

Modern interest in the collection and study of ancient Greek personal names began in the early 19th century. Almost all the evidence available at that time came from literature, which, even when it includes historical works, can paint only a partial picture of a society. The picture, however, was about to be transformed by the discovery and publication of documentary evidence provided by inscriptions, papyri (for Graeco-Roman Egypt), coins, and artefacts. Documentary evidence is important because it gives the names of relatively ordinary people, and because it is found in all parts of the Greek world, and not just the main centres of literary output, above all Athens.

Inscriptions on stone, by far the greater part of documentary evidence, record citizen lists, decrees, treaties, and judgements but also the more personal tombstones, religious dedications and curses, and the manumissions of slaves. New documentary evidence continues to be discovered, published, and analysed, but it is already clear that the names of upwards of half a million individuals have survived, and tens of thousands of different names. From the 8th century BC the volume of documentary texts increased steadily, reaching its first peak in the Hellenistic age. It is during this period that the fundamental features of ancient Greek naming practices can be observed and documented. It is, however, worth noting that two earlier sources, Mycenaean texts and the Homeric poems, push back the history of Greek onomastics, albeit partially, by a further 500 years.

Dating mainly from the 13th century BC, and written in Linear B, a pre-alphabetic script comprising ideograms, numerals, and syllabic signs, Mycenaean records have been found at Mycenae, Thebes, Tiryns, and Pylos on the mainland, and Knossos and Cydonia in Crete. There are many uncertainties in interpreting the names in these documents, because the spelling is ambiguous and because, being inventories, they supply no context, but Mycenologists are agreed that the basic formations of Greek names as described below were already in place, including familiar names such as Theodora and Alexandra. The same is true of the Homeric epic poems, the *Iliad* and the *Odyssey*, which are generally agreed to be the culmination of an oral tradition which may reach back to the 13th century BC. It is, however, interesting to note that the names of the main actors in the drama – Priam, Hector, Agamemnon, Menelaus, Helen, Cassandra, Odysseus, Penelope – thought of today as among the most famous of

"Greek" names, did not continue in use in the Archaic and Classical periods. They enjoyed a revival under the Roman empire, especially outside Greece, in Italy and in parts of Asia Minor.

Greek naming conformed to the Indo-European pattern found throughout most of Europe until relatively recent times, by which a child received one given name. In public contexts, and for legal purposes, the given name was followed by the name of the father (patronymic), very rarely by that of the mother (metronymic). In certain circumstances, an indication of citizenship (ethnic) would also be given. These three elements – given name, patronymic, and ethnic – are the fundamental elements of nomenclature. The last two are also the building blocks of a much later development, family names or surnames.

In antiquity, as today, there was a tradition of naming the firstborn son after the paternal grandfather, and the second after the maternal grandfather (there is less ancient evidence for the naming of daughters). In leading families whose tenure of public office is recorded, it is sometimes possible to trace this pattern over two or three hundred years. Conservatism in namegiving ensured the preservation of names even after the concepts embodied in them had passed away, sometimes against the tide of new forces.

The patronymic generally took the form of the father's name in the genitive case (thus, Alexandros Philippou); but in areas of the Aeolic dialect (especially Lesbos and the facing coast of Asia Minor, and Thessaly and Boeotia on the mainland) the patronymic adjective was used (and applied to wives as well as children), formed by making an adjective out of the father's name. This usage was common in Homer (e.g. Ajax Telamonios, Ajax the son of Telamon); a second form found in Homer, in which the father's name is given a termination with patronymic force -ides (Hector Priamides, Hector son of Priam), survived in the historical period, for example Simonides and Bacchylides, but as an independent form deprived of patronymic force.

While the patronymic was important in identifying and sometimes legitimizing the individual, its use varied according to place and context. The 2nd-century AD writer Pausanias (2. 7) commented that the citizens of Sicyon in the Peloponnese recorded on their tombstones the name but not the patronymic of the deceased. From this statement it might be inferred that the use of the patronymic was standard everywhere else, but tombstones, which survive in their thousands, show that in most parts of western Greece and in Boeotia the patronymic was not generally recorded, while in nearby Thessaly it usually was.

Use of the ethnic also varied, according to context. The purpose of nomenclature is to identify, and at home an individual did not need to indicate origin. The city or regional ethnic was, therefore, used only when abroad. By contrast, in a city with an internal political organization of demes, such as Athens, Rhodes, or Eretria in Euboea, the demotic was given. At Athens, in the late 6th century, Cleisthenes' reforms required that the demotic should replace the patronymic (*Athenaion Politeia*, 11. 4), but by the 4th century it had become standard practice to give both. Thus, at Athens, "Alcibiades son of Cleinias, of the deme Scambonidai", abroad "Alcibiades son of Cleinias, of Athens".

The Greek grammarians knew two ways of classifying names. They were either "simple" or "compound" in formation, and, as to content, they were either based on the names of gods, "theophoric", or they were secular.

Simple names consisted of a noun or adjective, alone or with a suffix: for example, from the adjective *aristos* ("excellent", "best"), the names Aristos, Arist-ion, Arist-ullos, etc., feminine Arista, Aristo, Arist-ulla, etc. Compound names were formed by combining nouns, adjectives, verbs, or adverbs in various patterns. Thus, Aristo-teles, Arist-ippos, Aristo-kles, Aristo-boulos, Aristo-damos. The order could be reversed: Aristo-nikos or Nik-aristos. Compounds were often turned into a so-called "hypocoristic" form which could be shorter (for example, Kleommas from Kleomachos) or longer (Sophroniskos from Sophron). Women's names could take neuter as well as feminine terminations, and covered broadly the same range of form and content as men's, including military and political connotations, for example Alexandra, Stratippa, Demostrata. Abstract names such as Harmonia ("harmony"), Eukarpia ("fertility"), Glukera ("sweet") did exist, but seem to have originated as slave names.

Within these broad rules, the Greeks showed almost limitless inventiveness; some components, such as *polis* ("city") appear in more than 50 different forms. The following are just a few examples: parts of the body (*kephalos* "head", making Kephalos, Kephal-ion), animals (*leon*, "lion", making Leon, feminine Leaina, Leont-iskos, Aristo-leon; *hippos*, "horse", making Hippo-stratos, Strat-ippos, Hippo-krates, Krat-ippos, Fil-ippos), plants (*ampelos*, "vine", making Ampelos, Ampel-ion, Ampel-ides), political institutions (*demos*, "sovereign people", making Demo-sthenes, Demo-stratos, Arche-demos, Dem-archos), defence or protection (the verb *alexo* making Alex-andros, Alexi-demos, Alexi-polis). Though usually laudatory, attributes could also be (at least to us) pejorative, and yet were passed down from generation to generation: thus, *aischros*, "ugly", making Aischr-ion, Aischr-a, *gaster*, "stomach", making Gastron.

Theophoric names could take the adjectival or the compound form. The most common of all Greek names were the adjectival forms based on Apollo (Apollonios), Dionysos (Dionysios), and Demeter (Demetrios); but a greater range was provided by compounds in which the name of the god was followed by -genes/geneia (birth), -dotos/dota and -doros/dora (giving/gift), -philos/phila (loved/loving), -kles/kleia (renown), -phanes/phaneia (manifestation), etc. Thus, from Zeus, root Dio-, Dio-genes/Dio-geneia, Dio-dotos, Dio-doros, Dio-philos, Dio-kles/Dio-kleia, etc.

Theophoric names could be formed from cult titles of gods, and from lesser deities such as nymphs and river gods; the river Asopus in Boeotia, for example, gave rise to names such as Asop-ios and Asopodoros, which are found only in Boeotia and Athens. There was also the generic type from *theos* ("god"): Theo-genes, Theo-dotos, Theo-doros, Theo-kles, etc. The arrival of new divinities was duly marked in nomenclature; thus, from the late 4th century BC, worship of the Egyptian goddess Isis gave rise to Isi-doros, Isi-dotos, Isi-genes, etc., that of the god Sarapis (later spelling Serapis) to Sarap-ion, Sarap-ias, Sarap-is, etc.

The first major disturbance to the pattern of Greek nomenclature came with the arrival of the Romans who had a wholly different system of nomenclature, with three names, *praenomen*, *nomen*, and *cognomen*. After the Romans conquered Greece, Greeks receiving Roman citizenship would adopt the *praenomen* and *nomen* of the donor (a conquering general, later the emperor or a governor); in this way, names like Julius and Flavius first made their way into Greek nomenclature. The third name, the *cognomen*, was usually Greek: thus, Tiberius Julius Alexander, Titus Flavius Alcibiades. The Romans indicated filiation in a brief formula which came between the *nomen* and the *cognomen*: for example, G(aius) Julius G(aii) f(ilius) Caesar. Greeks sometimes adopted this system, but often simply appended the patronymic to the *cognomen*. A new name-form developed, especially in Asia Minor, with the suffix *-ianus* (e.g. Herodianus from Herodes) which sometimes gave the name a patronymic force.

Christianity was destined to make a permanent impact on Greek nomenclature, but the change was neither sudden nor simple. Several different currents fed into the main stream. Some "Christian" names were in fact Jewish, for example John (Joannes), Anna, and Maria. In time, but not much before the 4th century, names incorporating new values appeared, such as Eusebius and Euphemia. Of the old names, the neutral theophoric names such as Theodora and Theophilos were retained, and some new compounds formed which had not occurred before, such as Theo-doulos (slave or servant of God), comparable to Christo-doulos (servant of Christ). More potent factors were at work, however. The appeal to parents by the 4th-century writer John Chrysostom to name their children after saints and not ancestors is a reminder of the inherent conservatism of naming, but also a background for the renewal of old pagan names with a new authority. Saints and martyrs were as likely as not to bear "pagan" names such as Demetrius, Dionysia, and Alexandra.

During and after the struggle between Christianity and paganism, Roman names, by now absorbed into Greek nomenclature, continued in general use. After AD 212, when citizenship was granted to all free inhabitants of the empire, Aurelius was the normal *nomen*; after the reign of Constantine (whose own name became a common "Christian" name after his conversion to Christianity), it was Flavius. In the correspondence of Libanius, in the 4th century, the names of recipients show a mixture of Roman names such as Marcus, Proclus, Modestus, Priscianus, and Ioulianus; old Greek names such as Andronikos, Alexandros, Dionysios, and Leontios; and a certain number of distinctly Christian names such as Eusebius, Eustathius, Euphemius, and Ambrosius. A century later, in the correspondence of the Christian Isidorus of Pelusium, Christian names such as Eulogius, Eulampius, Cyrillus, and Serenus account for a greater proportion, but there are also surprising survivals such as Isidorus, Serapion, and Apollonius. Overall, by this period, a general simplification in nomenclature had taken place, the patronymic had largely disappeared, and the ethnic fallen into disuse.

Invasions and political quarrels marked the end of the Roman empire, within which the Greek-speaking world was contained. The "Greek" world survived in the east, in the Byzantine empire. There began a period of transition in nomenclature. Biblical names and those with pious meaning, which marked the ascendancy of Christian values, remained in use, but names of new rulers, such as Basileios, Leon, Alexios,

also enjoyed a vogue. Family names began to be adopted, but only by ruling families. By the 13th century, however, the personal names Ioannes, Georgios, Demetrios, and Maria had established a lasting ascendancy. By that time, too, it was usual for monks to adopt a new name on entering the monastic life, and a class of names developed which was reserved for them, e.g. Gerasimos, Isaias, Iakovos, Makarios, though some continued to bear pagan names such as Dionysios, and even Hermes and Alcibiades.

The two main influences in post-Ottoman Greek nomenclature are Christianity and antiquity. Examples of the former are Ioannes/Yannis, Demetrios/Dimitri, Nicholas/Niko, Spiridon/Spiros, Konstantinos/Kostas for men, Eleni, Anna, Maria, Demetra, Konstantina for women, and of the latter, Aristoteles, Sokrates, Xenophon, Demosthenes, Leonidas, Miltiades, which were never forgotten but widely given from the 18th century onwards. Both male and female names are often familiarized by the addition of a hypocoristic termination such as *-aki*, *-oula*, or *-ita*, for example Petraki from Petros, Elenitsa from Eleni. The importance of the personal name is shown by the custom of celebrating name-days (the festival of the saint in question) rather than birthdays.

Hereditary family names or surnames developed sporadically from about AD 1000, at first mainly among ruling families, whose family names were often derived from locations, towns, and monasteries. The widespread use of surnames dates only from the War of Independence (c.1832). Many surnames take a patronymic form, with the terminations *-opoulos* or *-ides* (e.g. Konstantinopoulos, Apostolides), or are derived from trades (Metaxas, "silk weaver", Petalas, "blacksmith"), or physical characteristic (Kephalas, "head"). It is primarily in surnames that distinct local variations are to be found, reflecting past history, often occupation by foreign powers. Italian, especially Venetian, occupation left its mark in both personal and family names in Crete, the Ionian islands, and the Cyclades. Many surnames in Cephalonia, for example, have the termination *-atos* (Marinatos, Laskaratos), the Italian *-ato*. Surnames in *-oglou*, reflecting the Turkish "son of" and equivalent to Greek *-opoulos*, are particularly common among Greeks from the Pontic area of Asia Minor.

ELAINE MATTHEWS

Further Reading

Bechtel, Friedrich, *Die historischen Personennamen des Griechischen bis zur Kaiserzeit*, Halle: Niemeyer, 1917; reprinted Hildesheim: Olms, 1982 (fundamental study of the formation of names)

Daux, G., in *L'Onomastique latine*, Paris: Centre National de la Recherche Scientifique, 1977, p. 405ff. (on the impact of Roman nomenclature on Greek names)

Fraser, P.M. and E. Matthews, *A Lexicon of Greek Personal Names*, 4 vols to date, Oxford: Clarendon Press, and New York: Oxford University Press, 1987–2000 (comprehensive modern collection of names in the historical period, including literature except Homer)

Jones, A.H.M., J.R. Martindale, and J. Morris, *The Prosopography of the Later Roman Empire*, 4 vols, Cambridge: Cambridge University Press, 1971–92 (lists the important political figures)

Kamptz, Hans von, *Homerische Personennamen*, Gottingen: Vandenhoeck & Ruprecht, 1982

Masson, Olivier, *Onomastica Graeca Selecta*, 2 vols, Nanterre: Imprimerie Intégrée de l'Université de Paris X-Nanterre, 1990

Pape, Wilhelm and G.E. Benseler, *Wörterbuch der griechischen Eigennamen*, Braunschweig: Vieweg, 2 vols, 1863–70; reprinted

Graz: Akademische Druck und Verlagsanstalt, 1959 (names from antiquity in literature)

Robert, Louis, *Noms indigènes dans l'Asie-Mineure gréco-romaine*, Paris: Maisonneuve, 1963

Robert, Louis (editor), *Opera minora selecta: epigraphie et antiquités grecques*, 7 vols, Amsterdam: Hakkert, 1969–90

Smith, William and Henry Wace, *A Dictionary of Christian Biography*, 4 vols, London: John Murray, 1877–87; reprinted New York: AMS Press, 1974 (full listing of important figures in the Christian world)

Ventris, Michael and John Chadwick, *Documents in Mycenaean Greek: Three Hundred Selected Tablets from Knossos, Pylos and Mycenae*, 2nd edition, Cambridge: Cambridge University Press, 1973, chapter 4

Withycombe, E.G. (editor) *The Oxford Dictionary of English Christian Names*, Oxford: Clarendon Press, and New York: Oxford University Press, 1977 (good general introduction to names, including, briefly, Greek names)

Website

Prosopography of the Byzantine Empire, 641–1261, a collaboration between King's College, London and the Berlin-Brandenburgische Akademie's *Prosopographie der mittelbyzanischen Zeit*: http://www.kcl.ac.uk/humanities/cch/PBE/

Opera and Operetta

Modern musical drama, like other forms of European classical music, was transmitted to Greece primarily through the Ionian islands, which were ruled successively by Venice, France, and Britain during the Ottoman domination of the mainland. Yet ancient and even medieval Greek precedents for sung drama are not lacking. Classical tragedies were originally performed with melodies by their authors that were sung for centuries. After the decline of ancient theatre, some of its musicodramatic elements persisted in the imperial ceremonial, popular entertainments, and Orthodox worship of Byzantium. Nevertheless, despite the efforts of some commentators to find evidence for the existence of Byzantine musical theatre in such texts as the hymns of Romanos, only a single sacred drama from around the late 14th century has come to light, the strongly liturgical character of which has been affirmed by Symeon of Thessalonica and modern scholars. Contemporary Greek musical drama may therefore be linked to antiquity only indirectly through the medium of Italian opera, the late Renaissance creators of which were deeply influenced by the humanist rediscovery of Classical tragedy.

The earliest documented stagings of Italian opera in the Ionian islands were mounted in 1733 at the San Giacomo theatre in Corfu. Operatic performances by visiting Italian troupes became increasingly frequent over the next century, during which theatres were also constructed on the islands of Zakynthos (1813) and Cephalonia (1838). While it appears that local musicians did not participate to any significant extent in the production of opera before 1840, from the early decades of the 19th century Ionian-born composers were setting Italian libretti to music. The doyen of this first generation of native composers was Nikolaos Halkiopoulos-Mantzaros (1795–1872), whose early one-act comedy *Don Crepusculo* of 1815 is the oldest extant Greek opera. Invited to

Naples for study in the 1820s by Zingarelli, Mantzaros later returned to Corfu where, in addition to composing further operas and the music for the Greek National Anthem, he exercised considerable influence as a teacher. By the middle decades of the 19th century operas by such Greek composers as E. Lampelet, P. Carrer, and S. Xyndas were being performed alongside works by Donizetti and Verdi not only in the Ionian islands, but in Italy itself. Around this time Ionian composers and a few Italian expatriates introduced modern Greek themes to opera in a series of historical works based on the mainland's revolt against the Turks. These paved the way for the première in Corfu of Xyndas's *The Parliamentary Candidate* (1867), the first opera composed to a Greek libretto. Development along these lines continued until the outbreak of World War II, after which the musical culture of the Ionian islands went into a serious decline that was compounded by the destruction of several theatres in the earthquake of 1954.

The introduction of opera to mainland Greece occurred on 4 July 1837 when a group of Italian tightrope walkers employed an orchestra of ten to stage the first act of Rossini's *The Barber of Seville*. Despite the complete omission of Rosina's role due to the lack of a female singer, this performance was so enthusiastically received that an Italian opera company arrived the very next month to mount the entire work. After 1840 royal patronage and growing audiences stimulated increasingly frequent visits to Athens, Patras, Piraeus, and Syros by Italian and later French troupes, all of whom were evidently unaffected by the protests of Greek cultural conservatives incensed by what they perceived to be the immorality of many libretti. The mainland's growing operatic scene also soon attracted the attention of Ionian composers including Carrer, whose patriotic opera *Markos Botsaris* – which includes in its first act a lament sung by an old klepht ("O Yero Demos": Old Demos) that proved to be so popular that it virtually became a folk song – was previewed in Athens before the royal family in 1858 and premièred in Patras in 1861. S. Samaras, N. Lampelet, D. Lavrangas, and other members of the Ionian school would subsequently dominate Greek opera until the first decade of the 20th century. Ionians were also instrumental in the creation of the first Greek opera troupes at the end of the 1880s, one of which survived long enough to tour Egypt and Turkey. A more durable Athenian company, the *Helleniko Melodrama* founded by Lavrangas, inaugurated its existence with performances in 1900 of Puccini's *La Bohème*. These touched off an unprecedented wave of enthusiasm for opera that was sufficient to allow the troupe to serve as Greece's main operatic ensemble until the creation of the present National Opera (*Lyriki Skini*) in 1939.

Opera in the Italian tradition was gradually eclipsed on the mainland during the second decade of the 20th century by the rise of Greek operetta. Although French companies had been staging performances of operetta in Greece since the 1870s, the appearance of native operetta may be attributed more immediately to the Athenian revues of the early 1900s. The success of these pastiches of pirated foreign melodies encouraged the impresario I. Papaïonannou to found the *Hellinike Operetta* in 1909 to produce entire Viennese operettas in Greek translation. Other companies were soon founded, and in 1914 the veteran opera composers Samaras and Theophrastos I.

Sakellarides (1883–1950) wrote the first Greek operettas. The latter, who was the German-trained son of the famous cantor John Sakellarides and Papaïoannou's principal conductor, composed more than 103 musical works for the stage including the enduringly popular *O Vaphtistikos* (The Godson, 1918). His main compositional rival was the bass Nikos Hatziapostolou (1879–1941), who wrote music combining elements of French operetta with contemporary Athenian popular song. From the première of Hatziapostolou's *I Moderna Kamariera* (The Modern Chambermaid) in 1916 until the late 1920s, operetta reigned as the chief musical entertainment of Greece's westernized bourgeoisie. Other composers of operetta during this period included the classically trained Lavrangas, Lampelet, and Yiannis Konstantinides, who wrote popular music under the pseudonym Kostas Yiannides.

As the urban Greek public shifted its allegiance to operetta, Manolis Kalomiris emerged at the head of a so-called National School of composition to challenge the supremacy of Italianate classical music. While continuing the later Ionians' use of folk material in such operas as *To Dachtylidi tis Manas* (Mother's Ring, 1917), Kalomiris employed it in a manner derived from contemporary central European music. Greek opera thereafter began to fall along a spectrum running from the works of the National School to pieces firmly within the western mainstream such as *Soeur Béatrice*, composed in 1918 by Dimitri Mitropoulos (1896–1960) on a text by Maeterlinck. Despite the general decline of opera and operetta in Greece after World War II, T. Antoniou, A. Logothetis, Mikis Theodorakis, and many other Greek composers have continued to write significant musical dramas for production both at home and abroad.

ALEXANDER LINGAS

See also Song

Further Reading

Anogeianakis, Phoivos, "I Mousiki sti neoteri hellada" [Music in Modern Greece], in *Historia tis mousikis* [History of Music] by Karl Nef, translated by Phoivos Anogeianakis, 2nd edition, Athens, 1985 (original Swiss edition (in German), 1920)

Baroutas, Kostas, *I Mousiki Zoe sten Athena to 190 Aiona* [Musical Life in 19th-Century Athens], Athens, 1992

Chamoudopoulos, Demetrios A., *I Anatoli tis entechnis mousikis sten Ellada kai i Demiourgia tis Ethnikis Scholis: Anaskopoiseis kai skepseis* [The Rise of Art Music in Greece, and the Creation of the National School: Reviews and Reflections], Athens, 1980

Mylonas, Kostas, *Istoria tou Ellinikou Tragoudiou* [History of Greek Song], vol. 1: *1824–1960*, Athens, 1985

Sadie, Stanley (editor), *The New Grove Dictionary of Opera*, 4 vols, London: Macmillan, and New York: Grove, 1992

Symeonidou, Aleka, *Lexiko Ellinon Syntheton* [Dictionary of Greek Composers], Athens, 1995

Velimirović, Miloš, "Liturgical Drama in Byzantium and Russia", *Dumbarton Oaks Papers*, 16 (1962): pp. 351–85

West, M.L., *Ancient Greek Music*, Oxford: Clarendon Press, and New York: Oxford University Press, 1992

Zakythinos, Alexis D., *Discography of Greek Classical Music*, 2nd edition, Buenos Aires: Zakythinos, 1988

Oracles

Oracles were both utterances of (usually) gods, with or without an intermediary and in response to human questions, and the places where such utterances were made. At reputedly the oldest Greek oracular site, that of Zeus at Dodona in Epirus, the god was believed to make his response known through the rustling of the leaves of a sacred (probably Valonia) oak or the cooing of a dove (probably a ring-dove) perched there, which signs were interpreted by priests. By the 5th century BC, however, priestesses (later at least called "Doves") under the inspiration of Zeus simply gave affirmative or negative responses to questions scratched by enquirers on lead tablets, of which about 80 still survive (the most legible is in the museum at nearby Ioannina).

Far more is known about the oracle of Apollo at Delphi, which probably originated in the late 9th century BC (references to an earlier oracle of another deity on the site are subject to much modern debate). After a possible stage when its oracles, similarly to those at Dodona, merely involved interpretations of the rustling of the leaves of a laurel tree, already at the beginning of the Archaic age a local woman known as the Pythia was believed to act in a trance as Apollo's mouthpiece.

The procedure was as follows. Originally just once a year (according to Plutarch, *Moralia*, 292e), on Apollo's birthday, but from perhaps the 6th century BC on the seventh day of every month (except for the three months of winter when Apollo was believed to be among the Hyperboreans), consultation could take place, provided that the ominous behaviour of a goat sprinkled with cold water was favourable. Authorities (the Delphic Amphictiony) gave precedence first to Delphians and then favoured states and individuals. This was presumably often won by such costly gifts (most notably by the Lydian king Croesus) that some states even built treasuries at Delphi to house them (the best-preserved today is that of the Athenians). All enquirers had first to place on an altar an inordinately expensive cake (*pelanos*) as fee. Accompanied by the resident representative of his city (*proxenos*), the enquirer passed over the threshold of the temple, made blood-sacrifices, and entered the inner sanctuary, where he kept silence as a priest (*prophetes*) put the previously supplied question to the unseen Pythia, who was seated upon a tripod, and converted her response into intelligible, though often ambiguous, hexameters. The geology of the site and toxicology respectively prove untenable the ancient reports that the Pythia's trance was induced by mephitic vapours emanating from a chasm or by the properties of laurel leaves: it was probably merely self-induced by an uneducated and pious old woman of great religious susceptibility. The *prophetes*, we may assume, formulated responses on the bases of common sense, the desires of the enquirers, and Delphic interests (although the "Medizing of Apollo" during the Persian Wars has been much exaggerated, the oracle did later fall under the influence of both Philip of Macedon and the Aetolian League). A much cheaper and more common form of oracle at Delphi, and one that came to be practised on other days of the month, was cleromancy, by which one of two presumably differently coloured beans was drawn to give an answer of "yes" or "no".

Oracles: Attic red-figure krater showing Orestes as a suppliant at the shrine of Apollo in Delphi, 4th century BC, Louvre, Paris

Despite rivals, most notably the oracles of Zeus at Dodona and, from the 5th century BC, Ammon at Siwa in the Egyptian desert, the most famous oracle in the Archaic and Classical ages was that at Delphi. Although the vast majority of consultants were individuals, it played also a prominent political role (Sparta even maintained a standing commission of ambassadors called Pythii to transact Delphic business). Some evidence suggests that in early times it was consulted over the removal of unpopular rulers, but later it was never involved in internal politics. Although its public importance became most apparent in the belief of virtually all states that Apollo's approval was essential in the planting of colonies, it also both pronounced on the advisability of waging war and was involved in arbitration between states. In the 4th century BC, however, most public consultations were on cultic matters, and even these became rare after c.300 BC. In the Hellenistic period its functions were largely lost in the revival of local oracles, especially those of Asia Minor. Quintus Fabius Pictor enquired of Delphi in 216 BC about the proper rituals for ensuring victory over the Carthaginians, but after the Punic Wars the Romans usually had sufficient confidence in their own abilities to dispense with Greek oracular aid including Delphi's.

Other oracles offered a considerable variety in consultative practices, including the use of male spokesmen for the god, such as the *thespiodos* of Apollo's shrine at Claros in Asia Minor who drank from a sacred spring. At some sanctuaries priests interpreted "divine" signs such as those apparent in the flames (empyromancy) on Zeus' altar at Olympia. There were also oracles that dispensed with intermediaries, often giving their answers by lot (as with the beans at Delphi) and even dice but most notably by means of incubation, which was practised most commonly by those suffering from disease, insanity, or injury. In this, during a ritual sleep at a sanctuary, consultants were believed either to be healed by a god (often Asclepius) with or without divine helpers or sent a dream that prescribed treatment (Aristophanes describes in detail one such night at the Asclepieum in the Piraeus at *Plutus*, 653–747). Physicians were frequently in attendance subsequently to effect the cure. A bizarre, unmediated but non-medical parallel is afforded by the oracle of Trophonius at Lebadea in western Boeotia. Here the enquirer, after lengthy and elaborate preliminaries, had to thrust himself into a claustrophobic subterranean pit, where the chthonic deity made revelations to him and whence he emerged terrified and barely conscious to be questioned by priests and restored to sanity by relations (graphically described by Pausanias, 9. 39. 5–14).

Although Plutarch (d. after AD 120), himself a priest at Delphi for the last 30 years of his life, wrote on the decline of oracles (*De Defectu Oraculorum*, *Moralia* 409e–438e), inscriptions from the 2nd and 3rd centuries AD on the building of the oracle of Apollo at Claros prove its continued popularity for public consultations by neighbouring states. During this period too various charlatans sought to exploit human gullibility by oracle-mongering. The most notorious of these was Alexander of Abonuteichos in Paphlagonia, whose tricks, involving a live snake apparently attached to a lifelike artificial head (whose jaws he could manipulate) and a hot needle to remove the wax seals of consultants' written questions, are hilariously excoriated by Lucian (*Alexander* or *False Prophet*).

Some well-established pagan oracles certainly survived into the early Byzantine period (the emperor Julian consulted several, including Delphi and Dodona, before embarking on his war against the Sassanian Persians). However, their anti-Christian utterances, many of which had been collected by the Neoplatonist Porphyry in his lost *On the Philosophy of the Oracles*, hastened their suppression. Christians associated them with demons and witches, built churches on their sites, and even forged oracles, such as one of Apollo confessing that his temple at Cyzicus was now the home of the Theotokos. Although Constantine I closed the Asclepieum at Aegae in Cilicia, pagan incubation survived into the 5th century AD, and the practice itself continued throughout the Byzantine period (and has not completely died out today), Christian saints simply supplanting the older gods.

During their heyday the authority of oracles was such that no certain case of disobedience is known. Even among philosophers only the Epicureans denied their claims. Nevertheless, since typically an oracle did not initiate action but either merely expressed approval or disapproval or chose between alternatives put to it by consultants, it could be manipulated into giving apparent blessing to a dubious enterprise. Even the pious Xenophon was chided by Socrates for asking Apollo to which gods he should sacrifice before setting out as a mercenary on the expedition of Cyrus instead of enquiring if he should join it at all (*Anabasis*, 3. 1. 5–7). Bribery was also practised, but not as often as ancient authorities claim.

Collections of oracles had less authority except in the case of the most famous, the Sibylline oracles. Originally a single prophetess, the word sibyl (probably not Hellenic and therefore suggesting the existence of pre-Greek prophetesses) had become at least by the 4th century BC a generic term for such women throughout the Greek world and later beyond. They were believed to prophesy in the normal manner either under the influence of a god (Apollo for Virgil's sibyl in *Aeneid* 6) or through their own inspiration. Collections are first heard of in connection with the books offered to Tarquinius Priscus (traditionally king of Rome 616–579 BC), the last three of which he bought and had preserved in his new temple of Capitoline Jupiter. Upon its destruction in 83 BC a collection was made from scattered copies, and this was still being consulted as late as AD 363. The surviving Sibylline oracles, in Greek hexameters, date from the 2nd century BC to the 7th century AD and are of mainly Jewish origin with some pagan and some Christian material, which last claims the Sybil as an independent witness to the Christian faith, supports Christian morality, attacks paganism, and prophesies the suppression of certain pagan cults.

The Chaldaean oracles, again written in hexameters and surviving only in fragments, were traditionally ascribed to a father and son named Julian in the 2nd century AD. These offered a philosophical guide to how in a dualistic world believers might empty themselves of evil matter to ascend to a triune deity consisting of a monadic Paternal Intellect, a dyadic Second Intellect, and the Cosmic Soul, which was identified as Hecate. They were much used by the Neoplatonists (especially Porphyry and Iamblichus), fascinated Psellos in the 11th century and were known to Plethon in the 15th.

Among Byzantine collections of oracles is one written in iambics, purportedly by the emperor Leo VI (886–912), which predicted civil war in Constantinople and the rise of a saviour monarch. It had considerable popularity into the Tourkokratia, when messianic prophecies continued to appear. An interesting example of these appears in the massive *Book of Oracles* (containing both fulfilled examples and others awaiting fulfilment), which Païsios Ligarides dedicated in 1656 to tsar Alexis Michajlović who he wrongly predicted would be the liberator of the Greeks from Ottoman rule.

A.R. LITTLEWOOD

See also Divination, Necromancy

Further Reading

Fontenrose, Joseph E., *Python: A Study of Delphic Myth and its Origins*, Berkeley: University of California Press, 1959

Fontenrose, Joseph E., *The Delphic Oracle: Its Responses and Operations, with a Catalogue of Responses*, Berkeley: University of California Press, 1978; reprinted 1981

Lewy, H., *Chaldaean Oracles and Theurgy: Mysticism, Magic and Platonism in the Later Roman Empire*, new edition, Paris: Etudes Augustiniennes, 1978

Parke, H.W. and D.E.W Wormell, *The Delphic Oracle*, 2 vols, Oxford: Blackwell, 1956

Parke, H.W., *Greek Oracles*, London: Hutchinson, 1967

Parke, H.W., *The Oracles of Zeus: Dodona, Olympia, Ammon*, Oxford: Blackwell, and Cambridge, Massachusetts: Harvard University Press, 1967

Parke, H.W., *The Oracles of Apollo in Asia Minor*, London: Croom Helm, 1985

Parke, H.W., *Sibyls and Sibylline Prophecy in Classical Antiquity*, London and New York: Routledge, 1988

Parker, R.C.T., "Greek States and Greek Oracles" in *Crux: Essays Presented to G.E.M. de Ste. Croix on His 75th Birthday*, edited by Paul Cartledge and F.D. Harvey, Exeter: Imprint Academic, 1985

Potter, D.S., *Prophecy and History in the Crisis of the Roman Empire: A Historical Commentary on the Thirteenth Sibylline Oracle*, Oxford: Clarendon Press, and New York: Oxford University Press, 1990

Potter, David, *Prophets and Emperors: Human and Divine Authority from Augustus to Theodosius*, Cambridge, Massachusetts: Harvard University Press, 1994

Ševčenko, Ihor, "The Legend of Leo the Wise", *Zbornik Radova Vizantološkog Instituta*, 6 (1960): pp. 59–93

Oral Tradition

Oral tradition, since it is by definition not fixed by writing or recording, is continually in a state of change: rather like language itself, it is transmitted from person to person and created afresh in the course of every such transmission. There are two indirect routes to knowledge of oral tradition before our own day. The first is by way of authors who explicitly record tales or literature that reached them by word of mouth, or who depict the performance of oral texts. The second is by way of literature that we may judge for stylistic or comparative reasons to have oral origins.

Thus, although the oral literature and history of early Greece are unknowable to us by any direct means – we can have no real evidence that precedes the first written texts, those of Hesiod, Homer, and Archilochus – all three of these still have much to tell us, indirectly, of the oral literary milieux from which they evidently derive.

Hesiod tells us (*Works and Days*) of his victory in a poetry competition in the course of funeral games; it has been supposed that the *Theogony*, his other surviving genuine work, was the winning poem. Evidently other winning poems, in other similar competitions, were not necessarily written down. It has also been hypothesized that the Homeric poems were composed for competitive performance of a similar kind. Hesiod describes the origin of his poetic inspiration as a gift by the Muses; this is typical of the solutions offered by oral poets for the difficult question why some people are able to compose long narrative poems while others are not. His livelihood as a farmer – if we accept the autobiographical framework of *Works and Days* as true to life – is by no means unusual for epic poets in other cultures.

The two great Homeric epics say nothing at all about their own origin, except for brief invocations of a "goddess" or Muse. It was traditionally held, in later Greece, that they were composed for oral performance. Many have thought that the repeated scenes in the *Odyssey* in which singers perform at feasts are depictions of how the two epics themselves were performed. The use of stylized and repetitious formulas throughout these epics was imitated, with varying accuracy, by later authors of Greek and Latin literary epics, but it was viewed as little more than a curious quirk of the Homeric style until, in the 1930s, Milman Parry showed that these formulas were the building blocks with which long oral narrative poetry is typically, and necessarily, composed.

Parry's demonstration drew on his fieldwork among the oral epic poets of modern Bosnia. Equally important for those who wish to use the Homeric poems as historical sources was the evidence gathered by Parry and his co-worker, Albert Lord, demonstrating the rapid transformation of epic poems in the course of successive performances. It has been gradually accepted that poems recorded in the 8th century BC (or the 7th, as many now believe) could scarcely retain any accurate and identifiable historical detail concerning events of around 1200 BC, the traditional dating of the fall of Troy. The language and the social background would also predominantly reflect the period at which the epics were recorded.

In 5th- and 4th-century BC Greece the *Iliad* and *Odyssey* had become classics, learned by heart by many schoolboys. There were professional reciters whose business was to perform Homer; the main character of Plato's *Ion* is in this trade. Traditions of that kind can continue for a long time: the Sanskrit poems of the *Rig Veda* were transmitted similarly for many hundreds of years. In its fundamental aims, of accurate recitation and literal transmission, such a tradition differs entirely from those in which oral epics were originally composed.

The earliest non-epic Greek poetry now surviving is that of Archilochus. His iambic poems, and those of Hipponax, belong to a tradition of ritualized insult and obscenity that is not visible in the Homeric poems but for which there is some independent evidence from Classical Greece.

The Homeric poems do depict oral performances in various lyric genres that were soon to turn into written literature. The mythological and praise poetry of athletic games and banquets, as described in the *Odyssey*, may seem closer in style and occasion to that of Simonides and Pindar than to that of Homer himself. Wedding songs, depicted in the *Iliad*, are recorded in writing from Sappho onwards. Funeral laments are also described in the *Iliad* and *Odyssey*, and these have been a major genre of Greek oral poetry at many later periods. Working songs, too, have remained a feature of oral tradition: some later ones, such as the Rhodian "Swallow song", are directly recorded in Classical texts.

Thus, between 700 and 550 BC many poetic genres were turned over to literary composition and written transmission. In the 5th century BC prose was to follow. The sources of Herodotus' information, and of Thucydides', were almost wholly oral, the reliability of their narratives naturally varying – as oral tradition generally does – with the length of the period over which the information had been transmitted. History, from this point onwards, was written; records of local and genealogical history, in particular, help to show us how much had until then depended on oral transmission and collective memory. What of the stories of the gods? Greek mythological storytelling, although serving as a source for Hesiod, Homer, Pindar, and many other poets, may always have existed as a prose genre and as such remained essentially oral. Its wealth, even in Roman times, can be judged from the rich records of local mythology gathered by the scholar Pausanias of the 2nd century AD. A storyteller depicted in Longus' *Daphnis and Chloe*, a novel of about the same date, told an apposite mythological tale to the two lovers, and was rewarded for it (generously!) with a kid.

In Classical and Roman times epic narrative probably disappeared completely as a genre of Greek oral poetry. Later, it was to reappear. The 15-syllable "political" metre, whose earliest use may possibly have been in laments, emerges as the vehicle of Byzantine Greek popular verse, of which the best-known example is the *Digenis Akritis* epic. Like certain other medieval European epics, this was several times recorded in writing, in versions so radically different from one another that oral tradition (rather than a manuscript stemma) must be what separates them. The historical background to *Digenis Akritis* is the prolonged warfare between Byzantines and successive Muslim powers on the Anatolian plateau from the 10th to 12th century AD. Armenian, Turkish, and Arabian oral epics deal with the same historical nexus. Common features are the highlighting of local nobility rather than distant royalty, and the importance of intermarriage between opposing families – as in the parentage of Digenis, "the twice-born", himself.

There is much additional evidence for oral poetry and its context to be found in Byzantine literature. Examples include such major works as the *Chronicle of the Morea* – not necessarily oral in origin but linguistically, stylistically, and metrically close to oral texts and quite at odds with the classicism of high Byzantine culture.

The political verse is still ubiquitous in modern Greek oral poetry, *tragoudi*. Several genres can be distinguished nowadays, none of which attains epic length. They include the short-lived and still-imitated *rebetika* that were once symbolic of the criminal subculture of Athens. Typical, though, are poems of 12 to 40 lines, usually described by folklorists as "ballads", often evoking a figure or an incident of established tradition and thus already familiar to the audience. Some legends that recur in these ballads are shared by several neighbouring cultures. "The Bridge of Arta" tells of a wonderful structure that could not be successfully completed until the architect's young wife was immured in it: this story is known in all the Balkan countries – in Romania, for example, it is familiar as "Master Manole". Specifically Greek are the *klephtika*, tales of the brigands or freedom fighters of Turkish-ruled Greece; and Digenis Akritis remains one of the heroes of the songs that can still be heard in oral performance in parts of modern Greece.

ANDREW DALBY

Further Reading

Alexiou, Margaret, *The Ritual Lament in Greek Tradition*, Cambridge: Cambridge University Press, 1974

Beaton, Roderick, *Folk Poetry of Modern Greece*, Cambridge and New York: Cambridge University Press, 1980

Beaton, Roderick and David Ricks (editors), *Digenes Akrites: New Approaches to Byzantine Heroic Poetry*, Aldershot, Hampshire: Variorum, 1993

Dalby, Andrew, "Homer's Enemies" in *Archaic Greece: New Approaches and New Evidence*, edited by Hans van Wees and Nick Fisher, Swansea: Classical Press of Wales, 1998

Hesiod, *Theogony*, edited by M.L. West, Oxford: Clarendon Press, 1966 (see the editor's introduction and notes)

Jeffreys, E.M. and M.J. Jeffreys, "The Oral Background of Byzantine Popular Poetry", *Oral Tradition*, 1 (1986): pp. 504–47

Jeffreys, M.J., "The Nature and Origins of the Political Verse", *Dumbarton Oaks Papers*, 28 (1974): pp. 141–95

Nagy, Gregory, *Pindar's Homer: The Lyric Possession of an Epic Past*, Baltimore: Johns Hopkins University Press, 1990

Page, D.L., "Archilochus and the Oral Tradition", *Entretiens Hardt*, 10 (1965): pp. 119–79

Parry, Adam (editor), *The Making of Homeric Verse: The Collected Papers of Milman Parry*, Oxford: Clarendon Press, 1971; New York: Oxford University Press, 1987

Thomas, Rosalind, *Literacy and Orality in Ancient Greece*, Cambridge and New York: Cambridge University Press, 1992

Watts, Niki, *The Greek Folk Songs*, Bristol: Bristol Classical Press, and New Rochelle, New York: Caratzas, 1988

West, M.L., "Greek Poetry 2000–700 BC", *Classical Quarterly*, 23 (1973): pp. 179–92

Worthington, Ian (editor), *Voice into Text: Orality and Literacy in Ancient Greece*, Leiden and New York: Brill, 1996

Orchomenus

City in Boeotia

Orchomenus, cited by Homer as a paradigm of a wealthy city (*Iliad*, 9. 381), is often qualified as Minyan. The eponym Minyas is a shadowy, almost non-existent figure, but the place was real enough, and its reputation justified, at least in the Mycenaean period.

Situated in the northwest corner of the Copais, Orchomenus dominated the whole of this quadrant of Boeotia. Settlement was more or less constant from the Neolithic period. The most striking surviving monument is the Mycenaean tholos tomb (14 m in diameter) called the Treasury of Minyas. Also from the Mycenaean period isolated finds of pottery and fresco fragments have been found on the lower slope of the hill into which the tholos tomb was set. From the area of the convent east of the tomb have come numerous wall painting fragments. The economy of Mycenaean Orchomenus seems to have depended on crops grown in the Copaic basin. The Mycenaeans – like their British successors of the 19th century AD – constructed a system of hydraulic works to control the waters flowing into the basin in order to render the larger part of it free for cultivation. The canals were directed to a number of swallow holes – *katavothrai* – on the eastern shore and in the northeast corner of the Copais, which was protected there by the island fortress of Gla, which was both a control point – since the northeast bay of the Copais is the only part of the basin not visible from Orchomenus – and a refuge. Gla was abandoned at the end of Late Helladic IIIB. This suggests that the drainage works of Minyan Orchomenus were no longer functioning, the bureaucracy which maintained them having broken down. Nothing is known about relations between Mycenaean Thebes and Mycenaean Orchomenus: the legends concerning the war between Orchomenus and Thebes are more likely to reflect events during the 6th century BC than those of the Bronze Age.

In Archaic Boeotia there were still two major spheres of influence, one around the western half of the Copais under Orchomenus, the other covering the rest of the territory and more loosely tied, with no obvious dominant state. The power and influence of Orchomenus in the Archaic period may be reflected in the tradition that Orchomenus was a member of the Calaureian Amphictiony. This association was based at a sanctuary of Poseidon on the island of Calaureia (Poros) in the Saronic Gulf, for which evidence goes back to the 7th century BC. Eventually, Orchomenus, as it tried to extend its control to the east, and Thebes, moving westward, ran into each other, the result being the confirmation of Theban supremacy over the rest of Boeotia. This was assured by the fourth quarter of the 6th century, and is reflected not only in the literary traditions, but in contemporary inscriptions.

However, the new Boeotian League which emerged towards the end of the 6th century under the leadership of Thebes was by no means an autocratic association. One sign of this is the appearance late in the century of a distinctive Boeotian coinage, which means that there was not only an accepted common standard, but also a common economic policy. That the policy was consensual is shown by the facts that not only Thebes but at least nine other member states had their own mints, and that Orchomenus, although reduced, was allowed to issue its own small denomination coinage with a distinctive symbol of grain(s) of corn on the obverse, rather than the otherwise general Boeotian shield.

During the Persian invasion of 480/79 BC, Orchomenus joined Thebes and most of the rest of Boeotia in Medizing. In the period after the Battles of Tanagra and Oenophyta (456

Orchomenus: Church of the Dormition, built in 874 according to a Bulgarian style similar to that of Hagia Sophia at Ohrid

BC), when Athens dominated Boeotian affairs, Orchomenus may have been a member of the Delian League, but by 446 it had become a place of refuge for disaffected Boeotians of the oligarchic persuasion, who eventually defeated an Athenian force at nearby Coronea and threw the Athenians out of Boeotia.

Orchomenians fought on the left wing in the victorious battle of Delion (424), but it appears that, as the 5th century drew to its close, Orchomenus was being gradually stripped of its power and influence, with Thebes growing progressively more dominant within the Boeotian League. By the end of the century Orchomenus had lost control of Chaeronea and Lebadea, and was contributing only two of the 11 federal Boiotarchs.

It is not surprising that Orchomenus became a centre for anti-Theban sentiment. During the Corinthian war (which began in 395) it seceded to Sparta, and was protected by a Spartan garrison until at least 375. After the King's Peace (387/86 BC) Orchomenus, like the other poleis of Boeotia, formally regained its independence.

After the expulsion of the Spartan garrison from Thebes in 379/78, the Thebans gradually re-established themselves as the dominant power of Boeotia, and confirmed their status at the battle of Leuctra (371 BC). The Theban-led Boeotian League established the Basileia, games in honour of Zeus Basileus at Lebadea, which had formerly been dependent on Orchomenus. This Zeus was the original patron deity of Orchomenus, and

the location of his sanctuary on the hill of Profitis Elias was an open provocation to the Orchomenians, and a public proclamation to all who passed by – since the hill is clearly visible from the road to Delphi – of the political pretensions of the Boiotoi, that is, the Thebans. The Thebans went even further, and in 364 razed Orchomenus.

This destruction was not permanent, as Theban power waned after the death of Epaminondas, and hostility between Thebes and Phocis drew closer to open warfare. Orchomenus was functioning again as early as 359 BC, and during the Third Sacred War it was mostly in the hands of the Phocians. But at the end of this war (346 BC) Philip II of Macedon handed Orchomenus back to Thebes, when it seems to have been destroyed and the population dispersed.

However, after Chaeronea (338), Philip restored the city, and Alexander the Great even commissioned an engineer (Crates) to drain the Copais, but this enterprise was not completed, and Orchomenus never really recovered its former stature. During the Hellenistic period it fell upon bad times, was compelled to borrow money – which it had difficulty repaying – and relied increasingly on the generosity of individual citizens for its public operations. It is clear that under the Romans Orchomenus had shrunk to the status of a village, which indeed it has remained until relatively recently.

After antiquity, settlement persisted at the foot of the hill Akontion, focusing on the villages of Skripou and Petromagoula (now joined into one and called Orchomenus).

The outstanding monument surviving from this period is the church of the former convent of the Koimisis tis Theotokou (AD 874), one of the earliest cruciform churches in Greece. Its builders used blocks from an ancient temple and the nearby theatre (4th–3rd centuries BC).

Aside from the tholos tomb, theatre, and church, the most impressive remains are traces of city walls on the Akontion hill and, on the acropolis proper, fortifications built by the Macedonians late in the 4th century BC. No certain trace has been found of a Mycenaean palace, or of the sanctuary of the Charites – the Graces – whose cult Pindar mentions in *Olympian* 14, nor of the supposed tomb of Hesiod.

ALBERT SCHACHTER

Summary

A city in western Boeotia 11 km northeast of Lebadea, Orchomenus was important in the Bronze Age and famed in myth, but in historical periods was subordinated to and by Thebes. Its outstanding monuments are from the Bronze Age (the "Treasury of Minyas", a tholos tomb; the fortress of Gla in the northeast corner of Lake Copais), the early Hellenistic period (a theatre), and the 9th century AD (church of the Dormition).

Further Reading

Barber, Robin, *Greece*, 6th edition, London: A.&C. Black, and New York: Norton, 1995 (*Blue Guide* series)

Hansen, M.H., "An Inventory of Boiotian Poleis in the Archaic and Classical Periods" in *Introduction to an Inventory of Poleis*, edited by Mogens Herman Hansen, Copenhagen: Munsksgaard, 1996

Lauffer, Siegfried (editor), *Griechenland: Lexikon der historischen Stätten*, Munich: Beck, 1989

Lewis, D.M. *et al.* (editors), *The Fifth Century BC*, Cambridge: Cambridge University Press, 1992 (*The Cambridge Ancient History*, vol. 5, 2nd edition)

Lewis, D.M. *et al.* (editors), *The Fourth Century BC*, Cambridge: Cambridge University Press, 1994 (*The Cambridge Ancient History*, vol. 6, 2nd edition)

Schachter, Albert, *Cults of Boiotia*, London: Institute of Classical Studies, 1981–

Schachter, Albert, "Costituzione e sviluppo dell'ethnos beotico", *Quaderni Urbinati*, 52 (1996): pp. 7–29

Orgiastic Cults

The term *orgia* designated certain ceremonies and religious rites, with particular reference to initiation into a specific cult. Usually there were secret rites that had a symbolic function. The term "mystery" is also used. As Walter Burkert remarks, ancient mysteries were a kind of personal religion, since the initiation depended upon a person's decision to participate in a cult, and its practice enforced hope and belief in prosperity and future life. Such cults usually consisted of a variety of activities, such as purifications, processions, sacrifices, and dramatic enactments. The word mystery (*mysterion* in Greek) comes from the verb *myein*, meaning "to close". The *mystai*, those who participated, were required to keep their mouth closed and not to reveal secrets to those who had not been initiated. The word "orgiastic" in its modern sense probably best describes certain cults, particularly towards the end of the

Hellenistic time, when a fusion of religions from various origins took place. The most important cults of this kind were Eleusinia, Thesmophoria, Dionysia, Orphica, Cabeiria, and mysteries for the worship of Cybele, Isis, and Sabazius.

The general idea of passing beyond the limits of morality in as many directions as possible lies behind the existence and performance of many orgiastic cults. Moreover, the psychological need to ritualize all possible polarities of human nature, so as not to be excluded from a community but rather belong to one, is another factor that explains the wide reception they had in antiquity. Herodotus (8. 65) speaks of 30,000 people attending mysteries. The roots of many orgiastic cults are hidden in the mists of prehistory, since they developed from rural festivals that celebrated the power of nature and fertility. The notions of death and resurrection are associated with many principal figures of the mysteries, for example, Dionysus, Persephone, Adonis, Attis, Osiris, and the Mithraic bull.

The Eleusinia were a mystic cult centred around the myth of the rape of Persephone, daughter of Demeter, by Hades, and the search of the mother for her daughter. The explanation of the natural phenomena and the human hope for rich agricultural production and fertility were treated in a symbolic manner. A series of purification rites took place. Many citizens of Athens were initiated in these mysteries, and although there is some uncertainty as to what went on, there are plenty of literary and archaeological sources to help us reconstruct the image of the Eleusinian mysteries. They continued to exist throughout the Roman period, until the 4th century AD, when the emperor Theodosius abolished them.

The Dionysiac cults, which had more of an orgiastic character in the modern sense of the word, included much wildness and extravagance. The cult of Dionysus had many festivals, for example, the City and the Rural Dionysia, the Anthesteria, and the Oschophoria. Besides the official celebration in honour of the god, there were also private celebrations that involved ecstatic worshipping of the god and going beyond one's self. The phenomenon of maenadism, as described in Euripides' *Bacchae*, is one example of extravagant rites that, even if they are mythical, still retain the element of self-transcendence that orgiastic cults promoted. Women in a state of ecstasy abandoned their homes and joined frenzied dances on the mountains swinging thyrsi and torches. This cult involved as a sacramental meal the devouring of an animal as it was bleeding. There is evidence of *orgia* of this type on Mount Parnassus by women controlled by Apollo who admitted Dionysus to Delphi and assisted the establishment of his cult in a milder form.

The Orphic cult promised life after death, and was related to oriental and Egyptian ideas of the afterlife. It involved many expiation rites. The worship of Cybele, or the Great Mother, is the result of much religious syncretism. The orgiastic character is strongly associated with her due to the institution of eunuch priests, the self-castrating Galloi. As with the Eleusinian mysteries, there is a mythic narrative corresponding to the ritual practice. Attis, the young lover of the goddess, was castrated and became her follower. Various rites were associated with the worship of Cybele, such as the *taurobolia* (slaughter of a bull) and *kriobolia* (sacrifice of a ram), perhaps dating from the 2nd century AD, when the initiate had to be drenched in the blood of a sacrificed bull or ram.

The Cabeiria was a mystery cult that took place in Samothrace and acquired importance second only to the Eleusinian mysteries. Ancient writers talk about the cult of the "Great Gods" in Samothrace. It is possible that the Great Mother of the Gods as well as Hecate and a certain Zerynthia Aphrodite were worshipped in Samothrace. Archaeology reveals that the shrines were active until the 3rd and possibly 4th century AD. As at Eleusis, the two important stages were those of preparation and initiation. But whereas in the Eleusinian mysteries one had to wait for at least a year between the two, in Samothrace they could be achieved on the same day. All the initiation rites occurred at night. The most important buildings found are the Anaktoron, where the initiation took place, built in the 1st century BC (but replacing an earlier structure), the Hiera Oikia (sacristy) where all the preparations were made, the Arsinoeion, built between 289 and 281 BC by Arsinoe, the wife of Lysimachus, a place for sacrifices and gatherings, and the actual shrine (Hieron). Many votive offerings have been excavated as at Eleusis, and it is possible to see the ruins of a theatre.

Cults associated with foreign gods such as Mithras, Serapis, and Isis were important in Greek religious life until late antiquity. Orgiastic cults continued to exist even after pagan times and within Christianity, and some blended into Christian ceremonies, although there was conscious opposition, particularly by Church Fathers. After the establishment of Christianity, many of the places that were important for ancient mysteries were destroyed, as happened at Samothrace.

ANDROMACHE KARANIKA-DIMAROGONA

See also Festivals, Mysticism, Religion, Women's Cults

Further Reading

Burkert, Walter, *Greek Religion: Archaic and Classical*, Oxford: Blackwell, 1985
Burkert, Walter, *Ancient Mystery Cults*, Cambridge, Massachusetts: Harvard University Press, 1987
Meyer, Marvin W., *The Ancient Mysteries, a Sourcebook: Sacred Texts of the Mystery Religions of the Ancient Mediterranean World*, San Francisco: Harper and Row, 1987
Papageorgiou, Sophi N., *Samothrake: Historia tou Nesiou apo ta prota Christianika Chronia hos to 1914* [Samothrace: History of the Island from the First Years of Christianity to 1914], Athens, 1982

Origen AD 184/85–254/55

Christian writer

As a native of Alexandria, Origen encountered the thought of Philo and the Valentinian "Gnostics", though he does not admit to learning much from either. He may have succeeded Clement as the head of the Catechetical school, and one of his works, the lost *Stromateis*, derived its title from his predecessor. He also found time to study with a teacher of Greek philosophy named Ammonius. This may be the same Ammonius who taught the Neoplatonist Plotinus, but those who identify the Christian Origen with Plotinus' fellow pupil of that name are merely cherishing an indifference to the facts.

Origen's talents earned him first the patronage, then the enmity, of bishop Demetrius of Alexandria, and he migrated from the province to Caesarea, where his friends conferred on him the rank of presbyter. The breach with Alexandria was now irreparable, but in Caesarea Origen became an indefatigable teacher and a celebrated author, enjoying both the friendship of an empress and the general admiration of the Church.

Origen was the earliest Christian writer to make use of the Old Testament in Hebrew rather than Greek. The six columns of his *Hexapla* contained the Hebrew text, a transliteration of this into Greek characters, the Septuagint, and the later Greek translations or revisions made by Symmachus, Aquila, and Theodotion. Since he maintained the authority of the Septuagint against well-founded criticism, his object was more probably to establish the text of this than to replace it with a more accurate translation. Nevertheless, having had a "Hebrew" teacher, he acknowledged the Jewish canon (Eusebius, *Historia Ecclesiastica*, 6. 25), and his commentaries and homilies, which cover most of this and our New Testament, did not extend to the Apocrypha. The purpose of his exegetic writings was to bring every part of the Bible home to the thoughts and lives of his contemporaries; whereas his heretical precursors had appealed to uncanonical gospels, he applied the tools of allegory to the scriptures, introducing a distinction between the body, soul, and spirit of the text (*De Principiis*, 4. 2. 4 etc.). He argued that the spiritual sense was present everywhere, and might sometimes be the only one, as in the Song of Songs; but the bodily or literal sense was not discarded except when it appeared to condone absurdities, immoralities, or defections from the apostolic faith.

This faith he upheld at the greatest length in his eight books against the dead philosopher Celsus; they presented Christianity both as the heir of Judaism and as the philosophical antidote to the errors, pains, and vices of the world. This work, perhaps composed to mark the thousandth anniversary of Rome in 248, is largely orthodox, but in his earlier *De Principiis* (On First Principles), the first Christian experiment in systematic theology, he allowed himself more freedom in speculation. He appears to have held, for example, that our souls lived in a higher state with God before they descended into this world, where they must undergo a purifying chastisement for their sins (*De Principiis*, 1. 4 etc.). This process after death will be extended to the body, and, though each must attain perfection in his own time, the whole created order will eventually be saved (*De Principiis*, 2. 8–11 etc.). These views, whatever they owe to Platonism, rest on a fundamental tenet of Greek theology, that no one ever suffers more from God than he or she deserves. Equally seminal for Orthodox doctrine was his teaching on the Godhead, for he was the first to say that in this Trinity or triad of three hypostases the Spirit and the Son are coeternal with the Father, though their existence and activity depend upon his will (*De Principiis*, 1. 2, *Commentary on John*, 2. 10, etc.).

Origen undoubtedly saw himself as an exegetic theologian, whose reading of the scriptures was conditioned by the teachings and traditions of the Church. While he is glad from time to time to find a friend in Plato, he never takes a philosophical statement as his starting point or advances a conjecture that cannot be grounded on some sacred text. He takes it as an axiom that God the Word is present in every sentence of the scriptures (*Philokalia*, 5), and says that in his use of philosophical tools he was "spoiling the Egyptians" to enrich his own understanding (ibid. 13). Even his anthropology could not be independent of his Trinitarian doctrine. The Spirit first converts us by addressing the rational element, next the Son instructs our souls in virtue, and finally the Father gives us everlasting life, wherein the spirit and the soul will be united to the proper kind of body (*De Principiis*, 1. 3. 8 etc.). The germs of the threefold mystical way – the purgative, the illuminative, and the unitive – are discernible in this scheme, but it neglects the body less than many later speculations. The Spirit is our sole guide while our body is still at war with us; when this has been refined by immortality, we can be at last "one Spirit" with the Lord.

Among his disciples Origen numbered Eusebius of Caesarea, who profited greatly by his scholarship, and Gregory of Nyssa, who adopted his universalistic theory of salvation. In Gregory's time, however, it was already necessary to borrow silently, for Origen stood accused of many heresies: for example, of believing in the transmigration of souls, of denying the resurrection of the body, and of making the second person of the Trinity inferior to the first. His heresies were exposed in the *Ancoratus* and *Panarion* of Epiphanius of Salamis, who seemed disposed to condone the anthropomorphite heresy rather than follow Origen in abandoning the literal sense of scripture. He charged him with denying not only the bodily resurrection, but the fall of man in Adam, and his tract in defence of the Septuagint suggests that he saw an insidious purpose even in the *Hexapla*. Origen was condemned in 553 by the Second Council of Constantinople, and in consequence most of his writings were destroyed. All that survives in Greek is a number of homilies, passages from the *Commentary on Matthew*, the greater part of the *Commentary on John*, the *Contra Celsum*, the treatises *On Prayer* and *To the Martyrs*, the newly discovered *Dialogue with Heraclides*, and the *Philokalia*, a compilation of excerpts made by Basil the Great and Gregory of Nazianzus. We depend on the Latin renderings of Jerome and Rufinus for most of the rest, including the *De Principiis*; but in the West the uncertain status of the Constantinopolitan Council has allowed such theologians as von Balthasar to pay more open tribute to his *Commentary on the Song of Songs*, a seminal work of Christian mysticism. Jerome's regard for Origen and Rufinus turned to hatred under the spell of Epiphanius, but it was Origen's example that inspired his Latin translation of the Old Testament from the Hebrew. In eastern Christianity Origen's influence, where perceptible, is a testimony to his intellect, his honesty, and the many abiding merits of his work.

MARK EDWARDS

Biography

Born in Alexandria in AD 184 or 185, Origen was educated at the catechetical school under Pantaenus and Clement and learnt philosophy from Ammonius. He may have succeeded Clement as head of the school before moving to Palestine in 215. He wrote extensively about textual criticism, exegesis, and systematic theology and was ordained a priest. Recalled to Alexandria, he was later banished and settled at Caesarea. He died at Tyre in 254 or 255.

Writings

Werke, edited by P. Koetschau *et al.*, Leipzig: de Gruyter, 1899–1941
Contra Celsum, translated by Henry Chadwick, Cambridge: Cambridge University Press, 1953
On First Principles: Being Koetschau's Text of the De Principiis, translated by G.W. Butterworth, New York: Harper and Row, 1966
An Exhortation to Martyrdom, Prayer, First Principles: Book 4, Prologue to the Commentary on the Song of Songs, Homily 27 on Numbers, translated by Rowan A. Greer, London: SPCK, and New York: Paulist Press, 1979
Treatise on the Passover, and Dialogue with Heraclides, translated by R.J. Daly, New York: Paulist Press, 1992
Commentaries on Matthew and John, translated by John Patrick, in *Nicene and Post-Nicene Fathers*, 1st series, vol. 10, reprinted Peabody, Massachusetts: Hendrickson, 1994

Further Reading

Alviar, J. José, *Klesis: The Theology of the Christian Vocation According to Origen*, Dublin: Four Courts Press, 1993
Clark, E.A., *The Origenist Controversy: The Cultural Construction of an Early Christian Debate*, Princeton, New Jersey: Princeton University Press, 1992
Crouzel, Henri, *Origen*, San Francisco: Harper and Row, and Edinburgh: Clark, 1989
Crouzel, Henri, *Les Fins Dernières selon Origène*, Aldershot, Hampshire: Variorum, 1990
Danielou, Jean, *Origen*, London and New York: Sheed and Ward, 1955
Drewery, Benjamin, *Origen and the Doctrine of Grace*, London: Epworth Press, 1960
Hanson, R.P.C., *Origen's Doctrine of Tradition*, London: SPCK, 1954
Hanson, R.P.C., *Allegory and Event: A Study of the Sources and Significance of Origen's Interpretation of Scripture*, London: SCM Press, and Richmond: John Knox Press, 1959
Kannengiesser, Charles (editor), *Origen of Alexandria: His World and his Legacy*, Notre Dame, Indiana: University of Notre Dame Press, 1988
Scott, Alan, *Origen and the Life of the Stars: A History of an Idea*, Oxford: Clarendon Press, and New York: Oxford University Press, 1991
Torjesen, Karen Jo, *Hermeneutical Procedure and Theological Method in Origen's Exegesis*, Berlin and New York: de Gruyter, 1986
Trigg, Joseph Wilson, *Origen: The Bible and Philosophy in the Third Century*, Atlanta: John Knox Press, 1983; London: SCM Press, 1985
Widdicombe, Peter, *The Fatherhood of God from Origen to Athanasius*, Oxford: Clarendon Press, and New York: Oxford University Press, 1994

Orphism

The term "Orphism" is somewhat ambiguous, as it is not clear exactly what it refers to. The ancients never spoke of Orphism but only about Orpheus, the presumed author of Orphic books, and of certain Orphic rites. A book became Orphic simply by being ascribed to Orpheus. The question of whether Orphism existed as a religious movement or merely as a set of beliefs described in the Orphic literature remains controversial. The rise of Orphic ideas and the nature of Orphic practices remain obscure despite some recent discoveries. The unifying factor, Orpheus, is a mythical figure of Thracian origin whose main characteristic was a unique gift for music. This characteristic features in a number of ancient stories about Orpheus; he is said to have enchanted Hades with his song so that his prematurely dead wife Eurydice returned to life (cf. Plato, *Symposium*, 179d); to have taken part in the Argonauts' expedition and outsung the Sirens (cf. Pindar, Pythian 4. 167f.); and to have been beheaded by Thracian women while his head continued to sing (*Symposium*, 179d, *Republic*, 620a).

Through his achievements Orpheus appears as a great shaman – somebody whose spirit can affect the whole of nature, from plants and animals to souls and even gods or Hades. These achievements are often the subject of the Orphic poems, usually hymns or longer poems of theogonic or cosmogonic content, most of them now lost or only partially preserved. Such Orphic poems presumably started to circulate from the 6th century BC and they became popular in 5th and 4th centuries BC, as the testimony of various authorities suggests (e.g. Euripides, *Hippolytus*, 952ff.; Plato, *Republic*, 364e, *Cratylus*, 402b, *Philebus*, 66c, *Laws*, 829e). A relatively recent find, the Derveni papyrus, discovered in a tomb in northern Greece and dating from the late 4th century BC, contains a commentary on an Orphic theogony and proves that such Orphic poems were in circulation already in the 5th century BC. In the 6th century AD Damascius *(De Principiis,* 123–24), discussing the Orphic account of the beginnings of the world, talks of three Orphic theogonies, of which he had only indirect knowledge. According to the core of Orphic cosmogony Chronos, the primordial divinity, gives birth to Aether and Chaos and they generate a world-egg.

The link between these poems and a cult of Orpheus is difficult to determine. The Derveni papyrus, buried and burned with an unknown Greek, makes even clearer the close linking of religious practices to a specific text. Orphism seems to have been very much a book religion. Plato talks of purveyors of purifications and rituals which bring deliverance from unrighteousness, claiming that these people perform rites in accordance with books by Musaeus and Orpheus *(Republic,* 364e–365a). The most ancient testimony to Orphic practice comes from Herodotus. With reference to the prejudice against introducing woollen articles into temples or being buried in them, Herodotus says that this is an Egyptian custom and "in this they agree with the practices which are called Orphic and Bacchic, though they are actually Egyptian and Pythagorean" (2. 81). Herodotus is not the only one who identifies Orphic with Bacchic rites. In Euripides' *Hippolytus* (953) Theseus uses the verb *baccheuein* for Orphic rites. Archaeological evidence further supports the close relation between Orphic and Bacchic rites, and Orpheus often figures in artistic depictions of predominantly Dionysiac themes. Orpheus is sometimes said to be the initiator of the cult of Dionysus (Hecataeus), but at other times he is presented as having neglected the worship of Dionysus after his journey to Hades, instead venerating the sun (Aeschylus, *Bassarai*) for which his punishment was his assassination by a group of Thracian women. We hear of active *Orphikoi* in Athens and in southern Italy in the 5th century BC and we know of their distinctive views (e.g. Aristotle, *De Anima*, 410b28f.), but little is certain about their rites. Ancient sources speak of Orphic rites *(teletai)*, though without giving precise information (Aristophanes, *Frogs*, 1032, *Rhesus*, 943; Plato, *Protagoras*, 316d), and also of participants in these rites

(Orpheotelestai) (e.g. Theophrastus, *Characters*, 16. 11). Presumably the mysteries referred to, at least in some of those occurrences, are the Eleusinian mysteries. In some sources Orpheus is mentioned as their founder (Diodorus Siculus, 1. 23. 2f.), and Orphic mysteries are sometimes identified with the Eleusinian mysteries (Pausanias, 1. 37. 4). Orphic ideas indeed permeated the Eleusinian and also the Theban mysteries of the Cabiri. Orphics were particularly concerned with the purity of the soul, which was deemed to be imprisoned in the body. This purity was sought through an ascetic way of life with strict rules, especially about diet, such as abstinence from meat (Euripides, *Hippolytus*, 952–55; Plato, *Laws*, 782c–83c), but also from eggs, beans, and wine. Orphics believed in an afterlife and the transmigration of the soul, a feature which brings Orphism closer to Pythagorean ideas rather than to the Eleusinian mysteries. There is a certain common ground between Orphism and Pythagoreanism and perhaps some rivalry between them, to judge from such contradicting testimonies as that according to which Pythagoras and the Pythagoreans were the true authors of Orphic poems and that Pythagoras was indebted to Orpheus.

Orphic literature proliferated in the Hellenistic and the imperial eras. In the religious syncretism of late antiquity the name of Orpheus continued to fascinate, but now there was even less concern for demarcation between Orphic and other religious cults. A significant revival of interest in Orphic literature occurs with the Neoplatonists. Orpheus was now not only an inspired poet but also a theologian. The Orphic poems were interpreted allegorically and, under this interpretation, were held to be in accord with the doctrines of Platonic philosophy. The Orpheus legend had a considerable impact on Christianity. Although the Orphic rites were dismissed, the story of Orpheus charming nature with his music was interpreted as a prefiguration of Christ charming human souls with his teaching (Clement, *Protrepticus*, 7. 74. 3–6). Christ in his role of the Good Shepherd is said to be the new Orpheus (Eusebius, *Laus Constantini*, 244. 14–31). The figure of Orpheus which is often found in catacombs stands for Christ, who can also be depicted as Orpheus himself.

The Byzantines knew of the Orphic literature, which they still ascribed to Orpheus. The Orpheus legend was used as a metaphor of the power of poetry and music (Theophrastus of Ochrid, 1. 353. 3, cf. Arethas, *Scriptat Minora*, 2. 5. 27–6. 3, and Nicetas Choniates, *Orationes*, 129. 26–29). Psellos referred to Orphic rites *(Philosophica Minora*, II, opusc. 19. 48), while Anna Komnene contends that he emulates Orpheus in moving the souls of her readers *(Alexiad*, 1. 7. 14–20). In the 15th century Plethon showed vivid interest in the Orphic texts and Ficino translated some of them into Latin.

In modern Greek literature the presence of Orphism is striking. The impact of Orphic doctrines can be detected already in Palamas, but Orphism becomes prominent in the work of A. Sikelianos, who was very much inspired by ancient mystery religions. Orphic ideas permeate his early poems (e.g. his *Elaphroiskiotos*), but they become central in a series of lyric poems entitled *Orphica* (written between 1927 and 1942). Later in his life Sikelianos, engaged in the composition of tragedies, wrote *The Last Orphic Dithyramb* or *The Dithyramb of the Rose* (1932), a dialogue between Orpheus and the chorus, which was actually enacted in Athens in April 1933.

GEORGE E. KARAMANOLIS

Texts

Hermann, Gottfried (editor), *Orphica*, Leipzig: Fritsch, 1805

Kern, Otto (editor), *Orphicorum Fragmenta*, 2nd edition, Berlin: Weidmann, 1963

Laks, André and Glenn W. Most (editors), a provisional translation of the Derveni papyrus in their *Studies on the Derveni Papyrus*, Oxford: Clarendon Press, and New York: Oxford University Press, 1997, pp. 9–22

Quandt, William (editor), *Orphei Hymni*, Berlin: Weidmann, 1962

Further Reading

Brisson, Luc, *Orpheé et l'Orphisme dans l'antiquité greco-romaine*, Aldershot, Hampshire: Variorum, 1995

Burkert, Walter, *Greek Religion*, Oxford: Blackwell, and Cambridge, Massachusetts: Harvard University Press, 1985

Graf, Fritz, *Eleusis und die orphische Dichtung Athens*, Berlin: de Gruyter, 1974

Guthrie, W.K.C., *Orpheus and Greek Religion: A Study of the Orphic Movement*, 2nd edition, London: Methuen, 1952; reprinted Princeton, New Jersey: Princeton University Press, 1993

Keydell, R., Orphische Dichtung A.I: Die erhaltene Gedichte entry in *Real-Encyclopädie der klassischen Altertumswissenschaft*, edited by August Pauly *et al.*, vol. 18.3, 1942, 1321–41

Laks, André and Glenn W. Most (editors), *Studies on the Derveni Papyrus*, Oxford: Clarendon Press, and New York: Oxford University Press, 1997

Linforth, Ivan M., *The Arts of Orpheus*, Berkeley: University of California Press, 1941; reprinted New York: Arno Press, 1973

Nilsson, M.P., "Early Orphism and Kindred Religious Movements", *Harvard Theological Review*, 28 (1935): pp.181–230

Politis, Linos, *A History of Modern Greek Literature*, Oxford: Clarendon Press, 1973

West, M.L., *The Orphic Poems*, Oxford: Clarendon Press, 1983

Ziegler, K., Orpheus entry in *Real-Encyclopädie der klassischen Altertumswissenschaft*, edited by August Pauly *et al.*, vol. 18.1, 1939, 1200–1316

Ziegler, K., Orphische Dichtung B: Die verlorene Gedichte entry in *Real-Encyclopädie der klassischen Altertumswissenschaft*, edited by August Pauly *et al.*, vol. 18.3, 1942, 1341–1417

Orthodox Church

The Orthodox Church appears externally as a communion of self-governing jurisdictions – in 2000 the patriarchates of Constantinople, Alexandria, Antioch, Jerusalem, Moscow, Bucharest, Peć and Belgrade, Sofia, Georgia, and the archbishoprics of Cyprus, Athens, Warsaw, Tirana, and Prague (covering both the Czech and Slovak Republics). They are held together formally by mutual acceptance of each other's orthodoxy and canonical legitimacy; a common adherence to the decisions of the seven ecumenical councils, as also to the principle of conciliar and synodal government of the Church (going back to the apostolic council in Jerusalem) in general; rejection of the 8th-century (794) Frankish and 11th-century papal addition of the *filioque* ("and from the Son") to the affirmation in the Niceno-Constantinopolitan creed of 381 that the Holy Spirit proceeds from the Father; strong commitment to tradition, which includes both the Bible and much subsequent patristic teaching; and consequent opposition to any individual – whether the pope or other believers – altering or reforming that tradition without the consent of the ecclesial body at large.

Most important internally is a common manner of worship, centred around the eucharistic liturgies of St Basil and St John Chrysostom, but including numerous other service books, largely preserved as elaborated by the 9th century at the monasteries of Mar Saba near Jerusalem and the Stoudios in Constantinople. This shared tradition of worship represents for the Orthodox both a foretaste of God's kingdom and its already present reality. Even at a superficial level, committed Orthodox Christians almost certainly spend longer in ecclesial worship than most other Christians. Five examples of services of worship may illustrate some distinctive elements in the Orthodox tradition.

The *Chairetismoi* ("Salutations"), in the service books reserved to matins for the fifth Saturday in Lent, are in the Greek world sung partially on the four previous Friday evenings as well. The theological explanation for the service's popularity would be in terms of wonder at the Incarnation and devotion to the Mother of God. Furthermore, the rhetorical poetry is among the best in medieval Greek and still accessible to many Greeks today. Central to the service's creation historically, however, is the *Akathist* hymn (the title indicates that all remain standing throughout), written to celebrate the miraculous deliverance of Constantinople during the sieges by the Avars and Persians in 626, and by the Ummayads in 674 and 717–18. The central refrain – "To you, the general who fought for us, your city offers a hymn of victory" – retains such deep emotional resonance for Greeks that it is customarily chanted at moments of national exaltation or danger. Thus, whereas the service books transmitted to the Rus contained but one such service a year, today in the Greek world the hymn is central to five, an illustration of the close link between Orthodoxy and the history of those peoples who in their majority still adhere to it.

The matins service on four successive evenings from Palm Sunday announces Christ's arrival as bridegroom of the Church. Each believer acknowledges the absence of a wedding garment and hence unreadiness to join the wedding feast. No one who attends these services can doubt that Orthodox Christians share the common Christian insistence on personal responsibility. It is equally evident, however, that this is seen not primarily in terms of ethical norms (such as the Ten Commandments) but as an existential commitment and response to God (or lack of it), through such figures as the chaste Joseph and the unchaste but devoted harlot, the avaricious traitor Judas, and (on Good Friday) the repentant thief.

Western Christians have criticized Orthodox believers both as negligent of moral rules and as overly ascetic: the nub of any difference lies in the emphasis on personal response to God and one's neighbour, on the pattern of such parables as that of the Pharisee and the Tax-Farmer, the Prodigal Son, the Good Samaritan, and the Last Judgement, which are probably the Gospel passages most deeply etched in the ecclesial and individual consciousness of Orthodox Christians. Sin is seen less than in the West as a series of transgressions, and more as a falling-short from what is the best in human behaviour. This in turn is nothing less than the pattern set by Jesus, the Son of God incarnate. What God seeks of us then is what his Son

Orthodox Church: interior of the katholikon of the monastery of Chilandari, Mount Athos. Every available surface is decorated to create an image of heaven on earth

demonstrated on earth, namely fully human behaviour at the limit. This means sharing in the self-offering of his ministry, not acquring a sense of righteousness through the fulfilment of moral law.

The "Lamentation" service on Good Friday is the second most popular service in the Orthodox world. From Good Thursday the focus shifts to Jesus' Passion. Good Friday matins, sung late on Good Thursday, hymns Christ's action in redeeming us from "the curse of the law". There is also repeated emphasis on Jesus in his passion being simultaneously one of the passionless Holy Trinity. Furthermore the whole natural world is seen as participating in astonishment at the mystery of divine acceptance of such humiliation. The nub of the Lamentation itself, however, lies where Jesus' humanity joins with ours. We identify with someone who is betrayed by a friend; unjustly accused and condemned by his own people; condemned again, beaten, and executed by soldiers of a foreign power; and whose beloved ones, chiefly his mother, lament the deprivation of their most precious relationship through his death. The Orthodox Good Friday services dwell much less on the details of physical suffering than on the existential pain caused by death.

The fourth service, Paschal matins, is the most popular of all. Jesus' human experience was one of life lived, and in the end suffering endured, at its limits. What followed, namely the women's and then apostles' witness to his resurrection, implied something beyond a merely human drama, namely that God has involved himself in the human condition in order to encounter and heal its most basic problems. These are seen to be human subjection to physical, psychological, and conventional ethical law, with an ultimate end in physical death. The purpose of God's action is seen as making it possible for human beings to replace this bondage by a free and loving relationship with him and with other human beings, such liberation to be crowned by a life of eternal communion. Hence the Paschal hymn's repeated proclamation of Christ's defeat of death by death giving life to those in the tombs.

The Eucharist, less dramatic or obviously popular, has had the most continuous influence. It is not a meeting of individuals for common worship but the coming together of the local community to enter into communion with God, which explains why, in contrast to Western custom, there can be only one liturgy celebrated in any church by any priest on any one day. Each community is local but also universal, because through its presiding bishop it is in unity with all similar communities in the same thank-offering of praise.

The worshipping community approaches God both as creators in God's image, building, painting, adorning, preparing, serving, reading, and singing in the church; and as participants in its prayer of thanksgiving, praise, and self-offering.

God's response to this Eucharistic worship with the offering of the holy gifts of bread and wine, fruits of nature transformed by human hands, is, by giving himself, to bring those who pray into communion with him, revealed as three persons in an eternal communion of love, who calls human beings into communion among themselves as with God. This represents an even more fundamental sense in which human beings have been created in God's image, and can come to be in his likeness also.

It is from within the tradition of worship that one can best understand why certain issues that have exercised Western Christians have not much exercised Orthodox believers, whereas others are considered so vital that not a word may be added to or subtracted from the traditional formulation.

The Orthodox tradition did not develop a doctrine of predestination because it seemed at variance with Christ's ministry and the free response that this self-evidently demands from every human being. Neither is it seen as compatible with a loving Father, nor also is any concept of juridical satisfaction. Equally, long Western "either–or" debates on justification have frequently bemused Orthodox Christians, since to them the purpose of human life is to move into an ever closer relationship of communion with God.

It is indeed on the doctrine of God that Orthodox theology has concentrated. The first two ecumenical councils, of Nicaea (325) and Constantinople (381), elaborated a creed that is above all Trinitarian. In the earlier part of the 4th century St Athanasius of Alexandria taught that only if Jesus were as fully God as his Father could it be true that God had become man so that man might become God. In its latter part the Cappadocian fathers, St Basil, St Gregory of Nazianzus, and St Gregory of Nyssa, developed the doctrine of three persons and hypostases of God sharing a unity of nature. As St Basil expressed it, that unity of nature did not take priority: unity derived rather from the hypostasis of the Father, in a personal relationship of birth-giving with the Son and a personal relationship of procession with the Holy Spirit. In modern terms this means that ultimate reality lies in the eternal free and loving relationship of the divine persons, all three of whom are genuine subjects, not in the divine nature. The implications of this for life and liturgy have been illustrated above.

During the 5th to 7th centuries there were fierce disputes over the relationship between the divine and the human in the Son of God incarnate. The Council of Ephesus (431) determined that, since Jesus was Son of God at birth, Mary should be described as *Theotokos* or "Mother of God". The Council of Chalcedon (451), without denying that there might be legitimate use of one-nature language, elaborated what is for the West the classic statement of a two-nature theology. This caused ongoing schism in the East. The Fifth Ecumenical Council, in Constantinople (553), tried to bridge the divide. By accepting that a person of the Godhead had suffered in the flesh, it emphasized the priority of the divine person in relation to the two natures. This might have but did not heal the division, which had become ecclesial, dividing non-Chalcedonians from Chalcedonians in separate jurisdictions. Nor did the desperate attempt by emperors in the 7th century to assert that there were indeed two natures but only one will in Christ. Ultimately, and after the effective martyrdom of St Maximos the Confessor, one of the greatest Orthodox theologians, his

view prevailed in the Sixth Ecumenical Council in Constantinople (680–81), namely that Christ, together with his divinity, had a fully human nature, including a human will and mode of activity.

If the Fifth Ecumenical Council conformed to imperial plans, the Seventh, held in Nicaea (787), like the Sixth, represented the defeat of a previous imperial position imposed through persecution on an important section of the Church. Iconoclasm had been resisted above all by monks and women within the empire, and by the Church as a whole outside it. In justifying the veneration of icons, St John of Damascus emphasized that it was through matter that God had worked out mankind's salvation and that veneration for the person materially depicted was intended not for the material object but for the person represented. Later opponents of iconoclasm pointed out that since the Son of God had become incarnate he could be pictured. This had the beneficial consequence of balancing concern regarding the exact relationship between the divine and human natures in Christ with a vision of Christ as one of the divine persons, who had become human.

There were other beneficial consequences. The Orthodox Church became pre-eminently a Church with a positive and indeed Eucharistic attitude to matter, encouraging its use in harmony with God and his creation, rather than for utility or self-gratification. The relevance of such an attitude in relation to our century's ecological crisis is evident. Then again, while the conciliar tradition had long antedated Constantine, and while he himself in presiding at Nicaea had worked to achieve a decision representing a genuine consensus by the episcopate, it was inevitable that emperors would use their power and quasi-religious status to impose their view. After iconoclasm emperors could be and were more easily resisted, if they presumed to take doctrinal initiatives.

Theological debate did not end with the seven ecumenical councils. There are at least two more that are considered by many Orthodox to aspire to ecumenical status. The first is the council held in Constantinople (879–80) under patriarch Photios, when all, including the papal legates present, decided against any credal insertion (meaning the Frankish *filioque*). The other is the council in Constantinople (1341) that supported the Athonite monks led by St Gregory Palamas in their distinction, taken from the Cappadocians, between God's nature or essence, incommunicable to human beings, and his outgoing energies, which could be and are received by humans, sometimes indeed in experiences that resemble the Transfiguration of Christ. A remarkable feature of the 13th to 15th centuries is the strong bond that linked those who shared this "hesychast" theology across ethnic boundaries in a comradeship and service to the cause of Orthodox Christianity, buffeted as it then was by Islam from the East and the papacy from the West.

Apart from the distinction between God's essence and energies, the theological initiative from the 13th century to the 19th lay with the dominant West. Many Orthodox were attracted by elements of Western thought and spirituality but the combination of military and jurisdictional aggressiveness prevented their general acceptance. Jurisdictional expansionism by the papacy was indeed even more effective than particular doctrinal or ritual disagreements in spreading and cementing the schism. Latin military success in Antioch in 1100 and in

Constantinople in 1204 entailed the replacement of an Eastern by a Latin hierarchy under papal jurisdiction. This was unacceptable to local Christians.

If the later papal claim to universal jurisdiction has created the greatest problems between the traditional centres of Christendom, other jurisdictional disputes have not been far behind. The doctrinal history of the 5th and 6th centuries was scarred by rivalries between Constantinople and Alexandria, Rome and Constantinople, Alexandria and Antioch. And if its missionary efforts among the Slavs and resistance to papal ecclesiastical imperialism made the patriarchate of Constantinople generally acceptable as the moving force in Orthodoxy for several centuries, especially effective in nurturing emergent Muscovy, this did not remain true for ever – Moscow itself, effectively autonomous from 1448, was acknowledged as an autocephalous patriarchate in 1589. Still less was it true during the emergence of nation states in the 19th century, which led to autocephalous national jurisdictions, bitter nationalist hostility between Orthodox Christians, and indeed secular control of many Orthodox Churches.

Again, if the Orthodox were the first Christians to object to Rome's ecclesiological hegemonism, they were slow in developing theological alternatives and have been positively remiss in implementing them. It was in mid-19th-century Russia that Alexey Khomyakov argued for *sobornost* or "conciliarity" as the basis for an Orthodox ecclesiology. This has been theoretically accepted but too often practically ignored or limited to such a narrow group as to lack meaning for the body of the Church as a whole.

Today jurisdictional disputes still mar the worldwide witness of Orthodoxy. The patriarchate of Constantinople's coordinating role as primus inter pares is agreed, but little else. The diaspora from the Orthodox heartlands remains largely though not totally split along ethnic lines and jurisdictional disputes exist in several traditional Orthodox lands as well. Most important, the fundamental equality of bishops is often sacrificed in practice to theologically questionable direction by central patriarchal or archiepiscopal bureaucracies, while within their own dioceses many bishops display a parallel indifference to the spirit of conciliarity. There are also Orthodox countries where the weight of history leads many bishops and ordinary believers alike to assimilate responsibility to Christ and the Church with national loyalties.

If in jurisdictional and ecclesiological terms the Orthodox Church falls short of its own standards, it remains true that its witness in the 20th century has been notable. Few Christian Churches at any period could point to numbers of martyrs surpassing those under Soviet rule. None has faced the full force of a totalitarian state for so long, without external support, and yet survived. Since about 1960 there has been a remarkable revival of monasticism, of missionary spirit, and of theological reflection among the Orthodox in many parts of the world, while, contrary to some Western prejudice, Orthodoxy has not in general proved an obstacle either to democracy or to the civil society.

It was inevitable that Orthodox participation in the theological debate of the 20th century would lead to some reformulation, but not that Orthodox Christian theologians should be so creative or influential. Theological revival had begun in 19th- and early 20th-century Russia; after the Revolution of 1917 a series of powerful Russian theologians, patristic scholars, and pastoral leaders worked in the West, among them Nikolai Berdayev, Sergei Bulgakov, Georges Florovsky, Vladimir Lossky, Alexander Schmemann, John Meyendorff, and metropolitan Antony of Sourozh, who has also attempted to realize the vision of Orthodox ecclesiology in his diocese.

From the 1960s there has been a contribution to the restatement of Orthodox theology both by converts to Orthodoxy, such as Olivier Clement and bishop Kallistos (Ware), and by theologians from other Orthodox lands, especially Greece. Best known abroad are Christos Yannaras and John Zizioulas, whose attitude to the West differs although their theology, both belonging to the Cappadocian tradition of acknowledging the free and loving communion of the persons of the Holy Trinity as the fundamental reality on which all else should be based, is related. As metropolitan of Pergamum, John Zizioulas is the foremost exponent of Orthodox ecclesiology and ecology alike. This last has been strongly supported by two successive patriarchs of Constantinople, Demetrios and, since 1991, Bartholomaios. Metropolitan Anastasios of Tirana has set a notable example through the manner in which he began rebuilding the Church in Albania, a witness all the more valuable for coming at a time when a revived combination of religion and nationalism has become as dangerous to Orthodoxy as it was a century ago.

The Orthodox attitude to the worldwide ecumenical movement, despite the enthusiastic participation of the late patriarch Athenagoras, and the help it gave to Churches then under persecution behind the Iron Curtain, has been ambivalent, suspicious of politicization but effective in attempting to develop points of theological consensus. There are also dialogues with all the major communions, which proceed at the same deliberate pace as dialogue among the Orthodox themselves. Although there have been important agreements on specific issues, it is unlikely that dialogue will bear rich fruit until the Orthodox see their way towards a gradual implementation of their ecclesiology in practice and are able to work out the relative weight of history and theology in the interpretation of tradition. It is clear, however, that many Orthodox, not least members of the international youth movement Syndesmos, are looking in these directions.

It is also clear that the Orthodox combination of humanity, as for instance in the tradition of a married priesthood, forgiveness of divorce, and, in the recent debate, acceptance of contraception, with a liturgical, ascetic, and theological outlook uncompromised by modernism and self-proclaimedly based on Christian tradition, has drawn forth an answering chord from many Christians in the West, after centuries of ignorance and contempt.

COSTA CARRAS

See also Councils, Ecumenism, Liturgy, Schism

Further Reading

Worship
Lash, Ephraim (translator), *The Divine Liturgy of our Father among the Saints, John Chrysostom*, Oxford: Oxford University Press, 1995 (Greek and English texts)
Mother Mary and Kallistos Ware (translators), *The Lenten Triodion*, London and Boston: Faber, 1978

Schmemann, Alexander, *For the Life of the World: Sacraments and Orthodoxy*, Crestwood, New York: St Vladimir's Seminary Press, 1966

Schmemann, Alexander, *Introduction to Liturgical Theology*, 3rd edition, Crestwood, New York: St Vladimir's Seminary Press, 1966

Schmemann, Alexander, *The Eucharist: Sacrament of the Kingdom*, Crestwood, New York: St Vladimir's Seminary Press, 1987

Wybrew, Hugh, *The Orthodox Liturgy: The Development of the Eucharistic Liturgy in the Byzantine Rite*, London: SPCK, 1989; Crestwood, New York: St Vladimir's Seminary Press, 1990

Church History

Chitty, Derwas, *The Desert a City: An Introduction to the Study of Egyptian and Palestinian Monasticism under the Christian Empire*, Oxford: Blackwell, 1966; Crestwood, New York: St Vladimir's Seminary Press, 1977

Frend, W.H.C., *The Rise of the Monophysite Movement: Chapters in the History of the Church in the Fifth and Sixth Centuries*, Cambridge: Cambridge University Press, 1972

Hussey, J.M., *The Orthodox Church in the Byzantine Empire*, Oxford: Clarendon Press, 1986

Meyendorff, John, *A Study of Gregory Palamas*, Crestwood, New York: St Vladimir's Seminary Press, and London: Faith Press, 1964

Meyendorff, John, *Christ in Eastern Christian Thought*, Crestwood, New York: St Vladimir's Seminary Press, 1975

Meyendorff, John, *Byzantium and the Rise of Russia: A Study of Byzanto-Russian Relations in the Fourteenth Century*, Cambridge and New York: Cambridge University Press, 1981

Meyendorff, John, *Imperial Unity and Christian Divisions: The Church, 450–680 AD*, Crestwood, New York: St Vladimir's Seminary Press, 1989

Obolensky, Dimitri, *Six Byzantine Portraits*, Oxford: Clarendon Press, and New York: Oxford University Press, 1988

Papadakis, Aristeides and John Meyendorff, *The Christian East and the Rise of the Papacy: The Church, 1071–1453 AD*, Crestwood, New York: St Vladimir's Seminary Press, 1994

Pospielousky, Dimitry, *The Russian Church under the Soviet Regime, 1917–1982*, 2 vols., Crestwood, New York: St Vladimir's Seminary Press, 1984

Runciman, Steven, *The Eastern Schism: A Study of the Papacy and the Eastern Churches during the XIth and XIIth Centuries*, Oxford: Clarendon Press, and New York: Oxford University Press, 1955

Ware, Kallistos, *The Orthodox Church*, 2nd edition, London and New York: Penguin, 1993 (1st edition as Timothy Ware)

Zernov, Nicolas, *The Russian Religious Renaissance of the Twentieth Century*, London: Darton Longman and Todd, and New York: Harper and Row, 1963

Patristic, Pastoral and Theological Writings

Metropolitan Antony of Sourozh, *The Essence of Prayer*, London: Darton Longman and Todd, 1986

St Athanasios, *On the Incarnation: The Treatise "De Incarnatione Verbi Dei"*, Crestwood, New York: St Vladimir's Seminary Press, 1996

St Basil the Great, *On the Holy Spirit*, Crestwood, New York: St Vladimir's Seminary Press, 1980

Bishop Basil of Sergievo, *The Light of Christ: Sermons for the Great Fast*, Witney: St Stephen's Press, 1992

Florovsky, Georges, *Bible, Church, Tradition: An Eastern Orthodox View*, Belmont, Massachusetts: Nordland, 1972

Florovsky, Georges, *Christianity and Culture*, Belmont, Massachusetts: Nordland, 1974

St John of Damascus, *On the Divine Images: Three Apologies against Those who Attack the Divine Images*, Crestwood, New York: St Vladimir's Seminary Press, 1980

Lossky, Vladimir, *The Mystical Theology of the Eastern Church*, London: James Clarke, 1957; reprinted Crestwood, New York: St Vladimir's Seminary Press, 1976

Louth, Andrew, *Maximus the Confessor*, London and New York: Routledge, 1996

The Philokalia: The Complete Text, translated by G.E.H. Palmer, Philip Sherrard, and Kallistos Ware, London and Boston: Faber, 1979–

Sourozh, Diocese of, *Diocesan Statutes*, Witney: St Stephen's Press, 1998

Staniloae, Dumitru, *Theology and the Church*, Crestwood, New York: St Vladimir's Seminary Press, 1980

Walker, Andrew and Costa Carras (editors), *Living Orthodoxy in the Modern World*, London: SPCK, 1996

Yannaras, Christos, *The Freedom of Morality*, Crestwood, New York: St Vladimir's Seminary Press, 1985

Yannaras, Christos, *Elements of Faith: An Introduction to Orthodox Theology*, Edinburgh: Clark, 1991

Zizioulas, John D., *Being as Communion: Studies in Personhood and the Church*, Crestwood, New York: St Vladimir's Seminary Press, 1985

Orthodoxy and Hellenism

The encounter between Orthodox Christianity and Hellenism (traditional ancient Greek culture) was an event of great significance not only for European but also for world history. The intense, multi-faceted, and longstanding meeting of two different currents ranged from open hostility to dynamic interaction. Yet, it should be pointed out from the outset that in the so-called Helleno-Christian synthesis these currents were by no means equal partners, for Christianity was always in control of the situation. The appropriation or the rejection of the various elements that made up Hellenic civilization was carried out in most cases on the basis of Christian criteria and expediencies without taking into consideration the relevant Hellenic perspectives. This also explains the systematic Christian persecution of paganism in the Byzantine era as well as the understandable reactions of the followers of the Hellenic tradition.

Christianity, though initially a Jewish movement that originated in Palestine, soon came into contact with the prevailing Hellenic culture of the day, as evidenced by the "Hellenists", i.e. the Greek-speaking Jews, who might have adopted Hellenic customs as well (Acts 6: 1; 9: 29; 11: 20). Tension arose on the part of Jewish Christians when Gentiles were admitted to Christianity and the Christian Church started to expand in the non-Jewish world. Paul's confrontation with Hellenism at Athens provoked indifference and mockery (Acts 18: 32), for to preach Jesus crucified as the power and the wisdom of God was certainly a folly to the Gentiles (1 Corinthians 1: 23). These events marked the very early meeting of the emerging Christianity with the Hellenic world. Up to the era of emperor Constantine I (324–37), the Christian attitude towards Hellenism was conditioned by Christianity's delicate position in the Roman empire. The main intention of the Christian Church was to establish and legitimize itself in society as well as to evade Roman hostility and open persecution. Thus Hellenism was not initially the prime enemy, and Christian writers took varying stands on it. For example, in the 2nd century there were several Christian apologists (e.g. Justin Martyr, Athenagoras), who, among other things, tried to defend the new faith against the objections of the learned followers of Hellenism. Their interest also lay in discovering

Orthodoxy and Hellenism in harmony: a cenobitic brotherhood on Mount Athos

the positive aspects of Hellenic philosophy (e.g. Platonism) and incorporating them into Christian theology. In other cases, there were more systematic critiques and denigrations of Hellenic philosophy and religion from a Christian perspective (e.g. by Hermias, Theophilus of Antioch, Tatian, Clement of Alexandria, Origen, Athanasius of Alexandria). These attacks were in some cases caused by the reactions of pagan writers (e.g. Celsus, Lucian of Samosata), who tried to refute and ridicule Christianity.

The institutionalization of Christianity in the 4th century marked a decisive further development in its relationship with Hellenism. Paganism, as embodying the Hellenic religion and world view, was systematically criticized and attacked by Christian political and religious leaders. Despite some short-lived but unsuccessful pagan revivals (e.g. under emperor Julian, 361–63), the future of paganism was its inevitable extinction. Yet the 4th century also signified a turning point in the Christian appreciation of Hellenism. Secular wisdom, based on Hellenic philosophy, was deemed useful for Christian purposes. The Cappadocian Fathers, namely Basil of Caesarea, Gregory of Nyssa, and Gregory of Nazianzus, managed to incorporate Hellenic philosophy into the elaboration of Christian doctrine in their struggle against the various heresies. The articulation and systematization of "revealed Christian truth" was made possible through the use of the vocabulary of Hellenic natural philosophy, of words such as *logos*, *hypostasis*, and *ousia*. In this way, they successfully synthesized philosophical speculation with Christian teaching and dogmatics. The metamorphosis of Hellenic thought into the Christian

framework involved simultaneously a critique and rejection of Hellenic myth, polytheism, and practice. Basil of Caesarea is known for his speech to Christian youth on how to profit from the Hellenic tradition by avoiding its erroneous doctrines and pitfalls. In general, the Cappadocian strategy proved to be an important and productive innovation in the development of Christian thought that was followed by many theologians in the following centuries. From this perspective, the development of early Christian doctrine was seen in terms of a process of "Hellenization".

In the Byzantine period the noun "Hellene" was used in a pejorative sense mainly referring to paganism, but also to denote a polytheist of any sort. Although the Hellenic language and culture were present throughout Byzantium, the simultaneous opposition to paganism persisted as well. The Church always feared any potential revivals of pagan rites, traditions, and world views. The Hellenic element in certain views of Origen was condemned by the Fifth Ecumenical Council in 553. The search for truth and certainty in Hellenism was also condemned by the Seventh Ecumenical Council in 787. The Church viewed suspiciously any preoccupation with the Hellenic tradition, especially if such study was pursued independently of the ecclesiastical tradition. Byzantium experienced such a Hellenic renaissance from the 9th century onwards; the philosopher John Italos was condemned in 1082 for serious deviations from Orthodox doctrine, while Michael Psellos was also suspected of being influenced by Hellenism. The charge of "professing Hellenism" was often brought in Byzantium to condemn specific doctrines derived from ancient tradition, such as cosmology and anthropology. And the revival of the Hellenic tradition in the last days of Byzantium produced an important pagan thinker in George Gemistos Plethon, who hoped that the Hellenic religion would eventually replace Christianity. Nevertheless the term "Hellene" was used by the Byzantines to define themselves after the 13th century, despite the fact that the Church still disliked it. Yet the Orthodox critique of Hellenism was not blind and indistinctly articulated. Rather, the Byzantine Orthodox appropriation of Hellenism has been carried out in a gradual, careful, and very eclectic way on the basis of Christian principles. It is thus no accident that the portraits of several Greek philosophers (e.g. Socrates, Plato, Aristotle, Plutarch) are found in wall-paintings of some churches in the greater Balkan area and even on Mount Athos.

Under Ottoman rule the Church remained the principal bearer and promoter of the Byzantine tradition (*Romiosyni*) and its attitude towards Hellenism. It is true that an awareness of the ancient heritage existed among the Greek population at both a higher and a popular level throughout the Tourkokratia. The wide-ranging Hellenic revival, however, in pre-independence Greece, which was influenced by western interest in Hellenic antiquity, went hand in hand with a neglect of or even a critique of the Byzantine heritage in the context of the Greek Enlightenment. These events alarmed the Church, which feared an undermining of its authority and faced the threat of irreligion and atheism. It is no wonder therefore that in an encyclical of March 1819 patriarch Gregory V described the practice of giving Orthodox children Hellenic names as inappropriate. The same problem was encountered in the 19th century when religious decline and indifference towards Christianity were attributed to the widespread worship of antiquity. During that period there was also an antithesis between those who saw discontinuity in Greek history and those who supported the view that the Greek nation had continued uninterrupted throughout the ages. This controversy also touched on the debated correlation of Hellenism with Christianity, and the Hellenic and the Romaic models of identity, and was temporarily solved through the development of Greek historicism (e.g. in Konstantinos Paparrigopoulos's monumental *History of the Greek Nation*, 1864–75), while the term "Helleno-Christian" was first coined in 1852 by Spyridon Zampelios.

The relationship between Orthodoxy and Hellenism in modern Greece is an unresolved issue, and a matter of increasing complexity due to the serious problems of identity and orientation that Greek society continues to face. Apart from the difficulties with the West, an ideal synthesis of the Hellenic tradition with the Byzantine Orthodox Romaic heritage still remains a desideratum. Beneath the official rhetoric of the Church and the state about the allegedly harmonious Helleno-Christian synthesis, there lie a number of varying and even contradictory evaluations of both Hellenism and Orthodoxy, which attest to the persisting dichotomies of modern Greek culture. Thus, the various ways in which Hellenism and Christianity are correlated in modern Greece can be summarized in the following eight categories.

In the first place, there exists an extremely negative view of Hellenism from an Orthodox perspective and an emphasis on the incomparable superiority of Christianity. Hellenism is in

principle viewed as an enemy and no more than a few harmless elements from the Hellenic tradition are accepted. This negative evaluation of Hellenism, especially on the basis of moralistic criteria, was expressed at the turn of the 19th century by the hieromonk Athanasios Parios, who reacted against the Hellenic revival of the day. Such a mentality was evident later in the thought of the popular preacher Apostolos Makrakis (1831–1905), who argued against the re-establishment of the Olympic Games. Today it is exemplified by the metropolitan of Florina, Avgustinos Kantiotis, who fears a pagan renaissance and who manifests an extreme reaction to any remnants of the Hellenic tradition. For example, he is not only against giving Greek Orthodox children Hellenic names, but against anything that is reminiscent of Greece's heathen heritage. These views are also held by most Greek Orthodox fundamentalists.

In the second category there is a more positive and balanced appreciation of Christianity's encounter with Hellenism and their dynamic interaction in history. This general perspective is shared by the official Church as well as by various ecclesiastical and theological circles. Such an Orthodox policy towards Hellenism does not rule out the possibility of an eventual conflict with it, especially when certain Hellenic remnants appear independently of the predominant Christian context. This is the main reason for the Church's disapproval of the *Anastenaria*, the fire-walking rituals in northern Greece.

The third category refers to the most positive correlation between Christianity and Hellenism and their smooth historical continuity, which is the line officially propagated by the Greek state, by the Church, and by the politicians. In the context of this mythology, the harmonious synthesis of these two traditions is extolled, for having given rise to the Helleno-Christian civilization, an unprecedented worldwide cultural phenomenon. In this case, all differences between them are minimized and considered unimportant, while the Helleno-Christian ideology is also incorporated in the national expediencies of the Greek state.

The fourth category has to do with the Neo-Orthodox current, which criticized the aforementioned attempts to correlate Christianity with Hellenism and suggested a specific approach to this question. The Neo-Orthodox objective was to find the diachronic features of the Greek way of life over a span of 3000 years, patent and latent alike. Thus, apart from any discontinuities between Hellenism and Christianity, there is a great span of Hellenicity that remains to be discovered and instrumentalized in contemporary Greece.

The fifth category refers to the practical, unofficial correlation of Hellenic/pagan and Christian elements in popular worship and rituals all over Greece. In many cases, the Church tolerates this fusion between official and popular religiosity provided that the non-Christian elements do not function independently. Such survivals were earlier used by ethnologists to demonstrate the continuity of Greek culture from ancient to modern times.

The sixth category deals with the private, idiosyncratic, and particular interpretations of the relationship between Hellenism and Christianity on the part of various intellectuals, artists, and men of letters (e.g. Kostis Palamas, K. Tsatsos). These are usually syncretic views, which have little in common with the official state and Church ideology and belong to the personal worldview of these individuals alone.

In the seventh category we encounter various Hellenocentric currents, which promote the incomparable superiority of Hellenism over Christianity and criticize the latter as a Jewish religion. Christianity is accepted in some cases only if it discards its Jewish past and is Hellenized entirely in order to become truly the national religion of the Greeks.

In the last and eighth category there are various neopagan groups that emphasize the unbridgeable chasm between Christianity and Hellenism. They feel that they are in danger from the predominant Orthodox milieu in Greece, they intend to revitalize the Hellenic religion, and they ask for more freedom to express their ideals and visions.

This typology with regard to modern Greece attests to fundamental contradictions in the heterogeneous culture of the country. Despite the official propaganda and rhetoric by both Church and state, it is obvious that modern Greeks appreciate in quite varying and even contradictory ways their Hellenic and Christian past and the formation of Greek identity, which is still rent by major internal cleavages. In addition, the manifold influences coming from the West exacerbate this conflict and contribute to the serious identity crisis of modern Greeks in the contemporary global environment.

VASILIOS MAKRIDES

See also Paganism

Further Reading

Athanassiadi-Fowden, Polymnia, "The Idea of Hellenism", *Philosophia*, 7 (1977): pp. 323–58

Bees, Nikolaus, "Darstellungen altheidnischer Denker und Autoren in der Kirchenmalerei der Griechen", *Byzantinisch-Neugriechische Jahrbücher*, 4 (1923): pp. 107–28

Bratsiotis, Panayotis I., *Christianismos kai Ellinismos en antithesei kai synthesei* [Christianity and Hellenism in Antithesis and Synthesis], 2nd edition, Athens, 1967

Chadwick, Henry, *Early Christian Thought and the Classical Tradition: Studies in Justin, Clement and Origen*, Oxford: Clarendon Press, and New York: Oxford University Press, 1966; reprinted 1984

Clogg, Richard, "Sense of the Past in Pre-Independence Greece" in *Culture and Nationalism in Nineteenth-Century Eastern Europe*, edited by Roland Sussex and J.C. Eade, Columbus, Ohio: Slavica, 1985

Clucas, Lowell, *The Trial of John Italos and the Crisis of Intellectual Values in Byzantium in the Eleventh Century*, Munich: Institut für Byzantinistik, Neugriechische Philologie und Byzantinische Kunstgeschichte, 1981

Colpe, Carsten, Ludger Honnefelder and Matthias Lutz-Bachmann (editors), *Spätantike und Christentum: Beiträge zur Religions- und Geistesgeschichte der griechisch-römischen Kultur und Zivilisation der Kaiserzeit*, Berlin: Akademie, 1992

Danforth, Loring M., "The Ideological Context of the Search for Continuities in Greek Culture", *Journal of Modern Greek Studies*, 2/1 (1984): pp. 53–85

Daniélou, Jean, *Gospel Message and Hellenistic Culture: A History of Early Christian Doctrine before the Council of Nicea*, London: Darton Longman and Todd, and Philadelphia: Westminster Press, 1973

Dimitrakopoulos, Photis, *Vyzantio kai Neoelliniki Dianoisi sta Mesa tou Dekatou Enatou Aionos* [Byzantium and Modern Greek Thought in the Middle of the 19th Century], Athens, 1996

Dover, K.J., *Perceptions of the Ancient Greeks*, Oxford and Cambridge, Massachusetts: Blackwell, 1992 (articles by A. Garzya and K.T. Dimaras)

Garzya, Antonio, "Visage de l'hellénisme dans le monde byzantin, IVe–XIIe siècle", *Byzantion*, 55 (1985): pp. 463–82

Grodent, M., "Au-delà du christianisme et du paganisme" in *Philosophes non chrétiens et Christianisme*, Brussels: Institut de Philosophie et de Sciences Morales, 1984

Hanson, R.P.C., "The Christian Attitude to Pagan Religions up to the Time of Constantine the Great" in *Aufstieg und Niedergang der Römischen Welt*. 2. 23. 2, edited by Hildegard Temporini, Berlin: de Gruyter, 1980, 910–73

Hunger, Herbert, "Der Mythos der Hellenen in Byzantinischem Ambiente", *Byzantinische Zeitschrift*, 88 (1995): pp. 23–37

Ivánka, Endre von, *Hellenistisches und Christliches im frühbyzantinischen Geistesleben*, Vienna, 1948

Ivánka, Endre von, *Plato Christianus: Übernahme und Umgestaltung des Platonismus durch die Väter*, 2nd edition, Einsiedeln: Johannes, 1990

Jaeger, Werner, *Early Christianity and Greek Paideia*, Cambridge, Massachusetts: Harvard University Press, 1961; reprinted London and New York: Oxford University Press, 1969

Kakridis, John T., "The Ancient Greeks and the Greeks of the War of Independence", *Balkan Studies*, 4 (1963): pp. 251–64

Kakridis, John T., *Oi Archaioi Ellines sti Neoelliniki Laiki Paradosi* [The Ancient Greeks in Modern Greek Popular Tradition], 3rd edition, Athens, 1989

Lechner, Kilian, "Hellenen und Barbaren im Weltbild der Byzantiner" (dissertation), University of Munich, 1954

Mackridge, Peter A., "The Return of the Muses: Some Aspects of Revivalism in Greek Literature, 1760–1840", *Kampos*, 2 (1994): pp. 47–71

Mantouvalou, Maria, "Romaios - Romios - Romiossyni: La Notion de 'Romain' avant et après la chute de Constantinople", *Epistimoniki Epetiris Philosophikis Scholis Panepistimiou Athinon* [Academic Yearbook of the Philosophy Department of Athens University], series 2, 28 (1979/85): pp. 169–98

Meijering, E.P., *Die Hellenisierung des Christentums im Urteil Adolf von Harnacks*, Amsterdam: North Holland, 1985

Metallinos, Georgios, *Orthodoxia kai Ellinikotita* [Orthodoxy and Greekness], Athens, 1987

Orthodoxia kai Ellinismos: Poreia stin triti chilietia [Orthodoxy and Hellenism: A Way into the Third Millennium], vols 1–2, Mount Athos: Monastery of Koutloumousiou, 1995–96

Pelikan, Jaroslav, *Christianity and Classical Culture: The Metamorphosis of Natural Theology in the Christian Encounter with Hellenism*, New Haven, Connecticut and London: Yale University Press, 1993

Pheidas, Vlasios, "Domes tis Ellinochristianikis Paradoseos" [Structures of Greek–Christian Tradition] in *Oecumenica et Patristica*, edited by Damaskinos Papandreou, Stuttgart: Kohlhammer, 1989

Spetsieris, Konstantinos, "Eikones Ellinon philosophon eis ekklisias" [Likenesses of Greek Philosophers in Churches], *Epistimoniki Epetiris Philosophikis Scholis Panepistimiou Athinon* [Academic Yearbook of the Philosophy Department of Athens University], series 2, 14 (1963/64): pp. 386–458

Stewart, Charles, *Demons and the Devil: Moral Imagination in Modern Greek Culture*, Princeton, New Jersey: Princeton University Press, 1991

Stewart, Charles, "Syncretism as a Dimension of Nationalist Discourse in Modern Greece" in *Syncretism / Anti-Syncretism: The Politics of Religious Synthesis*, edited by Charles Stewart and Rosalind Shaw, London and New York: Routledge, 1994

Tabaki, Anna, "Byzance à travers des Lumières néohelléniques, début du XVIIIe siècle–1830" in *Byzantium: Identity, Image, Influence*, Copenhagen: Eventus, 1996

Trombley, Frank R., *Hellenic Religion and Christianization c.370–529*, 2 vols, Leiden and New York: Brill, 1993–94

Wada, Hiroshi, "Ellin als Seelenverderber in der frühbyzantinischen Gesellschaft?", *Byzantina*, 13 (1985): pp. 787–814

Warkotsch, Albert, *Antike Philosophie im Urteil der Kirchenväter*, Munich: Schöningh, 1973

Yannaras, Christos, "Thriskeia kai Ellinikotita" [Religion and Greekness] in *Ellinismos–Ellinikotita: Ideologikoi kai viomatikoi axones tis neoellinikis koinonias* [Hellenism–Greekness: Ideological and Experiential Axes of the Modern Greek State], edited by D.G. Tsaousis, Athens, 1983

Zizioulas, John, "Ellinismos kai Christianismos: I synantisi ton dyo kosmon" [Hellenism and Christianity: The Meeting of Two Worlds] in *Istoria tou Ellinikou Ethnous* [History of the Greek Nation], vol. 6, Athens, 1976

Orthodoxy and Nationalism

The interconnection between Orthodoxy and nationalism constitutes a much-discussed and debated issue, especially in the light of the radical changes in eastern Europe, the collapse of Marxism-Leninism, the conflicts in the former Yugoslavia, and the rise of previously suppressed ethnic groups. National awakening in eastern Europe including Greece has sought in the past as well as in recent times a necessary religious legitimation, for religion has often been used to harden national boundaries and to forge national aspirations. This poses the question of the relationship of the emerging nationalism to Orthodoxy. Nationalism in this context should be distinguished from ancient and later forms of patriotism, from love of one's own country, and from related visions and struggles. Nationalism as a modern phenomenon belongs to the new set of secular values that were germinated by the Enlightenment and the French Revolution and have been evident in the Balkans since the second half of the 18th century. There are a number of different ideas about Orthodoxy and nationalism in Greece today, promoted either by the Church and the state or by different religious, political, and intellectual circles.

Historically speaking, nationalism was always extraneous to Orthodox Christianity, which aimed to transcend racial boundaries and ethnic identities (cf. Galatians 3: 28) and become a universal religion (cf. Matthew 28: 19–20). The fact that Orthodoxy and Greek national identity are now closely related does not mean that this was always the case. The situation was quite different in the Byzantine empire, when Orthodoxy was officially used, among other things, as a means to unite this multiethnic sociopolitical unit. For this reason, nationalism has been repeatedly condemned by the Orthodox Church as a serious deviation from the authentic Christian spirit. Such a condemnation came from a synod of Eastern Orthodox patriarchs in Constantinople in August 1872, which castigated "phyletism" (nationalism) as a heresy. This calls into question a widespread opinion in modern Greece about the intimate relationship between Orthodoxy and nationalism, which regards Orthodoxy as the sole factor in safeguarding Greek ethnic identity under Ottoman rule and as the champion of nationalism. Such views, which are part of state propaganda and national mythology, often obscure the diversity of historical facts. Under Ottoman rule the supranational Orthodox Church, along with the communities and the family within the *millets*, preserved various ethnic identities mainly by distinguishing Christians from Muslims. This was a distinction of a religious and not of a national character. The Byzantine supranational ecumenicity was preserved by the spirit of the Orthodox Church, its great monastic centres, such as Mount Athos, and the Phanariots. Hence, the nationalization of the Orthodox Church is a much later phenomenon, while in certain Balkan areas (e.g. in Romania) the Orthodox Church, in isolation from the West, has clearly retarded national awakening.

The first serious encounter of the Orthodox Church with the nationalistic ideas coming from western Europe occurred during the Greek Enlightenment (1774–1821). The Church as well as the nobility of the Phanariots envisaged a restoration of Byzantium emerging from the fall of the Ottoman empire. What they had in mind was a supranational unit of Orthodox Christians, for example in the form of a Balkan Confederation or Commonwealth. In no way did they anticipate the foundation of a separate national Greek state such as the western powers and various Greeks, influenced by the Enlightenment, intended to bring about. This is the reason why the Church, in collaboration with the Sublime Porte, was generally against the spread of revolutionary ideas, which were given a strong impetus by the French Revolution, among Ottoman subjects. For the same reason, several Orthodox prelates did not regard the outbreak of the Greek War of Independence favourably.

Among the many influences of the Enlightenment on Greek thought were changes in the perception of history. Popular attention was directed away from the shared past of the Orthodox Christian peoples that had emerged after the fall of Byzantium to the search for a particular historical lineage in a remote and even mythical past as a means of distinguishing different peoples. In the case of the 18th-century Greeks, this meant their direct continuity from ancient Greece. In the area of political discourse, there was also a major change. The concept of the subject was replaced by the liberal notion of the citizen incorporated into a new sociopolitical and economic unit, the nation state, which led to the disappearance of localism and traditional communities.

All these profound changes, which were intensified by the French Revolution, had a destructive impact upon the tradition of the Byzantine Orthodox Commonwealth during the 19th century in the wake of the break-up of the Ottoman empire and the foundation of the modern Balkan nation states. The enmeshment of nationalist sensibilities in politics and religion even affected Mount Athos, a monastic centre where several ethnic traditions had coexisted harmoniously for centuries. It signified also the integration of Byzantium into the frame of specific national identities and aspirations, a development contrary to the spirit of that multiethnic empire. In the case of Greece, this happened after the foundation of the independent Greek state in 1832. The Orthodox Church was subjected to the state and was transformed into a national Church through a unilateral proclamation of its autocephaly after its separation from the patriarchate of Constantinople in 1833. Apart from this, it was later used in the service of a major nationalistic plan, the "Great Idea" (*Megali Idea*), that is, the restoration of the Byzantine empire and the liberation of many occupied lands (e.g. in Asia Minor) from the Ottoman yoke. The Greek Church, weakened by its structural defects and socially marginalized by the state, tried to acquire new ways of remain-

Orthodoxy and Nationalism: officers of the Greek Air Force take part in a religious procession on Mount Athos

ing vital and socially active. As a result, in attempting to revive the polymorphous role that it had played during the Ottoman domination, the Greek Church identified fully with the expansionist plans of the state and abandoned its traditional supranational character. This transformation took place in radical and diverse ways during the 19th century and continued into the 20th century as well.

Orthodoxy and nationalism are correlated in modern Greece in various ways. Mention must be made first of the specific perspective through which several Orthodox circles have viewed their history since the 19th century. In order to create an unbroken continuity from the past and to demolish the threat of Panslavist propaganda, they considered Byzantium and its civilization as "Greek" or as predominantly Hellenized. Such an interpretation of Byzantine history has triggered several heated debates. While the existence of Greek culture in the Byzantine empire cannot be denied, its "Greek character" should not be understood from a modern nationalistic viewpoint, for the Byzantines never considered themselves as Greeks in this sense.

Similarly, certain Orthodox circles in modern Greece think of the Orthodox *millet* during the Tourkokratia as Greek from a contemporary nationalistic perspective. The Greek control of the *millet-i-Rum* notwithstanding, this included Serbs, Romanians, Bulgarians, Vlachs, Albanians, and Arabs as well. The patriarchate of Constantinople, mainly in Greek hands,

promoted various elements of Greek culture, but it was not the centre of a Greek polity. In many instances, it tried to dilute Greek elements by incorporating them into a wider Orthodox identity. The aforementioned supranational and unifying character of the Church, imbued with the Byzantine tradition, remained crucial throughout this period, though in the long run it too fell victim to the inescapable forces of nationalism.

Another specific aspect of the correlation between Orthodoxy and nationalism can be observed in the idealized interpretation of Greek history as a whole that has been introduced by some modern Greek theologians and intellectuals (e.g. by the Neo-Orthodox current). They have tried to identify the alleged diachronic principles and constants underlying Greek Orthodox civilization as distinct from that of the West. But their emphasis upon the uniqueness, exclusiveness, and superiority of Greek Orthodox culture has served as a basis for promoting nationalistic sentiments and ideologies. In addition, their demonic view of the West creates a mentality of separatism, isolationism, and fear ill-suited to today's global environment. Orthodox singularity is thus used as a remedy for the many defects of contemporary Greek society in comparison with the West.

Additional nationalistic features can be observed in the way certain Orthodox circles and individuals, usually fundamentalist-orientated, consider Greek Orthodoxy. They think that Greek Orthodoxy is a more authentic form of the original

Christian tradition, because the New Testament and many patristic texts were written in Greek. Consequently, they consider that Greek Orthodoxy is superior to other related faiths (e.g. Russian/Slavic Orthodoxy) and the Greek nation as the "new Israel" with a monopoly of the truth, a burdensome heritage, and a universal mission to save the world. Orthodoxy is thus considered the most crucial element in Greece's superiority over other peoples.

The most significant manifestation of the correlation between Orthodoxy and nationalism in modern Greece can be seen in the numerous ways that the Church and state collaborate. Although there is often tension in their relations, both of them usually legitimize one another and try to preserve their coexistence. The Church is officially hailed as a crucial protector of Greek national identity. The state is also interested in gaining from the promotion of Orthodoxy worldwide (e.g. in the Orthodox patriarchates of the east, in many former Eastern bloc countries), which is asumed to be the bearer of Hellenism and of national interests as well. Public opinion is influenced by this and tends to conclude that without Orthodoxy Greece cannot survive. Furthermore, the alliance between Greeks and Serbs in the recent Yugoslav war was also due to their common Orthodox tradition. Such policies have often provoked neighbouring peoples (e.g. in Albania) into fearing an expansion of Greek nationalism through the influence of Orthodoxy.

Through its enmeshment in nationalism, the Church looked for other ways of remaining socially influential, despite the fact that its social presence today is limited by its largely conservative and reactionary policies. On the one hand, the Church has created its own mythology and promoted its image as a bastion of Greek national identity throughout history. An aspect of this mythology is the widespread theory that the Greek nation (ethnos/genos) and Orthodoxy were identified under Ottoman rule. Such a theory is often used to consolidate the diachronic unity between Orthodoxy and Greek national identity and to oppose a separation between Church and state. On the other hand, the Church's involvement in Greek nationalism proved to be very useful from another perspective. Thus the Church was able to counterbalance its numerous structural defects and polish its tarnished public image. And its strong participation in national issues (e.g. the Macedonian question) alleviates to some extent the negative image it usually conveys in other areas.

The use of Orthodoxy to promote Greece's national interests has been criticized by several Greek Orthodox theologians and intellectuals. Yet the vision of a renewed Orthodox Commonwealth in the Balkans, far removed from national differences and divisions, seems to belong to a distant past due to the inescapable forces of nationalism. It is thus highly unlikely that the future in the Balkans will include a universal Christian empire with one emperor and one patriarch ruling jointly according to the Byzantine model. The development of historical realities since the 19th century has seriously challenged and finally destroyed this Byzantine ideal. The fact that Orthodoxy and nationalism are inextricably intertwined in a variety of ways in modern Greece therefore serves to show that such a common Balkan Orthodox future is illusory.

VASILIOS MAKRIDES

See also Church–State Relations, Commonwealth, Enlightenment, Great Idea, Nationalism

Further Reading

Argyriou, Astérios, "Nationalismes et supranationalisme dans l'Église orthodoxe à l'époque turque" in *Aspects de l'Orthodoxie: structures et spiritualité*, Paris: Presses Universitaires de France, 1981

Arnakis, George G., "The Role of Religion in the Development of Balkan Nationalism" in *The Balkans in Transition: Essays on the Development of Balkan Life and Politics since the Eighteenth Century*, edited by Charles Jelavich and Barbara Jelavich, Berkeley: University of California Press, 1963

Begzos, Marios, *Orthodoxia i misallodoxia?* [Right Belief or Hatred of Other Belief?], Athens, 1996

Braude, Benjamin and Bernard Lewis (editors), *Christian and Jews in the Ottoman Empire: The Functioning of a Plural Society*, vol. 1: *The Central Lands*, New York: Holmes and Meier, 1982 (chapters by Richard Clogg and K. H. Karpat)

Clogg, Richard, "The Byzantine Legacy in the Modern Greek World: the *Megali Idea*" in *The Byzantine Legacy in Eastern Europe*, edited by Lowell Clucas, Boulder, Colorado: East European Monographs, 1988

Dvornik, Francis, "National Churches and the Church Universal" in his *Photian and Byzantine Ecclesiastical Studies*, London: Variorum, 1974

Georgiadou, Vasiliki, "Greek Orthodoxy and the Politics of Nationalism", *International Journal of Politics, Culture and Society*, 9 (1995): pp. 295–315

Halleux, A.D, "Une Vision orthodoxe grecque de la romanité", *Revue Théologique de Louvain*, 15/1 (1984): pp. 54–66

Jelavich, Charles and Barbara Jelavich, *The Establishment of the Balkan National States, 1804–1920*, Seattle: University of Washington Press, 1977

Karmiris, Ioannis, "Catholicity of the Church and Nationalism" in *Procès-Verbaux du Deuxième Congrès de Théologie Orthodoxe à Athènes 19–29 août 1976*, edited by S. Agouridès, Athens, 1978

Kitromilides, Paschalis M., "To Telos tis Ethnarchikis Paradosis" [The End of the Ethnarchic Tradition] in *Amitos: Sti Mnimi Photi Apostolopoulou* [Amilos: In Memoriam Photis Apostolopoulos], Athens, 1984

Kitromilides, Paschalis M., "'Imagined Communities' and the Origins of the National Question in the Balkans" in *Modern Greece: Nationalism and Nationality*, edited by Martin Blinkhorn and Thanos Veremis, Athens: Sage ELIAMEP, 1990

Kitromilides, Paschalis M., "Greek Irredentism in Asia Minor and Cyprus", *Middle Eastern Studies*, 26/1 (1990): pp. 3–17

Kitromilides, Paschalis M., "'Balkan Mentality': History, Legend, Imagination", *Nations and Nationalism*, 2 (1996): pp. 163–91

Kitromilides, Paschalis M., "Orthodox Culture and Collective Identity in the Ottoman Balkans during the Eighteenth Century", *Deltio Kentrou Mikrasiatikon Spoudon*, 12 (1997–98): pp. 81–95

Kitsikis, Dimitris, *I triti ideologia kai i Orthodoxia* [The Third Ideology and Orthodoxy], Athens, 1990

Lipowatz, Thanos, "Orthodoxia kai Ethnikismos: Dyo Ptyches tis Synchronis Ellinikis Politikis Koultouras" [Orthodoxy and Ethnicity: Two Aspects of Current Greek Political Culture], *Elliniki Epitheorisi Politikis Epistimis* [Greek Review of Political Studies], 2 (1993): pp. 31–47

Makrides, Vasilios, "Ortodossia e nazionalismo nella Grecia moderna: aspetti di una correlazione", *Religioni e Società*, 25 (1996): pp. 43–70

Maximos, Metropolitan of Sardis, *The Oecumenical Patriarchate in the Orthodox Church: A Study in the History and Canons of the Church*, Thessalonica: Patriarchal Institute for Patristic Studies, 1976, pp. 300–11

Metallinos, Georgios, *Politiki kai Theologia: Ideologia kai Praxi tou Rizospasti Politikou Georgiou Typaldou-Iakovatou, 1813–1882* [Politics and Theology: Ideology and Deeds of the Radical

Politician George Typaldos Iakovatos, 1813–1882], Katerini, 1990

Prodromou, Elisabeth, "Orthodoxia, Ethnikismos kai Politiki Koultoura sti Synchroni Ellada" [Orthodoxy, Ethnicity, and Political Culture in Contemporary Greece], *Elliniki Epitheorisi Politikis Epistimis* [Greek Review of Political Studies], 5 (1995): pp. 101–32

Sant Cassia, Paul, "Religion, Politics and Ethnicity in Cyprus during the Turkocratia, 1571–1878", *Archives Européennes de Sociologie*, 27/1 (1986): pp. 3–28

Schmemann, Alexander, *Church, World, Mission: Reflections on Orthodoxy in the West*, Crestwood, New York: St Vladimir's Seminary Press, 1979, pp. 85–116

Skopetea, Elli, *To "Protypo Vasileio" kai i Megali Idea: Opseis tou Ethnikou Provlimatos stin Ellada, 1830–1880* [The "Original Kingdom" and the Great Idea: Aspects of the Ethnic Problem in Greece, 1830–1880], Athens, 1988

Stokes, Gale, "Church and Class in Early Balkan Nationalism", *East European Quarterly*, 13 (1979): pp. 259–70

Stokes, Gale, "Dependency and the Rise of Nationalism in Southeast Europe", *International Journal of Turkish Studies*, 1 (1979/80): pp. 54–67

Suttner, Ernst, "Die orthodoxe Kirche und das Aufkommen der Nationalstaaten in Südosteuropa", *Ostkirchliche Studien*, 41 (1992): pp. 126–48

Suttner, Ernst, "Kirche und nationale Identität in Europa zur Zeit der Osmanenherrschaft über Südosteuropa", *Ostkirchliche Studien*, 43 (1994): pp. 41–53

Turczynski, Emanuel, "Nationalism and Religion in Eastern Europe", *East European Quarterly*, 5 (1972): pp. 468–86

Veloudis, Yorgos, *O Jakob Philipp Fallmerayer kai i Genesi tou Ellinikou Istorismou* [Jakob Philipp Fallmerayer and the Birth of Greek Historicism], Athens, 1982

Xydis, Stephen G., "Mediaeval Origins of Modern Greek Nationalism", *Balkan Studies*, 9 (1968): pp. 1–20

Ostracism

One of the most remarkable and at the same time controversial institutions of the Classical Athenian democracy was ostracism, a procedure whereby once a year any citizen (usually a leading politician), could be banished by a vote of the people. The term itself derives from the method of voting, which involved writing the name of the victim on a potsherd (*ostrakon*).

In the sixth prytany of every year the assembly voted by a show of hands whether or not to hold an ostracism; if it decided to do so, the ostracism took place in the Agora during the eighth prytany. The citizens voted by tribes in an enclosure, and if at least 6000 votes were cast, the man who received the highest number was obliged to leave Attica within ten days. He suffered no loss of citizenship (*atimia*) or property rights, but could not return to Athens for a period of ten years. The main ancient account of ostracism is found in the *Athenaion Politeia* (chapter 22), which attributes its introduction to Cleisthenes in 508/07 BC. Both attribution and date have been questioned, since ostracism was not in fact used for another 20 years; and a fragment of Androtion (Jakoby, *Fragmente de griechischen Historiker*, 324 fr.6, in Harpocration s.v. Hipparchus) has been taken to indicate an alternative tradition, that ostracism was introduced shortly before 487. However, the text of Androtion is very uncertain, and the *Athenaion Politeia* version is to be

preferred. Later sources, notably Aelian (*Varia Historia*, 13. 24), record that ostracism was originally held in the Boule (council) and that Cleisthenes was himself the first victim of his own procedure, but this third tradition is also to be rejected.

The purpose of ostracism was to end rivalry between politicians that could potentially be harmful to the interests of the state. According to the *Athenaion Politeia*, Cleisthenes' original intention was to prevent future tyrannies, and it was subsequently aimed against those who were too powerful. Its early victims, indeed, were "the friends of the tyrants": Hipparchus son of Charmus (487), a relative of the tyrant Hippias; Cleisthenes' nephew Megacles (486), a member of the Alcmaeonid family that was suspected of attempting to betray Athens to the Persians at the battle of Marathon; and probably Callias son of Cratius (485), another supporter of Hippias. One sherd bearing Callias' name has a drawing of a Persian archer on the reverse. However, it is unlikely that ostracism, even though it was introduced in the aftermath of the fall of the Pisistratid tyranny, was designed specifically as a check on the tyrants, for which more direct and secure action could have been taken, and this seems very much like an inference from the identity of the first victims. Rather, it will have been introduced by Cleisthenes as part of his political struggle against Isagoras.

Later victims of the 480s were also connected with the Persians, at least by the voters: Xanthippus, the father of Pericles (484), had married into the Alcmaeonid family, and one *ostrakon* bears an elegiac couplet possibly associating him with their curse; Aristides (482) appears on another which claims he was a "brother of Datis the Mede"; while other *ostraka* refer to their victims as Alcmaeonids and "one of the traitors". But both Xanthippus and Aristides were recalled early under an amnesty passed in 480 before the Persian invasion. Other prominent victims of ostracism were Themistocles (c.470), Megacles again (sometime in the 470s; 4647 of the Ceramicus *ostraka* bear his name), Cimon (461), the elder Alcibiades (c.460), and Pericles' rival, Thucydides son of Melesias (443). The last man to be ostracized was the demagogue Hyperbolus (probably 416); the practice subsequently fell into disuse, though the law remained in force, and was replaced by the *graphe paranomon* (indictment for unconstitutional activity).

Over 10,000 *ostraka* have been found, on the Acropolis, in the Agora, and in the Ceramicus cemetery, and these record the names of over 130 different men. This suggests that there were no lists of candidates; and while those actually exiled will regularly have been ostracized for their political policies, other citizens clearly featured in the voting as a result of personal enmities. Indeed, Plutarch records the occasion when a voter wished to cast his *ostrakon* against Aristides, because he was tired of hearing the latter being called "the Just" (*Aristides*, 7. 7). That this citizen was unable to write the name of his victim is evidence for illiteracy in Classical Athens, although the procedure seems to presuppose widespread literacy. One find, of 191 *ostraka* on the Acropolis with the name of Themistocles, also has a bearing on this question, since they are written in only 14 hands, but furthermore is clear evidence for a concerted campaign against him by political opponents.

The fourth speech in the corpus of Andocides purports to be an oration delivered at an ostracism. The occasion is, however, historically impossible, and it is extremely unlikely that speeches were made on the day of the voting. It is stated in section 6 of this work that ostracism was used only in Athens, but in fact there were similar procedures in other states, including Argos, Megara, and Miletus.

MICHAEL J. EDWARDS

Further Reading

Fornara, Charles W. (editor and translator), *Archaic Times to the End of the Peloponnesian War*, 2nd edition, Cambridge and New York: Cambridge University Press, 1983

Harding, Phillip, *Androtion and the Atthis: The Fragments Translated with an Introduction and Commentary*, Oxford: Clarendon Press, and New York: Oxford University Press, 1994, pp. 94–8

Lang, Mabel L., *The Athenian Agora*, vol. 25: *Ostraka*, Princeton, New Jersey: American School of Classical Studies at Athens, 1990

Rhodes, P.J., *A Commentary on the Aristotelian Athenaion Politeia*, Oxford: Clarendon Press, and New York: Oxford University Press, 1981, pp. 267–83; updated reissue 1993

Rhodes, P.J. in *Ritual, Finance, Politics*, edited by Robin Osborne and Simon Hornblower, Oxford: Clarendon Press, and New York: Oxford University Press, 1994, chapter 5

Thomsen, Rudi, *The Origin of Ostracism: A Synthesis*, Copenhagen: Gyldendal, 1972

Vanderpool, E., "Ostracism at Athens" in *Lectures in Memory of Louise Taft Semple*, 2nd series, Cincinnati: University of Cincinnati Classical Studies, 1973

Otho 1815–1867

King of Greece

Otho, the son of Ludwig I of Bavaria, of the house of Wittelsbach, was selected by the three guarantor powers, Great Britain, France, and Russia to be the first king of Greece at the age of 17 by the London Protocol of February 1832. As he was still a minor, during the first two years of his reign he was guided by a three-member regency appointed by his father, namely Armansberg, Heydek, and Maurer.

Otho landed at Nauplia, the Greek capital, in January 1833 and was enthusiastically received after the ravages of a civil war that followed the assassination of Count Ioannis Kapodistria. Ludwig of Bavaria played an active part in making appointments of leading Bavarian officials for service in the Greek kingdom, thus prejudicing the country's independent status and alienating the Greeks from the Bavarian dynasty.

The regents set about creating a centralized and secular state with rationally designed institutions. For instance, they unified the legal system, the administration, and the army and in 1833 they created a Greek national Church, subordinating it to state rule, and severed its administrative ties with the Patriarchate of Constantinople. However, this programme was perceived by the civilian and military leaders of the 1821 revolution as a restriction of their privileged position. Moreover, the enormous task of state-building, which fell initially upon the regents, later on proved far beyond Otho's mental capabilities.

In December 1834 the nation's capital moved from Nauplia to Athens, and the following year King Otho became of age and the regency was terminated. Nevertheless, the Bavarians Count von Armansberg and Rudhardt served successively as heads of governments (in 1834 and 1837 respectively). The Greek army was still extensively manned by Bavarian officers and this period has been dubbed "Bavarian rule".

King Otho's Roman Catholic faith became an additional source of irritation for the Greeks. This was later compounded by the absence of an heir, who was expected to join the Greek Orthodox Church, and entitled Russia to interfere in Greek affairs as defender of Eastern Orthodoxy. Otho married Amalia of Oldenburg in 1836. One of the high points of his reign was the founding of the University of Athens in 1837, an institution which filled all Greeks with expectations of national progress.

Once of age, King Otho, sovereign by divine right according to his own perception of monarchy, sought to take control of government by interfering in its daily business. He wished to neutralize the effect of party activities by sending party leaders as Greek diplomats abroad and by short-lived alternating alliances with all Greek parties. As the parties were under the patronage of Great Britain, France, or Russia, his policy also incurred the favour or hostility of the respective "protecting" power. He was ultimately forced to yield to a general demand for a constitution by a revolt staged in Athens on 3 September 1843.

The constitution of 1844 was a compromise between the king and the political parties and put an end to Otho's absolute regime. The period of his constitutional reign began with Alexander Mavrokordatos, the leading figure of the English party, as Prime Minister for a few months. Ioannis Kolettis, the leader of the French party, followed for a period of three years, until his death in 1847. Through his close collaboration with Kolettis, Otho was able to control parliament and obtain a stable if ineffective government. After Kolettis's death the monarch assumed personal control of state affairs.

The king inherited from Kolettis the idea of Greek irredentism, the *Megali Idea* or "Great Idea", the driving principle of his personal foreign policy. As a destabilizing factor in the regional balance of power, Otho further alienated the Great Powers. The Crimean War in 1853 between Russia, and the western allies, Great Britain and France, over the integrity of the Ottoman empire, constituted a test for Otho's foreign policy. Otho and the Greek nation could not turn down the opportunity for territorial expansion. Despite the opposition of France and Great Britain, the king personally encouraged insurgency in Thessaly and Macedonia. The outcome was an occupation of the country by France and Britain between 1854 and 1857 and the establishment of a pro-ally government in Athens under Mavrokordatos. Otho's resistance to foreign pressure earned him tremendous popularity. However, the Russian defeat was a setback for Greek national hopes and the king's irredentist activities.

British enmity towards King Otho persisted throughout the remaining years of his reign and undermined his authority. During the same years university students and young intellectuals challenged Otho's absolutist methods of government and questioned the sincerity of his nationalism in a spirit of liberalism. An abortive attempt on Queen Amalia's life in 1861 was followed by a revolt of the garrison in Nauplia in February 1862, which was suppressed by force. While the king toured the country to placate anti-dynastic sentiments, a rebellion spread from western Greece to the capital and on 10 October 1862 a revolutionary committee under Dimitrios Voulgaris declared the end of Otho's reign.

Thereafter Otho lived in exile in Bavaria, emotionally attached to Greece, and died in 1867. His reign is usually viewed in comparison to that of his successor, King George I. Posterity has tended to emphasize Otho's pedantry, stubbornness, and authoritarian methods of government. However, for his persistent irredentism he has been acknowledged as a patriotic ruler with the best interests of his country at heart, ready to stand up to foreign coercion. Finally, his state-building programme, with its distressing as well as its beneficial implications, has left a lasting contribution to the modernization of Greece.

KATERINA GARDIKAS

Biography

Born in Salzburg in 1815, the second son of Ludwig I of Bavaria, Otho was chosen at the age of 17 by the guarantor powers to be the first king of Greece. He landed at Nauplia, the capital, in January 1833. In 1834 the capital was moved to Athens. The country was ruled by a three-man regency until 1835. Otho ruled absolutely until 1844 when he was forced to accept a constitution. He married Amalia of Oldenburg in 1838 but she produced no heir. He was deposed in 1862 and lived in exile in Bavaria until his death in 1867.

Further Reading

Bower, Leonard and Gordon Bolitho, *Otho I, King of Greece: A Biography*, London: Selwyn and Blount, 1939

Economopoulou, Marietta, *Parties and Politics in Greece, 1844–1855*, Athens: Economopoulou, 1984

Petropulos, J.A., *Politics and Statecraft in the Kingdom of Greece, 1833–1843*, Princeton, New Jersey: Princeton University Press, 1968

Ottoman Period (Tourkokratia)

1453–1821

Tourkokratia, which literally translates as "Turkish rule", is the term used to designate the period during which the core territories that today comprise the Greek state were under the control of the Ottoman empire. Usually the dates given for this period are 1453–1821, that is, the year of the fall of Constantinople to the time of the first battles of the Greek War of Independence in the Peloponnese.

These dates are not wholly accurate, however. The year 1453, while by far the most symbolically evocative and memorable, was simply the moment that marked the definitive end of a centuries-long period of transition from Byzantine to Ottoman rule in Anatolia and southeastern Europe. The 1453 fall of Constantinople (described in the excellent eyewitness Greek accounts of Doukas, Chalkokondyles, Sphrantzes, and Kritoboulos) was merely the last of a long series of Byzantine defeats at the hands of the Ottomans. From at least the time of the 1204 sack of Constantinople during the course of the

Fourth Crusade, the Byzantine empire could be said to have been in a serious state of "decline"; territorial losses had been suffered at the hands of invading Turkomans as early as the 11th century, most notably at the 1071 Battle of Manzikert, following which the Byzantines lost control over much of Anatolia.

Under Osman (1280–1324), founder of the Ottoman dynasty, all territory surrounding Bursa was taken by the Ottomans; Osman's son Orhan (1324–59) took Bursa itself (1326) and went on also to capture Nicaea (1331), Nicomedia (1337), and Scutari (1338). Orhan's successors, Murad (1360–89) and Bayezit (1389–1402), consolidated and expanded Ottoman rule over central Anatolia, and moved into Europe. By the time of Mehmet II's (1451–81) conquest of Constantinople, the city was the sole remaining island of Byzantium in a vast sea of Ottoman holdings.

Similarly, 1821 is not an entirely accurate date to give as the end of Turkish rule of Greece. It marks rather the very beginnings of independent Greek rule in the region. The vast bulk of territory now contained within the Greek state remained under Ottoman control long after 1821. Epirus, Greek Macedonia, and the island of Crete were gained in the course of the Balkan Wars, Thrace in the aftermath of World War I; the Dodecanese islands were joined to the Greek state only as late as 1947.

Throughout the course of the 19th century the dominant guiding principle of the Greek nation state was the *Megali Idea* ("Great Idea"), a grandiose irredentist-expansionist programme that envisioned the recapture of Constantinople from the Turks, the recreation of the Byzantine empire, and the extension of Greek territories to include all Greeks. As the Greek prime minister John Kolettis put it in an 1844 speech to parliament, "The Greek kingdom is not the entirety of Greece, only a part of it, the smallest and poorest part of Greece." This ideology unwisely propelled Greece into war with Turkey in 1897, in which Greece suffered a humiliating defeat. Some 25 years later Greece again went into battle with the hopes of liberating further supposedly Greek territories from Turkish control. The result in this case was the psychologically and physically devastating Asia Minor "catastrophe" of September 1922, in which the Armenian, Frank, and Greek districts of Smyrna (Izmir) were destroyed and over 30,000 Christians killed, and as a result of which the Greek military presence in Asia Minor was completely eradicated. Four months later (January 1923) a treaty was negotiated providing for the exchange of populations between Greece and Turkey. The result was that some 1.5 million Orthodox Christians were sent from Turkey to Greece in exchange for 350,000 Muslims living in Greece. Arguably, the final end of Toukokratia came only with this definitive death of the *Megali Idea*.

That the period of Ottoman domination was so long (no matter how one chooses to demarcate its beginning and its end) brings to the fore one central question regarding the history of Greece and the Greek people, namely, how did so disparate a group of peoples emerge from so lengthy a period of foreign rule, with some sense of national identity and group cohesiveness intact? That is, how were notions of "Greece" and "Greekness" cultivated, propagated, and disseminated over the course of Tourkokratia?

The answer, of course, is complex, and involves questions both of Hellenic continuity and of assimilation and change.

The assumption of continuity between modernday Greece and the Classical period is now widespread, but it is, historically speaking, a fairly recent formulation. The notion that contemporary Greeks were the direct descendants of the Classical Greeks, most particularly those of the 5th century BC, was first articulated by Georgios Gemistos Plethon in the 15th century, just years before the fall of Constantinople to the Ottoman Turks. During this early period of Tourkokratia, however, the notion of continuity with the Classical past was a minority one. When, with the fall of Constantinople, many of the Greek community's intellectuals emigrated to the west (most notably to Venice and its holdings), the idea of Hellenic continuity went with them. For the first three centuries of Tourkokratia, the dominant factor in the unification of the Greek people was not a sense of continuity with the Classical past, but rather with the more recent past age of Byzantium. Thus the Orthodox Church was the central institution in the consolidation and propagation of ideas of Greek communal unity.

Political as well as cultural factors contributed to the establishment of the Orthodox Church as the pivotal instrument of Greek cultural survival during Tourkokratia. The Ottoman conquest brought the far-flung Greek populations of the south Balkans and the Levant under the jurisdiction of a single ecclesiastical authority, the ecumenical patriarchate. During the Ottoman period, the ecumenical patriarchate, according to the Ottoman bureacratic system, enjoyed wide-ranging authority (both ecclesiastical and secular) over the Greek Orthodox populations of the Ottoman empire. Moreover, the ecumenical patriarchate had jurisdiction over all other Orthodox Christian populations of the empire – which included Arabs, Albanians, Bulgarians, Romanians, Serbs, and Vlachs. This remained an accepted feature of the Ottoman hierarchical structure until the 18th and 19th centuries, when these other Orthodox populations came to resent not just Ottoman dominance, but Greek Orthodox hegemony as well. This administrative arrangement meant that the patriarch was, in effect, the ruler of an empire within an empire. Indeed, he enjoyed the imperial privileges of raising taxes and administering justice, along with a host of other secular as well as religious interventions in the lives of his Orthodox subjects.

This administrative arrangement worked side by side with the cultural climate of the day to guarantee the centrality of the Orthodox Church to the programme of Greek cultural survival during the Tourkokratia. At the time of the fall of Constantinople it was widely believed that the Ottoman invasions were best seen as the result of divine intervention, as a punishment for the Orthodox peoples' conciliatory attitude towards the Latin (Roman Catholic) Church during the late Byzantine period. According to this formulation, the rule of Muslims (who would leave the Orthodox Church to its own devices) was preferable to the rule of Catholics (who would force a heretical form of Christianity upon the Greeks). Thus Turkish rule was viewed as both punitive and protective, as an event that reflected the will of God. Indeed, one strong strand of early modern Orthodox apocalypticism argued that "it was the will of God for the City [Constantinople] to be Turkified." This belief that the Tourkokratia was in some way the product of God's will later provided a strong justification for the Church's opposition to the Greek revolutionaries of the late 18th and early 19th centuries.

The highest levels of the Orthodox hierarchy, then, clearly fared well under Ottoman control. Indeed, they enjoyed wider-ranging administrative powers than had the Church of the later Byzantine period, they had control over a wide array of subjects (not only the Greek Orthodox, but all Orthodox peoples within Ottoman territories), and they were largely left alone by the Ottoman state.

It is somewhat more difficult, however, to assess the state of the vast non-elite sector of the Greek community during the Tourkokratia. The primary reason for this, of course, is related to the problem of available sources: whereas the Church and other official institutions are mentioned in Ottoman records, and kept their own records as well, there is little literary record for the vast bulk of the Greek populace during the Ottoman period.

One sector of the Greek populace that clearly fared well during the Tourkokratia, particularly during the later Ottoman period, was the mercantile bourgeoisie. During the course of the 17th century the Greeks of the empire became the dominant force in trade, both domestic and international. Of particular consequence was the Greek mercantile community of the diaspora – Greek business outposts were to be found throughout the western Mediterranean, in northern Europe, and in Russia, and as far east as Calcutta. These diaspora communities maintained close contacts with the Greek trade centres of the Ottoman empire (Ioannina, Thessalonica, Istanbul), and were responsible for the transmission to the Ottoman Greeks not just of material goods, but of European intellectual and political ideologies as well. Indeed, the rise of this commercial bourgeoisie was arguably the most important direct precursor to the 1821 War of Independence. Greeks of the diaspora endowed schools in Greece; organized Greek presses which printed educational and, later, revolutionary materials for Ottoman Greek consumption; and also were an important point of contact for the increasingly large numbers of Ottoman Greeks who travelled to Europe in pursuit of a university education.

The rise of Greek mercantile success is directly correlated to the beginnings of Ottoman "decline", particularly in Europe. Following the reign of Suleyman (1520–66), there were no further serious imperial attempts at expansion in Europe, and Greeks came increasingly to be the bridge between the Ottoman east and the European west. Because of their growing wealth and commercial influence, Greeks also came to play an increasingly influential role in the political workings of the empire. This was most evident in the case of the so-called Phanariots, a small Greek Constantinopolitan elite on whom the Ottoman government began to rely heavily in the late 17th and early 18th centuries. Valued for their linguistic abilities, they were used as the official translators in Ottoman negotiations with the powers of Europe, and came through this function to have a significant influence on the diplomatic relationship between the Sublime Porte and the west. Their role as translators gave them high office in the Ottoman imperial fleet, as a result of which the fleet itself came to be manned largely by Greek sailors from the islands. Members of the elite Greek Phanariot class were also appointed to important provincial posts in the empire, most notably in the Danubian principalities (Moldavia and Wallachia), where they served as *hospodars*, or princes.

Ottoman Period: Athens during the Tourkokratia. By the 19th century the Acropolis was in ruins and the rest of the city had shrunk to little more than a village.

The tale of Greek life under Tourkokratia is not, however, one only of success and continuity. It must be kept in mind that while the historical record tends in general to tell us about the "winners" (commercial, political, and intellectual elites), usually far less is recorded about history's "losers". While it is quite remarkable that the Greek communities of the Ottoman empire maintained such a distinctive sense of identity and even flourished under Ottoman rule, the Greeks also suffered a number of economic and cultural losses as a result of Ottoman rule.

First and foremost, despite the relatively benevolent policies of early Ottoman sultans (most notably Mehmet II, under whose rule the city of Constantinople was captured by the Ottomans), sizeable numbers of Greek Orthodox Christians converted to Islam during the Tourkokratia. This tendency towards conversion was most marked in the 15th and 16th centuries, although it was a feature of Greek life throughout the Turkish period. In this early wave of conversions the greatest number occurred in the Greek Orthodox populations of Asia Minor, where it is thought that up to 50 per cent of the Greek population converted to Islam between the 13th and 15th centuries. Many of those who did not convert were assimilated linguistically, and used the Turkish language of their conquerors rather than the Greek of their ancestors. The result of this linguistic shift was one of the more interesting syncretisms of the Ottoman period, *karamanlidika*, a form of the Turkish language written (transliterated) in Greek script.

In addition to such gradually perceptible cultural shifts, conversions were also undertaken in dramatic and sudden fashion, at times by whole villages at a time. Such conversions were usually the result of financial pressures; Greeks who converted to Islam were spared the heavy tax burden of the empire's non-Muslim subjects, and could expect to enjoy other privileges as well. Some of these converts remained crypto-Christians (that is, in their private lives they continued to practise Orthodoxy, but for all official purposes called themselves Muslim), but the vast majority within the span of a few generations lost their connection with Orthodox Christianity.

During the final centuries of the Tourkokratia, when central Ottoman government was relatively weak, Greek subjects of the Ottoman empire became increasingly vulnerable to the predations of various provincial governors. Such governors, often of Albanian origin (as was the case with Osman Pasvanoglu of Vidin, Ali Pasha of Ioannina, and Mehmet Ali of Egypt), were, by the late 18th and early 19th centuries, far more interested in establishing their own political power than in acting as representatives of the Istanbul government. Greek populations living in their territories were thus subject not just to the usual imperial taxes, but also to whatever financial structures these governors chose independently to impose.

Thus, by the early revolutionary period Greek aspirations for independence were as likely to be articulated as opposition to such governors as to the Ottoman government itself. They also were likely to be articulated in anticlerical terms, for by the 18th century the Church hierarchy was widely regarded as a corrrupt entity which relished the privileges granted it by the Ottoman administrative system. Such resentments were cast in increasingly economic and class-based terms, as the Greek intellectual elites of the diaspora began in the wake of the French Revolution and the Napoleonic Wars to disseminate ideologies of nationalism and liberalism to the Ottoman Greeks.

The origins of Greek revolutionary thought are thus best identified as both external and internal, as a combination of factors accruing from the collective experience of the Tourkokratia, intellectual and political changes in Western Europe, Ottoman decline, and shifting perceptions of Greekness and Hellenic identity. The Tourkokratia has oftentimes been portrayed as a static, changeless period of Greek history, during which little economic, political, literary, or ideological evolution was seen. It is perhaps better understood as a fascinating time of Greek interaction with both the Islamic East and the Catholic and Protestant West; a time of gradual formulation of a new, distinct, Hellenic identity.

K.E. FLEMING

See also Conversion to Islam, Diaspora, Patriarchate of Constantinople, Phanariots, Rumeli

Summary

Dated from 1453 to 1821, the period of Ottoman domination of Greece in fact extended from early in the 14th century to well into the 20th. For much of the Ottoman period the ecumenical patriarchate in Constantinople exercised wide-ranging authority over the Orthodox peoples of the empire. Thus the Church was central to the survival of Hellenism, Greeks dominated trade in the empire. Diaspora communities also began to absorb ideas of Enlightenment from the West, leading to the formulation of a new Hellenic identity.

Further Reading

Fauriel, Claude, *Chants populaires de la Grèce moderne*, 2 vols, Paris: Firmin Didot, 1824–25

Finlay, George, *A History of Greece from its Conquest by the Romans to the Present Time*, BC 146 to AD 1864, revised by H.F. Tozer, 7 vols, Oxford: Clarendon Press, 1877; reprinted New York: AMS Press, 1970

Hasluck, F.W., *Christianity and Islam under the Sultans*, edited by Margaret M. Hasluck, Oxford: Clarendon Press, 1929; reprinted New York: Octagon, 1973

Henderson, G.P., *The Revival of Greek Thought, 1620–1830*, Albany: State University of New York Press, 1970; Edinburgh: Scottish Academic Press, 1971

Kypres, Konstantinos, "The Greeks of the Diaspora: A Review Article", *Balkan Studies*, 10/2 (1969)

Papadopoullos, Theodore H., *Studies and Documents Relating to the History of the Greek Church and People under Turkish Domination*, 2nd edition, Aldershot, Hampshire: Variorum, 1990

Runciman, Steven, *The Great Church in Captivity: A Study of the Patriarchate of Constantinople from the Eve of the Turkish Conquest to the Greek War of Independence*, London: Cambridge University Press, 1968

Stavrianos, L.S., *The Balkans since 1453*, New York: Rinehart, 1958

Sugar, Peter F., *Southeastern Europe under Ottoman Rule, 1354–1804*, Seattle: University of Washington Press, 1977

Zakythinos, D.A., *The Making of Modern Greece: From Byzantium to Independence*, Oxford: Blackwell, 1976

Ottomans

The Ottomans were a Turkish people who emerged in Asia Minor in the second half of the 13th century AD as the Seljuk empire declined. They rapidly became a threat to the Byzantine empire, but their expansion was momentarily checked by Timur, whose victory over the Ottomans at Ankara in 1402 gave a brief stay of execution to the weakening Byzantines by splitting the Ottoman territory between three rivals. When the Ottomans reunited under one ruler, they resumed their expansion at a slow rate designed to provoke response neither from Crusaders from western Europe nor from Timur's successors in Asia. Constantinople fell to the Ottomans in 1453, and they disputed the remnants of the Byzantine empire first with the Byzantine successor states and then with the Genoese and Venetians who had seized various ports and islands in the Aegean. Simultaneously they continued to absorb Syria, Palestine, Egypt, and north Africa, and to push northwards into the Balkans, until they were turned back at the gates of Vienna for the second and last time in 1685. Thereafter, the Ottomans went into a slow decline, exacerbated by the loss of the Peloponnese in the Greek War of Independence in the 1820s and cessions of Attica, Boeotia, and Euboea in the 1830s, Thessaly and Epirus in the late 1870s and the early 1880s, Macedonia and Crete in 1913, and Thrace after World War I. The last sultan was deposed after World War I, and Kemal Atatürk founded a secular republic which sought closer ties with Europe.

Osman, the eponymous founder of the Ottomans, was one of the beys who founded a *gazi* state on the marches of the Byzantine empire. As a *gazi* (warrior) state, his *beylik,* or principality, was devoted to waging *gaza* or holy war against the infidel, and this identification as a *gazi* state was to persist for many centuries, giving the Ottoman empire its raison d'être, at least until the conquests stopped. (Then, because the system had been geared to conquest and not to maintaining a static frontier, Ottoman institutions lost their dynamism and began to decay.) The Ottoman principality, like the other Turkish *beyliks* in Anatolia, was fostered by the pressure of population and need for expansion, the decay of the Byzantine frontier defence system, and the religious and social discontent in the Byzantine frontier areas. Additionally, the Byzantine empire, though substantially reunited after the fragmentation of the first part of the 13th century, never recovered from the Fourth Crusade in AD 1204, when the Crusaders, intervening at the instigation of the Venetians in a struggle for the succession to the Byzantine throne, took Constantinople and carved up the Byzantine empire among themselves.

Though the Ottomans formed only one of many Turkish principalities engaged in holy war against the Christians, they eventually outstripped their rivals as well as their enemies for several reasons. The other *beyliks* were fought to a standstill at the Aegean, so they turned from holy war to trade, and consequently developed commercial and cultural ties with western European peoples such as the Venetians. This replacement of *gaza* with trade allowed leadership to pass to the Ottomans, who could demand support from the other Turkish principalities against the common enemy. The other *beyliks* also suffered from dynastic wars, because each bey would divide his territory among his sons and try to rule over them from the centre, whereas the Ottomans, facing greater external pressure, better preserved their unity.

Osman's successors reached the Dardanelles by 1345, allowing the Ottomans to intervene in Byzantine internal politics and establish a foothold on the peninsula of Gallipoli, thus opening the door to Europe. Murad I took Adrianople in 1361, forcing the Byzantine emperor and various Balkan rulers to acknowledge Turkish suzerainty and defeating the Crusaders at Nicopolis on the Danube. Attempts to centralize the state, however, ceased when Timur defeated Bayezid I in 1402. The defeat created a decade-long interregnum during which Bayezid's three sons contended to see who would rule the Ottomans. Mehmet I re-established unity in 1413, conciliating local rulers in Anatolia and Rumelia, the land the Ottomans took from the Byzantines in Thrace. In restoring unity, he was helped by the "men of the sultan" (*gilman*), who ran the empire and the army and who had a vested interest in the return of centralized authority, since they were uncertain of their position and rights as long as rival sultans existed.

The waxing of Ottoman power, and the concomitant waning of Byzantine power, were two sides of the same coin. The Byzantines were prey to political, social, and religious divisions. Civil wars and lack of central authority allowed local lords to do as they pleased, and the central administration was unable to loosen their grip on the estates it wished to return to its own control. The Ottomans, for their part, won the allegiance of the Christian peasantry by abolishing feudal and manorial rights and commuting feudal service into payment of a tax directly to the state. They also took the politically shrewd step of supporting the Orthodox Church. This put them on the side of the peasantry and against that portion of the Byzantine nobility that sought help from the Catholic world, so that the peasantry disowned their ruling class. Indeed, on the eve of the fall of Constantinople, the Grand Duke Loukas Notaras is supposed to have said, "Better the turban of the Turk than the tiara of the pope", speaking in this for many Byzantines and displaying an attitude that doomed last-minute attempts to gain strong western European support against the Ottoman assault on the city. The Ottomans also sought to cement their hold on newly conquered territories by settling them with Turks who would form a landed aristocracy that was expected to fight in time of war (the *sipahis*). Furthermore, the Ottomans maintained their legitimacy, and their status as *gazis*, by proclaiming any Muslim rivals to be rebels against religion. The Ottoman sultan claimed to be caliph, "commander of the faithful", though he could not prove descent from the Prophet Muhammad as required by Islamic law. Such a claim was only one of many tensions between Ottoman political practice and Islamic political theory, along with the tensions between *Kanun*, Ottoman administrative law, and *Shariah*, Islamic religious law, and over the position of Islamic scholars in the state.

Mehmet II, the conqueror of Constantinople, saw himself as the heir to a world empire. This stemmed in part from the heritage of Osman, in part from the teachings of Islam on sovereignty, and in part from his claim to be emperor of the Romans as a result of his conquest of Constantinople. Other Islamic states henceforth hailed the sultan as *Qaysar-i-Rum* ("Caesar of Rome"). Mehmet wanted to have all the religions in his empire under his watchful eye and saw to it that the Greek Orthodox patriarch, the Armenian patriarch, and the Jewish chief rabbi lived in his capital, which he moved from Adrianople to Constantinople. In fact, he made the Orthodox patriarch the head of *Rum millet*, or the community of Orthodox Christians. As the new capital, he rebuilt and resettled Constantinople, whose population had sunk dramatically under the last Byzantine emperors, using forced resettlement to increase the number of its inhabitants. He also tried to recreate the Byzantine empire under his own rule, eliminating the empire of Trebizond and the despotate of Morea, two Byzantine successor states which had sprung up in the wake of the Fourth Crusade, and occupying ports in the southern Crimea and, briefly, Otranto in Italy which had once belonged to the Byzantines. He eliminated the family of Gattilusi, related to the last Palaiologoi emperors, and therefore possible pretenders to the Byzantine throne. Mehmet's attempt to establish himself as the heir to the Byzantine emperors, and the fact that he spoke Greek and maintained a library of Greek books, led 15th-century authors such as Laonikos Chalkokondyles and Kritovoulos Imvriotes to hope that Greece would culturally influence the Ottomans as it had the Romans 17 centuries before, when "captured Greece took captive its uncivilized conqueror", as the Roman poet Horace once said. Islam, however, disinclined the Ottomans to accept the cultural legacy of infidels, so these hopes died stillborn.

Mehmet centralized the Ottoman state, seeking to consolidate the gains of the previous half-century. He put the *yeniçeri* or Janissaries under his own control and made them the nucleus of his army. He chose the grand vizir, along with the other officers of the state, from among his own slaves. Although he left the administration of justice to the cadis, he entrusted its execution to his own slaves. Thus he retained for himself the last word on finance, justice, and military affairs, especially as the grand vizir, powerful as he was, could not give orders to the commander of the Janissaries, for example. Mehmet's policies in claiming the legacy of the Byzantine empire led him into conflict with Hungary in the Balkans and Venice in the Aegean and Morea.

Mehmet's successors continued the policy of expansion into mainland Greece, the Balkans, and the Near East. The Shiite Safavids came to power around the turn of the 16th century in Persia, providing a bulwark against Ottoman expansion to the east, but Mehmet II's grandson, Selim I, defeated the Mamluks and took Egypt. The most successful of these successors was Selim I's son, Suleyman the Magnificent (1520–66), who continued the Ottoman expansion in the Balkans against the Hungarians and Austrians, forced Venice to cede its last strongholds in the Aegean and the Morea, fought the Persians, waged a naval war in the Indian Ocean against the Portuguese over the spice routes to Syria and Egypt from southeast and east Asia, and intervened in European politics, allying with

Ottomans: the governor of Mount Athos with the insignia of his office. Karyes was reckoned to be a hardship posting.

Francis I of France and the corsairs of Algiers against the Habsburg Holy Roman Emperor Charles V.

After the death of Suleiman the Magnificent on campaign against Austria in 1566, the Ottoman empire went into a slow decline over the next three and a half centuries. There are many symptoms of this decline, which themselves had a pernicious effect on the empire. After Suleiman the Magnificent, sultans rarely took to the field with their armies, or indeed interested themselves in the great affairs of state. Up until the early 17th century Ottoman princes had been sent out to rule *sancaks* (military districts) in Asia Minor and thereby gain practical experience of administration. When the sultan died, his sons scrambled to be the first to reach the capital and become the new sultan, since the losers would be strangled to obviate future civil wars. Such a Darwinian approach to the succession, with the losing princes killed *pour encourager les autres*, produced an excellent series of sultans down to Suleiman the Magnificent, as princes were encouraged to prepare themselves as much as possible to rule. After the early 17th century Ottoman princes spent their lives in idleness in the palace in Istanbul, waiting for their turn to rule, and the long and enervating confinement sapped whatever abilities the princes might initially have had.

This lack of interest at the top in governing led to abuses by the sultan's underlings. When the sultan did not rule his officials, they conspired to rule him. Faction and intrigue among the great personalities of the imperial court, including the *Valide Sultan*, or sultan's mother, the *Haseki Sultans*, or women who had borne the sultan a male child, and the Ottoman princesses who sought to advance the careers of their husbands and children, increasingly determined policy and too frequent appointment, dismissal, or transfer of high officials made administration less efficient, because it encouraged them to capitalize on the offices while they held them, to the detriment of longterm policies. In addition, the abandonment of the *devshirme,* or levy of children from the conquered populations, which filled the ranks of the *gilman,* opened civil offices to those who could most successfully intrigue or bid for them, not those best qualified to hold them through training and experience.

The system also showed the strain of prolonged warfare, though *gaza* had been the original basis for the state, and the advancing frontier had not only yielded material rewards, but, perhaps more importantly, an ethos and purpose to the Ottomans. Formidable obstacles hindered campaigns against the Persians in the east and the Austrians in the north: time and distance, the opposite extremes of the arid climate of the desert in summer and the frozen climate of the Balkans in winter, and serious logistical problems attendant on operating armies far from Ottoman bases with 16th- and 17th-century methods of transport. The Habsburgs built a defensive barrier, further hindering the Ottoman advance, and the Ottomans in turn built their own defensive barrier, so war between them tended to become a conflict of sieges, shortened because an Ottoman army marching north from Istanbul at the beginning of the campaigning season in April would only reach the northern marches of Ottoman rule in late July or early August and so have only two or three months in the field before the end of the campaign season. In addition, the Ottoman army failed in the late 17th and 18th centuries to keep up with the tactical revolution in warfare brought about by the development of the mobile field gun and the flintlock musket. Furthermore, its budget was eaten up by pay increases for the Janissaries, who came to behave more and more like the Praetorian Guard in the Roman empire during the 3rd century AD, while the feudal landowners of Asia Minor and Rumelia, on which the Ottomans had relied for military manpower in earlier years, were hard hit by inflation and, from the beginning, excluded from the highest offices, which were only open to the *gilman*. Now the *gilman* intrigued for the estates which had supported the feudal aristocracy, and holders of these estates bought exemptions from service.

The position of Greeks under Ottoman rule was ambiguous. On the one hand, as a whole they were a conquered people, and mainland Greece languished in poverty, although the islands were slightly more prosperous, to the degree that Ottoman control was lighter. On the other hand, a small elite, inhabiting the Phanar quarter of Istanbul and therefore called the Phanariots, managed to win a privileged position for themselves under Turkish rule. They applauded the ultimately successful Ottoman efforts to expel the Genoese and Venetians from the Aegean and Morea, especially because the western Europeans were Catholic heretics who were preventing the revenues of their holdings from reaching the Orthodox patriarch in Istanbul and diverting the Moreot export trade for their own benefit. In addition, once the *devshirme* was given up and the *gilman* lost their grip on the civil offices in the state, Greeks took over from the Serbs and Croats who had filled such offices. Greeks filled the posts of Dragoman (translator) of the Porte and Dragoman of the Fleet, and the fleet itself was largely made up of Greek sailors. In addition, Greeks filled the offices of *hospodar* of Moldavia and *hospodar* of Wallachia, actually ruling those lands for the Ottomans. Both the Porte and the European embassies in Istanbul needed members of the relatively westernized Greek aristocracy to serve as go-betweens, and, by 1793, the permanent Ottoman diplomatic missions at Vienna, Paris, London, and Berlin had Greek Christian chargés d'affaires.

The Ottomans also did much to enrich Greek merchants by ruining their Italian rivals while themselves abstaining from commerce. Greek shipowners dominated the Black Sea and grain trades, and Greek business houses in Thessalonica developed a commercial network in Italy as well as in lands ruled by the Ottomans. The economy of the Ottoman empire as a whole, however, was stagnant, because it was based on agriculture and geared towards local self-sufficiency, not towards trade. In addition, despite repeated attempts at political and military reform throughout the 18th and 19th centuries, those running the empire found it difficult to solve the problems facing an empire that could not compete politically, economically, and technologically with the western European nations. The last of these reform attempts was led by the Young Turks in the early part of 20th century, and their miscalculations in foreign policy, which led them to support the Central Powers against the Allies and become involved in their defeat in World War I, brought an end to the Ottoman empire.

The War of Independence ended the relatively favoured position of the Phanariot elite in the Ottoman regime. Turkish reprisals against the Greeks can be symbolized by, though they did not begin or end with, the execution of the last Greek Dragoman of the Porte in 1821. British, French, and Russian intervention caused the Ottomans to grant independence in 1832 to a Greek state whose northern boundary ran from the Gulf of Preveza to the Gulf of Volos, though it was not until 1913 that a majority of Greeks lived under Greek rule.

ERIC KYLLO

See also Phanariots, Rumeli

Further Reading

Goodwin, Jason, *Lords of the Horizons: A History of the Ottoman Empire*, London: Chatto and Windus, 1998; New York: Holt, 1999
Lewis, Bernard, *The Emergence of Modern Turkey*, 2nd edition, London and New York, Oxford University Press, 1968
Toynbee, Arnold, *The Greeks and Their Heritages*, Oxford and New York: Oxford University Press, 1981

P

Paestum

Greek colony in Campania

Paestum (Poseidonia) was an important Greek colony in Campania in southern Italy and is the site of well-preserved Greek temples. Located about 80 km south of Naples, Paestum is about 700 m from the sea and just south of the Sele river.

The site saw human habitation as far back as the early Stone Age; roving hunters moved through the area, leaving behind tool artifacts. Neolithic farming is evidenced from the archaeological record, and recent excavations have recovered remains from the Bronze Age, e.g. a large graveyard 1.6 km north of the city, and houses in the southern sector of the ancient walls. Sherds of Mycenaean pottery suggest some, though probably indirect, contact with the Greek mainland. In the environs of Paestum 8th- and 7th-century sites have been recovered.

Paestum was founded between 650 and 600 BC by colonists from the Italian city of Sybaris, which was itself a colony established in 720 near Croton on the Ionian Sea by Greeks from Troezen and Achaea. The city was called Poseidonia, or the City of Poseidon. At about the same time, the sanctuary of Hera at Foce del Sele was established about 8.5 km north of Paestum; this sanctuary included a temple, altars, stoas, and a treasury. In the 6th century BC Paestum flourished through trade with the Etruscan cities to the north. Its political importance increased when Etruscan influence waned and the mother city Sybaris was destroyed in 510 BC. Many of the Sybarites fled to Paestum, and this, coupled with the great fertility of the plains and the city's strategic position on the trade routes, caused a further economic boom. Around 400 BC the Italian people called Lucanians descended from the interior mountains and invaded Campania, soon taking over Poseidonia. The city continued to prosper, however, and enjoyed a strong, vibrant industry and commerce. Soon the Lucanians' expansionist policies brought them into conflict with the Greek cities further south, especially Tarentum. The Greeks called upon Alexander, the Molossian king of Epirus and brother-in-law of Alexander the Great, for assistance. Alexander was initially successful, reaching as far north as Paestum where he defeated the Lucanians in 332 BC. The following year, however, Alexander died and Paestum fell again under the rule of the Lucanians. Soon another power appeared on the scene: Rome. Rome gradually became involved in Campania in response to the Greek cities' calls for help against the Lucanians. In 280 BC Tarentum reacted to this intrusion in their sphere of influence by calling upon Pyrrhus, king of Epirus, for assistance. Pyrrhus was soon defeated, abandoning Italy in 275 BC and thereby allowing Rome to assume control of the whole of southern Italy. Rome established a colony at Poseidonia in 275 and renamed the city Paestum. The city's status became *socius navalis*; this meant that Paestum, although nominally autonomous, supplied Rome with a quota of sailors and transport ships (as opposed to land troops, as in the case of other Italian cities).

Paestum proved very loyal to Rome, even in the darkest times. Throughout the First and Second Carthaginian Wars of the 3rd century BC Paestum's loyalty never wavered – even when much of Campania and all of Lucania defected to Hannibal after the disastrous Roman defeat at the battle of Cannae in 216 BC, and even as Hannibal feasted in the city of Capua, just a few days' march to the north. Paestum also maintained allegiance to Rome during the Social War of 91–88 BC, when many of Rome's allied cities in central and southern Italy revolted in an effort to achieve full Roman citizenship. As a reward for its unswerving loyalty, Paestum retained the right to mint its own coinage until the 1st century AD. Later in that century the emperor Vespasian settled a number of sailors at Paestum.

Paestum's gradual decline began as early as the 2nd century BC. The completion of the great highway, the Appian Way, diverted the major trade route away from the southeast coastal area to the ports on the Adriatic. Even a new local road, the Via Polilia, bypassed Paestum. Despite a somewhat renewed building programme in the 2nd or 3rd century AD, the city suffered malaria epidemics as well as flooding and swamping due to the silting of local rivers. By the 5th century the city had been reduced to a village of houses clustered around the temple of Athena, which by now had been converted to a Christian church. There are records of a bishop residing in the city as late as the 7th century, and an 8th-century basilica was erected. In the 9th century the inhabitants moved to the hills because of constant raids by the Saracens.

Paestum contains some of the best-preserved and most important Greek temples in the ancient world. The city walls, with a perimeter of nearly 5 km, date to the 5th century BC, with renovations done in the subsequent two centuries; 24 round and square towers ring the walls, with four main gates.

The Greek city was laid out with two sacred areas in the north and south, separate areas containing public buildings, and houses laid out in gridlike blocks. The south sacred zone contains two magnificent temples, both dedicated to Hera. The so-called "Basilica", dating to c.550 BC, is extremely well preserved. The adjoining, mid-5th-century temple, also dedicated to Hera but erroneously called in earlier literature the temple of Poseidon, is one of the best examples of Doric architecture. The two temples formed the centre part of a sacred precinct of Hera. The northern sacred area contains the 5th-century temple of Athena (originally thought to have been dedicated to Ceres); its design is radical, being the first Greek temple to incorporate both Ionic and Doric elements. The Greek agora, or marketplace, was situated just south of the Athena precinct, as recent excavations have shown. A circular meeting-house (bouleuterion) and an underground shrine flanked this area.

The Roman colonists radically restructured Paestum in accordance with typical Roman city planning. A large forum was mapped out between the two sacred zones, with the cardo maximus and decumanus roads leading into the forum (the cardo even replaced the Sacred Way that had run behind the two Hera temples). The open court of the forum was flanked by such buildings as theatres, markets, baths, an ampitheatre, a gymnasium, and smaller temples.

Paestum is surrounded by important archaeological sites, many of which are still being excavated. Three major necropolises have been located, ranging in date from the 3rd millennium to the 4th century BC. The paintings of early 5th-century BC tombs are important for the history of Greek art. At Santa Venera, 1 km south of the city, a large sanctuary has recently been discovered; dated to the 5th century BC, the complex was dedicated to Aphrodite (not Bona Dea, as once thought).

Paestum is an extremely important city for the study of ancient Greek architecture, south Italian tomb painting, Roman city planning, ancient religion, and pottery and burial customs.

STEVEN M. OBERHELMAN

Summary

Founded between 650 and 600 BC by Greek colonists from Sybaris in south Italy, Paestum (then called Poseidonia) flourished as a result of trade with Etruria. In the 4th century BC the city fell to the Lucanians and in 275 BC to the Romans who renamed it Paestum. It was reduced to a village by the 5th century AD. Paestum has some of the best-preserved Greek temples of the Archaic and Classical periods.

Further Reading

Coulson, William, Paestum entry in *The Princeton Encyclopedia of Classical Sites*, edited by Richard Stillwell, Princeton, New Jersey: Princeton University Press, 1976, pp. 663–65

Dunbabin, T.J., *The Western Greeks: The History of Sicily and South Italy from the Foundation of the Greek Colonies to 480 BC*, Oxford: Clarendon Press, 1968, reprinted 1999

Graham, A.J., "The Western Greeks" in *The Expansion of the Greek World, Eighth to Sixth Centuries BC*, edited by John Boardman and N.G.L. Hammond, Cambridge: Cambridge University Press, 1982 (*The Cambridge Ancient History*, vol. 3, part 3, 2nd edition)

Greco, Emanuele and Dinu Theodorescu, *Poseidonia–Paestum*, 3 vols, Rome: Bretschneider, 1980–87

Krauss, Friedrich, *Paestum: Die griechischen Tempel*, 3rd edition, Berlin: Mann, 1976

Lang, S., "The Early Publications of the Temples at Paestum", *Journal of the Warburg and Courtauld Institutes*, 13 (1950): pp. 48–64

Napoli, Mario, *Paestum*, Novara: Istituto Geografico de Agostini, 1970

Pedley, John Griffiths, *Paestum: Greeks and Romans in Southern Italy*, London and New York: Thames and Hudson, 1990

Pedley, John Griffiths, *et al.*, *The Sanctuary of Santa Venera at Paestum*, Rome: Bretschneider, 1993– (one vol. so far)

Sestieri, Pellegrino Claudio, *Paestum: The City, the Prehistoric Necropolis in Contrada Gaudo, the Heraion at the Mouth of the Sele*, translated by C.H. Pennock, 9th edition, Rome: Istituto Poligrafico dello Stato, 1968

Paganism

The word "paganism" derives from the Latin *paganus*, which literally means a peasant, villager, or rustic. Later on it came to signify the heathen, who drew their followers mainly from the rural population and thus were distinguished from the Christians, who were represented principally by the urban lower and middle classes. This article is concerned with the longstanding conflict between paganism and Christianity and with the passing from the ancient Hellenic world to the Christian Roman empire. The encounter of paganism and Christianity took place at various levels and exhibited different characteristics as it continued into the Byzantine period. Because the term "paganism" has also been used in modern times very broadly, objections have been raised to it. In the present context, however, it refers solely to the non-Christianized Hellenic world.

The institutionalization of Christianity as the official religion of the Roman empire by Constantine I (324–37) did not mean the immediate disappearance of paganism, which remained influential throughout the 4th century and had solid popular support. Under Julian (361–63) there was a short-lived, systematic, though unsuccessful attempt to revive paganism, which earned him perpetual Christian enmity. Outside politics, there were also a number of intellectuals who did not convert to Christianity and supported paganism, such as the rhetorician Libanius, who praised Julian's pagan revival. In addition, at the popular level people continued to adhere to pagan cults, sacrifices, and habits, especially in the country-side. These pagan survivals provoked the intervention of Theodosius I (379–95), who supported Orthodoxy, closed the oracle at Delphi, suspended the Olympic Games, and prohibited with harsh laws the celebration of pagan cults and the visiting of pagan temples. These measures resulted in the large-scale closure or destruction of pagan monuments.

Nevertheless, paganism did not become entirely extinct, and survived especially in rural areas. Sometimes there was a fusion between Christianity and paganism, manifested in syncretic religious remnants (e.g. in the northern Greek city of Philippi which was late entering the mainstream of Christian practice). It was Justinian I (527–65) who attacked the Hellenic past by forbidding the teaching of philosophy and law at the Academy of Athens in 529, and thus deprived paganism of a renowned school of higher education, in which Proclus, Simplicius, and Damascius had excelled as teachers. The systematic development of Christian missions also had a negative impact upon pagan survivals in the Byzantine empire. These radical events signified the social marginalization and even the extinction of pagans in many places. Yet, pagan elements were incorporated into Christianity in various open and covert ways. Many Church Fathers (e.g. the Cappadocians) had a thorough knowledge of Hellenic philosophy and used it selectively in the articulation of Christian dogma. The Hellenic tradition always formed part of Byzantine education and culture, notably after the 9th and especially after the 12th century when admiration for Classical authors was strong. Pagan cultic places were often transformed into Christian churches for various practical or artistic reasons. And pagan rituals in transmuted forms were incorporated into or replaced by relevant Christian ritual activity. These cases show that the meeting of paganism with Christianity was multifaceted and ambivalent and that under certain specific conditions remnants of the ancient religion coexisted with Christianity.

Certain aspects of paganism survived in the later centuries of Byzantium, manifested in everyday life and habits as well as in local cults, especially in the countryside. This continued to provoke Christian reactions. Canon 62 of the Council in Trullo of 692 explicitly condemned the continuation of pagan practices. In the 9th century the existence of some "Hellenes" is mentioned in the southern Peloponnese (Laconia) by Constantine VII Porphyrogennetos. In the 12th century the learned archbishop Eustathios of Thessalonica in his work *De emendanda vita monastica* (On the Improvement of Monastic Life) criticized the groups of monks who organized raiding parties in Greece and destroyed pagan temples. Paganism was defeated in the long run mostly for external reasons (e.g. persecutions, barbarian invasions), but also for internal reasons (e.g. stagnation and lack of innovation, the elitism of later pagan leading figures, isolation). The Church, despite its selective appropriation and conditional acceptance of Hellenic elements, always tried to keep them under control and feared their autonomous presence and function. During iconoclasm both parties accused one another of paganism. A preoccupation with the study of antiquity and ancient philosophy was often viewed suspiciously and led at times to accusations of professing paganism, especially during the 10th and 11th centuries, as the trial of the philosopher John Italos in 1082 demonstrates. The Church was particularly critical of any attempted revivals of paganism to the detriment of Christianity. The most conspicuous case from late Byzantium was that of the Neoplatonic philosopher George Gemistos Plethon in Mistra, who attempted to redirect Byzantine society and culture towards hitherto neglected Hellenic sources. Plethon believed in the Olympian gods and constructed a pagan system with a calendar, prayers, hymns, and liturgy. Yet his vision was not only unrealistic but was also met with Church reactions, and his book *On the Laws* was burned after his death by the patriarch of Constantinople Gennadios II Scholarios.

During the Tourkokratia there was an awareness of the Hellenic past at both the intellectual and the popular levels, albeit in many cases diffused and mixed with various beliefs and superstitions. However, growing signs of a Hellenic – but not strictly pagan – revival among the subjugated Greeks can be observed especially in the late 18th and early 19th centuries and in the Greek War of Independence, which had been given a strong impetus by European Philhellenism, Neoclassicism, and Romanticism. This renewed interest in Greek antiquity was viewed suspiciously by members of the Orthodox Church (e.g. patriarch Gregory V and the hieromonk Athanasios Parios), who feared that it would lead to indifference to Orthodox spirituality and tradition. This worship of antiquity was current in 19th-century Greece too and was closely connected with the conflict between the Hellenic and the Romaic–Byzantine models of Greek identity. It is no wonder therefore that various strategies were developed to overcome this cultural schism by attempting to view Greek history and culture diachronically as a unified system (e.g. the Helleno-Christian synthesis, which survives to this day). It should be noted, however, that in these attempts Hellenism was usually taken out of its pagan context and set up on the basis of Christian criteria. Yet, Orthodox fears of a pagan restoration were evident in the 19th century as the accusations against Theophilos Kairis in 1838–39 and A. Makrakis's opposition to the re-establishment of the Olympic Games in 1896 show. Such developments forced other Greeks in turn to emphasize the pagan character of the Hellenic tradition and the fierce confrontation of paganism with Christianity in history (e.g. the anti-Christian tragedy *Julian the Apostate*, written by Kleon Rizos Rangavis [1842–1917], which was entered for the Voutsinaios prize and provoked the Church's reaction).

In modern Greece elements of the pre-Christian Hellenic tradition still survive and are evident in popular customs, rituals, and worship, even within a Christian framework. These were identified from the late 19th century onwards by the now discredited "survivals" approach of folklorists in their attempt to show the diachronic unity of Greek culture. Idiosyncratic pagan trends and remnants can also be observed in several contexts, ranging from A. Papadiamantis's flirtation with paganism in the old sense and the continuing sanctity of place, to the Delphic festivals of A. Sikelianos. There have also been attempts to revitalize elements of Hellenic culture and its religious tradition in ways that would help the country to face the challenges of the modern world. This revival has nothing to do with the historical, patriotic, and national promotion of ancient Greece, which is done systematically by the state and others. Rather, it aims at a more serious acquaintance with the spiritual founts of Hellenic civilization with a view to re-establishing them. These Greek organizations and currents can be subsumed under two overlapping categories: "Hellenocentric" and "neopagan".

The term "Hellenocentric" refers generally to a wider Hellenic revival, expressed in various forms, with an emphasis on Greece's ancient heritage and usually at the expense of the Orthodox tradition. The most characteristic trend in this category is centred around the monthly journal *Davlos* (Torch), published since 1982 and devoted to all aspects of Hellenic culture. The common features of this trend include: the promotion of elements of Hellenic culture and the unique, unparalleled contributions of the Hellenes to universal civilization (in language, writing, politics, democracy, science, technology, philosophy, theatre, and athletics); the superiority of the Hellenic race, spirit, and culture worldwide as the only real alternative to the deep crisis of the West, since Hellenes are to be regarded as an autochthonous population designed to become leaders of the world; the fundamental antithesis and unbridgeable chasm between Hellenism and Judaism and the devastating criticism of the Old Testament and Zionism; the need to purge Christianity completely of its Jewish background and give to it a more Hellenic character; the sharp critique of Christianity's intolerance and persecution of dissidents over the centuries; and the rejection of hybrid combinations of Hellenism and Christianity (e.g. the Helleno-Christian synthesis, nationalistic Christianity, the *Romiosyni*-theorists, the Neo-Orthodox proposals) because of their artificial nature. Needless to say, similarly idiosyncratic views are expressed by other groups and journals as well as by individual authors.

The second category, which basically shares the features of the above groups, but is distinguished from them by its more explicit relation to paganism. It aims not only at reactivating the cultural values of ancient Greece, but at re-establishing the Hellenic religion as well. The traditional conflict between Christianity and paganism lies behind these efforts. The term "(neo) paganism" is used today to indicate various currents (e.g. in the USA and Britain), including an earth-respecting spirituality, goddess worship and spirituality, witchcraft, healing practices, magical rituals, various festivals, Gnostic elements, occultism, spiritualism, shamanism, ecology, nature religion, and other elements. It is, however, important to distinguish such broad esoteric movements from certain ethnic neopagan awakenings in various European countries (e.g. Odinism/Druidism in the Anglo-Saxon world, Romuva in Lithuania, Romanism in Italy). The ethnic character of this particular form of neopaganism points to the authentic, ancestral, and autochthonous traditions in various countries that existed long before the importation of Christianity and which differ fundamentally from revealed religions.

Modern Greek neopaganism has a predominantly ethnic character and remains in close relation to the Hellenic tradition and religion. The latter are considered comprehensive cosmogonic, psychological, and eschatological systems aiming to provide people with a serious religio-philosophical meaning of life. There are various independent neopagan groups, whose aim is the defence of the pre-Christian tradition and the creation of Hellenes in the literal meaning of the word. They criticize the pseudo-worshippers of antiquity, the Hellenized Christians, the New-Agers, and the Hellenized nationalists and fascists, because they all disregard the importance of the Hellenic religion and use antiquity for selfish purposes and objectives. The neopagan attempt to de-Christianize or de-Byzantinize modern Greece is evident in many instances (e.g. in the use of the Hellenic months and calendar of feasts as well as in the replacement of BC and AD by more neutral chronological indications). Thus, neopagans not only consider a correlation between Hellenism and Christianity as impossible, but they depict their multiple antitheses in the most negative way. They also organize some relevant festivities (e.g. to celebrate the summer equinox) and sometimes have their own private places of worship. There are several such groups and movements: the Diipetes, which publishes a journal of the same name with the subtitle "In the Defence of the Ancient Psyche"; the Ellines Eidololatres, the Megali Ethniki Ekklisia ton Ellinon, the Desmos ton Achaion, the Phaethnos Ethniki

Ekklisia, the Ypato Symvoulio ton Ellinon Ethnikon, and their related journals. It should be mentioned that these groups do not accept as their self-designation the terms "neopagans" and prefer some other terms such as "Gentile Hellenes" (Ellinikos Ethnismos) or "Followers of the ancestral Hellenic religion and way of life" (Archaiothriskoi, Archaiotropoi, or Ellinotropoi).

It goes without saying that these trends have met with the staunch opposition of the Orthodox Church, which has officially condemned the independent function of pagan ritual survivals (see the encyclicals 2565/24 January 1994 and 2598/19 June 1995 against the *Anastenaria*, the fire-walking rituals in northern Greece). Similar but more extreme is the reaction of Orthodox fundamentalists who are against anything that is reminiscent of the Hellenic past and religion (e.g. the ceremonial lighting of the flame at Olympia for the Olympic Games). This is because Orthodox Christianity has developed a specific understanding of and attitude towards Hellenism in general that is clearly incompatible with Hellenocentric or neopagan visions. Yet, the latter, though marginal and not especially influential until now, reveal a variety of orientation patterns that unavoidably contribute to the persisting crisis of modern Greek identity.

Vasilios Makrides

See also Antiquity, Identity, Orthodoxy and Hellenism

Further Reading

Abrahamsen, Valerie, "Christianity and the Rock Reliefs at Philippi", *Biblical Archaeologist*, 51 (March 1988): pp. 46–56

Anastos, Milton, "Pletho's Calendar and Liturgy", *Dumbarton Oaks Papers*, 4 (1948) pp. 183–305

Athanassiadi-Fowden, Polymnia, *Julian and Hellenism: An Intellectual Biography*, Oxford: Clarendon Press, 1981

Beatrice, Pier Franco (editor), *L'intolleranza cristiana nei confronti dei pagani*, Bologna: Dehoniane, 1990

Cameron, Alan, "The Last Days of the Academy of Athens", *Proceedings of the Cambridge Philological Society*, new series 15 (1969): pp. 7–29

Chuvin, Pierre, *Chronique des derniers païens: la disparition du paganisme dans l'Empire romain du règne de Constantin à celui de Justinien*, 2nd edition, Paris: Belles Lettres, 1991

Clogg, Richard, "Sense of the Past in Pre-Independence Greece" in *Culture and Nationalism in Nineteenth-Century Eastern Europe*, edited by Roland Sussex and J.C. Eade, Columbus, Ohio: Slavica, 1985

Clucas, Lowell, *The Trial of John Italos and the Crisis of Intellectual Values in Byzantium in the Eleventh Century*, Munich: Institut für Byzantinistik, Neugriechische Philologie und Byzantinische Kunstgeschichte, 1981

Dodds, E.R., *Pagan and Christian in an Age of Anxiety: Some Aspects of Religious Experience from Marcus Aurelius to Constantine*, Cambridge: Cambridge University Press, 1965; New York: Norton, 1970

Faber, Richard and Renate Schlesier (editors), *Die Restauration der Götter: Antike Religion und Neo-Paganismus*, Würzburg: Königshausen / Neumann, 1986

Fouquet, Claude, *Julien: la mort du monde antique*, Paris: Belles Lettres, 1985

Fowden, G., "The Pagan Holy Man in Late Antique Society", *Journal of Hellenic Studies*, 102 (1982): pp. 33–59

Gregory, T.E., "The Survival of Paganism in Christian Greece: A Critical Essay", *American Journal of Philology*, 107/2 (1986): pp. 229–42

Harvey, Graham and Charlotte Hardman (editors), *Paganism Today*, London: Thorsons, 1995

Herzfeld, Michael, *Ours Once More: Folklore, Ideology, and the Making of Modern Greece*, New York: Pella, 1986

Jones, Prudence and Nigel Pennick, *A History of Pagan Europe*, London and New York: Routledge, 1995

Kaegi, W.E., "The Fifth-Century Twilight of Byzantine Paganism", *Classica et Mediaevalia*, 27 (1966): pp. 243–75

Kantiotis, Avgustinos, *Epistrophi eis tin archaian eidololatreian?* [Return to Ancient Idolatry?], Athens, 1992

Kostopoulos, Tryphon, *Ellada: I athlia moira enos ierou topou* [Greece: The Sad Fate of a Holy Place], Athens, 1993

Kostopoulos, Tryphon, *Anthropoi tis gnoseos ginete epanastates!* [Men of Learning – Become Revolutionaries!], Athens, 1995

MacMullen, Ramsay, *Paganism in the Roman Empire*, New Haven and London: Yale University Press, 1981

Marinis, Panayotis, *I Elliniki thriskeia (To Dodekatheon): Kosmogonia – Psychogonia* [Greek Religion (The Twelve Gods): Cosmogony, Psychology], Athens, 1996

Marinis, Panayotis, *I Elliniki Thriskeia (To Dodekatheon): Theogonia* [Greek Religion (The Twelve Gods): Theogony], Athens, 1996

Mohtmann, C., "Encore une fois: 'Paganus'", *Vigiliae Christianae*, 6 (1952): pp. 109–21

Momigliano, Arnaldo (editor), *The Conflict between Paganism and Christianity in the Fourth Century: Essays*, Oxford: Clarendon Press, 1963, reprinted 1970

Paganisme, Judaïsme, Christianisme: influences et affrontements dans le monde antique, Paris: Boccard, 1978

Pagoulatos, Gerasimos, "The Destruction and Conversion of Ancient Temples to Christian Churches during Fourth, Fifth and Sixth Centuries", *Theologia*, 65 (1994): pp. 152–70

Puchner, Walter, *Akkommodationsfragen: Einzelbeispiele zum paganen Hintergrund von Elementen der frühkirchlichen und mittelalterlichen Sakraltradition und Volksfrömmigkeit*, Munich: Tudur, 1997

Rassias, Vlasis G., *Yper tis ton Ellinon Nosou* [For the Sickness of the Greeks], vols 1–3, Athens, 1992–94

Rassias, Vlasis G., *Zeus: Symvoli stin Epanakalypsi tis Ellinikis Kosmoantilipsis* [Zeus: A Contribution to the Rediscovery of the Greek World-View], Athens, 1996

Rassias, Vlasis G., *Eortes kai Ieropraxies ton Ellinon* [Feasts and Cultic Practices of the Greeks], Athens, 1997

Ricks, David, "Papadiamantis, Paganism and the Sanctity of Place", *Journal of Mediterranean Studies*, 2 (1992): pp. 169–82

Rochow, Ilse, "Zu 'heidnischen' Bräuchen bei der Bevölkerung des byzantinischen Reiches im 7. Jahrhundert vor allem auf Grund der Bestimmungen des Trullanum", *Klio*, 60 (1978): pp. 483–97

Saradi-Mendelovici, Helen, "Christian Attitudes toward Pagan Monuments in Late Antiquity and their Legacy in Later Byzantine Centuries", *Dumbarton Oaks Papers*, 44 (1990): pp. 47–61

Ševčenko, Ihor, "Byzantium, Antiquity and the Moderns", *Association Internationale des Études Byzantines: Bulletin d'Information et de Coordination*, 14 (1987–88): pp. 19–26

Trombley, Frank R., *Hellenic Religion and Christianization, c.370–529*, vols 1–2, Leiden and New York: Brill, 1993–94

Woodhouse, C.M., *George Gemistos Plethon: The Last of the Hellenes*, Oxford: Clarendon Press, 1986

Painting

Ancient

The origin of Greek painting is difficult to ascertain. Ancient literature is filled with references to famous painters and paintings, but very few paintings survive. Archaeological evidence provides some knowledge of the painter's craft and subject matter. There are specific descriptions by Aristotle, Plutarch, Pliny the Elder, Quintilian, Lucian, Cicero, and Pausanias. They extol the artistic talent of the Greeks, whose art was avidly collected and used to adorn public and sacred buildings. Among ancient painters, the most celebrated were male, yet it was not an exclusionary craft; Pliny names female artists as well. The gradual evolution from painted temple metopes and plaques, stelae, wooden panels, and pottery resulted in painting so illusionistic that horses were said to neigh when confronted with a painted image of another horse.

Antecedents of Greek painting occurred during the Bronze Age cultures of the Minoans and Mycenaeans. Murals on the palace walls of Crete and Thera were partly influenced by Egyptian art, but the subject matter and function appear to be completely different. There is an inherent liveliness and naturalism in the landscapes, figures, and animal motifs. Topics are religious (funerary or sacrificial rituals) or purely decorative. In both cultures marine and floral motifs were depicted on vases. Mycenaean painting is related to Minoan art, with military themes and abstraction becoming evident.

In Greece vase painting arose *c.*900 BC with the Geometric period. Figures were black silhouettes formed by circles, triangles, and squares. During the Orientalizing phase there was progress in distinguishing musculature and identifying facial characteristics. In Archaic black- and red-figure vase painting males and females are presented in mythological or everyday scenes. Overlapping figures indicate depth. Details are scratched into the dark figures for drapery, hair, and other features. Red-figure painting allowed for greater expressive freedom by using a brush loaded with paint for details rather than a stiff etching tool. From the second half of the 6th century BC artists' signatures are common, the painter writing *egrapsen* ("he drew") after his name.

According to one legend, drawing began in Greece when a woman traced the outline of her lover's shadow on the wall. Ancient writers relate that great achievements in Greek mural and panel painting occurred during the 5th and 4th centuries BC. The use of flat colours within an outline progressed to forms modelled in light and shade; buildings were depicted in perspective; and figures and objects were illusionistically set into space using cast shadows. The most celebrated painters, who included Polygnotus, Apollodorus, Zeuxis, Parrhasius, Pausias, Nicias, Apelles, and Protogenes, were renowned for their ability to create *trompe-l'oeil* effects on flat surfaces. Many paintings were on panels that could be transported to cities and art markets, thus spreading the fame and fortune of the artists.

In the early Classical period Polygnotus from Thasos was regarded as the "inventor of painting", completing huge murals depicting the lives of the Greek heroes. He used four colours in his palette: white, red, ochre, and black, and in various combinations. His most famous subject was a series of paintings of the Trojan War placed in the Propylaea on the Acropolis. His ethnic depictions were especially celebrated and spectators could read the thoughts of the characters from their expressions.

During the later 5th century BC Apollodorus of Athens developed the use of shadows and perspective. Pliny stated that Zeuxis "entered the gates of art which Apollodorus had opened". Pliny's description of the painted grapes of Zeuxis reveals a new peak in illusionistic art: birds flew at the panel to peck at the fruit, though his rival, Parrhasius, painted a curtain so convincingly that even Zeuxis was fooled. Parrhasius of Ephesus lived in an ostentatious manner, wearing a purple cloak and golden wreath around his head and singing as he worked.

An important representative of the school of Sicyon was Pausias, who is associated with improvements in colour. In an allegory of *Drunkenness*, a glass bowl was rendered so realistically that a woman's face was reflected in it. Many of his panels were taken to Rome by admirers to decorate the imperial capital and villas of aristocrats. In the Athenian school Nicias was highly esteemed and fits our contemporary picture of the passionate artist. He was so involved in his painting that he would forget to eat. Nicias was very particular about his subject matter as well, saying that what one painted was as important as how one painted. As with Pausias, many of his paintings were brought to Rome; one was placed in the Roman Senate, another in the temple of Concord.

Apelles, the favourite painter of Alexander the Great, is the artist who surpassed his contemporaries and predecessors in skill, fame, and fortune. He left his native Ephesus for Sicyon to complete his training and was taken by Philip of Macedon to his capital Pella when his talent was recognized. Upon Alexander's accession, Apelles became the court painter. He used a thin black glaze to unify his compositions and enhance the brilliance of the paints. Apelles was by all accounts a pleasant man and supportive of his friends. He apparently purchased several paintings by Protogenes at a high price to show his appreciation of his friend's work. Protogenes of Rhodes lived in poverty most of his life but remained dedicated to art, probably saved from starvation by the generosity of Apelles.

Several female painters also achieved a high level of success. Helena, daughter of an Egyptian, is credited with the *Battle of Issus* depicting Alexander's defeat of Darius from which the famous mosaic copy in Pompeii was made. Pliny names quite a few others: Timarete, who painted an Artemis at Ephesus; Eirene, painter of a maiden of Eleusis; Calypso, who painted portraits; Aristarte, who painted Asclepius. Iaia of Cyzicus mostly did commissioned portraits of women as well as a self-portrait with the use of a mirror. She was noted for the rapidity and excellence of her work. Her paintings sold for much higher prices than those of her contemporaries. Another painter, Olympias, is known only for her pupil, Aristobulus. In some cases, the women were daughters and pupils of other painters whom Pliny names. Iaia remained single all her life, devoted to her craft.

There are numerous Graeco-Roman murals in Pompeii, Herculaneum, and other small towns nearby which were perfectly preserved by the eruption of Vesuvius in AD 79. Unfortunately, the paintings are unsigned; some are possibly copies from famous compositions done by Greek painters. The murals themselves have been categorized into four basic styles ranging from simple reproductions of marble surfaces to elaborately conceived and depicted landscapes, architectural compositions, portraits, and panel paintings set within ethereal frames.

VIRGINIA M. DA COSTA

See also Pottery

Further Reading
Arias, P.E., *A History of 1000 Years of Greek Vase Painting*, London: Thames and Hudson, and New York: Abrams, 1962
Beazley, J.D. and Bernard Ashmole, *Greek Sculpture and Painting to the End of the Hellenistic Period*, Cambridge: Cambridge University Press, 1966
Devambez, Pierre, *Greek Painting*, New York: Viking, and London: Weidenfeld and Nicolson, 1962
Ling, Roger, *Roman Painting*, Cambridge and New York: Cambridge University Press, 1991
Rice, David Talbot, *Art of the Byzantine Era*, London: Thames and Hudson, 1963, reprinted 1997
Richter, Gisela M.A. (introduction), *Greek Painting: The Development of Pictorial Representation from Archaic to Graeco-Roman Times*, New York: Metropolitan Museum of Art, 1944
Robertson, Martin, *Greek Painting*, Geneva: Skira, 1959; New York: Rizzoli, 1979
Weir, Irene, *The Greek Painters' Art*, Boston: Ginn, 1905

Byzantium

The two arts of painting and mosaic may be separated in modern thinking, but in the Byzantine mind they were one, and such evidence as there is suggests that the same craftsmen practised in both media, using mosaic when money was available, and painting where it was not. Furthermore there is a lack of surviving painted church decoration between the 4th and 11th centuries. This account must therefore be read in conjunction with the article on Byzantine mosaic.

Byzantine painting can be defined as the painting of the Christian Roman empire that continued until the fall of Constantinople in 1453. Since Rome had more or less conquered Greece in the 1st century BC, and Roman culture was thoroughly Hellenized, it follows that the strongest influence on early Byzantine painting was the style of the Classical world. This can be seen in the surviving paintings of the catacombs in Rome, where the subject matter is derived mainly from the Bible, but the style shows simplified Classical figures and landscapes. A second influence, less well charted because less has survived, was Jewish and oriental. Scenes from the Old Testament can be seen painted on the walls of the synagogue of Dura Europus, a city on the Euphrates on the borders of modern Syria and Iraq.

Byzantine painting can be divided into three phases: early Christian and Byzantine up to the period of iconoclasm (726–843); middle Byzantine, from 850 to the sack of Constantinople by the Latins in 1204; and late Byzantine, from 1261 to 1453. The early years of Christian painting were clandestine and rudimentary, depicting symbolic images such as fish or peacocks and simple biblical scenes. The conversion of Constantine the Great in 311 heralded official church building on a grand scale, and all of the churches required painted or mosaic decoration. The usual form of church was the basilica, and the ruins of these can be found all over the territory of the late Roman empire. Little is left of their painting or mosaic decoration because of the widespread destruction of images during the iconoclast period of the 8th to 9th centuries.

The salient difference that emerges between the Classical temple and the Christian church is that the decoration of a temple was concentrated on the exterior of the building, whereas the decoration of a church was largely within it. A form of painting and mosaic that originates in the Classical world is the individual portrait or icon. Small portable icons executed in mosaic have been discovered from the Roman period, and portraits painted in encaustic from the Hellenistic period in Egypt are well known. These are the prototypes of the Christian icon which became as significant to the individual worshipper as were church decorations to the act of corporate worship. Another form of painting that was to assume even greater importance as the centuries passed by was the illumination of the Bible and of other Christian devotional manuscripts. Bible illustration seems to have provided the earliest subject matter, and while prototypes for Old Testament illustration may have been found in Jewish painting, an entirely new iconography was invented for New Testament scenes and figures. For the Old Testament, the Quedlinburg manuscript of the 5th-century AD provides evidence for what was expected of a painter. The actual illustrations have largely flaked away and underneath are simple written instructions directing the painter to make images of the people relevant to the biblical scene, and put in the buildings or landscape and animals relevant to the text. In this way a new iconography was evolved that changed little over the Byzantine period and the experienced observer can usually identify a scene even if only a small fragment of it remains. Another form of early Christian painting that must have been widespread is pilgrimage souvenirs, such as the Vatican Palestinian reliquary depicting the Crucifixion and other Christological scenes. This type of image may well have spread Byzantine iconography throughout the Christian world.

The Byzantine style of religious painting can be seen as already well evolved in a few surviving icons in the monastery of Mount Sinai, notably the 4th- or 5th-century panels of *Christ* and *St Peter*. In manuscript, the Rabbula Gospels (now in the Biblioteca Medicea Laurenziana, Florence) and the Rossano Gospels (in the cathedral museum at Rossano) already show the increasing use of gesture and linear drapery lines to exaggerate the sense of movement and emotion in a symbolic way. By contrast the survival of strongly Hellenistic elements can still be seen in manuscripts such as the Paris Psalter of 950–70, but in general the great 10th-century manuscripts show a fusion of styles with the figures developing increasingly linear effects but architecture, landscape, and other subsidiary elements retaining more from the Hellenistic past. The only painted church decoration of note from the 10th century is in Tokalı New Church in Cappadocia and this has a marked linear quality. In the early Christian period, Byzantine painting can thus be seen to inherit forms and techniques from the ancient world while constantly striving for liberation from them.

The encaustic technique of painting on panels with a wax medium was inherited from the Hellenistic art of Egypt, and it was commonly used for icon painting up to the 6th century. Thereafter it was superseded by the use of glues, egg, and oil media. On walls Byzantine painters used the fresco technique of painting on fresh lime plaster, and then finishing with an egg or glue medium for colours that were incompatible with lime. Fresco painting was known in ancient Egypt, Greece, and Rome but the Byzantines modified their inherited craft and adapted it to the increasing linear emphasis that appears in Christian painting from the 6th century onwards. Rome and

ancient Greece had striven for the softer effects of blended colour that gives the illusion of realistic depth in a painting. The Byzantines rejected this in favour of linear patterning that emphasized the otherworldly nature of images and placed them in a spiritual dimension suitable to a religious image. For this purpose the Byzantine technique evolved with a use of thick opaque colours that are often juxtaposed in contrasting sequences close to each other.

The conflicts of style and subject matter that characterize the early period of Byzantine painting more or less disappear in the period 850–1204. The Iconoclast controversy served to focus agreement in the mind of the Church hierarchy. A theological justification for the use of images was worked out by St John of Damascus, and the idea that a church represented heaven on earth became widely accepted. The acceptance of this premise meant that scenes depicting the life of Christ and the Virgin and images of the saints were not just didactic illustrations for the benefit of the congregation. The scenes and images were held to bear a constant and continuous reality by virtue of their illustrated presence and the congregation was absorbed within them and partook of the sacred drama. Christ was present by virtue of his image, usually in the dome, and from thence he looked down upon the congregation and was with them. Similarly it was possible to communicate directly with the saints through their painted image. This belief that the image provided a direct contact with the spirit of the figure portrayed may itself be seen as a continuing reflection of the ancient Greek belief that a god was directly accessible through his or her statue and in some magical way he or she was even present in the statue. A new architectural form evolved for this new conception of a church. Domes were added to the simple basilican plan, and the plan evolved into the centralized domed church usually in the form of a cross-in-square. The painted icon continued to serve its purpose as a focus of worship for the individual owner, but increasingly icons became a part of corporate worship in the altar screen or iconostasis of a church and in religious processions.

The continuity of Hellenistic illusionism can best be seen in the middle Byzantine period in the grander manuscript illustrations such as the Paris Psalter of 950–70, which was made under imperial or aristocratic patronage. Individual illuminations in such a manuscript might almost be mistaken for antique works, but elsewhere the surviving tradition was less obvious.

The best coherent survivals of church decoration of the period 950–1100 are in the crypt of the church of Hosios Loukas in Stiris, in the New Church of Tokalı in Cappadocia in Turkey, and in Hagia Sophia at Ohrid in Macedonia; there are a few provincial examples surviving in Italy, Egypt, and Cyprus. All of these churches bear witness to parts of the post-iconoclastic system of iconographic order: the image of Christ in the dome; the Mother of God in the semidome of the apse; the great feast days celebrating the life of Christ on the upper walls and in the vaults of the church; the first communion of the apostles on the apse walls; and the company of saints in the ground register or distributed wherever there might be a space such as in the soffits of arches or in decorative borders. In Cyprus good-quality examples of this orderly church decoration survive from throughout the 12th century. Another group of painted churches in Cappadocia represent provincial deco-

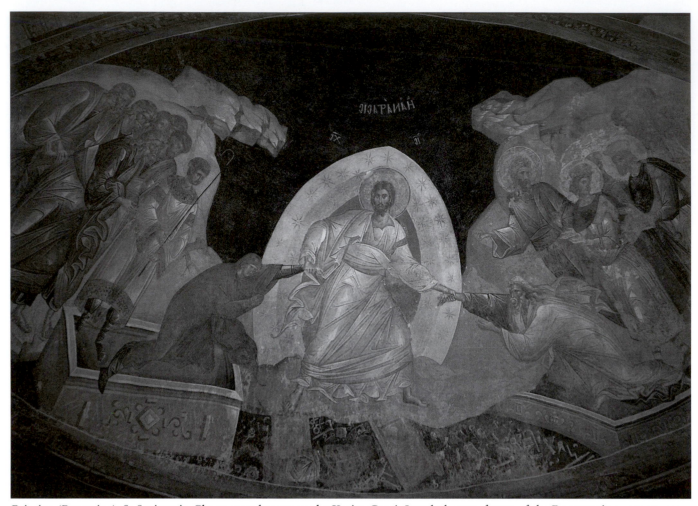

Painting (Byzantine): St Saviour in Chora, now known as the Kariye Cami, Istanbul, apse, fresco of the Resurrection, *c*.1315–21

rative work of the middle Byzantine period. The style of painting varies considerably throughout the Byzantine empire according to place and date, but all the quality work shows adherence to an orderly rule of figural proportion that makes for coherent unity in a decoration. The tendency to linear elaboration of draperies continued to develop from earlier centuries, culminating in the elaborate wind-blown style of the end of the 12th century, best seen in the churches of Nerezi in Macedonia, at Lagoudhera in Cyprus, and in fragmentary decorations elsewhere in Greece, Russia, and Turkey.

The Latin conquest of Constantinople in 1204 marks a century of uncertainty in the field of religious painting with an assumption on the part of some scholars that painting of the Byzantine style in this period is all by western artists. However that may be, it can be seen that surviving Byzantine painting from the late 13th and 14th centuries exhibits important changes. The most salient of these is the tendency towards narrative in the scenes rather than the monumental iconic approach. This may be compared with narrative in ancient Greek sculpture where a single scene may illustrate events that are separate in time, place, and action but which are related to the central character or happening. A good Byzantine example is the scene of the Nativity of Christ where the Mother of God and newly born child in the manger are surrounded by subsidiary events depicting the journeying Magi, the annunci-

ation to the shepherds, and the washing of the child by midwives. Another change in church decoration is the striking tendency to give figures greater bulk and weightiness so that they sometimes assume a sculptural quality. Painting of this period is best seen in Macedonia, Greece, and the Balkans, and in Constantinople.

There is a final flourish of late Byzantine painting of which good examples survive at Mistra in the Peloponnese and in Serbia. The narrative element became further developed in this late period and the weightiness of figures disappears in favour of an almost effeminate elegance and lightness that bears an affinity with the contemporary international Gothic style of western Europe. A variant of the late style in Russia moved in the opposite direction and developed the earlier Byzantine linear styles almost to a state of abstraction. Byzantine painting continued to thrive in the 16th and 17th centuries with vigorous schools of painting in Crete, Cyprus, Serbia, Dalmatia, and Russia. Its final impact in the West may be said to come in the works of El Greco, a Cretan by training.

In summary, Byzantine painting was born out of the pagan Classical world, and the continuity of Greek ideas can be seen in all the variations of the Byzantine style. Earlier scholarship tended to concentrate on finding Classical prototypes for features of Byzantine painting, but contemporary scholarship, while recognizing the influence of Classical work, stresses the individual character of the Byzantine achievement, so that the idea of a renaissance of Classical art in Byzantium is now less prominent. The continuity is rather to be sought in the sense of orderliness, proportion, and harmony in figural work that underlies the work of ancient Greece and which is present in all good Byzantine painting.

DAVID WINFIELD

See also Icon, Iconoclasm, Mosaic, Renaissance (Palaiologan)

Further Reading

Beckwith, John, *Early Christian and Byzantine Art*, 2nd edition, New Haven, Connecticut and London: Yale University Press, 1970

Buchthal, Hugo, *Art of the Mediterranean World*, AD 100 to 1400, Washington D.C.: Decatur House Press, 1983

Cormack, Robin, *Writing in Gold: Byzantine Society and Its Icons*, London: George Philip, and New York: Oxford University Press, 1985

Cutler, Anthony, *The Aristocratic Psalters in Byzantium*, Paris: Picard, 1984

Dalton, O.M., *Byzantine Art and Archaeology*, Oxford: Clarendon Press, 1911; reprinted New York: Dover, 1961

Demus, Otto, *Byzantine Mosaic Decoration*, London: Paul, Trench, Trubner, 1948; reprinted New Rochelle, New York: Caratzas, 1976

Grabar, André, *Christian Iconography: A Study of Its Origins*, Princeton, New Jersey: Princeton University Press, 1968

James, Liz, *Light and Colour in Byzantine Art*, Oxford: Clarendon Press, and New York: Oxford University Press, 1996

Kitzinger, Ernst, *Byzantine Art in the Making: Main Lines of Stylistic Development in Mediterranean Art, 3rd–7th Century*, Cambridge, Massachusetts: Harvard University Press, and London: Faber, 1977

Lazarev, Viktor, *Storia della pittura bizantina*, Turin: Einaudi, 1967

Lowden, John, *Early Christian and Byzantine Art*, London: Phaidon, 1997

Maguire, Henry, *Art and Eloquence in Byzantium*, Princeton, New Jersey: Princeton University Press, 1981

Mango, Cyril, *The Art of the Byzantine Empire, 312–1453*, Toronto: University of Toronto Press, 1986

Rodley, Lyn, *Byzantine Art and Architecture: An Introduction*, Cambridge and New York: Cambridge University Press, 1994

Talbot Rice, D., *Byzantine Art*, revised edition, Harmondsworth: Penguin, 1968

Walter, Christopher, *Art and Ritual of the Byzantine Church*, London: Variorum, 1982

Weitzmann, Kurt, *Late Antique and Early Christian Book Illumination*, New York: Braziller, and London: Chatto and Windus, 1977

Wharton, Annabel Jane, *Art of Empire: Painting and Architecture of the Byzantine Periphery: A Comparative Study of Four Provinces*, University Park: Pennsylvania State University Press, 1988

Winfield, June and David Winfield, *Proportion and Structure of the Human Figure in Byzantine Wall Painting and Mosaic*, Oxford: BAR, 1982

Tourkokratia and Modern

The fall of Constantinople in 1453 marks only a nominal break in the history of Greek painting, which continued to be predominantly ecclesiastical in function (wall paintings and icons) and Byzantine in stylistic character. But the scale of activity and its organization were considerably modified since, with the Orthodox community now poorer and oppressed, fewer and smaller churches were built, and painters were no longer located in major urban centres. The important monastic communities (e.g. Mount Athos, Meteora), however, retained their status and influence. The most important early school was in Crete, with another, less clearly defined, in Macedonia (perhaps in the region of Kastoria). (In the discussion that follows, representative works of the artists mentioned appear in brackets following the artist's name.)

But even at this early stage the seeds of stylistic change were being sown in those parts of Greece (Crete, the Ionian islands, and the Dodecanese) that were at the same time free from Ottoman control and in contact with western Europe (especially Venice). There Renaissance forms and subjects, foreign to the Byzantine tradition, influenced the development of painting. With the appearance of Cretan artists on the Greek mainland in the 16th century, such ideas spread more widely, and the trend was intensified when further emigration followed the fall of Crete in 1699. During the final phase (1700–1830) of post-Byzantine art (the term is used to refer to the period between the fall of Constantinople and the establishment of Greek independence) there was much activity in the field of church painting. This included both lively innovation and a determined adherence to tradition.

For some, at least, of the period so far discussed decorative painting plays an important role. Such work is found in the buildings of Rhodes during the rule of the Knights of St John (1309–1522). On the mainland most examples belong to the houses of wealthy merchants and are not earlier than the mid-18th century. But from then on they are plentiful.

At that time external contacts were increasing with the weakening of Ottoman control; artefacts in western taste were widely accessible; and western Europeans were increasingly interested in Greek culture and in visiting its country of origin. The ever-strengthening current of western influence – in the status of artists and the type of work demanded, as well as in style – was particularly evident in the Ionian islands. Thus, if the beginning of "modern" Greek painting is defined without strict reference to chronology but as the point when artists started seriously to move away from the conventions of Byzantine and folk art in favour of those of western painting, the late 18th and early 19th century hold the key.

With the installation of a Bavarian monarch (Otho, 1833) as king of Greece, the destination of the first Greek artists to study abroad was assured. Thus the Akademie der Bildenden Künste in Munich, with its tradition of academic realism, was the most influential institution in the formation of the artistic ideas of the first post-independence generation of "modern" painters. Formal teaching of painting in Greece was established around 1840 with the institution that was later (1863) to become the Polytechnic. To begin with, the teaching establishment was mainly foreign. From the turn of the century, however, artists studied in other countries (Austria, Denmark, France, Italy) as well. Thus new currents entered the world of Greek painting. Most significant was that of Impressionism, through Greek artists based in Paris. The consequent move away from strict realism of representation was a crucial one in the history of Greek painting. Subsequently, all the major developments in 20th-century western European art have been accessible to Greek painters and absorbed by them in varying degrees.

Sources and influences

The influences of the Renaissance from which Greece was largely isolated are most evident in Crete, the Ionian islands, and Rhodes, none of them initially under Ottoman control. The work of Michael Damaskinos (c.1535–92/93, *The Adoration of the Magi*, Hagia Aikaterini Sinaitiki, Herakleion), a member of the Cretan school who specialized in icons, shows a perceptibly increasing concern with the softer features and tones and less austere feeling of Italian painting as well as the use of some Italian subjects and motifs. Damaskinos, like other Cretan painters, worked in Venice for several years and would have executed commissions regularly for Catholic patrons. In the Ionian islands painters such as Panagiotis Doxaras (1662–1729, *The Holy Family*, Koutlidis Collection) and, later, Nikolaos Koutouzis (1741–1813, *Portrait of a Nobleman*, National Gallery, Athens) adopted a thoroughly western style for both religious and secular subjects. Particularly striking evidence of western influence is provided by a non-ecclesiastical aspect of their work – portraits; indeed the very development of portraiture demonstrates a new role for painting and a new social milieu.

In spite of the increasing infiltration of western forms, the prevailing climate remained (and has continued to be) overwhelmingly Byzantine. In the remote Agrafa region of northwestern Greece, Dionysios of Phourna (c.1670–after 1744), in his *Painter's Manual*, prescribed strict adherence to a traditional Byzantine approach in both subject and style. Among those who followed his precepts was George Markou of Argos (1719–46) who decorated several churches in Attica including Moni Petraki in Athens. A more informal approach displayed in the work of some Epirot painters (e.g. Panagiotis of Ioannina) stems from their background as artisans decorating house interiors in a "folk" style. More recent church decoration, not infrequently undertaken by major artists (Engonopoulos, Kontoglou, Kopsidis, Parthenis), usually has a strong and explicit undercurrent of tradition.

Apart from Frankish Rhodes, which is a special case because of its direct links with the crusader Knights of St John, the interior decoration of houses (*arkhontika*) and public buildings developed particularly in central or northern Greece and in areas with a prosperous merchant class (the shipowners of Pelion, the fur traders of Siatista). Greek traders carried on much of the commerce of the Ottoman empire. The painting was done by artisans, members of travelling bands of builders and craftsmen. The small village of Chioniades, near Konitsa in Epirus, was especially known for its painters. The style of such work is simple and direct, sometimes crude: the motifs are often largely decorative, but land- and seascapes – including actual places (a view of Chalcis in Euboea, 1832, by I. Pagonis is in the K. Makris collection in Volos) – are common, and there are occasional portraits. Decorative and ecclesiastical painting were often closely related and the interchange of motifs and style is evident. I. Pagonis, who came from Chioniades, worked extensively in the Pelion area between 1800 and 1838, and later lived there, decorating both houses and churches (such as Agia Marina in Kissos, Pelion, 1802). Foreign influences include elements derived from European rococo and baroque. The illustrations (1837–39, now in the National Historical Museum and the Gennadeion Library, Athens) for General Makriyannis's *Memoirs* of the 1821 upris-

ing by Panagiotis Zographos also fall into this category. Theophilos Chatzimichail (1873–1934), Greece's best-known "primitive", painted both panels and murals in an expansion of this tradition (*Limnios Kekhagias*, 1930, Theophilos Museum, Mytilini).

A "western" style of interior decoration, though copying ancient prototypes, can be seen in the paintings of Heinrich Schliemann's house, the Iliou Melathron in Athens (1879; following ancient "Pompeian" styles), or the original Athens University building (1839–49; king Otho in the company of personifications of noble qualities, ancient Greeks, etc.).

Mainstream secular painting

Although the hold of Byzantine art had been weakened through the influences of the West and of folk painters, it was only with the arrival of king Otho and his retinue in Greece that direct European contacts were possible for Greek artists as a whole and that mainstream, non-ecclesiastical painting became firmly established. In this context the influence of the Munich Academy (see above), where an academic approach with careful attention to accurate representation and an interest in genre subjects (cf. Nikephoros Lytras's *Return from the Panygyri of Pendeli*, Koutlidis Collection) were the dominant characteristics, was fundamental. Important Greek painters who studied there included Theodoros Vryzakis (1819–78), Nikephoros Lytras (1832–1904), Nikolaos Gyzis (1842–1901), and Georgios Iakovidis (1852–1932). Gyzis was subsequently a professor at Munich, and highly influential on Greek students, while Lytras and Iakovidis both taught at the Athens School of Fine Arts, thus encouraging the spread of the ideas of the Munich school from within Greece itself. The only indication of the Greek origins of these painters is (sometimes) the choice of subject – e.g. the historical events and portraits of Vryzakis (*Lord Byron at Missolonghi*, 1862, National Gallery of Athens) and the seascapes of Konstandinos Volonakis (1837–1907, *To limani tou Peiraia*, Piraeus Municipal Collection).

Increasing contacts with other centres – of which Paris was by far the most significant – radically changed the direction of Greek painting, away from academic realism and towards Impressionism. Here the important figures were Konstandinos Parthenis (1878–1967, *To limani tis Kalamatas*, 1911, National Gallery, Athens) and Konstandinos Maleas (1879–1928, *Topio Delfon*, National Gallery, Athens). Although European ideas were generally slow to be accepted in Greece, other subsequent 20th-century developments are all represented to varying degrees (e.g. the expressionism of Georgios Bouzianis (1885–1959) in paintings such as *Nude*, National Gallery, Athens).

The Greekness of Greek painting

This question became a central issue – indeed an aim – in the work of the so-called Generation of the '30s, a diverse group that included such artists as Iannis Moralis (1916–), Nikos Hadjikyriakos, known as Ghika (1906–94), and Ioannis Tsarouchis (1910–89), and can be examined most constructively in the context of their paintings.

As Lydakis has rightly pointed out, the definition of "nationality" in the painting of any country is a highly complex issue, although one that is often treated very superficially (to identify nationality on the grounds merely of subjects chosen, for instance, would be absurd). Major trends (Impressionism, abstraction) are international and the work of individual artists varies enormously in the extent to which it shows or does not show, universal, local, or individual features. "Nationality" can be defined only on the basis of a somewhat intangible blend of local atmosphere (including subject, treatment of light, topography, etc.), elements of style or subject derived from local tradition (whether continuous or retrospective), and attitude.

The role of tradition is crucial. Unsurprisingly, because of the unbroken continuity of icon painting and church decoration and the crucial role of the Orthodox Church in Greek national life, Byzantine subjects and style have exercised important influences on secular painting. In recent times this can be seen most clearly in the work of Photis Kontoglou (1898–1965, *Maria Kontoglou*, 1928, private collection; also paintings of Greek mythological and historical subjects in the Athens Dhimarkhion) and his pupils, including Rallis Kopsidis (1929–). It is interesting to note that Nikos Engonopoulos (1910–86), for all the surrealism of much of his work, also painted churches, including part of the Orthodox church of Hagios Spiridon in New York. Earlier Parthenis too had brought his distinctive style to bear on church painting (such as his panels for Agios Alexandros at Palaio Phaliro, Athens). The intermingling of folk and Byzantine styles, noted earlier in the context of post-Byzantine Epirot painters, is evident still in the work of Kopsidis in the monastery at Pendeli (scene of the *God-Protected Mountain of Pendeli*).

That folk art was still flourishing in the earlier 20th century is evident in the work of Theophilos Chatzimichail, who painted both murals and, less common in this tradition, panels, but its influences are evident also in the work of other artists. The most interesting case is that of Ioannis Tsarouchis, some of whose figures and decorative elements are clearly in this vein (*Sailor*, 1950, private collection, and *Protomayia*, 1965, National Bank of Greece). The artist expressed great admiration for Theophilos. In Tsarouchis's work are fused a range of elements including, apart from folk features, occasional references to Byzantium (he was for a time a pupil of Kontoglou), the Classical past (*Piraeus in Antiquity*, 1965), and Greek topography.

The use of ancient motifs and compositional forms, as found for instance in the grave monuments of Moralis (*Memorial Composition*, 1958, artist's collection), shows how such elements can be incorporated into work that is Classical in a much broader sense than of a simple reference to antiquity. Often, however, the use of ancient or archaeological motifs is retrospective rather than traditional since, with the exception of occasional features such as the Late Antique Fayum portraits which are clear antecedents to the Byzantine style, there is no continuity of use from antiquity.

Other more superficial but recurrent elements, which are local in the sense of reflecting the preoccupations of a sea-orientated people and traditional in that they occur sporadically in paintings of all periods, include a strong interest in ships and the sea. This is sometimes tied to naval battles of the War of Independence (Volonakis's *The Disembarkation of Karaiskakis at Phaleron*, National Bank of Greece), sometimes to ships themselves. Noteworthy also is a curiosity (Maleas's

Santorini, National Gallery, Athens) about the effects of light, shade, and colour, thrown into prominence by the vibrant Aegean atmosphere and encouraged by the influences of Impressionism. Artists have also been attracted to modern genre themes that represent endemic features of the Greek social scene such as family life, kafeneia (Tsarouchis's *To Kafeneion*, 1955, Methenitis Collection), etc.

Since the abstract movement of the 1950s and 1960s such tendencies have been less evident, in the context of a stronger internationalism and a greater concern with art theory. Nevertheless ancient and Byzantine art continues to inspire and provide subject matter for Greek artists (such as D. Mytaras's *Ap' to Ergastiri*, 1989), as do the unique landscape and atmosphere of Greece itself (as seen in K. Papatriandaphyllopoulos's *Coast of Attica*, 1988, Philaniotou Collection).

ROBIN L.N. BARBER

See also Renaissance (Veneto-Cretan)

Further Reading

Chatzidakis, Manolis, *Ellines Zographoi meta tin Alosi (1450–1830)* [Greek Painters after the Conquest (1450–1830)], 2 vols, Athens, 1987–97

Christou, Chrysanthos, *The National Gallery: 19th and 20th Century Greek Painting*, Athens, 1992

Christou, Chrysanthos, *Zographiki 20ou Aiona* [20th-Century Painting], Athens, 1996

Garidis, M., *Diakosmitiki Zographiki* [Decorative Painting], Athens, 1996

Ioannou, Andreas S., *Greek Painting: The 19th Century*, Athens: Melissa, 1974

Lydakis, S., *Istoria tis Neoellinikis Zographikis (16–20 aiona)* [History of Modern Greek Painting (16th–20th Centuries)], Athens, 1976

Makris, K., *Chionadites Zographoi* [Painters of Chios], Athens, n.d.

Papanikolaou, M.M., *Istoria tis Technis stin Ellada: Zographiki kai Glyptiki tou 20ou Aiona* [History of Art in Greece: Painting and Sculpture of the 20th Century], Athens, 1999

Turner, Jane, (editor), *The Dictionary of Art*, London: Macmillan and New York: Grove, 1996, vol. 13, pp. 351–53 (Greece. III. Painting entry)

A series of short exhibition catalogues (the English versions of the titles are given) published by and available from the Corfu Annexe of the National Gallery, Athens have useful Greek and English text and excellent illustrations:

Greek Painting: The 19th Century, n.d. (Corfu Annexe)

Greek Painting in the Early 20th Century, n.d. (Corfu Annexe)

Greek Painting: The Generation of the Thirties after the War, n.d. (Corfu Annexe)

Greek Painting: The Thirties, 1996 (Corfu Annexe)

Paisy Velichkovsky, St 1722–1794

Athonite monk

The Ukrainian St Paisy Velichkovsky was in the Greek-speaking world for only 17 years. He was on Mount Athos from 1746. He had been tonsured *rasophor* (novice) in the Pecherskaya Lavra of Kiev whence he came via the Danubian principalities of Moldavia and Wallachia. When he arrived on the Holy Mountain he walked northwards from the Great

Lavra. The exertions of journey on foot and the heat of the day caused him to fall seriously ill. He was cured by monks in the Pantokratoros skete, near which he then settled as a hermit, having searched in vain for a spiritual father. In 1750 he was visited by his former mentor, the Elder Vasily, who tonsured him with the small *schema* (habit) and after a while returned to Wallachia. Three months after Vasily's departure St Paisy was joined by another Wallachian, Monk Vissarion, who begged to be his disciple. St Paisy refused and they lived for some time sharing everything and submitting in spiritual obedience to each other. The two monks were soon joined by others from the Danubian principalities and Ukraine. Eventually St Paisy reluctantly agreed to be their spiritual leader. The brotherhood had to move into the larger cell of Sts Constantine and Helen, belonging to the Pantokratoros monastery. When he had 12 disciples, in 1757, St Paisy was granted a charter from Pantokratoros, to make another of its dependencies, the Prophet Elijah cell, into the Prophet Elijah skete. In under five years he was in charge of a brotherhood 60-strong. He had originally planned for a community of no more than 16 monks, but he was unable to turn people away. Eventually he was asked by the Holy Community to move to the debt-ridden monastery of Simonopetra, on the other side of the peninsula. He arrived there with 35 brethren on 15 April 1762. Unfortunately, Turkish creditors were clamouring for the 50,000 lei owing to them; and St Paisy, unable to cope with the debts, left the Holy Mountain the next year for Moldavia, whence he never returned.

This terse account of his all too brief sojourn on Athos gives little indication of the important role he played in Greek spiritual life and of his influence on subsequent Athonite history. The Prophet Elijah skete became the centre for Russians on Athos at the time, for the so-called "Russikon", or Russian monastery of St Panteleimon, was probably inhabited only by Greeks and southern Slavs in the latter half of the 18th century. The Russians whom the Greeks invited back to St Panteleimon in 1839, and whose successors took over the monastery, originated from the skete. Until 1992, when the last of its brethren representing the Russians were expelled, the skete was the oldest Russian Athonite house in modern times to be continuously in Russian hands.

During his 17-year stay St Paisy's renown spread all over the Holy Mountain. He had spiritual children of many nationalities, and was even confessor to Patriarch Seraphim I, who was living in retirement in Pantokratoros monastery. Word about St Paisy spread to other countries, particularly to the Danubian principalities, Ukraine, and Russia.

St Paisy's ability to attract pilgrims from abroad is remarkable because in the mid-18th century the Orthodox Church was undergoing a crisis. The Athonite community was having to cope with the increased *harach* (tax). Some monasteries, such as Simonopetra and St Panteleimon, were becoming depopulated and bankrupt; others were reverting to idiorrhythm and being abandoned by their senior monks, who were absent on alms-gathering missions. In post-Petrine Russia, which had tenuous links with the Holy Mountain, monasticism was hardly thriving. Perhaps the Orthodox world was yearning for such a luminary as St Paisy.

His personal qualities transcended ethnic barriers. Few Slavs had such good relations with Greek Athonites. The year after he left, the Greeks were extremely well disposed to the Russians because of him: the Holy Community offered to pay the *harach* that had been imposed on the skete by the civil authorities and apologized to the skete for the inconvenience that might have been caused. In the 1798 charter Pantokratoros granted the Prophet Elijah skete "substantial rights and privileges" in recognition for the "considerable benefit and help" received by the monastery from its "blessed and most venerable founder and father the Elder Paisios"; yet, somewhat less than a century later the monastery and its skete were embroiled in bitter quarrels and most of these privileges were taken away.

Paisy himself knew that facilitating harmonious international relations was a gift others did not have. When in later years he gave the Rule to Abbot George of Cherniça he told him to accept only Romanians into the brotherhood in order to avoid misunderstandings and conflicts. As the leader of a multinational community St Paisy was perforce a consummate linguist: Article 15 of the Rule he drew up in 1763 for the Dragomira monastery stipulated that "since our community is composed of three nationalities, then three languages, Greek, Slavonic, and Moldavian" must be known by the abbot. He learnt Moldavian before he came to Athos, when he and many other Small Russian monks were on the move between eastern Ukraine and the principalities in search of places where they could lead an eremitic existence under the guidance of spiritual fathers and without interference from the world outside. Acquiring Greek, however, required saintly dedication. In the tradition of the Elder Vasily and his other mentors, St Paisy sought out patristic texts and copied them, usually at night.

In his first years on the Holy Mountain he searched everywhere for these texts, but nobody knew of their whereabouts. Greek Athonites were so ignorant that they were not only incapable of reading them but many had never heard of them. He eventually found some of the texts he was looking for in a remote cell, copied them, translated them, used them as his spiritual guide, and taught from them. He was thus one of the first revivers of hesychasm on Athos and once again spread the teaching of Sts Gregory Palamas, Symeon the New Theologian, and Gregory of Sinai. There is evidence that St Paisy was a supporter of the Kollyvades, who sought to uphold an exact observance of the holy canons and the liturgical rules, and whose primary concern was to safeguard Orthodox faith and life in its total integrity. A little over a decade after St Paisy left Athos, the general Greek Orthodox revival of patristic traditions was further promoted on the Holy Mountain by Sts Nikodemos the Hagiorite and Makarios of Corinth, who published the *Philokalia*.

Although St Paisy began his Athonite life as a hermit, he was most influential as a leader of the cenobitic community. The admired harmony of his self-sufficient yet poor skete, the first on Athos to be a cenobium, counterbalanced the new trend of lax idiorrhythmic freedom, which seemed to be gaining the upper hand. St Paisy, the publishers of the *Philokalia*, and others, such as St Kosmas the Aetolian, were influential at the same time that feelings of revolutionary independence were stirring in all Greeks. Turkish oppression seemed at its worst; but just as in the Peloponnese, Church schools were opening and the Athoniada was founded. It is remarkable that St Paisy, a Slav, should be associated in this way with the resurgence of the Greek national Church.

NICHOLAS FENNELL

See also Athos, Kollyvades

Biography

Born in the Ukraine in 1722, Paisy studied at the theological academy in Kiev and was tonsured as a monk there before moving to the Danubian principalities. In 1746 he arrived on Mount Athos and settled as a hermit. In 1757 he was put in charge of the Prophet Elijah skete where by 1762 the brotherhood had grown to 60. He promoted hesychasm and translated the *Philokalia* into Slavonic. In 1763 he left Athos and founded a monastery in Romania where he died in 1794.

Further Reading

A Monk of the Brotherhood of the Prophet Elias Skete, Mount Athos [Ioanniky, Hieromonk], *Elder Basil of Poiana Murului*, Tennessee: St John of Kronstadt Press, 1996

Dmitrievskiy, A.A., *Russikie na Afone, ocherk zhizni i deyatel'nosti igumena russkago Panteleymonovskago monastyrya svyschenno-arkhimandrita Makariya (Sushkina)*, St Petersburg, 1895

Featherstone, J.M.E. (translator), *The Life of Paisij Velyckovs'kyj*, introduction by A.-E. Tachiaos, Cambridge, Massachusetts: Ukranian Research Institute of Harvard University, 1989

Gillet, Fr Lev [A Monk of the Eastern Church], *The Jesus Prayer*, 2nd edition, Crestwood, New York: St Vladimir's Seminary Press, 1987

Kallistos, Bishop of Diokleia, "The Spirituality of the *Philokalia*", *Sobortnost'*, 13/1 (1991): pp. 6–24

Panajoti, N., *The Holy Mount Athos and the Slavs*, Bern, 1963

Parfeniy (Aggeev), Inok, *Skazanie o stranstvii i puteshestvii po Rossii, Moldavii i Turtsii i Svyatoy Zemle*, Moscow, 1900

Seraphim (Rose), Hieromonk, *Blessed Paisius Velichkovsky*, Platina, 1976

Tachiaos, A.-E., *O Paisios Velitskofski kai i Askhitikophilologiki skholi tou* [Paisy Velichkovsky and His Ascetic-Philological School], Thessalonica, 1964

Tachiaos, A.-E., *The Revival of Byzantine Mysticism among the Slavs and Romanians in the XVIIIth Century: Texts Relating to the Life and Activity of Paisy Velichkovsky*, Thessalonica: University of Thessalonica, 1986

Palaiologos family

Byzantine imperial dynasty (1259–1453)

The earliest antecedents of the Palaiologoi are unknown but the family had emerged as an important member of the new landholding elite by the second half of the 11th century and was soon interconnected by marriage with other such families, in standard "aristocratic" practice. The first identified scion of the family was Nikephoros Palaiologos, a commander under the emperor Michael VII Doukas (1071–78). His son, George, was a loyal lieutenant of Alexios I Komnenos (1081–1118). Several members of the family served as generals and regional governors through the 12th century, and one of them, Alexios Palaiologos, rose to prominence at court on the eve of the Fourth Crusade by marrying Irene, daughter of emperor Alexios III (1195–1203). Their daughter, Theodora, married a cousin, Andronikos Palaiologos, who served as Grand Domestic (*Megas Domestikos*), or army chief, in the Byzantine government-in-exile of the Laskaris dynasty in Nicaea.

Their son, related by blood to three earlier families of emperors, was Michael Palaiologos, who followed his father in important military commands. Michael's restless personality and selfish machinations repeatedly won him the suspicion of the emperors John III Vatatzes (1222–54) and Theodore II Laskaris (1254–58). Exploiting the unstable regency for Theodore's young son, Michael boldly usurped the throne (1259). Defeat of rival forces at Pelagonia (summer–autumn 1259) and then the recovery of Constantinople itself (July 1261) gave him prestige as the restorer of rightful Byzantine sovereignty. But his ambitious programme of imperial recovery strained his realm's resources, while his abortive engineering of Church union with Rome for diplomatic purposes caused great dissension and hatred among his subjects.

His son and successor, Andronikos II (1282–1328), if well intentioned and good-hearted, was unequal to the task of adjusting the restored Byzantine empire to its reduced realities. A struggle for the throne between him and his grandson, Andronikos III (1321/28–1341), initiated the internal strife and dynastic conflict that repeatedly plagued the dynasty. Any hope for revival was further dispelled by renewed strife when, during the tumultuous minority of the legitimate successor, John V Palaiologos (1341/55–1391), the throne was contested by John VI Kantakouzenos (1341/47–1354). The latter's talents proved futile in the face of Serbian and Ottoman Turkish challenges; the achievement of sole rule by John V then brought to power a mediocre and hapless leader who presided in futility over the humiliating reduction of his dwindling realm to Turkish vassalage.

John V's son, Andronikos IV (1376–79), and then his grandson, John VII (1390), made shortlived efforts to seize the throne from him. Another of his sons, his legitimate successor Manuel II (1391–1425), was a man whose great abilities were wasted by the hopelessness of his situation, but who steered his wasted realm as well as he could between accommodation and hostility to the Turks. His eldest son and successor, John VIII (1421/25–1448), attempted to do the same, but his too-zealous commitment to Church union brought dissension without any reward of western aid. John's younger brother, Constantine XI (1449–53), was left to bear the ultimate burden, dying on the walls of Constantinople when the Turks stormed the city in May 1453 and ended the Byzantine empire.

Over the generations, diplomatic marriages gave the Palaiologoi a wide range of foreign connections, supplying them with Bulgarian, Russian, Serbian, Hungarian, Italian, Franco-Greek, Franco-Cypriot, diversely Levantine, Armenian, Trapezuntine, and even Turkish spouses. (By the same token, as with so many dynasties, such wide matrimonial mixing meant that the Palaiologoi could be considered a "Greek" family rather more in cultural than in strictly ethnic terms.) One case of such involvement was the north Italian house of Montferrat, with which Byzantium had long had a love-hate relationship. Theodore Palaiologos, a younger son of Andronikos II and his Latin wife Yolande-Eirene of Montferrat, was established in 1306 as marquis of Montferrat, and his descendants survived as an Italian dynasty until 1533, in the meanwhile producing a princess, Sophia, who was briefly (and unhappily) married to John VIII Palaiologos.

An important branch of the Palaiologan family became identified with the flourishing appanage of the Morea in the Byzantine Peloponnese. Following a younger son of John V, Theodore I (1388–1404), Manuel II's second son Theodore II (1407–43) ruled it in association with and then followed by his younger brother Constantine (1428/43–1448). It was also shared with Manuel's fifth and sixth sons, Demetrios (1449–60) and Thomas (1430–60).

This Moreot branch of the Palaiologan family was to play a curious role in the post-Byzantine Hellenic tradition. Following the Turkish capture of Constantinople (1453) and the final conquest of the Morea (1460), Demetrios surrendered to the sultan to become a Turkish dependant, dying in 1470, while Thomas fled to Italy where he became a pensioner of the pope and a diplomatic pawn, dying in 1463. Of Thomas's children, one daughter, Helena, married a Serbian prince, while the other, Zoe/Sophia, made a famous marriage (1472) to Ivan III of Moscow, becoming the mother of Vasili III and the grandmother of tsar Ivan IV "the Terrible", and helping to feed the Muscovite image of the "Third Rome". Of Thomas's two sons, the elder, Andreas, eked out a wretched existence at the papal and other courts, merchandising his titles and dying miserably and childless in 1502; while the younger, Manuel, fled to Constantinople in 1476 and became a Turkish subject, fathering two known sons.

At this point, the securely documented principal line of the Palaiologoi ends. But a vast number of genealogical claims have been made, asserting descent mostly from the sons of Manuel II (primarily Thomas and Demetrios but also the third son, the short-lived Andronikos), though some putatively linked to various earlier branches on the family tree. None of these claims can be proved conclusively, but their persistence – down into the international ex-nobility circles of our own time – is tenacious. There have been lively claimant branches in Romania, Malta, France, and England.

England, indeed, was most productive of would-be Palaiologoi. A curious claimant flourished until as late as 1988 on the Isle of Wight. On the other hand, we know something of a "Theodoro Palaeologos of Pesaro in Italye", who claimed descent from a supposed John, a putative son of Despot Thomas of the Morea. Born around 1560, Theodoro was a professional assassin and adventurer who, exiled from Italy, settled in England, saw military service in the Netherlands, and died in 1636: his tomb may still be found in the parish church of Landulph in Cornwall. Of his three known sons, one, Theodore, was born in 1611 and died in 1644 fighting in the English Civil War on the Parliamentary side, which won him a grave in Westminster Abbey still to be seen. The eldest, John, born in 1609, fought at the battle of Naseby in 1645 and subsequently settled on Barbados in the West Indies. There he joined his younger brother, "Ferdinando Paleologus", who, born around 1615, had left England before the Civil War to become one of the early colonists of the island; Ferdinando died there in 1678 and his grave is still visible, with a marker added in 1906.

Though most of the numerous pretensions to Palaiologan ancestry are dubious at best and clearly bogus at worst, it is not impossible that a few have merit, or derive from distant relatives or retainers of the family who conventionally adopted its name; but there is no secure way that any can be proved.

Nevertheless, the idea that descendants of the last family of Byzantine emperors survived in the West persisted over the centuries, even among the Greeks themselves. When they had won independence in the 1820s, the early leaders of the newly created nation of Greece sent a delegation to western Europe to locate any verifiable Palaiologoi. They returned without success in their quest, but it is a tribute to this family's historical reputation that Greeks, at that early stage of defining their Hellenic identity for the modern world, should still have thought of connecting themselves with the prestige of the Byzantine imperial tradition through a hoped-for dynastic survivor.

JOHN W. BARKER

See also Renaissance (Palaiologan)

Further Reading

Barker, John W., *Manuel II Palaeologos, 1391–1425: A Study in Late Byzantine Statesmanship*, New Brunswick, New Jersey: Rutgers University Press, 1969

Barker, John W., "The Problem of Appanages in Byzantium during the Palaiologan Period", *Byzantina*, 3 (1971): pp. 103–22

Bierbrier, M.L., "Modern Descendants of Byzantine Families", *Genealogists' Magazine*, 20/3 (1980): pp. 85–96

Bosch, Ursula Victoria, *Kaiser Andronikos III Palaiologos: Versuch einer Darstellung der Byzantinischen Geschichte in den Jahren 1321–1341*, Amsterdam: Hakkert, 1965

Dölger, Franz, "Johannes VII, Kaiser der Rhomäer, 1390–1408", *Byzantinische Zeitschrift*, 31 (1931): pp. 21–36

Gauci, Charles A. and Peter Mallat, *The Palaeologos Family: A Genealogical Review*, Hamrun, Malta: PEG, 1985

Geanakoplos, Deno John, *Emperor Michael Palaeologus and the West, 1258–1282*, Cambridge, Massachusetts: Harvard University Press, 1959

Gill, Joseph, "John VIII Palaeologus: A Character Study" in his *Personalities of the Council of Florence, and Other Essays*, Oxford: Blackwell, and New York: Barnes and Noble, 1964

Laiou, Angeliki E., "A Byzantine Prince Latinized: Theodore Palaeologus, Marquis of Montferrat", *Byzantion*, 38 (1968): pp. 386–410

Laiou, Angeliki E., *Constantinople and the Latins: The Foreign Policy of Andronicus II, 1282–1328*, Cambridge, Massachusetts: Harvard University Press, 1972

Nicol, Donald M., *The Immortal Emperor: The Life and Legend of Constantine Palaiologos, Last Emperor of the Romans*, Cambridge and New York: Cambridge University Press, 1992

Nicol, Donald M., *The Last Centuries of Byzantium, 1261–1453*, 2nd edition, Cambridge and New York: Cambridge University Press, 1993

Ostrogorsky, George, *History of the Byzantine State*, 2nd edition, Oxford: Blackwell, 1968; New Brunswick, New Jersey: Rutgers University Press, 1969

Papadopulos, Averkios T., *Versuch einer Genealogie der Palaiologen, 1259–1453*, Amsterdam: Hakkert, 1962 (as unpublished dissertation, 1938)

Philippides, Marios, *Constantine XI Dragas-Palaeologus: A Biography of the Last Greek Emperor*, New Rochelle, New York: Caratzas, forthcoming

Trapp, Erich, *et al.* (editors), *Prosopographisches Lexikon der Palaiologenzeit*, Vienna: Akademie der Wissenschaften, 1976–

Vakalopoulos, Apostolos E., *Origins of the Greek Nation: The Byzantine Period, 1204–1461*, New Brunswick, New Jersey: Rutgers University Press, 1970

Vannier, Jean-François, "Les Premiers Paléologues: Etude généalogique et prosopographique" in *Etudes prosopographiques,* edited by Jean-Claude Cheynet and Jean-François Vannier, Paris: Publications de la Sorbonne, 1986

Palamas, Kostis 1859–1943

Poet, critic, journalist, novelist, and dramatist

Palamas is the top-ranking representative of the so-called *Genia tou '80* (Generation of the Eighties) which gave new spirit to modern Greek literature after the period of Romanticism. The work of Palamas as poet and critic covers a span of more than half a century and represents a milestone in the history of letters of Greece by establishing a whole new set of literary values which find their expression in the *Nea Athinaiki Scholi* (New School of Athens) whose founder and foremost champion Palamas was.

After losing his parents at the age of eight he came into the custody of his uncle at Missolonghi and it was there that he spent his schooldays and part of his youth. In 1875 he began studies in law in Athens, but before long he broke them off and decided to devote himself to poetry and literature. Early literary endeavours were published in 1875 in the *Attikon Imerologion* (Attic Journal) of Irenaios Asopios, and a collection of poems titled *Eroton Epi* (Words of Love) was submitted in 1876 to the writers' Voutsinaios competition. Both works show the influence of Romanticism and are written in katharevousa.

The change occurred in 1886, the year of publication of a collection of poems by Palamas called *Tragoudia tis Patridos mou* (Songs of my Homeland). The poet had meanwhile fully adopted the message of Demoticism and by and by he would become one of the leading figures in the battle for its prevalence. The poems are the very incarnation of the values which the *Genia tou '80* had in mind: themes are taken from folk songs, popular traditions, and the history of the Greek nation, the linguistic instrument being Demotic. Quite evident is the influence of the *Eptanisiaki Scholi* (Ionian school), especially that of Dionysios Solomos, but also of Nikolaos Politis, the great champion of folklore research and founder of the new academic field of studies in modern Greek folklore. The folklore element quite often served as a basis in the works of Palamas, especially in the novel *Thanatos Pallikariou (*A Young Man's Death) (1897) and the play *Trisevgeni* (Thrice Noble) (1903). In 1889 he published *O Ymnos tis Athinas* (Hymn to Athena), a long poem which three years later won a prize at the writers' *Philadelphios* contest at the enthusiastic proposal of Nikolaos Politis.

Full recognition as a poet came in 1892 with the publication of a new collection of poems called *Ta Matia tis Psychis mou* (The Eyes of my Soul), the title being a line from a poem by Solomos. Linguistically the author is here strongly influenced by the views of Yannis Psycharis (the champion of Demoticism whose *To Taxidi mou* (My Journey) had been published in 1888), holding them in such high esteem as to focus in his prologue almost exclusively on the issue of national language. The collection was also awarded a prize at the writers' *Philadelphios* contest at the suggestion of Aristotelis Provellengios. A year later Georgios Kalosgouros emphasized

that the value of the poems lay in their Greek character, the author's orientation to the West, and his acknowledgement and acceptance of Solomos's legacy.

In 1895 Palamas accepted the challenge of writing the hymn for the first Olympic Games in modern times, a commission that confirmed his full recognition by the Greek learned upper classes.

In 1897 he was appointed secretary to the University of Athens (later he became secretary-general) and in the same year he published the collection of poems *Iamvi ke Anapesti* (Iambs and Anapaests), part of which was set to music by Manolis Kalomiris. Next followed the collections *Taphos* (The Grave) (1898), poems on the death of his four-year-old son Alkis, *I Chairetismi tis Iliogennitis* (Greetings to the Sunborn) (1900), and *I Asalevti Zoi* (Still Life) (1904) which contained the poems "Phinikia" (The Palm Tree) and "Askreos", both much discussed because of their content, as well as the famous "I Trilogia tou Thymou" (The Trilogy of Anger), a violent attack on the rigid attitude of the conservative circles of his time regarding matters of language. The first version of his trilogy was written in 1901 on account of the so-called *Evangelika*, dramatic events which had been caused by the translation of the New Testament into demotic by Alexander Pallis; it was revised in 1904 because of the *Orestiaka*, new wild demonstations directed against the translation of Aeschylus' *Oresteia* into a simplified katharevousa by Georgios Sotiriadis. Palamas, who had been a supporter of both these "revolutionary" events, consequently had to withstand the fierce attacks of the disciples of purism, thereby even losing his position as secretary-general to the university for 11 months.

Almost at the same time he worked on his two great epic poems, *O Dodekalogos tou Giphtou* (The Twelve Words of the Gypsy, 1907) and *I Phlogera tou Vasilia* (The King's Flute, 1910). Both works arise from the national humiliation brought about by the disastrous Graeco-Turkish war of 1897, each one expressing in its own way the yearning but also the hope for recovery. There is also a thematic blending of Classical, Byzantine, and modern history while, as for language, the wealth of the Byzantine vocabulary is apparent. In this connection it is interesting to note that in the field of historiography the first attempt to show the continuum in the sequence of antiquity–Byzantium–modern Greece was made in 1853 by Konstantinos Paparrigopoulos in his book *Istoria tou Ellinikou Ethnous apo ton Archaiotaton Chronon mechri Simeron* (The History of the Greek Nation from Antiquity to Today).

In *O Dodekalogos tou Giphtou* the poet identifies with the wandering hero who tries in vain to put down roots somewhere for good. The restless figure of the protagonist and the many adventures and sufferings he has to undergo reflect the state of the Greek nation. *I Phlogera tou Vasilia* on the other hand is centred on the Macedonian fight against the Bulgars, which is why the poet narrates the heroic deeds of the Byzantine emperor in such detail. Central to both works is the idea of the inner cohesion, the uninterrupted continuity, and the evolutionary progress of Hellenism in space and time, as well as the adoption of European values.

Palamas's lyrics comprise the following collections of poems: *I Kaimi tis Limnothalassas* (The Sorrows of the

Lagoon) (1912), *I Politia ke i Monaxia* (City and Loneliness) (1912), *Vomi* (Altars) (1915), *Ta Parakaira* (At the Wrong Time) (1919), *I Pentasyllavi* (Pentasyllabes) (1925), *I Lyki* (The Wolves) (1925), *Ta Pathitika Kryphomilimata* (Sentimental Whisperings) (1925), *Dyo Louloudia apo ta Xena* (Two Flowers from Abroad) (1925), *Dili ke Skliri Stichi* (Harsh and Timid Verses) (1928), *O Kyklos ton Tetrastichon* (The Cycle of the Tetrastichs) (1929), *Perasmata ke Chairetismi* (Passages and Greetings) (1929), *I Nychtes tou Phimiou* (The Nights of Phemios) (1931). As for his writing in prose, much of it is still unpublished and is preserved in the Palamas Archive in Athens.

Equal in importance to his lyrical work are the critical writings of Palamas: *Grammata* I (Letters) (1904), *Pezi Dromi* I, II (Prose Ways) (1928), III (1934), *I Poiitiki mou* (The Art of my Poetry) (1934), etc., in which he expresses his views on poetry and on literature in general and examines their relationship to society. These views were subject to change during his long career as an author but only with regard to aesthetic judgement, the stressing of certain aspects of the poet and his work, or the use of specific tools of criticism; the general pattern for evaluating the manifestations of Greek or world literature remained unchanged. In his view, literature expressed the national soul which is made up of the popular living language of the day (demotic and not katharevousa). Since the national soul finds its expression in the works of the Ionian school, especially in those of Solomos, all productions and writers of the modern Greek literary scene were evaluated in comparison to them. Palamas regarded Solomos as the poet who expressed best the national soul because his works are the very incarnation of the three nation-forming ideas, namely the idea of Beauty, the idea of Fatherland, and the idea of Language (*Idea tou Oraiou, Idea tis Patridos, Idea tis Glossis*). His critique of Solomos's work, written in 1901, is still regarded as a significant and substantial study of the subject.

The influence of Palamas's work on both the writers of his day and those that followed is evident. A number of minor poets (Konstantinos Manos, Miltiadis Malakassis, Lampros Porphiras, Ioannis Gryparis etc.) are to be found in his shadow and the upgrading of his work by later leading figures in the literary scene (George Seferis, Odysseus Elytis, Yiannis Ritsos) serves only to confirm the magnitude of the poet's lasting presence.

A large part of the lyrical and critical work of Palamas was edited by Georgios Katsimbalis and Konstantinos Kasinis. The latter completed his predecessor's research and in cooperation with the Foundation Kostis Palamas published his work in 16 volumes, together with a corresponding index. Also in collaboration with the Foundation the fourth volume of the correspondence was published in 1994.

ALEXANDRA-KYRIAKI WASSILIOU

Biography

Born in Patras in 1859, Palamas was brought up by his uncle in Missolonghi. In 1875 he began studying law in Athens but gave it up to devote himself to writing. He is the foremost representative of the so-called "Generation of the Eighties" which gave new spirit to modern Greek literature after the period of Romanticism. He was founder and champion of the "New School of Athens" and one of the leading figures in the battle for the prevalence of the demotic form of the language. He died in Athens in 1943.

Further Reading

Apostolidou, Venetia, *O Kostis Palamas Historikos tes Neollenikes Logotechnias* [Kostis Palamas, Historian of Modern Greek Literature], Athens, 1992

Chatzigiakoumis, Manolis, *Kostis Palamas, Dionysios Solomos*, Athens, 1970

Chourmouzios, Aimilios, *O Palamas kai i epochi tou* [Palamas and His Times], vols 1–4, Athens, 1944–60

Dimaras, K. T., *Kostis Palamas: He Poreia tou pros tin Techni* [Kostis Palamas: His Path to Technical Mastery], Athens, 1947

Dimaras, K. T., *Istoria tes Neoellenikes Logotechnias: apo tes Protes rizes os ten epoche mas* [History of Modern Greek Literature: From its First Roots to our Own Time], Athens, 1989

Emrich, Gerhard, *Antike Metaphern und Vergleiche im lyrischen Werk des Kostis Palamas*, Amsterdam: Hakkert, 1974

Fletcher, Robin A., *Kostes Palamas: A Great Modern Greek Poet, 1859–1943: His Life, His Work and His Struggle for Demoticism*, Athens: Kostes, 1984

He Lexe, 114 (March–April 1993), Palamas special issue

Hea Hestia, 34 (Christmas 1943), Palamas special issue

Kokolis, X.A., "Oi Problematismoi tis Kritikis kai o Palamas" in *I Kritiki stin Neoteri Ellada* [Palamas and Problems of Criticism in Modern Greece], edited by Giannes Dallas, Athens, 1980

Pouchner, Walter, *O Palamas kai to theatro* [Palamas and the Theatre], Athens 1995

Tziovas, Dimitrios, *The Nationism of the Demoticists and Its Impact on Their Literary Theory, 1888–1930: An Analysis Based on their Literary Criticism and Essays*, Amsterdam: Hakkert, 1986

Tziovas, Dimitrios, "*O Dodekalogos tou Giphtou*: To Dilemma tou Monternismou kai i Outopia tis Yperbatikis Synthesis" ["The Twelve Words of the Gypsy": The Dilemma of Modernism and the Utopia of Metaphysical Synthesis] in *Dimensionen griechischer Literatur und Geschichte: Festschrift für Pavlos Tzermias zum 65. Geburtstag*, edited by Gunnar Hering, Frankfurt: Peter Lang, 1993

Wassiliou, Alexandra-Kyriaki, "Biologische Grundpositionen zur Erklärung und Entstehung historischer Vorgänge bei Kostis Palamas" (dissertation), Vienna, 1995

Palestine

The name Palestine is derived from the Peleset (the biblical Philistines), a people settled on the coast of Palestine in the 12th century BC by the Egyptians to look after their interests; attempts to link them with the Mycenaean Greeks are highly speculative, though there are cultural similarities. There were contacts with Greece from the earliest period, but they were not especially significant, though the southern range of the cities of the Phoenicians, who had a decisive influence on the development of Greek culture from the 10th to the 7th centuries BC, overlaps into Palestine.

Palestine really enters Greek history with the conquest of the Persian empire by Alexander the Great of Macedon, who took it over on his way to Egypt in 332 BC. With the division of Alexander's empire on his death, Palestine was initially controlled by the Ptolemies of Egypt, and the attractions of Greek culture made themselves felt almost at once. In particular, Ptolemy recruited a large number Palestinian Jews to populate the new city of Alexandria. This new Jewish community became exclusively Greek-speaking (and was responsible for the translation of the books of the Old Testament into Greek – the Septuagint – with momentous consequences both for

Christianity and for the development of the Greek language), and its continuing contact with the Jews of Palestine was one of the means by which the international Hellenistic culture made its influence felt in Palestine. Thereafter, though the local Semitic language, Aramaic, continued to be the first language of most people in the region, knowledge of Greek spread very widely, and it seems likely that many people would have had at least some knowledge of the language. By 198 BC the Ptolemies had been driven out by the Seleucids, and subsequently one section of the population of Palestine, the Jews, reacted strongly against the spread of Hellenization (the issues are obscure, but seem to be related to the introduction of Greek institutions, such as athletics, into Jerusalem); the outcome was a rebellion which, thanks to the Seleucids' problems with the Parthians and the Romans, ultimately led to the setting up of a Jewish state under the Hasmonean dynasty. Though the ideology of the new state was "anti-Greek", the attractive influence of Hellenism continued to exert itself. The kings, for example, took Greek names (Aristoboulos, Alexander), and while the non-Jewish cities of Palestine were trying to establish ancient links with Greek culture (Joppa, for example, claimed to be the place where Perseus saved Andromeda from the sea monster, and other non-Greek cities invented Greek founders), the Jews went one better and claimed that Sparta was a Jewish colony (1 Maccabees 12: 5–23). Later, when Herod became king under the protection of the Romans, the Temple he built in Jerusalem was essentially in a Hellenistic style. Herod, indeed, founded a new city on the coast, Caesarea, which was entirely Hellenistic in nature, and equipped with the standard institutions of the Greek lifestyle, including theatres, statues, and temples.

The reduction of Palestine to a Roman province, and the crushing of two Jewish revolts in the 1st and 2nd centuries AD, removed the Jews from effective control of the region, and thereafter the process of Hellenization followed the same pattern as elsewhere in the Roman empire. The growth of Christianity, however, gave Palestine a new significance in the Greek world. Herod's foundation, Caesarea, was a particularly influential centre for the development of Christian thought. The Alexandrian theologian Origen worked there in the 3rd century towards the end of his life, and founded a school that played a decisive role in the formation of the eastern tradition of theology. In the next century the Christian historian Eusebius was bishop there. Later, with the establishment of Christianity as the official religion of the empire, Palestine became the home of a monastic tradition that was one of the roots of Orthodox monasticism. The patronage of the emperors from Constantine onwards resulted in the construction of major shrines in places important in Christian tradition, especially the Church of the Holy Sepulchre in Jerusalem. As a result, a long tradition of "religious tourism" had by the 4th century developed into pilgrimages proper, travel to sacred sites in the hope of accumulating spiritual benefits. The special position of Jerusalem is shown by the decision of the Council of Nicaea (325) to raise its bishop to the status of patriarch, fifth in precedence after the bishops of the politically more significant sees of Rome, Constantinople, Alexandria, and Antioch. Though politically a backwater, Palestine continued to be spiritually significant throughout the Byzantine period, and after the Arab conquests Byzantine emperors regarded the protection of religious communities there as one of their special responsibilities.

Under the period of Ottoman rule, Palestine remained an important goal for Greek Orthodox pilgrims and was, like most parts of the Ottoman empire, the home of a substantial population of Greeks engaged in trade and commerce. Most important of all, however, was the guardianship of the Holy Places, always a matter of contention between Greeks and Latins, and regarded as a matter of crucial importance by the Orthodox Church. The Grand Dragoman Alexander Mavrokordatos (died 1709) used his political leverage with the Turkish sultan to secure the transfer of many of the Holy Places of Jerusalem from Latin to Greek control (working with Dositheos, the patriarch of Jerusalem); to his great credit he also made every effort to ensure that unfettered access was given to Christians of all denominations. With the decline and break-up of the Ottoman empire, and with it the Ottoman economic system, the Palestinian Greek community dwindled. By the middle of the 20th century there were perhaps only about 5000 Greeks living within the Jerusalem patriarchate. There is a substantially larger (though still small) Greek Orthodox congregation in Palestine (though it is under increasing pressure), but most of its members are Arabic-speaking. The patriarch, however, and the higher clergy are still Greek (a fact that has recently caused some tension). Greeks still run a number of the holy places (most importantly, large sections of the Church of the Holy Sepulchre), and there are several Greek churches and monasteries, particularly in Jerusalem. Devout Greeks still go on pilgrimage to the Holy Land.

RICHARD WALLACE

See also Jews, Pilgrimage, Septuagint

Further Reading
Kuhrt, Amélie, *The Ancient Near East, c.3000–330 BC*, 2 vols, London and New York: Routledge, 1995
Wallace, Richard and Wynne Williams, *The Three Worlds of Paul of Tarsus*, London and New York: Routledge, 1998
Ware, Timothy, *The Orthodox Church*, 2nd edition, London and New York: Penguin, 1993
Wilken, Robert L., *The Land Called Holy: Palestine in Christian History and Thought*, New Haven and London: Yale University Press, 1992

Pallis, Alexandros 1851–1935

Scholar, poet, and translator

Known first as the "great demoticist", Pallis was an early advocate of the recognition of *dimotiki* or vernacular Greek as a viable language option for the modern Greek state. In the crucial decade of the 1890s he embraced and perpetuated the cause of demoticism and became "a perfect example of the chains of transmission so important in Greek literary life" (Bien, 1972).

Although spending most of his life away from Greece, in India and in England, Pallis remained closely associated with the language question in Greece. The complexity of the language problem itself – what was to be the official language of Greece – is staggering and has always been an integral part of the Greek struggle for self-determination. At least since the 1880s, the question has centred on the debate between the demoticists, who argue for a "living language", a form of Greek that mirrors the everyday speech of the people, and the "purists", who argue for katharevousa, the more purified Greek of the educated classes.

Pallis supported the linguistic and cultural theories of the influential demoticists, Dimitrios Vernardakis and especially Yannis Psycharis, remarking: "My eyes were first opened by Vernardakis and practically by Psycharis. The internal need which required me to change was common sense." The publication of the first substantial literary work written in demotic, *My Journey* by Yannis Psycharis, was a singular event, which demonstrated to Pallis that scholarly works could be successfully written in vernacular Greek. Remaining loyal to the tradition of Psycharis, Pallis produced numerous translations including Shakespeare's *The Merchant of Venice*, Euripides' *Cyclops*, book 1 of Thucydices, and some of the writings of Kant. He produced critical editions of the *Antigone* by Sophocles and book 18 of the *Iliad*. Of special note is an original work, *Brousos* (*Journey*), published in 1923, a satirical indictment of the conservative traditions of modern Greek society and its failure to respond to the needs of a modern generation.

Pallis's most significant and controversial achievements were his translations, into lively demotic, of the New Testament gospels (1901) and the *Iliad* (1904). His decision to translate these works was carefully considered. The gospels, written in "Byzantine Greek", formed the basis of the Orthodox faith. The writings of Homer were also important in the Greek consciousness. Although few modern Greeks could read either the *Iliad* or the *Odyssey* in the original, these epics provided a link to the ancient civilization of Greece. The translation of these revered works into demotic constituted a revolutionary act. In 1901, when the Athenian newspaper *Akropolis* began the serialization of Pallis's translation of the gospels, riots broke out in Athens. The translation was vehemently attacked in all sectors and was considered "anti-religious, anti-national, full of vulgar words, degrading the true meaning of the Gospel". Pallis was labelled a "traitor", and "an evil little creature that ought to be excommunicated". Despite all the controversy, the translation was clearly ahead of its time.

Pallis dedicated his translation of the *Iliad* (1904) to Psycharis, demonstrating his continued loyalty to his mentor. The importance of this translation cannot be overestimated. When composing his own translation of the *Iliad*, the novelist Nikos Kazantzakis acknowledged his debt to Pallis: "I want this translation to be at the same level as Pallis." In his translation Pallis does not treat the work as a single composition written by one author; indeed, he does not even mention Homer on the title page. He translates the poem into 15-syllable lines reminiscent of a collection of oral demotic folk ballads or heroic songs in the klephtic tradition. Pallis may have gone to extremes in this translation, but he remained steadfast in his support of Greek as a spoken language; he was interested above all in making this classic work accessible and familiar to the average Greek. Pallis's definitive translation became very popular and soon the preferred translation in Greece. It was adopted by the Ministry of Education in 1976 for use in high schools until it was replaced in the 1980s by the translation of Ioannes Kakridis and Nikos Kazantzakis.

In addition to his translations, Pallis was also an epigrammatist and a poet who published poems for both children and adults. His collection of poems for children, entitled *Little Songs for Children* (1889), is included, together with some of his other poems, in a second collection entitled *Empty Walnuts* (1915). In his poems he demonstrates his skills as an educator with a continuing interest in the impact of a living Greek language on future generations. He conveys a "freshness, a gaiety and a joy of life" that is especially appealing to young people. He was concerned to provide "a living education for neo-Hellenic youth" and to ensure that the transmission of Greek culture should not be mired in the past but remain a living tradition.

Pallis appears to have given and commanded great respect and admiration. He remained a loyal and steadfast colleague and friend, especially to Nikos Kazantzakis. When Kazantzakis was soliciting subscriptions for the publication of his work on Dante, Pallis seems to have been among the handful that responded. He died in England in 1935.

JANE JURGENS

Biography

Born in 1851 to a family from Epirus, Pallis studied philology in Athens. He lived most of his life in India and England pursuing a commercial career, but he remained closely involved with the Greek language question. Known as the "great demoticist", he produced translations of the gospels and the *Iliad* as well as poems of his own in the demotic form of the language. He died in England in 1935.

Further Reading

Beaton, Roderick, *An Introduction to Modern Greek Literature*, 2nd edition, Oxford: Clarendon Press, 1999

Bien, Peter, *Kazantzakis and the Linguistic Revolution in Greek Literature*, Princeton, New Jersey: Princeton University Press, 1972

Carabott, Phillip, "Politics, Orthodoxy, and the Language Question in Greece: The Gospel Riots of November 1901", *Journal of Mediterranean Studies*, 3/1 (1993): pp. 117ff.

Dimaris, K. T., *A History of Modern Greek Literature*, Albany: State University of New York Press, 1972

Gourgouris, Stathis, *Dream Nation: Enlightenment, Colonization, and the Institution of Modern Greece*, Stanford, California: Stanford University Press, 1996

Horrocks, Geoffrey, *Greek: A History of the Language and Its Speakers*, London: Longman, 1997

Kazantzakis, Helen, *Nikos Kazantzakis: A Biography Based on his Letters*, New York: Simon and Schuster, and Oxford: Cassirer, 1968

Kourvetaris, Yorgos A., *A Profile of Modern Greece: In Search of Identity*, Oxford: Clarendon Press, and New York: Oxford University Press, 1987

Legg, Keith R. and John M. Roberts, *Modern Greece: A Civilization on the Periphery*, Boulder, Colorado: Westview Press, 1997

Trypanis, C.A., *Greek Poetry: From Homer to Seferis*, Chicago: University of Chicago Press, and London: Faber, 1981

Website

Papaioannou, Sophia, "Translating Homer in 20th Century Greece: the 'Silent' Voice of a Revolution", 1998: http://www.hfac.uh.edu/mcl/faculty/armstrong/papa.draft.html

Palmyra

City in Syria

Palmyra is known today – as it was in very ancient sources – as Tadmor. It lies in the heart of the Syrian desert, 200 km northeast of Damascus, at an important oasis and astride major trade routes. The geographical location of the city provided an unprecedented opportunity for the commercial exploitation of its immediate and powerful neighbours, Parthia to the east and Rome to the west. Indeed, the city derived much of its fabled wealth from maintaining a monopoly on the luxury trade between east and west. In this respect it can be said that Palmyrene trade was also responsible for advancing western goods and cultural ideas into farther corners of the east.

Palaeolithic material has been found there and the site is mentioned in Assyrian sources of the 2nd millennium BC. Biblical references suggest that it was founded by Solomon but this has long been recognized as a confusion with Tamar. Nevertheless at the time of the writing down of 2 Chronicles – perhaps by the 4th century BC – it would seem that the site had become well enough known to have engendered this confusion. The story was even repeated by the 1st-century AD historian Josephus, who describes the grandeur of the site known as Tadmor by the Syrians and as Palmyra by the Greeks.

Throughout its later history Palmyrenes used the Seleucid calendar of 312 BC, although it is uncertain whether the city ever fell directly under Macedonian control.

Funerary monuments, architectural fragments (often incorporated into later monuments), and inscriptions are known from the 1st century BC, although the extent of the early city is not fully known. The earliest known attention by the western powers seems to have been an abortive cavalry attack against the city by Mark Antony in 41 BC. That this sortie was repulsed has led to the suggestion that the city was walled at this time, indicating a substantial settlement, although no archaeological proof has been forthcoming. However, inscriptions make it clear that from the reign of Tiberius (AD 14–37) Palmyra became part of the Roman world.

One of the most enduring aspects of Palmyra's cultural independence is the inscriptions which abound in its remains and record so much of its history. Palmyrene was a dialect of Aramaic but its script was related to Hebrew and Nabataean, developing into a mature monumental style by the 2nd century AD. However, from the 1st century AD Palmyrene inscriptions had become infiltrated by Greek administrative words such as *boule* (council), *strategos* (general or senator), *proedros* (president) and *grammateus* (secretary) transliterated into Palmyrene. In about AD 130 the emperor Hadrian visited the city and gave it the new epithet Palmyra Hadriane, and under the Severans it was made into a *colonia*. Even after this period,

Palmyra: remains of the Temple of Bel, dedicated in AD 32

Latin was rarely used and most inscriptions were in both Greek and Palmyrene. Palmyrene military units controlled the desert caravan routes as well as serving under Rome – as far away, indeed, as on Hadrian's Wall.

At the height of Palmyrene power and prosperity in the mid-3rd century AD, one of its leading citizens, Septimius Odenathus, was largely instrumental in saving Roman Syria from Persian aggression. He was rewarded with a string of titles and established almost royal power. After his death in AD 267 he was succeeded in all but name by his powerful widow Zenobia. Her "revolt" against Rome ultimately led to the downfall of the city when it was finally besieged and then sacked by the Roman emperor Aurelian in AD 272. After this the semi-independence of Palmyra and its brilliant culture were eclipsed and Palmyra was never again as important. Nevertheless a military garrison was set up in the late 3rd century and it had a large enough Christian community to elect a bishop by the mid-4th century.

This distinctive culture largely manifested itself in the 2nd and 3rd centuries AD but it was apparent earlier with the building of the great temple of Bel dedicated in AD 32. This building appeared to be Classical in design, resting on a Greek-style *krepidoma* (stylobate), and peripteral. However, the placing of a doorway off centre on one of its long sides was distinctly oriental as was some of its architectural decoration. Later, in the 2nd century AD, temples such as those dedicated to Baal Shamin and that to Nebo were in conventional eastern Roman style on a podium. However their *temenoi* (precincts) displayed an older repertoire; that of Baal-Shamin incorporated a distinctive Rhodian peristyle and the colonnade around that of Nebo was, unusually, Doric. Indeed most Corinthian decoration at the site was of a freer Hellenistic rather than severe Roman style. Such Greek-inspired ideas of civic munificence extended to the profusion of honorific statuary celebrating the great and good of the city. Many were placed on the brackets that adorned nearly every column of the great colonnaded street – itself a distinct element in eastern Roman architecture as was the *tetrakionion* (4-columned porch) that marked a major street junction. The agora (early 2nd century AD) contained a basilical building – unusual in the east – that is thought to have been a *kaisareion* of the imperial cult. Larger houses in the northern suburbs were of Hellenistic peristyle type, and even the earlier of the curious tower tombs are reminiscent of Hellenistic *hypogaia* (underground chamber).

It is with the sculptural arts of Palmyra that there is a more distinct break with Classical forms. There was a heavy emphasis on relief with humans and deities wearing distinctly oriental garb, the men with trousers and the women heavily veiled and bejewelled. The orientation was frontal and entirely lacks the realism of Roman portraiture. This was also usually the nature of religious reliefs; but it is interesting to note that the cult statue of the rebuilt 2nd-century AD temple of Allat was in fact a Roman copy of a 5th-century BC Greek statue of Athena. The Palmyrene pantheon remained oriental but was infiltrated by Graeco-Roman deities.

The striking ruins in the Syrian desert testify to the former grandeur of a city with the usual appurtenances of Graeco-Roman civilization. However, the city displays a unique position in the Hellenic east, one that preserved a measure of political, commercial, and above all cultural interdependence.

JULIAN M.C. BOWSHER

Summary

A city in the Syrian desert, Palmyra lies astride major trade routes between east and west. It formed part of the Roman world from the 1st century AD but retained its cultural independence. It reached the peak of its prosperity in the mid-3rd century AD when Septimius Odenathus saved Syria from the Persians. His widow Zenobia revolted against Rome, and the city was sacked by Aurelian in 272.

Further Reading

Colledge, Malcolm A.R., *The Art of Palmyra*, London: Thames and Hudson, and Boulder, Colorado: Westview Press, 1976

Gawlikowski, M., "Les Dieux de Palmyre" in *Aufstieg und Niedergang der römischen Welt*, edited by Hildegard Temporini, Berlin: de Gruyter, 1990

Matthews, J.F., "The Tax Law of Palmyra: Evidence for Economic History in a City of the Roman East", *Journal of Roman Studies*, 74 (1984): p. 157 ff.

Starcky, J. and M. Gawlikowski, *Palmyre*, revised edition, Paris: Librairie d'Amérique et d'Orient, 1985

Pamphylia

Region of southern Asia Minor

Pamphylia consists of a broad plain along the southern coast of Asia Minor, between the more difficult mountainous territories of Lycia to the west and Rough Cilicia (Cilicia Tracheia) to the east. It is framed by mountains to the north, through which passes give access to central Anatolia. The mountains are snow-covered in winter, and give rise to rivers, the most important of which is the Eurymedon, ensuring that the plain is well watered and fertile. It is a lush region (modern crops include cotton and bananas), and is obviously a desirable area in which to live.

In antiquity its population seems to have been of mixed origin, as, indeed, its name "all tribes" suggests. It would have been known in the Bronze Age to traders sailing from the Aegean to the Levant and Cyprus, and there is a tradition of Greek settlement in the area, though whether this goes back to that period, or, more likely, reflects something of the movement of peoples in the disturbed times at the collapse of the Bronze Age states is unclear. The legendary founders of this settlement include Mopsus, a seer who was the son of Manto, daughter of Teiresias. He drove the Carians from Clarus in Ionia, where he inaugurated the famous oracle. His name has been identified on Hittite documents, and on a Luwian Phoenician inscription at Karatepe, and may therefore be Anatolian in origin, assimilated into a Greek tradition of settlement. This all brings out the mixed origins of the peoples of Pamphylia, but by the Classical period Greek certainly was established as a language of the region, in a dialect which was related to Arcado-Cypriot, implying that the Greeks did arrive at the same time as they did in Cyprus, when the dialect indicates a unity between this region and the Greek homeland. An exception seems to have been the city of Side. Arrian, writing in the 2nd century AD, says this place was founded by settlers from Cyme, but once

Pamphylia: the main street of Perge looking north

they had arrived they promptly forgot their native Greek and began to talk in a foreign tongue, which was not the usual (and, by implication, non-Greek) language of Pamphylia, but a "new" dialect of their own. Such stories reflect the mixed origins of the Pamphylians of the Classical period. There is virtually no archaeological evidence to illuminate this very early period.

By the end of the 6th century Pamphylia was part of the Persian empire. The Ionian revolt, in conjunction with the rising in Cyprus, probably sought to exclude Persian influence in this strategically important area, but failed. This policy was revived by the Athenians under Cimon, culminating in the presence of an Athenian fleet in the waters off Pamphylia and the battle of the Eurymedon, when the Persian fleet was driven up the river and annihilated. This may have led to the inclusion of the Pamphylian cities in the Delian League. The evidence for this is slight; the Athenian tribute list of 425 BC, when the tribute paid by Athens' allies was sharply increased to pay the costs of the Peloponnesian War, includes Celenderis in Cilicia and in Pamphylia Perge and Sillyon, as well as another Pamphylian city the name of which is now missing from the inscription but which is generally identified as Aspendos. Pamphylia was hardly within Athens' area of interest or control at this date, but a reasonable explanation is that the list includes, rather optimistically, all places which were once part of the alliance, and for this the period following Eurymedon is

the most likely. What is clear is that when Athens and the Persian king, whether tacitly or by treaty agreement, recognized each other's sphere of influence, Pamphylia was in Persian hands; the inability of the Athenians to retain control is a reflection of the setbacks they experienced after Eurymedon, and the geographical difficulty of defending the Pamphylian communities.

Pamphylia remained under Persian control until the arrival of Alexander the Great. He first occupied Perge, where he was received by envoys from Aspendos, who surrendered their city to him, asking in return to be left free from the imposition of a garrison. Alexander agreed, but demanded in return 50 talents to pay his troops, and all the horses bred there as tribute to Darius the Persian king, implying that he did not recognize it as a Greek city to be liberated from Persian control. He also occupied Side, but had to besiege Sillyon, at which Aspendos reneged on its agreement; it was then forced to accept a governor and to give hostages. In the Hellenistic period Pamphylia first came under the control of the Ptolemies of Egypt. In the wave of Greek settlement in Egypt instigated by Ptolemy II many of the Greeks came from Pamphylia, the most distinguished of them being Apollonius of Perge, one of the greatest of Hellenistic mathematicians.

Pamphylia, however, remained vulnerable, Ptolemaic control being disputed by the Seleucid kings and by the neighbouring Pisidians. In the 2nd century BC it was taken over by the Pergamene kings, who founded the fifth of the great Pamphylian cities – Attaleia, the modern Antalya. Through this it was incorporated with the kingdom of Pergamum into the Roman province of Asia, eventually becoming part of a joint province with its western neighbour Lycia. Attaleia had by then lost territory through its support of the pirates in the troubled times of the 1st century BC, and was forced to accept under Augustus a settlement of legionary veterans of Italian origin.

It was the period of Roman peace which brought the greatest prosperity to the Pamphylian cities, though its inland mountainous areas seem to have remained more backward. Before this the cities were probably restricted places. Arrian desribes Aspendos when it rebelled against Alexander as built on a very steep hill, the base of which was washed by the river Eurymedon. Similarly Perge includes a steep-sided hill, which may be the original settlement; small-scale excavations (not yet published) which are being carried out here may throw light on its earlier development. In the Hellenistic period Perge was extended to include a large area of flatter ground below this hill, and this was surrounded by strong fortifications, with regular tall towers to accommodate the latest forms of torsion artillery, and an imposing main gate at its southern end. Even so the place was further extended in the Roman period, with a great theatre and adjacent stadium constructed outside the earlier limits.

Perge, above all, demonstrates the strength of the Hellenic city tradition in the Roman period, when it was the metropolis of Pamphylia. During the 2nd century AD, when the region was untroubled by any major historical occurrences, the architecture of Perge was greatly enhanced, not as a part of some remote imperial gesture of support but through the wealth of its local aristocracy. The main street, running from the acropolis to the southern gate, exemplifies this; broad, paved, lined with colonnades, and with an artfical stream down its centre fed by a splendid fountain at its northern end and running in a sequence of low waterfalls as it descends towards the city gate. The theatres of Pamphylia are equally spectacular. Perge has an auditorium built against a hillside, as does Aspendos. Aspendos is structurally complete, though the decoration of its stage building has gone. At Perge the stage building has collapsed (it is now, slowly, under reconstruction) but the elements of its elaborate facade survive. At Side the theatre stands on flat ground, its auditorium supported on a vaulted substructure, though this is built entirely in the local cut-stone tradition, not employing the Roman concrete technique.

Pamphylia escaped the worst consequences of Roman decline in the period of the late empire. It was the creation of an Arab fleet in the mid-7th century AD that exposed its weakness. Prosperity seems to have suffered as a result of the rise of Islam and the loss of whole sections of the Byzantine empire, and the population of the cities declined as a consequence. The great city walls enclosed areas too vast to be defended, and unnecessary for the population. The circuit of Side was reduced, the theatre being incorporated into an inner line of defence. But the decline continued, and further Arab threats in the 10th century resulted in a similar reduced fortification at Attaleia, much of which has been destroyed only recently. At the present time, only Antalya survives as a flourishing, rapidly expanding, but essentially non-Hellenic city.

R.A. TOMLINSON

Summary

A region of southern Asia Minor, Pamphylia ("all tribes") had a cosmopolitan population in antiquity. By the Classical period the Greek language was established but the region remained under Persian control until the arrival of Alexander the Great. The prosperity of the area is indicated by the size of the Hellenic cities of Perge, Sillyon, Side, Aspendos, and Attaleia.

Further Reading

Bean, George, E., *Turkey's Southern Shore*, 2nd edition, London: Benn, and New York: Norton, 1979

Beaufort, Francis, *Karamania*, 2nd edition, London: R. Hunter, 1818

Brewster, Harry, *Classical Anatolia: The Glory of Hellenism*, London and New York: Tauris, 1993

Jones, A.H.M., *Cities of the Eastern Roman Provinces*, 2nd edition, Oxford: Clarendon Press, 1971

Mansel, A.M., Report on excavations in Pamphylia, *Archäologische Anzeiger*, 49 (1975) (in German)

Niemann, G. and E. Petersen, *Städte Pamphyliens und Pisidiens*, 2 vols, Vienna: Tempsky, 1890–92

Panselinos, Manuel
Artist of the 13th–14th centuries

Manuel Panselinos is the name given to the master who made the important paintings in the church of the Protaton at Karyes, the capital of Mount Athos. Neither the exact date of the rebuilding of the Protaton nor the date of the paintings themselves is known. It is generally assumed that the church was rebuilt in the 13th century and it is likely that it was painted as soon as the building work was finished, since a Byzantine church could not function without its paintings.

The attribution of the paintings to Manuel Panselinos originates in oral Athonite tradition that was recorded only in the 17th century. In the 18th century the monk Dionysios of Fourna, author of the *Painter's Manual*, wrote down Panselinos's proportional rules for constructing the human figure, together with detailed measures for making the head and the face. He tells us that Panselinos came from Thessalonica and that he surpassed and eclipsed all ancient and modern painters in his abilities. There needs to be good reason to reject the Athonite attribution of the Protaton paintings to Panselinos, for oral tradition is enmeshed in the slow-moving, close-knit monastic community of Mount Athos. Two pieces of circumstantial evidence support this tradition. The first is that his proportional rules for painting, as written down by Dionysios, agree precisely with the proportions of the figures in the Protaton paintings. The second is the existence of an important series of church decorations of the late 13th and 14th centuries in southern Serbia and Macedonia, which are now termed works of the Macedonian school. The paintings in these churches follow the rules of Panselinos, as described by Dionysios, and they all show stylistic affinities to the paintings of the Protaton, while maintaining an individuality that makes it unlikely that they are by the same master.

Dionysios also tells us that many other churches on the Holy Mountain were painted by Panselinos, but these have either been overpainted with later work, or they have been destroyed. The sole surviving fragment that is certainly by Panselinos is the head of a saint from the Katholikon of the Great Lavra.

The church of the Protaton was transformed from a basilica and rebuilt as a cross-in-square at ground level, while retaining the basilican form at higher levels. This rather ungainly compromise made it difficult to give the church a standard Byzantine iconographic programme. Panselinos shows superb ability in overcoming these difficulties and has created painterly solutions in the placing of scenes and of figures that do much to unify the awkward spaces he had to decorate. Thus the upper register of the north and south walls is devoted to standing figures of the 46 forefathers of Christ descending from Adam to Joseph, the husband of Mary. The figures are enumerated as in the Gospel of St Luke. The majestic rows of figures emphasize the basilican shape and echo figural decorations of the 5th and 6th centuries, such as at Ravenna. The middle registers are devoted to scenes from the life of Christ and Mary, his mother. Here the painter innovates by sometimes leaving out the vertical red borders between scenes and by adding subsidiary if related episodes within the main scenes. Thus St John the Baptist is depicted preaching repentance in a preliminary episode to the main scene of the *Baptism of Christ*. The ground register is traditional in being devoted to standing figures with a strong emphasis on monastic and warrior saints.

In style Panselinos gives a dignity to his figures that owes much to the Hellenistic tradition of Byzantine painting. But he breaks with earlier developments in suppressing the excessive linear elaboration of 12th-century painting in favour of a much greater elegance and weightiness to his figures that recall developments associated with Giotto in Italian art of the 13th century. Similar comparisons can be made between Giotto and Panselinos with regard to the depiction of emotion in such scenes as the *Lamentation*.

Panselinos can also be distinguished as the finest painter of the Macedonian school of painting that flourished in Athonite monasteries and in Thessalonica, Macedonia, Serbia, and Constantinople in the first half of the 14th century. The earliest dated church of the Macedonian school is the Peribleptos (St Clement) at Ohrid, of 1295. More factual information about Panselinos will become available after the projected restoration of the church of the Protaton and its paintings.

DAVID WINFIELD

See also Painting

Summary

According to Dionysios of Phourna (18th century), Panselinos (*fl. c.*1300) was from Thessalonica, was the greatest artist of all time, and invented the proportional rules for constructing the human figure. Nothing else is known of him. But he is credited with having made the wall paintings in the church of the Protaton at Karyes on Mount Athos.

Further Reading

Chadjiphotis, I.M., *Macedonian School: The School of Panselinos*, Athens, 1995

Dionysios of Phourna, *The "Painter's Manual"*, translated by Paul Hetherington, London: Sagittarius Press, 1974, reprinted 1981

Kalomoirakis, D., "Erminevtikes paratiriseis sto eikonografiko programma tou Protatou" [Explanatory Remarks on the Iconographical Programme of the Protaton], *Bulletin of the Christian Archaeological Society*, 15 (1989–90): pp. 197–220

Mako, V., *The Proportional Distribution and Size of the Frescoes in the Church of St. Basil on the Sea at Hilandar*, Belgrade, 1997, pp. 75–97 (in Serbian)

Mako, V., *Figure and Number*, Belgrade, 1998 (in Serbian)

Torp, Hjalmar, *The Integrating System of Proportion in Byzantine Art: An Essay on the Method of the Painters of Holy Images*, Rome: Bretschneider, 1984

Winfield, David, *Proportion and Structure of the Human Figure in Byzantine Wall-Painting and Mosaic*, Oxford: British Archaeological Reports International Series, 154 (1982)

Xyngopoulos, Andreas, *Manuel Panselinos*, Athens, 1956

Papacy

The papacy is both an institution and a concept. It is as a concept that the papacy mainly figured in relations between the see of Rome and Byzantium. The patriarchal see of Rome was recognized as such at the Council of Nicaea in 325, clearly the outstanding bishopric in the western Roman empire. By tradition the see of Rome was founded by St Peter *c.*AD 40 and was hallowed by both his and St Paul's martyrdom in the city.

In 313 the Roman emperor became the protector and benefactor of the Christian Church. The idea soon emerged that a Christian empire should have spiritual aims, but who should define these aims? The Church Fathers, imbued with Roman law and an awareness of the needs for stability, hardly ever questioned the authority of the emperor and developed the idea of divine right. The transference of the capital from Rome to Constantinople in 330 threatened a diminution in the prestige and influence of the patriarch of Rome. The First Council of Constantinople in 381 gave the primacy of honour to Rome, but it also gave to the patriarch of Constantinople the same rights and privileges as the pope. This last point was restated at the Council of Chalcedon in 451 but not accepted in Rome.

After 330 the bishop of Rome was freed from the imperial presence and thus from direct imperial pressure. Distance and the role that the popes assumed in the 5th century – of defending, feeding, and administering the city in the face of barbarian attacks – meant that they were less inclined to acquiesce in imperial decisions and more inclined to adopt social and political theories that were never developed in Byzantium to even a remotely comparable extent. They were none the less theories and did not mean that the papacy, lacking an army of its own, behaved any more independently than did the Byzantine Church; but it did have the freedom and the necessity to look for other protectors than the emperor in distant Constantinople. In 753 and again in 773 the popes were to appeal to the Frankish kings for military support against the Lombards. The coronation of Charlemagne as emperor of the Romans by Leo III (795–816) in Rome in 800 outraged the Byzantine idea of one Roman empire.

Pope Gelasius I (491–96) had defined the limits of imperial and sacerdotal authority and had stated that, of the two responsibilities, the obligation of the bishops was the heavier since they were responsible to God for the souls of kings themselves. Until the 10th century the main question at issue was one of imperial interference in the ecclesiastical sphere. This had happened at Chalcedon in 451, and during the 8th century was marked by papal opposition to iconoclasm. The emperors sought to bring pressure on Rome by placing Illyricum under the jurisdiction of Constantinople. The 9th and 10th centuries were to see competition between Orthodox and Catholic missionaries to gain converts in Moravia, Bulgaria, and Scandinavia, while the issue of Illyricum remained unresolved.

The reform movement of the 11th century enhanced papal prestige in the west and raised once again the universalist claims of the papacy. These are summarized in a letter written by Pope Leo IX to the Byzantine patriarch Michael Keroularios in 1054 when use was made for the first time of that celebrated forgery the Donation of Constantine. This document, written in the 8th or 9th century, purported to record a grant by Constantine I to Pope Silvester of imperial powers in the west, jurisdiction over all clergy, and primacy over all patriarchates. The 11th century also saw a move on the part of the papacy for the union of the Greek and Latin Churches in one *respublica Christiana*. One manifestation was the proclamation of the First Crusade by Urban II in 1095. The drive for union was always on Western terms with the Greek Church seen as in error and, after 1054, as schismatic. No concession was made to Greek traditions or feelings. The scale of the task and the issues involved were never appreciated in the West and consequently led to failure and to increased tensions between the two communions. This was true of Innocent III's policy towards the Latin empire after 1204, of Gregory X at the Second Council of Lyon (1274), and of Eugenius IV at the Council of Ferrara-Florence in 1439. Fourteen years later the papacy was equally ineffective at raising western support for the beleagured city of Constantinople.

PETER LOCK

Further Reading

Barraclough, Geoffrey, *The Medieval Papacy*, London: Thames and Hudson, and New York: Harcourt Brace, 1968

Dvornik, Francis, *Byzantium and the Roman Primacy*, New York: Fordham University Press, 1966

Every, George, *The Byzantine Patriarchate, 451–1204*, London: SPCK, 1947; New York: AMS Press, 1980

Gill, Joseph, *Byzantium and the Papacy, 1198–1400*, New Brunswick, New Jersey: Rutgers University Press, 1979

Nicol, Donald M., *Byzantium: Its Ecclesiastical History and Relations with the Western World*, London: Variorum, 1972

Setton, Kenneth M., *The Papacy and the Levant, 1204–1571*, 4 vols., Philadelphia: American Philosophical Society, 1976–84

Papadiamantis, Alexandros 1851–1911

Short-story writer, novelist, translator, and journalist

Alexandros Papdiamantis is perhaps the best-known writer of prose fiction in Greece and occupies a legendary status as a writer. Although none of his writing was issued in book form during his lifetime, Papadiamantis's novels and numerous short stories have been frequently anthologized, and more recently, made available to younger readers in accessible, but controversial, demotic translations. A veritable industry has grown up around his life and work. His novella *I Phonissa* (The Murderess, 1903) has been adapted for the stage, as well as for the cinema in Kostas Ferris's award-winning 1974 feature, while his late "novel" *Ta Rodin' Akrogiala* (The Rosy Shores, 1907) has recently been adapted for the cinema by Efthimios Chatzis (1998). Papadiamantis's influence over subsequent Greek writers has been immense and the poet Odysseus Elytis has written extensively on his fiction (1977).

Papadiamantis was born on 4 March 1851 on Skiathos, one of the northern Sporades islands, then on the frontier of the newly established Greek kingdom. His father, Adamantios, was a priest (whence the writer's surname) and his mother's family were local landowners who came originally from the southern Peloponnese. On his mother's side he was a cousin, and close friend, of the writer Alexandros Moraitidis (1850–1929).

Papadiamantis's formal education was minimal. After attending school at Chalcis, he registered as a student in the Philosophical School of the University of Athens (1874) and for a time was a classmate of the writer Georgios Vizyinos (1849–96). Financial hardship, however, soon forced Papadiamantis to abandon higher education. He turned to a career in journalism, eking out a living as a translator for the newspapers *Ephimeris*, *Akropolis*, and *Asti*, and weighed down, after his father's death in 1895, with the responsibility of looking after his sisters. Together with Grigorios Xenopoulos (1867–1951), Papadiamantis was one of the first among the new generation of professional Greek writers to make a living from their writing. He died on 3 January 1911 in Skiathos where he had been living since 1908.

It is only in the last ten years, and due largely to the editorial diligence of Nikos Triandaphyllopoulos, that the full range and quality of Papadiamantis's translations have come to light. His translations include works by, among others, Mark Twain, Bret Harte, Jerome K. Jerome, and Alphonse Daudet. At the instigation of his friend, the writer and historian Yannis Vlachoyannis (1867–1945), Papadiamantis also translated the histories of the Greek revolution by George Finlay and George Gordon. Perhaps Papadiamantis's most remarkable translation, however, is a compelling version of Fyodor Dostoevsky's *Crime and Punishment*, translated from the French and serialized, with a preface by Emmanouil Roidis (1836–1904), in *Ephimeris*. In 1992 this translation was published in book form for the first time.

Papadiamantis's literary career was launched with the publication of the historical novel *I Metanastis* (The Emigration, 1879; published in English as *The Emigrant Woman*) in the Constantinopolitan newspaper *Neologos*. Set in the late 18th century, the romance centres on the adventures of a young Greek woman, Marina, who is left orphaned after a plague devastates Marseilles. In 1882 Papadiamantis's second novel, *Oi Emporoi tou Ethnou* (The Merchants of Nations), was published under the pseudonym Bohème, this time set in the 12th and 13th centuries. Two years later his third novel, *I Giftoula* (The Gypsy Girl), appeared in *Akropolis*. Papadiamantis's last novel takes place in the mid-15th century and explores the political and religious intrigues that divided Byzantium on the eve of Constantinople's capitulation to the

Ottomans in 1453. One of the central characters is the Neoplatonist philosopher Plethon.

In 1885 Papadiamantis published the novella *Christos Milionis*, based on a well-known folk poem and centring on Greek resistance to the Ottomans a century before. This novella is often taken to mark a bridge connecting the historical novels with the subsequent fiction. From 1887 onwards Papadiamantis, like many of the so-called 1880s generation, cultivated the short story, although *Vardianos sta Sporka* (Guardian of the Plague Ships, 1893), *I Phonissa* (The Murderess, 1903), and *Ta Rodin' Akrogiala* (The Rosy Shores, 1907) were described as novels on their publication. Numerous short stories evoke the historically rich texture of Greek rural life and the physical beauty of the Greek landscape. Papadiamantis belonged to a group of writers who gathered around the figure of Nikolaos Politis (1852–1921), the founder of folklore as a discipline in Greece and one of the chief advocates of the new ethographic literature. Writing in his autobiography about this folkloric movement, Papadiamantis's contemporary Georgios Drosinis (1859–1951) observed that the object was "to find themes from outside the cosmopolitan centres of city life in the freedom of the Greek life of the mountains and the sea". Many of Papadiamantis's short stories are, in fact, set on his native Skiathos and are replete with accounts of local traditions and customs. While the term *ithographia* remains one of the most controversial words in the Greek language, the designation is usually taken to refer to a current of folkloric realism which drew its inspiration from similar tendencies in Europe and Russia. The preferred genre of ethographic writing was the short story which centred on descriptions of local, contemporary life, with particular attention paid to rustic manners and customs. Yet, as the critic and novelist Alexandros Kotzias has pointed out, something in the region of a third of Papadiamantis's stories are set in Athens. Along with Michail Mitsakis (1863–1916) and Ioannis Kondylakis (1861–1920), he should be regarded as one of the most important Athenian writers.

Even within his lifetime, myths had accumulated around Papadiamantis. The photograph taken of him in Dexameni by his friend Pavlos Nirvanas with an early Kodak shows Papadiamantis dressed in his long overcoat (a gift sent to him from England by the writer Alexandros Pallis), and has become symbolic of the writer's otherworldliness. In his fictional biography of Papadiamantis (1948), Michalis Peranthis famously characterized the writer as a "worldly-monk" (*kosmokalogeros*). Papadiamantis continues to be promoted as a champion of Orthodoxy and traditional Greek values, in opposition to the disruptive impact of a cosmopolitan modernity. While it is certainly the case that in a number of his short stories and articles he deplores the slavish imitation of foreign ways, his fiction consistently undermines the sentimental idealism of the rural community celebrated by many of his contemporaries. Conversely, Papadiamantis's fiction tackles issues such as emigration, endemic poverty, social inequality, and prejudice. A number of his most memorable characters are neither Orthodox nor Greek, such as the kind-hearted Bavarian doctor in *Vardianos sta Sporka*. Many of his protagonists are both victims and victimizers. Papadiamantis's best-known work is *I Phonissa*, subtitled by the author "a social novel". First published in the journal *Panathenia* (1903), the narrative focuses on the activities of an old woman, Frangoyannou, who roams the island of Skiathos killing female infants and is eventually drowned in the sea "midway between divine and human justice".

Although much of Papadiamantis's fiction is written in katharevousa, his writing exploits the full range of the Greek language from the gruff demotic of the local Skiathos idiom, to liturgical Greek, back to antiquity. In a celebrated passage in his short story "The Black-Kerchiefed Woman" (1891), for example, the narrator quotes lines from the *Iliad* when he likens the wind rippling a cornfield to the waves of the sea.

Critical responses to Papadiamantis's fiction have not been unreservedly positive. In his *History of Modern Greek Literature* (1948), the influential critic K.T. Dimaras famously condemned Papadiamantis's myopic vision and the "closed world" which he depicted in his fiction. Critical assessments continue to be polarized between those who construe Papadiamantis as a deeply traditional writer and those who argue that his fiction is, in fact, highly experimental and questioning. In the first case, Papadiamantis's biography provides the overarching framework within which his work must be read, even while his fiction is scrutinized for any documentary evidence it might furnish. In the second case, an attempt is made to ignore extraneous material and concentrate exclusively on exhaustive textual exegeses. Georgos Kechayioglou's structuralist reading of the short story "Love in the Snow" (1981) and Georgia Farinou-Malamatari's pioneering study *Narrative Techniques in Papadiamantis* (1987), for example, draw attention to both the linguistic range of Papadiamantis's prose and to his fiction's innovative narrative strategies. Criticism of Papadiamantis has not been without its share of rancour, as in the acrimonious debate that followed the publication of Panayiotis Moullas's controversial anthology (1974) in which he argued that Papadiamantis's writing was symptomatic of the author's ungratified sexual impulses, and of an overriding feeling of impotence that derived from a dominant father and a suffocating environment. More recently, however, critics have sought to avoid the worst excesses of these formalist and biographical approaches by combining close readings of the texts with an awareness of the wider cultural and political contexts within which Papadiamantis's writing was produced and consumed. The bibliography of secondary work on Papadiamantis is immense. Between 1981 and 1992 a new five-volume edition of the *Collected Works* appeared, edited by Triandaphyllopoulos. In 1992 a Greek journal was established devoted to Papadiamantean studies.

ROBERT SHANNAN PECKHAM

See also Novel

Biography

Born in Skiathos in 1851, Papadiamantis was educated at Chalcis and enrolled at the University of Athens but was forced to abandon his studies. He became a journalist, and later a short-story writer, novelist, and translator. He wrote three historical novels and some 200 short stories and translated many works from French and English. He died in Skiathos in 1911.

Writings

The Murderess, translated by Peter Levi, London and New York:
    Writers and Readers, 1983
Tales from a Greek Island, translated by Elizabeth Constantinides,
    Baltimore: Johns Hopkins University Press, 1987

Further Reading

Beaton, Roderick, "Realism and Folklore in Nineteenth-Century
    Greek Fiction", *Byzantine and Modern Greek Studies*, 8 (1982):
    pp. 103–22
Chryssanthopoulos, Michalis, "Anticipating Modernism:
    Constructing a Genre, a Past, and a Place" in *Greek Modernism
    and Beyond: Essays in Honor of Peter Bien*, edited by Dimitris
    Tziovas, Lanham, Maryland: Rowman and Littlefield, 1997
Constantinides, Elizabeth, "Love and Death: The Sea in the Work of
    Alexandros Papadiamantis", *Modern Greek Studies Yearbook*, 4
    (1988): pp. 99–110
Coutelle, Louis *et al.*, *A Greek Diptych: Dionysios Solomos and
    Alexandros Papadiamantis*, Minneapolis, Minnesota: Nostos,
    1986
Dimitrakopoulos, Fotis, "The Continuing Search for Papadiamantis",
    Modern Greek Studies Yearbook, 7 (1991): pp. 532–38
Mackridge, Peter, "The Textualization of Place in Greek Fiction,
    1883–1903", *Journal of Mediterranean Studies*, 2/2 (1992): pp.
    148–68
Peckham, Robert Shannan, "Memory and Homelands: Vizyinos,
    Papadiamantis and Geographical Imagination", *Kambos*, 3
    (1995): pp. 95–123
Peckham, Robert Shannan, "Papadiamantis, Ecumenism, and the
    Theft of Byzantium" in *Byzantium and the Modern Greek
    Identity*, edited by Paul Magdalino and David Ricks, Aldershot,
    Hampshire: Variorum, 1998
Ricks, David, "Alexandros Papadiamantis and Thomas Hardy" in
    The Greek Novel AD 1–1985, edited by Roderick Beaton,
    London: Croom Helm, 1988
Ricks, David, "Papadiamantis and Homer: A Note", *Byzantine and
    Modern Greek Studies*, 16 (1992): pp. 183–87
Ricks, David, "Papadiamantis, Paganism and the Sanctity of Place",
    Journal of Mediterranean Studies, 2/2 (1992): pp. 169–82
Saunders, Rebecca, "Creating Content: Papadiamantis' *I Fonissa*
    [The Murderess] as an Allegory of Epistemological Treachery",
    Journal of the Hellenic Diaspora, 18I/2 (1992): pp. 55–65
Tziovas, Dimitris, "Diologism and Interpretation: Reading
    Papadiamantis' *A Dream Among the Waters*", *Byzantine and
    Modern Greek Studies*, 17 (1993): pp. 141–60

Papadopoulos, George 1919–1999

Leader of the military junta that seized power in 1967

Born and raised in the rural environs of Patras within a priest's
family, George Papadopoulos grew up in the spirit of middle-
class conservative ideals. An excellent student and cadet, he
had always distinguished himself with high marks and significant rankings. As a result, after graduation from the military
academy in 1940, he was appointed to good positions in the
army, especially in intelligence posts.

As a junior officer, he participated for a short period in the
Albanian campaign and afterwards, like many of his
colleagues, took part in the resistance movement against the
Axis. When Greece was liberated in late 1944, another series
of appointments in the intelligence service was supported by
special training in the USA.

Moving among officers of high standing and displaying
close understanding of the politics of Greece, Papadopoulos
soon became involved with serious-minded groups which were
concerned and worried by the political instability of the
postwar period. Meanwhile, all such groups expressed fears of
the communist threat that resulted from the state of flux of
Greek politics, a threat that was also prolonged by the Cold
War.

Papadopoulos had been a senior officer and had received
broad recognition of his qualities within the military, but he
was unknown to the general public, as he remained away from
the public eye. The only time that his name was publicly
mentioned was in 1964 when, serving in Thrace, he staged the
destruction of military matériel, blaming the incident on the
communists. Following this episode, which offered him
favourable exposure, he was assigned to the First Army group,
and shortly thereafter to the General Army Staff headquarters
in Athens. Political developments stimulated the military hierarchy to concerns about its future as well as the danger of a
liberal government assuming a leading role in national policy
making. This situation caused Papadopoulos and his
colleagues to fear that the eventual return of George
Papandreou to power could mean the restructuring of the
"ranking officers of the armed forces who were, in the main,
anti-communists and supporters of the monarchy".

Fear of the destabilization of the military status quo was the
primary reason on which the colonels moved in on the night of
20 April 1967. Rumours of an imminent coup had circulated
for several months, and it was no surprise to the Athenians,
when waking up on 21 April, to find that the parliamentary
government had been toppled. The race to power was won by
the colonels who, having formed the structure of the armed
forces, were capable of mobilizing them effectively. For some
years a number of groups had been toying with the idea of a
coup, which is why even the identity of those responsible for
21 April represented an enigma for the first few days. Swift
action by the armoured units combined with deployment of
selected personnel under Papadopoulos's instructions enabled
them to assume key positions in the capital, to take over
communication posts, and to detain several thousand citizens
involved in political movements. The coup d'état of April 1967
brought to power a small group of officers led by
Papadopoulos who managed quickly to secure the reins of
power through the imposition of martial law. The king had no
choice but to comply. He accepted the cabinet proposed by the
colonels and placed as its head the former attorney general of
the Supreme Court Konstantinos Kolias, a man who
commanded general respect. Brigadier Stylianos Patakos took
over the Ministry of Interior, and colonel Nikos Makarezos the
Ministry of Coordination. Papadopoulos maintained a low
profile, remaining minister to the prime minister's office.

While the new regime tightened its grip, relations with
representatives of the civil government as well as with foreign
governments continued to deteriorate. The situation in Cyprus
was no closer to a resolution and relations with Turkey became
strained due to the clashes on the island which reached critical
levels in October and November 1967, resulting in casualties.
Turkey threatened to land forces in Cyprus. In an attempt to
reach a compromise Athens recalled general George Grivas
from Cyprus, thereby arresting the guerrilla war against the

British, as well as reducing the Greek forces on the island from several thousand to 950.

The humiliation over Cyprus isolated Papadopoulos and his regime. King Constantine saw this as an opportunity to attempt a counter coup which he staged on 13 December 1967, assisted by the Third Army Corps of Thrace in east Macedonia. This attempt quickly collapsed and the king realized right away that he did not have the support needed for such an undertaking. He fled from the country while the junta began exercising tighter control of the government. This was the moment when Papadopoulos assumed the position of prime minister and minister of national defence.

Greece's isolation had a negative effect especially with regard to relations with the USA and the countries of the Common Market (now the EU). President Johnson suggested that the continuation of military aid to Greece would depend to a great extent on the return to a more democratic system of government. At the same time the Council of Europe threatened Greece with expulsion if steps were not taken towards installing a more democratic government. As a result of these pressures, in September 1968 the regime called for a plebiscite, attempting to legitimize the new constitution of the military government. Signs of weariness eventually began to appear in Papadopoulos's government. The student movement and the large demonstration at the Faculty of Law in Athens signalled the beginning of the end of the colonels' rule. Then discontent and disapproval in the navy, with the destroyer *Velos* under admiral Nikos Pappas defecting to Italy, showed strong evidence of the changing mood of the country, and alerted Papadopoulos and his colleagues who tried to gain a temporary victory by abolishing the monarchy and instituting a republic with Papadopoulos as president. Furthermore, he started meeting, secretly at first, and later publicly, old political figures who would be prepared to participate in an effort to bring democratic rule back to the country in preparation for parliamentary elections. Public opinion, however, did not seem to favour these attempts and the efforts of the junta to impose its authority were rapidly waning. It was then that a serious student demonstration occurred at the Athens Polytechnic which ended in bloodshed on 17 November 1973, halting the efforts of the regime to restore democracy. Papadopoulos was toppled by his colleague Dimitrios Ioanides whom he had appointed from the start of his regime as chief of the military police. Thus the reign of George Papadopoulos came to an end and the new junta took over.

The Ioanides government was even weaker than the Papadopoulos government of late 1973, and in 1974, in an effort to regain lost prestige, general Ioannides attempted to overthrow president Makarios of Cyprus and to bring about the union of the island with Greece. This fatal mistake not only brought about the dramatic fall of the junta, but also resulted in the invasion of the island by Turkey.

In those tragic days, all political parties joined together under the aegis of Constantine Karamanlis, and gradually normal life was resumed in Greek politics and society. As was to be expected, the members of the junta were tried and its leaders were sentenced to death, a penalty which by the personal intervention of premier Karamanlis was commuted to imprisonment for life.

Throughout the duration of his rule, George Papadopoulos proclaimed that Greece is the country of the Christian Greeks and this concept was no doubt well rooted in the dictator's mind. However, power obscured from him the crucial question of how the Greek people felt in their everyday lives about being governed by a man who had been unknown to the general public, but who more importantly had assumed office without the consent of the people.

STELIOS ZACHARIOU

See also Junta

Biography

Born in 1919 near Patras, Papadopoulos graduated from the military academy in 1940. After war service he became involved with right-wing political groups. Fearing destabilization of the military position, he led a coup on 21 April 1967 which resulted in the imposition of a military junta. After a failed counter-coup by the king in December 1967, Papadopoulos became prime minister. He was toppled in 1973 by his colleague Dimitrios Ioanides. The junta was ended in 1974 and its leaders were sentenced to death. Papadopoulos's sentence was commuted to life imprisonment, and he died in 1999.

Further Reading

Clogg, Richard and George Yannopoulos (editors), *Greece under Military Rule*, London, Secker and Warburg, and New York: Basic Books, 1972

Craig, Phylis, "The United States and the Greek Dictatorship", *Journal of the Hellenic Diaspora*, 3 (1976)

Gregoriadis, Solon, *Istoria tis Diktatorias 1967–1974* [History of the Dictatorship 1967–1974] Athens, 1975

Koliopoulos, John S., *Brigands with a Cause: Brigandage and Irredentism in Modern Greece, 1821–1912*, Oxford: Clarendon Press, 1987

Kremmydas, George, *Oi Anthropoi tis Chountas meta ti Dictatoria* [The Men of the Junta after the Dictatorship], Athens, 1984

Markezinis, Spiros, *Anamnisis 1972–1974* [Memoirs 1972–74], Athens, 1979

Meletopoulos, Meletis, *I Diktatoria ton Syntamatarchon* [The Dictatorship of the Colonels], Athens, 1996

Papachelas, Aleksis, *O Viasmos tis Ellinikis Dimocratias: O Americanikos Paragon, 1947–67* [The Rape of Greek Democracy: The American Factor, 1947–67], Athens, 1997

Schwab, Peter and George Frangos, *Greece under the Junta*, New York: Facts on File, 1970, reprinted 1973

Sulzberger, C.L., "Greece under the Colonels", *Foreign Affairs*, 3 (1973)

Woodhouse, C.M., *The Rise and Fall of the Greek Colonels*, London and New York: Granada, 1985

Papagos, Alexandros 1883–1955

Soldier and politician

The son of a lieutenant general, Alexandros Papagos surpassed his father by reaching the rank of field marshal. Following his retirement from the military, he felt compelled by the situation of the country to enter politics, becoming prime minister for the last three years of his life.

He received his basic training in Athens, and enjoyed further military studies in Belgium with the Brussels Military Academy and the Cavalry Institute between 1902 and 1906.

As a result of his brilliant student career he had no difficulty in achieving rapid promotion and important positions. As second lieutenant in 1910 he was assigned as adjunct to the Ministry of the Army, and by 1912, when the Balkan Wars erupted, he was promoted to lieutenant in the cavalry, having been among the officers close to prince Constantine, commander of the Greek armies in Epirus. For his dedication to duty and for his conduct in battle he was commended for bravery in the Bizzani campaign of February 1913, which resulted in the liberation of Epirus by Greek forces. Such distinctions enabled him to achieve high positions: in the first cavalry regiment of Thessalonica, as staff member of the Athens cavalry brigade, staff member of the third Greek army in Thessalonica, and finally, in 1917, a cavalry major.

In 1917 the clashes between royalists and Venizelists reached their peak, dividing the country into two camps and thus affecting the career of the royalist Papagos, who for a while received minor appointments in the Cyclades and Crete away from decision-making locations. In 1920, as lieutenant colonel, he fought in the disastrous Asia Minor campaign and after that, when an "ecumenical" government took over in 1926, he was promoted to the rank of colonel and given the command of the Larissa cavalry division, a position which he held until 1931. Thereafter he served as commander of the Larissa headquarters, and later, as major general, commander of the first and third army groups.

The career of general Papagos in the military was supported by his involvement in politics in which he always stood on the royalist side. In the company of his close colleagues, he became involved in small coups which were commonplace during the turbulent period 1926–1932 in Greece, serving as minister of defence in the governments of Icondilis (10 October 1935–30 November 1935) and Demertzis (19 December 1935–5 March 1936). This brought him membership of cabinets from time to time and, when the military regime of Ioannis Metaxas took over in 1936, the position of inspector general of the army was entrusted to Papagos. Soon thereafter, as the first clouds of World War II began to gather, he was named commander in chief of the army staff headquarters. This position gave him the opportunity to embark on a thorough and rapid restructuring of the Greek armed forces as well as to prepare the defence of the country against the (by then obvious) plans of the Axis to invade Greece through Albania. This sudden invasion was begun by Italy in October 1940, at a time when the greater part of Europe had already been occupied, or had capitulated to the Axis.

Much to the surprise of the military experts and students of history, the efforts to reorganize the army paid off when the Greek forces not only arrested the invasion by Italy, but by counterattacking managed to occupy half the territory of Albania. This represented the first victory of the Allied forces against the Axis, and part of that glory was recognized as being due to General Papagos. As expected, Germany could not ignore the defeat of the Italian forces; nor could Greece continue to be victorious in the Albanian campaign against the Italians. So Hitler helped Mussolini by attacking and occupying Greece in April 1941. The Greek army capitulated and the occupation of Greece followed, bringing immense problems to the people while numerous pockets of resistance sprang up throughout the country.

During the occupation (1941–44) Papagos was arrested and sent to concentration camps in Germany. Upon the defeat of the Axis powers he returned to Greece, devoting most of his time to writing, first his personal experiences in German concentration camps, and then his magnum opus which was an extended military study of the war in Greece of 1940–41 containing much valuable military information.

Highly appreciated for his accomplishments, but lacking popular recognition and high honours, Papagos was promoted to full general by the Greek parliament in 1947. Shortly thereafter, he was recalled to active duty by the national government and placed in charge of the campaign against the communist guerrilla forces.

By September 1949, under the leadership of Papagos, the Greek armed forces had managed to suppress the partisans. In recognition of his qualities and as an expression of the nation's appreciation, Papagos was promoted to field marshal, an honour which had never before been given to a member of the military.

An active and dynamic man like Papagos could not remain idle for very long. Conscious of the needs of his country, he assiduously dedicated himself to the creation of the Ministry of National Defence and the Academy of National Defence. He was also responsible for raising the moral and material standards of enlisted officers and for supervising Greece's membership of international alliances and finally NATO.

Greece, however, had been undergoing a period of political instability since the end of World War II. Antiquated political methods and the weak parliamentary multi-party system remained a barrier to the necessary social and economic development of the war-devastated country. A strong personality was needed to secure Greece in the Western camp, and it was found in marshal Papagos.

Though he had little experience of politics, he recognized the need for a powerful leader, and brought together the old political parties to form the Greek Rally party which in 1952 won a great electoral victory, using a system of proportional representation. Thus marshal Papagos formed a strong cabinet of distinguished personalities, quickly stabilizing the political environment in Greece during the following three years. The economy too showed signs of revival following the devaluation of the drachma on 9 April 1953, healing some of the wounds of the war.

Nevertheless, in 1953 he took the initiative in claiming the independence of Cyprus from Great Britain, resorting to various vague promises made to Greece both before and during World War II. He was also motivated by the British policy at the time of granting independence to countries that had been crown colonies. His claim embittered the British, creating a rift in diplomatic relations. In October 1955, following a period of illness, field marshal Papagos, prime minister of Greece, died. His memory is venerated by the Greek people in general and by the military in particular.

STELIOS ZACHARIOU

Biography

Born in 1883 the son of a soldier, Papagos was educated in Athens and pursued military studies in Brussels from 1902 to 1906. He served in the Balkan Wars of 1912–13 and in 1917 supported the royalist side against Venizelos. He fought in the Asia Minor campaign in 1920–1922. As chief of general staff under Metaxas he restructured the armed forces which gave him credit for the success in Albania in 1940. After the war he entered politics and became prime minister from 1952 until his death in 1955.

Further Reading

Charalambis, Dimitris, *Stratos kai Politiki Exousia: I Domi tis Exousias stin Metemphilaki Ellada* [The Military and Political Power: The Structure of Power in Postwar Greece], Athens, 1985

Close, David (editor), *The Greek Civil War: Studies of Polarization*, London and New York: Routledge, 1993

Papagos, Alexandros, *Dyo Chronia sta Stratopeda Synkentroseos tis Germanias* [Two Years in the Concentration Camps of Germany], Athens, 1945

Papagos, Alexandros, *The Battle of Greece, 1940–1941*, translated by Pat Eliascos, Athens: Alpha, 1949

Papagos, Alexandros, "Guerrilla Warfare", *Foreign Affairs*, 30/2 (1952): pp. 215–30

Papagos, Alexandros, *O Ellinikos Stratos kai pros Polemon Proparaskevi ton 1923–1940* [The Greek Army and Preparations for War 1923–1940], Athens, 1953

Stavrou, Nikolaos, *Symmachiki Politiki kai Stratiotikes Epemvaseis* [Allied Politics and Military Interventions: The Political Role of the Greek Military], Athens, 1976

Woodhouse, C.M., *The Apple of Discord: A Survey of Recent Greek Politics in their International Setting*, London and New York: Hutchinson, 1948

Papanastasiou, Alexandros 1876/79–1936

Founder and prime minister of the first Greek republic

Alexandros Papanastasiou was born in Tripolis, in the Peloponnese, the second son of a schoolmaster holding a PhD in philology who was later head of directory at the ministry of education. His studies at the law faculty of Athens University (1895–99) were followed by graduate studies in sociology, politics, and economics in Heidelberg and Berlin (1901–05) and further studies in London and Paris (1905–07). On his return to Athens Papanastasiou played the leading role in the foundation of the Sociological Society (1908) and its journal, *Social and Law Sciences Review*. He supported the modernization-motivated Goudi military coup of 1909, to whose leader colonel N. Zorbas the Sociological Society submitted a reform programme drafted by Papanastasiou. In 1910, with the members of the Sociological Society and on a reformative socialist platform, he founded the People's Party, which from 1915 was to become the left wing of Venizelos's Liberal Party.

Papanastasiou first entered parliament as a People's Party deputy for Arcadia in the first revisionary national assembly of August 1910 and again in the second one of November 1910, heading a seven-member group of the so-called Sociologists. He volunteered in the first Balkan War, taking part in campaigns on Chios and in Epirus. In the National Schism in 1916 he followed E. Venizelos in the establishment of a parallel/rival provisional government in Thessalonica. As its representative in the Ionian islands he succeeded in June 1917 in organizing the landing of Greek and French troops in Preveza, thus blocking the Italian advance in Epirus. He first held ministerial office as minister of communications (1917–20) in the

1917 Venizelos government formed in the wake of king Constantine I's departure and Venizelos's return to Athens as unopposed premier. In this capacity he worked hard for the reconstruction of Thessalonica and other damaged towns in Macedonia.

Following Venizelos's surprise defeat in the election of November 1920, and the return of Constantine to the throne, sanctioned by a rigged plebiscite, Papanastasiou expressed bitter criticism of the monarchy. With his *Republican Manifesto* of 12 February 1922 he pronounced against the return of Constantine as endangering the advantageous position Greece had attained by the Treaty of Sèvres (1920). Arrested for this and sentenced to three years' imprisonment, he was released in the wake of colonel Nikolaos Plastiras's military coup of 1922. Meanwhile, alienated from Venizelos and the Liberal Party, he founded the Republican Union in 1922 as a republican coalition of lower middle, agrarian, and working classes to pursue a purely anti-royalist policy. Following the election of December 1923, he entered the fourth Constituent Assembly as head of 70 deputies of his party (out of 398). In January 1924, within one month of the forced departure of king George II from Greece "on leave", Papanastasiou, as leader of the opposition in the national assembly, proposed the abolition of the monarchy and the establishment of a republic. This he effected as prime minister in his first government, formed on 12 March 1924, with the proclamation of the first Greek republic on 25 March 1924, fully ratified by plebiscite (receiving support of 69.95 per cent) the following month. Despite its parliamentary character, the Papanastasiou cabinet retained an authoritarian stance due to its distinct association with a group of "republican" army officers. Within four months the authority of his government had been sufficiently injured, especially because of the inextricable as well as troubled civil–military relationship, to step down on 19 July, after defiance broke out in the navy.

Initially tolerant, in fact conciliatory, towards general Pangalos's coup of 25 June 1925 and the general's early disingenuous maneouvres for a civil cabinet, Papanastasiou came out in time overtly against the dictatorship, and was banished to the island of Santorini in February 1926, as a result of his protests at the suppression of *Democracy*, his party's press organ. In the election of November 1926, following the restoration of the republic, the Republican Union, now subtitled "Agrarian and Labour Party", won 6.48 per cent of the vote and 17 seats in the assembly. Papanastasiou participated in the all-party government of Zaimis in December 1926, taking on the ministry of agriculture (1926–28). Within the term of office of the same assembly, he was elected head of the parliamentary committee on the promulgation of the republican constitution of 1927. In the election of August 1928 Papanastasiou's Republican Union / Agrarian and Labour Party cooperated with the Liberal Party and won 6.71 per cent of the vote and 20 seats in the assembly.

In October 1929 Papanastasiou presided at the peace conference held in Athens, where he expounded the idea of Balkan union as a model for that of the European states. One year later he chaired the first Balkan Conference in Thessalonica, achieving distinction for his dedicated work on the idea of Balkan cooperation. This initiative he pursued with unfailing interest at the ensuing Balkan conferences held from

1931 to 1933. In the same years he attended international congresses of agrarian and radical parties.

Papanastasiou formed his second ephemeral government in May 1932, but resigned eight days later over a quarrel with the Liberals relating to the social care issue. He became deputy for Mantinea in the election of September 1932, his Agrarian and Labour Party winning 5.89 per cent of the vote and 8 seats. He last held office as minister of national economy and (provisionally) agriculture in the last Venizelos government in January 1933. He was elected a senator in March 1933 but resigned a few weeks later. Persecuted and arrested in the abortive Venizelist coup in March 1935, he was eventually acquitted by a military court. He abstained with his party from the election of June 1935. He opposed the Kondylis dictatorship and pronounced publicly against the scheduled, and finally rigged, plebiscite of November 1935 for the return of king George II. He won a seat as deputy in the election of January 1936, his party commanding seven seats in the revisionary assembly. He died in Ekali, Attica, in November 1936 during the dictatorship established that August by General Metaxas, to whom, as president of a still parliamentary government in April, Papanastasiou had denied a vote of confidence.

Papanastasiou represents a revitalizing and socialist-oriented element in Greek political and social thinking of the first decades of the 20th century. His ideas were related to the rise of socio-economic and political radicalism before and during the interwar period; they may be traced back to the ideological and intellectual trend that began in the late 19th century with the inchoate efforts of the first Greek socialists. In the light of his sociological background he initiated a seminal discourse on the social question of Greece and drew attention to cardinal matters of social justice and economic development, notably land reform and the protection of the lower and working classes. His sociologists, combining academic prestige with political action, played a leading role within and outside the national assembly, and exerted influence on Venizelos's Liberals to promote the modernization of Greek society. The views he put forward, pioneering to a significant extent, came as a response to the country's vague quest for a renewal, which found its earliest expression in the Goudi military coup. Already in the programme he drafted then, unambiguously entitled "What is to be done?", he had comprised a constellation of measures to give substance to the call for a modern state, including distribution of çiftliks (large estates), general income tax, educational reform, proportional electoral system, compulsory social security for the workers, etc. In line with this, he aspired with increasing militancy in his political career to the reform of iniquitous institutions, democratization of the state, and to the elevation of the feebler social strata in all aspects of life. Education attracted his particular care, including training for former dropouts, and, as first republican premier, he founded the Thessalonica university, despite mounting reactions.

In foreign policy Papanastasiou stood for the union of the Balkan states, reviving the prerevolutionary vision of Rigas, and attended all four Balkan Conferences held from 1930 to 1933, behind which he was the driving force. Regarding Graeco-Turkish relations, in particular, he saw in the 1922 Catastrophe and the ensuing exchange of populations, which removed a perennial source of discord, an opportunity for a lasting understanding between the two countries, a policy that was realized shortly afterwards by Venizelos.

RENNOS EHALIOTIS

Biography

Born in the late 1870s in Tripolis in Arcadia, the son of a schoolmaster, Papanastasiou studied law at the University of Athens and continued his studies in Heidelberg, Berlin, London, and Paris. In 1910 he founded the People's Party and entered parliament that year as deputy for Arcadia. He served as minister of communications in Venizelos's government of 1917–20. Imprisoned for his *Republican Manifesto* in 1922, he became prime minister of the first Greek Republic in 1924–25. He was a supporter of Balkan union. He died in 1936.

Further Reading

Alexandros Papanastasiou: Oi Koinonikes, Oikonomikes kai Politike Apopseis tou [Alexandros Papanastasiou: His Social, Economic and Political Views], Proceedings of the Conference held at Panteion University, Athens, 1990

"Alexandros Papanastasiou: To Peirama tis Avasilevtis" [Alexandros Papanastasiou: The Experiment of the Republic], *Istorika*, 22 (16 March 2000), special issue

Christidis, C., *I Dekaetia tis Dimokratias: pou Vriskomaste, pou Pame; Dokimion politikis deontologias* [The Decade of the Republic: Where are We? Where are we Heading? Essay in Political Ethics], Athens, 1934

Dafnis, Grigorios, *I Ellas metaxy dyo Polemon, 1923–1940* [Greece between Two Wars, 1923–1940], Athens, 1955

Dafnis, Grigorios, *Ta Ellinika Politika Kommata, 1821–1961* [The Greek Political Parties, 1821–1961], 2 vols, Athens, 1961, reprinted 1997 (see especially vol. 1)

Grigoriadis, Foivos N., *Elliniki Dimokratia (1924–1935)* [Greek Democracy (1924–1935)], Athens, 1973

Istoria tou Ellinikou Ethnous [History of the Greek Nation], vol. 15, Athens, 1978, pp. 271–393

Kaltchas, Nicholas, *Introduction to the Constitutional History of Modern Greece*, New York: Columbia University Press, 1940

Kastrinos, Nikos S., *Al. Papanastasiou: O Anamorphotis kai i Dimokratia* [Al. Papanastasiou: The Reformer and Democracy], Athens, 1975

Kordatos, Yannis, *Istoria tou Ellinikou Agrotikou Kinimatos* [History of the Greek Agrarian Movement], Athens, 1963

Mavrogordatos, George T., *Stillborn Republic: Social Coalitions and Party Strategies in Greece, 1922–36*, Berkeley: University of California Press, 1983

Mazower, Mark, *Greece and the Inter-War Economic Crisis*, Oxford: Clarendon Press, and New York: Oxford University Press, 1991

Papanastasiou, Alexandros, *Meletes, Logoi, Arthra* [Studies, Speeches, Articles], edited by X. Levkoparidis, 2 vols, Athens, 1957, reprinted 1988

Vellay, C., "La République Hellénique: le declin de la dynastie et la formation de la République", *L'Europe Nouvelle* (16 August 1924)

Veremis, Thanos, *The Military in Greek Politics: From Independence to Democracy*, London: Hurst, 1997; Buffalo, New York: Black Rose, 1998

Waterlow, Sidney, "Decline and Fall of Greek Democracy, 1933–1936", *Political Quarterly*, 18 (April 1947): pp. 95–106; and 19 (July 1947): pp. 205–19

Papandreou family

Georgios Papandreou (1888–1968) was born in the village of Kalentzi in the Peloponnese and studied law at Athens and political science in Germany. A politician of the liberal centre, he became prime minister of the Greek government in exile in Cairo during the war and faced the communist insurrection upon his return to Athens in the winter of 1944. He found his true calling in Greek politics late in his life as the rallying force of a wide coalition that made up the Centre Union Party and challenged the authority of a conservative state. He defeated Constantine Karamanlis's ruling party in the elections of 1963 but resigned from his office as prime minister because of his disagreement with king Constantine II over the control of the military. This crisis of the mid-1960s caused the subsequent military intervention of 1967.

His flamboyant style and his turbulent family life left an indelible mark on his elder son, Andreas Papandreou (1919–96) who was born in Chios while his father was the prefect of the island. Andreas began his studies at Athens University and completed them at Harvard. He became part of the "new left" establishment in the USA during his career as professor of economics at Minnesota and Berkeley, and returned to Greece in 1961 to head the Centre for Economic Studies. He was elected deputy of Achaea in 1964 and served as minister of coordination in his father's Centre Union government between 1964 and 1965. As the left-wing advocate of his party he became a prime target of the military junta that took over in 1967. He was released from confinement through the intervention of US president Lyndon Johnson and allowed to leave the country. Throughout his years in exile he campaigned against the military regime and founded the Panhellenic Liberation Movement (PAK) which was later transformed into the Panhellenic Socialist Movement (PASOK). He returned to Greece two months after the fall of the junta and became a leading light of the political scene. He was a member of parliament from 1974 to 1996 and prime minister from 1981 to 1989 and 1993 to 1996.

Andreas Papandreou has been the most accomplished turncoat in Greek politics. A person of immense personal charm and with an intelligence quotient that towered over his own generation of politicians, he performed about-turns in policy without alienating his supporters. When the ratification of Greece's accession treaty to the European Community was brought before parliament for discussion in 1980, Papandreou and his PASOK deputies walked out of the debate and declared their unyielding opposition to the EC. Once in power (a year and half later), this negative attitude was dropped as $800 million from EC funds were directed to Greece's rural areas. In his second term he became the champion of the EC in Greece.

Papandreou's most significant action as premier *vis-à-vis* the EC was the Greek Memorandum which set conditions to future enlargement demanding the implementation of the "Intregrated Mediterranean Programmes" designed to finance and assist Mediterranean countries of the EC with structural impediments to development. At the December 1985 summit in Luxembourg, Papandreou withdrew his reservation for the amendment of the Rome Treaty which would facilitate the decision-making process in the EC by limiting the use of the veto. The measure was advantageous to the Community's larger members and Papandreou's cooperativeness was rewarded with the formal recognition of the "convergence" between the economic structures of member countries – a principle which favoured the weaker states, including Greece.

While in opposition (1974–81), Papandreou vowed that his future government would withdraw Greece from NATO and remove American bases from Greek soil. However, his defence policy after his October 1981 electoral victory did not deviate substantially from that of his predecessors. In 1983 he signed an agreement with the United States that renewed the tenure of American installations and then celebrated with his followers the beginning of the process of removing the US bases from Greece.

Papandreou's foreign policies, stripped of their more sensational declaratory aspects, were not as different from those of many other Western states as was widely believed. Yet he insisted on creating the impression of being a far greater maverick than his actions would seem to imply. In doing so he was addressing a Greek public that was thrilled with the prospect of attracting European attention after years of docile agreement on basic Western tenets of foreign and security policy. Furthermore, his tactics of appearing as an uncompromising champion of Greek interests, combined with widespread promises of social benefits, were the binding tissue that kept the wide spectrum of his followers together.

During Papandreou's terms in power, a significant income redistribution was effected but this was not accompanied by economic growth and was mostly financed by loans. The implication of this social policy was that its cost would burden future taxpayers.

As a politician who improvised from day to day, rather than planning ahead, Papandreou postponed confronting the mounting problem of Greece's debts until his final term in office. By then his health did not allow him more than a few hours of work per day, but somehow this last term proved to be the most constructive. After a bumpy start, Greece improved relations with Albania and FYROM (Former Yugoslav Republic of Macedonia) and the economic ministers imposed an austerity programme in line with European Union convergence requirements, which survived Papandreou's leadership.

He was survived by three sons and one daughter. His eldest, Giorgos, was in 1998 alternate foreign minister.

THANOS M. VEREMIS

Further Reading

Couloumbis, T.A., "Karamanlis and Papandreou: Style and Substance of Leadership", ELIAMEP, *Yearbook 1988*, 1989, pp. 129–49

Keramas, V., *To Aporrito Imerologio sto Kastri* [The Secret Diary of Kastri], Athens, 1989

Kouloglou, Stelios, *Sta Ichni tou Tritou Dromou: PASOK 1974–1986* [On the Tracks of the Third Way: PASOK 1974–1986], Athens, 1986

Papandreou, Andreas, *Democracy at Gunpoint: The Greek Front*, Harmondsworth: Penguin, 1973

Papandreou, Andreas, *I Ellada ston Kosmo: Exoteriki Politiki* [Greece in the World: Foreign Policy], Athens, 1994

Paraskevopoulos, Photis, *Andreas Papandreou: I Politiki Poria tou 1960–95* [Andreas Papandreou: His Political Path, 1960–95], Athens, 1995

Paparrigopoulos, Konstantinos 1815–1891

Historian

Konstantinos Paparrigopoulos is known as the national historiographer of Greece. He lived in a period of rapid changes in the Balkans, interminable political struggles, and ideological resurrections both outside and within the newly established independent Greek state. Born in Constantinople, he would have been raised and educated within the illustrious Phanariot society of rich merchants if the revolutionary events of 1821 had not left him an orphan and his family obliged to look for a safer environment in Odessa. It was not until 1830 that his family sought a permanent residence in Greece. The youthful Konstantinos never received a university education, but he had the advantage of attending classes given by the liberal Georgios Gennadios (1786–1854). Practically a self-made scholar, he became a polymath and a polyglot, as shown by his remarkable familiarity with the principal French, German, and English works on Greek history. From 1834 to 1845 he worked for the Greek Ministry of Justice, but resigned because of the rivalry between the native (*autochthones*) citizens, who were supposed to have actively participated in the revolution and thus the destinies of the nation, and the freshly settled immigrants, only nominally Greek (the *eterochthones*), the educated elite. This rivalry, indicative of the factional strife that plagued Greek society, was indeed a traumatic experience for Paparrigopoulos, but it convinced him that his compatriots needed to subscribe to a higher vision of national unity in order to override sectional interests. The propagation of such a vision in the 1840s, rooted in the irredentist Great Idea, provided the essential political and intellectual stimulus that turned him into the historiographer of Hellenism par excellence.

Before his appointment as professor of history at the University of Athens in February 1851, Paparrigopoulos published several studies related to historical issues either as monographs or as newspaper articles – some of them subsequently included in his *Istorikai Pragmateiai* (Historical Essays, Athens, 1858). The starting point of his literary career may be considered his work *Peri tis Epoikiseos Slavikon tinon Phylon eis tin Peloponnison* (On the Slavic Colonies in the Peloponnese, 1843), followed by his *To Teleutaion Etos tis Ellinikis Elevtherias* (The Last Year of Greek Freedom, 1844). The former was a critical reply to Jakob Philipp Fallmerayer, who in his *Geschichte der Halbinsel Morea während des Mittelalters* (2 vols, Stuttgart, 1830–36) maintained that after the extensive Slavic conquests at the close of the 8th century the original population of northern Greece had practically disappeared. Thus the modern Greeks, according to Fallmerayer, were Byzantinized Slavs. Coming at a time when the Greeks were seeking that necessary consciousness of their identity and pre-statehood nationality with a view to enlarging their frontiers to take in the huge non-liberated lands, which included (*inter alia*) Constantinople and the coastal regions of Asia Minor, such discouraging racist theories as Fallmerayer's naturally caused widespread resentment. For Paparrigopoulos, it was essential to show that casting doubts on the archaic origins of the modern Hellenes, and thereby depriving them of the distinction of having preserved and even consolidated

Orthodoxy during the Byzantine period, was wrong as a "scientific" historical account and pernicious for the nation's self-consciousness and development. In the latter work, Paparrigopoulos examined the fall of Greece to the Romans in 146 BC. The substance of his theoretical approach to the study of Greek history is there delineated clearly and unequivocally, and his faith in the continuity of the Greek nation is pervasive. Discord and division are recurrent themes in the traceable chain of Greek historical development, yet the concept of unity through evolution should predominate in any thoughtful examination of Greek history.

The aims and ideas presented throughout Paparrigopoulos's early writings place him directly in the camp of the conservative, anti-modernist Neohellenic intelligentsia, which was concerned with affirming the legitimacy of irredentism by invoking historical, broadly cultural, and religious factors. Romantic nationalism and religious fundamentalism contributed to the decline of the liberal tenets of the 18th- and early 19th-century Greek Enlightenment, and inevitably clashed with its enthusiasm for westernized educational and institutional reforms. Markos Renieris (1815–97) in his *Dokimion Philosophias tis Istorias* (Essay on the Philosophy of History, Athens, 1841) confidently declared the collapse of individualism and asserted the superiority of the Christian religion over the secularist tendencies of the 18th century, associating the failure of the Enlightenment with the historically justified political aspirations of Greece in the east. The genuinely ideological use of historiography becomes manifest in the works of Paparrigopoulos's predecessors. In his preface to *I Konstantinoupolis* (Constantinople, 1851) Skarlatos Byzantios (1798–1878), while arguing that medieval Hellenism and the Byzantine empire are part and parcel of Greek history, tried to establish the unbroken continuity of the Greek nation. Spiridon Zambelios (1815–81), in the Introduction to his *Asmata Dimotika tis Ellados* (Greek Popular Folk Songs, 1852) and *Byzantinai Meletai* (Byzantine Studies, 1857), highlighted the inexorable religious and ethnic bonds of the Byzantines with the modern Greeks. The national continuity was similarly emphasized by turning attention to the glorious – usually Christianized – Classical past, the defeat of the Persians, the Athenian empire, and the civilizing march of the Graeco-Macedonians in the east under Alexander the Great. In several texts replete with linguistic archaisms (serving as a proof of the diachronic unity of Hellenism), Alexander emerged as the symbol of Greek unity and provided the impetus for recovering the universal glory of the past. Konstantinos Asopios's speech of 1856 as the new rector of the university was characteristically devoted to Alexander. In introducing the new version of his speech (Athens, 1858), he stressed once again that the king of Macedon was the symbol of unity for the Greeks (*symbolon enotitos*). Not surprisingly, J.G. Droysen's *Geschichte Alexanders des Grossen* (Berlin, 1833) was very popular and a Greek translation by K. Frearitis was published in 1859.

The ground for Paparrigopoulos had been chalked out. Between 1849 and 1852 he issued a *General History of Greece* for use in schools, covering the Classical period and the Middle Ages, a prelude to the magnum opus that followed. In its two volumes he stands out prominently as the ideological spokesman for Greece. The ethnological continuity of the

Greek people is traced through three substantially interconnected stages of their historical development. At each stage, the nation had fulfilled a great mission: the Classical period gave to the nation (and indeed the whole of humankind) the institutional and normative framework of political existence; Byzantium fulfilled the apostolic duties of Christianity; during the third period, which started with the liberation from the Ottoman yoke, the nation is destined to fulfil the political and religious programme of the Great Idea. In his *Istoria tou Ellinikou Ethnous* (History of the Greek Nation, 5 vols, Athens, 1864–75) Paparrigopoulos went even further, arguing that the nation's pagan ancestors, and especially the Macedonians Philip and Alexander, were predestined by divine providence (*theia pronoia*) to pave the way for the Greek Christian empire that flourished in the Byzantine era.

The arguments put forward in the *History* are scholarly and the investigations conducted often exhaustive. But Paparrigopoulos was concerned with the development of national consciousness. He was a servant of Greek society and wrote history in a manner that had meaning and significance for his audience. He believed in progress from age to age, in which however the past was ineradicably embedded in the present. To some extent Paparrigopoulos followed contemporary historians in western Europe who envisaged the unfolding of the past as subject to a series of general laws. In his "Poion to ek tis Istorias Ophelos, kai Pos Deon na Spoudazomen autin" (What is the Use of History, and How We Must Study It, *Amyna*, 4 February 1872) he insisted on an "immutable and universal law of humanity", which he immediately resolved into a cofunctioning of "external change" with "a cluster of immovable ethical values". On another level, a nation is subject to its own particular historical laws such as those revolving around patriotism, religion, and language. The annals of history instruct that no nation can ever attain glory through the unchecked exercise of "infidelity, lawlessness, licentiousness, ignorance". Earlier Paparrigopoulos defined the "technical" qualifications required of a historian: precision, good judgement, ability to elaborate on the character of historical actors, imagination in recreating the past, excellent use of the linguistic apparatus (*History*, vol. 2, Athens, 1862, pp.106–07). Paparrigopoulos was well read in European historiography. The names of E. Gibbon, F. Guizot, the liberal utilitarian G. Grote, the representatives of the romantic school J. Michelet and A. Thierry, T.B. Macaulay, and many others are often mentioned in his narrative. Indeed his familiarity with scholars with diverse approaches to historical material is striking. Some of them were distinguished representatives of the interdisciplinary, empirical *Altertumswissenschaft* (science of antiquity). Paparrigopoulos was competent to apply the new streams to his subject, but Greece urgently needed a moralizing prophet and a dramatist of the achievement and the imperishable glories of the nation.

The "Epilogue" of the *History* was published independently in 1877, summarizing the major themes and arguments. A French version appeared as *Histoire de la civilisation hellénique* (Paris, 1878). A second and final edition of his *History* appeared between 1885 and 1887. During the last years of his life he was actively engaged in politics and diplomacy. He was involved in the Association for the Propagation of Greek Letters, which claimed on the basis of E. Stanford's new ethnological map (London, 1877) that Macedonia as far north as the Balkan mountains was predominantly Greek; he also presided over the Central Committee of the Council of National Defence, established to coordinate and support the revolutionary movements at the time of the eastern crisis, in which the irredentist ambitions of Greece culminated. At the close of his life he published another volume of *Istorikai Pragmateiai* (Historical Treatises, Athens, 1889), and left his "last will", *Ta Didaktikotera Porismata tis Istorias tou Ellinikou Ethnous* (The Didactic Conclusions of the History of the Greek Nation) to be published posthumously in 1899.

Paparrigopoulos's legacy was by any standard prodigious. His treatment of Classical Greece reproduced to a great extent the conclusions of European historiographers, but his handling of the Byzantine Greeks broke new ground. Ideology and erudition coalesce in his historical masterpiece. His successors at the University of Athens, especially Spyridon Lampros (1851–1919), Pavlos Karolidis (1849–1930), Konstantinos Amantos (1874–1960), and Sokratis Kougeas (1876–1966), persevered in exploring aspects of the "unity and continuity" of Greek history, with emphasis on the restoration and rehabilitation of Byzantium. Most importantly, Paparrigopoulos's scheme of the historical development of the Greek people (invested with moral and Christian overtones) which was designed to forge national consciousness and encourage irredentism, despite its obvious contextuality, still informs central aspects of contemporary cultural and political discourse: occasional idealization of historical figures, educational Hellenocentrism, the rhetoric over the unbroken line from the ancient to the modern Greeks, incidental resort to nationalist doctrines, and romantic historicism to distract from pressing social and economic problems are not uncommon in Greece today. It is not unrelated to the ever-pervasive appeal of Paparrigopoulos that the *History* passed through another edition, this time rendered in modern Greek, in 1983. Interestingly, the historian has lately become a source of constant reference. It is a common practice among social scientists who are searching into the origins of Greek nationalism to reduce Paparrigopoulos to a mere propagandist of the Great Idea whose prejudices fatally flawed his historical understanding. In doing so not only do they underestimate the copious scholarship and ignore the various influences that converge in his work, but they also misinterpret the ideological stance of the *History* as being the *History* itself.

KYRIACOS DEMETRIOU

See also Great Idea, Historiography

Biography

Born in Constantinople in 1815, Paparrigopoulos fled with his family to Odessa in 1821, then in 1830 they moved to Greece. He did not receive a university education but attended classes given by Georgios Gennadios and published a number of historical works before being appointed Professor of History at the University of Athens in 1851. His five-volume *History of the Greek Nation* appeared in 1864–75. In his last years he was involved in politics and diplomacy. He died in 1891.

Further Reading

Dimaras, K.T., *La Grèce au temps des Lumières*, Geneva: Droz, 1969

Dimaras, K.T., *Paparrigopoulos: Istoria tou Ellinikou Ethnous (i proti morphi: 1853)* [Paparrigopoulos: *History of the Greek Nation* (First Version: 1853)], Athens, 1970

Dimaras, K.T., *Paparrigopoulos: Prolegomena*, Athens, 1970

Dimaras, K.T., *A History of Modern Greek Literature*, Albany: State University of New York Press, 1972

Dimaras, K.T., *Konstantinos Paparrigopoulos: I Epochi tou, I Zoi tou, to Ergo tou* [Konstantinos Paparrigopoulos: His Times, Life and Work], Athens, 1986

Gooch, G.P., *History and Historians in the Nineteenth Century*, London and New York: Longman, 1928, 2nd edition, 1958

Henderson, G.P., *The Revival of Greek Thought, 1620–1830*, Edinburgh: Scottish Academic Press, 1971

Kitromilides, Paschalis M., "To Istoriographiko Ekkremes kai i Konst. Paparrigopoulos" [The Historiographical Pendulum and Konstantinos Paparrigopoulos], *Nea Estia*, 130/1546 (1991): pp. 1571–78

Kitromilides, Paschalis M., *Enlightenment, Nationalism, Orthodoxy: Studies in the Culture and Political Thought of South-Eastern Europe*, Aldershot, Hampshire: Variorum, 1994

Kitromilides, Paschalis M., *Neoellininikos Diaphotismos* [The Modern Greek Enlightenment], Athens, 1996

Kofos, Evangelos, *Greece and the Eastern Crisis, 1875–1878*, Thessalonica: Institute for Balkan Studies, 1975

Laios, G.A., "Konstantinos Paparrigopoulos", *Mnimosyni*, 5 (1974–75): pp. 284–324

Nes Estia, 130/1546 (1991), special issue: "Afieroma ston K.P.: ekato chronia apo to thanato tou"

Ricks, David and Paul Magdalino (editors), *Byzantium and the Modern Greek Identity*, Aldershot, Hampshire: Ashgate, 1998

Veloudis, G., *O Jakob Philipp Fallmerayer kai i Genesi tou Ellinikou Istorismou* [Jakob Philipp Fallmerayer and the Birth of Greek Historiography], Athens, 1982

Paphos

City in Cyprus

The kingdom of Paphos was already established in the 12th century BC, together with the other kingdoms of Cyprus which flourished mainly in the 1st millennium BC. The site of ancient Paphos (often referred to as Palaipaphos) lies about 15 km southeast of the modern town of Paphos, at a distance of about 1 km from the sea, under the houses of the modern village of Kouklia. In the 1950s the French archaeologist Jean Bérard tried to prove through excavation that ancient Paphos was situated near the northern outskirts of the modern town, but the results were negative.

The site of Old Paphos has been known since the 19th century, mainly because of the remains of the temple of Aphrodite which survived above ground. It was then that the first excavations were carried out, and the first inscriptions from the site of the temple were brought to light which mention the Great Goddess of Cyprus. According to legend the founder of Paphos was Kinyras, representing the indigenous population, but at the end of the Trojan War (soon after 1200 BC) the king of the Arcadians, Agapenor, came to the island with other Arcadians and founded a city of which he became the king. Behind these myths may lie the historical events which are attested by archaeological evidence, namely the beginning of the Achaean colonization of Paphos. Paphos must

have been an important urban centre during the 12th century BC. This is reflected by the magnificence of the architectural remains of the temple of Aphrodite and the wealth of the tombs excavated in the Evreti locality which yielded gold jewellery, carved ivory mirror handles, seals, and other artifacts. The Achaeans mingled with the local population and by the 11th century BC, when the process of colonization was completed, there is evidence for the use of the Greek language in the area. On a bronze skewer, found in a tomb of the 11th century BC, there is an engraved inscription with the Greek name Opheltes in the genitive in a form which is peculiar to the Arcadian dialect. Extensive excavations in the early Geometric cemeteries of Old Paphos have brought to light ample evidence for the influence which the Achaeans exercised on the material culture of Paphos (pottery, bronzes, and other objects) as well as on tomb architecture. It should be mentioned here that it is in the tombs of Paphos that there is material evidence for early contact with the Levantine coast, clearly the result of trade which may have been the source of wealth for the Paphians.

Recent archaeological excavations at the site of the temple of Aphrodite have proved beyond any doubt that the original temple was established early in the 12th century BC. It may have been dedicated to a local goddess of fertility, whose worship had a long tradition in the area of Paphos (since the Chalcolithic period). By the time of the Homeric epics, however, the temple is known as the temple of Aphrodite. It was to Paphos, according to Homer, that Aphrodite fled after she had been caught red-handed by her husband Hephaestus in her love affair with Ares. There she had a temple with a fragrant altar (*Odyssey*, 8. 360–66). The temple must have contributed considerably not only to the fame of Paphos as a religious centre throughout the Hellenic world and also the Levantine region, but also to the economic growth of the town. The goddess of Cyprus, Aphrodite, is referred to in Greek literature as Kypris or Paphia. Paphos is comparable to Delphi; the Greek lexicographer Hesychius (1st century AD) refers to Paphos and Delphi as the "omphalos of the earth".

The actual remains of the 12th-century BC temple are too scanty to allow an accurate reconstruction. Based on representations of the temple on seals and coins dating from the Hellenistic and Roman periods, it may be suggested that the original temple consisted of a large courtyard with a perimeter wall constructed of large well-hewn blocks of stone, some of which still survive in situ. There must have been a tripartite structure (as shown in later representations), a holy-of-holies, in the central part of which the sacred aniconic symbol of the goddess, a conical meteoric stone which actually survived, was kept.

The history of Paphos during the early decades of the 1st millennium BC is known mainly from archaeological discoveries in its rich cemeteries. In particular, a tomb of the 8th–7th centuries BC yielded not only rich tomb gifts, but also evidence of special funerary customs, namely the sacrifice of horses with their bronze gear; there were also iron firedogs and skewers, a bronze shield, pottery imported from the Aegean, bronze vessels, and other grave goods. This was not the tomb of an ordinary man. Both the architecture of the tomb and the wealth of the gifts which it contained justify comparison with the "royal" tombs of Salamis, where members of the royal family or prominent citizens, members of the aristocratic elite,

Paphos: interior decoration of a kalathos of the 11th century BC found in a tomb at Xerolimni

were buried. Numerous terracotta votive figurines have been found in the area of the temple of Aphrodite which betray the two cultural traditions to be found in Paphos, and also throughout the island, during the Archaic period, when the island was under the Assyrians: the Greek tradition illustrated by figurines of the goddess with uplifted arms, a type which was introduced from the Aegean in the 11th century BC, and figurines of a Phoenician type.

Assyrian rule over Paphos and the rest of Cyprus is reflected by the so-called prism of the Assyrian king Esarhaddon, which commemorated the reconstruction of the royal palace at Nineveh in 673/72 BC. Ten tribute-paying kings of Cyprus are mentioned, one of whom is "Ituandar, king of Pappa". His name is Greek, Eteandros, which is known also from other inscriptions. Other kings of Paphos with Greek names are also known from inscriptions of the 6th century BC, namely Stasis and his son Onasicharis.

Paphos suffered the same political fate as the other cities of Cyprus. After the Assyrians, the Egyptians ruled Cyprus for a while (669–545 BC). In 545 the kings of Cyprus submitted voluntarily to Cyrus, king of Persia, whose rule was ruthless. Paphos took part in the Ionian revolt against the Persians, together with the other cities of Cyprus, in 499. The Persian army besieged Paphos and a fierce battle was fought outside the northeast gate of the city. Archaeological excavation revealed some dramatic moments of this siege. The Persians built a mound outside the gate to reach the height of the city walls, but the besieged undermined it with countersiege works. To build the siege mound the Persians used stones and sculptures pillaged from a nearby Archaic sanctuary. The sculptures include fine heads of limestone, some of them illustrating Egyptianizing stylistic trends, but other sculptures such as a marble winged sphinx betray the influence of Greek art. Mention should be made of the discovery of a Greek bronze helmet, no doubt belonging to a Greek soldier who defended the city against the Persians. Paphos, together with the other cities of Cyprus, fell under the Persian yoke once more.

The names of several kings of Paphos of the Classical period are known from their coinage. One of the best known is king Nikokles. He seems to have objected to the lust of the cult of Aphrodite, and introduced to Paphos the cult of Hera, the goddess of family life. Finally, in about 320 BC, he transferred his throne from Palaepaphos to Nea Paphos, about 15 km to the northwest, near the coast, where he built a temple to Artemis Agrotera, demonstrating again his feelings against the cult of Aphrodite. Nikokles was responsible for the building of a harbour and the defences of the new city, remnants of which have been uncovered in recent years, in the western part of the city, with monumental gates and ramparts. The vertical rock face provided adequate protection against possible attacks from the seaward side.

Nea Paphos flourished under the Ptolemies. In the 1st century BC they transferred the seat of government from Salamis to Nea Paphos, which was more easily accessible from Alexandria. The mint of Paphos was quite important during the Ptolemaic period, as is illustrated by a hoard of 2484 silver tetradrachms found during recent excavations. Several Greek gods were worshipped at Nea Paphos including Zeus Polieus, Leto, Apollo Hylates, Artemis, Aphrodite, and Hera. The city had a gymnasium and a theatre. A playwright of the 3rd century BC who was a native of Paphos is known by name, Sopatros. Among the political-religious institutions of Paphos, the "Koinon Kyprion" (the confederation of the Cypriots) aimed at the promotion of the ruler cult. The city must have had monumental buildings, but none of these has survived. The splendour of the rock-cut "tombs of the kings", imitating those of Alexandria, echoes the importance of the Ptolemaic city.

Palaepaphos, with its temple of Aphrodite, continued as a religious centre during the Hellenistic and Roman periods, but its economy declined considerably, having lost the status of capital of the region.

The Romans favoured Paphos to a considerable extent and they retained it as their capital and as the headquarters of the Roman garrison. Culturally, however, as in the rest of Cyprus, the Hellenistic civilizations lingered on. The spacious and luxurious villas with their polychrome mosaics, which have been uncovered during recent excavations, illustrate the importance of Roman Paphos. In the Acts of the Apostles it is mentioned that St Paul and St Barnabas preached Christianity in Paphos, and Sergius Paulus, the governor of Paphos, was converted to Christianity in AD 45.

The repeated earthquakes of the 4th century AD destroyed the splendid buildings of the city, although some of them were repaired and continued to be used down to the 5th century. Christianity prevailed completely by the 4th century, in spite of some efforts to revive the old pagan religion. Paphos regained part of its old splendour during the early Christian period.

VASSOS KARAGEORGHIS

Summary

A city in southwest Cyprus, Paphos flourished mainly in the 1st millennium BC. It was an important centre in the 12th century BC when Achaean colonization began and the temple of Aphrodite was established. Greek culture mixed with Assyrian in the Archaic period, followed by periods of Egyptian and Persian rule. New Paphos flourished under the Ptolemies and became the island's seat of government, while Old Paphos declined.

Further Reading

Daszewski, Wiktor A., *Dionysos der Erlöser: griechische Mythen im spätantiken Cyper*, Mainz: Zabern, 1985

Gjerstad, E., *The Swedish Cyprus Expedition*, vol. 4, part 2: *The Cypro-Geometric, Cypro-Archaic and Cypro-Classical Periods*, Stockholm: Swedish Cyprus Expedition, 1948

Karageorghis, Vassos, *Cyprus: From the Stone Age to the Romans*, London and New York: Thames and Hudson, 1982

Karageorghis, Vassos, *Palaepaphos-Skales: An Iron Age Cemetery in Cyprus*, 2 vols, Konstanz: Universitätsverlag Konstanz, 1983

Maier, F.G. and V. Karageorghis, *Paphos: History and Archaeology*, Nicosia: Leventis Foundation, 1984

Maier, F.G., *Alt-Paphos auf Cypern: Ausgrabungen zur Geschichte von Stadt und Heiligtum, 1966–1984*, Mainz: Zabern, 1985

Masson, Oliver, *Les Inscriptions chypriotes syllabiques*, Paris: Boccard, 1961

Michaelides, D., *Cypriot Mosaics*, Nicosia: Cyprus Department of Antiquities, 1987

Nicolaou, Ino and Otto Mørkholm, *A Ptolemaic Coin Hoard*, Nicosia: Department of Antiquities, 1976

Vermeule, Cornelius C., *Greek and Roman Cyprus: Art from Classical through Late Antique Times*, Boston: Museum of Fine Arts, 1976

Papyrus, parchment, and paper

Stone, metal, clay, pottery, wood, wax, and other materials were all used as writing materials from an early date, but it was the lightness and convenience of papyrus, parchment, and paper that made writing a portable and accessible activity.

Evidence for the use of papyrus (from which we get our modern word paper) dates from the 3rd millennium BC in Egypt, and it was used in Greece from at least the end of the 6th century BC, as proved by its depictions on pots. An early Greek word for papyrus, *byblos*, may indicate that it came to Greece from Phoenician Byblos at the same time that the Greeks obtained their alphabet in the 8th century.

The papyrus plant, although cultivated in Palestine and Sicily in antiquity, was native to Egypt, where it was produced commercially for purposes as varied as material for boats, for sandals, and, of course, for writing. The primary production area was the lower Nile and delta, probably giving rise to Alexandria as its principal distribution centre later. Pliny (*Naturalis Historia*, 13. 74–78) provides the most extensive, if sometimes faulty, description for the manufacture of papyrus sheets in antiquity. The triangular-sectioned stalk was sliced into strips *c.*30–40 cm long, the centre pith providing the most prized grade of material, the outer strips the least prized. Strips of similar quality were set parallel to each other on a flat surface; a second layer was then placed at right angles on top and the two layers were pressed to release the natural gluten in the papyrus, which served as the bonding agent for the dried sheet. After drying, the sheets were smoothed with a smooth stone or shell before being attached to other sheets with a wheat paste and vinegar (probably to kill mould) by overlapping sheets by 1–2 cm. For writing from the left, the left sheet overlapped; for writing from the right, the right sheet over-

lapped. Individual sheets might be used for accounts and records, but literary works often used about 20 sheets in a book roll *c.*6–8 m long by 0.11–0.24 m wide. Customized rolls of different dimensions have produced examples more than 40 m long but customers generally bought a "regular" book roll and then cut or added according to need. One of these rolls would accommodate a dramatic text of *c.*1500 lines, two books of Homer, or one book of a prose writer such as Thucydides.

Most often the inside of the roll had the horizontal strips of papyrus. This helped to reduce the strain caused by rolling and unrolling but, more importantly, the horizontal grain aided writing and became the primary writing surface. The outside, composed of the vertical strips of papyrus, was not regularly employed as a writing surface although many exceptions exist. In addition, since the inks applied by reed pens were water soluble, the writing on the surfaces of both papyrus and parchment was often sponged or rubbed off and then reused (as a palimpsest). In order to protect the papyrus when rolled up, the first sheet, called the protocol (*protocollon*), was often attached at right angles to the grain of the next one. Occasionally parchment was used to reinforce the vulnerable sheet and the roll was wound around a cylinder to help protect it. Cedar oil was used to repel worms.

A variety of animal skins also served as writing materials. Two processes were used to procure a suitable surface although the initial stage was the same: the skin of the freshly slaughtered animal was temporarily cured to inhibit decay, allowing later processing, or the skin was immersed in a solution to help loosen flesh and hair, which were then removed. At this point the processes diverged. Hides steeped in tannins produced durable and flexible leathers. In the second process, hides were first slaked in lime and then rubbed with calcium oxide. Next they were stretched on a frame and gently air-dried in an environment that maintained a moderate temperature. At that point the hides were removed from the frames and smoothed with pumice or chalk to increase their whiteness. The final product, which might also be thinned by shaving, was parchment (goat or sheep) or vellum (kid or calf). The stiff and durable material was then cut into sheets and sewn into rolls with hair-sides on one surface and flesh-sides on the other. Later, in the 1st century AD, both parchment and papyrus were bound into codices (see below).

Papyrus was the favoured material throughout antiquity, even though hides were used as writing surfaces in Asia Minor from the beginning of the 1st millennium BC and in Greece probably from the 6th century at least. The theory that papyrus was eventually surpassed by parchment and paper since they have a better surface and are lighter in colour is not true. Pliny's (*Naturalis Historia*, 13. 21) statement that parchment was invented at Pergamum (*pergamena* is its name in Latin and Greek) also seems unlikely, but its surge in popularity probably arose in the first half of the 2nd century BC when problems with papyrus supply from Egypt gave the Pergamene rulers the opportunity to increase its prominence and distribution. During the Middle Ages parchment, even though more expensive, became the prized writing material largely as a result of its durability and wide availability, which was not governed by geographical restrictions and climate. Its use for liturgical purposes and then for legal and medical documents contributed to its success. Not until the 12th century did parchment begin to lose its position as the pre-eminent writing material, when the Moors introduced into Spain rag paper, an invention of ancient China that had steadily gained in popularity from the beginning of the 2nd century AD.

Book rolls were the most common medium for both papyrus and parchment throughout most of Greek and Roman antiquity. Wood tablets and hollowed wood tablets containing wax inserts, upon which accounts and temporary texts and exercises could be scratched or chalked, were joined together by a clasp or leather thong through holes and used as a type of notebook as early as the beginning of the 1st millennium BC in the Middle East and certainly by the early 5th century BC in Greece. The book roll, however, remained the preferred medium for longer, permanent texts. By the 1st century AD papyrus sheets and folded sheets of parchment began to replace the ungainly wood tablets. This produced a less cumbersome notebook that eventually, in its most common form, consisted of quires (gatherings) of four wide sheets of parchment folded along the vertical axis and sewn along the fold. The resulting codex (book) had eight leaves (folios) making sixteen pages, which were bound within a sturdy covering.

The new medium, however, did not win immediate acceptance among a seemingly conservative writing community. Doctors and astrologers may have promoted the use of such notebooks, but the acceptance and eventual domination of the codex over the ubiquitous book roll has been plausibly attributed to the newly emerging Christian religion. The codex provided a format that was clearly superior for recording and recovering information, and was convenient to carry, especially in contrast to the incredibly cumbersome book roll. For the first time it was possible to examine texts quickly and efficiently. The distinct format of the codex may also have been attractive to the new religion, which sought to set itself apart from the book roll of Jewish and pagan tradition.

From the 2nd century AD Christianity regularly employed the codex to record the Old Testament, New Testament, and Apocrypha. This use in conjunction with the growth of Christianity itself led directly to the acceptance of the codex as the standard format for the written word. Early Christian codices are all very utilitarian, but by the 4th century elegant volumes were being produced that contained elements foreshadowing medieval book illustration.

After the advent of writing, the innovation of the codex represents perhaps the most important advance to promote learning. Now real research could be recorded easily and efficiently.

ANDREW N. SHERWOOD

See also Books and Readers

Further Reading

Johnson, Richard R., "Ancient and Medieval Accounts of the 'Invention' of Parchment", *California Studies in Classical Antiquity*, 3 (1970): pp. 115–22

Kenyon, Frederic G., *Books and Readers in Ancient Greece and Rome*, 2nd edition, Oxford: Clarendon Press, 1951; reprinted Chicago: Ares, 1980

Lewis, Naphtali, *Papyrus in Classical Antiquity*, 2nd edition, Oxford: Clarendon Press, 1974

Maehler, Herwig, Papyrology: Greek and Books: Greek and Roman entries in *The Oxford Classical Dictionary*, 3rd edition, edited by Simon Hornblower and Antony Spawforth, Oxford and New York: Oxford University Press, 1996

Metzger, Bruce M., "The Making of Ancient Books" in *The Text of the New Testament: Its Transmission, Corruption, and Restoration*, 3rd edition, Oxford and New York: Oxford University Press, 1992

Reed, Ronald, *Ancient Skins, Parchments and Leathers*, London and New York: Seminar Press, 1972

Reed, Ronald, *The Nature and Making of Parchment*, Leeds: Elmete Press, 1975

Reynolds, L.D. and N.G. Wilson, *Scribes and Scholars: A Guide to the Transmission of Greek and Latin Literature*, 3rd edition, Oxford: Clarendon Press, and New York: Oxford University Press, 1991

Roberts, Colin H., "The Codex", *Proceedings of the British Academy*, 40 (1954): pp. 169–204

Roberts, Colin H. and T.C. Skeat, *The Birth of the Codex*, Oxford and New York: Oxford University Press, 1983

Rubicam, Catherine, "The Organisation of Material in Graeco-Roman World Histories" in *Pre-Modern Encyclopaedic Texts*, edited by Peter Binkley, Leiden and New York: Brill, 1997

Sanders, H.A., "The Beginnings of the Modern Book: The Codex", *University of Michigan Quarterly Review*, 44/15 (1938): pp. 95–111

Skeat, T.C., "Early Christian Book Production: Papyri and Manuscripts" in *The Cambridge History of the Bible*, vol. 2, edited by G.W.H. Lampe, Cambridge: Cambridge University Press, 1969

Skeat, T.C., "The Length of the Standard Papyrus Roll and the Cost-Advantage of the Codex", *Zeitschrift für Papyrologie und Epigraphik*, 45 (1982): pp. 169–75

Stephens, Susan A., "Book Production" in *The Civilization of the Ancient Mediterranean: Greece and Rome*, edited by Michael Grant and Rachel Kitzinger, New York: Scribner, 1988

Turner, Eric G., *The Typology of the Early Codex*, Philadelphia: University of Pennsylvania Press, 1977

Turner, Eric G., *Greek Manuscripts of the Ancient World*, 2nd edition, revised by P.J. Parsons, London: Institute of Classical Studies, University of London, 1987

Turner, Eric G., *Greek Papyri: An Introduction*, 2nd edition, Oxford: Clarendon Press, reprinted 1998

Weitzmann, Kurt, *Illustrations in Roll and Codex: A Study of the Origin and Method of Text Illustration*, Princeton, New Jersey: Princeton University Press, 1947; reprinted 1970

Parmenides *c.*515–*c.*440 BC

Philosopher

Parmenides was a Presocratic philosopher who lived in the southern Italian town of Elea (near the modern town of Agropoli). He was the first of a group of philosophers who are called Eleatics, the others being Zeno and Melissus. Parmenides also appears as a character in Plato's work *Parmenides* and is the probable inspiration for the character of the Eleatic Stranger in the same author's *Sophist* and *Politicus*, written a century after his death.

In the ancient world Parmenides and his successors were celebrated as opponents of the possibility of change. Just as Heraclitus was supposed to maintain, as a basic proposition, that everything is in constant change, so Parmenides and the

Eleatics were held to be committed to the denial of the possibility of any change. But as with Heraclitus, this characterization somewhat distorts the emphasis and focus of their concerns. It is more accurate to construe these philosophers as early metaphysicians. Their concern lay with the nature of what there is and what is real. Change comes into the discussion through this motivating interest.

Parmenides' words are preserved for us through extensive quotations in Simplicius, writing some 1000 years later in the 6th century AD. His work is a poem which, after a hieratic introduction invoking divine assistance, contains two notably contrasting parts. In the first part he expounds the truth, while in the second he relays the erroneous opinions of unenlightened speculators. In the Way of Truth (as it is often called) he argues that if something can be spoken and thought about, it must exist; nothing is not a possible subject for investigation. "You cannot say or think what is not there", is his controlling refrain. Any possible subject for investigation, *is*.

As the argument advances, he establishes further facts about this existent subject: it is without beginning or end, single, whole, and invariant. Parmenides establishes each of these conclusions on the same basis as his original argument: the position that he will endorse commends itself because it enables him to avoid thinking or talking about nothing. As the author of this ongoing argument, he insistently reminds us of the conditions for any rational communication. He concludes this part of his argument by comparing his subject to "a well-rounded sphere, everywhere equally balanced from the centre".

Parmenides then passes to an account of a less enlightened way of thinking, which he declares to be thoroughly false but still wishes to expound. This account differs from the Truth in being comprehensively dualistic. Opposing pairs – such as Night and Day – are admitted into the scheme of things, rather than the introduction of the one requiring the exclusion of the other. Yet even here the method of argument is resolutely hard-headed and rationalistic, bearing the stamp of the author of the Truth.

Was Parmenides' Way of Truth meant to be an account of the physical universe or of some quite different order of reality, or of some monadic element in either of these schemes? Some would regard the question as quite anachronistic, and certainly any detailed answer to it is underdetermined by his own words. His argument points in the direction of every one of these philosophical developments, while not favouring or excluding any of them. The comparison of reality to a sphere may indicate spatial extension but it need not.

Parmenides' originality and achievement consist in four points. First, he introduced questions concerning existence into the explicit agenda of philosophy; he is the father of ontology. Secondly, he grounded this ontological discussion in the conditions for successful talk and thought. This is a feature of method that he shares with Heraclitus; both philosophers thus deserve the credit for first raising issues in epistemology. But in Parmenides the control exercised by considerations of language is paramount. He is the first philosopher of language. Thirdly, he expounded profound paradoxes about the possibility of change; thereafter no philosopher could assume that change was an unproblematic phenomenon. Finally he was the first philosopher to use argument. He advances from one statement to another with the armoury of "therefore" and "since". According to some current conceptions of philosophy, this last feature of his work would suffice to establish him as the first philosopher.

Parmenides and his immediate Eleatic successors bequeathed a powerful agenda of problems to subsequent Greek philosophers. The sophists of the following generation of 5th-century BC philosophers included Gorgias, who wrote a nihilistic essay in the Eleatic style *On What There Is Not*. These thinkers also developed epistemological paradoxes of change – for example, that learning and enquiry are impossible because there is no intelligible way for someone to advance from a condition of ignorance to one of knowledge. This is a version of the paradox of enquiry, first adumbrated in Plato's *Meno*. In later works, notably *Sophist*, Plato confronts the central Parmenidean claim that *what is not* is unintelligible and undiscussable. His highly original analysis of this issue turns on securing a sense for "not" according to which it means "other than".

Aristotle's philosophy is greatly influenced by Parmenides, even though the influence appears to be negative. In his own ontology, the ability to bring about and undergo change is a deeply important fact about most things that exist; and his programme of philosophical enquiry is organized accordingly. Therefore he regards Parmenides, with his utter rejection of the significance of change for natural substances, as a wrongheaded maverick. But he is compelled to give an account of change that removes from it any air of paradox. Aristotle achieves this with analyses that involve his novel concepts of potentiality and actuality and of matter and form. The motivation for these influential doctrines is a desire to show that change, so far from being mysterious as Parmenides had argued, is intimately bound up with the nature of everyday substances.

Aristotle's anti-Eleatic polemic was in part directed against certain contemporary philosophers, sometimes known as "Megarians". These included Eubulides, Philo, and Diodorus Cronus, who were interested in modal logic. Their interest in rigorous argument, and their paradoxical theories about possibility and necessity, bear the stamp of Parmenides.

From this point on Parmenides' direct influence wanes; but his philosophical personality looms large as philosophers from Kant onwards have pondered the idea that there are – or may be – limits to what can enter the scope of rational enquiry and discussion. Are there truths that transcend human powers of ratiocination? Parmenides in effect replied "no" to this question; and even those philosophers who are inclined to reply otherwise, must acknowledge the posing of this fundamental philosophical question as Parmenides' greatest legacy.

J.D.G. EVANS

Biography

Born in Elea in southern Italy *c*.515 BC, Parmenides was the first of a group of philosophers known as the Eleatics. He was the first philosopher of language. He is said to have visited Athens when aged 65. He appears as a character in Plato's *Parmenides*. He wrote a philosophical poem which survives only through quotations in Simplicius (6th century AD). He died *c*.440 BC.

Further Reading

Gallop, David (translator), *Parmenides of Elea: Fragments*, Toronto: University of Toronto Press, 1984

Kirk, G.S., J.E. Raven and M. Schofield, *The Presocratic Philosophers: A Critical History with a Selection of Texts*, Cambridge and New York: Cambridge University Press, 1983, chapter 8

Mackenzie, M.M., "Parmenides' Dilemma", *Phronesis*, 27/1 (1982): pp. 1–12

Mourelatos, A.D.P., "Mind's Commitment to the Real" in *Essays in Ancient Greek Philosophy*, vol. 1, edited by John P. Anton and George L. Kustas, Albany: State University of New York Press, 1971

Owen, G.E.L., "Eleatic Questions", *Classical Quarterly*, 10 (1960): pp. 84–102

Parren, Callirrhoe 1859–1940

Feminist and journalist

Born to Stylianos and Sophia Siganos, in Platania Amariou Rethymnis, Crete, on 1 May 1859, Callirrhoe qualified as a teacher in 1878 and taught in schools in the Greek communities of Odessa and Adrianople. Back in Athens, she married, in 1886, the Constantinople reporter Ioannis Parren who was for years director of the Athens News Agency. Having observed the low intellectual level of women around her and their superficial and purposeless lives, especially when they had no children, Parren dreamed of working to raise women's level of awareness as social agents and in their role as mothers in the newly emerging modern Greek nation. With the encouragement of her husband, Parren published the first women's newspaper, on 8 March 1887, thus introducing female reportage to Greece. Through the *Ephimeris ton Kyrion* (Ladies' Newspaper, 1887–1917), Parren was soon established as one of the leading intellectuals of the country involved in the cultural discussions of the time. Through the pages of her weekly, Parren promoted women's issues and confronted governments with women's rights to education and equal employment opportunities. She soon had a number of talented women contributing to the paper which became a forum for the literary expression of women as well as a thesaurus of information on home economy, health, beauty, child rearing, world news, especially matters relating to the feminist movement and women's achievements in developed countries. Parren began receiving invitations to represent Greek women at international congresses of women (Paris 1889, London 1899, Chicago 1893, etc.).

Her desire to see her country a better place turned her into a social activist. Besides women's issues, her weekly articles addressed all the needs of Greek society and forced the government to pass appropriate bills. She mobilized women and organized fundraisers, often recruiting the support of the queen and the princesses of Greece, to redress social injustice, for which she was later decorated with the Silver Cross of the Phoenix (1921), the Silver Medal of the Academy of Athens (1936), and the Gold Cross of the Phoenix (1936). Her activities ranged from founding institutions – such as Sunday Schools for Poor Women and Girls (1890); Women's Hospital for Incurable Diseases (1892); St Catherine's Asylum (1893), offering needy

working girls and unmarried mothers accommodation and support; the Children's Asylum, a day-care centre (1896); the Association for the Protection of Animals (1896); St Sophia Children's Hospital (1896); The Epheveion (adolescent penitentiary) in the Averof Prison (1896), furnished with full grade-school and hospital – to making the government take protective measures such as banning the employment of under-age children and night shifts for children and women in factories, and to consider hiring women as state employees; and to pressing the University of Athens to open its doors to women in 1891 and the Polytechnic School in 1896. The causes to which Parren applied her social agenda were endless, her main goal always being to empower women, enforce social justice, and raise the awareness of Greek society to offering women equal opportunities. After her return from the Chicago World Congress of Representative Women, she founded the Association of Greek Women in 1896, offered relief to the refugees of the 1896 Cretan uprising. During the Graeco-Turkish War (1897) it organized surgical units at the front, directed and operated solely by women, and came to the succour of war widows and orphans. Parren is also remembered for founding the Lyceum of Greek Women (1911) whose purpose is the preservation of folk music, dances, and costumes from all over the country.

While promoting her social agenda, Parren realized that without the vote women had no real power to effect changes through legislation. Thus, although at the beginning she did not demand suffrage for women, in 1894 she presented prime minister Charilaos Trikoupis with a suffrage petition carrying thousands of women's signatures. She repeated the demand during the premierships of Theodoros Deliyannis (1897) and Demetrios Gounaris (1921). Although they received the petition favourably, none dared propose a women's suffrage bill. It was only in April 1949, and under pressure from the United Nations Charter, that women over 21 were granted the right to elect and be elected in municipal elections. In a 1952 amendment to the Constitution women were granted the vote in general elections, a right which they exercised for the first time in 1954.

Among her other activities, Parren adopted literary discourse as a means to promote her feminist and social agenda. All her novels are deeply enmeshed in the ongoing cultural debate about women and the changing concept of women's roles in the developing Greek society. Her first three novels – *I Cheiraphetimeni* (The Emancipated, 1900), *I Magissa* (The Sorceress, 1901), and *To Neon Symvolaion* (The New Contract, 1903) – comprise a trilogy under the title *Ta Vivlia tis Avgis* (The Books of Dawn) and refer to Parren's vision of a new era of equality and justice between the sexes, in which men and women, having had equal opportunities in education and the workplace, would develop responsible and honest characters which would lead to relationships of equality and happy lives together. At the same time, the three novels illustrate Greek society's vision of the messianic role women were expected to play in the regeneration of the nation in their role as mothers who would raise a generation of Greeks with a strong sense of national identity and ready to sacrifice themselves for their country. Parren also wrote *Choris Onoma* (Without a Name, 1905–06), *To Marameno Krino* (The Withered Lily, 1907–10), and *To Aspro Triantaphyllo* (The

White Rose, 1915–17), all serialized in her weekly. And she wrote plays: *I Nea Gynaika* (The New Woman, 1908), based on *Ta Vivlia tis Avgis* and performed in 1907, was the third of a trilogy of plays she intended to write in order to delineate the evolution of Greek woman from Homeric times to the present. *Penelope* and *Aspasia* would be representations of the perfect woman of Homeric and historical times but no manuscripts of these plays have been discovered so far. Consistent with her goal to raise Greek women's educational level, Parren researched and began to write but never completed the *Istoria tis Gynaikos* (History of Women, 1889) in three volumes: *Ai Gynaikes tis Proistorikis Epochis* (Women of Prehistoric Times); *Ai Gynaikes ton Indon kai tis Kinas* (Women of India and China); and *Ai Ellinides apo tou 1508 mechri Simerou* (Greek Women from 1508 to the Present). From the diaries of her travels, only *Ta Taxidia mou: Souidia* (My Travels: Sweden) was published. Accounts of her other trips appeared in the *Ephimeris ton Kyrion*.

Parren was admired and supported by men such as Gregorios Xenopoulos and Kostis Palamas who dedicated poem 95 from "Ekato Phones" (A Hundred Voices) in *I Asalevti Zoi* (Still Life) to her, the finest representative of "the new woman", capable of elevating man's world and human society. When Parren died on 16 January 1940, she was granted a state funeral. In 1991, the City of Athens offered a plot in the principal cemetery in Athens where Parren's bust, made by the well-known Greek sculptor Costas Valsamis, was erected. On this spot a memorial service for Parren has been held on International Women's Day every year since 1992. Her legacy, which was dimmed by the two World Wars, was reclaimed in the late 1970s and her literary works, forgotten for almost a century, are now being studied and reprinted.

MARIA ANASTASOPOULOU

Biography

Born in Crete in 1859, Parren qualified as a teacher and taught in schools in Odessa and Adrianople. In 1886 she married the journalist Ioannis Parren. She founded and edited the *Ephimeris ton Kyrion* (Ladies' Newspaper, 1887–1917), wrote novels and plays, and made Greece aware of women's issues. She died in 1940 and was granted a state funeral.

Further Reading

Anastasopoulou, Maria, "Feminist Discourse and Literary Representation in Turn-of-the-Century Greece: Kallirrhoe Siganou-Parren's *The Books of Dawn*", *Journal of Modern Greek Studies*, 15/1 (May 1997): pp. 1–28. A Greek version of this paper appeared in *Themata Logotechnias*, 8 (March–June 1998): pp. 110–36

Anastasopoulou, Maria, "Feminist Awareness and Greek Women Writers: The Case of Kallirrhoe Siganou-Parren and Alexandra Papadopoulou" in *Greek Society in the Making, 1863–1913: Realities, Symbols and Visions*, edited by Philip Carabott, Aldershot, Hampshire: Variorum, 1997

Barika, Eleni, *I Exegersi ton Kurion: I genisi mias pheministikis Suneidisis stin Ellada 1833–1907* [The Ladies' Revolt: The Appearance of a Feminist Awareness in Greece 1833–1907], Athens, 1987

Moschou-Sakorafou, Sassa, *I Istoria tou Ellinikou Pheministikou Kinimatos* [The History of the Greek Feminist Movement], Athens, 1900

Polykandrioti, Rania, "Callirrhoe Parren" in *I Palaioteri Logotechnia mas: apo tis Archis os ton proto Pangkosmio Polemo*, vol. 6: *1830–1880* [Our Older Literature: From its Beginnings to the First World War, vol. 6: 1830–1880], Athens, 1996

Psarra, Angelica, "To Mythistorima tis Cheiraphetisis, i 'syneti' Outopia tis Callirrhois Parren" [The Novel of Emancipation, or Callirrhoe Parren's "Reasonable" Utopia], essay introduction to new edition of *I Cheiraphetimeni* [The Emancipated] by Callirrhoe Parren, Athens, 1999

Xiradaki, Koula, *To Pheministiko Kinima stin Ellada: Protopores Ellinides 1830–1936* [The Feminist Movement in Greece: Pioneer Women 1830–1936], Athens, 1988

Parthians

The Parthians were originally the people who lived in the Achaemenid province of Parthia, (Parthava in Old Persian), which comprised the region of Chorasan in northeastern Iran and of southern Turkmenistan. The Parthians later came to be identified as the people of the Parthian empire, founded by the Parni, a nomadic people, who entered Parthia from the northeast in the mid-3rd century BC and adopted the name "Parthians" for themselves. Through gradual expansion the Parni / Parthians built an empire, which lasted for almost 500 years, from 246 or 238 BC to AD 224, and which stretched from the Euphrates to the Indus. Until the Parthians revolted against the Seleucid empire, Parthia remained a satrapy; during the reign of Antiochus III (223–187 BC) the Parthians were still regarded as vassals. Early Parthian coins bear a Greek legend and show that the Parthian kings did not always use a royal title; by the middle of the 1st century BC Parthian script was used and kings had adopted the Achaemenid royal title of "king of kings".

The expansion of Parthia from kingdom to empire was a gradual process which lasted over 100 years. After the death of Antiochus III in 187 BC, Parthian troops under Phraates I (176–171 BC) began campaigns against the mountain people north of the Elburz mountains, followed by campaigns south of the Elburz, led by his successors. Territorial conquest on a large scale was undertaken by Mithridates I (171–139/38 BC), who first secured the eastern lands for the empire, Bactrian territory in 160 BC, and eastern Iran in 150/145 BC. During the 140s BC Media was conquered and the Seleucids were driven out of Iran, allowing Mithridates to campaign against Babylonia and Elymais. With Adiabene, Gordyene, and Osrhoene, in northern Mesopotamia, as client kingdoms, and control of Dura-Europus won in 113 BC, the long period of Parthian conquest and expansion was completed.

The Parthians were ruled by the Arsacid dynasty, named after the founder of the empire, Arsaces I (c.248/238–217 BC). First establishing their power in the cities of Hecatompylos and Nisa, the Parthian kings then centred their power in Ctesiphon and Vologesocerta. The Parthian nobility was headed by the royal councillors (*ordo probulorum*), followed by the Parthian aristocracy (*pelatai*), the *douloi* (servants), and possibly a slave population. Organized in *regna*, client kingdoms of the Parthian king, which paid tribute and provided military service, the empire comprised a multitude of peoples who spoke different languages and dialects. Parthian became the administrative language of the empire, though other languages, such as Greek, Aramaic, Middle Persian, and Sogdian, were also used. Parthian culture shows distinctive features in art and architecture, most notably the vaulted *iwan* halls and the planning of cities and fortresses.

Parthian influence on the Classical world increased after 20 BC, with the establishment of diplomatic relations between Augustus and the Parthian king Phraates IV (38–3/2 BC). Phraates IV returned the standards taken from Crassus (54/53 BC), Decidius Saxa (40 BC), and Antony (36 BC), while Rome acknowledged the Euphrates as the border between the two empires, and returned Phraates' son to the Armenian throne. The diplomatic treaty marked Roman recognition of the Parthian empire, but Roman propaganda manipulated the event into a public demonstration of Roman superiority over the Parthians, expressed in literature and art. Parthia was considered to be yet another vast, oriental – and therefore inferior – empire, which Rome made little effort to understand.

In literature, the Parthians were stereotyped as cruel, uncivilized barbarians. They were on a par with the Scythians, and with the decadent Persians of the past, being interchangeably referred to as Medes, Persians, or Achaemenids. Roman art after 20 BC shows a preoccupation with the depictions of Parthians as typical barbarians. The statue of Augustus of Prima Porta, dated to 17 BC, prominently displays a Parthian on Augustus's breastplate, "offering" the Roman standards. Parthians were represented as kneeling subjects, as in the case of a huge bronze tripod, or standing as supporting figures in architectural designs. Bronze ornaments representing mounted or dead barbarians in Parthian dress were mass-produced. Statues of Parthian barbarians, first seen at the Basilica Aemilia in the Roman Forum, were sculpted from coloured marble, *marmor Phrygium* or *marmor Numidicum*, symbolizing oriental luxury and colour. Their un-Roman build and stature identified the Parthians as people who were not part of the civilized world of the *orbis Romanus*, but of the *orbis alter*. A Parthian arc was built after 20 BC, depicted on gold and silver coins. Trajan celebrated his shortlived victory over the Parthians with an *aureus,* describing himself as Rex Parthus, and a coin, bearing the legend "Parthia Capta", depicted two barbarians huddled together in front of a *tropaeum*. Blurring the distinction between Persians and Parthians, Roman emperors sought to compare the Greek–Persian wars of 490 BC and 480/79 BC with Rome's fight against Parthia, in an effort to legitimize Roman ambition to conquer Parthia. The restaging of the battle of Salamis in a vast *naumachia* (ship battle) by the Tiber in 2 BC to celebrate the opening of the temple of Mars Ultor was one of a number of public demonstrations hinting at the Greek–Persian wars, but implying Rome's fight against Parthia. According to Roman ideology, the Parthians were an eastern, barbarian power steeped in oriental luxury, military aggressors who threatened the western world. Roman propaganda was to demonstrate that Rome was dealing with defeated barbarians, not with a political and military power that was equal to Rome. The Romans upheld this view throughout the existence of the Parthian empire and then imposed it on the Parthians' successors, the Sassanians. The Sassanians, for their part, rigorously tried to erase Parthian culture, and it remained largely forgotten until the late 19th and 20th centuries when excavations began in the Near East and the past of the Persian empires was revived. First excavations at Nisa, undertaken by Russian scholars between 1948 and 1961, began to unearth archaeological evidence of the Parthian period, from which emerges, and continues to emerge, a picture of the Parthian empire independent of hostile Greek and Roman sources.

MARIA BROSIUS

Summary

Originally denoting the inhabitants of the Achaemenid province of Parthia, "Parthians" came to mean the people of the Parthian empire which lasted from 246 or 238 BC to AD 224 and stretched from the Euphrates to the Indus. For the Romans the Parthians were the stereotype of cruel, uncivilized barbarians. Recent excavation shows them in a different light.

Further Reading

Schneider, Rolf Michael, *Bunte Barbaren: Orientalenstatuen aus farbigem Marmor in der römischen Repräsentationskunst*, Worms: Wernersche, 1986
Shahbazi, A.S. *et al.*, "Arsacids" in *Encyclopaedia Iranica*, edited by Ehsan Yarshater, vol. 1, London: Routledge, 1982, pp. 525–46
Sherwin-White, Susan and Amélie Kuhrt (editors), *Hellenism in the East: Interaction of Greek and Non-Greek Civilizations from Syria to Central Asia after Alexander*, London: Duckworth, and Berkeley: University of California Press, 1987
Sherwin-White, Susan and Amélie Kuhrt, *From Samarkhand to Sardis: A New Approach to the Seleucid Empire*, London: Duckworth, and Berkeley: University of California Press, 1993
Sonnabend, Holger, *Fremdbild und Politik: Vorstellungender Römer von Ägypten und dem Partherreich in der späten Republik und frühen Kaiserzeit*, Frankfurt and New York: Peter Lang, 1986
Wiesehöfer, Josef, *Ancient Persia: From 550 BC to 650 AD*, London and New York: Tauris, 1996
Wiesehöfer, Josef (editor), *Das Partherreich und seine Zeugnisse / The Arsacid Empire: Sources and Documentation*, Stuttgart: Steiner, 1998
Ziegler, Karl-Heinz, *Die Beziehungen zwischen Rom und dem Partherreich*, Wiesbaden: Steiner, 1964

Pastoralism

Pastoralism, that is to say the phenomenon of animal husbandry, has tended to go hand in hand to a greater or lesser degree with an agrarian economy. Pastoralism can be linked to a farming economy or, at the other end of the scale, be associated with transhumance, the seasonal movement of flocks from one area to another. Pastoralist communities would have a high reliance on domesticated animals for their livelihood.

The first evidence for sheep and goats on Crete as well as mainland Greece comes in the early Neolithic period, that is to say the late 7th millennium BC. Evidence for pastoralism on Crete in the Bronze Age has been presented by excavation of the Early Minoan II site of Myrtos. Some 90 per cent of the animal bones were from ovicaprids, and the excavation suggested that the wool was being processed in individual homes. Indeed it has been suggested that the settlement of Myrtos was possibly seasonal. Also from Crete come some models of sheep from inside a Middle Minoan I bowl found at Palaikastro.

Pastoralism in Arcadia is reflected by the appearance of small bronze dedications during the 6th century BC. These can show shepherds wearing a distinctive conical hat, sometimes wearing a cloak and boots. Often the shepherds carry a sheep or ram under their arms, though one from Mount Lykeios had a small calf on his shoulders. One figure, now in the Metropolitan Museum of Art, New York and said to have been found near Andritsaina, carries an inscription, "Phauleas dedicated [this] to Pan". Many of these Arcadian figures were probably dedicated in the sanctuary of Zeus Lykaios or the sanctuary of Pan (described by Pausanias, 8. 38. 5). Such types are similar to the now lost dedication made by the Arcadians of Pheneus who commissioned a statue of Hermes by the Archaic sculptors Onatas of Aegina and Calliteles (Pausanias, 5. 27. 8). Pausanias described a statue of the god "in a tunic and a cloak with a peasant's cap on his head and carrying a ram under his arm". Such dedications may suggest specialized pastoral communities. On the island of Rhodes in the Classical period one of the social groups was called a *sunnoma* which suggests that the members had a common right of pasture.

Evidence for pastoralism appears in the faunal material from excavations at Greek sanctuaries. Sheep and goats appear to have been favoured for sacrificial victims at many sanctuaries. Ethnographic evidence shows that culling of flocks can take place in the early summer before there is a lack of suitable pasture for large flocks, or for younger animals in the spring. If pastoralism is geared to the production of milk, then males and ewes which have stopped lactating are likely culling victims.

Pastoralism can also be detected in the epigraphic record. For example, in the 5th and 4th centuries BC the Attic demes of Marathon, Thorikos, and Archia were sacrificing a number of wethers or ewes in their festivals. Such evidence for flocks makes up for the limited information for Attica available from literary sources. One such example may be the 4th-century BC legal case where sheep – the flock consisted of some 50 animals – were seized from a farm not far from the hippodrome (Demosthenes, 47. 52–53). A male lamb was sacrificed in the early summer on Mount Hymettos in Attica in the cult of Zeus Epakrios, presumably to coincide with the use of the higher winter pasture.

Pastoralism also makes its appearance in literary sources. For example, at the start of the *Theogony*, Hesiod was taught to sing as he tended flocks on Mount Helicon. Clearly the agricultural economy of Askra, so well known from the *Works and Days*, included a pastoral dimension; it should be noted that its pastures are only some 5 km from the lower slopes of Helicon. Aristotle (*Politics*, 1319a.19–23) noted pastoral communities as one of the best forms of democracy (after arable farmers). A more detailed account of sheep can be obtained from the Hellenistic writer Aeschylides (and recorded in Aelian, *On the Characteristics of Animals*, 16. 32), who noted that on the island of Ceos sheep were fed with the by-products of agriculture, such as fig leaves, olive leaves, and husks from pulses, to save on the poor pasture. Such reliance on agricultural products would keep the flocks close to the communities. The converse of this was that the flocks themselves were a ready source of dung which could be used to enhance the productivity of the cultivated plots and fields. However, one reason for the low profile of pastoralism in ancient sources is that shepherding was probably a humble occupation compared to that of arable farming.

The evidence from inscriptions and to a lesser extent literary sources suggests that flocks were usually owned by members of the social elite. For example, one of the mutilators of the herms in 415 BC at Athens had 84 sheep and 67 goats among his confiscated property. The flocks themselves appear to have been cared for by individuals of much lower status, sometimes slaves. Although there are some dedications known from herdsmen, they may have been hired.

One feature of pastoralism is the movement of flocks from summer to winter pasturage, transhumance. This may involve moving flocks from the summer pastures in the mountains to lower areas, sometimes over long distances. There are two main types: the first where the shepherds are drawn from lowland communities, but use the mountains for pasture in the summer; the second, so-called "inverse" transhumance, where the shepherds are themselves mountain dwellers, and only come to lower areas in winter or for markets. In recent centuries transhumance may involve the movement of whole communities, requiring winter and summer settlements. In medieval Crete the main community was often considered the winter one, often situated at less than 200 m, but by the mid-19th century the reverse was true with communities choosing to make the summer settlement their main centre. An ancient example detected in the literary sources is Sophocles' mention of the Theban and Corinthian shepherds on Mount Cithaeron in the story of Oedipus (*Oedipus Rex*, 1132ff.). However, such transhumance was over short distances; such pastures on Cithaeron lie only some 20 km from Thebes, and 30 km from the Corinthia. This can be contrasted with modern transhumance in the northern Peloponnese which might cover some 100 km. Another ancient example comes from the late 1st century AD on the island of Euboea where Dio Chrysostom (*Orations*, 7. 11–15) mentioned flocks and herds of cattle. Evidence from ancient border disputes suggests that such long-distance transhumance was unlikely.

Border disputes between neighbouring poleis could sometimes hinge on grazing rights. One such dispute in the 2nd century BC, marked by inscriptions giving details of the agreement, was between Epidaurus and Hermion in the southern Argolid. The text of the agreement indicates that pasturage was one of the issues at stake, along with cropping. The agreement records that there had already been a decision "concerning the payment of fees to tax collectors for the pasturage of goats". The border area in question was clearly delineated in the agreement, and on the ground it corresponds to an area of some 30 sq km with land rising to nearly 800 m. It may have been used for winter grazing, although it has been observed that in recent times the same area is traversed by transhumant shepherds taking flocks between Arcadia (Valtetsiotes) and the southern Argolid. Such recent patterns in Greece are thought to have been dependent on the landholding patterns developed during the Tourkokratia. The southern Argolid was thought to be a particularly attractive area for flocks, as there were ready markets on the offshore islands of Hydra, Spetsae, and Poros.

The number of goats using such land is hard to estimate, if only because other areas of grazing land would probably have been in use, but it has been suggested that something like ten herds each of 200 goats would not be unreasonable. If such numbers were using this area, it was clearly profitable to tax the land's use. A hint at the profits from such activity is

Pastoralism: shepherds pen goats for dawn milking near Paleokerasia, central Greece

revealed by a dedication made in one of the sanctuaries of the polis of Epidaurus by one Timainetos in the mid-4th century BC. Timainetos made an offering to the Dioscuri as "a tithe from the goats". Although Timainetos may have been one of the tax collectors, he is more likely to have been an owner.

Such disputes in the Argolid over such marginal territory were not unknown. Epidaurus had been in two further separate disputes with its neighbours, Corinth and Arsinoë (the renamed polis of Methana). It is perhaps significant that at the polis of Troizen in 146 BC there was a group of resident Arcadians. It has been plausibly argued that it was this group of individuals, who had been drawn to, and settled in, the marginal areas of the poleis of the southern Argolid, that was causing the tensions.

Such tensions may reflect the reasons for the 2nd-century BC boundary dispute between Delphi and its neighbour Ambryssos. The boundary between the two cuts across modern transhumance routes, and there is a possibility that grazing rights lay behind the ancient dispute. Such disputes emphasize the general view that mountain regions were considered to be the property of those dwelling in urban communities even though the majority of people chose not to dwell there.

The problem of neighbouring communities seizing flocks may explain the reason for the building of extensive walls for some cities in the Peloponnese. It has been argued, partly on the basis of Polybius' account of a raid on Messene in the 220s BC (4. 3. 8–4. 1), that one of the reasons for its new wall system in the 4th century was to serve as protection for flocks.

There seem to have been restrictions on grazing on land owned by some of the sanctuaries. For example, the inscription from Arkesine on Amorgos relates to some land which was the property of the sanctuary of Zeus and which restricted the pasturing of animals. A 4th-century inscription from Chios restricts pasturing and the spreading of dung on what must be considered sacred land. However, estates belonging to the temple of Delian Apollo on the islands of Delos and Mykonos included grazing land.

Grazing could be the prerogative of citizens who were given specific rights of pasture; such was the case at Tegea in Arcadia. Such rights could then be bestowed on specific individuals for services to the community. In the 1st century AD the citizens of Methana in the Argolid granted grazing rights to a resident of Corinth, L. Licinnius Anteros, in return for his acting on their behalf as *proxenos* ("consul") in the centre of Roman administration in the province. Such honours may in fact have become meaningless during the Hellenistic period, as sometimes they were bestowed on individuals who dwelt so far from the grazing areas that they are unlikely ever to have been in a position to take up the rights. In Hellenistic Boeotia the cities of Akraiphia, Kopai, and Orchomenus granted grazing rights on water meadows around Lake Copais as repayment for unpaid loans.

Pastoralism in Greece today is very different from what it is likely to have been like in antiquity. Rather than being linked to subsistence economies, flocks are intended to generate cash income. On contemporary Crete flocks can consist of some

400 sheep which require the care of two or three men. Flocks in antiquity are likely to have been used to produce wool and dairy products – sheep cheese from Ceos apparently sold for 90 drachmas a talent in the Hellenistic period – as well as meat. Traditional transhumant patterns are being disrupted. For example, the Sarakatsans of northwestern Greece used to exploit the plains around Ioannina until settlers from Turkey took over in 1927. Subsequently, the Sarakatsans have looked to large urban populations such as Athens for their markets.

DAVID W.J. GILL

See also Animals, Transhumance

Further Reading

Braudel, Fernand, *The Mediterranean and the Mediterranean World in the Age of Philip II*, 2 vols, London: Collins, and New York: Harper, 1972–73

Cherry, J.F., "Pastoralism and the Role of Animals in the Pre- and Protohistoric Economies of the Aegean" in *Pastoral Economies in Classical Antiquity*, edited by C.R. Whittaker, Cambridge: Cambridge Philological Society, 1988

Hodkinson, S., "Animal Husbandry in the Greek Polis" in *Pastoral Economies in Classical Antiquity*, edited by C.R. Whittaker, Cambridge: Cambridge Philological Society, 1988

Jameson, Michael H., Curtis N. Runnels, and Tjeerd van Andel, *A Greek Countryside: The Southern Argolid from Prehistory to the Present Day*, Stanford, California: Stanford University Press, 1994

Lamb, Winifred, "Arcadian Bronze Statuettes", *Annual of the British School at Athens*, 27 (1926): pp. 133–48

Lamb, Winifred, *Greek and Roman Bronzes*, London: Methuen, 1929; as *Ancient Greek and Roman Bronzes*, Chicago: Argonaut, 1969

Mee, Christopher and Hamish Forbes (editors), *A Rough and Rocky Place: The Landscape and Settlement History of the Methana Peninsula, Greece*, Liverpool: Liverpool University Press, 1997

Osborne, Robin, Jr., *Classical Landscape with Figures: The Ancient Greek City and its Countryside*, London: George Philip, and Dobbs Ferry, New York: Sheridan House, 1987

Rackham, Oliver and Jennifer Moody, *The Making of the Cretan Landscape*, Manchester: Manchester University Press, 1996, chapter 14

Sherratt, A., Pastoralism entry in *The Oxford Companion to Archaeology*, edited by Brian M. Fagan, Oxford and New York: Oxford University Press, 1996, pp. 557–59

Shipley, Graham and John Salmon (editors), *Human Landscapes in Classical Antiquity: Environment and Culture*, London and New York: Routledge, 1996

Skydsgaard, J.E., "Transhumance in Ancient Greece" in *Pastoral Economies in Classical Antiquity*, edited by C.R. Whittaker, 1988

Warren, P.M., *Myrtos: An Early Bronze Age Settlement in Crete*, London: British School of Archaeology at Athens, 1972

Whittaker, C.R. (editor), *Pastoral Economies in Classical Antiquity*, Cambridge: Cambridge Philological Society, 1988

Patmos

Island in the Dodecanese

The small island of Patmos, the most northerly of the Dodecanese and only 39 sq km in area, has achieved a world-wide fame out of all proportion to its size solely through its biblical associations. More than any other of the Greek islands it has, on account of its being where St John the Evangelist wrote the Apocalypse, become established as the one where the Hellenic world was integrated most closely with New Testament history.

Patmos lies some 56 km off the coast of Asia Minor and 34 km from its much larger neighbour, Samos, to the north. It was never blessed with good agricultural conditions, having poor soil and little water, and has no deep natural harbour; it is quite hilly, with its highest point rising to 270 m. In early Hellenic history it was recorded as being peopled first by Mycenaeans, and later by Dorians and Ionians, but was only mentioned once in passing by Thucydides.

During the Roman period Patmos was used as a place of exile for political prisoners, and it was for this reason that St John (also known as St John the Theologian or St John the Divine, in Greek St John Theologos) was banished to the island, probably in AD 95, during the reign of the emperor Domitian. This association of the island with a major New Testament figure received surprisingly little attention during the earlier Christian centuries, and there is evidence of only one basilica being built here before 1088. It was then that almost a millennium of neglect was ended when the emperor Alexios I Komnenos granted to a monk from Bithynia, Osios ("the holy") Christodoulos, permission to found a monastery here dedicated to St John Theologos. It is this foundation, accompanied by a chrysobull of the emperor (still held by the monastery) and the grant of many privileges, that permanently changed the fortunes of the island, with the monastery's fame and prestige growing with every century.

The island was not named in the Deed of Partition of 1204, and the Venetians, after they had taken it over, seem to have allowed it substantial independence and granted a number of privileges. In the same way the Knights of Rhodes (the Hospitallers) never used Patmos as a base for harassing Turkish shipping, and this may have been the reason for the Turks allowing the abbot to collect the taxes that formed the island's annual tribute after 1454, treating the island and its inhabitants with considerable tolerance. The growing fame of the island made it the target of many later attacks, although the fortifications of the monastery ensured that no assailant was ever able to take it by force. Like the rest of the Dodecanese, Patmos did not return to full Greek control until 1947, when Italian rule ended.

The association of Patmos with St John has been responsible for two major foundations: one is the monastery mentioned above; and the second is the theological college, founded in 1669 when refugees arrived from recently occupied Crete. Its position as one of the leading theological colleges of Greece gives it a continuing importance for the Hellenic world, while the cave of St Anne, which is the traditional site of the writing of the Book of Revelation, is a dependency of the college.

The visitors that come to the island in their thousands each year ensure that the monastery dominates not only the landscape and appearance of Patmos, but also the life of the island. Its most prominent feature is its sequence of massive walls which continued to be strengthened and rebuilt until at least the later 17th century, giving it the aspect of a major fortress. They effectively protected the monastery from the plague of pirates which were to be the bane of Aegean life throughout the later medieval period and well into the 19th century. Within them the monastic buildings have grown, developed,

Patmos: the monastery of St John, founded in 1088, is on the skyline in the middle of the picture

and expanded, undergoing constant modification, rebuilding, and refurbishment. The two earliest building periods of the monastery were from 1088 to 1093 (within the lifetime of the founder) and the mid- to later 12th century, but the process of expansion has continued into relatively recent times. The earliest surviving parts are the later 12th-century *parekklesion* (side chapel) of the *katholikon* (main church), dedicated to the Theotokos, of which the contemporary frescos are the earliest in the whole monastery, and the *trapeza* (refectory), also of comparable date.

The library of the monastery contains one of the greatest collections of manuscripts in Greece, second only to some of those in the monastic libraries of Mount Athos, while the many rich and interesting objects in the treasury well reflect the monastery's fame and prestige. Among them are an 11th-century miniature mosaic icon of St Nicholas with a silver frame and other exceptionally fine 13th-century icons. It is, of course, objects of this kind, many of them made from precious metal, that are most liable to dispersal. They were brought to Patmos by donors from many parts of Europe, with Russia, Georgia, Romania, Moldavia, and Italy among the countries represented. Almost all objects of metalwork that remain date from the 18th century or later, reflecting the large losses that are known to have occurred. Manuscripts, some of which are now to be found in major public collections, also left the library at different times.

The cave of St Anne, where St John traditionally wrote the book of the Apocalypse, was not mentioned by Osios Christodoulos, and seems only to have been adopted in the 12th century; some wall-paintings in the sanctuary, discovered in 1973, are thought to be of this date and constitute the best evidence for its first identification. Nevertheless, it is probably true that the image of St John Theologos dictating to the deacon Prochoros in the cave, which appears on countless icons and gospel illustrations, is the form in which Patmos became most widely known during the medieval period and later.

PAUL HETHERINGTON

Summary

The most northerly of the Dodecanese islands, Patmos has been occupied throughout Greek history but only achieved fame in the Christian period. It was on Patmos that St John composed the Book of Revelation. In his name a monastery was founded in 1088 and a theological college in 1669.

Further Reading

Chatzidakis, Manolis, *Icons of Patmos: Questions of Byzantine and Post-Byzantine Painting*, Athens, 1985
Komines, Athanasios D. (editor), *Patmos: Treasures of the Monastery*, Athens, 1988
Stone, T., *Patmos*, Athens, 1984

Patras

City in the northwest Peloponnese

Patras is a commercial and industrial city in the northwestern Peloponnese, the capital of Achaea prefecture, the largest municipality, and the most important cultural and spiritual centre of western Greece. It is also the major port of the country for passengers travelling to and from the western Mediterranean. Patras is the third largest municipality in Greece after Athens and Thessalonica with a population of about 300,000. The city is divided into an upper and a lower town (Ano and Kato Poli). The upper town is built on a hill, whereas the lower is on a slope that extends to the sea. The city is located at the foot of Mount Panachaiko or Vodias, which is about 9 km from the sea. Patras is one of few Greek cities to have been built according to a city plan; its roads are straight and at right angles to each other. The establishment in 1966 of the university reinforced the role of the city as an important cultural centre. Even from the years of Ottoman occupation, the city was a big export centre and a major port to the western Mediterranean. Because of its strategic geographical position it developed early industrial enterprises such as the cotton-spinning mill that was established in 1844.

The name of the city is believed to be derived from Patreas, a mythological hero who is regarded as its first settler c.1100–1080 BC, although other opinions exist, e.g. that the name is derived from Patrous a district of Egyptian Thebes and was given to the city by a tribe that came from there, or from Patar, a town in Asia Minor. The most probable explanation seems to be the first one. Patreas' father was a nobleman from the region of Laconia in the southeastern Peloponnese who took shelter near Patras after he was found guilty of conspiracy against the authorities. Patreas then conquered the nearby towns and villages and unified them under the name of Patras. Pausanias (2nd century AD) described the city as a cosmopolitan one with many temples, statutes, and groves.

Patras was one of the 12 cities that made up the Achaean League, an ancient Greek version of the contemporary European Union. The city followed the policy of the league and neither fought against the Persians nor took part in the civil wars between the Greek cities. During the Peloponnesian War, Patras was a passive ally of Sparta without being actively engaged in the conflict.

The Achaean League was dismantled in 338 BC by Philip II of Macedon because it supported Athens against him. In the wars against the Romans, Patras and the re-formed Achaean League supported Philip V. However, after the Romans had defeated him and declared the city independent, it joined the Roman camp. Patras, like all Greek cities, became subject to Rome in 146 BC. After the battle of Actium in 31 BC the city was granted many privileges. It was declared independent and had its own council. It did not pay any taxes and the only liability imposed on it was acceptance of the Roman judicial authority.

According to tradition, St Andrew spent his last years in Patras and suffered martyrdom there c.AD 60. Patras was Christianized during the reign of Constantine the Great (307–336). The city was destroyed twice by the Goths, during the Byzantine period it suffered many raids from pirates, and in 805 it withstood a formidable siege by Vandals.

In the 9th century Patras was a thriving commercial city, and had established itself as a silk- trading centre. In 1204 Patras was occupied by Franks and again became a prosperous city for about 200 years. In 1408 the city came under the aegis of Venice and flourished commercially but in 1446 it was burned by Sultan Murad as it resisted the Ottoman invaders. After a brief period of protection by Venetian and Greek nobles, the city was captured by the Ottomans in 1461 and remained under their rule until the eve of the Greek revolution (1821). A brief period of resistance against the Turks in 1769, when the Orloff brothers came with their fleet to liberate the town, ended with the killing of its residents and the torching of the city. Patras was rebuilt and at the time of the Greek revolution was the main port for agricultural exports to western Europe.

In the city was based the Peloponnesian branch of the Society of Friends (*Philiki Hetaireia*), the principal revolutionary organization. From the start of hostilities Patras was one of the first cities to act against Ottoman rule and one of the first to be liberated. Despite the bravery of the rebels, the Turks could not be dislodged from the castle. Turkish reinforcements occupied the city which remained under Turkish rule until 1828 when the French philhellene general Messeaun liberated the Peloponnese. In October 1828 Messeaun delivered the city to the first Greek governor, Count Kapodistria.

During the following years the city rapidly grew into a big municipality with dynamic industrial and commercial enterprises. Moreover, it became the country's gateway to western Europe, and the export centre of agricultural products such as olive oil, tobacco, and currants. After World War II its port was established as the main transit centre to Europe and handled increasing numbers of passengers to and from Italy as the country became a member of the European Community. In addition, Patras is considered to be the main centre of culture in western Greece, renowned for its carnival that takes place during the winter.

DIMITRIOS GKAMAS

Summary

A city in the northwest Peloponnese, Patras was probably named after the mythical hero Patreas. As a member of the Achaean League it took no part in the Persian and Peloponnesian Wars. Under the Romans it was granted generous privileges and prospered. It was among the first cities to join the revolution of 1821. It is now a major port, industrial centre, and university town.

Further Reading

Finlay, George, *A History of Greece from its Conquest by the Romans to the Present Time, BC 146 to AD 1864*, revised by H.F. Tozer, 7 vols, Oxford: Clarendon Press, 1877; reprinted New York: AMS Press, 1970

Freeman, Kathleen, *Greek City-States*, London, MacDonald: 1950

Sealey, Raphael, *A History of the Greek City-States, 700–338 BC*, Berkeley: University of California Press, 1977

Vournas, T., *Istoria tis sinxronus Elladas* [History of Modern Greece], Athens, 1977

Patriarchate of Constantinople

In the ancient Church certain cities with patriarchs (members of the episcopate enjoying a position of prominence and special regard) were designated patriarchates. Thus, some, but not all, patriarchs oversaw a patriarchate. As early as the 4th century, patriarchates functioned as jurisdictional centres over smaller ecclesiastical regions, such as provinces and metropolitanates, within the neighbouring territory of the patriarchate. (This organization was a rough adaptation of the structure of Roman civil government.) Constantinople was one such patriarchate, with jurisdiction over Asia, Pontus, Thrace, and Greece.

It was claimed that the apostle Andrew founded the see of Constantinople and ordained Stachys its first bishop. The claim is doubtful and seems to have been motivated by a desire to convey an ancient, apostolic authority to Constantinople equal to that of Rome, whose Church claims to have been founded by St Peter. Such apostolic status could help resolve disputes concerning ecclesial primacy – Constantinople's claim could prove ecclesial superiority over Rome, given that Andrew was the first called of the apostles. If Stachys was nominated patriarch, it implied that Constantinople was endowed with the nobility and honour of a bishop; patriarchy certainly did not have the formal ecclesiastical sense it later acquired – on a par with that of a bishop or archbishop of Rome, Constantinople, Alexandria, Antioch, or Jerusalem, with specific ecclesiastical jurisdiction and correlative duties. That ecclesiastical jurisdiction included the right to decide canonical and moral issues as well as to ordain bishops to the principal sees within the provinces of a patriarchate. Regardless of such claims to apostolicity in the early Church after the 4th century – the incomparable role the patriarchate played in the formulation of Christian dogma is beyond dispute – the patriarchate of Constantinople enjoyed a pre-eminence second only to Rome. This status was due, in part, to the fact that Constantinople became the capital of the Roman empire and the patriarch was given authority by imperial decree as well as by ecumenical council. Canon 28 of Chalcedon (451), for example, declares Constantinople a "New Rome" and gives its Church the "equal privileges" (*isa presbeia*) to those held by the Church of "Old Rome". See also Canon 3 of the Council of Constantinople (381).

Constantinople formed part of the important ancient pentarchy: five sees which enjoyed particular ecclesiastical status and authority. The pentarchy comprised Rome, Constantinople, Alexandria, Antioch, and Jerusalem, and in the east this organization was viewed as an alternative to Rome's claim of primacy. The patriarchs of each of these sees succeeded the apostles in their status as heads of the Church and they had, according to *novella* 109 of Justinian I, final authority to govern the Church. Such equality, though, was more hoped for than realized. While Justinian I nominated the patriarch of Constantinople "ecumenical", i.e. with authority over the entire Byzantine empire, the papacy continued to insist on primacy in ecclesiastical matters, along with jurisdiction over all the eastern patriarchs. (The papacy had previously refused to acknowledge Canon 3 of Constantinople (381), giving the patriarch of Constantinople honour second only to Rome.) After the 6th century the papacy became less able to contest primacy as Rome lost political autonomy and stability. Due to loss of other members of the pentarchy – Alexandria, Antioch, and Jerusalem – to Arab invasions, the power of the patriarchate of Constantinople continued to increase. In the 9th century, however, the papacy began to regain ecclesiastical power as it learned to accommodate regnant political forces. The papacy employed its new-found strength, along with a tradition of ecclesial independence from Constantinople, to reassert its primacy.

This rivalry between the patriarchs of Constantinople and the popes of Rome culminated in 1054 when papal legates placed a bull of excommunication on the altar of Hagia Sophia. The bull excommunicated patriarch Keroularios of Constantinople, who responded by excommunicating, in turn, the papal legates. (These excommunications were rescinded in 1965 by mutual agreement between Pope Paul VI and Patriarch Athenagoras.) Roman dominance culminated in the establishment of a Latin patriarch in Constantinople in 1204 when the incumbent Greek patriarch, John X Kamateros, recognized the authority of Pope Innocent III. Subsequent Greek patriarchs ruled in exile at Nicaea until 1261. After the restoration of Greek patriarchal rule, however, the patriarchate was weakened by internal controversies, e.g. reunion with the Latin Church, as well as by external political pressures. The external political pressures – the advance of the Turks – forced the emperor to take a politically and religiously divisive step: to solicit aid from the Church's theological rival, Rome. In response, the pope demanded a number of theological concessions – "innovations" in the Greek view – including acceptance of the *filioque* clause as well as observance of papal jurisdiction and the Roman rites. Proposals and counterproposals were made over the course of months at the Council of Florence (1438–39), and finally accepted by the Byzantine delegation. But much to the displeasure of the emperor John VIII, a majority of Orthodox believers were unwilling to abide by the terms and conditions of the agreement, believing that it required them to embrace heresy. The quip "Better to see the turban of the Turks reigning in our city than the Latin mitre" expressed common sentiment. Signatories of the Florentine reunion agreement, such as Gennadios II Scholarios, sensing the futility of their compromise as well as domestic political dangers, repudiated their signatures on returning home. The beginning of the end for the Byzantine patriarchate occurred in 1453 with the fall of Constantinople to the Turks.

Under the Turks the authority of the patriarchate was severely curtailed, and yet, paradoxically, also increased. The patriarch no longer had to share authority with the Christian emperor and thus the patriarch became the supreme religious figure of the Eastern Church. Furthermore, the sultan Mehmet II, conqueror of Constantinople, extended the patriarch's authority over all Greek- and non-Greek-speaking Christians under Turkish rule, giving the patriarch civil as well as religious authority. The patriarchate thus acquired both religious and civil power over more Christians under the Ottoman Turkish empire than it had under the Byzantine emperors, since the sultan (and the patriarch) now regarded previously independent Christian Churches as falling under the authority of the patriarch. The patriarch, in short, now also became the emperor of the Christian empire, and his vestments – a mitre in the shape of the imperial crown, among other insignia – reflected the accretion of authority.

At the same time, patriarchal authority was severely curtailed by the sultan's required subordination of the patriarchate to himself. This practice, which continued under subsequent sultans, allowed the patriarchs to serve only at the goodwill and pleasure of the sultans, who directly and indirectly influenced the selection and retention of patriarchs. The sultans, for example, levied heavy taxes on each succeeding patriarch and persecuted the patriarchs severely, often making them responsible for any political instability created by the general Greek population. (In the 18th century, for example, 48 patriarchs served in 63 years.) Additionally, the religious (and physical) survival of the patriarchate required a certain political legerdemain, which occasionally engendered suspicion concerning the fidelity of the patriarch to the Orthodox faith. Among the sacrifices required of the patriarchate by the sultan was the appropriation of Hagia Sophia, which he turned into a mosque.

Gennadios II Scholarios, who was captured by the Turks on the fall of Constantinople but later released, became the first post-Byzantine patriarch. He served intermittently; the sultan, not yet confident of how to deal with the patriarchate, had him removed and reinstated. Gennadios's policy of accommodation with the Turks was finally unsuccessful and he was removed in 1465. His tenure provided the paradigm for his successors: a precarious reign marked by varying success at finding a harmonious modus vivendi. The political control of the patriarchate reached its apogee in the 17th and 18th centuries, during which time Greek bishops were given control over Bulgarian and Slavic sees and the local patriarchates were dissolved. The centralization of control included imposing Greek as the liturgical language, and Orthodoxy became identified with Hellenism. This cultural and religious identification led to a rather destructive form of Greek nationalism, subsequently alienating many of the foreign sees. Resentment at Greek control and the breakup of the Turkish empire led the various branches of the Orthodox Church to declare themselves independent of the patriarchate of Constantinople. Likewise, after the Greeks won independence, the Church of Greece declared itself independent of the patriarchate.

In the 17th century the patriarchate found contact with Protestantism useful in its quarrels with Rome, though beyond this utilitarian alliance patriarch Cyril I Lukaris was thoroughly sympathetic with certain Protestant views. Though most branches of Orthodoxy asserted and gained their independence in the 19th and 20th centuries, today the patriarchate continues to be viewed as spiritual leader by all Orthodox Christians. It has direct jurisdiction over, among other sees, the Orthodox Churches in North and South America, Australia, and western Europe. Politically, the patriarchate exists precariously under control of the Turkish government, suffering from efforts to diminish its authority even further.

JAMES L. SIEBACH

See also Orthodox Church

Further Reading

Dvornik, Francis, *Byzantium and the Roman Primacy*, New York: Fordham University Press, 1966
Every, George, *The Byzantine Patriarchate, 451–1204*, London: SPCK, 1947; reprinted New York: AMS Press, 1980
Kazhdan, A.P. (editor), *The Oxford Dictionary of Byzantium*, 3 vols, New York and Oxford: Oxford University Press, 1991
Maximos of Sardes, *The Oecumenical Patriarchate in the Orthodox Church: A Study in the History and Canons*, Thessalonica: Patriarchal Institute for Patristic Studies, 1976
Meyendorff, John, *The Orthodox Church: Its Past and its Role in the World Today*, New York: Pantheon, and London: Darton Longman and Todd, 1962

Patronage

Patronage in the sense of established relationships between patrons and their clients is a common feature of many societies. The modern Greek nation state established in 1830 was based on a Western model of centralized administration under a monarchical government, whose autocratic powers were only partially checked by the introduction of a parliamentary constitution in 1844. This structure was imposed on a rural population of subsistence farmers. Inevitably the taxes levied on villages to support a distant administration of ministries, civil servants, and armed forces were seen as a regime of exploitation that drained resources from families and returned nothing.

That local communities seldom resisted, or negotiated with, central authorities was due to the segmented structure of such groups. Categorical obligations to their families that restricted individuals to forms of social and economic cooperation within a narrow circle of kinsmen and friends made corporate action on any scale difficult. It is true that in recent years producers' cooperatives have flourished but they are regarded, nevertheless, as organizations backed by the external authority of the state and villagers who act as their local officials are distrusted. Generally collective enterprises are undermined by consideration for the material interest and prestige of individual families. Instead, the heads of families have looked to form exclusive alliances in, or more often outside, the local community by offering their social, economic, and electoral support in exchange for a patron's influence in dealings with merchants, shopkeepers, or local agents of the state.

Typical patrons within the village are the elected president of the village council, whose signature and recommendation are needed on application forms to ministries and banks; the coffee shop owner, who may support a limited system of credit to his customers; and other men with wealth or outside connections. The client will refer to his patron as his "friend" to disguise the discomfort of his voluntary subordination. Nevertheless, if a "friend" uses his "means" (*mesa*) to protect and assist a man, the latter is under a general obligation to support his benefactor politically. Factions and clienteles loosely organized around relationships of friendship and patronage have historically been the basis for mobilizing support for national political parties in the Greek countryside.

If men cannot trust one another in their own community, the situation is much worse in their relations with people outside it. They expect to find that merchants exploit them and that public servants will be at least indifferent. Town Greeks, for their part, hold markedly ambivalent attitudes towards villagers. There is a nostalgia for the austere traditional values that to some extent still survive in the countryside, but a deep contempt for the material and social limitations of peasant life. Despite the fact that most are themselves migrants, or the children of migrants, from the villages, the myths of their own history in the ancient city state and Byzantium are principally urban, and the styles of Western city life are the models to which they aspire. Apart from that they themselves share the belief that the family must be the principal object of moral duty and financial aspirations, which leaves little margin for concern about others. Where civil servants are concerned, the authority of the service, and their own position in it, are best preserved by keeping a villager in his place. This proper social distance is destroyed if undue concern is shown for a villager's affairs that is based simply on his rights as a citizen. Much business in public offices is done in the presence of more than one official. The ethos tends to be one of conscious self-importance, and the fact that many civil servants are themselves sons of peasants only increases this sensitivity. Within the public service itself status and position are defended by a reluctance to delegate the right of decision to junior officials. This in turn makes it difficult for any official to use his own judgement without referring to his seniors. This attitude, aptly termed *evthynophovia*, fear of responsibility, is transmitted to the public as an indifference based on a mechanical and inflexible interpretation of administrative procedures. Even trivial questions may be referred to Athens for a ruling. If delays are to be avoided in relatively routine applications for pensions or licences of various kinds, or exemptions are to be obtained in more complex cases, the need for "friendly" intervention is believed to be essential.

The search for an intermediary begins with the relationships that a villager has already established. As has been suggested, he may look to the president or some other influential villager or kinsman who can find the intermediary for him. Another possibility is that a villager may sell produce, grain, tobacco, or milk to a particular merchant who advances him credit, keeps him in debt, buys his produce at less than the market price, but in exchange for these benefits of an economic and assured supply is prepared to protect the welfare of his commercial client with his patronage. Provincial town doctors and shopkeepers, to whom villagers often turn in difficulty, are competitive and anxious to build and hold clienteles; lawyers are even more numerous and of many grades. There is a considerable amount of litigation in Greek rural life. If a villager has confidence in his lawyer this may have developed into a persisting relationship and, as the professional "fixer" in Greek society, the lawyer may be the most satisfactory intermediary. To confirm any of these relationships a man may ask a patron to become the godfather of his child, seeking to raise their association above the level of mere reciprocal advantage.

A critical institution in these relationships is the *parea*, the informal gathering of the town's professional elite which is sometimes to be seen sitting drinking in a public place such as the lounge of the best hotel. This group may include the prefect, senior army and police officers and civil servants, lawyers, doctors, judges, and the more substantial merchants.

By their mutual acceptance and public recognition of one another they emphasize the exclusive status that they share. Not to respond to the reasonable requests of a friend in the elite circle is to threaten one's membership of it, even one's professional prospects and career. Friends and dependants of other members of the circle will not be sent for legal advice or as patients or customers. In the case of public servants there may be pressure to block promotion, or post a man elsewhere. Crucially, from time to time, the local member of parliament will arrive from Athens to enter into his notebook the favours asked of him, either directly by individual constituents or through the mediation of a member of the local elite.

Although the framework of party organization is based, to a considerable degree, on networks of friendship and patronage, it is not suggested that political behaviour is reducible simply to those kinds of personal relationship. Even in the countryside the personal obligations and relationships that at various removes link a deputy, or a candidate, to the voters are not, of course, unaffected by the scale and power of the national party he represents. A man is adopted as a candidate on a party list because he is influential and possesses an existing social or professional clientele. Equally the fact that he has been chosen by a party that may form the government adds considerably to his influence, particularly if the potential patronage is considerable. The traditional pattern of rural patronage is still the method of political recruitment in many country areas, but the considerable increase in agricultural incomes in more prosperous districts, where the greater part of the produce is sold in national and international markets, has greatly reduced the sense of insecurity which creates the need for the favours and protection of old-style personal patrons.

In urban areas the links between voters and the patronage of members of parliament have never been so comprehensive. But Greek towns are heavily populated with small family concerns of every kind. The need for loans and trading licences, negotiations with tax officials, the necessity of building a clientele of customers in a market generally too small to justify the proliferation of small competing businesses, draw him inevitably into relationships with professional, commercial, and political patrons and "friends" in terms not dissimilar to those already examined for rural patronage. The common feature in the two situations is the vulnerability of the client in defence of his independence. The principal difference is that in the city such relationships cannot provide a complete system of political recruitment. It remains true, however, that in the city political patrons work for their supporters, that a man with more than a routine difficulty in dealing with a government office, a hospital, a school, or any other institution will immediately attempt to find an influential friend or intermediary without whose aid he feels impotent and defeated, and that in any social or professional exchange when something is apparently conceded an obligation will be perceived and not forgotten. But any account of Greek patronage is inadequate that simply emphasizes reciprocal manipulation in an unequal relationship. The recognized ability to perform important favours is in itself the most significant and valued mark of status and prestige. Even when there is no reason to build a clientele, or mobilize votes, Greeks still need to demonstrate their social power and benevolence by the number and quality of their dependants. This is so in many societies, but in Greece values of honour and self-regard give this process a particular impetus.

J.K. CAMPBELL

Further Reading

Campbell, J.K., *Honour, Family and Patronage: A Study of Institutions and Moral Values in a Greek Mountain Community*, Oxford: Clarendon Press, 1964

Campbell, J.K., "Traditional Values and Continuities in Greek Society" in *Greece in the 1980s*, edited by Richard Clogg, London: Macmillan, and New York: St Martin's Press, 1983

Gellner, Ernest, and John Waterbury (editors), *Patrons and Clients in Mediterranean Societies*, London: Duckworth, 1977

Legg, Keith R., *Politics in Modern Greece*, Stanford, California: Stanford University Press, 1969

Meynaud, Jean, *Les Forces politiques en Grèce*, Montreal and Lausanne, 1965

Paul, St

Christian apostle of the 1st century AD

Little more is known of Paul, the second founder of Christianity, than of Jesus Christ, the first. His own letters inform us that he was born an Israelite of the tribe of Benjamin, that he became a rigorous Pharisee, and that he persecuted Christians with zeal (Philippians 3: 4–6). It is widely believed, on the evidence of Acts 21: 39, that he was a Roman citizen from Tarsus in Cilicia. His writings partly corroborate Luke's story, which appears in Acts three times with variations, that he encountered the risen Christ while he was carrying his instructions to Damascus. The remainder of Luke's narrative is, however, not so easily reconciled with Paul's allusions to his own history. Where his biographer states that he always preached the Resurrection in the synagogues before turning to the Gentiles, the letters show compassion for the Jews but never speak of them as an object of his own ministry. Paul boasts of eight beatings and three shipwrecks (2 Corinthians 11: 24–25), yet the one flogging and the one shipwreck recorded in Acts both occurred too late to have figured in his reckoning. Acts knows nothing of the 14 years between Paul's conversion and his appointment as the "Apostle to the Gentiles" (Galatians 2: 1–7); Paul's account of a meeting with the Apostles in Galatians 2 cannot be harmonized with Luke's description of the apostolic council in Acts 15. Luke knows nothing of Paul's escape from Damascus under the governorship of Aretas (2 Corinthians 11: 32); Paul claims none of the miracles that Luke attributes to him. Nevertheless, the two records may be complementary rather than contradictory, and a tentative chronology of the letters may be built on Luke's divisions of Paul's labours into four successive journeys, each beginning from Jerusalem. The first began and terminated in Asia Minor, the second included leading cities of Greece and Macedonia, the third retraced the first two with a protracted stay at Ephesus, and the fourth brought Paul to Rome.

If Paul and Luke are both reliable witnesses, the letter to the Galatians would have been written to the churches of south Galatia between Paul's first and second meetings with the Jerusalem elders, as recounted in Acts 11 and 15. The text is a fierce polemic against the "men from James" (Galatians 2: 12; cf. Acts 14: 19), who in Paul's view have betrayed the first agreement by demanding the circumcision of gentile Christians. Paul maintained that the law had been superseded by the new covenant in the death of Christ (Galatians 3: 15), the carnal circumcision by an inward crucifixion, and the "faith that works by love" (6: 14; 5: 6). The apostolic council ruled in favour of Paul (on circumcision at least), but in the course of his second journey he found that deaths in Gentile churches had raised fears about the salvation of the body. Writing from Corinth (1 Thessalonians 3: 6; cf. 18: 5), he told the Thessalonians that the imminent return of Christ would rouse the dead from "sleep" and then the living would be taken up to join them "in the air" (1 Thessalonians 4: 13–17). Soon after, while he was passing through the Troad and Macedonia, he developed a richer doctrine in three letters to the Corinthians (1 Corinthians 16: 5; 2 Corinthians 2: 13; Acts 20: 1–6), which now survive as two. Every believer, he argued, is a member of a new body, that of Christ, which is united by love and diversified by gifts of the Holy Spirit. We must therefore keep our own bodies free from sin, and commemorate that of Christ in a common Eucharist, where the rich share with the poor. After death our animal body will be transformed into a spiritual body, which, like the true Temple of Israel, will be a "house not made with hands". For the present, the hope of future glory must sustain us as we suffer in the flesh.

Paul's voyage to Rome, occasioned by his own appeal to Caesar after he suffered a Roman flogging, was pre-empted by the letter which he sent to that city while bearing a collection to Jerusalem at the end of his third mission (Romans 15: 25–26; cf. Acts 21: 17). Declaring that Greeks and Jews owed their salvation to one another, he exhorted them to renounce their external pieties, to acknowledge the universal reign of sin in our present bodies, to embrace the resurrection with its promise of inward and outward renewal, and thus to live according to the new law of the Spirit, which is fulfilled in love and purity of heart. His subsequent imprisonment is attested by three letters, though the causes remain obscure. Whether he is enjoining Christ's humility on the Philippians (Philippians 2: 5–12), or warning the Colossians not to follow manmade heresies (Colossians 2: 3–23), or sending back the runaway Onesimus to Philemon, his thoughts are now consumed by the glorious destiny that awaits the "slave of Christ" (Philippians 1: 1; Philemon 1: 1; Colossians 4: 3). According to tradition Paul was decapitated in the Neronian persecution of AD 64, though not perhaps before he achieved his goal of visiting Spain (Romans 15: 24).

Paul may have been the earliest writer to place the confession of Christ as Son of God at the heart of the gospel. He was also the first to offer any theory of atonement, describing Christ as a sacrifice (1 Corinthians 5: 7), as one who became a curse for us (Galatians 3: 15), and as a mercy-seat (*hilasterion*) for our sins (Romans 3: 24–25). His account of the Last Supper (1 Corinthians 11: 23–25) found its way into the liturgy, and his argument that it is better not to marry (1 Corinthians 7) seemed to justify the celibacy of monks. He was variously interpreted, and both Catholics and Gnostics can be reckoned among his heirs. It was therefore almost inevitable that those who wished to claim him should attach his name to spurious compositions. The letter to the Ephesians would appear to be a summary of Paul's mature doctrine by another hand. In the letter to the Hebrews his thoughts are encased in a carapace of arguments and expressed in texts more suited to its (supposed) recipients. The author of 2 Thessalonians was evidently desirous to acquit Paul of a false belief that the world was soon to end. The three "Pastoral Epistles", addressed to Timothy and Titus, were produced to lend authority to the episcopate which developed after his death. They already betray the legalistic, patriarchal, and anti-Jewish sentiments which mar many later readings of the apostle. Among early commentators, Origen took Paul's distinction between the inner and outer man as the key to an allegorical interpretation of scripture, while the Antiochene school of Theodore, Theodoret, and Chrysostom gave more weight to his personality, his audience, and the circumstances of his writing. All agreed, however, that he was preaching not so much freedom from the law as freedom to obey it in the Spirit; hence the Greek Church has resisted antinomian exegesis, with its concomitant beliefs in total depravity and irresistible predestination. Holding that Paul intended to change his hearers and not merely to formulate doctrine, Greek theology emphasizes the ethical and sacramental elements in his thought.

MARK EDWARDS

See also Christianity

Biography
Born (as Saul) at Tarsus in Cilicia, Paul was a Jew and a pharisee who persecuted Christians. Converted to Christianity c.AD 33, he became known as the "Apostle to the Gentiles". He undertook four missionary journeys and wrote epistles to many young churches. He was imprisoned in Rome and executed, probably in AD 64.

Further Reading
Barth, Karl, *The Epistle to the Romans*, London: Oxford University Press, 1933
Betz, Hans Dieter, *Galatians: A Commentary on Paul's Letter to the Churches in Galatia*, Philadelphia: Fortress Press, 1979
Bultmann, Rudolf, *Theology of the New Testament*, vol. 1, London: SCM Press, 1952
Davies, William David, *Paul and Rabbinic Judaism: Some Rabbinic Elements in Pauline Theology*, 2nd edition London: SPCK, 1965; New York: Harper and Row, 1967
Dodd, C.H., *The Meaning of Paul for Today*, London: G. Allen, 1920
Engberg-Pedersen, Troels (editor), *Paul in his Hellenistic Context*, Edinburgh: Clark, 1994; Minneapolis: Fortress Press, 1995
Gaston, Lloyd, *Paul and the Torah*, Vancouver: University of British Columbia Press, 1987
Harrison, Pery Neale, *The Problem of the Pastoral Epistles*, Oxford: Clarendon Press, 1921
Käsemann, Ernst, *Commentary on Romans*, London: SCM Press, and Grand Rapids, Michigan: Eerdmans, 1980
Lüdemann, Gerd, *Paul: Apostle to the Gentiles: Studies in Chronology*, London: SCM Press, and Philadelphia: Fortress Press, 1984
Minear, Paul S., *The Obedience of Faith: The Purposes of Paul in the Epistle to the Romans*, London: SCM Press, and Naperville, Illinois: A.R. Allenson, 1971
Raisanen, Heikki, *Paul and the Law*, Tübingen: Mohr, 1983; Philadelphia: Fortress Press, 1986
Ramsay, William Mitchell, *Paul the Traveller and the Roman Citizen*, London: Hodder and Stoughton, 1895
Robinson, John A.T., *The Body: A Study in Pauline Theology*, London: SCM Press, and Chicago: Regnery, 1952
Sanders, E.P., *Paul and Palestinian Judaism: A Comparison of Patterns of Religion*, Philadelphia: Fortress Press, and London: SCM Press, 1977
Sanders, E.P., *Paul, the Law, and the Jewish People*, Philadelphia: Fortress Press, 1982; London: SCM Press, 1985
Schweitzer, Albert, *The Mysticism of Paul the Apostle*, London: A. & C. Black, 1931; reprinted Baltimore: Johns Hopkins University Press, 1998
Theissen, Gerd, *The Social Setting of Pauline Christianity: Essays on Corinth*, Philadelphia: Fortress Press, 1982
Wright, N.T., *The Climax of the Covenant*, Edinburgh: Clark, 1991; Minneapolis: Fortress Press, 1992

Paulicians
Dualist sect

Paulicians was the name given to a group of militaristic dualist heretics who were active in Armenia, eastern Asia Minor, and later Thrace throughout the Byzantine era. There is still much scholarly debate over the nature of this sect due to the conflicting information contained in the sources. Peter of Sicily, who was sent as an ambassador by the Byzantine emperor to the Paulician state based in Tephrice in 869, is the most important source. According to Peter, the group originated with Paul of Samosata in the 3rd century, from whom they took their name. This identification has led to much confusion since there were two Pauls associated with Samosata, one a bishop of Antioch who promoted the Adoptionist doctrine and another, the son of a woman named Callinice, who was reputed to be a Manichaean. However, this woman could not have been a Manichaean since her son lived well before Mani's birth. It is more likely that she was a Gnostic, possibly even a Marcionite. Nevertheless, the confusion has led to the tradition of associating Paulicians with Manichaeanism.

The true origin of the sect probably goes no further back than the 7th century when an Armenian by the name of Constantine of Mananali learned the heretical doctrines in Syria and later took the name Silvanos, a companion of St Paul. He taught his followers to read only the New Testament and rejected those Manichaean doctrines which conflicted with Christianity. However, Peter of Sicily claimed that the sect used the teachings of the New Testament only for the ordinary members of the sect and had a secret teaching reserved for a select few in which dualist doctrines were taught. Dimitri Obolensky sees in this the influence of the Gnostic Marcionite sect with whom the Paulicians came into contact in Armenia. These contacts, coupled with the reforms of Constantine, made the Paulicians closer to Marcionism in doctrine than Manichaeanism. In addition, Obolensky notes some similarities with Messalian beliefs and concludes that Paulicianism arose under the combined influence of Manichaean, Marcionite, and Messalian sects. He also affirms that all the main tenets of Paulicianism, such as belief in the two principles, denial of the Incarnation, rejection of the Old Testament, anti-sacramentalism, etc., are derived from Manichaeanism and further argues that the absence of certain Manichaean doctrines, such as abstention from meat and sexual intercourse, as well as the Manichaean creation myth, were due to the reforms of Constantine-Silvanos. The Paulicians established themselves in Asia Minor under a succession of leaders who took Pauline pastoral names. The use of the name "Paulician" may actually be a reflection of the high regard in which the sect held the apostle Paul. The churches they founded were also named after places associated with St Paul.

Armenian sources, on the other hand, point to a tradition that the Paulicians were actually an Armenian sect dating back to the 5th century. The earlier sources do not mention them by name and scholars are not sure if they can be identified with these earlier heretical groups. However, in the 7th and 8th centuries they are specifically mentioned by name in the "Canons and Constitutions" of the Council of Albania, the Council of Dwin, and in the tract *Against the Paulicians* by John of Otzun. The Armenian sources also differ from the Greek in their characterization of Paulician doctrine by claiming that the Paulicians followed the Adoptionist doctrines of Paul of Samosata who argued that Christ was originally an ordinary man who was adopted by God as the Son of God for his extraordinary virtue, a condition which any equally righteous person can achieve. This argument was first advanced by Fred Conybeare who, in 1891, discovered a manuscript of the tract *The Key of Truth*. The theology of this work reflects Adoptionist Christian beliefs and even contradicts some known Paulician doctrines, such as dualism and rejection of the sacraments. Conybeare claimed that this work was a true manual of the Paulician Church and that it confirms that the Paulicians were Adoptionists, the descendants of Paul of Samosata, a position which has received more recent support from Nina Garsoïan. This argument was originally rejected by Steven Runciman, and later Paul Lemerle, who identified this Adoptionist Armenian group as the Thonraki, a sect which shared some doctrinal similarities with the Paulicians and were later confused with them. The Paulicians were also iconoclastic. Some of their number were later invited into the Byzantine empire by the iconoclastic emperors Leo III (717–41) and Constantine V (741–75). Garsoïan argues that it was during this time that they probably came under the influence of Gnostic dualism (which is how their beliefs are characterized by the Greek sources). Here they were then described as descendants of the Manichaeans who believed in the two principles of good and evil and equated the material world with the evil principle. All the sources agree that the Paulicians rejected the authority of the Orthodox Church and its sacraments and images, including the cross. The Paulicians were eventually driven from Constantinople by the empress Theodora in 842. They fled to eastern Asia Minor where they organized themselves militarily and established their own state centred around Tephrice. This fact in and of itself should cast doubt on the characterization of them as Manichaean, since Mani did not advocate warfare for his followers and even forbad the killing of any living thing. The Paulician state was eventually crushed by Basil I in 872 and a number of Paulicians were forcibly settled in Thrace around Philippopolis, where they are subsequently believed to have influenced the Bogomils.

The Paulicians would occasionally reappear in later Byzantine sources. Anna Komnene recounted the experiences of her father Alexios Komnenos (1081–1118) with this sect. The Paulicians revolted against the Byzantines in 1078, but were suppressed by Alexios Komnenos before he became emperor. Despite this experience, in 1081 the Paulicians made up part of Alexios's army in his campaign against Robert Guiscard. After Alexios's defeat at Dyrrachium the Paulicians deserted and returned to Philippopolis. Alexios had to wait until after his victory over the Normans at Kastoria (1083) to punish the Paulicians for their treachery. Unable to attack the Paulicians in their stronghold at Philippopolis, Alexios lured a delegation of Paulician representatives to appear before him at Constantinople. Once this delegation arrived in Constantinople, Alexios had the Paulician leaders arrested and imprisoned. Later, he agreed to pardon those heretics who apostatized and accepted baptism. Those who continued to resist conversion were exiled to some islands. Later that year (1084) a mutiny broke out under the leadership of a Paulician named Traulos, who was a servant in the imperial household, and was only suppressed with great difficulty. In 1114 Alexios established his headquarters at Philippopolis and took the opportunity to try personally to win the heretics over to Orthodoxy. Despite his failure to convert the leaders of the Paulicians, Anna reported that hundreds of their followers accepted conversion. The apostates were later settled in a new city located near Philippopolis called Alexiopolis or Neokastron. Alexios then returned to Constantinople where he resumed his theological debates with the imprisoned Paulician leaders. Only one of them relented and embraced Orthodoxy while the others were unregenerate and remained in prison until their deaths.

Another source which mentions the later activities of the Paulicians is the 14th-century account *The Life of Saint Hilarion of Moglena*, written by Euthymios of Trnovo, which includes a description of the saint's efforts to suppress the large number of heretics residing in his diocese, which included Bogomils, Paulicians, and Monophysites.

JOHN F. SHEAN

See also Heresy

Summary

A heretical sect of Armenian origin, the Paulicians appeared probably first in the 7th century and established themselves in Asia Minor. They were iconoclasts and dualists, but there is debate about the precise nature of their beliefs. In the 9th century they had their own state centred on Tephrice. They appear occasionally in the sources throughout the Byzantine period.

Further Reading

Conybeare, Fred C., *The Key of Truth: A Manual of the Paulician Church of Armenia*, Oxford: Clarendon Press, 1898

Garsoïan, Nina G., *The Paulician Heresy: A Study of the Origin and Development of Paulicianism in Armenia and the Eastern Provinces of the Byzantine Empire*, The Hague: Mouton, 1967

Obolensky, Dimitri, *The Bogomils: A Study in Balkan Neo-Manichaeism*, Cambridge: Cambridge University Press, 1948

Peter of Sicily, "The History of the Manichaeans called Paulicians" in *Patrologia Graeca*, edited by J.-P. Migne, vol. 104, columns 1239–1303.

Runciman, Steven, *The Medieval Manichee: A Study of the Christian Dualist Heresy*, Cambridge and New York: Cambridge University Press, 1955; reprinted 1982

Pausanias _c._AD 115–180

Travel writer

All our information about Pausanias' life has to be gathered from his work: he was not yet fully adult in AD 130 (8. 9. 7); the first book of his work must have been written before Herodes Atticus' great building programme in Athens, i.e. before AD 160; his historical references stop around AD 180. We know next to nothing about his personal life; his work lacks a prologue (where ancient writers usually introduced themselves) and a dedication; even his name is known only from the early Byzantine geographer Stephanus (who used Pausanias' work as a source around AD 535). Pausanias originated from Lydia, probably from Magnesia ad Sipylum, because he describes this region with extraordinary care and knowledge. He was born into a wealthy family of the city's elite; his work shows him to be a highly educated man, and he had the means to dedicate his life to extensive travelling (apart from Greece, he knows the whole of western Asia Minor, large parts of central Anatolia, Syria, Palestine, and Egypt). As he rarely mentions living people, we know nothing about his friends or the circles he associated with.

Pausanias' work, the _Periegesis Hellados_ (Guide to Greece) in ten books (about 900 printed pages), is very probably completely preserved. Because parts of Greece are missing in the description and the work has no epilogue, it was sometimes thought that it remained incomplete or that the last part had been lost; this, however, is unlikely, for numerous cross-references throughout show that it was written following an elaborate plan from the beginning. Periegesis as a genre arose in Hellenistic times (3rd and 2nd centuries BC), but before Pausanias these works were mostly monographs on very restricted themes. Pausanias' Greece comprises the Greek mainland on the Balkan peninsula; the ten books deal with: (1) Athens, Attica, Megara; (2) Corinth, Argolis, the island of Aegina; (3) Laconia; (4) Messenia; (5) and (6) Elis (with a detailed description of Olympia); (7) Achaea; (8) Arcadia; (9) Boeotia; (10) Phocis (above all Delphi), and parts of Locris. On the one hand, Pausanias aims to select the most valuable and remarkable from the abundance of curiosities that he saw, but on the other hand he also wants to be as comprehensive as possible; so he often describes small and remote places. Each book starts with an introduction about the legends and mythology of the region, and Pausanias also gives historical explanations concerning the monuments he describes.

In the 19th and early 20th centuries Pausanias was considered a third-rate author, harshly judged by, for example, the influential scholar Ulrich von Wilamowitz-Moellendorff, and accused of plagiarizing older works and not really having seen the things he described. Only since the beginning of the 20th century has it become clear how conscientiously Pausanias fulfilled the task he had set himself, and how astonishingly reliable he is. For a whole series of ancient places he was the decisive guide for modern excavators: at Mycenae, Heinrich Schliemann was the first to understand Pausanias' passage about the town and to draw the right conclusions – namely, that the graves must lie _behind_ the Lion Gate; when the monuments of Troezen were excavated in 1941, their identification was possible only because of Pausanias' precise report. His

systematic description of Messene, too, was confirmed by the finds; in the town of Callipolis, which according to Pausanias was totally destroyed by the Celts in 279/278 BC, excavations brought to light the completely burned buildings.

Pausanias was well versed in ancient Greek authors, above all lyric and epic poetry (which he often quotes) and, of course, the historians, of whom Herodotus was his great model. In his historical digressions he can be careless, and it is sometimes unclear whether he is giving his own interpretation or quoting from an older source and, if so, from which. On the other hand he is very reliable when he extracts historical facts directly from a monument: he reports hundreds of inscriptions, many of which have been confirmed by finds and have often proved very helpful for the transcription and historical setting of them.

Pausanias never explicitly states his personal preferences, but they become clear from his selection. First of all, it is its age that makes a site or cult interesting to him; this taste for the ancient is characteristic of the 2nd century AD and shared by many of his educated contemporaries. A more personal trait is his preferring religious monuments to profane ones. In matters of art, Pausanias again shows the high appraisal of the past characteristic of his epoch: he bestows the first place on Phidias, the second on Alcamenes (4. 10. 8); he appreciates some sculptures of the 6th and all of the 5th century BC, as well as the sculptors Cephisodotus and Praxiteles of the 4th century; but only Damophon of Messene of the later period; he has no regard for Polyclitus and Lysippus; nor does he even mention Hellenistic art or Pergamene "baroque". Similarly, the buildings that please him are from the 5th and 4th centuries BC.

Historically, Pausanias is interested in the period of independent Greece (mostly the 4th century BC); he judges Greek states according to their behaviour when Greek freedom was endangered; in his eyes, only Athens always did its duty. Though living in the Roman world, Pausanias feels totally Greek, as his work shows throughout. He exhibits no open resentment towards the Romans, but they are foreign rulers, and unlike some other contemporaneous writers (e.g. Aelius Aristides) he does not regard Roman world dominion as logical or natural; he points out the brutalities and pillagings of Roman generals, above all of Sulla. However, as things improved in the 2nd century AD, Pausanias several times praises the philhellene Roman emperors Hadrian, Antoninus Pius, and Marcus Aurelius, who showed respect and care for Greece and its heritage; but he never appreciated Greece's loss of freedom.

Unlike other "intellectuals" of his time, Pausanias did not catch the public eye and apparently failed to reach the readership for whom he wrote, perhaps (as Habicht suggests) because by the time of his writing the great wave of Roman "philhellenism" was already over. Another reason for this neglect may be the curiously mixed character of his work: for people who just wanted a traveller's guide the long historical digressions were boring, while those more interested in history did not want to read descriptions of buildings and works of art they did not have before their eyes. Apart from Stephanus of Byzantium (see above), the only attested reader of Pausanias in antiquity may have been Aelian (_c._AD 200). In Byzantine times, too, he is apparently ignored by Photios, but Arethas read him and probably commissioned a minuscule copy of the text (now lost), which in turn was read by Maximos Planudes (late 13th century) and Nikephoros Gregoras (14th century); some excerpts are already found in the *Suda* lexicon. Around 1400 Arethas's manuscript came to Italy, establishing Pausanias' presence in the west, which was to be so valuable for archaeologists in the 19th and 20th centuries.

BALBINA BÄBLER

Biography

Born c.AD 115 to a wealthy family in Lydia, probably at Magnesia ad Sipylum, Pausanias was well educated. He had the resources to spend his life travelling and writing about his travels. He knew Asia Minor, Syria, Palestine, and Egypt; but his only surviving work is a "Guide to Greece" in ten books. Nothing is known of his life but he probably died c.180.

Writings

Description of Greece, translated by J.G. Frazer, 6 vols, London and New York: Macmillan, 1898; reprinted New York: Biblo and Tannen, 1965

Further Reading

Arafat, K.W., *Pausanias' Greece: Ancient Artists and Roman Rulers*, Cambridge and New York: Cambridge University Press, 1996
Bingen, Jean (editor), *Pausanias historien*, Geneva: Fondation Hardt, 1996
Diller, Aubrey, "Pausanias in the Middle Ages", *Transactions of the American Philological Association*, 87 (1956): pp. 84–97
Habicht, Christian, *Pausanias' Guide to Ancient Greece*, Berkeley: University of California Press, 1985
Regenbogen, Otto, Pausanias entry in *Real-Encyclopädie der klassischen Altertumswissenschaft*, edited by August Pauly et al., supplement 8, 1956, 1008–97
Swain, Simon, *Hellenism and Empire: Language, Classicism, and Power in the Greek World AD 50–250*, Oxford: Clarendon Press, and New York: Oxford University Press, 1996, pp. 330–56

Pelagonia, Battle of

Battle fought between Nicaeans and an alliance of Epirots and Latins in 1259

The decisive battle of Pelagonia (near modern Bitola in former Yugoslavian Macedonia close to the Greek border) in 1259 saw Greek forces engaged on both sides to decide the future fate of the Latin empire in Constantinople. This empire was founded in 1204, when a joint enterprise of Venice and western knights, the so-called Fourth Crusade, conquered Constantinople. Although the crusaders had taken the capital, they did not succeed in gaining control over the whole territory of the collapsed empire in Asia Minor and the southern Balkan peninsula. Seljuk rulers and the newly refounded (1185/86) Bulgarian state seized their advantage. Greek resistance sprang up in various provincial areas and resulted in two regional powers, the despotate of Epirus and the empire of Nicaea (modern Iznik, c.160 km southeast of Istanbul). In armed rivalry they tried to reach a common aim, the recapture of Constantinople for the Greeks.

In 1258 the Epirot leader Michael II hoped that a change in Nicaean rulership might offer the opportunity to strengthen his position. By marriage ties he arranged an alliance with two

Latin powers also interested in Balkan affairs: Manfred of Sicily, the illegitimate son of Frederick II of Hohenstaufen, pursued plans similar to the Norman ambitions of the 11th and 12th centuries and had already (1257/58) occupied parts of the Albanian coastland; William (Guillaume) II of Villehardouin, prince of Achaea (Peloponnese), wanted to extend his influence beyond the Corinthian Gulf, thus finally becoming the leader of the Latin rulers in the entire region. Their common opponent, Michael VIII Palaiologos, now emperor of Nicaea, recognized the imminent danger. After diplomatic negotiations had failed (see Akropolites, 1978, p. 79), in the spring of 1259 Michael's general and brother John Palaiologos attacked Michael II's positions in western Macedonia (around Ohrid) and forced the despot himself to retreat to Valona (modern Vlore in Albania). Here he got reinforcements from Manfred (400 heavily armed cavalry). William's forces, who came from the south, met him at Arta (summer 1259). The united armies crossed the Pindus mountains and marched in an easterly ark (see *Chronicle of Morea*, 3618–39, 3672–95) northwards (via Servia and Soskos) towards Prilep, which apparently had to be relieved (Akropolites, 1978, p. 81) before an attack on Thessalonica. The advancing forces suffered from constant attacks by swift Cuman archers on horseback. When tempers were frayed a quarrel flared up among the allies (see Pachymeres, 1984, 1. 31). As they were encamped around Pelagonia one night, a secret messenger from the Nicaean army reached Michael and somehow convinced him that his Latin partners would soon desert the common cause for their own profit. (The weak points in the triple alliance from the very beginning – diverging interests and the different cultural backgrounds of its members, cf. Gregoras, 1978, 3. 5 – now caused its breakdown.) Immediately the despot retired, and most of his soldiers did so before dawn. On the following day John's army attacked the numerically shrunken and certainly shocked enemy and won a decisive victory (September 1259), in which once again archers played a major part (*Chronicle of Morea*, 3950–4091). William was taken prisoner and only released two years later in exchange for considerable territorial concessions in the Peloponnese, where a new Greek–Frankish frontier was drawn. Michael II – after a short setback due to Pelagonia – was able to regain his local dominion, backed by Manfred, for whom the Epirot despotate served as a protective shield against Nicaean attacks on his Albanian possessions. For Baldwin II, Latin emperor in Constantinople, the outcome of Pelagonia extinguished any hope of political survival. On 15 August 1261 Michael VIII Palaiologos solemnly entered the traditional capital of the renewed Byzantine empire.

EWALD KISLINGER

Summary

At Pelagonia (near Bitola in the Former Yugoslav Republic of Macedonia) a battle was fought in 1259 between an alliance of Michael II of Epirus, Manfred of Sicily, and William II of Villehardouin on the one hand and Michael VIII Palaiologos of the empire of Nicaea on the other. Palaiologos won a decisive victory on the strength of which he was able to recapture Constantinople from the Latins in 1261.

Texts

Akropolites, Georgios, *Opera*, edited by August Heisenberg, revised by Peter Wirth, 2 vols, Stuttgart: Teubner, 1978

Cronica de Morea, edited by J.M. Egea, Madrid, 1996

Gregoras, Nikephoros, *Historia*, edited by Ludwig Schopen, 3 vols, Bonn: Weber, 1829–55

Pachymeres, Georgios, *Relations historiques*, edited and translated into French by Albert Failler, Paris: Belles Lettres, 1984–

Further Reading

Asonitis, Spyros, "Pelagonia (1259): mia nea Theorisi" [Pelagonia (1259): A New Viewpoint], *Byzantiaka*, 11 (1991): pp. 129–65

Geanakoplos, Deno J., "Greco-Latin Relations on the Eve of the Byzantine Restoration: The Battle of Pelagonia, 1259", *Dumbarton Oaks Papers*, 7 (1953): pp. 99–141

Kravari, Vassiliki, *Villes et villages de Macédoine occidentale*, Paris: Lethielleux, 1989, pp. 46, 311–13

Nicol, Donald M., "The Date of the Battle of Pelagonia", *Byzantinische Zeitschrift*, 49 (1956): pp. 68–71

Nicol, Donald M., *The Despotate of Epiros*, Oxford: Blackwell, 1957, pp. 166–91

Pelion, Mount

Region in Thessaly

Mount Pelion, often referred to as the mountain of the centaurs, has been an inspiring place from antiquity to the present day. Its place in mythology is marked by many references in Homer, Pindar, the tragedians (especially Euripides), and Apollonius Rhodius. It is situated in central Greece, in Magnesia, north of Mount Ossa. It was believed to be the home of the centaur Chiron, the wisest of the centaurs, associated with the education of many heroes such as Heracles, Achilles, Jason, and Asclepius. In Hesiod's version of the Gigantomachy, Mount Olympus was challenged when the Giants tried to pile Pelion on Ossa. Jason used timber from Pelion in order to build the ship *Argo* for his voyage to Colchis with the other Argonauts to get the golden fleece. The marriage of Thetis and Peleus was celebrated on Mount Pelion. Although it has an eminent position in Greek mythology, it was most probably not settled extensively in ancient times, except for some areas on the coast, e.g. Pagasae, Iolkos, Aphetae, Orminion, and, in Hellenistic times, Demetrias. There are, however, archaeological remains of sanctuaries, such as the temples to Zeus Akraios on the Pliasidi peak and to Apollo Koropaios at Boufa (on the west coast).

In Byzantine times Pelion was a monastic mountain. Many monasteries were built on the western slopes in particular. Excavations in the village of Lafko have brought to light Byzantine ceramic objects. Pelion has also played an important role in modern Greek history. During the Ottoman period several villages were granted administrative privileges that encouraged the practice of trade. The village settlements date from the 16th century, as is the case with many mountain areas in Greece. A number of communities were first established around monasteries. The Ottomans preferred to be in the plains rather than the mountains and that was an important factor in the movement of the local population towards the mountains. Due to the rich vegetation and abundance of water it was easy to develop a strong agriculture, and later, with various capital investments, industry and trade. Soon Pelion's commercial interests spread not only to the rest of Greece but to important commercial centres of Europe and Asia. Until the end of the 18th century it was a centre not only of the textile industry but also of shipbuilding.

Many villages became exceptional intellectual centres in which famous schools were established, particularly in the period of Greek Enlightenment. Milies, one of the most famous cultural centres of Pelion, had a school and a library rich in rare books that survives until today. Intellectuals such as Anthimos Gazis and Gregorios Konstantas are associated with the place. Zagora, Pelion's largest village, also had a library and a school where many fathers of the Greek revolution studied, including Rigas Velestinlis. Most information concerning Pelion for the 18th and 19th century comes from scholars such as Dimitrieis, Daniel Philippides, Nikolaos Magnes, and Nikolaos Georgiades. Intellectual life was very lively and was particularly associated with the debate about the Greek language. Philippos Ioannou and Gazis argued for the archaizing form known as katharevousa, whereas Konstantas and Philippides (both directors of the Milies school) were zealous supporters of demotic. The above-mentioned scholars were also part of the Greek Enlightment movement that promoted the belief in a solid education and scientific research in all disciplines. Korais was associated with the views of Gazis in the linguistic debate, and Katartzes with those of Philippides. The late 18th-century patriarch Kallinikos was a native of Zagora.

Pelion is also of interest for the artistic trends that were developed there both in secular and in religious painting. Popular art adorned the interior of many mansions, particularly in the villages of Makrinitsa, Portaria, Zagora, Drakeia, and Hagios Laurentios. The famous folk artist Theophilos Chatzimichail lived and worked in Pelion for some time until 1927. Many villages have post-Byzantine churches such as St George and St Kyriaki in Zagora, the Dormition of the Virgin in Mouresi, and the church of Panagia in Portaria, and bear witness to a strong iconographic tradition in the area. What is more interesting for the art historian is the folk element that has been incorporated into the received Byzantine tradition. As with post-Byzantine iconography in general, particularly in the 17th and 18th centuries, there are obvious influences from the Western and Russian traditions. The local architecture is perhaps the most distinctive feature of Mount Pelion. The traditional "tower" type houses with many small, narrow windows and several storeys (an architectural style believed to have developed in wartime) cling to the slopes of the mountain. The roofs of the local grey or greenish stone have become typical of the mountain. Makrinitsa, perhaps the most famous village nowadays, is a fine example, one of many, of the traditional architecture. With its highly attractive landscape which combines both mountain and sea and distinctive traditional colour, Pelion has also become a major tourist centre.

Andromache Karanika-Dimarogona

Summary

Mount Pelion, in central Greece, was important in mythology as the home of the centaur Chiron, but the area was not much settled in antiquity. In Byzantine times many monasteries were built on its slopes. During the Tourkokratia it developed as a commercial centre (textiles and shipbuilding); as an intellectual centre (schools and libraries); and as an artistic centre (with folk art incorporated in the post-Byzantine tradition).

Further Reading

Bourberes, Konstantinos, *Morphai tes Magnesias* [Aspects of Magnesia], Volos, 1973

Chourmouziades, Giorgos C., *Magnesia: to Chroniko henos Politismou* [Magnesia: The Story of a Civilization], Athens, 1982

Liapes, Kostas, *Ores tou Peliou* [Hours on Pelion], Athens, 1985

Sisilianos, Demetres, *I Makrinitsa kai to Pelio: Historia, Mnemeia, Epigraphai* [Makrinitsa and Pelion: History, Monuments, Inscriptions], Athens, 1939

Tzamtzes, A.I, *I navtilia tou Peliou sten Tourkokratia: Mia Agnoste Ptyche tes Neoteres Nautikes mas Historias* [Pelian Shipping during the Turkish Domination: An Unknown Aspect of our Modern Naval History], Athens, 1980

Pella

City in Macedonia

The fortunes of Pella, which became the chief city of the Macedonian kingdom, mirror those of the kingdom itself. The city was situated in the region known as Bottiaea, to the north of what was until quite recently the lake of Giannitsa, the ancient lake Lydias. This was originally an inlet of the sea, but the major rivers which flow into it, the Haliacmon, the Loudias, and the Axios, gradually caused it to silt up, and it was finally drained in the 1930s. In Classical times, in the 5th and 4th centuries BC, the southern part, near the original Macedonian centre of Aegae, had already silted, but there was still open water to the north, accessible from the sea by boats. There was no dry route across it from the south at this time, and the land route had to skirt the silted, marshy area. The incorporation of Bottiaea into the Macedonian kingdom, at an uncertain date before 500 BC, gave the Macedonians access to the Axios valley and the lands beyond, where there were rich silver mines, certainly exploited by the Macedonians in the reign of Alexander I, in the first half of the 5th century BC, though their hold on this region was somewhat precarious. As a result, the old centre of Aegae was in effect at one end of the Macedonian kingdom, and gained access to the extended territories only by the roundabout overland route. When at the end of the 5th century the king Archelaus sought to modernize and so strengthen his kingdom, one of his most important actions was to develop a new capital at Pella, more in the centre of the extended state.

Not much is known about Archelaus' foundation. He built a palace on the low hill which seems to have functioned as the acropolis. The cemeteries of this city have been partly excavated, and their position suggests that the town extended only on the immediate slopes of this hill, to the south of it. The town was probably sacked (though there is no archaeological evidence for this as yet) by the Illyrians during their incursion in 359 BC, which almost destroyed the Macedonian state.

Under Philip II the Macedonian kingdom revived and reached unprecedented bounds, and with it, Pella. A new plan was laid out covering an area of at least 1.5 × 1.2 km, with the acropolis at the northern end, and the city extending down to the water's edge to the south. Within this a regular grid plan was laid out, with blocks measuring 110 × 48 m, running north to south and separated by streets some 6 m wide. On the flatter ground below the acropolis was the agora, a vast, near-square space 200.15 × 180.50 m. It was approached by a principal east–west street, noticeably wider than the others, an arrangement which seems to have been pioneered by the agora named after its town planner, Hippodamus, at Piraeus. This is town planning on a lavish scale. It is comparable, in general size, with the late 5th-century BC layout of Rhodes, but the detailed plan, with its repetition of blocks in the proportion 2:1, is not quite the same as Rhodes, where the blocks are subdivisions of square units demarcated by wider streets. The best antecedent for Pella seems to be the enlarged city of Olynthus (late 5th century) in Chalcidice, which is closer to hand and a more obvious model for town planners employed by Philip, even though he had destroyed the Greek city. Olynthus, however, does not have the large central agora. Evidence for the actual development of the city within this plan is as yet only partial. The agora was surrounded by stoas which seem to have been continuous on all four sides of it, with a double row of rooms behind them, some of which were certainly used as shops. The northern part may have been more official, the southern part commercial, the dividing line being the main road which passes through the colonnades into the central square. However, the architectural development of this agora appears to be relatively late, of the late 3rd century BC, the time of Philip V, rather than of the original layout by Philip II.

The most striking feature of Pella is undoubtedly a group of luxurious houses situated south of the agora. One of these, designated by its excavators the House of the Rape of Helen (from the subject of a scene depicted on one of its mosaic floors), occupied half of one of the street blocks. Its rooms were arranged round a large courtyard embellished by 8 × 8 Doric columns. The main rooms on the north side, with the mosaics, were surmounted by an upper floor, with a gallery of Ionic columns overlooking the court. The House of Dionysus, two blocks to the east, was even larger, taking up two-thirds of a street block. A doorway with a two-column porch gave on to an entrance hall running east to west between two courtyards, that to the north with 6 × 6 Ionic columns, that to the south with 8 × 8 Doric. The north side, again, was surmounted by an upper floor, with, probably, another gallery overlooking the court. All the mosaics in these houses are splendid examples, with figure scenes, made from complete pebbles, the earlier system, rather than the cut tesserae used in late Hellenistic floors at Delos and elsewhere.

These houses are of a particular magnificence, and, as far as the archaeological evidence goes, without parallel in the Greek world. Yet at Pella they are only two among others, and though this may well represent the wealthiest part of the city, they should not be regarded as special or public buildings. What they indicate is the degree of wealth achieved in Macedon as a result of the conquests of Philip and Alexander, to which period, from their architecture and contents, they undoubtedly date. The House of the Rape of Helen measures nearly 50 × 50 m (actually 2350 sq m), that of Dionysus about 50 × 65 m (3160 sq m), in contrast to the houses in Olynthus, which are approximately 15 × 15 m (215 sq m). Houses of a similar scale to those of Pella are implied by the street plan of Hellenistic Alexandria, but are there associated with a layout rather of Rhodian type. Houses in other Classical cities, where evidence exists, are only of the same size as those at Olynthus.

Pella thus indicates a level of luxury beyond that of the Classical cities, the benefits, doubtless, of conquest and empire, but demonstrating what the Macedonian kings had achieved. This, in turn, makes clear some of the motivation behind the fact that not all the citizens of Athens (to name only one of the Classical cities defeated by Philip) were inclined to oppose collaboration with the Macedonians.

The agora shows signs of sudden and unexpected destruction. One of the shops was a potter's workshop, containing moulds for terracotta vases decorated in relief. The systems of decoration depict, among a variety of subjects, scenes from the Homeric poems. That they remain as they were stacked in the shop, and also the overthrown columns of the luxury houses demonstrate that the city was destroyed by an earthquake, rather than the hostility of the Romans at the conclusion of the Third Macedonian War or the subsequent insurrection. But in the longer term Pella was ruined rather by the silting up of the lake, and the rise of Thessalonica, more conveniently placed by the sea, to serve as the principal harbour town of Macedonia. Pella was virtually extinguished. The Romans developed a new town a short distance to the west, but it never flourished. Thus Pella played only a brief part in the development of the Hellenic tradition. It was, however, a vital stage in a continuity which passed not only to Thessalonica, as its direct successor, but also to Alexandria as the outstanding city of the Hellenistic world.

R.A. TOMLINSON

Summary

The capital of the Macedonian kingdom from the end of the 5th century BC, Pella was sacked by the Illyrians in 359 BC and rebuilt by Philip II on a grand scale. The size of the city and the opulence of its houses indicate the benefits of empire won by Philip and Alexander. The city seems to have been destroyed at some point by an earthquake, but in the longer term it was eclipsed by the silting up of the lake and the rise of Thessalonica.

Further Reading

Akamatis, I.M., *Pelines Metres Angeion apo tin Pella* [Terracotta Vase Moulds from Pella], Athens, 1993 (with English summary)

Akamatis, I.M., "Agora Pellas" [The Agora of Pella], *Ancient Macedonia*, 6 (1999), pp. 23–43

Chrysostomos, P., *Makedonikoi Taphoi Pellas* [Macedonian Tombs at Pella], Thessalonica, 1998 (Greek and English text)

Hammond, N.G.L., *The Miracle that was Macedonia*, London: Sidgwick and Jackson, and New York: St Martin's Press, 1991

Lilibaki-Akamati, M., *Lachentoi Thalamotoi Taphoi tis Pellas* [Vaulted Chamber Tombs of Pella], Athens 1994 (with English summary)

Lilibaki-Akamati, M., "To Iero tis Miteras ton Theon kai tis Aphroditis stin Pella" [The Sanctuary of the Mother of the Gods and Aphrodite at Pella], *Ancient Macedonia*, 6 (1999): pp. 691–704

Makaronas, Y. and E. Giouri, *Oi Oikies Arpagis tis Elenis kai Dionysou tis Pellas* [The Houses of the Rape of Helen and of Dionysus at Pella], Athens, 1989

Peloponnese

Region of southern Greece

The Peloponnese (Peloponnesus) is the southernmost part of the Greek mainland, and has an area of 21,439 sq km, which is 16.24 per cent of the total area of Greece. An island originally, it was twice united and separated from the mainland by intense geological upheavals. It is thought to have been named after the legendary hero Pelops and, although it is called *nesos* (island), implying that the entire region was thought of as an "island", i.e. a separate part of Greece, it is actually a broad peninsula. On the west, south, and east it is bordered by the Ionian, Mediterranean, and Aegean seas respectively; but it is connected to the mainland of central Greece (Attica and Boeotia) by the isthmus of Corinth, formed by a subsequent retreat of the sea. In the 19th century this land bridge was cut to make the Corinth Canal, which almost made the Peloponnese into an island once again. Physically, the land is rugged and mountainous in its interior, and settlement is largely confined to the coastal plains and river valleys. Most villages cling to the steep mountainsides while the valley floors are reserved for farming. Products include wheat, citrus fruits, olives, tobacco, figs, and grapes. However, the greater part of the Peloponnese is mountainous, uncultivable, and poor. Sheep and goats of the pasturage and swine of the oakwoods are the main livestock that can be reared on about 50 per cent of the surface which consists of chalk and limestone. Climate and flora vary greatly according to the geographical and geological conditions: Arcadia and the east are almost entirely continental while the western parts are subject to maritime influences; the climate is purely Mediterranean along the coasts, but the centre has a relatively continental climate. In 1991 the population was 1,086,935, which is 10.59 per cent of the total population of Greece. It has been estimated that the civic population in 400 BC may have been 500,000 or 600,000.

The topography is complex. The north consists entirely of highland, from the lower mountain chains of the Argolid peninsula westwards successively through Cyllene (Ziria), Chelmos, Panachaicum, and to the south Erymanthus and Maenale towards the centre, all with extensive areas above 1500 m. Three chains run southwards from this mass, the lowest to the west beginning with Lykaion and running through Ithome to form the Messenian peninsula; Taygetus in the centre, with the highest summit of the Peloponnese (2409 m) forming the peninsula now called Mani, running to Cape Taenarum (Matapan); and Parnon to the east, running to Cape Malea. These parallel chains once formed part of the huge arc stretching from Albania through central Greece and Crete to Asia Minor. This original system was destroyed by the subsidence which created the large gulfs and most of the plains in the interior. In the Isthmian province and Argolid, as in the eastern parts of central Greece, the predominant direction of the ranges is west to east. The western and southern divisions of the Peloponnese are characterized by larger plains, forming a kind of counterweight to the smaller, closely enclosed plains, as around Tripolis, Mantinea and Arcadian Orchomenus, Pheneus, and Stymphalus. Along the north and west coasts are well-watered and well-drained terraces, the uplifted remnants of earlier coastal plains.

The eastern coastal plain, known as the Argolid, is dominated by the citadels of Argos and Mycenae. The fertile coastal strip in the north is divided into Corinth in the east and Achaea in the west; it includes Patras, the important port city and centre of tourism and the wine trade. The monotonous plain of Elis (Ilia), which extends down the west coast, is partially composed of the alluvium deposited by the river Alpheus. The southern coast is split into three promontories, the largest of which, Mani, is an extension of the Taygetus massif. Taygetus is flanked by Laconia round Sparta and Messinia round Kalamata. Both are alluvial plains and are free from winter frost.

In spite of its being a virtual island and with deeply indented gulfs between the mountain chains providing some good harbours, the Peloponnese had little communication with the sea. Arcadia, which is the most central of the regions, and whose pasturelands were 600–800 m above sea level, did not touch the sea at all and was nearly inaccessible. The Peloponnese had relatively few harbours and little or no hinterland except in the Argolid and Elis. Consequently, naval operations against the coast were rendered more difficult: hence the importance of Halieis for Athens and Argos during their alliance in the mid-5th century BC, and of Pylos and Methone. The capes were all dangerous, Malea notoriously so, as attested by authors belonging to different periods, such as Homer and Thucydides. The importance of Tiryns and Mycenae in Bronze Age Greece may have been due to the existence of an "isthmus" route from the Gulf of Argos to Corinth. Following the destruction of Tiryns and Mycenae, Argos began to develop and in the 7th century BC reached its peak as one of the most powerful cities in Greece.

The name Peloponnese does not appear in Homer, who knows the entire peninsula by the name of Argos, one of its well-known Mycenaean city states. The name is first attested in the *Cypria* (fr. 11, Allen), a poem belonging to the Trojan epic cycle and now preserved only in fragments. The next known occurrence is in the Homeric *Hymn to Apollo*. The philosopher Anaxagoras saw in it an appropriate unit to measure the size of the sun. The geographer Strabo, writing during the reign of the Roman emperor Augustus, devotes a considerable portion of his eighth book to the Peloponnese. During the latter part of the second millennium BC Mycenaean civilization flourished at centres such as Mycenae, Tiryns, and Pylos. The commercial and cultural influence of Crete, if not the political and military, began to be felt during the later part of the Mycenaean period, as shown by the Minoan-influenced design and decoration of palaces at Tiryns and Mycenae, and the impact of Minoan art revealed in the later shaft graves.

In historical times the Peloponnese consisted of six divisions: Achaea, Arcadia, Argolis, Elis, Laconia, and Messenia. These were separated from one another by mountains, and this fact hindered intercourse between them by land. Thanks largely to the landscape these regions maintained their identity throughout antiquity. Thus Elis was the region of the Alpheus plain and adjacent coasts. Achaea was made up of the steep northern valleys, their outfalls, and the coastal strip. Arcadia consisted of the central mountains and basins including the plain of Megalopolis. Messenia consisted of the southwestern peninsula and the Pamisus plain, while Laconia comprised the Eurotas valley and the southeastern peninsula. Corinth controlled the isthmus and its neighbourhood, while Argos dominated the plain. The Peloponnese was the home of several very powerful ancient city states, foremost among which were Sparta and Corinth. The decline of Greece's golden age has been traced to the Peloponnesian War (431–404 BC) fought between two factions led by Sparta and Athens, and admirably chronicled by Thucydides. The ensuing period was covered by Xenophon in his *Hellenica*. The complex and somewhat fragmentary topography may have been one factor that encouraged federalism and *sympoliteia* (union of states). The hegemony of Sparta promoted a regional solidarity, though it was never complete. Spartan domination of the Peloponnese was followed by Macedonian rule which ended with the Roman conquest of 146 BC. During the Hellenistic and Roman periods the southern coastal cities of Gythium and Methone played an increasingly important role as useful stations on long-haul east–west routes; and Methone, in particular, maintained its importance in this regard until the 19th century. It had been mentioned by Homer as being "rich in vines", and was famous for its wine and bacon under the Venetians, who built a fort to protect the shipping route around the Peloponnese.

In late antiquity the Peloponnese was part of the province of Achaea and retained its urban character: it contained 26 cities according to Hierocles. However, building activity practically came to a halt in the late 6th century AD either as a result of general decline or due to hostile invasions, primarily from the Slavs. In spite of the presence of Slavic toponyms, some of which are not beyond question, the extent of Slavic penetration of the Peloponnese is debatable. The Slavs apparently did not occupy the eastern cities which underwent rapid Hellenization. There were, however, independent Slavic communities in the peninsula as late as the 14th century.

From the late 7th century the Peloponnese constituted part of the theme of Hellas, and became a theme in its own right from the early 9th century. Its capital was at Corinth; and Leo Skleros may have been the first *strategos* (commander). Arab pirates ravaged the coasts of the Peloponnese in the 9th and 10th centuries, until Byzantium regained Crete in 961. Thereafter the region prospered with ample evidence of agricultural production, commerce, and industry in cities such as Corinth and Patras.

Although ancient geographers compared its peculiar shape to that of a leaf of the plane tree, in the Byzantine period the Peloponnese was often known as the Morea ("mulberry"). The name was first applied to the mulberry-growing northwestern district of Elis and then to the entire peninsula by the 14th century. Under the Byzantine empire the Peloponnese suffered repeated incursions by warrior tribes from the north. In the 13th century it was taken by the Franks, who held it for two centuries until it reverted to the last Byzantine emperors. In 1204 most of the Peloponnese had been taken over without serious struggle by the leaders of the Fourth Crusade, notably William I of Champlette and Geoffrey I Villehardouin. The land was divided into baronies, loosely under the authority of the principality of Achaea. By 1248 the conquest was complete, but the Frankish defeat at the battle of Pelagonia in 1259 and the surrender of Mistra and other territories by the Treaty of Constantinople in 1262 initiated the revival of Byzantine power in the Peloponnese which, from now on, was divided between the despotate of the Morea and the various Frankish states.

The Turks first entered the Peloponnese in 1446, and by 1460 they had conquered all of it except for the Venetian strongholds of Nauplia and Methone. One of its rulers, Thomas Palaiologos, brother of the last Byzantine emperor Constantine XI (1449–53), fled with his family to Corfu and thence by himself to Italy, where pope Pius II granted him a lodging and an annual pension which he enjoyed until his death in 1465.

With independence in the 19th century the Peloponnese became part of the new nation of Greece. Patras (Patrai), the major city in modern times, located in the northern Peloponnese, has continued to grow in commercial importance since the War of Independence and is today the third largest city in Greece.

Historically, the Peloponnese is one of the most famous parts of Greece. It includes such well-known sites as Corinth, Epidaurus, Mistra, Mycenae, Olympia, and Sparta. It has the most varied ruins of ancient Greece, making it one of the best-known centres of tourism. It is therefore not at all surprising that Pausanias, in the latter half of the 2nd century AD, devotes the greater part of his *Guide to Greece* (books 2–8) to a description of the Peloponnese and its historic sites. Blessed with abundant physical beauty and replete with important archaeological sites, the Peloponnese is a land every corner of which evokes some ancient myth. Its cities, towns, and spas were important centres in antiquity and remain so to the present day.

D.P.M. WEERAKKODY

Summary

The part of the Greek mainland south of the isthmus of Corinth, the Peloponnese (or Morea) is almost an island. In the Bronze Age Mycenae, Tiryns, and Pylos were flourishing centres, as were Sparta and Corinth in the Classical period. The Peloponnesian War (431–404 BC) marked the end of the Greek golden age. The last two centuries of Byzantine rule saw a cultural revival based on Mistra. Nauplia was the first capital of independent Greece (1833–34).

Further Reading

Bon, Antoine, *Le Peloponnèse byzantine jusqu'en 1204*, Paris: Presses Universitaires de France, 1951

Bon, Antoine, *La Morée franque: Recherches historiques, topographiques et archeologiques sur la principaute d'Achaïa, 1204–1430*, 2 vols, Paris: Boccard, 1969

Chrysostomides, J. (editor), *Monumenta Peloponnesiaca: Documents for the History of the Peloponnese in the 14th and 15th Centuries*, Camberley: Porphyrogenitus, 1995

De Jongh, Brian, *The Companion Guide to Southern Greece: Athens, the Peloponnese, Delphi*, London: Collins, 1972

Huxley, G., "The Second Dark Age of the Peloponnesos", *Lakonikai Spoudai* (1977): pp. 84–110

Jacoby, David, "The Encounter of Two Societies: Western Conquerors and Byzantines in the Peloponnese after the Fourth Crusade", *American Historical Review*, 78 (1973): pp. 873–906

Jacoby, David, *Recherches sur la Méditerranée orientale du XIIe au XVe siècle*, London: Variorum, 1979

Lemerle, P., "Une Province byzantine: le Peloponnèse", *Byzantion*, 21 (1951): pp. 341–53

Longnon, Jean, *L'Empire latin de Constantinople et la principauté de Morée*, Paris: Payot, 1949

McDonald, W.A., "Overland Communications in Greece during L.H.III", *Mycenaean Studies*, (1964): pp. 217 ff.

McQueen, E.I., "Some Notes on the Anti-Macedon Movement in the Peloponnese in 331 BC", *Historia*, 27 (1978): pp. 49–64

Malingoudis, P., "Toponymy and History", *Cyryllomethodiana*, 7 (1983): pp. 99–111

Miller, William, *The Latins in the Levant: A History of Frankish Greece, 1204–1566*, London: John Murray, and New York: Dutton, 1908; reprinted Cambridge: Speculum Historiale, and New York: Barnes and Noble, 1964

Miller, William, *Essays on the Latin Orient*, Cambridge: Cambridge University Press, 1921

O'Neil, J.L., "The Exile of Themistocles and Democracy in the Peloponnese", *Classical Quarterly*, 31 (1981): pp. 335–46

Runciman, Steven, *Mistra: Byzantine Capital of the Peloponnese*, London: Thames and Hudson, 1980

Westlake, H.D., "Xenophon and Epaminondas", *Greek, Roman and Byzantine Studies*, 16 (1975): pp. 23–40

Peloponnesian War 431–404 BC

The Peloponnesian War is the name given to the great conflict between Athens and Sparta and their respective allies that broke out in 431 BC and ended with the surrender of Athens in 404 BC. Warfare was not continuous: ten years of fighting (often called the Archidamian War after the the Spartan king Archidamus II, who led the first three invasions of Attica) were concluded by the Peace of Nicias in 421 BC; eight years of uneasy peace and occasional clashes followed, during which the Athenians' great Sicilian expedition was disastrously defeated (413 BC), before the peace was abrogated (also in 413) and the final phase, sometimes known as the Ionian War, began.

The Thirty Years' Peace of winter 446/45 BC, which had ended the earlier period of sporadic warfare between Athens and Sparta, had removed all Athenian footholds from the Peloponnese and the isthmus of Corinth and appeared to regulate relations between the two states for the future. But the Athenians' control of the subject allies that formed their empire was unimpaired and, when their continuing expansionism led them in 433 BC into actions over Corfu, Potidaea, and Megara that were not against the letter of the peace, but were seen by the Spartans' most influential allies, the Corinthians, as against its spirit and hostile to themselves, the Spartans decided to go to war if the Athenians did not back down (late 432 BC). Despite some busy Spartan diplomacy, Pericles persuaded the Athenians to stand firm and hostilities began in spring 431 BC, with the Spartans widening the issues by demanding that the Athenians free their subject allies (Thucydides, 1. 139).

At the start the Spartans expected to achieve their aims quickly by invading Attica, provoking the Athenians into battle and defeating them, an expectation shared, says Thucydides (7. 28), by most other Greeks. But, although they led Peloponnesian armies into Attica in five of the first seven years of the war and did a great deal of damage to Athenian agriculture, they could not draw the Athenians out to fight, an assault on their fortifications being out of the question. Meanwhile any hopes they had of challenging Athenian naval power proved groundless. Without the resources to build and man a large enough fleet, they tried to obtain Persian help, but the Persians were not interested so long as Athenian naval power was unimpaired, and the same factor deterred Athens' maritime allies from rebelling and transferring their money and rowers to support the Spartans; in the first ten years of the war just one of them, Lesbos, revolted in 428 BC and in 427 BC learned the hard way that the Spartans could do nothing effective to help them. One area of the Athenian empire, the Chalcidice peninsula, was vulnerable to the Spartans' land power, but they were slow to exploit this advantage, despite the fact that the Corinthians had been able to send a small army to the area in 432 BC to help Potidaea and that the Potidaeans did hold out under siege until winter 430/29 BC, while other smaller rebels nearby were never subdued. Eventually in 424 BC Brasidas did take a force to Chalcidice and, despite having only 1,700 hoplites, who were volunteers and liberated helots, won over a number of the Athenians' allies and their substantial colony at Amphipolis.

The Athenians' unassailable fortifications and their dominant fleet kept them safe from immediate danger provided that they avoided major battles on land, but, despite Pericles' public confidence in their financial strength (Thucydides, 2. 13), they were not adequately funded for a long war. It is possible that Pericles, who evidently directed their strategy, planned to use the fleet for offensive operations and that the attack he led on Epidaurus in spring 430 BC was the beginning of them, but the onset of the plague at that moment put an end to any such notions. Lasting two and a half years, its severity was exacerbated by the congestion caused by refugees from the countryside, where the longest of the Peloponnesian invasions, lasting 40 days, was in progress, and it seems that overall the Athenians lost from it up to a third of their fighting men. In the short term their war effort was brought to a standstill and they unsuccessfully sent envoys to Sparta to negotiate terms for peace, before Pericles rallied them; he himself died of the plague in autumn 429 BC and thereafter, in Thucydides' view (2. 65), his steadying influence was sorely missed. The Spartans, however, failed to exploit the Athenians' difficulties and their recovery was spirited. They reacted vigorously to the revolt of Lesbos in 428 BC, raising 200 talents from the first ever property tax on citizens, and crushed it the following spring.

After some small-scale offensive operations in 427 and 426 BC, including the dispatch of 20 ships to support their allies in Sicily against the Syracusans, in the summer of 425 BC the Athenians won a major victory near Pylos in the southwest Peloponnese. A fleet of 40 ships en route for Sicily was used by the enterprising general Demosthenes to fortify a small peninsula. A Spartan attack on the fortifications failed, the Spartan fleet that entered the bay was defeated, and a Spartan force that was put on the island of Sphacteria at the bay's entrance was cut off. The Spartans thereupon obtained a truce, so that they could send envoys to Athens about peace, and were evidently ready to ignore the interests of their allies on whose behalf they had claimed to go to war, in order to remove the Athenians and rescue their men. The Athenians, however, prudently demanded the concession of footholds on the isthmus and on Peloponnesian coasts that they had held before 446 BC as a guarantee that the Spartans would not renew the war within a few years once they had surrendered their advantage, and negotiations broke down. The Athenians then kept the Spartan ships that had been given as surety for the truce and later stormed Sphacteria, taking prisoner 292 hoplites, whom they held in Athens as hostages against any further invasions of Attica. Early the following summer (424 BC) they captured the island of Cythera, off the south coast of Laconia, and, using it and Pylos as bases for ravaging Spartan territory and as refuges for Spartan serfs, they had high hopes of victory; to pursue this, the previous winter they had decided to increase their revenue from their allies to about three times the prewar figure.

At this point, however, things went wrong for the Athenians. First, their 60 ships returned from Sicily unsuccessful after the Greek cities there had made peace with one another. Then an attempt to win over Megara, whose territory they had raided regularly since 431 BC, failed. This setback was not disastrous, but in the autumn an ambitious attack on Boeotia ended with a defeat in a pitched battle near the frontier close to Delium in which 1000 precious hoplites were lost. By this time Brasidas' small army had reached Chalcidice and was winning over allied cities, and, when he had crowned these successes with the capture of Amphipolis, the Athenians agreed to conclude a one-year truce (spring 423 BC). Although it did not lead, as the Spartans hoped, to a permanent peace, there was little fighting in southern Greece when it expired. The Athenians concentrated on trying to recover lost allies in Chalcidice; first Nicias and then Cleon had some success, but, when the latter was defeated and killed in a battle outside Amphipolis, in which Brasidas also perished, they too were ready to compromise.

The treaty as agreed in spring 421 BC, the Peace of Nicias, provided *inter alia* for the return of prisoners, the withdrawal of the Athenians from Pylos and Cythera, and the restoration to them of Amphipolis and their revenues from Chalcidice, but its terms were never fully implemented. The Athenians gave back the prisoners from Sphacteria, but, because the Spartans could neither force the Amphipolitans to return to their control nor persuade other important allies, including Corinth and Thebes, to ratify the treaty, they kept Pylos and Cythera. In a flurry of diplomatic activity, which led to some renewed warfare, it looked at one time as if Sparta and Athens might combine against the former's allies; and then that the Spartans might be defeated by a combination of the hitherto neutral Argives and other disaffected allies, Elis and Mantinea, backed to some extent by Athens; but the Spartans won a crucial battle near Mantinea in 418 BC and recovered the leadership of the Peloponnese, although the Argives remained allies of Athens.

Athenians had fought at Mantinea, but the peace remained in force with neither side eager to resume full-scale war. Nevertheless, the Athenians were still restless and, disinclined to do the hard work necessary to recover Amphipolis and their control of the north, their thoughts turned to Sicily, where, according to Thucydides (3. 86 and 4. 65), they had had conquest in mind when sending the ships in 427 and 425 BC. In the spring of 415 BC, lured by an appeal from non-Greek Segesta, they voted to send a fleet of 100 triremes and an army to the island under Nicias, Alcibiades, and Lamachus in the hope that they would conquer it and use its resources to achieve final victory over the Spartans at home.

Despite a slow and indecisive start, the recall of Alcibiades to face a charge of sacrilege and the death in battle of

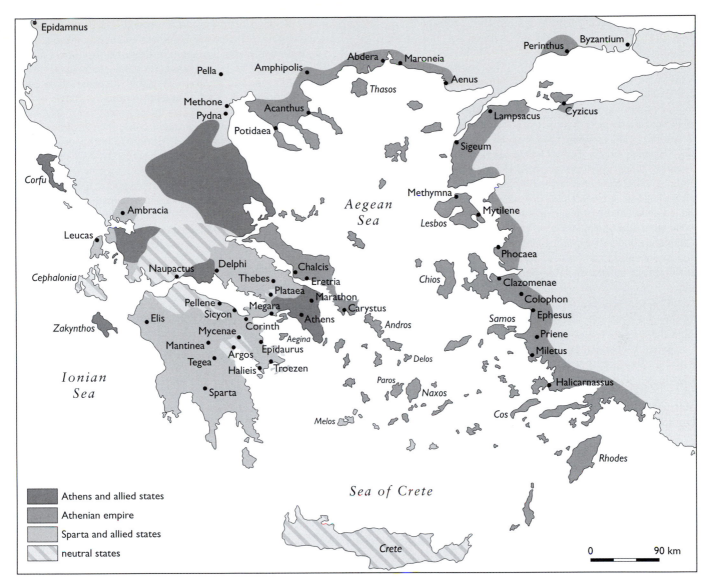

28. Alliances at the start of the Peloponnesian War, 431 BC

Lamachus, the Athenians in summer 414 BC were about to put Syracuse under siege and it seemed likely to surrender, but the arrival of Gylippus, sent out by the Spartans, on the advice of the exiled Alcibiades, to organize the city's defence, turned the tide and in the winter the Athenians became more besieged than besiegers. Nicias recommended the recall of the expedition, but the people at home preferred to send substantial reinforcements (spring 413 BC). This was to no avail, because the Athenians failed to regain the initiative and, with the Syracusans establishing naval superiority and Nicias unwilling to agree to withdrawal without the people's approval, the whole force was destroyed.

This defeat was catastrophic for the Athenians, not only for the losses of men, ships, and money, but also for its consequences in the Greek homeland. The Spartans had already declared the war renewed and established a garrison at Decelea in northern Attica that served as a base for year-round ravaging and a refuge for some 20,000 slaves over the remaining years of the war. They now began to send fleets into the Aegean, where the destruction of Athens' naval power was

encouraging its allies to revolt and the Persians to intervene in the hope of recovering control of the Asiatic Greeks.

The Athenians, however, despite internal discord, fought back, matching the Spartans almost ship for ship, limiting the revolts of allies and recovering some cities, while the Persians restricted their commitment to intermittent financial backing of the Spartan navy, even when in winter 412/11 BC the western satraps guaranteed their support in a treaty in which the Spartans recognized the Persian king's right to rule over all the Asiatic mainland. The Athenians indeed survived a short-lived oligarchic revolution in the summer of 411 BC and their fleet, which had remained loyal to democracy and had shrewdly accepted Alcibiades back from exile to join its leaders, won two battles, in the second of which, off Cyzicus in the Propontis (Sea of Marmora) in the summer of 410 BC, all the Spartan ships were destroyed or taken.

A Spartan peace offer was now rejected and the Athenians pressed on with the recovery of lost allies, but the process was incomplete in 407 BC, when the arrival in the eastern Aegean of a competent Spartan admiral, Lysander, coincided with the

Persian king's appointment of his son Cyrus to take charge in the west and make effective his support of the Spartans. Lysander's victory at Notium led to Alcibiades' withdrawal into exile, an indication of continuing dissension at Athens. This again showed itself in 406 BC, when, after the Athenians had defeated Lysander's successor off the Arginusae islands, eight of their victorious generals were prosecuted for failing to pick up the survivors in a storm and six of them were executed. Then in 405 BC Lysander was restored to the command, lured the Athenian fleet into the Hellespont (Dardanelles), and in a surprise attack took 170 of their 180 ships almost without a fight, as they were beached for the night near Aegospotami. It was the decisive blow. Up to this point the war could still have ended in stalemate or even victory for the Athenians, but these were their last ships and now Lysander cut their corn-supply lifeline, took over their allies, and expelled their colonists from the Aegean and then joined in the siege of Athens, which ended inevitably in surrender (spring 404 BC). Some of the Spartans' allies wanted Athens destroyed, but Sparta was content to reduce the Athenians to the status of a subject ally, with most of their fortifications demolished and, soon after, their democracy replaced by a repressive pro-Spartan oligarchy.

The war has always been seen as a turning point in the history of ancient Greece. Both protagonists, the victors as much as the vanquished, were irremediably weakened. A serious shortage of manpower combined with defects of character and judgement to bring down the Spartans' new Aegean empire within ten years and only Persian support enabled them to keep their control of the Peloponnese as far as 370 BC. The Athenians recovered remarkably and briefly were again the leading city, but they lacked not only the wealth, but also the vigour and dynamism of their 5th-century BC ancestors. Neither of these states nor the Thebans, whose strength and confidence grew significantly during the war, could effectively unite Greece against the expansion of Macedonian power under Philip II. In 338 BC he defeated the combined army of Athens and Thebes at Chaeronea and then could afford simply to ignore the Spartans' refusal to join in his settlement of Greek affairs.

This was certainly a sorry episode in Greek history not only for the long-term damage it inflicted on Greek freedom, but also for the extremes of cruelty practised by some of its participants. In 427 BC the Spartans killed all the surviving defenders of Plataea, an ally of Athens, when they surrendered; in 421 BC the Athenians did the same to Scione, a rebellious ally; and in 416 BC, during the formal period of peace and following no known act of recent hostility by the victims, they attacked Melos and on its surrender killed all the men of fighting age and sold the rest of the population into slavery; in 413 BC the Syracusans butchered many defenceless Athenians in the final disaster and sent the rest to the stone quarries. Other atrocities were committed when within cities the partisans of the two protagonists clashed in bitter civil strife (*stasis*), most notably at Corfu in 427 BC.

In contrast to these barbarities were the admirable doggedness and heroism of the defenders of Plataea (429–427 BC) and especially the remarkably resilient spirit of the Athenians that enabled them to recover from the plague of 430–428 BC and the Sicilian disaster of 413 BC. Remarkable too were their continued public patronage and enjoyment of art and drama through the times of crisis right to the end. The Erechtheum on the Acropolis was built during the war and many of the surviving tragedies of Euripides, some of those of Sophocles, and 9 of Aristophanes' 11 extant comedies come from these years, performed at public festivals at public expense. The war, however, provided the essential comic situations of Aristophanes' *Acharnians* (425 BC), *Peace* (421 BC), and *Lysistrata* (411 BC), and the tragic consequences of warfare were vividly echoed in Euripides' *Troades* (415 BC) and *Hecuba* (c. 424 BC). But its greatest contribution to the development of the Hellenic tradition was in inspiring Thucydides to write his history. With his strict sense of relevance and careful collection and treatment of information he set standards of objectivity and scientific analysis that no other ancient historian, Greek or Roman, could match, while at the same time being a master of dramatic narrative and at conveying the tragic quality of history.

T.T.B. RYDER

See also Political History 490–323 BC

Further Reading

Andrewes, A., "Thucydides and the Persians", *Historia*, 10 (1961): pp. 1–18

Brunt, P.A., "Spartan Policy and Strategy in the Archidamian War", *Phoenix*, 19 (1965): pp. 255–80

Cawkwell, George L., *Thucydides and the Peloponnesian War*, London and New York: Routledge, 1997

de Ste. Croix, G.E.M., *The Origins of the Peloponnesian War*, London: Duckworth, and Ithaca, New York: Cornell University Press, 1972

Kagan, Donald, *The Outbreak of the Peloponnesian War*, Ithaca, New York: Cornell University Press, 1969; reprinted 1989

Kagan, Donald, *The Archidamian War*, Ithaca, New York: Cornell University Press, 1974; reprinted 1990

Kagan, Donald, *The Peace of Nicias and the Sicilian Expedition*, Ithaca, New York: Cornell University Press, 1981

Kagan, Donald, *The Fall of the Athenian Empire*, Ithaca, New York: Cornell University Press, 1987

Lewis, D.M. *et al.* (editors), *The Fifth Century* BC, Cambridge: Cambridge University Press, 1992 (*The Cambridge Ancient History*, vol. 5, 2nd edition)

Meiggs, Russell, *The Athenian Empire*, Oxford: Clarendon Press, 1972

Thucydides, Works, translated by C. Forster Smith, revised edition, 4 vols, London: Heinemann, and New York: Putnam, 1928–30 (Loeb edition)

Thucydides, *History of the Peloponnesian War*, translated by Rex Warner, revised edition, Harmondsworth and Baltimore: Penguin, 1972

Xenophon, *Hellenica*, translated by Carleton L. Brownson, London: Heinemann, and New York: Putnam, 1918 (Loeb edition; many reprints)

Xenophon, *A History of My Times*, translated by Rex Warner, revised edition, Harmondsworth and New York: Penguin, 1978

Pergamum

City in northwest Asia Minor

Pergamum was the elegant capital of the Hellenistic kingdom of the same name that was founded by the Attalid dynasty in

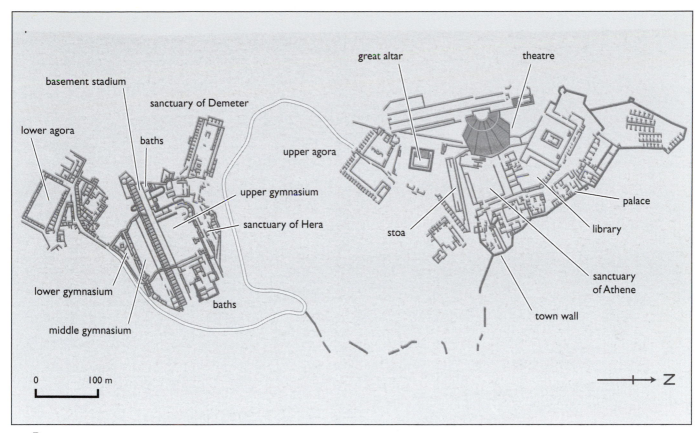

29. Pergamum

the early 3rd century BC. The city, in the region of ancient Mysia in northwestern Turkey, was c.20 km from the sea and was connected to its port at Elaea by the Caicus river. Pottery sherds show that there was Greek settlement at this site as early as the 8th century BC; in the early 5th century BC when the territory was under Persian control its governor was a Greek from Eretria. After the conquests of Alexander the Great in the late 4th century BC, Lysimachus, one of Alexander's successors, took Pergamum as part of his kingdom. He deposited a sizeable portion of his royal treasury there under the care of his general Philetaerus. In 281 BC Lysimachus was killed in battle, and Philetaerus, seizing the moment and the treasury, installed himself as ruler of the new kingdom of Pergamum and founder of the Attalid dynasty. With Athens having been in decline since the 4th century BC, the Attalids set as their goal the preservation of Classical civilization and Pergamum was to be a new Athens, the centre of Greek culture and art. During the reign of the fourth Attalid king, Eumenes II (197–159 BC), Pergamum was transformed from a modest Greek city into a magnificent Hellenistic metropolis with a population of more than 100,000 people. When the last king, Attalus III, ceded his estates to Rome in his will in 133 BC, Pergamum became the capital of the Roman province of Asia. The city continued to grow under the Romans and, at its peak in the 2nd century AD, the population was about 150,000.

The site is divided into two areas – a lofty acropolis (c.400 m high) and the plain surrounding it. Remains of numerous public buildings and private houses are found in both areas. The walled citadel was terraced from north to south providing building levels that were connected by a winding road. With

the exception of a few andesite structures, the view from the plain was of white marble Hellenistic and Roman buildings rising one above the other. At the summit, an aqueduct supplied water that was piped to public fountains, baths, and private dwellings. Nearby were military barracks, storerooms, a large temple honouring the deified Roman emperor Trajan (AD 98–117), and the "palaces" of the Attalid kings, which were merely large peristyle houses. On the second terrace was the sanctuary of Athena, honouring the patron deity of the city, which contained a small 3rd-century BC andesite Doric temple surrounded by spectacularly carved 2nd-century BC marble stoas. The north stoa provided access to the renowned Pergamene library. Behind the library and the Athena sanctuary, built into the steep southwest face of the citadel, is the precipitous theatre (it has the steepest *cavea* of all Greek theatres), with seating for 10,000 persons. The area at the base of the theatre is so narrow that the wooden stage building was removed when not in use so that it would not impede pedestrian movement. On the third terrace is the foundation of the Pergamum Altar (c.165 BC), arguably the most spectacular of all monuments from the Hellenistic period. This large square marble structure (c.35 × 35 m), which has been partially reconstructed in the Berlin Museum, consisted of a tall podium adorned with over-lifesized figures in very high relief depicting the Battle of the Gods and the Giants. A broad staircase led up to an Ionic peristyle court behind whose columns was a lengthy relief showing the life of the hero Telephus, mythic founder of Pergamum and adopted ancestor of the Attalids. The function of the "Altar" has been debated since its excavation in the late 19th century. Is it an altar, a victory monument, a dynastic

Pergamum: the Hellenistic theatre with seating for 10,000. It has the steepest cavea of all Greek theatres.

monument, or a *heroon* (i.e. a cult building for the worship of a hero)? The monument is in the form of a sacrificial altar (although it is much larger than all other examples) and the sculptural themes can be related to Attalid military victories and the political achievements of the dynasty. The lengthy relief telling the story of Telephus suggests most strongly, however, that its primary function was as his *heroon* (Webb, 1998). Among the remaining buildings on the terraced citadel are the *heroon* of the deified Attalid kings and several large complexes including the upper market or agora, the sanctuary of Demeter, the sanctuary of Hera, three gymnasia, large public baths, and the lower agora. There were also private houses, individual shops, small public baths, workshops, a tavern, and other establishments important to everyday life. At the base of the citadel was the main gate in the city wall.

The city in the plain was built primarily in the Roman period and contained a stadium, an amphitheatre seating 50,000, a theatre seating 30,000, various smaller public buildings, houses, tombs, and the vast temple of the Egyptian gods. From the area of the theatre a colonnaded street led to the famed healing centre, the sanctuary of Asclepius. The cult at Pergamum, founded in the 4th century BC, experienced continuous expansion and by the 2nd century AD the Asclepieum was the principal healing centre in Asia Minor. Medical treatment incorporated physical therapies, e.g. diet, exercise, baths, etc., but also spiritual procedures, e.g. incubation (dream therapy). The huge complex consisted of a large colonnaded court around and within which were temples, a library, a theatre seating 3500, fountains, pools, men's and women's latrines, sleeping rooms for incubation, and a large treatment building.

Pergamum declined as the power of the Roman empire waned in the 3rd century AD. The buildings on the lower acropolis, in the surrounding plain, and the sanctuary of Asclepius were abandoned with the exception of the temple of the Egyptian gods, which was converted into a Christian basilica. The upper acropolis continued in use, but comprised mostly modest houses built into and over the ancient structures. The city suffered severe damage from foreign invaders on a number of occasions, and the upper acropolis was refortified at least three times – in the 3rd, 7th, and 12th centuries. Even though Pergamum was home to one the "seven churches" of Asia Minor (Revelation 1: 11), was a major intellectual centre until the end of the 4th century, and was made a bishopric at the end of the 14th century, it had a small population and was relatively obscure throughout the Byzantine period. When the future emperor Theodore Laskaris visited the site in the mid-13th century, he recalled the greatness of the ancient city and equated the contemporary poorly constructed dwellings that lined the narrow streets to mouseholes in houses.

While the city of Pergamum as a whole was the glory of the Attalids, and the Pergamum Altar is the most important structure for modern admirers of the dynasty's accomplishments, the building that was central to Pergamum's role in the preservation of Classical civilization was the library. Second only to the library at Alexandria in the ancient world, it is estimated to have owned 200,000 volumes. Since the kings supported scholars in all the academic disciplines, one can assume that the holdings consisted of works representing the entire range of Greek learning. It is not clear what eventually happened to the contents of the library. In his *Life of Mark Antony* Plutarch relates a story that Antony gave the entire collection to Cleopatra as a gift. But Plutarch himself is unsure of the story's veracity, and there is no evidence that it is true. Since Pergamum continued as a centre of scholarly pursuits for four centuries after the deaths of Antony and Cleopatra, it is likely that at least a portion of the ancient collection remained intact during that period. In connection with the development of the library, Pergamum was also famous for the production of parchment, which eventually replaced papyrus as the preferred writing material in antiquity. Contrary to Varro's account (Pliny, *Naturalis Historia*, 13. 70), the Pergamenes did not invent parchment, for treated animal skin was used as a writing material very early in the Near East, and Herodotus (5. 58) mentions that it was used by the Ionian Greeks in the 6th century BC (Finegan, 1959, pp. 390–99). It is likely that Pergamum's reputation was based on the fine quality and large quantities it produced not only for consumption at home but also for export to Rome. The increased use of parchment facilitated the development of the more convenient and accessible codex (paged book), which supplanted papyrus and parchment rolls by the 4th century AD.

PAMELA A. WEBB

See also Attalids

Summary

Pergamum was the capital of the Attalid kings who controlled much of western Asia Minor in the 3rd and 2nd centuries BC. The city was a major centre of Greek culture and art. In 133 BC it became the capital of the Roman province of Asia. The library at Pergamum, along with that at Alexandria, owned the most important collection of Classical Greek works in the ancient world. Pergamene production and dissemination of fine-quality parchment facilitated the development of the more convenient codex book format.

Further Reading

Akurgal, Ekrem, *Ancient Civilizations and Ruins of Turkey*, 6th edition, Istanbul: Haset Kitabevi, 1985, pp. 69–111

Bean, George E., *Aegean Turkey*, 2nd edition, London: Benn, and New York: Norton, 1979, pp. 45–69

Finegan, Jack, *Light from the Ancient Past: The Archeological Background of Judaism and Christianity*, 2nd edition, Princeton, New Jersey: Princeton University Press, 1959, pp. 390–99

Foss, Clive, *History and Archaeology of Byzantine Asia Minor*, Aldershot, Hampshire: Variorum, 1990, pp. 479–81

Hansen, Esther V., *The Attalids of Pergamon*, 2nd edition, Ithaca, New York: Cornell University Press, 1971

Pfeiffer, Rudolf, *History of Classical Scholarship from the Beginnings to the End of the Hellenistic Age*, Oxford: Clarendon Press, 1968, especially pp. 234–51

Radt, Wolfgang, *Pergamon: Archaeological Guide*, 2nd edition, Istanbul: Türkiye Turing ve Otomobil Kurumu, 1984

Webb, Pamela A., *Hellenistic Architectural Sculpture: Figural Motifs in Western Anatolia and the Aegean Islands*, Madison: University of Wisconsin Press, 1996, especially pp. 55–71

Webb, Pamela A., "The Functions of the Pergamum Altar and the Sanctuary of Athena" in *Stephanos: Studies in Honor of Brunilde Sismondo Ridgway*, edited by Kim J. Hartswick and Mary C. Sturgeon, Philadelphia: Museum of the University of Pennsylvania, 1998

Pericles *c.*492–429 BC

Athenian statesman

Pericles was born around 492 BC. His mother's family, the Alcmaeonidae, had been prominent in Athenian politics throughout most of the 6th century BC. His maternal great-uncle Cleisthenes held the office of eponymous archon in 525 BC. The family spearheaded efforts to overthrow the tyranny held by Pisistratus' sons. That accomplished, Cleisthenes "took the common people into his political coterie" (to paraphrase Herodotus) and reformed the constitution.

Pericles' father Xanthippus was a hero of the Persian Wars. He showed himself to be firm, even ruthless, in siege operations against a Persian garrison at Sestos on the Hellespont. Earlier in his career he had prosecuted Miltiades, a prominent member of a rival family, and very nearly got him condemned to death. This antagonism between the two families was to continue into the next generation.

If we are to believe Plutarch, a certain shyness, a degree of social reticence, seems to have been one trait of Pericles' personality. For his entry into the public sphere Pericles acted as *choregos*, financial backer, for Aeschylus' drama about the Persian Wars, *Persians* (472 BC). Although Themistocles is not named, his spirit pervades the play. Themistocles had shrewdly foreseen the importance of maintaining an effective fleet of warships, and he persuaded the Athenian voters to forgo a one-time dole so that such a fleet could be built. Pericles was later to make maritime invulnerability the cornerstone of Athenian policy.

Pericles' first serious political opponent was Miltiades' son Cimon. As a general and public figure he garnered personal support through private largesse and especially by using war booty to improve the city's appearance and amenities. From him Pericles appears to have learned that such benefactions were a sure way to win votes.

Cimon was by disposition conservative and had a personal affinity for things Spartan. After a stunning series of victories against the Persian forces he made two serious mistakes. He laid himself open to charges of mismanagement after completing a lengthy campaign to bring a powerful rebel state, Thasos, back into the alliance. Pericles was among Cimon's prosecutors, but the attack failed (463 BC). Sparta was also reeling from the aftermath of an earthquake. Its numerous subject class, the helots, had revolted and the Spartans called on the Athenians for help. Cimon led a large Athenian force to aid Sparta, Athens' "yokemate", as he termed it, but when these troops were inexplicably sent away, the people's anger turned against him and he was ostracized, that is, obliged to leave Athens for a ten-year period. Pericles and a political associate, Ephialtes, saw their chance to carry out a reform of the senior judicial council at Athens, the Areopagus. This reform signalled a change in the direction of Athenian politics: from now on more power was to be wielded by the common people, and probably at this time the ordinary citizens who sat on the numerous Athenian juries were given a stipendiary daily allowance for the days when the courts were in session.

Athens' foreign policy suffered a serious setback in 454 BC. A revolt by a Libyan prince from the Persian empire failed, and two separate Athenian and allied support expeditions were lost. If Pericles supported the venture, the debacle appears not to have been brought up against him. During this period he was also taking careful note of the successes of other prominent Athenian commanders, such as Myronides and Tolmides. In 455 BC the latter led an Athenian naval force around the Peloponnese, and won some important victories. Not to be outshone, a few years later Pericles led a similar force that tried with only limited success to establish an Athenian presence in northwest Greece. Pericles may also have learned from Tolmides the advantages to be gained from the system of "cleruchies", pockets of Athenian settlers sent out to troublespots to prop up Athens' interests. In 451 BC Pericles sponsored a measure to restrict Athenian citizenship to those who could prove that both their mother and their father were citizens. What Pericles hoped to achieve by this measure is uncertain.

By the mid-5th century BC Pericles had a clearly formed vision of Athens as head of a maritime empire so powerful that the Spartans would have to concede superiority to the Athenians. His ambitions were fuelled by the huge financial surplus in the treasury of the Delian League, since 454 BC (probably) housed in Athens. Against strident opposition from such conservatives as Thucydides, son of Melesias, who was possibly related to Thucydides the historian, Pericles proposed that some of the money should be diverted to pay for an extensive building programme. The sources name Pericles himself in connection with a few of the projects, especially the statue of *Athena Parthenos* ("the Maiden"), executed by the Athenian sculptor Phidias, and an elaborate new odeum, a music hall that abutted the theatre of Dionysus, and it seems clear that he was the driving force behind the whole enterprise. These vast public works were intended not only to beautify Athens but also to give employment to its people. An estimated two to three thousand individuals were continuously employed over a period of 16 years, from 447 BC to the outbreak of the war with the Peloponnesians in 431 BC.

Some ancient sources assert that a formal peace was concluded between Athens and its allies and the king of Persia. A formal treaty around 449 BC would make it easier to explain the freedom that Pericles felt in applying to the building programme funds collected for military purposes. On the other hand, several ancient authorities claimed that the inscription purporting to record the peace was a forgery. Whatever the truth of the matter, there was a cessation of hostilities after some important successes against the Persians around 450 BC by league forces under Cimon (now returned from ostracism), so that Pericles would not have been taking a great risk in redirecting part of the league's war chest to other purposes.

In 449 BC or 448 BC the Spartans launched a "Sacred War" to defend (as they claimed) the Delphians' claims to be supervisors of Apollo's shrine. Pericles responded with a counterexpedition that restored control to the original claimants, the Phocians, with whom Athens had entered into an alliance some years before. Inscriptional and other evidence suggests serious disaffection among the allies, especially in Ionia, in the late 450s BC. In every case Athens was quick to react, by armed intervention and other means. Although the sources do not connect Pericles' name directly with any of these measures, there can be little doubt that he was prepared to take all necessary steps to see that the allies were kept tightly under Athens'

Pericles, elected ruler of Athens during the city's golden age. Roman copy of a Greek original, Vatican Museum

control. In 446/45 BC two important nearby states, Megara and Euboea, rebelled. Pericles responded with quick military action and both revolts were quashed. A Peloponnesian force that had advanced as far as Eleusis to lend support to the rebels returned home without having accomplished anything, and in the upshot a treaty of peace for 30 years was signed between the two superpowers: Athens repudiated claims to certain areas in the Peloponnese and Acarnania in northwest Greece, and in effect agreed to extend its empire only by sea. A sop had been thrown to the Spartan Cerberus, but it was becoming increasingly clear that it would not remain permanently quiescent.

In 440 BC Athens' powerful island ally Samos revolted. Again, Pericles' response was quick and tough. After several naval engagements and a protracted siege, the rebels were brought to heel. One of Pericles' colleagues for the first year of the campaign was the dramatist Sophocles, and several anecdotes survive of the shared command. Samos' longterm rival, Miletus, had figured in the preliminaries to the war, and this gave the gossipmongers and the comic poets a golden opportunity to spread the report that Pericles had got Athens involved as a personal favour to his mistress, Aspasia, who had originally come from Miletus; he had been in a relationship with her for some years after his own marriage to an aristocratic lady, not named by our sources, had broken down. By Aspasia Pericles had an illegitimate son, Pericles the Younger.

By the early 430s BC war between Athens and Sparta and their respective allies appeared inevitable. Athens responded to various provocative incidents with increasing firmness, and Pericles himself threw down the gauntlet with one or more decrees intended to cripple commercially the neighbouring state of Megara, an erstwhile ally of Athens but whose culture and language linked it firmly with Dorian Sparta. The Spartan side voted for war in the spring of 432 BC and invaded Attica a year later. Pericles himself survived the war's outbreak by only two years, succumbing in the autumn of 429 BC to the effects of a plague of a now unspecifiable type. Pericles' own strategy of defence was partly to blame. He persuaded the Athenians who lived in the countryside – a substantial portion of the populace, according to Thucydides – to move to the city and refuse any challenge to a land battle. Such an encounter would inevitably be to the advantage of the Spartans, who had a near-perfect record in infantry fighting. Although the Athenians did not abandon Pericles' defensive strategy, out of intense frustration at their sufferings they briefly removed him from the generalship, only to reinstate him shortly afterwards. With a break of only a few years after 421 BC, when a peace treaty between the combatants was nominally in effect, the war dragged on until the Athenians had to witness not only defeat but the humiliation of looking on as their fortifications were dismantled by a Spartan occupying force in 404 BC.

The sources make out Pericles to have been a competent and popular general, but probably not a brilliant one. He had rivals, generals such as Tolmides and Myronides, whose achievements might have become part of the permanent record had they had their own eulogists, and he had colleagues in the generalship, men such as Hagnon and Phormion, in whose selection Pericles perhaps had a hand and on whose abilities and loyalty he knew he could rely. But the real reasons for Pericles' enormous popularity – he was reportedly re-elected to the generalship continuously from about 443 BC until his death – was that he had a vision of Athens' potential for greatness and he knew how to achieve it in practice. He possessed outstanding oratorical skills, a speaker on whose lips, to paraphrase the comic poet Eupolis, a kind of persuasiveness settled enabling him to outstrip his rivals like a champion runner. Above all, he was acknowledged as a man of personal and financial integrity. Plutarch crowns his praise by remarking that Pericles "did not increase the property left to him by his father by one drachma", in marked contrast to what was believed about other popular leaders. His death at a critical moment in the history of Athens was a cruel stroke, with parallels on the contemporary Athenian tragic stage.

"The Periclean age" has become a useful label for Athens in the period 460–430 BC, a time of outstanding achievement in drama, philosophy, architecture, and the plastic arts. It may be an overstatement to say that Pericles was personally responsible, but it can hardly be denied that Athens' accomplishments were due in large part to the high degree of material prosperity that control of its empire had brought to the city, to his vision of what could be achieved through wise use of public funds, and to his firm hand at the tiller of the city's affairs. His carping critics might call it a tyranny, but in fact it was responsible democratic government in which the individual most fitted to lead was given a mandate by the citizens to lead them, and for a period of sufficient duration that his best expectations of them were given the chance to be realized.

ANTHONY J. PODLECKI

See also Athens, Classical Period, Peloponnesian War, Political History 490–323 BC

Biography

Born *c.*492 BC the son of Xanthippus and great-nephew of Cleisthenes, Pericles was *choregos* (financial backer) for Aeschylus' *Persians* in 472 BC. In 463 he was among the prosecutors of Cimon. After the ostracism and death of Ephialtes, Pericles became popular leader of Athens. His vision was of Athens at the head of a maritime empire. He instituted a vast programme of public building works. His ambitions for Athens led to the outbreak of the Peloponnesian War. He died of plague in 429 BC.

Further Reading

Boegehold, Alan L., "Perikles' Citizenship Law of 451/0 BC" in *Athenian Identity and Civic Ideology*, edited by Alan L. Boegehold and Adele C. Scafuro, Baltimore: Johns Hopkins University Press, 1994

Burn, A.R., *Pericles and Athens*, London: Hodder and Stoughton, 1948

Connor, W. Robert, "Vix Quandam Incredibilem: A Tradition Concerning the Oratory of Pericles", *Classica et Mediaevalia*, 23 (1962): pp. 23–33

Eddy, Samuel K., "Athens' Peacetime Navy in the Age of Perikles", *Greek, Roman and Byzantine Studies*, 9 (1968): pp. 141–56

Ehrenberg, Victor, *Sophocles and Pericles*, Oxford: Blackwell, 1954

Farrar, Cynthia, *The Origins of Democratic Thinking: The Invention of Politics in Classical Athens*, Cambridge and New York: Cambridge University Press, 1988

Frost, Frank J., "Pericles, Thucydides, Son of Melesias, and Athenian Politics before the War", *Historia*, 13 (1964): pp. 385–99

Henry, Madeleine M., *Prisoner of History: Aspasia of Miletus and her Biographical Tradition*, Oxford and New York: Oxford University Press, 1995

Kagan, Donald, *Pericles of Athens and the Birth of Democracy*, London: Secker and Warburg, 1990; New York: Free Press, 1991

Markle, M.M. III, "Jury Pay and Assembly Pay at Athens" in *Crux: Essays Presented to G.E.M. de Ste. Croix on his 75th Birthday*, edited by Paul Cartledge and F.D. Harvey, Exeter: Imprint Academic, 1985

Meiggs, Russell, *The Athenian Empire*, Oxford: Clarendon Press, 1972

Neils, Jenifer, *Worshipping Athena: Panathenaia and Parthenon*, Madison: University of Wisconsin Press, 1996

Ober, Josiah, "Thucydides, Pericles, and the Strategy of Defense" in *The Craft of the Ancient Historian: Essays in Honor of Chester G. Starr*, edited by John W. Eadie and Josiah Ober, Lanham, Maryland: University Press of America, 1985

Ostwald, Martin, *From Popular Sovereignty to the Sovereignty of Law: Law, Society, and Politics in Fifth-Century Athens*, Berkeley: University of California Press, 1986

O'Sullivan, Neil, "Pericles and Protagoras", *Greece and Rome*, 2nd series 42 (1995): pp. 15–23

Patterson, Cynthia, *Pericles' Citizenship Law of 451–50 BC*, New York: Arno Press, 1981

Podes, Stephan, "The Introduction of Jury Pay by Pericles: Some Mainly Chronological Considerations", *Athenaeum*, 82/1 (1994): pp. 95–110

Podlecki, Anthony J., *The Political Background of Aeschylean Tragedy*, Ann Arbor: University of Michigan Press, 1966, reprinted Bristol: Bristol Classical Press, 1999

Podlecki, Anthony J., *Perikles and his Circle*, London and New York: Routledge, 1998

Powell, Anton, "Athens' Pretty Face: Anti-Feminine Rhetoric and Fifth-Century Controversy over the Parthenon" in *The Greek World*, edited by Anton Powell, London and New York: Routledge, 1995

Rhodes, P.J., *The Athenian Empire*, Oxford: Clarendon Press, 1985, reprinted 1993

Robkin, Anne Lou Hawkins, "The Odeion of Perikles: The Date of its Construction and the Periklean Building Program", *Ancient World*, 2 (1979): pp. 3–12

Romily, Jacqueline de, *The Great Sophists in Periclean Athens*, Oxford: Clarendon Press, and New York: Oxford University Press, 1992

Schubert, Charlotte, *Perikles*, Darmstadt: Wissenschaftliche Buchgesellschaft, 1994

Schwarze, Joachim, *Die Beurteilung des Perikles durch die attische Komödie und ihre historische und historiographische Bedeutung*, Munich: Beck, 1971

Shear, Theodore Leslie Jr., "Studies in the Early Projects of the Periklean Building Program" (dissertation), Princeton University, 1966

Stadter, Philip A., *A Commentary on Plutarch's Pericles*, Chapel Hill: University of North Carolina Press, 1989

Starr, Chester G., *The Birth of Athenian Democracy: The Assembly in the Fifth Century BC*, New York and Oxford: Oxford University Press, 1990

Stockton, David, *The Classical Athenian Democracy*, Oxford and New York: Oxford University Press, 1990

Travlos, John, *Pictorial Dictionary of Ancient Athens*, New York: Praeger, and London: Thames and Hudson, 1971

Walker, Henry J., *Theseus and Athens*, New York and Oxford: Oxford University Press, 1995

Westlake, H.D., "Seaborne Raids in Periclean Strategy" in *Essays on the Greek Historians and Greek History*, edited by H.D. Westlake, Manchester: Manchester University Press, and New York: Barnes and Noble, 1969

Wet, B.X. de, "The So-Called Defensive Policy of Pericles", *Acta Classica*, 12 (1969): pp. 103–19

Yunis, Harvey, "How do the People Decide? Thucydides on Periclean Rhetoric and Civic Instruction", *American Journal of Philology*, 112/2 (1991): pp. 179–200

Persian Wars

The Persian Wars are usually taken to refer to the two Persian expeditions to Greece in 490 BC and 480/79 BC. They imply that a continuous state of war existed between Greece and Persia during this period, thus portraying Persia as being preoccupied with the subjection of Greece. In fact, a distinction should be made between the campaign of 490 BC, under the command of two Persians, Datis and Artaphernes, and the invasion of 480/79 BC, led by the king, Xerxes. The campaign of 490 BC should be seen as a direct reaction to the involvement of Athens and the Euboean city of Eretria in the uprising of the Greek cities of Ionia, known as the Ionian Revolt (499–492 BC); the expedition of 480/79 BC was a Persian invasion, prepared on a large military scale and led by the king himself. The term "Graeco–Persian war" would perhaps more accurately describe the military aggression of 480/79 BC.

In 499/98 BC, under the leadership of Aristagoras, tyrant of Miletus, some of the Greek cities of Ionia revolted against Persia. By the time of the Ionian Revolt, tyrannical rule in the Greek cities of Asia Minor, which were under the control of the Lydian kingdom, was already established as the favoured form of government, and it continued after the Persian conquest of Lydia in 546 BC. This was in line with the Persian policy of allowing local forms of government, language, culture, and religion of the different peoples of the empire to continue, and through this policy of political tolerance limiting resistance to Persian rule. Aristagoras had been approached by exiles from Naxos to help them regain power on the island; after having obtained the approval of the Persian king Darius I (522–486) and of Artaphernes, the Persian satrap of Lydia and brother of Darius I, he left for Naxos. If successful, this campaign would increase Persian political influence in the Aegean, and establish Aristagoras' personal standing with the king. However, after an unsuccessful siege, which lasted four months, the Persians were forced to leave Naxos, and Aristagoras, faced with the personal consequences of the failed expedition, revolted against Persia, abandoning tyrannical rule in favour of *isonomia* (equal rule), with the intention of gaining popular support from other Greek cites for his revolt. His attempts to win Spartan support for his movement failed when the Spartan king Cleomenes refused to become involved in a military conflict overseas. Only Athens and the Euboean city of Eretria offered support, sending 20 and five ships respectively. This fleet arrived in Miletus in the spring of 498 BC, and a first attack was directed against the Lydian capital Sardis. The city was successfully defended by Persians and Lydians, but when a fire broke out the city quickly burnt down. A battle near Ephesus initiated by the Persians and Lydians against the Ionians forced the Ionians to retreat to their respective cities (Herodotus, 5. 102). After this defeat the Athenians and Eretrians abandoned the revolt and returned to Greece.

Gathering momentum, the revolt now spread to cities in the Hellespont, Caria, and Cyprus. Here the rebel Onesilus was killed, probably in the summer of 497 BC, forcing the Ionian ships to leave the island. Between 497 BC and 496 BC Daurises and Hymaees, both sons-in-law of Darius I, successfully fought the rebellious cities in the Hellespont, while Artaphernes and Otanes launched attacks in Caria. Aristagoras, having lost control over the revolt, fled to Myrcinus in Thrace, where he was killed (Thucydides, 4. 102. 2–3).

Persian military and naval forces retaliated with a battle off the coast near Lade and an attack on Miletus, which was taken in 494/93 BC. Its inhabitants were taken to Susa and resettled near the Red Sea. Following Miletus' defeat, other cities surrendered, and part of their population likewise was taken to Persia. In 493 BC Artaphernes began the reorganization of Ionia, and in the spring of 492 BC Mardonius, son-in-law of Darius I, was sent to Asia Minor to continue implementing political reforms of the cities of Ionia (Herodotus, 6. 43). Although Herodotus tells us that Mardonius introduced democracy to the cities of Asia Minor, we know of at least two cities, Lampsacus and Samos, which continued their tyrannical rule after 492 BC.

In preparation for a punitive campaign to be led against Athens and Eretria, the Persian king sent an embassy to Greece in 491 BC demanding from the individual states earth and water, the symbolic signs of the recognition of Persian supremacy. Thrace, Macedon, Thasos, Aegina, and other islands complied with this demand, but neither Athens nor Sparta submitted. In 490 BC the campaign was led by Datis and Artaphernes, the son of Artaphernes (Herodotus, 7. 74). Their first target was Naxos, which, offering no resistance, was burnt and looted. From there they proceeded to Eretria and took the city after a seven-day siege (Herodotus, 6. 100–01). A few days later the Persian fleet landed near Marathon, upon the advice of Hippias, the former Athenian tyrant who had found exile in Persia, and who now acted as adviser to the Persians. In the ensuing battle the Persians were defeated by the Athenians, who were under the command of Miltiades. Retreating to Phalerum, the Persians then decided to abandon the attack and to return home. Neither Herodotus' account of the battle nor his casualty figures (6400 Persian dead, but only 192 Athenians) can be given any credibility. While Plataea had sent 600 soldiers in support of the Athenians, Spartan forces arrived a day after the battle.

The Battle of Marathon marked the first military encounter between Greeks and Persians on the Greek mainland, and, although it was won through favourable circumstances and good fortune rather than by military superiority, it had a huge ideological impact on the Greeks. For the Persians, their punitive mission had been successful as far as Naxos and Eretria were concerned. Persian interest in Naxos in 499 BC and the retaliation of 490 BC in fact identify the Persian objectives for their military action, i.e. to assert Persian control in the Aegean. In this regard the campaign of Datis and Artaphernes had been successful. The limited military force used in this campaign, the fact that Darius I had sent envoys to demand earth and water from the Greek cities in order to avoid involving other Greek states, and the fact that the king himself did not participate in this campaign do not allow us to argue that the Persian campaign of 490 BC had been an attempt to subject Greece as part of an expansionist plan.

Nevertheless, Athens still had to be punished, and it meant that a new expedition was prepared over the next four years in which Darius I gathered an army from all parts of the empire, while the king's fleet was prepared and transport vessels were built (Herodotus, 7. 1). But in 486 BC a revolt which broke out in Egypt claimed priority; because Darius had died, aged 66, in

December of that year, it fell to Darius' son and successor Xerxes to quash this revolt, which he successfully did by 485/84 BC. Xerxes then turned his attention to the expedition to Greece, carrying out his father's military plans. In 482/81 BC he probably also quashed a revolt in Babylonia under Belshimanni. In Greece the victory at Marathon had not resulted in the political unity of Greek states. A war between Athens and Aegina had broken out and lasted until 481 BC. Themistocles' proposal of 483/82 BC to built an Athenian fleet was accepted as a military plan against Aegina, and was on a par with the fortification of the Piraeus, the Athenian harbour, which Themistocles had advocated during his archonship ten years previously. The discovery of the silver mines at Laurium in 483/82 BC meant that Themistocles now possessed the finances to back his plan. At the same time Persian preparations for a military attack on Greece began. First, Persian envoys were sent to Greece to demand earth and water, which were offered by Thessaly, the people from the Malian Gulf, Locris, Thebes, and Boeotia. No ambassadors were sent to either Sparta or Athens. After Xerxes had gathered his army in Sardis, he crossed the Hellespont and marched via Dorsicus to Therma in Thessaly (Herodotus, 7. 127–31). At the battle of Thermopylae, which was fought on land, the Persians defeated the Spartan troops under the command of Leonidas, but a naval battle fought off Cape Artemisium on the same day was indecisive, the Persian fleet having suffered heavy losses in a storm, and the Athenians withdrawing their ships to Salamis after three days of battle. The Persian army advanced through Phocis and Boeotia to Attica and seized the Acropolis of Athens, the inhabitants already having been evacuated to Salamis and Troezen. With Attica under Persian control the Peloponnesians began building fortifications at the isthmus of Corinth, and those Peloponnesians who were still in Attica abandoned their positions. In September 480 BC Xerxes attacked the Greek navy at Salamis but the narrow straits made it impossible for the large Persian vessels to operate and they suffered heavy losses. Xerxes withdrew his naval forces, which returned to Cyme and Samos, but Mardonius and 10,000 elite soldiers were left to continue the war on land, and to destroy the Peloponnesian fortifications in the next campaigning season. Through a Persian ally, Alexander of Macedon, Mardonius offered the Athenians a peace agreement, including the promise to rebuild the destroyed temples, but the Athenians refused. In the spring of 479 BC, after wintering in Thessaly, Mardonius proceeded through Boeotia without any opposition and retook Athens. The Athenians, having received no support from Sparta, had to evacuate the city again. A second envoy, Murychides, was sent to the Athenians, but he also failed to persuade them to accept the peace. Faced with an Athenian ultimatum, the Spartans finally sent 5000 Spartiates, 35,000 helots, and 5000 perioikoi (dwellers in dependent towns). At the ensuing Battle of Plataea Mardonius was killed and his death decided the outcome of the battle. The Spartans took the Persian camp and forced Thebes, who had remained loyal to Persia, to surrender. Their main Persian supporters were sent to Corinth and killed. The Persian troops, now led by Artabazus, returned via Thrace, Macedon, and Byzantium to Persia.

In Asia Minor Chios and Samos began a revolt when the Spartan king Leotychidas was asked by six Chians to assist in

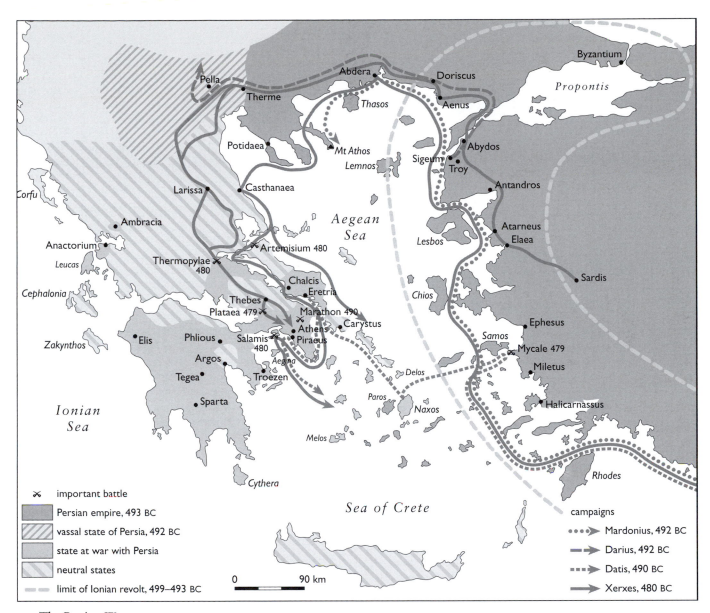

30. The Persian Wars, 499–479 BC

a conspiracy against the tyrant Strattis, while on Samos people turned against Theomestor. In the face of the approaching Greek fleet on Samos Xerxes withdrew his naval forces to Mycale, where a battle with the Greek forces caused the defeat of the Persian army. The battle of Mycale marked the end of the Greek–Persian war of 480/79 BC. Over the next three years Samos, Byzantium, and the Hellespont were taken by the Greeks. For Xerxes his unsuccessful expedition to Greece had no repercussions in the Persian empire, where he continued to rule until his death in 465 BC, while for the Greeks the Persian Wars soon acquired the status of myth, laden with ideological propaganda. This was the beginning of Greek nationalism, marked by the Greeks' identification of themselves as Hellenes and the Persians as barbarians. In fact, neither during the period of 490 to 480/79 BC nor during the actual war of 480/79 BC had Greek political unity ever existed. Some Greek states had remained allies of Persia throughout that period, and during 480/79 BC the Greek states hardly acted as a unified

force against Persia. The political rift between the anti-Persian Aristides, who initiated the Delian League, and the anti-Spartan Themistocles after 479 BC showed that even within Athens political opinion towards Persia was divided. Yet ideologically the Battle of Marathon and the victories at Salamis and Mycale boosted Greek morale beyond reality. In retrospect the war between Greece and Persia had become the symbol of the fight for freedom fought by small states against the might of an empire.

The Greek–Persian wars quickly acquired a mythical dimension. Aeschylus' play *The Persians*, performed in 472 BC, shows a Hellenized version of the Persian court, the decadence of Persia, and the hubris of Xerxes, while an earlier play by Phrynichus, *The Fall of Miletus*, performed in 493 BC, was an embarrassing reminder for the Athenians of their half-hearted efforts to defend the freedom of the Greeks of Asia, and the author was fined 1000 drachmas. Herodotus' *Histories*, written around 430 BC, used the huge figures given for the

Persian forces, in contrast to the small number of Greek forces, to demonstrate how successful a united Greece could be. Yet in his account Corinth, which fought against the Persians alongside the Greeks, was discredited, perhaps already in light of the political climate of the 430s BC in which Corinth emerged as an enemy of Athens. In antiquity itself the terms "Persians" and "Persian Wars" became powerful means of political propaganda. Augustus staged the Battle of Salamis in a specially excavated arena by the Tiber in 2 BC, the opposing sides being called "Athenians" and "Persians". In AD 39 Caligula's bridge across the bay of Naples was an imitation of the bridge which Xerxes had built over the Hellespont, used for a demonstration of military manoeuvres, during which the emperor paraded the son of the Parthian king Artabanus II (Josephus, *Antiquitates Judaicae*, 19. 5–6). Following Augustus, Nero also staged a sea battle in Rome, casting shadows on his intended war against Armenia in AD 57/58 (Dio, 61. 9. 6). In the later empire Lucius Verus in AD 161 and Caracalla in AD 214 took contingents of Spartan auxiliaries on their eastern campaign—symbolic gestures which were to reflect the Roman fight against the Persian/Parthian power. In AD 235 Gordian III staged a festival for the goddess Athena Promachus for the Athenians at Marathon, again a symbolic gesture made prior to his eastern campaign. In modern times the fight between the Greeks and the Persians received an additional propagandistic note. It became symbolic of the fight of Western Europe against the Orient. Greece, seen as the birthplace of democracy, architecture, literature, and philosophy, and which had defended its values against the oriental despotism of the Persian king, now represented European and Western values upheld against the perceived threat of the Orient, which became equated with despotism, decadence, and effeminacy.

MARIA BROSIUS

See also Persians, Political History 490–323 BC

Further Reading

Briant, Pierre, *Histoire de l'empire perse: de Cyrus à Alexandre*, Paris: Fayard, 1996

Burn, A.R., *Persia and the Greeks: The Defence of the West, c.546–478 BC*, 2nd edition, London: Duckworth, and Stanford, California: Stanford University Press, 1984

Miller, Margaret Christina, *Athens and Persia in the Fifth Century BC: A Study in Cultural Receptivity*, Cambridge and New York: Cambridge University Press, 1997

Osborne, Robin, *Greece in the Making, 1200–479 BC*, London and New York: Routledge, 1996

Sancisi Weerdenburg, Heleen and Jan Willem Drivers (editors), *The Roots of the European Tradition: Proceedings of the 1987 Groningen Achaemenid History Workshop*, Leiden: Nederlands Instituut voor het Nabije Oosten, 1990

Sancisi Weerdenburg, Heleen, Amélie Kuhrt, and Margaret Cool Root (editors), *Continuity and Change: Proceedings of the Last Achaemenid History Workshop, April 6–8 1990*, Leiden: Nederlands Instituut voor het Nabije Oosten, 1994

Schneider, Rolf Michael, *Bunte Barbaren: Orientalenstatuen aus farbigem Marmor in der römischen Repräsentationskunst*, Worms: Wernersche, 1986

Sonnabend, Holger, *Fremdenbild und Politik: Vorstellungen der Römer von Ägypten und dem Partherreich in der späten Republik und frühen Kaiserzeit*, Frankfurt and New York: Peter Lang, 1986

Wiesehöfer, Josef, *Ancient Persia: From 550 BC to 650 AD*, London and New York: Tauris, 1996

Persians

The Persians were an Iranian people, identified by their language as Indo-Europeans. Earliest written records identify three different regions of ancient Iran inhabited by Persians: Parsua, southwest of Lake Urmia; Parsumash, in the central Zagros mountains in northwestern Iran; and Parsa, in the southwest. Persian settlement in Parsa (Greek Persis, modern Fars) is first attested in the 7th century BC, and was the result of a migration process which had begun early in the 1st millennium BC, followed by a gradual process of acculturation, in which Persians lived alongside the indigenous Elamite population. It is this region that gave its name to the first Persian empire, which stretched from Egypt and the eastern Mediterranean to the Indus river, and which lasted from 559 BC to 331 BC.

In an exceptionally short but successful period of military expansion Cyrus II, who held the royal title of "king of Anshan", an adaptation of the Elamite royal title, built the Persian empire, first conquering the Median empire of Astyages in 550 BC, followed by the conquests of Lydia in 547/46 BC and Babylonia in 539 BC. With Cyrus II's annexation of the countries of eastern Iran and Central Asia, probably in the 530s, and the conquest of Egypt by his son Cambyses II (539–522 BC), the expansion of the Persian empire was concluded. Though Darius I (522–486 BC) undertook an expedition against the Scythians (518/17 BC) and maintained control over the Aegean (490 BC), his main concern was the consolidation of the empire, focusing on the administration of the provinces of the empire, the satrapies, established in the time of Cyrus II.

The Persians were organized in tribes, among them the Pasargadae, Maraphians, and Maspians. Prominent families of the Persian nobility formed the political elite under the Persian kings. As satraps, they represented the king in the lands of the empire, and were responsible for collecting tribute, levying military troops, and executing the political will of the king. The term "Persians" was first used in the royal inscriptions of Darius I to identify an ethnic class of people, while the king identified himself and the royal family as Achaemenids, descendants of the eponymous founder of the empire, Achaemenes. Though Darius' claim to an Achaemenid lineage might be pure creation in order to legitimize his kingship, the identification of the Persian dynasty as Achaemenids was recognized by Greek and Roman writers. Darius I defined the ethnic term "Persians" further to classify a Persian nobility, who also may have been identified by a common script and language, Old Persian, introduced by Darius I, and by the common worship of Ahura Mazda, the principal god of the Persian kings. The many peoples of the empire were permitted to maintain their distinctive character through their own language, culture, and religion, a latitude by which the Persians aimed to minimize the risk of revolt against their rule in the satrapies. The presence of the satrap, who represented the splendour of the king in the provinces, nevertheless influenced the local elite to adopt and imitate Achaemenid values, which were expressed in architecture as well as in luxury goods such as gold and silverware, jewellery, and Persian-style fabrics and fashion.

The Greeks used the term "Persians" as a general reference to the peoples of the Persian empire, regardless of their ethnic identity. Greek contact with the Persians began as early as the 6th century BC, when the Ionian Greeks under Cyrus II were part of the workforce which built Pasargadae, the first royal city of the Persians, and later Persepolis. In the same century the domestic chicken was introduced to mainland Greece; it was known as the Persian bird (Cratinus, 259; Aristophanes, *Birds*, 485, 707). Achaemenid gold and silver vessels served as models for the "Achaemenid *phialai*" (libation bowls) in the late 6th and early 5th century BC, but Persian influence on Greece increased significantly after the Greek–Persian wars of 490 BC and 480/79 BC, when Greek awareness of the Persians and Persian culture was reflected in literature, art, and architecture. Persian luxury goods became a desired commodity among the Greek elite. Persian garments, imported as well as imitated, were luxury items for wealthy Greeks, and pottery reflecting Persian-shaped vessels was increasingly used. Athenian buildings like the Odeum were built after the Achaemenid model of a hypostyle hall. With the establishment of the Athenian empire in the mid–5th century BC, Athens regularly summoned its allies to Athens to celebrate the Great Panathenaea, during which the latter offered a cow and a panoply, while at Eleusis they were required to present first fruits during the Eleusinia. The procession of the allies can be seen as the Greek adaptation of the tribute or gifts being brought by peoples of the Persian empire, as depicted on reliefs at Persepolis. Intriguingly, during the Panathenaea, the *kanephoroi* ("basket-carriers") carried parasols, a distinctive attribute of the Persian king.

After the collapse of the Persian empire in 331 BC, first Alexander and then the Seleucids adopted many Persian practices, maintaining the satrapal division of the empire, Persian administration, collection of tribute, and the levying of military forces. Adopting Persian dress and royal court ceremony, Alexander even saw himself as the legitimate successor to the Achaemenid throne. In the Hellenistic period the close cultural contact in Asia Minor between the Greek/Lydian community and the local Persians probably led to the Greek assimilation of the cult of Artemis with that of the Persian goddess Anahita, when inscriptions refer to the Greek goddess as "Artemis Anaitis" and "Artemis Persike".

In the Roman period the term "Persians" acquired an extended meaning, generally referring to the people of both the Parthian and the Sassanian empires. European knowledge about the Persians was gradually all but forgotten, except for the names of kings and geographical places, preserved in the books of the Old Testament. Here Cyrus II was perceived as a benign ruler, who allowed the return of the Jewish exiles in Babylon, and who supported the rebuilding of the temple of Jerusalem. Early accounts of ancient Persian ruins were due to individuals travelling through Persia, though their identification was not always possible. Knowledge about the Persians began early in the 19th century with the decipherment of the cuneiform script by Georg Grotefend and Henry Rawlinson and the archaeological excavations of the Persian royal cities of Susa, Pasardagae, and Persepolis.

MARIA BROSIUS

Summary

The Persians were an Iranian people whose empire stretched from Egypt and the eastern Mediterranen to the Indus and lasted from 559 to 331 BC. Provinces of the empire were ruled by satraps. Greek contact with the Persians dated from the 6th century BC. Persian influence on Greece increased after the Persian invasions of 490 and 480/79. After the fall of the empire in 331 BC many Persian practices were adopted by Alexander and the Seleucids.

Further Reading

Briant, Pierre, *Histoire de l'empire perse: de Cyrus à Alexandre*, Paris: Fayard, 1996

Brosius, M., "Artemis Anaitis and Artemis Persike", *Achaemenid History*, 11 (1998): pp. 227–38

Burn, A.R., *Persia and the Greeks: The Defence of the West*, *c.546–478 BC*, 2nd edition, London: Duckworth, and Stanford, California: Stanford University Press, 1984

Hansman, J., "Elamites, Achaemenians and Anshan", *Iran*, 10 (1972): pp. 101–25

Kuhrt, Amélie, *The Ancient Near East, c.3000–330 BC*, 2 vols., London and New York: Routledge, 1995

Miller, Margaret Christina, *Athens and Persia in the Fifth Century BC: A Study in Cultural Receptivity*, Cambridge and New York: Cambridge University Press, 1997

Miroschedji, P. de, "La Fin du royaume de Ansan et de Suse et la naissance de l'empire perse", *Zeitschrift für Assyriologie*, 75 (1985): pp. 265–306

Root, Margaret Cool, "The Parthenon Frieze and the Apadana Reliefs at Persepolis: Reassessing a Programmatic Relationship", *American Journal of Archaeology*, 89 (1985): pp. 103–20

Root, Margaret Cool, "From the Heart: Powerful Persianisms in the Art of the Western Empire", *Achaemenid History*, 6 (1991): pp. 1–29

Wiesehöfer, Josef, *Ancient Persia: From 550 BC to 650 AD*, London and New York: Tauris, 1996

Petra

City in modern Jordan

The city of Petra (in modern Jordan) lies approximately 85 km south of the Dead Sea, in a mountain valley close to Wadi Araba. In the Hellenistic period the city was the capital of the Nabataeans, an Arabic people first mentioned in 312 BC. The Nabataeans were renowned for trade, and Petra was well positioned as a focus for long-distance transport.

The city was in contact with the Greeks from, probably, the 4th century BC onwards, and the Nabataeans became somewhat Hellenized at least as early as the 2nd century BC. Their earliest coins, dating from the 1st century BC, derive from Greek models and show figures in Greek dress. However, the Nabataeans never became wholly part of the Greek world and, instead, showed a remarkable cultural conservatism. Thus, while they adopted Greek (instead of their own Semitic language, related to pre-Islamic Arabic) as a written and legal language after the 4th century, Nabataean names remained commonplace for settlements and other aspects of the environment into the early Byzantine period.

The earliest mention of Petra by name (also in 312 BC) is in a Greek source – written by the author Diodorus Siculus – and coincides approximately with the earliest datable material archaeologically associated with structures in the city. This

Petra: the so-called Treasury has the most ornate façade of all the rock-cut tombs

material comprises sherds of 4th-century BC Greek pottery and the earliest occupation of the city may well date from that period. The city was then occupied through the Nabataean, Roman, and early Byzantine periods.

Although Petra was a flourishing commercial centre and an important city, probably the most famous aspect of its archaeology is the series of c.800 rock-cut tombs with monumental façades, some in "Classical" style. These were carved in the sandstone cliffs around the town and included rows of tombs with their façades lining narrow natural rifts in the rock, which provide very spectacular settings. They were probably constructed in the Nabataean and Roman periods, although only one of these is closely datable by an inscription – the "Sextius Florentinus tomb", which can be ascribed to the early 2nd century AD.

The rock-cut tombs are today known by modern names, such as the "Treasury", "Deir", and the "Urn Tomb", but although some tombs show indications of reuse, such names need have no bearing on their early history. Although these façades look like buildings, the town itself was not rock-cut; the façades represent an elite cemetery for its inhabitants.

In AD 106 the Nabataean realms, including the city, were peaceably annexed by Rome. In the early Roman period it continued to thrive as a trading town and was elevated to the status of a *colonia* in the early 3rd century. Romanizing facilities – such as a theatre, monumental fountain, and colonnaded street – were constructed, and the city's elite became partially Romanized. The importance of the city in the Roman world appears to have continued into the 4th century AD, when it became the seat of a bishop, later a metropolitan.

Petra retained its status as a city, and was under effective Byzantine administration, into the 6th century. It was elevated to the role of capital of Palestina Tertia and new walls were built. As in other early Byzantine provincial cities, older constructions were reused and remodelled: for example, the shops along the colonnaded street were replanned and an inscription shows that one of the Nabataean tombs (the "Urn Tomb") was consecrated as a church (perhaps the first cathedral of Petra) in 447. These modifications have often been misinterpreted as indications of decline, but this interpretation is not sustainable in the light of newly available evidence.

Until recently, conclusive evidence regarding the character of early Byzantine Petra was lacking. But the discovery of 50 rolls of papyri, comprising a 6th-century archive, has transformed modern understanding of the later phases of the town's history. These were found in the storage room of an elaborate 5th- and 6th-century church, probably the cathedral, destroyed by fire. The archive provides a great amount of information about the town in the 6th century, demonstrating that it was still a focus of administration and occupation and the population included soldiers, clerics, farmers, a doctor, and craftspeople. The city was densely populated and there were houses with terraced roofs and internal yards.

Although this has clarified the situation in the 6th century, the end of the city is very obscure. Nevertheless, claims that it ceased to be used in the mid-6th/early 7th century have been shown wanting. New archaeological and textual information suggests that Petra may have survived in some form into the 7th century, and the church archive contains papyri of late 6th-century date. The city may have been bypassed by invading Islamic forces, perhaps because of its highly defensible location, and then peacefully abandoned. The probable cathedral was disused after having been set on fire, although whether this was by attackers, by chance, or by inhabitants unwilling to see it fall into enemy hands is uncertain. So, too, is the date at which the fire occurred: 7th-century pottery found in the church is attributed to "squatters" occupying the site following the fire, but ceramics found in Byzantine churches are generally associated with continuing use. Once its Byzantine inhabitants departed, the city was deserted, only to be rediscovered by European archaeologists in the 19th century.

KEN DARK

Summary

A Nabataean city 85 km south of the Dead Sea in modern Jordan, Petra had contact with Greeks from the 4th century BC and was to a degree Hellenized by the 2nd century BC. Greek language and Greek-style coinage were adopted, but other cultural features remained Nabataean. It became a bishopric in the 4th century but was deserted in the 7th. Today it is most famous for its rock-cut tombs.

Further Reading

Bowersock, G.W., *Roman Arabia*, Cambridge, Massachusetts: Harvard University Press, 1983

Browning, Iain, *Petra*, 3rd edition, London: Chatto and Windus, 1989

Fiema, Z.T., R. Schick, and K. 'Amr, "The Petra Church Project" in *The Roman and Byzantine Near East: Some Recent Archaeological Research*, edited by J.H. Humphrey, Ann Arbor, Michigan: Journal of Roman Archaeology, 1995

Gutwein, Kenneth C., *Third Palestine: A Regional Study in Byzantine Urbanization*, Washington D.C.: University Press of America, 1981

Koenen, L., "Phoenix from the Ashes", *Michigan Quarterly Review*, 35/3 (1996): pp. 513–31

Lindner, Manfred, *Petra und das Königereich der Nabatäer*, 5th edition, Munich: Delp, 1989

McKenzie, Judith, *The Architecture of Petra*, Oxford and New York: Oxford University Press, 1990

Millar, Fergus, *The Roman Near East, 31 BC–AD 337*, Cambridge, Massachusetts: Harvard University Press, 1993

Segal, Arthur, *From Function to Monument: Urban Landscapes of Roman Palestine, Syria and Provincial Arabia*, Oxford: Oxbow, 1997

Taylor, Jane, *Petra*, London: Aurum, 1993

Wenning, Robert, *Die Nabatäer: Denkmäler und Geschichte*: Göttingen: Vandenhoeck & Ruprecht, 1987

Phaestus

City in Crete

Phaestus is located in the Mesara plain in south central Crete. The Mesara is the largest fertile plain outside the Greek mainland and has always been a focus for cultivation and settlement. Its edges are defined to the north by the Ida range (Mount Psiloriti) and to the south by the Asterousia ranges, which block access to the southern coast; the plain runs into the Libyan Sea to the west at the bay of Mesara. Phaestus, along with Hagia Triada, is located on a ridge rising some 100 m above the plain and running east–west in the middle of it. Phaestus is set on the eastern summit of this ridge, with a commanding view of the plain below and to the east, while Hagia Triada is located at the west end, overlooking the Ieropotamos river where it runs into the sea.

Occupation of the Phaestus site is attested by deposits of pottery and by scraps of architecture from as early as the late Neolithic period (c.4000–3500 BC) and also in the Early Minoan period (c.3500–2150 BC). However, the principal architectural remains uncovered by the extensive excavations attest to the grandeur and importance of the site during the "palatial" period of Minoan civilization (c.2000–1450 BC). As at Mallia and Knossos, Phaestus went through two principal periods of use at this time, the protopalatial (c.2000–1700 BC) phase and the neopalatial (c.1700–1450 BC) phase, thus around 550 years during which a great deal of continuity of social structure and religious practice is evidenced at the site.

Although second in size to Knossos, Phaestus is the principal site in Crete for the study of the protopalatial period. At Knossos and Mallia, reconstruction work in the neopalatial phase obscures much of the earlier history of the building complexes, but careful excavation by the Italian team at Phaestus since 1900 has revealed much detail about the earlier period. Principal architectural features are a massive western facade of cut ashlar blocks, clearly forming the public face of the building, which fronts on to a west court that is built on three levels. The preservation of the protopalatial court and facade is due to the removal of the facade wall some 8 m to the east and the raising of the central part of the court by at least 1 m during the neopalatial rebuilding phase.

The west court is paved with flagstones and marked by characteristic "raised walkways", present at the other palaces and plausibly interpreted as defining processional routes. One branch of these walkways leads to the "theatral area", a flight of low steps backed by a wall, interpreted as a place for people to stand or sit while watching or participating in events in the west court. A shrine has been identified in the immediate vicinity. A second branch leads to the protopalatial entrance to the palace, considerably simpler than its neopalatial successor and located further south. A third branch leads by a winding route to the lower west court, where the facade of the palace continues, behind which lie rooms interpreted as workshop and possibly domestic areas.

The principal effect of the neopalatial remodelling of the western area was to create a massive propylon leading off the west court, apparently to serve as a monumental entrance to the palace. This entrance may also have served to limit access to the palace, since exits from it were small. Beyond lie the storage areas and the central court. Both features were present, in slightly differing forms, in both protopalatial and neopalatial periods. The storage areas consist of rooms containing massive pithos storage jars, for storing grain, oil, or wine; caches of Linear A tablets and clay sealings found in this area, principally of the protopalatial phase, have revealed much of the workings of the bureaucracy of the palace. In particular, not only jars but also doors seem to have been sealed, and seals often bore the impression of multiple seals, perhaps an indication of hierarchy in the palace personnel.

The paved central court was colonnaded and furnished with a fine north entrance. The possible functions of the central courts of Minoan palaces remain obscure, with suggestions ranging from a simple place of gathering to the possibility of bull-leaping ceremonies (also given as suggestions for uses of the west court). The court is aligned with the remote Kamares cave in the mountains to the north, where excavation revealed characteristic sacred cave deposits, including examples of the old palace pottery style now called "Kamares" ware. North of the court is a series of rooms forming the characteristic "Minoan hall complex" of the neopalatial period, with two halls and anterooms, light wells, corridors, and a lustral basin. This area seems to form an equivalent to the "domestic quarter" at Knossos. Other sections of the palace have been identified with workshop, ceremonial, public, or private space.

Although the size of Phaestus is not great, it is spectacular by prehistoric standards, and not all of the area has been excavated. The palace buildings represent a flourishing and highly complex centre, whose relationship to its hinterland is still far from clear. The storage facilities seem impressive, but probably do not represent the whole output of the Mesara, so it seems likely that only partial concentration of harvest at the centre was occurring. By the neopalatial period a number of lesser centres ("villas") had sprung up in the countryside and seem similarly concerned with the organization of agricultural production. But in the protopalatial period, archaeology has revealed little infrastructure that can be associated with the palaces in the countryside. It seems likely that the symbolic and ideological aspects of the palaces were always primary and that the coming into being and flourishing of these places depended on the importance attached to such aspects by most, if not all, of the population. The difficult question of what portion of the population might have lived in a town around the palace has not been resolved for either phase.

Phaestus suffered, with much of Crete, at the end of the neopalatial period, as a result of either natural catastrophe or human intervention, or both. Some LMIII occupation is attested, and it is assumed that the site is signified by the Linear B *pa-i-to*, but in this last period of the Bronze Age the focus of occupation was the west end of the ridge, at the site of Hagia Triada. In the neopalatial period a large Minoan villa was constructed here, with characteristic features such as a "Minoan hall complex" and storage areas. Neopalatial finds from Hagia Triada are in many ways more impressive than those from Phaestus itself in this period, including a Linear A archive associated with storage areas, frescos, copper ingots, and objects regarded as high art. In the later Bronze Age a large building, interpreted by some as a Mycenaean megaron, was built at the site. This has been taken as an indication of Mycenaean control of the area at this time; it certainly points to new occupation in the area with a complex organization. The surrounding area includes a large number of houses and a large open space with a complex of storage places or perhaps of shops.

Evidence for post-Bronze Age occupation at Phaestus has come to light in various excavations on the ridge. At the palace site a temple, probably dedicated to Rhea, has been investigated at the southwest edge of the excavations. This was founded in the 8th century and used throughout the Classical and Hellenistic periods. Other geometric remains including houses were located west and southwest of the palace, and elsewhere on the ridge. Occupation certainly continued through the Archaic and Classical periods, although historical and archaeological evidence is rare. The Hellenistic period represents something of a revival. Phaestus was one of the city-states of Crete, and both the palace site and other sites on the ridge, including Hagia Triada, have revealed substantial remains of settlement. Apart from the temple of Rhea, there was also a temple to Apollo or Asclepius, a city wall, and paved roads. Phaestus remained independent, though subject to Gortyn, until the mid-2nd century BC, when it was sacked by Gortyn and not reoccupied.

Roman remains are few, but in Byzantine and Venetian times churches and a monastery were founded on the ridge, including the church of Hagios Georgios Galatas with 14th-century frescos, and tombs have been located in some excavations. The site of Hagia Triada was occupied by an Ottoman Turkish village until 1897.

MICHAEL J. BOYD

See also Minoans

Summary

The site of Phaestus in the Mesara plain of south–central Crete has been occupied since the late Neolithic period but its principal remains are of the Minoan palatial period (*c*.2000–1450 BC). Though second in size to Knossos, it is the chief site for the study of the protopalatial period. It continued to be occupied until the mid-2nd century BC

when it was sacked by forces from Gortyn. The Minoan villa at nearby Hagia Triada has yielded impressive finds.

Further Reading

Beschi, Luigi *et al.*, *Creta antica: centro anni di archeologia italiana, 1884–1984*, Rome: De Luca, 1984

Levi, Doro, *Festòs e la civiltà minoica*, 3 vols (vol. 1, vol. 2 part 1, vol. 2 part 2), Rome: dell'Ateneo, 1976–88 (vol. 2 part 2 with F. Carinci)

Pernier, Luigi, *Il palazzo minoico di Festòs: scavi e studi della Missione archeologica italiana a Creta dal 1900 al 1950*, 2 vols, Rome: Libreria dello Stato, 1935–51 (vol. 2 completed by Luisa Banti)

Phanariots

A social, economic, and political elite under Ottoman rule

The Phanariots were an influential nobility that was especially active in the last two centuries of the Tourkokratia. They were named after the Phanar district in Constantinople on the south sea-front of the Golden Horn, where these families settled and lived. The area also became a significant centre of Greek presence at that time due to the transfer of the Ecumenical Patriarchate from the Pammakaristos monastery to the church of St George in Phanar at the turn of the 17th century. In the course of time, the Phanariot oligarchy managed to distinguish itself by its educational and cultural status, its commercial and financial activity, and its concomitant prosperity. This enabled the Phanariots to form a distinct social class within the society of Constantinople and to hold vital positions in the Ottoman administration from the second half of the 17th century onwards. From the Phanariot milieu came also a few patriarchs (e.g. Samouil Chantzeris). The Phanariots' intimate relationship with the Orthodox Church, in whose affairs they often interfered, is evident from their numerous benefactions. These developments attest to their great influence in the Ottoman empire, a fact that had significant repercussions for the Greek subjects too.

The Phanariots were not descendants of old, eminent Byzantine families who had remained in Constantinople after the fall of Byzantium, as some Phanariots later claimed and as is still erroneously believed. The Phanariots came mostly from provincial elite families who had moved to Constantinople later. Nor were they ethnically exclusively Greeks: some Romanian and Albanian families were included in their ranks. The Phanariots acquired an enhanced social status when important changes were made in the structure of post-Byzantine Greek society. In fact, there was an internal rivalry between the decaying old Greek aristocracy of Constantinople and the emerging class of new rich Phanariot families looking for positions of power and privilege within Ottoman society. Among Phanariot family names the following may be mentioned as prominent: the Aristarchis, the Mavroyenis, the Chantzeris, the Mourouzis, the Rangavis, the Racovitza, the Ypsilantis, the Neroulos, the Mavrokordatos, the Ghika, the Kallimachi, the Soutsos, the Karatzas, the Rosetti.

The first high office held by Phanariots was that of principal interpreter (*megas dierminevs*) to the Sublime Porte, which needed capable and skilled diplomats with a knowledge of western languages for its negotiations with European states. The first interpreter to be appointed was Panayotis Nikousios (1613–73), who was succeeded by Alexander Mavrokordatos (1641–1709) known as the Exaporite (*ex Aporrhiton*, "of the Secrets"), a man of remarkable erudition and skill, who negotiated the Treaty of Karlowitz in 1699. In fact, this office became a Phanariot monopoly throughout the 18th century until 1821. The last interpreter, Konstantinos Mourouzis, was executed in 1821 at the outbreak of the Greek War of Independence. Another office held by the Phanariots was that of interpreter to the High Admiral of the Ottoman Fleet (*dierminevs tou stolou*). The holders of these two offices were often in a position to extend their influence far beyond their immediate duties. Thus, as principal interpreters, they managed to influence the direction of Ottoman foreign policy in a decisive way and had contacts with many Western leaders, noblemen, and state officials. Further, as interpreters for the Ottoman fleet, they followed the *kaptan pasha* (admiral) and had the opportunity as intermediaries to deal with various issues pertaining to the Greek population in the Aegean islands.

Aside from these two offices, the most important post held by the Phanariots was that of prince (*hospodar*) of the Danubian principalities of Moldavia and Wallachia from the beginning of the 18th century. These regions belonged to the Ottoman empire, but retained their autonomy and were ruled by local princes. Although this office had already been given to Greeks (e.g. the Kantakouzenos family) in the 17th century, Moldavia from 1709/11 and Wallachia from 1715 were governed until 1821 exclusively by Phanariots drawn from a total of 11 families. In the capitals of these principalities, Jassy and Bucharest respectively, the Phanariots established their own courts with an entourage of courtiers and officials comparable to the imperial court in Constantinople. Due to the opportunities for wealth and power offered by these fertile regions, the competition between the Phanariot families for this post was particularly strong and there were constant plots and intrigues among them in Constantinople either to secure it or to overthrow an incumbent. In this way, the corruption of the Ottoman governmental system permeated also the Phanariot milieu in its various dealings with Ottoman authorities. It is no wonder then that Phanariot princes usually remained in office for a short time (an average of less than three years), though they often tried to incapacitate their rivals in the capital by various means, e.g. through their confidential agents (capuchehaia) in Constantinople.

An important contribution of Phanariot rule in the Danubian principalities had to do with the promotion of Greek culture through education. The organization and reform of the princely academies of Bucharest and Jassy transformed these cities into great centres of Greek culture, where numerous eminent, western-educated Greek intellectuals lived and taught (e.g. Nikolaos Zerzoulis, Nikephoros Theotokis, Josephos Moisiodax, Daniel Philippidis, Benjamin Lesvios, Stephanos Doungas, Konstantinos Vardalachos, Nikephoros Doukas, Stephanos Kommitas). Thus, the principalities became important channels through which Western ideas and influences reached the Greek world. Some Phanariots showed a particular predilection for making contacts with 18th-century Western intellectuals, for translating Western books into Greek, for publishing their own contributions in various fields (e.g. medicine, poetry, political thought and ethics), for stocking libraries, and for supporting intellectual endeavours (e.g. publishing books, inviting scholars to teach). The debt owed to these activities becomes evident from the dedications of many books by Greek scholars to Phanariot princes.

Other Phanariots (e.g. Dimitrios Katartzis) were supporters of the Ottoman empire and introduced certain social and intellectual reforms in the principalities without, however, calling into question the existing status quo. After the start of the French Revolution many Phanariots expressed certain reservations towards Western philosophy and some even collaborated with the patriarchate of Constantinople (e.g. at the patriarchal press) to suppress its impact in the East, though they acted out of their own interests too (e.g. in order to castigate the ambitious mercantile class supporting the Greek Enlightenment and the restructuring of society). But again, the Phanariots never resorted to blind reactionism and counter-Enlightenment, as many Orthodox clerics did; and some of them translated French works into Greek. The impact of the Phanariots is evident from the statement of a Greek intellectual in 1719 that the Phanar was no longer found in Constantinople, but was transferred to Bucharest. A large Greek merchant community had also settled in the principalities and did good business with central and western Europe. The establishment of Phanariot rule in the Danubian principalities thus facilitated the coexistence of a Greek bourgeoisie with Romanian boyars.

The Phanariots were strongly influenced by various elements of Greek culture, which they promoted through their writings and in other ways during their rule in the Danubian principalities. On the other hand, they were also influenced by the cherished heritage of Byzantine Orthodoxy. Some of them actually dreamed of recreating the Byzantine empire. Due to their involvement in the Ottoman administration, their social status, and their alliance with the Orthodox Church, the Phanariots were not bound to any specific national tradition, which explains why they did not favour the revolutionary ideas coming from the West.

The Phanariots and their wide influence in the Ottoman empire were viewed – even during their lifetime – from differing perspectives. In popular sentiment they were often identified with the Ottoman rulers and were criticized for having served principally their own interests in wealth, power, and prestige, and indirectly those of the Ottomans. As such, they were portrayed as oppressors of the Greek people (e.g. in the satirical poem *Rossanglogallos* at the beginning of the 19th century, which was directed against all the ruling elites of pre-independence Greece). They were also thought to have complete control of the Orthodox Church. From the middle of the 18th century there was an attempt to marginalize the Phanariots, initiated by an emerging Greek social class, led principally by merchants, who during the Greek Enlightenment sought positions of power and influence within society. There were also other critiques of Phanariot policies at a more sophisticated level, e.g. by Adamantios Korais. The most devastating attack on the Phanariot aristocracy was that by the physician Marc-Philippe Zallony in 1824, who depicted them as intriguers, ambitious, greedy, and totally neglectful of the Greek population of the Ottoman empire. It is no wonder then that the designation "Phanariot" was sometimes used pejoratively to indicate a love for intrigue and rapacity. It is true that the Phanariots in the principalities were influenced by the feudal traditions of the previous Romanian landowners, a fact that changed the early bourgeois character of their social class and transformed them into a feudal aristocracy. Aside from these, the Phanariots were accused by Romanian historians and others of neglecting the individuality of the Romanian lands and of serving Greek interests by the imposition of Hellenism. Thus, they failed to identify with the aspirations of the Romanian people. Yet, it is also argued that the intellectual endeavours of the Phanariots exerted a major impact upon other Balkan peoples generally (e.g. the Romanians), since the Hellenization process in southeastern Europe was of utmost importance for the cultural development of these regions. Moreover, to spread the Greek language and education at that time in the greater Balkan area was not the same as the promotion of a Greek national identity.

Despite these negative assessments of the Phanariots and their social class, it cannot be denied that their rise to high positions in the Ottoman administration did not serve Ottoman interests alone, but had beneficial repercussions for the Greek population too. It should not be forgotten that court machinations and illicit give-and-take were the principal means of survival within the corrupt Ottoman system. The Phanariots were no exception to this prevailing tradition. And indirectly, they played a significant role in the articulation of political and intellectual aspects of Greek life. In the Phanariots the subject Greek people acquired an influential political entity that functioned both as a shelter for the development of letters and as a source of considerable prestige. Nor should it be forgotten that many Phanariots were executed by the Ottomans in retaliation for their activities and those of other Greek subjects. This proves that the Ottoman authorities considered the Phanariots as being close to the Greek people and their cause. As mentioned above, the Phanariots envisaged a restoration of the Byzantine empire with its centre in Constantinople. But this does not mean that the Phanariots were entirely against the Greek War of Independence. After all, it was Alexandros Ypsilantis (1792–1828) who started the unsuccessful Greek uprising in the principalities in 1821. Several other Phanariots (e.g. Dimitrios Ypsilantis, 1792–1832; Alexandros Mavrokordatos, 1791–1865) played a significant role later in the Greek War of Independence. The outbreak of this war led to a massacre of many Phanariots in Constantinople and brought an end to their power. Of those that survived, some remained in Turkey, some settled in Greece and Romania, while others emigrated to the West.

All in all, the Phanariots, aside from their caste system and their various ambitions, did act as catalysts for significant developments in the Ottoman empire vis-à-vis the Greek Orthodox population, and it was through their mediation that the first substantial encounter of the Greek world under Ottoman rule with western Europe before the Greek Enlightenment took place. Generally, they showed a bipolarity in their overall orientations and activities, oscillating between preserving traditions and introducing innovations in various fields. Their many critics and their undeniable flaws notwithstanding, the Phanariots represented a distinguished chapter in the history of post-Byzantine Hellenism that left an indelible mark upon eastern Europe.

VASILIOS MAKRIDES

See also Ottoman Period

Summary

The Phanariots, originally Greek Christian residents of the Phanar district in Constantinople, formed a social, economic, and political elite under Ottoman rule. From the 17th century on they held important positions in the Ottoman administration, notably as interpreters to the Sublime Porte and as princes of the Danubian principalities of Moldavia and Wallachia. They played a significant role in the survival of Hellenism both politically and culturally.

Further Reading

Apostolopoulos, Dimitris G., *La Révolution Française et ses répercussions dans la société grecque sous domination ottomane: Réactions en 1798*, Athenes, 1997

Berindei, Dan, "Princes Phanariotes des Principautés roumaines: une forme de résurrection de Byzance?", *Byzantinische Forschungen*, 17 (1991): pp. 71–84

Bouchard, Jacques, "Les Relations épistolaires de Nicolas Mavrocordatos avec Jean le Clerc et William Wake", *O Eranistis*, 11 (1974): pp. 67–92

Bouchard, Jacques, "Les Lettres fictives de Nicolas Mavrocordatos à la manière de Phalaris: une apologie de l'absolutisme", *Revue des Études Sud-Est Européennes*, 13 (1975): pp. 197–207

Bouchard, Jacques, "Nicolas Mavrokordatos et l'époque des Tulipes", *O Eranistis*, 17 (1981): pp. 120–29

Bouchard, Jacques, "Nicolas Mavrokordatos et l'aube des Lumières", *Revue des Études Sud-Est Européennes*, 20 (1982): pp. 237–46

Camariano, Nestor, *Alexandre Mavrocordato, le Grand Drogman: Son activité diplomatique, 1673–1709*, Thessalonica: Institute for Balkan Studies, 1970

Camariano-Cioran, Ariadna, *Les Académies princières de Bucarest et de Jassy et leurs professeurs*, Thessalonica: Institute for Balkan Studies, 1974

Deletant, Dennis J., "Some Aspects of the Byzantine Tradition in the Rumanian Principalities", *Slavonic and East European Review*, 59 (1981): pp. 1–14

Dimaras, Konstantinos T., "Peri Phanarioton" [On the Phanariots] in his *Ellinikos Romantismos* [Greek Romanticism], Athens: Ermis, 1985

Florescu, Radu, "The Fanariot Regime in the Danubian Principalities", *Balkan Studies*, 9 (1968): pp. 301–18

Georgescu, Vlad, *Political Ideas and the Enlightenment in the Romanian Principalities, 1750–1831*, Boulder, Colorado: East European Quarterly, 1971

Gottwald, Joseph, "Phanariotische Studien", *Leipziger Vierteljahrsschrift für Südosteuropa*, 5 (1941): pp. 1–58

Grassi, Lauro, "Per una storia della penetrazione dei 'lumi' nei Principati Danubiani, 1740–1802: Note e appunti", *Nuova Rivista Storica*, 63 (1979): pp. 1–32

Iorga, Nicolae, *Byzance après Byzance: continuation de l'"histoire de la vie byzantine"*, Bucharest: Institut d'Etudes Byzantines, 1935, esp. pp. 220–41

Mango, Cyril, "The Phanariots and the Byzantine Tradition" in *The Struggle for Greek Independence: Essays to Mark the 150th Anniversary of the Greek War of Independence*, edited by Richard Clogg, London: Macmillan, and Hamden, Connecticut: Archon, 1973

Marinescu, Florin, *Étude généalogique sur la famille Mourouzi*, Athens, 1987

Mavrokordatos, Nicolas, *Les Loisirs de Philothée*, edited by Jacques Bouchard, Athens: Association pour l'étude des Lumières en Grèce, and Montréal: Presses de l'Université de Montréal, 1989

Papacostea-Danielopulu, Cornelia, "État actuel des recherches sur 'l'Époque phanariote'", *Revue des Études Sud-Est Européennes*, 24 (1986): pp. 227–34

Pippidi, Andrei, "Phanar, Phanariotes, Phanariotisme", *Revue des Études Sud-Est Européennes*, 13 (1975): pp. 231–39

Sturdza, Mihail-Dimitri, *Dictionnaire historique et généalogique des Grandes Familles de Grèce, d'Albanie et de Constantinople*, Paris: Sturdza, 1983

Symposium l'époque phanariote, 21–25 octobre 1970: à la mémoire de Cléobule Tsourkas, Thessalonica: Institute for Balkan Studies, 1974

Völkl, Ekkerhard, "Die griechische Kultur in der Moldau während der Phanariotenzeit, 1711–1821", *Südost-Forschungen*, 26 (1967): pp. 102–39

Zallony, Marc-Philippe, *Essai sur les Fanariotes, où l'on voit les causes primitives de leur élévation aux hospodariats de la Valachie et de la Moldavie, leur mode d'administration, et les causes principales de leur chute [...]*, Marseille: Ricard, 1824

Zepos, Panagiotis, "La Politique sociale des princes phanariotes", *Balkan Studies*, 11 (1970): pp. 81–90

Zervos, Socrate C., "Recherches sur les Phanariotes: À propos de leur sentiment d'appartenance au même groupe social", *Revue des Études Sud-Est Européennes*, 27 (1989): pp. 305–11

Phidias

Athenian artist of the 5th century BC

Phidias, son of Charmides, was Athens' most prominent artist in the period between the start of the radical democracy and the beginning of the Peloponnesian War (c.462–431 BC). He was probably born around 490 BC. He was reputedly a pupil of Hegias and Hageladas of Argos (who also were supposed to be the teachers of Myron and Polyclitus), who introduced him to the new technique of bronze casting.

His earliest works can be dated only approximatively: they are a group of bronze statues in the sanctuary of Delphi, showing the victorious Athenian general Miltiades surrounded by gods and heroes (Pausanias, 10. 10. 1); an over-lifesize statue of *Athena Areia* (with a height of more than 3 m), whose clothes were of gold and flesh of marble, for a newly built temple at Plataea (Pausanias, 9. 4. 1; Plutarch, *Aristides*, 20; probably recognizable in the so-called Athena "Medici" type); and a giant bronze statue (about 9 m) of *Athena Promachos* ("front-fighter") on the Acropolis of Athens (Pausanias, 1. 28. 2). All these monuments were commissioned by the Athenian state as memorials of the victories at Marathon (490 BC), Plataea, and Salamis (480/79 BC); today it is widely believed that they were constructed around 460 BC, when because of its foreign policy situation (tensions with Sparta and Thebes) Athens was very much inclined to point to its leading role in the Persian Wars.

These works must already have won Phidias great fame by the middle of the 5th century BC; he apparently had connections with influential people in the city (above all Pericles) who decided what was to be built at Athens and by which artist. So when in 448 BC the city decided to rebuild the Parthenon with a huge statue of Athena Parthenos, Phidias was again commissioned to create this statue. More controversial is the question of how big a role Phidias really played in the building of the Parthenon itself and how many of its pediments, metopes, and friezes were really made by him: Plutarch (*Pericles*, 13) calls him "overseer" (*episkopos*) and credits him with a near-omnipotent role as leader and organizer; this, however, does not fit very well with our knowledge of democratic Athens, where many people had a surprisingly large say even in matters of art. On the other hand, the coherent conception of the building's exterior sculpture and its many connections with Athena Parthenos indicate that Phidias must have been at least a very influential supplier of ideas.

Phidias' fame rested chiefly on his *Athena Parthenos* and his *Olympian Zeus* (see below). Both were made of gold and ivory laid over a wooden core and additionally decorated with other precious materials. The *Athena* was 12 m high and her garments consisted of more than a ton of gold (consuming a sizeable part of the state treasury of Athens); her extended right hand held a Nike (goddess of victory), her left a spear and a shield embellished on the outside with an Amazonomachy, on the inside with a Gigantomachy; furthermore, a snake (the symbol of the mythical Athenian king Erechtheus) was curled up inside the shield. Lapiths and Centaurs adorned Athena's sandals, and her pedestal displayed the birth of Pandora in relief. At the centre of her aegis a Gorgon was displayed, and the triple crest of her helmet sported a sphinx and two Pegasi, its cheek-pieces griffins. The statue was finished in 438 BC, the exterior sculpture of the Parthenon in 432 BC. During this time Phidias had several other, minor public commissions: the statue of *Athena Lemnia*, also on the Acropolis; the so-called *Mattei Amazon* for a contest in Ephesus; and a cult statue of *Aphrodite Ourania* ("the heavenly") for Elis near Olympia.

Plutarch (*Pericles*, 31f.) reports that Pericles' enemies prosecuted Phidias for allegedly embezzling ivory from *Athena Parthenos* and for blasphemy (because he allegedly included his and Pericles' portrait on the *Parthenos*' shield); but the evidence for this trial (about 434 BC) is very contradictory, and Phidias' death in prison is almost surely a later fiction, for his workshop at Olympia, which has been found (with tools, terracotta moulds, and even a cup bearing his name), must be dated to the 430s BC. The *Olympian Zeus* (Strabo, 8. 353f.; Pausanias, 5. 10. 2ff.) was even bigger than the *Parthenos*: enthroned, he held a Nike in his right hand and a sceptre in his left; the throne itself was richly embellished with Graces, Seasons, Nikai, Sphinxes, the slaughter of the children of the Theban queen Niobe, and an Amazonomachy; Phidias' brother or nephew Panaenus decorated the screens between the legs of the statue with paintings of *Hellas and Salamis*, some of the *Labours of Heracles*, *Hippodamia and Sterope*, and *Achilles and Penthesilea*. Another Amazonomachy could be seen on Zeus' footstool, and the statue's pedestal showed the birth of Aphrodite. At some point in the 420s BC Phidias disappears from our sources; according to some, he was killed by the people of Elis, but there is no real evidence for this.

Reliable sources for Phidias' life are few; brief mentions by Aristophanes (*Peace*, 605–18) and Plato (*Meno*, 91d; *Protagoras*, 311c) provide the only contemporary written testimony; more informative, but not always reliable, is Plutarch's *Life of Pericles* (late 1st century AD). In his *Olympic Discourse* of AD 97 Dio Chrysostom stages an imaginary defence of the *Olympian Zeus* by Phidias himself against those who doubt

Phidias: copy of the statue of Athena (the Minerva with Collar) by Phidias, Louvre, Paris

that the majesty of a god can be rendered in human form; and in the 3rd century AD the Neoplatonist philosopher Plotinus pays an even more handsome tribute to this statue, which became one of the seven wonders of the world: he says (*Ennead*, 5. 8. 1) that Phidias did not make it from any earthly model, but that his imagination grasped what Zeus would look like if he wanted to make himself visible.

We do not really know what happened to Phidias' works in later antiquity. By the end of the 5th century AD most of them had probably already been destroyed; what at this time still survived of valuable artwork was in most cases transferred either to Rome or to Constantinople (the Neoplatonist Marinus (*Vita Procli*, 30) records that *Athena Parthenos* was taken out of the Parthenon during the lifetime of his teacher Proclus, but says nothing about the further fate of the statue). Probably the last mention of a work of Phidias may be found in the account of Niketas Choniates (*c.*1155–1217) that a statue of Athena (possibly the Promachos from the Acropolis)

was destroyed by a raging mob who believed that her outstretched hand had lured foreign enemies into the city of Constantinople.

BALBINA BÄBLER

See also Ivory, Sculpture

Biography

Born *c.*490 BC the son of Charmides, Phidias was the most famous artist of 5th-century Athens. He was said to have been a pupil of Hegias and Hageladas of Argos. His fame rested largely on his statues of Athena Promachos for the Parthenon and of Zeus for Olympia. The extent of his role as overseer of the Parthenon as a whole is uncertain. He died probably in the 420s BC.

Further Reading

Boardman, John, *Greek Sculpture: The Classical Period*, London and New York: Thames and Hudson, 1985, p. 96ff., p. 203ff.

Borbein, Adolf H., "Phidias-Fragen" in *Beiträge zur Ikonographie und Hermeneutik: Festschrift für Nikolaus Himmelmann*, edited by Hans-Ulrich Cain *et al.*, Mainz: Zabern, 1989, p. 99ff.

Cook, B.F., *The Elgin Marbles*, London: British Museum Publications, and Cambridge, Massachusetts: Harvard University Press, 1984; 2nd edition 1997

Himmelmann, Nikolaus, "Phidias und die Parthenon-Skulpturen" in *Bonner Festgabe: Johannes Straub zum 65. Geburtstag*, edited by Adolf Lippold and Nikolaus Himmelmann, Bonn: Rheinland-Verlag, 1977

Höcker, Christoph and Lambert Schneider, *Phidias*, Hamburg: Rowohlt, 1993

Spivey, Nigel, *Understanding Greek Sculpture: Ancient Meanings, Modern Readings*, London and New York: Thames and Hudson, 1996, pp. 152–70

Weber, Martha, "Zur Überlieferung der Goldelfenbeinstatue des Phidias im Parthenon", *Jahrbuch des Deutschen Archäologischen Instituts*, 108 (1993): pp. 83–122

Philhellenes

The term "philhellene" was first used in ancient Greece with regard to allies of the Greeks or to foreign rulers who imitated Greek ways. With the revival of interest in Greek culture and civilization during the Renaissance the term began to be used of any admirer of the ancient Greeks.

However, the established sense of philhellenism focuses on a multi-faceted yet specific 19th-century historical phenomenon, the manifold support by foreigners for the struggle of the Greeks for independence, particularly during the war years 1821–30. Philhellenism in this sense is sometimes defined in vague or contradictory terms; despite some good monographs on the subject, there is still room for an in-depth analysis and new interpretations.

Philhellenism should be seen in the context of 19th-century European cultural and political trends, notably Clacissism, Romanticism, and above all liberalism and radicalism. An all-embracing analysis of the phenomenon must take account of all the forms in which support for the Greek struggle for liberation and the establishment of a modern Greek state expressed itself.

Philhellenes: memorial to the philhellenes in the church of the Transfiguration, Nauplia. Nauplia played a major part in the War of Independence.

Up to the late 18th century interest in Greece was confined to an admiration for classicism by members of the educated middle and upper classes of western Europe. There was a steady stream of foreign travellers visiting the very lands where Greek civilization was born and flourished, and their numbers increased considerably in the early years of the 19th century. On their return home many of them published their impressions from the Levant, but – significantly and in contrast with earlier accounts – the new emphasis was not only on the material remains of ancient Greek civilization but also on the modern inhabitants of the region, who were now presented as having a direct link with the celebrated figures of antiquity. Manifestations of continuity with the Classical past were eagerly sought and publicized; the degenerate state of the contemporary Greeks was attributed to their harsh fate under the domination of infidels, while their aspirations for independence found a sympathetic response. The wave of sympathy was inflamed by the romantic movement and its widely circulating literary products with an oriental theme, the most influential being those by Byron (*Childe Harold's Pilgrimage* and *The Giaour*) and Chataubriand (*Les Martyres* and *Itinéraire de Paris à Jerusalem*).

Coming as it did soon after the national/liberal insurrections in other parts of Europe, the outbreak of the Greek revolution was viewed with great hostility by the European powers which, ever since the Congress of Vienna (1815) had been striving to maintain the status quo and not challenge the legitimacy of sovereigns. Predictably, this negative reaction on the part of a repressive establishment united the opposing forces in a common front supporting the Greek cause. They came from all walks of life: there were liberal and radical university students, Classical scholars and intellectuals; decommissioned soldiers of the now underactive European armies, persecuted Bonapartists, political refugees from repressive regimes, and former fighters of the failed risings in Spain, Portugal, and Italy; Christian philanthropists, social reformers, and even plain adventurers, dropouts, and speculators.

A great number of the philhellenes who would take active part in the conflict headed for Greece in the first year of the war. They generally had unrealistic expectations of the situation in the field and of the role they were destined to play themselves. Many were soon to be disillusioned by the almost total absence of planning and organization, the lack of pay, and the shortage of supplies. They could not understand or participate effectively in the traditional method of warfare practised in the region, which was based on undisciplined irregulars and had little use for regular soldiery of the European type. The harsh conditions, the war atrocities, and the infighting for dominance among the Greek factions compounded their disappointment. Although westernized leaders of the Greeks made repeated attempts to organize a regular corps of foreign volunteers, such corps were shortlived and made little impact on military developments. After the decimation of a philhellenic battalion at the Battle of Peta (September 1822) the first phase of philhellenic activity in the field virtually came to an end.

Nevertheless, the movement continued and philhellenic committees were founded by philhellenes and Greeks of the diaspora in many European and American cities. Their aims were to promote the Greek cause with publications and appeals, to make collections, and organize military and humanitarian aid. Meanwhile the stream of new volunteers arriving in Greece was never interrupted, but it increased dramatically following the revival of philhellenic feeling in 1825, in the aftermath of Byron's death at Missolonghi and the subsequent heroic struggle and dramatic fall of the town of Missolonghi itself. In the meantime, the staying power of the insurgents had made the European governments reconsider the status quo in the eastern Mediterranean, where there was an increasing antagonism between Russia, France, and Britain, as each of the three wanted to expand its influence and trading interests in the region. This resulted in an uneasy triple alliance which, following the Battle of Navarino (1827), negotiated the establishment of the modern Greek state.

The number of people who helped the Greek cause systematically, many of them without ever having set foot in Greece, is impossible to estimate, but it is thought that around 1200 foreign volunteers participated in the war. These last came from all over Europe, but mostly from Germany, followed by France, Italy, and Britain, with a strong presence of Irish and Scots. Smaller numbers came from Switzerland, Poland, the Low Countries, and the United States; there were also Scandinavians and Spaniards. Some of the foreign professional officers – for example, Karl Normann, Charles Fabvier, Richard Church, Frank Abney Hastings, and Thomas Gordon – assumed roles of military leadership and participated in major battles, but on balance the military contribution of foreign volunteers was not a decisive factor in the outcome of the war. Their symbolic contribution to the Greek cause far outstripped their practical help.

While in most cases of philhellenism it is difficult to disentangle genuine affection for the Greeks and a sincere solidarity with their cause from other considerations, this is not the case with politicians of that period who pursued policies favourable to the Greek cause (a notable example is George Canning); therefore, they should not strictly be ranked among the philhellenes. However, in the category of philhellenes belong, along with the soldiers, a great number of others who supported the Greeks in many different ways. There were prominent figures who gave financial, moral, and ideological support, such as Charles James Napier and Frederick North (later Earl of Guildford) or Samuel Gridley Howe, who not only offered his services as a doctor during the war, but also toured America to collect donations for the Greek cause and organized relief for the war refugees. There were academics who became the guiding force in Greek committees, such as Professor Thiersch. There were theorists such as Jeremy Bentham, who prepared a draft for the Greek constitution, and

reformers such as Leicester Stanhope, who promoted liberal and educational reforms in Greece. There were businessmen and philanthropists, such as Jean-Gabriel Eynard, who worked indefatigably, using his international contacts, personal funds, and organizational skills for the regeneration of Greece, both before, during, and after the liberation. Many of these people have left histories of the war, or first-hand accounts of their efforts and experiences in Greece (e.g. Maxime Raybaud, Howe, Gordon, George Finlay, or William Humphreys).

Most of the survivors who had come to Greece as volunteers did not stay in the country for long and, with few exceptions, left after the liberation. However, the philhellenic movement did not die with the end of the War of Independence. Ardent philhellenes, such as King Ludwig I of Bavaria, continued to show an active interest in the country. In the years to come philhellenic sentiments, generating humanitarian relief and even military aid, likewise kept surfacing during insurrections in the unliberated parts of Greece throughout the 19th century. As late as 1896–97 there was a philhellenic legion composed of Polish and German volunteers.

AGLAIA KASDAGLI

See also Independence (War of), Romanticism

Further Reading

Dakin, Douglas, *British and American Philhellenes during the War of Greek Independence, 1821–1833*, Thessalonica, 1955

Dimaras, A., "The Other British Philhellenes" in *The Struggle for Greek Independence: Essays to Mark the 150th Anniversary of the Greek War of Independence*, edited by Richard Clogg, London: Macmillan, and Hamden, Connecticut: Archon, 1973

Droulia, Loukia, *Philhéllenisme: ouvrages inspirés par la guerre de l'indépendance greque 1821–1833*, Athens 1974

Larrabee, Stephen Addison, *Hellas Observed: The American Experience of Greece, 1775–1865*, New York: New York University Press, 1957

Rosen, F., *Bentham, Byron and Greece: Constitutionalism, Nationalism and Early Liberal Political Thought*, Oxford: Clarendon Press, and New York: Oxford University Press, 1992

St Clair, William, *That Greece Might Still Be Free: The Philhellenes in the War of Independence*, London and New York: Oxford University Press, 1972

Woodhouse, C.M., *The Philhellenes*, London: Hodder and Stoughton, and Rutherford, New Jersey: Fairleigh Dickinson University Press, 1969

Philip II 383/82–336 BC

King of Macedonia

The famous historian Theopompus said of Philip II that "Europe had never produced such a man at all as Philip, the son of Amyntas." Yet the same sentence can also be translated "Europe had never endured such a man at all as Philip, the son of Amyntas." The enigma reflects the mixed views of both Theopompus and other Greeks of the 4th century BC. Moreover, the conundrum persists today. Philip's dubious reputation stems from the hostility shown towards him by many of the ancient writers who treated his life and deeds. His mortal enemy was the eloquent Demosthenes, whose portrait of him entirely in black has had the greatest impact on the historical imagination from antiquity to the present.

Philip was born in either 383 or 382 BC to Amyntas, king of Macedonia, and Eurydice, a princess of Lyncus. The northern connection proved vastly important to him, for the Illyrians in the northwest, the Paeonians in the north, and the Thracians in the northeast posed continual threats to Macedonia. The Greeks too exploited Macedonian weakness whenever possible. Philip spent three of his early years as a hostage in Thebes during the hegemony. There he learned much from Epaminondas and Pelopidas about Greek life. In 359 BC he returned home, and at the age of 24 ascended the throne.

At the outset Philip defeated the invading Paeonians and Illyrians, and coped with Athens, which supported the pretensions of Argaeus to the throne. This was the first of many Athenian acts of aggression against Philip. Success freed him for intervention in Thessaly at the request of the noble Aleuadae family. This friendly connection served him well by protecting his southern border and later allowing him direct entry into the mainstream of Greek affairs. Hence, by 358 BC Philip had confronted all his enemies by a combination of might and diplomacy.

Philip next built a new, mobile, formidable army, and in 357 BC he used it to conquer Amphipolis, which secured his eastern border and gave him command of the riverine commerce of the Strymon valley. Declaration of war by Athens failed to stop his move into the rich mining region of Mount Pangaeus. In 356 BC he seized Crenides, also rich in gold and silver, the income from which provided him with more than 1,000 talents a year. Now freed from economic worries, in 356 BC he suppressed discontent among the Thracians, Paeonians, and Illyrians, and obstructed Athenian ambitions in the northern Aegean. With his conquest of Pydna, Potidaea, Anthmus, and Methone by 354 BC he gained control of the entire Macedonian coast. Victories in the north and peace in the south gave Philip a secure kingdom, which he further consolidated by winning the complete allegiance of the nobility and moving Macedonians from their mountain fastnesses to newly established cities in the plain. Urban life thereby flourished, and many of these cities survive today in altered form.

Philip entered the main current of Greek affairs by invitation, not by design. In 355 BC Greece had become embroiled in the Sacred War, sparked when the Phocians illegally seized the sanctuary of Apollo at Delphi, whereupon they systematically plundered it. The members of the Amphictyonic Confederacy, which included Thessaly and Thebes, had vainly striven to dislodge the temple robbers. In 354 BC the Phocian general Onomarchus attempted to drive Thessaly from the war by supporting the rebellious tyrants of Pherae. The Thessalians appealed to Philip for help, and he proved so successful that Pherae entreated Onomarchus for relief. After hard fighting, Onomarchus drove Philip from Thessaly, but in the following year Philip defeated Onomarchus at the Battle of the Crocus Plain. Philip added a symbolic meaning to his victory, for he announced that he came to Greece as a champion of Apollo, whose sanctuary he intended to liberate. He came to Greece not as a foreign invader but as the pious defender of Greek religion.

Philip used his victory in Thessaly wisely by bringing it and its federal government completely over to his side. He systematically conquered the strategically vital harbour of Pagasae, next won Pherae, and reduced the rest of Thessaly to his will, the culmination of which was his election as archon of the Thessalian Confederacy. His new position in Thessaly permanently altered the face of Greek politics. He was now the most powerful man in Greece, and no single state could stand against him.

Alarmed by Philip's success in Thessaly, Athens strengthened its position in Thrace. In 352 BC it gained the Chersonese from Cersebleptes. After a campaign in the northwest that took him nearly to the Adriatic, Philip in 351 BC made sweeping gains in Thrace that threatened Athenian designs more closely. In the following spring Philip attacked Olynthus to remove the last major impediment in his political road. In 352 BC Olynthus had made peace with Athens, a breach of its earlier treaty with Philip. In 349 BC Philip declared war, whereupon Olynthus concluded an alliance with Athens. Yet an Athenian relief force proved too small to accomplish anything. Forgoing a direct attack on Olynthus, Philip instead reduced 32 surrounding allied cities, most of them scattered throughout the region. In 348 BC he conquered Torone and Mecyberna, the port of Olynthus, thus closing the trap. Athenian help availed nothing, and in 346 BC Philip took and razed Olynthus. Athens had none the less openly declared war on Philip.

The years 347–346 BC proved fruitful for Philip. At the request of Thessaly and Thebes he marched into Phocis to end the Sacred War. His presence intimidated Athens into making peace. In 346 BC Philip and his allies and Athens with its naval allies concluded the Peace of Philocrates. All other states were excluded. While the negotiations were still pending, Philip defeated Cersebleptes, thus giving him control of the Chersonese. He now stood on the western side of the Hellespont, where he anchored the eastern flank of his empire both militarily and diplomatically.

After the peace Philip campaigned in the north from 344 to 340 BC, during which he subdued the Illyrians as far north as Albania, Epirus, and Thrace, where he established Philippopolis. These expeditions took Macedonian power north of the Great Balkan range. In the northeast he attacked Perinthus and Byzantium in 340 BC, but Athenian and Persian aid foiled his plans. In 339 BC Philip decided that Athens' time had come. Entering central Greece through the Dhema pass, he outflanked Thermopylae and reached Elatea, just three days' march from Attica. Demosthenes rallied first Athens and then Thebes to war. Throughout the year they parried Philip's thrusts, but in 338 BC he reached the small plain of Chaeronea unopposed. The ensuing battle was marked by hard fighting on both sides, but the Macedonians cut through the stubborn front of the Thebans and smashed the Athenians. Even though Philip had not vanquished all of Greece, he was nevertheless *hegemon* (commander) of it.

Military victory was crowned with political consolidation. In 337 BC Philip summoned the Greeks to a congress at Corinth. There he established the so-called League of Corinth that forged a general alliance of Greeks and Macedonians. Each member state received protection from external attack and freedom from outside interference in local affairs. Delegates of the cities met in common assembly to formulate policy, and Philip was elected *hegemon* to implement its resolutions in peace and lead it in war. One of his first acts was to summon the Greeks to a great crusade against Persia under his leadership. Contingents were assigned and muster ordered for the following spring.

His work in Corinth done, the lord of Greece returned to Macedonia to celebrate his seventh marriage and to prepare for the Persian expedition. His last wedding proved to be his last act. Philip entered the theatre at Aegae at the head of the wedding procession only to be struck down by an assassin. The party who instigated the deed was never discovered. All tracks had been too carefully covered. Alexander, soon to be called the Great, quickly and effortlessly ascended the throne. Philip was buried with great pomp, but his achievements did not die with him.

Philip's legacy reached from his day to this. He inspired the Macedonians to resist Rome, and even Roman victory did not erase his memory. As late as the 19th century his fame remained alive in Macedonian legends, and numerous myths perpetuated the memory of his famous kingdom. Folklore also attributed many of the ruins of antiquity to him. During the Greek War of Independence he served as an inspiration but in a mixed fashion. Although some Greeks compared him to various Turkish leaders, most saw him as a champion against the barbarians. Since World War II the communists and their successors have tried to establish a Slavic state of Macedonia, against which the Greeks have reasonably objected. In the midst of this controversy Philip returned to uphold the Greek cause. In 1978 Greek archaeologists discovered at Vergina a royal tomb that was almost certainly Philip's. Whosesoever it was, it is purely Greek, dating from the late 4th century BC, incontestable proof of Philip's success in cultivating Hellenism in northern Greece. That heritage is as strong today as it was at his death.

JOHN BUCKLER

See also Macedonia

Biography

Born in 383 or 382 BC the son of Amyntas and Eurydice, Philip spent three early years as a hostage at Thebes where he learnt much about Greece from Epaminondas and Pelopidas. Returning home in 359 he became king of Macedon at the age of 24. By a series of campaigns he established Macedonian supremacy and at Chaeronea in 338 he defeated an alliance of Athenians and Thebans. He was assassinated at Aegae in 336 BC.

Further Reading

Buckler, John, *Philip II and the Sacred War*, Leiden and New York: Brill, 1989

Buckler, John, "Philip II's Designs of Greece" in *Transitions to Empire: Essays in Greco-Roman History, 360–146 BC*, edited by Robert W. Wallace and Edward M. Harris, Norman: University Press of Oklahoma, 1996

Cawkwell, George, *Philip of Macedon*, London and Boston: Faber, 1978

Ellis, J.R., *Philip II and Macedonian Imperialism*, London: Thames and Hudson, 1976

Hatzopoulos, Miltiades B. and Louisa D. Loukopoulos (editors), *Philip of Macedon*, London: Heinemann, 1981

Wirth, Gerhard, *Philipp II*, Stuttgart: Kohlhammer, 1985

Philip V 238–179 BC

King of Macedonia

The young prince Philip was left fatherless as a boy of 9 in 229 BC upon the death of his father Demetrius II. He was placed in the care of a regent, a royal relative named Antigonus Doson, and was sent to Aratus of Sicyon, a Greek statesman and head of the Achaean League, in order to learn about Greek affairs. The effects of this education on Philip's later behaviour are impossible to calculate. He acceded to the throne in his own right in 221 BC, and quickly became embroiled in the Social War in which he and the Hellenic League faced the Aetolians, Sparta, and their allies. This war (217–200 BC) marked his transition into a mature king.

Philip was a brilliant military commander whose flair got him further than the odds against him should have allowed (although he experienced some spectacular setbacks), but he was reckless and foolhardy. The destruction of the kingdom of Macedonia and the eventual domination of northern Greece by Rome must in large measure be laid at Philip's door. He became alienated from Aratus (and his possible moderating influence) when he fell under the influence of Demetrius of Pharos, an Illyrian dynast whom Rome had placed in control of the Adriatic island of Pharos (Hvar in modern Croatia) and then displaced. Demetrius therefore harboured a deep-seated grievance against Rome, and incited Philip in the same direction. The final break came with Aratus' death in 213 BC, after Philip had seduced Aratus' daughter-in-law. Aratus died, claiming that Philip had poisoned him.

Philip irritated Rome by interfering in Illyria by land and sea, and by staging campaigns in Greece against Roman allies and on behalf of its enemies. Rome's declaration of war on Philip was probably inevitable. Three Macedonian wars against Rome and its allies ensued. Philip's military successes, continued meddling in the affairs of other Greek states, and alliances with various other Hellenistic monarchs increased Rome's suspicions of his political motives and led it to regard him as a dangerous threat. Paradoxically, the Romans claimed to be protectors of Greek freedom against Philip. The appointment of the great Roman general Flamininus to the command in the Second Macedonian War led to Philip's decisive defeat at the Battle of Cynoscephalae (in Thessaly) in 197 BC.

Philip was allowed to remain king, but a fine of 1,000 talents was levied on Macedonia, and his elder son Demetrius was taken to Rome as a hostage. Philip was confined to his kingdom and concentrated on rebuilding his country, with considerable success. He needed to be seen as an active ally of Rome in its further campaigns in Greece while in reality he bridled at his treatment. He continued to pursue an active foreign policy in Thrace, which only fuelled Rome's continued suspicions against him. After Demetrius had returned from Rome, his dubious actions and demeanour led his father to fear him as a Roman-inspired pretender to the throne. Perhaps encouraged by his younger son Perseus (who stood to benefit), Philip had Demetrius killed, thereby clearing the way for the accession of Perseus to the Macedonian throne.

Philip set forth on a great tour of his kingdom, but fell seriously ill in Amphipolis in 179 BC and died soon after. Perseus inherited a kingdom that was far stronger than it had been at the beginning of Philip's reign. The irony of Philip's reconstruction of Macedonian manpower and its economy lies in the fact that Perseus thought that the country was strong enough to face Rome a third time – this time with fatal results.

It is not easy to assess Philip V's place in the Hellenic world. He is one of the last larger-than-life figures to emerge from the Hellenistic monarchies, but, his dynamic personality aside, this is due to the abundant ancient evidence about his life and career. Given his unique place in history between Greece and Rome, he was an object of fascination to Greek as well as to Roman historians. The flaws in Philip's character are clear and his military genius is undoubted, but hindsight shows that this dangerous combination ultimately opened northern Greece to Roman rule. The final assessment of F. W. Walbank still cannot be bettered:

> But perhaps the greatest irony of all lies in this, that the king of Macedon, who was renowned above all for his energy, speed and enterprise, who opened his reign as the "darling of Greece" ... should claim his place in world history, not for any of these things which he initiated, but solely as the unwitting instrument that enabled the culture of Greece to spread along the paths of the legions to Rome, and so to the western civilisation that grew up after her.

> (Walbank, 1940, p. 275)

E.E. RICE

See also Antigonids

Biography

Born in 238 BC the son of Demetrius II, Philip was adopted (after his father's death in 229) by Antigonus Doson and sent to Aratus in Sicyon to be trained. He succeeded Antigonus as king of Macedonia in 221 BC. He was a brilliant commander and restored the fortunes of his kingdom, but he antagonized Rome. Fearing the treason of his elder son Demetrius, Philip had him killed. Philip died at Amphipolis in 179 BC.

Further Reading

Astin, A.E. *et al.* (editors), *Rome and the Mediterranean to 133 BC*, Cambridge: Cambridge University Press, 1989 (*The Cambridge Ancient History*, vol. 8, 2nd edition), chapters 8–9

Errington, R. Malcolm, *A History of Macedonia*, Berkeley: University of California Press, 1990, pp. 184 ff.

Gruen, Erich S., *The Hellenistic World and the Coming of Rome*, Berkeley: University of California Press, 1984, chapters 11–14

Hammond, N.G.L., and Walbank, F.W., *A History of Macedonia*, vol. 3: *336–167 BC*, Oxford: Clarendon Press, 1988, part 3

Hammond, N.G.L., *The Macedonian State: The Origins, Institutions and History*, Oxford: Clarendon Press, and New York: Oxford University Press, 1989, chapters 13–14

Walbank, F.W., *Philip V of Macedon*, Cambridge: Cambridge University Press, 1940; reprinted Hamden, Connecticut: Archon, 1967

Walbank, F.W. *et al.* (editors), *The Hellenistic World*, Cambridge: Cambridge University Press, 1984 (*The Cambridge Ancient History*, vol. 7, part 1, 2nd edition), pp. 473ff.

Philo

Jewish philosopher of the 1st century AD

Philo, born in the latter half of the 1st century BC, belonged to a wealthy priestly family in the large Jewish community in Alexandria. Of the course of his life we know nothing save that in AD 39/40, as an old man, he was part of an embassy to Rome to plead the religious rights of the Jews with the emperor Caligula. He was the author of a large number of predominantly philosophical works, many of them taking the form of a commentary on passages from the Pentateuch in the Alexandrian Greek translation known as the Septuagint, in which he sought to reconcile God's revelation to Moses, in which he deeply believed, with the Platonic philosophy of his day (nowadays known as Middle Platonism). Because he believed in the inspired nature of the Septuagint translation, he had no need for recourse to the original Hebrew text, and there is no real evidence of his knowledge of the Hebrew language. His Hellenized Judaism was probably typical of many Greek-speaking Jews of his day, but stands at a distance from the contemporary emerging Rabbinic tradition, in which form Judaism was transmitted to the Middle Ages and beyond to the present day. There are consequently no explicit traces of Philonic influence on subsequent Jewish tradition, and no Jew mentions him by name until Azariah de Rossi in the 16th century. His writings were treasured and preserved by Christians, especially of the Alexandrian tradition.

As with the Stoics in their reconciliation between philosophy and the Homeric epics, Philo's method of reconciliation was allegorical exegesis. His Platonic reading of the divine revelation to Moses in the Pentateuch yields a metaphysical view of God and the cosmos, and of the place of the human within it, that is in many respects typical of the Middle Platonism of his day. His God is one and transcendent and consequently utterly beyond any human comprehension: Philo has a good claim to the title of "the father of negative theology". This one transcendent God is manifest in the universe through his "powers" (*dynameis*), in which his kingly rule and beneficent providence are manifest. The highest of these powers (and sometimes apparently distinct from them) is the Word, or *Logos*, which has some of the characteristics of the Stoic *logos*, some of the Platonic *nous* (or intellect), but is uniquely regarded by Philo (responding to the language of the scriptures) as the utterance of God, as the one who speaks, pre-eminently to Moses. Here, and in other ways, we find in Philo a sense of God's personhood, lacking in his Middle Platonic contemporaries. In his understanding of creation, the account of Genesis is read in the light of Plato's *Timaeus*, and the cosmos, informed by the world-soul, is modelled on the soul–body unity of the human person. In his ethics Philo for the most part follows the Stoics.

Because so much of Philo's work survives, compared with contemporary Middle Platonists, he is an important witness to the philosophical matrix from which Neoplatonism developed, even though his own influence on the Neoplatonists themselves may not be very great. His Platonized Hebraism, however, paved the way for Christian Platonism; it is for his influence on

Christian thinkers that he is important, beginning with Clement of Alexandria and Origen in Alexandria in the 2nd and 3rd centuries AD, and manifest in the 4th century in exegetes such as Didymus the Blind, also an Alexandrian, and the Cappadocian Fathers, especially Gregory of Nyssa. In his *Life of Moses* Philo provided a two-part interpretation of the biblical account of Moses' life: the first part tells the biblical story of Moses, and the second part, through an allegorical account of events from that life, provides an account of how the mind relates to God and the world. Gregory of Nyssa's own *Life of Moses* is clearly inspired by Philo's, and presents Moses' life in the second part as an allegory of the Christian life, understood as the ascent of the soul to God. Through Gregory's version, Philo's *Life of Moses* became one of the models for the *Lives* of the saints, perhaps the most popular form of literature in the Byzantine world. Philo's fundamentally contemplative ideal of the philosophical life had a profound influence on Christian monasticism (already with the Cappadocian Fathers, the "philosophical life" is a synonym for monasticism), and his work *On the Contemplative Life*, in which he gives an account of the life of a Jewish community called the *therapeutae* ("servants" or "worshippers" [of God]), was taken by Eusebius and many after him to be an account of an early Christian monastic community.

ANDREW LOUTH

See also Jews

Biography

Born in Alexandria in the second half of the 1st century BC, Philo was a leading exponent of Jewish culture. He accompanied an embassy to Rome in AD 39/40 to the emperor Caligula. He wrote many philosophical works in the form of commentaries on scripture. His writings paved the way for Christian Platonism and were more influential on subsequent Christian thought than Jewish.

Writings

Philo, translated by F.H. Colson and G.H. Whitaker, 10 vols, London: Heinemann, and Cambridge, Massachusetts: Harvard University Press, 1929–62 (Loeb edition); supplementary volumes, *Questions and Answers on Genesis* and *Questions and Answers on Exodus*, translated by Ralph Marcus, 2 vols, 1953 (translation only, from the extant Armenian version)

Further Reading

Goodenough, Erwin Ramsdell, *An Introduction to Philo Judaeus*, New Haven, Connecticut: Yale University Press, and London: Oxford University Press, 1940; 2nd edition, Oxford: Blackwell, 1962; New York: Barnes and Noble, 1963

Radice, Roberto and David T. Runia, *Philo of Alexandria: An Annotated Bibliography, 1937–1986*, 2nd edition, Leiden and New York: Brill, 1992

Sandmel, Samuel, *Philo of Alexandria: An Introduction*, New York and Oxford: Oxford University Press, 1979

Wolfson, H.A., *Philo: Foundations of Religious Philosophy in Judaism, Christianity and Islam*, 2 vols, Cambridge, Massachusetts: Harvard University Press, 1947

Philodemus *c.*110–40 BC

Philosopher and poet

Philodemus of Gadara studied philosophy in Athens, choosing Epicureanism from the several schools there as the doctrine he would follow for the rest of his life. After Athens, and perhaps after a stay in Alexandria, he lived in and around the bay of Naples, where Greeks had settled earlier but whose pleasant surroundings were attracting Romans; many of them were eager to be instructed in the ways of Epicureanism by Siro and Philodemus, both of whom made the acquaintance of Virgil and his circle of friends. Philodemus seems also to have attracted L. Calpurnius Piso Caesoninus, the father-in-law of Julius Caesar, as his patron. When Mount Vesuvius erupted in AD 79, covering Pompeii and nearby towns, the impressive villa on the shore of Herculaneum was found upon excavation in the 18th century to contain the charred papyrus remains of a library comprising, for the most part, Greek Epicurean texts, many by Philodemus. It is usually assumed that Piso was the villa's original owner. Since Philodemus refers in one of his works to his own house as "a humble cottage", he would not have lived in the villa himself, as is sometimes thought.

In addition to the papyrus remains found at Herculaneum, we also have about 35 Greek epigrams written by Philodemus which were preserved in the manuscripts containing the *Greek Anthology*. Although Epicurus discouraged his followers from writing poetry, Lucretius, Philodemus, and some others found ways to justify their poetic activities. What makes Philodemus particularly interesting is that among his prose treatises are several concerned with the composition of poetry and music, which prove to be among the most important theoretical writings on these subjects from Greek antiquity. In his *On Poems* Philodemus argues that poetry is to be judged not by its didactic or instructional value but rather by criteria that are largely but not entirely aesthetic. Poetry, that is, should play with ideas; but if one truly desires to be instructed in the ways of philosophy, there is no substitute for lectures and prose argument. Other writings by Philodemus on literary subjects are *On Music*, *On the Good King According to Homer*, and a *Rhetoric*. In these, as in most of his prose, Philodemus typically reviews and criticizes the various views proposed by others before offering his own views. This methodology is welcome in that it provides information otherwise unknown about obscure theorists of the Hellenistic period. Unfortunately, however, the fragmentary nature of the Herculaneum papyri is often such that isolated sentences, even if largely comprehensible in themselves, cannot be assigned to their proper authors.

Much of Philodemus' writing is ethical in nature. From one large work, *On Vices and Virtues*, and substantial fragments from several other books are extant: *On Flattery* (book 7), *On Household Management* (*Oeconomicus*, book 9), and *On Arrogance* (book 10). Other works preserved to varying degrees are *On Frankness*, *On Anger*, *On Death*, and an untitled ethical work now called, after its first editor, the *Comparetti Ethics*. Philodemus' writings thus nicely complement those of Lucretius, who concentrated almost exclusively in his Epicurean poem on the nature of matter and the causes of natural phenomena, with almost no attention paid to ethical concerns.

Only on the most important subject of death do Philodemus and Lucretius overlap to any appreciable extent, for Epicurus was convinced that only by learning to live without fear of death could mankind achieve and maintain the state of *ataraxia* (lack of disturbance) necessary for happiness. The Epicurean view, denying that there is any life after death or any reincarnation, or that the gods have any concern for our welfare (see Philodemus' *On the Gods*), was used to argue that we should be happy with what little is required to satisfy the basic needs of the body. Philodemus' personal and gentle treatment contrasts noticeably with Lucretius' harsh way of dealing with this subject.

Other ethical works by Philodemus are *On Piety*, *On Frankness*, and *On Anger*. Frankness, or freedom of speech, is not to be taken too literally: Philodemus is here concerned with the appropriate language that one should use in various circumstances, which often calls for caution rather than complete truth. In *On Anger* Philodemus argues, against the Stoic position, that there are indeed times when a display of anger is appropriate.

Philodemus also wrote a work on scientific method, *On Signs*, and some histories of philosophy. It seems, however, that most, if not all, copies of his prose were destroyed in AD 79, although Diogenes Laertius (3rd century AD) may have organized his biographies of Greek philosophers (which end with a lengthy, favourable life of Epicurus) along the lines he found in Philodemus' history of philosophy. Philodemus' poetry, however, which had a much wider audience than his prose, survived on its own to influence contemporary Roman poets (Virgil, Catullus, Horace) and their immediate successors (Ovid, Tibullus, Propertius). Selected epigrams were incorporated by Philip of Thessalonica into his *Garland* of epigrams, which in turn found its way into the *Greek Anthology*, where Philodemus was read and admired from the Renaissance until the present day.

DAVID SIDER

Biography

Born at Gadara in Syria *c*.110 BC, Philodemus studied philosophy in Athens and became a follower of Epicureanism. Moving to Italy, he settled near Naples. Through L. Calpurnius Piso Caesoninus he was acquainted with many students of Greek literature including Horace and Virgil. Some 35 poems of his survive in the *Greek Anthology*. Some of his prose writings survive in charred papyri rescued from Piso's villa in Herculaneum. He died *c*.40 BC.

Writings

On Methods of Inference, edited and translated by P.H. De Lacy and E.A. De Lacy, revised edition, Naples: Bibliopolis, 1978

On Piety, part 1, edited by Dirk Obbink, Oxford: Clarendon Press, and New York: Oxford University Press, 1996

The Epigrams, edited by David Sider, New York: Oxford University Press, 1996

Further Reading

Gigante, Marcello, *Philodemus in Italy: The Books from Herculaneum*, Ann Arbor: University of Michigan Press, 1995

Obbink, Dirk (editor), *Philodemus and Poetry: Poetic Theory and Practice in Lucretius, Philodemus, and Horace*, Oxford and New York: Oxford University Press, 1995

Philokalia

Anthology of Christian texts

The title "Philokalia" is an ancient one. It means, literally, "love of the beautiful"; beauty being understood, on the basis of the Platonic tradition, as coincident with the Good on the highest level. In Christian usage it was employed by St Basil and St Gregory of Nazianzus as the title of their compilation drawn from the works of Origen. It became a familiar designation of works of compilation in later centuries. The most famous such compilation is that edited and published by St Makarios of Corinth and St Nikodimos of the Holy Mountain: *The Philokalia of the Holy Neptic Fathers* (Venice, 1782).

It is likely that this anthology was based in part on earlier Athonite compilations. This was certainly the view of the Slavonic translator of the *Philokalia*, St Paisy Velichkovsky. No one manuscript or group of manuscripts has, however, been satisfactorily identified as the source. The material was gathered by St Makarios on Mount Athos and presented to Nikodimos in 1777. Nikodimos revised and corrected the text, providing a preface and notes for each of the authors represented. It was Makarios who arranged for its publication in Venice.

The material dates from the 4th to the 15th centuries and provides an excellent summary of the eastern Christian spiritual tradition. The earliest material is from Evagrius of Pontus (*c*.345–99). There are also significant works of (Pseudo-)Macarius (4th century), St Diadochus of Photice (5th century), St Mark the Monk (5th century), St Maximos the Confessor (580–662), St Hesychios of Batos (?8th century), St Peter of Damascus (?12th century), and many texts from the 13th- and 14th-century hesychasts. The anthology covers a great range of writers, virtually all from a monastic background. The selection may have been partly influenced by the availability of texts. The *Apophthegmata Patrum* and the *Ladder* of St John Klimakos, works that would have been available in abundance on Athos, are absent. The selection from (Pseudo-)Macarius is from the less familiar Collection IV of his works. Among the authors selected, St Maximos the Confessor and St Gregory Palamas carry particular weight. There are no texts from western writers, with the one exception of St John Cassian who, in fact, stands very much in the eastern Christian tradition.

The focus of the texts is prayer. They deal primarily with the inner life of the monk. The writings are a school of *nepsis* (vigilance) and *hesychia* (stillness). Later texts put special emphasis on the practice of the Jesus prayer as a means of attaining true prayer of the heart. The writings have as their aim, as the title page puts it, "the purification, illumination, and perfection of the spiritual intellect through moral philosophy on the levels of action and contemplation". The tradition of the *Philokalia* is deeply experiential: theology is never separated from the living experience of God. As Abba Evagrius puts it: "If you are a theologian, you will pray truly. If you pray truly, you are a theologian." This is a sentiment echoed nearly a millennium later by St Gregory Palamas: "Our devotion lies not in words, but in realities." The *Philokalia* has as its aim the achievement of such perfect union between man and God that man may be said to be deified: all else is subordinated to that goal.

Despite the monastic provenance of the texts, the *Philokalia* was aimed at monastics and laypeople alike, as the title page states: "for the common benefit of the Orthodox". They are intended to be read within the context of the living tradition of the Church and under the guidance of a spiritual father. More than that, these texts were published to reanimate and reinvigorate the genuine tradition of the Orthodox Church. Both Makarios and Nikodimos belonged to the movement for liturgical and spiritual renewal known collectively as the Kollyvades. Against the prevailing mentality of the Enlightenment and the spiritual decline of Greece under the Tourkokratia, the Kollyvades looked to a patristic and Byzantine *ressourcement*, to a recovery of the ascetic and mystical tradition of the Church. Even Athos had not been immune to the mindset of the Enlightenment, as witnessed by the establishment of the Athonite Academy under Evgenios Voulgaris (1716–1806). The *Philokalia* represents a kind of response to the dry scholasticism of Enlightenment-influenced theology. It stands as a call to reacquire the experiential, lived theology of the eastern Christian tradition. It provides an alternative to the divorce between theology and mysticism, nature and supernatural, time and eternity, implicit within the modern western mentality. It is perhaps for this reason that it has proved so attractive to the contemporary West.

The influence of the *Philokalia* in the Greek-speaking lands was not initially very great. Its early influence was most palpable in Romania and Russia. It was reissued in Greek only in 1893, and not published again for more than 60 years, in 1957–63. The fact that no translations appeared in modern Greek until the 1960s may also have restricted its influence. As St Paisy Velichkovsky observed: "These books are written in the purest Greek tongue, which few among the Greeks understand much of now, except for learned people, and many do not understand it at all; therefore such books have fallen into all but complete oblivion." There are echoes of a response to the call of the *Philokalia* in writers such as Alexandros Papadiamantis, but it is only in the latter half of the 20th century that the kind of *ressourcement* urged by and typified in the *Philokalia* has begun to take hold in Greece. Much of the stimulus to this response has come from outside, most notably from the "Paris school" of the Russian Orthodox diaspora. Figures such as Demetrios Koutroublis have acted as catalysts in this process. It is a renaissance that is now firmly rooted in Greek soil. The monastic revival of modern Greece, in particular, owes a great debt to the "mystical school of noetic prayer" that is the *Philokalia*.

MARCUS PLESTED

See also Kollyvades

Summary

In Christian usage the term *Philokalia* was applied to compilations of spiritual writings. Most famously it is applied to the compilation made by St Makarios of Corinth and St Nikodimos of the Holy Mountain and published in 1782 with the title *The Philokalia of the Holy Neptic Fathers*. It incorporates a wide range of mystical writings from the 4th to the 15th centuries which form a summary of the Eastern Christian spiritual tradition.

Text

The Philokalia: The Complete Text, translated by G.E.H. Palmer, Philip Sherrard and Kallistos Ware, London and Boston: Faber, 1979–

Further Reading

Sherrard, Philip, "The Revival of Hesychast Spirituality" in *Christian Spirituality: Post-Reformation and Modern*, edited by Louis Dupré and Don E. Saliers, New York: Crossroad, 1989
Ware, Kallistos, "The Spirituality of the *Philokalia*", *Sobornost*, 13/1 (1991): pp. 6–24

Philopoemen *c.*252–182 BC

Achaean statesman

Philopoemen, son of Craugis of Megalopolis in the Peloponnese, grew up against the background of the political activities of the Achaean League (a federation of Greek cities in the Peloponnese) under its most famous leader Aratus of Sicyon. He became the pupil of Demophanes and Ecdelus, the liberators of Megalopolis from the tyrant who ruled the city in the mid-3rd century BC. Since Demophanes and Ecdelus had been pupils of the famous philosopher Arcesilaus of Pitane, head of the Academy in Athens, theories have been put forward about their philosophical influence upon the young Philopoemen. It can at least be said that they were staunch opponents of tyrannical government wherever they found it, and Philopoemen's predilection for federal government stayed with him throughout his life.

Philopoemen espoused the policies of the Achaean League, especially its strong anti-Spartan bias. He fought with the league against Sparta at the Battle of Sellasia in 221 BC, playing a prominent role that was lavishly praised by the historian Polybius (see below), and spent the next 11 years in Crete apparently furthering Macedonian interests there. His return to the Peloponnese coincided with the power vacuum in league politics left by the death of Aratus in 213 BC. He began holding league offices in 210 BC, and was elected its general for the first time in 208 BC.

Philopoemen finally helped to defeat the Spartan usurper Nabis, and forcibly united Sparta to the Achaean League in 192 BC, and he fought for its continued membership despite attempts to detach it by rival factions supported by Rome. His harsh treatment of Sparta alienated even some Achaean supporters and led to Spartan complaints in the Roman Senate. Philopoemen fell out of favour with Rome when he and his supporters maintained that various suggested solutions to Peloponnesian problems were none of Rome's concern but internal league affairs. He furthered his beliefs through league policies in the face of growing Roman involvement in the Peloponnese, although his intransigence caused a rift in the league. The political situation was unresolved when Philopoemen was captured in battle in Messenia in 183/82 BC and he died in prison, perhaps poisoned by his captors; poison was, of course, alleged by his political heirs.

Before his dramatic public funeral, Philopoemen's ashes were borne in an emotional procession back to Megalopolis by the young Polybius (later the historian), whose father Lycortas had been a friend and close political ally of Philopoemen (Lycortas succeeded Philopoemen as general of the league and continued to carry out his policies vigorously). In his later *Histories* Polybius, understandably profoundly affected by these earlier events, depicted Philopoemen as a great folk hero of the Achaean League and a great Greek patriot standing firm against the threat of Rome. Because the writings of Polybius are our best historical source for this period, his picture of Philopoemen has coloured later appreciation of him. Most modern scholarship would now argue that Philopoemen's vision was parochial and his policies blinkered by his opposition to Sparta and Rome. With the benefit of hindsight it is clear that the Achaean League could not in the end resist the power of Rome, and Philopoemen's activities led to greater Roman interference in Greek affairs and to the ultimate defeat of the Achaean League in 146 BC.

In his *Life of Philopoemen* Plutarch (1. 4) says that a certain Roman called Philopoemen "the last of the Greeks". Plutarch himself interprets this to mean that "Greece produced no great man after him, nor one worthy of her" (Loeb translation), but this is clearly a banal observation that is manifestly untrue. The explanation of this enigmatic statement has been widely debated by modern scholars. The most plausible interpretation is that Philopoemen was the last Greek in this turbulent age to achieve local political independence – albeit temporary – for his state. In this case it was the Greek Achaean League against the dominant power of Rome. Like Aratus before him, who had achieved similar freedoms, and because no later Greek was to have equal success in this regard, Philopoemen was thus worthy of extravagant praise and the accolade "the last of the Greeks" (see Errington, 1969, pp.216–27).

E.E. RICE

Biography

Born *c*.252 BC the son of Craugis of Megalopolis, Philopoemen was a pupil of Demophanes and Ecdelus. He fought for the Achaean League against Sparta at the Battle of Sellasia (221 BC) and then served 11 years in Crete. Returning to the Peloponnese on the death of Aratus, he became general of the league in 208. In 192 he brought Sparta into the league but lost favour with Rome. Captured by Messenians, he died in prison in 182 BC.

Further Reading

Errington, R.E., *Philopoemen*, Oxford: Clarendon Press, 1969
Gruen, Erich S., *The Hellenistic World and the Coming of Rome*, Berkeley: University of California Press, 1984
Plutarch, *Plutarch's Lives*, translated by Bernadotte Perrin, 11 vols, London: Heinemann, and New York: Macmillan, 1914–26 (Loeb edition; vol. 10)
Walbank, F.W. *et al.* (editors), *The Hellenistic World*, Cambridge: Cambridge University Press, 1984 (*The Cambridge Ancient History*, vol. 7, part 1, 2nd edition), chapter 7

Philoponus, John

Philosopher of the 6th century AD

John Philoponus was born in Caesarea around 490 and died in Alexandria after 567, perhaps even after 574. The biographical information about him is extremely scanty. The name

"Philoponus" is a nickname, presumably given to him either because he was a "lover of work" or because he belonged to the Alexandrian guild of *philoponoi* or church helpers. He was also called "Grammarian", a title that is usually taken to imply that he never succeeded in obtaining the chair of philosophy. He seems to have been a Christian by birth. He was a student of Ammonius, who was a son of Hermeias and head of the Alexandrian Neoplatonist school.

Philoponus' activities extend into several fields, but his chief claim to fame is his massive attack on the Aristotelian science of the time, in particular Aristotle's assumption of the eternity of the world. He wrote at least three treatises for this purpose. The first, *De Aeternitate Mundi contra Proclum*, was written in or shortly after 529 and is thought to have been intended as a demonstration to the authorities that it was unnecessary to extend their measures against the Neoplatonists of Athens to Alexandria because the Neoplatonists there had reached an understanding with the Christians. Most of the surviving fragments of the second work, *De Aeternitate Mundi contra Aristotelem*, are preserved by Simplicius, but some more fragments have also been found in Arabic and Syriac sources. In *De Opificio Mundi* Philoponus argues that there is no inconsistency between the cosmogony of the Bible and science.

In all these treatises Philoponus' arguments are primarily based on a central contention, which springs from the Christian conception of creation, namely that the universe had a beginning. The object of his attack was the dominant Aristotelian view that postulated the eternity of the universe and the dichotomy of heaven and earth, according to which the celestial region has an invariable structure whereas things in the sublunar region may be contingent. Philoponus refuted Aristotle's doctrine that the celestial bodies are made of indestructible aether – i.e. the fifth element whose natural movement is circular – by referring to astronomical observations that prove that the stars have specific motions not homocentric with the universe. In fact, he argued that the sun and the stars must be composed of fire, and that the different colours indicate differences in material composition. Thus, he inferred that the heavenly bodies are not distinct from the terrestrial ones, and hence are not eternal. Philoponus moreover argued, against the Aristotelian and Neoplatonic belief in the eternity of the world, that the universe, like every organic entity, is composed of parts that actually change at different rates, which may be extremely low.

In addition, Philoponus criticized Aristotle's explanations of dynamics, and proposed his own innovative theories on velocity in a void and on impetus. He believed, unlike Aristotle, that void is possible and that velocity in a void need not be infinite. Of great importance also is his doctrine of the impetus, in which he developed earlier ideas of Hipparchus and Ptolemy and rejected the Aristotelian conception that a body can perform a motion other than its natural one only as long as a force acts on it; it was supposed, for example, that a projectile is kept moving by the constant push of the air behind it. Philoponus, on the other hand, advocated that an immaterial kinetic power is imparted by the thrower to the object thrown and keeps the projectile moving until the power is consumed. Later, Philoponus expanded impetus theory into a unifying system by claiming that God impressed different kinds of impetus into bodies at the time of the Creation. Philoponus' theory of light is also related to his concept of the impetus, in that he regards light as an impetus emitted from the luminous body and propagated to the eye according to the laws of geometrical optics. This conception is opposed to that of Aristotle, who regarded light as the actualization of a potential state of a transparent medium, thus in no way associating it with motion.

Though not all of these ideas were entirely new, they were argued by Philoponus with great detail and thoroughness, and were often to prove more influential in Philoponus' version than in those of his predecessors. In particular, Philoponus' theory of the impetus was very influential, even if his eventual influence was delayed by theological controversy. For since he was anathematized in 600 for his views on Christology, his theories were marginalized and first taken up by Islamic philosophers in the 12th century. They became known in the Latin west only in the 13th century, some by direct translation, but most as filtered through Arabic sources, so that they were not attributed to him, with the result that modern scholars have believed them to be discoveries of the philosophers of the 13th century. He finally came fully into his own with the extensive Latin translations of the Renaissance, so that he came to be acknowledged by such thinkers as Galileo, and his ideas contributed to the breakaway from Aristotelian science.

Similar views are expressed in Philoponus' commentaries on Aristotle's physical works, namely in his commentary on the *Physica*, the *De Generatione et Corruptione*, and the *Meteorologica*. In addition, Philoponus composed commentaries on Aristotle's logical works, the *Categoriae* and the *Analytica Priora et Posteriora*. Simplicius accuses him of not being competent in logic, and modern logicians may agree. However, it is still the case that Philoponus' logical commentaries often record interesting views that are not preserved by his predecessors, and which proved to be quite influential to the Byzantine logical tradition. Finally, we also have Philoponus' commentary on Aristotle's *De Anima*, part of which was translated into Latin in 1268 by William of Moerbeke. There is no doubt that all these commentaries constitute, to a large extent, Philoponus' revised version of the notes taken at Ammonius' lectures. However, careful comparison with the commentaries attributed to Ammonius himself suggests that Philoponus was an independent thinker, who at times even points out that he is dissenting from his teacher's doctrines.

In the later part of his life Philoponus turned to controversial issues of Christian doctrine. Several theological treatises have been attributed to him, but the evidence for his authorship in some cases does not seem to amount to proof. Most of these works are transmitted in Syriac. According to the notice of him in the *Suda*, he was declared by the doctors of the Church to have fallen into the heresy of Monophysitism and Tritheism. Several of his early theological works, including the *Arbiter* or *Diaetetes* and the *Letter to Justinian*, prove that he was a supporter of the monophysite view that Christ had only one nature, not two, one human and one divine. A treatise entitled *On the Trinity* or *On Theology*, which was written in 567, and a later one *Against Themistius*, reveal his tritheistic doctrines, according to which the Trinity should be viewed as three substances.

Philoponus' other works include the oldest extant account in Greek of the plane astrolabe and a commentary on Nicomachus' *Introduction to Arithmetic*, which was a standard text used in the quadrivium. Grammatical treatises on accentuation are also ascribed to him (*De Vocabulis Quae Diversum Significatum Exhibent Secundum Differentiam Accentus* and *Tonika Parangelmata Ailiou Herodianou peri Schematon* [Accentual Rules of Aelius Herodianus on Logic]); probably none of these works has come down to us in its original form, because their utility invited alterations and abridgements by other teachers. Finally, some manuscripts attribute to him writings on medicine, but that is most probably a mistake, though an influential one, for it seems to have earned him a great reputation as a physician among Arabic authors.

KATERINA IERODIAKONOU

Biography

Born in Caesarea c.AD 490, Philoponus was apparently a Christian and a pupil of Ammonius, head of the Neoplatonist school in Alexandria. He became a teacher in Alexandria. As a philosopher he attacked Aristotle on the eternity of the world. As a theologian he supported the Monophysite view of creation. He died probably in the 570s.

Writings

In *Commentaria in Aristotelem Graeca*, edited by H. Vitelli *et al.*, Berlin: Reimer, 1887– , vols 13.1–3, 14.1–2, 15–17
Corollaries on Place and Void, translated by David Furley, London: Duckworth, 1991 (*Ancient Commentators on Aristotle*)
On Aristotle on the Intellect (De Anima 3. 4–8), translated by William Charlton, London: Duckworth, 1991 (*Ancient Commentators on Aristotle*)
On Aristotle's Physics 2, translated by A.R. Lacey, London: Duckworth, 1993 (*Ancient Commentators on Aristotle*)
On Aristotle's Physics 5–8, translated by Paul Lettinck and J.O. Urmson, London: Duckworth, 1994 (*Ancient Commentators on Aristotle*)

Further Reading

Blumenthal, H.J., "John Philoponus: Alexandrian Platonist?", *Hermes*, 114 (1986): pp. 314–35
Böhm, Walter, *Johannes Philoponos: Grammatikos von Alexandrien*, Munich: Schöningh, 1967
Evrand, E., "Jean Philopon: son 'commentaire sur Nicomaque' et ses rapports avec Ammonius", *Revue des Etudes Grecques*, 78 (1965): pp. 592–98
Saffrey, H.D., "Le Chrétien Jean Philoponus et la survivance de l'école d'Alexandrie au VIe siecle", *Revue des Etudes Grecques*, 67 (1954): pp. 396–410
Sorabji, Richard (editor), *Philoponus and the Rejection of Aristotelian Science*, London: Duckworth, and Ithaca, New York: Cornell University Press, 1987
Wildberg, Christian, *John Philoponus' Criticism of Aristotle's Theory of Aether*, Berlin and New York: de Gruyter, 1988
Wolff, Michael, *Fallgesetz und Massebegriff: Zwei wissenschaftshistorische Untersuchungen zur Kosmologie des Johannes Philoponus*, Berlin: de Gruyter, 1971

Philosophy

Ancient Greeks were the first to practise philosophy – that is, they did not just provide world views or narratives, but arguments and reasons. Greeks were highly competitive and fond of adversarial, critical debate. To do this effectively, the philosophers abstracted and analysed, which led them to distinguish specialized areas of inquiry or method. They considered nothing exempt from scrutiny. Philosophy was universal in scope, inclusive of politics, physics, astronomy, cosmology, mathematics, ethics, psychology, religion, and literature. On the whole, epistemology (how and what we know) was closely connected with metaphysics (what are the nature and causes of things), while ethics (literally habits and conduct) was an extension of psychology (theory about life).

The philosophers were small groups of dedicated individuals, usually conscious of their difference from ordinary citizens. The Pythagoreans first organized a philosophical society, which distinguished between occasional followers and more permanent members, and had its own rules of conduct. Plato established his Academy (387 BC) with the benefit of the Pythagorean example, and made it an autonomous fellowship for advanced universal study. In the Roman empire philosophy schools were centres of higher learning, passing this heritage to Europe and Islam. Thus, the Greek philosophical methods and practices became international and intrinsic to university education.

Greek philosophy is summarized here in the following periods: early philosophers (Presocratics, Sophists, and Socrates); Plato and Aristotle; the schools (Sceptics, Epicureans, Stoics, Lyceum, Academy); break, new trends, and state recognition (Middle Platonists, Aristotelians, Sceptics, Neopythagoreans, Plotinus); Neoplatonists and the end of the independent schools; Byzantines; and post-Byzantine and modern Greek philosophers.

Early Philosophers

The first philosophers (6th–5th century BC) abstracted for the purpose of understanding, provided varied accounts of their ideas, and tested their conclusions and common sense by taking them to logical extremes (e.g. paradox-making). They were disparate individuals or small circles of friends known by their home town or leader. Their generic labels, however, serve an ulterior bias. Aristotle called them "physicists", because he wanted to show that they were limited to studying only one of his four causes, the material. Moderns call them "Presocratics". Yet, all were interested in ethics, too, and several were Socrates' contemporaries. Moreover, Socrates' reputation as a philosopher is owed completely to Plato's genius for philosophical writing and foresight in establishing a self-perpetuating school.

Greek philosophy until Plato is very fragmentary and doxographical. Some (e.g. Socrates, Pythagoras) preferred not to write, and the rest left records that did not survive intact. Our two main sources are Aristotle and the Neoplatonist Simplicius.

The Milesians (flourished 6th century BC) proposed parsimony. The world as one experiences it is due to one principle (arche) taking many shapes and forms. For Thales this principle was multiphase water, for Anaximander infinitude, and for Anaximenes diffuse air. The Pythagoreans (6th–4th century BC) asserted that pure numbers are the permanent principles of physical things. They also arrived at the peculiar doctrine of

the transmigration of psyche, not just from religious belief but from logical conclusion: the principle of life, psyche, cannot not-live.

Heraclitus (late 6th century), the "riddler", alluded to the interrelatedness of things and their constant change by employing paradoxical ("everything is and is not") or obscure ("everything flows") sayings. Fire exemplifies the variety and contradictions of things. Philosophers, therefore, have to pay closer attention to reason and account (logos). On the other hand, the Eleatic Parmenides (early 5th century BC) made the startling claim that certainty in word, thought, or existence can only apply to something positive, unitary, and unchanging. Zeno followed this by showing the paradoxes entailed by change and plurality in ordinary events.

The Athenian Anaxagoras (5th century) responded to Parmenides with the theory that the world is a mixture of all substances, and change is just the rearrangement of stuffs. Nous (intellect), the stirrer of the mixture, alone is incomposite. Empedocles (influenced by Pythagoreans) was the first to invent the notion of fundamental cosmic constituents, the elements. He suggested four: Fire, Air, Water, and Earth. Democritus theorized that all things, including souls, are really temporary regroupings of an infinite number of tiny, invisible "indivisibles" (atoma). Thus what truly is and what appears are different.

Socrates (5th century BC) also upheld that there are invariable principles of things but sought them through the "right reason". Ordinary conversations on ethics and knowledge are soon transformed into probing tests how to define things (virtue, etc.), so they are valid for all possible occasions. For his purpose Socrates employed extensively counter-argumentation. This was typically practised by the Sophists (lit. "the clever ones"), mainly for the purpose of winning lawsuits for their paying clients. Prominent sophists, however, such as Protagoras and Gorgias, were philosophically interested in the problems of communicable account (logos), ethics, and the origins of human judgement.

Plato and Aristotle

Plato and Aristotle (5th–4th century BC) consolidated earlier thought (Parmenides, Heraclitus, Anaxagoras, Empedocles, Socrates), and originated an unprecedented advance in conception and expression. They were responsible for a basic division in philosophy.

Plato was Socrates' most eloquent follower. What survives are his public treatises, the dialogues, which were written as Socratic debates on key philosophical problems. Plato was also influenced by the Pythagoreans, when he was involved with power-politics at a Greek colony in Sicily. The later Plato shifted his attention, but towards what: logic, politics, or Pythagorean-type metaphysics? Plato remains controversial, for every party wants to claim the first major philosopher as their own.

Aristotle was a student at the Academy for 20 years until Plato's death. After empirical studies on the natural world, he returned to Athens to start his own philosophy and school, the Lyceum, or Peripatos. Aristotle's philosophy bears some similarities with Plato's, but in other respects it contradicts it, and in the fundamentals it is different in scope. Unlike Plato, what survives are his internal school lectures (see below on the Lyceum and on Andronicus).

For Plato, truth is found in reality, which to be unfailingly valid has to be separate from the changeable world around us. Reasoning and mathematics point the way to full, precise knowledge (*episteme*) of the "true realities", the "Forms". One of these, the Good, is ultimate. Physical things, properties, and sensations are merely the "appearances" (*phainomena*) of the Forms.

For Aristotle, reality lies in nature. The "forms" are merely the essential definitions of things. Change can be philosophically known because it involves the "actualization" of the "potential" to gain the thing's proper definition (e.g. for an oak seed to become an oak tree). However, a thing may be logically stripped, abstracted, of its various physical and mathematical properties until the philosopher examines only its essential substance, and ultimately the pure being (*on*).

The elements of the physical world for Plato are minimal shape-quantities, since mathematical properties underlie physical qualities. But for Aristotle, they are minimal qualities (hot, dry, moist, cold), because the constituents of sense-perceived things must be sensations.

In logic, Plato developed the "dialectical" analysis, but Aristotle constructed the formal "syllogism" and critically distinguished the terms of scientific knowledge. In ethics, Plato boldly prescribed the ideal virtues of both individual and society, but Aristotle analytically described the problems of choice, constantly relying on the opinion of the moderate majority.

The Schools

The period from the 4th to the 1st century BC saw the establishment of philosophical schools at Athens, their proliferation, and greatest rivalry. Unfortunately, of their thousands of books, few survive complete, and scholars must rely on collections of fragments and reports.

The first new talent was Pyrrho (360–270 BC). He pointed out that neither reason nor sense-perception can form knowledge, leaving the suspension of all judgements. Psychologically and ethically it offers "well-being" as relief from all theories. This "sceptical" approach did not survive as an independent school, but was adopted by the Academics.

Epicurus established the main branch of his school at Athens in 306 BC. He followed Democritus' atomism, but went far further. Philosophy is practical wisdom gained empirically. Ethics shows that the natural impulse of living beings is to gain pleasure and avoid pain. Happiness is the autonomous pursuit and holding of enduring pleasure. This is found in philosophy, companionship, and modest delights. Knowledge is attained with the veridicality of sense perception, assisted by natural conceptions. Such is the "yardstick" (*kanon*) and "discerning mean" (*kriterion*) of truth.

The highly acclaimed Stoic school was founded in 300 BC by the Cypriot Zeno. He was succeeded by Cleanthes, and Chryssipus (head, 232–206 BC). They subdivided philosophy into logic, physics, and ethics, after the Old Academician Xenocrates. For Stoics, philosophy is practical, based on the world as it is. The natural world is analysed into one continuous body causally joined by a universal *pneuma* and organized by reason-principle (*logos*), which can be worshipped as divinity. Ethics shows how to lead a life according to nature, guided by reason. The "psychotherapeutic" benefit is "apathy", freedom from troublesome passions, which brings the "well-being" of happiness. Physics and logic show how natural things are constituted, and become known through the presentation (*phantasia*) on the physical senses. Stoics developed sophisticated distinctions about substance, knowledge, and logic, and their terminology influenced subsequent philosophy.

Of the older schools, Aristotle's Lyceum fell into decline. His successor Theophrastus continued the interest in natural science and philosophy. Yet, it seems that its philosophical naturalism and rationalism were better explored by Epicureanism and Stoicism, while science was better served at the new science school, the Museum of Alexandria. Strato rejected a good deal of Aristotle's physics.

Plato's Academy underwent the greatest transformation. His immediate successors (Speusippus, Xenocrates) elevated mathematics and considered the Forms as mathematical objects. But Arcesilaus (Middle Academy) abandoned systematic philosophy, and returned decidedly to the Socratic critical questioning, using it to attack Stoicism. With Carneades (New Academy), the Platonic school became the champion of scepticism, extending and formalizing it. Carneades' refutation of Stoicism proved lasting.

Break, New Trends, and State Recognition

The first break happened in 86 BC, when the Roman consul Sulla sacked Athens. Institutions, including the Academy and the Lyceum, were destroyed. Philosophy diffused outside Athens and Greece, and freelancers advanced new trends. New schools often claimed succession from the original.

The Platonist Antiochus of Ascalon (1st century BC) reacted against the sceptical Academy. Instead he endorsed the positive value of Socratic thought, and showed that Aristotle and the Stoics developed particular views of Plato. Eventually this dealt the final blow to independent Stoicism: from now on there emerged Stoic Platonizers, such as Posidonius, the proponent of "universal sympathy". Nevertheless, Stoicism flourished among Romans, from Seneca and Epictetus (1st century AD) to Emperor Marcus Aurelius (2nd century AD).

Plutarch of Chaeronea (AD 45–125), head of a Platonic school at Athens, promulgated the dualism of good and evil cosmic agents. He and the Neopythagorean Numenius proved the most influential of this period's Platonizers; their doctrines entered Gnosticism, and similar Near Eastern religions. Moreover, in the 2nd-century *Handbook of Platonism* by one Alcinous, the Aristotelian forms were incorporated as the objects of sense perception. Alexandrian Platonists included the Jewish theologian Philo (who originated the Bible's agreement with Plato), and the famous physician Galen. The 2nd- and 3rd-century AD Alexandrians St Clement and Origen pioneered Christian philosophy while arguing continuity with Platonism.

Around 60 BC Andronicus of Rhodes recovered Aristotle's lectures, and edited them in the systematic form known to this day. He also started writing commentaries, amending and criticizing the doctrines as he saw fit. The Aristotelian Aristocles (2nd century AD) advocated Plato's agreement with Aristotle, so long as the latter remained the fulfilment of the former. He taught Alexander of Aphrodisias.

Scepticism found a new exponent in Sextus Empiricus (c.AD 200). He showed that every philosophical position has equally strong but opposite arguments, which leads to the suspension of judgement (later employed in negative theology).

Hadrian and the Antonine Roman emperors inaugurated a series of state recognitions of Athenian learning. In AD 176 the emperor Marcus Aurelius established four Athenian professorships ("successors") in Platonism, Aristotelianism, Stoicism, and Epicureanism. They were the highest-paid teachers in the empire, attracting 50 per cent more salary than the equivalent rhetoricians. However, the 3rd-century Roman civil wars starved imperial funding. Of the independent successors only the Platonists endured.

The Platonic professor was probably Atticus. He maintained dualism, and was fiercely anti-Aristotelian. The Aristotelian professor of about AD 198/209 was Alexander of Aphrodisias. He was the great systematizer of Aristotelianism, and the proponent of influential interpretations. Particularly, he identified the object of thinking with the thinking activity and intellect. This strongly attracted Platonists, such as Plotinus, who made the Forms both objects and contents of intellect.

Individual Neopythagoreans especially flourished in the 2nd century AD. For them, the pure Plato was Pythagorean. Nicomachus, author of the *Introduction to Arithmetic* (later a textbook), held unity to be the ultimate principle of the Forms as numbers. Numenius of Apamea differentiated God the creator from God supreme, and asserted that matter is both active and evil. An allied Neopythagorean was possibly Ammonius Saccas, the Alexandrian teacher of Plotinus and the Christian Origen.

Plotinus (3rd century) settled in Rome, where he attracted a wide circle of followers, including senators. He saw reality as a continuum emanating from a transcendent One, made identical to Plato's Good. It becomes differentiated into Intellect and Soul, as degrees of being. Matter is informed by them but itself is a privation, the source of evil. For Plotinus, Plato was the philosopher who came closest to this truth. Plotinus entrusted his student Porphyry to edit and publicize his works. Porphyry had already left because he disliked Plotinus' diminishing of Aristotle.

Neoplatonists and the End of the Schools

After his departure from Plotinus (AD 268), Porphyry elevated Aristotelian studies and assimilated Stoic ethics and logic, all within a revised Platonism. Iamblichus (4th century) increased dramatically the popularity of this "harmonization", and added Neopythagorean ideas: mathematics is the reliable basis of knowledge, embracing theology. With this merger of most of Greek sectarian thinking (Epicureanism alone was rejected) into a new, unified Hellenic philosophy came the domination of higher education of the Mediterranean world.

Single schools of philosophy appeared at Apamea, Pergamum, and at the chief place of learning, Athens, where the new school called itself the "Academy" (Plutarch of Athens, Syrianus, Proclus). From Athens, philosophy schools spread to Alexandria (Hierocles, Hermeias, Ammonius), and through Alexandria even to a Christian Platonic school at Gaza.

The philosophers of the 4th to 6th centuries AD bear the modern, inadequate label "Neoplatonists". They rejected dualism, whether Gnostic, Christian, or Platonic/Pythagorean. They proposed that knowledge, reality, matter, religion, and ethics are multimodal, founded on One unqualified principle. Aristotelian logic and metaphysics are valid for the modes relating to sense perception, and to things referenced to or abstracted from body and senses. Platonism is valid for the modes fixed by intellect, for the incorporeal, permanent realities, and the One.

The Neoplatonic schools were centres for research and teaching. Accordingly, they offered an encyclopaedic education. It encompassed science (physics, mathematics, astronomy, medicine), the study of literature, interpretation (exegesis), and politics.

However, in AD 529 came the second break in the history of Greek philosophy. Emperor Justinian banned public teaching by pagans. This and the increased enforcement of state-regulated teaching ended the millennium of independent schools of philosophy.

The Athenian school closed, and after an unsuccessful trip to the Persian court, its scholars dispersed. However, Simplicius flourished after the ban as a private writer. Continuity in private would account for the story that the 7th-century Greek monk, Theodorus, who became archbishop of Canterbury, studied philosophy at Athens.

The Alexandrian school survived the ban by compromising with local authority. One of its later members, Stephanus, occupied the prestigious, sole philosophy professorship at the Imperial Academy of Constantinople (610).

Byzantines

Byzantine philosophy from the 6th to 9th century was largely a continuation of the late antique but applied to the rational grounding of Christian doctrines, such as God's transcendence and immanence, and the coexistence of divine and human natures in Christ. Due to the Neoplatonic transmission, both Aristotle and Plato were taught at the Imperial and Patriarchal Academies. Maximos the Confessor (a saint in the Greek and Latin churches) clarified the Orthodox tenets, particularly the relation of God to being and generation. John of Damascus elucidated the function of divine representations in the controversy against iconoclasm.

The value of Hellenic philosophy having been demonstrated, 9th- to 12th-century Byzantines turned increasingly to the ancients. Patriarch Photios and bishop Nicholas of Methone championed Aristotle, while the university professor Michael Psellos promulgated Plato, Plotinus, and Proclus. The autonomy of philosophy was enhanced.

Despite the territorial decline of 13th- to 15th-century Byzantium, philosophical study increased. The reorganizer of education, Nikephoros Blemmydes, returned to the Neoplatonic programme of harmonizing Aristotle with Plato, which was further cultivated by his student the emperor Theodore Laskaris, and by George Pachymeres. Nikephoros Choumnos fostered an Aristotelian mainstream in the university and the Church. Theodore Metochites, however, employed scepticism against both religionists and rationalizers, and pointed to the limits of knowledge. George Gemistos Plethon rejected all religious dogmatism and saw philosophy (Neoplatonism) as the sole guarantor of truth. With his visits to Medici Italy he inspired the founding of the Florentine Academy. His student Bessarion later settled in Italy, where he became cardinal and envoy to European courts, promoting Platonic and Aristotelian studies.

Outside the Greek world, Islamic thought grew after its direct contact with Greek philosophy at Alexandria. Jewish thinkers profited from Greek philosophy first in 1st-century cosmopolitan Alexandria (Philo) but mainly during the Islamic period. Western European philosophy was born through Latin Neoplatonism (including Boethius) and Augustine. Aristotelianism flourished in the 13th–16th centuries. The 17th-century "mechanical philosophers" and empiricists rejected both Aristotle and Platonists, and instead took for a model the neglected Greek atomism of Democritus and Epicurus. Eventually this led to the separation of science from philosophy. From the 18th century onwards, Aristotelianism and Platonism influenced idealist philosophers (Hegel, Kant, *et al.*), while 19th- and 20th-century phenomenologists and existentialists often build on or react against the Hellenic-based views of intellection, being, and existence.

Post-Byzantine and Modern

The Turkish conquest of Greece and Constantinople (1453) was followed by a dark age. Intellectuals, such as Bessarion, John Argyropoulos, Dimitrios Chalkokondylis, and the Laskaris brothers, emigrated to Italian universities. At home, encouraged by special Ottoman privileges, education survived under the auspices of the Church at the Patriarchal Academy, schools in the Aegean and Ionian islands, Ioannina, and Asia Minor.

The revival of Greek higher learning formally starts with the return from Padua of an Athenian émigré, Theophilos Corydalleus. He had been in Galileo's circle, and studied Aristotle and the commentators. Corydalleus taught at Athens *c.*1610–20, then in the Ionian islands, and finally became head of the Patriarchal Academy. He exerted a lasting influence on the philosophy (logic and neo-Aristotelianism), education, and language of post-Byzantine Greece, but also precipitated the tensions over its identity: secular or religious; Classical, contemporary, or traditional; homegrown or imported?

From 1670s to 1770s, Mavrokordatos and other members of the Phanariot community (the administrative class at Constantinople) introduced more western European influence with their liberal education. Some adhered to rationalism and neo-Aristotelianism (from Padua), others advocated John Locke's empiricism, which broke ties with ancient tradition. The Ionian Evgenios Voulgaris, head of the shortlived Academy on Mount Athos (1750s), unusually combined avant-garde empiricism with Classical Greek expression.

The period leading to Greek independence (1820s) brought a deepening in professional philosophy and a confidence to debate home-grown material, influenced by Locke and Kant. Josephos Moisiodax rejected all scholasticism and authority (particularly Corydalleus), and defined "sound philosophy" to be practical. Athanasios Psalidas courageously arrived at the

philosophical impossibility of knowledge, which leaves ineffable revelation. Benjamin Lesvios promulgated the unity of empiricism with mathematics, and the human self-licence for free action. Adamantios Korais rejected the Byzantines and scholastics as grammarians void of philosophy. He promoted emancipation through rational education and the study of Classics. Daniel Philippidis expounded language philosophy, where philosophical meaning derives from word usage, and argued for the "analytic" against the "synthetic". He also put philosophy at the basis of education. Nikephoros Doukas, however, pointed to the coherence of ancient Greek, and urged the teaching of philosophy in that language. Konstantinos Koumas went further in favour of experimental science, against didactic philosophy.

The first decades of modern, independent Greece (1830s to 1870s) saw the great philosophical activity of the Ionian Academy, and the establishment of the Athens University (1837-) where the Ionian Neophytos Bambas was the first philosophy professor. The Ionian Academy used French rationalism and Scottish psychology for a new philosophy of self-consciousness. Peter Braïlas-Armenis (Ionian Academy, 1824–64) introduced a conciliation of idealism with realism, and Spyridon Komnos (later director of the National Library 1870–75) advanced the philosophy of Victor Cousin, including his Neoplatonism. Nineteenth-century Greek thought also bore the influence of Hegel. Several considered German idealism (e.g. problems of One and Many, being and existence) as the return of philosophy to its Greek roots. Supporters of idealism included Paul Kalligas and Philipp Ioannou.

In the 20th century positivism was promoted by Theophilos Voreas (philosophy chair at Athens), who was also an influential sponsor of philosophy in education. Neo-Kantianism and Platonism were championed by Charalambos Gieros, Ioannis Theodorakopoulos, and Konstantinos Tsatsos. The election of Tsatsos as the first constitutional president (1975–80) of the new Greek Republic honoured the free-loving engagement with intellectual argument for itself and for the benefit of individual and civic life, which has characterized Greek philosophy since the beginning.

Lucas Siorvanes

See also Academy, Aristotelianism, Astronomy, Atomism, Cosmology, Ethics, Government, Logic, Lyceum, Mathematics, Medicine, Neoplatonism, Physics, Scepticism, Stoicism, Theology

Further Reading

Argyropoulos, Roxane, *I Philosophiki skepsi stin Ellada* [Philosophical Thought in Greece], 2 vols, Athens, 1995–98 (covers the period 1828–1922)

Barnes, Jonathan, *The Presocratic Philosophers*, London and Boston: Routledge, 1982

Barnes, Jonathan (editor), *The Cambridge Companion to Aristotle*, Cambridge and New York: Cambridge University Press, 1995

Benakis, Linos G. (series editor), *Byzantine Philosophers*, Athens: Academy of Athens; Paris: Vrin; and Brussels: Ousia, 1984–

Dillon, John, *The Middle Platonists: A Study of Platonism*, 80 BC to AD 220, revised edition, London: Duckworth, and Ithaca, New York: Cornell University Press, 1996

Frede, Michael, *Essays in Ancient Philosophy*, Oxford: Clarendon Press, and New York: Oxford University Press, 1987

Furley, David, *The Greek Cosmologists*, Cambridge and New York: Cambridge University Press, 1987–

Henderson, G.P., *The Revival of Greek Thought, 1620–1830*, Albany: State University of New York Press, 1970; Edinburgh: Scottish Academic Press, 1971

Jordan, William, *Ancient Concepts of Philosophy*, London and New York: Routledge, 1990

Kraut, Richard (editor), *The Cambridge Companion to Plato*, Cambridge and New York: Cambridge University Press, 1992

Lloyd, G.E.R., *The Revolutions of Wisdom: Studies in the Claims and Practice of Ancient Greek Science*, Berkeley: University of California Press, 1987

Long, A.A. and D.N. Sedley (editors), *The Hellenistic Philosophers*, 2 vols, Cambridge and New York: Cambridge University Press, 1987

O'Meara, Dominic J., *Plotinus: An Introduction to the Enneads*, Oxford: Clarendon Press, and New York: Oxford University Press, 1993

Papanoutsos, E., *Neoelliniki Philosophia* [Modern Greek Philosophy], 2 vols, Athens, 1953–56

Psimmenos, N., *I Elliniki Philosophia, 1453–1821* [Greek Philosophy 1453–1821], Athens, 1988–89

Sharples, R.W., *Stoics, Epicureans and Sceptics: An Introduction to Hellenistic Philosophy*, London and New York: Routledge, 1996

Siorvanes, Lucas, *Proclus: Neo-Platonic Philosophy and Science*, Edinburgh: Edinburgh University Press, and New Haven, Connecticut: Yale University Press, 1996

Sorabji, Richard (editor), *Aristotle Transformed: The Ancient Commentators and their Influence*, Ithaca, New York: Cornell University Press, and London: Duckworth, 1990

Tatakis, Basile N., *La Philosophie byzantine*, Paris: Presses Universitaires de France, 1949; updated bibliography in *Bibliographie Byzantine*, Athens: Association Internationale des Etudes Byzantines, 1991

Vlastos, Gregory, *Platonic Studies*, 2nd edition, Princeton, New Jersey: Princeton University Press, 1981

Phoenicians

"Phoenicians" is a term used first in Classical sources to describe the people occupying the cities of the Levant coast between Syria and Israel. It was a term developed by the Greeks and its origins may be a Greek form of "Canaan" or, as is more usually assumed, it derived from the word for purple dye with which Phoenicians were associated. Linear B tablets contains a word *po-ni-ka* which probably referred to this dye.

The Phoenicians were inextricably linked to the sea; their cities were those independent Canaanite states which had not been absorbed by the Aramean or Israelite expansion. Among the Phoenician cities were Arvad, Beirut, Byblos, Sidon, Tyre, and Tarsus. The names of the coastal cities became synonymous with the Phoenicians; so in the *Odyssey* Eumaeus describes the Phoenician sailors who took him captive as Sidonian, from the city of Sidon (Homer, *Odyssey*, 4. 84). Phoenician also describes the descendants of colonial populations which the people of the Levant established elsewhere in the Mediterranean. Among their better-known colonies are Citium (in Cyprus: see Michaelidou-Nicolaou, 1987) and Carthage.

The Phoenicians are best known in ancient Greek literature for their commercial enterprise which paved the way for their foundation of new settlements, the majority of which were located in the western half of the Mediterranean (Frankenstein, 1979). The major colonization phase predated the emergence of Greek colonies; Thucydides (6. 2. 6) realized that Phoenician settlements in Sicily predated Greek activities on the island.

The Phoenicians transmitted much of their own culture and that of others from the Near East to Greece with the diffusion of their settlements and their highly developed trading activities. However, the Greek image of the Phoenicians has done much to limit the popular image of their culture: rich in religion, craftsmanship, and writing. It is easy to forget that the Greek figure Heracles is in fact a reincarnation of the Phoenician god Melaurt. The poor survival of Phoenician writing makes it difficult to trace other influences. Few literary texts have survived, and the majority are brief religious dedications, honorific cult decrees, or funerary monuments inscribed on stone. The Phoenicians were also famous for their glassware (Pliny, *Naturalis Historia*, 36. 65) and their metalwork – they are said to have discovered the silver mines of Cadiz in southern Spain (Diodorus Siculus, 5. 20).

The spread of the Phoenicians westwards throughout the Mediterranean diffused an important orientalizing influence. The Phoenicians had absorbed many cultural aspects of the Assyrian and Mesopotamian civilizations, and so their influence on Greek civilization was not restricted to the transmission of their own culture. Communities on Cyprus display considerable absorption of Phoenician culture. The building styles, metalwork, and ivory objects indicate the degree of Phoenician presence; even the designs and decoration on indigenous pottery imitate Phoenician ware. Citium, in northeast Cyprus, and its inhabitants were described as Phoenician up to historical times; their most famous citizen was Zeno the Stoic philosopher.

Probably the most important legacy of the Phoenicians was the adoption of their alphabet by the ancient Greeks. The Greek alphabet developed out of the Semitic alphabet perhaps as late as the 8th or early 7th century BC. Herodotus had first suggested that the Greeks learnt their alphabet from the Phoenicians (Herodotus, 5. 58. 1–2). The word "alphabet" is derived from the first two letters of the Phoenician alphabet, *aleph* and *beta*.

The trading activities of the Phoenicians brought them into contact with the Greek world very early on. Many Greek communities may have had an element of Phoenician population; Herodotus describes how Euboea was originally settled by Phoenician travellers. Representations in Greek literature of Phoenician traders conjure up pictures of hostile pirates or pacific merchants. Their trading movements required sailing skill and well-constructed ships. The shipbuilding timber of the Levant coast was famous in antiquity. It is quite likely that the Phoenicians invented the bireme sometime in the 8th century BC: their warships were fitted with rams and must have influenced Greek shipbuilding technology. In the 6th to 4th centuries BC the Phoenicians supplied fleets to the Achaemenid kings whilst under Persian rule, and later to Alexander the Great when he overran the coastal cities in the 330s.

Phoenician presence within Greek communities expanded from the 5th century onwards. From the end of the 4th century the Phoenicians themselves were absorbing different aspects of Greek culture. This is best seen in the bilingual inscriptions of the Hellenistic period set up to worship Phoenician deities.

More is known about the Phoenicians from their own colonies in the Mediterranean (e.g. Sicily, Sardinia, Malta, Spain, and North Africa) than is known from their native coastal cities (Bunnens, 1979). Some sites, apparently known in antiquity as Phoenician, suggest a different ethnicity from their inscriptions in Aramaic. It is almost certain that the Greek idea of "Phoenician" was very broad, and may have been applied to traders from the eastern Mediterranean seaboard rather than the identifiable Phoenician centres (Morris, 1992). Their cultural presence outlived any political strength in the Hellenistic and Roman periods.

GRAHAM OLIVER

See also Alphabet

Summary

A seafaring people from the cities of what is now Lebanon, the Phoenicians established trading settlements throughout the Mediterranean (Cyprus, Sicily, Sardinia, Malta, Spain, north Africa). They brought to Greece not only their own culture and alphabet but also the cultures of their Assyrian and Mesopotamian neighbours. Few texts survive but they were famous for glassware, metalworking, and shipbuilding.

Further Reading

Aubet, Maria Eugenia, *The Phoenicians and the West: Politics, Colonies and Trade*, Cambridge and New York: Cambridge University Press, 1993

Bonnet, C., E. Lipiński, and P. Marchetti (editors), *Religio Phoenicia*, Namur: Société des Etudes Classiques, 1986

Bunnens, Guy, *L'Expansion phénicienne en Méditerranée*, Brussels: Institut Historique Belge de Rome, 1979

Clifford, R.J., "Phoenician Religion", *Bulletin of the American School of Oriental Reseach*, 279 (1990): pp. 55–64

Frankenstein, S., "The Phoenicians in the Far West: Function of Neo-Assyrian Imperialism" in *Power and Propaganda: A Symposium on Ancient Empires*, edited by Mogens T. Larsen, Copenhagen: Akademisk, 1979

Gras, M.P. Rouillard and J. Texidor, *L'Univers phénicien*, Paris: Arthaud, 1989

Kuhrt, Amélie, *The Ancient Near East c.3000–330 BC*, 2 vols, London and New York: Routledge, 1995

Lipiński, E. (editor), *Phoenicia and the East Mediterranean in the First Millennium BC*, Leuven: Uitgeverij Peeters, 1987

Michaelidou-Nicolaou, I., "Repercussion of the Phoenician Presence in Cyprus", *Studia Phoenicia*, 5 (1987): pp. 331–38

Morris, Sarah P., *Daidalos and the Origins of Greek Art*, Princeton, New Jersey: Princeton University Press, 1992

Moscati, Sabatino, *The World of the Phoenicians*, London: Weidenfeld and Nicolson, and New York: Praeger, 1968

Moscati, Sabatino, *The Phoenicians*, Milan: Bompiani, and New York: Abbeville Press, 1988

Muhly, J., "End of the Bronze Age" in *Ebla to Damascus: Art and Archaeology of Ancient Syria*, edited by Harvey Weiss, Washington, D.C.: Smithsonian Institution, 1985 (exhibition catalogue)

Shaw, J.W., "Phoenicians in Southern Crete", *American Journal of Archaeology*, 93 (1989): pp. 165–83

Tritsch, F.J., "Sackers of Cities and the Movements of Populations" in *Bronze Age Migrations in the Aegean: Archaeological and Linguistic Problems in Greek Prehistory*, edited by R.A. Crossland and Ann Birchell, London: Duckworth, 1973; Park Ridge, New Jersey: Noyes Press, 1974

Photios *c.810–c.893*

Patriarch of Constantinople, statesman, scholar, and writer

Born around 810, or a little later, into an upper-class family which had been persecuted by the iconoclasts but which had a tradition of public service, Photios himself rose to the position of *protasekretis* (head of the imperial chancellery) and took part in an embassy to Baghdad (in 838, 845, or 855). Upon the forced resignation of Ignatios as patriarch in 858, Photios, the neutral candidate, was chosen to succeed him with the backing of Bardas, the uncle of the youthful emperor Michael III. For the next eight years Byzantium enjoyed one of the most successful periods in its history, effective rule being in the hands of Bardas and Photios. Among their most far-reaching triumphs were the baptism of the Bulgar tsar Boris-Michael and the mission of Constantine (Cyril) and Methodios to Moravia. Photios's speedy election from layman through all the degrees of the priesthood to patriarch in a mere five days was, however, uncanonical though not unprecedented (it is strikingly similar to the election of, among others, his uncle Tarasios) and embroiled him with the papacy. After initially accepting with reluctance the validity of Photios's election, pope Nicholas I condemned it, a move repeated in Constantinople in 867 when the new emperor Basil I, siding with the extremist Ignatian party and desiring western help against the Arabs, deposed Photios and restored Ignatios. However, after Ignatios's death in 877, Photios was recalled from exile, reinstalled as patriarch, and reconciled with the papacy. Later, having taken the part of Basil in the emperor's quarrel with his son Leo, Photios was once more both deposed and exiled on Leo's succession to the throne in 886. Photios's death is unrecorded, but it probably occurred after 891.

In the "Photian schism" both political and ecclesiastical factors were involved in the pope's claims to authority over Illyricum and Bulgaria and in the doctrine of papal supremacy. To bolster his position, however, Photios brought up a purely theological point in his condemnation of the western Church's unofficial addition to the creed of the *filioque*, which gives a double procession to the Holy Spirit from the Son as well as from the Father. The *filioque* and papal supremacy remain today the two main obstacles to the reunion of the Roman Catholic and the Orthodox Churches. Photios's principal exposition of his arguments, the lengthy treatise *On the Mystagogy of the Holy Spirit*, entitles him to be classed as a theologian. This claim may be strengthened by the theological discussions in his *Amphilochia*, by some of his *Homilies* and *Letters* (in particular an encyclical to the oriental patriarchs), and by a polemical treatise on the Paulicians which is, however, based upon a work by Peter of Sicily. Regarded in the East as a saint and the upholder of true doctrine, Photios was vilified for centuries by Catholics in the West who suppressed or were ignorant of his reconciliation with the pope. They regarded him simply as the villainous opponent of the papacy and the arch-destroyer of Church unity. His rehabilitation came as recently as the middle decades of the 20th century through the meticulous research of the Czech Byzantinist Father Francis Dvornik.

Whether or not Photios was ever a teacher at an institution of higher education in Constantinople before his elevation to the patriarchate is fiercely debated by scholars, but that he and his older contemporary Leo the Mathematician were the leading intellectuals of their day there can be no doubt, and they can be regarded as the prime movers in the cultural revival of the middle Byzantine period. The tradition of Byzantine humanism, which can be said to have continued until the fall of the capital in 1453, was in its inception largely due to them and especially to Photios. Both men immersed themselves in and encouraged a study of ancient texts, but Leo had more a scientific and philosophical bent, Photios a literary one. Photios's own writing aims at a harmonious combination of levels dictated largely by his subject matter, but he never descends to the vulgar and shies away from the pretentiousness of indulging in figures of speech for their own sake. Although he has a tendency to abstraction, he can be graphic and some of his descriptions are brilliant. His use of Classical (and biblical) allusions is often subtle and employed in imaginative ways, and it is notable that he has the courtesy to avoid them when addressing an audience that would presumably have been unable to appreciate them. His vocabulary is varied and shows evidence of his enormously wide reading, a by-product of which is his surviving *Lexikon*, probably a youthful work, which he entitles *Alphabetical List of Words which Lend Particular Elegance to the Compositions of Orators and Prose-writers*. This was written ostensibly for the benefit of a friend reading Classical authors, but Photios's lexical interests continued into his later career when he made additions to the *Etymologicum Genuinum*.

Some of his 19 *Homilies* are traditional in form, but others are innovative in introducing into sermons secular aspects of political speeches and the *ekphrasis* (rhetorical description). The most notable examples of the former are two homilies on the attack by the Rus on Constantinople in 860, and of the latter one on the church of the Virgin of the Pharos and its symbolism and another on an image of the Virgin (most probably the surviving mosaic in Hagia Sophia), both of which are of inestimable value in depicting a Byzantine's emotional reaction to a work of art.

Photios's 299 *Letters* are addressed almost exclusively to emperors, civil and ecclesiastical leaders, and foreign dignitaries. Some are tracts, such as that on the duties of a monarch addressed to Boris-Michael of Bulgaria and that on the heresy of the Theopaschites sent to Ashot of Armenia. Others cover the whole range of epistolary topics from recommendation to consolation to reprimand. Many were written in exile defending his position and encouraging his friends who were suffering because of their support for him. The *Amphilochia* consists of answers to 329 theological, philosophical, linguistic, and even scientific problems addressed to Amphilochios, metropolitan of Cyzicus. Some of these answers are to be found also among his *Letters*.

Photios's most famous work is the *Myriobiblon* or *Bibliotheca*, a collection of 280 chapters containing reviews of 386 books allegedly requested by his brother Tarasios. It is an astonishing work, but there has been no scholarly consensus on its date, purpose, and manner of composition. Slightly more than half the texts are of theology, hagiography, and ecclesiastical history. Others are scientific – geographical, agricultural,

medical, lexical, and grammatical. The remainder are of secular literature with an emphasis on historiography and oratory, but including six romances. "School texts" such as Homer, the tragedians, Aristophanes, Plato (and Aristotle) are omitted, presumably because they were well known, and there are only two chapters on poets (one on the 5th-century poetess Eudocia and one on five Egyptian poets). The reviews vary greatly in size, but typically contain the author's name, title, dedication, biography, summary (often including quotation), and evaluation which both corrects errors of fact and doctrine and comments on stylistic features. Of the books mentioned 78 survive today only in part (51 of these only in fragments) while 110 are completely lost, of which 81 are nowhere else even attested. Photios thus remains the sole witness to the existence of a sizeable quantity of Classical and Byzantine literature.

A.R. LITTLEWOOD

See also Humanism

Biography

Born *c*.810 to a distinguished family, Photios served as head of the imperial chancellery and participated in an embassy to Baghdad. When Ignatios resigned as patriarch of Constantinople in 858, Photios was chosen to succeed him though he was still a layman. Basil I deposed him in 867 and restored Ignatios; but on Ignatios's death in 877 Photios was reinstated. Deposed again by Leo VI in 886, Photios died in exile *c*.893. As a scholar he was one of the instigators of the 9th-century cultural revival.

Writings

In *Patrologia Graeca*, edited by J.-P. Migne, vols 101–04
Bibliotheca
    Bibliothèque, edited and translated by René Henry, 9 vols, Paris: Belles Lettres, 1959–91
    The Bibliotheca: A Selection, translated by N.G. Wilson, London: Duckworth, 1994
Homilies
    Homiliai, edited by B. Laourdas, Thessalonica, 1959 (Greek text)
    The Homilies, translated by Cyril Mango, Cambridge, Massachusetts: Harvard University Press, 1958
Epistulae et Amphilochia [Letters and Amphilochia], edited by B. Laourdas and L.G. Westerink, 6 vols, Leipzig: Teubner, 1983–86
Lexicon, vol. 1, edited by Christos Theodoridis, Berlin: de Gruyter, 1982

Further Reading

Beck, Hans-Georg, *Kirche und theologische Literatur im byzantinischen Reich*, Munich: Beck, 1959, esp. pp. 520–28
Dvornik, Francis, *The Photian Schism: History and Legend*, Cambridge: Cambridge University Press, 1948
Dvornik, Francis, *Photian and Byzantine Ecclesiastical Studies*, London: Variorum, 1974
Haugh, Richard, *Photius and the Carolingians: The Trinitarian Controversy*, Belmont, Massachusetts: Nordland, 1975
Hunger, Herbert, *Die hochsprachliche profane Literatur der Byzantiner*, 2 vols, Munich: Beck, 1978
Kustas, G.L., "The Literary Criticism of Photius: A Christian Definition of Style", *Hellenika*, 17 (1962): pp. 132–69
Lemerle, Paul, *Byzantine Humanism: The First Phase*, translated by Helen Lindsay and Ann Moffatt, Canberra: Australian Association for Byzantine Studies, 1986 (French edition 1971)
Treadgold, Warren T., *The Nature of the Bibliotheca of Photius*, Washington, DC: Dumbarton Oaks, 1980
White, Despina Stradoudaki, *Patriarch Photios of Constantinople: His Life, Scholarly Contributions, and Correspondence Together*

with a Translation of Fifty-two of His Letters, Brookline, Massachusetts: Holy Cross Orthodox Press, 1981

Wilson, N.G., *Scholars of Byzantium*, revised edition, London: Duckworth, and Cambridge, Massachusetts: Medieval Academy of America, 1996

Photography

The ancient monuments of Greece were an obvious subject for photographs, from the very first moments when the practical techniques of photography were invented. This occurred in 1839, with the separate processes developed by Louis Daguerre in France and William Henry Fox Talbot in England. Daguerre's process produced a positive image of the subject photographed on a silvered copper plate. The resulting pictures were of a very high quality, but suffered from the distinct disadvantage that only the single original photograph was produced (called, after its inventor, a daguerrotype). Fox Talbot's system (called talbotype, or, more generally, calotype) produced in the first instance a negative image on paper, which was then used for the second stage to produce a paper positive. The results of Fox Talbot's system did not, at first, have the quality of the daguerrotypes; the double process, the texture of the paper, and the patent restrictions demanded by Fox Talbot (unlike Daguerre, who encouraged the use of his process) militated against them. But calotypes did have the immense advantage that a large number of prints could be made from each negative, while the only way to reproduce the results of Daguerre's system was to make engraved copies, which inevitably put the skills of the engraver between the published result and the original photograph.

The earliest photographs of Greece were daguerrotypes. They followed in a tradition of artists' images of Greece and its antiquities that went back to the 18th-century travellers and artists. A French publisher, Noel Lerrebour, sent trained daguerrotypists to various parts of the world, to secure images as the basis for engravings published in a work entitled *Les Excursions Daguerriennes*. The photographer sent to Athens was Pierre Joly de Lotbinière, a French Canadian. His original photographs do not survive, but the published engravings include, inevitably, a view of the Parthenon, with the little Turkish mosque still standing within it, photographed in September 1839. Others are a view of the temple of Olympian Zeus, with the column later blown down in a gale still standing, and the "stylite's hut" still in position on the entablature, and a view looking out through the ruins of the Propylaea.

The oldest original daguerrotypes of Greece to survive are now in the Gernsheim collection in the University of Texas. They were made in 1842 by Girault de Prangey. One of them shows the Byzantine "Little Metropolis", with the modern cathedral of Athens under construction in the background. The best early calotypes were made in 1848 by the Revd. G.M. Bridges, and were sold in a portfolio, together with a variety of other photographs from different regions. The production of such portfolios became the favoured method of selling photographs, and, with improvements in the technique of making the original negative, put an end to the daguerreotype system, which was obsolete by the 1850s. The new negative system was developed in 1851 by Frederick Scott Archer, who used glass plate negatives, which were coated with a wet collodion emulsion. The process was still cumbersome (the plate had to be prepared and exposed before the emulsion dried) and in practice could be used only by professionals, who thus had a ready market in the increasing numbers of travellers to Greece, or artists, such as Sir Lawrence Alma Tadema, who made a vast collection of photograph prints, including the Classical monuments of Athens, as a basis for his Neoclassical paintings.

The last calotypes were made in the early 1850s, and include excellent photographs by Alfred Normand, now in the library of the French School of Archaeology at Athens, showing among other subjects the west end of the Acropolis before the excavation of the Beulé gate, and the temple of Olympian Zeus, again with its "stylite's hut", just before the gale that felled one of its columns. Then the wet-collodion process led to what has been justly termed the golden age of photography in Greece. Many photographs were produced by foreigners and sold elsewhere. An early example is James Robertson, employed by the Ottoman mint in Constantinople, who began photographing in Athens (as well as elsewhere) in 1853: he is probably responsible for a series of photographs of Athens of that date collected by field marshal Sir John Lintorn Simmons. Photographers based in London who made and sold excellent photographs of Greece include Francis Frith, whose first Greek photographs date from 1859 or 1860, and Francis Bedford, who visited Greece and other countries in the east Mediterranean at the express command of queen Victoria, accompanying the prince of Wales in 1862.

The climax of this phase came in the late 1860s and early 1870s, and is associated above all with three photographers, William Stillman, former American Consul in Canea and subsequently correspondent in Rome for *The Times*, who made photographs for his great album *The Acropolis of Athens* in 1869; Pascal Sebah, who had his photographic establishment in Constantinople; and Felix Bonfils, who worked from Beirut. Using very large glass plates, all three took photographs of unsurpassed quality, which found a ready market both in the form of albums and as individual prints. Those of Stillman were eventually sold by the Society for the Promotion of Hellenic Studies in London, who still possess an original negative of 1869, as well as the negatives of a later series taken by Stillman in 1882.

All this stimulated the development of photographic establishments in Greece itself. The earliest Greek photographer, Kostas Makedonas, began experimenting with the techniques in 1848, but the first fully professional studio in Athens was that of Phillippos Margaritis, who won prizes in international exhibition, for his photographs of the Acropolis and Athens in the mid-1850s. He also found a ready market for portrait photographs made for individuals in Athens. A slightly later photographer, Petros Moraitis, worked for an extended period in the 1860s, 1870s, and 1880s, and was the first holder of the title of Photographer to the King of Greece; again, much of his work comprises photographs of individuals, as well as views of the monuments. Other important Greek photographers included the Rhomaides brothers, in the later part of the 19th century. They took the usual views of ancient sites for tourists, but also worked specifically for archaeologists; they were the

Photography: view of Athens from the southeast by William Stillman, 1869

photographers for the Athens Archaeological Society, and took the photographs of the German excavations at Olympia in the mid-1870s.

By the late 19th century photography had become a much simpler and faster process. Ready-made dry photographic plates removed the necessity for working with wet chemicals while taking the actual photographs. Stillman's second series of Athenian views were made with dry plates, though the results lack something of the quality of the earlier series. The subsequent development of roll film put photography within the reach of virtually every tourist, and though the professional photographers continued to flourish, they are now too numerous even to list.

R.A. TOMLINSON

Further Reading
Benaki Museum, *Athens, 1839–1930: A Photographic Record*, Athens, 1985
Çizgen, Engin, *Photography in the Ottoman Empire, 1839–1919*, Istanbul: Haset Kitabevi, 1987 (for Robertson, Sebah and Bonfils)
Ehrenkranz, Anne *et al.*, *Poetic Localities: Photographs of Adirondacks, Cambridge, Crete, Italy, Athens*, New York: Aperture, 1988 (photographs by William J. Stillman)
Gernsheim, Helmut, *The History of Photography: From the Camera Obscura to the Beginning of the Modern Era*, revised edition, London: Thames and Hudson, and New York: McGraw Hill, 1969
Tomlinson, Richard A., "The Acropolis of Athens in the 1870s: The Evidence of the Alma-Tadema Photographs," *Annual of the British School at Athens*, 82 (1987): p. 297
Tomlinson, Richard A., *The Athens of Alma Tadema*, Stroud: Sutton, 1991
Tomlinson, Richard A., "Ten Early Photographs of Athens", *Annual of the British School at Athens*, 87 (1992): p. 447

Physics

Physics is one of the basic sciences in the development of human civilization. The semantic framework that defines modern physics was formulated through a series of procedures and modifications that are themselves studied by historians of science.

For many, the foundations of physics are based on the formulations proposed by certain ancient Greek philosophers concerning the interpretation of the world and the phenomena that evolve in it. These philosophers included Pythagoras, who attempted to pinpoint the physical principle of sight *c*.500 BC; Parmenides, who denied the reality of motion; and Anaxagoras, whose thoughts were directed in the opposite direction. Certain atomistic philosophers should also be mentioned, such as Leucippus, Epicurus, and Democritus. But it was Aristotle who formulated a system of physical philosophy that dominated Western civilization up to the 17th century, when the so-called "scientific revolution" took place and many Aristotelian views were rejected or reformulated, notably by Isaac Newton and his successors.

Aristotelian natural philosophy was the basis for further research about natural phenomena through observation. The main contribution of Aristotle was that he created a cohesive framework of principles and rules which govern the world, including both living creatures and non-living matter. For Aristotle there was no dispute about the reality and objectivity of the material world that is understood through human senses. He argued that there is no vacuum, a concept which he considered problematic to the way he tried to explain physical phenomena, and especially to the way he determined the movement of bodies. Aristotle made a distinction between natural motions and violent motions.

Another significant contribution of Aristotle was to transmit the hypothesis of Empedocles that the fundamental elements of all bodies are fire, air, water, and earth. These four elements were considered to be the only simple bodies for centuries, until modern chemistry proved that air was a mixture of several gases and water a compound of hydrogen and oxygen. This supposition was also compatible with the theory expressed by Aristotle that all bodies move in a way that brings them to their physical place. Lighter bodies move upwards, heavier ones downwards towards the centre of the earth. This was an example of natural motion, while the motion of a projectile was a violent one. Concerning the fall of heavy bodies Aristotle stated that they are attracted by means of their heaviness. The closer the bodies come to the earth's surface, the more the property increases. The impossibility of a vacuum, incidentally, led Aristotle to formulate a principle analogous to that of inertia.

During the Hellenistic period physics retreated as a discipline of science and other, more descriptive fields, such as geography and natural history, became more popular. Meanwhile, the influence of the Neoplatonic school was maintained. At Alexandria several scholars, such as Ammonius and his student Philoponus, tried to link ancient Greek natural philosophy with the Christian faith.

Little is known about the understanding and development of physics in Greek Orthodox Byzantium. The absence of detailed texts does not necessarily mean that physics was not studied during this period. Indeed, the Fathers of the Church such as St Basil the Great and his brother Gregory argued that it is not possible for man fully to understand God, and accordingly the laws he gave to the universe. Therefore physics, as the science responsible for finding out what these laws are, took the form of a commentary on what the scriptures say on related subjects.

Nevertheless during the reign of Herakleios (610–41), Stephanos of Alexandria taught Plato, Aristotle, and the subjects of the quadrivium, namely arithmetic, geometry,

music, and astronomy in the "university" of Constantinople. In the 7th century Kallinikos of Heliopolis in Syria is said to have invented Greek fire. In the following centuries a number of works were written dealing with mathematics, medicine, astronomy, and astrology but few may be considered as relevant to physics. In the 12th century Michael of Ephesus published a commentary on the *Generation of Animals* and other works of Aristotle.

During the Latin occupation of Constantinople (1204–61) the sciences developed in the empire of Nicaea. One of the most prominent figures of that period is Nikephoros Blemmydes (1197/98–1272). Blemmydes taught in his own monastery at Ephesus and his writings include an *Epitome of Physics*. But the main subjects of interest during this very creative period were once again mathematics and astronomy.

Throughout the Byzantine period, Aristotelian philosophy constituted the dominating "paradigm", acquiring a characteristic that prevented the expression of criticisms and speculations. At the same time, the Church also accepted it, both in the West and in the East, since theologians believed that the Aristotelian model of the world coincided with the writings of the Holy Scriptures. Therefore the support for Aristotelian philosophy shown by the official Churches made it even more difficult to contradict it.

It should be noted that – as with all works that endure the passage of time – ideas and views that were not initially expressed by Aristotle but were due to medieval annotators were gradually incorporated into the corpus of Aristotelian ideas. Commentary on Aristotle's works was also the first direction taken by Greek scholars concerned with physics after the fall of Constantinople in 1453. Of significance were Gerasimos Vlachos, Nikolaos Koursoulas, and Alexandros Mavrokordatos, with Theophilos Corydalleus also playing a leading role. Corydalleus influenced the thought of the period to such an extent that it became known as the Corydallic period and its methodological approach formulated a new school – that of Corydallism. In his work he tried to escape from strict adherence to Aristotelianism and to develop a more creative approach to it. The influence of Aristotelian thought is also evident in the way that Alexander Mavrokordatos determined the procedure for teaching physics. But a wave of doubt about Aristotelianism arose from the middle to the end of the 18th century.

A new way of thinking about physics, which was formed in 17th-century Europe – especially in the theories of Isaac Newton, René Descartes, and Gottfried Leibniz – reached the Greek intellectual scene via Italy. There, at the University of Padua, Nikiphoros Theotokis, Nikolaos Zerzoulis, Evgenios Voulgaris, and Josephos Moisiodax were taught experimental physics by the distinguished Italian scholar Giovanni Poleni. At the same time, they came into contact with the literature of international scholarship and thus had the opportunity to acquire and to study the most significant physics books of that period, which would later be used as sources for their own writings.

Of the four scholars mentioned above, Theotokis, with the publication of his work *Elements of Physics*, was responsible for introducing physics at that period to southeastern Europe. The most radical was Moisiodax, who believed that Aristotelian thinking poisoned the hearts of the young since it rejected evolution. In practice, however, European physics was successfully combined with certain basic principles of Aristotelianism, such as the maintenance of the inductive method, and Greece has continued to play a full part in the subsequent development of physics as an academic discipline in the international tradition.

GEORGE N. VLAHAKIS

See also Aristotelianism

Further Reading

Karas, Giannes, *Oi Thetikis-Physikis Epistimis stin Elliniko 18o aiona* [The Natural-Physical Science in the Greek 18th Century], Athens, 1977

Karas, Giannes, "Physics in the Greek Area during the 18th Century", *Physikos Kosmos*, 63 (1977): pp.19–22

Karas, Giannes, "The Structures of the Physical Science during the Period of the Ottoman Domination: The Physical Thought in the 18th Century", *Themelia ton Epistimon*, (1979) pp. 31–52

Karas, Giannes, "The Physical Thought of Theophilos Kairis and of his Time: the Theory of 'Enylon'" in *Panellenio Symposio "Theophilos Kaires", Andros, 6–9 Septemvriou 1984: Praktika / Epimeleia* [Proceedings of the Panhellenic Congress on Theophilos Kairis, Andros, 6–9 September 1984], edited by Giannes Karas, Athens, 1988

Karas, Giannes, *Oi Epistimis stin Tourkokratia: Cheirographa kai Entypa* [Sciences in Tourkokratia: Manuscripts and Books], 3 vols, especially vol.2: *Oi Epistimis tis Physis* [The Sciences of Nature], Athens, 1993–

Vlahakis, George N., "Physics in Balkan Region during the Period of the Greek Enlightenment (1750–1821): A General Approach" in *Proceedings of the First General Conference of the Balkans Physical Union*, Thessalonica, 1991

Vlahakis, George N., "The Introduction of Classical Physics in Greece: The Role of the Italian Universities and Publications", *History of Universities*, 18 (1998): pp. 157–80

Vlahakis, George N., "Dissemination and Development of Non-Aristotelian Physics in Aristotle's Land" in *The Spread of the Scientific Revolution in the European Periphery, Latin America and East Asia*, Turnhout: Brepols, 2000

Pikionis, Dimitris 1887–1968

Architect

Distinguished architect, city planner, and painter, Dimitris Pikionis merged in his work the basic tenets of modern architecture with essential elements of Greek tradition.

Pikionis was born in Piraeus and studied civil engineering at the Athens Polytechnic. There he was the contemporary of such future celebrities as painter Giorgio de Chirico, Byzantinist Anastasios Orlandos, and the historian of Athens Dimitris Kambouroglou. He studied painting and architecture in Paris and returned to Greece in 1912 to join the campaigns of Balkan Wars and World War I. In 1925 he became associate professor at Athens Polytechnic.

In 1932 he designed the primary school complex in Pevkakia at the foot of the Lykabettos hill. A stark functional structure, it maintained the scale that was appropriate for its fragile environment. After 1935 Pikionis began to combine the universality of modernism with the particular aspects of Greek tradition, ancient, Byzantine, and folk. In 1943 he was elected

full professor in Athens and after the war he worked for the Ministry of Reconstruction by travelling all over Greece in search of the authentic features of Greek architecture. In time he gave up modernity for tradition.

The period 1950–57 was his most creative. Among other works he designed the Xenia hotel in Delphi, the Potamianos home in Philothei (suburb of Athens), and his masterpiece, the unification of the archaeological site around the Acropolis, the hill of Philopappos, and the tourist kiosk of St Demetrios Loumbadiaris. The work involved the creation of two spiral paths, one leading from the main road of Dionysios Areopagitis to the Acropolis and the other to the Philopappos monument on the opposite hill. Pikionis made these paths with a mixture of marble and stone fragments that cancel out all reference to the industrial present. This most conclusive of Pikionis's creations is not a work of reconstruction but a journey into the collective cultural subconscious (as Jung would put it). At a time when the Athenian landscape and its natural environment were disappearing under the onslaught of the postwar construction boom, Pikionis designed this monumental walk around the ancient citadel to preserve the fading memory of a pre-industrial habitat.

In 1961 he became honorary professor of the Munich Academy of Fine Arts and designed a children's playground in Philothei, the town hall of Volos, and an ecclesiastical centre of learning on the island of Tinos. In 1966 he became a member of the Academy of Athens. Pikionis was a figure in Greek architecture with a profound influence on a select number of Greek intellectuals. His attachment to the Greek landscape and local tradition defied the universality of modernism, but he equally rejected the elements rooted in the land and in human dwellings.

THANOS M. VEREMIS

Biography

Born in Piraeus in 1887, Pikionis studied civil engineering at the Athens Polytechnic and painting and architecture in Paris. He fought in the Balkan Wars and in World War I. In 1925 he became an associate professor at Athens Polytechnic. As an architect his principal works were the Xenia hotel at Delphi, the Potamianos home in Philothei, and the landscaping of the Acropolis. He died in 1968.

Further Reading

Dimitris Pikionis, Architect 1887–1968: A Sentimental Topography, London: Architectural Assocation, 1989 (exhibition catalogue)

Ferlenga, Alberto, *Pikionis, 1887–1968*, Milan: Electa, 1999

Kounenaki, Pegy (editor), *Dimitris Pikionis*, issue of the *Kathimerini* supplement, "Epta Imeres", 16 October 1994

Pikionis, Agni (editor), *Dimitris Pikionis, 1887–1968*, Athens, 1994

Pilgrimage

Pilgrimage, in the Greek context, is an awkward term for the "journey of a pilgrim". The Latin word for "pilgrim", *peregrinus*, a foreigner living outside the territory of Rome and travelling to a shrine or sacred place (to fulfil a religious duty, to pray, and to receive blessings or some other religious benefits), refers specifically to the aspect of travelling, the journey. The

Pilgrimage: pillar of St Symeon the Stylite at Qalat Seman, Syria. Pilgrims have removed so much of the stone that little remains

Greek words for pilgrimage (*proskynisis*, literally "veneration") and pilgrim (*proskynitis*), however, come from the verb *proskyneo* meaning "I kneel and worship", which has an entirely different connotation. Greeks go to shrines and sacred centres for the purpose of veneration: to kiss the icons, to venerate the relics, to make confession, and to discuss personal matters with their spiritual fathers. In the Greek context, therefore, the core meaning of pilgrimage is not the "journey" but the "veneration".

Holy place, in the Greek context, is an equally awkward term for a "sacred centre". The early Christians did not attribute holiness to places, and indeed had no holy places for the first three centuries. There is no evidence that Jewish Christians or other Christians designated sites as holy or sacred before the beginning of the 4th century. Their attitude towards holy places and pilgrimages was, in fact, negative. Eusebius of Caesarea (c.260–339), for example, was extremely reluctant to countenance any talk of holy places. Moses had promised a holy land to the Jews. Holy places were what Jews and pagans had. On the other hand, Christianity was a spiritual religion and Jesus had promised his followers a "much greater land, truly holy and beloved of God, not located in Judea". Only a heavenly Jerusalem could be the holy city for the Christians. Pilgrimage was prescribed neither in the Bible nor by the Church Fathers.

The Greek pilgrimage tradition originates in remote antiquity, when the population of every town honoured their tutelar deity in solemn processions to his or her temple. At the time of the original Olympic Games, the temple of Zeus at Olympia became the "pilgrimage" centre for multitudes from every Hellenic country. The shrines of the oracular divinities, that of Apollo at Delphi in particular, attracted private and official visitors all year round. Visiting cult centres was also common among the ancient Israelites. With the restriction of Yahweh worship to Jerusalem, the sanctuary on Mount Moria became the principal centre of Jewish pilgrimage.

Cyril of Jerusalem (d. 386) was the first bishop to embrace the emperor Constantine's enthusiasm for building churches on biblical sites in Jerusalem, which he did after the Council of Nicaea in 325. "Others merely hear", Cyril told his catechumens; "we see and touch." Historical curiosity combined with pious zeal began to motivate an ever-increasing number of Christians to go and see the biblical sites where Jesus was born, lived his earthly life, and was crucified and resurrected.

To Cyril, Jerusalem was a holy city not because God had been involved there in the past, but because it had "a specific quality in the present". The ritual processions around the churches and the related sites replaced the prevailing pagan, Jewish, and Samaritan cults in places that had a biblical association. This brought the physical sites and the narrating of the corresponding biblical events into close proximity. In Jerusalem, story, liturgy, and site became one; the past became the present. The commemoration of the life of Christ thus affected the choice of biblical narrative to be read, so that it suited not only the site, but also, and in the course of time more exclusively, the liturgical season.

Before the end of the 4th century Jerusalem as a holy city evoked mixed feelings. Gregory of Nyssa, for example, considered it necessary to excuse his visit to Jerusalem by stating that travelling there did not bring man closer to God. The early Christians did not consider their churches as temples of a divinity. They were rather built for the specific purpose of congregating and gathering "the living temples" (i.e. Christians) of God into one. It was the gathered community and their liturgy that were holy, not the church that housed it nor the place per se.

Attitudes towards relics were also hesitant at first. Jerome, responding to the attack on the cult of relics and holy places in Palestine by Vigilantius (born 370), realized that the means used to honour God were similar to those already used for honouring gods, and that martyrs were now honoured in ways that were previously considered idolatrous.

The decisive and final shift in attitude corresponds to Augustine's own acceptance of the prevalent belief in the everyday occurrence of miracles, which arose in the two first decades of the 5th century. His change in attitude was brought about when, almost daily in his pastoral work among his congregations, he was witnessing miracles wrought by the relics of St Stephen which had recently been discovered and brought to Africa.

In her account (c.381–84) of the prevailing custom of visiting *martyria*, or churches that had been built on the tomb of a martyr or a saint, the pilgrim Egeria remarks that specific passages from scripture became attached to specific sites and the events associated with them: readings *apta diei et loco*. She also notes that the monks in the region of Charra of Mesopotamia lived in seclusion and came out only occasionally, notably at Easter and for the feast of the martyr, to participate in the liturgy in the *martyrium*.

The cult of martyrs prepared the way for the idea of holy places, and gave the place a new sacred significance; it bridged the need to make the present (in post-Constantinian conditions) the past of the persecuted Church. It abolished the gap between the generation of martyrs and later generations. The places were derivatively rather than intrinsically holy, however, being the sites of historical events of sacred significance. The miracles witnessed in the *martyria* in particular seem to have been the cause of the rapid growth of the pilgrimage movement in the early 5th century. The cult of images became popular, too, due to the miracle-working icons.

Since it was not the place but the congregation and the relics that were originally regarded as holy in the early eastern Churches, visitors or pilgrims did not need to make the journey to the temple or to the "holy places" of Christendom. To them, pilgrimage implied spiritual participation in the life of Christ, as expressed in the liturgy. This attitude gave rise to another kind of pilgrimage, namely that of visiting holy men and women who had dedicated their lives to perpetual prayer: monks and ascetics. When Basil of Caesarea, for example, visited Palestine in 351, he went there to stay with the monks and ascetics to unlock the secret of their holy lives. He wanted to learn about personal spiritual pilgrimage; the destination was the heavenly city of God, as experienced on an internal level.

With the growth of the ascetic movement, the monasteries in 4th-century Egypt soon gave it the status of a second Holy Land. Travellers who visited Jerusalem felt the need to visit the ascetic houses of the Nile too. Most monasteries became pilgrimage centres in the following centuries. Notable among these were St Catherine's on Mount Sinai, built in the 6th century on the site of the Burning Bush at the foot of the craggy peak where God delivered the Tablets to Moses, and the great monastery of Stoudios in Constantinople. This development went hand-in-hand with the cults of relics and images, and with the veneration of holy men and women. All newly founded monasteries had some relics, which also became objects of veneration on the death of well-known hermits and spiritual fathers.

Between the early 4th and the mid-7th centuries, men and women, young and old, rich and poor came to the biblical sites in the Holy Land, following in the footsteps of Constantine's mother Helena. At first it was the Old Testament site of Mount Sinai in particular that attracted the pilgrims, but these were later superseded by the sites associated with the life and Passion of Christ. The pilgrimages turned into a circuit of sites starting from the tomb of Christ at the Holy Sepulchre. Pilgrims descended from the Mount of Olives on Palm Sunday and formed a citywide procession during which thousands of visitors were entertained and exploited by the many commercial fairs and festivals.

The growth of pilgrimage was accelerated by the belief that sanctity was somehow transferable through physical contact. Some pilgrims therefore came to the Holy Land to intensify their faith by means of prayer and through revelation, others brought offerings and votives. Many came for miraculous healing of various diseases and illnesses, and there were those who came to seek advice, and to do penance.

Travel was slow. It was speedier by sea and more comfortable. Most pilgrims went overland by donkey or on foot, the daily distance being around 30 km. The Bible, maps, guidebooks, and letters of introduction were the prerequisites of every pilgrim. Letters of transit were needed at the frontiers before permission was granted to join the official highway system known as the *cursus publicus*. Along the pilgrimage routes were local guides who pointed out the sites and assisted in dealing with hostile natives, bandits, and robbers. Travelling in groups was more or less obligatory under these circumstances.

A pilgrimage could be made at little expense, because the local Christian community was obliged to take care of travellers. There were both Church- and state-endowed hostels as well as commercial hotels and camping grounds. The indigent and the sick found their haven in the church hostels, as did monks, nuns, and theologians. The merchants traded as they travelled. The aristocrats could afford themselves some comfort during the journey, and the soldiers were used to camping. The bureaucrats were always welcomed at the state-endowed hostels. In principle, therefore, a pilgrimage could be made by anyone.

When pilgrimage became part of popular religion, it inspired the production of a wide variety of minor pilgrims' *evlogia* ("blessing") artefacts, such as small pieces (diameter 1–10 cm) of sanctified earth, identifiable by the stamped impression. The token of Symeon the Stylite the Younger (521–92), in which the seal impression shows the saint on his column flanked by angels with crowns or palm fronds, and a monk climbing a ladder towards him, was the most common *evlogia* at the time. These pieces of portable pilgrims' tokens, "the *evlogia* made from dust and blessed by him", were carried home for their apotropaic and medicinal powers. In the hour of need they were crumbled into dust and applied externally, either dry or in a paste. The effect was believed to be both prophylactic and curative.

With Palestine and Sinai in Arab hands, pilgrimage to the Holy Land became virtually impossible. Constantinople, the heart of Byzantium, became the new pilgrimage centre. The great monastery of Stoudios and the other 350 monasteries in the capital soon became havens for thousands of pilgrims and visitors. Pilgrimage to the tombs of famous spiritual monks, notably those of the healer monk Theodore of Sykeon (died 613) and the wandering hermit Luke the Stylite (died 953), became an important Byzantine religious phenomenon, and continued to be so throughout the era.

With Constantinople in Turkish hands from 1453, Mount Athos became the new heart of Byzantine monasticism and pilgrimage. The Athonites were attracting monks and pilgrims from non-Greek lands, including the various Balkan countries and Russia, as early as the 10th century. During Ottoman rule (1430–1912), the monasteries of Mount Athos became pan-Orthodox centres of pilgrimage, with a large network of benefactors among the wealthy Serbs and Russians in particular. European bibliophiles visited it too, in search of lost manuscripts and rare books, but also for spiritual reasons. Today more than 40,000 men from all over Europe visit the Holy Mountain every year. In the modern Greek context a visit there is by definition a pilgrimage in the sense of venerating the icons and relics, as well as making confession to a spiritual father, receiving his advice for the future, and experiencing, with the monks, the presence of God in the services. This is also why the tomb of the famous spiritual Athonite monk of our time, Father Paisios, near Thessalonica, is rapidly becoming a pilgrimage centre. Other significant centres include the convent of the Annunciation at Ormylia on the Chalcidice peninsula, and the Kechrovouni convent on the island of Tinos, renowned for the increasing number of educated women visiting the shrine of the Mother of God.

RENÉ GOTHÓNI

See also Martyrdom, Relics

Further Reading

Davies, J.G., *Pilgrimage Yesterday and Today: Why? Where? How?*, London: SCM Press, 1988

Dillon, Matthew, *Pilgrims and Pilgrimage in Ancient Greece*, London and New York: Routledge, 1997

Gothóni, René, *Tales and Truth: Pilgrimage on Mount Athos Past and Present*, Helsinki: Helsinki University Press, 1994

Hellier, Chris, *Monasteries of Greece*, London: Tauris Parke, 1996

Kazhdan, A.P. (editor), *The Oxford Dictionary of Byzantium*, 3 vols, New York and Oxford: Oxford University Press, 1991

Markus, R.A., "How on Earth Could Places Become Holy? Origins of the Christian Idea of Holy Places", *Journal of Early Christian Studies*, 2/3 (1994): pp. 257–71

Ousterhout, Robert, *The Blessings of Pilgrimage*, Urbana: University of Illinois Press, 1990

Pakkanen, Petra, "The Religiosity of the Sacred Island of Tinos in Greece: History, Monasticism and Pilgrimage", *Byzantium and the North / Acta Byzantina Fennica*, 7 (1995): pp. 55–86

Walker, P.W.L., *Holy City, Holy Places? Christian Attitudes to Jerusalem and the Holy Land in the Fourth Century*, Oxford: Clarendon Press, and New York: Oxford University Press, 1990

Wilken, Robert L., *The Land Called Holy: Palestine in Christian History and Thought*, New Haven and London: Yale University Press, 1992

Wilkinson, John, *Egeria's Travels to the Holy Land*, Jerusalem: Ariel, and Warminster: Aris and Phillips, 1981

Pindar *c.*518–*c.*438 BC

Lyric poet

Pindar is best known today for his four books of epinician (victory) odes which were written on commission to celebrate victories at the great games of ancient Greece. By a mixture of direct praise and the interweaving of heroic legends, they glorify the aristocratic life, whose pinnacle is victory at the games and recognition for it.

In the 2nd century BC Pindar's work was divided into 17 books, roughly according to genre. Of these the four books of epinician odes survive virtually complete. Fragments of poems in other genres survive: hymns, paeans, dithyrambs (two books), processional hymns (two books), maiden songs (three books), choral songs (two books), praise songs, and dirges. These poems, where the evidence allows of an opinion, were, like the epinicians, written on commission. In the circumstances, it is difficult to disentangle the poet's own sentiments and autobiographical material from the restrictions and demands imposed by the conventions of the medium. Many of the opinions and value judgements expressed are revealed, on comparing the epinician odes of Bacchylides, as part of the baggage carried by a writer in this genre: it celebrates victory through toil, but victory and toil appropriate to aristocrats who have the time to exhaust themselves in the non-productive pursuit of kudos. Nevertheless, it is possible, by judicious examination of internal allusions and external sources (e.g. victors' lists), to get some idea of the progress of Pindar's career, at least as a writer of epinicia.

The epinician odes are divided into *Olympians* (14), *Pythians* (12), *Nemeans* (11), and *Isthmians* (8 as well as fragments). Not all celebrate victories in these games: *Nemeans* 4 and 9 record victories at the Adrasteia in Sicyon; *Nemean* 10 a victory at the Argive Heraia; *Pythians* 2 and 3 are epistles to Hieron of Syracuse; *Isthmian* 2 an epistle to Xenocrates of Acragas, and *Nemean* 11 celebrates the appointment of Aristagoras of Tenedos to a magistracy. Almost all of the latter, however, make some allusion to the games, and follow the same overall pattern as a typical epinician.

This pattern – very roughly speaking – is, at some point in the poem, to give the details of the victory or set its scene briefly and, as soon as possible, to present one or a series of stories associated with the legendary traditions of the home-land of the victor and/or patron. The linking passages are often tenuous. Consider for example the very earliest epinician (*Pythian* 10, for a Thessalian winner in the boys' double foot race), where Pindar compares his technique to that of a bee, which flits from one theme to another (lines 53–54). Early as the ode is, it already fixes the mould in which most were cast: the victor and his family are introduced and praised, especially his father, whose good fortune extends as far as a mortal's can; but even farther are the Hyperboreans, with whom Perseus once feasted; there follow praise of the Hyperboreans and a brief allusion to the slaying of the Gorgon, whose severed head turned men to stone; no miracle is beyond belief; the finest victory hymn flits like a bee from one theme to another; the poet hopes that his poem will glorify the victor in the eyes of others, and praises the ruler of Thessaly (who seems to have commissioned the poem from him).

The victors range from the very rich who entered victorious chariots to boxers and wrestlers. There is even one *aulos* player (*Pythian* 12 for Midas of Acragas). But all are encompassed within the aristocratic ideal of nobility and noble deeds. Pindar's most distinguished patrons were the Sicilian tyrants Hieron and Theron and members of their entourages. It is clear that the poet spent several months at least in Sicily, during the Olympic year 476 BC. He wrote three odes (*Pythians* 9 in 474 BC, 4 and 5 in 462 BC) for Arcesilas of Cyrene, in which he alludes to his own family connection with the Spartan clan of Aegeidae. But those for whom he wrote the largest number of victory odes (11) were victors from Aegina: he may have spent the years immediately before and after the Persian invasion of 480–479 BC on this island (*Isthmian* 5 of 480 BC refers to the battle of Salamis, and *Isthmian* 8 of 478 BC to the removal of the danger threatening Hellas). At *Nemean* 7. 61 he calls himself a *xenos* (guest) of the Aeginetans. It is to be remembered that not all Thebans supported the dominant faction of Medizers: 400 fought with Leonidas at Thermopylae

(Herodotus, 7. 202), and after the Battle of Plataea the victorious Hellenes punished only the leading Medizers at Thebes. If it is true that Pindar was later criticized at Thebes for writing in praise of Athens, this must also be seen in the same context of divided loyalties.

Pindar's epinician career began when he was 20 in 498 BC, with a commission from Thessaly (*Pythian* 10). In the year of Marathon he had his first commission from Sicily (*Pythians* 6 and 12 for Acragas). During the 480s and early 470s BC he wrote for Boeotian Orchomenus (*Olympian* 14), Athens (*Pythian* 7 for an Alcmaeonid), Attic Acharnae (*Nemean* 2), and Aegina (*Nemean* 5, *Isthmians* 5, 6, 8). The decade or so following the Persian invasions marks the high point of his popularity and production in this genre: three odes for Thebans (*Isthmians* 1, 3, 4), three for Aeginetans (*Isthmian* 8, *Nemeans* 3, 4), one for Cyrene (*Pythian* 9), and an impressive thirteen for Sicily and southern Italy (*Olympians* 1, 2, 3, 6, 10, 11, 12, *Pythians* 1, 2, 3, *Nemeans* 1, 9, *Isthmian* 2). There are signs, however, that towards the end of this period Pindar found it harder to get patrons (*Isthmian* 2 of *c.*470 BC is a letter to Xenocrates of Acragas which seems to be a request for payment). For the rest of his epinician career, he cast his net more widely: there were still Aegina (*Olympian* 8, *Nemeans* 6, 7, 8), although that island's conquest by Athens almost completely cut off this source (only *Pythian* 8 of 446 BC comes from after the conquest), and Thebes (*Pythian* 11, *Isthmian* 7), but also, on the mainland Opous (*Olympian* 9), Corinth (*Olympian* 3), and Argos (*Nemean* 10), and overseas Rhodes (*Olympian* 7), Cyrene (*Pythians* 4 and 5), Tenedos (*Nemean* 11), and Camarina (*Olympians* 4 and 5).

Pindar's poems were probably meant to be sung, and many to be accompanied by dancing. The music and choreography have been lost, and only the words remain. His poetry, regardless of the genre, is characterized by a controlled extravagance of language, and a skill and agility in linking apparently disconnected themes into a satisfying whole, which is unmatched by any other poet (one has only to compare the epinician odes of Pindar and Bacchylides to see how pedestrian the latter appear by contrast).

The epinician genre more or less died with Pindar, or rather with the drying-up of the supply of patrons. The tyrannical regimes of Sicily and Cyrene had been replaced by more broadly based governments, and in general rich individuals had other claims upon their resources, particularly in the unsettled conditions that prevailed throughout the second half of the 5th century BC. The result is that Pindar's poetry, when it was used as a model by later poets, was mined only for its extravagance of imagery and apparent convolution of expression. The poets of the Pléiade, for example, wrote so-called Pindaric poetry, which fails because it completely misses not only the music and dance, which were integral features of the original, but also the occasion to which the epinician genre is bound.

It was Aristophanes of Byzantium who divided the text of Pindar into 17 books; Aristarchus (2nd century BC) subsequently worked on the text, and Didymus (1st century BC) produced extensive commentaries. By the 3rd century AD only the epinicia were still circulating widely, perhaps, as Eustathios later claimed, because they had more of human interest and less of mythology than the other genres, and were also less obscure (Drachmann, 1926, Praefatio, 34). They were thus more suitable to be used as school texts. Later, in Byzantium, Pindar was studied more for his language than for his qualities as a poet. Eustathios (d. 1194) heralds a revival of scholarly interest, to be followed by editions made by Thomas Magister, Moschopulos (both 13th–14th centuries), and Triclinius (14th century).

ALBERT SCHACHTER

See also Poetry (Lyric)

Biography
Born *c.*518 BC at Cynoscephalae in Boeotia, Pindar wrote lyric poetry in several genres, divided later into 17 books. Of these, four books of epinician (victory) odes survive. These were written on commission to celebrate victories at the great games. By mixing direct praise with references to heroic legend, they glorify the aristocratic life, of which victory at the games was the pinnacle. Pindar died *c.*438 BC.

Writings
Pindar, translated by William H. Race, 2 vols, Cambridge, Massachusetts: Harvard University Press, 1997 (Loeb edition)

Further Reading
Bowra, C.M., *Pindar*, Oxford: Clarendon Press, 1964
Drachmann, Anders Björn (editor), *Scholia Vetera in Pindari Carmina*, 3 vols, Leipzig: Teubner, 1903–27, reprinted Stuttgart: Teubner, 1997
Highet, Gilbert, *The Classical Tradition: Greek and Roman Influences on Western Literature*, Oxford: Clarendon Press, and New York: Oxford University Press, 1949; reprinted 1985
Irigoin, Jean, *Histoire du texte de Pindare*, Paris: Klincksieck, 1952
Race, William H., *Pindar*, Boston: Twayne, 1986
Weiden, M. J. H. van der (editor), *The Dithyrambs of Pindar: Introduction, Text, and Commentary*, Amsterdam: Gieben, 1991

Pindus

Mountain range in northern Greece

The Pindus mountain range stretches like a backbone through northern Greece in a position roughly analogous to the Pennine chain in England, with the difference that the Pindus is far higher and more impenetrable. Its highest peak, Smolikas, is over 2600 m above sea level, and the central Zygos or Katara pass is over 1700 m. There is now one other road over the Pindus through Konitsa, and a tunnel is being built to get over the difficulty that the Zygos pass is often closed by snow. In ancient times great generals such as Alexander the Great and Caesar won praise for their daring and leadership in crossing the Pindus, and up until modern times travellers crossing the mountains found it a hazardous experience.

The Pindus is not one range, but a series of limestone and greenstone ranges with high plateaux in between. These plateaux provide excellent summer pasturage, but are obviously difficult of access. Hence transhumance has been practised in the Pindus from ancient times until the present day with shepherds driving their flocks into the mountains each spring, returning them to the plains of Epirus and Thessaly in the winter. Such transhumance has been particularly associated with the Vlachs. There is no certain evidence linking the Vlachs with the Pindus until the 14th century, although it is known that there were Vlachs in Thessaly and Vlachs practising transhumance before this date. The Pindus is the place where the largest concentration of Vlachs in the Balkans can be found, but there are also Greek villages in the area.

In Classical times there are references to tribes such as the Tymphaei living in the Pindus, but little is known about them. Strabo, perhaps going back to Hecateus, is well informed about the rivers which rise in the mountains (the Haliacmon, Peneus, Aous, Aspropotamus, and Arachthus) but is vague about the people of this area. In the Roman era there was no road across the Pindus, the roads in Epirus and Thessaly going from north to south rather than east to west. Strabo mentions towns at Tricca (modern Trikkala), Aeginium, Aethicia, and Chalcis (possibly modern Chaliki), all on the Thessalian side of the Zygos pass. The western side would appear to have suffered from the brutal Roman punishment of the Molossian defection in 168 BC.

The harsh climate of the Pindus and the absence of east–west routes are likely to have protected the mountains from barbarian invasions. The emperor Justinian (527–65) may have included some fortifications in the Pindus as part of his grand plan to defend the Balkans, and this might explain the presence of Latin speakers in the area. The ethnology of northern Greece is a difficult subject, since in spite of the remarkable survival of Greek there was undoubtedly a Slav invasion to the west of the Pindus in the 7th century, a Vlach presence in Thessaly in the 11th century, and in the 14th century incursions of both Albanians and Vlachs into the central Pindus area.

Under the Ottomans the economy of the Pindus mountains would appear to have taken on a more settled pattern. Villages like Samarina and Perivoli appear to have been founded as summer settlements; in return for tax privileges the inhabitants of such villages, themselves used to making long journeys, became the guardians and guides of other travellers making these journeys. The summer pastures provided a rich source of revenue, and merchants from Pindus villages travelled all over the Balkans, becoming very wealthy in the process. With the collapse of Ottoman authority, inhabitants of the Pindus including *armatoloi* (militia) and klephts continued to profit from their key position in the mountain passes, alternatively keeping the law and breaking it. In general the Pindus suffered at the end of the 19th century through brigandage, guerrilla war, and the creation of new boundaries which played havoc with the economy of the region. Brigandage was not unknown between the wars. In World War II control of the Zygos pass was a key factor in the Italian invasion (which failed to reach it), in the subsequent German occupation, and in the Civil War which followed. In all this warfare Pindus villages suffered badly, as the flocks which had been their livelihood were sacrificed for food, and the move from winter to summer pastures became impossible.

In the last half century the Pindus has revived. New roads have made travel much easier. Metsovo, in the heart of the Pindus, has become a minor tourist resort with skiing in winter, a pleasant climate in summer, and picturesque ethnic costumes for the visitor. Smaller villages have become more accessible, although it still takes a rugged bus ride to reach famous Pindus villages such as Samarina and Sirrakou, and electricity did not reach Chaliki until the 1980s. The biannual migration on foot from summer to winter pastures has now almost vanished, although the higher villages are still abandoned by car and lorry before the winter. The extensive pine forests provide, through timber merchants, an alternative form of employment to the sheep and goat breeding of the past, although wool products are plentiful in the tourist shops and mutton and cheese are staple items in Pindus meals.

T.J. WINNIFRITH

See also Armatoloi, Brigandage, Vlachs

Summary

A mountain range stretching through northern Greece like a backbone, the Pindus represents a barrier between east and west. The rugged terrain and harsh climate protected the mountains, though Albanians and Vlachs penetrated the central Pindus in the 14th century. During the Ottoman period merchants from the Pindus villages prospered but in the late 19th and early 20th centuries the economy was disrupted by brigandage.

Further Reading

Hammond, N.G.L., *Migrations and Invasions in Greece and Adjacent Areas*, Park Ridge, New Jersey: Noyes Press, 1976
Koltsidas, A.M., *Oi Koutsovlachoi* [The Koutslovaks], Thessalonica, 1976
Salmon, Tim, *The Unwritten Places*, Athens: Lycabettus, 1995
Weigand, Gustav, *Die Aromunen*, Leipzig: Barth, 1845

Piracy

Ancient sources show that piracy has always coexisted with sea voyages and maritime trade. In the age that Homer described in the *Odyssey*, piracy was a profession that men entered as a recognized way of making a living. It was so widespread, and the consequences to its victims so disastrous, that settlements often moved away from coastal areas (where they were a target for raids) to locations further inland and were surrounded by protective walls (Thucydides, 1. 7).

War and piracy have always had much in common. The acquisition of booty was a vital element in ancient Greek warfare and in ancient sources it is frequently very difficult to distinguish between warfare and piracy. At the end of the Archaic period, however, with the development of organized states with mercenary armies, a distinction emerges. In the 5th century BC opportunities for plunder provided the impetus for several military offensives. During the Peloponnesian War each side plundered the other's territory by both land and sea. Several generals even used the methods of pirates to help finance their wars. These practices continued in the Hellenistic period. For example, Philip II of Macedon used the proceeds of piracy to finance the building of his navy. Another incentive to piracy lay in the custom of reprisals against an enemy.

As means of accumulating wealth, trade and piracy have much in common. Piracy posed a considerable threat to merchants: the pirates of Zancle were ideally placed to attack and seize ships passing through the straits of Messina between

Italy and Sicily. The Taurian tribes in the Crimea and the Thracians developed an organized system of wrecking ships for plunder (Diodorus, 20. 25; Xenophon, *Anabasis*, 7. 5. 12). This system became so widespread in Roman times that the Romans were obliged to impose penalties on wreckers. Illyrian pirates were another source of trouble. According to Polybius (2. 5), the Illyrians had always been in the habit of pillaging along the extensive Roman seaboard; as the principal cities were located in the interior, help against such raids was distant and slow to arrive, allowing the Illyrians to overrun and plunder the surrounding territory unmolested.

Piracy and the slave trade were also closely connected. The largest centres for both activities were Crete and Cilicia, and pirates would often sell their captives into slavery. This was not always the case. Strabo, writing about the northeastern Black Sea coast, says of the local population that they lived by robbery at sea. Their boats were slender, narrow, and light, holding only about 25 people, rarely as many as 30. The Greeks called them *kamarai* (11. 2. 12). Their cruellest practice was to wander on foot night and day looking for people to kidnap but "they readily offer to release their captives for ransom, informing their relatives after they have put out to sea" (Strabo, 11. 2. 12). In this part of the Pontus pirates would attack Greek cities.

The control of piracy is usually considered to have been one of the prime functions of the Roman garrisons established along the eastern coast of the Black Sea under the principate. In the middle of the 3rd century AD large bands of marauders from the Pontus would make their way into the Aegean, plundering both shores, penetrating as far south as the coast of Lycia and Pamphylia, and forcing their way inland as far as Cappadocia (Zosimus, 1. 28; Ammian Marcellinus, 31. 5. 15).

The authorities of Greece and of countries on the Black Sea tried to fight piracy to make the sea safe for voyagers and merchants. The king of the Bosporan kingdom, Eumelus (310/09–304/03 BC) "in order to protect those sailing through Pontus Euxinus ... waged war against the Heniochi, Tauri, and Achaei who were engaging in piracy and cleansed the sea of such pirates, for which he was praised not only in his own kingdom, but also throughout the universe, for traders everywhere spread the word about his determination" (Diodorus, 20. 25).

Piracy in the Black Sea was a matter of concern to the rulers of non-Pontic countries as well. Even Pericles was aware of these dangers, and it is possible that one of the reasons for his Pontic expedition was to protect Athenian interests and trade in the Black Sea from local pirates (Plutarch, *Pericles*, 50; Diodorus, 20. 25). An inscription (228–225 BC) from a temple wall in Samothrace gives us some details of Egyptian methods there: the *strategos* (commander) of the Hellespont and Thrace is thanked for the precautions taken to safeguard the island against marauders who regularly threatened to seize the temple treasures: a detachment of horse, foot, and catapult men had been dispatched to the island (*Sylloge Inscriptionum Graecarum*, 3. 502).

In the Archaic and Classical periods the aim of pirates had been to satisfy their own needs through plunder. Rulers had resisted this. In the Hellenistic period there was a gradual change in the nature of piracy: it became more concerned with supplying the demand for slaves throughout the Greek world.

Rulers began to come to an accommodation with pirates and the slave trade became one of the sources of revenue for their states. From the 3rd/2nd centuries BC local rulers were no longer concerned about piracy. On the contrary: in the Pontus, for example, they colluded with them. As Strabo reports: "[Achaei, Zygi, and Heniochi] sailing sometimes against merchant vessels and sometimes against a country or even a city ... hold the mastery of the sea. And they are sometimes assisted even by those who hold the Bosporus, the latter supplying them with mooring places, with a marketplace, and with means of disposing of their booty" (11. 2. 12). At this time Tanais became a large and famous marketplace in the Bosporus, where slaves, hides, and other goods of the sort possessed by nomads were brought for exchange for clothing, wine, and other trappings of civilized life (Strabo, 11. 2. 3).

Piracy in the Byzantine and Ottoman periods continued to be a source of wealth and slaves. A distinctive feature of the Ottoman system was the formation of the Mamluks, Christian slaves taken as children and trained to form an elite military caste, who long ruled in Egypt and exerted considerable influence in Constantinople.

GOCHA R. TSETSKHLADZE

See also Slavery

Further Reading

Casson, Lionel, *The Ancient Mariners: Seafarers and Sea Fighters of the Mediterranean in Ancient Times*, 2nd edition, Princeton, New Jersey: Princeton University Press, 1991

de Sonza, P., "Greek Piracy" in *The Greek World*, edited by Anton Powell, London and New York: Routledge, 1995

Garlan, Yvon, "War, Piracy and Slavery in the Greek World" in *Classical Slavery*, edited by M.I. Finley, London: Cass, 1987

Garlan, Yvon, *Slavery in Ancient Greece*, revised edition, Ithaca, New York: Cornell University Press, 1988

Ormerod, Henry A., *Piracy in the Ancient World: An Essay in Mediterranean History*, Liverpool: University of Liverpool Press, 1924; reprinted Baltimore: Johns Hopkins University Press, 1997

Pritchett, W. Kendrick, *The Greek State at War*, 5 vols, Berkeley: University of California Press, 1971–91

Piraeus

The Piraeus (in Greek: Peiraieus) is a rocky limestone peninsula situated at the northeastern end of the Saronic Gulf about 10 km southwest of the centre of Athens. Its chief features are the hill of Munychia (modern Kastella or Kastellon), which rises abruptly in the northeast, and Akte, a lower plateau that extends southwest towards the sea. According to Strabo (*Geography*, 1. 3. 18) Piraeus derives from *peran* meaning "opposite" because the peninsula was originally detached from the mainland. It possesses three harbours: from east to west these are Zea (modern Limen Zeas or Pasolimi), Munychia (modern Tourkolimani or latterly Mikrolimani), and Cantharus or Goblet (modern Kentrikos Limen). Cantharus was also known as Megas Limen or Great Harbour in antiquity. There is little archaeological evidence for any settlement that predates the 5th century BC. The region entered history in 510 BC when Munychia was fortified by the tyrant Hippias, who intended to make it the seat of his government after being driven out of Athens ([Aristotle], *Constitution of Athens*, 19. 2).

The Piraeus became important in 483 BC when, on the initiative of the politician Themistocles, the Athenians voted to allocate the proceeds from a new strike at the silver mines of Laurium to finance the building of a fleet. At the same time work began on a fortification wall to safeguard the Piraeus against attack. Previously the sandy bay of Phalerum, which lies to the east and which is "the place where sea and city are nearest" (Pausanias, 1. 1. 2), had served as a roadstead for the Athenian navy, though it afforded little shelter. Thanks to Themistocles' initiative the Athenian fleet was able to play a decisive part in the defeat of the Persians in the straits of Salamis in 480 BC. Without the development of the Piraeus, Athens would never have acquired its maritime empire. Naval inventories reveal that in the 4th century BC Zea was the largest naval port with no fewer than 196 shipsheds, while the Great Harbour accommodated 94, and Munychia 82. The naval headquarters are likely to have been concentrated in the Great Harbour.

The fortification of the Piraeus was also destined to have profound consequences for its political development since it was the *thetes*, the lowest property-holding group, who served as rowers and who, when Athens became dependent on its sea power, came to acquire a leading position in foreign-policy decisions. From this evolved the intimate association between democracy and the Piraeus, whose population, in Aristotle's phrase, was "more democratic" than that of Athens (*Politics*, 5. 1303b10–12). As an administrative unit the deme of Piraeus was "a law unto itself" (Whitehead 1986, p.122). One of the clearest indications of its anomalous nature is the fact that its demarch was appointed by lot by the entire citizen body of Athens, whereas all other demarchs were appointed by their demes.

In 458/57 BC the city of Athens became linked to the Piraeus by the construction of two diverging long walls that incorporated the Piraeus and Phalerum. This wedge-shaped area could now be sealed off from the rest of Attica in time of war. Shortly afterwards a middle wall, known as the southern Long Wall, was built parallel to the western one, thereby eliminating the bay of Phalerum. Around the middle of the 5th century BC, and probably at Pericles' suggestion, the town planner Hippodamus of Miletus was invited to "cut up the Piraeus" (Aristotle, *Politics*, 2. 1267b23), which he did according to a grid pattern.

The Piraeus now began to develop as an urban entity that came to rival Athens in size. It also became the leading commercial port in the eastern Mediterranean. Since Athens was now very largely dependent on imported corn, the commercial quarter, which was known as the Emporion, was vital to its survival. The Emporion was situated along the eastern and northern shorelines of the Great Harbour. In 431 BC Pericles could boast with justification that "all the produce of every land comes to Athens" (Thucydides, 2. 38). A duty of 2 per cent was levied on all cargoes passing through the Emporion. We receive some indication of the volume of goods that it handled from the fact that in 399 BC, when trade can have barely recovered from the crippling effects of the

Peloponnesian War, the state collected 1,800 talents in harbour dues.

The Piraeus was home for a very large number of metics who came from all over the Greek world and beyond. Their presence, which is evident from a variety of foreign cults established around the port, must have lent it a very cosmopolitan flavour. Among the most prominent of these cults was that of the Thracian goddess Bendis, situated on Munychia (Plato, *Republic*, 1. 327a). Others include the Egyptian gods Isis and Sarapis, and the Phoenician Baal. It was here, too, that the cult of the healing god Asclepius was first introduced into Attica around 420 BC. According to Pausanias the most notable sight in the Piraeus was the Diisoterion or shrine of Zeus Soter and Athena Soteira (1. 1. 3).

Like any thriving port, the Piraeus possessed its sleazy underworld. Aristophanes' description of the spectacle of a man defecating in a brothel, as observed by Trygaeus as he flies over the Piraeus, was evidently intended to convey the distinctive flavour of the region (*Peace*, 164f.). Though many prosperous Athenians and metics lived in the Piraeus, given the size of its population, it is plausible to suppose that it also contained a large number of multiple dwellings or *synoikiai*, the ancient Greek equivalent of the modern tenement.

The Piraeus was critical to Athenian strategy during the Peloponnesian War when, on Pericles' advice, the decision was taken to abandon the countryside of Attica, turn Athens into an island, and coop up the entire population within the fortified area of Athens, the Long Walls, and the Piraeus. This led to a very severe outbreak of the plague, which reduced Athens' population by perhaps as much as one-third. The peace terms to which Athens agreed at the end of the war required the destruction of the Long Walls and the Piraeus circuit (404 BC). The Piraeus subsequently played a leading part in resistance to the Spartan-backed Thirty Tyrants when exiles under the command of Thrasybulus seized Munychia and drove out the Thirty.

The circuit walls and shipsheds were rebuilt by the Athenian general Conon in 393 BC. Before long the Piraeus resumed its importance as a naval and commercial port of first-rank significance. In the middle of the 5th century BC it was able to accommodate more than 350 triremes. In 330 BC Philon's so-called Arsenal was built in Zea, described by Pliny (*Historia Naturalis*, 7. 37. 135) as one of the most admired buildings of antiquity. This was not an arsenal as such but a warehouse for the storage of the sails, oars, and tackle that were removed from triremes when they were at berth. No traces of the building remain and it can be reconstructed only from the precise specifications that are preserved in an inscription authorizing the work to be undertaken. Ironically, within a decade of its completion, Athens had suffered a defeat at the hands of the Macedonians that eclipsed its naval power for ever.

Under Macedonian domination (322–229 BC) the garrison on Munychia Hill became one of the four "fetters of Greece". The Piraeus now began to decline steadily in size and importance. In the 2nd century BC it served as a Roman base for naval operations against the Macedonians. Lacking the glamour that attached to the name of Athens, the Piraeus never attracted royal patronage in the Hellenistic era. The only evidence of building activity is the impressive and well-preserved theatre overlooking Zea Port, which was constructed around the middle of the 2nd century BC. In around 120 BC several major festivals were revived and celebrated on a grandiose scale, notably the Diisoteria and Munychia, whose festivities incorporated nautical manoeuvres performed by ephebes.

In 86 BC the Piraeus was ruthlessly destroyed by the Roman general Sulla who spared "neither Philon's Arsenal nor the docks nor any of its other famous architectural works" (Appian, *Mithridatic Wars*, 41). One of the few buildings to escape destruction was the Diisoterion, though all traces of the shrine have since disappeared. A number of important bronze statues, including those of *Apollo*, *Artemis*, and *Athena*, which were deliberately buried at this time, came to light in 1959. Though it continued to function as a port, notably for the flourishing trade in neo-Attic sculpture that the Roman market demanded, the Piraeus never recovered its importance in antiquity. When Pausanias visited it in the 2nd century AD, very few buildings of note were standing. In 1040 Harald Hardraade, who later became the king of Norway, captured the port on behalf of the Byzantine emperor. In the Middle Ages it was merely a fishing village.

When Athens became the capital of Greece at the end of the Greek War of Independence, the ancient name of Piraeus had been forgotten. The port was then known as Porto Leone, after the figure of a lion that had been removed by the Venetians in 1687. It was now renamed, and from 1835 onwards it came to be furnished with quays and other modern harbour facilities. It also acquired many impressive Neoclassical buildings, though sadly many have either been destroyed or are in disrepair. In 1923, following the destruction of Smyrna, more than 100,000 Greek refugees fled to the Piraeus from Turkey. In World War II the port was destroyed by German bombs. It was subsequently rebuilt with US aid.

Today the Piraeus is the largest port in the eastern Mediterranean. More than half the country's imports and exports pass through it. It is also Greece's third largest city with a population of close to 200,000. The Kentrikos Limen functions as both a commercial and a passenger port, whereas Mikrolimani and Pasolimani handle only yachts. Many major industries, notably engineering, cigarettes, paper, textiles, and chemicals, are situated on the outskirts of the city. The Piraeus is also the headquarters for the Greek navy and an important fishing centre. Thanks to railway and road connections, it is once again closely linked to Athens.

The only traces of the ancient city that are visible today include portions of the 4th-century BC circuit wall, the theatre at Zea, some shipsheds, and the restored tomb of Themistocles on the promontory of Alkimos. Virtually all that remains of the Hippodamian layout is confined to a series of boundary markers, though the modern street plan follows the course of its ancient predecessor.

ROBERT GARLAND

See also Harbours, Navy, Ships and Shipping

Summary

The port of Athens, Piraeus possesses three harbours. It was fortified in 483 BC when Athens began to build a fleet. In 458/57 BC it was linked to Athens by the Long Walls. In the mid-5th century BC the city was planned by Hippodamus of Miletus. The harbour could accommodate 350 triremes. Piraeus declined in the Macedonian period and was destroyed by the Romans in 86 BC. Its importance returned in the 19th century.

Further Reading

Garland, Robert, *The Piraeus: From the Fifth to the First Century* BC, London: Duckworth, and Ithaca, New York: Cornell University Press, 1987

Lorenzen, Eivind, *The Arsenal at Piraeus: Designed by Philo and Reconstructed after His Description*, Copenhagen: Gads, 1964

Panagos, Chrestos, *Le Pirée*, Athens, 1968

Travlos, John (editor), *Bildlexikon zur Topographie des antiken Attika*, Tübingen: Wasmuth, 1988

Whitehead, David, *The Demes of Attica 508/7–ca. 250 BC: A Political and Social Study*, Princeton, New Jersey: Princeton University Press, 1986

Pisistratus

Tyrant of Athens in the 6th century BC

Solon's reforms had (perhaps inevitably) left none of the contending parties completely satisfied. He himself had proudly proclaimed that he was taking up his position "amidships" in the ship of state, i.e. that he would not go to either extreme, satisfying neither the demands being made by those without property that the ancestral land of Attica be redivided so that all would literally have a portion of it, nor the insistence of the aristocrats that the running of the city's affairs should be left entirely in their hands: "to each side what it deserved". The years 590/89 and 586/85 BC were designated in the official records as (literally) "anarchic", because no chief magistrate had been elected, due to internal dissension. In 582/81 BC an otherwise unknown individual named Damasias attempted to hold on to the archonship for an illegal period beyond his official tenure, and there are indications of an experiment with some kind of block election of archons by social and economic grouping. With continuing unrest of this kind, it was only a matter of time before some opportunist succumbed to the temptation that Solon himself said that he had been strong enough to resist, of initiating a coup d'état and taking all power effectively into his own hands. (This had already happened in many other Greek states in the preceding two generations, and for a man in such a role the Greeks themselves had borrowed, possibly from the Lydians, the term "tyrant".)

The later tradition remembered, and even thought it had evidence, that Solon himself both foresaw and tried to warn the Athenians of an impending coup by his kinsman (and, the gossipers said, former lover), Pisistratus. The men were related on the side of their mothers, both tracing their descent from an early king, Codrus, and thus from a junior branch of the royal house of Pylos. What can safely be asserted is that the remains of Solon's poems have a scattering of dark hints that, if civil unrest should continue, Solon himself envisaged that an unscrupulous would-be autocrat would emerge to try to respond to the people's demands; but in what survives of his work Solon nowhere mentions Pisistratus by name; nor does it seem likely that he would have overlapped with Pisistratus' early, tentative gropings for power by more than a year or two.

Our earliest and fullest account of Pisistratus' coup comes from Herodotus (the chronology for the early Pisistratean period is uncertain, but we are in the late 560s BC). What gave Pisistratus his chance was the fact that the city was beset by factional strife, the "Men of the Shore" being led by Megacles, son of Alcmaeon (Megacles had married into the "tyrant" family of Sicyon), and the "Men of the Plain" by a certain Lycurgus. Pisistratus organized his own followers under the title "Men from beyond [or "across"] the Hills". Attempts have been made to discover here a classification beyond the merely geographical, perhaps according to some division along ideological or economic lines, but no suggestion has been entirely convincing. It seems most probable that the names were chosen to give a rough indication of where the leaders lived and where they derived their support. Herodotus' flair for the dramatic may be leading him astray, but what he reports is that Pisistratus staged an attack on himself by his enemies, even going so far as to wound himself and claim that his enemies had done it. He reminded the Athenians of his services to them in earlier hostilities against Megara, and asked for a bodyguard. Thus reinforced, he established himself in power on the Acropolis, where the Athenian kings had resided in the Mycenaean period. His opponents put aside their squabbling and joined forces to drive him out, but Pisistratus was able to outmanoeuvre them by entering into a marriage alliance with Megacles. The alliance, like the marriage that was its surety, proved shortlived, and Pisistratus once again went into exile, this time for a ten-year period (on the likeliest chronology, c.557–547 BC). He took the opportunity to make sure that he had the resources, financial and in manpower, to gain a secure grip on power. He turned to northern Greece, founding a colony on the Thermaic gulf and exploiting sources of silver near Mount Pangaeus; with this wealth (perhaps converted into a personal coinage) he hired mercenaries and called for additional support from Thebes, Argos, and the island of Naxos. Pisistratus and his troops landed near Marathon, near his family holdings and original power base in Attica at Brauron, and marched on Athens, to good omens and, if not exactly token opposition, at least a resistance that was only half-hearted; his sons were able to reassure the Athenians of their father's good intentions. To all but the disgruntled leaders of the aristocratic faction and their immediate coteries it must have appeared that a period of stability, no matter whose hand was at the tiller, was far preferable to the almost half-century of turmoil and the politics marked by family rivalries that had preceded it.

Greek writers of later periods invariably looked back on a time of autocracy as distasteful; the personal performances as well as the character of these early tyrants tended to be blackened, their shortcomings if not invented then considerably exaggerated and turned into bizarre perversions and even crimes. It is all the more surprising, therefore, that in our major sources Pisistratus comes off with a relatively clean record. Herodotus comments that Pisistratus ruled "without disturbing the previously existing offices or altering any of the laws; he administered the state according to the established usages and his arrangements were wise and salutary". Of course there was no office of "tyrant", nor do we have any indication that he assumed an actual title, such as "Protector of the Constitution", but Thucydides reports that he "took care to

see that one of his own men was in the archonship". The writer of the *Constitution of Athens* remarks: "his rule was more like a constitutional government than a tyranny".

Pisistratus may have started as just another faction leader, but he seems to have grown in his rule. He took particular care to introduce measures that would perhaps not unify Attica in a literal sense (a role that political myth assigned to Theseus), but would at least make residents of outlying districts of the city itself feel loyalty to Athens as an integrated political entity. One especially strong weapon he had was that the religious cults tended to be situated locally and were invariably organized by the aristocratic families of the particular area. Archaeological and other evidence indicates that Pisistratus sponsored new or revitalized cults that broke down these local and class barriers and fostered a sense of unity. Thus at neighbouring Eleusis, where people of every class (including slaves) could be inititiated into the mysteries of Demeter, which promised some kind of personal survival after death, a new *telesterion* or initiation house was built, and a shrine to Demeter was established in the city itself as a kind of district office of the cult. The career of the poet-dramatist Thespis (himself a somewhat legendary figure) was launched at Athens in the 530s BC, and it is possible that from this date there were regular performances there of some kind of proto-tragedy in honour of Dionysus. Probably another shrine to Dionysus, the Lenaion, was built in the Agora during this period. There were also various new cults of the god Apollo with separate cult titles (Hypoakraios on the west slope of the Acropolis, Patroos on the west side of the Agora), and one in particular, Apollo Pythios, appears to have been designed to compete with Delphi, with which Pisistratus was on rather cool terms. Pisistratus undertook a ritual purification of Apollo's sacred island of Delos (by removing graves, making sacrifices etc.) immediately upon his final, firm assumption of power. This should probably be seen as an attempt to shift people's attention away from Delphi, and is an anticipation of the centrality of Delos in Athenian imperial propaganda a century later.

There is no concord among archaeologists as to specifics, but most agree that an ambitious building programme was undertaken on the Acropolis. There was a large temple to the city's patron goddess, Athena (variously styled the "Hekatompedon" or Athena's "Old Temple"), and architectural sculpture survives – including the lively and amusing sea monster dubbed "Bluebird" in the Acropolis museum – that suggests that there are other "shrines" on a more modest scale. There was also a temple to Athena Nike, the "Bringer of Victory", at the west end of the Acropolis, on the site where a later temple greets today's visitors to the precinct. Nor were sacred structures the only ones in this building scheme (whether by Pisistratus or his sons – it is often difficult to be sure that the remains predate Pisistratus' death in 528 BC). A fountain house named Enneakrounos, "Nine Spouts", was built southeast of the Agora to bring fresh water down from the hills northeast of the city, guaranteeing an efficient and orderly water supply for the residents of Athens. The name of Pisistratus' son Hipparchus is associated with an improvement in the road system connecting the central city, specifically the Altar of the Twelve Gods in the Agora which Hipparchus is said to have dedicated, with the outlying districts. Hipparchus was also remembered as an artistic entrepreneur; he is said to have invited the poets Anacreon and Simonides to take up residence in Athens, and to have been responsible for collecting manuscripts of Homer's epics, perhaps as some kind of official text for competitions at the Panathenaic festival, which was probably not founded by Pisistratus, but may have been expanded under his patronage.

The Athenians were thus encouraged to be proud of their city and to visit it, if they lived in the countryside, as often as possible. Realistically, however, a rural Athenian spent most of his or her time on the family farm in the 6th century BC, even as later in the 5th century BC. Sculptors and artisans might be based in the city itself, and the upsurge in exports of fine black-figure Attic pottery suggests a thriving industry of production and export, but Pisistratus seems also to have taken to heart the plight of the Athenian farmer. He is reported to have made loans to the poor so that they could make a living by farming (but he also charged a land tax of 5 or 10 per cent), and he set up a system of circuit judges who travelled the Attic countryside and settled legal disputes. As already noted, Pisistratus appears to have been careful in his observance of the forms of Athenian civic life, and, if a story told by the *Constitution of Athens* can be believed, he once even came before the Areopagus court to answer a charge of homicide; we are told that the plaintiff, perhaps not surprisingly, failed to appear. His rule was later remembered as a golden age, the "age of Cronus" (in contradistinction to the rather harsher Olympian rule of Cronus' son and successor, Zeus). There is probably a good deal of truth to this, although the foreshortening of time and dimming of collective memory may have done something to enhance his reputation with later generations of Athenians.

The evidence of his dealings with the other aristocrats is somewhat ambiguous. The Alcmaeonidae, Megacles' family, chose to play the role of martyrs. When Pisistratus died (probably 528 BC), there was no rush to substitute a different form of government or damn his memory, as happened with other Greek tyrannies; his eldest sons, Hippias and Hipparchus, may have been worried about possible competitors to succeed Pisistratus, and Herodotus reports that they had arranged for the assassination of the elder Cimon, who had won multiple victories in the Olympic Games and so might have appeared as a plausible contender for supreme power. What appears to have been the sons' preferred tactic of neutralizing opposition, however, was diplomacy and cooption. There is inscriptional evidence that in the years immediately after Pisistratus' death the chief archonship was held by his son Hippias (526 BC), Cleisthenes the Alcmaeonid, the later lawgiver (525 BC), Miltiades, future victor at Marathon (524 BC), and the younger Pisistratus, the tyrant's grandson (523 BC).

The family's control of Athenian government finally came to an end in 510 BC after a period of turmoil. An assassination attempt in 514 BC was only partly successful: the tyrant Hippias' younger brother Hipparchus was killed though Hippias himself escaped. The sources uniformly report that the Pisistratids' rule (to give the family the name by which ancient writers refer to them) became much harsher. The aristocrats saw an opportunity to dislodge the family that had held the dominant position at Athens for 36 years, but this was managed only after several failed attempts, and with the assistance of some formidable propaganda from the Delphic oracle as well as an armed invading force led by a Spartan king.

Pisistratus' reign was crucial to the development of Athenian democracy. Under Pisistratus Athens' leading and ever-contentious families were either exiled or reduced to political impotence. If he had tampered with the Solonian institutions, much (though perhaps not all) would have been lost; Cleisthenes in 508 BC would have had to start, so to speak, from scratch. As it was, the Athenians were given a tantalizing taste of the fruits of political stability and peace (no foreign engagements of any consequence are recorded for the period of Pisistratus' rule, and it is a continuing puzzle whether he even maintained a standing army and navy). Athenian manufacture and trade flourished, and the fruits of this increased prosperity went to enhance life in both city and countryside. Local workers and craftsmen were given employment, and designers and artists were imported from the more artistically advanced regions of the Near East, such as Ionia. Athenians came to see that the advancement of Athens' interests was best viewed as a community enterprise and that, as their city prospered, so did their own individual circumstances. A century later, under Pericles, Athenians of all stripes and classes were to discover how advantageous a full public treasury could be.

ANTHONY J. PODLECKI

See also Tyranny

Biography

Born in the early 6th century BC, Pisistratus first seized power in Athens in the 560s BC. After a ten-year exile (*c.*557–547) in Macedonia, he returned to Athens in 546 and established a tyranny. The city flourished and the period of his rule was remembered as a golden age. He died *c.*528 BC and was succeeded by his sons Hippias and Hipparchus.

Further Reading

Andrewes, A., "The Tyranny of Pisistratus" in *The Expansion of the Greek World, Eighth to Sixth Centuries BC*, edited by John Boardman and N.G.L. Hammond, Cambridge: Cambridge University Press, 1982 (*The Cambridge Ancient History*, vol. 3, part 3, 2nd edition)

Boardman, John, "Herakles, Peisistratos and Sons", *Revue Archéologique* (1972): pp. 57–72

Davies, J.K., *Athenian Propertied Families, 600–300 BC*, Oxford: Clarendon Press, 1971, pp. 444–55

French, A., "The Party of Peisistratus", *Greece and Rome*, new series 6 (1959): pp. 46–57

Frost, Frank J., "The Athenian Military before Cleisthenes", *Historia*, 33/3 (1984): pp. 283–94

Frost, Frank J., "Peisistratos, the Cults and the Unification of Attica", *Ancient World*, 21/1–2 (1990): pp. 3–9

Holladay, James, "The Followers of Peisistratus", *Greece and Rome*, new series 24 (1977): pp. 40–56

Hurwit, Jeffrey M., *The Art and Culture of Early Greece, 1100–480 BC*, Ithaca, New York: Cornell University Press, 1985, pp. 234–53

Manville, Philip Brook, *The Origins of Citizenship in Ancient Athens*, Princeton, New Jersey: Princeton University Press, 1990, pp. 162–209

Parker, Robert, "The Sixth Century: New Splendours" in his *Athenian Religion: A History*, Oxford: Clarendon Press, and New York: Oxford University Press, 1996

Podlecki, Anthony J., "Solon or Peisistratus - A Case of Mistaken Identity?", *Ancient World*, 16/1–2 (1987): pp. 3–10

Rhodes, Peter J., "Pisistratid Chronology Again", *Phoenix*, 30 (1976): pp. 219–33

Ritook, Z., "The Pisistratus Tradition and the Canonization of Homer", *Acta Antiqua Hungarica*, 34 (1993): pp. 39–53

Shapiro, H.A., *Art and Cult under the Tyrants in Athens*, Mainz: Zabern, 1989; supplement 1995

Plants

Greece is a very diverse country, with high mountains and a varied climate. Like other Mediterranean countries, it escaped the worst ravages of the ice ages. Its flora is the richest in Europe after Spain's. Most of the plants do their growing in the winter or spring, and are dormant through the harsh dry summers.

Typical Mediterranean vegetation is supposed to be dominated by evergreen trees such as prickly oak, phillyrea, and arbutus. These are very adaptable: they exist in either a tree or a shrub form according to the degree of browsing, burning, and woodcutting, and can change from one to the other (see the article on Landscape). However, in less arid places, deciduous oaks and other deciduous trees are prevalent and increasing. There are also conifers, such as Aleppo pine, mountain fir, and Cretan cypress. The aromatic, sticky, and spiny plants of dry hillsides – cistus, thyme, Jerusalem sage – are undershrubs, which cannot turn into trees. There are innumerable grasses, annual and perennial legumes, and orchids. Colourful weeds of cultivation, such as wild gladiolus, now rarely seen in the rest of Europe, frequent old-fashioned olive groves.

Nearly all crop plants in Greece, except the olive, are introduced rather than indigenous. Cereals, vines, legumes, and some vegetables were familiar to the ancient Greeks, but many other crop plants have been introduced from other continents. Greek agriculture and cuisine were transformed by the introduction from the Americas of plants such as tomato, potato, maize, tobacco, and most beans. Although most wild plants were known to the ancients, some weeds have been brought in along with exotic crops. The yellow *Oxalis pes-caprae*, now one of the commonest plants, arrived from South Africa a little over a century ago. Irrigated cultivation has produced a universal set of tropical, weedkiller-resistant weeds.

Many Greek plants are generically Mediterranean: Aleppo pine is found almost everywhere from Spain eastwards, except in Crete. Most evergreen trees and shrubs and grey-green undershrubs also prevail in other Mediterranean countries, though the species may differ. However, Greek vegetation has its own peculiar character. The common evergreen oak is the prickly oak, *Quercus coccifera*, not holm oak or cork oak as in other countries. One of the common deciduous oaks is *Quercus macrolepis*, whose huge acorn-cups were exported for tanning leather.

Many species are restricted to particular altitudes. Mediterranean plant communities tend to form zones at various heights above sea level, with deciduous oakwoods predominating in the lower mountains, fir- and pinewoods above these, and special alpine plants above the tree line. This zonation, however, is relatively weak in Greece, and in Crete there are really only two zones: the alpine desert and the rest.

Greece has outliers of Central European vegetation, extending southwards in the mountains. Beechwoods, for example, extend in the Pindus mountains well within modern Greece; they are accompanied by wild strawberry and even primrose.

Endemic plants are those found nowhere else but Greece. Some are common: the Greek fir tree, abundant in the mountains to within sight of Athens, is peculiar to Greece. Many others are confined to a particular mountain or group of mountains: Macedonia is particularly rich in them.

Crete is a miniature continent with high mountains, deserts, and jungles, and a profusion of cliffs and gorges. Some Greek plants, such as Aleppo pine, do not extend to Crete, and the island has many species of Asian rather than European affinities, with a few African. In misty ravines in the western mountains are royal fern and bog pimpernel, more characteristic of cool damp Ireland; not far away are spiny shrubs outlying from the Sahara. Crete also has the largest concentration of endemic plants in Europe. Cliffs, gorges, and the alpine desert are full of strange specialized plants. Others, often of arresting beauty, are common and conspicuous.

Examples of Cretan plants are cypress, an Asian tree native nowhere else in Europe; Cretan pine, which is also Asian and different from Greek pines; *Origanum dictamnus*, a Cretan endemic famous since antiquity as a medicinal herb, still common in the gorges; *Ebenus cretica*, one of the most beautiful plants in Europe, common in Crete and found nowhere else; the glorious blue *Petromarula pinnata*, an endemic on cliffs and Venetian walls; and *Hyoscyamus aureus*, golden henbane, common on the city walls of Herakleion (where it has been for at least 400 years), its only European locality.

Greek plants are at their best between March and May, when the annuals, the wonderful bulbs, and the many species of orchids are in bloom. Later in the year visitors should explore the high mountains.

OLIVER RACKHAM

See also Botany, Landscape

Further Reading

Bauman, Hellmut, *The Greek Plant World in Myth, Art, and Literature*, translated by William T. Stearn and Eldwyth Ruth Stearn, Portland, Oregon: Timber Press, 1993

Huxley, Anthony J. and William Taylor, *Flowers of Greece and the Aegean*, London: Chatto and Windus, 1977, reprinted London: Hogarth, 1989

Polunin, Oleg, *Flowers of Greece and the Balkans: A Field Guide*, Oxford and New York: Oxford University Press, 1980, reprinted 1987

Rackham, Oliver and Jennifer Moody, *The Making of the Cretan Landscape*, Manchester: Manchester University Press, 1996

Planudes, Maximos *c.1255–c.1305*

Scholar and translator

Typical of the best Byzantine polymaths, Planudes's range of scholarly activities paralleled the traditional disciplines of the Byzantine educational curriculum. He wrote not only treatises on grammar, rhetoric, and the correct usage of vocabulary but also commentaries on and texts of literary, rhetorical, mathematical, and astronomical works, as well as original rhetorical pieces exemplifying good prose style. As director of a school in Constantinople, he energetically provided texts and treatises for his students, who included scions of prominent families and some nascent scholars or public officials. Planudes's interests and energies, however, transcended the needs of a school curriculum.

Planudes extended the scientific knowledge of his time through his activity with texts. With the help of the patriarch of Alexandria and of the emperor Andronikos II Palaiologos (1282–1328), he obtained a text of Ptolemy's *Geography*, then reconstructed its missing maps himself. He copied out Aratus' *Phaenomena*, which was regularly used as an astronomical textbook, and also used Ptolemy to correct its factual information, neatly excising the obsolete sections of Aratus and substituting passages in the same style and metre. Although Planudes violated the integrity of the original, he maintained and enhanced its literary quality and scientific purpose.

Planudes extended traditional literary studies beyond the mere copying and annotation of Classical authors. He collated different manuscripts of the same text and attempted to make emendations, thus producing a modest critical edition in the modern sense of the word. He and his younger associate Demetrios Triklinios are regarded as "the latest Byzantines whose activities had any lasting effect on classical texts" (Reynolds and Wilson, p. 77). Planudes also searched out rare but interesting literary texts. He selected, adapted for school use, and copied in his own hand an anthology of epigrams, systematically arranging and subdividing them. This collection, which was frequently recopied, was the only one to preserve the so-called *Greek Anthology* until the larger *Palatine Anthology* was discovered in the 19th century (380 epigrams still survive only in Planudes's anthology). He confided in a letter that he was undertaking the task of producing a complete collection of Plutarch's writings "because, as you know, I am completely devoted to the man" (Letter 106). This massive task would not be completed by Planudes's associates until after his death, when the last section of the *Moralia* was finally located and copied. His circle reintroduced nine plays of Euripides that had been omitted from the traditional school curriculum and were preserved in a single manuscript, now lost (this contained part of the entire works of Euripides in alphabetical order; the plays we owe to this circle are *Helen, Electra, Heraclidae, Heracles, Suppliant Women, Iphigenia at Aulis, Iphigenia among the Taurians, Ion,* and *Cyclops*). Although the discovery of this manuscript has been credited to Dimitrios Triklinios in Thessalonica, new evidence suggests that Planudes may have been responsible for finding it.

Planudes advanced the development of arithmetic and geometry by editing texts and by adapting an earlier anonymous essay (1252) on Indian calculation. His adaptation improved the process of extracting square roots, contained the first use of zero as a place holder in Byzantine arithmetic, and demonstrated Persian scholarly influence through the use of eastern Arabic number forms. (His source used western Arabic forms.) He annotated Euclid's *Elements* and also collated an edition and produced a commentary for Diophantes's *Arithmetic*, a notoriously difficult work studied by advanced mathematicians among Planudes's contemporaries. His edition improved the text of Diophantes and his commentary provided explication of some vexed problems more clearly than Diophantes's original. The recent discovery that Byzantine scholars in the circle around Planudes accomplished a vast recension of astronomical and mathematical texts sometime after 1296 suggests that he participated in an effort so significant that manuscripts owned by Bessarion in the 15th century were influenced by it.

In his broad literary and scientific interests, Planudes exemplifies the late Byzantine polymath. In his commitment to translating Latin literary works into Greek, however, he was extremely unusual and perhaps even unique in his time.

Some of Planudes's translations figured in the religious and political controversies surrounding the union of the Eastern and Western Churches. His translation of Augustine's 15-book philosophical treatise *On the Trinity* drew criticism from both parties. In 1305 an anonymous Dominican in Constantinople labelled the work "not a translation but a falsification"; in the 15th century the anti-unionist patriarch Gennadios I Scholarios complained that Planudes's translation failed to clarify the nature of the procession of the Holy Spirit, while Cardinal Bessarion, a fervent supporter of ecclesiastical union, warmly commended him as a translator. Planudes also translated "one of the most read books of the Middle Ages" (Schmitt, p. 132), the anonymous theological treatise *On the Misdeeds of the Age*, erroneously attributed to both Cyprian and Augustine.

The translation of Latin theological writings into Greek involved the risk that he would raise suspicions of anti-Orthodox sympathies. Was it to counter such suspicions that Planudes became a monk? Curiously, the only other Byzantine of this period who may have translated Latin literary works into Greek was also a monk, Manuel Holobolos, an Aristotle scholar and teacher in the Patriarchal Academy under Michael VIII. The Greek translations of two rhetorical works by Boethius, *On Various Topoi* and *On the Hypothetical Syllogism*, are attributed in manuscripts both to Planudes and to his less famous senior colleague. Only stylistic analysis and comparison can determine which scholar produced these translations, probably the first from Latin literature in 13th-century Constantinople.

Whatever Planudes's reasons for becoming a monk, the volume and variety of his translations from Latin indicate that his activities as a translator extended throughout his scholarly career. Some of these translations served pedagogical purposes. He translated part of Priscian's *Grammatical Instruction* in his own essay *On the Syntax of Parts of Speech*, and he selected and translated aphorisms from the *Sayings of Cato*, a collection preserved in numerous manuscripts and cited in the 14th-century novel *Imberios and Margarone* and in Emmanuel Georgillas's 15th-century poem, *The Plague of Rhodes*. Planudes may also be the anonymous Byzantine translator of the pseudo-Aristotle's *On Plants*, a work that survived only in Latin.

Planudes's remaining translations from Latin were purely literary in their appeal – Boethius' *Consolation of Philosophy* with a *Life of Boethius* appended, Cicero's *Dream of Scipio* with Macrobius' *Commentary*, Ovid's *Heroides*, his *Metamorphoses*, and perhaps a selection from his *Amores* as well as four lines of Juvenal's *Satires*. Except for the metrical translations of Juvenal and of the *Sayings of Cato*, these are prose paraphrases, embellished with rhetorical figures and preserving a slightly foreign flavour in diction. They were extremely popular among early western humanists, who used them as aids to learning Greek; Petrarch, for instance, owned a copy of the Cicero / Macrobius translation with marginal references to the Latin text, and in the 15th century Ambrogio Traversari reported reading both Latin and Greek versions of Boethius' *Consolation*.

The works translated by Planudes represented staples of a good Latin library. Planudes may have encountered educated Latins conversant with these works and a library containing them in the Franciscan and Dominican friaries that probably operated in Constantinople during the Latin occupation. He acquired both his knowledge of Latin and the texts he translated in the east, for he had mostly completed his translations by 1296, when he made his only visit to the west.

Planudes's translations from Latin endorsed the value of this foreign tradition for cultured Greek readers. An interest in Latin literature as evidenced by translations had faded at Constantinople until its revival during the early Palaiologan period, which also valued Arabic and Persian science and literature. Translation then languished until the mid-14th century, when the controversy over ecclesiastical union prompted such scholars as Demetrios and Prochoros Kydones, Manuel Kalekas, and George Scholarios to translate Latin theological writings. In this period Planudes was credited with translations of works by Caesar, Cicero, pseudo-Donatus, Augustine, Thomas Aquinas, Petrus Hispanus, Hilarius, and Macrobius. These false attributions, still quoted in the scholarly literature, provide eloquent if flawed testimony to the enduring fame as a translator that the Byzantine polymath Planudes achieved.

ELIZABETH A. FISHER

See also Translation into Greek

Biography

Born *c.*1255 in Nicomedia and baptized with the name Manuel, Planudes worked as a scribe in the imperial palace from 1283. On becoming a monk, he took the name Maximos and, though abbot of the monastery at Mount Auxentios, he remained in Constantinople. His pupils included Manuel Moschopoulos and George Lekapenos. In 1296 he visited Venice on an imperial embassy. He translated many Latin authors and made important contributions to Greek scholarship. He died *c.*1305.

Further Reading

Decorps-Foulquier, Micheline, "Un Corpus astronomico-mathématique au temps des Paléologues: essai de reconstitution d'une recension", *Revue d'Histoire des Textes*, 17 (1987): pp. 15–53

Fisher, Elizabeth A., "Ovid's *Metamorphoses*, Planudes and Ausonians", in *Arktouros: Hellenic Studies Presented to Bernard M.W. Knox on the Occasion of his 65th Birthday*, edited by Glen W. Bowersock, Walter Burkert, and Michael C. J. Putnam, Berlin and New York: de Gruyter, 1979

Fisher, Elizabeth A., *Planudes' Greek Translation of Ovid's Metamorphoses*, New York and London: Garland, 1990

Fisher, Elizabeth A., "Innovation Through Translation: The Greek Version of Ovid's Amatory Poems", in *Originality in Byzantine Literature, Art and Music: A Collection of Essays*, edited by A.R. Littlewood, Oxford: Oxbow, and Oakville, Connecticut: David Brown, 1995

Hunger, Herbert, *Die hochsprachliche profane Literatur der Byzantiner*, 2 vols, Munich: Beck, 1978

Labowsky, Lotte, "Aristoteles *De plantis* and Bessarion: Bessarion Studies 2", *Medieval and Renaissance Studies*, 5 (1961): pp. 132–54

Nikitas, Dimitrios Z., "Boethius, *De differentiis topicis*: Eine Pachymeres-Weiterbearbeitung der Holobolos-Übersetzung", *Classica et Mediaevalia*, 38 (1987): pp. 267–86

Reynolds, L.D. and N.G. Wilson, *Scribes and Scholars: A Guide to the Transmission of Greek and Latin Literature*, 3rd edition, Oxford: Clarendon Press, and New York: Oxford University Press, 1991

Schmitt, Wolfgang O., "Lateinische Literatur in Byzanz: Die Übersetzungen des Maximos Planudes und die moderne Forschung", *Österreichische Byzantinische Gesellschaft Jahrbuch*, 17 (1968): pp. 127–47

Stadter, Philip A., "Planudes, Plutarch and Pace of Ferrara", *Italia Medioevale e Umanistica*, 16 (1973): pp. 137–62

Thorndike, Lynn, "Relation between Byzantine and Western Science and Pseudo-Science before 1350", *Janus*, 51 (1964): pp. 1–48

Wendel, Carl, Planudes entry in *Real-Encyclopädie der klassischen Altertumswissenschaft*, edited by August Pauly *et al.*, vol. 40, 1940, 2202–53

Wilson, N.G., *Scholars of Byzantium*, revised edition, London: Duckworth, and Cambridge, Massachusetts: Medieval Academy of America, 1996

Plastiras, Nikolaos 1883–1953

Politician

Nikolaos Plastiras played a leading role in the events of the revolution of 1922, and, serving on several occasions as premier during the post-World War II era, upheld the democratic principles of his country.

As a young man, Plastiras lived in Karditsa in central Greece. When he completed his schooling, he enlisted in the Greek national army (1903) and, as a commissioned officer, participated in the Macedonian struggle of 1905. Before the outbreak of the First Balkan War (4 October 1912), Plastiras was admitted to the cadet school (1910–12), graduating with the rank of second lieutenant. During the Balkan Wars Plastiras showed great courage and leadership in the battlefield and was highly respected by his fellow officers and his superiors.

At the outbreak of World War I, Plastiras had already been promoted to the rank of lieutenant. The political and ideological friction between King Constantine I and Eleftherios Venizelos led to a division in both the political and the military ranks. The Venizelists believed that Greece should enter the war on the side of the Allies, while the Royalists supported a more neutral stance, hoping to avoid armed opposition against Germany. In September 1916 Plastiras joined the supporters of Venizelos and assumed the command of one of the battalions of the 6th regiment of the Archipelagos division. While commanding his battalion, Plastiras participated in the military operations on the Macedonian front, and proved once again his leadership and valour. He was promoted to lieutenant colonel in 1919 and given the command of the 5/24 regiment which fought in the Ukrainian campaign against the Bolsheviks, showing the same qualities that he had exhibited during the Balkan Wars. After the end of this campaign, and with the rank of colonel, Plastiras was reassigned to Asia

Minor, where the campaign against the Ottoman empire was under way.

In Asia Minor Plastiras was recognized for his contributions in every phase of the military campaign, especially the period 1921–22, when the Greek forces, having overextended their supply lines, came under heavy fire from the troops of Mustafa Kemal and the Turkish nationalists. During that period Plastiras conducted an orderly retreat, supporting the general exodus of the Greeks from Asia Minor. Plastiras remained on the coast of Asia Minor and was a witness to the disaster of Hellenism in Ionia. Immediately after the humiliating defeat in Asia Minor, Plastiras, in collaboration with colonel S. Gonatas and captain D. Phokas, succeeded in forcing king Constantine I to flee by instigating a coup. As a member of the powerful triumvirate that ruled Greece, Plastiras played a leading role in the political developments and financial difficulties that Greece had to face following the influx of refugees from Asia Minor. He assumed responsibility for the verdict that was passed on the six high-ranking personnel who were accused of being responsible for the Asia Minor disaster, and worked diligently for the rapid reformation of the Greek national army. Plastiras also made every effort to tackle the socioeconomic problems created by the inflow of the refugees. After the elections of 22 November, when Gonatas assumed the presidency, Plastiras continued to play a key role in political decision-making. He supported the negotiations in Lausanne, and was responsible for the final ratification of the decisions of the Greek delegation which led to the signing of the agreement in July 1923.

Exhausted by the events of the past several years, Plastiras withdrew from the political scene. However, a few months later, in October 1923, as a result of the movement of general P. Gargalidis and general G. Leonardopoulos, Plastiras once again became fully involved in politics in the effort to stop the Royalists from returning to power. Although successful in preventing another dictatorial government from taking over, Plastiras realized the importance and necessity of a return to parliamentary democracy. He called for elections, which were promptly held in December 1923, and shortly thereafter, despite his popularity, he quietly withdrew from the political foreground.

A decade later, and anxious about the future of his country's national identity, Plastiras perceived as a major threat the anti-Venizelist government that was voted into office following the elections of 5 March 1933. He acted decisively against the new government by instigating a military coup. The failed coup was criticized by the public and by Venizelos himself, and Plastiras went into voluntary exile in Paris until 1935. That year, however, the Royalist cause had gathered sufficient momentum to secure the return of the king, despite the efforts of the Venizelists in support of parliamentary democracy. This effort reached its pinnacle with the institution of the Metaxas dictatorship in 1936. In exile Plastiras maintained a very distant and at times hostile stance to the Metaxas regime, and did not return to Greece until after the end of World War II. However, he continued to be politically active and was a strong supporter of the National Democratic Hellenic Union (EDES).

World War II devastated the socioeconomic foundations of Greece. The tragedy continued as liberated Greece fell under the shroud of a brutal civil war. Archbishop Damaskinos and the British government recalled Plastiras to Greece, inviting him to assume the premiership in place of George Papandreou. During his shortlived first period in political office (3 January–8 April 1945) Plastiras succeeded in bringing the National Liberation Front (EAM) to the negotiating table in Varkiza to reach a peace agreement. An adamant supporter of peaceful solutions, Plastiras always spoke out against the violence of the civil war and campaigned strongly for a cessation of hostilities.

The conclusion of the civil war brought hope of a new beginning in rebuilding the devastated nation. In this optimistic environment Plastiras returned to the political foreground by creating the National Progressive Centre Party (EPEK). In the elections of 5 March 1950 his party secured 45 seats, winning 16.4 per cent of the popular vote. Shortly thereafter Plastiras entered a coalition with Sophokles Venizelos and George Papandreou in order to strengthen his government and initiate a campaign of national unity, essential for the future of Greece. The desire which Plastiras expressed to breach the social gap resulting from the civil war came under increasing scrutiny by the parliamentary opposition. He was criticized by members of his own coalition government and less than six months after his assumption of the premiership Plastiras was forced to resign. Despite personal attacks, Plastiras was returned to power in the elections of 9 September 1951, when he won 23.5 per cent of the popular vote and increased his party's representation in parliament by 29 seats.

Once again his political career was short-lived. Now 68, weary, and ailing, Plastiras was no longer capable of defending his political beliefs. On 16 November 1952 Alexandros Papagos and the Greek Rally Party defeated EPEK, forcing Plastiras to resign. He died a few months later on 26 July 1953, having valiantly represented his country and upheld his moral values in both the political and the military sphere at transitional and crucial moments of Greek history.

STELIOS ZACHARIOU

Biography
Born in 1883 and brought up in Karditsa in central Greece, Plastiras graduated from the Cadet School in 1912 and fought with distinction in the Balkan Wars. In World War I he joined the Venizelists and in 1919 fought in the Ukraine against the Bolsheviks. In 1921–22 he organized the Greek army's retreat from Asia Minor and instigated the coup that overthrew King Constantine. He was briefly prime minister in 1945 and again in 1950–52. He died in 1953.

Further Reading
Markezinis, Spiro, *Politiki Istoria tis Neoteras Ellados, 1936–75* [Political History of Modern Greece, 1936–75], Athens, 1994
Mbastias, Ioannes, *I Istoria tou Ellinikou Ethnous* [History of the Greek Nation], vol. 15, Athens, 1975
Veremis, Thanos, *The Military in Greek Politics: From Independence to Democracy*, London: Hurst, 1997; Buffalo, New York: Black Rose, 1998

Plataea
City in Boeotia, site of a battle in 479 BC

Plataea was a city of southern Boeotia situated in the plain between Mount Cithaeron and the Asopus river. As the result of an attempt by Thebes to force it into the Boeotian Confederacy, the city joined an alliance with Athens in 519 BC. It subsequently provided support to the Athenians against the Persians at Marathon (490), Artemesium, and Salamis (480), before being sacked by the Persians in 479.

After the Greek victory over the Persian fleet in the bay of Salamis and Xerxes' subsequent withdrawal, the Greek forces still had to confront a substantial Persian army under the command of Mardonius. Plataea became the site of the great final battle between the Persian forces and the assembled Greek resistance in 479. The Greek victory ended the threat of Persian domination of Greece.

Mardonius, who had retired to Attica after Salamis, moved his forces to the plains of Boeotia, probably to provide more favourable terrain for his cavalry. The Peloponnesian forces, which had assembled at the isthmus, marched first to Eleusis where they were joined by the Athenians under Aristides, and then moved across the Cithaeron range along the main road and the pass of Eleutherae (Gyphtokastro).

Perhaps before engaging the Persians, the Greek allies swore the "Oath of Plataea", a pledge to fight to the death against the Persians, remain loyal to one's allies, and not rebuild the temples destroyed by the Persians. Denounced even in antiquity as a forgery (Theopompus, FGrH 115 F 153), scholars still debate its authenticity and its location and date of swearing.

At the battle the Spartan regent, Pausanias, led the Greek forces to victory against a numerically superior Persian foe. Herodotus' estimate for the Persian force (300,000 Persians and 50,000 Medizing Greeks, i.e. Greeks who sided with the Persians) is not accepted, although his numbers for the Greek forces (38,700 hoplites and 71,300 light or unarmed auxiliaries) are given more credence. Modern estimates give the Persians a cavalry of 10,000 with 50,000 to 70,000 infantry (plus support), perhaps 20,000 Medizing Greeks, and another Persian force of 40,000 under another commander, Artabazus.

Many details of the battle itself are still not agreed upon. After more than two millennia, changes to topographical features have made troop positions and movements impossible to prove. Even the specific date of the engagement is unknown, although mid-August of 479 is widely accepted. The general strategies of the two sides, however, seem clear: the Persians wished to employ their cavalry on the plain, while the Greek force, using hoplites in phalanx formation, preferred not to give them that advantage.

With the main Persian force assembled along a front, perhaps 8 km long, north of the Asopus with a 2-km square wooden stockade (c.900 acres/360 ha) to their rear, Pausanias utilized the rough terrain of his position on the lower slopes of Mount Cithaeron successfully to fight off the Persian cavalry, killing their majestic commander Masistius. Pausanias then shifted his line westward towards Plataea and the Asopus, perhaps in need of better water supplies, and moved further down the slopes. The Persians were able to deny the Greeks the river by employing their mounted archers to harass parties sent to collect water. Eventually the Persians also choked up the Gargaphia spring, a major water source for the entire Greek force; this may have forced the Greeks to attempt a more desperate course of action.

For eight days the two forces faced each other across the Asopus, neither side willing to give up its favourable terrain to attack. But after four days of raids by Mardonius' cavalry, which cut the Greeks' supply lines, Pausanias made the decision to attempt a night withdrawal to secure provisions. Confusion during the withdrawal resulted in the division of the Greek forces: the Athenians were isolated on the left, the centre just outside Plataea itself, and the Lacedaemonians and Tegeans on the right.

Mardonius, sensing that the advantage was his, ordered a general assault but, after a furious battle, the Spartans defeated his Asiatic and allied troops. The Athenians held his Boeotian allies, who fought well but disengaged under the protection of the Theban cavalry once the battle against the Greek right had been lost. Mardonius himself died in the battle, triggering a Persian retreat into the stockade where they were slaughtered once the Greeks breached its walls. Artabazus, who had maintained his troops in reserve, watched the battle develop into a rout, then retreated to Byzantium without fighting. Attempts have been made to depict the Greek victory as a brilliant ploy on the part of Pausanias, but it is impossible now to determine whether the victory was a result of luck or a clever plan.

Casualties are difficult to estimate, but the Persians probably lost about 10,000 non-European warriors and 1000 Medizing Greeks; the Greek forces suffered casualties of perhaps just over 1000 men. The Greeks had won a resounding victory that demonstrated they could inflict tremendous punishment upon a numerically superior Persian force. The Persians were no longer a military threat to the Greek mainland.

Booty from the battle was tremendous. Dedications from the spoils were made at Olympia, the isthmus, and Delphi (the triple entwined serpent-column, the remains of which is now in Istanbul, was erected on a gold tripod at Delphi). So luxurious were the spoils that this is the moment cited in antiquity when the Greeks became enamoured of wealth.

To complete their victory, the Greeks turned to punish Thebes for its support of the Persians. After a short siege, several ringleaders were surrendered to allies, who quickly removed them to the isthmus where they were executed. Theban hegemony over Boeotia was also broken.

Even more than Marathon or Salamis, the victory over the Persians at Plataea determined the course of European history. Xerxes had been defeated at sea and on land. Instead of becoming a Persian satellite, the Greeks formed the Delian League and went on the offensive.

Plataea faded in significance after the battle until the middle of the 5th century when it joined the new Boeotian Confederacy with control of two votes. The Theban assault on the city in 431 is regarded by many as the real beginning of the Peloponnesian War and, although most inhabitants had fled to Athens for refuge, the remaining inhabitants only surrendered in 427 when the city was razed to the ground. Plataea was rebuilt after the war and remained independent until seized by the Thebans in 372, when refugees once again fled to Athens. Philip II of Macedon restored the city after the battle of Chaeronea (338) and the Plataeans exacted revenge against Thebes in 335 when they helped Alexander the Great destroy their old enemy. Although loyal to Rome during the Third Macedonian War, the city suffered along with the other Boeotian cities during the campaigns of Sulla in 86 BC.

Two cults, the Homonoia and the Eleutheria, which celebrated the great victory over the Persians, provided some fame for the city in the Hellenistic and Roman periods, but other than the restoration of its walls under Justinian (527–65) little else of significance is known about the city.

ANDREW N. SHERWOOD

See also Persian Wars

Summary

A city in Boeotia, Plataea was an ally of Athens and supported the Athenians at Marathon and Salamis before being sacked by the Persians in 479 BC. It was the site of a decisive Greek victory over the Persians in that year which finally removed the Persian military threat to Greece. The city continued to exist into the early Byzantine period.

Further Reading

Amit, M., *Great and Small Poleis: A Study in the Relations between the Great Powers and the Small Cities in Ancient Greece*, Brussels: Latomus, 1973

Badian, E., *From Plataea to Potidaea: Studies in the History and Historiography of the Pentecontaetia*, Baltimore: Johns Hopkins University Press, 1993

Barron, J.P., "The Liberation of Greece" in *Persia, Greece and the Western Mediterranean, c.525 to 479 BC*, edited by John Boardman *et al.*, Cambridge: Cambridge University Press, 1988 (*The Cambridge Ancient History*, vol. 4, 2nd edition)

Bengtson, Hermann, *The Greeks and the Persians: From the Sixth to the Fourth Centuries*, New York: Delacorte Press, 1968; London: Weidenfeld and Nicolson, 1969

Boucher, A., "La Bataille de Platées d'après Hérodote", *Revue Archéologique*, 2 (1915): pp. 257–320

Bradford, A.S., "Plataea and the Soothsayer", *Ancient World*, 23/1 (1992): pp. 27–33

Burn, A.R., *Persia and the Greeks: The Defence of the West, c.546–478 BC*, 2nd edition, London: Duckworth, and Stanford, California: Stanford University Press, 1984

Green, Peter, *The Greco-Persian Wars*, Berkeley: University of California Press, 1996

Grundy, G.B., *The Topography of the Battle of Plataea: The City of Plataea, The Field of Leuctra*, London: John Murray, 1894

Hignett, Charles, *Xerxes' Invasion of Greece*, Oxford: Clarendon Press, 1963

Lazenby, J.F., *The Defence of Greece 490–479 BC*, Warminster: Aris and Phillips, 1993

Munro, J.A.R., "Some Observations on the Persian Wars", *Journal of Hellenic Studies*, 24 (1904): pp. 144–65

Nyland, R., "Herodotos' Sources for the Plataiai Campaign", *L'Antiquité Classique*, 61 (1992): pp. 80–97

Prandi, Luisa, *Platea: momenti e problemi della storia di una polis*, Padua: Programma, 1988

Pritchett, W. Kendrick, "New Light on Plataia", *American Journal of Archaeology*, 61 (1957): pp. 9–28

Pritchett, W. Kendrick, *Studies in Ancient Greek Topography*, parts 4–5, Berkeley: University of California Press, 1969

Pritchett, W. Kendrick, *The Greek State at War*, 5 vols, Berkeley: University of California Press, 1971–91

Pritchett, W. Kendrick, "Plataiai", *American Journal of Philology*, 100 (1979): pp. 145–52

Raubitschek, A.E., "The Covenant of Plataea", *Transactions and Proceedings of the American Philological Association*, 91 (1960): pp. 178–83

Siewert, Peter, *Der Eid von Plataiai*, Munich: Beck, 1972

Wallace, P.W., "The Final Battle at Plataia" in *Studies in Attic Epigraphy, History and Topography Presented to Eugene Vanderpool*, Princeton, New Jersey: American School of Classical Studies at Athens, 1982

Woodhouse, W.J., "The Greeks at Plataiai", *Journal of Hellenic Studies*, 18 (1898): pp. 33–59

Wright, Henry Burt, *The Campaign of Plataea (September 479 BC)*, New Haven, Connecticut: Morehouse and Taylor, 1904

Plato 429–347 BC

Philosopher

Plato was destined for an active life in Athenian politics. He was a member of an Athenian family that traced its origins back to the famous lawgiver Solon, and although his close relatives Crito and Charmides were discredited by their actions during the constitutional disturbances of the last decade of the 5th century BC, Plato could have carved out his own path. As Plato himself tells us in his *Seventh Letter* (now taken to be genuine by most scholars), he indeed began adult life with the usual political ambitions and was invited by his relatives to join them. Their actions were repellent, but what finally deterred Plato from ever taking part in conventional political life was the way in which powerful people brought charges against Socrates that led to his death, an action that in Plato's mind condemned both the oligarchic forces and the democratic masses. He would now devote his life to unconventional politics; that is, "having decided that all existing cities are badly governed", he would investigate "the nature of justice in both the individual and the state".

Plato would have had very few models for his own investigations. Greeks by and large looked to poets for ethical paradigms and heroes. Heraclitus wove ethical doctrines into an intentionally enigmatic prose text that lacked the detail and argumentative rigour that Plato desired. Some of the Sophists dealt with ethical matters but did so less with a desire to learn the truth and more in order to train students to come out on top in any morally ambiguous situation. Plato found his model in what was then a minor genre, the Socratic dialogue; that is, a prose drama in which Socrates and one or more fellow speakers (dialogists) would raise and analyse, or at any rate discuss, ethical matters. According to Aristotle, the first to write Socratic dialogues was a certain Alexamenos of Teos. There is also credible evidence that an Athenian, Simon the cobbler, would scribble notes for himself that he would later work up into a more polished form. How philosophical these earlier dialogues were we can only guess. They may have been similar to the chatty and anecdotal Socratic dialogues of Xenophon that are still extant. But whereas Xenophon was chiefly interested in retelling those conversations in which Socrates expressed his own views, Plato was more drawn to the Socrates who, when it came to the most important qualities of ethical life, preferred to withhold his own opinions, frequently willing to bring the discussion to an impasse (*aporia*) rather than impose upon his fellow dialogists a conclusion that he himself could not fully endorse.

Socrates did this in part because, as he himself is made to say in Plato's *Apology*, the profession of one's own ignorance is a necessary first step on the way to the truth. He also, again according to Plato, believed that whatever truth one does attain will occur only as a result of one's having actively

Plato, Roman copy of a Greek original

of how fathers can educate sons in bravery quickly becomes an investigation of the very meaning of bravery. The *Euthyphro*, *Lysis*, and *Charmides* deal likewise (and respectively) with the other commonly recognized virtues of piety, friendship, and *sophrosyne* (for which "temperance, prudence, moderation" are but inadequate translations). The *Hippias Major* (whose authenticity is still doubted by some) seeks to define *kalon* ("good" or "beautiful"), a term that comprises both aesthetic and moral values. Perhaps most aporetic of all is the *Hippias Minor*, which manages to shock even Socrates when the dialogue leads him and Hippias to the statement that the man who does wrong willingly is superior to the man who does so only involuntarily. And while not aporetic, the moral message of the *Crito* is clear: Socrates owes a debt to Athens that will not allow him to escape from prison, where he lies under sentence of death.

A question that is raised more than once in these early dialogues, most noticeably in the *Laches*, is how, supposing that we can ever attain a sufficiently correct opinion concerning these individual virtues, can one generation instil them in the next. This is an important question at any time, but Plato's 4th-century BC Athens was still feeling the effects of Socrates' 5th-century BC Sophists, the professional teachers who come off so badly in Plato's dialogues not so much for their pretentious ways and their love of money as for their claim to be able to teach virtue. Whereas Hippias in the *Hippias Minor* is artfully led to an immoral conclusion unwillingly, the Sophists of the *Euthydemus* with malicious glee delight in their ability to twist the normal ambiguities of ordinary language into startling paradoxical statements, a skill that they claim will enable a citizen to excel in the law courts or wherever such "eristic" skills are valuable. The question of whether virtue can be taught at all is addressed head on in the *Protagoras*. At first, Protagoras understandably argues with a sceptical Socrates that virtue (*arete*) can indeed be taught, and by no one so well as he. In the course of the discussion, however, they somehow change sides so that by the end it is Socrates who now believes that virtue is teachable, Protagoras arguing against his earlier position. This aporetic turnabout, artfully stage-managed by Socrates and Plato, has the desired result that Socrates' young friend who had been on the point of paying Protagoras his huge fee to learn virtue is now almost certainly deterred from doing so.

Whereas up to this point Plato was content to reveal the essentially immoral nature of sophistic teaching by indirection, in the *Gorgias* he starkly reveals the results of these ill-thought-out doctrines. Gorgias himself is shown merely to be morally purblind. His students, however, Polus and Callicles, provide examples of the totalitarian political character who embraces the idea that might makes right. Another student of Gorgias reveals in the *Meno* how little he knows about the nature of virtue (as opposed to its many manifestations in different people and situations).

Having shown in so many dialogues both the existence of widespread ignorance on ethical matters and the necessity for exposing its many forms, it was time for Plato to flesh out some of the many hints he dropped in the aporetic dialogues of a more positive doctrine. In the deathbed setting of *Phaedo*, Socrates not only elaborates on his earlier statements in the *Apology* and *Crito* on the necessity of devoting one's life to the

wrestled with the matter and elicited it out of one's own soul – a difficult matter, to be sure, but possible for a bright person who is asked the right questions. Plato, who no doubt often found himself in this situation with Socrates, proceeded to shape both real and imagined dialogues with this intriguing old man into a powerful literary form. There is therefore no voice within the dialogues that declares itself to be that of the author arguing his own cause; nor does Plato even put himself forward as narrator of any dialogue. The reader is thus put on constant guard, never sure at first or perhaps even after consideration whether any particular idea expressed by Socrates or anyone else comes with Plato's own endorsement. This is Plato's way of reproducing Socrates' habit of encouraging would-be philosophers to work things out as much as possible by themselves.

Quite naturally, therefore, apart from the speech that forms the *Apology*, Plato's earliest dialogues tend to end in the doubt that earns them the label "aporetic". Plato brings Socrates together somewhere in Athens with one or more acquaintances. Whether or not they have a specific question for him, Socrates soon raises the level of discussion from the ordinary to the philosophical. In the *Laches*, for example, the question

study of wisdom (which is the very serious meaning he gives to the word *philosophia*), he describes the immortality of the soul and those entities he calls Ideas or Forms. (In the *Meno* real learning was said to be the immortal soul actually recollecting what it had known before.) Although the metaphysical nature of the Forms is often studied by itself, when viewed in their contexts the Forms clearly represent an essential part of Plato's overarching ethical programme. While it is not difficult to enumerate the qualities of these unchanging, eternal, and immanent Forms, it is quite another thing to explain how one might attain direct apprehension of them for oneself.

The *Phaedo* shows how even Socrates' own most devoted followers can accept the immortality of the soul (not a difficult thing for a Greek) and yet prove incapable of absorbing it into their philosophical belief. The immortality of the Forms is even more difficult to incorporate. The *Symposium*, primarily about love, likens the apprehension of the Forms to the initiation into a mystery religion, which cannot be revealed to an outsider. In the *Republic*, however, Plato took the plunge, sketching out (his metaphor) an elaborate scheme for instituting and governing a state where justice would prevail in both its own constitution and in the very souls of its citizens. Its first book (of ten) is modelled on an aporetic dialogue in which the object of discussion is justice. Socrates, however, not allowed to run off after having dispelled various mistaken notions, is compelled to continue with a more positive doctrine of justice, which, it turns out, governs some of the cardinal virtues treated in earlier dialogues. Maintaining the proper relationship among the parts of the soul makes for a just individual, who in turn along with a like-minded citizenry will serve the state – whether as ruler or follower – so that all elements work together in a harmony that Socrates calls justice. Rulers can come only from that elite group of men and women who have pursued a course of education so rigorous that they are able to apprehend the Form of the Good, the nature of which demands that they work for the good of the state. Complementary to the idea that Good demands good is the Socratic paradox that nobody does wrong willingly.

The *Phaedrus*, like the *Symposium*, seeks to understand love through speeches; here, however, Socrates emphasizes less the content of a speech than its form, which, it is argued, should be clearly and naturally articulated. This notion of proper composition calls for a discussion of what Plato will develop in later dialogues, namely analysis of the subject to be defined by a process of collection (of all similar things) and division (of the whole into its parts). The *Phaedrus* is one of Plato's great literary accomplishments. On the whole, however, it may be said that after having considered, with some justification, the *Republic* as the culmination of all of his earlier virtue-oriented writings, Plato now felt free to explore and develop some of the logical consequences of his theory of Forms. This is not to say that the later dialogues lack all literary touches – the *Theaetetus*, for example, is informed by metaphors of pregnancy and birth that illuminate the process whereby Theaetetus is questioned on the meaning of knowledge – but it must be admitted that the *Sophist*, *Statesman*, and *Philebus* have far fewer readers (outside philosophy departments) than the earlier dialogues. Among late dialogues, perhaps only the *Timaeus*, with its fascinating attempt to describe the cosmos by marrying Greek science and religion,

commands a wide readership. The *Laws*, the longest dialogue, both complements and, as an older and more conservative Plato must have imagined it, corrects the picture of the ideal state described earlier in the *Republic*.

Plato's influence on later thought was felt immediately and has lasted until the present. The school he founded in the sacred grove known as the Academy lasted until the 6th century AD. Aristotle, denied advancement with the Academy, continued with his own school in Athens and in his writings continued until the end of his life to argue with his teacher. Nor could any other school of western philosophy ignore him; they either adopted, adapted, or overtly rejected the basic doctrines of Plato.

DAVID SIDER

See also Academy, Aesthetics, Philosophy, Socrates

Biography

Born in Athens in 429 BC to an ancient and wealthy family, Plato was destined for a political career but decided to devote himself to philosophy after the death of Socrates. He founded a philosophical school known as the Academy whose original aim was to train prospective statesmen. He visited Syracuse several times in a vain attempt to convert Dionysius II to his philosophical ideas. He published his theories in the form of dialogues, dramatic conversation pieces, of which some 30 survive. He died in 347 BC.

Writings

Opera (texts in Greek), edited by John Burnet, 5 vols, Oxford: Clarendon Press, 1900–07

The Dialogues, translated by Benjamin Jowett, 4 vols, Oxford: Clarendon Press, and New York: Scribner, 1868–71; new edition, edited by D.J. Allan and H.E. Dale, 4 vols, Clarendon Press, 1953

Dialogues, translated by H.N. Fowler *et al.*, 15 vols, London: Heinemann, and Cambridge, Massachusetts: Harvard University Press, 1914–35 (Loeb edition; many reprints)

Collected Dialogues, edited by Edith Hamilton and Huntington Cairns, New York: Pantheon, 1961

The Dialogues, translated by R.E. Allen, New Haven and London: Yale University Press, 1985–

The Collected Dialogues, edited by John Cooper, Indianapolis: Hackett, 1997

Further Reading

Friedländer, Paul, *Plato*, 2nd edition, 3 vols, Princeton, New Jersey: Princeton University Press, 1958–69

Gould, John, *The Development of Plato's Ethics*, Cambridge: Cambridge University Press, 1955

Griswold, Charles L., Jr (editor), *Platonic Writings, Platonic Readings*, London and New York: Routledge, 1988

Guthrie, W.K.C., *A History of Greek Philosophy*, vols. 4–5, Cambridge and New York: Cambridge University Press, 1962–65

Kahn, Charles H., *Plato and the Socratic Dialogue: The Philosophical Use of a Literary Form*, Cambridge and New York: Cambridge University Press, 1996

Kraut, Richard (editor), *The Cambridge Companion to Plato*, Cambridge and New York: Cambridge University Press, 1992

Mackenzie, Mary Margaret, *Plato on Punishment*, Berkeley: University of California Press, 1981

Nightingale, Andrea Wilson, *Genres in Dialogue: Plato and the Construct of Philosophy*, Cambridge and New York: Cambridge University Press, 1995

Price, A.W., *Love and Friendship in Plato and Aristotle*, Oxford: Clarendon Press, and New York: Oxford University Press, 1989

Robinson, Richard, *Plato's Earlier Dialectic*, 2nd edition, Oxford: Clarendon Press, and New York: Oxford University Press, 1953

Robinson, T.M., *Plato's Psychology*, Toronto: University of Toronto Press, 1970; 2nd edition, 1995

Ross, D., *Plato's Theory of Ideas*, Oxford: Clarendon Press, 1951

Rutherford, R.B., *The Art of Plato: Ten Essays in Platonic Interpretation*, Cambridge, Massachusetts: Harvard University Press, and London: Routledge, 1995

Vlastos, Gregory, *Platonic Studies*, Princeton, New Jersey: Princeton University Press, 1973

Plethon, George Gemistos c.1360–1452

Philosopher

The philosopher George Gemistos (he adopted the pseudonym Plethon around 1439) was both one of the most original thinkers of the Byzantine period and also a significant influence on the development of Platonic studies in Italy during the Renaissance. Little is known of the first 50 years of his life, but from an early stage he held unorthodox views, taking an interest in Neoplatonism and Zoroastrianism. Around 1410 he was exiled from Constantinople by the Byzantine emperor Manuel II Palaiologos, on suspicion of heresy and paganism, and sent to Mistra in the Peloponnese where he spent most of the remainder of his life, attached to the court of the despots of the Morea.

In spite of his relegation to a distant province, Gemistos's powerful personality soon attracted a number of promising students to study under him, including the future cardinal Bessarion, George Hermonymos, Laonikos Chalkokondyles, and Demetrios Rhaoul Kavakis. He became the centre of a lively literary circle and acquired a reputation as the most brilliant exponent of Platonism.

Gemistos also appears to have regarded himself as an adviser to the young despot of the Morea, Theodore II Palaiologos (1408–43), perhaps in conscious imitation of the similar role played by Plato at the court of the tyrant Dionysius II of Syracuse. Between 1415 and 1418 he wrote a series of rhetorical works that drew heavily on Platonic ideas and which offered solutions to the ills then afflicting the Byzantine empire. His *Advisory Address to the Despot Theodore on the Peloponnese* and his *Address to the Emperor Manuel on Affairs in the Peloponnese* proposed various reforms to improve the condition of the Byzantine province of the Morea. He urged the establishment of a standing army, composed of Greeks rather than of mercenaries. To encourage recruits soldiers should be exempt from taxation, but the monastic vocation was to be discouraged because it burdened society with idle mouths. Some of his proposals reflect the utopianism of Plato's *Republic*, notably his suggestions that the Morea should be ruled, under the despot, by a council of dedicated, moderate men, and that all property should be held in common. Both works advanced the idea of Hellenic nationalism as opposed to the traditional universalism of the Byzantine empire.

A turning point in Gemistos's life occurred in 1438 when, at the age of nearly 80, he joined the retinue of the Byzantine emperor John VIII to attend the Council of Florence. He played little part in the union of the Churches but engaged in lively debate with Florentine scholars on the relative merits of the philosophies of Plato and Aristotle. Gemistos naturally took Plato's side, even going so far as to adopt the pseudonym Plethon, with its connotations of "a second Plato". During his stay Plethon circulated his Greek treatise *On the Differences of Plato and Aristotle*, in which he rejected the philosophy of Aristotle and championed that of Plato. The work was interpreted by many as an attack on Christianity, largely because Plethon made no secret of his admiration for those aspects of Plato's thought that were incompatible with Christian doctrine, particularly the concept of *metempsychosis*, the transmigration of souls. Others, however, were deeply impressed by his work, especially the Florentine humanist Marsilio Ficino who later played a leading role in the Platonic Academy established by Cosimo de' Medici at Careggi near Florence in 1462. Plethon can therefore be credited with having aroused the initial interest in Platonism that was later to have a profound influence on the development of Florentine political thought.

Plethon's latter years were spent teaching and writing at Mistra. He produced an essay on Strabo that adopted a sceptical approach to the ancient geographer, rejecting monsters and mythical realms. However, his last work, *On the Laws*, was his most controversial, advocating a new religion based on a synthesis of Neoplatonism and Classical paganism, stating that Zeus was the supreme god, and containing hymns, prayers, and liturgies to pagan deities. Not surprisingly, the work caused considerable offence to the Church authorities, and the patriarch of Constantinople George Scholarios later ordered that all copies be burned on pain of excommunication.

Nevertheless, some fragments of *On the Laws* survive, including a few autograph manuscript sheets. These, along with the *On the Differences*, ensured that the debate on the relative merits of Plato and Aristotle that Plethon had initiated in Florence would be continued after his death in 1452. The controversy was revived in earnest in 1458 when George of Trebizond wrote his *Comparisons of Plato and Aristotle* with a view to exposing Plethon as a heretic, and provoked a series of responses by the members of the Academy of cardinal Bessarion in Rome. Bessarion's *Against the Calumniator of Plato* (1469) which, unlike Plethon's book, was available in Latin, completed the work of his teacher by convincing the Italian humanists that Plato's philosophy was compatible with Christianity and worthy of study in its own right.

Thus it was in Italy, rather than his native land, that Plethon's influence was to be most lasting. By a curious turn of events, it was to Italy that his remains were to return. In 1464, during a campaign against the Turks in the Morea, Sigismondo Malatesta, hereditary ruler of Rimini, came across Plethon's grave at Mistra and had the philosopher's bones exhumed and transported back to Italy. They were reinterred in the Tempio Malatestiano in Rimini, where Plethon's tomb can still be seen.

JONATHAN HARRIS

See also Mistra

Biography

Born in Constantinople c.1360, Gemistos taught in the city until c.1410 when he was exiled to Mistra on suspicion of heresy and paganism. There he remained for the rest of his life attracting a large number of distinguished pupils. He promoted Platonism and Hellenic nationalism. In 1438 he attended the Council of Florence where his teaching had a profound impact on humanist scholars. He died at Mistra in 1452.

Further Reading

Anastos, Milton V., "Pletho, Strabo and Columbus", in his *Studies in Byzantine Intellectual History*, London: Variorum, 1979

Brown, Alison M., "Platonism in Fifteenth-Century Florence and Its Contribution to Early Modern Political Thought", *Journal of Modern History*, 58/2 (1986): pp. 383–413

Keller, A., "Two Byzantine Scholars and Their Reception in Italy", *Journal of the Warburg and Courtauld Institutes*, 20 (1957): pp. 363–70

Masai, François, *Pléthon et le platonisme de Mistra*, Paris: Les Belles Lettres, 1956

Monfasani, John, "Platonic Paganism in the Fifteenth Century", in his *Byzantine Scholars in Renaissance Italy: Cardinal Bessarion and Other Emigrés*, Aldershot: Variorum, 1995

Runciman, Steven, *The Last Byzantine Renaissance*, Cambridge: Cambridge University Press, 1970

Setton, Kenneth M., "The Byzantine Background to the Italian Renaissance", *Transactions and Proceedings of the American Philosophical Society*, 100 (1956): pp. 1–76

Wilson, N.G., *From Byzantium to Italy: Greek Studies in the Italian Renaissance*, London: Duckworth, and Baltimore: Johns Hopkins University Press, 1992

Woodhouse, C.M., *George Gemistos Plethon: The Last of the Hellenes*, Oxford: Clarendon Press, 1986

Plotinus AD 205–269/70

Philosopher

Plotinus was the most influential and important philosopher of ancient Greece after Plato and Aristotle. His philosophical system, though based primarily on Plato, was deeply influenced by Aristotle. Stoicism, too, was an important ingredient as well as the ideas of those intervening philosophers and scholars who commented on, developed, and frequently sought a rapprochement between the thought of their great predecessors. His influence, at first direct, on his sucessors Porphyry, Iamblichus, and Proclus and, subsequently, indirectly through them, on later thinkers had a profound and lasting impact on the way in which Greek philosophy, and particularly Plato, was viewed and on the development of Christian theology, particularly in the Orthodox tradition, which was more receptive of Platonic ideas than the western Church. It is, then, important to grasp some of the basic tenets of Neoplatonism that were given their classic shape by Plotinus, though refined and systematized by later Neoplatonists.

Although Plotinus was deeply imbued with the philosophy of Aristotle as well as that of the Stoics, he regarded himself primarily as a follower of Plato, the hidden implications of whose works he sought to explicate and develop. The term Neoplatonist is modern and Plotinus would have regarded himself simply as a Platonist. He came from Lycopolis in Egypt and was educated in the philosophical schools of Alexandria. Political circumstances brought him to Rome where he founded a school in a private house. He did not start to write down his ideas until he was 50 years old and his system was well thought out, but his treatises give the impression of a lively philosophical dialogue, at times almost of a seminar, in which problems, issues, and objections are thoroughly aired. His treatises were not published until many years after his death by his pupil Porphyry who arranged them in sets of nine: hence the curious title *Enneads*. One result of Porphyry's diligent work as an editor is that Plotinus is the only philosopher of antiquity whose works survive in their entirety.

Plotinus laid great emphasis on the two-world view of Plato, who regarded the physical world as an image of a transcendent world of archetypal Forms and the true home of the soul which, during its earthly life, may be considered to be in exile. Plotinus, however, gave far greater stress to this sense of exile and the necessity for the soul to divest itself of its earthly burdens and return to its original home by a process of moral and intellectual effort leading to mystical union with the supreme principle. At the same time, however, he could see the physical world, in the optimistic context of Plato's *Timaeus*, as the best possible image of its divine maker, indeed as a god in its own right. The idea of return to God as father from exile in this world and the spiritual earnestness with which it was expressed by Plotinus were naturally appealing to Christian writers such as Basil. For Plotinus, however, this return of the soul was not dependent on the grace of God but on the innate capacity that we all have, if only we would use it, to recognize our own worth, our kinship, and ultimate identity with the divine. Plotinus himself had little time for religious cults and even less time for those such as the Gnostics who denigrated the physical universe as the creation of a fallen God.

Equally appealing and influential was Plotinus' complex development of Plato's transcendent world into three levels: above all is the One, the source of all, which gives rise to Intellect (*nous*) from which Soul derives. Although these levels of reality are subordinate to each other, they provided a fertile source for Christian Trinitarian theology. Less obvious but more subtly influential were his complex speculations about the relationships within Intellect which provided a model and a language that Christian theologians could employ to describe mutual relationships within the Godhead. For Plotinus thinker, thinking, and object of thought are substantially identical, though conceptually distinct. The concept of the One also proved influential. For Plotinus this ultimate principle, source of all unity, was beyond all description. It could be indicated only by affirming what it was not. This so-called negative or apophatic theology was to have a long following, including Gregory of Nyssa and pseudo-Dionysius. Equally influential was the way in which Plotinus attempted to describe and analyse his personal mystical union with the One, "the flight of the alone to the alone".

The *Enneads* were read and quoted by Eusebius of Caesarea, Basil the Great, and Gregory of Nyssa. They became fashionable again in the 11th century partly through the interest of Michael Psellos, who also knew Proclus' commentary on them. In the 15th century Gemistos Plethon's Neoplatonic religion owed much to Plotinus and it was his pupil Bessarion who brought manuscripts of Plotinus to the west. But the indirect influence of Plotinus is probably of even greater importance for the Greek east. Although Plotinus had never been official head of the Academy or even visited Athens, his interpretation of Plato gradually became accepted and more systematically developed under a sequence of Academy heads including Plutarch of Athens, Syrianus, and, most importantly of all, Proclus, whose works had a profound influence on pseudo-Dionysius the Areopagite. The great pagan philosophical and Christian centre of Alexandria was also influenced both directly and through the Academy at Athens, as scholars moved freely between the two cities. Although this form of later Neoplatonism was in many respects quite different from that of Plotinus, the *Enneads* remain the vital source and the most dynamic exposition of Neoplatonic ideas and thus the essential text to which all subsequent Neoplatonists have returned and from which all modern study of Neoplatonism takes its start.

ANDREW SMITH

See also Neoplatonism

Biography

Born at Lycopolis in Egypt in AD 205, Plotinus was educated in Alexandria where he was a pupil of Ammonius Sacas. In 245 he moved to Rome where he founded a school and taught philosophy. His pupils included Porphyry. Plotinus was the greatest of the Neoplatonists and wrote philosophical treatises which were published after his death by Porphyry as *Enneads*. He died in Campania in 269/70.

Writings

Plotinus, translated by A.H. Armstrong, London: Heinemann, and Cambridge, Massachusetts: Harvard University Press, 1966–88; revised edition 1989– , (Loeb edition)

The Enneads, translated by Stephen MacKenna, 4th edition, revised by B.S. Page, London: Faber, 1969; abridged by John Dillon, London and New York: Penguin, 1991

Further Reading

Armstrong, A.H., *The Architecture of the Intelligible Universe in the Philosophy of Plotinus: An Analytical and Historical Study*, Cambridge: Cambridge University Press, 1940

Armstrong, A.H. (editor), *The Cambridge History of Later Greek and Early Medieval Philosophy*, London: Cambridge University Press, 1967, chapters 12–16

O'Meara, Dominic J., *Plotinus: An Introduction to the Enneads*, Oxford: Clarendon Press, and New York: Oxford University Press, 1993

Rist, J.M., *Plotinus: The Road to Reality*, Cambridge: Cambridge University Press, 1967

Plutarch *c.*AD 50–120

Prose writer

Plutarch came from the Boeotian town of Chaeronea where he lived for most of his life. In his writings there are regular references to various local landmarks, such as the tomb of Lysander on the road leading from Delphi to Chaeronea (*Lysander*, 29. 3). These details cumulatively suggest his fondness for his birthplace, which he once wryly said that he did not wish to leave, for fear of making a small place even smaller (*Demosthenes*, 2. 2). In addition we have an inscription from the base of a statue which was found in Chaeronea: "Philinus dedicated to the gods [this statue of] Plutarch the benefactor"

(W. Dittenberger, *Sylloge Inscriptionum Graecarum*, 3rd edition, 1915–24, 843B). This inscription shows that Plutarch had a warm relationship with his home town, but it is clear from his writings that he still found time to travel. Thus at Ravenna Plutarch claims to have seen a statue of Marius (*Marius*, 2. 1), and in northern Italy, when he was travelling with his friend the ex-consul Mestrius Florus, he visited the civil war battlefield at Bedriacum (*Otho*, 14. 2). For the last 30 years of his life Plutarch was a priest at the Greek sanctuary of Delphi (*Moralia*, 792F) and the knowledge of antiquities that he acquired there can be seen throughout his works. For example, Plutarch notes that there existed at Delphi a statue of *Aphrodite of the Tomb* and he uses this fact to suggest why the Romans used to sell items for funerals in the precinct of Libitina/Venus (*Moralia*, 269B). In addition he wrote whole essays that draw on his knowledge of Delphi, including *On the Pythia's Prophecies* and *On the Delphic E*.

Plutarch undoubtedly loved Greece, but at the same time he was a Roman citizen, as we know from an inscription that refers to him as Mestrius Plutarch (Dittenberger, 843B). This name suggests a link between his acquisition of citizenship and his friendship with Mestrius Florus, who was one of a circle of influential Plutarchan contacts that also included Sosius Senecio, to whom the *Parallel Lives* are dedicated. Thus Plutarch was a Janus figure, a Roman citizen who retained a strong Greek identity, but who could see positive qualities in both cultures. Plutarch valued the stability that came with the Roman imperial system (*Moralia*, 317C), but saw the influence of Greek culture on Rome as valuable and even as necessary: "for the time in which Rome reached its greatest success was the time when it welcomed Greek studies and education" (*Cato the Elder*, 23. 3).

Plutarch's most remarkable achievement lies in his vastly rich and varied body of written work. The Catalogue of Lamprias, which is itself incomplete, lists 227 different works. Today we possess 78 essays by Plutarch on a range of topics, which are known collectively as the *Moralia*, and 50 *Lives*. Subjects that Plutarch addresses in the *Moralia* include philosophical questions, historical issues, religious antiquities, rhetoric, and literary themes. Plutarch's most popular works, however, are the *Parallel Lives*, in which he presents pairs of biographies, one of a Greek and one of a Roman protagonist, including in most cases a brief comparison or *synkrisis* at the end. These *Parallel Lives* were not Plutarch's first attempt at writing biography. Probably before AD 96 he had composed the *Lives of the Caesars* about the eight Roman emperors from Augustus to Vitellius. Unfortunately, only the *Galba* and the *Otho* have survived, although there is some material in the *Moralia* that it is tempting to think may have appeared in the other lost imperial *Lives of the Caesars*. For a man who claims that his knowledge of Latin was acquired later in life (*Demosthenes*, 2. 2. 4) researching these imperial biographies cannot have been easy and Plutarch certainly did not have the advantages of the later imperial biographer Suetonius, whose post as imperial secretary gave him access to some unique documents and archives about the emperors. However, Plutarch persevered with his reading of Latin sources when researching the subjects of his *Parallel Lives*. This strategy of pairing Greek and Roman lives was innovative and symptomatic of an era when interaction between Greek and

Roman cultures was gaining momentum: the *Parallel Lives* appear to have been written early in the 2nd century AD under the more enlightened principates of Trajan (emperor AD 98–117) and Hadrian (emperor AD 117–38). Previously, biographers such as Cornelius Nepos and Varro had certainly written groups of lives centring on men of a particular profession, such as orators, poets, and generals, but Plutarch allowed himself the potential for developing vivid and subtle portraits by restricting himself to delineating only two subjects at a time in the *Parallel Lives*, apart from the one double pairing of *Agis and Cleomenes* and *Tiberius and Gaius Gracchus*. His biographical corpus as a whole was extensive, but he kept his readers' interest alive by his tremendous powers of description and by his astute eye for detail. As Plutarch famously says: "Nor is it always the most famous actions which reveal a man's good or bad qualities: a clearer insight into a man's character is often given by a small matter, a word or jest, than by engagements where thousands die" (*Alexander*, 1. 1–2). Rather than offer long authorial analysis of an individual's personality, Plutarch often allows character to emerge from carefully chosen anecdotes, which enable readers to draw their own conclusions about the subject of the biography. Moreover, Plutarch often devotes considerable attention to characterizing other protagonists in his biographies. For example, his portrait of Cleopatra in the *Antony* is unforgettably vibrant, and by serving as a foil to Antony, the Egyptian queen further deepens our understanding of the Roman general.

Plutarch's writings rapidly became popular. In the Byzantine era there were more transcriptions made of Plutarch than of any other ancient author. Strikingly, one scholar, John Tzetzes (died *c*.1180), when he fell on hard times, resigned himself to selling almost all his library but refused to part with his Plutarch. The individual to whom we owe the greatest debt for the preservation of Plutarch's works is undoubtedly Maximos Planudes. In 1294/95 Planudes, who was devoted to Plutarch, assembled a group of scribes whose task was to make copies of a large portion of the *Moralia*, as well as the *Galba* and the *Otho*. The *Parallel Lives* and the remaining essays from the *Moralia* were added to the project in 1296. Without Planudes's determination to collect the scattered pieces of the Plutarchan corpus we would almost certainly have had a much more fragmentary knowledge of Plutarch's work today. Testimony to the continuing interest in Plutarch can be found in the pervasive but inaccurate medieval tradition that the author had served as tutor to the emperor Trajan, just as Aristotle taught Alexander. There is even a Latin version of a "letter" supposedly written by Plutarch to Trajan and consisting of a compilation of quotations from the surviving works. During the Renaissance Plutarch was translated into French by Amyot (*Lives* 1559 and *Moralia* 1572) and into English (via the French) by North (*Lives* 1579). Material from Plutarch was also used by William Barker in 1578 to supplement the incomplete text of Appian on the civil wars. Such translations provided crucial inspiration for Shakespeare and Montaigne. More recently Mary Shelley made Frankenstein's monster a devotee of Plutarch's *Lives* and Harry S. Truman allegedly learned some valuable political lessons through reading the *Lives*. Today Plutarchan studies are thriving on a global level: not only is there *Ploutarchos*, the journal of the International Plutarch Society edited by Dr F.

Titchener, but one can also access *Chaironeia*, a lively site devoted to Plutarch on the World Wide Web maintained by the University of Texas.

RHIANNON ASH

See also Biography and Autobiography

Biography

Born in Chaeronea *c*.AD 50, Plutarch spent most of his life there, though he was a Roman citizen and he did travel to Egypt and Italy. For 30 years he was a priest at Delphi. His writings were copious and varied: 78 essays (*Moralia*) and 50 *Lives* survive. He died soon after AD 120.

Writings

Plutarch's Lives, translated by Bernadotte Perrin, 11 vols, London: Heinemann, and New York: Macmillan, 1914–26 (Loeb edition; many reprints)

Moralia, translated by F.C. Babbitt *et al.*, 15 vols, London: Heinemann, and Cambridge, Massachusetts: Harvard University Press, 1927–69 (Loeb edition)

Further Reading

Brenk, Frederick E., *In Mist Apparelled: Religious Themes in Plutarch's Moralia and Lives*, Leiden: Brill, 1977

DeBlois, L., "The Perception of Politics in Plutarch's Roman *Lives*" in *Aufstieg und Niedergang der römischen Welt*, edited by Hildegard Temporini *et al.*, vol. 2. 33. 6, Berlin: de Gruyter, 1992, 4568–615

Geiger, J., "Nepos and Plutarch: From Latin to Greek Political Biography", *Illinois Classical Studies*, 13 (1988): pp. 245–56

Georgiadou, A. "Idealistic and Realistic Portraiture in the *Lives* of Plutarch" in *Aufstieg und Niedergang der römischen Welt*, edited by Hildegard Temporini *et al.*, vol. 2. 33. 6, Berlin: de Gruyter, 1992, 4616–23

Hirzel, Rudolf, *Plutarch*, Leipzig: Dietrich, 1912

Jones, C.P., *Plutarch and Rome*, Oxford: Clarendon Press, 1971

Momigliano, Arnaldo, *The Development of Greek Biography*, expanded edition, Cambridge, Massachusetts: Harvard University Press, 1993

Mossman, Judith (editor), *Plutarch and his Intellectual World: Essays on Plutarch*, London: Duckworth, 1997

Muir, Kenneth, *The Sources of Shakespeare's Plays*, London: Methuen, and New Haven, Connecticut: Yale University Press, 1977

Pelling, C.B.R., "Plutarch's Method of Work in the Roman Lives", *Journal of Hellenic Studies*, 99 (1979): pp. 74–96

Pelling, C.B.R., "Plutarch's Adaptation of his Source Material", *Journal of Hellenic Studies*, 100 (1980): pp. 127–40

Pelling, C.B.R., "Plutarch and Roman Politics", in *Past Perspectives: Studies in Greek and Roman Historical Writing*, edited by I.S. Moxon *et al.*, Cambridge: Cambridge University Press, 1986

Pelling, C.B.R., "Aspects of Plutarch's Characterisation", *Illinois Classical Studies*, 13/2 (1988): pp. 257–74

Pelling, C.B.R., "Is Death the End? Closure in Plutarch's *Lives*", in *Classical Closure: Reading the End in Greek and Latin Literature*, edited by Deborah H. Roberts, Francis M. Dunn and Don P. Fowler, Princeton, New Jersey: Princeton University Press, 1997

Russell, D.A., *Plutarch*, London: Duckworth, and New York: Scribner, 1973

Scardigli, B. (editor), *Essays on Plutarch's Lives*, Oxford: Clarendon Press, and New York: Oxford University Press, 1995

Stadter, Philip A. (editor), *Plutarch and the Historical Tradition*, London and New York: Routledge, 1992

Swain, S.C.R., "Character Change in Plutarch", *Phoenix*, 43 (1989): pp. 62–68

Swain, S.C.R., "Plutarch *De Fortuna Romanorum*", *Classical Quarterly*, 39/2 (1989): pp. 504–16
Wardman, Alan E., *Plutarch's Lives*, London: Elek, and Berkeley: University of California Press, 1974

Poetry, Epic

Ancient

"Homer is enough for everyone", remarked Theocritus (16. 20), and interestingly this is true: the Homeric poems stand at the beginning of extant Greek literature, and the scope of their achievement is such that they constitute defining examples of what came to be known as epic poetry, as well as becoming a fixed standard against which all subsequent epics were assessed. An epic on the Homeric model is a substantial narrative poem that is composed in dactylic hexameters, that has an elevated tone, and that concerns the exploits of gods and heroes, the subject matter being drawn from traditional myth. Epic poetry also had numerous conventional features: formulaic language, frequent archaisms, extensive use of parataxis, ring-composition, type-scenes (e.g. describing arming, dining, etc.), digressions, and extended similes. This picture is consistent with modern notions of what constitutes epic; the ancient understanding of the genre, however, remains uncertain in important respects. The word "epic" – derived from *epos*, literally "word" – seems originally to have been used chiefly of poetry composed in dactylic hexameters (not only the Homeric poems), but also didactic poetry in the Hesiodic tradition and of philosophical poems by early philosophers, such as Parmenides and Empedocles. In later antiquity the term was applied more narrowly to the genre exemplified by the Homeric poems. It is not clear precisely when *epos* became "epic" in the modern sense, although it seems that some idea of an epic genre is implicit in Aristotle's treatment of poetry.

Aristotle's *Poetics* was enormously influential in consolidating and determining ancient views of the genre. Although ostensibly concerned with tragic poetry, the *Poetics* refers to the Homeric poems more often than to any tragic text, and Aristotle's keen engagement with epic is everywhere in evidence (chapters 23 and 24 are particularly relevant). Central for Aristotle is the organic unity of plot (*mythos*), which must comprise a "beginning, middle, and end". As in the case of tragedy, epic plots should be compact, and their unity should reside in events, not character. In this light he called attention to the conspicuous superiority of the Homeric poems and compared them favourably with other products of the early epic tradition. Later critics occasionally offered a broader definition of epic, suggesting, for example, that didactic and pastoral poetry be included (Quintilian, 10. 1. 46, 10. 1. 85), but the view implicit in Aristotle's *Poetics* remained dominant, constituting a point of departure for later poets.

As early as Aristotle (e.g. *Rhetorica*, 1406b3; *Poetics*, 1459b35), commentators had regularly viewed many of the conventional features as simply characteristic of epic dignity; during the 20th century scholars have determined that the style of Homeric poetry and the character of its narrative were indicative of the oral nature of epic poetry in early Greece, and that many apparently idiosyncratic features of these poems were rooted in a tradition of at least partially improvised song. This has led to a widely accepted distinction between "primary", or traditional oral epic and "secondary", or literate epic, the familiar tradition of epic poetry composed with the aid of writing by a literate poet.

It is important to note that the *Iliad* and the *Odyssey* were not the sole products of the early epic tradition. There is evidence for a series of poems called the Epic Cycle, which seem to have offered an account of the world from the beginning to the close of the heroic age. None of these poems is extant, but fragmentary evidence – most notably summaries of a number in various late mythographers (of especial importance are those by Proclus) – allows us to form some impression of the series. Best attested are the poems describing the Trojan War. The *Cypria* provided the background to the war and events leading up to the point at which the *Iliad* begins. There is some evidence to suggest that the beginning and the end of the *Iliad* were adapted to fit more comfortably in the sequence. The sequel to the *Iliad* was provided by the *Aethiopis*, the *Little Iliad*, and the *Iliou Persis*. These poems follow the Trojan myth from the death of Hector to the sack of Troy and the departure of the Greeks. The *Nostoi*, which detailed the homeward journeys of some of the central Greek warriors, marks a transition to the *Odyssey*, the action of which was followed by *Telegonia*, which brought an end to the story of Odysseus' life. In addition to the Trojan War epics, the Epic Cycle is known to have comprised shorter poems on largely unrelated mythic themes: a *Theogony* and *Titanomachy*, covering ground familiar from Hesiod; and an *Oedipodia*, *Thebais*, and *Epigonoi*, providing influential treatment of Theban myths. Other early epics were no doubt in circulation in antiquity, and some may have been included in the Epic Cycle, but no trace of such an ascription can be found among extant ancient sources. We are aware of a number of other poems from the 7th and 6th centuries BC that are often described as epics, although that term may simply mean that they were hexametric. Some of these shadowy poems, such as the *Naupactia* and the *Theseis*, seem to have treated traditional myths; others, like the *Arimaspea* ascribed to Aristeas of Proconnesus, seem to have had affinities with other poetic traditions.

The whole Epic Cycle was ascribed to Homer by many, but other poets are frequently named. Among them are Stasinus, Arctinus, Lesches, and Thestorides, although today these poets are at best little more than names. The Homeric ascription is none the less telling, for it reflects the character of these poems and the way in which they complement the *Iliad* and the *Odyssey*, and in this latter point we can discern the underlying motivation for the formation of the Epic Cycle. As the adjustments made to the beginning and end of the *Iliad* suggest, the cycle's sequence is not natural and indicates some kind of editorial intervention. The precise nature and date of this intervention, however, remain uncertain. Whereas explicit mention of the cycle as a whole is not found until late antiquity, the Trojan cycle seems to have been current at least as early as the 4th century BC, when the alternative beginning of the *Iliad* is first attested.

Although evidence of the existence of the Epic Cycle is too fragmentary to allow any certainty, it is likely that the cycle, along with the Homeric poems, represented a fixing of the oral tradition of epic in textual form, and this may be true of the other epics known from the early period. The transition to "secondary" epic seems to begin in the 5th century BC. Panyassis of Halicarnassus, who was a kinsman of the historian Herodotus, wrote a *Heraclea* that was well regarded by ancient critics. Although the few surviving fragments seem to reflect the conventional language of oral epic, we seem for the first time to be confronted with a poet who was clearly a historical personage. More noteworthy was the *Thebais* of Antimachus of Colophon, who flourished at the end of the 5th century BC. Although few fragments of any length survive, it is clear both from what little remains and from the ancient *testimonia* that Antimachus' work was characterized by a new sensibility that manipulated the language of epic in a selfconscious way. For subject matter Antimachus looked back to the Theban myths of the *Thebais* from the Epic Cycle, but his treatment seems to have anticipated the learned and allusive manner of Alexandrian poetry. Another notable development from about the same time is the work of Choerilus of Samos, whose *Persica* treats a historical subject, the Persian invasion of Greece. Hexametric poetry on historical subjects is first attested in the second half of the 8th century BC with the *Corinthiaca* ascribed to Eumelus, but Choerilus' *Persica* is the first known work to present what is clearly an epic treatment of such a theme. Although this poem survives only in brief fragments (some of them on papyrus), we are fortunate in having a few lines (fr. 317 *SH*) that seem to derive from a passage (possibly the proem) in which the poet addressed the issue of stylistic innovation.

It is difficult to gauge with certainty the degree to which epic flourished in the post-Classical world. There is considerable evidence for poems in hexameters – a number clearly of some length – and this has led many to conclude that the literary landscape of the Hellenistic world was richly populated with many epic poems that are now lost. Other scholars are more sceptical, arguing that hexametric poetry is not necessarily epic; these lost poems could easily have been accounts of historical events or panegyrics. Whatever the truth of the matter, it remains nonetheless true that the Hellenistic world provides some striking responses to the challenge posed by the Homeric poems. The most obvious of these is the *Argonautica* of Apollonius of Rhodes, a product of the scholarly world of the royal library at Alexandria and the only epic extant from the period between the Homeric poems and the imperial period. Apollonius' epic is a creative reworking of the Homeric poems that recounts the expedition of Jason and the Argonauts in quest of the golden fleece. Apollonius' response to Homer is flexible and subtle, drawing on Homeric language and narrative manner yet producing an epic very different from the Homeric poems, one that is very much rooted in the tastes and preoccupations of the literary circle of the Alexandrian court.

Equally notable was the epic written by Apollonius' contemporary, Callimachus, whose (now fragmentary) *Hecale* represented a striking attempt to produce a new kind of epic. The poem recounted the reception of Theseus by a humble old woman named Hecale on the night before the hero was to face the bull of Marathon. The time-frame of the poem seems to have covered little more than a single day, but through the careful use of digression, flashback, and foreshadowing, the poet offered considerable insight into the two central figures.

The focus on Hecale's humble hospitality rather than the celebrated combat with the bull seems to indicate a deliberate attempt to reposition epic tone; it is as though the *Odyssey* were to be retold from the point of view of Eumaeus or Erycleia.

The most influential successors to the Alexandrians were Roman poets such as Virgil, Ovid, and Lucan. But Greek epic continued to be composed in the imperial period. Quintus of Smyrna, writing in the 3rd century AD, produced the *Posthomerica* in 14 books, which dispenses with the familiar epic proem and continues directly from the last line of the *Iliad* to treat the Trojan myth that originally formed part of the Epic Cycle. On a more ambitious scale was the *Dionysiaca* of Nonnus of Panopolis. Composed in 48 books – the aggregate total of the *Iliad* and the *Odyssey* – this poem narrated the birth of Dionysus and his battles in India. Nonnus' elaborate language and highly rhetorical manner constitute an attempt to forge a new kind of epic style; in his detailed literary and mythological learning Nonnus is reminiscent of the Alexandrians. The influence of Nonnus can be detected in the small-scale epics on Trojan themes by Colluthus and Tryphiodorus.

CHRISTOPHER G. BROWN

See also Oral Tradition

Further Reading

Cameron, Alan, *Callimachus and His Critics*, Princeton, New Jersey: Princeton University Press, 1995

Hainsworth, J.B., *The Idea of Epic*, Berkeley: University of California Press, 1991

Huxley, G.L., *Greek Epic Poetry from Eumelos to Panyassis*, London: Faber, 1969

Koster, Severin, *Antike Epostheorien*, Wiesbaden: Steiner, 1970

Newman, John Kevin, *The Classical Epic Tradition*, Madison: University of Wisconsin Press, 1986

Ziegler, Konrat, *Das hellenistische Epos: ein vergessenes Kapitel griechischer Dichtung*, 2nd edition, Leipzig: Teubner, 1966

Byzantine and Modern

Epic is a notoriously difficult genre to define. It would be possible to argue that medieval and modern Greece have had no epic after the first Byzantine centuries, making this article a very short one. The medieval *Digenis Akritis* is as much a romance as it is an epic, while the epic deeds of the heroes of the revolution of 1821 were sung in the brief framework of the klephtic ballads. The most characteristic Greek epics of the 20th century, those of Kostis Palamas and Nikos Kazantzakis, also have a lyrical intensity (Palamas) and a philosophical depth (Kazantzakis) which would lead many to exclude them from the genre. However, if one retreats a little from the demand for fully fledged epics and looks for the characteristics of epic in poems which are shared with other genres, a considerable number may be found. The major characteristics of epic will here be assumed to be length, narrative, heroism, a number of books divisible by 12 (in the tradition of Homer and Virgil), and a sense that the poem concerned represents, in some totalizing way, a community at an important stage of its history.

In early Byzantium the literary tradition of the ancient epic was still alive, being used for histories of cities and encomia of famous personalities. There was also a genre of epic on mythical subjects, which reached its climax in the 4th century with the *Dionysiaca* of Nonnus of Panoplis, recounting in 48 books of hexameters the story of the god Dionysus in India. Despite their refined Classical form and subject matter, these poems show an increasingly medieval world view. After Nonnus, poems with epic tendencies abandoned the hexameter, which linguistic developments had made increasingly difficult to write in and restricted to an audience of a small caste of literati. Epic came to be composed in the Byzantine 12-syllable line: the best-known examples are a series of poems by George of Pisidia celebrating the achievements of the emperor Herakleios. After the 7th century the epic dimension of poetry is lost, to reappear, probably in the 12th century, in *Digenis Akritis*. The metre then used was the 15-syllable political verse – the national metre of modern Greece, used in all the poems discussed below until the end of the 19th century. During this period it may with some justification be felt that any medieval or modern Greek epic could only have been written in that metre.

At the beginning of the 20th century, when several of its manuscripts had been found, the medieval poem *Digenis Akritis* was hailed as the "national epic of the modern Greeks". However, it was soon discovered that such nationalist labels were inappropriate. The society represented in the poem is that of the Byzantine-Arab borders, and its hero acts as a policeman against bandits, mainly Christians. One may speculate that oral epics played some role in the genesis of the poem, and that at least one of them, the "Lay of the Emir" (Digenis's father), celebrated the exploits of an Arab raider against Byzantium. However, the axis of the poem's narrative and the inspiration of much of its heroism is the relationship between Digenis and his wife, whom most of the bandits are seeking to steal from him – and this is the basis for the categorization of the poem as a romance. It is unfortunate that neither of the surviving medieval manuscripts of *Digenis Akritis* is internally convincing, while later versions, based on a fusion of the two medieval poems, move steadily away from the epic.

The *Chronicle of the Morea* also deserves to be examined as an epic. The society concerned is that of the Greek Peloponnese under a ruling caste of western crusaders. The poem is expressly written to remind a generation growing up in the early 14th century of the exploits of their ancestors, who won the principality in 1205 after the Fourth Crusade. The poem is very long and has many heroic passages, together with others which suggest that the author was more at home with administration and documents than on the battlefield. No modern society is able to sympathize with the anti-Byzantine and anti-Orthodox spirit which pervades the Greek text of its oldest manuscript. There is a later text of the same type, the *Chronicle of the Tocco*, which celebrates the exploits of a family of Italian origin which ruled parts of the Ionian islands and Epirus in the early 14th century.

The *Erotokritos* of Vitsentzos Kornaros presents itself as a romance, a categorization that is uncontested. However, in this long poem there is also much that is heroic, and other epic characteristics (like the long parade of the champions in book 2), reminiscent of many epic catalogues. It is also plain that the choice of cities and areas from which the champions hail is made with care to represent a version of the thoughtworld of the mixed Venetian-Greek society of 17th-century Crete.

Primary epic has usually existed in close connection with the oral poetry of the area where it arises, and we must turn to Greek oral poetry of the late Turkish period, the first date at which it is possible to study surviving collected material. The chief tradition of the *demotika tragoudia*, the name by which Greek folk songs have come to be known, consists of short ballads, rarely exceeding 100 or so lines in length. Some of the most intense of these, as stated above, celebrate the klephts, the bandit freedom fighters who caused great troubles to the Turkish rulers of Greek lands and were to play a major role in the revolution of 1821. These are intensely heroic, but anti-epic in their brevity.

The prehistory of Greek folk song is, of course, a matter for speculation, for live oral traditions constantly change. This has not prevented a series of historians of Greek literature from linking a number of heroic ballads collected in the last two centuries with the epic romance *Digenis Akritis*, and calling them the Akritic Cycle. Jumping back half a millennium or more, these ballads have been judged in close proximity to the medieval poem, often as its source. As a result, it was once traditional to begin histories of modern Greek literature with a chapter on an epic cycle of Akritic ballads, most of the earliest surviving examples of which date from the 19th century. There are indeed many features which link these ballads to the world of Digenis, not least the appearance in some of them of the names Digenis and Akritis, though other names, like Konstantinos and Porphyrios, are just as common. But the medieval elements are combined with many later features, and the Akritic cycle certainly does not form a cohesive group. A few poems like the *Lay of Armouris* (which survives in a manuscript of similar date to the later of the medieval *Digenis Akritis* manuscripts) form a useful bridge between medieval literature and modern folk song. About most of the Akritic Cycle, however, though some distant relationship to the epic may be admitted, it is unwise to attempt precision over the nature of the connection.

At the margins of the ballads there survives a separate tradition of historical songs, chiefly found in the 20th century in Crete and Cyprus. It is tempting to link this tradition with a few post-Byzantine narrative poems with heroic themes, particularly that on Michael the Brave of Romania. One could make the hypothesis that these were imitations of oral narrative poetry, and trace the genre further back to the chronicles of *Tocco* and the *Morea*, which may well be in traditional Greek form in spite of their non-Greek stance. But this hypothetical narrative oral tradition, with its promise of an epic dimension, is as tenuous as the medieval Akritic Cycle of ballads.

When one turns from folk song to the written poems of the 19th century that are closest to the epic definition, two names stand out, Gerasimos Markoras and Athanasios Valaoritis. Both are among the demoticist successors of Solomos in the Ionian islands. Both take the brief form of the klephtic song and expand it, keeping the epic ideology and atmosphere. Markoras was inspired by the heroic self-sacrifice of the defenders of the Cretan monastery of Arkadi (1866) to write the poem *The Oath*, a moving example of the genre. Valaoritis used this style for several poems, including *Athanasios Diakos*, a poem with a klephtic subject to match its style. Valaoritis's work is often regarded as more verbose and less successful than that of Markoras.

Greece ended the 19th century in the grip of the Great Idea, the desire to extend the kingdom to cover all areas where Greeks lived. This was at times combined with weak political leadership, leading to crises culminating in that of 1897, a humiliating defeat at the hands of the Ottoman empire. The resultant mixture of aspiration and shame was the motive which led Palamas to write his two great "epico-lyrical" poems *The Dodecalogue of the Gypsy* (1907) and *The King's Flute* (1910). Both poems link the Great Idea to Byzantium and both are in 12 sections, though only the second is in 15-syllable verse. The first makes the astonishing choice of a gypsy hero, who in the first half rejects the foundations of Greek civilization and in the second presides over their rebuilding in a radically new form. The Byzantine setting gives opportunities for prophecy of the degradation of the Greece of Palamas's time. The gypsy hero is able to examine Hellenism with a ruthless external eye, without special interests or preconceived ideas: his portrayal is clearly influenced by Nietzsche's Superman, though Marxist ideas are also present. The poem demands radical change, if Greece's politics are to fulfil the national purposes. The scope is certainly epic, but there is also a smaller-scale lyric dimension, assisted by a free and flexible metrical form, which provides most of the best moments. *The King's Flute* portrays Byzantium at the height of its glory, and narrates a symbolic journey made by the emperor Basil II from Constantinople to Athens, clearly foreshadowing the continuation of Hellenic Byzantine tradition in modern Greece. There are many opportunities to refer to and quote early poetry in modern Greek, and especially folk song. These literary echoes are in the end a significant anti-epic feature of the poem.

The Great Idea led to the Asia Minor disaster, and a need to rethink Greece's place in the world, within the universal ideological ferment which followed World War I. In the years between 1924 and 1938 Nikos Kazantzakis was writing his epic *Odyssey*, in which all the competing currents of the time and all the varied sides of the poet's complex personality and intellect play major roles. There are 24 books and 33,333 lines. The plot begins with Odysseus' return to Ithaca, and continues with his further travels, events which are too many and complex for summary here. The scale is cosmic, the narrative subordinated to the poem's profound philosophical dimension, the language full of abstract and extreme demoticist forms, and the initial impact rather bewildering for most readers. In fact it has often been said that, despite its obvious epic claims, the *Odyssey* is an intensely personal poem, reflecting not so much the tortured world between the wars as the tortured reaction to that world of its creator, whose personality holds together many disparate elements. The poem was well served by its translator Kimon Friar, who made it somewhat more accessible in English than in the original.

The problems of the same period were faced by George Seferis in a quite different way, though using some elements of the epic framework. His poem *Mythistorema* was composed in 24 units and makes constant reference to the Homeric stories. But each unit is only a few lines in length, and the narrative

elements are fractured and distorted by various modernist techniques. Seferis obviously feels that this is as close to epic as his degenerate times could come.

MICHAEL JEFFREYS

Further Reading

Beaton, Roderick, *Folk Poetry of Modern Greece*, Cambridge and New York: Cambridge University Press, 1980

Jeffreys, Elizabeth (editor and translator), *Digenis Akritis: The Grottaferrata and Escorial Versions*, Cambridge and New York: Cambridge University Press, 1998

Kazantzakis, Nikos, *The Odyssey: A Modern Sequel*, translated by Kimon Friar, London: Secker and Warburg, and New York: Simon and Schuster, 1958

Palamas, Kostis, *The Twelve Lays of the Gipsy*, translated George Thomson, London: Lawrence and Wishart, 1969

Palamas, Kostis, *The King's Flute*, translated Theodore P. Stephanides and Georgios C. Katsimbalis, Athens: Kostes Palamas Institute, 1982

Vincent, A.L., "From Life to Legend: The Chronicles of Stavrinos and Palamidis on Michael the Brave", *Thisavrismata*, 25 (1995): pp. 165–238

Poetry, Lyric

Ancient

"Lyric" is a term commonly used to describe a wide range of Greek poetry; it is in fact applied to most poetic forms, excluding stichic hexameters and drama. The word itself suggests a more precise meaning: it is derived from *lyra* ("lyre"), and this indicates that lyric poetry was originally performed to the accompaniment of a stringed instrument, its range later being broadened to include iambic and elegiac poetry. The modern usage of the word can be imprecise. Lyric poetry was not considered a literary genre until the Hellenistic period; in early texts we occasionally find the word *melos* ("song"), and so "melic" is a convenient modern term often employed to designate lyric proper, although this obscures the fact that elegy also was sung. Greek lyric comprises both solo song (often called monody) and choral poetry, although it is unlikely that ancient scholars made this distinction. Apart from the victory odes of Pindar, no early Greek lyric poetry survives in an independent manuscript tradition, so that we are forced to work with fragmentary texts, some of which are preserved on lacunose (mutilated) pieces of papyrus and others quoted by later authors. Complete poems are all but nonexistent. Still, despite such incomplete evidence, considerable variety can be discerned in the extant lyric texts. These poems are characterized by elaborate metrical patterns, often organized in strophes consisting of three or four lines, sometimes in larger units of corresponding strophe and antistrophe followed by an epode of a different metrical character.

The performance of song can be imagined as taking place in a variety of settings, the performers being no doubt either soloists or communal groups. In the celebrated scene in the *Iliad* Achilles may be giving such a performance when he sings "the glorious deeds of men" while accompanying himself on the lyre (9. 186ff.), although that passage has regularly been understood as referring to heroic song in the epic tradition (the songs of Demodocus in *Odyssey*, 8 are similar). The *Iliad* also mentions songs that are familiar from the later lyric tradition: the paean, most familiar as a hymn to Apollo (1. 472–73, 22. 391), the *threnos* or formal lament (24. 720ff.), the *ailinos* or dirge (18. 570), and the *hymenaios* or wedding song (18. 493). These songs are all rooted in the religious traditions of Greek communities, and cult seems to have constituted one of the commonest settings for the performance of song, and, perhaps more important, the religious context seems to have influenced the character and development of principal lyric genres. This is not to say that song was confined to sacred occasions; doubtless it featured in many secular settings too. Brief fragments of soldiers' marching songs (*Poetae Milici Graeci*, edited Page, 1962, frr. 856 and 857) and songs sung at work (*PMG*, fr. 869) suggest that Greek life was alive with song – in fact, early Greek society has been characterized as a "song culture".

Modern knowledge of Greek lyric begins in the 7th century BC, and the period from then down to the 5th century BC witnessed an extraordinary flowering of lyric; in fact, this period is often called the Lyric Age of Greece. It is sometimes said that lyric poetry was "invented" at this time, but there was clearly already a long tradition of popular song, and the preservation of poetry beginning in the 7th century BC no doubt coincides with the relatively recent introduction of writing and its use for recording poetry, a process that also brought about the preservation of the Homeric poems. These early lyric texts became the objects of considerable scholarly interest, first in the school of Aristotle, and later in the great library at Alexandria, where the texts of the central poets were edited and annotated. It is largely through the eyes of Hellenistic scholarship that we today view the fragmentary remains of the work of these poets, and we still make considerable use of that system of classification and categories, although it is clear that it imposed distinctions that obscure as well as clarify the issues. Perhaps the most pernicious is the rigid formal distinction between monody and choral song. Stesichorus and Pindar are classified as choral poets, and their surviving works have been seen to reflect a tradition of choral song that also stands behind the choral poetry of Greek drama; but recent discussion has challenged this view, and it now seems likely that this firm classification may be misleading, and that both monodic and choral performance were possible.

Working from the texts preserved in the library at Alexandria, scholars established a canon of nine lyric poets of the Archaic and Classical period. This list is avowedly selective, purporting to include only the finest exponents of lyric poetry, and we know incidentally of a number of lesser figures. Nevertheless the Alexandrian canon gives some impression of the character and range of the poetic activity in the early period. In chronological sequence, first comes Alcman, who was active in Sparta in the mid-7th century BC. He is best known from an extensive papyrus fragment containing a portion of a long *partheneion* ("maiden song"), a genre for which the poet was well known, in which a chorus of nubile young girls sing a song that strikingly combines both traditional myth and self-presentation at a local religious festival. Much remains teasingly uncertain, and we are reminded of how closely bound much of early Greek poetry was to the occasion for which it was intended. Next we encounter Alcaeus and Sappho, who both composed monody on the island of Lesbos and represent what was clearly a distinctive Aeolic tradition of song. Alcaeus' poems seem to have been sung against the backdrop of the political factions in Mytilene at the close of the 7th century BC. Sappho lived during the same period, and the remains of her work afford a tantalizing glimpse into the private world of young women as they prepared for marriage. Stesichorus was born in Himera, in the western part of the Greek world. He seems to have been a contemporary of the Lesbian poets, but the fragments of his work betray little of his world; he composed large-scale lyric treatments of traditional myth, and his strongest affinities seem to be with the epic tradition. It has generally been assumed on formal grounds that Stesichorus' poetry was choral, but recent scholarship has increasingly been inclined to see these poems as the products of a tradition of solo song. Ibycus and Anacreon both seem to have moved in the world of the tyrants of the 6th century BC, and we can gain from the extant passages of their poetry an arresting impression of the aristocratic symposium. Simonides of Ceos, his kinsman Bacchylides, and the Theban Pindar are the great lyric voices of the Classical age; they composed in an impressive range of genres, but it is the surviving victory odes by Pindar and Bacchylides that give us the clearest picture of their art.

The latter part of the Classical period witnessed the decline of lyric poetry. The bold experiments of dithyrambic poets of the "new music" led to the subordination of poetry to music. In the Hellenistic period changes in social organization seem to have led to a severing of that important connection between occasion (especially religious festivals) and specific poetic forms. Once free of the need to produce the familiar forms for traditional occasions, poets were able to reconsider the established genres and give them new expression. During this period the epigram emerged as a remarkably flexible form, and quickly became the favoured medium of small-scale poetic expression. Lyric poems, however, continued to be composed, although many seem to have been prompted by special occasions and there is little impression of a continuous tradition of lyric song. From the imperial period little survives of importance. The *Anacreontea*, a collection of poems written after the manner of Anacreon, are variable in quality, but exerted considerable influence on western poetry. More interesting is Hadrian's freedman, Mesomedes, who lived in the 2nd century AD. A collection of 13 poems survives in a manuscript tradition that also preserves musical notation for four of them; there are also two poems preserved in the *Palatine Anthology* (14. 63 and 16. 323). Mesomedes employed a number of metres and attempted to produce novel verbal effects and colouring in poems on a striking range of subjects.

CHRISTOPHER G. BROWN

See also Song

Further Reading

Campbell, David A., *The Golden Lyre: The Themes of the Greek Lyric Poets*, London: Duckworth, 1983

Fowler, R.L., *The Nature of Early Greek Lyric: Three Preliminary Studies*, Toronto: University of Toronto Press, 1987

Gerber, Douglas E. (editor), *A Companion to the Greek Lyric Poets*, Leiden and New York: Brill, 1997

Johnson, W.R., *The Idea of Lyric: Lyric Modes in Ancient and Modern Poetry*, Berkeley: University of California Press, 1982

Byzantine and Modern

Byzantine poetry is Christian poetry. Although educated men of the eastern Roman empire continued to display their erudition and training in the writing of Attic Greek on ancient (mythological or historical) themes, even they knew that their tradition was suffocating them. In fact the Greek language had played a crucial role in the diffusion of Christianity after 313 and slowly the simple style of the Septuagint and New Testament began to be used for poetry of religious feeling.

The pagan traditions were dealt a near-death blow when the emperor Justinian I closed the schools of Athens in 529, and so this is a good date to start calling Greek literature "Byzantine"; it lasted until 1453, when Constantinople fell to the Ottoman Turks. Classical mythology was supplanted by the rapidly developing Christian mythology, and Byzantine poetry, even of the most formal kind, could appeal to the average citizen, for whom religion was meat and drink.

The change of the metrical system from Classical quantity to modern stress and syllable count caused poets more trouble than changes in diction and grammar. Amazingly, the poems of the influential George of Pisidia observed both systems simultaneously; no wonder his production was limited. His most popular poem praised the victory of his patron, emperor Herakleios (610–41), over the Persians. Since George, the rhythm of spoken Greek has been the rule.

Formal Byzantine poetry took three main forms, all lyrical. In the 4th and 5th centuries short hymns, or *troparia*, were most popular. In the 6th and 7th centuries these yielded to long metrical sermons, called kontakia. And in the 8th and 9th centuries cycles of hymns, called canons, were the rule. Much religious poetry was set to music and it is poorer read silently on the page. Luckily, some of it, such as the magnificent *Akathistos* hymn (date unknown, but early) is still sung in church.

The greatest of the kontakia poets was Romanos the Melodist, possibly a converted Jew from Emesa, living in the 6th century. His music, now lost, was as renowned as his verses, which are lyrical, clear, rich in metaphor, and dramatic. But the flaws that make Byzantine poetry less popular than it deserves are evident in him: grandiloquence and love of size.

The canon, which usually consists of eight or nine long odes, did nothing to curb this inflation. Probably the greatest writer of canons was St John of Damascus (*fl.*730); deeply religious, he nevertheless revived Classical metres, perhaps because music was flooding the poetic tradition. Also important was Kassia (*fl.*840), Byzantium's only poetess. Her great poem on Mary Magdalene is sung for the evening of Tuesday in Holy Week. It concludes:

who will trace out my multitude of sins and the abysses
of thy judgements, my saviour of souls?
Do not pass by thy slave
in thy boundless mercy.

Symeon the New Theologian (949–1022) is often considered Byzantium's greatest poet after Romanos. Though overlong, his hymns are full of undoubted feeling. Symeon introduced the metre which now became the rule for 800 years.

This is the so-called "political verse", a 15-syllable iambic line similar to the English fourteener. But after Symeon, it seems, there was nowhere to go.

Among the educated, the refined Hellenistic tradition maintained its appeal, and it still breathed in the epigram. The *Palatine Anthology*, comprising poems from the 1st century BC to the 10th century AD, was compiled in the 10th century and added to in the 14th. Poems worthy of their predecessors were composed by Agathias Scholasticus (536–82) and Paul the Silentiary (*fl.*563), and personal lyric poetry never vanished entirely. But after Symeon inner necessity in general gave way to rhetorical display.

The importance of anonymous folk poetry kept growing and came to a rich flowering during the Tourkokratia; because Ottoman domination forestalled the Renaissance and intellectual and religious development ceased, the common ancestral roots thrust deeper. Perhaps the earliest and most remarkable of these productions was the epic cycle *Digenis Akritis*, about a heroic Byzantine borderguard fighting the Saracens. The cycle's origins – before the 10th century – are lost in time, and many of its folk songs were not written down until the 19th century. After the Venetians conquered Constantinople in 1204, many popular verse romances were turned out. The folk poetry of Turkish Greece is extensive: love songs, satiric comments on politics, laments, imitations of foreign models, evocations of place, wrestlings with death, and much more: it is from this fertile loam that modern Greek poetry was waiting to spring. It needed only one more nutrient: freedom.

It might have started in Crete, which evaded Ottoman domination until 1669, and where higher education was in Italian. Vitsentzos Kornaros (1553–1617), who wrote Greek in Latin letters, composed a long romance, *Erotokritos*, that became for the Cretans what the *Iliad* was for Classical Greece; Cretan folk musicians perform it to this day. Though based on a French work, its diction is the most fluent, lyrical, and natural since the Hellenistic age. The ease and variety of the flow in strict metre and rhyme keep it fresh and delightful throughout its elaborate plot turnings. A medieval love story, it is full of wisdom:

The Cycles with their circling paths that rise and fall aright;
Time's Wheel that comprehends the Whole, from depth up
    to the height,
And bears the whims of Destiny and never then turns back,
But as it whirls all Good and Evil whirl within its track,
The clanging clash of angry war, the spur of hate and spite,
The rapturous embracing and the languorous kiss by
    night ...

Erotokritos remained Greece's national poem until Elytis' *Axion Esti*. Had the Turks not stifled this remarkable efflorescence (it includes poetic drama and El Greco), Cretan dialect might have prevailed.

Erotokritos, klephtic ballads, vigorous folk songs, heroic narratives, and freedom – something had to come of this. Dionysios Solomos (1798–1857), the father of modern Greek poetry, lived in Corfu, which was never under the Turks. Critics call the poets of the Heptanese, of whom he was chief, the School of the Ionian islands. Like his model Kornaros, he was educated in Italian; as an adult he learned to write Greek from Greece's first prime minister, Charilaos Trikoupis.

However imperfect, a more limpid Greek has never been written. It is no coincidence that his output coincided with the War of Independence of 1821. Though he never visited free Greece, its spirit suffuses his work much more than it does that of the Romantic poets of Constantinople, who relocated to form the Old School of Athens. The first stanzas of Solomos's *Ode to Liberty* are now the Greek national anthem, and his *The Free Besieged*, about the heroic resistance at Missolonghi, is often accounted the greatest modern Greek poem. His lines on the Turkish massacre of Chios rival Simonides.

> On the deepblack ridge of Psara
> Glory walking in solitude
> meditates on the bright young heroes
> and on her hair she wears a wreath
> woven of the scanty grasses
> remaining on that desolate land.

Solomos also introduced European metres new to Greek. Though his work is mostly fragments, every line has proved a seed for the future.

The new poetry was an adventure, but what were its influences, diction, forms, and themes? Like Solomos, whom he did not know, Andreas Kalvos (1792–1869) was educated in Italian, and lived for a while in Corfu; born in Zakynthos, he also lived in Italy, France, Switzerland, and England. He published only two books, of ten odes each, and they are so original that, though he was long neglected, modern poets continue to turn to him for a genuine exaltation of Greek; he devised one way to write Greek poetry when nobody was quite sure how to do it. His freedom from fixed metre helped too. As an imagist, Kalvos is supreme and startlingly original:

> The circlechasing sun
> enriches the sea
> with the scent
> of golden citrons

Elytis wrote of him: "He was – both for the uncompromising line of his life and for his original poetics – the only one who could be considered our distant forerunner."

Aristotle Valaoritis (1824–79) continued the values of the Ionian School. Rigorously demotic and exuberantly romantic, he had a deep and immediate influence, especially on the New School of Athens, which produced much enduring poetry. The New School, which dominated the later 19th century, made a conscious attempt to be both Parnassian and demotic, both classicist and folkloristic; it took the whole tradition of Greece for its subject. Though many fine poets wrote under its banner, its great figure was Kostis Palamas (1859–1943), who went beyond the parameters of the school in theme and time and whose funeral was a state affair. His huge output includes long poems (his masterpiece is *The Twelve Books of the Gypsy*), songs, meditations on philosophical, historical, and social themes, and critical works. His great poetry collection, *Life Immovable*, is both intensely lyrical and vigorously masculine. With Palamas we enter the 20th century, which has produced as much and as various first-rate Greek poetry as any.

Like Solomos and Kalvos, Constantine Cavafy (1863–1933) had imperfect Greek. He was born in Alexandria of a Constantinopolitan family, was educated mostly in England, and was not a Greek citizen. Spending his life as a minor official in Alexandria, he produced a small body of work that, for all its hard diffidence, first strikes the modern note, influencing dozens of modern writers. "I am not a Greek", he said, "but a Hellene." Though he clearly learned something from Robert Browning, he sounds like no previous poet; Seferis thought he got it from Suidas. If Solomos introduced a singing folk-like language, new themes, and high vigour, Cavafy was a dry, scholarly poet of the Greek diaspora, whose careful rhythms resemble prose and who, eschewing imagery (simile and metaphor) entirely, relies on direct statement. The notes of alienation, irony, and isolation later struck by Eliot and Seferis were first struck by him.

> No new lands will you find, you'll find no other seas.
> The city will follow you. To the same streets you will
> turn again. And you will age in the same neighbourhoods;
> and in these same houses you will grow grey.

W.H. Auden wrote that Cavafy had "a unique perspective on the world", and that perspective, though it carefully cherishes and builds on Hellenism, has travelled everywhere.

Influenced by French Symbolism and later Surrealism, modern Greek poetry developed rapidly in Athens; for all its being a tiny country, Greece has produced an extraordinary number of world-class poets. Although Seferis and Elytis – both recipients of the Nobel Prize for Literature – are deservedly the most famous, such fine poets as the suicidally gloomy Karyotakis (1896–1928), the exuberantly dithyrambic Sikelianos (1884–1951), and the imagistic and much-translated Ritsos (1909–90) are only the apex of an immense pyramid of poetic activity. And the novelist Kazantzakis wrote, among other works in verse, a frenzied philosophical continuation of the *Odyssey*, longer than the original. As with nearly all Greek writers, the care and passionate advocacy of the Greek language was of first importance to him.

The middle of the 20th century, during which Greece suffered so much from war and foreign occupation, was dominated by the diplomat-poet George Seferis (1900–71), a symbolist who, through essays, translation, and his own masterpiece *Mythistorema* (1935), brought T.S. Eliot's influence into Greek. Overburdened with exile and hopelessness, Seferis's poetic protagonist continually finds salvation in aesthetic values:

> We brought back
> these carved reliefs of a humble art.

A very erudite man, constantly wrestling with his heritage, he wrote the leanest Greek of all, and helped fix its Protean slipperiness.

Where Seferis was chaste in diction, pessimistic in theme, ironic and allusive in tone, and faint in rhythm, Odysseus Elytis (1911–96), for all his craft, seems to be overflowing with Greece, its eros, landscapes, traditions, language. His book-long poem, *Axion Esti*, especially as set to music by Theodorakis, has helped Greeks to engage their tradition as a living organism. Although Elytis is full of the Aegean – its islands, girls, skies, depths, flora – he also wrote about the war, about history, about childhood, about love. In his long career he kept experimenting, writing mostly in free verse, but also in various species of closed measures, in slang, in formal diction – he changed strategy with every book. So great was his presence that today's young poets have had to avert their eyes from him for a long while before yielding. A song from his *Axion*

Esti has become for Greeks an anthem of independence and is the best-known contemporary poem:

A solitary swallow * and Spring's great worth is found
It takes a lot of work * to make the sun turn round
Their shoulders to the Wheels * it takes a thousand dead
It also takes the living * to offer up their blood.

God my greatest Masterworker * high in the mountains
   You built me
God my greatest Masterworker * You have surrounded
   me with sea!

Sensuous in his youth, in old age he wrote profound meditations on death.

Throughout the Byzantine and modern periods – some 1500 years – Greece produced little dramatic or satiric verse of value. But the fount of lyricism has never ceased flowing, and an astonishingly prolific record of a people's and a language's intense joys and sorrows remains for us to read for ever.

JEFFREY CARSON

See also Epigram, Hymnography

Further Reading

Baldwin, Barry, *An Anthology of Byzantine Poetry*, Amsterdam: Gieben, 1985

Bien, Peter, *Three Generations of Greek Writers: Introductions to Cavafy, Kazantzakis, Ritsos*, Athens: Efstathiadis, 1983

Cavafy, Constantine, *Collected Poems*, translated by Edmund Keeley and Philip Sherrard, Princeton, New Jersey: Princeton University Press, and London: Hogarth Press, 1975; revised edition Princeton, New Jersey: Princeton University Press, 1992

Cavafy, Constantine, *The Complete Poems of Cavafy*, edited and translated by Rae Dalven, New York: Harcourt Brace, 1976

Elytis, Odysseus, *Open Papers*, translated by Olga Broumas and T. Begley, Port Townsend, Washington: Copper Canyon Press, 1995

Elytis, Odysseus, *The Collected Poems of Odysseus Elytis*, translated by Jeffrey Carson and Nikos Sarris, Baltimore: Johns Hopkins University Press, 1997

Friar, Kimon (editor and translator), *Modern Greek Poetry*, New York: Simon and Schuster, 1973

Kazantzakis, Nikos, *The Odyssey: A Modern Sequel*, translated by Kimon Friar, London: Secker and Warburg, and New York: Simon and Schuster, 1958

Kazhdan, Alexander P. (editor), *The Oxford Dictionary of Byzantium*, 3 vols, New York and Oxford: Oxford University Press, 1991

Keeley, Edmund and Peter Bien (editors), *Modern Greek Writers: Solomos, Matesis, Palamas, Cavafy, Kazantzakis, Seferis, Elytis*, Princeton, New Jersey: Princeton University Press, 1972

Liddell, Robert, *Cavafy: A Critical Biography*, London: Duckworth, 1974; New York: Schocker, 1976

Lorenzatos, Zissimos, *The Lost Center and Other Essays in Greek Poetry*, Princeton, New Jersey: Princeton University Press, 1980

Mackridge, Peter A. (editor), "Greece: The Modern Voice", special issue of *Review of National Literatures*, 5/2 (Fall 1974)

Preminger, Alex *et al.* (editors), *The New Princeton Encyclopedia of Poetry and Poetics*, 3rd edition, Princeton, New Jersey: Princeton University Press, 1993 (articles on Byzantine poetry and Greek poetry)

Ricks, David, *Byzantine Heroic Poetry*, Bristol: Bristol Classical Press, and New Rochelle, New York: Caratzas, 1990

Ritsos, Yannis, *Ritsos in Parentheses*, edited and translated by Edmund Keeley, Princeton, New Jersey: Princeton University Press, 1979

Romanos le Melode, *Hymnes par Romanos le Mélode*, edited by J. Grosdidier de Matons, Paris: Cerf, 1964–81 (French and Greek)

Seferis, George, *On the Greek Style: Selected Essays in Poetry and Hellenism*, Boston: Little Brown, 1966; London: Bodley Head, 1967

Seferis, George, *Collected Poems*, edited and translated by Edmund Keeley and Philip Sherrard, Princeton, New Jersey: Princeton University Press, 1981; London: Anvil Press Poetry, 1982

Sherrard, Philip, *The Marble Threshing Floor: Studies in Modern Greek Poetry*, London: Vallentine Mitchell, and Fair Lawn, New Jersey: Essential, 1956

Stanford, W.B., *The Ulysses Theme: A Study in the Adaptability of a Traditional Hero*, 2nd edition, Oxford: Blackwell, 1963; New York: Barnes and Noble, 1964

Trypanis, C.A. (editor), *The Penguin Book of Greek Verse*, Harmondsworth: Penguin, 1971

Viljamaa, Toivo, *Studies in Greek Encomiastic Poetry of the Early Byzantine Period*, Helsinki: Fennica, 1968

Political History to 490 BC

Although a preoccupation with defining personal and collective relationships both within and between communities can be assumed to date back at least as far as the Neolithic period, the current state of knowledge makes it impossible to write a coherent political "prehistory" of Greece prior to the emergence of the polis (city state). While archives of Linear B tablets are now known from Mycenae, Tiryns, Midea, Thebes, Pylos, Knossos, and Chania, they are chiefly administrative records and inventories of commodities stored in the palaces; no texts have yet emerged that parallel the royal decrees and diplomatic documents of the Near East. What is known is that the Mycenaean palaces employed large workforces of specialized labourers (including slaves) dominated by an administrative hierarchy under a *wa-na-ka*, sometimes assisted by a *ra-wa-ke-ta*. The Pylos tablets reveal that the "kingdom" of Pylos was divided into two provinces, governed by a *da-mo-ko-ro* and a *du-ma*, and that each province was further subdivided into districts under the authority of a *ko-re-te* who was assisted by a *po-ro-ko-re-te*. Nothing is recorded about the relationships that existed between palatial centres, though a recent tablet from Thebes appears to attest the presence of a Lacedaemonian.

Even less is known about the succeeding Dark Age due to the complete absence of literary material prior to the adoption of the Phoenician alphabet in the 8th century BC. Inferences for this period are largely based on archaeological investigation or analysis of institutional forms and social structures in the Homeric epics (though there is considerable debate as to whether Homeric society is in any sense historical and, if so, whether it reflects the social and political conditions of the Dark Age, the 8th century, the 7th century, or an amalgam of each). Scholarly opinion is divided as to whether Dark Age society was predominantly hierarchical or egalitarian and whether the communities of this period were subject to individuals whose authority derived from personal charisma and social standing or – as the Homeric poems and later political theorists suggest – to hereditary monarchies. Consensus remains elusive, though recent interpretations of the archaeological evidence incline towards the view that Dark Age communities were not as small as previously assumed and may have been characterized by a weak form of ranking, though

31. Principal sites of the Dark Age and Geometric period

political leadership was probably an achieved rather than ascribed status.

The political history of Archaic Greece is essentially the history of the polis (plural: poleis), though in western Greece the prevailing form of organization was the *ethnos* – a large territorial entity characterized by scattered settlement and loose "federal" ties between communities, particularly in the religious and military domains. The word polis is conventionally translated as "city state" to indicate its dual status as both (1) an urban centre housing a single, unitary decision-making body whose authority extends over not only the settlement itself but also the surrounding territory (including second-order habitation sites) and (2) a community of citizens, fully enfranchised or not, who are entitled to own property within the territory of the polis and whose citizen status is predicated on either agnatic (patrilineal) descent from a citizen or a grant of citizenship from the central authority. While some possible

continuities with features of the Mycenaean states cannot entirely be discounted and although poleis continued to be founded throughout the whole period of Greek antiquity, the crucial era for the formation of this type of organization would appear to be the 8th century BC. Archaeological evidence in particular indicates that this was a time of increasing settlement nucleation – perhaps accompanied by a more sedentary way of life and demographic increase which would itself necessitate a greater division of labour and specialization – as well as of a new preoccupation with defining territoriality through the foundation of sanctuaries in both urban settings and marginal rural areas.

The 8th century also witnessed the commencement of colonization of areas outside the Aegean and a symbiotic relationship has been posited between this and the emergence of the polis. The processes of social exclusion through which the polis was forged may have created a new group of outsiders who decided to form communities overseas, but the immediate imperatives of colonial foundation – settlement planning, allotment of land, and procedures for decision making – probably exerted a feedback effect on the communities of the Greek mainland.

The rise of the polis should not be confused with the advent of democracy (the Athenian democracy hardly predates the reforms of Cleisthenes at the end of the 6th century BC, or in its more familiar "radical" form the measures undertaken by Ephialtes and Pericles in the middle of the 5th century) and ultimate authority in the poleis of the Archaic period invariably rested with the elite. The provisions of the Spartan "Great Rhetra" (conventionally – though not uncontroversially – dated to the mid-7th century BC) imply that deliberation and the right of veto lay with the two kings and their advisory council of 28 elders, drawn from the wealthier families, while the function of the popular assembly was merely to accede to the motions placed before it. A law from the temple of Apollo at Cretan Dreros, dated to 650–600 BC and stipulating that the office of kosmos could not be held by the same individual twice within a ten-year period, makes it clear that the function of early legislation was concerned less with defining rights and privileges within the citizen body as a whole than it was with regulating the distribution of power within the elite classes.

The word demos, which in democracies of the Classical period signified the entire citizen body, is in this period employed to denote those who are not of elite status, and the poetry of Hesiod, Theognis, and Solon testifies to a sharp division between elite and non-elite groups as well as to the growing importance of wealth (as opposed to birth) in recruitment to the governing classes. One of the many grievances which the demos held against the "bribe-devouring lords" who governed them (Hesiod, *Works and Days*, 38–39) appears to have been the fact that there was no clearcut dividing line between poor citizens and slaves: among the social problems that the Athenian statesman Solon had to address in the early 6th century BC was the practice whereby poorer citizens took out loans on the security of their person, risking enslavement in the event of default.

From the 7th century BC onwards certain members of the elite recognized that popular discontent could be mobilized for political ends and appealed to the demos for support against their rivals in establishing tyrannical regimes (the thesis that tyrannies emerged as a result of a sudden radical reorganization of military equipment and tactics – the so-called "hoplite reform" – is less religiously held today). The earliest tyrannies are attested in the area of the Corinthian isthmus: at Corinth itself Cypselus seized power *c.*655 BC; at about the same time Orthagoras gained control at Sicyon; and at Megara Theagenes established a tyranny *c.*640 BC. Towards the end of the 7th century, tyrannies were established at Mytilene on the island of Lesbos and Miletus on the coast of Asia Minor and in the middle of the 6th century Polycrates seized power on the island of Samos. A tyranny is attributed to Pheidon at Argos, though dates for this enigmatic figure range from the 8th to the 6th century BC. About 630 BC Theagenes of Megara assisted his son-in-law Cylon in a coup at Athens, but the attempt was unsuccessful and Athens remained free from tyranny until *c.*546 BC when, on his third attempt, Pisistratus established himself as tyrant. The reason for Cylon's failure and

Pisistratus' two failed attempts is probably that the vast and differentiated territory of Attica militated against any unified sentiments of collective consciousness among the Athenian demos (Pisistratus' eventual success was achieved through a mercenary force rather than the support of the demos). Popular support for tyrannical regimes was often shortlived as rival elite claimants also joined in courting the favour of the demos. Alternatively, elite factions might call upon outside help: the Spartan expulsion of Pisistratus' son Hippias in 510 BC was reputedly instigated by the wealthy Athenian family of the Alcmeonidae.

Relationships between poleis in the early Archaic period are characterized by the counteracting tendencies of aggregation and competition and conducted mainly at the level of the elite – the majority of citizens constituted a landbound peasantry whose horizons rarely exceeded the territorial limits of the polis, though specialist craftsmen, merchants, and mercenaries would often seek employment in other (Greek and non-Greek) cities. The elite classes maintained more cosmopolitan networks of support through guest friendships (*xenia*) and intermarriage (*epigamia*). This policy is demonstrated most clearly by the tyrants: guest friendships existed between Pisistratus and Lygdamis of Naxos (Herodotus, 1. 61), between Periander of Corinth and Thrasybulus of Miletus (Herodotus, 1. 20), and between Polycrates of Samos and Amasis, pharaoh of Egypt (Herodotus, 2. 182), while intermarriage guaranteed bonds of friendship between Periander and Procles of Epidaurus (Herodotus, 3. 50) and Theagenes and Cylon (Thucydides, 1. 126). The practice was not, however, limited to the tyrants alone: Isagoras, the Athenian archon (chief magistrate) for 508/07 BC, was a guest friend of the Spartan king Cleomenes (Herodotus, 5. 70); the Athenian Alcmeonidae contracted a guest friendship with King Croesus of Lydia (Herodotus, 6. 125); and among suitors from the most important families of Greece, it was the Alcmeonid Megacles who won the hand of Agariste, daughter of the Sicyonian tyrant Cleisthenes (Herodotus, 6. 130).

Aside from forging bonds of friendship, the elites also competed among themselves to win *kleos* (repute) and *kudos*. Archaeological evidence from Olympia indicates that the origins of the sanctuary date back to the 10th or even 11th century BC, long before the formal institution of the Olympic Games (traditionally dated to 776 BC), and that the sanctuary originally served as an arena for competitive display through the dedication and circulation of prestige goods. Such conspicuous consumption served to assert an individual's status in the eyes of his peers as well as to guarantee his authority in his home community.

In the 6th century BC, however, elite habits came to be increasingly integrated within the more collective framework of the polis. The practice of contracting individual guest friendships was usurped and institutionalized at a civic level by appointing an official *proxenos* ("consul") in another city (a Locrian is already described as a *proxenos* of Corfu on a limestone cenotaph dated to 625–600 BC). New regulations regarding *epigamia* stipulated the communities into which one might marry, and the glory that individuals won in agonistic competitions at the Panhellenic sanctuaries of Olympia, Delphi, Isthmia, and Nemea was now redirected to reflect credit on the victor's polis. Cities, alongside individuals, vied with one another to dedicate expensive offerings and treasury buildings at the most important sanctuaries of Greece. These shared cult places provided a locus for the proclamation of common bonds between Greek cities, but it was those perceived commonalities that provided a defined framework for poleis to publicize not only their parity but also their distinct identities.

Warfare was simply a more violent manifestation of this agonistic spirit which employed shared rules and ritualized norms within which poleis might assert their independent identities. One of the earliest wars of which we hear is the Lelantine War fought between the neighbouring Euboean cities of Eretria and Chalcis, probably towards the beginning of the 7th century BC. Thucydides (1. 15) asserts that the rest of the Hellenic world participated in the conflict through alliances with one of the main protagonists, and isolated notices from Hesiod, Archilochus, Theognis, Herodotus, Plutarch, and Strabo have been ingeniously marshalled to draw a picture of a conflict between two massive trading leagues; in reality, however, it is far from clear that each of the sources refers to the same war and it is more likely that the story of an original conflict between two neighbouring cities was exaggerated over time by a tradition that cast the Lelantine War in similar terms to the Trojan War. Certainly wars in the Archaic period generally involved powerful neighbours – for instance, the mid-6th-century "Battle of the Fetters" between Sparta and Tegea (Herodotus, 1. 66) or the long-running dispute between Argos and Sparta over the Cynourian region of the Peloponnese, which may already have run intermittently for about a century by the time of the mid-6th century when each side put forward 300 picked men to fight a "Battle of Champions" (Herodotus, 1. 82). Warfare in this period required the preselection of a time and place (generally a level plain) at which two armies of citizen hoplites (heavy infantry) confronted one another; in conforming to prescribed rules and rites both as preliminaries to the battle and in the conduct of the battle itself, hoplite armies played out a regulated (if lethal) game to determine which city was the victor.

Polis autonomy was also guaranteed within the leagues and amphictionies ("dwellers around") that are said to have emerged during the Archaic period. Though its origins are hazy, one of the earliest is said to have been the amphictiony of central Greek states, organized around the sanctuary of Demeter at Anthela, which is thought to have been the predecessor of the Delphic Amphictiony charged with administering the sanctuary of Pythian Apollo. Strabo (8. 6. 14) refers to a Calaurian amphictiony, centred on the sanctuary of Poseidon on Calauria (modern Poros) and including the cities of Hermione, Epidaurus, Aegina, Athens, Prasiae, Nauplia, Orchomenus, and, later, Sparta and Argos, though there is no independent testimony for this amphictiony prior to the Hellenistic period. By the beginning of the 6th century, if not earlier, six Dorian cities in Asia Minor had organized themselves into a league (the Dorian Hexapolis) centred on the sanctuary of Apollo Triopios near Cnidus, while 12 Ionian cities constituted a similar federation (the Ionian Dodecapolis) focused on the sanctuary of Poseidon Heliconius at Mycale. Towards the end of the 6th century BC Sparta created a new hegemonic Peloponnesian league in which allies were required to follow wherever Sparta led by land or sea.

It is likely that an increase in the incidence of hostilities between poleis, together with the need to field larger citizen armies, contributed to growing calls for a broader base of political inclusion. An inscription from the island of Chios attests to a "popular council" (as opposed to an aristocratic council) by 575–550 BC, and a few decades earlier the Athenian Solon is said to have established a new probouleutic council (boule) of 400 which coexisted with the aristocratic council of the Areopagus, though it is unclear exactly how powerful this council was prior to its reconstitution as the Council of 500 under Cleisthenes in the last decade of the 6th century and the reorganization of the Areopagus under Ephialtes in the 460s. Solon also established the right of appeal to popular jury courts and formalized the admission of the lowest property class of Athenian citizens (the thetes) to the popular assembly, though the aristocracy continued to exert considerable influence – particularly in rural areas – until Cleisthenes engineered a radical reorganization of the citizen body into demes distributed among ten new tribes.

The rise of Lydia and especially Persia in the 6th century BC had profound consequences for the cities of eastern Greece. By 546 the cities of Colophon, Magnesia, Smyrna, and Ephesus had fallen to the Lydians, and following the defeat of Croesus of Lydia the Greek cities of Asia Minor became the possession of the Persian king Cyrus the Great. In about 520 Cyrus' successor Darius I assessed the cities for tribute within the new satrapies that he had established and launched attacks on the islands of the Aegean as well as advancing into Thrace, where he accepted the submission of the Macedonian king Amyntas c.500 BC. In 499 the Ionians initiated their ill-fated revolt from Persian dominion, and Herodotus (5. 97) argues that it was the support afforded the Ionian rebels by Athens and Eretria on this occasion that provoked Darius' successful assault of Eretria and unsuccessful landing at Marathon in 490. The Athenian victory against overwhelming forces at Marathon served as a key founding-myth of Athenian identity throughout the 5th and 4th centuries BC.

JONATHAN M. HALL

See also Archaic Period, City State, Colonization, Dark Age, Mycenaeans, Sanctuaries, Tyranny, Warfare

Further Reading

Jeffery, L.H., *Archaic Greece: The City-States, c.700–500 BC*, New York: St Martin's Press, 1976; London: Methuen, 1978

Morgan, Catherine, *Athletes and Oracles: The Transformation of Olympia and Delphi in the Eighth Century BC*, Cambridge and New York: Cambridge University Press, 1990

Murray, Oswyn, *Early Greece*, 2nd edition, Cambridge, Massachusetts: Harvard University Press, 1993

Osborne, Robin, *Greece in the Making, 1200–479 BC*, London and New York: Routledge, 1996

Settis, Salvatore (editor), *I Greci: Storia, Cultura, Arte, Società*, vol. 2: *Una Storia Greca*, part 1: *Formazione*, Turin: Einaudi, 1996

Snodgrass, Anthony, *Archaic Greece: The Age of Experiment*, London: Dent, and Berkeley: University of California Press, 1980

Starr, Chester G., *Individual and Community: The Rise of the Polis, 800–500 BC*, Oxford and New York: Oxford University Press, 1986

Political History 490–323 BC

The immediate effect of the Athenian victory at Marathon was to prompt Darius' son Xerxes to launch a new and greater invasion in 480 BC. His force, incorporating various Greek contingents including the Thebans, was repulsed by the Greeks, under the hegemony of the Spartans but without the Argives, in the battles of Artemisium, Salamis (both 480), Plataea, and Mycale (both 479). These victories, and the glorious defeat at Thermopylae (where the fighting on land coincided with the naval battle at Artemisium), were of utmost importance in the fostering of Greek self-belief and were commemorated in verse, prose, art, and architecture for centuries afterwards. But they are also indicative of two of the major themes of Greek history in the 5th and 4th centuries BC: the persistent external threat posed to the Greeks by the Persian empire, and the constant internal, interstate rivalries which served to undermine Greek political stability.

Athens was the first state to assert this new-found confidence, when the Spartans withdrew from the command of the Greek forces in 487. The Spartan king Pausanias captured Byzantium, but his arrogant behaviour led to his recall to Sparta. A new alliance was formed, comprising the Ionian states, most of the Aegean islands, and cities of the Hellespont and Propontis regions, with a base on Apollo's island of Delos (hence the modern title "Delian League") and under the leadership of Athens, which claimed to be the Ionians' mother city. Delos housed the treasury of the league, to which most of the members paid an annual tribute (others, most notably Chios, Lesbos, and Samos, provided ships). The history of the *pentekontaetia* (roughly the 50-year period 480–430 BC) is dominated by the Athenians' increasing hold on the Delian League and its transformation into an Athenian empire, and the largely ineffectual opposition to Athens by the Spartans and their allies (loosely termed the Peloponnesian League). Although the early campaigns of the league were aimed at dislodging the Persians from western Asia Minor, culminating in the Athenian general Cimon's victory at the river Eurymedon (466), almost from the start Athenian ambitions were barely disguised. Cimon's coercion of Skyros (c.475) was followed by that of Carystus in Euboea (c.472), Naxos was forcibly prevented from seceding (c.467), and Thasos was harshly dealt with after revolting in protest against Athenian interference in Thasos' mainland possessions (465). Athenian confidence was further fuelled by the development of the democracy. Cleisthenes' democratic reforms of 508/07 BC were buttressed by the rising importance of the board of ten elected generals at the expense of the archons, and by the reforms of Ephialtes in 462, in which the powers of the Areopagus were divided between the assembly, the council, and the law courts. Soon after, Pericles introduced pay for the jurors and members of the council, and in 451 he passed a law which restricted citizenship to those who were the legitimate sons of an Athenian mother as well as father.

The Spartans, meanwhile, were unable to check the expansion of Athens. Although the threat of Argos, Sparta's main rival in the Peloponnese, had been crushed in 494, internal problems with the Arcadians were followed by a serious helot revolt after an earthquake c.465. Cimon led a force of Athenians to assist the Spartans, but in his absence Ephialtes passed his reforms and Cimon was dismissed. After subduing the revolt, Sparta finally took action to secure its interests in central Greece, but Athens' main opponents during the First Peloponnesian War (c.461–446) were the Corinthians. Corinthian aggression led Megara to leave the Peloponnesian League and side with Athens, and Corinth suffered heavy losses in the early stages of the war. Athenian power now reached its peak in Greece and the Aegean under the leadership of Pericles: Aegina was forced into the league (458), and after an initial defeat at Tanagra had been reversed at Oenophyta, Boeotia came under Athenian control (457–446). The Athenians were confident enough to pursue war on two fronts, dispatching an expedition to Cyprus in 460 which was sent on to Egypt to support Inarus' revolt against Persia, but this force was destroyed in 454. The league treasury was subsequently transferred from Delos to Athens, and the Peace of Callias was concluded with the Persians in 450, ending open hostilities until 413 (it is not quite certain that a formal peace was made). Back in Greece, the war ended in 446 as Boeotia revolted and the Athenians were defeated at Coronea. Megara returned to the Spartan fold and was used as the base for a Spartan invasion of Attica, and Euboea also rebelled. The Thirty Years' Peace was concluded, by which Athens lost control of Boeotia (whose major cities formed the Boeotian Confederacy) and other recent acquisitions, and which satisfied the Corinthians, who prevented Peloponnesian intervention against the Athenians when Samos revolted in 440. The peace held until 431, despite continued Athenian expansionism (e.g. the establishment in 437–436 of the strategically important colony of Amphipolis on the east bank of the river Strymon) and increasing oppression of the allies, especially by means of cleruchies (settlements on conquered territory). But in Thucydides' view war was inevitable, and in his opinion Spartan fear of the growth of Athenian power was the truest cause of the outbreak of the main Peloponnesian War (431–404). It was precipitated by a series of grievances among Sparta's allies, including the Athenian alliance with Corfu against Corinth (433), the Megarian Decree (?432), which restricted access to the Athenian agora and to harbours of the Athenian empire, and Aeginetan complaints that their autonomy under the terms of the peace had been infringed. The Spartans and the Peloponnesians now attempted to liberate Greece from Athenian domination, but the first ten years (the Archidamian War) resulted in stalemate and the Peace of Nicias (421). On the resumption of hostilities Athens suffered various setbacks, including the disastrous failure of the great expedition to Sicily (415–413), the subsequent secessions of Chios, Miletus, Thasos, and Euboea, the renewal of Persian interference in Greek affairs (413) and their commitment to the Spartans (407), and the temporary overthrow of the democracy by the oligarchy of the Four Hundred (411). Nevertheless, the fighting continued (the Ionian War) with some notable Athenian successes until they were finally defeated at Aegospotami (405). Persian money was no small influence here. The city itself fell in 404, and the Spartans installed the shortlived and hated regime of the Thirty Tyrants (404–403).

Sparta's victory in the Peloponnesian War, far from curtailing hostilities, was only the beginning of a series of struggles in the 4th century, as various states in turn asserted their claim to supremacy and were overthrown. The victorious Spartan

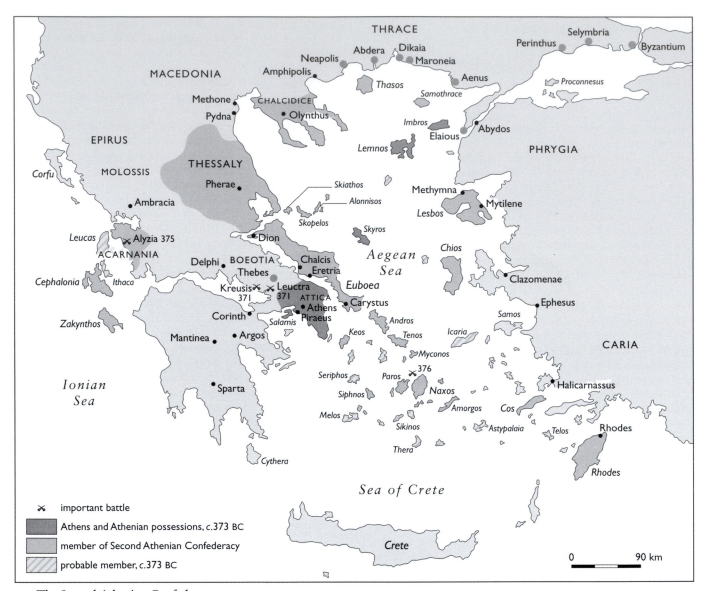

32. The Second Athenian Confederacy, 377–355 BC

general, Lysander, quickly made himself and his country unpopular with his policy of establishing oligarchic decarchies in numerous cities, and fear of Sparta's expansionist policies in Asia Minor, central and northern Greece, and the west led to the Corinthian War (395–386). Athens, with a restored but less radical democracy, had recovered remarkably from defeat and now joined in an anti-Spartan alliance with Thebes (which had gained control of the Boeotian Confederacy during the Peloponnesian War, but had fallen out with Sparta and received Athenian democratic exiles during the rule of the tyrants), Corinth (whose relations with Sparta had also deteriorated in 404 when the Spartans refused to destroy the defeated Athens), Argos (Sparta's old enemy), and Persia (reversing the former alliance). The Athenian Conon led a Persian-sponsored fleet to victory at Cnidus (394), but despite much fighting around Corinth the allies were unable to inflict a fatal reverse on the Spartans and the war was ended by the King's Peace. This treaty, negotiated by the Spartan Antalcidas and imposed by King Artaxerxes II, guaranteed the Greeks'

autonomy, but in exchange for Persian control of the cities of Asia, Clazomenae, and Cyprus. The peace had the additional effect of strengthening Sparta's position in central and northern Greece, enabling the coercion of Olynthus and dissolution of the Chalcidian Confederacy. The Boeotian Confederacy was also dismantled, but the Spartans, whose king Agesilaus II was implacably hostile to Thebes, went too far in occupying the Theban acropolis, the Cadmea (382), which the Athenians helped liberate in 379. Thebes subsequently joined the Second Athenian Confederacy (378), which was formed to ensure the Spartans' compliance with the terms of the King's Peace. Athens was careful not to repeat the mistakes of the 5th-century empire, guaranteeing no internal political interference or tribute, and membership grew rapidly in the period 378–373. But so too did Theban power, as it re-established the Boeotian Confederacy under Theban control, and the Spartans' military dominance was ended for good at the Battle of Leuctra (371). A decline in the number of full Spartan citizens (*homoioi*) had set in during the 5th century, as changes in the pattern of landholding deprived many Spartans of the ability to contribute to the common messes on which their citizenship depended. Now Athens and Sparta were forced to forget past differences and unite in opposition to Thebes, which tried to supplant Athens at sea and to undermine Sparta's position in the Peloponnese by the foundation of Megalopolis in Arcadia (c.370–367) and Messene in Messenia (369). While the Peloponnesian League finally collapsed (366), the Thebans, led by Epaminondas and Pelopidas, enjoyed a brief period of hegemony, which ended with Epaminondas' death at the Battle of Mantinea (362).

One other major player in the 370s was Jason, the tyrant of Pherae in Thessaly, who made an alliance with Thebes after 375, captured Pharsalus (375/4), and became *tagos* (supreme magistrate of Thessaly). His unification of Thessaly provoked Phocis (373–371), but he went on to gain control of Perrhaebia and was planning a Persian invasion when he was assassinated (370).

Athens, meanwhile, was beginning to return to its old ways. Attempts to recover Amphipolis (from 368), which had surrendered to the Spartan general Brasidas in 424 and had since remained independent, the installation of cleruchies, especially that in Samos (366), and increasing political and judicial interference in confederate states made the Second Athenian Confederacy unpopular; and eventually Byzantium, Chios, and Rhodes rebelled in the Social War (357–355). Athens and Sparta also became involved in the Third Sacred War, backing Phocis against the Delphic amphictiony (355). All the time a new threat to Greek independence was growing, as Philip II of Macedon (ruled 359–336) first consolidated his position and then began expanding his kingdom. Amphipolis was captured in 357 while Athens was involved in the Social War, other northern Greek states were annexed, and Philip secured Thessaly in 352. Athens finally began to wake up to the threat, and opposition to Philip was promoted by Demosthenes. It was too late, however, to save Olynthus (349–348), and without Greek support the Athenians were forced to negotiate the Peace of Philocrates (346). Before ratifying the treaty Philip accepted the invitation of the Delphic amphictiony to lead resistance to Phocis, which was destroyed. Further expansion in Illyria and Thrace, and the besieging of Perinthus and Byzantium, delayed the final attack on Greece, which culminated in the destruction of the Theban, Corinthian, and Athenian forces at Chaeronea (338). This was the end of Greek political independence: the League of Corinth was formed the next summer (337) with a common peace which provided for the autonomy of member states, prohibited constitutional change, and put Philip at the head of the governing council (*synedrion*). At the foundation meeting Philip announced his plan to invade Persia, but he was assassinated before he could carry it out (336).

Philip's successor was Alexander III the Great, who accomplished his father's plan in a series of brilliant campaigns (334–323). Before departing on his great expedition Alexander made a show of strength in southern Greece, and when Thebes revolted during Alexander's campaign on the Danube, he returned to destroy the city and enslave its inhabitants (335). Alexander left Greece under the control of Antipater, who crushed a Spartan rebellion led by Agis III, supported by Elis, Tegea, and the Achaean Confederacy (331). Athens refused to support Agis and remained subdued in the 330s and 320s, its leading politician being Lycurgus. He was responsible for re-establishing the city's finances, increasing the navy, and a rebuilding programme, which included an arsenal, docks, and the theatre of Dionysus. Alexander's death sparked the struggles of the successors and in the Greek sphere the Lamian War (323–322), in which a coalition led by the Athenians and Aetolians was almost successful. But the crushing defeat at Crannon resulted in the suppression of the Athenian democracy by Antipater, which was temporarily restored in 318 by Polyperchon before the tyrannical rule of Demetrius of Phalerum (318–307).

The momentous struggles of mainland and eastern Greece in the 5th and 4th centuries should not be allowed to overshadow the events in the western Greek world, in Sicily and southern Italy. Here too the Greek communities faced the double threat of external powers and internal rivalries. Those in Italy had local, indigenous rivals (e.g. the Messapians massacred the Greek Tarentines c.470), as well as the major power of the Etruscans; while those in Sicily faced the threat of the Carthaginians. The main western Greek state was Syracuse, whose power rose greatly under Gelon, the tyrant of Gela, who seized Syracuse in 485 (his brother Hieron becoming tyrant of Gela). He was prevented from helping the mainland Greeks in 480 by the Carthaginian Hamilcar's invasion of Sicily, but won a crushing victory at Himera. Gelon was succeeded in 478/77 by Hieron, who defeated the Etruscans in a naval battle with the help of Cumae (474). Democracy was restored after Hieron's death (466), but Syracuse became involved in wars with another leading Sicilian state, Acragas, and with the Sicels, who under Ducetius defeated the joint forces of Syracuse and Acragas in 451. Ducetius himself was in turn defeated by the Syracusans in 450 and exiled, but returned to found the colony of Caleacte, which resulted in another war between Syracuse and Acragas. Syracusan victory was later followed by successes against Athens (427–424, 415–413), but further interference by the Carthaginians resulted in the destruction of Himera and other cities (409). The democracy was overthrown in 406 by Dionysius I, who fought four wars against the Carthaginians and extended Syracusan power over most of Sicily and much of southern Italy. He died in 367 and his successor, his eldest son Dionysius II, was opposed by Dion (356) in a civil war which was ended by the intervention of the Corinthian Timoleon on behalf of exiled opponents of Dionysius. Timoleon put down tyranny in Sicily, defeated the Carthaginians (341), and re-established stable government, but after his retirement (c.336) an oligarchic government was installed until Agathocles became tyrant (317) and once again subdued most of Sicily.

MICHAEL J. EDWARDS

See also Classical Period, Delian League, Democracy, Macedonia, Pelopponesian War, Persian Wars, Sicily

Further Reading

Buckler, John, *The Theban Hegemony, 371–362 BC*, Cambridge, Massachusetts: Harvard University Press, 1980

Boardman, John *et al.* (editors), *Persia, Greece and the Western Mediterranean, c.525 to 479 BC*, Cambridge: Cambridge

University Press, 1988 (*The Cambridge Ancient History*, vol. 4, 2nd edition), pp. 592–622

Boardman, John, *The Greeks Overseas: Their Early Colonies and Trade*, 4th edition, London and New York: Thames and Hudson, 1999

Cargill, Jack L. Jr, *The Second Athenian League: Empire or Free Alliance?*, Berkeley: University of California Press, 1981

Cartledge, Paul, *Sparta and Lakonia: A Regional History, 1300–362 BC*, London and Boston: Routledge and Kegan Paul, 1979

Cartledge, Paul, *Agesilaos and the Crisis of Sparta*, London: Duckworth, and Baltimore: Johns Hopkins University Press, 1987

Caven, Brian, *Dionysius I: War-Lord of Sicily*, New Haven and London: Yale University Press, 1990

Davies, J.K., *Democracy and Classical Greece*, 2nd edition, Cambridge, Massachusetts: Harvard University Press, 1993

Hamilton, Charles, *Agesilaus and the Failure of Spartan Hegemony*, Ithaca, New York: Cornell University Press, 1991

Larsen, J.A.O., *Greek Federal States: Their Institutions and History*, Oxford: Clarendon Press, 1968

Lewis, D.M. *et al.* (editors), *The Fifth Century BC*, Cambridge: Cambridge University Press, 1992 (*The Cambridge Ancient History*, vol. 5, 2nd edition)

Lewis, D.M. *et al.* (editors), *The Fourth Century BC*, Cambridge: Cambridge University Press, 1994 (*The Cambridge Ancient History*, vol. 6, 2nd edition)

Meiggs, Russell, *The Athenian Empire*, Oxford: Clarendon Press, 1972

Salmon, J.B., *Wealthy Corinth: A History of the City to 338 BC*, Oxford: Clarendon Press, and New York: Oxford University Press, 1984

Political History 323–31 BC

The chaos resulting from the unexpected death of Alexander III the Great in Babylon in 323 BC lasted for several decades before the establishment of the three major Hellenistic Greek kingdoms which form the focus of the history of the next three centuries. The kingship fell jointly to the son and half-brother of Alexander, the satrapal appointments were rearranged, and the successors (the name traditionally used for Alexander's generals) fought each other and jockeyed for positions of ever greater power. Some were killed early on in this power struggle, and successive regents of the two kings died. The kings were returned to mainland Greece (which in effect signalled the end of Alexander's Asian empire) where they became pawns in the hands of those seeking to establish mastery over Macedonia and Greece, and the remaining successors continued to fight each other in Asia Minor.

It was probably inevitable that both kings would be murdered, as also were eventually all the immediate members of Alexander the Great's family, thereby extinguishing the Argead dynasty of kings of Macedonia (to which Alexander and his father Philip II belonged). In 306–305 BC the surviving successors assumed the title of "king", thus acknowledging finally that Alexander's kingdom was now split among several rulers even if they did not yet have fixed geographical kingdoms. A major landmark of this period was the Battle of Ipsus (in Phrygia) in 301 BC, in which the Macedonian general Antigonus the One-Eyed was defeated and killed by a coalition of the other successors, who divided the spoils of the territories he controlled among themselves.

Antigonus' ambitious son Demetrius (known as Poliorcetes, "the Besieger", because of his siege of Rhodes in 305/04 BC) unsuccessfully tried to re-establish his father's Asian empire while also intervening in Greece. It was only when his son Antigonus Gonatas securely established himself on the throne of Macedon in 277/76 BC that the Antigonid dynasty of kings of Macedon was created.

Third-century Macedonian history is characterized by warfare on the northwestern borders with Illyria and by attempts to control mainland Greece by both diplomacy and guile. Judging from the low numbers of Macedonian troops recorded in various encounters, it appears that the country suffered the effects of severe depopulation as a result of Alexander the Great's removal of some 40,000 men in their prime in the 4th century BC. Finally, in 229 BC, the accession to the throne of the boy king Philip V under the care of a regent left the country potentially vulnerable. When he assumed control in his own name in 221, Philip unwisely thought that he could prevail against the growing power of Rome, whose suspicions about Greece were becoming ever stronger. Three Macedonian Wars were fought, leading to Philip's defeat at Cynoscephalae in 197, and to his son Perseus' even more catastrophic defeat at Pydna in 168. After Pydna, Macedonia was ruthlessly sacked and the kingship abolished. The region became a full province of Rome in 146 BC.

Mainland Greece suffered various vicissitudes during this period. Athens, usually under Macedonian control, was constantly split between pro- and anti-Macedonian factions and experienced severe internal political stasis. A major revolt against Macedonia is attested in 287 BC, and the Chremonidean War in the 260s signalled the final unsuccessful attempt of Athens (this time allied to Sparta) to overthrow the Macedonian yoke. A Macedonian garrison was imposed, Macedonian officers were installed in Athenian political posts, and the activity of the Assembly was curtailed. This was a severe humiliation to a city which was the birthplace of Greek democracy. Athens became politically unimportant after this period, but remained culturally pre-eminent, even if eclipsed by the new Greek city Alexandria in Egypt. During the next centuries many notable figures of both Greek and Roman origin came to study in Athenian philosophical and rhetorical schools.

During this period politics in the Peloponnese revolved around the Achaean League (a powerful federation of Peloponnesian cities), a stubbornly independent Sparta, the interference of both Macedonia and Rome, and the attempts of the league to manipulate all parties to its advantage. Despite some flirtations with social and economic reform in the 3rd century, Sparta was finally forcibly united with the Achaean League in 192 BC, which was in turn defeated by Rome in 146 BC. The Greek city of Corinth was sacked with a savagery which shocked the Greek world. The region was first incorporated into the Roman province of Macedonia but became the separate province of Achaea under the Roman empire.

Events in mainland Greece in the Hellenistic period arguably take second place to events in the new Greek kingdoms established in Asia after the wars of the successors. Ptolemy, a Macedonian general of Alexander the Great, received the satrapy of Egypt after Alexander's death and developed it into a wealthy and powerful kingdom to be ruled

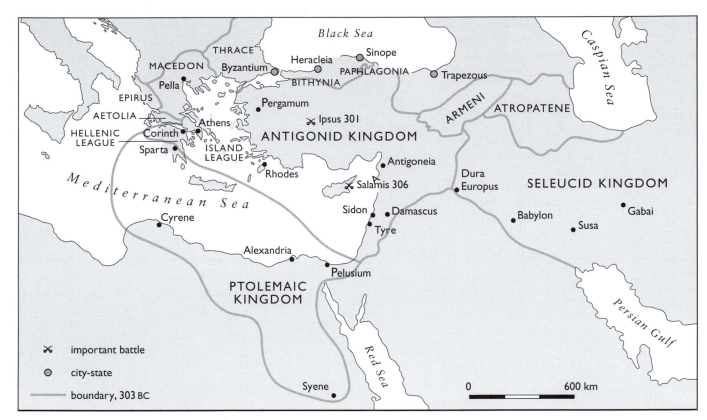

33. The successor kingdoms to Alexander's empire

by himself and his descendants. Being content with Egypt, Ptolemy wisely avoided any temptation to extend his territory at the expense of the other successors, but he displayed a defensive strategy by establishing control over nearby Cyprus and Cyrenaica (a large region in modern Libya). His capital was the coastal city of Alexandria in the north of the Nile delta, founded by Alexander during his visit to Egypt in 331 BC. Alexandria – superbly situated for east–west trade – quickly became the jewel of the Mediterranean, taking over from Athens in cultural terms, and grew into a great city as a result of encouraged immigration from the rest of the Greek world.

Third-century Ptolemaic Egypt is characterized by good kings, relatively stable government, and enormous prosperity. Although there were brief interventions in mainland Greece, Egypt's major foreign problem was an ongoing dispute with the Seleucids (see below) over the area called Coele (in Greek "Hollow") Syria, the region comprising much of the modern Middle East. A series of Syrian wars were fought during the 3rd and 2nd centuries BC, with varying outcomes. By the middle of the 3rd century Ptolemy II had developed the largest and most powerful naval fleet ever known in the ancient Greek world (although the navy did experience a few defeats in battle), and Egypt became the protector of the Mediterranean, securing the safety of trade and travel against the threat of pirates. At the end of the 3rd century the kingdom was shaken by a native revolt in which Nubia (southern Egypt) seceded for a time.

In the 2nd century the growing interest of Rome in eastern Greek politics was combined with weak Ptolemaic kings and continued Syrian wars. The Ptolemaic habit of brother–sister marriage led to even worse cases of incest, resulting in several multiply interrelated claimants to the throne at various periods. Rivals were murdered, princesses were married off to foreign kings to seal temporary alliances, and the support of Syria and Rome was sought by different factions. The last Ptolemaic queen was Cleopatra VII, descended from an illegitimate royal line. Julius Caesar came to Egypt in the mid-1st century BC in the course of his war with Pompey the Great, and fought on Cleopatra's behalf a war against her brother-husband (the so-called "Alexandrian War"). Their love affair resulted in the birth of a son. Cleopatra turned to Mark Antony after Caesar's assassination, and their even more famous love affair ended with a naval defeat at the Battle of Actium in 31 BC at the hands of Octavian (later the emperor Augustus). Both committed suicide, the Ptolemaic dynasty ended, and Greek Egypt became a province of Rome.

The Seleucid empire was established by Seleucus, a Macedonian general of Alexander the Great who had received the satrapy of Babylon during the various divisions of Alexander's empire. He was eventually confirmed as ruler also of the territories east of the Euphrates – the huge Asian empire of Alexander which included modern Iran, Iraq, Afghanistan, and Pakistan as far as India. Seleucid control over much of this vast territory was nominal, with several royal expeditions during the next three centuries in not always successful attempts to reconquer or pacify various regions. After the battle of Ipsus in 301 Seleucus received the area of greater Syria (the northern part of the Middle East, not to be confused with the boundaries of the modern state of Syria), and this became the heartland of his empire, now with an outlet to the Mediterranean. A new capital city was founded at Antioch on the Orontes river (the city of Antakya in modern Turkey), with a seaport on the coast at Seleuceia in Pieria. Antioch became one of the greatest and most important Greek cities of later antiquity. Seleucus also encouraged Greeks from all over the Mediterranean to inhabit his kingdom, and the early Seleucid kings were enthusiastic city founders, founding several cities throughout their empire in which Greek urban lifestyle, institutions, culture, and language were established and continued for centuries.

During the 3rd and 2nd centuries the Seleucids fought several wars against the Ptolemies for the control of adjoining Coele Syria (see above), and suffered dynastic disputes and revolts by brothers, cousins, and eastern satraps. Expansion into Asia Minor came up against the growing power of the Attalid kingdom of Pergamum, and in the 2nd century Rome's unfavourable attention focused on king Antiochus III the Great because of his troublemaking alliances with other Hellenistic kings and forays into mainland Greece. In 191 BC Roman forces defeated Antiochus at the Thermopylae pass in central Greece (the site of the famous battle of the Persian War in the 5th century BC). He refused harsh Roman demands and an ultimatum that he withdraw to Syria. Risking all in battle, he was decisively defeated by a Roman army at the Battle of Magnesia in 189 BC. The resulting Peace of Apamea in 188 meant that the Seleucid empire was no longer a Mediterranean power, and successful revolts in the eastern territories decreased the extent of its influence.

Later Seleucid history is dominated by catastrophic dynastic disputes and the rise of pretenders to the throne which led to constant civil wars (much of the conflict was aided and abetted by Ptolemaic kings who intervened in devious ways in order to weaken their main rivals). The situation deteriorated to the extent that the Syrian people offered the throne to the king of Armenia in 83 BC. After appealing to Rome, the last Seleucid king, Antiochus XIII, was temporarily restored to the throne in Antioch under Roman protection in 69 BC, but in 64 BC Syria was made a Roman province.

The rise of the kingdom of Pergamum also lies in the age of Alexander's successors. Philetaerus, of mixed Macedonian and Paphlagonian background, is first seen in the entourage of Antigonus the One-Eyed, then in that of Lysimachus of Thrace, and finally in that of Seleucus I. He had been put in charge of the stronghold of Pergamum, a city in northwest Asia Minor (now Bergama in modern Turkey), as well as a substantial treasury. The descendants of Philetaerus gradually established their independence from the Seleucids, and deprived the Seleucid empire of large areas of Asia Minor by cunningly intervening in Seleucid civil wars. Attalus (after whom the Attalid kingdom of Pergamum is named) was the first ruler to take the title of king in the late 230s BC, as a result of his military victories over Celtic mercenaries (called Galatians) in Seleucid employ. By means of lavish sculpted dedications, Attalus depicted his victories as important achievements, and himself as the champion of Greek freedom against a renewed barbarian threat. The Attalids early on were allies of Rome against Philip V of Macedon, and established the beginnings of an overseas empire in the Greek islands of Aegina, Andros, and Euboea. Attalus I's sons continued as Rome's allies against various Greek foes, and Pergamum was rewarded with vast grants of territory in the reassignment of territory in the Peace of

Apamea in 188 BC. After the Galatians were finally decisively defeated, Pergamum became the most powerful kingdom in Asia Minor, and extensive building operations on the acropolis transformed Pergamum into a magnificent Greek city. A library of Greek literature rivalled those of Athens and Alexandria (some scholars say that parchment, called in Greek *pergamena* after the city, was invented there to remove dependence on Egyptian papyrus), and monuments proclaiming in mythological terms the Attalids as the defenders of Hellenism and civilization against barbarism were erected. These are among the greatest creations of Hellenistic art. In order to reinforce their place in the Hellenic world, the Attalids also dedicated lavish buildings at Delos, Delphi, and Athens (the stoa of Attalus II in the Athenian Agora is a famous example of their beneficence towards Greek cities).

The Attalid dynasty came to an end in 133 BC upon the death of its last king, Attalus III, who for uncertain reasons bequeathed his kingdom to Rome, thereby giving Rome a free rein to intervene in Greek Asia Minor.

During the Hellenistic period the Greek cities of Asia Minor and the islands suffered different fates under the shifting control of various Hellenistic monarchs. The Dodecanesian island of Rhodes maintained its democratic independence for some time despite attempts by the kings to control it, and it gained a position of considerable power and prestige in the Greek world at this period. Its position on the east–west trade routes and the facilities provided by five harbours in the capital guaranteed considerable economic prosperity. Bravely resisting a year-long siege by Demetrius Poliorcetes against immense odds in 305/04 BC, Rhodes built up its navy and gradually replaced the Ptolemies as protector of Greek cities in the Aegean against marauding pirates. Friendship with Rome ensured rewards for Rhodes in the Peace of Apamea in 188 BC, and it was granted extensive territory on the mainland of Asia Minor. The democratic system of government on Rhodes allowed for the development of anti-Roman factions, however, and Rhodes was punished for its support of Macedonia in the Third Macedonian War. It was forced into an unequal alliance with Rome in 164 BC, and thereafter ceased to be an independent political power, although it remained a prosperous and highly cultured city.

The Hellenistic age saw the expansion of Greeks and the Greek way of life into Asia Minor, the Middle East, Egypt, Iraq, Iran, Afghanistan, and Pakistan as far as India. Some settlements were not as successful and long-lasting as others, depending upon the fortunes of the Hellenistic empires, but Greeks and the Greek language lasted in these areas throughout the Roman empire until it phased into the world of Byzantine Greece. It could be maintained that the Hellenistic period had a more cosmopolitan Greek culture than that of the parochial city-states in the Classical period. Unfortunately, the Greek world was ultimately unable to resist the power of Rome in political terms, but, far from extinguishing Greek culture, Rome itself became captivated by Greek scholarship, philosophy, and literature.

E.E. RICE

See also Antigonids, Attalids, Hellenistic Period, Ptolemies, Rhodes, Seleucids

Further Reading

Allen, R.E., *The Attalid Kingdom: A Constitutional History*, Oxford: Clarendon Press, 1983

Astin, A.E. *et al.* (editors), *Rome and the Mediterranean to 133 BC*, Cambridge: Cambridge University Press, 1989 (*The Cambridge Ancient History*, vol. 8, 2nd edition)

Berthold, Richard M., *Rhodes in the Hellenistic Age*, Ithaca, New York: Cornell University Press, 1984

Bickerman, Elias J., *The Jews in the Greek Age*, Cambridge, Massachusetts: Harvard University Press, 1988

Bilde, Per, *et al.*, *Centre and Periphery in the Hellenistic World*, Aarhus: Aarhus University Press, 1993

Boardman, John, Jasper Griffin, and Oswyn Murray (editors), *The Oxford History of the Classical World*, Oxford and New York: Oxford University Press, 1986, chapter 13

Bowman, Alan K., *Egypt after the Pharaohs, 332 BC–AD 642: From Alexander to the Arab Conquest*, 2nd edition, London: British Museum, 1986

Cartledge, Paul and Anthony Spawforth, *Hellenistic and Roman Sparta: A Tale of Two Cities*, London and New York: Routledge, 1989

Crook, J.A., Andrew Lintott, and Elizabeth Rawson (editors), *The Last Age of the Roman Republic, 146–43 BC*, Cambridge: Cambridge University Press, 1994 (*The Cambridge Ancient History*, vol. 9, 2nd edition)

Davies, W.D. and Louis Finkelstein, *The Cambridge History of Judaism*, vol. 2: *The Hellenistic Age*, Cambridge and New York: Cambridge University Press, 1989

Errington, R. Malcolm, *A History of Macedonia*, Berkeley: University of California Press, 1990

Finley, M.I., *Ancient Sicily*, revised edition, London: Chatto and Windus, and Totowa, New Jersey: Rowman and Littlefield, 1979

Fraser, P.M., *Ptolemaic Alexandria*, 3 vols, Oxford: Clarendon Press, 1972

Green, Peter, *Alexander to Actium: The Historical Evolution of the Hellenistic Age*, Berkeley: University of California Press, 1990

Gruen, Erich S., *The Hellenistic World and the Coming of Rome*, Berkeley: University of California Press, 1984

Habicht, Christian, *Athens from Alexander to Antony*, Cambridge, Massachusetts: Harvard University Press, 1997

Hammond, N.G.L. and F.W. Walbank, *A History of Macedonia*, vol. 3: *336–167 BC*, Oxford: Clarendon Press, 1988

Hammond, N.G.L., *The Macedonian State: The Origins, Institutions and History*, New York: Oxford University Press, and Oxford: Clarendon Press, 1989

Hansen, Esther V., *The Attalids of Pergamon*, 2nd edition, Ithaca, New York: Cornell University Press, 1971

Mossé, Claude, *Athens in Decline, 404–86 BC*, London and Boston: Routledge and Kegan Paul, 1973

Narain, A.K., *The Indo-Greeks*, Delhi: Oxford University Press, 1957; reprinted 1980

Potts, D.T., *The Arabian Gulf in Antiquity*, vol. 2: *From Alexander the Great to the Coming of Islam*, Oxford: Clarendon Press, and New York: Oxford University Press, 1990

Roebuck, Carl Angus, *A History of Messenia from 369 to 146 BC*, Chicago: University of Chicago Libraries, 1941

Sherwin-White, A.N., *Roman Foreign Policy in the East, 168 BC–AD 1*, London: Duckworth, and Norman, Oklahoma: University of Oklahoma Press, 1984

Sherwin-White, Susan M., *Ancient Cos: An Historical Study from the Dorian Settlement to the Imperial Period*, Göttingen: Vandenhoeck & Ruprecht, 1978

Sherwin-White, Susan M. and Amélie Kuhrt, *From Samarkhand to Sardis: A New Approach to the Seleucid Empire*, London: Duckworth, 1993

Spyridakis, Stylianos V., *Ptolemaic Itanos and Hellenistic Crete*, Berkeley: University of California Press, 1970

Tarn, W.W., and G.T. Griffith, *Hellenistic Civilization*, 3rd edition, London: Arnold, 1952; Cleveland, Ohio: World, 1961

Walbank, F.W. *et al.* (editors), *The Hellenistic World*, Cambridge: Cambridge University Press, 1984 (*The Cambridge Ancient History*, vol. 7, part 1, 2nd edition)

Walbank, F.W., *The Hellenistic World*, revised edition, London: Fontana, and Cambridge, Massachusetts: Harvard University Press, 1992

Woodcock, George, *The Greeks in India*, London: Faber, 1966

Yarshater, Ehsan (editor), *The Cambridge History of Iran*, vol. 3, parts 1–2: *The Seleucid, Parthian, and Sasanian Periods*, Cambridge: Cambridge University Press, 1983

Political History 31 BC–AD 330

Many discussions of the history of Roman Greece begin with the famous line from Horace: "Graecia capta ferum victorem cepit" ("Greece, the captive, took her savage victor captive", *Epistulae*, 2. 1. 156). It is true that Greek ideals and language captured and dominated the eastern Mediterranean world, but politically Greece became part of the Roman sphere of influence long before the triumphs of Augustus and the poems of Horace. As early as 229 BC the Romans had established protectorates over Greek towns, such as Corcyra, Apollonia, Dyrrachium, and Issa, and in the mid-2nd century BC the Romans arrived to stay in the eastern Mediterranean region. In 146 BC the Romans, led by L. Mummius, destroyed the Achaeans near Corinth. Corinth was razed, its treasures were shipped to Rome, men were massacred, and other inhabitants were sold into slavery. The Achaean League was dissolved, and Greece ultimately became the site of much bitter Roman warfare throughout the 1st century BC. The Civil Wars brought Pompey and Caesar and then Octavian and Mark Antony to Greece, where the combatants depended upon men and material aid from the Greeks, putting significant psychological and economic burdens on the population.

Once the east was conquered, the Romans needed to manage their new territories. The organization of political control in Greece was complicated by Roman respect for Greek culture and traditions, so that the province's administrative status underwent several changes throughout the centuries of Roman rule. Shortly after the Battle of Actium (31 BC) Octavian created the new province of Achaea (roughly the area of modern Greece without Crete, Macedonia, and Thessaly). The idea of a unified Greece rather than politically independent city states took root in this era, even though parts of what we now consider Greece remained separate. Epirus was eventually (though temporarily) made into a separate province as well. The province of Achaea was at first under the control of the Senate (i.e. "proconsular"), but both Achaea and Macedonia were, according to Tacitus (*Annales*, 1. 76), officially turned over to the emperor in AD 15. After AD 44 "proconsul" and "praeses" are both used to describe the governor of Achaea, and the province seems to have, de facto, reverted to proconsular rule. The Greeks briefly enjoyed some independence under a grant from Nero. At the Isthmian Games in AD 66/67 he declared Achaea free, though this status was overturned by Vespasian only a few years later. Achaea was formally made proconsular again in either Diocletian's or, more likely, Constantine's reign, after which the governors of

34. The Hellenic world in the Roman empire

Achaea are known only as proconsuls or consuls until they disappear from the record in the 5th century AD.

After the conquest the Hellenistic leagues endured (at least 12 are known), but they were of little bureaucratic importance. Instead, the Greek provinces were ruled through their well-established cities where small groups of local elites played important roles as Roman managers and representatives, and ran the day-to-day provincial business. Among the most important duties of the cities and their managers was the collection of imperial revenues. It was likely that as early as the reign of Augustus (as Octavian was styled from 27 BC onwards) regular taxation was levied. Both a "head tax" (*tributum capitis*) and a "land tax" (*tributum soli*) are attested under the Principate. Other levies included customs and port taxes, sales taxes, and special levies in times of need. Though statistically relatively low (probably less than 10 per cent), taxation was despised by the provincials and felt to be oppressive, and may well have been devastating to subsistence farmers and other poorer provincials. Not all cities, however, were subject to regular taxation and control by the provincial governor. Pliny (*Epistles*, 8. 24. 2–3) states that the cities most revered for their Classical history were granted freedom and immunity from levies (these included Amphissa, Athens, Corinth, Delphi, Elateia, Pallanteion, and Sparta). But even these cities were sometimes asked to provide contributions from a sense of "friendliness" to the Romans. Strabo (*Geography*, 8. 5. 5) notes that the Spartans "were held in

particular honour, and remained free, contributing to Rome nothing else but friendly services [*philikon leitourgion*]". Of particular importance to the economic health of Greece, however, is the crucial fact that, whether regular or sporadic, resources were drained away from Greece into the coffers of the larger empire.

In addition to any economic burdens, the Greeks experienced a mixed blessing from their location at the centre of the empire. Technically, Achaea was an unarmed province with little military presence, so the influence of the empire may often have been a degree less obvious and oppressive in Greece than on the frontiers. Only small contingents of soldiers, rather than significant garrisons, were found in the territory during the early empire. On the other hand, the economic stimulation that the frontier provinces experienced was missing in Greece, where insulation brought a measure of economic stagnation.

For the most part Greek citizens and cities were unmolested and enjoyed the fruits of the *pax Romana*, but there were examples of violent strategies in the imposition of early imperial control. The arrival of the Romans sometimes meant territorial and demographic manipulation. Particularly in the early years of Roman control under Caesar and Augustus, land was taken and redistributed to show pleasure or displeasure with one city over another. These were considered the rights of the victor over the vanquished. Cities and colonies were founded at will. Corinth, for example, was rebuilt, colonized, and grew under the support of Caesar and then Augustus. Augustus also founded Nicopolis in Epirus, and Dium and Cassandreia in Macedonia, while Caesar was known to have created the city of Patras in Achaea and possibly Dyme nearby. Augustus not only manipulated territories, he moved people. Men were transferred, for instance, into Patras where the emperor "united them with the Achaeans also from Rhyope, which town he razed to the ground" (Pausanias, 7. 18. 7).

Recent archaeological and historical work supports ancient claims, such as those of Pausanias, that there was significant movement of populations and realignment of states under the emperors. Results from archaeological survey in Aetolia show a clear pattern of site abandonment in the Roman era which reflects the claims of Pausanias (7. 18. 8–9) that the province was "laid waste" by the emperor Augustus. Epirus, too, was depopulated – so much so that Strabo claims all remaining Epirots in Augustus' time would fit into a single city (7. 7. 6).

Over the course of the 1st and 2nd centuries AD in Greece, as elsewhere, there was a trend towards larger, but fewer, administrative centres such as Corinth, where the provincial governor and his staff were based. Corinth itself did not formally control other Achaean cities, or even mediate between them and the Romans, but it did show a particularly close connection to Rome. Corinthian coinage was modelled on Roman, its pottery showed clear western influences, and Corinth was the site of one the earliest overseas capitolia (though its precise location is still disputed). Clear benefits of empire also accrued to regions outside Corinth. As is well known, one way to emphasize one's political power and prestige was through patronage. The emperor Augustus began a long-imitated trend when he made Greece the beneficiary of such largesse. He continued to rebuild Corinth, which probably became the provincial capital at that time (and which remained Latin-speaking until the reign of Hadrian). Roman Messenia also shows signs of growing prosperity with the coming of empire. Pausanias (4. 31. 5–33. 2) lists numerous Roman-period structures, both civic and religious, which testify to an affluent way of life.

Many Roman emperors evinced a personal interest in Greek culture and history (sometimes, of course, this meant despoiling Greece of its art and antiquities). Nero, for example, was a devoted philhellene. He spoke Greek, attempted to cut a channel through the isthmus of Corinth (to improve communications and trade routes), became an Athenian archon, and was initiated into the mysteries of Demeter. Imperial dedications to Greece could be substantial, including buildings, roads, and other physical manifestations of their concern for Achaea and their own prestige. Trajan had built the Library of Pantaenus in Athens. Hadrian supported numerous projects including buildings at Delphi, many structures in Athens – creating a "New Athens" in the process – as well as stoas, temples, aqueducts, bridges, and baths throughout Achaea. In AD 131/32 Hadrian founded the "Panhellenion", a largely cultural organization of Greek cities (from Greece, Asia Minor, and north Africa) centred in Athens. The respect for Greek culture supported by the creation of this organization lasted well into the 3rd century AD. Throughout these years the Greeks kept their language, culture, and traditions, and continued to maintain control over their cities, which may help explain why, for the most part, the Greeks were loyal to Rome.

The late 2nd and 3rd centuries AD brought unwelcome changes to the Roman world as a whole. Civil wars, economic woes, migrations, and invasions from the north characterize this era in Roman history. Revolts erupted periodically in the 2nd century AD, including at least one in Greece: A small abortive rebellion occurred under the relatively benevolent rule of Antoninus Pius. The chaotic 3rd century AD brought civil wars and extensive Gothic raids to the Balkans. Greek territories were not immune. The restless northern peoples were no longer stopped at the borders of the empire after the death of Severus Alexander (AD 235). Thrace suffered the first assaults from Gothic invaders and related tribes. The emperor Decius was eventually killed by these invaders, which led to further raids and a civil war. The Danube and Rhine regions were the locations of most of this raiding activity, but in AD 254 raiders made their way as far south as Thessolonica. Many parts of Greece, especially coastal areas such as Athens, were severely damaged by these incursions. In the AD 260s further raids occurred. Gallienus repelled the intruders in AD 262, but he was soon forced to return to protect Greece again. Gallienus, just like Hadrian, was a philhellene, held the archonship in Athens, and was initiated into the Eleusinian mysteries. His support for Greece was sorely needed when in AD 268 the Heruli captured and wrought considerable destruction upon Athens. Eventually Gallienus expelled the Heruli, but such attacks were only slowed and would happen again in the future (most notably in the 5th, 6th, and 7th centuries).

In the 3rd century AD the empire was also faced with fiscal crises. Inflation worked to wreak havoc on urban financial structures. The content of silver coinage (the denarius) had become debased, while at the same time imperial mints were producing ever-growing quantities of money in an attempt to keep up with fiscal demands. The situation grew particularly painful for Greek cities and their elite, the *curiales* or *bouleutai* ("councillors"), who had drawn their revenues from civic lands, from taxes, and from local dues and tolls. Those leaders with access to goods, rather than money, were able to increase prices and rents, but they became hard pressed if they depended upon debased and devalued revenues. The *curiales*, thus, began to feel unable to carry out their administrative duties. The needs of the imperial treasury, as expressed by the Roman *correctores* (regional governors, normally senators) who now governed Achaea, led to the loss of autonomy for any remaining free Greek cities. Increasing demands on the province as a whole required new strategies for production, which strategies would eventually result in a late Roman (4th- and 5th-century) resurgence of economic prosperity in Greece.

Upon Diocletian's accession to the throne in AD 284, the empire was temporarily at peace and the emperor set about solving the more serious economic and social problems in the provinces. To fix the problem of ruling vast territories, Diocletian reorganized provincial administrative units. There were 45 official districts in AD 117, but 108 districts by the end of the 4th century. Diocletian had expanded the number of Severan provinces by creating smaller provinces for easier administration and methodically divided the empire into clear eastern and western sections. The province of Achaea (with its capital still at Corinth) was incorporated into the administrative structure of the east. Diocletian placed Achaea into the diocese of Moesia, though Constantine moved the province under the jurisdiction of Macedonia in Illyricum. Northern Greece included the provinces of Epirus, Thessaly, and Macedonia. Crete remained a separate province. These provincial divisions continued to separate what we think of as "Greece" into several administrative units, but provided smaller territories that allowed for more efficient management and tighter control.

Once Diocletian stepped down from his office, conflict began again and the Balkans, Greece included, became a recruiting ground for Constantine's civil war with Licinius. Constantine, once in power, set about moving his capital to "New Rome" or Constantinople. In the tradition of earlier emperors, he felt it his right to remove art and artefacts from his provinces, including Achaea, to beautify his new capital. Nevertheless, 4th-century Achaea generally saw a renewal of building activity, an invigorated economy, and another revival of Greek letters after the hiatus of the civil wars. Subsequently, Achaean political, religious, and economic orientation was focused on the east and thus began the transition to the later Roman empire, or early Byzantine era in Greek history.

CYNTHIA K. KOSSO

See also Christianity, Roman Period

Further Reading

Alcock, Susan E., *Graecia Capta: The Landscapes of Roman Greece*, Cambridge and New York: Cambridge University Press, 1993

Bommejlé, Sebastiaan *et al.*, *Aetolia and the Aetolians: Towards the Interdisciplinary Study of a Greek Region*, Utrecht: Parnassus Press, 1987

Cartledge, Paul and Anthony Spawforth, *Hellenistic and Roman Sparta: A Tale of Two Cities*, London and New York: Routledge, 1989

Davis, Jack L. (editor), *Sandy Pylos: An Archaeological Survey from Nestor to Navarino*, Austin: University of Texas Press, 1998

Engels, Donald, *Roman Corinth: An Alternative Model for the Classical City*, Chicago: University of Chicago Press, 1990

Hopkins, K., "Taxes and Trade in the Roman Empire", *Journal of Roman Studies*, 70 (1980): pp. 101–25

Oliver, James H., *The Civic Tradition and Roman Athens*, Baltimore: Johns Hopkins University Press, 1983

Owens, E.J., *The City in the Greek and Roman World*, London and New York: Routledge, 1991

Walker, Susan and Averil Cameron (editors), *The Greek Renaissance in the Roman Empire*, London: University of London, Institute of Classical Studies, 1989

Political History AD 330–802

The period AD 330–802 is dominated in its early phase by the dynasties of Constantine the Great and Theodosius the Great. The middle period contains the spectacular rule of Justinian followed by his less fortunate successors. The years from 610 to 802 witness the rise of two relatively long-ruling houses founded by Herakleios and Leo III the Isaurian, respectively. Each of these epochs is characterized by internal and external troubles, some being an outgrowth of unresolved earlier problems, while others were unique to their times. The history of these roughly 500 years reflects the efforts of the imperial government to find practical solutions to these difficulties, and at the same time to maintain the fiction of an empire undiminished in authority and power.

When Constantine the Great (324–37) inaugurated his new city of Constantinople on the Bosporus in AD 330, he set in motion a movement that would end with the two halves of the empire forming a Latin-speaking west and a Greek-speaking east, each with its own government and cultural life. If Constantine, who was the first ruler to protect the Christians among his subjects, had hoped to unite the empire under the banner of the new religion, he was to be disappointed. His reign and the reigns of his immediate successors were beset with Christological controversies and bickering within the ranks of the Church.

It was left to Theodosius I (379–95) to found the orthodox state, enforce uniformity, and in consequence deny toleration to pagans and heretics. Questions of dogma and definitions of the right faith were hammered out in ecumenical councils, of which the first dealt with the Arian heresy at Nicaea in 325 under Constantine, and the second with the establishment of Christianity as the state religion under Theodosius at Constantinople in 381.

The enemies threatening the security of the empire during this time were the Persians on the eastern borders, and the invading Germanic barbarians who had earlier threatened the Rhine frontier and later overrun the hinterland of Constantinople. The terrible defeat of a Roman army by a Gothic force at Adrianople (378) and the death of the emperor Valens in this battle brought Theodosius to the throne. He settled the Gothic threat by making the Visigoths *foederati* (confederates) of the empire, and he was able to secure a peace with Persia which ended for a time the ceaseless warfare in that region. This peace, however, depended on sacrificing the independence of Armenia which had been the apple of discord between Persia and the empire and was now divided between the two powers. It was timely, since the empire faced new dangers on its borders with the advance of the Huns.

In Church affairs there was bitter discord between Alexandria and Constantinople, both struggling for ecclesiastical supremacy. The matter was finally resolved in 451 at the Fourth Ecumenical Council at Chalcedon which decided in favour of Constantinople. The same council, in addition, was sowing the seeds of further conflict with its definition of the Orthodox faith. From now on the Eastern Church would find it impossible to please Rome as well as Syria and Egypt.

The reign of Justinian (527–65) is distinguished by the emperor's efforts to restore the Roman empire to its former size and to re-establish Roman authority in the territories lost during the barbarian invasions. The emperor's general, Belisarius, in quick succession wrested North Africa from the Vandals and began the conquest of Italy. Finally, a strip of territory in southern Spain was taken from the Visigoths.

In the internal affairs of the empire, Justinian quelled the rowdy circus factions in Constantinople when he put down the Nika uprising. The destruction that had been done in the capital during the rebellion allowed the emperor to embark on an ambitious building programme, the most impressive result of which was the church of Hagia Sophia. All of this activity needed money, and for this reason Justinian tolerated the excesses of his minister of finance, John of Cappadocia.

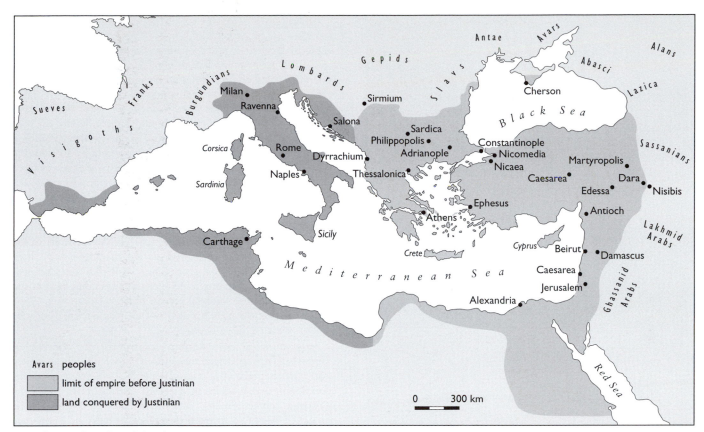

35. The empire of Justinian in AD 565

New dangers for the empire arose in the Danubian provinces with the first appearance of the Slavs and Bulgars. At the same time, an outbreak of plague in 542 created a serious shortage of recruits for the army. In the reigns of Justin II (565–78) and his successors the resources of the empire were unequal to the demands made on them. Justin himself became insane, unable to carry the burden of his responsibilities. He had provoked an outbreak of hostilities by his arrogant treatment of the Persians. At the same time, the Avars, a people of Turkic origins, together with hordes of Slavs, attacked the Balkans, and Italy was overrun by the Lombards.

The emperor Maurice (582–602) was able to obtain a favourable peace with Persia in 590 when he helped Khusrau, the heir to the throne, to regain his kingdom after a rebellion that had killed his father. Before Maurice could turn his attention to the dangerous situation in the Balkans, however, he himself was overthrown and killed in 602 in an army rebellion that elevated Phokas, an insignificant officer, to the throne. Phokas initiated a reign of terror that bled the aristocracy until in 610 he too became the victim of a revolt. The exarch of Carthage rebelled and sent his son, Herakleios, at the head of an army against Constantinople, where he founded a dynasty that was to last till 717.

Herakleios (610–41) came to the throne of an empire that was in mortal danger. The Avars and Slavs continued to be a threat, and the Persian king broke the peace on the pretext of avenging the murder of the emperor Maurice. Herakleios, leaving his capital in the care of the patriarch, went to Asia Minor to gather and train an army for the defence of his realm. For six long years the emperor campaigned against the Persians

with great success, breaking the power of the Persian king. The benefit of his victory, however, was to be reaped by another. The reign of Herakleios saw the tribesmen of Arabia, possibly driven out by the increasing desiccation of their lands, and steeled by the new faith of Islam, overrun both Persian and Byzantine territories. Sassanian Persia succumbed to the new power in 628, to be followed in quick succession by Syria, Palestine, and Egypt. At the death of Herakleios in 641 the Byzantine empire was territorially more compact, comprising Asia Minor, some Balkan coastlines, north Africa, and Sicily.

With the loss of the eastern provinces came greater religious homogeneity. In the future, the Orthodox Church and the Orthodox empire were to be closely intertwined. The heart of the empire now lay in Asia Minor, and with Italy mainly in the hands of the Lombards, the eastern empire became distinctly Greek in language and culture. This was not necessarily clear at the time, and Constans II, Herakleios's grandson, attempted to move the seat of government once more to the west. The experiment ended when he was murdered in Sicily in 668. The last member of the house of Herakleios, Justinian II, reigned twice from 685 to 695 and again from 705 to 711. His arbitrary government became unpopular, and he was banished to Cherson after having been mutilated. In spite of this he was able to regain his throne with the help of the Bulgar khan Terbel, but was killed in an uprising in 711.

The importance of the Herakleian dynasty lies in the fact that it stayed the Arab invasions and preserved Asia Minor. When the Arabs built a fleet and became expert sailors, Constantinople was in grave danger from repeated attacks. Its strong walls, however, withstood the sieges, and in 678 the

Political History AD 330–802: silver votive platter showing the emperor Arcadius and two guards, 388. The son of Theodosius I, Arcadius reigned from 395 to 408, Academia de la Historia, Madrid

caliph Muawiya made peace. Three short reigns followed after the Herakleian dynasty, but in 717 the general of the Anatolikon theme, Leo III the Isaurian (or Syrian), ascended the throne, inaugurating the Isaurian dynasty that was to last until 802.

In 717 the Arabs returned to mount an assault by land and sea on the capital. The siege was abandoned the following year when a discomfited enemy withdrew after an exceptionally hard winter, and Leo's victory at Akroinon in 740 temporarily ended the Muslim advances in Asia Minor. Applying diplomacy, the Byzantines had been able to draw both Bulgars and Chazars to their side in the fight against the Arabs.

Internally, Leo, who had himself been brought to the throne by an army revolt of the Anatolikon and Armeniakon themes, understood the danger these large units posed for the ruler. He, therefore, restructured these territories creating smaller units that were less likely to provide any would-be usurper with the necessary resources. He is thought to have applied the same principle to the Karabisianon theme which housed the fleet.

In 726 Leo issued the *Ecloge* (literally "selection"), reforming the law of the empire. Far more than a mere compilation, this body of legislation reflects the influences of both custom and the orient. In family law, the *Ecloge* curbed the power of the *paterfamilias* by distributing rights and obligations more evenly between spouses; and in criminal law mutilation largely replaced the death penalty.

Leo's reign is remembered as the beginning of the conflict over the use of icons. Icons had a special place in popular worship but were opposed in some theological and intellectual circles. The motives for the emperor's sudden move against the veneration of icons are no longer understood, and possibly were not clear to his contemporaries either. It has been suggested by some that Leo, who came from the eastern provinces of the empire, had fallen under the influence of Arab culture. It is of some significance that the first order forbidding the veneration of pictures was issued in 723 not by a Byzantine ruler but by the caliph Jezid who ordered the removal of pictures from Christian churches in his domain. Others detect in the emperor's fight against icons purely political motives, proposing that Leo, in his bid for autocratic rule, hoped to liberate the people from the influence of the Church. The sources of this period are biased since only the accounts of the iconodules (supporters of icons) survive, making it difficult to grasp the intellectual background to iconoclasm in its totality. Leo tried to gain converts to his ideas by preaching against the veneration of icons which he saw as idolatry. He wrote to Pope Gregory II that this was his duty not only as emperor but also as high priest to his subjects.

Persecution of icon worship began with the removal of Christ's image from above the gates of the Chalke, the entrance to the Great Palace in Constantinople. The officer sent on this commission was lynched by a crowd. Significantly, it was the European theme, Hellas, that immediately revolted at the news. Leo was able to quell the rebellion but could convince neither the pope nor the patriarch of his move against icons. Leo's most formidable opponent, however, was John of Damascus, regarded as the greatest theologian of his time. As a Greek in the service of the caliph at Damascus, he was out of reach of the emperor. John wrote three speeches in defence of holy icons arguing in Neoplatonic terms that icons were merely symbols and a means to communicate with the sacred. His writings were to become the basis for the defence of icons.

With his edict of 726 Leo gave imperial sanction to the destruction of pictures, and the persecutions of the iconodules began in earnest. The emperor could not enforce his will in the west, however, and Pope Gregory III condemned iconoclasm. In a counter move, Leo placed the Churches of Calabria, Sicily, and Illyricum under the patriarchate of Constantinople which meant that the incomes from these territories would now flow directly to the eastern capital.

Leo died in 741 and was succeeded by his son Constantine V (741–75) who had been associated in his father's reign since the age of two. The *strategos* (commander) of the Opsikion theme, Artabasdos, who was related to the imperial house, immediately contested Constantine's succession. He posed as a restorer of images but was defeated in 743. Constantine then took advantage of unrest in the Caliphate, where the Abbasids had replaced the Umayyads and moved the centre from Damascus to Baghdad, to recapture territory in Asia Minor that had been lost in earlier campaigns. For some time, the fight between Arabs and Byzantines was to take on the character of border conflicts, a fact which was later immortalized in the epic of *Digenis Akritis*.

The danger facing the empire was now no longer to be seen in Asia Minor but in the rising power of Bulgaria. Constantine V fought nine campaigns against the Bulgars. In 763 he won a great victory over the khan Teletz who in consequence became the victim of a revolt at home. After this the Byzantines interfered frequently in Bulgaria, which entered a phase of internal upheavals. While Constantine was thus engaged in the Balkans, Ravenna, Byzantium's outpost on the Adriatic, fell to the Lombards. With the eastern empire no longer an important power in Italy, in 754 Pope Stephen II crossed the Alps to seek an alliance with the Frankish monarchy which marked the beginning of a lasting relationship between the papacy and the Carolingians.

In his iconoclast policies Constantine was more radical than his father had been. The "headless synod" of 754 ordered the destruction of pictures, and was followed by renewed persecutions and executions reaching into the highest strata of society. Monasteries were closed down, and their lands were confiscated. Those monks that could escape fled to southern Italy where they founded monasteries and schools, thereby reinforcing the surviving Greek culture of the region.

Hated by the Orthodox Church for his heavy-handedness, the body of Constantine V Kopronymos was later removed from the church of the Holy Apostles where it had been buried. He was, however, also remembered for his great military successes by the people who, in times of danger, would pray at his grave for deliverance from their enemies.

The reign of his son Leo IV (775–80) was characterized by a much more restrained form of iconoclasm. Iconodules were left largely undisturbed, and monks returned to high positions in the Church. When Leo died prematurely in 780, his ten-year-old son became emperor Constantine VI with the iconodule empress Irene as regent. She systematically began to change the officials at court, advancing her own family. The monasteries flourished again under Irene, and she tried to achieve reconciliation with both the papacy and the Frankish power now under Charlemagne. An ecumenical council in 787 anathematized the iconoclast synod of 754 and re-established the veneration of icons. Irene herself signed the canons to that effect in the Magnamara palace in the presence of papal legates. Her name was invoked as a token of peace, and her government was hailed as the bringer of it.

The young Constantine was kept in the background, and his mother arranged several marriages for him. These were the cause of irreconcilable differences between them and in 797 Irene had him imprisoned in the palace and blinded in the very room where he had been born.

The subsequent reign of Irene (797–802) was marked by renewed hostilities and losses in warfare with both Arabs and Bulgars. The latter received tribute payments from that time on. Internally, Irene did much damage to the finances of the empire with a taxation policy that aimed to win her popularity. The most important event of her reign, however, came from the outside. Pope Leo III took the opportunity presented by her rule to crown Charlemagne emperor of a reconstituted western empire on Christmas Day 800 since, so the pope reasoned, there was now no longer an emperor in Constantinople. This signalled the end of the long-maintained fiction of a universal Christian empire with its centre at Constantinople.

In autumn of 802 a palace revolution ended the rule of Irene and she died a year later in exile on the island of Lesbos. It fell to her successor, Nikephoros I (802–11), to undo the damages

of her reign and he addressed himself energetically to restoring the financial and military needs of the empire.

FRANZISKA E. SHLOSSER

See also Arabs, Bulgars, Byzantine Period (Early), Councils, Goths, Slavs

Further Reading

Bryer, Anthony and Judith Herrin (editors), *Iconoclasm*, Birmingham: University of Birmingham, 1977

Bury, J.B., *A History of the Later Roman Empire from Arcadius to Irene, 395 AD–800 AD*, 2 vols, London and New York: Macmillan, 1889

Cameron, Alan, *Circus Factions: Blues and Greens at Rome and Byzantium*, Oxford: Clarendon Press, 1976

Fine, John V.A., *The Early Medieval Balkans: A Critical Survey from the Sixth to the Late Twelfth Century*, Ann Arbor: University of Michigan Press, 1983

Haldon, J.F., *Byzantium in the Seventh Century: The Transformation of a Culture*, Cambridge and New York: Cambridge University Press, 1990; revised edition 1997

Hussey, J.M. (editor), *The Byzantine Empire*, 2 vols., Cambridge: Cambridge University Press, 1966–67 (*The Cambridge Medieval History*, vol. 4, parts 1–2, 2nd edition)

Kaegi, Walter Emil, *Byzantine Military Unrest, 471–843: An Interpretation*, Amsterdam: Hakkert, 1981

Leo III and Constantine V, *A Revised Manual of Roman Law: Founded upon the Ecologa of Leo III and Constantine V, of Isauria, Ecologa Privata Aucta*, translated by Edwin Hanson Freshfield, Cambridge: Cambridge University Press, 1927

Leo III, *Ecloga: Das Gesetzbuch Leons III. und Konstantinos' V.*, edited and translated into German by Ludwig Burgmann, Frankfurt: Löwenklau, 1983

Mango, Cyril, *Byzantium: The Empire of New Rome*, London: Weidenfeld and Nicolson, and New York: Scribner, 1980

Obolensky, Dimitri, *The Byzantine Commonwealth: Eastern Europe, 500–1453*, New York: Praeger, and London: Weidenfeld and Nicolson, 1971

Ostrogorsky, George, *History of the Byzantine State*, 2nd edition, Oxford: Blackwell, 1968; New Brunswick, New Jersey: Rutgers University Press, 1969

Treadgold, Warren, *A History of the Byzantine State and Society*, Stanford, California: Stanford University Press, 1997

Vasiliev, A.A., *History of the Byzantine Empire, 324–1453*, revised edition, 2 vols, Madison: University of Wisconsin Press, 1952

Political History 802–1204

In 802 Byzantium was still recovering from the crises of the previous two centuries. Its realm, of Asia Minor, parts of Greece, Sicily, and toeholds in Italy, was threatened on every side. The vast and far richer Abbasid caliphate, then at its height, was the most obvious threat as Arab forces continued to harry Asia Minor, but the Bulgarian kingdom posed an equally serious threat close to the capital, and the rising empire of Charlemagne loomed in the west. Nikephoros I (802–11), who made important reforms that strengthened the administration after the extravagant reign of his predecessor Irene, recovered the Peloponnese, strengthened the Hellenic population of Greece, and hoped for greater success in the Balkans. Instead, his huge army met with disaster at the hands of the

36. The empire of Basil II in 1025

Bulgars, with Nikephoros becoming the first emperor to fall in battle since Valens in 378.

Although the Bulgars inflicted more defeats and advanced up to the walls of Constantinople, the death of their khan removed the immediate threat. These military setbacks provoked Leo V (813–20) to revive iconoclasm, remembering the great military successes of iconoclastic emperors in the 8th century. His murder, however, was followed by the devastating revolt of Thomas the Slav during which the Arabs landed in Sicily and – a more immediate threat to imperial naval supremacy close to home – occupied Crete in 828. Theophilos (829–42) laid the basis for recovery by tightening the administrative system based on military districts called themes, and improving the army. He issued new coinage, was an active builder, and presided over a cultural revival. Nevertheless, he suffered the humiliation of seeing Amorium, home of the dynasty, fall to Arab attack in 838.

The tide turned under Michael III (842–68). His victory in Asia Minor in 863 brought the centuries of Arab raids to an end, while his extensive fortifications laid the basis for advances to the east. He had restored veneration of images in 843, ending a long period of ecclesiastical turmoil. Byzantine influence now spread to the Slavic world thanks to the missionary efforts patronized by the highly learned patriarch Photios (858–67, 877–86). Although at first directed to Moravia, they soon led to the conversion of the Bulgars and Serbs to Orthodox Christianity. In 860, however, a potential new threat, a Russian fleet, appeared at Constantinople.

Basil I (867–86), an Armenian of humble origins, founded Byzantium's most successful dynasty, which presided over

triumphant expansion, prosperity, and cultural flourishing for two centuries. Basil himself rebuilt the army and moved on the offensive in the east. He conquered much of southern Italy, which became a refuge for the Greek population of Sicily, finally lost with the fall of Syracuse in 878. Basil's work of reforming the laws and making them available in Greek was continued by his son Leo VI (886–912), a ruler famed for his learning, but also for his four marriages which caused serious dissent with the Church. External troubles also were not over: an Arab raider sacked Thessalonica, second city of the empire, in 904 and the Russians attacked in 907, but the greatest danger came from the Bulgars. To weaken them, Leo called in the Hungarians whose settlement permanently changed the map of Europe. Nevertheless, this was a flourishing time for the Bulgars whose king Symeon aimed at ruling the empire. During the regency that succeeded Leo, Symeon's victorious forces approached Constantinople and almost assured his aims of an imperial title and marriage, but the usurpation of Romanos I Lekapenos (920–44) saved the day for Byzantium. In the east Romanos extended Byzantine territory to Armenia and Mesopotamia, where in 944 Edessa fell and one of Christianity's most sacred relics, the sacred towel that bore the imprint of Christ's face, was transferred to Constantinople. He also gained significant victories over pirates and the Russians. Romanos began a legislative assault on great landowners who had been acquiring land from their smaller neighbours, a tendency that could weaken the system of military landholdings; the effort continued through the next several reigns. Meanwhile the legitimate emperor Constantine VII Porphyrogennetos (913–59) devoted himself to the learning that reached its height in this period. During the short reign of his son Romanos II (959–63) the great general Nikephoros Phokas finally reconquered Crete in 961, re-establishing Byzantine naval supremacy in the Aegean and making further advances possible.

Byzantium reached its apogee under Basil II (976–1025). During his childhood, the regents Nikephoros Phokas (963–69) and John Tzimiskes (969–76) annexed eastern Bulgaria after inflicting a signal defeat on the Russians, and extended imperial power ever further east, bringing much of Syria under control. Tzimiskes, perhaps the greatest general the empire ever had, conquered Damascus and Beirut and even approached Jerusalem in a movement that had many aspects of a crusade. Byzantine influence took deeper root in the west when Tzimiskes married his niece Theophano to the future Holy Roman emperor Otto III. The sole rule of Basil II began with a devastating series of civil wars, 976–89, which finally established imperial supremacy over the powerful landed magnates of Asia Minor, and ended their efforts to submerge their smaller neighbours. Thereafter expansion was rapid on all fronts: in the east Basil annexed much of Armenia; in the west he secured his position in Italy. Basil is most famous, however, for his unrelenting Balkan campaigns that brought Bulgaria under complete control and extended the empire to the Danube. His savage but effective victories earned him the name of Bulgaroktonos, "Slayer of the Bulgars". He was planning a campaign to reconquer Sicily when he died after the longest reign in Byzantine history. By then, the empire was the most powerful state in Europe and the Near East. Of the powers that threatened Byzantium in 802, the caliphate had collapsed, Bulgaria was reduced to insignificance, and the western empire was concerned with its own problems. The empire also enjoyed its greatest influence as the centre of the Orthodox world, vastly expanded in 988 when the conversion of prince Vladimir of Russia brought his country into the Byzantine sphere.

The glory of Byzantium faded with incredible rapidity. Within 50 years of Basil's death, new enemies had struck mortal blows from which the empire never recovered. Although the Komnenoi (1081–1185) effected a partial restoration, the state never regained the extent, wealth, or power it had under Basil II. Incompetent rulers, strife between military and civil factions, increasing decentralization, and frequent conspiracies and revolts combined with changing external circumstances to weaken the empire. In 1040 it was still strong enough to attempt the reconquest of Sicily and to annex further territory in Armenia, but these were the last gains. In the mid-11th century the Seljuk Turks appeared in the east, and the Normans in Italy. Both soon exerted pressure on a state in serious financial trouble. Extravagance had led in 1050 to the debasement of the gold coinage, which had maintained its purity since the time of Constantine and served as a universal standard. In 1054 the Byzantine Church split definitively with Rome, leaving a legacy of hostility that would never be repaired. Two years later the empress Theodora, last descendant of Basil II, died.

The military revolt that brought Isaac Komnenos (1057–59) to the throne in an effort to suppress corruption failed to solve the problems that the ineffectual regimes of his successors only compounded. Finally, Romanos IV (1068–71) made a major attempt to reform the army and to crush the constantly encroaching Seljuks. He met disaster at Manzikert in 1071. The Seljuk victory left Asia Minor open to the Turks who were soon ravaging every part of it, and could never be dislodged. In the same year the Normans took Bari, the empire's last outpost in Italy. During the next decade Turkish attacks combined with constant revolts to destabilize the empire and bring the almost total loss of Asia Minor. Economic collapse was not far away since the currency was drastically debased.

When Alexios I Komnenos (1081–1118) came to the throne, the empire was in ruins. Turks had occupied most of Asia Minor and the Normans landed in Albania and rapidly advanced into Greece. Recognizing the western threat as the most immediate, Alexios turned to Venice, long a subject, then an ally of Byzantium. In exchange for extensive concessions that gave them virtually free trade in the empire, the Venetians sent their fleet to rescue Alexios. This combined with the death of the Norman leader to allow Alexios to turn to the interior of the Balkans where he suppressed revolts and neutralized the invading Cuman and Pecheneg tribes. By 1094 the Danube was once again the imperial frontier. At the same time Byzantium advanced further towards feudalism as the emperor made considerable grants of land with immunity from taxation, especially to his relatives.

Alexios was ready to turn east when the uncontrollable forces of the First Crusade arrived in 1096. He sent them on to Asia Minor where their victories enabled the empire to regain considerable territory. The crusaders' reluctance to submit to imperial authority or to surrender Antioch, however, led to further conflicts, especially with the Normans. Finally in 1110 Alexios was free to move against the Seljuks, who now ruled a state in central Asia Minor. His successes ensured control over the rich coastal region and laid the base for further advances by his son John (1118–43), who consolidated Byzantine Asia Minor by acquiring additional territory and establishing a network of strategic fortresses that served as bases for advance. He campaigned successfully against the Seljuks, whom he confined to the Anatolian plateau. Much of his effort was directed to Cilicia, which he conquered, and to Antioch, which recognized his authority. In the west he consolidated Byzantine control and neutralized the threat from Hungary. His one failure was a war against Venice, after which he was obliged to renew their trading privileges.

During the reign of Manuel I (1143–80) Byzantium was renowned as a centre of wealth and culture, but also saw the beginning of a fatal decline. This was a time of considerable influence from the rapidly advancing West, reflecting the taste and preoccupations of the emperor who tended to neglect the ultimately much greater danger from the east. The immediate threat, though, came with a renewed war with the Normans and the unwelcome arrival of the Second Crusade in 1147. Manuel hurried the crusaders across into Anatolia where they met total defeat. With the expensive help of Venice, he defeated the Normans but failed in the last attempt to establish a Byzantine foothold in Italy. Manuel fought two successful wars with Hungary, which recognized his suzerainty, thereby gaining Dalmatia and the enmity of Venice, which felt threatened. In the subsequent war (1170–77) Manuel had once again to renew all the Venetian privileges. To balance them, he had made similar concessions to Genoa as his father had to Pisa. As a result, most of the empire's trade was in the hands of the Italian states.

Manuel extended the practice of granting lands to subordinates who would collect taxes and contribute to the army. In this he strengthened his military (though at the price of an increasingly powerful aristocracy) while his new system of fortifications bolstered Byzantine Anatolia preparatory to a major advance against the Turks. He had already made a triumphal entry into Antioch, and entered into alliance with the crusaders of Jerusalem against Egypt. His ambitions in the east, however, came to disaster at Myriokephalon in Asia Minor in 1176. The imperial army that hoped to solve the Seljuk problem once and for all was completely crushed. In the aftermath major bastions fell permanently to the Turks, whose nomads encroached further on imperial territories. Although Byzantium was still the greatest regional power in 1180, Manuel had spent much of its treasury and prestige and his death was followed by a rapid collapse.

Resentment against the Italians and their privileges culminated in 1182 when traders were massacred and their quarters looted. Manuel's cousin Andronikos I (1183–85) seized power during the crisis, cleaned out corruption, and attacked the over-powerful aristocracy, but the disastrous Norman sack of Thessalonica led to his overthrow and murder by the urban mob. Isaac Angelos (1185–95) proved incapable of maintaining central control in the face of external threats and major revolts. Although the Normans were defeated, and the Third Crusade passed through without disturbance in 1189, a successful revolt that established a new Bulgarian empire in 1186 fatally undermined the Byzantine position in the Balkans. Revolts and widespread disorder increased under Alexios III (1195–1203) who had deposed and blinded his brother Isaac. When plans for a new crusade were announced, Isaac's son Alexios appealed for aid against his uncle, making fabulous promises to the crusaders. The Venetians agreed, despite the denunciations of the pope, to divert the crusade to Constantinople, where they arrived in 1203. The young Alexios IV assumed the throne but was unable to pay off the crusaders. When his efforts on their behalf provoked a revolt that deposed him, the crusaders attacked. On 12 April 1204, for the first time ever, Constantinople was taken by a foreign army. The city was mercilessly looted, a Latin empire established, and Byzantium permanently finished as a great power.

CLIVE FOSS

See also Bulgars, Byzantine Period (Middle), Commonwealth, Crusades, Iconoclasm, Normans, Russia, Schism, Seljuks, Venetians

Further Reading

Choniates, Nicetas, *O City of Byzantium: Annals of Niketas Choniates*, translated by Harry J. Magoulias, Detroit: Wayne State University Press, 1984

Hussey, J.M. (editor), *The Byzantine Empire*, Cambridge: Cambridge University Press, 1966–67 (*The Cambridge Medieval History*, vol. 4, parts 1–2, 2nd edition)

Jenkins, Romilly, *Byzantium: The Imperial Centuries, AD 610–1071*, London: Weidenfeld and Nicolson, 1966; New York: Random House, 1967

Komnene, Anna, *The Alexiad of Anna Comnena*, translated by E.R.A. Sewter, Harmondsworth and Baltimore: Penguin, 1969

Magdalino, Paul, *The Empire of Manuel I Komnenos*, Cambridge and New York: Cambridge University Press, 1993

Psellos, Michael, *The Chronographia*, translated by E.R.A. Sewter, London: Routledge, and New Haven, Connecticut: Yale University Press, 1953; as *Fourteen Byzantine Rulers*, Harmondsworth and New York: Penguin, 1966

Runciman, Steven, *The Emperor Romanus Lecapenus and His Reign: A Study of Tenth-Century Byzantium*, Cambridge: Cambridge University Press, 1929; reprinted 1988

Treadgold, Warren, *The Byzantine Revival, 780–842*, Stanford, California: Stanford University Press, 1988

Treadgold, Warren, *A History of the Byzantine State and Society*, Stanford, California: Stanford University Press, 1997

Whittow, Mark, *The Making of Orthodox Byzantium, 600–1025*, Basingstoke: Macmillan, 1996

Political History 1204–1261

The sack of Constantinople in April 1204 marked the end of the Byzantine empire, at least temporarily. The French and Venetian Crusaders who had brought this about, whether by luck or by accident, sought to carve out lordships in Greece and the Aegean, and in so doing appropriated for their use the name Romania, which from thence fell from Greek usage as a geographic identification of the Byzantine empire. The partition committee of 24 men – 12 Franks and 12 Venetians – based their division on Byzantine tax registers compiled for Alexios IV in 1203. Possession and effective defence of the newly acquired territories were critical. While Niketas Choniates marvelled at the task that lay ahead for the crusaders, the latter sought to make a quick conquest by taking advantage of Greek demoralization and confusion, as well as the continued presence of the crusader army until March 1205.

By September 1204 the area south of the Rhodope mountains between Constantinople and Thessalonica was reported subdued. Up to March 1205 Greek resistance was light and an army led by Boniface of Montferrat, the ruler of Thessalonica, encountered little opposition in taking Thebes, Athens, and the island of Euboea. In much of central Greece the Latins were welcomed as liberators and, after they made concessions to Greek *archontes* (rulers) guaranteeing their own position in the new order and the continuance of Greek inheritance practices and the Orthodox religion, they were even hailed as the bringers of some hope of stability following the destabilization and disintegration which had characterized the provinces of the Byzantine empire in the last 20 years of the 12th century. This first campaign came to a halt before the fortresses of Acrocorinth, Argos, and Nauplia, where the first serious Greek opposition was led by Leo Skouros. Boniface had carefully avoided any trespass on potential Venetian territories in Epirus and he continued to avoid a possibly hostile encounter in the Morea too, when he allowed William de Champlitte and Geoffrey de Villehardouin to conquer that area. The conquest proceeded from Corinth west and south via Patras and Andravida. Three sieges and one battle are mentioned by the western chroniclers; they emphasize the ease with which the conquest proceeded and compromise was reached with the Greeks. There is much that is obscure here. The southeastern corner of the Peloponnese, the Skorta region, was not

37. The Greek world in 1214

conquered until the late 1240s, while many Greek landowners who saw no chance of reaching an accommodation with the Franks sought refuge in Epirus. By contrast, Latin expeditions to Nicomedia and Cyzicus in Asia Minor and up the Maritza valley to Philippopolis (modern Plovdiv) were contained and repulsed by the Nicene Greeks and the Bulgarians respectively.

When they captured Constantinople, the crusaders had not expunged all Greek resistance, as they clearly believed at the time. In July 1203, as the crusaders arrived on the Bosporus and his father-in-law, Alexios III (1195–1203), was deposed, Theodore I Laskaris (d. 1222) established himself at Nicaea; in the summer of 1205, following Latin defeat at the hands of the Bulgarians at Adrianople, he was proclaimed emperor. This Byzantine government in exile was eventually to recapture Constantinople in July 1261, but for now it contained Latin expansion into Asia Minor by securing its power base in Bithynia. The immediate and most serious threat to the Latin position came from the Vlacho-Bulgarians led by Kalojan. Eager to gain papal recognition for a Bulgarian empire, Kalojan had sought coronation as emperor and recognition of a Latin Church from pope Innocent III as early as 1203. Though his initial approaches to the crusading army had been friendly, they had been rebuffed and followed up by Latin incursions into his territory.

In April 1205 Kalojan inflicted a serious defeat on the crusaders at Adrianople and went on to launch raids into Thrace. On Kalojan's death in 1207 the Latin empire was granted a respite, and the subsequent power struggle among his successors was not resolved until the emergence of John II Asen as tsar of the Bulgars (1218–41). Asen contested control of Thrace with the Greeks of Epirus, whom he defeated at the Battle of Klokonitsa in 1230. Thereafter it was his proud boast that the Latins only survived in Constantinople by his leave. Certainly the Greeks rulers of Nicaea were to profit from his

death, gaining many Bulgarian territories in Thrace and Macedonia and in 1246 capturing Thessalonica from the Greeks of Epirus.

Michael I Komnenos Doukas (1205–15) was the illegitimate son of John Doukas and the cousin of Alexios III. For a short time in 1204 he was in the army of Boniface of Montferrat, but left to lead Greek resistance in Epirus. Epirus had become a refuge for many who could not come to terms with the Franks and there was something of the fanatic about Michael's attack on the Latins in Thessaly. By 1210 he had recovered many towns from Latin control and had treated captured Latins with marked brutality. His brother and successor Theodore (1214–30) captured Ochrid (1216) and Thessalonica (1224). The Latin emperor Peter de Courtenay sought to relieve Epirot pressure on Constantinople by proceeding to his capital along the Via Egnatia with his force of 5000 troops. Somewhere along the way he was captured by Theodore and died in prison. Until defeated at Klokonitsa the Epirot Greeks seemed poised to recapture Constantinople itself. Their loss of Thessalonica to the Greeks of Nicaea effectively left the leadership of the Greek resistance in Nicaean hands.

Despite this instability in the north Aegean states, the principality of Achaea and the lordship of Athens and Thebes enjoyed some stability, with secure frontiers and an uninterrupted succession of rulers. The principality of Achaea certainly flourished and in the 1240s was able to offer substantial naval and financial support to the beleaguered Latin empire. In 1259 Prince William of Achaea (1246–78) formed an alliance with the rulers of Epirus to counter Nicene Greek expansion into Macedonia. At Pelagonia his army was deserted by the Epirots and was surrounded and defeated by the Greeks of Nicaea. William and many of his leading knights were captured. On 25 July 1261 the Byzantines recaptured Constantinople itself. Prince William ceded the towns of

Monemvasia, Mistra, and Maina. From then onwards the Frankish position in Greece was to be a defensive one, down to the extinction of the principality of Achaea in 1430.

The Venetians too gained much territory by the partition of 1205. In 1206 they began the conquest of Crete and licensed scions of noble Venetian families to set themselves up as rulers of the Aegean islands. Marco Sanudo became Duke of the Archipelago based upon the islands of Naxos, Paros, and Syros, while his cousin Marino Dandolo set himself up as lord of Andros. In Constantinople itself the Venetian *podestà* (chief magistrate) took the title of "*podestà* and despot of the empire of Romania and lord of a quarter and a half of a quarter of the same empire". There were plans at least among some of the Venetians in Constantinople for independence from the mother city, but such moves were quashed, and the title passed to the doge by 1217. In the Aegean the Venetians maintained two sorts of possessions – colonies like Crete, Corfu, Korone, and Methone, which were administered by officials sent out from Venice, and the *condominia*, which were conquered by private enterprise but ruled by Venetian noble families. The former saw the Greeks treated as subjects, with occasional revolts against Venetian rule. The latter were marked by the policy of accommodation and concession prevalent in the Frankish states of mainland Greece. With the exception of Corfu (lost to Epirus in 1214) Venetian occupation of these territories lasted well into the 15th century and in the case of Crete was to persist until 1669.

There was a third Greek successor state to the Byzantine empire, namely the empire of Trebizond, set up in 1204 by Alexios and David Komnenos with the help of Tamara of Georgia. The new empire was more a symptom of the fragmentation of Byzantine power in the late 12th century than a reaction to the Latin conquest. Alexios fled from Constantinople in September 1185 when his relative Andronikos I (1183–85) was dethroned. Alexios was criticized by Niketas Choniates for taking no action against the Latins in Constantinople. Isolated as they were and surrounded by enemies, the emperors of Trebizond concentrated their energies on survival, acknowledging the suzerainty of Seljuks, Mongols, and Ottomans in turn. The empire was to last until 1461, when it was incorporated in the Ottoman empire.

PETER LOCK

See also Epirus, Latin Empire, Nicaea, Trebizond, Venetokratia

Further Reading

Bon, Antoine, *La Morée franque*, 2 vols., Paris: Boccard, 1969

Fine, John, V.A., *The Late Medieval Balkans: A Critical Survey from the Sixth to the Late Twelfth Century*, Ann Arbor: University of Michigan Press, 1987

Lock, Peter, *The Franks in the Aegean, 1204–1500*, London and New York: Longman, 1995

Miller, William, *Trebizond: The Last Greek Empire*, London: SPCK, 1926

Setton, Kenneth, *The Papacy and the Levant, 1204–1571*, vol. 1, Philadelphia: American Philosophical Society, 1976

Thiriet, Freddy, *La Romanie vénitienne au Moyen Age*, Paris: Boccard, 1975

Vasiliev, A.A., "The Foundation of the Empire of Trebizond, 1204–1222", *Speculum*, 11 (1936): pp. 3–37

Political History 1261–1453

In the period 1261–1453 the Byzantine empire was beset by a variety of internal problems and external crises which eventually led to the disintegration of the state and to the fall of Constantinople to the Ottoman Turks in 1453. It is necessary, however, to make a distinction between the first part of the period (1261–c.1350), when the state was relatively strong and prosperous, and the second half (c.1350–1453), when Byzantium was reduced to an "empire of the straits" as a result of civil wars and loss of territory to both Turks and Serbians.

The period began with high hopes following the triumphal entry into Constantinople of Michael VIII Palaiologos (1261–82) who removed form the throne the last Laskarid emperor, John IV (1258–61), and established the rule of the longest-lasting dynasty in Byzantine history, the Palaiologans (1261–1453).

The recovery of Constantinople had some important political consequences for Byzantine foreign policy. For one, it displaced the focus of interest of the Byzantine rulers from Asia to Europe. The papacy, Charles of Anjou, the French royal house of Valois, and the Venetians all became engaged between 1261 and 1314 in various efforts to retake Constantinople. In Michael Palaiologos' day, Charles of Anjou, brother of the French king Louis IX and master of Sicily, led a coalition including the despot of Epirus Michael II Angelos (c.1231–71) and the kings of Serbia and Bulgaria. Michael VIII deflected the coalition through a major concession on his part and masterful diplomacy. The concession was the Union of Lyons in 1274, according to which Byzantium recognized the primacy of the Roman Church. The papacy forced Charles of Anjou to abandon his plans for a time, but in 1281 pope Martin IV decided that Michael VIII had not really implemented the union and gave his full support to Charles of Anjou. The diplomacy of Michael VIII again prevented a Western expedition against Constantinople; he entered into negotiations with the king of Aragon and others, contributing significantly to the attack of Aragon on Sicily occasioned by the Sicilian vespers in 1282. Michael VIII's heir, Andronikos II (1282–1328), who repudiated the Union of Lyons, had to face yet another Western coalition in 1308–14, but good diplomacy and sheer luck saved the day. The matrimonial policy of the Palaiologan emperors also served the purpose of thwarting a possible Western attack on Constantinople. Andronikos II took as a second wife Irene/Yolanda of Montferrat, and his heir Andronikos III (1328–41) married Anne of Savoy.

The increasing involvement of the Byzantine empire in the West meant a more active Balkan policy vis-à-vis the despots of Epirus and Thessaly. It was, however, only in the first half of the 14th century that the emperors of Constantinople succeeded in subjugating the despotate of Epirus and the independent rulers of Thessaly. The city of Ioannina recognized Byzantine overlordship in 1318 and the rest of Epirus submitted in 1340. Thessaly was acquired piecemeal in 1333. In 1348, however, both Thessaly and Epirus fell into the hands of the Serbian emperor Stephan IV Dushan, and were never again fully reunited with Constantinople. In the Peloponnese the process of reconquest from the Latin principality of Achaea continued throughout the period; after 1349 the Byzantine

38. The Byzantine empire and its neighbours in 1350

possessions were organized as the despotate of the Morea, which became one of the most vital parts of the state.

The necessity for an active policy in the west led to neglect of the eastern boundaries of the empire that proved to have disastrous consequences in the long run. Michael VIII overtaxed the border soldiers (*akritai*) on the Byzantine–Turkish frontier and even withdrew troops from there for his western campaigns. The Turks themselves were in a condition of political and social turmoil after the collapse of the Seljuk sultanate of Rum under Mongol pressure. A powerful Turkish migratory thrust led to the collapse of the Turkish–Byzantine frontier in the late 13th century. The emperors in Constantinople became

seriously involved with the problem too late and could do too little. Andronikos II made a number of efforts to remedy the situation: he personally campaigned in Asia Minor in 1282 and tried to mitigate the pro-Laskarid sympathies of the population of Asia Minor by visiting the blind John IV in his prison in 1290. The military successes of the able general Alexios Philanthropenos were shortlived and the rebellion that he led in 1295 ended his career. The Byzantine defeat at Bapheus, near Nicomedia, in 1302 by a Turkish force led by Osman brought the Ottomans to the fore for the first time. The Ottomans took Bursa in 1326, Nicaea in 1331, Nicomedia in 1337. Further to the south Ephesus, Miletus, and Sardis fell to the Seljuk emirates in the first decade of the 14th century. In a misguided effort to halt the advance of the Turks, Andronikos II in 1303 hired the Grand Catalan Company, a group of undisciplined Spanish mercenaries who soon turned against their Byzantine masters, laying waste to Thrace, Mount Athos, and Thessaly, and eventually establishing the Catalan Duchy of Athens (1311–88) in place of the Frankish lords who had hitherto ruled Attica and Boeotia.

The territorial contraction of the empire and the decrease of its tax resources led to a feeling of restlessness among the powerful landed aristocracy. The Byzantine political elites became increasingly prone to support rival candidates for the imperial throne who promised high material rewards and tax exemptions to their followers. This competition for the diminishing resources of the state fuelled two major civil wars in the first half of the 14th century and exacerbated succession conflicts in the second half. The first civil war (1321–28) between the two Andronikoi, Andronikos II and his grandson Andronikos III, began when the former decided to disinherit the latter because of an amorous escapade that had led to the murder of his brother. Andronikos III was joined in his struggle against his grandfather by prominent aristocrats, such as the future emperor John Kantakouzenos, and succeeded in 1328 in ousting the old Andronikos. Andronikos III (1328–41) achieved the annexation of Thessaly and Epirus to the empire, and in 1333 joined an anti-Turkish alliance with Venice and the Latin lords of the Aegean. The promise of his short reign, however, remained unfulfilled after his death due to the onset of the second civil war (1341–48) which had even more disastrous consequences for the body politic than the first one. It was fought between the regency government of John V (1341–91), including his mother Anne of Savoy, the patriarch John XIV Kalekas, and the admiral of the fleet Alexios Apokaukos, on the one hand, and John VI Kantakouzenos (1347–54), on the other. Both parties in the conflict claimed to represent the rights of the young John V Palaiologos and, when John Kantakouzenos eventually entered Constantinople in triumph, he ruled in the name of the legitimate Palaiologan emperor.

The second civil war saw social conflicts on a scale unprecedented in Byzantine history. Before declaring himself co-emperor in the Thracian town of Didymoteichon, John VI Kantakouzenos had sent letters to prominent men in the cities, seeking their support; when his letter was read on 27 October 1341 in Adrianople, three men, one of whom was certainly a merchant, aroused the people of the city, who attacked the aristocrats and burned their houses. The civil war spread rapidly to the cities of Thrace and Macedonia. The most acute aspects of social conflict were visible in Thessalonica, where the opposition to Kantakouzenos was led by the Zealots, a group with radical social views that ruled the city from 1342 until 1349. Although the social alignments in this civil war are not always easily drawn, the main lines of division are clear. The merchants, perhaps the bankers, certainly the sailors, and in general the people whom contemporary authors call *mesoi*, i.e. the middle classes, supported the regency government. The landed aristocracy sided primarily with John VI Kantakouzenos, the winner of the civil war. Kantakouzenos was crowned co-emperor again in Constantinople in February 1347 and married his daughter Helen to John V Palaiologos. His victory was, however, bittersweet.

In his brief reign (1347–54) Kantakouzenos failed to stop the advance of the Serbians, his erstwhile allies during the civil war. By the middle of the 14th century the empire of Stephan IV Dushan (1331–55) stretched from the Danube to the gulf of Corinth, with only the city of Thessalonica remaining in Byzantine hands. In the second civil war and during his rule as a sole emperor, Kantakouzenos regularly used Turkish mercenaries, who thus became familiar with the rich resources offered by the Balkans. Kantakouzenos had employed first the emir of Aydin, Umur pasha, but subsequently concluded an alliance with the Ottoman house that was cemented by the marriage of his daughter Theodora to the Ottoman ruler Orhan (1326–62). In 1354 John V forced Kantakouzenos's abdication and assumed sole power over the greatly reduced territory of the empire consisting of Constantinople, Thrace, Thessalonica, parts of the Peloponnese, and Philadelphia and its immediate surroundings in Asia Minor. Both financially and politically the Byzantine empire was a ruined state.

The middle of the 14th century marks a break not only because of the territorial reduction of the Byzantine state, but also due to the rise in political influence and prestige of the Orthodox Church. Unlike the imperial office, the Church emerged unscathed and even strengthened from the period of the civil wars. The heightened prestige of the Orthodox Church enabled it not only to command the spiritual allegiance of the people, but also to fill the political vacuum left by the decline of the state's institutions. The Church had grown as a judicial institution since the reign of Andronikos II, who reformed the supreme court in 1296 to include ecclesiastical judges. In the second half of the 14th century the ecclesiastical courts grew in power and met much more regularly than the imperial ones. The rise of Church power in this period was, however, chiefly due to the revival of monasticism. The monasteries of Mount Athos had been detached from imperial control since November 1312, but it was the hesychast belief in the possibility of contemplating the divine light through rigorous asceticism that gave a new impetus to Orthodox monasticism. The monastic theology of hesychasm triumphed in two councils of Constantinople, the first in 1341 pronouncing the orthodoxy of the teachings of Gregory Palamas and condemning those of Barlaam and Gregory Akindynos, the second one in 1351 denouncing the opposition of Nikephoros Gregoras. Hesychast monks, such as Kallistos I (1350–54 and 1355–63), Philotheos Kokkinos (1354–55 and 1364–76), and Neilos (1380–88), captured the patriarchate during the second half of the 14th century and often influenced the will of emperors.

The middle of the 14th century marks also a new stage in the advance of the Turks. In 1354 the Ottomans acquired their first permanent foothold in Europe, the fortress of Tzympe in the Gallipoli peninsula. A fortunate accident allowed the Ottomans to capture the fortress of Gallipoli itself in 1356 after an earthquake had damaged its walls. From this time onwards, the Ottomans assumed control of the Dardanelles and crossed regularly into Europe. Philippopolis was conquered in 1363 and Adrianople c.1369. The most that John V could do was to seek closer ties with the West in the hope of a crusade. He journeyed to Hungary in 1366 and in 1369 to

Rome, where he declared his personal conversion to Catholicism. On his way home he was detained in Venice because of his debts and was forced to promise the cession of the island of Tenedos in the Sea of Marmara to the Venetians. The only result of John V's diplomatic efforts was the expedition of Amadeo of Savoy which restored Gallipoli to the Byzantines for ten years (1366–76).

The Ottoman advance, however, did not propel Byzantium into coalitions with other Balkan powers. In 1371 the brothers Vukasin and John Uglesa, rulers of Slavic principalities in Macedonia that emerged after the disintegration of Stephan Dushan's empire, were defeated by the Ottomans at the battle at Chernomen on the Maritza river. This Turkish victory opened up the Balkans for further Ottoman conquest. After the Battle of Maritza John V sought an accommodation with the Turks and became an Ottoman vassal obliged to join the sultan in his military campaigns. The desperate situation in the last years of John V's rule was further aggravated by the rebellions of his son Andronikos IV (1373, 1376–79) and his grandson John VII (1391). Thessalonica submitted to the Ottomans in 1387 and Thessaly in 1393. As an Ottoman vassal, the future emperor Manuel II (1391–1425) had to accompany Sultan Bayezid I "the Thunderbolt" (1389–1402) on campaigns in Anatolia and witnessed the conquest of Philadelphia, the last independent Byzantine city in Asia Minor. The Ottoman blockade of Constantinople began in 1394 and seemed to spell the imminent fall of the imperial capital.

Nevertheless, the life of Byzantium was prolonged almost miraculously for 50 more years. A Mongol army under the leadership of Timur invaded Asia Minor from the east and dealt a crushing blow to the Ottomans at the battle of Ankara on 28 July 1402, taking into captivity Sultan Bayezid himself. The civil war that broke out among Bayezid's four sons allowed Byzantium a much-needed breathing space. Manuel II Palaiologos, who had been in the west since 1399, returned immediately to Constantinople. An energetic ruler as well as author of numerous literary works, Manuel II negotiated the recovery of Thessalonica and supervised the reconstruction of the barrier walls across the isthmus of Corinth protecting the despotate of the Morea. In the first half of the 15th century the Morea became the most viable part of Byzantium and a centre of Hellenic revival exemplified in the ideas of the philosopher and political thinker George Gemistos Plethon (c.1360–1452). Its capital Mistra witnessed a remarkable cultural and artistic renaissance similar to the one that had occurred in Constantinople in the early 14th century. While the capital of the empire was slowly dying, the despots of the Morea managed to extend their boundaries. Manuel II's three sons, the despots Theodore, Constantine, and Thomas, succeeded in conquering the Latin principalities in the northern part of Peloponnese in 1430–32.

In the meantime, the Ottomans had renewed their expansionist policies. Constantinople was besieged in 1422 and the Byzantine empire became a vassal state of the Ottomans again in 1424. Thessalonica fell for a second and last time to the Turks in 1430. Manuel's son and heir John VIII (1425–48) again pursued a rapprochement with the West in order to ward off the Ottoman advance. He personally participated in the Council of Ferrara-Florence in 1438–39, where he signed the decree of union recognizing the primacy of the Roman Church.

The Union of Ferrara-Florence, like the Union of Lyons a century and a half earlier, met with strong popular opposition. Moreover, the crusade of 1444 triggered by the union never reached Constantinople, but was crushed by the Turks at Varna. John VIII's brother Constantine XI Palaiologos (1449–1453), the last ruler of the Byzantine empire, accepted the Union of Ferrara-Florence in the hope of gaining military assistance from the West. He did not implement the union, however, until the eve of the Ottoman conquest, on 12 December 1452. Constantine XI Palaiologos fought bravely during the Ottoman siege of Constantinople and perished in the final battle on 29 May 1453. The despotate of the Morea survived the conquest of Constantinople by exactly seven years; Mistra fell to the Ottomans on 29 May 1460. Trebizond, the last outpost of independent Hellenism, submitted to the Turks in 1461.

DIMITER G. ANGELOV

See also Byzantine Period (Late), Hesychasm, Mistra, Ottomans, Renaissance (Palaiologan), Serbs

Further Reading

Barker, John W., *Manuel II Palaeologus, 1391–1425: A Study in Late Byzantine Statesmanship*, New Brunswick, New Jersey: Rutgers University Press, 1969

Geanakoplos, Deno John, *Emperor Michael Palaeologus and the West, 1258–1282: A Study in Byzantine-Latin Relations*, Cambridge, Massachusetts: Harvard University Press, 1959

Laiou, Angeliki E., *Constantinople and the Latins: The Foreign Policy of Andronicus II, 1238–1328*, Cambridge, Massachusetts: Harvard University Press, 1972

Nicol, Donald M., *Church and Society in the Last Centuries of Byzantium*, Cambridge and New York: Cambridge University Press, 1979

Nicol, Donald M., *The Last Centuries of Byzantium 1261–1453*, 2nd edition, Cambridge and New York: Cambridge University Press, 1993

Nicol, Donald M., *The Reluctant Emperor: A Biography of John Cantacuzene, Byzantine Emperor and Monk, c. 1295–1383*, Cambridge and New York: Cambridge University Press, 1996

Ostrogorsky, George, *History of the Byzantine State*, 2nd edition, Oxford: Blackwell, 1968; New Brunswick, New Jersey: Rutgers University Press, 1969

Runciman, Steven, *The Fall of Constantinople, 1453*, Cambridge: Cambridge University Press, 1965

Political History 1453–1832

Those who seek the unbroken thread of the Hellenic tradition may find it at its most tenuous, and therefore vital, in the Ottoman period, when the Greeks had no political history. Even the conventional dates are unhelpful. True, in May 1453 the 21-year-old Sultan Mehmet II conquered Constantinople, when Constantine XI, last Byzantine emperor "of the Romaioi", died. True, in August 1832 the 16-year-old Bavarian prince Otto accepted the throne as king Otho of the "Hellenes" of Greece. But the dates are inconsequential and all the two Christian rulers had in common was that they acknowledged the ecclesiastical supremacy of Rome, while most of their Orthodox subjects did not. In fact most "Greek"

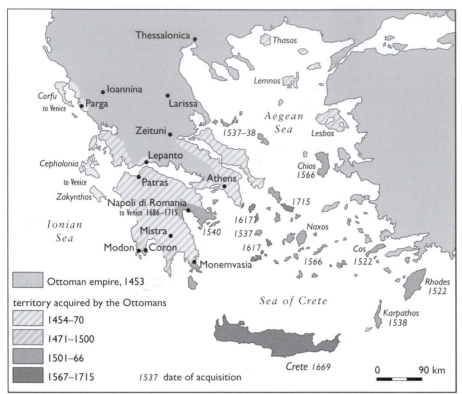

39. Greece under the Ottomans

Map legend:

Ottoman empire, 1453

territory acquired by the Ottomans
- 1454–70
- 1471–1500
- 1501–66
- 1567–1715

1537 date of acquisition

0   90 km

Orthodox had been secular subjects of the Ottoman state for some decades before 1453 and were to remain so for some decades after 1832. But that did not make the Ottoman empire Byzantium with a turban either, despite their common lands and peoples. A surer link between the Byzantine and Ottoman empires was an attitude to empire. In a pre-nationalist world, neither existed for the convenience of its subjects. Each used an administration in Constantinople with the simplest aim of best exploiting its resources: to maintain or extend its empire by diplomacy, threat, or so far as a summer campaign could be supplied – which for the Ottomans stopped at Vienna in 1529 and 1683. In both the Byzantine and Ottoman empires the capital was the source of patronage. For example, Cyprus was for Byzantine administrators until 1191 and for Ottoman administrators from 1571 neither "Greek" nor "Turkish", but a medium-rank posting from the capital, like Bengal in the Indian Civil Service in the British empire.

Along with an administrative capital, Mehmet II (1451–81) also inherited religious and legal duties as a Muslim sultan, one of which was the recognition and protection of his *dhimmis*, or non-Muslim subjects. In 1454 Mehmet came to a settlement with his first chosen patriarch, Gennadios II Scholarios (three reigns between 1454 and 1465), who, unlike the last emperor, had rejected the union of the Roman and Orthodox Churches signed at Florence in 1439. The arrangement in effect defined a Greek as a religious subject of the patriarch who was responsible to the sultan, and in return for economic concessions gave the patriarchate extensive legal control of its flock. This settlement came only just in time to save the Greeks, for while those areas which the Turks had conquered since the 11th century had been largely Islamicized with the loss of the economic base

of the Byzantine Church and state, the areas conquered after the settlement (e.g. much of the Balkans, the Morea in 1458, the Pontus in 1461, Cyprus in 1571, Crete by 1669) remained largely Christian. But for the momentous settlement of 1454, and subsequent ones between the Ottomans and the Armenian and Jewish communities, no contemporary documents survive. What is known only emerges in retrospective Greek tradition by 1520, and probably owes as much to wishful thinking of the benevolence of Mehmet II on the part of all parties (Ottoman included) as to its codification by the lawgiving sultan Suleyman I (1520–66), during whose reign the settlement largely worked its way through.

The tradition, and, until recently, modern historiography, is that Mehmet II and Gennadios created a *Millet-i Rum*, or semi-autonomous non-Muslim community, governed through the ecumenical patriarch. Neither sultan nor patriarch can really be described as Renaissance figures. Mehmet may have collected icons, employed Bellini, and discussed theology with Gennadios in Greek, but his "mightiest war", as he put it, was to make Constantinople a Muslim capital. Similarly, Gennadios may have been willing to compromise (he could do no other), but his writings are of conventional polemic impartially against Islam and Rome, and also demonstrate that the end of the world was to come in 1492 – a date then understandably postponed in popular Greek tradition to 1772. The mindset that sultan and patriarch shared was medieval. History is about practice rather than origins and all parties have found it convenient to let sleeping myths lie, for the *Millet-i Rum* worked that way in the end, and sounds logical, for Mehmet had the example of centuries of Islamic experience of dealing with non-Muslim minorities (and majorities) under the caliphate behind him.

However, the settlement was not preordained. Mehmet's first action on taking Constantinople was to execute his own prime minister, an almost hereditary post in the Anatolian Candaroğlu dynasty – henceforth his ministers were mostly converts who tried ever harder to please. His second action was not to turn to the patriarch (who in any case was in Rome) as his agent to deal with his Greek subjects, but to the last Byzantine prime minister, Luke Notaras, who famously preferred the turban of the sultan to the tiara of the pope. Notaras, however, was executed, and only then did the sultan seek out Gennadios as his patriarch and agent. Armenian and Hebrew traditions have it that he made similar arrangements to set up an Armenian patriarch of Constantinople in 1461, and a Jewish *haham* is claimed by 1492 – dates certainly too early, but such officers were in place by 1520. The point is that the Ottomans created Christian and Jewish institutions which had not hitherto existed, in order to keep their eye on a head of community in the capital. The very patriarchate of

Constantinople must be put in this category. In 1454 it was an Ottoman recreation on Ottoman terms. It is not known what Mehmet and Gennadios discussed, but they cannot have called it a *millet*, for the term was unknown to them. The conqueror and canonist may have been talking past each other, but in effect they seem to have made up a *Millet-i Rum* as they went along. The determinants were Constantinople and *Rum*. Constantinople makes the political history of the Greeks from 1453 to 1832 quite literally the history of the polis, or of the City; but while all Greeks, and by definition no Armenians, Jews, or Latins (who were without the law), were *Rum*, not all *Rum* were Greeks, for they included Slav, Arab, and other Orthodox subjects of the sultan and patriarch in Constantinople – to an extent that national risings after 1832 were as much against patriarchs as sultans, for the sees and churches of Jerusalem (1520), Antioch (1720), Peć (1760), and Ohrid (1767) fell in turn to the patronage of Constantinople. While the settlement of 1454 defined who a *Rum* was, it allowed a Greek-writing mandarin class to enter Orthodox service, whatever their origins – just as the Byzantine empire had done. But while terms such as "Hellene" only meant something on paper after 1832, Mehmet and Gennadios knew, without using it, what a "Greek" was in 1454, and the Greeks learned how to use the Ottoman patriarchate to establish a cultural control over other Orthodox subjects of the sultan.

Among the arts of the underdog, Ottoman patriarchs soon learnt how to use, if not raise, the *peşkeş*, or bribe of office, first voluntarily offered to the sultan by patriarch Symeon of Trebizond (three reigns between 1467 and 1486). The system percolated down to equivalent bribes offered for patriarchal patronage of his own sees and led to a spiralling of the cost of Constantinople, which did not produce many great shepherds in the revolving post, whose *peşkeş* their lay flock largely paid. Among the most impressive was Cyril I Lukaris (six reigns between 1612 and 1638) whose great rival was Cyril II Contari (three reigns between 1633 and 1639). If the Church was for auction, rival Western commercial and political interests found it a way into the Ottoman system. Cyril Lukaris, the so-called "Protestant Patriarch", was sponsored by Protestant, and Cyril Contari by Catholic, powers, who encompassed Lukaris's murder in 1638, of which Archbishop William Laud of Canterbury was concerned for further details before he was in turn executed in 1645.

Greeks outside Constantinople found opportunities within the Venetian empire, in Cyprus until 1551, Crete until 1669, the brief Venetian reconquest of the Morea thereafter, and in the Ionian islands until 1797, contributing, like El Greco (Domenikos Theotokopoulos), to a European culture which knew the Renaissance, Reformation, and Counter-Reformation. But this entry concerns their political history in Constantinople, not just the polis but the patriarchal quarter in the Phanar on the Golden Horn, where Phanariots entered the Ottoman civil as well as patriarchal service, as Grand Dragomans from 1661 and as rulers of the Danubian tributary provinces of Moldavia (from 1709) and Wallachia (from 1714) on the same, if more elaborate, terms that the patriarchate could obtain. All such slave princes endowed the Orthodox Church at the expense of their Romanian subjects, and some caught and promoted the Enlightenment too. But in Constantinople both Phanar and Church, Porte and *ulema* (the body of religious scholars) were at one, not with the *Revolutionary Proclamation* of Rigas Velestinlis (1797), but with the *Paternal Exhortation* under the name of the patriarch Anthimos of Jerusalem (1798): "When the last emperors of Constantinople began to subject the Eastern Church to papal thraldom, the particular favour of heaven raised up the Ottoman empire to protect the Greeks against heresy, to be a barrier against the political power of the Western nations, and to be a champion of the Orthodox Church."

If there had been any Greek readers of both Rigas and Anthimos, they would have been found among such burgeoning Greek commercial centres as Marseilles, Odessa, Bucharest, and Smyrna (where at nearby Kydonia (Ayvali) there was indeed a rising). But in 1821 the revolution began with the crossing of the river Pruth from Russia to modern Romania by Prince Alexander Ypsilantis to restore a "Great Idea" of Byzantium. The Romanians would not have it. On 25 March 1821 the metropolitan of Patras raised another banner in the Morea, where factors were quite different. It looked as if the southern Balkans were to fall apart under local warlords, such as Ali Pasha of Ioannina (1741–1822). Patriarch Gregory V (three reigns between 1797 and 1821) could only condemn the rising in the Morea and sultan Mahmud II (1808–39) could only hang his patriarch from his gate in the Phanar on Easter Sunday, 15 April 1821. In 1827 the untoward Battle of Navarino led to the independence of Greece, and in fact of Egypt, then unwanted by all parties. Politically, the upstart new state of king Otho was excommunicated by Constantinople until 1850, by when whatever understandings had been made between sultan and patriarch in 1454 entered a final phase. Patriarch Gregory V was canonized as a saint in Athens in 1921, but patriarchs Gennadios Scholarios and Cyril Lukaris await similar recognition.

ANTHONY A.M. BRYER

See also Ottoman Period, Patriarchate of Constantinople, Phanariots, Renaissance (Veneto-Cretan), Rumeli, Independence (War of)

Further Reading

Anonymous [E. Ritzos-Rhangabes], *Livre d'or de la Noblesse Phanariote*, Athens, 1892

Clogg, Richard C., *A Concise History of Greece*, Cambridge and New York: Cambridge University Press, 1992

Frazee, Charles A., *Catholics and Sultans: The Church and the Ottoman Empire, 1453–1923*, Cambridge and New York: Cambridge University Press, 1983

Kitromilides, Paschalis M., *Enlightenment, Nationalism, Orthodoxy: Studies in the Culture and Political Thought of South-Eastern Europe*, Aldershot: Variorum, 1994

Loucaris, C., *Confessio Christianae Fidei*, Geneva, 1633

Runciman, Steven, *The Great Church in Captivity: A Study of the Patriarchate of Constantinople from the Eve of the Turkish Conquest to the Greek War of Independence*, London: Cambridge University Press, 1968

Ypsilantes, A.K., *Ta meta ten Alosin, 1453–1789* [Events after the Capture, 1453–1789], Constantinople, 1870

Zakythinos, D.A., *The Making of Modern Greece: From Byzantium to Independence*, Oxford: Blackwell, 1976

Political History since 1832

Greek political history since 1832 has indeed been turbulent. During these 170-odd years Greece has had six constitutions, the form of the regime changing from authoritarian regency and monarchy (1832–44), to constitutional monarchy (from 1844), to republic (1924–35), back to monarchy (1935–74), and again to republic (from 1974). The country's political history is further studded with around half a dozen successful or attempted coups, military or with military involvement (1909, 1922, 1923, 1925, 1933, 1935), two periods of dictatorship totalling a little over 11 years (1936–41, 1967–74), a long and destructive civil war (1946–49), and other periods of anomalous or irregular democracy. Yet, despite these events, Greek political history shows that the democratic system adopted by the country during the 19th century has enjoyed great legitimacy and popular support and has exhibited considerable resilience. Of course, this does not make Greece into an exemplary democratic state: repression, vote-rigging, even intimidation of opponents have at times been features of Greek political life, even up to the 1960s. This is explainable if it is taken into account that the system of government imported into Greece in the 19th century had to coexist with a much older and deeply embedded system where patronage and clientelism were the norm; and at the same time it was subject to "royal intrusions". The nature of Greek society (traditional and pre-industrial in the 19th century) and the lack of a staged evolution of democracy, along with the inevitable (regional and world) wars, economic crises, and internal upheavals, were to create tensions that manifested themselves as regime instability and turbulence in Greek political history.

The Treaty of London (1832) established an independent and "monarchical" Greek state whose crown was given to Otho, second son of king Ludwig of Bavaria. A three-man Bavarian regency ruled Greece until 1835 (when Otho came of age) in a highly authoritarian manner, showing little respect for Greek tradition and customs. Their rule (not least their handling of religious issues) caused resentment both among the common people and to the political and military elites, which considered themselves entitled to a share of power. A further problem was the constitutional question. A constitution had been promised by the Protecting Powers, and confirmed again in 1832; yet both the regents and Otho, despite domestic and external pressure, refused to grant it. However, on 3 September 1843 a popular uprising forced Otho to grant a constitution. The 1844 constitution established Greece as a democracy. Constitutional government did not significantly improve Otho's popularity; nor did it at first significantly alter the rules of the political game: elections in 19th-century Greece were often conducted in an atmosphere of irregularity and even violence, and Otho continued to intervene in politics.

Otho was deposed in 1862, by an uprising in the capital. His fall was the result of popular discontent with both his foreign policy and his domestic governance. He left Greece in October 1862. Otho's deposition was followed by a period of anarchy, while the Protecting Powers were looking for a suitable replacement. Prince Christian George of Denmark accepted the throne and in 1863 became George I, king of the Hellenes. Greek politics remained unstable: between 1864 and 1910 there were 42 general elections and 140 governments;

Charilaos Trikoupis became prime minister seven times between 1875 and 1895. Between 1863 and 1909 Greece suffered a bankruptcy (1883) and a disastrous war with Turkey (1897), but also acquired the Ionian islands (1864) and Thessaly (1881). The Great Idea remained the main theme of Greek politics, but was now joined by the need for modernization. This period is characterized by an expansion of democracy, though the king retained considerable powers that provided the means for royal interventions. An important political development was the consolidation and regularization of democracy and its institutions. For a sizeable part of his reign a bipolar party system operated, with a stable if frequent alternation of the major parties in power. Another major development was the adoption of the principle of *dedilomeni*, a stipulation that the king has to invite the leader of the party with a majority in Parliament to form a government.

The year 1909 marks the first significant military intervention in politics. Pressure for modernization at home, exasperation at royal patronage, and fear of the effects of the Young Turk revolution in the Ottoman empire had been building up. In the summer of 1909 officers belonging to the Military League staged a pronunciamento. The army's demands and grievances were expressed in very moderate terms; surprisingly, the people quickly and openly embraced them, and the government and king equally quickly surrendered to the coup. Lacking the experience to govern, the Military League invited the Cretan politician Eleftherios Venizelos to assume the government of Greece (January 1910). Venizelos presided over a period of intense preparation for the conflict with the Ottoman empire that everybody expected. Venizelos's party, the Liberals, was dominant in parliament in all electoral contests between 1910 and December 1915. The successful conduct of the Balkan Wars was as much the result of careful preparation as of cooperation between Venizelos and George I. The assassination of the latter and the succession of Constantine were to end this. Constantine's intervention in politics in 1915 led to the painful period of the national schism. Venizelos and the king became two mutually exclusive poles. The nation and the country were deeply divided, and even a physical division took place when Venizelos formed the provisional government. The division of the country (but not the people) ended in 1917, when Constantine was deposed by Entente forces. He appointed his second son, Alexander, to succeed him.

Upheaval continued during the period 1917–36. Greece participated in World War I, and gained considerable territories in Thrace and Asia Minor, bringing closer the realization of the Great Idea. However, the country was still deeply divided between royalists and Venizelists; after Constantine's departure in 1917 Venizelos had recalled the parliament elected in June 1915. The death of king Alexander (October 1920) caused a political and constitutional crisis; Venizelos's fateful decision to find a solution by elections led to his defeat in November 1920. The victorious Populist Party quickly organized a referendum for the return of Constantine (December 1920), where the Liberals abstained. Constantine returned to Greece the same month. Purges of Venizelos's supporters now took place.

The Populists were to preside unwillingly over the territorial liquidation of the Great Idea. While the Gounaris govern-

40. Development of the Greek state, 1832–1947

In the map legend:

Greece, 1832

territory acquired by Greece in
1864
1881
1913
1920
1947

territory lost to Turkey, 1922

0   90 km

ment decided to continue the war against Mustafa Kemal's nationalists in Asia Minor (begun in 1919), war fatigue, the withdrawal of financial support by the Entente, and Italian and French hostility led to the collapse of the front in Asia Minor and the 1922 disaster, with over a million destitute refugees arriving in Greece.

The defeat and the subsequent exchange of populations further radicalized Greece. In September 1922 the army revolted in Chios under the leadership of colonel Nikolaos Plastiras and marched on Athens; the government collapsed. A revolutionary committee, formed by a group of officers, assumed power. King Constantine abdicated and left Greece; crown prince George briefly became king. Six politicians (among them Dimitrios Gounaris, the former prime minister) and a general were accused of high treason, tried by a revolutionary court martial, sentenced to death, and executed in November 1922. The revolutionary committee defeated a royalist coup, following which George II had to leave Greece "on leave" (December 1923). The same month elections (from which the Populists abstained) produced a Liberal-dominated parliament, with a strong republican minority that pressed for the abolition of the monarchy. In January 1924 the revolutionary committee handed power back to civilians and dissolved itself. Government instability as well as popular anti-monarchist feeling (the monarchy had been associated with the Asia Minor debacle) allowed the republican minority to advance its aims: Greece was made a republic on 25 March 1924, an act retrospectively confirmed by a referendum three

weeks later. Two-thirds of the electorate voted in favour of the republic; however, the royalist parties (as well as George II) refused to accept the regime change.

Instability continued under the republic. In June 1925 general Theodoros Pangalos overthrew the government and concentrated power in his own hands. He was himself overthrown by general Georgios Kondylis in August 1926. An all-party government was formed in November 1926 and surprisingly survived in different forms until the summer of 1928. However, the return of Venizelos to Greece in March 1928 hastened its fall. Venizelos resumed the leadership of the Liberal Party, and in July 1928 was invited to form a government. He won the elections held in the same month and those of September 1932 and January 1933. Venizelos governed Greece until March 1933. Another period of instability followed, laced with two abortive republican coups (March 1933 and March 1935). Venizelos, declared the nominal head of the second coup, had to leave Greece for France, where he died a year later.

Liberal and republican abstention in the elections of June 1935 produced a parliament monopolized by the royalists. Panayis Tsaldaris, the leader of the Populist Party, formed a government, but a putsch replaced him by Kondylis (October 1935), who hastily organized a referendum for the return to monarchy. The referendum of November 1935 was clearly rigged: 97 per cent of the votes were in favour of the monarchy and there were many reports of irregularities. Nevertheless, George II returned to Greece the same month. The January 1936 elections produced a hung parliament, with the balance held by the 15 communist deputies. The Communist Party of Greece (KKE) had been making limited progress since it was founded in January 1918; now it assumed centre stage. Workers' unrest in May 1936 and a general strike announced for 5 August 1936, both endorsed by the KKE, provided Ioannis Metaxas with the pretext for establishing a dictatorship.

Metaxas, leader of a marginal political party, had been appointed caretaker prime minister in April 1936, while negotiations for the formation of a coalition government were taking place. Metaxas's appointment had been aided by the death (by natural causes) of several major politicians (Kondylis, Demetzis, Venizelos, and Tsaldaris all died between January and May 1936) and also by the army's confidence in him. With considerable naivety the parliament had allowed him to rule by decree, initially for five months. On 4 August 1936, using as pretext the "communist danger", Metaxas with the consent of the king dissolved parliament, suspended the constitution, and declared martial law.

The "Regime of 4 August" which Metaxas founded proved quite durable. It remained in power until his death (January 1941) and even afterwards its rule was only relaxed. It was characterized by political repression all round, with communists singled out for particularly harsh treatment.

The mainstream political parties remained in suspended animation throughout the 1936–44 period; the Metaxas dictatorship and the war and Axis occupation that followed did not allow for traditional political activity. The one exception was the KKE which, through its role in the resistance, emerged as a major player in the political game.

In 1944, after a series of crises in the Greek government-in-exile, an agreement (brokered by the British) was reached, creating a coalition government with communist participation, under George Papandreou. The coalition broke up in December 1944, during what is often seen as the half-hearted communist attempt to seize power. A series of weak and short-lived governments followed.

The single most serious political issue that dominated Greek politics during the Axis occupation was the future of the monarchy. Until 1944 George II had refused to accept a referendum as the means to decide the issue; nevertheless, the referendum was held in September 1946, after the national elections in March 1946 (where the KKE had abstained) had given a clear majority to the Populist Party. The referendum, held in a climate of disorder, resulted in the restoration of the monarchy. George II returned to a country sliding quickly into a bloody civil war that lasted until August 1949.

The post-1945 political scene briefly saw the resurrection of the pre-1936 Liberal/Populist division. The Civil War was fought by a series of governments formed by either or both groups. However, it was becoming clear that the division was weakening. New political forces were emerging: in the 1951 elections a new party, the National Rally (*Ethnikos Synagermos*) under marshal Alexandros Papagos displaced the Liberals and Populists as the largest single party in parliament; another new party that contested the elections was the United Democratic Left (*Enomeni Dimokratiki Aristera*), which was to act as an umbrella for communists and leftists until 1974. The election of 1952 ushered in a decade of rule by the Right. The National Rally ruled until Papagos's death in 1956 and was succeeded by Constantine Karamanlis whose Greek Radical Union (ERE) used National Rally cadres and support. Liberalization, begun under Papagos, continued alongside economic development and reconstruction. The political system came close to a breakdown in 1959, when EDA surprisingly became the largest opposition party in parliament. Though on that occasion the crisis was defused, the army and the Right were seriously alarmed. However, the catalyst that probably deepened the crisis was the victory of George Papandreou's Centre Union in the elections of 1963 and 1964. The army as well as the palace had been alarmed by the prospect of loss of power by the Right; the army felt that anti-communism (almost an institutional ideology after the Civil War) was being questioned by Papandreou. Furthermore, the palace considered the armed forces its exclusive domain and felt threatened by the attempts of the elected government to control them. The protracted government crises of 1965–67 were as much an attempt by the palace to influence politics as the result of multiple fragmentation of the Greek political parties.

The army seized its chance on 21 April 1967, when a group of officers staged a coup. Though the king was probably not informed of the coup, he cooperated with the new regime, swearing in a new puppet government. In December 1967 the king organized his own (abortive) coup. Its failure forced him to leave Greece and allowed the Colonels (after a period of regency lasting until 1973) to proclaim Greece a "presidential parliamentary republic".

The Colonels' regime ruled Greece repressively until July 1974, when the Cyprus debacle forced them to hand power to a civilian government. Karamanlis returned from France to a hero's welcome. He formed a centre-right coalition, presiding over a highly successful transition to democracy. Among his first actions was to legalize the KKE (illegal since 1947). Elections were called for November 1974 (the first in ten years) and were won overwhelmingly by Karamanlis's New Democracy. A plebiscite to decide on the regime issue in December 1974 resulted in favour of abolishing the monarchy. Throughout the 1974–81 period modernization of both society and politics continued apace; a major achievemat of Karamanlis was the entry of Greece to the European Economic Community in January 1981.

The elections of November 1974 and November 1977 were won by New Democracy. However, it became obvious that the Greek political scene was changing rapidly. PASOK, a new party led by Andreas, the son of George Papandreou, contested both elections on a radical leftwing platform, with strong anti-Western overtones. PASOK enjoyed a meteoric rise, becoming the main opposition party in 1977 and coming to power in a landslide victory in 1981. This was the first time a left-of-centre party had come to power since 1944. PASOK rule lasted until 1989. Beginning quite radically, it settled down and by 1986 anti-Westernism had been largely abandoned. PASOK rule quickened the pace of reconciliation and the ending of the Civil War divide, not least by recognizing all national resistance movements. PASOK's main failings were the introduction of rampant populism and reckless economic policies.

A political crisis erupted in 1985 over the election of the president of the republic. Karamanlis had moved to the presidency in May 1980, but resigned in May 1985 when in a surprise move PASOK announced it would not support his re-election. However, despite fears, both the political system and the ruling party proved durable. PASOK's downfall was the result of serious economic problems and corruption scandals involving top-level members of the government. Elections in June 1989 and Novernber 1989 resulted in hung parliaments and produced first a coalition government of the conservative New Democracy and the far-left Alliance of the Left, and then an "ecumenical" grand coalition governmment. New Democracy won the elections of April 1990 and formed a government with a very slim majority; surprisingly it lasted over three years.

In the summer of 1993 Antonis Samaras, a former foreign minister, broke away and formed his own party. The government fell in September. The elections of October 1996 were the last victory for PASOK leader Papandreou. He fell seriously ill in the following month and resigned the premiership in January 1997. He was succeeded as both leader of PASOK and prime minister by Costas Simitis.

GEORGE KAZAMIAS

See also Asia Minor Campaign, Balkan Wars, Civil War, Constitution, European Community, Graeco–Turkish War, Great Idea, Junta, Modern Period, Monarchy, Refugees, Republic, World War I, World War II

Further Reading

Clogg, Richard, *Parties and Elections in Greece: The Search for Legitimacy*, London: Hurst, and Durham, North Carolina: Duke University Press, 1987

Clogg, Richard, *A Concise History of Greece*, Cambridge and New York: Cambridge University Press, 1992

Featherstone, Kevin and Dimitrios Katsoudas, *Political Change in Greece: Before and after the Colonels*, London: Croom Helm, 1987

Featherstone, Kevin and Kostas Ifantis (editors), *Greece in a Changing Europe: Between European Integration and Balkan Disintegration?*, Manchester: Manchester University Press, 1996

Kourvetaris, George A. and Betty A. Dobratz, *A Profile of Modern Greece: In Search of Identity*, Oxford and New York: Clarendon Press, 1987

McNeill, William Hardy, *The Metamorphosis of Greece since World War II*, Oxford: Blackwell, and Chicago: University of Chicago Press, 1978

Mavrogordatos, George T., *Stillborn Republic: Social Coalitions and Party Strategies in Greece, 1922–36*, Berkeley: University of California Press, 1983

Mazower, Mark, *Inside Hitler's Greece: The Experience of Occupation, 1941–44*, New Haven and London: Yale University Press, 1993

Mouzelis, Nicos P., *Modern Greece: Facets of Underdevelopment*, London: Macmillan, and New York: Holmes and Meier, 1978

Psomiades, Harry J., *The Eastern Question, the Last Phase: A Study in Greek–Turkish Diplomacy*, Thessalonica: Institute for Balkan Studies, 1968

Sarafis, Marion, *Background to Contemporary Greece*, 2 vols, London: Merlin, and Savage, Maryland: Barnes and Noble, 1990

Woodhouse, C.M., *Karamanlis: The Restorer of Greek Democracy*, Oxford: Clarendon Press, and New York: Oxford University Press, 1982

Woodhouse, C.M., *The Rise and Fall of the Greek Colonels*, London and New York: Granada, 1985

Woodhouse, C.M., *Modern Greece: A Short History*, London and Boston: Faber, 1991

Politis, Nikolaos 1852–1921

Anthropologist

Nikolaos Politis is considered the founder of folklore studies in Greece. He founded the Laographiki Etaireia (Folklore Society) in 1905 when the first volume of the journal *Laographia* was also published, in which Politis published an article setting down the epistemic and disciplinary parameters of folklore and delineating the basic operating principles of the discipline.

Politis's life spans the time of the solidification of the modern Greek state, a time during which the basic foundations for the state apparatus and national institutions were laid, alongside the institutional establishment and development of the arts. It was also the period when the most violent and heated debates over the Hellenic character of the modern Greeks were taking place, initially in western Europe and subsequently in Greece itself. These debates, which though resolutely rooted in the development of Enlightenment thought, were precipitated by the political changes and ethnic uprisings that were taking place in the Balkans in the 19th century. The developments in Greece, in particular, were met with a combination of suspicion and philhellenism. Suspicion, because there were many Europeans, ranging from politicians to intellectuals, who believed that modern Greece had no reason to exist because it lacked an organic connection with ancient Greece. Of these intellectuals, Jakob Philipp Fallmerayer was not the only one, although his theory (espoused in his *Geschichte der Halbinsel Morea*, 1830) was the one most vehemently refuted. Philhellenism, because there were just as many European politicians and intellectuals who believed that Greece had an absolute reason for existence despite the fact that it did not have an organic connection with ancient Greece. In either case the end result was the same, namely that ancient and modern Greece comprised two different civilizations, two different nations, two different languages, two unconnected (and not simply disconnected) entities. The debate was not simply academic, as it touched upon issues of the sovereignty of the modern Greek nation state, the political existence of which was debated and seriously threatened.

In this climate modern Greece had to prove that its civilization was indeed a continuation of the ancient one. Initially, the Greek state comprised only a small part of what is Greece today and every expansion and addition was achieved with war, after which the acquired portion had to prove that it belonged culturally and racially with the rest of Greece. This was a problem faced by all newly established nation states, that of Germany included. Germany became important in this framework for three reasons: first because that was the starting point of Fallmerayer; secondly because the most complete and crystallized articulation of folklore came from Germany, through the studies of Herder, Schmidt, Waschmuth, and the Grimm brothers; and finally because Politis studied in Germany, under Bernhard Schmidt, from whom he borrowed the methodology, while he turned to the British, especially Sir James Frazer and Edward Tylor, for the development of his own theory of folklore. Frazer's comparative theory, based on Darwinian evolutionism, and Tylor's theory of cultural survivalism provided the cornerstones of Politis's theory of folklore.

While Politis concerned himself with Fallmerayer's theory, which maintained that modern Greeks were not Greek at all but rather a blend of Slavs and Albanians, it would be a mistake to see Politis's efforts and contributions as exhausting themselves in a battle against Fallmerayer. This was a battle fought by his Greek colleagues in folklore research, primarily Spyridon Zambelios, Emmanouil Vyvilakes, Michail Lelekos, and many more, along with a large number of European and American philhellenes, such as Claude Fauriel, Lord Byron, Grindley Howe, and Edgar Quinet. What Politis effectively managed to do, with regard to Fallmerayer's theory, was to elevate the discussion and the debate from a purely national and political level to one of epistemology. Politis was engaged in a discussion with his European colleagues. It was through the example of Fallmerayer that Politis tried to advance the folklore studies and research already undertaken by the early (and untrained) Greek folklorists. Politis managed to place Greek folklore within the disciplinary framework that had been established by the European folklorists. Nineteenth-century folklore tried to establish first the universality of the human psyche and secondly the theory that all civilizations operate within an evolutionary scale of their own which allows them to keep their cultural cohesion through the survivals (*epiviomata* was Politis's translation of the term proposed by Tylor) of behaviours and beliefs which, while belonging to earlier times, have divested themselves of their original meanings and have survived as cultural gestures. This process Politis understood as the one that leads to the attainment of truth and reason. He understood the comparative method as the key that would open the dialogue between the previous (barbaric) and later (civilized) points in the process of human civilization.

Prior to Politis's theories, the constructions of the cultural and racial continuities of the Greek nation had been situated within its diachronic linguistic cohesion. Politis, however, who was an erudite and scientifically informed researcher, knew only too well that there was more than one language spoken within the Greek state. He also knew, equally well, that the German romantic theories that viewed national and ethnic cohesion through the framework of linguistic homogeneity had already been tested and disproved in Greece, where many of the various ethnic groups that comprised the Greek nation were at least bilingual. For instance, the Arvanites spoke both Greek and Arvanitika, the Sarakatsans Greek and Romany, the Greeks in Asia Minor and the rest of the Ottoman empire spoke Greek and Turkish, without any dispute or uncertainty as to their Greekness. Politis turned elsewhere for his constructions of the continuities of the Greek nation. He turned to the idea of a common descent of the Greeks, which could be researched and proved through their character, the continuity of which could be shown through a comparison of modern folk models of behaviour with the corresponding ancient ones. In this manner Politis coordinated the orientation of Greek folklore theory with the German and British theories while attributing to it the archaeological texture that still circumscribes folklore as a discipline.

By establishing folklore as a discipline Politis set its epistemological parameters, so that some sort of order would be placed over the practice of folklore, thus guiding future research while delimiting the unscientific and highly individualistic nature of its the practice until then, which had resulted in research of dubious quality and relevance. Politis set out to teach folklorists in Greece what constituted their research object and the principles of classification and recording. The definition of folklore, as suggested by Politis in 1909, occurred in a political climate decidedly different from the one that had marked the beginnings of the discipline in the mid-19th century. The year 1909 was politically marked by Charilaos Trikoupis and his Liberal Party, of which Politis was a member. Ideologically this period was framed not by the archaeolatry which had marked the previous century but by a move forwards, towards the restitution of the state. This promising Greek reality was considered to be the achievement of the people, not of the scholars, and was appropriated by the rising middle classes. By this time the orientation had turned towards folk tradition, and the language of that tradition was the vernacular, the Demotic. The Greek countryside became the point of reference of the intellectuals and the scholars, and the demoticist movement found fervent supporters among the members of the philological circle established by Politis, despite the fact that he was not a demoticist himself. Besides the project of introducing demotic to the curriculum of primary and secondary schools, Politis was very much interested in modern Greek history, especially the period from the revolution of 1821 onwards. As a result of the combination of these interests came the establishment of the Historical and Ethnological Society of Greece which tried to combine historical and folklore research.

These were the official gestures of Politis. Unofficially he coordinated the first attempts at the creation of a demoticist literature in Greece. The poet Georgios Drosinis mentioned in a letter that he sent to Stilpon Kyriakidis that Politis had returned from Germany exhorting Greek intellectuals to apply themselves to a type of art that would be Greek in all of its expressions. With that in mind they established weekly Saturday evening meetings at a German beer tavern where, besides those who belonged to the circle of Hestia, many more came, among them Georgios Vizyinos, Antonis Meliarakis, Dimitrios Kambouroglous, Aristotelis Kourtidis, the gymnast Ioannes Phokianos, and the painter Nikephoros Lytras, among others. From that circle, which also included sculptors and architects, developed the Historical and Ethnological Society. Drosinis also mentioned that Politis encouraged him to write the *Agrotikes Epistoles* (Peasant Letters) and the *Eidyllia* (Idylls) and to make systematic use of his own *Paradoseis tou Ellinikou Laou* (Traditions of the Greek People).

Politis introduced and systematized the scientific approach to the study of Greek culture; he established or edited important journals which provided a forum for scholars and intellectuals of his day to publish their theories and research; and he legitimized the demotic as the medium of communication between the intellectuals and the people.

NENI PANOURGIÁ

See also Folklore, Identity, Language

Biography

Born in Kalamata in 1852, Politis while still a student wrote a study of the manners and customs of the Greek people, comparing the modern with the ancient, entitled *Modern Greek Mythology* (1869). He devoted his life to the establishment of folklore as a discipline. He published collections of *Proverbs* and *Traditions* and a *Selection from the Songs of the Greek People* and edited the journal *Laographia*. He died in Athens in 1921.

Further Reading

Herzfeld, Michael, *Ours Once More: Folklore, Ideology, and the Making of Modern Greece*, Austin: University of Texas Press, 1982

Kyriakidou-Nestoros, Alki, *I Theoria tis Ellenikes Laographias: Kritiki Analysi* [The Theory of Greek Folklore: A Critical Analysis], Athens, 1978

Pollution

Pollution is related to the intensive exploitation of natural resources and raw materials to meet the needs mainly of industry, agriculture, and transport. It has occurred on a scale large enough to cause serious environmental damage only following the industrial and technological revolutions of the 19th century and has today become a matter of major global concern. Incidents of pollution in earlier historical periods are scarce. A rare occurrence was the pollution caused by residues of silver, lead, and iron from the mine of Laurium in southern Attica, which were exploited from the 6th to the 1st century BC, the residues significantly affecting the biodiversity of the locality. Philosophical ideas on nature, resources, and the economic activity of man were, however, fundamental to ancient Greek thought and infiltrated everyday activities. In contrast to the anthropocentric principles of Judaism and Christianity, the gods of ancient Greek mythology were part of nature, bestowing a sacred aspect on its protection. The unity of nature was a paradigm for social behaviour, and moderation, the ruling standard in the ancient Greek world, influenced Greeks' attitude towards the environment as well as to every human pursuit. The irreversibility route of natural processes was emphasized by Heraclitus, and both Xenophon and Aristotle related economic activity and productivity to conservation of natural resources, and conceived of the ethical risk pertinent to overproduction. Such views were reflected in social organization; special rules applied to the cheese and leather industry, to the protection of vegetation from overgrazing by goats, and to the conservation and treatment of water. In Byzantium, although human activities and ideas did not revolve around ancient concepts of moderation and the unity of nature, water was also protected and treated with care, for its connection with hygiene was understood.

Industrial development and the intensification of agricultural production reached modern Greece later than other European countries, and never reached a comparable scale. As a result the effects of pollution are localized and often largely reversible. Variation in topography and climatic conditions and the geographical position of Greece in the Mediterranean basin have led to the development of a multitude of small habitats that are sensitive to pollution. They are extremely important for biodiversity and the protection of rare species, particularly birds and wild flowers. It is estimated that there are between 5000 and 6000 different species of vascular plants in Greece, of which 730 are endemic and more than 100 threatened by extinction. Bird species exceed 400, of which one in four is threatened. Both Greek and EU legal frameworks and guidelines for environmental protection are satisfactory, but implementation, coordination, and monitoring are poor. Adequate protection and monitoring are, however, achieved in 11 natural water reserves that fall under the umbrella of the international Ramsar convention, and the protection of ten forest habitats is assured by their status as national reserves.

Pollution of seawater is a major concern in Greece. The Greek coastline stretches for 16,000 km; it is not only the longest in the EU but one of the longest national coastlines in the world. Some 40 per cent of agricultural activity, 70 per cent of industrial activity, and 90 per cent of tourism are based on the coastal areas, resulting in a conflict of interests and making environmental protection hard to implement. However, seawater quality is generally good and less than 3 per cent of the waters fail to meet bathing quality standards. The greatest cause of organic pollution in coastal waters is the disposal of urban wastewater. Industrial heavy-metal pollution is local-ized, but data are lacking on local occurrence and levels of various xenobiotics (non-natural synthetic pollutants). Large areas of the Saronic and Thermaic gulfs are heavily polluted by both urban and industrial activities in Athens and Thessalonica respectively. Oil transport through the Aegean and the Ionian seas reaches 100,000,000 tonnes per year of which 10,000–60,000 tonnes are estimated to be disposed of in the sea either by tank cleaning or by naval accidents. This makes the Aegean Sea, together with the northern Adriatic and the Ligurian Sea, one of the three areas most heavily polluted by hydrocarbons in the Mediterranean. Although this does not usually affect coastal areas, the gulf of Pylos in the southern Peloponnese suffered two serious oil transport accidents in the 1980s. A special water-pollution problem for Greece derives from the disposal of olive-mill wastewaters during winter. This occurs particularly in olive-oil-producing areas such as the Peloponnese and the islands of Lesbos and Crete. Although non-toxic in the long term, olive-mill wastewaters may induce eutrophication (an excess of organic substrate overstimulating plant growth and in turn leading to anoxic conditions and death of organisms) in both seawaters and freshwaters.

Use of fertilizers in agriculture has tripled since 1950 but is still lower than in other EU countries. However, occasional occurrences of seawater eutrophication have been attributed to phosphate and nitrate fertilizers; rivers used for farm irrigation, like the Peneus in the plain of Thessaly, have been heavily polluted. The permeability of chalk rock, which is abundant in Greek subsoils and allows for solute leaching, contributes largely to such conditions, so that strict guidelines are needed to protect water from fertilizer and pesticide pollution.

Waste production per capita is among the smallest in the EU, but disposal is poorly organized and planned since only one in three designated disposal areas operates under full official licence. Waste increases dramatically in environmentally sensitive regions preferred by holidaymakers during the summer months; not only is it unsightly but rapid waste decomposition under high temperatures is often also a fire risk and threat to hygiene.

Energy consumption is directly related to pollution, particularly air pollution. Energy consumption per capita in Greece is less than 50 per cent of the mean consumption in the EU, and Greece contributes only by 0.3 per cent to the universal carbon dioxide production responsible for the greenhouse effect. However, energy consumption for transport is rising fast. Air pollution as a result of energy consumption is serious in Athens and its suburbs, where about half the population of Greece lives. The fact that the city is surrounded by mountains, except for the Saronic gulf outlet to the south, prevents the rapid dispersal of air pollutants, which are produced mainly by motor cars (60–70 per cent of smoke, nitrogen oxides, and hydrocarbons, and nearly 100 per cent of carbon monoxide). Measures to reduce traffic jams and improve petrol quality during the 1980s and 1990s have not been particularly successful and under certain weather conditions air pollution levels exceed safety limits. Acid rain, directly related to air pollution in Athens, has affected the marbles of the Acropolis, causing irreversible chemical calcination of their external surfaces. Most of the original pieces, however, have already been transferred to the Acropolis museum, their presence on the Acropolis being replaced by replicas.

Public opinion is very sensitive to the issue of radiation pollution in Greece and, since most regions of the country are vulnerable to earthquakes, no nuclear power plant operates (other than for purely scientific purposes). Technologically outdated nuclear power stations still operate, however, in Bulgaria near the northern Greek border, raising fears of a nuclear accident.

CONSTANTINOS EHALIOTIS

Further Reading

Bonazoundas, M. and A. Katsaiti, *Epilegmena Themata Diacheirisis Perivallontos* [Selected Works on Environmental Conservation], Athens, 1995

Clarke, Robin, *Europe's Environment: The Dobris Assessment, An Overview*, Copenhagen: European Environment Agency, and London: Earthscan, 1994

European Environment Agency, *Europe's Environment: The Second Assessment*, Oxford and New York: Elsevier, 1998

Fytianos, K.K. and Samanidou B.F., *I Rypansi ton Thalasson* [Sea Water Pollution], Thessalonica: University Studio Press, 1988

Kirkitsos, F., K. Pelekasi, and N. Chrysogelos, *Meiosi Aporrimaton: mia Stratigiki gia to Paron kai to Mellon* [Waste Reduction: A Strategy for the Present and the Future], Athens, 1995

Organization for Economic Cooperation and Development, *Environmental Policies in Greece*, Athens, 1983

Papaspiliopoulos, S., T. Papagianis, and S. Kouvelis, *To Perivallon stin Ellada, 1991–1996* [The Environment in Greece, 1991–1996], Athens, 1996

Pelekasi, K. and M. Skourtos, *I Atmosfairiki Rypansi stin Ellada* [Air Pollution in Greece], Athens, 1992

Scoulikidis, T. (editor), *I Epidrasi tis Atmosferikis Rypansis stin Ypobathmisi ton Arxaion Mnimeion* [The Influence of Air Pollution on the Deterioration of Ancient Monuments], Thessalonica, 1982

Stanners, David and Philippe Bourdeau (editors), *Europe's Environment: The Dobris Assessment*, Copenhagen: European Environment Agency, 1995

Tskouras, G., "Olokliromeni Diaxeirisi Akton kai Nhsion" [Integrated Conservation of Coasts and Islands], *Nea Oikologia* [New Ecology] (December 1996): pp. 20–23

Valkanas, G., *Rypansi Perivallontos* [Environmental Pollution], Athens, 1992

Varela, E. and M. Korma, "To perivallon" [The Environment], *Archaiologia*, 35 (1990): pp. 48–52

Polybius *c.200–c.118* BC

Historian

Polybius is an invaluable contemporary witness of the rise of Rome in the 3rd and 2nd centuries BC. Where so much is now lost, Polybius' history, at least in part, survives. He was a member of a prominent Megalopolitan family; his father Lycortas held the chief magistracy (*strategia*) of the Achaean League and was a strong advocate of Achaean autonomy in the face of the growing power of Rome. Polybius' own political career was terminated by the Roman victory over Macedon in 168 BC; he was among 1000 Achaeans deported to Italy, not to be released until 150 BC. In Rome he formed a friendship with P. Scipio Aemilianus, which was to bring him into closer contact with the workings of the Roman state and later enabled him to accompany Scipio abroad, for instance on campaign to Carthage.

During this period of enforced leisure in Rome he began his history, an ambitious work in 40 books that took the whole Mediterranean as its subject. After two introductory books the history proper begins with the 140th Olympiad (220–216 BC), the date at which Polybius believed the history of Italy and Libya merged with that of Greece and Asia (1. 3). He was concerned to explain to his fellow Greeks "how and by what sort of government in less than 53 years the Romans came to conquer and rule almost the whole inhabited world" (1. 1. 5, cf. 1. 3. 7–10 for Greek readership). The 53 years ended with the demise of the Macedonian kingdom in 168/67 BC. At some point, however, perhaps after reflecting on the Roman destruction of Carthage and Corinth, he decided to extend his history so that it covered not only Rome's acquisition of power (books 3–29) but also the years that followed, up to 145/44 BC (books 30–39). His purpose was to provide the information that would allow the reader to pass judgement on Roman rule; thus contemporaries could determine whether it should be avoided or welcomed and future generations whether it should be praised or condemned (3. 4). Polybius' own attitude to Rome has been variously interpreted, pro-Roman, anti-Roman, cynical, embittered, impressed; it is perhaps safest to say that he was ambivalent.

The first five books are complete, but the rest exist only in fragments, some quite substantial (in particular the remains of book 6). These are largely the work of Byzantine excerptors, although numerous citations can also be found in Strabo, Athenaeus, and Plutarch, a sign of Polybius' importance for later writers. The "Excerpta Antiqua", which date from no later than the 10th century AD, offer an abridgement of books 1–18, though without book 17. The remaining excerpts survive due to the thematic collections compiled under Constantine VII Porphyrogennetos and reflect the interests of 10th-century Byzantium. They fall under the following headings: *de legationibus* (on embassies), *de sententiis* (on sayings), *de virtutibus et vitiis* (on virtues and vices), *de insidiis* (on plots or ambushes), and *de strategematis* (on military stratagems). Some idea of what is missing can often be obtained from the Roman historian Livy who used Polybius extensively for events in the east in books 31–45 of his own history. None of Polybius' minor works is extant (on tactics, Philopoemen, the Numantine War, and perhaps one on the habitability of the equatorial region).

Polybius had strong views on the writing of history. He frequently breaks off to point out the failings of other historians, attacking the practitioners of sensationalist history (Phylarchus, Timaeus, Zeno of Rhodes) and scorning those who spend their time immersed in the library (Timaeus again, the subject of an extended critique in book 12). He himself stressed the importance of experience and autopsy; only someone with experience of war and politics could write satisfactorily on those subjects. For Polybius the study of history was of practical value, both for the politician and for anyone trying to cope with the vicissitudes of fortune; knowledge of the past helps in the present (1. 1). Polybius' outlook has been described as "utilitarian" and therefore distinct from his Hellenistic contemporaries (Walbank), but recently an attempt has been made to discern a moralizing tendency in his work (Eckstein).

Book 6 was a digression on the Roman state, with particular emphasis on the constitution and army, both of which he considered fundamental to Roman success and especially to their recovery after the disastrous defeat by Hannibal at Cannae in 216 BC. His analysis of the constitution was very much the work of an outsider, depending heavily on the concepts and categories of Greek political thought. The strength and stability of the constitution, he argued, lay in its combination of kingship (consuls), aristocracy (senate), and democracy (people). However inappropriate this may have been as a model to interpret the Roman constitution, it has had an enormous influence on subsequent western political thought from Cicero to Machiavelli, Montesquieu, and beyond. Its impact in the east is less evident; it was worth excerpting but its theory of the value of divided power was hardly compatible with Byzantine autocracy.

In the Greek world from late antiquity onwards the influence of Polybius appears to have been limited, although he is frequently cited in reference works such as Stephanus' *Ethnica* and the *Suda*. His subject may have appealed, but his style and length deterred. He had long before been damned by Dionysius of Halicarnassus who numbered him among those writers no one reads to the end (*De Compositione Verborum*, 4). Of the historians of late antiquity Zosimus is probably the only one to show any significant awareness of Polybius, but even here the influence is formal and superficial rather than substantial. Echoes of Polybius have been detected in Byzantine historians such as Procopius, Agathias, and Anna Komnene, but nothing is explicit. Byzantine lack of interest is evident in his absence from Photios's *Bibliotheca* and the truncated state of the text.

ANDREW W. ERSKINE

See also Historiography

Biography

Born in Megalopolis *c.*200 BC, Polybius was the son of Lycortas, a wealthy aristocrat who was a leading figure in the Achaean League. Polybius went on an embassy to Alexandria in 180 and served as Hipparch of the Achaean League in 170/69. After the Battle of Pydna (168 BC) he was deported to Rome where he remained and became the friend of Scipio Aemilianus. He wrote a history of Rome's rise to power in 40 books of which 1–5 survive intact and the rest in fragments. He died *c.*118 BC.

Writings

The Histories, translated by W.R. Paton, 6 vols, London: Heinemann, and New York: Putnam, 1922–27 (Loeb edition)

Further Reading

Davidson, James, "The Gaze in Polybius' *Histories*", *Journal of Roman Studies*, 81 (1991): pp. 10–24
Derow, P.S., "Polybius, Rome, and the East", *Journal of Roman Studies*, 69 (1979) pp. 1–15
Eckstein, Arthur M., *Moral Vision in the Histories of Polybius*, Berkeley: University of California Press, 1995
Erskine, Andrew, *The Hellenistic Stoa: Political Thought and Action*, London: Duckworth, 1990, chapter 8
Momigliano, A., "Polybius' Reappearance in Western Europe" in *Polybe*, edited by Emilio Gabba, Geneva: Hardt, 1974
Moore, John M., *The Manuscript Tradition of Polybius*, Cambridge: Cambridge University Press, 1965
Paschoud, F., "Influences et échos des conceptions historiographiques de Polybe dans l'antiquité tardive" in *Polybe*, edited by Emilio Gabba, Geneva: Hardt, 1974
Pédech, Paul, *La Méthode historique de Polybe*, Paris: Les Belles Lettres, 1964
Sacks, Kenneth, *Polybius on the Writing of History*, Berkeley: University of California Press, 1981
von Fritz, Kurt, *The Theory of the Mixed Constitution in Antiquity*, New York: Columbia University Press, 1954
Walbank, F.W., *A Historical Commentary on Polybius*, 3 vols, Oxford: Clarendon Press, 1957–79
Walbank, F.W., *Polybius*, Berkeley: University of California Press, 1972

Polygnotus

Painter of the 5th century BC

Polygnotus was the son and pupil of Aglaophon of Thasos; his brother Aristophon and a younger Aglaophon, probably his son or his nephew, were also painters. Polygnotus, a distinguished artistic figure of the early Classical period, worked in Athens at the time of Cimon, the leader of the Athenian democracy from 472 to 461 BC. In the absence of any surviving fragments of his monumental painting, literary texts – and Pausanias in particular – are the sole source of evidence, giving often lengthy descriptions of Polygnotus' works.

Much of Polygnotus' painting in Athens was in buildings associated with Cimon. According to Pausanias, who lived in the 2nd century AD, the wall paintings that decorated the shrine of the Dioscuri, the Anakeion, located south of the Agora towards the Acropolis, and the Stoa Poikile on the south side of the Agora were attributed to Polygnotus (he was said to have refused a fee for painting the latter). His work in the Stoa or in the Anakeion gained him Athenian citizenship.

These paintings were on view in late antiquity when Pausanias travelled to Athens, but are not preserved today. Polygnotus represented the wedding of Castor and Polydeuces with the daughters of Leucippus in the Anakeion and painted a scene of *Iliou Persis* (Troy Taken) on the interior back wall of the Stoa Poikile. In the latter, he was said to have given to Laodice, Priam's daughter, the features of Cimon's sister Elpinice, who was the artist's mistress, an element implying the idea of individual portraiture in the works of art of the time. The scene was painted on wooden panels secured to the wall, a common practice among painters of murals in Classical Greece.

Pausanias also mentions a set of pictures from the Trojan cycle by Polygnotus in the Pinakotheke (picture gallery) of the Periclean Propylaea. He had painted wooden panels to replace those decorating the Archaic gateway to the Acropolis, which was destroyed by the Persians and later reconstructed under Cimon. Thus, his paintings were earlier than the Periclean building. *Achilles in Skyros* and *Nausicaa* were also in the Pinakotheke. Another painting attributed to Polygnotus was in Rome in Pliny's time, in the 1st century AD, and depicted a man with a shield. This was a fragment of a larger composition, most probably a wall painting on wooden panels, which had been transported to Rome.

Polygnotus' most famous works, however, were at Delphi, in the Lesche (club-house), which was dedicated to the sanctuary by the people of Cnidus. Although the date of this dedication is unknown, it is usually assumed that the building was put up after the liberation of the city from the Persians, as a result of Cimon's Eurymedon campaign, and that the paintings were executed between 458 and 447 BC. Only the foundations of the building survive, on a terrace near the top of the sloping sanctuary, and it would have been impossible to reconstruct the paintings without Pausanias' description. Two scenes on wooden panels, including some 70 figures (humans and animals), often named, in a scale half lifesize, decorated the interior of the building, which consisted of a rectangular room with a roof supported by wooden pillars set round a central area where athletic exercises took place. One represented the *Iliou Persis* in a more detailed version than that in the Stoa Poikile at Athens, and the second was a depiction of the *Nekyia*, the Underworld. The scenes met in the centre of the north wall and each occupied half of it; it is possible that they extended over the short walls. Besides a detailed description of the composition, Pausanias also refers to the problems with which Polygnotus had to deal and his way of tackling them.

Recent reconstruction has suggested that the *Iliou Persis* and the *Nekyia* formed three self-contained compositions, each spreading over three walls. The former consisted of the sea scene, the altar scene, and the land scene, while the latter included the sacrifice of Odysseus on the north, Achilles and Patroclus in the centre of the western wall, and groups of heroes from both sides of the Trojan War on the south wall. This arrangement of the individual groups was no doubt intentional, so as to enable Polygnotus to focus on the main emphasis of the various subjects in his painting.

He is also said to have worked in Boeotia. He painted *Odysseus after the Slaying of the Suitors* in the temple of Athena Areia at Plataea, the foundations of which are dated after the battle of 479 BC. He also worked at Thespiae, not far from Plataea, where his wall paintings were restored in the 4th century BC by Pausias of Sicyon. One of his paintings portrayed Salmoneus, the king of Elis, with a thunderbolt, a rare subject in the art of the period, which might have been part of a larger scene.

The composition represented an important departure from the established principles of Archaic painting. The figures were not set down on the baseline of the picture, but were scattered on various levels, demonstrating a new concept for the representation of pictorial space, which is associated with the name of Polygnotus. The innovation is reflected in contemporary vase painting, as on the Niobid Painter *krater* (mixing bowl) from Orvieto, now in the Louvre, Paris. Moreover, Polygnotus' compositions were built up from figures in groups of two, three, or more. According to Pausanias, his paintings were characterized by a liking for quiet scenes with little action, often adaptations of earlier action themes to the new ideal of passivity, as in the change from the Sack of Troy into Troy Taken, as well as for the stillness of the figures. Ancient literary sources also attest that Polygnotus had a distinguished ability in the rendering of physiognomy, anatomy, and drapery to reveal the *ethos* (character) and *pathos* (emotion) of his

figures. He presented them either before the action – in the process of taking a decision – or in their reaction after it. Another source for Polygnotus' art is Pliny's *Natural History*, compiled in the 1st century AD, which mentions that he painted women wearing transparent drapery and gave them headdresses of various colours, and also showed the mouth open and the teeth visible. Although certain elements of his art had appeared sporadically earlier, their combination by Polygnotus was pioneering.

ELENI ZIMI

See also Painting

Biography

The son and pupil of Aglaophon of Thasos, Polygnotus was a renowned painter who worked in Athens at the time of Cimon (*fl.*472–461 BC). Nothing of his painting survives. Pausanias and Pliny are our only sources. At Athens he painted for the shrine of the Dioscuri, the Anakeion, the Stoa Poikile, and the Pinakotheke. He also worked at Delphi and in Boeotia.

Further Reading

Kebric, Robert B., *The Paintings in the Cnidian Lesche at Delphi and Their Historical Context*, Leiden: Brill, 1983

O'Donnell Stansbury, Mark D., "Polygnotos' Iliupersis: A New Reconstruction", *American Journal of Archaeology*, 93/2 (1989): pp. 203–215

O'Donnell Stansbury, Mark D., "Polygnotos's Nekyia: A Reconstruction and Analysis", *American Journal of Archaeology*, 94/2 (1990): pp. 213–35

Robertson, Martin, *Greek Painting*, Geneva: Skira, 1959; New York: Rizzoli, 1979

Robertson, Martin, *A History of Greek Art*, Cambridge: Cambridge University Press, 1975, pp. 240–70

Pomaks

Bulgarian-speaking minority in Greece

The Pomaks are Bulgarian-speaking Muslims to be found in Greece around Echinos in the Rhodope mountains northeast of Xanthi. In the 1951 Greek census 18,671 Pomaks were recorded, about 500 more than in the corresponding census of 1940. Every other minority in Greece shows a decline during these years. Both figures are likely, however, to be an underestimate. Pomaks are confused about their identity, and could have registered as Greeks, Slavs, or Turks. The census of 1951 was the last to show any interest in any minority apart from the Muslim minority, a blanket term to cover Pomaks, Turks, and Gypsies. A figure of 30,000 Greek Pomaks in 1998 is likely to be an overestimate, since assimilation has proceeded apace since 1951.

In Bulgaria there are about 200,000 Pomaks, equally confused about their identity. In the 1980s, when there was a strong Bulgarian national movement, Pomaks were persuaded to think of themselves as Bulgarians, and changed their Islamic names accordingly. In the 1990s a Turkish political party for a time held the balance of power in the Bulgarian parliament, Islam was supported from abroad, and the Pomaks began changing their names back again. There are Slav- speaking Muslims in the former Yugoslav republic of Macedonia where they are called Torbeš and in Albania where they are called Poturs. None of these groups has had much contact with any other since World War II. Even the Greek and Bulgarian Pomaks, though both living in the Rhodopes, are not contiguous with each other, the Bulgarian Pomaks living northwest of Xanthi over a border that was very strictly guarded.

The origin of the Pomaks is shrouded in mystery and obscured by political prejudice. The Bulgars assert that they are native Bulgarians lured over to Islam in the early years of the Ottoman occupation. The Turks maintain that they are Turks who somehow learnt the language of their subjects. The Greeks, always anxious to prove the antiquity of a Greek presence in Macedonia and Thrace, suggest that the Pomaks are descendants of some ancient Greek tribe. An alternative theory is that they derive from pre-Ottoman Turks, who had entered the service of the Byzantine empire, and are thus in some sense part of the Greek commonwealth. There is little evidence to support any of these theories; in a curious way the Pomaks with their fair hair and blue eyes seem equally remote from Bulgarians, Turks, and Greeks.

Though the Rhodope mountains were outside the orbit of Classical Greece, their proximity to Constantinople meant that even in the darkest days of the Byzantine empire they were usually under Byzantine control. It is therefore surprising to find this area inhabited by a non-Greek non-Orthodox people. A possible explanation is that the Rhodopes, like Albania and Bosnia, were an area where the Paulician heresy was strong, being indeed the kind of place where heretics could be banished to keep them out of the way. For political and theological reasons such heretics would be ripe for conversion to Islam, particularly when the form of Islam on offer was Bekhtashism, tolerant and mystical. There may also have been less altruistic and more commercial reasons for conversion, in the shape of reduced taxes. Bulgarian speech is easier to explain. A strong Bulgarian empire in the 10th and 13th centuries was not far from the Rhodopes, and even in the 11th and 12th centuries there were many Slav-speakers in the restored Byzantine empire. The Rhodopes are a high mountain range, but not an impenetrable barrier as there are several passes through it. Indeed it looks as if the Pomaks – as cattle and sheep rearers, like the transhumant Vlachs and Sarakatsans – regularly moved across the mountains in search of summer or winter pastures, each preserving their identity through their separate language.

This image of the Pomaks as peaceful pastoralists receives a rude shock with their first definite appearance in history as partly responsible for the Bulgarian atrocities of 1876. It is fairly clear that the irregular Turkish troops or Bashibazouks against whom Gladstone contemptuously inveighed were Pomaks. The peace treaties of 1878 left the the Pomaks under nominal Turkish control, although they seem at the end of the 19th century to have achieved virtual independence. There were further atrocities in 1912. The Balkan War started and the Bulgarians took revenge. Pomak villages still remember this revenge, as Bulgarian villages remember 1876.

In 1913 western Thrace passed to Bulgaria, giving it an outlet to the Aegean. Ethnological maps and statistics of the area show some Greeks in the towns and along the coast, very

few Bulgarians, and a large number of Muslims. A different picture would have been shown if language rather than religion had been used as a criterion, since the Pomaks would then have counted as Bulgarian, hard though this would have been in view of the recent massacres. After World War I western Thrace was awarded to Greece, as was eastern Thrace which had a higher proportion of Greek speakers. After the Asia Minor disaster Greece lost eastern Thrace, and there were exchanges of population which dramatically increased the proportion of Greeks in western Thrace. The Pomaks did not, however, take part in these exchanges. Western Thrace was exempted from the exchanges of Muslims and Christians which took place between Greece and Turkey; it would indeed have been difficult for the Slav-speaking Pomaks to have settled in Turkey. Nor did the Pomaks join in the exchanges between Bulgaria and Greece; recent hostilities between Pomaks and Bulgarians would have made this difficult, and the Greeks in Bulgaria lived along the Black Sea coast in an area very different from the Rhodope mountains. Thus the Pomaks remain in Greece as an uncomfortable and rather unhappy fragment since neither Bulgarians nor Muslims are exactly popular, the Rhodopes though beautiful are harsh, the border area is a sensitive one, and it requires a special permit to visit it.

T.J. WINNIFRITH

See also Muslims

Summary

Pomaks are Bulgarian-speaking Muslims who live in the Rhodope mountains of northern Greece. Their origins are obscure. They are probably transhumant pastoralists. They were unaffected by the exchange of populations with Turkey in the 1920s and today probably number fewer than 30,000 in Greece. There are about 200,000 in Bulgaria.

Further Reading

Angelopoulos, A., "Population Distribution of Greece Today According to Language, National Consciousness and Religion", *Balkan Studies*, 20 (1979): pp. 123–32

Asdracha, Catherine, "La Region des Rhodopes aux XIIIe et XIVe siècles: étude de géographie historique" in *Texte und Forschungen zur Byzantisch-neugriechischen Philologie*, Athens, 1976

Photea, P., *Oi Pomakoi tis Dytikis Thrakis* [The Pomaks of Northern Thrace], Komotini, 1978

Seypell, J. "Pomaks in Northeastern Greece: An Endangered Balkan Population", *International Institute of Muslim Minority Affairs*, 10/1 (January 1989): pp. 41–49

Winnifrith, T.J., *Shattered Eagles: Balkan Fragments*, London: Duckworth, 1995

Pontus

The Greek *Pontos* (Latin *Pontus*) has at least seven meanings or connotations, general and specific.

(1) In Greek mythology Pontos personifies the Sea, son of Gaia, the Land, who by Thalassa fathered another ancient sea god, Nereus. Hence (2) the *Euxeinos Pontos*, or Black Sea and,

by extension, the southeastern littoral of that sea, called (3) the Pontus.

How the sea became a land is no mystery. Greeks approached and named the land from the sea. But from the land, on which it turns its back, the Pontus is one of the most strikingly distinct regions of Anatolia. Geography and climate, economy and settlement conspire to make the Pontus as obvious a maritime enclave as the Lebanon is of Syria. The territorial boundaries of the Pontus run for over 500 km from Sinope in the west to the mouth of the Akampsis (Çoruh) river to the east. Often less than 50 km inland this strip is hemmed to the sea by the Pontic Alps. Sinope is the hub of the Black Sea, where the seafaring cult of Poseidon was replaced by that of St Phokas. The Akampsis marks one of the oldest and most stable divisions in the world, traditionally between Europe and Asia, actually between Byzantium and Persia, the Ottoman and Russian empires, and today between Turkey and Georgia. The Pontic Alps rise gently south of Sinope, where they are broken by the Halys (Kizilirmak) and Iris (Yeşilirmak) rivers, which allow access to an Inner Pontus along the Lykos (Kelkit) valley. South of Trebizond (the modern Turkish city of Trabzon) a pass through the Pontic Gates near Zigana at about 2500 m carries the most easterly practicable land route to Persia, until the Pontic Alps reach the Paryadres (Kaçkar Dağ) at almost 4000 m, before falling into the gorges of the Akampsis. The Pontic Alps offer extensive summer pastures for nomads from the interior and transhumants from coastal Pontus, a region streaked by steep, well-wooded, and densely populated valleys, each with its own dialect and tartan, which connect to a chain of Classical Greek colonies along the coast. Here Greeks encountered barbarians, such as Jason found, represented in fable and fact by peoples such as the Amazons to the west and the monstrous Mossynoikoi to the east. Perhaps the most persistent of local identities is that of Chaldia, a basin on the southern side of the Pontic Gates around modern Gümüşhane, which takes its name from the Urartu sun god Haldi. Chaldia was a Byzantine theme (military province) from the 9th century AD and a surviving Orthodox metropolitan bishopric thereafter. To Turks *Halt* indicates people on the other, or "wrong", side of the mountains. The Pontus is surrounded by less well-defined boundaries: Paphlagonia to the west, Cappadocia to the south, and Armenia to the east.

(4) As a political unit a kingdom of the Pontus first emerged in the late 4th century BC, in the aftermath of the conquests of Alexander the Great. Its focus lay inland along the Lykos and Iris valleys, particularly at Comana Pontica (Gömenek), with a great temple economy, and a royal capital at Amaseia (Amasya), where the rock-cut tombs of the Pontic kings over-look a gorge of the Iris. A series of six Pontic kings called Mithridates extended the Pontic state from the 3rd century BC. Pharnaces I moved the capital from Amaseia to Sinope in 183 BC whence Mithridates VI Eupator (120–63 BC) conquered the Crimea and challenged Rome, with disastrous results. Mithridates VI died old and in despair in the Crimea and was buried by Pompey at Sinope. The last Pontic king, Pharnaces II, was defeated at Zela (Zille) by Julius Caesar in 47 BC. These Hellenized kings and their feudal nobility were of Persian origin and ruled a mixed indigenous population, traditonally settled in the *Chiliakomon*, thousands of nucleated villages.

(5) The Roman province of Pontus retained much of this local character and at various stages was subdivided by Diocletian into two provinces: Hellenopontus (Diospontos) based on the city of Amaseia, and Pontus Polemoniacus, also based inland, at Neocaesarea (Niksar) on the Lykos, but with access to Polemonium (Boloman) beside a cape still named after Jason (Yasun). The civil and military division became part of the primary Byzantine theme of Anatolikon. The Roman province is reflected in ecclesiastical dioceses. The evangelist of the Pontus was St Gregory the Wonderworker of Neokaisareia (Neocaesarea) (d. *c.*270), himself converted by Origen, whose life was written by St Gregory of Nyssa. Neokaisareia remained the mother church and metropolis of the Pontus long after the Danishmendids took its great castle and Monastery of the Wonderworker at the end of the 11th century.

(6) With Turkish pressure from the interior, the political focus of the Pontus moved back to the ancient Greek coastal settlements and to Trebizond, capital of the Byzantine theme of Chaldia during the 12th century. The Gabras family, semi-hereditary and semiautonomous dukes of Chaldia, made a political entity of coastal Pontus before it was given political title with the dismemberment of the Byzantine empire, when in 1204 Alexios and David Komnenos aimed to restore the rule of their dynasty in Constantinople, but found themselves pre-empted by members of the Fourth Crusade. Frustrated by another, Laskarid, empire in exile at Nicaea, the Komnenoi settled for the original coastal Pontus, from Sinope to the Akampsis, including high Chaldia, with Trebizond as their capital. The Grand Komnenoi, "emperors and autocrats of all the East [Anatolia], of the Iberians [Georgians], and of the Land Beyond [perhaps the Crimea]", ruled the so-called empire of Trebizond as a Byzantine state, upon which their legitimacy depended, until 1461, when Cardinal Bessarion (*c.*1400–72), perhaps the best-known native of Trebizond, bewailed the loss of this last outpost of Hellenism. Indeed the patronage of such emperors as the Grand Komnenos Alexios III (1349–90) made the Pontus a flourishing part of the late Byzantine world, more populous than the Morea, with a cultural capital to match Mistra. Alexios III endowed Dionysiou on Mount Athos and his own great pilgrim monastery of Soumela. But, like Bessarion, he looked west too. The wealth of Trebizond partly depended on its natural resources and partly on the reopening of the route east through the Pontic Gates to Italian traffic with the Mongol empire from the mid-13th century. But for their security the Grand Komnenoi depended upon the intense local separatism of the Pontus, which the steep valleys engendered along with their own dynasties of warlords, of which the Gabras family were forerunners. The neighbours of the empire were now Turkmen, Mongol and Georgian, with whom the Grand Komnenoi inter-married. They fought their minor wars over summer pastures in the Pontic Alps which divided them. The Ottoman state was not a neighbour until Sultan Mehmet II's conquest of Trebizond (taking the emirate of Sinope on the way) in his summer campaign of 1461, when Bessarion heard of the fate of David, the last Grand Komnenos.

(7) The Ottoman conquest left a Pontic identity alive. From the 18th century local warlords (*derebeys*) controlled the valleys again, but the Pontic Greeks probably found greater economic reward running the revived silver mines of Chaldia

around Gümüšhane (Argyropolis). The mines were exhausted by 1829 when the Russians reached Gümüšhane, but the Treaty of Adrianople reopened the Black Sea to western shipping and subsequent Ottoman reforms brought civil order to the coast. By the 1840s the Pontic Gates were carrying most of Persia's overland trade to the west again through Trebizond. Greek bankers and merchants of Trebizond helped fund an astonishing revival of Pontic Greek culture, but this time schoolmasters from Athens taught villagers that they were descendants of Xenophon's Ten Thousand. Athens, not Constantinople, was the promised city. In fact, since the 1790s many Pontic Greeks found promise in the new cities of southern Russia, such as Odessa and Mariupol, and Pontic Greeks left in the wake of successive Russian invasions to recolonize the Caucasus. The opening of the Suez Canal in 1869 marked the end of the laborious overland route east through the Pontic Gates, but by then the economic focus of the Pontus had already shifted west to Amisos (Samsun), promised railhead of the Berlin–Baghdad railway. Amisos mushroomed as the last major Greek city of the coast, on the scale of Smyrna, where Pontic Greeks cornered the Ottoman tobacco monopoly. The exchange of populations of 1923, when 164, 641 Pontic Greeks left Trebizond alone for Greece seemed to be the final migration. It was not. After an initial honeymoon in the Soviet Union, Pontic Greeks were deported under Stalin in the 1940s, during and after World War II, from the Ukraine, Russia, and Georgia to Central Asia, where in Uzbekistan and Kazakhstan they were joined by Greeks from a very different background – that of the Civil War in Greece. From 1991 the Pontic Greeks (the name by which they refer to themselves) of the former Soviet Union started coming home in what promises to be the last and largest of all Greek migrations: it is potentially a matter of millions. For most, Athens is no more home than Ohio or Melbourne, where many had already settled. *Patrida*, or "home", is still the distinct green land and concept of the Pontus, which few Pontic Greeks have ever seen. Yet, both in Turkish Trabzon and in innumerable Greek colonies in Australia or America, a Pontic identity remains obdurately alive.

ANTHONY A.M. BRYER

See also Black Sea

Summary

Pontus is the land bordering the *Euxeinos Pontos* (Black Sea), specifically the southeast littoral from Sinope in the west to the modern border with Georgia in the east. The coast was colonized early by Greeks. A kingdom of Pontus emerged in the 4th century BC. The Roman Pontus was subdivided into two provinces. The area was part of the Byzantine theme of Anatolikon, but from 1204 to 1461 formed the independent "empire" of Trebizond. Many Greeks remained during the Tourkokratia who even in the diaspora refer to themselves as Pontic Greeks.

Further Reading

Bruneau, Michel (editor), *Les Grecs pontiques: diaspora, identité, territoires*, Paris: Centre National des Recherches Scientifiques, 1998

Bryer, Anthony, "The Pontic Greeks before the Diaspora", *Journal of Refugee Studies*, 4 (1991): pp. 315–34

Magie, David, *Roman Rule in Asia Minor, to the End of the Third Century after Christ*, Princeton, New Jersey: Princeton University Press, 1950

Porphyry AD 234–c.305
Philosopher

Porphyry was one of the most influential philosophers and scholars of late antiquity, although from his vast output of more than 70 works only a handful survive. He was probably born in Tyre and bore the Syrian name Malchas. His international career is typical of many Greek-speaking Syrians of this period who made a considerable impact on the whole of the Graeco-Roman world. He was educated in Alexandria, at the Platonic Academy (under Longinus) in Athens, and finally in Rome where he studied under Plotinus. Perhaps his most enduring legacy was the introduction of Plotinus' philosophy to a wider world, achieved both by his careful edition of Plotinus' philosophical treatises under the title *Enneads* and his explanatory commentaries, which are now lost. Among others, Longinus, his former teacher, was grateful to Porphyry for sending him copies of Plotinus' work. A short and probably incomplete work popularly known as the *Sententiae* or *Ideas Leading to the Intelligibles*, which is the only substantial survival of Porphyry's metaphysics and which consists of paraphrases, summaries, and restatements of Plotinus' ideas, may have formed a part of these commentaries or of an introduction to Plotinus.

Porphyry's scholarly commentaries on the logical works of Aristotle and on some of the major Platonic dialogues (*Parmenides*, *Cratylus*, *Phaedo*, *Republic*, *Philebus*, *Sophist*, *Timaeus*) were so valued by his Neoplatonic successors that they were absorbed into their own works. Through Iamblichus, a fellow Syrian who may have studied with Porphyry, these works survive in the great commentaries of Proclus and later Neoplatonists. Porphyry was, in particular, responsible for securing a firm place in the Neoplatonic school curriculum for Aristotle's *Organon*, a virtually canonical set of his logical works. His *Isagoge* became, in both east and west, the standard introduction to Aristotelian logic and is frequently found in manuscripts of Aristotle's logical works. It is through Porphyry, too, that the ideas, and often the actual words, of earlier Aristotelian commentators (e.g. of Aspasius, Herminus, and Alexander of Aphrodisias) were handed on.

His vast learning, which provided an important source for Byzantine scholars, may be discerned in the fragmentary remains of bulky commentaries on Homer and other philological works on Pindar and Thucydides and, not least, in a *Chronology* that was an important source for Christian writers in their attempts to prove the greater, or at least equal, antiquity of the Jewish, compared with the pagan, tradition. But Porphyry fell foul of the Christians with the publication of his treatise *Against the Christians*. The work proved so damaging that it was publicly condemned in a number of imperial edicts and was fated to survive in fragmentary form, ironically, in the works of Christian polemicists seeking to counter its claims (e.g. Eusebius of Caesarea). Although Porphyry attacked a number of Christian doctrines (the divinity of Christ, the resurrection of the body), he reserved his chief criticism for the worldly quarrelling of Christ's disciples, especially Peter and Paul, and their distortions of his teaching. Most serious of all, however, was his devastating and scholarly attack on the authority of scripture itself and particularly that of the book of Daniel, which he proved to have been written after the events it was claimed to have prophesied. Porphyry is commonly referred to by Christian writers as the enemy of Christianity and his name was effectively invoked against the Arians who were dubbed Porphyrians, probably because of their subordination of Christ to the Father.

Unlike Plotinus, Porphyry was deeply interested in religion, to which he devoted several large works including a collection of oracles, *Philosophy from Oracles*, in which he apparently explored the philosophical content of oracles mainly from oracular centres in Asia Minor (Didyma and Claros). The attempt to relate philosophy to religion was one of his abiding interests. Realizing that the philosophical road to what he called "salvation" was open only to the few, he sought among the various religions (including Judaism) a common way of salvation open to all men. His failure to find such a way involved him in addressing serious questions about the assumptions of traditional religious practice and in expressing concern about its limited spiritual horizons. His *Letter to Anebo*, a probably fictitious Egyptian priest, raises these issues and was answered by Iamblichus in *On the Mysteries*, a work that can lay claim to being the first systematic attempt to grapple with the philosophy of religion. This work of Iamblichus was to be a momentous point in the reconciliation of pagan religious practice, particularly the salvific rites of theurgy, with philosophy. Iamblichus set the tone for Proclus who in this respect had a profound influence on pseudo-Dionysius and Michael Psellos, who tried to adapt his views to Christian sacramental theology. But, despite his more reserved views about such subjects as the effect of theurgic rites or the presence of the divine in statues, some of Porphyry's pious philosophical tracts survived as popular reading: for example, the *Letter to Marcella*, written to his wife, whom he married late in life, and in which he apologizes for an enforced absence with the explanation that physical separation means nothing to those whose true self is set at the level of "intellect" which is beyond all spatial restrictions; or *On Abstinence*, which advocates vegetarianism and a spiritualized religious practice. The charming essay *On the Cave of the Nymphs*, which presents a number of differing philosophical allegorical interpretations of Homer's depiction of the cave in which Odysseus hid his Phaeacian treasures (*Odyssey*, 13. 102–12), had an enduring influence as a model of Neoplatonic metaphysical allegory despite its unsystematic approach compared with the rigours of Proclus' method.

ANDREW SMITH

See also Neoplatonism

Biography

Born probably at Tyre in AD 234 with the Syrian name Malchas, Porphyry studied at Alexandria, at Athens under Longinus, and at Rome where he was a pupil of Plotinus. He wrote more than 70 works, of which few survive. He also edited the *Enneads* of Plotinus. His commentaries on Aristotle and Plato are much valued. He died *c.*305.

Writings

On Abstinence from Animal Food, translated by Thomas Taylor, edited by Esme Wynne-Tyson, London: Centaur Press, and New York: Barnes and Noble, 1965
The Cave of the Nymphs in the Odyssey, Buffalo: Department of Classics, State University of New York at Buffalo, 1969
Porphyry, the Phoenician Isagoge, translated by Edward W. Warren, Toronto: Pontifical Institute of Mediaeval Studies, 1975

Further Reading

Bidez, J., *Vie de Porphyre, le philosophe Néo-Platonicien*, Ghent: Van Goethem, 1913; reprinted Hildesheim: Olms, 1964
Smith, Andrew, "Porphyrian Studies since 1913", in *Aufstieg und Niedergang der römischen Welt*, edited by Hildegard Temporini et al., 2. 36. 2, Berlin: de Gruyter 1987, 717–73

Portraiture

Realistic likenesses of individuals originated in the 4th century BC in Greece, although portrait prototypes had appeared two centuries earlier as dedication statues. An example of this type is the seated figure of *Chares* (British Museum, London), a hereditary priest from the temple of Apollo at Didyma. Similar categories of images from the later Archaic period are commemorations honouring victorious athletes, mainly at Olympia. In the 5th century BC the cult of the hero was prominent, but portrayals of athletes continued. There was a high degree of realism, although the works reflected an idealized picture of youth. Between 480 and 450 BC the practice of honouring the great citizens of Athens with portrait statues became acceptable, although only posthumously. During the Classical period images of military and political leaders, poets, and other heroic men were created so as to reflect their super-human qualities.

With the end of the Peloponnesian War in the early 4th century BC a novel approach in rendering portraits evolved. Contemporary heroes and intellectuals were now honoured in public locations by private donors. A portrait of the philosopher Plato by the sculptor Silanion (Vatican Museum, Rome) was commissioned by a former student for the Academy in Athens. The sculpture is more of a mask, individual features that reveal nothing of the inner workings of the mind. Towards the middle of the 4th century BC, when the Greeks were encountering rising Macedonian power under Philip II, father of Alexander the Great, Lycurgus, appointed virtual dictator of Athens for 12 years, systematically commissioned a large number of public buildings decorated with portrait statues; he wished to revive the great heroes of the past as examples for modern Athenians to emulate. A large number of portraits were set up at public sites such as the theatre of Dionysus, where bronze statues of the great tragic playwrights Aeschylus, Sophocles, and Euripides were installed. The likenesses of these individuals have an added quality of character and personality that contrasts with the idealized and detached countenances of the 5th-century examples. As full-length statues, their gestures and pose were as important as the features, reminding viewers

Portraiture: mummy portrait of a woman named Aline, Fayum, Egypt, *c.*AD 50, Aegyptisches Museum, Berlin

of their personality, character, and physique. Such statues were frequently inscribed with the subject's name, but rarely with the sculptor's. Portraits of women were rare before this time and restricted to generic statues of maidens, or as female types engaged in everyday activities on vase paintings. An exception to this trend is a portrait of an elderly priestess of Athena by the sculptor Demetrius who specialized in depicting elderly people.

In the last third of the 4th century BC Alexander the Great chose Lysippus as the official sculptor for his court portraits. The heroic ideal of the beardless young general became a standard mode of representation for the Macedonian king. The famous mosaic of *Alexander the Great and Darius* at the Battle of Issus (Museo Archeologico Nazionale, Naples) is a Roman copy of a Hellenistic painting probably painted in Egypt, perhaps by Helen, who trained under her father Philoxenos, in the 4th century BC. It is also known that Alexander commissioned the great painter Apelles and the gem engraver Pyrogoteles to portray him, in addition to the sculpted likenesses by Lysippus. Despite literary descriptions of the beautiful young general, no great images remain for posterity.

Subsequent Hellenistic rulers emulated this portrait type but eventually added their own distinctive style and individual characteristics to the mass-produced likenesses. The most significant change in the portrait tradition reflected the philosophical changes that had taken place. Aristotle, teacher of Alexander, identified men according to personality rather than

classifying them according to their occupation, the practice of the 5th century BC. In sculptural portraits, therefore, there was a marked change from emphasizing external features to showing the characteristics that mirrored the psyche of the individual and reflected his or her inner life. Changing attitudes towards the physical and spiritual world are identified in the portrait of *Aristotle* commissioned by Alexander. The new biographical portrait encompassed the entire life of the individual and, as such, became a milestone in the development of the history of portraiture and art in the western world.

The portraits of Alexander's successors are more individualized, with the three major kingdoms in Egypt, Syria, and Asia Minor assimilating distinctive artistic traditions. General categories of portraits still persisted, that of the ruler and the intellectual. A desire to portray strong emotions resulted in a new emphasis in portrait-making that emphasized a kind of hyper-realism in depicting anti-heroic types. Drunken old women, defeated boxers, dancing dwarves, emaciated men, and languid lovers all promoted art and its spread, not only in public places of gathering, but at a popular level. Because of the vast numbers of portraits produced, there is ample evidence for multiculturalism and diversity in the ancient Greek world, shedding light on ordinary people as well as the aristocracy. With the Roman conquest of Greece, the changing tradition of creating and commissioning portraits of private citizens as well as public heroes was an important artistic and philosophical legacy passed on to Rome by the Greeks. Unfortunately, surviving painted portraits and likenesses created in mosaic are rare in the Greek world. As a result of the eruption of Mount Vesuvius in AD 79, however, several personalities have been brought to light by archaeological discoveries at Pompeii, Herculaneum, and Stabiae. A 25 ¥ 20 cm mosaic of an unidentified Pompeiian woman of the 1st century BC (Museo Nazionale, Naples) reflects the psychological portrait type popular in the Hellenistic era. Her likeness is formed with very small pieces of coloured stone, called tesserae, in a manner that mimics the subtle shading of the facial features. Likewise, the double portrait of a man and his wife (Museo Nazionale, Naples), discovered next door to a bakery in Pompeii, is painted with the cultural symbols of the middle class. He is holding a scroll and his wife, in her red-dyed robe, holds a wax tablet and stylus, perhaps for the accounts. For the merchant classes, it was important to show one's occupation and status in addition to a rather naturalistically rendered likeness.

In Egypt the painters of the Fayum were either Greek residents dating from the Ptolemaic period of the late 4th century BC, or those who had inherited the Greek artistic tradition. The art school established at Alexandria was an extension of Graeco-Macedonian art, a tradition that melded with the Egyptian manner of creating body doubles to which the spirit of the deceased could return. Culture was much the same under the Romans as it had been under the Hellenistic rulers, with the chain of artistic knowledge remaining unbroken for many years. The Fayum portraits bridged the gap between Hellenistic portraits and the abstract likenesses of Byzantine icons.

The wax portraits completed during the life of the individual and displayed in the home belonged to the traditions of Greek art. After death, the portrait panel was placed over the Egyptian mummy's face. Gold wreaths, jewellery, and hair ornaments were painted on, contrasting with the impressionistic quality of the portrait. What is unique about the Fayum portraits is the way in which the personality is reflected through the faces of men and women in a psychologically compelling way. The Christian emphasis on the spirit with the body as a vehicle for the soul found a parallel in the Fayum portraits, particularly the eyes, which convey spirituality; they were the ideal stepping stone for the transition from painted portrait to icon. Portraits underwent a series of transformations from idealized image to the abstracted faces of Byzantine emperors and members of their court, which were represented in paintings, mosaics, coins, and jewellery.

By the end of the 3rd century AD true realism gave way to greater expressiveness, sometimes with an almost caricature-like effect. Yet the eyes maintained their dominant emphasis and spiritual character in the sacrifice of physical beauty in order to convey the beauty of the soul. The kind of artistic symbolism apparent in these and subsequent portraits persisted for a millennium. Sixth-century mosaic portraits in San Vitale, Ravenna, of the emperor Justinian and his wife Theodora reflect the pomp and ceremony of the court. The tesserae are larger in size, making the images bolder, brighter, and heavily resplendent with the trappings of their office as Christian rulers. Even coin portraits revealed the shift to abstraction, with bejewelled empresses and emperors in the regalia of Christian monarchs. The new frontality and enlarged eyes that had once been the realm of lower-class portraiture in the early empire were adopted by the Church and state as proper vehicles of expression in a new world of spirituality, ceremony, and status. Image was everything, naturalism secondary.

This new world order made a ready transition in portraiture to Byzantine icons and has been maintained to this day, in the icons of Virgin and Child, saints, and other holy figures prevalent in monasteries, churches, and homes. The custom of preserving the image of the deceased persists but in the more naturalistic manner of the Classical age. While modern technology has allowed for photographic likenesses, other grave memorials with relief carvings or portrait statues maintain the sculptural tradition of the past. One has only to visit the cemeteries and churches to glimpse the art of the portrait still celebrated in Greece.

VIRGINIA M. DA COSTA

See also Icon, Painting, Sculpture

Further Reading

Ackland Art Center, *Ancient Portraits*, Chapel Hill: University of North Carolina, 1970 (exhibition catalogue)

Breckenridge, James D., *Likeness: A Conceptual History of Ancient Portraiture*, Evanston, Illinois: Northwestern University Press, 1968

Doxiadis, Euphrosyne, *The Mysterious Fayum Portraits: Faces from Ancient Egypt*, London: Thames and Hudson, and New York: Abrams, 1996

Harrison, Evelyn B., *Ancient Portraits from the Athenian Agora*, Princeton, New Jersey: American School of Classical Studies at Athens, 1960

Hinks, R.P., *Greek and Roman Portrait Sculpture*, 2nd edition, London: British Museum Publications, 1976

Thompson, David L., *The Artists of the Mummy Portraits*, Malibu, California: J. Paul Getty Museum, 1976

Walker, John., *Portraits: 5,000 Years*, New York: Abrams, 1983

Posidonius *c.*135 BC–*c.*51 BC

Philosopher and scientist

To call Posidonius a "historian" would be unduly reductive. Posidonius was a Stoic philosopher and a scientist, with a wide world-view that integrated cosmic, natural, and human phenomena. More than 400 testimonia and fragments testify to his contribution to knowledge, which ranges from mathematics, astronomy, and geology, to ethics, anthropology, and history. He meditated on the universe, seen by him as an animated organism, and on its generation and destruction. He studied the solar system, envisaged a lunar theory to explain the periodicity of tides and a new method of measuring the circumference of the earth, suggested "ethnic criteria" for naming the earth zones, and outlined a history of the circumnavigation of Africa. In human sciences his curiosity was stimulated mainly by customs, an essential element of what he called "ethology" (fragment 176 in the Edelstein-Kidd edition, E-K), i.e. character formation and characterization of people. He might be defined as a "primitivist" who idealizes the primeval stages of mankind as a golden age; but he was convinced that the ascent of man from barbarism to civilization was determined ultimately by "wise men" – legislators, inventors, imitators, or importers of foreign arts and techniques (testimonium 6; fragments 265–67 in the Jacoby edition; fr. 284 E-K) – as if there was an element of "progress" in his thought. Undoubtedly, he admired the presumed simplicity of "noble savages" and had no praise for the luxury and extravagances prevailing in his time either in decadent cities and royal courts (especially in the east: e.g. frr. 56, 58, 61a, 65, 77 E-K) or among the ruling elites of tribal societies (frr. 67, 152 in the Theiler edition, D-F). He eulogized the presumed virtues, frugality, justice, and religious devotion of the ancient Romans (frr. 256–61 and 265–67 E-K, with the exempla of Brutus, Marcellus, and Scipio), as against the current intemperance and corruption. Following Polybius, he probably looked at the crucial year of 146 BC as the completion of Roman imperialism and the beginning of its moral decline. Like Polybius, he was a Greek thinker who tried to explain the merits of Roman rule to his fellow countrymen and to persuade them to accept it, at the same time doing his best to persuade the Roman ruling class to behave in a way that was attractive to most of the subject peoples. He fully justified imperial rule, even the exaction of tribute by more intelligent nations, in return for protection and security for the weak, on the model of the relationship between the Pontic Heracleotes and the Mariandynians, who were allegedly reduced to serfdom by consent (fr. 60 E-K). He believed that riches spur men to do evil, and was ready even to acknowledge that tyrannical rule may provoke rebellions; yet he never justified revolts and described vividly the immoral and extravagant behaviour of rebel leaders (e.g. Athenion, tyrant of Athens: fr. 253 E-K; Demophilus, the leader of the rebel slaves in Sicily: fr. 59 E-K). In the light of such views it is not easy to decide whether

Posidonius sided with the Roman Optimates or with the Populares. His romantic view of the past invites comparison with the Gracchan tradition, but unlike it, his conservatism was definitely anti-revolutionary (fr. 51 E-K; cf. Jacoby, frr. 87, 110–12).

Posidonius' direct predecessors were Panaetius and Polybius, the first as his Stoic teacher, the second as chosen universal historian to continue his work. Yet Posidonius was not dogmatic, and continuation did not imply identification with the views and methods of his predecessor. He criticized Chrysippus (fr. 34 E-K), the grand master of 3rd-century Stoicism, and attacked Polybius for his biased report of Tiberius Gracchus' activities in Spain (fr. 271 E-K). In sciences and philosophy he used Plato extensively, and Aristotle, and occasionally many others, for example, the "astrologer" Bion (a disciple of Democritus), the philosopher Crates, the historian Callisthenes, the peripatetic statesman Demetrius of Phaleron, and the geographer Timosthenes. In ethnography Posidonius was comparative and moralistic in spirit. He valued autopsy no less than Herodotus, whom he mentions together with Heraclides Ponticus on the circumnavigation of Africa, and shared with him the main didactic purpose of pointing out the contrast between *Naturvölker* and civilization. An oriental Greek like Herodotus, Posidonius was no less inclined to ascribe to ancient eastern sages discoveries conventionally attributed to later Greek scientists – for example, the atomic theory, invented according to Posidonius not by Democritus of Abdera but by the Phoenician Mochos of Sidon before the Trojan War (fr. 286 E-K). In his repetitive descriptions of luxury banquets and receptions, drinking habits, etc., Posidonius echoes the Hellenistic motif of trust, best represented before him by Phylarchus of Athens and Agatharcides of Cnidus. He also probably used Ephorus, Polybius' main predecessor in universal history, and Timaeus; and he knew of Eudoxus of Cnidus' observation of Canopus when making his own (fr. 204 E-K). Finally, Artemidorus of Ephesus, who travelled in Gaul and Spain around 100 BC, was known to Posidonius, who occasionally disagreed with him (Jacoby, frr. 119, 223).

Posidonius was unquestionably the greatest Stoic philosopher of his age. Among his closest friends and admirers were some prominent Romans, such as Rutilius Rufus, Cicero, and Pompey, and his prestige in Latin literature is well attested (e.g. in Vitruvius, Seneca, Pliny, Quintilian, Tertullian, Lactantius, St Augustine, Macrobius, and Boethius). The Hellenic tradition starts with his disciple Jason, who succeeded him at Rhodes, and with Diodorus Siculus, who used Posidonius (with other sources) on the period covered by his *Events after Polybius* (146–*c*.86 BC). Posidonius' influence as an intellectual must have been extensive in his generation, but he soon began to be consulted, quoted, and at times criticized by scientists and philosophers mainly for specific points of their interest. Thus, for instance, his disciple Geminus, an astronomer, compiled an "epitome" of, or a commentary on, his *Meteorologica* (t 42, 72 E-K), and the philosopher Arius Didymus included in his doxography Posidonius' definitions of cause, substance, and matter, origin, destruction, and so on. Strabo, a great admirer of Posidonius, made full use of his geographic works, though criticizing his "aetiology"

("precisely what our school [i.e. the Stoic] avoids") and his rhetorical style (fr. 239 E-K).

Plutarch quotes Posidonius both on scientific and moral issues in the *Moralia* (and in his *Lives* of great Romans (Marcellus, Fabius Maximus, Marius, Cicero, Pompey, and Brutus). Galen used Posidonius extensively but critically, especially on ethics; Athenaeus, our main authority on Posidonius' historical works, aptly understands the relationship between his ethnography and his Stoicism; and Diogenes Laertius quotes his views on many topics, especially in book 7 (on the Stoics). Among later readers the most prominent is perhaps Cleomedes (now dated to the 4th century AD), who was interested in astronomy and physics. The *Suda* has an entry on Posidonius, and in the 12th century Eustathios made full use of his scientific and ethnological work in his commentaries on Homer and Dionysius Periegetes.

Surprisingly enough for a man of such reputation, with nearly 70 recorders, none of Posidonius' 30 or so works has reached us in its entirety. But perhaps modern evaluations of his achievements have been too high. The claims that in the history of ancient thought Posidonius can be compared to no one but Aristotle, or that he was the most important critic and philosopher of culture in the ancient world, are patent and unwarranted exaggerations, partly resting on questionable reconstructions of Posidonius' thought allegedly retrievable from later authors supposed to be his followers or even his plagiarists. At any rate, in the Hellenic tradition of Roman and Byzantine times Posidonius' place seems assured among the great thinkers of second rank – still a very high station.

DAVID ASHERI

Biography

Born at Apamea in Syria *c*.135 BC, Posidonius was educated in Athens under Panaetius but lived mostly in Rhodes. He participated in an embassy to Rome in 87/86 BC and travelled extensively in the west. His school in Rhodes was a centre for Stoicism. He wrote on a wide range of subjects including science, mathematics, geography, and history as well as philosophy. He died *c*.51 BC.

Writings

In *Die Fragmente der Griechischen Historiker*, edited by Felix Jacoby, vol. 2a.87, Leiden: Brill, 1961 (only historical and ethnographic fragments)

Posidonius, edited by L. Edelstein and I.G. Kidd, 3 vols, Cambridge University Press, 1972–99 (text, commentary, and translations)

Die Fragmente, edited by Willy von Theiler, 2 vols, Berlin: de Gruyter, 1982

Further Reading

Crawford, M.H., "Greek Intellectuals and the Roman Aristocracy in the First Century BC" in *Imperialism in the Ancient World*, edited by P.D.A. Garnsey and C.R. Whittaker, Cambridge and New York: Cambridge University Press, 1978

Edelstein, L., "The Philosophical System of Posidonius", *American Journal of Philology*, 57 (1936): pp. 286ff.

Ferrary, Jean-Louis, *Philhellénisme et impérialisme: aspects idéologiques de la conquête romaine du monde hellénistique*, Rome: École Française de Rome, 1988, pp. 370ff., pp. 382ff., pp. 573ff.

Kidd, I.G., "Posidonian Methodology and the Self-Sufficiency of Virtue", *Entretiens Hardt*, 32 (1986): pp. 1ff.

Kidd, I.G., Posidonius entry in *The Oxford Classical Dictionary*, 3rd edition, edited by Simon Hornblower and Antony Spawforth,

Oxford and New York: Oxford University Press, 1996, pp. 1231–33

Laffranque, Marie, *Posidonius d'Apamée: essai de mise au point*, Paris: Presses Universitaires de France, 1964

Malitz, Jürgen, *Die Historien des Poseidonius*, Munich: Beck, 1983

Meister, Klaus, *Die griechische Geschichtsschreibung: Von den Anfängen bis zum Ende des Hellenismus*, Stuttgart: Kohlhammer, 1990, pp. 166 ff.

Momigliano, Arnaldo, *Alien Wisdom: The Limits of Hellenization*, Cambridge and New York: Cambridge University Press, 1975, chapter 2

Nock, A.D., "Posidonius", *Journal of Roman Studies*, 49 (1959): pp. 1 ff.

Reinhardt, Karl, *Poseidonios*, Munich: Beck, 1921; reprinted Hildesheim: Olms, 1976

Reinhardt, Karl, Poseidonios entry in *Real-Encyclopädie der klassischen Altertumswissenschaft*, edited by August Pauly *et al.*, vol. 22. 1, 1953, 558ff.

Strasburger, H., "Poseidonios on Problems of the Roman Empire", *Journal of Roman Studies*, 55 (1965): pp. 40ff.

Tierney, "The Celtic Ethnography of Posidonius", *Proceedings of the Royal Irish Academy*, 60 (1959–60): pp.189 ff.

Treves, Piero, Posidonius entry in *The Oxford Classical Dictionary*, 2nd edition, edited by N.G.L. Hammond and H.H. Scullard, Oxford: Clarendon Press, 1970, pp. 867–68

Pottery

The introduction of pottery vessels is one of the defining features of the Neolithic period (*c*.7000 BC). Although at this time it was handmade, some Greek Neolithic pottery reached high standards of fabric, form, and decoration, the last mostly in geometric patterns. The products of the Neolithic cultures of Thessaly (Sesklo, Dimini) are particular noteworthy.

There was only limited continuity of features into the Early Bronze Age (*c*.3500 BC), when quite different types appeared and some early influence was exerted by Anatolian forms. The most interesting innovations are found in Crete (Vasiliki "teapots", the mottled colouring produced by manipulating the firing process) and the Cyclades (incised "frying pans" with representational motifs; painted patterns).

The Middle Bronze Age saw the rise of the Cretan palaces (*c*.2000 BC), the first widespread use of the wheel for pottery-making, and highly sophisticated ceramics. Some Cretan wares were extremely fine ("eggshell") and motifs, in the "light-on-dark" technique characteristic of the time, were subtly accommodated to the shapes. Potters on the mainland had some distinctive fabrics (Minyan, Matt-painted ware) but less decorative imagination, while Cycladic craftsmen derived their inspiration from Crete, at the same time showing individual enterprise in the development of shapes (panelled cup) and motifs (goblins).

The Late Bronze Age (*c*.1600 BC) was dominated, both politically and culturally, first by the later Cretan palaces, then by the Mycenaeans of the Greek mainland. In Crete a new system of decoration ("dark-on-light") succeeded, and was used at first for a combination of geometric motifs (spirals) and floral and grass designs, then also for a highly distinctive "marine" style. The Myceneans inherited all these features but imbued the pottery and other products of their material culture with distinctive stylistic and thematic features. In particular

they simplified and stylized the decorative elements, which in Crete had been relatively naturalistic, to a high degree. Some shapes are also distinctive of their taste (*kylikes*, or high-stemmed goblets; deep bowls). A "pictorial style", the motifs of which are mainly birds, animals, and warriors in chariots, was less widespread. In the last phase of the Bronze Age (12th and early 11th centuries BC) a pictorial strain continued (including the new "Octopus style" of the Aegean) but pottery subsided into a more limited range of shapes with little or no decoration. In the sub-Mycenaean phase (mid-11th century BC) the pottery produced was poor in quality and restricted in variety.

Although little Cretan pottery was exported beyond the Aegean in the Palace periods, within that area it was strongly influential. Mycenaean products reached a much wider audience – Cyprus (for which market much of the pictorial style was manufactured), the Near East, Egypt, southern Italy, and Sardinia. Philistine pottery of a late phase of the Bronze Age is derived from Mycenaean.

During the Protogeometric period (*c*.1025–900 BC) there was a great revival of quality, if not range, with new taut shapes and precise, often compass-drawn motifs, and craftsmen showed a fine sensitivity for the harmonizing the two. This characteristic quality continued to prevail in the subsequent Geometric period, when zones of decoration tended to multiply until they covered the whole surface of the vase. Schematic figures, geometric in character, also appeared, and some of the scenes in which they were shown may be the earliest pictorial versions of Greek myths. The largest vases (*c*.1.5 m high) were used as grave markers, and mourning and funerary scenes are common.

The Geometric style lasted to *c*.725 BC and beyond, but, in its later stages, enlargement of and greater concentration on the figured scenes brought a decline in the relationship of decoration to shape. This trend was partly due to the increasing interest of Greek vase painters in the arts of the east Mediterranean, where a fuller and non-geometric treatment of the human form was current (although not in pottery decoration). "Orientalizing" features (*c*.725–625 BC) are most evident in the adoption and treatment of bird and animal motifs.

Corinth was the most innovative centre at the time, and a new technique was introduced there *c*.700 BC. This was the so-called "black figure" method, which involved painting the figures in a clay slip (the black colour was achieved by the firing process) on the vase surface and incising details of anatomy, drapery, etc. with a sharp point; other colours were sometimes added. The precision of this method suited the fine detail required for the decoration of the tiny perfume flasks (*aryballoi*) which were the staple of the Corinthian industry.

The Athenians, with a preference for larger vases, initially drew their figures in outline, painting in the detail, but around 625 they too adopted the black-figure technique and used it increasingly for large-scale mythological scenes. Their pottery rapidly superseded that of Corinth in popularity. The stately magnificence of the work of the best Athenian black-figure painters (such as Execias and the Amasis Painter) of the mid-6th century BC is astonishing. Interest continued to be focused on the figured scenes (see below), although the elegance and symmetry of the shapes and the surface finish were also of excellent quality. Black-figure pottery was widely exported,

Pottery: stirrup jar from Knossos, 2nd millennium BC, Ashmolean Museum, Oxford

especially to the Greek colonies, and regional styles developed, in the case of the Etruscans even outside the Greek-speaking world.

Around 530 BC another new technique ("red-figure") was introduced and gradually became dominant. The vase surface itself was now covered with paint, the figures being left "reserved" to take on the natural colour of the clay when fired. Interior details were painted. The more natural body colour, and the greater fluidity that the painted line gave to dress and anatomy, allowed artists to depict more complex scenes in a more naturalistic way, but the otherworldly quality of black-figure was lost. During this period the art of wall painting was becoming prominent in Greece and there is good reason for thinking that vase painters adopted on occasion certain features (variable ground lines, landscape and background elements) that were better suited to the broad sweep of large panel pictures than to vase decoration.

Although there is no convincing explanation why pottery decorated with figured scenes in the red-figure technique ceased to be produced much after c.300 BC, it may be that the aesthetic effect had become much less satisfying, now that the importance of the relationship between shape and decoration had been forgotten in the quest for exciting narrative and spectacular effects, and borrowings from the world of free painting had proved counterproductive. Red figures were also less

appropriate for vase decoration than black since, while the latter stay visually on the surface of the vessel and emphasize its volume and structure, the former seem to recede into the shape and deny its solidity.

From the time when the Greeks started to establish colonies and trading centres overseas (as early as the 8th century BC, but more intensively from the later 7th century BC), especially in south Italy and Sicily but also in other areas (the north Aegean, the Black Sea, Asia Minor), their pottery became more widely distributed, more influential on other cultures, and, in theory at least, more open to modification by the adoption of foreign ideas. In fact the influence of Greek pottery on that of other traditions was strictly limited (Etruscan vases are a marked exception) and the Greeks, whether at home or abroad, seem to have adopted little directly (the rhyton shape is one example) apart from a few superficial features, although exotic stylistic features were transformed into local idioms in the Orientalizing period. In particular, the black- and red-figure styles that are so admired today had no further influence until the Neoclassical movement of the 18th century (see below).

Although the red-figure style lasted longer (till the early 3rd century BC) in the Greek colonies of south Italy, in the Hellenistic period it was superseded by other forms of decoration. Painted figured scenes were less prominent, but minor decorative elements were applied in this way (West Slope ware). Figures were now depicted in relief on vases made in moulds (Megarian bowls). The tradition of relief decoration continued in the most widely known varieties of Roman figured pottery (Arretine and Terra Sigillata, the latter sometimes known as "Samian", although it has no significant connection with the island of Samos). Many Roman shapes were also inherited from the Hellenistic world.

Greece, as part of the Roman empire, succumbed to Roman forms in the field of pottery and, if the Hellenistic influences are discounted, the products of this period are Greek only in the sense that they were manufactured in the Aegean, where some local variants of more widespread types naturally appeared. Only relatively recently has serious scholarly attention begun to be focused on pottery of the late Roman and subsequent periods. The first synthetic work on Greek pottery after 1700 (with discussion of the late Roman and Byzantine background), an excellent study by K. Korre-Zografou, appeared in 1995. Treatment of these phases here is therefore more summary.

Byzantine pottery, which was based initially on late-Roman forms but later developed highly distinctive features with new decorative techniques (glaze from the 7th century, and sgraffito, or incised designs), was the pottery not only of Greece in its ancient or modern territorial sense, but of the Byzantine world as a whole. Much of it was made in Constantinople and exported. During the post-Byzantine period, after the fall of Constantinople in 1453 and the spread of the Ottoman empire, there was at first little change in the pottery produced in the Greek world, though eventually there was a coarsening of style and an increase in local rather than centralized production. But Greek traders were involved in wide international contacts that resulted *inter alia* in the arrival, increasing popularity, and imitation of foreign wares in the Aegean. These came from both east and west.

Islamic influence was first passed into Greece through the products of the Asia Minor centre of Iznik (Nicaea), active *c.*1490–*c.*1700. The so-called Rhodian plates and other forms, whose attractive and colourful designs included flowers, human and animal figures, and ships, were widely distributed in the Aegean and further afield in the 16th and 17th centuries. In spite of the name these are now known to have been produced at Iznik but were mostly distributed through the island of Rhodes. In the 19th century and at the beginning of the 20th century products of the Koutalhaya potteries (established 17th century) were also distributed in Greece, and another important centre was Çannakale (18th and 19th centuries, surviving until 1922).

From the other direction, westerners (Venetians, Genoese, crusader Franks, etc.) had been involved in the Aegean from at least the 11th century, and more intensively after the establishment of the Latin empire at Constantinople in 1204. Some Greek merchants were resident in Italy (especially from the 16th century). There are occasional signs of the influences of knightly taste (falconry, armed combat) in the figured decoration of late-Byzantine pottery. Italian majolica was extensively imported and imitated from the 16th century; protomajolica is found in Greece in the 13th century.

In shapes, colours, and decorative techniques the late-Byzantine tradition remained strong, particularly in northern Greece (Epirus, Macedonia, Thrace) where the characteristic colouring and sgrafitto decoration are found into the 20th century. In the 19th century many regions and places in Greece developed their own distinctive products and styles and there was a good deal of exchange. Island potteries were particularly active (Samos, Siphnos). The spread of ideas and techniques was facilitated by travelling potters, especially those from the island of Siphnos. At the same time foreign products were popular and some types were specially ordered from abroad (Syros commemorative plates from Britain; others from France and Italy) for the Greek market. Many of the products (e.g. storage pithoi) of these potteries fulfilled purely practical functions, but fine wares were increasingly demanded for the table and for interior decoration, a special stimulus being given by the emergent bourgeois society that developed after the establishment of the kingdom of Greece in 1833. Ceramic decoration (especially antefixes) in a Neoclassical style was also popular for buildings of the 19th and earlier 20th centuries. After the exchange of populations in 1923, refugee potters from Asia Minor set themselves up in Greece, establishing workshops and factories and introducing new ceramic features. Although a few local potteries survive and some of the larger factories (e.g. Kerameikos in Athens) continue to turn out fine pottery, some of which reflects earlier traditions, most regional production has been superseded in recent years by featureless mass-produced or imported products.

Greek pottery, especially that of antiquity, has contributed to the spread and understanding of the Greek tradition in various ways. Perhaps the most striking example of its influence on a foreign ceramic tradition is a somewhat anachronistic one. From the late 18th century the British Wedgwood potteries made extensive use of shapes, decorative motifs, and figured styles directly derived from ancient black- and red-figured and mouldmade pottery. Apart, however, from one or two attempts to imitate black- and red-figure effects using

modern techniques (the ancient methods were not then understood), the materials and techniques were different, even though the connections in style and subject are very marked. This trend of course was part of a much wider Neoclassical movement.

As regards the scholarly investigation of ancient Greece, pottery of the black- and red-figure styles has played a major role in the study of Greek mythology and everyday life as well as in disseminating knowledge, since it is by far the most abundant, as well as an exceptionally attractive, pictorial source. The vast amount of material available and the equally vast amount of academic effort devoted to ancient pottery have resulted in a detailed understanding of types and phases of development and of the precise origins of many classes and features. Invaluable for establishing both relative chronology and interconnections between different centres in antiquity, such material is fundamental to historical reconstruction. Recent research has greatly extended its usefulness in this way in the Byzantine and later periods.

In more general terms, ancient Greek pottery has come to be regarded, if often implicitly, as providing classic examples of ceramic quality and style. In fact, however, interest in its archaeological and thematic value has almost entirely overshadowed discussion of its merit as an integrated art form. Here, there are good grounds for arguing that the Geometric was the most successful period and that, however subtle and skilful the figured scenes depicted in the black- and red-figure styles, the very impact of these and their neglect of the structure of the vessel distorted that balance between decoration and shape that is essential to make a vase a work of art.

ROBIN L.N. BARBER

See also Painting

Further Reading

Arias, P.E., *A History of Greek Vase Painting*, translated and revised by B.B. Shefton, London: Thames and Hudson, 1962

Boardman, John, *The Greeks Overseas: Their Early Colonies and Trade*, 4th edition, London and New York: Thames and Hudson, 1999

Boardman, John (editor), *The Oxford History of Classical Art*, Oxford and New York: Oxford University Press, 1993

Boardman, John, *The Diffusion of Classical Art in Antiquity*, London: Thames and Hudson, and Princeton, New Jersey: Princeton University Press, 1994

Cook, R.M., *Greek Painted Pottery*, 3rd edition, London and New York: Routledge, 1997

Hayes, J.W., *Late Roman Pottery*, London: British School at Rome, 1972

Johns, Catherine, *Arretine and Samian Pottery*, London: British Museum, 1971

Korre-Zographou, Katerina, *Ta kerameika tou Hellenikou Chorou* [Pottery of the Hellenic Region], Athens, 1995

Lacy, A.D., *Greek Pottery in the Bronze Age*, London: Methuen, 1967

Lane, Arthur, *Style in Pottery*, 2nd edition, New York: Oxford University Press, 1948; reprinted London: Faber, 1973

Lane, Arthur, *Greek Pottery*, 3rd edition, London: Faber, 1971

Mankowitz, Wolf, *Wedgwood*, 3rd edition, London: Barrie and Jenkins, 1980

Marinatos, Spyridon and M. Hirmer, *Crete and Mycenae*, London: Thames and Hudson, and New York: Abrams, 1960

Noble, J.V., *The Techniques of Painted Attic Pottery*, revised edition, London: Thames and Hudson, 1988

Sparkes, Brian A., *Greek Pottery: An Introduction*, Manchester: Manchester University Press, 1991

Talbot Rice, D., *Byzantine Glazed Pottery*, Oxford: Clarendon Press, 1930

Trendall, A.D., *Red Figure Vases of South Italy and Sicily: A Handbook*, London and New York: Thames and Hudson, 1989

Praxiteles

Sculptor of the 4th century BC

Praxiteles was an Athenian sculptor active in the 4th century BC; Pliny (*Naturalis Historia*, 34. 50) places him in the 104th Olympiad (364–361 BC). It is likely that he came from a family of sculptors; his father was probably Cephisodotus, who created a famous statue of *Peace* (perhaps dedicated after 374 BC when Athens came to terms with Sparta). Praxiteles is likely to have been born around 400 BC and had probably died before 326 BC, when his son is known to have been responsible for naval liturgies at Athens. He was celebrated in antiquity, along with Lysippus, for achieving "realism" (Quintilian, *Institutio Oratoria*, 12. 10. 1–10).

Praxiteles made statues in both bronze and marble, and was, according to Pliny (*Naturalis Historia*, 34. 69), "more successful" in the latter medium. Marble was the medium used for his most celebrated statue, the *Cnidian Aphrodite*, which in Pliny's day attracted people to the city of Cnidus (*Naturalis Historia*, 36. 20). Praxiteles had apparently been commissioned by the people of Cos to make a statue of Aphrodite, and he created two, one draped, and the other naked. The people of Cos rejected the former, while the naked statue was acquired by Cnidus and displayed in a circular temple so that the goddess could be viewed from all sides. One of the best descriptions was made by Lucian of Samosata (*Amores*, 13–14) in the 2nd century AD, who described it as "an exceedingly beautiful work of Parian marble". The original is likely to have had parts that were gilded or painted to enhance the work. There was a tradition that Praxiteles used his mistress, Phryne, as the model for the statue. Roman copies of a naked Aphrodite, clearly just concluding a wash, are thought to be representations of this work. The original was carried off to Constantinople where, according to the Byzantine chronicler George Kedrenos, it was displayed in the basilica of Lausus – along with many other statues of the ancient world including the chryselephantine cult statue of *Zeus* from Olympia – until its destruction in a fire in AD 476.

Praxiteles also made a comparable *Aphrodite* in bronze. This was carried off to Rome and was subsequently destroyed in a fire that consumed the temple of Felicitas where it was displayed. Praxiteles' continuing popularity in the Roman period is reflected by the way that his works were carried off to Rome. These were displayed in the gardens of Servilius, on the Capitoline, and in the collection of Asinius Pollio. Praxiteles' fame led him to be associated with the creation of the Mausoleum of Halicarnassus, one of the wonders of the ancient world.

Praxiteles: statue of Hermes attributed to Praxiteles, Olympia Museum

Phryne was celebrated in a gold statue made by Praxiteles at Delphi (Athenaeus, 13. 591b). Phryne herself came from Thespiae in Boeotia, and it was there that Praxiteles made a marble statue of *Eros*; Strabo records the tradition that Praxiteles had given it to his mistress as a gift. This statue was removed by the Roman emperor Caligula, returned by Claudius, and then snatched by Nero; in Pliny's day it was displayed in the lecture rooms of Octavia in Rome. Pausanias, writing in the 2nd century AD (9. 27. 3–5), recorded that, although the original had been destroyed by fire in AD 80, a copy of Praxiteles' work made by Menodorus of Athens could still be seen at Thespiae.

At Olympia Pausanias (5. 17. 3) saw a marble *Hermes* carrying the infant Dionysus in the temple of Hera that was attributed to Praxiteles. A *Hermes* was in fact discovered in the temple in 1877 and was accepted as Praxiteles' original until questioned in 1927. Although there is a possibility that it is an original that was touched up by later sculptors, scholars now tend towards the view that the Olympia piece – perhaps the one seen by Pausanias – is in fact a work of the Hellenistic period, either by a member of Praxiteles' school or by somebody working in his style.

Pausanias (8. 9. 1) also recorded statues of *Apollo*, *Leto*, and *Artemis* in the temple of Leto at Mantinea. Although these statues have not survived, the base showing the *Muses* and *Marsyas*, mentioned by Pausanias, is preserved. These statues were dated to "the third generation after Alcamenes" who was active, according to Pliny (*Naturalis Historia*, 34. 49), in the 83rd Olympiad (448–445 BC).

Another of Praxiteles' works known from later Roman copies as well as representations on Roman coins is the *Apollo Sauroctonus* ("Lizard Killer"). This statue was described by Pliny as showing a young Apollo waiting to kill a lizard with an arrow. Altogether almost 70 works have been associated with Praxiteles, though some may be the works of members of his school or workshop.

Praxiteles' sons Cephisodotus (probably named after his grandfather) and Timarchus were also sculptors. Pliny (*Naturalis Historia*, 34. 51) places their activity in the 121st Olympiad (296–293 BC), although an inscription from a statue base shows Cephisodotus II was active in the year 344/43 BC (because it names the priest of Asclepius for that year). Further generations of sculptors can be traced into the Roman period.

DAVID W.J. GILL

See also Sculpture

Summary

Born probably *c*.400 BC Praxiteles was the son of Cephisodotus of Athens, himself a sculptor, and was active *c*.375–330 BC. He worked in bronze and marble and specialized in portraits, notably of gods. No surviving statues can be attributed with certainty to him, though several are ascribed to his school. His sons Cephisodotus and Timarchus were also sculptors. He died *c*.326 BC.

Further Reading

Ajootian, A., "Praxiteles" in *Personal Styles in Greek Sculpture*, edited by Olga Palagia and J.J. Pollitt, Cambridge and New York: Cambridge University Press, 1996, pp. 91–129

Boardman, John, *Greek Sculpture: The Late Classical Period and Sculpture in Colonies and Overseas*, London and New York: Thames and Hudson, 1995

Loewy, Emanuel, *Inschriften Griechischer Bildhauer: Greek Inscriptions Recording Names and Works of Ancient Sculptors*, reprinted Chicago: Ares, 1976 (originally published 1885)

Love, I.C., "A Preliminary Report of the Excavations at Knidos, 1970, 1971", *American Journal of Archaeology*, 76 (1972): pp. 61–76, 393–405

Mango, C., M. Vickers, and E.D. Francis, "The Palace of Lausus at Constantinople and Its Collection of Ancient Statues", *Journal of the History of Collections*, 4/1 (1992): pp. 89–98

Pollitt, J.J., *The Art of Ancient Greece: Sources and Documents*, Cambridge and New York: Cambridge University Press, 1990

Ridgway, Brunilde Sismondo, *Hellenistic Sculpture*, vol. 1: *The Styles of c. 331–200 BC*, Bristol: Bristol Classical Press, and Madison: University of Wisconsin Press, 1990

Stewart, Andrew, *Attika: Studies in Athenian Sculpture of the Hellenistic Age*, London: Society for the Promotion of Hellenic Studies, 1979

Stewart, Andrew, *Greek Sculpture: An Exploration*, New Haven: Yale University Press, 1990

Prehistory

Prehistory is the term used to describe societies which did not have written records. In Greek archaeology the term is sometimes used to include the Bronze Age, but more frequently (as here) it refers to the three periods of the Stone Age: Palaeolithic, Mesolithic, and Neolithic.

Because of its geographical position between Africa, Asia, and Europe, Greece is an area of great significance for the study of the movement of the earliest human groups between these areas, yet the discovery of the Greek Palaeolithic is very recent, dating from the late 1950s and early 1960s, when the first finds of stone tools were made in Thessaly and Epirus. The earliest and most important discovery to date is the human skull found in 1960 in the cave of Petralona, 75 km northeast of Thessalonica. The skull, which was initially thought to be that of a Neanderthal man (who lived in the middle Palaeolithic period) is now believed to belong to an archaic *Homo sapiens* (a more advanced, though earlier human being than Neanderthal) and to be at least 200,000 years old, much older than any of the stone tools found on Palaeolithic sites in Greece.

The earliest stone tools recovered from excavations and surveys are 50,000–30,000 years old and belong to the Levallois-Mousterian industry characteristic of the middle Palaeolithic. This industry, which is characterized by bifacial leaf points, is generally associated with Neanderthal man, who probably penetrated into northern Greece from central and southeastern Europe after the beginning of the last glaciation (a Neanderthal skull has been reported from the Mani peninsula in the Peloponnese). During the glacial periods northern Greece was positioned between the extremes of cold in the north and aridity in the south, and because it may have supported larger pockets of tree cover than areas further south, it was a favourable habitat for animals, and hence for hunter-gatherers. The groups which populated northern Greece are believed to have been small (about 25 people on average), and an extensive area such as Epirus may have had a total population of no more than 50 people at any one time.

In Epirus investigations in rock shelters (Asprochaliko, Kastritsa, Klithi) and open sites (Kokkinopilos and Grava on Corfu, which would have been attached to the mainland at the time) have yielded substantial quantities of middle and late Palaeolithic flint tools, animal bones (particularly of red deer and caprines), fish bones, sea molluscs, and plant foods. Research carried out by British archaeologists has highlighted the importance of the environmental setting of sites, such as their altitude and orientation. The use of the different sites by the highly mobile hunter-gatherer groups would have been conditioned by the time of the year, which affected the seasonal movement of animals, and by the specialized function of any one site. Subsistence strategies would have changed over time, following climatic and environmental changes. Conditions were at their most unfavourable during the glacial maximum (*c*.18,000 BC), but gradually gave way to a warmer, wetter climate, leading to the spread of deciduous forests and the downcutting of rivers around 10,000 BC.

In Thessaly middle and late Palaeolithic tools and fossilized animal bones were found on the banks of the Peneus river, while caves appear to have remained uninhabited. In the

Peloponnese the most important upper Palaeolithic site is the large cave of Franchthi, where occupation started about 20,000 BC and continued into the Mesolithic and Neolithic periods.

The Mesolithic (8th millennium BC) is a period of change, which is particularly noticeable in the greater dependence on seafood, but in Greece sites dating from this period are very rare, probably because many were coastal sites and may have been swamped by the rising sea levels in later periods. At Franchthi the range of plant foods (nuts, legumes, and, for the first time, cereals) suggests a year-round occupation of the cave. The sea was the most critical resource for the provision of food, and for communications, as shown by the presence in the cave of obsidian from Melos. The earliest burials in Greece are also found in the cave in this period.

The momentous change to a subsistence economy based on agriculture and animal herding and the birth of the farming village in Greece date from the 7th millennium BC, in Thessaly, the Argolid (Franchthi cave), and Crete (Knossos). Except for Franchthi, the earliest Neolithic sites had not previously been occupied (Crete had not been occupied at all), and because the animal and plant species used by the earliest farmers were not indigenous to these areas, it seems likely that the settlers came from lands where farming was already established, most probably Anatolia, sailing across the sea with the first domesticated animals and seeds on board their boats. Some pioneering explorations must have been carried out prior to full settlement, as the farmers seem to have identified advantageous environments for farming. The major areas of occupation and subsequent expansion were in Thessaly, particularly the Larissa basin, and they attracted settlement because of their good arable soil and possibly the natural irrigation system, through river valleys and flood plains, which prevailed at the time.

The Greek Neolithic (7th–4th millennia BC) is divided into early Neolithic, middle Neolithic, and late Neolithic. Between the early and late Neolithic settlement expanded steadily and increased in density. It was particularly successful in Thessaly; just over 100 sites were established in the Larissa basin in the course of the 1000-year duration of the early neolithic, and the number had increased to 150 by the end of the late Neolithic. Some sites did not survive from one phase to the next, but several new ones were founded in their place. All areas of mainland Greece, including Macedonia and central and southern Greece, were occupied by the end of the early neolithic, and island settlement, previously confined to Crete, Alonisos, Corfu and Antiparos (Saliagos), increased during the late Neolithic to include Aegina, Ceos, Mykonos, and Naxos. Although it has been suggested that successive waves of farmers arrived from the east throughout the Neolithic, it is more likely that the initial influx of people into the area was not followed by any equally significant number of immigrants.

The characteristic site in this period is the farming village, situated on a ridge or knoll and numbering a few hundred inhabitants. The dwellings were initially flimsy, but by the middle Neolithic the prevailing building type was a structure which, although only one storey high, could be fairly large, had a stone foundation, a superstructure of mudbrick or *pisé* (layers of clay) faced with plaster, and a flat or pitched roof of wattle and daub. Buildings with a megaron plan (rectangular with two rooms of uneven size) make their appearence in Thessaly (Otzaki, Sesklo) in the middle Neolithic.

The main means of subsistence was the cultivation of plant foods: cereal (wheat, barley, millet) and pulses (lentils, peas, vetch). Of less importance was the herding of domesticated animals; sheep and goats predominate on excavated sites, with pigs and cattle in smaller numbers. Fish or game could play a supplementary role in the diet depending on the location of the settlement. Neolithic society is largely believed to have been egalitarian, with the whole community involved in food production. A move towards social differentiation may have taken place in the late Neolithic with the establishment of settlements on marginal lands.

Among the crafts, pottery making was the single most important innovation of the period. For a time the farmers of the earliest villages did not produce ceramic vessels (the phase is known as the preceramic Neolithic), but made extensive use of perishable materials such as wickerwork, matting, wood, and hide. Once introduced, pottery reached very high artistic and technical standards, though the potter's wheel was still unknown, and it was made in a considerable variety of styles; the surfaces were painted in one or more colours (polychrome), were impressed or incised, and the patterns were mostly geometrical (chevrons, triangles, spirals, etc.). There are both chronological and regional differences between the styles. Much of the fine decorated pottery must have been non-utilitarian. Tools were made of bone and stone (both polished and chipped), as were beads, pendants, and other ornaments.

Clay figurines are among the most attractive artifacts of Neolithic Greece. The largest group consists of steatopygic female figurines of different types, but there are also seated male figurines, and models of houses and furniture. Once thought to be fertility goddesses, the steatopygic figurines are today believed to have had a variety of functions, as their use for one specific cult cannot be inferred from their contexts in graves and houses. Ritual was an important element in the life of Neolithic communities. Although no structures have been unequivocally connected with ritual ceremonies, these may have taken place in open spaces, as in other cultures. The nature of Neolithic religion is unknown. Suggestions have been made that it was an "animistic religion" and, if so, the figurines may represent the spirits of ancestors.

The Neolithic was a period of increased communications, by sea as well as land. Similarities between pottery styles and the movement of materials from one area to the other reveal contacts between settlements and regions. The most frequently imported material, and one which travelled in great quantities over great distances, was obsidian from Melos, out of which the sharpest cutting tools were made.

The greatest strides in the study of Greek prehistory have taken place in the last decades. New sites are being discovered with every new survey, and ongoing research is taking place into artefacts, as well as other areas relevant to the understanding of prehistoric man: strategies of exploitation of the environment, transmission of agricultural economy, seafaring, and human colonization of the islands. Progress has been made through the use of scientific techniques for dating deposits and sites, and for reconstructing the palaeoenvironment, but there is much scope for work leading to a better knowledge of important environmental aspects, such as the configuration of the Greek shoreline, particularly during the Palaeolithic, and changes in climatic conditions and vegetation cover. More accurate dating of neolithic sites would lead to a better understanding of the divisions between periods, and of the correlations between the different local cultures and assemblages during the period.

In modern Greece the Neolithic period arouses a fair amount of interest, among both archaeologists and the general public. It is regarded as the period when many of the "good things" in our modern civilization first appeared, including art, religious thought, and above all farming and the village way of life, both of which have remained fundamentals of Greek life to this very day. Moreover, figurative art appears for the first time in this period, as do other more specifically "Greek" forms, like the megaron building plan. By contrast, the study of the Palaeolithic (and the Mesolithic) has yet to be assigned the position and given the support it enjoys in other countries. That it has not achieved such status may be due not only to the fact that it is still in its infancy or to the more impressive character of the products of later Greek cultures, but also to the fact that the achievements of man in this period are seen as having more significance at a global rather than at a national, Greek level. One of the leading archaeologists in the field, Geoff Bailey, made a plea in 1992 for increased support for training and research in Palaeolithic archaeology within Greece, stressing that this is the period when our species "acquired those most fundamental characteristics by which we define our humanity". It therefore deserves, and let us hope will receive, greater recognition in the future.

CHRISTINA SOUYOUDZOGLOU-HAYWOOD

See also Archaeology

Further Reading

Bailey, G., "The Palaeolithic of Klithi in its Wider Context", *Annual of the British School at Athens*, 87 (1992): pp. 1–28

Cherry, J. F., "The First Colonization of the Mediterrannean Islands: A Review of Recent Research", *Journal of Mediterranean Archaeology*, 3 (1990): pp. 145–221

Jabobsen, T. W., "Franchthi Cave and the Beginning of Settled Village Life in Greece", *Hesperia*, 50/4 (1981): pp. 303–19

Papathanassopoulos, George A. (editor), *Neolithic Culture in Greece*, Athens: Goulandris Foundation, 1996

Weinberg, S. S., "The Stone Age in the Aegean" in *Prolegomena and Prehistory*, edited by I.E.S. Edwards, C.J. Gadd, and N.G.L. Hammond, Cambridge: Cambridge University Press, 1970 (*The Cambridge Ancient History*, vol. 1, part 1, 3rd edition)

Prespa, Lake

Lake Prespa is one of the most remarkable natural phenomena in the Balkans. The most northerly border of Greece passes through the lake, as do those of the Former Yugoslav Republic of Macedonia and of Albania. With Lake Ohrid, 30 km to the north, to which it is linked by underground water channels, it forms the Prespa World Heritage Park, as designated by UNESCO. There are actually two lakes in the region, Great Prespa and Small Prespa, divided by a narrow causeway. Great Prespa is an important wildlife refuge, although bird life has been adversely affected by falling water levels in the lake in recent years.

In ancient times there were Greek fishing settlements around the lake, but populations were small until the Roman period, when larger villages sprang up in connection with trade along the Via Egnatia that ran to the north of Lake Prespa. Prespa was an early centre for the growth of Christianity, and in the medieval period played a seminal role in the spread of Christianity to the Slav-speaking world. There are some important rock icons painted in caves above the lake that were once occupied by hermits, and many small churches and shrines in the vicinity. This Christian activity continued while Ohrid was an important town and religous centre under the Bulgarian empire. In Ottoman times the vicinity of the lake fell into economic decline and the extensive forests became notorious as centres of banditry and outlaws. The Prespa villages suffered badly in the Ilinden uprising in 1903, and in the First Balkan War in 1912. The lake remained within European Turkey until 1913.

Today the area of the lake has a complex ethnic mosaic, with most inhabitants in all three countries being of basically Slav descent. The Macedonian language is widely understood and spoken, but there are also substantial numbers of Vlachs, along with a few Albanian-speakers who have crossed the border in recent years. The main Greek element consists of people who were moved to this area after the influx into Greece of Asia Minor refugees after 1922, and others of a "national consciousness" who were moved here after the end of the Civil War in 1949. From 1946 to 1949 the headquarters of the Democratic Army of Markos Vafiades was situated near the lake, and it was bombed by the RAF and the United States Air Force in 1948–49.

The main village on the Greek side of the lake is Psarades, a fishing settlement of about 400 people. There is a very fine church, financed by a Russian philanthropist in 1906. Before the Civil War, Psarades was known as Nivica. Many inhabitants fled to Yugoslavia or Russia after 1949, and only returned in 1982 after the PASOK government amnesty for Civil War participants. In recent years some small-scale ecotourism has developed in the region. The main Vlach villages near the lake are Pili and Vronderon.

JAMES PETTIFER

Summary

Lake Prespa lies on the border between Greece, Albania, and the Former Yugoslav Republic of Macedonia. It is connected to Lake Ohrid by underwater channels, and together they form the Prespa World Heritage Park. The area saw heavy fighting in the Greek Civil War. Most inhabitants today are of Slav descent, though there are Vlachs and Albanian-speakers too.

Further Reading

Pettifer, James, *Albania*, 2nd edition, A. & C. Black, London 1996 (*Blue Guide* series)

Prevelakis, Pantelis 1909–1986

Novelist and poet

Pantelis Prevelakis, one of the most prominent Greek authors of the 20th century and a member of the so-called 1930s generation, was distinguished in many different genres of writing. He was born in the city of Rethymnon in Crete in 1909. Although he went to Athens to study law, he in fact studied art and literature in the universities of Athens and Paris. From 1935 he was a professor of art history at the School of Fine Arts in Athens. Very well educated, he was a prolific writer. His works include poetry, novels, plays, and critical essays.

He first appeared as a writer in 1928 with a collection of poems entitled *Soldiers* and in 1930 with a historical monograph, *Domenico Theotokopoulos*, in which his writing skills and his knowledge of art history are well combined. In 1939 he produced his first historical novel, *The Death of the Medici*. He was a loyal student of his teacher Nikos Kazantzakis, whose influence on Prevelakis is so strong that it puts him in the shade. The comparison with Kazantzakis is almost self-evident and has done undue damage to the reputation of Prevelakis. His critical volume *Nikos Kazantzakis and his Odyssey* is an excellent piece of literary criticism. With *The Naked Poetry* (1941) and *The Hours on a Greek Island* (1945) he reached his poetic maturity, enhanced by an ideological development associated with World War II.

Prevelakis began exploring his Cretan roots in prose in the novels *The Chronicle of a Town* (1938) and *Desolate Crete: The Chronicle of the Rising of '66* (1945) which, as the subtitle suggests, is about the 1866 rising in Crete, and the trilogy entitled *The Cretan: The Tree* (1948), *First Liberation* (1949), *The City* (1950). His work embodies the uncompromising struggle for liberty. In *The Cretan* he focused on the personality of Eleftherios Venizelos, the new political hero of the time who was charged by his Cretan soul to lead the Greek people. This work revealed the strength of Prevelakis's writing skills and his deep interest in contemporary reality. Another trilogy followed: *The Sun of Death* (1959), *The Head of Medusa* (1963), and *The Bread of Angels* (1966). His memories of his Cretan past were very important and there is often a sensitive autobiographical tone in his writing. The historical element was also an important aspect. His town of origin, Rethymnon, held a key position in his work: it represented all the ideological and emotional tensions that Prevelakis went through while trying to define himself. He was haunted by a crystallized idea of a certain lifestyle that he had known in Crete and wanted to know again whether or not he was still defined by the same place and lifestyle after all his travels and experiences. He sought to bridge the gap between his youth and maturity, with a need to refer to his own "Ithaca". He also published books on art history early in his career as an academic: *Italian Renaissance and Art* (1935), *Art in Modern Greece* (1938), *El Greco in Rome* (1941).

As many of Prevelakis's titles suggest, Crete and his notion of heroism were cardinal motifs in his work. It is often said that history outweighs fiction in his writings. He chose historical subjects for his plays as well, such as Florence under the Medici or the blowing up of the monastery of Arkadi. Once again the tragic aspect of life is the one that appears on his stage. All of his theatrical works – *The Sacred Massacre* (1952), *Lazaros* (1954), *The Hands of a Living God* (1955) – describe a moment of inner crisis and present a soul in constant dialogue with death. His faith in his heritage and the concept of tradition in a time of transition marks not only his humanism but also the path he chose as a writer. He did not believe in a modernity that denied its roots; on the contrary the tradition that he drew on proves to be in a constant state of dynamic renewal. His work *The Hands of a Living God* is overtly indebted to Dostoevsky, reflecting the dramatic process of a conscience. In his last work, *The New Erotokritos* (1971), using the traditional 15-syllable verse, he discovers a new lyric identity. With this work Greek poetry regained its link with tradition, creating at the same time a marriage between the traditional and the innovative. This is not the only marriage, however, since he also united the personal with the national, the fictional with the historical, the real with the symbolic. The complexity of this work reflects the synthetic mind of its writer. It is written in rhyming couplets, like its predecessor by Vintsentzos Kornaros, yet every couplet has a lyric autonomy, being in this way close to the folk-song tradition. The language in his novels and poetry owes much to the Cretan dialect of his time, although it is more polished. He published more than 30 books, poems, novels, essays, biographies, plays, and translations of other works, and was elected a member of the Academy of Athens.

ANDROMACHE KARANIKA-DIMAROGONA

Biography

Born in Rethymnon in Crete in 1909, Prevelakis was destined for a legal career. But instead he studied art and literature in the universities of Athens and Paris. He became a professor of art history at the School of Fine Arts in Athens and also studied under Kazantzakis, with whom he is often compared as a novelist. He also wrote poetry, drama, and criticism. He was a member of the Academy of Athens. He died in 1986.

Further Reading

Decavalles, Andonis, *Pandelis Prevelakis and the Value of a Heritage: A Talk*, edited by Theophanis G. Stavrou, St Paul, Minnesota: North Central, 1981

Decavalles, Andonis, *Eisagogi sto logotechniko ergo tou Panteli Prevelaki* [Introduction to the Literary Output of Pantelis Prevelakis], Athens, 1985

Kasdagles, Emmanouel C., *Symvoli sti vivliographia tou Pandeli Prevelaki* [A Contribution to the Bibliography of Pantelis Prevelakis], Athens, 1967

Mastrodemetres, P.D., *O Neos Erotokritos tou Panteli Prevelaki* [The New Erotokritos of Pantelis Prevelakis], Athens, 1987

Tsatsos, Konstantinos, *I neoelliniki kritiki gia ton Pandeli Prevelaki* [Modern Greek Criticism of Pantelis Prevelakis], Athens, 1979

Vitti, Mario, *Ideologik Leitourgia tis hellinikis ithographias* [The Ideological Function of Greek Ethnography], Athens, 1980

Priene

City in Ionia

Priene was a small Greek city (population *c.*4000) on a peninsula in Asia Minor *c.*30 km south of Ephesus that flourished

Priene: temple of Athena, dedicated in 334 BC

from the mid-4th century BC throughout the Hellenistic and early Roman periods. It is notable for being one of the most intelligible examples of ancient town planning, and its remains include most forms of public and domestic Greek architecture. The buildings, which are laid out on a grid plan, sit on the southern slope of Mount Mykale overlooking the Meander valley, c.15 km from the sea. In antiquity Priene was connected by a branch of the Meander river to its seaport at Naulochos on the bay of Latmos. The river silted up over time, however, causing the bay to become landlocked, and the city diminished in importance in later Roman times without access to a harbour.

Priene seems to have been founded originally at a different location, perhaps as early as the 2nd millennium BC, but its early history is known almost entirely from ancient authors, including Strabo, Herodotus, and Pausanias. In the 7th century BC it was one of the 12 major cities of Ionia and a member of the Ionian League. In the 6th and 5th centuries BC Priene was variously under the influence of the Lycians, Carians, Lydians, Phrygians, Athenians, and Persians. The city was refounded, probably by the Persian satraps the Hekatomnids, at its present location c.350 BC, and it is from this date and throughout the Hellenistic period that most of the extant remains come. Priene, along with the other Greek cities of Ionia, was freed from Persian domination in 334 BC by Alexander the Great, who lived there while he laid siege to Miletus on the other side of the bay of Latmos. After Alexander's death Priene came under the control of various Hellenistic kings – Lysimachus, the Ptolemies, the Seleucids, and the Attalids. Upon the death of the last Attalid king in 133 BC, Priene passed into Roman hegemony along with the rest of the kingdom of Pergamum. By the 3rd century AD, with the river silted up, the city dwindled to a town half its original size.

Priene was designed according to the philosophy of orthogonal town planning that was promoted by the renowned 5th-century BC architect Hippodamus of Miletus. Facing south to provide maximum light during winter, it was surrounded by a defensive wall with the main gate on the northeast and subsidiary gates on the southeast and west. High above and behind the city on the summit of Mount Mykale was a walled acropolis that was a permanent station for a military garrison. The urban water supply flowed down from the summit by aqueduct to reservoirs on the northeast of the city, and then was piped to public buildings and fountains. The streets were laid out as a grid, the six major streets on the east–west axis comprising a main thoroughfare 7.36 m wide and five others 4.44 m wide. These were intersected at right angles by narrower streets, 3.5 m wide, most of which incorporated steps because they lay on the north–south slope of the hill. The standard city block (insula) was 120 × 160 Attic feet. In the public areas of the city the buildings often took up an entire block or more, while in the domestic quarters each insula usually accommodated four houses.

Priene displays all the components necessary to the Classical Greek city (polis). At its heart was its major monument, honouring the city's patron, the 4th-century BC temple of Athena. An inscription states that it was dedicated in 334 BC in the name of Alexander the Great, who furnished the funds that were needed to complete basic construction. The temple was built by the renowned Carian architect Pytheos, who was esteemed as well for his work on the Mausoleum at Halicarnassus, one of the seven wonders of the ancient world. As was common practice among famed architects in antiquity, Pytheos wrote about his general architectural theories and he used as illustration the temple of Athena at Priene. His book, unfortunately, survives only in the commentary of Vitruvius. The ceiling of the peristyle was highly unusual in that it contained coffers carved in very high relief with scenes depicting gods fighting Giants and Amazons. The statue of Athena that stood within the cella was a replica of the colossal figure of Athena from the Parthenon in Athens. In front of the temple was the altar of Artemis, an ornate rectangular structure adorned with nearly life-sized figures carved in high relief set between attached columns.

To the east of the sanctuary of Athena was the commercial and social centre of the city, the agora. This large, open rectangle (75.64 × 35.40 m) contained various shops and was the site of many public meetings and festivals. To the north and south of the agora were other public buildings: the bouleuterion, the council house; the prytaneion, a smaller administrative building; stoas; gymnasia; a stadium; various temples and sanctuaries; and the theatre, whose ruins are impressive especially since they preserve the 2nd-century BC stage building more completely than at most other sites of the period. Filling the insulae on the west and east sides of the city were private dwellings. The large number of houses surviving at Priene is particularly propitious, for ancient Greek domestic architecture can be studied to this extent at few other sites. The houses were relatively small, with several rooms surrounding an open court. While most appear to have been of one storey, some preserve stairs that would have led to an upper level.

Although Hippodamus was esteemed by Hellenistic Greeks as the inventor of formal city planning, Priene as a visual expression of his ideas was a relatively late example of orthogonal urban design. In the 2nd millennium BC Egyptian workers' villages at Kahun and Tell el-Amarna consisted of housing built in rectangular blocks along parallel streets. In the 5th century BC Herodotus (1. 180) describes the streets of Babylon as a grid, all being either parallel or perpendicular to the Euphrates river. In the Greek-speaking world, in the 7th century BC, both Smyrna in Asia Minor and Megara Hybleia in Sicily were built with parallel streets on orthogonal plans. Priene's position in the heart of the Hellenistic world provided it with greater influence than its size might otherwise have inspired. The fact that it was the site of an important temple built by a major architect also brought the city an extra measure of attention. Cities that were built or rebuilt under the Hellenistic kings or Roman emperors, e.g. Miletus, most assuredly were influenced by knowledge of orthogonal town planning at Priene.

Priene's influence seems not to have continued beyond the 3rd century AD when the city lost half its population and fell into disrepair. From that time it consisted primarily of poorly built houses and shops – constructed of materials from Hellenistic ruins – that extended over the original city streets destroying the grid plan. Priene was deserted from the 7th to the 10th centuries. Between the 10th and 13th centuries the site was reoccupied and Priene was a bishopric of the Metropolitan of Ephesus. But as with other bishoprics of impoverished Ephesus (e.g. Pergamum, Didyma), it was merely a small village of modest houses and chapels, and the bishop must have been little more than the equivalent of a parish priest. By the end of the 13th century Priene was deserted.

PAMELA A. WEBB

Summary

Priene was a small Greek city on the Meander river in Ionia (western Asia Minor) that flourished from c.350 BC to the later Roman empire. It is most notable as an example of Hippodamian town planning on the grid system, and for its wide variety of remains of public and domestic architecture. In late antiquity the river silted up and Priene lost its harbour and with it its importance.

Further Reading

Akurgal, Ekrem, *Ancient Civilizations and Ruins of Turkey*, 7th edition, Istanbul: NET Turistik Yayinlar, 1990, pp. 185–206

Bayhan, Suzan, *Priene, Miletus, Didyma*, Ankara: Keskin Color Kartpostalcilik, 1989, pp. 15–62

Bean, George E., *Aegean Turkey: An Archaeological Guide*, 2nd edition, New York: Norton, and London: Benn, 1979, pp. 161–178

Carter, Joseph Coleman, *The Sculpture of the Sanctuary of Athena Polias at Priene*, London: Society of Antiquaries, 1983

Foss, Clive, *History and Archaeology of Byzantine Asia Minor*, Aldershot: Variorum, 1990, p. 479

Ridgway, Brunilde Sismondo, *Fourth-Century Styles in Greek Sculpture*, Madison: University of Wisconsin Press, and London: Duckworth, 1997, pp. 135–41

Vitruvius, *The Ten Books on Architecture*, translated by Morris Hicky Morgan, Cambridge, Massachusetts: Harvard University Press, 1914; reprinted New York: Dover, 1960 (see especially 1. 1. 12, 4. 3. 1, 7. praef. 12)

Ward-Perkins, J.B., *Cities of Ancient Greece and Italy: Planning in Classical Antiquity*, New York: Braziller, 1974, pp. 8–14, 24

Webb, Pamela A., *Hellenistic Architectural Sculpture: Figural Motifs in Western Anatolia and the Aegean Islands*, Madison: University of Wisconsin Press, 1996

Wycherley, R.E., *How the Greeks Built Cities*, 2nd edition, London: Macmillan, and New York: Norton, 1962

Priesthood

In Mycenaean Greece the king discharged religious functions that, for want of a better term, may be identified with those of a high priest. In Athens these functions came in time to be invested in an elected magistrate known as the *archon basileus* or king archon. However, in no period in antiquity did there exist any institution exactly comparable to our notion of priesthood. The word *hiereus*, which comes closest to "priest", denoted an official attached to a particular sanctuary who supervised the *hiera* (sacred objects) stored within that sanctuary and who conducted the sacred rites connected with the cult. The most important of these were the performing of sacrifice, the purification of the sanctuary, the punishment of those who violated sanctuary regulations, and maintaining the buildings in good repair.

Since Greek religion did not concern itself much with morality, priests never functioned as spiritual advisers; their duties were primarily those of a liturgical and administrative nature. They were debarred from playing any part in the ceremonies connected with birth, marriage, and death because of the pollution that was believed to be associated with these events. Priests also lacked the technical competence and skill to pronounce upon matters arising from the practice of religious ritual; instead, when problems arose, particularly those having to do with pollution, religious experts known as *exegetai* were consulted.

Eligibility for priestly office was based on external qualifications. The most important qualification was the absence of any blemish or deformity, since it was believed that a blemish constituted evidence of divine disfavour. So far as we know, priests did not have to undergo any formal training, though they obviously had to be adept in the performing of their religious ritual. Since most temples were open to the public only a few days of the year, the holding of a priesthood was generally a part-time occupation. Priests were not paid for their services, though they were entitled to portions of meat from all the sacrifices performed in the sanctuary over which they had charge. Some had special seats of honour in the theatre of Dionysus. The more important priests were distinguished by their dress; the Hierophant of the Eleusinian Mysteries, for instance, wore a mantle, probably of purple, a headband surmounted by a wreath of myrtle, and carried a staff.

As a general rule, gods were served by priests, goddesses by priestesses. Some priesthoods were hereditary, others were for a fixed term. In democratic Athens the newer priesthoods were annual appointments for which all members of the citizen body were eligible. The more venerable ones, such as that of Athena Polias or Poseidon Erechtheus, were reserved for members of a particular *genos* or noble kin-group. With few exceptions the powers of a priest were strictly curtailed and there is no evidence for any involvement *qua* priest in politics. Even in matters that had to do with religion, it was the citizen body as a whole, rather than the priesthood, that took all major decisions, without consulting the priesthood, at least in any formal way. Priests were not in a position to challenge the legal or political authority of the state because they never acknowledged any corporate identity. Thus when Socrates was accused of violating religious law in 399 BC, a group of individual citizens conducted the prosecution. Even so, it is probable that the major priesthoods carried considerable prestige. The priestess of Hera in Argos was so important that the Greeks based their system of chronology on the number of years that she had been in office (Thucydides, 2. 1).

The concept of the Christian priest emerges towards the end of the 2nd century AD, largely due to the teachings of Cyprian. Priests now became celebrants of the Eucharist, a role previously confined to bishops. During the period of Turkish occupation, priests often served as intermediaries between the Turkish authorities and the Greek people. It was a priest, Germanos of Patras, who began the revolt against the Turks in the Morea in 1821, thereby instigating the War of Independence. Priests receive little money for their services and in order to supplement their salary they may charge for the baptisms, liturgies, exorcisms, and other services that they perform. They are permitted to marry before (but not after) ordination. The Greek Orthodox priesthood falls under the jurisdiction of the four patriarchs, those of Constantinople (properly known as the ecumenical patriarch), Alexandria, Antioch, and Jerusalem.

ROBERT GARLAND

See also Cult, Women's Cults

Further Reading

Beard, Mary and John North, *Pagan Priests: Religion and Power in the Ancient World*, London: Duckworth, and Ithaca, New York: Cornell University Press, 1990
Ware, Timothy, *The Orthodox Church*, 2nd edition, London and New York: Penguin, 1993

Printing

The beginnings of Greek printing are inextricably linked with the humanist current predominant in the period of the Italian Renaissance, and in particular with the desire of humanists, most of them Italian, to preserve works of ancient Greek literature, either in the original or in Latin translation. Byzantine scholars had begun to teach Greek in the West as early as the late 14th century, and Italian printers were the first to turn to the printing of Greek.

Greek incunabula (works printed before 1500) form a corpus of 80 books, published in three main cities: Milan, Florence, and Venice. The rest come from cultural centres of lesser importance, such as Parma, Vicenza, Brescia, and Reggio nell'Emilia. These works were for the most part grammars and dictionaries, though some of the monuments of Classical literature were also published, among them the five-volume series of the entire corpus of Aristotle's writings (Venice: Aldus Manutius, 1495–98), the complete works of Homer (Florence, 1488–89), the comedies of Aristophanes (Venice, 1498), and others.

The first endeavour to print a Greek book is dated around 1471, in Venice, and was due to the German printer Adam de Ambergau. The work in question was the *Erotemata* of Manuel Chrysoloras, in a Latin version by Guarino Veronese, which included extensive extracts in Greek. The first continuous Greek text was again Chrysoloras's *Erotemata*, which was printed with no indication of the date, place of publication, or printer, though probably in Bologna or Florence around 1475. The first dated Greek book was printed by Dimitrios Damilas of Crete in 1476, at the press of Dionigi Paravicino in Milan. It contains the *Epitome of the Eight Parts of Speech* by Constantine Laskaris, another grammar for the teaching of the Greek language to westerners.

Two Greek presses were established, both of them in Venice, before 1500, by Cretan men of letters and printers. The first operated in the house of two priests, Laonikos and Alexandros, for about a year, in 1486, and produced the

Psalter and the *Battle of Frogs and Mice*. The second, which was one of the most famous of the early presses, functioned from the beginning of 1499 to the end of 1500 and published the following works: the *Etymologicum Magnum* and the *Commentary on the Ten Categories of Aristotle* of Simplicius in 1499, and the *Commentary on the Five Voices of Porphyry* by Ammonius and the *Therapeutics* of Galen in 1500. To print these books, one of the most elegant character sets ever designed was cut by Zacharias Kalliergis; the texts were edited in part by Nikolaos Vlastos, who also financed the publications.

The Italian presses that published Greek books included those of Giovanni da Reno, Lorenzo de Alopa, Pellegrino de Pasquali, Uldericus Scinzenzeler, and others; the most famous of all, however, was that of Aldus Manutius in Venice. From 1494 Aldus collaborated with Greek scholars to print a large number of Greek books, totalling 18 incunabula, the first of which was the *Hero and Leander* of Musacus.

From the early decades of the 16th century, after the deaths of Aldus (1517) and Kalliergis (after 1523), the production of Greek books ceased to depend on Greek teachers and their pupils. The Italian presses, and also those in the north (Basle, Paris, Lyons, Strasbourg, and Frankfurt), were staffed by a considerable number of fine Hellenists and published important works of Greek literature, as well as first editions of the Church Fathers, in this way lending support to local humanist studies. The Greeks of the diaspora and Venice, for their part, realized that it was essential to publish "tools" for the teaching of Greek to the scattered Greek population, as well as liturgical books for the needs of the hundreds of Orthodox monasteries and churches to be found in the territories of the Ottoman empire. In view of the prohibition on the practising of the printer's art, though not the distribution of books, in the territory of the Sublime Porte, the Greeks of the diaspora successfully established publishing houses in Venice that functioned without interruption down to the early decades of the 19th century.

The presses founded in Venice were the fruit of the cooperation of Greek merchants, men of letters, and printers, and also Italians who owned printing workshops and the appropriate materials to print Greek texts, and who possessed the necessary permits. The most important establishments to emerge were those of Andreas Kounadis, Damiani di Santa Maria, Andrea Pinelli, Nicolini da Sabio, Nikolaos Glykys, Nikolaos Saros, Antonio Bortoli, Dimitrios Theodosiou, and many others. Commercially, many printers collaborated with these publishing–printing centres and businesses frequently changed hands or were financed by different supporters.

For their subject matter these presses relied mainly on the contents of liturgical books, such as gospel books, Menaia, anthologies, lives of saints, intercessions, books of hours, and prayer books. Nevertheless, a significant role was also played by many publications of a popular nature, which began to appear in the second decade of the 16th century with texts written by members of learned circles in Crete – books such as the *Apokopos* by Bergadis, the *Mourning for Death*, the *Story of Sossana*, and others. Another major source of material for the publishing programmes of these houses consisted of new editions of grammar books, mainly the *Grammar* of Manuel Chrysoloras, and those of Constantine Laskaris and of Theodore Gaza. These were aimed at the learned Greek public and the teaching staff of the private and monastery schools in the East.

In addition to the major centres of Greek printing such as Venice, efforts began in the early decades of the 17th century to establish presses in other centres of Hellenism. The first of these attempts was by the ecumenical patriarch of Constantinople, Cyril I Lukaris who, beginning in Lvov, Poland, and thereafter in collaboration with Nikodemos Metaxas in Constantinople, endeavoured to set up a press in the Phanar, in 1627. Lukaris's purpose was to circulate Greek books whose content would counter the proselytizing policy of the Catholic Church and Jesuit propaganda directed at Orthodox Christians.

Between this time and the end of the 18th century, Greek presses were founded in Mount Athos, Moschopolis, Bucharest, Jassy, Vienna, Trieste, Moscow, and St Petersburg, as well as Constantinople. The ulterior motive of these centres was to produce books not only to educate Greeks everywhere and to maintain Orthodox beliefs, but, from the beginning of the 18th century, also to disseminate the ideas of the European Enlightenment.

The most important centre of the Neohellenic Enlightenment was Vienna. Here the output of the Greek and Viennese presses was completely different from the traditional publishing map of Greek books: translations of European literature, scholarly treatises, new grammars and dictionaries, texts giving expression to modern Greek literature and poetry, as well as newspapers, literary journals, and single-sheet pamphlets of a nationalist revolutionary content. Printers of the calibre of Georgios Ventotis and the Markidis Pouliou brothers were active in Vienna, which not only developed into the most important publishing centre of Hellenism from the late 18th century on, but was also the centre from which the distribution of Greek books to the length and breadth of the countries around the Mediterranean was efficiently organized through a system of prior enrolment and permanent subscription.

Printing presses began to be established systematically in Greece from the early decades of the 19th century, as a result of the various historical circumstances that stamped this period. Presses were set up successively on Corfu (1798), Zakynthos (1819), Chios (1819), at Kydonies (1819), Kalamata (1821), Corinth (1821), on Hydra (1823), and at Missolonghi (1823). The pamphlets published by these presses were related to administrative decisions and decrees, and their revolutionary or informative content was associated with the Greek national uprising in 1821.

Printed works began to appear in Athens in 1824, at the instigation of the British colonel Leicester Stanhope, who believed that a press ought to be established in the seat of the new government to meet its needs for newspapers and other printed matter. Since that time, especially after Athens was proclaimed capital of the newly founded Greek state, important publishers and printers have honoured the age-old tradition of Greek books, and there are still some functioning presses that perpetuate the art of Gutenberg, such as those of C. Manousaridis, A. Kaliakatsos, and others. Athens and Thessalonica virtually monopolize the production of Greek books, which in recent decades has been aimed at the publication not only of original works, but also of a good many translations of international literature.

KONSTANTINOS STAIKOS

See also Books and Readers

Further Reading

Barker, Nicolas, *Aldus Manutius and the Development of Greek Script and Type in the Fifteenth Century*, Sandy Hook, Connecticut: Chiswick Book Shop, 1985; 2nd edition, New York: Fordham University Press, 1992

Koumarianou, Aikaterine, Loukia Droulia, and Evro Layton, *To Helleniko Vivlio, 1476–1830* [Greek Books, 1476–1830], Athens, 1986

Proctor, Robert, *The Printing of Greek in the Fifteenth Century*, Oxford: Bibliographical Society, 1900

Staikos, Konstantinos S., *Charta of Greek Printing: The Contribution of Greek Editors, Printers and Publishers to the Renaissance in Italy and the West*, vol. 1: *Fifteenth Century*, Cologne: Dinter, 1998

Proclus AD 410/11–485

Philosopher

Proclus was head of the philosophy school at Athens from AD 435/36 until 485. By this time Neoplatonism had covered most of ancient Greek thought, including Aristotelianism, so there was no other philosophical school. Proclus taught and wrote on logic, theories of being, properties and causation (metaphysics); on knowledge, perception and truth (epistemology), theology and revelation, mathematics, physics, astronomy; and on the literature of Homer and Hesiod.

He was born in Constantinople but his family soon left for their family home, Xanthus in Lycia, probably around AD 415, to avoid the persecution of "Hellenes" (pagans) by the empress Pulcheria. He was sent to Alexandria to study law and to follow in his father's career, but underwent a conversion to Athenian philosophy while on a temporary visit to Byzantium at the time of the empress Eudocia's patronage of Hellenic learning and the institution of a university there (AD 425). At the age of 19 he went to Athens, where he studied Aristotle and Plato. He was elected head of the richly endowed Athens Academy at the age of 25; there he remained until his death aged 75, in the reign of the emperor Zeno.

Proclus asserted that the analysis of being leads to more simple and universal principles: from *physis* (nature) and *psyche* (soul) to *nous*, Life, and Essence. The simple are also more deep and fundamental: that renders them less explicit. Ultimately there is an unconditioned principle which can only be referred to as "the One" (*to hen*), but cannot be captured by any word or definition. Every entity, a stone, a human, or the world as a whole, is composed of the appropriate levels, plus its own "one" (*henas*). Each analytical level is known with befitting means: physical phenomena with the senses; mental images with imagination, conceptions, scientific laws, and mathematical objects with the reasoning mind; permanent, atemporal realities with direct intellection; the transcendent with faith (*pistis*), an intimate but incommunicable union between knower and object.

Things are defined and known by their properties. The latter originate in exempt, "imparticipable" realities (*hypostaseis*), but become known when they are correlated with, "partaken" by mind or experience. A "manifest" property is thus an "image" (*eikon*), representation, or a phenomenon. Proclus conceived of properties dynamically. A property in its "imparticipable" state "remains" unqualified. It spontaneously "proceeds", thereby informing others. It recovers its identity by "returning". Creation is a "procession"; contemplation and salvation are "returns".

Philosophy and theology have the same objects, just as metaphysics is the study of God (since Plato and Aristotle). For Proclus, the "ones" of self-sufficient realities are the deities of philosophical or popular religion. The scale of unity correlating with being is also the scale of divinity. The principal One is the all-transcendent God, but, for example, the "one" of principal Essence is God the Father, the "one" of principal *nous* (Intellect) is God the Creator, and the "ones" of subsidiary entities are the angels or incarnate saviours. The "procession" from reality to phenomena is thus accompanied by the descent of divine light to matter. This makes possible the salvation of mortal beings, which is the recovery of their unity. However, Proclus stressed that divinity is not fully fathomed by thinking, because it is indefinable. Theology needs something more, an active sympathy, *theourgia* ("divine work").

All beings, down to the lowest matter, partake of the Good God, but each in their own qualified manner. Evil results from ignorance, weakness, or some deficiency. According to Proclus, evil itself is nothing, a privation subsisting parasitically (*parhypostasis*: a "parallel existence").

Platonists reasoned that personal life, *psyche*, is a substance capable of life independent of the body. *Psyche* acts purposely, which implies rationality and volition. So psychology extends to metaphysics, life, mind, and ethics. For Proclus, *psyche* is in essence incorporeal and atemporal but its activities occur in some space or time. *Psyche* causes the body to move this way or that. Internally, it makes manifest dimensional images: the process of imagination. Images formed by the reasoning mind can be compared to those impressed by the senses, and correct them. However, for *psyche* to have full awareness of its unlimited source of inspiration, the *nous*, it must "return" by "ascending" to its proper level. From this level it "descends" when it becomes embodied. It falls because of its "daring" (*tolma*) generated by the individuality of its consciousness.

Science bridges the senses with reality, and provides understanding. Studying mathematics integrates reasoning with imagination, and trains the mind to contemplate. Mathematics mirrors the grand scale of being and knowledge. It extends from concrete things (mechanics and other applied mathematics) to abstractions, and then from models of reality to the hidden reality itself. Proclus was an observational and theoretical astronomer, and a physicist. He had the courage to reject Ptolemy's cosmology and Aristotle's physics. By applying his graded metaphysics, he proposed that the heavens and the earth are made of the same elements, except that they are in different modalities. Thus he reunified the scope of physical science. Further, he concluded that the place occupied by a mass-body, or by the visible universe as a whole, is a three-dimensional volume-interval. He advanced the novel theory that this "space" is a massless body, consisting of pure, invisible light.

Proclus taught many prominent figures, including Byzantine statesmen. His student Ammonius became head of the Alexandrian school, and using Proclus' lectures taught Simplicius and the Christian Philoponus. Simplicius went to Athens with another Alexandrian, Damascius, subsequently the last head of the Athenian school. After Justinian closed it (AD 529) Simplicius wrote his influential commentaries on Aristotle. Philoponus proved the greatest philosophical critic of Proclus. Nevertheless, Proclus' teachings were maintained by the Alexandrian philosophers, including Stephanus, the appointee to the imperial university of Constantinople.

Proclus' hierarchy of being and divinity was adapted by pseudo-Dionysius the Areopagite, and became central to Orthodox theology with Maximos the Confessor (7th century) and John of Damascus (8th century). Proclus' writings themselves continued to be studied by Byzantines through Psellos (11th century) to Plethon (15th century), or were deemed dangerous enough for renewed Christian refutation (Nicholas Methone, 12th century).

In Islam, Proclus influenced the Ikhwan al-Safa (10th century), a cornerstone of Shiite theology. In philosophy, the Arabs drafted compilations of Proclus' works under Aristotle's name. They were transmitted to the west as the *Liber de Causis*, and became an important source of Greek philosophy.

In the Latin west, Eriugena (9th century) promulgated the pseudo-Dionysian corpus. William Moerbeke, bishop of Corinth in the Latin occupation (13th century), translated Proclus' works and made them available to his friend, the Dominican theologian Thomas Aquinas. Proclus attracted great interest among western theologians, especially Nicholas of Cusa. During the Renaissance (Ficino, *et al.*) Neoplatonism and Proclus were important influences. Elizabethan literary figures such as Edmund Spenser also read Proclus. The trend continued to the 19th-century Romantics.

Proclus' mathematical science was valued by Galileo's circle, and profoundly influenced the 17th-century astronomer Kepler. In modern philosophy the editions of Proclus by the Frenchman Victor Cousin and the German Friedrich Creuzer opened him to the chief Idealists, particularly Hegel, who respected Proclus above Plotinus. In America Proclus was read by the Transcendentalists, notably Ralph Waldo Emerson.

LUCAS SIORVANES

See also Neoplatonism

Biography

Born in Constantinople in 410 or 411 to a family from Lycia, Proclus first studied law at Alexandria. In 430/31 he went to Athens to study Plato and Aristotle. At the age of 25 he became head of the Athenian Academy and remained there until his death. In addition to teaching he wrote widely on logic, metaphysics, epistemology, theology, mathematics, physics, astronomy, and literature. He died in 485.

Writings

The Elements of Theology, edited and translated by E.R. Dodds, 2nd edition, Oxford: Clarendon Press, 1963

Théologie platonicienne, edited and translated by H.D. Saffrey and L.G. Westerink, 6 vols, Paris: Belles Lettres, 1968–97

A *Commentary on the First Book of Euclid's Elements*, edited and translated by Glenn R. Morrow, Princeton, New Jersey: Princeton University Press, 1970; reprinted 1992

Commentary on Plato's Parmenides, edited by John M. Dillon, translated by Dillon and Glenn R. Morrow, Princeton, New Jersey: Princeton University Press, 1987

Further Reading

Gersh, Stephen, *From Iamblichus to Eriugena: An Investigation of the Prehistory and Evolution of the Pseudo-Dionysian Tradition*, Leiden: Brill, 1978

Lloyd, A.C., "Athenian and Alexandrian Neoplatonism" in *The Cambridge History of Later Greek and Early Medieval Philosophy*, edited by A.H. Armstrong, Cambridge: Cambridge University Press, 1967

Nicholas of Methone, *Refutation of Proclus' Elements of Theology*, edited and translated by Athanasios D. Angelou, Leiden: Brill, and Athens: Akademia Athenon, 1984

O'Meara, Dominic J., *Pythagoras Revived: Mathematics and Philosophy in Late Antiquity*, Oxford: Clarendon Press, and New York: Oxford University Press, 1989

Pachymeres, George, *Commentary on Plato's Parmenides* (anonymous sequel to Proclus' commentary), edited by Thomas A. Gadra, Paris: Vrin, 1989

Saffrey, H.D. and Jean Pépin (editors), *Proclus: lecteur et interprète des anciens*, Paris: Centre National des Recherches Scientifiques, 1987

Siorvanes, Lucas, *Proclus: Neo-Platonic Philosophy and Science*, Edinburgh: Edinburgh University Press, and New Haven, Connecticut: Yale University Press, 1996

Procopius of Caesarea

Historian of the 6th century AD

Procopius, "a writer who must be accounted the most excellent Greek historian since Polybius" (Bury, 1958, vol. 2, p. 419), was born in Caesarea, Palestine, in the early 6th century AD. Appointed the *assessor*, or legal adviser, of the emperor Justinian's chief general Belisarius in 529, he accompanied him on his campaigns until the early 540s. The stirring events he witnessed, combined with his Classical education, inspired him to write a detailed account of the wars waged by Justinian. Divided geographically into *Persian Wars* (books 1–2), *Vandalic Wars* (books 3–4), and *Gothic Wars* (books 5–7), his history narrates the progress of Roman campaigns in these three theatres of conflict. In the year 550 he not only completed the first seven books of the *Wars*, but also the *Anecdota* or *Secret History*. This latter work disappeared from circulation almost immediately, it seems, not to reappear again until c.1000, when it is mentioned in the *Suda* as a piece of *psogos* (invective) and *komodia* (satire) about Justinian, Theodora, Belisarius, and Antonina. Procopius continued working in the 550s, producing one more book of *Wars* (book 8), covering the ongoing campaigning in Italy and the Transcaucasus. He also composed a panegyric, the *Buildings* or *De Aedificiis*, detailing the building work undertaken by Justinian in Constantinople, the east, the Balkans, and north Africa. Both these works were probably produced around 554, although some scholars have preferred to place them later in the 550s. Procopius died soon afterwards, and should not be identified with the homonymous prefect of Constantinople in 562.

Procopius is among the very few Greek historians of the Roman empire whose works have survived in their entirety (as far as is known), and it is clear that he was quickly recognized as the leading authority on the events he relates. Agathias of Myrina, who continued his history of Justinian's wars for the period 552–59, mentions that "he [Procopius] who was so learned ... had read the whole of history, so to speak" (*Histories*, 4. 26. 4, translated Cameron). Both Agathias and, slightly later, Evagrius Scholasticus made use of Procopius' *Wars*: clearly this work enjoyed wide distribution (as Procopius himself notes at *Wars*, 8. 1. 1), although the *Buildings*, like the *Anecdota*, vanishes from view until much later. Before the hiatus that overtook Byzantine historiography in the early 7th century, a considerable number of historians, such as Menander Protector, John of Epiphania, and Theophylaktos Simokattes, continued to write "classicizing histories" similar to those of Procopius.

Procopius is but one in a long sequence of what are known as classicizing historians, so called because they wrote in a style which strove to emulate the historians of the 5th century BC, Herodotus and Thucydides. Although some classicizing historians may have had only a limited knowledge of these historians' works, it seems clear that Procopius at least was well acquainted with them. He owes a greater debt, perhaps, to the latter than the former: he aims to write in an "Atticizing" style, adopts a Thucydidean formula for dating campaigns, and on numerous occasions echoes Thucydidean phrases and sentiments (most notably in his description of the plague that struck Constantinople in 542 (*Wars*, 2. 22–23, modelled on Thucydides, 2. 46–53, a passage that influenced several later Byzantine historians)). But the interest in the esoteric and anecdotal visible in the *Anecdota* and the *Wars* is more reminiscent of Herodotus, as is the preface to the *Wars*.

In later times Procopius, as a successful exponent of the Atticizing style of historiography, remained popular among the Byzantine elite. The *Wars* were highly regarded, but some books more so than others: the patriarch Photios summarized only the *Persian Wars* in his *Bibliotheca*, while the chronicler Theophanes preferred to incorporate into his work a résumé only of the *Vandalic Wars*. One scholar has referred to a "Procopius renaissance" in the 12th century; certainly his works were used extensively by the historian Zonaras, and influenced the style of John Kinnamos. Around the same time he is among the authors recommended by the bishop of Corinth, Gregory, who praises the political and deliberative oratory in his work. Belisarius, in many ways the main focus of Procopius' narrative, became a heroic figure in popular literature of the later Byzantine period, although many of the stories concerning him do not come from Procopius. The contrasting depiction of events in the *Wars* and *Anecdota*, which initially led scholars to doubt the attribution of the latter to Procopius, has proved fertile ground for writers of fiction. The first modern scholar of Procopius, Felix Dahn, based his nationalistic novel *Der Kampf um Rom* (1876) on the *Gothic Wars*, while Robert Graves's *Count Belisarius* (1938) is little more than an imaginative reworking of the *Wars* and *Anecdota*.

Although Procopius' reputation as a historian has declined since Bury's time, he remains probably the most valuable primary source concerning the reign of Justinian; and his works continue to provide the framework for modern accounts of the period.

G.B. GREATREX

See also Historiography

Biography
Born in Caesarea in Palestine early in the 6th century AD, Procopius accompanied Belisarius on his campaigns until the early 540s as his secretary and legal adviser, visiting north Africa, Italy, and the east. He wrote an account of the wars of Justinian which survives in eight books. He also wrote the *Buildings* (on Justinian's public works) and the *Secret History* (a piece of satire). He died *c*.560.

Writings
Procopius, translated by H.B. Dewing, 7 vols, London: Heinemann, and New York: Putnam, 1914–40 (Loeb edition)
Opera Omnia, edited by Jakob Haury, revised by Gerhard Wirth, 3 vols, Leipzig: Teubner, 1962–64
History of the Wars, Secret History, and Buildings, translated by Averil Cameron, New York: Washington Square Press, 1967

Further Reading
Adshead, K., "The Secret History of Procopius and its Genesis", *Byzantion*, 63 (1993): pp. 5–28
Bury, J.B., *History of the Later Roman Empire from the Death of Theodosius I to the Death of Justinian*, 2 vols, London: Macmillan, 1923; reprinted New York: Dover, 1958
Cameron, Averil, *Procopius and the Sixth Century*, London: Duckworth, and Berkeley: University of California Press, 1985
Evans, J.A.S., *Procopius*, New York: Twayne, 1972
Greatrex, Geoffrey, "Procopius the Outsider?" in *Strangers to Themselves: The Byzantine Outsiders*, edited by Dion Smythe, Aldershot, Hampshire: Ashgate, 2000
Rubin, Berthold, *Prokopios von Kaisareia*, Stuttgart: Druckenmuller, 1954
Whitby, M., "Greek Historical Writing after Procopius: Variety and Vitality" in *The Byzantine and Early Islamic Near East*, vol. 1: *Problems in the Literary Source Material*, edited by Averil Cameron and Lawrence I. Conrad, Princeton, New Jersey: Darwin Press, 1992

Procopius of Gaza c.475–c.538
Christian rhetorician and teacher in the humanities

Procopius was very proud of the ancient city of Gaza where he was born and spent most of his life, a place to which he added distinction. Among the most prosperous cities of Palestine, at the crossroads of trade routes in all directions, Gaza was a major trading post and port, a provincial centre, and a meeting point of peoples and languages. By the time of Procopius it had become prominent in Christian terms as the site of an important episcopal see. At the same time, Gaza saw the existence, in a period of decline, of a late-flourishing school of rhetoric where the Christian context allowed the coexistence of traditional expressions of pagan Greek culture, a school that attained a distinction that drew students from a wide area.

Procopius came to be regarded as the most important of the "Triad of Gaza", the other members being his brother Zacharias and the rhetorician Aeneas whom he probably succeeded as head of the school (c.491–95). Also notable in the school was Choricius, a student of Procopius, from whose funeral oration, together with Procopius' own letters (166 survive), may be derived a patchy account of his life. The dates are subject to debate, with c.475–538 emerging as more probable than c.465–528. (He was said to have died at the same age as Demosthenes.) Starting with a good Classical education in his native city, he went on to Alexandria and perhaps elsewhere before returning to a salaried post in Gaza. He remained as a rhetorician with public duties and as a teacher, despite attempts to lure him away to Antioch, Tyre, and Caesarea. His letters show a man of wide acquaintance, including distinguished and influential contemporaries in the spheres of medicine, law, and the Church, as well as among professional colleagues and students. His correspondence includes personal communications and letters of recommendation and consolation. They contain elements of personal concern, social awareness, and learned humour, revealing aspects of city life and, on occasion, verging on the light-hearted. Written in a highly polished, rather artificial style, these letters exemplify a continuity of Attic prose. Not only in style, but in content, is to be found continuity, a generous range of pagan Classical allusion being juxtaposed with aspects of Christian belief.

Alongside the teaching activity of which Choricius spoke highly, Procopius left examples of his rhetorical skill, in particular his celebratory oration on the emperor Anastasius I (491–518). In a forceful work of panegyric, following a pattern set by many predecessors, he achieves a measure of individuality within the bounds of conventional form. Tracing the emperor's career and emphasizing his vital part in the war against the Arabs, he looks for a wider context. As the city is set within the empire, so the empire itself has its place in the life of the human race, as the orator adumbrates a view of world history and a theory of government. Anastasius is depicted as a strong ruler, concerned for his subjects, especially the poor, and accessible to all classes in his pursuit of universal harmony. He represents a living law and exemplifies morality. Though there are discreet omissions, as when Procopius passes over various controversial episodes and disputes on religious matters, he contrives to maintain some balance within his idealized account.

Within the Christian sphere Procopius is more noted for an activity very different from any so far considered. The bulk (and it is extensive) of what has come down to us consists of catenae (seirai) of commentary on books of the Bible, composed of lengthy excerpts from established writers who include Philo Judaeus, Origen, Basil, Gregory of Nyssa, Clement of Alexandria, and Theodoret. He compiled comments on the books from Genesis to Ruth, in longer and shorter forms, together with collections on Isaiah, Song of Songs, and Proverbs. These display little evidence of shaping by a mind conscious of exegetical principles. Procopius adheres to no interpretative school, merely setting down side by side comments in an eclectic mass.

Yet another aspect of his interests is found in the account he gives of a series of pictures, all on traditional pagan themes.

Introducing them with a rhetorical flourish on the all-pervading power of love, he vividly describes mythological motifs, involving figures such as Theseus, Ariadne, Phaedra, and Hippolytus, with a strikingly sensitive evocation of scenes from the *Iliad*, where the reader is brought to stand in emotional involvement with the defeated Priam before Agamemnon. The grouping of figures and the subtle variations of landscape emerge in telling detail. In a rather different mode are a stylized set of declamations on Classical subjects, such as Venus, Adonis, and Spring.

Though the attribution has been disputed, it may well be that the fragments of a work in which the writer disputes views held by the Neoplatonist Proclus come from Procopius. Proclus had connections with Gaza and Aeneas wrote of the influence of Neoplatonism, selective in acceptance and rejection.

It is not easy to form a unified view of Procopius, the elements of his interest being so diverse. It has been suggested that the large number of pagan references point to a preconversion phase in his life. This is not a necessary supposition. It is quite conceivable that a Christian layman, sitting lightly to exegetical principles in his understanding of a Christian past, might have found himself able to draw in purely literary terms upon the imagery as well as the style of a pagan past. If he considered that the religious struggle was over, he could feel at ease with the richness of that literary and rhetorical heritage which he felt to be his.

D.A. SYKES

See also Rhetoric

Biography

Born in Gaza c.AD 475, Procopius received a good Classical education and travelled to Alexandria. He spent his life teaching rhetoric at the school in Gaza where his pupils included Choricius. He wrote widely – letters, panegyric, and biblical exegesis – in a polished Attic style. He was a member of the "Triad of Gaza", the others being his brother Zacharias and the rhetor Aeneas. He died c.538.

Writings

Spätantiker Gemäldezyklus in Gaza: des Prokopios von Gaza "Ekphrasis eikones", edited by Paul Friedländer, Vatican City, 1939; reprinted Hildesheim: Olms, 1969

Epistolae et declamationes, edited by Antonio Garzya and R.J. Loenentz, Ettal: Buch-Kunstverlag, 1963

Further Reading

Aly, W., Prokopius von Gaza entry in *Real-Encyclopädie der klassischen Altertumswissenschaft*, edited by August Pauly et al., vol. 23. 1, 1957, 259–73

Bardenhewer, Otto, *Geschichte der altkirchlichen Lieratur*, vol. 5, Freiburg: Herder, 1932, pp. 86–91

Chauvot, Alain, *Procope de Gaza, Priscien de Césarée: Panégyriques de l'empereur Anastase Ier*, Bonn: Habelt, 1986

Choricius of Gaza, *Opera*, edited by Richard Foerster and Eberhard Richtsteig, Leipzig: Teubner, 1929; reprinted, 1972

Cross, F.L. and E.A. Livingstone (editors), *The Oxford Dictionary of the Christian Church*, 3rd edition, Oxford and New York: Oxford University Press, 1997

Prodromos, Theodore

Poet of the 12th century

Theodore Prodromos, also called Ptochoprodromos ("poor Prodromos"), lived at the time of the Komnenoi emperors, Alexios Komnenos (1081–1118), John II (1118–43), and Manuel I (1143–80), a contemporary of John Tzetzes. He was renowned for a strong satirical touch in his work and a propensity for complaining and begging. There is much philological debate as to how many people are referred to under the name Prodromos, some scholars arguing that there are two different people, others that there is only one. Various kinds of literature are believed to have been written by him, both prose and poetry, the content ranging from philosophical and rhetorical texts to satiric dialogues, religious, and even astrological poems.

Six poems are preserved under his name, known as the *Prodromika*, with a total of 2259 verses, all in the 15-syllable folk metre and in a language close to modern Greek syntax and morphology. They are petitions to the emperor, either John II or Manuel I Komnenos or other members of the imperial family. In the first poem the writer talks about his married life, contrasting his demanding wife with his stoic personality. In the second he complains about his poverty and requests some help from the emperor; there is no reference to his wife. In the third and fourth it seems clear that he has become a monk, and his barbs have as their target the monastic life. Again his descriptions are addressed to the emperor, whose patronage he seeks. In the fifth and sixth poems he complains about the misery that intellectuals have to go through, in comparison with other more lucrative professions. The strong autobiographical tone that he employs in his poems present an intense social reality and poses many questions, both from a narratological and from a historical point of view. Dimaras suggests that this is a hero of urban folk poetry, "who was presented each time by a different author and placed by him in social situations with different professions". The language contains many vernacular elements, and some works are believed to preserve the spoken language of the 12th century. If this is the case, and if Prodromos indeed came from an urban and even scholarly environment, then his choice is very significant for the history of the Greek language. A kind of popular wisdom is represented in the poems, revealing that, whatever his educational background, he was in contact with the oral tradition of his time. He mentions *Digenis Akritis* in two places in his work. His works are also an important source for the social history of his time. The "Prodromic" poems, even if they were not written by Prodromos, seem to be part of an extremely popular tradition. They circulated widely until late in Byzantine times, in many copies and in various versions. Adamantios Korais, a representative of the Greek Enlightenment, edited some of the poems in his collection *Atakta* (1828). Korais was proposing his own solution to the Greek language problem, with the archaizing and the folk language competing strongly against one another, and the combination of the two in the Prodromic poems might well have provided him with some inspiration.

Although it has many defects from an aesthetic point of view, the *Rodanthe and Dosicles*, a romance written in 12-syllable verse (4614 trimeters), is a very interesting piece and is important for the history of the Greek novel. There was a revival and transformation of the Greek novel at this period and a protorenaissance in literature, which have been neglected by scholars. There was a rich novel tradition at the time of the Second Sophistic and in late antiquity that had a great influence on the 12th-century renaissance of the novel, both from the thematic and the linguistic point of view. Prodromos is also believed to be the author of a semi-philosophical dialogue on friendship in exile, and of an astrological poem of 593 political verses. Also attributed to him is a satiric poem, *Katomyomachia* (battle between cat and mice), written under the influence of the *Batrachomyomachia* (battle between frogs and mice) of the archaic Homeric corpus. He is associated with court poetry, verses that were recited at official celebrations and ceremonies. It is highly unlikely that all the above categories were part of one man's work, and the literary identity of Prodromos is unclear.

ANDROMACHE KARANIKA-DIMAROGONA

See also Romance

Biography

A variety of works written in the 12th century at the time of the Komnenoi emperors are ascribed to Prodromos (or Ptochodromos). It is unlikely that they were all written by one man. They include six autobiographical poems known as the *Prodromika*, the romance *Rodanthe and Dosicles*, the satirical *Katomyomachia*, an astrological poem, and a philosophical dialogue on friendship.

Further Reading

Dimaras, K.T., *Istoria tis Neoellinikis Logotechnias*, Athens, 1948–49; translated as *A History of Modern Greek Literature*, Albany: State University of New York Press, 1972; Oxford: Clarendon Press, 1973

Polites, Linos, *Istoria tis Neas Hellinikis Logotechnias* [History of New Greek Literature], 2nd edition, Thessalonica, 1969

Voutierides, Elias P., *Syntome Istoria tis Neoellinikis Logotechnias (1000–1930)* [Short History of Modern Greek Literature (1000–1930)], 3rd edition, Athens, 1976

Proselytism

The Greek term "proselytism" denotes the process of conversion from one belief to another and is mostly used in a religious context. The adjective "proselyte" signified initially the Gentile convert to Judaism; the newcomers to Christianity were also called proselytes. Christianity as a prophetic, missionary religion had a message to deliver to the world and stressed the radical changing of one's life. The Christian notions of sin, repentance, and the need for salvation signified the renunciation of all one's previous beliefs and ways of life, which had to be replaced by the wholesale adoption of the Christian faith and mode of living, either through conversion or adhesion.

In contemporary Greek usage the term "proselytism" has overtones of coercion. According to a law dating from the Metaxas government in 1938, it denotes the process of intrusion into an individual's religious belief and conversion through secretive, devious, and fraudulent means. Conversion may thus occur in exchange for material goods, job and education opportunities, upward social mobility, and related promises. Proselytism may also take place by betraying a person's confidence or by taking advantage of his or her mental deficiency, naivety, inexperience, ignorance, or an emergency. Proselytism is considered to be an act of unfair religious or ideological competition and constitutes a violation of the individual's own conscience.

Theoretically, proselytism should be distinguished from genuine conversion after a fair dialogue. It is also vital to distinguish proselytism from the freedom to teach non-Christian religions, either in schools or to the public. But historically speaking, it is not always easy to distinguish clearly between proselytism and genuine conversions to Christianity. Under the wider umbrella of Christian missionary efforts, there was a variety of conversion methods including those that followed in the wake of colonialist invasion and conquest. Furthermore, Christianity's own proselytizing practices were to a large extent felt to be self-justified: since it was about the spread of the sole true faith, almost anything was allowed.

In Byzantium the establishment of Orthodoxy was of utmost importance for its political ideology. Conquered people were Christianized in order to be smoothly integrated into the empire. It goes without saying that any deviation from Orthodox standards was forbidden. All dissidents, whether pagans or heretics, especially when these engaged in proselytizing efforts, were prohibited or faced various penalties and repressive measures.

A similar situation can be observed under Ottoman rule, when the Church was particularly interested in safeguarding Orthodoxy. This period was marked by the systematic proselytism by Roman Catholics in the Levant, especially by the Jesuits. In 1577 pope Gregory XIII (1572–85) founded the Collegio Greco in Rome to initiate Greek students into Roman Catholicism and to employ them later in the East. The Sacra Congregatio de Propaganda Fide, founded in 1622, and the Uniate Church worked towards the same ends. These acts often provoked a reaction from the patriarchate of Constantinople (e.g. in 1722) and even from the Ottoman authorities (e.g. in 1702). Despite these religious conflicts, it was in this period that the Greek term for religious freedom and toleration, *anexithriskeia*, was coined by Evgenios Voulgaris, but its semantic content differed from its western counterparts.

After the foundation of the Greek state the Orthodox Church, though deprived of its previous broad responsibilities, managed to retain its ideological authority, especially with regard to non-Orthodox currents and ideas. While its repressive potential was less strong than it had been before 1821, it was still in a position to condemn and occasionally to take harsh measures against proselytizing acts. A well-known case is that of Theophilos Kairis (1784–1853), who was condemned as the founder of a new religion to the detriment of Orthodoxy. From the beginning of the 19th century onwards, the most serious cases of foreign proselytism were undertaken by various British and American Protestant organizations, which developed wide missionary activities in Greece, ranging from translating the Scriptures and publishing to the founding of

schools and mission stations. This provoked an Orthodox reaction, as manifested in patriarch Gregory VI's anti-Protestant encyclical of 1836, which, among other things, prohibited the Orthodox faithful from attending Protestant schools. Similar encyclicals were issued by the Church of Greece (e.g. on 22 March 1891). In Greek state legislation proselytism was also considered a major offence against Orthodoxy, the dominant religion (e.g. in the Constitution of 1844, Article 1, and that of 1864/1911, Article 1).

At present, Orthodoxy is still acknowledged as the dominant, established religion of the Greek state (Constitution of 1975/86, Article 3). The Church intends to keep the Orthodox faith that has been vouchsafed to it unaltered. Claiming a unique handle on truth, the Orthodox Church regards the existence of non-Orthodox on its exclusive Greek territory with disfavour. Its intention is to control them, defend itself, and warn its members through related encyclicals and long lists of heretical groups. These antiheretical measures are supported by the state and its legal system. This situation can be attributed to the close relationship between Church and state in Greece and the mythology about the inextricable historical connection of Orthodoxy with Greek national identity.

The privileged status that the Orthodox Church enjoys obviously implies certain restrictions regarding the circulation and dissemination of non-Orthodox systems and ideas. Proselytism is forbidden (Constitution of 1975/86, Article 13(2)) as a penal offence. Yet the simple right to be informed about or to teach non-Orthodox religions is hardly distinguished from proselytism. The latter is not confined to conversion through improper means, but is interpreted broadly and applied to a variety of cases, often leading to convictions. Discrimination against religious minorities is thus not uncommon, because of the fear that they might undermine the established religion and alienate Greece's traditional culture. While the freedom of conscience is accepted and "known religions" are allowed, religious rights for minorities are in practice restricted (e.g. concerning the establishment of their "houses of worship"). The related legal terminology is ambiguous and can be interpreted and applied inconsistently. Proselytism by non-Orthodox minorities is strictly prohibited; but proselytizing for Greek Orthodoxy through individual means or institutional mechanisms is encouraged. In some cases, though, legal measures against certain religious movements and their proselytizing methods are deemed justified, as was the case with Scientology (in Greece since 1983), which was forbidden in 1997 through a decision (no. 10493) of the Court of Appeals of Athens.

In fact, the Orthodox Church considers that all non-Orthodox religions are unacceptable, i.e. either as heresies or as erroneous beliefs. It is therefore not surprising that religious minorities (e.g. Jehovah's Witnesses, Roman Catholics, Protestants) feel endangered by this milieu, and some have appealed to international organizations (e.g. the European Human Rights Commission and Court) for protection, which have often decided in their favour. Yet the Church, supported by the state, does not intend to renounce its traditional exclusive rights on Greek territory. Such ambiguities create tension between the Orthodox Church and the religious minorities and subsequently between Greece and its European partners, while the demand for Greece's relative deconfessionalization and greater liberalization in religious matters is repeatedly being voiced.

Vasilios Makrides

See also Conversion to Islam

Further Reading

Alivizatos, Nicos C., "A New Role for the Greek Church", *Journal of Modern Greek Studies*, 17 (1999): pp. 23–40

Argyropoulos, Roxane, "La Diaspora protestante et les lumières en Grèce au début du 19e siècle", *Folia Neohellenica*, 8 (1987/89): pp. 7–18

Beck, Hans-Georg, *Vom Umgang mit Ketzern: Der Glaube der kleinen Leute und die Macht der Theologen*, Munich: Beck, 1993

Beis, Costas E. (editor), *I Thriskevtiki Elevtheria: Theoria kai Praxi stin Elliniki Koinonia kai Ennomi Praxi* [Religious Freedom: Theory and Practice in Greek Society and Legal Practice], Athens, 1987

Christopoulos, Dimitris (editor), *Nomika Zitimata Thriskevtikis Eterotitas stin Ellada* [Legal Questions Concerning Non-Orthodox Religions in Greece], Athens, 1999

Christopoulos, Panayotis, *To vivlio I Alitheia Kritis kai i Tychodioktiki drasi tou Syngraphea tou Leandro Lombardi ston Elliniko Choro* [The Book Alitheia Kritis and the Daring Acts of its Author Leandro Lombardi in Greece], Athens, 1984

Clogg, Richard, "The Publication and Distribution of Karamanli Texts by the British and Foreign Bible Society Before 1850", *Journal of Ecclesiastical History*, 19 (1968): part 1, pp. 57–81, part 2, pp. 171–93

Clogg, Richard, "Some Protestant Tracts Printed at the Press of the Ecumenical Patriarchate in Constantinople 1818–1820", *Eastern Churches Review*, 2 (1968): pp. 152–64

Hefner, Robert W. (editor), *Conversion to Christianity: Historical and Anthropological Perspectives on a Great Transformation*, Berkeley: University of California Press, 1993

Hering, Gunnar, *Ökumenisches Patriarchat und europäische Politik, 1620–1638*, Wiesbaden: Steiner, 1968

Hofmann, Giorgio, "Apostolato dei Gesuiti nell'Oriente Greco (1583–1773)", *Orientalia Christiana Periodica*, 1 (1935): pp. 139–63

Knapp, Martin von, *Evgenios Vulgaris im Einfluss der Aufklärung: Der Begriff der Toleranz bei Vulgaris und Voltaire*, Amsterdam: Hakkert, 1984

Konidaris, Ioannis, *Nomiki theoria kai praxi gia tous "Martyres tou Iechova"* [Legal Theory and Practice on "Jehovah's Witnesses"], 3rd edition, Athens, 1991

Loverdos, Andreas, *Prosylitismos* [Proselytism], Athens, 1986

Maltezou, Chrysa A. (editor), *Oi perithoriakoi sto Vyzantio* [Fringe Elements in Byzantium], Athens, 1993

Mamoni, Kyriaki, "Agones tou Oikoumenikou Patriarcheiou kata ton Missionarion" [Struggles of the Ecumenical Patriarchate Against Missionaries], *Mnimosyni*, 8 (1980–81): pp. 179–212

Mango, Cyril, *Byzantium: The Empire of New Rome*, London: Weidenfeld and Nicolson, and New York: Scribner, 1980, chapter 4

Marinos, Anastasios N., "I Thriskevtiki Elevtheria" [Religious Freedom] (dissertation), Athens, 1972, pp. 195–244

Metallinos, Georgios, *To Zitima tis Metaphraseos tis Agias Graphis eis tin Neoellinikin kata ton 19 aiona* [The Question of the Translation of the Holy Scriptures into Modern Greek in the 19th Century], Athens, 1977

Metallinos, Georgios, "'I kata tin Anatolin Dysis': O 'metakenotikos' rolos ton Dytikon Missionarion sto Elliniko Kratos" ["West Against the East": The "Disturbing" Role of the Western Missionaries in the Greek State], *Synaxi*, 8 (1983): pp. 23–55

Metallinos, Georgios et al., *I Ounia Chthes kai Simera* [The Unia Yesterday and Today], Athens, 1992

Nock, A.D., *Conversion: The Old and the New in Religion from Alexander the Great to Augustine of Hippo*, Oxford: Oxford University Press, 1961

Panagopoulos, Theodor J., "Die Religionsfreiheit in Griechenland", *Orthodoxes Forum*, 5 (1991): pp. 73–79

Pollis, Adamantia, "The State, the Law, and Human Rights in Modern Greece", *Human Rights Quarterly*, 9/4 (1987): pp. 587–612

Pollis, Adamantia, "Greek National Identity: Religious Minorities, Rights, and European Norms", *Journal of Modern Greek Studies*, 10/2 (1992): pp. 171–95

Pollis, Adamantia, "Eastern Orthodoxy and Human Rights", *Human Rights Quarterly*, 15 (1993): pp. 339–56

Saloutos, Theodore, "American Missionaries in Greece, 1820–1869", *Church History*, 24 (1955): pp. 152–94

Salt, Jeremy, "A Precarious Symbiosis: Ottoman Christians and Foreign Missionaries in the Nineteenth Century", *International Journal of Turkish Studies*, 3 (1985–86): pp. 53–67

Simon, Dieter (editor), *Religiöse Devianz: Untersuchungen zu sozialen, rechtlichen und theologischen Reaktionen auf religiöse Abweichung im westlichen und östlichen Mittelalter*, Frankfurt: Klostermann, 1990

Sotirelis, Yorgos C., *Thriskeia kai ekpaidevsi kata to Syntagma kai tin Evropaiki Symvasi: Apo ton katichitismo stin polyphonia* [Religion and Education According to the Constitution and the European Treaty: From Catechism to Pluralism], Athens, 1993

Stavros, Stephanos, "O prosilytismos kai to dikaioma sti thriskevtiki elevtheria" [Proselytism and the Right to Religious Freedom], *Poinika Chronika*, 43 (1993): pp. 964–97

Stavros, Stephanos, "The Legal Status of Minorities in Greece Today: The Adequacy of Their Protection in the Light of Current Human Rights Perceptions", *Journal of Modern Greek Studies*, 13 (1995): pp. 1–32

Stavros, Stephanos, "Human Rights in Greece: Twelve Years of Supervision from Strasbourg", *Journal of Modern Greek Studies*, 17 (1999): pp. 3–21

Troianos, Spyros N., ed., *Egklima kai Timoria sto Vyzantio* [Crime and Punishment in Byzantium], Athens, 1997

Tsirpanlis, Zacharias, *Oi Makedones Spoudastes tou Ellinikou Kollegiou Romis kai i drasi tous stin Ellada kai stin Italia* [Macedonian Students of the Hellenic College at Rome and their Activities in Greece and Italy], Thessalonica, 1971

Tsirpanlis, Zacharias, *To Elliniko Kollegio tis Romis kai oi Mathites tou (1576–1700): Symvoli sti meleti tis Morphotikis Politikis tou Vatikanou* [The Greek College at Rome and its Pupils (1576–1700): A Contribution to the Study of Vatican Educational Policy], Thessalonica, 1980

Vegléris, Phédon, "Quelques Aspects de la liberté de religion en Grèce", *Revue trimestrielle des droits de l'homme*, 24 (1995): pp. 555–66

Voulgarakis, Ilias A., *I Ierapostoli kata ta Ellinika Keimena apo tou 1821 mechri tou 1917* [Missionaries in Greek Texts, 1821–1917], Athens, 1971, pp. 72–78 and passim

Prostitution

In ancient Greece the sex trade was not illegal and there was a ready market for prostitutes who, in contrast to later Christian sexual ethics, were not regarded as improper objects of male desire. For Athenian men, who usually married in their thirties and for whom marital fidelity was not a requirement anyway, females under the protection of citizens, whether unmarried girls or married women, were, at least formally, strictly off limits and erotic relationships with such women could attract the severest penalties. Sex with prostitutes was much less risky and provided an outlet for "releasing the pressure of lust" (Xenophon, *Memorabilia*, 2. 2. 4).

Male prostitutes (*kinaidoi*) were much in demand; there was no overarching moral stricture on same-sex behaviour in antiquity and, while a man was expected to be the active sexual partner, the object of his desire could be male or female. However, just as relationships with respectable women were restricted, so too there were formal restrictions regarding male partners; men of actual or potential citizen status were considered improper objects of a fully sexual relationship. Indeed, there could be serious civic consequences for citizen prostitutes; those who subsequently exercised their civic privileges invited prosecution and civic dishonour (a good example is the case of Timarchus in the 4th century BC, documented in Aischines, 1). However most prostitutes in antiquity, male and female, were slaves, and thus had no status to compromise.

While the all-embracing term of *ergasia* ("trade") denoted prostitution in Hellenic antiquity, prostitutes did not comprise a homogeneous category and there existed a broad spectrum of practice and status for those involved in selling sex. At the bottom of the heap were common prostitutes (*pornai*) who walked the streets and worked in the brothels of the Piraeus and the Kerameikos, still Athens' red-light district today. For brothel workers (always female) life could be grim; in one 5th-century BC text a concubine who fears her lover may send her to the brothel resorts to poisoning him (Antiphon, 1. 14). Other prostitutes, male and female, sat in cubicles (*oikemata*) open to the street, displaying themselves Amsterdam-style to prospective clients.

The Athenian state involved itself in the regulation of prostitution: *pornai* paid tax to the state, while Philemon (fr. 4) claimed that Solon established state-run brothels for the provision of cheap sex to all citizens as a democratic measure. The state also controlled the fees of flute girls and male kithara players, hired to provide musical and erotic entertainment at symposia, often the site of sexual dalliance; the mere appearance of an Athenian woman at a symposium could bring her reputation into question (Isaeus, 3. 13–14). In later periods too public entertainers were assimilated to prostitutes, perhaps because of their public visibility.

Courtesans (*hetairai*), on the other hand, exercised at least some choice in the bestowal of their favours and were hired for companionship as well as sex. Courtesans who commanded extravagant fees (*megalomisthoi*) could become rich and famous; Phryne, possibly the model for Praxiteles' *Aphrodite of Cnidus*, was reputedly rich enough to rebuild the city wall of Thebes (Callistratus, *On Courtesans*). Sometimes permanent attachments to men resulted and it can be difficult to distinguish the courtesan from the concubine (Aspasia and Theodote, the mistresses respectively of Pericles and Alcibiades, are two examples). Prostitution could even provide a way out of slavery and there are many examples of men buying the freedom of a favourite girl; Herodotus (2. 178) claims that Rhodopis of Thrace was redeemed from slavery by Sappho's brother and became rich. However, Neaira of Corinth (a city renowned for its prostitutes) started life as a slave, was freed by her lovers, and then, following a legal prosecution, was sold again ([Demosthenes], 59). The sex trade offered a chance of social mobility to some but it was a precarious existence; prostitutes could come up in the ancient world, but they could also go down.

Certainly many ancient writers vilified prostitutes and condemned them for their extravagance and use of artifice; in the 4th century BC Alexis sneered at girls who compensated for their lack of natural charms with high heels, make-up, false breasts, and the ancient equivalent of a bustle (fr. 18). Men who frittered their money away on prostitutes or fought over them in the street also attracted criticism. Yet in pre-Christian Hellenic society it was not unacceptable for men to patronize prostitutes, who were regarded as a cure for dangerous desire, nor was the profession the object of religious disapproval; indeed Aphrodite was the tutelary goddess of prostitutes and temple prostitution in her honour is attested for Corinth (Strabo, 8. 6. 20), although this was unusual for Greece. Christianity, however, introduced a radically different slant on sexual continence. Marriage became the only proper outlet for male sexual desire and, indeed, a "defence against desire" (Brown, 1988). Paul advised one Greek community to marry rather than to burn (1 Corinthians 7. 9), while in the 4th century John Chrysostom, hugely influential in the Orthodox Church, envisaged marriage not as a celebration of sexual love but as a method of avoiding fornication (*De Virginitate*, 19. 1. 1–2). One consequence of this was the outlawing of same-sex behaviour between men; an imperial edict of 390 demanded that male prostitutes in Rome should be burnt. Orthodox theology regards desire as the spiritual effect of original sin and the Church still censures fornication and male homosexual acts.

Another effect of Christian teaching was the shifting of anxiety and blame concerning male desire on to female prostitutes. For medieval society all women were potential Eves, the embodiment of lust, but the prostitute represented the epitome of sexual temptation, the ruination of married men and celibate clergy. Religious anxieties about fornication were exacerbated by the large number of prostitutes in medieval society, driven into the sex trade through poverty. One (rather unsuccessful) solution was the attempt to redeem "fallen women", a social programme influenced perhaps by the example of the Magdalene. One ex-prostitute, Martha, sat in a shrine outside Byzantium exhorting women to avoid temptation (for the repentant prostitute theme see Ward, 1987). Attempts were made to redeem prostitutes by placing them in monastic homes, notably by the empress Theodora in the 6th century. From the 9th century this practice was established as law and female sexual subversives (prostitutes and adulteresses) were forced into convents to learn from the example of their betters and perform menial tasks, perhaps more a matter of punishment than salvation. In contrast, prostitution was used as a punishment for one early Christian martyr at least: Irene of Thessalonica was placed in a public brothel by the Roman prefect Dulcitius for her subversive religious behaviour (*Acts of the Christian Martyrs*, 22).

Finally, it is worth noting that in more recent times sex workers have born the brunt of moral panics about sexually transmitted diseases and perceived moral declines. As ever, the prostitute is at the sharp end of society's concerns about sexual behaviour and her image is a reflection of both cultural anxieties and religious ethics.

EUGÉNIE FERNANDES

See also Homosexuality, Women

Further Reading

Brown, Peter, *The Body and Society: Men, Women, and Sexual Renunciation in Early Christianity*, New York: Columbia University Press, 1988; London: Faber, 1990

Brown, Peter, "Plots and Prostitutes in Greek New Comedy", *Papers of the Leeds International Latin Seminar*, vol. 6, Leeds: Cairns, 1990

Brundage, James A., *Law, Sex and Christian Society in Medieval Europe*, Chicago: University of Chicago Press, 1987

Carey, Christopher (editor and translator), *Apollodoros against Neaira: [Demosthenes] 59*, Warminster: Aris and Phillips, 1992

Clark, Elizabeth A., *Women in the Early Church*, Wilmington, Delaware: Glazier, 1983

Cohen, David, *Law, Sexuality and Society: The Enforcement of Morals in Classical Athens*, Cambridge and New York: Cambridge University Press, 1991

Davidson, James N., *Courtesans and Fishcakes: The Consuming Passions of Classical Athens*, London: HarperCollins, 1997; New York: St Martin's Press, 1998

Dubisch, J., "Greek Women: Sacred or Profane?", *Journal of Modern Greek Studies*, 1 (1983): pp. 185–202

Foucault, Michel, *The History of Sexuality*, vol. 3: *The Care of the Self*, translated by Robert Hurley, New York: Pantheon, and London: Allen Lane, 1988, reprinted 1990

Gould, G., "Women in the Writings of the Fathers: Language, Belief and Reality" in *Women in the Church*, edited by W.J. Shiels and Diana Wood, Oxford, and Cambridge, Massachusetts: Blackwell, 1990

Halperin, David M., "The Democratic Body: Prostitution and Citizenship in Classical Athens" in his *One Hundred Years of Homosexuality and Other Essays on Greek Love*, London and New York: Routledge, 1990

Konstan, D., "Between Courtesan and Wife: Menander's Perikeiromene", *Phoenix*, 41/2 (1987) pp. 122–39

Leontsini, Stavroula, *Prostitution im fruehen Byzanz*, Vienna: VMGO, 1989

Otis, Leah Lydia, *Prostitution in Medieval Society: The History of an Urban Institution in Languedoc*, Chicago: University of Chicago Press, 1985

Payer, Pierre J., *Sex and the Penitentials: The Development of a Sexual Code, 550–1150*, Toronto: University of Toronto Press, 1984

Pomeroy, Sarah B., *Goddesses, Whores, Wives, and Slaves: Women in Classical Antiquity*, New York: Schocken, 1975; London: Hale, 1976

Richlin, Amy (editor) *Pornography and Representation in Greece and Rome*, Oxford and New York: Oxford University Press, 1992

Rousselle, Aline, *Porneia: On Desire and the Body in Antiquity*, Oxford and New York: Blackwell, 1988

Starr, C.G., "An Evening with the Flute-Girls", *Parola del Passato*, 33 (1978): pp. 401–10

Ward, Benedicta, *Harlots of the Desert: A Study of Repentance in Early Monastic Sources*, Oxford: Mowbray, and Kalamazoo, Michigan: Cistercian Publications, 1987

Weeks, Jeffrey, *Sex, Politics, and Society: The Regulation of Sexuality since 1800*, 2nd edition, London and New York: Longman, 1989

Winkler, John J., "Laying Down the Law: The Oversight of Men's Sexual Behaviour in Classical Athens" in his *The Constraints of Desire: The Anthropology of Sex and Gender in Ancient Greece*, New York and London: Routledge, 1990

Protestantism

On 31 October 1517 Martin Luther's 95 theses ignited the Reformation. While defending his theology at the Disputation of Leipzig (1519) he was surprised to hear that his views resembled those of Jan Hus, who had been burned at the stake by the Council of Constance in 1415. Scholars have debated whether the origins of the Hussite (the *Unitas Fratrum*) opposition in Bohemia and Moravia to the Roman Catholic Church arose from dim memories of the missionary work of the Greek Orthodox brothers Cyril and Methodios. Whatever the truth of that, in 1450 an individual named Constantine Platris Anglikos (probably of Lollard origins) arrived in Constantinople claiming to represent the Hussite Churches and seeking communion between them and the Greek Orthodox Church. With the fall of Constantinople in 1453 nothing came of this proto-Protestant contact with the Greek Church.

Luther himself did not make any direct contacts with the Eastern Orthodox, but in debates with Rome he did cite them as examples of Christians who did not conform with Roman beliefs and practice. A common opposition to the papacy soon led Protestants – Lutheran, Calvinist, and Anglican – to cite the example of eastern Christians and to seek contacts with them. While Luther did not engage in direct talks with the East, others did. His younger protégé Philipp Melanchthon made a Greek translation of the *Augsburg Confession*. This Lutheran summary of beliefs was sent to Constantinople with a request for further contacts. Melanchthon died in 1560 awaiting a reply. Embarrassed by the doctrinal differences, the patriarch had merely ignored the request.

Continual Lutheran requests for closer ecclesiastical relations eventually gained a response when a delegation of Lutheran scholars visited Constantinople in 1573. Unable to avoid the issue, patriarch Jeremias II wrote a point-by-point response to the *Augsburg Confession* explaining Greek agreements and disagreements with its 21 articles. The reply reached Germany in 1576, and further correspondence ensued. While no Lutheran–Orthodox union was achieved, the correspondence between Tübingen and patriarch Jeremias II was the first ecumenical approach by the West to the East.

The second major attempt to link Protestantism with Greek Orthodoxy occurred during the stormy ministry of Cyril I Lukaris, the Calvinist patriarch of Constantinople (1572–1638). Born on Crete, which was controlled by the Venetians at the time, he studied for a while in Venice. Travelling in Europe in the summers, Lukaris may have met Franciscus Portus in Geneva. Portus was a Cretan and a convert to Calvinism, who became the master of the scholarly production of Classical and biblical texts in Greek at Geneva. While serving as patriarch of Alexandria (1602–20), Lukaris was increasingly influenced by Calvinism through contacts with English and Dutch ambassadors and others. He carried on an extensive correspondence with many western Protestants, both Reformed, such as Antoine Léger, a Genevan minister, and Anglicans including archbishop William Laud. When he became patriarch of Constantinople (1621–38), he strove to reform the moral and spiritual conditions in the Church along Calvinist lines.

Lukaris's *Eastern Confession of the Christian Faith* (1629) was published in Geneva. It contains a mild Calvinism in its doctrines regarding scripture, justification, the sacraments, and predestination. Opposition to it was widespread. Lukaris was denounced and forced to resign five times by Greek clerical opponents who were often incited by the Jesuits. However, the sultan continued to restore him to office. He was finally falsely accused of inciting the Cossacks against the Turks and was executed by strangling upon the order of sultan Murad IV. The ecclesiastical opposition to Lukaris's doctrines produced a series of synods that officially repudiated them. A synod in 1638 anathematized both Cyril and the confession attributed to him. The synod of 1642 condemned the confession and Calvinism without mention of Cyril. The Synod of Jerusalem (1672) eliminated Calvinism from the eastern Church. The ultimate effect of Lukaris's ministry was that it forced the wider Greek Church to define itself more carefully in relation to both Latin Catholicism and Protestantism.

The third major attempt to establish ecumenical relations between Greek Orthodoxy and Protestantism was made with Anglicans. Patriarch Lukaris's correspondence with Anglicans led him to send to England the New Testament *Codex Alexandrinus*. He also sent Metrophanes Kritopoulos to study at Oxford and London (1617–24) and other Greeks to study at the request of the English. In the 17th century numerous commercial contacts between the English and Greeks in the eastern Mediterranean encouraged some to believe that closer ties might be possible. Many in England hoped that similarities in liturgy, ordination, sacraments, and views on church–state relations would make full communion possible. Eventually the theological distances proved too great.

In the 19th century Protestant missions, mainly American, became active in the Balkans and Greece, but with little success. Eventually small Protestant churches were established in Greece. At the end of the 20th century the Greek Evangelical Church (30 congregations, Presbyterian in polity) and the Free Evangelical Church (Congregational) were the largest Protestant churches in Greece. Pentecostals, the Church of England, and others had small congregations. Many of the Protestant congregations were composed of expatriates and American military personnel. After 1945 a neo-Pentecostal or charismatic movement spread widely in the Greek Church, growing to several hundred thousand in number.

In the latter half of the 20th century the main vehicle of contact between Greek Orthodoxy and Protestants has been through the ecumenical movement and the World Council of Churches. Mutual understanding has continued to grow, but deep theological differences remain.

A.J.L. WASKEY, JR

See also Ecumenism

Further Reading

Anderson, Gary F., *A Study of Greek Protestantism*, St. Peter, Minnesota: Gustavus Adolphus College, 1962

Bainton, Roland H., *Here I Stand: A Life of Martin Luther*, New York: Abingdon Press, 1950

Chatzeantoniou, Georgios A., *Protestant Patriarch: The Life of Cyril Lucaris 1572–1638, Patriarch of Constantinople*, Richmond, Virginia: John Knox Press, and London: Epworth, 1961

Dillenberger, John and Claude Welch, *Protestant Christianity Interpreted through Its Development*, 2nd edition, New York: Macmillan, and London: Collier Macmillan, 1988

Fey, Harold E. (editor), *A History of the Ecumenical Movement*, 2nd edition, vol. 2: *1948–1968*, Philadelphia: Westminster Press, 1970

Geanakoplos, Deno John, *Byzantine East and Latin West: Two Worlds of Christendom in Middle Ages and Renaissance*, Oxford: Blackwell, and New York: Harper and Row, 1966

Latourette, Kenneth Scott, *A History of Christianity*, New York: Harper, 1953; revised edition, 1975

Legrand, Emile, *Bibliographie Hellénique*, reprinted New Rochelle, New York: Caratzas, 1977

McNeill, John T., *The History and Character of Calvinism*, New York: Oxford University Press, 1954

Pelikan, Jaroslav, *The Christian Tradition: A History of the Development of Doctrine*, vol. 2: *The Spirit of Eastern Christendom, 600–1700*, Chicago: University of Chicago Press, 1977

Piepkorn, Arthur Carl, *Profiles in Belief*, vols 1–2, New York: Harper and Row, 1978–79

Rouse, Ruth and Stephen Charles Neill (editors), *A History of the Ecumenical Movement*, 2nd edition, vol. 1: *1517–1948*, Philadelphia: Westminster Press, 1967

Runciman, Steven, *The Great Church in Captivity: A Study of the Patriarchate of Constantinople from the Eve of the Turkish Conquest to the Greek War of Independence*, London: Cambridge University Press, 1968

Schlier, Richard, *Der Patriarch Kyrill Lukaris von Konstantinopel: Sein Leben und Sein Glaubensbekenntnis*, Marburg: Bauer, 1927

Zernov, Nicolas, *Eastern Christendom: A Study of the Origin and Development of the Eastern Orthodox Church*, London: Weidenfeld and Nicolson, and New York: Putnam, 1961

Psellos, Michael 1018–after 1081

Statesman, historian, and polymath

Born to a middle-class family in Constantinople in 1018, Psellos was baptized Constantine, but is better known under his monastic name of Michael. Extemely well educated by the scholar and later court rhetorician and bishop John Mauropous, Psellos embarked early upon a career in the civil administration when he was appointed judge of a theme before the age of 20. He was one of a group of young intellectuals (including his friends the future patriarchs Constantine III Leichoudes and John VIII Xiphilinos) who gained some real political power as advisers to Constantine IX Monomachos (1042–55). When, however, the emperor was forced to abandon some of the salutary reforms of the early part of his reign, the group's power rapidly declined. The liberally adaptable Psellos stayed on as long as was possible until he was ultimately forced to take refuge as a monk on Bithynian Mount Olympus in 1054 when the emperor lost his struggle for supremacy with the rigorously rigid patriarch Michael I Keroularios. Nevertheless, Psellos's return and revenge were swift, for in 1058, as chief minister of Isaac I Komnenos, he was given the role of principal prosecutor in the patriarch's trial, although his surviving speech was never delivered owing to Keroularios's sudden death. Upon Isaac's illness in 1059 Psellos ensured his own safety by persuading the emperor to abdicate in favour of Constantine X Doukas. He was, however, never again an important political figure, despite his own claims and the fact that he became private tutor to the imperial children. He even had to retreat for a second time to a monastery, but this time to one in Constantinople and under his own patronage. After the accession of Michael VII Doukas in 1071 he fades from history. The date of his death is unknown, but some of his works were probably written after 1081 and he may have been still alive in 1095.

When in 1047 Constantine IX opened a law school headed by John Xiphilinos, protests by students of rhetoric that their opportunities to enter the civil service would now be curtailed persuaded the emperor to satisfy their interests as well. Psellos was consequently appointed "consul of the philosophers" (*hypatos ton philosophon*). Although it is unclear precisely what this position entailed, Psellos probably gained supervision of the private schools in the capital and taught rhetoric and philosophy under some form of imperial patronage. He makes many claims for himself as a teacher, most notably that he revived in Byzantium the study of philosophy, and especially of Plato, and introduced the new teaching method of *schedographia* (parsing) that involved the grammatical, stylistic, and historical analysis of a piece of dictation which was either taken from literature or composed for the purpose by the teacher. Psellos boasts that "people tug and pull at me, loving to hear my voice above all others because I know more than everyone else" and that his fame attracted as students Celts, Arabs, Persians, Egyptians, and Ethiopians. Despite a few surviving short addresses to students who did not pay attention, squabbled, or arrived late or not at all because of a shower, we know that he inspired at least one outstanding student, the philosopher John Italos, who succeeded him as "consul of the philosophers".

Psellos's main interest was philosophy, on which he wrote extensively and could rarely keep out of his work, whatever its subject. Despite his proclaimed attachment to Plato, and his genuine familiarity with his works, he frequently sees the philosopher through the medium of Neoplatonism (especially that of Proclus). This accords with his fascination for the occult – magic, alchemy, astrology, and Chaldaean theurgy. Although the treatise *De Operatione Daemonum* (*On the Working of Demons*) is almost certainly spurious, his interest in those subjects as well as his Platonism led to accusations of paganism, which he was more successful in fending off than was his student John Italos. Many of his philosophical works are derivative, especially his commentaries for students on Plato and Aristotle (whom he knew as well as he did Plato), and a collection of miscellaneous learning, often drawn from Plutarch, known as *De Omnifaria Doctrina*. Although he was not as original a thinker as John Italos, some of his works show an independent mind that wedded theology with philosophy and science in positing a divinely created *physis* (Nature) that works in accordance with immanent laws.

Psellos's chief claim to fame today, however, is as a historian. Although he wrote, probably in his youth, a brief traditional and only recently discovered chronicle, this claim rests on his *Chronographia*, an account of the reigns of 14 emperors from 976 to 1078. The *Chronographia* is a revolutionary piece of historiography based largely on his own observations. It is largely a series of often subtle and perceptive psychological studies of character, which are never stereotypical but frequently both complex and fluid. In denying providential causation Psellos attributes events to personal emotions and ambitions which he explores at length, and he presents his material in such a way that the reader gains vivid pictures of an unfolding drama. His reliability as a historian is generally admitted, but with the reservations that he is aware of little of what happened outside the capital, has sparse military interest, and exaggerates his own role in events (the most extreme example of egocentricity is his rewriting of the *Life* of St Auxentios to include details of his own biography). Although the *Chronographia* is idiosyncratic and inimitable and was not widely read, at least after its author's death, it expanded the horizons of subsequent Byzantine historiography, most notably in the works of Anna Komnene and Niketas Choniates.

Psellos's oratorical style was modelled especially on Plato, Aelius Aristides, and Gregory of Nazianzus. Among his surviving speeches are many addresses to the reigning emperors, for whom he also wrote speeches for them to deliver themselves, and a number of masterly funeral orations. Two of these, for his mother and his young daughter, are notable for his deep affection, which comes through also in many of his more than 500 letters and a touching little essay addressed to his infant grandson.

Literary interests are shown in many works: essays on the styles of the Church Fathers John Chrysostom, Basil of Caesarea, Gregory of Nazianzus, and Gregory of Nyssa, whom he compares with writers of the Classical period and the Second Sophistic; comparisons between the novelists Heliodorus and Achilles Tatius, and between Euripides and George of Pisidia; allegorical interpretations of Homer; explanations of contemporary phrases; occasional literary essays often of a humorous or satirical nature; and poems (37 genuine ones survive) on a variety of topics and which range in length from 2 to more than 1400 lines. Linguistic studies are further seen in essays on etymologies and grammar. Numerous other treatises attest to his interest in jurisprudence, mathematics, medicine, mathematics, music, geography, etc. On the practical side he asserts that he experimented with mechanical devices described by the ancient inventor Heron of Alexandria, and in an encomium on wine claims that he successfully extracted a friend's tooth.

Unfortunately some of Psellos's works still remain unpublished and many are available only in poorly edited form in widely scattered books and periodicals. To remedy this situation, since 1985 the German publishing house of B.G. Teubner has been issuing a series of newly edited volumes in a uniform scholarly edition. Very little has been translated into any modern language. Nevertheless, enough is known of Psellos to call him the "Cicero of Byzantium" in his combination of a political life with one as an intellectual and writer; but the range of his interests was far more extensive than the Roman's.

A.R. LITTLEWOOD

See also Historiography

Biography

Born in Constantinople in 1018, Psellos was a pupil of John Mauropous. He became an adviser to Constantine IX Monomachos but had to resign in 1054, becoming a monk. He returned later to Constantinople but played little part in politics after 1059. He wrote extensively on many subjects, notably philosophy, literature, and theology. But he is best known as a historian of the period 976–1078. He died after 1081.

Writings

Scripta Minora, edited by E. Kurtz and F. Drexl, 2 vols, Milan: Vita e Pensiero, 1936–41

Mesaioniki Bibliotheke / Bibliotheca graeca medii aevi, edited by K.N. Sathas, vols. 4–5, 1874–76; reprinted Hildesheim: Olms, 1972

Chronographia

 Imperatori di Bisanzio: Cronografia, edited by Salvatore Impellizzeri and Ugo Criscuolo, translated into Italian by Silvia Ronchey, 2 vols., Milan: Valla / Mondadori, 1984

 The Chronographia, translated by E.R.A. Sewter, London: Routledge, and New Haven, Connecticut: Yale University Press, 1953; as *Fourteen Byzantine Rulers*, Harmondsworth and New York: Penguin, 1966

De Omnifaria Doctrina, edited by L.G. Westerink, Nijmegen: Centrale Drukkerij, 1948

The Essays on Euripides and George of Pisidia and on Heliodorus and Achilles Tatius, edited by Andrew R. Dyck, Vienna: Akademie der Wissenschaften, 1986

Philosophica Minora, edited by J.M. Duffy and D.J. O'Meara, 2 vols, Leipzig: Teubner, 1989–92

Poemata, edited by L.G. Westerink, Stuttgart and Leipzig: Teubner, 1992

Oratoria Minora, edited by A.R. Littlewood, Leipzig: Teubner, 1985

Orationes Panegyricae, edited by George T. Dennis, Leipzig: Teubner, 1994

Orationes Forenses et Acta, edited by George T. Dennis, Leipzig: Teubner, 1994

Orationes Hagiographicae, edited by Elizabeth A. Fisher, Leipzig: Teubner, 1994

Theologica, vol. 1, edited by Paul Gautier, Leipzig: Teubner: 1989

Further Reading

Angold, Michael, *The Byzantine Empire, 1025–1204: A Political History*, London and New York: Longman, 1984, especially pp. 43–57, pp. 77–85, pp. 88–90; 2nd edition, 1997

Beck, Hans-Georg, *Kirche und theologische Literatur im byzantinischen Reich*, Munich: Beck, 1959, especially pp. 538–42; 2nd edition, 1977

Hunger, Herbert, *Die hochsprachliche profane Literatur der Byzantiner*, 2 vols, Munich: Beck, 1978, especially vol. 1, pp. 372–82

Karahalios, G. "Michael Psellos on Man and His Beginnings", *Greek Orthodox Theological Review*, 18 (1973): pp. 79–96

Ljubarskij, J.N., *Michail Psell. Ličnost' i tvorčestvo* [Michael Psellos: The Man and His Works], Moscow, 1978

Wilson, N.G., *Scholars of Byzantium*, revised edition, London: Duckworth, and Cambridge, Massachusetts: Medieval Academy of America, 1996

Psycharis, Yannis 1854–1929

Philologist

Yannis Psycharis is one of the most important figures of Greece's intellectual history. His influence, which was radical and fundamental, concerns mainly the direction of the development of the Greek language. He entered Greece's intellectual history at a time when the young Greek nation was searching for its identity and when it was deeply divided on the question of which language form should be the official one. The options were (1) a more archaic Greek aspiring to restore the Attic, (2) the demotic, i.e. the common language of the people, and (3) katharevousa ("purified") an artificial compromise solution advocated by Adamatios Korais. From his first publication, *Études de philologie néo-hellénique* (1885), and for the rest of his life, Psycharis became the most dynamic and persuasive supporter of the demotic.

From early childhood Psycharis was exposed to a number of different languages: the demotic Greek from his grandmother and the servants, Italian from friends, French from his family and from the schools in Paris, and later German. He also studied ancient Greek and Latin as well as the katharevousa. This rich language experience made Psycharis linguistically sensitive and gave him a better perspective. He studied historical and comparative linguistics at the universities of Paris and Bonn (in spite of the fact that his father sent him to Bonn in order to study law), when the predominant linguistic theory was that of the Neogrammarians. This theory demonstrates scientifically that language change is not degeneration caused by ignorance, but rather a natural development brought about by natural phonetic laws supplemented by analogy and borrowing. His teachers were the eminent linguists Michel Breal, Arsène Damsteter, Louis Havet, Gaston Paris, and Émile Legrand. He also attended lectures given by the founder of structural linguistics, Ferdinand de Saussure, while his philosophical views were shaped by his father-in-law Ernest Renan, and by the European positivist Hippolyte Taine. Taine and especially Renan encouraged Psycharis to direct his studies to the Greek language to which Psycharis turned decidedly in 1885. Psycharis was also influenced by his friend, the great literary figure Victor Hugo, and was inspired by the work of Dante. Psycharis had a very successful career as professor of Modern Greek at the École des Langues Orientales of the Sorbonne after succeeding Legrand. He held this chair until his death in 1929 when he was succeeded by another important Hellenist, André Mirambel.

Psycharis was a complex, passionate, and ambitious personality. He was both French and Greek, but with his native Greek side stronger than the French. He was also a scientist with literary aspirations. His work consists of an impressive number of scientific analyses of the Greek language and its dialects as well as of poetry, short stories, and a novel.

Given his background and his temperament it is not surprising that Psycharis entered the linguistic battle of Greece on the side of the demotic. Of his works the one which had the greatest impact was *To Taxidi Mou* ("My Journey", 1888), which is a novel, a travelogue, a philosophical treaty, and most importantly a linguistic manifesto. In it Psycharis expresses most clearly the arguments in support of the demotic and the charges against katharevousa. The book also contains extremely lyrical sections on love as well as insightful comments on historical and current figures from the Greek intellectual scene, but most importantly it constitutes the first attempt to use the demotic in prose. This step was very daring because, in spite of the fact that the demotic had made inroads into poetry (the Ionian school earlier with its major representative Dionysios Solomos and the Athenian school during Psycharis's time with Kostis Palamas and Angelos Sikelianos), prose writers hesitated to use it. Even demoticists such as Emmanouil Roidis, who had advanced important scientific arguments for the demotic in his book *Ta Eidola* ("The Idols"), refrain from using it in their work. Thus *To Taxidi Mou* becomes a major turning point in Greece's literary development.

Psycharis's work and views on language met with a great deal of hostility in Greece. One of his critics was the linguist and first occupant of the chair of linguistics in Athens, George Chadzidakis, who, in spite of his early positive views on the demotic and his extensive studies of it, came to embrace katharevousa on the grounds that the demotic lacked a systematic grammar and richness of its vocabulary. Psycharis was also criticized for his extreme views on which forms should be considered licit in the modern Greek language. Because he believed that a language must operate on a pure system and that the only natural and thus legitimate system is that of the demotic on the grounds that it has emerged from the ancient language via natural diachronic phonetic laws, he proposed that katharevousa words which had entered the common language in their archaic morphology should be modified so as to follow the demotic rules. This purification programme in the direction of the demotic went against the sensibilities of most Greeks and Psycharis was attacked from many quarters. His supporters, who were referred to as *malliari* ("the hairy ones"), were ridiculed by attributing to them gross hyperdemoticisms. However, Psycharis also inspired a number of significant literary figures, the most important of whom was the highly respected poet Palamas, the leader of the Athens school of intellectuals whose demoticism found in Psycharis strong scientific support. Nikos Kazantzakis, later on, also considered Psycharis as his inspiration and his mentor on language matters.

Psycharis may not have been the only person to argue the case for the demotic. Indeed, Psycharis's arguments can be found almost intact in Solomos 50 years earlier. Nevertheless, Psycharis was the first to provide the demotic with a persuasive scientific basis and to demonstrate by his novel *To Taxidi Mou* that the demotic can be used in all forms of discourse.

IRENE PHILIPPAKI-WARBURTON

See also Language

Biography

Born in 1854 to a Greek family from Chios, Psycharis studied linguistics at the universities of Paris and Bonn and lived mostly in Paris where he became professor of Modern Greek at the Sorbonne. His chief contribution was to support demotic in the language question; but he also wrote poetry, short stories, and a novel. He died in 1929.

Further Reading

Holton, David, (editor) "O Psycharis kai to kinima tou dimotikismou" [Psycharis and the Demotic Cinema], *Mandatoforos*, 28 (December 1988), Psycharis special issue

Kriaras, Emmanouil, *Psycharis, Idees, Agones, O Anthropos* [Psycharis, Ideas, Struggles, Man], Athens, 1981

Mandilaras, B.G., "John Psichari and his Contribution to the Modern Greek Language" in *Studies in the Greek Language*, edited by B.G. Mandilaras, Athens, 1972

Ptolemies

Greek rulers of Egypt

The Ptolemies, Greek kings of Egypt, formed a dynasty that ruled the country from 305 BC to 30 BC. The Ptolemaic dynasty takes its name from the first such king, Ptolemy the son of Lagus, a Macedonian childhood friend and later general of Alexander the Great. Alexander conquered Egypt (then part of the Persian empire, which he set out to destroy) in 332 BC, during the early stages of his great expedition to the east. While in the country, he founded the city of Alexandria on the western branch of the Nile delta on the coast of the Mediterranean Sea. As Alexander passed on, the city was left in the hands of an architect and a financial administrator and it appears to have functioned as a Greek city from early on. It later became the royal capital of the Ptolemies, and among the greatest cities of the ancient world.

When Alexander died in 323 BC, his empire was divided for purposes of administration among his generals; Egypt passed into the control of this same Ptolemy, first as satrap (the Persian term for a provincial governor) and then as king. Ptolemy ousted the financial administrator Cleomenes, and finally had him killed for peculation in the grain trade. The country remained firmly under Ptolemy's control throughout the power struggles that took place among Alexander's successors during the next 20 years. Generally he concentrated on consolidating his power in Egypt, eschewing the territorial ambitions of his fellow successors in Asia and Greece. In 305 BC Ptolemy declared himself king, as did other successors in their own territories.

Ptolemy I Soter ("Saviour", an epithet he received after helping the island of Rhodes during a siege) established a secure kingdom, which for the next three centuries was to be ruled by his direct descendants. A mark of his political acumen was the fact that he was the only one of Alexander's successors not to die a violent death in battle. Greek civilization and culture came to Egypt, and settlers from Greece and Macedonia were actively encouraged. Alexandria and other cities in Egypt grew with the influx of the new ruling class. Certainly it can be maintained that a veneer of the Greek way of life was imposed on the native civilization of Egypt. To Ptolemy I's early patronage can probably be attributed the foundation of the famous library of Alexandria, in which the works of Greek literature were codified, copied, studied, and therefore preserved for posterity. Attached to the library was the museum ("Shrine of the Muses", the patronesses of intellectual arts), a residential study facility which attracted the finest Greek scholars and writers of their day. Alexandria became the capital of Greek culture, overtaking Athens as its centre.

Ptolemy I made his son co-regent in 285 BC, and the latter on his father's death in 283 became Ptolemy II (later to receive the cult title Philadelphus, "sister-loving"). During his long reign Ptolemy II presided over the growth of Alexandria into a famous and rich capital. The library and museum flourished, the wealth of Alexandria and its kings became proverbial among contemporary writers, and Ptolemy II amassed the greatest navy ever known in the Greek world. The largest political clouds on the horizon were Egypt's constant dispute with the Seleucid kings over Coele ("Hollow") Syria, the area known as the Middle East today. Two wars were fought over this territory in Ptolemy II's reign. In the mid-270s BC Ptolemy married his full sister Arsinoe (known as Arsinoe II Philadelphus), a clever woman who abetted his political schemes. This established the custom of royal brother–sister marriage in Ptolemaic Egypt, although at the time the Greeks were scandalized at the notion of incest.

Ptolemy III, known as Euergetes ("Benefactor"), succeeded his father in 246 BC. His reign is best known for the Third Syrian War, in which he invaded the Seleucid Syrian empire to support the claims of his sister Berenice Syra ("the Syrian") as queen to the Seleucid throne. (The Greek poet Callimachus wrote a poem called "The Lock of Berenice" to describe the dedication of a lock of hair by Ptolemy's queen, also named Berenice, to ensure his safe return from the war. The lock was, according to the poem, apotheosized into a constellation and subsequently spotted in the heavens. Although only fragments now remain of Callimachus' poem, it was translated into Latin by the Roman poet Catullus and is one of the most famous ancient poems.) The sister Berenice Syra had already been murdered when Ptolemy arrived. Although he captured some important cities in Asia Minor, this appears to have been the limit of Ptolemaic expansion.

So far the 3rd-century Ptolemaic empire had been characterized by good kings and stable government. With the accession of Ptolemy IV Philopator ("Father-loving") in 221 BC, the situation changed. Ptolemy IV's predilections were more for intellectual and dilettante pursuits than for politics, and he succumbed to the control of unscrupulous ministers. Although he won a great victory in the Fourth Syrian War at the Battle of Raphia in 217 BC, he failed to press for any concessions in the peace treaty. After Raphia, Egypt was shaken by severe internal revolts, and in 206 BC by the secession of Upper Egypt for 20 years. The lack of any positive foreign policy continued, and Ptolemy IV and his sister-wife were eventually murdered by his ministers in 205 BC, their deaths being kept secret for some time.

Ptolemy V Epiphanes ("Made Manifest") acceded to the throne as a child following his father's murder. Other Greek Hellenistic kingdoms unsuccessfully colluded to divide Egypt between them. The end of the Fifth Syrian War brought him a wife of the Seleucid house, the first of the Ptolemaic queens to be called Cleopatra. Ptolemy V was crowned in traditional Egyptian fashion at the old dynastic capital Memphis, south of Cairo. He was the first of the Ptolemies to be crowned pharaoh, although all had been depicted in native dress in statues and temple reliefs. The priestly decree of 196 BC which followed his coronation is the famous trilingual Rosetta Stone (now in the British Museum) written in outmoded Egyptian hieroglyphics, current Egyptian demotic, and Greek. The Greek part of the Rosetta decree enabled translators for the first time to decipher Egyptian hieroglyphics, one of the most important advances ever made in latterday understanding of ancient Mediterranean history.

Ptolemaic Egypt of the 2nd century BC was a fundamentally different world from that of the 3rd century BC. All the Hellenistic Greek empires were affected by the growing power of Rome and its increasing interest in the Greek east, and Egypt was no exception. Beginning with Ptolemy VI (a child

Ptolemies: hypostyle hall, nucleus of the temple of Horus begun in the reign of Ptolemy III at Edfu, Egypt

king like his father), who acceded to the throne in 180 BC, successive Ptolemies warred among themselves and collateral relatives, reunited, ruled jointly, and fell out again. The practice of incestuous marriage between siblings may have had adverse genetic effects over generations. Fraternal civil wars, exile, incest, murder, and even matricide are well-documented features of Egypt in the 2nd century BC. A prime example of the rulers of this period is Ptolemy VIII Euergetes II, also called Physkon ("Potbelly"). He succeeded his brother Ptolemy VI, killed his nephew Ptolemy VII (the son of his brother Ptolemy VI and sister), married Ptolemy VI's widow, who was also his own full sister, and concurrently married the daughter of his brother and sister (his double niece). He produced children by both wives, and also an illegitimate son. It is almost inconceivable to imagine how this complex marital situation functioned, with a man married at the same time to both his sister and her daughter, but inscriptions attest to a triple joint rule for at least some of the period, although civil war did break out intermittently.

After Ptolemy VIII the situation did not improve. Quarrelling brothers found that the temptation to invoke Rome to support their side against their rival proved too difficult to resist. No strong king emerged to bring the matter under control, and the Alexandrian populace, increasingly disgusted with the dynastic debacle, seized power. Finally, in the early 1st century BC either Ptolemy X or Ptolemy XI bequeathed the kingdom of Egypt to Rome, ensuring that the last half-century of Ptolemaic rule was inextricably entwined with the history of Rome.

The legitimate line of the Ptolemies died out with the deaths of Ptolemy IX, X, and XI. Ptolemy XI was actually established on the throne by the Roman dictator Sulla in 80 BC, but he soon murdered his stepmother (to whom he was then married), and was in turn himself murdered by the Alexandrian mob, who resented Rome's interference in their country as well as the murder of their queen. The succession passed to the illegitimate son of Ptolemy IX, who became Ptolemy XII, known as "Auletes" ("Flute player", indicating his frivolous tendencies). Auletes and his sister-wife Cleopatra V probably had six children together, among them the girl destined to become Cleopatra VII, the last Ptolemaic ruler of Egypt.

Far from secure on his throne, Ptolemy XII depended on the firm support of Rome. In 59 BC he paid a huge sum of money to be formally declared a friend and ally of Rome, but the wrath of the Alexandrian mob drove him into exile in 58 BC. Auletes fled to Rome to the protection of Pompey, one of the triumvirs (three generals who jointly ruled in Rome), and then to the city of Ephesus in Asia Minor. The two eldest daughters of Auletes appear to have ruled Egypt in his absence; one soon died, but the marriage of the other to the alleged son of Rome's Parthian enemy Mithradates VI caused consternation in Rome. From a Roman point of view, Ptolemy XII seemed preferable to his maverick second daughter; in 55 BC, with the help of Roman troops, he was escorted back to Egypt by Aulus Gabinius, the Roman governor of Syria, and reinstated on the throne. He had his second eldest daughter killed, and ruled until his death in 51 BC.

The eldest surviving child of Auletes was now Cleopatra, who was declared queen and who as Cleopatra VII Philopator ruled jointly with her younger brother Ptolemy XIII (then no more than a boy), whom she married in accordance with Ptolemaic custom. Ambitious ministers contrived to control the boy king and divide him from his sister, who even as a girl of 18 was showing signs of political cunning. Cleopatra was forced to flee Egypt. She then became involved in the consequences of the civil war between Pompey and his rival Julius Caesar. Caesar came to Egypt in pursuit of Pompey, and decided to support the claims of Cleopatra against her brother. The so-called Alexandrian War of 48–47 BC ensued in which Caesar and Cleopatra were victorious, and Ptolemy XIII killed. Cleopatra was reinstated on her throne by Caesar and married her younger brother Ptolemy XIV, ostensibly ruling jointly with him.

A legendary Nile cruise was then enjoyed by Cleopatra and Caesar, a married man some decades older than the queen. When he left Alexandria she was pregnant, and bore a son (probably Caesar's child) named Caesarion. Cleopatra spent the years 46–44 BC in Rome with Caesar and their son, but had no option but to return to Egypt after his assassination in 44 BC. Caesar's supporter Mark Antony and adopted son Octavian (later to become the Roman emperor Augustus) initially joined forces to defeat Caesar's assassins, but Antony and Octavian later became rivals for ultimate power in Rome. Antony's agreed control of the eastern part of Roman territory set the stage for Cleopatra's cataclysmic meeting with him in 41 BC, when he summoned her to meet him at Tarsus in Cilicia.

For 11 years Cleopatra was intermittently associated with Antony (who at the time was married to a succession of Roman women including, finally, Octavian's half-sister), and she bore him three children. Antony's political differences with Octavian, his liaison with a foreign queen deemed dangerous by the Romans, and Antony's and Cleopatra's apparent dynastic ambitions for their children meant that war was inevitable. Rome declared war upon Egypt. At the battle of Actium in 31 BC the combined forces of Antony and Cleopatra were defeated by Octavian, who pursued the couple back to Alexandria. With defeat now inescapable, Antony committed suicide, followed by Cleopatra some days later.

With the death of Cleopatra the Ptolemaic dynasty ended (her son Caesarion was killed, and the fates of her two sons by Antony are unknown). Egypt lost its independence and became a province of Rome until its conquest by the Arabs in AD 642. Despite the gradual decline of the Ptolemies from their glorious beginning in the 3rd century BC through to the petty internecine squabbles of the 1st century BC, Ptolemaic Egypt remained independent from Roman control longer than the other Hellenistic empires. The upper echelons of Greek society made it a Greek kingdom which can be credited with the creation, preservation, and transmission of Greek culture and ways of life.

E.E. RICE

See also Alexandria, Egypt

Further Reading

Bagnall, Roger S., *The Administration of the Ptolemaic Possessions outside Egypt*, Leiden: Brill, 1976

Bell, H. Idris, *Egypt from Alexander the Great to the Arab Conquest: A Study in the Diffusion and Decay of Hellenism*, Oxford: Clarendon Press, 1948

Bevan, Edwyn, *A History of Egypt under the Ptolemaic Dynasty*, London: Methuen, 1927

Bouché-Leclercq, A., *Histoire des Lagides*, 4 vols., Paris: Leroux, 1903–07

Bowman, Alan K., *Egypt after the Pharaohs 332 BC–AD 642: From Alexander to the Arab Conquest*, Berkeley: University of California Press, and London: British Museum, 1986

Bowman, Alan K., Edward Champlin, and Andrew Lintott (editors), *The Augustan Empire, 43 BC–AD 89*, Cambridge: Cambridge University Press, 1996 (*The Cambridge Ancient History*, vol. 10, 2nd edition), chapter 1

Ellis, Walter M., *Ptolemy of Egypt*, London and New York: Routledge, 1994

Foss, Michael, *The Search for Cleopatra*, London: O'Mara, 1997

Fraser, P.M., *Ptolemaic Alexandria*, 3 vols, Oxford: Clarendon Press, 1972

Gruen, Erich S., *The Hellenistic World and the Coming of Rome*, Berkeley: University of California Press, 1984

Longega, Gabriella, *Arsinoe II*, Rome: Bretschneider, 1968

Macurdy, Grace Harriet, *Hellenistic Queens: A Study of Woman-Power in Macedonia, Seleucid Syria, and Ptolemaic Egypt*, Baltimore: Johns Hopkins Press, and London: Oxford University Press, 1932

Rice, E.E., *The Grand Procession of Ptolemy Philadelphus*, Oxford and New York: Oxford University Press, 1983

Rice, E.E., *Cleopatra*, Stroud, Gloucestershire: Sutton, 1999

Smith, R.R.R., *Hellenistic Royal Portraits*, Oxford: Clarendon Press, and New York: Oxford University Press, 1988

Volkmann, Hans, *Cleopatra: A Study in Politics and Propaganda*, London: Elek, 1958

Walbank, F.W. *et al.* (editors), *The Hellenistic World*, Cambridge: Cambridge University Press, 1984 (*The Cambridge Ancient History*, vol. 7, part 1, 2nd edition)

Ptolemy

Astronomer and geographer of the 2nd century AD

Claudius Ptolemaeus (more usually known to English-speakers as Ptolemy) worked in Alexandria, and the astronomical observations he records suggest that he was active in the middle of the 2nd century AD. We know virtually nothing else about him.

Ptolemy's principal astronomical work, the *Mathematike Syntaxis* (Mathematical Treatise), is usually known in the modern world as the *Almagest*, which is derived from the Greek *megiste* ("greatest") with the Arabic definite article added to it, a name that bears witness both to the dominant position the *Almagest* established in ancient astronomy, and to its influence on later astronomers. The *Almagest* is the culmination of the attempts of Greek astronomers to create a mathematical model that would account for and predict the observed movements of the heavenly bodies (the fixed stars, the sun, the moon, and the five known planets), on the basis of regular movements in circles and taking the earth as the fixed point. This is indeed mathematically possible, but, looked at on this basis, the movements are very complex, and incorporate many very small variations, so that the weaknesses of any particular model might become apparent only when errors had accumulated over centuries of observation. Ptolemy's great achievement was to devise a model that not only produced a very close match to what was observed, but was also capable of modification and could be refined as new inconsistencies were identified. For this reason it was not seriously challenged for 1300 years; it was only in the 16th century that it was realized that the mathematics could be simplified enormously by taking the sun as the fixed point and having the earth as well as the planets move round it in orbits which were elliptical, not circular. Ptolemy builds principally on the work of Hipparchus, active some three centuries earlier, and uses the epicycles (orbits around the circumference of a circle whose centre is itself moving round the circumference of another circle) and eccentric circles (circles whose centre is not the sun) that were the basis of Hipparchus' system. Book 1 incorporates a Table of Chords which is in fact the equivalent of a modern sine table, and reveals considerable knowledge of trigonometry; Ptolemy certainly did not invent trigonometry (for it had already been used by Hipparchus), but his full and clear exposition of its principles is one of the foundations of the modern development of the subject. Book 2 deals with the geometry of the heavenly sphere; book 3 is on the sun; books 4 and 5 are on the moon; book 6 discusses eclipses; books 7 and 8 are on the fixed stars, and include a catalogue of stars; the rest of the work (books 9–13) deals with the complex problems of the movements of the planets. It is difficult to be sure which elements of the system described in the *Almagest* are Ptolemy's own, and which are derived from his predecessors (and indeed many of the observational data he uses must have come from earlier astronomers). It is, however, the sophistication and adaptability of the system that guaranteed that it would dominate subsequent astronomical thought, and for this Ptolemy can clearly claim the credit.

Almost as important and influential is his other main work, the *Geography*, an attempt to systematize and map everything known about the world at the time. We cannot tell whether Ptolemy himself ever produced such a map (the maps that are found in surviving manuscripts are certainly derived from Byzantine originals), but the material in the *Geography* is presented in such a way that drawing a map from it would be relatively easy. Ptolemy had predecessors in this (he himself acknowledges his dependence on Marinus of Tyre, who is otherwise unknown), but it is likely that the use of lines of latitude and longitude to define positions on the earth's surface may be Ptolemy's own original contribution. Impressive though the mathematical and geographical concepts in the work are, the factual basis on which the *Geography* rests was inadequate (and could hardly be otherwise, since for most of his information Ptolemy would have been dependent on the reports of others, and sometimes he would have had nothing to use but travellers' tales). Within the Roman empire his information is reasonably accurate, but further afield it is completely unreliable. Errors in some of the astronomical data on which he relies (observations of the time at which eclipses were observable in different places, for example) inevitably produce distortions. Nevertheless it was not until the 16th century that it was entirely superseded.

Less well known in the modern world, but almost as influential, was Ptolemy's *Harmonics*, which built on the work of Aristoxenus, and is most notable for the balance it strikes between empirical and mathematical approaches. It is an invaluable source of information on the views of earlier writers, and on ancient musical practice, and had great influence on the theory of music in the Middle Ages (through Boethius) and in the Renaissance.

Among Ptolemy's others works are: the *Tetrabiblos* (so called because it is in four books), an astrological work based on the principles of the *Almagest* and perhaps an attempt to put astrology on a scientific footing; the *Optics* in five books (surviving only in part, in a Latin version of an Arabic translation) which deals with reflection and refraction, and represents a substantial advance on Euclid's *Optics*; the *Planispherium* (surviving in Arabic and Latin translations) dealing with the geometry of the celestial sphere and in particular the system of stereographic projection of the heavenly sphere on to the plane of the equator; the *Analemma* (surviving only in Latin translation, with some fragments in Greek) on the orthogonal projection of the sphere on to a single plane; and the *Phaseis Aplanon Asteron* (of which only the second book survives) on the weather associated with the heliacal risings and settings of prominent stars. He is also said to have written a rather unimpressive minor philosophical work, *On the Criterion and the Ruling Faculty*. Proclus tells us that he tried to prove Euclid's controversial parallel postulate (Postulate 5) and gives us excerpts from the proof. Ptolemy is also credited with works on dimensions and on mechanical problems.

RICHARD WALLACE

See also Astronomy, Cartography, Geography

Summary

Ptolemy (Claudius Ptolemaeus) lived in Alexandria in the 2nd century AD but nothing else is known of his life. He wrote on astronomy (the *Almagest*), on geography, and on music (the *Harmonics*), and a variety of other subjects. His astronomical work went unchallenged until the 16th century.

Writings

Geography, translated and edited by Edward Luther Stevenson, New York: New York Public Library, 1932, reprinted Mineola, New York: Dover, Toronto: General Publishing, and London: Constable, 1991

Tetrabiblos, translated by F.E. Robbins, London: Heinemann, and Cambridge, Massachusetts: Harvard University Press, 1940 (Loeb edition; several reprints)

Almagest, translated by G.J. Toomer, London: Duckworth, and New York: Springer, 1984

Harmonics, translated by Jon Solomon, Leiden: Brill, 2000

Further Reading

Britton, John Phillips, *Models and Precision: The Quality of Ptolemy's Observations and Parameters*, New York: Garland, 1992

Grasshoff, Gerd, *The History of Ptolemy's Star Catalogue*, New York: Springer, 1990

Heath, Sir Thomas Little, *A History of Greek Mathematics*, 2 vols, Oxford: Clarendon Press, 1921, reprinted New York: Dover, 1981

Heath, Sir Thomas Little, *Greek Mathematics and Science*, Cambridge: Cambridge University Press, 1921

Neugebauer, O., *A History of Ancient Mathematical Astronomy*, Berlin and New York: Springer, 1975

Newton, Robert R., *The Origins of Ptolemy's Astronomical Tables*, Baltimore: Johns Hopkins University Applied Physics Laboratory, 1985

Smith, Mark A., *Ptolemy and the Foundations of Ancient Mathematical Optics*, Philadelphia: American Philosophical Society, 1999

Taub, Liba Chaia, *Ptolemy's Universe: The Natural, Philosophical, and Ethical Foundations of Ptolemy's Astronomy*, Chicago: Open Court, 1993

Purple

In ancient Greece the colour purple was an emblem of conspicuous consumption, a symbol of wealth and prestige. The most favoured dye was extracted from shellfish found in the Mediterranean, a process that was developed in the Near East by the Phoenicians around 1400 BC. They searched every coast known to them – from the Sea of Marmara to Asia Minor, from Greece to southern Italy, from Lebanon to north Africa – for murex shellfish, establishing factories and trade centres. Common species producing sea purple were *Murex trunculus*, with a blue-purple hue, and *Murex brandaris*, known to the Venetians as Turk's Blood because of its dark red stain. Producing purple was a painstaking and costly process despite cheap labour. Enormous quantities of the molluscs were needed for the potent colourfast pigment, which was extracted from the mucus glands of freshly killed sea snails. They yielded an almost black liquid called *anthos* (blossom) by Greek dye workers. Exposure to air and sunlight developed the purple hue. Modern experiments using 12,000 *Murex brandaris* and a high extraction technique have yielded 1.5 g of dye. Though it is difficult to equate ancient costs with modern currencies, the price of sea purple in Greece around 200 BC might be estimated at $28,000 a kilo. Dye workshops, with their spoil heaps of discarded shell fragments and bits of decaying shellfish, were neither clean nor savoury places of employment. The Greek geographer Strabo said that the Phoenician dye centres of Tyre and Sidon were so putrid that they were "unpleasant for residence". One could easily identify dye workers by their brightly coloured hands and arms as well as the smell that clung to their bodies and clothing.

The demand for purple exceeded its supply and in the ancient world cheaper and more plentiful substitutes were developed by diluting the true organic dye with water, urine, or honey, or by using animal or vegetable material that approximated to the desired colour. One such source came from the kermes insect called *coccus ilicis* which produced a colour between blue and red. There were industries devoted to the production of counterfeit purple from cheap materials such as mulberry juice, amaranth blossoms, and crushed bloodstone. Papyrus fragments found in Egypt containing dyeing recipes are based on four books attributed to the Greek philosopher Democritus, who reportedly dabbled in alchemy, converting substances that yielded the desired colour and lustre to textiles that would fool even connoisseurs of the coveted hue.

Ancient historians and poets wrote about purple textiles and their production. The most famous dye centre in Greece was at Hermione in Argolis; its textiles were in demand throughout the Mediterranean and coveted by the Persian court. Robes made at Hermione were entirely purple with a broad vertical white stripe. In Thessaly the workshops of Meliboea were praised by ancient writers for the quality of the dyes produced there. The town of Bulis in the Gulf of Corinth engaged more than half the population in harvesting and processing the molluscs. Spartan law prohibited dyers from the region as falsifiers of nature. Yet, with time, Pliny claimed that the shellfish along the Laconian coast and on the island of Cythera provided the best purple dye in the world. The islands of Euboea, Chios, Rhodes, Cos, and Cyprus yielded an excellent quality of purple. In the west the cities of Syracuse and Tarentum were also noted for their purple dye centres. In fact, a hill in Tarentum named Mount Testaccio is made up entirely of broken murex shells, both the *trunculus* and *brandaris* types.

The *Iliad* makes numerous references to garments of purple worn by kings and generals. In the *Odyssey* the hero Odysseus is given a cloak dyed sea purple by his wife, Penelope. Purple robes were deemed worthy offerings to Apollo at Delphi by king Croesus of Lydia, according to Herodotus. The poetry of Sappho relates the high esteem of purple garments as gifts for gods and goddesses. Greek lyric poets of the 5th century BC equated purple with the garments of heroes and gods. Parrhasius of Ephesus was notorious for his luxurious tastes including a purple cloak, which was considered to be well above his status as a painter. Plato, one of the Athenian moral majority, considered purple to be a decadent emblem of wealth and an effeminate article of clothing. However, despite the conservative views of Athenian philosophers, by the 4th century BC the use of purple was fairly widespread in Greece.

What had previously been a mark of Persian tyranny and decadence was transformed by Alexander's defeat of Darius in 330 BC into an accepted status symbol, when he exchanged his white Macedonian robes for the coloured trappings of royalty brought to the Mediterranean world by Phoenician tradesmen.

The Greeks did not associate the colour purple with the same mystical qualities as it enjoyed in the Near East. However, they too dressed their deities in purple and the ancient association of the colour with war persisted. Its psychological and aesthetic peculiarities were of the utmost importance. Greek generals wore purple and its significance was promoted in the dress of singers at festivals in honour of the gods. In the Classical and Hellenistic periods purple enjoyed a sacrosanct and noble status, adorning distinguished people. It was common, therefore, for great statesmen, actors, courtesans, and wealthy citizens to wear purple as a rather blatant show of power and status. A 4th-century BC grave of a woman in south Russia yielded some purple cloth that was painted on with a brush. The colour was frequently used as paint, rather than as a dye, and was also employed as a cosmetic.

The Romans, like the Macedonians, originally wore white or natural-coloured garments. However, over the course of time certain robes became associated with specific officials or priests for wear on festivals and other sacred occasions. One of these was the purple pallium of the priesthood. An old Roman family, named after Furius Purpureo, had the purpura shellfish as its insignia. Centres of international trade included the dye workshops of Greece, which were especially important in promoting a desire for the exotic and expensive colour. The first official documented to have worn a purple robe was an aedile named P. Lentulus in 63 BC. Purple stripes were worn on the togas of officials and eventually became the privilege of senators. As the colour became more popular, the purple trade flourished in Rome and dealt in many items, mainly textiles but also leather, ivory, pottery, marble, and stone. Porphyry, a deep purple stone imported from Egypt, was used as the material for sarcophagi for the royal family of Constantine the Great and for statuary of the Tetrarchs, to name a few examples.

In AD 383 an imperial decree was issued establishing a monopoly on the most costly purple dyes known as *blatta*. Only the emperor could wear robes dyed with the colour; private individuals who ignored the new law were charged with treason. Several late antique tombs, one from a necropolis near Nero's Circus in Rome and another from a Palmyrene tomb in Syria, have yielded shrouds and other garments woven in purple and gold threads. Entire garments have been preserved in the hot, dry climate of Egypt, in graves from the Fayum and Panopolis dating from the 3rd to the 8th centuries AD. Though Christianity had been established for centuries, the embroidered and painted scenes are direct quotations from the mythology of ancient Greece and Rome. According to modern research the colours were based on imitation purple extracts rather than genuine sea purple dyes.

During the Byzantine period the colour purple underwent a tremendous rise in prestige. The offspring of Byzantine emperors were born in the palace at Constantinople in a purple room that was swathed in purple drapes and were wrapped in purple swaddling clothes. The title *Porphyrogennetos* was added to the name of those born in this manner. Mosaics at San Vitale in Ravenna reveal the emperor Justinian and the empress Theodora with their respective attendants wearing gold-embroidered purple robes. Yet the tradition was not completely lost. The 6th-century Codex Porphyrius at Patmos with 33 purple parchment pages illuminated with silver and gold script can still be seen. Wilfred of Ripon, a late 7th-century Church Father, commissioned the four gospels on purple-dyed parchment. His altar at Ripon Minster in England was decorated in purple interwoven with gold thread, a custom that persisted in the medieval period for sacred purposes just as it had in antiquity. The crusaders were credited with bringing back to England some of the ancient art.

With the fall of Constantinople to the Turks in 1453 purple commerce ended and the secrets of its manufacture were lost until modern times. Pope Paul II permitted his cardinals to wear scarlet made with the kermes insect for their vestments, which was a great deal less expensive than true sea purple. The secret of the ancient craft was rediscovered in 1858 by a French zoologist named Henri Lacaze-Duthiers who was studying animal life in the Mediterranean. He noted that fishermen stained their clothing with the juice of a shellfish, initially yellow in colour, which turned a brilliant and colour-fast purple upon exposure to the sunlight. Earlier scholars had inquired into the problem of purple production based on the writings of Pliny and Aristotle but it took a scientific mind to correlate the methodology with the philology for a reproducible result. The chemical composition of purple was discovered in 1909 by Paul Friedlander of Vienna and since that time it has been possible to produce purple synthetically.

Purple still maintains its association as a colour used by priests and leaders of the Orthodox Church in Greece and other areas particularly during Lent, Advent, and other periods of preparation and mourning. Purple today is also identified with healing, fantasy, insanity, and passion throughout the western world.

VIRGINIA M. DA COSTA

Further Reading

Barber, Elizabeth Wayland, *Women's Work, The First 20,000 Years: Women, Cloth, and Society in Early Times*, New York: Norton, 1990

Born, Wolfgang, "Purple Shell-Fish" and "Purple in Classical Antiquity", *Ciba Review*, 4 (December 1937): pp. 106–17

Edey, Maitland E., *The Sea Traders*, New York: Time Life Books, 1974

Faber, G.A., "Dyeing in Greece", *Ciba Review*, 9 (May 1938): pp. 284–90

Jenkins, G.K., *Ancient Greek Coins*, 2nd edition, London: Seaby, 1990

Jensen, Lloyd B, "Royal Purple of Tyre", *Journal of Near Eastern Studies*, 22 (January–October 1963): pp. 104–18

Plant, Richard, *Greek Coin Types and Their Identification*, London: Seaby, 1979

Reinhold, Meyer, "On Status Symbols in the Ancient World", *Classical Journal*, 64 (October 1968–May 1969): pp. 300–04

Reinhold, Meyer, *History of Purple as a Status Symbol in Antiquity*, Brussels: Latomus, 1970

Ziderman, I. Irving, "Seashells and Ancient Purple Dyeing", *Biblical Archaeologist*, 53 (June 1990): pp. 98–101

Pydna

City in Macedonia

Pydna was a Greek city founded on the east coast of Pierian Macedonia on the Thermaic Gulf in the 7th–6th centuries BC. An acropolis site on the coast south of the modern village of Makriyialos is now thought to have been its original location. The city played an occasional role in political events in Greece in the 5th and 4th centuries BC, and, as such, is attested by Greek historians of the period. The 5th-century king Alexander I of Macedonia was known as the "Philhellene", but his interests inevitably clashed with those of Athens in northeastern Greece. When the Athenian general Themistocles fell out of favour and fled from Athens, he was given refuge at Pydna by Alexander in the early 460s BC before escaping to Asia. In the build-up to the Peloponnesian War and the revolt of Potidaea in 432 BC, Athens briefly besieged Pydna, hoping to establish a base there for operations in the north.

In 410 BC the Macedonian king Archelaus I captured Pydna and refounded the city as a Macedonian town some distance inland to the northwest, probably to guard it from attack from the sea. This was the site of Macedonian and Roman Pydna, near the modern village of Alonia. The inland site continued to be inhabited after the coastal site was reoccupied after Archelaus' death in 399 BC. In the late 360s BC, during the establishment of the Second Athenian Confederacy, Pydna was among the cities seized by the Athenian general Timotheus to provide bases against Macedon and Chalcidice, but the Macedonian king Philip II, in the course of his campaign to subdue Greece, captured Pydna, probably in 357 BC, along with other Greek cities along the Macedonian coast. Pydna was treated harshly and garrisoned.

At the end of the 4th century BC Pydna briefly took centre stage in the violent political struggles that followed the death of Alexander the Great. Alexander's Epirot mother, queen Olympias (the first wife of king Philip II of Macedon), was a formidable woman and a dangerous opponent. She championed the claim to the Macedonian throne of her grandson, Alexander's posthumous child, and, to this end, engineered the deaths of the rival claimant Philip III Arrhidaeus (an illegitimate son of Philip II) and his powerful wife Eurydice. She thereby incurred the fury of Cassander, the son of the old regent Antipater, who had supported Philip III as the legitimate king. In the face of Cassander and a large army, in 317 BC Olympias and her royal retinue went to Pydna, whereupon the town was besieged by land and sea. Relieving forces from outside were persuaded to abandon Olympias, and many inside Pydna deserted to Cassander when a grievous famine incapacitated the besieged. In the spring of 316 BC Olympias surrendered to Cassander and was condemned to death in absentia by the general assembly of the Macedonians. Although she refused proffered exile, and Cassander's troops were too awestruck to kill her as ordered, Olympias was eventually murdered at Pydna by the relatives of some of her past victims. (The story of the siege of Pydna and the death of Olympias is told in Diodorus Siculus, 19. 35–36, 49–51.)

Three important inscriptions of a later date were found in the vicinity of Pydna which refer to the tomb of Olympias and the nearby burial of descendants of the Aeacidae, the royal house of Epirus to which Olympias herself belonged. These texts indicate, surprisingly, that members of this family were living at Pydna in the 2nd century BC after the Roman conquest of Macedonia (see below), and that the tomb of Olympias was revered. Pydna therefore occupies a complex place in the Hellenic tradition: on the one hand, it witnessed the first of many brutal deaths of Alexander the Great's immediate family, but, on the other, it sheltered Alexander's maternal Epirot descendants long after the Antigonid dynasty of Macedonian kings had been destroyed by Rome.

The tomb of Olympias has never been found, and a suitable historical context for its construction can only be surmised, but burials in typical Macedonian chamber tombs are known from this area (for example the so-called Tomb of Pydna, an elaborate multiroomed chamber tomb probably dating from the end of the 3rd to the beginning of the 2nd century BC).

Pydna is best known as the site of the great battle between the forces of the Macedonian king Perseus (son of Philip V) and the Roman general Lucius Aemilius Paullus in June 168 BC. The decisive Roman victory, in which some 20,000 Macedonians were killed and some 11,000 taken prisoner, brought to an end the Third Macedonian War and had catastrophic consequences for the future of Macedonia and northern Greece. Perseus and his family were eventually captured and sent to Rome. The king marched in chains in Paullus' triumph and died soon after in captivity, thus ending the Antigonid dynasty of Macedonian kings. The vast wealth of Macedonia, especially the royal palace at Pella, was plundered and taken to Rome to be paraded in the three-day triumph (see Plutarch's *Life of Aemilius Paullus*, 30–35, for an account of the staggering number of art treasures borne along on waggons). Paullus embarked on a "reign of terror" by allowing Epirus to be sacked (as many as 150,000 citizens were enslaved) and condoning other reprisals, even as he himself embarked upon an archaeological tour of Greece. The kingdom of Macedonia lost its independence as a nation, was divided into four republics with elected magistrates, and paid heavy taxes to Rome. It became a Roman province in 146 BC.

The aftermath of the Battle of Pydna had two unexpected consequences for the spread of the Hellenic tradition. The first was that a young man named Polybius, son of Lycortas of Megalopolis in Achaea, was taken to Rome among the hostages deported after Pydna and became a close friend of the influential Roman Scipio Aemilianus, in whose circle he travelled widely and became privy to Roman political life at a high level. Polybius returned to Greece in 146 BC and became a distinguished historian. His *Histories* cover the years 264–146 BC (focusing on the period 220–168 BC) when Rome established its control over most of the inhabited world, which Polybius – given his background – saw as a unique event and sought to explain. His lucid narrative remains the main historical source for the period when Rome became master of the Greek east.

The spread of the Greek artistic tradition was also a by-product of the Battle of Pydna. Plunder brought to Rome made the Roman people aware of masterpieces of Greek art in the media of bronze and marble statuary, painting, and toreutic art. Greek art had a profound effect on the style of Roman art because of this contact. It is perhaps a historical irony that Paullus commandeered for a statue of himself a pillar erected at Delphi that was originally intended for a statue of Perseus. It was topped with a bronze equestrian statue of himself above a sculpted frieze depicting a battle between Romans and Macedonians, that is, a real rather than a mythological battle. The Greek tradition of this type of monument was adapted by the Roman general for his own purposes, and was perhaps the first in the great tradition of Roman historical reliefs.

The site of Pydna at Kastro continued to be occupied in Byzantine times (known then as Kitros; the modern village of Kitros is nearby). Fortifications dated originally from the time of Justinian, and there are remains of early Christian churches and a later 10th-century basilica. It was captured by the Franks in the early 13th century, and finally by the Turks at the end of the 14th century.

E.E. RICE

See also Macedonia

Summary

A city in Macedonia founded in the 7th–6th centuries BC, Pydna was the site of the death in 316 BC of Olympias, mother of Alexander the Great. It was also the site of a battle in 168 BC at which Macedonian forces were decisively defeated by the Romans, ending the independence of Macedonia.

Further Reading

Borza, Eugene N., *In the Shadow of Olympus: The Emergence of Macedon*, Princeton, New Jersey: Princeton University Press, 1990

Derow, P.S., chapter 9 in *Rome and the Mediterranean to 133 BC*, edited by A.E. Astin *et al.*, Cambridge: Cambridge University Press, 1989 (*The Cambridge Ancient History*, vol. 8, 2nd edition)

Edson, C.F., "The Tomb of Olympias", *Hesperia*, 18 (1940): pp. 84–95

Errington, R. Malcolm, *A History of Macedonia*, Berkeley: University of California Press, 1990

Gruen, Erich S., *The Hellenistic World and the Coming of Rome*, Berkeley: University of California Press, 1984

Hammond, N.G.L., *A History of Macedonia*, vol. 1: *Historical Geography and Prehistory*, Oxford: Clarendon Press, 1972

Hammond, N.G.L. and G.T. Griffith, *A History of Macedonia*, vol. 2: *550–336 BC*, Oxford: Clarendon Press, 1979

Hammond, N.G.L., "The Battle of Pydna", *Journal of Hellenic Studies*, 104 (1984): pp. 31–47

Hammond, N.G.L. and F.W. Walbank, *A History of Macedonia*, vol. 3: *336–167 BC*, Oxford: Clarendon Press, 1988

Hammond, N.G.L., *The Macedonian State: Origins, Institutions and History*, Oxford: Clarendon Press, and New York: Oxford University Press, 1989

Sakellariou, M.B. (editor), *Macedonia: 4000 Years of Greek History and Civilization*, Athens: Ekdotike Athenon, 1983; reprinted 1995

Pylos

City (or cities) in the western Peloponnese

Pylos now refers to four distinct places in the western Peloponnese, largely as a result of the attempts to identify the site of Nestor's palace as described by Homer. These are discussed from north to south.

In 1907 the German archaeologist Wilhelm Dörpfeld discovered and excavated three tholos tombs and the ruins of a building at *Kakovatos*, *c.*40 km south of Pirgos. He therefore concluded the site was Pylos as, following Strabo, many Alexandrian scholars had postulated that the Homeric site lay in Triphylia, an area also notable for the sandy beaches characterized in the epics.

The site at *Ano Englianos* (50 km south of Kiparissia) was identified in 1938 by a Hellenic–American expedition and excavated in 1939 and 1952–64 by Carl Blegen of the University of Cincinnati. A Mycenaean palace on a low hill with associated tholos and chamber tombs has been uncovered. It is the most comprehensible of all the Mycenaean palaces, though it is less impressive with its mudbrick walling and low elevation. The most important discovery was an archive room beside the entrance containing over 1000 tablets inscribed in the Linear B script; others and other types of administrative records were found elsewhere on the site. The palace was decorated with wall paintings in fresco; it had a central hearth in the megaron surrounded by four fluted columns in wood with clay chimney above. In the private wing was a bathroom with small tub. Copious evidence of pottery in functional contexts as well as stores of wine and oil contributes with the texts to a still unique picture of Mycenaean elite life. There are remains of a lower town at the base of the hill but little excavation has been carried out here. Since 1990 further study of the site and the region in general has been carried out by the American School of Classical Studies. Finds are to be seen in a small museum at nearby Chora with the most important items in the National Museum in Athens.

The rocky promontory of *Koryphasion* lies at the north end of the bay of Navarino. This bay (like that of Methone to the south) was, and still is, an important feature in the safe navigation of the west coast of the Peloponnese and the history of the area reflects this importance. Heinrich Schliemann in 1888 (after a preliminary visit in 1874) investigated the acropolis area, which was known as Old Pylos, and the cave of Nestor at the north end. In 1896 a French expedition also undertook some exploration in the cave. Ancient pottery (Middle Helladic to Roman) came to light. The small rounded bay to the north may have been the Mycenaean harbour. The southern tip of the promontory was fortified in 425 BC by the Athenians under Demosthenes and Cleon in order to cut off the Spartan contingent on the island of Sphacteria which closes the large southern bay on the west. The engagement is described in detail by Thucydides (4. 3ff.) and by Peter Green in a modern semifictional account. One of the shields, captured from the Spartans on their surrender after the dramatic siege of 72 days and later dedicated in the Stoa Poikile in Athens, came to light in the excavations of the Athenian Agora and is displayed in the Agora Museum.

From the 6th to 9th century AD the site was the home of a colony of Slavs or Avars from which it acquired the name of Avarinos or Navarino as the bay has become known. In the late 13th century AD Nicholas II of St Omer built a castle, generally known at this period as Port-de-Jonc, on the acropolis which featured in various engagments thereafter. In 1423 the castle was purchased by the Venetians. After the northern entry to the bay began to silt up and Don John of Austria bombarded the site in 1572, a new castle (Neokastro) was built on the southeast side of the bay overlooking the southern entry and what became known as Palaikastro diminished in importance. It was taken by the Turks in 1501. Morosini recaptured it in 1686 and effected a few repairs.

The charming modern Neoclassical town, also known as *Pylos*, was built by the French in 1829. It lies at the foot of Mount St Nicholas on which stands the handsome and well-preserved Neokastro, built by the Turks in 1572. Plans have been put forward for several museums to be organized within the castle, notably one for underwater archaeology. In 1825 Ibrahim Pasha made Neokastro the centre of his operations and proceeded to devastate the province of Messenia. Two years later, under the Treaty of London, Britain, France, and Russia agreed to demand an armistice as a preliminary to a settlement of the Greek revolt against the Turks. After some months of unsatisfactory demands and manoeuvres, a letter of expostulation was sent to Ibrahim asking him the refrain from his actions against the Greeks on land. When it was returned with the manifestly false answer that he had left Navarino, the three admirals (Codrington, de Rigny, and Heiden) decided to sail into the bay on 20 October. The combined allied fleet consisted of 26 vessels, the Turkish fleet of 18 larger vessels and a mass of smaller ones, totalling about 80. Following a small incident in which a Turkish fire ship opened fire, a full-scale battle ensued. By the end of the day the Turks had lost over 50 vessels and over 6000 lives. No single allied ship was lost. European reaction to the victory was mixed from jubilation to puzzlement: it was referred to in the king's speech to parliament of the following year (the work of the Duke of Wellington) as "an untoward event". It did however lead directly to the evacuation of the Morea by the Turks and the full establishment of an independent Greece.

ELIZABETH FRENCH

See also Independence (War of), Mycenaeans, Peloponnesian War

Summary

The ancient settlement of Pylos has been identified with four different places in the western Peloponnese: Kakovatos, 40 km south of Pirgos, site of tholos tombs; Ano Englianos, 50 km south of Kiparissia, site of a Mycenaean palace; Koryphasion, at the north end of the bay of Navarino, site of an ancient acropolis; and Pylos, the modern town. The area was the site of famous battles in 425 BC (on the island of Sphacteria) and 1827 (in the bay of Navarino).

Further Reading

Blegen, Carl W. and Marion Rawson, *The Palace of Nestor at Pylos in Western Messenia*, 3 vols, Princeton, New Jersey: Princeton University Press, 1966–73

Mylonas, George E., *Mycenae and the Mycenaean Age*, Princeton, New Jersey: Princeton University Press, 1966

Pyrrho *c.*365–275 BC

Philosopher

Pyrrho of Elis is regarded as the founder of Greek scepticism. He is said to have studied with a certain Bryson and the Democritean Anaxarchus with whom he travelled to India in the campaign of Alexander the Great. His acquaintances with the "gymnosophists" and the "magi" are said to have influenced his thought. Pyrrho did not leave any writings, but some knowledge about his teaching comes from his disciple Timon of Phlius (*c.*325–235 BC), a literary man who wrote satires (*Silloi*) parodying all dogmatic philosophers and contrasting them with Pyrrho. Pyrrho did not establish a school of philosophy in the institutional sense. There were no successors after Timon, although ancient doxography tried to invent a succession down to Aenesidemus (1st century BC). Pyrrho's teaching as transmitted by Timon enjoyed a revival several centuries later with Aenesidemus and Sextus Empiricus (2nd century AD), who systematized it. Our main sources for his philosophy are a substantial *Life* by Diogenes Laertius (9. 61–108), fragments from the Peripatetic Aristocles' *History of Philosophy* (1st century AD?) preserved by Eusebius (*Praeparatio Evangelica*, 14. 8), and the writings of Sextus Empiricus (especially his *Outlines of Pyrrhonism*).

However, these later sources do not always represent Pyrrho's teaching and there is some evidence that his later followers imposed a certain interpretation on his philosophy. Yet, given the state of evidence, it is extremely difficult to distinguish Pyrrho's original teaching from the later interpretations of it.

Pyrrho was primarily a moralist. His aim was to live a life of tranquillity (*ataraxia*). He apparently argued that everything was utterly indifferent. He maintained that there is no difference between good and bad things, just and unjust, and the like, and argued that it is only a matter of convention or habit that people believe things to be good or bad. Pyrrho was concerned to refute any natural basis for evaluating a thing as good or bad, but apparently he did not make the further move to dispute the possibility of knowing whether things are good or bad. On the contrary, he dogmatically asserted that things are neither good nor bad, and that they are only designated as such by convention. He seems to have expressed his ideas using a language such as this: "*x* is no more [*ou mallon*] this than *y*." Using such a non-committal language (already used by Democritus), he avoided making any value judgements. Yet this is not tantamount to the sceptic suspension of judgement (*epoche*) with which he was later accredited. Although Pyrrho may have distinguished sharply between *x appearing y* and *x being y*, he was concerned with the evaluation of things and not with the perceptual experience of them, i.e. with the question of the possibility of knowing them or with the nature or their apparent characteristics; and as far as their evaluation was concerned he found them indifferent. Dispensing with value judgements, Pyrrho liberated himself from all the anxieties that conventional value judgements impose on us and thus he was able to live a life of tranquillity and lack of affection (*apatheia*). Pyrrho's aim of achieving detachment from human concerns is confirmed by a number of anecdotes. He took no precautions against dogs, carts, and precipices and he was always saved by his friends. Again Pyrrho did not seem to act in this way because he disputed the evidence of the senses but because he considered that things were indifferent to him and that whatever might happen was of no account to him. Although Pyrrho found it hard to be entirely indifferent, he did attain a remarkable degree of imperturbedness.

So Pyrrho's main thesis was apparently neither epistemological nor metaphysical but primarily ethical. Yet his attitude was interpreted as a sceptical one by his followers, Timon, and by the later Pyrrhonians who relied on Timon. Timon reports that Pyrrho argued that things in themselves are indifferent, unmeasurable, and inarbitrable. Hence our perceptions are neither true nor false, their testimony is unreliable, and we should think that something is no more this than that. The moral to draw was that we should not commit ourselves to views about the nature of things on the basis of our senses since things are elusive and undetermined. This attitude may lead us first to speechlessness and then to imperturbability, which finally makes up a good life – admirably achieved by Pyrrho. Timon obviously understands the "no more this than that" formula as concerning the trustworthiness of perceptions and beliefs. According to this interpretation indifference is a result of diffidence to perceptions and beliefs and not to the value of things themselves. This interpretation is patterned on the main idea underlying the history of Greek scepticism and it could easily be imposed on Pyrrho's teaching. Yet there might well have been aspects of Pyrrho's teaching that encouraged such an interpretation.

Pyrrho's scepticism enjoyed a revival with Aenesidemus, who seceded from the sceptical Academy under Philo of Larissa and appealed to Pyrrho's radical scepticism because he wanted to restore scepticism in its pure form, castigating Academic scepticism, which tended to become more and more dogmatic. With Aenesidemus and later Pyrrhonians the focus shifts clearly to epistemology. Aenesidemus disputed the anecdotes about Pyrrho's life and maintained that Pyrrho's philosophy was based on suspension of judgement. He also added that suspension of judgement may lead us to pleasure too. Aenesidemus is well known for the systematization of the Pyrrhonian arguments against holding a belief in ten modes. By means of these modes the Pyrrhonian sceptic would be able to question any dogmatic claim or demonstration and to show how ill-founded they were.

Many Pyrrhoneans after Aenesidemus were physicians of the empirical school of medicine. Most prominent among them was, of course, Sextus Empiricus. Sextus is for us today the major exponent of Pyrrhonian scepticism, but it is evident that he relies much on Aenesidemus. In his main expository work of Pyrrhonian philosophy, the *Outlines of Pyrrhonism*, Sextus makes interesting distinctions between the Pyrrhonian and the other philosophies and he devotes a long section on the significance of standard sceptical phrases.

Pyrrhonian scepticism, like all forms of scepticism, was polemicized by Christian intellectuals in the Middle Ages since it undermined Christian dogma. Photios obviously had access to some of Aenesidemus' works and he reports on them in his *Bibliotheca*. In the Renaissance Pyrrhonian scepticism, like most ancient philosophical systems, enjoyed a revival, but there is little trace of a considerable impact on modern Greek philosophy. Recently, though, Pyrrhonian scepticism has been found appealing and modern Greek intellectuals such as Nikos Demou have stressed that it offers an honest alternative to philosophical discussions.

GEORGE E. KARAMANOLIS

See also Scepticism

Biography

Born *c.*365 BC, Pyrrho of Elis was a pupil of Bryson and Anaxarchus. With Anaxarchus he travelled to India with Alexander the Great, where he was influenced by local sages. Pyrrho returned to Elis and lived quietly. He is regarded as the founder of scepticism but he left no writings and did not establish a school. Knowledge of his teaching derives from the writings of his pupil Timon of Phlius. He died in 275 BC.

Writings

Testimonianze, edited by F.D. Caizzi, Naples: Bibliopolis, 1981
In *The Hellenistic Philosophers*, edited and translated by A.A. Long and D.N. Sedley, 2 vols, Cambridge and New York: Cambridge University Press, 1987 (text, translation, and philosophical commentary)

Further Reading

Frede, Michael, "The Skeptics' Beliefs" in *Essays in Ancient Philosophy*, Oxford: Clarendon Press, and New York: Oxford University Press, 1987, pp. 179–200
Frede, M., Scepticism entry in *Routledge Encyclopedia of Philosophy*, edited by Edward Craig, London: Routledge, 1998
Hankinson, R.J., *The Sceptics*, London and New York: Routledge, 1995
Long, A.A., *Hellenistic Philosophy: Stoics, Epicureans, Sceptics*, 2nd edition, London: Duckworth, and Berkeley: University of California Press, 1986

Pyrrhus 319–272 BC
Ruler of Epirus

Pyrrhus became king of the Molossians and created the kingdom of Epirus. As ruler of Epirus, he became one of the most respected military leaders of the Hellenistic age. He was revered in his own lifetime and later in antiquity for his expertise and military knowledge: Hannibal described him as the greatest of generals in both experience and ability. He is most renowned for his military successes which he achieved at the expense of heavy casualties to his own army – the so-called "Pyrrhic victory". However, while his career as a general and king was spectacular, he failed to fulfil the potential he promised. He fought against the rising power of Rome in southern Italy and in Greece against the Macedonian monarchs Demetrius Poliorcetes and Antigonus Gonatas. His career falls into three main phases: the establishment of his power in Greece (307–285 BC), his expedition in southern Italy (285–274 BC), and his return to and death in Greece (275–272 BC).

Pyrrhus, the son of Aeacides and Phthia, was born to a line that traced its ancestry back to Neoptolemus, son of Achilles. His career became wrapped up in the intrigues and intricacies of the early Hellenistic era known as the period of the successors. He became king of the Molossians in 307/06 BC while still only 12 years old when he was installed by Glaucias, king of the Illyrians, but he reigned for only five years before being expelled by Cassander in 302 BC.

In these early years Pyrrhus was embroiled in some way or other with Demetrius Poliorcetes, whom Deidameia, his sister, had married in 303 BC and with whom he sought refuge. In 302 BC he served as a lieutenant to Demetrius Poliorcetes and Antigonus Monophthalmus on what was to be the losing side at the Battle of Ipsus in 301 BC, but remained loyal to Demetrius, acting as caretaker in Greece.

In 299 BC Pyrrhus was handed over as a political hostage to Ptolemy I. He married Antigone, the daughter of Berenice and Ptolemy I, and with the support of Egypt and Agathocles, tyrant in Syracuse, in the early 290s BC he became co-regent of Epirus with Neoptolemus. He soon removed his co-regent and consolidated his Epirot kingdom. He founded a city named Berenice (modern Preveza) in honour of his mother-in-law. On his wife's death, Pyrrhus married Larnassa, daughter of Agathocles, and received the islands of Corfu and Leucas as a dowry. A series of additional political marriages secured further territory around Epirus.

Following his success against Demetrius Poliorcetes' lieutenant Pantauchus, Pyrrhus added territory to his kingdom. He was given the title "Eagle" by the Epirots and began to decorate his helmet with a high crest and goat's horns at the side. The rift between Demetrius – who had declared himself king of Macedon – and Pyrrhus was widened by the death of Deidameia. In addition, Demetrius married Pyrrhus' estranged wife Larnassa, and took control of Corfu.

The rising power of Demetrius was met by the concerted efforts of Pyrrhus and other Hellenistic kings in the early 280s BC. Ptolemy sailed to Greece "to persuade the cities there to revolt", Lysimachus invaded the north of Macedonia from Thrace, and Pyrrhus attacked southern Macedonia (Verroia). The kingdom of Macedon was partitioned by Pyrrhus and Lysimachus, but Pyrrhus' successes were short-lived. The Aetolians shifted their support to Lysimachus, and Ptolemy ended his aid to Pyrrhus, who was forced to withdraw back to Epirus.

In 284 BC a request came from the people of Tarentum (and other Greek cities in Italy) to Epirus for help against Rome. Pyrrhus took up the invitation and fought for the cause of Greek cities in southern Italy. Early success at Heraclea with an army of infantry, cavalry, and elephants secured the support not only of Greek cities in Italy but also Italian tribes, the Bruttians, Lucanians, and Samnites. Pyrrhus then marched on Rome. Another victory was secured at Asculum in 279 BC, but again with some loss on the Greek side. Before he was able to consolidate these successes, he was distracted by another appeal, this time from the city of Syracuse in Sicily. There he fought in 278 BC the allies of Rome, the Carthaginians, and the Mamertines. In 276 BC Pyrrhus was recalled to southern Italy, was defeated by Rome in 275 BC, and returned to Epirus with a severely depleted army. He left a garrison in Tarentum but was never to return.

In Greece Pyrrhus embarked on a campaign in Macedonia in 274 BC before marching into the Peloponnese in 273 BC to respond to an appeal from Cleonymus. At Megalopolis he declared that he was fighting to liberate the Greek cities from Antigonus Gonatas, king of Macedon. His intentions are doubted by the ancient sources. Whatever Pyrrhus' plans, they were ended abruptly in 272 BC. During an attack on the city of Argos, he was killed: struck on the head by a tile thrown from the roof, he was beheaded by one of Antigonus' men.

Pyrrhus fought on behalf of the Greek cause for the cities of southern Italy and Sicily and had tried to liberate Greek cities from the king of Macedon, Antigonus Gonatas. At the time of his death he had established Epirus as a major power, and he had transformed Dodona into a major cultural outpost. However, his lasting legacy to Hellenic culture is his military exploits. His prowess as a military leader went before him, but his inability to secure victory without heavy losses has outshone his strategic and tactical expertise.

GRAHAM OLIVER

Biography

Born in 319 BC, Pyrrhus became king of the Molossians at the age of 12 but was expelled by Cassander in 302. He served Demetrius Poliorcetes but in 299 was given as a hostage to Ptolemy I. With the help of Agathocles of Syracuse he became ruler of Epirus and founded Berenice (modern Preveza). In 284 he supported the Greek cities of south Italy against Rome but was defeated in 275. He died at Argos in 272 BC.

Further Reading

Brown, Blanche R., *Royal Portraits in Sculpture and Coins: Pyrrhos and the Successors of Alexander the Great*, New York: Peter Lang, 1995

Garonfalias, Petros, *Pyrrhus, King of Epirus*, London: Stacey, 1979

Hackens, Tony *et al.* (editors), *The Age of Pyrrhus*, Providence, Rhode Island: Center for Old World Archaeology and Art, Brown University, 1992

Hammond, N.G.L., *Epirus: The Geography, the Ancient Remains, the History, and the Topography of Epirus and Adjacent Areas*, Oxford: Clarendon Press, 1967

Hammond, N.G.L. and F.W. Walbank, *A History of Macedonia*, vol. 3: *336–167 BC*, Oxford: Clarendon Press, 1988

Lévêque, Pierre, *Pyrrhos*, Paris: Boccard, 1957

Plutarch, *The Age of Alexander: Nine Greek Lives*, translated by Ian Scott-Kilvert, Harmondsworth: Penguin, 1973

Walbank, F.W. *et al.* (editors), *The Rise of Rome to 220 BC*, Cambridge University Press, 1989 (*The Cambridge Ancient History*, vol. 7, part 2, 2nd edition)

Pythagoras

Philosopher and mathematician of the 6th century BC

It is extraordinarily difficult to make any definite statement about Pythagoras, although he, and the philosophical tradition he founded, was clearly of the greatest importance in the development of Greek thought. He was born in Samos in the first half of the 6th century BC, son of Mnesarchus, a gem engraver. He moved to Croton in southern Italy around the middle of the 6th century, supposedly to escape the tyranny of Polycrates, and there formed a sort of society of followers ("Pythagoreans"), which involved itself in the politics of the Greek cities of Italy until there was a violent reaction, the Pythagoreans were massacred, and Pythagoras was driven from Croton; he died an exile in Metapontum. Nevertheless, there is clear evidence that in some places the Pythagoreans remained politically active in Italy well into the 4th century BC. The earliest reports represent him (sometimes in a negative sense) as a sage and wonderworker; he was reputed to have had a golden thigh, the ability to be in two places at once, and

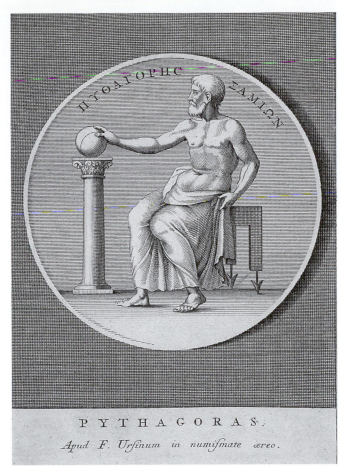

Pythagoras

Apud F. Urſinum in numiſmate æreo.

Pythagoras

the power of prophecy. By the time that reasonably reliable reports become available (from the late 5th century BC onwards), he has already become a rather shadowy figure to whom a great variety of ideas could be attributed (and the situation is further confused by the reported practice of his followers of attributing all of their own ideas to him); Aristotle, who wrote an account (now lost) of Pythagoras, in his surviving works prefers to discuss "the Pythagoreans" rather than Pythagoras himself. Nevertheless, the fact that there was a group of serious thinkers who called themselves Pythagoreans (e.g. Philolaus, who composed a cosmology of which fragments survive, and Archytas, who did impressive work in mathematics and harmonics) confirms that Pythagoras' contribution to the development of thought, whatever it was in detail, was substantial and fruitful.

The ideas attributed to Pythagoras fall into two quite distinct categories (and indeed some ancient writers believed that this meant that he had two different sets of followers). First, he is said to have to have been a religious teacher, whose doctrines were based on the idea that souls migrate to new bodies (both human and animal) after death, and that by observing a series of rules and prohibitions the believer may achieve a better reincarnation in future lives. The most notorious of these rules were vegetarianism and abstinence from beans, and among others mentioned by various authorities are not picking up things that fall from the table, not touching a white cock, and not breaking a loaf of bread; they were as

inexplicable in antiquity as they are now, and various attempts were made to interpret them allegorically as containing philosophical and moral truths.

It is, however, for his supposed contributions to mathematics and science that Pythagoras is remembered today. He and his followers are credited with making a crucial contribution to the early development of Greek mathematics, but it is very difficult to say precisely what this was, since it is to non-Pythagoreans (such as Thales and Anaximander) that most actual mathematical developments are attributed; the story that Pythagoras discovered the famous proof of the proposition that the square on the hypotenuse of a right-angled triangle is equal to the sum of the squares on the other two sides, the so-called theorem of Pythagoras, is found no earlier than Plutarch, who wrote in the 1st and 2nd centuries AD quoting one Apollodorus as his source (Plutarch tells us that on making the discovery Pythagoras sacrificed an ox to celebrate), and it is probable that the proof most often used today was devised by Euclid (*Elements*, 1. 47) rather than Pythagoras. Aristotle reports that the Pythagoreans claimed that "things are number" (though he could not understand what they meant by it), and certainly number played an important part in the Pythagorean picture of the world. Pythagoras is said to have discovered that the concordant musical intervals are produced by strings under the same tension whose lengths are in simple numerical ratios involving the first four integers (1:2 produces the octave, 3:2 the fifth, and 4:3 the fourth). Whether or not this is true (the reports come only in late authors), it began a process of applying the principles of ratio and harmony to the structure of the cosmos. So, the first four integers, represented by dots and arranged in a triangle, and their sum, 10, were thought to have special significance, and the Pythagoreans swore oaths by the *tetractys*, the diagrammatical representation of the relationships between these numbers in the form of an equilateral triangle. In some way, the generation of numbers, beginning with an original One, was the key to the understanding of the universe; the number of heavenly bodies was assumed to be 10 (because 10 was the perfect number), and their movement generated a musical harmony (which only the enlightened, like Pythagoras, could hear). Whatever Pythagoras' role in all of this, the idea that mathematics was fundamental to the universe, and that its study brought spiritual benefits, was undoubtedly a factor in encouraging the development of Greek mathematics beyond purely practical applications.

By the end of the 4th century BC Pythagoras had come to be regarded as the archetypical philosopher, and his supposed ideas had been incorporated into the mainstream of philosophy by the followers of Plato and Aristotle. We hear of very few philosophers who identified themselves as Pythagoreans, although preachers promulgating a popularized form of his religious ideas appear in new comedy. From the 3rd century BC onwards, however, he was sufficiently important a figure for a considerable number of forged documents to be produced under his name, a process that accelerated in the 1st century BC, when the school was refounded (the revived school is referred to by modern scholars as Neopythagoreanism, but is really a form of Platonism with a mathematical orientation); this later recreation and reinterpretation of Pythagoreanism makes the task of reconstructing the doctrines of the early school considerably more complicated. Later, with the rise of Christianity, Pythagoras became a sort of pagan counter-Christ, and Iamblichus' *On the Pythagorean Life* (4th century AD) presents him as a semidivine sage and miracleworker, to whom the philosophical basis of a challenge to Christianity could be attributed. Interest in him continues well into the Byzantine period, and much of our information on later Pythagoreanism depends on the work of Michael Psellos (1018–after 1081), to whom we owe the survival of most of Iamblichus' work.

RICHARD WALLACE

See also Mathematics

Biography

Born in Samos in the first half of the 6th century BC, Pythagoras moved to Croton in south Italy in the mid-6th century. There he founded a society of "Pythagoreans" whose members were involved in the politics of Magna Graecia. His name is associated with reli-gious teaching and important contributions to mathematics and science. He died in exile in Metapontum.

Further Reading

Barnes, Jonathan, *The Presocratic Philosophers*, vol. 1, London and Boston: Routledge and Kegan Paul, 1979

Burkert, Walker, *Lore and Science in Ancient Pythagoreanism*, Cambridge, Massachusetts: Harvard University Press, 1972

Guthrie, W.K.C., *A History of Greek Philosophy*, vol. 1, Cambridge and New York: Cambridge University Press, 1962

Iamblichus, *On the Pythogorean Life*, edited and translated by Gillian Clark, Liverpool: Liverpool University Press, 1989

Kirk, G.S., J.E. Raven, and M. Schofield, *The Presocratic Philosophers: A Critical History with a Selection of Texts*, 2nd edition, Cambridge and New York: Cambridge University Press, 1983

O'Meara, Dominic J., *Pythagoras Revived: Mathematics and Philosophy in Late Antiquity*, Oxford: Clarendon Press, and New York: Oxford University Press, 1989

Philip, J.A., *Pythagoras and Early Pythagoreanism*, Toronto: University of Toronto Press, 1966

R

Railways

The historical evolution of Hellenic railways is closely related to the economic and social development of the country. Their evolutionary phases can be broadly classified in two periods: from mid-19th century to the end of World War II and from the end of World War II till today. A major characteristic of the first period is the development of many independent networks that served local needs for the transportation of goods and people. The reason for that development was mainly the geographical shape of Greece. The distinctive characteristic of the second period is the consolidation of the industry under a state monopoly. The changing conditions in the transportation industry made the operation of local networks inefficient, and subsequently required the state to take over the management of all the rail networks.

The first railway line was opened in 1869 between Athens and Piraeus and was operated by the "Athens to Piraeus Railway Company". During the 1870s no new network was constructed but by the beginning of the 1880s the need for new railways was apparent. The road network was underdeveloped and transportation was efficient only by sea. The construction of railways at that time was seen as a means of accelerating economic development and further integrating Greece into the world market.

In the spring of 1882 the parliament made a detailed examination of the plans for the construction of long-distance railways. Lengthy discussions took place about the width of the gauge. The government insisted on the construction of tracks with a gauge of 1 m, whereas the opposition favoured the so called "international" line that had a gauge of 1.4 m. This disagreement may seem to be irrational but was justified because of the cost of the technology: the larger the gauge, the more expensive the associated works, such as bridges and tunnels. The advantage of the so-called "international" line was the higher travelling speed. In the end, the government's proposal was accepted because of the lower financial expenditure, and because the travelling speed was not so crucial at that time.

The peculiar physical shape of Greece together with the established routes for transportation by sea led to the construction not of a large, compact, national network that would connect the principal cities with each other, but of many small, regional, autonomous networks that connected the flat regions of the country with the major ports. It should be noted that before the 1920s communication between Greece and other countries was conducted exclusively by sea; the railway line that connected Greece with the Balkans and consequently with the rest of Europe was not operational until 1913. The main railway networks, apart from the Athens–Piraeus railway, were as follows.

Piraeus–Athens–Peloponnese Railways. One of the first networks in the country, 650 km long, its construction started in 1882 and was finished in 1904 after many difficulties. It followed a circular route around the Peloponnese and connected the majority of the Peloponnesian cities with the capital. The first section to be opened to the public connected the Corinthian Gulf with the Saronic Gulf. Thus there was no need to sail all the way round the Peloponnese in order to arrive in Piraeus. The passengers or merchandise arrived by boat in Corinth and were carried by the railway across the isthmus to the other side where waiting ships transported them to Piraeus.

Thessaly Railways. Construction started in 1882, after Thessaly was liberated from the Turks, and was finished in 1886. The network had two lines: the first was from Volos to Larissa and the second from Volos to Kalambaka, a total of 220 km. The opening of railways made the transportation of agricultural products from the plains of Thessaly to the rest of Greece and abroad from the port of Volos more efficient and accelerated the modernization of Greece's economic infrastructure.

Hellenic Railways. This was the major railway network with international standards that finally connected Greece with the rest of Europe. Construction lasted from 1900 to 1909. It connected Piraeus with Larissa and the then Greek–Turkish borders. Its construction was considered a priority for at least two reasons. The first was the ability to move troops quickly and efficiently from southern Greece to the Turkish borders; the second was the opportunity for the Greek network to be linked to the European railways.

In Macedonia the Ottomans constructed the first railway in 1871. It connected Thessalonica with Skopje and it had a length of 243 km. One year later the line from Constantinople to Alexandroupolis was completed. The connection of these two cities to the international network was important because for the first time it was possible to transport goods and people easily and efficiently by land to Central and Western Europe.

The Eastern Railways Company had the responsibility of managing these lines and had a monopoly in the ports of Thessalonica and Alexandroupolis. These two cities became the gates of the Ottoman empire not only to Europe but also to the Mediterranean. During 1892 construction began of the line from Thessalonica to Monastiri (modern Bitola), the second centre of commercial and strategic importance in Macedonia. In 1896 Thessalonica was connected with Constantinople. The railway connection between Greece and Macedonia was delayed for many years by the Turks who were conscious of the strategic importance of railways in the event of a conflict. It was finally achieved with the liberation of Macedonia in 1912–13.

In 1920 the Greek State Railway Company was founded and began to acquire the international lines of the country, and in July of the same year the Athens–Paris intercity connection was established. During the years 1920–40 no major construction of new railway lines took place except for some small extensions to the Macedonian network.

The construction and operation of railways in the context of a traditional economy and society such as Greece inevitably brought with it a series of changes. The presence of railways in the flat areas of the country accelerated a large-scale economic and social transformation, especially after the connection with the rest of Europe. Although in the years preceding railway construction the society and economy were by no means static, the underdeveloped state of the road network had kept the rate of economic and social modernization extremely low, given that the only efficient means of transportation was by sea. Despite the fact that migration was already an established social characteristic and urbanization was also in progress, and although agriculture in the regions of the Peloponnese, Thessaly, and Macedonia had already been integrated with the world market, such social features and economic developments were confined within certain geographical limits or social groups. The agricultural and industrial potential of the country had not been fully realized and commerce was heavily restricted to the coastal areas. Seasonal migration, excluding islanders, was a venture engaged in only by transhumant shepherds and a class of artisans. The advent of railways established close contacts between towns and villages, the ports and the hinterland, the country and Europe. This supported industrial development, increased commerce, and accelerated social transformation. In addition, railways contributed significantly to the defence of the country. During the Balkan Wars the deployment of troops to the front line, was extremely rapid, given the circumstances.

The end of World War II found the country's railways seriously damaged. Their repair began at once and was finished in a relatively short period. Meanwhile, the construction of an adequate road network changed dramatically the pattern of communications. The regional rail networks could no longer survive because the transportation of goods and people by road was more efficient. The only way for them to continue in business was by merging with the larger networks. After a period of industrial consolidation in 1971 the Organization of Railways of Greece (OSE) was founded, a state monopoly that took over all independent railway companies.

Unlike the railways in Europe, the development of Greece's railway network after World War II was relatively modest, despite initial efforts. The reasons for this can be traced partly to the automobile's domination of the country's transportation and partly to the management of the organization. Instead of focusing on customer satisfaction, on the provision of adequate services, and on the modernization of equipment, the company simply became one more organization of an inefficient state. Evidence of this is the fact that 70 per cent of rolling stock and locomotives are between 20 and 35 years old. In the 1990s some effort was made to modernize and expand the network and introduce new trains. Moreover, plans have been put forward for privatization.

DIMITRIOS GKAMAS

See also Industry

Further Reading

Gounaris, Basil C., *Steam over Macedonia, 1870–1912: Socio-Economic Change and the Railway Factor*, Boulder, Colorado: East European Monographs, 1993

Matzaridis, D., *Sinoptiko Istoriko ton Ellinikon Sidirodromon* [A Brief History of the Greek Railways], Athens, 1984

Papagianakis, O., *Oi Ellinikoi Sidirodromoi, 1882–1910* [The Greek Railways, 1882–1910], Athens, 1982

Simms, W., *The Railways of Greece*, Rustington: Simms, 1997

Ward, M., *The Railways of Greece: Their Inception and Development*, Athens, 1997

Ravenna

City in north Italy

Ravenna, particularly in the 5th and 6th centuries AD, was the site of a culture which, while largely Latin-speaking and involved in Italian affairs, also absorbed much from the Greek east; Byzantine rule after 540 acted "as an incubator, which helped preserve Ravenna's own traditions and made possible its development as a dynamic and independent society" (Brown, 1988). The nearby harbour of Classis, especially in the earlier part of this period, maintained trade and communications routes with the east. (This was one of the main reasons why the western emperor Honorius moved his capital to Ravenna from Milan in 402 and why it continued in use as capital of the Ostrogothic kings Odoacer and Theodoric, and of the Byzantine Exarchs.)

During the Ostrogothic period close contacts with the empire were maintained. Theodoric himself had spent much of his youth in Constantinople (as a hostage) and acknowledged Byzantine sovereignty – his coins continue to bear the emperor's head; eastern involvement in the affairs of Ravenna increased during the regency of Amalasuntha (526–34). Greek influence is already evident in the churches of this time, and particularly at the basilica of Sant' Apollinare Nuovo, begun as the palace church c.490. The plan remains that of the traditional Roman basilica but there are conspicuous eastern elements, most obviously the exterior polygon of the apse, the articulation with pilasters of the outer walls, and marble columns imported from the imperial workshops of Proconnesus. The mosaic saints of the nave (mid-6th-century Byzantine replacements for the originals of Theodoric's time),

Ravenna: interior of S. Apollinare in Classe, consecrated in 549, with an apse mosaic of the Transfiguration

processing from the palace to Christ and from Classis to the Virgin, are a departure from the separable panels and more naturalistic figures of earlier mosaic and may be the work of craftsmen either from the east or at least trained by eastern mosaicists. (In Ravenna it is never entirely clear, however, what was the balance between imported eastern expertise and evolving local tradition.)

San Vitale, the only building in Ravenna which is eastern in plan as well as decoration, was also founded under Ostrogothic rule (*c*.525) and Cyril Mango has suggested that even before 540 it was designed to make a pro-Byzantine statement. Its completion in the late 540s under Justinian I's appointee as the first archbishop of Ravenna, Maximianus, unambiguously asserted imperial dominance (and the victory of Orthodoxy over the Arian Ostrogoths). This is most evident in the mosaics of the apse where Justinian and his consort Theodora, in their most famous surviving representations, lead their courtiers (including Maximianus) in an offering to the church. These confident, bejewelled, glittering figures, emphatically present yet, in their lack of depth and volume, otherworldly, suggest at least an awareness of recent developments in eastern floor mosaics. Losses as a result of iconoclasm mean that the mosaics at San Vitale are the best surviving indication of what contemporary church decoration in Constantinople was like, although as ever there will have been room for local variation. Certainly there are significant differences between San Vitale and the church of Sts Sergius and Bacchus in Constantinople, overall the most similar in design: in Ravenna the emphasis is more vertical and the whole drawn together by factors including the "placement of arcades in both the upper and lower zones of the niches ... the slenderness of the surmounting arches" and "the flood of light from rows of huge windows in the ambulatory, gallery, and the clerestory zone of the centre room" (Krautheimer and Ćurčić, 1986).

No expense seems to have been spared in the construction and decoration of San Vitale. It is known to have cost the considerable sum of 26,000 *solidi*, dispensed by the banker Julianus, either on his own account or on behalf of Justinian's treasury. Julianus is also recorded as patron of the contemporary basilica of Sant' Apollinare in Classe which was enriched, like San Vitale, with mosaics, marble revetments, and Proconnesian capitals and column shafts. To this day the buildings of Justinian's time, glinting with gold, semi-precious stone, or silver tesserae, give the impression that Ravenna was a splendid and closely integrated Greek imperial city. But in a number of ways the Justinianic survivals are unrepresentative, a brief Byzantinizing interlude; it is easy to exaggerate subsequent Greek influence on Ravenna. Brown has gathered the evidence: no Greek literature connected with Ravenna is known (although there were four Greek monasteries), Latin remained the dominant official language, the archbishops after Maximianus emanated from the see itself, eastern immigrants appear to have been rapidly assimilated, and the city is rarely mentioned in eastern sources. After Justinian's time there was little by way of magnificent church building or decoration; lack of resources and weakened trade and communication routes ended imports from the imperial workshops and restricted or redirected the movements of craftsmen between east and west. (Mosaic work at Sant' Apollinare in Classe was, however, undertaken in the later 7th century, including representations of Constantine IV, his brothers, and his son Justinian II.)

Partly as a result of this cultural divide, relations with the Exarchs and with Constantinople were sometimes difficult. Local and fiscal disputes resulted in the murder of several Exarchs and there was lasting resentment at the savage reprisals taken against prominent citizens of separatist sympathies by Justinian II in 709. Both fierce opposition to iconoclastic decrees and the perception that Constantinople could or would do little to protect the Exarchate from the Lombards contributed to the revolt of 727, and the latter impression was confirmed both by Liutprand's capture of Ravenna in 732 and by the fact that it fell to Venice to expel him soon afterwards. By the time the Lombards under Aistulf took the city again in 751, it must long have been obvious to many that Ravenna's future lay in different directions from Constantinople. By 757, with Frankish aid, it was part of the pope's domain. Eclipsed as a trading power by Venice, especially once the harbour silted up, the city soon became relatively obscure.

MARTIN GARRETT

See also Italy, Mosaic

Summary

Ravenna became the capital of the western Roman empire in AD 402 and later the capital of Ostrogothic Italy. During this time it absorbed much cultural influence from the Greek east. Captured by Belisarius for Justinian in 540, Ravenna remained a Byzantine possession until 751 when it fell to the Lombards. Ravenna's mosaics are among the best surviving examples of pre-iconoclastic Byzantine art.

Further Reading

Brown, Thomas S., "The Interplay between Roman and Byzantine Traditions and Local Sentiment in the Exarchate of Ravenna", *Settimane di Studio del Centro Italiano di Studi sull'Alto Medioevo*, 34 (1988): pp. 127–60

Deichmann, F.W., *Ravenna: Hauptstadt des spätantiken Abendlandes*, 4 vols, Wiesbaden: Steiner, 1958–89

Kitzinger, Ernst, *Byzantine Art in the Making: Main Lines of Stylistic Development in Mediterranean Art 3rd–7th Century*, London: Faber, and Cambridge, Massachusetts: Harvard University Press, 1977, reprinted 1995

Krautheimer, Richard and Slobodan Ćurčić, *Early Christian and Byzantine Architecture*, 4th edition, New Haven, Connecticut and London: Yale University Press, 1986

Mango, Cyril, *Byzantine Architecture*, New York: Rizzoli, 1985; London: Faber, 1986

Nordhagen, Per Jonas, "The Penetration of Byzantine Mosaic Techniques into Italy in the Sixth Century AD" in *III Colloquio internazionale sul mosaico antico: Ravenna*, edited by R.F. Campanati, Ravenna: Girasole, 1983

Refugees

Refugees have always played a significant role in the history of Greece. Even before the fall of Constantinople in 1453 groups of refugees from Greek lands conquered by the Ottomans sought refuge in Venetian-occupied Crete, the Ionian islands, and even the Italian states themselves. The flow intensified in the half century before the fall of Constantinople, when numerous Greeks (among them many intellectuals) emigrated to Italy, bringing with them the scholarship which helped underpin the Renaissance. The best-known example is the philosopher Plethon (who spent a year in Florence) but also Chrysoloras and Bessarion and Isidore of Kiev, of whom the last two became cardinals. Emigration continued after 1453: there is for example some evidence that a group of Greeks from Constantinople settled on the island of Patmos, probably in the second half of the 15th century. Following the fall of Crete in 1669 and the wars between the Ottomans and Venice, groups of Greeks (usually associated with revolts in favour of a western power) took refuge in the Ionian islands but also further west, in Italy, France, and even Britain; smaller groups went to Spain (Domenikos Theotokopoulos, known as El Greco, was such a refugee). A few hundred Greeks from Rhodes settled in Malta with the Hospitaller Knights of St John in 1530; between 1532 and 1534 several thousand inhabitants of the Peloponnese settled in southern Italy and Sicily after the failure of the campaigns of Charles V in the Peloponnese. Similar waves of refugees were generated after the Russo-Turkish wars of the 18th century, usually towards the Ionian islands but also further north (to Venice, Trieste, Austria, and Hungary) and west (to Naples, Livorno, even Minorca). Large numbers, mostly from the Black Sea coast (the Pontus), also settled in the Ukraine and the Crimea. In the second half of the 17th century groups of Greeks from Mani (in the southern Peloponnese) settled in Italy but also in Corsica. Still in pre-independence Greece, groups of refugees escaping from Turkish depredations left the plains and colonized much of the mountain uplands of the Greek mainland, forming virtually autonomous enclaves. Their relative freedom allowed them to play a major role in the spread of learning and the Greek Enlightenment, which in turn paved the way for the struggle for independence.

Refugees from throughout and beyond the modern-day Greek frontiers participated in the Greek struggle for independence (1821–30). The operations of the struggle created considerable upheavals throughout the Greek mainland, as well as the archipelago, Asia Minor, and Cyprus; large numbers of people were made refugees; several thousand Cypriots left the island in 1821. Some of these refugees (perhaps most) settled in Greece, but others emigrated to southern Russia, the Caucasus, western Europe, and the United States, where (among others) orphans from the War of Independence were settled or rehomed. Once the Greek state was formed, war refugees from throughout the Greek world settled within the new state, in large enough numbers to create the question of the *eterochthones* (or foreign-born Greeks) that was to remain controversial for some time.

However, the largest groups of refugees arrived in Greece in the course of the 20th century, usually (but not exclusively) as a result of the antagonisms of the Balkan states.

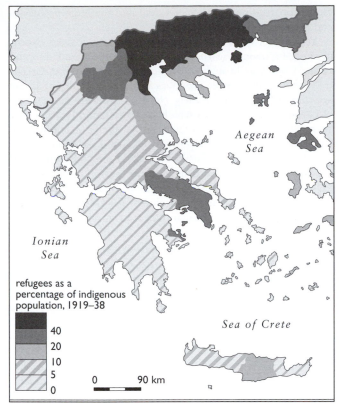

41. Density of refugees settling in Greece from 1919 to 1938

Chronologically the first wave of such refugees to arrive in Greece was from Bulgaria; the thriving Greek communities of eastern Rumelia, incorporated in the principality of Bulgaria in 1885, suffered during the early years of the 20th century. An example is the city of Anhialos (Anhiolu) on the Bulgarian Black Sea coast: almost exclusively Greek in 1900, it was destroyed in the course of a Bulgarian pogrom against the Greeks of Bulgaria in 1905, in retaliation for Bulgarian reverses in the Macedonian struggle. Numerous Greeks from Bulgaria subsequently sought refuge in Greece; most were settled in Thessaly.

The policy of Ottomanization pursued by the Young Turk regimes, especially after 1914, created a wave of some 90,000 refugees from Asia Minor, eastern Thrace, Pontus, and Constantinople; they sought refuge in Greece. The outbreak of World War I caused an intensification of the process of Ottomanization, and even more Anatolian Greeks were made refugees, often to allow for the settlement of Muslim refugees from the Balkans.

The largest wave of refugees was, however, yet to come to Greece, in the wake of the Greek army defeat in Asia Minor, in August 1922. The immediate aftermath of the defeat included the destruction of the Greek and Armenian quarters of the city of Smyrna, burnt by Turkish troops. Many of the Greek male inhabitants of the city faced death or deportation to work camps in the interior of Asia Minor; few were eventually to survive. Virtually all other Greek inhabitants of the city had to be evacuated to Greece; most arrived destitute, some with the clothes they were wearing their only possession. This was followed by a more orderly, but equally comprehensive evacuation of the coast of the Sea of Marmara and eastern Thrace,

handed to the Turks following the Chanak affair in October 1922. The Lausanne Treaty of 1923 included a clause on the compulsory exchange of populations between Greece and Turkey; all Orthodox Christians of Turkey (with the exception of inhabitants of Constantinople) were exchanged for the Muslims of Greece (with the exception of the Muslims in western Thrace and some Albanians). The exchange began in 1922 and was completed by 1924.

The precise number of refugees is not known; little effort was made at the time to provide statistics of the mostly destitute populations coming into Greece. A considerable number of them also succumbed to disease shortly after arrival. It is estimated that between 1.2 and 1.5 million refugees entered Greece after 1922, while some 350,000–400,000 Muslims left. Over 45 per cent of the refugees were populations of rural origin, the rest urban.

The vast majority of incoming rural refugees were settled in northern Greece, in rural areas of Macedonia and Thrace; for the urban refugees, resettlement originally meant living in houses vacated by Muslim city dwellers, while a considerable proportion of them had to live in shanty towns created in the outskirts of large towns and cities. The settlement of the refugees was a colossal task. That of the rural refugees proceeded relatively quickly, and was almost complete by 1938. The urban refugees' resettlement proceeded at a much slower pace and was not completed until the 1950s. For both the urban and rural refugees, the process was highly bureaucratic, painful, and often humiliating.

The Asia Minor refugees contributed to the economic development of Greece in many ways: some of them (especially those coming from Smyrna) had enjoyed under the Ottomans a standard of living that was considerably higher than that of mainland Greece in the years before 1922. They brought with them much-needed entrepreneurial, industrial, and agricultural skills, but also a degree of political and cultural sophistication often higher than that of the mainland. They also became a ready pool of cheap labour for Greece's fledgeling industry. At least some of them became a target group for the – then new – ideas of communism: some of the most prominent-ranking members of the Greek Communist Party at the time were refugees. Greece's first Nobel Prize winner, George Seferis, as well as numerous other writers (Yorgos Theotokas, Ilias Venezis) and painters (such as Photis Kontoglou) that were to make a major impact in the country's cultural life were also refugees.

In politics, the refugees provided a relatively stable source of electoral support for the Venizelist side throughout the interwar years. It was the numerical strength of the refugees and their support for Venizelos that made it possible for him to return to power in 1928. The large numbers and relatively compact pattern of settlement (almost 90 per cent of the rural refugees were settled in whole villages in Macedonia and Thrace) also created a divide between refugees and non-refugees in the countryside; this divide (also mirrored to a lesser extent in cities) repeatedly degenerated into violent conflict in the interwar years and would endure for many decades.

The refugees from Asia Minor and eastern Thrace were by no means the last refugees to arrive in Greece. Greeks from Bulgaria continued to emigrate to Greece as prescribed by the voluntary exchange of populations under the Neuilly Treaty signed in 1919 between Greece and Bulgaria. It is estimated that around 70,000 Greeks came to settle in Greece from Bulgaria between 1919 and the late 1930s. An estimated 100,000 Greeks from southern Russia, the Crimea, the Caucasus, and the Ukraine also came to Greece between 1920 and the outbreak of World War II, most arriving in the wake of the upheavals caused by the Bolshevik Revolution and the Civil War. Further numbers of Greeks also became refugees during the Axis occupation of Greece (1941–44) and the Civil War (1946–49). Over 100,000 Greeks were forced to leave Bulgarian-occupied eastern Macedonia and Thrace between 1941 and 1944. The refugees from Asia Minor that had been settled in the region after 1922 were specially targeted for expulsion by the Bulgarian occupation authorities. Some of the refugees from the Bulgarian-occupied areas never returned, settling in other parts of Greece after the liberation in 1944.

The Civil War resulted, among other things, in further numbers of refugees. During the Civil War a practice was developed by the National (Government) Army by which whole villages from areas controlled by the insurgents were evacuated and their inhabitants resettled. They were often moved to shanty towns, always near larger cities under government control. These were the *antartopliktoi* (victims of the guerrillas) or *kataphygontes* (those who sought refuge); it is estimated that some 700,000 persons or approximately 10 per cent of the population fell into this category. Once the hostilities were over, many did not return to their home villages, thus creating the first wave of the postwar population movement from the countryside that greatly increased the population of urban centres.

On the other side of the Civil War divide, both during the hostilities and following the communist defeat, considerable numbers of supporters of the communist guerrillas left Greece, some forcibly, most voluntarily; initially most went to Albania and Yugoslavia. They were subsequently resettled in the countries of the Eastern bloc and in the USSR, creating a string of Greek settlements ranging from the German–Polish border to Tashkent in Soviet Central Asia. They were banned from returning to Greece, at least until 1974; the bulk of them were only repatriated in the early 1980s.

In the 1950s and 1960s the Turkish authorities forced or "encouraged" tens of thousands of Greeks from Istanbul, as well as the Greek inhabitants of the islands of Imbros and Tenedos (given to Turkey in 1923), to emigrate to Greece; the pressure was especially strong during periods when relations between Greece and Turkey were tense, typically over differences related to Cyprus. Such an incident took place on 5–6 September 1955, when large numbers of Greek homes and businesses in Istanbul were looted by mobs, with some loss of life and massive destruction of property. The anti-Greek riots were organized with the connivance if not the support of the Turkish authorities and were the trigger for the large-scale exodus of the once thriving Greek community of Constantinople. While some Constantinopolitan Greeks emigrated to other countries, most settled in Greece. A considerable number of Greeks that had been living in Egypt also came to Greece following the Nasser revolution of 1956 and the nationalization of the Suez Canal and the large businesses and private estates that followed.

Yet another wave of refugees arrived in Greece from Cyprus in 1974, following the Turkish invasion of the island. The end of the Cold War brought more refugees into Greece: Greeks from the former Soviet republics (especially Georgia) began arriving in Greece in the early 1990s. They were descendants of Greeks from the Pontus who had emigrated to Russia in the 19th century. They had suffered at the hands of Stalin (who had had many of them deported to Central Asia); and while perestroika brought a revival in their fortunes, the collapse of the Soviet Union created a much more unstable environment for relatively small minorities such as theirs. An estimated 100,000 Greeks emigrated from the former USSR to Greece in the early 1990s, and this emigration continues.

The collapse of the Stalinist regime in Albania also resulted in a new wave of refugees: numerous ethnic Greeks from southern Albania streamed into Greece, also beginning in the early 1990s. While many are simply seasonal migrant workers, a number of them have settled in Greece more or less permanently. Finally, a number of political refugees fleeing from repressive regimes (most Kurdish, but also others from African and Asian countries) have sought and been granted asylum in Greece.

In the short term, the successive waves of refugees has invariably caused considerable economic and social problems to Greece: their resettlement and absorption has required and still requires considerable economic and social capital; and social division and tensions have also arisen, sometimes to boiling point. Similar tensions are to be observed today, with the large number of economic migrant workers and refugees in residence in Greece, some in a highly precarious economic state; the legal position of considerable numbers of them is also not very clearly defined. Yet, in the long run, the refugees have traditionally proved highly beneficial for Greece: not only have they contributed to the economic development of the country not least by bringing new skills and increasing the workforce; they have also given Greece a high degree of ethnic homogeneity, making it the most homogeneous national state of the Balkans.

GEORGE KAZAMIAS

See also Asia Minor Campaign

Further Reading

Hassiotis, I., *Episkopisi tis Istorias tis Neaellinikis Diasporas* [Survey of the History of the Modern Greek Diaspora], Thessalonica, 1993

Hirschon, Renée, *Heirs of the Greek Catastrophe: The Social Life of Asia Minor Refugees in Piraeus*, New York: Oxford University Press, 1989

Kourvetaris, G.A., "Greek–American Professionals, 1820s–1920s", *Balkan Studies*, 18/2 (1977)

Ladas, Stephen P., *The Exchange of Minorities: Bulgaria, Greece, and Turkey*, New York: Macmillan, 1932

League of Nations, *Greek Refugee Settlement*, Geneva: League of Nations, 1926

Pentzopoulos, Dimitri, *The Balkan Exchange of Minorities and Its Impact upon Greece*, Paris: Mouton, 1962

Sandis, Eva E., *Refugees and Economic Migrants in Greater Athens: A Social Survey*, Athens: National Centre of Social Research, 1973

Relics

The veneration of relics (the physical remains of the saints, or articles closely associated with them) became a part of active Christian devotion from the 4th century onwards, and remains a distinctive aspect of the Greek Christian tradition to the present day. The practice also marks western Catholic Christianity, from its shared historical and doctrinal roots, but was decisively rejected by the Protestant Churches of the Reformation.

Biblical roots of the religious practice can be traced in the Old Testament narratives of Elisha assuming Elijah's cloak as an effective symbol of the transference of divine charismata to the new prophet (2 Kings 2: 14), or in the story of how the bones of Elisha raised a corpse to life when laid upon them (2 Kings 13: 21). The New Testament continued this oriental tradition of seeing even material objects as capable of being imbued with divine charisma, as for example in the stories of Jesus curing the woman who merely touched the fringe of his garment (Matthew 9: 20), the wonderworking talismans of Paul (Acts 19: 12), and the thaumaturgical shadow of Peter (Acts 5: 15). The standard Jewish-Christian practice of exhumation of the dead, and the subsequent reburial of the bones in an ossuary, perhaps also created a positive environment for the formation of a Christian cult of the dead. This was certainly alien to the widespread contemporary Roman mentality which regarded the relics of dead with distaste and fear (akin to modern European attitudes) .

The beginnings of the Greek Christian cult of relics have usually been referred to the devotion offered to the early martyrs, especially those of the 3rd and 4th centuries. Already the description of the martyrdom of Polycarp (mid-2nd century) speaks of the faithful gathering up his relics, "more valuable than precious stones and finer than refined gold", which were then taken back to a martyrium where his memory could be commemorated regularly. A similar aspect is seen in the account of Ignatius of Antioch's martyrdom, after which fragments of his body were "put into a coffin like an inestimable treasure". The cult of the martyrs became powerful and popular within the Church. The early martyria shrines were focuses of regular commemorations throughout the Christian world (eventually to become the Christian liturgical calendar) where Eucharistic celebrations and feasts were held around the tombs of the saints. The martyrs were believed to be immediately admitted to heaven with the power to intercede for the earthly Church, and to act as powerful patrons in adverse times. The cult of martyrs, obviously attached to their tombs and physical remains from the very logic of its origins, eventually spread in Christian practice to encompass other Christian heroes: notably confessors (those who had courageously witnessed but survived) and hierarchs. The holy ascetics of the 4th and 5th centuries became new focal points of Christian devotion.

By the time of the mid-4th century the cult of the relics of the saints was so widespread that a series of *inventiones* was taking place. The relics of past Old Testament prophets or other historic saints, such as John the Baptist, were discovered to popular acclaim. The form of the *inventio* usually followed a revelatory dream to a significant figure. In the 5th century Cyril of Alexandria had revealed to him the whereabouts of

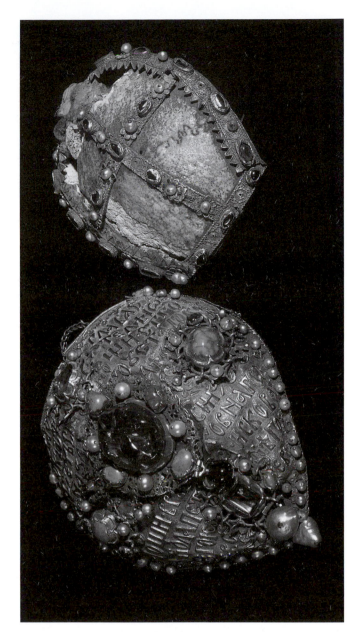

Relic: two pieces of the skull of St John the Baptist, decorated with gold and semi-precious stones, Topkapi Palace Museum, Istanbul

powerful relics of martyrs who would do battle with Isis in his own generation. Ambrose of Milan discovered the relics of Sts Protasius and Gervase. The empress Eudoxia in the Holy Land discovered the relics of St Stephen and had a triumph in bringing them back to Constantinople. Dominant figures in the newly ascendant Christian empire thus sought to associate themselves with the mediatory efficacy of the saints in a political culture where intercession with the throne was viewed as the primary avenue to power. The discovery of relics also extended to the finding of notable objects of the Passion. The stories of the discovery of the True Cross, the nails from Calvary, and other sacred objects belong to this era. The *inventio* was often followed by a "translation" to a suitable place of worship, or the establishment of a new and splendid oratory. One of the most famous of these early translations was that of

St Babylas the Martyr, whose remains were brought by Caesar Gallus in 351 to a shrine adjacent to the great temple of Apollo at Daphne in Antioch. Later, when Julian learned that the oracle there had ceased to function, he indignantly sent back the saint's bones. Julian scornfully denigrated Christian churches at this time as having become little more than charnel houses.

Christian Constantinople, just as it rose in the ascendancy of political influence, also became a veritable repository of the most venerable cult objects of the ascendant religion. Up to the time of the Fourth Crusade (which had among its policies of depredation the explicit aim of forcibly taking famous relics to disseminate them among the princes of the west) Constantinople was a famous pilgrimage centre. It possessed two pieces of the True Cross (one taken from Jerusalem, one from Apamea), the pillar of scourging, the crown of thorns, the sponge, and the lance. Among its relics of the Blessed Virgin was the famous robe kept at the palace of Blachernae and used as a palladium for the imperial city (evidenced in the famous Greek hymn of the *Akathist*, and in the cultic celebration of the feast of the Protecting Veil). The shrines of saints in the city, with their relics, were innumerable. Demand for relics of the saints became so widespread that dismemberment of their bodies became commonplace in the East (though discouraged until much later in the Roman Church), and eventually the liturgical service of dedicating a new church was forbidden without the practice of placing relics of saints under (now within) the main altar. To this day, apart from relics within the altar in all consecrated Orthodox churches, the relics of saints must also be sewn into the *antiminsiou* (the cloth on which the sacred mysteries stand during the eucharistic liturgy), and without the *antiminsiou* no liturgy may be celebrated.

Some Christian writers in antiquity attacked the potential abuses of the veneration of relics. The first to do so was the 5th-century presbyter Vigilantius of Aquitaine, who was lambasted for his pains by Jerome. At this time Jerome enunciated the principle that the relics of the saints were venerated, but not worshipped, for the sake of reverence to the Lord whose martyrs they were. This was to remain, substantially, the central Christian theological principle of the cult. It is a matter of current debate whether relic veneration was attacked by the iconoclasts in 9th-century Byzantium, but John of Damascus certainly defended the practice of relic veneration, refining the standard Greek theology of relics in the process. The second Council of Nicaea in 787, and that of Constantinople in 1084, confirmed the basis of the doctrine for the eastern Church. Relics are henceforth regarded as sacred objects, veneration of which passes directly to the saint involved. As the saints in life were special vehicles of the divine grace of sanctification, so now those saints have access to the throne of God, and offer continuing patronage to their new kin groups, those within the Church who gather around their earthly remains. The relics themselves, like the icons, were regarded as possessed of particular grace. On the feast of the saint, or on the occasion of the translation, works of grace were expected from the saint, and, from ancient times even to the present in Orthodox practice, pilgrimages were made to the shrines on such special occasions.

Some modern commentators have regarded the Christian cult of saints' relics as a by-product of the ancient Hellenistic cult of the heroes, whose tombs were often located in the most notable ancient temples, and from whom benefits were often sought (such as the relics of Theseus translated to Athens in 469 BC, found by virtue of an oracle and a prodigy, at whose tomb the poor prayed for relief). It is difficult to speak collectively, or entirely to disregard numerous instances of superstitious abuse within Christian history, but it should be noted that the cult of the saints in antiquity was always carefully distinguished from the cult of the dead heroes by its literate defenders (usually monks or hierarchs). Apologetical writers such as the Syrian bishop Theodoret in the 5th century ruefully ask why the Christian practice has aroused so much antagonism in the Hellenistic world, when the temples themselves encourage the cult of heroes. Eusebius of Caesarea in the 4th century is also at pains to distance Christian devotion from Hellenistic superstitions. The refined Byzantine theology of the period after iconoclasm elevated the attitude towards relics (and icons) as illustrative of a Christian's whole attitude to sacramental efficacy – the principle at stake being to what extent a material form can act as a valid medium of spiritual grace. The east, with its firm belief in the direct incarnation of God in the flesh, took a positive view on that matter, and this is mainly why its active veneration of the relics of the saints is closely bonded with its very concrete theology of the deification of the flesh by Christ. For this reason, unlike western Christianity, the Greek Christian tradition saw relics as substantive to the true faith rather than peripheral.

JOHN A. MCGUCKIN

See also Canonization, Dead

Further Reading

Brown, Peter, "Relics and Social Status in the Age of Gregory of Tours" in his *Society and the Holy in Late Antiquity*, Berkeley: University of California Press, and London: Faber, 1982

Brown, Peter, *The Cult of the Saints: Its Rise and Function in Latin Christianity*, Chicago: University of Chicago Press, and London: SCM Press, 1987

Delehaye, Hippolyte, *The Legends of the Saints: An Introduction to Hagiography*, London and New York: Longman, 1907; Notre Dame, Indiana: University of Notre Dame Press, 1961

Delehaye, Hippolyte, *Les Origines du culte des martyrs*, 2nd edition, Brussels: Société des Bollandistes, 1933, reprinted New York: AMS Press, 1980

Kazhdan, A.P. (editor), *The Oxford Dictionary of Byzantium*, New York and Oxford: Oxford University Press, 1991: Relics entry, vol. 3

Leclercq, Henri, Reliques et reliquaires entry in *Dictionnaire d'archéologie chrétienne et de liturgie*, edited by Fernand Cabrol and H. Leclercq, vol. 14, part 2, Paris: Letouzey & Ané, 1948

Maraval, Pierre, *Lieux saints et pèlerinages d'Orient: Histoire et géographie des origines à la conquête arabe*, Paris: Cerf, 1985

Mercati, S.G., "Sanctuari e reliquie Constantinopolitane: rendiconti", *Atti della Pontificia Accademia Romana di Archeologia*, 12 (1937): pp. 133–56

Pfister, Fredrich, *Der Reliquienkult im Altertum*, 2 vols., Giessen: Töpelmann, 1909–12, reprinted Berlin: de Gruyter, 1974

Rothkrug, L., "The Odor of Sanctity, and the Hebrew Origins of Christian Relic Veneration", *Historical Reflections, Reflexions Historiques*, 8/2 (1981): pp. 95–142

Segourné, P., Reliques entry in *Dictionnaire de théologie catholique*, vol. 13, Paris: Letouzey & Ané, 1937

Religion, Ancient

In attempting to describe Classical Greek religion, it is necessary to state at the outset that the Greeks themselves had no word to describe our concept of "religion", no comparable conception of a sphere of life marked out from the "political" or the "secular". Greek religion, moreover, did not – like modern Christianity – focus upon a set of dogmas or principles to which a man or a woman consciously chooses (or declines) to adhere. Nevertheless, even without a body of sacred texts, without an organized Church with the professed purpose of ensuring uniformity, the Greeks shared a roughly coherent set of beliefs and ritual practices that merit description together.

Greek religion was polytheistic. A core group of so-called Olympian divinities (those who were held in myth to live on Mount Olympus) was often numbered 12, but the identity of the 12 varied: the Parthenon frieze featured Aphrodite, Apollo, Ares, Artemis, Athena, Demeter, Dionysus, Hephaestus, Hera, Hermes, and Zeus. Though some of these divinities would have been familiar to all Greeks – Zeus, Demeter, and Hermes, for example – there was great variation both in the deities worshipped and in the relative emphasis given to different deities in different Greek cities and regions. Poseidon was associated particularly with the city of Corinth, Athena with Athens, Hera with Argos and Samos. Different cult titles or epithets were applied to divinities in different areas: Athena Polias (or "of the city") in Athens or Zeus Lykaios (named after a local mountain) in Arcadia.

These relationships between cities and divinities were not exclusive or monogamous ones: Poseidon also held a central place in Athens, Athena in Sparta (even under the title "Polias"). Other local deities, however, such as the Arcadian goddess Despoina (or "mistress") or the Spartan Helen (though they may have shared certain attributes, or even sometimes fused, with Panhellenic deities), were more or less restricted to particular localities. In addition, there were a large number of lesser divinities such as nymphs (believed to inhabit and somehow to embody rivers, trees, and mountains) and heroes. The latter, a particularly disparate group, included the Panhellenic Heracles (also worshipped as a god); mythological characters, for example from the Trojan War; and historical individuals worshipped after their deaths, such as the Spartan Brasidas, the antagonist in the Peloponnesian War of the Athenian historian and general Thucydides. In Athens, the city that is best documented, we know of the existence of hundreds of heroes.

How are we to understand this confusion of deities? Were the Argive and Samian Hera, say, or the Spartan and Athenian Athena Polias, one god or two? The answer is probably that they were believed to be both different and the same. That the names of so many divinities, and the stories of their exploits, were common across the Greek world clearly means something, even if the devotees of a god's different cults were distinct. In his odes in honour of the victors of Panhellenic festivals, when a victor's home city possessed no cult of the Panhellenic deity in question, Pindar addressed himself to a different local manifestation of that god. In describing an instance of divine intervention, Herodotus will sometimes ascribe it at one moment to a named divinity, at another to a generalized divinity, "the divine", or "the god". A powerful principle in Greek religious thought was that the nature of the gods was fundamentally unknowable, and that the distinctions between divinities, and their characterizations through myth, were traditional, even arbitrary. Far from leading to widespread scepticism concerning the existence of the gods, this "uncertainty principle" seems, however, to have cushioned the individuated gods of myth and ritual from challenge.

The relationship between men and gods in Greek religion is often portrayed in modern accounts as more contractual than personal: the proper observation of ritual duties – especially of sacrifice, accompanied by prayer – was rewarded by good fortune in the form of, for example, a good harvest, the birth of children, or through negative blessings such as the absence of disease or a journey free of shipwreck. (The idea of personal salvation after death was not widespread, being limited largely to the mystery cults such as that of Eleusis.) Though a greater emphasis perhaps was given to ritual than in many other religious systems, the exchange was not quite so crudely commercial. In literature emphasis is often placed on the spirit in which propitiation of the gods was performed. A man's past actions may make his sacrifice unwelcome. Xenophon's account in his *Anabasis* of his journey into Asia with a group of Greek mercenaries, the so-called Ten Thousand, reveals also an extraordinarily warm piety.

Other differences between Greek religion and Christianity have also perhaps been exaggerated. The existence of sacred texts or an organized Church demonstrably fails to ensure more than a degree of uniformity in belief and practice. Though there was never in the Greek world any identifiable core set of beliefs to which adherence was demanded, there were limits to diversity and toleration: a number of prosecutions for impiety took place in the late 5th and early 4th centuries BC in Athens; the grant of divine honours to rulers such as Alexander encountered opposition. Though we cannot talk in a Greek context of "belief" in the sense of a personal leap of faith, the reality of Christian belief reveals a number of similarities to Greek religion. Just as Christian belief in an everloving and just god must explain the appearance of injustice, so Greek belief in the gods' unfailing response to propitiation must incorporate similar strategies for explaining exceptions. A similar pattern can be seen underlying other areas of Greek belief. The belief that gods punish unjust or impious actions – there was a considerable overlap between the ideas of the pious (*hosion*) and the just (*dikaion*) – is maintained by means of a number of such "let-out clauses": that retribution may occur through human agency, that it may follow immediately or be delayed even for a number of generations, or that, while the divine is, in general, just, it may also be capricious. The Greek belief in the reliability of oracular prophecy (from shrines such as Delphi, Dodona, and Didyma) similarly relies on a number of explanations for prophecies that are patently never fulfilled: that the correct interpretation was not discovered, that undue influence had been exerted (or even that the priestess had been bribed), that the consultant at the oracle had committed some error in procedure, or that some prophecies are simply misleading or dud.

A consequence of the lack of a clear separation of "sacred" and "secular", the lack of a distinction of Church and state, is that it is perhaps less easy to generalize on the political implications of Greek religion. A number of activities or aspects of life that we would casually class as secular were in the Greek world coloured or shaped by religious practices or beliefs. The political relationships between Greek cities were regulated through religion: when one city founded a colony, the flame for the sacred hearth of that colony was taken from its mother city; the relationship of colonizer and colonized was a relationship of religious duty. Treaties between cities, termed in Greek *spondai* (or "libations"), were marked by oaths sworn by the gods, accompanied by sacrifice: Thucydides records how in the Peloponnesian War the Spartans ascribed a number of military reversals to their breaking of a treaty. Many official aspects of city life – politics, the administration of justice – were touched by religion: as the comic playwright Aristophanes reveals through a parody, the assembly meeting started with a prayer. Oracles and prophecies were also clearly introduced into arguments in the assembly. Greek tragedy and comedy themselves were performed in the context of religious festivals such as the festival of Dionysus. Though there were professional oraclemongers and diviners, priests never formed a separate caste in Greek society. Rather they were drawn from the population at large, sometimes by virtue of family, but increasingly by election or by lot. The magistrates of Athens or the kings of Sparta performed functions that we would classify as a mixture of sacred and secular.

Religion was also central to the Greeks' perception of their identity in relation to foreign peoples and one another. The Greeks represented their gods as universal and found equivalents for them among foreign peoples, saying, for example, that Dionysus was the Greek name for Osiris or that the Ethiopians worshipped Zeus and Dionysus "alone of the gods". There was consequently no need felt to "evangelize" foreign peoples; for a Greek to proclaim a "war of religion", a crusade, was unthinkable. Herodotus describes as madness the action of the Persian king in mocking the rites of the Egyptians. Nevertheless, it is arguably no coincidence that such, often imaginary, religious crimes are ascribed to foreign peoples (so-called "barbarians") rather than to Greeks. Stories of the punishment of such actions are often reported with relish. Moreover, though they may have espoused an ideal of toleration of foreign practices, and though they may have thought most foreign gods had equivalents in the Greek pantheon, the line was drawn at common worship. Though the long-standing Greek god Dionysus was perceived as of eastern origin, genuine newcomers such as Adonis, Sabazius, Bendis, and Asclepius (from within the Greek world) were assimilated into the cult system of a city only with difficulty and some reluctance. Panhellenic festivals such as the Olympic Games were closed to non-Greeks. Those Greeks who settled in Egypt built their own temples: the Hellenion for common use and other shrines of Zeus, Hera, and Apollo for settlers from Aegina, Samos, and Miletus respectively.

As this last example demonstrates, the citizens of different Greek cities were conscious of their distinct religious identities. Just as the Olympic Games were barred to non-Greeks, so certain city festivals were barred to non-citizens. Citizens belonged, however, to more than one religious community: phratries (or brotherhoods – groups based on, at least perceived, common descent), tribes, demes (or villages), and families, all had religious rituals associated with them and all were doubtless the focus for some feeling of community.

Perhaps the hardest issue in the study of Greek religion is the assessment of change. During the 5th century BC there was a particular upsurge in religious scepticism: the development of natural, "scientific", explanations of disease or madness, observations of the injustice of the gods, that the gods were created as a form of social control, or that the belief in divination was a popular superstition. It is important, however, not to see scepticism on such issues as heralding a general or widespread reaction against religious belief. A certain degree of questioning and doubt was integral to Greek religion in all periods. Many of these sceptical positions – the injustice of the gods, for example – were rooted in traditional attitudes. Such changes as occurred as a consequence of events – the failure of Athenian diviners during the Peloponnesian War, for example – were probably largely piecemeal. The Greeks to a large extent had prepared answers for such eventualities: most diviners are charlatans; not all forms of divination are equally reliable. There is no reason, or evidence, for supposing that such reversals sparked a general decline in divination or in religiosity. Perhaps the clearest changes in Greek religion occurred as a consequence of Alexander's conquest of the Persian empire. Not only were new gods such as Isis and Serapis absorbed, but the pattern of worship changed in response to new political realities: Greek cities came to terms with the powerful and distant rulers of the Hellenistic kingdoms, or with the growing power of Rome, by integrating them in their pantheons as gods.

THOMAS HARRISON

See also Afterlife, Cult, Divination, Festivals, Gods and Goddesses, Heroes and Heroines, Oracles

Further Reading

Alcock, Susan E. and Robin Osborne (editors), *Placing the Gods: Sanctuaries and Sacred Space in Ancient Greece*, Oxford: Clarendon Press, and New York: Oxford University Press, 1994

Bremmer, Jan N., *Greek Religion*, Oxford and New York: Oxford University Press, 1994

Bruit Zaidman, Louise and Pauline Schmitt Pantel, *Religion in the Ancient Greek City*, Cambridge and New York: Cambridge University Press, 1992

Burkert, Walter, *Greek Religion: Archaic and Classical*, Oxford: Blackwell, and Cambridge, Massachusetts: Harvard University Press, 1985

Buxton, Richard, *Imaginary Greece: The Contexts of Mythology*, Cambridge and New York: Cambridge University Press, 1994

Connor, W.R., "'Sacred' and 'Secular': *Iera kai Osia* and the Classical Athenian Concept of the State", *Ancient Society*, 19 (1988): pp. 161–88

Gould, J., "On Making Sense of Greek Religion" in *Greek Religion and Society*, edited by P.E. Easterling and J.V. Muir, Cambridge and New York: Cambridge University Press, 1985

Lloyd, Alan B. (editor), *What Is a God? Studies in the Nature of Greek Divinity*, London: Duckworth, 1997

Murray, Oswyn and Simon Price (editors), *The Greek City from Homer to Alexander*, Oxford: Clarendon Press, and New York: Oxford University Press, 1990

Parker, Robert, *Miasma: Pollution and Purification in Early Greek Religion*, Oxford: Clarendon Press, 1983

Parker, Robert, "Greek States and Greek Oracles" in *Crux: Essays Presented to G.E.M. de Ste. Croix on His 75th Birthday*, edited by Paul Cartledge and F.D. Harvey, Exeter: Imprint Academic, 1985

Parker, Robert, *Athenian Religion: A History*, Oxford: Clarendon Press, and New York: Oxford University Press, 1996

Parker, Robert, "Pleasing Thighs: Reciprocity in Greek Religion" in *Reciprocity in Ancient Greece*, edited by Christopher Gill, Norman Posthlethwaite and Richard Seaford, Oxford and New York: Oxford University Press, 1998

Price, S.R.F., "Gods and Emperors: The Greek Language of the Roman Imperial Cult", *Journal of Hellenic Studies*, 104 (1984): pp. 79–95

Price, S.R.F., *Rituals and Power: The Roman Imperial Cult in Asia Minor*, Cambridge and New York: Cambridge University Press, 1984

Rudhardt, Jean, "Sur la Possibilité de comprendre une religion antique" in his *Du Mythe, de la religion grecque et de la compréhension d'autrui*, Geneva: Droz, 1981

Rudhardt, Jean, "Comprendre la religion grecque", *Kernos*, 4 (1991): pp. 47–59

Rudhardt, Jean, *Notions fondamentales de la pensée religieuse et actes constitutifs du culte dans la Grèce classique*, 2nd edition, Paris: Picard, 1992

Versnel, H.S., *Inconsistencies in Greek and Roman Religion*, vol. 1: *Ter Unus*, Leiden and New York: Brill, 1990

Religious Brotherhoods

Missionary organizations in 20th-century Greece

Religious brotherhoods constitute an important feature of religious life in 20th-century Greece. Their appearance was due to the inability of the official Church to deploy a necessary missionary programme in the country. Their spiritual antecedents must be sought in various religious movements in Greece from the late 18th century onwards, which originated out of private initiative and remained in tension with the Church. The best-known brotherhoods are Zoe ("Life"), Sotir ("Saviour"), and Stavros ("Cross"), but there are some recent ones too (e.g. Lydia). Though there are several notable differences between them, they have some common characteristics.

The most influential brotherhood has been Zoe. It was founded by archimandrite Evsevios Matthopoulos (1849–1929) in 1907 in Athens. Its initial nucleus consisted of theologians and a few working men. The purpose of Zoe was the spiritual growth of its members and the expansion of Orthodoxy all over Greece. Its eponymous journal has been published regularly since 1911. Zoe was a semi-monastic organization and its members, some clerics but mostly lay theologians, had to accept the monastic vows of chastity, poverty, and obedience while living a cenobitic life. However, Zoe did not retreat from the world, but was based in urban centres across the country, engaging in religious activism in order to transform Greek society.

Zoe expanded rapidly and soon needed a more effective organization. Between 1927 and 1947 its influence all over the country under the leadership of archimandrite Serapheim Papakostas was impressive. Its many-sided activities included the publishing of the Bible, religious books, and journals; preaching, Sunday schools, and Bible study groups; charitable work; summer camps; various affiliated sisterhoods of devoted celibate women and numerous other associations for various social groups (e.g. parents, students, workers). In this way, Zoe brought about a revival in Greek religious life, which left its imprint in the years to come. After the end of World War II and the ensuing Civil War (1946–49), Zoe contributed to Greece's restoration. With the support of the state and the help of the "Christian Union of Professional Men" and its monthly magazine *Aktines*, edited by the law professor Alexandros Tsirintanis, its activities were incorporated in the 1950s into a broader quasi-messianic vision of creating a wholly new Orthodox Greece within the frame of a "Helleno-Christian Civilization". This led to the culmination of its power and prestige in that decade.

Between 1958 and 1960, however, an internal split appeared within Zoe. Three of the oldest founding members, including P. Trempelas (1886–1977), professor of theology at the University of Athens, decided to leave Zoe and create a new brotherhood, Sotir. Sotir claimed a return to the authentic spiritual heritage left by E. Matthopoulos and exhibited more conservative orientations than Zoe. Despite initial difficulties, Sotir managed to develop a stable organization and to expand its activities across the country. However, this schism had a negative impact upon the brotherhoods' influence. Numerous previous members dissociated themselves completely from them and criticized them for deviating from the true Orthodox tradition.

In the case of the brotherhood Stavros, things are different. It appeared first in 1959 and in a more organized form in 1966. Its founder was archimandrite Avgustinos Kantiotis, who in 1967 became bishop of Florina. Born in 1907, Kantiotis undertook extensive missionary activity in many dioceses and made headlines with his militant and uncompromising views on issues pertaining to Orthodox dogma and ethos. As a result, his conflicts with Church and state officials were numerous, but he did not change his attitude even after his elevation to a bishopric. Stavros has been influenced to a certain extent by Zoe, but exhibits some differences too. Kantiotis's charismatic personality remained of paramount importance for his movement, while the other brotherhoods were not dependent on one particular person. Furthermore, Kantiotis's critique was fierce and fanatical, whereas the other brotherhoods were generally milder in their overall attitude. Finally, as far as the Lydia brotherhood is concerned, it is based in northern Greece and was founded by archimandrite Theophilos Zisopoulos.

The most serious problem of the brotherhoods has been their relationship with the official Church. Although they belonged to the Church and their founders were Orthodox clerics, the Church hierarchy has always been critical of their independence, their social influence, and their elitism. In addition, the official Church organization for internal mission, the Apostoliki Diakonia ("Apostolic Service"), became active from the late 1940s onwards; in other words, relatively late in comparison to Zoe, which had been far more successful. Various accusations were brought against Zoe as early as 1914 and later in 1923, but without repercussions. The "cold war" between the Church and Zoe continued. Serious criticism of the brotherhoods appeared after the split between Zoe and Sotir, and was made known to a wider public through newspaper articles and the media. The brotherhoods were labelled as sectarian, puritanical, pietistic, and activist movements, modelled upon western religious orders such as Opus Dei. They distanced themselves from authentic Orthodoxy and genuine ecclesiastical life through their independence from parish life and the local bishops. They were regarded either as being parasitic upon the Church or as lying entirely outside the Church body. Their political preferences and social conservatism, manifested in their general support of the military junta (1967–74) and of the policies of archbishop Ieronymos Kotsonis, a former Zoe member, provoked biting criticism. The brotherhoods were accused of attempting to control the Church and holding politicians under their religio-ideological influence. More recently, the brotherhoods were officially held responsible for spreading fundamentalist attitudes within the Greek Church in various long-standing violent conflicts, as manifested in the diocese of Larissa.

The brotherhoods have tried repeatedly to refute these accusations and show their historical roots in the Orthodox tradition. They have pointed to their contributions to Greek religious life, especially regarding the revival of sacramental practices and mission. They have also emphasized that their members remain in the Orthodox Church, since there has never been a schism between them. Clerics belonging to the brotherhoods are employed in several dioceses across the country. Their sectarian features (e.g. elitism, pietistic morals, tension with the surrounding secular culture) have not yet transformed them into full-fledged sects. Their intention to remain within the Church is evident in many ways. After all, Stavros's founder and leader A. Kantiotis is an Orthodox bishop. Two other eminent and learned hierarchs, the archbishop of Albania, Anastasios Yannoulatos, and the bishop of North and South America, Dimitrios Trakatellis, were previously members of Zoe. Nevertheless, the brotherhoods' independence and elitism may eventually lead them to separate from the Church, especially if they think that the Church is making dangerous compromises regarding the Orthodox faith. The emergence of Old Calendarists in 20th-century Greece through a schism shows that such developments can happen.

VASILIOS MAKRIDES

Further Reading

Angelopoulos, Athanasios, "Selides Ekklisiastikis Istorias" [Pages of Ecclesiastical History] in *Xenia Iakovo Archiepiskopo Voreiou kai Notiou Amerikis* [A Greeting to Iacovos, Archbishop of North and South America], Thessalonica, 1985

Bratsiotis, Panagiotis, "Die Theologen-Bruderschaft 'Zoë'", *Zeitschrift für Religions- und Geistesgeschichte*, 12 (1960): pp. 371–84

Constantelos, Demetrios J., "The Zoe Movement in Greece", *St Vladimir's Seminary Quarterly*, 3 (1959): pp. 11–25

Diamantopoulos, Leonidas, *Ekklisia kai Thriskevtikai Organoseis* [The Church and Religious Societies], 3rd edition, Athens, 1988

Giannakopoulos, Angelos, *Die Theologen-Bruderschaften in Griechenland*, Frankfurt: Peter Lang, 1999

Gousidis, Alexandros, *Oi Christianikes Organoseis: I Periptosi tis Adelphotitos Theologon i "Zoi": Koinoniologiki Prosengisi* [The Christian Societies: The Case of the Theologians' Brotherhood "Zoe": A Sociological Approach], 2nd edition, Thessaloniki, 1993

Hammond, Peter, *The Waters of Marah: The Present State of the Greek Church*, London: Rockliffe, and New York: Macmillan, 1956, pp. 125–40

Harakas, Stanley, "Alexander N. Tsirintanis on the Present Age", *Greek Orthodox Theological Review*, 2 (1956): pp. 75–82

Jioultsis, Basil, "Religious Brotherhoods: A Sociological View", *Social Compass*, 22 (1975): pp. 67–83

Kalyvas, Christophoros, *Monachismos kai Ierapostolikai Adelphotites* [Monasticism and Apostolic Brotherhoods], Athens, 1985

Maczewski, Christoph, *Die Zoi-Bewegung Griechenlands: Ein Beitrag zum Traditionsproblem der Ostkirche*, Göttingen: Vandenhoeck & Ruprecht, 1970

Makrides, Vasilios, "The Brotherhoods of Theologians in Contemporary Greece", *Greek Orthodox Theological Review*, 33 (1988): pp. 167–87

Mantzaridis, Georgios, *Koinoniologia tou Christianismou* [Sociology of Christianity], 4th edition, Thessalonica, 1990, pp. 302–14

Moustakis, Yorgos, *I Gennisi tou Christianofasismou stin Ellada* [The Birth of Christian Fascism in Greece], Athens, 1983

Papakostas, Seraphim, *Eusebius Matthopoulos, Founder of Zoe: A Biography*, London: SPCK, 1939

Psilopoulos, Emmanuel, "Le Mouvement 'Zoë' dans l'Église orthodoxe de Grèce", *Revue des Sciences Religieuses*, 40 (1966): pp. 258–89

Rinvolucri, Mario, *Anatomy of a Church: Greek Orthodoxy Today*, London: Burns and Oates, and New York: Fordham University Press, 1966, pp. 81–101

Yannaras, Christos, *Kataphygio Ideon: Martyria* [The Refuge of Ideas: Testimony], Athens, 1987

Renaissance, Palaiologan

During its politically weak and socially decadent final two centuries (1261–1453), the Byzantine empire underwent a cultural renaissance that revitalized art, architecture, philosophy, music, religion, and other manifestations of the intellect and spirit. This flowering, a true renaissance fostered by Byzantium's last dynasty, the Palaiologoi, crucially influenced the Italian Renaissance and so all subsequent western culture. The Orthodox Balkans and Russia, whose conversion and religion depended on the Greeks, have a strong Byzantine character to this day, and the Palaiologan achievement properly includes their art. Many monuments and objects of Palaiologan art and religion (these two were the same to them) remain, though they represent a mere fraction of what was produced by the imperial workshops and under private patronage (what Greeks called the "poetic" cause). These prove that the empire's final weakness was political and financial only, and that under the Palaiologoi Byzantine culture was not at its last gasp, as older historians, following Gibbon in his magisterial *The History of the Decline and Fall of the Roman Empire* (1776–88), tended to assert, but rather in a period of spectacular renewal till near the end. Greek high culture thus evolved for more than 2,000 years without a break.

Byzantine culture properly begins during the reign of the emperor Constantine the Great (died 337), who made it eastern (based on Constantinople) and Christian. Thus Byzantium developed a culture that was compounded of Classical and oriental elements, with an emperor as its heart and a patriarch as its soul. In this, Palaiologan culture is no different from that of Justinian's age. Though the Fourth Crusade, in 1204, was a disaster from which the Greeks never fully recovered – Venice carried off so much booty that its artistic tradition remained Byzantine for 250 years – from the embers the Palaiologan dynasty eventually rose in splendour. Michael VIII Palaiologos (1259–82), scion of an old Byzantine family, reconquered Constantinople in 1261 and, despite reduced circumstances, undertook the restoration of houses, fora, market places, theatres, law courts, and churches, and encouraged the astonishing late flowering that we rightly call the Palaiologan Renaissance.

In ways unavailable to the West, this renaissance was a continuation; Greek intellectuals did not have to discover Plato and Euripides, for they had never forgotten them. And there was no Byzantine century without poetry, history, theology, and the copying and illuminating of manuscripts. The Italians, for their revival, were dependent on Byzantium for their Hellenism, just as the Byzantines had to look to the West for military succour, which never came, though several Palaiologan emperors were ready to submit to Rome for it.

Intellectual activity remained much higher in Byzantium than in the West. George Pachymeres (died c.1310), for example, wrote a *Roman History*, a 13-volume work that is accurate and emphasizes the theological nature of recent events. He also composed a theological treatise on the doctrine of the Trinity. His collection of lectures (*Compendium of Four Mathematics*) on mathematics, music, geometry, and astronomy, which became the standard academic text in Byzantine culture, was one of the first to use Arabic numbers, and his compendium of the philosophy of Aristotle was also for school use. Theodore Metochites' *Philosophical and Historical Miscellany* is an encyclopaedic collection of tracts and essays on Classical thought, history, and literature, comprising more than 70 Greek authors; he also produced treatises on physics, astronomy, physiology, and Aristotelian psychology. His commentaries on Plato's *Dialogues* were an important influence on Neoplatonic thought, and his *Embassy Papers* an invaluable history. The emperor John VI Kantakouzenos (1341/47–54) retired to a monastery to compose his *Histories* and theological works. Their volume and quality are astonishing.

Byzantine art had always striven to reflect the divine shadow on earth, and to open a window on heavenly permanencies and the theological mystery of transcendent reality. Severely Platonist, it sought the divine lineaments, usually as a setting for the liturgy; secular art, though it existed, was minor. The art of the Palaiologan Renaissance, as developed in mosaic, fresco, and icon-painting – to say nothing of ivory carving, liturgical music, and textiles – continued this, but was gentler than its predecessor; it strove to please and observe as well as to inspire, and so is easier for us to enjoy.

Probably the greatest surviving masterpiece of Palaiologan art is the church of St Saviour in Chora at Constantinople, also known by its Turkish name, the Kariye Cami. Michael's son and heir, Andronikos II Palaiologos (1282–1328), was not fierce and calculating like his father but rather amiable and intellectual; he fostered the golden age of the great monastery complex on Mount Athos. One of his chief ministers, the same rich and pious scholar Theodore Metochites (died 1332), had the church built and decorated to his own excellent, classicizing taste. It is full of glittering mosaics of the highest quality, one of which shows Theodore himself in an immense oriental hat and rich robe offering his church to Christ. But perhaps the church's high point is the Resurrection fresco in the side chapel. These works, while they maintain traditional spiritual power, are replete with humanism, colour, movement, and

narrative, attributes often associated with the Italian Renaissance.

After the plague of 1346 killed a third or more of the population of Constantinople, such an expensive, elaborate project was not attempted again; civil war and foreign threats worsened the situation. With the rise of the Ottoman Turks, Byzantines could see the end coming, and their art and thought turned inwards. Icons, often for personal adoration, now became the chief mode, and the one that best continued the tradition after the fall.

This inward turn was intensified by heschyasm, the religious cause célèbre of the day. Though inextricably intertwined with politics in the violent Byzantine way, this quietist doctrine became dominant on Mount Athos and its chief apologist, Gregory Palamas, was canonized. As the empire grew poorer, Athos's monasteries grew richer, and much Byzantine scholarship, so coveted by the West, was encouraged and preserved there. There frescos were painted, church decoration schemes formalized, and Byzantine chant developed to its present form.

Constantinople was not the only venue for the Palaiologan Renaissance. The prosperous city of Thessalonica was always an artistic centre. And the empire's last outpost was at Mistra in the Peloponnese, whose churches with their elaborate brickwork and richly coloured frescos can still be visited. The jewel of Mistra, however, was the philosopher Gemistos Plethon, who was celebrated throughout Europe; the manuscript of his last work, a strange amalgam of Christianity, Platonism, the Classical pantheon, and Zoroastrianism, was destroyed on his death in 1452 for its dangerously baffling thought.

When the peaceable sultan Murad II was succeeded by his brilliant and bellicose son Mehmet II (1451–81), the end was inevitable. On 29 May 1453 Constantinople fell for ever. No more a separate entity, its civilization became an element, indeed a crucial element, in the emerging culture of the West. The last emperor, Constantine XI Palaiologos (Odysseus Elytis hymned him as "the last Greek"), went down heroically fighting alongside his people; his body was never found.

JEFFREY CARSON

See also Byzantine Period (Late), Historiography, Mistra, Mosaic, Music, Painting

Further Reading

Baynes, N.H., *Byzantine Studies and Other Essays*, London: Athlone Press, 1960

Boyd, Susan A., *Byzantine Art*, Chicago: University of Chicago Press, 1979

Geanakoplos, Deno John, *Emperor Michael Palaeologus and the West, 1258–1282: A Study in Byzantine–Latin Relations*, Cambridge, Massachusetts: Harvard University Press, 1959

Geanakoplos, Deno John, *Byzantium: Church, Society, and Civilization Seen through Contemporary Eyes*, Chicago: University of Chicago Press, 1984

Gibbon, Edward, *The History of the Decline and Fall of the Roman Empire*, 6 vols, 1761–88; edited by J.B. Bury, 7 vols, London: Methuen, 1926–29

Godfrey, John, *1204: The Unholy Crusade*, Oxford and New York: Oxford University Press, 1980

Haussig, H.W., *A History of Byzantine Civilization*, New York: Praeger, and London: Thames and Hudson, 1971

Hussey, J.M., *The Byzantine World*, 4th edition, London: Hutchinson, 1970

Miller, William, *The Latins in the Levant: A History of Frankish Greece, 1204–1566*, London: John Murray, and New York: Dutton, 1908; reprinted Cambridge: Speculum Historiale, and New York: Barnes and Noble, 1964

Norwich, John Julius, *Byzantium: The Decline and Fall*, London and New York: Viking, 1995

Ostrogorsky, George, "The Palaeologi" in *The Byzantine Empire*, part 1, edited by J.M. Hussey, Cambridge: Cambridge University Press, 1966 (*The Cambridge Medieval History*, vol. 4, 2nd edition)

Ostrogorsky, George, *History of the Byzantine State*, 2nd edition, Oxford: Blackwell, 1968; New Brunswick, New Jersey: Rutgers University Press, 1969

Kazhdan, A.P. (editor), *The Oxford Dictionary of Byzantium*, 3 vols, New York and Oxford: Oxford University Press, 1991

Rice, D. Talbot, *Art of the Byzantine Era*, London: Thames and Hudson, and New York: Praeger, 1963

Rice, D. Talbot, *The Byzantines*, revised edition, London: Thames and Hudson, and New York: Praeger, 1964

Runciman, Steven, *The Fall of Constantinople, 1453*, Cambridge: Cambridge University Press, 1965

Runciman, Steven, *The Last Byzantine Renaissance*, Cambridge: Cambridge University Press, 1970

Runciman, Steven, *Byzantine Style and Civilization*, Harmondsworth and Baltimore: Penguin, 1975, reprinted 1990

Runciman, Steven, *Mistra: Byzantine Capital of the Peloponnese*, London: Thames and Hudson, 1980

Underwood, Paul A., *The Kariye Djami*, 3 vols, New York: Bollingen Foundation, 1966; London: Routledge and Kegan Paul, 1967

Vasiliev, A.A., *History of the Byzantine Empire, 324–1453*, revised edition, 2 vols, Madison: University of Wisconsin Press, 1952

Renaissance, Veneto-Cretan

The successful colonial development of Crete by the Most Serene Republic of Venice from 1211 until 1669 overlapped culturally with the period of the Renaissance in Italy. The island consequently became one of the most significant locations in Greek lands where new Western developments penetrated into the visual arts, literature, and music. The townscape of the capital city Candia (modern Herakleion) was soon developed into a vista of churches and houses of Gothic and Renaissance appearance, and the other two major ports of Rethymnon and Chania (called La Canea) were equally visibly westernized, and endowed with ornamental fountains and other amenities. The Venetian possessions in previously Byzantine lands after the Fourth Crusade had disrupted the empire in 1204 were, of course, extensive, but Crete, particularly after the fall of Constantinople in 1453, acted as a key cultural centre, and, through its maritime connections with Venice, was the recognized place of transit for Byzantine refugees and scholars between Byzantium and Italy.

An issue in understanding the westernization of Cretan painting is to what extent artists travelled backwards and forwards between Candia and Venice and to what extent western objects and artists came to the island. Precise information on artists, artist objects, patronage, and the intermarriage of Cretans and Venetians is available in the notarial archives of the dukes of Candia who, under the treaty of 16 September 1669 between Francesco Morosini and the Ottoman Turks, were given the concession of transport together with other valuables to Venice. The continuing study of these documents

has allowed more precise discussion of the working practices and nature of artistic organization in Crete than in any other Byzantine or Hellenic community. Equally the existence of the Greek community in Venice which maintained contacts with Crete gave a permanent place in Italy where itinerant artists could expect support and patronage. From the archival documents we can construct a time sequence of the main artists and their families who worked in Crete (and some in Venice and elsewhere in Italy as well). Some of the most prominent names over the period are Nicholas Philanthropenos (active 1375–1440), Angelos Akatantos (*fl.*1436–*c.*1457), John Akatantos (*fl.*1435–77), Andreas Ritzos (1422–*c.*1492), his son Nikolaos Ritzos (*fl.*1460–*c.*1507), his son Maneas Ritzos (*fl.*1528–54), Andreas Pavias (d. after 1504), Nikolaos Tzafouris (d. before 1509), Angelos Bitzamanos (1467–1532), Theophanes Strelitzas Vathas (often known as Theophanes of Crete, *c.*1490–1559), Michael Damaskinos (1530/35–92), Georgios Klontzas (*c.*1530–1608), and El Greco (Domenikos Theotokopoulos, *c.*1541–1614). But there are many more documented artists, both during this period and in the 17th century. What is important for the Veneto-Cretan Renaissance is that these names can be connected with extant works, many with signatures, and so can be appreciated as distinctive artistic personalities during the period. This means that in Crete we can characterize the architectural nature of the built environment, both secular and ecclesiastical; we can track the careers of icon painters, manuscript painters, and wall painters; and we can also see how Cretan artists spread their ideas both as a result of other commissions in the Orthodox world (the most notable case being the wall paintings and icons of Theophanes the Cretan and his sons in monasteries at Meteora and Mount Athos) and through sales of icons in Italy and elsewhere in western Europe (some mass-produced in Crete and exported).

Politically Venetian Crete was administered by a governor, the duke, based in Candia. This was a short-term post for two or three years only, after which the holder was expected to go back to Venice. A high proportion of Cretans remained loyal to their Byzantine past and traditions, and although the Venetians expelled the bishops, the Orthodox parish churches and monasteries were maintained and developed, even if stripped of their estates. The head of the Christian Church in Crete was the Latin archbishop. Orthodox priests could be ordained only outside the island and the movement of monks and priests was controlled. Venice after the Council of Florence of 1439 tried to impose on Crete the union of the Orthodox and Catholic Churches, but while their efforts were in the long term unsuccessful such activities are reflected in a number of works of art of this period that ostentatiously merge Byzantine and Renaissance styles and subject matter (for example a panel by Andreas Ritzos of the monogram IHS, standing for *Jesus Hominum Salvator* (Jesus Saviour of Men), the emblem of the Franciscan saint Bernardino of Siena (1380–1444) who was notable for his attempt to unite the Churches). While institutionally the attempted unification of the Churches was a failure in Crete, in cultural terms the westernization of Byzantine art which became so conspicuous a feature of the products of Cretan artists did radically transform the character of Orthodox art.

It is also clear that, despite the failure to unify the Churches, congregations in the Catholic and Orthodox churches on the

Veneto-Cretan Renaissance: church of the Arkadi monastery near Rethymnon, built in 1587

island were mixed, with Catholics present at Orthodox services. Catholic churches no doubt contained decorations carried out by Cretan artists and both Latin and Greek inscriptions are found on Cretan icons. Renaissance musical settings for the Mass, religious processions, and secular occasions were composed on Crete. The demography of the island inevitably became less polarized over the course of the period. When the Venetians took over at the beginning of the 13th century, the island was divided up into large estates owned either by the Greek aristocracy (*archontes*) or by the Orthodox monasteries. This situation soon changed (despite some opposition), and by 1300 the countryside had been organized into four administrative districts which consisted of properties now in large part owned by Venetian colonists who had been given land in return for military duties. Cretan society had now developed into four categories: *nobili veneti*, the Venetian colonists; *nobili cretensi*, the new assimilated group of intermarried Venetian and Greek aristocracy; a bourgeoisie; and the peasants. The Latins preferred to live in towns, and so village churches remained Orthodox. With few exceptions, new church buildings in the villages were relatively small, usually with barrel vaults over the nave; western architectural features might occur in the exterior in the window mouldings or architectural carvings, particularly on the apse. The buoyant nature of patronage is shown in western Crete by the fact that eight

churches were decorated there between 1313 and 1347. The work was entrusted to one artist who signed the wall-paintings as John Pagomenos.

The architectural development of the cities was substantial (and has only become less obvious today through earthquake and war damage and through neglect and destruction in the first half of the 20th century). Candia was dominated by the spire and high Gothic nave of the church of San Marco (now St Mark's Hall, converted from use in the Turkish period as a mosque), and in front of this church has survived the fountain built by Morosini the Elder in 1626–28. Other important churches were those of St Peter and St Titus. The inner harbour is guarded by the Venetian fortress (1523–40), and the 16th-century arsenals have survived (the Venetian loggia is a modern reconstruction). The Venetian population could describe their city as having a Palazzo Ducale and Palazzo del Capitan Generale on the Piazza del Biada, while on the Piazza del Signore were the Palazzo del Capitan Grande and the Loggia. The third piazza contained the church of San Marco. The Venetians built the imposing walls and fortress at Rethymnon (the latter was constructed in the years 1573–83 by the Venetian engineer Pallavicini), and they fully developed Chania with a cathedral, rector's palace, walls, and bastions, and with a protected harbour and arsenal. These ports became ostentatious Venetian fortress cities, but the vocabulary of

Renaissance architectural forms spread throughout the island also as a result of church building. This operated in two distinct ways. First, as a result of the encouragement of missionary activities to convert Cretans to Catholicism, impressive churches were built over the island to house the monastic orders (Franciscans, Dominicans, and Augustinians). The Dominicans built St Peter Martyr close to the port of Candia, and its surviving shell shows that it was a large single-naved church with a flat sanctuary, pointed wooden roof, and ribbed vaults. The rich church of St Francis at Candia disappeared in the Turkish period, and the mendicant church of S. Salvador where many prominent Venetians were buried was demolished in 1970, but the smaller church of St Mary of the Crusaders has survived and indicates the nature of a simple Italianate church of the early Venetian period. The monuments of Chania give a much better record of the Italian workmanship of the period, with the Dominican church of St Nicholas (c. 1300), San Salvador, and the church of St Francis (now the archaeological museum) which is a grand church of the 14th century (and later additions) with rib vaults, capitals, and a bell-tower with window tracery, closely copied from Venetian models. The second way in which the environment was westernized was through the adoption by Orthodox monasteries and other civic buildings of the ornamental and structural features of Italian architecture: the west front of the church of the Arkadi monastery (near Rethymnon) built in 1587 is a complex mix of Classical orders and Renaissance ornamentation, and on the Akrotiri peninsula near Chania both the monastery of Hagia Triada (built in the 17th century by two Venetian monks of the family Zangaroli who had converted to the Orthodox faith) and the Gouverneto monastery of St John are built in stone with Renaissance mouldings and Classical façades.

The atmosphere of the Veneto-Cretan Renaissance is therefore consciously proclaimed by its Italianate civic environment, but the intellectual climate was equally strongly influenced by humanist interests, communicated in part through the new printing presses of Venice and the development of literary societies or academies in each of the three main cities of Crete. All Cretan writers used some form of the vernacular, and in their poetry and prose covered a range of modes. The masterpiece of religious drama is *The Sacrifice of Abraham*, a short and very popular play in rhyming couplets, generally attributed to Vitsentzos Kornaros (1553–1613/14), who was also the author of a poetic romance, the *Erotokritos*, in which the two separate strands of Greek and Western narrative fiction have been described as coming together. From the same period of production comes the *Erofili*, a classicizing tragedy of 3205 verses written in Rethymnon around 1600 by Georgios Chortatsis. The miniature drama *Fortounatos* by Markos Antonios Foskolos (1597–1662) supplies a literary work from this period by a writer of Venetian origin and Catholic faith who in language and culture was integrated with the Greek-speaking majority.

While the literary scene flourished in the last century of the Venetian period, the pace of the transformation of the pictorial arts in Crete can be succinctly measured over the whole period. In the initial phase of conservatism the 14th-century wall-paintings of the church of Panagia Kera at Kritsa exhibit a strongly traditional nature; they relate closely in style to such

Byzantine works as the Peribleptos church at Mistra in the Peloponnese. Among the innovators of the 15th century, one of the most prolific artists was Angelos Akotantos (whose career is well documented in his will of 1436 which is preserved in the Venetian archives). He worked in Crete and visited Constantinople, and among his signed icons ("Hand of Angelos") are paintings in both a decorative Byzantine style and also a more narrative and naturalistic style which exhibits a knowledge of Venetian and Tuscan quattrocento interests in landscape and perspective. Other 15th-century artists show a considerable ability to use Italian themes and expressive forms. A century later, when the literary scene was so highly prominent, the paintings of Michael Damaskinos and the young El Greco, who both worked in Venice as well as Crete, fully integrated the developments in colour and tone of Venetian Renaissance artists, while their contemporary Georgios Klontzas worked in a more miniaturist and decorative manner.

The Veneto-Cretan Renaissance was a reflection of contact with the Italian Renaissance and not a separate autonomous movement. It came to an end with the departure of the Venetian colonists. However, the result of eastern contacts with the west in this impressively creative environment was permanently to transform eastern Christian art into a new form of expression and to change the horizons of Orthodox society and thinking. As a cultural unit on the periphery of the Renaissance world, Crete selectively appropriated Italian ideas, and thereby also offers a contemporary critical assessment of the values of that Renaissance.

ROBIN CORMACK

See also Architecture (religious), Crete, Music, Painting, Venetokratia, Venice

Further Reading

Acheimastou-Potamianou, Myrtali (editor), *From Byzantium to El Greco: Greek Frescoes and Icons*, London: Royal Academy of Arts, 1987 (exhibition catalogue)

Bourboudakis, Manolis, Klaus Gallas, and Klaus Wessel, *Byzantinisches Kreta*, Munich: Hirmer, 1983

Bourboudakis, Manolis (editor), *Eikones tis Kritikis Technis* [Icons of Cretan Art], Herakleion and Athens, 1993 (exhibition catalogue)

Chatzidakis, Manolis, *Etudes sur la peinture postbyzantine*, London: Variorum, 1976

Chatzidakis, Manolis and E. Drakopoulou, *Hellenes zographoi meta ten Halose, 1450–1830* [Greek Painters after the Fall, 1450–1830], 2 vols, Athens, 1987–97

Chatzidakis, Nano, *From Candia to Venice: Greek Icons in Italy, 15th–16th Centuries*, Athens: Foundation for Hellenic Culture, 1993

Chatzidakis, Nano, *Icons: The Velimezis Collection*, Athens, 1998

Cormack, Robin, *Painting the Soul: Icons, Death Masks, and Shrouds*, London: Reaktion, 1997

Georgopoulou, M., "Late Medieval Crete and Venice: An Appropriation of Byzantine Heritage", *Art Bulletin*, 77 (1995): pp. 479–96

Gerola, Giuseppe, *I monumenti Veneti nell'Isola di Creta*, 4 vols, Venice: Istituto Veneto di Scienze, Lettere ed Arti, 1905–32

Hadjinicolaou, N. (editor), *El Greco of Crete*, Herakleion, 1995

Holton, David (editor), *Literature and Society in Renaissance Crete*, Cambridge and New York: Cambridge University Press, 1991

Panagopoulos, Beata Kitsiki, *Cistercian and Mendicant Monasteries in Medieval Greece*, Chicago: University of Chicago Press, 1979

Republic

Meaning a political system in which supreme power is vested in the people, a republic is the modern equivalent of an ancient democratic city state. Since the birth of the modern Greek state in 1830 experience of republican government has been considerable, but interrupted. There were declarations by Greek national assemblies in republican directions even before the establishment of the Greek state, during the War of Independence. Hence the period of the War of Independence and the first years in the life of the new state have been regarded as the First Republic (1821–32). Despite clear indications of an increasing preference for a republican model, geostrategic realities, foreign influences, and the complex domestic situation eventually led to the imposition of monarchy in 1832. After the 1830s, however, it became evident that different sociopolitical factions championed different models of government. Those who aimed to initiate a process of state-building in the western tradition pushed for a centralized state with strong executive and rationalized administrative structures. On the other hand, those who wished to retain the power of local notables had a preference for more decentralized governmental structures.

The westernizers prevailed in the end, despite the power of the conservative local oligarchies. Still, the state apparatus soon became colonized by the so-called *tzakia*, influential families whose origins can be traced to those local notables (*proestoi*) who had played a critical role during the War of Independence. By and large, the *tzakia* increasingly favoured a loose parliamentary model, since the latter, adapted to 19th-century Greek conditions, would simultaneously constrain the capacities and the reach of central authority and assist the patrician families to strengthen their role in the state, based on their local power resources and their extensive presence in parliament. In 1875 the king accepted the parliamentary principle in government formation, against the background of the liberal constitution of 1864 and of the early (1844) declaration of parliamentarism. The balance thus achieved survived until 1909, when a coup set in motion developments that favoured the ascendancy of liberal statesmen and the prevalence of liberal institutions. The formation of a modernized and operational political system, a rationalized bureaucracy, and a professional army was a slow and difficult process, and it was not until the 1920s that the Greek state can be said to have acquired modern structures of government.

The political regime of the Second Republic (between 1924 and 1935) represents a remarkable combination of a liberal institutional edifice and political uncertainty. The revision in 1911 of the Constitution of 1864 had as a main objective the establishment of a modern constitutional state based on respect for parliamentary government and the rule of law. In brief, there were strong liberal elements in the Constitution of 1864/1911 and these were extended and acquired a republican form in the Constitution of 1927. Venizelos, the liberal statesman, aimed to steer the Second Republic towards liberal consolidation on the domestic front and in foreign policy. In 1930 Greece and Turkey signed the Atatürk–Venizelos agreements, which were largely the culmination of Venizelos's efforts to put an end to the irredentist drive, which had suffered a massive blow in 1922 with Greek defeat in Asia Minor and the expulsion of the Greek population, and to redirect Greek policy. At the same time, the Second Republic bears the marks of the conflict between the republicans and the royalists, a conflict that acquired considerable dimensions and became a crucial parameter in Greek politics in the early decades of the 20th century (see Mavrogordatos, 1983). One aspect of the legacy of the cleavage over the regime was the politicization of the military, which participated in various royalist or republican coup and counter-coup activities throughout the early decades of the century (see Veremis, 1997).

The restoration of the monarchy after World War II and the Civil War took place in a context of political turmoil and institutional uncertainty. It was only with the Constitution of 1952 that a new institutional equilibrium was reached, based on the consolidation of a political regime with several authoritarian aspects. The Constitution of 1952 was, in many respects, "an authoritarian version of the liberal constitution of 1864/1911" (Alivizatos, 1979). First, it was based on and confirmed a political regime that excluded the left, mainly through the extension of various measures and decrees from the period of the Civil War into the postwar period. Second, it provided for a strong executive which was later used in another direction, namely the conservative modernization efforts of the late 1950s and early 1960s under Constantine Karamanlis (Charalambis, 1985). The Constitution of 1952 remained in place until 1967, when a military coup installed an authoritarian regime. The coup was apparently aiming to block the possibility of a centre-left government emerging from the planned elections of 1967. The regime's attempts to institutionalize itself proved unsuccessful. The main feature of the regime was "a blind and militant anticommunism and a conscious attempt to secure its political base by resuscitating the polarization of the civil war. Its dismal failure was due as much to its anachronistic message as to the inability to appreciate the enormous transformation that Greek society had undergone since the 1940s" (Diamandouros, 1995, p.287). The authoritarian regime collapsed in 1974 amid foreign-policy crisis and domestic upheaval.

The Third Republic (since 1974) represents the most successful period of sustained democratic government in the history of the modern Greek state. In 1974 a referendum abolished the monarchy, whose ambivalent role in domestic politics in the 1960s was widely seen as a crucial factor in causing the political instability that paved the way for the coup in 1967. The republican Constitution of 1975 is a modern democratic constitutional document. From the perspective of a comparison with similar documents in countries that went through comparable political processes in the 1970s, such as Portugal, the Greek constitution included aspects that manifest a clear break with the recent past without necessarily incorporating elements that marked the particular mode of regime change (such as the constitutional role of the Council of the Revolution in the Portuguese Constitution of 1976, which was later amended). The authoritarian potential in conservative rule having exhausted itself, the new equilibrium which was reflected in the 1975 Constitution allowed the operation of liberal institutions, lifted the ban on the communist left, and sought to reorient the role of the military in the political system. But there were also elements of continuity with the situation before the coup. The emphasis on a strong executive essentially represented a continuity from political and institutional strategies before 1967, only this time the organization of relationships between the head of state, the government, and the parliament revealed the influence of French semi-presidentialism. Also, the regime change in 1974 did little to challenge the inherited corporatist structures which govern the participation of organized interests in the making and implementation of policy. The transformation of interest politics was gradual and took place in the 1980s and 1990s through the shifts and the revisions in the structures of policy making and collective action, largely as a response to the process of Europeanization (see Lavdas, 1997).

The limited constitutional revision of 1986 eliminated most of the extensive powers of the president of the republic. Despite its opportunist aspects, which reflected the government's political priorities, the limited constitutional revision of 1986 marked an important shift in the institutional balance of power. The revision's institutional net result has been to enhance further the role and powers of the prime minister and to constrain the president of the republic, whose role became largely ceremonial. To some extent, the revision was consistent with the socialist (PASOK) analysis of the 1975 Constitution arming the president with extensive powers and distorting parliamentarism. It can be argued that the revision reduced the president's capacity "to exercise initiative in moments when it is most needed, that is, during political uncertainty or crisis", while at the same time helping to create a unitary power circuit centring on a powerful prime minister and his government majority (Diamandouros, 1995, p.295). In this sense, the revision represented an unnecessarily drastic reduction of the powers of the head of state. A more reasoned revision might have resulted in a more efficient organization of constitutional relationships.

Under the Third Republic Greece has been able to reach considerable levels of affluence and political stability. The processes of democratization and Europeanization led to changes in the practice of government in terms of both form (governmental and administrative structures) and content (public policies). Since 1981 membership in the EC/EU has given a new sense of direction to the Greek state. New orientations in public policy have included the spatial reorganization of government and the emergence of a new pluralism of policy-making centres at various levels: local, regional, national, European. It can be argued that, despite rhetorical assurances to the contrary, the political system has been slower to respond to the process of Europeanization in comparison to the economic and even the administrative and policy-making systems. Persistent clientelist linkages have resulted in parties and political leaderships often being unable to set priorities and act in a coherent way. On the other hand, both PASOK and New Democracy have been able to avoid extensive fragmentation and, crucially, have been able to play reasonably well their institutional roles in government and in opposition since 1974. More generally, republican government has ceased to be a divisive issue. Against the background of a successful regime change in 1974, the Third Republic has been able to consolidate itself as a modern democracy.

KOSTAS A. LAVDAS

See also City State, Constitution, Government, Monarchy

Further Reading

Alivizatos, Nicos, *Les Institutions politiques de la Grèce à travers les crises, 1922–1974*, Paris: Librarie Générale de Droit et de Jurisprudence, 1979

Blinkhorn, Martin and Thanos Veremis (editors), "Modern Greece: Nationalism and Nationality", *European History Quarterly*, special issue, 19 (1989)

Charalambis, Dimitris, *Stratos kai Politiki Exousia: I Domi tis Exousias stin Metemphilaki Ellada* [The Military and Political Power: The Structure of Power in Postwar Greece], Athens: Exantas, 1985

Clogg, Richard (editor), *Greece, 1981–89: The Populist Decade*, London: Macmillan, and New York: St Martin's Press, 1993

Coutogeorgis, Georgios (editor), *Koinonikes kai Politikes Dynameis stiin Ellada* [Social and Political Forces in Greece], Athens: Exantas, 1977

Dertilis, George, *Koinonikos Metaschimatismos kai Stratiotiki Epemvasi: 1880–1909* [Social Transformation and Military Intervention, 1880–1909], Athens: Exantas, 1977

Diamandouros, Nikiforos, "Politics and Constitutionalism in Greece: The 1975 Constitution in Historical Perspective" in *Politics, Society and Democracy: Comparative Studies*, edited by H.E. Chehabi and Alfred Stepan, Boulder, Colorado: Westview Press, 1995

Henderson, G.P., *The Revival of Greek Thought 1620–1830*, Edinburgh and London: Scottish Academic Press, 1971

Kaltchas, Nicholas Stavrou, *Introduction to the Constitutional History of Modern Greece*, New York: Columbia University Press, 1940, reprinted New York: AMS Press, 1970

Kitromilides, Paschalis M., *Enlightenment, Nationalism, Orthodoxy: Studies in the Culture and Political Thought of South-eastern Europe*, Aldershot, Hampshire: Variorum, 1994

Lavdas, Kostas A., *The Europeanization of Greece: Interest Politics and the Crises of Integration*, London: Macmillan, and New York: St Martin's Press, 1997

Makridimitris, Antonis, *I Organosi tis Kivernisis* [The Organization of Government], Athens: Sakkoulas, 1992

Malefakis, Edward, "The Political and Socioeconomic Contours of Southern European History" in *The Politics of Democratic Consolidation: Southern Europe in Comparative Perspective*, edited by Richard Gunther, P. Nikiforos Diamandouros, and Hans Jürgen Puhle, Baltimore: Johns Hopkins University Press, 1995

Manessis, Aristoboulos, *Syntagmatiki anatheorisi tou 1986* [The Constitutional Revision of 1986], Thessalonica: Paratiritis, 1989

Mavrogordatos, George T., *Stillborn Republic: Social Coalitions and Party Strategies in Greece, 1922–1936*, Berkeley: University of California Press, 1983

Mouzelis, Nicos P., *Modern Greece: Facets of Underdevelopment*, London: Macmillan, and New York: Holmes and Meier, 1978

Pantelis, Antoine M., *Les Grands Problèmes de la nouvelle constitution hellénique*, Paris: Librairie Générale de Droit et de Jurisprudence, 1979

Petropulos, John Anthony, *Politics and Statecraft in the Kingdom of Greece, 1833–1843*, Princeton, New Jersey: Princeton University Press, 1968

Veremis, Thanos, *The Military in Greek Politics: From Independence to Democracy*, London: Hurst, 1997

Rhetoric

Rhetoric is commonly understood to have to do with persuasive speaking – when, that is, it is not thought of as verbal deception or coercion. It is important to realize, however, that rhetoric has a long and complex history as a discipline taught in schools and as a way of doing things with words in the public sphere.

As a cultural practice, the resolution of disputes and the formation of policy decisions by means of discourse can be traced back to preliterate Greek society, as is evident from numerous episodes in epic poetry, for example the assembly early in book 2 of the *Iliad* and the debate at the beginning of *Odyssey* 2. From these it is clear that there were strict conventions governing the conduct of debates, and of what was considered adequate and relevant evidence. From the mid-5th to the end of the 4th century BC, one can see the development in Athens of competing systems for the teaching and practice of speaking persuasively in court and in public assemblies, where institutional frameworks had been erected in the wake of judicial and political reforms. An old tradition has it that the teaching of rhetoric began in Sicily; but it is clear that the earliest significant lessons were given in Athens by two non-Athenians, the so-called sophists Protagoras and Gorgias. We see, next, in Plato's *Gorgias* and *Phaedrus*, a scathing critique of sophistic teaching, which, in Plato's view, would include that of Isocrates. Plato's pupil Aristotle composed a systematic treatment of rhetoric which takes issue with Plato and the sophists alike. During this same period, independently of the others, Anaximenes of Lampsacus composed another handbook, the *Rhetorica ad Alexandrum*. Its orientation is quite pragmatic, but its origins and intended audience are not clear.

Reduced to their basic elements, the rhetorics produced in Classical Greece differ from one another in important ways. The sort of rhetoric taught by Gorgias, so it seems from Plato's testimony and from the *Encomium to Helen* attributed to Gorgias, gave almost unlimited power to the speaker, who used language as a means to condition the emotions of his audience to achieve its compliance. Plato, by contrast, allowed as legitimate only a rhetoric that communicated to its audience truth arrived at by means of dialectic. The rhetoric of Aristotle's *Rhetoric* is one based on a method of arguing from "what usually happens" – i.e. "probabilities" – using rhetorical syllogisms (*enthymemata*) to provide audiences with grounds for judgement on legal, political, and moral issues. For Isocrates, the teaching of rhetoric would produce eloquent speakers with the ability to bring about consensus (*homonoia*) among the citizens of the state. The Gorgianic and Platonic models are both unilateral and asymmetric, because the only function of the audience is to attend to the speaker. The Aristotelian and Isocratean models of the speech situation tend more towards a collateral relationship between speaker and audience; and it is the audience that provides the grounds for argument and makes the decisions. These four notions of rhetoric – all developed in the same place over less than a century – have persisted down to our own time, sometimes in competition with one another, with one becoming dominant at one time, another at another time.

Only Isocrates continued to exert any significant influence over succeeding generations in antiquity, and only in the context of a rhetoric curriculum that had been developed in schools all across the Greek world after the conquests of Alexander the Great as part of the standard programme of basic education, the *enkyklios paideia*. This curriculum, designed to train boys to succeed in a range of discursive activities from letter writing to diplomacy to the practice of political and forensic oratory, was the one inherited both by Cicero (see, e.g., *De Oratore*, 3. 23ff., 59ff., 86ff.; and *Epistulae ad Familiares*, 1. 9), who continued to dominate rhetorical education in the west until well into the 17th century, and by Hermogenes (d. AD 225), whose refined versions of it virtually defined rhetoric in the eastern, or Byzantine, tradition.

The school curriculum consisted of, first, a set of elementary exercises (*progymnasmata*) and, at a later stage, declamations on assigned questions, usually of a fictitious nature. The lessons that were inculcated and repeated performance aimed at producing "the good man skilled in speaking". The art, as it was taught, consisted of five parts: invention (the techniques for discovering arguments); arrangement (consideration of order and amplitude in making the argument); expression (deploying the techniques for composition and ornamentation); memory (techniques for remembering both one's own speech and the body of accepted opinions on every subject); and delivery (the rules for the control of voice and gesture). At the heart of the process of invention is the so-called *stasis* system, a methodical way of determining the issue in dispute – is it the issue of fact, of definition, or of quality? – and of developing appropriate argumentative strategies. Students were taught a standardized format for speeches, usually based on a conventional courtroom argument, that consisted of the exordium (in Greek, *prooimion*), or introduction; the narration (*diegesis*); the argument (*pistis*) and refutation (*lysis*); and the peroration (*epilogos*). With minor variations, this standard format persisted in school rhetorics, in both the Latin and Greek traditions, throughout late antiquity, the Middle Ages, and the Renaissance.

To the school curriculum, Cicero (or perhaps his rhetoric masters) added a philosophical dimension borrowed from Academic scepticism as taught by Carneades, the idea that, in the absence of certain knowledge, it is necessary to be able to produce the arguments on both sides (*in utramque partem*) of an issue. An issue addressed by this "multivoiced method" (*multiplex ratio dicendi*), *controversia*, is resolved only in so far as one decides to adopt one of the positions in conflict as having more *probabilitas* or to modify it or to formulate a new position. It is precisely this method that Cicero uses in *De Oratore* and in such philosophical works as *De Natura Deorum*. As with Isocrates, "philosophy" is assimilated to rhetoric.

The persistence of the Isocratean–Ciceronian tradition in the west is evident in such works as Augustine's *De Doctrina Christiana* (completed c.AD 325), the last book of which is devoted to the principles of eloquence in a Christian setting; the brief dialogue on rhetoric composed by Alcuin (c.800); and the many handbooks on preaching, letter writing, and poetic composition that were in circulation during the later Middle Ages. In the east we find the tradition of Greek eloquence as defined by the likes of Isocrates and Demosthenes and systematized by Hermogenes in the productions of the so-called Second Sophistic, the works of Church Fathers, and in Byzantine diplomatic and court literature up to the fall of Constantinople in 1453.

As Christianity moved from being a persecuted sect and became the official religion of the Roman empire under Constantine, rhetoric became the vehicle both of public policy and of religious discourse. Perhaps the most important figure in the reconciliation of Classical rhetoric and Christianity was the 4th-century theologian Gregory of Nazianzus, who became in the Byzantine world the model of Christian eloquence. Commentaries on Gregory's speeches appear as early as the 6th century; and Byzantine commentaries on Hermogenes regularly cite passages from Gregory. John Chrysostom ("The Golden-Mouthed"), roughly contemporary with Gregory, was perhaps the most prolific of the Church Fathers; and his homilies were likewise looked upon as models.

During the late 10th and early 11th centuries there was a surge of scholarly production in the field of rhetoric, partly due to the recovery of near-forgotten texts under Constantine VII Porphyrogennetos and the consequent need for new commentaries. In this, John Sikeliotes and John Doxapatres (both late 10th or early 11th century) were probably the most productive and influential scholars, producing extensive commentaries on Aphthonius and Hermogenes. (Byzantine rhetoricians were not much interested in Aristotle's *Rhetoric*.) Rhetoric played a central role in the imperial court from the 11th century on, and the office of *maïstor ton rhetoron* (director of the rhetoricians) became one of the most prestigious in the bureaucracy.

Byzantine Greek rhetoric arrived in the west even before the fall of Constantinople, smuggled in, as it were, by George of Trebizond (1395–1472), who used Hermogenes extensively (but cited him seldom) in his *Rhetoricorum Libri Quinque*. But it was after the fall that the deluge of Greek rhetorical manuscripts truly began; and Aldus Manutius' publication of the two-volume *Rhetores Graeci* in 1508/09 guaranteed that Greek rhetorics would be widely disseminated throughout Europe. The Reformation played an important role in this too. Frankiskos Portos's editions of Hermogenes and of Longinus (Geneva, 1569), Sturm's editions and commentaries on Hermogenes (Strasbourg, 1570, 1571, 1575), and Margounios's 1595 Augsburg edition and translation of the *Epitome of Rhetoric* by Matthaios Kamariotes (d. *c.*1495) were all part of a short-lived programme to provide the foundations for a counter-curriculum in Protestant schools.

By the beginning of the 17th century Greeks were teaching rhetoric in the College of St Athanasios in Rome and at Padua to the many Greek students who, in the absence of such opportunites in Greece during the Tourkokratia, were sent there by their families. These teachers sought to achieve a synthesis of the Latin western and Greek eastern rhetorical traditions, and the results can be seen in, for example, the bilingual sermons of Cyril I Lukaris (d. 1638) and in the *Techne Rhetorike* (Art of Rhetoric) by Theophilos Corydalleus (London, 1625). Corydalleus (1565–1646) turns for authority to both Aristotle and Cicero in his exposition.

Rhetoric was also taught at the Flanginian Academy in Venice, founded in 1626, where, likewise, Aristotle was read alongside Cicero and Hermogenes. One of the teachers there, Frankiskos Skoufos (1644–97), drew upon his experience of Classical authors, Church Fathers, and Byzantine writers in composing his *Techne Rhetorike* (Art of Rhetoric, Venice, 1681). Significantly, he borrows also from the *De Eloquentia Sacra et Humana* of the Jesuit Nicolas Caussin and from the sermons of Segneri and Bossuet. The organization of the book is fairly conventional. Book 1 contains introductory matters and the fundamentals of invention, drawing on, among others,

Aristotle's *Topics* and doctrine of four causes. Book 2 treats of arrangement, taking each part in order. Book 3 is on style, with copious attention to metaphor and the other tropes. Book 4 continues the subject, treating at length the figures of speech and figures of thought. These latter two books make up well over half of the treatise as a whole. Book 5 treats, comparatively briefly, memory and delivery. All of this theoretical doctrine was given life in the practice of Corydalleus's student, Elias Miniates (1669–1714), one of the most famous preachers in the history of Europe.

Rhetoric, Skoufos writes, is the art of speaking well in such a way as to agitate the souls of the hearers (*Techne*, 1. 2). This conception of rhetoric is in full correspondence with other 17th-century works on the subject that, in the wake of Reformation and Counter-Reformation struggles and the relegation of morals to the realm of emotion by Cartesians and Empiricists alike, emphasized the centrality of affect, or feeling, in persuasion. Not that Skoufos neglects to treat of argumentation; but affect plays an immeasurably more important part in his rhetoric. This, in turn, explains why he draws almost indiscriminately from both Aristotle and Cicero, and holds Bossuet (whom he calls "the Gallic Hercules") and Segneri in such high regard. His goal, after all, is to give instruction on how to "move souls". Although training in rhetoric could prepare students for careers in law or government, the more intense interest in rhetoric centred on its use from the pulpit.

Many of the rhetorics produced by diaspora Greeks in the late 17th and early 18th centuries, consequently, have a distinctly homiletic focus. Gerasimos Palladas (d. 1714), who became patriarch of Alexandria, composed a treatise on rhetoric, as did Nikolaos Mavrokordates (1670–1730), who draws from Aristotle, Cicero, and St Ambrose. Anastasios Gordios (1654–1729) composed a rhetoric handbook for his students; and Ephraim the Athenian (d. 1771), metropolitan of Jerusalem, saw his rhetoric as a continuation of the tradition of the great Greek Fathers. Makarios Patmios supplemented his *Ekthesis Kanonon Rhetorikon* (Exposition of the Rules of Rhetoric, Venice, 1755) with *Evangellike Salpinx* (Evangelical Trumpet, Leipzig, 1758).

Rhetoric also continued to be taught at a more elementary level in general liberal arts curricula in schools all over the Balkans. In the National Library in Athens, for instance, there is a manuscript copy of the *Rhetorike Leucheimonousa* (White-Robed Rhetoric) composed by Anastosios Papavasilopoulos while he was teaching in Trnavo around 1700. It is a short introductory treatise composed in catechetical form that emphasizes not style, but invention. The Leichoudis brothers, Joannikios (1633–1717) and Sophronios (1652–1730), taught Latin and Greek rhetoric in a variety of schools, including one in Novgorod. Manasses Eliades (died 1785) lectured on the *Rhetoric* of Corydalleus and on Hermogenes at the Academy in Bucharest; and Països Paramythias (*fl.*1770) taught from his *Rhetorical Exercises* in schools in Moldavia, Hungary, and Corfu. Vikentios Damodos (1700–52), who had trained at the Flanginian Academy and at the University of Padua, composed at least three separate treatises on rhetoric for his students in Cephalonia, none of which was published in his lifetime. And Demetrios Darvaris, who studied philosophy at Halle and went on to become a teacher in Budapest and Vienna, included a modern Greek rendition of Isocrates' *Pros Demonikon* (To Demonikos) in his *Guide to Happiness* (Vienna, 1796).

Rhetoric, in both its ecclesiastical and secular forms, continued to be taught during the Tourkokratia. The generation before the War of Independence recognized another important aspect of rhetoric, however – its role in the formation of national identity. It is no coincidence that authors of rhetoric texts such as Spyridon Vlantis (1765–1830) and Konstantinos Bardalachos (1755–1830) were also deeply involved in the publication and translation of major Classical and Byzantine poets, historians, and philosophers, and translations into Greek of some Latin writers as well (e.g. Vlantis's translation into modern Greek of Ovid's *Metamorphoses* (Venice, 1798). Most of them were also involved in the debates about the Greek language itself. Vlantis, who taught at the Flanginian Academy, produced several grammatical works in addition to his editions of Hermogenes (Venice, 1799) and Longinus (Venice, 1802); and so, too, Bardalachos, who published his grammar in Odessa in 1830, 15 years after the appearance of his *Rhetorike Techne* (Art of Rhetoric, Vienna, 1815). Coincidentally, it was also in 1830 that Konstantinos Oikonomos (1780–1857) published in St Petersburg his treatise on the correct pronunciation of Greek. Oikonomos had published a major work on rhetoric in Vienna in 1813, drawing on Aristotle, Cicero, and borrowing much from Hermogenes, particularly in the area of *stasis* and topics of invention.

However important rhetoric seemed to the founders of modern Greece, their successors found little place for it in schools. Greek education in the mid-19th century – and indeed, to this day – modelled itself on its European counterparts, particularly France and Germany. Rhetoric in Greece, as in those other countries, was not very prominent in the curriculum; and there are no chairs of rhetoric in Greek universities – as is the case in Europe generally. Yet the tradition clearly lives on in Greek literature and jurisprudence.

THOMAS M. CONLEY

See also Education, Second Sophistic, Sophists

Further Reading

Aristotle, *Art of Rhetoric*, translated by John Henry Freese, in *Aristotle*, London: Heinemann, and New York: Putnam, 1926 (Loeb edition, many reprints)

Enos, Richard Leo, *Greek Rhetoric Before Aristotle*, Prospect Heights, Illinois: Waveland, 1993

Heath, Malcolm, *Hermogenes on Issues: Strategies of Argument in Later Greek Rhetoric*, Oxford: Clarendon Press, 1995

Johnstone, Christopher Lyle (editor), *Theory, Text, Context: Issues in Greek Rhetoric and Oratory*, Albany: State University of New York Press, 1996

Kennedy, George Alexander, *Greek Rhetoric under Christian Emperors*, Princeton, New Jersey: Princeton University Press, 1983

Kennedy, George Alexander, *A History of Classical Rhetoric*, Princeton, New Jersey: Princeton University Press, 1994

Knös, Börje, *L'Histoire de la littérature néo-grecque: la période jusqu'en 1821*, Stockholm: Almqvist & Wiksell, 1962

Kournoutou, Georgiou (editor), *Logioi tes Tourkokratias* [Orators of the Turkish Domination], Athens, 1956

Sathas, Konstantinos N., *Neoellenike Philologia: Viographiai ton en tois grammasi dialampsanton Hellenon, apo tes Katalyseos tes Vyzantines Autokratorias mechri tes Hellenikes Ethnegersias, 1453–1821* [Modern Greek Philology: Biographies of Distinguished Greek Men of Letters from the Fall of the Byzantine Empire to the Rise of the Greek State, 1453–1821], Athens, 1868, reprinted 1969

Schiappa, Edward (editor), *Landmark Essays on Classical Greek Rhetoric*, Davis, California: Hermagoras, 1994

Tatakis, Basil N., *Skouphos, Meniates, Voulgaris, Theotokes*, Athens, 1957

Worthington, Ian (editor), *Persuasion: Greek Rhetoric in Action*, London and New York: Routledge, 1994

Rhodes

Island in the Dodecanese

The largest of the Dodecanese group of islands, Rhodes lies in the eastern Aegean a few miles off the southwest corner of modern Turkey. Habitation on the island extends back as far as the neolithic period, and pre-Greek and early Greek settlements are attested in the 2nd millennium BC. The Minoans, a highly civilized seafaring people from Crete, had founded a trading post at Trianda (on the west coast about 9 km south of modern Rhodes town) by the 16th century BC, and the Mycenaean Greeks who succeeded the Minoans as the main power in the Aegean appear to have established prosperous colonies on the island some two centuries later, judging from the presence of chamber tombs and rich finds from the cemetery near Ialysus (not far from Trianda).

After the collapse of the Mycenaean civilization, the Dodecanese islands were inhabited in the so-called Dark Age of Greece by Dorian-speaking Greeks emigrating eastward from mainland Greece. The island had various names in antiquity, but finally "Rhodos" (in Greek) became standard. Mythological legend held that Rhodos was the child of the sun god Helios and the nymph Rhoda. Other traditions associated it with the Greek work for rose, *rodon* (whether or not this etymology is true, the rose appeared as a symbol on Rhodian coinage in the Classical and later periods, and Rhodes is popularly known as "the Island of Roses" in modern times). Three city states were founded: Ialysus (see above), Camirus (also on the west coast some 35 km south of Rhodes town), and Lindus (about halfway down the east coast). These three cities are mentioned in the Homeric Catalogue of Ships as sending ships to the Trojan War (*Iliad*, 2. 656).

The cities flourished in the 7th–6th centuries BC and, like many other cities in archaic Greece, sent out colonies (Lindus founded Phaselis on the east coast of Lycia *c*.690 BC, and, in association with Cretans, Gela on the south coast of Sicily in 688 BC). The cities on Rhodes were on the whole ruled by tyrants from local aristocratic families. The most famous of these was Cleobulus of Lindus in the early 6th century BC, who was one of the "Seven Sages" – men renowned for their wisdom in political and practical matters – in Greek literary tradition (an impressive round structure on the headland just north of Lindus is traditionally known as the tomb of Cleobulus, but it is of pre-Hellenic date).

Rhodes: view of the harbour, Rhodes town. The walls were built by the Hospitaller Knights of St John in the 15th and 16th centuries

Rhodes was caught up in the political situation affecting the rest of the Greek world in the 5th century BC. In common with the rest of east Greece, the island became subject to the growing power of the Persian empire in 490 BC. After Greece – under the leadership of Athens – finally defeated the Persian empire in 479 BC, the cities of Rhodes, like most of the other Greek cities, joined the Delian League, a confederation of cities which paid tribute to Athens in return for protection against a possible new Persian threat (all three cities of Rhodes are recorded in the Athenian Tribute Lists). The Rhodian cities remained under Athenian influence until they revolted in 412/11 BC during the Peloponnesian War and switched their allegiance to Sparta. The revolt is often attributed to the encouragement of a prominent aristocrat from Ialysus named Dorieus, who had been exiled by Athens some years previously and had turned to Sparta.

The most important political event in the history of ancient Rhodes occurred in 408/07 BC, when the three independent city states formed a single community and founded a federal capital city, also called Rhodes, at the north tip of the island. The three old cities thereby lost their independent status, and together formed a single political unit run by federal officials and legislative bodies. The reasons for this dramatic political rearrangement are not known, but an economic motive seems likely. Rhodes island occupied an ideal position between east and west, and a city at the northern tip of the island provided easy access to both seas. The economic prosperity of Rhodes in years to come proves the wisdom of the synoecism. The old cities continued to be inhabited, had local governments, and controlled their own local religious cults, but, from now on,

the capital city of Rhodes controlled the federated island's foreign policy.

The political life of Rhodes in the 4th century BC is complex. A revolt from Sparta in 395 led to the return of Athenian influence, despite continuing internal unrest, and within the next decades to the establishment of a democratic government which was the hallmark of Rhodes throughout the rest of its independent life. It was during the 4th century that Rhodes consolidated overseas territory and incorporated it into the Rhodian state. This consisted of the so-called *peraia* ("the land opposite"), the area of southwest Turkey immediately opposite Rhodes, as a result of which Rhodes gained a firm foothold in Asia Minor between Caria and Lycia. Various nearby islands were also incorporated (Chalki, Symi, Tilos, Nisyros, Karpathos, Kasos, and Megiste [Kastellorizo]). As an Athenian ally, Rhodes joined the Second Athenian Confederacy in 378/7 BC, but the growing influence of the Persian satrap Mausolus of Caria upset the political equilibrium in the eastern Aegean. His meddling led to the "Social War" against Athens in 357, and the consequent emancipation from it of several former allies, including Rhodes. Nonetheless, Rhodes remained under the domination of Caria until the arrival of Alexander the Great in 332. The island submitted to the conqueror, and its "liberation" from Persian influence consisted in the installation of a Macedonian garrison whose removal after Alexander's death was a cause for celebration.

Alexander's conquests and the activity of his successors created the conditions in which Rhodes was to thrive. The foundation of Greek cities in the new Hellenistic empires transferred the centre of trade to the east. The new trade routes converged on Rhodes, and it rapidly became the chief commercial entrepot of the Levant, with consequent enormous economic prosperity. Furthermore, Rhodes managed to maintain its system of democratic government and independence even in the face of the warring Successors.

When the Successors Ptolemy of Egypt and Antigonus Monophthalmus were engaged in a power struggle in the eastern Aegean, Rhodes refused to join Antigonus against Ptolemy, thereby preserving its alliance with Egypt (Antigonus was interested in Rhodes because of its naval capacity – a considerable navy, impressive harbour installations, and shipbuilding timber). This was the occasion which led in 305/4 BC to the famous year-long siege of Rhodes by Antigonus' son Demetrius (who was to receive his nickname "Besieger" (in Greek, "Poliorcetes") as a result of this action; the siege is vividly described in Diodorus Siculus, 20. 82–88, 91–100). Demetrius did not take Rhodes despite ferocious assaults by land and sea, and in thanks for their salvation the Rhodians erected a 33-m-high bronze statue of their patron god Helios which was paid for from the sale of Demetrius' abandoned siege equipment. The Colossus of Rhodes was one of the most famous statues of all antiquity and was reckoned as one of the seven wonders of the ancient world. It stood until toppled by an earthquake in the early 220s BC.

In the first half of the 3rd century the friendship between Rhodes and Egypt was the mainstay of Rhodian policy and responsible for its rise to pre-eminence in both the political and commercial spheres. Under the benevolent eye of Egypt, Rhodes began to play an active role in the Aegean, beginning its crusade against the marauding pirates who threatened economic stability. Rhodes kept the pirates contained through special naval techniques, and this activity enhanced its prestige and the confidence felt towards it by seafaring communities.

Some time around the middle of the 3rd century, Rhodes appears to have distanced itself politically from an Egypt which had suffered loss of face on land (in the Chremonidean War) and sea (at the battles of Cos and Andros) at the hands of the Antigonids. For the rest of the 3rd century Rhodes stands on its own feet as the paramount Aegean power, stepping into the position of naval supremacy vacated by Egypt. At the same time these political differences do not seem to have led to a rupture of commercial relations between Rhodes and Egypt, since these ties were economically essential to both. Rhodes continued to win for itself the recognized position as protector of the island communities, and this was achieved when it refounded the "Nesiotic League" ("League of the Islanders") by the end of the 3rd century. The earthquake of the early 220s which toppled the Colossus (see above) also destroyed much of the ancient city. Significantly, all of the Greek kings of the east and west contributed lavishly to the cost of reconstruction, and even assisted in money and kind for the rebuilding of the Rhodian fleet – a sure sign of the high prestige and pacific intentions of the independent democracy at the time.

At this period Rome began to interfere in Greek affairs, and Rhodes was an active Roman ally in the wars against the Macedonian Philip V and the Seleucid Antiochus III. As a result, the Treaty of Apamea in 188 BC rewarded Rhodes with the possession of Caria and Lycia. Internal dissension between the pro- and anti-Roman factions within Rhodes led to political equivocation, for which Rhodes paid the price in the aftermath of the Third Macedonian War when it was deprived of Caria and Lycia. It was further punished in 167 BC by Rome's declaration of Delos as a free port, which gave Rhodes overwhelming competition as the centre of transit trade in the Aegean. Rhodes finally became an ally of Rome in 164 BC, thereby ending its political independence. From then on it shared the consequences of Roman intervention in the east, notably the Mithradatic War of 88 BC, and the Roman civil wars of the second half of the 1st century BC.

Ancient Rhodians famous for their cultural achievements include the 2nd-century BC Stoic philosopher Panaetius and his pupil Posidonius (a Syrian granted Rhodian citizenship); the sculptor of the Colossus of Rhodes, Chares of Lindus, a pupil of the great Greek sculptor Lysippus of Sicyon; and the 3rd-century BC epic poet and author of the *Argonautica*, Apollonius Rhodius (who may have been a native of Alexandria who settled in Rhodes).

Christianity came to Rhodes early. The apostle Paul records that he stopped in Rhodes on his way to Jerusalem (Acts 21: 1), local tradition maintaining that he came to a small harbour at Lindus. The importance of the early Church is attested by the fact that it had a bishop from early times, and the title of metropolitan was bestowed upon Rhodian bishops in the 4th century AD. Rhodes became part of the eastern empire after the Roman empire was divided in AD 395, and was subsumed into the history of the Byzantine empire for the following centuries. The Greek governor of Rhodes declared the island's independence during the troubled times of the Fourth Crusade, but in the early 14th century it was taken by force and occupied for the following two centuries by the Hospitaller Knights of St John of Jerusalem, having fled Cyprus en route from the Holy Land. The Knights constructed in western European style the medieval city which is a remarkable example of the military and domestic architecture of the period, and is the chief glory of Rhodes town today. Evidence of their relations with the local Greek population is still being researched, but the continuation of Orthodox traditions is clear from the evidence of Rhodian religious icons and frescos of the 13th–16th centuries AD.

The Knights of St John were expelled from Rhodes in 1523 after a formidable siege mounted by the Ottoman sultan Suleiman I ("the Magnificent") and eventually established themselves in Malta. Rhodes was garrisoned and became part of the Ottoman empire for the next four centuries. The conversion of several churches in Rhodes town into mosques during this period has given the surviving city a curious blend of western and eastern medieval architecture.

In the political turmoil leading up to the collapse of the Ottoman empire and World War I, Italy (then at war with Turkey) invaded and captured Rhodes and the other Dodecanese islands in 1912. The islands became part of Italy's Aegean empire, and Rhodes town in particular retains some extraordinary public buildings erected in a distinctive style during the next decades. The Italians were in turn expelled by the German forces during the later stages of World War II. Rhodes was then occupied yet again but was liberated by British and Greek forces in a daring commando raid in 1945. Rhodes was finally united with the state of Greece in 1947. Over the past 50 years Rhodes has become a thoroughly modern Greek island, and Rhodes town a sophisticated cosmopolitan city. The 2400th anniversary of the foundation of Rhodes town was commemorated with great fanfare in 1992–93. The success of Rhodes as a major tourist resort has ensured that knowledge of the island – ancient, medieval, and modern – has spread throughout the westernized world.

E.E. RICE

See also Dodecanese

Summary

Largest of the Dodecanese islands, Rhodes has been settled since the neolithic period and has traces of Minoan and Mycenaean presence. Three city states were founded (Ialysus, Camirus, and Lindus) which together established a federal capital, also called Rhodes, in 408/07 BC. It prospered as a trading centre and retained its independence and democratic government until 164 BC. From the 14th to the 16th century Rhodes was occupied by the Knights of St John of Jerusalem.

Further Reading

Barber, Robin, *Rhodes and the Dodecanese*, London: A.&C. Black, and New York: Norton, 1997 (*Blue Guide* series)

Berthold, Richard M., *Rhodes in the Hellenistic Age*, Ithaca, New York: Cornell University Press, 1984

Clayton, Peter A. and Martin J. Price (editors), *The Seven Wonders of the Ancient World*, London and New York: Routledge, 1988, reprinted 1996, chapter 6

Durrell, Lawrence, *Reflections on a Marine Venus: A Companion to the Landscape of Rhodes*, London: Faber, 1953; New York: Marlowe, 1996

Fraser, Peter Marshall, and George Ewart Bean, *The Rhodian Peraea and Islands*, London: Oxford University Press, 1954

Gabrielsen, Vincent, *The Naval Aristocracy of Hellenistic Rhodes*, Aarhus: Aarhus University Press, 1997

Gruen, Erich S., *The Hellenistic World and the Coming of Rome*, 2 vols, Berkeley: University of California Press, 1984

Karouzos, Chrestos I., *Rhodos: History, Monuments, Art*, Athens: Hesperos, 1973

Kollias, Elias, *The City of Rhodes and the Palace of the Grand Master: From the Early Christian Period to the Conquest by the Turks (1522)*, translated by William Phelps, Athens: Archaeological Receipts Fund, 1988

Mee, Christopher, *Rhodes in the Bronze Age: An Archaeological Survey*, Warminster, Wiltshire: Aris and Phillips, 1982

Merker, Gloria S., *The Hellenistic Sculpture of Rhodes*, Gothenburg: Åström, 1973

Sherwin-White, Adrian Nicholas, *Roman Foreign Policy in the East, 168 BC to AD 1*, London: Duckworth, and Norman: University of Oklahoma Press, 1984

Ritsos, Yiannis 1909–1990

Poet

Ritsos was one of the most eloquent and prolific modern Greek poets. Displaying an extraordinary ability to combine the realistic, lyric, dramatic, and epic elements in his poetry and drawing on a surprisingly wide gamut of ideas, he has been recognized not simply as the poet of sensation but, most importantly, as the bard of the spontaneous and impulsive response to any kind of intuition. Being endowed with a genuine and effortless sense of compassion, possessing pure poetical gifts, and exercising the most remarkable skills, he was considered to be the initiator of cinematographic picturization and the personification of reality in modern Greek poetry. With his sharp and alert political spirit, Ritsos was capable of both conveying his own political experiences and reflecting the contemporaneous Greek political situation in his verse. His poems are filled with personal visions, individual denunciations and apologies, and enduring messages. Ritsos's poetry enabled him to express his doubts and hesitations, to voice his biting criticism, to phrase his disillusionment, and, finally, to convey his deeper concern for man and society. Thus, he is rightly numbered among the prominent representatives of Greek surrealist poetry able to express the subconscious mind, the irrational juxtaposition of things, and the illogical dimension of everyday reality.

The poetic legacy of Ritsos is huge in quantity and outstanding in quality. He began to write poetry from a very young age, and poetry soon became his dominant interest. Ritsos's formal debut in the literary milieu of his time took place in 1934 when his first collection was published under the title *Tractor*. His published *oeuvre* amounts to seven volumes (*Poems* in four volumes, *Fourth Dimension*, *Chronicles*, *Being*), while a significant number of his poems remain uncollected and some unpublished.

Ritsos treated the art of poetry as a means to approach the social and personal problems of his time and to propose possible solutions. He led a tumultuous and active political life stigmatized by personal deprivations, serious health problems, exile, and imprisonment due to his espousal of socialist ideas. Meanwhile a number of historically important events exerted a profound influence on the poet's work: the Balkan Wars, World War I, the Russian Revolution and the rise of socialism, the Asia Minor disaster of 1922. Not surprisingly, all those political transformations together with his involvement in the Greek Communist Party and his participation in the National Liberation Front (EAM) inspired his poetry.

Ritsos's principal contribution to the Hellenic literary tradition is twofold: on the one hand, through the thematic framework of his poetry; and on the other hand, through the art of poetry itself which he treated as the means to pronounce on the national accord, harmony, fellowship, and consensus among his compatriots. It is on that point that Ritsos's message acquired a universal quality emphasizing the principles of love, freedom, concord, and peace throughout the world. One of the recurrent themes of his poetry is the idea of his homeland, Greece. Ritsos's Greece is perceived as both the country and the people who are always striving to overcome the barriers, to heal their wounds, to surpass their difficulties in order to validate their enduring tradition. It is the same theme that had dominated the wider spectrum of Greek poetry, starting from ancient Greek epic and lyric poetry, transmitted to the Byzantine literary tradition, culminating in the literary production of the years after the Greek War of Independence, and transplanted to modern Greek poetry. Ritsos's Greece can be seen in its entirety, as the diachronic Greece, the living Hellenic heritage thriving throughout its long history.

Another main theme, closely related to that of Greece, is the worship of one's homeland. Nevertheless, Ritsos's passion for his native land is accompanied by a commensurate feeling of sorrow, agony, and pain. He insisted on a Greek landscape drawn with the simplest, palest colours while at the same time depicting it as wild, barren, and infertile, permeated with perpetual light and inexhaustible sounds. In many respects, it resembled Homer's plain, bright, fierce panorama.

Of equal importance in Ritsos's perspective is the idea of the vigilant soldier, enhanced by his deep admiration for all those who never betray their principles, withdraw from the battlefield, or yield before the enemy. The poet seems to identify himself with the persona of the fighting man, when referring either to his ideological comrades or to the protagonists in any sort of struggle that validates life. In this respect Ritsos's contribution to the Hellenic tradition is indisputable. He recognizes the essential role of tradition in fusing the present, past, and future into an organic whole and in ensuring its continuity. Tradition operates as a powerful spiritual force that encourages man to look ahead to the future, and to make his return to the simple, archetypal way of life. Following the example of Socrates, he posed crucial philosophical questions and rhetorical dilemmas without offering any real answers to them.

Ritsos's meditative style and analytical interpretation are ratified in the theme of falsehood. He tends to disapprove of and express his aversion to any sort of hypocrisy. In fact, he attempts to emphasize the difference between the reality and the appearance of falsehood by standing between them. The philosophical treatment of this theme made a tremendous impact on the thought of other modern Greek poets and appealed to the general public.

As for his technique, Ritsos's verse is marked by vivid original imagery. His powerful pictures recall Homer's descriptive picturization of landscape, nature, and people. By making extensive use of a personified depiction of reality, he utters his personal cry. In this way, the inanimate reality automatically receives a real substance, undergoes psychological crisis, reacts, feels, suffers, and performs. Ritsos's cinematographic pictures come to replace words. His supreme ideas are heard distinctly from the mouth of an inanimate cosmos. His favourite imagery has to do with an extremely diverse landscape: on the one hand, it carries within it the elements of Andreas Kalvos's mute landscape; one the other hand, it is diffused by a blissful light which monopolized Odysseus Elytis' poetry.

Ritsos was capable of interweaving the world of dreams and fantasies with the world of factual reality. In this way, he presented his readers with a multidimensional reality. To understand such a reality, the reader has to set in motion his imagination and his insight.

Ritsos's persistence on a meditative, interior monologue in blank verse, the continual use of the collective first person plural, his apparent tendency towards introspection, his enlarged vision and philosophical manner led him to compose a kind of poetry which commanded a wide appeal and which could be addressed to all generations. Inspired by the most elementary objects of reality, he revealed an astonishingly mature vision of life and art. His first appearance in the literary world was greeted enthusiastically by Kostis Palamas, and his incorporation in the body of the Hellenic tradition was immediate. In 1956 he was awarded the Lenin Prize for literature, and he received numerous other international awards. His work has been translated into many languages. His contribution to the Hellenic tradition is of twofold importance. First,

he succeeded in revitalizing the art of poetry by renewing its basic elements and by proposing a reality fused with traditional and new structures. Secondly, he made an enormous contribution to the revival of Hellenic poetry as a whole by introducing and exploring a number of striking poetic expressions and philosophical ideas. His influence on other Greek poets is considerable and will continue to be so. Passages from his poetry, particularly his distinctive long poem *Romiosini*, have been set to music by the composer Mikis Theodorakis in an attempt to marry modern Greek verse with folk music.

MARIA ROUMBALOU

See also Poetry (Lyric)

Biography
Born at Monemvasia in 1909, Ritsos moved to Athens in 1925. His health was poor and he suffered from tuberculosis. Moved by the political events of his time, he became a communist and was exiled during the Civil War. He was prolific as a poet – his published work runs to more than 5000 pages of poetry. He was awarded the Lenin Prize for literature in 1956. He died in Athens in 1990.

Writings
Selected Poems, translated by Nikos Stangos, Harmondsworth: Penguin, 1974
In *Six Modern Greek Poets*, edited and translated by John Stathatos, London: Oasis, 1975
Scripture of the Blind, translated by Kimon Friar and Kostas Myrsiades, Columbus: Ohio State University Press, 1979
Exile and Return: Selected Poems, 1967–1974, translated by Edmund Keeley, New York: Ecco Press, 1985
Selected Poems, 1938–1988, edited and translated by Kimon Friar and Kostas Myrsiades, Brockport, New York: BOA, 1989
Repetitions, Testimonies, Parentheses, translated by Edmund Keeley, Princeton, New Jersey: Princeton University Press, 1991
The Fourth Dimension, translated by Peter Green and Beverly Bardsley, London: Anvil Press, and Princeton, New Jersey: Princeton University Press, 1993
Late into the Night: The Last Poems of Yannis Ritsos, translated by Martin McKinsey, Oberlin, Ohio: Oberlin College Press, 1995

Further Reading
Bien, Peter, *Antithesi kai Synthesi stin Poiisi Gianni Ritsou* [Antithesis and Synthesis in the Poetry of Yiannis Ritsos] Athens, 1980
Bien, Peter, *Three Generations of Greek Writers: Introductions to Cavafy, Kazantzakis, Ritsos*, Athens: Efstathiadis, 1983
Dialismas, S., *Eisagogi stin Poiisi tou Gianni Ritsou* [An Introduction to the Poetry of Yiannis Ritsos], Athens, 1981
Papandréou, Chrysa, *Yannis Ritsos: Etudes, choix de texte, et bibliographie*, Paris: Seghers, 1968
Piera, Zerar, *Giannis Ritsos: I Makria Poreia Henos Poiete* [Yiannis Ritsos: The Long Way of a Poet], Athens, 1978
Prevelakis, P., *O Poiitis Giannis Ritsos: Synoliki Theorisi tou Ergou tou* [The Poet Yiannis Ritsos: An In-Depth Examination of His Work], Athens, Kedros, 1981

Roidis, Emmanouil 1836–1904
Critic, novelist, short-story writer, and translator

Emmanouil Roidis is remembered today chiefly for his satirical novel *I Papissa Ioanna* (Pope Joan, 1866), which provoked an outcry in the Athenian press on its publication and was vigorously condemned by the Orthodox Church in a synodical encyclical. Subtitled "A Medieval Study", Roidis's novel is characterized in the book's lengthy preface as "a narrative encyclopedia of the Middle Ages". The narrator self-consciously evokes the apparatus of academic scholarship, including extensive footnotes, in order to present his fiction as an erudite study grounded in irrefutable historical fact. The narrative that follows, however, is a ribald adventure that draws upon an obscure medieval legend which claimed that the 9th-century Pope John VIII was, in fact, a woman.

The novel begins with Joan's "miraculous" birth, following her father's castration and her mother's rape by two soldiers, and proceeds to describe her relationship with the young monk Frumentius, her arrival in Rome, and her subsequent journey to Constantinople. On her return to the papal city Joan is elected as pontiff and conducts an illicit affair with the Chamberlain. It is only with her death in childbirth that the plague which is ravaging Rome is finally assuaged.

On the one hand, Roidis's novel engages ironically with the conventions of the historical novel which had become popular in Greece, partly through the translations of Sir Walter Scott's fiction into Greek from the 1840s. The riotous, indecorous ecclesiastical world Roidis evokes is far from being an idealized milieu of chivalrous deeds and romance. Significantly, it was during this period in the 1860s that Byzantium was being rediscovered by Spyridon Zambelios (1815–81) and the historian Konstantinos Paparrigopoulos (1815–91) as a vital link that established the historical continuity of modern Greece with the ancient world. On the other hand, the novel questions the assumptions that underlie realism by presenting outrageously fictional material as if it were documentary evidence and by consistently drawing the reader's attention to the rhetorical strategies which are mobilized in fiction to produce the illusion of verisimilitude. Recent scholarship has tended to emphasize the experimental, self-reflexive, and ironic nature of Roidis's fiction which, it could be argued, prefigures the exploratory narrative techniques of writers such as Kostas Tachtsis (1927–88) in the late 20th century. It was doubtless this interrogative aspect of Roidis's novel that prompted the satirical dramatist and author of Ubu Roi Alfred Jarry (1873–1907) to translate the novel into French. Indeed, Pope Joan is the only 19th-century Greek novel to have entered the European canon. First translated into English in 1886, a version was also produced by Lawrence Durrell in 1960 (reissued in 1999).

The fame of Pope Joan, which the author later dismissed as a "youthful sin", has tended to eclipse Roidis's major contribution in other fields. As the poet and critic Kostis Palamas (1859–1943) observed in 1899, Roidis's fame was a result of his notoriety following the publication of the novel, rather than of any deep acquaintance with his work. Yet Roidis was arguably the most perceptive and wide-ranging critic of his generation, a translator of versatility who produced short stories towards the end of his life, as well as making an important intervention in the language debate. Although the first attempt to anthologize his work took place within his own lifetime, in 1885, it was not until after Roidis's death in 1904 that an attempt was made by his nephew A.M. Andriadis and D. Petrokokkinos to collect his writings together in seven volumes

(1911–14). Yet, with a few exceptions, notably Kleonas Paraschos's laudatory biography (1942, 1950), Roidis's reputation continued to wane and critics, taking their lead from K.T. Dimaras's summary treatment of the writer in his History of Modern Greek Literature (1948), tended to view his work (which, with a few exceptions, was written in katharevousa, or purist Greek) as obscure, superficial, and uninspiring, even while they conceded his enlightened intervention in the language debate on the side of the demoticists. The reassessment of Roidis which began in the 1970s and 1980s, after a long period of neglect, has at last brought the variety and percipience of Roidis's writing to the attention of a wider reading public. A decisive step along the way of Roidis's rehabilitation was the publication in 1978 of Alkis Angelou's authoritative Collected Works.

Roidis was born into a well-to-do family in Ermoupolis on the island of Syros in 1836, one of the commercial hubs of the eastern Mediterranean with a lively cultural life. Although the family moved to Genoa in 1841, Roidis returned to his native island in 1849 where he attended school and was a classmate of the writer Dimitrios Vikelas (1835–1908). Subsequently he studied literature and philosophy in Berlin, before working in the family business of his mother, Cornelia Rodokanaki. He travelled extensively before returning to Athens in 1859 and the following year published a translation of Chateaubriand's Itinéraire, which was followed two years later by a study of the critic Sainte-Beuve. During his career Roidis translated work from such diverse authors as Edgar Allan Poe, Charles Baudelaire, and Thomas Macaulay, whose History of England appeared in Greek between 1898 and 1902. Roidis also contributed numerous articles and reviews to journals and newspapers such as Estia, Parnassos, Asti, Ora, and Avyi. In 1873 Roidis lost the bulk of his family fortune through bad investments; with the help of friends, however, he secured a position at the National Library in Athens where he worked from 1880.

The combative, sometimes vituperative style of Roidis's writing offended many of his contemporaries. The writer Georgios Drosinis (1859–1951), for example, recalled in his autobiography how Roidis was known as "the policeman of Art" who was apt to censure others without offering a positive alternative to the positions being criticized. No doubt Drosinis had in mind Roidis's criticism of contemporary Greek ethographic writing in the preface to Konstantinos Metaxas-Vosporitis's collection of short stories entitled Skinai tis Erimou: Ithi Vedouïnou (Scenes of the Desert: Customs of the Bedouin, 1899). Contemporary Greek writers, Roidis asserted, had become monotonous in their preoccupation with an idealized rural setting and the public had grown weary of fishermen and shepherds. It is undoubtedly true that, as in his famous exchange with Angelos Vlachos (1838–1920) in 1877, Roidis revelled in controversy. On the occasion of a drama competition organized by the Parnassos literary society, Roidis, who was on the competition's committee, published an article in which he maintained that poetry reflected the cultural and social concerns of the society in which it was produced. He concluded, devastatingly, that: "it is impossible for a poet to be born and to exist outside of any poetic atmosphere; we do not have such an atmosphere in Greece today, since, on the one hand we forsake our local traditions, and on the other, we still play no part in the intellectual life of Western nations." Roidis's bold assertions were attacked by Vlachos, who vehemently rejected what he construed as Roidis's deterministic view of culture. Poetry, for Vlachos, was born of the imagination; the influences of the poet's surroundings hindered rather than nourished his creativity. This essentially Romantic conception of poetry was in turn condemned by Roidis who went on to develop his ideas in a sharp-witted article entitled "On Contemporary Criticism in Greece". Here he evoked Darwinian thinking and quoted Herbert Spencer as saying that great men must be classified as part of the society which produced them. For Roidis all cultural expressions were historically contingent and a complex reciprocal relationship existed between artistic creation and social and political environments. This comparative interest in a more broadly defined notion of culture is evident in the range of Roidis's articles that touch upon all aspects of Greek society from women's emancipation to food, urban living, and the treatment of animals. His journalistic sketches vividly evoke the texture of everyday life in late 19th-century Athens and, ironically, in so doing are reminiscent both of Vlachos's sketches as well as the tales of Michail Mitsakis (1863–1916).

With the principal exception of a fairy tale entitled "The Apple Tree" most of Roidis's texts are written in a purist Greek. Ironically, however, he was a supporter of Yannis Psycharis (1854–1920) and celebrated the poetry of demoticists such as Athanasios Christopoulos (1772–1847), Ioannis Vilaras (1771–1823), Dionysios Solomos (1798–1857), and Aristotelis Valaoritis (1824–79). In his study *Ta Eidola* (The Idols, published in 1893), Roidis supported the cause of the spoken language, although he expressed himself in an elegant katharevousa. The term *diglossia* (bilingualism) first seems to have been used by Roidis in his review of Psycharis's controversial book *To Taxidi mou* (My Journey, 1888).

ROBERT SHANNAN PECKHAM

See also Novel

Biography

Born on Syros in 1836, Roidis moved with his family to Genoa in 1841 but returned in 1849 to Syros where he attended school. He studied literature and philosophy in Berlin, returning to Athens in 1859. He is best known as the author of the satirical novel *Pope Joan* (1866) and as one of the most perceptive critics of late 19th-century Greek culture. He produced several short stories and translations. He died in Athens in 1904.

Writings

The Curious History of Pope Joan, translated by Lawrence Durrell, London: Verschoyle, 1954; revised edition as *Pope Joan: A Romantic Biography*, London: Deutsch, 1960, New York: Dutton, 1961, reprinted London: Peter Owen, 1999
Apanta [Collected Works], edited by Angela Alkes, 4 vols, Athens, 1978

Further Reading

Macrides, Ruth, "'As Byzantine Then as It Is Today': Pope Joan and Roidis's Greece" in *Byzantium and the Modern Greek Identity*, edited by David Ricks and Paul Magdalino, Aldershot, Hampshire: Ashgate, 1998

Paraschou, Kleonas, *Emmanouil Roidis: I Zoi, to Ergo, i Epochi tou* [Emmanouil Roidis: His Life, Works, and Times], 2 vols., Athens, 1942–52
"The Fabrication of the Middle Ages: Roidis's Pope Joan", *Kambos: Cambridge Papers in Modern Greek*, 4 (1996)
Yeorganda, Athina, *Emmanouil Roidis: I Poria pros tin "Papissa Ioanna"* [Emmanouil Roidis: The Way to "Pope Joan"], Athens, 1993

Roman Catholic Church

In Greek lands the Roman Catholic Church was distinct from the Greek Orthodox Church in that its members, known as "Latins" (*Latinoi*), recognized the authority of the Roman Church in ecclesiastical matters and because they used Latin as their liturgical language. It is therefore in everyday events and in personal relationships that the Roman Church is important in the Levant. Generally, tolerance and mutual cooperation between lay members of the Roman and Orthodox faiths existed in the face of political and doctrinal disputes at the level of popes and patriarchs. The Great Schism of 1054 led to the mutual excommunication of pope Leo IX and patriarch Michael Keroularios, but both sides had been careful to limit their mutual censures, and the dispute seems to have affected individual Greek and Latin Christians little. There was no general excommunication of either the Greek or the Latin Church and indeed much cooperation is evident.

Amalfitan merchants had established a Benedictine monastery on Mount Athos in the 10th century. This, one of the oldest Athonite houses, was to maintain an independent existence down to 1393. In 1212 the patriarch of Alexandria had ordained a Latin deacon to the Latin priesthood in the absence of any Latin bishop, while his clergy had a tradition of giving spiritual succour to Latin prisoners in Alexandria. In the Crusader states set up in the 12th century, Latin patriarchs in Jerusalem, Antioch, and (later) Constantinople saw themselves as successors to their Greek predecessors, even if this perception was not shared by their Greek subjects. In their day-to-day dealings Greek and Latin Christians in the Levant paid little or no heed to papal pronouncements and patriarchal opinions. The pope or the patriarch might disapprove at an official level of such cooperation between members of the two communions, but they were after all coreligionists.

This general mood of cooperation and mutual toleration could be upset by specific political and military causes which might in turn be affected by demographic factors. Thus the Norman conquest of southern Italy and Sicily in the late 11th century not only brought an effective end to the Byzantine patriarchate in the region but was also marked by considerable pressure on Greek priests in the area to acknowledge the ecclesiastical primacy of Rome. In return, considerable flexibility over the Latin tonsure and rules of celibacy was allowed but Greek religionists were enjoined to conform to Latin practices. This, together with the encouragement of Latin immigration from northern Italy, resulted in the virtual extinction of Greek culture in Sicily by the beginning of the 13th century.

Before 1204 the presence of western merchants, pilgrims, mercenaries, and other Latins in the Byzantine empire necessitated the availability of Latin priests to minister to their spiritual needs according to the Latin rite. However, Latin priests were few and the materials needed for their ministrations – such as a church building, candles, chrism, and bread – had in practice to be obtained locally and with the cooperation and assent of the Greek host community. In the cities of the Levant most concern at an official level was focused on the relations of the minority Latin Christians to the Byzantine patriarch. This usually took the form of attention to minor differences in practice such as the use of unleavened bread at the Eucharist, certain dietary issues, the observance of particular fast days, and the fingers used in signing with the cross. These were differences that would be evident in daily practice. Interestingly, Latin clerical celibacy and the tonsure received scant attention at patriarchal level. It is also notable that so much was said about *azymes* (unleavened bread) and virtually nothing about the *filioque* which was to be the major sticking point of Church union debates at papal/patriarchal level in the 13th century and later.

In practice there seem to have been few problems with the establishment of the Benedictine monastery on Mount Athos around 985. Similarly, all the trading outposts granted to the Almifitans, Genoese, Pisans, and Venetians were endowed with the grant of a church for their use. Latin burials were also respected by the host communities. Political disputes that culminated in the Great Schism might result in local difficulties. The patriarch Michael Keroularios closed Latin churches in Constantinople, but this ban was difficult to enforce and at the time of his death in 1058 all churches were open and functioning. There was concern in Rome that Latins resident in the Byzantine empire might conform too readily to Greek rites. Around 1200 Innocent III banned Latin priests from confirming children by chrismation in accordance with Orthodox practice and was uneasy about Latin communities obtaining chrism from the patriarch. On the eve of the Fourth Crusade there was no clear line distinguishing Roman Catholics from Greek Orthodox.

Even with the fall of Constantinople in 1204 and the subsequent establishment of Latin lordships in Greece and the Aegean there appears to have been no plan on the part of Innocent III to set up a separate Latin Church in the conquered territories. It was the Crusaders themselves who had elected a Latin patriarch. Although Innocent acquiesced, he was much more concerned with this election as a gross example of lay intervention in clerical appointments. He was also particularly concerned with the protection of the rights and lands of the Greek Church, for which the Crusaders had made no provision in their division and subsequent conquest of the Byzantine empire. Innocent III viewed the fall of Constantinople as a just judgement on the proud and schismatic Greeks, who would now see the error of their ways and acknowledge the ecclesiastical supremacy of Rome. Greek lands were to be preserved and Innocent's legate in Constantinople was to conduct seminars to persuade and instruct the Greek clergy in their error and in the way forward. In fact only a handful of Greek bishops became Latinized. Union did not follow conquest. Pressure was brought on the Greeks within the city by the closure of their churches, but was ineffectual. In the provinces where the Latins formed a very small minority of the population it was never even tried. Accommodation based on mutual toleration was reached with local notables. Despite occasional

fulmination from Rome during the course of the Latin occupation, this situation held firm. It was only on the island of Cyprus that there were Greek martyrs to the division of the churches. Latin bishops were appointed in the former Greek diocese; the motivation for these appointments came from the new Latin lords themselves, concerned both for the spiritual needs of their Latin followers and for their own status. The presence of the bishops persisted only as long as Latin control held firm. In some areas like Thessaly and Thrace this was not very long at all. The extreme violence shown by Michael of Epirus to Latin priests who fell into his hands in 1210 is a sign that a new element of intolerance was appearing between the Roman Catholics and Orthodox Christians. This manifested itself in the writings of propagandists at the court of the Greeks in Nicaea, eager to condemn anything Latin and in particular Roman Catholic religious practices. After the loss of Constantinople by the Latins in 1261 attempts on the part of the papacy to lend support to the former Latin emperor exacerbated this polarization. The capture and sack of Constantinople would never be forgotten or forgiven. The Latins were no longer coreligionists to be tolerated but heretics who were now enemies of the Hellenes and targets to be attacked. Such attitudes can be detected in the village of Galaxdi in 1404, yet even there hostility did not result in violence but in legerdemain at the expense of certain Hospitaller knights.

The new Hellenism of the late 13th century defined itself in large part by its religion, and the differences between Roman and Orthodox Christianity became more clearly defined. This was certainly evident at an official level: the Orthodox Church of Cyprus was banned from communion with the Orthodox Church until the Turkish conquest in 1571 because it was deemed to have submitted to Rome during the years of Lusignan rule, while the Great Schism of 1054, which had gone largely unnoticed at the time, took on such significance that the rift was not to be healed until 1965.

The Ottoman conquest of Greece and the Aegean (Greece 1450–1500, Rhodes 1523, Chios 1566, Cyprus 1571, and Crete 1669) led to the reduction of Roman Catholic communities by emigration and deportation. It appears from the island of Chios that this particularly affected the availability of Latin priests. Nevertheless, pockets of Latin Christians persisted in Constantinople and other cities of the Ottoman empire and on the Aegean islands. The Catholic communities had powerful protectors in the west, particularly the kings of France, and to some extent this set them apart from the other religious groups, or *millets*, within the empire. Interestingly, at a local and personal level, there are many examples of cordial relations, mixed marriages, and common services. Again such behaviour might be disapproved of at an official level on both sides but it persisted. It was as an institution and as an idea that Roman Catholicism was unacceptable in Greek lands. At a personal and practical level Christians from both communions had always coexisted with and assisted each other as neighbours in Christ.

PETER LOCK

See also Orthodox Church, Papacy, Schism, Uniates

Further Reading

Argenti, Philip P., *The Religious Minorities of Chios: Jews and Roman Catholics*, Cambridge: Cambridge University Press, 1970

Every, George, *The Byzantine Patriarchate, 451–1204*, London: SPCK, 1947

Hussey, J.M., *The Orthodox Church in the Byzantine Empire*, Oxford: Clarendon Press, 1986

Lock, Peter, *Franks in the Aegean, 1204–1500*, London and New York: Longman, 1995

Setton, Kenneth M., *The Papacy and the Levant*, 4 vols, Philadelphia: American Philosophical Society, 1976–84

Ware, Timothy, *Eustratios Argenti: A Study of the Greek Church under Turkish Rule*, Oxford: Clarendon Press, 1964

Roman Period 31 BC–AD 330

Long before Roman political control of Greece began in the 2nd century BC, contact between Greece and Rome had already wrought cultural and economic changes in both regions. Scholars have found evidence of a Greek presence in Italy from as early as the Mycenaean era and throughout the period of colonization in the 8th and 7th centuries BC. Within 50 years of colonizing southern Italy and Sicily (Magna Graecia), Greek communities began to engage in a flourishing trade and an exchange of ideas with the Italians. The Romans adopted some Greek gods, their temples took on aspects of Greek architectural styles, Greek artisans produced pottery for the Italian market, and Greek historians wrote about the origins of the Italians and Romans. Writers such as Timaeus made genuine efforts to understand the history of Italy, in light of the growing power and influence of Rome. While these writers tended to Hellenize Roman history and origins, their views were accepted by the Romans themselves.

Gradually there began a fusion of Greek and Roman cultures. The Romans entered into more formal relations with the local Greek city states, while the mainland Greeks became actively involved in conflicts in Magna Graecia. The merging of Roman and Greek politics and culture began in earnest with the military interference in Greek affairs by the Romans, in particular during the Achaean War (146 BC). After the Achaean War Corinth was levelled, vast amounts of booty were shipped to Rome, the men were massacred, and the rest of the inhabitants sold into slavery – leaving the once bustling town empty and in ruins. The events that followed this war are unclear, but over the course of the next century these events slowly reshaped the Hellenistic east into provinces of the expanding Roman empire, and Greek city states into Graeco-Roman municipalities.

This contact, while certainly important politically and economically, at first had only limited influence on the essence of Greek civilization. The Greeks themselves, and the Romans too, had a profound respect for the language, literature, and culture of the Hellenic world, which would remain unshaken by political conquest, devastation by Roman legions, and economic turmoil of the 1st century BC. Elite Romans continued to send their sons to Greece for the finishing touches on a proper education. Cicero and then his son went to Athens, as did Ovid and Horace – who saw that Greece had captured its captors ('Graecia capta ferum victorem cepit et artis intulit agresti Latio' [*Epistulae*, 2. 1. 156–57]). Colonies of veterans were founded, especially by Julius Caesar and Augustus, some nine or ten in Greece, and included the revival of cities such as Patras and Corinth. Yet these colonies were quickly assimilated to Greek culture, and the Greek language superseded Latin. Indeed, the administrative language in the east generally was Greek; edicts and legal proceedings were in Greek. The eastern legions were largely recruited from among the Greek-speaking peoples. Roman citizenship remained rare in the Greek east (until AD 212 when Caracalla proclaimed the *Constitutio Antoniniana*), and only a few citizens were created by their enrolment in these legions.

This is not to say that no Romanization occurred. Greek art, which the Romans greatly admired, was influenced by Roman patronage. The Romans showed their affection for things Greek both by carrying off treasures to Italy and by buying copies of the Classical and archaic works that were in vogue. But the Romans also controlled the economic life of Greece by providing a market and consumer demand thus dictated artistic output. Among the distinctive forms of Roman art was realistic portraiture, rather than the pure idealization found in Greek art. New subjects were explored by Greek artists as a result of Roman interest in recreating a strong sense of psychological reality. Stricter realism was appealingly combined with an attempt to convey character. Common themes investigated youth and age, hermaphrodites, groups suggesting a complex set of emotions (e.g. the *Laocoön*), or physiological studies (e.g. the *Belvedere Torso* and the *Boxer*).

During the principate, Roman building techniques were widely adopted in Greece (for example, in the use of fired brick and brick with mortar construction, as well as, occasionally, podium-style temples). Other Roman amenities, such as baths, became a common feature of any well-appointed Greek town, while mosaics, wall paintings, marble revetments, and Roman-style garden sculptures became an integral part of costly homes and public buildings. For reasons of both economy and an archaizing spirit, reuse of architectural materials was common throughout the Roman period (for example, 12 unfluted Ionic columns were brought from the temple of Athena at Sunium for use in Athens for a podium temple in the Agora).

Since Greece had lost its ability to compete through war, the centuries of Roman rule provoked a new competitive spirit. Abandoning the old political rivalries, cities were now transformed by cultural battles. Citizens strove to build ever more beautiful buildings, and, with Roman direction and encouragement, they offered expensive prizes to their victors in the Panhellenic games. During the 2nd and 3rd centuries AD Achaea held a privileged position in the world of these athletic competitions. Celebrating such contests in the Greek manner became a popular pastime throughout the Graeco-Roman east. The games were expanded and an elite circuit of festivals was established that included the four ancient Panhellenic festivals, as well as newer games such as the Asclepian games at Epidaurus, the Olympia Commodea at Sparta, and at Athens the Panhellenia, the Olympia, and the Hadriana. Other popular games, off the most common circuit, were found at Sparta (the Urania) and in Boeotia (the Eleutheria at Plataea, Trophonea at Lebadea, and Heraclea at Thebes). Regional games also existed and, though these were locally popular, they tended to have fewer out-of-town visitors and very small prizes (such games included the Gorgas festival at Ambryssus and the Euryclea at Sparta). Nearly every city had its own gymnasium where the young men could train for the games.

Likewise drama, music, and even religion provided an arena for competition, not only through the building of temples and theatres, but also through the professionalization of actors, singers, and poets, who toured throughout their regions. Religious festivals generally became elaborate affairs, particularly with the introduction of popular new cults into the Graeco-Roman world. The mystery cults of Isis, Mithra, Judaism, Christianity, and the imperial cult of Roma and Augustus were among the most common of these. The imperial cult was, of course, also a means to express loyalty and support for the rulers of Rome. This cult was introduced very early in Greece; for example in Athens the cult was founded in 27 BC. In fact, religious fervour seems to have been on the rise throughout the Graeco-Roman world and can be seen even in philosophical movements such as Neopythagoreanism and Neoplatonism, both of which evoked strongly emotional and spiritual reactions. Cities also demonstrated their importance through their support of education: higher education was paid for out of public funds and even smaller cities had teachers on salary.

Many Roman emperors showed an active interest in Greece (sometimes, of course, this meant despoiling Greece of its art and antiquities). Pausanias reports that Claudius restored to Greek cities the artworks and statues that his predecessor Caligula had looted. He also remodelled the entrance way to the Athenian Acropolis. Nero was a devoted and active Philhellene. He spoke Greek, attempted to cut a channel through the isthmus of Corinth (to improve communications and trade), and he declared Achaea free at the Isthmian Games in AD 66/67, though this status was overturned by Vespasian only a few years later.

While the emperors clearly felt it their right to remove whatever objects from Greece they wished, imperial dedications to Greece could be substantial, including buildings, roads, and other physical manifestations of their concern for Achaea (as well as concern for their own prestige). The Flavian and Trajanic ages particularly marked an increase in both local and imperial benefices to Greek cities. Trajan built the Library of Pantaenus in Athens and instituted a competition in Sparta for the "best citizen". Sparta's competition relied on a citizen's "love of honour" and the prize was the right to take over the city's costly liturgical offices in a generous way.

Some Roman benefits had a profound effect on the appearance of Greek cities. Among the most dramatic of these was introduction of the colonnaded street – broad avenues flanked by matching porticoes and often paved in marble (such as at Athens and Corinth). Hadrian supported numerous costly projects including buildings at Delphi and many structures in Athens – transforming and restoring Athens in the process (Hadrian's Library in Athens was closely modelled on the temple of Peace in Rome and helped to create a new sense of space in the centre of one of Greece's oldest cities). The emperor also had constructed stoas, temples, aqueducts, bridges, and baths throughout the province of Achaea. Private benefactors participated in such largesse as well. One of the most famous of these was the wealthy Athenian, Herodes Atticus. A Sophist, Roman senator, and a friend of Hadrian's,

he used his wealth and power to beautify Greece (for instance, he built a music hall and stadium in Athens, replaced statues at Olympia, and remodelled a music hall in Corinth).

In 131/32 Hadrian founded the "Panhellenion", an organization of Greek cities (from Greece, Asia Minor, and north Africa) centred in Athens. By creating this organization he implicitly joined himself to the traditions of Classical Greece and the legends of Athens' founder, Theseus. Hadrian's behaviour was set neatly within a cultural context that generally idealized and tried to revive the Greek past. A specific feature of this 2nd-century Greek revival was known as the Second Sophistic, a movement in which Sophists, or teachers of rhetoric, sought a public reputation. References to the past were central to their approach and were integral in their performances. Most Roman elites, even many of the emperors, had been schooled by such rhetoricians. Thus, rhetorical and philosophical schools flourished in many Greek cities, including Athens and Sparta. (Marcus Aurelius eventually endowed philosophy chairs in the cities of Achaea, in part because of the respect instilled by his own training.) This education and the fairly common activity of tourist travel to Greece – a fashion encouraged by Hadrian's own travels in Greece – combined with the foundation of the Panhellenion, created a climate favourable to merging both the "Greek past and the Roman present". This lively and pro-Greek atmosphere, though archaizing, benefited Greece both materially and intellectually. Roman respect for Greece and its traditions lasted well into the 3rd century AD.

At the same time, Greek elites were beginning to infiltrate the Roman aristocracy, by being admitted increasingly to the senate and equestrian classes. Local elites continued to play important roles as Roman administrators and representatives. These men formed a part of the empire's governing body. This is not to say, however, that the Greeks accepted Roman authority without resistance. Revolts erupted periodically throughout the period of Roman rule into the 2nd century AD. Indeed, a small abortive rebellion occurred even under the relatively benevolent rule of Antoninus Pius. Less overt forms of resistance were also present in Greek behaviour through, for example, continued local control of religious icons, rituals, and sacred space.

The late 2nd and 3rd centuries AD brought unwelcome changes to the entire Roman world. Civil wars, economic woes, migrations, and invasions from the north characterize this era in Graeco-Roman history. The needs of the imperial treasury increased economic and material demands on the provinces. Ambitious building projects and artworks were neglected in favour of defensive structures and strategies, especially since the northern peoples were no longer held back at the borders of the empire, forcing the Greeks to defend themselves from invaders such as the Goths in AD 262 and the Heruli in AD 268 (these latter were expelled by the Philhellene emperor Gallienus). According to tradition, the Herulians destroyed nearly every building in Athens (except perhaps the area around the southern slope of the Acropolis). These attacks did leave tangible remains, both in the numerous destruction layers of Greek towns, and in the visible response of the inhabitants of Greece. The citizens of the unarmed province of Achaea, Zosimus recalls (1. 29. 3), fell into a panic at first, but evidence also suggests that inhabitants fought the invaders off and then, in some regions, hurried to restore and/or build fortifications both in urban areas and on the frontiers. An inscribed poem in Athens records this building effort after the Herulian attack: "As Amphion raised the walls of Thebes by the music of his cithaera so now do I, Illyrius, follower of the sweet voiced muse build the walls of my native city." Claudius Illyrius was the governor of Cyprus and was honoured with statues on the Acropolis of Athens, perhaps for the gift of walls to his native city.

Upon Diocletian's accession to the throne, the empire was temporarily at peace and the emperor set about solving the more serious economic and social problems in the provinces. Some regions in Greece enjoyed a brief building boom, but when he stepped down, conflict began again, and the Balkans, Greece included, became a recruiting ground for Constantine's civil war with Licinius. Constantine, once in power, moved his capital to Byzantium, "New Rome" or Constantinople. In deference to Greece's illustrious past, Constantine encouraged another revival of Greek letters and renewed support for educational institutions after the hiatus of the civil wars. Thus, during the early 4th century Achaea generally saw a renewal of building and literary activity, rejuvenation in the decorative arts (Christian sarcophagi were the medium of some of the best sculptural artists of the times), and an invigorated economy. Nevertheless, in the tradition of earlier emperors, Constantine felt it his right to remove art and artefacts from his provinces, including Achaea, to beautify his new capital. Despite the emperor's respect for Greek traditions, and his desire for its art, there was a widespread decline in the dominance of Hellenic culture among the Latin ruling classes. The court at Constantinople, for example, was predominately Latin-speaking, forcing ambitious Greeks to learn Latin and Roman law in order to get ahead. Increasingly too, after the 4th century, Greeks became Christianized. Hellenic political, religious, and economic orientation turned east and thus began the transition in earnest to the later Roman empire, or early Byzantine era, in Greek history.

CYNTHIA K. KOSSO

See also Political History 31 BC–AD 330

Summary

Dated 31 BC to AD 330, the Roman period follows the Hellenistic and precedes the early Byzantine. The annexation of Egypt in 31 BC completed the Roman conquest of the Hellenistic world. Greek culture was widely admired and imitated by the Romans. Many Greek works of art were removed to Italy but Greece was also the recipient of much imperial munificence. Roman and Greek cultures merged, revealing the power of Greek traditions.

Further Reading

Alcock, Susan E., *Graecia Capta: The Landscapes of Roman Greece*, Cambridge: Cambridge University Press, 1993

Alcock, Susan E., "Nero at Play? The Emperor's Grecian Odyssey" in *Reflections of Nero: Culture, History, and Representation*, edited by Jás Elsner and Jamie Masters, London: Duckworth, and Chapel Hill, North Carolina: University of North Carolina Press, 1994

Arafat, Karim, *Pausanius' Greece: Ancient Artists and Roman Rulers*, Cambridge: Cambridge University Press, 1996

Barker, Graeme and John Lloyd (editors), *Roman Landscapes: Archaeological Survey in the Mediterranean Region*, London: British School at Rome, 1991

Cartledge, Paul and Antony Spawforth, *Hellenistic and Roman Sparta: A Tale of Two Cities*, London and New York: Routledge, 1989

Garnsey, Peter and Richard Saller, *The Roman Empire: Economy, Society and Culture*, Berkeley: University of California Press, and London: Duckworth, 1987

Greene, Kevin, *The Archaeology of the Roman Economy*, Berkeley: University of California Press, and London: Batsford, 1986

Jones, A.H.M, "The Greeks under the Roman Empire", *Dumbarton Oaks Papers*, 17 (1963)

MacMullen, Ramsey, *Roman Social Relations, 50 BC–AD 284*, New Haven, Connecticut: Yale University Press, 1974

Macready, Sarah and F.H. Thompson (editors), *Roman Architecture in the Greek World*, London: Society of Antiquaries, 1987

Oliver, James H., *The Civic Tradition and Roman Athens*, Baltimore: Johns Hopkins University Press, 1983

Petrochilos, Nicholas, *Roman Attitudes to the Greeks*, Athens: National and Capodistrian University of Athens, Faculty of Arts, 1974

Shear, T.L., "Athens: From City-state to Provincial Town", *Hesperia*, 50/4 (1981): pp. 356–77

Spawforth, Antony and S. Walker, "The World of the Panhellion", parts 1–2, *Journal of Roman Studies*, 75 (1985): pp. 78–104 and 76 (1986): pp. 88–105

Spawforth, Antony, "Agonistic Festivals in Roman Greece" in *The Greek Renaissance in the Roman Empire*, edited by Susan Walker and Averil Cameron, London: University of London, Institute of Classical Studies, 1989

Syme, Ronald, "The Greeks under Roman Rule" in his *Roman Papers*, vol. 2, Oxford: Clarendon Press, and New York: Oxford University Press, 1979

Vermeule, Cornelius C., *Roman Imperial Art in Greece and Asia Minor*, Cambridge, Massachusetts: Harvard University Press, 1968

Wallace, Robert W. and Edward M. Harris (editors), *Transitions to Empire: Essays in Greco-Roman History, 360–146 BC, in Honor of E. Badian*, Norman, Oklahoma: University of Oklahoma Press, 1996

Wardman, Alan, *Rome's Debt to Greece*, London: Elek, 1976; New York: St Martin's Press, 1977

Wilkes, J.J., "Civil Defence in Third-Century Achaia" in *The Greek Renaissance in the Roman Empire*, edited by Susan Walker and Averil Cameron, London: University of London, Institute of Classical Studies, 1989

Romance, Byzantine

The reign of Manuel I Komnenos (1143–80) saw the revival of both satire and romance, the latter dormant since the 4th century AD. A tiny quantity of fiction had been written in the intervening years, most notably the romantic epic *Digenis Akritas*, recensions of such things as Aesop's fables and the *Alexander Romance*, and innovative adaptations from the Arabic of, in the 8th or 9th century, the immensely popular *Barlaam and Ioasaph* (originally a Buddhist fable in Sanskrit) and, in the late 11th century, *Stephanites and Ichnelates* (mainly animal fables, again originally in Sanskrit), while around 1100 a series of largely sexual tales in a narrative framework (of probably Persian origin) had been reworked from the Syriac as the *Book of the Philosopher Syntipas*.

Pure fiction had, however, been largely supplanted as entertaining literature by the saints' Lives, which were also uplifting. These, like the romances, often entail exciting adventures and end in the much-desired union of the hero with the beloved. It is perhaps more than merely coincidental that the revival of the romance followed close upon the decline of hagiography. The collapse of military, territorial, and economic strength, and the growing concomitant doubt that the Byzantines were the favoured recipients of divine providence, probably also encouraged a genre whose theme was largely the subordination of man to the cosmic forces of Love and Chance. The ancient novels were still known (the five surviving examples today are the result of Byzantine choice), their popularity being in part due to the metaphorical interpretation of their plots as struggles for salvation. Most often read seem to have been those of Achilles Tatius and Heliodorus, the subject of reviews by Photios and of a comparison by Michael Psellos. This ancient inheritance became the inspiration for the 12th-century "learned" romances, which are nonetheless no slavish imitations. All four are written in the high language, with only very few and minor intrusions of the vernacular, and are clearly intended for an educated readership that must have been familiar with the prototypes in order to appreciate their literary allusions. All four are again traditional in that they retain an antiquarian and pagan setting, but three break new ground by being in verse.

The earliest is almost certainly *Rhodanthe and Dosikles*, which was written in the 12-syllable accentual metre by the court poet Theodore Prodromos, perhaps in the 1140s. Though imitating Heliodorus' *Aethiopica*, it is more skilfully constructed, more rhetorically sophisticated, and more intellectual and, while keeping the excitement of piratical and other adventures, it probably reflects through them contemporary military and diplomatic preoccupations.

Clearly modelled on this romance, and written in the same metre, is *Drosilla and Charikles*; the author, Niketas Eugeneianos, wrote an epitaph on Prodromos and was either a younger friend or his disciple. Like his predecessor, Niketas does not completely avoid his own world, and his *ekphrasis* (description) of Drosilla coincides verbatim with that of the ideal bride in his own *epithalamium* on the wedding of the court official Stephen Komnenos. Nevertheless, Niketas's tone is more pastoral, with an obvious debt to Longus' *Daphnis and Chloe*, and on occasion he introduces a note of pure comedy as in his description of Maryllis's drunken dancing upon the table or the literary pretensions of the bumpkin Kallidemos.

Constantine Manasses is best known as the author of a popularizing verse chronicle, and his romance *Aristandros and Kallithea* survives unfortunately only in fragments. Despite an interest, new to the romance, in fabulous beasts, it is most noteworthy for its choice of the 15-syllable metre known as "political", which became standard for vernacular poetry until the late 17th century.

The last romance written in the high language, and also the only Byzantine example to revert to the ancient precedent of prose, is Eustathios (or Eumathios) Makrembolites's *Hysmine and Hysminias*. This is modelled on Achilles Tatius' *Leucippe and Clitophon* and, especially, the romances of Prodromos and Eugeneianos. More interestingly, Makrembolites appears to draw also on the novel *progymnasmata* (preparatory exercises)

of his contemporary Nikephoros Basilakes, especially in abandoning the traditional narrative style for the character study. His romance is highly charged with eroticism, although in conformity with the still-unbroken rule of romances the heroine miraculously preserves her chastity to the end. This eroticism is largely realized in the early books by allegorical paintings and Hysminias's own dreams. No other surviving romance is as psychologically subtle, and no other makes such demands on the reader to appreciate the often humorous parody created by quotation and covert allusion to a wide range of ancient literature. It is innovative also in using a first-person narration.

With the sack of Constantinople in 1204 the era of the "learned" romances in the high language came to an end. The 11 surviving romances of the 14th to 16th centuries are all written in some form of the vernacular, but with a widely differing lexical and grammatical admixture of the high language. Since, however, most of their manuscripts date from *c*.1500 or later and exhibit considerable divergences in language, it is a matter of much scholarly debate as to what was their exact original form and consequently readership. That, for some of these works, this must have included the intellectual elite is shown not only by literary subtleties but also by the fact that the single one that is not anonymous, admittedly the least "vernacular", was actually written by a member of the imperial family and received a religious exegesis from the court poet Manuel Philes. One feature common to most of these compositions is an exuberant enthusiasm for the coining of multiple compound words, especially adjectives. They all exhibit also a varying and at times dominating degree of influence from western romances. Five are original Greek works, six are adaptations or translations. Whereas the verse romances of Prodromos and Eugeneianos numbered just over 4600 and 3600 lines respectively, the "vernacular" romances tend to be considerably shorter.

The earliest original work, possibly dating to the very early 1300s, may be the *Tale of Achilles*, which has been preserved in three separate versions. It is best described as a romance of chivalry that is indebted not only to *Digenis Akritas* but also to more conventional romances. It reveals the contemporary Graeco-Frankish world of tournaments, jousting, and a knightly abduction, and retains from Homer no more than the names of Achilles, Patroclus, and the Myrmidons. Unlike other romances, which conclude happily with the union of the lovers, the *Tale of Achilles*, like *Digenis Akritas*, ends in a death, this time of the heroine who is mourned inconsolably by her husband.

Kallimachos and Chrysorrhoe (2607 lines) was written by Andronikos Palaiologos, a nephew of the first Palaiologan emperor, Michael VIII (1259–82). Although it shows considerable acquaintance with earlier romances, both ancient and Byzantine, it contains many folkloric elements. The hero is the youngest of three princely brothers who set out to prove themselves worthy of succeeding their father. He penetrates a castle perched on a mountain, rescues a damsel from an ogre, loses her to an abduction by a neighbouring king, feigns death through a witch's magic apple, and works in disguise as a gardener in the king's palace grounds. The ending is unexpected: when the two are caught together Chrysorrhoe wins their freedom with a well-composed speech.

In the much shorter *Belthandros and Chrysantza* (1348 lines), most probably from the 14th century, the hero follows a magical river of fire and water to the castle of Eros the king, where he reads a prophecy that he will fall in love with the heroine. Unfortunately, just after he has adjudicated her the winner of a beauty competition which is reminiscent of a bride show, she vanishes. However, a few exciting adventures later, they are permanently united. Like *Kallimachos and Chrysorrhoe* this romance moves from the world of fantasy to that of a fictional reality.

The five surviving manuscripts of *Libistros and Rhodamne* differ so greatly in length, language, and even sequence of episodes that it is impossible to reconstruct exactly what the 14th-century original was like. The probably most reliable manuscript gives a length of 4407 lines. Alone of the vernacular romances it interweaves two love stories, one of the eponymous couple, which ends with their union, and the other of the narrator Klitobos, the result of whose courting of Myrtane, a widow and his former mistress, is left uncertain. Realistic elements again appear in combination with the fantastic, which latter take the form of a magic ring, flying horses, and erotically prophetic dreams.

Because of its familiarity with other literature and its use of Italian loanwords the *Tale of Troy* (1166 lines) may perhaps be dated as late as the fall of Constantinople or even later. It begins as a romantic tale of Paris. To prevent the destruction of Troy should he reach manhood, he is put to sea in a basket, but, having been rescued, shut up in a tower, and shipwrecked, he eventually gains access to Helen in the disguise of a monk and takes her back to Troy. Thereafter Paris recedes into the background as the emphasis shifts to Achilles, the lamentation over whose death at the hand of Paris concludes this poorly constructed story.

A further work of fiction, though not strictly a romance, depends upon the romantic tradition. In the late 14th century Theodore Meliteniotes, possibly the same as a writer on theology and astrology, composed in 3062 lines an astonishing allegorical poem in the high language entitled *To Chastity*, in which may be found allusions not only to Greek authors but even to Pliny the Elder, Boccaccio, and Dante. In its attack on entertaining literature it mercilessly parodies Byzantine and western romances. The late 14th-century verse *Romance of Belisarius* is a largely legendary history of Justinian's general rather than a true romance. Emphasizing the workings of envy and revealing tension between classes, a feature rarely found in Byzantine literature, it proved sufficiently popular to gain two rhymed redactions during the Tourkokratia.

Of the Greek adaptations and translations the closest to their originals are the 14th- or 15th-century *Phlorios and Platzia-Phlora* and the probably late 15th-century *Theseid*. The former is a translation of *Il Cantare di Fiorio e Biancifiore*, the Tuscan version of a widespread western medieval tale of ultimately eastern origin. The latter is a translation of Boccaccio's *Teseida*. The monstrously long *War of Troy* of perhaps c.1350 is at 14,369 lines still slightly less than half the length of its immediate source, Benoît de Saint-Maure's *Roman de Troie*. The tale thus goes full circle since the French version derives from the pseudo-autoptic Latin accounts attributed to Dictys Cretensis and Dares Phrygius, the former of which for certain and the latter probably were translated from Greek in the 4th and 5th or 6th centuries respectively. The Byzantine version oddly omits exotic details, but, indicative of the less warlike nature of the Greeks, it also omits the prolix battle scenes. The omission of the judgement of Paris probably reflects its suppression in Manasses' influential chronicle. The short *Imberios and Margarona* is a translation from either French or Catalan which probably predates the oldest surviving French version from 1453 of *Pierre de Provence et la Belle Maguelonne*. *The Old Knight* is the modern title for an incomplete 14th-century poem of only 307 lines very freely taken, perhaps through an Italian intermediary but with added Homeric allusions, from the Arthurian prose romance *Guiron le Courtois*. Its theme is Branor le Brun's challenge to the younger knights of the Round Table. Uniquely in the post-12th-century romances it is written in the high language. The 14th- or 15th-century *Apollonios of Tyre* is an adaption of a 14th-century Tuscan translation of a Latin tale, itself possibly dependent upon a Greek original of the time of the early romances. Its main interest is in the Christianization of the pagan setting of its model. It also is thus unique among Byzantine romances. The verse redaction of Callisthenes' *Alexander Romance* is, like the *Romance of Belisarios*, fabulous history rather than romance. It, *Imberios*, and *Apollonios* also share the fate of later reworkings into rhyming verse.

The greatest Greek literary production of the Tourkokratia is the *Erotokritos*, written in Crete around 1600 by Vitsentzos Kornaros, a poet of noble Venetian descent. Despite its debt to Pierre de la Cypède's *Paris et Vienne*, it is an original work in its own right. Set in ancient Athens, it unfolds in just over 10,000 lines the ultimately successful love affair of king Heracles' daughter Aretousa and Erotokritos, the son of a royal counsellor. Possibly aware only of the *Theseid* and *Imberios* among Byzantine romances, Kornaros nonetheless suffuses a romance of western chivalry, replete with long speeches and psychological exploration, with the hues of a poetic and chronologically composite Greek world.

Traditionally castigated by scholars, when not completely ignored, for being paltry imitations of ancient exemplars of a second-rate genre, Byzantine romances are now enjoying a sensitive re-evaluation. Their *ekphraseis* are no longer regarded as wearisome rhetorical irrelevancies but as integral parts of a whole, their literary borrowings are being appreciated as frequently subtle or even humorous parody, and, in the best of them, artistic construction and psychological characterization are being carefully revealed. They can now claim a small, but not contemptible, place in the history of world literature.

A.R. LITTLEWOOD

See also Novel

Collections

Betts, Gavin (translator), *Three Medieval Greek Romances*, New York: Garland, 1995 (contains *Belthandros and Chrysantza*, *Kallimachos and Chrysorrhoe*, *Libistros and Rhodamne*)

Conca, Fabrizio (editor), *Il romanzo bizantino del XII secolo: Teodoro Prodromo, Niceta Eugeniano, Eustazio Macrembolita, Costantino Manasse*, Turin: UTET, 1994 (with Italian translation)

Cupane, Carolina (editor), *Romanzi cavallareschi bizantini*, Turin: UTET, 1995 (includes *Achilleid*, *Belthandros and Chrysantza*, *Kallimachos and Chrysorrhoe*, *Phlorios and Platzia-Phlora*, *Apollonios of Tyre*, with Italian translation)

Individual Works

Alexander Romance: *Das byzantinische Alexandergedicht*, edited by Siegfried Reichmann, Meisenheim: Hain, 1963; rhymed version *The Tale of Alexander* edited by David Holton, Thessalonica, 1974 (text in modern Greek, introduction and commentary in English)

Belisarios: *Istoria tou Belisariou*, edited by W.F. Bakker and A.F. van Gemert, Thessalonica, 1988

Erotokritos: *Erotokritos*, edited by Stylianos Alexiou, Athens, 1980, shorter version, 1985; as *Erotocritos: circa 1640 AD*, translated into English by Theodore P. Stephanides, Athens: Papazissis, 1984

Imberios and Margarona: *To mythistorema tou Imperiou kai tes Margaronas* in *Byzantina Hippotika Mythistoremata*, edited by Emmanouel Kriaras, 1955, pp. 199–249; as *Il romanzo di Beltandro e Crisanza*, edited and translated into Italian by Fabrizio Conca, Milan: Cisalpino Goliardica, 1982

Libistros and Rhodamne: *Le Roman de Libistros et Rhodamne*, edited by J.A. Lambert, Amsterdam: Noord-Hollandsche, 1935

Old Knight: "La Table ronde en orient: Le poème grec duvieux chevalier", edited by P. Breillat, *Mélanges d'archéologie et d'histoire*, 55 (1938): pp. 308–40

On Chastity: *Sophrosyne*, edited by E. Miller, *Notices et extraits des Manuscrits de la Bibliothèque Impériale*, 19. 2, Paris: Académie des Inscriptions et Belles-Lettres, 1858, pp. 1–138

Theseïd: *Il Teseida neogreco*, book 1, edited by Enrica Follieri, Rome: Istituto di Studi Bizanti e Neoellenici, 1959

The War of Troy: *O Polemos tes Troades / The War of Troy*, edited by M. Papathomopoulou and E.M. Jeffreys, Athens, 1996

Further Reading

Alexiou, M., "A Critical Reappraisal of Eustathios Makrembolites' *Hysmine and Hysminias*", *Byzantine and Modern Greek Studies*, 3 (1977): pp. 23–43

Beaton, Roderick, *The Medieval Greek Romance*, 2nd edition, London and New York: Routledge, 1996

Beck, Hans Georg, Fabrizio Conca and Carolina Cupane (editors), *Il romanzo tra cultura latina e cultura bizantina*, Palermo: Enchiridion, 1986

Conca, Fabrizio, "Il romanzo di Niceta Eugeniano: modelli narrativi estilistici", *Siculorum Gymnasium*, 39 (1986): pp. 115–26

Garland, L., " 'Be Amorous, but Be Chaste ... ': Sexual Morality in Byzantine Learned and Vernacular Romance", *Byzantine and Modern Greek Studies*, 14 (1990): pp. 62–120

Holton, David, *Erotokritos*, Bristol: Bristol Classical Press, 1991

Hunger, H., "Un Roman byzantin et son atmosphère: Callimaque et Chrysorrhoè", *Travaux et Mémoires*, 3 (1968): pp. 405–22

Plepelits, Karl, *Eustathios Makrembolites: Hysmine und Hysminias*, Stuttgart: Hiersemann, 1989 (with German translation)

Romania

Romania is situated on the western shore of the Black Sea at a point where routes from Central Europe to the east and south-east converge. Its southern and southwestern frontier is marked by the Danube (ancient Istrus); its western and north-western frontier extends far into the Hungarian plain; and its northeastern boundary is the Prut river, although from time to time it stretched to the Dniester by the incorporation of all or part of Bessarabia. Dobrudja abuts its Black Sea coastline, and this too has been attached to the core of modern Romania – the principalities of Moldavia and Wallachia – within varying boundaries at different times. The Carpathian mountains cut an arc through the country from northeast to southwest, sepa-

rating those parts long under the influence of Constantinople and those which, looking to the Black Sea from Transylvania, the Banat, and Maramures, belong to the Danube basin and formed part of millennial Hungary before 1919.

The territory of modern-day Romania has been populated from the Palaeolithic period. The country's historical period begins in the 9th–8th centuries BC and is connected in south-western Europe with the so-called Thracian Hallstatt period (c.600–550 BC), which corresponds to European Hallstatt C. Basarabi culture is considered the most representative of this new period within Romanian territory: the population was formed of mainly agricultural tribes living in fortified or open villages whose dwellings were constructed of timber.

The middle Danube was populated by the Tribali, a Thracian tribe, and Dobrudja by the Crobyzi and Getae. In Dobrudja the assimilation of the Getae and other Thracian tribes by the Dacians (from the second half of the 6th century BC) led to the creation of a Geto-Dacian culture. In addition to these tribes, Scythians inhabited both Dobrudja and Transylvania, introducing certain types of iron weapon, contributing to the development of art, and bringing certain features of Greek civilization to Transylvania. Greek influence reached the Geto-Dacian peoples more directly—via Greek colonies established on the Romanian Black Sea coast. The lands south of the Carpathians have yielded very fine examples of metalwork (helmets, greaves, goblets and other vessels, and a gilt rhyton), decorated mainly with zoomorphic figures, although human figures and floral and geometric ornament are not entirely absent. Some of these objects may have come from native workshops (Thracian or Getic); most, however, are from Asia Minor or the Pontic region, or are of Persian workmanship.

Histria was the first Greek colony on the Romanian Black Sea coast. It was founded by Milesians in the last quarter of the 7th century BC at the mouth of the Danube, and named accordingly. In the archaic period it was a small settlement of modest wattle-and-daub houses, surrounded by defensive walls. From the Classical period it grew: stone temples were built in the city's sacral area; stone dwellings were constructed, many with fine masonry, some with an upper storey; and the city minted its own coins. Histria became the centre of Hellenic culture in Getic lands. It was a centre of trade through which Greek goods penetrated deep into the hinterland. Its agricultural territory (*chora*) was populated by local people, who also formed a small part of the city's own population. In the Hellenistic period Histria doubled in size; new city walls were built, as were new temples. In the Roman period the city was enlarged further and yet new city walls and new temples were built. It remained a craft and trade centre until its destruction in the 4th century AD.

Another two Greek colonies, Tomis (modern Constanta) and Callatis (modern Mangalia), were established on the Romanian coast. Tomis, Ovid's place of exile, was established, also by Milesians, at the end of the 6th century BC. Excavation is very difficult, as the modern city lies directly above the ancient settlement; chance finds, however, demonstrate that it was an important craft and trading centre. In the Roman period it was decorated with marble sculptures, and mosaics were also found there. Callatis was established by Heraclea Pontica, itself a Dorian colony on the south coast of the Black

Romania: monks at the skete of Lakkou, which is reserved for Romanians, on Mount Athos. Romanians form the largest ethnic minority on the Holy Mountain today.

Sea. Archaeological material and inscriptions demonstrate that Callatis, sited in a fertile cereal-growing region, was a prosperous city.

At the end of the 4th century BC the Celts entered Transylvania, bringing with them a more advanced iron-working technology and the potter's wheel. Celtic tombs in this area contain fine metal objects and pottery. North of the Carpathians Celtic influence played a role of similar importance to that of the Greeks in the southern and eastern regions.

Under Greek influence the Geto-Dacians minted their first coins in the 3rd century BC, imitating those of Philip II and Alexander the Great. Assimilation of the different tribes and cultures was gradually completed. A similar process affected Scythians of the Dobrudja, who exacted tribute from neighbouring Greek cities in exchange for military protection: by c.AD 100 they had disappeared, the memory of their presence retained in the Roman name for Dobrudja – Scythia Minor.

In c.80 BC Burebista established the kingdom of Dacia and became its first ruler. Dacia reached its peak under King Decebalus, who fought against the Romans. The second Dacian War (AD 105–106) brought about the destruction of the Dacian kingdom and Roman conquest of the entire region. The importance of this to the Romans is shown by the erection of Trajan's column (*Tropaeum Traiani*) at Adamclisi in AD 109; this, the most important Roman monument on the lower Danube, depicts scenes of Roman victory in the war. Trajan made Dacia a Roman province. Because of its strategic impor-

tance, an outpost of empire in the hostile region north of the Danube, it was placed under direct imperial authority. Three legions reinforced by various auxiliary troops, a force of some 50,000 men, were permanently stationed there. Here Roman culture had a clearly military character. New Roman cities (such as Sarmizegetusa, Apulum, Napoca, and Drobeta) were established, as well as military settlements. The Danubian *limes* was strengthened by the construction of fortresses at such points as Axiopolis, Carsium, and Capidova. New cities (Tropaeum Traiani and Troesmis) were also founded in Scythia Minor.

The province of Dacia, extremely hostile to the Romans, could be held against frequent invasions by aggressive neighbours only at enormous cost in terms of money and manpower. In 271 the emperor Aurelius decided to evacuate the province. This led to a cultural retreat and Dacia's return in the 4th century to its old agrarian lifestyle. The departure of the Romans provided an opportunity for fresh tribes to fill the vacuum and invade this fertile region. This culminated in a period of mass migration by (seriatim) the Huns, Gepids, Ostrogoths, Avars, Slavs, and Protobulgarians, who fought each other as well as the Byzantines. Justinian was the last emperor to guarantee protection of the border on the Danube; it gave way in 602.

Byzantine remains are found in Histria and other Romanian Black Sea coastal cities and settlements. The history of post-Roman art in the region is closely linked with protonational historical developments. Features of Roman and Byzantine origin were assimilated with Dacian tradition, whose wooden buildings gave way to stone architecture. The spread of Christianity over the course of the 4th century throughout the region south of the Carpathians, Dobrudja, and Transylvania exerted a deep influence on the art and artistic language of the Middle Ages, but interacting with historical factors peculiar to particular areas this common inspiration yielded a rich diversity of results. The influence of Byzantine Orthodox culture came to the area indirectly through a Serbian intermediary. This was of considerable importance for the development of indigenous Romanian art and architecture. No stone churches predating the 14th century survive in Romania, earlier ones being built of wood. Early stone-built examples have the usual Byzantine cross-in-square arrangement and basilican ground plans. The typical Romanian church has a distinctive form, Morava style, that developed in Serbia in the 14th and 15th centuries. Church painting echoed the techniques of 15th-century Byzantine art, and in later centuries was in keeping with late Byzantine trends (scenes are multifigured and small scale, with many tiers of paintings covering the walls from top to bottom). Jewellery and church utensils were either Byzantine or locally produced under Byzantine artistic influence. This was especially the case before the Tatar invasion of 1247.

Richly embroidered and adorned ceremonial garments dating from the 14th and 15th centuries are found, as well as jewellery of Byzantine craftsmanship (although western jewellery had also been introduced). The ladies of the ruling families were depicted in contemporary murals and embroidery wearing gold crowns of a characteristic shape decorated with pearls and precious stones, their shoulders and upper torsos draped in richly ornamented pendants, the whole redolent of Byzantine imperial dress.

The question of the ethnic origins of the modern Romanians has, in recent times, become embroiled with the rival national and territorial claims of Hungary and Romania in Transylvania. There is long gap in written sources, especially between the Roman/Byzantine collapse on the Danube and the re-establishment of Byzantine domination there 300 years later. Two rival theories have gained currency: that developed by Roessler holds that the modern Romanians have their origin outside the Carpathian area, while that known as continuous development holds that they are the descendants of the Daco-Roman population and the Slavs who through fusion and assimilation in the 7th–9th centuries, developed a "proto-Romanian" language.

The foundations of the modern Romanian state rest on a number of small feudal states (*terrae valachicae*), governed by chieftains, which were established in the 10th century. Over the succeeding centuries those to the west of the Carpathians were overrun by the kingdom of Hungary and settled by Saxon colonists. Those to the south and east, after two centuries of exposure to further invasion by Cumans and Tatars, and intermittent Hungarian involvement, were consolidated in the 14th century to form two large and independent principalities (Moldavia and Wallachia) with elected rulers. Dobrudja, formerly part of Wallachia, was conquered by the Ottoman Turks at the end of the 14th century. The two principalities, despite spirited resistance and the manoeuvring common in

buffer states (seeking to play off Hungary, Poland, and the Ottomans), ultimately fell under Ottoman suzerainty (in the generation after the fall of Constantinople) but retained their separate identities, considerable autonomy (politically and culturally), and an appetite for using Hungary and Poland as some counterbalance to the Ottomans – who interfered in princely elections and might eliminate overambitious or restive princes. From the 17th century Phanariot Greeks (native or adoptive) became ever more prominent in both principalities, with families such as the Mavrogordato furnishing some 90 per cent of the ruling princes in the century up to 1812. Thereafter, modern nationalism, Ottoman weakness, and great-power patronage ushered the principalities towards *de facto* independence and unity in the 1850s under the native prince Alexander Ion Cuza, and full independence and the acquisition of Dobrudja in 1877 under his German successor. The creation of greater Romania followed in the aftermath of World War I (with the acquisition of Transylvania, parts of the Banat, Maramures, etc. from Hungary, Bukovina from Austria, Bessarabia from Russia, and various unreconciled minorities from all of them); various territorial amputations (some temporary – to Hungary; some permanent – southern Dobrudja returned to Bulgaria, and Bessarabia to the USSR) occurred during and as a result of World War II.

GOCHA R. TSETSKHLADZE

See also Moldavia, Wallachia

Further Reading

Castellan, Georges, *A History of the Romanians*, Boulder, Colorado: East European Monographs, 1989
Condurachi, Emil and Constantin Daicoviciu, *Romania*, London: Barrie and Jenkins, 1971
Glodariu, Ioan, *Dacian Trade with the Hellenistic and Roman World*, Oxford: British Archaeological Reports, 1976
Halbertsma, R.B., "The Doom of the Dacians: Archaeological Discoveries from Romania, 7000 BC–AD 600", *Minerva* (November/December 1994): pp. 26–31
Isaac, Benjamin, *The Greek Settlement in Thrace until the Macedonian Conquest*, Leiden: Brill, 1986
Teodor, Dan G., *The East Carpathian Area of Romania in the V–XI Centuries AD*, Oxford: British Archaeological Reports, 1980
Treasures from Romania, London: British Museum, 1971 (exhibition catalogue)

Romanos I Lekapenos c.870–948

Emperor

Romanos I Lekapenos (920–44) was a Byzantine emperor whose reign coincided with a period of military success and territorial expansion, a process that continued throughout the 10th century and reached its culmination during the reign of Basil II (976–1025). Romanos Lekapenos's family took its name from the town of Lakape, near Melitene, and was ethnically Armenian. Although of peasant background, Romanos had a successful military career as a naval officer. He held the post of *strategos* (commander) of Samos and eventually became *droungarios* or commander-in-chief of the fleet. Because of this important military command, he became a

ROMANOS 1465

pivotal figure in the struggle for the regency after the death of the emperor Alexander in 912. Romanos's political support was solicited by Theodore, the tutor of Constantine VII Porphyrogennetos (913–59), for help against rival claimants to the regency. In May 919 Romanos secured his position by repudiating the marriage pact already arranged by the patriarch Nicholas between Constantine VII and the daughter of the Bulgarian king Symeon by having his own daughter Helen marry Constantine instead, for which Romanos took the title *basileopator* (royal father-in-law), previously held by Symeon. Romanos also ordered the patriarch Nicholas to hold a Church council in 920 to reconcile differences between the proponents of Nicholas and the former patriarch Euthymios. This council issued canons condemning Leo VI's fourth marriage as illicit and allowing the third only under certain circumstances. Later, after the death of Nicholas, Romanos replaced him with one of his own sons, Theophylact. Following the conclusion of the council, Romanos charged the empress Zoe Karbonopsina, widow of Leo VI (886–912) and mother of Constantine VII, with trying to poison him and had her tonsured. Finally Romanos secured control of the regency by having the tutor Theodore exiled. After being declared Caesar, Romanos further strengthened his position by having himself crowned co-emperor with Constantine on 17 December 920. In 921–22 he decided to push the child emperor into the background and reserved most of the responsibility for governing the state to himself. Romanos would eventually have three of his sons, Christopher, Stephen, and Constantine, crowned as co-emperors, with Constantine VII remaining as the most junior of them.

Romanos was an effective emperor who initiated legislation that helped to protect small landholders against the encroachments of the *dynatoi* (magnates), who would buy out poor farmers and then use their position to obtain tax exemptions for themselves. Romanos believed that reform was necessary to protect the recruiting base for the army and to secure revenues for the state. In 922 he reversed the legislation of Leo VI by reinstating the right of preemption for relatives or neighbours in the sale of soldiers' land. The law enumerated five categories of neighbours who had preemptive rights in any alienation of peasant land. This was designed to prevent the transfer of land to large landowners unless they fitted into one of these categories. All soldiers' holdings that had been previously alienated had to be returned without compensation. The legislation created more problems than it solved. Many peasants were not interested in assuming control of this land again because of the onerous obligations it entailed. Of course, the local nobility were opposed to any legislation that expropriated them of their property. Eventually the situation in the countryside became worse as the famine of 927–28, resulting from bitter winter weather, imposed more hardships on the smallholders and led to the transfer of more land to the *dynatoi*. In 932 the rebel Basil attempted to take advantage of this discontent by staging an uprising in the Opsikion theme, for which he was eventually executed. In response, in 934 Romanos issued another decree that denounced the *dynatoi* and required the return of all land transferred since 928.

Romanos also enjoyed success in dealing with the empire's many enemies, especially Bulgaria. In 924, after receiving news of Romanos's usurpation and the cancellation of Nicholas's marriage pact, Symeon marched on Constantinople, but Romanos confronted him personally and successfully turned him away. After Symeon died in 927, Romanos was able to manipulate his successor Peter by having him marry one of his own granddaughters, Maria. On the eastern front the Armenian general John Kourkouas conducted several successful campaigns against the Hamdanids of Aleppo, the leading Islamic state at this time. John's victories eventually aroused the jealousy of Romanos which resulted in his replacement by the less talented Pantherios, a relative of the Lekapenoi. Romanos also suppressed revolts in Italy, the Peloponnese, and Chaldia.

A major change in Romanos's fortunes occurred after the death of his son Christopher, a bitter blow that seemed to sap his will to carry on. He later specified in his will that Constantine VII (son of Leo VI) would succeed him ahead of his own two sons, Stephen and Constantine. Fearing their impending loss of power these two brothers, with the backing of some courtiers, organized a coup against their father in 944. Romanos was overthrown and sent to a monastery; however, a month later, the two Lekapid sons met the same fate when they tried to assassinate Constantine VII, and were exiled to the same monastery as their father. Despite a plot to restore Romanos to power in 946, he spent the rest of his life on the island of Prote, eventually dying there on 15 June 948.

JOHN F. SHEAN

Biography

Born in Lakape *c.*870, the son of Armenian peasants, Romanos had a naval career. He became *strategos* of Samos and commander-in-chief of the Byzantine fleet. He married his daughter Helen to Constantine VII Porphyrogennetos. After being declared Caesar, Romanos had himself crowned co-emperor in 920. He was dethroned by his sons in 944 and sent in exile to Prote where he died as a monk in 948.

Further Reading

Nicholas I, *Letters*, edited and translated by R.J.H. Jenkins and L.G. Westerink, Washington, D.C.: Dumbarton Oaks, 1973
Nicholas I, *Miscellaneous Writings*, edited and translated by L.G. Westerink, Washington, D.C.: Dumbarton Oaks, 1981
Runciman, Steven, *The Emperor Romanus Lecapenus and His Reign: A Study of Tenth-Century Byzantium*, Cambridge: Cambridge University Press, 1929, reprinted 1963
Symeon the Logothete (revised by Leo Grammaticus), *Chronographia*, edited by Immanuel Bekker, Bonn: Weber, 1842 (*Corpus scriptorum historiae byzantinae* 31)
Theodoros Daphnopates, *Correspondance*, edited and translated into French by J. Darrouzes and L.G. Westerink, Paris: Centre National des Recherches Scientifiques, 1978
Theophanes Continuatus, *Works*, edited by Immanuel Bekker, Bonn: Weber, 1838 (*Corpus scriptorum historiae byzantinae* 45)
Vasiliev, A.A. *et al.*, *Byzance et les Arabes*, 2 vols, Brussels: Institut de Philologie et d'Histoire Orientales, 1935, 1968

Romanos the Melodist, St

Hymnographer of the 6th century

Honoured on 1 October by the Orthodox Church as its patron saint of music, St Romanos the Melodist is also revered by modern scholars as Byzantium's greatest sacred poet. The primary sources for his life and career are the short summaries of his lost *Life* transmitted in Byzantine Synaxaria and Menologia, to which one may also add the autobiographical references and other historical evidence found in his poetic works. These indicate that Romanos was born in the Syrian city of Emesa during the late 5th century, most probably to a Semitic (possibly Jewish) family. After his ordination to the diaconate, he was assigned to the church of the Resurrection in Beirut, where he spent several years before journeying to Constantinople during the reign of Anastasius I (491–518). In the capital Romanos served at the church of the Mother of God of the Kyros district, while also frequenting the all-night vigil (*pannychis*) at the city's important Marian shrine and stational church of Blachernae. According to the *Life*, his poetic gift was revealed when the Virgin Mary appeared to him during the vigil of Christmas at his home parish in Kyros with a scroll that she asked him to swallow. After acceding to her request, he mounted the ambo of the church and began to sing his famous hymn "Today the Virgin Gives Birth". The *Life* then records that Romanos went on to compose more than 1000 such hymns, the manuscripts of which were preserved in the church of Kyros, where he was eventually buried.

Today the figure of more than 1000 hymns is held to be a superlative form of praise for the Melodist. Only 85 texts bearing attributions to Romanos have survived, of which the editors of the Oxford edition of his works selected only 59 for inclusion in their volume of his *Cantica Genuina*. All of the latter belong to the early Byzantine genre of hymnography known anachronistically as the kontakion (the term refers to the scrolls from which the hymns were later sung), which Romanos is generally acknowledged to have brought to its apogee. The kontakia of Romanos are metrical homilies consisting of a short prologue (originally called a *koukoulion*, but later confusingly referred to as a kontakion) which serves to introduce the subject and refrain of the work, followed by a series of up to 40 longer and metrically identical stanzas known as *oikoi* that are united by an acrostic. Although the structural affinities between the kontakion and earlier forms of Syrian liturgical poetry have long been recognized, recent scholarship has also revealed cases of direct borrowing by Romanos from such Syriac sources as the *Diatesseron* of Tatian and the hymns of St Ephraim the Syrian, thus indicating that he may have been fully bilingual. The significance of other concordances noted earlier in the 20th century between the works of Romanos and Greek works that circulate under the name of St Ephraim, however, remains to be determined by future study.

The language of Romanos's genuine kontakia is an Atticized form of koine that, despite the poet's frequent use of rhetorical devices, remains fresh and direct. Particularly appealing are the many episodes of dialogue between historical or symbolic figures that occur in his hymns, in which Romanos demonstrates both a keen sense of drama and considerable psychological insight. These kontakia cover a variety of subjects: 34 are on the person of Christ, five relate other episodes from the New Testament, seven commemorate figures from the Old Testament, three praise martyrs and saints, and the remaining ten address other topics. Considered together, they constitute an almost complete cycle of hymns for the major fixed Christological and Marian feasts of the liturgical year, many of

which were created or positioned in the Byzantine calendar during the reign of Justinian (527–65). To this fixed cycle may be added a second group of hymns for the movable seasons of Lent – notably including kontakia for the original Sunday cycle of Old Testament commemorations – and Easter. A number of the poems falling outside these main cycles of feasts were inspired by contemporary events. The hymns *On Earthquakes and Fires* and *On Baptism* relate, respectively, to the Nika rebellion of 532 and to the imperial edict issued in or around 528 requiring the baptism of all remaining pagans. Similarly, the only two genuine hagiographic kontakia of Romanos commemorate the Forty Martyrs of Sebastea, saints who were personal favourites of Justinian.

The discovery of a 6th-century papyrus containing a fragment of an authentic hymn by Romanos would seem to indicate that he became famous in his own lifetime. In the centuries following his death, his continuing popularity is attested to by the frequency with which the metrical patterns (and therefore the melodies) of his hymns were borrowed by later composers of kontakia, the existence of a body of (mostly hagiographical) hymns posthumously attributed to him, and his canonization at an unknown date. It also appears that for some time his hymns continued to be performed in their entirety within their original context of the Constantinopolitan service of *pannychis*. An episode in the 7th-century *Miracles of St Artemios*, for example, refers to the chanting of hymns by Romanos during a popular all-night vigil, while the 10th-century *Typikon of the Great Church* contains hints of similar practices at Hagia Sophia and its dependent stational churches.

During the 9th century the kontakia of Romanos were adopted by St Theodore of Stoudios for use within the monastic rite of St Savas as *mesodia*, i.e. compositions to be sung between the biblical odes and poetic canons of the Palestinian psalter. Although St Theodore and other Middle Byzantine hymnographers initially continued to draw on the poetry of Romanos as a source for their own hymns (mostly *stichera* and canons), whole kontakia began to disappear from the active repertory. Whatever the causes of this curtailment, one result was that Romanos's reputation as the Orthodox east's patron saint of music came to rest increasingly on the miraculous origins of his gift, which became the centrepiece for icons of the Protection of the Mother of God. In the 14th century, for example, Nikephoros Kallistos Xanthopoulos attributes the origins of the kontakion to Romanos by retelling the story of the Virgin's appearance during the vigil of Christmas. Echoed in the lives of the 14th-century musical saints John Koukouzeles and Gregory the Domestikos, this episode is cited directly in the post-Byzantine period by Agapios Landos in his devotional collection *Amartolon Soteria* (The Salvation of Sinners, Venice, 1641). Indeed, it is only with the publication, study, and translation of his works over the course of the late 19th and 20th centuries that Romanos has again become firmly established as Byzantium's preeminent sacred poet.

ALEXANDER LINGAS

See also Hymnography

Biography

Born at Emesa in Syria in the late 5th century, perhaps to a Jewish family, Romanos served as a deacon in Beirut before moving to

Constantinople where he served in the church of the Mother of God in the Kyros district. According to tradition he composed over 1000 hymns. In fact just 85 survive, of which only 59 are considered genuine. He is revered as the Orthodox Church's patron saint of music and Byzantium's greatest sacred poet. He died after 555.

Writings

Cantica, edited by Paul Maas and C.A. Trypanis, Oxford: Clarendon Press, 1963

Kontakia of Romanus, Byzantine Melodist, translated by Marjorie Carpenter, 2 vols, Columbia: University of Missouri Press, 1970–73

On the Life of Christ: Kontakia, translated by Archimandrite Ephrem Lash, London: AltaMira, and San Francisco: HarperCollins, 1995

Further Reading

Alexiou, Margaret, "The Lament of the Virgin in Byzantine Literature and Modern Greek Folk-Song", Byzantine and Modern Greek Studies, 1 (1975): pp. 111–40

Brock, Sebastian P., "From Ephrem to Romanus" in Studia Patristica, vol. 20, edited by Elizabeth A. Livingstone, Leuven: Peeters, 1989

Grosdidier de Matons, José, Romanus le mélode et les origines de la poésie religieuse à Byzance, Paris: Beauchesne, 1977

Levy, Kenneth, "An Early Chant for Romanus' Contacium Trium Puerorum?", Classica et Mediaevalia, 22 (1961): pp. 172–75

Lingas, Alexander, "The Liturgical Place of the Kontakion in Constantinople" in Liturgy, Architecture and Art in Byzantine World, edited by Constantin C. Akentiev, St Petersburg: St Petersburg Society for Byzantine and Slavic Studies, 1995

Mitsakis, K., The Language of Romanus the Melodist, Munich: Beck, 1967

Petersen, William L., "The Dependence of Romanus the Melodist upon the Syriac Ephrem: Its Importance for the Origin of the Kontakion", Vigiliae Christianae, 39/2 (1985): pp. 171–87

Raasted, Jørgen, "Zur Melodie des Kontakions I Parthenos Simeron", Cahiers de l'Institut du Moyen-Age Grec et Latin, 59 (1989): pp. 233–46

Strunk, Oliver, "Some Observations on the Music of the Kontakion" in his Essays on Music in the Byzantine World, New York: Norton, 1977

Topping, Eva Catafygiotu, Sacred Songs: Studies in Byzantine Hymnography, Minneapolis: Light and Life, 1997

Trypanis, C.A., "On the Musical Rendering of the Early Byzantine Kontakia" in Studies in Eastern Chant, vol. 1, edited by Miloš Velimirović, London and New York: Oxford University Press, 1966

Wellesz, Egon, A History of Byzantine Music and Hymnography, 2nd edition, Oxford: Clarendon Press, 1961

Romanticism

The protagonists of the Romantic movement drew their inspiration from themes connected with the revival of an idealized past. Chateaubriand's Le Génie du christianisme rallied the French Romantics around ideas associated with the sentimental reawakening of medieval Catholicism, while the Germans sympathized with Herder's rediscovery of a Gothic past. Although the German Romantics wished to break free from the heavily weighing tradition of Classical Hellenism, they owed a great debt to the forerunners of the Romantic movement, Hölderlin and Goethe, who remained unequivocally Hellenists throughout their poetic career.

The central Romantic themes of struggle with invincible powers, freedom, self-determination, and divinely inspired creativity were formidably expressed in the most significant works of Romanticism inspired by the Greek struggle for independence. Shelley's Hellas, Byron's Giaour and some cantos of Childe Harold, Delacroix's Massacre of Chios and Greece Lamenting on the Ruins of Missolonghi, Ary Scheffer's antagonistic treatment of similar themes accompanied by Victor Hugo's Les Orientales (Chio ... tout est désert), Beethoven's The Ruins of Athens, and Keats's New Hellenism dominated the cultural landscape of the first two decades of the 19th century and contributed to easing the controversy waged between the Classical and the Romantic. In this way a balance was restored between the Romantic Hellenism of Hölderlin, the Weimar Classicists, and the Romantic Philhellenism associated with the sympathizers to the Greek cause.

Romanticism, as an emotional reaction to the rationalistic spirit of the Enlightenment, infused the rediscovery of Hellas with the power of the sensation of Gefühl, understood as an intense feeling capable of producing interior states of revelatory insight in the mind and soul of the person who would surrender to its influence. The setting of the stage in the Greek War of Independence helped to resolve the conflict between the traditional-Classical and the modern-Romantic formulations as set forth by A.W. Schlegel. In both the Jena (1798) and the Berlin lectures (1801–04) Schlegel had contrasted the Classical literature of antiquity with the modern Romantic literature in which he included Shakespeare, Goethe, the folk poetry of the Spanish romances, the Scottish ballads, as well as the medieval romances of Charlemagne and the Nibelungen. A few years earlier, in the spirit of Sturm und Drang, Hamann and Herder had stressed the vitality of folk poetry, contrasting it with the dead letter of Classical poetry. The latter's collection of German popular poetry, Stimmen der Völker in Liedern (1778–79), advanced the notion that the folk poetry of a nation is imbued with the spirit of the people, the so-called Geist des Volkes, and that the national poetry expressed in vernacular speech is the authentic expression of the spirit of a nation, Geist der Nation.

Madame de Staël, greatly influenced by Schlegel, was instrumental in the dissemination of Romantic ideas in France. In 1813 De l'Allemagne was published in London, and two months later Schlegel's lectures were published in a translation done by her cousin, Madame Necker de Saussure. C.C. Fauriel had a first-hand knowledge of these ideas through his intimate association with Madame de Staël. His Preface to the Chants populaires de la Grèce, the Discours préliminaire, reproduced the pattern of thought of the German Romantics.

Set against this background, Solomos's Romanticism acquires a particular colouring inherited by the German Romantics. Even his impassioned defence of the demotic language, opposed to the dubious reforms of Korais, as presented in his Dialogos (1824), and the emulation of popular poetry in his own compositions point to Herder's unmistakable influence. From his correspondence it transpires that he was familiar with K. Ludwig Michelet's "neo-Christian spiritualism" and that he had studied attentively Hamann, Schelling, Manzoni, Speroni (who had also written a Dialogo sopra le lingue), and the circle of Italian Romantics associated with the literary review Conciliatore. Solomos had already put together a collection of popular songs which were later offered to Nicolò Tommaseo, who included them in his three-volume *Canti popolari toscani, corsi, illirici, greci* (1841–42). However, what is of paramount importance is not Solomos's debt to the popular Muse, but rather the role that the German and, to a lesser degree, the Italian Romantics played in the consolidation of the arguments for the encouragement given to the predominance of the demotic language as the authentic medium for the expression of the Greek version of *Volksgeist*.

This particular streak of Romanticism associated with the authentic expressions of national idiosyncracies left its distinctive marks on all facets of Greek cultural, social, and political life in the 19th century. Linked to the theme of the revival of the past, it created a particular style in architecture known as the Neoclassical Romantic style in which Athens, Aegina, Nauplia, and other urban centres were built. Its main exponents, who were responsible for designing and building Athens as the new capital of the Greek state, E. Schaubert, C. and T. Hansen, E. Ziller, and S. Kleanthis, were all steeped in the tradition of German Romanticism. Both L. von Klenze and F. von Gärtner, who were responsible for some of the most representative works of German Romanticism in Ludwig I's Bavaria, were instrumental in giving Athens its Neoclassical look. This distinctive style was original enough to be imitated throughout the world's great cities, from Paris to Moscow and from Cape Town to New York. The same spirit, which had dictated a return to the forms of the past, penetrated other disciplines and influenced, through the pioneering work of K. Paparrigopoulos's national historiography, the theories about the uninterrupted continuity of the Greek nation – *to Hellenikon ethnos*, notwithstanding the incomprehensibility of this term to a Byzantine Greek – in the ancient, Hellenistic, medieval, and modern periods. It was also responsible for creating the new discipline of folklore (*laographia*) which under Nikolaos Politis was elevated to the rank of an authoritative branch of knowledge and painstakingly sought to find the origins of popular customs in antiquity.

An infinitely more complex form of Romanticism was cultivated in Greece by the Phanariots. The 18th-century *Mismagia* collections of poetry glorifying unrequited love are certainly the precursors of the melancholic mood with its despairing *Weltschmerz*, which thoroughly permeated the entries in the diary of P. Kodrikas, where the first instances of all gradations of sultry sentiment, sensation, and feeling – *aisthesis, aisthema, aisthetikon* – are tirelessly recorded in an endless succession for the years 1790–97. P. Soutsos, whom Hugo respected sufficiently to quote him in *Le Derviche*, is responsible for the first Greek novel, *Leandros* (1834), one more variation on the perennial theme of unrequited love, which ends in death and suicide, but in reality forming an elaborate pastiche made up from plagiarized paragraphs from Goethe's *Werther*, Lamartine's *Lac*, and mainly Chateaubriand's *René*.

Irrespective of the influences brought to bear on Romanticism from the Ionian or the Phanariot schools, the Romantic movement exercised a lasting power on Greek thought in the 19th century and tipped the scales in favour of the demotic language, the unquestionable sovereignty of the popular taste in poetry, song, dance, and discourse, the adoption of the distinctive Neoclassical style in architecture, and the idea of the uninterrupted continuity of the Greek nation. It was

to this last concept that modern Greece owed one of the most tragic chapters of its recent history – the ideological deployment of the Great Idea and its disastrous conclusion in Asia Minor. In spite of its infelicitous ramifications on political thinking Romanticism infused the vision of new Greece with a dynamic vitality and produced some of the most representative works in literature and the arts, their echo still resonating with intensity well into the 20th century.

LAMBROS KAMPERIDIS

See also Folklore, Great Idea, Neoclassicism

Further Reading

Deutschbein, Max, *Das Wesen des Romantischen*, Cöthen: Schulze, 1921

Honour, Hugh, *Romanticism*, London: Allen Lane, and New York: Harper and Row, 1979

Mastrodemetres, Panagiotes D., *Eisagogi ste Neoelliniki Philologia* [Introduction to Modern Greek Philology], 4th edition, Athens, 1983

Neoelliniki Poli: Praktika tou Diethnous Symposiou Istorias [The Modern Greek City: Proceedings of the International History Symposium], Athens, 1985

Praz, Mario, *The Romantic Agony*, London: Oxford University Press, 1933; 2nd edition, London and New York: Oxford University Press, 1970

Rotolo, Vincenzo, *Il dialogo sulla lingua di Dionisio Solomòs*, Palermo, 1970

Solomos, Dionysios, *Allelografia* [Letters], edited by Linos Politis, Athens, 1991

Rome

Largely through Magna Graecia, Greek influence on Roman life began to be felt at least as early as the 5th century BC. The *Sibylline Books* early acquired importance: kept beneath the temple of Jupiter Optimus Maximus, they are first recorded as being consulted in 496 BC. The cult of Apollo was introduced to Rome in 431 BC, and his oracle at Delphi was consulted in 398. As Rome's empire expanded, contact with the western Greeks increased; Greek art – particularly statues – arrived in large quantities on the capture of Syracuse, Capua, and Tarentum (211–209 BC).

Extensive Hellenization, however, began mainly in the 2nd century BC and chiefly as a result of Roman military conquest of the east, climaxing in Perseus of Macedon's defeat at Pydna in 168 BC and the sack of Corinth in 146 BC. More works of art came to Rome. (Polybius reports that in 146 Roman soldiers used Corinthian paintings as gaming boards, but more often captured artefacts were reverently or ostentatiously displayed in temples, villas, and public buildings.) Whole libraries also came: Aemilius Paullus took Perseus', and in the 1st century victors' spoils included libraries which had once belonged to Aristotle and Theophrastus; Pompey brought the medical works collected by Mithridates. And also, most importantly, there came the Greek personnel – refugees, political detainees like Polybius, educated slaves, many of whom were later manumitted – who could organize libraries and give instruction at all levels in Greek language, rhetoric, and philosophy. Other visitors who whetted an appetite for such learning included Crates of Mallus, who lectured in Rome probably during the 160s, and the three philosophers who came as ambassadors from Athens in 155 BC. The presence of such figures contributed to an already strong Greek element in Roman education; increasingly in the 1st century BC Latin equivalents to Greek teaching materials were produced, but the principles remained Greek and knowledge of the language from an early age continued throughout the Roman period to be regarded as essential for members of the ruling class. (In literature Greek influence was also pervasive, as for instance in Plautus' adaptations of material from New Comedy in his plays.)

Some prominent Republican Romans were evidently philhellenic: for example Aemilius Paullus (d. 160 BC) and his son Scipio Aemilianus (185/4–129 BC), friend of Polybius. On the other hand Cato the Censor (234–149 BC) was one of those who publicly associated Hellenization with moral degeneracy, and the stereotype of fickle, unreliable Greeks – used on occasion for forensic purposes, for instance, by the otherwise generally philhellenic Marcus Tullius Cicero (106–43 BC) – remained commonplace into imperial times. But even Cato was fearful only, according to the usual modern view, of excessive Hellenization; he was himself well versed in Greek literature. By the 1st century BC Hellenism had clearly acquired an irresistible momentum. (On the other side, it seems to be in the late Republican and early imperial centuries that the double meaning of *Rhome* in Greek – Rome and strength – gave the city, and increasingly the cult of the goddess Roma, as Erskine has suggested, "a special aura in the eyes of the Greeks".)

Under the principate (as often earlier) it is not always possible – or profitable – to separate Roman and Hellenic elements in Roman culture. But there are some episodes and periods where one can be more specific. Augustus' rebuilding of Rome relied heavily on Greek expertise in working with marble and Athenian craftsmen in particular led the "neoclassical 'purification' of architectural decoration" (Torelli, 1996). Some of the most evidently Hellenic work was for Gaius Sosius' restoration of the temple of Apollo in the Circus Maximus. Nero indulged in public, in Rome as in Greece itself, in Greek athletics and singing to the lyre. The notably philhellene Hadrian (whose early nickname *Graeculus* indicates that resistance to such immersion was not yet dead) introduced many Greek elements into the decoration of his villa near Tibur (Tivoli) and brought a fresh wave of artists from the east to work there and on projects including the temple of Venus and Roma in the Forum Romanum. At the same time the status of non-Italians was changing: senators with origins in the Greek east, occasionally admitted since Augustus' day, were numerous by the reign of Trajan.

Once Constantinople was established as the Second or New Rome (terms in common use by the 6th century AD) Rome gradually declined in importance for the Greek world. Until final separation in the 8th century, however, the city's history is often dominated by its uneasy relationship with its eastern overlords. For a time, after the third and final recapture of Rome from Ostrogothic control by Justinian's general Narses in 552, the much-ravaged city benefited from Byzantine reorganization and repair. But in the absence of any lastingly effective imperial involvement, it was the popes (especially from Gregory I the Great (590–604) onwards) who came in practice to administer Rome and pay its soldiers. Nevertheless, in the early 650s the emperor Constans II could still (if not without resistance from Rome and Ravenna) arrest and later dethrone pope Martin I for non-compliance with his edict of 648 banning discussion of the imperially approved doctrine of Monotheletism (the single will in Christ); the papacy acknowledged Byzantine suzerainty and papal elections were, nominally at least, subject to imperial approval until the 8th century. (Byzantine coinage may have been minted in Rome as late as 781.)

A more broadly eastern influence was felt as a result of a long line of popes of Syrian or Greek background or descent between Theodore I (642–49) and Zacharias (741–52), and by the arrival of several waves of refugees: many fled the Arab incursions of the 630s onwards, and many fled iconoclasm, mainly in the mid-750s or after 816. (The papacy was by now sufficiently powerful to resist stoutly the iconoclastic edicts.) These new arrivals were mostly Greek-speakers and many of them were monks. Greeks had their own church in Rome at Santa Maria de Schola Graeca (subsequently Santa Maria in Cosmedin); Pope Paschal I (817–24) founded a monastery for them at Santa Prassede. Partly because of the presence of the refugees, the use of icons became more widespread in the city and other Eastern customs, notably the translation of martyrs' bones, gained acceptance.

As in earlier periods, Greek and Roman art can easily be too rigidly divided – some work was carried out by refugees from the East, but some, in styles more loosely inspired by Byzantine work, derived from common early Christian sources, or was distinctively adapted by local artists. In a number of cases, however, Byzantine influence seems to be generally agreed: in the fragmentary 8th-century frescos of Santa Maria Antiqua, for instance, and above all in the resplendent 9th-century mosaics of the chapel of San Zeno at Santa Prassede. With a few exceptions (there are, for example, evidently Byzantine elements in the late 13th-century mosaics at Santa Maria Maggiore and Santa Maria in Trastevere), such influences declined fairly rapidly once the papacy sought the aid of the Frankish kings against the Lombards from the 750s; this movement westward culminated in the crowning of Charlemagne as emperor in St Peter's in 800.

MARTIN GARRETT

See also Roman Period

Summary

Greek influence reached Rome as early as the 5th century BC, and large-scale Hellenization began in the 2nd century BC. Roman art, literature, philosophy, rhetoric, and education were heavily Hellenized. Rome was less important to the Greek world after the foundation of Constantinople, but it remained theoretically subject to Byzantium until the 8th century AD.

Further Reading

Astin, Alan E., *Scipio Aemilianus*, Oxford: Clarendon Press, 1967
Astin, Alan E., *Cato the Censor*, Oxford: Clarendon Press, and New York: Oxford University Press, 1978
Erskine, Andrew, "Rome in the Greek World: The Significance of a Name" in *The Greek World*, edited by Anton Powell, London and New York: Routledge, 1995

Griffin, Miriam, "The Intellectual Developments of the Ciceronian Age" in *The Last Age of the Roman Republic, 146–43 BC*, edited by J.A. Crook, Andrew Lintott and Elizabeth Rawson, Cambridge: Cambridge University Press, 1994 (*The Cambridge Ancient History*, vol. 9, 2nd edition)

Gruen, Erich S., *The Hellenistic World and the Coming of Rome*, 2 vols, Berkeley: University of California Press, 1984

Gruen, Erich S., *Culture and Identity in Republican Rome*, Ithaca, New York: Cornell University Press, 1992

Krautheimer, Richard, *Rome: Profile of a City, 312–1308*, Princeton, New Jersey: Princeton University Press, 1980

Nordhagen, Per Jonas, "Italo-Byzantine Painting of the Early Middle Ages: An 80-Year Old Enigma in Scholarship", *Settimane di Studio del Centro Italiano di Studi sull'Alto Medioevo*, 34 (1988): pp. 593–626

Polybius, *The Rise of the Roman Empire*, edited by F.W. Walbank, translated by Ian Scott-Kilvert, Harmondsworth and New York: Penguin, 1979

Rawson, Elizabeth, *Intellectual Life in the Late Roman Republic*, Baltimore: Johns Hopkins University Press, and London: Duckworth, 1985

Torelli, Mario, "Roman Art, 43 BC to AD 69" in *The Augustan Empire, 43 BC–AD 89*, edited by Alan K. Bowman, Edward Champlin and Andrew Lintott, Cambridge: Cambridge University Press, 1996 (*The Cambridge Ancient History*, vol. 10, 2nd edition)

Wardman, Alan, *Rome's Debt to Greece*, London: Elek, 1976; New York: St Martin's Press, 1977

Rumeli

The Ottoman name for the Balkan peninsula

Rumeli was the name given to the Balkan peninsula by the Ottomans. The Byzantine empire understood itself to be the inheritor of the Roman empire and Byzantine Christians called themselves Romans. Among the Muslims this translated into *Rum*, and the Arabs referred to the Byzantine empire as the *Bilad al-Rum* (Land of the Rum) or *Mamlakat al-Rum* (Country of the Rum). When Turkish Muslims conquered Byzantine Anatolia, they referred to this new territory as *Rum*, since it had belonged to the Byzantines. Once they had gained possession of the Balkan peninsula as well, they began referring to the Balkans as *Rum-ili*, a name they borrowed from the Latin term *Romania*, which originally designated the Byzantine empire as a whole. Anatolia was now more commonly called Anadolu, in order to distinguish it from Rumeli. As with the Byzantines before them, the Ottomans considered the northern boundary of Rumeli to be the Danube and the Drava rivers.

Although Anatolian Turks began settling in the Balkans as early as 1264, the Ottomans did not begin their conquest of the peninsula until the middle of the 14th century. The chaotic conditions obtaining at that time in both the Byzantine empire and the various Balkan states were of enormous help in allowing the Ottomans to extend their rule. Taking advantage of the Byzantine civil wars that pitted the supporters of John V Palaiologos (1341/55–91) against John VI Kantakouzenos, the Ottoman leader Orhan came to the aid of the latter. Orhan's troops routed the Serbian-Greek forces supporting John V and it was this victory, in 1352, that allowed the Ottomans to begin settling in Rumeli. Just three years later, in 1355, Stephan

Dushan, the Serbian ruler whose state covered a vast area of the Balkans, died and the Ottomans were once again able to benefit from the civil wars that broke out after his death. By 1400, apart from the Dalmatian coast and some cities in the Morea, most of the Balkans were under Ottoman rule. Serbia, Bosnia, and Wallachia were vassal states and Byzantine possessions in the Balkans barely extended beyond the walls of Constantinople.

But Ottoman control of the Balkans was not yet assured. The Mongol defeat of sultan Bayezid at Ankara in 1402 dealt them a severe blow and handed the Balkan Christian princes the opportunity to reconstruct their states. They were not able to do so. Nor were the Europeans able to form a successful alliance against the Ottomans once the latter's fortunes recovered after 1413. It was the great victory at Varna, on 10 November 1444, that sealed the fate of both the Balkans and Constantinople. Murad II came out of retirement to defeat a Hungarian-Wallachian army, which had crossed the Danube and was marching towards Edirne, the Ottoman capital. With this defeat the European threat to Ottoman rule in the Balkans was effectively extinguished. Rumeli would remain an integral part of the empire until the early 20th century.

Significant numbers of Turkish settlers from Anatolia, both sedentary and nomadic, followed in the footsteps of the military beys who were constantly extending the borders of the Ottoman principality. Thrace, eastern Bulgaria, the valley around the Maritsa river, and the Dobrudja – all fertile areas which were conquered early by the Ottomans – were the regions of most extensive colonization. All received large numbers of immigrants from Anatolia in the 14th century. Turks would continue to form a large part of the population in these areas throughout the centuries of Ottoman rule. Turkish settlement was important not only in the countryside but in the cities as well. In fact, after the 15th century, Turkish immigrants from Anatolia settled almost exclusively in the cities, or else along the major military roads, so much so that the cities came to be associated with the ruling Muslim elite, while the countryside was the stronghold of Orthodoxy. Religious fraternities (*akhis*) played an important role in the founding of new cities, or, more commonly, the revitalization of existing ones. As the fraternities established themselves in urban centres, they petitioned the sultan for land that would sustain their religious and commercial activities in the city. Through these endowments (*waqfs*), which supported inns, baths, hospitals, fountains, bridges, and markets, the cities came to control substantial amounts of income from large rural estates. Such endowments were responsible for the transformation of Sarajevo, for example, from an obscure village into a major city in the 16th century. Edirne, Serres, Sofia, and Monastir, among others, owed their rapid development to this system of religious endowments.

Despite significant Turkish settlement in the eastern part of the Balkans, the Ottoman conquest of Rumeli did not dramatically alter the region's ethnic composition. There were no mass migrations similar to those of the Slavs during the Byzantine era, although Jewish refugees from Christian Europe in the 15th and 16th centuries did transform Thessalonica into a town with a Jewish majority. But certain demographic shifts, however minor in a relative sense, did come to acquire great significance during the period of nationalism and nation-state creation. Building upon the Ottoman–Habsburg peace at the very end of the 17th century, Greek merchants established a series of trading posts stretching from the northern Balkans through Hungary, and into southern Russia. Greek commercial and then intellectual florescence in the 18th century accelerated the process of Hellenization in the Balkans, whereby Balkan Christians from other ethnic backgrounds became Hellenized through their contact with Greek culture. The vibrant Greek communities that developed in Wallachia and Moldavia at this time help to explain why the initial focus of the Greek revolution was the Danubian lands, not the Peloponnese which was very marginal to Greek life in the Balkans. The Serb lands had the misfortune of being right on the border between the Ottoman empire and its various Christian opponents. Serbs often took flight as a result of war, the most famous example being the large migration into southern Hungary at the end of the 17th century; more than 200,000 Serbs followed the metropolitan of Pec into Habsburg lands. The cumulative effect of Serbian migration was that, by the 19th century, Serbs had spread far to the north and west – into Croatia, Bosnia, and Hungary – of their original homeland and this fuelled the hope for a greater Serbia which would include the far-flung Serbian population in both the Habsburg and Ottoman empires. At the same time that the Serbs and the Greeks were moving north and west, mountaineers from the Albanian lands moved down into the recently vacated plains. "Old Serbia" came to have a majority Albanian population – those few Serbs who had remained became assimilated – and large numbers even made their way to southern Greece. The famous merchants and sailors of the island of Hydra were recent Christian Albanian immigrants.

If Turkish settlement did little to disturb the ethnic balance of the Balkans, Ottoman policy encouraged the maintenance of the religious status quo. The Ottomans in Rumeli were never concerned to convert the Christians to Islam. In fact, they moved decisively to protect the Orthodox Church, as part of a policy of encouraging the hostility that already existed beween eastern and western Christianity. The Balkan Christian peasants, who were, of course, the majority of the population, were already well disposed towards the Ottomans because the latter abolished the most onerous demands of the feudal system in the areas they controlled. Their sympathy for the Ottomans could only have grown as they watched their own landlords and princes bring in various Latin armies, such as the Hungarians, to help roll back the Ottoman advance. As the Hungarians waved the flag of Catholic crusade and made it clear that they considered the Orthodox to be schismatic, the Ottomans offered recognition and protection to the Orthodox Church, including generous terms for the monasteries on Mount Athos. Certainly the Orthodox patriarch of Constantinople benefited from the Ottoman conquest of Rumeli. Prior to 1453 the patriarch had had to watch helplessly as the Byzantines were pushed out of the Balkans and independent Serbian and Bulgarian Churches were established. His jurisdiction dwindled to the immediate environs of the capital city. After 1453 the Balkans were once again ruled from Constantinople and the sultan showed himself willing to let the patriarch move against autonomy-seeking bishops and metropolitans, although the Serbians, it should be noted, were able to regain their ecclesiastical independence in the 16th century.

Ottoman policy towards the Orthodox Church in Rumeli is of the utmost importance in understanding why the Balkan peninsula remained largely Christian, despite 500 years of rule by a Muslim empire. A very different situation obtained in Anatolia where successive waves of Turkish conquest and immigration, beginning in the 11th century, succeeded in gradually changing Anatolia from a Christian to a Muslim peninsula.

Despite this relatively generous attitude towards the Orthodox Christians, conversion to Islam did occur in the Balkans and remains a hotly debated topic. The largest number of converts were to be found in Bosnia and Albania, where significant Muslim populations remain to this day. The inhabitants of certain parts of Bulgaria also accepted Islam and came to be known as Pomaks (as distinct from ethnic Turks, who were also Muslim, living in the Bulgarian lands). Not all conversions followed immediately upon the Ottoman conquest. The Albanians, for instance, did not convert in extensive numbers until the 17th century, while the Muslim population in Bosnia-Hercegovina was already strong by the time of the Ottoman provincial census of 1520–30. The *kaza* (district) of Bosnia was 18.4 per cent Muslim in 1489; in 1520 that number had soared to 46 per cent. Sarajevo was 100 per cent Muslim. Clearly a phenomenon that stretched out over many centuries cannot be explained by one factor alone. Historians have traditionally emphasized some balance of the legal and economic advantages that stemmed from conversion, the prestige of Islam, the willingness of Muslim missionaries to accommodate folk belief, and, finally, fear. Much empirical work remains to be done, however. For a long time, for example, historians believed that conversion to Islam in Bosnia-Hercegovina was explained by the prevalence of Christian heretical beliefs in this mountainous remote district. Conversion from one heresy to another, as it were, was relatively easy to do. Subsequent research, however, has thrown serious doubt on this theory.

Although the Ottomans had already lost Hungary by the end of the 17th century, they managed to hold on to Rumeli proper until the early 19th century. This did not preclude certain cities on the border – such as Belgrade – from going back and forth between the Ottomans and the Habsburgs with an almost monotonous regularity, nor did it prevent the Russians from making serious inroads on Ottoman sovereignty in Moldavia and Wallachia. Yet the first serious loss of territory came not from yet another clash with the Habsburgs or the Russians, but rather from a peasant uprising in 1821 on the southernmost tip of the peninsula that doggedly refused to go away. This turned into, of course, the Greek revolution and ultimately involved the Great Powers at the highest levels of diplomacy. With the Treaty of London (1830) the Ottomans lost this territory for ever. A long period of calm followed, but in just one short decade – the 1870s – the Ottomans were obliged to recognize the independence of Montenegro, Romania, and Serbia, as well as the entirely new state of Bulgaria. By the eve of World War I, all that remained of Ottoman Rumeli was the city of Constantinople itself and most of eastern Thrace. With the loss of Ottoman political control, Balkan Muslims began fleeing their homeland for the greater safety of Constantinople and Anatolia.

MOLLY GREENE

See also Conversion to Islam, Ottoman Period, Ottomans

Summary

Rumeli was the Ottoman term for the Balkan peninsula as far north as the Danube and Drava rivers. By 1400 most of the Balkans were Ottoman territory and remained so until the late 19th century. Despite almost 500 years of Ottoman rule most of Rumeli remained Christian thanks to generous treatment of the Orthodox Church. By 1914 all that remained was Constantinople and eastern Thrace.

Further Reading

Birnbaum, Henrik and Spiros Vyronis, Jr (editors), *Aspects of the Balkans: Continuity and Change*, The Hague: Mouton, 1972

Chirot, Daniel (editor), *The Origins of Backwardness in Eastern Europe: Economics and Politics from the Middle Ages until the Early Twentieth Century*, Berkeley: University of California Press, 1989

Hasluck, F.W., *Christianity and Islam under the Sultans*, edited by Margaret M. Hasluck, 2 vols, Oxford: Clarendon Press, 1929, reprinted New York: Octagon, 1973

Inalcik, Halil, *The Middle East and the Balkans under the Ottoman Empire: Essays on Economy and Society*, Bloomington: Indiana University Turkish Studies, 1993

Kiraly, Bela K. and Gale Stokes (editors), *Insurrections, Wars and the Eastern Crisis in the 1870s*, Boulder, Colorado: Social Science Monographs, 1985

McGowan, Bruce, *Economic Life in Ottoman Europe: Taxation, Trade and the Struggle for Land, 1600–1800*, Cambridge and New York: Cambridge University Press, 1981

Stavrianos, L.S., *The Balkans since 1453*, New York: Holt Rinehart, 1958

Stoianovich, Traian, *Between East and West: The Balkan and Mediterranean Worlds*, 4 vols, New Rochelle, New York: Caratzas, 1992–95

Stoianovich, Traian, *Balkan Worlds: The First and Last Europe*, Armonk, New York: Sharpe, 1994

Sugar, Peter F., *Southeastern Europe under Ottoman Rule, 1354–1804*, Seattle: University of Washington Press, 1977

Russia

"Russia" is the designation customarily applied to (1) territories once constituting the Russian empire or the Union of Soviet Socialist Republics (USSR) in Europe and Asia; (2) those areas of Eastern Europe inhabited by Eastern Slavic populations (Great Russians, Ukrainians, White Russians); and (3) those areas of Europe and Asia constituting republics of the Russian Federation excluding Ukraine, Belarus, Moldova, and the Baltic republics. For the purposes of the following discussion, "Russia" shall designate that area of eastern Europe predominantly inhabited by peoples of Eastern Slavic origin on the territories of the Russian Federation, Ukraine, and Belarus, bounded on the east by the Ural Mountains and Caspian Sea; on the south by the Caucasus and the Black Sea; on the southwest and west by the present political borders of the Russian Federation, Ukraine, and Belarus; and on the north by the Arctic Ocean. Similarly, "Russians" shall denote persons of Eastern Slavic ethnic origin, including the Russians, Ukrainians, and White Russians.

The English "Russia" is a Latinized form deriving from Russian *Rossiya* and Greek *Ros* or *Rosia,* both coming ultimately from the Old Slavic *Rus',* the exact etymology of which remains controversial, being said by some to derive from the Finnish *Ruotsi,* a corruption of Swedish *Rothsmenn,* "rowers", hence "seamen", or, by others, from the name of the *Roxolani,* a steppe people of Indo-Iranian origin known from the Greek and Latin sources.

Humans appeared in Russia about 30,000 years ago and several early to late Stone Age sites attest to this settlement. The transition from stone to copper occurred during a time that a highly advanced culture, called Tripolye or Cucuteni from the sites of its first discovery in Ukraine and Romania, began producing exquisite ceramic wares. This represents the northeasternmost of the cultural provinces of Old Europe, predating Indo-European settlement by two millennia. Fragments of Tripolyan ceramics have been unearthed in Greece and Palestine, indicating well-developed systems of commerce, while patterns used in Tripolyan art suggest parallels in contemporary Greece.

Beginning about 4000 BC, incursions of stock-breeding peoples, ethnically distinct from the Tripolyans, and possessing domesticated horses, carts, wooden ploughs, and bronze instruments and weapons disrupted the Tripolyan culture: these people, probably of Indo-European origin, belong to the corded-ware culture and introduced new social, cultural, and religious ideas. With them begins the Bronze Age in Russia. Evidence of continued connection with the Aegean cultural region is widespread: carvings and paintings of bulls' heads in graves and homes, characteristic ritual vessels, and clay statuettes of females with wide, pleated dresses recall parallels in Minoan Crete. In southeastern Russia, along the north Black Sea coast, related nomadic tribes settled down to stock breeding and simple agriculture, beginning intense production of bronze weapons using techniques learnt in Transcaucasia. These people, possibly identical with the Cimmerians mentioned in the *Odyssey* as living on the edge of the world, settled a broad area north of the Black Sea. Their *kurgans,* or burial mounds, have yielded rich finds of gold and silver objects showing the influence of Transcaucasian cultural centres.

Iron, first imported from Asia Minor, came into widespread use about 800 BC. Simultaneous advances in agriculture and architecture and in social and administrative practices were facilitated by the local occurrence of iron in Russia. Beginning in the 7th century BC, incursions of Indo-Iranian Scyths displaced the Cimmerians, whose invasion of Asia Minor was described by Herodotus in the 5th century BC. The Scyths, to whom Herodotus devotes a large part of his *Histories,* were divided into the "ploughmen" and "royal" Scyths, the former representing the local agricultural populations who had enjoyed several centuries of contact with the Aegean/Greek and the Caucasian/Asiatic cultural spheres. Contacts with the Greeks became more intense. Mentioned by Homer, Hesiod, Eumelus, and Artcinus in the 7th and 6th centuries BC, the peoples of the north Black Sea coastline came into the cognizance of Greek explorers and merchants. The tale of Jason and the Argonauts represents a mythic retelling of the expeditions of Greek mariners to new lands in search of gold and riches.

The Scyths established a kingdom between the Danube and Kuban and their raiders ranged into Asia Minor and beyond. In 513 BC the Persians under Darius I mounted an attack on the Scyths, who, though not entirely subdued, sustained sufficient

Russia: monastery of St Panteleimonos, Mount Athos. There has been a Russian presence on the Holy Mountain since the 11th century.

losses to stop their raids on Asia Minor. North of the Black Sea, in a climatic zone quite different from the Mediterranean climate to which they had been accustomed, Greeks established colonies, beginning around 650 BC. Of these, the most important were Olbia, called "the rich", located at the mouth of the Dnieper and Bug, and Panticapaeum, later capital of the kingdom of the Bosphorus (with Nymphaeum), predecessor of modern Kerch at the Cimmerian Bosphorus, providing access to the Sea of Azov (Lake Maeotis); the other cities commanded the mouths of the Dniester (Tyras), the Don (Tanais), and the Kuban (Phanagoria). Developing close commercial and social ties with neighbouring territories, these colonies drew them into the cultural and economic sphere of Hellas. Following their defeat by the Persians, the Scyths entered a period of decline, ultimately being replaced in their hegemony of the northern Pontic regions by the Sarmatians, an Iranian people, who held sway from the 2nd century BC to the 2nd century AD.

The kingdom of the Bosphorus, profiting from the trade of the district, became the major power in the area and a centre of culture and the arts, its coins being prized down to our own times for their beauty. The rich soil made the area an important source of wheat, the control of which had already become vital to Athens at the time of Herodotus. In return, the Scyths purchased Greek wares, which, traded far inland, reached finally into Prussia, whence the prized amber was imported. Together with the Scyths and Sindians, a so-called Bosphoran

group emerged, whose influence spread westward into the Crimea. First under the Archaeanactids and, after 438 BC, under the Spartocids of Panticapaeum, a type of military tyranny was founded, which, developing into a Hellenistic monarchy, flourished for two centuries. Beginning around 250 BC, the Greek colonies entered a long period of decline. In the face of the influx of Sarmatians, the kingdom sought the protection of Pontus, whose king, Mithridates VI, defeated the barbarians, but also captured Panticapaeum and in 106 BC founded a new Pontic-Bosphoran state, which remained semi-autonomous under Roman rule, finally succumbing to the attacks of the Huns.

As elsewhere, the Romans were content to control this area through local powers, taking care that these local powers remained adequately strong and loyal. The ravages of the Germanic Skirians and Bastarnae and of the Getae in the 3rd to 1st centuries BC were checked by Roman arms and it was this protection which helped preserve the Greek colonies through difficult times to come. In the 2nd and 3rd centuries AD the region experienced significant prosperity, deriving from trade with the neighbouring barbarian tribes and with Asia Minor and the Caucasus. Much of the grain required for the Roman legions guarding the Danube was obtained from the area. Relations with the barbarians, such as the Sarmatians and Alans, appear to have been favourable, though this seems to have contributed to increased cultural influence by the

Sarmatians among the inhabitants of the coastline. The alliance of the Goths and Alans directed against Roman authority in the 3rd century was felt at Panticapaeum, which became a Sarmato-Gothic settlement.

The Greeks themselves do not seem to have penetrated far inland, since their geographical knowledge, beginning with Aristeas of Proconessus and Hecataeus of Miletus, is sketchy and often flawed. Herodotus provides a description of the Russian hinterland but includes fantastic descriptions of the tribes and conditions in those regions. Though Herodotus himself questioned the accuracy of what he had heard, later authors received and embellished these data with new inventions. Beyond the Scythian tribes and regions inhabited by strange races of men and monsters, there were the Rhipaeans, an impenetrable range of mountains, or a snowy desert punctuated with ill-defined lakes, and finally the Outer Sea or Ocean. The sole tangible highways were the large rivers at the mouths of which the Greeks had settled. The ancient geographers, including Herodotus, Ptolemy, and others, knew of a so-called Scythian route leading up the Don (Tanais) and Volga (Oarus), past Kazan, Orenburg, and Perm toward Central Asia and China, but the details are very confused and identifications depend on conjectures not always well taken.

Christianity in Russia dates to the 1st century, thus predating the conversion of the Slavs by eight centuries. The legendary *Lives* of St Andrew, one of the patron saints of Russia, affirm that the apostle reached the site of present-day Kiev, and Eusebius states that St Andrew did indeed preach among the Scyths. Whether the apostle did reach the northern shore of the Black Sea is not known, though contact with both Judaism and Christianity through the Bosphoran kingdom occurred at an early date. Early traditions state that pope Clement I, martyred under Trajan, was first banished to the Tauric Chersonese in southern Russia. The Pannonian *Lives* of Sts Constantine (Cyril) and Methodios tell of the translation of St Clement's relics to Rome, while some late Russian chronicles report that some of these relics were presented to the Kievan prince St Vladimir (?956–1015) after his conversion to Christianity. The Greek Fathers mention the Scyths and Sarmatians repeatedly, and bishops from Cherson or from the eparchy of "Gothia", that region inhabited by the Ostrogoths, are mentioned in the acts of the ecumenical councils beginning with Nicaea in 325. It is obvious that Christianity spread rapidly throughout the Hellenized regions of the north Black Sea coast and that even the Scyths and Sarmatians may have embraced the new religion.

Beginning in the 2nd and 3rd centuries, there were great movements of tribes from the east (Alans, Roxolani, etc.) and from the northwest (Germanic tribes such as the Gepids and Goths) into the north Pontic region. By about 200 the Goths had reached the Black Sea and begun to dominate large areas to the north. They destroyed Olbia, Tyras, and other cities in 251. Once the Goths had divided into the Ostrogoths and Visigoths, the Ostrogoths formed a large kingdom centred in southern Russia on the Dnieper. This kingdom reached its height under Hermanaric (reigned 350–75), who united all the Goths under his rule.

The appearance of the Huns in AD 375 led to the disruption of the Gotho-Alanic alliance and begins a new epoch in the history of the lands north of the Black Sea. From this time, hordes of barbarians, who had previously been checked in the north Pontic steppe, including the Avars and, later, the Khazars, Bulgars, and Magyars, found their way into Pannonia and the Balkans. While some of these tribes, such as the Avars, Bulgars, and Magyars, dissipated or settled beyond the borders of southern Russia, the Khazars were to remain a significant factor in the history of the region, ruling the left bank of the Dnieper and exacting tribute from the citizens of Kiev. The memory of their suzerainty over Kiev forms the basis of the story of the summoning of the Varangians out of Scandinavia by the Kievans, given as the central event in the founding of the state of Kievan Rus'. The immense wealth and strength of the Khazars derived from their control of the rivers Volga and Don and of the trade of the Black and Caspian Seas. Their power was finally broken by the Kievan grand prince Svyatoslav about 965.

Under Justinian and throughout the succeeding centuries, Byzantine policy had attempted to maintain some control over possessions north of the Black Sea. This was maintained, sometimes by military force, sometimes by treaties and tribute. Though these territories had never been fully integrated into the provincial system, cities sometimes quartered imperial garisons. The interest of Byzantium focused more keenly on the area because of the migrations of barbarians, such as the Bulgars, who passed through southern Russia in the late 7th century. By the mid-9th century both the Byzantine empire and its allies, the Khazars, found themselves confronted with dangerous developments in the region. Under Theophilos (reigned 829–42), the *klimata*, Byzantine possessions in southern Russia, were reorganized. Cherson was made their centre, and, as a theme, was governed by a *strategos*, or military governor. At the same time, Byzantine architects aided the Khazars in designing the fortress of Sarkel, which commanded the entrance to the Don from the Sea of Azov. The cause for this concerted action remains disputed, though there is much to favour the hypothesis that these measures were taken because of the appearance and expansive potential of the Kievan Rus'.

The north Pontic regions became an outpost of the empire against the Turkic steppe tribes, such as the Pechenegs (10th century) and Polovtsians (11th century), as well as against the Rus', both from Kiev and from their southern centre at Tmutarakan. In the 13th century the area came under the influence of the Grand Komnenids of Trebizond. The population was made up of diverse nationalities, including Greeks, Alans, Armenians, and Jews. In the 14th century the Genoese made inroads in the regional economy, establishing commercial centres along the northern Black Sea coast. The region was ravaged by the Mongols, first in 1222–23, then again in 1299, when Cherson was destroyed. After the fall of Constantinople (1453) and of Trebizond (1461), the area passed finally under the cultural and political influence of the Ottoman Turks and their subject Crimean Tatar khanate.

With the rise of the Slavs and, in particular, with the formation of the state of Kievan Rus', the influence of Byzantium in Russia becomes less political and more pronounced in the realm of culture, religion, and the arts. The conversion of Kiev to Christianity in 989 was a major success for both Byzantine political and ecclesiastical policy, since, with Vladimir's baptism, the last pagan and, at the same time, largest Slavic nation came under the cultural influence of Constantinople. The energetic politics of Basil II, during whose reign this event occured, strove to maintain and increase the strength of the state; indeed, his political survival was due, in no small part, to the assistance of Vladimir and his Varangians. Nevertheless, the advent of the Turks in Anatolia in the second half of the 11th century turned the political attention of Byzantium towards the east, though the cultural development of the Kievan state was to remain under Byzantine influence for years to come.

The Russians belong ethnically and linguistically to the Eastern Slavic branch of peoples. Their language, together with those of the Ukrainians and White Russians, belongs to the eastern branch of the Slavic group of the Indo-European family of languages. Deriving from the "proto-Indo-Europeans", a grouping of seminomadic pastoralists who from about 4000 to 2300 BC had infiltrated the north Pontic regions, subduing and becoming assimilated with the resident populations, the Slavs arose as an Indo-European group distinct from neighbouring Baltic and Indo-Iranian tribes in a circumscribed area between the Vistula and the Dnieper, comprising Galicia, Volhynia, Podolia, and the middle Dnieper region. This corresponds with the development of the North Carpathian culture in this same area during the Bronze and early Iron Ages. In historical records the Slavs appear at the beginning of the Christian era, when their ancestral lands had already been penetrated by Germanic and Sarmatian invaders from the west and south. The "Veneti" were known to Pliny and Tacitus, while Claudius Ptolemy mentions the "Soubenoi", derived by Moszyński from *Slovene,* a tribe said vaguely to be living north of the Scythian lands and before the Imaos (Ural?) mountains. Only about AD 500, however, when the Sclavini are repeatedly mentioned by Procopius and Jordanes, is it possible to speak of an expanding, clearly Slavic culture. The state of the Antes, which occupied the regions of southern Russia and Ukraine, flourished from the late 4th to early 7th centuries, and was distinguished for its attacks on both Byzantium and on the Avars and Bulgars. By about 900, Slavs filled the large tracts between the Oder and the sources of the Dnieper and Don.

By this time development of distinctly Eastern Slavic culture had begun, coinciding with the growth of political centres at Kiev and Novgorod and the beginnings of the state of Kievan Rus'. The 11th-century *Primary Chronicle,* or *Tale of Bygone Years,* composed by Nestor, a monk of the Cave Monastery at Kiev, tells of the distribution of the Slavic tribes, such as the Polianians, the Severians, and the Derevlians, among many others, stretching from the region of Novgorod in the north to the delta of the Kuban river in Ciscaucasia. Bordering these tribes to the north were peoples of Finnish origin, who once occupied lands as far south as the upper reaches of the Desna and the Dnieper. In the west they bordered on Polish lands, on Great Moravia (which formed at the beginning of the 9th century), and on lands occupied by Magyars from the end of the 9th century. In the south their neighbours were the Bulgars across the Danube and the north Pontic regions, under Byzantine sway.

From the mid-9th century, with the legendary calling of the Scandinavian Ryurik to Kiev, the Rus' state grew to encompass the lands occupied by the Eastern Slavs. Their princes Oleg (d. 912) and Igor (d. 945) concluded commercial treaties with Constantinople, guaranteeing the rights of their merchants in Byzantine territories and including a pact of non-aggression. Igor's widow Olga, embracing eastern Christianity about 955, was baptized at Constantinople in the presence of the emperor Constantine VII Porphyrogennetos. Her son Svyatoslav dreamt of expanding his realm into the Balkans, but reverses against the Byzantines and his murder by the Pechenegs ended this phase of Rus' history. Svyatoslav's son, Vladimir I, acted to consolidate Kievan Rus' by unifying the Slavic tribes in a process begun by Igor and Olga. Vladimir himself was baptized around 989. Because of the increasing power of the emperor in the Byzantine Church and the implications of political subordination inherent in receiving Byzantine Christianity, Vladimir attempted to establish an autocephalous Church, even entertaining overtures from the Latin west. Vladimir's son, Yaroslav the Sage, received a metropolitan, Theopempt, from Constantinople in 1037, though a war in 1043 against the Byzantines and later disturbances (such as the appointment of independent metropolitans in the 11th and 12th centuries) show that neither Yaroslav nor his successors recognized the absolute political supremacy of the Byzantine emperors.

Though the Christian religion had been present in Russia since the 1st century, the conversion of the Slavs was a phenomenon of the 9th and 10th centuries. Beginning with the missions of Cyril (Constantine) and Methodios to the Khazars and their later activity in Moravia, Greek Christianity reached out to the nations of eastern Europe. While the patriarchs Photios and Ignatios stood in communion with a Russian eparch (probably at Tmutorokan) as early as 867, it was only the baptism of Olga and the later conversion of her grandson Vladimir that made Rus' a Christian state. Ecclesiastical exchanges proved the strongest link in the chain of Russo-Byzantine relations. With only two exceptions (Hilarion in 1051 and Kliment in the 12th century), all metropolitans of Kiev were Greeks. Similarly, about half of the other eparchs came from Constantinople, accompanied by their retinues of clerics and secretaries. These churchmen were instrumental in importing Greek artists, whose influence in determining the style of Russian art is obvious. However, despite the immense importance of Greek artists, the native Russians were not totally subservient to Byzantine tastes and developed a style uniquely their own. Similarly, the use of the old Slavonic language in Church literature and the liturgy was symbolic of the independent tendencies arising in Russia and of the ecclesiastical mentality, which differed in many respects from the spirit pervading Byzantine Christianity.

Beside the presence of Greek, later Byzantine, colonies along the north Black Sea coast, merchants established an interface of contact which comprised the so-called "great waterway from the Varangians to the Greeks". Beginning at the Baltic Sea and taking advantage of the numerous navigable rivers throughout Russia, traders ascended the Neva and Volkhov and then crossed overland to the headwaters of the Dnieper, which they descended in boats to the Black Sea. This route is described by Constantine VII Porphyrogennetos in *De Imperio Administrando.* Merchants traded in the emporia of the north Black Sea coast, such as Cherson (Korsun'), or went on to Constantinople, where their activities were regulated by commercial treaties. The major wares acquired at Constantinople included gold, silver, and glass vessels, jewellery, ornaments, gold and silk textiles, as well as wine and dried fruits. The main Russian exports included furs, wax, and slaves, commodities also traded with western Europe, the Khazars, and the Arab world. The desire to secure the trade routes to the Black and Caspian Seas against the steppe nomads and the Khazars and Byzantines was probably one of the greatest motives behind expansive moves by the early Russian state, beginning with the attack on Constantinople by Askold and Dir in 860 and a later one by Oleg around 907.

Parallel to the commercial treaties, Byzantine law exerted no small influence on everyday life. The *Kormchaya Kniga*, the body of ecclesiastical law, was derived from the Byzantine *nomokanons*, the digests of canon law and imperial edicts touching on the Church. The ecclesiastical ordinances of Vladimir and Yaroslav also show Byzantine influence in some of their provisions. In the civil law the *Russkaya Pravda* is based in form and content on the systematic digests of Byzantine law, such as the *Procheiros Nomos,* or "handy law". As elsewhere, the Church did not attempt radically to change the law of the land in which it had been recently established, and many provisions of Byzantine law had to be modified or experienced lax enforcement.

As elsewhere in the sphere of eastern Christianity, monasticism proved to be a powerful cultural force in Russia. The first monasteries were founded in the 11th century, the most famous being the Cave Monastery near Kiev, in which St Theodosios (d. 1074) introduced the rule of St Theodore the Studite. Monasteries exercised notable social functions, for monks went abroad, recommending people to penance and devotion; they served the poor, but became important landholding entities in their own right. Furthermore, their influence was magnified, for it was from the ranks of unmarried monastic priests that bishops were chosen. Monasteries were also involved in the colonization of the Russian north. Beginning with the earliest higumens of the Cave Monastery, monks travelled to the Christian east and there was early contact with Mount Athos. The first Russian monastery on the Holy Mountain was founded in 1169. The invasions of the Tatars interrupted these connections, but they were renewed at the end of the 14th century.

The beginnings of literature in Russia were also closely related to the Church and, with it, to Constantinople. Translations of the scriptures, of edifying works, and histories formed the models upon which original works were composed. Beginning with the *Primary Chronicle*, one is confronted with the use by Nestor of Byzantine sources and with the very fact of his compiling a work constituting a continuous, annalistic account of Russian history. Further examples are seen in the immense body of hagiographical literature, it too based on Byzantine models. Book illustration was also a monkish art with Byzantine roots, which developed luxuriantly on Russian soil.

The invasion of the Tatars in the early 13th century radically changed the political and cultural landscape of Russia. The destruction of Kiev resulted in displacement of political power to the northeast (Yaroslavl, later Moscow) and to Galicia, where a branch of the Rurikide line established itself at Galich and later in Lvov, before incorporation into Poland in the mid-14th century. The years of struggle against the Tatars reached fruition in the victory of the Russian armies at Kulikovo Pole in 1380. Over the next 100 years Russian policy slowly developed a theory of royal sovereignty, culminating in the marriage of Ivan III to Sophia, niece of the last Byzantine emperor, in 1472 and the adoption in 1480 by the same monarch of the title "tsar", renouncing the Tatar yoke and proclaiming the autocrat's independence of any foreign power. Within this time frame Bulgaria fell to the Ottoman Turks (1393), resulting in the emigration of Bulgarian intellectuals to Russia, one of whom, Kiprian, became metropolitan of Moscow. Constantinople, seeing the advance of the Turks, entered into a union of the Eastern and Western Churches at the Council of Florence (1438–39), but its fall in 1453 opened the way for Russian claims of its Church being the single, true representative of Orthodoxy. In 1551 the *Stoglav*, or Council of the Hundred Chapters, proclaimed Moscow's Orthodoxy as a model for the whole Eastern Church and in 1589 Jeremiah, the Ecumenical Patriarch, recognized Moscow as the Third Rome and its tsar as the "only Christian sovereign in the world".

The fall of Constantinople and the subjection of both the Greeks and their Church to the Ottomans after 1453 of necessity changed the relationship between Russia and the Greek world. While earlier Russian policy had centred on inheriting the spiritual legacy of the Byzantine empire, later tsars, beginning especially with Peter the Great at the turn of the 18th century, began looking to the Orthodox, primarily the Greek population of the empire, as a sort of "fifth column", potentially useful to Russia in the case of territorial expansion at the expense of the Turks. After 1764 the Russian government took an active role, portraying itself as the liberator of the Greeks, while, as a result of treaties, beginning with that of Küçük Kainarci (1774), Greek merchants came under the protection of Russian consuls with the privilege of flying the Russian flag. Later, the Ionian islands stood briefly under Russian protection, forming a nidus for the crystallization of interest in an autonomous or sovereign Greek state. Young Greeks, selected from principal Levantine families, were educated in Russia, many of them gaining wealth and often high rank in Russian service. Russian officers, among whom were several Greeks who had entered Russian service, including Count Ioannis Kapodistria, later president of the provisional Greek republic, became involved with efforts of the Greeks to throw off the Turkish yoke. In Odessa the so-called *Philiki Hetaireia* ("Friendly Society") was formed which, though the Russian government did not directly sanction or support it, became a major force in the organization of the Greek movement for independence. In general, however, Greek sympathy for and reliance on Russia was motivated by questions of religion and, throughout the late 18th and the 19th centuries, the Greeks were often disappointed by Russian policy resulting from changes in the tsars' political aims.

With the consolidation of the kingdom of Greece, Russian influence in Greek affairs declined throughout the 19th and early 20th centuries. During the Crimean War, despite British efforts, Greek public opinion, seconded by King Otho, supported the Russian cause and the Greeks invaded Thessaly and Epirus until a landing by French and English forces at the Piraeus forced Otho to abandon the Russian alliance. The Russo-Turkish conflict of World War I centred in the Caucasus and the end of Russian participation in the war in 1918 was followed by large emigrations of ethnic Greeks from portions of Turkish territory into lands controlled by the nascent Soviet state. Russian influence now took the form of supporting revolutionary and leftist groupings in Greece, and Greek communists based their policies in part on ideas formulated by the Cominform. With the German invasion of the Soviet Union in 1941, Greek communists (KKE) formulated the fundamental duty of Greeks to participate in the defence of the Soviet motherland, forming the National Liberation Front (EAM) in September 1941. In 1943 agreements between Churchill and Stalin delineated Britain's and the Soviet Union's "interests" in Greece at 90 per cent and 10 per cent, respectively. In the Civil War (1946–49) which followed the close of World War II, communist support for political allies in Greece did not receive Stalin's complete backing, since a victory by communists in Greece was seen potentially to strengthen Tito's hand in gathering the Balkans under Yugoslav influence, while the importance of Greece to both the United States and Britain, the lack of a sufficient Soviet navy to aid the partisans, and the fact that the Soviet Union could not afford a confrontation with the West convinced Stalin that there was little hope of avoiding an eventual crushing of the revolt.

Greek influence in southern Russia continued into the 20th century. Living as they did along the shores of the Black Sea, Greeks gradually came under the political domination of the Russian empire. Some Greeks had been settled by Catherine the Great in the region of Mariupol in southern Russia (so-called "New Russia"), while others (mostly Pontic Greeks) migrated into Russian territory upon the withdrawal of Russian armies at the end of the Russo-Turkish wars of the 19th and early 20th centuries, settling mainly in port cities, such as Odessa, Sevastopol, and Rostov, in the Kuban steppe, and in Abkhazia and Georgia. After the Revolution of 1917 Greeks made notable cultural progress and Greek autonomous regions were established in some parts of the Ukraine and southern Russia. Beginning in the mid-1930s and continuing to 1949, Greek populations were decimated and up to 170,000 Greeks were exiled from southern Russia (especially the Crimean and Kuban regions) and the Caucasus, their lands were collectivized, and the people dispersed among Muslim communities in Central Asia. Following Stalin's death in 1953, some of these exiled Greeks began to return westwards and,

after the dissolution of the Soviet Union in 1991, many Greeks, most of them of Pontic origin, began to emigrate to Greece. It is estimated that about 500,000 Greeks lived in the Soviet Union in the mid-1980s, at least half of them in Central Asia.

RICHARD A.E. MASON

See also Black Sea, Bulgars, Colonization, Commonwealth, Crimea, Hetairists, Slavs

Further Reading

Boba, Imrie, *Nomads, Northmen and Slavs: Eastern Europe in the Ninth Century*, The Hague: Mouton, 1967

Bury, J.B., *A History of the Eastern Roman Empire from the Fall of Irene to the Accession of Basil I, AD 802–867*, London and New York: Macmillan, 1912, reprinted New York: Russell, 1965

Bury, J.B., *History of the Later Roman Empire from the Death of Theodosius I to the Death of Justinian*, 2 vols, London: Macmillan, 1923; reprinted New York: Dover, 1958

Clogg, Richard, *A Short History of Modern Greece*, 2nd edition, Cambridge and New York: Cambridge University Press, 1986

Dakin, Douglas, *The Unification of Greece, 1770–1923*, London: Benn, and New York: St Martin's Press, 1972

Davidson, H.R. Ellis, *The Viking Road to Byzantium*, London: Allen and Unwin, 1976

Dvornik, Francis, *The Making of Central and Eastern Europe*, London: Polish Research Centre, 1949

Haussig, H.W., *A History of Byzantine Civilization*, New York: Praeger, and London: Thames and Hudson, 1971

Minns, Ellis H., *Scythians and Greeks: A Survey of Ancient History and Archaeology on the North Coast of the Euxine from the Danube to the Caucasus*, Cambridge: Cambridge University Press, 1913, reprinted New York: Biblo and Tannen, 1965

Obolensky, Dimitri, *The Byzantine Commonwealth: Eastern Europe, 500–1453*, London: Weidenfeld and Nicolson, and New York: Praeger, 1971

Obolensky, Dimitri, *Byzantium and the Slavs*, London: Variorum, 1971; Crestwood, New York: St Vladimir's Seminary Press, 1994

Ostrogorsky, George, *History of the Byzantine State*, 2nd edition, Oxford: Blackwell, 1968; New Brunswick, New Jersey: Rutgers University Press, 1969

Thomson, J. Oliver, *History of Ancient Geography*, Cambridge: Cambridge University Press, 1948, reprinted New York: Biblo and Tannen, 1965

Vernadsky, George, *Ancient Russia*, New Haven, Connecticut: Yale University Press, 1943

Vernadsky, George, *Kievan Russia*, New Haven, Connecticut: Yale University Press, and London: Oxford University Press, 1948

S

Sacrifice

Thought to be an important means of communication between divinity and mortals, sacrifice is a central feature of religious practice. In antiquity, although animal sacrifice was predominant, the offering of fruit and vegetables was also considered to be sacrifice. The mythological *aition* (origin) of the idea of sacrifice is believed to be the story of Prometheus in Hesiod's *Theogony* (521–616). Prometheus, representing mortals, hosts a dinner at Mekone (Sicyon) and purposely deceives Zeus by assigning for him a good-looking portion that consists of nothing but bones. There are references to sacrifice throughout ancient Greek literature, and with the help of archaeological finds such as vase paintings and votive reliefs we are able to reconstruct approximately what went on. The sacrifice probably consisted of three stages. There was a procession that led the animal to the altar, and a purification ritual in which the animal's head was cleaned with water and sprinkled with barley grain. Then followed the cutting of the throat, and finally the burning of the meat. The gods' portion was bones covered with fat; then the entrails and the meat were given to the participants for consumption. The entrails were observed by the priests because their condition was supposed to provide omens. That is why sacrifices were often made at critical moments in mythology as well as in history, before mounting an expedition or taking an important decision. Most cults and festivals (such as the Dionysia, the Bouphonia, and the Eleusinian mysteries) involved some form of sacrifice. Besides the official celebrations in honour of a god or goddess, where sacrifice plays a central role, sacrifices were made at major events in private life, such as marriage, childbirth, death, and were often accompanied by libations. Sacrifices could be organized at various levels, by a city, a deme, a family, or an individual. Young people of both sexes would offer sacrifices to Artemis before they got married. Pindar tells us about fireless sacrifice (*Olympian*, 7. 47). Burned sacrifices were believed (Philostratus, *Eikones*, 2. 27) to have first appeared in Athens, where they were conducted gloriously. The altar was the site of the sacrifice. The Classical Greek altar was stone-built and often decorated at the sides. As for human sacrifice, some scholars have argued that it was practised by the Minoan civilization, citing examples from myths such as that of Iphigeneia; but this is a theory that requires more research before it can be accepted.

Sacrifice was conducted to honour not only the gods but also heroes and heroines in corresponding cults. Very often the word *enagizein* ("make sacrifice to the dead") is used for heroic cults in contrast with *thuein* ("make offering to the gods"). Many heroes featured in the deme calendars that regulated the sacrifices that were to take place during the year. Most often the sacrifice was followed by a banquet, as in the cult of gods. In addition to blood sacrifice, libations were performed at the tomb of a hero, as on a funerary occasion, and votive offerings would be dedicated to heroic figures, most often objects (vases, shields, etc.) with artistic depictions inspired from the life of the hero. Some scholars have argued that there was sometimes ritual antagonism in sacrifice between gods, or between heroes and gods, as in the case of Erechtheus and Poseidon in Attica.

The concept of sacrifice and offering is believed to have survived in the Christian religion, as we know from the writings of the early Church Fathers. The notion of sacrifice exists in Greek Orthodox liturgical practice, at the Eucharist, in a reverse means of communication between the divinity and mortals. The concept that the Son of God was sacrificed in order to save mankind from sin creates a different model of communication, in which the divine initiates sacrifice and invites human participation. The sacrifice of Christ is symbolized in Holy Communion, in which the faithful receive his body and blood.

In modern Greek folklore tradition sacrifice is an important feature, reflecting the importance it had in antiquity. Sometimes it is done at important feasts, or in private life, particularly to mark certain rites of passage (at weddings, births, deaths), or in order to avert an evil. The ritual and the ideological form that it assumes justify labelling the act as a sacrifice and distinguish it from normal animal killing for the purpose of food. The act of sacrifice today is often seen as a clash between paganism and Christianity that has survived from the past, whereas in truth it shows the need of humans to express their feelings and convey a message to the divinity in material terms.

ANDROMACHE KARANIKA-DIMAROGONA

Further Reading
Aikaterinides, Georg N., *Neoellenikes Aimateres Thysies: Leitourgia Morphologia Typologia* [Modern Greek Bloody Sacrifices: Liturgy, Morphology, Typology], Athens, 1979

Sacrifice: worshippers of Artemis are shown offering sacrifice on this 4th century BC votive relief from the sanctuary of Artemis at Brauron, Brauron Museum

Burkert, Walter, *Homo Necans: The Anthropology of Ancient Greek Sacrificial Ritual and Myth*, Berkeley: University of California Press, 1983

Burkert, Walter, *Greek Religion: Archaic and Classical*, Oxford: Blackwell, and Cambridge, Massachusetts: Harvard University Press, 1985

Grottanelli, Cristiano and N. Parise, (editors), *Sacrificio e società nel mondo antico*, Rome: Laferza, 1988

Larson, Jennifer, *Greek Heroine Cults*, Madison: University of Wisconsin Press, 1995

Vernant, Jean Pierre, *Mythe et société en Grèce ancienne*, Paris: Maspero, 1974

St Catherine's Monastery, Sinai

The monastery of St Catherine at Sinai is located in the southern part of the triangular Sinai peninsula, between the continents of Asia and Africa. It is unique in many ways: it is one of the oldest Orthodox monasteries, with an uninterrupted life of more than 14 centuries, during which it was never totally destroyed or abandoned. It is the only Orthodox monastery that is also the seat of an archbishop; it is also the smallest Orthodox diocese.

St Catherine's has the oldest monastic library in the Christian world and has preserved some of the best examples of early Christian icons (the earliest dating from the first half of the 6th century). The Sinai peninsula has been a monastic centre since the early days of monasticism. The proximity to Egypt as well as Palestine, the fact that it is sparsely populated, and the harshness of conditions made it ideally suited as a centre for anchorites, the early Christian monks who sought a life of isolation and prayer. The community of monks in Sinai (and neighbouring Raitho, now El Tor) was already in place during the reign of the emperor Diocletian (AD 284–305), when a number of them were slaughtered by the Blemmyes, a local marauding tribe. According to tradition (recently partly confirmed by archaeological evidence), St Helena ordered a fortified tower and church to be built on the site of the Burning Bush, in order to protect the monks living in the area from raids. Travellers and visitors of the 4th century refer to a small church and a fortified tower on the plain of the Burning Bush. (Egeria in 400 also reports the existence of a church on top of the mountain and on Mount Horiv.) In any event the tower already existed by 381 and pottery of the early Christian period confirms the existence of communities of monks.

The life of the monastery as we know it today began during the reign of the emperor Justinian (527–65). It is probable that the monastic community had grown in size and the earlier buildings were no longer sufficient. Justinian ordered a large basilica to be built near or on the site of the earlier structures and also a rectangular fortified protecting wall surrounding the church and the other buildings. The historian Procopius refers to the need to protect not only the monks but also the route from Egypt to Palestine as a motive behind the building of the fortress-monastery. The walls and the church (as well as some

St Catherine's Monastery, Sinai, where there has been an unbroken tradition of asceticism since the 6th century

of the buildings inside the walls) were designed and built by Stefanos, from nearby Aila (now Eilat). Apart from imperial funds, Stefanos also had at his disposal a contingent of soldiers. Some 200 of them with their families settled around the monastery to help protect it, but also the imperial communications. The monastery soon became well known: pope Gregory Dialogos (590–604) financed the building of a hospital; and other dignitaries in East and West also endowed it with property.

The monastery found itself outside imperial jurisdiction quite soon; the Arab conquest of Sinai (633) and the conversion of the inhabitants of the peninsula to Islam left the monks the only Christian population in the region. However, on the whole neither the monastery nor the monks were greatly affected: they had secured from the Prophet Muhammad himself the *Ahtiname*, a document signed by Muhammad with the imprint of his hand, in which his followers were asked not to molest the monastery, which was also given tax privileges. Moreover, being outside the empire, the monastery escaped the depredations of iconoclasm in the 8th and 9th centuries. While the monastery has had periods of trouble (e.g. in the reign of the caliph Hakeem, 1101–06), the *Ahtiname* has always been recognized as genuine by Muslims. This and the diplomatic conduct of the monks have ensured a largely peaceful coexistence between the dominant faith in the region and the monastery.

Originally named after the Burning Bush, the monastery changed its name to St Catherine in the 9th century, when the saint became known in the West. Greater prominence was achieved in the 11th century largely through the efforts of a monk from Sinai, Symeon Pentaglossos ("of the five tongues"), who took some relics of St Catherine to western Europe. Following this and other tours, the monastery received donations of property throughout Europe and other privileges, confirmed by papal bulls of Honorius III (1217), Gregory I (1271–76), and John XXII (1316–34). Venice granted tax exemptions to the monastery for its dependencies in Crete; and after the Turkish conquest of Egypt and Sinai (1517) sultan Selim confirmed the privileges. He also took the original *Ahtiname* to Constantinople, leaving copies in the monastery. Even Napoleon issued an edict confirming the monastery's privileges in 1798; his army also repaired one of the walls of the monastery which had collapsed following heavy rain that year. The monastery received considerable patronage from Russia as well; apart from gifts of land, both Catherine the Great and Alexander II donated reliquaries for the relics of St Catherine.

Within the formidable walls of the fortress lies the complex of monastic buildings. These include the main church and numerous chapels, the old refectory, the library, a mosque (for the local bedouin), a mill, and many other buildings. The monastery church was probably originally built in honour of the Transfiguration, as the magnificent mosaic in the apse attests. Evidence from inscriptions on the beams supporting the ceiling suggests that it was built at some time after the death of empress Theodora (548) and before the death of Justinian (565). It is a three-aisled basilica with a narthex at the west end. On the east, south, and north sides it has nine other chapels dedicated to various saints. Of particular interest is the chapel of the Burning Bush on the eastern wall of the church, behind the chancel. Among its many remarkable features are the doors to the main church dating from the 6th century and the doors to the narthex (from the period of the crusades).

Other notable buildings include the mosque (a Byzantine building, formerly the monastery's refectory and turned into a mosque early in the 12th century) and another building of unknown use from the 12th or 13th century. This has Gothic arches and a fresco of the Second Coming (dated 1573). Graffiti in Latin on its arches seem to imply that it was used as quarters for pilgrims from the West. The monastery of St Catherine of Mount Sinai has preserved priceless architectural, artistic, and cultural treasures as well as its Greek Orthodox tradition. It has also been and continues to be a unique (if lonely) Greek and Orthodox Christian beacon in the Sinai wilderness.

GEORGE KAZAMIAS

See also Monasteries

Summary

Founded in the mid-6th century by the emperor Justinian I on the traditional site of the Burning Bush, the monastery has enjoyed good relations with neighbouring peoples throughout its existence. It changed its name to St Catherine in the 9th century. Still functioning as a Greek Orthodox house, it preserves a unique collection of architectural, artistic, and cultural treasures.

Further Reading

Amantou, K., *Syntomos Historia tes Ieras Mones tou Sina* [Short History of the Holy Monastery of Sinai], Thessalonica, 1953

Baddeley, Oriana, and Earleen Brunner (editors), *The Monastery of Saint Catherine*, London: Saint Catherine Foundation, 1996

Galey, John, *Sinai and the Monastery of St Catherine*, Cairo: American University in Cairo Press, 1985

Manafis, K. (editor), *Sina: Oi Thisavroi tis Ieras Monis Agias Aikaterinis* [Sinai: The Treasures of the Holy Monastery of Saint Catherine], Athens, 1990

Nektariou, Ierosolymon, *Epitomi tis Ierokosmikis Istorias* [Epitome of Sacred World History], 7th edition, Athens, 1980 (1st edition 1677)

Nikolaou, Glyky, *Perigrafi Iera tou Agiou kai Theovadistou Orous Sina* [Sacred Description of the Holy and God-Trodden Mount of Sinai], Venice, 1817, reprinted Athens, 1978

Weitzmann, Kurt and George H. Forsyth, *The Monastery of St Catherine at Mount Sinai: The Church and Fortress of Justinian*, Ann Arbor, Michigan: University of Michigan Press, 1973

Weitzmann, Kurt, *The Monastery of St Catherine at Mount Sinai: The Icons*, vol. 1: *From the Sixth to the Tenth Century*, Princeton, New Jersey: Princeton University Press, 1976

Weitzmann, Kurt and George Galavaris, *The Monastery of St Catherine at Mount Sinai: The Illuminated Greek Manuscripts*, vol. 1: *From the Ninth to the Twelfth Century*, Princeton, New Jersey: Princeton University Press, 1990

Sakellarides, John Theophrastos

*c.*1853–1938

Composer and teacher of music

The life and work of John Theophrastos Sakellarides, teacher, arranger, and reformer of Byzantine chant, is of fundamental importance for understanding the development of sacred music in the Greek Orthodox Church since the late 19th century. Born *c.*1853 in Litochoros, Olympus, outside the Greek kingdom, he received his first instruction in Byzantine chanting from his father, a priest. Sent to secondary school in Thessalonica, he continued to study chant under the noted cantor Papa-Theodoro Mantzourani, a former Constantinopolitan, who also taught the young Sakellarides Arabo-Persian music. He then enrolled in the medical school at Athens university, transferring later to its school of philosophy. During this period he secured the first of his many cantorial positions in the Athens area, while also studying Western musical theory under a German teacher at the recently founded Athens conservatory.

Sakellarides's encounter with Western music proved decisive, causing him to reject many elements of the received tradition of Byzantine chanting as relics of Turkish domination. He began to view the repertories of florid chant as bodies of formless creations in which the meaning of the text was obliterated by senseless melismas, and to criticize traditional vocal production as barbaric *rhinophonia* (nasal singing). Thereafter he cultivated a more Western manner of singing and embarked on a mission to purify Byzantine chant through a radical recomposition of the central repertory. He simplified or eliminated most melismatic chants, while rewriting many of the less florid chants to conform to his classicizing theories of metre and punctuation. In 1880, while still at university, he published his *Christomatheia Ekklesiastikis Mousikis* [Handbook of Church Music], a book of liturgical music in modern Byzantine notation containing a theoretical prologue recommending the adoption of equal-temperament tuning, followed by a compendium of the most frequently encountered chants for the Divine Liturgy and major offices. This volume was soon followed by others in both Byzantine and Western staff notation, some of which also contained elementary harmonizations in two, three, and occasionally four parts. Sakellarides justified the latter innovation with citations of Classical and patristic texts, dubiously interpreting references to *harmonia* as evidence for harmonized singing in the modern Western sense. Moreover, he defended his harmonizations – often little more than parallel thirds or sixths over a rudimentary bass part – as *triphonia* (three-voice music) not subject to the recent synodal and patriarchal proscriptions of *tetraphonia* (polyphonic compositions, usually in four parts). These rationalizations did not prevent his censure in 1886 by the Holy Synod of the Church of Greece for breaking the ban on polyphony with his choir at the church of Hagia Eirene, as well as for having introduced female voices into his ensemble. Although the synod's action forced him to resign from Hagia Eirene, it did little to stem his rapidly growing popularity. The subsequent accession of a new archbishop from the Ionian islands brought Sakellarides toleration followed by official sanction as he successively assumed musical directorships at the most prominent churches of Athens, including its cathedral. Attracting large crowds wherever he went, he was renowned for the clarity of his tenor voice, his diction, and for inviting the congregation to participate in certain of his simplified chants with the command *"Laos!"* ("People!"). He eventually returned to Hagia Eirene, where he remained *protopsaltes* (chief singer) until his death on 15 December 1938.

Prior to the Asia Minor disaster of 1922, Sakellarides worked vigorously as a composer and teacher to reconcile the musical cultures of ancient Greece, Byzantium, and the contemporary West. In addition to producing a comprehensive repertory of reformed chant that was constantly republished, he wrote incidental music for three Classical dramas and composed a large number of patriotic songs intended for use in schools, many of which appear in his nationalistic collection *Tyrtaios* (1907). Sakellarides personally taught his music to nearly two generations of Athenian clergy and laity (both men and women) at such institutions as the Rizarios seminary and the Arsakeion school for girls. His firm belief in the fundamental unity of Greek musical culture through the ages took him and his three children to Munich in 1903, where they presented lecture-recitals of sacred and folk music. These included a concert featuring the participation of the Munich Philharmonic Orchestra under the direction of his son Theophrastos, a composer of operetta who had orchestrated the music performed on that occasion. Back in Athens, from 1904 to 1907 he instructed the young H.J.W. Tillyard, a future cofounder of the *Monumenta Musicae Byzantinae*, in the received tradition of Byzantine chanting, thereby influencing the subsequent course of Byzantine musicology in the West with his reformist views.

Sakellarides continued to clash with traditionalists even after his *Hiera Hymnodia* [Sacred Hymnody] – which contains among its chants for the Orthodox wedding service such curiosities as a Greek adaptation of Wagner's famous march from *Lohengrin* – was recommended for general use by the Holy Synod and ministry of education in 1902. In that same year he provoked a public disturbance by attempting to provide piano accompaniment for the public final examination of one of his chant students. His 1904 transcription of an acclamation for the last Byzantine emperor from a medieval manuscript precipitated a bitter debate in the periodicals of Athens and Constantinople regarding the true nature of chant in Byzantium. This was also the first of many conflicts with the newly arrived Constantinos Psachos (c.1866[–]1949), another student of Mantzourani who had just been sent by the ecumenical patriarchate to direct a school of traditional Byzantine music at the Athens conservatory.

The influence of Sakellarides on liturgical music in Greece began gradually to wane after the 1950s. By the late 1980s a revival of traditional Byzantine and folk music had relegated the vast majority of Sakellarides's reformed chants to the musical periphery. An exception to this trend is his melody for the vesper hymn *Phos Hilaron* [Hail Gladdening Light] which has all but completely displaced the ancient chant even on Mount Athos. For a variety of cultural and historical reasons, the music of Sakellarides has proved far more durable in the Greek Orthodox churches of the West. This is particularly true of the United States, where his reformed melodies were so widely disseminated during the heaviest periods of Greek immigration that they have since come to be regarded by most people as traditional. Yet with the rise of professionally trained Greek-American musicians, Sakellarides's elementary harmonizations have largely given way to more sophisticated modal arrangements by such composers as Frank Desby, Anna Gallos, and Tikey Zes.

ALEXANDER LINGAS

Biography
Born *c.*1853 at Litochoros on Mount Olympus, Sakellarides was educated in Thessalonica and Athens where he was a student at both the university and the conservatory. He introduced Western elements into Byzantine chant which brought him censure from the Holy Synod of the Church of Greece but great popularity. His influence on liturgical music has waned since the 1950s. He died in 1938.

Writings
Hymns and Odes, translated by Philolaus Kalavros, Hollywood: Angelos Desfis, 1949 (widely distributed reprint of the 1930 edition of *Hymnoi kai Odai*, with an edited English translation of Sakellarides' preface)

Further Reading
Desby, Frank Harry, "The Modes and Tuning in Neo-Byzantine Chant" (dissertation), University of Southern California, 1974

Desby, Frank Harry, "Growth of Liturgical Music in the Iakovian Era" in *History of the Greek Orthodox Church in America*, edited by M.B. Ephthimiou and G.A. Christopoulos, New York: Greek Archdiocese of North and South America, 1984

Filopoulos, Giannes, *Eisagogi stein helliniki polyphoniki ekkelsiastiki mousiki* [Introduction to Greek Polyphonic Church Music], Athens, 1990 (includes brief summary in English)

Lingas, Alexander, "Performance Practice and the Politics of Transcribing Byzantine Chant" in *Le Chant byzantin: état des recherches*, edited by Christian Hannick and Marcel Pérès, Grâne: Créaphis, forthcoming

Tillyard, H.J.W., "The Rediscovery of Byzantine Music" in *Essays Presented to Egon Wellesz*, edited by Jack Westrup, Oxford: Clarendon Press, 1966

Salamis (city)

City in Cyprus

Unlike Paphos, which had a predecessor in the Bronze Age and even earlier at the same location, Salamis is a relatively new foundation, dating to the 11th century BC. Its Late Bronze Age predecessor Enkomi lies *c.*2 km inland, to the southwest. Around the beginning of the 11th century BC the inner harbour of Enkomi silted up, perhaps as a result of earthquakes, and the town was gradually abandoned; its inhabitants chose a site near the sea, which was provided with a natural harbour, and the town of Salamis developed around this harbour. Judging from the perimeter of the 11th-century BC fortification wall, the early town was small, with its necropolis situated *extra muros* to the west. Of the 11th century BC only one sanctuary has been excavated, as well as a portion of the city wall, but there is ample ceramic evidence that the town originated at that time. This is also supported by the discovery of a tomb of the same period, west of the harbour, with a long narrow *dromos* (entrance passage) and a rectangular chamber, of a

Salamis: the ancient city viewed from the air. In the foreground the gymnasium and to the right the theatre which dates from the 1st century AD.

type which was introduced to the island from the Aegean. According to mythical tradition the founder of Salamis was Teucer, the son of Telamon, king of the island of Salamis (near Attica) and brother of Ajax, who came to the island after the end of the Trojan War. Underlying this myth may be the phenomenon of the foundation of new towns by Achaean immigrants of the 12th century BC, after they finally established themselves on the island and gained political power.

Salamis of the Dark Ages (10th and 9th centuries BC) is not represented in the archaeological record, but the 8th–7th centuries BC are represented by a number of large built tombs with monumental *dromoi*. Although the chambers of these tombs have been found looted or half-looted, many important objects were found in the spacious *dromoi* which the looters left intact. The size of the tombs, their style, and the wealth of objects which they have yielded justify their identification as "royal", although not all of them were used for the burial of members of the royal family. As in other tombs, at Salamis too there must have been an aristocratic elite, probably the descendants of the Achaean immigrants of the 12th–11th centuries BC. The burial customs which have been observed for these "royal" burials are remarkable: the dead person was placed in a ceremonial chariot or hearse, drawn by two or four horses, and was carried to the tomb. The chariots and horses were richly adorned with bronze plaques and gear respectively, all decorated in repoussé with Egyptianizing scenes. The chariot was drawn down the slope of the *dromos* to near the entrance of the chamber. There the horses were ceremonially killed. The

sacrificing of horses in honour of the dead recalls Mycenaean burial customs. In one case there is evidence for the burial of slaves in the *dromos* of a tomb to serve their master in the afterlife. Among the tomb gifts there were weapons and ivory furniture (a bed and a throne were found in Tomb 79). There were also iron skewers (*obeloi*) and firedogs of a type known on Crete and in the Argolid during the same period. The burial customs of the "royal" tombs of Salamis, as well as the gifts offered to the dead, recall customs and objects mentioned by Homer in the *Iliad* (book 23, where the burial of Patroclus is described). This has led some scholars to interpret the appearance of such burial customs at Salamis as the result of the reciting of the Homeric epic in the court of Salamis. The most plausible explanation, however, is that such "heroic burials" also existed on the Greek mainland, and it was quite natural for the aristocratic elite of Salamis to imitate these burial customs.

Salamis maintained close relations with Greece throughout its history. In a "royal tomb" of the 8th century BC a large number of Greek Geometric bowls and dishes were found, as well as a *krater* (mixing bowl). The dead person, a woman, was cremated and her incinerated remains together with her necklace were put in a bronze cauldron. Gjerstad ingeniously proposed that this was the tomb of a Greek princess who had married into the royal court of Salamis.

Salamis of the late-Archaic and Classical periods is known from tombs as well as the votive offerings belonging to a sanctuary on the western outskirts of the town. The style of the limestone statues, most of them female, imitates that of the

Greek *korai* of the end of the 6th and the beginning of the 5th century BC.

The earliest king of Salamis whose name is known is Euelthon (560–525 BC). He was the first to issue silver coins on the island in 530 BC. Herodotus (4. 162) records that queen Pheretima of Cyrene visited Euelthon in 530 and asked for his assistance in re-establishing her son on the throne. Herodotus also mentions Euelthon as having dedicated an incense burner at Delphi, which could be seen in the treasury of the Corinthians. Another Salaminian who offered a *peplos* (robe) at Delphi, woven by himself, was Helicon, son of Acesas.

Herodotus describes very vividly the dramatic events connected with the Ionian revolt and the active participation of the Salaminians under their king Onesilus (5. 104, 108–16). The latter managed to dethrone his brother, the pro-Persian king, and lead the revolt. He died while besieging the pro-Persian kingdom of Amathus.

One of the most famous kings of Salamis was Evagoras I, probably a member of the Teucrid royal family and a great supporter of Athenian policies. He was honoured by the Athenians, who erected his statue in the Agora of Athens next to the statue of Zeus Eleutherios. His ideal was to unite all the Greeks under the leadership of Athens. In Cyprus his efforts were to unite all Cypriot kingdoms under the leadership of Salamis in order to free the island from the Persians. Neither of these ideals was fulfilled. He fought against the Persians and helped the Athenians against the Lacedaemonians. He died in 374/73 BC, a few years after the Peace of Antalcidas was signed in 386, which decreed that all cities of Asia and Cyprus should belong to the Great King. The Greek orator Isocrates praised Evagoras in one of his orations; Isocrates was the tutor of his son, Nicocles.

A funerary monument, the cenotaph of the last king of Salamis Nicocreon, was excavated in the necropolis of Salamis. On the funerary pyre, under the tumulus of earth, the Salaminians buried rich gifts for the brave king and the members of the royal family who preferred to die rather than surrender to the Ptolemies. This event, narrated by Diodorus, is dated to 311 BC. The burial may have been effected by Demetrius Poliorcetes, who became the ruler of Cyprus in 306 BC.

Salamis continued to be one of the most important cities of Cyprus, but with the transfer of the capital to Paphos in the 1st century BC the city must have lost some of its glamour. Its harbour and its rich hinterland, however, contributed to its continued prosperity. During the Roman period the city enjoyed the favours of Trajan and Hadrian, who erected public buildings such as the gymnasium and the theatre, which they adorned with marble statues. The temple of Zeus Salaminios was considered to be one of the most important religious centres in the island. Recent excavations have revealed some of the splendours of Salamis in the northern part of the town including a gymnasium, a theatre, an amphitheatre, a *xystos* (colonnade), and spacious baths.

The city was destroyed by the earthquakes of the 4th century AD, after which it was reconstructed on a smaller scale as a Christian city, named Constantia in honour of the emperor Constantius II, who assisted in its reconstruction.

VASSOS KARAGEORGHIS

Summary

The largest city of ancient Cyprus, Salamis was said to have been founded by Teucer, brother of Ajax, after the Trojan War. Remains date from the 11th century BC. Relations with Greece were close throughout antiquity. Evagoras I, king of Salamis in the 4th century BC, was honoured by the Athenians for his support. The city lost some of its importance when the capital was moved to Paphos in the 1st century BC.

Further Reading

Chavane, Marie-José, *Testimonia Salaminia*, vol. 1, Paris: Boccard, 1978

Gjerstad, E., *The Swedish Cyprus Expedition*, vol. 4, part 2: *The Cypro-Geometric, Cypro-Archaic and Cypro-Classical Periods*, Stockholm: Swedish Cyprus Expedition, 1948

Karageorghis, Vassos and Cornelius Vermeule, *Sculptures from Salamis*, 2 vols, Nicosia: Department of Antiquities, 1964–66

Karageorghis, Vassos, *Excavations in the Necropolis of Salamis*, 2 vols, Nicosia: Department of Antiquities, 1967–78

Karageorghis, Vassos, *Salamis: Recent Discoveries in Cyprus*, London and New York: McGraw Hill, 1969

Karageorghis, Vassos, *Cyprus: From the Stone Age to the Romans*, London: Thames and Hudson, 1982

Karageorghis, Vassos, *Excavating at Salamis, 1952–1974*, Athens: A.G. Leventis Foundation, 1999

Mitford, Terence B. and Ino K. Nicolaou, *The Greek and Latin Inscriptions from Salamis*, Nicosia: Department of Antiquities, 1974

Pouilloux, J. and G. Roux, *Testimonia Salaminia: Corpus épigraphique*, Paris: Boccard, 1987

Vermeule, Cornelius, *Greek and Roman Cyprus: Art from Classical through Late Antique Times*, Boston: Museum of Fine Arts, 1976

Yon, Marguerite, *La Tombe T.1 du XIe siècle avant J.C.*, Paris: Boccard, 1971

Yon, Marguerite, *Un Dépôt de sculptures archaïques*, Paris: Boccard, 1974

Yon, Marguerite, *Salamine de Chypre: histoire et archéologie, état des recherches*, Paris: Centre National des Recherches Scientifiques, 1980

Yon, Marguerite (editor), *Kinyras: French Archaeology in Cyprus*, Paris: Boccard, 1993

Salamis (island)

Island in the Saronic gulf

The island of Salamis sits off the western coast of Attica. It is the northernmost island of those which lie in the Saronic Gulf. The island is approximately 100 sq km in area. The terrain is mountainous, with some arable plains. There are no rivers running on the island today. The vegetation consists largely of pine, scrub oak, and olive.

The island was inhabited from at least the Neolithic period. Excavation in a cave on the south coast of the island has produced numerous stone implements. In addition, prehistoric pottery has been found at various spots on the island. The Bronze Age is well represented by tombs and pottery, both of which have been found all over the island. The remains of a Bronze Age settlement may be seen at Ginani in the southern part of the island. A large sub-Mycenaean cemetery was excavated on Salamis around the start of the 20th century. It yielded much pottery, some of which came from Attica. There was thus a connection of some kind between the two places from an early period.

Although the centuries between 1000 and 800 BC are less well represented, there is some evidence of habitation, and from the Archaic period through to the present there is clear, continuous habitation. While the area most heavily inhabited in the Bronze Age seems to have been the southern section of the island, in the Archaic and Classical periods the settlement moved north to the middle of the island. The Classical city sat on a peninsula on the east which juts out towards Attica. Later, at a date which is still not certain, the principal settlement moved to the west coast of the island, and this city (modern Salamina) is still the principal city on Salamis.

The mythology of the island is related by the 1st-century BC historian Diodorus Siculus, among others, who says that Telamon and Peleus killed their brother Phocus on the island of Aegina, and then Peleus fled to Thessaly and Telamon to Salamis. Telamon, according to one version of the story, was then married to the daughter of the king of Salamis, and they had a son, Ajax. When the old king died, Telamon inherited the island, and one of his grandsons in turn gave it to the Athenians. (Peleus married Thetis and she bore him Achilles. Thus Achilles and Ajax are cousins.)

The close ties between Athens and Salamis are further demonstrated by the earliest Athenian decree (late 6th century BC), which deals with regulations for those living on the island, and by the use of Ajax as one of the ten eponymous heroes chosen by Cleisthenes in 508 BC for the Athenian tribes. Ajax was the only non-Athenian in the group.

In 480 a critical naval battle in the Persian Wars was fought in the straits between Salamis and Athens. The smaller, swifter ships of the Athenians outmanoeuvred the large Persian ships, and the Athenians and their allies defeated a larger power. This battle became a legend in Athenian history, and a topos in Athenian literature. Thus later writers who refer to Salamis often do so with reference to this battle. The island itself served as a refuge for women and children during the Persian invasion of Athens.

At least two major figures in the 5th century had connections with Salamis. Towards the end of the Peloponnesian War democratic sympathizers took refuge on the island, and they were pursued there by the Thirty Tyrants. An incident involving one such individual, a certain Leon, is mentioned by Socrates in the *Apology*. Socrates was meant to retrieve Leon from Salamis, but he refused to do so. Also there was a tradition that the playwright Euripides was born on the island, and that he used to write his plays there in a cave overlooking the sea.

Mention must be made of two groups of people who lived on the mainland of Attica and called themselves Salaminioi, i.e. men from Salamis. These men from Salamis were dubbed the Salaminioi of the Heptaphylai, and the Salaminioi from Sunium. It is unclear when, where, and why they had their origins, and furthermore we have little idea of their purpose. They are known through fragmentary inscriptions, and study of those is still ongoing. They were apparently a kinship group with a civic function.

Aristotle tells us that Salamis had its own archon, although no remains of any inscriptions concerning archons on the island have been identified. It is also known (from the *Athenaion Politeia*) that Salamis had its own dramatic festival, but no remains of the ancient theatre have been found.

The island changed hands in the late 4th century, when Demetrius was in control at Athens, but there is little other solid information about the status of the island in the literature of the Hellenistic period. It is known through inscriptional evidence that the Ephebes, Athenian (and later, wealthy Roman) young men in military training, performed some of their activities on and around the island. Numerous honorific inscriptions attest to their good behaviour while on the island.

Roman pottery is visible at many sites on the island and it is thus clear that Salamis remained active in the waning years of the pre-Christian era, and the subsequent centuries of the empire. Chapels from the Byzantine period, as well as the occasional mention of the island in literature, are evidence that Salamis was inhabited in the medieval period. Turkish and Albanian place names on the island attest to the presence of those peoples, and much later, during the War of Independence, Salamis served as a base of operations in Attica. It was from Salamis that George Karaiskakis set out on the mission to take the Acropolis. Karaiskakis lost his life just as the battle was beginning. In May 1997 a monument was erected on the island in Salamis town to commemorate this event.

TIMOTHY F. WINTERS

See also Persian Wars

Summary

The northernmost of the islands in the Saronic gulf, Salamis has been inhabited since the Neolithic period. There are mythological as well as historical connections with Athens. An important battle was fought in 480 BC in the straits between Salamis and Athens in which the Persian fleet was defeated. Salamis was a base of operations in the War of Independence in the 1820s.

Further Reading

Burn, A.R., *Persia and the Greeks: The Defence of the West, c.546–478 BC*, 2nd edition, London: Duckworth, and Stanford, California: Stanford University Press, 1984

Christensen, K.A., "Athens and the Conquest of Salamis: Crisis, Competition and Innovation in the Saronic Gulf" (dissertation), Princeton, New Jersey: Princeton University, 1993

Culley, G.R., "The Restoration of Sanctuaries in Attica: IG II² 1035", *Hesperia*, 44 (1975): pp. 207–23

Hignett, Charles, *Xerxes' Invasion of Greece*, Oxford: Clarendon Press, 1963

Lambert, S., "The Genos Salaminioi and the Island of Salamis", *Zeitschrift für Papyrologie und Epigraphik*, 119 (1997): pp. 85–106

Legon, Ronald P., *Megara: The Political History of a Greek City-State to 336 BC*, Ithaca, New York: Cornell University Press, 1981

McCleod, W., "Boudoron: An Athenian Fort on Salamis", *Hesperia*, 29 (1960): pp. 316–23

Pallas, D., "Archaiologikes Episimanseis sti Salamina" [Archaeological Sites on Salamis], *Archaiologikon Deltion* [Archaeological Bulletin], 42 (1987)

Pritchett, K., "Toward a Restudy of the Battle of Salamis", *American Journal of Archaeology*, 63 (1959): pp. 251–62

Styrenius, C.G., "The Vases from the Submycenaean Cemetery on Salamis", *Opuscula Atheniensia*, 4 (1962): pp. 103–23

Taylor, M.C., *Salamis and the Salaminioi: The History of an Unofficial Athenian Demos*, Amsterdam: Gieben, 1997

Samos

Island in the east Aegean

Samos is one of the larger of the Aegean islands, with an area of 492 sq km, and it lies closest of all of them to the coast of Asia Minor: the channel dividing it from Turkey is today only 3 km wide, and in prehistoric times it was joined to the mainland. In antiquity it was known as both Parthenia and Anthemus, but as Samos from at least the 5th century BC. Pausanias (10. 12) claimed that the island had an early distinction as the home of one of the first of the Sybils. It is quite mountainous, well watered, and heavily wooded, and has always been known principally for the fertility of its land; the island still exports olive oil and tobacco. While for later centuries the fineness of Samian muscat wine was much famed, and was later to be extolled by Byron, it was not always thus. Strabo (*Geography*, 14) emphasized the poor quality of the island's wine compared with other islands in the region, but praised its other products, and quoted Menander as saying that "it even produces birds' milk".

Throughout the pre-Christian period from the 3rd millennium BC the island was populated, but it was only in the 6th century BC that Samos knew real fame and power, when the tyrant Polycrates established himself as sole ruler. He built up a powerful fleet, annexed other islands, and established a famous court that attracted artists of all kinds. A tunnel more than 900 m long that was completed in 524 BC under the direction of Eupalinus of Megara, ensuring a water supply to the city of ancient Samos in time of siege, remains to this day a unique monument to another aspect of his reign. To Polycrates is also attributed the construction of a man-made harbour and breakwater. The success with which the Samians resisted a siege by the Lacedaemonians for 40 days (Herodotus, 3. 56) during the reign of Polycrates, when they were unable to bring about the city's subjection, was no doubt due in part to this tunnel. The tyrant's eventual death at the hands of Oroetes is described by Herodotus (3. 125): "He slew him in a way too horrible to describe, and then crucified him."

At least one and a half millennia of the history of Samos can be traced in the extensive coastal site of the sanctuary of Hera, known as the Heraion. Its earliest remains date from the Bronze Age, but its most impressive feature, which was known all over the Hellenic world, was the great temple built during the 6th century BC; its size (it was almost 100 m in length) caused Herodotus to state that it was the largest of all the temples he had seen. "Its first architect was Rhoecus, the son of Phileas, who was a Samian" (3. 60). Burnt down in the later 6th century BC, it was rebuilt, with numerous other structures added at various dates, before an early Christian basilica was built at its east end during the 5th century AD; a cistern here was in use into the 6th century AD. Pausanias also credited the same Rhoecus with being one of the first Greeks to make images by casting molten bronze (8. 14). Another 6th-century BC artist of great fame was Theodorus of Samos, who was a sculptor and architect, and made a magnificent ring of gold and emeralds for the tyrant Polycrates. He was credited by Pliny (*Naturalis Historia*, 34. 83) with creating the first self-portrait to be made in bronze.

Further evidence of the vigorous developing life of Samos in late antiquity and the early Christian centuries is provided by several excavations, such as that at Pithagorio, where an early Christian basilica was built on the site of a Roman villa; at Panagitsa another basilica and baptistery were built over Roman baths. Churches were built in various parts of the island between the 4th and 6th centuries, showing that a vigorous island life persisted until Arab raids began in the 7th century, but this must have continued because a bishop of Samos attended the important Church council of 787 in Nicaea at which iconoclast edicts were revoked. The island's position continued to dominate its history, since it was chosen as the base from which Nikephoros Phokas would reconquer Crete in 960.

In the 10th century Samos was the only Aegean island to be named as the centre of a theme, when it became a subdivision of the theme of the Aigaios Pelagos; this importance was probably due to its geographical location close to the mainland, and it was governed from Smyrna. The island's prosperity continued into at least the early 12th century, when a Russian traveller, the *higumen* (abbot) Daniil, wrote admiringly of his visit here, noting that "the sea abounds with fish, and the island is very fertile."

In the Deed of Partition of 1204 Samos was listed as being allocated to the new Latin emperor, but he never occupied it and from c.1225 it was taken into the empire of the Byzantine government in exile in Nicaea. In the 14th century, with weakening Byzantine power, the island suffered Turkish raids, and then was occupied briefly by the Genoese in 1304 and again in 1346 for some 30 years. Samos, like so many other islands, began to suffer from the incessant plague of piracy, and after a little more than a century of Western government the population was moved to the more secure Genoese island of Chios. The proximity of Samos to the mainland meant that it was thereafter one of the earliest islands to come under direct Turkish rule, probably during the 1470s.

Samians became known during the early history of the Greek War of Independence for their bravery and dedication, and Samiots joined the revolution in 1821 at the earliest possible moment, taking up arms in April of that year and murdering the entire local Turkish population. Samos contributed more than any of the other smaller Aegean islands to the cause of independence, and was given exceptional status at several stages in the development of the Hellenic state during the 19th century. A substantial castle, known as the Kastro tis Logothitis, was built in 1824 and it still occupies the hill to the west of Pithagorio; no other island is able to demonstrate the assertion of its independence at such an early date with a building of this kind. At the London Conference of 1829–30 it was proposed that Samos, with Crete, should be excluded from the geographical division of the rest of Greece, but the island was granted special privileges, and from 1834 to 1859 was governed by a Greek ruler, Stephanos Bogaridas. This autonomous status only came to an end in 1913 when, in the distribution of territories after the Balkan wars, Samos came under fully greek rule; from that point it received the same treatment and status as any other Aegean islands that were not then still under Turkish or (from 1912 in the case of the Dodecanese) Italian, rule.

PAUL HETHERINGTON

Summary

The closest of all Greek islands to the Turkish mainland, Samos first claims attention in the 6th century BC when it was ruled by the tyrant Polycrates. Monuments of this date include a tunnel (900 m long) ensuring the supply of water to the city of Samos, and the temple of Hera. Samos was very active in the War of Independence in the 1820s.

Further Reading

Barron, J.P., *The Silver Coins of Samos*, London: Athlone, 1966

Finlay, George, *A History of Greece from Its Conquest by the Romans to the Present Time, BC 146 to AD 1864*, revised by H.F. Tozer, 7 vols, Oxford: Clarendon Press, 1877; reprinted New York: AMS Press, 1970

Miller, William, *Essays on the Latin Orient*, Cambridge: Cambridge University Press, 1921; reprinted New York: AMS Press, 1983

Shipley, Graham, *A History of Samos, 800–188 BC*, Oxford: Clarendon Press, and New York: Oxford University Press, 1987

Woodhouse, C.M., *Modern Greece: A Short History*, 5th edition, London and Boston: Faber, 1991

Samothrace

Island in the northern Aegean

Samothrace lies in the northern Aegean, at a point approximately equidistant from Thasos, Alexandroupolis, and the Gallipoli peninsula. It covers an area of 176 sq km and is well watered and quite fertile, although it has a ruggedly mountainous interior. It was from the "topmost peak of wooded Samothrace" that Poseidon was said by Homer to have watched the fighting on the plains of Troy (*Iliad*, 13. 12). Pausanias (7. 4) records that it was first called Dardania, a name perpetuated in the important sea channel nearby of the Dardanelles. Samothrace has been populated from earliest times, but controversy surrounds the place of origin of its inhabitants. It was peopled initially by Thracians from the nearest part of the mainland of what is now northern Greece. In the Classical period colonists were said to have come to the island from Samos in the 8th century BC, hence its name. However, archaeological evidence tends to support Lesbos or the Troad as the source of these new settlers, though the Thracian dialect continued to be used until the end of the pre-Christian era.

The outstanding importance and fame of Samothrace in the Hellenic world was due to its being the focus of a cult, which caused the island to become the foremost religious centre in the northern Aegean from the 6th to the 1st century BC. The sanctuary of the Great Gods, excavation of which has continued for over a century, reveals that a complex process of initiation rites took place there. The mysteries that were enacted here are referred to by Plato and Aristophanes, and it is known that the historian Herodotus (among many others) underwent them. The physical remains of the sanctuary are immensely impressive; the rotunda, dedicated to the Great Gods by queen Arsinoe in the late 3rd century BC, is the largest circular structure known to have been built by Greek architects. The world-famous statue of the Winged Victory, also known as the Nike of Samothrace and now in the Louvre,

was found here in 1863. With the statue of Venus found on Melos it perhaps shares the distinction of representing the essence of the Hellenic artistic spirit of its age.

The prosperity of the island must have continued into the early medieval period, as an inscription records the restoration of baths here by the emperor Justinian; it formed part of the eparchy of Thrace in the 10th century. After 1204 it was awarded to the Latin emperor, and as its location was not as favourable as that of Lemnos, it was retained by his successors until 1261. Subsequently it was the Genoese dukedoms of the northern Aegean that were to leave the most substantial remains on Samothrace after the sanctuary of the Great Gods.

The Gattilusi dynasty, from Genoa, became more closely integrated into Greek life than almost any other of the Italian families that settled in the Aegean, and so have a place in the Hellenization of western European culture. The *kastro* (castle) that Palamede Gattilusi built in the 1430s at the Chora on Samothrace carries an inscription in Greek that states that "the fortress will strike fear into his enemies". The family was proud of having married into the Palaiologos dynasty in 1355, and the monogram of the imperial family figures on this inscription. When the antiquarian Cyriacus of Ancona visited the *kastro* in 1444, he called it "the new inland town". He also visited the towers that Palamede Gattilusi had built near to the sanctuary of the Great Gods, and mentioned the Classical inscriptions in both Latin and Greek that the Genoese lord had assembled in his tower, where "he loved greatly to hear learned discussions".

The victorious sultan Mehmet II dispossessed Palamede Gattilusi in 1456, but in the same year the island (with Lemnos and Thasos) was annexed by an Italian cardinal, Ludovico Trevisan, who had been sent as part of a crusade against the Turks by pope Callixtus III. For three years the banner of St Peter was flown from the *kastro* until Mehmet II retook the island, and it was to remain in Turkish hands (except for a brief Venetian hiatus of 1466–79) until 1912. Only then was the island able to resume its full place in the Hellenic island tradition.

PAUL HETHERINGTON

Summary

An island in the northern Aegean, Samothrace was traditionally colonized from Samos, though this is not supported by archaeology. The island's fame rests on the mystery cult of the Great Gods (Cabiri), the remains of whose sanctuary survive. The *kastro* (fortress) built by the Genoese duke Palamede Gattilusi dates from the 1430s.

Further Reading

Lehmann, Phyllis Williams and Karl Lehmann, *Samothracian Reflections: Aspects of the Revival of the Antique*, Princeton, New Jersey: Princeton University Press, 1973

Miller, William, *Essays on the Latin Orient*, Cambridge: Cambridge University Press, 1921; reprinted New York: AMS Press, 1983

Setton, Kenneth M., *The Papacy and the Levant, 1204–1571*, vol. 2: *The Fifteenth Century*, Philadelphia: American Philosophical Society, 1978

Sanctuaries

In the context of Classical Greece a "sanctuary" is best defined as a sacred space, formally bounded and set aside for ritual activity. In historical times at least, such centres usually provided sanctuary in the sense of asylum for refugees from human or divine persecution.

Most of the important sanctuaries of Classical Greece were founded or underwent major development from the 8th century BC. The traditional date of 776 BC for the foundation of the Olympic Games is a good benchmark. The evidence is at first provided chiefly by sacrificial debris and small-scale votive offerings (among which pottery and terracotta and bronze figurines are prominent) at sites such as the sanctuary of Zeus at Olympia. Modest temples were sometimes built, but the most prominent structural and ritual component of the sanctuary was always the altar where sacrifical victims were burned.

Although ritual activity in sanctuaries was standardized to a degree (public and private sacrifice, votive offerings, some components of festivals), there were numerous local variations corresponding to the character of the individual cults.

Greek sanctuaries developed an increasingly monumental character after 700 BC, with first temples, then other buildings, constructed of ashlar masonry. These tended to accumulate slowly and haphazardly (e.g. at Olympia) in and around the sacred area. Only in the Hellenistic period did formal regular planning become the norm and then it could be effectively applied only to new or previously undeveloped sites (e.g. the Asclepieum on Cos).

The architectural character of sanctuaries, such as that of Apollo at Delphi in the late-Classical and Hellenistic periods, when structural development was most intense, provides the clearest indication of the major aspects of the festivals – athletic competitions (stadia, gymnasia, baths, offerings of victors), theatrical events (theatres, offerings). Their administration and the importance of the major sanctuaries (especially the Panhellenic centres of Olympia, Delphi, Isthmia, and Nemea) as international meeting places are indicated by other elements, such as *bouleuteria* (council chambers) and treasuries, as well as significant sculptural and architectural dedications, which often had a propaganda intent. Some of these functions are likely to go back to the period of expansion of the sanctuaries in the 8th century BC, although (unless the large bronze tripods from Olympia are athletic prizes, as is sometimes thought) there is little direct evidence, since most of them can be carried on without the need for any formal structures (races can be run on open ground: a stadium is a luxury).

In the Roman period the use of the Greek sanctuaries continued uninterrupted, although new buildings (the bath houses are particularly common and striking) were regularly added in the new and distinctive building style of concrete and brick. The appearance of temples to house the imperial cult (there was a temple to Rome and Augustus on the Athenian Acropolis) is another distinctive feature.

As Christianity gradually took hold of the Roman world, especially after its adoption in AD 313 by the emperor Constantine, the pagan sanctuaries went into decline, although they continued to be patronized at least until closed by edict of Justinian in AD 529.

The fact that many ancient sanctuaries have later Christian churches within their boundaries (at Olympia the workshop of Phidias was converted into a church in the 5th century AD), and particularly that some of these (the basilica at the sanctuary of Asclepius, Epidaurus, c.AD 400) seem to have been built before the pagan complex became defunct, shows that sometimes paganism and Christianity intermingled and that the places retained their sacred character, even when the formal nature of the religion changed. Some later monasteries (e.g. at Daphni, on the outskirts of Athens) are even built on the sites of ancient sanctuaries, and the modern buildings incorporate material from the ancient.

While the sanctuary in the sense defined at the beginning of this entry seems essentially a creation of the Geometric period and to have died with the banning of pagan religion, various similarities of form and function can be identified at sites of both earlier and later periods. In Greece some prehistoric sites have been designated sanctuaries, with varying degrees of probability and correspondence to the above definition. Although the Neolithic period is a blank, in the Early Bronze Age the Cycladic island of Keros has sometimes been thought a sanctuary on the grounds of unusually rich discoveries of marble artefacts, but this is disputed. More plausible is the rustic shrine at Korfi t'Aroniou on Naxos, which was uniquely adorned by decorated stone blocks.

In Minoan Crete the most convincing candidates are the peak sanctuaries, remote hilltop sites with clear evidence of exclusively ritual activity (sacrifice, votive offerings). The Middle Minoan complex at Anemopsilia, near Archanes, is perhaps a temple rather than a sanctuary, but its ritual use is undoubted. Sacred groves are sometimes identified in scenes in art (seal stones, the "sacred grove" fresco from Knossos). Some houses (especially Xeste 3) at Akrotiri on the Cycladic island of Thera have extensive and clearly ritual painted scenes but their assignation as sanctuaries is difficult, since the focus again seems to be on the individual building rather than a sanctuary area; the same is true of other ritual structures, such as the "temple" on the island of Kea, the Mycenaean-type "sanctuary" at Phylakopi on Melos, the "cult centre" at Mycenae itself (a stronger candidate), or the shrine area at Mycenaean Tiryns.

It is impossible to say how far the elaborate festivals, often involving athletic and dramatic competitions, so characteristic of Classical sanctuaries, may have existed in prehistoric times, but there is so far no evidence for the sort of installations that later became the norm. One could however appeal to the funeral games mentioned in Homer or the scenes of chariots on Mycenaean gravestones and vases as hints of similar activities in earlier times.

While a few important later sanctuaries (Hera on Samos, Apollo Maleatas at Epidaurus, etc.) have produced virtually certain evidence of continuous use from prehistoric times into Classical antiquity, the extent to which this reflects continuity of religious belief and practice in detail is obscure. As well as these possible prehistoric predecessors, the continued use of parts of some sanctuary sites after AD 529 has already been mentioned. Several aspects of ancient practice associated with sanctuaries find echoes even up to the present day, although the degree of genuine continuity is hard to assess, partly because people look for similar relationships with their gods, whether Christian or pagan, and may approach them with similar rituals.

Votive plaques seem to have lasted from antiquity, through Byzantine times, to the present day. Representations of diseased limbs etc., similar to those that used to be offered to Asclepius, can still be seen in Orthodox churches.

The annual patronal festival of each Orthodox church takes on a festive character that involves the sharing of a meal. In several parts of Greece animals are slaughtered on the spot. One example of this is on Imbros (now under Turkish control), where the festival of the Dormition on 15 August is accompanied by the blessing and slaughtering of animals, and the cooking and consumption of the meat. Patronal festivals are still occasions for reunion of émigré locals from all over the world and, as in antiquity, larger festivals are used as occasions for secular activities (fairs etc.). They may also be the occasion for political pronouncements. In Cyprus, up until quite recent times, cattle markets took place at some festivals.

Occasionally too contemporary religious festivals are accompanied by competitive events, such as that at Hagios Soulas on Rhodes, described by Lawrence Durrell in *Reflections on a Marine Venus* (1953), where the saint is honoured *inter alia* with athletic contests and horse and donkey races. On Lesbos, at Hagia Paraskevi, the festival of Hagios Charalambos includes the slaughter of bulls and an equestrian parade and races.

ROBIN L.N. BARBER

See also Architecture (Religious), Festivals, Healing Cults, Votive Offerings

Further Reading

Bergquist, Birgitta, *The Archaic Greek Temenos: A Study of Structure and Function*, Lund: Gleerup, 1967
Burkert, Walter, *Greek Religion: Archaic and Classical*, Oxford: Blackwell, and Cambridge, Massachusetts: Harvard University Press, 1985
Desborough, V.R.d'A., *The Greek Dark Ages*, London: Benn, and New York: St Martin's Press, 1972
Durrell, Lawrence, *Reflections on a Marine Venus: A Companion to the Landscape of Rhodes*, London: Faber, 1953; New York: Marlowe, 1996
Hägg, Robin and Nanno Marinatos, *Sanctuaries and Cults in the Aegean Bronze Age*, Stockholm: Svenska Institute i Athen, 1981
Hägg, Robin and Nanno Marinatos (editors), *Greek Sanctuaries: New Approaches*, London and New York: Routledge, 1993
Lawson, John Cuthbert, *Modern Greek Folklore and Ancient Greek Religion: A Study in Survivals*, Cambridge: Cambridge University Press, 1910, reprinted New York: University Books, 1964
Megas, Georgios A., *Greek Calendar Customs*, 3rd edition, Athens, 1982
Nilsson, Martin P., *The Minoan-Mycenaean Religion and Its Survival in Greek Religion*, 2nd edition, Lund: Gleerup, 1950; reprinted New York: Biblo and Tannen, 1971
Petropoulos, D.A., "Survivances de sacrifices des animaux en Grèce", in *Papers of the International Congress of European and Western Ethnology, Stockholm, 1951*, edited by Sigurd Erixon, Stockholm: International Commission on Folk Arts and Folklore, 1955
Peatfield, A.A.D., "Minoan Peak Sanctuaries: History and Society", in *Opuscula Atheniensia*, 18 (1990): pp. 117–31
Psychogiou, E., "Thysia Tavron kai Nekrika Ethima st' Agridia tis Imbrou" [Bull Sacrifices and Funerary Customs at Agridia on Imbros], *Archaiologia*, 41 (1991): pp. 83–91 (includes short summary in English and useful bibliography)
Tomlinson, R.A., *Greek Sanctuaries*, London: Elek, and New York: St Martin's Press, 1976

Santorini

Island in the Cyclades

This form of the island's name is Frankish, from Santa Irini, one of the local churches. In antiquity, as often nowadays, it was called Thera, also at times Kalliste and Strongyle. At the southeast of the Cycladic group, it is geologically the most remarkable of the Cyclades, since it contains an active volcano.

Although there have been numerous recorded volcanic episodes over the last 4000 years, sometimes severe, the most violent concluded with the explosion and collapse of the crater in a massive catastrophe during the Bronze Age (*c.*1500 BC, or 1628 BC if recent scientific analyses are correctly interpreted). During the eruption phases at that time the volcano disgorged pumice and tephra (volcanic ash). The latter covered the island with a layer up to 50 m thick. This extraordinary event is thought by some to have been the source of the myth reported by Plato of the submerged city of Atlantis. Research has shown that tephra was also deposited in substantial quantities on Crete, Rhodes, and the mainland of Asia Minor, with potentially serious consequences for the agriculture of those areas. The massive tidal wave which followed the collapse of the crater almost certainly inflicted heavy damage on coastal sites in the southern Aegean. The psychological consequences of this catastrophe cannot now be accurately assessed but were surely profound, and must have played a part in the transfer of political and cultural authority in the Aegean from Minoan Crete to the Mycenaeans of mainland Greece, by weakening the former.

At the time of the eruption the material culture of Thera was spectacular. Archaeological work near Akrotiri since 1967 has uncovered a town with many buildings in fine ashlar masonry and richly decorated with frescos. If the unusually good state of preservation has not led to an overestimation of the significance of Late Bronze Age Thera, it may well have been a centre of architecture and the arts whose influence spread throughout the Aegean. Even if, as seems more probable, the artistic and technical achievements of the Therans were learnt from the Cretan palaces, it was nonetheless probably a centre of Cretan authority in the Aegean and must have acted as a conduit through which ideas and techniques were exchanged.

In later mythology Thera got its name from Theras, who supposedly came there with a group of settlers from Sparta. This would explain the Dorian character of the island. Thera seems to have had significant settlement from the Geometric period and produced locally distinctive Geometric and Orientalizing pottery. The earliest remains of the ancient town, on an impressive but remote site high on Mesa Vouno, belong to the Archaic period. The nearby cemetery (Sellada) has produced finds from the Geometric period onwards, including three archaic *kouroi* (nude statues of standing young men). Therans founded the colony of Cyrene in 631 BC, according to Herodotus because their homeland was devastated by a long drought. The place flourished particularly in Hellenistic times, to which many of its surviving remains belong and when it was a forward naval station under the Ptolemies. It does not seem to have been particularly important in the Roman or Byzantine periods, although there are remains of both, including the painted church of the Panagia Episkopi, reputedly founded by the emperor Alexios I Komnenos (1081–1118).

From 1207 (apart from a brief interlude in 1269 when it was retaken by the Byzantines), it was in the hands of various Frankish families – the Sanudi, the Barotsi, the Crispi, etc. In the 15th century the island's prosperity was curtailed by pirate raids and it became impoverished and depopulated. Several hundred families fled to Crete. In 1537 it was captured by Barbarossa and became part of the Ottoman empire, though without much direct interference. In 1821 the Greek flag was raised.

ROBIN L.N. BARBER

Summary

Santorini (or Thera) was a flourishing centre of prehistoric civilization of which remarkable artistic remains survive. The volcanic eruption of the island which brought that to an end may be the source of the legend of Atlantis. In early antiquity the island was prosperous and took part in the colonizing movement. In the medieval and later periods its history was similar to that of the other Cyclades.

Further Reading

Doumas, Christos G., *Thera, Pompeii of the Ancient Aegean: Excavations at Akrotiri, 1967–79*, London and New York: Thames and Hudson, 1983

Fouqué, F., *Santorini and Its Eruptions*, edited and translated by Alexander R. McBirney, Baltimore: Johns Hopkins University Press, 1998 (original edition, 1879)

Hiller von Gaertringen, Friedrich, *Thera*, vols 1–4, Berlin: Reimer, 1899–1909; vol. 5, Berlin: Mann, 1997

Koukkou, Helene, *Oi Koinotikoi Thesmoi stis Kyklades kata ten Tourkokratia* [Social Institutions in the Cyclades during the Tourkokratia], Athens, 1980

Lock, Peter, *The Franks in the Aegean, 1204–1500*, London and New York: Longman, 1995

Luce, J.V., *The End of Atlantis: New Light on an Old Legend*, London: Thames and Hudson, 1969; New York: Bantam, 1978

Marinatos, Spyridon, *Some Words About the Legend of Atlantis*, 2nd edition, Athens, 1971, reprinted 1972 (first published 1950)

Page, D.L., *The Santorini Volcano and the Destruction of Minoan Crete*, London: Society for the Promotion of Hellenic Studies, 1970

Papamanolis, I., *I Nisos Thira-Santorini* [The Island of Thera-Santorini], Piraeus, 1932

Sappho

Poet of the 7th–6th centuries BC

Born probably at Eressos on Lesbos around 630 BC, Sappho was a contemporary of Alcaeus and of Pittacus, the tyrant of Lesbos. Her family may have been involved in the same upheavals among aristocratic factions that feature prominently in Alcaeus, since sometime before 595–594 BC she is said to have been exiled to Syracuse, where there was a statue of her

down to the 1st century BC. She seems otherwise to have spent most of her life in Mytilene.

The remains of Sappho's poetry consist of one whole poem (poem 1), preserved by Dionysius of Halicarnassus as an example of the "smooth and exuberant" style, in which she invokes Aphrodite to assist her in love; about ten substantial fragments, including five stanzas (poem 31) preserved by "Longinus", describing the physical symptoms of love; 100 short citations from ancient writers; and around 50 papyrus fragments. The poems are written in the Aeolic dialect native to Lesbos. Unlike that of Alcaeus, Sappho's extant poetry barely mentions contemporary politics, and her focus of interest instead is on individual emotion, and the traditional female concerns of love, marriage, and beauty. This focus accords with the general tendency of the early lyric poets to reject the Homeric role of poet as impersonal narrator. No more than the other lyricists, however, did Sappho ignore Homer, and some of her poetry seems to recast Homeric themes from a female perspective.

Her poetry indicates intense romantic and probable sexual involvement with some of the young women of whom she writes. The exact nature of these relationships must remain uncertain because our evidence is so fragmentary: possibly as early as Anacreon, but certainly by the time of Ovid's *Heroides*, the affairs were assumed to be sexual. Female same-sex love is rarely mentioned, though not unattested, in early Greece, and may have become taboo later on, but one may assume that such relationships and sentiments were acceptable in the Lesbos of Sappho's time. A relatively large number of her poems concern young girls, marriage, or farewells. It is therefore sometimes suggested that her poetry reflects a social structure in which young girls came to Sappho prior to marriage for some kind of education in music and other arts, and romantic or sexual involvement was part of the educative process. If so, one may compare the better-attested educational relationships between men and boys in the ancient world. Sappho's passionate descriptions of female beauty may be intended to inspire male desire for the girls in marriage – the destination of all Greek girls – as much as it expresses any personal feelings of Sappho herself. Some of the content of Alcman's *Partheneia* may be comparable.

Lesbos was home to an unusually large number of early poets – Terpander and Arion as well as Alcaeus and Sappho. It was also known for the beauty of its women, and as both a gifted poet and a celebrator of female beauty Sappho may be regarded as typical of her island. In later tradition she is regarded as anomalous precisely because of these two features. Although she was not the only female poet in the ancient world, she seems to have outshone others to such a degree that Galen states that "the poet" is Homer, and "the poetess" Sappho. Again, the intense passion of the poems has had a clear effect on her later reputation: one may guess that such passion was unusual, at least from a woman. One late tradition divides Sappho into two people – one a remarkable lyric poet, the other a sex-crazed courtesan. Down to Roman times, emphasis is less on the female objects of her passion than the passion itself, with the result that in Greek comic traditions she is portrayed as heterosexually voracious. Popular tradition recounts that she fell in love with a fisherman called Phaon and threw herself off the Leucadian rock when her passion was unrequited. The story probably derives from mistaken extrapolation from her verse: it appears on vases of the late 5th century BC, and was popular among comic poets from the 4th century BC. Roman attitudes to sexuality focused more on the female objects of her passions, and the concerns of the late 20th century have made Sappho's perceived lesbian sexuality nearly as important as her poetry.

Ancient sources unanimously praise her brilliance. She is a subject of vase painting from the late 6th century BC. She found favour with Solon and Plato's Socrates, and she is the subject of treatises from at least the 4th century BC. The Alexandrian scholars included her in the canon of the ten lyric poets, arranging her songs in nine books, according to metre. Theocritus, Callimachus, Apollonius, Moschus, and Bion all show her influence. Epigrams honour her: Dioscorides in the late 3rd century BC calls her the tenth Muse, and this honorific title becomes conventional for her thereafter. Her fame in her native island was such that coins from Mytilene of the 1st to 3rd centuries AD bear her portrait.

Sappho's poetic reputation has survived on progressively slimmer evidence, since she suffered the fate of all those writers whose subject matter or dialect did not suit the educational requirements of the later ancient world. Her difficult dialect rendered her writing unsuitable for inclusion in a canon that increasingly favoured Attic Greek: the lyric poets are notoriously under-represented in the body of texts that came to form the educational canon. Moreover, her passionate subject matter, like that of many other lyricists, did not suit the prevailing preference for texts suitable for the classroom.

As the canon came to dominate textual production, fewer and fewer noncanonical texts were copied, especially in the 2nd–4th centuries AD when the transition from the book roll to the codex took place. Even so, some of Sappho's poems did make that transition, and in the 2nd century AD the poems seem to have been popular as after-dinner entertainment. Most surviving papyrus fragments of her poetry may be dated to the 2nd and 3rd centuries AD. Gradually, however, Sappho came to be quoted in short citations more for grammatical or metrical peculiarities than for literary reasons, although writers down to the 6th century AD quote her and show some familiarity with her works. A parchment from Egypt shows that she still had an audience even in the 7th century AD.

After this the trail starts to go cold. This is more likely to be due to a general decline in circulation of all but the most standard authors than to Christian distaste for her subject matter. It is sometimes asserted that her books were burned, for example by Gregory VII in 1073, but the evidence for this is far from conclusive. Although the 9th-century lexicographer Photios cites her, the *Etymologicum Magnum* of *c.*1000 mentions her only five times and later encyclopaedias after the *Suda* ignore her. Byzantines of the 12th century and later mention her, but it is impossible to determine whether their knowledge derives directly from texts or from reference works. Tzetzes even claims that her work had disappeared by his time, although this may be an exaggeration. Certainly after the sack of Constantinople in 1453 rare texts such as hers are unlikely to have survived. In 1546 Robert Estienne published the first edition of Dionysius of Halicarnassus, which contains

Sappho's only complete surviving poem, and in 1554 there followed the edition of "Longinus".

SOPHIE MILLS

See also Poetry (Lyric)

Biography

Born at Eressos on Lesbos *c.*630 BC, Sappho was a contemporary of the poet Alcaeus. She may have been involved in local politics, for she was exiled to Syracuse in the 590s, but she spent most of her life in Mytilene. Very little of her poetry survives but it was much admired in antiquity. Her passionate subject matter may not have endeared her to the Byzantines.

Writings

In *Greek Lyric*, vol. 1, translated by David A. Campbell, Cambridge, Massachusetts: Harvard University Press, and London: Heinemann, 1982 (Loeb edition)

Further Reading

Hallett, J.P., "Sappho and Her Social Context", *Signs*, 4 (1979): pp. 447ff.
Johnson, W.R., foreword to *Sappho's Lyre: Archaic, Lyric and Women Poets of Ancient Greece*, edited and translated by Diane J. Rayor, Berkeley: University of California Press, 1991
Lardinois, Andre, "Lesbian Sappho and Sappho of Lesbos" in *From Sappho to de Sade: Moments in the History of Sexuality*, edited by Jan Bremmer, London and New York: Routledge, 1989
Lefkowitz, Mary, "Critical Stereotypes and the Poetry of Sappho", *Greek, Roman and Byzantine Studies*, 14 (1973): pp. 113ff.
Page, D.L., *Sappho and Alcaeus: An Introduction to the Study of Ancient Lesbian Poetry*, Oxford: Clarendon Press, 1955; reprinted 1979
Reynolds L.D. and N.G. Wilson, *Scribes and Scholars: A Guide to the Transmission of Greek and Latin Literature*, 3rd edition, Oxford: Clarendon Press, and New York: Oxford University Press, 1991
Robinson, D.M., *Sappho and Her Influence*, New York: Cooper Square, 1963
Snyder, Jane McIntosh, *The Woman and the Lyre: Women Writers in Classical Greece and Rome*, Carbondale: Southern Illinois University Press, 1989
Stigers, Eva S., "Sappho's Private World" in *Reflections of Women in Antiquity*, edited by Helene P. Foley, New York and London: Gordon and Breach, 1981
Williamson, Margaret, *Sappho's Immortal Daughters*, Cambridge, Massachusetts: Harvard University Press, 1995

Sarakatsans

Nomadic people of northern and central Greece

Up until 30 years ago it was possible to find in Greece a shy breed of nomads living in straw huts, known as Sarakatsans. In Bulgaria similar nomads, also speaking Greek, were called Karakatchans, but their way of life had been regulated, although not abolished, by communist bureaucracy. There were over 4500 Karakatchans in the 1965 census, and this number is almost certainly an underestimate. In the 1980s the Karakatchans seemed to be doing rather well in Bulgaria, the authorities having decided that collective farming in winter and summer pasturage was best left in their hands, but the

Sarakatsans: a traditional straw hut of the Sarakatsans. A hut such as this houses a family of six or seven adults and is erected by five or six women in two to three days.

collapse of communism has led to much emigration to Greece. In Greece the forces of capitalism and bureaucracy have led to collapse in the Sarakatsan way of life. Sometimes wandering families of Sarakatsans were settled in Greek villages, causing a certain amount of resentment from the villagers, some of whom as semi-nomadic transhumants like the Vlachs felt that they had a better claim to the land being settled. Alternatively the Sarakatsans, used to travelling long distances, made with other emigrants from the Balkans the pilgrimage to Germany in search of employment as *Gastarbeiter*. Here they rapidly lost their distinctive identity and gave up their way of life, so different from that practised in western Europe. Sarakatsans used to be found in the mountain ranges of Macedonia, Epirus, Thessaly, and even Boeotia and Attica. In Bulgaria they roamed the Rhodopes and the Haemus mountains. Now one can occasionally find them in mountain villages, frequently confused with the Vlachs. Because of their nomadic habits it is hard to tie them down to one place, and their lack of regional identity is a further factor which will probably lead to their disappearance.

If the future of the Sarakatsans seems dim, their past is yet more obscure. Scholars are divided as to whether they are Hellenized Vlachs or pure Greeks. The former theory rests on certain common habits like transhumance with a biannual journey beginning on St George's Day (23 April) and ending on St Demetrius' Day (26 October), and certain common words like *tselnik*, the leader of a tribe, and *kalivi*, a hut. On the other hand, Vlachs, though confused with Sarakatsans, are contemptuous of them. Customs in such matters as marriage ceremonies and the construction of huts are different in the two groups. Most scholarly opinion holds that the Sarakatsans are purely Greek, indeed more purely so than the average Greek. An occasional straight nose, reminiscent of a Minoan fresco, seen on a Sarakatsan, and the geometric pattern of their costume lend support to the theory, well argued by Hoeg and Hadjimichalis, that the Sarakatsans are an ancient Dorian tribe who somehow never became incorporated in the life of ancient and medieval Greece. Leigh Fermor, who travelled among the Sarakatsans of western Thrace, put a romantic gloss on this theory, imagining a people who somehow managed to escape from history, bypassing the Persian invasion, the empire of Alexander the Great, the Roman conquest, the Slav invasions, and even the fall of Constantinople in the same way that their modern descendants by being constantly on the move have managed to bypass the apparatus of the modern state.

Such a theory, as Kavadias has pointed out, flies in the face of linguistic and historical evidence. There is no mention in ancient or medieval sources of a fully nomadic Greek tribe like the Sarakatsans, although there are references to non-Greek nomads, such as the Scythians, and of transhumance as practised by shepherds in *Oedipus Rex* and by the medieval Vlachs. Nor does the language spoken by the Sarakatsans, although it contains several archaic features, show like Tsakonian any resemblance to the pre-koine dialect. It seems more likely that the Sarakatsans were Greeks settled in the Byzantine empire who, when this empire collapsed in the 13th century, took to a wandering life in the mountains in order to preserve their Greekness and their ancient customs.

It is in their customs rather than their language that the Sarakatsans show their ancient roots. Many of their rituals display a strange syncretism between Christianity and perhaps pre-Classical paganism. Campbell establishes well the Sarakatsan subordination of women to men, combined with a protective reverence to the female sex. In Sarakatsan marches the place of honour at the rear of the column is taken by the last woman to be married; the Vlachs give this post to an old man. Any offence against female chastity is severely punished, particularly if it is the woman who is the sinner. As with so many minority groups, the moral values that kept Sarakatsans together as a close-knit community receive scant respect in the modern world.

T.J. Winnifrith

See also Transhumance

Summary
A nomadic Greek-speaking people, the Sarakatsans used to inhabit the mountainous areas of Macedonia, Epirus, Thessaly, Boeotia, and Attica. In Bulgaria they were known as Karakatchans. Their origins are obscure and the subject of debate. In recent decades they have mostly lost their identity.

Further Reading
Campbell, J.K., *Honour, Family and Patronage: A Study of Institutions and Moral Values in a Greek Mountain Community*, Oxford: Clarendon Press, 1964
Hoëg, Carsten, *Les Saracatsans: une tribu nomade grecque*, Paris: Champion, 2 vols, 1925–26
Kavadias, Georges B., *Pasteurs-nomades méditeranéens: les Saracatsans de Grèce*, Paris, 1965
Leigh Fermor, Patrick, *Roumeli: Travels in Northern Greece*, London: Murray, and New York: Harper and Row, 1966
Marinov, V., *Die Schafzucht der Nomadisierenden Karacakatschanen in Bulgarien*, Budapest, 1961

Sassanians

Persian dynasty

The name Sassanians, given to the royal dynasty which ruled the third Persian empire from AD 224 to 651, derives from Sasan, possibly the grandfather of the first Sassanian king, Ardashir I (224–39/40) (Tabari 1. 814). Ardashir's family ruled as local dynasts of the Parthian empire in Istakhr, near Persepolis, but he extended his power to Elymais and Kerman, forcing the submission of local kings and vassals. On 28 April 224 Ardashir defeated the Parthian king Artabanus IV in a battle on the plain of Hormazdjan in Media and, after the capture of the Parthian capital Ctesiphon, celebrated his official enthronement there as "king of kings". At its utmost extent the empire of the Sassanians stretched from Syria to India, and from the Caucasus to the Persian Gulf, but borders changed frequently in its 427-year existence. Middle Persian was the principal language of the Sassanians, though Parthian, Greek, Aramaic, and Bactrian, among others, were also used.

Throughout Sassanian rule the Persian empire was faced with two principal enemies, the Romans in the west, and invading tribes from the north and northeast. Though written Greek and Roman sources focus predominantly on the Persian–Roman aggressions, the constant threats to the Sassanian empire from nomadic peoples were equally serious and have to be taken into account. Relations between Rome and Persia were characterized by their respective ideologies. As with their attitude towards the Parthians, the Romans saw their fight against Persia in the ideological light of the Graeco-Persian wars of 490 BC and 480/79 BC and Alexander's conquest of Persia in 331 BC. Alexander Severus, like Caracalla, regarded himself as a "second Alexander" (Dio, 79. 17. 3) while Gordian III celebrated a festival in honour of Athena Promachos for the Athenians at Marathon prior to his eastern campaign. The Sassanians, though they lacked any direct knowledge of the first Persian dynasty, laid claims to the heritage of the Achaemenids. Politically this was manifested in the use of Achaemenid sites in Fars, and militarily in their claim to Achaemenid domains, which in particular meant the region west of the Euphrates river. This was the prime motivation for their western campaigns, though the reconquest of this region was never achieved.

Hostilities against Rome began with raids into Syrian territory in AD 230, and escalated under Shapur I (239/40–70/72), who claimed victories over Gordian III (244), Philip the Arab (244), and Valerian (260). Roman–Persian aggression continued under Shapur's successors, and Ctesiphon was briefly taken by the Romans (283). Between 337 and 363 the Persians under Shapur II (309–79) fought intermittently against the Romans, but a peace settlement agreed under Shapur III (383–88) led, with one brief exception in 421–22, to a long period of peace, which lasted until the beginning of the 6th century. Shapur II undertook a campaign against the Arabs, and settled Arab tribes in Iraq as protection against the desert Arabs and those Arab tribes who supported Rome. The threat of invading nomads became reality in 395 when Huns invaded Armenia and even reached Syria and Cappadocia.

After a period marked by seven years of famine during the reign of Peroz (459–84), by Sassanian defeat by the Hephtalites (White Huns), and by inner revolt, a phase of revival began with Chosroes I (531–79). Though his reign also saw Persia at war with Byzantium, Chosroes I reached several peace settlements with Justinian I in 545, 551, and 561. The 6th century was a period of close cultural exchange between Persia, China, and Byzantium. The three thrones, which stood beneath the throne of Chosroes I in Ctesiphon, ready to receive the emperors of Rome and China and the great khan of Central Asia as his subjects, are perhaps the best demonstration of the fact that the Sassanians were well aware of their central position between the eastern and western empires. Cultural exchange between the Far East and the Mediterranean was transmitted through merchants and traders as well as the Syriac-speaking Christians of Mesopotamia. Through them Byzantine medicine and philosophy became known in Ctesiphon, while in 527 Nestorian Christian scholars from Nisibis were received in Constantinople. In 638 Nestorians explained their religious beliefs to the emperor of China, while Indian science and knowledge found their way into the west via Ctesiphon.

Chrosroes I defeated the Hephtalites in 568, an achievement which he commemorated on specially minted coins. Chosroes II (590–628) undertook major campaigns, invading Byzantium (603), taking Antioch and Jerusalem (614), and Egypt (619), but he was met with an equally strong opponent, Herakleios (610–41), who marched against the Sassanian king in 622. The fall of the Sassanian empire, however, was brought about by a third power, which both Byzantium and Persia had neglected with grave consequences—the Arabs, who invaded Persia and the Roman Near East in the mid-7th century.

The cities of Ctesiphon, Firuzabad, and Bishapur were the main seats of Sassanian power. At its centre was the king, who ruled as a god-king (*bay*) with the divine sanction of Ahura Mazda (*yazd*), together with his queen, whose public role is well documented on rock reliefs and on coins. The king was the guardian of the Zoroastrian religion, though other religions—Judaism, Christianity, and Manichaeism—were, depending on the respective king, tolerated. The aristocracy consisted of four groups, the local dynasts (*shahrdar*), the princes (*vaspuhragan*), the heads of the noble houses (*vuzurgan*), and the Persian nobility (*azadan*). These were followed by a middle class of merchants, craftsmen, and traders, as well as peasants and slaves, about all of whom very little is known. In the 4th century high offices emerged in religion and politics: the head of the high priests (*mobad*), the great priest (reconstructed term: *vuzurg mobad*), and the priests themselves (*mobads*), and in the political sphere the head of the farmers (*vastaryoshan salar*) and the head of the army (*arteshtaran salar*).

Frequent military aggression between the Romans and the Sassanians undoubtedly led to reciprocal influence in weaponry and military tactics. Under Chosroes I Sassanian fortifications seemed to follow the prototype of the Roman *limes,* while it is thought that equipment of the heavily armoured Sassanian cavalry, the cataphract, which had been developed in their wars against the nomads, was adopted by the Roman army (*clibanarii*; Ammianus Marcelinus, 16. 10. 8). The claim that a mutual influence existed in the respective administration and fiscal policy of the Sassanian and Roman empires has yet to be convincingly demonstrated, but in art and architecture reciprocal inspiration is well attested. Sassanian artistic elements can be traced in Byzantine decorative motifs, and it is thought that the Persian dome-structured buildings provided the prototype for Byzantine architecture. The find of a silver jug with Classical figures in China, and a silver gilt *rhyton* (drinking horn) from Tibet decorated in a Classical/Sassanian style, are evidence that Persia was the transmitting power of western and Sassanian culture.

MARIA BROSIUS

Summary

The Sassanians were the royal dynasty which ruled the Persian empire from AD 224 to 651. Hostilities with Rome were frequent for the first 150 years. Revival came with the reign of Chosroes I (531–79). In the 6th century there was close interchange between Persia, China, and Byzantium. The Sassanians were defeated by Herakleios in 622. Their empire fell to the Arabs in the mid-7th century.

Further Reading

Boardman, John, *The Diffusion of Classical Art in Antiquity*, Princeton, New Jersey: Princeton University Press, 1994

Brown, Peter, *The World of Late Antiquity*, London: Thames and Hudson, and New York: Harcourt Brace, 1971

Cameron, Averil, *The Mediterranean World in Late Antiquity*, AD 395–600, London and New York: Routledge, 1993

Cameron, Averil and Peter Garnsey (editors), *The Late Empire*, AD 337–425, Cambridge: Cambridge University Press, 1998 (*The Cambridge Ancient History*, vol. 13, 2nd edition)

Ettinghausen, R., "A Persian Treasure", *Arts in Virginia*, 8 (1967–68): pp. 29–41

Frye, Richard N., "The Political History of Iran under the Sasanians" in *The Seleucid, Parthian, and Sasanian Periods*, edited by Ehsan Yarshater, Cambridge: Cambridge University Press, 1983 (*The Cambridge History of Iran*, vol. 3, part 1)

Frye, Richard N., *The History of Ancient Iran*, Munich: Beck, 1984

Garsoïan, N., "Byzantium and the Sasanians" in *The Seleucid, Parthian, and Sasanian Periods*, edited by Ehsan Yarshater, Cambridge: Cambridge University Press, 1983 (*The Cambridge History of Iran*, vol. 3, part 1)

Harper, P.O., "Art in Iran, 5: Sasanian", *Encyclopaedia Iranica*, vol. 2, London: Routledge, 1987

Herrmann, Georgina, *The Iranian Revival*, Oxford: Elsevier / Phaidon, 1977

Huff, D., "Archaeology, 4: Sasanian", *Encyclopaedia Iranica*, vol. 2, London: Routledge, 1987

Kröger, J., "Ctesiphon", *Encyclopaedia Iranica*, vol. 6, 1993

Millar, Fergus, *The Roman Near East, 31 BC –AD 337*, Cambridge, Massachusetts: Harvard University Press, London: Routledge, 1993

Schippmann, Klaus, *Grundzüge der Geschichte des sasanidischen Reiches*, Darmstadt: Wissenschaftiche Buchgesellschaft, 1990

Tabari, *The History of Al-Tabari*, edited by Ehsan Yarshater, vol. 5: *The Sasanids, the Byzantines, the Lakhmids, and Yemen*, translated and annotated by C.E. Bosworth, Albany: State University of New York Press, 1999

Wiesehöfer, Josef, "Iranische Ansprüche an Rom auf ehemals achaimenidische Territorien", *Archäologische Mitteilungen aus Iran, Neue Folge*, 19 (1986): pp. 177–85

Wiesehöfer, Josef, "Ardašīr", *Encyclopaedia Iranica*, vol. 2, London: Routledge, 1987

Wiesehöfer, Josef, *Ancient Persia: From 550 BC to 650 AD*, London and New York: Tauris, 1996

Satyr Play

The satyr play was a type of Classical Greek drama that stood midway between tragedy and comedy. Satyr plays were composed by tragedians and performed with tragedies at dramatic festivals in Athens; the rules of these contests required that each tragedian present three tragedies followed by a satyr play. Satyr plays also resembled tragedies in being concerned with mythological subjects for the most part, rather than with contemporary ones, as were comedies. Like comedies, however, satyr plays were humorous, irreverent, and frequently obscene. The chorus was always composed of satyrs, mythological servants of Dionysus who were partly human but had horses' hooves, ears, and tails and wore enormous erect phalluses.

Satyrs were known for their wildness, drunkenness, cowardice, sexual appetite, and total lack of the virtues of civilization. The one satyr play that survives intact, Euripides' *Cyclops*, makes use of these attributes to produce a very funny

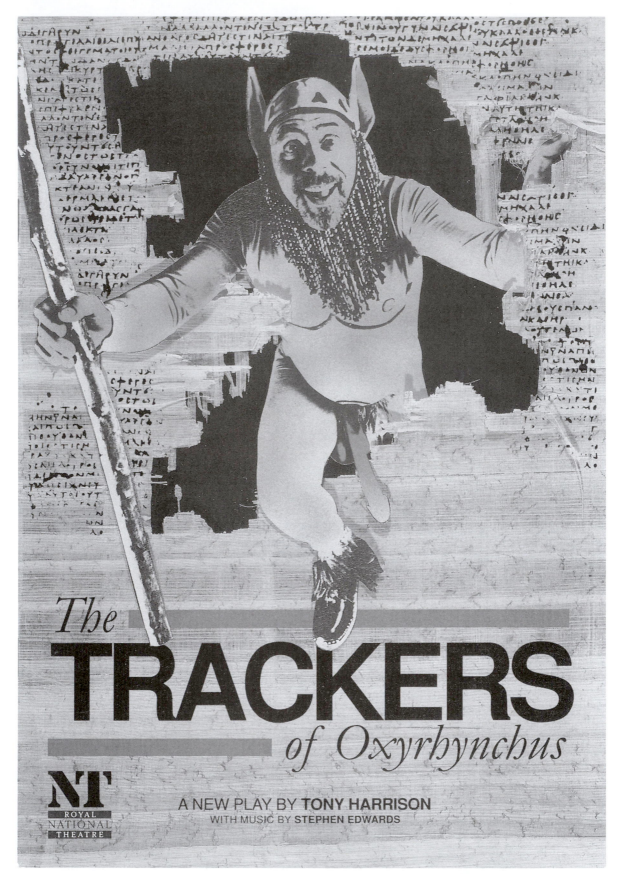

Satyr: programme of Tony Harrison's satyr play *The Trackers of Oxyrhynchus*, based on Sophocles' *Ichneutae*, National Theatre, London, 1990

parody of Homer's tale of Odysseus and the Cyclops, a one-eyed giant named Polyphemus. In Homer's version Odysseus and his men land on the Cyclops' island and are captured after they take some of his food. Polyphemus locks them in his cave and promises to eat a few of them every day for dinner, but Odysseus gets him drunk and blinds him, enabling the men to escape. In Euripides' version Silenus, an old man who cared for Dionysus in his youth, has been shipwrecked on the Cyclops' island with the band of satyrs he leads, and all of them are serving as slaves when Odysseus and his men turn up on the island. Silenus sells them the Cyclops' property in exchange for wine, of which he has long been deprived, but when Polyphemus returns unexpectedly Silenus is terrified and pretends that the Greeks have robbed him by force. The Cyclops imprisons Odysseus' men and eats two of them, but Odysseus plies him with wine, while Silenus does all he can to get some of the wine for himself. Eventually Polyphemus becomes drunk enough to think that he is Zeus and Silenus Ganymede, and carries the frantic Silenus off into the cave. While he is gone Odysseus prepares a burning stake for blinding the giant, but the satyrs, who have promised to help him, prove to be too cowardly to do so. Odysseus gets his crew to help instead, and they blind the Cyclops and escape, taking the chorus with them.

The origins of the satyr play and those of tragedy are probably linked. Aristotle says both that tragedy grew out of the dithyramb and that it emerged from satyric drama; this satyric drama is probably not the Classical satyr play but its ancestor. The link between dithyramb and satyr play may have been made (sometime around 600 BC) by the poet Arion, who is said to have been the first to have his dithyrambs sung by choruses of satyrs. The word "tragedy" itself, which means "goat song", may come from the satyrs of such choruses; although depictions of satyrs on Greek pottery suggest that at an early period their non-human features were those of horses rather than goats, the satyrs in drama may well have disguised themselves as goats or acted like goats.

One ancient explanation for the development of satyr plays into their Classical form is that as tragedy developed from the dithyramb (originally a hymn to Dionysus), the tragedians started to use plots that had nothing to do with Dionysus; this annoyed the audience, and to satisfy them the poets invented the satyr play. More modern ideas are that the satyr play started from a humorous part of a tragedy (functioning to relieve tension like the grave-diggers in *Hamlet*) that was gradually split off, or that satyr plays were a genre parallel to tragedy that evolved somewhere in the Peloponnese while tragedy was emerging at Athens. In any case, the structure of satyr plays seems to be much like that of tragedies, though the length of the *Cyclops* suggests that such plays were in general much shorter than tragedies. They were probably performed, like tragedies, by three actors and a chorus of 12 (later 15).

According to legend, the first writer of satyr plays in their classical form was Pratinas of Phlius at the beginning of the 5th century BC; he was one of the most important and prolific writers of such works, but almost none of his output survives. Pratinas' son Aristias was another great writer of satyr plays, as was the tragedian Aeschylus, parts of whose satyr play *Dictyulci* have survived on papyrus. Euripides had a tendency to replace satyr plays with tragedies that had happy endings,

such as the *Alcestis*, or with humorous pieces that did not use a chorus of satyrs; it is possible that Sophocles too may have written such "prosatyric" plays. Both dramatists, however, also wrote a number of satyr plays; Euripides' *Cyclops* survives intact, and a large portion of Sophocles' *Ichneutae* has been found on papyrus.

In the 4th century BC the production of satyr plays declined, and their number was reduced to one per tragic festival, rather than one per trilogy. The genre was revived in the Alexandrian period and still kept its chorus of satyrs, although these late satyr plays seem to have been concerned with contemporary events as well as with mythology. Eventually the genre inspired a type of Latin satyr play in Rome but died out in Greece. The satyr play has remained essentially a dead form to the present day, though the *Cyclops* and the *Ichneutae* are occasionally performed, the latter sometimes with a good deal of modern creativity supplying the missing portions.

ELEANOR DICKEY

See also Dithyramb, Tragedy

Further Reading

Euripides, *Cyclops* in *Euripides*, vol. 1, translated by David Kovacs, Cambridge, Massachusetts: Harvard University Press, 1994 (Loeb edition)

Sophocles, *The Searchers* (*Ichneutae*) in *Sophocles*, vol. 3, translated by Hugh Lloyd-Jones, Cambridge, Massachusetts: Harvard University Press, 1996 (Loeb edition)

Sutton, Dana F., *The Greek Satyr Play*, Meisenheim: Hain, 1980

Scepticism

The philosophical denial of the possibility of human knowledge

There are varieties of scepticism. Natural scepticism is simply asking for sufficient evidence before trusting some claim. This mode of doubting protects people from ignorance or credulity. Philosophical scepticism goes far beyond this.

Scepticism comes from *skeptomai*, which means "I inquire, consider, reflect". Inquiry can lead to answers (*dogma*), or to confusion when there is no reliable way to decide between competing answers.

Philosophical scepticism challenges all claims to knowledge by seeking to show that all is confusion. Philosophical scepticism challenges all epistemologies. Doubting, or withholding belief, until satisfactory reasons to believe are offered is the core of the sceptical method.

The Greek sceptics claimed they were the intellectual descendants of Socrates. They believed that the Socratic claim to ignorance, "I only know that I do not know", was not due to inadequate inquiry. Socrates could not know because no inquiry will ever find any answers.

Actually the real fountainhead of scepticism lay not in Socrates, but in his opponents, the Sophists. These teachers had expressed the confusion felt by many Greeks at the contradictory answers of the Presocratic metaphysicians, and the scepticism implicit in their thought. In addition, the flood of conflicting ideas challenging traditional belief after Alexander the Great's conquests and the loss of meaning in public life with the end of independence of the city state made despair common.

The sceptics attacked the claims to knowledge made by the dogmatic philosophers, especially the Stoics and Epicureans, by raising the problem of the criterion (Sextus Empiricus, *Outlines*, 1. 21). To answer questions about how a person has acquired knowledge of something, rules of evidence need to be offered. Reasons need to be given. The reasons which support a truth claim (or a value judgement) need in turn to be supported. This eventually leads to an infinite regress, or to circular argument, and not knowledge, they claimed.

Ethically the sceptics rejected positive knowledge of ethical values. For practical reasons they usually adopted a strategy of behaviour that accommodated them to the values prevailing in the community.

Philosophical scepticism began in the Hellenistic age with the teaching of Pyrrho of Elis (*c.*363–273 BC). His goal was peace through an apathetic state of mind (*artaraxia*). Freedom from care through an indifferent attitude was the goal of the sceptics in general (Sextus Empiricus, *Outlines*, 1. 8–12).

Pyrrho's ideas were popularized in Athens by his student, Timon of Phlius (320–230 BC). He used lampoons (*silloi*) to attack dogmatic claims. This form of scepticism claimed to be unable to decide if the dogmas of the Stoics and Epicureans could be proved. Since he was unable to decide if something was fact or error, the wise man should suspend judgement until proof could be offered.

In the 3rd century BC a more radical form of scepticism appeared. The Middle or New Academy of Plato became the centre of Academic scepticism. The first of the Academic sceptics was Arcesilaus of Pitane (*c.*316–240 BC). His arguments attacked the Stoic criterion of knowledge.

The most important of the Academic sceptics was Carneades of Cyrene (*c.*215–129 BC), who also headed the Academy in Athens. He taught that nothing can be known with certainty, but that there are degrees of probability which will assist the wise when deciding how to act. He was succeed by Clitomachus (Hasdrubal) of Carthage (*c.*270–200 BC). Clitomachus was a dedicated popularizer of the arguments of Carneades. Little remains of his 400 works.

The later sceptics revived Pyrrhonism at Alexandria. They include Aenesidemus of Cnossus (*c.*80 BC–AD 30), Agrippa (dates are unknown), and Sextus Empiricus (*c.*AD 163–210). The last of these preserved the sceptic tradition. In his works Sextus discusses the methods of his predecessors including the use of modes (tropes) of doubting used to attack empirical claims. Essentially these pile enough differences in sense impressions to create doubt, so suspension of judgement is warranted. He also presents arguments for attacking rationalist claims to knowledge.

Eventually Greek teachers and Roman students of the Academy, such as Cicero, were to spread scepticism to Roman literature where it would be refuted by Plotinus and Augustine. The success of these critiques of scepticism was to last for over a thousand years.

The Renaissance introduced western Europe to the Hellenistic philosophies. By the 1500s Greek editions of Sextus' books were being printed. These printed editions were based on manuscripts preserved in the Greek-speaking east since the advent of Christianity.

Sceptical thought had played some role in the theology of the east. The early Church Fathers had made some use of it. Usually they were opposed to the sceptics because the latter were seen as a threat to Christianity. Gregory of Nazianzus (*c.*330–89) argued that the sceptics were to be lumped with Greek philosophers in general as incompatible. The Fathers occasionally used sceptical arguments to advance the faith.

In the following centuries occasional references to the sceptics can be found in Byzantine thought. In the 14th century a few Byzantine thinkers revived sceptical arguments. Their thought was opposed by Theodore Metochites (1260–1322) in his *Miscellanea Philosophica et Historica*. Others also worked on sceptical issues, including Gregory Palamas (1296–1359). Little use was made of scepticism after the fall of Constantinople in 1453.

A.J.L. WASKEY, JR

See also Philosophy

Further Reading

Annas, Julia and Jonathan Barnes, *The Modes of Scepticism: Ancient Texts and Modern Interpretations*, Cambridge and New York: Cambridge University Press, 1985

Bevan, Edwyn R., *Stoics and Sceptics: Four Lectures*, Oxford: Clarendon Press, 1913; New York: Barnes and Noble, 1959

Bréhier, Émile, *The Hellenistic and Roman Age*, Chicago: University of Chicago Press, 1965

Burnyeat, Myles, *The Skeptical Tradition*, Berkeley: University of California Press, 1983

Chisholm, Roderick M., *Theory of Knowledge*, Englewood Cliffs, New Jersey: Prentice Hall, 1966; 3rd edition, 1989

Copleston, Frederick, *A History of Philosophy*, vol. 1: *Greece and Rome*, part 2, revised edition, Garden City, New York: Image, 1962

Diogenes Laertius, *Lives of Eminent Philosophers*, translated by R.D. Hicks, 2 vols, London: Heinemann, and New York: Putnam, 1925 (Loeb edition; many reprints)

Hankinson, R.J., *The Sceptics*, New York and London: Routledge, 1995

Mates, Benson (editor and translator), *The Skeptic Way: Sextus Empiricus's Outlines of Pyrrhonism*, New York: Oxford University Press, 1996

Naess, Arne, *Scepticism*, London: Routledge and Kegan Paul, and New York: Humanities Press, 1968

Popkin, Richard H., *The History of Scepticism: From Erasmus to Descartes*, New York: Harper and Row, 1964; revised 1979

Sextus Empiricus, *Outlines of Pyrrhonism*, translated by R.G. Bury, London: Heinemann, and New York: Putnam, 1933 (Loeb edition, vol. 1)

Sextus Empiricus, *Against the Logicians*, translated by R.G. Bury, London: Heinemann, and Cambridge, Massachusetts: Harvard University Press, 1935 (Loeb edition, vol. 2)

Sextus Empiricus, *Against the Physicists; Against the Ethicists*, translated by R.G. Bury, London: Heinemann, and Cambridge, Massachusetts: Harvard University Press, 1936 (Loeb edition, vol. 3)

Sextus Empiricus, *Against the Professors*, translated by R.G. Bury, London: Heinemann, and Cambridge, Massachusetts: Harvard University Press, 1949 (Loeb edition, vol. 4)

Sharples, R.W., *Stoics, Epicureans and Sceptics: An Introduction to Hellenistic Philosophy*, New York and London: Routledge, 1996

Stough, Charlotte L., *Greek Skepticism: A Study in Epistemology*, Berkeley: University of California Press, 1969

Zeller, Eduard, *Outlines of the History of Greek Philosophy*, 13th edition, revised by Wilhelm Nestle, New York: Meridian, 1967

Schism

Schism is a term designating the separation of a group from the main body of the Church due to disagreements on doctrinal, administrative, or other issues. This separation, however, is not absolute and irreconcilable but rather, as pointed out in the definition of "schism" given by Basil the Great, "capable of mutual solution" (J.B. Migne, *Patrologiae Cursus Completus, Series Graeca*, 32. 665). The term is first found in the New Testament and, although in patristic writings "schism" is distinguished from "heresy" – a much stronger term denoting a deviation from "correct faith" – schismatics have often come to be regarded as heretics.

The long history of Christianity displayed many schismatic tendencies. Some of them, particularly those of the 5th and 6th centuries, concerning the interpretation of Christological doctrine, resulted in permanent splits, such as that of the Nestorians and Monophysites who subsequently maintained a separate existence. These earlier schisms were mostly a natural consequence of heresies. From the 9th century onwards, however, the causes of schisms assumed a more personal character and the usual motives were the attempts of the emperors to exceed their prerogatives and privileges. Yet most of these schisms – such as the Photian schism of the 9th century, the schism known as "the affair of the tetragamy" of Leo VI in the 10th century, and the Arsenite schism of the 13th century – were temporary rifts and were eventually resolved. In many ways, however, all these ecclesiastical conflicts, from the 4th century onwards, may be regarded as the onset of an estrangement that was taking place within the main body of Christians and that was to widen century after century.

This estrangement reached its climax with the so-called Great Schism of 1054 between the Latin and Byzantine Churches. In the history of Christianity the Great Schism is considered to be the most significant one, and the term "schism" is most habitually employed to denote this particular split. The alienation of eastern and western Christians was not a synchronic historical event that took effect everywhere at once. It was rather a lengthy and perplexing process, the origins of which can be dated back to the 4th, 5th, and 6th centuries, while its final stage did not occur until the middle of the 15th century. In this extended process two incidents are explicitly acknowledged by historians as reflecting the widening gulf.

First there was the conflict between pope Nicholas I of Rome and patriarch Photios of Constantinople in 863–67. The appointment of Photios as patriarch and the deposition of his predecessor Ignatios were clearly connected with the papal controversy. Different interpretations concerning the primacy of Rome and other important ecclesiastical centres were apparent already in the 4th century and were related to the crisis over Arianism and the Acacian schism (485–519). The dispute between the two patriarchs, Photios and Ignatios, was used by Nicholas I to enforce his claim for universal papal jurisdiction. Although Nicholas's legates had acknowledged Photios as the legitimate patriarch, Nicholas repudiated their decision and demanded a retrial. A council was held in Rome under his presidency in 863. Here Photios was declared deposed and Ignatios was restored as patriarch. This approach was unacceptable to the Byzantines, who regarded the Church not as a monarchy, as the Latins did, but rather as conciliar in structure. The Council of Chalcedon (451) had attributed to the bishop of "Constantinople which is New Rome" equal privileges, in keeping with those of Old Rome, which was the imperial city (canon 28). Thus Byzantines saw Nicholas's actions as an intolerable interference in the affairs of another patriarchate. Photios also caused an additional strain to Byzantine–papal relations by adding a doctrinal dimension to the jurisdictional conflict through the questioning of the so-called *filioque* clause. This came at a time when a strong political rivalry existed between the Roman and Byzantine Churches over the control of the newly converted tsar of Bulgaria, Boris (852–89). Photios then in an encyclical to the Eastern patriarchs presented a list of Latin errors, the most important of which was the *filioque*. He went so far as to suggest that it was heretical, since to affirm that the Spirit "proceeds from the Father and the Son" was to admit of two principles. Although the *filioque* was not used at that time in Rome, German missionaries had introduced the creed in Bulgaria with this addition. By this act Photios was aiming to persuade Boris to embrace the Eastern rather than the Western form of Christianity. Boris received baptism from the Byzantines and, despite the fact that he negotiated with Rome when Constantinople refused to grant autonomy, Bulgaria remained Eastern in its polity. Photios in his second patriarchate (877–86) remained in communion with Rome. But even though it appeared that the Photian schism came to an end, its underlying causes were never really solved.

At the beginning of the 11th century relations between Rome and Constantinople were allowed to backslide once more. Rome in 1014 added the *filioque* to the creed. Moreover, at that time, for reasons that still remain unclear, patriarch Sergios II excluded from the Diptychs (i.e. excommunicated) the name of the new pope Sergius IV. This meant that the loss of communion was there even before the second incident, which is recognized by historians as leading to the final rupture between the two parts of Christendom.

This new incident took place in the mid-11th century when Constantinople was at the peak of its medieval power, and the see of Rome had just reformed itself, after passing through a century of decadence and confusion. At the same time the Normans were invading the Byzantine provinces in south Italy, thus complicating the already fragile political and ecclesiastical relations between Rome and Constantinople. The matter became even worse when the Normans compelled the Greeks living in Byzantine Italy to comply with Latin practices. The patriarch, Michael Keroularios, retaliated by closing down all the Latin churches in Constantinople. A reconciliation effort was made by Constantinople, which included an invitation to a papal delegation. In 1054 pope Leo IX sent cardinal Humbert as his legate to Constantinople. Humbert was annoyed by the uncooperative attitude of Keroularios and excommunicated him in a bull, which was left on the altar of the church of Hagia Sophia. Keroularios, in turn, anathematized Humbert. These mutual anathemas have been identified as the incident from which we may date the consummation of the schism. After these anathemas, however, relations between the two Churches continued to be unclear for many years. The quarrel was perceived by many as a simple misunderstanding, which would be easily resolved. Furthermore, it appeared not to have had a great impact on the Byzantines, who continued communion with the Latins on a local basis. Yet, doctrinally, culturally, and institutionally, the two sides had drifted so far apart that their estrangement proved to be intractable.

It was the sack of Constantinople on Good Friday 1204 by the Fourth Crusade that made even the laity aware that the split between the two sides was profound and decisive. For three days the crusaders were allowed to kill their fellow Christians as well as burn and ruin the sacred city of the Christian East. This act initiated a spirit of abiding bitterness and hatred. Thereafter the Latins were considered by most Byzantines as enemies of their Church and nation. Nevertheless, since then, efforts have been made to reestablish full communion between Eastern Christianity and the Roman Church. The attempts at union of the councils of Lyon (1274) and Ferrara-Florence (1438–39) failed: first because they were politically rather than spiritually motivated; and second because the overwhelming majority of the clergy and laity throughout the Orthodox world were not ready to accept the Latin doctrine of the *filioque* and the papal claims. Even in the last days of Byzantium, when the political situation became desperate due to the advances of the Ottomans, the animosity between western and eastern Christians was not lessened; many of the latter even came to look upon the Ottoman advance as a lesser evil than submission to the Latins.

At first sight, the whole story of the Great Schism seems to be one of political and personal conflict, often rooted in human folly and narrow-mindedness. Recently, however, historians looking at the underlying causes of the schism have stressed the importance of historical, cultural, and even ethnic factors. It is important to point out that the breach of communion between pope and patriarch occurred when the Church of Old Rome was under the influence of Germans. In fact, it was the Normans who made the restoration of communion between the two sides impossible. This led some writers to view the schism as a conflict not between the Latin and Orthodox Churches, but between Franks and (east) Romans, and to go so far as to suggest that the Franks used the institutional aspects of Christianity to keep the conquered (west) Romans in a submissive state (cf. J. Romanides, 1981). However, all the aforementioned factors found a suitable expression in religious and doctrinal differences. Nevertheless, many writers still hold that the schism was above all a matter of theology and doctrine.

Although geographically the Christian East and West could not be clearly delimited, differences in modes of thinking and theologizing were (and still are) very apparent. Orthodox theology was a patristic one based on the writings of the Greek Fathers of the 4th century. It was a theology that was lived and taught liturgically, principally through Eucharistic worship. Western Christianity, on the other hand, until the 12th and 13th centuries when it was influenced by the rationalism of Scholasticism, had a more rudimentary theology. It subsequently became common to consider Orthodoxy as more conservative, ritualistic, mystical, personal, and existential in comparison with Western Christianity, which was seen as more rationalistic, "scientific", and systematic. The two wings of Christianity, therefore, developed a very different outlook as far as church life was concerned. Their difference in theological outlook coloured not only the two fundamental issues of their controversy, which still remain unsolved, i.e. the teaching concerning the procession of the Holy Spirit and the limits of papal power, but also the less important issues involved in the conflict, such as the celibacy of the clergy, the use of the *azymes* or unleavened bread in the Eucharist, the manner of conferring confirmation, and the Western teaching on Purgatory.

The schism of 1054 is regarded as one of the greatest tragedies in Church history with far-reaching consequences for both Eastern and Western Christianity. It is connected to the fall of the Byzantine empire and the advance of Islam, to the failure of the crusades, to the Reformation, which divided the West into two hostile camps, and to the rivalry between Russia and Western Europe. Even the schism of 1923 that took place within the Church of Greece and resulted in the excommunication of a group of Greek Orthodox known as the "Old Calendarists", can be seen as part of the aftermath that followed the breach of communion between the Orthodox and Western Churches. The Old Calendarists refused to follow the Gregorian calendar, introduced by pope Gregory III in 1572, which the Greek Church officially adopted, and still continue to adhere to the Julian reckoning.

In the course of the centuries various attempts have been made to restore unity between East and West. On 7 December 1965 the mutual anathemas were revoked by both sides. Yet such efforts resulted in further tensions and oppositions because of the fear of many Orthodox of losing their identity and autocephaly, and also because of the additional Latin innovations made after the schism of 1054, specifically the dogma of the infallibility of the pope and his immediate and universal jurisdiction over the entire Church. Further complications in the relations between East and West were also added by Uniatism, which appeared in eastern Europe in the 16th and 17th centuries, the consequences of which are still apparent today. The Uniates follow the Byzantine ritual in their worship, but recognize the supremacy of the pope. Such partial unions have been regarded by Orthodox as imbued with proselytism and as an unacceptable form of "missionary apostolate" on the part of the Latin Church.

ELENI SOTIRIU

See also Heresy, Old Calendarists, Roman Catholic Church, Uniates

Further Reading

Dvornik, Francis, *The Photian Schism*, Cambridge: Cambridge University Press, 1948

Geanakoplos, Deno J., *Byzantine East and Latin West: Two Worlds of Christendom in Middle Ages and Renaissance*, Oxford: Blackwell, and New York: Barnes and Noble, 1966

Gill, Joseph, *The Council of Florence*, Cambridge: Cambridge University Press, 1959

Gill, Joseph, *Byzantium and the Papacy 1198–1400*, New Brunswick, New Jersey: Rutgers University Press, 1979

Hussey, J.M., *The Orthodox Church in the Byzantine Empire*, Oxford: Clarendon Press, 1986

Pelikan, Jaroslav, *The Spirit of Eastern Christendom, 600–1700*, Chicago: University of Chicago Press, 1974

Podskalsky, Gerhard, *Theologie und Philosophie in Byzanz*, Munich: Beck, 1977

Romanides, John S., *Franks, Romans, Feudalism, and Doctrine: An Interplay Between Theology and Society*, Brookline, Massachusetts: Holy Cross Orthodox Press, 1981

Runciman, Steven, *The Eastern Schism: A Study of the Papacy and the Eastern Churches During the XIth and XIIth Centuries*, Oxford: Clarendon Press, and New York: Oxford University Press, 1955

Sherrard, Philip, *Church, Papacy and Schism: A Theological Enquiry*, London: SPCK, 1978

Ware, Timothy, "Scholasticism and Orthodoxy: Theological Method as a Factor in the Schism", *Eastern Churches Review*, 51 (1973): pp. 16–27

Ware, Timothy, "Eastern Christendom" in *The Oxford Illustrated History of Christianity*, edited by John McManners, Oxford and New York: Oxford University Press, 1992

Ware, Timothy, *The Orthodox Church*, 2nd edition, London and New York: Penguin, 1993

Yannaras, Christos, "Orient-Occident: la signification profonde du Schism", *Service Orthodoxe de Presse*, 150 (1990): pp. 29–35

Zernov, Nicolas, "Christianity: The Eastern Schism and the Eastern Orthodox Church" in *The Hutchinson Encyclopedia of Living Faiths*, 4th edition, edited by R.C. Zaehner, London: Hutchinson, 1988

Scholarship, History of

Whether there is any Greek word that corresponds to the English "scholarship" may be doubted. Nevertheless it is clear from what is known of men of letters in antiquity that they engaged in activities that would fall within any ordinary definition of the term. The understanding and criticism of literature were stimulated by the existence of schools where Homer and other poets formed a substantial part of the syllabus, and the teacher was forced to explain the texts and answer questions. Apart from the numerous minor linguistic difficulties arising from archaic words in Homer there were bigger questions: how could one interpret suitably such passages as Hera's approaches to Zeus in *Iliad* 14 or the tale of Hephaestus catching Ares and Aphrodite in flagrante delicto in *Odyssey* 8? For that difficulty it seems probable that the method of allegorical interpretation was invented, apparently by Theagenes of Rhegion (*c*.525 BC).

A desire to illuminate literary history and the origins of genres becomes visible in Aristotle's circle in such works as his *Homeric Questions* or the lists of dramatists who had won victories in the competitions at the Athenian state festivals, and a teleological view of the world was naturally conducive to such inquiries. But most of what would nowadays be considered literary scholarship (I leave out of account philosophical monographs and commentaries on Plato and Aristotle) appears to be the invention of men working in Alexandria in the 3rd and 2nd centuries BC. The librarians at the Museum collected Greek literature systematically, and they must soon have been puzzled and dismayed by the number of texts that had unintelligible passages resulting from careless transcription, or – worse still – by serious discrepancies between copies of the same text, a problem very noticeable in the case of

Homer. There were also questions of authenticity. Though our sources of information on all these matters are very fragmentary, it is clear that discussions in the Museum led to the development of a number of aids for the reader, some of them mundane, such as the possibility of marking the accents so as to facilitate reading or the insistence on dividing lines of lyric verse so as to respect the metrical units, and others more sophisticated, such as the use of symbols in the left-hand margin of texts to advise the reader of certain problems raised by the passages in question. And with all this there had to be a second-order literature, i.e. books about books. Some of these were detailed commentaries on the texts, in others the critic expounded a topic and offered solutions to the problems, sometimes with an explicit mention of the principles by which puzzles might be solved. An enormous quantity of such literature was produced in antiquity. The most important scholars and critics were Zenodotus, Callimachus, Aristophanes of Byzantium, and Aristarchus. None of their work survives in its original form; at best we have brief citations, more usually a substantially rephrased and abbreviated version of their views, often not specifically attributed to the original author. So it is not always clear to whom we owe the best ideas; it is for instance a matter of debate whether Aristarchus is to be credited with the important maxim that "Homer should be illuminated from Homer", in other words that one needs to explain difficulties as far as possible by looking elsewhere in the writings of the same author. The question then arose whether a unique feature could be accepted, and one anonymous scholar formulated the necessary principle that in Homer there are many unique words, without which there would have been a temptation to deal drastically with the text. As it was, some critics declared a number of passages "improper" for one reason or another, but fortunately they did not go so far as to delete the lines in question, which would have had disastrous consequences, since their judgement now seems to us to have been at fault in most cases. Nevertheless there are many stimulating observations to be found in the surviving sources, for example the note that remarks that in the first book of the *Iliad* there are no similes, or the statement attributed to both Aristophanes of Byzantium and Aristarchus that the end of the *Odyssey* is to be placed at line 296 of book 23. It is therefore extremely unfortunate that the only critical monographs to survive from antiquity in their original form are not by the leading scholars of the period *c*.275–150 BC but works of later date or of marginal interest. The earliest appears to be a discussion of Aratus' and Eudoxus' *Phaenomena* by the astronomer and geographer Hipparchus (*c*.150 BC); the most famous, assuming it to be genuine, the brief *Techne Grammatike* of Dionysius Thrax (*fl. c*.150–90 BC); others are an essay by one Heraclitus (1st century AD?) on allegory in Homer and part of a commentary by Didymus (1st century BC) on speeches 9–11 and 13 of Demosthenes; this is a careless and unimpressive piece of work by a man whose fluent pen made him almost proverbial.

Any author of reasonably high quality could become the subject of a commentary, especially if his works were adopted for the school curriculum. But the lion's share of attention went to Homer, a fact reflected in the bulk of the surviving scholia, that is, notes written in the margins of medieval manuscripts but deriving from ancient monographs. One especially famous manuscript of the *Iliad* (Venice, Biblioteca Nazionale Marciana, gr. 454) has preserved a quantity of material not known from any other source, with many snippets of information or judgements attributed to their authors. This manuscript gives us an idea of the specialized and detailed nature of studies devoted to Homer, including a great deal of a book by a certain Nicanor (*fl.* *c.*AD 130), on the correct way to punctuate the more complex sentences in Homer; what was presumably a series of notes presented as a running commentary has been divided into tiny sections and inserted into the rest of the commentary at the appropriate places. A similar fate befell an equally specialized monograph on the lyric metres in Aristophanes' comedies: quite a few excerpts of work by Heliodorus (lst century AD) are embedded in the scholia to Aristophanes.

In the expanding and changing cultural world of the late Hellenistic period and the Roman empire, the types of scholarship developed in Alexandria continued to flourish and prove their value. In the Greek-speaking Jewish community of Alexandria the Old Testament was studied in the Greek Septuagint version. Difficulties in the text had already been expounded by one Aristobulus (*c.*150 BC), and he may have had some connection with the Museum, since he shows occasional awareness of Greek poetry. When the Christians began to study their sacred texts they too availed themselves of the tools of pagan culture. The most notable figure is Origen, active in Alexandria from 202 until 223, then in Caesarea until 253. He and some of his successors were keen exponents of allegory as a means of interpreting the scriptures, but he was also aware of other scholarly methods, and in his remarkable *Hexapla* he produced an edition of the Old Testament set out in six columns, a somewhat clumsy forerunner of the critical apparatus typical of modern scholarly editions. Origen was not unwilling to use the techniques of the pagan scholars of Alexandria in dealing with the Bible; the same is true to a greater extent of the members of what is generally treated as a rival school in Antioch, whose leading exponents Diodore of Tarsus (d. 394) and Theodore of Mopsuestia (350–428), though ignorant of Hebrew, showed an acute awareness of the problems of translation.

Just as there had been commentaries on Homer and other pagan classics, so too there were commentaries on books of the Bible, and by the early 6th century the number of such texts, though probably not equal in bulk to what had been written about the leading pagan classics, was substantial. But it was difficult, especially in an age of declining economic resources, for readers to find copies of all the commentaries they might wish to consult, and frequently there was repetition of material. A solution was found by selecting and amalgamating notes from existing commentaries or monographs; the new collections of material, generally known as scholia on pagan texts and catenae on books of the Bible, could be fitted into the margins of the codex form of book that had replaced the roll and become standard since *c.*AD 400. It is not known exactly when and where this important and time-consuming operation took place, but catenae are perhaps the invention of Procopius of Gaza (*c.*475–538), a leading member of an intellectual circle in which devout Christians continued the study of the pagan classics as part of the educational curriculum. Catenae and scholia, though very similar, exhibit one important difference:

whereas material on pagan texts rarely gives the name of the scholar who is being quoted, many catenae make a point of naming the authors of each extract, and it is interesting to note that catenae preserve a fair number of observations by Church Fathers such as Origen and Theodore of Mopuestia who subsequently fell out of favour.

Since the 2nd century AD Greek literature had been dominated by the archaizing Atticist movement, which obliged authors to imitate as best they could the language of acknowledged masterpieces written when Athens was at its peak. Manuals of correct usage were produced in abundance; we still have those compiled by Moeris, Phrynichus, and Pollux. The fashion lasted much longer than might have been expected. Classical texts were studied as much for their stylistic qualities as their power to instruct or edify, and their place in the school syllabus was barely affected by the spread of Christianity. Authors were equipped with scholia so that teachers should never be at a loss when questioned by pupils, and what had been done for pagan authors was replicated for the one significant addition to the corpus of *Kunstprosa*, a selection of 16 orations by St Gregory of Nazianzus. No other substantial alterations seem to have been made to the curriculum and essentially the educational system remained unchanged until the end of the Byzantine empire.

The fragmentary nature of our sources makes it hard to discern any scholarly achievement of note in the period of Justinian (the preparation of the *Digest* falls outside the scope of this article). It is perhaps worth noting one specific controversy: at a church council held in 532 Hypatius, bishop of Ephesus, put forward a properly argued case against recognizing the works of Dionysius the Areopagite as genuine. Unluckily this pioneer of rational thought was a millennium ahead of his time and his view did not gain acceptance.

After the Dark Ages, which may be reckoned as falling between the death of the emperor Herakleios in 641 and the end of the 8th century, we find a literary scene not much changed except geographically, for some centres of cultivated urban life had been lost to the empire. Yet the libraries of Constantinople still contained many texts that have not come down to the modern world, and these were exploited by one outstanding figure, the patriarch Photios (*c.*810–?after 893), especially in his so-called *Myriobiblon* or *Bibliotheca*. The title is misleading and not authentic, and the habit of referring to each chapter as a "codex" is unfortunate, because it suggests that a personal library is being described. The work is in fact a series of notes and essays compiled for the benefit of his brother, describing books he had read. Poetry is barely represented, but there are accounts of many texts now lost, for which Photios is the best or the only source; his comments on their stylistic merits or failings, while couched in vocabulary he may have acquired from predecessors, are not just plagiarism and show a well-developed literary sensibility. He was also alert to problems of authenticity and interpretation of texts, for example in one passage ("codex" 230, p.270 a 17) he uses an adapted form of a principle cited earlier when he says "Who could be more suitable to interpret St Cyril than Cyril himself?" A more remarkable statement occurs in his *Amphilochia* (chapter 152) where, basing himself at least in part on an earlier patristic writer, he states that heretical doctrine can arise from small faults in texts such as the loss or addition of a single letter, or a faulty accent or inadequate punctuation.

No later Byzantine scholars quite equalled Photios. But much energy was devoted to preserving the Classical literary heritage. In the 10th century the emperor Constantine Porphyrogennetos and his circle attempted an encyclopaedic compilation of useful knowledge arranged in categories, which survives only in part and may never have been completed. From much the same period comes the *Suda* or *Suidas*, a large dictionary and encyclopaedia designed to help the reader of the classics of pagan and patristic literature. The polymath and professor of philosophy Michael Psellos (1018–78?) has left a number of essays on literary themes, including one on the ancient novels by Achilles Tatius and Heliodorus, and another on the respective merits of Euripides and George of Pisidia (the latter too poorly preserved to be properly assessed). Archbishop Eustathios of Thessalonica (1115–95) was an indefatigable compiler of commentaries on Homer and other authors. He and his fellow bishop Michael Choniates of Athens (1138–1222) had access to some texts that did not survive the onslaught of the Crusaders in 1204, and their quotations from such works are valuable; their own contribution to scholarship, however, probably amounted to little more than maintaining tradition in the schools.

That tradition had to be restored when the Byzantines recovered their capital in 1261, and during the Palaiologan period that followed, despite a deepening economic crisis, there was much scholarly activity of a high calibre. Particular credit is due to Maximos Planudes for his wide interests. *Inter alia* he prepared a recension of Plutarch and a somewhat bowdlerized edition of the *Greek Anthology*, and tried to improve the text of Aratus' poem *Phaenomena* by substituting lines of his own for passages that were now known to be astronomically erroneous. Less wide-ranging but in a way more important was the work of the 14th century scholar Dimitrios Triklinios on Greek tragedy and comedy. Triklinios understood Classical metre much better than anyone else in Byzantium, and he used this knowledge to correct many faulty verses; his corrections in many cases are accepted by modern editors, a fact that distinguishes him from other Byzantine scholars.

The final stages of Byzantine scholarship can be said to have taken place in Italy. The diaspora of refugees began well before the Turkish capture of Constantinople, and many educated men came to Italy in the hope of making a living as teachers. The most notable refugee was a clerical member of the delegation sent to the Council of Florence, Bessarion, who soon after settled in Italy and was made a cardinal. His astonishing personal library became the basis of the Marciana in Venice through his donation of 1468. But he was not simply a bibliophile, and though his marginal annotations to the texts he read do not demonstrate a particularly happy touch in making suggestions to heal corrupt passages, his pamphlet dealing with the disputed verse in St John's Gospel (21: 22) is important for the way it casts doubt on the wording found in the Vulgate.

Once the study of Greek took root in Italy it could spread to other western countries, especially with the aid of the printed book. Many of the early editions are due to Aldus Manutius, who did not always succeed in finding in Venice plentiful manuscript sources and collaborators of high ability. But he had great success with one of the Greek refugees,

Markos Musuros (1470–1517), who prepared editions of Aristophanes and other authors, and at his best did excellent work towards the restoration of corrupt texts. From the middle of the 15th century onwards, however, Greek scholarship gradually became an international activity, with various western countries in turn producing a crop of eminent scholars, while Greece itself languished under Ottoman rule. The most remarkable personality from Greece in early modern times was Adamantios Korais (1748–1833), born in Smyrna but resident in Paris for much of his life; in addition to contributing to the Greek language question he published editions of the classics and made many acute conjectures that have won the admiration of modern critics. But he does not seem to have had close contacts with the German scholars of the day who were transforming the study of the classics into a science of antiquity, the study of ancient civilization as a whole.

NIGEL WILSON

See also Books and Readers, Education, Humanism, Libraries, Museum of Alexandria, Printing, Renaissance (Palaiologan)

Further Reading

El-Abbadi, Mostafa, *The Life and Fate of the Ancient Library of Alexandria*, 2nd edition, Paris: Unesco / UNDP, 1992

Pfeiffer, Rudolf, *History of Classical Scholarship from the Beginnings to the End of the Hellenistic Age*, Oxford: Clarendon Press, 1968

Pfeiffer, Rudolf, *History of Classical Scholarship from 1300 to 1850*, Oxford: Clarendon Press, 1976

Reynolds, L.D. and N.G. Wilson, *Scribes and Scholars: A Guide to the Transmission of Greek and Latin Literature*, 3rd edition, Oxford: Clarendon Press, and New York: Oxford University Press, 1991

Sandys, J.E., *A History of Classical Scholarship*, 3 vols, Cambridge: Cambridge University Press, 1903–08; 3rd edition, 1921

Vogt, E., in *Einleitung in die griechische Philologie*, edited by Heinz-Günther Nesselrath, Stuttgart: Teubner, 1997, pp. 117–32

Wilamowitz-Moellendorff, Ulrich von, *Geschichte der Philologie*, Lepizig: Teubner, 1921, reprinted 1998; translated by Alan Harris as *History of Classical Scholarship*, edited by Hugh Lloyd-Jones, London: Duckworth, and Baltimore: Johns Hopkins University Press, 1982

Wilson, N.G., *From Byzantium to Italy: Greek Studies in the Italian Renaissance*, London: Duckworth, 1992

Wilson, N.G., *Scholars of Byzantium*, revised edition, London: Duckworth, and Cambridge, Massachusetts: Medieval Academy of America, 1996

Wilson, N.G., in *Einleitung in die griechische Philologie*, edited by Heinz-Günther Nesselrath, Stuttgart: Teubner, 1997, pp. 87–116

Schools and Universities

The word "school" is of Greek origin: *schole* means "leisure, liberty from waged work and affairs of state". This leisure time could be devoted to scholarly studies. In this way the place where such occupations were practised received the same name. Through Latin (*schola*) the term then passed into many European languages. The "university" (from Latin *universitas*, "totality, teaching staff"), however, is a product of medieval western Europe; it did not exist in an institutionalized form in the Byzantine empire. Nevertheless facilities for a higher schol-

Schools: primary school in Athens. There is compulsory education for nine years in Greece today.

arly education already existed in Classical times (and later in the Byzantine period), but one should rather speak of academies or colleges.

An essential aspect of schools and academies in antiquity and in Byzantium is that they were mostly organized on a private basis. The state was not responsible for education and therefore there was no compulsory schooling or any continuous support for academies – it happened only occasionally that some project received support – or any permanently employed teachers. On the other hand, society as well as state authorities had an interest in passing on the cultural values of their civilization to the younger generation to make good citizens of them. In addition, the state was intent on getting good staff for its civil service and thus had a natural interest in enabling children and young people to obtain a comprehensive general education.

Fixed educational forms existed from approximately the 6th century BC. One of the few organized schools of this period was to be found in Sparta. Boys there were educated under state control between the ages of 7 and 29. In addition to elementary teaching in the basic principles of reading and writing, music and sports were taught. To a large extent the education was oriented towards the military in order to prepare boys for a life as soldiers. Girls received a similarly regulated education meant to prepare them for their social roles as mothers and educators of their children.

These elementary schools, which were mostly private, were also found in other regions of Greece. In Athens this educational form must have existed from at least the 6th century BC, as widespread writing skills demonstrate (e.g. written votes for citizens). Normally, elementary schools were run by a single teacher (the so-called *grammatistes*, from Greek *gramma*, "letter") who taught children between the ages of 7 and 14 in his private room. The furnishing was scanty: an easy chair for the teacher, simple benches or stools for the pupils, no tables. Wax tablets and slate pencils or papyrus and ink served as writing materials. The lessons at the *grammatistes* consisted of writing, reading, and arithmetic. Children learned to write by a strictly systematic, bottom-up method: first single letters, then syllables, and finally whole words. Reading was practised in the same way. Memorizing and reciting texts went together with reading them. The pedagogical method was limited to passive instruction, and corporal punishment often used. Since the elementary schoolteacher had to support himself from grants by his pupils' parents, his social standing was not very high. Nor was there any special training for teachers; anybody who could write and read was allowed to act as a teacher. There were no fixed holidays, but no lessons took place on the numerous monthly feasts and holidays.

In the 5th century BC it was the sophists (primarily philosophers and scholars who truly distinguished themselves as educationists) who, more than any others, helped to raise education to a higher level. They gathered young people around them to offer them a more ambitious intellectual training that lasted several years. This was, however, a collective instruction rather than an institutionalized schooling. The sophists were "travelling teachers" who went to different regions and villages demonstrating their knowledge in order to gain new trainees.

From about the 4th century BC true schools were created instead of individual educational schemes. They provided a secondary education that lasted two years. Boys especially, after finishing elementary school, i.e. at about the age of 14, were instructed – sports and military training apart – in theoretical subjects to achieve the so-called *enkyklios paideia* ("all-round, general education"). Besides scientific subjects (viz. geometry, arithmetic, music, astronomy) literary studies were mostly pursued. The Classical Greek writers – mainly poets, but also historians – were read, and their works were analysed and explained from a lexical and a grammatical perspective as well as in relation to their contents. The theory of grammar, which was an independent discipline, was treated too. Moreover, pupils had to do practical exercises in the form of literary essays.

These educational institutions, the so-called ephebic colleges (from Greek *ephebos*, "boy who has reached puberty"), were dependent on the particular town or municipality, which undertook to pay the teachers (Greek *grammatikos*, "grammar teacher"), though often private donors had to help out. Originally, these schools were compulsory for young men but over the centuries they gradually became elite schools for rich parents' children in the same measure as instruction in the humanities became more significant. The teaching place was the so-called *gymnasion* (the German term *Gymnasium* corresponds to the English "college") which originally meant sports field. There were comparable higher schools for girls, but here instruction was limited to music and literature.

In the Classical and Hellenistic periods it is impossible to draw a clear line between secondary and higher education. But scholarly instruction concentrated on such subjects as rhetoric and philosophy, which were seen as the main pillars of education. Specialized teachers, i.e. rhetoricians or sophists, gathered groups of pupils around them and trained them – over a period of up to five years – in theoretical and practical rhetoric in a private and friendly atmosphere. From the 2nd century BC Rhodes was particularly famous for its rhetorical schools. There were schools for philosophy as well, as in Athens, where teachers conveyed their philosophical opinions in lectures and personal conversations with the pupils, together with explanations of Classical authors. The two kinds of higher education competed with each other, but also mutually influenced each other. Teachers in these institutions had a high social standing, often occupying honorary state positions. It is striking that no professional training conveying practical skills (except for medicine) was offered in the higher schools. Special skills could only be acquired by practising with a specialized instructor.

In late antiquity the state, represented by the emperor, increasingly intervened in educational policy in order to induce the towns and municipalities to open new schools and to ensure the teachers' payment. There were practical reasons for this, since the state needed trained civil servants for administrative tasks. Christianization did not have any far-reaching influence on school education since religious education was regarded as the responsibility of the parental home. Schools continued to pass on Classical "pagan" values. As to higher education, centres for special subjects arose in different towns of the empire: Antioch for rhetoric, Athens and Alexandria for philosophy; Berytus (Beirut) for the new subject jurisprudence (under the influence of Roman legislation).

In the Byzantine period educational structures from antiquity were in general adopted almost without any change, but with certain individual developments. From the 5th century Constantinople became the centre for education, retaining this status until the 15th century. Elementary teaching could be obtained in almost every town, even in provincial ones, while secondary education was available only in the larger towns. Of course, not every member of every social class was able to do so. Girls especially received a rudimentary education in reading and writing at best. Primary-grade schoolmasters still had a bad reputation. Secondary-grade private tutors however were appreciated socially, living on payments by their pupils or partly supported by patrons. In this period, as in late antiquity, support for secondary schools and academies for the education of civil servants (and of clerics for Church offices), doctors, and jurists is noticeable. Apart from private schools public ones were founded and maintained by the state (i.e. by the emperor or by the Church), which ensured that the state and the Church retained substantial control of education. The founders won great fame, not to speak of the practical benefits, for themselves because by training people they could expect to have loyal civil servants and clerics. Nevertheless, one cannot speak of state institutions since they were connected to an individual, after whose death they stopped functioning.

The *grammatikos* or secondary-school teacher instructed his pupils mainly in Classical Greek. As the written and spoken languages drifted apart, the schoolmaster's task of teaching the grammar and literature of antiquity became more important.

The last stage of education was rhetorical training in reading the Classical and post-Classical orators and also in writing and giving lectures. At least in Constantinople there were several schools of grammar and rhetoric. The pressure of competition among teachers was sometimes high and schoolmasters were often tempted to woo pupils away from each other.

A formal institution, however, that today we would call a "university", cannot be found in this period. Over the centuries different emperors made isolated attempts to guarantee a higher education – for the above-mentioned reasons – by intervening personally. In the 5th century, for example, there was a higher school in Constantinople that offered Greek (and also Latin) rhetoric, grammar, philosophy, and jurisprudence. But in the 6th century it was already beginning to decline. During the following centuries individual foundations were again and again patronized by emperors to support higher education. In the 11th century under emperor Constantine IX Monomachos schools for philosophy and jurisprudence were created for the training of high-ranking civil servants, lawyers, and notaries. In the 12th century a Church academy, the so-called Patriarchal School, was founded in Constantinople that particularly offered lessons in theology, as well as in grammar and rhetoric for future clerics and monks. The sources give no clue as to whether it still existed in later centuries. In the late Byzantine period new educational centres arose in places other than Constantinople, e.g. in Thessalonica and in Mistra. Imperial patronage, however, decreased as the state became more and more impoverished, which is why many scholars emigrated to western Europe.

After the fall of the empire the Orthodox Church as the only official Greek institution made it its duty to maintain and to pass on the traditions of Byzantine education during the long period of the Tourkokratia. A newly founded school in the vicinity of the patriarchate (perhaps a revival of the Patriarchal School) covered secondary education. Elementary teaching, in former times mostly delivered by parish priests, remained almost unchanged over the centuries. New methods, particularly educational reforms, gradually came in from the West.

After the establishment of the free Greek nation (1821) the educational system was also structured anew. In the course of the 19th and 20th centuries a three-tier system was established that was essentially adopted from western Europe: the lower or primary level at primary school (six years of education) which is followed by higher schools divided into the so-called secondary level 1 or *gymnasion* (three years of education) and the secondary level 2 or *lykeion* (again three years of education). The third level finally is university. There is general compulsory education for nine years, i.e. for primary and secondary level 1. Secondary level 2, apart from schools providing a general education, includes specialized and professionally oriented educational branches. It also serves to prepare pupils for university. There are also private schools as well as church high schools that admit only boys. Teacher training is now regulated by the state and primary teachers are trained in pedagogical academies. Graduates of different university faculties, who are not compelled to acquire didactic skills, are engaged as teachers for the secondary levels. Recently, however, these posts have been given only to the best performers in a competitive examination.

In 1837 the first university (Greek *panepistimion*) in the modern sense was founded in Athens with originally four faculties: theology, philosophy (humanities and sciences), law, and medicine. Technological academies such as the polytechnic university (1836) gradually sprang up. In the course of the 20th century more universities were founded, in Thessalonica, Patras, Ioannina, Thrace, on Crete, in the Aegean, on Corfu, and in Thessaly. As a member of the European Union, Greece is now involved in many cultural programmes that support the exchange of university lecturers and students.

ASTRID STEINER-WEBER

See also Education, Rhetoric, Sophists

Further Reading

Beck, A.G., *Greek Education, 450–350 BC*, London: Methuen, and New York: Barnes and Noble, 1964

Browning, Robert, *Studies on Byzantine History, Literature and Education*, London: Variorum, 1977

Browning, Robert, School entry in *The Oxford Dictionary of Byzantium*, edited by A.P. Kazhdan, New York and Oxford: Oxford University Press, 1991, vol. 3

Davidson, Thomas, *The Education of the Greek People and its Influence on Civilization*, New York: AMS Press, 1971 (first published 1894)

Drever, James, *Greek Education: Its Practice and Principles*, Cambridge: Cambridge University Press, 1912

Freeman, Kenneth John, *Schools of Hellas: An Essay on the Practice and Theory of Ancient Greek Education from 600 to 300 BC*, 3rd edition, London and New York: Macmillan, 1922; reprint of 1st edition (1907), Port Washington, New York: Kennikat Press, 1969

Greek EURYDICE Unit, *The Greek Education System*, Luxembourg: Office for Official Publications of the European Communities, 1987

Lemerle, Paul, *Byzantine Humanism, the First Phase: Notes and Remarks on Education and Culture in Byzantium From its Origins to the 10th Century*, translated by Helen Lindsay and Ann Moffatt, Canberra: Australian Association for Byzantine Studies, 1986

Marrou, Henri-Irénée, *Histoire de l'éducation dans l'antiquité*, 6th edition, Paris: Seuil, 1965

Monroe, Paul, *Source Book of the History of Education for the Greeek and Roman Period*, New York and London: Macmillan, 1939, reprinted New York: Macmillan, 1948 (first published 1901)

Speck, Paul, *Die Kaiserliche Universität von Konstantinopel: Präzisierungen zur Frage des höheren Schulwesens in Byzanz im 9. und 10. Jahrhundert*, Munich: Beck, 1974

Scopas *fl.*360–335 BC

Sculptor

Though Scopas is counted as one of the greatest of Classical Greek sculptors, our definite knowledge of him, as with all named ancient sculptors, is slight and partially suspect. What we can reasonably guess from suggestive but unreliable traditions and remains widens our discernment but is also more hazardous. The remaining sculpture and testimonia, however, are so important for our understanding of ancient Greek art and so beautiful that we must make the effort: unreliability is not negation. And the ancient Greeks were excellent judges of their art, so that the traditions, even if unverifiable, can lead our eyes and minds to a just appreciation. Because Scopas was traditionally one of the three great sculptors of the late Classical age – the decades before Alexander's conquests – there are old traditions, modern attributions, and influences. Out of them an artistic personality emerges.

After the triumphs of the 5th century BC, 4th-century BC artists, while maintaining the basic Classical stylistic criteria of idealism combined with realism, felt the need to change and experiment. Where Praxiteles of Athens (Scopas' main rival) was sensuous and soft in his development of the female nude, and Lysippus of Sicyon interested in reforming the proportions of the male nude (providing, for example, a longer body and a smaller head) in portraits and increasing movement, Scopas of Paros was famed for emotional intensity, for a tragic, which means noble, sense of man's intense struggle. These three sculptors dominated the 4th century BC in the way that Myron, Phidias, and Polyclitus had dominated the 5th century BC, and determined much ancient art for hundreds of years – to Hadrian and beyond. Like their contemporary Plato, they looked to the towering past for their ideals and to the uncertain future in their ideas.

According to Pliny, Scopas was the son of the Parian sculptor Aristandros (working in 405 BC); Scopas is documented as active between 360 and 335 BC. Probably because it is the source of the world's most translucent marble for sculpture, Paros had a long sculptural tradition, including Aristion in the Archaic age and Phidias' pupil Agoracritus in the high Classical age. Scopas, who worked mostly in marble, was to be the greatest in this unbroken line.

We know that Scopas was as esteemed in his own age as in succeeding ages, because he was employed to work on the great projects of the period, including the temple of Athena Alea at Tegea, the Mausoleum of Halicarnassus, and the temple of Artemis at Ephesus. It is from the first of these that we get the best idea of his style.

At Tegea in the Peloponnese Scopas was an architect as well as a sculptor. The original temple had burned down in 395 BC and Scopas was at work some decades later. (The nearby temple of Nemea is so close in style and date that it seems that Scopas was active in the neighbourhood.) Pausanius says of Tegea: "The present temple is far superior to all other temples in the Peloponnese on many grounds, but particularly as regards its embellishment and size" (8. 45). The temple is the best example of 4th-century BC Doric; it was peripteral with a pronaos and opisthodomos and very narrow. Though it was Doric, Scopas brought from his home island a new spirit of lightness and delicacy: the columns were slender, and the interior columns were very early Corinthian with Ionic elements. On one of the pediments Scopas sculpted the *Hunt of the Calydonian Boar* (whose hide the temple displayed), and on the other the *Battle of Telephus and Achilles in the Kaikos Plain*. Many fragments of these sculptures survive and can be admired in the local museum and in the National Archaeological Museum in Athens. For the temple, Scopas also sculpted an *Asclepius* and a *Hygeia*, whose head, with its expression of divine sweetness, survives (National Archaeological Museum). He also made another *Asclepius* for a temple of Gortys in Arcadia. The squarish warriors' heads from the pediment, though battered, show brooding, deep-set eyes and furrowed brows – the new emotionalism of the 4th century BC.

The Mausoleum of Halicarnassus was the most ambitious monument of its day (355–330 BC), and all good sculptors were eager for employment there. According to Pliny (36. 30) Scopas worked on the frieze of the east side. The panel most usually attributed to him, now in the British Museum, depicts an animated *Battle of Greeks and Amazons*.

Pliny also says (34. 95) that Scopas carved and decorated one of the columns from the famed temple of Artemis at Ephesus, but the remains are too scanty to form a judgement. Of the other statues or copies of statues attributed to him, the finest are probably the deep-eyed *Meleager* (perhaps original) in the gardens of the Villa Medici and the copy of the *Pothos* ("Longing") in the Museo dei Conservatori, both in Rome. For his *Pothos*, Scopas sculpted a youth with crossed legs; his head looks longingly up with melting gaze. The Romans, who starting with Augustus carted off many of his sculptures to their capital, often copied this work, indicating its popularity. The lovely *Dancing Maenad* (a copy) in Dresden is thought to be an example of Scopas' new swirling movement. Callistratus wrote at length about it:

Scopas, as if moved by some inspiration, imparted to the making of his statue the divine frenzy that possessed him ... The Maenad wrought from Parian marble has been transformed into a real Maenad ... You would have seen that, hard as it was, it became soft to resemble the feminine, though its vigour corrected the femininity, and that, though it lacked the power to move, it knew how to dance in Bacchic frenzy, responding to the god as he entered within ... (*Descriptions*, 2. 1–4)

Hellenistic critics considered that Scopas' forte was statues of the gods, a genre unfortunately very poorly represented among the surviving monuments. We know of a *Heracles* for Sicyon, an *Apollo* for Rhamnous, a bronze *Aphrodite Pandemos Riding a Goat* for Elis, an *Artemis Eukleia* for Thebes, a *Dionysus* for Cnidus, a *Hecate* for Argos, and many more: it seems that Scopas was in demand everywhere.

Given his popularity, originality, and skill, it is not surprising that his influence on the ensuing Hellenistic age was pervasive. It has been especially remarked on in the great *Gigantomachy* frieze from the altar at Pergamum (c.180 BC), now in Berlin. Although it can be frustrating trying to recreate the work and thought of a great artist from toppled stones, hopeful assumptions, and guesswork, Scopas will no doubt continue to provoke lovers of ancient art to do so, in the hopes that he may become for us ever clearer and closer.

JEFFREY CARSON

See also Sculpture

Biography

Born in Paros, Scopas was active as a sculptor and architect *c*.360–335 BC. With Praxiteles and Lysippus he dominated Hellenic art of the 4th century BC. He is known to have worked on the temple of Athena Alea at Tegea, the Mausoleum of Halicarnassus, and the temple of Artemis at Ephesus. In antiquity he was famous for statues of gods.

Further Reading

Bieber, Margarete, *The Sculpture of the Hellenistic Age*, New York: Columbia University Press, 1961

Boardman, John (editor), *The Oxford History of Classical Art*, Oxford and New York: Oxford University Press, 1993

Boardman, John, *Greek Sculpture: The Late Classical Period and Sculpture in Colonies and Overseas*, London and New York: Thames and Hudson, 1995

Boardman, John, *Greek Art*, London and New York: Thames and Hudson, 1996

Brilliant, Richard, *The Arts of the Ancient Greeks*, New York and London: McGraw Hill, 1973

Hanfmann, George M.A., *Classical Sculpture*, Greenwich, Connecticut: New York Graphic Society, and London: Joseph, 1967

Pollitt, J.J., *The Art of Ancient Greece: Sources and Documents*, Cambridge and New York: Cambridge University Press, 1990

Richter, Gisela M.A., *A Handbook of Greek Art*, 9th edition, Oxford: Phaidon Press, 1987

Ridgway, Brunile Sismondo, *Fourth-Century Styles in Greek Sculpture*, Madison: University of Wisconsin Press, and London: Duckworth, 1997

Ridgway, Brunilde Sismondo, *Prayers in Stone: Greek Architectural Sculpture, ca. 600–100 BCE*, Berkeley: University of California Press, 1999

Robertson, Martin, *A History of Greek Art*, 2 vols, Cambridge: Cambridge University Press, 1975

Stewart, Andrew F., *Skopas of Paros*, Park Ridge, New Jersey: Noyes Press, 1977

Stewart, Andrew, *Greek Sculpture: An Exploration*, 2 vols, New Haven, Connecticut: Yale University Press, 1990

Sculpture

The mythical Daedalus was viewed in the ancient world as being one of the earliest sculptors in the Greek world. Although he had associations with Crete, he was later thought to have been an Athenian and a member of the Erechtheid family. His name has been linked to "daedalic" statues, which were recognized by Pausanias in the 2nd century AD. These included a statue of *Aphrodite* on the island of Delos which Pausanias (9. 40. 3) believed had been given to Ariadne by Daedalus.

Daedalus' influence was seen by ancient art historians as giving birth to the Sicyonian school of sculpture in the Peloponnese, which in the fullness of time was to see the appearance of the master sculptor Lysippus. Pliny the Elder (*Naturalis Historia*, 36. 9) retains the tradition that the marble sculptors Dipoenus and Scyllis – thought by Pausanias (2. 15. 1) to be either the pupils or even the sons of Daedalus – settled in Sicyon and made the city a centre of the arts.

Some have seen the creation of monumental sculpture in the Greek world as deriving from contact with Egypt. This tradition, cited by the historian Diodorus Siculus (1. 97. 5–6) in the 1st century BC, links the composition – the Greek term is *rhythmos* – of Daedalus' work with that found in Egypt. Certainly the establishment of a Greek settlement at Naucratis, according to Herodotus during the reign of the pharaoh Amasis, may have facilitated such contact. Whether or not Greek sculpture was derived from Egyptian proportions, it has long been recognized that *kouroi* – naked male statues of the Archaic period – had been carefully designed with set proportions. Such statues were used both as dedications within a sanctuary as well as for placing on tombs. An example of a funerary *kouros* comes from Anavyssos in Attica, where it was erected over the grave of one Croesus who had been killed in battle. *Kouroi* were a regular dedication in the Archaic Ptoan sanctuary in Boeotia.

The Peloponnese, and especially Argos and Sicyon, seems to have been innovative in sculpture, particularly monumental bronzes. Some of the key personalities, fulfilling commissions from both the western and the eastern Greeks, were the sculptors Ageladas of Argos and Canachus of Sicyon. The former is known to have accepted both private and public commissions from the Greek colony of Taras in southern Italy for statues which were erected at Olympia and Delphi, and the latter made a bronze statue for the important sanctuary of Apollo at Didyma in western Asia Minor. Argive sculptors were responsible for a pair of archaic *kouroi* which were dedicated to the Anakes (the Argive version of the Dioscuri) at Delphi; the pair were formerly known as Cleobis and Biton after the sons of the Argive priestess of Hera who according to Herodotus (1. 31) were commemorated by statues at Delphi.

Other schools of sculpture in the Archaic period were located on the islands of Aegina and Naxos. Aeginetan sculptors seem to have been in demand for making victory monuments at Olympia. Marble versions of their work can be glimpsed in the marble pediments, showing the two separate expeditions to Troy, from the temple of Aphaea on the island. The Naxians seem to have had one of the earliest schools of sculpture. Their sculptors made such works as the colossal Naxian *kouros* dedicated at Delos, as well as the statue of the Naxian Nicander who dedicated a *kore* (statue of a young woman) to "the far-shooter of arrows" in the sanctuary of Artemis on Delos. The Naxians also seem to be responsible for a large marble sphinx dedicated at Delphi, where it rested on a 10-m-high Ionic column.

Due to the habit of signing works, a more detailed picture can be derived from Attica in the 6th century BC. It is clear that both Attic and non-Attic sculptors (such as Aristion of Paros) were active in creating funerary monuments (*kouroi* and stelae) as well as dedications in sanctuaries such as the Athenian Acropolis; for example some 17 sculptors – identified by name, and not all of them from Attica – are known to have worked on the Acropolis alone in the late Archaic period. It seems that around the end of the 6th century BC there may have been a move towards specialization either in funerary sculpture or in religious dedications.

The Archaic period also saw the increased appearance of architectural sculpture. One of the earliest uses was on the temple of Artemis at Corfu where the sculptor has conceived of the triangular pediment as a frame for a series of scenes of differing scales, dominated by a large central gorgon. The temple of Apollo at Delphi received new pediments thanks to the generosity of the exiled Alcmaeonid family in the late 6th century BC (Herodotus, 5. 62). The pediments featured rather static individuals, the *korai* differing little from the freestanding figures found dedicated in Greek sanctuaries or as funerary monuments. The late Archaic period also saw the appearance of highly decorated treasuries at the Panhellenic sanctuaries. One of the best known was the treasury of the Siphnians at Delphi, which was noted by both Herodotus (3. 57) and Pausanias (10. 11. 2). The building identified as the Siphnian treasury was decorated with monumental caryatids, a continuous frieze, and pedimental sculpture. After the Battle of Marathon Athens celebrated its victory over the Persians with a small treasury decorated in the Doric style with metopes of the heroes Theseus and Heracles (Pausanias, 10. 11. 4).

After the Persian Wars there was a move away from the static pose of *kouroi* and *korai*. For example, the replacement group of the tyrannicides (Harmodius and Aristogeiton) made by the sculptors Critios and Nesiotes and erected in the Athenian Agora, showed the pair of "heroes" in the process of striking down the "tyrant" Hipparchus in 514 BC; he was in fact the son of Pisistratus and the younger brother of the actual tyrant Hippias. An attempt was made to distinguish between their ages by showing one of the figures bearded, the other beardless. From the 470s BC comes the hollow-cast statue of a charioteer – part of a larger group – dedicated by the Sicilian tyrant Polyzalus of Gela to celebrate a chariot victory at the Pythian games at Delphi.

During the 5th century BC, perhaps due to the increasing use of bronze casting, there were numerous innovations in sculpture. One of the key figures who can be identified in this process was Myron of Eleutherae (in Attica). He is perhaps best known for his discus-thrower (or *Discobolos*) where the

Sculpture: Greek youth fighting a centaur on a metope from the Parthenon, 5th century BC, British Museum, London

sculptor has captured a moment in the swing which would never normally be seen by the human eye. The statue itself, though lost, has been recognized in a number of Roman copies. Before this, victors in the discus competition are likely either to have been shown standing holding a discus, or the nature of their victory would have been identified by the inscription accompanying the statue. Such action poses seem to have been the hallmark of Myron. For example, the victory monument for the runner Ladas was celebrated for capturing the runner leaning forward in anticipation of his prize (*Anthologia Graeca*, 16. 54).

A sense of proportion in sculpture was created by Polyclitus of Argos, apparently a pupil of the Argive sculptor Ageladas. He is known to have been interested in the theory of sculpture and was said to have written a treatise on the subject whose tenets were then put into practice by his creation of the canon or spear-carrier (*Doryphoros*). Certainly the distinctive Polyclitan pose – straight and flexed arms, head turned to one side, and straight and flexed legs – suggests the formation of a new style which was to have great influence on subsequent generations of Greek sculptors as well as the creation of an image for the Roman emperor Augustus.

Greek victories against the Persians, notably at Salamis and Plataea but also at the Battle of Eurymedon in the 460s BC, led to the production of a number of monuments to celebrate Greek prowess. This civic patronage may have given opportunity to gifted sculptors such as Phidias who not only became one of the chief overseers for the Pericleian building programme at Athens, but also produced some monumental chryselephantine sculptures. Two of his most famous statues served as cult images for the temples of Athena Parthenos at Athens, and Zeus at Olympia. At Olympia itself the remains of the workshop where Phidias did his work have been found. Neither statue has survived, though both are known from contemporary images, such as the Attic Baksy krater, or from Roman copies. Phidias himself also created a monumental bronze statue of Athena Parthenos, apparently made to celebrate the Athenian victory at Marathon in 490 BC, which was dedicated on the Athenian Acropolis; the tip of the spear could apparently be seen as far away as Cape Sunium.

A number of highly sculpted marble buildings were raised in Athens in the 5th century BC as part of the Pericleian building programme. The most notable was the Parthenon, which housed Phidias' chryselephantine statue. This highly decorated building, with a continuous frieze, sculpted metopes, and two pediments, must have required teams of sculptors to complete it. Detailed accounts indicate the progression of the temple. At the same time the Acropolis was given a monumental entrance, the Propylaea, and in the 420s BC the bastion above the entrance received a new temple dedicated to Athena Nike and designed by Callicrates. This Ionic building was decorated with a continuous frieze, and the parapet around the temple was decorated with reliefs. This period also saw the erection of the Erechtheum.

Although much attention is focused on Athens of the 5th century BC some major sculptural schemes were being created elsewhere in Greece. At Olympia Phidias' chryselephantine statue of *Zeus* was placed in a Doric temple which was decorated with a sophisticated pair of pedimental sculptures depicting, respectively, the mythical origins of the games and the battle between the Lapiths and the Centaurs. The temple itself must have been nearly complete in 457 BC, as in that year the Spartans and their allies placed a dedication on the roof to celebrate their victory at Tanagra (Pausanias, 5. 10. 4). One of the architects of the Parthenon, Ictinus, was also apparently involved in the creation of the temple of Apollo Epikourios at Bassae near Phigaleia in Arcadia; although some would dispute this connection, the temple carried an internal frieze showing a centauromachy and an amazonomachy.

This tradition of architectural sculpture produced one of the seven wonders of the ancient world, the Mausoleum of Halicarnassus. This monumental tomb was built for Mausolus of Caria, a former Persian satrap. Although this was in western Turkey, technically beyond the Greek world, Mausolus' widow Artemisia engaged notable Greek sculptors to create an elaborate tomb after his death in 353 BC. The tomb was later dismantled, but it is clear that it had a continuous frieze showing an amazonomachy and a chariot race. Individual portrait statues may have stood between columns and the top was decorated with a chariot. Ancient writers such as Pliny the Elder and Vitruvius associate several Greek sculptors with the project: Leochares, Bryaxis, Scopas, Timotheus, and even Praxiteles.

During the 4th century BC a number of personalities in Greek sculpture emerged. In Athens Praxiteles came to prominence and was particularly celebrated for his creation of a naked Aphrodite displayed in a circular temple at Cnidus in western Asia Minor. Scopas, from the island of Paros, was regarded in antiquity as a rival of Praxiteles, no doubt due in part to having his name associated with the Mausoleum of Halicarnassus. One of the most innovative sculptors of the 4th century BC was Lysippus of Sicyon, who can perhaps be considered the creator of portraiture.

Although the literary sources, especially Pliny, allow us to identify a number of individual artists during the 4th century BC, many extant works are in fact anonymous. These include a group of bronzes from the Piraeus which may have been lost when Sulla destroyed the port in 86 BC. These fine works include an *Athena* and two statues of *Artemis*. Another high-quality bronze of this period is the statue of a youth found in the sea off Marathon.

Attic sculptors continued to make copies of famous Greek works in the Roman period to meet the tastes of the elite in the areas bordering the Mediterranean. A batch of marble reliefs from the Piraeus contains scenes copied from the amazonomachy on the shield of the Athena Parthenos; presumably some educated Roman wished to enhance his villa with elements from this major Athenian monument. An Athenian sculptor, Apollonius son of Archias, signed the bronze herm representing Polyclitus' *Doryphoros* which was found in the Villa of the Papyri at Herculaneum.

Sculpture continued to be created in the Greek east during the period of late antiquity, particularly under the patronage of Constantinople. It includes portraits of local governors, such as those erected at Megara and Athens. Some of the late antique sculpture is in marble, such as the relief of the archangel Gabriel at Antalya in southern Anatolia, derived from the quarries of Proconnesus which had been heavily exploited in the Roman imperial period. Low reliefs continued to be made in the Middle Ages, including representations of the Virgin Orans and Virgin Hodegetria.

DAVID W. J. GILL

Further Reading

Adam, Sheila, *The Technique of Greek Sculpture in the Archaic and Classical Periods*, London: British School of Archaeology at Athens, supplementary vol. 3, 1966

Ashmole, Bernard, *Architect and Sculptor in Classical Greece*, London: Phaidon, and New York: New York University Press, 1972

Barber, R., "The Greeks and Their Sculpture: Interrelationships of Function, Style and Display" in *Owls to Athens: Essays on Classical Culture Presented to Sir Kenneth Dover*, edited by E.M. Craik, Oxford: Clarendon Press, and New York: Oxford University Press, 1990

Barron, John, *Greek Sculpture*, London: Studio Vista, 1965

Boardman, John, *Greek Sculpture: The Archaic Period*, London: Thames and Hudson, and New York: Oxford University Press, 1978

Boardman, John, *Greek Sculpture: The Classical Period*, London and New York: Thames and Hudson, 1984

Boardman, John, *Greek Sculpture: The Late Classical Period and Sculpture in Colonies and Overseas*, London and New York: Thames and Hudson, 1995

Lullies, Reinhard and Max Hirmer, *Greek Sculpture*, London: Thames and Hudson, and New York: Abrams, 1960

Palagia, Olga and J.J. Pollitt (editors), *Personal Styles in Greek Sculpture*, Cambridge and New York: Cambridge University Press, 1996

Richter, Gisela M.A., *The Sculpture and the Sculptors of the Greeks*, New Haven, Connecticut: Yale University Press, and London: Oxford University Press, 1930; 4th edition, Yale University Press, 1970

Ridgway, Brunilde Sisimondo, *The Severe Style in Greek Sculpture*, Princeton, New Jersey: Princeton University Press, 1970

Ridgway, Brunilde Sisimondo, "The Setting of Greek Sculpture", *Hesperia*, 40, (1971): pp. 336–56

Ridgway, Brunilde Sisimondo, *Fifth Century Styles in Greek Sculpture*, Princeton, New Jersey: Princeton University Press, 1981

Ridgway, Brunilde Sisimondo, *Hellenistic Sculpture 1: The Styles of c.331–200 BC*, Bristol: Bristol Classical Press, and Madison: University of Wisconsin Press, 1990

Ridgway, Brunilde Sisimondo, "The Study of Classical Sculpture at the End of the 20th Century", *American Journal of Archaeology*, 98 (1994): pp. 759–72

Smith, R.R.R., *Hellenistic Sculpture: A Handbook*, London and New York: Thames and Hudson, 1991

Spivey, Nigel, *Understanding Greek Sculpture: Ancient Meanings, Modern Readings*, London and New York: Thames and Hudson, 1996

Stewart, Andrew, *Greek Sculpture: An Exploration*, New Haven, Connecticut: Yale University Press, 1990

Second Sophistic

Literary movement of *c*.AD 60–410

Philostratus (d. AD 249) coined the term "Second Sophistic" to create a connection between current rhetorical practice and the sophists of the Classical period. He marks the beginning of this "movement" during Nero's reign (*c*.AD 60), in the speeches (now lost) of Nicetas of Smyrna. This "Second Sophistic" continued until the sack of Rome in AD 410, and included such rhetoricians as Dion of Prusa, Herodes Atticus, his student Aristides (d. *c*.AD 181), Polemon, and Libanius. Much of the activity of these rhetoricians was in the realm of public performances in aristocrats' mansions, lecture-rooms, libraries, and amphitheatres, mainly in provincial cities such as Smyna, Ephesus, Antioch, and Pergamum, where their displays were often greeted by large, enthusiastic audiences.

Some idea of the variety of occasions for such performances can be gained from the two treatises on "epideictic" attributed to Menander Rhetor (3rd century AD) and from the *Techne* traditionally attributed to Aristides. These include instructions on how to compose speeches in honour of a city, at birthday and wedding celebrations, or to the emperor or other dignitaries. A very important part of a rhetorician's repertoire consisted of "political" declamations recreating mythological or historical situations, for example, a member of the delegation sent to persuade Achilles to return to the ranks (Aristides, *Orationes*, 52). Set-piece descriptions (*ekphraseis*), too, were popular and influential in other areas of literary production, for example in the works of the "novelists" Longus and Achilles Tatius, who are both described as "Sophists" in the manuscripts. The influence of these rhetoricians extends also to the great Church Fathers, almost all of whom were converts who had studied or taught rhetoric, for example, Gregory of Nazianzus (d. 390) and John Chrysostom (d. 407), who was a student of Libanius.

Many of the rhetoricians in this movement were active in state affairs, as ambassadors, as envoys sent to the emperor to speak in his praise or to secure privileges for their cities. So important was their eloquence that Vespasian established a salaried chair of Greek rhetoric, and Marcus Aurelius sponsored a chair of rhetoric that was worth 10,000 drachmas per year. Many later emperors reserved important offices for distinguished rhetoricians, some of whom moved up in the ranks of the imperial court to achieve even higher honours and more powerful positions.

The display speeches of the new "Sophists" were more than mere entertainment. Aristides, for instance, delivered speeches at festivals in all the great cities of the Greek-speaking parts of the empire, bringing to widely disparate audiences a common set of cultural themes and standards of taste and behaviour, fulfilling, in a way, Isocrates' dream of Panhellenism. The Church Fathers found in the rhetoric of the Second Sophistic a way of rehabilitating the eloquence of scripture and, in doing so, of helping their fellow Christians to achieve an identity of their own. What is perhaps most striking about this rhetorical movement is the fact that it was almost exclusively Greek, in spite of the dominance of Latin Rome over the entire Mediterranean basin. Even Favorinus, from the Gallic city of Arles, composed and delivered his speeches in Greek. In the Second Sophistic, then, we see no attempt to adapt to the culture of Rome, but a reassertion of Greek cultural values as a unifying force in an empire that was becoming more and more fragmented in the centuries before it collapsed in the west.

THOMAS M. CONLEY

See also Rhetoric, Sophists

Summary

A term coined in the 3rd century AD by Philostratus to demonstrate the link between contemporary rhetoric and the sophists of the Classical period, the Second Sophistic was a literary movement that began in the 1st century AD and continued until AD 410. It influenced all Greek literature of the day and represented a reassertion of Greek cultural values.

Further Reading

Anderson, Graham, *The Second Sophistic: A Cultural Phenomenon in the Roman Empire*, London and New York: Routledge, 1993

Bowersock, G.W., *Greek Sophists in the Roman Empire*, Oxford: Clarendon Press, 1969

Cassin, Barbara, *L'Effet sophistique*, Paris: Gallimard, 1995

Reardon, B.P., *Courants littéraires grecs des IIe et IIIe siècles après J.-C.*, Paris: Belles Lettres, 1971

Secularization

Secularization is one of the most commonly debated issues not only in sociology, but in philosophy, theology, history, and other disciplines as well. Originally, the term "secularization" was used in early modern times to signify the passing of ecclesiastical and monastic property to the control of a secular institution. The concept has since been incorporated into several theories, whose aim was to examine the role of religion in society in the wake of the continuing sociocultural evolution and change, especially with regard to modern times. There have been various secularization theories relating to specific aspects of this process across the centuries. Thus secularization was aptly described as a "multidimensional concept", while some scholars considered the secularization thesis as a modern myth. It is possible, though, without turning secularization into an ideology, to single out its basic postulates, which are useful for examining religious evolution and change in various contexts.

Generally speaking, secularization refers to the decline of religion either in theory and practice or in the public and private spheres. This phenomenon should be not equated, however, with the (hypothetical) complete disappearance of religion, since religion seems to belong somehow inherently to the human condition. Further, although there exist certain historical antecedents of secularization, this process is basically connected to developments in the western world in modern times. For example, the massive de-Christianization of western Europe in the 19th century was related to the specific socioreligious background and evolution of this particular geographical and cultural unit. Though exceptional in their secularity, these changes in western Europe have also influenced significantly the non-western world.

With regard to the Greek world, early forms of secularization can be located in the development of rationalism and scientific inquiry in ancient Greece, which contributed to an understanding of the world from a causal perspective and consequently to a relative desacralization of nature. Apart from this, the passing from pagan polytheism to Christian monotheism has also been considered as a major shrinkage of the supernatural realm from its numerous deities and supernatural beings to their replacement by the one God as the sole lord of the entire universe. Such developments did not signify a direct decline of religion, but opened the door for subsequent religious changes. After all, these were premodern societies in which religion played a vital role in all spheres of life as well as in the entire world order. The same is true with regard to the Byzantine empire, in which Orthodoxy as the official state religion was a most crucial parameter in the articulation of political ideology and permeated all societal sectors in a decisive way. Of course religious changes did take place during that period too, but they did not undermine the dominant role of Orthodoxy in society.

As far as the Greek world and its Orthodox tradition in modern times are concerned, the period of Ottoman domination is of paramount importance. Due to the privileges bestowed on the Orthodox Church after the fall of Byzantium, the patriarch became the head of the Orthodox *millet* ("community"). His jurisdiction was not confined to the religious domain alone, but concerned various other spheres (e.g. educational, judicial, social-communal, economic). This new status of the patriarchate of Constantinople enhanced substantially its role within Ottoman society. This may be also interpreted as a kind of worldliness due to the relative loss of its religious specificity and its involvement in manifold mundane activities and dealings with the Sublime Porte. Yet the patriarchate's religious role remained its most basic and characteristic feature throughout this period.

The main challenge for the Church appeared from the second half of the 18th century onwards under the influence of the Enlightenment. The Greek diaspora and students in western Europe as well as the merchant and trading communities initiated a major shift towards societal liberalization and modernization. Despite anticlericalist criticism, their intention was not to destroy the Church, but to limit its influence to the religious domain. Its polysemic role was of utmost importance at that time, thus social innovators tried to reform the Church partially rather than collide with it frontally. During the period of the Greek Enlightenment several such secularizing trends

can be observed: the separation of various sectors (e.g. education, communities) from religious control and their independent development; the deflecting of interest from metaphysics and otherworldliness to worldly, practical, and socially useful issues; and the explanation of natural phenomena scientifically and empirically and not by reference to supernatural factors. These trends, though influential enough, did not alter radically the socioreligious establishment of the day and were met with the staunch reaction of the Church, which feared losing its privileges. But they acted as catalysts for subsequent change in the newborn Greek state.

The 19th century was marked by several important developments concerning the Church's role in Greek society. In the wake of social differentiation the Church lost its previous broad societal responsibilities and was subjected to the state. This shrinkage of religious influence, which resulted in the autonomous evolution of various sectors (e.g. education), was mitigated later due to popular reactions and the Church's worldliness, i.e. through its transformation into an organ of the state and its involvement in vital national issues (e.g. the Great Idea). The social marginalization of the Church was effected also through the pluralization and cultural differentiation of Greek society under western influences, which allowed the existence and dissemination of anti-Orthodox and antireligious ideas by scientists and intellectuals despite ecclesiastical countermeasures. Yet, the consequences of secularization remained ambiguous, a fact attributed to the cultural specificity and idiosyncrasy of eastern Orthodoxy as distinguished from western Christianity. Despite the serious changes and problems created for the Church, secularization in Greece was limited and adapted to its specific exigencies. Orthodoxy, both as a personal belief system and as an institution, continued to exercise a powerful authority over the collective mentality of the Greeks. The same situation continued mutatis mutandis in the 20th century when the Church, despite the pervasive impact of westernization and modernization, still constitutes a crucial parameter of Greece's sociopolitical and cultural environment. This is clearly manifested in the fact that Church and state, despite numerous disagreements and conflicts, are still strongly bound together, and no separation between them is in prospect.

Modern Greece, despite its alliance with the western world, is a country continuously oscillating between its own traditions and the multifaceted challenges of modernity. This situation creates numerous paradoxes and contradictions. On the whole, popular sentiment remains close to the Church. Greeks may be very critical of their Church, but they do not intend to annihilate its power, but rather to ameliorate its condition and modernize it in certain ways. Although they do not follow meticulously the Church's directives, its influence permeates their entire cultural ethos – the phenomenon of "diffused religion". Historically, Greek society never wanted to sever its relationship entirely with the Orthodox Church, as has happened in many western countries with Roman Catholicism. This explains why secularization, despite its limited success, cannot neutralize the Orthodox factor.

VASILIOS MAKRIDES

See also Anti-westernism, Enlightenment

Further Reading

Alivisatos, Hamilcar S., *Saecularismus und Saecularisation und ihr neuer Sinn vom Orthodoxen Standpunkt aus gesehen*, Athens: Sonderdruck von der "Theologia", 1967

Argyropoulos, Roxane D., "Modifications du monde de vie et rôle des mentalités dans les Balkans, XVIIIe–XIXe siècles", *Études Balkaniques*, 27 (1991): pp. 52–60

Begzos, Marios P., *Elevtheria i Thriskeia? Oi Aparches tis Ekkosmikevsis sti Philosophia tou Dytikou Mesaiona* [Freedom or Religion? The Beginnings of Secularization in the Philosophy of the Western Middle Ages], Athens, 1991

Dobbelaere, Karel, *Secularization: A Multi-Dimensional Concept*, London: Sage, 1981

Kitromilides, Paschalis, "Modernization as an Ideological Dilemma in Southeastern Europe: from National Revival to Liberal Reconstruction" in *The Southeast European Yearbook 1992*, edited by T.A. Couloumbis and T.M. Veremis, Athens: ELIAMEP / Hellenic Foundation for Defense and Foreign Policy, 1993

Kokosalakis, Nikos, "Religion and Modernization in 19th Century Greece", *Social Compass*, 34/2–3 (1987): pp. 223–41

Kokosalakis, Nikos, R. Cipriani and R. van Boeschoten, "Aspects of Cultural and Religious Life in a Corfiote and a Sardinian Village" in *Secularization and Religion: The Persisting Tension*, Lausanne: CISR, 1987

Kokosalakis, Nikos, "Religion and the Dynamics of Social Change in Contemporary Europe", *Archives de Sciences Sociales des Religions*, 81 (1993): pp. 133–48

Kokosalakis, Nikos, "The Historical Continuity and Cultural Specificity of Eastern Orthodox Christianity" in '*Religions sans frontières?' Present and Future Trends of Migration, Culture, and Communication*, edited by R.Cipriani, Rome: Dipartimento per l'Informazione e l'Editoria, 1994

McNall, Scott G., "Value Systems that Inhibit Modernization: The Case of Greece", *Studies in Comparative International Development*, 9 (1974): pp. 46–63

Makrides, Vasilios N., "Orthodoxy as a *conditio sine qua non*: Religion and State Politics in Modern Greece from a Socio-Historical Perspective", *Ostkirchliche Studien*, 40 (1991): pp. 281–305

Makrides, Vasilios N., "The Orthodox Church and the Post-War Religious Situation in Greece" in *The Post-War Generation and Establishment Religion: Cross-Cultural Perspectives*, edited by W.C. Roof, Jackson W. Carroll and David A. Roozen, Boulder, Colorado: Westview Press, 1995

Makrides, Vasilios N., "Secularization and the Greek Orthodox Church in the Reign of King George I" in *Greek Society in the Making, 1863–1913: Realities, Symbols and Visions*, edited by Philip Carabott, Aldershot: Variorum, 1997

Martin, David, "Sociology, Religion and Secularization", *Religion*, 25/4 (1995): pp. 295–303

Nissiotis, Nikos, "Church and Society in Greek Orthodox Theology" in *Christian Social Ethics in a Changing World: An Ecumenical Theological Inquiry*, edited by John C. Bennet, London and New York: Association Press, 1966

Papapetrou, Konstantinos, "Die Säkularisation und die Orthodox-Katholische Kirche Griechenlands", *Kyrios*, new series 6 (1966): pp. 193–205

Savramis, Demosthenes, "Griechenland zwischen Tradition und Fortschritt", *Die Dritte Welt*, 1 (1972): pp. 101–18

Tschannen, Olivier, "The Secularization Paradigm: A Systematization", *Journal for the Scientific Study of Religion*, 30/4 (1991): pp. 395–415

Seferis, George 1900–1971

Diplomat and poet

The title of Seferis's first collection, *Turning Point* (1931), was intended to suggest his own "turn towards the world": that is, away from the introvert and nihilistic tendencies which characterized much of the poetry of the 1920s and, indeed, his own juvenilia. It also proved to be a turning point for Greek poetry as a whole, heralding a period of literary experiment and innovation. The collection consists of 13 short poems in a variety of rhyming patterns and metrical forms, and the large-scale "Erotikos Logos", cast mainly in the traditional 15-syllable verse (*politikos stichos*) which dates back to Byzantine times. As such, it draws and builds on the tradition of the folk song but also of earlier poets who cultivated this verse form, particularly Vitzentzos Kornaros, Dionysios Solomos, Kostis Palamas, and Angelos Sikelianos. The theme of love, a recurrent one in Seferis's poetry, plays a dominant role in the collection. Likewise, the extensive use of myth and literary allusion he was to make later is already adumbrated here. Although poetically accomplished, *Turning Point* is the product of Seferis's apprenticeship in the Symbolist tradition. The same is true of *The Cistern* (1932), his poem closest to Paul Valéry's work and to the ideal of *poésie pure*, and of the early poems in the *Book of Exercises* (1940), a collection the coherence of which, as he saw it, is none other than "that provided by ten years of continuous effort towards poetic expression". It was the publication of the poem sequence *Mythistorema* (1935) – marking his abandonment of an indisputably masterful handling of strict metre and rhyme in favour of free verse – that established him as a key exponent of Modernism in Greece.

If the example of the Symbolists fostered in Seferis a proper regard for the aural quality of poetry, it also made him wary of the dangers to the language inherent in their wish to attain the condition of music. Like T.S. Eliot and Ezra Pound, he sought to revivify poetic diction which he believed should be an enriched form of contemporary speech; the notorious "language question" made this an even more daunting task for a Greek poet. A desire for clear, precise, more objective expression and the need to give voice to collective rather than personal feelings, already discernible in his earlier verse, grew more imperative. He thus turned to less personal and inscrutable symbols and was increasingly drawn towards dramatic modes, realistic forms of expression, personae, and myth. It was at this stage that he became acquainted with Eliot's work which functioned as a catalyst in the completion of *Mythistorema*. A tension between past and present runs through the 24 sections of this many-voiced poem, set in a Greek landscape, employing ancient myth and conveying a contemporary outlook. More than just relating to the Asia Minor disaster – for the Greeks the tragic aftermath of World War I – it is a powerful comment on, and exposition of, life in modern times: an atmosphere of fracture, of futility and cultural collapse, a sense of acute loneliness, of rootlessness and lost wholeness characterize the world it describes. The same mood prevails in the twin-poemed *Gymnopaidia* (1936).

Written between 1937 and 1940, *Logbook I* (1940) concludes with one of his best-known poems, "The King of

George Seferis, poet and diplomat

Asine". Characteristically, specific events are at most only alluded to, but an atmosphere of apprehension and anxiety about the looming menace of World War II permeates the collection. The drama of this war, its tragic consequences, and the internal politics of the Greek government-in-exile form the background to *Logbook II* (1944/45). Yet, even in this most diary-like of his collections, his poetry also goes beyond a situation in time. For example, while "Last Stop" focuses on the topical reality of wartime and "An Old Man on the River Bank" contains references to it, the former also involves profound, if depressing, musings on human psychology, and the latter a number of quintessentially Modernist themes: the poetic medium and the process of poetic creation, or the contrast between a more wholesome past and 20th-century life with its sense of nullity and lost signification. Above all, however, it is an agonizing cry of the heart for the need to find a way of preserving human qualities – man's humanism.

Logbook II was followed, in 1947, by the large-scale composition *Thrush* which draws on the Odysseus and Oedipus narratives and concludes with the poem's modern Odysseus experiencing a moment of transcendence or, in Seferis's words, "an affirmation of a moment of dazzling and eternal life". Another moment of visionary transcendence, during which love again has a central role, is the subject of "Engomi", which closes *Logbook III* (1955). The main bulk of the poems in this collection were written after Seferis's visit to Cyprus in 1953, a time when the Cypriot struggle for self-determination was rapidly moving towards a climax. They

relate to the island's past and present, to its landscape and people. Rich in its appeal to the senses, *Logbook III* arguably contains the most extensive use of literary allusion by a poet in whose work a creative dialogue with the literary tradition, from Homer and the ancient tragedians down to contemporary poetry, is a constant and distinctive feature. This wealth of literary evocation is supplemented here by recourse to religious tradition and an intensified use of inherited popular culture. Myth is not abandoned, but poetic elaboration of historical themes is also introduced. Distilled from the island's reality (past and present) are those elements which at the same time transcend it, for they bear upon human experience more generally. Even in those poems relating to the Cyprus situation at the time the emphasis is still on the sense of belonging or its opposite ("Details on Cyprus" and "In the Kyrenia District", respectively), on the hubris of acting against nature ("Salamis in Cyprus"), and on the tribulation involved in the quest for ideals unrealized ("Helen").

The Three Secret Poems (1966) is the last collection to appear in Seferis's lifetime. Likewise exploiting literary, religious, and folk tradition, it is marked by references to accumulated experience, by allusions to his earlier poetry, and by a reflective mood. Concern with poetic practice emerges as a key theme. Others are the portrayal of a "ravaged" present and a vision of the end approaching, but also of a happier future for coming generations. They bear out the strongly held humanist belief, informing much of his poetry from at least *Mythistorema* onwards, that for all the bleakness of the present there is still hope and promise for mankind.

Seferis's first act of protest at the Greek coup d'état in 1967, and the censorship it imposed, was to refrain from publishing anything in his own country. Two years later he issued, through the BBC, his much-acclaimed "Declaration" against the Greek junta calling on the Colonels to restore democracy. Moreover, he produced two poems ("The Cats of Saint Nicholas" in 1969, and "On Aspalathoi..." in 1971) which, obliquely but unmistakably, warn of inherent dangers and condemn the political reality of the time.

Although three more collections came out posthumously, Seferis's poetic output remains relatively small in size. His oeuvre as a whole, however, was always considerably more extensive and proved to be dramatically so after his death. A novel, *Six Nights on the Acropolis*, begun in the later 1920s and reworked in 1954, appeared in 1974. Seven volumes of his private diaries and two of his political ones (covering the years 1926–60 and 1935–52 respectively) have been published to date as well as much of his vast correspondence. Fascinating in their own right, they add to our understanding of Seferis as man and poet, always open to stimuli from outside, yet deeply rooted in his own language, landscape, and tradition.

His concern with the Greek language, its limits and potentialities, lay behind his decision to translate a variety of texts into modern Greek. Conscious as he was of linguistic continuity, when rendering from an earlier form of the Greek language (passages from the Greek classics, the Revelation of St John, etc.) he insisted on the term "transcription" rather than "translation". In translating Eliot's *The Waste Land*, one of his many renderings of English and French texts into Greek, he prefaced it with an extensive introduction (1936). This was subsequently included in his essays (*Dokimes*), becoming the first of several in which, with the sensibility of the practitioner, he examined the direction and complexities of contemporary poetic production, the nature of poetry, and its relation to language. Mostly Greek in their focus, his essays also cover a variety of topics as diverse as the *Homeric Hymns*, the Byzantine rock-cut churches of Cappadocia, and the *Memoirs* of general Makriyannis, *Erotokritos*, the poetry of Andreas Kalvos or Constantine Cavafy, and the painting of Theophilos Chatzimichail. For all their ostensible diversity, they constitute facets of Hellenism, a subject Seferis spent a lifetime exploring. Offering new insights and written in a style admirable for its clarity, precision, and economy, *Dokimes* form, with his poetry, a lasting legacy.

KATERINA KRIKOS-DAVIS

Biography

Born in Smyrna in 1900, Seferis moved with his family to Athens in 1914 where he completed his schooling. He studied law in Paris (1918–24) and then spent some months in London to improve his English. Entering the Greek diplomatic service in 1926, he spent most of his professional life outside Greece. His last appointment was as Greek Ambassador to London (1957–62). As a poet he attracted attention from an early stage. He won the Nobel Prize for Literature in 1963. He died in 1971.

Writings

On the Greek Style: Selected Essays in Poetry and Hellenism, translated by Rex Warner and T.D. Frangopoulos, London: Bodley Head, 1967; reprinted 1992

A Poet's Journal: Days of 1945–1951, translated by Athan Anagnostopoulos, Cambridge, Massachusetts: Harvard University Press, 1974

Complete Poems, translated by Edmund Keeley and Philip Sherrard, London: Anvil Press, 1995

Further Reading

Beaton, Roderick, *George Seferis*, Bristol: Bristol Classical Press, 1991

Capri-Karka, C., *War in the Poetry of George Seferis*, New York: Pella, 1985

Daskalopoulos, Dimitris, *Ergographia Seferi, 1931–1979* [Works of Seferis, 1931–1979], Athens, 1979

Daskalopoulos, Dimitris (editor), *Eisagogi stin Poiisi tou Seferi: Epilogi Kritikon Keimenon* [Introduction to the Poetry of Seferis: A Selection of Cretan Texts], Herakleion, 1996

Hadas, Rachel, *Form, Cycle, Infinity: Landscape Imagery in the Poetry of Robert Frost and George Seferis*, Lewisburg, Pennsylvania: Bucknell University Press, 1985

Keeley, Edmund, *Modern Greek Poetry: Voice and Myth*, Princeton, New Jersey: Princeton University Press, 1983

Kiourtsakis, Yannis, *Ellinismos kai Dysi sto Stochasmo tou Seferi* [Hellenism and the West in Seferis's Thought], Athens, 1979

Kohler, Denis, *L'Aviron d'Ulysse: l'itinéraire poétique de Georges Séféris*, Paris: Belles Lettres, 1985

Kokolis, X.A., *Seferika Mias Eikosaetias* [Twenty Years' Writings on Seferis], Thessalonica, 1993

Krikos-Davis, Katerina, *Kolokes: A Study of George Seferis' Logbook III (1953–1955)*, Amsterdam: Hakkert, 1994

Labrys, 8 (April 1983) (Seferis issue; guest editor John Stathatos)

Mackridge, Peter (editor), *Ancient Greek Myth in Modern Greek Poetry: Essays in Memory of C.A. Trypanis*, London: Cass, 1996

Maronitis, D.N., *I Poiisi tou Giorgou Seferi* [The Poetry of George Seferis], Athens, 1984

Pieris, Michalis (editor), *Giorgos Seferis: Philologikes kai Ermineftikes Prosengiseis* [George Seferis: Philological and Interpretative Approaches], Athens, 1997

Ricks, David, *The Shade of Homer: A Study in Modern Greek Poetry*, Cambridge and New York: Cambridge University Press, 1989

Savidis, G.P. and Leonidas Zenakos (editors), *Gia ton Seferi* [For Seferis], Athens, 1961

Tsatsos, Ioanna, *My Brother George Seferis*, translated by Jean Demos, St Paul, Minnesota: North Central, 1982

Vayenas, Nasos, *O poiitis kai o Chorevtis* [The Poet and the Dancer], Athens, 1979

Vitti, Mario, *Phthora kai Logos: Eisagogi stin Poiisi tou Giorgou Sepheri* [Decay and Intellect: An Introduction to the Poetry of George Seferis], Athens, 1978

Seleucids

Dynasty of Macedonian kings

The name Seleucids refers to the dynasty of Macedonian kings founded by Seleucus I Nicator (*c*.355–281BC), one of the successors of Alexander the Great. The dynasty dated its beginning to 312 BC (the start of the "Seleucid era") when Seleucus recaptured his original province of Babylon and started on a long career of expansion, during which he assumed the royal title in 305/04 BC. The dynasty lasted until 64 BC when it was overthrown by the Roman general Pompey, who created the Roman province of Syria. The name Seleucids is used by only one ancient author (Appian, *Syriake*, 48–50, 65, 67). More commonly the rulers are referred to in ancient writers from the 2nd century BC onwards as either "the kings descended from Seleucus Nicator", or most frequently as "the kings of Syria", the "Syrian kings", the "kings of the Syrians", but also as the "kings of Asia"; other designations are found as well. None of these territorial designations originates with the rulers, who never described themselves as kings of any particular country or people: the Seleucid empire thus never had a precise territorial definition. The Seleucids are also frequently referred to collectively as "the Macedonians".

Starting from his province of Babylonia, Seleucus I went on to enlarge his territories steadily, first towards the east and then towards the west. By the time of his death in 281 BC his empire extended from Bactria and the borders of India in the east to north Syria and the eastern Mediterranean, Asia Minor, and even a foothold on the European mainland across the straits. This large empire proved difficult to maintain as a unit, and subsequent rulers were frequently on the defensive against internal and external challenges. Under Antiochus III the Great the empire was able to stage a spectacular recovery, though Antiochus then clashed with the Romans and was defeated by them. The Treaty of Apamea that followed his defeat (188 BC) excluded the Seleucids from Asia Minor north of the Taurus and imposed heavy penalties on them. Of subsequent rulers the best known is Antiochus IV because of his attack on Egypt and rebuff by the Romans (168 BC), and especially because of his failed attempt in 167 BC to ban Judaism at Jerusalem. This is recounted at length in the Jewish tradition (Daniel, 1 and 2 Maccabees) on which Antiochus IV made a profound impact, but receives scant mention in the extant Classical sources

(Diodorus, 34. 1; Tacitus, *Histories*, 5. 8. 4–5). After his death in 164 BC the dynasty was increasingly prey to internal dynastic conflicts as well as external intervention. With the defeat and death of Antiochus VII in his Parthian expedition of 130–129 BC the dynasty ceased to play a significant role on the international scene.

The Seleucid contribution to the Hellenic tradition is not easily assessed. The court history that once existed is lost, and other contemporary accounts are incompletely preserved if at all; hence reliance must be placed on later and thus derivative writers, whose ultimate sources are largely unknown. Only two of these give a continuous, but sketchy, account of the history of the dynasty as a whole (Appian's *Syriake*, 2nd century AD; Justin's *Epitome* of the *Philippic Histories* of Trogus Pompeius, 3rd century AD). Whereas Alexander the Great attracted much attention under the Roman empire, the Seleucids were apparently largely neglected apart from their continued reputation in north Syria, especially at Antioch, and were often thought of as kings who had not stood up to Rome. Plutarch's general lack of sympathy for the kings after Alexander is also a relevant factor, as shown by his choice of biographies. The presentation of the Seleucids in the extant literary sources diverges. In one tradition, most clearly represented in the 4th century AD by Libanius of Antioch (*Antiochicus*, 11 especially 100–04; written in AD 360), Seleucus I in particular is presented encomiastically as having extended the Greek world in the east through his city foundations (notably Seleuceia on the Tigris, and the four cities of Antioch, Seleuceia in Pieria, Laodicea, and Apamea in north Syria). Among these, Antioch in particular continued to flourish after the end of the Seleucids as one of the leading cities of the eastern Roman empire. Other writers, dating from the 3rd century BC onwards (Phylarchus, later Posidonius), presented the dynasty negatively as an example of "oriental despotism" and "eastern decadence". This pejorative colouring was further emphasized by Roman propaganda at the time of the conflict with Antiochus III (cf. the speech of the Roman commander Manlius Vulso in 189 BC in Livy, 38. 17: "the Macedonians who hold Alexandria in Egypt, who dwell in Seleuceia and Babylonia and in other colonies scattered throughout the world, have degenerated into Syrians, Parthians, Egyptians"). The presentation in Justin's *Epitome* follows this predominantly negative view of post-Alexander history. In practice it is very unlikely that the Seleucids had any general programme of "Hellenizing" their empire; the action of Antiochus IV at Jerusalem seems to have been strictly local in character (despite 1 Maccabees 1.41), and was in any case soon rescinded. The aims of the kings were probably imperial and dynastic rather than specifically Hellenic. Modern approaches to the Seleucids have fluctuated. In the early 20th century they were presented as champions of Hellenism in the east (E.R. Bevan, A. Bouché-Leclercq, E. Meyer). After World War II Seleucid history was studied increasingly from an eastern perspective, and the Seleucids were presented as continuators of the Persian empire whose centre of gravity lay in Babylonia rather than in the west (P. Briant, A. Kuhrt and S. Sherwin-White), though the approach is controversial. The true identity and orientation of the Seleucids thus remain a matter of dispute.

Macedonian in origin but Greek in culture, the Seleucids used Greek as the language of the court. Their abundant coinage is purely Greek in style, types, and inscriptions, and makes no concession to the eastern world. On the other hand the Seleucids were able to identify at Babylon with native traditions of kingship, and there is much Babylonian evidence for their activity there, though unlike Alexander they made no attempt to connect themselves directly with Persian royal traditions. The Seleucid record in the patronage and promotion of Greek culture appears to be much more limited in all fields than that of the Ptolemies (their rivals) or of the Attalids, and there was no Seleucid equivalent in the cultural field to Ptolemaic Alexandria or Attalid Pergamum. No Seleucid ruler acquired the reputation of being a patron of the arts. This in itself may help to account for their more modest reputation in the general Hellenic tradition.

The last extended mention of the Seleucids in antiquity is in the *Chronography* of John Malalas (8. 197–213) in the 6th century AD; he is fullest on Seleucus I and his foundations, though the reliability of this work is often questionable and there are numerous gaps and confusions. The modern rediscovery starts with Erasmus Fröhlich's *Annales Compendiarii Regum et Rerum Syriae* (Vienna, 1744; 2nd edition 1754), though the stimulus for that was the Jewish tradition on Antiochus IV and the evidence of coinage, rather than the Seleucid reputation in Greek literary sources.

MICHEL AUSTIN

Further Reading

Astin, A.E. *et al.* (editors), *Rome and the Mediterranean to 133 BC*, Cambridge: Cambridge University Press, 1989 (*The Cambridge Ancient History*, vol. 8, 2nd edition)

Austin, Michel, "War and Culture in the Seleucid Empire", forthcoming; German translation published as "Krieg und Kultur im Seleukidenreich" in *Zwischen West und Ost: Studien zur Geschichte des Seleukidenreichs*, edited by Kai Brodersen, Hamburg: Kovac, 1999

Bevan, E.R., *The House of Seleucus*, 2 vols, London: Arnold, 1902; reprinted London: Routledge and Kegan Paul, and New York: Barnes and Noble, 1966

Bikerman, Elias Joseph, *Institutions des Séleucides*, Paris: Geuthner, 1938

Bilde, Per *et al.* (editors), *Religion and Religious Practice in the Seleucid Kingdom*, Aarhus: Aarhus University Press, 1990

Bouché-Leclercq, A., *Histoire des Séleucides, 323–64 avant J.-C.*, 2 vols, Paris: Leroux, 1913–14

Briant, Pierre, *Rois, tributs et paysans: études sur les formations du Moyen-Orient ancien*, Paris: Belles Lettres, 1982

Brodersen, Kai, *Appians Abriss der Seleukidengeschichte (Syriake 45, 232–70, 369)* and *Appians Antiochike (Syriake 1, 1–44, 232)*, 2 vols, Munich: Maris, 1989–91 (text and commentary)

Edson, C.F., "Imperium Macedonicum: The Seleucid Empire and the Literary Evidence", *Classical Philology*, 53 (1958): pp. 153–70

Fraser, P.M., "The Career of Erasistratus of Ceos", *Rendiconti Istituto Lombardo Accademia di Scienze e Lettere – Classe di Lettere e Scienze Morali e Storiche*, 103 (1969): pp. 518–37

Habicht, C., "Athen und die Seleukiden", *Chiron*, 19 (1989): pp. 7–26

Holleaux, Maurice, *Etudes d'épigraphie et d'histoire grecques*, vol. 3, Paris: Boccard, 1942

Grainger, John D., *The Cities of Seleukid Syria*, Oxford: Clarendon Press, and New York: Oxford University Press, 1990

Grainger, John D., *A Seleukid Prosopography and Gazetteer*, Leiden and New York: Brill, 1997

Kuhrt, Amélie and Susan Sherwin-White (editors), *Hellenism in the East: The Interaction of Greek and non-Greek Civilizations from Syria to Central Asia after Alexander*, London: Duckworth, and Berkeley: University of California Press, 1987

Malitz, Jürgen, *Die Historien des Poseidonios*, Munich: Beck, 1983

Meyer, Edward, *Blüte und Niedergang des Hellenismus in Asien*, Berlin: Curtius, 1925

Musti, Domenico, "Lo stato dei Seleucidi: dinastia, popoli, città da Seleuco I ad Antioco III", *Studi classici e orientali*, 15 (1966): pp. 61–200

Robert, Jeanne and Louis Robert, *Fouilles d'Amyzon en Carie*, vol. 1, Paris: Boccard, 1983

Rostovtzeff, M.I., *The Social and Economic History of the Hellenistic World*, 3 vols, Oxford: Clarendon Press, 1941; revised 1953

Sherwin-White, Susan and Amélie Kuhrt, *From Samarkhand to Sardis: A New Approach to the Seleucid Empire*, London: Duckworth, and Berkeley: University of California Press, 1993

TOPOI: Orient-Occident, vol. 4. 2, Lyon: Maison de l'Orient Méditerranéen, 1994 (collected articles commenting on Sherwin-White and Kuhrt 1993)

Walbank, F.W. *et al.* (editors), *The Hellenistic World*, Cambridge: Cambridge University Press, 1984 (*The Cambridge Ancient History*, vol. 7, part 1, 2nd edition)

Will, Edouard, *Histoire politique du monde hellénistique*, 2nd edition, 2 vols, Nancy: Presses Universitaires de Nancy, 1979–82

Seljuks

Turkish dynasty

The Seljuks were a Turkish dynasty that in the mid-11th century dominated the Caliphate at Baghdad to form what is now known as the Great Seljuk empire. While this empire, based in Mesopotamia, existed in one form or another till the end of the 12th century, a sibling state, the Seljuk Sultanate of Rum (the land of the "Romans", primarily discussed here), developed in Anatolia at the very end of the 11th century and was to remain an important factor in Byzantine and Crusader history till its demise at the beginning of the 14th century

Tradition has it that the primogenitor Seljuk was the leader of an Oghuz tribe that appears in history for the first time in the latter half of the 10th century in the region of the Caspian and Aral Seas. Seljuk (d. *c.*1000) was probably the first tribal leader to embrace Islam, ostensibly in its Sunni form.

The Seljuks were originally a nomadic and warrior-like Turkoman people amongst whom there was little political organization. This began to change during the 1020s when they made their presence felt as mercenaries for local warlords and became increasingly ambitious for territory. At the Battle of Dandanquan in 1040 Seljuk's grandsons, the brothers Chaghrï (d. 1058) and Tughrï I (d. 1063), captured Khorasan and effectively destroyed the power of the Turkoman empire of the Ghaznavids. By 1055 Tughrï I had captured Baghdad and was proclaimed sultan (or temporal ruler) by the Caliph, who was largely a religious rather than a political leader.

An influx of Turkoman tribes into Mesopotamia followed, and by the 1050s Turkoman raids were posing a threat to Byzantine possessions in eastern Anatolia where important towns such as Artze, Caesarea, Sebasteia, Ani, and Chonae had been sacked by 1070. Rivalries at home ensured that the Byzantines were unable to offer consolidated opposition. In 1071, at the Battle of Manzikert (Armenia), the emperor Romanos IV was defeated and captured by the Seljuks under the sultan Alp Arslan. The debacle of Romanos's capture, his release to collect a ransom, his deposition, and blinding created a military vacuum in Anatolia which the Turkoman troops of the Seljuks came to fill. Alp Arslan himself, however, was more concerned with establishing his position against fellow Muslims in Mesopotamia and Egypt rather than waging war on the empire.

In 1072 the son of the now late Alp Arslan, sultan Malikshah, placed the prince Sulayman Ibn Kutlumush in charge of the Anatolian front. By 1081 Sulayman, who first styled himself sultan, managed to establish himself at Nicaea, some 160 km from Constantinople. In 1084 the important city of Antioch at the other extremity of Anatolia was also taken. Events in the east led to Sulayman's withdrawal from Anatolia, but his son Kilij Arslan I returned to establish himself at Nicaea in 1092. Although some fortified *kastra* were taken in Anatolia, it was in the rural areas that the Turkomans made themselves particularly felt.

Here a distinction has to be made. The embryonic Seljuk state that was developing in Nicaea and other towns regarded the Byzantine empire as an eternal entity: "Rome". Accommodation with Constantinople and the development of a stable state system were the keystones of official Seljuk policy. This sometimes clashed with the many independent-minded Turkoman soldiers-of-fortune (or *ghazi*) on whom the Seljuk state mostly relied. The *ghazi* were interested in booty and fired by Islamic notions of holy war. A third group can also be identified: Turkoman nomads, interested more in grazing lands rather than settled state systems or "holy war". The *ghazi* Turkomans were to prove both a bane and an ally for the Seljuks, and a constant nuisance to the Byzantines throughout the next two centuries. Some managed to establish a powerful state, the Danishmendid, which proved a formidable foe in later years to Greek, Latin, and Seljuk.

Political turmoil in Byzantium after 1070 led to a situation where Byzantine rebels increasingly made use of Turkoman mercenaries, including the armies of the Seljuks, to achieve their aims. In 1092 Alexios I Komnenos had made an agreement with the Nicaean Seljuks to assist him in attacking the *ghazis*. The same emperor, however, is alleged to have invited contingents from the West (which eventually took the form of the First Crusade) to assist him in removing the Turkomans from Asia Minor.

The Seljuks were forced out of Nicaea in 1097 by the First Crusade, but soon reorganized themselves at Iconium (Konya, south central Asia Minor) which became the capital of the Seljuk state. The activities of the crusaders and the Byzantines in Asia Minor had pushed Seljuks and Turkomans from the coasts, and thus the 12th-century Seljuk state was confined mostly to the interior. In 1116 the Seljuks were defeated at the Battle of Philomelion, and a period of relative peace followed between Konya and Constantinople. This was terminated by the Seljuks' defeat of the Byzantine emperor Manuel I at the Battle of Myriokephalon in 1176. Thereafter, turmoil in Asia Minor ensued with Seljuks, Byzantines, Armenians of Cilicia, Turkoman emirs, and crusaders fighting among themselves.

The creation of the Byzantine empire in exile at Nicaea following the capture of Constantinople by the Fourth Crusade

Seljuks: illustration from the 11th-century chronicle of Skylitzes showing a battle between Byzantine and Seljuk cavalry, Biblioteca Nacional, Madrid

in 1204 led, ironically, to a period of relative peace and prosperity for both the Byzantines and Konya. Indeed, the two states enjoyed almost intimate relations. In 1243, however, the Mongol hordes crushed the Seljuks at Köse Dagh, initiating a period of instability that the Seljuks would never fully recover from. In one form or another the sultanate existed till the beginning of the 14th century, when it disappears in obscurity.

The Seljuk state, which developed in virtual isolation from its parent Great Seljuk empire in Iraq-Iran, rapidly drew on Byzantine and Islamic-Persian traditions to establish a permanent state system. The Persian element was especially prevalent. Arabic was used only for Qur'anic and legal matters, and was virtually unknown by the majority of Seljuks. This led to the development of a very different type of Islamic state in Anatolia, one which had no Arab cultural base to speak of. This distinction assisted in the development of a uniquely "Turkish blend" of Islamic, Persian, and Byzantine traditions that would culminate in the Ottoman empire.

By the reign of Kilij-Arslan II (1155–92), an efficient administrative, military, and fiscal machine was perfected and the trappings of the sultanate were firmly established at court. The sultan, however, increasingly lost power to his ministers, especially after 1243, when the famous *pervane* (a sort of chief minister) Muin al Din Sylaman held the reins of power.

Art and letters at Konya from about 1150 up to 1243 were characterized by a strong Persian influence. There is no native Turkish literature from the Seljuk period. Writers, mystics, and artists from Mesopotamia increasingly came to Rum as Mongol pressure on Mesopotamia increased. The most famous was the poet and mystic Jalal al-Din Rumi (1207–73) whose followers developed the whirling Dervishes. (The revolt of the "false prophet" Baba Ishak *c.*1240, however, proved how great a danger these men could be to the state.) Mystic and spiritual traditions (notably Sufism) – sometimes with Shiite overtones – established themselves in Seljuk Anatolia prior to flourishing later in Ottoman times. The study of law was also encouraged, and some great Islamic jurists could be found in Konya. The institution of the *madrasa* (orthodox Sunni school of preparation for the "official classes") was found throughout the sultanate.

Seljuk architecture is justly singled out as an admirable development in that field, while the decorative arts involved mostly relief carving (some of it figural), tile and textile making, and some book illumination.

The Seljuks played an ambivalent role in the history of medieval Hellenism. Despite obvious tensions, the official state was not consistently hostile to the existence of the Byzantine empire and at times allied with it. Kilij Arslan II made a state visit to Constantinople in 1162. Seljuk troops often fought for Byzantium (even in Europe) and vice versa, especially against unruly *ghazis* and the crusader states. Relations were peaceful from 1211 to 1243, and many Seljuks fled to Nicaea in the wake of the Mongol attack. Some of these espoused Christianity and were resettled by the Byzantines. The so-called Gagauz, now living in Bulgaria, may have originally been Seljuk followers of the half-Greek sultan Izz a-Din (Kaykaus II, d. 1289) who was himself openly sympathetic to Christianity and had a Christian chancellor. Many Byzantine nobles, furthermore, served the sultan in many capacities, and many did not convert to Islam.

There is no doubt, however, that the demographic picture of Anatolia was slowly but irreversibly changed in the 12th and 13th centuries. Ecclesiastical administration simply collapsed in many provinces, cutting off a vital lifeline to the Byzantine world. Many people converted to Islam, some of them preferring this to the constant hardships under Christian rule. Islam, as a consequence, was a given fact in Anatolia by the time the Ottomans appeared and this made the eventual Islamization of the region easier than in the Balkans, where Islam for the most part was not adopted by the local Orthodox populations.

DAVID R. TURNER

Summary

Originally a nomadic Turkoman people, the Seljuks dominated the Baghdad Caliphate in the mid-11th century and formed the Great Seljuk empire. This was a threat to Byzantine territory in eastern Anatolia and in 1071 the emperor Romanos IV was defeated by the Seljuks at Manzikert. By 1081 they had reached Nicaea but were pushed back by the Crusaders in the following decade. Centred on Konya, a Seljuk state flourished from the mid-12th to the mid-13th century when it was defeated by the Mongols.

Further Reading

Cahen, Claude, *Pre-Ottoman Turkey: A General Survey of the Material and Spiritual Culture and History, c.1071–1330*, London: Sidgewick and Jackson, and New York: Taplinger, 1968

Cahen, Claude, *A History of the Crusades*, edited by Kenneth M. Setton, vol. 2, Madison: University of Wisconsin Press, 1969, chapter 19

Hillenbrand, Carole, *The Crusades: Islamic Perspectives*, Edinburgh University Press, and Chicago: Fitzroy Dearborn, 1999

Holt, P.M., *The Age of the Crusades: The Near East from the Eleventh Century to 1517*, London and New York: Longman, 1986, chapter 19

Vryonis, Speros, *The Decline of Medieval Hellenism in Asia Minor and the Process of Islamization from the Eleventh through the Fifteenth Century*, Berkeley: University of California Press, 1971

Septuagint

The ancient Greek translation of the Old Testament

The translation of the Hebrew scriptures into Greek first occurred in Egypt. According to the *Letter of Aristeas*, the pharaoh Ptolemy II Philadelphus (285–246 BC) wanted a translation for the library at Alexandria and sent a request to Jerusalem for translators. The chief priest responded by sending 72 scribes with Hebrew scrolls of the Pentateuch (the first five books of the Old Testament). On their arrival in Egypt they were housed on an island in the Nile where they worked. When completed, their version was approved by the synagogue at Alexandria, and a copy was delivered to Philadelphus. Somehow the original 72 scribes were slightly reduced to 70, and their translation acquired the name "Septuagint", which is Latin for 70; it is usually cited in biblical studies as the LXX, after the Roman numerals for 70.

At first (c.250 BC), the Septuagint included only the Pentateuch, but eventually, by c.130 BC, all the other Old Testament books had been translated, at different times and by a wide range of hands. This piecemeal translating into a developing Hellenistic Greek, mixed with many Hebraisms, produced translations that varied greatly in style and quality.

Additional Jewish works, probably written in Greek in the Hellenistic Jewish community of Egypt, were added to the Septuagint; they are known as the Old Testament Apocrypha. They were accepted as canonical by the early Church and included in the Septuagint; they were also included in the Latin Vulgate. During the Reformation, however, Protestants segregated the Apocrypha as uncanonical, and in the 19th century it was generally dropped from Protestant Bibles. It remains in Orthodox and Roman Catholic Bibles.

Translating from Semitic Hebrew into Hellenistic Koine Greek forced scholars to take account of the great philosophical critiques of the anthropomorphic Olympian gods. Consequently they frequently suppressed the overt anthropomorphism of the Hebrew stories in favour of the more abstract thought of the Greeks. This anti-anthropomorphism is apparent in many verses. For example, when Moses at the burning bush asks God for his name, the Hebrew says the "one who is present"; the Greek for "I am" becomes an abstract *en an* (the Being). Other Hellenistic thought patterns were also accommodated.

Widely used as the scriptures of the Greek-speaking Jews of the diaspora, the Septuagint soon became the first scriptures of the Church. The writers of the New Testament books drew from the Septuagint. Perhaps as much as 5 per cent of the New Testament is composed of direct quotations from the Old Testament. In addition, there are many allusions, indirect quotations, and paraphrases of the Old Testament in the New. Almost all of these references are drawn from the Septuagint; this is almost always the "scriptures" referred to in the New Testament. (The Nestle-Aland version prints the direct quotations in bold type in its critical apparatus.)

When debates developed between Jews and Christians over the truth of the Christian interpretations of the Septuagint, the Jews argued that the Christians were quoting from translations; the Christians responded that the Septuagint was a Jewish translation. These debates led at first to new Jewish translations into Greek from Hebrew sources. Finally, after the destruction of Jerusalem in AD 70, the reorganization of Judaism under the rabbis involved the abandonment of all versions of the Old Testament except for the Hebrew one.

In order to make the Hebrew scriptures the sole authority for Jews, rabbinic Judaism found it necessary to establish one final version from the various Hebrew ones. Eventually the stabilized Hebrew text was known as the Masoretic text (MT). Meanwhile, in general, synagogues continued to use bulky scrolls for the individual books. Christians abandoned scrolls for the more convenient and "modern" form of the codex, which pulled the books together into a single volume. The books in the Hebrew scriptures soon differed in order of arrangement from that in the Septuagint. The Hebrew scriptures were grouped into the law, the prophets, and the writings; the Septuagint was arranged as law, histories, poetry, and prophets, with the Apocryphal books scattered among the latter three groups according to their character.

The discovery of the Dead Sea Scrolls at Qumram from 1947 has revealed that earlier Hebrew text families underlie both the Masoretic Hebrew text and the Septuagint. This has meant that the Septuagint can now be viewed as equal, superior, or inferior to the Masoretic text depending on the books in question. In addition, the discoveries of fragments of the Septuagint have now pushed scholarship back close to the original. It should also be noted that the Septuagint is currently the only source for understanding a number of obscure Hebrew words. Modern study of the Septuagint is now being aided by the use of computers for textual analysis. Major centres of study are in Germany, Finland, France, and Spain.

The value of the Septuagint has been immense. From the beginning the Septuagint has been the official version of the Old Testament for the Greek Orthodox Church. It paved the way for Christian missionaries. And it was the basis for the translations into Armenian, Georgian, Coptic, and other languages.

A.J.L. WASKEY, JR

See also Jews

Summary

The Septuagint is a translation of the Hebrew scriptures into Greek made at the request of Ptolemy II Philadelphus (285–246 BC). A monument of Hellenistic Greek, it is the oldest and most influential of the ancient translations of the Old Testament. It has always been the standard text of the Old Testament for the Greek Orthodox Church.

Further Reading

Aejmelaeus, Anneli, *On the Trail of Septuagint Translators: Collected Essays*, Kampen: Kok Pharos, 1993

Archer, Gleason L. and Gregory Chirichigno, *Old Testament Quotations in the New Testament*, Chicago: Moody Press, 1983

Barrett, C.K. (editor), *The New Testament Background: Selected Documents*, London: SPCK, 1956; New York: Harper and Row, 1961

Charlesworth, James Hamilton (editor), "Letter of Aristeas" in *The Old Testament Pseudepigrapha and the New Testament: Prolegomena for the Study of Christian Origins*, Cambridge and New York: Cambridge University Press, 1985

Danker, Frederick W., "History of the Septuagint" and "The Use of the Septuagint", in his *Multipurpose Tools for Bible Study*, revised edition, Minneapolis: Fortress Press, 1993

Dogniez, Cecile, *Bibliography of the Septuagint, 1970–1993*, Leiden and New York: Brill, 1995

Eissfeldt, Otto, *The Old Testament: An Introduction*, New York: Harper and Row, and Oxford: Blackwell, 1965

Ellis, E. Earle, *Paul's Use of the Old Testament*, Edinburgh: Oliver and Boyd, 1957; Grand Rapids, Michigan: Baker, 1981

Ewert, David, *From Ancient Tablets to Modern Translations: A General Introduction to the Bible*, Grand Rapids, Michigan: Zondervan, 1983

Goodspeed, Edgar J., *The Apocrypha*, New York: Vintage, 1959

Greenspoon, L., "'It's All Greek to Me': Septuagint Studies Since 1968", *Currents in Research: Biblical Studies*, 5 (1997): pp. 147–74

Jellicoe, Sidney, *The Septuagint and Modern Study*, Oxford: Clarendon Press, 1968

Jellicoe, Sidney, *Studies in the Septuagint: Origins, Recensions, and Interpretations: Selected Essays, with a Prolegomenon*, New York: Ktav, 1974

Katz, P. "Septuagintal Studies in the Mid-Century" in *The Background of the New Testament and Its Eschatology*, edited by W.D. Davies and David Daube, Cambridge: Cambridge University Press, 1956

Nestle, Eberhard *et al.*, *Novum Testamentum Graece*, Stuttgart: Deutsche Biblestiftung, 1979

Rahlfs, Alfred (editor), *Septuagint*, Stuttgart: Deutsche Biblegeschellschaft, 1979

Schiffman, Lawrence H., *Reclaiming the Dead Sea Scrolls*, Philadelphia: Jewish Publication Society, 1994

Wurthwein, Ernst, *The Text of the Old Testament: An Introduction to the Biblia Hebraica*, Grand Rapids, Michigan: Eerdmans, 1979; revised 1995

Serbia

The boundaries of Serbia have altered during the 14 centuries since the first arrival of Serbs in the Balkan peninsula. The emperor Herakleios (610–41) is supposed to have granted them territory in the northwest Balkans, and also to have settled some Serbians in the north of Greece at Servia, but both grants of territory may be legal fictions. For a long time contacts between Serbia and Greece were limited owing to the presence of the intervening Bulgarian empire. In the 9th century the Serbs were converted to Christianity, adopted the Cyrillic alphabet, and entered the world of Orthodoxy if not of the empire. The emperor Constantine VII Porphyrogennetos (913–59) wrote a good deal about the Serbs in *De Adminstrando Imperio*. Basil II's defeat of the Bulgarians brought the Serbians in Raška and Dioclea under Byzantine control, and the Komnenoi were keenly interested in the Serbians as potential allies or enemies in the face of invasions from Italy or against it. Crusading armies, entering the Byzantine empire at Belgrade, found some kind of Byzantine presence there, but northern Serbia was largely uninhabited and Byzantine control really began at Niš.

After the Fourth Crusade the situation changed. The Nemanjid dynasty steadily extended their power southwards at the expense of Byzantium. They built Byzantine churches and married Byzantine princesses. In return Byzantine chroniclers like Gregoras and Pachymeres commented on the uncouth manners and crude dwellings of the Serbs. Stephan IV Dushan (1331–55) called himself emperor of the Greeks as well as the Serbs and wished to become emperor at Constantinople. He also occupied northern Greece, but on the collapse of his empire Serbs appear to have made little impression in this area, although there were briefly petty Serbian dynasties in Thessaly and Epirus.

The Ottoman invasion again drove a wedge between Serbia and Greece. Each nation fell to the Turks in a catastrophic way, celebrated thereafter in song. The Greeks gave no help to the Serbs at the battle of Kosovo in 1389, the Serbs no help to the Greeks at the siege of Constantinople in 1453. In between these two events, Greeks and Serbs helped the Turks at the battle of Ankara in 1402. While history linked and divided Greeks and Serbs in this way, legend provided more glorious links with each nation carrying with it during years of subservience memories of a heroic defeat, a martyred ruler, and hopes of an eventual triumph.

The Serbs had established an autocephalous Church as early as 1219. A patriarchate at Peć was founded in 1346, but met with opposition from the Greeks. In the early part of the period of Ottoman domination it was Turkish policy to manage ecclesiastical affairs through Greek control, but an independent patriarchate at Peć was re-established from 1557 to 1766. Even outside these years Greek religious influence was never very strong except perhaps in the south, and Greek efforts to set up schools in Serbia were equally unsuccessful. Where Greeks did achieve success and influence was through trade. Greek and Vlach merchants travelling through Serbia to the markets of the Habsburg empire set up warehouses and trading posts in Serbia, sometimes settling to build houses and churches. At one time, Belgrade almost looked like a Greek city. It contained a flourishing Greek school for which Serb government funds were allocated in the 1840s, although it became a private school in 1847. Strong family ties kept Greek merchants in touch with their native villages, to which they often returned, bringing part of their wealth with them. Those who stayed behind in Serbia were eventually assimilated, although they contributed to a feeling of friendship between their adopted country and Greece. There was some contact between the Greek revolutionaries who sought independence from Turkey and those who fought for the same cause in Serbia. Iordakis, also known as Olympiotis, had fought in Serbia and with the Russians before taking part in the abortive rising of 1821 in Romania. Milos Obrenovic, however, adopted a rather pacific role around 1830.

When in 1913 Serbia was awarded the territory now known as the Former Yugoslav Republic of Macedonia, it found substantial quantities of Greeks in towns like Titov Veles, Bitola, and Strumica. Many of these Greeks were in fact Vlachs, harbouring pro-Greek sentiments. It is impossible to find such Greeks any longer, as they have either left or been assimilated. Occasionally a building or an old family name is a reminder of the Greek past, although this past is not remote, going back no further than the mercantile expansion of the 18th and 19th centuries.

After World War II a new kind of emigrant entered Serbia in the shape of fighters for the Communist side in the Greek Civil War, but many of these were sent to other Communist countries or were already Slavophones, and the only real Greek-speakers in Yugoslavia after the war were a few elderly Hellenized Vlachs. The emergence of Macedonia as an independent state between Serbia and Greece has made communi-

42. The Serbian empire of the Nemanjids

cation between the two countries difficult, although Macedonia like Bulgaria and Turkey has served as a common enemy to link Serbs and Greeks.

T.J. WINNIFRITH

See also Commonwealth, Serbs, Vlachs

Further Reading

Karanovich, Milenko, *The Development of Education in Serbia and Emergence of Its Intelligentsia, 1838–1858*, Boulder, Colorado: East European Monographs, 1995

Obolensky, Dimitri, *The Byzantine Commonwealth: Eastern Europe, 500–1453*, London: Weidenfeld and Nicolson, and New York: Praeger, 1971

Serbia: the Serbian monastery of Chilandari on Mount Athos, founded in 1198 by Symeon (formerly Stefan Nemanja)

Stoianovich, T, "The Conquering Balkan Orthodox Merchant" ,
   Journal of Economic History, 20 (1960): pp. 234–313
Wilkinson, Henry Robert, *Maps and Politics: A Review of the
   Ethnographic Cartography of Macedonia*, Liverpool: Liverpool
   University Press, 1951

Serbs

The origin of the Serbs is obscure. It has always been suggested that like both the Bulgars and the Avars they and the Croats were originally of non-Indo-European stock, dominating a subservient Slav population. Alternatively, though they are apparently quintessentially Slav with their Orthodox religion, Cyrillic alphabet, and attachment to Russia, it has been suggested that most Serbs like Vlachs and Albanians are the descendants of the indigenous Illyrian tribes. In the 7th century Serbs are said to have moved from Czechoslovakia to modern Serbia. They are thought to have acknowledged the authority of the Byzantine emperor in the time of Herakleios (610–41), although such authority, if it existed, must have been both nominal and ephemeral. The rise of a powerful Bulgarian kingdom acted as a barrier between Serbia and Byzantium in the early Middle Ages. It is a recurring feature of the relation-ship between Greeks and Serbs that, through not clashing with each other and clashing instead with the intervening Bulgars, they have been generally on friendly terms with each other.

The Serbs were originally pagans, organized as extended families or *zadrugas*, then as clans, then as tribes. In the middle of the 9th century these tribes were united under one župan (governor), and Cyril (St Constantine) and Methodios intro-duced Christianity and the Cyrillic alphabet. After the final defeat of the Bulgarians in 1018 the Byzantine empire controlled the Balkan peninsula, and the Serbs once again acknowledged Byzantine rule, although again this rule cannot have been too strictly enforced, especially after the defeat of Manzikert and the arrival of the Crusaders when the empire had trouble on other fronts. The main area of Serb strength was in Dioclea or Zeta, roughly corresponding to modern Montenegro, and Raška, roughly corresponding to the south-ern part of Serbia and the northern part of Kosovo. Interestingly and tragically, neither area has been the hub of the modern Serbian state.

In 1167 Stephan Nemanja became župan of Raška. The Nemanjis were to dominate Serbian history for the next 200 years. They soon obtained independence from Byzantium after the death of Manuel I Komnenos, and gradually extended their power southwards and northwards until in the reign of Stephan IV Dushan (1331–55) Serbs ruled from the Danube to the Gulf of Corinth. The Nemanjids were bloodthirsty but pious. It was rare for rulers to suceed to the throne without slaughter of rival claimants or their predecessors. Yet they were builders of beautiful churches, modelled on Byzantine architecture. St Sava, the son of Stephan Nemanja, was a man of conspicuous piety who established an autocephalous Serbian Church. The Byzantines despised the Serbs as rude barbarians, but for political reasons Byzantine princesses often married into the Serbian royal family, and Dushan aspired to become emperor at Constantinople.

On Dushan's death his ramshackle empire fell to pieces. Serbian princelings ruled for a time in Thessaly, Epirus, and Macedonia, but the Ottoman advance soon put an end to them. Further north, Serbian resistance coalesced under prince Lazar with his capital at Kruševac. On 15 June 1389 the Serbs fought the Turks on the Field of Blackbirds in the plain of Kosovo. In Serbian oral poetry, often compared to the work of Homer, this battle is celebrated as a heroic defeat for the Serbs. prince Lazar certainly died. In the west bells were rung for a glorious victory. The sultan was certainly slain. Probably the battle was indecisive. In Serbia prince Lazar's son Stephan and great nephew George Branković continued to have a certain degree of autonomy, but both were forced to help the Turks in their campaigns. In 1459 the Ottomans captured the Serb capital of Smedrevo and ruled Serbia for the next 350 years.

This period was not one of complete stagnation. The Serbian Church was a focus for national feeling. Between 1557 and 1776 there was an independent patriarchate at Peć; before and after these dates Greek influence was strong in the Church. Patriarch Jovan II led a revolt known as the insurrection of St Sava between 1593 and 1609.

In 1691 patriarch Arsenye III led a great emigration of about 30,000 families to the north of the Danube away from the traditional homelands of the Serbs. This was an important if eventually tragic move as it meant that Serbia had a less good claim to areas like Kosovo and Macedonia, and it involved Serbia in a difficult relationship with Austro-Hungary. Serbs in the Voivodina, north of the Danube, were in the 18th century at the forefront of the movement for Serb emancipation, but the Catholic Habsburg empire which briefly occupied Belgrade was not always on good terms with its Orthodox Serb subjects.

In 1804, under the leadership of Kara George, the Serbs revolted against the Turks. This revolt has little to do with similar movements in Greece for independence. Kara George, an illiterate dealer in pigs, has not much in common with lofty idealists like Rigas Pheraios. One of the reasons for discontent was the rapacity of the Greek clergy, dominant since the abolition of the patriarchate of Peć in 1766. Kara George's rebellion failed, but in 1817 Serbia gained a limited form of independence for a small area south of Belgrade. For the next 100 years the Karageorgevic and Obrenovic dynasties were to reign over Serbia in uneasy succession, with no fewer than four rulers meeting untimely deaths.

Milos Obrenovic, who reigned from 1817 to 1839 and then again from 1869 to 1870, did much for the organization of the state. In education he took a strongly nationalistic line. The Serbian language was standardized by the great scholar of the Kosovo epic, Vuk Karadžić. The influence of Serbs in the Voivodina was also marked. Although ancient Greek was part of the curriculum, little help was sought from Greece, although

the two countries, recently liberated from the Turk, and proud of their ancient traditions, had much in common. Closer links and also rivalries were established in the latter half of the 19th century when Serbia, Greece, and Bulgaria all became claimants to what remained of the Turkish empire, an area ruled in the past by all these countries. Linguistic claims were equally difficult to determine since, in addition to Albanians, Vlachs, and Turks complicating the issue, the central district under dispute was inhabited by people who spoke a language somewhere between Bulgarian and Serbian, although closer to the former. Bulgaria was indeed awarded this land at the Treaty of San Stefano, but the Treaty of Berlin reversed this decision and left Macedonia in the hands of the Turks. Serbia made some gains around Niš.

In the Balkan Wars of 1912 and 1913 the Serbs and the Greeks were on the winning side, and thus able to divide the bulk of Macedonia between them. The Serbian gains, known as south Serbia, became an integral part of Yugoslavia, and only Serbo-Croat was taught in the schools. Relations with Greece were generally friendly, although there was some tension about Serbian access to a free port at Thessalonica. The Greeks and Serbs had been somewhat uneasy allies during World War I when after a gallant resistance the Serbian army retreated through Albania to Corfu and joined the Allied front at Thessalonica. During World War II the two countries were again briefly allied when in 1941 the German armies drove through Serbia on their way to Greece.

Resistance in Greece and Yugoslavia followed a similar pattern with a right-wing faction supporting the monarchy pitted against a communist faction, both officially fighting the Germans, but sometimes fighting each other. The result of this struggle was, however, different. Yugoslav support for the communists in the Greek Civil War led to much tension between the countries. Tito's break with Russia eased this tension, but his recognition of Macedonia inflamed Greek nationalist feelings. The disintegration of Yugoslavia increased the pressure with an independent state under the name of Macedonia being anathema to the Greeks. Paradoxically Serbs, now dominant in the rump of Yugoslavia, although ruled by a communist and repressive regime, became oddly popular in Greece as a beleaguered Orthodox nation, facing dangers from unreliable Macedonia, Muslim Albanians in Kosovo, Catholic and German-backed Croatia, and a host of other enemies.

T.J. WINNIFRITH

See also Macedonia, Slavs

Summary

Originally pagans, the Serbs became Christian and literate in the 9th century. From 1167 to 1355 the Nemanjids dominated Serbia and ruled an empire that eventually reached from the Danube to the gulf of Corinth. Under the Turks the Serbian Church maintained national feeling. Limited independence was gained in 1817.

Further Reading

Clissold, Stephen (editor), *A Short History of Yugoslavia from Early Times to 1966*, Cambridge: Cambridge University Press, 1966

Dvornik, Francis, *The Slavs: Their Early History and Civilization*, Boston: American Academy of Arts and Sciences, 1956

Malcolm, Noel, *Bosnia: A Short History*, London: Macmillan, and
    New York: New York University Press, 1994; revised 1996
Temperley, Harold W.V., *History of Serbia*, London: Bell, 1919
West, Rebecca, *Black Lamb and Grey Falcon: A Journey Through
    Yugoslavia*, 2 vols, New York: Viking, 1941; London: Macmillan,
    1942

Serres

City in Macedonia

With a population of 50,390 according to the 1991 census,
Serres is one of the most populous towns of Greek Macedonia,
the second largest in east Macedonia after Kavalla, and capital
of the administrative department of the same name. The town's
position remains the same as when it was first recorded in
antiquity; it occupies the southern slopes of Mount
Menoikion, while a vast plain extends to the west and south.
Not far from the town, at a distance of about 12 km, flows the
Strymon river, a dominant feature of the region. Serres lay
close to the Via Egnatia, one of the most important land routes
in Roman, Byzantine, and Ottoman times, which linked
Thessalonica to Constantinople (modern Istanbul). The development of Serres was much affected by its proximity to that
major route.

The first record of the town is connected with events of the
4th century BC. It was probably founded by the Thracian tribe
of Odomantes under the name of Sira or Siris, which was later
transformed in Serrai/es (the Ottoman Turks knew it as Siroz).
Originally a Thracian settlement, it was open to the influences
of Hellenic civilization that came from the Greek colonies on
the east Macedonian coast. The process of Hellenization was
accelerated and finally completed after the region was annexed
to the Macedonian state by Philip II between the years 358 and
355 BC. From 146 BC onwards the region of Serres was incorporated in the Roman province of Macedonia. Christianity
was introduced to the region by St Paul, who visited the nearby
towns of Philippi and Amphipolis and established a Christian
church there. In late antiquity the bishop of Serres was a subordinate of the metropolitan of Thessalonica.

Little is known about Serres in the 7th and 8th centuries AD.
The collapse of Byzantine authority in most of the Balkans
during that period affected eastern Macedonia as well. The
Slavic tribes of Strymonitai and Ryghinoi who settled in this
region lived an independent existence and were often hostile to
Byzantium. However, the Byzantine emperors were keen to re-
establish control of the routes between Constantinople and
Thessalonica and they seem to have taken some measures in
that direction. There is evidence of a campaign by Constantine
IV (668–85) against the Ryghinoi Slavs; and Justinian II
(565–78) is said to have settled a garrison of Scythian mercenaries at the Strymon defiles, northwest of Serres. Whether
Serres continued to be a centre of organized urban life during
that period, and what role it might have played in those events,
is not known. Byzantine authority was definitely re-established
there in the 9th century. Serres too re-emerged from obscurity.
By the late 9th century the region of eastern Macedonia was
organized into the Byzantine province (theme) of Strymon with
Serres as its capital. The rest of the Middle Ages saw Serres as

the most important administrative and economic centre in
eastern Macedonia, a position which it retained in modern
times as well, despite the serious damage it suffered during a
Bulgarian raid in the early 13th century from which it quickly
recovered. The church of Serres re-emerged in the early 10th
century as a separate archbishopric and was later in the same
century elevated to a metropolitan see. The town was under
Byzantine rule for most of the Middle Ages. The Franks were
established there in the aftermath of the Fourth Crusade
(1204), to be followed by the Epirot Greeks and then the
Bulgarians, until the Byzantines retook the land c.1242. The
Serbs came a century later and occupied the town in 1345, as
a result of their involvement in the Byzantine civil war between
the regency of John V Palaiologos and John Kantakouzenos.
Serres held an important position in the administration of the
short-lived empire of Stephan IV Dushan. The latter's death
and the subsequent disintegration of his empire were followed
by the establishment of a semi-independent Graeco-Serbian
principality centred at Serres, which was first governed by
Dushan's widow Elisabeth, then by John Ugljesa until 1371.
The years between 1371 and 1383 were the last period of
Byzantine rule in Serres; the town fell to the Ottoman Turks on
19 September 1383 and so began the Ottoman period of the
town's history which lasted for more than five centuries.

The late medieval and early modern years are a well-documented period for the social and economic life of the town. A
wealth of documents from the archives of the Athonite monasteries, which owned a great deal of land in the surrounding
region, and from the local monastery of St John Prodromos on
Mount Menoikion, which prospered during the 14th century,
show that the fertile and well-irrigated plain of southeastern
Macedonia was populous and productive enough to create the
conditions for the town's development. More about the population and economy of the town itself can be found in the
Ottoman fiscal registers of the 15th century.

Agricultural activities in the region were oriented towards
cereal cropping and viticulture. The cultivation of textile
substances, mainly flax, had a less important role to play and,
it seems, was limited to serving local demands, while cotton
was only a marginal product in those years. Mining was
another significant economic activity of this region with iron
being extracted from the (now worked-out) mines of
Siderokastro, Vrontou, and Trilision. Serres was the marketplace of the region and also a centre of handicrafts. Merchants
and artisans were organized in corporations (guilds) and were
able in the course of the 14th century to influence local government. The opposition which the town of Serres raised against
the party of John VI Kantakouzenos (who was himself a
wealthy landowner in that region), during the Byzantine civil
war of the 1340s, was probably a reflection of the anti-aristocratic tendencies of the local mercantile and artisan classes.

The earliest figures for the town's population are derived
from the Ottoman fiscal registers of the 15th century: about
6200 people are recorded in Serres in 1454/55 (3450 Christian
and 2750 Muslim), and about 4896 in 1478/79 (1706
Christian and 3190 Muslim). The Muslims were introduced
into the town straight after the Ottoman conquest, and soon
made up a large proportion, often becoming the majority, of
the population, as is shown by these figures. They were in part
immigrants from Anatolia, in part the product of Islamization.

The emergence of this new element of the population was accompanied by the topographic expansion of Serres, as they established their own quarters outside the old fortified section of the town. This provides good evidence of a voluntary surrender of the town to the Ottomans, because it was against their usual practices to allow the Christian population of places taken by force to remain in the fortified sections; the same can be deduced from the fact that the cathedral church of the town, the church of St Theodore, remained in Christian hands after the Ottoman occupation. The majority of the Christians of the town were ethnically Greek (the early 17th-century chronicle of Papasynadinos is a characteristic text in the local Greek dialect), while the population of the surrounding countryside was mixed, Greek and Slavic. Another ethnic element present in Serres were the Sephardic Jews who were settled there at the end of the 15th century. In 1519 the population of Serres consisted of approximately 6847 people (3157 Christian, 3420 Muslim, and 270 Jewish). Sephardic Jews were settled in other towns of Macedonia as well (about 120 persons are recorded in Giannitsa for the same year), but the largest group of them was to be found in Thessalonica where they numbered 15,715 in 1519.

The following centuries were marked by new developments in the economy of the region. The establishment of large private estates (*çiftliks*) in the 18th century was accompanied by the commercialization of agriculture. As a result, the cultivation of highly commercial products, such as cotton and tobacco, which was strongly favoured by the abundance of water and the quality of the soil in this region, soon gained ground and became the most profitable agricultural activity.

The Ottoman conquest of the land in the late 14th century had brought about the collapse of the local Christian landowning nobility, which was not to reemerge again. During the long period of Ottoman rule the rural estates were in the hands of either Muslim individuals or pious foundations (*waqf*). Nevertheless, several members of the Greek community did make their fortunes through trading. The good economic standing of many local Greeks, as well as contact with central and western Europe, brought a revival of intellectual life to the town. Efforts to promote a form of Greek education in Serres were made throughout the centuries of Ottoman rule (this is indicated even in the early 17th-century chronicle of Papasynadinos), but the earliest known Greek school at Serres was founded by the metropolitan Gabriel in 1735 and was subsidized by many wealthy Serrean merchants. Throughout the 18th century the influence of the ideas of the Enlightenment gave rise to Greek national sentiment. Many prominent members of the Greek community joined the *Philiki Hetaireia* ("Friendly Society"), including the metropolitan Chrysanthos and the rich merchant Emmanuel Papas (1772–1821). The Greek people of Serres remained inactive during the War of Independence, the main reason for this being the large number of Muslims in the town and their readiness to deal ruthlessly with any revolutionary action. Nevertheless, several Serrean individuals either supported the Greek forces or took part in the fighting. Most prominent among them was Emmanuel Papas who organized and led the unsuccessful uprising in Chalcidice between May and November 1821.

Ottoman rule in Serres lasted until the Balkan Wars. The Bulgarian army occupied the town on 25 November 1912 and held it until the 28 June 1913 when it was driven out by Greek forces, after the former members of the anti-Turkish alliance came to blows. The region of Serres and the rest of southeastern Macedonia were officially assigned to Greece by the Treaty of Bucharest (1913) which ended the Balkan Wars. Yet the town of Serres and the surrounding region were occupied twice again by the Bulgarian army during World Wars I and II.

The history of Serres in the 20th century is marked by significant changes in its demographic and economic conditions. First, the Muslims of the region departed as a result of the 1923 exchange of populations between Greece and Turkey and were replaced by Greek refugees from Anatolia. Then the large number of newcomers, the distribution of land to every individual peasant, the expansion of arable land by drainage, and the introduction of modern agricultural techniques resulted in an unprecedented increase in agricultural production (which continues with the cotton and tobacco crops). Contemporary Serres is a large provincial town with a lively economy based on the agricultural production of the surrounding region, commerce, and services.

KONSTANTINOS P. MOUSTAKAS

Summary

Serres is the second largest city of eastern Macedonia after Kavalla and lies close to the ancient Via Egnatia. It has a documented history from the 4th century BC. Christianity was brought to the region by St Paul. Serres was the capital of the Byzantine theme of Strymon. It was taken by the Serbs in 1345 and by the Ottomans in 1383. Agriculture and iron mining were the principal activities of the region. There was a large Muslim population until 1923.

Further Reading

Balta, Evangelia, *Les Vakifs de Serrès et de sa région*, Athens: National Research Foundation, 1995

Karanastasis, T., "Ehas Neomartyrs stis Serres sto Deutero Misy tou 15ou Aiona: O Agios Ioannis o Serraios kai i Akolouthia tou, Ergo tou Manouil Korinthiou" [A Neomartyr of Serres in the Second Half of the 15th century: St. John the Serrean and his Sermon via the work of Manuel the Corinthian], *Byzantina*, 16 (1991): pp. 197–262

Papazoglou, Fanoula, *Les Villes de Macédoine à l' époque romaine*, Paris: Boccard, 1988

Pennas, Petros T., *Historia tou Serrou* [History of Serres], 2nd edition, Athens, 1966

Sakellariou, M.B. (editor), *Macedonia: 4000 Years of Greek History and Civilization*, Athens: Ekdotike Athenon, 1983

Vacalopoulos, Apostolos, *History of Macedonia, 1354–1833*, translated by Peter Megann, Thessalonica: Institute for Balkan Studies, 1973, reprinted 1988

Sèvres, Treaty of 1920

Treaty of the Allied Powers with Turkey

The Treaty of Sèvres was the last of four treaties ancillary to Versailles that imposed terms on Germany's defeated allies in World War I, after St Germain (Austria), Neuilly (Bulgaria), and Trianon (Hungary). Presented to the Ottoman government on 11 May and signed at Sèvres on 10 August 1920, the settlement was never enforced and was ultimately replaced by the Treaty of Lausanne (1923).

The treaty confined the Turkish state to a part of Asia Minor. The sultan's government was allowed to continue at Constantinople, but the city was included with the Dardanelles, the Sea of Marmara, the Bosporus, and adjacent lands in a Zone of the Straits. This zone was placed under the administration of an international commission, so as to ensure access "to every vessel of commerce or war without distinction of flag". Kurdistan was given local autonomy, with the right to secede within a year. Armenia was made an independent state with boundaries drawn by president Wilson to include Trebizond, Erzurum, and Van. Syria, Mesopotamia, and Palestine were granted independence subject to mandatory powers appointed by the League of Nations. Turkey renounced all claims to the Hejaz, Egypt, Sudan, and Libya, and recognized the French protectorate over Tunis and Morocco, the British protectorate over Egypt, the British occupation of Cyprus, and Italian control of the Dodecanese. The finances of the Turkish state were placed under the control of a financial commission appointed by the Allied Powers. The capitulations affording extraterritorial status to non-Turkish nationals were extended to all the Allied Powers. Also stipulated were the protection of minorities, disarmament of the Turkish military, and the prosecution of war criminals.

The terms of the treaty were particularly favourable to Greece. The exercise of Turkish sovereignty in Smyrna and a large surrounding region was delegated to Greece, with the prospect of annexation to Greece after a plebiscite in five years. The islands of Imbros and Tenedos and the whole of European Turkey outside the Zone of the Straits were ceded to Greece, while Greek possession of other Aegean islands was confirmed.

Five other agreements were signed at Sèvres on the same day. Greece and Armenia both signed treaties for the protection of minorities within their borders. A tripartite pact between Britain, France, and Italy recognized their respective zones of influence within Turkey. Italy agreed to cede the Dodecanese, excepting Rhodes, to Greece. But the only enduring geographical outcome of Sèvres was the transfer of western Thrace from Bulgaria to Greece by a treaty between Greece and the Great Powers.

The treaty of Sèvres proved unworkable. The Greek military presence in the Smyrna region which it codified provoked a resurgence of Turkish power. The Allied signatories were divided among themselves, leaving the Greeks alone to enforce the treaty. But perhaps decisive to its failure was its identification with the political fortunes of the Greek prime minister, Eleftherios Venizelos.

The treaty was signed almost two years after the Turkish surrender. This delay resulted from British resistance to French claims in Syria and Cilicia, Wilson's temporizing over proposed American mandates for Armenia and the Straits, and from consequences of the Greek landing at Smyrna on 15 May 1919. The Greek presence gave coherence to what had heretofore been desultory Turkish resistance to Allied occupation; the British high commissioner commented that "the Greek occupation of Smyrna has stimulated a Turkish patriotism probably more real than any the war was able to evoke." In the summer of 1919 Mustafa Kemal, appointed inspector of the eastern provinces by the Sublime Porte, emerged as the leader of a Turkish nationalist movement. Already a year before Sèvres the National Pact formulated at Erzurum and Sivas defied Allied

pretensions in Asia Minor. The Allied occupation of Constantinople on 16 March 1920 led Kemal's Grand National Assembly to denounce the sultan's regime, and swelled the ranks of the nationalist army, already victorious over the French at Marash. The signature of Riza Tevfik, the Ottoman legate at Sèvres, was more representative of an Allied protectorate than of the Turkish nation.

The Greek position at Smyrna and the emergence of Kemal exacerbated differences among the Allies. At the Paris peace conference the Italians, with their interests in the Adalia (Attalia) region, opposed Greek claims in Asia Minor – the Smyrna landing itself was dictated more by Lloyd George's and Wilson's pique over Italian claims than by a concerted strategy. On 13 March 1921 count Sforza signed an accord with the Nationalists pledging opposition to the Sèvres awards to Greece in Thrace and Asia Minor. The report of the Interallied Commission of October 1920 investigating atrocities in the Smyrna region led the French prime minister to criticize the Greek presence. Economic interests disposed France to make a separate peace with Kemal; the Franklin–Bouillon accord ceded Cilicia to Turkey while protecting the French position in Syria. Nor would the British government fight to uphold the Treaty of Sèvres. Although Lloyd George saw the greater Greece it stipulated as a prop to British interests in the eastern Mediterranean, his cabinet was divided – Churchill urged a return to the traditional policy of supporting Turkey against Russia. Venizelos secretly hoped for a Turkish rejection of the Sèvres terms that might force Britain into a larger war, but assured Lloyd George that Greece could enforce the treaty without allied armies.

The Treaty of Sèvres reflected the Allies' desire to support the political position of Venizelos, whom the Entente had installed as prime minister by overthrowing the neutralist king Constantine in June 1917. Venizelos hoped that gains in Asia Minor and Thrace might mitigate popular discontent over his use of foreign intervention against his political opponents, since acquisitions in Epirus and Macedonia had won him popularity after the Balkan Wars. When Venizelos lost the elections of November 1920, the Allies placed an embargo on economic credits to the new government, and by April of the next year they declared neutrality in the Greek–Turkish conflict. Kemal's forces drew the Greeks into the interior, routed them at Sakarya in August 1921, and one year later drove them from Smyrna. In November 1922 Venizelos was at Lausanne negotiating recognition of Kemal's Turkey, while six of his political enemies – including the prime minister, Gounaris – were executed in Athens.

The Treaty of Sèvres was intrinsically untenable. Marshal Foch's commission had estimated that 27 divisions would be necessary to enforce its terms – the Greeks had 6. "To maintain M. Venizelos in power in Greece for what cannot in the nature of things be more than a few years at the outside", the British adviser de Robeck observed, the Allies were "prepared to perpetuate bloodshed indefinitely" and to violate their own principle of self-determination. The census of the ecumenical patriarchate of 1912 (taken before the arrival of thousands of Turkish refugees from the Balkan Wars) had found Greeks a minority on the mainland; the Interallied Commission of 1919 found Greeks a minority everywhere but Smyrna and Aivali. In rejecting the prime minister Gounaris's request to lead the Asia

Minor campaign general Metaxas commented that "we are an ethnological minority even in the area round Smyrna". But more importantly, he recognized, the Turks had developed a national feeling.

Greece and Turkey are the only two countries to have waged their respective wars of independence against one another. As Toynbee observes, the Greek war of 1821 had been the first thoroughgoing application of the Western national idea in Ottoman lands; the Turkish war against the terms of Sèvres a century later was fought for the same principles. The Treaty of Sèvres was the apex of the recrudescence of the Great Idea – the dream of a restoration of Greek hegemony in the heartland of Byzantium. This aspiration, spawned by the romantic nationalism of the French Revolution, corresponded little to the reality that inspired it. In its polyethnic character and the liberty afforded to local administrative, social, and economic structures Byzantium had more in common with the Ottoman regime than with modern Greece. In addressing the Paris peace conference Venizelos used maps showing the historic persistence of Greek settlement in Asia Minor to argue for the introduction of a national regime of a kind the region had never known. His attempt to extend the modern Greek state into Asia Minor fostered a Turkish leviathan. For the Turkish state *Sèvres fobisi* – fear of Sèvres – remains an abiding anxiety. For Greeks the treaty of Sèvres represents the phantom culmination of a century of territorial expansion, precipitating the catastrophe of 1922 and foreshadowing that of 1974.

C.G. BROWN

See also Asia Minor Campaign, Great Idea, World War I

Further Reading

The text of the Treaty of Sèvres can be found in *The Treaties of Peace 1919–1923*, vol. 2, New York: Carnegie Endowment for International Peace, 1924

Davison, Roderic H., "Turkish Diplomacy from Mudros to Lausanne" in *The Diplomats: 1919–1939*, edited by Gordon A. Craig and Felix E. Gilbert, Princeton, New Jersey: Princeton University Press, 1953

Fromkin, David, *A Peace to End all Peace: Creating the Modern Middle East 1914–1922*, London: Deutsch, and New York: Holt, 1989

Helmreich, Paul C., *From Paris to Sèvres: The Partition of the Ottoman Empire at the Peace Conference of 1919–1920*, Columbus: Ohio State University Press, 1974

Howard, Harry N., *The Partition of Turkey: A Diplomatic History 1913–1923*, Norman: University of Oklahoma Press, 1931, reprinted New York: Fertig, 1966

Llewellyn Smith, Michael, *Ionian Vision: Greece in Asia Minor 1919–1922*, London: Allen Lane, and New York: St Martin's Press, 1973

Montgomery, A.E., "The Making of the Treaty of Sèvres of 10 August 1920", *Historical Journal*, 15 (1972): pp. 775–87

Sonyel, Salahi Ramsdan, *Turkish Diplomacy, 1918–1923: Mustafa Kemal and the Turkish National Movement*, London and Beverly Hills, California: Sage, 1975

Toynbee, Arnold J., *The Western Question in Greece and Turkey*, London: Constable, 1922, reprinted New York: Fertig, 1970

Zurrer, Werner, "Der Friedensvertrag von Sèvres: ein kritischer Beitrag zur Problematik der Neuordnung des nahostlichen Raumes nach dem ersten Weltkrieg", *Saeculum*, 25 (1974): pp. 88–114

Ships and shipping

The Greeks of antiquity lived mostly near the sea; the fact and its significance were not ignored (Aristotle, *Politics*, 1271b34). The influences that formed their culture were seaborne as was its own diffusion; their literature from its earliest pages has references to the sea, to ships, and cargoes. The Greeks of the Middle Ages have been described as suspicious of the sea and of commerce. Nevertheless a Byzantine of the 14th century reportedly considered that his city should become a purely maritime commercial power (John Kantakouzenos, *Histories*, 2. 537). In the contemporary world merchant shipping is one (perhaps the only) commercial activity in which Greece is internationally prominent. The Greek-owned merchant fleet is now the largest on earth; members of a nation accounting for about 0.2 per cent of the world population apparently control about 15 per cent of its maritime carrying capacity.

Such facts create an understandable temptation to see a continuity of maritime genius and to stress its importance in the history of the Greeks. To this some writers have succumbed despite difficulties that should encourage resistance. A number of centuries before the 18th are an almost complete blank. From other facts (these include the Italian basis of the modern Greek maritime argot, the very unsettled conditions in the Aegean during part of the period, the feeble representation of maritime Greeks in surviving commercial documents of late Byzantine times, the known maritime strength of other nations, and the beginnings, so far as documented, of the maritime adventure of the 18th century) it may be suspected that the blank reflects reality rather than lack of evidence or diligence in collecting it. In addition it is not only difficult to assess the importance of shipping but the approach to the difficulty must differ for different ages. Antiquity, therefore, and the modern period will be described separately. Between them there will be an intermission of about a thousand years.

The physical characteristics of ancient ships may be inferred from surviving descriptions, depictions, and wrecks. By the 5th century BC merchantmen and warships were clearly distinguished. The former were known as "round ships" (*strongyla ploia*) or *holkades* or (in the Phoenician context) *gauloi*, the latter simply as ships (*nees*) or long ships (*nees makrai*) or with reference to a specific type *pentekontoroi* (ship with 50 oars) or *triereis* (trireme). The distinction was not only in beam but also the principal means of propulsion, which for merchantmen was sail and for warships, at least in battle, oars. Use of pentekonters by the Phocaeans on their journeys to the west seemed to the 5th century remarkable (Herodotus, 1. 163) and reference to oared merchantmen (Thucydides, 4. 118. 5) is extremely unusual. The date of this functional specialization between speed and capacity is obscure. The earliest surviving picture of a round ship on a pot is from the late 6th century BC (British Museum, London); if the surprise of Herodotus was shared by contemporaries of the events, then round ships should have existed by its earlier years.

The construction of Mediterranean ships, as appears from their wrecks, had certain common features between the late Bronze Age and the end of antiquity. The hull planking is held together by mortice and tenon joints locked with tree nails. In construction the shell would have been built first and the frames added afterwards. The advantage of this method is a

Ships: Kavalla in Macedonia is a major port and entrepôt for the export of tobacco

very firm hull. Its disadvantage is the skill and time required for the adzing and jointing of the timbers. It seems to have given way to skeleton-based construction (in which the integrity of the hull depends on fixing its planking to the frames) by the 7th century AD, Oak was used for the keel and frequently the frames, fir or pine for the hull planking. Hulls were caulked and often sheathed in metal, lead being found more than copper.

Most merchantmen were single masted with a single square (strictly, rectangular) sail. The sail's angle to the mast could be adjusted and it could be flexibly brailed. Some later ships also had a foremast with a smaller sail. Three-masted vessels must have been very rare. Rudders were oar-shaped and projected astern from one or both sides of the hull.

The capacity of merchantmen may be judged from indications of their cargoes or their dimensions. The stone for some archaic statuary or masonry was carried by sea; there are surviving statues of more than 20 tons and blocks of more than 30. Round ships could carry considerably more. Gifts of grain to Athens in the late 4th century BC are attested in quantities of 3000 *medimnoi* (*c.*120 tons) and less frequently of 4000 *medimnoi* (*c.*160 tons) and they are plausibly whole shiploads. The 3000 wine jars that were the cargo intended in [Demosthenes] 35 are likely to have exceeded 100 tons. A decree from Thasos of the 3rd century BC excludes ships carrying less than 3000 talents (*c.*80 tons) from one harbour and less than 5000 talents (*c.*130 tons) from another. There is evidence of much larger cargoes. Privileges in the Roman period were available in respect of vessels carrying at least 50,000 *modii* (*c.*340 tons) of grain (*Digest*, 50. 5. 3) and there are wrecks of the Roman period with more than 400 tons aboard. The vessel that brought the Vatican obelisk to Rome must have been able to carry around 1300 tons (for the ballast see Pliny, *Naturalis Historia*, 16. 201); vessels with such dimensions seem from the tone of Pliny's reference to have been unusual enough to provoke wonder (cf. The *Navigium* of Lucian for the wonder that a ship of enormous dimensions could provoke). The largest vessel that is known (through a description reproduced by Athenaeus, 206ff.) from antiquity was built in the 3rd century BC for Hiero of Syracuse; its size has been estimated at around 2000 tons. The largest vessels of antiquity thus approached the limits of purely timber construction. It was not until the 19th century that ships became substantially larger. Passengers in considerable numbers are recorded on long-distance voyages: 600 from Palestine to Rome (Josephus, *Vita*, 15) and 276 (including crew) on the ship that took St Paul as far as Malta (Acts 27: 37), this at the extremity of the sailing season.

The speeds of which ancient ships were capable were less important than the fact that they were at the mercy of the winds and weather (the discovery of the periodicity of the monsoon was for this reason very important for Indian Ocean traffic) and that in winter navigation generally stopped (this defined what journeys could be undertaken). A replica of the Kyrenia wreck (c.300 BC) has reached 9 knots under sail and records of remarkably fast voyages show that speeds of 5 knots or more could be averaged over several hundred miles. Conversely on a voyage against the prevailing wind a ship was doing well to average 2 knots. The prevailing direction of the winds defined the expected journey times of ancient travel (e.g. fast from the northwest towards Egypt but slow in the opposite direction) and the superimposition of a short sailing season further limited the possibilities. The risks in pushing one's luck with the seasons are accessibly exemplified by Acts 27–28; the story of Paul's journey to Rome is one of the most vivid records (Synesius, *Epistles*, 4 vies with it) of the vagaries of an ancient sea voyage.

As in the modern world, it was much cheaper in antiquity to transport goods over water than over land; to quote a classic inference from the Diocletianic price edict, "it was cheaper to ship grain from one end of the Mediterranean to the other than to cart it 75 miles". Nevertheless, the function and significance of shipping in antiquity are controversial; the divisions in the controversy are aligned with those on the nature of the ancient economy generally. That contradictory accounts of, say, trade in the Archaic period or lending in Classical Athens are pressed on the public with equal conviction is partly due to the nature of the evidence: fragments that may be fitted into different pasticcios whose shape owes more to the restorer than to them. Even apparently elementary questions (e.g. how many of the maritime lenders known from Athens in the 4th century BC were Athenians and/or merchants?) receive different answers because of the opacity of sources that were not composed to satisfy the curiosity of modern scholars. By and large, rival interpreters have not attempted a reconciliation of their differences and the diversity of their views cannot be conveyed in a brief entry.

From the 4th century BC organizational features of shipping that were to endure for centuries (even to the present day) are clearly discernible. Much less can be discerned about earlier periods; this is doubly unfortunate because Greek seafaring created its most important and enduring monument in the vast diffusion of people and culture of the Archaic period. The mere existence of maritime adventures is easy to establish from a variety of sources: stories in Herodotus (e.g. the fabulous wealth gained by Colaeus of Samos and his crew as a result of an unintended voyage to Spain at 4. 152 or the journeys of the Phocaeans in the far west at 1. 163), the remains of trading settlements at, for example, Naucratis in Egypt (see also Herodotus, 2. 178f.) or Al Mina on the Orontes, fragmentary business documents recovered from trading posts of the outer fringes (Berezan on the north coast of the Black Sea and Pech Maho in the west). Since colonists did not set out for the unknown (Herodotus, 4. 150. 4), their choice of destination depended on information brought back by seafaring adventurers.

To picture their adventures, scholars have turned to the *Odyssey* (the earliest reference to seafaring, Hesiod's advice at *Opera et Dies* 618–94 being concerned with less ambitious journeys) assuming that it is, even when the characters are

telling lies as at 14. 192–359, in background realistic. Attention is drawn to the commonality of the enterprise (necessary when a leader needed oarsmen and linked to a historical datum such as the dedication of Colaeus and his crew together) and its close association with the exchange of gifts or prestige goods on the one hand and raiding and abduction on the other. A precisely focused picture is impossible; despite elaborate attempts, the basis, for example, of the distinction between the high status of a Mentes (actually Athena in disguise) in search of copper in exchange for iron at 1. 179ff. and the low status of a trader mindful of his cargo (8. 159ff.) is elusive. It has been suggested that by the end of the Archaic period the wealth of some cities (e.g. Aegina) depended on seaborne commerce.

The 4th century BC reveals a clear separation between hull and cargo interests and the finance of cargo by bottomry loans (under which repayment was contingent on the safe arrival of ship and cargo), a financial device that was to endure into the modern world. There is evidence of elementary economic rationality in, for example, the stipulation of maritime lenders that the cargo was to be worth twice the loan and that the borrower was to borrow no additional sums from others, or the diversion of a grain cargo to a port at which prices were higher (Demosthenes, 56). That hardy perennial, the maritime fraud, also heaves into view (Demosthenes, 32). The status and wealth of the participants and the scale and significance of their activities have been much debated. By and large, throughout antiquity, the masters of vessels and the merchants who travelled with them were of low status and for the most part their means were also modest. When, in the case of late antiquity, comparisons are possible, even the largest merchant fortunes are dwarfed by landed wealth. Arguments from silence indicate the same for earlier periods. The capital, though, for the business either in the form of bottomry loans or even ownership of vessels seems throughout antiquity to have been provided by persons (and later institutions such as the Church) of wealth and status. The amount of maritime activity in antiquity cannot be quantified. On the demand side certain large cities (in chronological order Athens, Alexandria, Rome, and Constantinople) imported a significant proportion of their grain needs over water and attracted delivery of luxuries over considerable distances. On the supply side it is difficult to identify cities for which maritime activity was in itself significant. In the Classical period Aristotle names Aegina and Chios (*Politics*, 1291b24); Phaselis is also possible. Later Rhodes is a clear example; with cities such as Alexandria (or for instance Nicomedia in the Roman period) it is hard to tell the relative importance of the maritime activity attested.

The strictly economic effect of maritime activity in antiquity may have been slight, the social status of its participants low by comparison with their counterparts today, and most detail of its organization obscure. These facts do not contradict the assumption of a much wider significance for shipping in antiquity. Already by the 4th century BC a city's access to the sea had effects notable enough for its merits to be the subject of debate (Aristotle, *Politics*, 1327a11ff.). Throughout antiquity ships were the uniting link in the Mediterranean world.

If we pass over the thousand years ending around AD 1700, it is not because maritime activity ceased completely. People continued to travel on ships, the so-called Rhodian Sea Law was recopied presumably because it had a use, references to maritime loans and cargoes occur. But it is extremely difficult to synthesize this scattered material into a general picture. When with the Italian archival material at the end of the Byzantine period the available documentation becomes richer, the Greek representation is found to be very small. The Ottoman conquest was followed by chaos and depopulation in the Aegean and such Turkey trade as there was was carried in western ships. There are glimmers of revival in the 17th century (in the relative prosperity of settlements such as Lindos and Patmos or passing references in Evliya Çelebi to rich Greek shipowners at Yenikoy) but the scale is very small. A significant revival began only with the stabilization of Ottoman relations with the west from the end of the 17th century (notably through the Treaty of Karlowitz, 1699, and the Treaty of Passarowitz, 1718) and the increasing access to western markets of produce from the southern Balkans.

For this reason the first sizeable merchant fleets were formed in western Greece, chiefly at Missolonghi (whose connections were with the Ionian islands, then Venetian, and Epirus) and Galaxidi (whose connections were with the Morea). The development of these fleets is obscure, but it was extremely rapid after about 1740, and by the 1750s they dominated the trade between the west coast of Greece and Italy. In the Aegean, development was a little slower. While 40 to 50 indeterminately "large" ships are attributed to Mykonos in the early part of the 18th century, Hydra, which was to become preeminent by its end and has the best-documented history, created a vessel of more than 100 tons (a *latinadiko*, twin masted with lateen sails) only in 1745. Up to that time the predominant vessel had been the *sakhtouri*, a small vessel of up to 15 tons engaged solely in Aegean traffic. It has been suggested that a stimulus to the development of Greek shipping after the middle of the century was the weakness of its chief rival, France, during the Seven Years' War.

Notable features of Hydra's development include: its original poverty, which pushed the inhabitants to sea; the favour it enjoyed as a supplier of crews to the Ottoman navy; its astuteness in keeping in with both sides during the Russo-Turkish War of 1770–74 so that unhindered by either it overtook other islands such as Mykonos; and the windfall of the continental blockade during the Napoleonic wars, which the Hydriots had the pluck to run to phenomenal gain. At first the Hydriots did not have the resources to take risks with cargoes and so ships were let on charter to merchants. Later maritime loans would be raised from financiers (*cambiadori*) and later still cargoes were financed by the resources of the owners. To disperse risk, a rich man's wealth would be spread over several vessels and maritime loans, and it was extremely uncommon for a vessel to be in single ownership. The crew (which exceeded 60 on larger vessels) was generally paid out of a profit share. Success led to a gradual increase in the size of vessels. By 1812 the most common size was between 250 and 300 tons and some vessels exceeded 450 tons. At this time Hydra had the largest merchant fleet in the Greek world, twice as large as its neighbour and nearest rival, Spetses. Notable for its weak presence in shipping at the time was the richest island of the Aegean, Chios. The Greek merchant fleet seems to have continued to grow even after the end of the Napoleonic boom and to have reached about 700 vessels on the eve of the War of Independence.

During the war 80 per cent of the fleet (which doubled as a navy) was obliterated, and it did not regain its prewar capacity until the 1840s. By this time the centre of gravity had shifted to Syros (which was also the most important centre of Greek shipbuilding in the 19th century). Greek ships seem to have operated almost exclusively in the eastern Mediterranean and the Black Sea and to have been losing ground to western vessels of greater capacity. The fleet, nevertheless, continued to grow and almost doubled its capacity by the mid-1850s, partly in response to the stimulus provided by the Crimean War.

Conversion to steam was the most significant trend in 19th-century navigation. This was relatively slow because substantial improvements in engine technology and ship construction were required for the steamship to become a competitive carrier over large distances. Even in the most developed fleet, the British, steamships did not provide a majority of capacity until the late 1880s. At this time Greece had hardly started its conversion to steam and did not reach a similar stage till after 1900.

The first Greek steamships belong to 1857, but the fact (despite the efforts made to create them) was not of enduring significance. The ships served as domestic packet boats and the owning company folded after an inglorious history. Around 1860 two Greeks based in Britain began steamship operations, but these belong to the history of British shipping. The start of Greek steam shipping was due to merchant families active in the Black Sea. The first steam cargo ship to enter the Greek registry was the *Chrysovelonis* (of M. Chrysovelonis of Vraila) in 1874 and it was soon followed by others. Rapid growth in steam navigation came after 1890 partly with the development of a financial structure from the same source (specifically the trading houses of P. Vagliano and M. Zarifis) which was to survive until World War II. The trading house provided half the capital for the purchase at interest and with priority on repayment and also undertook the management. This provided capital to those to whom it was otherwise inaccessible but at the same time provided a high return on invested funds and additional commissions from management. Funds for shipping were also raised from domestic investors whose interest was excited by the extremely high returns available during the Boer War. By 1906 Greeks were the largest purchasers of second-hand British tonnage and between 1890 and the eve of World War I the steam fleet had grown tenfold. Greek shipping already had a character it was to retain for the rest of the 20th century, as a low-cost competitor in the general cargo trades; the fleet was still very small, only 3 per cent of Britain's (which then accounted for 45 per cent of world tonnage) and well behind the US, Germany, Norway, Italy, and Japan.

During World War I the Greek merchant fleet shrank by about 70 per cent, but more than half of this reduction was due to sales at inflated war prices. Compensation was also available for some losses with the result that funds for reinvestment were plentiful. Those who succumbed quickly to the temptation regretted it, for ship prices fell abruptly after 1920 and collapsed altogether in the early 1930s. Yet the Greek flag fleet more than trebled in the inter-war period. The stimulus was obviously cheap prices (as shown by the peak years for acquisition, 1933 and 1934, and the advanced age of the vessels acquired). But it was remarkable that the risk was taken. An explanation is in the small scale and informal constitution of many Greek shipping enterprises. The savings required for acquisition could be pooled by family members, many of whom would have made up the crew. This made for great flexibility on costs by comparison with competitors, as indeed they complained. By 1939 the Greek flag fleet at 1.8 million tons GRT was the third largest in the Mediterranean and the ninth in the world; significantly for the coming war the fleet was to a greater extent than any other (86 per cent) composed of general cargo vessels over 2500 GRT and in this capacity Greece was second only to Britain. There was also about 0.6 million of tonnage under foreign flag.

During the war the Greek flag fleet was requisitioned by Britain and about three-quarters of it was sunk. Some 2000 seamen lost their lives, proportionately as great a loss as Britain's. The war years were also marred by tension between the owners and the Greek government in exile on the one hand and the seamen's union on the other. A consequence was that the expansion of Greek shipping after the war took place mostly outside the Greek registry.

The defining characteristic of shipping in the half-century or so since World War II is an unprecedented increase in demand. The volume of maritime trade increased about tenfold and individual vessel sizes did much the same. The result, with important consequences, was not only that shipping became more capital intensive than ever before but that the capital required for entry rose dramatically. The period since the war can be divided into two halves. The first, during which the increase in demand for shipping was not fully matched by an increase in shipyard capacity, was generally profitable and during certain episodes (the Korean War, the closures of the Suez Canal in 1956 and 1967) exceptionally so; this ended in 1974. The reputation of shipping as a creator of fabulous wealth lingers from this period. In the ten years that followed, the volume of seaborne trade hardly grew at all with the consequence, since vessels (particularly oil tankers) had been built on the presumption of continuing growth, of appalling results. From the mid-1980s growth in seaborne trade has resumed, but the profitability of shipping has been restrained by oversupply.

In consequence expansion was extremely rapid after the war. Greek-owned tonnage regained its prewar level by 1948 and continued to grow at well over 10 per cent per annum. By the early 1950s Greece outside its flag was already talked of as the third maritime power. In 1952 alone Greek owners were reported as having taken delivery of more tonnage from shipyards than was represented by the entire prewar fleet, and by the mid-1950s were said to control more than 50 per cent of the tramp and about 15 per cent of the tanker market.

Successive Greek governments, meanwhile, attempted to entice Greek-owned vessels into the Greek register by assuring freedom of capital movement and low taxation (related at first to gross income and then to tonnage). These measures began in 1951 and reached the apogee of favour during the dictatorship of 1967–74, after which the tonnage tax was substantially increased. The measures (together with the growing inconvenience of flags of convenience) resulted in the proportion of Greek-owned tonnage under the Greek flag growing fairly steadily from about one-third in 1952 to about three-quarters in 1980/1. Since then the process has gone into reverse because, despite concessions on the manning of Greek flag ships,

crewing costs can be much lower with fewer Greeks in other registries. The result of growing prosperity in Greece is that Greek shipping is now Greek chiefly in a managerial sense. At sea Greeks serve only as officers (the number of active seamen has halved over the last 20 years and in respect of ocean-going vessels there are now only about 20,000) and with a vanishing interest on the part of the young in sea-based employment there is doubt about how they will eventually be replaced.

Providing even an economic assessment of Greek shipping is not easy. An account of the number and size of ships is no more a history of shipping than an account of the number and square footage of branches a history of banking. Yet a full history of Greek shipping is unlikely to be written. By a curious parallel with Classical Athens, shipping in modern Greece is "unseen" wealth of which no direct knowledge exists. Its most visible economic manifestation is the figure for invisible earnings from shipping in the balance of payments. This consists of seamen's remittances, pension contributions, taxes, and declared dividends to Greek nationals. It currently runs at about $2 billion per annum; in proportional terms it has appeared to wax and wane with the Greek flag fleet and the employment of Greek seamen. As a proportion of GDP it appears to have grown from about 3 to 5 per cent in the 1970s and to have declined to about 2 per cent since then. To name only other invisibles, it was overtaken by tourism in the mid-1980s. Two per cent is not a negligible proportion (it is the estimated contribution of "the City" to the UK's gross domestic product); but it may be misleading since Greek GDP figures are widely assumed to be incomplete and the figure for invisibles does not include all inflows from shipping activities.

A consensus (based on theoretical considerations and empirical evidence from better-documented cases such as the British) holds that general or bulk shipping is a business yielding low average returns and exhibiting high volatility. Some people can be successful some of the time in such activities, which is why they can attract, as do lotteries, a lot of people a lot of the time. But on the whole people do badly out of them and would be better advised to do something else. A useful analysis of Greek shipping would attempt to answer why it has expanded despite this fact. There are many possible explanations. A better choice might not be available (true of barren islands); ship operators might consistently make foolish choices (the lottery analogy) or have motives in which economic rationality plays an insignificant part; they may be the lowest cost supplier or extraordinarily lucky; they may to their own advantage be dividing risks and rewards asymmetrically with less-involved and worse-informed lenders and passive investors; there may be truly hidden returns at or beyond the boundaries of legality (e.g. blockade running, smuggling, or insurance fraud); and so forth. The information for such an analysis is unlikely to be forthcoming; its absence means that a good understanding of Greek shipping will remain elusive.

In the 8th century BC Hesiod's father went to sea leaving behind not wealth and prosperity but poverty (*Opera et Dies*, 637–38). The earliest passage on ships and shipping in Greek literature expresses an enduring truth. Poverty pushed the

Greeks to sea in the modern period as well, and is now pushing others to replace them.

GEORGE LEMOS

See also Navy, Trade, Travel, Woodworking

Further Reading

Casson, Lionel, *The Ancient Mariners: Seafarers and Sea Fighters of the Mediterranean in Ancient Times*, 2nd edition, Princeton, New Jersey: Princeton University Press, 1991

Casson, Lionel, *Ships and Seamanship in the Ancient World*, 2nd edition, Baltimore, Maryland: Johns Hopkins University Press, 1995

Damianides, Kostas, *Hellenike Paradosiake Navpigiki* [Greek Traditional Shipbuilding], Athens, 1998

Garnsey, Peter, Keith Hopkins, and C.R. Whittaker (editors), *Trade in the Ancient Economy*, London: Chatto and Windus, and Berkeley: University of California Press, 1983

Harlaftis, Gelina, *A History of Greek-Owned Shipping: The Making of an International Tramp Fleet, 1830 to the Present Day*, London and New York: Routledge, 1996

Kardases, B., *Apo tou Istiou eis ton Atmon: Helleniki Emporike Navtilia 1858–1914* [From Sail to Steam: Greek Merchant Shipping 1858–1914], Athens, 1993

Khlomoudes, K., *Synergasia kai Symploioktesia sten Helleniki Phortego Navtilia: I Periodos tou Mesopolemou* [Cooperation and Shared Ship Purchase in the Greek Merchant Navy: The Years Between the Wars], Athens, 1996

Papadopoulos, Stelios (editor), *The Greek Merchant Marine (1453–1850)*, translated by Timothy Cullen, Athens: National Bank of Greece, 1972

Parker, A., *Ancient Shipwrecks of the Mediterranean and the Roman Provinces*, Oxford: Tempus Repartum, 1992

Shrines, Wayside

The wayside shrines (*proskynitaria* or *eikonostasia ton dromon*) scattered along most rural roads in Greece and occasionally found in urban locations are both a familiar part of the landscape of contemporary Greece and an inherent part of Greek popular religious devotion. They may well represent a development of Byzantine practices involving the veneration of icons, but while it may be superficially attractive to link them with rather similar phenomena in the ancient Greek tradition, such as herms or shrines to Hecate located at crossroads, there is no firm evidence to suggest a genuine continuity of religious expression.

With some rare exceptions, almost all wayside shrines may be considered primarily as markers, whether of accident sites or of turns and boundaries. Most contemporary wayside shrines stand at the sites of traffic accidents and are thus found particularly beside dangerous stretches of road, on steep mountain bends for example. Such shrines are erected either as memorials by relatives at the scene of fatal accidents or else as tokens of thanksgiving by victims or relatives at the site of accidents in which someone is believed to have been miraculously preserved. Other shrines that fulfil a related function may be placed not at the site of a particular accident, although a number of accidents may have occurred there, but at a location that is thought to be inherently dangerous in spiritual terms and where malign forces are believed to make themselves manifest.

Although most shrines erected in recent decades are of the accident marker type, it would be wrong to assume as a result that this is the original or only purpose of the *proskynitaria*. A substantial number of shrines are thus positioned at the junction of main roads with side roads or tracks that lead (almost always) to a church, monastery, or chapel. The primary function of these shrines is to indicate the presence of the adjacent holy place to the passer-by, although it may also be of practical use to a traveller in providing directions in areas where roads are generally unsigned. Closely related in function are the *proskynitaria* which, typically, act as boundary markers on the outskirts of villages; sometimes four shrines may "cross" the village, being set at the points of the compass, or more shrines may form a circle around it. To the minds of the local inhabitants these shrines delineate an area of sacred protection and aid, as well as of "civilized" as opposed to "wild" space.

A recent study of the shrines of the Argolid region has revealed that, at least in their present form, almost none is more than 40 years old and most have been erected within the last two decades. This is not to say that wayside shrines are a recent phenomenon in the Greek world, but is rather evidence of the fact that, due to the frequently flimsy nature of their construction and their dangerous location, they are essentially ephemeral things, vulnerable to decay and accidental destruction. There is plentiful evidence that the wayside shrines that serve as turn or boundary markers are constantly being replaced (although this does not appear to be the case with accident markers) and this indicates not only that the tradition is flourishing but also that it may well be a long one.

Within some basic parameters, the construction and design of Greek wayside shrines exhibits an enormous variety, and there are many distinctive regional and, indeed, very local features to be observed. The shrines, too, display a range from complex, professional, and extremely artistic creations to simple, sometimes ramshackle structures; it is clear that the purpose rather than the appearance of the shrine is paramount in many cases. Almost all shrines consist of a box (varying in size within a fairly standard range from c. 30 × 30 × 45 cm up to 60 × 45 × 60 cm) supported some 120 cm off the ground. Most contemporary shrines are constructed out of metal with a rectangular box (which may sometimes contain glass "windows") set on a post or legs; there may be considerable elaboration in the metalwork and also in the paint and decoration. Many others are made of masonry or concrete, and recent shrines are frequently faced with or built from marble, sometimes elaborately worked after the fashion of the funerary monuments to which they are related in design; here the box is either set on a rectangular plinth or forms part of a square column that may be topped by a dome. Shrines are occasionally constructed on or in walls, rocks, or the hollows of trees; with the masonry ones, these may perhaps reflect the oldest traditions of design. Almost all shrines have at least one cross set on their roof, while a fair number imitate (to varying degrees) aspects of typical church design. As a practical feature, many incorporate some sort of storage cupboard or niche, and a number, particularly older ones, include a money box.

Wayside shrine in western Crete

shrines the lamp burns constantly, but more usually it is lit only at night or on a saint's day or other occasion particularly associated with the shrine. Quite often there is also a small incense burner to be used on such special days, when the shrine may be further decorated or wreathed with fresh or artificial flowers. Functioning shrines are usually tended by neighbouring households that have a personal connection to them, but devout passers-by in general will acknowledge their presence by some simple act of devotion, such as making the sign of the cross.

RICHARD P.H. GREENFIELD

Further Reading

Chatziphotis, Ioannis M., *Ta Proskynitaria ton Hellinikon Dromon* [Greek Wayside Shrines], Athens, 1986

Greenfield, Richard P.H., "The Wayside Shrines of Argolis: a Preliminary Study" in *Argolo-Korinthiaka I*, edited by John M. Fossey, Amsterdam: Gieben, 1999

Hurlbutt, R.C., "The Phenomonology of 'Proskinitaria'" (dissertation), St Paul, Minnesota: Hamline University, 1985

Konstantinides, Demetrios E., "Eikonostasia tis Hellinikis Ypaithrou" [Shrines of the Greek Countryside], *Nees Morphes*, 6 (November–December 1962): pp. 22ff.

Konstantinides, Demetrios E., Proskyinitarion [Shrine] entry in *Thrisevtiki kai Ithiki Engkyklopaideia* [Religious and Ethical Encyclopedia], vol. 10, Athens, 1966

Konstantinides, Demetrios E., "Merika endiapheronta 'proskynitaria' tis Argolidos" [Some Interesting Shrines of the Argolid] in *Praktika tou A' Synedriou Argolikon Spoudon, Navplion, 4–6 Dekemvriou, 1976* [Acts of the First Conference of Argolid Studies, Navplion, 4–6 December, 1976], Athens, 1979

Kyriakidou-Nestoros, Alki, "Simadia tou Topou i I Logiki tou Hellinikou Topiou" [Place-Markers, or the Logic of the Greek Landscape] in his *Laographika Meletimata*, Athens, 1975

Almost all wayside shrines include the same basic elements used for the devotional practices connected with them, although there is great variety in their elaboration and in the care that is taken of them. The most important items in the shrine are undoubtedly the icons, most shrines containing one or two, with some having considerably more. These icons range from cheap card reproductions to more expensive copies of Byzantine originals, some with elaborate silver and gilt frames or covers; hand-painted icons are, however, very rare. A single icon is generally placed against the back wall of the shrine but, when there are a number of icons, that which is the most important (to attendant or location) occupies this position with the others flanking it; smaller icons are sometimes stacked in front of the larger ones. The subject of the icons follows traditional general and local patterns of popular veneration, with the Theotokos (Mother of God) being the figure most frequently represented. Understandably, the dedication of shrines, as exemplified by their icons and occasionally by an inscription, also corresponds in many cases to the association of local churches, monasteries, and natural features with particular holy figures; the same is true of occupations and thus, for example, shrines dedicated to St Nicholas (the patron of sailors) are more common by the sea. There is almost always a simple lamp (*kandili*) of some kind in each shrine, along with the various materials required to tend it (matches or lighter, wicks, a cloth, and bottles of water and oil). In some

Sicily

Greek colonization of Sicily began in the second half of the 8th century BC. Information about Sicily's indigenes is based upon archaeology and the untrustworthy evidence of later Greek and Roman writers. Thucydides (late 5th century BC), who took his information from an earlier contemporary Antiochus of Syracuse, whose history of Sicily stretched from the earliest period to 424 BC, relates that the first settlers, if Homer's Cyclopes and Laestrygones are excluded, were the Sicans, who claimed to be autochthonous, though Thucydides considered them migrants from Iberia. After them came refugees from Troy who settled at the western end of the island, where they later intermarried with Phocian Greeks driven there by gales at sea and became the Elymians, whose cities were Eryx (now Erice) and Segesta. Then, some three centuries before the Greek colonists arrived, the Sicels migrated from Italy, and gave the island its name.

Archaeology shows modest trade for 1400–1200 BC between mainland Greece and eastern Sicily, and yields no evidence for connections with Minoan Crete, in spite of the legend of King Minos' expedition against the Sican king Kokalos, which resulted in a settlement on Sicily by Cretans who found their retreat cut off. The period of destruction and migration c.1200 BC which affected the whole eastern

Legend

● Greek colony
◆ Elymian city
■ Phoenician city

Tyrrhenian Sea

ITALY

Drepana (Trapani)
Panormus (Palermo)
Zancle (Messina)
Rhegium
Eryx
Segesta
Taormina
Naxos
Mt Etna 3323
Motya
Sicily
Catane
Mediterranean Sea
Selinus
Leontini
Megara Hyblaea
Acragas
Syracuse
Gela
Acrae
Carthage
Malta
Camarina
Casmenae
AFRICA

0   60 km

43. Sicily

Mediterranean and Italy left traces on Sicily as well. But the "Urnfield" culture which is found in central Italy c.1000 BC does not appear in Sicily, and archaeology fails to corroborate the tradition of Sicel emigration from the mainland.

The first Greek settlement in the west was not in Sicily, but on the island of Ischia off the bay of Naples c.770 BC, followed on the mainland some two decades later by Cumae, some 14 km west of Naples. About the same time, the first colony in Sicily, Naxos, was founded on a headland below Taormina, which was the first landfall a sailing ship coasting eastward along the toe of Italy would reach. Then in rapid succession colonies were planted at Leontini, Catana (modern Catania), Syracuse, Zancle (soon renamed Messina), and Megara Hyblaea. Finally, in 688 BC, Gela was founded on the south coast. The founding city states were Chalcis on Euboea, which founded the four most northerly colonies, Corinth, which founded Syracuse (734–733 BC), Megara (Megara Hyblaea), and in the case of Gela the settlers were Greeks from Rhodes and Crete.

The subsequent history of these settlements varied: Syracuse with its splendid harbour became the greatest city in Sicily, while little Megara Hyblaea was razed c.483 BC and its population deported to Syracuse, the wealthy to be absorbed as citizens and the poor to be sold as slaves. Colonies themselves, once established, might send out colonies: Megara Hyblaea founded Selinus (modern Selinunte) in 628 BC, a century after its own foundation, and Gela founded Acragas (modern Agrigento) in 580 BC. Messina founded Himera on the north shore, and Syracuse founded Camerina on the south coast and two inland colonies, Acrae and Casmenae.

The two chief reasons for a city to send out a colony were the promotion of trade and the attraction of arable land, though there were subsidiary reasons in some instances, such as repeated crop failures, or an effort to dispose of potentially troublesome citizen groups. The 8th century BC saw a surge in population in Greece, as well as increased urbanization, marked by the development of the Classical polis (city state) as the unit of government. The pacesetters were the Greeks on the island of Euboea, where the two chief poleis, Chalcis and Eretria, cooperated in founding the first colony in the west on Ischia; but by mid-century Chalcis and Eretria were at war over ownership of the Lelantine Plain in Euboea, and Eretria, the loser, was sidelined. Corinth, an ally of Chalcis in the Lelantine War, was not far behind, and pottery from Corinth was to dominate Sicilian markets until the mid-6th century BC, when imports from Athens displaced it. Colonial foundations were state ventures: the government of the founding city organized the venture, usually consulting Apollo's oracle at Delphi first, and, with the oracle's approval and advice, it chose the colonists, generally unmarried men, and selected a "founder" (*oikistes*) who brought coals from the altar of Hestia in the mother city to light the hearth fire of the new foundation. Once arrived in Sicily, the colonists would acquire territory for themselves, preferably by peaceful means, and divide it into parcels (*kleroi*) for themselves. An urban centre was laid out with an agora as a place for commerce and city government, which, like contemporary polities in Greece, would be an aristocracy. The colony became itself a polis, politically independent, though it might be bound to its mother city by ties of sentiment, and if it in turn founded a colony, it generally invited a citizen from the mother city to serve as *oikistes*. Religion, too, came to the colonies as aristocratic possessions; at Megara Hyblaea, for instance, a century passed before a public temple was built in the agora.

The attitude of the native Sicels and Sicans to the Greek invasion varied. At Megara Hyblaea a Sicel king, Hyblon, helped the colonists find a site on his territory after their first attempts failed. Possibly he hoped for a buffer between his kingdom and Syracuse, for the Corinthian colonists led by their *oikistes* Archias seized their site by force, and once established, Syracuse reduced the Sicels in their territory to serfs called Killyrioi. The native policies of the Dorian Greeks differed from those of the Chalcidian foundations, which maintained generally friendly relations with the Sicels. But both Syracuse and Gela were assimilationist: Gela expanded at the expense of the Sican chiefdoms, and Hellenized as it expanded, and its foundation of Acragas in 581 BC marked the culmination of its westward advance into Sican territory along Sicily's southern shore. There was little overt native resistance to Hellenization, though in the mid-5th century BC a Sicel chief named Ducetius tried to launch a national movement, and captured an outpost of Acragas c.450 BC. But Syracuse came to Acragas' aid; Ducetius was defeated and exiled to Corinth, and though he returned and founded a city at Caleacte (modern Caronia Marina), he was no further threat to the Greeks.

The physical remains of Greek Sicily furnish impressive evidence for great wealth in the 6th and 5th centuries BC. On the acropolis of Selinus are the ruins of four Archaic temples and on a low hill to the east are three more, of which the 5th-century "Temple G", measuring 50 × 110.4 m, is one of the largest temples ever built. Yet it was rivalled by the great temple of Olympian Zeus at Acragas. The growing wealth and population brought with it social unrest, and the names of various early tyrants have survived: Acragas had the dictator Phalaris (c.570–555? BC) whose cruelty was legendary: he was said to have a hollow bronze bull in which he roasted his enemies, and their cries issuing from the bull's mouth sounded like lowing! Historical sources become firmer by the end of the 6th century BC. At Gela two brothers, Cleander and Hippocrates, sons of an Olympic victor, ruled in succession from 505 to 491 BC, and after Hippocrates died in battle with the Sicels, his cavalry commander Gelon, son of Deinomenes (hence the name "Deinomenid" for the dynasty), succeeded, first as protector of Hippocrates' sons and then as tyrant in his own right. In 485 BC Gelon captured Syracuse where the aristocratic landowners, the Gamoroi, who had been driven out by the commons allied with the Killyrioi, had appealed to him, thereby giving him an opening. Then he transferred to Syracuse more than half the population of Gela which he entrusted to his brother Hiero, and rapidly added Camarina and Megara Hyblaea to his empire as well. Theron, tyrant of Acragas (488–472 BC), became an ally early in Gelon's career and gave his daughter Demarata to him as wife. The Theron–Gelon power bloc was ominous enough that when Theron took Himera, expelling its pro-Carthaginian tyrant Terillus, Carthage, which had planted footholds in western Sicily first at Motya, then at Panormus (modern Palermo) and Drepana (modern Trapani), reacted by mounting a major invasion which was utterly defeated at Himera by Gelon and Theron. A temple of Victory was built on the battle site at Himera, and a twin was built in Syracuse, where it still survives as the cathedral of the city. The Carthaginian attack took place in the same year, 480 BC, as the Persian invasion of Greece, and Pindar in his first *Pythian* written ten years afterwards in honour of a victory by Gelon's heir, Hiero, in the chariot race in the Pythian Games at Delphi, associates the victory at Himera and the Persian naval defeat at Salamis under the common motif of saving Hellas from slavery, while Herodotus reports a Sicilian tradition that the two victories were on the same day. This seems to have been the beginning of the myth that made Carthage a western outpost of orientalism, which in concert with Persia sought to extinguish western civilization at its birth.

Under Hiero, the Deinomenid dynasty rapidly lost its popular support, and his brother Thrasybulus, the next tyrant, was expelled by the Syracusans with support from Acragas, Himera, Gela, and Selinus, with some Sicel help. The following years in Sicily marked a democratic interlude, though political life remained turbulent, and there was sporadic warfare among the cities. In Greece itself, Athens emerged from the Persian Wars with a sea-based empire which showed an interest in Sicily, but it was not until after the Peloponnesian War between Athens and Sparta broke out in 431 that Athens undertook military intervention. In 427 BC it sent 20 warships to help Leontini against Syracuse; apparently its motive was to block grain exports to Sparta's allies in the Peloponnese. In 415 BC Athens again dispatched a large expedition on a Sicilian venture, ostensibly to help the Elymian city of Segesta against its neighbour Selinus. But its forces became bogged down in a siege of Syracuse and in 413 BC they were completely destroyed. Yet the Athenian intervention had disturbed the balance of power in Sicily, and Carthage, which after its defeat

at Himera had remained at peace, intervened, whether from opportunism or because it thought its interests were threatened. In 410 BC it grasped an appeal from Segesta which was again menaced by Selinus. The Carthaginian invasion force destroyed Selinus and Himera in 409 BC, and three years later Acragas fell, followed by Gela and Camarina. In Syracuse, which had been torn by civil strife between the democrats and the moderate oligarchs, the defence was led by Dionysius, who had been a young lieutenant of Hermocrates, the leader of the Syracusan resistance against the Athenian expedition. Hermocrates had been exiled for oligarchic sympathies, and died in a failed coup d'état in 407 BC. Dionysius I was to emerge as the most famous of Sicily's tyrants.

From 405 BC, when Dionysius' career began, until the Roman conquest, Sicily's political history centres around a group of colourful tyrants. Dionysius, whose rule lasted 38 years, was a precursor of the Hellenistic monarchs who dominated the Greek world after Alexander the Great. Like them, he exploited dynastic marriages: he himself took two wives, one a Syracusan and the other from Locri in Magna Graecia, and he arranged political marriage alliances with his daughters. He converted the oldest section of Syracuse, the island of Ortygia, into a fortress for his courtiers and mercenary soldiers, and Greek tradition preserved legends about his elaborate precautions against assassination. He treated neighbouring cities ruthlessly, and bolstered Syracuse's defences with a rampart surrounding the Euryalus ridge which runs westwards from the city for several kilometres and at its western point built a fort which survives as the Castello Eurialo, though it has been much altered since Dionysius' day.

Against Carthage Dionysius fought with varying success: in 396 BC he won an overwhelming victory, aided by plague which broke out among the Carthaginian troops, and he turned back fresh attempts in 393 and 392 BC. But some five years later he suffered a defeat and he was in the midst of a new campaign against Carthage when he died and was succeeded by his son by his Locrian wife. Dionysius II preferred a softer, less active life and made peace.

The involvement of the philosopher Plato with the regime of Dionysius II is a curious adventure, described by Plutarch and by Plato's own *Seventh Letter*. Plato visited Syracuse in 388 or 387 BC and met Dion, the brother of Dionysius I's Syracusan wife. After Dionysius' death, Dion persuaded Dionysius II to invite Plato to instruct him on kingship. Plato made two trips to Syracuse; the first achieved nothing and he left for home in 366 BC, and his second visit, five years later, was equally unsuccesful. He failed to persuade Dionysius to recall Dion whom he had exiled to Greece.

However in 357 BC Dion returned with 3000 mercenaries and expelled Dionysius, but Dion's government rapidly became a disguised tyranny, and in 354 BC he was overthrown and killed by his own soldiers. Sicily lapsed into anarchy which not even the return of Dionysius II in 347 BC could quell, and, faced with a renewed Carthaginian threat, a group of Syracusan exiles appealed to their mother city Corinth, which dispatched the Corinthian citizen Timoleon with ten ships and 700 men to Sicily.

Timoleon's public career in Sicily lasted only from 344 until 337 BC, when he resigned his powers, but during this period he defeated Carthage and forced it back into the west corner of

Sicily: illustration from the 11th-century chronicle of
Skylitzes showing the Arab siege of Messina in 842–43,
Biblioteca Nacional, Madrid

the island, deposed the tyrants in the Greek cities, and set up a
moderate democracy in Syracuse. Exiles were recalled, 60,000
new colonists were recruited in Greece, and the ruined Sicilian
economy revived. In retirement he continued to be a respected
counsellor of the new regime, but his intervention checked
Sicily's decline only briefly. In 317 BC an unscrupulous demagogue, Agathocles, led an uprising against the Syracusan aristocrats, who were massacred or exiled and their lands redistributed. He was an astute and restless tyrant; in 310 BC, when
Syracuse was faced with a new Carthaginian invasion,
Agathocles mounted a brilliant counterattack in north Africa
itself, which was initially successful, though in the end
(November 307 BC) he had to abandon his army there and
return home without it. The following year Carthage retreated
to its corner of the island and made peace, and Agathocles
spent the rest of his life consolidating his power in Sicily and
south Italy.

Agathocles' empire disintegrated at his death (289 BC) and
he left an unhappy legacy. His Italian mercenaries, who called
themselves Mamertines after their war-god Mamers (Mars),
seized Messina and used it as a base to ravage eastern Sicily.
When they allied themselves with Carthage against Syracuse,
the Syracusans appealed to the king of Epirus, Pyrrhus, who
had just defeated the Romans in two costly victories in southern Italy in the employ of Tarentum, but had failed to achieve
a profitable settlement and was ready for a new adventure. But
Pyrrhus, brilliant tactician though he was, failed to expel
Carthage from the island, and the Sicilian cities rapidly grew
weary of his pretensions. Pyrrhus retired to Italy, where he lost
his last battle against Rome at Beneventum, and Syracuse
turned for salvation to one of his former lieutenants, Hiero, by
origin a Syracusan. He was proclaimed king after he defeated
the Mamertines in 269 BC and his reign lasted until 215 BC.

Rome's first clash with Carthage began in Sicily in 264 BC
and the cause was once again the Mamertines. The First Punic
War was long and destructive, and Rome suffered terrible
manpower losses, but at the end Carthage departed from Sicily,
which became Rome's first province. Syracuse, however,
remained independent, for Hiero had shrewdly thrown in his
lot with Rome, and it was not until the Second Punic War that
Hiero's son Hiero II broke off the alliance and switched
support to Carthage. The Romans thereupon laid siege to the

city, captured it, and plundered it thoroughly. In the last years
of the war Sicily became the base for Publius Scipio the
Younger's attack on north Africa which culminated in the
defeat of a Carthaginian army led by Hannibal at Zama, and
when the war was over, all Sicily became a Roman province,
paying tribute to Rome and governed by a Roman praetor
(later a *pro praetore*), who installed himself in Hiero's palace
in Syracuse.

Rome increased Sicilian grain production enormously, but
the profits flowed into the pockets of Roman and Italian businessmen who built up large estates worked by slave labour.
Two slave revolts, which were rare in the ancient world, broke
out in Sicily under the Roman Republic, one in 139 BC which
lasted seven years, and the other in 104 BC. The revolts did
little damage to the cities, however, but the same cannot be
said for the misrule of the propraetor Gaius Verres (73–70 BC)
whose spoliation of Sicily is described vividly in Cicero's
Verrine Orations which were published after Cicero prosecuted
Verres for corruption before a senatorial court and forced
Verres to go into exile without attempting a defence. The civil
war which followed Julius Caesar's assassination also hurt
Sicily, which was held by Sextus Pompeius for seven years
during his struggle with Caesar's heir Octavian, the future
emperor Augustus, and this was one factor in the decline of
Sicilian wheat production, for Sicilian grain was cut off from
its market in Rome. With Augustus, Sicily drew closer to Italy:
he gave the Sicilians "Latin rights" and planted colonies of
Latin-speaking army veterans at Syracuse, Palermo,
Tauromenium, Tyndaris, Catana, and Thermae. In AD 212 all
the islanders became Roman citizens.

In late antiquity the Vandals, who captured Carthage in AD
439, plundered the island and finally annexed it in 468, only
to yield it eight years later to Odoacer who had deposed the
last western Roman emperor and needed Sicily's grain. The
Ostrogoths under Theoderic, who crushed Odoacer in AD 490,
took Sicily the following year and held it until the Byzantine
reconquest under the emperor Justinian (527–65). Justinian's
war against the Ostrogoths in Italy was long and costly, but
Sicily escaped the worst of it. It was not made part of the
prefecture of Italy; instead it was governed by an imperial
appointee with the title of "patrician" who was responsible to
the "Quaestor of the Sacred Palace" in Constantinople, and
the armed forces were commanded by a duke likewise responsible to Constantinople. But after the Lombards overran Italy
and the Arab menace became acute, Sicily evolved into a
"theme" commanded by a *strategos* (commander) and civil
government withered. The emperor Constans II (641–68) came
to Sicily and seems to have intended to move his capital there
from Constantinople, but his oppressions led to his murder in
Syracuse. Greek culture and language revived, however, particularly after the emperor Leo III the Isaurian (717–41) attached
the Sicilian Church to the patriarchate of Constantinople, and
Greek became once again the language of the streets.

The Arab conquest was sparked by the revolt of a Byzantine
officer, Euphemios, who sought help from the Aghlabid emir of
Kairouan. In AD 827 an expeditionary force from Tunisia, said
to number 70 ships and 10,000 men, landed at Mazzara on the
south coast. The conquest was slow: Syracuse fought off the
initial attack, but in 831 Palermo fell to the invaders who were
reinforced by a second fleet of 300 vessels from Spain. In 878

Syracuse was captured at last and sacked so thoroughly that it never recovered its position as the first city of the island. Constantinople could give little help, and in 902 the Aglabid emir captured the last Byzantine stronghold, Taormina, burned it, and killed its population. For over two centuries Sicily was to be under Saracen rule, and perhaps as many as half a million Muslims from Africa, Spain, and the Levant settled there. Christians and Jews were granted the rights reserved for infidels under Islamic law: those who were not enslaved by right of conquest became *dhimmis* (non-Muslim subjects), liable to a polltax (*djizya*) and a tax on their land (*karadj*), but they were allowed freedom of religion. Sicily prospered as a locale where Arab, Greek, and Latin cultures met, and if it were not for the Norman conquest, Sicily's subsequent history might have belonged to the orbit of north Africa. As it was, the Aglabid Caliphs at Kairouan fell in 910 and were succeeded by the Shiite Fatimids; and when the Fatimids moved their capital to Cairo in 969, Sicily became virtually independent under the Kalbid family, descendants of an able emir, al-Hassan, who had been appointed to Sicily in 947. Sicilian agriculture prospered: wheat was still the mainstay, but the Arabs introduced lemons, bitter oranges, cotton, the date palm, the mulberry tree, and papyrus, and reintroduced Roman irrigation technology which they themselves had mastered in north Africa. The Kalbid capital, Palermo, became a city of some 300,000 souls, a brilliant centre famous for its mosques, where Islam met both the Latin west and the Byzantine east. But by the 1030s rival Arab families in Sicily were challenging Kalbid rule, and the emir sought an alliance with the emperor in Constantinople who dispatched a Byzantine army led by George Maniakes to Sicily. For four years (1038–42) Maniakes led a successful offensive, capturing Messina first, followed by many other cities including Syracuse, which he attempted to restore as a Byzantine stronghold before he ran foul of court intrigues; his successor, the emperor Michael's brother-in-law, lost the conquests. Thus when Roger the Norman landed near Messina in 1060, Arab strength was sapped by internal division.

A half-century before the Norman conquest of England, Norman adventurers arrived in southern Italy, where at first they sold their services in turn to the Byzantines, Lombards, and Saracens, and then their ambitions extended to acquiring land for settlement: the first Norman to do so was Rainulf who got the county of Aversa from the duke of Naples, Sergius, in 1030, in return for help against the Lombard prince of Capua. In 1059 pope Nicholas II invested Robert Guiscard, the sixth of the 12 sons of a lesser Norman noble, Tancred de Hauteville, as duke of Apulia and Calabria and future ruler of Sicily. However, it was Guiscard's youngest brother Roger who led the conquest of Sicily. Palermo was taken in 1072 after a six-month siege, and in 1091 the last important Muslim stronghold, Noto, fell.

Count Roger's government restored Byzantine traditions; court ceremonial and protocol were borrowed from Constantinople, and since the Christians who survived the Arab regime were Greek Orthodox, Roger endowed more Greek than Latin monasteries. But he gave fiefs to Norman, French, and Italian immigrants who brought colonists from their homelands, and thus by the 13th century the dominant speech in Sicily had become a dialect of Italian. Count Roger's son, Roger II, added Apulia, which he incorporated into his realm on the death of his cousin, Capua, Naples, and the Abruzzi, and had won a foothold in Africa, and his admiral George of Antioch took Corfu and transplanted silk-workers from Greece to Sicily. Palermo became the most brilliant capital in Europe under Roger's son, Roger II, who was crowned king in the cathedral there in 1130 by a representative of the antipope Anacletus II, though it was more than eight years before pope Innocent II acknowledged the title. Arabs, Greeks, and Latins all served in the royal bureaucracy, though the chief officers were Greek and the flavour of the court was Byzantine. Sicily was a medley of cultures, held together by a monarchy which blended concepts of kingship taken from both Byzantium and Ottonian Germany.

But power was shifting towards the feudal barons; William I (the Bad) faced a baronial uprising in 1155 which he suppressed with help from his Muslim subjects, and when William II (the Good) died childless, the barons divided their support between William's aunt Constance, wife of the Hohenstaufen emperor Henry VI, and an illegitimate grandson of King Roger, Tancred of Lecce. Tancred secured the throne, but in 1194 he died, leaving only a boy to succeed him; when Henry invaded the island, the barons hurried to submit, and on Christmas day Henry was crowned king of Sicily in Palermo. His avarice and despotism soon alienated Sicily which rebelled, and while he was suppressing the revolt mercilessly, he died (1197), probably of malaria, at the age of 32, leaving behind a three-year-old son, Frederick.

During Frederick's minority Sicily fell into anarchy; the Muslim population rebelled and set up an independent principality and the German barons to whom Henry had granted fiefs took possession of Palermo and of the young king, in defiance of pope Innocent III who became Frederick's guardian on his mother's death. Frederick had to leave for Germany in 1212 to defend his election as emperor of the Holy Roman empire against the Welf candidate Otto of Brunswick, but he returned in 1220 and rapidly restored royal authority. The *Liber Augustalis*, the new law code he promulgated, defined a new concept of kingship: the emperor received his royal power from God; clerics were barred from interference in secular affairs; and criminal justice was reserved for the king. Self-government in the cities was disallowed, which had the result of forestalling the rise of any independent merchant class strong enough to counterbalance the landowning aristocracy. Significantly, the *Liber Augustalis* was in Latin, though a Greek translation was provided for the surviving Greek communities.

Frederick presided over a semi-oriental court; the popes, who found him altogether too rationalist and secular, referred to him as a baptized sultan. He claimed to love Sicily more than all his other possessions; yet he used its wealth to support his ambitions in Italy and Germany, and the long decline of Sicily began with his death in 1250. He had been excommunicated twice, and in 1245 he was formally deposed by pope Innocent IV; and upon his death, Innocent hawked the crown of Sicily around the courts of Europe.

Frederick's only legitimate son Conrad survived his father by only four years, but the heir of his Sicilian interests was his illegitimate son Manfred, first regent and then king of Sicily (1250–66). But the papacy would not accept a hated Hohenstaufen, and when a Frenchman became pope as Urban

IV in 1261, he determined to secure Sicily for a French ally. In 1266 Charles, count of Anjou and brother of St Louis, defeated and killed Manfred at Benevento. Two years later the 16-year-old son of Conrad, Conradin, made a last attempt to secure Sicily for the Hohenstaufen, but Charles defeated him and put him to death after a mock trial at Naples.

Angevin rule came abruptly to an end with a massacre known as the "Sicilian Vespers" which takes its name from the incident which sparked it: an insult offered on Easter Monday, 30 March 1282, to a young married Sicilian woman by a French soldier outside the church of San Spirito in Palermo and promptly avenged by her husband. At the beginning of the year Charles of Anjou was Europe's greatest sovereign: he was king of Sicily, Jerusalem, and Albania, Count of Provence, Forcalquier, Anjou, and Maine, regent of Achaea in Greece, Lord of Tunis, and a Roman senator, and in the first week of April his fleet was due to sail against the emperor Michael VIII Palaiologos (1261–82) in Constantinople. Messina, where the Angevin fleet lay at anchor, hesitated at first, but on 28 April it joined the revolt; the fleet was destroyed, and Charles's Vicar, Herbert of Orléans, was allowed a safe conduct out of the city for himself and his staff. Angevin oppression had united Sicily, and a personal affront supplied the incitement, but in the background were the intrigues of the emperor Michael and Pedro of Aragon, who had inherited the Hohenstaufen claim, and the go-between was John of Procida who had been Frederick II's physician and remained a Hohenstaufen loyalist. Legend has exaggerated his role, but there is no doubt that Aragonese agents were active in Sicily and smuggled in arms; and the emperor supplied money. Five months after the Vespers, Pedro landed in Sicily and on 4 September he was acclaimed king at Palermo.

Both Charles and Pedro died in 1285 and Pedro's son James inherited Sicily and, after the death of his elder brother, Aragon as well. James appointed his younger brother Frederick his viceroy in Sicily, although according to Pedro's disposition Sicily should have gone to him if James became king of Aragon. Yet it was Frederick who restored the island's independence. The Sicilians crowned him king in 1296 and he defended his kingdom successfully against both the Aragonese and the Angevins. Thus there were two kingdoms and two kings of Sicily, one with his seat at Naples who for convenience is called the king of Naples, and the other at Palermo. War followed by the Black Death was to exhaust Sicily in the next century. The last remnants of the island's Greek population were absorbed, though Sicily had one last encounter with Greece: a temporary peace in 1302 freed Sicily from pillage by foreign soldiers of fortune and the most formidable of these armed bands, the Catalan Company, moved east and in 1311 conquered Athens and attached it temporarily to the Sicilian kingdom. But the heritage of Greece had passed into history.

JAMES ALLAN EVANS

See also Arabs, Carthage, Colonization, Normans

Further Reading

Amari, Michele, *Storia dei Musulmani di Sicilia*, 2nd edition, 3 vols, Catania: Prampotini, 1933–39

Bérard, Jean, *La Colonisation grecque de l'Italie méridionale et de la Sicile dans l'antiquité*, 2nd edition, Paris: Presses Universitaires de France, 1957
Boardman, John, *The Greeks Overseas: Their Early Colonies and Trade*, 4th edition, London and New York: Thames and Hudson, 1999
Finley, M.I., *Ancient Sicily*, revised edition, London: Chatto and Windus, and Totowa, New Jersey: Rowman and Littlefield, 1979
Freeman, E.A., *The History of Sicily from the Earliest Times*, 4 vols, Oxford: Clarendon Press, 1891–94; New York: Franklin, 1965
Holloway, R. Ross, *The Archaeology of Ancient Sicily*, London and New York: Routledge, 1991
Mack Smith, Denis, *A History of Sicily: Medieval Sicily, 800–1713*, London and New York: Chatto and Windus, 1968
Matthew, Donald, *The Norman Kingdom of Sicily*, Cambridge and New York: Cambridge University Press, 1992
Runciman, Steven, *The Sicilian Vespers: A History of the Mediterranean World in the Later Thirteenth Century*, Cambridge: Cambridge University Press, 1958
Sanders, L.J., *Dionysius I of Syracuse and Greek Tyranny*, London and New York: Croom Helm, 1987
Sjöqvist, Erik, *Sicily and the Greeks: Studies in the Interrelationship between the Indigenous Populations and the Greek Colonists*, Ann Arbor: University of Michigan Press, 1973
Takayama, Hiroshi, *The Administration of the Norman Kingdom in Sicily*, Leiden and New York: Brill, 1993
Woodhead, A.G., *The Greeks in the West*, London: Thames and Hudson, and New York: Praeger, 1962

Siegecraft

Whatever its historical validity, the Trojan War and its traditional length of ten years argue for an almost total lack of siegecraft in the Late Greek Bronze Age. That determined attempts were made to take cities, however, is indicated by the massive fortifications of the time (most notably at Tiryns), and that these attempts were mainly directed at the weakest points, the gates, is demonstrated by the existence, as at Mycenae, of a bastion to enable the defenders to hurl missiles at the unshielded left side of the attackers. Furthermore, although the battering ram is first known from Assyrian reliefs of the 9th century BC, it has reasonably been speculated that one with a reinforced head and slung beneath a wooden frame may lie behind the tale of the wooden horse.

Whereas in the Late Bronze Age only the king's palace and its immediate vicinity were fortified, the polis (city state) that emerged at the end of the Dark Age demanded protection for its much larger urban centre. It was, however, only in the late 6th century BC, against the Persian threat to Greek settlements in Asia Minor, that attempts were made to embrace with walls whole cities (and by the 4th century BC agricultural land as well), and not until the 5th century BC that numerous towers were built to facilitate the hurling of greater concentrations of missiles. However, even insubstantial walls were generally sufficient to withstand most hostile attacks. With the exception of a few very small places (e.g. those captured by Brasidas in Chalcidice), treachery and starvation consequent on circumvallation were the engines of capitulation. This situation was probably due to contemporary emphasis upon the hoplite at the expense of archers and slingers who could have afforded covering fire for the attackers. Nevertheless, expertise in the design and placing of walls and counterwalls by besiegers and besieged made considerable advances (well illustrated in the Athenian siege of Syracuse in 415–413 BC, Thucydides, 6. 63–7. 87).

Siege engines, however, did make a tentative appearance. Rams and "tortoises" (protective sheds) built by a certain Artemon of Clazomenae were introduced by Pericles at the siege of Samos in 440 BC, but Diodorus (12. 28. 3) gives no details. Similarly Thucydides merely mentions (2. 58. 1) "machines" used unsuccessfully by the Athenians at Potidaea in 430 BC. He does, however, describe at great length (2. 75–78) the siege of Plataea in 429–427 BC. The mound built by the attackers against the city wall was countered by the erection on that wall of a wooden frame filled with bricks by workmen protected against flaming arrows by screens of hides. The defenders also knocked a hole through the bottom of their wall to withdraw earth from the mound (an action countered by the Peloponnesians' plugging of the gap with heavy reed baskets of clay), and subsequently they tunnelled underneath to remove loose earth from the bottom of the mound. They further built a crescent-shaped inner wall at this point, a tactic which was to become standard. The blockading Peloponnesians for their part failed to break through with battering rams, because the Plataeans raised up the heads with nooses or snapped them off with beams let down from chains. The attackers' incendiary attempt with faggots piled up against the wall and kindled with brimstone and pitch failed, however, only through rain and the absence of a favourable wind. They consequently resorted, ultimately with success, to circumvallation and resultant starvation. "Machines" on board ships were nevertheless instrumental in capturing two towers on the Megarian island of Minoa in 427 BC (Thucydides, 3. 51. 3); and fire was successfully employed, though only against the palisade of a garrison, at Delium in 424 BC when it was driven through a pipe by bellows (Thucydides, 4. 100).

Huge advances were made in the 4th century BC in siege engines and artillery. Siege towers, possibly learned from the Carthaginians, and arrow-firing catapults, possibly an Assyrian invention, were already being used by Dionysius I of Syracuse at Motya in 397 BC (Diodorus, 14. 48–53), and by the time of Alexander's sieges of Tyre and Gaza in 332 BC siege techniques and machines, including stone-throwing catapults, almost always gave the attackers the upper hand. An eminently sane treatise from the middle of the 4th century BC by an author known today as Aeneas Tacticus (probably the Stymphalian general Aeneas) gives a sobering picture of the strains of a city under siege. It details such things as the organization of guards, scouts, patrols, sorties, and passwords, the smuggling in of weapons, proclamations to the citizenry, the threat of plots, the allaying of panic, and the contrivances needed to counter siege engines, artillery, and sapping. This formidable legacy of technical knowledge was further developed throughout the Hellenistic period. This can be seen, for instance, in Diodorus' account (20. 81–88, 91–100) of the siege of Rhodes in 305–304 BC, which gave its protagonist Demetrius I of Macedon his soubriquet Poliorcetes ("Besieger"), and descriptions (Polybius, 8. 3–7; Plutarch, *Marcellus*, 4–17) of Archimedes' innovations at Syracuse in 213–211 BC.

Technical details of artillery come from four ancient authors. The earliest, a treatise of *c.*240 BC by Biton, supplies instructions for mechanics and includes valuable details on advanced non-torsion catapults. The work of Philon of Byzantium from *c.*200 BC gives critical descriptions of standard and novel torsion catapults. Vitruvius, the Roman architectural writer (*c.*25 BC), is useful for giving highly detailed dimensions, which he probably found in Greek sources. Of Heron of Alexandria in the late 1st century AD there survive two works, one (*Belopoiika*, probably derived from the lost works of Ctesibius of Alexandria) mainly valuable for its descriptions of early non-torsion and torsion catapults, the other (*Cheiroballistra*, but the title may be corrupt) detailing a contemporary torsion weapon with an all-metal frame.

The earliest catapult, the *gastraphetes* ("belly-bow"), had a concavity at the end of the stock which was held against the stomach. An arrow placed in a groove was fired by means of what amounted to a composite bow, whose manipulation was aided by ratchets, pawls, and a triggering mechanism. Its effective range of possibly 200–250 m was somewhat superior to that of the hand-held composite bow (itself known from the Bronze Age). It was subsequently enlarged and furnished with a base to stand on the ground, a universal joint for efficient aiming, and a winched pull-back mechanism, and it could be adapted for stone-throwing. Though superseded by the late 3rd century BC, non-torsion machines reappeared in the 4th century AD and spawned the medieval crossbow.

Probably around 340 BC there appeared also the superior torsion weapons in which, effectively, the composite bow was replaced by wooden arms inserted into "springs" of twisted sinews (and occasionally hair). Of two sorts, the *euthytone* to fire arrows, and the *palintone* to hurl rocks, these swiftly became superbly engineered machines, each being optimally designed for the length of arrow or weight of shot. They could project also incendiary bombs consisting of pitch, sulphur, tow, etc. packed into pots (and, if sources are to be believed, on one occasion, by Hannibal, even live poisonous snakes). The *polybolos* ("multithrower") described by Philon had an ingenious ammunitionfeed for rapid firing. Such engines were used by besiegers and besieged from the ground, walls, siege towers, and ships. The maximum range, at which point accuracy was much impaired, was probably around 500 m. The main defence was padding on the walls to soften the impact of rocks, while the Tyrians erected on their walls mechanically rotating multi-spoked wheels to deflect Alexander's arrows.

Although circumvallation was still commonly practised, sometimes (and often by the Romans) with an outer wall to protect the attackers from a relieving force, offensive weapons besides artillery were also improved. Siege towers reached massive proportions under Demetrius Poliorcetes, his nine-storey monster at Rhodes being *c.*45 m high. On huge pivoted wheels, it was strongly protected and even furnished with mechanical shutters over the catapult ports. His rams too were massive, the largest being *c.*55 m long. Rams were frequently sheathed in iron and their points could be specifically designed to wreak maximum damage on stone walls or wooden gates. The larger ones were sometimes mounted on rollers and many were slung from a penthouse roof by ropes. One such early penthouse of Alexander was surmounted by a 9-m tower to house a small catapult and pots of water to extinguish fires.

Scaling ladders were improved, some being protected by attached shields and others mechanically operated. Sapping and counter-sapping techniques developed, including timbered galleries and devices for detecting tunnels, while at the siege of Ambracia in 189 BC pungent smoke was driven in the diggers' faces through an iron tube by means of bellows. Against blockading ships defenders could use submarine stakes in the virtually tideless Mediterranean and fire-ships (as famously at Tyre) while, according to a perhaps over-imaginative tradition, Archimedes employed grappling hooks on chains to lift and catastrophically release ships' prows and also set smaller boats on fire by concentrating on them the sun's rays reflected from shields.

Apart from improvements in architecture the main advances in siegecraft during the Roman period were in artillery, in the introduction of the *cheiroballistra*, and, by the 4th century AD, the one-armed stone-throwing torsion *onager*.

The Byzantines' most important contribution was in architecture, most notably the superb walls of their capital, which were never properly broken through by any enemy. Artillery saw the invention in the 7th century of Greek fire, which was employed in siege warfare as well as at sea. The adoption from the peoples of the steppes of the immensely powerful trebuchet or mangonel in place of torsion engines increased the range of artillery, but at some expense in accuracy. The motive force in the trebuchet was the weights attached to the butt end of a pole which was placed over a crossbar, furnished with a cup or sling for the missile, and pulled down by ropes which were released for firing. Cannon were used at the siege of Constantinople in 1453, but only by the Turks after Constantine XI had through poverty rejected the assistance of Urban, the Hungarian gunsmith. Byzantine military manuals (see Dennis, 1985) largely repeat inherited knowledge, which was frequently put to good practical use. An anonymous 10th-century treatise, known today under the Latin title of *De Obsidione Toleranda*, details the stockpiling of various foods and other materials and the choice of personnel most useful in withstanding a siege, while Eustathios, archbishop of Thessalonica, memorably relates the siege of his city by the Normans in 1185, in which he himself took a valiant part. The choice by Constantine XI of a famed expert in siege warfare, the Genoese soldier Giovanni Giustiani Longo, to supervise the defences in 1453 proved to be the immediate cause of the taking of the city (through his retirement from the battle upon injury despite the emperor's entreaties); but it also dramatically demonstrates that Greek contributions to the science had by then come to an end.

A.R. LITTLEWOOD

See also Architecture (fortifications, military), Technology, Warfare

Further Reading

Aeneas Tacticus, *How to Survive under Siege*, translated by David Whitehead, Oxford: Clarendon Press, and New York: Oxford University Press, 1990

Berg, Hilden van den, *Anonymus de obsidione toleranda*, Leiden: Brill, 1947

Connolly, Peter, *Greece and Rome at War*, Englewood Cliffs, New Jersey: Prentice Hall, 1981, pp. 274–303

Dennis, George T. (editor and translator), *Three Byzantine Military Treatises*, Washington, D.C.: Dumbarton Oaks, 1985

Garlan, Yvon, *Recherches de poliorcétique grecque*, Athens: Ecole Française d'Athènes, 1974

Landels, J.G., *Engineering in the Ancient World*, London: Chatto and Windus, and Berkeley: University of California Press, 1978, pp. 99–131

Marsden, E.W., *Greek and Roman Artillery: Historical Development*, Oxford: Clarendon Press, 1969

Marsden, E.W., *Greek and Roman Artillery: Technical Treatises*, Oxford: Clarendon Press, 1971 (with translations)

Sikelianos, Angelos 1884–1951

Poet

Angelos Sikelianos is one of the major poets of modern Greece. His creative period stretched from 1902, when he first began publishing poems in literary magazines, until shortly before his death, in 1951. All the influential poets of his time, including representatives of its two main literary movements, Symbolism and Surrealism, acknowledged him as a leading voice. Sikelianos does not, however, belong to any single school or generation and does not even fit into the broader division of modern Greek poetry into two main schools, the Athenian and the Heptanesian, since he combines both traditions in his poetry. Literary historians place Sikelianos in a category of his own, like Constantine Cavafy.

Born on the Ionian island of Leucas, the son of a schoolteacher and the youngest of seven children, Sikelianos was educated locally and at Athens University (where he failed to complete his studies in law). Since there was no family money available, Sikelianos had no clear idea of how he was to support his ambition to become a poet until, through the agency of his sister Penelope, he met and married the American biscuit heiress Evelina (Eva) Palmer (1874–1952). The marriage took place in 1907, when Sikelianos was 19.

The year 1909 saw the birth of Eva and Angelos's only child, Glavkos, and the publication, at Eva's expense, of Sikelianos's first major poem, *Alaphroïskiotos* (The Light-Shadowed One), together with the sequence of short lyric poems, *Ionian Rhapsodies*. This pattern of long and short lyric poems was to be repeated, and Sikelianos was to publish a further eight collections of short lyric poems (*Songs of Victory* I and II, *Descent into Hades* I and II, *Sonnets*, *Heavenly Aphrodite*, *Orphic Songs*, and *Desires*) and four extended poems (*Prologue to Life*, *Mater Dei*, *Easter of the Greeks*, and *Delphic Word*).

The poetry of Sikelianos is a product of painstaking craftsmanship, based on a complex system of poetics. It draws for its inspiration on two main sources: nature and other texts. Based on a close and accurate observation of the natural world of rural Greece, Sikelianos works with a system of nature metaphors, often very extended, to parallel the experience of the poet as individual and as visionary. At the same time, extensive creative use is made of intertextuality, and Sikelianos draws on ancient Greek poets and philosophers in his attempt to present time in cyclical, rather than linear, terms. Homer, Heraclitus, Pindar, and Aeschylus are particular favourites, but Sikelianos also makes use of the Septuagint, Byzantine liturgy, and modern Greek folk poetry. Ancient, Byzantine, and dialect words coexist with standard modern Greek in his poetry, underlining his belief in the unity of the Greek language.

A consistent, stated aim of the poetry of Sikelianos is to bridge gulfs. In the first of the early *Ionian Rhapsodies*, the poet's persona speaks of "commingling" the Ionian sea with the Greek mainland, which may be read as a metaphor for combining the Heptanesian and Athenian traditions. In a poem from the late collection *Desires* ("Letter III"), the ability of poetic thought to conjoin incompatible elements is compared to the bridging of unfordable rivers by the god Dionysus, who "hung vines across the chasms of the world". Here, as elsewhere in his poetry, Sikelianos places the poet at the centre. The theme of return is also deeply entrenched in the form and content of Sikelianos's writing, promoting a cyclical view of life and art. A recurring metaphor for the poet is the returning Odysseus.

Sikelianos was the first poet of modern Greece to experiment with free verse. In *Alaphroïskiotos* he adopts and extends the approach of the French poets who first experimented with loosening the Alexandrine by using enjambment and overriding the caesura. Most of the poem is based on the commonest modern Greek metre, the 15-syllable line. *Prologue to Life* represents a far more extreme experiment in free verse, based on lines of differing lengths and differing metrical forms, and completely dispensing with rhyme. Originally printed (privately) in four volumes, a fifth part was added in 1946. It is characterized, like much of Sikelianos's work, by immense syntactic complexity which, in combination with its metrical freedom, sometimes gives an impression of incoherence. For *Mater Dei*, inspired by the illness and death of Penelope Sikelianou Duncan, Sikelianos returned to a strict metrical form: rhymed 15-syllable couplets. *Easter of the Greeks* (which remained unfinished) and *Delphic Word* also employ strict metrical forms and rhyme. All Sikelianos's poetry exploits the acoustic potential of language and is unusually dense in sound-patterning.

Between 1924 and 1936 Sikelianos produced very little poetry. During this period he was working to promote his "Delphic Idea": the establishment of a world spiritual centre and university at Delphi. In this project he was inspired by the religious syncretism of the French writer Edouard Schuré, but it was Eva Palmer Sikelianou who assumed practical responsibility for the two Delphic festivals of 1927 and 1930. At these festivals ancient drama was presented in its original setting for the first time since the inception of the modern Greek state; the stadium was used for athletic contests, and traditional handicrafts were exhibited in local houses. Largely inspired by the work of Isadora Duncan, who attempted to restore a classical simplicity to dance, and her brother Raymond (husband of Penelope Sikelianou), who affected ancient Greek dress, Eva choreographed the plays and set the choral odes to Byzantine-style music. Under her direction, ancient-style costumes were woven on traditional hand looms. The festivals directed international attention to Greece and inaugurated the reuse of ancient theatres. They may also be seen as the inspiration behind present-day arts festivals in Athens and elsewhere.

The Delphic project ultimately led to public ridicule, financial ruin, and the effectual break up of Sikelianos's marriage. Eva returned to the United States in 1933, ostensibly to raise funds to continue with the Delphic project. She did not return to Greece until 1952. Throughout her life Eva Palmer Sikelianou continued to promote Sikelianos's work, translating some of it with her daughter-in-law Frances Lefevre Sikelianos, and sending him money. She also continued to make suggestions for literary projects, encouraging Sikelianos to experiment with ancient Greek drama, a suggestion which he was to pursue, with mixed results, in his last years.

During the later 1930s Sikelianos wrote most of the poems of the two great collections of his maturity, *Orphic Songs* and *Desires*. In 1938 he met Anna Karamani, and the couple married in 1940, following divorces from their respective spouses. Although too old to serve in World War II, Sikelianos engaged in public acts of symbolic resistance during the German occupation. He read a specially composed poem at Kostis Palamas's funeral, and circulated the collection *Akritic Songs* (later assimilated into *Songs of Victory* II).

In 1946 Sikelianos collected his poems in the three-volume *Lyrikos Vios* (Lyric Life), which was republished posthumously in five volumes by G.P. Savidis (Athens, 1966; 2nd edition 1981). A sixth volume contains unpublished poems and juvenilia. The planned seventh volume, which was to have contained the editor's notes and a glossary, unfortunately never materialized. Sikelianos's plays and prose writing have also been collected and edited by Savidis.

Sikelianos died in 1951, after drinking Lysol (a disinfectant) in mistake for Nujol (prescription medication).

SARAH EKDAWI

See also Tragedy

Biography

Born on the island of Leucas in 1884, Sikelianos began (but did not complete) studies in law at Athens University. Ambitious to become a poet, he married the American heiress Evelina (Eva) Palmer in 1907. His first collection of poems appeared in 1909. Between 1924 and 1936 he and Eva devoted themselves to his "Delphic Idea", a project to establish a spiritual centre and university at Delphi. Ancient plays were performed but the project failed and with it the marriage. He died in 1951.

Writings

Selected Poems, translated by Edmund Keeley and Philip Sherrard, Princeton, New Jersey: Princeton University Press, 1979; London: Allen and Unwin, 1980

Lyrikos Vios [Lyric Life], edited by G.P. Savidis, 2nd edition, Athens, 1981

Further Reading

Keeley, Edmund, *Modern Greek Poetry: Voice and Myth*, Princeton, New Jersey: Princeton University Press, 1983

Palmer-Sikelianos, Eva, *Upward Panic: The Autobiography of Eva Palmer-Sikelianos*, edited by John P. Anton, Philadelphia: Harwood Academic, 1993

Sherrard, Philip, *The Marble Threshing Floor: Studies in Modern Greek Poetry*, London: Vallentine Mitchell, and Fair Lawn, New Jersey: Essential, 1956

Silk

Silk is a luxurious fabric; it was called *serikon* because it was made by the Seres, the Indian people from whom wild silk was first purchased by the ancient Greeks. The Latin word *Seres* later came to mean the Chinese, when domesticated silk began to be imported from that country as well.

One type of silk fabric from northern India is called "tussah", or wild silk, and comes from the silkworm called the *Antheraea mylitta* of the family *Saturnidae*. This caterpillar, not needing to be domesticated, feeds on different types of leaves, including oak, and produces short fibres of a brown or yellow colour, that result in a fabric less fine and strong than domesticated silk. The date at which silk was first worn or produced in the ancient Near East and Greece remains a mystery, due to the perishable nature of cloth and the lack of precision in the ancient references about it. Biblical references (Ezekiel 16: 10 and 13) to silk and Herodotus' remarks (1. 135) about Median cloth probably refer to wild silk from India. Aristotle seems to have known something of silk processing (*Historia Animalium*, 5. 19. 6). In Hellenistic times a fine transparent cloth was produced called mussel silk, alluding to the threads by which a mussel attached itself to rocks, and most likely made from a mixture of Egyptian linen and Indian wild silk.

The thread of "true" silk, from China, is produced from the cocoon of the domesticated caterpillar, or silkworm, of the moth species *Bombyx mori* of the family *Bombycidae*. This thread is extremely long since the cocoon is spun with one continuous filament and can be woven into a fabric that is prized for its ability to be smooth, thin, and flexible, as well as strong and readily acceptable of dye. According to Chinese tradition, silk production was known from the Neolithic period and originated with Hsi-ling-shi (or Lei-tsu), the 14-year-old bride of the emperor Huang Ti. The legend credits her with the first knowledge of sericulture or the raising of silkworms. Silkworms were selectively bred until they were enfeebled, easily susceptible to temperature changes, unable to walk, and dependent on human attendants to feed them large quantities of fresh chopped mulberry leaves. At maturity the caterpillar spins a cocoon consisting of one very fine, long (500–1000 m) silk thread. The cocoon is then steamed with the caterpillar inside to prevent it from emerging and chopping through the thread. Six or eight cocoons are spun together through a water bath with an elaborate reel-and-pulley system to form a thread thick enough for weaving. It takes about 35,000 worms to produce 5 kg of silk.

Sericulture was successfully kept secret and guarded by the Chinese until the Japanese learned about it in AD 300. In the 6th century AD, during the reign of Justinian, two Nestorian monks were reputed to have concealed silkworms in a hollow cane and smuggled them into Byzantine territory, along with the procedures of sericulture.

The silk trade between China and the west cannot be traced with confidence before 115 BC. In that year the emperor Wu-ti of the Han dynasty initiated trade with Mithridates II of Parthia. Silk thread and cloth, although not the knowledge of its production, would thereafter be exported from China through the Tarim basin, across the top of the Kushan empire in India and, with the Parthians as middlemen, on to the Near Eastern coast, Asia Minor, Greece, and Italy. In exchange for the cloth, according to the annals of the Later Han dynasty, the *Hou-han-shu* (from the 1st century AD), the Chinese traders received gold, silver (both highly desirable due to the lack of such metals in China), precious stones, amber, glass, gold-embroidered rugs, gold-coloured cloth (from Syria and Alexandria), silk cloth of various colours, and fine cloth made from wild silkworms. The reason why the Chinese bought back silk at Merv is because their own silk was a heavy brocade and densely woven. Silk weavers in Syrian cities and Greek islands, such as Cos, specialized in unravelling the Chinese silk cloth and reweaving it into a lightweight, transparent gauze, thereby multiplying the lengths of fabric for sale in Roman cities, increasing their profit, and satisfying the upper-class desire for erotic, sensational fashion. Other fabrics such as flax and wool could also be mixed with it, which the Romans called *subserica* or *transerica*. Cos, in particular, specialized in a purple-dyed silk, famous enough to be called the "Coan purple" by Augustan poets (Horace, *Odes*, 4. 13).

Trade increased with the peaceful conditions of the Augustan era, but Roman authors from the time of the early empire were scandalized by wearers of silk, "clad in which no woman can honestly say she is not naked" according to Seneca. Although Caesar had silk curtains and Caligula, later, was rumoured to have worn silk clothing, many agreed with Tacitus (*Annals*, 2. 33) that "men should not disgrace themselves with silk clothing from the East" and an edict of the Roman Senate in AD 16 prohibited such dress for men. But the gulf between moralistic intellectuals and public desire was vast, and since all four territories along the silk route – China, India, Parthia, and the Roman empire – were peaceful from AD 90 to 130, the Roman empire acquired plentiful supplies of domesticated silk from China during this period, even though it was said to be worth its weight in gold, due to its difficult manufacture, middlemen fees, and long transport from China.

Strabo (15. 693) thought that silk grew on trees and had to be scraped off the leaves. Pausanias (6. 26. 6–9), however, knew that silk came from an eight-footed insect, called by the Greeks the *ser*, and that they were taken care of by the Chinese in special houses; he mistakenly thought that they were fed millet for four years. Missions were sent to China by Maes Titianus and Marcus Aurelius in the 3rd century to acquire more silk and information.

During the Byzantine empire the meaning of wearing silk, particularly coloured purple and gold, changed from defining women who lived off their beauty to distinguishing men of authority – the emperor, aristocracy, and ecclesiastics. The rarity and glitter of silk, purple dye, and gold embroidery were restricted to those at the top of the Byzantine hierarchy and separated them from common citizens and barbaric aliens.

Complicated monopolistic regulations enforced state control over the production, manufacture, trade, and export of silk cloth. There were two types of guilds in Constantinople that could work silk – imperial guilds (*demosia somata*) and private ones (*somata*). The imperial guilds were directly controlled by the state and manufactured textiles only for the emperor and his court, officers, and for gifts to foreign powers. During the late Roman empire in the 4th century AD rulers had frozen workers in their occupations, obliging them to remain in their guilds as part of a hereditary caste system. By the 6th

Silk: the Epitaphios of Thessalonica, a representation of Christ administering the eucharist to the apostles, in silk with gold and silver thread, 14th century, Byzantine Museum, Athens

century, in the time of Justinian, there were too many textile workers in the imperial guild, so restrictions and examinations were enforced. The head of the *Eidikon*, a branch of the state treasury, was the administrative supervisor of the imperial factory, which was largely housed in a wing of the imperial palace in Constantinople. The three types of imperial silk workers included tailors, purple-dyers, and gold-embroiderers.

The private guilds had begun to decline in the 4th century due to a shortage of labour and a limited supply of higher-priced imported silk because of the war with Persia. The labour shortage was adjusted by legislation that obliged workers to remain in their craft. Emperors tried to find alternative silk routes bypassing Persia, but were not very successful. The restriction on purchases of silk in the Byzantine empire by anyone other than a single imperial officer, the *Comes Commerciorum per Orientem*, however, was effective in keeping prices down.

Justinian took a further series of steps to increase the state monopoly on silk manufacture, which depressed the private guilds during his reign. First he legislated that imperial silk cloth could be purchased by the public but worn only by women, thereby increasing the market for the imperial guild.

He also fixed a low price for raw silk at 8 *nomismata* per pound, which may be related to the introduction of the Chinese silkworm and sericulture into Constantinople in 553–54. The result was that foreign merchants refused to sell at such a low price, so the independent private guilds had their supply of silk cut off, and they either left Constantinople for Persia or tried to gain admittance to the imperial guild, which was doing quite well since retail prices for silk clothing had been raised to 6–24 *nomismata* per ounce.

By the late 6th century the single buyer was replaced by the *kommerkiarioi*, who could purchase raw silk at 15 *nomismata* per pound, but had to resell it at the same price to private merchants of raw silk, one of the private guilds, so that the state monopoly created by Justinian loosened. By the 9th century sericulture was thriving in the Byzantine empire and the guilds of merchants of raw silk and spinners could purchase silk without state intermediaries or price limits. The only legislation left concerning the wearing of silk clothing stated that purple cloth could not be manufactured or worn by the public. Besides the private guilds, noblemen were authorized for the manufacture of silk for their own households and certain workers of low status could buy soiled or damaged silk.

The *Book of the Prefect* (911–12), a collection of state-approved by-laws from the time of Leo VI, described the duties and rights of the private guilds and industry. The five guilds in Constantinople, by this time, were merchants of raw silk, silk spinners, clothiers and dyers, merchants of domestic silk garments, and merchants of imported silk garments. These workers were independent of the state and sold cloth to the public, but prerequisites for membership ranged from the necessity of a sponsor to large entrance fees. The goals of guild legislation were to stabilize prices, the amount of work, and the supplies of raw material.

Some Byzantine examples of imperial silk are still in existence, such as the Textile of Liège of the emperor Herakleios (610–41), the Textile of Siegburg of the emperors Romanos I and Christopher (921–31), the Textile of Düsseldorf of the emperors Basil II and Constantine VIII (976–1025), the Textile of Aix-la-Chapelle placed in the tomb of Charlemagne by Otto III (1000), and the Pallium of the emperor Michael VIII Palaiologos (1261). The types of weave included twill, typical until the 11th century; lampas weave, developed then; tabby, damask, and tapestry. The fabric was dyed in vivid yellow, red, blue, or dark purple with designs of heraldic lions, elephants, human figures, geometric patterns, arabesques, leaves, or flowers. Byzantine mosaics, such as the portrait of Theodora and her court at S. Vitale in Ravenna, supply additional evidence for patterns and colours used in royal silk.

Guild conditions continued to loosen until the 12th century when Jewish manufacturers of gold, silk, and purple garments were allowed to work in Constantinople, Thessalonica, and in Thebes. In 1147 Roger II captured Corfu, Corinth, and Thebes, and moved silk workers to Palermo in Sicily. Thebes was still producing silk in 1170, as reported by Benjamin of Tudela who numbered the Jewish silk workers at 2,000 in Thebes and 2,500 in Pera, when the Genoese were denied a licence to buy silk fabric in Thebes.

The Byzantine emperors had used their silk monopoly as a tactical weapon against Europe, guarding the secrets of sericulture as had the Chinese before them. Western rulers capitulated to the power of Byzantine ceremonial dress and its concept of "hierarchy through silk clothing". They tried to imitate purple silk, but never succeeded in producing the highly refined quality of Byzantine fabric.

The Genoese reintroduced the craft of silk production in the 15th century to the island of Chios, whose velvets and brocades remained popular in Europe until the 18th century. Silk embroidery was essential for regional, traditional Greek dress. Girls working on their dowry linens and hangings embroidered in predominantly red and blue silk floss. Designs were conservative and localized so that three main groups can be distinguished – the Aegean islands, with varied designs from figural groups to geometric patterns; Ionia, dominated by Epirus on the mainland with Ottonian-influenced vegetal designs; and Crete, with Venetian-influenced foliage, mermaids, vases, and birds in the Cretan feather stitch. Silk fabric, yarn, and floss for embroidery continued to be exported from Greece until the 1830s, when the mulberry trees in Greece became diseased and political instability increased.

In modern times silk is still produced on a small scale. Refugees from Asia Minor came to Athens and Thessalonica in the 1920s, reintroducing the techniques of silkworm breeding and the production of silk. It continues today as a localized industry, but the competition from cheap, mass-produced, and man-made cloth has lessened demand for it in the 20th century.

CATHERYN CHEAL

See also Dress, Textiles

Further Reading

"Byzantine Silks", *Ciba Review*, 75 (1949)
Cultural and Commercial Exchanges between the Orient and the Greek World: Athens: Centre for Neohellenic Research / NHRF, 1991
Johnstone, Pauline, *Greek Island Embroidery*, London: Tiranti, 1961
Johnstone, Pauline, *The Byzantine Tradition in Church Embroidery*, Chicago: Argonaut, and London: Tiranti, 1967
Lopez, R.S., "Silk Industry and Trade in the Byzantine Empire", *Speculum*, 20 (1945): pp. 1–42
Muthesius, Anna, "A Practical Approach to the History of Byzantine Silk Weaving", *Jahrbuch der Osterreichischen Byzantinistik*, 34 (1984): pp. 235–54
Muthesius, Anna, *Studies in Byzantine and Islamic Silk Weaving*, London: Pindar Press, 1995
Muthesius, Anna, *Byzantine Silk Weaving*, AD 400 to AD 1200, Vienna: Fassbaender, 1997
Oilonomides, Nicolas, "Silk Trade and Production in Byzantium from the Sixth to the Ninth Century: The Seals of Kommerkiarion", *Dumbarton Oaks Papers*, 40 (1986): pp. 33–53
Starensier, Adele La Barre, *An Art Historical Study of the Byzantine Silk Industry*, Ann Arbor, Michigan: University Microfilms International, 1982
Starr, J., "The Epitaph of a Dyer in Corinth", *Byzantinish-neugriechischen Jahrbucher*, 12 (1936): pp. 45ff.
Thorley, J., "The Silk Trade between China and the Roman Empire at its Height, *c*.AD 90–130", *Greece and Rome*, 5, series 2/18 (1971): pp. 71
Werblowsky, R.J., "Contacts of Continents: The Silk Road", *Diogenes*, 144 (1988): pp. 52–64
Wild, John Peter, "The Roman Horizontal Loom", *American Journal of Archaeology*, 91/3 (July 1987): pp. 459–71

Silver and Lead

Silver and lead were probably among the first metals to be smelted and were used throughout the Copper, Bronze, and Iron Ages. The association of these two metals is fundamentally geological. Silver was valued and used in ancient Greece in exactly the same way as other cultures: for coins, plate, and statuary. Lead was used in its metallic form for anchoring the iron clamps used to secure stone blocks, for covering the hulls of ships, and as sinkers for fishing lines and standard weights. It was added to bronze to improve fluidity in casting and for the patina that such alloys develop. In Roman times large quantities were used for plumbing, cooking vessels, and other purposes. Indeed, lead poisoning may have been a significant problem for the wealthier sectors of the population. White lead (lead carbonate-hydroxide) was used in cosmetics, salves, and medicaments.

The most abundant ore of silver and lead is the lead sulphide called galena, which usually contains 0.1 to 0.4 per cent silver and some gold. This silvery-grey mineral, which breaks easily into cubes, may occur on its own, or associated

Initially, weathered ores were extracted, but later shafts were sunk into the primary galena ore. The silver produced in these mines was used in the minting of coins which were the source of much of the wealth of ancient Athens. The lead by-product was widely exported throughout the ancient Greek world, and has been found in western Turkey and Egypt. More than 2000 shafts produced about 8000 tonnes of silver and between 1 and 2 million tonnes of lead during antiquity. Activity ceased by the time of Christ, and was only revived late in the 19th century, but this time for zinc and manganese. The mines are now idle.

The primary ore at Laurium occurs as a replacement of marble near contacts with schists. The ore was formed during Miocene times (between 22 and 6 million years ago) from the watery solutions expelled during the crystallization of a granite. These solutions circulated along cracks in the rock until they reacted with the marble and crystallized galena and other minerals. The ore contained up to 50 per cent galena, but little can now be found in the area, testifying to the efficiency of ancient mining.

Siphnos was another source of silver and lead from the Early Bronze Age, a long time before Laurium, but production reached a peak at about the same time. The wealth of the island at that time is borne out by the opulence of their treasury at Delphi, which they built around 530 BC. During the 6th and 5th centuries BC silver, lead, and gold were produced in large quantities, but the mines were soon exhausted, and from then on Siphnos was poor and unimportant. As at Laurium, the ore formed as a replacement of marble by circulating watery fluids. The source of the fluids may have been metamorphism, or a granite pluton that does not crop out on the island.

The mines at Balya Maden (Asia Minor) have been active since Phoenician times. They may have supplied lead and silver to nearby Troy. They were particularly active from 1880–1940 and have produced about 400,000 tonnes of lead since Roman times.

There were other silver and lead deposits of lesser importance that were exploited in antiquity at Thera, Kimolos, Thasos, Mount Pangaeus, Mount Samsun, and Balya Maden (Asia Minor). Minor amounts of silver were produced from the natural gold–silver alloy electrum, especially at Sardis in Asia Minor.

MICHAEL D. HIGGINS

See also Coinage, Metalwork, Mines and Quarries

Further Reading

Conophagos, Constantin E., *Le Laurium antique et la téchnique greque de la production de l'argent*, Athens, 1980

Craddock, Paul T., *Early Metal Mining and Production*, Edinburgh: Edinburgh University Press, 1995

de Jesus, Prentiss S., *The Development of Prehistoric Mining and Metallurgy in Anatolia*, Oxford: BAR, 1980

Gale, N.H. and Stosgale, Z., "Lead and Silver in the Ancient Aegean", *Scientific American*, 244/6 (1981): pp. 176 ff.

Higgins, Michael Denis and Reynold Higgins, *A Geological Companion to Greece and the Aegean*, London: Duckworth, and Ithaca, New York: Cornell University Press, 1996

Nriagu, Jerome, *Lead and Lead Poisoning in Antiquity*, New York and Chichester: Wiley, 1983

Silver: hexagonal silver vessel with representations of Christ, the Virgin, Peter, Paul, John, and James, from Kyrenia, Cyprus, early 7th century, British Museum, London

with copper or iron ores. However, in antiquity the ore first exploited may have been the minerals cerussite or anglesite, earthy, pale-coloured, surface-weathering products of galena. These oxidized ores are commonly richer in silver than galena. Some silver may have also occurred as the native metal, silver chloride and sulphide. However, these more easily smelted ores were probably exhausted by the Iron Age.

The raw ore was first purified by washing – a current of water was directed over the powdered ore and the associated minerals, which are lighter than the lead minerals, were removed. Lead and silver were then extracted from the ore concentrate by roasting with charcoal. If the smelting was done at high temperatures under reducing conditions, the silver in the ore was also extracted into the lead. It was then separated by cupellation – molten lead was exposed to a stream of air, whereby the lead and other base metals were oxidized. The silver remained as a molten bead on the lead-oxide slag (lithage). This simple process can yield almost pure silver. The lithage was resmelted with charcoal to recover the lead. Gold is also extracted with the silver but seems to have been rarely separated, although the technology certainly existed. The provenance of silver and lead can be determined from the isotopic composition of lead, which is used as a "fingerprint" for different ore regions.

Lead and silver mines were worked at Laurium, south of Athens, as early as Mycenaean times, but the really rich veins were not discovered or exploited before the 5th century BC, when this area became the principal source of silver for Greece.

Wagner, Gunther A. and Gerd Weisgerber, *Silber, Blei und Gold auf Sifnos: Prehistorische und antike Metallproduktion*, Bochum: Deutschen Bergbau-Museums, 1985

Simokattes, Theophylaktos

Historian of the 7th century

Theophylaktos Simokattes was born in Egypt, and wrote his major historical work of the reign of the emperor Maurice (582–602) in the early 7th century. This military, diplomatic, and political history takes the Classical historians from Herodotus to Arrian as an example. The *History* continues from where Procopius, Agathias, and Menander Protector ended their accounts. Theophylaktos's *History* was later extended by the patriarch Nikephoros, who wrote a brief account of the 7th and 8th centuries.

There are three other surviving minor works of this author. One, the *Quaestiones Physicae*, is written in the form of a Platonic dialogue, and belongs to a pseudo-scientific genre of literature. The other, *Ethical Epistles*, is a collection of 85 fictitious letters, ranging from ethical to amatory subjects. Michael and Mary Whitby consider them to be juvenilia, literary exercises composed in testimony to the author's cultural attainments.

The third minor work of Theophylaktos is a discussion of the theological question of whether the duration of human lives is predetermined. The book, *On Predestined Terms of Life*, consists of a dialogue between two speakers, with another set of speakers pronouncing their verdict at the end. This work reflects the rhetorical education that Theophylaktos had no doubt received in his youth. It mirrors the *controversiae* which were a standard exercise in this type of education. In their discussion of *On Predestined Terms of Life* Michael and Mary Whitby point out that the conclusion reached by Theophylaktos in this work has relevance for his judgements of events in the *History*. He admires moderation in good and bad times, and he criticizes immoderation in both triumph and despair.

None of Theophylaktos's works can be dated precisely. His main work, the *History*, covers the 20-year reign of the emperor Maurice. It begins with his coming to the throne in 582, and reports as the last important event the death of the Persian king Khusrau on 25 February 628. Thus it seems reasonable to consider this date as the *terminus ante quem*. The eight books into which the *History* is divided have for their main theme the many wars that the emperor Maurice had to fight against the Persians on the eastern frontier, and the Avars and Slavs in the Balkans. Theophylaktos recognizes that there was little that Maurice could do in the earlier years of his rule, being confronted with war on two sides most of the time. He rejoices when finally a revolt in Persia led to the overthrow of the Persian king in 590, and his successor Khusrau II fled to the Romans asking for help. The situation brightened for Maurice with this event, and so, records Theophylaktos, he was able to return Khusrau to his kingdom, concluding a favourable treaty with him that lasted to the end of the emperor's reign. In general, Theophylaktos's account of Maurice's reign concentrates on the affairs of the empire in the east and Africa, neglecting Italy and the other provinces, which are hardly mentioned.

Theophylaktos's *History* is introduced with a dialogue between a personification of philosophy and history. According to Herbert Hunger, this is unique in Byzantine historical literature. Hunger thinks that Theophylaktos Simokattes used this rhetorical device indirectly to show reverence to the then emperor Herakleios by declaring the reign of his predecessor Phokas as an aberrant episode in history; and also to parade his own scholarliness.

On balance, the author of the *History* is considered to be objective and truthful. On the one hand, he is censured for his confusing chronology; and Photios later considers his heavy-handed use of rhetorical gags as immature tastelessness. On the other, Theophylaktos's work is considered valuable for the many references to peoples such as the Huns and Avars, since his sources are now mostly lost.

Although Theophylaktos seldom makes reference to his sources, it has been assumed that in his elevated position as *scholastikos* ("intellectual") and *antigraphevs* (assistant quaestor) he had access to documents and oral information. The sources used for the *History* that can be verified are mainly Menander Protector, and for books 4 and 5 John of Epiphaneia, with occasional help from the ecclesiastical history of Evagrios. The Whitbys postulate, besides the above, a "Herakleios source", a "Priskos source", the *Constantinople Chronicle*, and the hagiography of Maurice. The latter is used for describing the final days of the emperor during which various portents foreshadowed his tragic end. Hunger sees in the uncritical use of this hagiographical material a clear indication that a new historical epoch was beginning in 7th-century Byzantium.

The *History* of Theophylaktos Simokattes was used by later writers. Of these writers, Theophanes is the most essential for the reign of Maurice. His *Chronographia* treats the events from 284 to 813, and is partly based on works now lost.

FRANZISKA E. SHLOSSER

See also Historiography

Biography

Born in Egypt in the late 6th century, Simokattes had a civil service career rising to be *scholastikos* ("intellectual") and *antigraphevs* (assistant quaestor). His main work is a history in 8 books of the reign of the emperor Maurice (582–602). This continues where Procopius, Agathias, and Menander Protector left off. He also wrote philosophical and scientific dialogues and a collection of letters.

Writings

Quaestiones Physicae et Epistolae, edited by J.F. Boissonade, Paris: Mercklein, 1835; reprinted Hildesheim: Olms, 1976

Historiae, edited by Carl de Boor, Leipzig: Teubner, 1887; revision edited by Peter Wirth, Stuttgart: Teubner, 1972

Quaestioni naturali, edited by Lydia Massa Positano, Naples: Libreria Scientifica, 1965

On Predestined Terms of Life, edited and translated by Charles Garton and L.G. Westerink, Buffalo: Department of Classics, State University of New York at Buffalo, 1978

The History, edited and translated by Michael Whitby and Mary Whitby, Oxford: Clarendon Press, 1986

Further Reading

Haussig, H.W., "Theophylacts Excurs über die skythischen Völker", *Byzantion*, 23 (1953) pp. 275–462

Higgins, Martin Joseph, *The Persian War of the Emperor Maurice, 582–602*, vol. 1: *The Chronology with a Brief History of the Persian Calendar*, Washington, D.C.: Catholic University of America Press, 1939

Hunger, Herbert, *Die hochsprachliche profane Literatur der Byzantiner*, vol. 1, Munich: Beck, 1978, pp. 313–19

Olajos, T., "Données et hypothèses concernant la carrière de Théophylacte Simocatta", *Acta Classica Universitatis Scintarium Debreceniensis*, 17–18 (1981–82): pp. 39–47

Shlosser, F.E., *The Reign of the Emperor Maurikios (582–602): A Reassessment*, Athens: Historical Publications St. D. Basilopoulos, 1994

Stein, Ernest von, *Studien zur Geschichte des byzantinischen Reiches: vornehmlich unter den Kaisern Justinus II und Tiberius Constantinus*, Stuttgart: Metzler, 1919

Veh, O., "Untersuchungen zu dem byzantinischen Historiker, Theophylaktos Simokattes", *Jahresbericht des Humanistischen Gymnasium Fürth im Bayern* (1956–57)

Whitby, L.M., "Theophylact's Knowledge of Languages", *Byzantion*, 52 (1982): pp. 425–28

Whitby, L.M., "The Great Chronographer and Theophanes", *Byzantine and Modern Greek Studies*, 8 (1982–83): pp. 1–20

Whitby, L.M., "Theophanes' Chronicle Source for the Reigns of Justin II, Tiberius and Maurice (AD 565–602)", *Byzantion*, 53 (1983): pp. 312–45

Whitby, L.M., *The Emperor Maurice and His Historian: Theophylact Simocatta on Persian and Balkan Warfare*, Oxford: Clarendon Press, 1988

Simonides

Lyric poet of the 6th–5th centuries BC

Simonides was probably born at Iulis, the chief town of Ceos. Most sources set his birth around 557–556 BC (and some *c*.532 BC). Both he and his nephew Bacchylides, also a lyric poet and also born in Ceos, around 510 BC, were steeped in a cultural tradition marked by the worship of Apollo and Dionysus, which most probably accounts for the intellectual rigour and Bacchic enjoyment that marks their poetry in a way characteristic of lyric poetry of the 5th century BC in its entirety.

Simonides' poetry belongs to the new wave of choral lyric that flourished in the first half of the 5th century BC and which is represented mainly by the extant poems of Pindar, and the fragments of Bacchylides and Simonides himself. Simonides' artistic production, spanning the second half of the 6th and the first half of the 5th centuries BC, is situated at the point of transition from late Archaic to Classical art and so registers the developments triggered by this shift, especially in the field of choral lyric. That is, while the poetry is still heavily dependent on religious and other social occasions for its delivery, it also gradually ceases to preoccupy itself mainly with religious themes, and adopts wider political, moral, intellectual, and literary concerns.

No poem of Simonides survives in its entirety. But the extant fragments indicate that he was an expert in a wide range of lyric expression. We have evidence that he composed epinicians, dithyrambs, dirges, paeans, encomia, partheneia, elegies, and epigrams. His elegies included traditional sympotic pieces as well as some historical ones, such as the elegy on the Battle of Artemisium and the one on Plataea, a portion of which turned up in a papyrus published in 1992 (*Oxyrhynchus Papyri*, 3965).

Simonides was a professional poet with great scope and range. Ancient critics praised his elegant lyricism and his colourful and decorative diction, but they also admired his balanced discourse and the smoothness of his composition. The typical noble features of Archaic lyric are juxtaposed in his work with new ethical preoccupations, and sensuous details with gnomic austerity, just as the heroic absolutes of the aristocratic tradition are framed by a more tolerant and flexible world view that is willing to take into consideration inner conflicts and the uncertainties of fortune.

Simonides' work was an important influence on the poetic production of the two other major choral poets of the 5th century BC, Bacchylides and Pindar. And it was especially Simonides and Pindar who persistently incorporated in their poems reflections on the significance of their craft. Simonides regularly quoted and commented on the earlier poetic tradition and is believed to have explicitly compared himself to Pindar. Aligning himself with a strand of the tradition that goes back to Homer and Hesiod and looks forward to Plato and further down to the Hellenistic poets, he also stresses the alluring enchantment, and even falsehood, of song.

The complex relation of Simonides' art to both the preceding and the subsequent poetic tradition is best celebrated by the new fragments of *Plataea* discovered in *Oxyrhynchus Papyri*, 3965. These findings give us a proem to what seems to have been an elegy on an epic-like heroic event, which also happens to be of contemporary historical significance. A proemial hymn to Achilles suggests a parallelism between the Trojan and the Persian wars, thus striking a Panhellenic note that anticipates later historians and rhetoricians such as Herodotus, Thucydides, and Isocrates. Moreover, through this parallelism the Trojans are depicted as barbarians, thus foreshadowing their tragic counterparts in 5th-century Athens. And the connections are not yet exhausted: the new Simonides fragments combine features of Pindaric encomium, Homeric diction and narrative technique, and heroic historiography, all laced with elements of the epitaph and organized by a performer with a remarkably developed persona who dominates the short elegiac poem in a strikingly un-epic way. It is little wonder indeed that critics have detected in Simonides' work a primitive model of the famous Hellenistic features of miniaturization and crossing of genres.

Throughout his long life Simonides was commissioned to work in the courts of many tyrants. He also lived and worked in the cities of the new 5th-century BC democracy. He was notorious for demanding high fees: ancient sources describe him as a money-grubber and Pindar scornfully calls his muse "Muse for hire" (*Isthmian*, 2. 6). However, this mercenary attitude also indicates an emerging professionalism. The poet ceases to be the inspired mouthpiece of the Muses or other divinities and poetic creation is no longer or not mainly their inspired gift: it is rather the combined outcome of skill and practice for which the poet deserves remuneration. Simonides may have been frowned upon for his attitude to money, but his legendary high fees, together with his less solemn tone and a certain deviousness scattered in his poems, make him an important precursor of the secularized art of the sophists of the Classical period.

EFROSSINI SPENTZOU

See also Poetry (Lyric)

Biography

Born at Iulis on Ceos *c*.557/56 BC, Simonides may have been employed at the court of Hipparchus. Only fragments of his poems survive but he wrote on a wide range of lyric themes. He was the uncle of Bacchylides. He died at the court of Hieron and was buried at Acragas.

Writings

In *Greek Lyric*, vol. 3, translated by David A. Campbell, Cambridge, Massachusetts: Harvard University Press, and London: Heinemann, 1991 (Loeb edition)

Further Reading

Arethusa, 29/2 (1996) (special issue: "The New Simonides")

Bowra, C.M., *Greek Lyric Poetry from Alcman to Simonides*, 2nd edition, Oxford: Clarendon Press, 1961

Calame, Claude, *The Craft of Poetic Speech in Ancient Greece*, Ithaca, New York: Cornell University Press, 1995

Carson, A., "Simonides Negative", *Arethusa*, 21/2 (1988): pp. 147–57

West, M.L., "Simonides Redivivus", *Zeitschrift für Papyrologie und Epigraphik*, 98 (1993): pp. 1–14

Simplicius

Neoplatonist philosopher of the 6th century AD

Simplicius was one of the most important Neoplatonists of 6th century AD, and one of the last representatives of Greek philosophical thought, as he has often been described. Agathias informs us (*History*, 2. 30. 3) that he was born in Cilicia around AD 500. He was first educated in the philosophical school of Alexandria under the direction of Ammonius. He continued his studies in philosophy at the school in Athens under the leadership of its last director, Damascius, and remained there until 529, when the emperor Justinian closed the school. Then he moved with his master and five other philosophers to Persia, to the school of Gundi-Sapur that was established by the Persian king Chosroes I. There he remained for two years (531–32); but after a treaty of peace was signed between the Byzantine state and the Persians, he returned to the empire with guarantees that he would not be compelled to leave against his will, as Agathias tells us (*History*, 2. 31. 4).

The earliest preserved work of Simplicius is his commentary on Epictetus' *Enchiridion*, written after 529, for he refers to "tyrannical circumstances" (*Enchiridion*, 138. 17–19). He wrote a series of influential commentaries on Aristotelian works after his stay in Persia, in which he endeavoured to harmonize and reconcile Aristotle and Plato. His first commentary was on *De Caelo*, followed by *Physics*, and finally *Categories*. The authenticity of a fourth commentary, on *De Anima*, preserved under the name of Simplicius, was questioned as long ago as the 17th century and is nowadays regarded as spurious. The first Latin translations of his commentaries by William Moerbeke appeared in 1266. The complete Greek text was published in the *Commentaria in Aristotelem Graeca* series of the Berlin Academy between 1882 and 1907.

Another question relates to where Simplicius wrote his commentaries. Although it has been suggested that he composed them at Athens or Alexandria where he would have had access to the libraries, modern scholars such as H. Hadot propose Harran, a city in Mesopotamia where Hellenism remained active and powerful, situated close to the Persian border, 30 km from Edessa.

Simplicius' commentaries are a very helpful source for later scholars because they include accurate information about earlier works that have since been lost. For example, his commentary on *De Caelo* (264. 25) tells us of Hipparchus' attempt to justify forced motion with the earliest version of impetus theory. Simplicius' contribution to this problem was outstanding for, although he was himself influenced by Aristotle, he incorporated his objections to the Aristotelian view. He discusses forced motion in his commentary on *Physics* (1348. 36–1351. 13), where he introduces his objections to the pure Aristotelian interpretation with some questions. These questions show that he did not fully accept Aristotle's view of the propelling role of air during forced motion and that he preferred to invoke physical causes as being responsible for a projectile's propulsion. In conclusion, we can say that Simplicius' attempt to interpret forced motion was a cautious one. Meanwhile his contemporary John Philoponus introduced a radical theory for it.

John Philoponus was a Christian Neoplatonist of the 6th century. Simplicius seems to have been a little older than Philoponus (he calls him a "young man" in *In De Caelo*, 42. 17) and he informs us that they did not meet. It seems that a major difference arose between these two great commentators that centred on their different religious beliefs, for Simplicius was not a Christian while Philoponus was (or became one during his lifetime). This difference strengthened after 529, a turning point in the history of ideas. It was the year in which the school of Athens (which Simplicius attended) was closed by Justinian, and Philoponus wrote the essay *De Aeternitate Mundi* that indicates his return to Christian belief. Simplicius was strongly opposed to the principle asserted by Philoponus regarding the origin of the world through divine creation. Nor did Simplicius accept the linear conception of time that sprang from Philoponus' view of a beginning point for the creation of the cosmos, but instead he asserted a cyclical conception for it.

MANOLIS KARTSONAKIS

See also Neoplatonism

Biography

Born in Cilicia early in the 6th century AD, Simplicius was educated at the philosophical schools of Alexandria and Athens where he was a pupil of Ammonius and Damascius respectively. When Justinian closed the school at Athens in 529, Simplicius was one of the seven philosophers who moved to the court of the Persian king Chosroes I. He was later permitted to return and wrote commentaries on the works of Epictetus and Aristotle. The place and date of his death are unknown.

Writings

Commentarius in Enchiridion Epicteti, in *Theophrasti Characteres*, edited by Friedrich Dübner, Paris: Firmin Didot, 1877

In Aristotelis Physicorum Libros Quattor Priores Commentaria, edited by Hermann Diels, in *Commentaria in Aristotelem Graeca*, vol. 9, Berlin: Reimer, 1882

In Aristotelis de Anima Commentaria, edited by H. Hayduk, in *Commentaria in Aristotelem Graeca*, vol. 11, Berlin: Reimer, 1882

In Aristotelis de Caelo Commentaria, edited by J.L. Heiberg, in *Commentaria in Aristotelem Graeca*, vol. 7, Berlin: Reimer, 1894

In Aristotelis Physicorum Libros Quattor Posteriores Commentaria, edited by Hermann Diels, in *Commentaria in Aristotelem Graeca*, vol. 10, Berlin: Reimer, 1895

In Aristotelis Categorias Commentarium, edited by Karl Kalbfleisch, in *Commentaria in Aristotelem Graeca*, vol. 8, Berlin: Reimer, 1907

On Aristotle's Physics 6, translated by David Constan, Ithaca, New York: Cornell University Press, and London: Duckworth, 1989

Further Reading

Cameron, Alan, "The Last Days of the Academy at Athens", *Proceedings of the Cambridge Philological Society*, new series 15 (1969): pp. 7–29

Franz, A., "Pagan Philosophers in Christian Athens", *Proceedings of the American Philosophical Society*, 119 (1975): pp. 29–38

Hadot, I., "The Life and Work of Simplicius in Greek and Arabic Sources" in *Aristotle Transformed: The Ancient Commentators and their Influence*, edited by Richard Sorabji, London: Duckworth, and Ithaca, New York: Cornell University Press, 1990

Hoffmann, P., "Simplicius' Polemics" in *Philoponus and the Rejection of Aristotelian Science*, edited by Richard Sorabji, London: Duckworth, and Ithaca, New York: Cornell University Press, 1987

Sambursky, Samuel, *The Physical World of Late Antiquity*, London: Routledge and Kegan Paul, and New York: Basic Books, 1962; reprinted 1987

Sorabji, Richard, *Matter, Space and Motion: Theories in Antiquity and their Sequel*, London: Duckworth, and Ithaca, New York: Cornell University Press, 1988

Sorabji, Richard, "The Ancient Commentators on Aristotle" in *Aristotle Transformed: The Ancient Commentators and their Influence*, edited by Richard Sorabji, London: Duckworth, and Ithaca, New York: Cornell University Press, 1990

Sinope

City on the north coast of Asia Minor

Sinope is the most northerly point on the Pontic coast of Asia Minor, lying west of the river Halys. On a coast which afforded little shelter, it was praised from at least the time of Strabo for its harbour, a double bay divided by an isthmus on which the city itself stood. In later periods storm-driven travellers were grateful for its haven. These included the Trapezuntine *archon* (governor) of the Crimea in the 13th century, the great Arab traveller Ibn Battuta and bishop Ignatios of Smolensk in the 14th century, Vincenzo Alessandri, the Venetian ambassador to Persia, in the 16th century, and the patriarch of Antioch, Makarios, in the 17th century. From antiquity to early modern times, links with the Chersonese (Crimea) were important, as well as coasting traffic in indigenous products such as timber, iron, and the arsenical compound *miltos* (Sinop red, cinnabar, realgar) for dyeing, while its fish, especially tunny and mullet, were celebrated.

Sinope has traditionally been seen with Trebizond as a colony of Miletus established in the 7th century BC. In recent times an 8th-century date has been proposed and Corinth is credited with its foundation. Perhaps there was a refoundation after the Cimmerian incursion of the early 7th century. From the 6th century connections with Athens were strong, especially after the visit of Pericles about 436/35 which saw the establishment of 600 Athenian settlers at Sinope. Herodotus remarked on its position on the trans-Anatolian route to Cilicia. The coins of Sinope, which circulated widely in the Pontus, typically have the head of the nymph Sinope and an eagle and dolphin. Diogenes the Cynic was a native of Sinope, where his father was a moneyer. Trade with Colchis flourished, as roof tiles and amphorae from Sinope found there show. Sinope provided the ships and supplies for the return voyage of Xenophon and the survivors of his 10,000. After a period under Persian overlordship in the 4th century, Sinope became part of the kingdom of Pontus in 183 BC. King Mithridates V was murdered at Sinope but his son and successor Mithridates VI Eupator (120–63 BC) embellished its buildings and restored its walls. Sinope fell to the Romans under Lucullus and Pompey (the former displayed sculptures looted from Sinope in his garden) and in 45 Julius Caesar renamed the city, which became Colonia Iulia Felix. Under Trajan, Pliny the Younger surveyed the area and built an aqueduct.

In legend St Andrew evangelized Sinope, but in fact the cult of St Phocas, reputedly its first bishop, eclipsed that of the apostle. The 2nd-century heresiarch Marcion was a shipbuilder in Sinope before, it is alleged, his father (who was a bishop) excommunicated him for immorality. East of Sinope at Çiftlik a large basilica with a fine mosaic in a 4th-century style has recently been discovered.

After some rebuilding in the 6th century by Justinian I, centuries of decline followed, culminating in the taking of the city by the Turks about 1081. The newly established empire of the Grand Komnenoi of Trebizond recovered the city for the Greeks from about 1204 to 1214, when it fell to the Seljuk Turks. Its capture enabled the sultan to claim among his titles "Lord of the two Seas", for the Seljuks now had access to the northern as well as to the southern shores of Anatolia. The Seljuk period saw further rebuilding under the direction of a Greek called Sebastos, commemorated in a bilingual Arab/Greek inscription which survives. Genoese and Venetian merchants increasingly frequented its harbour. Perhaps the most intriguing episode in the period is the assault by Ghazi Çelebi on Genoese shipping in the harbour which was attacked by swimming underwater to hole the vessels. Çelebi's tomb is still to be seen. In 1324 Sinope was taken by the emirate of Kastamonu and in 1461 by the Ottomans. Some of the town's Jewish community moved to Istanbul. An attack by Russia on the Turkish fleet at Sinope in 1853 precipitated the Crimean War (1853–56). The wrecks of the Turkish vessels were reportedly still a hazard to shipping at the end of the 19th century.

Sinope retains traces of its Hellenistic gridiron plan and the remains of the Hellenistic temple of Serapis. The museum has sarcophagi, altars, and jewellery from antiquity, some late icons, and a very representative sequence of coins. The ruinous building known as "Mithridates' Palace" is Roman, perhaps a

Sinope: the walls are mainly Byzantine but incorporate both earlier and later work

bath complex. Its walls, so often attributed to the Genoese, in reality incorporate work of almost every other phase from Hellenistic to Ottoman.

The "Sinope Gospels" are a copy of St Matthew's gospel written in gold uncials on purple vellum with a number of miniatures. They date perhaps to the 6th century. The manuscript was bought from an old Greek woman in Sinope in December 1899 by a French officer and is now in the Bibliothèque Nationale.

The title of duke of Sinope was taken by Konstantinos Ioannes Alexios Laskaris-Komnenos who was born in Saragossa in 1923, the second son of prince Eugenios Laskaris-Komnenos, a claimant to the Greek throne. Prince Konstantinos was professor of philosophy in the National University of Costa Rica.

M.E. MARTIN

See also Black Sea, Pontus

Summary
A city on the Black Sea coast of Anatolia, Sinope was first colonized by the Greeks in the 8th or 7th century BC. It had strong connections with Athens. Its excellent harbour made it a focus for trade. In the 2nd century BC it formed part of the kingdom of Pontus before falling to Rome. It was taken by the Seljuks in 1081, was briefly Byzantine again c.1204–14, and Ottoman from 1461.

Further Reading
Boardman, John, *The Greeks Overseas: Their Early Colonies and Trade*, 4th edition, London and New York: Thames and Hudson, 1999

Bryer, Anthony and David Winfield, *The Byzantine Monuments and Topography of the Pontos*, Washington D.C.: Dumbarton Oaks Research Library and Collection, 1985

Drews, R., "The Earliest Greek Settlements in the Black Sea", *Journal of Hellenic Studies*, 96 (1976): pp. 18–31

Robinson, David M., *Ancient Sinope: An Historical Account*, Baltimore: Johns Hopkins University Press, 1906

Tsetskhladze, Gocha R., "Greek Penetration of the Black Sea" in *The Archaeology of Greek Colonisation: Essays Dedicated to Sir John Boardman*, edited by Gocha R. Tsetskhladze and Franco De Angelis, Oxford: Oxford University Committee for Archaeology, 1994

Skalkottas, Nikolaos 1904–1949

Composer

The author of more than 110 finely crafted musical works, Nikolaos Skalkottas is generally considered to be one of the outstanding Greek composers of the 20th century. He was born on 8 March 1904 in the town of Chalcis to a family with a strong musical tradition. His great-grandfather Alekos had been a famous folk musician, while both his father and his uncle Kostas were instrumentalists in the town band. When Nikolaos was 2 years old the family moved to Athens, where his uncle began to teach him the violin in 1910. Four years later he enrolled in the Athens Conservatory, graduating in 1920 with a diploma in violin and a gold medal. An Averoff scholarship for study abroad enabled him to continue his violin studies in 1921 with Willy Hess at the Hochschule für Musik in Berlin. Despite continuing success as a violinist, Skalkottas was increasingly drawn towards composition, which he began to study under a distinguished succession of teachers beginning with Paul Juon, Robert Kahn, and Kurt Weill. During this period he produced his first surviving works, a jazz-influenced *Greek Suite* for piano (1924) and an atonal *Sonata* for solo violin (1925). Overruling the protests of Hess, in 1925 Skalkottas renounced his aspirations for a career as a solo violinist in order to concentrate on composition. For the next two years he studied under Weill's teacher Philipp Jarnach while continuing to support himself with work as a pianist in bars and cinemas.

Shortly after switching to the tutelage of Arnold Schoenberg in 1927, Skalkottas received an Emmanuel Benaki scholarship (1928–31) that enabled him not only to refine his personal style of atonal composition, but also to direct his works at the Singakademie and collaborate with other students in performances of modern chamber music. Schoenberg came to think highly of his Greek pupil, later listing him as one of his few students worthy of the appellation "composer". Meanwhile, Skalkottas's artistic productivity was complemented by a happy personal life centred around cohabitation with the violinist Mathilde Temko, with whom he produced two children (only one of whom survived). Outside the home, he was popular with his fellow musicians, among whom were a significant group of Greek expatriates that at various times included the pianists Marika Papaionannou and Spyros Farantatos, the singers Tito Xirellis and Kostas Mylonas, and the composers Yiannis Konstantinidis and Dimitri Mitropoulos, whose piano piece *Fête crétoise* Skalkottas orchestrated in 1928. He further refreshed his ties with Greece during a brief visit that featured his inauguration of the 1930–31 season of popular concerts in Athens with a performance of his *Concerto for Wind Orchestra* (1929).

The year 1931 was marked for Skalkottas by a series of traumatic events: his departure from Schoenberg's circle, the conclusion of his relationship with Temko, and the end of his scholarship. He composed little during a subsequent period of depression (1932–34), which permanently introverted his formerly sociable personality. In the wake of Hitler's rise to power, Skalkottas left Berlin in May 1933 – the very month of Schoenberg's flight from Nazism – and returned to Athens, leaving behind the scores of his musical works together with most of his possessions. For the remainder of his life he toiled in relative obscurity as a back-desk violinist, initially for the State Orchestra of Athens, and later for the orchestras of the National Opera and Greek Radio. Interestingly, however, Skalkottas's misfortune coincided with a renewal of his interest in Greek folk music. In 1931 and 1932 he produced a few tonal settings of folk songs for voice and piano, while after his arrival in Athens he transcribed a body of Cretan songs for the ethnomusicologist Melpo Merlier. Working with her provided Skalkottas with access to the raw material for his most enduringly popular work, the *36 Greek Dances* for orchestra (1933–36, with later reorchestrations and arrangements). Elements of folk music continued to surface occasionally after 1935 as he returned forcefully to composing atonal orchestral and chamber music in a dense polyphonic style, employing both free atonality and ingenious variations on Schoenberg's method of 12-tone composition. Yet the advent of his most

prolific period, during which he wrote many large-scale works in the traditional genres of western art music, passed almost without notice. Faced in Greece with indifference and even hostility towards his progressive music, he composed in radical isolation a substantial body of work that remained mostly unperformed and unknown at the time of his death.

Although World War II brought him such additional hardships as two months in a German prison camp, Skalkottas continued to develop musically, reaching an impressive level of formal complexity with the one-movement symphony *The Return of Ulysses* (1944–45). This massive work, which was originally conceived as the overture for a projected opera, deploys an astonishing 18 different 12-note rows in various combinations over the course of an extended essay in sonata form. In 1946, the year of his marriage to Maria Pigali, Skalkottas entered a new creative phase characterized by greater textural transparency and a partial return to tonality. Shortly before the birth of his second son, however, on 19 September 1949 he died unexpectedly of an untreated hernia.

Without neglecting his musical heritage, Skalkottas was the second Greek composer after Mitropoulos to eschew the musical folklorism of Kalomiris and the National School in favour of a direct confrontation with European modernism. Yet his little-known music exercised only a marginal influence on Greece's post-World-War-II generation of composers, whose more adventurous members were inspired directly by the contemporary international avant-garde. Devotees of Skalkottas's music nevertheless succeeded in establishing an archive of his scores in Athens, while various efforts have been made both in Greece and abroad to perform and record his works. The harpsichordist Maria Lalandi was a particularly successful advocate, organizing numerous overdue premières within the context of the English Bach Festival she cofounded in 1963. Most recently a project has been initiated by Margun Music of Newton, Massachusetts, to publish critical editions of the complete works of Skalkottas.

ALEXANDER LINGAS

Biography

Born in Chalcis in 1904, Skalkottas studied violin at the Athens Conservatory and then at the Hochschule für Musik in Berlin. Turning to composition, he became a pupil of Arnold Schoenberg in 1927. In 1933 he returned to Athens where he supported himself as a violinist but continued to compose. He died suddenly in 1949.

Further Reading

Anogeianakis, Phoivos, "I Mousiki sti neoteri hellada" [Music in Modern Greece], in *Historia tis mousikis* [History of Music] by Karl Nef, translated by Phoivos Anogeianakis, 2nd edition, Athens, 1985 (original Swiss edition (in German), 1920)

Keller, Hans, "Nikos Skalkottas: An Original Genius", *Listener*, 52 (1954): p. 1041

Papaioannou, John G., "Skalottas's 'Ulysses'", *Musical Times*, 90 (1969): p. 615

Stein, Leonard (editor), *Style and Idea: Selected Writings of Arnold Schoenberg*, Berkeley: University of California Press, and London: Faber, 1984

Symeonidou, Aleka, *Lexiko Ellinon Syntheton* [Dictionary of Greek Composers], Athens, 1995

Thornley, John, Skalokottas entry in *The New Grove Dictionary of Music and Musicians*, edited by Stanley Sadie, vol. 17, London: Macmillan, 1980, pp. 361–64

Zakythinos, Alexis D., *Discography of Greek Classical Music*, 2nd edition, Buenos Aires, 1988 (an updated Greek-language edition was published in Athens and Ioannina by Dodoni in 1993)

Recording

Mayday Spell, Double Bass Concerto and Three Greek Dances, Iceland Symphony Orchestra, conducted by Nikos Christodoulou, BIS compact disc, CD-954 (see especially the booklet notes by Nikos Christodoulou and Jason Dimitriades)

Skopje

City in Macedonia

The city of Skopje lies along the Vardar river in mountainous country on the north–south route between Thessalonica and Belgrade at a distance of 320 km from Belgrade. The valley near Skopje is flanked by the Sar Planina mountain range, which extends into Thessaly east of Trikkala. In the Roman period the town was called Scupi, an outpost town, which would eventually become the capital of the district of Dardania in the 4th century AD. In AD 518 two events occurred that altered the town's location and name: barbarians sacked it and a disastrous earthquake struck. The town was rebuilt on the Vardar river and given its Slav name of Skopje, which is said to be derived from the Greek word for "episcopal". To this day, many Skopjans and Macedonians deny any significant cultural debts to Hellenism or neighbouring cultures. Linguistic, archaeological, and historical evidence, however, affirms strong Hellenic cultural influence in the Skopje area.

Linguists have traced the influence of Greek over three millennia. As early as 900 BC the area was known to be Greek-speaking. The word "Macedonian" can be traced to the Greek "Makedones", high (tall people) or highlanders. The debate is particularly focused on what language(s) inhabitants of the Skopje area spoke. The Macedonian alphabet, primarily Cyrillic, was established as a language in May 1945, and the first primer appeared in 1946 from the University of Skopje. Others debate the extent to which Macedonian is a dialect of Greek. Since the early 19th century, linguists (H. Ahrens, O. Hoffman, G. Buck, J. Chadwick, and G. Babinoitis) have considered the Macedonian language a form of pre-stage Greek, or a dialect related to northwestern ancient Greek.

Artefacts collected from the Skopje area provide evidence of Hellenic cultural continuity. Archaeological finds housed at the museum in Skopje date from the Neolithic period with artefacts such as the "Great Mother". Habitation continued through the Iron Age (1050–650 BC). The Skopje Museum's collection of substantial Hellenistic artefacts, as exemplified by figures such as *Dionysius the Laurel Bearer*, from the 1st century BC, attests to Greek cultural influences. Recent archaeological excavations have revealed more than 5000 inscriptions in Greek on grave stelae and votive offerings. Coinage and sanctuaries dedicated to the 12 Olympian gods supply evidence of Greek influence in Skopjan Macedonia, even when allowing for cultural distinctions.

Historical documents confirm the Hellenicity of the Skopje area and Macedonia. Thucydides (2. 99) wrote that the Macedonian state was founded in the 7th century BC. The historian Polybius documented flourishing Greek culture between 280 and 160 BC. He recognized the importance of Macedonian cooperation with the Greeks: "The Greeks would be for ever the greatest danger, if we did not have as a bulwark the Macedonians and the ambition of their kings."

The inhabitants of the area, as Macedonians, have claimed ancestral links in turn with Illyrians, Dorians, Thracians, Dardanes, and Paenones. The ancient royal house is traditionally said to be derived from Argive origins when descendants of Temenus and Heracles migrated and ruled as a Macedonian dynasty up to the 4th century BC (Thucydides, 2. 99). Herodotus (5. 22) affirmed that the Macedonian tribes were of Greek descent: "And the people originating from Perdiccas are Greeks". Some question the Hellenicity of Macedonia because Demosthenes labelled Philip a barbarian. From this antique name-calling, it was presumed that Macedonians were non-Hellenes. This presumption does not take into consideration the fact that the word could refer merely to an uncultivated person. Plutarch (*Life of Aratus*) called the Macedonians *allophyloi* (foreigners); but Alexander the Great's ardent support and exportation of Hellenism during his reign is evident.

Skopje's history reflects the sociopolitical movements that affected much of Europe from Byzantium until the Ottoman occupation and the 20th-century reorganization. Skopje was close to the birthplace of the emperor Justinian (527–65). The Serbs took Skopje in 1189, and the coronation of Stephan IV Dushan, emperor of the Serbs, took place here in 1346. The Ottoman Turks held control from 1392 to 1912. In 1913 Skopje was again incorporated into Serbia and from 1918 was under the control of Yugoslavia. German troops occupied Skopje from 1941 until its liberation in 1944. After World War II the Socialist Federal Republic declared Skopje to be the capital of Macedonia. An earthquake struck the city on 26 July 1963, causing over 1000 fatalities and leaving more than 120,000 homeless. As a result 80 per cent of Skopje's infrastructure had to be rebuilt, depriving the city of much of its Turkish character.

Macedonian nationalism and ethnogenesis continue to play a powerful role in Skopje. In 1968 the independent Macedonian Orthodox Church was founded in Skopje. This Church remains unrecognized by the patriarchates of Constantinople and Serbia. In 1977 two Skopje citizens, Lazar Krajnichanes and Angel Miterev, were sentenced to five years' imprisonment for asserting that Macedonians were Bulgarians. Sporadic trials of those who resist the notion of an ethnically pure and long-lived Macedonian nation continue. Skopje's population today is about 500,000.

KATHERINE V. WILLS

See also Macedonia, Serbia

Summary

The capital of the Former Yugoslav Republic of Macedonia, Skopje was known to the Romans as Scupi. It became the capital of the district of Dardania and was the birthplace of Justinian. Skopje was taken by the Serbs in 1189. From 1392 to 1912 it was part of the Ottoman empire. In 1918 it was incorporated in Yugoslavia.

Further Reading

Arrian, *Alexander the Great*, translated by J.G. Lloyd, Cambridge and New York: Cambridge University Press, 1981

Austin, M.M., *The Hellenistic World from Alexander to the Roman Conquest: A Selection of Ancient Sources in Translation*, Cambridge and New York: Cambridge University Press, 1981

Barr-Sharrar, Beryl and Eugene N. Borza, *Macedonia and Greece in Late Classical and Early Hellenistic Times*, vol. 10, Washington, D.C.: National Gallery of Art, 1982

Borza, Eugene N., *Makedonika*, Claremont, California: Regina, 1995

Bosworth, A.B., *From Arrian to Alexander: Studies in Historical Interpretation*, Oxford: Clarendon Press, and New York: Oxford University Press, 1988

Burstein, Stanley M. (editor and translator), *The Hellenistic Age from the Battle of Ipsos to the Death of Kleopatra VII*, Cambridge and New York: Cambridge University Press, 1985

Dimitrov, Evgeni *et al.*, *Macedonia and its Relations with Greece*, Skopje: Macedonian Academy of Sciences and Arts, 1993

Ginouvès, René, *Macedonia: From Philip II to the Roman Conquest*, Princeton, New Jersey: Princeton University Press, 1994

Godolphin, Francis R.B., *The Greek Historians*, 2 vols, New York: Random House, 1942

Kypriandis, A. (editor), *On Scientific Truth about Macedonia*, Athens: National Technical University of Athens, 1993

Martis, Nicolaos, K., *The Falsification of Macedonian History*, Athens: Alexander S. Onassis Foundation, 1984

Poulton, Hugh, *Who Are the Macedonians?*, Bloomington: Indiana University Press, and London: Hurst, 1995

Tomovski, Ivan, *Skopje: Between the Past and the Future*, Skopje: Macedonian Review, 1978

Vacalopoylos, A.E., *History of Macedonia, 1354–1833*, Thessalonica: Institute for Balkan Studies, 1973

Slavery

Slavery was apparently known already in Mycenaean times, but it is not quite clear to what extent the Mycenaean *doero* meant the same condition as the Greek word *doulos*. Various kinds of unfree people are also to be found in Homer: prisoners of war, women as booty of war, domestics, and servants in agriculture. The origins of slavery lay probably in war and/or indebtedness; the occurrence of the latter greatly increased after about 600 BC, when money was introduced and trade and business expanded. A real slave trade seems to have been established first in eastern Greece and the areas bordering on northern and eastern barbarian countries; from there it quickly spread to commercial centres such as Athens, Corinth, and Aegina. From the 5th century BC onwards, slavery was an established social institution in Greece, and the laws of this institution were (with minor local variants) more or less the same everywhere. A slave was the property of his master and could be sold and bought like cattle; the price (between a half and ten *minae*) depended on his skills and his physical condition. Slaves toiling in workshops, at public buildings, in mines, etc. received the same salary as free workers and could eventually buy their freedom. They had no political rights, but were in some measure protected by the law; they were allowed to marry and have their own money. In Athens a stranger was not allowed to mistreat or beat a slave who was not his property. Slaves often retained the cults of their native countries; in Athens they were even allowed to take part in the mystery cults.

In Classical Greece slaves were mostly "barbarians", including many from Asia Minor, but also Thracians and Scythians; trading places in the Black Sea and cities such as Byzantium and Ephesus were big suppliers of slaves for Greece. Grave stelae, lists of slaves in the Athenian fleet, lists of the workers on the Athenian Acropolis, and inscriptions of slaves who bought their freedom at Delphi show a wide range of countries from which slaves came: Egypt, Caria, Illyria, Lydia, Mysia, Paphlagonia, Persia, Phoenicia, Phrygia, Syria, and others. Pseudo-Aristotle's *Oeconomica* gives the telltale advice not to have too many slaves from the same nation (ch. 4).

The circumstances that brought people into slavery are not always clear; a great number of them were certainly prisoners of war; armies must have been one of the most important sources of supply in Greece (during his invasion of Scythia in 339 BC Philip II of Macedon enslaved and sold 20,000 women and children). Slave traders apparently accompanied armies on their campaigns and instantly bought prisoners as well as other booty. Sometimes barbarian tribes even seem to have exchanged their own people against urgently needed goods; the sentence "You are a noble Thracian, sold for salt" (Menander, fr. 891 Kassel-Austin) was proverbial in Greece. Another source was piracy, which reached a peak in the middle of the 4th century BC (in 334/33 BC the general Diotimus was honoured in Athens for his fight against pirates). The Attic slave trade was centred in Athens and Sunium, the harbour of which played an important role in the import of goods since the beginning of the 5th century BC; from there the slaves could be brought directly into the silver mines of Laurium.

In the ancient world a slave could work in every kind of profession, not just as "mean slave labour"; there were slave doctors, stonemasons at official buildings, soldiers, enterpreneurs, wetnurses, teachers, musicians, artisans (potters and painters), etc. Household slaves made up the majority of the slave population in Greece; considerable numbers were also employed in agriculture. In Athens minor public positions (the police among them) were filled by slaves; these so-called "state slaves" had a salary and their own dwelling. Astonishingly, the police in Athens consisted of Scythians, who were famous for their skills as archers; several times Aristophanes makes fun of them as stupid, stammering, and randy barbarians. State slaves able to write and calculate were also used in the army; if they were killed in action, they were given a state funeral like free citizens, and the survivors were often set free. The many slaves working in the silver mines were an important factor for the Athenian economy; often they were not the property of the state (who owned the mines), but were hired in groups from private masters (the Athenian general and politician Nicias cleverly employed such slave groups to further his own income). Some of these people must have been highly specialized to do the more difficult work (probably they had already been imported as skilled workers from countries such as Thrace and Paphlagonia which were also renowned for their mines), and they at least had a chance of rising to the post of an overseer; for the great majority, however, working in the mines was by far the worst, most horrible, and most humiliating fate (in this manner the Athenian army captured in Sicily in 413 perished in the quarries of Syracuse). Still, several grave stelae and votives (mostly for gods of Asia Minor and Thrace) found in Laurium show that it must have been possible even for these people to preserve something of their own life and their native cults.

Serving as nurses and pedagogues was another important "profession" of ancient slaves; in Classical Athens Thracian wetnurses seem to have been very popular. From the middle of the 4th century BC on, numerous grave stelae and grave epigrams were dedicated for nurses by their foster children and their families, often containing the same laudatory epithets as for their next of kin. It is remarkable that the Greeks entrusted their children to barbarian slaves and gave them duties with so much responsibility.

It is still an unsolved question how many slaves lived in Classical Attica (assessments range from one quarter to half of the whole population), to say nothing about other regions; it is also disputed how many slaves lived in an average Greek household, as ancient evidence on this question is almost completely lacking. Still, some remarks in comedies of Aristophanes seem to show that a "normal" citizen had at least one slave; even the poor farmer Chremylus has one (*Plutus*, 253ff.), as do the birds (*Aves*, 70, 1579f.), and to have none means utmost poverty for Praxagora (*Ecclesiazusae*, 593). A middle-class family may have had between three and twelve slaves, but this number certainly varied according to place and epoch. In the later 5th century BC there must have been a considerable number of slaves in the silver mines of Laurium, for according to Thucydides (7. 27. 5) 20,000 of them went over to the enemy after the Spartans occupied Deceleia in 413 BC. Compared with other Greek states, Classical Athens (with its leading role in the Delian League) may have had the largest proportion of slaves in relation to its citizens; in any case they always held an important place in the economy.

From the later 5th century onwards, Greek thinkers developed something like a theoretical concept of slavery. Its institution was usually justified by the notion that barbarians were slaves by nature because they had no political institutions for free and equal citizens and because the monarchies in which they often lived were themselves a kind of slavery; therefore, as Euripides put it (*Iphigeneia at Aulis*, 1400f.), "it is right that Greeks rule over barbarians". The thesis of barbarian inferiority and a legitimate Greek claim of dominion over them is also found in Aristotle (who reportedly advised Alexander the Great to treat barbarians like animals and plants), Isocrates, and Plato, who outlined precise laws of slavery in his *Laws*. These sources, of course, primarily reflect political tendencies after the Persian Wars and do not necessarily tell us how slaves were perceived or treated in reality; many grave stelae with touchingly personal inscriptions were set up for loyal slaves and faithful nurses by their masters and show that their relationships were more complex in the real world than in philosophical theory. The Sophists and later the Stoics and Cynics declared that all people were equal and free by nature, and noble slaves can also be found in the plays of Euripides; even the slaves themselves, however, apparently did not question the institution of slavery and had no "class-consciousness" of their own.

In Hellenistic times new areas of trade and new markets (e.g. Delos) led to an increase of slavery; the legislation concerning slavery saw new developments (taxation of slave trade, intensified search for runaway slaves, but also extended asylum rights). Menander's comedies show that there was often a very familiar relationship between master and slave.

During the Roman empire mass enslavement of free people (as a consequence of wars and conquests) increased; but slave revolts (among other places in Attic mines and on Delos) remained unsuccessful. Many Greek slaves (and freedmen) worked in the imperial household and held important administrative posts. The sources (among others Libanius, Justinian's law corpus, Egyptian papyri, the letters of Sidonius Apollinaris) show that slavery was still an important factor in the economy of the late Roman empire; in Byzantine law, slaves still had almost no civil rights, but at least the intentional killing of a slave was now treated as homicide.

The Church's attitude to slavery was ambiguous: while some (e.g. Gregory of Nazianzus) condemned it, others (e.g. Basil the Great) tolerated it as a necessary evil. The Church (following St Paul) usually pointed out that slaves and free men alike were servants of Christ, so that worldly freedom was irrelevant; nevertheless, Christian masters were advised to treat their slaves as brothers.

There are only a few sources about slavery in Byzantium between the 7th and the 9th centuries AD; during the 10th century slavery apparently expanded once more. After the victories of Nikephoros II Phokas (963–69) numerous prisoners of war were to be found in Byzantine households and fields. A great number of slaves then worked above all in the imperial workshops and in the establishments of goldsmiths and silk weavers of Constantinople. From the 12th century on, slavery declined; and in the 13th century it largely vanished. A new increase followed the fall of Constantinople in 1453, but slavery in Muslim countries was very different from that in the ancient and Byzantine world, because slaves in the fields, industry, or mines were almost unknown; nearly all of them were employed in rich families and usually well treated. In the Ottoman empire slavery was abolished rather late, so that the final end of slavery in Greece itself came only with the wars of liberation.

BALBINA BÄBLER

See also Mines and Quarries, Piracy, Trade

Further Reading

Cartledge, Paul A., "Serfdom in Classical Greece" in *Slavery and Other Forms of Unfree Labour*, edited by Léonie J. Archer, London and New York: Routledge, 1988

Collins Reilly, Linda, *Slaves in Ancient Greece: Slaves from Greek Manumission Inscriptions*, Chicago: Ares, 1978

Davis, David Brion, *The Problem of Slavery in Western Culture*, Ithaca, New York: Cornell University Press, 1966; revised 1988

Finley, M.I., "Was Greek Civilisation Based on Slave Labor?", *Historia*, 8 (1959): pp. 145–164

Finley, M.I., (editor), *Slavery in Classical Antiquity: Views and Controversies*, Cambridge: Heffer, 1960; New York: Barnes and Noble, 1968

Finley, M.I., "The Black Sea and Danubian Regions and the Slave Trade in Antiquity", *Klio*, 40 (1962): pp. 51–59

Finley, M.I., *Ancient Slavery and Modern Ideology*, London: Chatto and Windus, 1980; New York: Viking, 1981

Finley, M.I., (editor), *Classical Slavery*, London: Cass, 1987

Fisher, N.R.E., *Slavery in Classical Greece*, London: Bristol Classical Press, 1993

Garnsey, Peter, *Ideas of Slavery from Aristotle to Augustine*, Cambridge and New York: Cambridge University Press, 1996

Jameson, M.H., "Agriculture and Slavery in Classical Athens", *Classical Journal*, 73 (1977–78): pp. 122–45

Kazhdan, A., "The Concept of Freedom (eleutheria) and Slavery (douleia) in Byzantium" in *La Notion de liberté au moyen âge: Islam, Byzance, Occident*, Paris: Belles Lettres, 1985

Köpstein, Helga, *Zur Sklaverei im ausgehenden Byzanz*, Berlin: Akademie, 1966

Lauffer, Siegfried von, *Die Bergwerkssklaven vom Laureion*, 2nd edition, Wiesbaden: Steiner, 1979

Marinovic, L.P., *Die Sklaverei in den östlichen Provinzen des römischen Reiches im 1.-3. Jahrhundert*, Stuttgart: Steiner, 1992

Morrow, Glenn R., *Plato's Law of Slavery and its Relation to Greek Law*, Urbana: University of Illinois Press, 1939

Osborne, Robin, "The Economics and Politics of Slavery at Athens" in *The Greek World*, edited by Anton Powell, London and New York: Routledge, 1995

Patterson, Orlando, *Slavery and Social Death: A Comparative Study*, Cambridge, Massachusetts: Harvard University Press, 1982

Phillips, William D. Jr, *Slavery from Roman Times to the Early Transatlantic Trade*, Minneapolis: University of Minnesota Press, 1985

Pomeroy, Sarah B., *Goddesses, Whores, Wives, and Slaves: Women in Classical Antiquity*, New York: Schocken, 1975; London: Hale, 1976

Sargent, Rachel L., "The Size of the Slave Population at Athens during the Fifth and Fourth Centuries BC" (dissertation), Urbana: University of Illinois, 1923

Schlaifer, Robert, "Greek Theories of Slavery from Homer to Aristotle", *Harvard Studies in Classical Philology*, 47 (1936): pp. 165–204

Vogt, Josef, *Ancient Slavery and the Ideal of Man*, Oxford: Blackwell, and Cambridge, Massachusetts: Harvard University Press, 1974

Westermann, William L., "Athenaeus and the Slaves of Athens", *Harvard Studies in Classical Philology*, supplement 1 (1940): pp. 451 ff.

Westermann, William L., *The Slave Systems of Greek and Roman Antiquity*, Philadelphia: American Philosophical Society, 1955; reprinted, 1984

Wiedemann, Thomas (editor), *Greek and Roman Slavery*, London: Croom Helm, and Baltimore: Johns Hopkins University Press, 1981 (a selection of translated excerpts from ancient sources; bibliography of works up to 1980)

Wiedemann, Thomas, *Slavery*, Oxford: Clarendon Press, and New York: Oxford University Press, 1987

Slavs

According to the 6th-century historian Procopius Slav incursions into Byzantine territory began in the reign of emperor Justinian I (527–65) whose policy of expansion had clearly strained the resources of the empire. A number of ancient sources confirm that these invasions grew more frequent and severe in the last quarter of the 6th century, although there is disagreement among modern historians about their nature, extent, and duration. It is fairly clear that the Slavs, themselves Indo-European speakers, were dominated by non-Indo-European speakers such as the Avars and Bulgars, although it was the Slav language which eventually prevailed. Although there are references to invasions of Hellas, this was an elastic term. The evidence of proper names suggests that there were more Slavs in western than in eastern Greece. The Slavs did

reach the Peloponnese and there were Slavonic tribes – the Ezeritae and Melingi – there as late as the 13th century. The *Chronicle of Monemvasia* with unusual precision says that the Peloponnese was occupied for 231 years after an Avar invasion of 581, but the authority of this chronicle has been doubted by Greek historians anxious to prove the continuity of Greek occupation, for which the survival of the Greek language provides some testimony. Pointing to the Slav domination by the Avars, they like to think of the Slavs as peaceful, pastoral immigrants, fairly rapidly absorbed by the surviving Greek population.

By the 9th century some kind of absorption had begun in southern Greece, but in the north Slav tribes more naturally fell under the powerful sway of the Bulgarian kingdom. The activities of Cyril (St Constantine) and Methodios in inventing the Cyrillic script and the establishment of a separate Bulgarian Church, though civilizing influences, were an obstacle to the work of the Greek Church in re-establishing Greek. Bulgaria was defeated at the beginning of the 11th century and once again Byzantium ruled the Balkans, but in this multilingual empire Slav-speakers dominated in the north and central Balkans, and there were still pockets of them further south.

With the collapse of Byzantine authority after the Fourth Crusade (1204) the Serbs and Bulgars reasserted their independence and occasionally occupied northern and central Greece. The turbulent two centuries until the Ottoman invasion produced many movements of population, Latins, Vlachs, and Albanians all adding to the racial mix of Slav and Greek, and nationalist advocates of ethnic purity or continuous occupation would find it difficult to make sense of these years. The Ottomans were not particularly interested in the ethnic composition of their subject populations, but the long years of Turkish rule did something to restore the balance of Greek against Slav, since Greek was the language of the Church, of commerce, and of education.

It was not until 1870 that the Ottoman authorities sanctioned the founding of the Bulgarian Exarchate and did something to tilt the scales yet again. By this time, apart from some pockets of Greeks or Greek-speaking Vlachs in towns of the central Balkans, the boundary between Greek speakers and Slav speakers stood slightly to the south of the present northern Greek frontier. For the next 40 years Greeks and Bulgars fought a guerrilla campaign with each other and the Turks over the disputed territory. The battle was largely fought in religious terms between exarchists, supporters of the Bulgarian Church, and patriarchists, supporters of the Greek Church. The Serbs were rarely in competition with the Greeks, but as a result of being on the winning side in the Second Balkan War, it was the Serbs who were awarded the territory which now calls itself Macedonia, while Greece gained a large section to the south which confusingly they too call Macedonia. Both areas contained large numbers of people speaking a Slav language akin to Bulgarian.

After World War I, in which again Greece and Serbia were on the winning side and gained territory from Bulgaria as a result, the problem of the Slav-speakers in Greece was solved in a number of ways. There was a series of population exchanges involving Greek-speakers from Bulgaria replacing Bulgarian-speakers in Greece. The much larger exchanges between Turkey and Greece resulted in the population of

Macedonia becoming much more Greek. Assimilation was encouraged and the speaking of the local Slav dialect discouraged. During World War II part of northern Greece was occupied by the Bulgarians and in the Civil War the communist forces had a considerable Slav-speaking element: the defeat and consequent unpopularity of first the Bulgarians and then the communists cannot have helped the Slav cause.

Nevertheless in 1951 the Greek census included 41,017 Slav-speakers and 18,671 Pomaks, Slav speakers near Xanthi who had adopted Islam and in subsequent censuses are recorded as Muslims. Slav-speakers were not recorded as such after 1951 on the grounds that assimilation was likely to take place very rapidly. In the 1970s and 1980s, with relations between Greece and Tito's Yugoslavia fairly amicable, it was possible to find Slav-speakers near Florina chatting with their counterparts near Bitola as they made social or shopping visits to the other country, but with the dismemberment of Yugoslavia and the independence of the Former Republic of Macedonia the Slav-speakers of Greece have again become a topical issue. Their numbers are clearly not great, but minorities all over Europe are the cause for controversy and concern. Greeks see the name Macedonia and the existence of the Slav-speakers as a threat to their northern borders. Such a threat, present at the time of the Civil War and in the Cold War that followed it, is hardly very potent now, but it has affected the attitude of Greeks to the history of the Slavs and to Slav-speakers in Greece.

T.J. WINNIFRITH

See also Bulgars, Pomaks, Russia, Serbs

Further Reading

Dakin, Douglas, *The Greek Struggle in Macedonia, 1897–1913*, Thessalonica: Institute for Balkan Studies, 1966; reprinted Thessalonica: Museum of the Macedonian Struggle, 1993

Karakasidou, Anastasia N., *Fields of Wheat, Hills of Blood: Passages to Nationhood in Greek Macedonia, 1870–1990*, Chicago: University of Chicago Press, 1997

Lemerle, P., "Invasions et migrations dans les Balkans", *Revue Historique*, 211 (1954): pp. 265–308

Pentzopoulos, Dimitri, *The Balkan Exchange of Minorities and its Impact upon Greece*, Paris: Mouton, 1962

Toynbee, Arnold, *Constantine Porphyrygenitus and his World*, Oxford and New York: Oxford University Press, 1973

Vasmer, Max, *Die Slaven in Griechenland*, Berlin: de Gruyter, 1941; reprinted Lepizig: Zentralantiquariat, 1970

Smyrna

City in western Asia Minor

The first ancient Greek settlement of Smyrna was founded in about the 10th century BC on the northeastern shores of the gulf of Smyrna, in what is now the modern Izmir suburb of Bayrakli. Aeolian Greek migrants established their colony here on the site of an earlier Anatolian settlement, but were soon themselves displaced by Ionian Greeks. From this time on Smyrna was considered part of Ionia, though it was not incorporated into the Panionium, or organization of the original 12 Ionian colonies, until the 3rd century BC, following the refoundation of the city. Fortified by at least the 9th century BC, Old Smyrna boasted a fine archaic temple of Athena. It was most famous, however, for its claim, strongly contested by neighbouring Chios, to be the birthplace of Homer. Indeed, still today, Classical scholars generally agree that the Homeric poems underwent their early development in the Smyrna-Chios region: the mixed Ionic-Aeolic dialect of the poems belies their origin in this part of the Greek world, as does also their description of the topography of the Smyrna region. The ancient tradition linking Homer and Smyrna proved to be long-lived and widespread across the Hellenic world: Aristotle, Pindar, Aristides, and Dio Chrysostom, among others, all mention Homer's Smyrnaean roots. By the 2nd century BC coins of Smyrna could be identified by their pictorial device of the seated figure of Homer, shown together with his name. At the turn of the 1st century BC–1st century AD Strabo also details the existence of a Homereion, or shrine to Homer, in the refounded city of Smyrna.

The first Greek city of Smyrna at Bayrakli grew and prospered until c.600 BC, when it suffered destruction at the hands of the powerful Lydians. It was never to recover from these destructions, and declined further throughout the Classical period, until by the late 4th century BC it lay more or less abandoned. At this time the second Greek city of Smyrna was founded on the slopes of Mount Pagus, on the opposite (southeastern) shores of the Smyrnaic gulf. The refoundation of the city can perhaps be attributed to Alexander the Great, or alternatively to Antigonus I and Lysimachus. It is this site, gradually and considerably enlarged over the centuries, which has remained in continuous urban use until the present day. Fortified from the beginning, the new city soon prospered and, during the Hellenistic period, attracted the interest of both the Seleucids and the Attalids, to whom it reacted with vacillating loyalty. The increasing power of Rome further served to increase Smyrna's prosperity and prestige as it emerged as one of the major cities of the Roman province of Asia, well placed on routes of trade and communication and functioning as a Roman administrative centre. As such it was graced with many fine public buildings, and Strabo claims it to be the most beautiful Roman city of his day. In AD 178, however, disaster struck in the form of a powerful earthquake, which resulted in grave damage to the city and necessitated much rebuilding. The imperial favour and generous benefactions of Marcus Aurelius, nevertheless, made this reconstruction work possible, the extant remains of the state agora still today bearing testimony to the suitably grand scale on which the refurbishments were carried out. By the mid-1st century AD Christianity seems already to have been established at Smyrna. From this point onwards, the city played a significant role in the development of the early Christian Church, a role perhaps recognized in the book of Revelation by the identification of Smyrna as one of the seven Churches of Asia. As elsewhere, the early Christian Church at Smyrna was subjected to much persecution, and in AD 155 Polycarp, bishop of Smyrna, was martyred.

Smyrna continued as a prosperous trading centre until the onset of the Arab raids in the 7th century AD. Towards the end of the 11th century the city fell briefly into the hands of the Seljuk Turks, until retaken by the Byzantines in 1097. Thereafter, for some 300 or so years, Byzantines, Crusaders, Genoese, and Turks all fought over it. In 1415 it was taken by the Ottoman Turks and in 1472 was sacked by the Venetian fleet. However, for the most part, Smyrna during the Middle Ages, at least until 1600, had lost the wealth and importance which it had so enjoyed in earlier times. Nevertheless, by 1600 its fortunes were again changing with the establishment of French, Venetian, English, and Dutch factories and consulates in the city. Throughout the centuries which followed, Smyrna reasserted itself as one of the most dynamic and attractive mercantile centres in the Mediterranean, a position greatly assisted and enhanced by the arrival of the railway in the mid-19th century, a development which now linked the city effectively with the Anatolian hinterland. The trade and population of Smyrna expanded rapidly, particularly so in the case of the Greek element for, attracted by the growing wealth of the city, many Greeks migrated there from the islands and Greek mainland. While in 1800 the Greeks comprised under one-third of the city's total population, by the end of the century the figure had risen to almost half, thus giving them the status of the majority population. Even prior to this Hellenic population explosion, the growing wealth and influence of the Greek merchants in Smyrna had led to a revival of Hellenism in western Anatolia. This focused on the Evangelic School of Smyrna, which possessed a fine library of books and manuscripts, and which taught its pupils not only the ancient Greek classics but also a sense of pride in their language and national identity. This sentiment, naturally, was boosted by the 1821 revolt of the mainland Greeks against the Ottoman Turks, and the subsequent creation of the independent Greek state in the Western Aegean. Smyrna now became the lifeblood of Hellenism in the east.

The Smyrna Greek community was organized as a recognizable and, as far as possible, autonomous unit within the Ottoman system: not only its schools, but also its hospitals, were funded by the Greeks for the Greeks, and the community appointed its own representatives to handle its relations with the Ottoman state. All of this was subject to the authority of the bishop of Smyrna and, through him, to that of the ecumenical patriarch in Constantinople. For many decades this arrangement provided mutual benefits to both Asia Minor Greek and Turk. But in the early years of the 20th century, the Young Turk revolution and the First Balkan War undermined the symbiotic balance in Graeco-Turkish relations. Ethnic and religious differences were highlighted and came to be wielded by each side as blunt weapons against the other. World War I compounded matters further. Greece was courted for its participation in the war on the side of the Entente, in return for which Britain promised it territorial compensation on the coast of Asia Minor: the bait, of course, was Smyrna. In this offer Eleftherios Venizelos, prime minister of Greece, saw the ideal opportunity to incorporate the Asia Minor Greeks and their territory into the Hellenic state. When the war ended in September 1918, the victorious Allied Powers duly rewarded Greece for Venizelos's loyalty with the gift of Smyrna: in May 1919 Greek troops entered the city, a Greek High Commissioner was appointed, and the Greeks occupied a zone extending inland from Smyrna. This action provoked Turkish nationalist sentiments; these soon found a focus in Mustafa Kemal, a Turkish army officer who, establishing his base in Turkey's eastern provinces, set about organizing resistance to the occupation. In 1920 the signing of the Treaty of Sèvres brought the Ottoman empire to an end and granted the administration of Smyrna to Greece: if after a five-year period the local populace confirmed this arrangement to be acceptable, Smyrna would then be annexed to Greece. Beginning in June 1920, the Greek army had begun to advance northeast from Smyrna towards Ankara, its goal being to defeat Kemal's Turkish forces. The latter, however, proved too powerful, and in August 1922 the Greek front collapsed and the Greek forces retreated to Smyrna. Troops, civilians, and officials, including the Greek High Commissioner, fled Smyrna for the Greek islands and mainland, ahead of the advancing Turks. When in September the Turkish troops entered Smyrna, the pen stood poised to write one of the blackest pages in Hellenic history and memory. Archbishop Chrysostom, among others, was seized and killed by the angry Turkish mob, in an incident reminiscent of the martyrdom of bishop Polycarp almost 2000 years earlier. A few days after the death of Chrysostom a great fire swept through the city, destroying the Greek and other foreign quarters. Hellenic Smyrna, almost 3000 years in existence, was no more.

Following the Greek defeat, a Convention concerning the Exchange of Greek-Turkish Populations was signed by Greece and Turkey at Lausanne in January 1923. This provided for the compulsory exchange of the, now vastly reduced, Greek Orthodox population still remaining in Turkey, and the Muslim population of Greece. The resulting total of Asia Minor Greeks arriving in mainland Greece in 1922–23 numbered something approaching 1,500,000 refugees. Uprooted from their homeland, they attempted to recreate the familiar in their new surroundings: names such as Nea Smyrna and Menemeni still today identify suburbs in the mainland Greek cities which now became home to these eastern Greeks. With them they also brought their Hellenic Asia Minor culture, including a particular kind of oriental-style café music (*café aman*) and dance which greatly shaped the Greek *rebetika* (popular music) tradition. The influx of such a large number of refugees also made a profound contribution to Greece's interwar economic and political development: with their arrival, the pace of industrialization and agricultural mechanization quickened and the electoral outcomes of the period, too, reflect their considerable influence.

Modern Smyrna, rebuilt after the 1922 destructions as the bustling Turkish port of Izmir, is still regarded with great affection and nostalgia by the Greek people. A Greek consulate still survives today at Izmir, a lonely and isolated reminder of the long Hellenic contribution to the history of the city and of western Asia Minor.

LESLEY A. BEAUMONT

See also Asia Minor Campaign

Summary

Smyrna (modern Izmir, from Greek "I Smyrni") was first colonized by Greeks in about the 10th century BC. It claimed to be the birthplace of Homer. Destroyed by the Lydians *c.*600 BC, it was refounded in the early Hellenistic period on a different site and flourished. After a period of decline in the Middle Ages it prospered again after 1600 as a trading centre and many Greeks migrated there, making it once again a focus of Hellenism. In the break-up of the Ottoman empire it was given to Greece, but a Greek advance into the hinterland was defeated in 1922 resulting in the destruction of Smyrna and the expulsion of its Greek population.

Further Reading

Akurgal, Ekrem, *Alt Smyrna*, vol. 1: *Wohnschichten und Athenatempel*, Ankara, 1983

Apostolidis, S., I. Apostolidis, and I. Kapantai, *Ionia: Oi Ellines sti Mikrasia* [Ionia: The Greeks in Asia Minor], Athens, 1997

Augustinos, Gerasimos, *The Greeks of Asia Minor: Confession, Community, and Ethnicity in the Nineteenth Century*, Kent, Ohio: Kent State University Press, 1992

Cadoux, Cecil John, *Ancient Smyrna: A History of the City from the Earliest Times to 324 AD*, Oxford: Blackwell, 1938

Cook, J.M. and E. Akurgal, "Excavating Old Smyrna", *Illustrated London News* (28 February 1953): pp. 328–29

Cook, J.M. *et al.*, "Old Smyrna, 1948–1951", *Annual of the British School at Athens*, 53–54 (1958–59): pp. 1–181

Cook, J.M. and R.V. Nicholls, *Old Smyrna Excavations: The Temples of Athena*, London: British School at Athens, 1998

Hasluck, F.W., "The Rise of Modern Smyrna", *Annual of the British School at Athens*, 23 (1918–19): pp. 139–47

Housepian, Marjorie, *Smyrna 1922: The Destruction of a City*, London: Faber, 1972; Kent, Ohio: Kent State University Press, 1988

Llewellyn Smith, Michael, *Ionian Vision: Greece in Asia Minor, 1919–1922*, London: Allen Lane, and New York: St Martin's Press, 1973; 2nd edition, London: Hurst, and Ann Arbor: University of Michigan Press, 1998

Socrates 470–399 BC

Philosopher

Socrates was born in Athens, the son of a stonemason and a midwife; he was executed by the Athenian democracy in 399 BC. He did not leave any written work; and yet Karl Marx rightly called him the embodiment of philosophy (*Rheinische Zeitung*, no. 179, 1842; Karl Marx–Friedrich Engels, *Werke*, vol. 1, Berlin, 1956, p. 91). For Socrates lived his entire life for philosophy. He learned his father's craft, but the political service of his polis and the education of his fellow-citizens were more important for him. Such a way of life was possible, for everyday life was simple and thus not expensive. He strove to be a good citizen and served his native city several times as a brave and persevering soldier, but he refused to act wrongly when ordered to do so by the authorities of the pseudo-democracy. He considered that his first duty was to seek the truth and he tried to show it by the maieutic method of his mother, the midwife. He made enemies by questioning the knowledge and opinions of his fellow-citizens in chance meetings. But he himself confessed that he knew nothing. Wishing to be taught, he became an ideal teacher; rejecting the sexual pederasty that was common in Classical Greece, he developed the pedagogical ethos. He was familiar with the doctrines and writings of the natural philosophers, especially of Anaxagoras, but their answers did not satisfy him. More important for him was the individual and social morality that was directed by the demonic, which was more powerful than the human conscience: it was a divine voice. Socrates was a deeply religious man. He made use of the sophistic dialectics, not for his personal advantage, but in the search for truth. He was not interested in establishing a philosophical system or in labori-

ously propagating them by writing. Already in his lifetime there were thus very different views about his personality and his doctrines. He was known as an odd man, and became an object of mockery and caricature (for instance in the comedies of Aristophanes), and, as we have seen, he made enemies for various reasons. He was thus subjected to a political trial, charged with impiety and corrupting young men, and was condemned to death by the Athenian radical democracy.

According to the customs of his time Socrates' wife and sons were in the background of his life. This was the cause of many anecdotes about the character of his wife Xanthippe and his relations with her. Indeed, his relationships with his friends and pupils were particularly important for him. Socrates, the man without riches or power, attracted a circle of aristocratic young men which occasionally attracted criticism from some democrats. Members of this circle included the two authors whose writings about Socrates survive: Xenophon and Plato. Xenophon was a competent officer, a successful farmer, and a good chronicler, but he was more a man of action than of theory. What he reports in his *Memorabilia* is very valuable, but it represents only part of Socrates' philosophical speculations. For Plato the figure of Socrates was a pretext to formulate his own opinions, and it is difficult to fix the boundary between Socratic inheritance and Plato's continuation. It should be noted that neither Xenophon nor Plato mention each other.

Socrates did not participate in Athenian politics, but some of his pupils were celebrated as the founders of various philosophical schools, such as Plato of the Academy, Aristippus of the school of Cyrene, Phaedo of the school of Elis, and Antisthenes of the school of the Cynics. The Hellenistic doxographers did not reflect the doctrines of Socrates, but preserved a tradition of anecdotes and apophthegms, of which we find traces in the writings of Diogenes Laertius of the 3rd century AD.

In the Roman period a new and different interest in Socrates awoke. A collection of fictitious letters of Socrates appeared (edited by L. Koehler, Berlin 1928). Plutarch, the popular philosopher, priest at Delphi, and archon at Chaeronea, wrote *On the Divine Socrates* and *On the Condemnation of Socrates* and produced an *Apology for* Socrates. A friend of Plutarch, Favorinus of Arelate (2nd century AD), rhetorician and polymath, wrote a (lost) book *On Socrates and His Erotic Art*, which drew the criticism of the contemporary physician and philosopher Galen of Pergamum. The archaizing orators Dio Chrysostom and Maximus of Tyre treated Socratic problems in their speeches, such as the demonic or the erotic, and influenced their colleagues. The Neoplatonists celebrated the birthdays of Socrates and Plato with sacrifices, solemn dinners, and speeches.

At Rome the life and work of Socrates were read more in Xenophon than in Plato. The most important mediator was Panaetius (c.185–109 BC), the director of the Middle Stoa. Cicero called Socrates the father of philosophy and praised him for bringing philosophy down from heaven to everyday life (*Academica Posteriora*, 1. 415). The philosopher Seneca the Younger (1st century AD), when speaking of Socrates, utters only commonplaces. Valerius Maximus (early 1st century AD) in his *Factorum et Dictorum Memorabilia* sometimes mentions

Socrates: antique marble copy of a bust from the 4th century BC attributed to Lysippus, Louvre, Paris

Socrates as a praiseworthly example of virtue and wisdom with sound character and self-control.

For the Christian Apologists, and especially for Justin (*c*.AD 100–*c*.165), Socrates was a forerunner of Christ; for Socrates the *logos* (intellect) was necessary, while Christ is in possession of the *Logos* (governing principle of the universe). The Alexandrian theologians held this view, but it was rejected by western Christian writers; for St Augustine all the virtues of the pagans were no more than splendid vices.

During the Middle Ages Socrates was nearly forgotten in the West. His name signified the wise man par excellence, but it remained a mere name. The anonymous poem *Causa Pauperis Scolaris cum Presbytero* was ascribed to him; the "doctor universalis" Alanus ab Insulis (*c*.1125/30–1203) in his *Distinctiones Dictionum Theologicalium* had Socrates conversing with Christ. Godefridus of Breteuil (12th century) calls Socrates the "fons philosophiae". In the *Divina commedia* of Dante Alighieri Socrates is to be found in Purgatory (4. 135) beside Plato and Aristotle.

The situation in the Byzantine east was little better. The chapter (2. 5) about Socrates in the *Lives* of Diogenes Laertius (3rd century) is full of anecdotal material, and the lexicon known as the *Suda*, from the 10th/11th centuries, made wide use of it. The *gnomologia* (collections of maxims) are in the same tradition, more interested in biographical dates than in the doctrines of Socrates. But the portrait of the Athenian wise man was also present. In the paintings of the tree of Jesse in the late medieval churches of Greece and Bulgaria Socrates is often portrayed among other pagan philosophers. In the last period of the Byzantine empire Xenophon's *Memorabilia* were again read, and in the controversy over hesychasm the writings of Plato played an important role. Some of the Renaissance humanists revered Socrates extravagantly. Marsilio Ficino, the translator of Plato, was ready to equate Socrates with Christ, and Desiderius Erasmus, the leader of the northern humanists, formulated the prayer: "Sancte Socrates, ora pro nobis!"

But the real Socratic century was the 18th. All branches of philosophy made use of the figure of Socrates, at first leaning on Xenophon, and after the publication of the *Phaedo* by Mendelssohn, more on Plato. Socrates became the type of the popular philosopher. In the 19th century the Danish thinker Sören Kierkegaard admired and interpreted Socrates as a "subjective" (not idealistic) philosopher, whose mode of life he imitated in his own. Friedrich Nietzsche, the philological specialist on Diogenes Laertius, considered Socrates as the philosopher of *décadence*. In the 20th century the Greek publicist Kostas Varnalis in his *True Apology of Socrates* criticized the falsification of Classical ideals by bourgeois society, and in a similar manner Bertolt Brecht wrote about the "wounded Socrates" (*Geschichten*, Frankfurt, 1962, pp 109ff.).

JOHANNES IRMSCHER

See also Dialectic, Philosophy

Biography

Born at Athens in 470 BC the son of a stonemason and a midwife, Socrates served as a soldier in several battles. He was married to Xanthippe and had two sons. He played little part in public life and devoted himself entirely to philosophical debate. He wrote nothing, but his pupils included the founders of several philosophical schools, including Plato. When ordered to arrest an innocent man he refused to comply. He was charged with impiety and with corrupting young men and condemned to death in 399.

Further Reading

Böhme, Gernot, *Der Typ Sokrates*, Frankfurt: Suhrkamp, 1988

Chroust, Anton-Hermann, *Socrates, Man or Myth: The Two Socratic Apologies of Xenophon*, London: Routledge, and Notre Dame, Indiana: University of Notre Dame Press, 1957

Döring, Klaus, *Exemplum Socratis: Studien zur Sokratessnachwirkung in der kynisch-stoischen Popularphilosophie der frühen Kaiserzeit und im frühen Christentum*, Wiesbaden: Steiner, 1979

Ferguson, John, *Socrates: A Sourcebook*, London: Macmillan, 1970

Field, Guy Cromwell, *Plato and his Contemporaries: A Study of Fourth-Century Life and Thought*, 3rd edition, London: Methuen, 1967

Gigon, Olaf, *Sokrates: Sein Bild in Dichtung und Geschichte*, Bern: Francke, 1947

Irmscher, Johannes, *Sokrates: Versuch einer Biografie*, 3rd edition, Leipzig: Reclam, 1989

Irwin, T.H., *Plato's Moral Theory: The Early and Middle Dialogues*, Oxford and New York: Clarendon Press, 1977

Lesky, Albin, *Geschichte der griechischen Literatur*, 3rd edition, Bern: Francke, 1971, pp. 537 ff.

Montuori, Mario, *The Socratic Problem: The History, the Solutions, from the 18th Century to the Present Time*, Amsterdam: Gieben, 1992

Navia, Luis and Ellen Katz, *Socrates: An Annotated Bibliography*, New York: Garland, 1988

Robinson, Richard, *Plato's Earlier Dialectic*, 2nd edition, Oxford: Clarendon Press, 1953, reprinted Oxford: Clarendon Press, and New York: Oxford University Press, 1984

Seebeck, Hans Günther, "Das Sokratesbild vom 19. Jahrhundert bis zur Gegenwart" (dissertation), Göttingen, 1947

Vilhena, Vasco de, *Le Problème de Socrates: le Socrate historique et le Socrate de Platon*, Paris: Presses Universitaire de France, 1952

Vlastos, Gregory, *Socrates: Ironist and Moral Philosopher*, Cambridge and New York: Cambridge University Press, and Ithaca, New York: Cornell University Press, 1991

Vlastos, Gregory, *Socratic Studies*, Cambridge and New York: Cambridge University Press, 1994

Solomos, Dionysios 1798–1857

Poet

Born on the island of Zakynthos to Count Solomos, a tobacco merchant, and his young maid Angeliki, Dionysios Solomos was raised in the privileged manner of the Zakynthian nobility. In 1808, a year after his father died, Dionysios was put in the charge of his tutor, the liberal-minded priest Don Santo Rossi, who is thought to have exercised considerable influence on the young boy's artistic and political ideas. After a ten-year sojourn in Italy, where he acquired a solid classical education and became acquainted with Italian Neoclassicism and the emergent Romanticism of his day, Solomos returned to his native island in 1818 to begin a career as a poet. His early poems, written in Italian, are mostly of a devotional nature and show him a competent and skilful versifier, though lacking in originality. Within a couple of years of his return to Zakynthos, Solomos began to write in Greek, a language he is said to have "imbibed with his mother's milk". In a bid to encourage the young poet's use of his native language, Spiridon Trikoupis told him upon meeting him that "Greece is waiting for its Dante". Solomos turned for inspiration to the rich vein of Greek demotic songs, dirges, and pastoral idylls which had formed an anonymous oral tradition since Byzantine times. He wrote lyrics, elegies, odes, and satires, as well as a prose work in defence of vernacular poetry modelled on the Platonic dialogue and probably inspired by Dante's *De Vulgari Eloquentia*.

Solomos's poetry is nearly always fast-moving and melodious. He made use of various metrical forms, Greek and Italian. The most important of these was the 15-syllable line, a distant descendant of the Classical dactylic hexameter, used by Cretan bards throughout the 16th and 17th centuries. Solomos's early poems display a Romantic's preoccupation with death, especially the death of young innocents. Later, as his poetic vision matured, he combined bold lyricism with an ethical outlook rooted in the idea of spiritual freedom. Among Solomos's most important works are *Lambros*, an almost Gothic narrative of betrayal, incest, and suicide; *The Cretan*, a haunting lyric tale set at sea; and his monumental *The Free Besieged*, in which the long, tragic siege of Missolonghi by the Turks shows man defying the sufferings without and the temptations within until he has finally achieved a dignity commensurate with his highest ideals.

The *Hymn to Liberty*, his best-known work, written in 1823 during a month-long outpouring of political and lyrical enthusiasm, is a stirring account of the Greek War of Independence and the ideals it embodied for patriots and philhellenes alike. The poem is made up of 158 four-line stanzas, the first two of which were later adopted as the fledgeling country's national anthem. Thus at the age of 25 Solomos became the country's national poet. His own youth seemed to be consonant with the youth of the nation. The hymn's role in Greek emancipation is rightly deemed inestimable. It was quickly translated into all the major European languages and widely disseminated among foreign politicians and men of letters. The sympathy which it aroused on behalf of Greek independence has prompted one biographer to characterize its political contribution as equivalent to numberless frigates and regiments. Solomos, however, did not see himself as a man of action but as a poet whose first duty was to his art. A restless perfectionist, he set himself the impossible task of single-handedly adapting demotic Greek as a vehicle for the highest philosophical and artistic ideas.

One consequence of this incessant perfectionism was Solomos's inability to complete any of his longer poems. Solomos's continual artistic development invariably tended to outstrip the pace of his work, leaving many of his projects unfinished. Most of his mature work comes to us in what have been wrongly labelled "fragments"; however, nearly all of Solomos's extant poems are complete in themselves, even if the larger work for which they were intended never came to fruition. In this respect Solomos resembled other Romantic poets such as Byron, Shelley, or Keats. It should be remembered that modern Greek was still in its infancy as a literary language, a point well observed by the poet George Seferis, who repeatedly acknowledged his own debt to the Zakynthian bard. Solomos's success can be measured by the fact that vernacular Greek was never again seriously challenged by

katharevousa as the natural language of poetry. No one ever again doubted that the everyday speech of the people could articulate the loftiest ideas. But for Solomos this was never an axiom. The many discarded drafts in his extant manuscripts show him wrestling with the problem of finding the right form and register for his ideas.

Solomos believed earnestly that the poet has to be a profound thinker as well as a skilful versifier. He found the technical perfection of Italian Neoclassicism wanting and turned to German aesthetic philosophy for direction. In his later poetry he was greatly influenced by Schiller's ideal of *das Erhabene*, the sublime. The aim of poetry, in Solomos's view, was to elevate men's souls, an artistic virtue he greatly admired in ancient poetry, especially the Homeric epics. Unlike his Neoclassical forerunners, however, Solomos did not dress up his poetry with Classical lore in a bid to make it seem dignified or grand; instead he made sparing use of the motifs of ancient epic, lyric, and tragic verse. He believed that the poets of ancient Greece had struck a perfect balance between form and content. Nevertheless, Solomos refused to subordinate his poetry to the forms of Classical models but sought rather to emulate the spirit in which they had been composed. His translation of book 18 of the *Iliad* was the first truly poetic rendition of the work into modern Greek and it spurred many of his disciples to do the same for other classics.

In his last years Solomos began to write poetry in Italian once more, but by then his contribution to Greek letters had been decisive. Nearly all subsequent Greek poetry owes something to Solomos. Kostis Palamas, who succeeded Solomos as Greece's national poet, paid tribute to the Zakynthian in his own poems and in many articles about Solomos's poetry. The free lyricism of Solomos's later works anticipated the lyrical experimentation of Seferis and Elytis, while the almost prosodic commitment to ideas can be seen in the work of Cavafy. Ironically, Solomos's most lasting contribution may lie in his revisions, aborted poems, and notes to himself. In these one sees the first great modern Greek poet struggling to harness the fleet rhythms of the vernacular to lofty themes which had been the exclusive preserve of classicizing Greek since late antiquity. "With Solomos," Zisimos Lorentzatos has written, "the problem of artistic expression enters our cultural life, as the problem of independence entered our national life."

EMMANUEL C. BOURBOUHAKIS

Biography

Born on Zakynthos in 1798, Solomos was educated in Italy from 1808 to 1818. Returning to Zakynthos in 1818 he wrote his first poems in Italian. Then turning to demotic Greek he wrote lyrics, elegies, odes, and satires. His most famous work is the *Hymn to Liberty* (1823), the first two stanzas of which later became Greece's national anthem. He died in 1857.

Writings

Neugriechisches Gespräch: Der Dialog des Dionysios Solomos, translated by Rudolf Fahrner, Munich: Bohm, 1943
Introduction, Prose et Poèmes, translated by Robert Levesque, Athens: Institut Français d'Athenes, 1945
Apanta [Complete Works], edited by Linos Polites, 2 vols, Athens, 1948–60 (vol. 1: *Poiemata* [Poems]; vol. 2: *Peza kai Italika* [Prose and Italian Works], and supplement (translations) to vol. 2; 2nd edition of vol. 1, 1961

In *The Penguin Book of Greek Verse*, edited by C.A. Trypanis, Harmondsworth: Penguin, 1971, pp.501–04

Further Reading

Canna, Giovanni, *Dionisio Solomos: uno studente dell'Università di Pavia negli anni 1815–1818*, Pavia: Successori Bizzoni, 1896

Kriaras, Emmanuel, *Dionysios Solomos: Ho vios, to ergo* [Dionysios Solomos: His Life and Work], Athens, 1969

Polites, Linos, *Gyro sto Solomo: Meletes kai Arthra, 1938–1958*, [Studies and Articles Concerning Solomos], Athens, 1958

Raizis, Byron M., *Dionysios Solomos*, New York: Twayne, 1972

Tomadakes, Nikolaos, *O Solomos kai Oi Archaioi* [Solomos and the Ancients], Athens, 1943

Solon *c.640–c.560* BC

Poet, statesman, and philosopher

Solon lived and worked in Athens in the late 7th/early 6th century BC. His poetry survives only in fragments. The biographical tradition is late and not completely reliable, but one may draw a general picture of Solon's life and activity. He was an aristocrat, and became active in Athenian politics probably at an early age.

Solon's entry on to the political stage appears to have occurred in the following way. Athens and its neighbour to the west, Megara, had been fighting for some time over the possession of the island of Salamis, which lies between the two cities in the Saronic gulf. When Solon was a young man, the island was in the possession of Megara and the Athenians had passed a law forbidding discussion of reopening the war for possession. If the sources can be believed, Solon rushed into the marketplace feigning madness and recited a long poem about the recovery of the island (frr. 1–3). The war was resumed and ultimately Athens regained possession. The story reveals something about the way people perceived Solon's character: fiercely Athenian, he was full of bravado, and very clever. He was a good enough poet and speaker to persuade his audience, and he made his appeal directly to the people rather than going through official channels. All these traits seem characteristic of Solon, even though the story is probably apocryphal.

Having acquired a reputation for wisdom, Solon was given the task of reconciling two opposing forces in Athenian politics: the tyrannical rulers, and the people who were on the verge of revolt. To accomplish this task, Solon composed a set of laws which effectively ushered in democratic ideals (frr. 4a–c). Among his reforms were the *seisachtheia*, or shaking off of debts, the introduction of a representative council of 400 Athenian citizens, the abolition of debt slavery, a grant of amnesty for all those who had left Athens on account of excessive debt, and other measures (see *Athenaion Politeia*, 5–12). These laws were apparently meant to replace the stern measures contained in the code of Draco, the earlier and harsher legislator of Athens. After putting the reforms into place, Solon was said to have left Athens for ten years.

Although Solon clearly opened a door to representative government for the people, the reforms were not entirely effective and ultimately Athens slipped back into a modified tyranny which it would not escape until the late 6th century BC.

In spite of this, Solon's name became linked with democracy and remains so to this day. The Attic orators of the 4th century BC (Demosthenes and others) commonly invoked Solon as the founder of democracy, and the mid-4th-century BC text referred to as the *Constitution of the Athenians* (*Athenaion Politeia*) attributes virtually all democratic reform to either Solon or Cleisthenes. Solon was a reform-minded conservative who tried to address the concerns of the people while at the same time maintaining a firm power base for the aristocracy.

So little of Solon's poetry has survived (about 300 lines out of a total output of well over 5000) that it is difficult to draw many firm conclusions about it. His poetry treats various themes, including politics (fr. 4), the dangers of excessive wealth (fr. 13), the notion that there are seven ages to a man's life (fr. 27), and even food (frr. 38–40). He is the first Athenian poet, indeed the first firmly established figure in Athenian history, although he did not write in the Athenian dialect. This poet of Archaic Athens wrote on a variety of topics central to the life of the individual and the polis. In doing so, he foreshadowed the flowering of the Classical period.

Many of the themes which Solon addressed became standard in later literature, particularly in Athenian tragedy. Specifically, fr. 13 contains, among other themes, the notions that one must guard against excess and that one must take care not to offend the gods by obtaining wealth unjustly lest they exact vengeance. This paradigm, excessive wealth (*koros*), leading to an act of overweening pride (*hybris*), which brings on justice (*dike*) and ultimately divine retribution (*ate*), is at the core of much Greek tragedy of the 5th century BC. Solon clearly saw Zeus as the driving force of the paradigm. He is not only the principal deity, but a guide to correct action. One can easily imagine that the early 5th-century BC tragedian Aeschylus had read Solon's poetry. In another poem (fr. 5) Solon spoke of the need to find the middle way, much as Aeschylus did in the final play of the Oresteia, *Eumenides*.

The wisdom for which Solon's poetry and political acumen made him famous is epitomized in his meeting with the Lydian king Croesus (Herodotus, 1. 29–33). After showing Solon his vast wealth, Croesus asked Solon who he believed was the happiest man. Solon replied that Tellus the Athenian was happiest because he had a good family and had died defending his country. Croesus asked who would be second, and Solon chose Cleobis and Biton. These two Argive heroes had yoked themselves to an oxcart and pulled their mother, a priestess, to a festival of Hera. On entering the temple of Hera, the mother prayed that her sons should receive the greatest gift the gods could give. She emerged to find the two lying on the temple steps, dead. Solon then told Croesus to count no man happy until he has passed the limit of his life, i.e. one cannot judge that a man's life has been happy until he has lived all of it. The story and its attendant proverb, often misinterpreted as though the Greeks thought death a good thing, demonstrate the insight for which Solon was famous.

Although Solon's poetry has received some scholarly attention, discussion of it generally focuses not on its technical innovation but on the thoughts that it contains. Through the ages Solon has been cited principally as a statesman, a wise legislator, and one of the seven sages. His most important legacy has been the ideals of democracy.

TIMOTHY F. WINTERS

See also Democracy

Biography
Born *c*.640 BC, Solon was an Athenian aristocrat who became active in politics. He was renowned for his wisdom and enacted a number of reforms to address the concerns of the people. He also wrote poetry of which little survives. He died *c*.560 BC.

Writings
In *Iambi et Elegi Graeci ante Alexandrum cantati*, vol. 2, edited by M.L. West, 2nd edition, Oxford: Clarendon Press, 1992

Further Reading
Adkins, A.W.H., *Poetic Craft in the Early Greek Elegists*, Chicago: University of Chicago Press, 1985

Anhalt, Emily Katz, *Solon the Singer: Politics and Poetics*, Lanham, Maryland: Rowman and Littlefield, 1993

Bowra, C.M., *Early Greek Elegists*, Cambridge, Massachusetts: Harvard University Press, and London: Oxford University Press, 1938

Easterling, P.E. and Bernard M.W. Knox (editors), *Cambridge History of Classical Literature*, vol. 1: *Greek Literature*, Cambridge: Cambridge University Press, 1985

Falkner, T.M., "The Politics and Poetics of Time in Solon's Ten Ages", *Classical Journal*, 86 (1990–91): pp. 1–15

Fraenkel, Hermann, *Early Greek Poetry and Philosophy: A History of Greek Epic, Lyric, and Prose to the Middle of the Fifth Century*, New York: Harcourt Brace, and Oxford: Blackwell, 1975

Freeman, Kathleen, *The Work and Life of Solon, with a Translation of His Poems*, London: Oxford University Press, 1926

Hignett, C., *A History of the Athenian Constitution to the End of the Fifth Century* BC, Oxford: Clarendon Press, 1952

Lattimore, R., "The First Elegy of Solon", *American Journal of Philology*, 68 (1947): pp. 161–79

Linforth, Ivan M., *Solon the Athenian*, Berkeley: University of California Press, 1919

Martina, A., *Solon: Testimonia Veterum*, Rome, 1968

Plutarch, *The Rise and Fall of Athens: Nine Greek Lives*, translated by Ian Scott-Kilvert, Harmondsworth and Baltimore: Penguin, 1960

Podlecki, A.J., "Three Greek Soldier Poets: Archilochus, Alcaeus, Solon", *Classical World*, 63 (1969): pp. 73–81

Rexine, John E., *Solon and His Political Theory: The Contemporary Significance of a Basic Contribution to Political Theory by One of the Seven Wise Men*, New York: William Frederick Press, 1958

Vlastos, G., "Solonian Justice", *Classical Philology*, 41 (1946): pp. 65–83

Woodhouse, W.J., *Solon the Liberator: A Study of the Agrarian Problems in Attika in the Seventh Century*, London: Oxford University Press, 1938

Song

The corpus of Hellenic song includes a broad range of repertories for amateurs and professionals that reflect the ubiquity of singing in Greek society from antiquity to the present day. This diversity reflects not only processes of stylistic development, but also the varied ways in which vocal music has served to punctuate nearly every aspect of public and private life. The study of repertories antedating the 19th century, however, is limited by the historical tendency of Greek singers to rely heavily on oral methods of transmission. Despite the existence of ancient Greek musical notation, for example, we possess only an unrepresentative handful of melodies from antiquity. One consequence of these losses is that songs originally viewed as a union of verse, melody, and, in the case of choral lyric, dance are today primarily viewed from a literary perspective. Yet even if the pitches for ancient songs are lost, their rhythm may be partially recovered from the study of their quantitative metres, elements of which have been shown to survive in modern Greek folk music.

The written history of Greek song begins with the *Iliad* and the *Odyssey*, two relics of oral traditions of sung epic which mention the performance of such forms of vocal music as paeans, laments, and wedding songs. While certain repertories continued to be transmitted entirely through oral means, the texts of others gradually became subject to literary transmission. The inclusion of singing competitions in the festivals sponsored by Greek cities – e.g. the funeral games held in Chalcis around 700, at which Hesiod won a prize for song – was evidently a major stimulant to the development of cultivated forms of song, as was cultural interchange between the Aegean and the mainland. An important link between the latter was Terpander (700–650 BC), who left his native Lesbos to embark on a career as a prize-winning poet and *kithara* (lyre) player that has earned him general recognition as the father of lyric poetry. Such cultural interchange, however, did not prevent the emergence of distinct regional schools of composition during the 7th century BC. Lesbos gave birth to the Aeolian lyric of Sappho and Alcaeus, both of whom wrote solo songs of modest scale intended for private or semi-private performance. On the mainland the remarkable mix of religious and state ceremonial with competition and mass entertainment featured at such festivals as the Carneia in Sparta and the Pythian games in Delphi promoted the growth of increasingly complex forms of solo and choral lyric, most of which were accompanied on either the *kithara* or the *aulos*. Particularly significant was the emergence in Corinth around the year 600 BC of the dithyramb, a choral dance to Dionysus with *aulos* accompaniment that later played a seminal role in the development of tragedy.

Over the course of the 6th century BC poet-musicians received increasing levels of state support, particularly from dictators seeking to heighten the prestige of their city states. Athens, for example, witnessed the enlargement of the Panathenaia and Dionysia festivals, followed later by the Pisistratids' sponsorship of such composers as Lasus, Simonides, and Alcaeus. The succeeding generations of 5th-century BC Athenians, which included Pindar and the great tragedians, brought song to its apogee as an integrated art form encompassing verse, music, and dance. Soon, however, the old categories regulating the form and content of compositions began to break down under the strain of constant innovation and ever-increasing technical virtuosity. Consequently, music and poetry drifted apart not only from the civic and religious contexts that had raised them to prominence, but also from each other, relegating the poets and musicians of later antiquity to separate professional fields.

Harsh criticism of the allegedly decadent state of song began during the 5th century BC with Plato and continued throughout the Hellenistic and Roman periods. This critique was eventually adopted by the Fathers of the Christian Church, who broadened it to include funeral laments and licentious wedding songs. In place of the music of pagan society, St Basil, St John Chrysostom, and other Church Fathers offered psalms, the singing of which was initially popularized by Egyptian desert monks. The rapid development in cathedrals and urban monastic communities of melodically interesting psalmody and hymnography laid the foundations for Byzantine chant and other regional traditions of Christian liturgical song.

With the exception of a few acclamations, notated sources for medieval Greek secular music are completely absent, leaving unknown the extent to which ancient song survived among either the common people or the Classically educated elite of Byzantium. Manuscripts and theoretical treatises of Byzantine chant, however, bear witness to the introduction of new organizational principles for the composition of vocal music. Reflecting the effects of both organic growth and external influence, these innovations included accentual metre – the general adoption of which was stimulated by changes in the pronunciation of the Greek language – and the system of eight modes (octoechos) attributed to St John of Damascus. The broader significance of these developments is shown by the presence of cognate modal and metrical structures in Greek folk songs. Indeed, despite the linguistic gulf between the patristic Greek of liturgical chant and the vernacular, Greek sacred and secular song have maintained strong musical and textual affinities to the present day.

The oldest surviving vernacular song texts are the *akritika*, a repertory describing the exploits of the Byzantine empire's border guards during the 9th to the 11th centuries, which are transmitted in 14th-century manuscripts. Four Athonite codices of liturgical music ranging in date from 1562 to the beginning of the 18th century contain the first songs preserved with their melodies, which are notated in Byzantine neumes. Probably transcribed by Cretan monks, these works include both folk and art songs. The fact that one of the latter – the single Greek song of MS Iviron 1189, held on Mount Athos – was recorded alongside two Persian compositions is indicative of the extensive participation of Greeks in the musical cultures of their rulers and neighbours during the centuries of their domination by Ottomans and Italians. One result of this involvement, which extended into the early decades of the 20th century, was the creation of such hybrid repertories of cultivated Greek song as the *kantades* (serenades for male chorus) of the Ionian islands and the *amanedes* (songs with an "aman" refrain) of Constantinople and Smyrna.

Since the 19th century the systematic study of the received tradition of Hellenic folk song as practised from Corsica to Asia Minor has been taken up by scholars employing diverse methodologies. Philologists, musicologists, and ethnographers have discerned in the metres, subjects, and melodies of Greek folk songs a degree of continuity with antiquity and Byzantium, as well as innovation and close relationships with other cultures. Some have grouped the repertories by textual content and social function into such broad categories as life-cycle songs (lullabies, wedding songs, laments, etc.), narrative ballads (*paraloges*), historical songs (e.g. *klephtika* praising the bands of outlaws who resisted Turkish authority), songs for the seasons and Christian feasts of the year (*kalanda*), and dances. Meanwhile, Chianis and others studying the regional traditions of song from a more strictly formal perspective have observed certain shared characteristics differentiating, for example, the repertories of the islands and Asia Minor from those of the Greek mainland. In particular, Baud-Bovy has noted that these families differ according to (a) poetic metre and strophic form; (b) the presence or absence of rhyme, the former being more typical of island songs; (c) their preference for improvised poetry (as in the *mantinades* – improvised couplets – of Crete) or melodic ornamentation; (d) their dance rhythms; and (e) the composition of their instrumental ensembles. Also of signal importance are the melodic and scalar (diatonic, pentatonic, and chromatic) patterns employed in each area and their degree of kinship to the modes (*echoi*) of Byzantine chant or the *maqams* of Ottoman and Arabo-Persian music.

Although the foundation of the modern state of Greece and the subsequent administrative reforms of the Ottoman empire provided many of the necessary preconditions for the recording and preservation of Greek folk songs, they also fostered the growth of the popular repertories that have progressively replaced them. Disseminated at first through public performances and printed musical scores in western and Byzantine notation, these urban songs became ubiquitous in the 20th century through gramophone records and electronic broadcasting. The prosperous Phanariots of Constantinople and the residents of the Ionian islands preceded the cities of the new Greek kingdom in their development of distinct popular repertories. Eventually the influence of Ionian *kantades* and performances of Italian music by visiting opera troupes contributed to the emergence of a highly westernized form of Athenian song in the last decades of the 19th century. Among the Greek bourgeoisie, popular songs composed in western styles remained in the ascendant until the onset of World War II. Much of this music was intended for the stage, including revues (*epitheoreseis*) dominated by Greek adaptations of foreign arias and popular songs. The arias of Greek operas enjoyed a period of popularity during the early years of the 20th century, before they were overshadowed by the songs featured in the phenomenally successful operettas of such composers as Nikos Hatziapostolou (1879–1941) and Theophrastos I. Sakellarides (1833–1950). Meanwhile, non-dramatic songs employing varying mixes of native and western musical elements continued to be composed, notable among which were the songs of Attik (pseudonym of Kleon Triantaphyllou, 1895–1944), Michalis Souyioul (1906–58), and Kostas Yiannides (pseudonym of Yannis Konstantinides, 1903–84).

The rise of westernized popular song in late 19th-century Athens was complemented by the emergence of orientalizing Greek repertories in the cities of the Ottoman empire. Exported to the west through the harmonizations of Bourgault-Ducoudray and Ravel, these songs were performed for middle-class Greeks along with Turkish and western popular music in cafés that often featured female vocalists and dancers, many of whom were Jews or Gypsies. After musicians from Smyrna founded the first so-called *Café aman* in Athens in 1873, similar establishments began to appear in Greek communities around the world, provoking denunciations from those who rejected the oriental style on aesthetic and patriotic grounds. The forced migration of Asia Minor's Greek population to the Hellenic kingdom in 1922 brought the essentially bourgeois music of the *Café aman* into close contact with a repertory viewed with even greater distaste by westernized Greeks, namely the *rebetika* of the urban underclass. Frequently compared to the American blues, these songs of hardship and alienation were originally created in prisons and the hashish dens (*tekedes*) of Piraeus. Typically accompanied on such fretted stringed instruments as the bouzouki and the baglamas, *rebetika* featured an evolving mix of modes (*dromoi*) related to Turkish *maqams*, western tertian harmony, and dance rhythms (e.g. the *zeimbekiko* in 9/4 and the *tsifteteli* in 4/4) shared with the songs of the *Café aman*. A more general convergence with the oriental style of the refugees during the 1930s gradually brought *rebetika* greater social respectability while also subjecting their future development to commercial pressures. Vassilis Tsitsanis (1915–84) then led a new generation of musicians who oversaw the transformation of *rebetika* during the 1950s and early 1960s into *laika* (popular song), a hybrid style characterized by technical virtuosity, generally lighter texts, and eclectic borrowing from foreign popular musics, including those of Latin America and India.

Western-oriented Athenian popular song also underwent major changes after World War II. Although ephemeral adaptations of the latest American hits were never lacking, during the 1950s there emerged the distinctly Greek phenomenon of "popular art-song" as a group of composers, many of them classically trained, began to set texts of often outstanding literary merit in a finely crafted popular musical idiom. Pioneered by Manos Hadjidakis in songs and works for the stage transcending the boundaries that existed in Greece between "high" and "low" culture, the style was firmly established by Mikis Theodorakis with a setting of selections from the *Epitaphios* of the poet Yiannis Ritsos in 1958. Over the next two decades Theodorakis, who was grounded ideologically in socialist realism and musically in Byzantine and folk music, and Hadjidakis, who eschewed political involvement, were joined in their efforts to expand the artistic horizons of Greek popular song by, among others, Stavros Xarhakos, Yannis Markopoulos, Christodoulos Halaris, and Thanos Mikroutsikos. In addition to individual songs, these composers produced ambitious song cycles and cantatas setting poetry by Kornaros, Elytis, Kampanellis, Gatsos, Neruda, and Seferis for ensembles often incorporating the bouzouki and other Greek instruments. A refreshing alternative to the increasing historical and political self-consciousness of "popular art-song" was provided by Dionysios Savvopoulos in his relatively unpretentious songs of social critique.

The lifting of censorship in Greece that followed the collapse of the colonels' dictatorship in 1974 temporarily strengthened the links between singing and left-wing politics as the songs of communist guerrillas from the 1940s, the works of Theodorakis, and other suppressed repertories were revived. Nevertheless, within a few years it became apparent that neither leftist ideology nor the return to folk music advocated by Markopoulos could succeed in rejuvenating "popular art song". As Theodorakis, Hadjidakis, and Mikroutsikos turned to focus on the composition of art music, the leadership of Greek popular music passed to Giorgos Dalaras and other celebrity performers. Radical stylistic diversification ensued over the last two decades of the 20th century as foreign influence competed with renewed interest in traditional forms, giving rise to a fragmented culture of song in which orientalism and Europop coexisted with authenticist revivals of folk music and *rebetika*.

ALEXANDER LINGAS

See also Dance, Dithyramb, Opera, Poetry (Lyric), Tragedy

Further Reading

Alevizos, Susan and Ted Alevizos, *Folk Songs of Greece*, New York: Oak, 1968

Barker, Andrew (editor), *Greek Musical Writings*, 2 vols, Cambridge and New York: Cambridge University Press, 1984–89

Baud-Bovy, Samuel, *Essai sur la chanson populaire grecque*, Nauplia: Fondation Ethnographique du Péloponnèse, 1983, 2nd edition, 1994

Bourgault-Ducoudray, L.A., *Trente mélodies populaires de Grèce et d'Orient*, 4th edition, Paris: Lemoine, 1876, reprinted Katerini, 1993

Conomos, Dimitri E., "The Iviron Folk-songs: A Re-examination" in *Studies in Eastern Chant*, vol. 4, edited by Miloš Velimirović, Crestwood, New York: St Vladimir's Seminary Press, 1979

Feldman, Walter, *Music of the Ottoman Court: Makam, Composition and the Early Ottoman Instrumental Repertoire*, Berlin: Verlag für Wissenschaft und Bildung, 1996

Frye, Ellen (editor), *The Marble Threshing Floor: A Collection of Greek Folk Songs*, Austin: University of Texas Press, 1973

Gauntlett, Stathis, *Rebetika Carmina Greciae Recentioris: A Contribution to the Definition of the Term Rebetiko Tragoudi through a Detailed Analysis of its Verses and of the Evolution of its Performance*, Athens: Denise Harvey, 1985

Georgiades, Thrasybulos, *Greek Music, Verse and Dance*, translated by Erwin Benedict and Marie Louise Martinez, New York: Merlin, 1956, reprinted New York: Da Capo, 1973

Lampelet, Georgios, *I Helliniki Dimodis Mousiki: 60 Tragoudia kai Choroi* [Greek Popular Music: 60 Songs and Dances], [n.p.], 1933, reprinted Katerini, 1995

McKinnon, James, *Music in Early Christian Literature*, Cambridge and New York: Cambridge University Press, 1987

McKinnon, James (editor), *Antiquity and the Middle Ages: From Ancient Greece to the 15th Century*, London: Macmillan, 1990; Englewood Cliffs, New Jersey: Prentice Hall, 1991

McKinnon, James, *The Temple, the Church Fathers, and Early Western Chant*, Aldershot, Hampshire: Ashgate, 1998

Mazarake, Despoina B., *Mousiki Ermeneia Demotikon Tragoudion apo Agioreitika Cheirographa* [The Musical Interpretation of Folk Songs from Athonite Manuscripts], 2nd edition, Athens, 1992

Mitsakis, Kariofilis, *Neoelliniki Mousiki kai poiisi: Anthologia / Modern Greek Music and Poetry: An Anthology*, Athens: Grigoris, 1979

Mylonas, Kostas, *Istoria tou Ellinikou Tragoudiou* [History of Greek Song], vols. 2–3, Athens, 1985–92

Pennanen, Risto Pekka, *Westernisation and Modernisation in Greek Popular Music*, Tampere: University of Tampere Press, 1999

Quasten, Johannes, *Music and Worship in Pagan and Christian Antiquity*, translated by Boniface Ramsey, Washington, D.C.: National Association of Pastoral Musicians, 1983

Touliatos, Diane, "The Traditional Role of Greek Women in Music from Antiquity to the End of the Byzantine Empire" in *Rediscovering the Muses: Women's Musical Traditions*, edited by Kimberly Marshall, Boston: Northeastern University Press, 1993

Trypanis, Constantine A. (editor), *The Penguin Book of Greek Verse*, Harmondsworth: Penguin, 1971, reprinted 1979

Tsiamoulis, Christos and Pavlos Evrenidis, *Romioi Synthetes tis Polis, 170s–200s ai.* [Greek Composers of Constantinople, 17th–20th Centuries], Athens, 1998

Watts, Niki, *The Greek Folk Songs*, Bristol: Bristol Classical Press, and New Rochelle, New York: Caratzas, 1988

West, M.L., *Ancient Greek Music*, Oxford: Clarendon Press, and New York, Oxford University Press, 1992

Winnington-Ingram, R.P. *et al*, Greece entry in *The New Grove Dictionary of Music and Musicians*, edited by Stanley Sadie, London: Macmillan, and Washington, D.C.: Grove, 1980, vol.7, pp. 659–82

Sophists

"Sophist" is a general name given to a variety of (mainly rhetorical) intellectuals and virtuosos who appeared in Athens in the mid- to late 5th century BC. It was a term of opprobrium that, while recognizing that these men were all competent at what they did, carried with it many of the connotations of the American phrase "wise guy" when used by such contemporaries as Aristophanes and Plato. Most Sophists that are known about were not Athenians, but flocked there because there was a market for what they had to teach, public speaking skills that would be effective in political life and in litigation. As there is very little extant that might enlighten modern scholars, there have been many efforts to reconstruct their teachings, particularly since G.W.F. Hegel's *Lectures*. Fragments of and *testimonia* relating to the Sophists were included in Hermann Diels's *Die Fragmente der Vorsokratiker* (1896, with many subsequent editions), which remains the standard reference in spite of long-recognized problems with the texts he published.

Among the most famous are Protagoras of Abdera (*c*.490–420 BC?), Gorgias of Leontini (483–*c*.400 BC), Prodicus of Cos (*c*.470–399 BC), and Hippias of Elis (b. 433 BC?). Protagoras and Gorgias were both active in official capacities, the former as the author of the laws governing the Athenian colony at Thurii (in 443 BC) and the latter as ambassador to Athens in 427 BC. Gorgias is perhaps the best known, since some works attributed to him have survived in their entirety, e.g. the famous *Encomium to Helen*. Only a few lines of alleged quotations of Protagoras are extant. Prodicus and Hippias were polymaths, with interests extending from natural science and mathematics to rhetoric and semantics. Others often named as "Sophists" include Thrasymachus, Antiphon of Rhamnos, and the Athenian aristocrat Critias, a prominent leader of the antidemocratic faction active in Athens in the last decade of the 5th century.

In later antiquity, particularly in the setting of the New Academy, the Sophists were admired, along with Isocrates, for their eloquence and their efforts to systematize the teaching of rhetoric. Since then, the Sophists have been consistently placed on the margins of the philosophical establishment. Their apparent challenges to traditional values and their divergences from intellectual orthodoxy attracted the notice of later philosophers similarly situated; and so their champions tend to be the dissenters: Denis Diderot and Friedrich Nietzsche, for instance. In recent years there has been a resurgence of interest in their ideas, one doomed, perhaps, by the sparse record left to us and by the variety of ideas the Sophists expounded.

THOMAS M. CONLEY

See also Rhetoric, Second Sophistic

Summary

A term of abuse, the word "sophist" was applied to an intellectual circle that appeared in Athens in the 5th century BC. Most were not native Athenians. They set themselves up as teachers of rhetoric. In later antiquity they were admired for their eloquence. The term was revived by the movement known as the Second Sophistic.

Further Reading

Classen, Carl Joachim, "Aristotle's Picture of the Sophists" in *The Sophists and Their Legacy*, edited by G.B. Kerferd, Wiesbaden: Steiner, 1981

Diels, Hermann and Walther von Kranz, *Die Fragmente der Vorsokratiker*, 6th edition, 3 vols, Berlin: Weidmann, 1951–52

Hegel, G.W.F., *Lectures on the History of Philosophy*, translated by E. Haldane, London: Routledge, 1963

Kerferd, G.B., *The Sophistic Movement*, Cambridge and New York: Cambridge University Press, 1981

Sprague, Rosamond Kent (editor), *The Older Sophists*, Columbia: University of South Carolina Press, 1972

Sophocles *c*.496–406 BC

Tragedian

Sophocles was born at Colonus near Athens in about 496 BC and died in 406 BC. Living through the glorious Persian Wars, and the increasingly inglorious Peloponnesian War, he was spared the sight of Athens' final defeat at the hands of Sparta, when it had to dismantle its walls in 404 BC.

He was a model citizen. He acted as a treasurer in the league Athens organized against Persia. He studied dance and was said to have danced round the trophy after the battle of Salamis. He also served as a general dealing with the Samian revolt in 441. After the Sicilian defeat he was one of the *probouloi* (Committee of Ten) elected to deal with the disaster.

Like Aeschylus, Sophocles acted in his own plays. In extreme old age he is said to have been sued by a son, who claimed he was no longer capable of managing his own affairs. He read lines from the recently written *Oedipus at Colonus*, and was acquitted. After his death Sophocles became a sacred hero like Oedipus, and was worshipped as *Dexion*, roughly translatable as "he who receives", because of his association with the cult of Asclepius, which he had helped to introduce into Athens after the plague (430–426 BC).

In Aeschylus, god can confront god and major questions are raised about conflicting rights. Sophocles shows man confronting god and a world he claims can never be knowable. As one fragment says (871 Radt), the fate given to us by god is as changeable as the moon; "it never can maintain one shape for two nights, ... just when it is at its fullest and most beautiful, it flows away and ebbs to nothing." All that can be known is something transient, like the moon in one of its phases. In spite of this, man struggles nobly. Truth, loyalty, and commitment to one's chosen path, all characterize the Sophoclean hero

Sophocles: scene from a modern production of *Antigone*, with Amy Greenfield in the title role

and condemn him or her to isolation. But often in his isolation he redeems society. For the Sophoclean hero, the love of the impossible proves to be a redemptive love.

Sophocles is said never to have taken third place when he competed. He wrote about 123 plays, more than the other two playwrights, and is said to have won 24 times (18 at the City Dionysia). Aristotle tells us he added one actor to the two that existed; this created additional possibilities for interchange and conflict. Aristotle tells us he increased the chorus from 12 to 15. He also used scene painting to enhance the visual background. He abandoned the practice of the connected trilogy, allowing him to highlight a major character, in contrast to Aeschylus' practice which allowed the development of a concept such as the workings of divine justice over several generations.

Of the plays that survive, only the *Philoctetes* and the *Oedipus at Colonus* can be dated with certainty, and the *Antigone* approximately, with reference to the Samian war. The following chronology is tentatively suggested: *Antigone* 443 or 441 BC; *Ajax* c.442 BC; *Trachiniae* c.432 BC; *Oedipus*

Tyrannus c.427 BC; *Electra* c.413 BC; *Philoctetes* 409 BC; *Oedipus at Colonus* 401 BC (posthumous). There are many fragments, including a large part of the satyr play, the *Ichneutae*.

Antigone, *Oedipus Tyrannus*, and *Oedipus at Colonus* are often called "the Theban Cycle", but do not make up a trilogy, performed on one day. Instead they span Sophocles' life, and seem to reflect his own developing values. The *Antigone* shows a type of idealism which implies a belief in higher values to the point of sacrificing one's life to achieve them; Antigone opposes civic authority. G.W.F. Hegel said the *Antigone* was "one of the most sublime and in every respect the most consummate work of art human effort ever produced". The *Oedipus Tyrannus* seems to justify the struggle itself, as a type of self-affirmation, rather than the pursuit of an ideal. The last play shows sparks of the earlier struggle, but there is a final capitulation to death, prized as an end to suffering (*Oedipus at Colonus*, 1777–79).

Aristotle sees Sophocles as the greatest of the ancient playwrights and uses his *Oedipus Tyrannus* as a model of the way a play should be written. Sophocles is a master of character, and of the language which creates character. He steers a path between the grandeur of Aeschylus and the witty colloquialisms of Euripides. He is also skilled at plots, and his *Oedipus Tyrannus* has been called the greatest detective story ever written. His lyrics are superb, and his characters often sing at dramatically important moments. He varies his rhythms and uses words percussively. Sophocles is also master of symbols and imagery, such as the use of blindness in *Oedipus Tyrannus*: when Oedipus can see he is blind, and when he is blind he can see. The bare island of Lemnos is also a wonderful symbol for the craggy hero Philoctetes. Sophocles has brilliant descriptions of nature, such as the ode to fair Colonus, a land of fine horses where the nightingale sings her melodious songs in the wine-dark ivy and sacred foliage (*Oedipus at Colonus*, 668–719).

The City Dionysia in 386 BC instituted a revival of the great plays of the 5th century. Around 330 BC the Athenian politician Lycurgus prescribed that copies of the texts of the plays should be deposited in the official archives, and that future performances should conform to these texts. The purpose was to safeguard the plays from adaptation and interpolation by actors and producers, of a kind to which they had already become vulnerable. These copies were lent to the Egyptian king Ptolemy I Euergetes, and will have passed into the library at Alexandria, to form the basis of the critical edition made by the librarian Aristophanes of Byzantium (*c*.257–180 BC). Aristophanes divided the lyrics (previously written as continuous prose) into metrical cola. He also added brief introductory comments, probably making use of Aristotle's lost *Didaskaliai* (production records). Part of these comments survive in the *hypothesis* (plot summaries) which were prefixed to the plays by later scholars in the Roman period. The composition of commentaries (*scholia*) on the plays was began in the Hellenistic period (by scholars such as Aristarchus of Samothrace, ?217–145 BC, and Didymus, ?80–10 BC). Further scholia were added in the Byzantine period.

The Theban plays were also popular in Rome: Accius (170–?86 BC) wrote a *Thebais* and *Antigona* (besides *Philocteta*) and Seneca (?AD 1–65) a particularly bloody *Oedipus Tyrannus*. The selection of the seven plays that survive was probably made in the 2nd or 3rd century AD and scholia were included for school use. After parchment replaced papyrus (around the 4th century AD), the unselected plays gradually passed out of use. After the Athenian Academy was closed in 529, the Classical texts disappeared from sight for several centuries and did not re-emerge until the revival of learning in the middle Byzantine period, when they were copied from the uncial into the new cursive script. Among the scholars who wrote commentaries and handled the texts of the plays the most important are Thomas Magister (late 13th century), Manuel Moschopulus (*fl.*1300), and Demetrios Triklinios (early 14th century). Triklinios brought a new metrical awareness to the amendment of the text, in particular the lyrics. Sophocles' *Oedipus Tyrannus* was one of the Byzantine triad along with *Electra* and *Ajax*. The oldest manuscript of Sophocles' plays is L (in the Laurentian library in Florence), written in the 10th century, and there are many others from the 12th to the 15th centuries. The first printed edition was published by Aldus Manutius in Venice in 1502.

There was a famous revival of *Oedipus Tyrannus* in 1585 in Palladio's Teatro Olimpico at Vicenza. The music for the odes was by Andrea Gabrieli. There were many European revivals and reworkings for the next 400 years. Notable ones were by Pierre Corneille, Voltaire, John Dryden, Heinrich von Kleist, Friedrich von Schiller, Hugo von Hofmannsthal, André Gide, Jean Cocteau, and others, to say nothing of how Sigmund Freud used both Oedipus and Electra to represent universal drives. *Antigone* is often used to express a country's political unrest.

Constant revivals are given in Greece. *Ajax* has been performed since 1868, with notable productions in 1961 (directed by Takis Mouzenidis, with music by Mikis Theodorakis) and 1983 (directed by Nikos Charalambous); *Trachiniae* in 1960, 1970 (directed by Alexis Solomos), and 1984 (Charalambous). *Antigone* has always been popular and performances date from 1863, with an outstanding one in 1965 (directed by G. Sevastikoglou, with Anna Synodiou as Antigone), 1990 (M. Volanikis, with music by Mikis Theodorakis), and 1994 (Theodoros Terzopoulos). *Oedipus Tyrannus* was performed in Greece from 1878, with excellent productions in 1951 (with Alexis Minotis directing and playing Oedipus), 1958 (also at the Théâtre des Nations with Alexis Minotis and Katina Paxinou as Jocasta), 1969 (directed by Karolos Koun), 1978 (directed by Robert Mitchell, costumes and masks by Dionisios Photopoulos), and 1984 (Koun, sets and costumes by Photopoulos).

Electra is considered a great vehicle for acting and has been done in Greece since 1899, with exceptional performances in 1959 (directed by Dimitris Rondiris, with Aspasia Papathanasiou as Electra), 1960 (with Katina Paxinou as Electra), 1963 at Delphi (Rondiris / Papathanasiou), 1978 (Rondiris, music by D. Metropoulos), 1980, and 1984 (Koun / Photopoulos). *Philoctetes* has been done since 1818, and notably in 1967 (with Alexis Minotis directing and playing Philoctetes), 1988 (two, one with Christos Tsakas directing and starring with sets by Yannis Tsarouchis, the other with Giorgos Lazanis directing and starring with sets and costumes by Photopoulos). *Oedipus at Colonus* has been done since 1907, with an excellent performance in 1975 (dir. Alexis Minotis, also starring) and 1986 (dir. Alexis Minotis, who starred, with sets by Yannis Tsarouchis and costumes by Dion Photopoulos).

There have been several films based on *Electra*, namely Ted Zarpas's in 1962, and *Electre* by Jean-Louis Ughetto in 1972, and a revolutionary *Elektreia* by Miklós Jancsó in 1975. There was also an *Oedipus Rex* by Tyrone Guthrie in 1957 with a screenplay adapted from W.B. Yeats, which emphasized the monumental in its use of masks, a version by Philip Saville in 1968 (*Oedipus the King*) which was more naturalistic in its approach, and an adaptation by Pier Paolo Pasolini (*Edipo Re*) in 1967. George Tzavellas made a politically charged film on *Antigone* starring Irene Papas in 1961, and Liliana Cavani's *I Cannibali* (1970) was also based on this play. Thodoros Angelopoulos's *The Travelling Players* wove its political theme around the Electra legend.

MARIANNE MCDONALD

See also Tragedy

Biography

Born at Colonus near Athens *c*.496 BC, Sophocles played his part in public life. He was a treasurer of the Delian League, a *strategos* (general) at the time of the Samian revolt, and a *proboulos* (member of the Committee of Ten) after the failure of the Sicilian expedition. He wrote more than 120 plays and won at least 20 victories, the first in 468 BC. He died in 406 BC. After his death he was revered as a hero.

Writings (in translation)

The Plays and Fragments, edited and translated by R.C. Jebb, 7 vols, Cambridge: Cambridge University Press, 1883–1900; reprinted Amsterdam: Servio, 1963, St Clair Shores, Michigan: Scholarly Press, 1972

The Fragments, edited by R.C. Jebb and A.C. Pearson, 3 vols, Cambridge: Cambridge University Press, 1917; reprinted Amsterdam: Hakkert, 1963

Oedipus the King, translated by Bernard M.W. Knox, New York: Washington Square Press, 1957

The Complete Greek Tragedies (Centennial Edition), edited by David Grene and Richmond Lattimore, vol. 2: *Sophocles*, Chicago: University of Chicago Press, 1992

Sophocles, translated by Hugh Lloyd-Jones, 3 vols, Cambridge, Massachusetts: Harvard University Press, 1994–96 (Loeb edition)

Texts and Commentaries

Davies, Malcolm (editor), *Trachiniae*, Oxford: Clarendon Press, 1991

Dawe, R.D. (editor), *Oedipus Rex,* New York and Cambridge: Cambridge University Press, 1982

Dawe, R.D. (editor), *Tragodiae*, 2nd edition, 2 vols, Stuttgart: Teubner, 1984

Diggle, James (editor), *Tragicorum Graecorum Fragmenta Selecta*, Oxford: Clarendon Press, 1998

Kamerbeek, J.C. (editor), *Philoctetes*, Leiden: Brill, 1980

Kells, J.H. (editor), *Electra*, London: Cambridge University Press, 1973

Lloyd-Jones, Hugh and N.G. Wilson (editors), *Fabulae*, Oxford: Clarendon Press, and New York: Oxford University Press, 1990; reprinted with corrections, Clarendon Press, 1992

Radt, Stefan (editor), *Tragicorum Graecorum Fragmenta*, vol. 4: *Sophocles*, Göttingen: Vandenhoeck & Ruprecht, 1977

Webster, T.B.L. (editor), *Philoctetes*, Cambridge: Cambridge University Press, 1970

Further Reading

Albini, Umberto, *Viaggio nel teatro classico*, Florence: Monnier, 1987

Albini, Umberto, *Nel nome di Dioniso: Vita teatrale nell'Atene classica*, Milan: Garzanti, 1991

Blundell, Mary Whitlock, *Helping Friends and Harming Enemies: A Study in Sophocles and Greek Ethics*, Cambridge and New York: Cambridge University Press, 1989

Burton, R.W.B., *The Chorus in Sophocles' Tragedies*, Oxford: Clarendon Press, 1980

Easterling, P.E. (editor), *The Cambridge Companion to Greek Tragedy*, Cambridge: Cambridge University Press, 1997

Elledt, Friedrich and H.F. Genthe (editors), *Lexicon Sophocleum*, Hildesheim: Olms, 1965

Flashar, Hellmut, *Inszenierung der Antike: Das griechische Drama auf der Bühne der Neuzeit*, Munich: Beck, 1991

Flashar, Hellmut (editor), *Tragödie: Idee und Transformation*, Stuttgart: Teubner, 1997

Hegel, G.W.F., *Hegel on Tragedy*, translated by Anne and Henry Paolucci, Garden City, New York: Anchor, 1962, reprinted New York: Harper and Row, 1975

Knox, Bernard M.W., *The Heroic Temper: Studies in Sophoclean Tragedy*, Berkeley: University of California Press, 1964; reprinted 1983

Knox, Bernard M.W., *Word and Action: Essays on Ancient Theater*, Baltimore: Johns Hopkins University Press, 1979

Long, A.A., *Language and Thought in Sophocles: A Study of Abstract Nouns and Poetic Technique*, London: Athlone Press, 1968

McDonald, Marianne, *Ancient Sun, Modern Light: Greek Drama on the Modern Stage*, New York: Columbia University Press, 1992

MacKinnon, Kenneth, *Greek Tragedy into Film*, London: Croom Helm, and Rutherford, New Jersey: Fairleigh Dickinson University Press, 1986

Moorhouse, A.C., *The Syntax of Sophocles*, Leiden: Brill, 1982

Pfeiffer, Rudolf, *History of Classical Scholarship*, 2 vols., Oxford: Clarendon Press, 1968–76

Pucci, Pietro, *Oedipus and the Fabrication of the Father: Oedipus Tyrannus in Modern Criticism and Philosophy*, Baltimore: Johns Hopkins University Press, 1992

Reinhardt, Karl, *Sophocles*, translated by Hazel Harvey and David Harvey, introduction by Hugh Lloyd-Jones, New York: Barnes and Noble, and Oxford: Blackwell, 1979

Reynolds, L.D. and N.G. Wilson, *Scribes and Scholars: A Guide to the Transmission of Greek and Latin Literature*, 3rd edition, Oxford: Clarendon Press, and New York: Oxford University Press, 1991

Rosenmeyer, Thomas G., *The Masks of Tragedy: Essays on Six Greek Dramas*, Austin: University of Texas Press, 1963; reprinted New York: Gordian Press, 1971

Segal, Charles, *Tragedy and Civilization: An Interpretation of Sophocles*, Cambridge, Massachusetts: Harvard University Press, 1981

Segal, Charles, *Oedipus Tyrannus: Tragic Heroism and the Limits of Knowledge*, New York: Twayne, 1993

Segal, Charles, *Sophocles' Tragic World: Divinity, Nature and Society*, Cambridge, Massachusetts: Harvard University Press, 1995

Walton, J. Michael, *Living Greek Theatre: A Handbook of Classical Performance and Modern Production*, New York: Greenwood, 1987

Whitman, Cedric Hubbell, *Sophocles: A Study of Heroic Humanism*, Cambridge, Massachusetts: Harvard University Press, 1951

Winnington-Ingram, R.P., *Sophocles: An Interpretation*, Cambridge and New York: Cambridge University Press, 1980

Souli

Region of northwest Greece

Souli is the name of a region comprising a group of inland Epirot villages, located between Ioannina and Parga (on the Adriatic coast). It has stood alongside such places as Mani in the Peloponnese and Sfakia in Crete as a territory symbolic of bravery, freedom, and, particularly, resistance against foreign rule. The name "Souli", while technically that of the principal village of the region, is used more generally for the territory encompassed by the group of villages.

Like Mani and Sfakia, Souli is situated in rugged terrain, which provides a natural barrier from outside invaders. In the Cassiopian mountain range, the villages of Souli perch on mountain crags and beside the gorge formed by the Glykys river. Surrounded by rocky peaks, ravines, and precipitous drops, Souli's remote location has historically allowed for a large degree of independence and autonomy for its inhabitants. Vast panoramas from many strategic locations make it possible to spot anyone approaching from afar, while the distinctive ethnic background of the Souliots has provided a cultural isolation that parallels their geographic seclusion.

The origins of the Souliots are debated. Within the Souliot population, one tradition maintains that the Souliots are Orthodox Christians of Albanian ethnic descent who fled to their remote, rocky district to avoid Turkish domination following the death of Skanderbeg (Iskander Bey) in 1468. Others claim that the territory was founded in the early 17th century by shepherds looking for both unclaimed pasturage for their animals and relief from Ottoman rule.

By all accounts it seems clear that by the mid-17th century the territory was made up of four core villages, known as the *tetrahorion*: Kako Souli, Avarikos, Samoniva, and Kiafa. By 1700 seven more villages in the region had been founded; they comprised the *heptachorion*, and were situated further down the mountain and thus served as defensive outposts for the *tetrachorion*. In times of war the inhabitants of the lower villages sent their families up to the four villages above, and then defensively staked out the entrance to the narrow ravines that gave access to Souli. The 11 villages together comprised a "warrior confederacy", which came at the peak of its powers to control more than 60 villages on the plains below.

The villages of Souli thus managed to exist as a functionally independent island surrounded by a vast sea of Ottoman-held territory. Their primary, if not sole, territorial allegiance was to Souli itself, and they seem to have had little more loyalty or sympathy towards the Greek Orthodox peoples under Ottoman rule than they had to the Ottoman Turks themselves. Their inaccessibility allowed them to remain clear of the administrative, fiscal, and cultural reach of Ottoman rule. Their legal system was tribal, and all disputes were adjudicated by tribal headmen on the basis of traditional precedent.

For close to two centuries the Souliots remained largely untouched by any outside ruling influence. In 1790, however, Ali Pasha of Ioannina began a series of campaigns against them, with the intention of bringing them and their territories fully under his control. His initial attempt, in the spring of that year, was a disaster, and the following year he recruited the assistance of the neighbouring pasha of Berat, Ibrahim, to whose daughter his second son Veli was married. In July of 1792 Ali sent a message to two Souliot leaders, George Botsaris and Kitsos Tzavellas, ostensibly to gain their favour, but in reality to lure them into a trap. In the ensuing battle Ali managed to take Tzavellas's son hostage, but suffered great losses when he again attacked Souli.

Not until more than ten years later was Ali finally able to subdue the Souliots, and even then he did so only because of the betrayal of the Souliots by Botsaris, and not before losing many men over the course of a long-drawn-out battle with Souli, during which its residents were virtually starved by a blockade imposed on them by Ali's troops. In the course of the final rounds of battle between Ali's troops and the Souliots, the Souliot women inscribed themselves in folk memory through several acts of tremendous bravery and martyrdom. In the most famous instance, 50 women, who had been cut off from their men, and were certain to be captured by Ali's forces, threw their children off the edge of a cliff, then danced in turn over the precipice after them. Another group of women drowned themselves, along with their babies, in the White river on the way to seeking asylum in Parga, while a third group of women blew themselves up. All preferred death to falling into the hands of Ali Pasha, and personified Greek folklore's depiction of the Souliots as a fiercely independent people who preferred death to subjugation to any external power.

K.E. FLEMING

Summary

A group of villages in Epirus, Souli achieved a degree of independence during the Tourkokratia. Ali Pasha of Ioannina set out to subdue them in 1790 but it took him more than ten years to do so. The women of Souli are commemorated in folklore and song for their many acts of bravery and martyrdom.

Further Reading

Davenport, R.A., *The Life of Ali Pasha of Tepeleni, Vizier of Epirus, Surnamed Aslan, or the Lion*, London: Tegg, 1837

Fleming, K.E., *The Muslim Bonaparte: Diplomacy and Orientalism in Ali Pasha's Greece*, Princeton, New Jersey: Princeton University Press, 1999

Perraivo, Christophorou, *Istoria tou Souliou kai Pargas* [History of Souli and Parga], Athens, 1857

South Africa

The 80,000-strong Greek community in South Africa today has a long history. According to existing South African archival records, there were at least 11 known Greeks in the country in 1860 and more than 30 in the early 1800s. At the turn of the 20th century Cape Town attracted growing numbers of Greeks, many of them sailors as well as tobacconists, small entrepreneurs, and adventurers. By 1905 there were over 1500 Greeks throughout South Africa. Greeks fought on both sides during the Anglo-Boer War (1899–1902). A large number of the pioneers in the Transvaal Province became miners and most of them died of miners' phthisis, a deadly progressive disease. The numbers of Greeks grew after World War II and reached a peak of over 120,000 in the mid-1970s.

Due to the "Liberal White Policy" of the apartheid regime of the National Party (which came to power in 1948) many Greek artisans and professionals arrived in the country with one-year contracts. Most of them established themselves later as entrepreneurs and contributed greatly to the economic development of the country. They brought with them individual and collective skills and entrepreneurial spirit of a high calibre. The crisis of the apartheid government and the Soweto riots of 1976 persuaded several sections of the Greek population to return to Greece, where they have established well-organized associations of a philanthropic nature.

Initially they started as small traders in the services and distributive spheres (fruiteries, cafes, general shops, etc.). There were also several small pioneer manufacturers of tobacco, mineral water, confectionaries, bricks, etc. Few were active in agriculture and farming. Many of their businesses were destroyed physically by large hostile crowds in the anti-Greek riots of 1917. These were caused by faction fighting among sections of the community over the attitudes of

Venizelos and King Constantine towards World War I. Political passions ripped the community apart during that period.

The development of the productive forces in the country was instrumental in shaping an ever-increasing upward mobility among Greeks in South Africa. Thus there was a notable transformation of the Greek entrepreneurs from a predominantly service and distribution mould into the broader spheres of the South African economy (building development, shipping, mining, high technology, financial services, etc.). Greeks still have wide control of the restaurant and leisure sectors, many Greek-led companies have entered the Johannesburg Stock Exchange, and it has been calculated that Greek-owned businesses produce over 8 per cent of the country's GDP. Over 200,000 people of all colours and creeds are directly employed by Greek-owned enterprises. There are several Greek and Cypriot banks operating in South Africa, the oldest being the South African Bank of Athens which was established in 1947. Intellectually, the Greek community in South Africa has produced a wide range of academics, researchers, and professionals in all spheres of society, many of them of international standing and reputation.

There is also a surprisingly rich tapestry of Greek culture in South Africa with large numbers of dance groups, theatre groups, musicians, poets, novelists, and the like.

In terms of communal organization, the Greek community associations (koinotites) are the stalwarts of development. The first was established in Cape Town in 1898 and the second in Johannesburg in 1908 following the amalgamation of several benevolent and nationalist groups. The Federation of Hellenic Communities and Associations of South Africa was established in 1975. Today there are 20 Greek communities in South Africa whose main aims are the preservation of the Greek language, Orthodox religion, culture, and traditions. There are also 14 brotherhoods and associations of people from different geographical areas, the first of which, for Ithacans, was established in 1906.

Greek education has a long history of struggle in South Africa. Today Greek language, tradition, culture, and history are taught in all community schools throughout the country and also in the South African Hellenic Educational and Technical Institute (SAHETI), which is a private school and one of the best in the country. The community school follows the programmes of the Greek National Education Ministry, which provides the bulk of the teachers.

The Greek press has played an important role in the social and national life of Greeks in South Africa. The first newspaper (Apokalypsis, later Nea Hellas) was established in 1902 in Johannesburg. Afrikanis was established in 1918 and is called today Hellenikos Typos (Greek Press, incorporating Nea Hellas).

Although the first pioneers were mainly from Ithaca and the Peloponnese, the composition today has changed radically. There are large numbers of Greek Cypriots as well as people from throughout Greece living and working in South Africa. Historically South Africa's Greek population has played an active part in all Greece's national struggles. A large number of Greek pioneers fought in the Balkan Wars, World War I, and World War II. Millions of dollars have been collected and sent to Greece and Cyprus during difficult times, especially the 1974 Cypriot tragedy.

EVANGELOS MANTZARIS

See also Diaspora

Further Reading

Mantzaris, Evangelos, "Ellines Logotechnes sti Notia Aphriki" [Greek Writers in South Africa], *Diavazo*, 37

Mantzaris, Evangelos, "Social Structure and the Process of Assimilation of the Greek Community in South Africa" (MA thesis), University of Cape Town, 1978

Mantzaris, Evangelos, "Class and Ethinicity: Politics and Ideology of the Greek Community in South Africa, 1890–1924" (dissertation), University of Cape Town, 1981

Mantzaris, Evagelos, "I Avchanomeni Aphomoiosi tis Mikroastikis Taxis sti Notia Aphriki" [The Increasing Assimilation of the Greek Middle Class in South Africa], *Greek Review of Social Research*, 42–43 (May–December 1981): pp. 37–49

Mantzaris, Evangelos, "Greek Workers in South Africa: The Case of Railway Workers and the Cigarette-makers, 1905–1914", *Journal of the Hellenic Diaspora*, 14/3–4, (1987): pp. 28–43

Mantzaris, Evangelos, "Oi Ellines Ergates stin Notia Aphriki 1890–1930" [Greek Workers in South Africa 1890–1930], *Syllogikes Ekdosis*, 1995

Mantzaris, Evangelos, *South African Workers Struggles: The Forgotten Pages*, Collective Resources, 1995

Nicolaides, Constantines, *Ai Ellinikai Paroichiai tis Notioteras Aphrikis* [Guide to the Greek Communities of Southern Africa], Johannesburg: New Hellas, 1923

Papamichael, Michael, *O ana tin Aphriki Ellenismos* [Hellenism across Africa], 1951

Soutsos, Mikhail 1778–1864

The last prince of Moldavia

Soutsos was a descendant of one of the most famous families of Epirus with a long history reaching back at least to the late Byzantine period. The family was first recorded as being settled in Constantinople well before the fall of Constantinople to the Ottomans in 1453. However, after the fall of Constantinople, the Soutsos family among many others was obliged to leave Constantinople and return to Epirus. Yet, following the sultan's decree of 1470, the family once more made its way back to Constantinople. The Soutsos family was to produce a variety of celebrated figures who played an active role or offered their services either to the Orthodox patriarchate or to the Sublime Porte from the 17th century on. Other members of the family took on high office or became distinguished as diplomats, rulers, princes, military officers, or scholars.

Mikhail Soutsos was the grandson of M. Soutsos (b. 1730) who settled in the principalities across the Danube and served as ruler of Wallachia in the years 1783–86 and later as prince of Moldavia in the period 1793–95. Soutsos was born in 1778 at his grandfather's court in Wallachia where he was educated by private tutors. Having received the necessary qualifications and theoretical knowledge, he proceeded to put them into practice by undertaking important political and administrative duties and finally by presiding over the political department of the court. There he witnessed the beheading of his uncle, A.

Soutsos (1807), as well as the execution of the son of the grand interpreter of the princely court. The tragic deaths of these two eminent officers marked a turning point in Soutsos's political career. Almost immediately he succeeded them in their high positions and showed himself to be a resourceful and prudent leader in public affairs and diplomacy. In the meantime, he was appointed as the Wallachian prince's representative to Constantinople. In 1815 he was promoted to the office of the grand ambassador to the Sublime Porte, which he held until 1818 when he entered the advisory body of the sultan Mahmut II. In 1819 he accepted the throne of Moldavia and retained it till the outbreak of the Greek War of Independence (1821).

Soutsos made an enormous contribution to the inception, progression, expansion, and final fulfilment of the Greek cause, which he supported financially and morally. Not only did he encourage it but he supported it by whatever means were available to him. Soutsos, as prince of Moldavia, played an active role in and encouraged the sacred mission of the Society of Friends (*Philiki Hetaireia*), namely the liberation of Greece from the Ottoman yoke. For the attainment of that goal Soutsos was willing to sacrifice his own life and not only did he adopt the principal ideas of the Society of Friends but also he jeopardized his throne and his wealth. Soutsos joined the society in 1820, in the wake of Alexander Ypsilantis's revolutionary movement in Moldo-Wallachia and his subsequent triumphal entry into Jassy that signalled the beginning of the revolution. Since Moldavia occupied a strategic location, it was well suited to carry the seeds of the revolution which erupted there. Moreover, Soutsos could mobilize a significant military force consisting of Serbs, Vlachs, and Bulgars to assist Ypsilantis. It should be noted that, in addition to being a member of the Society of Friends and prince of Moldavia, Soutsos enjoyed the high esteem and support of the sultan.

Soutsos's moral contribution to the Greek revolution is incalculable. He followed the example of Constantine Ypsilantis, the prince of Wallachia some years earlier, who had supported the Serbian revolutionaries in the hope that their regional revolt would develop into a revolutionary movement throughout the Balkans against the Turks. When he joined the Society of Friends Soutsos offered a large amount of money to the revolution. By his example he persuaded other Moldavian princes and governors to contribute financially, militarily, and morally to the success of the revolution. In addition, he put his garrison troops at the disposal of the society and made himself responsible for their overall preparation as well as for supplying the Greek army with food, equipment, and other provisions. By risking his crown he succeeded in mollifying the Boyars, the Romanian notables who were against the revolution, as well as the uncooperative members of the society. When Ypsilantis's troops crossed the river Pruth and arrived in the capital of Moldavia, Soutsos announced his decision to abdicate, since there was no reason to keep his throne once the Greek revolution against the Turks had commenced. However, after Ypsilantis intervened, he remained prince of Moldavia for a while in order to prevent a possible scattering of his population. At the same time he collaborated with the leader of the society and undertook personally to recruit volunteers and to stockpile weaponry and munitions. Immediately after the failure of the revolution in the Danubian principalities and the public burning of the regal insignia, Soutsos was deported to

Bessarabia, having been excommunicated by the ecumenical patriarch Gregory V for his involvement in the revolution. Meanwhile, the Sublime Porte repeatedly asked for Soutsos to be expelled from Russian soil in order to prevent the outbreak of a new Russo-Turkish war. Thus Soutsos was forced to live in exile in Austria where he was imprisoned for four years and was then banished to the neutral territory of Switzerland.

Soutsos's contribution to the Greek cause did not stop there but continued until his death. When in Switzerland he still served the Greek revolution he cooperated with Count Kapodistria and the philhellene community there, and he devoted his life to charities and the development of Swiss philhellenism. At the same time, he contributed to the spiritual renewal, enlightenment, and education of Greek refugees there.

After the end of the war and the establishment of peace in Greece, Kapodistria appointed Soutsos as the Greek representative to Paris. In that capacity he persuaded the king of France to give economic and military support to Greece. In fact, he sent 20,000 French soldiers to the Peloponnese to drive out Ibrahim's army. From Paris, Soutsos moved as Greek ambassador to St Petersburg (until 1835) and London (until 1839). That year he returned to Athens where he was appointed a member of the advisory body of the newly established Greek state.

Soutsos saw his dreams come true when the Greek people won their independence. Residing now in Athens, he bought a large area of land in one of the most fashionable suburbs of Athens which even today bears his name, and he built a mansion in which he lived till his death and which he bequeathed posthumously to the Greek state.

MARIA ROUMBALOU

See also Hetairists, Phanariots

Biography

Born in Moldavia in 1778, Soutsos was educated privately at the court of his grandfather. At an early age he undertook political and administrative duties, becoming ambassador to the Sublime Porte and in 1819 prince of Moldavia. He assisted the Greek revolutionary movement in Moldavia and Wallachia. He abdicated in 1821 and was deported to Bessarabia. He later served as Greek ambassador to Paris, St Petersburg, and London. He died in Athens in 1864.

Further Reading

Clogg, Richard (editor and translator), *The Movement for Greek Independence, 1770–1821: A Collection of Documents*, London: Macmillan, 1976

Dakin, Douglas, *The Greek Struggle for Independence, 1821–1833*, London: Batsford, and Berkeley: University of California Press, 1973

Draghici, M., *Istoria Moldovei*, Iasi, 1857

Erbiceanu, C., *Istoria Mitropoliciei Moldovei si Sucevei*, Bucharest, 1888

Istoria tou Ellinikou Ethnous [History of the Greek Nation], Athens, 1994

Kordatos, G., *I Megali Istoria tis Ellados* [The Great History of Greece], Athens, 1985

Panaitescu, P.P., *Corespondenta, Iui Constantiu Ipsilanti cu guvernul Rusesc, 1806–1810: Pregatirea Eteriei si a remasterii politice rominesti*, Bucharest, 1933

Petridis, P., *Synchroni Elliniki Politiki Istoria* [Modern Greek Political History], Athens, 1996

Phillips, W. Alison, *The War of Greek Independence, 1821 to 1833*, London: Smith Elder, and New York: Scribner, 1897

Roussos, G., *Neoteri Istoria tou Ellinikou Ethnous* [Modern History of Greek Nation], Athens, 1975

Vournas, T., *Istoria tis Synchronis Elladas* [History of Modern Greece], Athens, 1977

Woodhouse, C.M., *The Greek War of Independence: Its Historical Setting*, London: Hutchinson, 1952, reprinted New York: Russell, 1975

Zakythinos, D.A., *The Making of Modern Greece: From Byzantium to Independence*, Oxford: Blackwell, 1976

Spain

Spain occupies the major part of the Iberian peninsula. Iberia is the ancient name of the country and Iberians the name of the people who inhabited the peninsula in ancient times and who became urbanized from the 5th century BC. The first Phoenician settlement in Iberia, Gades (modern Cadiz, northwest of Gibraltar), is traditionally dated to *c*.1100 BC. However, archaeological finds demonstrate that this flourishing Phoenician trading settlement was not established until the 8th century BC. It minted coins down to the 1st century BC and initially traded for metals with Tartessus, a cultural agglomeration in southern Spain. Tartessus developed out of local roots, and from *c*.750 BC was exploiting the rich metal resources in the hinterland of Onoba (Huelva). These were traded with Phoenician settlements on the coast in exchange for metalwork, jewellery, ivory, and ceramics, all of which were in turn traded within Iberia. As a result of its close links with Phoenicians and Greeks in Iberia, Tartessus developed a unique orientalizing culture (expressed in sculpture, jewellery, and architecture, for example). Tartessus collapsed in *c*.550 BC for reasons that are still a matter of academic dispute.

Greek presence in the Atlantic regions of Iberia is traceable from the second half of the 7th century BC, especially in the Huelva region, where it is linked to Tartessian culture; it may also be identified in the same period in the northeastern regions of Iberia. From the last third of the 6th century BC, Greek presence in Huelva diminished and remained at a low ebb for the next 100 years. The Greek colonies in Spain were established by the Phocaeans. Of the three known colonies – Emporion, Rhode, and Maenace – the first, which was indeed the major Hellenic centre in Spain, has received the most detailed archaeological study.

Emporion, northwest of modern Barcelona, was founded *c*.600 BC at about the same time as Massalia (modern Marseilles). Initially a small settlement was established on an island, and in *c*.575 BC it moved to the shore of the mainland, an area populated by local people and set amid marshes. It is clear from finds of local pottery in the Palaiapolis and study of the city's necropolis that the population of Emporion included local people from its very beginnings. Emporion was also surrounded by the settlements of the local population; peaceful relations between colonists and natives were very important for ensuring the survival of the Greeks in the region. Iberian society was highly organized but not centralized. The Ullastret settlement, about 20 km from Emporion, housed the Iberian elite of the hinterland. Situated atop a hill, it controlled the whole of the territory surrounding Emporion. In consequence, the relationship between Emporion and Ullastret was not merely mercantile but political as well. It may be remarked that the city walls of Ullastret were constructed only about 500 BC, long after the final establishment of Emporion. In almost every house in Ullastret large quantities of Greek pottery were found. Greek influence is clearly discernible in the planning of the settlement, in features such as an acropolis with its own inner walls and small temples, and a porticoed marketplace.

Tivisa is another native Iberian settlement. It overlooks the Ebro river, controlling access to the Iberian interior. It has very strong fortifications and a gateway closely modelled on Greek plans of the 4th century BC. Here more Greek pottery was found. These two settlements are evidence of the close and peaceful relationship which the Greeks enjoyed with the Iberian elite who, from well-fortified settlements, controlled the hinterland so vital for Greek trading activity. The Emporitans could expect little benefit from the marshy territory immediately around them. In the southeast of the Iberian peninsula the most important illustrations of Graeco-Iberian relations are the local settlements of Porcuna and Castulo, as well as Huelva.

Although strongly indigenous, Tartessian/Iberian culture was more Phoenicianized than Hellenized. Further Greek influence can be traced from the 4th century BC when, with the fall of the Punic world to Rome, Iberian–Phoenician links became sparse. Ionian influence on Iberian stone sculpture is obvious. Most probably, local, very Hellenized sculpture workshops existed in Castulo and Obulco. In them it is possible that Greek and local craftsmen worked alongside each other, the former adapting their artistic skills to the tastes of the local elite, and the latter working under Greek instruction. Tomb monuments show Anatolian influence (which came via the Ionians); important in this respect are funeral stelae which carry depictions of Ionic columns. Iberian small bronze figures as well as silver gilt *phialai* (libation bowls) from Tivisa and Santiesteban show Greek influence.

Graeco-Iberian script is another aspect of the Hellenization of the Iberian elite and society at large. It uses the Ionian alphabet. The earliest inscription dates from the second quarter of the 5th century BC. The script was widespread in the Hellenistic period, especially after the 2nd century BC. It is found not only at local sites but also in Emporion, on both Greek and local pottery.

Spain first experienced a Roman presence at the very end of the 3rd century BC. In 197 BC Rome divided its possessions in Iberia (or Hispania, as it was known to the Romans) into two provinces: Hispania Citerior, the eastern coastal strip; and Hispania Ulterior, the southeast coast and the Guadalquivir valley. The conquest of the peninsula was completed by Augustus in the Cantabrian Wars (26–19 BC). Twenty-two colonies were founded under Caesar and Augustus. In the 1st century AD many provincial Roman senators came from the colony of Hispania; and several emperors – Trajan, Hadrian, and Marcus Aurelius – could boast Spanish ancestry. The barbarian invasion of 409 resulted in the rapid loss of Roman control of all the Spanish provinces. By 475 Spain was finally lost to Rome. Visigothic control was established in 586 and lasted until the early 8th century, although part of the south of Spain was held by the Byzantines from 552 to 624. In consequence some Greek traditions survived. However, the south of Spain was to be that part of the peninsula which remained longest under Arab control (from the 8th to the late 15th century) and it is that which has left a stronger legacy.

GOCHA R. TSETSKHLADZE

See also Colonization

Further Reading

Arribas, Antonio, *The Iberians*, London: Thames and Hudson, 1963; New York: Praeger, 1964

Boardman, John, *The Greeks Overseas: Their Early Colonies and Trade*, London: Thames and Hudson, 1980

Boardman, John, *The Diffusion of Classical Art in Antiquity*, London: Thames and Hudson, and Princeton, New Jersey: Princeton University Press, 1994

Bonet, P.C. and C.S. Fernandez, *Los Grigos en Espana*, Athens and Madrid, 1998 (English text pp. 429–605)

Collins, Roger, *Early Medieval Spain: Unity in Diversity, 400–1000*, London: Macmillan, and New York: St Martin's Press, 1983

Harrison, Richard J., *Spain at the Dawn of History*, London and New York: Thames and Hudson, 1983

Richardson, J.S., *Hispaniae: Spain and the Development of Roman Imperialism, 212–82 BC*, Cambridge and New York: Cambridge University Press, 1986

Sparta

City in the Peloponnese

Sparta was the controlling city of Laconia, the southeastern part of the Peloponnese, situated in an extremely fertile area well watered by the river Eurotas. There was a Mycenaean settlement in the vicinity, on the hills above the opposite bank of the river, quite substantial, but hardly comparable with the great palaces of Mycenae, Tiryns, or Pylos. It may or may not have been the residence of the Mycenaean king who is personified in Homer's *Iliad* and *Odyssey* as Menelaus, the husband of Helen and brother of Agamemnon himself.

Classical Sparta was founded by Dorian settlers who moved in during the confused period after the collapse of the Late Bronze Age political systems. They avoided the previous settlement, which was later marked by a sanctuary dedicated to Menelaus and Helen (the Menelaion) and instead occupied a series of sites on the west bank, where they founded four villages. These merged, by some totally unknown process, into a single political entity which, along with a fifth village at Amyclae a short distance to the south, became the city, though for a long time – certainly until the 5th century BC when Thucydides wrote – it remained in physical terms a cluster of villages. According to Thucydides, it is clear that in his time it was distinctly a non-monumental place, in contrast to his own and other cities of his day.

The Dorian settlers brought with them a primitive constitution, paralleled by those of other settlements, particularly in Crete, which were founded or refounded at the same time as a result of the Dorian migration. It aimed to confirm the military effectiveness of the political body. In adolescence, young men were taken from their families and lived in communal groups, where they underwent a rigorous regime of physical and mili-

tary, rather than intellectual or academic, training. The effectiveness of this was enhanced by the development of the heavy infantry armour and fighting method of the hoplite type of warrior. By the 6th century BC the Spartan army was generally recognized as the most efficient fighting force in Greece, a reputation which was confirmed by the part it played in defeating the Persian invasion. The total normal strength of the army was 5000, all full citizens of the city. Citizenship was restricted to those who underwent the training regime and served in the army, in effect the adult male population of the five constituent villages. Its function was not so much to ward off external enemies (not merely the Persians, but other Greek city states, particularly Argos) as to maintain a supremacy over Laconia and, by conquest, the district to the west, Messenia. This involved another distinctive element in the Spartan system, the allocation of landed estates away from the city itself to its citizens, who were entitled to the products of their estates, but which were farmed for them by subservient workers, the helots ("captives"), who were tied to the land. This freed the Spartan citizens from the necessity to work for their living, and allowed them instead to dedicate themselves to military training. Part of the food produced by their estates had to be given to the military group to which they belonged, and where they normally ate, rather than at home.

The reason for this system is unclear. In the training and communal meals there is a primitive, tribal element; but when it first emerges, it is devoted to a supremacy which enabled the Spartans to trade agricultural produce for luxury items imported especially from the east, a phenomenon to be found in other contemporary Greek cites, Corinth most clearly. Items such as pottery, metalware, and so forth were also produced in Laconia itself: examples have been found in the Archaic levels at the sanctuary of Artemis Orthia on the banks of the Eurotas, and at the Menelaion, along with ivories and other imports. There must therefore have existed an artisan class, though who they were and where they lived is uncertain. They are usually attributed to a third political category, the "dwellers round" or *perioikoi*, communities which enjoyed local independence (i.e. they were not tied helots), but were under political obligations, particularly of rendering military assistance, to the Spartans. Their numbers, when called upon, seem to have doubled the size of the Spartan army. However, the Spartan army was needed more and more, particularly after rebellion by the Messenian helots, to police and maintain the Spartan constitutional supremacy. It became self-devouring: military supremacy was needed to maintain the training and living systems, which were themselves needed to maintain military supremacy. Thus it had become an end in itself. This led to a tightening of the regime, and in particular a rejection of luxury and personal wealth. Strengthening the system meant its maintenance, and innovations were frowned on: Sparta notoriously did not issue its own coins, since coinage had been invented to facilitate commercial development.

As a result, Sparta emerges as the natural antithesis of Athens: restricted constitution in contrast to democracy, military prowess as opposed to naval development, self-sufficient instead of relying on trade and imperial exploitation. It even kept its curious institution of a dual kingship, at a time when most Greek states no longer had kings. It is a contrast which, in its political application, led to war.

Sparta: view of the plain of Sparta from the castle of Mistra

Sparta failed because it was not equipped to deal with the problems which faced the wider Greek world, particularly the need to maintain a constant defence against the possibility of a Persian resurgence. The consequences of this can be seen in the strains imposed on Sparta when it tried to sustain this role in the first half of the 4th century BC. The loss of Messenia, liberated by the new- style Boeotian army, crippled it permanently. This and other strains led to a steady decline in numbers of the citizen population able to draw from their estates to contribute to their military groups: the problem may have been exacerbated by a primitive system for deciding inheritances. The number of subordinate helots (except for those lost with Messenia) and *perioikoi* does not seem to have declined, and a new group, the "inferiors", grew up in Sparta itself, former citizen families who had lost the necessary property qualifications.

At first, this diminished Sparta stands outside the new order created by Philip II and the Macedonians, largely ignored because it was unimportant, though generally managing to remain independent. Land passed into the hands of an extreme few, usually through female inheritance, and Sparta was regarded as a mere has-been. All this ended with social reform introduced by King Cleomenes III. In this he confiscated all the land and redistributed it into new estates, on the pretext that he was restoring the original Spartan system. The new land-holders were, at the same time, liable to military service, and so a new and briefly powerful Spartan army was created. It failed, at the Battle of Sellasia in 222 BC against the superior Macedonian army of Antigonus Doson, and Sparta relapsed into insignificance.

However, it was an insignificance with a distinguished past. As part of the Roman empire Sparta flourished, in the form of a small but prosperous provincial city. It traded on its traditions. The training regime was partly revived, though the harshness, which included whipping the youths, became something of a spectacle, and a theatrical structure was built at the sanctuary of Artemis Orthia so that an audience could observe. The town itself included wealthy families, some of them newly arrived, and houses with lavish mosaic floors have been excavated. A substantial theatre was built in the 1st century BC and subsequently enlarged. In the troubled times of the late empire, and for the first time, fortifications were constructed, delimiting a much-reduced area, and these maintained the place into the Middle Ages until the population was transferred to the stronghold of Mistra, away from the river in the foothills of Mount Taygetus. Such, however, was the reputation of ancient Sparta that, with the freeing of Greece from the Turks, Mistra was abandoned and new Sparta refounded yet again in its old place.

R.A. TOMLINSON

Summary

A city in the southern Peloponnese, Sparta was the site of a Mycenaean settlement, in Homer the residence of Menelaus. The Classical city, originally a collection of villages, was a Dorian foundation. By the 6th century BC the Spartan army was the best in Greece. But the military system could not deal with wider political problems and ultimately failed. In the Middle Ages the population was transferred to Mistra, but in the 19th century Sparta was refounded on its original site.

Further Reading

Cartledge, Paul, *Sparta and Lakonia: A Regional History, 1300–362 BC*, London and Boston: Routledge and Kegan Paul, 1979

Cartledge, Paul and Antony Spawforth, *Hellenistic and Roman Sparta: A Tale of Two Cities*, London and New York: Routledge, 1989

Dawkins, R.M. (editor), *The Sanctuary of Artemis Orthia at Sparta, Excavated and Described by Members of the British School at Athens, 1906–1910*, London: Macmillan, 1929

Forrest, W.G., *A History of Sparta, 950–192 BC*, 2nd edition, London: Duckworth, 1980

Lane. E.A., "Lakonian Vase Painting", *Annual of the British School at Athens*, 34 (1936): p. 99

Spells

The vocabulary of casting spells comprehends the terms *epoide*, literally a "singing over", and *pharmakon*, a broad designation that straddles the notions of incantation and drug (medicine or poison, possibly enchanted) and which could be extended to describe any psychagogic force: Plato in particular assimilated the power of the spellbinding word to the power of poetry or rhetoric, both of which deprive their objects of the capacity for autonomous action (*Charmides*, 157a; *Republic*, 607d; *Meno*, 80a; cf. Gorgias, *Encomium of Helen*).

Spells were ubiquitous in ancient Hellenic society. More than 1500 incised tablets associated with spellbinding survive from antiquity as do many incised ostraka and amulets, while the *Papyri Graecae Magicae* (*PGM*) of Hellenistic Egypt, dating from the 3rd and 4th centuries AD but informed by long-established practice, constitute a veritable magician's handbook. Individuals seeking supernatural aid could buy spells from professionals; Aristophanes claims that the witches of Thessaly (an area famous for witchcraft) charged a fee (*Clouds*, 749–52) and Plato suggests that such specialist services came cheap (*Republic*, 364c).

Incantations were accompanied by various practices that served to reinforce the power of the spoken word. One important supplement to the oral spell from the Classical period onward was the process of inscription – the performance of writing down the name of the victim and that of the god or demon invoked to work the spell lent greater efficacy to the accompanying words. Inscriptions could be empowered further by the addition of the inscribed images of humans, animals, and demons and of arcane astrological symbols and mystical numbers; often the words themselves were written backwards, mixed up, or repeated. The language of spells was highly formulaic and sometimes specifically magical; "nonsense" words comprehensible only to demons could be used, such as "abracadabra", attested for the 1st century AD,

and the Ephesian *grammata* ("letters"), recited or inscribed in apotropaic rituals.

Herbs and plants, often pharmacologically active, were used in spells, as were minerals and the body parts of animals – the *PGM* record many charming recipes; and personal effects of the victim such as hair, nails, or clothing were employed synechdochically. Magic tools were used, for example the *iunx* (a bronze whirling disc), bull-roarer, and gong, while in the *Odyssey* Hermes, Circe, and Athena have magic wands (13. 429, 16. 172, 456). Voodoo dolls of wax, mud, or dough representing the victim of the spell and often inscribed with his or her name were a common feature of spellbinding. These figurines could be placed in graves, burnt, melted, or transfixed with nails (*PGM*, 1. 83–87 suggests the insertion of 13 needles) and sometimes had their hands tied behind their backs. Indeed the vocabulary of bondage, such as *katadein* (tie down) and *katechein* (restrain), is prevalent in spells – more than 1000 examples of ancient binding spells (*katadesmoi*) have been found, and as late as the 12th century AD Eustathios was familiar with the idea. The concept of binding the victim is important, a notion perhaps related to the bonds of fate and a demonstration of the appeal of sympathetic magic – the victim is bound to the speller's will and rendered powerless. The frequency of curses resulted in their corollary – antidotes: *PGM* 4. 2177 offers a spell to break the power of a curse tablet; many inscriptions suggest remedies to ward off the anger of one's enemies (for example *PGM*, 7. 940–68, 4. 831–32); others have a more general apotropaic function. Of course the notion of magic could be used as a method of saving face: failure in anything from litigation to love could be ascribed to a malignant spell.

Often spells are agonistic in context. Many Athenian *katadesmoi* relate to lawsuits and represent an attempt to silence opponents in court: an inscription on a lead tablet from the 5th century BC calls down a curse upon Aspasia and her legal helpers (*Inscriptiones Graecae*, 3. 3106), while the "binding song" (*hymnos desmios*) of Aeschylus' Erinyes occurs in a legal context (*Eumenides*, 306ff.). Other spells relate to success in athletics, the theatre, and business, while many promise to endow the speller with a more general appeal and success (e.g. *PGM*, 12. 397–400). Another important locus of enchantment was love, and *agogai* – rituals designed to lead the beloved to the speller's bed – form a large part of the literature on spelling. Theocritus' *Pharmaceutria* (3rd century BC), a portrait of an abandoned woman attempting to bewitch a former lover, echoes the sympathetic erotic magic of contemporary practice – the melting of a wax dummy, the burning of a thread from the victim's cloak, the use of magical tools, and an incantatory refrain.

In Greek literature it is women in particular who cast spells and are skilled in the use of *pharmaka*, while bewitchment is often troped in terms of the characteristically female activity of weaving – Medea, ancient literature's most infamous witch, weaves spells and invokes demons (Apollonius Rhodius, *Argonautica*, 4. 1635–90). Yet the spells in the *PGM* are addressed more often to male practitioners, and their use crossed the boundaries of gender and status.

Spells were not used only to harm: some of the earliest references to incantation in Greek literature occur in a medical context. In the *Odyssey* Autolycus and his sons bind Odysseus' wound and sing incantations over the dark blood (19. 457) and Pindar's Cheiron heals with incantations, *pharmaka*, and surgery (*Pythian*, 3. 43–54). Indeed the distinction between magic and medicine in antiquity is blurred: amulets (*periapta*, *periammata*) applied with incantations were worn as remedies for or prophylactics against disease (e.g. as a cure for headache, Plato, *Charmides*, 155e–156e); healing with spells is mentioned (and disparaged) in a text belonging to the Hippocratic corpus (*On the Sacred Disease*, 1–2); Plato says midwives use *pharmaka* and *epoidai* to induce labour (*Theaetetus*, 149c–d). The distinction between magic and religion is arbitrary too: many spells were in prayer form. Plato claims that sorcerers persuade the gods to serve them by prayers (*euchai*) and *epoidai* (*Laws*, 909b; cf. *Republic*, 364c) and Sappho's prayer to Aphrodite has the tone of an erotic magical spell (fr. 1 L-P). Indeed the whole pantheon of Greek gods was invoked in incantations in which supernatural powers were compelled to serve the speller, although Hecate, Persephone, Selene, and Hermes figure most prominently.

In ancient Greece religion and "magic" were not mutually exclusive categories and no legislation of pagan antiquity relates directly to spells (although Plato suggested that "black magic" should be criminalized, *Laws*, 933a). The Church, however, ideologically mandated against all non-Christian "magic", and spells fell outside its orthodox circumscriptions. Paul made the Ephesians burn their magic books (Acts 19: 18–20) and the use of spells was condemned by patristic writers such as Basil (*Epistles*, 188. 8), Eusebius (*Laus Constantini*, 13), and Jerome (*Life of Saint Hilarion the Hermit*, 21), while the Theodosian code (9. 16. 4) outlawed the use of magic and prescribed death for its practitioners. The Church's proscription of practices it labelled un-Christian led many to seek supernatural consolation in Christianity but a belief in pagan magic, the efficacy of spells, and the power of the evil eye persisted in Hellenic society throughout the medieval period and beyond into the modern era; indeed Dionisopoulos-Mass records a tale of magical intrigue which took place on the Aegean island of Nisi in 1968 when a husband, rendered impotent by a malicious spell, successfully sought help from a professional witch in Athens.

EUGÉNIE FERNANDES

See also Magic

Further Reading

Barb, A.A., "The Survival of the Magic Arts" in *The Conflict between Paganism and Christianity in the Fourth Century*, edited by Arnaldo Momigliano, Oxford: Clarendon Press, 1963

Betz, Hans Dieter (editor), *The Greek Magical Papyri in Translation, Including the Demotic Spells*, vol. 1: *Texts*, 2nd edition, Chicago: University of Chicago Press, 1992

Brown, Peter, *Religion and Society in the Age of Saint Augustine*, London: Faber, and New York: Harper and Row, 1972

De Romilly, Jacqueline, *Magic and Rhetoric in Ancient Greece*, Cambridge, Massachusetts: Harvard University Press, 1975

Dionisopoulos-Mass, R., "The Evil Eye and Bewitchment in a Peasant Village" in *The Evil Eye*, edited by Clarence Maloney, New York: Columbia University Press, 1976

Douglas, Mary (editor), *Witchcraft: Confessions and Accusations*, London: Tavistock, 1970

Edelstein, L., "Greek Medicine in its Relation to Religion and Magic" in *Ancient Medicine*, edited by Owsei and C. Lilian

Temkin, Baltimore, Maryland: Johns Hopkins University Press, 1967

Faraone, Christopher and Dirk Obbink, *Magika Hiera: Ancient Greek Magic and Religion*, Oxford and New York: Oxford University Press, 1991

Flint, Valerie I.J., *The Rise of Magic in Early Medieval Europe*, Oxford: Clarendon Press, and Princeton, New Jersey: Princeton University Press, 1991

Gager, John G., *Curse Tablets and Binding Spells from the Ancient World*, Oxford and New York: Oxford University Press, 1992, reprinted 1999

Galatariotou, C., "Holy Women and Witches: Aspects of Byzantine Conceptions of Gender", *Byzantine and Modern Greek Studies*, 9 (1984–85): pp. 55–94

Jordan, D.R., "New Archaeological Evidence for the Practice of Magic in Classical Athens" in *Praktika of the 12th International Congress of Classical Archaeology*, vol. 4, Athens, 1988

Lloyd, G.E.R., *Magic, Reason and Experience: Studies in the Origin and Development of Greek Science*, Cambridge and New York: Cambridge University Press, 1979

Luck, Georg, *Arcana Mundi: Magic and the Occult in the Greek and Roman Worlds*, Wellingborough, Northamptonshire: Crucible, and Baltimore, Maryland: Johns Hopkins University Press, 1985, reprinted 1987

Parry, Hugh, *Thelxis: Magic and Imagination in Greek Myth and Poetry*, Lanham, Maryland: University Press of America, 1992

Preisendanz, Karl, *Papyri Graecae Magicae*, 2 vols, Leipzig: Teubner, 1928–31, reprinted Stuttgart: Teubner, 1973

Segal, C.P., "Eros and Incantation: Sappho and Oral Poetry", *Arethusa*, 7/2 (1974): pp. 148–50

Walsh, George B., *The Varieties of Enchantment: Early Greek Views of the Nature and Function of Poetry*, Chapel Hill: University of North Carolina Press, 1984

Winkler, John J., "The Constraints of Desire: Erotic Magical Spells" in his *The Constraints of Desire: The Anthropology of Sex and Gender in Ancient Greece*, London and New York: Routledge, 1990

Sphrantzes, George 1401–1477/78

Diplomat and historian

As a young man George Sphrantzes entered the service of the emperor Manuel II (1391–1425) and later of Constantine XI (1449–53), whom he accompanied and served as a friend and adviser until the emperor's death during the capture of Constantinople. Sphrantzes carried out several diplomatic missions, to the Turks, Georgia, Trebizond, the Morea, and the Aegean islands. He saved Constantine's life during the siege of Patras, but was captured and imprisoned (1429). After his release and the final surrender of the inhabitants of Patras, he became governor of the city. He was appointed *protovestiarites* (chief of the sovereign's bodyguard) in 1432 and governor of Mistra in 1446. After the fall of Constantinople in 1453 and his release from captivity by the Turks, he joined Constantine's brother Thomas in the Morea and after the final Byzantine defeat followed him to Corfu, where at the end of his life, tired and sick, he entered a monastery. There, Sphrantzes wrote down a personal account of the events that took place during his lifetime, the so-called *Chronicon* (*Minus*). His work is based on a diary and annalistic source material as well as on oral tradition. Sphrantzes focuses on his own experiences and on the person of Constantine Palaiologos, his devotion to whom is obvious in the whole account. The language of the *Chronicon* is remarkable because it is surprisingly simple and colloquial. Some narrative passages, such as the account of the events that led to his appointment as governor of Patras and the biography of his godmother Thomais, may be regarded as early examples of modern Greek prose writing. The *Chronicon* has some characteristics in common with traditional Byzantine historiography, but differs substantially through the use of informal language and in the extraordinary density of autobiographical elements. Because no addressee is mentioned, we can surmise that the *Chronicon* was intended for members of the former Byzantine ruling elite living in exile after the fall of Constantinople, probably for the circle of refugees around the despot Thomas Palaiologos. Sphrantzes's original work is preserved in a slightly revised version represented by six independent manuscripts, two of which originated in the 1570s, one in the 17th century, and three deriving directly from one of the two 16th-century copies. Through the centuries of Ottoman rule Sphrantzes's account proved a "living text" that was changed and reshaped according to the needs of the period.

In Naples, between 1573 and 1578, Makarios Melissenos (Melissourgos), metropolitan of Monemvasia, composed a historiographical work for the years 1258–1477 in four books. For this compilation he used several authentic, and some forged, sources. Melissenos's text is primarily based on Sphrantzes and supplemented by material from Byzantine and post-Byzantine historiography, for example Georgios Akropolites, Nikephoros Gregoras, and Manuel Malaxos. He presented it as the work of Sphrantzes, so that the true identity of the author was unknown until the research of Ioannis V. Papadopoulos in the 1930s revealed it; previously it was, and sometimes still is, referred to as "pseudo-Sphrantzes". Traditionally Sphrantzes's authentic work has been known as the *Chronicon Minus* to distinguish it from Melissenos's *Chronicon Maius*. A large part of book 3 of Melissenos's compilation is formed by the famous so-called siege section, an account, purportedly by an eyewitness, of the last days of Constantinople. This passage is probably based on the eyewitness account of Leonard of Chios (d. 1459?; originally composed in Latin), though the authorship is still disputed.

Melissenos's compilation may claim independent value because of the author's critical use of the material but also because of his obvious effort to reshape Sphrantzes's original text according to the norms of Byzantine chronography, expanding the chronological frame, and enriching the text with material concerning ecclesiastical history and dogmatic questions as well as natural phenomena. The compiler also attempted to make the language look more like ancient Greek, replacing demotic forms with archaic ones, and occasionally intervened to try to improve the understanding of the text – it is also because of these changes that among historians of Byzantium Melissenos's compilation has often enjoyed higher authority than Sphrantzes's unpretentious original text. We may surmise that Melissenos's ultimate aim was to alert the western powers to the Turkish threat and the suffering of Greece after the victory at Lepanto (1571) when they seemed inclined to a peaceful arrangement with the Ottoman Porte. Instead of being regarded as nothing but a forgery Melissenos's

work deserves to be viewed as a creative reworking and a link between Byzantine and modern Greek literature.

Melissenos's creation, due to its historiographical content, literary form, and not least the fact that in the forged additions to the authentic material the author ascribed a prominent role in history to members of influential Neapolitanian families, obviously met the taste of his time as well as of later centuries, and therefore attracted a wide and continuing readership. As many as 27 manuscripts of pseudo-Sphrantzes have been discovered so far. These can be divided into two groups: 7 date to the end of the 16th century and are directly or indirectly connected to the circle of scribes around Makarios Melissenos, representing different stages of a continuous process of reworking of the original text; 15 date to 18th century – a fact that might be linked to intensified literary activities at this time (in particular at the Phanariot courts of Bucharest and Jassy) and growing interest in the history of the Greek nation, in particular in the fate of the Palaiologan dynasty and other families of the Byzantine aristocracy.

Besides being a major source for Greek history of the last 50 years before and the first years after the Ottoman conquest of Constantinople, in the 20th century Sphrantzes' *Chronicon* also exerted some influence on modern Greek literature. The politician, sociologist, and writer Panagiotis Kanellopoulos used his text (in the form of the *Maius*) and other contemporary sources for the composition of his novel *Gennithika sto Chilia Tetrakosia Dyo* (*I Was Born in 1402*, first published in 1957).

MARTIN HINTERBERGER

See also Historiography, Political History 1261–1453

Biography

Born in 1401, Sphrantzes served Manuel II and later Constantine XI as a diplomat and adviser. He became governor of Patras and later of Mistra. After the fall of Constantinople he travelled widely and finally settled in Corfu. There he wrote his *Chronicon* (*Minus*), an account of the events of his lifetime from 1413 to 1477. The expanded version, *Chronicon Maius*, is probably the work of a 16th-century bishop of Monemvasia. Sphrantzes died in Corfu in 1477/78.

Writings

Memorii 1401–1477: In anexa, Pseudo-Phrantzes, Macarie Mellisenos, Cronica 1258–1481, edited by Vasile Grecu, Bucharest, 1966
The Fall of the Byzantine Empire: A Chronicle, translated by Marios Philippides, Amherst: University of Massachusetts Press, 1980
Cronaca, edited by Riccardo Maisano, Rome: Accademia Nazionale dei Lincei, 1990

Further Reading

Carroll, Margaret, *A Contemporary Greek Source for the Siege of Constantinople, 1453: The Sphrantzes Chronicle*, Amsterdam: Hakkert, 1985
Chasiotis, Ioannes K., *Makarios, Theodoros kai Nikephoros oi Melissenoi* [Makarios, Theodoros, and Nikephoros Melissenos] Thessalonica, 1966
Kanellopoulos, Panagiotis, *Gennetheka sto Chilia Tetrakosia Dyo* [I was born in 1402], 3rd edition, Athens, 1980
Kazhdan, A.P. (editor), *The Oxford Dictionary of Byzantium*, 3 vols, New York and Oxford: Oxford University Press, 1991, vol. 2 pp. 1212 and 1335–36; vol. 3 p. 1937

Maisano, Riccardo, "L'opera memoralistica di Sfranze dentro e fuori i confini della storia", *Italoellinika: Rivista di cultura greco-moderna*, 1 (1988): pp. 111–22

Maisano, Riccardo, "Il manoscritto Napoletano II. E. 25 e la storia della tradizione dello pseudo-Sfranze", *Italoellinika: Rivista di cultura greco-moderna*, 2 (1989): pp. 121–34

Philippides, Marios, "The Fall of Constantinople: Bishop Leonard and the Greek Accounts", *Greek, Roman and Byzantine Studies*, 22/3 (1981): pp. 287–300

Philippides, Marios, "Patriarchal Chronicles of the 16th Century", *Greek, Roman and Byzantine Studies*, 25/1 (1984): pp. 87–94

Sporades

Islands in the northwest Aegean

The Sporades comprise a cluster of four islands and a number of rocky islets in the western Aegean Sea, extending in longitude from Thessaly to Euboea. The three main islands – Skiathos, Skopelos, and Alonnisos – lie southeast of the Magnesia peninsula, while Skyros is situated further south, northeast of the midpoint of the island of Euboea. Their geographical location has determined their administrative position, making Skyros part of Euboea while the other three belong to Magnesia.

Although the islands have a common history, each is known for its own character. Skiathos has a cosmopolitan ambiance; Skyros is well known for its rich local folklore; Skopelos is famous for its outstanding churches; and Alonnisos for its scenery.

Skiathos is the closest of the four to the mainland, situated opposite Mount Pelion about 43 nautical miles from the port town of Volos. It covers a surface of 48 sq km and is populated by little more than 4000 people. Endowed with a large number of lovely beaches and a pine-filled landscape, it has long been one of the most attractive tourist destinations of Greece. Of the nine small islands surrounding its coastal waters, two with the name Tsougries lie across the main harbour, making it a safe haven for small boats and yachts.

The island's strategic location was a principal reason for its being conquered by a long succession of rulers since antiquity. During prehistoric times, it was inhabited by Pelasgoi who came from Thrace in northern Greece around the 12th century BC. It is hypothesized that Cretans of the Minoic age also inhabited the island. This idea is supported by the name of the island, which is very similar to "Skianthios", the Cretan name for the god Dionysus. Thessalians of the Mycenean age may also have been among the early settlers. Ionians and later Chalcidians colonized it by the 6th century BC. In 477 BC Skiathos became a member of the Delian League to gain protection from Persian invasion. Initially city members of the alliance were autonomous and had a democratic administration, but Skiathos came increasingly under the direct rule of Athens, until it passed into the control of Sparta following its victory in the Peloponnesian war in 404 BC. The Antalkidios peace treaty in 386 BC gave the island its official independence, but Sparta violated the agreement and Skiathos was again under their hegemony. In 378 BC the island regained its autonomy by becoming an ally of Athens and taking part in the second Athenian Alliance. During almost 40 years of this alliance, Skiathos enjoyed a remarkable economic prosperity, a sign of which was the privilege of minting its own coins. The Macedonian victory in the battle of Chaeronea in 338 BC signalled the beginning of Macedonian occupation. During the second Macedonian war in 199 BC, Philip V completely destroyed Skiathos and Skopelos so they would not fall into the hands of the enemy Roman fleet, which nevertheless reached Skiathos and completed its devastation. A quick recovery followed and the island obtained a democratic regime in 197 BC. When Greece was subjugated by Rome in 146 BC, Skiathos followed the fate of the rest of the country. In 42 BC, after the battle of Philippi, Mark Antony handed the island over to the Athenians as a token of appreciation for their assistance.

After centuries in the Roman empire, Christianity came to Skiathos in AD 325 and in 530 the first church, Agia Triada, was built. The history of the island in the Byzantine years has not been documented in detail, though it is known that it belonged administratively to the province of Thessaly. During the 7th century the island suffered much from Saracen pirate raids. When Constantinople was seized by the Fourth Crusade in 1204, Skiathos, like most of the Aegean islands, was taken by the Venetians. From 1207 to 1454 Skiathos was the property of the Venetian Ghisi family, which built a fortress in 1270 in Bourtzi, a charming quarter of the capital. In 1537 the island was conquered by Haradin Barbarossa and the Turkish navy. Skiathots, like all Greek islanders, used their naval resources and creativity to aid the struggle for independence that started in 1821. Two years later the island was liberated.

Its capital Skiathos has stood in the same position since antiquity. It was briefly abandoned when its inhabitants moved north to a fortress for security during the precarious times of the Turkish dominance of the Aegean. This fortified capital, Kastro, is best visited today by boat. It provided respite to the Allied forces on their way to the Middle East during World War II. Of the 30 churches once inside the castle, only 3 remain. Several other churches and monasteries dot the island. An unspoiled strip of coast is known as "the port of Xerxes" because during the campaign of the Persian king in 480 BC three Greek ships were waiting here to confront his fleet. The island was the home of two short story-writers, Alexandros Papadiamantis (1851–1911), whose birthplace may be visited, and Alexandros Moraitidis (1851–1929), who towards the end of his life found refuge in the 18th-century monastery of St Charalambos on the north side of the island.

Skopelos (Greek for "steep rock from the sea" because of its rugged coastline) is almost twice as large as Skiathos and has about the same population. It is situated between Skiathos and Alonnisos and, like Skiathos, has frequent connections with Volos and Euboea. Its land is mostly flat with only a few low mountains. Pine trees abound and the local prunes are famous. The verdant landscape, the domestic architecture, and the churches are the chief attractions of this island.

Its present name appeared first in the Hellenistic period. Previously the name Peparithos was used. Legend has it that Peparithos with his brother Staphylos, sons of Ariadne and Dionysus, landed on the island with a group of Cretans in the bay known as Staphylos to this day. Staphylos, who became the first king, was buried there in a grave which was discovered in 1927. The finds – a gold crown, funerary offerings, and weapons – are displayed in the museum of Volos. During historical times Skopelos was inhabited first by Mycenaeans between 1600 and 1100 BC and later by Chalcidians between 700 and 500 BC. As a member of the Delian League it was ruled by Athenians until 340 BC when it came under Macedonian dominance, which continued until 168 BC when Athenians took over once again. The Ghisi family owned the island during the Venetian occupation and built a castle with a magnificent view over the ruins of the ancient citadel. In 1537–38 Skopelos shared the fate of Skiathos, being sacked by Barbarossa and by the Turks under whose occupation it remained until the revolution, during which its fleet played an active part in the struggle for liberation.

Its main town, Skopelos (Chora), is built on a bay in the southeast, winding in tiers from the quarter of Kastro down to the shore with its gleaming white two- or three-storeyed houses, narrow cobbled streets, quaint alleys, and a plethora of churches, chapels, monasteries, and convents. Chora alone has 123 churches; there are 360 on the island as a whole. Notable also are its 12 whitewashed 17th- and 18th-century convents.

Alonnisos to the east of Skopelos is an oblong island with a hilly landscape covering an area of 64 sq km and is populated by slightly more than 1500 people. It is the least developed of the Sporades and therefore the least visited. The sea surrounding the coastline is designated a marine conservation park to protect the Mediterranean seals which have chosen the coves of smaller islands near Alonnisos as a haven. An earthquake in 1965 damaged the earlier capital, Alonnisos, and most of the inhabitants abandoned it and resettled 5 km to the east near the sea. The present port capital of Patitiri is on the southeastern side, 68 nautical miles from Volos and 35 from Euboea. The same earthquake split the centre of the island into two small islets – Psathoura (the remains of ancient Alonnisos) and Psatharopoula. Both lie submerged.

Signs that Alonnisos was inhabited in prehistoric times were found at Kokkinokastro and on the islet near it. The earliest palaeolithic finds in the Aegean were discovered here: animal bones and stone tools dating from 100,000 to 33,000 BC (Middle Palaeolithic period). The island was known as Ikos in antiquity, and the names Chelidromia and Diadromia were used later. A variation of these, Liodromia, is heard even today. According to mythology Peleus, father of Achilles, spent the last years of his life in Ikos and was buried on the island. Statues, tombstones, potsherds, and wine bottles from Ikos have been preserved at Kokkinokastro. The Athenians maintained a naval base there, stimulating the interest of Philip II of Macedon to bring the island under his rule. In 1538 Barbarossa and the Turks did not spare the island from plunderous attacks.

Alonnisos is surrounded by a host of tiny islands, the largest of which are Peristera and Lehoussa on its eastern side. On the small island of Youra to the northeast the Cyclops' cave with multicoloured stalactites and stalagmites is worth visiting.

Skyros, the largest in the group with an area of 209 sq km and a population of almost 2800, is the closest to Euboea, which is only 24 nautical miles away. Its capital, Skyros (Chorio or Chora), is close to the sea on the northeastern coast, while its port, Linaria, is located on the western side 11 km from the capital. The stark antithesis between the northern

and southern parts of the island creates a natural divide connected by a narrow isthmus. Most of the population is concentrated in the northern, verdant part, since the southern, rocky side is virtually inaccessible. The island's vernacular architecture, its rich local folklore, and the diversity of its scenery give Skyros its unique character.

Archaeological finds reveal that the island has been inhabited since the neolithic period (5000 BC). Ancient legend considers its citadel to be the place where Thetis, Achilles' mother, hid her son disguised as a maiden among the daughters of king Lycomedes so that he could avoid the draft in the Greek campaign against Troy. Another legend claims this as the place where Theseus, king of Athens, met his death. Between 469 and 340 BC Athenians colonized the island and during Cimon's rule they divided the land in lots. Macedonians succeeded in taking over the island and kept it until 196 BC; the Athenians took it back and later passed it over to the Romans. Like Skopelos it served as a place of exile in the Byzantine period. The Ghisi family owned it during the Venetian rule until Barbarossa sacked it in 1537 and facilitated the Turkish conquest. It was liberated in 1829. A witness of its continuous history since prehistory is the fortified acropolis around which the present capital is built. A castle was erected on the site of the ancient citadel. At the castle the restored church of St George has dominated the island since its foundation in 963 by the emperor Nikephoros Phokas as a *metochion* (dependency) of the monastery of the Great Lavra on Mount Athos. The houses of the island with their carved wooden furniture and decor, the pottery, the handwoven household items and embroideries exhibit a faithful continuation of a strong tradition in folk art. Beyond the castle to the north in a square overlooking the sea stands the bust of the British poet Rupert Brooke (1887–1915) who is buried on the south coast at Treis Boukes. In the south one may chance upon some of the indigenous ponies that can be found only on this island.

CELIA KAPSOMERA

Summary

A group of four islands and numerous rocky islets in the northwest Aegean. The main islands are Skiathos, Skopelos, Alonnisos, and Skyros. In the 5th century BC they belonged to the Delian League. From 1207 to 1454 they were owned by the Venetian Ghisi family. In 1537 they were sacked by Barbarossa. Though sharing a common history, each island preserves its own character.

Further Reading

Ephstratiou, Nicholas, *Agios Petros: A Neolithic Site in the Northern Sporades*, London: BAR, 1985

Graindor, Paul, *Histoire de l'ile de Skyros jusqu'en 1538*, Paris: Belles Lettres, 1906

Graves, Robert, "The Death of Theseus" in *The Greek Myths*, Harmondsworth: Penguin, 1960, reprinted 1992

Held, Marc, *Skopelos: The Landscapes and Vernacular Architecture of an Aegean Island*, translated by Ros Schwartz, Thessalonica: Reprotime, 1994

Karpodini-Dimitriadi, E., *The Greek Islands: A Traveller's Guide to all the Greek Islands*, Athens, 1995

Sampson, Adamantios, *He nesos Skopelos*, Athens, 1968

Trudel, Jean-Paul, *Sporades*, Ottawa: Avila Lacoursière, 1946

Stephan IV Dushan

Ruler of Serbia in the mid-14th century

A Serbian king and self-styled emperor, Stephan IV Dushan (1331–55) led the southward expansion of the Serbian state and tried to build a Graeco-Slavic empire modelled on Byzantium. He had spent seven years of his youth in Constantinople with his exiled father Stephan III Decanski (1321–31), and he had obtained there a first-hand knowledge of Byzantium. After the assassination of his father by Serbian nobles in 1331, he acceded early to the Serbian throne. The land-hungry Serbian nobility was both the motive force behind Serbia's expansionist drive and the main cause for the rapid disintegration of the Serbian empire after Dushan's death.

The internal difficulties of Byzantium and the Black Death that struck in 1348 greatly facilitated the Serbian success. At the onset of the second civil war (1341–47) in Byzantium, the imperial pretender John Kantakouzenos allied himself with the Serbians against the regency government of John V Palaiologos. When Kantakouzenos found military support among the Greeks in Thessaly, he abandoned the alliance with Dushan, but the Serbs continued to plunder Byzantine territories on their own. Southern Macedonia fell into Serbian hands in 1345, and was followed by Thessaly and Epirus in 1348. After the fall of the city of Serres in 1345, Stephan Dushan began to style himself emperor of the Serbs and Romans. In the following year, on Easter Sunday, he had himself crowned emperor at Skopje by the archbishop of the Serbian Church whom he had elevated to the rank of a patriarch. Dushan sought legitimacy for his title among both the Greek and the Slavic population living under his rule. The coronation was witnessed by the Protos (head of the community) and the abbots of the monasteries of Mount Athos. Dushan generously endowed the Athonite monasteries with lands and privileges and he himself spent several months in the Serbian monastery of Chilandar in 1347–48.

As *basileus* (king) and *autokrator* (emperor) of the Serbs and Romans Dushan intended to take over Constantinople and make himself master of the Byzantine empire. The seriousness of his intentions is seen in the fact that he offered Venice possession of Galata and the whole of Epirus if the Italian republic would help him to storm Constantinople with its fleet. The dream of the conquest of Constantinople was never realized and Dushan died in the last stage of his preparation for assault on the imperial capital. Nevertheless, his advance into the Balkans in the late 1340s and early 1350s met with extraordinary success. By 1355 the Serbs controlled Albania, Epirus, Thessaly, Aetolia, and Acarnania. Their empire stretched from the Danube to the Gulf of Corinth and from the Adriatic to the Aegean Sea. Byzantium lost half of its territory, retaining only Thrace, the Peloponnese, Thessalonica, and Constantinople.

Stephan IV Dushan introduced Byzantine influence into Serbian administration, court ceremonial, and law. The process of Hellenization of Serbian court life and administration had begun already in the late 13th century when the Byzantine princess Simonis came to the Serbian court as wife of Stephan II Milutin (1282–1321). In Dushan's day, Serbian administrators became increasingly adorned with Byzantine titles. Dushan minted silver coins that closely followed the Byzantine model. Churches and monasteries in his empire were decorated in the best Byzantine style. Furthermore, the emperor attempted to merge the legal traditions of the Serbs and the Byzantines. By his order, the *Syntagma* of Matthew Blastares (a collection of both secular and ecclesiastical rulings), written in 1335, was translated into Serbian shortly after its composition. Dushan's code of law, the *Zakonik*, promulgated in 1349 and reissued in 1354, was based partly on Byzantine legal models. It proclaimed the equality of Byzantines and Serbs, and reconfirmed privileges conferred on Greek cities by past Byzantine emperors.

Still, Stephan Dushan was less successful as a state-builder than as a conqueror. This was due primarily to the ambitions of his nobles, but also to the ethnically heterogeneous character of his empire. The Serbian conquest was too rapid and too violent, while the conquered Byzantine population could hardly accept an emperor of the Romans outside Constantinople. Although Dushan tried to accommodate Greeks in his state, the important administrative offices in the conquered territories were held by Serbian nobles or by members of Dushan's family, all decorated with Byzantine titles. His son and heir Stephan V Uroš (1366–77) lacked the energy of his father and saw the disintegration of the Serbian empire into a medley of small states. Stephan IV Dushan's half-brother Uroš carved for himself a principality in northern Greece with a capital at Trikkala and proclaimed himself tsar of the Romans, Serbs, and Albanians. Uroš was a generous benefactor of the monasteries of the Meteora, which would become an important centre of Orthodoxy during the period of the Tourkokratia. Other relatives of Dushan or noblemen established themselves as princes elsewhere. When the Ottomans started their incursions into Europe after 1354, two local lords in Macedonia, the brothers Vukasin and John Uglesa, led the resistance against the Turks and perished in the fateful Battle of Chernomen on the Maritza river in 1371. Soon thereafter Byzantium became a vassal tributary state of the Ottomans. The victory of the Turks in 1371, more than the Battle of Kosovo in 1389, opened up the Balkans for Ottoman conquest.

The empire of Stephan IV Dushan represents the second unsuccessful attempt at the creation of a Graeco-Slavic empire modelled on Byzantium after the one led by king Symeon of Bulgaria (893–927). Like Symeon, Dushan lacked the military and economic resources for such a grand endeavour. The long-term effects of Dushan's empire lay elsewhere, particularly in his patronage of the Orthodox Church, which was revitalized in this period by hesychast monasticism. Hesychasm spread rapidly among the southern Slavs and strengthened the bonds of the Graeco-Slavic cultural commonwealth just before the Turkish conquest of the Balkans. The expansion of the Serbs in the mid-14th century had serious political effects on the Greek peninsula. The breakdown of Dushan's empire left northern and central Greece in a state of extreme political fragmentation and decentralization, a circumstance that eased the Ottoman conquest of this area in the late 14th and the 15th centuries.

DIMITER G. ANGELOV

See also Serbia

Biography

The son of Stephan III Decanski, Stephan Dushan spent some years as a youth in Constantinople. He came to the Serbian throne in 1331 after his father's assassination. He conquered much Byzantine territory south of Serbia and in 1345 proclaimed himself emperor of the Serbs and Romans. His conquests contributed to the Hellenization of Serbia. He died in 1355.

Further Reading

Fine, John V.A., Jr, *The Late Medieval Balkans: A Critical Survey from the Late Twelfth Century to the Ottoman Conquest*, Ann Arbor: University of Michigan Press, 1987

Nicol, Donald M., *The Last Centuries of Byzantium, 1261–1453*, 2nd edition, Cambridge and New York: Cambridge University Press, 1993

Obolensky, Dimitri, *The Byzantine Commonwealth: Eastern Europe, 500–1453*, London: Weidenfeld and Nicolson, and New York: Praeger, 1971

Soulis, George Christos, *The Serbs and Byzantium during the Reign of Tsar Stephen Dušan (1331–1355) and his Successors*, Washington: Dumbarton Oaks, 1984

Stoicism

Stoicism was a philosophical movement that took its name from the Stoa Poikile, or Painted Porch, in the Agora at Athens, the central public place where philosophers used to meet, to lecture, and to engage in discussions. The school was founded by Zeno of Citium (335–263 BC), who came to Athens around 313 BC and studied under the Academic Polemo and the Cynic Crates. He was succeeded as the head of the school by Cleanthes of Assos (331–232 BC), who in turn was succeeded by Chrysippus of Soli (c.280–207 BC), perhaps the greatest Stoic philosopher, Diogenes of Babylon (c.240–152 BC), and Antipater of Tarsus (2nd century BC). Zeno divided philosophy into three parts: logic, physics, and ethics. His followers took up and developed his doctrines in different directions. Zeno's student Aristo of Chios stressed ethics to the exclusion of physics and logic, whereas Herillus emphasized knowledge at the expense of moral action. Cleanthes, on the other hand, advocated a religious view of the world, and his contributions to Stoicism lay especially in the areas of theology and cosmology. It was Chrysippus more than anyone else who advanced and systematized the doctrines of the school; thus his works came to be regarded as offering the standard formulation of Stoicism. The so-called Middle Stoa attempted to make Stoic doctrine more accessible to a wider audience, and was more hospitable to ideas from other philosophical schools, particularly Plato's and Aristotle's. Panaetius from Rhodes (c.185–109 BC) changed the emphasis of the school's teaching to make it more directly relevant to the practical concerns of everyday life. Panaetius' pupil Posidonius of Apamea (c.135–50 BC) also modified the traditional doctrine of the school in some areas, but his main interest seems to have been the sciences, including geography and ethnography. Of the writings of the Stoics down to Posidonius almost nothing remains except for a hymn by Cleanthes and a few papyrus fragments. We have, though, numerous reports in later writers, some of them clearly hostile to Stoic philosophy, and many simply failing to grasp fully the Stoic doctrines. Thus reconstructing the philosophical ideas of the earlier Stoics proves to be a difficult, if not at times impossible, scholarly task.

Stoic philosophy was a major influence on political and moral thought in the Roman empire in the last century BC and the first two centuries AD. The treatises and letters of Seneca (c.4 BC–AD 65), the lectures of Epictetus (c.AD 55–135), and the meditations of the emperor Marcus Aurelius (AD 121–80) laid particular emphasis on the ethical teachings of the school. Seneca and Roman expositors of Stoic philosophy such as Cicero facilitated the transmission of diffuse accounts of Stoic ethics into the writings of the Latin Fathers, such as Lactantius, Ambrose, Augustine, and Martin of Braga, and subsequently into the medieval world. We find a kind of medieval Stoicism, represented by such scholars as Petrarch, and focused mainly on ethics. During Humanism the main sources for ancient Stoicism were all translated into Latin, and in the 15th century scholars such as Justus Lipsius made an attempt to reconstruct and to some extent revive Stoicism, presenting it as compatible with Christian theology. Early modern thinkers of the 16th century such as Jean Pena, Tycho Brahe, Juan Luis Vives, and Guillaume du Vair already show the influence of Stoic ideas. Some of the most important philosophers of the 17th and 18th centuries such as Hobbes, Descartes, and Spinoza incorporated into their philosophy Stoic elements, just as scientists such as Newton also drew on Stoic ideas.

Although it may be true that especially in the later phases of Stoicism ethics became the vital concern, this does not mean that the other parts of philosophy, namely logic and physics, had a subordinate place in Stoic doctrine. On the contrary, the Stoics viewed philosophy as a whole and repeatedly emphasized the close interdependence of the three parts of philosophical discourse. For though the highest aim of the Stoic was to learn how to conduct himself in life, Stoic philosophers never doubted that this was to be based on a firm grasp of the truth and on an adequate understanding of the world. This is the reason why they used to compare parts of philosophy to the parts of an egg or an animal; the shell or the bones are logic, the white or the flesh are ethics, while the yolk or the soul are physics. The tripartite division of Stoic philosophy as well as the different orders that were suggested for the study of the three parts served only as the most appropriate way of expounding or learning the theorems of Stoic philosophy.

Logic, according to the Stoics, was the study of everything to do with rational discourse. It was divided into dialectic and rhetoric; dialectic included logic in the modern sense, but also grammar, semantics, philosophy of language, and epistemology. The Stoics believed that knowledge ultimately is based on sense experience. Human beings start as irrational animals with no mind at birth, and it is only because they receive repeated impressions from the outside world that give rise to concepts that their rationality grows, by the continuous formation of concepts and beliefs. They also claimed that in principle it is possible for human beings to have solid knowledge. For there are certain impressions, the so-called cognitive impressions (*kataleptikai phantasiai*), which by their nature indicate in a clear and distinct way a fact about the world. Hence they can be regarded as criteria of truth, i.e. as instruments for judging whether our opinions are true or false. Needless to say, the ancient sceptics questioned whether there are such criteria on which the whole of our knowledge may securely rest, and the Stoics, who engaged in a continuous controversy with them, tried to refine and develop their theory in order to meet their objections.

The basis of Stoic logic is a theory about significant speech, in which the Stoics distinguish between the sound uttered, that which is said or meant, the *lekton*, and the external referent. Although this Stoic doctrine is often highly praised, because it seems to resemble recent theories of meaning and, in particular, to anticipate the modern distinction between sense and reference, there are significant differences. For instance, in Stoic logic a *lekton* does not correspond to any expression, say a noun, but only to a complete utterance. So some *lekta* may be questions or commands, whereas others are propositions that may be true or false. The Stoic logical system was concerned with the interrelations of non-simple propositions, in particular of propositions of the form of conditionals, exclusive disjunctions, and negated conjunctions. It was mainly Chrysippus who, also under the influence of Diodorus Cronus and Philo of Megara, advanced the logic of propositions to its highest point in antiquity, presumably independently of Aristotle's logic of terms. According to Chrysippus, this logic can be construed as an axiomatic system in which all arguments are reducible to five basic kinds of indemonstrable arguments (*anapodeiktoi*) whose validity does not admit of proof. The form of the first two indemonstrables, for instance, was as follows: (1) if the first, then the second; but the first; therefore the second; and (2) if the first, then the second; but not the second; therefore not the first. These two indemonstrables became known later in antiquity and in the Middle Ages as the *modus ponendo ponens* and the *modus tollendo tollens* respectively.

Stoic physics was based on the presupposition that there is one world (*kosmos*) which constitutes a single living being, and that there are only two principles from which everything is constituted; an active principle, which is named God, *Logos* (Intellect), or Nature, and a passive principle, which is understood as unqualified substance or matter. The Stoics stressed that these principles are always joined and never exist separated from one another. The active principle is present in the whole universe and gives to every part of it its character. It is therefore the ruling principle of the whole world, a ruling principle itself of the form of a rational living being that is both intelligent and intelligible. Materiality, on the other hand, is not equivalent to corporeality, but just one aspect of it, as any body is already formed. The world is a continuous object and it cannot be divided into discrete particles, as in Epicurus' physics. The Stoics confined existence to bodies, and vehemently rejected claims of earlier thinkers concerning incorporeal entities. Even God was identified with a special form of fire, which gives shape and life to the world. Following Heraclitus, the Stoics claimed that the transformations of fire, which correspond to the designing or creative activities of God, bring about the alternating phases of a cosmic cycle. For the Stoics did not maintain that the present world is ungenerated and indestructible; they rather believed that it will end in a total conflagration (*ekpyrosis*), but will then be reconstituted again as the conflagration subsides. Only God persists through the conflagration as the fire into which everything is absorbed. As the world order again emerges from this fire, God's presence in earthly things is in the form of breath or spirit (*pneuma*), a fiery form of air. Organic and inorganic things alike owe their identity and their properties to it; its two constituents, fire and air, are blended in different proportions in different things. In the case of human beings, it is the human soul that constitutes part of the all-pervasive *pneuma*. Thus within the world order *pneuma* has two related functions: it gives internal coherence to individual bodies, and it also, because it permeates everything, makes the world as a whole a single coherent body.

In this rational world order, which is ruled by God or *Logos*, the interactions of bodies occur according to exceptionless laws; these laws constitute "fate" and are identified by the Stoics with providence. They held the view that for everything that happens there are causes such that, given these causes, nothing else could happen; for the Stoics "chance" is simply a name for undiscovered causes. That is why they claimed that all future events in principle are predictable, and that astrology and divination should be regarded as empirical disciplines. However, in this deterministic world there still is a place for what is just possible and not necessary. Chrysippus understood the possible as that which admits of being true and is not prevented from being the case. He moreover developed a complex theory of causation to explain how human action is free in a sense required if human beings are to be responsible for their actions. According to his view, fate is the set of external causes that act upon the individual and work to bring about their destined effects; but these external causes only trigger things to happen, whereas the primary cause is in the individual itself. Thus the external antecedent cause by itself does not necessitate the action. Now, although for the Stoics all people are responsible for their actions, only the wise man is free; for freedom consists of acting of one's own choice as one is providentially ordained to act for the best of the universe as a whole. Thus Stoicism is not a fatalistic philosophy of inaction, and the wise man will act in whatever way seems appropriate given the understanding he has; to decide to act in the way one is destined to act is in our own power, even if it is settled by fate how we are going to act, given the sort of person we are.

Stoic ethics presents the most demanding account of virtue in antiquity. Virtue alone is the good, while all wrong actions are equally wrong. We acquire the notion of the good as a crucial part of our reason, and this transforms our motivation in such a way as to be attracted by what we judge to be good. Virtue is sufficient for happiness, which is defined as life in accordance with nature; the nature with which one is to live in agreement is both one's own rational constitution as a person, human nature, and the rationality of universal Nature or God. That we are meant to live in agreement with Nature is also expressed by the Stoics in talking about the common law, or a natural law, which demands that we do what is natural and refrain from doing what is against Nature. This gave rise to a theory of natural law that was taken up by the Christian Fathers, notably Augustine, and exerted considerable influence on discussions of human rights throughout modern times. For the Stoics the possible conflict between particular and universal Nature is only apparent; the virtuous man will have no preference of his own in conflict with the good of the world. Passions are the source of unhappiness, for a person in such a state, by assenting to a certain kind of false impression, has himself generated an excessive impulse to pursue or avoid something that in reality is indifferent. Passions as false judgements are thus not a feature of non-rational animals, but characterize only human beings who should be blamed for them. So there is no conflict between reason and desire in an individual soul free of passion, and apparent conflicts are explained as rapid waverings of our judgement.

Happiness does not in the least depend on the possession or absence of things only conventionally regarded as good or bad, such as health, reputation, wealth, beauty, etc.; these things are regarded as "indifferent", since they make no difference to virtue and true happiness. Now among things indifferent some things are in accordance with nature and others contrary to nature; both lack goodness, but the first should be selected on the grounds of their natural preferability, and that is why they are called "preferred indifferents". Furthermore, "proper actions" are all the actions that are natural to a mature human being. "Right actions" are a special kind of proper actions, the perfect proper actions, which are the peculiar province of the unfailingly wise or virtuous man. The difference lies in the motivation. A right action is a proper action done with the motivation only a wise man can have. A wise person realizes that the important thing is not to attain a particular preferred indifferent but to try to do so, because it is good to do it. For the Stoics there is a sharp distinction between the virtuous or wise person and everybody else, who is regarded as foolish. It is very difficult to be wise, and that is why the Stoics never claimed that they had achieved wisdom.

KATERINA IERODIAKONOU

See also Philosophy

Texts

Arnim, H.F.A. von, *Stoicorum Veterum Fragmenta*, 4 vols, Leipzig: Teubner, 1903–24

Long, A.A. and D.N. Sedley, *The Hellenistic Philosophers*, vols. 1–2, Cambridge and New York: Cambridge University Press, 1987

Further Reading

Bobzien, Susanne, *Determinism and Freedom in Stoic Philosophy*, Oxford: Clarendon Press, and New York: Oxford University Press, 1998

Frede, Michael, *Die stoische Logik*, Göttingen: Vandenhoeck & Ruprecht, 1974

Hahm, David E., *The Origins of Stoic Cosmology*, Columbus: Ohio State University Press, 1977

Ierodiakonou, Katerina (editor), *Topics in Stoic Philosophy*, Oxford: Clarendon Press, and New York: Oxford University Press, 1999

Inwood, Brad, *Ethics and Human Action in Early Stoicism*, Oxford: Clarendon Press, and New York: Oxford University Press, 1985

Long, A.A. (editor), *Problems in Stoicism*, London: Athlone Press, 1971

Rist, John M., *Stoic Philosophy*, Cambridge: Cambridge University Press, 1969

Rist, John M. (editor), *The Stoics*, Berkeley: University of California Press, 1978

Sandbach, F.H., *The Stoics*, London: Chatto and Windus, and New York: Norton, 1975

Strabo *c.*64 BC–*c.*AD 19

Geographer, philosopher, and historian

Strabo is the author of two monumental works: a universal history in 47 books, which has not survived, and his famous *Geography* in 17 books, which has. As a young man Strabo studied philosophy and was particularly drawn to Stoicism. He knew, and was apparently influenced by, the famous philosopher Posidonius. Strabo believed, with the Pythagoreans, that the universe was geocentric, and that the earth was a sphere with a single land mass surrounded by water. He travelled to Italy three times, visited Greece and Asia Minor, and lived in Egypt for about six years. This combination of travel and philosophical study resulted in a work of geography which is noteworthy for the exposition of a philosophy of geography and for its wealth of historical and mythological information.

Strabo held that the study of geography belongs to the realm of philosophy. He states in book 1 of his *Geography* that, although it is primarily useful to commanders and statesmen, geography is also invaluable for philosophers who investigate everything on land and sea. The study of geography presupposes "the man who busies himself with the investigation of the art of life, that is of happiness" (1. 1. 1). Given this purpose, Strabo's methodology was to interlace clear and accurate descriptions of geographical features with a broad range of cultural information. He saw himself as writing in a tradition of literary, historical geography whose origins went back to Homer, and included Hecataeus and Herodotus.

The value of Strabo's work also lies in the fact that it fills certain gaps in our knowledge of his predecessors. He opens his *Geography* with a history of geographical writing from Homer down to his own day, providing critiques of earlier geographers such as Eratosthenes, Eudoxus, Artemidorus, and Hipparchus. The first two books thus provide us with an invaluable survey of ancient geographical practice, including, among other things, details about ancient mapmaking practices and attempts by Aristotle and Eratosthenes to measure the earth.

In the remainder of the work Strabo describes particular regions. He begins with Europe and works his way east to Asia, ending with north Africa. Within that range he discusses Spain (book 3); Gaul, Britain, and the Alps (book 4); northern Italy (book 5); southern Italy and Sicily (book 6); northern, eastern, and central Europe (book 7); Macedonia and Greece (book 8); Athens, Boeotia, and Thessaly (book 9); and Aetolia, Crete, and certain Greek islands (book 10). His coverage of Asia Minor is divided into four books: Caucasus and Armenia (book 11); Galatia, Bithynia, and Lycia (book 12); the Troad, including the island of Lesbos (book 13); and Ionia, Caria, Samos, Chios, Rhodes, and Cyprus (book 14). The remaining three books describe India and Parthia (book 15); Assyria, Babylonia, Mesopotamia, Syria, Phoenicia, Palestine, and Arabia (book 16); and finally Egypt, Ethiopia, and Libya (book 17).

The books which deal with Greece contain more mythological and historical information than any others. The section on Olympia (8. 3. 30), for example, has as much discussion of Homer as it does of geography. With regard to his reliability, there are times when it is clear that Strabo has visited the locations under consideration. He describes the coast of Attica in such a way that it seems likely that he circumnavigated it. At other times he seems to have relied largely on other sources. The passages on Boeotia are apparently taken largely from earlier writings, most notably the catalogue of the ships in book 2 of the *Iliad*. Most scholars would agree that Strabo probably never visited the interior of Attica, and perhaps that is true for the rest of mainland Greece as well.

We have no way of knowing whether Strabo's work ever fulfilled its task of aiding some ancient general or politician. We do know that the geography did not find a wide audience in antiquity. Strabo's work was apparently not known to the Romans, not even to Pliny the elder, although the Jewish historian Josephus referred to it. His work was apparently not much used in the Byzantine and medieval periods, but the first translation of his text into Latin (1472) preceded Columbus's voyages by only 20 years. For the next 400 years Strabo's work was in the public eye. As an exemplar of idiographic, or descriptive, geography he was much admired. A prominent German geographer of the 16th century, Sebastian Munster, was referred to as the German Strabo. His *Cosmographia Universalis* was a standard work for over a century. By the mid-19th century such universal geography had become impossible for one man to compile. The trend was toward specialization, and from that point on, Strabo was forgotten as more modern methods of geographical research evolved.

For all that, Strabo's approach to geography is remarkably modern, a suitable predecessor to the current integration of physical and cultural geography. His prose does not, perhaps, reach the heights of literary achievement, but it is serviceable and he does not claim to be writing a literary masterpiece. A. Lesky's harsh judgement (*History of Greek Literature*, London, 1966, p. 890), that Strabo is "not important in any way", is surely unmerited. The value of his work as a compendium of cultural information, a historical geography, and a philosophy of geography is inestimable.

TIMOTHY F. WINTERS

See also Geography

Biography

Born at Amaseia in Pontus *c.*64 BC, Strabo was a pupil of Aristodemus of Nysa and later studied philosophy at Rome. He knew the philosopher Posidonius from whom he may have developed the idea of writing a historical geography. He wrote two major works: a universal history in 47 books (lost) and a *Geography* in 17 books which survives. He died *c.*AD 19.

Writings

The Geography, translated by H.L. Jones, 8 vols, London: Heinemann, and New York: Putnam, 1917–33 (Loeb edition; several reprints)
De Strabonis Codice Rescripto, edited by Wolfgang Aly, Vatican City: Biblioteca Apostolica Vaticana, 1956
Geographica, edited by Wolfgang Aly, Bonn: Habelt, 1957–

Further Reading

Aly, Wolfgang and E. Honigman, Strabon entry in *Real-Encyclopädie der klassischen Altertumswissenschaft*, edited by August Pauly *et al.*, vol. 4A, 1931, 76–155
Bunbury, E.H., *A History of Ancient Geography*, 2nd edition, London: John Murray, 1883; reprinted New York: Dover, 1959
Diller, Aubrey, *The Textual Tradition of Strabo's Geography*, Amsterdam: Hakkert, 1975
Engels, Johannes, *Augusteische Oikumenegeographie und Universalhistorie im Werk Strabons von Amaseia*, Stuttgart: Steiner, 1999
James, Preston E. and G.J. Martin, *All Possible Worlds: A History of Geographical Ideas*, 2nd edition, New York: Wiley, 1981
Thomson, J. Oliver, *History of Ancient Geography*, Cambridge: Cambridge University Press, 1948; New York: Biblo and Tannen, 1965
Tozer, H.F., *A History of Ancient Geography*, Cambridge: Cambridge University Press, 1897
Waddy, L., "Did Strabo visit Athens?", *American Journal of Archaeology*, 57 (1963): pp. 296–300
Wallace, P., "Strabo on Acrocorinth", *Hesperia*, 38 (1969): pp. 495–9
Weller, C.H., "The Extent of Strabo's Travel in Greece", *Classical Philology*, 1 (1908): pp. 339–56

Sublime Porte

Ottoman centre of government, 1789–1922

The term "Sublime Porte" is a western description of the Ottoman centre of government from 1789 to 1922. Sublime Porte is an English adoption of the French phrase "La Sublime Porte", derived from the Turkish expression "Bab-I Ali". The literal translation of both phrases is "High" or "Exalted Gateway", representing the elevated western opinion of the Ottoman capital. Central to the effective administration of the Ottoman empire was the efficient bureaucracy that directed the actions of government at every level. An imported system imitating the Byzantine model, the Ottoman government of the late 18th, 19th, and early 20th centuries was one of the most effective administrations in the world.

Denoting the centre of government through description of a physical term is a western tradition similar to that of identifying the king's "court" with the centre of government of a kingdom. The Porte, or actual governmental headquarters of the Ottoman empire, changed location over the period 1789–1922, but the term consistently referred to the building or collection of buildings that housed the principal administrative agencies of the empire. In the 18th century the Porte referred to the actual court of the Grand Vizier; however, by the 20th century the term included the Grand Vizier's household and the multiple dispersed bureaux attached to him.

A lasting legacy that permeated many forms of government in the post-Byzantine world was dependence upon a trained, efficient bureaucracy to regulate and administer empires. The organization of the Porte, and the personnel assigned to it, was distinguished by the education of its workers and their dedication to specific government functions. Bureaucrats were selected by their aptitude for specific duties. Scribes dedicated themselves to the routine and monotonous functions of government record. Derived from this condition was a lack of concern for events beyond those related to the completion of official business. The Hellenic tradition, forming the base of the Ottoman administration, demanded servitude to government needs and duties with a lack of regard to social or societal disposition. This tradition further demanded a highly skilled and dedicated workforce.

Ottoman bureaucratic efficiency remained constant through the period of significant government change that occurred between 1789 and 1922. In the 18th century patrimonial appointment regulated duty assignments within the government and the Turkish system reflected lingering trends of the Hellenic tradition. Ottoman rulers, faced with the daunting task of administering distant and diverse populations, employed Greek civil servants in an attempt to replicate the efficiency of the Greek model. Greek bureaucrats, likewise, found employment within administrations in Europe and the Middle East. Imperial administration required specialized skills and disciplined dedication to duties, two qualities found in Greek civil servants.

It was not until the 19th century that the Sublime Porte reached its peak of efficiency. Imbued with the ideals of government servitude and possessing a great literary tradition, the Ottoman bureaucracy began a slow but distinct rise to prominence within the Ottoman empire. Most scribes dedicated themselves to a life presenting few opportunities for advancement; however, some civil servants found themselves employed in the highest positions in the state. Bureaucratic personnel in the 19th century came, in large part, from the ruling class. Gradually, Greek professionals lost opportunities to more politically attuned Turkish bureaucrats. Turkish civil servants encouraged a series of changes that resulted in the ability to enforce government policy, a condition absent in the period of Greek domination. No longer were the qualities of servitude and dedication in demand, as the Sublime Porte of the 19th century strove to align itself with changes in society and politics.

The Ottomans created a well-regulated bureaucratic apparatus capable of administering the empire with great efficiency through periods of significant political change. Disregarding political concerns, the civil service as an institution possessed the flexibility to meet the evolving needs of a changing nation. The personnel policy of the 20th century replaced the paternalism of the imperial system. This change facilitated a gradual shift in the balance of power from the government heads to the government as a whole. No longer were the imperialist tendencies of irrational and immediate changes in policy possible. The well-established bureaucracy of the 20th century efficiently carried out policy and administered law and order in a manner that was consistent with tradition but flexible enough to survive contemporary demands. The Sublime Porte represented the continuity of a Greek legacy adapted to the needs of a foreign government and system.

SCOTT BLANCHETTE

Summary

The Sublime Porte (literally the High Gateway) is a western term for the Ottoman centre of government in Constantinople from 1789 to 1922. Its bureaucracy (a system inherited from the Byzantines) formed the heart of the Ottoman administration and managed the empire with great efficiency. Its location changed several times.

Further Reading

Armstrong, John A., *The European Administrative Elite*, Princeton, New Jersey: Princeton University Press, 1973

Berger, Morroe, *Bureaucracy and Society in Modern Egypt: A Study of the Higher Civil Service*, Princeton, New Jersey: Princeton University Press, 1957

Berkes, Niyazi, *The Development of Secularism in Turkey*, Montreal: McGill University Press, 1964, reprinted New York and London: Routledge, 1998

Dodd, C.H., *Politics and Government in Turkey*, Berkeley: University of California Press, and Manchester: Manchester University Press, 1969

Findley, Carter V., *Bureaucratic Reform in the Ottoman Empire: The Sublime Porte, 1789–1922*, Princeton, New Jersey: Princeton University Press, 1980

Frey, Frederick W., *The Turkish Political Elite*, Cambridge, Massachusetts: MIT Press, 1965

Lewis, Bernard, *The Emergence of Modern Turkey*, 2nd edition, London: Oxford University Press, 1968

Superstition

Superstition, taken to refer to a mechanical application of ritual without regard for or knowledge of either the outcome or the reasons underlying the act, can be said to exist in one form or another in every culture and society. In this sense the term is derisive and negative. For that reason one would be hard pressed to find any person or group of persons who jealously claimed that they were superstitious or that their beliefs amounted to superstition. Nevertheless, the word does have a certain currency in discussions of religion and magic. Modern scholarship has yet to purge it of its purely negative connotations or to arrive at any adequate definition of it.

The Greek term for superstition is *deisidaimonia* which roughly means "fear of the divine". The adjectival form of the word, *deisidaimon*, entered the language in the early part of the 4th century BC and bears a neutral, if not positive, meaning. Thus in the *Cyropaedia* Xenophon uses it to designate the piety of Cyrus' soldiers. Writing a few decades after Xenophon, Aristotle in the *Politics* also uses the word in a positive sense, saying that a populace takes comfort in a leader who is pious.

Deisidaimonia is far more commonly used in a derogatory sense, and the ancients commonly supposed that women were especially susceptible to it. The most famous discussion of *deisidaimonia* occurs in the *Characters*, a short tract by Aristotle's student and successor Theophrastus, whose purpose was to present the reader with a catalogue of various personality types. Among those enumerated is the type that suffers from *deisidaimonia* or superstition, which, in his words, is a form of cowardice with respect to the divine. People of this type are mechanical and fastidious in their observance of ritual. They live in a state of anxiety and are for ever concerned with the proper observance of rituals no matter how trifling or strange. To cite one example, "upon seeing a crazy person or an epileptic, with a shudder he spits into his bosom."

Writing some 400 years later, Plutarch informs us in an essay devoted to table talk that belief in the evil eye was a superstition that could be ridiculed by the educated classes of his day. In a separate tract *On Superstition* he discusses more fully the meaning of *deisidaimonia*. In his view, it is akin to atheism, the latter resulting from the former, but not vice versa. Furthermore, *deisidaimonia* arises from false reasoning and is characterized by an almost pathological fear of the divine.

Accordingly, a fundamental tenet of *deisidaimonia* is a belief that the gods are evil and visit misfortune upon man, whereas the atheist attributes such misfortunes to chance.

For Christian writers *deisidaimonia* was a convenient term with which to attack traditional pagan belief. In this way Clement of Alexandria, writing his *Exhortation to the Greeks* during the last half of the 2nd century AD, labels non-Christian belief *deisidaimonia* and calls its believers superstitious. In this work, *deisidaimonia* has a sense of demon worship characterized by festivals and sacrifice. While exceptional, it is worth noting that the author of Acts depicts Paul applying this word to the Athenians in the positive sense of "godfearing". Despite this, the general trend throughout antiquity for Christian and pagan alike was to view *deisdaimonia* as negative. In more modern times it is worth noting that the *Didaskalia Patriki* from the 18th century equates superstition with a belief that Christianity depends upon its Churches for survival. Here the emphasis on symbol over faith appears to be the distinguishing mark of superstition.

The modern belief in the evil eye is an oft-cited example of superstition, although this concept is obviously of very ancient origin and not unique to Greece. As manifested in Greek culture, the evil eye is a complex idea that misfortune can accrue to an individual, animal, or object through the mere glance of one who possesses it. Thus, the evil eye entails not only the idea that someone falls victim to it, but also that someone may acquire it as an attribute. The number of qualities that cause an individual to become vulnerable to it are many and at times contradictory. The belief that the beautiful and ugly alike can fall prey to the evil eye is one example of this. Curiously, mothers who have recently given birth, but have not yet been purified, can suffer its effects, while their babies are immune until after their baptism. A variety of defences are available to protect oneself from the evil eye, the most widely used of which is the protective amulet. Once afflicted by it, the victim may seek treatment from spiritual healers, whether in the form of "wise women" or even the clergy.

C.A. HOFFMAN

See also Atheism, Evil Eye, Magic

Further Reading

Clogg, Richard, "The 'Dhidhaskalia Patriki' (1798): An Orthodox Reaction to French Revolutionary Propaganda", *Middle Eastern Studies*, 5/2 (May 1969): pp. 87–115

Dickie, Matthew W., "The Fathers of the Church and the Evil Eye" in *Byzantine Magic*, edited by Henry Maguire, Washington, D.C.: Dumbarton Oaks, 1995

Dodds, E. R., *The Greeks and the Irrational*, Berkeley: University of California Press, 1951

Hardie, Margaret M., "The Evil Eye in Some Greek Villages of the Upper Haliskamon Valley in West Macedonia" in *The Evil Eye: A Folklore Casebook*, edited by Alan Dundes, New York: Garland, 1981

Jones, A.H.M., *The Later Roman Empire, 284–602: A Social, Economic, and Administrative Survey*, 3 vols, Oxford: Blackwell, and Norman: University of Oklahoma Press, 1964, reprinted Oxford: Blackwell, and Baltimore, Maryland: Johns Hopkins University Press, 1986

Syllabary, Cypriot

The syllabic writing system used on Cyprus from the Bronze Age to the Hellenistic period

It is more precise to speak of "Cypriot syllabaries" than "the Cypriot syllabary", for there have been discovered many forms of syllabic scripts on Cyprus, corresponding to at least two distinct languages (probably more), and dating from the 16th to the 3rd centuries BC.

The earliest syllabic script on Cyprus, the vehicle of a language commonly called "Cypro-Minoan", remains undeciphered. This script has been found on objects dating from the 16th to the 12th centuries BC, including clay tablets, vases, cylinders, and balls, various objects of bronze, copper, and silver, and cylinder seals. The script generally runs from left to right, though a few short inscriptions run from right to left, and at least one is written in boustrophedon fashion ("as the ox plows", running alternately right to left and left to right). At least 85 distinct signs have been identified, each probably representing a complete syllable – i.e. a vowel sound or a consonant–vowel combination, but not an unvocalized consonant (as in a true alphabet). The subject matter of the Cypro-Minoan inscriptions is obscure, of course, since the script is undeciphered, but the inscriptions appear to serve practical purposes: personal names to identify ownership, records of economic transactions, and lists of names and objects. Even in the present state of ignorance about the language underlying these inscriptions, the fact of there being so many inscriptions on such a variety of objects, all distributed over a wide area, conveys the idea of a general population on Cyprus that had achieved at least a limited degree of literacy by this early period.

The Cypro-Minoan script and the Linear B syllabic script of the Greek mainland stand in equal relation to the Linear A syllabic script of Crete, both Cypro-Minoan and Linear B being offshoots of the even more ancient Linear A. The relationship between these three syllabic scripts was not understood at first, but it is now generally accepted that even the earliest Cypro-Minoan inscription, a small fragment of a clay tablet from Enkomi (on the east coast of Cyprus) containing three lines of text with 20 distinct signs and dated to the late 16th century, is derived directly from Minoan Linear A. Perhaps as many as 18 of the 20 distinct signs on the Enkomi tablet have parallels in Linear A, while none of the 20 signs has been found in any Near Eastern script. This confirms what had been well known from other archaeological evidence: that Cyprus during this period was within the orbit of Minoan Crete. It implies further that epigraphic contact between Crete and Cyprus may date as far back as the late 17th century BC. As this is well before the arrival of Greek-speaking Mycenaeans on Cyprus, the source of the early Cypro-Minoan script can now be confidently ascribed directly to Minoan Linear A, without the intermediation of Mycenaean Linear B.

The script of the Enkomi tablet is the prototype of the three subcategories of Bronze Age Cypro-Minoan (CM) script, which have been classified by type of text, location of find, and writing style: CM 1 (the local script from all over Cyprus), CM 2 (from Enkomi), and CM 3 (from the region of Ugarit in Syria). As such, it is also the ancestor of the second major cate-

Cypriot Syllabary: inscription found on a bronze obelos (spit) in a tomb at Skales, Cyprus

gory of syllabaries on Cyprus: the later Archaic and Classical Cypriot syllabary.

While the Archaic and Classical Cypriot syllabary is epigraphically the natural evolution of the Cypro-Minoan, the language conveyed by the Cypriot syllabary has been understood for over 100 years, its decipherment having been initiated by George Smith in 1871. The language is Greek. Mycenaean Greek traders had begun to focus their attention on Cyprus from as early as the late 15th century BC, and trade between the two countries – as evidenced by the vast quantity of Mycenaean pottery that continues to be found on Cyprus, as well as by the juxtaposition of Mycenaean and Cyprian goods recently discovered in the underwater excavation of a Bronze Age trading vessel wrecked off the coast of Ulu Burun – grew enormously in the 14th and 13th centuries BC. Finally, in the wake of the disturbances that inundated the Mediterranean at the end of the 13th century BC, large numbers of Mycenaean Greeks, displaced from their palace states on the Greek mainland, fled both westward and eastward, one of the more attractive destinations being Cyprus.

These Mycenaean refugees brought with them their language – a dialect of Greek now designated Arcado-Cypriot – which they began to transcribe in the writing system already in place on Cyprus. Like the Linear B syllabary on the Greek mainland, the Cypriot syllabary served this purpose adequately; and the fact that some of the later Cypriot signs – *na*, *se*, *pa*, *po*, *to*, *ti*, *ta/da*, and *lo/ro* – are nearly identical to Linear B signs of the same value shows that some crossfertilization occurred. The Cypriot syllabary has the same five vowel sounds as Linear B, and the consonant sounds are only slightly different (the labio-velars are absent; *t* and *d* are not distinguished, while *l* and *r* are). But unlike Linear B, the final consonants *-n*, *-r*, and *-s* are noted, and consonant clusters and diphthongs are fully spelled out. The ideograms that are so common on the Linear B tablets are absent in the Cypriot inscriptions, and, unlike Linear B, the writing direction of the Cypriot script is usually from right to left, perhaps owing to Semitic influence. The system as a whole is somewhat more streamlined, with only 56 distinct signs in the Cypriot script in comparison to the 87 distinct signs of Linear B.

The earliest inscription in the Cypriot syllabary, found in Palaipaphos in southwestern Cyprus and dating from the 11th century BC, is on a bronze spit; it contains five signs – *o-pe-le-ta-u* – which can be recognized as the genitive case of a Greek name, presumably that of the owner of the spit. The next earliest extant inscription does not occur until the 8th century BC, and inscriptions do not become common until the 6th. These are mostly funerary and dedicatory inscriptions on stone, metal, and clay. A very long inscription dating from 480–470 BC, containing more than 1000 signs, has been found in the city of Idalium, in central Cyprus. It is a large bronze tablet engraved with a promise from the king of Idalium to grant plots of land as a reward to a family of physicians who had operated without pay on those wounded in battle during a siege of the city by the Medes. The corpus of Cypriot inscriptions continues to grow as excavations on Cyprus continue, and it can now boast around 1000 members.

It is a matter of some surprise that although the Greek alphabet, modelled on the Phoenician, was apparently current on Cyprus from the 8th century BC on, the syllabic system continued to be preferred until at least the Classical age. But eventually inscriptions began to be written digraphically, with the Cypriot syllabary and the Greek alphabet written side by side, until the spread of Hellenization under Alexander the Great tipped the scales in favour of the alphabetic system.

As an addendum, it should be noted that several inscriptions in the Classical Cypriot syllabary, some as late as the 4th century BC, found especially in the city of Amathus on the south coast of Cyprus, cannot be deciphered as Greek. This unknown, non-Greek, perhaps native language is conventionally called Eteo-Cypriot. Its relation to the undeciphered Cypro-Minoan of the Bronze Age remains obscure.

STEVE REECE

See also Linear B

Further Reading

Best, Jan and Fred Woudhuizen (editors), *Ancient Scripts from Crete and Cyprus*, Leiden and New York: Brill, 1988

Casson, Stanley, *Ancient Cyprus: Its Art and Archaeology*, Westport, Connecticut: Greenwood Press, 1970

Catling, H.W., "Cyprus in the Late Bronze Age" in *History of the Middle East and the Aegean Region, c.1800–1380 BC*, edited by I.E.S. Edwards *et al.*, Cambridge: Cambridge University Press, 1973 (*The Cambridge Ancient History*, vol. 2, part 2, 3rd edition)

Chadwick, John, *Linear B and Related Scripts*, Berkeley: University of California Press, and London: British Museum Publications, 1987

Egetmeyer, Markus, *Wörterbuch zu den Inschriften im kyprischen Syllabar*, Berlin: de Gruyter, 1992

Heubeck, Alfred, *Schrift*, Göttingen: Vandenhoeck & Ruprecht, 1979, pp. 54–64

Hintze, Almut, *A Lexicon to the Cyprian Syllabic Inscriptions*, Hamburg: Buske, 1993

Karageorghis, Jacqueline and Olivier Masson (editors), *The History of the Greek Language in Cyprus*, Nicosia: Pierides Foundation, 1988

Masson, Emilia, *Étude de vingt-six boules d'argile inscrites trouvées à Enkomi et Hala Sultan Tekké (Chypre)*, Gothenburg: Åström, 1971

Masson, Emilia, *Cyprominoica*, Gothenburg: Åström, 1974

Masson, Olivier, *Les Inscriptions chypriotes syllabiques*, Paris: Boccard, 1961; 2nd edition, 1983

Masson, Olivier and Terence B. Mitford, *Les Inscriptions syllabiques de Kouklia-Paphos*, Konstanz: Universitätsverlag Konstanz, 1986

Mitford, Terence Bruce, *Studies in the Signaries of South-Western Cyprus*, London: Institute of Classical Studies, 1961

Mitford, Terence Bruce, *The Inscriptions of Kourion*, Philadelphia: American Philosophical Society, 1971

Mitford, Terence Bruce and Olivier Masson, "The Cypriot Syllabary" in *The Expansion of the Greek World, Eighth to Sixth Centuries BC*, edited by John Boardman and N.G.L. Hammond, Cambridge, Cambridge University Press, 1982 (*The Cambridge Ancient History*, 2nd edition, vol. 3, part 3)

Mitford, Terence Bruce and Olivier Masson, *The Syllabic Inscriptions of Rantidi-Paphos*, Konstanz: Universitätsverlag Konstanz, 1983

Symeon of Thessalonica, St d. 1429

Archbishop and liturgist

Until quite recently, Symeon has been known to scholars and the Orthodox faithful mainly as the author of seven works of pastoral and liturgical theology printed in volume 155 of Migne's *Patrologia Graeca*. These texts, which were first published in 1683 by patriarch Dositheos of Jerusalem and later translated into the vernacular languages of Orthodox Christians, have earned Symeon both recognition as a great authority on Byzantine worship and notoriety for his strong anti-Latin bias. Yet very little was known about either his life or his activities as archbishop of Thessalonica during a particularly turbulent period of that city's history until a substantial body of previously unknown historical, dogmatic, and liturgical writings by Symeon came to light in the last third of the 20th century. In addition to providing a biographical context for the archbishop's previously known work as a theologian and mystagogue, these recently discovered texts also contain valuable information about such events in the history of Thessalonica as the long siege of Murad II and Byzantium's transfer of the city to Venetian rule.

Symeon's spiritual formation apparently began in the last quarter of the 14th century within the circles of hesychast monks who, ever since the vindication of Gregory Palamas, had controlled the patriarchate of his native Constantinople. Tonsured as a monk and later ordained to the priesthood, he preached publicly in the capital and wrote a short treatise *On the Priesthood*. While gaining a reputation for erudition, Symeon evidently became acquainted with high officials of the Byzantine court and Church. Although the exact nature of these contacts is unknown (Balfour suggests that he may even have served as the confessor of Manuel II Palaiologos), they doubtless contributed to his elevation to the archiepiscopal see of Thessalonica sometime between June 1416 and April 1417.

As the archbishop of Byzantium's second city, Symeon immediately sought to put into practice the strong and simple faith in God, Orthodoxy, and empire that he had acquired as a monk in his beloved Constantinople through bold initiatives to raise moral and liturgical standards within his archdiocese. After issuing as his first official act an encyclical urging his entire flock to repent, he began to combat what he saw as moral laxity through a combination of preaching repentance and judicial activism. This course of action, which he pursued vigorously despite being beset by frequent and severe illnesses, soon alienated many members of his flock. Opposition to the rigorous application of the law in the ecclesiastical and civil courts under Symeon's jurisdiction was particularly strong, leading to successful appeals against his harsher decisions on matrimonial impediments to the patriarchal synod. Somewhat less controversial were his efforts to improve worship at his cathedral of Hagia Sophia, which was the last church in the empire to celebrate daily the liturgy of the hours according to the archaic Constantinopolitan "Sung" Office (*asmatiki akolouthia*). Recognizing the desire of worshippers to hear popular hymns from the monastic offices of Mar Saba, Symeon introduced a reformed cathedral Typikon and prayerbook that systematized borrowings of texts and music from the dominant Palestinian monastic rite. These two service books – which have survived incompletely as MSS. 2047 and 2065 in the National Library, Athens – show that Symeon further enriched the liturgy of his cathedral by supplementing the pre-existing liturgical texts of both rites with a considerable number of hymns and prayers of his own composition.

Political events overshadowed Symeon's work as the chief liturgist and moral guardian of Thessalonica when the peace that had held since the city's first Turkish occupation in 1403 began to deteriorate. In opposition to strong civic factions that favoured either a transfer of sovereignty to Venice or outright surrender to the Turks, Symeon preached a policy of total loyalty to Constantinople and Orthodoxy backed up by repentance and faith in the miraculous powers of the city's patron St Demetrius. Already deeply unpopular, this idealistic stand provoked severe criticism that caused the near total breakdown of his health, despite which he embarked on an abortive personal mission to the capital in 1422. After reaching only as far as Mount Athos, Symeon returned to Thessalonica and witnessed the despot Andronikos hand over the city to the Venetians in September 1423. Remarkably, with the transfer accomplished, Symeon began to recover from his illnesses and bargained successfully with his new Roman Catholic masters to safeguard the rights of Thessalonica's Orthodox Christians. During the following six years of constant Turkish siege, he regained the respect of his dwindling flock for his efforts to alleviate their material suffering. These contributions to the maintenance of morale greatly impressed the city's Venetian governors, whose Senate recognized him as *fidelissimus noster* for his determined resistance to the Turks. When Symeon died unexpectedly in the autumn of 1429, some months before Murad II's capture of Thessalonica, his death was recorded by the historian John the Reader as presaging the removal of God's protection from the city.

After the fall of Thessalonica, Symeon's personal and literary reputation went into steep decline. The vast majority of his texts for the archaic public liturgy of Thessalonica probably fell out of use immediately, becoming useless after the city's great secular churches were converted into mosques. His dogmatic and hortatory writings, highly topical and full of temporarily unfashionable anti-Latin sentiments, similarly passed into obscurity. By contrast, the seven mystagogical and didactic works mentioned above were extremely influential as textbooks for priests throughout the period of Turkish domination. The greatest of these is the monumental *Dialogue in Christ*, an extended treatise on doctrine and liturgy set as a dialogue between Symeon and an unnamed lower cleric. Beginning with a section refuting various heresies, the *Dialogue* proceeds systematically to describe and interpret the symbolism of the major liturgical services – both cathedral and monastic – of the Orthodox Church, achieving in its course a valedictory synthesis of the two main streams of Byzantine liturgical theology: the "cosmic" tradition of Maximos and the "life of Christ" tradition of Germanos. In recognition of this and his other achievements, Symeon was finally proclaimed a saint of the Orthodox Church on 3 May 1981.

ALEXANDER LINGAS

Biography

Born in Constantinople in the later 14th century and educated by hesychast monks there, Symeon was tonsured as a monk and ordained a priest. He became archbishop of Thessalonica in 1416/17. He witnessed the handover of the city to the Venetians in 1423. His writings concern pastoral and liturgical theology but also the history of Thessalonica in the 1420s. His didactic works were used as textbooks for priests. He died in 1429.

Writings

Treatise on Prayer: An Explanation of the Services Conducted in the Orthodox Church, translated by H.L.N. Simmons, Brookline, Massachusetts: Hellenic College Press, 1984

Further Reading

Balfour, David, *Politico-Historical Works of Symeon, Archbishop of Thessalonica (1416/17 to 1429)*, Vienna: Akademie der Wissenschaften, 1979

Balfour, David, "St. Symeon of Thessalonica: A Polemical Hesychast", *Sobornost*, 4 (1982): pp. 6–21

Balfour, David, "Saint Symeon of Thessalonike as a Historical Personality", *Greek Orthodox Theological Review*, 28 (1983): pp. 55–72

Lingas, Alexander, *Sunday Matins in the Byzantine Cathedral Rite: Music and Liturgy*, Amsterdam: Harwood Academic Publishing, forthcoming

Schulz, Hans-Joachim, *The Byzantine Liturgy: Symbolic Structure and Faith Expression*, New York: Pueblo, 1986, pp. 114–24

Wybrew, Hugh, *The Orthodox Liturgy: The Development of the Eucharistic Liturgy in the Byzantine Rite*, London: SPCK, 1989; Crestwood, New York: St Vladimir's Seminary Press, 1990

Symeon the Logothete

Chronicler of the 10th century

Symeon the Logothete is the name of a 10th-century chronicler who worked in the revived tradition of Byzantine chronicle writing. The tradition of the world chronicle (that is, spanning the period from Creation to present memory) had stalled in the 7th century, only reviving (or surviving) at the start of the 9th century with the world chronicle of Theophanes, which ended in the year 813. Other 9th-century chronicles are Nikephoros's *Short History*, which covered the period from Phokas (602–10) to Constantine V (741–75), and the *Scriptor Incertus de Leone Armenio* covering up to a few years after 813, but it was George the Monk who next took up the mantle of the world chronicler, covering from creation to 842. After George the next surviving chronicle is that of our Symeon. Unfortunately no edition of the original text exists, and the problematic nature of producing one is not in doubt; it is universally acknowledged that Symeon's chronicle presents severe difficulties, for the primary text was soon the object of redactional alterations that have modified its original character (see for instance Markopoulos, 1979, p. 83).

It is however generally agreed that the chronicle covers world history up to 948, that it shows a positive bias towards the emperor Romanos I Lekapenos (920–44) at the expense of the Macedonian dynasty, and extends an earlier chronicle that originally covered from Adam to 713 (see however Markopoulos, 1983, p. 279). The chronicler's hand seems to appear first in the reign of Michael III (842–67), and from this point on the chronicle appears to fall into three distinct parts: the reign of Michael III, the reigns of Basil I, Leo VI, and Alexander (867–913), and a personal account of the period 913–48 (Jenkins, 1965). For the reign of Michael III, the author has apparently united an account of the accession of Basil the Macedonian, a Basilian résumé, and some interpolations, rather than a single hostile account of the life of Basil (Karlin-Hayter, 1991). As for the middle section, it seems that the author has used an annalistic source, with the result that the order of events for this period is chronologically accurate, in contrast to the chronological errors for the periods 856–67 and 913–48 (Jenkins). Following Jenkins's method for the period 867–913 Treadgold argues that Symeon is also chronologically accurate for 813–45, having used accurate chronicles that are now lost, thus making him a very significant source for early 9th-century history. For the four reigns before Leo V the *Chronographia* of Theophanes is used.

The textual history of the chronicle is not, however, so simple; in fact there appear to be two versions of the chronicle: the deemed-authentic A, which is philo-Lekapene and close to the original text; and B, the long version, with interpolations from Genesios (Markopoulos, 1979; Karlin-Hayter, 1971, pp. 454–55). Logothete B is notable for its favouring of the Phokas family, and is extended to 963. There also appears to be a linguistic difference between the two versions. B is more "purist", with methods akin to those of the Metaphrast, but may have been written by the Logothete too, using a pro-Phokas text (Markopoulos, 1979, p. 89).

As noted above, the original text was soon subject to redactions by other authors, notably those of Theodosios Melissenos (once thought to be "Melitenos") and Leo Grammatikos. It is also known as the continuation of the chronicle of George the Monk (Georgius Monachus Continuatus), perhaps done by Symeon the Logothete himself (Moravcsik, 1958, p. 270). There is also another version of Georgius Monachus Continuatus (marked by insertions from Genesios), so there are in fact two redactions under this name also. Thus developed the different redactions of the "Epitome" (the name given to the hypothesized original base text), which appeared under diverse author names or anonymously.

It is interesting to note the different bias of the two other mid-10th-century chroniclers, Theophanes Continuatus (whose chronicle consists of the sections 813–67, the *Life of Basil*, and the later extension from 886 to 961) and Genesios (who spans the years 813–86), who are essentially pro-Macedonian (though all the chroniclers show the preference for the arrangement by reign rather than by year). These two chroniclers continued Theophanes directly, from 813. While Theophanes Continuatus is distinct from Symeon up to the famous book 5, the *Life of Basil*, he does turn to Symeon (via the second recension of Georgius Monachus Continuatus) for material for book 6 (886–961), namely the period 886–948. The later chroniclers Skylitzes and Zonaras were to turn directly to Theophanes Continuatus rather than to Symeon the Logothete. Another chronicler worth noting in connection with Symeon the Logothete is pseudo-Symeon, whose chronicle covered from the creation up to 963, and is in fact largely copied from other sources, including Symeon the Logothete. His chronicle is marked by the insertion of regnal years (which seem to have no validity), and also by a striking anti-Photios streak.

As to the person of the original Symeon magister and logothete, some seek to identify him with other known 10th-century homonyms, notably Symeon Metaphrastes, thus making a single figure who was "a high imperial official, hagiographer, lawyer, legal writer, chronicle compiler – and poet" (Ševčenko, 1969–70, p. 218). However some still doubt this conjecture. Metaphrastes was famous for his systematized collection of saints' lives, which he reworked in a higher literary style. There are also poems (on the deaths of Stephen son of Romanos I and of the emperor Constantine VII) and letters in the name of Symeon magister and logothete.

SHAUN TOUGHER

See also Chronicles

Biography

The name given to the author of a 10th-century world chronicle covering the period from the Creation to AD 948. Extending the received tradition, the chronicler seems to have contributed three sections covering (1) the reign of Michael III (842–67), (2) the reigns of Basil I, Leo VI, and Alexander (867–913), and (3) a personal account of the period 913–48.

Writings

Chronographia (revised by Leo Grammaticus), edited by Immanuel Bekker, Bonn: Weber, 1842 (*Corpus scriptorum historiae byzantinae* 31)

Further Reading

Jenkins, R.J.H., "The Chronological Accuracy of the 'Logothete' for the Years AD 867–913", *Dumbarton Oaks Papers*, 19 (1965): pp. 91–112

Karlin-Hayter, P., "Les Deux Histoires du règne de Michel III", *Byzantion*, 41 (1971): pp. 460–68

Karlin-Hayter, P., "Le *De Michaele* du logothète: construction et intentions", *Byzantion*, 61 (1991): pp. 365–95

Kazhdan, A.P., "Khronika Simeona Logofeta", *Vizantijskij Vremennik*, 15 (1959): pp. 125–43

Kazhdan, A.P. (editor), *The Oxford Dictionary of Byzantium*, 3 vols, New York and Oxford: Oxford University Press, 1991

Markopoulos, A., *I Chronographia tou Pseudosymeon kai oi Peges tis* [The *Chronographia* of pseudo-Symeon and its Sources], Ioannina, 1978

Markopoulos, A., "Le Témoignage du Vaticanus Gr. 163 pour la période entre 945–963", *Symmeikta*, 3 (1979): pp. 83–119

Markopoulos, A., "Sur les Deux versions de la chronographie de Symeon Logothete", *Byzantinische Zeitschrift*, 76 (1983): pp. 279–84

Moravcsik, Gyula, *Byzantinoturcica*, vol. 1, Berlin: Akademie, 1958

Moravcsik, Gyula, "Sagen und Legenden über Kaiser Basileios I", *Dumbarton Oaks Papers*, 15 (1961): pp. 61–126

Oikonomidès, N., "Two Seals of Symeon Metaphrastes", *Dumbarton Oaks Papers*, 27 (1973): pp. 323–26

Scott, R., "The Byzantine Chronicle after Malalas" in *Studies in John Malalas*, edited by Elizabeth Jeffreys *et al.*, Sydney: Australian Association for Byzantine Studies, 1990

Ševčenko, Ihor, "Poems on the Deaths of Leo VI and Constantine VII in the Madrid Manuscript of Scylitzes", *Dumbarton Oaks Papers*, 23–24 (1969–70): pp. 185–228

Treadgold, W.T., "The Chronological Accuracy of the *Chronicle* of Symeon the Logothete for the Years 813–845", *Dumbarton Oaks Papers*, 33 (1979): pp. 157–97

Symeon The New Theologian, St 949–1022

Mystic

Symeon was a highly controversial figure in his time. His works are among the most vivid of the eastern Christian Church's tradition, with their rhapsodic appeal to direct personal experience. His title "New Theologian" began, in all probability, as a denigration, suggesting an "innovator", but his disciples turned it to their advantage, elevating him to the rarefied heights of only two others who were given that designation – the Apostle John and St Gregory of Nazianzus. He was afterwards to be regarded as a forefather of the hesychast movement, although the influential treatise assigned to his name, concerning the physical method of hesychastic prayer, so highly prized among the Athonites, is not by him; nor can certain noted characteristics of later hesychastic method be found in his work, such as devotion to the Jesus prayer. Nevertheless, his ecstatic light-centred mystical enthusiasm set a standard to which later writers aspired. In a real, but qualified sense he can be regarded as a founder of what later came to be Byzantine hesychasm.

Symeon was born to a wealthy Byzantine family, provincial aristocrats from Asia Minor. His father brought him to Constantinople for his education in 960. In the revolution of 963, as Nikephoros Phokas seized the throne, Symeon's uncle and patron met his end and the child's education was interrupted. After a short setback he reappeared once more in an elevated social setting. An unknown senator had taken him on to his household staff. Symeon attended the palace daily, and soon assumed senatorial rank himself.

In his twenties he described himself as a somewhat rakish youth, travelling to and from court on business. He first encountered the Studite monk Symeon Eulabes at this time, and, like other aristocrats, he was drawn to this odd but generously charismatic figure who served as father confessor to an elite group. He visited him whenever he was in the city, and the monk gave him spiritual books to read, but clearly there was little more to the connection until the occasion, around 969, when he had an experience that he described (much later) as highly significant for him. He tells us of a vision of lights – one light in the presence of another. He interpreted the event as his spiritual father interceding for him before Christ. Nothing much seems to have changed in the outward circumstances of his life subsequent to that first visionary experience, but it would be decisive in retrospect. Seven years after this, in 976, when he was 27 years of age, another palace coup initiated a sequence of events that changed his life permanently. The *parakoimomenos* (guardian of the bedchamber) Basil seized the throne on behalf of the prince (Basil II) and Symeon's family seem to have been clearly marked out by the new power as a hostile element. His political career was definitively terminated at this point, and he seems to have taken temporary refuge with his spiritual father at the Stoudios monastery in Constantinople. Here he tells us that once again he experienced an overwhelming vision of light. He saw the radiance of Christ, directly, and this became for him a definitive conversion point. It marked his permanent entrance into the monastic state.

In a short time Symeon was moved to the St Mamas monastery at the Xylokerkos gate in the capital (not far from the Stoudios monastery). The hagiographer, and those following him too trustingly (for the *Life* is tendentious and often confused over details), have seen this as an "expulsion". It ought to be read as his promotion and his permanent protection by sympathetic patrons outside the court. Three years later, in 979–80, Symeon was elected *hegoumenos* (abbot) of the same household. It was an event that indicated the significant patronage he could still bring to bear as a powerful aristocratic leader, even though now a monk.

Symeon substantially refurbished the site of St Mamas, and at this time began to deliver the traditional morning Catecheses to the monks of the community, which have survived as the central body of his work. Much of his approach in the Catecheses is traditional Stoudite observance, but he has his own style and emphasis, and so he places a particularly strong emphasis on the dedicated obedience that he expects should be given to the spiritual father by all monks. He stressed the necessity for direct personal experience in the life of the Spirit, underlining the need for tears, even insisting that without tears a monk should not approach the divine mysteries. This telescoping of the roles of spiritual father and *hegoumenos* seems to have caused no little conflict among his subordinates. Between 986 and 989 Byzantine society was disrupted by serious civil dispute. The emperor Basil II took measures to restrict his enemies, and regarded Symeon with more and more suspicion. In the same period (986–87) Symeon Eulabes died at the Stoudios monastery, leaving Symeon as the new head and leader of his school of disciples, a circle that included both monastics and aristocrats.

Some time between 995 and 998 the growing opposition to Symeon's discipline and teaching broke out in the form of a revolt by a large number of his community. They threatened him at morning service and lodged an official complaint against him at the patriarchal court, a plea that was eventually dismissed. The *Life* attempts to minimize the whole affair, but the uprising probably coincided with the death of patriarch Nicholas Chrysoberges and the installation of the first appointment of Basil II in his own right, patriarch Sisinnios II (995–98). Sisinnios was succeeded by Sergios II Manuelites (999–1019) and the latter's court also instituted legal proceedings against Symeon. These processes were more vigorously pursued and eventually would result in his exile. The first formal arraignment turned around the issue of the unofficial cult of the master that Symeon had instituted in memory of his teacher. The elder's reputation was attacked, in an attempt to discredit the younger Symeon, and after 995 his cult (veneration of his icon) was forbidden at St Mamas. The emperor thus began to move against Symeon by means of the ecclesiastical court process, employing his long-time confidant bishop Stephen of Alexina, the patriarchal chancellor. In 1003 an attempt was made to entangle Symeon in a more formal theological debate concerning his Trinitarian orthodoxy. He returned a satisfactory answer to the charges but also took the opportunity to lambaste Stephen for attempting to theologize without first having experienced impassibility and the divine light. It was tantamount to a declaration of war. The attrition carried on for six years in all, culminating in a sentence of deposition issued against Symeon in 1005 with house arrest, then exile.

On 3 January 1009 Symeon was forcibly exiled to Paloukiton, near Chrysopolis. His circle soon supplied the money to buy the oratory of St Marina and nearby lands. Here Symeon wrote some of his most famous works, including the exquisite *Hymns of Divine Love* which are a classic of Byzantine religious writing. They mark him out as one of the Christian tradition's leading mystics. On his last journey, while returning to his monastery, he was worn out by an attack of dysentery, and nearing Chrysopolis he died at the age of 73, in 1022.

Symeon was received as a great master of the inner life by the Athonite monks, and his reputation was championed on the Holy Mountain. In recent decades he has also attracted increasing scholarly attention. His writing is important both for the historical light it throws on a dark period of Byzantine affairs, and more so for the spiritual and mystical themes it treats with such freshness and authority. In a more restricted sense Symeon is also a highly influential figure for the doctrine of spiritual fatherhood that he represented to such a strong degree, and which has had so marked an impact on Orthodox spiritual praxis.

JOHN A. McGUCKIN

Biography

Born in Paphlagonia in 949, Symeon was brought to Constantinople in 960 by his father for his education. He initally embarked on a career in public life and became a senator. But under the influence of Symeon Eulabes he changed course and entered the Stoudios monastery. He became head of his own monastery in 979, but was exiled in 1009. His writings include catecheses, hymns, and treatises. He died near Chrysopolis in 1022.

Writings

The Discourses, translated by C.J. de Catanzaro, New York: Paulist Press, 1980

On the Mystical Life: The Ethical Discourses, translated by Alexander Golitzin, 3 vols, Crestwood, New York: St Vladimir's Seminary Press, 1995–97

The Practical and Theological Chapters, and Three Theological Discourses, translated by Paul McGuckin, Kalamazoo, Michigan: Cistercian Publications, 1982

Hymns of Divine Love, translated by George A. Maloney, Denville, New Jersey: Dimension Press, 1975

The Philokalia, vol. 4, translated by G.E.H. Palmer, Philip Sherrard and Kallistos Ware, London: Faber, 1995, pp. 11–75

Further Reading

Fraigneau-Julien, B., *Les Sens spirituels et la vision de Dieu selon Syméon le Nouveau Théologien*, Paris: Beauchesne, 1985

Gouillard, J., "Syméon le Jeune, le théologien, ou le nouveau théologien", *Dictionnaire de théologie catholique*, 14/2, Paris: Letouzey & Ané, 1941

Gouillard, J., "Constantin Chrysomallos sous le masque de Syméon le Nouveau Théologien", *Travaux et Mémoires*, 5 (1973): pp. 313–28

Hausherr, Irénée, *Un Grand Mystique byzantin: vie de Syméon le Nouveau Théologien*, Rome: Pontificum Institutum Orientalium Studiorum, 1928

Holl, Karl, *Enthusiasmus und Bussgewalt beim griechischen Mönchtum: eine Studie zu Symeon dem Neuen Theologen*, Leipzig: Hinrich, 1898, reprinted Hildesheim: Olms, 1969

Krivocheine, Basil, "The Brother-Loving Poor Man", *Christian East*, new series 2, (1953–54): pp. 216–27

Krivocheine, Basil, "The Writings of S. Symeon the New Theologian", *Orientalia Christiana Periodica*, 20 (1954): pp. 323–26

Krivocheine, Basil, "The Most Enthusiastic Zealot", *Ostkirchliche Studien*, 4 (1955): pp. 108–28

Krivocheine, Basil, *In the Light of Christ: Saint Symeon, the New Theologian*, Crestwood, New York: St Vladimir's Seminary Press, 1986

McGuckin, J.A., "Symeon the New Theologian: His Vision of Theology", *Patristic and Byzantine Review*, 3/2 (1984): pp. 208–14

McGuckin, J.A., "St. Symeon the New Theologian and Byzantine Monasticism" in *Mount Athos and Byzantine Monasticism*, edited by Anthony Bryer and Mary Cunningham, Aldershot, Hampshire: Variorum, 1996

McGuckin, J.A., "St. Symeon the New Theologian (d. 1022): Byzantine Theological Renewal in Search of a Precedent" in *The Church Retrospective*, edited by R.M. Swanson, Woodbridge, Suffolk: Ecclesiastical History Society, 1997

McGuckin, J.A., "The Notion of Luminous Vision in 11th-century Byzantium: Interpreting the Biblical and Theological Paradigms of St. Symeon the New Theologian", *Acts of the Belfast Byzantine Colloquium, Portaferry 1995*, Belfast: Queens University Press, 1997

Maloney, George A., *The Mystic of Fire and Light*, Denville, New Jersey: Dimension, 1975

Pelikan, Jaroslav, "The Last Flowering of Byzantium: The Mystic as New Theologian", in *The Spirit of Eastern Christendom, 600–1700*, Chicago: University of Chicago Press, 1974

Rosenthal-Kamarinea, I., "Symeon der Neue Theologe und Symeon Studites", *Oekumenische Einheit*, 3 (1952): pp. 103–20

Rosenthal-Kamarinea, I., "Symeon Studites: ein heiliger Narrativ" in *Akten des XI Internationale Byzantinisten Kongresses, 1958*, edited by Franz Dölger and Hans-Georg Beck, Munich: Beck, 1960, reprinted Nendeln: Kraus, 1978

Turner, H.J.M., *St. Symeon the New Theologian and Spiritual Fatherhood*, Leiden and New York: Brill, 1990

Völker, Walther, *Praxis und Theoria bei Symeon dem Neuen Theologen: Ein Beitrag zur byzantinischen Mystik*, Wiesbaden: Steiner, 1974

Symi

Island in the Dodecanese

The Aegean island of Symi lies to the north of Rhodes, of which the nearest point is 24 km away, and almost equidistantly between the two rocky mainland peninsulas of Cnidus and Dorakis, the latter some 10 km to the south; with an area of 64 sq km it is one of the smaller islands of the Dodecanese.

Symi is mentioned briefly in the writings of Herodotus, Strabo, and Pliny, but it was the 6th-century AD grammarian Stephanus Byzantinus, drawing on Classical authors, who provided most of the early information on the island's origins. Initially called Metapontis and Aegle, the island apparently obtained the name Symi from the daughter of Ialysus, called Syme; it was she, with Chthonius, a son of Poseidon, who was held to have first populated the island. At several points in its history the island was deserted, but was finally (according to Diodorus Siculus, 5. 33) populated by Argives and Lacedaemonians. In the *De Thematibus* of Constantine VII Porphyrogennetos (913–59) the island is listed in the 14th theme, named Cibyrreote. When Christopher Buondelmonti wrote of the island in his *Liber Insularum* of c.1420 he claimed

that its name derived either from Simatis, who had been king of the island, or from *sima*, the Greek vernacular for "near", in reference to its proximity to Asia Minor.

The island's history is dominated by its involvement with the sea, the Symiots being renowned boat builders, sponge fishers, and swimmers. The prowess of the men at building boats was already acknowledged in Homeric times, since during the Trojan War the hero Nireus, the son of Aglaia and king Charopus, is reported (*Iliad*, 2. 671) to have gone with a contribution of three ships from Symi to assist Agamemnon in the Trojan expedition.

The small harbour-side village of Nimporeio offers interesting traces of early Christian building activity. Mosaics from the floor of the north aisle of a basilica can be seen there; dated to the 6th century, the inventiveness of the designs, which include a man leading a camel and a stag being chased by a hound, suggests a relatively prosperous phase in the island's history. If so, this would probably have been brought to an end with the widespread Arab raids of the 7th century. Symi is not mentioned by any of the medieval Byzantine historians.

The Hospitaller Knights of St John of Jerusalem, based at Rhodes, were certainly in possession of the island by 1351, since in that year the inhabitants complained to the Order that they could not afford to pay the *mortuaria* (a tax comparable to death duties), but it is probable that the knights were already in control by 1320, as was certainly the case on the nearby island of Nisyros. The castle that the knights built at Symi on the ancient acropolis of the harbour town of Egalio made use of pre-existing Cyclopean walling, and it must have played a significant part in their developing defences against the Turks. In 1457, and so only four years after he had taken Constantinople, the young sultan Mehmet II launched an assault on the castle as part of his campaign of intended subjugation of the Aegean, but his forces were driven off by the boiling oil and liquid pitch that the defenders poured down; the attackers withdrew after ten days. The importance that successive grand masters placed on the castle of Symi is shown by the escutcheons that can still be seen there; one is of the grand master Pierre d'Aubusson (1476–1503), and is dated 1507 (four years after his death), suggesting continued rebuilding.

The natural resources of the island, which has a mild climate although only a modest rainfall, included plentiful trees that for centuries were the source of timber for the construction of boats. This supply was much depleted when many ships were being built during the War of Independence. The land is generally rather infertile, but wine was certainly produced there in the later medieval period.

Symi did not play any major strategic role in Hellenic history, being dominated either by the nearby promontories of Asia Minor or by the much larger island of Rhodes to the south. Thus, with the capitulation of the Hospitallers to the Turks in January 1523, Ottoman rule was inaugurated in Symi. The island was to remain in Turkish hands until 1912, when the Italians occupied all the Dodecanese. The 18th-century monastery of St Michael Panormitis on the south coast played a part as a staging post at the end of the World War II, providing shelter for refugees who were returning to Greece from Asia Minor. Symi returned to being within Greek governance only in 1947.

PAUL HETHERINGTON

Summary
One of the Dodecanese, Symi is renowned for its connection with the sea. Boat building has been an important industry since Homeric times. The Hospitaller Knights of St John, based at nearby Rhodes, controlled Symi from c.1320 to 1523 when it fell into Ottoman hands. Since then its history has followed that of the rest of the Dodecanese.

Further Reading
Luttrell, Anthony, *The Hospitallers of Rhodes and their Mediterranean World*, Aldershot, Hampshire: Variorum, 1992

Symposium

A *symposion* was a drinking party. It was also the setting from which much of early Greek poetry and philosophy emerged.

The focus of research on symposia is on Greek cities of the 7th to 4th centuries BC: during that period, several forms of evidence concur in demonstrating their crucial importance in Greek culture. They are to be observed in the archaeology of private houses and of temples, in sculpture, in the form and the iconography of vases, and in poetic and prose literature. But if we look for origins, the different kinds of evidence lead us in different directions.

Symposia took place in purpose-built rooms, *andrones* ("men's rooms"), easily recognized by archaeologists because they were designed to take a certain number of couches (usually 5, 7, or 11) around the walls. Sometimes there are surviving floor markings to show the placing of the couches and of the small serving tables. Participants reclined, one or two to a couch. The custom of reclining at banquets and drinking parties is traced to the 7th or 8th century BC in Greece, to the 6th or 7th century BC in Etruscan Italy, and to the 8th century BC or earlier in the Levant and Mesopotamia. The idea thus appears to have spread westwards, and has been linked with Phoenician trading contacts.

Symposia followed an evening meal. Food did not mix with conversation or with cultural pursuits. After eating, a libation of neat wine marked the beginning of the drinking; the libation was mainly for the gods, however. Wine, in large quantities, was then mixed with at least equal volumes of water for the symposium itself. The ideal strength of the mixture was a matter of argument: it was decided on each occasion by the host or by a participant who was chosen as *symposiarchos* ("party ruler"). Mixing was done in a large vase (*krater*). Vase paintings show how attendants ladled wine from the *krater*

Symposium: relief showing a participant holding out his drinking bowl to have it replenished, National Archaeological Museum, Athens

into individual cups. *Krateres*, accompanied by drinking cups, are well known from Classical Greece (and Greek vases were exported in great numbers to Etruria, where they are found as grave goods), but there are also vases of similar forms from much earlier sites in Greece and the southern Balkans, suggesting that the wine-mixing ritual is to be traced back locally to prehistoric times.

Vase paintings depict many other details of the typical or ideal symposium. Sweets, dried fruit, and nuts accompanied the wine. Toasts were drunk, often praising the beauty of boys; some vases appear to have been commissioned as mementos of this. Music was played, both by participants and by slave entertainers such as the ubiquitous "flute-girls" (*auletrides*). Philosophy, politics, and many other topics were discussed; poems and songs were recited. Dancers, acrobats, and prostitutes might be hired. Drunkenness supervened – slowly, since the wine was diluted – but almost inevitably, since not to drink was a cause for mockery and the proceedings might well last all night. Symposia allowed free speech and the release of inhibitions: proverbially, things said and done there were to be forgotten, or at any rate not to be betrayed, the next day.

In Greece the symposium was essentially an activity for those of citizen status, and for men only. The latter was apparently not true of Levantine drinking parties and certainly not of Etruscan ones. In Greece any women who were present were slave entertainers or *hetairai* (courtesan) and in either case sexually available; participants' wives and daughters were not to be seen. The presence of adolescent boys, under the aegis of a parent or a lover, may be regarded as a form of initiation into adult male society.

There was a genre of short poems composed specifically for recitation at symposia, *skolia* or drinking songs. There is persuasive evidence that much of the rest of early Greek poetry, including elegy, iambus, and monodic lyric, was typically performed at symposia too. As a setting for philosophical discussion symposia appear in different, but complementary, lights in the *Symposium* of Plato and the *Symposium* of Xenophon, in both of which Socrates is depicted as a participant. These two works mark the beginning of a literary genre of dialogues with a sympotic setting and, in general, with moral, philosophical, or scholarly themes; examples survive by several much later authors, including Lucian and Plutarch.

While feasting might often be a municipal, and an essentially public, activity, symposia may be seen as essentially private. How far the practice was common to different social classes must have varied from place to place. In the Archaic period, for example, symposia are integral to the aristocratic society depicted in the lyrics of Alcaeus and Anacreon; they are not apparent at all in Homer or Hesiod, though aspects of sympotic behaviour have been observed in the feasts of the *Odyssey* and *Iliad*. In Classical Athens, if we may judge by the written sources, people who went to symposia consisted of a fashionable, cultural, and political elite; others did not know how to behave at such a gathering, or even how to recline elegantly, as Streptocleon teaches his father Bdelycleon to do in an amusing scene from Aristophanes' *Wasps*. Some participants were wealthy enough to act regularly as hosts, while others were perpetual guests or *parasitoi*, tolerated or welcomed for their entertainment value.

It is far from clear how long into Hellenistic or Roman times the symposium remained a living institution. In the 2nd century AD Plutarch's *Symposium Questions* claim to be based on social gatherings that were similar to Classical symposia in their intellectual content if not in their sexual freedom. This is the latest significant source for symposia as a feature of contemporary society.

ANDREW DALBY

Further Reading

Bowie, E.L., "Early Greek Elegy, Symposium and Public Festival", *Journal of Hellenic Studies*, 106 (1986): pp. 13–35

Lissarrague, François, *The Aesthetics of the Greek Banquet: Images of Wine and Ritual*, Princeton, New Jersey: Princeton University Press, 1990

Murray, Oswyn (editor), *Sympotica: A Symposium on the Symposion*, Oxford: Clarendon Press, and New York: Oxford University Press, 1990

Murray, Oswyn and Manuela Tecuşan (editors), *In vino veritas*, London: British School at Rome, 1995

Murray, Oswyn, "Forms of Sociality" in *The Greeks*, edited by Jean-Pierre Vernant, Chicago: University of Chicago Press, 1995

Slater, William J. (editor), *Dining in a Classical Context*, Ann Arbor: University of Michigan Press, 1991

Wees, Hans van, "Princes at Dinner: Social Event and Social Structure in Homer" in *Homeric Questions: Essays in Philology, Ancient History, and Archaeology*, edited by Jan Paul Crielaard, Amsterdam: Gieben, 1995

Synesius AD 370–413

Administrator and philosopher

Synesius, an aristocrat of Cyrene, proud of the city's Doric past, was educated at Alexandria among other places by the philosopher Hypatia, from whom he acquired his deep love of Plato mediated through the writings of the Neoplatonists. Thanks to his letters (156 survive) we have one of the fullest and most sympathetic depictions of the life of a late 4th-century amateur philosopher and administrator. For nearly three years (AD 397–400) he represented his city in Constantinople on an embassy to secure tax concessions. His essays *On Kingship* and *On Providence* reveal this involvement with contemporary politics in the imperial capital. No doubt this practical experience and the high regard in which he was held by his fellow citizens as well as his own virtuous life were among the reasons why Theophilus, the patriarch of Alexandria, asked him to become bishop of Ptolemais (Cyrene and the Pentapolis) even though he was not yet a Christian. In a long and eloquent letter (105) he attempted, clearly in vain, to dissuade the patriarch, arguing his loyal devotion to his wife and family and his deep attachment to the philosophy of Plato. On three issues in particular he felt he could not compromise: the eternity of the world, the resurrection, and the creation of soul at birth. He was willing to accept certain Christian dogmas as "mythical" truth presented to the faithful in general, so long as he might continue to hold his own, true view, in private. This is how he puts it himself:

It is difficult if not impossible for doctrines to be shaken which have entered the soul through knowledge and proof. You know that philosophy in many ways opposes these doctrines that are on everyone's lips. To be sure, I will never think it right to consider the soul to be generated after the body. I will not say that the cosmos and its parts will perish. The resurrection that everyone speaks about I consider to be something sacred and inexpressible and I am far from agreeing with the ideas held by the masses. The philosopher's mind which has a vision of the truth can agree to a necessary lie.

Synesius served as bishop from 410 to 413, a number of his letters giving details of some of the difficulties he faced with corrupt officials and of some of his pastoral duties. His last days were not happy, because he vainly sought to protect Cyrene from the incursions of marauding tribesmen from the interior.

Although a man who enjoyed the active life – he was particularly fond of hunting – his temperament was also deeply spiritual as is testified by nine surviving metrical hymns that are completely pagan in content. They betray the influence of Orphic, Hermetic, and Chaldaean ideas and expressions grafted onto a metaphysical structure that owes much to a tradition taking its rise in speculations begun by Porphyry. Despite their pagan ethos, the personal engagement and passion of the author as he contemplates his place as an exile in the beguiling and dangerous physical world ensured their popularity among Christians. Synesius, however, and here he was again following in the footsteps of Porphyry, rejected in his work *On Dreams* the sacramental (theurgic) rituals of salvation espoused by Iamblichus and Proclus. This tendency he probably owed to Hypatia's version of Neoplatonism that emphasized science more than ritual religion. The treatise *On Dreams* extols personal moral and intellectual effort in the ascent and return of the soul to God.

The figure of the incorruptible and indefatigable bishop caught the imagination of Christian writers of the 6th and 7th centuries such as Evagrius and John Moschos, whereas from the 9th century onwards the philosophical content of his essays is of greater importance to his readers. Photios praises him as having brought glory again to Cyrene. Synesius' own programme to unite literature (rhetoric) and philosophy, expounded in his essay *Dion*, found a resonance in the similar programme of Michael Psellos who, like Synesius, could also regard the study of Plato as the best of all preparations for Christianity. In the 14th century Nikephoras Kallistes cites with approval a large passage of letter 105, included perhaps as a disguised claim for freedom of thought.

Synesius appealed, too, as a model of Attic style and as an example for the genre of epistolography in which he was admired by Theophylact of Ohrid. Although Synesius was one of the most popular authors of the Byzantine period, he can scarcely be described as an original or fundamental thinker; the later wide circulation and influence of his works can best be ascribed to the fact that he lived at a period of transition from a pagan to a Christian world, a transition that he encapsulated in his own life and thought. It was all too tempting to find together in one person Christian bishop, pagan philosopher, Greek stylist, and an engaging and likable character. Too unorthodox to have been proclaimed a saint, he has neverthe-

less served as a model for the double ideal of traditional Hellenist and devout Christian.

ANDREW SMITH

Biography
Born at Cyrene in AD 370, Synesius was a pupil of Hypatia in Alexandria. He went to Constantinople on an embassy in 397–400. Though not yet a Christian, he was elected bishop of Ptolemais in 410. His writings include letters, hymns, and essays. He died in 413.

Writings
The Essays and Hymns, translated by Augustine FitzGerald, London: Oxford University Press, 1930
Hymni et opuscula, edited by Nicolaus Terzaghi, Rome, 1939–44
Epistolographi Graeci, edited by Rudolf Hercher, Paris: Didot, 1873; reprinted Amsterdam: Hakkert, 1965

Further Reading
Bregman, Jay, *Synesius of Cyrene, Philosopher-Bishop*, Berkeley: University of California Press, 1982
Cameron, Alan, *Barbarians and Politics at the Court of Arcadius*, Berkeley: University of California Press, 1993

Syracuse
City in Sicily

Syracuse (modern Siracusa) was the leading city of Sicily virtually from its foundation in 733 BC until its sack by the Arabs in AD 878. It was founded by Corinthian colonists led by Archias, one of the Bacchiad aristocracy of Corinth, who placed his settlement on the island of Ortygia which was well supplied with water: the spring of Arethusa on the waterfront was potable until an earthquake early in the 19th century allowed sea water to seep in. Myth related that, as the nymph Arethusa fled from her lover Alpheus, Artemis saved her from rape by changing her into a spring and her wooer into a river. Strabo claimed that the Alpheus river in the Peloponnese flowed underground to Syracuse where its water mingled with the spring.

The earliest settlers monopolized the land, reducing the native Sicels to serfs, and they became a landowning aristocracy called the Gamoroi. The city prospered, pulling ahead of its nearest rivals Gela and Acragas. It had outgrown Ortygia by the mid-6th century BC, when the island was connected to the mainland by a mole and the population spilled into the Neapolis area. A temple to Apollo was built c.565 BC (it is considered the earliest of Sicily's great Doric temples), and it was soon followed by a temple of Olympian Zeus outside the city, south of the river Ciane. In 485 BC the Gamoroi, who had been expelled by a popular uprising of the Syracusan commons and the Sicel serfs, appealed to Gelon, tyrant of Gela, who took Syracuse easily and transferred his headquarters there, conscripting new citizens from Gela and expanding at the expense of Syracuse's neighbours. In 480 BC he destroyed a Carthaginian invasion force at Himera on the north coast, and one monument of this is the Doric temple of Athena which was transformed into the cathedral of Syracuse in AD 640 and is still in use.

Syracuse: the columns of the ancient temple of Athena are embedded in the north wall of the cathedral

Gelon's brother Hiero (478–467 BC) succeeded him as tyrant, but he was a harsh, unpopular ruler, and a year after his death a general uprising ousted his brother and successor Thrasbylulus, and founded a democracy. Yet Syracusan politics were still unsettled at the time of the ill-fated Athenian attack (415–413 BC) which ended with the annihilation of the Athenian forces. Hermocrates, the hero of the Syracusan resistance, was no supporter of democracy, and after the Athenian debacle, when he left Syracuse to lead a squadron of warships to help the Peloponnesian allies, the democratic statesman Diocles persuaded the city to adopt a new constitution and lawcode. Hermocrates was banished in 409 BC, but he returned to Sicily, and in 407 BC he was killed attempting to force re-entry into Syracuse.

Yet one of his followers, Dionysius "the Elder", did manage eventually to seize power and he held it until his death 38 years later. Early in his tyranny Syracuse narrowly avoided capture by a Carthaginian army, which was first weakened by pestilence and finally utterly defeated by a Syracusan attack. Refugees from Acragas, Gela, and Camerina enlarged the city's population, and Dionysius strengthened its defences with walls along the triangular Epipolae ridge and the Euryalus fort (modern Castello Eurialo) at its apex. Dionysius' son and namesake was of a different stripe. Good-natured, impractical, and ultimately oppressive, he toyed with the idea of becoming a Platonic statesman with Plato as his adviser, and for three years (357–354 BC) his step-uncle Dion, having seized power, tried to play the philosopher king and succeeded only in

becoming a despot. He was killed by his own soldiers in 354 BC and Syracuse lapsed into anarchy which not even Dionysius II's return to power seven years later could remedy. Finally, with Greek Sicily depressed and Carthage threatening again, Syracusan exiles appealed to Corinth, which sent Timoleon who ousted Dionysius, defeated Carthage, and revived Syracuse.

After Timoleon's death another revolution in Syracuse brought in an oligarchy, and in 317 BC Agathocles seized power, backed by mercenaries from Campania and exiles from the Greek cities. He vigorously resisted the encroachment of Carthage, even invading Carthaginian territory in Africa itself, while at home the conduct of affairs seems to have been peaceful. Disorder followed his death in 289 BC until around 270 BC, when Hiero II began his reign of more than 50 years. Hiero II was a paternalistic despot who shrewdly allied himself with Rome in the First Punic War, and consequently, when Sicily became a Roman province, Syracuse remained a free Roman ally and a centre of Greek culture which could claim the poet Theocritus and the scientist Archimedes. Hiero's successor, his grandson Hieronymus, reversed his policy, but did not live to see the result. A coup overthrew him, and out of the bloodshed that ensued, a pro-Carthaginian faction seized control and Rome laid siege to the city. Syracuse resisted valiantly, helped by the ingenious devices designed by Archimedes, and Carthage sent help, but disease carried off much of the Carthaginian army. Hope vanished by the autumn of 212 BC, and traitors opened one of the gates of Ortygia. In the pillage that followed, Archimedes was killed by a Roman soldier who failed to recognize him.

Syracuse now became the seat of the praetor or governor of the Roman province of Sicily, and we get a glimpse of the city under Roman rule in Cicero's orations against Verres, a corrupt governor who looted the province. It suffered in the civil war following Julius Caesar's assassination in 44 BC, and the emperor Augustus planted a colony there in 21 BC. In AD 665 the Byzantine emperor Constans II moved his capital there, but he was assassinated in 668 and his plan to remove the imperial capital from Constantinople died with him. The bishops of Syracuse were under papal jurisdiction until the 8th century, but around 733 the emperor Leo III placed them under the patriarch of Constantinople, and the head of the diocese became archbishop of Syracuse, then archbishop of Sicily and, probably from the second half of the 9th century, metropolitan of Sicily. Cultural links with Byzantium were close, and aspiring Syracusan youths sometimes went to Constantinople for their education.

The Arabs raided Syracuse frequently and in 878 they took the city. We have an account of the siege by an eyewitness, Theodosios the Monk, who described it in a letter to the deacon Leo, which has survived complete in Latin translation. The Byzantines recaptured the city in 1040 under George Maniakes, but after his recall the Arabs recovered it, and held it until the Normans took it in 1085. The Arab notables fled when the city fell, and the Normans restored papal jurisdiction and the Latin rite. The Arabs, however, left one memorial: they introduced papyrus, which still grows beside the river Ciane, the only place north of the Equator where it still grows wild.

Modern Syracuse is rich in monuments of the Graeco-Roman past. In Ortygia there are the badly damaged temple of Apollo, c.565 BC, and the temple of Athena, now the cathedral, c.480 BC. There are also remains of a large unfinished Ionic temple, which would have borne comparison with the great Ionic temples of Hera on Samos and Artemis at Ephesus. On the mainland is the temple of Olympian Zeus, c.550 BC, where two columns still stand. The great Greek theatre was remodelled frequently for different uses, and there is a small, unexcavated Roman theatre that was probably used for drama when gladiatorial games became the staple of the Greek theatre. The fortifications of the Epipolae ridge have been extensively modified since they were built by Dionysius I. The great altar of Hieron II was built between 241 and 215 BC for mass sacrifices of victims when the festival of Zeus Eleutherios was held, and the Roman amphitheatre (3rd century AD) is one of the largest still in existence. The Christian catacombs are more extensive than in any other city except Rome. The early Christian churches attest to a vibrant community: one of them, the basilical S. Giovanni Evangelista (6th century?), is the largest church in Byzantine Sicily.

JAMES ALLAN EVANS

See also Sicily

Summary

The chief city of ancient Sicily, Syracuse was founded by Corinthian colonists in 733 BC. In 485 BC Gelon, tyrant of Gela, moved his capital to Syracuse and in 480 defeated the Carthaginians at Himera. After a period of democracy in the 5th century tyranny returned to

Syracuse with Dionysius I who continued to fight Carthage. The city prospered in the 4th century BC. It fell to Rome after a long siege in 213–211 BC and became the seat of government of the province. It was taken by the Arabs in 878.

Further Reading

Berve, Helmut and Gottfried Gruben, *Greek Temples, Theatres and Shrines*, photographs by Max Hirmer, London: Thames and Hudson, and New York: Abrams, 1963

Burns, Alfred, "Ancient Greek Water Supply and City Planning: A Study of Syracuse and Acragas", *Technology and Culture*, 15 (1974): pp. 389–412

Drögemüller, Hans-Peter, *Syrakus: Zur Topographie und Geschichte einer griechischen Stadt*, Heidelberg: Winler, 1969

Guido, Margaret, *Syracuse: A Handbook to Its History and Principal Monuments*, 4th edition, London: Parrish, 1965

Guido, Margaret, *Sicily: An Archaeological Guide*, 2nd edition, London: Faber, 1977

Holloway, R. Ross, *The Archaeology of Ancient Sicily*, London and New York: Routledge, 1991

Loicq-Berger, Marie Paule, *Syracuse: Histoire culturelle d'une cité grecque*, Brussels: Latomus, 1967

Talbert, R.J.A., *Timoleon and the Revival of Greek Sicily, 334–317 BC*, London and New York: Cambridge University Press, 1974

Whittaker, C.R., "Carthaginian Imperialism in the Fifth and Fourth Centuries" in *Imperialism in the Ancient World*, edited by P.D.A. Garnsey and C.R. Whittaker, Cambridge and New York: Cambridge University Press, 1978

Winter, F.E., *Greek Fortifications*, Toronto: University of Toronto Press, and London: Routledge and Kegan Paul, 1971

Syria

The name Syria is variously used in ancient sources. At its widest it is applied to the whole area from the Egyptian border to the Taurus mountains covering modern Israel, Phoenicia, Jordan, Lebanon, and a small part of Turkey. More often Palestine and Phoenicia are excluded from it. In late antiquity Syria was subdivided into ever smaller provinces. Greek traders were active at the Syrian trading centre of Al Mina at the mouth of the Orontes river from around 825 BC. At first they shared it with Phoenicians; later they almost monopolized the emporium. In the late 8th century BC Euboeans predominated. In the 7th century BC the most common pottery was Corinthian, from the later 6th century BC Athenian. Through this trade oriental skills came to Greece at the end of the Geometric period: gold workers learned techniques of granulation, filigree, and inlaying; craftsmen, especially potters, decorated their wares with oriental imagery, with sphinxes, griffins, roaring lions, and lions fighting men. Greeks heard stories about the origin of the world and the birth of the gods that were to be reshaped by Hesiod and to become part of the Greek heritage.

Al Mina remained an important centre until after the conquest of Syria by Alexander the Great (331–333 BC), when it was replaced by Seleuceia, founded 6 km to the north in 301 BC by king Seleucus Nicator, founder of the Macedonian Seleucid dynasty that was to rule Syria until Pompey turned it into a Roman province in 64 BC. At the time Syria had few and small towns and as part of his policy of settling veteran soldiers and immigrants from Greece Seleucus founded ten cities: the

Syria: the church at Qalaat Semaan was a centre of pilgrimage built in the late 5th century around the pillar of St Symeon the Stylite

biggest was Antioch; second-order cities were Seleuceia, Apamea, and Laodicea; others were Beroea (Aleppo), Chalcis, Cyrrhus, and Zeugma. All were laid out on a grid plan and were given the political institutions of a Greek city. Subsequently Greek culture became exceedingly popular all over greater Syria, and ruling groups everywhere gradually adopted Greek ways. Local gods were identified with Greek deities. Young men took up athletics. Wealthy men spent money to provide Greek-type civic amenities for their fellow citizens. So the Greek way of city life spread from the Greek colonies to native towns and larger settlements. Only among the Jews, thanks to the revolt led by the Maccabee family (168/67 BC), was Hellenization checked.

When the Romans took over Syria they divided the province into city territories and delegated most administrative tasks to the civic authorities. So cities flourished under Roman rule and Hellenism in the cities. While a large part of the country population, and a considerable part of the urban population as well, must have retained their Aramaic language and traditional customs, all visible aspects of their way of life, the architecture of temples and houses, the images of gods, the language of monuments and tombstones, came to be almost exclusively Greek. The earlier literary traditions of the area, except those of the Jews, appear to have faded out. What knowledge we have, for instance about the Phoenicians, has been transmitted

through Greek writers. By the 2nd century AD all Syrian inscriptions, except at Palmyra which had a bilingual culture, were in Greek or occasionally in Latin. It was only in late antiquity that Aramaic inscriptions were once more displayed in Syria. This was a consequence of Syriac becoming a literary language in Mesopotamia, especially at Edessa and Nisibis, in an environment that was bilingual in Greek and Aramaic. Syriac was used by Christians in Mesopotamia, and became the liturgical language of the Monophysites in Mesopotamia and Syria, and of the Nestorians in Persian Mesopotamia. Some works composed in Greek have survived only in Syriac translation and Syriac hymnography strongly influenced the development of the Greek kontakion, or short hymn.

The rise of Syriac marks the turning of the tide of Hellenization. The retreat of Greek was accelerated by the Arab conquest of Syria in 638, which resulted in the flight of many inhabitants and the settlement of Muslims, perhaps mainly in cities. For the next two centuries or so, many of the cities nevertheless continued to have large Christian populations. Between 969 and 1084 part of Syria was again under Byzantine rule. In the latter year it was occupied by the Seljuks, but soon after it was conquered by the Christian armies of the First Crusade. The Crusaders established the princedom of Antioch, which in 1108 was forced to recognize the suzerainty of the Byzantine emperor. The link with Byzantium was finally broken in 1268. Subsequently Syria was governed first by Mamluks and then by Turks.

J.H.W.G. LIEBESCHUETZ

See also Arabs, Colonization, Phoenicians, Seleucids

Further Reading

Bowersock, G.W., *Greek Sophists in the Roman Empire*, Oxford: Clarendon Press, 1969

Bowersock, G.W., *Hellenism in Late Antiquity*, Cambridge: Cambridge University Press, and Ann Arbor: University of Michigan Press, 1990

Brock, S., "Syriac Culture AD 337–425" in *The Late Empire*, AD 337–425, edited by Averil Cameron and Peter Garnsey, Cambridge: Cambridge University Press, 1998 (*The Cambridge Ancient History*, vol. 13, 2nd edition)

Cameron, Averil, "The Eastern Provinces in the Seventh Century AD: Hellenism and the Emergence of Islam" in *Hellenismos: quelques jalons pour une histoire de l'identité grecque*, edited by Suzanne Said, Leiden: Brill, 1991

Dentzer, Jean-Marie and Winifried Orthmann (editors), *Archéologie et histoire de la Syrie*, vol. 2: *La Syrie de l'époque achéménide à l'avènement de l'Islam*, Saarbrücken: Saarbrücker Druckerei, 1989

Grainger, John D., *The Cities of Seleukid, Syria*, Oxford: Clarendon Press, and New York: Oxford University Press, 1990

Griffith, S.H., "Images, Islam and Christian Icons" in *La Syrie de byzance à l'Islam: VIIe–VIIIe siècles*, edited by Pierre Canivet and Jean-Paul Rey Coquais, Damascus: Institut Français de Damas, 1992

Jones, A.H.M., *The Cities of the Eastern Roman Provinces*, 2nd edition, revised by Michael Avi-Yonah *et al.*, Oxford: Clarendon Press, 1971, chapter 10

Kuhrt, Amélie and Susan Sherwin-White (editors), *Hellenism in the East: The Interaction of Greek and Non-Greek Civilizations from Syria to Central Asia after Alexander*, London: Duckworth, 1987

Millar, Fergus, *The Roman Near East, 31 BC–AD 337*, Cambridge, Massachusetts: Harvard University Press, 1993

Rey-Coquais, J.P., "La Culture en Syrie à l'époque romaine", *Electrum*, 1 (1997): pp. 139–60

Schick, Robert, *The Christian Communities of Palestine from Byzantine to Islamic Rule: A Historical and Archaeological Study*, Princeton, New Jersey: Darwin Press, 1995

Tate, Georges, *Les Campagnes de la Syrie du Nord du IIe au VIIe siècle*, vol. 1, Paris: Geuthner, 1992

Tchalenko, Georges, *Villages antiques de la Syrie du Nord*, 3 vols, Paris: Geuthner, 1953–58

T

Tarentum

City in south Italy

The city of Tarentum (modern Taranto), a colony of Dorian Sparta, was situated on the north coast of the gulf of Tarentum facing the Ionian Sea. The acropolis is perched on a peninsula between two harbours – a main outer harbour and an inland tidal lagoon. It was one of the best ports in southern Italy, with access to good cornlands in the interior.

The literary tradition records that the site was founded in 706 BC (Eusebius, *Chronica*, 91b Helm); the archaeological evidence supports this date. Myth relates that the settlement was established by a group of *Partheniai*, the illegitimate offspring of helots, or slaves, and Spartan women, led by their founder, the *oikistes* Phalanthus. The Delphic oracle directed the settlers to found a colony on the south coast of Italy, rather than closer to home in the Peloponnese, in effect legitimizing colonization by means of war and conquest. What is certain is that this was a group of dissatisfied Spartans, perhaps remnants of the pre-Dorian population or others disenfranchised in the aftermath of the First Messenian War (743–724 BC), affected by a social crisis involving land and status. The site was established through the conquest and expulsion of the native inhabitants – Iapygians, Peucetians, and Daunians. Tarentum is unusual in that it had a "double" founder; the second was the eponymous hero Taras, the mythical leader of the pre-Greek Iapygian settlement.

The area was known to the Greeks, especially the Rhodians, from the Mycenaean period on through trade. Despite this long history of contact, the original settlement expanded only slightly to the southeast in the Archaic period, as the inhabitants were afraid of the native tribes. In the late 6th or early 5th century BC Aristophilides appears to have ruled according to a constitutional model based on that of Sparta, with kings and ephors – officials elected both by lot and by vote. The colony retained Spartan cults in their new homeland, continuing to worship Apollo Hyacinthus, and Spartan rituals, such as the burial of the dead within the city walls. It also continued to maintain close ties of kinship with its mother city. There are few remains of the Greek city today because modern Taranto occupies the same site, but Strabo (6. 3. 1) mentions an Archaic Doric temple thought to be dedicated to Poseidon (late 6th century BC), an altar to Aphrodite, a sanctuary of Demeter and Persephone (containing terracotta votive offerings from the 7th and 6th centuries), and other religious structures.

In the early part of the 5th century BC Tarentum enjoyed victories over its Messapian and Peucetian neighbours (c.490 and 460 BC), taking slaves and expanding along the coast to the southwest. The city commemorated these events with the erection of a monument at Delphi. In c.475 BC, though, it suffered a crushing defeat at the hands of a native confederation led by the Iapygians, and much of the aristocracy was destroyed, providing the impetus for the establishment of democracy (Herodotus, 7. 170). At the end of the 5th century BC the settlement began to expand once again, filling the vacuum left by the destruction of its rival Croton, a powerful city to the west. This expansion brought Tarentum wealth and power, and it now became the leading Greek centre in southern Italy. In 433 BC the city founded a colony itself at Heraclea (Policoro) on the west coast of the gulf, which acted as a counterweight to the Athenian colony at Thurii, and served as the new head of a league of Italiot Greeks. It was allied with Syracuse in the Peloponnesian War, contributing ships to the cause and sending corn to Sparta, in an attempt to offset Athenian power in the region as well as support its mother city. Consequently it was invaded by the Athenians.

Tarentum began to develop a reputation for possessing many great works of art. Among others, Pythagoras of Rhegium created a famous statue of *Zeus and Europa* which graced the city centre. In the same period the Apulian school of pottery, founded by Greeks who came from Thurii to Tarentum, established its centre in the city (c.420 BC). This school was known especially for its representations of myth and comic parodies on the vessels it produced. Much of what we know about Greek theatre today is illustrated by the images painted on these vases. Terracotta figurines and antefixes were also widely exported from the city.

Tarentum attained its greatest wealth and power in the 4th and 3rd centuries BC, at which time it became the pre-eminent city in Magna Graecia, renowned for its luxuriousness. The extent of its wealth and political power is indicated by the great number of goods produced in the city, as well as its attractive series of coins, which were distributed widely around the shores of the Mediterranean Sea. In the early 4th century BC politics were dominated by Archytas, a Pythagorean philosopher-mathematician and friend of Plato, who expanded Tarentine influence in the area. After the mid-4th century BC the city's difficulties with the surrounding native tribes increased, and it requested help first from Sparta, and then from a series of mercenary princes and kings. Initially it called upon Archidamus III of Sparta (338 BC), who died in battle. Then Alexander I of Epirus came to its aid. In the beginning he was successful, but was eventually slain c.330 BC. The next call for help was directed to Cleomenes of Sparta, who also ultimately failed.

Tarentum was host to many famous residents and visitors in this period. Aristoxenus, a philosopher and musician, developed his theory of harmonics there. Rhinton was a comic dramatist who popularized *phylax* farces – local productions that drew on daily life for their inspiration. It was famous as well for its fine works of art, both large and small. At this time Lysippus of Sicyon created a large bronze statue of *Zeus and Hera* for the city. It was a major centre of production for votive figurines of terracotta, primarily religious in nature, which were precursors of the well-known Athenian and Tanagran types. It was also known for its limestone architectural sculpture adorned with human figures.

Towards the end of the century, the inhabitants of the city became fearful of the growing power of Rome, and felt threatened by Roman aid to the nearby cities of Thurii, Locri, and Rhegium. Despite having signed a treaty in 303 BC, in the early 3rd century Tarentine forces attacked Roman ships in the harbour and insulted the Roman ambassador. These actions precipitated war with Rome. Tarentum once again enlisted the help of an Epiriot ruler, Pyrrhus, who responded to its request in 281 BC. The Tarentines were soon joined by the native tribes of the Bruttians, Lucanians, and Samnites. At first Pyrrhus enjoyed a number of successes, especially against the Carthaginians in Sicily, but the city felt threatened by the king's growing power and his plan for a united kingdom of Sicily and lower Italy, and withdrew its support. Upon Pyrrhus' departure, the Romans took over in 272 BC, forcing territorial concessions from the Tarentines. The city became an ally of Rome in 270 BC and the struggle for the control of central Italy was over, with Roman domination of lower Italy now assured. Many of its art treasures were carried off to Rome. At this time the city was the home of Livius Andronicus, a Greek-born slave, who produced comedies, tragedies, and a Latin translation of the *Odyssey*. He played an important part in the creation and development of Latin literature.

A group of Tarentine aristocrats revolted in the Second Punic War (218–201 BC) and went over to Hannibal (213 BC), who fortified the lower city, but it was retaken by Rome in 209 BC. The extension of the Via Appia and the founding of Brundisium (Brindisi) undercut its trade, and part of its territory was confiscated. The city declined from this period on, although it probably regained allied status in 180 BC. It subsequently received colonial status and became a provincial Italian town, but there is much epigraphical evidence of civic activity and mention of the importance of its products – wool, textiles, purple dye made from the processing of murex shells, and agricultural produce. Strabo maintained that the city was still linguistically and culturally Greek in his time (6. 1. 2), but this is controversial. Horace (*Odes*, 3. 5. 53–56) described it as a suitable holiday place for a tired businessman.

From the late-6th and early-7th centuries AD, Tarentum was fought over by the Lombard princes operating from their stronghold at Beneventum (Benevento), and the Byzantine Greeks inhabiting the heel of Italy to the south. After the Italian dukes and the Greeks together took Muslim pirates into their employ in the early 9th century, Saracens from north Africa and Spain entered the fray. The city was destroyed by the Saracens in 927, but was rebuilt by Nikephoros Phokas, who re-established Greek as the common language, and brought the city back into the Greek fold. The southwards-expanding Normans, under the adventurer Robert Guiscard, were invited into the region as mercenaries to fight against the marauding Arabs. The Normans benefited from continual dissension in the area, and finally took control of the city themselves in the 1060s.

KATHLEEN DONAHUE SHERWOOD

See also Magna Graecia

Summary

Founded as a colony of Dorian Sparta, traditionally in 706 BC, Tarentum played an important part in establishing a Greek presence in southern Italy. It was a centre of Greek culture and power in Magna Graecia, renowned for its fine works of art and luxurious lifestyle attained through the benefits of trade. It fell to Rome in 272 BC. It was destroyed by the Saracens in 927 and rebuilt by Nikephoros Phokas.

Further Reading

Belli, Carlo, *Il tesoro di Taras*, Milano: Bestetti, 1970

Boardman, John, *The Greeks Overseas: Their Early Colonies and Trade*, 4th edition, London and New York: Thames and Hudson, 1999

Brauer, George C., *Taras: Its History and Coinage*, New Rochelle, New York: Caratzas, 1986

Christie, Neil, *The Lombards*, Oxford and Cambridge, Massachusetts: Blackwell, 1995

Dunbabin, T.J., *The Western Greeks: The History of Sicily and South Italy from the Foundation of the Greek Colonies to 480 BC*, Oxford: Clarendon Press, 1968, pp. 87–93

Falkenhausen, V. von, "Taranto in epoca bizantina" in *Studi Medievali*, 39 (1968): pp. 133–66

Holmes, George, *Oxford Illustrated History of Medieval Europe*, Oxford and New York: Oxford University Press, 1988, reprinted 1996, pp. 209–15

Hussey, J.M. (editor), *The Byzantine Empire*, Cambridge: Cambridge University Press, 1966 (*The Cambridge Medieval History*, vol. 4, part 1, 2nd edition)

Kazhdan, A.P. (editor), Tarentum entry in the *Oxford Dictionary of Byzantium*, vol. 3, New York and Oxford: Oxford University Press, 1991

Lo Porto, F.G., "Topografica antica di Taranto" in *Taranto nella civiltà della Magna Grecia*, Naples: Arte, 1971

Lomas, H. Kathryn, Tarentum entry in *The Oxford Classical Dictionary*, 3rd edition, edited by Simon Hornblower and Antony Spawforth, Oxford and New York: Oxford University Press, 1996, pp. 1473–74

Malkin, Irad, *Myth and Territory in the Spartan Mediterranean*, Cambridge and New York: Cambridge University Press, 1994

Nenci, G. and G. Vallet, *Bibliografia topografica della colonizzazione greca in Italia e nelle isole tirreniche*, Pisa: Scuola Normale Superiore, and Rome: Ecole Française de Rome, 1977–

Purcell, N., "South Italy in the Fourth Century BC" in *The Fourth Century BC*, edited by D.M. Lewis *et al.* Cambridge: Cambridge University Press, 1994 (*The Cambridge Ancient History*, vol. 6, 2nd edition)

Reuter, Timothy (editor), *The New Cambridge Medieval History*, vol. 3: *c.900–c.1024*, Cambridge: Cambridge University Press, 2000

Stillwell, Richard (editor), *Princeton Encyclopedia of Classical Sites*, Princeton, New Jersey: Princeton University Press, 1976, pp. 878–80

Vallet, Georges, *Le Monde grec colonial d'Italie du Sud and de Sicile*, Rome: École Française de Rome, 1996

Taxation

Taxes are compulsory levies imposed by the state primarily for the purpose of financing government expenditure. They are commonly classified as either direct or indirect. Direct taxes are levied on an individual's income or personal wealth (e.g. imposts on income) while indirect taxes are assessments on transactions or services (e.g. customs duties). Since taxes are imposed by the state, the nature of the levies collected by each government reflects the interests of the group in power. Thus any treatment of taxation involves discussing the nature of the government imposing the levies in question.

The earliest Greek taxation system that can be discussed in detail is that used by the kingdoms that ruled Greece in the Mycenaean period. In this system each village was responsible for producing specific amounts of individual commodities such as wool and wheat. Taxes were thus of the direct variety and were paid in kind, i.e. with produce rather than with money.

The simpler forms of government that arose after the collapse of Mycenaean civilization adopted equally simple forms of taxation. The ruler (a relatively weak king) was given the use of a piece of public land, the produce of which supported the royal household and paid for the few public functions that were undertaken.

The more complex forms of political organization that arose around 800 BC made use of three basic taxation systems. The simplest of these was used exclusively by Sparta, which was ruled by a fairly numerous military elite. The members of this group were exempt from all taxes and were fully supported by mandatory contributions in kind levied on the serfs assigned to each individual's estate. Apart from small gifts presented to royalty, no other regular taxes existed.

The second system of taxation of interest here was used primarily in cases where the state was ruled by a limited number of individuals. Examples include Corinth under the Cypselid family (*c.*650 BC) and Athens under Pisistratus and his sons (*c.*540 BC). This system relied on direct taxes imposed on the entire population. The most important imposts were a 10 per cent levy in kind on agricultural produce and a yearly fee (a head or poll tax) due from each individual. Indirect imposts, including customs duties and sales taxes, also played a role. The payment of direct taxes by the entire population was a reflection of the concentration of political power.

The link between political power and taxation is also evident in the third system, which is most clearly known from its manifestation in democratic Athens (510–322 BC). Democracy entailed the participation of a substantial number of citizens, who expected to be compensated for their services. At the same time, the obligation to pay direct taxes was seen as a form of subservience. The existence of a democratic government thus meant that a significant revenue stream had to be generated without the imposition of direct levies on most of the state's residents.

A vast variety of indirect taxes were levied on all Athenians. These included customs duties, sales taxes, and levies on banking transactions. Direct taxes in the form of a head tax were paid only by resident aliens. However, the limited number of non-citizens made direct taxation on citizens unavoidable. This taxation took the form of "liturgies". A liturgy was a governmental expense, such as the maintenance of a warship, that was assigned directly to an individual. The liturgist was responsible for providing all necessary funds to complete the designated project. In Athens the wealthiest residents, both citizens and aliens, served as liturgists. This practice was politically expedient since it provided government financing without the use of a direct tax.

The practice of imposing liturgies also simplified the state's administrative duties. The vast number of individual taxes that were imposed and the fact that Athenian taxes were due in the form of money rather than in kind made the collection and supervision of revenue a complicated process. Liturgies provided one solution to this problem by uniting taxation and expenditure. Tax farming was another solution.

Rather than appointing agents to collect taxes, the Athenian state auctioned off ("farmed") the right to procure the revenues generated by a particular impost. In exchange for an advance payment to the state, the tax farmer was granted the right to collect a specific impost for a specific period of time. This practice had two advantages. First, the administrative demands placed on the state were greatly reduced. Second, the yield of each impost was known and acquired in advance. This greatly simplified the process of planning and financing government expenditure.

This system of taxation was shaped by the diffusion of political power engendered by democracy. Other Greek states with democratic government structures took a similar approach to taxation. The political evolution of Greece, however, moved in a direction that made such situations unusual. By the end of the 4th century BC most of Greece was ruled by large kingdoms. The taxation system used by these kingdoms bore a striking resemblance to that used in earlier Greek states ruled by a limited number of individuals. Direct taxes in the form of levies on agricultural produce and a head tax were the primary sources of government revenue. The needs of the kingdoms were such that taxes were levied in monetary form, which again complicated the process of collection. This prompted the use of tax farming.

In spite of the fact that the identity of the state controlling Greece changed on numerous occasions over the course of the centuries, this system of taxation remained in operation with only minor changes well into the 19th century AD. The Byzantine empire (*c.*330–*c.*1453) drew a substantial portion of its revenues from two different direct levies, both of which were payable in cash on an annual basis. A land tax was collected in the form of a flat charge per unit of acreage owned (the *modius*, equal to 0.08 hectares), with some allowance for varying soil fertility and the use to which the land was put. Each household also paid a hearth tax (in essence a collective head tax imposed on each family unit). Non-Christians were obligated to pay a special yearly impost in addition to the hearth tax. Indirect levies in the form of customs duties and market and inheritance taxes were also collected. As was the case earlier, tax farming was extensively employed during the Byzantine period.

During the Tourkokratia (c.1453–c.1832) the Ottoman empire, which took control of Greece after the collapse of the Byzantine empire, left the pre-existing taxation system largely intact. The most important differences between the Ottoman system and that of their Byzantine predecessors consisted of the collection of a significant amount of taxes in kind (rather than in cash) and the imposition of special head taxes on non-Muslims rather than on non-Christians. The high degree of continuity between the Byzantine and Ottoman periods is also observable at the end of Ottoman rule in that the newly inde-pendent Greek state made relatively few immediate modifica-tions to the extant tax structure.

Over the course of time, however, two major changes took place. First, the gradual construction of a revenue collection system based on western European models made it possible for the Greek government to phase out tax farming. The first sustained effort in this direction began in 1847. Second, there was a distinct trend away from direct levies. Imposts of this kind were strongly associated with political subjection and were thus largely replaced by a variety of indirect alternatives. By the mid-1980s Greeks were paying more than 500 different indirect taxes.

Greece's reliance on indirect taxes continues to the present. About 65 per cent of the national budget (excluding social insurance) is still provided by indirect levies. This is at variance with the practice of most other European states, which finance most of their expenses with direct imposts. Direct taxes are widely used outside Greece because they are relatively easy to collect and because they can be used to reduce the inequality of income distribution, an important goal in many countries. Whereas indirect taxes are imposed at a uniform rate on all individuals regardless of their income, direct taxes can be tailored so as to take a progressively larger share as the total income rises. Rich individuals are thus obliged to turn over a larger percentage of their wealth than poor ones. The ability of direct taxes simultaneously to raise revenue and to reduce income inequalities makes this form of impost highly attrac-tive. During the 1990s the Greek state initiated a series of reforms intended gradually to replace most indirect taxes with direct alternatives.

PAUL CHRISTESEN

See also Finance

Further Reading

Andreades, A.M., *A History of Greek Public Finance*, 2nd edition, Cambridge, Massachusetts: Harvard University Press, 1933

Andreades, A. M., "Public Finances: Currency, Public Expenditure, Budget, Public Revenue" in *Byzantium*, edited by N. H. Baynes, Oxford: Clarendon Press, 1948

Darling, Linda T., *Revenue-Raising and Legitimacy: Tax Collection and Finance Administration in the Ottoman Empire, 1560–1660*, Leiden: Brill, 1996

Eulambio, Michel S., *The National Bank of Greece: A History of the Financial and Economic Evolution of Greece*, Athens: Vlastos, 1924

Finlay, George, *A History of Greece from its Conquest by the Romans to the Present Time, BC 146 to AD 1864*, revised by H.F. Tozer, vol. 7, Oxford: Clarendon Press, 1877; reprinted New York: AMS Press, 1970

Forrest, W.G., *A History of Sparta, 950–192 BC*, 2nd edition, London: Duckworth, 1980

Goldsmith, Raymond W., *Premodern Financial Systems: A Historical Comparative Study*, Cambridge and New York: Cambridge University Press, 1987

Hammond, N.G.L., G.T. Griffith, and F.W. Walbank, *A History of Macedonia*, 3 vols, Oxford: Clarendon Press, 1972–88

Legg, Keith R. and John M. Roberts, *Modern Greece: A Civilization on the Periphery*, Boulder, Colorado: Westview Press, 1997

National Bank of Greece, *Economic and Statistical Bulletin*, published 1975– (annual statistical survey)

Petropulos, John Anthony, *Politics and Statecraft in the Kingdom of Greece, 1833–1843*, Princeton, New Jersey: Princeton University Press, 1968

Sealey, Raphael, *A History of the Greek City States, c.700–338 BC*, Berkeley: University of California Press, 1976

Treadgold, Warren T., *The Byzantine State Finances in the Eighth and Ninth Centuries*, Boulder, Colorado: East European Monographs, 1982

Webber, Carolyn and Aaron Wildavsky, *A History of Taxation and Expenditure in the Western World*, New York: Simon and Schuster, 1986

Technology

Technological discoveries and importations from elsewhere are notoriously hard to date in the ancient world. Many tech-niques leave little or no archaeological evidence and literary mention is sporadic and incidental before the Hellenistic period. Even then from the 3rd century BC we have little other than the Aristotelian *Mechanical Problems* (perhaps by Straton, the head of the Lyceum from c.287 to 269 BC) which, though primarily theoretical, does deal with problems in applied mathematics involving levers, compound pulleys, etc. The inventor Ctesibius wrote a treatise on pneumatics (now lost but used by later authors), while his contemporary Archimedes, apart from a lost treatise on how to build a spher-ical planetarium, chose deliberately to write only theoretical mathematical treatises. Around 200 BC Philon of Byzantium composed a compendium of technology whose main concern was the construction of mechanical devices: surviving books deal mainly with pneumatics and war machines. More remains from the Roman period. The tenth book of Vitruvius' Latin treatise *De Architectura* (c.25 BC) details relevant technical devices largely drawn from Greek predecessors. The great *Natural History* of the Elder Pliny (mid-1st century AD), despite its title, ignores virtually no field of human endeavour and preserves much information from lost Greek sources. His contemporary Heron of Alexandria is our principal authority for ancient technology, although his books on mechanics survive only in an Arabic translation and in extensive quota-tions by the 3rd- to 4th-century Pappus of Alexandria. From the Byzantine period little of use was written and even less survives: in the 4th century Oribasius described mechanical constructions for resetting dislocated limbs; the 5th-century alchemist Zosimus described chemical apparatus and recipes for smelting, dyeing, etc.; while, unfortunately, most of the treatises on mechanics and hydraulics by Anthemius of Tralles (the innovative architect of Hagia Sophia, Constantinople) are lost. Later works are almost entirely mere reworkings of inherited knowledge.

Until the Hellenistic period the Greeks largely used technology that was already existing in the eastern Mediterranean at the time of their arrival in the late 3rd millennium BC, and remarkably few advances were made. The conservative attitude of the Classical period, known in many other areas for exuberant originality, is sometimes attributed to the existence of slavery, but is more probably due to a cultural attitude of the intellectual elite which elevated "pure" far above "applied" knowledge. Even the famous black- and red-figure Attic pottery in the Archaic and Classical periods depended upon a refinement of a technique known as early as the Middle Helladic age (c.2000–1500 BC). The Attic potters placed their pots, painted with a clay slip containing iron oxides, in a wood-fired kiln which with the air vents open produced an oxidizing phase, thereby turning both painted and unpainted parts red, up to a temperature of 800°C, between which and 945°C closure of the vents and the introduction of smoke-producing green wood created a reducing phase in which the whole pot turned black. Subsequently the temperature was allowed to decrease and at about 900°C the vents were reopened to create the final, reoxidizing, phase in which the unpainted parts became red again while the sintered areas remained black.

The most advanced technology before the Hellenistic period was probably metallurgy: alluvial gold was caught in fleeces; gold and silver were extracted from lead by cupellation; and ore-bearing rocks were pounded and washed or heated in a blow- and later bellows-heated furnace to separate metal from gangue. The ability to attain a temperature sufficiently high to form iron blooms for hot-hammering (first managed perhaps by the Hittites c.1400 BC) was the single most important technological change in Greek history and may have been partly responsible for the downfall of the mainly bronze-using Mycenaeans. Alloys, especially of copper, were developed for specific purposes and soldering was practised. Implements were made by hot- and cold-hammering or casting (including the lost-wax process). Decorative processes included repoussé work and niello inlays (both known in the Mycenaean period), filigree, and granulation. Metal tools in the Classical and especially Hellenistic periods became increasingly precise. Notably carpentry was provided with hammers, chisels, saws (including the frame saw), and planes, while surgery benefited from a wide range of specialized implements. Locking devices also became increasingly ingenious.

The farmer raised water with the *shaduf* (swing-beam with compensating weight). Tillage of the soil was accomplished through the hoe and the usually ox-drawn ard-plough; seed was broadcast by hand from a container slung round the neck; harvesting was done with sickles; grain was separated from chaff by flailing or threshing, in which centrally tethered animals were driven round a threshing floor and the chaff carried away by a breeze when tossed in the air by hand with the grain from a winnowing basket or by a winnowing fan; milling was done in querns. There was little change in agricultural methods until the addition of the threshing sledge, animal- and water-powered mills, and the rare animal-driven reaping machines in the Hellenistic and Roman periods.

Raw, wetted pelts were moulded over hard cores into containers which became stiff when dry. Cleansed pelts cured with salt or sun-dried were rendered imputrescible and water-resistant by numerous vegetal tanning agents with varying resultant colouration, but there is also some evidence for tawing by minerals. Malleability could be achieved by chamoising, the subsequent rubbing with animal fat, which is mentioned already in the *Iliad*.

Spinning was done most commonly by twisting carded wool (or other fibres) drawn from a distaff on to a suspended spindle to which was attached a whorl to steady rotation. Weaving was done on a warp-weighted vertical loom, the threads alternately hanging straight down or passing over a horizontal shed-rod. Different weaves were attained by manipulation of heddle-rods. During the Roman period the loom at which a standing weaver pushed the weft upwards with the weaving sword gave way to one at which a seated weaver pressed it down with a comb, which was itself replaced in turn by a horizontal version. Specific looms for specific fibres were also being designed.

The Hellenistic and Roman periods were by far the most productive time of technological development in Greek history. Nevertheless, despite important practical advances, especially in the areas of building and war machines, even then a love of theory resulted in the invention and description of many contrivances of such great inefficiency that, even if models were ever built, they could not have served any practical purpose. Most notable in this respect are Heron's descriptions of a ball revolving on its own axis through the emission of steam from angled vents, and his device for covertly opening (and closing) temple doors by the pressure of air heated by fire on an altar forcing water to flow into a bucket which in turn tugged cords wrapped around a subterranean extension of the door-posts. On the other hand his related description of figurines making libations when a fire was lit on an altar is eminently feasible, as is Philon's automaton that alternately handed guests a pumice stone and poured water for washing, which led ultimately to similar but far more complex robots in the Islamic world. Toys, such as Heron's automatic theatre which could mechanically produce a puppet show in several acts, were probably made for amusement, while ingenious hydraulic devices that gave moving figures to fountains were to have a long history. One Athenian device of the mid-4th century BC was certainly of practical benefit: the stone *kleroterion* precluded jury-rigging by enabling black and white balls to fall randomly from a hopper down a tube at the side of a series of rows in which potential dicasts had inserted their metal tickets.

In mechanics we find that the lever, which had been known since the Neolithic age, had multifarious applications (e.g. for raising objects and as a steelyard). While the lever-press became common (the wedge-press was also invented), perhaps the most surprising anticipation of the modern world to employ the lever was a slot machine for dispensing ritual water upon insertion of a coin (but whether this was ever constructed or is merely theoretical is not known). The winch and the pulley (both known much earlier separately) were combined in hoisting- and pulling-engines, while compound pulleys became increasingly effective (often incorporated into cranes powered by human treadwheels). The endless rope or belt, however, seems not to have been employed for transmitting power but only when itself driven, as in the bucket chain for the raising of water (activated by a treadwheel). Both horizontal and vertical capstans were widely used, while Drachmann (1973) believed that the crank had been invented by Archimedes and underwent subsequent experiments, although strangely this simple but efficient mechanism never enjoyed widespread application until the later Middle Ages, and certainly never appeared in antiquity with a connecting rod.

Of great importance was the invention of the screw-line ("the snail on the cylinder"), attributed to Apollonius of Perge, a younger contemporary of Archimedes who promptly employed it in his *cochlea* ("water-snail") for the raising of water. Screws were used more for moving and adjusting than for holding down (in which role they first appear in goldsmithery). Corresponding female screws made large presses (e.g. fullers' and olive-presses) more efficient than the alternative lever- and wedge-presses. Female screws were first cut into a split block which was then rejoined, but Heron describes a machine for their manufacture. The impossibility of making them small, however, meant that many instruments (e.g. the gynaecological *specula matris*) had to use the inferior method of a screw with an engaged peg.

Cogwheels, of wood for large machines and of metal for small, were employed for transmission in four ways. The rack and pinion is first attested in a water clock made by Ctesibius, but is not found again until Heron's toys (e.g. a self-snuffing lamp). Archimedes is credited with both inventing and employing in war machines the endless screw (the worm-and-wheel gear), but it does not appear again until Heron, who used it for, among other devices, his surveying instruments the *dioptra* (theodolite) and hodometer. Chronologically next probably comes the use of parallel engaging wheels. Although these were generally inefficient owing to an inability to find the optimum shape, there has been found in a shipwreck off the island of Anticythera a calendarial celestial computing mechanism from *c*.80 BC (the sole surviving machine from antiquity) containing three brass dials and 31 cogwheels of different sizes with teeth in the shape of equilateral triangles: that this was actually used is proved by the evidence of repairs. Toothed wheels engaging at right angles are not attested until Vitruvius, who describes an undershot water wheel that gives motive force to a corn mill, a device of longterm practical benefit. (An overshot wheel is depicted in the Roman catacomb of S. Agnese in a representation of probably the 3rd century AD, probable remains of one from the 5th century have been found in the Athenian Agora, and a certain example has been recently excavated from 9th to 10th century Byzantine Thebes. The wind-driven wheel, mentioned for Seistan, Afghanistan, in the 10th century AD, did not appear in the Greek world until the 14th apart from a miniature experimental usage by Ctesibius.)

In hydraulics and pneumatics the most important advance was in the increasing application of the syphon (used earlier for mixing liquids), which led not only to ingenious toys and drinking vessels (such as one still made in a Chiot village) but to the ability to force water to rise in aqueducts (at Pergamum in the 2nd century BC the citadel was served at 155 m above the lowest level of the aqueduct). Ctesibius' experiments in pneumatic machines, such as his organ (operated from a keyboard) in which water pressure forced air through pipes, led him to the invention of the force pump with cylinders and plungers operated by horizontal levers and vertical connecting rods. One adaptation for fire fighting had a nozzle that could be swivelled in any direction and tilted both ways. Surviving examples of pumps have both flap valves and the superior spindle valves. Ctesibius also improved the accuracy of timekeeping by ensuring a uniform flow in the *klepsydra* (water clock), to which he attached, in addition to all manner of entertaining automata, a figure with a pointer to indicate the hours on a column. Vitruvius describes a later water-driven clock which more efficiently adjusted the varying length of ancient hours on a revolving disc engraved with the zodiacal constellations.

Of great practical value was the development, probably in Hellenistic Syria *c*.100 BC, of glass blowing. Hitherto only modelled around a core of sand or poured into a mould when molten or carved when cold by hand or lathe, glass now became a common and relatively cheap material for vessels of daily use. More expensive articles were subject to an exuberant range of decorative processes including marvering, trailing, engraving, and painting, while openwork cage cups were carved from thick blanks. Gold glass, in which gold leaf carved into patterns or figures was placed between layers of transparent glass, appears to be an early Hellenistic innovation. Lenses are known from the Bronze Age onwards, but they remained a craftsman's (engraver's) tool and are not mentioned in any theoretical treatise on optics. By the 5th century BC they were being employed also as burning mirrors. Glass was used in addition for reflecting mirrors (sporadically from *c.* 600 BC as cosmetic aids and later both for signalling and in lighthouses), for lamps (from the Hellenistic period), in small panes for windows, and in sheets cut into tesserae for mosaics (both from the Roman period). Stained glass was developed, if not perhaps invented, by the Byzantines.

Its Classical inheritance allowed Byzantium to remain the most technologically advanced state in Europe and the eastern Mediterranean until at least the 12th century. It acted, moreover, as a conduit for ancient knowledge to the Islamic world and of Islamic (e.g. of damascening) and even barbarian knowledge (e.g. of the stirrup from probably the Avars) to the West. Nevertheless, Byzantine technology did suffer from the subordination of mundane to heavenly affairs. Apart from a few minor improvements to existing machines (e.g. water mills and a geared quern), ingenuity was largely expended on the making of automata, notably in the 9th and 10th centuries when there was a rivalry with the caliphal court: water-driven clocks indicated the hours with an impressive display of moving figures; compressed air from bellows or water power lifted an imperial throne into the air, caused lions to roar and wag their tails, birds in golden trees to warble and flutter their wings, and figures on fountains to make appropriate movements. Atypically, in the mid 6th century, Anthemius is reputed to have driven away a neighbour and personal enemy with a powerful reflector and contrivances that created artificial thunder and, by steam power, a mock earthquake; the emperor Theophilos in the 9th century was praised for his construction of organs (pneumatic rather than hydraulic as in Heron's original instrument); while in the 11th century Psellos claims to have repeated some of the experiments of Heron.

The most famous invention was Greek fire (which nonetheless may possibly have been of Arab origin) and the most bizarre a paddle boat driven by pairs of oxen attached to capstans in the hold of the vessel, which is described in a Latin treatise of probably the late middle of the 4th century AD, the anonymous author of which was probably a westerner despite some scholars' belief that he was a native Greek-speaker. While useful progress was mostly made in pharmacological and chemical technology, a few other discoveries, improvisations, and technical improvements are known or suspected. The general Belisarius mounted wheels between pairs of boats furnished with mills when the besieging Goths had cut the supply of water to Rome in AD 537; by the 6th century wooden stamps for printing fabrics were employed in Byzantine Egypt and at that time and subsequently refinements were made in silk-weaving looms; Leo the Mathematician devised a beacon system in the 9th century (at which time mention was also made of a water clock with an alarm to awake the monk deputed to rouse his brethren); from the 9th to the 13th century great advances were made in enamelling techniques; an ox-driven mechanism for kneading dough appeared in the 10th; new techniques improved the staining of glass in the 10th and made it more durable in the 11th and 12th; and a more efficient method of stacking pots inside each other and separating them by tripod-stilts facilitated mass-production in the 12th century.

The period of foreign occupation that followed the fall of Constantinople in 1453 allowed little scope for technological innovation. The independent modern state of Greece preferred to establish its literary rather than scientific credentials before the 1980s, since when the Ministry of Education has made a determined effort to promote technology at the secondary and tertiary levels.

A.R. LITTLEWOOD

See also Fire, Glass, Metalwork, Pottery, Siegecraft, Textiles, Water Management

Further Reading

Aristotle, *Mechanical Problems*, translated by W.S. Hett in *Aristotle: Minor Works*, London: Heinemann, and Cambridge, Massachusetts: Harvard University Press, 1936

Brumbaugh, Robert S., *Ancient Greek Gadgets and Machines*, New York: Crowell, 1966

Drachmann, A.G., *Ktesibios, Philon and Heron: A Study in Ancient Pneumatics*, Copenhagen: Munksgaard, 1948

Drachmann, A.G., *The Mechanical Technology of Greek and Roman Antiquity: A Study of the Literary Sources*, Copenhagen: Munksgaard, and Madison: University of Wisconsin Press, 1963 (contains many translations, including *Mechanics* by Hero of Alexandria)

Drachmann, A.G., "The Crank in Graeco-Roman Antiquity" in *Changing Perspectives in the History of Science*, edited by Mikuláš

Teich and Robert Young, London: Heinemann, 1973

Forbes, R.J., *Studies in Ancient Technology*, 3rd edition, 3 vols, Leiden: Brill, 1993

Hero of Alexandria, *The Pneumatics*, translated by J.G. Greenwood, London: Whittingham, 1851; reprinted London: Macdonald, and New York: Elsevier, 1971

Hero of Alexandria, *Opera*, edited by Wilhelm Schmidt *et al.*, 5 vols, Leipzig: Teubner, 1899–1914

Hill, Donald, *A History of Engineering in Classical and Medieval Times*, London: Croom Helm, and La Salle, Illinois: Open Court, 1984

Landels, J.G., *Engineering in the Ancient World*, London: Chatto and Windus, and Berkeley: University of California Press, 1978

Noble, J.V., *The Techniques of Painted Attic Pottery*, revised edition, London: Thames and Hudson, 1988

Oleson, J.P., *Bronze Age, Greek, and Roman Technology: A Select, Annotated Bibliography*, New York: Garland, 1986

Pappus, [Works] edited by Friedrich Hultsch, 3 vols, Berlin: Weidmann, 1876–78; reprinted Amsterdam: Hakkert, 1965

Pavlovskis, Zoja, *Man in an Artificial Landscape: The Marvels of Civilization in Imperial Roman Literature*, Leiden: Brill, 1973 (contains much information on automata in the Graeco-Roman world)

Philo of Byzantium, *Belopoeica*, edited and translated by Eric William Marsden in *Greek and Roman Artillery*, Oxford: Clarendon Press, 1971; reprinted Ann Arbor: UMI Books on Demand, 1997

Philo of Byzantium, *Pneumatica: The First Treatise on Experimental Physics*, translated by Frank David Prager, Wiesbaden: Reichert, 1974

Pliny the Elder, *Natural History*, translated by H. Rackham, W.H.S. Jones and D.E. Eichholz, 10 vols, London: Heinemann, and Cambridge, Massachusetts: Harvard University Press, 1938–63 (Loeb edition; many reprints)

Price, Derek de Solla, "Gears from the Greeks: The Antikythera Mechanism, a Calendar Computer from ca. 80 BC", *Transactions of the American Philosophical Society*, new series 64/7 (1974)

Vitruvius, *On Architecture*, translated by Frank Granger, 2 vols, London: Heinemann, and Cambridge, Massachusetts: Harvard University Press, 1931–34 (Loeb edition; many reprints)

Vogel, K., in *The Byzantine Empire*, edited by J.M. Hussey, Cambridge: Cambridge University Press, 1966 (*The Cambridge Medieval History*, vol. 4, part 2, 2nd edition), pp. 299–305, 465–70

White, K.D., *Greek and Roman Technology*, London: Thames and Hudson, and Ithaca, New York: Cornell University Press, 1984

White, Lynn, Jr, *Medieval Religion and Technology: Collected Essays*, Berkeley: University of California Press, 1978

Textiles

Textiles are highly perishable and rarely survive the ravages of time. Our knowledge of them comes from a variety of sources, including archaeological finds, pictorial representations, and written sources.

In the Near East the use of flax to make linen cloth predates silk, cotton, and the domestication of sheep for wool by several millennia. The oldest textile in the world, a woven linen fabric adhering to a tool excavated at Cayonu in southeastern Turkey in 1993, is dated to about 7000 BC; wool did not appear in the Balkans until about 3500 BC.

The history of textiles in Greece begins in early Minoan Crete (*c.*2300 BC) where excavations at the prehistoric village of Myrtos turned up the first evidence for cloth production: sheep bones, tubs for washing wool, bowls for wetting linen thread, and clay spindle whorls. These finds indicate that the Minoans knew how to spin both flax and wool. Remnants of cloth from other sites in Bronze Age Greece and Turkey reveal the human penchant for decorating cloth. At Troy, for example, Schliemann found a linen textile embellished with tiny blue-green faience beads from *c.*2600 BC.

Evidence from later Minoan Crete and Mycenae (1600–1150 BC) tells the story of a flourishing textile industry. The men tended flocks of sheep in the countryside; women spun yarn and wove cloth in the palaces. The sheep were caught and plucked, because shears had not yet been invented to cut the wool from the sheep's back. Early breeds of sheep moulted fine wool from their coats, leaving the bristly kemp hairs, which moulted later. The wool was brought to the palace and weighed, then distributed for cleaning, combing, and spinning. The oils and fats were removed from the wool and retained for use in perfumes and ointments. Spinners worked in groups; weavers worked in pairs. Greek women did not spin on wheels, but on spindles. The spinner held the fibre-laden distaff in her right hand; from this she drew out the fibre and twisted it into thread with the aid of a spindle weighted with a whorl. Large numbers of ancient spindles and whorls have been found in archaeological digs.

The warp-weighted loom, for which ancient Greece is well known in textile history, was apparently already in use among Mycenaean weavers around 1400 BC. The Linear B script lists "cloth with white edges" or "cloth with coloured edges", indicating the use of starting bands typical for weaving on warp-weighted looms. (The starting bands were made by specialists who wove on small band looms.) These bands stabilized the warps which were suspended from a horizontal bar on vertical supports. The warps were anchored at the lower end with clay weights. A shed rod divided the warps, half in front, half at the back. The rear warps were attached to a heddle rod which, when lifted, created a shed through which the weft was inserted. The weft was beaten upwards, towards the horizontal bar, with a sword-like shuttle. Herodotus wrote of "pushing the woof [weft] upwards". Generally the looms were no taller than the weaver's reach, although one depiction of a warp-weighted loom shows the weavers wearing platform shoes to gain height. With warp-weighted looms, the length of the cloth was limited to the height of the loom. However, the loom allowed the manufacture of wide cloth with three finished edges.

Minoan artwork depicts elaborately patterned and coloured textiles, implying advanced weaving skills and a knowledge of dyeing. Patterns include rosettes, grids of tiny diamonds, and spirals. Such patterns could have been embroidered, painted, or woven. Wool, the most common fibre, was easy to dye. The known dyestuffs included two classes of dyes, direct and vat. Direct dyes, unlike vat dyes, required the addition of a mordant, probably alum, to fix the dye to the fibre. Minoans and Greeks used direct dyes such as madder roots and scale insects called kermes to obtain reds; saffron lilies yielded yellow. Woad and murex shells were the two main vat dyes, the former yielding blue, the latter purple. The Minoans may have exported their patterned textiles to Egypt where, according to Barber (1991), they were copied and used for canopies and banners.

Textile making was women's work in Greece. Homer's *Iliad* and *Odyssey* suggest that weaving was a task fit for queens in Mycenae and Troy. While living in Troy, Helen wove "a purple double-layered cloak" depicting the struggles of the Trojans and Achaeans. Odysseus' wife Penelope spent three years weaving a complicated pictorial cloth by day, unravelling it at night in an attempt to dissuade suitors who believed her long-absent husband was dead. Women were so important to the Mycenaean textile industry that raiding soldiers captured them to weave as captive labourers. So many were brought to Mycenae that they most likely made textiles for export. In Classical Greece women of all ranks spun and wove. Mastery of such household tasks signified a virtuous female. A 6th-century BC vase in the Metropolitan Museum of Art in New York shows women participating in all phases of textile work from weighing the wool fibre to folding the finished cloth. Woven textiles were used for clothing, bedding, hangings, cushions, towels, banners, burial shrouds, and sails. Greek women were proficient at other textile techniques besides weaving, including a type of knotless netting called "sprang". Vase paintings show women working with small frames to make elastic-like fabrics, probably for hairnets.

Only a few textile fragments survive from Classical Greece. The royal tomb at Vergina in Macedonia, believed to be the final resting place of Philip II of Macedon, father of Alexander the Great, contained a fragment of a purple cloth embroidered with gold. A funerary urn from Koropi, near Athens, held a fragment of linen embroidered in gilt silver in a diaper pattern with small lions in the centre of each lozenge. Several specimens unearthed in a Greek colony in the Crimea comprise tapestry-woven, embroidered, painted, or resist-dyed textiles incorporating either scenes from Greek mythology or geometric motifs.

Cotton, hemp, and silk appeared by the 5th century BC, attesting to the extensive trade networks developed by the Greeks. Cotton originated on the Indian subcontinent, hemp in northern Europe, and silk in China. Several purple and white silk textiles found in a late 5th-century BC tomb in Athens raise questions about when silk arrived in Greece. Silk is the only filament-length fibre in nature, and silk fabrics were thus prized for their smooth, lustrous surfaces. China, Korea, and Japan kept knowledge of sericulture, the raising of silkworms for fibre, a closely guarded secret while exporting both fibre and finished fabrics to the Mediterranean world. Although wild silk was known in the Classical era, was not until trade routes were developed across Asia that cultivated silk was brought to Greece and Rome during the Hellenistic period. According to legend, around AD 550 two Byzantine monks smuggled silkworm eggs and mulberry leaves out of China and presented them to the emperor Justinian, who subsequently established the cultivation of silk in Byzantium.

During the Graeco-Roman period an important technical change occurred. Around the 4th century AD weavers began to work on horizontal looms that had two rigid bars, one for warp and the other for finished cloth. This loom allowed for longer, but narrower fabrics. The transition from vertical, warp-weighted looms to two-bar horizontal looms can be seen in the changing construction of numerous tunics that survive from Coptic Christian burials in Egypt (3rd to 12th centuries AD). These tunics were made of undyed linen with tapestry sections of dyed wool.

Byzantine Greece supplied silk and skilled weavers to the imperial workshops of Constantinople, which had incorporated techniques and motifs from the great silk-weaving centres of Persia and Syria. Constantinople was renowned in the 10th, 11th, and 12th centuries for compound silk textiles. The trade was strictly regulated, but the city exported silk to

Europe where a substantial number of fragments remain in church treasuries. Perhaps the best known is the Quadriga cloth in Aachen cathedral which depicts a charioteer driving four horses. Silk weaving in Byzantium degenerated in the 13th century, but the art of embroidery continued to flourish for church vestments.

Embroidery also flourished in the Greek islands and in some parts of the mainland. Major museums in Greece, Britain, and North America have magnificent examples of needlework including bed tents and valances, cushion covers, spreads, and women's bridal and festival clothing. The embroideries are grouped stylistically by region, because the preferred motifs and stitches reflect local cultural influences. Italian-inspired designs prevailed in Crete and the Ionian islands; Byzantine eagles and mythological creatures were found in the Sporades. Ottoman floral motifs dominated the work of Epirote embroideries, while geometric designs deriving from the Neolithic era were seen on bridal dresses from the mainland. The embroideries of the Dodecanese and the Cyclades featured stylized motifs from nature (i.e. birds, flowers) which are reminiscent of Italian textiles of the same period.

Lace, which originated in Renaissance Italy, was introduced to the Greeks by nuns in Catholic monasteries in the mid-17th century. The technique of making lace, or *danteles*, quickly spread throughout the islands where it flourished during the 1700s. Using needles, bobbins, or drawn threadwork, Greek women created lace borders for bedcovers and other household linens as well as a narrow lace trim known as *bibiles* for the edges of chemises and headscarves.

Greece inspired the textiles of other countries centuries after the eclipse of the Hellenistic world. About the time that democratic ideals arose in Europe and America in the 18th century, designs from Classical Greece and Rome began to appear in French and English textiles. From 1790 to 1830 motifs incorporating ancient ruins, Greek keys, palmettes, Classical drapery, pillars, and columns were printed on, or woven into, textiles indiscriminately labelled "Grecian", "Etruscan", or "Pompeian". Generally large in scale, these textiles were widely used for bed hangings, draperies, and upholstery in Neoclassical interiors.

Fibre production, spinning, and weaving took place in every Greek village until recently. Women used wool, goat's hair, cotton, linen, and hemp. They wove sheets, blankets, cushion covers, and yardage for clothing to stock their dowries. The industrial revolution brought new factory-made textiles and chemical dyes to Greece. Villagers selectively absorbed these commercial products (especially cotton calico and muslin), eventually laying aside their homemade textiles in favour of manufactured cloth. Today women make handwoven textiles for tourists including *tagari* shoulder bags and the fluffy wool rugs known as *flokati*. Greece has several textile factories, but textiles are not an important industry for the country.

Today few Greek women spin or weave, although the love of textile crafts remains. On a warm summer night the visitor to Greece can see women sitting outside their homes crocheting, knitting, or tatting – continuing the long tradition of textile handwork.

LINDA WELTERS

See also Dress, Purple, Silk

Further Reading

Barber, Elizabeth Wayland, *Prehistoric Textiles: The Development of Cloth in the Neolithic and Bronze Ages with Special Reference to the Aegean*, Princeton, New Jersey: Princeton University Press, 1991

Barber, Elizabeth Wayland, *Women's Work, The First 20,000 Years: Women, Cloth, and Society in Early Times*, New York: Norton, 1994

Birrell, Verla Leone, *The Textile Arts: A Handbook of Fabric Structure and Design Processes*, New York: Harper, 1959

Brunello, Franco, *The Art of Dyeing in the History of Mankind*, Vicenza: Pozza, 1973

Harris, Jennifer (editor), *5000 Years of Textiles*, London: British Museum Press, 1993; as *Textiles, 5,000 Years: An International History and Illustrated Survey*, New York: Abrams, 1993

Hefford, Wendy, *The Victoria and Albert Museum's Textile Collection: Design for Printed Textiles in England from 1750 to 1850*, London: Victoria and Albert Museum, 1992

Hoffman, Marta, *The Warp-Weighted Loom: Studies in the History and Technology of an Ancient Implement*, Oslo: Universitetsforlaget, 1964

Jenkins, Ian, *Greek and Roman Life*, Cambridge, Massachusetts: Harvard University Press, and London: British Museum Publications, 1986

Johnstone, Pauline, *A Guide to Greek Island Embroidery*, London: HMSO, 1972

Papantoniou, Ioanna, *Folk Art Museum, Nafplion: Catalogue*, Nafplion: Peloponnesian Folklore Foundation, 1988

Polychroniades, Helen, *Greek Embroideries*, Athens: Benaki Museum, 1989

Richter, Gisela M.A., *A Handbook of Greek Art*, 9th edition, Oxford: Phaidon Press, 1987

Taylor, Roderick, *Embroidery of the Greek Islands and Epirus*, Yeovil, Somerset: Marston House, 1998

Trilling, James, *Aegean Crossroads: Greek Island Embroideries in the Textile Museum*, Washington, D.C.: Textile Museum, 1983

Wilson, Kax, *A History of Textiles*, Boulder, Colorado: Westview Press, 1979

Thasos

Island in the north Aegean

Thasos is the most northerly of all the Aegean islands, lying only some 7 km from the Thracian coastline of northern Greece, where the mouth of the Nestos river forms a low promontory. Its ties with the mainland were always close, and it is today governed from the port town of Kavalla. The mountainous interior of Thasos, rising to more than 1100 m, is thickly wooded, and the whole island has an area of just under 400 sq km. Its rich endowment with mineral wealth has been a source of contention throughout its history: from its mines of gold, silver, and marble that were particularly famous in antiquity, to the substantial installation of a German mineral mining and exporting complex at Limenaria still in operation after World War II, to offshore oil deposits discovered in 1974, the natural mineral endowments of the island have shaped its history.

Both Herodotus (6. 47) and Pausanias (5. 25) claimed that the first people to occupy Thasos were Phoenicians, traditionally led by Thasos, son of Poseidon, but archaeological

Thasos: fishing boats are still being built to traditional patterns on Thasos

evidence has not supported this, and Parian settlers were in occupation by the early 7th century BC. The wealth that they accumulated, deriving from the island's gold mines, was the cause of the island twice being attacked during the 5th century BC, by a tyrant of Miletus and, in 463 BC, by Athens. Herodotus wrote that he had seen the mines "where a huge mountain has been overturned in the search for *metalla*". In 340 BC Philip II of Macedon occupied Thasos, and it remained in Macedonian hands until the Romans took over the island in 196 BC.

Thasos was the birthplace of several personalities of cultural importance in antiquity: the 8th- to 7th-century BC poet Archilochus was among the colonists from Paros; the 5th-century BC rhapsodist and historian Stesimbrotus was a native of the island, as was also the famous athlete Theogenes. But the most famous of all the natives of Thasos was Polygnotus, who was to be numbered among the most distinguished of all Classical Greek painters. Pliny (*Naturalis Historia*, 35. 58) described how he was the first artist to "represent the mouth as open, showing the teeth, and relaxing the rigidity which had been usual before", and he also introduced the painting of women in transparent drapery. Descriptions of his paintings, by Pausanias and other writers, which could be seen all over the Greek world, provide ample evidence of his fame.

The extent of early Christian remains on Thasos demonstrates continuing prosperity well into the 6th century AD.

There are the substantial remains of five basilicas in or near the main town of Thasos, and even more impressive are the two adjacent basilicas at Alyki on the south coast; an Archaic sanctuary has been excavated nearby, and the quarries that supplied the marble for these three structures are close at hand.

Thasos passes almost completely unmentioned by Byzantine historians; although Procopius tells of the Vandals under Genseric ravaging the mainland and nearby islands in 467–68, this island is not named; it was just off Thasos that in 829 an Arab fleet from Crete completely defeated the Byzantine navy, but the island itself played no part. Later, under Byzantine administration, it was allocated to the Thracian theme, and so was identified (as was the case with other islands situated closer to the mainland than to other island groupings) with a mainland authority. This absence of any particular identity continued after the Fourth Crusade, when even the Venetians decided that Thasos was too remote from the Cyclades to be of interest to them, and later in the 13th century its port was used by the Byzantines as a naval base for their operations against the Latin invaders. The Genoese presence later became too powerful in the north Aegean, and from 1307 to 1313 Tedisio, of the Zaccaria family, was in control. Although the island was recovered by the Byzantines, its bishopric being raised to metropolitan status, by 1434 the Gattilusi were in overall control. It would have been under this family that the Classical acropolis above the town of Thasos was partly rebuilt and adapted to form a coastal fortress for the Genoese that over-looked the harbour. They also built a small inland castle in the centre of the island, installing a member of the Grimaldi family as the local captain at the village which is still called Kastro.

Succumbing to Ottoman rule in 1455, the following year Thasos was occupied, like the other north Aegean islands of Lemnos and Samothrace, by a papal force under cardinal Lodovico Trevisan. It was retaken for sultan Mehmet II three years later, and until 1470 he generously made all three islands over to Dimitrios Palaiologos, the dispossessed Byzantine despot of the Morea. Thereafter Turkish control continued until 1760, when the sultan Mahmud II ceded it to the family of the Egyptian pasha Mohammed Ali; in this way Thasos became unique among the Greek islands in having the status, from 1813 to 1920, of an appanage of Egypt, and even having its own president. During World War I it was occupied by the Allies, and in 1941 by the Bulgarians.

Just as its mineral riches were the cause of the island's first colonization, and of its being coveted by other powers at different periods, so its oil deposits in commercial quantities must ensure its importance in the contemporary Hellenic world.

PAUL HETHERINGTON

Summary

The most northerly island in the Aegean, Thasos is only 7 km from the coast of Thrace. Its mineral deposits (gold, silver, marble) made the island sought-after throughout history, and today oil is being extracted in commercial quantities. It was the birthplace of Polygnotus. Ceded to Mohammed Ali of Egypt in 1760, Thasos was an appanage of Egypt from 1813 to 1920.

Further Reading

Miller, William, *Essays on the Latin Orient*, Cambridge: Cambridge University Press, 1921; reprinted New York: AMS Press, 1983

Salviat, François (editor), *Guide de Thasos*, Paris: Boccard, 1967

Setton, Kenneth M., *The Papacy and the Levant, 1204–1571*, vol. 2: *The Fifteenth Century*, Philadelphia: American Philosophical Society, 1978

Sodini, P., *Thasos du IVe au VIIe siècle*, Paris, 1975

Woodhouse, C.M., *Modern Greece: A Short History*, 5th edition, London and Boston: Faber, 1991

Theatres

The rituals of Classical Greek religion involved, above all, the observation by worshippers of actions performed for the gods. In addition to the crucial sacrifices at an altar, there were athletic activities, and the singing and dancing of choral odes, normally as part of a contest. Evidence for this survives from a wide variety of city states; even at Sparta choruses of young maidens danced and sang odes composed for them by poets of the highest calibre, a marked contrast to the superficially dour impression that is attached to that state. The area in which this activity took place formed part of the sanctuary of the god to whom it was dedicated, and in most instances no more was required than a space, usually circular, on which the dancers could perform their movements of turn and counterturn, and round about this, space from which the spectator-worshippers could observe the ritual.

It was out of this that the Greek theatre developed. Drama formed an elaboration of the choral ode, by the separating out of individual characters, performed by actors, from the body of the chorus. This did not happen in all the city states, and is most clearly associated with Athens; the plays whose texts survive were all written for performance at the religious dramatic festivals of Dionysus there. Nevertheless theatres form an extensive and widespread category of building, whatever precisely the type of production that took place in them. The form, however, is best understood in relation to the development of drama as we perceive it from the Athenian examples.

The principal theatre of Classical Athens is situated on the south side of the Acropolis, in the sanctuary dedicated to Dionysus. The circular dancing floor for the chorus was placed between the small temple and the lower slopes of the Acropolis itself, which provide a most suitable area for viewing. The architectural elaboration of this into a developed theatre was protracted in time, and the earliest phases are inextricably obscured by the later, more permanent forms. Though the chorus remained an essential element in 5th-century BC drama, the separating out of actors would have required a distinct area for their performance, which we know took place in front of a structure that provided the setting. Much later accounts (in Vitruvius) talk of actual scenery and scene painting, but this may be something of an anachronism. There are, however, ample references to what are translated as stage buildings, the *skenai*, which may at first have been temporary. In the front of this (usually referred to by the Latin *scenae frons*) were doors through which actors emerged or disappeared. The convention seems to have been a single, central door for tragedy (which might serve, for example, as the palace of Agamemnon or the cave of Polyphemus), and probably three doors for comedy. These gave on to a stage, the height of which above the level of the dancing floor (the orchestra), failing the survival of material evidence from the 5th century BC, is perennially disputed by modern scholars. Actors, particularly those taking the role of messengers, could also come on to the stage from either side without going through the stage building. Within that structure there was provision for ancillary apparatus, particularly the "machine" (*mechane*) used for the sudden appearance of deities (hence the "god from the machine", the *deus ex machina*) which often brought to an end the otherwise insoluble dilemmas created in the plays of Euripides. In Athens in the 5th century BC the auditorium was provided with wooden seating, presumably removable, which seems to have been arranged in a polygonal rather than curved plan.

Everything became more durable in the 4th century BC. The size of the auditorium was enhanced by extensions from the natural slope on terraces supported by massive end walls. Permanent stone seating was placed on this, a development attributed to the statesman Lycurgus, in 346 BC, and the stage building was also translated into stone. This general arrangement is now found in other places, and culminates in the construction of the great theatre at Epidaurus. This was begun, probably, in the 330s BC, though development was slow, and work was still being carried out in the following century. There is a large circular orchestra, with a stage building behind, the

Theatre of Dionysus, the principal theatre of Classical Athens

details of which unfortunately are lost, only the foundations surviving. The seating is on a natural hillside, extended out with terraces on support walls and in plan occupying more than a semicircle. The rows of seats are divided into "wedges" by stairs. Twelve wedges form a semicircle, with a further wedge each side to the terrace walls. There is a middle walkway dividing the seating into lower and upper sections, the upper being possibly an addition to the original plan; here each wedge is further subdivided by an additional stairway, but with only a half-wedge beyond the semicircle. The resulting acoustic qualities are superb, as can be attested in modern performances, although such qualities are more a natural consequence of the layout than the result of deliberate planning. Though small roofed auditoria (*odeia*) were built specifically for musical performances, theatres remained essentially open-air, and so could accommodate large numbers. Epidaurus holds more than 10,000, and this is not unusual. Some later theatres, such as those at Ephesus, Miletus, and Pergamum, are even larger.

There is an interesting theatre of *c*.300 BC at Sicyon, where access to the auditorium was facilitated by two tunnels under the upper section of seating, leading to the walkway dividing the upper from the lower area. These were roofed with tunnel vaults, indicating a Macedonian design and the work of Demetrius Poliorcetes, who ruled over a reduced kingdom here following the defeat and death of his father at the Battle of Ipsus in 301 BC. In Macedon itself there had been a theatre a century earlier, for king Archelaus, who had enticed Euripides

to his court, but the surviving theatre at Aegae has only the lowest row of seats in stone, the remainder being wooden on an earth bank. This was the scene of the great wedding procession in which Philip II was murdered. This procession demonstrates how theatres were used for activities that were not, in themselves, dramatic in character. Theatres also served as meeting places for political assemblies, and there is evidence for such use even at the theatre of Dionysus in Athens.

The best-preserved stage building is that of the theatre at Priene in Ionia, which is probably 2nd century BC in date. The stage platform is raised high above the orchestra level, and has in front a row of engaged Doric half-columns, with openings between. Behind the stage the *skene* rose for another storey, with the traditional doorways. Such a stage separated the actors from the chorus, and presumably reflects a decline in the importance of the chorus, which can be seen clearly in the Athenian comedies by Menander of the late 4th century BC. Even so, as well as these plays, the Athenian drama of the 5th century BC was still performed; a guild of professional actors, the "tradesmen of Dionysus", based in the Ionian city of Teos, seems to have gone on tour with such productions, and every self-respecting Greek city now required a theatre for them.

This continued after the Greek cities were assimilated into the Roman empire. It is possible to distinguish Greek from Roman theatres by the later truncation of the auditorium to a strict semicircle, and linking its ends to a high *scaenae frons*, usually with two or three storeys of attached columnar decoration framing the traditional three doors. Such theatres were built in Rome itself and the western provinces, but those in the Greek areas usually kept enough space for the choruses, even if one suspects that they were not always used solely for revivals of classical drama. But the distinction is primarily a chronological one, and the semicircular plan was evolving already in late Hellenistic theatres. Improved Roman construction methods, particularly vaulting techniques, made it simpler to build theatres on flat ground, though if a suitable hillside was available it would be used; even in the 4th century BC Greek architects could build auditoria with seats resting entirely on artificial terraces, as at Mantinea and Eretria.

By the time of the Roman empire the religious significance of the theatres had largely passed. In the troubled times of the late empire theatres were often incorporated, by virtue of their massiveness, into fortifications. In Byzantine times plays were still written, but as literary exercises, rather than for performance. Theatrical performances in the Greek world continued only with the travelling players who still entertained in villages even in the early years of the 20th century, though without dedicated buildings. The new theatres of independent Greece, like the splendid example at Piraeus, were based rather on western and specifically Italian models.

R.A. TOMLINSON

See also Comedy, Satyr Play, Tragedy

Further Reading

Bieber, Margarete, The History of the Greek and Roman Theater, 2nd edition, Princeton, New Jersey: Princeton University Press, 1961

Fiechter, Ernst R., Die baugeschichtliche Entwicklung des antiken theaters, Munich: Beck, 1914

Gerkan, Armin von and Wolfgang Muller-Wiener, Das Theater von Epidauros, Stuttgart: Kohlhammer, 1961

Greek National Tourism Organization, Greece, Cultural Heritage: Ancient Theatres, Athens, 1996 (a picture book)

Green, Richard and Eric Handley, Images of the Greek Theatre, London: British Museum Press, and Austin: University of Texas Press, 1995

Izenour, George C., Theater Design, 2nd edition, New Haven, Connecticut: Yale University Press, 1996 (contains a section on ancient theatres)

Thebes

City in Boeotia

Thebes was the capital of Boeotia, set in its eastern basin with an area of some 12,400 sq km. Centrally located within this basin, Thebes commands the large, fertile Aonian plain to the north, and is near the Asopus valley to the south. The Teneric plain lies only some 7 km to the west. The area is also blessed with ample springs, rivulets, and rivers. Hence Thebes controlled a large, cohesive area of rich, arable land, which meant that it could easily extend its power throughout Boeotia. The city also enjoyed access to the Aegean by way of Aulis. Thebes itself was likewise endowed with a constant, dependable supply of good water. The acropolis of Thebes was the Cadmea, a plateau that rises gently from north to south, reach-

ing a height of 63 m. It has always been the principal site of inhabitation.

Thebes did not become a major city until the Mycenaean period (c.1600–1250 BC). Archaeology has revealed two palaces, other buildings, and walls pierced by the famous seven gates of Thebes. The Mycenaean city appears early in the realm of Greek legend. Some ancient traditions attribute its founding to the Phoenician Cadmus, but other legends tell of founders who preceded him. No modern evidence supports the Cadmus legend: even though Cadmus gave his name to the citadel, the settlement was purely Greek.

Thebes entered the historical era in the Archaic period (c.600–500 BC). The city grew until it spread its influence abroad in Boeotia. By the middle of the 6th century BC it had helped to forge a loose confederation that was originally a religious amphictyony, marked by a festival in honour of Poseidon. The confederacy gradually served as the inspiration for political unity, and as such its members repulsed a Thessalian attack around 520 BC. Succeeding it was a rejuvenated league that came into conflict with Athens, an enmity that became traditional. These events show a clear and growing Theban policy that sought to strengthen the confederacy and to oppose Athenian ambitions in the region.

The bleakest moment in Theban history occurred when the city sided with the invader during the Persian Wars. Although in 480 BC Thebes defended Thermopylae against the Persians, the other Greeks suspected it of harbouring Persian sympathies. Abandoned by its allies after the loss of Thermopylae, Thebes fought with the Persians against the Greeks at Plataea in 479 BC. Thereafter, Thebes was branded as a traitor to the Greek cause. Following the Greek victory, it fell to a successful siege, but the rest of Boeotia was spared. The aftermath of the defeat was an eclipse of Theban power and authority. The confederacy survived, but only in 457 BC did Sparta strengthen Thebes by making an alliance with it, reaffirming its hegemony of the confederacy, and enlarging its circuit wall. Seeing these developments as a threat, Athens immediately attacked Boeotia, only to be repulsed by Sparta and Thebes at Tanagra. Later that year Athens struck again, routed Thebes at the battle of Oenophyta, and overran Boeotia. The unpopularity of Athenian rule prompted a successful rebellion in 447 BC that resulted in a Boeotian victory at the Battle of Coronea and the expulsion of the enemy from Boeotia. The victory led the major cities of Boeotia to create a new confederacy that conducted all federal business. It was the most innovative, comprehensive, and successful federal government of the Classical period, and helped to make Boeotia a major power in Greece.

Thebes played a disreputable role at the outbreak of the Peloponnesian War, attacking Plataea before the formal beginning of hostilites. Ally and enemy alike considered Thebes guilty of having violated the yet unbroken peace. Nevertheless, in 424 BC Thebes defeated a major Athenian army at the Battle of Delium, and afterwards contributed significantly to the ultimate defeat of Athens. Victory in 404 BC brought the submission of Athens and strife with Sparta: Sparta insisted on a hard but fair peace with the vanquished; Thebes, on the contrary, demanded the complete destruction of Athens. It also unsuccessfully demanded from Sparta a tenth part of the spoils of war. Thebes thenceforth displayed coldness to Sparta and warmth to Athens. Antagonism gave way to open hostilities during the Corinthian War (395–386 BC). With the encouragement of the Persians, Thebes banded together with Athens, Argos, and Corinth to overthrow Spartan power in Greece. Fighting was at first fierce, with Thebes and its allies defeating Sparta at the Battles of Haliartus (395 BC) and Coronea (394 BC) and holding their own at the Battle of the Nemea River (394 BC). The war thereafter dragged on until Sparta, with vast Persian support, forced its enemies to accept peace. The King's Peace of 386 BC dismantled the Boeotian Confederacy and weakened Thebes.

Not content with humbling Thebes, Sparta sought to enfeeble it. In 382 BC a Spartan army seized Thebes in time of peace, and held it with a garrison. After four years of military occupation the Thebans overthrew the Spartans and rebuilt the confederacy. In 371 BC Thebes, under its two brilliant generals Epaminondas and Pelopidas, annihilated the Spartan army at Leuctra, thus inaugurating the era of the Theban hegemony, a decade when Thebes stood at the pinnacle of Greek politics. During that time it destroyed Sparta as a major power, frequently invaded the Peloponnese, and spread its influence northwards to Thessaly and Macedonia. In 366 BC Thebes won the friendship of the Persian empire. After a fruitless attempt to win naval superiority, Epaminondas made one last effort to reassert control over an unruly Peloponnese, but failed. At the battle of Mantinea in 362 BC Thebes won the victory but lost Epaminondas. That victory, ironically, ended the hegemony.

If the years after the Theban hegemony were anticlimatic, they were nonetheless eventful. In 355 BC Thebes came to the defence of the sanctuary of Pythian Apollo at Delphi. Seized by a band of Phocians whom the Amphictyons had found guilty of sacrilege, the shrine was militarily occupied and systematically plundered. Thebes and many other Amphictyons struggled to liberate Delphi from the Phocian temple robbers in a conflict known as the Sacred War (355–346 BC). Exhausted after years of unavailing warfare, Thebes and Thessaly turned to Philip II, king of Macedon, for succour. Together with the Amphictyons, Philip freed Delphi in 346 BC. His triumph propelled him to prominence throughout the Greek world, on the heels of which came a conflict with Athens that drew him further south to confront his enemy. Thebes and a few other Greek states now saw Philip as a threat to Greek freedom. In 338 BC Thebes, Athens, and some other allies suffered disaster at the Battle of Chaeronea. In its heroic resistance to this threat from the north, Thebes redeemed itself for having earlier sided with the Persians.

Chaeronea marked the end of Thebes' greatest days. In their place came a long period of twilight. Under the Macedonian kings it was generally at the mercy of greater powers. In 335 BC Alexander the Great punished a rebellious Thebes by utterly destroying it. Rebuilt in 316 BC by the Macedonian king Cassander, the city fell to Demetrius Poliorcetes in 290 BC. From 315 to 86 BC the fortunes of the city changed with those of Hellenistic and Roman commanders. Thebes and Boeotia alike suffered years of decline and decadence. The worst came in 86 BC, when the Roman Sulla reduced it to little more than a village.

Under the Roman emperors Thebes enjoyed renewed material prosperity. Its spiritual inspiration came with the espousal of Christianity, and its first bishop, Rufos (AD 81–96), was also its first martyr. Thebes was reputedly the burial site of the evangelist Luke, and in AD 325 it became an established bishopric. Devastated by Alaric the Goth in AD 397 and levelled by an earthquake in 551, it was rebuilt by Justinian. Thereafter it became economically important because of its voluminous industry in silk and purple dye, which not even the plundering of the Norman king Roger II totally ruined. In 1205 Thebes became the capital of the Duchy of Athens. The Turks, becoming predominant by 1447, reduced Thebes to insignificance. In 1829 Demetrios Ypsilantis besieged it. Again rebuilt after the earthquakes of 1853 and 1893, the city grew in 1923 owing to the influx of Greeks from Anatolia. Today Thebes is most prominent as a market city, but bauxite works have also grown on its outskirts.

Thebes has left a rich legacy. From the realm of legend come Heracles, Cadmus, Oedipus, the cycle of the Seven against Thebes, Antigone, and Tiresias. Indeed, Athenian drama would have been much the poorer without the seven-gated city. Pindar and Corinna wrote exquisite poetry, and Pindar's sophisticated verses are masterpieces of metre, variety, and content. In the Middle Ages Thebes became a steadfast seat of Chrstianity, a fundamental ingredient in the heritage of modern Greece and the world at large.

JOHN BUCKLER

See also Boeotia

Summary

The capital of Boeotia, Thebes was an important city in the Mycenaean period and also in Greek legend. For much of the Archaic and Classical periods it was the head of a Boeotian confederacy. It fought alongside the invader in the Persian Wars. Defeated by Sparta in 386 BC, Thebes had its revenge at Leuctra (371 BC) and for ten years enjoyed hegemony over Greece. Defeated by Philip II of Macedon at Chaeronea (338 BC), Thebes went into decline. Famous for its silk industry in the Middle Ages, it was capital of the Duchy of Athens after 1205.

Further Reading

Amit, M., *Great and Small Poleis: A Study in the Relations between the Great Powers and the Small Cities in Ancient Greece*, Brussels: Latomus, 1973

Buckler, John, *The Theban Hegemony, 371–362 BC*, Cambridge, Massachusetts: Harvard University Press, 1980

Buckler, John, *Philip II and the Sacred War*, Leiden and New York: Brill, 1989

Cloché, Paul, *Thèbes de Béotie: des origines à la conquête romaine*, Namur: Secrétariat des Publications, 1952

Demand, Nancy H., *Thebes in the Fifth Century: Heracles Resurgent*, London and Boston: Routledge and Kegan Paul, 1982; also review by J. Buckler, *Gnomon*, 55 (1983): pp. 554–57

Symeonoglou, Sarantis, *The Topography of Thebes from the Bronze Age to Modern Times*, Princeton, New Jersey: Princeton University Press, 1985

Theme System

Themes were primary divisions of the armed forces, provincial administration, and land or sea territory in the Byzantine empire. As a concept of government they had a remarkable

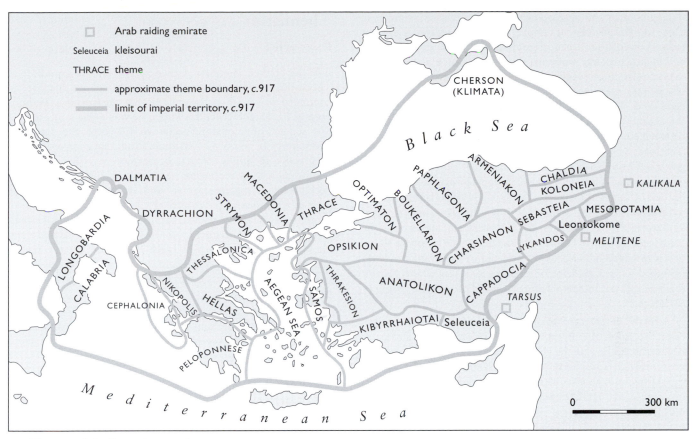

44. Themes of the Byzantine empire c.917

lifespan, from around AD 600 to 1300, although towards the end of this period they were mostly abandoned in practice. Their complex history remains controversial in many respects, but they did acquire a systematic character that reflected both the organizational strengths and individual weaknesses of Byzantine leadership. On the whole, they played a major role in stabilizing the empire, and in enabling it to shield Europe from eastern aggressors, especially the Arab Muslims.

The first Byzantine rulers, striving to protect borders against barbarians from every direction, gradually found that the traditional Roman emphasis on a civil administration with centralized armies was no longer the most effective way to maintain soldiers and defend exposed regions. An improvement was made by the emperor Maurice who, late in the 6th century, subordinated civil to military authority in the Exarchate of Ravenna and imposed a similar regime at Carthage. This measure was not yet extended to other areas that it might have saved, notably continental Greece in the face of Slav invasions. But soon Maurice's successors, from Herakleios (610–41) to Leo III (716–41), reconquered Asia Minor and began settling troops there, more or less permanently and independently prepared for war.

Men who gained a hereditary right to land that could support them in peacetime were thus expected not only to fight when needed, but to do so at best in defence of their own homes, and to demand little payment from the capital. Such reasoning was not unprecedented, as citizen farmers had been the core of armies a thousand years earlier both in the majority of classical Greek city states and the Roman republic. What

distinguished the Byzantine approach was its elaboration, flexibility, martial-law institutions, and focus on survival rather than expansion. It also stimulated local economic life, and agreed with a fundamental tendency in this multiethnic society to feel regional solidarity as opposed to national identity. In some ways anticipating a modern collective security alliance such as NATO, it turned the empire's military efforts into a many-headed monster that often had nothing to fear but changes of heart in Constantinople.

Each province was termed a theme due to the resident army corps (*thema*) and could be named for its particular corps. Its governor, appointed by the emperor, was the corps commander (*strategos*). Beneath him, an intricate hierarchy of officers (chiefly entitled, in ascending order, *droungarios*, *tourmarchis*, and *komis* or count) was responsible for corresponding subdivisions of the theme. *Kleisoura*, meanwhile, was the name given to some frontier districts of the empire, of lesser status than the themes. Themes were not static units with rigid borders, and while the forces in Anatolia usually had greatest importance, further themes were created continually. From a few in the mid-7th century, they proliferated as far as Italy and the Caucasus, numbering nearly 40 before the Crusades. Concurrently they spread to the surrounding waters: in a versatile navy including imperial, local, and thematic fleets, the last were the most autonomous and covered a vast range of east Mediterranean and Black Sea coasts. Maritime themes, led by admirals instead of generals, resembled the terrestrial ones in management, but were based upon many supply ports or islands.

The control and development of themes varied as much as their topography. For example, their very existence invited mutual discord and they occasionally attacked each other or revolted against the emperor. Since the western and maritime themes were more rooted in Graeco-Roman culture than those of the east, the system also worsened relations between the navy and army, contributing to conflicts such as that of 8th-century iconoclasm. Nor did it bridge the social gap between city and countryside. In Greece the key areas came to comprise a single theme of Hellas and the Peloponnese, governed from Thebes or Athens, with self-supporting administrators who collected revenues rapaciously, adding to a burden of imperial taxation. Yet thematic organization helped to recolonize the Aegean in the wake of the Slavs, and persisted in dreams of its rescue from the crusaders. As late as 1300 the historian Pachymeres seemingly imagined that a district somewhere in Laconia had been surrendered by the Franks and still belonged to the old theme or might become a new one, though the place stayed in Slavic hands according to the *Chronicle of the Morea*.

Already at the turn of the millennium, however, success began to spoil the Byzantines and two contrary processes began the decline of the themes. First, the sprawling empire was consolidated by recentralizing authority in a refined, anti-militaristic bureaucracy that neglected the regional defences, promoting civil ministries and local judges (*krites*). Second, its resources were being fragmented through feudalization, eventually under western influence: officials and churches amassed huge estates, while freeholding soldiers and sailors sold out. The 11th- and 12th-century emperors favoured direct systems that gave command to dukes or domestics (*domestikoi*, "commanders"), bought the loyalty of potentates and troops with grants of land or produce (*pronoia*), and defined the provinces differently, reducing "themes" to a vague geographic and fiscal term.

Thus, again like their ancient predecessors, and despite correctives by some Komnene and Palaiologan rulers, the themes largely succumbed to the rise of aristocrats competing at the expense of the peasantry, who increasingly merged with the urban proletariat and were replaced on the battlefield with costly, unreliable mercenaries. All this was soon proved unwise by the Turkish invasions, which can be seen as a legacy in default of the theme system.

JON VAN LEUVEN

Further Reading

Ahrweiler, H., *Byzance et la mer: la marine de guerre, la politique et les institutions maritimes de Byzance aux VIIe–XVe siècles*, Paris: Presses Universitaires de France, 1966

Kaegi, W.E., Jr., *Byzantine Military Unrest, 471–843: An Interpretation*, Amsterdam: Hakkert, 1981

Pertusi, Agostino, "La Formation des thèmes byzantins" in *Berichte zum XI. Internationalen Byzantinistenkongress*, Munich: Beck, 1958

Shahid, I., "Heraclius and the Theme System: Further Observations", *Byzantion*, 59 (1989): pp. 208–43

Themistius *c.*AD 317–*c.*388

Philosopher

Like his father, his first father-in-law, and a grandfather, Themistius was a philosopher, and throughout his life he continued to regard philosophy as his chief calling. Perhaps born in Paphlagonia like his father, he was made a member of the senate of Constantinople in 355 by the emperor Constantius II, son of Constantine. From that time on, he was very active in public affairs. In the late 350s he played an important role in recruiting new senators for what was fast becoming the "eastern capital" and almost certainly held the high urban office of proconsul of Constantinople. His rise to prominence in the senate was rapid; he served as a spokesman for the city and its aristocracy and frequently represented them abroad. Office came to him again in the mid 380s, when he assumed the urban prefecture, which had replaced the Constantinopolitan proconsulship in 359. He died soon after holding this office.

In addition to serving Constantinople and its senate, Themistius was a panegyrist and adviser of emperors. He gave the usual general advice of the philosopher on how to govern well. On specific issues a reconciling tone prevails. A flexible pagan who worked well with Christian emperors, he urged the pagan emperor Julian (361–63) not to persecute Christians and later tried to moderate the Arian emperor Valens' persecution of Nicene Christians. He encouraged emperors to show clemency to their domestic foes. The Goths, who were threatening the Roman empire in the north under Valens (364–78) and Theodosius (379–95), should, in Themistius' view, be offered peace and admission into the empire. Themistius' influence at court was probably strongest in the late 350s under Constantius and in the 380s under Theodosius. Ironically, he may have been somewhat marginalized under his fellow pagan Julian. The two men had disagreed on certain issues of political philosophy, as Julian's *Letter to Themistius* reveals, and Themistius could not have been comfortable with Julian's religious fanaticism. Themistius' closeness to Constantius, against whom Julian revolted, may have caused an initial awkwardness. And it is hard to imagine the irenic Themistius approving of Julian's military campaign against the Persians.

Before he became involved in public affairs in 355, Themistius devoted all his time to the pursuit and teaching of philosophy. Although he was open to a variety of philosophical influences, he regarded himself mainly as a follower of Aristotle. His so-called *Paraphrases* or explications of Aristotelian works were a project of his early career. Some of the *Paraphrases* have not survived; but we do have those on Aristotle's *Analytica Posteriora*, the *Physica*, and the *De Anima* in Greek and those on the *De Caelo*, *Metaphysica* book 12, and the *Analytica Priora* (excerpts only) in Arabic and especially in Hebrew. Most if not all of these commentaries were completed before 355. After 355 public affairs as well as philosophy would have a claim on Themistius' time.

In his *Oration* 23 Themistius says that his *Paraphrases* attempted nothing more than to clarify Aristotle's words, have nothing new in them, and were never intended for publication. He was being excessively modest. The *Paraphrases* were cited by subsequent Greek Aristotelian commentators, from

Ammonius in the 5th and 6th centuries to Eustratios of Nicaea in the 11th and 12th centuries. According to his modern editor G. Vitelli, John Philoponus (6th century) in his commentary on Aristotle's *Physica* not only explicitly cited Themistius' commentary on the same work some 15 times, but also tacitly drew from it 600 times!

We have, in addition to the Aristotelian commentaries, a collection of Themistius' orations. Thirty-three have survived in Greek and, along with them, an oration in Latin that has been proved to be a forgery of the 16th century. We also have a Themistian work on virtue that survives only in Syriac and a work, addressed to Julian, on governing the state that survives only in Arabic; these may also be orations. The Greek orations have traditionally been divided into "public" or "official" (*politikoi*) addresses (1–29 minus the spurious Latin *Oration* 12) and "private" ones (20–34). It is in the public orations that one finds Themistius praising and advising emperors. These orations make it clear that, for Themistius, the central imperial virtue is *philanthropia*, the benevolence of which the emperor is uniquely capable and through which he becomes like God. The private orations consist of apologetics, cultural (i.e. rhetorical and philosophical) programmatics, material of autobiographical interest, and philosophical discourses. In these orations Themistius argues, against his critics, that the philosopher should be involved in public affairs. He also argues that the lessons of philosophy should be broadcast, in an appropriate form, to the masses, not reserved for a few select pupils. Holding this view, he was in disagreement with the contemporary Neoplatonist circles to which Julian was drawn; in these circles esoteric learning was shared with an elite corps of disciples. It was rhetorical skill, Themistius contended, that allowed the philosopher to present his teachings to the general public in an attractive and persuasive manner. The philosopher's use of rhetoric was not "sophistical", not merely for show, pleasure, or gain.

The Byzantines admired Themistius' orations. They belong to the long tradition of classicizing Greek oratory in the Roman empire that produced Dio Chrysostom and Aelius Aristides in the 1st and 2nd centuries AD, included Themistius' contemporaries Julian and Himerius, and had its final florescence in late antiquity in the so-called school of Gaza.

ROBERT J. PENELLA

See also Philosophy, Rhetoric

Biography

Born *c.*AD 317, perhaps in Paphlagonia, Themistius became a senator in Constantinople in 355. He was urban prefect in the mid-380s. His fine rhetoric attracted imperial attention. As a philosopher he wrote commentaries on various Aristotelian works; also public and private orations. He died *c.*388.

Writings

Discorsi, translated into Italian by Riccardo Maisano, Turin: Unione Tipografico Editrice Torinese, 1995 (all the *Orations*)

The Private Orations, translated by Robert J. Penella, Berkeley: University of California Press, 1999 (*Orations* 17 and 20–34)

On Aristotle On the Soul, translated by Robert B. Todd, Ithaca, New York: Cornell University Press, and London: Duckworth, 1996

Further Reading

Dagron, G., "L'Empire romain d'orient au IVe siècle et les traditions politiques de l'hellénisme: le témoignage de Thémistios", *Travaux et Mémoires*, 3 (1968): pp. 1–242

Daly, L.J., "Themistius' Plea for Religious Tolerance", *Greek, Roman and Byzantine Studies*, 12 (1971): pp. 65–79

Daly, L.J., "The Mandarin and the Barbarian: The Response of Themistius to the Gothic Challenge", *Historia*, 21 (1972): pp. 351–79

Daly, L.J., "Themistius' Concept of *Philanthropia*", *Byzantion*, 45 (1975): pp. 22–40

Downey, G., "Themistius and the Defense of Hellenism in the Fourth Century", *Harvard Theological Review*, 50 (1957): pp. 259–74

Vanderspoel, John, *Themistius and the Imperial Court: Oratory, Civic Duty, and "Paideia" from Constantius to Theodosius*, Ann Arbor: University of Michigan Press, 1995

Themistocles *c.*525–459 BC

Athenian statesman

Themistocles first appears in our sources as archon of Athens for 493/92 BC, when he began fortifying the Piraeus, as a much superior replacement for Athens' former harbour at Phaleron. This first appearance exemplifies the central preoccupation of his career, that Athens should become a great naval power. It also exemplifies the legendary intelligence that all the sources emphasize. Similarly, in 483 BC, when a rich seam of silver was discovered at Laurium, he urged that it be used not for the short-term individual gain of the citizens, but to augment the Athenian fleet, which then numbered only 50, but would number 180 at Salamis. Whether Athens' ongoing dispute with Aegina or rumours of a Persian invasion were his focus, his policy was directly responsible both for Greece's unexpected victory against Persia and the thalassocracy on which the Athenian empire was based.

The climax of Themistocles' Greek career was his performance as commander of the Greek fleet at Salamis in 480 BC. Aeschylus himself fought at this battle, and his *Persians* and Herodotus are our most contemporary sources for what happened. Though there are different emphases in each, they agree that Themistocles forced the battle – in Herodotus, against the will of the Peloponnesians – by sending word to Xerxes that the Greeks were planning to retreat by night: Xerxes blocked off the escape routes and the Greeks and Persians were forced to fight. Themistocles' motives and the exact details of what happened are disputed, but his plan enabled the Greeks to fight in narrow waters, which were advantageous to them, but detrimental to the Persians, because of their superior numbers. It was widely acknowledged in Athens that the Battle of Salamis was decisive in saving Greece, and in Simonides' poem on the battle Themistocles' wisdom was especially praised. A sanctuary of Artemis and a trophy for the victory on Salamis were discovered in the 19th century, though little is visible today.

Themistocles foresaw that Athens' new prestige and power would eventually damage its relations with Sparta. When the Athenians began to rebuild their ruined city, and the Spartans suggested that refortification was unnecessary, Themistocles

Themistocles: marble portrait bust, Museo Ostia, Italy

outmanoeuvred them as he had outmanoeuvred Xerxes. Ordering the Athenians to finish the rebuilding as quickly as possible, he went to Sparta, allegedly to discuss the issue there. By delaying and making excuses, he kept Sparta uncertain of what was happening in Athens until it was too late and the fortifications were established: Athens' credit was too good in Greece for the Spartans to complain openly, but they were not pleased, and this is an early sign of the tensions that would ultimately lead to the Peloponnesian War.

In the spring of 478 BC Themistocles returned to the fortification of the Piraeus that he had begun in his archonship. Although events ultimately proved the wisdom of his plan, in the short term the decision worked against him. While Cimon and Aristides pursued glamorous foreign campaigns of revenge against Persia, Themistocles presided over the valuable but dreary and exhausting work of fortification at home. His desire for continuous expressions of gratitude for his services at Salamis also harmed him among the people, who became resentful, especially when he constructed a temple of Artemis of the Best Advice (Aristoboule) which contained his own statue. One of his supporters, however, may have been Aeschylus, whose *Persians*, performed in 472 BC, is sometimes interpreted as an attempt to remind Athens of Themistocles' services at a time when he was unpopular, although only a few lines concern him and he is never actually named. At any rate, Aeschylus was not enough to save him and, perhaps in 471 BC, he was ostracized. In fact, ostraca dating back to the mid-480s BC indicate that he had always had many enemies, and it is surprising that he had managed to avoid ostracism for so long.

He went to Argos, and it may be significant that Elis and Mantinea acquired democratic governments at this time. If he was stirring up democratic anti-Spartan feeling in the Peloponnese, it is not surprising that the Spartans wanted his removal. An opportunity presented itself when they put to death their own general Pausanias under suspicion of treason with Persia. Letters were allegedly found that implicated Themistocles, but before he could be arrested, he fled to Corfu. A strongly romanticizing strain, which seduced even Thucydides, colours the rest of his story: it probably derives from Themistocles himself and his descendants. Thucydides tells a stirring tale of hair's breadth escapes from capture, as Themistocles' ship was carried by a storm straight into the Athenian fleet besieging Naxos, until he finally landed in Persia, where he seems to have lived a life of obscurity for several years before approaching the Persian king. The dating for this part of his career is uncertain, for the obvious reason that his actions had to be so clandestine.

Later accounts describe his meeting with Xerxes' successor Artaxerxes, in which he won him over. Themistocles reminded the king that he had persuaded the Greeks not to break the bridges that had conveyed the Persians into Europe, thereby saving Xerxes. The story is told first in Herodotus, who interprets it – implausibly – as a sign that Themistocles was already planning to defect after Salamis, and the story may derive from Themistocles' own fertile imagination. Tradition recounts that he learned Persian in a year and became a friend and adviser to the king, who gave him control of several towns, including Magnesia. He settled there happily, keeping up with his origins by introducing Athenian festivals into Magnesia, and issuing his own coinage on the Attic standard, of which some examples are extant. Aristophanes already knew of a tradition in which Themistocles committed suicide by drinking bulls' blood when the king insisted that he should repay his kindness by leading an expedition against Greece: this too may come from Themistoclean sources, eager to erase any stain of disloyalty to Greece, and a natural death is more likely. For his descendants, honours were maintained in Magnesia even down to the time of Plutarch. It is likely that Themistocles' relatives eventually brought his body back to Athens: monuments to him in both Magnesia and Attica are recorded.

Though quite abundant, all accounts of Themistocles are shaped by the strong reactions, both positive and negative, that he elicited from his fellows. In Herodotus his greed and deception predominate, though his services to Greece are also acknowledged; for Aeschylus and Thucydides his "deceit" is cleverness, and Thucydides may deliberately have rehabilitated a man whose outstanding intelligence he regarded as equal only to that of Pericles. The life of Themistocles, with its exceptional triumphs and reverses, generated tremendous interest in later tradition. Some information on his life is historically valuable, though much is also of a purely anecdotal variety: strands of both types are clearly evident in Plutarch's *Life*. Because of his part in building the Athenian navy, he is regarded as Pericles' forerunner as a democrat, and sources tend to speak well or ill of him according to their judgements of democracy. Among philosophers, his character was a favourite test case on the relative roles of nature and nurture in creating intelligence, and rhetorical schools used incidents from his thrilling life as material for debates: these factors exacerbated the tendency for traditions to be embroidered even more as time went on, even to the extent of the forgery, probably in the late 1st or 2nd century AD, of 21 letters, allegedly written by Themistocles to friends from various stops along his escape route.

SOPHIE MILLS

Summary

Born c.525 BC, Themistocles was archon at Athens in 493/92, when he began fortifying Piraeus. When silver was discovered at Laurium in 483, he urged that it be used to enlarge the fleet. In 480 he commanded the fleet at Salamis. Ostracized in c.471, he went to Argos and then Corfu; then he fled to Persia and settled at Magnesia. According to tradition he committed suicide in 459 BC.

Further Reading

Forrest, W.G., "Themistokles and Argos", *Classical Quarterly*, new series 10 (1960): pp. 221–41

Frost, Frank J., *Plutarch's Themistocles: A Historical Commentary*, Princeton, New Jersey: Princeton University Press, 1980

Jameson, Michael, "A Decree of Themistocles from Troezen", *Hesperia*, 29 (1960): pp. 198–223

Lenardon, Robert J., *The Saga of Themistocles*, London: Thames and Hudson, 1978

Meiggs, Russell and David Lewis, *A Selection of Greek Historical Inscriptions to the end of the Fifth Century* BC, revised edition, Oxford: Clarendon Press, and New York: Oxford University Press, 1988

Podlecki, A.J., *The Life of Themistocles: A Critical Survey of the Literary and Archaeological Evidence*, Montreal: McGill–Queen's University Press, 1975

Theocritus

Poet of the 3rd century BC

Theocritus lived and worked in the first half of the 3rd century BC. A native of Syracuse, he was probably also active in Cos and in Alexandria under Ptolemy II Philadelphus. This peripatetic poetic career may be considered as characteristic of a period in which old loyalties to individual cities were eroded under the larger governmental units that were their successors. Theocritus is typical of his time also in his movement away from the older literary forms native to the Greek polis, such as epic and drama, and for his preference instead for creating new combinations within traditional genres out of his intimate knowledge of the Greek literary heritage, and mixing "high" and "low" literary forms, to create new poetic blends designed to appeal to a highly sophisticated audience.

Theocritus is best known for bucolic poetry, whose setting is the countryside and whose subject matter is herdsmen, their animals, their loves, and above all their songs. The countryside is highly idealized: specific indications of places and times are generally ignored in favour of timeless scenes that emphasize the abundance and beauty of the countryside, the sensual pleasures of its colours, smells, and sights, and the leisurely lives of the herdsmen. Theocritus likes to contrast the world of nature and simplicity with a larger world of civilization beyond it. His herdsmen partake of both worlds, being simultaneously portrayed with amusement as representatives of rustic simplicity, yet also admired as artists and creators of exceptional poetry. Thus his portrayal of them is never consistent and somewhat detached, and the tone of the poems moves constantly between the realistic and the idealized. This shift is also reflected in their form and language. Theocritus writes in Doric, but not the Doric actually spoken by Sicilian herdsmen, but a stylized mixture of contemporary and poetic forms, and while an occasional bawdiness colours the poems to give some illusion of reality, mostly he prefers a formal elegance and motifs that look unceasingly to his great predecessors for their inspiration. Although superficially his thought seems straightforward, with only occasional ventures into symbolism or obscure myths, these poems of simple country life are as much a product of Alexandrian literary taste as the more obviously learned poetry of Theocritus' library-dwelling contemporary Callimachus.

The relation of Theocritus' bucolic poetry to contemporary practice in the countryside is unclear, but the repetitions and use of refrains that are such a notable stylistic feature in his poems are attested in other traditions of pastoral poetry. Furthermore, the singing contests of which he writes still exist – in a less self-consciously literary form – in modern-day Sicily, Crete, and Rhodes, and the capping of stanzas, the use of phonological and syntactical parallelisms, and the general spirit of display and mockery that Theocritus' herdsmen exhibit all feature in modern songs of this type. In ancient tradition there is also a consistent association of shepherds and herdsmen with music making, as is seen in the biographical traditions attached to Archilochus and Hesiod. Theocritus may possibly have been the first poet to make higher literature from traditions of popular song. If so, he is again typical of his time,

since the high poetry of the Hellenistic age tended to rework elements from popular culture into new, literary modes.

Theocritus is best remembered for his poems of country life, largely because, via Virgil's adaptations of them in the *Eclogues*, they influenced later European pastoral poetry so strongly, but his extant corpus extends beyond these in subject matter, tone, and dialect. He addressed poems to the great men of the day, such as Hieron II of Syracuse, from whom he may, probably unsuccessfully, have hoped for patronage, and to Ptolemy II Philadelphus (who may have been more generous). Some poems are set in the city, such as poem 2, which is a monologue by a young woman using magic to retrieve her errant lover, and 15, a dramatic dialogue of two women in Alexandria and their day out at the festival of Adonis. The amusing realism of this poem and its interest in the lives of ordinary people reflect general tendencies in Hellenistic literature and art. These poems have an antecedent in the work of Sophron, a writer of mimes of the 5th century BC, a "low", but popular, genre of entertainment, and a parallel in the rather earthier mimes of Theocritus' contemporary Herodas.

Other poems are written in epic dialect, or in a mixture of epic and Doric, and Theocritus even seems to have imitated the Lesbian of Alcaeus and Sappho. Twenty-seven epigrams are preserved under his name, as is the novelty poem "Syrinx" written in the shape of panpipes. In his handling of epic themes, such as stories of Heracles and the Dioscuri, he shows the normal tendencies of this time to retell lesser-known stories in a domesticizing, small-scale style. His treatments of the myths of Heracles and Hylas and of the Dioscuri may be compared with those of Apollonius, which, by contrast, are in a more traditional epicizing mode. It would appear from these and other evidence that Theocritus was a devotee of Callimachus' small-scale aesthetic, rather than that of Apollonius.

At least one Theocritean poem, the *Berenice*, has not been preserved, while several poems transmitted in the Theocritean corpus are the work of later imitators. Little bucolic poetry between Theocritus and Virgil survives, but Moschus in the mid-2nd century BC and Bion, c.50 years later, show a strong Theocritean influence. The first ancient collection of Theocritus was gathered by Artemidorus of Tarsus (1st century BC), and from the writings of Lucian, Longus, and others it is clear that bucolic poetry remained popular in the next century. Our papyri range from the 1st to the 7th centuries AD. A maintenance or revival of interest in bucolic is evident in the 4th to 6th centuries in the poems of Quintus, Nonnus, Tryphiodorus, and epigrammatists, some Christian writers, and also in the numerous papyri datable to the 5th century AD. To the pastoral renaissance in the Greek world from the 12th century on we owe a large number of Theocritean manuscripts – nearly 180 in all – and Byzantine scholars such as Planudes, Moschopoulos, Triklinios, and probably Tzetzes all wrote commentaries on his poems.

Although Theocritus' secure place in the Byzantine canon has ensured that relatively substantial remains of his work have come down to us, the Byzantine enthusiasm for Attic Greek has wreaked havoc with Theocritus' Doric forms, and has caused problems for modern editors trying to restore his original language. Throughout the 15th century Byzantine manuscripts came to Italy and Theocritus was one of the first

Greek poets to be produced in printed form, in Milan c.1480. More people continued to read translations of Theocritus than the original, however, and he has been translated into many languages throughout Europe, including modern Greek. No other Greek author was as often and as successfully imitated as Theocritus, but his influence on western literature is primarily through Virgil whose Latin was more acccessible to many more people than Theocritus' Greek.

SOPHIE MILLS

See also Poetry (Lyric)

Biography

A native of Syracuse, Theocritus was active in Cos and Alexandria in the 270s BC. He is famous for his bucolic poetry, which was the model for Virgil's *Eclogues*; but he also wrote mimes, epigrams, and minor epics. He was much read in Byzantium and has been translated into many modern languages.

Writings

Select Poems, edited and translated by K.J. Dover: London: Macmillan, 1971
Theocritus, edited and translated by A.S.F. Gow, 2nd edition, 2 vols, Cambridge: Cambridge University Press, 1952 (includes commentary)

Further Reading

Gutzwiller, Kathryn J., *Theocritus' Pastoral Analogies: The Formation of a Genre*, Madison: University of Wisconsin Press, 1991
Halperin, David M., *Before Pastoral: Theocritus and the Ancient Tradition of Bucolic Poetry*, New Haven, Connecticut: Yale University Press, 1983
Herzfeld, Michael, *The Poetics of Manhood: Contest and Identity in a Cretan Mountain Village*, Princeton, New Jersey: Princeton University Press, 1985
Hunter, Richard, *Theocritus and the Archaeology of Greek Poetry*, Cambridge and New York: Cambridge University Press, 1996
Hutchinson, G.O., *Hellenistic Poetry*, Oxford: Clarendon Press, and New York: Oxford University Press, 1988, pp. 142–213
Lawall, Gilbert, *Theocritus' Coan Pastorals: A Poetry Book*, Washington D.C.: Center for Hellenic Studies, 1967
Rosenmeyer, Thomas G., *The Green Cabinet: Theocritus and the European Pastoral Lyric*, Berkeley: University of California Press, 1969
Walker, Steven F., *Theocritus*, Boston: Twayne, 1980

Theodora c.497–548

Empress and wife of Justinian I

Theodora grew up in an impoverished environment that contrasted sharply with the glamour and power of her adult life as empress and wife of the Byzantine emperor Justinian I. Her unprecedented power as Augusta and her deep influence over Justinian were bound to attract attention and mixed reactions from contemporary observers in an age when the political role of the empress was neither well received nor formally spelled out. Our main source on Theodora's early years as well as on her public life is the contemporary historian Procopius, whose *Wars* and *Buildings* attempt to be an official history of the reign of Justinian and Theodora, while his *Secret History* engages in an exhaustive and often vitriolic examination of Theodora's origins, morality, and private life. Procopius' work is valuable evidence of the reception of female political power in the early years of the Byzantine empire; however, its involved character makes a reliable reconstruction of Theodora's life particularly difficult, especially since no other contemporary source enlightens us much on the subject.

In Procopius' account of events, Theodora is presented as the daughter of Akakios, a bear keeper employed by the Greens in the Hippodrome in Constantinople, whose family was put under the protection of the Blues after his death. Procopius is not sparing with scurrilous descriptions of Theodora's allegedly profligate youth in the rough culture of the Hippodrome. Other sources, however, point at Paphlagonia as her birthplace and suggest that she made her way to Constantinople as a lowly spinner of wool. Reading between the lines of Procopius' account, we can be fairly sure that Theodora was a rather successful comic actress, a kind of courtesan with considerable popularity in the capital, as well as in Alexandria and Antioch, before her meeting with Justinian around 520 and her subsequent marriage to him in 525.

To make things appear more seemly Justinian persuaded his uncle, the emperor Justin, to confer upon Theodora the dignity of the patriciate. Additionally, a special edict had to be issued allowing senators to contract a legal marriage with actresses who had abandoned their former life. Both acts signify the highly unconventional character of Theodora's ascent on to the public stage, which in fact was bound to have far-reaching repercussions on the way that power was distributed and important decisions were made throughout Justinian's long reign, which began in 527 and ended with his death in 565.

The sources describe Theodora as a woman with remarkable compassion for the unprivileged, no doubt related to the destitution of her early life. This compassion triggered what should be seen as the first important social reform programme in the empire, involving welfare programmes for the poor, rehabilitation projects for former prostitutes, and endowment schemes for hospitals, orphanages, and schools. Her public role is, however, more difficult to ascertain.

Procopius draws our attention to Theodora's conspiratorial palace politics, which nevertheless appear rather unavoidable given that the political status of the Byzantine empress was never explicitly defined. He presents her as a forceful and domineering woman constantly meddling in state affairs and dominating an impressionable and weak-willed Justinian. Her most notable interventions were her fervent support of Monophysitism throughout her life, her outspoken and courageous attitude during the riot of Nika (11–19 January 532), her manipulative intervention in the rupture of the empire with the Ostrogoths in Italy in the early 530s, her involvement in the removal of pope Silverius (536–37), her hostile attitude to pope Vigilius (537–55), and her plotting against John of Cappadocia, a high-ranking official, which led to his deposition in 541.

In the light of the above, it is not surprising that Theodora's political role has always been deemed ambivalent. Modern historians have often pointed to her inability to grasp the main weaknesses and needs of the expanded but also fragile and

Theodora: mosaic of the empress in San Vitale, Ravenna, 6th century

rather loosely integrated Byzantine empire of the 6th century, and have held her accountable for letting her personal preferences and aversions interfere with judgements on sensitive matters of state. Charges of political ineptitude seem to apply, at least in certain cases, and one need not underestimate the fact that, having been catapulted into her royal position by marriage, Theodora, just like Irene in the 8th century and the second Theodora in the 9th century, was certainly never properly prepared for her imperial duties. On the other hand, reading between the lines of the contemporary hostile accounts, we perceive her as an exceptional individual with remarkable personal courage. We also realize that she was perhaps the first, most highly eccentric and vivid example of a small but not insignificant series of Byzantine imperial women who wielded considerable, even if often indirect, power, against the background of a highly militarized and largely male-dominated society that tacitly accepted but never felt at ease with the female influence exercised by the empresses. Theodora died in Constantinople on 28 June 548, perhaps of cancer, and was buried in the church of the Holy Apostles.

EFROSSINI SPENTZOU

Biography

Born *c*.497, perhaps in Paphlagonia, Theodora was allegedly the daughter of Akakios, a bear keeper in the Hippodrome of Constantinople. In 525, after a career as an actress, she married the emperor Justinian I and played an active part in politics. She died in Constantinople, perhaps of cancer, in 548.

Further Reading

Allen, P., "Contemporary Portrayals of the Byzantine Empress Theodora" in *Stereotypes of Women in Power: Historical Perspectives and Revisionist Views*, edited by Barbara Garlick, Suzanne Dixon, and Pauline Allen, New York: Greenwood Press, 1992

Browning, Robert, *Justinian and Theodora*, revised edition, London: Thames and Hudson, 1987

Fisher, E.A., "Theodora and Antonina in the *Historia Arcana*: History and/or Fiction?" in *Women in the Ancient World*, edited by John Peradotto and J.P. Sullivan, Albany: State University of New York Press, 1984

Procopius of Caesarea, *History of the Wars, Secret History, and Buildings*, translated by Averil Cameron, New York: Washington Square Press, 1967

Runciman, Steven, "Some Notes on the Role of the Empress", *Eastern Churches Review*, 4 (1972): pp. 119–24

Theodora d. 867

Empress and saint

Born at Ebissa (Paphlagonia), the daughter of an Armenian in the service of the empire, Theodora married (either in 821 or in 830) the iconoclast emperor Theophilos, becoming regent at his death in 842. According to the chronicler, the loveliest girls in the empire had been brought to Constantinople for Theophilos to choose a bride: he chose Theodora. (The same is told of half-a-dozen other empresses. Ryden, 1985, convincingly suggests that in each case the story is a "stylized" description of imperial weddings, popular for a time, rather than a realistic account.) Five daughters (Thekla, Anna, Anastasia, Pulcheria, Maria) and one son (Michael) were born of the marriage.

After Theophilos's death in 842 there is little doubt that a small number of men, of imperial blood or with other claims, envisaged bidding for the throne. Theodora relished power, and, as regent, she meant to keep it. Connected to her plans, but in what manner can only be conjectured, is the pardon of Theophilos. Was Theodora motivated by love for her dead husband or was she aware that the Church's curse on him for having prohibited the cult of icons, publicly renewed yearly, might be damaging for his son – and for the regent?

The different accounts of the "Restoration of Orthodoxy" (i.e. the cult of icons) are perhaps best understood as reflecting the positioning and the initial moves made by the parties in confrontation. Theodora relied on the civil service and certain elements of the Church, including holy men from the hills in considerable numbers, whose presence in Constantinople made any attempt to seize the throne far more risky, and took as a symbol of her assumption of power a change of religious policy, presented merely as a return to the former state, in fact imposing the contrary option as iconoclasm had never been imposed. At the same time the whole episcopate was changed.

Not all the sources mention the pardon of Theophilos, but the number of variants suggests that great importance was attached, not only to obtaining it, but also to having this known. As justification for it, in most sources, he is alleged to have repented and venerated images before his death, in the presence, according to one version, not only of Theodora. But in general Theodora is presented requesting the new patriarch, Methodios, and the new hierarchy – as she is granting them restoration of icons and showing them every possible favour – in return, to grant her, their sovereign, a favour: God's forgiveness, pardon, and amnesty for her husband for his sins with respect to images. "Your request is just", they reply. "It is right to repay benefactors and rulers freely, so let it be not a tyrant's hand that rules, but a God-fearing mind. But we cannot snatch from God's judgement one already departed to the other life. Those who died manifestly condemned, their guilt we cannot remove." The empress, "telling the truth or out of love for her husband", related on oath to the sacred assembly that he had abjured on his deathbed, and embraced icons that she had supplied; on the strength of this she asked for "a written forgiveness of his sin". They accept her story. In an alternative version the patriarch Methodios lays a list of heretics' names, including Theophilos's, on the altar, and he and all the Orthodox metropolitans, monks, and laymen pray earnestly. An angel appears to Methodios saying: "Your prayer has been heard, Theophilos is pardoned." When the list is checked, Theophilos's name, and his alone, has disappeared; all the other names are still on it. The historian Genesios makes Theodora bargain more crudely: "If this is not granted me, you will not find me on your side, nor will you obtain from me the restoration of icons, nor the direction of the Church."

However, the advantage of having witnesses is obvious – and not only for Theophilos. The principal witness apart from Theodora was Theoktistos, who had been Theophilos's right-hand man, and whom Theodora intended to keep as her principal collaborator and supporter. How fortunate that he was able to pull an image of the Virgin out from under his clothes for Theophilos to adore! So he had been a crypto-iconodule! It suited both Theoktistos and Theodora to propagate this image of him, and this may well have been the final official story, once everything was settled. Possibly the other stories reflect what happened more faithfully.

Theodora's investment in the bureaucracy and suspicious attitude towards generals enabled her to retain power but did not lead to success in war. She also made Theoktistos, her principal minister for home affairs, a general for campaigns; he seems to have been defeated more often than he was victorious, but remained in position till his murder was organized by Theodora's brother Bardas, assisted by Michael, in 856.

Bardas left the empire to Michael, and himself founded the College of the Magnaura (where the syllabus included philosophy, geometry, astronomy, and grammar, in a much broader sense than it has today). He was also active in the law courts, representing the emperor and reviving the tradition of justice being meted out by him. Theodora did not appreciate being set aside and participated in a plot against Michael. It was uncovered, the other leading participants were executed, and Theodora and her daughters were sent to a convent. Her relations with Michael seem, however, to have remained good, and the picture of her mourning over his corpse is surely at least figuratively true.

Theodora's canonization was purely political. There was no canonically defined process for achieving that state. Recognition by a sufficient number of people and, after death, having a hagiographer, or at this date having been father-superior of one of the more powerful monasteries, were in the Eastern Church the normal stepping stones to becoming a saint.

PATRICIA KARLIN-HAYTER

See also Iconoclasm

Biography

Born in Paphlagonia the daughter of an Armenian civil servant, Theodora married the iconoclast emperor Theophilos. She became the mother of five daughters and one son, later Michael III. After Theophilos's death in 842 she ruled as regent for Michael. In 843 she restored the cult of icons. She was deposed in 856 by Bardas and sent to a convent. She died in 867.

Further Reading

Bury, J.B., *A History of the Eastern Roman Empire from the Fall of Irene to the Accession of Basil I, AD 802–867*, London: Macmillan, 1912; reprinted New York: Russell, 1965
Ryden, Lennart, "The Bride-Shows at the Byzantine Court: History or Fiction?", *Eranos*, 83 (1985): pp. 175–91

Theodorakis, Mikis 1925–

Composer

Mikis Theodorakis is not only the leading modern Greek composer of his generation, but an internationally acclaimed artist who became a symbol of resistance to the 1967–1974 dictatorship in Greece. Outside his own country he is probably best known for his film scores for *Zorba the Greek*, *Z* , *State of Siege*, and *Serpico*. His popular songs, many of them settings of well-known poetry, inspired a generation of Greeks, many of whom shared the composer's left-wing political beliefs. In the 1960s Theodorakis established a new style of song that combined elements of low-class popular music with sophisticated poetry. Less well known but equally impressive are Theodorakis's achievements as a classical composer. From his first symphony, begun in a prison camp in 1948, to the trio of operas – *Medea*, *Electra*, *Antigone* – completed in 1996, Theodorakis has composed a large body of classical works, many of which have had successful performances in Europe. As a political figure Theodorakis has always been controversial. Persecuted and tortured, like so many Greeks of his generation, for his loyalty to the communist-led resistance during World War II, he was never a doctrinaire politician and even became, for a brief period in the early 1990s, a minister for the conservative New Democracy Party. Despite the unpopularity of many of his political decisions, Theodorakis remains a legendary figure in Greece, a hero to many, and a composer whose songs are familiar to an entire population.

Theodorakis's life has been shaped by the tumultuous events of his country's history. He was born in 1925 on the island of Chios, where his parents had fled following the burning of Smyrna in the Graeco-Turkish war of 1920–21. His father was a Cretan civil servant and loyal supporter of the anti-monarchist leader Eleftherios Venizelos. At the outbreak of World War II Theodorakis senior was posted to Tripolis, in the Peloponnese. The young Theodorakis was already composing his first choral works when the Germans occupied Greece. He soon joined a youth group allied to the partisan resistance and in 1944 became a captain in the partisan army ELAS. He continued his musical studies at the Athens Conservatorium but was arrested and tortured in 1945 and 1946. During the Greek Civil War Theodorakis spent months in prison camps on Greek islands where he began to compose his first symphony.

In 1952 Theodorakis married a medical student, Myrto Altinoglou. The young couple both won scholarships to study in Paris, she to study radiology at the Curie Foundation, he, composition at the Paris Conservatoire. Despite his initial success as a composer, including a commission for the ballet score *Antigone* from Covent Garden, Theodorakis was dissatisfied with the esoteric world of classical music and he longed to play an active part in the political life of his own country. When the well-known Greek poet Yiannis Ritsos sent him his poem *Epitaphios*, a lament for a young man killed by police in a street demonstration, Theodorakis immediately set the verses to music. Influenced by the popular music he had come to know while in prison, he deliberately wrote the songs in a style that he knew would be accessible to working-class Greeks. He then returned to Greece to record his song cycle, which would change the course of Greek music for ever.

The furore that erupted over Theodorakis's first popular song cycle *Epitaphios* centred on his use of the bouzouki and of a popular singer of the low-class *rebetika* music associated with the instrument, to perform his settings of sophisticated poetry. Both conservative and left-wing intellectuals thought Theodorakis had taken leave of his senses, to try to combine "highbrow" poetry with such low-class music, but the success of *Epitaphios* was immediate and lasting. In the years between 1960 and 1967 Theodorakis produced an astonishing volume of songs, setting the poetry of George Seferis, Odysseus Elytis, Nikos Gatsos, Federico García Lorca, and Brendan Behan to music. At the same time he and his fellow artists, many of whom had suffered persecution for their left-wing views, were engaged in ambitious programmes to bring art to the working-class areas of Athens. Theodorakis formed a chamber orchestra in Piraeus and wrote a number of scores for the theatre. He was also active in politics and became a deputy for the United Left Party. When his fellow-deputy Grigoris Lambrakis (hero of the novel and film Z) was murdered, Theodorakis became the leader of the left-wing Lambrakis Youth Movement.

During these seven years of frantic political and musical activity, Theodorakis was always looking for texts that expressed the Greek struggle for a contemporary national identity. It was Elytis, who later won the 1979 Nobel Prize for literature, who seemed to the composer to speak for his generation in his long poem *Axion Esti*. Taking the poem as his text, Theodorakis created what is considered by many Greeks to be his finest composition. The musical divisions of his setting mirrored the formal structure of the original, employing elements from all the genres with which he was familiar: the music of the Orthodox Church, contemporary classical music, folk music, and popular bouzouki music. Despite the difficulties of the classical sections of the composition, the performances of *Axion Esti* attracted a broad audience. Like Elytis's poem, the music material is rich in traditional echoes, in melodies, and rhythms deeply embedded in modern Greek culture.

The exciting blend of music and poetry that Theodorakis, together with fellow composers such as Manos Hajidakis, had established in the early 1960s, was interrupted by the military coup of 1967. One of the first acts of the dictatorship was to ban performances of Theodorakis's music and prevent sales of his recordings. The international fame brought by his film score for *Zorba the Greek* ensured that Theodorakis was only briefly imprisoned during the dictatorship, but when the regime failed to silence the composer, he and his family were placed under house arrest in a remote mountain village in Arcadia. While there, he continued to compose and managed to smuggle tapes of his work to the outside world. In 1970, suffering from severe health problems, Theodorakis was allowed to leave Greece. He and his family settled in Paris for the remainder of the dictatorship. He began touring the world to protest against the dictatorship, giving concerts of his music wherever he went and attracting, for the first time, an international audience for his songs.

With the fall of the dictatorship in 1974, Theodorakis returned to a hero's welcome in Greece, but soon became involved in bitter political controversies. The compositions he had produced in exile, including a large-scale setting of Pablo Neruda's *Canto General*, were not nearly as popular as his pre-dictatorship works. Disillusioned with his reception in Greece, Theodorakis returned briefly to Paris and talked of leaving Greece permanently. Instead, he began to compose classical music again. In the 1980s he composed four symphonies, a liturgy, a cantata, and an opera: *Kostas Kariotakis*. In 1988, following the enormous success of his ballet score *Zorba* at

Verona, he decided to write a trilogy of operas based on ancient Greek drama, beginning with *Medea*. Theodorakis's *Medea* received its premiere at the Bilbao opera house in 1991. Its richly melodic score, often drawing on the composer's early songs, contributed to its success. His second opera *Electra* was performed at the Municipal Theatre of Luxembourg in May 1995, a few days before the composer's 70th birthday. Theodorakis had always been attracted to the character of Electra, and had composed what he considered his finest film score for Michael Cacoyannis's 1962 film of *Electra*. Using some of the same melodic material but with greatly expanded orchestral resources, he produced an impressive, moving version of Sophocles' tragedy. Theodorakis was pleased by the reception of his operas in Europe, but he was determined that the premiere of the third opera of the trilogy, *Antigone*, would take place in Greece – this eventually took place in an enthusiastically received production at the Athens Music Hall in 1999.

Theodorakis has often been frustrated by the lack of appreciation of his classical compositions in his own country. Greek audiences still think of him as a writer of popular songs. In addition, his political activities, including his support for a dialogue with Turkey and his collaboration with the Turkish composer Zülfü Livaneli, have alienated many Greeks who once idolized him. Recognition of the breadth of Theodorakis's achievements as a composer and as a force for international cooperation has tended to come from outside Greece rather than inside. It was not surprising to Theodorakis that his highest honour should come from abroad: in 1996 Theodorakis was awarded the Légion d'Honneur by the French government

GAIL HOLST-WARHAFT

See also Song

Biography

Born in 1925 in Chios, Theodorakis began composing his first choral works during the German occupation. He joined the communist resistance and became a captain in ELAS. After the war he studied at the Athens Conservatorium and the Paris Conservatoire. Returning to Greece, he set Ritsos's poem *Epitaphios* to music and won instant acclaim. He has composed classical music (including four symphonies and several operas) as well as film scores and popular music. He was awarded the Légion d'Honneur in 1996.

Further Reading

Giannaris, George, *Mikis Theodorakis: Music and Social Change*, New York: Praeger, 1972; London: Allen and Unwin, 1973

Holst, Gail, *Theodorakis: Myth and Politics in Modern Greek Music*, Amsterdam: Hakkert, 1980

Theodorakis, Mikis, *Journals of Resistance*, translated from the French by Graham Webb, London: Hart Davis, 1973

Theodorakis, Mikis, *Les chemins de l'archange* (translation from the Greek of the first two volumes of the composer's 4-volume autobiography *Oi Dromoi tou Archangelou* [The Roads of the Archangel]), Paris: Belfond, 1986

Wagner, Guy, *Mikis Theodorakis: Ein Leben für Griechenland*, Luxembourg: Reihe Musik, 1995

Theodore of Stoudios, St 759–826

Politician and monastic reformer

Born into a family in the upper ranks of the civil service, in 781 Theodore entered the family monastery of Sakkoudion in Bithynia which was administered by his uncle Plato. In 794 Plato made way for Theodore to become abbot and in 798 the community transferred to the Stoudios monastery in Constantinople.

Of the seven rulers whose reigns are spanned by Theodore's active life, two enjoyed his support: Irene (797–802) and Michael I (811–13). When Irene overthrew her son Constantine VI in a palace coup and had him blinded, on the pretext of his "adulterous" marriage – in fact a marriage contracted after divorce, which was legal and usually celebrated religiously in the Byzantine empire – she knew she could count on the support of Theodore, who was in exile because of his campaign against the emperor.

The remarkable aspect of Theodore's campaign against the "adulterous" marriage is that it took place ten years after Constantine's death. Nikephoros I (802–11) had seized the throne, shutting Irene up in a convent. He was probably never as ready as she had been to take Theodore's advice, but there was no open opposition until the patriarchate became vacant. Theodore, backed by his uncle Plato, had aimed at it; but when it became clear that the emperor intended to appoint a namesake, Theodore and Plato set about some underground activity (the text says no more than that) which led to Theodore's being flogged and their both being jailed until all the rites of enthronement were accomplished, whereupon they were released. Shortly after, the priest who had blessed Constantine's marriage was restored to communion and to his priestly function, in recognition of his important role in ending the war with Bulgaria. This provided Theodore with grounds for attacking the patriarch. He himself informs us that this was seen at the time as the real significance of his action: he is "accused falsely", he claims, of intending, once the priest who had celebrated the marriage had been removed from the ministry, to "seize on the excuse for bringing down the patriarch on the grounds of having concelebrated with him". Since restoring a deposed priest was authorized by the leading canonical authorities of the eastern Church, St Basil and the Council in Trullo of 691–92, Theodore unearthed a canon from an African council of 419 that prohibited the restoration of a priest who had been deposed for more than a year. This had no success, and he decided to change tack. The letter in which he informs his uncle Plato of this decision is a singularly opaque exercise in Aristotelian syllogisms, perhaps deliberately opaque in case it fell into the wrong hands. The basis is Aristotle, but the wording is in places clearly that of John Philoponus' 6th-century commentaries on Aristotle, possibly also those of Alexander of Aphrodisias (a pagan philosopher of the late 2nd/early 3rd century AD). The *Organon* is the main work drawn on, and a few quotations from the *Topica* and the *Physica* are also exclusively concerned with distinguishing between "necessary" and "contingent". Renouncing canonical attack, Theodore proclaimed it heresy to lift the ban on the priest and share communion with those who had lifted it. His closest supporters, including Plato, almost without exception, drew the line here; the Synod said he was babbling; he promptly excommunicated the Synod. He persisted in this incredible campaign till the death of the emperor Nikephoros in Bulgaria.

In Michael I (811–13) he again found a submissive sovereign who, in disregard of his advisers but obedient to Theodore, led his armies against the Bulgars; the result was disaster. With Leo V (813–20) Theodore no longer had much say, and when Leo revived iconoclasm in 815, Theodore, who in a letter probably of 809 had defended the re-establishment of the iconoclast bishops after the Seventh Ecumenical Council of 787, since "their sin [iconoclasm] had not been over essentials", promptly reversed his views. As well as letters, three tracts against iconoclasm by him survive. The first two take the form of dialogues with an iconoclast, the third consists simply of a string of 102 syllogisms.

Homer and Euclid are the only pagan writers with which Theodore appears to have had direct acquaintance – the other references are simply jargon of the educated, though this does not prove that he had no acquaintance with those authors. His main contribution to the history of the Hellenic tradition, and perhaps to history, is the information that he supplies on the fantastic loss of documents for his period: his 556 preserved letters represent slightly less than three-quarters of the collection preserved in his monastery. Some 250 named correspondents wrote to him. Naukratios quite probably wrote as much as Theodore; one of his letters survives, 20 or so for them all. But from the many important monasteries and abbots in communion with the iconoclast hierarchy, not to mention the hierarchy itself, there is not one. One of Theodore's letters and his *Life* bear witness to a genre of which no trace is left: versified biographies. Arethas of Caesaraea speaks of beggars singing ballads relating the deeds of great men to win their favour; one can imagine some of these sending out a secretary to take the words down. But for Theodore it is stated that his first biographies were written in verse, and in one of his letters he calls for the *Lives* of the "martyrs of iconoclasm" to be written in verse.

Theodore endeavoured to enlist papal support for his battle against patriarch Nikephoros, and for his proclamation of the sharing of communion with the priest who had married Constantine VI as heresy. Two letters from him to the pope survive. The second and a letter to a "monk Basil" show that the appeal did not meet with success: "What is it to me that the pope should act this way or that? ... When he says he is not impressed by the manifest crimes of the priest, he mocks and shames [in himself] the very Head of the Church."

PATRICIA KARLIN-HAYTER

Biography

Born in 759 into a family that served the empire and venerated icons, Theodore entered the monastery of Sakkoudion in Bithynia in 781. In 794 he became abbot. In 795 he was exiled for opposing the marriage of Constantine VI. In 798 he moved to the Stoudios monastery in Constantinople and restored it. Exiled again (twice) he was recalled by Michael I in 821. His writings include hymns, homilies, and treatises against iconoclasm. He died in 826.

Further Reading

Gouillard, Jean, "La Femme de qualité dans les lettres de Théodore Stoudite", *Jahrbuch der Österreichischen Byzantinistik*, 32/2 (1982): pp. 446–51

Karlin-Hayter, Patricia, "A Byzantine Politician Monk: Saint Theodore Studite" in *Andrias: Herbert Hunger zum 80 Geburtstag*, edited by Wolfram Hörandner *et al.*, Vienna: Akademie der Wissenschaften, 1994

Kazhdan, A.P. (editor), *The Oxford Dictionary of Byzantium*, 3 vols, Oxford and New York: Oxford University Press, 1991, Theodore of Stoudios entry

Theodore the Studite, St, *On the Holy Icons*, translated by Catherine P. Roth, Crestwood, New York: St Vladimir's Seminary Press, 1981

Theodoret *c.393–c.466*

Christian writer

Translated from his monastery to the bishopric of Cyrrhus in 423, Theodoret became conspicuous only when he sided with Nestorius against Cyril of Alexandria after the Council of Ephesus in 431. The Alexandrian delegates, pre-empting the arrival of John of Antioch with the easterners, had announced the deposition of Nestorius and declared the Second Letter of Cyril canonical – this urged that whatever is true of Christ as God was also true of him as man. In the Third Letter Cyril denounced Nestorius for refusing to accept that God could suffer in the Incarnate Christ or that Christ the man could be worthy of divine honours. The dispute turned on a hair, and in 433 a Formula of Reunion, asserting both the unity of Christ's person and the distinction between his natures, was accepted by both parties, though Nestorius gained no relief from this. On his behalf Theodoret continued to write vehemently against Cyril, whom he accused of being a follower of the Apollinarian heresy. Cyril of course demanded that the emperor Theodosius II depose him from his see, but this object was achieved only by Cyril's successor Dioscorus, whose violent partisans overwhelmed the moderates at the so-called Robber Council of 449. The subsequent controversy was resolved in 451 by the Council of Chalcedon, when Theodoret, though greeted at first with jeers and hissings by the Cyrilline party, was finally restored with acclamation.

He owed his vindication to his dialogue *Eranistes*, the first work of its kind in which the speakers' names are indicated only in the margins. The form is more dramatic than the content, for all the best lines are awarded to Orthodoxus, as he responds to the inquiries of a sceptical but deferential pupil. The premiss of his orthodoxy (one that Cyril would not have disputed) is that the Godhead must remain changeless and impassible in its union with humanity. The epithets that the manuscripts give as titles to the three parts of the dialogue are *atreptos* (immutable), *asynchytos* (unconfused), and *apathes* (impassible). Each part is succeeded by an eclectic florilegium, drawing on eastern and western sources, which illustrates both the learning of Theodoret and his eirenic disposition. For him, as for all theologians of his time, the chief authority is scripture: drawing a metaphor from John 2: 21, he argues that the body of Christ is his temple, not his person, and that the manhood is what God assumed, but not what he became. The resultant thesis, like that of Nestorius, belongs to the

Antiochene tradition in Christology, which declines to add speculation to the statements of the Bible, and insists upon the inconvertibility of the human and divine. Theodoret is careful, however, not to ascribe two persons or *prosopa* to the incarnate Christ, as Nestorius seems to have done, and therefore the fourth anathema of Cyril's Third Letter could not apply to him. His formula "one person in two natures" was adopted by the Chalcedonian Council in the teeth of the Monophysites, who soon fell into schism. Nevertheless, the party of Cyril continued to rage against him, and in 553 he was posthumously condemned by the Second Council of Constantinople, along with the great Antiochene exegete Theodore of Mopsuestia, who is often thought to have been the mentor of Nestorianism.

His works, however (unlike most of Theodore's), survived his condemnation. The *Ecclesiastical History*, one of many continuations of Eusebius, covers the interval from Constantine to the outbreak of the Nestorian controversy in 428. It is, like all its rivals, a mixture of good and bad reporting, punctuated by original documents that retain their value for the modern scholar. A combination of hearsay and first-hand knowledge produced his *Religious History*, an anecdotal record of the Syrian Desert Fathers. Competing with the popular *Lausiac History* of Palladius, this work proved that the extremes of self-denial, and even novel forms of it such as living on top of pillars, could be practised outside Egypt. There is more polemic than scholarship in his *Curatio Omnium Affectuum Graecorum* (*Therapy for All the Greek Diseases*), which purports to be a therapeutic guide to the philosophic roots of heresy. The biographical details are of more interest to modern readers than his summaries of doctrine, and one could almost say the same of his commentaries on the Pauline letters. These are a stock example of the Antiochene exegesis, which treated the letters not (in the Alexandrian way) as libraries of prooftexts, but as pedagogic documents designed to meet peculiar circumstances. Most of Theodoret's comments are abridged from the more eloquent and copious observations of John Chrysostom, but he offers an original contribution in his prefaces, which explain the situation of both the apostle Paul and his audience in each letter. Rather than allegorize a difficult passage, he is more likely to commend the rhetorical flattery (*psychagogia*) by which the apostle works upon the feelings of his hearers. It is only in recent times that biblical scholarship has retrieved his sense of history, though the King James Bible incorporates the epigraphs in which he states each letter's place of origin. Unfortunately, most of these are no more credible than his attempts to prove, against the obvious meaning of Galatians 1: 19, that James was not the brother of the Lord.

Theodoret has rarely detained the attention of either scholars or theologians, though Protestant controversialists have quoted him against the doctrine of transubstantiation. He was neither saint nor heretic, neither scholar nor ignoramus, but a pious churchman snatched from willing obscurity by the troubles of his age.

MARK EDWARDS

Biography

Born *c.*393 in Antioch, Theodoret received a Classical education and entered a monastery in Syria. In 423 he became bishop of Cyrrhus and was frequently involved in controversy, supporting Nestorius against Cyril in 431. In 449 Theodoret was exiled, but later recalled. His writings include the dialogue *Eranistes*, the *Ecclesiastical History*, the *Religious History*, and other discourses. He died *c.*466.

Writings

In *Patrologia Graeca*, edited by J.-P. Migne, vols 80–83

Kirchengeschichte, edited by Léon Parmentier, revised by Felix Scheidweiler, Berlin: Akademie, 1954

Thérapeutique des maladies helléniques, edited and translated by Pierre Canivet, 2 vols, Paris: Cerf, 1958 (Sources Chrétiennes, 57)

Eranistes, edited by Gérard H. Ettlinger, Oxford: Clarendon Press, 1975

A History of the Monks of Syria, translated by R.M. Price, Kalamazoo, Michigan: Cistercian Press, 1985

On Divine Providence, translated by Thomas Halton, New York: Newman Press, 1988

Ecclesiastical History, Eranistes, translated by R.B. Jackson, in *Theodoret, Jerome, Gennadius, Rufinus: Historical Writings*, vol. 3 of *Nicene and Post-Nicene Fathers*, 2nd series, edited by Philip Schaff and Henry Wace, reprinted Peabody, Massachusetts: Hendrickson, 1994

Further Reading

Young, Frances M., *From Nicaea to Chalcedon: A Guide to the Literature and Its Background*, London: SCM Press, and Philadelphia: Fortress Press, 1983, pp. 265–89

Theology

"Theology, study of the highest problems in the universe by means of philosophical reason, is a specifically Greek creation. It is the loftiest and most daring venture of the intellect" (Werner Jaeger in *Paideia*, vol. 2, Oxford: Blackwell, 1944). Plato was the first great theologian, and he appears to be the first to use the term *theologia*; the speculations of the Presocratic philosophers about the origin of everything, however, were regarded as "theologizing" by Aristotle, who ranks their speculations with the cosmogonic notions of poets such as Hesiod and Homer, whom he called "theologians", *theologoi*. For Plato, theology was the study of eternal realities, that is the realm of the Forms or Ideas. For his pupil Aristotle, theology was the study of the highest form of reality, the "first substance", which he seems to have regarded at different times as being the "unmoved mover" or as "being *qua* being"; he spoke of three theoretical, or speculative, ways of knowing, the mathematical, the physical, and the theological, theology being the "most honourable". Such a notion of theology as the study of, or contemplation (*theoria*) of, the highest form of reality was a commonplace in the Hellenistic philosophy of the Roman world in which Christianity first emerged. But that was a world in which the quest for God had for many, besides Christians, a certain urgency: the realization of the highest contemplative exercise of the mind acquired a religious colouring. The "lower" studies of logic, ethics, and the understanding of the natural order became a sequence of preparatory training for communion with the divine, seen as fulfilment. These ideas very quickly found acceptance among Christian thinkers, so that in the 3rd century Origen saw three stages in the Christian's advance to communion with God, the ethical, the physical, and the "epoptic" or visionary, a triad that found its classical form in the 4th century with Evagrius, the theorist of the monastic asceticism of the Egyptian desert: *praktike* (ascetic struggle), *physike* (contemplation of the natural order), and *theologia* (theology as contemplation of God). Such an understanding of theology as essentially prayer or contemplation, the highest exercise of the human mind or heart, the fruit of sustained ascetic struggle, quickly established itself in Greek Christianity, and is still fundamental in Orthodox theology. It is expressed succinctly in Evagrius' oft-quoted assertion: "If you are a theologian, you will pray truly; if you pray truly, you will be a theologian."

Alongside such an understanding of theology as a state to be attained, theology is also used among Christian thinkers to mean study of the nature of the divine, in a way very similar to its Classical Greek usage. The God of the Christians is not, however, some remote principle, but one who has revealed himself, not only through the works of nature, but also in his dealings with his chosen people, Israel, and pre-eminently in the incarnation of the Son or Word of God: in those events to which the writings of the Old and New Testaments bear record. In patristic and Byzantine thought a distinction is often made between *theologia* and *oikonomia*, *theologia* referring to the doctrine of God himself, and *oikonomia* to God's dealings with his creation, especially in the Incarnation. *Theologia*, in this restricted sense, means the doctrine of the Holy Trinity, and the names (or properties) of God. Within theology in this sense a distinction is further made between kataphatic and apophatic theology, that is between theology that makes affirmation (*kataphasis*) of what is revealed of God through the created order and scripture, and theology that points to the transcendent nature of God by denial (*apophasis*) of any of the concepts or images by which we seek to express an understanding of God. The idea that God is most surely approached by denial of our concepts and images of him can be traced back to the roots of both the Classical tradition (e.g. Plato's assertion that the Idea of the Good is "beyond being and knowledge") and the Hebrew tradition (e.g. God's riddling revelation of himself to Moses as "I am that I am"), and is strongly asserted in the 4th century by the Cappadocian Fathers and St John Chrysostom. The terminology of *apophatic* and *kataphatic*, in a theological context, is first found in the Neoplatonist Proclus, and was introduced into Christian theology by Dionysius the Areopagite in the 6th century. It quickly became popular in Byzantine theology. Of the two, apophatic theology is understood to be more fundamental, undergirding the theology of affirmation, while appearing to undermine it. In the idea that God is most truly known, not in concepts or images that the human mind can grasp, but in a movement beyond them in which God is acknowledged in silent wonder as transcendent, theology as doctrine is united with the notion, more fundamental to the Orthodox mind, of theology as prayer.

The consequences of the conviction of the more fundamental nature of apophatic theology are profound. A realization of the ultimate inadequacy of the human intellect paves the way for a recognition of the place of poetry and imagery of the most diverse kinds in any attempt to express human understanding of the reality of God. It is no coincidence that the great theologian of apophatic theology, Dionysius the Areopagite, speaks not of predicating terms of God, but of praising him by ascribing names to him; nor is it a coincidence that the same theologian devotes much space to exploring the nature of the liturgical action in which the sacraments of the Church are celebrated, seeing in this liturgical action a reflection of the heavenly liturgy of the angelic beings. Orthodox tradition grants the title *theologos* to only three people: John the Evangelist, Gregory of Nazianzus, and Symeon the New Theologian. John's Gospel is the one that most aspires to the form of poetry, and the other two "theologians" were both poets. The liturgical poetry of the Orthodox Church is a vast repository of theological reflection: theology presented in the form of song.

The theology of the Orthodox Church, in the broader sense, including both *theologia* and *oikonomia*, is an attempt to express in terms of Greek intellectual culture the revelation of God that found its fullest form in the Incarnation and to which the canonical scriptures bear witness. At its most fundamental level, theology is a sustained meditation on the scriptures, read in a "sophianic" way, that is, read as a confirmation of the witness to God found in the cosmos, created through his wisdom (*sophia*), and especially in the human person created in God's image and likeness. Such an approach finds different levels of meaning in scripture, and sees in the advance through these levels to deeper forms of understanding an adumbration of the Christian life. Christian thinkers departed from such a pondering on scripture only in order to meet challenges from outside, in defending Christianity from attacks by pagan and Jewish critics, and from within, from heretics. In due course this process led to dogmatic definitions, intended not so much to define what ultimately lies beyond human understanding (in dogmatic theology, too, the apophatic principle applies), as to prevent human misunderstanding of the nature of God and his ways with humanity and the cosmos. The most important of these definitions were endorsed by church councils, or synods, especially "ecumenical" councils (from *oikoumene*, "the inhabited [world]"), called in Byzantine times by the emperor. The Orthodox Church recognizes seven such ecumenical councils. The decisions of these councils represent for the Orthodox Church a further level of authority, irrefragable, though open to interpretation, beyond that of scripture, on which it reposes. The decisions of the councils themselves make it clear that they represent a crystallization of the authority of the Fathers (conciliar definitions are commonly prefaced by the phrase "Following the holy fathers").

The first two ecumenical councils (held at Nicaea in 325 and Constantinople in 381) defined the doctrine of the Trinity, which holds the three persons to be co-equal, the Son and the Spirit each *homoousios* ("consubstantial", i.e. "having the same essence") with the Father. The next four councils (Ephesus 431, Chalcedon 451, Constantinople II and III, 553 and 680–81) were principally concerned with defining Orthodox belief in the Incarnation, affirming that the Son of God, being perfect God, assumed a perfect humanity, "*homoousios* with us" and like us in all respects save for sin: these two natures (*physeis*) being united in the person (*hypostasis*) of the Son. A consequence of this definition is that the Virgin Mary is truly *Theotokos* ("one who gave birth to God") and, as Constantinople III affirmed, that the natures, being perfect, both possess their natural activity (*energeia*) and will (*thelema*). The Seventh Ecumenical Council (Nicaea II,

787) defended the veneration of icons or images of Christ, the Mother of God, and the saints, as entailed by God's assumption of a material human form in the Incarnation. The witness of the ecumenical councils is, then, to the fundamental doctrines of *theologia*, the Trinity, and of *oikonomia*, the Incarnation, the veneration of icons being regarded as a matter of Christology.

Thereafter, theological concern in the Byzantine world, apart from some controversy about the doctrine of the Trinity (including the question of the procession of the Holy Spirit, whether from the Father "alone", as Photios defined it in the 9th century, or from the Son also (*filioque*), as the West came to affirm), the reality of Christ's presence in the Eucharist, and the nature of the Eucharistic sacrifice, focused on matters directly affecting the spiritual life. These concerned the reality of the experience of God in prayer, and how such experience of the presence of God himself could be reconciled with the apophatic assertion of God's transcendent ineffability. Controversy broke out in the 14th century in which solitary monks known as "hesychasts" (from *hesychia*, meaning stillness), who claimed in prayer to experience transfiguration in the uncreated light of the Godhead, were defended from charges of hallucination by St Gregory Palamas, archbishop of Thessalonica from 1347 to 1359. Central to Palamas's defence of hesychasm was his distinction (based on earlier Fathers) between God's essence and his energies: both essence and energies are God, and therefore uncreated, but in his essence God is unknowable, whereas in his energies (or activities) God makes himself known. Palamite doctrine was endorsed by synods held in Constantinople between 1341 and 1351.

After the fall of Constantinople in 1453, Orthodox theology, whether among the Greeks or the Slavs, became defensive, and ultimately entangled in the concepts and terminology of western theology (notably in the "Symbolic Books", endorsed at the synods of Jassy, 1642, and Jerusalem, 1672). A decisive moment in the renewal in modern times of Orthodox theology, based on the theology of the Fathers, was the publication of the *Philokalia* in 1782 by St Nikodimos of the Holy Mountain and St Makarios of Corinth. This anthology of largely ascetic writings from the Fathers, notably St Maximos the Confessor and St Gregory Palamas, soon translated into Slavonic and Russian, is the inspiration behind the "Neo-patristic synthesis" that Father Georges Florovsky (1893–1979) hoped modern Orthodox theology might become. Perhaps the most comprehensive attempt to explore what such a synthesis might be can be found in the works of the Romanian theologian, archpriest Dumitru Stăniloae (1903–93). In a complementary way, the Philokalic vision found poetic expression in the writings of the uneducated Russian peasant St Silouan (1866–1938) who became a monk of the Holy Mountain.

ANDREW LOUTH

See also Councils, Hesychasm, Orthodox Church, *Philokalia*

Further Reading

Clément, Olivier, *The Roots of Christian Mysticism*, 5th edition, New York: New City Press, 1998

Lossky, Vladimir, *The Mystical Theology of the Eastern Church*, London: James Clarke, 1957; Crestwood, New York: St Vladimir's Seminary Press, 1976

Meyendorff, John, *Byzantine Theology: Historical Trends and Doctrinal Themes*, London: Mowbray, and New York: Fordham University Press, 1974

Pelikan, Jaroslav, *The Spirit of Eastern Christendom, 600–1700*, Chicago: University of Chicago Press, 1974

Podskalsky, Gerhard, *Theologie und Philosophie in Byzanz*, Munich: Beck, 1977

Podskalsky, Gerhard, *Griechische Theologie in der Zeit der Türkenherrschaft, 1453–1821*, Munich: Beck, 1988

Sofrony (Sakharov), Archimandrite, *The Undistorted Image: Staretz Silouan, 1866–1938*, London: Faith Press, 1958

Sophronii, Archimandrite, *Starets Silouan, moine du Mont-Athos, 1866–1938: vie, doctrine, écrits*, Paris: Présence, 1973, reprinted 1989 (fuller French version of the previous item)

Stăniloae, Dumitru, *Orthodoxe Dogmatik*, 3 vols, Zurich: Benziger, and Gütersloh: Mohr 1985–95

Stăniloae, Dumitru, *The Experience of God*, Brookline, Massachusetts: Holy Cross Orthodox Press, 1994 (English translation of first half-volume only of Stăniloae's *Orthodox Dogmatics*)

Theophanes of Crete *c.*1490–1559

Monk and painter

Theophanes of Crete (also known as Theophanes Strelitzas and Theophanes Bathas), Greek monk and painter, was a native of Candia, the modern Herakleion. He became one of the foremost representatives of the Cretan school of wall and icon painting that flourished in Venetian- and Ottoman-ruled Greece during the 16th century. His distinctive style is characterized by an ability to fit balanced compositions into available wall spaces, and by dramatic and realistic figures. The primary influence on his work appears to have been the Constantinopolitan painters of the 14th-and 15th-century Palaiologan renaissance, some of whom worked on Crete for a time, especially after the fall of Constantinople in 1453. Examples of their wall paintings survive in a number of Cretan churches, so that it is likely that Theophanes had seen them and that they provided a starting point for his own.

It would seem, however, that Theophanes was also influenced by contemporary Italian art, no doubt as a result of his being brought up on Crete which was then under Venetian rule. The similarity of some of his compositions to the work of the engraver Marcantonio Raimondi, particularly in his depiction of the Massacre of the Innocents, has been noted, and the influence of the Venetian painter Giovanni Bellini has been discerned in some of the figures in Theophanes's *Supper at Emmaus* (now in the katholikon of the Great Lavra on Mount Athos), particularly that of a shepherd in a fur hat. Theophanes's interest in using white highlights to achieve a realistic depiction of clothing and drapery also suggests Italian influence.

Theophanes's earliest known work is to be found in the *katholikon* or monastery church of St Nicholas Anapavsas at Meteora in Thessaly. His frescos, which according to an inscription over the door were completed in October 1527, cover the walls and vaults, inserting small-scale scenes into restricted spaces. Particularly impressive is his large scene showing the death of the Syrian monk Ephraim, and his burial with an icon laid on his breast.

In 1535 Theophanes became the first Cretan to be invited to

work at the Great Lavra on Mount Athos. Taking his sons Symeon and Niphon/Neophytos with him, he worked on the much larger expanses of wall in the *katholikon* there for about five years. The result was some of his finest work, especially his depiction of the *Massacre of the Innocents*, the *Supper at Emmaus*, and the *Transfiguration*, all of which are distinguished by hard-edged drapery and a dramatic impression of movement. Theophanes may also have participated in the decoration of the refectory of the Great Lavra between 1535 and 1540.

Together with his son Symeon, Theophanes also painted the walls of the *katholikon*, refectory, and tiny side chapel of the monastery of Stavronikita on Athos in 1545–46. Although these frescos have since been overpainted, enough remains to identify Theophanes's style, for example in the carefully executed creases in the tablecloth in the depiction of the *Last Supper*. In 1552 he returned to Meteora, where he supervised the painting of the dome of the *katholikon* in the Great Meteoron.

Apart from his work as a fresco painter, Theophanes is also thought to have been a painter of icons. Although those icons that are attributed to him are not signed, they show all the hallmarks of his style, when compared to his known mural work. The icon of Christ Pantokrator in the modern marble iconostasis in the *katholikon* of the Great Lavra, for example, is very similar to the figure in the dome in the *katholikon* in the Great Meteoron. The surviving 11 icons in a series of 12 depicting the *Dodekaorton*, or 12 great feasts of the Christian Church, also at the Great Lavra, are likewise attributed to him. That which depicts the Nativity has a great deal in common with Theophanes's treatment of the same subject at St Nicholas Anapavsas.

Another series of 28 icons, in the monastery of Stavronikita, is thought to be Theophanes's work, and to date from around 1546 when he was working on the monastery's *katholikon* and refectory. In the Protaton, the chief church of Karyes, the administrative centre of Athos, a series of seven icons makes up a Deësis, a depiction of Christ with the Virgin and John the Baptist interceding on either side. An inscription on the icon of John the Baptist dates the composition to around 1542, and the treatment of the figures suggests the hand of Theophanes of Crete.

After Theophanes's death his work remained an important influence on subsequent Greek wall painters, especially those working on Mount Athos. The influence of his workshop can be seen in numerous other decorations on the Holy Mountain, such as the refectory of the Philotheou monastery (1539–40). As late as 1730, when the monk Dionysios of Phourna published a *Hermeneia*, or manual of painting, it was to Theophanes's work that he turned to provide examples of perfection in the painter's art.

JONATHAN HARRIS

See also Painting, Renaissance (Veneto-Cretan)

Biography

Born in Candia (modern Herakleion) c.1490, Theophanes was a monk who became one of the principal representatives of the Cretan school of painting. He was influenced by both Constantinopolitan and Italian painters. His work, in the form of both wall and icon painting, is to be found in the monasteries of Meteora and Mount Athos. He died in 1559.

Further Reading

Chatzidakis, Manolis, "Recherches sur le peintre Théophanes le Crétois", *Dumbarton Oaks Papers*, 23–24 (1969–70): pp. 311–52

Chatzidakis, Manolis, *O Kritikos Zographos Theophanis: I Televtoia phasi tis Technis stis Toichographies tis Ieras Monis Stavronikita / The Cretan Painter Theophanis: The Final Phase of His Art in the Wall-Paintings of the Holy Monastery of Stavronikita*, Athos: Holy Monastery of Stavronikita, 1986

Dionysios of Phourna, *The "Painter's Manual" of Dionysios of Fourna*, London: Sagittarius Press, 1974

Hetherington, Paul, *Byzantine and Medieval Greece: Churches, Castles, and Art of the Mainland and the Peloponnese*, London: John Murray, 1991

Nicol, Donald M., *Meteora: The Rock Monasteries of Thessaly*, London: Chapman and Hall, 1963

Yiannis, John J., "The Refectory Paintings of Mount Athos: An Interpretation" in *The Byzantine Tradition after the Fall of Constantinople*, edited by John J. Yiannis, Charlottesville: University Press of Virginia, 1991

Theophanes the Confessor, St *c.*760–818

Monastic leader and historian

Theophanes's main claim to fame is the historical opus entitled the *Chronography* (*Chronographia*). He was also a leading monastic figure, earning the epithet Confessor for his support of the icons during the first years of the second period of iconoclasm (815–43).

Theophanes was born into a wealthy family. His father, Isaac, was *droungarios* (commander) of the imperial fleet in the Aegean under Constantine V (741–75) and a close friend of Constantine's son and successor Leo IV (775–80). Leo was Theophanes's godfather and, after Isaac's death, his guardian. In Leo's reign the youth was made a *strator* (or subaltern officer) and then *spatharios* (sword bearer), becoming engaged to and then marrying Megalo, the daughter of a prominent patrician and confidant of the emperor.

Despite their fortune, Theophanes and Megalo decided not to consummate their marriage, preferring the monastic life instead. Each went their separate ways after having sold or given away their possessions, much to the horror of their families. In about 780/81 Theophanes left Constantinople and entered the monastery of Polichnion on the slopes of Mount Sigriane near ancient Cyzicus on the Asian side of the Sea of Marmara, where he may have been tonsured. This monastery appears to have been on one of his father's estates, but Theophanes left it to build a monastery on land he owned on the nearby island of Calonymus. Resisting attempts by the monks there to elect him *higoumenos* (or abbot), Theophanes spent six years in relative seclusion reading and writing. None of his works from this period appears to have survived and their nature remains unknown. At the end of this period he returned to Sigriane and entered the monastery of the renowned monk Christopher (patriarch Methodios's *Life* of Theophanes suggests that he was only then tonsured). Around 786/87, however, he purchased a tract of land nearby and built his most famous monastery, the Agros, soon to became known as Megas Agros to distinguish it from Christopher's monastery (now the Mikros Agros).

Theophanes's *Lives* state that he accompanied Christopher to the Seventh Ecumenical Council of Nicaea II (787), where the empress Irene restored the icons. While unsubstantiated, the claim is not impossible. He remained in the Megas Agros monastery until the outbreak of the second period of iconoclasm in 815.

The monastery of Megas Agros appears to have been a thriving coenobitic community by the first decade of the 9th century, with its own estates and daughter monasteries (*metochia*), all under the ultimate guidance of Theophanes. His reputation as well as his family links to powerful people in the capital appear to have brought him into close contact with the patriarch Tarasios (784–806) and high state and church officials, including the patriarch's *synkellos* (cell companion), George (see below). He supported the patriarch in his stand against Theodore of Stoudios and his monks during the controversies over the "adulterous" second marriage of Constantine VI (795–99 and 808–11) and is at times negative in his *Chronographia* about Stoudite conduct between 790/91 and 813. Nevertheless, Theodore's own letters (edited Fatouros, 1991–92, nos 319, 333) indicate that Theophanes was Theodore's spiritual father and that Theodore and many others held him in especially high regard. (Two of Theodore's letters are addressed to Theophanes: Fatouros, nos 214, 291.) Theodore even wrote an encomium for him around 820 on the translation of his relics back to the Megas Agros monastery (see Vorst, 1912). This text includes our only physical description of Theophanes, who seems to have been of a robust, soldier-like build. Constantine VII (913–59) proudly claimed in his *De Administrando Imperio* that on his mother's side he was related to Theophanes.

Theophanes and Theodore both refused to accept the restoration of iconoclasm by Leo V (813–20) in 815. Both were among the *hegoumenoi* of the empire's most distinguished monasteries, whom Leo was particularly keen to recruit to his cause. One of the few who resisted the emperor's bribes and threats, Theophanes was consequently imprisoned in the Hormisdas monastery (Sts Sergius and Bacchus) and then in the Eleutherios palace, both in Constantinople, prior to exile on the island of Samothrace in 818, where he died on 12 March, just 23 days after arrival.

Theophanes was a close friend of George, a *synkellos* of the patriarch Tarasios, who was writing a history from the creation to his own day when he fell ill around 810. George asked Theophanes to complete the work, and the result was Theophanes's *Chronographia* which recounted events from 284 to the beginning of the reign of Leo V.

The resulting work is mostly a collation of the edited works of previous chroniclers and historians, and scholars have debated whether Theophanes's own hand can be found therein. Cyril Mango's assertion (*Zbornik Radova–Vizsantološkog Instituta*, 18 (1978): pp. 9–17) that Theophanes had very little to do with the compilation process, and that hardly any comments of his own are to be found in the work, is not widely accepted; this despite Theophanes's own self-deprecating words to that effect in his preface, a topos that would become typical in the prefaces of later chroniclers.

The *Chronographia* is arranged in strict chronological order, with years highlighted by various dating systems, ranging from the Alexandrian *Anno Mundi* to the regnal years of emperors, shahs, caliphs, popes, and patriarchs. A few serious chronological oversights appear but the dating is usually accurate.

Theophanes's sources may have included summaries of important historical works rather than the originals themselves, a good many of which are still extant (e.g. Socrates's *Ecclesiastical History*, Malalas, Theophylaktos Simokattes, George of Pisidia, and others). The sources for the 7th century to 813 are less easy to trace, and this part of the book remains the most significant source for that period. A hypothetical Great Chronographer may have served as one of many sources for the historical works of both Theophanes and the patriarch Nikephoros (806–15). The period after 713 also appears to contain imperial, ecclesiastical and even military documents (iconoclast ones for the campaigns of Constantine V). Theophanes is surprisingly informed about affairs in the Caliphate and the east, but less so on western matters.

The *Chronographia* was compiled or written between 810 and 814. The most fascinating part is therefore the last section, from about 780 to 813. Theophanes seems at times to have included his own personal observations as well as records of oral sources (e.g. de Boor, 1998, p. 490). His negative picture of the emperor Nikephoros I has been interpreted by scholars as a reflection of a monkish resentment of the emperor's purported attack on the landed wealth of the rich and the Church and a sign of the author's resentment at the emperor's apparent toleration of iconoclasts. But far from representing a fanatical "monk's chronicle" for this period, Theophanes has left us with the only contemporary text expressing the bewilderment caused by the events surrounding the disastrous Bulgar war of Nikephoros I and the subsequent turmoil in Constantinople. In many respects, his account is the iconophile flip side of the reaction that restored iconoclasm in 815 precisely because of widespread dissatisfaction with the previous regimes.

The 9th-century translation of the *Chronographia* into Latin by the Roman scholar Anastasios is literal, and of great importance since it was made from a Greek manuscript earlier than any that now survive, the earliest of which comes from the late 9th century (Oxford, Bodleian Library, Wake 5). The *Chronographia* served as a major source for virtually all later Byzantine histories dealing with the period it covers, and a demoticizing Greek version exists in a post-Byzantine manuscript (Austrian National Library, Vienna, Vindob. Hist. gr. 76).

DAVID R. TURNER

See also Chronicles

Biography

Born in Constantinople *c.*760 into a wealthy family, Theophanes was godson of Leo IV. He embarked on a career at the emperor's court and married well. But both Theophanes and his wife chose instead the monastic life. Theophanes founded the monastery of Megas Agros. Refusing to accept the restoration of iconoclasm in 815, he was exiled to Samothrace in 818, where he died in the same year. His chronicle, the *Chronographia*, covers the years 284–813.

Writings

Epistulae, edited by Georgios Fatouros, 2 vols, Berlin: de Gruyter, 1991–92

The Chronicle of Theophanes the Confessor: Byzantine and Near Eastern History, AD 284–813, translated by Cyril Mango and Roger Scott, Oxford: Clarendon Press, and New York: Oxford University Press, 1997 (with complete bibliography)

Chronographia, edited by Carl de Boor, 2 vols, Leipzig: Teubner, 1883–85; reprinted Turnhout: Brepols, 1998

Further Reading

Bibliotheca Hagiographica Graeca, vol. 2, 3rd edition, edited by François Halkin, Brussels: Société des Bollandistes, 1957 (contains the *Lives* of Theophanes at 1787z–1792e)

Hunger, Herbert, *Die hochsprachliche profane Literatur der Byzantiner*, 2 vols, Munich: Beck, 1978

Markopoulos, A., *I Chronographia tou Pseudo Symeon kai oi Piges tis* [The *Chronographia* of Pseudo-Symeon and its Sources], Ioannina, 1978

Pargoire, J., "Saint Théophane le Chronographer ets ses rapports avec Saint Théodore Studite", *Vizantijskij Vremennik*, 9 (1902): pp. 31–102

Vorst, C. van de, "En Quelle Année mourat S. Théophane?", *Analecta Bollandiana*, 31 (1912): pp. 148–56

Theophilos 812/13–842

Emperor

Born possibly at Amorium in 812 or 813 to Michael II and Thekla, the emperor Theophilos (829–42) was brought up in Constantinople. He was crowned co-emperor in the spring of 821 and succeeded his father in October 829 at the age of 16, but, in accordance with the latter's wishes, as co-emperor with his stepmother Euphrosyne, daughter of Constantine VI. After arranging his marriage through a bride show (if this is indeed a genuine historical event and not merely a rhetorical device) perhaps in May 830 (though possibly in 821) at which Theophilos chose Theodora, daughter of the late tourmarch (squadron commander) of Paphlagonia, Euphrosyne retired to a monastery of her own founding. After some years of poor health Theophilos died in Constantinople of dysentery on 20 January 842, leaving the crown to his 2-year-old son Michael and the empire in the hands of his wife and the logothete of the post (*logothetes tou dromou*, an officer in the imperial bodyguard), the eunuch Theoktistos.

In military affairs Theophilos's main task was to preserve the empire against Arab incursions. His efforts in Sicily and southern Italy were sporadic and hampered both by a lack of ships (a problem which he later took pains to remedy) and by the fact that the loss of Crete to expatriate Spanish Arabs shortly before his accession had created another hostile base for Muslim control of the seas. In Asia Minor he campaigned himself with personal bravery and no little success, but ultimately his destruction of Sozopetra provoked substantial Arab retaliation from the caliph Mutasim in 838. Theophilos was badly defeated, and nearly killed, in the ensuing Battle of Dazimon which opened the way to the Arab destruction of Amorium, a major blow since the city was the capital of the important theme of Anatolikon. Elsewhere Theophilos in 836 rescued from Bulgar rule Macedonian Byzantines who had

been deported by Krum 25 years before to the area between the Danubian delta and the Dniester; and in 839 he built the fortress of Sarkel in the Crimea to protect his Khazar allies against the Rus. His military reorganization included the creation of further subdivision of the thematic *droungoi* (units) into *banda* (detachments), thereby improving control over his troops, and the establishment of the new themes of Cherson (in the Crimea), Paphlagonia, and Chaldia (both on the southern coast of the Black Sea) and the *kleisourai* (minor themes) of Charsianon, Cappadocia, and Seleuceia facing Arab-held territory to the east. He also increased the soldiers' pay and strengthened Byzantine forces by recruiting military detachments of Khurramite rebels (mainly Kurds) from what is now Azerbaijan, who converted to Christianity and served under their own leaders, and by forming a band of Ethiopian soldiers.

In domestic affairs Theophilos fully deserved his description by an anonymous historian of the first half of the 10th century as "a fiery lover of justice and a strict guardian of civil laws" (*Theophanes Continuatus*, 85. 1–2). He frequently demonstrated his willingness to punish even the most influential without favour, most notoriously by executing his father's accomplices in the assassination of Leo V (his godfather whom he seems to have admired and perhaps tried to imitate) and by having his brother-in-law Petronas publicly flogged for illegally building a palace that cut off the sunlight from a widow's house. An unfortunate tendency to assume guilt too hastily on insufficient evidence was partly compensated by contrite efforts at restitution, as is demonstrated by the elaborate plans to help Manuel, a former *strategos* (commander) of Asia, escape from the caliphate whither he had fled when slanderously accused by another official of treason. His reputation in this sphere persisted in Byzantium, since the anonymous 12th-century satirical *Timarion* presents Theophilos as a judge in the underworld together with the mythical Aeacus and Minos.

His highly developed social conscience, which won him considerable popularity, was publicly shown also in his weekly rides around Constantinople, when he checked the quality and prices of merchandise and heard petitions from the people. His fiscal policies were generally sound and the treasury consequently benefited considerably. Under his rule provincial economies began a slow recovery, profiting from both the establishment of regional mints and the issue of large quantities of *folleis*, the principal copper coins, a measure which contrasted with his predecessors' undue preoccupation with gold, and which was probably intended to facilitate daily shopping in the capital.

The principal domestic strife that disturbed his reign was occasioned by his increasingly enthusiastic promotion of iconoclasm, which had been pursued rather half-heartedly in recent years. He had probably been schooled in this by his former tutor, John the Grammarian, himself a convert to the cause. Despite, however, his religious convictions, his language suggests that his hostility to iconodules stemmed principally from the fact that they were breaking the law. The increasing zeal of his persecution (an initial policy of toleration has perhaps been overemphasized by historians) seems to have been exacerbated by attacks on him in iconodule pamphlets, but according to Eutychios, a Melkite patriarch of Alexandria writing in Arabic, it was ignited by his disgust at the charlatanry of a church administrator who, by means of a lead tube, caused an image of the Virgin to lactate. Until the disastrous loss of Amorium he was encouraged in his policy by a remarkable coincidence of his military fortunes with the severity of his persecutions. The latter, nevertheless, continued and on occasion took bizarre forms, as when he ordered 12 iambic lines to be tattooed on the foreheads of two Palestinian brothers, Theodore and Theophanes (hence known as the "graptoi"), to advertise their propagation of heresy. During his reign he issued two iconoclastic edicts, one forbidding the manufacture and use of all sacred images, the other barring iconodule monks from public places and even their own monasteries. His religious problems penetrated his home life as well, for both his stepmother Euphrosyne and Theodora, the wife whom she had encouraged him to choose, were both iconodules (as was the only other known contestant at his bride show, the future poetess Kassia). In mid-839 he learned from Pulcheria, the youngest of his five daughters, that Euphrosyne was secretly teaching them to venerate icons by kissing "dolls" that she kept in a box. Nevertheless, Theodora permitted the restoration of icons in 843 only after fabricating the tale of her husband's recantation on his deathbed, whereby she saved him from condemnation. The posthumous rehabilitation of Theophilos, with the accretion of several fictitious tales, continued into the late 10th century, most notably in Theophanes Continuatus and the anonymous *De Theophili Imperatoris Absolutione* and *De Theophili Imperatoris Benefactis*.

Unlike his provincial and uncultured father, Theophilos was well educated, most notably by John the Grammarian. As emperor he encouraged learning and extended his patronage to three of the most influential scholars of his day, his former tutor, John, whom he elevated to the patriarchate in 837, John's cousin (or nephew) Leo the Mathematician, and the future patriarch Methodios I, whom he released from the imprisonment imposed upon him by Michael II and brought to court, though apparently not trusting him completely because of his iconodule position. Theophilos himself delighted in intellectual conversation and wrote hymns that were sung in Hagia Sophia. His artistic interests extended to architecture, for he was not only responsible for the restoration of the capital's sea walls and a hospital but was also by far the most influential figure in the development of the Great Palace. His additions there included a small but refined residence for himself (the "Pearl"), which was adorned with mosaics and was perhaps constructed for his bride show, and later some adjoining domestic buildings (one of which probably included a nursery for his children), a palace for his daughters ("Karianos"), business and ceremonial halls (the "Triconch" and "Sigma"), which were splendidly decorated with marble inlays, a chapel, and a large courtyard adorned with elaborate fountains. His beautification of other more public buildings within the complex was further enhanced by the making of two huge golden organs, a golden plane tree with golden birds, and two golden lions which chirped and roared respectively in rivalry with similar technological marvels in Baghdad. At Bryas on the Asiatic shore of the Sea of Marmara he built a new palace which, with the exception of a church and a chapel, was entirely Arab in style.

Theophilos's faults were due mainly to an excess of zeal, but his energy, his willingness to learn from his mistakes, and his

warm personality, well exemplified by his loyalty to and fondness for both his old tutor and his iconodule stepmother, suggest that but for a premature death his could have been a truly memorable reign. At the very least it provided or consolidated the bases for the economic, military, and cultural successes of the Macedonian dynasty which were soon to follow.

A.R. LITTLEWOOD

See also Iconoclasm

Biography

Born in 812 or 813 the son of emperor Michael II and Thekla, Theophilos was brought up in Constantinople. He was crowned co-emperor in 821 with his step-mother Euphrosyne. He married Theodora. He campaigned against the Arabs but lost Amorium. He improved the thematic organization of the empire and strengthened its defences. He was a popular ruler and he encouraged learning but he promoted iconoclasm. He died of dysentery at Constantinople in 842.

Further Reading

Markopoulos, A., "The Rehabilitation of the Emperor Theophilos" in *Byzantium in the Ninth Century: Dead or Alive?*, edited by L. Brubaker, Aldershot, Hampshire: Ashgate, 1998
Rosser, J., "Theophilus (829–842): Popular Sovereign, Hated Persecutor", *Byzantiaka*, 3 (1983): pp. 37–56
Treadgold, Warren, *The Byzantine Revival, 780–842*, Stanford, California: Stanford University Press, 1988, 263–384
Vasiliev, A.A., *Byzance et les Arabes*, vol. 1, *La Dynastie d'Amorium, 820–867*, Brussels: Institut de Philologie et d'Histoire Orientales, 1935, pp. 89–190

Theophrastus c.371–c.287 BC
Philosopher

Theophrastus succeeded Aristotle as the head of the Lyceum in Athens. More than 200 works are attributed to him. Allowing for duplications because of confused titles and some works that are excerpted from larger ones, the volume of his writings spanning numerous subjects is enormous. Diogenes Laertius wrote Theophrastus' biography and related the testimony of numerous later authors who preserved quotations from lost works. Only a few of his works survived intact. Theophrastus' influence is measured in differing ways: the accomplishments of his students; the indirect influence through intermediary writers who summarized his ideas; the knowledge in his scientific works on mineralogy and botany; and his writings on philosophy and religion.

Among the 2,000 students taught by Theophrastus were Strato of Lampsacus (physics), Erasistratus (physiology), Demetrius of Phalerum (librarian at Alexandria), and Arcesilaus (philosophy). In the turmoil of Athens in the 320s and 310s BC, the works of Aristotle and Theophrastus did not circulate widely. In the arrangement of Aristotle's works by Andronicus of Rhodes (c.70 BC), some of Aristotle's writings may have been confused with Theophrastus' in what is now called the *Corpus Peripateticum*. At the very least, during the Middle Ages a number of small works and fragments of larger works circulated under Theophrastus' name, some of which are not now regarded as genuine. Conversely some works attributed to Aristotle (e.g. *On Colours* and *On Sounds*) were probably written by one or more of Aristotle's or Theophrastus' students or by Theophrastus himself.

While accepting most of Aristotle's ideas, Theophrastus broke with his mentor in a number of ways important in later Hellenistic, Islamic, and Christian theology and natural philosophy. He challenged Aristotle's notion that to all things nature imparted a final cause, a direction towards which action takes place. Theophrastus said that nature does many things "at random" and that there is no discernible purpose for such things as the tides, breasts on men, and horns on deer. He also raised doubts about fire as an element: it alone generates and destroys itself; there are numerous ways in which it is born; it requires a substratum (something to burn); thereby, it cannot exist by itself. On motion, Theophrastus questioned why, if there was one mover (*primum mobile*), all heavenly bodies did not have similar motions; if such bodies have a desire for circular motion, does that not imply a soul in them?

Theophrastus' major surviving works now regarded as genuine are: the *Enquiry into* Plants (*Historia Plantarum*, 9 books: morphology, classification, habitats, uses including medicinal); *Plant Explanations* (6 books: generation, propagation, environmental factors including cultivation, seeds, degeneration, juices); *Minerals* (2 books: formation and differences among minerals and stones such as by visual and tactile qualties); *Metaphysics* (1 book which questioned some of Aristotle's ideas but was published in Aristotle's works); *Characters* (1 book: 30 profiles of personality types); and short works: *Odours*, *Meteorology* (preserved only in Syriac and Arabic), and *Senses* (in manuscript with Aristotle's treatises).

Theophrastus' importance is perhaps greater because of his influence on other writers than because of the direct knowledge from his surviving treatises. Some patristic writers knew him and, especially, Jerome quoted Theophrastus' work on *Marriage*, but he disapproved of Theophrastus' negative opinion, and Chaucer's Wife of Bath agreed with Jerome. Strangely, Theophrastus was less influential on Byzantine writers than on those in Arabic and later Latin. Eustathios referred to *Characters* and Michael of Ephesus knew of several of his works. Cicero said that Theophrastus placed more emphasis than Aristotle on the importance of fortune and wordly goods. Arabic writers knew of Theophrastus' philosophy and discourses on botany and minerals. In the west Theophrastus' works on minerals had indirect influence on lapidaries. The biggest impact came in the 15th and 16th centuries when a rediscovery of Theophrastus began with Lupus Castilliunculus's translation of *Characters* (*c.*1430s) and Theodore Gaza's rendering of the botanical works (1453/54). The fields of botany (including pharmaceutical uses) and minerals were the centres of Theophrastus' considerable impact on the Latin Renaissance. Appropriately the first printed edition, by Aldine (Venice, 1497) combined both Aristotle's and Theophrastus' works.

JOHN M. RIDDLE

See also Lyceum

Biography

Born in Lesbos *c.*371 BC, Theophrastus succeeded Aristotle as head of the Lyceum in Athens. His pupils included Strato, Erasistratus, Demetrius of Phalerum, and Arcesilaus. His writings ranged over many subjects including mineralogy, botany, philosophy, and religion. He died in Athens *c.*287 BC.

Writings

Enquiry into Plants and Minor Works on Odours and Weather Signs, translated by Arthur Hort, 2 vols, London: Heinemann, and New York: Putnam, 1916 (Loeb edition; many reprints)

Metaphysics, edited and translated by W.D. Ross and F.H. Fobes, Oxford: Clarendon Press, 1929; reprinted Chicago: Ares, 1978

On Stones, edited and translated by Earle R. Caley and John F.C. Richards, Columbus: Ohio State University, 1956 (includes commentary)

The Characters, edited by R.G. Ussher, London and New York: Macmillan, 1960

De Causis Plantarum [Plant Explanations], translated by Benedict Einarson and George K.K. Link, 3 vols, London: Heinemann, and Cambridge, Massachusetts: Harvard University Press, 1976–90 (Loeb edition)

Theophrastus of Eresus (projected 9 vols of texts, translations, and commentaries)

   1–2. *Sources for His Life, Writings, Thought, and Influence*, edited and translated by William W. Fortenbaugh, Pamela Huby, R.W. Sharples and Dimitri Gutas, 2 vols, Leiden, Brill, 1992

   3.1. *Sources on Physics (Texts 137–223)*, edited and translated by R.W. Sharples and Dimitri Gutas, Leiden: Brill, 1998

   4. *Psychology (Texts 265–327)*, edited and translated by Pamela Huby and Dimitri Gutas, Leiden: Brill, 1999

   5. *Sources on Biology (Human Physiology, Living Creatures, Botany: Texts 328–435)*, edited and translated by R.W. Sharples, Leiden: Brill, 1995

Further Reading

McDiarmid, J.B., "Theophrastus on the Presocratic Causes", *Harvard Studies in Classical Philology*, 61 (1953): pp. 85–156

McDiarmid, J.B., Theophrastus entry in *Dictionary of Scientific Biography*, edited by Charles Coulston Gillespie, vol. 13, New York: Scribner, 1976, pp. 328–34

Regenbogen, Otto, Theophrastos von Ersos entry in *Real-Encyclopädie der klassischen Altertumswissenschaft*, edited by August Pauly *et al.*, supplement 7, 1940, 1353–1562

Schmitt, Charles B., Theophrastus entry in *Catalogus Translationum et Commentariorum*, edited by Paul Oskar Kristeller, vol. 2, Washington, D.C.: Catholic University of America Press, 1971, pp. 239–322

Theopompus 378/77–*c.*320 BC

Historian

Theopompus of Chios, son of Damasistratus, was one of the most important historians and public men in the years leading up to and including the reigns of Philip of Macedon and Alexander the Great. Not much is known for certain about his life. Photios (9th century AD) wrote a detailed biography (*Bibliotheca*, 176 = T2): he was exiled from Chios with his father; he later returned, thanks to a letter written by Alexander to the Chians; on the death of Alexander he fled to Egypt, where Ptolemy I Soter almost had him killed. While some of these details may be doubted, he did in fact write letters to Alexander, and Alexander did restore exiles to Chios.

Although there are good reasons for doubting it, Theopompus is widely credited with being one of the pioneers of "oratorical" or "tragic history", in part due to the alleged influence of the Athenian rhetorician Isocrates whose student he was later thought to have been. Certainly for his Roman readers he was thought of as a combination of historian and orator. In the Byzantine period his writing was known chiefly by lexicographers and grammarians, arising from the fact that he was not a canonical author. His work survives to us only in the form of later paraphrase and quotation (F. Jacoby, *Fragmente der griechischen Historiker*, 115).

According to ancient testimonia, Theopompus was the author of a number of historical works and minor treatises: the *Epitome of Herodotus*, *Hellenica*, and *Philippica* on the one hand, and *On the Funds Plundered from Delphi*, *Against the Teaching of Plato*, and encomia of both Philip and Alexander on the other. Given the propensity in antiquity to epitomize works and then view those epitomes as different productions from the material from which they came, it is probable that Theopompus did not in fact write all of the above works. Far and away his most important contributions were the *Hellenica* and *Philippica*.

According to Marcellinus' biography of Thucydides (chapter 45), both Xenophon and Theopompus completed their great predecessor's history of the Peloponnesian War, which breaks off in the year 411 BC: in both cases, these works were entitled *Hellenica* or *Greek Affairs*. However, unlike Xenophon's text, which reports events down to 362 BC (the second Battle of Mantinea), Theopompus took his narrative down only to the year 394 BC (the Battle of Cnidus). A claim by Porphyry that Theopompus plagiarized a portion of Xenophon's history in his own work places its composition in the late 350s BC. A papyrus published in 1908 and subsequently called the *Hellenica Oxyrhynchia* was thought by some to be Theopompus' *Hellenica*, though this claim has not won general acceptance. The two fragments of any real substance that survive from the *Hellenica* deal with the moral characters of the Spartan leaders Lysander and Agesilaus, in the same spirit as much of what survives from the *Philippica*.

The *Philippica* treated events between Philip II's assumption of the Macedonian throne in 359 BC and his death in 336 BC; it comprised 58 books, and must have been massive in scale. As the title suggests, it is an account of Greek history understood as unified by the activities of Philip; according to Polybius (2nd century BC), Theopompus chose to organize his text around Philip because "Europe had never before produced such a man as Philip, son of Amyntas" (8. 11. 1 = fr. 27). While Theopompus recognized the king's importance for shaping the events of his age, he did not take a positive stance towards him. Indeed, quite the contrary: Philip is simultaneously a corrupting force in the Hellenic world, and his victory over the Greeks is proof of their decadence. Theopompus frequently engages in an analysis and evaluation of the characters of men and states, and he is especially interested in the detrimental effects of luxury: so, for example, famous Athenian statesmen are criticized for their personal failings (frr. 97, 99), and whole populations such as the Ardiaeans (fr. 40) and the inhabitants of Byzantium (fr. 62) are singled out for scorching moral censure. Some of Theopompus' criticisms stem from personal bias as well as a dislike for democratic institutions. He can also offer positive evaluations of character: the portraits of Lysander and Agesilaus from his *Hellenica* are good examples.

With the exception of a few Hellenistic historians who were also interested in the question of moral decay and luxury (Timaeus, 4th–3rd centuries BC; Duris of Samos, 4th–3rd centuries BC; Phylarchus, 3rd century BC), Theopompus' influence on subsequent historiography was not great. However, ancient readers were broadly familiar with his work. Critics such as Dionysius of Halicarnassus, Cornelius Nepos, and Lucian all point to Theopompus' acerbity and censorious stance: he is, as Nepos describes him, "maledicentissimus" – the most abusive writer.

Theopompus' work was known in some form by late anti-Atticist writers and lexicographers. Several of his fragments are taken from Stephanus of Byzantium (6th century AD); and, as noted above, the patriarch Photios provides an important biographical notice, as well as fragments of his work. Krumbacher (*Geschichte der byzantinischen Literatur*, 1. 232) adduces Theopompus as a precedent for the court historian Procopius of Caesarea (5th–6th centuries AD), but does not claim any direct influence.

JOHN DILLERY

See also Historiography

Biography

Born in Chios in 378/77 BC, Theopompus was exiled from Chios with his father for sympathizing with Sparta. Allowed back by Alexander the Great in 333/32, he was exiled again on Alexander's death and fled to the court of Ptolemy I Soter. According to tradition he was a pupil of Isocrates and worked as an orator. In addition to various speeches and treatises, his principal works were historical: *Epitome of Herodotus*, *Hellenica*, and *Philippica*. He died *c*.320 BC.

Further Reading

Connor, W. Robert, "History without Heroes: Theopompus' Treatment of Philip of Macedon", *Greek, Roman, and Byzantine Studies*, 8 (1967): pp. 133–54

Connor, W. Robert, *Theopompus and Fifth-Century Athens*, Cambridge, Massachusetts: Harvard University Press, 1968

Flower, M.A., *Theopompus of Chios: History and Rhetoric in the Fourth Century BC*, Oxford: Clarendon Press, and New York: Oxford University Press, 1994

Lane Fox, Robin, "Theopompus of Chios and the Greek World" in *Chios: A Conference at the Homereion in Chios, 1984*, edited by John Boardman and C.E. Vaphopoulou-Richardson, Oxford: Clarendon Press, and New York: Oxford University Press, 1986

Shrimpton, Gordon S., *Theopompus the Historian*, Montreal: McGill–Queen's University Press, 1991

Theotokis, George 1844–1916

Politician

Few Greeks today recall the name of George Theotokis, prime minister of Greece four times between 1899 and 1909. Unlike his predecessor Trikoupis, the ardent reformer, and his successor, Venizelos, the unmatched diplomat, Theotokis was a moderate politician but by no means mediocre. He was not a passionate man (at least not passionate for power) but he had sophistication and natural nobility. He was descended from the Byzantine family of Theotokis who had eventually settled in Venetian-held Corfu. In the 16th century they were registered in the Venetian *Libro d'Oro*. In the following centuries several members of the Theotokis family distinguished themselves in the humanities and sciences, the most famous being Nikiphoros Theotokis, an 18th-century representative of the Greek Enlightenment.

George Theotokis was the grandson of John-Baptist, the Greek minister of justice in 1824, a man of religion, strongly anti-British, and a keen supporter of king Otho. He was the son of Nikolaos, a low-profile judge at the Court of Appeals of the Ionian islands, a landowner of average income. There is evidence that the influence exercised by John-Baptist's ideas about God, king, and country on the young George was even stronger than his own extravagant life and law studies in Paris, where he received his baccalaureate in 1863 and eventually his doctorate in 1868.

In mid-19th-century Greece all men educated in Europe were expected to play a role in politics and Theotokis was no exception. Local society in Corfu was experiencing a difficult transitional period from a British colony into a Greek province tormented by social controversies and little respected for its lost nobility. Having failed to enter parliament in 1873 and 1874, Theotokis was elected mayor twice (1879 and 1883) and contributed much to Corfu's infrastructure. Better roads, gas lighting, the demolition of the city walls, and the installation of sewage works restored the lost European glamour of Corfu and secured for Theotokis an easy election to parliament (April 1885) as a deputy of the Trikoupis party.

A year later, when Deliyannis's government resigned, Trikoupis, the new premier, appointed Theotokis minister for the navy, to implement the armament programme he had launched five years earlier. At a period when the Greek nation's most fervent desire was to free Crete from the Turks and Macedonia from Bulgarian infiltration Theotokis was justified in devoting most of his efforts to bargaining for three French-built cruisers and introducing measures for the better training of the crews. In early 1889 he was also assigned the Ministry of Education and Religious Affairs, but under constant pressure from the opposition he did not manage to introduce any legislative measures at all.

Trikoupis remained in opposition from 1889 to 1892. When he resumed office, he appointed Theotokis his minister of the interior. He was then assigned (1893) the mission to contract a new British loan, which was expected to save the government and prevent the country's bankruptcy. The tough terms demanded by London bankers were eventually accepted by the premier but declined by king George I in May 1893 under heavy pressure from the opposition. In 1894 Greece's bankruptcy was officially announced. Theotokis was among the few of Trikoupis's deputies who survived the electoral disaster of 1895.

Bankruptcy was followed by the Cretan revolution in 1896 and the gradual involvement of the National Society (*Ethniki Hetaireia*) in Greek military and political affairs, encouraging a war against Turkey. Theotokis tried to strike a balance between war and peace. He criticized the government for its lack of determination and approved the dispatch of Greek troops to Crete in 1897; but he also suggested that encounters

at the Thessalian border should be avoided. He refrained from siding with the National Society "hot-shots", as he called them, but when, amid Greek military disaster and humiliation, he was again appointed minister of interior of the short-lived Dimitrios Rallis government (April–September 1897), he failed to bring about the Society's dissolution. In November 1898 he was elected head of the Trikoupis party and in February 1899 he won the elections. In early April Theotokis became prime minister, an office he held until November 1901 and three more times in the following years: 14–28 June 1903, December 1903–December 1904, and December 1905–July 1909.

At the turn of the century the Eastern Question was entering its last stage and Greece was approaching the climax of irredentism. Armaments were again the chief priority if the disaster of 1897 was not to be repeated. Under pressure from the opposition and the army Theotokis eventually succeeded in passing and implementing a series of laws providing for the reorganization of the General Staff, the reserve officers' training, mobilization plans, and military medical services. He also ensured the purchase of modern rifles and artillery, and a significant increase of both serving and reserve forces. His choices were justified by the Greek victories in the Balkan Wars of 1912–13.

Meanwhile foreign policy required caution. Theotokis was known for his "blameless position" (*apsogos stasis*) towards Turkey but in fact he had few options. Alienated from Russia, the patron of Bulgaria, rejected more than once by Britain and France, which supported Ottoman integrity, he occasionally sided with Germany, Turkey, and Romania in order to protect Greek interests in Macedonia. But, on the other hand, he provided diplomatic and financial support for the Greek bands to counterattack Bulgarians and Romanians. He also tried (in vain) to play the Turks and the Great Powers against each other during several crises over Crete, Macedonia, and Samos.

In domestic affairs his achievements were inferior to his intentions and abilities. He contributed in particular to administrative decentralization, tramway and railway communications, and Athens' infrastructure; he established a bank for raisin producers and a fund for retired seamen. He might have done even more had more of his laws been approved by parliament. But like most premiers of his time, Theotokis had just as many problems with keeping his party together as with defending his policy against the opposition. Certainly he was most unwilling to exert pressure in order to prolong his tenure of office; and he gave in rather easily to the pressure of the Church, to social riots, the raisin producers, the guilds, and army officers, resigning with dignity because he was a man of honour, loyal to his king, but not a conservative by conviction.

Theotokis was in favour of the king's interference in foreign policy but not at any cost. When he was called to ministerial office again in 1915, he advised king Constantine to no avail not to defy Venizelos's majority in parliament. He was elected deputy for the last time in December 1915 but did not enjoy an easy comeback. He died in January 1916 worrying over the disasters looming on the horizon, which eventually came in the form of a national schism, the Asia Minor catastrophe, and the execution in 1922 of his own son, Nikolas Theotokis, after the famous "trial of the six" (the scapegoating of prominent anti-Venizelists following the Asia Minor Catastrophe). It was in fact his grandson, another Greek premier, George Rallis

(1980–81), who pointed to Theotokis's mildness as his chief contribution to Greece's public affairs. If that was the case, then his chances of qualifying for the Greek national pantheon, crowded with passionate heroes, were very slim indeed.

BASIL C. GOUNARIS

Biography

Born in Corfu in 1844, the grandson of a minister of justice and the son of a judge, Theotokis was educated in Paris. Twice mayor of Corfu, he was elected to parliament in 1885 as a deputy of the Trikoupis party and became a minister in 1886. He was prime minister four times between 1899 and 1909. He was elected to parliament again in 1915 but died in January 1916.

Further Reading

Rallis, Georgios, *Georgios Theotokis: O Politikos tou Metrou* [George Theotokis, the Moderate Politician], Athens, 1986

Theotokis, Nikiphoros 1731–1800

Scientist and theologian

Nikiphoros (baptized Nikolaos) Theotokis was one of the brightest scholars of the modern Greek Enlightenment. His multidimensional contribution classifies him as one of the pioneering representatives of modern Greek scholasticism who during the century before independence battled against ignorance and superstition to develop a national conscience within the Greek population of the Balkans and Asia Minor.

According to the official record in the *Libro d' Oro*, Nikiphoros was born in Corfu on 15 February 1731. He studied initially in his own country under Jeremia Kavvadias, who also taught during the same period the other great Corfiot scholar, Evgenios Voulgaris. Kavvadias's overpowering personality steered the young student towards the Church, so in 1748 at the age of 17 – in spite of objections from his family and various bureaucratic obstacles – he was ordained a deacon. But since he was not allowed to practise his religious duties until he came of age and since he had completed his basic studies, Theotokis travelled to Italy around 1749 – which was then the centre of studies for the majority of Greeks who wanted to enrich their knowledge – where he studied philosophy, physics, and mathematics at the universities of Bologna and Padua. Here the teachings of modern physical theories already prevailed, theories that questioned Aristotelian authority.

Even though his attendance at the University of Padua has been questioned, reports by Theotokis himself as well as the scientific content of his work verify the fact that he actually did study at Padua under Giovanni Poleni. Poleni, a pioneering leader of the scientific reformist movement in Italian universities, also taught other significant scholars of the first period of Greek Enlightenment, such as Voulgaris, Josephos Moisiodax, and Zerzoulis, scholars who generally supported the introduction of modern scientific thought into the wider Balkan region. The young Theotokis was especially impressed by the value of experiments in the sciences and this can be seen in his books. At the same time he acquired an adequate knowledge of higher mathematics, a knowledge that was among the best for a Greek of that period. His biographers mention that he also studied medicine and E. Sarafidis tells us that Theotokis practised medicine in Jassy in 1775.

He returned to Corfu after three years of studies and at his own expense founded an educational centre where he taught philosophy, mathematics, and physics, while his former teacher Kavvadias taught all other subjects. During this period, vice-admiral Iakovos Nanis of the Venetian navy asked Theotokis for his advice concerning the repair work being carried out at the port of Gouvion. Nanis accepted and recognized his scientific knowledge – especially in hydraulics – since Poleni (Theotokis's teacher) was considered then to be one of the greatest experts in Europe in these matters.

In conjunction with the founding of his educational centre, Theotokis was appointed a priest at the church of Sts John the Baptist and Paraskevi in 1758 and for the next three years he delivered inspiring Christian sermons.

During this period Theotokis received an invitation from patriarch Ioannikios to assume the management of the academy on Mount Athos, which had been closed since 1761 when Voulgaris had left it. But objections were raised on the Holy Mountain to his assumption of these duties.

Theotokis therefore travelled to Constantinople where he developed close ties with Grigorios Gikas, a leading person among the aristocracy of Constantinople. It should be noted that during his stay in Constantinople Theotokis replaced Voulgaris as head of the patriarchal school but, since he worked in a climate that negated progressive thought, he soon came into conflict with the conservative Phanariot groups. Theotokis eventually resigned after clashing with the patriarch himself. When Gikas assumed the throne of Moldavia, he invited Theotokis to head the academy at Jassy and to teach mathematics, physics, and geography. In 1765 Moisiodax succeeded Theotokis as head of the academy and the latter travelled to Leipzig where after a number of years he published the first volume of his work *Stichia Physikis* (Elements of Physics), which even today is considered to be a milestone for science in Greece. At the same time, he was being systematically informed about all recent scientific developments. His activities soon became known to other European scientists and their respect is confirmed by the fact that J.J. Reisck dedicated the eighth volume of his work *Analekta ton Ellinon Ritoron* (Outstanding Greek Orators, Leipzig, 1773) to Theotokis.

In 1772 he persistently refused the archbishopric of Philadelphia in Venice since he did not want anything to do with the Catholic Church. Returning to Jassy in 1773, Theotokis assumed the directorship of the academy (a three-form school for children aged 10–13), teaching there until 1776 and thus contributing to the introduction of modern scientific theories to the principalities along the Danube. He travelled to Russia at the end of 1776 at the invitation of Voulgaris. When Voulgaris resigned, Theotokis was ordained archbishop of Cherson on 6 August 1779, and later assumed the archbishopric of Stavroupolis, which he resigned in 1792 after clashing with Potemkin. Theotokis lived in the monastery of St Daniel in Moscow until his death on 31 May 1800. Evidence of his pastoral work in Russia includes the conversion of a good many Muslim Tartars to Orthodoxy.

His published work may be classified under two main headings: ecclesiastical and scientific. With regard to the first, Theotokis was one of the clerics who made Christian doctrine more easily understood by the people. His most valuable book on that subject was *Kyriakodromion* (Sunday Cycle, Moscow, 1796), in which he tried to explain New Testament passages by means of the interpretation and annotations of the early Church Fathers. He also wrote sermons, a guide to the ascetic life, and a treatise on the conversion of the Jews. With regard to the second, Theotokis the scientist showed a restless and investigative spirit and had a complete understanding of the Hellenic Enlightenment of which it would not be an exaggeration to consider him a co-founder.

GEORGE N. VLAHAKIS

See also Enlightenment

Biography

Born in Corfu in 1731, Theotokis was a pupil of Jeremia Kavvadias who steered him into the Church. He was ordained a deacon in 1748 at the age of 17. He continued his studies of philosophy, physics, mathematics, and medicine at the universities of Bologna and Padua. Returning to Corfu, he founded a school. Moving to Constantinople, he succeeded Voulgaris first as head of the patriarchal school and in 1779 as archbishop of Cherson. He died in Moscow in 1800.

Further Reading

Mourouti-Genakou, Zoe, "Nikephoros Theotokis (1731–1800) and his Contribution to the Education of the Nation" (dissertation), Athens University, 1979

Vlahakis, George N., "Nikephoros Theotokis and Education in the District of Thessalia: References to his Work by Thessalian Teachers", *Proceedings of the Congress "Physical Sciences in Greece and Especially in Thessalia before the Revolution"*, Larissa, 1985: pp. 111–16 (in Greek)

Vlahakis, George N., "L'Oeuvre scientifique de Nikiphoros Theotokis: tentative d' approche fondée plus particulierement sur les *Stichia Physikis* (Elements de Physique)", *Revue des Etudes Sud-Est Européennes*, 25/3 (1987): pp. 251–61

Vlahakis, George N., "The *Physics* of Nikephoros Theotokis: A Turning Point in the Scientific Thought of the 18th Century" (dissertation), National Polytechnic University of Athens, 1991 (in Greek)

Vlahakis, George N., "A Note for the Penetration of Newtonian Scientific Thought in Greece", *Nuncius*, 2 (1993): pp. 645–56

Vrokinis, Lavredios, essays in *Kerkyraika Chronika*, vol. 16, 1972

Theotokopoulos, Domenikos (El Greco) *c.*1541–1614

Painter

Domenikos Theotokopoulos, usually known as El Greco ("the Greek"), was one of the most original and innovative painters of 16th-century Europe. The curiously elongated figures that people his later compositions are instantly recognizable, as are the brilliant and contrasting colours in which he clothes and surrounds them. So unusual are his portrayals of the human figure that they have even been attributed to mental illness or to the distorted vision caused by astigmatism. In the same way, so unique is his style of painting that no consensus has emerged on exactly how to categorize it. He has been described as a member of the Castilian school, as a follower of the Venetian master Titian, and as a representative of the fervour of the Counter-Reformation. Yet, while each of these categories may have some claim to authenticity, the origins of El Greco's art lie in the Byzantine tradition and in the Cretan school of icon painting.

Like another famous representative of that school, Theophanes of Crete, El Greco was a native of Candia, the modern Herakleion, on Crete. His family were Roman Catholics and a number of his relatives worked as officials in the service of the Venetian government of the island. It used to be thought that he had trained under Titian in Venice, but it is now clear from documentary evidence that he had learnt his trade long before he left Crete. One document dated 1563 describes him as a master painter, and evidence of the value placed on his work as early as 1566 is given by another which prices one of his paintings at the considerable sum of 70 ducats. A number of works from this early period have now been identified. They include a signed *Dormition of the Virgin*, painted in about 1567, in the church of the Koimesis on Syros, and an *Adoration of the Magi*, now in the Benaki Museum in Athens. Both works are in the post-Byzantine style, although Italian influence is already noticeable in the mobility and corporeality of the figures.

Had El Greco remained on Crete, he might perhaps have continued to work in this unremarkable style, but in about 1568 he left the island, never to return. He went first to Venice, where he seems to have had some contact with Titian. By the end of 1570 he had moved on to Rome, where he operated a workshop for some years. He left Italy altogether in 1577 and moved to Spain, first to Madrid and then to Toledo, where he remained for the rest of his life.

The move westwards was accompanied by a profound change in El Greco's style, transforming him into a fundamentally Western painter. The change is plain to see in the public commissions that he carried out during his early years at Toledo, such as his *Disrobing of Christ* (1577–79) in the cathedral sacristy, and his famous *Burial of the Count of Orgaz* (1586–88) in the church of Santo Tomé. As his fame as a painter spread, his workshop produced scores of religious paintings for private clients and he was unanimously acclaimed by his contemporaries as a portraitist. His portraits tend to be austere in tone and usually on a neutral background, but they show an ability to convey character and physique. Perhaps the best known is the full-length depiction of the bespectacled inquisitor, cardinal Fernando Niño de Guevara, in his red robes and biretta, now in the Metropolitan Museum of Art, New York. A number of self-portraits also survive.

His later work became increasingly impressionistic, as he adopted an ever freer style. In the *Immaculate Conception* of 1607–13, in the Museo de Santa Cruz, Toledo, the Virgin floats upwards, supported by spindly angels. The *Adoration of the Shepherds*, painted in 1612–14 for his own burial chapel in Toledo, displays vivid, dissonant colours and distorted physical shapes. These compositions puzzled contemporaries and were regarded as eccentric, but they were to be a powerful influence on painters of the early 20th century.

Yet, in spite of his move to Spain and the radical development of his painting style, El Greco did not lose touch with his Greek origins. He tended to associate mainly with the Greek community in Toledo, and had little to do with local Spanish life. He continued to sign his paintings in Greek, and on a

Domenikos Theotokopoulos: *The Crucifixion* (1600–1605), National Gallery, Athens

number of occasions came forward to support his fellow Greeks when they were involved in cases in Spanish law courts.

It is therefore not surprising that elements of Byzantine iconography still occur in his later work. His depictions of Mount Sinai, painted in the 1570s, contain the same angels, tombs, and camels, in the same places, as a treatment of the same subject painted in traditional style in Thessalonica around the same time. The *Disrobing of Christ* in Toledo Cathedral preserves some Byzantine feeling in the superimposition of the heads of the figures in the background to the main scene. Other works display not so much elements from Byzantine imagery as a mystic vision, similar to that of icons venerated in the Orthodox Church. His *Christ as Saviour of the World*, in the National Gallery of Scotland, Edinburgh, exemplifies this tendency. The figure of Christ is placed in no definite time or space, in stark frontality, with light and dark colours used to enhance the effect. It would, of course, be easy to make too much of these Graeco-Byzantine influences in El Greco's work, and David Talbot Rice was surely exaggerating when he described the painter as "the last of the Byzantines". Nevertheless, such influences remained an aspect of his work, up to the very end of his life.

Thus El Greco's idiosyncratic style should not be seen as the product of any particular school, Byzantine or Western, any more than it should be dismissed as the result of madness or myopia. Rather it grew out of his physical and artistic journey westward: the fusion of Greek, Italian, and Spanish influences with his own unique creativity and genius.

JONATHAN HARRIS

See also Painting

Biography

Born *c.*1541 in Candia (Herakleion), Crete, to a Roman Catholic family, El Greco was trained as a painter in his home island. Some works survive from his Cretan period. He left Crete *c.*1568 and went first to Italy (Venice, then Rome) and in 1577 moved to Spain (Madrid, then Toledo). He was admired by his contemporaries as a portraitist. He died in Toledo in 1614.

Further Reading

Davies, David, *El Greco*, Oxford: Phaidon, and New York: Dutton, 1976

Davies, David, "The Byzantine Legacy in the Art of El Greco" in *El Greco of Crete: Proceedings of the International Symposium held on the Occasion of the 450th Anniversary of the Artist's Birth*, edited by Nicos Hadjinicolaos, Herakleion: Municipality of Herakleion, 1995

Kelemen, Pál, *El Greco Revisited: Candia, Venice, Toledo*, New York: Macmillan, 1961

Marías, Fernando, El Greco entry in *The Dictionary of Art*, edited by Jane Turner, vol. 13, London: Macmillan, 1996

Papadaki-Oekland, Stella, "El Greco's 'Byzantinism': A Re-evaluation" in *El Greco of Crete: Proceedings of the International Symposium held on the Occasion of the 450th Anniversary of the Artist's Birth*, edited by Nicos Hadjinicolaos, Herakleion: Municipality of Herakleion, 1995

Rice, David Talbot, "Five Late Byzantine Panels and El Greco's Views of Sinai", *The Burlington Magazine*, 89 (1947): pp. 93–4

Rice, David Talbot, *Byzantine Painting: The Last Phase*, London: Weidenfeld and Nicolson, and New York: Dial Press, 1968

Wethey, Harold E., *El Greco and his School*, 2 vols, Princeton, New Jersey: Princeton University Press, 1962

Thessalonica

City in Macedonia

Thessalonica is the second largest city of Greece, with a population of 750,000 according to the census of 1991. Founded by decree in 316 BC by Cassander, who subsequently became king of Macedonia, the city was named after his wife Thessalonica, half-sister of Alexander the Great. It comprised 26 older towns and hamlets of the region, whose inhabitants were encouraged to resettle at the new location. Some of these towns survived the foundation of Thessalonica, while others disappeared entirely. Thessalonica was to serve as the harbour of Pella, the Macedonian royal capital, which had become landlocked as a result of the sedimentation deposited by the four large rivers of western and central Macedonia. The city plan followed the Hippodamian system applied to contemporary cities, a grid of streets at right angles to each other. Despite its long and turbulent history since the Hellenistic era, through periods of great

Thessalonica: the Rotonda of Galerius, late 3rd century AD

prosperity and times of hardship and instability, Thessalonica has preserved the main features of the original orthogonal layout, corrupted in times of overcrowding. Furthermore, the walls, which have defended Thessalonica since late antiquity, defined an area of 330 hectares, which – with some alterations mainly on the eastern side – became the confines within which the city developed until its expansion after the mid-19th century.

Owing to its geographical position Thessalonica prospered as a centre of commerce and industry and was already a wealthy city when the Romans conquered Macedonia in 168 BC after the battle of Pydna. Its inhabitants remained loyal to the imperial party during the civil wars that followed the assassination of Julius Caesar in 44 BC. Under the Romans Thessalonica acquired an additional military importance, since it often hosted army units on their way to defend the empire against enemies in the east or against hostile tribes of migrating peoples from the north. Indeed, the very routes that carried trade, ideas, and wealth in times of stability were to bring raids, armies, and violence in times of instability, both on a large scale, as the Pax Romana, the lengthy period of peace inaugurated and secured by the Romans, was drawing to an end in the mid-3rd century AD.

The Romans provided the city with public works. Many public buildings came down in the earthquake that shook the city in AD 620 and their materials were either reused in Byzantine constructions or served as landfill. By contrast, however, a small number of Roman public works outlasted the

Roman era, most notably the Via Egnatia, the road constructed by the vice-consul Gnaeus Egnatius in the 2nd century BC to connect the Adriatic coast to the eastern regions of the Roman empire. The main highway, which branched off the Via Egnatia and ran across the city from west to east, was named Via Regia in antiquity, Leoforos in Byzantine times, Broad Street under the Ottomans, and Egnatia today.

At the end of the 3rd century AD Thessalonica became the residence of the tetrarch, or quarter-emperor, Galerius, who constructed a palace, a triumphal arch to commemorate his victories against the Persians, a hippodrome, and a round building, the Rotonda, whose original use is still an issue of debate among scholars. It is the oldest surviving building in continuous use in the Balkans, was converted to a Christian church, then to a mosque in 1591 by the Ottomans. In 320 emperor Constantine replaced the ancient harbour at the southeast end of the wall with an artifical harbour at the western end of the city limits. This harbour served the city during the Byzantine era. Even after it had fallen out of use, the harbour has remained in the same area.

Among the foreigners who had settled in the ancient city, probably since pre-Roman times, was a community of Jews. They retained their religion but became linguistically assimilated and later became known as Romaniot Jews. It was among this early Jewish community of Thessalonica that St Paul preached his new faith when he visited the city in AD 40. He then kept contact with his Jewish and Gentile converts through his letters to the Thessalonians.

Christianity became important as a force of ideological cohesion in the subsequent history of the city, which gradually assumed a truly Christian character during the 4th century. The focus of this new identity was the cult of St Demetrius, a young Roman officer, who had died for his faith in 305. The new cult was a Christian substitute for the older mystic cult of the Cabiri brother-gods, who, like their Christian counterpart, had also been the city's patrons. The first church to St Demetrius was built on the site of the Cabiri shrine in the 5th century. It burned down after the earthquake of 620, was rebuilt, then became a mosque in 1491, and was reconverted to a Christian church when Thessalonica became Greek again in 1912. It burned a second time in the great fire of 1917 and was rebuilt once more.

Throughout the 6th century the Avars and Slavs raided the environs and besieged the city. They never succeeded in capturing Thessalonica, but drove large numbers of the rural population inside its walls. After the emperor Justinian II put an end to these attacks at the end of the 7th century prosperity returned, while peaceful exchanges began with the Slavic settlers in the area. The church of St Sophia was constructed during this period. In the 9th century the monks Cyril and Methodios set off from Thessalonica to convert the Slavs to Christianity and introduce literacy by creating a suitable alphabet.

In 904 the Saracen Arabs from their pirate state in Crete, which thrived on plunder, piracy, and the slave trade, attacked and sacked the city, and killed and captured its inhabitants, carrying them off to be sold as slaves. John Kameniatis, who was among the captives, wrote a gruelling account of the incident.

Thessalonica withstood the clash between the Byzantine empire and the Bulgarian state in the 10th century, but had once more to take in large numbers of destitute peasants. In 1185, however, it fell into the hands of the Normans from Sicily, who sacked it, killed and plundered, held it for a year, and then left. When the city fell to the Latin crusaders in 1204, after the sack of Constantinople, the city elders negotiated their surrender and were thus able to retain some of their traditional rights of self-government. The Byzantines recaptured the city 20 years later, while the imperial capital was restored to Byzantine rule in 1261.

The empire was weak and fragmented. Nevertheless, Thessalonica experienced its last period of greatness: the Palaiologan renaissance of the 14th century. Profiting from the overall economic decline of the state, the Venetians had expanded their commercial business, acquired trading privileges, and settled in Thessalonica, thus contributing to intense economic activity and prosperity to the benefit of the arts. Several of the surviving Byzantine churches with their paintings and mosaics (Holy Apostles and St Catherine) date from that period and illustrate the artistic achievements of the Macedonian school of architecture and painting.

During this period of social cleavage, economic inequity, civil war, and foreign attacks, some scholars found new values in Classical Greek literature, began to speak of justice and freedom, and chose a western political and philosophical orientation. By contrast, their opponents developed the mystical movement of hesychasm of eastern inspiration, which became attractive to the wealthy and the nobility. They

Thessalonica: illustration from the 11th-century chronicle of Skylitzes showing the Thessalonians repelling a Bulgar siege in the 10th century, Biblioteca Nacional, Madrid

supported the pretender to the Byzantine throne, John Kantakouzenos. The middle classes and the poor took the opposing side in the ideological controversy, that of the Zealots, and supported the legitimate heir to the throne, John V Palaiologos. In 1342 they rebelled, assumed control of the city, held it for seven years, and established a republic, confiscating the estates of the Church and of the nobility.

Throughout this period the neighbouring Serbs, Bulgarians, and Turks were also drawn into the conflict. Finally, in 1387, Thessalonica surrendered to the Ottoman Turks; in exchange for tribute to sultan Murad I it retained some of its communal privileges – as it turned out, only in name. The city returned to Byzantine rule for a short while until, in 1423, unable to defend itself against the Turks, it voluntarily capitulated to the Venetians. In 1430, after a long siege that left Thessalonica virtually depopulated and defenceless, the second largest city of the empire fell unconditionally to the Ottomans under sultan Murad II and was incorporated into his private domain.

The Ottomans established a military guard of Janissaries and proceeded immediately to resettle the city. The great population influx, however, occurred two generations after the fall of Thessalonica, in 1492, when the Ottoman sultan Bayazid II welcomed the Sephardic Jews expelled from Spain by king Ferdinand and queen Isabella. Approximately 20,000 of them settled in Thessalonica, which became a predominantly Jewish city and began to thrive once again in trade and industry. Until the beginning of the 19th century the relative proportions of the three main ethnic groups were approximately half Jews and, of the remaining half, slightly more Turks than Greeks.

The principal occupation of the Jews of Thessalonica was connected with the production and trade of woollen textiles for military uniforms. Thanks to its importance for the army their community acquired the monopoly in this field, in exchange, however, for the economic protection of the Janissaries. The heyday of the Jewish community of Thessalonica was the 16th century. Thereafter, with the decline of Venice as the Mediterranean trade lost its international importance in favour of the Atlantic routes, the Jews in Thessalonica entered a period of crisis, accompanied by a serious rift when, in the 1660s, large numbers converted to Islam and became known as "Dönme".

New circumstances in the 18th century proved favourable for the rise of the Greek community of Thessalonica, when French merchants settled in the city to trade in grain, wool, cotton, and hides from the Macedonian hinterland, and were followed by other European nationals. However, as a consequence of the Greek national uprising of 1821 the Greeks of Thessalonica suffered atrocities at the hands of the Turks and their community entered a period of decline. Furthermore, the destruction of the Janissaries as a result of the reforming efforts of sultan Mahmud II in 1826 disrupted the overall economy of the city, which had been in Janissary hands to a great extent.

Although there was no institutionalized segregation, each ethnic group lived in a more or less distinct neighbourhood, whose boundaries varied over the years. The Turks lived mostly in the higher section of the city in large and more hygienic housing. The Greeks lived lower down and towards the eastern parts of the city in smaller houses, while the Jews lived in the city centre and closer to the harbour and the marketplace in confined, occasionally overcrowded conditions, in narrow streets, more exposed to the hazards of epidemics and fire. Each group was governed by a communal body of elders with legal jurisdiction led by its religious head.

A new age of prosperity came to Thessalonica after the mid-19th century with the age of steam, accompanied by a great interest among the European powers in the economic and political reforms of the Ottoman empire. The Greeks had profited from the support of the Greek kingdom and they as well as the other nationalities from the benefits of secular education, economic progress, and modern banking. The affluent members of all ethnic groups were acquiring larger houses beyond the city walls, which the enlightened regional authorities began to pull down, since they no longer served the city's defence. Construction of a railway line from Thessalonica to Mitrovica began in 1871 and, as a result of new transportation requirements, the harbour had to be modernized. Public works began on a large scale. However, in 1890 an extensive fire burned down a large section of the town centre, which was redesigned and rationalized.

Thessalonica was liberated by the Greek army on 26 October 1912, at the beginning of the First Balkan War. During World War I it became the quarters of large numbers of Entente army units and the temporary seat of the pro-Entente Greek government of Eleftherios Venizelos in 1916. In August 1917 the last major fire destroyed the centre of the city and left approximately 15,000 families homeless. A new town plan was devised by the French city planner Ernest Hébrard, which created the outline of Thessalonica as it is today through a significant reallocation of properties.

Dramatic changes were to occur in the following years, which affected the ethnic composition of the city, namely the arrival of thousands of destitute Christian refugees from Asia Minor in 1922 and 1923 and the fall of Greece to the Nazis in April 1941. In March 1943 the German authorities deported the Jewish population of Thessalonica by train loads to the Nazi extermination camps, from which only a few were to survive. Of the 50,000 Thessalonica Jews 95 per cent perished. The city suffered the disruptive consequences of the Civil War (1946–49) and was able to begin its economic recovery only in the early 1950s.

KATERINA GARDIKAS

See also Jews, Macedonia, Renaissance (Palaiologan)

Summary

Founded by Cassander in 316 BC, Thessalonica was an amalgam of 26 older towns and villages. It was the port of Macedonia and prospered as a centre of commerce and industry. It lay on the Via Egnatia which connected Constantinople with the Adriatic. It had a Jewish community in antiquity and was visited by St Paul. It was raided by Slavs and Avars in the 6th century, sacked by Arabs in the 10th, and taken by Latins in 1204. Finally taken by the Ottomans in 1430, it received an influx of Spanish Jews in 1492. It was liberated by the Greek army in 1912.

Further Reading

Papagiannopoulos, Apostolos, *A History of Thessaloniki*, translated by Pantazidou Anastasia, Thessalonica: Rekos, 1982
Vacalopoulos, Apostolos, *A History of Thessaloniki*, translated by T.F. Carney, Thessalonica: Institute for Balkan Studies, 1972

Thessaly

Region of central Greece

Thessaly is an easily identifiable area, bounded by the Pindus mountains on the east, Pelion and Ossa to the south, and Mount Olympus to the north. In between there are two large plains, divided by a range of hilly country. These plains, at the centre of which lie Larissa and Trikkala, are much larger than any other comparable area in Classical Greece, and perhaps explain why Thessaly in both ancient and modern times has not followed the pattern of the rest of Greece. The climate is a little harsher. Thessaly never really developed the city state. The territory became Greek in 1881, well before Macedonia and Epirus, but long after the rest of Greece. Though more clearly Greek than either Macedonia or Epirus, it used to contain a large Turkish element in its population and still contains many Vlachs. It has an extensive coastline and a major port in Volos, but is far less bound to the sea than most of Greece. The olive and the vine grow less well, but traditionally Thessaly has been rich in horses, cattle, and grain.

Thessalians figure in the Homeric catalogue, and Achilles came from Pthiotis in the southeastern portion of Thessaly. The Thessalians of the Classical period appear from their dialect to have been a mixture of the original Homeric element and invaders such as the Dorians from the northwest. The latter appear to have ruled as an oligarchy with one of their number elected as *tagos* or leader of the whole of Thessaly. An early family to achieve prominence were the Aleudae, based on Larissa, but they lost favour through supporting the Persians. In the Peloponnesian War the Thessalians were generally on the Athenian side, but not very effectively. Jason of Pherae in the 4th century BC gained considerable power, but his assassination prevented him from anticipating Philip of Macedon, who easily gained control of a divided Thessaly. Thessalian cavalry formed an important part of Alexander's army, and Thessaly generally remained loyal to Macedon until the Roman victory at Pydna in 168 BC.

While the rest of Greece on the whole suffered under Roman rule, there are complimentary references in Latin literature to Thessaly's plains, mountains, and rivers. Lucan, though mainly concerned with mythology, gives a glowing tribute in his *Pharsalia*. A Roman colony at Dium and a good road from Thessalonica to Athens ensured a plentiful Roman presence, well attested by inscriptions. Larissa and Tricca (Trikkala) were the main towns. Towards the end of the 2nd century AD Apuleius paints a gloomier picture of brigandage and witchcraft. The barbarian invasions in the Roman empire's declining years sometimes reached as far as Thessaly, and when the Danube frontier finally broke in 602, western Thessaly was soon lost to the invaders with Byzantium maintaining a precarious control only over the coastline. As late as the end of the 10th century Larissa was sometimes in the hands of the Bulgarian tsar Samuel. Even after the conquest of the whole of the Balkans by Basil the Bulgar slayer there was always a threat from rebellious Vlachs in the mountains and from western invaders like the Norman Bohemund, who crossed the Pindus mountains and besieged Larissa before being defeated by Alexios Komnenos in 1083.

After the Fourth Crusade of 1204 Thessaly passed under various rulers before the Turks arrived at the end of the 14th century. Originally it was part of the subordinate Latin kingdom of Thessalonica which Boniface of Montferrat had carved out for himself after failing to gain the throne of Constantinople. Then in 1224 it was captured by Theodore Doukas of Epirus and, in spite of Byzantine successes at Pelagonia in 1259 and the reconquest of Constantinople in 1261, it remained under the rule of a member of the Doukas family, being independent of Epirus from 1271. In 1318 the Catalans gained possession of southern Thessaly, while Stephen Gabrieloupolos preserved a precarious independence in the north. The frequent changes of ruler and the presence of so many external threats cannot have made Thessaly a peaceful place, and it was in the 14th century that the extensive monastic foundations of the Meteora were established, no doubt as a place of refuge from the strain of the internal and external strife. In 1335 the Palaiologoi briefly under Andronikos III regained both Thessaly and Epirus, but there was a new danger in the north in the shape of the Serbs. A disastrous civil war (1341–47) between John Kantakouzenos, a great landowner in Thessaly and a benefactor of the Meteora, and John Palaiologos gave the Serbs their opportunity and in 1348 Stephan IV Dushan conquered both Thessaly and Epirus. On his death his half-brother Symeon Uroš ruled for a time; his mother was a Palaiologos and wife a Doukas. But Symeon's son did not rule in his place, retiring instead to the Meteora to end his days as Father Iosaaph. The Turks conquered Thessaly in 1393, although Manuel II Palaiologos (1391–1425) briefly recovered the eastern coastline after the Battle of Ankara.

The Turks were rulers of Thessaly for nearly 500 years. Arriving early in the rich plains with a similar climate to Anatolia, they settled there in considerable numbers, often reducing the original inhabitants to near serfdom, forced to work the land with few rights and heavy taxes. In the mountains the Greeks and Vlachs had more independence, often gaining special privileges in return for nominal duties as guardians of passes. As the central authority became weaker we have evidence from western travellers and from Greek and Vlach folk song of how the independent mountain villagers were able to deceive the Turks by adopting a dual role as *armatoloi*, guardians of law and order, and klephts, disturbers of the peace. No doubt the success of these heroic manoeuvres is exaggerated in our sources, and other Thessalians played a more pacific part. In the 18th century the villages of Pelion with their distinctive houses became an intellectual centre of Hellenism, while the cotton merchants of Ambelakia on the slopes of Mount Ossa established a thriving trade.

Thessaly remained in Ottoman hands after the rest of Classical Greece had been granted independence in 1830. Greece was not formally represented at the Congress of Berlin in 1878, and it needed a general mobilization in 1880 to secure the cession of Thessaly in 1881. In 1897 a disastrous war against Turkey resulted in a major defeat for the Greek forces in Thessaly and there were small frontier rectifications in Turkey's favour. Between 1881 and 1912 Thessaly was a frontier province and a haven for freedom fighters in Macedonia and Epirus.

The Balkan Wars, World War I, and the Greek disaster in Asia Minor of 1922 brought about a major change in Thessaly's position. It was no longer a frontier province. Population exchanges meant that there was no longer a substantial Turkish element in the area. Immigrants from Asia Minor who replaced them were sometimes rich merchants who took over the privileged position of the Turkish landowners, sometimes landless refugees with left-wing sympathies. In World War II and the Civil War that followed it Thessaly played a crucial part since through it lay the life-line from Athens to Thessalonica. Forces of ELAS (*Ellinikos Laikos Apelevtherotikos Stratos*, the Greek Popular Liberation Army) were strong in the area, hindering first the German occupation and then the royalist government. Support for ELAS was strong, as was resentment against it. The head of Ares Velouchiotis was exhibited briefly in Trikkala after his death in 1945.

Such a bloodthirsty episode seems at variance with the position of modern Thessaly, peaceful if unexciting. With little in the way of Classical sites and few beaches except in more remote Pelion, Thessaly has escaped the perils of modern tourism, but has prospered from European Union support for agriculture. Volos and Larissa are among Greece's six largest towns, but well below Athens and Thessalonica in population. The slightly provincial note about Thessalian society is perhaps best shown by the fact that it features in modern Greek literature very infrequently, although there is a novel, *The Beggar* by Andros Karkavitsas, written in 1896 and set at the foot of Mount Olympus.

T.J. WINNIFRITH

Summary

A region of central Greece, Thessaly did not develop into city states but was ruled by an oligarchy in the Classical period. Its plains were famous for horses. Invaded by Slavs in the 7th century and Bulgars in the 10th, Thessaly changed hands many times between 1204 and the Ottoman conquest in 1393. It was united with Greece in 1881.

Further Reading

Abbott, G.F., *Turkey, Greece and the Great Powers: A Study in Friendship and Hate*, London: Scott, 1916

Abramea, A., *I Byzantini Thessalia mechri tou 1204* [Byzantine Thessaly to 1204] Athens, 1974

Chirol, Valentine, *Twixt Greek and Turk, or, Jottings during a Journey Through Thessaly, Macedonia, and Epirus, in the Autumn of 1880*, Edinburgh: Blackwood, 1881

Miller, William, *The Latins in the Levant: A History of Frankish Greece, 1204–1566*, London: John Murray, 1908

Nicol, Donald M., *The Last Centuries of Byzantium, 1261–1453*, 2nd edition, Cambridge and New York: Cambridge University Press, 1993

Rose, W. Kinnaird, *With the Greeks in Thessaly*, London: Methuen, 1897

Vacalopoulos, Apostolos E., *Origins of the Greek Nation: The Byzantine Period, 1204–1461*, New Brunswick, New Jersey: Rutgers University Press, 1970

Westlake, H.D., *Thessaly in the Fourth Century BC*, London: Methuen, 1935, reprinted Groningen: Bouma, 1969

Zakythinos, D.A., *The Making of Modern Greece: From Byzantium to Independence*, Oxford: Blackwell, 1976

Thrace

Region bordering the north Aegean

Thrace and Thracians are the names given by the ancient Greeks to the territory and the people living in the region bordering the north Aegean. Neither the origin of the name nor the local name for this large territory is known. Over time the boundaries of Thrace changed. It was at its greatest extent in the 5th century BC when the Odrysian kingdom was established, stretching over present-day Bulgaria, east of the Hebrus (Turkish Thrace), and Greece between the Hebrus and Strymon, except for the coastal areas from the Danube to north of the Hellespont, and from Constantinople to Strymon in southwest Bulgaria. The territory was rich in fertile plains, forests, fish, precious metals, and iron and copper ores. The Thracians who are mentioned by Homer (*Iliad*, 6. 130, 9. 5, 14. 227, etc.; *Odyssey*, 8. 361) were agricultural tribes. Ancient writers give the names of many Thracian tribes: Tribali, Odrysae, Dardani, etc. They were a warlike, rural people, ruled over by various dynasties. The king of Odrysae was the dominant figure in the Classical period, until Philip II of Macedon invaded Thrace in the 4th century BC and established various cities including Philippopolis (Plovdiv). After the death of Alexander the Great in 323 BC Thrace fell to Lysimachus.

Greek colonies were established on the shores of Pontic Thrace from the end of the 7th century BC (Apollonia Pontica, Mesembria, Odessus) and from the middle of the 7th century BC in Aegean Thrace (Abdera, Maroneia, Aenus, Perinthus). Orpheus, the mythical singer, son of Apollo and a Muse, is generally called a Thracian and Thrace was considered to be his home. His grave and cult belong not to Thrace but to Pierian Macedonia, northeast of Mount Olympus, a region that the Thracians had once inhabited. Orpheus' song had superhuman powers and an important consequence of his miraculous song was his creation of Orphic poetry. The image of Orpheus was very popular in Greek and Roman art. In Attic vase painting he was represented in oriental as well as Greek costume. Several vases show him being killed by Thracian women.

The close links between Greece and Thrace are demonstrated not only by the depiction of Thracians in Attic vase painting but also by the introduction of the cult of the Thracian goddess Bendis to Athens in the 5th century BC.

Greek artists represented her as a booted huntress, like Artemis. A priestess was assigned to her by one of the decrees of 413/12 BC and a great festival was established in Piraeus, at which twin processions of native Thracians and Athenians were followed by a torch race on horseback, and celebrations continued all through the night.

Thracian religion is a much-debated subject. The information given by ancient writers, especially Greeks, presents the Greek interpretation of local religious beliefs. Herodotus (5. 7) states that the Thracians worshipped Ares, Dionysus, Artemis, and Hermes. The similarities between the worship of a Great Goddess and the cult of Artemis in Asia Minor or of Cybele are obvious. The idea of heroization was restricted to members of the nobility and royal family. The existence of a cult of Helios is attested not only in Greek literature (Sophocles, *Tereus*, fr. 582) but by archaeological and numismatic data. The most popular cult was that of the so-called Thracian Rider, represented by about 2500 votive stone monuments, often of the rider hunting.

Little is known about Thracian culture of the Archaic period. We have much more evidence from the period of the establishment of the Odrysian kingdom in the 5th century BC, although our knowledge of Thracian culture is confined to that of the ruling elite. The Thracians were very advanced metalworkers, and many metal objects made of gold or silver, especially drinking vessels, are known from the tombs of local rulers and nobles; Greek and Achaemenid or Achaemenid-type vessels are also known. Stylistically, there is a mixture of Greek, Achaemenid, and local elements. The quantity of vessels and pieces of jewellery found in tombs is quite impressive. The information provided by Thucydides (2. 37) concerning gift giving and tribute collected from Greek cities and from "all the barbarous nations" in the reign of Seuthes (424–c.408 BC), the king of the Odrysae, makes it clear that the Odrysian kingdom was similar to the Achaemenid empire in that the king exploited Greek craftsmen to create his culture. Excavation of the settlement at Vetren, in the Thracian hinterland not far from Plovdiv, shows that this practice began in Thrace in the mid-5th century BC. This settlement, the residence of the local ruler, was built entirely by Greek architects and masons, as the planning and layout, paved streets, and, most importantly, city-gate and fortification system demonstrate.

Greek influence on local elite culture was strong. The nobility used the Greek alphabet, as seen on a ring and vessels from the Rogozen Treasure (now in the National History Museum, Sofia). In the Hellenistic period the Greeks became even more heavily involved; for example, the town planning and architecture of Seuthopolis (which had an agora), as well as its fortifications, are examples of Greek craftsmanship and masonry, as in Vetren. Inscriptions, legends on coins, and stamps and graffiti on Thracian pottery all indicate that the Greek language was very much used in Seuthopolis. In this royal city, built and decorated entirely by Greeks, temples as well as Thracian clay altars were found. The religion shows very strong Greek influence. Another royal city, Cabyle, archaeologically less well known, has an inscription in ancient Greek which is identical to that found in Seuthopolis. The Getic capital at Sboryanovo, which has been studied since the late 1980s, has also revealed a stone fortification system, stone architecture, and inscriptions in Greek.

Greek masons were further employed to build and decorate tombs. In the chamber of the barrel-vaulted tomb at Sveshtari a Doric entablature is supported on the raised hands of women, with the help of five Corinthian half-columns: this is redolent of Greek caryatids. There are impressive murals in a tomb at Kazanluk: chariot races, a Greek decorative frieze of bowls and bucrania, and figures approaching the dead prince and his consort seated at a table. All the trappings and furniture are Greek. Since the 1980s excavations in the Shipka area have brought to light several dozen rich tombs, some decorated with very impressive murals.

Roman involvement arose from Thrace's links with Macedonia. After the Macedonian revolt of 149 BC (in which Thrace was heavily involved) was put down, Rome aimed to stabilize the area by establishing client kings in Thrace. These continued until AD 46 when the country was annexed and made into a province. It became one of the most important Danubian provinces of the Roman empire, and protected the lines of communication from Macedonia to Bithynia and Asia Minor via Byzantium. Barbarian ravaging of Thrace, which began with the Goths passing through in a swathe of destruction, continued in the 4th and 5th centuries AD.

Under Byzantium, Thrace, especially along the Black Sea littoral, continued to be an area of Hellenic culture, as it had been in the Graeco-Roman period. Bulgarian churches show strong Byzantine influence. The earliest surviving example, dating from the 5th century AD at Nessebur (Greek Mesembria), was constructed as a conventional basilica, with aisles added in the 8th century when the main arcade columns were changed to square piers. Medieval churches exist throughout Bulgaria, many dating from the second Bulgarian empire (late 12th–13th centuries), and most have the typical Greek cruciform plan. Many contain frescos demonstrating very strong Byzantine influence, particularly the Ivanovo rock churches. Monasteries, 150 at the peak, flourished as centres of Christian culture and literacy, Rila and Bachkovo among the most prominent. They house very fine collections of illuminated manuscripts and icons, which, once again, betray the closeness of links with Byzantium. Many Bulgarian monks lived and worked on Mount Athos.

The Bulgars, a non-Indo-European people, had a long migrant history before entering Europe in the wake of the Huns. They crossed the Danube in the second half of the 7th century AD and settled in Moesia (modern Bulgaria), gradually fusing with the resident Slavs and spreading further to the south and west. From khan Krum's defeat of the Byzantine emperor Nikephoros I in 811, Byzantium's most disastrous defeat for a considerable time, until the overwhelming victory of Byzantium at Kleidion in 1014, the first Bulgarian empire was a power with wide dominion over the mid-Balkans. Christianity was accepted in 865 at the hands of Sts Cyril and Methodios, the former devising the Glagolitic alphabet, based on Greek characters, which is the ancestor of most modern Slav scripts. Although all of Bulgaria passed back to Byzantine control, the Church remained autonomous. The second Bulgarian empire lasted from the late 12th century for less than a hundred years. The centre of Balkan power moved into Serbia and the whole of Bulgaria passed under Turkish control in the 14th century.

In the first half of the 19th century many monasteries were restored: Rila, Troyan, Bachkovo, and Preobrazhenski were repainted by Zakhari Zograph from Samokov, who also worked on Mount Athos. This reflects the importance of the Church in stimulating a "national revival". Modern Bulgaria arose from a nationalist revolt in the 1870s, combined with the Ottoman decline and strong pan-Slavist Russian support. The other Great Powers intervened to prevent the Bulgaria (including most of Macedonia and part of the Thracian seaboard) envisaged in the San Stefano treaty of 1878 disappearing. Northern Bulgaria achieved de facto independence under nominal Turkish suzerainty; Eastern Roumelia, newly autonomous within the Ottoman empire, joined it in 1885 (a position not regularized until formal Bulgarian independence in 1908); and other territories were added from Turkey (including western Thrace) and lost (to Greece – western Thrace; Romania and Serbia) as a result of the two Balkan Wars of 1912–13 and World War I. Between the wars a limited population exchange of Greeks and Bulgarians took place. Until 1944 Bulgaria skilfully avoided participation in World War II but used its German alliance to reoccupy many lost territories and much of its San Stefano inheritance. Disaster struck in September 1944: the country found itself simultaneously at war with Germany and Russia and undergoing a communist-backed putsch. Territory was lost again and the Bulgarian elite cut down on a scale not seen since Kleidion.

GOCHA R. TSETSKHLADZE

See also Bulgaria, Bulgars

Summary

The boundaries of Thrace, a region bordering the north Aegean, have changed much over the centuries. Greek colonies were established on the Black Sea coast from the 7th century BC. From the Classical (Odrysian) period much metalwork and jewellery of Greek craftsmanship survives. Thrace was even more Hellenized in the Hellenistic period. It became a Roman province in AD 46. Under Byzantium it remained an area of Greek culture. Its borders have changed frequently since the creation of modern Bulgaria in the 1870s.

Further Reading

Archibald, Z.H., *The Odrysian Kingdom of Thrace*, Oxford: Clarendon Press, and New York: Oxford University Press, 1998

Boardman, John, *The Diffusion of Classical Art in Antiquity*, London: Thames and Hudson and Princeton, New Jersey: Princeton University Press, 1994

Cook, B.F. (editor), *The Rogozen Treasure*, London: British Museum, 1989

Dimitrov, Bojidar, *Bulgaria: Illustrated History*, Sofia: Borina, 1994

Fol, Alexander and Ivan Marazov, *Thrace and Thracians*, London: Cassell, and New York: St Martins Press, 1977

Ganev, Stefan and Aleksandur Vulchev, *Sreshti s neprekhodnite bogatstva na Bulgariia* [Aspects of the Cultural Heritage of Bulgaria], Sofia: Kiril i Metodii, 1995

Isaac, Benjamin, *The Greek Settlements in Thrace until the Macedonian Conquest*, Leiden: Brill, 1986

Marazov, I. (editor), *Ancient Gold: The Wealth of the Thracians: Treasures from the Republic of Bulgaria*, New York: Abrams, 1998

Stancheva, Magdalina (editor), *The Bulgarian Contribution to the World Cultural Heritage*, Sofia: Technika, 1989

Venedikov, Ivan and Todor Gerassimov, *Thracian Art Treasures*, Sofia: Bulgarski Houdozhnile, 1975

Thucydides

Athenian historian of the 5th century BC

Thucydides was a member of an Athenian aristocratic family which owned gold mines in Thrace and was connected at least by friendship, possibly also by marriage, with the local Thracian aristocracy. In 424 BC, during the Peloponnesian War between the Athenian empire and the alliance headed by Sparta, he held an amphibious command on the Thracian coast, but went into exile in consequence of his failure to prevent the Spartan capture of a strategically valuable city. He returned to Athens in 404 BC, when all the exiles were recalled, and died probably about 395 BC.

According to his own account, when the Peloponnesian War began in 431 BC he decided to write its history. This ambition was not completely realized, because his work, which survives, ends abruptly in the winter of 411 BC, though passages elsewhere refer clearly to the end of the war in its 27th year. His account (book 8) of the 20th and 21st years differs in character from books 1–7, and may represent a stage intermediate between a first draft and a final version. Histories of the last six years of the war were written by others in the 4th century BC.

Thucydides was not the first major Greek historian, for Herodotus' history of the Persian invasion of Greece appeared a generation earlier, but he was nevertheless a pioneer who did much to shape the form and nature of subsequent historiography. In particular, he put speeches, condensed in language and thought, into the mouths of his personages on critical or otherwise memorable occasions. The most famous has long been the funeral speech of his Pericles in book 2, at the burial of the war dead of 431 BC. The speeches are sophisticated in language and replete with moral, political, and psychological generalizations. There are, of course, abundant speeches in Homeric epic, and quite a number in Herodotus, but Thucydides is peculiar in that he had been present on some of the occasions which he adorns with speeches, and could have learned much about the rest from contemporaries. Aware of the role of the spoken word in determining the decisions of the Greek city states, in his preface he divides the content of his work into "what was said" and "what was done", and claims that he had recourse to inventing what speakers "needed" to say only when he could not recall or discover what they actually said. The extent to which this claim is compatible with what we read in his text (in books 1–3 speeches amount to nearly a third of the whole) is a focus of controversy which is likely to continue. Whatever his own intention, he unwittingly set a bad example to later historians, Greek and Roman alike, who, writing for a culture devoted to the art of oratory, assumed the right to invent speeches.

In narrative his style is usually simpler than in speeches, and sometimes vivid and dramatic, but his generalized descriptions of situations (for example, the moral effects of the plague in book 2 and the disastrous spread of civil strife in book 3) are hard going. He experiments with syntax, deploys a stock of unusual abstract nouns (some probably coined by him), and often seems to be trying to convey too much in too few words. Our problems as readers might well be solved if we could hear him reading his own text aloud and could note his placing of stress and pause. Since ancient literary critics could no more do that than we can, they found him a difficult author and often disagreed over his meaning.

Such experimental language is one aspect of the tendency among intellectuals in his time to innovation and rejection of tradition. Save in one doubtful instance, he is sceptical about oracles, never attributes historical events to divine intervention, and gropes after scientific explanations of natural phenomena. In these respects he is much nearer to early medical writers than to Herodotus; indeed, he seems to have modelled his description of the plague on them, though differing from them in terminology. In a few articulate intellectuals the shift from a religious to a scientific world view generated the idea that the good and admirable person is the one who (following the law of nature) imposes his will on others for his own self-aggrandizement. Thucydides certainly does not think that. The belief that he does, still widespread, is generated by the error of treating arguments put forward in this or that speech as if they were his own.

He is undeniably an impressive, magisterial writer, professing strong attachment to accuracy and adopting a detached view which only rarely wavers under pressure from his emotional reactions and predilections. A sombre tone manifest in some of his observations on human behaviour may also be inferred from some of his apparently "deadpan" statements, and this has given him, over the centuries, a reputation for integrity, profundity, and wisdom. He was extensively read and studied in Byzantium; Procopius in the 6th century AD borrowed whole passages, and in the 12th century, while the scholar Tzetzes was exasperated by Thucydides' obscurity, Anna Komnene strewed her history with unusual Thucydidean expressions, thereby enlarging the gulf between classicizing language and the vernacular of her time. Thucydidean language and style (with some injections from Herodotus and Polybius) continued to serve as a model for Byzantine historiography; a notable example is the work of the emperor John VI Kantakouzenos in the 14th century. He was translated into Latin by Lorenzo Valla in 1452, and into English in 1628 by Thomas Hobbes, who idolized him, not least for his exposure of what Hobbes regarded as the follies of democracy.

In Greece, Neophytos Doukas prepared an edition of Thucydides with Latin translation, published in Vienna in 1805. Korais in his *Hellenic Library* ignored Thucydides, either because Doukas had got in first or because Thucydides was unedifying and insufficiently philosophical. The difficulty of the language came to be recognized as a serious obstacle to Thucydides' attainment of the central place in educational curricula that his fame might seem to justify, and in 1920 the statesman Eleftherios Venizelos embarked on a translation into a somewhat literary demotic Greek, published posthumously in 1937. Venizelos believed (as Thucydides himself did, to judge from what he says in his preface) that constants in human behaviour are such that a careful and wise account of an ancient war abounds in political lessons which are still valid.

But *is* Thucydides "careful and wise"? Is he even a reliable authority on the details of his narrative? In the 20th century no other Greek author has been subject to so heavy a revisionist onslaught. A general decline in reverence reminds us that a gifted writer can profess devotion to truth and then compose a narrative that is largely fiction. Modern standards of historiography make us aware that a narrative such as Thucydides' comprises many thousands of data, of which only a very small fraction can be checked against other relevant evidence. On topographical matters he is sometimes wrong; and when what he says is irreconcilable with what is said by later historians patently drawing on independent sources, we cannot simply assume that he, the master, must be right. No later historians, of course, can be treated as "confirming" him, because they may be drawing on him. He virtually never reveals, let alone discusses, his sources, but expects us to trust him to have put the right questions to his informants and to have pursued them until he got what we would regard as adequate answers. He very often makes firm statements about the hopes, fears, plans, and ambitions of individuals, and it is a failure of historical curiosity on our part if we do not ask, "How did he know?" There is a certain arrogance in his declaration that he begins his history with an account of the causes of the war "so that no one need ever seek to discover how so great a war arose"; little did he know how much would be written in our time on precisely that question.

Historians are necessarily selective, for otherwise their task would never be done, but selection presupposes at least a tentative interpretation, no matter what may be added or subtracted in the definitive interpretation. Given massive evidence, it is easy to discern what underlies a particular historian's selectivity, but our evidence for the Peloponnesian War is far from massive. The most interesting aspect of Thucydides' selectivity is his allocation of space: four lines on the massacre at Scione, six pages for the dialogue between Athenian and Melian negotiators preceding the siege and eventual massacre at Melos. Selection apart, it is suspected that Thucydides on occasion went beyond mere exaggeration, beyond an illegitimate slide from "must have been" to "was", and had recourse to fiction in order to assimilate his narrative to the theatrical unfolding of a Greek tragedy. The implausible role which he consistently assigns to pure chance in the account of the fighting at Pylos (in book 4) is notably vulnerable to this suspicion. However, the evidence that he embraced fiction on that occasion and may possibly have done so on others falls far short of proving that he had any intention of turning historical exposition systematically into myth. A chain of tragic events must necessarily resemble tragedy, and before denying Thucydides the status of historian we would need to discount the immense quantity of down-to-earth details which constitute by far the largest ingredient of his work.

KENNETH DOVER

See also Historiography, Peloponnesian War

Biography

Born to an aristocratic Athenian family which owned gold mines in Thrace, Thucydides fought as a general in 424 BC. After a period of exile he returned to Athens in 404. His history of the Peloponnesian War survives but is incomplete, ending in 411. He died *c.*395 BC.

Writings

Thucydides, translated by Benjamin Jowett, revised by W.H. Forbes and Evelyn Abbott, 2 vols, Oxford: Clarendon Press, 1900; Jowett's translation revised and abridged by P.A. Brunt, as *The Peloponnesian Wars*, New York: Twayne, 1963

Thucydides, translated by C. Forster Smith, revised edition, 4 vols, Cambridge, Massachusetts: Harvard University Press, 1928–30 (Loeb edition; many reprints)

History of the Peloponnesian War, translated by Richard Crawley, edited by W. Robert Connor, London: Everyman, 1993

Further Reading

Adcock, F.E., *Thucydides and his History*, Cambridge: Cambridge University Press, 1963; reprinted Hamden, Connecticut: Archon, 1973

Connor, W. Robert, *Thucydides*, Princeton, New Jersey: Princeton University Press, 1984

Dionysius of Halicarnassus, *On Thucydides*, edited and translated by W. Kendrick Pritchett, Berkeley: University of California Press, 1975

Dover K.J., *Thucydides*, Oxford: Clarendon Press, 1973; with addenda, 1978

Finley, John H., Jr., *Thucydides*, Cambridge, Massachusetts: Harvard University Press, 1942

Finley, John H., Jr., *Three Essays on Thucydides*, Cambridge, Massachusetts: Harvard University Press, 1967

Gomme, A.W., Antony Andrewes and K.J. Dover, *A Historical Commentary on Thucydides*, 5 vols, Oxford: Clarendon Press, 1945–81

Hornblower, Simon, *Thucydides*, London: Duckworth, 1987

Hornblower, Simon, *A Commentary on Thucydides*, 2 vols, Oxford: Clarendon Press, 1991–96 (vol. 1: books 1–3; vol. 2: books 4–5.24)

Hunter, Virginia J., *Thucydides: The Artful Reporter*, Toronto: Hakkert, 1973

Rawlings, Hunter R. III, *The Structure of Thucydides' History*, Princeton, New Jersey: Princeton University Press, 1981

Romilly, Jacqueline de, *Histoire et raison chez Thucydide*, Paris: Belles Lettres, 1956

Romilly, Jacqueline de, *Thucydides and Athenian Imperialism*, translated by Philip Thody, Oxford: Blackwell, 1963, reprinted New York, Arno Press, 1979

Stahl, Hans-Peter, *Thukydides: Die Stellung des Menschen im geschichtlichen Prozess*, Munich: Beck, 1966

Timaeus

Historian of the 4th–3rd centuries BC

Timaeus of Tauromenium in Sicily, a Greek historian of the front rank, was born in the middle years of the 4th century BC and died in the late 260s BC in advanced old age. Naxos, the original home city of his family, was destroyed by Dionysius I of Syracuse in 403 BC. In 358 BC Timaeus' father Andromachus gathered together all the surviving Naxians and settled them at Tauromenium. There Timaeus was born and there he lived until the mid-310s BC when he was exiled by the tyrant Agathocles of Syracuse. He took refuge in Athens where he spent the next 50 years, first studying under a former pupil of Isocrates, and subsequently researching and writing in that city's libraries, for which he was derided by Polybius as a pedant and an armchair historian par excellence. Possibly he died at Athens.

As a preliminary to his historical work he researched (at Olympia) and published a study of Olympic victors to which he appended, apparently in the form of tables, the corresponding sequences of Spartan kings and ephors, Athenian archons, and priestesses of Hera at Argos. Greek chronology at the time was a highly complex and bewildering affair that hampered the task of serious historians. Timaeus' system of reckoning by Olympiads, though by no means perfect, marked a definite advance and was a commendable effort to impose order on chaos. It was adopted by Polybius, who otherwise had no kind words for Timaeus. Though he lived and worked at Athens, like many another émigré, Timaeus' attention was constantly turned towards the country of his origins, his concern as a historian being the history and achievements of western Hellenism. His *Histories*, in 38 books, were a detailed study of the Greeks of the west, of Sicily in particular, from earliest times until the death of Agathocles in 289/88 BC. To this magnum opus he added a further composition that dealt with the wars in Italy against Rome of king Pyrrhus of Epirus, and which brought events in the west in general down to 264 BC. And this therefore became Polybius' starting point.

As one of the earliest and best of Hellenistic historians, Timaeus' work seems to have combined with some success the various strands and tendencies of Greek historical writing that had been developing since the late 6th century BC. Into a framework of straightforward political and military history (what Polybius called a "pragmatic" history) he incorporated much else of diverse nature, very much in the mould of Herodotus and Ephorus. On the other hand, the unwelcome tendency to dramatize, and indeed sensationalize, historical narratives by, for instance, emphasizing and developing further appropriately pathetic elements in a story, a characteristic of much of Hellenistic historiography, appears to have been a feature of Timaeus too. Furthermore, his Sicilian background and experiences clearly conditioned his work and help to explain certain aspects of it that gained its author notoriety. One such aspect was the extreme hostility with which he dealt with the tyrannies of Dionysius I, Dionysius II, and Agathocles at Syracuse, which took up most of the 4th century BC, a most important period for western Hellenism. As Polybius and Diodorus Siculus pointed out, blinded by personal hatred Timaeus seriously distorted the record of history. The other side of the same coin, which Polybius likewise criticized as a falsification of history, was Timaeus' propensity, when the above tyrants and their associates were not involved, to idealize Siceliots and their achievements.

Yet even when his personal feelings were not involved, Timaeus, it would seem, was far readier to censure than to praise, a trait that earned him the epithet (a play on his name) of "Epitimaeus", meaning the "fault-finder". He was not a respecter of persons, the greatest writers and thinkers being criticized alongside persons of humbler accomplishments. The surviving fragments do not enable us to draw any firm conclusions as to his motives, but in some instances certainly a passion for accuracy appears responsible, as when he criticized Ephorus' arithmetic. Diodorus has preserved for us the respective figures for Carthaginian armaments given by Ephorus and Timaeus and we see that in every instance Timaeus' numbers are far more moderate and realistic. The merits of the *Histories*, therefore, outweighed the flaws and it is not surprising that such a detailed and readable account, one moreover set against a firm and lucid chronological framework of Olympiads, quickly established itself as the standard account

of western Hellenism and the western Mediterranean in general, and so it remained for centuries. Undoubtedly a contributory factor here was what Timaeus said about Rome. He was not the first Greek historian to refer to Rome, but he was one of the first to appreciate the city's significance and certainly the first to present a fairly detailed and connected account of Rome's early steps on the international scene. As such he exerted considerable influence on Roman historiography.

P.J. STYLIANOU

See also Historiography

Biography

Born in the mid-4th century BC at Tauromenium in Sicily, Timaeus was the son of Andromachus of Naxos who refounded Tauromenium in 358 BC. Timaeus was exiled by Agathocles of Syracuse in the mid-310s and moved to Athens where he studied and wrote his *Histories*, a study of the Greeks of the west in 38 books. He died c.260 BC.

Writings

In *Die Fragmente der griechischen Historiker*, no. 566, edited by Felix Jacoby, Leiden: Brill, 1923–

Further Reading

Brown, Truesdell S., *Timaeus of Tauromenium*, Berkeley: University of California Press, 1958
Momigliano, Arnaldo, *Essays in Ancient and Modern Historiography*, Oxford: Blackwell, and Middletown, Connecticut: Wesleyan University Press, 1977, pp. 37 ff.
Pearson, Lionel, *The Greek Historians of the West: Timaeus and his Predecessors*, Atlanta: Scholars Press, 1987

Tinos

Island in the Aegean

The small island of Tinos lies to the northwest of the main group of the Cyclades, with an almost equal distance separating it from Andros to the northwest and Mykonos to the southeast; it has an area of 60 sq km. The interior is hilly, with a major mountain formation, called Mount Tsiknia, rising to 713 m in the east of the island; where crops can be grown, often by means of terracing, it is mainly fertile. The silk grown here was the most prized throughout the Cyclades, and for several centuries in the post-Byzantine period it was exported to Italy and France where it was widely bought as a Tiniot speciality.

According to an early tradition, the island abounded with snakes, and due to this it was known as Ophiousa; by tradition, Poseidon sent storks to eliminate the snakes, and the grateful Tinians built a famous temple dedicated to him. In 480 BC Xerxes forced the islanders to serve in his navy in the war with Greece, but before the battle of Salamis one of their ships was able to desert and tell the Greeks of the Persian plans. "For this reason the Tinians were inscribed upon the tripod at Delphi among those who overthrew the barbarians" (Herodotus, 8. 82). In 378 BC the islanders joined the Athenian confederation and fell under Macedonian control in 338 BC after the Battle of Chaeronea.

Like most of the Aegean islands Tinos suffered from Arab raids in the 9th and 10th centuries, but medieval sources do not mention the island until 1204, when it appears in the Deed of Partition as being one of the eight islands awarded to the Latin emperor; but Venetians, in the persons of Andrea and Geremia Ghisi, were already in occupational control by 1207 as vassals of the emperor. This association with Venetians was to last longer in the case of Tinos than with any of the other Aegean islands, and it was to be more than 500 years before they finally left, being forced by the Turks to evacuate their castle of Exobourgo only in 1715. The Venetian attitude to their last Aegean colony seems to have been equivocal, because an 18th-century engraving of the castle indicates that its fortifications could not have been extensively modernized, and that their commander could never have been expected to hold it against the overwhelming might of the Turkish forces; yet on his return to Venice he was tried and imprisoned for his act of supposed cowardice. In the peace agreed with the Turks in 1540 Tinos, with Crete, Cyprus, and some of the Ionian islands, had been even then the only Aegean island still to remain in Western hands.

Due to this long Western presence Tinos always had (and continues to have) the largest Roman Catholic population of any of the Aegean islands; in the 17th century their number was greater than all the rest of the Cyclades together. Tinos also came to be linked closely with Mykonos, and for centuries the two islands shared a Latin bishop. Today a large Roman Catholic Neoclassical church (renamed in 1895 as the church of the Sacred Heart), and an Ursuline school for girls at Loutra, remain as evidence of the continued Western involvement here.

Tiniots, both Orthodox and Catholic, became known in the 17th and 18th centuries for their industry and honesty, in contrast to the Naxiots. The islanders took part in the War of Independence with other islands of the Cyclades, but in 1833 their individualism took the form of a minor insurrection against the regency, which resulted in the imposition of martial law. The event that may have ultimately contributed more to the modern fame of Tinos, both within the Hellenic sphere and in the world outside, and has certainly brought substantial wealth to the island, was the "discovery" in 1822 of an icon of the Virgin which is believed to have miraculous powers. It was made by a nun, Pelagia, and every year on 25 March and 15 August the island is visited by thousands of pilgrims coming to honour it, many climbing the street from the harbour to the large church of the Panagia Evangelistria on their knees.

PAUL HETHERINGTON

See also Cyclades

Summary

One of the Cyclades, Tinos was occupied by the Mycenaeans. In antiquity it was said to be famous for snakes. In later periods it was famous for its silk. It was in Venetian hands from 1207 to 1715, longer than any other Aegean island, which accounts for its large Roman Catholic population. It has been a centre of pilgrimage since the "discovery" in 1822 of an icon to which miracle-working powers have been attributed.

Further Reading

Miller, William, *Greek Life in Town and Country*, London: Newnes, 1905

Miller, William, *The Latins in the Levant: A History of Frankish Greece, 1204–1566*, London: John Murray, and New York: Dutton, 1908; reprinted Cambridge: Speculum Historiale, and New York: Barnes and Noble, 1964

Miller, William, *Essays on the Latin Orient*, Cambridge: Cambridge University Press, 1921; reprinted New York: AMS Press, 1983

Setton, Kenneth M., *The Papacy and the Levant, 1204–1571*, vol. 2, Philadelphia: American Philosophical Society, 1978

Slot, B.J., *Archipelagus Turbatus: Les Cyclades entre colonisation latine et occupation ottomane, c.1505–1718*, 2 vols., Leiden: Nederlands Historisch-Archaeologisch Instituut te Istanbul, 1982

Woodhouse, C.M., *Modern Greece: A Short History*, 5th edition, London and Boston: Faber, 1991

Tiryns

Bronze Age city in the Argolid

Tiryns is described by Homer as "wall-girt" and, in the catalogue of ships, it formed part of the realm of Diomedes, ruler of Argos. The north/south division of the Argive plain that this implies may now be justified on recently expanded evidence of the Bronze Age road system. In myth Tiryns was the seat of Eurystheus who inflicted the 12 labours on Heracles, and thus features in several of Pindar's odes.

The site lies in the southeast of the Argive plain on an isolated limestone knoll rising some 20 m above the surrounding area; it divides naturally into three sections known as the Oberburg, Mittelburg, and Unterburg. Geomorphological work indicates that in the Late Bronze Age the sea lay only 1 km from the foot of the knoll. Tiryns may thus have been the main port for the Argolid at a period when boats were beached rather than moored or anchored. In the 12th century BC the settlement extended widely around the site. Lack of evidence for this feature from earlier periods is thought to be the result of deep deposition from a flash flood that buried the settlement under alluvium. To prevent further inundation an extensive barrage was built higher up the valley to divert the torrent into another streambed. A hill to the southeast has two tholos tombs built into the west face and a series of chamber tombs (15 fully excavated) on the east. Further cemeteries for the 15th to 12th centuries BC remain to be found.

Excavation was begun in 1831 by Friedrich Thiersch and Alexander Rizos Rangabé and continued by Heinrich Schliemann in 1876. From 1884 Schliemann with Wilhelm Dörpfeld carried out a systematic exploration for the Deutsches Archäologisches Institut, which continued at intervals until 1929. Restoration of the walls was initiated by the Greek Archaeological Service in the late 1950s and led to discoveries requiring further excavation. In 1965 the DAI resumed its work under the direction of Klaus Kilian; the work of publication and clarification continues despite his early death.

Settlement on the site dates back to the Neolithic period (5th millennium BC) but the earliest architectural remains of importance belong to the Early Helladic period. A round building was built on the top of the citadel; it is considered to be one of the series of large monumental buildings built for public or elite use in the EH II period (early 3rd millennium BC) but is the only one of this particular type known to date.

The site was continuously occupied but there are only scattered remains of structures before the Mycenaean period. Then a series of major buildings, usually known as palaces, were constructed on the Oberburg and fortifications of Cyclopean type built around each of the three sections of the site. Several features are particularly notable. A room floored with a single slab of limestone is identified as a bathroom. The so-called galleries are passages that led to storerooms, all corbel-vaulted and built within the thickness of the fortification walls. A similar passage, this time curving, led through a bastion to a small west gate. On the west side of the Unterburg two similar passages led through the wall and underground at a distance of c.30 m to sumps where water collected, thus affording an emergency supply of water approachable only from within the walls.

In post-Mycenaean times, probably in the Geometric period, the central megaron was divided and a small temple created. This was dedicated to Hera. To the same period may be assigned the final square phase of an altar in the inner courtyard. Well-equipped tombs of the Protogeometric and Geometric periods have been excavated from immediately south of the citadel. A notable find has been identified as a helmet of Protogeometric date. To the Archaic period can be assigned a group of unique votive offerings including terracotta shields painted with scenes of warfare and gorgon masks as well as many more usual small terracotta figures of women. Also of the Archaic period are inscriptions carved on the upper outer face of the stones that roofed the passages leading to the underground water supply. These indicate that the partially destroyed wall was used at this point as seating for the population in an assembly. Tiryns joined with Mycenae in sending troops to fight the Persians at Platea in 479 BC, and a decade later suffered a similar destruction at the hands of the Argives. The population is said to have migrated to Haleis (modern Porto Cheli) at the southern end of the Argive peninsula, where numismatic evidence supports the claim.

Strabo describes Tiryns in terms similar to those he uses for Mycenae, as a site once famous and now without significant habitation. Pausanias mentions only the walls. In Roman times an olive press was constructed inside Tholos I. A small Middle Byzantine church was built over the inner side of the outer wall at the south of the Oberburg. Around it were several graves. Both church and graves as well as a threshing floor that had been built above them were removed in excavation to reveal the Mycenaean site.

The first description of the site by European travellers is by the French envoy de Monceaux in 1668. Around the start of the second Venetian occupation of the Morea (1686), Piero Antonio Pacifico states that the site was barely inhabited; unfortunately he does not give a description. It appears correctly placed on the maps of Barbié de Bocage (late 18th century) and is mentioned by many 19th-century travellers. Among the illustrations that they made, a watercolour by Rottmann (now in the Graphische Sammlung, Munich) and a sketch by Edward Lear (J. Fitton collection) are particularly attractive. Others indulge in a rather Gothic interpretation of the massive masonry.

Finds from all periods, though mainly pottery, are exhibited in Nauplia while the outstanding finds of the Mycenaean period, including frescos, the carved stone base of a throne, and a group of small objects of various dates known as the Tiryns Treasure are on display in the National Museum in Athens. Following structural damage there is only restricted access to the site for visitors.

ELIZABETH FRENCH

See also Mycenaeans

Summary

Located in the southeast of the plain of Argos, Tiryns was inhabited from the Neolithic period. A series of major buildings (palaces) dates from the Mycenaean period when it was (in myth) the seat of Eurystheus. It may have been the port for the Argolid. There are some remains from the Archaic period but Tiryns was destroyed by Argos in the 5th century BC.

Further Reading

Iakovidis, Spyros E., *Late Helladic Citadels on Mainland Greece*, Leiden: Brill, 1983
Iakovidis, Spyros E., "Das Werk Klaus Kilians", *Athenische Mitteilungen*, 108 (1993): pp. 9–27
Jantzen, Ulf (editor), *Führer durch Tiryns*, Athens: Deutsches Archäologisches Institut, 1975 (with full bibliography)
Mylonas, George E., *Mycenae and the Mycenaean Age*, Princeton, New Jersey: Princeton University Press, 1966
Schliemann, Heinrich and Wilhelm Dörpfeld, *Tiryns: The Prehistoric Palace of the Kings of Tiryns*, London: John Murray, and New York: Scribner, 1886
Zangger, E., "Landscape Changes around Tiryns during the Bronze Age", *American Journal of Archaeology*, 98/2 (1994): pp. 189–212

Tobacco

Tobacco was first cultivated in Greece during the early years of 17th century. Because Greece is a mountainous country with a climate marked by long dry periods in summer, the cultivation of tobacco was a natural choice. The regions that are major tobacco producers are Macedonia, Thrace, to a lesser extent Thessaly, and some parts of western Greece where the weather and soil conditions are ideal for the cultivation of the product.

Before the First Balkan War (1912–13), the districts that accounted for much of the production of tobacco were under Turkish occupation and most tobacco farms were in the hands of few Turkish landlords. Many of the landlords were nobles with limited agricultural education. They usually resided in Constantinople or Thessalonica, and had very little knowledge of or interest in the technological developments that might have enabled them to intensify and modernize the cultivation of the product. Absent from their lands, they relied entirely on the uncertain productive capacity of their tenants. These tobacco growers, working under various restrictive practices, inadequately equipped, using traditional methods of cultivation, having to bear various tax abuses and extortionate credit terms, were heavily dependent on weather conditions. There was little incentive to increase tobacco output since any additional profits were unlikely to end up in their pockets. Small independent tobacco growers, on the other hand, although more efficient as producers, suffered from similar disadvantages and were probably more vulnerable to bad crops than tenants since they were not always self-sufficient in labour, given the manpower that tobacco production requires. The harvest was sold mainly to Greek and foreign merchants, at prices dictated by them, to be exported.

With the annexation of Macedonia to Greece and after the Asia Minor disaster of 1922, a number of laws were passed redistributing most of the fertile land to the impoverished tenants and refugees. The arrival of refugees, many of whom were tobacco growers, resulted in an increase of the skilled labour force and the introduction of modern cultivation methods. The cultivation of tobacco was one of the main activities of the refugees, especially in Macedonia and Thrace. The revenue gained from selling the crop greatly mitigated their hardships in those difficult times and accelerated the restoration of their livelihood in their new home.

The tobacco industry greatly benefited in the early 1930s from an increasing demand for the oriental type of tobacco that Greece produced in large quantities. Prices doubled and tripled in a few years, a development that significantly improved the living conditions for both cultivators and retailers. According to some estimates, 10 per cent of an area cultivated with wheat, if planted with tobacco, could give an export value 10 times greater than the whole of the area under wheat cultivation. Greek firms were gaining ground in the international markets not only with the trading of tobacco but also with the production of cigarettes, at home and abroad.

The presence of Greek cigarette manufacturers in Egypt is particularly notable. The majority of them settled in the country after a monopoly granted by the Porte in 1897 to a firm in Constantinople for the production and sale of tobacco. Egypt had the advantages of a very cheap labour force, easy access to a great variety of Greek and Turkish leaf tobacco needed for the production of superior-quality cigarettes, and a dry climate which, although unsuitable for growing anything but low-quality tobacco, was ideal for processing the imported leaf into cigarettes. Despite their dynamism, the Greek cigarette manufacturers in Greece and abroad before the start of World War II faced a number of internal and external problems such as lack of modernization and fierce competition from foreign capital. Most Greek manufacturers in Egypt in the late 1930s were unable to compete efficiently with the foreign firms and sold their factories. The same to a lesser extent was true of manufacturers in Greece.

Until the early 1930s, state policy with regard to the tobacco industry and the agricultural sector in general suffered from a lack of coordination of means and ends. This reflected in part the emphasis of the national economic policy towards the development of a sufficient industrial base. The tobacco industry was seen only as a source of income, as is evident from a series of laws relating to control of production and tax evasion. Gradually the importance of the tobacco industry, which employed more than a sixth of the working population, was recognized, and the state took measures to support it. One of the plagues from which producers suffered greatly, given the unavailability of credit, was usury. Banks were reluctant to take over the extremely risky business of financing the small farmers, since commerce was a far more remunerative occupation. For this reason, in 1929, the state established the Agricultural Bank of Greece which set favourable credit conditions for farmers in general and tobacco producers in particular.

After World War II the Greek tobacco industry, with its structural inefficiencies (such as the small size of farms for historical reasons and the low level of modernization), suffered a great setback from the changing tastes of the world market. Oriental tobacco went out of fashion and the American blend was preferred, so Greek tobacco farmers lost their competitive advantage as they had specialized in the former. The foundation of cooperatives was promoted in order to resolve the problems of the size of farm holdings and the low bargaining power that individual producers had in the market. In 1957 the National Board for Tobacco was founded in order to implement and coordinate the state policies with respect to the tobacco industry.

The state increasingly supported the tobacco industry and the agricultural sector in general which was important for social as well as economic reasons. The principal objectives with respect to the tobacco industry included the raising and stabilizing of income and living standards of the farming population, the increase of productivity, and the cultivation of new varieties in accordance with international demand. Because of the political influence of the rural population, subsidies and price supports had been used as income aids. Gradually the policy concentrated increasingly upon support for the tobacco producers through intervention in the market rather than through direct income aids. The National Board for Tobacco became the means of supporting tobacco growers by its marketing and trading operations.

The admission of Greece to the EEC (now the European Union) gave tobacco cultivators, through the Common Agricultural Policy (CAP), great benefits and opportunities to modernize their business in order to compete more efficiently in the marketplace. But the CAP failed to achieve its targets not only because of the farmers' complacency but also because of an escalating antismoking campaign and changing consumer tastes. Nowadays, the Greek tobacco industry is gradually losing the subsidies provided by the state and the CAP as the result of World Trade Organization treaties, and it faces its greatest challenge. If radical measures are not taken soon, the economic survival of tobacco cultivators in Greece without any state support is questionable.

DIMITRIOS GKAMAS

See also Agriculture, Industry

Further Reading

Agra Europe, *Greek Agriculture since Accession: Situation and Outlook*, Tunbridge Wells, Kent: Agra Europe, 1981

Avdelidis, P., *To Agrotiko Synergistiko Kinima stin Ellada* [The Co-operative Movement in Greece], Athens, 1986

Choumanidis, L., *Oikonomiki Istoria tis Ellados* [Economic History of Greece], Athens, 1990

Gounaris, Basil C., *Steam over Macedonia, 1870–1912: Socio-economic Change and the Railway Factor*, Boulder, Colorado: East European Monographs, 1993

Kitroeff, Alexander, *The Greeks in Egypt, 1919–1937: Ethnicity and Class*, London: Ithaca Press, 1989

Zographos, D., *Istoria tis Ellinikis Georgias* [History of Greek Agriculture], Athens, 1976

Tourism

Tourism, in the sense of travel undertaken for pleasure, was probably not a common feature of ancient Greece, or in fact of the ancient world as a whole, where the conditions of travel must generally have been far from pleasant. Poor and dangerous roads, uncomfortable inns, expensive and inconvenient transport, and rampant piracy must all have contributed to discourage travel as a pastime.

Ancient travellers, however, the wealthy ones in particular, shared many of the objectives of tourism as we know it today: rest, recreation and relaxation, education, religious, cultural, and aesthetic experience, sports, food, shopping, and social contact. They may have retreated to the mountains or the seaside in summer to get away from the congestion or the boredom of the city, as suggested, for instance, by Lucretius (*De Rerum Natura*, 3. 1301–1318). Others probably visited curative thermal spas in search of relief from ill health. In the absence of diplomatic establishments, they relied on guest-friendships between families of different regions.

Although mass tourism is a relatively modern phenomenon, travellers throughout the ages have reacted as tourists, whatever the original purpose of their journeys may have been. From early times seaborne trade, in particular, was closely associated with sightseeing, even though the Greeks, at least those of the Homeric epics, did not show much enthusiasm for seagoing. Yet Odysseus, the ancient traveller par excellence, was admired as one who had seen many cities and visited many nations. Roman country estates and watering places and medieval centres of religious pilgrimage no doubt represent the small beginnings of a tourist industry. Some of the spas frequented by the Romans attracted pleasure seekers as centres of luxury, gambling, and high living. Due to its prestige as a cultural centre Athens, even after losing political importance, continued to attract Romans with pretensions to learning. The Greek and Latin graffiti on pharaonic monuments and the papyrus (*Tebtunis Papyri*, 1902–38, 1. 33, p. 58 in Bagnall and Derow's edition) detailing instructions to prepare for a Roman senator's visit to the Fayum prove that in Roman Egypt sightseeing had come into its own. Memphis and the Fayum, Thebes, and the Valley of the Kings were popular destinations. On the Nile the Ptolemies employed great luxurious houseboats known as *thalamegi*. With the growing popularity of Panhellenic sanctuaries and the growth of academically prestigious centres, travel for spiritual and intellectual purposes must have become more common; in any case, sightseeing received monumental conceptualization in the idea of the seven wonders of the world. These consisted of the greatest achievements of ancient technology, architecture, and art known to Greek and Roman writers, which were visited during the Hellenistic age and remained the most famous attractions of the Roman world. The list first appeared around 130 BC in a poem by Antipater of Sidon included in the *Greek Anthology*, and a treatise on the subject (probably from the time of the Roman empire) has been attributed to the engineer Philo of Byzantium (*fl.* 146 BC). The canon originally consisted of the pyramids of Giza in Egypt, the city walls of Babylon, the hanging gardens of Babylon, the temple of Artemis at Ephesus, the statue of Zeus at Olympia, the Mausoleum at Hallicarnassus, and the colossus of Rhodes. Listings from Pliny's time onwards generally substitute the Pharos lighthouse at Alexandria for the city walls of Babylon.

One of the earliest Greeks known to have gone abroad (at least ostensibly) for the purpose of seeing the world was the Athenian statesman and poet Solon (*c.*640–*c.*558 BC). Although he belonged to an aristocratic family, he was poor in his young days and travelled as a merchant to enrich himself. But after promulgating his laws he travelled to Egypt and Lydia as a tourist (Herodotus, 1. 30). Herodotus (*c.*480–*c.*425 BC) himself travelled widely in order to gather material for his *Histories*. He was intrigued by the customs of Egypt, where nothing was done as in Greece. His theme was the conflict between the Greeks and the Persians, and he personally visited many of the regions that made up the Persian empire. He was preceded in this respect by the geographer Hecataeus of Miletus (*fl. c.*500 BC) who compiled a book entitled *Journey round the World* (*Periodos Ges*), a sort of itinerary, based partly on his own travels, in which he described countries, their inhabitants and customs, animals, and curiosities, and included local fables. A map (which may have been an improvement on an earlier one by Anaximenes) was appended to it. The authenticity of this book, which survives only in fragments, has sometimes been questioned, but is now generally accepted. Fragmentary also is the descriptive work *On the Cities in Greece* by Heraclides Criticus of the 3rd century BC (ed. F. Pfister, 1951). The Roman elite, and above all emperors, pursued travel as a pastime. Hadrian (AD 117–38), a Hellenist who spoke Greek better than Latin, travelled in all the provinces, and built at Tivoli near Rome a vast villa in which the finest buildings he had seen on his travels were reproduced on a small scale.

The only work of ancient travel literature that has come down to us in its entirety is the *Description of Greece* (*Hellados Periegesis*) of Pausanias who, in the middle of the 2nd century AD, travelled throughout the Greek mainland visiting the principal cities (including Athens) and religious sanctuaries such as Olympia and Delphi. His work is a guidebook for tourists, in which he describes in succession various parts of Greece, and he enumerates their most worthy possessions including statues, pictures, tombs, and sanctuaries, giving their etymology, narrating anecdotes, legends, and historical episodes. He related in detail what he saw, and his book is particularly valuable for information about Classical works of art and buildings no longer extant. He also provides much information about customs, religion, and social life in Greece under the Roman empire. He mentions rivers, roads, and villages, curious customs and superstitions, but references to scenery and natural products are rare, and he shows little interest in economic aspects of the country or in its inhabitants.

The extirpation of piracy by Pompey and Augustus and the unification of the Roman empire by the latter gave greater security to travel, though it was still vulnerable to weather conditions, the menace of robbers and brigands, and the many discomforts of ancient transport. The development of travel necessitated the growth of infrastructure, which in its turn encouraged voluntary travel by the provision of support in the form of inns, eating places, etc., though the elite often preferred to rely on reciprocal hospitality. Travelling for pleasure was no doubt enhanced by geographical writing which grew in parallel with mobility in general.

Tourism: a group of visitors view the remains of Mycenae

There was a marked shrinking of the scope of travel in the Byzantine world after the 7th century and the horizons of mobility rarely spread beyond Baghdad in the east, Alexandria in the south, France in the west, and the northern coast of the Black Sea, although we occasionally hear of journeys to India, the Baltic regions, and England. Although Constantinople was visited by travellers from the east and the west (especially after the 11th century), the Byzantines themselves did not travel much. The travellers mainly comprised merchants, officers on government business, ambassadors, and pilgrims and patients visiting shrines of healing. Travel was rarely undertaken for education or pleasure. In the *Lives* of saints we hear of monks travelling to Jerusalem or Rome. Unlike merchants, however, who preferred to travel in groups employing professional ass drivers, these holy men liked to travel by themselves or in pairs. Travellers went on foot or rode horses, mules, or donkeys, or carts drawn by horses and oxen, and the rich were sometimes carried on a litter. But the preferred mode of travel was by ship, which was easier, faster, and cheaper. The travel literature of the period concentrated mainly on Palestine, Egypt, Constantinople, and Rome. It comprised mainly *hodoiporiai* or guidebooks for pilgrims and descriptions of pilgrimages. Their interest was largely directed to religious monuments and relics, sometimes including tales of wonder-working, accounts of diplomatic missions, and the adventures of captives.

In more recent times tourism has been encouraged by changes in aesthetic thought that awakened fresh enthusiasm for the beauties of untamed nature. This change was accompanied by a newfound enthusiasm for antiquity and its ruins and remains. Thus, in 1788 the 72-year-old Abbé Jean-Jacques Barthélémy published, after working on it for 30 years, *Voyage du jeune Anacharsis en Grèce*, which purported to describe the physical appearance, antiquities, institutions, customs, and coins of Greece in the 4th century BC as seen by a Scythian traveller. Much of its success was due to its vividly detailed topographical descriptions, but its author had never set foot in Greece. The clear and intense sunlight of Greece was one of the favourite topics of the numerous visitors to the country in the 19th century who recorded their experiences in an unprecedented proliferation of travel memoirs.

This romantic sensibility stimulated the craving for viewing and sightseeing that is the prerequisite for the evolution of modern tourism. Thanks to the industrial revolution long-distance travel has become comfortable and attractive through safer and faster modes of transport on both land and sea, and Greece and the Greek islands are among today's most popular holiday resorts and centres of tourism.

Tourism has benefited many of Greece's industries, chief among them being the service industry. Since the 1950s many hotels have been built to cater for the rapid increase in tourism. Athens, which is one of the most historic cities in the world, attracts about 90 per cent of all travellers to the country at some point in their stay. In 1998 nearly 11 million foreign visitors came to Greece, the greatest numbers coming from (in descending order) Germany (some 2.1 million), the United Kingdom, Italy, the Netherlands, and France (nearly half a million). The most popular primary destinations for these visitors were (in descending order) Rhodes (with nearly 9 million), Herakleion, the remaining Dodecanese (excluding Rhodes), Athens, and Corfu (with just over 3 million).

D.P.M. WEERAKKODY

See also Travel

Further Reading

André, Jean-Marie and Marie-Françoise Baslez (editors), *Voyager dans l'antiquité*, Paris: Fayard, 1993

Angelomatis-Tsougarakis, Helen, *The Eve of the Greek Revival: British Travellers' Perceptions of Early Nineteenth-century Greece*, London and New York: Routledge, 1990

Augustinos, Olga, *French Odysseys: Greece in French Travel Literature from the Renaissance to the Romantic Era*, Baltimore, Maryland: Johns Hopkins University Press, 1994

Bagnall, Roger S. and Peter Derow, *Greek Historical Documents: The Hellenistic Period*, Chico, California: Scholars Press, 1981

Burkart, A.J. and S. Medlik, *Tourism: Past, Present and Future*, 2nd edition, London: Heinemann, 1981

Casson, Lionel, *Travels in the Ancient World*, London: Allen and Unwin, 1974; reprinted Baltimore: Johns Hopkins University Press, 1994

Clayton, Peter A. and Martin Price, *The Seven Wonders of the Ancient World*, London and New York: Routledge, 1988, reprinted New York: Routledge, 1996

Eisner, Robert, *Travelers to an Antique Land: The History and Literature of Travel to Greece*, Ann Arbor: University of Michigan Press, 1991, reprinted 1993

Stoneman, Richard, *Land of Lost Gods: The Search for Classical Greece*, London: Hutchinson, and Norman: University of Oklahoma Press, 1987

Stoneman, Richard, *A Literary Companion to Travel in Greece*, revised edition, Harmondsworth: Penguin, and Malibu, California: Getty Museum, 1994

Stoneman, Richard, *A Luminous Land: Artists Discover Greece*, Malibu, California: Getty Museum, 1998

Town Planning

In the Neolithic settlement of Chirokitia on Cyprus (c.5500 BC) we encounter one of the first examples of a street. It runs uphill from the bank of the Maroniou river, crosses the settlement, and descends on the opposite side. In modernday Athens archaeologists can trace the path of ancient roads under some of the paved streets. Clearly streets are among the earliest signs of town-planning efforts, underscoring the element of continuity in human settlements. Our experience of the urban environment, however, is not limited to the street layout and its two-dimensional representation on a map. Towns also gain their character from their governing institutions, their civic and religious buildings, their residential quarters, their open spaces, the goods they produce and trade, and their relationship to the surrounding regions.

The plan of ancient Athens, one of the best-studied cities of antiquity, was largely consolidated in the 6th century BC. At that time the Acropolis, once a defensive fort, became dedicated to the deities, and the first administrative buildings were erected in the Agora, the city's political and social centre. By the end of the 6th century BC the Agora defined a quadrilateral area, bounded by magnificent buildings. Other public works were carried out throughout the city, including water and sewer networks. A new road system was established, originating from the Agora. Outside the city there existed three gymnasia, for the military, athletic, and academic training, respectively, of the male youth. Urban legislation, dating also from the 6th century BC, forbade burials inside the city and controlled new building, while the city architect was charged with the maintenance of temples and other public structures. There was, therefore, an already established town-planning tradition that dictated the city's urban affairs, even though the street network remained irregular – "Attic", as it was often called – following closely the site's topography, rather than a prescribed orthogonal geometry. After the destruction of Athens by the Persians in 480 BC the Athenians could have redesigned their city in a regular manner. Instead, they adhered to tradition and rebuilt it along the same lines, this time surrounding it by a new set of walls. The Persians were finally defeated in 479 BC and the Athenian statesman Pericles marked this victory by initiating a completely new building programme on the Acropolis, with the erection of the Parthenon (447–432 BC), the Erechtheum (421–405 BC), and the temple to Athena Nike (427–424 BC), all dedicated to the goddess Athena.

Unlike Athens, the city of Miletus in Asia Minor, which was also destroyed by the Persians, was rebuilt in 479 BC following a regular plan of orthogonal blocks. Possibly the earlier settlement there was also regular. One of its residents, Hippodamus, who was fairly young at the time, might have participated in the city's rebuilding. Later he undertook the design of Piraeus (c.460 BC), Thurii in southern Italy (444–43 BC), and, allegedly, of Rhodes in 408–407 BC. In 432 BC the city of Olynthus in Chalcidice was laid out according to the Hippodamian manner. Its grid of parallel and perpendicular streets defined mostly identical building blocks, with some variations among the individual property lots.

Hippodamus is the only architect and planner whose name has come down to us from Greek antiquity. He certainly did not invent regular, orthogonal planning, since there are several earlier examples of regularly planned settlements from around the world. Greek colonial settlements in southern Italy and Asia Minor also adhered to regular, orthogonal planning. According to Aristotle:

> he was the first who, not being actually engaged in the management of public affairs, set himself to inquire what sort of government was best; and he planned a city state, consisting of 10,000 persons, divided into three parts, one consisting of artisans, another of husbandmen, and the third of soldiers; he also divided the lands into three parts, and allotted one to sacred purposes, another to the public, and the third to individuals.

(*Politics*, 2. 8)

Hippodamus was one of the first urban theorists and philosophers to reflect on the relationship between a society and its urban environment. His legacy has been associated primarily with regularly planned cities, made up of streets that follow an orthogonal grid.

According to Plutarch, Alexander the Great founded approximately 70 new cities. After his death his successors continued to establish numerous new cities in northern Greece, Egypt, Asia Minor, and Anatolia. They all followed the regular, Hippodamian plan, the simplicity of which facilitated expeditious settlement and land allocation. Thessalonica, an important Hellenistic centre, was founded by Cassander in 316 BC, and laid out in orthogonal building blocks measuring 100 ¥ 50 m. Two major east–west roads, on the site of modern Agiou Dimitriou and Egnatia Streets, traversed the city and led to the city gates. Open public areas contained the ancient agora, a sacred precinct, a stadium, a gymnasium, and a Serapeum. The modern city was redesigned after a catastrophic fire in 1917, but a careful examination of the pre-1917 plan allows us to recognize the Hellenistic grid that ordered it originally. Other prominent Hellenistic cities included Alexandria in Egypt, Pergamum and Priene in Asia Minor, and Damascus, Palmyra, and Dura Europus in modern Syria.

We can also gather significant information on the town-planning practices of the Hellenistic period from *De Architectura,* the only surviving architectural treatise from antiquity. Written by the Roman architect Vitruvius (*c*.90–*c*.20 BC), it makes reference to famous Greek architects and their building methods. Vitruvius outlined site considerations for a new city: healthy location, moderate climate, protection from hot winds, and examination of the animals living on the site. "I cannot too strongly insist upon the need of a return to the method of old times", he wrote. "Our ancestors, when about to build a town or an army post, sacrificed some of the cattle that were wont to feed on the site proposed and examined their livers" (*De Architectura*, 1. 4).

After Greece became a Roman province in 146 BC, some of its cities became the beneficiaries of imperial building programmes, while others fell into oblivion. In Athens under Julius Caesar and Augustus the Roman Agora and the Library of Hadrian – both structures located east of the ancient Greek Agora – were erected. Hadrian, the philosopher-emperor (AD 117–38), endowed Athens with a number of buildings and laid the foundations for a new city, Hadrianopolis, on the site of the modern National Garden, Zappeion, and Constitution Square. As a sign of gratitude, the Athenians erected a dedicatory triumphal arch that marked the city of Theseus, on one side, and the city of Hadrian, on the other side. Roman town planning was also based on an orthogonal grid, punctuated by the *cardo* and *decumanus*, the two main streets meeting at right angles at the Roman forum. Thessalonica, which retained its Hellenistic grid, enjoyed a building boom in the years of the Antonines (end of the 2nd century AD), as is evident from the Roman forum, the stoa of the Incantadas, the exedra, and other epigraphic evidence. Also significant is the imperial complex of Galerius Maximianus, built around AD 305, in the southeastern part of the Roman city. It consists of the Rotunda, the arch of Galerius, the palace, the octagon building, and the hippodrome. The north–south axis of the complex follows the orientation of the already established street network.

During the Byzantine era most cities preserved their earlier street network and continued to maintain their public buildings, often adding new structures that included aqueducts, cisterns, baths, hospitals, and churches. New defensive city walls were erected, protecting not only the urban but also the rural population in case of enemy attacks. The ancient Greek gymnasia, stadia, and theatres were gradually replaced by the hippodrome. Used for race tracks but also for political meetings and rallies, the hippodrome came to replace the ancient Greek agora. Eventually, the singular focus of the ancient agora was superseded by the multiple focal points of the neighbourhood, the parish churches. Parishes became administrative divisions that were preserved in the subsequent Ottoman period and are in effect to this day.

Important Byzantine urban centres such as Thessalonica maintained their significance under Ottoman rule. Although the street network was not altered, cities acquired an Ottoman physiognomy with the addition of new religious and civic buildings. The outlines of the minarets and the prominently positioned mosques signalled to both visitors and residents the presence of a new political and religious power. Baths, khans, caravanserais, poorhouses, fountains, and coffee shops brought together the diverse population and forged a common lifestyle among them. Travellers during the Ottoman period were often unable to distinguish between the houses of Christian and Muslim inhabitants. Travelling building groups were responsible for the most complicated structures – bridges, inns, etc. These groups often worked throughout the empire and adapted their building vocabulary to regional practices, working for both Christian and Muslim patrons.

The War of Independence (1821–27) and subsequent formation of the modern Greek kingdom in 1833 marked a break with the existing conditions. Originally, the new kingdom did not contain any of the major urban centres of the Greek world, namely Thessalonica, Ioannina, Constantinople, Smyrna, and Alexandria. The liberated territory was primarily agrarian, none of its small towns and villages containing more than 15,000 inhabitants. Following the destruction of the war, many of these settlements had been ruined or abandoned, the population seeking refuge in the countryside. One of the main intentions of the 19th-century administrations was the establishment of a unified, rational, urban network throughout the country, initiated by the capital and comparable to prevailing western models. Newly imposed grid lines sought to erase most historical particularities of existing towns and villages that had developed along irregular street systems. Planning legislation also aimed at establishing homogeneity among the rebuilt or newly built towns and villages. The territorial expansions of the state in 1864 and 1881 offered further opportunities for regularized town-planning projects, while generous contributions from wealthy Greeks of the diaspora endowed the capital and other cities with new and imposing civic buildings. By the end of the 19th century more than 170 plans were approved for the foundation of new towns and the restructuring of existing ones. Planning alone, however, did not guarantee a town's economic and cultural prominence. The cities that flourished the most were well-established commercial centres such as Piraeus, Athens, Patras, and Hermoupolis.

In the 20th century the borders of Greece expanded to incorporate Macedonia, western Thrace, and the Dodecanese, while its population grew dramatically after the arrival of 1.2 million Greek refugees, mainly from Asia Minor. The urgent needs for housing and accommodation dictated the state's planning efforts, while the powerful post-1960s wave of urbanization tested the state's ability to control and direct future growth. The issues facing Greek planners today are global, rather than regional or national. Cities and towns have to accommodate local, immigrant, and transient populations, balance the needs of economic growth with the protection of the natural and cultural environments, and pursue the goals of a unified Europe while showing respect for local histories, traditions, and aspirations.

ELENI BASTÉA

See also Cities, Urbanization

Further Reading

Bastéa, Eleni, *The Creation of Modern Athens: Planning the Myth*, Cambridge and New York: Cambridge University Press, 2000

Bierman, Irene A., Rifa'at A. Abou-el-Haj, and Donald Preziosi (editors), *The Ottoman City and Its Parts: Urban Structure and Social Order*, New Rochelle, New York: Caratzas, 1991

Hastaoglou-Martinidis, Vilma, "City Form and National Identity: Urban Designs in 19th-Century Greece", *Journal of Modern Greek Studies*, 13/1 (May 1995): pp. 99–123

Hoff, Michael C. and Susan I. Rotroff (editors), *The Romanization of Athens*, Oxford: Oxbow, 1997

Kostof, Spiro, *A History of Architecture: Settings and Rituals*, 2nd edition, Oxford and New York: Oxford University Press, 1995

Travlos, John, "Poleodomia" [Town Planning] in *Istoria tou Ellenikou Ethnous* [History of the Greek Nation] vol. 3b, Athens, 1972, pp. 328–33

Travlos, John, "Poleodomia" [Town Planning] in *Istoria tou Ellenikou Ethnous* [History of the Greek Nation] vol. 5, Athens, 1974, pp. 469–77

Vitruvius, *Ten Books on Architecture*, translated by Morris Hicky Morgan, New York: Dover, 1960; also translated by Ingrid D. Rowland, Cambridge and New York: Cambridge University Press, 1999

Wycherley, R.E., *How the Greeks Built Cities*, New York: Norton, and London: Macmillan, 1962; 2nd edition, 1976

Trade

Trade has always played an important role in the economic and social life of Greece. The earliest evidence for some kind of formal trade (both national and international) comes from the Bronze Age, when the Minoans and the Mycenaeans were interacting with Asia Minor, Cyprus, the Levant, Egypt, and Italy. This is mainly attested by several exotic materials found on Crete and the Greek mainland and by Aegean pottery found in the areas mentioned above. In addition, there are numerous references in Egyptian 18th-Dynasty sources to "Keftiu", which appears to be the equivalent of Caphtor and to be associated with Crete and the Aegean. Whether these exchanges were palace-administered or "free-enterprise" is not easy to say. The Linear B tablets (in the Mycenaean script) do not even mention the word "trade" but the shipwrecks of Ulu Burun and Cape Gelidonya (off the Turkish coast) indicate that some sort of free entrepreneurs were "tramping" from port to port,

making various goods available to Greeks, Cypriots, Syrio-Palestinians, and Egyptians. Both the Minoans and the Mycenaeans mainly imported luxury goods such as gold, ivory, ostrich eggs, and lapis lazuli, but also copper, which was very important for them.

After the fall of the Mycenaean civilization around 1200 BC these exchanges did not cease completely, but became less organized than previously. The period from 1200 to 800 BC, which is widely known as the Greek Dark Ages, is considered as a time of poverty, isolation, and illiteracy. One would therefore expect a complete breakdown of such exchanges. The sites of Lefkandi in Euboea and Knossos in Crete, however, have yielded large numbers of high-value Near Eastern imports such as gold jewellery and ivory objects, indicating frequent contacts with the eastern Mediterranean.

It is not a coincidence that the Euboeans were the first Greeks to establish colonies in the west (such as Pithekoussai) and to participate in the development of multinational emporia in the east (Al Mina) during the 8th century BC. The commodities most sought after in the west were metals – iron, copper, and tin. Soon other Greek cities, such as Corinth, Rhodes, and Chios, founded colonies in the west (mainly in southern Italy and Sicily). These colonies, although politically independent, still kept close trade links with their mother city.

By 600 BC Greek trade was flourishing, mainly due to the establishment of permanent trading posts in Egypt (Naucratis), the Levant, and Etruria. In Greece some of the most important trading cities were Corinth, Megara, and the island of Aegina. It was during this time that Athens started to develop as a major commercial centre. The distribution of black-figure ware is the clearest indication of the growth of Athenian trade. In the period 560–520 BC Attic pottery reached most of the Aegean islands, Asia Minor, Cyprus, the coasts of the Black Sea, Egypt, southern Italy, Sicily, and southern France. The most important Athenian import was corn.

The conquest of the east by Alexander the Great in the 4th century BC widened the field of operation open to Greek trade. His successors carried exploration even further and we see, for example, the Seleucids securing the route to India and the Ptolemies encouraging the development of the trade route around southern Arabia. The most traded goods were grain from Egypt and the Crimea, silk from China, gold from Nubia, silver from Asia Minor and Iberia, wine from north Syria, and slaves. Most of our information about trade patterns during the Hellenistic period comes from the distribution of large pottery containers known as amphorae which survive in huge numbers and whose handles used to be stamped with a state's symbol. Many of them are Rhodian and are found in Alexandria. From this we can infer that Rhodes was a major exporter of liquids, with Alexandria being a major recipient.

By the 2nd century BC Delos had become one of the most important commercial centres, especially after 166 BC when the Romans made it a free port. Unfortunately, the most traded commodity was slaves, something that attracted large numbers of Roman businessmen there. It is said that tens of thousands of slaves could pass through Delos in a single day.

During the Byzantine era trade increased. Few cities have enjoyed so magnificent a commercial site as the capital of the empire, Constantinople, located on the sea channel between the Aegean and the Black Sea and the land bridge between

Europe and Asia. From the earliest years of the Byzantine empire most of its emperors took a keen interest in trade. Especially from the 5th century onwards, emperors such as Anastasius and Justinian managed to gain control of the most sensitive areas for trade near the Red Sea. By the 6th century Byzantium had become the principal intermediary between east and west. The main trade goods were silk from China, aloes, cloves, and sandalwood from Indo-China, pepper from Calliara, various herbs from India, and precious stones from Sri Lanka. It was the trade in silk, however, that made the Byzantine empire so wealthy. All these goods arrived at Constantinople both by land and by sea. The land route passed through Persia and the sea route through Sri Lanka. Most of the goods were carried by Abyssinian ships to the Red Sea, and from there by imperial ships to the Byzantine customs station at Jotabe near Suez.

In the 9th and 10th centuries Byzantine trade was at its height. Far Eastern and Indian goods continued to reach Constantinople in large quantities. At the same time, trade with the north started to develop. Furs, dried fish, amber, and slaves were the main imports from Russia and central Europe. In the west Bari was the principal Byzantine trading post. Gradually, however, the Italian merchant fleets took over, and by the end of the 10th century the Adriatic was in the hands of the Venetians.

The 11th century marked the beginning of the decline of Byzantine trade. The Seljuks conquered most of Asia Minor, destroying the organization and infrastructure of the imperial commerce in the area. Norman invaders captured important trade centres such as Corinth and Thebes and carried off silk-worms to Italy, breaking the Byzantine monopoly. Finally, the crusades changed the trade routes of the east, to the detriment of Constantinople. Goods no longer travelled through the Byzantine capital but were shipped at the ports of Latin Syria and carried by the Italians directly to the west, avoiding the customs dues of the empire. After that, Byzantine trade never managed to recover.

After the fall of Constantinople in 1453 and for the next two centuries Greek merchants mostly interacted with central Europe and especially Austria, Hungary, Serbia, and Romania. During the 16th century the most traded goods were cotton, wine, and tobacco, which were mainly distributed by the Macedonian traders located in Budapest and Temesvar. This Greek presence in central Europe had some very important implications for the Greek economy. The inflow of money from these traders back to their places of origin stimulated the underdeveloped mountainous areas of the Greek mainland, and created opportunities for further development. For example, in areas such as Epirus and western Macedonia, small cities started to develop that gradually became commercial and cultural centres.

For the 18th century most of the information available to us comes from the French archives. The most common Greek exports were agricultural products and especially grain and cotton from the Peloponnese and Crete. Imports consisted of industrial products mainly coming from western Europe, food supplies from Russia, and wax from Romania.

In the 19th century and during the reign of king Otho foreign trade flourished. According to Thiersch (quoted in Christopoulos, 1970–79), in 1832 Greece had a merchant fleet consisting of 2000 ships and about 30,000 families working in the business. The main trade centres were Nauplia and the islands of Spetsae, Syros, and Hydra. In the years 1855–60 a new increase in trade occurred. Corinthian raisins were the primary export, with Britain being the main recipient. Greece imported iron from Britain, timber from Austria, cereals from Turkey, and coffee from France. From 1858 onwards it started to export large quantities of wine and olive oil, mainly to Russia, Austria, and Turkey.

Greek trade experienced some growth during 1906–07, a slight fall during 1908–09, and a new rise in 1910. At the same time, the Greek merchant fleet acquired large numbers of steamships. In 1915 it consisted of 475 steamships with a capacity of about 893,650 tons; it was the 11th largest fleet in the world with 2 per cent of world tonnage. During World War I and despite the great difficulties, the Greek merchant fleet not only survived but produced huge profits. It is estimated that in a normal year the Greek merchant fleet produced profits of about 30 million francs (the common currency of Greek trade at the time). In the first year and a half of the war profits rose to about 200 million francs. After the end of the war, Greek trade continued to grow both in quantity and in value. The main exports were tobacco, raisins, olive oil, and wine which accounted for 75 per cent of the total exports during 1919–23. The main destinations were Britain, the United States, and Germany. Imports consisted of cereals, linen, coal, and metals, with the United States being the main supplier.

During the early 1930s a new trade policy was implemented in Greece. Its basic principal was that imports should be paid for by the profits from exports. Under this system, known as "clearing", Greece imported goods only from those countries that accepted Greek products of the same value. By 1936 76.5 per cent of Greek trade was carried out in this way. The period from 1940 to 1950 was very problematic for Greek trade due to World War II and the Civil War that followed. By the early 1960s, however, the total volume of Greek foreign trade had increased by more than 50 per cent over that of the 1930s. Exports still consisted mainly of agricultural products (about 81 per cent of all exports in 1963) and imports mainly of industrial products such as machinery and transportation equipment. During that period Greece was heavily dependent on eastern Europe for trade expansion.

The acceptance of Greece into the European Economic Community (EEC) in 1981 offered significant economic improvement through wider markets for Greek products. Exports now included textiles, clothing, fruits, and vegetables, primarily going to Germany, Italy, and France. Imports included crude petroleum, ships and boats, and chemicals, mainly from Germany, Japan, Italy, and Saudi Arabia. Since the early 1970s Greek-owned merchant shipping has ranked first in the world fleet in terms of tonnage, a distinction it still holds today with 16 per cent of world tonnage.

IOANNIS GEORGANAS

See also Colonization, Ships and Shipping, Slavery

Further Reading

Casson, Lionel, *Travel in the Ancient World*, London: Allen and Unwin, 1974; Baltimore: Johns Hopkins University Press, 1994

Casson, Lionel, *Ships and Seafaring in Ancient Times*, London: British Museum Press, and Baltimore: Johns Hopkins University Press, 1995

Tsigakou, F.-M., *The Rediscovery of Greece: Travellers and Painters of the Romantic Era*, New York: Caratzas, 1981

Xenophon, *The Art of Horsemanship*, translated by Morris H. Morgan, Boston: Little Brown, 1893; London: J.A. Allen, 1962; as "On Equitation" in *Ancient Greece Horsemanship* by J.K. Anderson, Berkeley: University of California Press, 1961

Tragedy

Greek tragedy matured in Attica in the 5th century BC. With one possible exception, all of the surviving plays date from this time and were written by Athenians for competitive performance at dramatic festivals, notably the City (or Great) Dionysia (from at least the end of the 6th century BC) and the Lenaea (from the 430s BC). There were also performances at the Rural Dionysia. Productions were not confined to Attica and there are traditions that earlier forms of tragedy originated in the northern Peloponnese. The main festivals were important civic and political occasions with a strong religious framework expressed in sacrifice, ritual, and processions. There were performances of dithyramb and comedy as well as tragedy. The tragedy competition was part of the Athenian culture of public display, also evidenced in the gymnasium, law courts, and Assembly. Each contestant entered a trilogy followed by a satyr play. Judges were selected by lot from across the tribes and their votes were delivered by secret ballot. Victories were listed in public records (*didaskalia*). These records, although fragmentary, help with dating.

The origins of tragedy are somewhat obscure. Aristotle (*Poetics*) put forward an analysis that has strongly influenced subsequent debate. He suggested that early tragedy was improvised by the leading performers of the dithyramb, a choral song and dance in honour of Dionysus, and that it was also influenced by the satyr play. Aristotle also gives an account of 5th-century BC developments affecting staging, the balance between choral and spoken words, and the increase in the number of actors from two to three. He emphasized the concept of the tragic hero and argued that tragedy inspired in the audience the emotions of pity (for suffering that was largely undeserved) and fear (because the hero represented the human condition). As a result, the audience would experience catharsis or relief of these emotions, tempered by a sense of satisfaction at recognizing and learning about moral and spiritual truths.

This combination of powerful emotions and the political context of popular democracy was thought by Plato to be dangerous. In the *Republic* he associated tragedy with his criticisms of poetry, especially Homer. Drama and poetry were to be banished from education in Plato's ideal state because he thought that they were concerned with representation rather than reality. He held that their appeal to the imagination and their portrayal of the extremes of divine and human behaviour were morally and politically subversive.

Greek tragedy is a prime example of the theatre of convention. These conventions cover staging, subject matter, and form. The main contextual conventions are that the plays were staged in large, open-air theatres as part of a performance culture embedded in civic and religious life. All actors were male. The City Dionysia had a tradition of competition by choruses. The financing of the chorus (including its maintenance and training) was undertaken as a liturgy (or public service) by a wealthy citizen, appointed by the eponymous archon who also chose the three tragedians who were to be "granted a chorus". The visual nature of the theatre spectacle, with its large audiences (perhaps in excess of 14,000 at the major festivals), had considerable impact on performance styles, especially masks, costume, gesture, and movement. The archaeological evidence for the orchestra, the part of the theatre where the chorus performed, between the stage and the audience, dates from the 4th-century BC theatre at Epidaurus. In the 5th century BC the stage and its buildings (*skene*) were probably wooden with steps down to the orchestra. Stage machinery for tragedy included the *ekkyklema*, a wheeled platform for set-piece displays (such as Sophocles' Ajax surrounded by the carcasses of the animals he had slaughtered in mistake for the Greek leaders). The *mechane*, a crane, enabled "flying" entrances and exits of the gods. Literary sources and vase paintings suggest that masks had stock features according to the character represented. Taken together, masks and the size of the theatre precluded the use of facial expression, thus putting more emphasis on grand gesture, costume, music, and choreography, as well as on the rhetorical force of the dialogue. Masks also facilitated the doubling of roles.

The subject matter of tragedy was also bound by conventions. With one exception all the surviving plays are based on stories from myth. These were part of the common culture of Greece, expressing values often shaped by the Homeric poems and transmitted by the rhapsodes' performance of epic, particularized in vase painting and sculpture, and given local associations through cult. However, these myths, with their stories about the relationships between gods and heroes and their dilemmas of rivalry, revenge, murder, and betrayal in peace and war, were not presented by tragedians as fixed icons of the past. They were reworked and reinterpreted and, because of their indeterminate historical provenance, they provided a distanced but culturally influential setting for the exploration of suffering and the examination of moral and religious imperatives. The selection of particular myths and contrasts in the ways in which they were treated provide important insights into changes in attitude and artistic aims as well as a commentary on Greek perceptions of the relation of myth to the contemporary world and its problems. The surviving exception (others are lost) to the convention of mythological setting is Aeschylus' *Persians* (472 BC), which depicts the aftermath to the Persian defeat by the Greeks at the Battle of Salamis, although the Persian setting maintains the remoteness from Athens that is a feature of most tragedy. A striking feature of tragedy, created in a society that subordinated and marginalized women, is that a significant proportion of the protagonists are female (e.g. Antigone, Medea, Hecuba) and that issues of gender and power are presented from a variety of perspectives.

The formal conventions within which the plays were constructed also served to distance tragedy from over-ready identification with everyday life. Of these conventions, the most important are the chorus, the various types of verbal

Tragedy: a performance of Euripides' *Suppliant Women* at one of the Delphic Festivals staged by Angelos Sikelianos and Eva Palmer, late 1920s

exchange, and the lament. The chorus consisted of 12 or 15 singers and dancers who performed in the orchestra, providing for the audience a collective mediation of the moral and religious implications of the action of the tragedy. Their entry song (*parodos*) was supplemented by lyric exchanges with the actors and by the choral ode (*stasimon*). Reconstruction of the music and dance in tragedy is speculative and so presentation of the chorus has been difficult for modern productions, especially those that take place in a commercial or studio theatre. There were normally five choral performances in a tragedy and the episodes between these were the focus of sung or spoken exchanges. These might include the narration, often in a messenger speech, of vital events, including violence, which by convention took place off stage. Even more important was the formal debate or *agon* between two main characters. This usually included the dramatic device of *stichomythia*, in which actors spoke alternate lines or pairs of lines. Conventionally, a sung lament (*kommos*) expressed the pent-up emotions produced by the dramatic tension and the suffering of the hero. The ways in which these formal conventions are refined or varied provide significant insights into the work of the different writers.

Major parts of the work of three 5th-century BC tragedians have been preserved, while others are represented only by fragments. Aeschylus has seven plays extant and records indicate that he gained 13 victories. Sophocles wrote more than 120 plays and won at least 20 victories, 18 of them at the City Dionysia. Seven plays survive. Euripides had a less consistent record, with four victories at the Dionysia. He wrote about 90 plays, of which 19 survive.

The reception and transmission of tragedy in antiquity from the 4th century BC onwards shaped the responses of later ages. Fifth-century plays were performed and read in the 4th, when there was legislation to prevent wholesale changes to the text. In 386 BC a competition for revivals was established at the City Dionysia, but the 4th century BC also included important new work, and tragedians such as Archestratus, Astydamas, Carcinus, Chaeremon, and Theodectes are either mentioned by Aristotle or were themselves the subject of revivals in the 3rd century BC. The "family" archives of theatre practitioners were a significant means of preserving previously unperformed plays and an influential feature of the widespread demand for performance was the development of powerful guilds for actors (Craftsmen or Artists of Dionysus) with their own institutions and privileges.

Adding to the early demand for Athenian tragedy in Sicily and Macedonia, Alexander the Great's policy of establishing Greek cities in the east both spread Hellenic culture and exposed it to the contributions of non-Greeks. At Alexandria in Egypt the process of canon formation intensified from the 3rd century BC onwards with the collection together of selected plays of Aeschylus, Sophocles, and Euripides and the addition of commentaries. Demand for the availability of texts for education may have helped to make this a self-replicating operation. Greek tragedy also entered the culture of the Roman Republic through the plays of Ennius, Accius, and Pacuvius. In the 1st century AD Seneca's tragedies, nine of which survive, violently orchestrated the situations and some of the formal elements of the Greek corpus. Senecan tragedy strongly influenced Renaissance theatre, especially in Italy, France, and England.

Once the Roman empire was Christianized and the centre of power shifted to Byzantium, tragedy was again regarded as dangerous, because it was a pagan art form and part of a theatre culture that the Church regarded as obscene (since it involved cross-dressing) and blasphemous (since it invoked the name of Dionysus). State funding for the traditional dramatic festivals was withdrawn and drama exiled to the melange of popular events in the Hippodrome. The alternative to suppression was appropriation and some features of the language and rhetoric of tragedy were absorbed into political and religious life. There was, however, continued artistic interaction between the tradition of tragedy and new work. For example, an undated Byzantine tragedy *Christos Paschon* drew heavily on Euripides, particularly the *Bacchae*, in its exploration of the suffering of Christ.

In Greece itself cultural activities that attracted crowds were forbidden during the 400-year period of Turkish domination after the fall of Constantinople, but tragedy continued to be performed in the Greek communities on the Danube and in Bucharest, Odessa, and Jassy, cities controlled by Russia. The ancient theatre became an icon of Hellenic identity and a symbol of the desire for freedom, notably in the Hellenic Carta, designed by Rigas Pherraios (1797) at a time when translations of tragedy were being widely circulated among Greeks, especially in the diaspora. More radically, the *Philiki Hetaireia*, which promoted rebellion against the Turks, regarded the establishment of a Greek theatre as a means of ensuring the translation of historical and cultural awareness into revolutionary action. After Greek independence (1821) the association between Greek tragedy and freedom influenced drama and poetry in other literatures, including the work of Byron and Shelley.

In 1867 the (Roman) theatre of Herodes Atticus in Athens was used for a revival of *Antigone*, performed by students with music by Mendelssohn, and in the early 20th century Angelos Sikelianos and his wife Eva Palmer developed the "Delphic Idea". This aimed at establishing at the *omphalos* (the navel of the earth at Delphi) a university based on a spiritual and communal ideal of world peace. A festival was held in 1927 at which tragedy was performed, together with athletics and folk dancing. Part of the performance of Aeschylus' *Prometheus Bound* has been preserved on film. In 1930 another festival was held, which also included Aeschylus' *Suppliants*. There was some criticism from the radical press that such festivals were inaccessible to the public and encouraged cultural nostalgia, but the staging of the plays stimulated debate about performance styles and there were further productions at Constantinople and Alexandria.

Regular productions of tragedy were also instituted by the Greek National Theatre (founded 1930), which in 1938 performed Sophocles' *Electra* at Epidaurus, where a festival was instituted in 1954. The Piraiko Theatre and the Theatro Technis also established distinct traditions in the performance of tragedy, as did the National Theatre of Northern Greece and the innovative Amphi-Theatro. More than 20 ancient theatres have been brought into use, with regular productions at the Athens and Epidaurus festivals.

Discussion and experiment were further encouraged by the European Cultural Centre at Delphi, founded in 1964 to encourage cultural exchange among all nations. In recent years performances of tragedy in Greece have included *Antigone* by an Inuit company, *Oedipus Tyrannus* by the Central Academy of Drama of Beijing as well as Noh- and Kabuki-inspired productions directed by Tadaski Suzuki (Japan), and the Epidaurus Festival performance of Aeschylus' *Oresteia*, directed by Peter Hall and translated into English by Tony Harrison.

Following the Sikelianos *Prometheus in Chains*, film has presented tragedy in both realistic and experimental forms, using myth as a catalyst for invention, as did the tragedians. Work by Greek artists includes *Electra* (Sophocles, directed by Zarpas, 1962), *Antigone* (Tzavellas, 1961), *Electra* (Euripides, directed by Cacoyannis, 1961), *Orestes* (Fotopolous, 1971, shot in Mani), *Iphigenia* (Cacoyannis, 1976), *Phaedra* (Dassin, 1961, joint USA/Greece production), the experimental *Prometheus Second Person Singular* (Costas Ferris, 1975), and *A Dream of Passion*, based on Volonakis' modern Greek version of *Medea* (Dassin, 1978, Swiss/Greek production). Cacoyannis also made a version in English of *The Trojan Women* in Spain (1971) while the Junta was in power in Greece and this was perhaps influenced by his staging of the play, which had more than 650 performances. In 1994 Nikos Koundouros directed *Antigone*, subtitled "A cry for peace", in no man's land between northern Greece and the former Yugoslavia, with a backdrop of troops and armoured weapons.

In contrast to the fear expressed by some modernist theatre practitioners, 20th-century work on ancient tragedy has not led to a mood of nostalgia and cultural fossilization. The themes and ethos of tragedy have continued to figure in novels, poetry, and drama, notably in the work of Nikos Kazantzakis, where they are mediated both by Homer and by Byzantine traditions. Such works, together with modern films, versions, and performances, have explored, both aesthetically and politically, that theme of reinterpretation of myth in the context of debate about the present with which the ancient tragedians were themselves engaged.

LORNA HARDWICK

See also Comedy, Dithyramb, Festivals, Satyr Play, Theatres

Further Reading

Beacham, Richard C., *The Roman Theatre and Its Audience*, London and New York: Routledge, 1991

Council of Europe and the Greek Ministry of Culture, *A Stage for Dionysos: Theatrical Space and Ancient Drama*, Athens: Capon, 1998

Csapo, Eric and William J. Slater, *The Context of Ancient Drama*, Ann Arbor: University of Michigan Press, 1995

Easterling, P.E. (editor), *The Cambridge Companion to Greek Tragedy*, Cambridge: Cambridge University Press, 1997

Goldhill, Simon, *Reading Greek Tragedy*, Cambridge and New York: Cambridge University Press, 1986

Green, J.R., *Theatre in Ancient Greek Society*, London and New York: Routledge, 1994

Green, Richard and Eric Handley, *Images of the Greek Theatre*, London: British Museum Press, and Austin: University of Texas Press, 1995

Hall, Edith, *Inventing the Barbarian: Greek Self-Definition through Tragedy*, Oxford: Clarendon Press, and New York: Oxford University Press, 1989

MacKinnon, Kenneth, *Greek Tragedy into Film*, London: Croom Helm, and Rutherford, New Jersey: Fairleigh Dickinson University Press, 1986

Mavromoustakos, Platon (editor), *Productions of Ancient Greek Drama in Europe during Modern Times*, Athens, 1999

Patsalidis, Savas and Elizabeth Sakellaridou (editors), *(Dis)placing Classical Greek Theatre*, Thessalonica: University Studio Press, 1999

Pelling, Christopher (editor), *Greek Tragedy and the Historian*, Oxford: Clarendon Press, and New York: Oxford University Press, 1997

Pickard-Cambridge, A., *The Dramatic Festivals of Athens*, 2nd edition, revised by John Gould and D.M. Lewis, Oxford: Clarendon Press, and New York: Oxford University Press, 1988

Rehm, Rush, *Greek Tragic Theatre*, London and New York: Routledge, 1994

Seaford, Richard, *Reciprocity and Ritual: Homer and Tragedy in the Developing City-State*, Oxford: Clarendon Press, and New York: Oxford University Press, 1994

Silk, M.S. (editor), *Tragedy and the Tragic*, Oxford: Clarendon Press, and New York: Oxford University Press, 1996

Sommerstein, Alan H. *et al.* (editors), *Tragedy, Comedy and the Polis*, Bari: Levante, 1993

Taplin, Oliver, *Greek Tragedy in Action*, London: Methuen, and Berkeley: University of California Press, 1978

Walton, J. Michael (editor), *Living Greek Theatre: A Handbook of Classical Performance and Modern Production*, New York: Greenwood Press, 1987

Wiles, David, *Tragedy in Athens: Performance Space and Theatrical Meaning*, Cambridge and New York: Cambridge University Press, 1997

Winkler, John J. and Froma I. Zeitlin (editors), *Nothing to do with Dionysos? Athenian Drama in its Social Context*, Princeton, New Jersey: Princeton University Press, 1990

Transhumance

Transhumance is a form of herding organized around the movement of livestock between lowland pastures in the winter and mountain pastures in the summer. Herding of this type is a recurring feature of Greek life because year-round maintenance of substantial numbers of animals in either the plains or the mountains of Greece is difficult. The plains must be avoided during the summer months because a nearly complete lack of rainfall makes it impossible to find forage. The mountains must be avoided during the winter months because deep snows and extreme cold make it impossible for flocks to graze. Greek transhumants, drawn by relatively abundant vegetation and mild temperatures, spend the months from October to April in various coastal plains. As summer approaches, they move to upland areas where melting snow produces rich forage. Greek transhumants rely almost exclusively on sheep and goats; the nimbleness and size of these animals make them much better suited to the rough topography of the country than cattle.

Transhumance can take one of two very different forms. In some cases it involves nothing more than individual shepherds migrating with their flocks. Typically such shepherds are employed by large landowners who provide the animals and grazing lands. In other cases transhumance is a form of societal organization in which large, independent family groups migrate with and organize their lives around the care of their flocks.

While the latter form of transhumance is the more common and probably the more ancient, the earliest documented instance of transhumance in Greece is an example of the former. During the Mycenaean period (c.1600–1100 BC) Greece was divided into a number of kingdoms, each with a ruler and an elaborate bureaucracy. These rulers controlled very large numbers of sheep that were assigned, flock by flock, to individual shepherds. In return for sustenance provided by the royal household, the shepherd was responsible for tending the animals assigned to him and for producing a specified amount of wool each year. Extant records indicate that the ruler of Crete owned 80,000 sheep which produced nearly 68,000 kg of wool each year.

This system of transhumance broke down with the collapse of Mycenaean civilization. The highly unsettled conditions that ensued were an ideal environment for group transhumance. The ability of transhumants to move out of the way of danger was an important aid to survival in a period of societal disintegration. In addition, the steep decline in population levels and in agricultural activity that marked the post-Mycenaean period made extensive areas of Greece newly available as pasture land. Animal bones from this period found at the site of Nichoria in the southwest Peloponnese show that the composition of herds differed from that found in the Mycenaean period in such a way as to increase the production of meat and milk and at the expense of wool production. This change reflects the transition from individual transhumants supported by the Mycenaean state to group transhumance and direct reliance on flocks for sustenance.

While the collapse of society and population levels encouraged transhumance in the years immediately after 1100 BC, the gradual restoration of society and rise in population levels that took place in the 8th and 7th centuries BC did the reverse. In settled conditions the advantages of mobility were considerably lessened. More importantly, the fact that herding, relative to agriculture, is a non-intensive land-use pattern that is capable of supporting a limited number of people meant that as population densities in Greece increased, so did the importance of agriculture. Even so, transhumance continued to be practised throughout antiquity. Sophocles' *Oedipus Tyrannus* (lines 1133–40), for instance, includes a scene involving two shepherds who spent summers with their flocks on Mount Cithaeron and then returned to lowland pastures in the winter.

Group transhumance returned to prominence during the confused period of the 12th–15th centuries AD which was brought about by the gradual collapse of Byzantine rule in Greece. Albanians and Vlachs moved into Greece from the north, bringing their families and flocks with them, displacing though not entirely destroying native Greek transhumants in the process. One of the more enduring results of this migration was the division of transhumants in Greece into two groups, Vlachs and Sarakatsans. After this period and right up to the present day, ethnic Vlachs who speak their own language and who descend directly from these migrants have remained separate and distinct from the Greek-speaking Sarakatsans, who are descended from the native transhumants resident in Greece as early as the Byzantine period. The Albanian and Vlach migrants found a depopulated countryside ideal for transhumant herding. A 14th-century document describes a group of Albanian transhumants who wintered in the coastal plain of Elis (northwestern Peloponnese) because the area "had good grazing and was deserted by men" (cited and translated by Hammond, p. 61).

The imposition of Turkish rule in the 15th century did not bring an end to group transhumance because much of Greece was divided into large estates under the control of powerful Turks or of monasteries. These estates were not as a rule intensively cultivated and significant areas were thus available as pasturage, which was rented out on a seasonal basis. This pattern continued even after Greece achieved independence from the Ottoman empire. Throughout the 19th century most of the large estates continued in existence despite changes in ownership brought about by the departure of the Turks. Group transhumance continued much as before.

This situation was drastically altered as a result of the population exchange undertaken by Greece and Turkey beginning in 1922. The Greek government settled the people arriving from Turkey on smallholdings carved out of the large blocks of land mentioned above. This made winter grazing lands very much more difficult to find and resulted in a significant decrease in the number of transhumants active in Greece. In order to ameliorate the situation, a law of 1930 gave shepherds the right of protected leasing of grazing land. Under the provisions of this law, grazing leases had to be offered for yearly renewal at prices set by the government. Further relief was given to transhumants in 1938 when legislation permitted them to register as official residents of the mountain villages where they spent their summers. Registration brought with it the right of free access to public grazing lands held by these villages.

Despite these measures, during the 20th century there has been a continued marked decline in the numbers of transhumants in Greece. Most transhumants are now confined to the less densely settled, more mountainous regions of Greece such as Epirus. Increases in settlement density and the advent of heavy motor traffic have made migration across the countryside increasingly difficult. The steady economic development that Greece has experienced since World War II presents a real and growing threat to the continued existence of transhumance within its borders.

PAUL CHRISTESEN

See also Sarakatsans, Vlachs

Further Reading

Aschenbrenner, S.E. and George Rapp, Jr (editors), *Excavations at Nichoria in Southwest Greece*, 3 vols, Minneapolis: University of Minnesota Press, 1978–83

Boserup, Ester, *The Conditions of Agricultural Growth: The Economics of Agrarian Change under Population Pressure*, New York: Aldine, and London: Allen and Unwin, 1965

Campbell, J.K., *Honour, Family, and Patronage: A Study of Institutions and Moral Values in a Greek Mountain Community*, Oxford: Clarendon Press, 1964

Hammond, N.G.L., *Migrations and Invasions in Greece and Adjacent Areas*, Park Ridge, New Jersey: Noyes Press, 1976

Killen, J.T., "The Wool Industry of Crete in the Late Bronze Age", *Annual of the British School at Athens*, 59 (1964): pp. 1–15

Koster, Harold, "The Thousand Year Road", *Expedition*, 18/1 (Fall 1976): pp. 19–28

McDonald, William A. and George Rapp, Jr (editors), *The Minnesota Messenia Expedition: Reconstructing a Bronze Age Regional Environment*, Minneapolis: University of Minnesota Press, 1972

Primentas, N., "Greek Sheep and Their Wool", *Wool Knowledge*, 4 (1959): pp. 20–23

Whittaker, C.R. (editor), *Pastoral Economies in Classical Antiquity*, Cambridge: Cambridge Philological Society, 1988

Translation from Greek

Translations, together with adaptations and imitations, have been an important vehicle in the diffusion of Greek literature and thought. In certain instances, translations from the Greek represent the earliest examples of written literature. This is the case in particular with the Christian literature in Armenian and Georgian, where translations from Greek and Syriac played a formative role. Similarly, Roman literature is believed to have begun in 240 BC when a Greek schoolmaster named Livius Andronicus translated into Latin a tragedy, a comedy, and an epic, the last being the *Odyssey* which he rendered into Saturnian verse. New Comedy (and possibly Middle Comedy) provided the sources for the earliest literary comedies in Latin, of which we have surviving examples by Plautus and Terence, on whose work we have to depend for our knowledge of many lost works by poets of New Comedy such as Philemon, Diphilus, and Menander. The plays of Seneca are the only surviving examples of Latin adaptations from the great Classical Greek tragedians. Latin poets did sometimes translate Greek lyrics, Catullus 51 being a well-known example; but no one today would wholeheartedly agree with Aulus Gellius who held that Virgil in his *Eclogues*, *Georgics*, and *Aeneid* translated Theocritus, Hesiod, and Homer respectively, his debt to these poets being best described as one of inspiration and imitation.

Most educated Romans were bilingual, and many of them endeavoured to make the literature and learning of the Greeks available to Romans by translation and adaptation of Greek works into Latin. Thus, Cicero translated the *Phaenomena* of Aratus, a Hellenistic didactic poem on astronomy (this work was translated once again in the 7th century). But the Romans, and especially their poets, were quite conscious of the limitations of the Latin language in matching the richness and subtlety of Greek (cf. the complaint of Lucretius in 1. 139 about the poverty of the language).

The Romans conceptualized the process of translation and established the framework and norms which endured in the west until the end of the 18th century. The younger Pliny (*Epistulae*, 8. 9. 1) recommends translation from Greek to Latin and vice versa as an exercise for developing verbal fluency and critical discernment. There was also advice against undue literalism. Horace (*Ars Poetica*, 133–34 tr. Dorsch) says:

> A theme that is familiar can be made your own property
> as long as you do not waste your time on a hackneyed
> treatment; nor should you try to render your original
> word for word like a slavish translator, or in imitating

another writer plunge yourself into difficulties from which shame, or the rules you have laid down for yourself prevent you from extricating yourself.

On translating from Demosthenes and Aeschines, Cicero's advice is "not the words of the orators". "To explain not word by word but sense by sense", says St Jerome, who produced the Latin Bible known as the Vulgate.

During late antiquity translators into Latin concentrated mainly on science, military exploits, and adventures, and Christian works on theology, hagiography, and ecclesiastical history. Among scientific writings, the *Periegesis* of Dionysius was rendered into Latin by both Rufus Festus Avienus and Priscian. The gynaecological works of Soranus of Ephesus were translated by Mustio during the 6th century. The metrological treatise of Epiphanius of Salamis, written around AD 392, was translated in the 5th or 6th century. The alleged memoirs of Dares of Phrygia (6th century BC) and the story of Apollonius of Tyre are representative of military exploits and adventures. Translations of hagiography began quite early: Athanasius' *Life of St Antony* appeared in Latin as early as AD 373, and the story of *Barlaam and Joasaph* was translated into Latin during the 11th century.

Theology became the main focus of attention from the 9th century onwards. In 824, at the request of Louis the Pious, Erigena translated the Greek manuscript of *The Celestial Hierarchy*, attributed to Dionysius the Areopagite, and was deeply influenced by it. The result was the unofficial establishment in Christian theology of the Neoplatonist picture of a universe evolving or emanating out of God through different stages or degrees of diminishing perfection, and slowly returning through different degrees back into the deity. John Chrysostom and John of Damascus were among the authors translated by Burgundio of Pisa in the 12th century, while Moses of Bergamo translated a treatise attributed to Epiphanius of Salamis and a florilegium on the Trinity.

Greek science and philosophy had so far been rendered into Latin mainly from Arabic versions which were themselves sometimes made from Syriac versions. But the desire for more accurate renderings led to such productions as Aristotle's *Topics*, *Sophistici Elenchi*, and *Posterior Analytics* by one James, known to us only as "a clerk of Venice", at some time before 1128. Eugene "The Emir" of Palermo translated the *Optics* of Ptolemy in 1154, and in 1160 shared in a Latin translation of the *Almagest* directly from the Greek. Before this, Aristippus of Catania had translated (*c.*1156) Diogenes Laertius' *Lives of the Philosophers* as well as Plato's *Meno* and *Phaedo*.

The revival of interest in Greek philosophy that began in the 13th century resulted in Latin renderings of the Aristotelian corpus and its commentaries. Notable in this regard are William of Moerbeke, the Flemish archbishop of Corinth and friend and fellow Dominican of Thomas Aquinas (he also translated works by Hippocrates, Galen, Heron of Alexandria, Proclus, and Archimedes), and the circle of scholars at Lincoln headed by Robert Grosseteste (who also translated works of pseudo-Dionysius the Areopagite and John Argyropoulos), Theodore Gaza, and George of Trebizond (who also translated Plato and some Church Fathers). Several writers including Demosthenes and Plutarch were translated by Nicholas Sekoundinos. These Latin translations exerted a profound influence on developments in grammar and philology, medicine, astronomy, and mathematics as well as theology and philosophy. They enlarged the curriculum of the schools and contributed to the growth of European universities in the 12th and 13th centuries.

The only Latin translation of Homer known to Europe in the 14th century was the inaccurate and prosaic version by Leon Pilatus, a pupil of Barlaam of Calabria and an acquaintance of Bocaccio and Petrarch. Pope Nicholas V commissioned Francesco Filelfo to prepare a fresh translation; but this commission, like that given to Manetti and his aides for a new translation of the Bible, was terminated by the pope's death in 1455. He also made liberal grants for translations of Classical Greek texts: to Lorenzo Valla for Thucydides, to Guarino da Verona for Strabo, to Niccolo Perotti for Polybius, to Poggio Bracciolini for Diodorus Siculus, to Theodore Gaza for Aristotle, to Gianozzo Manetti and George of Trebizond for Cyril, Basil, Gregory of Nazianzus, Gregory of Nyssa, and other patristic texts. Though hurried and imperfect, these Latin translations opened these Greek authors for the first time to students who could not read the originals. In February 1516 the printer Froben brought out Erasmus' critical revision of the Greek New Testament with a new Latin translation and a commentary, and this was reprinted in 1518.

Next in importance to Latin translations in the conveying of Greek ideas to the west are the translations into Arabic. The earliest instances were of Christian origin, and the translations were made mainly through Syriac versions. Here, too, the emphasis was on religious, philosophical, medical, and scientific works. The earliest religious translations were of biblical and liturgical texts whose dating, however, is uncertain, especially whether any of them predate the coming of Islam. Both hagiographical works and the writings of Church Fathers and ascetics came to be translated in the monasteries of southern Palestine by the 9th century. Medical material most probably came initially through Syriac before direct translations from the Greek were made. The case of astronomy and mathematics may have been the same except that the Syriac versions appear to be contemporaneous with the Arabic, being largely the work of Hunayn Ibn Ishaq al-'Ibadi (died 873 or 877) or his school. It does not appear that the translations of Euclid and Ptolemy were made until after the reign of Harun al-Rashid (786–809), so the story that they were suggested to the caliph by Jafar Ibn Barmak as a remedy for the Arabs' inability to understand a version of the Indian *Siddhanta* of Brahmagupta cannot be trusted.

In astronomy and mathematics, where absolute accuracy of terminology was imperative, direct reference to the Greek originals appears to have taken place earlier than in medicine, whose terms, when borrowed from the Greek, suggest a greater degree of Syrian intermediation. The desire for more accurate scientific knowledge led to more careful translations or revision of existing versions, as well as commentaries and original works based on Greek authorities. The best-known translator of Greek scientific works into Arabic is Hunayn Ibn Ishaq al-'Ibadi, whom the caliph al-Mamun placed in charge of the House of Wisdom (*Bayt al-Hikmah*) that he established in 830 at Baghdad at a cost of 200,000 dinars as a scientific academy, an observatory, and a public library. Here he installed a body of translators and paid them from the public treasury in order to foster the preparation and propagation of translations from Greek scientists. The resulting translations included the greater part of the works of Galen, Hippocrates, Ptolemy, Euclid, Aristotle, and other Greek authorities. The desire for greater accuracy is reflected in the preparation of Syriac translations in addition to the Arabic to replace defective versions already in use. A Syrian Christian named Qusta Ibn Luqa al-Balbakki (*fl. c.*912) translated several works including Hypsicles (later revised by al-Kindi), Theodosius' *Sphaerica* (later revised by Thabit Ibn Qurra), Heron's *Mechanics*, Autolycus, Theophrastus' *Meteora*, Galen's catalogue of his books, and John Philoponus on the *Physics* of Aristotle. He also revised the existing translation of Euclid. Aristotle's *Poetics* was translated by Matta Ibn Yunus al-Qunnai (d. 940). Among the medical and logical works translated by the monophysite logician Abu Zakariya Yahya Ibn Adi al-Mantiqi (d. 974) was the *Prolegomena* of Ammonius and an introduction to Porphyry's *Isagoge*. Thereafter, translation gave way to revisions, commentaries, and expositions.

The literatures of the eastern Christians owed their formation to a large extent to translations of Greek texts into Syriac, Armenian, Georgian, Arabic, Coptic, Ethiopic, and the Slavonic languages. These translations of biblical, theological, and liturgical texts represent the common cultural debt of eastern Christianity to Hellenistic civilization, whose impact transcended linguistic, cultural, and even theological differences and was not confined to religious literature. Thus translations from the Greek works on theology, philosophy, rhetoric, and science not only laid the foundation for Syrian learning in those spheres, but also served as the principal medium for the transmission of Greek thought to the Muslim world. Throughout the Byzantine period Armenian literature was enriched by translations from the Greek. Of particular significance was the impact of the Hellenistic Jewish writers Josephus and Philo, and of the church historians Socrates and Eusebius. Georgian translations have preserved the liturgical traditions associated with Jerusalem that were later subordinated to the Byzantine rite. Since they remained Chalcedonian, the Georgians were in touch with Greek scholars at monastic centres such as Mount Athos (Iviron in particular), Mount Sinai, and the Black Mountain (in the Karakorum near Peshawar in Pakistan).

Because the Slavonic translations made by Cyril and Methodios for their Moravian mission (863–85) have not survived, the earliest examples are those belonging to the Christian period of the first Bulgarian empire (864–971). These were mainly religious in character (biblical, exegetical, homiletic, historical, and liturgical writings as well as hagiography, gnomologia, florilegia, works on canon law, and the like), as were those from the 12th to 15th centuries made in Bulgaria, Serbia, and on Mount Athos (e.g. at Hilandar). Many of these were literal translations, in keeping with the medieval insistence on preserving both the content and the form of the original.

The immense popularity of certain works is indicated by the number of translations into various languages. As examples may be cited the story of *Barlaam and Joasaph*, the fables of Aesop, and the *Alexander Romance*. The last-mentioned work was translated into Armenian and the Slavonic languages.

During the second half of the 16th century a large number of English translations of the classics were made, including

Theocritus' *Idylls*, Musaeus' *Hero and Leander*, Epictetus' *Enchiridion*, Aristotle's *Ethics* and *Politics*, Xenophon's *Cyropaedia* and *Oeconomicus*, the speeches of Demosthenes and Isocrates, the histories of Herodotus, Polybius, Diodorus Siculus, Josephus, and Appian, and the novels of Heliodorus and Longus. In 1579 Sir Thomas North translated Plutarch's *Lives* using Amyot's French translation. These translations exerted such an immense influence upon Elizabethan literature that, during the next two centuries, English poetry and prose were fraught with Classical allusions. There were no Greek plays in English for quite some time, however, and Homer had to wait till the verse renderings of George Chapman (1611) and Alexander Pope (*Iliad*, 1715–20; *Odyssey*, 1725–26).

Some recent collections of Classical texts are accompanied by translations into modern languages. Thus, the Budé edition (named after the well-known French humanist Guillaume Budé, 1467–1540) includes a French translation, while the collection known as the Loeb Classical Library, founded in 1912 by the American banker James Loeb, presents the original text with an English translation on opposite pages. Meanwhile, in 1946, under the general editorship of the late E.V. Rieu, the Penguin Classics series was launched with Rieu's own translation of the *Odyssey*. This series has been instrumental in popularizing the Classics among the English-reading public throughout the world by providing highly readable translations at affordable prices.

D.P.M. WEERAKKODY

Further Reading

Gutas, Dimitri, *Greek Thought, Arabic Culture: The Graeco-Arabic Translation Movement in Baghdad and Early 'Abbasid Society, 2nd-4th/8th-10th Centuries*, New York and London: Routledge, 1998

Kelly, L.G., *The True Interpreter: A History of Translation Theory and Practice in the West*, Oxford: Blackwell, and New York: St Martin's Press, 1979

O'Leary, De Lacy, *How Greek Science Passed to the Arabs*, London: Routledge and Kegan Paul, 1949

Rosenthal, Franz, *The Classical Heritage in Islam*, London: Routledge and Kegan Paul, 1975

Thompson, F., "Sensus or Proprietas Verborum: Mediaeval Theories of Translation as Exemplified by Translations from Greek into Latin and Slavonic" in *Symposium Methodianum*, edited by Klaus Trost *et al.*, Neuried: Hieronymus, 1988

Walzer, Richard, *Greek into Arabic: Essays on Islamic Philosophy*, Cambridge, Massachusetts: Harvard University Press, and Oxford: Cassirer, 1962

Translation into Greek

Translation in the west goes as far back as the Septuagint – the translation, in the 3rd century BC, of the Old Testament from the original Hebrew into Greek Koine. Yet, it was only in the last decades of the 20th century that translation practice and theory became objects of systematic enquiry with histories of translation attempting to unearth and organize them into a distinct field of knowledge. Although references to Greece in such works of reconstruction are conspicuously absent, there exists, nevertheless, a long and particularly interesting tradition of practice and thought regarding translation into Greek; a tradition that brings into focus three distinct yet interrelated contexts where translation constitutes a key issue: Greek Orthodoxy, Greek national identity, and the so-called Language Question. Modern Hellenism's relation to its ancient past, the much-debated question of continuity, and, more generally, the definition of the modern Greek state's national and cultural identity (tradition, religion, educational system, form of government, form of language, etc.) are all issues that, directly or indirectly, translation brings to the fore as Greek translators, at different historical moments, have had to decide whether, what, how, and for whom to translate.

Although by no means an exclusively Greek phenomenon, no other European nation has practised or debated more intensely the category of translation that Roman Jakobson (1959) has termed "intralingual": translation, that is, that brings into contact different phases of the history of a language as opposed to interlingual or translation proper. Intralingual translation in Greece has, traditionally, concerned the rendering of the Classical and biblical texts into a more or less simple katharevousa or into demotic and the existence of various terms to describe this practice – *metaphrasi, metagraphi, metaglotisi, metaphora, devteri graphi, morphi* – testifies to the different ways of conceiving it. As early on as the first stages of the Tourkokratia, Greek scholars faced the question of whether to adapt the biblical texts to a more accessible form of language, creating, thereby, two opposed traditions. The one, represented by the Greek Orthodox Church, remained hostile to and deeply suspicious of such adaptations maintaining that the original Greek language of the texts was the only language of Orthodoxy, that any form of interference with it was fraught with doctrinal and political dangers – altering the true letter and spirit of the texts and subverting the authority of the Church – and that the Greek vernacular was too poor and vulgar to express the divine meaning of the texts. For the Church hierarchy, translation of the holy scriptures into the spoken language amounted to treason and heresy or, as expressed by Konstantinos Oikonomos, a leading conservative theologian in the first decades of independence, to a futile, damaging, and useless activity. To this day, the Greek Constitution does not recognize any translation of the scriptures that does not have the authorization of the Church. But the very fact that the Greek Constitution is itself written in two versions – katharevousa and demotic – testifies to the importance and still unresolved status of intralingual translation.

In opposition to this ultraconservatism, however, there runs a liberal tradition which goes as far back as 1544, in which year Nikolaos Sophianos printed in Venice his version of pseudo-Plutarch's *Peri Paidon Agoges* in the "common language". The tradition inaugurated by Sophianos began by recognizing translation as a means of making knowledge accessible to all social layers and thus contributing to the construction of the nation – an idea that was to remain a constant throughout this tradition. For Sophianos, compiler of *A Grammar of the Common Language of the Greeks*, concern with translation went hand-in-hand with concern for language and education; just as five centuries later, in 1938, translation, particularly of the ancient texts, was to be seen as a key to the construction of a modern national education and language system by Manolis Triandaphyllidis, author of a *Neoelliniki*

Grammatiki, this time in demotic. But even within the Church hierarchy there have been enlightened figures who defended (sometimes with their own lives) the value of intralingual translation. Cyril I Lukaris (1572–1638) who, within a more general context of reforms and innovations which included the setting up of a Greek printing house and the translation into spoken Greek of the New Testament, is a case in point. And, continuing with this tradition, two centuries later Neophitos Vamvas (1776–1855), a Greek liberal intellectual and close collaborator of Adamantios Korais, was to play a crucial role in the translation (published in London in 1836) from Hebrew to modern Greek of the Old Testament. By then, however, the equation of Orthodoxy with Hellenism, with the question of a national identity, and with the consolidation of a modern national state, linked to the Church's anxiety to maintain the power and independence gained during the Tourkokratia, had converted Greek intralingual translation into a key doctrinal as well as national issue while marking profoundly, and for centuries to come, the Language Question. The conflict was to reach dramatic dimensions in the so-called *Evangelika*, the bloody street incidents in 1901 that forced the interruption of the newspaper publication of Alexandros Pallis's translation into demotic Greek of the Gospels, and again in 1903 (*Orestika*) following the performance of Aeschylus' tragedy as translated into a "mixed" Greek by G. Sotiriadis.

It was in the 18th century, however, the century of the Enlightenment and a period marked by intense intellectual curiosity, that translation into Greek began to acquire full-scale dimensions embracing an unprecedented variety of fields of knowledge: from works with a moral, pedagogical, and didactic purpose to works of narrative, theatre, philosophy, history, geography, law, mathematics, medicine, astronomy, psychology, political theory, and others. Evgenios Voulgaris (translator of Voltaire and pioneer of a Greek theory of translation), Josephos Moisiodax (pioneer of the spirit of Enlightenment in Greece and especially interested in translation), Dimitrios Katartzis (whose Prologue to Réal de Curban's *La Science du gouvernement*, 1784, constitutes the first attempt at a systematic theory of translation), Korais, and Rigas Pherraios are landmark figures in this tradition for whom translation theory and practice constituted an intrinsic part of the projects of national rebirth and emancipation to which they were committed. Questions of why, what, for whom, and how to translate began to be rigorously posed. Translation became a means for the introduction of new ideas and knowledge, a means of satisfying the need for a new code of moral and social values, of transferring to Greece the secularizing spirit of the Enlightenment. It was recognized as a crucial instrument of moral instruction and as a means for the cultivation of the spoken language as an instrument of written expression. Translation became a means whereby Greek people might become aware of, recover, and transplant to their own soil their rightful cultural inheritance, a means of elevating their educational and cultural level and of bringing the emerging nation into line with achievements in the west. Having access, through translation, to the ideas already available in other languages, developed by other nations, was a way of laying the foundations for Greece's own intellectual production, since no original intellectual production can take place without a constant cultivation and elaboration of the language in which it is to be expressed. Translation for Korais, for example, was a crucial means of combating the Church's obscurantist hold on people's consciousness and education and, of course, people's education is directly linked to its emancipation as a nation. Thus, it is no accident that his calls for financial support of translation were made in patriotic terms; nor can it be doubted, as he argued in his *Mémoire sur l'état actuel de la civilisation dans la Grèce* (1803), that translations of works by Molière, Voltaire, Condillac, Montesquieu, Locke, and other scientific, philosophical, and historical works testify to the emerging nation's rapid progress and development. Every nation needs a model on which to base itself and, for all these men, the model of modern Greek cultural identity could not be other than that of Classical Greece as discovered and reconstructed in Europe. The decade 1790–99, marked by the ideals of the French Revolution, was exceptionally fruitful for translation into Greek and Rigas occupies an outstanding place in it. For him, translation was not only a means of struggle against ignorance but an efficient way of disseminating the most emancipatory and revolutionary ideas of his period: Voltaire and the Encyclopaedists D'Alembert and Diderot, Restif de la Bretonne, Montesquieu, Metastasio, Marmontel, Salomon Gessner, Abbé Barthélemy, selections of texts from astronomy, the natural sciences, and physiology.

The question of what to translate was obviously closely linked to the question of why translate. Translating not just any but those worthy works capable of transmitting knowledge as well as moral and ethical instruction became a conscious criterion of choice. To this was added the requirement for clarity and pleasurable reading, aiming as the Greek translators did at the widest possible circulation of the translated printed work. Equally important were the twin questions of whom should the translations be addressed to and how should the task of translation (methods, procedures, and form of target language) be carried out. If translation were to serve the pedagogical and national emancipatory aims of these men and provide the ideological elements out of which the modern Greek national identity was to emerge, it should address itself to the widest possible readership, to the emergent nation. And, naturally, its language could not be but the closest form to the Greek vernacular (even if purged of all foreign and vulgar elements, as in the case of Korais). Being conscious of translation's crucial role in introducing new concepts and terminology into the Greek language (and mentality) also made the 18th-century translators highly conscious of the additional difficulties facing the Greek translator: the lack of infrastructure (finance, dictionaries, and reference books), the lack of established linguistic norms, the poor state of spoken Greek as a result of the absence of sufficient experience and experimentation with it as a vehicle of written expression. And this consciousness produced another: the realization that translation was not only a source of knowledge and ideas but also, crucially, a space for the creation of language itself. Thus, as from the late 18th century, it is possible to speak of the beginnings of a Greek theory of translation that underlines the singularity of each text and the need of translation to respect and reflect it by adopting the appropriate form of language and style that demands precision and clarity, that introduces the concept of translation as faithful recreation, and, alongside the concept of usefulness, the aesthetic requirement of a "good"

translation. Influential views on translation practice are encountered in Emmanouil Roidis's prologue to his translation of Chateaubriand's *Itinéraire* in 1860, in Iakovos Polylas whose translation activity embraced ancient Greek (Homer), Latin, and western classics (*Hamlet* and *The Tempest*), in Stamatios D. Valvis's outstanding essay *Peri Metaphraseos Poiiton* (On Translating a Poet, 1878) which poses many of the issues that still concern modern translation theory – the questions of translatability and ethnocentrism, among others – in Ioannis Kambouroglou's insightful prologue to his translation of Zola's *Nana* in 1880 (commenting on what is today known as dynamic or functional equivalence) and whose naturalist realism was to exercise a great influence on Greek literary writing, or in Ioannis Kakridis's *To Metaphrastiko Provlima* (The Translation Problem, 1936), an important source of information, moreover, regarding the history of Greek translation.

The role played by both intra- and interlingual translation in the construction of a modern Greek national literature cannot be overestimated. The methods, interventions, and statements, the works chosen, and, of course, the form of language used in translation provide a guide to the different – and changing – ways of conceiving the history and identity of Hellenism. For Andreas Kalvos and Dionysios Solomos the experience of translating from ancient Greek, koine, and modern European languages, especially Italian, not only helped them to find their own approach to the Greek language, to dig into Greek tradition and combine it with the European, but also provided them with elements that proved essential in their own poetry, thereby marking the subsequent course of modern Greek literature. George Seferis and Odysseus Elytis in the 20th century, both of whom translated the Revelation of St John, followed in their footsteps. Seferis's translations of T.S. Eliot (particularly *The Waste Land* in 1936) and Elytis's translations of, especially, French poetry played a key role in their poetics and, consequently, in the configuration of Greek postwar poetry. To this day, translation from katharevousa to demotic (Alexandros Papadiamantis is a case in point) remains a controversial issue, demonstrating that translation not only reflects but also generates ideas, conflicts, ideological and political stakes, and that the history of modern Hellenism is inextricably tied to the problem of translation. Today, Greece possesses a rapidly developing field of translation studies with interlingual translation, in which literature in English holds the lead, occupying one third of the total book publication. The fact that, in 1997, the European Prize for Translation was awarded to the Greek translation of James Joyce's *Ulysses* is undoubtedly an indication of the distance covered by Greek translation since its beginnings.

IOANNA A. NICOLAIDOU

See also Enlightenment, Language

Further Reading

Constantinidou, E.I., *Ta Evangelika: To Provlima tis Metaphraseos tis Agias Graphis stin Neoellinikin kai ta Aimatira Gegonota tou 1901* [The Gospels: The Problem of the Translation of Holy Scripture into Modern Greek and the Bloody Events of 1901], Athens, 1976

Dimaras, I.T., *Neoellinikos Diaphotismos* [The Modern Greek
Enlightenment], Athens: Ermis, 1977

Dimaras, I.T., *Istoria tis Neoellinikis Logotechnias* [History of
Modern Greek Literature], 7th edition, Athens: Ikaros, 1985

Iliou, Philippos, *Elliniki Vivliographia, 1801–1818* [Greek
Bibliography, 1801–1818], vol. 1, Athens: ELIA, 1997

Jakobson, Roman, "On Linguistic Aspects of Translation" in *On
Translation*, edited by Reuben A. Brower, Cambridge,
Massachusetts: Harvard University Press, 1959

Kakridis, Ioannis, "Oi Archaioi Hellines kai oi Xenes Glosses" [The
Ancient Greeks and Foreign Words] in *Meletes kai Arthra* [Studies
and Articles], Thessalonica, 1971

Kakridis, Ioannis, *To Metaphrastiko Provlima* [The Translation
Problem], 5th edition, Thessalonica: Panepistimion, 1979

Katartzis, Dimitrios, *Ta Evriskomena* [Findings], edited by I.T.
Dimaras, Athens: Ermis, 1970

Koutsivitis, Vasilis, *Theoria tis Metaphrasis* [Translation Theory],
Athens: Ellinikes Panepistimiakes, 1994

Patsiou, Viki, "Metaphrastikes Dokimes kai Proypotheseis sta Oria
tou Neoellinikou Diaphotismou" [Theories and Attempts at
Translation at the Beginning of the Modern Greek
Enlightenment], *O Eranistis*, 19 (1993)

Seferis, George, *Metagraphes* [Transcriptions], Athens: Leschi, 1980

Triandaphyllidis, M., *Apanta* [Collected Works], vol. 5, Thessalonica:
Institouto Neoellinikon Spoudon, 1963–65

Tsaknias, Spyros, "I Metaphrasi tis *Nanas* tou Zola apo ton Ioanni
Kambouroglou" [The Translation of Zola's *Nana* by Ioanni
Kambouroglou], *Grammata kai Technes*, 60 (1990)

Valvis, Stamatios D. "Peri Metaphraseos Poiitou" [On Translating a
Poet], *Athinaiou*, 7 (1878): pp. 167–68

Vayenas, Nasos, *Poiisi kai Metaphrasi* [Poetry and Translation],
Athens: Stigmi, 1989

Vranousis, Leandros, "Rigas kai Marmontel" [Rigas and Marmontel]
in *Ellinogallika: Aphieroma ston Roger Milliex / Mélanges offerts
à Roger Milliex*, Athens: ELIA, 1990

Travel

Long-distance travel was widespread in all periods of Greek antiquity. Already in the *Odyssey* we encounter itinerant experts, including seers, physicians, builders, and bards, who, as Homer tells us (17. 386), were "invited from the ends of the earth". Questions such as "Who are you? Where do you come from? What is your city? Who are your parents?", which occur frequently in the *Odyssey*, no doubt reflect the realities of Homer's own world where travel for military or commercial purposes was commonplace. In later times sophists and – a much larger category – mercenaries travelled extensively. In addition, many individuals occasionally made long journeys, either to attend a distant festival or celebration of the games, consult an oracle, or visit a healing sanctuary. It is unlikely that anyone ever undertook a long journey purely for pleasure, however. The most widely travelled Greek in antiquity was probably Herodotus, who in the 5th century BC visited Babylon, the Black Sea region, Egypt, and Phoenicia while researching his historical account of the Persian Wars, which is also the world's first travel book. The only guidebook that has survived is Pausanias' *Description of Greece*, written c. AD 150, which claims to describe "all things Greek".

Since no part of the Greek mainland is more than 100 km from the coast and since safe harbours abound, the most common method of long-distance travel as well as of transportation was by sea. Owing to the frequency of storms in the Aegean, however, seafaring was regarded as a dangerous undertaking. As today, it was largely confined to the months from May to October. In the winter very few voyages were undertaken, except in the case of an emergency such as that resulting from a desperate food shortage. A further hazard was piracy, which was endemic throughout the Aegean from early times onwards. Passenger ships were unknown and those who wanted to take a sea voyage would generally have had to stand on the waterfront and request a place on a cargo ship that happened to be travelling in the right direction, if not to their actual destination. No food or bedding was provided on board, so passengers had to come supplied with their own. The perilousness and unpredictability of the sea is a central motif in the *Odyssey*, since it is due to the wrath of the sea god Poseidon that Odysseus, who is returning home to Ithaca at the end of the Trojan War, loses all his companions and is delayed for nine years. Poseidon's enmity reflects a genuine paranoia about sea travel, notwithstanding its importance.

From early times the sea played a vital part in shaping Greek history and in moulding the Greek character. There is evidence of settlement in several of the hundreds of islands dotted around the Aegean already in the Early Bronze Age. Homer's world extended from Sicily in the west to the Hellespont in the east. It was surely due to their familiarity with this element that seafaring Greeks came to develop a flexible response to the challenges of the outside world. Almost all the most important city states possessed seaports and those that were landlocked remained conservative. The dichotomy is exemplified by the difference in character between the Athenians and the Spartans, the dominant powers in the Classical era. Whereas Sparta, an inland state, was reactionary and unenterprising, Athens, whose might and wealth were based on the sea, was innovative and progressive.

None of Greece's rivers is navigable and only a few have estuaries wide enough to serve as ports. Hence travel on the mainland was generally by road or track. Owing to the unevenness of the terrain, this tended to be slow, arduous, and difficult. Most people travelled on foot with a slave or two to carry their baggage because horses were not capable of travelling long distances or of negotiating the steep mountain paths that often provided the only means of access from one community to another. Likewise chariots and other wheeled vehicles were useful only over short distances. The island of Ithaca, which is described as "rugged and unfit for driving horses" (*Odyssey*, 13. 242), is typical of much of Greece and the suggestion that the road between Pylos and Sparta was sufficiently smooth to permit Telemachus to traverse it in a chariot is a sublime fantasy on Homer's part (*Odyssey*, 3. 482–86). Even so, horses remained important status symbols throughout antiquity.

It follows that in all periods up until the present day Greeks would have been accustomed to walking considerable distances. Socrates in Xenophon's *Memorabilia* (3. 13. 5) talks nonchalantly of undertaking a five to six days' walk from Athens to Olympia. Even though the distance from Athens' furthest demes to the capital is no more than 50 km, it is unlikely that its rural population would have regularly travelled to the city to attend meetings of the assembly, however. Probably women, the elderly, and the infirm hired wagons drawn by horses, mules, or oxen to convey them short distances, where the roads permitted. In later times a litter or sedan chair, known as a *phorelon*, was available to the wealthy.

The dangers of moving about in a world where no protection was offered to travellers gave rise to the image of the culture hero, whose task was to clear the roads of brigands and wild beasts. Examples include Theseus and Heracles. One of the brigands eliminated by Theseus was Sciron who, after robbing travellers, ordered them to wash his feet before kicking them over a cliff into a ravine below. Though we hear of highwaymen only occasionally, they must have presented a constant danger on land, as did pirates on the high seas. To safeguard the interests of their compatriots, many states appointed officials called *proxenoi* in foreign cities. *Proxenoi* were resident aliens who lived permanently abroad.

In times of emergency a city might call upon the services of a professional runner to bear a message to an ally. The stamina of such runners was prodigious. A famous example was the Athenian Pheidippides, who according to legend ran from Athens to Sparta – a distance of 240 km – to request military assistance against the Persians in 490 BC. Pheidippides then ran a similar distance to Marathon and followed up this feat by running to Athens, whereupon, after delivering his report of the Athenian victory, he expired. In the Hellenistic era the Greek kings took over the highly efficient network of roads and communications maintained by the Persians throughout their vast empire.

A number of Greek roads that were used in historical times had their origins in the Mycenaean period. Very few were paved, but the Greeks developed a number of sophisticated roadbuilding techniques. These included ramps, switchbacks, and pulloffs, for which there is evidence already in the archaic era. All roads, however, were local, their purpose being to facilitate travel within a state's territory rather than to join communities to one another. Mule and drovers' tracks provided the only link between communities. It was common to bury the dead in family plots adjoining major roads, for which reason epitaphs frequently address the wayfarer.

Many sanctuaries were served by sacred ways, though these usually extended only a short distance. As Pausanias reports, however, even an international sanctuary like Delphi was difficult to approach on foot. The principal paved road in Athens was the Panathenaic Way, which began at the Dipylon Gate on the west side of the city and ended up on the Acropolis, barely 1.5 km away. A more functional paved road extended from the marble quarries on Mount Pentelikon to Athens. Goods were conveyed to and from the port of Piraeus along a paved cart road. During the Peloponnesian War, when it was no longer safe to travel outside the city, a road running the entire length of the Long Walls joining Athens to its port served in its place. The most impressive road-building project in Greece was the *diolkos* or slipway, which was constructed by the Corinthians in around 600 BC. The *diolkos* enabled ships to be towed across the isthmus of Corinth, rather than having to circumnavigate the Peloponnese. It remained in use until the 9th century AD.

Though Agamemnon supposedly conveyed his mighty army to Troy by sea, in historical times armies travelled to the theatre of war by land. Homer's warriors are usually conveyed to the battlefield in chariots, though they fight almost exclusively on foot. Their chariots remain parked while their owners engage, ready to provide a means of escape if their owners are forced to retreat or when they go off in search of a new opponent. Cavalry, though frequently mentioned in our sources, played a relatively minor part in Greek warfare.

In the absence of inns and hostelries, aristocrats in the Archaic period operated a system known as guest-friendship or *xenia*. This facilitated long-distance travel by providing hospitality on a reciprocal basis. The guest–host relationship was judged to be so sacred that its supervision was placed under the protection of Zeus Xenios. Homer suggests that guest-friendship transcended what passed for national boundaries. In the *Iliad* (6. 230f.) the Greek Diomedes and the Trojan Glaucus refuse to fight against one another once they have discovered their parentage "so that everyone will realize that our families have provided hospitality for one another in days of old". Not until the 5th century BC do we hear of facilities offering accommodation for travellers. These remained basic throughout antiquity. Even in a major commerical centre like the Piraeus, accommodation was limited. Aristophanes (*Frogs*, 112–15) indicates that its inns had a reputation for discomfort and bedbugs. By the middle of the 5th century BC the lack of decent facilities led Xenophon (*Revenues*, 3. 12) to recommend the construction of more facilities, though whether his advice was followed is not known. By the Roman period the situation seems to have deteriorated further. Cicero (*Letters to Friends*, 4. 12. 3) states that when a certain Servius Sulpicius journeyed to the Piraeus to collect the body of a friend, he found the latter stretched out under a tent, evidently because he had been unable to find more suitable accommodation in the port. Throughout antiquity the wealthy continued to find hospitality in one another's houses or brought tents and other gear in their entourage.

Under Roman rule the provinces of Macedonia in the north of Greece and Achaea in the south became linked by an efficient network of roads like the rest of the empire, with Thessalonica, Athens, and Corinth representing the principal hubs. The most important road in the region was the Via Egnatia, which ran in an east–west direction through Thessalonica, parallel to the northern border of the empire. It was strategically important in the late Republic at the time of the Civil Wars but declined in military significance from the 1st century AD onwards when the frontier moved north to the river Danube. In this period, too, Roman tourists began to visit Athens and other major sites. The first guidebook on Greece, which was essentially limited to the province of Achaea, was written by Pausanias (fl. AD 150).

The early Christians, notaby St Paul, travelled extensively through the Greek-speaking half of the empire, seeking to convert its population. When the Roman empire fell, the road system remained largely intact and travel continued. Guest houses known as *xenodochia*, which were run by monks, provided accommodation for pilgrims visiting holy places. Some Christians even adopted a wandering life-style and journeyed perpetually throughout the Mediterranean. With the advent of the Dark Ages, much forced migration took place throughout the region. Under the Ottoman Turks Greece became something of a backwater and long-distance travel became less frequent.

When the Ottoman empire began to fragment at the end of the 17th century, Greece became increasingly accessible to European travellers. Henceforth, the story can be told largely from the perspective of foreigners, many of them British, who were lured to Greece in part by the desire to acquire antiquities. Now, too, Athens became the focal point of any tour of Greece – a position which it retains to the present day, due not only to its incomparable treasures but also to its location as a convenient point of departure for travel within the mainland. In addition, the Piraeus, Athens' port, provides easy access to the Aegean islands, many of which, including Aegina, Hydra, Poros, and Salamis, can be visited in a day. The decision to establish Athens as the capital of the fledgeling kingdom of Greece following the Greek War of Independence in 1829 ensured that the city would be laid out on modern lines with broad thoroughfares. Shortly afterwards the Piraeus was provided with modern harbour facilities. It was also at this time that the first detailed maps of Greece were made.

Today large hotels dominate the islands and coastal towns of Greece and the needs of the tourist often prevail over those of the local residents. All the occupied islands of the Aegean are served by ferries, many of which originate from the Piraeus, Greece's busiest port. In addition, some islands are served by hydrofoils, known popularly as "Flying Dolphins". Recently catamarans have also been introduced to some routes. The Aegean is host to numerous cruise liners in the high season. Athens Airport has two main terminals, East and West, which handle a vast amount of international and domestic air traffic in the summer months. Greece's national airline is Olympic Airways; its affiliate, Olympic Aviation, provides domestic flights. The road system still remains somewhat rudimentary by the standards of other European countries. The only major highways are those that run between Athens, Thessalonica, Volos, and Patras. The train service is very limited, the most efficient line being the one that runs between Athens and Thessalonica. There is also a narrow-gauge railway that connects Athens to stations in the Peloponnese. By contrast, Greece's bus service is excellent and virtually every village, no matter how remote, is provided with a service. Travel in Athens tends to be slow, owing to the heavy congestion. In an attempt to ease the congestion and pollution, cars with an odd-number licence plate are permitted to enter the central area only on dates with an odd number and those with even-number licence plates on even dates. Athens' metro, however, which began in the 1930s with one line running from Kifisia to the port of Piraeus, now has two further lines, opened in January 2000.

ROBERT GARLAND

See also Tourism

Further Reading

Casson, Lionel, *Travel in the Ancient World*, London: Allen and Unwin, 1974; Baltimore: Johns Hopkins University Press, 1994

Casson, Lionel, *Ships and Seafaring in Ancient Times*, London: British Museum Press, and Baltimore: Johns Hopkins University Press, 1995

Tsigakou, F.-M., *The Rediscovery of Greece: Travellers and Painters of the Romantic Era*, New Rochelle, New York: Caratzas, 1981

Xenophon, *The Art of Horsemanship*, translated by Morris H. Morgan, Boston: Little Brown, 1893; London: J.A. Allen, 1962; as "On Equitation" in *Ancient Greece Horsemanship* by J.K. Anderson, Berkeley: University of California Press, 1961

Trebizond

City on the southeast coast of the Black Sea

Trebizond is the English name for the Greek Trapezous, modern Turkish Trabzon, a city in the Pontus, on the southeastern shore of the Black Sea. The port was a Greek colony, daughter of Sinope and granddaughter of Miletus, from the 7th century BC (its traditional foundation date of 753 BC is much too early). Historically Trebizond owes its importance to two factors. First, as Xenophon found as early as 400 BC, it is the political capital of a distinct and persistent local identity, a combination of indigenous, especially Caucasian (including Laz), people and of Greek colonists and culture (Pontic Greek is one of the oldest spoken examples of the language). Second, Trebizond is the furthest port east through which European shipping could once reach an overland route that penetrates Central Asia. This combination of factors made Trebizond both a local provincial capital and, intermittently, a port of intercontinental strategic and commercial importance. The periods of the city's commercial importance (especially from 1258 to 1475 and from 1829 to 1869) coincided with its local autonomy (particularly under the Grand Komnenoi, emperors of Trebizond from 1204 to 1461) and with the patronage of most of its major monuments.

The city basically consists of two settlements, hemmed between the sea and Mount Minthrion (Boz Tepe). On the west is a naturally defensive site, wedged between two deep ravines that narrow to an acropolis 1 km inland, on which the Upper City bears the accumulated masonry of an administrative citadel and palace of the Grand Komnenoi. Below it the Middle City is dominated by the domed basilican cathedral of the Chrysokephalos, remodelled as a coronation church in the 13th century, now the Orta Hisar Camii and principal mosque of Trabzon. Trebizond was an episcopal see from the 3rd century AD and Justinian dedicated its aqueduct to St Eugenios, its patron martyr. The Lower City reaches the sea to embrace an artificial harbour, the Molos, plausibly attributed to the emperor Hadrian (AD 117–38).

The second settlement lies about 1 km east of the walled city and acropolis, around the commercial harbour of Daphnous. Trebizond appears to have lacked many of the conveniences of a Hellenistic city, such as a theatre, although the cathedral probably stands on the site of a temple. But the modern street plan that links the city with the eastern suburb reveals a Milesian or Hippodamian grid, such as in Sinope, Histria, and Cherson, of blocks of about 100 ¥ 60 m, complete with a *cardo*, or main street. Four empty blocks suggest an agora, today the *meydan* or main square of Trabzon, around which all the Classical inscriptions have been found. This open space overlooking Daphnous is the oldest monument of Trebizond in continuous use; it became the supply base of the Roman campaign against Armenia in AD 58, from AD 64 of the legion XV Apollinaris, stationed at Satala (Sadak), of Justinian's 6th-century Laz and Persian wars, and of 9th- and 10th-century

Trebizond: 17th century engraving of the city which was the last Byzantine outpost to fall to the Turks, in 1461

Byzantine campaigns on the eastern frontier, when Trebizond was capital of the theme of Chaldia. From the 13th century it became the ceremonial square of the Grand Komnenoi and assembly point of caravans going south. Venice and Genoa built their own castles on the seaward side – the latter, Leontokastron (now Güzel Hisar), rivals that of their host emperors. The *cardo* (now Meraş Caddesi) remains the principal commercial quarter and bazaar of the city. The overland route to Tabriz, 32 staging posts away, reaching eventually to Central Asia, was already in decline after the break-up of the Mongol and Timurid empires before sultan Mehmet II conquered Trebizond in 1461. The *meydan* was reanimated after 1829, when western traders returned to exploit the overland route to Persia, but declined after 1869 when the Suez Canal offered a more convenient alternative. Trebizond is not a convenient port. Although Daphnous faces east, before the 20th century all goods had to be beached or taken ashore by double-ended lighters, including the first Ford motor car, rowed ashore in 1921. Until then pack animals assembled in the *meydan*; today the stables on its corner have been replaced by the garage of the Ulusoy Bus Company. Marco Polo was not the last to mislay his luggage on the square.

The Greek monuments of Trebizond reflect its periods of prosperity before the exchange of populations of 1923, since when its demography has been transformed. Of the first period of prosperity under the Grand Komnenoi, from 1204 to 1461, the Chrysokephalos in the Middle City and St Eugenios (Yeni Cuma Camii) in the eastern suburb are preserved as mosques,

their paintings and *opus sectile* floors safely hidden. The paintings and mosaic floor of the 13th-century monastic church of St Sophia in the western suburb are preserved as a museum. Of the final period of Trapezuntine Greek prosperity the exotic house that Constantine Kapayiannides built in the summer resort of Kryonero (Soğuksu) above Trebizond in 1903 is happily preserved as a museum too, because Mustafa Kemal Atatürk wrote part of his will there in 1937. But, after the *meydan*, the most impressive surviving monument of Greek culture in the city is the Phrontisterion, which still stands between the square and the sea, beside the site of the colossal and now dynamited cathedral of St Gregory of Nyssa. Founded by Sebastos Kymenites in 1683, this institute of higher education could claim to be the first of its kind in the Black Sea – Kymenites went on to regulate others in modern Romania. The elegant 19th-century building of the Phrontisterion now houses the Anadolu Lisesi, which retains its function of enlightenment.

ANTHONY A.M. BRYER

See also Pontus

Summary
A city on the southeastern shore of the Black Sea, Trebizond was founded as a Greek colony in the 7th century BC. Its position on the land route to Central Asia made it an internationally important port. Commercially it flourished especially under the Grand Komnenoi from 1204 to 1461, and in the 19th century. Several Greek buildings

survive, having been converted for use as mosques, museums, or schools.

Further Reading

Bryer, Anthony, *The Empire of Trebizond and the Pontos*, London: Variorum, 1980

Bryer, Anthony and David Winfield, *The Byzantine Monuments and Topography of the Pontos*, 2 vols, Washington, DC: Dumbarton Oaks, 1985

Kayaoğlu , G., O. Civaroğlu, and C. Akalin (editors), *Bir Tutkudur Trabzon*, Istanbul, 1997 (in Turkish)

Miller, William, *Trebizond: The Last Greek Empire*, London: SPCK, 1926

Papadopoulos-Kerameus, A. (editor), *Fontes Historiae Imperii Trapezuntini*, vol. 1, St Petersburg, 1897, reprinted Amsterdam: Hakkert, 1965

Philippidis, Chrysanthos (metropolitan of Trebizond), "I Ekklisia Trapezountos" [The Church of Trebizond], *Archeion Pontou* [Pontus Archive], 4–5 (1933)

Uspenzkij, F.J. and V.V. Beneshevich (editors), *Vazelonskie Akty*, Leningrad, 1927

Trikkala

City in Thessaly

Trikkala has had a long and varied history. As Trikka or Trike it appears in the *Iliad* as the home of the sons of Asclepius, one of whom, Machaon, was the chief physician of the Greeks. There are signs of Mycenaean and early Iron Age settlements in the area. In Classical times the town did not figure very prominently, situated as it was in a remote part of Thessaly, itself on the periphery of the Hellenic world. It appears occasionally in inscriptions. There is a shrine to Asclepius in the area. In 352 BC it suffered during the war between the Phocians and Philip of Macedon. It played a part in the wars between Rome and Macedon and that between Caesar and Pompey, occupying a strategic position at the foot of the high Zygos pass that provides the only route between Epirus and Thessaly. It was one of the cities that according to Procopius was fortified by Justinian (527–65), and there are traces of masonry from this period in the Turkish fortress, which is a conspicuous feature of the modern town. There is also one church that is of 6th-century origin.

After Justinian Trikkala passed from Byzantine control. In the 11th century, after Basil II (976–1025) had regained the Balkans, we still find Kekaumenos referring to Trikkala as a Vlach town. He is the first person to give the town its modern name, which may have a Vlach origin; as in Homer, there has always been some doubt as to whether it had two *k*s or one. Briefly captured by the Normans in 1082, Trikkala after the Fourth Crusade was sometimes in Byzantine, sometimes in Epirot control. The Serbs occupied it in 1348, and the last Serbian ruler in the region, Symeon Uroš, made it for a short time the capital of the fragment of the empire that he had inherited from his brother Stephan IV Dushan. The 13th and 14th centuries in spite of, or more probably because of, the frequent changes of ruler were great periods for church building, and most of Trikkala's Byzantine churches date from this period.

The Turks made Trikkala a provincial capital, the seat of a bey, and many Turks moved into the town. Remains of a picturesque Turkish quarter including a graceful mosque can be seen to this day, although all the Turks left after World War I and the exchange of populations. A third element of the population were the Vlachs from the villages of the Pindus who came down to the town in winter. Writing at the beginning of the 19th century, Leake comments on the mixed population, noting that many of the Turks were absentee landlords. At the time he wrote, Trikkala was controlled by Ali Pasha from Epirus, and the town had been sacked by marauding Albanians in 1770. Holland, writing of a journey in 1810, said that the population was mainly Turkish, and enumerates ten churches, seven mosques, and two synagogues. In 1853 Tozer talks of gleaming minarets, but these have vanished.

In 1881 Trikkala became Greek. Possibly because of the Turkish element in the population it did not play a particularly prominent part in the war of 1897 or the campaign to free Macedonia or the Balkan Wars, as might have been expected from a town that was on the borders of the unliberated areas of Macedonia and Epirus. The Balkan Wars moved back the frontier, and the exchange of populations removed the Turkish element. There was some brigandage between the wars, and the town suffered in World War II and the Civil War that followed it. The severed head of Ares Velouchiotis was displayed there in 1947. These not very distant events seem a far cry from the present state of Trikkala, pleasantly situated on the banks of the Lethaios river with the plains of Thessaly on the one side and the Pindus mountains on the other. Although only the third town of Thessaly after Larissa and Volos, to which it is attached by an erratic rail service, Trikkala acts as the centre for both the villages of the west Thessalian plain, and for the villages, many of them Vlach, of the east Pindus, the local bus station being a hive of activity.

T. J. WINNIFRITH

See also Thessaly

Summary

The third city of Thessaly after Larissa and Volos, Trikkala has existed since the Bronze Age and is mentioned by Homer. It had a shrine to Asclepius. As the gateway to the Zygos pass it was fortified by Justinian. Occupied by the Serbs in 1348, it was briefly the capital of their empire. Under the Ottomans it was a provincial capital. It became Greek in 1881.

Further Reading

Holland, Henry, *Travels in the Ionian Isles, Albania, Thessaly, Macedonia, etc., during the Years 1812 and 1813*, London: Longman Hurst Rees Orme and Brown, 1815

Leake, William Martin, *Travels in Northern Greece, Albania, Thessaly, Macedonia, etc., during the Years 1812 and 1813*, 4 vols, London: Rodwell, 1835; reprinted Amsterdam: Hakkert, 1967

Tozer, H.F., *Researches in the Highlands of Turkey, including Visits to Mounts Ida, Athos, Olympus, and Pelion, to the Mirdite Albanians and other Remote Tribes*, 2 vols, London: John Murray, 1869

Triklinios, Dimitrios *c.1280–c.1340*

Scholar

Triklinios was born in Thessalonica probably around 1280. He began his scholarly career in his home town under the guidance of Thomas Magistros. One of his early editions is a rhetorical corpus (Hermogenes and Aphthonius) contained in an autograph of 1308, in which Triklinios still calls himself Triklines. In his edition of Hesiod (another autograph, dated both 1316 and 1319) Triklinios for the first time subscribes as Triklinios; before this he may already have undertaken an edition of Theocritus. He also corrected the text of what is our chief manuscript witness for the fables of Babrius. Compared with his later work, however, these are mere preliminaries.

During the second decade of the 14th century Triklinios came into contact with the school at Constantinople of Manuel Moschopoulos, who had become the successor of Maximos Planudes; Triklinios either stayed longer in the capital himself or at least visited it several times during those years. At Constantinople he worked with manuscripts written by Planudes and revised the Planudean Anthology. Moreover, the contacts with Moschopoulos and his school apparently stimulated Triklinios's interest in ancient metre and set him on his way to his most decisive contribution to scholarship: Triklinios in fact came furthest of all Byzantine scholars in grasping some basic principles of ancient Greek lyric metre. In this area scholars before Triklinios could draw upon not much more than the metrical handbook of Hephaestion and more or less ancient notes (scholia) connected with the poems of Pindar. Moschopoulos had already made a start in further elucidating the structures of Pindaric metre (he was the first to discover the triadic structure in Pindar's *Olympian Ode* 5), but Triklinios in time surpassed Moschopoulos considerably. He developed a firm understanding of the triadic strophic systems in Pindar's choral songs (in which the first two parts of a triad are characterized by elaborate response) and after that probably turned his attention to the lyric passages of the Attic dramatists, which (apart from some metrical scholia on Aristophanes) were almost totally devoid of any help with the metre. Working on the tragedians Triklinios gradually discovered that the lyrics in Greek drama had structures similar to Pindaric odes (i.e. triadic and internally responding), a really fundamental insight; by 1319 he seems to have come to a full appreciation of response in tragic lyrics.

Working with Moschopoulos apparently induced Triklinios to produce his first commentary on Pindar, which contained only the *Olympian Odes*. After returning to Thessalonica – where he was to stay until his death (around 1340) – he embarked on annotating and editing the Greek dramatists (his work on Euripides probably started only after he had already worked on Aristophanes and Sophocles, with Aeschylus probably coming last, i.e. not before 1330); he also expanded his commentary on Pindar beyond the *Olympian Odes*. Careful study of manuscripts connected with Triklinios (e.g. Triklinios's autograph of the "Byzantine triad" of the plays of Aristophanes, i.e. *Plutus*, *Clouds*, and *Frogs*, discovered by Koster in the 1950s) has shown how he proceeded: he copied a manuscript of Thomas Magistros, revised its text several times, added metrical notes and excerpts from the old scholia

to Thomas's commentary, and thus created a new edition. Triklinios proceeded similarly in the case of the Euripidean triad: he based his own edition on Thomas's so-called second edition of Euripides and supplemented it over the years with additional notes; he also rewrote a number of pages, especially those containing choral parts, which he corrected considerably. Triklinios's "work in progress" on this and other authors well shows how he moved from a more primitive metrical annotation to a more complex one.

It is important to note that Triklinios also moved beyond the very restricted number of plays tackled by his predecessors as part of the normal Byzantine school curriculum – the "triad" of Aeschylus (*Prometheus*, *Persians*, *Seven against Thebes*), of Sophocles (*Ajax*, *Electra*, *Oedipus Tyrannus*), of Aristophanes (see above), and seven plays by Euripides. Thus, among the five tragedies of Aeschylus edited by Triklinios there were two (*Agamemnon* and *Eumenides*) that had previously been ignored. Of Sophocles, Triklinios edited all seven plays still extant, basing this edition on a text by Thomas Magistros (who had supplied only four tragedies with notes), on Moschopoulos's recension of the Byzantine triad, and on one or two "old" (i.e. pre-Palaiologan) manuscripts. Triklinios's edition of Aristophanes contained eight plays instead of the former three. Most important, however, was his edition of all the surviving plays of Euripides: he found the sole surviving manuscript of the so-called alphabetic plays of Euripides and revised and annotated it.

By this indefatigable activity over many years, Triklinios became the greatest of all Byzantine editors of Classical Greek texts. He wrote introductions and explanatory notes for the metre of each part of the plays he commented upon, and he usually tried to base his editions on several manuscripts, a practice not yet very common in his time (or afterwards). It was in these editions of dramatic texts that Triklinios reaped a rich harvest of corrections based on his superior knowledge of metre; Triklinios in fact is the only Byzantine scholar whose name still appears in the critical apparatus of modern editions of ancient texts. Apart from his editorial work, Triklinios had other scholarly interests as well, for example in astronomy (he wrote an essay on lunar theory) and in geography (he annotated a manuscript of Ptolemy's *Geography*).

In the later decades of his life, contacts between Thessalonica and Constantinople became much more precarious (due to the constantly deteriorating political situation of the dwindling empire and Thessalonica's growing isolation), so that Triklinios's final editions with their remarkable philological achievements apparently remained unknown in Constantinople until the beginning of the 15th century. Between 1423 and perhaps 1432 an increased interest in Triklinios's philological contributions is documented by some manuscripts written then (in the circle of John Chortasmenos); another such period already postdates the fall of the empire (1489–95: manuscripts produced in Crete, where the material remains of Triklinios's scholarship had been transmitted). Every time, however, that Triklinios's work was brought to the attention of scholars, they have been justifiably enthusiastic about his mastery of the principles of ancient Greek metre, the level of which had not been attained since Alexandrian times and was reached again only several centuries afterwards in western philology. Already one of Triklinios's pupils in his awe called him a "mystagogue", Wilamowitz (1889) acclaimed him as the first modern critic of tragedy, and still today his achievement is judged as "admirable on any count" (Zuntz, 1965).

HEINZ-GÜNTHER NESSELRATH

See also Scholarship

Biography

Born in Thessalonica c.1280, Triklinios was a pupil of Thomas Magistros. Visiting Constantinople he had contact with the school of Manuel Moschopoulos and worked on manuscripts copied by Maximos Planudes. He developed an unprecedented understanding of ancient lyric metre and wrote a commentary on Pindar. He also edited the texts of the three great tragedians of Classical Athens, and of Aristophanes. He died c.1340.

Further Reading

Günther, Hans-Christian, *The Manuscripts and the Transmission of the Palaeologan Scholia on the Euripidean Triad*, Stuttgart: Steiner, 1995, pp. 115–17, pp. 128–32, pp. 187–97

Günther, Hans-Christian, *Ein neuer metrischer Traktat und das Studium der pindarischen Metrik in der Philologie der Paläologenzeit*, Leiden: Brill, 1998, pp. 167–85

Koster, W.J.W., *Autour d'un manuscrit d'Aristophane écrit par Démétrius Triclinius: Etudes paléographiques et critiques sur les éditions d'Aristophane de l'époque byzantine tardive*, Groningen: Wolters, 1957

Langwitz Smith, Ole, "Tricliniana", *Classica et Mediaevalia*, 33 (1981–82): pp. 239–62

Langwitz Smith, Ole, "Tricliniana II", *Classica et Mediaevalia*, 43 (1992): pp. 187–229

Wilamowitz-Moellendorff, Ulrich von, *Euripides: Herakles*, vol. 1: *Einleitung in die attische Tragödie*, Berlin: Weidmann, 1889, reprinted Darmstadt: Wissenschaftliche Buchgesellschaft, 1981–85; vol. 1 printed separately as *Einleitung in die griechische Tragödie*, Berlin, Weidmann, 1907, reprinted 1921

Wilson, N.G., *Scholars of Byzantium*, 2nd edition, London: Duckworth, and Cambridge, Massachusetts: Medieval Academy of America, 1996

Zuntz, Günther, *An Inquiry into the Transmission of the Plays of Euripides*, Cambridge: Cambridge University Press 1965, pp. 27–125

Trikoupis, Charilaos 1832–1896

Politician

Charilaos Trikoupis was the most important Greek reformer of the 19th century. His contribution was multifaceted. He was responsible for ensuring that the royal head of state would refrain from granting a mandate to governments that lacked the confidence of parliament, he introduced legislation that secured the tenure of civil servants, he created a modern political party based on liberal democratic principles as well as discipline, he improved the readiness of the armed forces and military education, and, most of all, he attempted the monumental task of creating the infrastructure necessary for the take-off of the Greek economy. His thrust, however, was impeded by unfavourable international circumstances and his foreign loans therefore were instrumental in inflicting bankruptcy on the state. Although he did not live to witness the

fruition of his strategy for growth, subsequent generations of politicians reaped the harvest of his labour.

Son of Spyridon Trikoupis (historian and prime minister), he studied law in Athens and Paris and entered the diplomatic service in 1856. While serving in London he was elected representative of the city's Greek community in the Hellenic parliament. As a parliamentarian, Trikoupis made good use of his diplomatic skill during the negotiations for the 1864 accession of the Ionian islands to Greece. In 1865 he resigned from the diplomatic service and was elected representative of Missolonghi, his parental home-town. In 1866 he became foreign minister in a government headed by his future political opponent, Alexander Koumoundouros, and signed a treaty with Serbia. During the 1874 constitutional crisis his famous article, "Who is to blame?", criticizing royal interventions in parliamentary politics, earned him a brief prison sentence, but his position was vindicated. He was foreign minister again in the 1877 grand coalition under Constantine Kanaris and in 1880, after the fall of a Koumoundouros government, he became prime minister. His 1882 government was the first of several, the duration of which allowed his reforms to take effect. His defeat in 1885 by his populist opponent Theodoros Deliyannis reflected public discontent with his austerity programme. The see-saw of victory and defeat between Trikoupis and Deliyannis continued during the decade of 1886–96, but with the bankruptcy of 1893 the former's popularity waned until his abject electoral defeat in 1895. He died in a Parisian hotel a year later while Greece was hosting the first modern Olympic Games.

Trikoupis's times constitute an interlude between two eras of modern history. The transition from steam to electricity was accompanied by a protracted recession of the more developed Western economies with a concomitant dearth of domestic demand for capital. In their quest for customers many Western banks turned to the states of the developing periphery of Europe and Trikoupis was quick to embrace the opportunity of available credit to spur the growth of his country's economy. His substantial investment in the construction of railway networks was aimed at unifying disparate agricultural regions into an expanded market. In this project Trikoupis was repeating the experiment of western European industrial prototypes. His venture however yielded fewer economic results in the short term than was anticipated. Domestic markets were still in their infancy and could not be induced technologically to a state of development that required a few decades of growth and social transformation. Although this and other public works laid the infrastructure of a transportation system that proved invaluable for the future take-off of the Greek economy, the railways of Trikoupis were in his time perceived as a premature and costly undertaking that benefited speculators, financiers, and international middlemen. Such people became a familiar spectacle in the Greek capital and the object of criticism by Trikoupis's chief political opponent, Deliyannis. The latter was an exponent of splendid isolation from international financial influences and a firm believer in an agrarian economy that aspired to self-sufficiency, rather than economic growth. Deliyannis's major flaw, however, was his predilection for irredentist adventures that proved inconsistent with his pipe dream of independence from foreign creditors and great-power involvement. His views in fact caused more foreign intervention in Greek affairs than Trikoupis's own policy of growth.

At about the same time, Russia's return to Balkan politics after a long period of absence, following its Crimean misadventure, revived the slumbering Eastern Question. The Russo-Turkish war that ended in 1878 with the San Stefano treaty encouraged the irredentist debate in the Balkans, and Greek governments were faced with the dilemma between Trikoupis's priority of domestic development and Deliyannis's agenda of territorial aggrandizement. Trikoupis had visited Serbia, Bulgaria, and Romania in an abortive attempt to forge a Balkan alliance in 1891 but was soon disappointed and thereafter pursued a policy of abstaining from confrontations with Turkey. In the Cretan uprising of 1889 he went as far as to discourage the insurgents and was for that reason defeated in the elections.

The Graeco-Turkish war of 1897 was largely created by the political camp that considered irredentist priorities more pressing than development and growth. The disastrous outcome of the war nevertheless vindicated Trikoupis.

THANOS M. VEREMIS

Biography

Born in Nauplia in 1832 the son of prime minister Spyridon Trikoupis, Charilaos Trikoupis studied law in Athens and Paris. He entered the diplomatic service in 1856. In 1865 he became MP for Missolonghi and in 1866 foreign minister. He was five times prime minister: 1880, 1882–85, 1886–90, 1892, 1893–95. He modernized the economy and the armed forces. He died in Paris in 1896.

Further Reading

Andreadis, A., *Ta dimosia oikonomika tis Ellados* [The Public Economy of Greece], Athens, 1924

Gardika-Alexandropoulou, K., "I Elliniki Koinonia tin Epochi to H. Trikoupi" [Greek Society in the Times of Trikoupis] in *Opsis tis Ellinikis Koinonias tou 19ou Aiona* [Aspects of Greek Society in the 19th Century], edited by D. Tsaousis, Athens, 1984

Papayannakis, Lefteris, *Oi Ellinikoi Sidirodromoi, 1882–1910* [Greek Railways, 1882–1910], Athens, 1982

Peri Charilaou Trikoupi, ek Dimosievmaton [Published Sources on Charilaos Trikoupis], vols 1–16, Athens, 1907–12 (from October 1862 to May 1884)

Stassinopoulos, E., *O Stratos tis protis ekatontaetias* [The Army in the First Hundred Years], Athens, 1935, pp. 55–60

Tsokopoulos, G., *Charilaos Trikoupis: Viographia* [Charilaos Trikoupis: A Biography], Athens, 1896

Woodhouse, C.M., *Modern Greece: A Short History*, 5th edition, London and Boston: Faber, 1991

Tripolis

City in Arcadia

Tripolis, the capital city of Arcadia, lies at the foot of Mount Mainalon, in the centre of the Arcadian plain at an altitude of 655 m above sea level, surrounded by Mainalon, Ktenias, Artemision, Parthenion, Taygetus, and the mountains of Dimitsana. Due to its geographical position, it is the administrative centre of the Peloponnese and has between 30,000 and 35,000 inhabitants. The city's economy depends on several industrial units related to leather dressing, carpet making, weaving, cheese manufacture, etc. Its inhabitants are also engaged in trade, cattle breeding, and agriculture. In the vicinity there are marble quarries as well as local iron ores. In the 20th century Tripolis suffered the greatest mass emigration of all Greek regions.

In 1476 Stefano Magno in his *Estratti degli Annali Veneti* referred to "Dropoliza" as one of the deserted castles of the Peloponnese and we find the same toponym on maps dating from the 16th century. As far as the provenance of the name is concerned, it is generally accepted that the name Dropoliza, which changed in the 19th century to the literary form Tripolis, derived from the Slavonic word *dabr*, which means oak tree. This agrees with Pausanias' description (c.AD 150) which confirmed that the place was full of oak trees. The originally obscure settlement began to develop after the conquest of Mouchli(on) by the Ottoman Turks in 1458, but the name Dropoliza is rarely mentioned during the first two centuries of Ottoman rule. In the middle of the 17th century sources refer to revolutionary activity by several people originating from Tripolis, and references become more frequent after the end of the Turko-Venetian war (1686–99), when the Peloponnese was occupied by the Venetians. The *teritorrio* of Tripolitza had a population of no more than 8000, including 1200 inhabitants of the town of Tripolis and also about 50 large villages.

The reoccupation of the Peloponnese by the Turks in 1715 was an important event for the history of the town. At first it was one of the 17 *vileatia* (provinces) into which the region was divided and after 1719 it became the seat of the pasha of the Peloponnese. Its population increased gradually and by the end of the 18th century it had reached 10,000 inhabitants, of whom one quarter were Turks. During the Orloff rebellion (1770) the town was besieged by the Russians and the Peloponnesians and was badly damaged. Until 1799 Tripolis suffered continuous disasters and plunderings by Albanian troops. From 1807 to 1812 Veli Pasha, the second son of Ali Pasha, was commander of the town. In the last decade before the revolution it was the most important military base in southern Greece. The siege of Tripolis by the Greeks started in the first days of April 1821 and lasted five months, resulting in its capture by Theodore Kolokotronis and his men on 23 September 1821; this victory was the first important prize of the Greek revolution. After the liberation, Patras, Nauplia, Kalamata, and Tripolis became the most significant administrative centres of the Peloponnese, which was then divided into five prefectures. Tripolis – the name was established at that period – was the capital of the prefecture of Messenia. In February 1822 it became the seat of the Peloponnesian Senate. In June 1825 Ibrahim conquered Tripolis, and destroyed it completely on 16 February 1828. In 1834 the Court of First Instance was installed there, as well as one of the two courts of appeal in Greece. During the 19th century Tripolis showed important progress in the cultural and economic fields.

The town of Tripolis, although totally destroyed in 1828 by Ibrahim, still preserves important architectural monuments. The cathedral of Hagios Vasileios and the church of Hagioi Taxiarches, the Neoclassical Malliaropouleion Municipal Theatre, Mantzouneios Municipal Library, town hall, and court of justice are some of the most important traditional buildings in the town. The Archaeological Museum (1895–1905), which was designed by the famous Austrian architect Ernst Ziller, houses the cultural and archaeological treasures of Arcadia. Many important personalities were born in Tripolis, including the poet Konstantinos Karyotakes, the writer Nikos Gatsos, the academic Nikos Veis, the philologists G. Mystriotes and D. Goudes, and the writers T. Valtinos, Y. Panou, B. Benopoulos, G. Lambrakis, A. Petronotes, and the Angelopoulos brothers.

CHRYSANTHI GALLOU

See also Arcadia

Summary

The capital of Arcadia, Tripolis is the administrative centre of the Peloponnese. The town was of little importance before the 17th century. In 1719 it became the seat of the pasha of the Peloponnese. It was liberated in 1821 and became the seat of the Peloponnesian Senate. It was destroyed by Ibrahim in 1828 but recovered later in the 19th century.

Further Reading

Gritsopoulos, Tasou A., *Istoria tes Tripolitsas* [The History of Tripolitsa], 3 vols, Athens, 1972–76

Moutsopoulos, N., *Arkadikes Spoudes: To Rhythmistiko Schedio tis Tripolis* [Arcadian Studies: The Overall Plan of Tripolis], 2 vols, Thessalonica, 1974

Tsakopoulos, Panayotis, *Tripolis: Poleodomic, Morphological Study of the Transition from the Ottoman to the Neo-hellenic City*, vol. 1, Athens: Society for the Study of New Hellenism, 1985, pp. 297–325 (in Greek)

Tsakopoulos, Panayotis, "L' Urbanisme dans le Péloponnèse au XIXe siècle: de la ville ottomane à la ville néohellenique" (dissertation), University of Paris X, 1986

Zacharopoulos, I.Z., *Arkadia*, Tripolis, 1987 (in Greek)

Trojan War

The Trojan war was a legendary expedition undertaken by the Mycenaean Greeks against the people of Troy, the modern Hisarlik which lies in northwest Asia Minor, 6.5 km from the Aegean coast. This military operation was made famous mainly through the *Iliad* and *Odyssey*, two epic poems attributed to the Archaic poet Homer.

Hisarlik's identification with the Homeric Troy has never been proved, but it is generally assumed that the legends relating the Trojan War also encompass elements of historical truth. It is plausible that the Mycenaean Greeks could have destroyed Troy between 1270 and 1190 BC; Troy VIIa – which lasted until 1190 BC – is considered by Carl Blegen to be the Homeric city, but others push the date of the sack back to *c.*1270 BC, the time that coincides with the peak of power of both Mycenaean Greece and Troy. According to Thucydides, the Achaeans' sack of Troy led to no permanent settlement in the Troad; instead the Greeks returned home with their plunder to face destructions connected with the Dorian invasion, which put an end to the Mycenaean period.

Neither the *Iliad* nor the *Odyssey* gives a comprehensive account of the events related to the Trojan War. The *Iliad* concentrates on only four days of fighting in the tenth and last year of the war and its major theme is Achilles' anger over

Briseis, who was given to him as booty and subsequently taken away from him by Agamemnon. The *Odyssey* includes consecutive flashbacks of Odysseus' adventurous trip home, and its second half is devoted to Odysseus' cunning restoration of order in Ithaca.

Several other aspects of these events were covered by the cyclic epics, subsequent hexameter poems reproducing the repertoire of the oral bards and indicative of the heroic poetry before Homer. Among them, the *Cypria* narrates the causes of the Trojan War, the judgement of Paris, the abduction of Helen, and the gathering of the Greeks in Aulis; the *Aethiopis* recounts the story of Amazon Penthesileia and the death of Achilles; the *Sack of Ilium* deals with events connected with the Greek victory such as the ruse of the wooden horse and the deaths of Priam and Astyanax; the *Telegonia* narrates the later adventures and the death of Odysseus.

The Trojan War is widely represented on Greek vases, sculpture, and architecture. Among the earliest Archaic representations of scenes from the Trojan War are the wooden horse on the 7th-century pithos of Mykonos (still in situ), the pediments of the temple of Aphaia Athena in Aegina, and several black-figure vases from Athens and elsewhere. Famous later representations include the metopes from the north side of the Parthenon and the temple of Asclepius in Epidaurus.

Subsequent Greek literature gives centre stage to the Trojan War. Both Herodotus and Thucydides attempt to provide rational accounts of the war, but Stesichorus' famous *Palinode* and Sappho's ode to Helen's passion for Paris (fr. 16 L-P) are indicative samples of the poets' early fascination with the legendary beauty of the queen of Sparta. Helen, the dehumanizing power of the war, and the ambiguities of military heroism are also some of the main themes developed further in the Athenian tragedies of the 5th century BC. Famous among those surviving are Aeschylus' *Agamemnon*, Sophocles' *Philoctetes*, and Euripides' *Hecuba*, *Andromache*, *Troades*, and *Iphigeneia in Aulis*. In post-Classical times *Hecuba* was one of the three tragic plays of the Byzantine academic canon. In early modern times the earliest attempts at the revival of tragedy include P. Katsaitis' *Tragedy of Iphigeneia* (1720) and Metastasios' *Achilles en Skyro* from the period of the Greek Enlightenment (1794).

The Trojan War and its deeply human conflicts have survived in Greek literature to the present day. Modern literature, mainly of the late 19th and the 20th century, has given remarkable centrality to the Trojan myth. Constantine Cavafy's famous *Ithaca* (1905–1915) is the first in a series of symbolic interpretations of Odysseus' wanderings as an inexhaustible source of self-learning and self-renewal; Nikos Kazantzakis' *Odysseia* (1938), with Odysseus involved in a revolt against Pharaoh in Egypt and in an uprising of workers and slaves in Knossos, is another striking example.

Ancient Troy is rooted in the poets' subconscious life. It is part of a continuum: in Angelos Sikelianos's *Lyrikos Vios* the epic coexists with folk elements and Odysseus is linked with Solomos and Palamas. In poems such as George Seferis's *King of Asine* (1940) and *Helen* a series of images evocative of the nation's past becomes the means that captures the mood of current historical moments. The Homeric themes give depth to modern Greek worries and visions and the Homeric figures are anachronistically revived in modern Greek society. So Takis

Trojan War: Sophia Schliemann wearing the so-called Treasure of Priam, discovered by her husband at Troy

Sinopoulos portrays Helen and Elpenor in a taxi or on the train from Larissa; similarly, Yiannis Ritsos' Agamemnon, Heleni, and Iphigeneia, even though explicitly evoking their mythical past, are familiar figures of modern Greek reality, whose disturbingly disrupted lives reflect the political and social turbulence of this reality that Ritsos wants to denounce.

Alongside the existential projection of the Trojan myth into modern Greek poetry, the Trojan War has had a separate revival with a wider social impact in many modern performances of Greek tragedy. Even though several Trojan plays – such as Euripides' *Helen* – were not properly re-established until the 1960s, the Trojan saga was the subject of engagingly powerful performances; notable among them were Marika Kotopouli's acclaimed Hecuba in the Panathenaic Stadium (1927), when the chorus of the defeated Trojan women-refugees recalled recent poignant memories of the Asia Minor defeat, and Anna Synodinou's moving Andromache in the theatre of Dodona (1963).

EFROSSINI SPENTZOU

Further Reading
Bianchi Bandinell, Ranuccio, *Hellenistic-Byzantine Miniatures of the Iliad*, Olten: Graf, 1955

Blegen, Carl William, *Troy and the Trojans*, London: Thames and Hudson, and New York: Praeger, 1963
Emlyn-Jones, C. (editor), *Homer: Readings and Images*, London: Duckworth, 1992
Finley, M.I., *The World of Odysseus*, 2nd edition, London: Chatto and Windus, and New York: Viking, 1978
Foxhall, Lin and John K. Davies, *The Trojan War: Its Historicity and Context*, Bristol: Bristol Classical Press, 1984
Friar, Kimon, *Modern Greek Poetry*, New York: Simon and Schuster, 1973
Kakridis, Johannes T., *Homeric Researches*, Lund: Gleerup, 1949
Keeley, Edmund, *Modern Greek Poetry: Voice and Myth*, Princeton, New Jersey: Princeton University Press, 1983
Mackridge, Peter (editor), *Ancient Greek Myth in Modern Greek Poetry: Essays in Memory of C.A. Trypanis*, London: Cass, 1996
Mylonas, George E., *Mycenae and the Myceanean Age*, Princeton, New Jersey: Princeton University Press, 1966
Prevelakis, Pandelis, *Nikos Kazantzakis and His Odyssey*, New York: Simon and Schuster, 1962
Scherer, Margaret R., *Legends of Troy in Art and Literature*, New York and London, Phaidon Press, 1963
Stanford, W.B. and J.V. Luce, *The Quest for Ulysses*, New York: Praeger, 1974; London: Phaidon, 1975
Woodford, Susan, *The Trojan War in Ancient Art*, London: Duckworth, and Ithaca, New York: Cornell University Press, 1993

Tsakonians

Ethnic group from the eastern Peloponnese

There are still today on Mount Parnon in the eastern Peloponnese a few villages where Tsakonian is spoken. This is a language of Greek origin, but it is virtually unintelligible to other Greeks. Alone among modern Greek dialects Tsakonian appears to derive not from the Attic koine, but from Doric, the dialect of ancient Sparta, which is parodied by Aristophanes, appears on inscriptions, and is recorded in the 5th century AD by Hesychius. The most obvious feature of the dialect is the substitution of alpha for eta. Thus "day" in Tsakonian is *hamera* (instead of *hemera*), "mother" is *mate* (instead of *metera*). Another feature of ancient Spartan apparent in Tsakonian is the rhotacism that turns *tes hemeras* into *tar ameri*. The dialect has other peculiarities that owe nothing to Spartan origins, in particular the fact that the present and imperfect tenses can only be found in a periphrastic form. Thus "I see" is *emi horu* or *emi horua* if the speaker is feminine, and "I was seeing" is *ema horu*.

The similarity between the words *Tsakones* and *Lakones* has led both ancient and modern writers to claim a further proof of this remarkable survival, but the similarity may be coincidental. The Spartans called themselves Lakedaimonians rather than Lakonians and the change from *l* to *ts* is not explicable, although other consonants do change to *ts*, *kai* becoming *tse*. The first reference to Tsakonians is in the *Chronicle of Monemvasia* (c.1000 AD). This describes them as living in the neighbourhood of that town, simultaneously claiming that the Lakonians, still preserving their dialect, had fled to Italy; one version of this chronicle expressly links Lakonians and Tsakonians. Other medieval sources are less specific about the Lakonian origins of the Tsakonians, and indeed do not necessarily describe them as an ethnic group or place them in the

Peloponnese. Thus Constantine VII Porphyrogennetos (913–59) among others mentions Tsekones as a kind of military corps, and we find Tsekones and Tsakones referred to in Thessaly and Macedonia. Sometimes the term is used with a derogatory religious sense to describe Paulician heretics.

In the 14th century the *Chronicle of the Morea* places Tsakonia in the Peloponnese without any very precise location, and in the 15th century Theodore Palaiologos mentions Tsakonia and the names of some existing Tsakonian villages such as Prastos and Kastanista. In 1668 the Turkish traveller Evliya Çelebi appears to place Tsakonia to the west rather than the north of Monemvasia. This may be a mistake, but it might suggest that the dialect was once spoken more widely. When philologists discovered Tsakonians at the end of the 18th century, they were confined to Cynouria, a small area of northeastern Laconia, and perhaps numbered about 10,000 people. In the past few years, with new roads in the interior and Leonidion on the coast more accessible by sea, Tsakonians have been subject to the modern pressures that destroy minority languages.

Sparta was a conservative state and tried to preserve its particular constitution even in the Hellenistic age. There is evidence, however, that in the towns koine rapidly prevailed, and 2nd-century AD inscriptions in Sparta do not differ from those in Athens. It was different in remote rural areas. Two other factors combined to keep a Dorian dialect going. Laconia was reluctant to accept Christianity with its centralizing tendency, and we hear of paganism in Mani as late as the 8th century. Moreover the Slav invasions of the 6th and 7th centuries would cut off Dorian pockets from their fellow Greek speakers. The slow reclamation of mainland Greece from the Slavs would require special bodies of soldiers, and it is therefore not surprising that we find Tsakones both in the Peloponnese and elsewhere, although only in the former did the name last and only in the former did they speak a dialect derived from ancient Spartan. Attempts to link the language of the Tsakonians in Cynouria with other odd dialects such as the language of Silli in Asia Minor (Pernot, 1934) and even the language of the Vlachs in the Pindus (Katsanes, 1989) seem far fetched, although there were Tsakonian colonies in the Propontis that after the transfer of the populations managed to preserve their dialect for a time in the Macedonian village of Chionades. The number of those stubbornly speaking Tsakonian now is about 300, and the fate of the language seems as doomed as that of the 300 who fought at Thermopylae.

T.J. WINNIFRITH

See also Dorians

Summary

Tsakonians are a people who live in the eastern Peloponnese and speak a language that appears to derive from Doric. Attempts to link this Tsakonian language with Lakonian are unproved. Today Tsakonian speakers number about 300.

Further Reading

Browning, Robert, *Medieval and Modern Greek*, London: Hutchinson, 1969

Caratzas, Stamatis C., *Les Tzacones*, Berlin and New York: de Gruyter, 1976

Charalampoulos, A., *Phonologiki analysi tis Tsakonikis dialektou* [Phonological Analysis of the Tsakonian Dialect], Thessalonica, 1980

Katsanes, N., "Koutsovlachica kai Tsakonika" [Koutslovachian and Tsakonian], *Helleniki Dialektologia* [Greek Dialectology], 1 (1989): pp. 41–61

Pernot, Hubert, *Introduction a l'étude du dialect Tsakonien*, Paris: Belles Lettres, 1934

Scutt, C., "The Tzakonian Dialects", *Annual of the British School at Athens*, 19–20 (1912–14): pp. 133–73 and 18–31

Tsarouchis, Ioannis 1910–1989

Painter, stage designer, and director

The painter Ioannis Tsarouchis was born into an affluent merchant family. Tsarouchis's talent extended to many fields, but it is no exaggeration to style him the father of postwar Greek painting. His first period proper as a professional painter began in 1936 following his studies under Konstantinos Parthenis at the School of Fine Arts in Athens from 1928 to 1934. He had also been an apprentice, from 1930 to 1934, in the workshop of the painter Photis Kontoglou who introduced him to the secrets of Byzantine painting and to the whole culture of Byzantium in general. Tsarouchis's second period, highly influenced by the European Renaissance, may be said to have begun in 1969 and terminated with his death.

For Tsarouchis, as for many Greek artists, Paris was to become a second home. In 1936, on his first period of travels abroad, he met Matisse, Laurens, and Giacometti in Paris. His first one-man show was held in Paris in 1951 and in London later that year. Moreover, from 1967 to 1984 Paris was Tsarouchis's home. Between 1951 and 1957, he established a fruitful relationship with the Iolas Gallery in New York. Tsarouchis was probably the first Greek painter that could be classed as a European artist, but he by no means abandoned the long and multifarious artistic tradition of his homeland.

From Kontoglou, Tsarouchis learnt that inspiration is something totally different from tradition. In the 1930s one recognizes in Tsarouchis's works powerful influences from contemporary European painting, especially Matisse. Such influences, however, were harmoniously blended with elements drawn from the traditional Greek shadow theatre (*Karaghiozis*), from the art of the Greek folk painter Theophilos Chatzimichail, from Byzantine art, ancient Greek Classical art, and, of course, from the Egyptian Fayum portraits. All these influences are recognizable in most of Tsarouchis's output. His first main period is marked by youthful vitality and new ideas. His second period, however, from 1969, is more contemplative and attains a certain maturity, with memories of Renaissance art and, more particularly, of the art of 17th-century Italy. His canvases combine the formality of Byzantine style with a use of colour and a freedom typical of the Renaissance. He also executed several works of a distinctive baroque flavour, and was particularly aware of Dutch painting as represented by Vermeer, but also of ancient Greek art via the Pompeii wall paintings.

Much has been said and written about the "Greekness" of Tsarouchis's work, especially of that executed in the 1930s. But nothing can replace the simple contemplation of the works themselves. Since Greece itself lies on the border between East and West, Tsarouchis strongly believed that national traditions could be used in a fecund combination with outside influences. He explains: "Do not accept it with enthusiasm nor reject it with hate, treat it as something inevitable." The artistic expression of this belief is evident in both periods in the thousands of variations he made on individual themes. Here, according to Tsarouchis, the world could be faithfully reflected. All his work, except for a short period of experimentation with cubism, surrealism, and abstract art, falls within this category.

Tsarouchis introduced Greek painting to a new repertoire of subject matter which reflected his basic thinking. Different types drawn from the life of the people: soldiers, sailors, and village women among the most popular. His central subject was the human being, most importantly the male nude. Much later, when he had isolated himself from people, he painted more and more landscapes and still lifes. He painted a disappearing world: the large Neoclassical houses and the grand coffee houses of Athens. In his works there is a tenacious sadness in the eyes of his fellow man. His art is a painted story, quite uneven, conservative yet revolutionary, somewhere between nostalgia and reality, imbued with a positive moral bearing and a conscious miniaturism.

Tsarouchis was also closely involved with stage design and the theatre in general. In 1935 he was stage designer of the National Theatre in Athens. Other theatres he worked with included the Theatro Khun, the ancient theatre at Epidaurus, the Dallas Civic Opera of Texas, Covent Garden in London, La Scala at Milan, the Olympico at Vicenza, and the National Popular Theatre of Paris. Tsarouchis designed the decor and costumes for Cherubini's opera *Medea*, which became a leading success for Maria Callas. Under his direction, Euripides' *Women of Troy* was staged in 1978 in the centre of Athens. With good sense and a new outlook on ancient drama, Tsarouchis transformed stage design in this field. In 1983 Aeschylus' *Seven against Thebes* was directed by him in Thebes. Both plays were performed in his translations from the ancient Greek. He also wrote humorous pantomimes.

Besides painting, the young Tsarouchis between 1935 and 1937 wrote surrealist poems that were published as a collection in 1980. In December 1986 a book of some 300 pages was published with articles he had written over the years about art and artists. Within two months it was in its third printing.

HANS HENDRIKX

Biography
Born in Piraeus in 1910, Tsarouchis was a pupil of Konstantinos Parthenis at the School of Fine Arts in Athens (1928–34). He was also an apprentice in the workshop of Photis Kontoglou (1930–34). He specialized in painting the male nude, landscapes, and still lifes. He lived in Paris 1967–84. He also designed and directed for the theatre. He died in Athens in 1989.

Writings
Translation (into modern Greek), *Trojan Women* by Euripides, Athens, 1978
Poems, 1934–1937, Athens, 1980 (in Greek)

Translation (into modern Greek), *Seven against Thebes*, by Aeschylus, Athens, 1983

Further Reading
Anadromiki Ekthesi Gianni Tsarouchi 1928–81 [Retrospective Exhibition: Ioannis Tsarouchis, 1928–81], Archaeological Museum of Thessalonica, 1981 (exhibition catalogue)
Tsarouchis (in Greek and French), Athens, 1978 (exhibition catalogue)

Turkey

The modern republic of Turkey was born from the ruins of the Ottoman empire after World War I, in 1923. Established partly in Europe (area of 23,623 sq km) and mostly in Asia (area of 756,953 sq km), it has a population of 60.8 million. European Turkey lies west of the Dardanelles, the Sea of Marmara, and the Bosporus; these link the Black Sea with the Mediterranean, giving the country control of important waterways. Asian Turkey, known also as Anatolia, with its fertile coastal plains constitutes the mainland. The geostrategic importance of the country "at a multifold crossroads between East and West, North and South, Christendom and Islam", and the fact that it was the main obstacle to Soviet expansion in the Mediterranean, "the southeast keystone of NATO during the Cold War", facilitated its integration into the Atlantic Alliance and its ties with western Europe and the United States.

There had been a close relationship between Greeks and Turks inside the Ottoman empire where Greeks lived for more than four centuries under Turkish domination. In 1923 Mustafa Kemal (later Atatürk) proclaimed the end of the Ottoman empire and created the nation state of Turkey. Encouraged by the hostility of some of the Allies (notably the French and the Italians) to Greece's presence in Asia Minor, Kemal refused to accept the Treaty of Sèvres signed by the sultan's delegation in August 1920. Receiving support from the Soviets who considered that the Greeks were acting on behalf of British imperialism, Kemal gained control of Anatolia. Abandoned by the British after Lloyd George's resignation, the Greeks were forced in August 1922 to evacuate Smyrna, which was sacked and looted. Greece had to absorb about a million and a half refugees under the terms of the exchange of populations. The Turks who were evacuated from Greece to Turkey amounted to fewer than 400,000. With the abandonment of the Treaty of Sèvres Greece lost Asia Minor, Eastern Thrace, and the islands of Imbros and Tenedos. Under the Treaty of Lausanne, signed in 1923, which confirmed these losses for Greece, Turkey renounced its claims on Cyprus in favour of Britain.

The debacle of 1922 remains a trauma for Greeks, the greatest national disaster since the fall of Constantinople in 1453. The Greek culture and population that had been established in Asia Minor for 3000 years were driven out. But the Lausanne treaty led to a normalization of Graeco-Turkish relations and a brief period of friendship followed.

Relations between the two countries later became hostile, however, and came dangerously close to a clash. A number of factors account for the deterioration of relations: the Turkish invasion and occupation of northern Cyprus, the Aegean dispute, and the question of minorities.

As far as minorities are concerned, the exchange of populations was not applied to the Muslims of western Thrace or to the Greeks of Constantinople. About 250,000 Greeks remained in Constantinople and on the islands of Imbros and Tenedos, while about 120,000 Muslims stayed in western Thrace. The Greek minority in Constantinople suffered continual harassment. For instance, in November 1942 the emergency tax called *varlik vergisi* (wealth tax) was imposed upon the community, a measure that caused distress and loss of property. In September 1955 anti-Greek riots encouraged by government officials led to the destruction of many churches as well as Greek businesses and properties. Thousands of Greeks were forced to leave Constantinople in an exodus that marked the end of the Greek community there. After the coup d'etat of 1960 the Turkish prime minister Menderes and the foreign minister Zorlu were subsequently charged and found guilty of inciting the riots.

Nevertheless the harassment of the tiny Greek minority continued. In 1964–65, 9000 Greeks were expelled and the Turkish government confiscated their property. In addition, the Turkish authorities placed restrictions on Greek educational establishments and in some cases closed them. From the 250,000 Greeks living in Constantinople in 1923, their number has declined to an anaemic 3000 consisting mostly of elderly people, while the Muslim minority in Western Thrace has not only prospered but is represented in the Greek parliament. Greece and the Greek diaspora in the US have also raised the case of the mistreatment and harassment of the ecumenical patriarchate of Constantinople and the restrictions imposed on it contrary to the Treaty of Lausanne and international law.

Even though relations remain tense, Greece and Turkey are allies inside NATO and under American influence. Efforts are made from time to time to reduce tension and improve the relationship. Yet these efforts are hampered by several factors: the political instability in Turkey, the Kurdish situation, and the rise of Islamic fundamentalism. Movements towards a "re-Islamization" and "re-Ottomanization" of Turkey's foreign policy also hinder these efforts.

Only increased democratization in Turkey and a respect for human rights may help to establish better relations with Greece. As long as the country remains under military supervision with what is considered from a Greek point of view to be an expansionist foreign policy – in Cyprus, in the Aegean, and even in the Balkans – relations between the two countries will continue to be tense and may become worse. Nevertheless, if we take the example of Franco-German reconciliation in the postwar period, there is no reason to assume that Greece and Turkey will be rivals for ever and that beneficial cooperation between the two countries is impossible.

STEPHANOS CONSTANTINIDES

Further Reading

Bahcheli, Tozun, *Greek–Turkish Relations since 1955*, Boulder, Colorado: Westview Press, 1990

Barchard, David, *Turkey and the West*, London and Boston: Routledge and Kegan Paul, 1985

Bozarslan, Hamit, *La Question Kurde: états et minorités au Moyen-Orient*, Paris: Presses de Sciences-Po, 1997

Chase, S. Robert, B. Emily Hill, and Paul Kennedy, "Pivotal States and US Strategy", *Foreign Affairs* (January/February 1996): pp. 37ff.

Constantinides, Stephanos, "Turkey: The Emergence of a New Foreign Policy, the Neo-Ottoman Imperial Model", *Journal of Political and Military Sociology*, 24/3 (Winter, 1996): pp. 323ff.

Constantinides, Stephanos and Paris Arnopoulos (editors), "The Aegean Dispute", special issue of *Etudes helléniques / Hellenic Studies*, 4/2 (Autumn 1996)

Rouleau, Eric, "Turkey: Beyond Atatürk", *Foreign Policy* (Summer 1996): pp. 71ff.

Vaner, Semih, Deniz Akagül, and Bahadir Kaleagasi, *La Turquie en mouvement*, Brussels: Complexe, 1995

Tyranny

The word "tyranny" was almost certainly Lydian in origin. From its first use in Greek – in a fragmentary poem of the 7th century BC by Archilochus of Paros – it was associated with the kingdoms of the Near East. The speaker in Archilochus' poem denies any ambition for the wealth of the Lydian king Gyges or for a great tyranny: "these things are far from my eyes". The term was subsequently applied, however, to a number of Greek figures – Pheidon of Argos, Polycrates of Samos, Cypselus and Periander of Corinth, Cleisthenes of Sicyon, Pisistratus and Hippias of Athens – who came to exercise dominant positions within their cities in the Archaic period of Greek history (7th to 6th centuries BC). These men were, characteristically, fringe members of a ruling elite of their city who took power with the help of a faction of supporters. In some cases it is possible that they represented a body of those who felt excluded – due to their status or their geographical position within the city's territory – from the political constitution. The common view, however, that the Archaic tyrants were the product of a newly wealthy class of hoplites (or heavily armed soldiers) who felt that their contribution to the city merited a share in its political offices, is, at the very least, a caricature. Many tyrants seized power with no sign of any great ground-swell of support, sometimes with only a handful of men. Arguably tyrants were motivated by little more than a desire for glory and power.

There are some signs of the contemporary popularity of the Archaic tyrants. Stories of miraculous escapes from death or of their usurpation being forecast by miracles may suggest that their rule was seen as divinely sponsored. Later writers often dwell on the mild and constitutional nature of tyrannical rule: tyrants are seen as exercising an excessive influence on the selection of magistrates but allowing such magistrates to rule according to the constitution of the city – even though such constitutions were themselves probably very ill defined. Tyrants seem often to have initiated massive building projects; such largesse must have bought them popularity. Tyranny, nevertheless, came to be seen as archetypally unconstitutional, often contrasted with kingship, the archetypally constitutional form of monarchy. This view of tyranny was first defined in theoretical terms by the historian Herodotus in his *Debate on the Constitutions*, a discussion between three Persians, shaped also by a stereotypical image of oriental kingdoms, on the relative merits of oligarchy, democracy, and tyranny. The tyrant, according to the Persian Otanes, "disturbs the ancestral laws, rapes women, and kills men without trial"; the unaccountability of a monarch will necessarily breed hubris and violence. Stories abounded of the crimes of tyrants, perhaps most colourfully of the bronze bull in which Phalaris of Acragas roasted his enemies.

Though some such stories may have a historical kernel, to a large extent they probably derive from the backlash subsequent to the fall of a tyranny. Tyrannical rule rarely lasted more than two generations. Inherited rule seemed perhaps more patently unjust. Stories of cruelty tend to be focused on the second rather than the first generation. In some cities – Corinth is the most prominent example – tyranny was replaced by a broader oligarchic clique. In Athens, however, the city for which there is the best evidence, tyranny was followed by democracy. The idea of tyranny indeed seems to have been defined in opposition to the ideal of accountable, democratic government. When the early 6th-century BC Athenian reformer Solon had warned of the threat of tyranny in Athens, he seemed to conceive that men might aspire to tyranny. The imaginary tyrant was an ever-present bogeyman of the democracy. The institution of ostracism (a period of ten years' exile imposed on leading politicians) was probably introduced, for example, as a safeguard against the excessive power of individuals in response to the expulsion of the Athenian tyrants. The charge of aiming for tyranny was one that was frequently laid against Athenian leaders, most famously Alcibiades.

The distinction between tyranny and democracy took on an additional sharpness of focus, and a patriotic gloss, in the light of the Persian Wars fought between the Persian kings Darius and Xerxes and the cities of Greece (490–479 BC). The Persians had been responsible for maintaining a number of petty tyrants in power within their sphere of influence in Asia Minor. The association of tyranny with the Persian enemy was ensured in Athens by the participation of Hippias, the expelled Athenian tyrant, in the Persian campaign that culminated in the battle of Marathon (490 BC). Already in Aeschylus' play the Persians, performed in 472 BC, the superiority of the Athenian system of government is seen as a crucial factor in the Greeks' victory. Like the tyrants of Archaic Greece, Darius, Xerxes, and subsequent Persian kings down to Darius III (the defeated opponent of Alexander the Great) were portrayed in an almost consistently lurid light: whimsically cruel, sexually decadent, surrounded by powerful queens and a population of slavish "yes-men".

In addition to the Archaic tyrants, another group of rulers are commonly referred to as tyrants: Gelon and Hieron of Syracuse in the 5th century BC and Dionysius I and II in the 4th. These Classical tyrants are usually seen as being very different in character from their Archaic counterparts: essentially military dictators, in the size of their power bases they preshadowed the rule of the Hellenistic kings who followed on from Alexander's conquest of the Near East. But just as in the case of the Archaic tyrants – where, however, the simultaneous appearance of so many figures lends the group an artificial coherence – tyranny is essentially in the eye of the beholder, an accusation rather than a position. The charge of tyranny was one that could even be turned against Athens. The Athenian writers Aristophanes and Thucydides (as well as the pamphlet often known as the Old Oligarch) reflect in their work the idea that the Athenian dominance over their allies in the 5th century BC also constituted a tyranny. A compelling argument makes

out that Herodotus, writing his Histories in the early years of the Peloponnesian War, draws parallels between the empires of the Athenians and the Persians before them.

In the period of the Roman empire the charge of tyranny was regularly laid against imperial usurpers. A hostile tradition could even brand a successful emperor a tyrant: the Byzantine historian Socrates terms Constantine a tyrant. The same extremes of tyranny and freedom were predictably potent – though they took on a different colouring – in the period of the independence movement: the anonymous Hellenic Nomarchy of 1806 gave two explanations – the Church and the Greek diaspora – for why Greece was "bound with the fetters of tyranny". As Ypsilantis crossed the river Pruth between Bessarabia and Moldavia at the launch of the War of Independence in March 1821, he invoked the shades of Themistocles and Leonidas, the generals of the Persian Wars, in the struggle to bring "liberty to the classical land of Greece". Even today the assertion in Aeschylus' Persians that the Athenians are "slaves to no man", by implicit contrast to the Persians, is met in performance in Athens by rapturous applause – the result, arguably, of an equation of the Persians with a more recent enemy.

THOMAS HARRISON

Further Reading

Andrewes, Antony, The Greek Tyrants, London: Hutchinson, 1962; New York: Harper and Row, 1963

Berve, Helmut, Die Tyrannis bei den Griechen, 2 vols, Munich: Beck, 1967

Cawkwell, G.L., "Early Greek Tyranny and the People", Classical Quarterly, 45/1 (1995): pp. 73–86

Ehrenberg, Victor, Alexander and the Greeks, Oxford: Blackwell, 1938

Lavelle, Brian M., The Sorrow and the Pity: A Prolegomenon to a History of Athens under the Peisistratids, c.560–510 BC, Stuttgart: Steiner, 1993

Lewis, David M., Sparta and Persia, Leiden: Brill, 1977, pp. 155–58

McGlew, James F., Tyranny and Political Culture in Ancient Greece, Ithaca, New York: Cornell University Press, 1993

Osborne, R., "Archaeology, the Salaminioi, and the Politics of Sacred Space in Archaic Attica" in Placing the Gods: Sanctuaries and Sacred Space in Ancient Greece, edited by Robin Osborne and Susan E. Alcock, Oxford: Clarendon Press, and New York: Oxford University Press, 1994

Podlecki, A.J., "Festivals and Flattery: The Early Greek Tyrants as Patrons of Poetry", Athenaeum, 58 (1980): pp. 371–95

Raaflaub, Kurt, Freedom in the Ancient World entry in The Oxford Classical Dictionary, 3rd edition, edited by Simon Hornblower and Antony Spawforth, Oxford and New York: Oxford University Press, 1996, pp. 609–11

Rosivach, V.J., "The Tyrant in Athenian Democracy", Quaderni Urbinati di Cultura Classica, 30/3 (1988): pp. 43–57

Wiesehöfer, Ancient Persia: From 550 BC to 650 AD, London and New York: Tauris, 1996

Tzanes, Emmanuel c.1610–1690

Painter and man of letters

Emmanuel Tzanes, whose surname was Bounialis, was a notable 17th-century figure. Known mainly as a painter, he also wrote poetry (verses by him were published in Venice in 1668 and 1684) and composed religious services (for the saints Govdelaas, 1661; Joseph the Hymnographer, 1665; Theodora, 1671; Photini, 1671; and Alypios, 1679). He was distantly descended from a noble Cretan family and was brother of the poet Marinos Tzanes, who composed the extensive narrative poem *Cretan War*, and of Konstantinos Tzanes, also a painter. He was also connected to the Cretan priest and man of letters Kalliopios Kallergis.

Tzanes was ordained a priest before 1637. He probably fled from his native Rethymnon in 1646, the year in which that city was captured by the Turks. Between 1648 and 1656 he was in Corfu, executing numerous icons and collaborating with the painter Philotheos Skoufos. By 1658 he was in Venice, where he remained for the rest of his life. In 1660 he was elected parish priest of the Greek Orthodox church of San Giorgio dei Greci, which he served for approximately 20 years; for a short time he was also supervisor of pupils at the Flanginian School of the Greek Confraternity in Venice.

Tzanes had an active career of about 60 years (dated works range from 1636 to 1689), which came to an end only a few months before his death in March 1690. His oeuvre is large, comprising some 130 known works, and paintings by him are to be found in museums and other public foundations, private collections, churches, and monasteries in Greece (most of them in Athens, though some also on the mainland and the islands) and abroad (most in Venice, with a few in other European cities, St Catherine's, Sinai, and Baltimore in the US). Some works formerly thought to be by him have been shown to bear forged signatures, such as *St Anne Holding the Young Mary*, which is actually a 15th-century icon, and the icon of the *Allegory of the Holy Eucharist*, both in the Benaki Museum in Athens.

Tzanes executed paintings of differing sizes, shapes, and styles, ranging from small icons and triptychs to monumental paintings and large sanctuary doors. A conscientious and methodical craftsman, he had a strong grounding in the tradition of Cretan painting, which he had studied at Rethymnon before his flight to Corfu. Equally competent in both miniature painting and monumental art, and trained in both the traditional and more modern style, his artistic background enabled him to respond to the demands of a public of varying social status and tastes. His clientele came from both the secular and the religious world and included Greek Orthodox and Catholics. Among the latter was the Venetian overseer (*proveditore*) of Rethymnon, Andrea Corner, for whom an icon of the Virgin was commissioned from Tzanes in 1645 (Venice, Giudecca, Santa Trinità).

Tzanes sometimes depicted his patrons in his works (*St Demetrios on Horseback*, 1656, Loverdos Collection, Byzantine Museum, Athens; *St James*, 1683, Museo dell'Istituto Ellenico, Venice; *Triptych*, Kanellopoulos private collection, Athens), rendering these secular figures quite successfully with personal features and wearing contemporary dress. He frequently includes a date on his icons, contrary to usual custom, which enables us to trace the enviable continuity of his output virtually year by year from 1640 to 1689, and to document the various phases of his work. His art does not exhibit any spectacular development.

Tzanes brought a rather different approach to a tradition that covered about two centuries of Cretan artists painting in the Byzantine manner, adopting Western iconographic and stylistic elements. He shows a marked preference for iconographic innovations, although he also executed a large number of traditional subjects. Sometimes he returns to subjects that were very popular in the 15th century, repeating them with minor changes or additions (*Virgin with the Symbols of the Passion*, *Christ Enthroned*, a full-length *St John the Baptist*). He also makes use of details from much earlier Cretan painting, such as the characteristic dotted haloes, though he gives them richer floral decoration. Essentially he is an exponent of the Byzantine tradition, which he attempts to enrich with new elements. At the same time, he created new iconographic types, modifying and varying the traditional elements and enriching his repertoire by selecting and transforming features borrowed from works of the late Renaissance and Mannerism, and also from engravings by the Flemish Sadeler brothers and other artists. Architectural and sculptural elements are derived from Renaissance and Baroque art, but the poses and movements of his figures show Mannerist features.

Tzanes had a varied repertoire, despite the fact that he painted individual saints much more often than narrative scenes. Some of these saints were clearly favourites, such as *St Alypios the Stylite*; *St Govdelaas the Persian*, whose iconographic type he created and established, and was even the subject of an engraving executed in Venice in 1681; and *St Demetrios on Horseback*. He also painted many icons of the Virgin and of Christ, enthroned or bust-length, and in a variety of iconographic types. Icons notable for their monumental size or of particular iconographic interest include: the icon of *St Spyridon*, with charming miniature scenes from the saint's life – the earliest (1636) dated work by Tzanes (Museo Correr, Venice); the *Annunciation*, flanked by ten other scenes in a smaller scale (1640, Berlin); the *Tree of Jesse* (1644), an old subject given a new treatment (Museo dell'Istituto Ellenico); the *Virgin and Child Enthroned* (1664) and the corresponding icon of *Christ Enthroned* (1664) in the Byzantine Museum in Athens, which repeats, with minor additions, the type used by the painter Angelos (first half of the 15th century, according to recent research); the *Adoration of the* Magi (1667; Loverdos Collection, Byzantine Museum, Athens), obviously based on an engraving (1585) by J. Sadeler after a composition by Martin de Vos; *Sts Constantine and Helen with the Cross* (1669, Loverdos Collection, Byzantine Museum, Athens); *Christ Pantocrator Enthroned* (1678, Kato Panayia Monastery, Arta); the *Virgin Lambovitissa Enthroned* (1684, Loverdos Collection, Byzantine Museum, Athens); the *Miracle of the Holy Girdle of our Lady* (Benaki Museum, Athens); and the *Virgin between Sts John the Baptist and Philip* (Baltimore). Three large sanctuary doors preserved in Corfu and dated 1654 (St John of Damascus, St Cyril, St Gregory Palamas) contain inscriptions with a reference to the procession of the Holy Spirit from God the Father.

Works of interest for their narrative character and the treatment of the background, with the scenes set in a landscape or accompanied by buildings include two scenes of Christ's miracles: the *Healing of the Paralytic* and the *Healing of the Blind Man* (1682 and 1686), and also *Christ and the Samaritan Woman* (1689), the *Incredulity of Thomas*, and the

Appearance of Christ to the Holy Women Bearing Myrrh, the two last undated (all in the Museo dell'Istituto Ellenico). This group of five paintings is also of iconological interest, in that it is a visual representation of the Gospel passages for the five Sundays after Easter, until Ascension Sunday, which come from St John's Gospel. The *Entombment* (1677, San Giorgio dei Greci, Venice) has an unusual form: it is painted on both sides and the background is cut away around the figures. The work is still used as a processional icon during Good Friday of the Orthodox Easter.

Tzanes follows the traditions of the Cretan school, but his modelling is more calligraphic and he includes picturesque details; his use of line is distinctly decorative, occasionally producing a dry style, or a sweetish expression and loose gestures. He clearly admired the compositions of Michael Damaskinos, though he lacked this painter's compositional abilities, and his drawing and painting were weaker. His technique is flawless and he gave great attention to detail, leading to a degree of pedantry, and his style recalls that of Emmanouil Lambardos, an older fellow-Cretan artist. The decorative charge that inundates many of his works is often carried to the point of affectation: great attention is paid to the treatment of fabrics and the details of thrones (*Enthroned Virgin and* Child, 1650, Corfu; *St Cyril, St Gregory Palamas,* and *St John of Damascus,* all 1654, Corfu; *St Basil,* 1667 and *St James,* 1683, both in the Museo dell'Istituto Ellenico), and there is distinct eclecticism in the western elements. His workmanship, with its delicate modelling and large number of white highlights (*psimmythies*), produces meticulous results (e.g. the *Holy Mandylion,* 1659, formerly in a private collection and now in the Benaki Museum), and bright icons that are nevertheless rather academic in style. Among the most positive features of Tzanes's paintings are the brilliant colour combinations that create pleasing, though occasionally cold, ensembles. Generally speaking, he prefers symmetrical compositions. He essays a few timid steps in the articulation of space and the perspective rendering of buildings, though without fully grasping the problems. In this, too, he follows the line of Damaskinos, though not particularly successfully.

A bearer of the Byzantine tradition in his calling as priest, and also as composer of religious services and an individual with a genuinely religious character, Tzanes reveals himself as a more complex personality through his painting. Though a conservative at bottom, his leaning towards western European art and iconographic amalgams makes him a representative of certain regenerative trends in Greek 17th-century painting. His work was accordingly much appreciated and his style exercised a great influence on post-Byzantine religious painting.

MARIA CONSTANTOUDAKI

See also Renaissance (Veneto-Cretan)

Biography

Emmanuel Tzanes, whose surname was Bounialis, was born to a cultivated family at Rethymnon in Crete c.1610. He was ordained a priest before 1637, and in 1646 (when Rethymnon fell to the Turks) he fled to Corfu. By 1658 he was in Venice where he remained for the rest of his life, serving as parish priest of the church of San Giorgio dei Greci c.1660–80. He had a long and distinguished career as a painter. He died in Venice in 1690.

Further Reading

Acheimastou-Potamianou, Myrtali, *Eikones tou Vazantiyou Mouseiou Athinou* [Icons of the Byzantine Museum in Athens], Athens, 1998

Chatzidakis, Manolis, *Ellines Zographoi meta fin Alosin (1450–1830)* [Greek Painters after the Conquest (1450–1830)], vol. 1, Athens, 1987

Drandakes, Nikolaos Basileiou, *O Emmanouel Tzane Mpouniales theoroumenos ex eikonon tou sojzomenon kurios en Benetia* [Emmanuel Tzanes Bounialis Considered on the Basis of his Icons Mainly Preserved in Venice], Athens, 1962

Drandakes, Nikolaos Basileiou, "Notizie supplementari su Emanuele Zanes: due sue icone ignote", *Thisavrismata*, 11 (1974): pp. 36–72 (in Greek with Italian summary)

Vocotopoulos, P., *Eikones tis Kerkyras* [Icons of Corfu], Athens, 1990

Tzetzes, John

Scholar of the 12th century

John Tzetzes was a Byzantine scholar and teacher who has a certain importance for the tradition of Classical Greek literature, because he preserved some otherwise unknown fragments of ancient authors. His writings also provide rich biographical material.

Tzetzes was born in Constantinople around 1110. His mother's family originated from Georgia (Caucasus); his great-grandmother had accompanied the princess Mary of Alania from Georgia to the capital. His father was a Greek, whose "Hellenic" roots Tzetzes proudly mentioned in a letter. He had several brothers, of whom only Andronikos and Isaac are known by name. John's father appears to have been an educated man, because he acquainted his son with a wide range of Classical literature (Tzetzes later compared him to the elder Cato, who had instructed his son in a similar way). His brother Isaac was also interested in ancient literature and a commentary on Pindar is evidence of his scholarship; he died at Rhodes returning from a military campaign in the eastern parts of the empire. Tzetzes first found employment in the provinces as a secretary in the office of the governor Isaac Komnenos in Verroia (Macedonia), but he had to give up his job because of an affair he seems to have had with his employer's wife.

He later referred to this experience several times, accusing the woman of having ruined his career. Leaving Verroia, he returned to Constantinople, where financial necessity forced him to sell his library piece by piece – a manuscript of Plutarch's *Parallel Lives* was the last remaining book, as he laments. He started to earn his living by teaching (parents who could afford it would send their children to a grammarian for primary lessons). In one of his letters he describes a scene in his classroom: some pupils are reading and interpreting a passage of Homer; they are divided into different levels, from beginners to advanced students. In addition he gave lectures on various Classical topics. The scholar became a respected teacher and a tutor to members of distinguished families. Finally he was chosen by the emperor Manuel I Komnenos (1143–80) to instruct his wife Irene, the former German princess Bertha of Sulzbach. Tzetzes had to acquaint her with the literature of her new home and was charged to prepare a commentary on the Homeric poems. But he did not finish this work: discontented with the delay in his payment, he gave up this position. He finished the commentary only several years later, encouraged by his friend Konstantinos Kotertzes.

We do not know exactly why Tzetzes moved to the Pantokrator monastery in Constantinople. It seems likely that he had run into trouble by joining the supporters of patriarch Kosmas II Attikos who was deposed at the synod of 1147 because of his contacts and sympathies with heretics. At the monastery of the Pantokrator, founded by John I Komnenos in 1136, Tzetzes continued to teach monks. Some of his last letters deal with the monastic life. He died there after 1165.

The main source for reconstructing Tzetzes's life – besides some autobiographical notes in other works – is his correspondence, which he arranged himself and put into chronological order. He also commented on various topics mentioned in his letters and published them as the *Histories* (*Historiai*). N. Gerbel, the first editor of this commentary, divided it into 12 parts, each containing 1000 verses, and titled it *Chiliades* (from *chilioi*, "thousand"). This work, written in political verse (the Byzantine 15-syllable metre), is a thesaurus of Tzetzes's enormous knowledge of Classical literature and history.

There are also commentaries on Homer. Tzetzes wrote a hexameter poem describing the situation before, during, and after the fall of Troy (*Antehomerica*, *Homerica*, *Posthomerica*). He also interpreted Homer by allegories (*Chronike Biblos*). Finally he commented on Aeschylus, Aristophanes, Euripides, Hesiod, Lycophron, Nicander, Oppian, and Porphyry.

As far as we know, Tzetzes gave no public lectures, but he composed some funeral orations for members of the emperor's family and high officials. Although he is often accused of quoting inexactly, he remains an authority on Classical literature.

MICHAEL GRÜNBART

Biography

Born in Constantinople *c.*1110, Tzetzes's mother's family was Georgian but his father was Greek. His father taught him ancient literature. Tzetzes first worked for Isaac Komnenos in Verroia. Returning to Constantinople he lived by teaching. Later he moved to the Pantokrator monastery where he taught the monks. He wrote letters which he prepared for publication with a verse commentary. He also commented on Homer and other poets. He died after 1165.

Writings

Antehomerica, Homerica et Posthomerica, edited by F. Jacobs, Leipzig: Weidmann, 1793
Historiae, edited by P.A.M. Leone, Naples: Libreria Scientifica, 1968
Epistulae, edited by P.A.M. Leone, Leipzig: Teubner, 1972

Further Reading

Grünbart, M., "Prosopographische Beiträge zum Briefcorpus des Ioannes Tzetzes", *Jahrbuch der Österreichischen Byzantinistik*, 46 (1996): pp. 175–226
Wendel, C., Tzetzes entry in *Real-Encyclopädie der klassischen Altertumswissenschaft*, edited by August Pauly *et al.*, vol. 7. A2, 1948, 1959–2010 (includes list of works)
Wilson, N.G., *Scholars of Byzantium*, revised edition, London: Duckworth, and Cambridge, Massachusetts: Medieval Academy of America, 1996

U

Ukraine

It is now thought that Greeks from Miletus first settled in the Ukraine in the course of the 6th century BC, though a century earlier has been claimed. Settlement was either coastal or along the banks of the major rivers of the region and their estuaries. By about 550 BC the town of Olbia was established near the modern village of Parutino, on the west shore of the estuary of the river Bug (the Greek Hypanis), when an agora and religious precinct were laid out. Numerous minor Greek settlements fringed the whole estuary around Olbia, while the islet of Berezan just beyond the mouth of the estuary had been settled at the same time as Olbia itself, if not a little earlier. The island was named Borysthenes by the ancient Greeks, as was the great river Dniepr which emptied into the Black Sea immediately to its east, beside the Bug. The name Borysthenes was also attached to Olbia itself, especially in more literary accounts of the town, such as that of Dio Chrysostom, composed about AD 100 (*Oration* 36). Dio's gloomy account is not to be taken at face value, as archaeology now shows: it is designed to make a philosophical argument about civic culture and harmony, for presentation at Prusa in northwest Asia Minor. Later, in the 10th century, the Byzantine emperor Constantine VII Porphyrogennetos (913–59) in his famous survey of his realm looked upon the Dniepr as the principal highway to the first Russian state, the Rus of Kiev, and beyond as far as the Baltic. It was down this river that furs, amber, and mercenaries came into the Byzantine world, including the Varangian bodyguard of the emperor himself.

The hinterland of the Crimea was a continuation of the Ukrainian steppe to the north: Greek settlement followed its coast. The largest Greek cities were Chersonesus (modern Sebastopol) in the southwest Crimea and the cities of the Bosporan kingdom that formed its eastern part, especially Panticapaeum (Kerch) and Theodosia. Recent work has indicated Greek settlement also on the northeast coast, on the shallow Sea of Azov, which was dominated by the Bosporan kingdom as far as the Don (the Greek Tanais). The Greeks reasonably treated Azov as a lake and named it Maiotis.

Chersonesus offered excellent harbours, but seems not to have been established as a Greek settlement until about 422 BC, when settlers came from Heraclea Pontica. No doubt the local Tauri, famously ferocious, were a main reason for earlier neglect of the site. It was here that Euripides set his *Iphigeneia in Tauris*, first performed in Athens about 412 BC and a very popular theme in art thereafter. Euripides' version of the myth stresses that the cult of Artemis at Halai Araphenides (modern Loutsa in Attica) took its origin and ritual from the Taurian form of the cult.

Chersonesus (then Kherson) remained a strong outpost of the Byzantine empire after much else in the region had been lost. It was here that Cyril and Methodios wintered in AD 860/61 en route to the Volga Khazars. Here too in 989 prince Vladimir of Kiev was baptized and married to a Byzantine princess: this was the beginning of the Russian Orthodox Church. Not far from Chersonesus lay the promontory that gave its Greek name to the Crimea, the Ram's Head (Kriou Metopon).

Theodosia was founded by Milesian Greeks in the 6th century BC on the southeast coast of the Crimea; for the Byzantines it was Theodosioupolis, and later for the Genoese the great trading port of Kaffa. In the 4th century BC much of the grain imported into Athens seems to have come from Theodosia and its hinterland. At the eastern extremity of the Crimea lay Panticapaeum, the capital of the Bosporan kingdom. It too was established in the 6th century BC by Milesian Greeks. About 438 BC the Spartocid dynasty formed the Bosporan kingdom, which embraced both the eastern Crimea and the Taman' peninsula across the straits of Kerch to the east. It was to last into the 3rd century AD. Pericles, who led an expedition to the Black Sea in the 430s BC, may have played a role in creating the dynasty. Certainly, Athens subsequently developed close social and economic ties with the kingdom, whose rulers could even receive Athenian citizenship in the 4th century BC. Although Bosporan rulers had other cultural allegiances (Iranian and perhaps Thracian), the language and principal culture of their realm were firmly Greek throughout its history.

Across the whole region and through most of their history Greek communities of the Ukraine had to come to arrangements with local populations who were often nomadic – Scythians, Sarmatians, Goths, and others. For the most part, the Greek literary tradition stresses hostility with these peoples, while epigraphic and archaeological evidence reveals also more friendly or at least structured interaction and exchange, including formal treaties. The great ramparts across the breadth of the eastern Crimea, with which the Bosporan kingdom shielded itself, indicate the significant threat of assault by land. However, in surveying the region in book 4 of his *Histories*, Herodotus observes the existence of Scythian–Greek intermarriage and mixed populations, as near Olbia. He also describes a Hellenized settlement in the Ukrainian hinterland (perhaps modern Bel'sk), settled by the Geloni, whom he regards as of Greek descent, but as in his day speaking a language that is a mixture of Scythian and Greek (4. 108–09). No doubt Greeks of the region mediated exchange between the Scythians and the Aegean world: it was presumably through the Greek settlements of the region that the Scythian archers came who maintained public order for 5th-century Athenian democracy. For the Greeks of the Aegean the whole region was a reservoir of resources (slaves, grain, leather, and other goods).

From the perspective of the mainland Greeks the Ukraine was viewed as significant also for its peculiar geography and climate. The flat grassy steppe was contrasted with Greek landscapes, while the great rivers of the region had few parallels among the rivers of Greece. The climate was imagined as very cold, rather colder than it was in fact. The medical writers in particular viewed the region as a source of enlightenment about the effects of severe cold on the human body, for example in reducing fertility. The fate of Greeks in the Ukraine in modern times replicates that of Georgia.

DAVID BRAUND

See also Black Sea, Colonization, Crimea, Georgia

Further Reading

Ascherson, Neal, *Black Sea*, London: Cape, and New York: Hill and Wang, 1995

Bortoli-Kazanski, A. and M. Kazanski, "Les Sites archéologiques datés du IVe au VIIe siècle au nord et au nord-est de la Mer Noire: état des recherches", *Travaux et Mémoires*, 10 (1987): pp. 437–89

Braund, D.C., "Greeks and Barbarians: The Black Sea Region and Hellenism under the Early Empire" in *The Early Roman Empire in the East*, edited by Susan E. Alcock, Oxford: Oxbow, 1997

Danoff, Chr., Pontos Euxeinos entry in *Real-Encyclopädie der klassischen Altertumswissenschaft*, edited by August Pauly *et al.*, supplement 9, 1962, 866–1175

Gaidukevich, V.F., *Das Bosporanische Reich*, revised edition, Berlin: Akademie, and Amsterdam: Hakkert, 1971

Hind, John, "Greek and Barbarian Peoples on the Shores of the Black Sea", *Archaeological Reports*, 30 (1983–84): pp. 71–97

Hind, John, "Archaeology of the Greeks and Barbarian Peoples around the Black Sea", *Archaeological Reports*, 39 (1992–93): pp. 82–112

Hind, John, "The Bosporan Kingdom" in *The Fourth Century BC*, edited by D.M. Lewis *et al.*, Cambridge: Cambridge University Press, 1994 (*The Cambridge Ancient History*, vol. 6, 2nd edition)

Koromila, Marianna (editor), *The Greeks in the Black Sea from the Bronze Age to the Early Twentieth Century*, Athens: Panorama, 1991

Minns, Ellis H., *Scythians and Greeks*, Cambridge: Cambridge University Press, 1913

Rolle, Renate, *The World of the Scythians*, London: Batsford, and Berkeley: University of California Press, 1989

Treister, M.J., and Y.G. Vinogradov, "Archaeology on the Northern Coast of the Black Sea", *American Journal of Archaeology*, 97/3 (1993): pp. 521–64

Vasiliev, A.A., *The Goths in the Crimea*, Cambridge, Massachusetts: Medieval Academy of America, 1936

Vinogradov, Yuri G. and Sergej D. Kryzickij, *Olbia: eine altgriechische Stadt im nordwestlichen Schwarzmeerraum*, Leiden: Brill, 1995

Uniates

"Uniates" is the name given to the entirety of the flock of those Churches of eastern Christendom that are in communion with Rome. In their ecclesiastical life they still retain their own respective rites, languages, and customs. After the great schism between the Churches of the East and the West (1054) several attempts were made at reunification. But they were not successful, and the gap between the Churches widened after the sack of Constantinople by the Latins of the Fourth Crusade (1204). The latter dismembered the empire into numerous Frankish territories, while the Church of Rome established Latin patriarchates in Constantinople, Antioch, and Jerusalem, under its jurisdiction. The Franks, the political rulers, forced the Orthodox clergy to take an oath of devotion to the Roman pontiff. A number of Orthodox clergymen took this oath; others refused; while a third group among them rejected the unilateral solution of the oath and suggested the convocation of an ecumenical council. The council was convened in 1215 in the Lateran, but no Orthodox clergy were present. Evidently no discussions took place, as the intermediate faction had hoped. But since the Catholics had prior knowledge of the Orthodox reaction, they decided not to impose the Latin rite on them. The Orthodox would be allowed to keep their doctrine, liturgy, language, and customs in their ecclesiastical life. Nothing would change in their traditions, except for a fundamental element: their subjugation to the pope of Rome. This decision of the Lateran Council constituted the beginning of the Unia.

The advance of the Ottomans into Asia Minor gave a political and a military dimension to the move towards the unification of the Churches. Despite the favourable decisions taken in this direction in the context of several councils (e.g. the Council of Lyon in 1274 and the Council of Ferrara–Florence in 1439) convened by the political and ecclesiastical authorities of the East and the West, the union of the Churches that was decided on remained temporary. Already before the fall of Constantinople to the Turks (1453) prominent clerics and a large number of lay persons denounced the unification. Besides, the West failed to provide military assistance. Immediately after the fall, Turkish policy was hostile to unionist tendencies. Apart from that, the sultan Mehmet II the Conqueror selected as patriarch George/Gennadios Scholarios, who had become anti-unionist, following the Council of Ferrara–Florence.

Rome practised proselytism even towards the followers of other Orthodox Churches using the same method, that of Unia. On several occasions, in fact, its politics were backed up by military action, as well as by alliances with other states. Poland, for example, having the Ukraine under its rule, protected the Jesuits in their efforts to force the Orthodox inhabitants into a unification with Rome. In Poland the term "Uniati" was used for the first time. The synod in Brest (1596) was divided into two camps: the Orthodox and the Uniates.

The Polish king Sigismund ratified the decisions of the latter, while he launched a persecution against the Orthodox, who asked the Greek patriarchates of the East to help them. It was then that Cyril Lukaris was sent to Poland, where he recommended the founding of schools and printing houses. The Jesuits attempted to proselytize the Russians. As their pawn, they used a Russian monk, who because of his resemblance to Dmitri, the deceased last descendant of the Rurik dynasty, managed to ascend the Russian throne with the help of the Poles (1604–06). (He is better known as False Dmitri.) The people revolted and executed him. Sigismund of Poland invaded Russia, occupied Moscow (1607), annexed Russian territories, and imposed unification with Rome on the Russians. A period of upheavals followed, until Michael Romanov became tsar (1613) and put an end to Western intrusions.

The Uniate tactic of proselytizing the Orthodox was also employed towards other confessions of the East. Thus, several oriental rites were formed, which are distinguished as: the Alexandrian rite (for Copts and Ethiopians); the Antiochene rite (Malankarese, Maronite, and Syrian Churches); the Chaldean rite (Chaldeans and Malabar Christians); and the Armenian rite. The Uniates who come from the ranks of the Orthodox call themselves Greek Catholics or followers of the Constantinopolitan or Byzantine rite. The individual faithful are divided into national community Churches, such as the Albanians, Byelorussians, Bulgarians, Georgians, Greeks, Italo-Albanians (in southern Italy), Serbs (in Croatia), Melkites (in the Near East), Romanians, Russians, Polish Ruthenians (now called Ukrainians), and Podcarpathian Ruthenians. Among the Greek Catholics, there are also a number of Chinese, Estonians, Latvians, Finns, Japanese, Slovaks, and Hungarians. After World War II the Greek Catholics of the Ukraine and Romania were forced by the state to join the Orthodox Church. They were legalized in 1989 and 1990 respectively. In 1990 a Code of Canons for the Oriental Churches was issued in Rome. According to data that were published in Rome by the Sacred Congregation for the Oriental Church in 1962, the total number of Uniates was estimated at 8 million. In Greece the Greek Catholics number approximately 2,500 and are subject to the Apostolic Exarchate in Athens.

CHARALAMBOS K. PAPASTATHIS

See also Papacy, Roman Catholic Church

Summary

Uniates are members of those Churches in predominantly Orthodox societies that are in communion with Rome. They retain their own rites, languages, and customs but take an oath of devotion to the pope. Those Uniates who come from the ranks of the Orthodox call themselves Greek Catholics. In Greece itself they number today about 2500.

Further Reading

Catholic Church, *Oriente Cattolico: Cenni storici e statistiche*, Vatican City: Sacra Congregazione per la Chiesa Orientale, 1962

Janin, Raymond, *Les Eglises orientales et les rites orientaux*, 4th edition, Paris: Letouzey & Ané, 1955

Metallinos, G.D., D. Gonis, I. Fratsea, E. Morarou, and Bishop Athanasios of Banat, *The Unia: Past and Present*, Athens: Armos, 1992 (in Greek)

Stephanidis, B., *Ecclesiastical History*, 2nd edition, Athens, 1959 (in Greek)

Valognes, Jean-Pierre, *Vie et mort des Chrétiens d'Orient: des origines à nos jours*, Paris: Fayard, 1994

Urbanization

When Aristotle famously described man as a political animal the strict meaning of the Greek – *politikon zoon* – is "an animal that lives as part of a polis", that is, a member of what is usually translated as a "city state". Latinized he would be an urban creature. The implication is that urbanization, the forming of cities, is the natural way of life for a Greek community. In its simplest form, this is true. In both ancient and modern Greece people prefer to live together, forming communities, rather than isolated in individual homesteads. An obvious original reason for this is the need for security; isolation is potentially dangerous, particularly in unsettled times. On top of this, though, come the social reasons: the need to belong, to be part of the whole, rather than a self-contained individual. Human fulfilment required the larger grouping.

This in turn requires an understanding of the communities, the poleis. There is no implication of great size. Many of the city states in Classical Greece are more readily defined as villages, rather than cities in the sense of modern urban sprawl, while at the same time the population was not necessarily concentrated in a single urban centre; in the largest of them, Athens, the majority of the citizens lived not in the city of Athens, as defined by its encircling fortifications, but in outlying villages scattered throughout the various regions of Attica. It was the village that formed the essential starting point. It was from this that urbanization, in the strict sense, started.

Urbanization was a response to the political condition of the times. The earliest urban communities of Greece developed in the Middle and Late Bronze Age, initially in Crete. They vary in size, from Gournia, no more than a village in modern terms, to the much larger (and still mostly unexplored) communities at places such as Knossos. All centred on the architectural complexes usually termed palaces, presumably the residences of monarchs but including the administrative (in all senses), economic, and religious functions that their owners represented. Similar urban groupings, some much larger then the Cretan examples, are, of course, found in the Near East at an even earlier date; there is every likelihood of direct influence on Crete, just as in the same way the Cretan examples influenced similar developments in mainland Mycenaean Greece. What is uncertain, in what is essentially a prehistoric context, is the relationship between the palaces and the urban areas surrounding them. Some of the "villas" or "mansions" (terms applied by the archaeologists who have explored them) round the palace at Knossos are substantial and opulent, but it is unclear whether they were "official" buildings or the residences of well-to-do individuals. Similarly, houses outside the palace at Mycenae have been attributed to merchants, though again the ownership is unclear.

What is certain is that with the destruction of the palaces and their organization the urban centres collapsed; in the succeeding Dark Age it is assumed – there is little archaeological evidence – that a village pattern resumed. Some of these villages were the settlements of newcomers. Those that coalesced into the city state of Sparta, which retained their village form long into the Classical, historical period, are a good example. Others were formed by survivors from the earlier populations, and for these, in mainland Greece, the heavily fortified citadels that surrounded the sites of the former palaces often became the urban nucleus. Some (Mycenae) hardly outgrew their citadel. Others (Athens) from an early date spread over the lower ground below the Mycenaean citadel walls of the Acropolis. It was all this that developed as the urban centre for the enlarged city state, which came to include the other villages of Attica.

Thus in Classical Greece urbanization meant the provision of an urban centre rather than simply a place of residence for an enlarged population. Compared with a modern city, a much greater proportion of the area within a city's defined boundaries was devoted to public building, religious, economic, administrative. It included places, which may or may not be actual buildings in the architectural sense, where the citizens could gather for political or religious purposes. The central "gathering place", the agora, in Athens was the place where in the 5th century BC the citizens collected when they voted to banish (ostracize) politicians who had lost their favour, while on the adjacent hill of the Pnyx was the open-air location for the political assembly, the Ekklesia. Those who attended came from the whole of Attica, not merely the city itself. Within the urban area the Acropolis (now demilitarized, the city fortifications instead now including the whole town) formed the gathering place for the entire population of Attica when they came to worship Athena at her annual festival. With the growth of wealth and the desire for prestige that came with it, the city was embellished with fine buildings, to modern thinking completely out of scale compared with the size of the actual population dwelling within the walls.

A further stage in urbanization was the deliberate, planned construction of cities. This started in the colonies that the Greeks founded overseas, where the settler community was concentrated in the urban centre, the outlying land being allotted to them, often with non-Greek inhabitants to work it for them. Such artificial cities are easily recognized by the use of a regular grid plan for their street system, facilitating the allocation of equal-sized individual plots to the settlers. Himera, in Sicily, is an excellent example of such a city. The concepts involved in this were elaborated into theories of urban planning and the proper form a city should take, with the emergence of individual town-planning experts, the most famous of whom was Hippodamus of Miletus. He may have been responsible for the planning of his native city when it was recreated after its destruction by the Persians; he certainly planned the new harbour city of the Athenians at Piraeus. The basis of his theories was the inevitable grid plan of streets, but planning extended also to the proper location of the different areas and structures a city requires.

Thus during the 5th and 4th centuries BC a new category of urbanization developed, the deliberate bringing together of people from a wider area and its villages into a large, planned urban centre. The motives were various, but the underlying purpose was to create more powerful communities. The city of Rhodes, formed by the amalgamation and transfer of population from three older poleis, Lindus, Ialysus, and Camirus, embraced a large area within strong fortifications, though it seems never to have been fully built up. Other cities were moved to new, planned sites, such as Priene and Cnidus, these perhaps at the behest of a foreign ruler, Mausolus of Caria. By the 4th century BC urbanization, often on a substantial scale, was considered an ideal; it formed a crucial element in propelling backward areas, such as Macedon, into the forefront of up-to-date powers, even if politically they adhered to the older concept of monarchy. A culmination comes with the laying out of Pella as the Macedonian capital. Here urbanization created a spacious city, with broad streets, proper drainage and water supplies, and opulent houses. No doubt it represented a considerable improvement in the standard of living for the people who came to inhabit it; at the same time they were content with a regime that controlled them, rather than a political system under which they governed themselves.

So the Greek city was transformed from a political to an urban organization. In the Hellenistic period, and following the conquests of the Macedonian Alexander the Great, this was extended, and many more urbanized places were organized. Some of these were too artficial, too remote from a natural raison d'être, and failed (though one of the remotest, Aï Khanum in Afghanistan, was remarkably successful). Others prospered. In Greece itself Cassander's foundation of Thessalonica was one of the triumphs of the urbanization movement. In the newly conquered areas the greatest of the Alexandrias founded by Alexander the Great, that "next to" (rather than "in") Egypt, to use the official nomenclature, became one of the greatest cities of the whole ancient world. Urbanization was a policy that was synonymous with the concept of Greek political superiority and domination.

Even after the collapse of the Hellenistic monarchies, the Romans continued the policy of urbanization, using the cities as an essential method of local political control, extending the policy to the non-Greek parts of their empire. The Hellenistic and Roman periods thus saw the apogee of Greek urbanization. The cities played a vital role in the political and economic order of things, and were rewarded accordingly. Where the Classical cities had built for the gods, the Hellenistic and Roman cities built for man; or at least, those men who were privileged to be part of them. Public buildings were constructed on a magnificent scale. The agoras were lined all round with stone colonnades (stoas), behind which were shops, offices, rooms for dining and feasting. Each city had its theatre; its gymnasia – which became places of education – were no longer mere open fields, but colonnaded courtyards, with assembly rooms and running courses (that at Cyrene roofed to provide shade from the African sun). Streets were wide, and paved; in late Hellenistic and Roman cities they were monumentalized with long lines of columns. Water supplies were, where necessary, piped in (Priene affords a 4th-century BC example of this), or, where suitable springs were not available, stored in specially built and often cavernous cisterns (Alexandria). Much was done at the expense of the kings and the Roman emperors who succeeded them. Where cities fell back on their "own" resources, this often meant the pockets of the well-to-do, from whom lavish public expenditure was an expected duty.

In many senses the heyday of Greek urbanization was the 2nd century AD; the worsening conditions of the 3rd century brought an end to much urban development (it has been suggested that excessive expenditure on urban amenities hastened, or even created, the economic collapse of the mid-3rd century AD). Even so, the concept of the urbanized ideal continued, so that when the emperor Constantine founded his New Rome at Constantinople, it was conceived on the grand urbanized scale, with the same lavish amenities, as in earlier times. Constantinople flourished as the new imperial centre. Other Greek cities declined, impoverished by the Byzantine financial system, or the victims of political change. A few survived right through the Middle Ages, though often much reduced, such as Thessalonica. But even the greatest, Alexandria, dwindled to a small town, though the ghost of its vast Hellenistic grid plan was still discernible in the sands as late as the early 19th century. Under the Turks, Athens was a small, squalid town huddled against the north slopes of the Acropolis.

The revival of urbanization came with the liberation of Greece from the Turks. Athens was deliberately extended as the capital of free Greece (though the inevitable grid plan, despite the magnificent broad main street, Panepistemiou, is now a traffic nightmare). Other Classical cities were revived, as centres for the new Hellenism. None of these places reached any great size in the 19th century. Athens continued to be separated from its (equally revived) harbour town of Piraeus by open country and olive groves as late as the 1950s. A new and unplanned impetus for urbanization was the Asia Minor disaster of 1922, when refugees arrived at the principal centres, creating new, unplanned extensions to the existing cities, particularly Athens and Thessalonica. But on top of this, modern economic pressures, the creation of factories and employment, turned the cities into magnets, drawing ever-increasing populations from the rural areas, and putting enormous strain on what must now be termed the urban infrastructure. Now, Greek urbanization needs to be rescued from its own success.

R.A. TOMLINSON

See also Cities, City State

Further Reading

Effenterre, Henri van, La Cité grecque: des origines à la défaite de Marathon, Paris: Hachette, 1985
Fraser, P.M., Cities of Alexander the Great, Oxford: Clarendon Press, and New York: Oxford University Press, 1996
Hoepfner, Wolfram and Ernst-Ludwig Schwandner, Haus und Stadt im klassischen Griechenland, 2nd edition, Munich: Deutscher Kunstverlag, 1994
Jones, A.H.M., The Cities of the Eastern Roman Provinces, Oxford: Clarendon Press, 1937; revised by Michael Avi-Yonah et al., 1971
Jones, A.H.M., The Greek City from Alexander to Justinian, Oxford: Clarendon Press, 1940, reprinted 1966
Martin, Roland, L'Urbanisme dans la Grèce antique, 2nd edition, Paris: A. & J. Picard, 1974
Osborne, Robin, Classical Landscape with Figures: The Ancient Greek City and Its Countryside, London: George Philip, and Dobbs Ferry, New York: Sheridan House, 1987
Travlos, J., Poleodomike Exelixis ton Athenon [The Planned Development of Athens], Athens, 1960
Wycherley, R.E., How the Greeks Built Cities, 2nd edition, London: Macmillan, 1962; New York: Norton, 1976

USA

In spite of the scarcity of relevant records, it is widely believed that several Greek immigrants landed in America – mostly as members of Spanish crews – in the very early years of its colonization, mainly driven by a spirit of adventure. The first Greek recorded to have arrived in the New World with the Spaniards was a certain Theodoros who landed at Tarpon Springs in Florida in 1528. The records have also registered that the first Greek coffee house was established in New England in 1652.

The first organized settlement comprising about 500 Greeks, as well as Minorcans and Italians, was established in the 1760s in the wilderness of Florida by John Turnbull, a British citizen, with generous help from his king and government. The colony was named New Smyrna, after the birthplace of Turnbull's Greek wife, but it hit difficulties from the very beginning mainly due to the hostile wilderness that surrounded it, as well as insufficient provisions, short supplies of food, malaria, excessive labour demands, and a general mismanagement and lack of human consideration for the settlers. However, a significant number of Greeks survived the hardships and carried on as an ethnic group in the region with John Giannopoulos as their teacher; his house – subsequently restored – is registered as the first schoolhouse in America.

However, these first Greeks seem to have disappeared by the early 19th century. The new century brought new arrivals – the records give 20 for 1821–30, 49 for 1831–40, 16 for 1841–50. The Greek War of Independence against Turkey, which had started on 25 March 1821, had also attracted a lot of attention in the New World which offered substantial help for the cause of Greece either by sending fighting troops or by bringing many Greek orphans to America. As a rule, the Greeks who settled in the United States before the mid-19th century made little effort to retain their ethnic identity. Yet, many among them managed to develop unusually successful careers and so they helped foster a positive image of Greece and of Greek identity in other Americans. Examples include Evangelidis Apostolidis Sophocles who became professor of Ancient, Byzantine, and Modern Greek at Harvard University in 1842, Georgios Perdikaris who was appointed United States consul in Athens in 1845, John Rodonaki who was Greek consul in Boston from 1850 to 1872, and Michael Anagnos who married into a highly respectable Boston family and became director of the Perkins Institute for the Blind in 1872.

From 1880 onwards, Greek immigration rates to the United States started rising sharply and reached a peak between 1890 and the late 1920s with a mass exodus of what is estimated to be one third of the total labour force of Greece at the time. Statistical figures give 173,513 immigrants for 1900–10, 196,119 for 1911–20, 91,369 for 1921–30, and 9138 for 1930–34 – although one has to take the figures only indicatively.

The earliest waves of this systematic immigration came from the Peloponnese, especially Laconia and Messenia, as early as the mid-1860s. However, the point of exodus soon spread to the mainland (mainly Attica, Boeotia, Phthiotis, and Phocis), and in the 1900s and early 1910s emigration from the northern parts of Greece, which were fighting their own war for independence, was particularly heavy. The last massive wave of immigrants was about to surge during the years following the defeat of the Greeks in Asia Minor (1922), when masses of Greek refugees from the wider area were directed to the States, just as Greece itself was unable to accommodate them all. But American views and laws on immigration had already toughened: by 1917 Greek and other immigrants realized that admission into the USA was no longer based on the individual concerned, but was based on racial and ethnic discrimination, while the Immigration Act of 1921 – limiting the number of each country's new immigrants to 3 per cent of its natives already living in USA – was a further blow to Greeks, who had only recently begun to enter the country in substantial numbers.

In fact, the Greek immigrants of the late 19th and early 20th centuries were part of the second substantial immigration wave which is associated with the USA during the second half of the 19th century and which supplied the country with newcomers from southern and eastern Europe, mostly fleeing depressed economies and oppressive governments. They were thus faced with a certain anti-foreign sentiment, which had developed against them not only among long-established Americans but also among the many immigrants of the first wave who were on their way to becoming Americanized. This first large-scale immigration had taken place in the mid-19th century and comprised immigrants coming primarily from Germany, the British Isles, Norway, and Sweden. Fair-skinned and usually Protestant, these new inhabitants blended fairly quickly into the American mainstream and gained relatively easy acceptance from their American neighbours.

The great majority of the Greek immigrants were men in their late teens or early twenties, most of them shepherds, farmers, merchants, and fishermen with minimal education who were mainly seeking to escape the compulsory military service in those turbulent times, or the dire economic conditions currently prevailing in Greece, especially after the humiliation of the 1897 war and the economic sanctions imposed by the European forces. There was also a small proportion of women among them seeking husbands without demand of dowry. Even though from a rural background, almost all felt a strong aversion for agriculture, due to their painful recollections of it, and so they gathered in the northeast (New York, Chicago, Washington, Massachusetts) facing the hard competition for industrial jobs and troubles connected with their ignorance of the English language and with the antagonism from the earlier immigrants mentioned above. Some of the earliest arrivals peddled cigars, flowers, or sweets from push-carts, or became bootblacks or dishwashers. Some more adventurous newcomers headed for the western frontier, to Nevada, Utah, and California, taking jobs in the mines or laying track for the transcontinental railway that was being constructed.

In spite of the hardships, America remained for years the dream destination for thousands of impoverished Greeks, most of whom were seeing their immigration to the US as a temporary stay that would earn them enough money to pay off debts or the mortgage on the family property before coming back home. With the exception of the period just before and during the Balkan Wars of 1912–13, when restrictions were imposed on the emigration of Greek males capable of fighting, the Greek government directly or indirectly encouraged emigration, often misleadingly glorifying the achievements of the Greeks in the New World and avoiding references to their failures, for obvious reasons: according to a bulletin issued by the Bank of Greece in 1921, $114,010,259 was received through immigrant remittances, most of them from Greeks living in the United States.

Of course, some Greeks did return to the homeland, especially in periods of economic depression in America: according to the Annual Report of the Commissioner General of Immigration, 197,088 Greeks had returned to Greece between 1908 and 1931. However, for many Greek immigrants the prospect of returning to their family and home country with pockets full of new wealth soon turned out to be untenable. Realizing that their stay in the country was being indefinitely prolonged, they started organizing themselves around a society of Greek character and structure that would help them preserve their Greek identity. One of their first steps was the establishment of Greek Orthodox churches that were initially ministered by priests sent from home. The first Greek Orthodox congregation was formed in New Orleans, Louisiana. Several churches and communities centred around them were established in the following years, while Greek newspapers soon made their appearance with a double aim: to create a bridge to English-speaking society for the mostly Greek-speaking immigrants and to keep them updated with events in the homeland. *Neos Kosmos* started up in Boston in 1892 but closed after only eight years. *Atlantis* was founded in New York City in 1894 and lasted until the mid-1970s. *Ethnikos Kiryx* appeared in New York City in 1910 and has been in circulation ever since.

However, these communities did not always conduct their affairs harmoniously. Intragroup differences would often plague them, frequently kindled by similar divisions in the home country. That was the case with the friction around Eleftherios Venizelos and the loyalists in Greece, especially during the 1910s, which brought severe conflict to the Greeks in America and thus encouraged anti-Greek sentiments amongst the American press and public who were dismayed at this divisive behaviour. Even the churches were for a long time at the centre of a fierce controversy over their jurisdiction, into which the Holy Synod of Greece and the Ecumenical Patriarchate were both drawn, and which formally ended in 1930–31 when the Archdiocese of North and South America was definitively attached to the Patriarchate. The new archbishop of North and South America, Athenagoras, then started his long tenure during which he worked persistently and efficiently towards uniting the Greek communities in the United States.

The wake of the defeat of the Greeks in Asia Minor in 1922 saw the onset of a gradual withdrawal of the concern of the American Greeks for affairs in the homeland. Disillusioned with the vices tormenting Greek political and economic life and accepting the indefinite nature of their stay in America, they started to feel a need for further integration into and for a deeper commitment to their new homeland. The Greek entrepreneurial spirit had already worked miracles throughout America and many Greeks were known to own small and successful business in the places where they started as cheap labourers. In September 1922 AHEPA (the American Hellenic Educational Progressive Association) was formed in Atlanta, Georgia, with the explicit aim of uniting the Greek communities and promoting Americanism among the Greeks of the United States.

World War II had a significant effect on the Greek communities in the United States. The heroic resistance of Greece against the Axis powers attracted attention and much admiration in the United States, also filling the Greek Americans with a renewed sense of pride in their homeland and a renewed concern for its plight. The Greek War-Relief Association was founded less than a fortnight after Greece was invaded, and within a few months it was reported that $5,250,000 had been collected. In February 1943 the Friends of Greece announced a plan to finance the reconstruction of Greek cities and towns, with blueprints to be drawn up at the School of Architecture of Columbia University. Additionally, throughout the war, numerous organizations fundraised continually towards shipping foods, medicine, and clothing to Greek war victims. In the aftermath of the war these Greek-Americans' support for Greece was reflected in the favourable terms of the Marshal Plan, while their pressure was instrumental in the decision for the return of the Dodecanese islands to Greece in 1947.

In the years after the war new waves of emigrants departed for America. This immigration pattern involved well-educated people, many of whom are now enjoying highly respectable positions in American society. Lobby groups have been created in Washington, promoting in Congress the concern of Greek-Americans for issues related to their mother country; notable among them are the United Hellenic Congress and the American Hellenic Institute. These and other lobbying groups staged substantial opposition to the 1967 dictatorship in Greece and the Turkish invasion of Cyprus in 1974, enlisting important academic and professional people in their campaigns.

Nowadays, Americans of Greek descent for the most part enjoy an integrated position in American society, with many of them retaining a keen interest in the affairs of Greece. Several Greek-Americans have held influential political positions, notably Spyro Agnew, John Brademas, Paul Sarbanis, and Michael Doukakis. Greek- Americans as a whole enjoy professional success: it is estimated that their income falls only 4 per cent below the average for the total American population. The latest immigration wave from the late 1960s onwards has established the new type of Greek-born university-educated student immigrants, who have subsequently moved on to occupy respectable positions in American academia.

EFROSSINI SPENTZOU

See also Emigration

Further Reading

Fairchild, Henry Pratt, *Greek Immigration to the United States*, New Haven, Connecticut: Yale University Press, 1911

Fenton, Heike and Melvin Hecker (editors), *The Greeks in America, 1528–1977: A Chronology and Fact Book*, Dobbs Ferry, New York: Oceana, 1978

Kontargyris, T., *O Apodemos Ellenismos tis Amerikis* [Greek Emigration to America], Athens, 1964

Psomiades, Harry and Alice Scourby (editors), *The Greek American Community in Transition*, New York: Pella, 1982

Saloutos, Theodore, *The Greeks in the United States*, Cambridge, Massachusetts: Harvard University Press, 1964

Seaman, P. David, *Modern Greek and American English in Contact*, The Hague: Mouton, 1972

V

Varnalis, Kostas 1884–1974

Poet, prose writer, and critic

Kostas Varnalis's work – more than the work of his contemporaries Angelos Sikelianos and Nikos Kazantzakis – could be read as a striking paradigm of "the anxiety of influence", with the persona of blind Oedipus in his poem *Proskynitis* ("Pilgrim", 1919) functioning as an emblem of this anxiety. His most important texts constitute a disciplined distortion of powerful precursors such as Aeschylus, Plato, Xenophon, Aristophanes, Solomos, Rabelais, Goethe, and Flaubert, in the name of a truth they failed to discover. The historical and ideological conditions at the end of the 20th century encourage an evaluation of Varnalis as a poet who was defeated in his struggle to assert himself against his renowned precursors. Furthermore, literary ideologies that dismiss traditional poetics or the ideals of human emancipation and solidarity as tedious anachronisms classify Varnalis as an overvalued writer, while ideologies that resist the modernist and postmodernist "prejudices" consider him as either a twilight hero or a pioneering figure. Irrespective of the validity of such value judgements, the relationship of his oeuvre with the ancient Greek tradition and the poetics of the demoticist school remains a significant and appealing issue in the history of modern Greek letters.

Varnalis's work is usually separated schematically into two periods: the first (1902–19) includes all the poems he wrote before he embraced dialectical materialism, and the second (1922–74) his lyrical and satirical texts written from a revolutionary, demystifying perspective. His long idealistic poem *Proskynitis* does not belong to either period because of its transitional character.

After the Graeco-Turkish War of 1897, the relative uniformity of the demoticist attitude towards antiquity broke down. The older generation of demoticists headed by Kostis Palamas continued to regard the ancient past as a reviving symbol which was to serve the present. For the younger demoticists however, and among them Varnalis, ancient tradition in their early poetry was to function as an "independent", autonomous symbol of beauty and vitality, apparently devoid of any social and political preoccupations. Contrary to established literary practice at that time, they adapted the Parnassian and Nietzschean readings of antiquity to their own aspirations in order to deliver Greek poetry from any social and political associations, from long-winded lyricism and ornate language. Whereas in Palamas's mature work Parnassianism and Nietzscheanism served the modern Greek search for a historical and cultural self-identity, in Varnalis's early poetry these were related to the attainment of beauty and the celebration of the Dionysian spirit.

The centrality of the category of the beautiful, the perception of art as the supreme value in life, the cult of instincts, the liberation of poetic language from the bonds of conventional morality, the lack of any nationalistic mystique, all constitute dominant features of the Varnalian use of ancient tradition up to 1919. It was mainly because of his "unpoetic" language and coarse realistic imagery that he was acclaimed by many critics of his time as the initiator of new and unconventional elements in Greek poetry and a champion of the so-called "poetic revolution of 1910".

The period of painfully wrought, impeccable sonnets came to an end when Varnalis went to Paris in 1919. There, in an extraordinary atmosphere of ideological and literary effervescence, the need for a renewal of his poetic practice became self-evident. At this crucial point, the national literary tradition performed an important role in the transition from the aesthetic/hedonistic Hellenism of his first period to the idealistic Hellenism of *Proskynitis*. It was in the light of the Parisian experience that Varnalis decided to follow Dionysios Solomos's example and become a national bard. In *Proskynitis*, for the first time, an interest in the national collective psyche enters the domain of his poetic practice. The ideological representation of Hellenism as the incarnation of "the human Essence" is central to the poem. Thematic subdivisions devoted to the Homeric world, the cult of Dionysus, the folk songs, Cretan poetry, and Solomos stress the continuity and "eternal greatness" of the Hellenic historical-cultural tradition. Nevertheless, this embellished and idealized picture of the Greek nation is undermined by the anticlimactic epilogue where the tension between the real and the ideal appears unresolved.

Varnalis's idealism achieved its full embodiment in *Proskynitis*, but the poem already adumbrates an opposite standpoint. *To Phos pou Kaiei* ("The Burning Light", 1922), *Sklavoi Poliorkimenoi* ("Enslaved Besieged", 1927), and *I Alithini Apologia tou Sokrati* ("The True Apology of Socrates", 1931) are the three major works of his artistic maturity. They all oscillate between bitter scepticism about the human condition and the expectation of a classless society as a historical imperative. *Sklavoi Poliorkimenoi* – a refutation in verse of Solomos's *Elevtheroi Poliorkimenoi* ("Free Besieged") – is the only one which does not draw on symbols from antiquity. The demystification of war, religion, and Solomos's idealist notion of freedom is effected through the radical reappropriation of Christian myth and folk tradition.

To Phos pou Kaiei is a symbolic dramatic composition in the manner of Goethe's *Faust* and Flaubert's *La Tentation de Saint Antoine*. The assimilation of traditional material from the standpoint of internationalism and class humanism is achieved through the dialectical tripartite organization of the work, the reinterpretation of mythological archetypes as familiar human figures, and the intensity of satirical unmasking. The symbols of Prometheus and Jesus were used to point out the deficiencies of Hellenic and Christian thought, while ancient sources (Hesiod, Aeschylus, Aristophanes, Nicander, Lucian) were treated in such a way as to present a demystified antiquity. The poetics of unmasking reached its culmination with *I Alithini Apologia tou Sokrati*, one of the three major satirical texts of modern Greek literature, the other two being Solomos's *I Ginaika tis Zakynthou* ("The Woman of Zakynthos") and Emmanouil Roidis's *I Papissa Ioanna* ("Pope Joan"). The tension and synthesis between the ancient and the modern, the radical and the regressive, the realistic and the symbolic, satire and lyricism, emerge as the ideological and formal principle of the work. The Varnalian Socrates, functioning simultaneously as an apostle of idealism and a social rebel, an advocate of social discriminations and a prophet of the classless society, a sensitive lover of nature and a relentless critic of the Athenian polis, reenacts and defies in a Rabelaisian fashion the Socrates of Plato, Xenophon, and Aristophanes.

This highly dialectical combination of antitheses based on ambivalence is absent in Varnalis's two postwar prose works, *To Imerologio tis Pinelopis* ("The Journal of Penelope", 1947) and *Attalos o Tritos* ("Attalus III", 1972). The first, a satirical demythologization of Penelope and the Homeric world, does not achieve the balanced combination of symbolism and satire found in *Alithini Apologia*. The second, the poet's sole play, reveals the network of power relationships in Hellenistic Pergamum as similar to that in postwar Greece, but is lacking in ambivalence and suggestiveness.

With the exception of *Proskynitis*, the relation of Varnalis's oeuvre to the Hellenic tradition never entailed a notion of Greece as a hypostasized essence. During the poet's first creative period Hellenism was a source of symbols and metaphors for the celebration of aesthetic life. From 1922 onwards its artistic assimilation subserved a twofold objective: to unmask and censure the dominant readings of past and present alike. The Varnalian use of tradition, far from constructing an ahistorical concept of "Greekness", exposes the recurrence of relations of power and exploitation in different forms. And in doing so, it indirectly demonstrates intertextuality as a poetic device, as a critical practice, as much as an inherent property of writing itself.

THEANO MICHAILIDOU

Biography

Born in Burgas in 1884, Varnalis studied classics at the University of Athens and was a militant member of the demoticist movement. In 1919 he won a state scholarship to study in Paris, where he attended courses on aesthetics and modern Greek literature. He worked as a teacher but was relieved of his post in 1926 on the grounds of being a communist. From then onwards he lived as a journalist and translator. The inter-war years were the most creative period of his life. In 1959 he was awarded the Lenin Prize for peace. He died in Athens in 1974.

Further Reading

Beaton, Roderick, *An Introduction to Modern Greek Literature*, Oxford: Clarendon Press, and New York: Oxford University Press, 1994

Dallas, Giannes, *I Demiourgiki Dekaetia sten Poisi tou Kosta Varnali* [The Creative Decade in the Poetry of Kostas Varnalis], Athens, 1988

Politis, Linos, *A History of Modern Greek Literature*, Oxford: Clarendon Press, 1973

Yatromanolakis, Yorgis, "The Prometheus Myth in Modern Greek Poetry and Drama: An Outline and Two Examples" in *Ancient Greek Myth in Modern Greek Poetry*, edited by Peter Mackridge, London: Cass, 1996

Velestinlis, Rigas *c.*1757–1798

Revolutionary and martyr

Rigas (as he is usually known) was born at Velestino, ancient Pherae (hence his cognomen Velestinlis or Pheraios) about 1757. According to one tradition his father was a rich landowner and Rigas was educated in Thessaly and worked for some time as a schoolmaster. To improve his financial situation he went to Constantinople and from there to Bucharest, the capital of Wallachia, which was governed by Greek Phanariots under the dominion of the sultans. Rigas had close relations with some of these Phanariot princes and also with representatives of the incipient Greek Enlightenment. He acquired a large holding of land and cattle. In 1788 he joined the service of the Baron de Langenfeld, whom he accompanied to Vienna in 1790. In the Austrian capital he published three books as an essential contribution to the enlightenment of his people: (1) *Scholeion ton Delikaton Eraston* ("The School for Discerning Lovers": six love stories from the collection of the French author Nicolas Edmonde Rétif de la Bretonne, 1734–1806, as an example of "modern" European literature and of the new relations between the sexes); (2) *Physikis Apanthisma* ("Physics Anthology": an introduction to physics on the basis of European works, to stimulate the legacy of Plato and Aristotle); (3) a translation of *L'Esprit des lois* by Charles de Montesquieu.

In 1791 Rigas returned to Bucharest in order to administer his property and to continue his activity as a translator and writer. He made contact with French revolutionaries residing in Wallachia, especially the diplomat Émile Gaudin; from these friends Rigas obtained the latest news and literature about the French Revolution. Rigas developed the idea of a national and social uprising of the Greek people, and although it is not certain, it is possible that he founded a secret society. In 1796 he returned to Vienna, which was also a centre of the Greek intelligentsia and offered him the opportunity for political agitation in Austria and neighbouring countries. At the start of 1796 the *Thourios Ymnos* ("War Hymn") was published; it

Rigas Velestinlis

analysed the political and military situation of the time and called for an insurrection not only of the Greeks, but of all the peoples of the Balkans, including the Turks. In 1797 the Viennese publishing house of the brothers George and Poulios Pouliou printed the following works by Rigas: (1) *O Ithikos Tripous* ("The Ethical Trilogy"), a collection of three belletrist works of the European Enlightenment, translated into Greek: the drama *Olympia* by the versatile Italian Pietro Antonio Metastasio (Rome 1698, Vienna 1782), the novelette by the member of the Paris Academy and favourite of Voltaire, Jean François Marmontel (1723–99), *La Bergère des Alpes*, and the idyll *Der erste Schäfer* by the Swiss poet and painter Salomon Gessner (1730–88); (2) *To Taxidion tou Neou Anacharsidos, IV*, a translation of part of the fourth volume of the famous work *Voyage du jeune Anacharsis en Grèce*, a kind of *Kulturgeschichte* of Classical Greece, published by the French antiquary Jean Jacques Barthélemy (1760–95) in 1788; for Rigas it was an aid to the formation of the national consciousness of his people; (3) *Megali Charta tis Ellados* ("Great Map of Greece"), a geographical map of the territories with Greek settlements: Greece and the Aegean, Asia Minor, southeast Europe; many placenames are given in ancient and modern Greek forms; important historic places have special illustrations in the margin; (4) *Geniki Charta tis Moldavias* ("General Map of Moldavia"); (5) *Nea Charta tis Vlachias* ("New Map of Vlachia"); (6) *Eikon tou Megalou Alexandrou* ("Likeness of Alexander the Great"), with marginal sketches illustrating the life of Alexander and an explanatory text in modern Greek and in French; (7) *Enkolpion Stratiotikon* ("Military Handbook"), a translated extract from the writings of the Austrian field marshal Count Ludwig Andreas Khevenmüller (1683–1744), as a help in the preparation of the armed insurrection (no copy of this work has survived); (8) *Epanastatiki Prokiryxis* ("Revolutionary Manifesto"); the original text has not survived, but it can be reconstructed in its four parts: the *Nea Politiki Dioikisis* ("Modern Civil Government") provides an introduction to Rigas's political programme, which applies to all regions where Greeks are living together with "non-Christians", i.e. Turks; the second part contains 35 articles on human rights according to the French *Déclaration des droits de l'homme*, but adapted to the Greek situation; there follows a plan for a constitution of this region in which several peoples are to be found but the Greeks are dominant; the last part repeats the *Thourios Ymnos*, a kind of poetic interpretation of the constitution. Separately Rigas published two other political poems, the *Ymnos Patriotikos* ("Patriotic Hymn") and the *Paian i Ethnikos Ymnos* ("Paean or National Hymn").

On 17 October 1797 France and Austria concluded the Treaty of Campoformio. This treaty ceded the Venetian possessions in Albania and in the Ionian islands to Napoleon. The changed political situation seemed to Rigas to be the right moment for the insurrection. He wrote a letter to Napoleon (which was confiscated by the Austrian police) and without waiting for an answer he went to Trieste with his revolutionary material in order to travel to Greece. But he was betrayed and arrested by the Austrian police. He was taken to Vienna and from Vienna to Belgrade in the spring of 1798. Here he was strangled by the Turks on 28 June 1798 together with seven comrades.

Rigas was one of the most eminent representatives of the Greek Enlightenment and the most important forerunner of the Greek uprising of 1821. His poems were very popular and he himself became a martyr not only in Greece but throughout the Balkans. His politics were geared to the liberation of all Balkan peoples and to the formation of a Balkan state under Greek hegemony. But in the wave of Greek nationalism after 1821 his intentions were misunderstood. The Patriarchate of Constantinople condemned his actions and Greek chauvinism later falsely made him into a precursor of the *Megali Idea* ("Great Idea") of the reconstruction of the Byzantine empire. His unfettered patriotism was based on the memory of Greek antiquity and influenced by the ideas of the European Enlightenment and the French Revolution.

JOHANNES IRMSCHER

See also Enlightenment

Biography

Born at Velestino (ancient Pherae in Thessaly, whence his alternative name Pheraios) *c*.1757, Rigas was educated in Thessaly and worked for a while as a schoolmaster. He moved first to Constantinople and then to Bucharest where he befriended the Phanariots and representatives of the Enlightenment. Inspired by the French Revolution with ideas for Balkan liberation he published revolutionary tracts for which he was arrested in Trieste. Strangled to death by the Turks in Belgrade in 1798, he became a martyr throughout the Balkans.

Further Reading

Enepekidis, P.K., *Rigas Velestinlis: Epistrophi ap' ton Thrylo stin Istoria* [Rigas Velestinlis: A Return from Legend to History], Athens, 1958

Mantouvalou, Maria, *O Rigas sta Vimata tou Megalou Alexandrou* [Rigas in the Footsteps of Alexander the Great], Athens, 1996

Pantazopoulos, Nikolaos I., *Meletemata gia ton Riga* [Essays on Rigas], Athens, 1994

Velestinlis, Rigas, *Ta Epanistatika* [Revolutionary Writings], edited by Dimitrios A. Karamperopoulos, Athens, 1994

Veloudis, G., Velestinlis entry in *Biographisches Lexikon zur Geschichte Südosteuropas*, vol. 4, edited by Mathias Bernath and Felix V. Schroeder, Munich: Oldenbourg. 1981, p. 398 ff.

Velouchiotis, Ares 1905–1945

World War II resistance leader

Ares Velouchiotis was the nom de guerre of Thanasis Klaras, leader of ELAS (*Ellinikos Laikos Apeleftherotikos Stratos*, or the Greek Popular Liberation Army) which spearheaded the resistance to the German and Italian occupation forces during World War II and later became the military wing of the Communist Party in the Civil War against the combined Greek and British royalist forces. Velouchiotis's life has been obscured by countless layers of ideologically driven calumny from both the left and the right in Greece. He has been variously portrayed as a self-serving renegade, a merciless terrorist, or communist pawn. To many, however, he remains a shining example of patriotism and idealism during one of the country's darkest hours. He led one of the most effective resistance movements in all occupied Europe and his military prowess was legendary.

Born in Lamia to a middle-class family, Klaras demonstrated from a young age a nonconformism and iconoclasm that would mark his entire adult life and would eventually lead to his death. Although undoubtedly intelligent, he was refused entry into high school because of his ungovernable temperament. Since he was unwilling to follow in the footsteps of his father and older brother, who were both lawyers, his family arranged for him to be trained as an agronomist. After a brief tenure in the Ministry of Agriculture, Klaras left for Athens where he sought the company of like-minded young idealists who had grown impatient with the rising poverty of the masses and the government's authoritarian methods. This led him to join the motley coalition of leftists who then made up the emergent Communist Party of Greece. He became a member and served the party in a wide variety of functions, including journalist, courier, and political agitator. On one notable occasion he risked his life to save that of the party's leader, Nikos Zachariadis, who, ironically, was to betray him years later in the name of party discipline. Unrepentantly irreverent, Klaras smoked, drank, and sang popular songs, refusing to toe the party's puritanical line that forbade most forms of entertainment as degenerate. Klaras was jailed repeatedly for his political activities and suffered torture at the hands of the state security services until, in 1939, disillusioned with the party's inflexibility on the issue of signed renunciations of communist ideology, he won his release from prison by signing such a declaration. His membership in the party was revoked and he was ostracized by his former comrades, many of whom had always viewed his boldness and nerve with suspicion. After his release from prison he became isolated and dejected, eventually taking to drink, until the declaration of war in October 1940.

With the onset of the German-led occupation in 1941, Klaras began secretly organizing resistance. A gifted orator, he made speeches in which he invoked the heroic achievements of the revolution of 1821 against the Turks. He held that the key to effective resistance was armed struggle in the mountains, the traditional haven of the Greek klephts, the rebels who had won independence for the nation by fighting a war of attrition against the Turks. In a bid to remove this agitator from their midst, the Communist Party sent him to central Greece with the mission of exploring the possibilities for armed resistance. Slowly at first and against great difficulties, Klaras, now known as Ares Velouchiotis (a name derived from his ancestral village of Velouchi), began recruiting men from villages across the mainland. Velouchiotis's manner quickly won over the rural population and his resistance force gradually grew. His partisans struck at the Italian and German occupiers with swiftness and daring, often defeating numerically superior forces with great displays of courage and audacity. In November 1942 Velouchiotis's men, together with a smaller force from the rival resistance organization EDES (*Ethnikos Dimokratikos Ellinikos Syndesmos*, the National Democratic Hellenic Union) and a small detachment of British commandos, blew up the Gorgopotamos rail bridge. The most important European sabotage operation up to then, the destruction of the bridge cut off the principal supply line to Rommel's forces in North Africa for nearly five weeks, thus giving the British Eighth Army the upper hand in what became the first Allied victory, at El-Alamein.

Under Velouchiotis's leadership ELAS grew into a formidable, agile, and uniquely effective resistance movement with a broad popular base. By the spring of 1943 they had liberated nearly a third of Greece, from Kastoria to the Corinthian Gulf. Velouchiotis's guerrilla tactics had forced the Germans and Italians to withdraw to a handful of small cities. His success was viewed with amazement and suspicion by the political classes of Athens and by the British who cooperated with him nominally while financing independent, right-wing resistance forces in an effort to ensure Greece became a pro-British monarchy after the war. He in turn was deeply suspicious of politicians and openly hostile to most foreigners, especially the British, whose political intentions he rightly mistrusted. Velouchiotis showed brazen disregard for party policies, a fact often overlooked by critics who accuse him of having blindly served the communist cause. He cared little for ideology and was noted for invoking the glorious achievements of the ancient and 19th-century Greeks rather than the militant ideas of Marx or Lenin. His success as a partisan leader among the mountain villagers of Greece can be partly attributed to his profound respect for rural customs and the often harsh discipline he imposed on his men. Although he had no military training, he was a peerless tactician and charismatic leader who earned the loyalty of his men through humility and fairness. Demotic songs composed in his honour still survive.

Velouchiotis nevertheless made many enemies, especially among those on both the left and the right who saw their own political prospects in postwar Greece threatened by his popularity and military might. The communists began a secret smear campaign against him in the cities, implicitly supporting the accusations of theft and savagery levelled by rival right-wing partisan groups. On a number of occasions Velouchiotis's men came into open conflict with right-wing partisans supported by the British. These conflicts foreshadowed the Civil War that followed the liberation of Greece and resulted in the transformation of Velouchiotis's resistance force into an armed wing of the Communist Party. Velouchiotis did not live to see this. He broke ranks with the party over the controversial agreement with the British-backed Royalists, signed at Varkiza in the winter of 1944. Accompanied by a core group of his most loyal fighters, he went into hiding in the mountains of central Greece, pursued by right-wing militias. Driven to despair over the country's political situation and his own increasing isolation, Velouchiotis took his own life on 16 June 1945 near the Acheloos river. His head was cut off by right-wing militiamen and set on display in the town of Trikkala as proof of his death. His memory remains a source of vociferous political debate and attempts to recognize his decisive role in the liberation of Greece continue to provoke contention.

EMMANUEL C. BOURBOUHAKIS

See also EAM and ELAS

Biography

Born in Lamia in 1905 to a middle-class family, Velouchiotis (whose real name was Thanasis Klaras) was trained as an agronomist. At the age of 19 he joined the Communist Party in Athens and was often jailed. In World War II he became the charismatic leader of the ELAS resistance movement. Accused of treachery, he took his own life on 16 June 1945.

Further Reading

Charitopoulos, Dionysis, *Ares o Archigos ton Atakton* [Ares, Leader of the Disobedient], 2 vols, Athens, 1997

Demetriou, D.N., *Antartes sta Vouna tis Roumelis* [Partisans in the Mountains of Greece], Athens, 1978

Klaras, Mpampis, *O Adelfos mou o Ares* [My Brother Ares], Athens, 1984

Kousoulas, George D., *Revolution and Defeat: The Story of the Greek Communist Party*, London and New York: Oxford University Press, 1965

Mazower, Mark, *Inside Hitler's Greece: The Experience of Occupation, 1941–44*, New Haven, Connecticut: Yale University Press, 1993 (especially pp. 297–322)

Tsoukalas, K., *I Elliniki Tragodia* [The Greek Tragedy], Athens, 1981

Woodhouse, C.M., *The Struggle for Greece, 1941–1949*, London: Hart Davis MacGibbon, 1976; New York: Beckman Esanu, 1979

Zaousis, Aleksandros, *I Dyo Ochthes* [The Two Solitudes], Athens, 1987

Venetians

The region at the head of the Adriatic – Venetia and Istria – formed one of the imperial provinces. In the early Byzantine period, as the barbarian invaders moved into Italy, the islands of the Venetian lagoon were settled by refugees. The newcomers retained their imperial links: their dukes or doges had portentous Byzantine titles, frequent embassies passed between Venice and Constantinople, and Venetian chroniclers concerned themselves with events in Byzantium. Venetian churches were dedicated to Greek saints and were enriched with Greek relics, such as those of St Sabas, St Donatus, and St Nicholas of Myra, some received as gifts, others filched by raiding parties. The church of St Mark in Venice, which served as the palatine chapel of the doge, was adorned with a succession of rich altarpieces made up of pieces of Constantinopolitan workmanship reaching their final form in the Pala d'Oro of the 14th century. The third rebuilding of St Mark's in the years 1063–94 was in conscious imitation of the church of the Holy Apostles in Constantinople. A set of doors made in Constantinople graced its portals. As for ecclesiastical traffic the other way, a Venetian chronicler claimed that Greek use of church bells began with a gift of bells from Venice. The coincidence of Venetian and Greek interests in opposing Dalmatian piracy and Saracen advances in the Adriatic strengthened the relationship, prefiguring the Venetian-Byzantine resistance to the Normans in the next two centuries. Venetian merchants became increasingly active in trade between Italy and the empire, importing even silk textiles, despite imperial prohibition, and competing with the Greeks for the carrying trade within the empire itself.

From 992 comes the first of a series of privileges that further mark the stages in the relationship between the empire and Venice. An imperial bull of that year established a favourable scale of tariffs for Venetian merchants and, by excluding them from the jurisdiction of certain officials, gave them an advantage from which their Amalfitan and other rivals were explicitly excluded. Almost a century later under the emperor Alexios I Komnenos (1081–1118), a bull, or perhaps a series of bulls, exempted the Venetians from payment of duties throughout the empire. The concession further made over to the Venetians a number of properties on the Golden Horn, which later became the Venetian quarter of Constantinople where the Venetians enjoyed rights of extraterritoriality. During the 12th century Venetian privileges were confirmed and extended. The survival of several hundred private Venetian commercial contracts shows how active the Venetians were in the empire at this time. They had their own churches, monasteries, domestic and commercial properties, not only in Constantinople but also elsewhere in the empire, for example at Corinth and Almyros. Olive oil is the commodity most often the subject of these contracts. By the second half of the 12th century the numbers of Venetians resident in Constantinople, said to be 10,000, inflamed anti-western feeling in the capital. In a famous passage Niketas Choniates refers to Venetian arrogance, to the affront caused by Venetian marriages into Greek families, and to the great temperamental gulf that divided the two peoples. The tension exploded in 1171 when the emperor Manuel ordered the arrest of all Venetians in the empire. The disruption of life in the empire must have been severe and this, perhaps combined with Venetian retaliation and their pact with the Normans, led Manuel to negotiate, but at his death in 1180 negotiations were still incomplete. Under the Angeloi emperors the old Venetian privileges were confirmed and more fully enumerated while their legal status was enhanced.

The Fourth Crusade of 1202–04 delivered Constantinople to the westerners. The story, perhaps not literally true, that the doge Enrico Dandolo had lost his sight in the struggle with the

Greeks in 1171 was at any rate expressive of the residue of bitterness against the Greeks that those events had produced in Venice. In the division of the spoils the Venetians took three-eighths of the city and the Balkan coast south of Dyrrachium. They obtained Crete by purchase from the Crusaders, and the Ionian Islands and others such as Euboea, Andros, Naxos, and Santorini fell to Venice or Venetian citizens in the course of the next century. The doge took the title of lord of a quarter and a half of a quarter of Romania, that is of the "Roman lands" or Byzantine empire. A Venetian *podestà*, or governor, was appointed in Constantinople and rivalled the Latin emperor and the doge himself in influence. The monastery of the Pantokrator became his headquarters. It took years for the abundant loot to be transported to Venice. The plunder included antiquities such as the great bronze horses from the Hippodrome destined to adorn the loggia of St Mark's, church plate for the treasury of St Mark's, innumerable architectural trophies, some to adorn the exterior of St Mark's and some, like so many columns, to be sliced into roundels for the decoration of *palazzi*. Relics included the icon of the Hodegetria, said to be the work of St Luke, carried off to the Venetian Pantokrator, while others such as the head of John the Baptist, an arm of St George, the headless body of St Paul the hermit, and the body of St Eutychios ended up in Venice. Even the Crown of Thorns, initially appropriated by the Latin emperors, was pawned to a consortium of Venetian business-men in 1238. Gleeful Venetian chroniclers catalogued the extent of the spoils while Niketas Choniates mournfully recorded the losses.

In 1261 the Greeks once more took Constantinople, with the help of Venice's great rival, Genoa. During the period between 1261 and 1381 there were four Venetian–Genoese wars, some of great intensity, which were often fought off the Byzantine coast or on Byzantine seas. Neither the restoration of Greek power in Constantinople nor the enmity of the Genoese inhibited the progress of Venetian commerce so much as might have been expected. In the 14th century Venice, like Genoa, made agreements with the Grand Komnenoi in Trebizond, modelled on the concessions in Constantinople, which gave them an enclave and commercial advantages. Throughout the Byzantine lands and through those lands to distant destinations beyond them, Venetian commercial enter-prise continued to prosper. The two centuries between 1261 and the fall of Constantinople to the Ottomans in 1453 were dominated by conflicts in which the two Italian states, Byzantium, and the emerging Ottoman power were the leading protagonists in an intricate and changing set of alliances and counter-alliances, seldom made with regard to religion or to the interests of western Christendom as a whole. A series of short-term treaties between the Greek emperors and Venice gave the Venetians new quarters in Constantinople and Thessalonica, protection for their ecclesiastical usages, and their own weights and measures. These rights were extended to those of mixed parentage who classed themselves as Venetians. A commission was established to examine the many demands for compensation for losses that the Venetians claimed to have suffered in the empire. Concessions and agreements constantly broke down under the pressure of threats, squabbles over alleged infringements, and disputes over the regulation of corn sales or taxing wine. In 1343 the poverty of Byzantium compelled the empress Anna, regent for her son John V, to pawn the crown jewels to Venice to secure a loan of 30,000 ducats. Four years later, at the coronation of John VI, glass baubles had to be substituted, while Venice became restless at the failure to repay the interest. In the 1370s Venice seized the strategic island of Tenedos when negotiations to buy it from the emperor were stalled by dynastic disputes and Genoese subversion. After the Peace of Turin in 1381 ended the Venetian–Genoese wars, Venice was principally concerned with the protection of its trade and possessions in Greece from the rising Ottoman power. In 1453 some individual Venetians fought bravely against the Turks, but the Venetian state made an alliance with the sultan. Venice had already written off Byzantium.

Under the Ottomans Venice struggled, not unsuccessfully, to retain some of its outposts and even to take new ones, such as Monemvasia. Crete remained Venetian until 1669 and the Ionian islands until the fall of the Venetian republic in 1797. The visible remains of the Venetian presence include loggias and fortifications in Crete and on the coast of the Peloponnese, such as Modon and Monemvasia, while Venetian architectural features appear in the churches of the Ionian islands and the Argolid. A scattered Roman Catholic population in some Aegean islands such as Naxos and Santorini is attributable to the Venetian presence.

In the early centuries a knowledge of Greek had been rare, almost unknown, in Venice, but even before 1453 Greeks had begun to arrive in the city. Famous scholars included Demetrios Kydones and Bessarion, while the Cretan painter El Greco was numbered among the artists. Some 4000 Greeks were resident there before 1500. Bessarion made a gift of his library to Venice. For Aldus Manutius Venice was the best city for the foundation of his Greek press, although some may claim that his founts, based on the Greek script of the day with ligatures and accents, were less successful than the typeface of Nicolas Jenson who himself had worked in Venice. From 1573 the church of S. Giorgio dei Greci was the focus of the Greek community in Venice and became a centre for Hellenic studies.

M.E. MARTIN

See also Venetokratia, Venice

Further Reading

Borsari, Silvano, *Venezia e Bisanzio nel XII secolo: i rapporti economici*, Venice: Deputazione, 1988

Chrysostomides, Julian, "Venetian Commercial Privileges under the Palaeologi", *Studi Veneziani*, 12 (1970): pp. 267–356

Geanakoplos, Deno John, *Greek Scholars in Venice: Studies in the Dissemination of Greek Learning from Byzantium to Western Europe*, Cambridge, Massachusetts: Harvard University Press, 1962; as *Byzantium and the Renaissance*, Hamden, Connecticut: Archon, 1973

Maltezou, Chryssa A., "Venetian *Habitatores, Burgenses* and Merchants in Constantinople and Its Hinterland, 12th–13th Centuries" in *Constantinople and Its Hinterland*, edited by Cyril Mango and Gilbert Dagron, Aldershot, Hampshire: Variorum, 1995

Manoussacas, M.I., "The History of the Greek Confraternity (1498–1953) and the Activity of the Greek Institute of Venice (1966–1982)", *Modern Greek Studies Yearbook*, 5 (1989): pp. 321–94

Nicol, Donald M., *Byzantium and Venice: A Study in Diplomatic and Cultural Relations,* Cambridge and New York: Cambridge University Press, 1988

Venetokratia 1204–1797

Venetokratia is the term given to the period of Venetian rule in the areas of Greek-speaking, formerly Byzantine-controlled territories. The period begins with the Fourth Crusade (1204) and closes essentially with the formal end of the Venetian Republic in 1797. Those Greek lands that were divided between Frankish and Venetian rule experienced over this period – some for a longer and others for a shorter length of time – foreign domination that varied in character. Some, for example, passed directly from Byzantine to Venetian rule, others became feudal fiefs according to the pattern of the medieval West, while yet others had to undergo a process of feudalization before finally becoming Venetian dominions. These differing historical circumstances affected the local populations of each region in various ways.

After the Latin conquest of Constantinople in 1204, Crusaders and Venetians divided among themselves the territories of the dismembered Byzantine empire. According to the terms of the agreement known as the *Partitio Terrarum Imperii Romaniae,* the Byzantine lands were divided into six lots, of unequal size, two of which were given to the Latin emperor, two to the Crusaders, and two to the Venetians. In reality, however, the *Partitio* was of little practical worth since the lands that were assigned to the Crusaders had not as yet been conquered.

One of the Greek lands that was to experience a long period of Venetian rule was Crete. The island is not mentioned in the *Partitio* because it had ceased to be part of the Byzantine state just prior to the Crusade. Among the terms of the agreement made between Alexios Angelos, son of Isaac II, and the Crusaders, whereby Alexios secured the Crusaders' support in his efforts to put his father back on the throne of Byzantium, was the cession of Crete to Boniface, marquis de Montferrat, the leader of the Fourth Crusade. Since the island already belonged to Boniface before the conquest of Constantinople, it was not mentioned in the *Partitio.*

A few months after the conquest of the Byzantine capital, however, on 12 August 1204, in his efforts to win the support of Venice in his dispute with the Latin emperor of Constantinople, Baldwin of Flanders, Boniface signed a treaty ceding Crete to the most Serene Republic of Venice. At first Venice was too involved with establishing control over its newly won Greek-speaking territories to push ahead with a full takeover of the island of Crete as well. Thus when Genoese pirates, led by Enrico Pescatore, titular count of Malta, attempted to seize the island, they succeeded in taking control of it relatively quickly. Venice reacted immediately by sending its fleet to Candia. Pescatore was eventually compelled in 1211 to come to terms with Venice, though he was not sent away empty-handed. The withdrawal of the Genoese marked the beginning of Venetian rule in Crete, which was to last until 1669.

Another island that had been prised from Byzantine control on the eve of the Fourth Crusade was Cyprus. The island had originally been conquered in 1191 by king Richard the Lionheart of England, one of the leaders of the Third Crusade, who subsequently gave his dominion first to the military Order of the Temple, and then to Guy de Lusignan, king of Jerusalem. The French Lusignan dynasty was to remain in Cyprus for the next 300 years. The marriage of Giacomo II (1460–73) to Caterina Cornaro, the daughter of a noble Venetian family, signalled the beginning of Venetian mercantile domination of the island. Venice meanwhile prepared the ground for outright control of the island and in 1489, after the death of Giacomo, compelled Caterina, now queen regent of Cyprus, to resign her right to sovereignty of the island and to hand it over to Venice. The Venetian period in Cyprus lasted until 1571, when the island was conquered by the Turks.

Thessalonica also experienced a short period of Venetian rule. In 1423 the despot Andronikos Palaiologos found himself unable to defend the city against the Turkish threat and consequently ceded control of it, with the approval of the Byzantine emperor and the local population, to the Venetians. Ever with an eye to its commercial interests, Venice snatched up the offer and rushed to take over the city. Venetian control lasted until 1430, when the Turks captured it.

Athens was initially conquered by the French and ruled by the la Roche Burgundians. Later, however, it came under the control of the Catalans and then the Florentines, before succumbing to the Turks in 1456. Two centuries later Athens experienced further misfortune. In 1687, in their efforts to contain the Turkish military threat, the forces of the Venetian Francesco Morosini and of the Swede Königsmarck decided to invade and take control of Attica. During the course of the siege of the Acropolis by the Venetians, explosives fell on the Parthenon, which the Turks were using as a magazine, and the Classical monument was severely damaged by the enormous explosion that resulted. Despite initial successes, Morosini was eventually forced to abandon his siege of the city, taking a number of important Classical sculptures back to Venice with him as a consolation prize.

The Venetian period in the Peloponnese can be divided into two phases: the first extends from 1204 to 1540, and the second from 1685 to 1715. During the first period the Venetian territories consisted of Modon and Coron (1206), Nauplia (1388), Argos (1388), and Monemvasia (1464). During the course of the second and third Turko-Venetian wars (1499–1502, 1572–73) Venice lost its dominions in the Peloponnese, together with Lepanto (Naupactus), its sole dominion in mainland Greece. The Venetian flag was not raised again in the Peloponnese until the end of the 17th century when Venice joined the Holy League (*Sacra Lega*) and declared war on the Turks. The second period of Venetian rule in the Peloponnese was not to last long: in 1715 the Turks replied to the blow dealt them earlier by the Venetians by recapturing the entire peninsula.

After the Fourth Crusade, Euboea (Negroponte) was divided between Boniface, marquis de Montferrat, who took the central part, and Venice, which took the northern and southern ends – Oreos and Carystus – of the long island. A little later Boniface gave his share to three nobles from Verona, who came to be known as the *terzieri* since they each took a

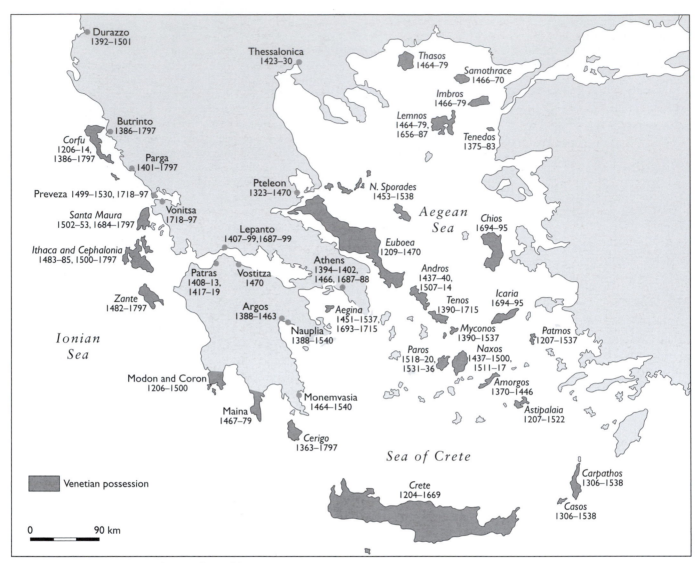

45. Venetian possessions in the Greek world

third. In 1390, following the death of the Latin feudal lord Giorgio Ghisi, the Venetians annexed the entire island. With the first Turko-Venetian war, however, the island fell under Ottoman control in 1470.

The Ionian islands were only gradually absorbed into the overseas dominions of Venice. Corfu was granted to Venice during the first period of Venetian rule, being placed under the control of ten Venetian nobles. This regime, however, lasted for less than ten years (1206–14) after which the island passed first to the Despotate of Epirus and then to the Angevins. Later, in the 14th century, the local population consented to being brought under Venetian rule, and were granted various privileges by the Serenissima. Venetian administration on the island survived to the end of the Venetian Republic in 1797. Zante became a Venetian dominion in 1482, and Cephalonia and Ithaca in 1500, while Leucas (Santa Maura) came under Venetian rule much later, in letter in 1684 and in practice in 1699, with the treaty of Karlovich. With the annexation of Leucas Venice also acquired Vonitsa and Preveza. Lastly, Cythera became Venetian in 1363, when Venice declared its virtual rulers – the members of the Venier family – personae

non gratae because of their involvement in the St Titius rebellion in Crete. The two smaller islands of Paxos and Anticythera followed the fortunes of neighbouring Corfu and Cythera respectively. It was under the flag of St Mark that, for the first time in their troubled history, the Ionian islands acquired a specific political and geographical identity, when the whole group was treated as a clearly defined entity. The Venetian state, as early as the 14th century and long before gaining formal control of the Ionian islands, "desired", as a Venetian chronicler succinctly put it, "to acquire the configuration of islands comprised of Corfu, Zante, and Cephalonia". This "configuration" later comprised the principal feature of the Venetian presence in the Ionian Sea.

The Aegean islands, with their capital on Naxos, comprised the duchy of the "Arcipelago", and were divided into feudal domains governed as family fiefs by Venetian nobility, some for longer, others for shorter periods of time. Often the names of the families came to be linked with the local history of the various islands, such as the Sanudi in Naxos, Paros, Antiparos, Melos, Ios, Kythnos, and Siphnos; the Dandoli in Andros; the Querini in Astypalaia; the Barozzi in Santorini; and the

Cornari in Karpathos. The decline in power of the various Latin fiefdoms began in 1537 when Barbarossa crushed the strength of many of the Latin dynasties in the Aegean. The consolidation of Turkish power throughout the Aegean, however, was not effected until 30 years later, in 1566.

In the first centuries of Venetian rule in Greek lands the elements of the distinctly foreign culture established themselves only very slowly, faced as they were by a tightly knit Greek social body, and succeeded in influencing only a limited number of areas of local life. Nevertheless Hellenism, presented as it was with an open road of communication with the West, came under the influence of the European Renaissance and began to assimilate the values of the Western world. With the gradual meeting of these two worlds, over time relations between what had originally been mutually hostile communities became warmer. Greek society not only assimilated foreign influences but also blended older and newer cultural traditions. The fusion of the foreign with the Greek reached its quintessence perhaps in Crete, where a fertile cultural dialogue between the Byzantine tradition and western Europe gradually led to a common, Veneto-Cretan form of cultural expression, particularly in painting and literature. Despite the unpleasant aspects of foreign occupation, and despite the unusual blend of conditions under which the Greeks lived throughout the course of Venetian rule, they nevertheless managed to maintain their own cultural character and potential and to make of this a new, exciting fabric.

CHRYSSA A. MALTEZOU

See also Renaissance (Veneto-Cretan), Venetians

Summary

Dating from the Fourth Crusade in 1204 to the end of the Venetian Republic in 1797, *Venetokratia* denotes Venetian rule in former Byzantine territory. The principal areas were Crete (1204–1669); Cyprus (1489–1571); Thessalonica (1423–30); the Peloponnese (1204–1540 and 1685–1715); Euboea (1390–1470); the Ionian islands (various dates from 1206 to 1797); and the Aegean islands (various dates from the 13th to the 16th centuries). The two cultures merged to form a generally harmonious and often creative blend.

Further Reading

Holton, David (editor), *Literature and Society in Renaissance Crete*, Cambridge and New York: Cambridge University Press, 1991

Koder, Johannes, *Negroponte: Untersuchungen zur Topographie und Siedlungsgeschichte der Insel Euboia während der Zeit der Venezianerherrschaft*, Vienna: Akademie der Wissenschaften, 1973

Lock, Peter, *The Franks in the Aegean, 1204–1500*, London and New York: Longman, 1995

Papadopoulos, T. (editor), *Istoria tis Kyprou* [History of Cyprus], vols 4–5: *Messaionikon vassileion Enetocratia*, [The Medieval Kingdoms and the Venetokratia] Nicosia, 1996

Thiriet, Freddy, *La Romanie vénitienne au Moyen Age*, 2nd edition, Paris: Boccard, 1959, reprinted 1975

Venice

Of all the maritime cities of Italy it was Venice that had the greatest impact on the fortunes of the Byzantine and modern Greek world. Itself a creation of Byzantium, it developed into

Venice: San Giorgio dei Greci and its 16th-century leaning bell tower

a major economic power, rising from the status of a Byzantine province to be the ruling master of formerly Byzantine territories. With the reconquest of Italy by the Byzantine emperor Justinian in the 6th century, Venice became a part of the Byzantine empire. The governor of the *provincia Venetiarum* was the *magister militum*, later *dux*, who was under the direct authority of the exarch of Ravenna. A fine example of the Byzantine presence in the lagoon of Venice in this period is the inscription, dated 639, in the cathedral of Torcello, in which mention is made of the emperor Herakleios, the exarch Isaacius, and the *magister militum* Mauricius.

The fall of the exarchate of Ravenna in the mid-8th century marked the beginning of Venetian autonomy. However, the theoretical bond of vassalage that continued to unite Venice with Byzantium in fact served its interests. Thus the dukes, or *doges*, of Venice continued in this early period to use such titles as consul, *spatharius*, *protospatharius*, patrician, and *protosebastus*, awarded them by the Byzantine emperor. From the 10th century onwards the power and prestige of Venice increased. Following a request by the doge, the Byzantine emperors Basil II and Constantine VIII issued a *chrysobull* in 992 granting Venetian merchants tax exemptions in exchange for transporting Byzantine troops to Italy in Venetian vessels. This *chrysobull* was the first in a series of imperial documents defining relations between Byzantium and Venice. Political and commercial relations between Byzantium and the maritime power resulted ultimately in the penetration of Venice into the sphere of Byzantine influence. Byzantine saints were worshipped, their relics were brought to Venice, doges were wedded to the daughters of Byzantine nobles, and Byzantine artistic styles were adopted or imitated. The earliest mosaics in the basilica of St Mark, whose architectural plans were based on the church of the Holy Apostles in Constantinople, together with the mosaics in the cathedral of Torcello, are among the finest examples of Byzantine art in the region of the lagoon.

In 1082 the emperor Alexios I Komnenos was hard pressed by the Norman invasions of Byzantine territories in the Balkans. In order to deal with the threat he sought the help of Venice, in exchange for which he granted the city far-reaching privileges that allowed Venetian merchants free access to all Byzantine ports. These served to open the way for Venetian expansion into the lucrative trade of the Levant. It has often been claimed that the seed of the Fourth Crusade that was to take place in 1204 was in fact planted with the *chrysobull* of 1082. In the words of Fernand Braudel, as termites eat away at the structure of a building invisible to the outside observer, so too Venice managed gradually to consume the vast Byzantine edifice. In 1204 the Venetians, with the help of the Crusaders, conquered the city of Constantinople and became masters of the lands of the dismantled Byzantine state. For a large part of the Greek world the period of Venetian rule had begun, to last in some areas for many centuries.

After the final fall of Constantinople to the Turks in 1453, Venice became a great cultural centre for the subjugated Greek world. In 1498 the Greeks of Venice, merchants, craftsmen, sailors, and soldiers (*stradioti*) set up the Greek Orthodox Contraternity of Venice, which was to be the most renowned of all the Greek confraternities of the diaspora. The Orthodox church of San Giorgio dei Greci, built in the years 1539–73, was decorated with beautiful works of art. Later, some of the greatest figures in the world of modern Greek learning were to study and teach at the college set up thanks to funding from Thomas Flanghinis in 1665. The Greeks of Venice maintained a hospital and a convent, and provided major bequests for schools in the Turkish-ruled Greek east (such as in Patras, Athens, and Ioannina). Numerous Greek books were printed in the Greek printing houses of Venice, and were then sent for sale and distribution in the Orthodox centres of the East. Besides the printing houses, Venice also played host to numerous scribes and copyists of manuscripts, editors and correctors of ancient texts, and painters and artists who contributed not only to the development of Greek cultural styles and values but also, more generally, to European culture and learning. Such figures included Ianos Laskaris, Markos Moussouros, and Domenikos Theotokopoulos, known as El Greco.

CHRYSSA A. MALTEZOU

See also Venetians

Summary

Venice became part of the Byzantine empire with the conquests of Justinian in the 6th century. It became autonomous after the fall of Ravenna in the mid-8th century. Its merchants were first granted tax concessions by the Byzantine emperor in 992 and further privileges in 1081. Venetian rule of much of the Greek world began with the Fourth Crusade in 1204. After the fall of Constantinople in 1453 expatriates made Venice a centre of Greek culture and learning.

Further Reading

Geanakoplos, Deno J., *Byzantine East and Latin West: Two Worlds of Christendom in Middle Ages and Renaissance*, Oxford: Blackwell, and New York: Harper and Row, 1966

Martin, M.E., "The Venetians in the Byzantine Empire before 1204" in *Byzantium and the West, c.850–c.1200*, edited by J. D. Howard-Johnston, Amsterdam: Hakkert, 1988

Nicol, Donald M., *Byzantium and Venice: A Study in Diplomatic and Cultural Relations*, Cambridge and New York: Cambridge University Press, 1988

Thiriet, Freddy, *La Romanie vénitienne au Moyen Age*, Paris: Boccard, 1959, reprinted 1975

Venizelos, Eleftherios 1864–1936

Politician

Eleutherios Venizelos was eight times prime minister of Greece. His legacy is a mixed one. An advocate of *enosis* (union) of the unredeemed Greeks with Greece, in the aftermath of World War I he came closer than any other Greek leader to achieving the *Megali Idea* (Great Idea). When this new empire was subsequently lost after his fall from power, Greece again turned to him to salvage what could be saved from the ruins. One of his last achievements was to inaugurate an unusually long period of Graeco-Turkish amity. Domestically he was a reformer, modernizing the government services and constitution, but his disputes with the king would begin the national schism which would dominate Greek political life for decades to come.

Venizelos was born on 23 August 1864 near Chania on the island of Crete to a Greek family which had migrated to Crete in the late 18th century. He graduated from the university in Athens in 1886 and returned to Crete to practise law. Venizelos became active in the political life of the island, was a leader of the local Liberal party, and a strong advocate of *enosis* of the Ottoman-ruled island with independent Greece. In 1888 he was elected to the Cretan assembly, but was forced to flee the following year after an unsuccessful insurrection against Ottoman rule. He was later allowed to return and was again elected to the assembly, becoming minister of justice. He was one of the leaders of a revolt against the Ottomans in 1897 and was one of the Cretan delegates sent to meet the admirals of the Great Powers dispatched to mediate a settlement. As a result of this mediation, Crete achieved autonomy within the Ottoman empire, under a high commissioner selected by the powers. The new high commissioner was prince George of Greece, son of king George I. Venizelos became head of the new island executive in 1899, but quarrelled with prince George, and they fell out by 1904. When Venizelos was defeated at the polls in 1905, he organized a revolt, proclaiming *enosis* with Greece. The revolt failed but it contributed to the departure of prince George and the appointment of a new high commissioner. During the years 1906–09 Venizelos served as either head of the Cretan government or leader of the opposition.

Venizelos's career was transformed as a consequence of the Goudi coup in Greece, which saw a significant faction within the army demanding reforms. Venizelos, who had become widely known because of his role in Cretan politics, was seen by many in metropolitan Greece as a politician who could implement reform, unsullied by close contact with the ruling elites of Athens. In 1909 king George invited Venizelos to Athens to advise him, in 1910 he was elected to parliament as a member for Athens, and then became prime minister, combining it with the war and naval portfolios. With tremendous energy, Venizelos set about modernizing the public services, including both the army and the navy. He also helped shape a new constitution, and in the elections of 1912 held under this new constitution he won a significant majority.

Venizelos displayed great shrewdness throughout his career in foreign policy. In 1912 he engineered Greece's role in the Balkan League, and in the Balkan Wars which followed (1912–13) he accomplished a significant expansion of territory for the Greek state, including *enosis* with his home island of Crete. Venizelos had worked well with king George, but the king was assassinated at the peak of Greece's victories, and his son and successor, Constantine I, did not enjoy as easy a relationship with Venizelos. The two fell out in particular over Greece's response to the outbreak of World War I in 1914. The entry of the Ottoman empire into the war on the side of the Central Powers led Venizelos to advocate support of the Allied cause, seeing an opportunity to acquire much of Greece's *irredenta* with Allied support. Throughout 1914–15 the king and Venizelos disagreed as to policy, the king advocating neutrality, Venizelos anxious to join the Allies. The dispute came to a head in 1915 over Greece's reaction to the Gallipoli campaign, with Venizelos advocating support for the Allies. The result was Venizelos's forced resignation. In the elections which followed, Venizelos's supporters won 190 out of 316 seats in parliament. This election can be seen as the beginning of the national schism which would bedevil Greek political life for decades to come, drawing sharp divisions through Greek life. Despite this commanding electoral victory, Constantine delayed as long as possible in appointing Venizelos as prime minister. Once this was done he reluctantly followed his prime minister's advice and allowed the Allies to land at Thessalonica (1 October 1915), which they wished to do in order to assist their beleaguered Serbian allies. The king still refused to countenance entering the war, backed by such figures as the chief of the general staff, General Metaxas. The king's unhappiness with Venizelos finally led to his dismissal. In the elections which followed, the Venizelists, who claimed the king's action to be unconstitutional, boycotted the elections and as a result a neutralist government was elected.

Venizelos now embarked on a dangerous course. At the end of September 1916 he and some supporters sailed for Crete, his original base of support. From there they sailed through the Aegean islands to Thessalonica, rallying support. On reaching Allied-occupied Thessalonica Venizelos proclaimed a Provisional Government of National Defence, which was quickly recognized by Britain and France, and which declared war on Germany and Bulgaria. king Constantine, who was rapidly losing support, left the country in June 1917, passing the throne to his son Alexander. Venizelos returned in triumph to Athens, and Greece as a whole now declared war on the Central Powers. Venizelos's acquisition of power with foreign support would turn many against him, and deepened national divisions.

Greece now reaped the benefit of Venizelos's earlier overhaul of the military. Venizelos was one of the great war ministers of the early 20th century, on a par with such figures as Britain's Lloyd George. Venizelos's energy saw the creation of a highly effective 11-division army, which performed with great effectiveness in the last offensive of the war. The collapse of both the Ottoman empire and Bulgaria in the autumn of 1918 opened the way for Venizelos to launch a diplomatic offensive to achieve the *Megali Idea*.

At the Paris peace conference summoned to settle the issues of World War I Venizelos, a consummate diplomat, emerged as one of the key figures, wielding influence out of all proportion to Greece's power. In the Treaties of Neuilly and Sèvres Greece acquired western Thrace and a substantial district around Smyrna in Asia Minor. Venizelos's fortunes now suffered a sudden reverse. The unexpected death of the young king Alexander, continued fighting in Asia Minor which necessitated continued mobilization, and the persistence of martial law led to an upsurge in favour of the return of the soldier-king Constantine. In a general election in November 1920 Venizelos was decisively defeated, the king returned, and Venizelos went into self-imposed exile.

The Greek armies suffered from these national divisions, with Venizelist officers now being purged in favour of royalists, and this contributed to Greece's defeat in 1922 and the evacuation of Asia Minor. The country now turned to Venizelos to save what he could from the wreckage, and in the 1923 Treaty of Lausanne he undoubtedly accomplished what could be done in such adverse circumstances. He returned to Greece briefly in 1924, serving as prime minister for one month, before once again going abroad to live. Shortly after this the monarchy was abolished and a military regime for a while dominated the country. Venizelos re-entered political life in 1928, winning a majority in the general election, and embarked on a four-year premiership. During this period he established good relations with Italy, Yugoslavia, and Turkey, making a highly successful visit to Ankara in 1930. His government, however, suffered from the impact of the world economic crisis which began in 1929, and he had to resign in 1932, serving again briefly as prime minister that year and again at the start of 1933. He ended his political life much as he had started, by taking part in an abortive revolt based on Crete, this time aimed at preventing a restoration of the monarchy. After its failure Venizelos went into exile in Paris where he died in 1936, his body being brought back to Crete for burial.

ERIK GOLDSTEIN

See also Lausanne (Treaty of), World War I

Biography

Born in Crete in 1864, Venizelos studied in Athens and returned to Crete to practise law. He became active in Cretan politics and was made head of the island's executive in 1899. In 1909 King George I invited Venizelos to Athens. In 1910 he was elected to parliament and became prime minister. His disagreement with King Constantine over Greece's involvement in World War I led to his resignation. He secured Smyrna for Greece at the Paris Peace Conference but was defeated in elections in 1920. After the Asia Minor disaster in 1922 he negotiated the Treaty of Lausanne. After several more terms of office he went into exile in Paris where he died in 1936.

Further Reading

Alastos, Doros [Evdoros Joannides], *Venizelos: Patriot, Statesman, Revolutionary*, London: Lund Humphries, 1942, reprinted Gulf Breeze, Florida: Academic International, 1978

Leon, George B., *Greece and the Great Powers, 1914–1917*, Thessalonica: Institute for Balkan Studies, 1974

Llewellyn Smith, Michael, *Ionian Vision: Greece in Asia Minor 1919–1922*, London: Allen Lane, and New York: St Martin's Press, 1973, reprinted London: Hurst, and Ann Arbor: University of Michigan Press, 1998

Papacosma, S. Victor, *The Military in Greek Politics: The 1909 Coup d'État*, Kent, Ohio: Kent State University Press, 1977

Petsalis-Diomidis, N., *Greece at the Paris Peace Conference (1919)*, Thessalonica: Institute for Balkan Studies, 1978

Zavitsianos, K.G., *Ai Anamniseis tou ek tis Istorikis Diaphonias* [Recollections of the Historic Dispute of King Constantine and Eleftherios Venizelos], 2 vols, Athens, 1946–47

Verroia

City in Macedonia

This large town of south central Macedonia is one of the few in the region that has enjoyed a more or less continuous existence from antiquity to the present day and has retained its original name over the centuries (the same is also true of Thessalonica and Serres). Verroia stands on the site where it was originally founded, i.e. on the slopes of a hill at the eastern extremities of Mount Vermio, overlooking the vast coastal plain of central Macedonia. In antiquity Verroia lay much closer to the sea than it does now, for the Thermaic Gulf extended so far inland as to include the area of the future lake of Giannitsa. Located in the heart of Macedon, in the neighbourhood of the royal residence and cemetery of Aegae (modern Vergina, where the tombs of the Argead dynasty have been excavated), Verroia was already in existence in the 5th century BC, if not earlier, and was one of the main urban centres of the ancient Macedonian state. The town's name is believed to derive from Veres, a hero of the Macedonian religious tradition.

Being the birthplace of Antigonus I, the renowned general and one of the successors of Alexander the Great, Verroia was particularly favoured by his descendants who ruled in Macedonia as the Antigonid dynasty between 294 and 288 BC and from 277 BC to the end of the Macedonian kingdom in 168 BC. The town's prosperity continued during the Roman era, when Verroia is attested as a place of significant commercial activity and also the centre of the *concilium* (*koinon*) of the Macedonians, an ethno-religious league of the Macedonian towns and districts under Roman rule. A Jewish mercantile and artisanal community existed there by the 1st century AD, a fact that attracted St Paul to visit the town and preach there. The only obscure period in Verroia's history coincides with the so-called Byzantine dark age (7th and 8th centuries). The serious demographic crisis and urban decline that mark the Byzantine Balkan provinces during that period must have affected life in Verroia and the development of the town. This probability is supported by the absence of any record of the town's existence for that period, and also by the fact that the surrounding district was occupied by the Slavic tribes of the Drogouvites and Sagoudatoi that were independent for a long time and had uneasy relations with the Byzantine authorities.

The history of medieval Verroia actually begins in the 9th century when the town reemerged from obscurity. The early 10th-century text of John Kameniatis makes reference to Verroia, which is described as a prosperous town (Böhlig, p. 8), at a time when the Byzantines had reestablished control over that area of Macedonia and placed the Slavic tribes under their yoke. In the same period the bishop of Verroia was a subordinate of the metropolitan of Thessalonica.

Verroia remained under Byzantine rule for most of the Middle Ages, save for rather short intervals of Bulgarian (985–1001, 1205–07), Latin (1204/05, 1207–15/16), and Serbian (c.1345–50, 1351–56) occupation. The town was finally occupied by the Ottoman Turks around 1385 and, like the rest of Macedonia, remained under their control until 1912. Byzantine and Ottoman Verroia was one of the largest towns in Macedonia, although its oldest surviving records date from as late as 1519. Its diocese was promoted to the rank of a metropolitan see late in the 13th century.

Verroia was an important centre of Byzantine and post-Byzantine art. Its artistic development is represented in its surviving monuments, namely the old cathedral church of SS Peter and Paul (which was later converted into the Hunkyar Camî, the principal mosque of the town), the churches of St John the Theologian, St Paraskevi (also converted into a mosque by the Ottomans), St Vlasios (13th century), SS Kerykos and Julieta (13th century), and the Resurrection church which was painted in 1315 by the famous Thessalonian artist George Kalliergis. Verroia's development was based on the resources of the surrounding region, particularly on the agricultural production of the coastal lowlands (mainly grain, wine, and fruits), as well as on livestock and timber from Mount Vermio. Moreover, Verroia lay close to an important junction where the coastal road from Thessaly met the route of the Aliacmon, which led to Kastoria and Albania. As a result of the Ottoman conquest, most of the landed estates in Verroia's vicinity passed under the possession of Muslims – in fact many of those estates became *waqf* (i.e. pious endowments) of the family of Evrenos – though Christians could still make their fortune out of trade.

From the 15th century onwards Verroia's history ran in parallel to that of the newly founded town of Naousa, which stood on higher ground on Mount Vermio and is traditionally believed to have been settled by people who left the lowlands of Macedonia in order to escape Ottoman rule. These neighbouring towns were different in many respects. While Verroia became a typical Ottoman Balkan city, which housed every kind of institution that represented Ottoman authority and had a significant Muslim population (approximately 1155 Muslims to 3874 Christians in 1519), Naousa was an exclusively Greek Christian town in a state of self-government. For this reason Greek education and the Greek national ideas, which took shape in the 18th century, found a more hospitable environment in Naousa than in Verroia. During the War of Independence the restless elements of Mount Vermio (a retreat of the renowned klephts and *armatoles* ("armed men") throughout the centuries of Ottoman rule) and the inhabitants of Naousa were urged to revolt by the town's patriots – Zapheirakis was the most notable among them – which resulted in a military failure accompanied by massacres and the destruction of the town in April 1822. Meanwhile, Verroia remained calm due to the size of its Muslim population – a big proportion of the town's 18,000 people at the end of the 18th century (Cousinéry, 1831, p. 69) — and to its less revolutionary background.

Verroia was finally annexed to Greece in 1912, as a result of the Balkan Wars. The subsequent departure of the Muslim population and the assimilation of whatever other ethnic elements had existed in the town (Evliya Çelebi wrote in the 17th century of a Christian population consisting of Greeks, Bulgarians, and Vlachs) gave Verroia the image of a typical provincial Greek town. Yet contemporary Verroia is one of the biggest towns in Greek Macedonia, with 37,858 people according to the census of 1991, and is particularly wealthy due to the agricultural resources of the surrounding countryside (cotton and fruits being the main products today) and to the development of a considerable industry specializing in food processing.

KONSTANTINOS P. MOUSTAKAS

See also Macedonia

Summary

The principal town of south central Macedonia, Verroia has had a continuous existence on the same site since antiquity. It was established by the 5th century BC and received favourable treatment as the birthplace of Antigonus, founder of the Antigonid dynasty. Several Byzantine churches survive. It fell to the Ottomans in 1385. Unlike nearby Naousa, which was a hotbed of Greek nationalism, Verroia had a large Muslim element in its population and played little part in the War of Independence.

Further Reading

Caminiate, Ioannis, *De Expugnatione Thessalonicae*, edited by Gertrud Böhlig, Berlin: de Gruyter, 1973

Chionides, Georgios, *Historia tes Veroias: Tes Poleos kai tes Perioches* [History of Verroia: The Town and the Countryside], 2 vols, 1960–70

Cousinéry, E.M., *Voyage dans la Macédonie*, Paris: Imprimerie Royale, 1831

Kravari, Vassiliki, *Villes et villages de Macédoine occidentale*, Paris: Lethielleux, 1989

Papazoglou, Fanula, *Les Villes de Macédoine à l' époque romaine*, Athens: Ecole Française d'Athènes, 1988

Vakalopoulos, A.E., *History of Macedonia, 1354–1833*, Thessalonica: Institute of Balkan Studies, 1973

Vasdravellis, I.K., *Historical Archives of Macedonia*, vol. 2: *Archives of Verroia-Naousa*, Thessalonica, 1954 (Ottoman Turkish documents published in Greek translation)

Village Society

The first traces of permanent human settlement on the Greek peninsula date back to the early Neolithic era, long before its penetration by Greek-speaking tribes around the end of the 3rd millennium BC. Archaeological excavations have revealed remains of permanent settlements of agriculturalists and sedentary pastoralists consisting of densely built single-room habitations surrounded by gardens. Their burial customs indicate a society organized in clans, while the absence of sizeable buildings denotes an egalitarian society without centralized forms of government or administration. Excavations of large private buildings of the Bronze Age with ample storage areas and numerous yards possibly designate the emergence of social stratification.

As we advance into historical times, social stratification became increasingly complex as did the interrelations between the different echelons of the social ladder. The formation of the city state in the 8th century BC, in particular, defined a situation where villages became dependent on urban centres. Village society at the time consisted of independent households of free peasants. The family unit was the economic and social nucleus of a society whose economy depended on agricultural production. However, the majority of peasants were owners of small plots of land that were often insufficient for the subsistence of the household. While peasants were faced with poverty, large landed properties began to form, increasing the social distance between villagers and aristocrats. Peasant contributions, furthermore, were appropriated by the aristocracy, who thus augmented their wealth.

Byzantine villages were fiscal and legal units that consisted of independent land holders. The peasants were poor, but their plot of land secured them their subsistence. Furthermore, village life was far more healthy than life in the city. Monasteries provided education for peasant offspring, while religious celebrations provided the opportunity for feasting. Local festivals held considerable importance for the peasant economy since their open markets were a focus for economic transactions. An important principle in Byzantine village society was that of collective tax liability. Taxes were allotted to whole villages, not to individual landowners, so that if a peasant had had a bad year the rest of the village community had to make up for his share in the taxes. However, in actual fact peasants were overtaxed, and punishment for those in debt to the state was particularly harsh. Village life was further aggravated by invading troops of the empire's enemies, as well as by natural causes, such as drought. This led great numbers of peasants to sell their land, and, during the decline of the Byzantine empire, large landed properties began to form, thus transforming the character of rural Byzantium.

The Ottoman conquest halted these changes. State ownership of the land replaced both family and communal property. Peasants were able to secure their plot of land, but had to pay excessive taxes to the sultan's tax collectors. For reasons of fiscal effectiveness the sultan retained the system of collective tax liability at the level of the community. The village community was further strengthened as it was granted relative administrative autonomy. Local communities were ruled by an elected council of elders. Since land accumulation was not possible, participation in local administration became the new basis for social stratification within villages; the council of elders represented the wealthier sector of the village households who, moreover, often took advantage of their position in order to augment their wealth.

Village Society: two women load a mule in the village of Olimbos

On the eve of Greek liberation village society was characterized by relative autonomy and self-sufficiency; it had its own distinctive social and cultural character and an ethos peculiar to it. Towards the end of the 17th century the Ottoman empire entered a prolonged phase of crisis with repercussions for village communities. The centralized state gradually took over the authority of the semi-autonomous local communities, while the local council of elders became mere functionaries of the state.

The kind of village society that emerged as the continuation of the semi-autonomous communities of the Ottoman era is what has been referred to by folklorists and others as traditional society. Its basic productive and reproductive unit was the extended family household. The family was the primary source of identification for villagers. Village families related through blood or affinity formed a network of relations of cooperation and solidarity within the village. Outside this circle of relatives and affines lay the world of strangers: unrelated, potentially hostile families competing for prestige in the village hierarchy.

What bound unrelated families together into a relationship of solidarity and cooperation, making them transcend possible causes of friction and rivalry, was the sense of belonging to a community. The village community provided the second most important source of identification for the villagers. The relationship of the villager with the community was mediated by the neighbourhood. The neighbourhood provided an important network of relations of cooperation outside the immediate circle of the kindred.

Traditional village society was a society of relative self-sufficiency. It was an endogamous society. Likewise most goods needed for its sustenance were produced within the village itself. Despite the introduction of monetization and the cultivation of cash crops in the 19th century, the production was basically subsistence-orientated.

Traditional village society was a community bound by a set of moral values and beliefs observed by all. Central to its identification as a moral community has been the Orthodox Christian religion. As such, the Church and the religious calendar have played, and still play, an important role in village life. What is particularly revealing of the role of the Church and the Orthodox faith for village society is the annual feast or *panegyri*. This feast, held on the name day of the saint to whom the local church is dedicated, is important because it draws together not only those resident in the village, but their migrant relatives as well, in a celebration of village identity.

The processes of modernization and urbanization that were at work in Greece after the Civil War (1945–49) deeply affected the character of traditional village society. The most profound changes were brought about by the process of rural exodus, which became particularly intense during the 1960s and 1970s. As a result, numerous mountain and island communities became depopulated and heavily dependent on resources coming from centralized state mechanisms, such as the Ministry of Agriculture, the Agricultural Bank, and recently the European Union. Social relations within villages have been disrupted due to depopulation. Village youth have left for urban centres, leaving villages with ageing populations; houses have been abandoned, impairing the structure and function of the neighbourhood. On the other hand, villages in the plains have developed as satellite communities to urban centres, functioning more and more as city suburbs.

GABRIELLA-EVANGELIA ASPRAKI

Further Reading

Allen, Peter, "Social and Economic Change in a Depopulated Community in Southern Greece", dissertation, Providence, Rhode Island: Brown University, 1973

Campbell, J.K., *Honour, Family and Patronage: A Study of Institutions and Moral Values in a Greek Mountain Community*, Oxford: Clarendon Press, 1964

Damianakos, Stathis (editor), *Aspects du changement social dans la campagne Grecque*, Athens: Centre National de Recherches Sociales, 1981

Dimen, Muriel and Ernestine Friedl (editors), *Regional Variation in Modern Greece and Cyprus: Toward a Perspective on the Ethnography of Greece*, New York: New York Academy of Sciences, 1976, pp. 1–465

Du Boulay, Juliet, *Portrait of a Greek Mountain Village*, Oxford: Clarendon Press, 1974

Friedl, Ernestine, *Vasilika: A Village in Modern Greece*, New York: Holt Rinehart, 1962

Greger, Sonia, *Village on the Plateau: Magoulas, a Mountain Village in Crete*, Studley: Brewin, 1985

Hart, Laurie, *Time, Religion, and Social Experience in Rural Greece*, Lanham, Maryland: Rowman and Littlefield, 1992

Herzfeld, Michael, *The Poetics of Manhood: Contest and Identity in a Cretan Mountain Village*, Princeton, New Jersey: Princeton University Press, 1985

Hussey, J.M. (editor), *The Byzantine Empire*, part 2: *Government, Church and Civilization*, Cambridge: Cambridge University Press, 1967 (*The Cambridge Medieval History*, vol. 4, 2nd edition)

Laiou-Thomadakis, Angeliki E., *Peasant Society in the Late Byzantine Empire: A Social and Demographic Study*, Princeton, New Jersey: Princeton University Press, 1977

Ostrogorsky, G, "La Commune rurale byzantine", *Byzantion*, 32 (1962): pp. 139–66

Papataxiarchis, Efthymios, "Kinship, Friendship and Gender Relations in Two East Aegean Village Communities", dissertation, University of London, 1988

Schein, Muriel, "Change and Continuity in a Greek Mountain Village", dissertation, New York: Columbia University, 1970

Vakalopoulos, A.E., *Origins of the Greek Nation: The Byzantine Period, 1204–1461*, New Brunswick, New Jersey: Rutgers University Press, 1970

Vine

Viniferous species of grapes (*vitis vinifera sativa*) were known to the Mycenaean Greeks. The mythological account of Dionysus' importation of the vine from Asia Minor, the evidence of wine on the Linear B tablets, and the remains of storage vessels make it clear that by the 2nd millennium BC grape growing was firmly entrenched on the Greek mainland.

Yet only with the rise of the polis (800–300 BC) did domesticated cultivars, which produce larger and better-quality fruits, become truly ubiquitous. The Classical Greeks planted vineyards from the Black Sea to Crete, and from southern Italy to northern Asia Minor, where, along with olives and grains, they became part of the great triad of Greek agronomy – an agricultural diversity that helped to make the ancient rural household self sufficient and the city state prosperous. Vines could grow well on difficult terrain and produce on poor soils; they were resistant to extremities of temperature and humidity, and provided the farmer with in-season fresh fruit and juices, storable raisins, and non-perishable wine. That versatility of the grape prompted the 7th-century BC poet Alcaeus to advise: "Plant no other tree before the vine."

The wide variety of soil and weather conditions in Greece and Italy allowed for regional specialization, as the Aegean islands, the bay of Naples, and Rhodes earned a Mediterranean-wide reputation for premium vintages. There is some practical advice found in Greek agricultural writers such as Theophrastus on establishing the vineyard, but the full sophistication of the Greek art of viticulture can be appreciated only in extant and derivative Latin texts such as Cato, Columella, and Varro. It is clear from these authors that the Greeks translated empirical observation into a more abstract and theoretical knowledge of the proper combination of climate, soil, and vine species necessary to produce premium grapes. Such scientific treatises attest to the Greek mastery of viticulture from the arts of vine trellising, fertilization, pruning, and pest management to the intricacies of wine pressing and processing – a level of expertise not surpassed until the 19th century with the rise of bacteriology, soil chemistry, and plant biology.

The polis Greeks saw viticulture as emblematic of Classical culture at large, whose stable populations, local councils, sturdy yeomen, and fiercely independent rural communities were the natural dividends of the time, patience, expertise, and investment necessary to grow good grapes. Thus vine growers are idealized as dependable, though crusty sorts, in the comedies of Aristophanes and Menander. The livelihood of entire communities might depend on the success of the autumn vintage, and during wartime it was a crucial factor in state policy. In Thucydides' history, for example, the small northeast-Greek city state of Acanthus sued for peace when its grape harvests were threatened by Brasidas and his Spartan invaders; similarly the Acharnian viticulturalists outside Athens were especially critical of the Athenian leaders when their vineyards were left unprotected before the annual Spartan invasions of Attica (431–425 BC).

In Hellenistic and Roman times, agriculture in general and viticulture in particular in the Greek world became increasingly divorced from the Classical ideal of agrarianism and evolved more into a cash enterprise, where large absentee estate holders, through the use of slave gangs and skilled overseers, grew grapes aimed at particular specialized wine markets, often at great distances and throughout the Mediterranean. Athenaeus (*c.*AD 200), for example, provides a comprehensive catalogue of choice regional wines that attests to the sophisticated commercial nature of Greek viticulture in

Vine: interior of a bowl by Execias showing a vine growing above a ship in which Dionysus sails, mid-6th century BC, Antikensammlung, Munich

commutes and made mechanization nearly impossible. However, during the 1980s there was a veritable revolution in the practice of Greek vine growing. The entry of Greece into the European Common Market in 1981, together with strong government programmes to supply agricultural expertise, capital, and machinery, increased the subsidized export of Greek wines and raisins throughout the world – even as grape growing became no longer one of the central cultural experiences of the small Greek village. Currently, Greece is the world's third largest producer of raisins and there are well over 200,000 hectares planted to various species of grapes. Such guaranteed export profits have sparked a remarkable spread of vineyards on to marginal lands, together with an increase in irrigation in otherwise unfarmable arid soils. At the millennium, the danger grows that historically unprecedented levels of Greek grape production may not be sustainable – given the age-old limitations of rocky soil, difficult terrain, and shallow aquifers. And should lucrative European subsidies be withdrawn, Greek wines and raisins may lose many of their markets to higher-quality and less expensive grape products from America, South Africa, and Turkey. Thus a decline of vine acreage is probably inevitable, part of the boom-and-bust cycle of Greek viticulture that has characterized the past four millennia of Hellenic history.

VICTOR DAVIS HANSON

See also Agriculture

Further Reading

Amouretti, Marie-Claire, *Le Pain et l'huile dans la Grèce antique: De l'araire au moulin*, Paris: Belles Lettres, 1986

Amouretti, Marie-Claire and Jean-Pierre Brun (editors), *La Production du vin et de l'huile en Méditerranée*, Paris: Ecole Française d'Athènes, 1993

Burford, Alison, *Land and Labor in the Greek World*, Baltimore: Johns Hopkins University Press, 1993

Hanson, Victor Davis, *The Other Greeks: The Family Farm and the Agrarian Roots of Western Civilization*, New York: Free Press, 1995

Hehn, Victor and O. Schräder, *Kulturpflanzen und Haustiere in ihrem Übergang aus Asien nach Griechenland un Italien sowie in das übrige Europa*, Berlin: Borntraeger, 1911

Isager, Signe and Jens Erik Skydsgaard, *Ancient Greek Agriculture: An Introduction*, London and New York: Routledge, 1992

McGovern, Patrick E., Stuart J. Fleming and Solomon H. Katz (editors), *The Origins and History of Wine*, Philadelphia: Gordon and Breach, 1995

Roman times. Yet even as exports grew, viticulture ceased to be part of a vibrant countryside, which for the most part suffered continual depopulation due to emigration, banditry, and oppressive taxation.

With the collapse of the Roman empire and during the subsequent Byzantine protectorate, viticulture returned to a more subsistence and local enterprise. There was some renewed commercial prosperity during the Frankish and Venetian occupations of the Peloponnese (13th–15th centuries), when the export of wine and raisins to western Europe increased. The name *currant* (extremely small, dark purple grapes used for raisin production and now variously known internationally as Black Corinth or Zante Currant) is a corruption of the word Corinth itself (*raison of Couraunte*), attesting to the popularity of such raisins that were grown near the isthmus and from the Middle Ages were shipped throughout western Europe. The distinctive resinated flavours of many Greek wines – which often hampered their export value – are an acquired taste and may date back to antiquity, when herbal, spice, and resin preservatives were first used to maintain wine quality during storage and transport. Problems of security and high taxation under the Ottoman empire, along with the continuance of large monasteries and estates with absentee landlords, depressed Greek viticulture, which returned to subsistence levels, largely to provide in-season table grapes, local wines, and a few raisins for export.

Until very recently, Greek viticulturalists have suffered from technological stagnation and the increasing fragmentation of farmland; both developments tended to reduce vineyards to dispersed plots of tiny acreages that involved lengthy

Vizyinos, Georgios 1849–1896

Short-story writer

Being a distinguished craftsman of lyricism, a skilful and exceptionally competent author of manners, Georgios Vizyinos devoted his short life to the perfection of psychoanalytical writing. Exhibiting an extraordinary ability to describe in every possible detail ordinary events as well as to portray and explore the psychological dimensions and moral tenets of his characters, he shattered old orthodoxies in Greek literature and erected new ones. He pronounced on cultural and social questions and played a central role in the evolution of modern Greek fiction. He is regarded as one of the forerunners of the modern Greek novel. His tentative experimentation in style, structure, and diction contributed to the development of Greek moral and psychological writing and laid the foundations of modern Greek fiction.

Vizyinos had an adventurous life tinted with energy, spirit, uncommonly romantic visions, moments of great passion and sometimes unfulfilled love. However, paradoxically enough, the last years of his life were spoiled by disillusionment, pessimism, and psychological problems, which turned into a fatal, chronic paranoia. It is no exaggeration to say that Vizyinos is numbered among the less fortunate writers of Greek literature. He was not simply a tender, nostalgic poet but also a gifted author of philosophical, aesthetical, and psychological essays, teaching textbooks, and folklore documentaries. As far as his fiction is concerned, it consists of six stories: "Metaxy Pirea ke Napolis" ["Between Piraeus and Naples"], "To Amartima tis Mitros mou" ["My Mother's Sin"], "Pios Ito o Phoneus tou Adhelphou mou" ["Who was my Brother's Killer?"], "Monon tis Zois mou Taxidiou" ["The Only Journey of my Life"], "I Sinepie tis Palaias Istorias" ["The Consequences of an Old Story"] were all published in *Estia* during the years 1883–84 and a sixth, "Selim Moskov" ["Selim the Muscovite"], though written earlier, was published in 1895. Vizyinos's primary concern in these stories is the depiction of the rural way of life in his native Thrace. In this way, he became the spiritual stimulus and mentor for two of the most distinguished authors of manners, namely Alexandros Papadiamantis and Andreas Karkavitsas, and inaugurator of a whole generation of literature dominated by the figures of George Drosinis, Kostis Palamas, and other representatives of the so-called New Athenian school of poetry.

Vizyinos was born in 1849 in a small village in Thrace with a rich historical past and living folklore traditions which are revived and reflected in his work. With the patronage and support of a wealthy man from Constantinople, Vizyinos completed his higher education in Germany where he became acquainted with classical German literature. He also paid visits to London and Paris. In his stories, he analysed the outward behaviour and manners of his characters but, most importantly, he aimed to expose the conscious and unconscious motives affecting that behaviour. The same psychoanalytical perspective was endorsed later by Papadiamantis, Karkavitsas, Nikos Kazantzakis, Demosthenes Voutiras, and Nikolaos Politis. Moreover, his work was pervaded by a genuine feeling of patriotism which he inherited from Andreas Kalvos and Dionysios Solomos, and a deep religious faith would be passed on later to Photis Kontoglou. By relying on a Pindaric lyricism and sensual appeal, he delivered a precise depiction of the Greek natural landscape with specific reference to his home and the cordial relations of its people, who were in close contact with Turks. In this way, his work gives a credible historical account of his time while simultaneously it epitomizes the ancient Greek ethos.

Vizyinos's main persona, dominating his work, is that of an unfortunate mother figure, a common theme in the Hellenic literary tradition. The same motif appears first in the pages of ancient Greek tragedy, is fashioned in popular culture, and is transplanted to modern fiction. Another topos that repeatedly occurs in his stories is that of the mystery of human psyche. In other words, he professed the unpredictability of human behaviour, which is dependent on the psychological condition and the special external circumstances affecting the actions of human beings. Thus, it is not accidental that the most sensitive people sometimes display ill-mannered behaviour. Vizyinos had undergone a similar psychological metamorphosis when personal troubles transformed him into a gloomy unconfident man.

An equally important place in his work is occupied by the phenomenon of emigration (expatriation) with specific emphasis given to its emotional parameter. Vizyinos wrote about the classic model of the reluctant exile that prevails in the Hellenic literary tradition from Homer to Kalvos till today. It is the idea of diaspora combined with the nostalgia for return. Vizyinos's stories also contain the idea of the human soul seeking revenge for any injustice as well as the notion of humanity's power to replace dissension and enmity with harmony and unity. With reference to the first idea, he was reproducing one of the pivotal dilemmas of ancient tragedy. As far as the second idea is concerned, he glorifies the principle of altruism, generosity, and humanitarianism.

Finally, he commented on much more difficult philosophical themes such as the eternal conflict between reason and emotion, mind and soul, and logic and sensation. Each of them represented a completely diverse world: the first represents the world of critical mind and rational thinking, of strong arguments and scientific thought, while the other is that of spontaneous emotions, sentiments, and passions. Once more, Vizyinos pays homage to the world of ancient tragedy and reemphasizes the theme of Sophocles' *Antigone*. Closely related to these ideas in Vizynos's work is the notion of human mania (frenzy), the turbulent and disordered state of mind. He considers such a theme either by stressing its tragic dimension or its comical alternative. This double treatment of human mania is endorsed by Papadiamantis.

Vizyinos's works overflow with a lively, animating imagery, and are marked with elegance and clarity of style, elaborate, effective dialogues, and rich, vibrating plots. All of his characters undergo an inner conflict and suffer a personal ordeal. Their tragic element is intensified by their ignorance (like that of Oedipus) of their fate. Vizyinos insisted also on an unusual idiom. Whereas his narrative is written in a dense, archaic, but pleasant idiom, his dialogue is enriched with a vernacular language enlightened with local expressions and jargon. In this way, Vizyinos's idiom stands as a bridge between the old-style language of the past and the vernacular of the future without neglecting the accents of the periphery.

Vizyinos was a tragic figure and at the same time a gifted writer who made a profound contribution to the Hellenic literary tradition. He was considered the renovator of the Greek literary model and the founder of psychoanalytic modern Greek fiction. His work is filled with national folk-traditions and is inspired by nostalgia for the past. His task was to present customs and emotions as well as high ideas to his own generation and to impart knowledge of them to the next. His stories appeared in a transitional period for Greek literature marked by spiritual stagnation, conventional ideas, and decline. In the face of bitter criticism from his opponents and the conventional literary milieu of his time, which could not understand his lasting message, he became disillusioned and disappointed, and his work was destined to receive only posthumously the recognition it deserved.

MARIA ROUMBALOU

Biography

Vizyinos (whose real name was Michaelides) was born in Vizyi, a small village in Thrace, in 1849. With the support of a wealthy bene-factor he was educated in Athens and later in Germany where he studied philosophy and psychology. He became a professor of philos-ophy at the University of Athens and wrote essays and textbooks as well as short stories. In 1892 he was confined to a mental hospital and died in Athens in 1896.

Writings

My Mother's Sin and Other Stories, translated by William F. Wyatt, Jr, Hanover, New Hampshire: University Press of New England, 1988

Further Reading

Charis, P., *Ellines Pezographoi* [Greek Novelists], vol. 3, Athens, 1968

Daphnis, S., "G. Vizyinos, o Rapsodos tis Thrakis" [G. Vizyinos: The Rhapsodist of Thrace], *Lexi*, 135 (1996)

Doukas, M., "Ena Gramma apo tin Avstria" [A Letter from Austria], *Lexi*, 135 (1996)

Mamonis, K., *Vivliographia tou G. Vizyinou* [Bibliography of G. Vizyinos], Athens, 1963

Paganos, Y., *Mathimata Neoellinikis Pezographias* [Studies in the Modern Greek Novel], Athens, 1980

Sahinis, A., *To Neoelliniko Mythistorima* [The Modern Greek Novel], Thessalonica, 1958

Vlachs

Ethnic group from the Balkan mountains

The Vlachs, who call themselves Aroumanians and in Greece are known as Koutzovlachs or by a host of regional names, are found in scattered pockets throughout the Balkan peninsula. In Greece they are principally settled in the Pindus mountains around Metsovo. At the beginning of the 20th century there were in the Balkans about half a million people speaking Vlach, a Latin language akin to Romanian. Now this number has been reduced to about 100,000 with only a third of this total living in Greece. Exact numbers have always been diffi-cult to calculate owing to the political dimensions of the ques-tion, the migratory habits of the Vlachs, and the fact that almost always Vlachs will be fluent speakers of the language of the country in which they are located.

It is equally hard to be exact about Vlach history. Almost all are staunch members of the Orthodox Church, and most Vlachs have followed a Greek nationalist line. Greek and Vlach historians are therefore anxious to prove the long asso-ciation of the two ethnic groups, and have therefore concluded that Vlachs are the descendants of Roman legionaries, guard-ing the mountains and marrying Greek speakers. There is little evidence for this theory, which is inherently improbable. Romanian historians, anxious to use the Vlachs as counters in Balkan politics, assume that they left Romania in the Middle Ages, although again we have no evidence or explanation why difficult areas like the Pindus mountains should be attractive to migrants from the Danube.

Even after the collapse of the western Roman empire there were Latin speakers in the eastern half of the empire, mainly settled along the Danube frontier and in the province of Illyricum, roughly corresponding to modern Yugoslavia. The emperor Justinian (527–65) was such a Latin speaker. Just before the collapse of the Danube frontier we hear of an inci-dent in 586 in which two muleteers in a Byzantine army appear to be speaking Vlach. When in 602 most of the Balkan penin-sula was lost to the empire and there were massive Slav incur-sions, Latin speakers must have been involved in these move-ments of populations, journeying southwards with the invaders or to escape from them. They could thus have reached their present dwellings by the 7th century, although it is diffi-cult to talk of dwellings with any confidence since in both medieval and modern times the Vlachs have been associated with transhumance, moving to the mountains in summer and the plains in winter.

There are no references to Vlachs between 586 and 976. This lack of evidence is hardly surprising in view of the almost total silence of Byzantine sources about events in the western and central Balkans when these areas passed out of the empire's control. With the 10th-century recovery the Vlachs are mentioned quite frequently, although some references to Vlachs may be to shepherds or nomads rather than to Latin-speakers. Most Byzantine sources comment on the Vlachs' migratory habits, their connection with sheep, and a tendency to treachery, perhaps engendered by the fact that as transhu-mants they were hard to fit into any administrative system. Transhumants make poor taxpayers.

In 976 certain Vlach *hoditai* ("road-men") killed David, the brother of the future Bulgarian emperor Samuel, in the area between Kastoria and Prespa. *Hoditai* is ambiguous; it is not certain whether the Vlachs so described were there to guard the roads or to pillage them as highwaymen. Perhaps as with *armatoloi* ("armed men") and klephts, the distinction was not a precise one. As with the muleteers of 579, the *hoditai* of 976 were involved in trades that Vlach merchants of the 18th and 19th centuries sending baggage trails of mules along the high-ways of the Balkans would easily recognize. It is not clear whether on this occasion the Vlachs by killing David were acting on the Byzantine side, the position being made more obscure by the fact that it is not certain whether David and Samuel were themselves originally in the Byzantine service. It is just possible that David and Samuel may themselves have been Vlachs.

There are Vlachs today between Kastoria and Prespa. More can be found in Thessaly where in the 11th century Benjamin of Tudela speaks harshly of their unreliable behaviour. There was a scandal on Mount Athos involving Vlach women. In 1194 a revolt in the Haemus mountains led by the Asen broth-ers brought into being the second Bulgarian empire. Most contemporary sources refer to this as a Vlach empire, although Bulgarian historians play this down. Romanian historians like to think of the Vlachs as being really Romanians, and the Haimos mountains are fairly close to the Danube, although at its greatest extent the second Bulgarian empire would have included a great deal of territory now inhabited by Vlachs.

Vlachs: portrait of a Vlach man in Voskopje, eastern Albania

With the collapse of the Byzantine empire at the end of the 12th century the lawless Vlachs would seem to have profited. Thessaly became known as Vlachia, and there were ephemeral Vlach states. We also hear of Vlachs joining the Albanian incursions into Greece. Our sources are not particularly helpful about ethnological matters. A certain Boncoes in the early 15th century is called *Serbalbanitobulgarovlachos*, suggesting that in the Middle Ages, as at the present time, many Vlachs spoke more than two languages. Metsovo is referred to for the first time in 1380. By this time the Turks had entered the Balkans. On the whole the Turks were not too interested in the ethnology of their various subject races, but there are some mentions of specifically Vlach villages in Ottoman records.

Most Vlachs remained under Ottoman rule until the Balkan Wars of 1912–13. On the whole they prospered. The Ottoman authorities tended to favour local arrangements over taxes, and the Vlachs made several advantageous bargains in this respect. A strong central government protected trade, and as merchants the Vlachs with raw materials from their sheep and transport with their mules were in a good position to take advantage of this trade. In the 17th century the Ottoman empire began to decline, and its frontiers to recede, but this meant new markets and avenues for trade, particularly in central Europe, where Vlachs established prosperous businesses.

It is to the 17th century that we can date the formation of many Vlach villages. Such villages now seem poor and remote, although occasionally a large if battered mansion hints at former prosperity. As merchants and as owners of large flocks of sheep some Vlachs became extremely wealthy and such houses reflect this wealth. A particularly wealthy Vlach centre was Voskopoje in southern Albania where as well as large houses and fine streets there was also an academy and a printing press.

In the late 18th century Voskopoje incurred the wrath of Ali Pasha, the virtually independent ruler of southern Albania and Epirus. His Albanians destroyed the city, and the inhabitants fled to other Vlach centres in the Balkans. This diaspora probably strengthened the presence of Vlachs in the Balkans, but the story of Voskopoje illustrates the difficulties that they faced when Ottoman authority collapsed. With the breakdown of law and order Vlach prosperity was reduced. The future might seem to lie with the new national states, but here the Vlachs were in something of a dilemma. Though speaking Vlach at home, the merchants of Voskopoje would naturally use Greek in commercial business, and Greek was the language of the academy and printing press. Vlach was rarely written, and there was no standard grammar or orthography. Greek schools and priests encouraged Greek and discouraged Vlach.

Not surprisingly many Vlachs became fervent Greek nationalists, most notably Rigas Velestinlis, a visionary poet and patriot, author of the Greek national anthem, but a Vlach from Velestino. The first prime minister of Greece, John Kollettis, was a Vlach from Sirrakou. Some of the finest buildings in Athens were erected owing to the munificence of Vlach families such as the Averoffs from Metsovo and the Sinaias, originally from Voskopoje. Other Balkan nationalities were slower than the Greeks in asserting their claims, and it was not until the end of the 19th century that the Romanians started to promote the idea that Vlachs were really Romanians.

Their campaign was not very successful. Schools, though they cost the Romanian government a great deal of money, were not well attended, attracting perhaps a quarter of the population, generally the poorest quarter. There was no real Vlach church, although eccentrically and heroically Apostol Margarit (1832–1903) tried to start one. There were differences between Vlach and Romanian and between different dialects of Vlach. Romania was a long way away from the Pindus mountains.

Economic problems were as pressing as political ones. Vlachs, accustomed to lengthy journeys, found new boundaries and customs dues a barrier to migration and trade. Metsovo, just to the north of the Greek border of 1887, experienced a period of economic decline. The guerrilla campaigns in Macedonia led to hardship and persecution. Generally Vlachs were on the Greek side, but we sometimes find them supporting Bulgarians, taking a pro-Romanian line, or even allying themselves with the Turks. The Ilinden rising of 1903 began in the Vlach town of Kruševo north of Bitola and spread to the Vlach villages now in Greece of Neveska and Pisoderi. Though some Vlachs were involved in the revolt, and severe damage was done to the Vlach quarter in Kruõevo, the Ilinden rising was not a Vlach rebellion any more than it was an uprising of the Slav Macedonian nation or the proletariat against the bourgeoisie. In 1905 the Ottoman authorities recognized the Vlachs as a separate *millet* (community), a move probably intended to divide their subject races in order to rule them, but the days of Ottoman rule were almost over.

The Balkan Wars were fought over Vlach territory and the subsequent peace treaties divided the Vlachs among the various Balkan states. World War I produced new battles and new frontiers. None of these wars was good for the Vlachs. Their attempts to win a hearing in the peace treaties were generally unsuccessful, although Greece did allow Romanian-sponsored schools in its territory. Some pro-Romanians in Greece left for Romania, others to America. The Greek refugees from Turkey made northern Greece much more ethnically homogeneous, and the assimilation of the Vlachs proceeded apace.

World War II and the Greek Civil War did further damage to Vlach mountain villages. Attempts by the Italians to show friendship to the Vlachs as fellow Latins were fairly futile, and did not help the Vlach cause. Material progress after World War II, bringing non-Vlachs to Vlach villages, making some villages inaccessible, and turning the biannual migration into a summer holiday, increased the process of assimilation. It is remarkable that Vlach has survived so long. The census of 1951 recorded that there were 39,855 Vlach speakers in Greece. This is probably an understatement, but numbers would have declined in the next 40 years, perhaps to be revived by an interest in minorities and the discovery of Vlachs in other parts of the Balkans and among the Vlach diaspora.

T.J. WINNIFRITH

See also Transhumance

Summary

Vlachs are a transhumant people speaking a Latin language that is similar to Romanian. Their origins are obscure. They inhabited the mountainous regions of the central Balkans and northern Greece, where they prospered as merchants and muleteers. They have declined in numbers since World War II. The census of 1951 recorded fewer than 40,000 Vlach speakers in Greece.

Further Reading

Keramopoulos, A., *Ti Einai Hoi Koutsoblachoi* [Who Are the Koutsovlachs], Athens, 1938

Lazarou, Achille G., *L'Aroumain et ses rapports avec le Grec*, Thessalonica: Institute for Balkan Studies, 1986

Peyfuss, Max Demeter, *Die aromunische Frage*, Vienna: Böhlau, 1974

Wace, A.J.B. and M.S. Thompson, *The Nomads of the Balkans: An Account of Life and Customs among the Vlachs of Northern Pindus*, London: Methuen, 1914, reprinted New York: Biblo and Tannen, 1972

Winnifrith, Tom, *The Vlachs: The History of a Balkan People*, London: Duckworth, and New York: St Martin's Press, 1987

Volcanoes

Humanity has always had an ambiguous relationship with volcanoes. Volcanic eruptions can be tremendous forces of destruction, but soils produced by the weathering of volcanic rocks are very fertile in the right climate. For the archaeologist, eruptions can preserve aspects of communities almost instantaneously. The earliest record of a volcanic eruption is a wall painting from Çatal Hüyük, central Turkey, dating from 6200 BC. This is beyond the scope of this volume and here only the volcanoes of post-Stone-Age Greece and Italy will be discussed.

The recently active volcanoes of Greece lie along an arc from Corinth to Nisyros, near the Turkish coast. They are produced by the melting of the Mediterranean sea floor as it is subducted beneath the Aegean region. The sea floor descends at an angle of about 45 degrees until parts of it melt at a depth of 150 km. The magma (molten rock) then rises and is stored in chambers at depths of 5 to 10 km before eruption.

The most famous Greek volcano is Thera (Santorini). It had been dormant for a long period before the famous "Minoan" eruption in 1450 or 1650 BC – the exact date is still disputed. Before the eruption the present bay was probably almost filled with a volcano, similar to but larger than the present Kameni islands. The eruption started on this volcano and quickly destroyed it, creating a caldera (giant crater) 8 km in diameter. At its maximum the cloud of volcanic ash rose to more than 35 km in the atmosphere and was dispersed as far as Turkey, Israel, and Egypt. On the island the ash was up to 40 m deep and buried all the settlements, including the well-preserved village now known as Akrotiri. Towards the end of the eruption parts of the island collapsed into the caldera. These giant landslides, or particularly violent episodes of the eruption, produced a tsunami (tidal wave) more than 40 m high. Such a wave must have caused considerable erosion, damage to coastal communities, and the salination of agricultural land on nearby islands. These destabilizing effects may have led to the collapse of the Minoan civilization on Crete.

Since then, sporadic minor lava eruptions have created the Kameni islands. The only violent eruption was in AD 726, when so much pumice was produced that it reached Constantinople. There it was noticed by Leo III who interpreted it as a sign of divine displeasure and imposed icono-

clasm. The last eruption was a minor one, in 1950. Another volcano 15 km northeast of Thera erupted in 1650. It started underwater and built up a small island, which was rapidly eroded below sea level. Gas from this eruption killed animals and people on Thera.

The largest volcano of this arc is Melos and its archipelago. Volcanism started 3 million years ago, but essentially finished 100,000 years ago. In antiquity the most important volcanic product of the island was obsidian, a natural glass that occurs in ancient lava flows. It was used for knives from the 9th century BC. Recently, exploitation has turned to clay (kaolinite and bentonite) and volcanic ash (perlite). The easternmost volcano of the chain is Nisyros, a small island that has not had any eruptions of lava during historical times. However, there have been a number of steam explosions caused by the interaction between rainwater and magma at shallow depths. These made an impressive series of craters in the interior of the island, the last in 1887. Another small volcano is the peninsula of Methana, in the Saronic gulf. Fresh lavas in the northwest may have been erupted in the 3rd century BC.

In Italy there are recently active volcanoes around Naples (Vesuvius and the Phlegraean fields), on the Aeolian islands, and in eastern Sicily. As in Greece, this volcanism is related to the subduction of the Mediterranean sea floor. Here, however, the geometry is more complex and no single arc has formed. Mount Vesuvius is probably the best-known volcano in the world. The oldest parts, known as Mount Somma, started to form some 12,000 years ago. Construction continued intermittently until 1100 BC, when the volcano was about 2,000 m high. A long period of repose ended with the famous eruption of AD 79, when the top of the mountain was completely removed in three days. A cloud of volcanic ash rose to 30 km and fell on the surrounding countryside: Pompeii was buried to a depth of 7 m. Rain falling on the ash near the vent transformed it into hot mud flows that swept down and engulfed Herculaneum. Eruptions of ash since that time have partly filled the crater to form the present cone of Vesuvius. Most of these were small, except that of 1631. The last eruption was in 1944.

The Phlegraean ("burning") fields volcanic area lies just to the west of Naples. It comprises more than 50 small ash cones, some under the gulf of Pozzuoli. A large magma chamber underlies this region at a depth of a few kilometres. Magma movements can produce rapid changes in the height of the land. The effects of these changes can be seen in the Roman market place (Serapheum), where marine molluscs drilled holes in the columns at a height of several metres above the present sea level. The most recent eruption produced Monte Nuovo in 1538.

Most of the Aeolian islands are volcanic, but only three are of interest. Lipari was a major source of obsidian in the western Mediterranean. It was obtained from lava flows erupted during the 4th millennium BC. The last eruption was in AD 729, when up to 200 m of pumice was deposited in the north, burying the Roman acropolis. The eruption terminated with new flows of obsidian. The island of Vulcano has two independent volcanoes, Fossa and Volcanello, which were linked by an isthmus during the 16th century. Fossa has generally been more active with explosive eruptions about twice a century. The last eruption was in 1886–89; hence we can

Volcanoes: view of the caldera of Nisyros-Stephanos

expect a new eruption soon. Stromboli is a small, almost perfect, volcanic cone that has been active for at least 2,500 years. However, the activity is not generally intense and consists of small explosions every 5 to 10 minutes from the summit craters. These are caused by large gas bubbles that rise up the narrow conduits and burst, scattering parts of the bubble wall.

Mount Etna, the mythical forge of Vulcan and also home of the Cyclopes, is the largest volcano in Europe but also one of the youngest – it was mostly formed during the last 150,000 years. The volcano has been almost permanently active for at least 2,500 years. The lava flows from fissures or small ash cones on the flanks of the volcano and more rarely from the summit craters. At other times there are explosions and small eruptions within the craters.

MICHAEL D. HIGGINS

See also Geology, Santorini

Further Reading

Chester, D.K., *Mount Etna: The Anatomy of a Volcano*, London: Chapman and Hall, and Stanford, California: Stanford University Press, 1985

Doumas, Christos (editor), *Thera and the Aegean World*, vol. 2, London: Thera and the Aegean World, 1980

Hardy, D.A., *et al.* (editors), *Thera and the Ancient World*, vol. 3, London: Thera Foundation, 1990

Higgins, Michael Denis and Reynold Higgins, *A Geological Companion to Greece and the Aegean*, London: Duckworth, and Ithaca, New York: Cornell University Press, 1996

Krafft, Maurice and François-Dominique de Larouzière, *Guide des volcans d'Europe et des Canaries: France, Islande, Italie, Grèce, Allemagne, Canaries*, 2nd edition, Lausanne: Delachaux & Niestlé, 1991

Stothers, R.B. and M.R. Rampino, "Volcanic Eruptions in the Mediterranean before AD 630 from Written and Archaeological Sources", *Journal of Geophysical Research*, 88 (1983): pp. 6357–71

Volos

City in Thessaly

Volos is the capital of the nome of Magnesia, the chief port of Thessaly, and a regional commercial and industrial centre (particularly during the period 1860–1980). It stands in the deepest recess of the gulf of Pagasae, between Mount Pelion and the coast, on slightly sloping ground. It is the sixth biggest municipality in Greece with a population of some 100,000.

In the Bronze Age the site was occupied by the city of Iolcus, from where the Argonauts set out on their quest to bring the golden fleece back to Greece. Homer reports that Iolcus was a city in the kingdom of Eumelos and Herodotus records that the city was given as a present to the tyrant Hippias when he was exiled by the Athenians. Despite the importance of the place, systematic archaeological excavations have not been performed because the site is inhabited. Also close to modern Volos was the ancient city of Pagasae (600–353 BC) and on the same site flourished from AD 393 to 1423 the town of Dimitrias, built by Demetrius Poliorcetes. The first dwellings of the modern city of Volos were constructed in 1833. A small pre-existing residential area was occupied by the Turkish authorities.

The derivation of the city's name is not known with certainty. There are two prevalent opinions. The first argues that the name is derived from the Slavic *gol* (deserted) or *golos* (administrative centre); the second that it is a corruption of the name Iolcus, in Turkish Giolkaz, from Giolkas, Golos, and finally Volos. The problem is that until the 12th century the region was known as Iolcus, but after 150 years the ancient name disappears and the area is mentioned as Golos. At Volos the Byzantines erected a great castle that fell to the Turks in 1389. The Christian population took refuge in Mount Pelion and the Turkish army and a few Turkish families occupied the city. Despite having been destroyed by the Venetians, the castle was fortified and rebuilt by the Turks and became one of the most powerful in Greece. During the revolution of 1821 it was defended vigorously and was not taken by the Greeks. A squadron of the Turkish navy, stationed in the port of Volos, was destroyed in 1827 by the Greeks, but again the castle prevented the capture of the city.

The economic development of Volos began at the end of the 16th century, beginning with the fair that took place twice a week outside the castle walls. The country people from the Pelion area traded their merchandise there. Because of the restricted area and the arrival of merchants from all over Greece, the need arose for a suitable harbour from which to export the products of Pelion. A port was built on the beach beside the castle and during this period the first European merchant ships arrived in Volos.

The city started to flourish after the end of the Greek revolution, when its port became the trading centre for Greeks from all over Thessaly. In 1833 the first coastal dwellings were built. In a few years, the seashore had been transformed into a fine residential area following European models. Consulates from Austria, Britain, France, Italy, and Greece were located there. In 1860 Volos had 80 dwellings and, by 1880, more than 1,000 European-style residences had been built. After the annexation of Thessaly to Greece in 1881 the Turks surrendered the castle. This was later abandoned by the Greek authorities and finally destroyed. Once part of the Greek state, Volos quickly became a commercial and industrial centre, and its cultural activities were equal to those of Athens. By the start of the 20th century, the city was a focus of progressive thought and one of the first places in Greece where socialist ideas found fertile ground. At the city's girls' school (Parthenagogion) innovative educational methods were applied. The acute agricultural problems, particularly over the redistribution of land from the aristocracy to the peasantry, led to many revolts and confrontations with the state in the years before 1920. Volos was the birthplace of the principal revolutionary ideas. The poor working conditions and the inadequate income of industrial workers made the city one of the first in Greece where a Labour Centre (1908) was established. This became one of the founding members of the Confederation of Greek Labourers (Geniki Sinomospondia Ergaton Ellados). The predecessor of the Labour Centre was the Panergatikos Syndesmos Volou (All-Labour Association of Volos) (1907) which reinforced the notion of workers' solidarity in a town that was experiencing a steady process of urbanization. Its aims were the promotion of the workers' moral and cultural development, the bolstering of their consciousness as regards their rights as citizens and as working class, the enactment of protective social legislation, and the proffering of mutual support to any of the workers' material and moral needs. The city accepted many refugees from Asia Minor after the disaster of 1922, and these were employed in Volos's thriving spinning mills and cigarette factories. The port, which suffered severe damage during World War II, handled most merchandise arriving from the Middle East.

Nowadays Volos is well placed to benefit from the development of tourism in the Pelion region and the islands of the northern Sporades but it has lost its preeminence as an industrial and commercial centre.

Dimitrios Gkamas

See also Pelion

Summary

Volos is the chief port and commercial centre of Thessaly. As ancient Iolcus it was the point of departure for the Argonauts. Ancient Pagasae was also nearby. During the Tourkokratia the Christian population fled to Mount Pelion. Commerical development began in the late 16th century and expanded in the mid-19th. In the early 20th century Volos was a focus of revolutionary ideas.

Further Reading

Apostolakou, L., "All for One and One for All: Anarchists, Socialists and Demoticists in the Labour Centre of Volos, 1908–1911" in *Greek Society in the Making, 1863–1913: Realities, Symbols and Vision*, edited by Philip Carabott, Aldershot, Hampshire: Variorum, 1997

Clogg, Richard (editor and translator), *The Movement for Greek Independence, 1770–1821: A Collection of Documents*, London: Macmillan, 1976

Finlay, George, *A History of Greece from Its Conquest by the Romans to the Present Time, BC 146 to AD 1864*, revised by H.F. Tozer, 7 vols, Oxford: Clarendon Press, 1877, reprinted New York: AMS Press, 1970

McGrew, William W., *Land and Revolution in Modern Greece, 1800–1881: The Transition in the Tenure and Exploitation of Land from Ottoman Rule to Independence*, Kent, Ohio: Kent State University Press, 1985

Petridis, P., *Modern Greek Political History*, Athens, 1996 (in Greek)

Roussos, G., *Modern History of Greek Nation*, Athens, 1975 (in Greek)

Vournas, T., *History of Modern Greece*, Athens, 1977 (in Greek)

Votive Offerings

Strictly speaking, the term "votive offering" signifies something dedicated in consequence of a vow. Partly because the exact circumstances of a dedication are not always known, partly because a gift to the gods can almost always be taken to imply some kind of a vow, the category is elastic.

Comparison of the modest tin votive plaques readily available to worshippers in Greece today with the terracotta plaques or representations of parts of the human body from the ancient (4th century BC) sanctuary of Asclepius at Corinth or, on a larger scale, with the stone relief of a leg from Epidaurus demonstrates the identity of practice. Furthermore the existence of early Christian votive plaques supports the idea of a continuous tradition.

More substantial gifts to churches from the early Christian period onwards (furniture, church plate, icons) can often be seen to be votive from accompanying inscriptions, and the votive dedication of churches themselves in Byzantine and later times is demonstrated by the known origins of numerous chapels in the Greek countryside and elsewhere. Similar gifts to sanctuaries, deities, or other superhuman authorities are attested in antiquity by inscriptions and literary sources as well as the objects themselves. Ancient figurines and statues are regularly inscribed ("Mantiklos dedicated me to Apollo"; "The Messenians and Naupactians dedicated [this statue] to Olympian Zeus as a tithe of the spoil of their enemies").

The custom of making votive offerings may well go back into prehistory, since some of the objects found in prehistoric shrines, such as the terracotta animals in Minoan peak sanctuaries and in other sacred places, seem certainly votive. The subject is best presented with primary reference to antiquity.

Since the definition of a votive offering is by the intent of the donor, whether an individual or a group, and is dependent also on economic circumstances, the range of types, sizes, material, and value is immense. The material may be perishable (vegetable), cheap (wood, terracotta), or more valuable (stone, metal, precious metal). The type may be anything from a wreath, a candle, or a tiny object to a building. The treasuries (small temple-like buildings but without colonnades) that individual Greek states erected in sanctuaries to house the ritual equipment that their representatives used on ceremonial occasions were a kind of votive offering, intended to glorify the sanctuary and its patron deity. Temples such as the Parthenon, which were additional to the temple that housed the cult statue of the sanctuary, could be votives. If the item concerned was itself representational, or else decorated with figures, possible subjects include images of the deity addressed, images of the worshipper (often with the intention of making permanent an act of piety depicted, e.g. the bringing of an animal for sacrifice), images of sacrificial animals, or sacred objects. Otherwise, attractive or precious items of any kind at all could be offered. Occasions of offering can be summarized by quoting the chapter headings of Rouse (1902), with some additional comments.

Rouse's categories are: (1) to the dead, heroes, chthonian deities (in anticipation of or gratitude for help or favours); (2) tithes, first fruits, kindred offerings (whether crops or the products or profits of trade or business); (3) war (spoils, commemorative statues, etc.); (4) games and contests (prizes, instruments, commemorative statues); (5) disease and calamity (models of the diseased part; an inscription relating a cure); (6) domestic life (items relating to marriage and childbirth); (7) memorials of honour or office (herms, honorific statues or reliefs); (8) memorials of feasts and ceremonials (inscribed

Votive Offerings: clay heads of deities offered at altars, Calabria

vases, representations of the animal sacrificed or the votary carrying a sacrificial animal or object); (9) propitiation (offerings given in redress for impiety, such as the "Zane" statues at Olympia); and (10) rarities and valuables (as the due of deities).

ROBIN L.N. BARBER

Further Reading

Burkert, Walter, *Greek Religion: Archaic and Classical*, Oxford: Blackwell, and Cambridge, Massachusetts: Harvard University Press, 1985, pp. 68–70

Lang, Mabel, *Cure and Cult in Ancient Corinth: A Guide to the Asklepeion*, Princeton, New Jersey: American School of Classical Studies at Athens, 1977

Linders, Tullia, *Studies in the Treasure Records of Artemis Brauronia Found in Athens*, Lund: Åström, 1972

Linders, Tullia and Gullög Nordquist (editors), *Gifts to the Gods*, Uppsala: Academia Ubsaliensis, 1987

Raubitschek, A.E., *Dedications from the Athenian Acropolis: A Catalogue of the Inscriptions of the Sixth and Fifth Centuries BC*, Cambridge, Massachusetts: Archaeological Institute of America, 1949

Rodley, Lyn, *Byzantine Art and Architecture: An Introduction*, Cambridge and New York: Cambridge University Press, 1994 (see pp. 47–48 for early Christian votives)

Roebuck, Carl, *Corinth: The Results of Excavations Conducted by the American School of Classical Studies at Athens*, vol. 14: *The*

Asklepieion and Lerna, Princeton, New Jersey: American School of Classical Studies at Athens, 1951

Rouse, W.H.D., *Greek Votive Offerings: An Essay in the History of Greek Religion*, Cambridge: Cambridge University Press, 1902, reprinted New York: Arno Press, 1975

Voulgaris, Evgenios 1716–1806

Intellectual

Voulgaris was one of the most eminent ecclesiastical and learned figures of the Greek world in the 18th century. Born in Corfu in 1716 as Eleftherios, Voulgaris assumed the name Evgenios upon his ordination as a deacon. His initial studies were completed in the Ionian islands. Between 1740 and 1742 he stayed in Italy studying and serving the Greek community of Venice as a preacher. From 1742 to 1761 he taught at various schools in Ioannina, in Kozani, on Mount Athos (Athonias Academy), and finally in Constantinople (Patriarchal Academy). His innovative teaching as well as the western ideas that he introduced provoked the reaction of several Orthodox traditionalists, who, apart from personal rivalries, accused him of heresy and even of atheism. He was thus forced to resign or to escape in order to avoid further confrontations with this conservative religious and social establishment.

In 1763 Voulgaris finally left for Germany (Leipzig and Halle) to continue his studies. There he familiarized himself with German rationalism and the latest scientific developments. He also published some of his writings and translations including his influential *Logic* (Leipzig, 1766). In 1771 Voulgaris was invited to Russia by the empress Catherine II to become librarian and curator of antiquities at her court in St Petersburg. Voulgaris accepted this invitation, which should be understood in the light of the growing Russian interest in Greek antiquity and in the Orthodox populations of the Balkans. After the end of the Russo-Ottoman war of 1768–74 and the treaty of Kuchuk-Kainardji, Voulgaris was appointed from 1775 to 1779 archbishop of the diocese of Kherson and Slaviansk in Novorossia, the strategic new frontier of the Russian empire. After his retirement Voulgaris stayed in Poltava and Kherson until late 1788 when he returned to St Petersburg. There he lived for the rest of his long life, studying as well as revising his previous works. Many of them were published in the early 1800s through the financial support of the Zosimades brothers, a wealthy Greek merchant family. Voulgaris died in 1806 in the Aleksandr Nevskii monastery in St Petersburg.

Voulgaris is rightly considered an outstanding intellectual and theologian of the 18th century. Although he has had many enemies and opponents, his numerous contributions to the Greek people were highly appreciated even during his lifetime. Voulgaris was usually referred to and known at that time only by his first name (Evgenios). It was deemed a great honour for someone to have been a pupil of the "celebrated Evgenios", whose definitive flight to Germany was considered an irreparable loss for Greece. Adamantios Korais called Voulgaris the doyen of the Greek intellectuals of his age, while Josephos Moisiodax considered him "the living library of polymathy".

Voulgaris was a real polymath and polyglot. His interests were manifold and encyclopedic, ranging from philosophical and scientific to theological and historical, as manifested in the wide range of his numerous publications (see Batalden, 1982, pp. 148–72). He attempted to combine the religious humanism of the Orthodox east with western philosophy and rationalism. Among other things, Voulgaris contributed especially to the renewal of Greek philosophical thought on the basis of western developments including the work of Francis Bacon, René Descartes, Gottfried Wilhelm Leibniz, John Locke, C. Wolff, J.B. Duhamel, E. Purchot, J.F. Wucherer, A. Genovesi, W.J.S. Gravesande, and others. Proclaiming the freedom of thought from the chains of outdated authorities (e.g. Scholastic Aristotelianism), Voulgaris moved Greek thought beyond the Neoaristotelianism which was established in Greek schools. He introduced an eclectic form of philosophical inquiry in order to profit from the major systems and move towards the construction of a "sound philosophy", but without upholding them as absolute and infallible authorities. In a similar manner, Voulgaris's influence was instrumental in renewing the scientific thought of Greece on the basis of new theories and discoveries (e.g. by Galileo, Newton, and Andreas Segner). Yet, in some cases Voulgaris showed a reluctance to accept novel theories and criticized them. Motivated probably by religious concerns, he rejected heliocentrism and resorted to the compromising Tychonian world system that posed no threat to the authority of the Bible.

Voulgaris's religious thought was firmly anchored in the Orthodox tradition. He repeatedly defended the Orthodox Church against the Roman Catholics and against the anti-Christian atheistic trends of western Enlightenment. He wrote a compendium of dogmatic theology, polemical and exegetical works as well as a treatise on religious tolerance. Voulgaris was fond of Voltaire and translated some of his works into Greek, but he did not share his antireligious sentiments. Generally, Voulgaris's preoccupation with western ideas did not alienate him from his Orthodox background. He accepted a moderate Enlightenment in which religion occupied a central role and determined his overall objectives. He never intended to compromise his highly valued Orthodox faith. He also tried to distinguish clearly between the areas of jurisdiction of faith/revelation and reason. After all, from his youth Voulgaris was a cleric and remained loyal to the Church until his death.

Voulgaris also took a keen interest throughout his life in the cause of his compatriots against Ottoman rule. Before moving to Russia, he had translated into Greek the *Nakaz* of Catherine, namely the Instructions to the Legislative Commission, and published it, with the Russian text attached, in St Petersburg in 1771. In his dedication to Catherine, Voulgaris wished that the Greek nation one day might be governed by the same laws as Russia was. During this period Voulgaris wrote and translated other works into Greek (e.g. some philhellenic pieces by Voltaire) hoping to persuade Catherine to liberate his Orthodox brethren. This was in the context of the widely circulating apocalyptic literature of the time. One of his works, published in 1772, contained an assessment of the political situation in the Ottoman empire in the light of the Russo-Ottoman war of 1768–74. There Voulgaris opined that, aside from France which had strong commercial interests in the Levant, all other European nations could easily undertake a common struggle against the Ottomans. Otherwise, the Ottoman menace would be always imminent for Christian Europe. Probably aware of Catherine's "Greek Project", Voulgaris also followed closely the political developments and the growing role of Russia in Balkan politics. He was particularly thrilled by the treaty of Constantinople (May 1800) between Russia and the Ottomans, which acknowledged the independence of the Ionian islands, including his birthplace Corfu, and by the creation of a "Heptanesian Republic" under Ottoman suzerainty and Russian protection with a moderate constitutional government from 1800 to 1807.

Given the wide range of Voulgaris's activities and interests, it is no wonder that he was regarded as an authority by some of his admirers, a phenomenon comparable to the adoption of Theophilos Corydalleus's Neoaristotelianism a few decades ago. Such a development drew various criticisms from his contemporaries, ranging from the moderate of Moisiodax to the sharp from Athanasios Psalidas, who tried to demonstrate certain drawbacks in Voulgaris's character, teaching methods, archaic Greek style of writing, as well as ideas. These criticisms notwithstanding, it is generally held that Voulgaris's overall contributions to the Greek nation and prodigious output of writings were seminal and almost unparalleled in his time.

VASILIOS MAKRIDES

See also Enlightenment

Biography

Born in Corfu in 1716 as Eleftherios, Voulgaris took the name Evgenios when he was ordained deacon. Educated first in the Ionian islands, he lived in Venice from 1740 to 1742 and from 1742 to 1761 taught at schools in Greece and Constantinople. His teaching displeased the Orthodox establishment and he fled to Germany in 1763. Invited to St Petersburg by Catherine II in 1771, he was appointed archbishop of Kherson and Slaviansk (1775–79). In 1788 he returned to St Petersburg where he died in 1806.

Further Reading

Angelou, Alkes, *Ton Photon: Opseis tou Neoellinikou Diaphotismou* [Bringing the Light: Aspects of Modern Greek Enlightenment], Athens, 1988

Angelou, Alkes, "I madame Tyaniti", *Ellinika*, 44 (1994): pp. 369–98

Arsh, Grigorii L., "Evgenii Bulgari v Rossii", *Voprosy Istorii*, 4 (1987): pp. 103–13

Batalden, Stephen K., "Notes from a Leningrad Manuscript: Eugenios Voulgaris' Autograph List of his Own Works", *O Eranistis*, 13 (1976): pp. 1–22

Batalden, Stephen K., *Catherine II's Greek Prelate: Eugenios Voulgaris in Russia, 1771–1806*, New York: Columbia University Press, 1982

Henderson, G.P., *The Revival of Greek Thought, 1620–1830*, Albany: State University of New York Press, 1970, pp. 41–75

Kitromilides, Paschalis M., "I Politiki Skepsi tou Evgeniou Voulgari" ["The Political Thought of Evgenios Voulgaris"], *Ta Istorika*, 7/12–13 (1990): pp. 167–78

Kitromilides, Paschalis M., "John Locke and the Greek Intellectual Tradition: An Episode in Locke's Reception in South-East Europe" in *Locke's Philosophy: Content and Context*, edited by G.A.J. Rogers, Oxford: Clarendon Press, and New York: Oxford University Press, 1994

Kitromilides, Paschalis M., "Athos and the Enlightenment" in *Mount Athos and Byzantine Monasticism*, edited by Anthony Bryer and Mary Cunningham, Aldershot, Hampshire: Variorum, 1996, pp. 257–72

Kitromilides, Paschalis M., *Neoellinikos Diaphotismos: Oi Politikes kai Koinonikes Idees* [The Modern Greek Enlightenment: Political and Social Concepts], Athens, 1996, pp. 53–65

Knapp, Martin, *Evjenios Vulgaris im Einfluss der Aufklärung: Der Begriff der Toleranz bei Vulgaris und Voltaire*, Amsterdam: Hakkert, 1984

Makrides, Vasilios, *Die religiöse Kritik am kopernikanischen Weltbild in Griechenland zwischen 1794 und 1821: Aspekte griechisch-orthodoxer Apologetik angesichts naturwissenchaftlichert Fortschritte*, Frankfurt: Peter Lang, 1995, pp. 231–97

Noutsos, Panayotis, "I Leitourgia tou Neoterikou Pneumatos sti *Logiki* tou Voulgari" [The Function of the Spirit of Innovation in the *Logic* of Voulgaris], *Dodoni*, 13 (1984): pp. 139–46

Podskalsky, Gerhard, *Griechische Theologie in der Zeit der Türkenherrschaft, 1453–1821: Die Orthodoxie im Spannungsfeld der nachreformatorischen Konfessionen des Westerns*, Munich: Beck, 1988, pp. 344–53

Wallachia

A principality on the lower Danube that joined
Moldavia in 1859 to form the state of Romania

Roughly corresponding to the southern half of Trajan's Dacia,
the territory of Wallachia (named after the Vlachs and known
to the Byzantine chancellery as Oungrovlachia) lay between
the Danube and the Transylvanian Alps. It had enjoyed an
indigenous Romanized culture despite being overrun in the 4th
to 6th centuries AD by Goths, Huns, Gepids, Avars, and Slavs.
When a major part of it was incorporated into the Bulgarian
state in the 9th century it came increasingly under largely
second-hand Byzantine influence, which persisted sporadically
during subsequent invasions by Pechenegs, Cumans, and
Tatars. It became a political entity in its own right during the
early years of the 14th century through the unification of
various small states by Basarab I, who established its independence by defeating his overlord, the Hungarian king Charles I,
at the battle of Posada in 1330. With the accession of the
Dobrudja it reached its acme under Mircea the Old
(1386–1418) despite increasing pressure from the Ottomans,
to whom Wallachia was paying tribute by 1391. Although
enjoying internal self-government and never becoming an
Ottoman *pashalik*, it was forced to recognize Ottoman
suzerainty until well into the 19th century (the sultan abandoned his claims as late as 1878), despite the occasional briefly
successful attempt to break free.

From its beginning Basarab's state was open to Byzantine
influence. This came at first mainly through trade and the
Church. Though having first reached the area much earlier,
Christianity had been spread by Byzantine missionaries in the
mid-10th century, so Wallachia had followed Constantinople
rather than Rome in the schism of 1054 and remained firmly
Orthodox despite Hungarian pressure. The principal medium
of this influence was texts in Old Church Slavonic, the
language of both Church and administration until late in the
17th century and the only language of the approximately
2,000 manuscripts known from Romania prior to the 16th
century. These texts included translations from Greek of
euchologia (prayerbooks) and numerous saints' lives and
patristic works, and also of secular works, mainly chronicles
and legendary tales such as the ever popular *Alexander
Romance*. Law was at first largely orally transmitted Roman

law, but Byzantine influence was seen here too, most notably
in translations of Matthew Blastares's *Syntagma* of 1335 (a
legal handbook for clergy that included material from both
ecclesiastical and secular sources) and the slightly later compilation of secular laws (*Hexabiblos*) of Constantine
Harmenopoulos.

After repeated requests from the Wallachian *voievod* (ruler)
Nicolae Alexandru, the ecumenical patriarch in 1359
appointed a metropolitan, Iachint, to the state, a practice that
continued until the fall of Constantinople to the Turks in 1453
(the metropolitanate's authority extended to Transylvania,
where Hungarian domination allowed Orthodoxy only a tolerated status). Thus encouraged, Wallachian *voivode* both established in their own country many monasteries, which attracted
a number of Byzantine monks to administer them, and became
patrons of Greek monasteries elsewhere, most notably on
Mount Athos, where Alexandru and his son Vladislav
completely rebuilt the monastery of Koutloumousiou (whose
abbot Chariton later became metropolitan of Wallachia).

Byzantine artistic influence had long been apparent in
pottery (in both imports and imitations) and, through
Bulgarian intermediaries, in ecclesiastical architecture (e.g. the
11th–12th-century church in the cemetery of Dinogetia), but
the reign of Basarab I saw the beginning of much more extensive and closer links. Although his princely church at his first
capital, Cîmpulung, was Romanesque, the church of S.
Nicolae-Domnească at his new capital, Curtea de Argeş, was
not only architecturally dependent upon Byzantine models but
contains frescos remarkably similar to those in the narthex of
the celebrated church of the Chora (Kariye Djami) in
Constantinople. Later in the century Byzantine influence was
often more in a Serbian guise (most notably at Cozia) owing to
the half-Serbian Athonite monk Nikodemos, who established
two monasteries and probably served as the principal conduit
into Wallachia of the spiritual movement known as hesychasm
which long persisted there.

Under Ottoman vassalage the Wallachian boyars prided
themselves upon their Byzantine culture, and after the fall of
Constantinople in 1453 they and their Moldavian counterparts, as the ruling class in the only self-governing Orthodox
states in southeastern Europe, supported the faith throughout
the Balkans: many Greek (especially Athonite), Bulgarian, and
Serbian monasteries owed their enhancement and even survival
to Wallachian benefactions; influence was exercised even in the

appointment of the ecumenical patriarch (e.g. Niphon II and Pachomios I); and late in the 17th century polemical treatises were published in Greek. Wallachian (and Moldavian) independence naturally attracted Greek churchmen and scholars, who in turn fostered a Byzantine culture in their new homeland (one, Ignatios Petritzis, founded a Graeco-Latin college at Tîrgovişte, the capital in 1646). The Byzantine-Slavonic literature, both religious and secular, also became better known through its translation into Romanian during the 16th and 17th centuries, in the latter of which it received an additional impetus from the establishment of printing presses. Among the enthusiastic promoters of this neo-Byzantine renaissance were the *voivode* Şerban Cantacuzino (1678–88) and Constantin Brâncoveanu (1688–1714), who respectively founded and reorganized at the new capital of Bucharest a Greek academy of such quality that it attracted students from throughout the Greek-speaking world.

From 1714 to 1821 Wallachia was ruled by Phanariot Greeks (or part-Greeks) from Constantinople and members of two families of Hellenized Romanians, who were appointed, dismissed, and often reappointed, like their native predecessors, by the Sublime Porte. The average length of reign for this period was two and a half years, while between 1730 and 1769 Konstantinos Mavrokordatos precariously enjoyed no fewer than six terms in Wallachia and four in Moldavia. Both greed and the need to disburse lavish bribes to gain reappointment ensured that a major preoccupation of their reigns was the amassing of wealth. Since they alone could elevate to the class of boyar, their frequent acceptance of bribes from ambitious members of their accompanying Greek entourage created a strong Greek element among the Wallachian aristocracy. On the other hand, Mavrokordatos weakened their power by granting personal freedom to the serfs in 1746 (although the land was still owned by boyars and monasteries) and limiting to 12 the number of days that they had to work without pay.

Greek language and culture now became dominant for all classes down to the artisanate, as large numbers of Greeks entered the country as both courtiers and merchants. Also, many boyars imitated the Phanariots in having their children educated at home by Greek tutors, who were often priests; and Greek schools were established in provincial centres, although the quality of pedagogy there was frequently very poor. Nevertheless western news, ideas, and culture increasingly penetrated the country, a result of both the importation by traders of Greek newspapers and books printed in Vienna and the Italian education enjoyed by most of the Phanariots, one of whom, Alexandros Ypsilantis, introduced science into the curriculum at the academy in Bucharest. In religious matters, however, the Phanariots continued to be staunch upholders of Orthodoxy and patrons of monasteries both inside and outside the country. The end of their rule came through a conflict of interests in the Greek War of Independence, but Romanians have remained very conscious of their Byzantine Greek inheritance and enjoy a growing presence on Mount Athos, which was revitalized in the 1990s through a reversal of the policy of the communist leader Nicolae Ceauşescu.

A.R. LITTLEWOOD

See also Moldavia, Phanariots, Romania, Vlachs

Summary

The land between the Danube and the Transylvanian Alps, Wallachia was named after the Vlachs and was known to the Byzantines as Oungrovlachia. Part of the Byzantine Commonwealth from the 9th century, it became an independent state in the 14th century. Though forced to recognize Ottoman suzerainty, it remained a self-governing state until 1859 when it joined Moldavia to form the state of Romania.

Further Reading

Bodea, N., *Mănăstiri şi Biserici Româneşti*, 2nd edition, Bucharest: Scripta, 1991

Deletant, D.J., "Some Aspects of the Byzantine Tradition in the Rumanian Principalities", *Slavonic and East European Review*, 59/1 (1981): pp. 1–14

Elian, A., "Les Rapports byzantino-roumains", *Byzantinoslavica*, 19 (1958): pp. 212–25

Iorga, Nicolae, *Byzance après Byzance: continuation de l'"Histoire de la vie byzantine"*, Bucharest: Institut d'Etudes Byzantines, 1935, reprinted Bucharest: Association Internationale d'Etudes du Sud-Est Européen, 1971

Warfare

Antiquity

Civilized warfare on a grand scale in Greece began with the rise of Mycenaean civilization during the 2nd millennium BC. From roughly 1600 to 1250 BC palaces at Mycenae, Pylos, Tiryns, Thebes, and elsewhere fielded well-equipped forces that put a high premium on the use of the horse, chariot, and bow. By the last century of Mycenaean civilization well-protected foot soldiers with spear and sword were fielded in response to seaborne attackers. From the evidence of the Linear B tablets, painted pottery, engraved jewellery, and the physical remains of the vast fortifications of the citadels, the Mycenaean palace armies were probably small, tightly controlled by royal dynasts, and generally inflexible in their response to less well-organized raiders and plunderers, who posed a far greater threat to their stratified societies than did other royal armies in Asia Minor and Egypt. By 1200 BC most of the palaces were destroyed, the population had plummeted, and material culture was impoverished. For the next four centuries Greek warfare of the Dark Ages was probably characterized by the haphazard raiding and skirmishing of mounted grandees accompanied by small bands of attached light-armed foot soldiers.

The rise of the Greek polis – by 700 BC there were probably more than 1,000 city states in the Greek-speaking world – was probably the result of an emerging middling class of adroit and independent small farmers. Their peculiar practice of phalanx warfare was inseparable from their own agrarian chauvinism and political autonomy, and marks the true beginning of western infantry practice. The predominately agrarian character of these citizen militias tended to define hoplite war as a single collision between phalanxes of heavily armed infantry – a decisive engagement in which casualties were limited, victory and defeat clear-cut, and damage to the surrounding countryside and civilian population limited. Such fighting did not require taxation, public investment in war material, or fortifications, and thus helps to explain the astonishing rise of the Archaic city state itself.

Infantrymen were known as hoplites, due to their cumbersome gear (*hopla*): bronze breastplate, greaves, and helmet; a wooden double-grip concave shield; a spear about 2.7 m long; and a secondary short iron sword. The large shield, more than 7 kg in weight and 90 cm in diameter, also explains the nature of hoplite fighting. The infantryman depended on the man next to him to shield his own unprotected right side and to maintain the cohesion of the entire phalanx, military service now reinforcing the solidarity of the citizenry. The shield's unique double grip allowed its weight to be held by the left arm alone, and its concave shape permitted the rear ranks to rest it on their shoulders as they pushed on ahead. The weight of the panoply – ranging anywhere from 20 to 30 kg – meant that hoplite battle would be short and decisive: infantrymen massed into the columns of the phalanx and charged each other head-on, soldiers seeking cover from the array of shields and victory through the sheer force generated by spearmen pushing against the backs and sides of their friends and family ahead. On flat ground, hoplites in formation were usually invulnerable to mounted assault by the more wealthy and the harassment of poorer skirmishers.

Generals fought in the front rank and their tactical options were exhausted with the prebattle placement of particular contingents along the battle line and the choice of terrain. Before the 6th century BC fleets were rare and sea battles essentially non-existent. Armies were challenged to fight by formal notification and occasionally coerced to action by the ravaging of local crops. Battle itself was not much longer than a half-hour or so; pursuit was haphazard. The Persian (490–479 BC) and Peloponnesian (431–404 BC) wars changed all that, and revealed the tactical limitations of hoplite armies when faced with forces that did not share the same protocols of warfare and fought in theatres and on terrain far removed from flat plains. During the 5th century BC Athens turned to its fleet and soon developed sophisticated methods of defensive and offensive naval manoeuvres, attacking through or around an enemy line of ships to achieve easy ramming. In contrast, the Spartans sought to improve on the simple collision of hoplite battle by mastering outflanking movements on the right wing, made possible by the superior drill and training of their professional corps. Thucydides' magnificent description of Mantinea (418 BC) reveals how such tactical competence might shatter an enemy line and change the entire course of battle. At the battle of Delium (424 BC) the Theban general Pagondas first employed reserves, massed phalanxes deeper than the standard eight shields, and used horsemen for more than just preliminary skirmishing. Cleon, Brasidas, and Demosthenes during the Archidamian War (431–421 BC) experimented with light-armed troops to attack hoplites, through manipulation of terrain, darkness, and sheer surprise. No-one sought decisive confrontation through traditional hoplite pitched battles, since warfare was now beginning to be governed more by military necessity than by cultural restraint.

Epaminondas the Theban (d. 362 BC) is often considered the father of Greek infantry tactics. In fact, none of his "discoveries" – a deepened phalanx, the use of superior troops on the left, the oblique order of march, the incorporation of elite units, and the combined use of horsemen – was novel per se. Rather his originality lay in combining these previously known tactical options into a unified battle plan – one uniquely suited for his phalanx of dour Theban agrarians who had a reputation in antiquity for physical prowess and infantry ferocity. Epaminondas' victories at Leuctra (371 BC) and second Mantinea (362 BC) proved that an innovative heavy infantry might alone still clear a battlefield of the enemy. Yet, his grand invasion of Laconia (370–369 BC) that freed the Messenian helots did more to emasculate Sparta than did his defeats of Spartan hoplites in pitched battles, proving that victory now required the use of infantry as part of larger economic and cultural strategies. More abstract 4th-century BC reactionaries also sought to maintain infantry superiority through more innovative use. Plato and Aristotle, for example, speculated on novel ways of preserving the noble tradition of hoplite supremacy within the city state; their advice ranged from the employment of infantry in expanded roles on the borders to the incorporation of stockades and fortifications within the old civic idea of a hoplite militia defence.

Nevertheless, throughout the 4th century BC most generals worried less about the tactical possibilities of infantry employment than learning the new uses of artillery, missile troops, peltasts, and cavalry, both for the attack on and defence of fortified positions. The more utilitarian philosophers and rhetoricians of the 4th century BC reflect this growing tactical renaissance, as they sought to apply dialectic and induction to generalship (*strategika*), the arrangement of troops (*taktika*), and weapons training (*hoplomachia*). War was no more a question of bravery or a reflection of values, but simply an art (*techne*), teachable like any other. Xenophon (428–354 BC), as author of monographs such as *The Cavalry Commander* and *On Horsemanship*, is the best example of this mixture of battlefield experience and philosophical training. His contemporary, the pragmatic Aeneas the Tactician, follows in the same utilitarian tradition. Aeneas' apparently vast *Military Preparations* is lost, but an extant monograph about survival under siege covers everything from the mundane (e.g. passwords, reveille, codes, tunnelling, fire-signals) to the broader employment of mercenaries, sorties, and plans of evacuation.

Philip II (359–336 BC) and his son Alexander III (336–323 BC) of Macedon sought to combine infantry innovation with light-armed, missile, and mounted troops to form a true symphony of forces. Battle became longer, as much as several hours in duration. The general – nearly always mounted – now had a host of options and different troops at his command, which allowed the much smaller Macedonian armies to create havoc at particular spots in the enemy's battle line, through which poured heavy cavalry and infantry, causing psychological terror and general collapse – as the Greek confederates learned at Chaeronea (338 BC), the last battle by truly independent city states. Perhaps Alexander's greatest tactical contribution was the idea of rapid and unceasing pursuit, as part of his overall aim of destroying the enemy outright on the battlefield. Heretofore, battle tactics had not been closely integrated with larger strategic issues. But Alexander saw troop arrangement as merely a part of grand strategy – his aim was not only to win on the battlefield, but to destroy both materially and spiritually the enemy's will to resist. Infantry battle would then logically lead to the invaded surrendering its territory and very culture to Macedonian royal control.

In that regard, Alexander entirely reinvented the notion of Greek tactics, which in the 4th century BC had evolved from, but not replaced, the original emphasis on formal infantry engagements to resolve border disputes. The original purpose of Greek battle had been to limit casualties and resolve disagreement through the simple and often economic use of force. With the decline of the agrarian city state in the 4th century BC, however, the Greeks enhanced decisive battle with auxiliary troops to make fighting longer and more elaborate – but not necessarily all-destructive. Under the Macedonians the West at last applied its full scientific and rational arsenal to the battlefield, as part of a larger effort to destroy a culture, rather than to defeat an enemy. Tactics at last now fully served strategy and Hellenic warfare became the most lethal in the history of civilization up to that time.

During the subsequent Hellenistic era (323–146 BC) Greek-speaking mercenaries were prized throughout the Mediterranean as pike-carrying phalangites that could rout indigenous tribal armies and alone stand up to the Roman legions. Pikes lengthened to nearly 6 m in length and were wielded by both hands, as body armour and the shield shrank or disappeared altogether – the safety of Greek mercenaries' lives was now less important than their ability to kill. After the failure of Pyrrhus in Italy (280–279 BC), the Greeks spent a century and a half resisting Roman invasions. Some of the great battles of the age – Cynoscephalae (197 BC) and Pydna (168 BC) – pitted Greek hired infantry on Greek soil against republican legionaries. But the inflexibility of Greek tactics, the cumbersome nature of the Macedonian phalanx, the greater manpower reserves of Italy, and the superior élan of agrarian Italian recruits led to the doom of the Greek-speaking armies. With the final subjugation of Corinth (146 BC) Greek military forces per se ceased to exist and the phalanx became the curiosity of pedantic armchair strategists. In some sense, Roman republican militias with their emphasis on group solidarity, patriotism, and belief in a superior culture had become more Greek than the Hellenistic dynastic armies they conquered. The forces of Alexander's successors were every bit as despotic, top heavy, and corrupt as the old Persian imperial levies, whom the Greeks had conquered almost two centuries earlier.

Under the Roman empire Greece suffered from high taxation and general depopulation, ensuring that organized military rebellion was out of the question. Most Greek soldiers fought anonymously as hired soldiers in the legions on the northern and eastern frontiers of the empire. Yet except for a few horrific battles between rival Roman dynasts, Roman control brought Greece a half-millennium of general tranquillity (100 BC–AD 400) – the longest period free of major wars in Hellenic history. With the collapse of the western empire, Byzantine armies took over the exclusive protection of Greece. For the first time since the 2nd century BC, there were now to be independent Greek-speaking armies in Italy, North Africa, and Asia Minor. Under Justinian's skilled generals Narses (478–573) and Belisarius (500–65), Greek soldiers ranged from Italy to Persia, trying in vain to reconsolidate the western empire under the aegis of Hellenism and Orthodoxy. Sound tactics and the Byzantines' technological edge in shipbuilding, fortifications, and armament compensated for a general absence of manpower and hardy rural infantry. Still, small

mobile Greek armies would keep foreigners out of Greece until the arrival of the Franks in the 13th century. The ancient and modern history of Greek warfare is characterized by remarkable success when local, highly motivated militias are used for defence, but eventual failure when Hellenic armies are sent far overseas without adequate material and spiritual support from home.

VICTOR DAVIS HANSON

See also Architecture (Fortifications), Architecture (Military), Siegecraft

Further Reading

Anderson, J.K., *Military Theory and Practice in the Age of Xenophon*, Berkeley: University of California Press, 1970

Dawson, Doyne, *The Origins of Western Warfare: Militarism and Morality in the Ancient Greek World*, Boulder, Colorado: Westview Press, 1996

Delbrück, Hans, *History of the Art of War within the Framework of Political History*, vol. 1: *Antiquity*, Westport, Connecticut: Greenwood Press, 1975

Drews, Robert, *The End of the Bronze Age: Changes in Warfare and the Catastrophe ca. 1200 BC*, Princeton, New Jersey: Princeton University Press, 1993

Hanson, Victor Davis, *The Western Way of War: Infantry Battle in Classical Greece*, London: Hodder and Stoughton, and New York: Knopf, 1989, 2nd edition, Berkeley: University of California Press, 2000

Hanson, Victor Davis (editor), *Hoplites: The Classical Greek Battle Experience*, London and New York: Routledge, 1991

Hanson, Victor Davis, *Warfare and Agriculture in Classical Greece*, 2nd edition, Berkeley: University of California Press, 1998

Lloyd, Alan B. (editor), *Battle in Antiquity*, London: Duckworth, 1996

Pritchett, W.K., *The Greek State at War*, 5 vols, Berkeley: University of California Press, 1971–91

Rich, John and Graham Shipley (editors), *War and Society in the Greek World*, London and New York: Routledge, 1993

Byzantium

Peace was not the expected norm for the Byzantines, who inherited traditions of planning and practising warfare from their ancient and Hellenistic predecessors and from the Romans, although usually reported through the medium of the later Greek military writers. Yet the Byzantines were not primarily a warlike people nor was Byzantium a martial state, even though it inherited and adapted some Roman traditions. Caution, resort to cunning, and confidence in the value of mental expedients to compensate for the lack of numbers were vital features of Byzantine military strategy. Byzantine military manuals owe much to Hellenistic models, such as the 1st-century AD treatise of Onasander. In the early Byzantine period some generals found advantage in using or adapting ancient and Hellenistic Greek battle formations to their own situations. A close examination of the historical narratives indicates that such exercises were not merely theoretical, but were occasionally used in reality.

There are many gaps in the sources. Byzantine historical narratives about warfare seldom provide detailed reports on combat, except for some stereotypical flourishes about the feats of arms of a few prominent individuals. Military manuals provide some of the best information concerning battle,

Warfare (Byzantium): illustration from the 11th-century chronicle of Skylitzes showing troops of Basil I (right) fleeing from the Arab army, late 9th century, Biblioteca Nacional, Madrid

manoeuvre, and logistics, but they are abstract. Speeches, letters, and other literary works are usually unhelpful on the subject of battles and campaigns. Autobiographical reminiscences are rare in themselves and seldom useful. There are no memoirs or other autobiographical accounts by Byzantine warriors, whether at the top of the military hierarchy or in the ranks. These omissions limit our understanding of warfare and soldiers' experiences of it. Archaeology provides some evidence concerning arms and armour, and occasionally on topography and the appreciation of its contribution, but it cannot resolve many serious questions about actual battles or campaigns. Representations of combat and military dress in illuminated manuscripts and frescos may appear to be important but they are problematic, because they may depend on non-contemporary prototypes and models.

Opponents of the Byzantines, both western European and Muslim, have left important narrative accounts of their military encounters. These external accounts are valuable for the 10th century and later, and especially for the 12th century and beyond. Warfare changed measurably during this long period. In the early Byzantine periods, the armies fought in different kinds of terrain and were subject to the vagaries of very different climates.

Whenever possible, irrespective of period, Byzantine strategists preferred to avoid pitched battles and their attendant risks of human and material losses, and instead to resort to their intellect. Because human and material resources were limited, they tended to try to avoid risking what they had. The Byzantines seldom enjoyed numerical superiority in the field. Instead, they often sought to destabilize their opponents through assassination, diplomacy, delay, craft, deception, and the exploitation of internal divisions, to cause them to desert, switch sides, or flee. They tried to take advantage of the impetuousness, recklessness, and thoughtless greed of their opponents. They sought to gain intelligence about their opponents through any possible means and they developed refer-

ence works about the weaknesses and strengths of the fighting techniques and practices of various contemporary ethnic groups. They sought to adjust warfare to the practices of their foes, whose psychological vulnerabilities they tried to exploit. This prudent avoidance of gambling everything on the outcome of a single battle or campaign contributed to the longevity of the empire, although it did result in some humiliating and serious territorial losses, and ultimately there were situations in which there was no choice but war. The Byzantines became overconfident in their ability to use intelligence instead of raw power to prevail, and there were occasions in which superior power determined the outcome.

More difficult to trace but nonetheless valuable was another Byzantine inheritance from ancient Greek and Hellenistic practices: the passing down and modification of lore from the Balkans and from Anatolia about fortifying and exploiting mountain passes in warfare. Mountain passes could permit small forces to check or destroy much larger numbers of opponents. Techniques for trapping raiders reached their perfection in the early 10th century. The Byzantines developed techniques for observing, tracking, trapping, and destroying the Arab raiders who penetrated on to the Anatolian plateau, especially between the mid-7th and 10th centuries. These techniques may have originated in unrecorded practices of guarding and using mountain passes in earlier warfare against the Persians, and to some extent they may even have derived from lessons learned in defending rough terrain and passes in Byzantine Africa against Berber raiders.

Byzantium had no military academy. Soldiers learned by apprenticeship, direct and third-party experience, and for a few of the elite, by reading military manuals from the larger corpus of military literature. Likewise there was no general staff in some centralized location. Although Constantinople was the nerve centre for the reception and filtering of military and political intelligence, given the slowness of communications, many important decisions had to be made by commanders on the spot, especially in the early and middle periods when the empire's perimeters were vast and conditions poor on many of the routes. Local situations could not be micromanaged from faraway Constantinople; local commanders therefore enjoyed considerable discretion.

Civilians and the ecclesiastical hierarchies probably had little accurate understanding of the realities of warfare, so that although popular support and input might be valuable at times, it was rarely useful. No great effort was made to bridge this gap, apart from some late theoretical treatises, such as a memorandum of George Gemistos Plethon. Morale-building was important to the Byzantines. What has been called a liturgy of war had already appeared by the 6th century. Exhortation to Christian as opposed to ethnic solidarity was fundamental in some cases of Byzantine combat. However the efforts by such emperors as Nikephoros II Phokas (963–69) to obtain patriarchal approval for promises of salvation for those who died in combat failed; concepts of holy war were alien to the Byzantines.

Success in warfare met with both appreciation and fear. Victorious commanders might win popular adulation but they might also become objects of fear and envy – fear (especially on the part of emperors and their bureaucratic counsellors) that they might attempt to seize power for themselves. Because of their perpetual fear that generals might be tempted to revolt and covet the imperial throne for themselves, the officials of the imperial government often sought to deny them large amounts of funds and supplies and discretion and imposed rigid bureaucratic controls.

The Byzantines relied on both horse and foot. Field armies seldom exceeded 15,000 or 20,000 men, and were usually smaller. Although cavalry may have been dominant, infantry was important in many actions. Archery, especially mounted archery, gave the Byzantines an asymmetrical advantage over some Germanic opponents in the 6th-century reconquests of the era of Justinian I (527–65). Heavily armoured horse became predominant by the late 10th century. Throughout their history the Byzantines made extensive use of a combination of naval and land forces. Their extensive coastlines and islands and their maritime heritage made the naval dimension an important one in their ability to wage war. Siegecraft was a particular speciality of the Byzantines, and owed much to its Hellenistic and Roman heritage.

The zenith of Byzantine skills in actual combat, as opposed to the containment and destruction of Muslim raiders, may well have occurred in the late 10th century, contemporary with and an essential ingredient of the Byzantine reconquest of eastern Anatolian and north Syrian territories from the Muslims. This was the era of heavily armoured (cataphract) Byzantine cavalry, armoured themselves as well as their mounts, and also the era in which Byzantine expertise in shock in mounted combat peaked. One difficult aspect of such combat, as in earlier Roman and Byzantine warfare, was the coordination of horse and foot: hollow squares might be formed from which horse would sally and foot would open and then close ranks. It was easy for such formations to make mistakes that led to costly losses in men and beasts.

In the early centuries the Byzantines drew on a vast repertory of ancient and contemporary military experience from many regions, climates, and ethnic groups. They adapted manoeuvres, weapons, and techniques from the best of the array of contemporary friends and foes. What might be effective in the Balkans might be impractical in North Africa or Syria. The Byzantine Balkans, with their marshes, mountains, and severe winters and greater precipitation than Asia, offered challenges and opportunities. Booty, including prisoners, was an important aspect of warfare. Exchanges of prisoners took place from time to time. Noncombatant casualties were high, and although some effort was made to evacuate the wounded, losses from wounds were probably very high throughout Byzantine history.

Byzantine armies were not homogeneously Hellenic, for at all periods of the empire there were substantial numbers of non-Greeks serving in the armies. Latin remained the language of command until the end of the 6th century, but presumably it gave way permanently to Greek in the 7th. The core of the officers who dominated the Byzantine army and organization of warfare were of mixed Greek-Armenian background and, between the 6th and 11th centuries, largely from Anatolia. Belisarius (died c.AD 565?) was the greatest master of Byzantine warfare, for he waged war competently and successfully against the Persians in western Asia, in North Africa against the Vandals, and in Italy against the Goths.

The greatest Byzantine innovation in warfare was the invention and use of Greek fire, an igneous petroleum mixture, which is first attested in the late 7th century, although it may owe something to traditions of Hellenistic techniques. Eventually, most notably by the time of the Crusades, other peoples learned and mastered these techniques. Fortification and siegecraft consumed many financial resources as well as much mental effort. Special attention was given to problems of selecting, creating, and securing camps, a process that owed much to adaptations from earlier Roman traditions. In principle, conforming to Roman tradition, emperors ideally were soldier-emperors and leaders in war. The reality was often different.

The Byzantines relied heavily on the gathering of intelligence to aid their military and tactical decision-making and performance in warfare. They developed skills in fighting against diverse peoples in diverse terrain and weather. They made use of climate (darkness, cold weather) in fighting certain peoples. Expeditions into enemy territory involved different problems from arranging local defences against raids. Elaborate preparations were necessary for expeditions. Some extant treatises describe expeditions that included the emperor, which were, of course, very special cases.

By the middle of the 11th century the Byzantines began to lose their superiority in expertise in warfare. Innovation in technology, weapons, tactics, and in military theory took place outside the borders of the empire, which henceforth had to hire external specialists. Norman men at arms in the west and Turkic horsemen in the east simultaneously proved superior in combat by 1100. The reasons for this loss of initiative and innovation are unclear. Resort to diplomacy became even more important than before. The Byzantines drew heavily on Turkish and western manpower and specialized foreign skills in warfare in the 11th to the 15th centuries. They failed to internalize either the gunpowder revolution or newer techniques of drilling and deploying infantry that were emerging in Europe and in the Levant in the 14th and 15th centuries, such as training infantry to develop cohesive formations using the pike. This helps to explain the increasing Byzantine dependence on foreign mercenaries, although soldiers of foreign origin existed in every century of Byzantine history. Their specialized skills were valued. But mercenaries were an expensive option for the fisc and also brought in their wake political costs, for they were unpopular with many of the empire's subjects, including significant parts of the elite.

Traditions of Byzantine warfare became an important and lasting Hellenic legacy to early modern military thought, that is, in continental Europe in the 17th and 18th centuries. Even the modern term "strategy" derives from a late-18th-century inspiration from a Byzantine military treatise, the *Strategikon* of Maurice. That treatise, as well as the *Tactica* of Emperor Leo VI the Wise and some writings of emperor Nikephoros II Phokas, marked the apogee of Byzantine military writing. It is unclear to what extent later estradiots (light cavalry), who were prominent in early modern warfare of the late 15th and 16th centuries, consciously inherited and perpetuated Byzantine traditions.

WALTER E. KAEGI

See also Architecture (Fortifications), Army, Brigandage, Fire (Greek), Navy, Siegecraft

Further Reading

Bartusis, Mark C., *The Late Byzantine Army: Arms and Society, 1204–1453*, Philadelphia: University of Pennsylvania Press, 1992

Haldon, John, *State, Army, and Society in Byzantium: Approaches to Military, Social, and Administrative History, 6th–12th Centuries*, Aldershot, Hampshire: Variorum, 1995

Haldon, John, *Warfare, State and Society in the Byzantine World, 560–1204*, London: UCL Press, 1999

Kaegi, Walter E., *Army, Society and Religion in Byzantium*, London: Variorum, 1982

Kaegi, Walter E., *Some Thoughts on Byzantine Military Strategy*, Brookline, Massachusetts: Hellenic College Press, 1983

McGeer, Eric, *Sowing the Dragon's Teeth: Byzantine Warfare in the Tenth Century*, Washington, D.C.: Dumbarton Oaks, 1995

Water management

Use and distribution of water

Whenever more than a handful of human beings settle permanently in one spot the availability of water becomes one of the parameters that determines their survival. Water for drinking must be reliable and potable. Water for crops must be available at the right time and in the right quantities. For the Greeks, the availability of water is itself largely determined by the Mediterranean climatic regime and the limestone-dominated geology of Greece, which allows for the formation of many subterranean sinkholes and channels.

Perpetual streams and springs are rare, with even major rivers shrinking to trickles or dry stream beds in the summer, only to become rushing torrents when the winter rains arrive. Across the millennia the Greek farmer needed to be opportunistic with regard to the use of water. Along with wells, cisterns for catching and storing rainwater are a regular feature of ancient houses, whether they stand in town or in the country. Terracing of fields is also a product of the rainfall regime of the Mediterranean climate; it simultaneously prevents erosion and ensures that more water saturates the agricultural land. Cereals must go into the ground in the winter to take advantage of the period of maximum moisture and be harvested at the beginning of the summer. Grapes, on the other hand, need the long dry weeks to ripen and become sweet. After picking, fruit that the farmer intends to dry for raisins can safely be left to bake in the open under the sun. The chances that sudden rain will ruin the harvest are slim.

The Aegean cultures were not like the "hydraulic civilizations" of Mesopotamia and Egypt which depended on the construction and coordination of a vast network of irrigation canals and dykes. Water management, whether rural or urban, tends to be small-scale and locally controlled. A simile from Homer's *Iliad* (21. 257–59) gives a vivid picture of the typical irrigation technology of ancient and medieval Greece:

> as a man running a channel from a spring of dark water
> guides the run of the water among his plants and his gardens
> with a mattock in his hand and knocks down the blocks in the channel...

An important exception to this rule can be observed through the history of Lake Copais in Boeotia. Historically, it was more of a swamp than a continuous expanse of water, waxing and waning with the seasons. The ancient Greeks believed that the Minyans, a legendary people of the heroic age, had drained the water and turned it into arable land. When drainage operations were begun in the late 19th century, the truth behind the tradition was revealed. The lake had been drained in Mycenaean times by a series of canals and earthen dykes, reinforced by Cyclopaean masonry, which conveyed the water to natural fissures in the earth. Perhaps this work was overseen by the rulers of the citadel of Gla which overlooks the Copaic plain. There were attempts at drainage in classical and Roman times, but none was carried through to completion. Even the modern efforts were not completed until well into the 20th century.

If the Mycenaean rulers were capable of envisioning and carrying out the draining of the Copaic basin, it should not be surprising to find that they had a sophisticated infrastructure for providing for the water needs of the palaces and surrounding settlements. Large populations living in close quarters had to be provided with drinking and washing water, while waste water and sewage had to be drained away from areas of habitation. In this technology, as in so many other things, they borrowed heavily from their Minoan predecessors.

Given the high level of luxury and elegance in the palace of Knossos, it should come as no surprise that much care and ingenuity were devoted to the area of personal hygiene. This is seen most strikingly in the suite of rooms known as the Queen's Megaron. Besides the bathroom proper, furnished with a soaking tub, there was a separate chamber with an elaborate system of interconnected cisterns, drains, and sewers. This running water was apparently used for a lavatory and, perhaps, a shower (Pendlebury, 1933, p. 52). At one of the outbuildings of the palace complex, dubbed the Caravanserai, there were provisions for travellers to wash their feet and bathe in tubs filled with water heated by wood fires. Even at this level of society, however, water was not wasted: the water from the footbath flowed out into a drinking trough for animals.

Mycenaean palaces and towns have produced evidence of aqueducts and public drainage systems. The most impressive Mycenaean water projects date from the late 13th century BC. This was a time of increased fortification at major citadels such as Mycenae and Tiryns. If, as seems likely, the rulers of these towns felt the need to prepare to face external threats, their efforts to secure the water supply can be seen as part of that preparation. At Athens, Tiryns, and Mycenae tunnels or passages were opened to secret springs, so that they could be reached even in the event that the city walls were besieged. Despite all these precautions, the Mycenaean civilization collapsed in the 12th century BC. With the administrative structure of the palaces gone, the Mycenaean drains and aqueducts fell into disrepair.

The depopulation and devolution of the Dark Ages saw the loss of many of the technological achievements of the preceding centuries. Although people may have been aware of the principles behind the construction of systems for water transport and drainage, there seems to have been little incentive and/or logistical support for carrying out such projects. This situation changed in the Archaic period when many Greek cities were ruled by tyrants. Dependent on popular support in their conflicts with aristocratic factions, these despots often undertook major public works projects for the improvement of their cities. In the late 6th century BC Polycrates, the tyrant of Samos, was responsible for what Herodotus would later call three of the greatest feats of building and engineering in the Greek world: the great temple of Hera, the island's artificial harbour and breakwater, and a tunnel driven straight through a mountain to bring water to the city.

This tunnel, called the tunnel of Eupalinus after its architect, was inspired by the same desire that we saw in the Mycenaean citadels: to provide the city with a hidden and secure water source in times of siege. What sets Eupalinus' achievement apart is that he drove his tunnel straight through a mountain for approximately 1 km. Even then the water had to be brought from its source more than 800 m away through an underground conduit. Water did not flow through the tunnel itself, but through a covered conduit that ran below the level of the tunnel floor and at a steeper gradient. It is not known whether this secondary excavation was part of the original plan or was added when it became clear that the slope of the tunnel was inadequate to maintain the flow of water. How exactly the line of the tunnel was laid out and followed with such remarkable accuracy by the workmen is another mystery (Goodfield, 1964).

Although none of the other tyrants attempted anything so grandiose, many of the famous fountain houses of antiquity had their first architectural elaboration in the 7th and 6th centuries BC. For the ancient Greeks, even natural springs had an aura of sanctity about them because of their importance and rarity. Obviously a settlement could not be contemplated where there was no source of water, but the built-up area might be some distance from the spring itself, perhaps because of concerns about contamination. Transporting the water to a more convenient location became an objective. Pisistratus of Athens, for example, laid an aqueduct that ran into the Agora, as well as building Athens' famous nine-spouted fountain called Enneakrounos. The location of this fountain is still uncertain, although a contemporary fountain house was found in the southeast corner of the Agora.

Archaic and Classical fountain houses tended to be relatively simple. The first modifications to the natural spring might be simply to carve out a basin or storage cisterns from the surrounding rock. After that came the roofing over of the cisterns, and then the construction of a columnar porch under which the people drawing water might stand. Other amenities might be a parapet on which to rest one's jar, or a spout to fill it. Fountain houses, along with government buildings, a theatre, an agora, etc. were among the marks of a polis, according to Pausanias. This public supply of water had several advantages over what might be available in private homes. Well water, though fresh, was difficult to draw up and might disappear in times of drought. Runoff water was collected and stored in underground cisterns, but was used for purposes other than drinking if at all possible. By bringing water from the fountains, women (and it was almost always women who performed this task) got better-quality drinking water as well as a chance to meet friends. Many depictions on vases make it clear that going to the fountain house was a time for socializing.

Classical cities, by the end of the 6th century BC, also had provisions for draining away storm and waste water. These sewers ran in large channels through public open spaces and in smaller pipes beneath the streets of residential areas. Private houses were equipped with a small room holding a drain leading into the sewer lines. By the 4th and 3rd centuries BC, Greek latrines progressed to wooden benches or terracotta seats. Bath tubs were still free-standing containers without drainage holes, so drawing and emptying a bath must have been tedious work. Public baths had individual tubs which in some cases were filled by running water from a channel that ran by them at shoulder height. These baths were connected with gymnasia or shrines of Asclepius and thus generally for the use of men only (Crouch, 1993, pp. 26–29).

Aqueducts, fountains, and baths from the Roman period show a much higher degree of elaboration than earlier structures. Roman rule brought an end to endemic warfare, so it was possible to run above-ground aqueducts for great distances without fear of exposure to enemy forces. Large public baths open to both sexes are a prominent feature of Roman urbanism throughout the provinces. During this period fountains become nymphaea – ornate, usually multistorey constructions which were only secondarily places to get water. With their sculptural decoration, multiple fountains and pools, and rich materials they existed mostly as a stage for the display of the interplay of light, water, and stone which is such a hallmark of the architecture of the empire at its height.

As conditions deteriorated in the empire, bringing water to cities and towns over long distances became more problematic. Constantinople was largely dependent for water on an aqueduct originally built by Hadrian and restored by Valens in the 4th century AD. More aqueducts were constructed around this time, but both the capital and provincial towns became increasingly dependent on cisterns. This was especially true after the wave of destructions in the 7th century when many aqueducts were destroyed and never replaced. Urban need for water may in fact have been less in the 7th century, since by this time most of the large public baths had fallen into disuse. Declining population and rising maintenance costs were no doubt a factor in this decline, but there was also a change in attitude towards the public baths. Attendance at the baths was no longer considered part of one's daily routine but a rare luxury, or something undertaken as part of a medicinal regimen. Monasteries, on the other hand, constructed baths that were specifically associated with healing throughout the Byzantine period. During this time there was an increase in the use of water, instead of oxen, to power mills. Remains of several examples from the late 5th century AD, along with the aqueduct that brought water to them, are preserved in the Athenian Agora.

Changes in Greece's economy and society since the late 19th century have raised a whole new set of problems connected with water. The reorientation of the agricultural sector towards the commercial exports of crops such as citrus, tobacco, and cotton which require extensive irrigation has led to a depletion of groundwater and the salinization of farmland that often accompanies irrigation. The generation of hydro-electric power has resulted in the draining of many lakes. Greece's population is inadequately served by waste-water treatment plants, with the result that industrial wastes and untreated sewage have rendered the inner Saronic Gulf almost lifeless in recent years (Curtis, 1995, p. 106). Water management is a subject that will loom large in planning for future development in Greece.

BARBARA FIEDLER

See also Canals, Climate, Technology

Further Reading

Broneer, O., "A Mycenaean Fountain House", *Hesperia*, 8 (1939): pp. 317–433

Burford, Alison, *Land and Labor in the Greek World*, Baltimore: Johns Hopkins University Press, 1993

Camp, John M., *The Athenian Agora: Excavations in the Heart of Classical Athens*, London and New York: Thames and Hudson, 1986, revised 1992

Crouch, Dora P., *Water Management in Ancient Greek Cities*, New York and Oxford: Oxford University Press, 1993

Curtis, Glenn E. (editor), *Greece: A Country Study*, 4th edition, Washington, D.C.: Government Printing Office, 1995

Dickinson, Oliver, *The Aegean Bronze Age*, Cambridge and New York: Cambridge University Press, 1994

Frantz, Alison, *Late Antiquity*, AD 267–700, Princeton, New Jersey: American School of Classical Studies at Athens, 1988 (The Athenian Agora, vol. 24)

Goodfield, J., "The Tunnel of Eupalinus", *Scientific American* (June 1964): pp. 104–12

Hanson, Victor Davis, *The Other Greeks: The Family Farm and the Agrarian Roots of Western Civilization*, New York: Free Press, 1995

Karpozilos, A. *et al.*, Baths entry in *The Oxford Dictionary of Byzantium*, edited by A.P. Kazhdan, New York and Oxford: Oxford University Press, 1991

Pausanias, *Description of Greece*, translated by J.G. Frazer, 6 vols, London and New York: Macmillan, 1898, reprinted New York: Biblo and Tannen, 1965

Pendlebury, J.D.S., *A Handbook to the Palace of Minos, Knossos, with Its Dependencies*, London: Macmillan, 1933, reprinted Chicago: Ares, 1979

Rackham, O., "Observations on the Historical Ecology of Boeotia", *Annual of the British School at Athens*, 78 (1983): pp. 291–351

Symeonoglou, Sarantis, *The Topography of Thebes from the Bronze Age to Modern Times*, Princeton, New Jersey: Princeton University Press, 1985

Vermeule, Emily, *Greece in the Bronze Age*, Chicago: University of Chicago Press, 1964

Wycherley, R.E., *How the Greeks Built Cities*, 2nd edition, London: Macmillan, 1962; New York: Norton, 1976

Women

There is little certain information about women in Bronze Age Greece and Crete so that most of our knowledge of them during this period is speculative. The two main sources of information are art and the Linear B tablets.

While feminine figures play an important role in both Minoan and Mycenaean art, their identity is not clear. They may be goddesses, priestesses, nobility, or common women. It appears that in many instances females portrayed in Bronze Age Aegean art are goddesses. Feminine statues are shown adorned with snakes, birds, or floral motifs, often with arms upraised in a possible pose of prayer or benediction (the "Goddess with Upraised Arms"). One small ivory figurine from Mycenae shows two women seated together with a small child on the lap of one of them. Some scholars have interpreted this as an early portrayal of Demeter, Persephone, and Plutus. In glyptic art, especially from Crete, females are shown in the centre of outdoor religious scenes, often engaged in dances. Women were represented in the frescos that adorned houses and palaces. In some instances they are depicted gathering crocuses in idyllic scenery, while in others they are shown socializing in the company of men. In Crete they participate in scenes of ritual procession, while one fresco from Mycenae shows two females together driving a chariot.

Linear B texts, while fragmentary and of a "shopping list" nature, give clearer glimpses into the everyday lives of women: they appear as queens (*wanassa*), priestesses (*hiera*), landowners, temple servants, and slaves. While only the surface of the roles of women in Linear B has been scratched, it appears that on the Greek mainland a patriarchal system was already in place. Among women, only religious functionaries owned land. Conversely, texts from Knossos in Crete show women owning fruit orchards independently of men, possibly indicating their higher status in the wake of the Minoan civilization. In both regions female slaves were common, usually identified by a proper name and the land of origin. This may be indicative of the seizure of women as war booty as portrayed in Homer's *Iliad*.

Beginning with Homer and Hesiod, literary and historical texts and art provide information concerning the lives of women in the historical period. Unfortunately, most of these texts and images were rendered by men, and thus they offer a view of women from the male perspective. While women had extremely limited political and economic powers, they played active roles in the cultural life of ancient Greece. Prominent literary names that have survived are of the poets Sappho of Lesbos (6th century BC) and Telesilla of Argos (5th century BC).

Women were most active in the religious life of the polis. The two most important fertility rites, the Thesmophoria and the Skirophoria, were administered solely by women. Since the former was a three-day-long affair involving all Greek women (except virgins – Callimachus, fr. 63), it is evident that considerable planning was involved, all controlled by women. In Aristophanes' *Lysistrata* (640ff.) the chorus of women recounts bearing the basket in the Arrhephoria, milling flour for the Athenaion festival, "playing the bear" for Artemis at Brauron, and serving as basket-bearers in the Athenaion festival. While such roles were often reserved exclusively for the upper classes, other important religious positions were not. The priestess of Athena Nike on the Athenian Acropolis was chosen by lot from the female population of Athens. For her services she received an annual salary of 50 drachmas and the hides and legs from the public sacrifices. On the more human side of religion, literature and art show that it was women who were responsible for the care and remembrance of the dead. Women prepared corpses for burial, were the chief mourners during funeral processions, and brought offerings of garlands and funerary libations to the dead after burial (*Choephori*).

Beyond religious duties, women's lives consisted of marriage and motherhood, textiles, and household management. The clearest picture of household life comes from Xenophon's *Oeconomicus* and Lysias' *Murder of Eratosthenes*. Combining the two, a picture of married life emerges. The woman is married very young to an older husband chosen by her parents. Once married, she cares for the organization of the household, spinning and weaving, and, in the case of more affluent brides, supervises the household slaves. Women wore lead cosmetics to make themselves appear pale, the ideal shade for those expected to remain indoors. They travelled outside the house for religious events, funerals, and to meet neighbours. These forays outside the home were viewed with suspicion by men, who were apparently in chronic fear of adultery (*Eccleseazusae*). Lower-class women also worked outside the home (Demosthenes, 57. 31–35; *Thesmophoriazusae*, 446–52). Between the "respectable" and working classes were the *hetairai* (courtesans), the most famous of whom were Aspasia, Neaira, and Lais.

From the end of the 5th century BC into the 4th, women's lives became increasingly constricted. Pericles claimed that the best that could be said of any woman was that her name was never mentioned in public either for praise or blame (Thucydides, 2. 45). In the 4th century BC gynaecology, and thus women's bodies, fell increasingly into the hands of male doctors, while philosophers such as Plato ascribed the roles of midwife and mother to males and their progeny of the mind.

In the Hellenic period, while many general aspects of life such as religion and motherhood remained the same, women of all classes made greater contributions to politics, culture, and society than previously, and women experienced greater freedoms than at the end of the Classical period. In the aristocracy, women ruled as queens, either side by side with their consorts or independently. Notable at the head of dynasties were Olympias, queen of Macedon and Alexander's mother; Berenice II (3rd century BC), queen of Cyrene and Egypt; queen Arsinoë of Egypt (*c.*270 BC); and Cleopatra VII (1st century BC), queen of Egypt and final monarch of the Hellenistic dynasties.

Nonroyal women also enjoyed social, legal, and economic benefits in the Hellenistic age. In the 2nd century BC a woman called Archippe was publicly honoured in Cyme (Asia Minor) for financial contributions made to the polis (Pleket, no. 3), while an inscription from Histria records the existence of a female archon (ibid., no. 2). In the 1st century BC Phile of Priene held the office of *stephanephoros* ("garland bearer") for building, at personal expense, the city aqueduct and reservoir (*Inschriften von Priene*, 208). Economic independence, if not wealth, was possible for lower-class women. Documents preserved from Egypt reveal: a marriage contract sworn between Heraclides and Demetria to regulate their claims to property and means of redress in case of violation (*P. Elephantine*, 1); a lawsuit enacted by Philista, "a working woman", in a case of personal injury (*P. Enteuxis*, 82); and the complaint of one father whose daughter Nike was expected to support him financially through her labour (ibid. 26).

In the cultural sphere, this was the age of the female intelligentsia. Poets such as Erinna (4th century BC) and Nossis (3rd century BC) were likened to Sappho (Antipater, 9. 26), while Aristodama of Smyrna was made *proxenos* ("patroness"), citizen, and benefactor of Lamia for her verses (W. Dittenberger, *Sylloge Inscriptionum Graecarum*, 1915–24, 3. 532). Anyte of Tegea, among other works, wrote epigrams for dead maidens, noting their wisdom as well as their beauty (*Anthologia Palatina*, 7). Some women became painters, with Laia of Cyzicus renowned as the finest portrait painter of her day (Pliny, *Naturalis Historia*, 35. 147ff.). In philosophy, women studied at Plato's Academy (Diogenes Laertius, 3. 46, 4. 2, 6. 96ff.), while in the 4th century BC women began formal practice of medicine (Hyginus, *Fabula*, 274. 10–11).

Like the Hellenistic age, the Byzantine period is punctuated by prominent women in politics and the intelligentsia. Earlier female aristocrats, such as St Helena and Pulcheria, functioned mainly through the offices of their male relatives (the emperors Constantine I and Theodosius II respectively). Empress Theodora (*c.*497–548), wife of Justinian, was the first woman co-autocrat of Byzantium, with her own functions within government and the power to legislate reforms. Many of these reforms benefited women, such as an edict of 535, interdicting procurement and brothels in all major cities of the empire. At the pinnacles of female political power were empress Irene (fl. 800), and Anna Dalassene (fl.1090). The former, having blinded her son and rival to the throne, ruled as sole autocrat of Byzantium, prompting the coronation of Charlemagne in the West. Dalassene was chief adviser to her son, emperor Alexios I Komnenos (1081–1118), and she ruled Byzantium with full administrative powers when her son was on campaign.

Female intellectuals were rare but significant. The most famous is Hypatia of Alexandria (*c.*AD 370–415), scientist, mathematician, and Neoplatonic philosopher. In the 12th century lived Anna Komnene, the only female historian of the Byzantine era, who wrote the *Alexiad*, her father's biography.

The Church Fathers of the now Christian empire proclaimed that women were inferior and weak; even sins acquired feminine personifications (Neophytos Enkleistos). Thus women were barred from priestly functions and teaching. The ideal role of woman was, of course, wife and mother, with this latter occupation receiving high praise in panegyrics from such notables as Theodore of Stoudios and Psellos. While virginity was considered a high virtue, its inappropriate loss was not as severely punished as in the days of Solon; a girl who lost her virginity to a man other than her betrothed could simply be repudiated by the bridegroom (Leo VI, *novels* 93).

Women wielded considerable economic power at all levels of society for which data exist. From the days of Theodora, sisters shared equal inheritance rights with brothers, and widows kept full control of their dowries. From the 11th century at least a significant portion of legal cases concerned women's control of their property (Laiou, 1992, vol. 1, p. 239). Abbesses who wrote typika (or rules) for their monasteries had full economic powers and deliberative control (ibid p. 242). As for employment, although women were expected to work only in textiles, it is evident that they were occupied in other fields. One typikon of the Pantokrator monastery in Constantinople refers to female doctors and nurses (ibid, p. 245), while the 14th-century traveller Ibn Battuta wrote that most artisans and merchants in the Constantinople bazaar were women.

In most respects, Greek women's lives today differ little from those of other western women. They have the right to education, property, and equal representation in law. Specifics of life, as always, are determined by class and region of habitation. The lives of upper-class women and villagers are more restricted before marriage than those of the lower classes and urban residents. A "proper" upper-class young woman travels with a chaperone until she is married. After marriage, and especially after divorce, however, these women are free to travel and spend their time as they will. While divorce is a more difficult matter for less affluent rural denizens, marriage does nevertheless allow a new freedom for women. Even adultery may be acceptable should the husband not be present for extensive periods of time (Loizos and Papataxiarchis, 1991, p. 229).

Bourgeois and urban women travel, socialize, work, study, and live freely although, as in the villages, they usually live with their families until marriage. Since approximately half the population of Greece now resides in Athens, most Greek women have considerable freedom (although disapproval of this "wanton" lifestyle is often expressed when city-dwellers return to the family village).

Two aspects of women's lives in Greece are distinctive from other western cultures. First is the continued use of the dowry (despite 20th-century legal sanctions) given by the bride or her family to the groom upon marriage. The bride's age and social position, especially relative to the groom's, determine the size of the dowry. In rural communities the dowry often takes the form of a house (Dubisch, in Loizos and Papataxiarchis, 1991, p. 36) located in the wife's area of residence. Thus, while Greece itself is essentially patriarchal (if not sexist) in its attitudes towards women, the dowry creates a matrilocal structure whereby women have greater familial support after marriage than men necessarily do.

Second is the general segregation of the sexes, especially after marriage, in non-urban areas. As in previous ages, outside the home is male territory, notably the *kafeneia* (cafés) where women are very rarely found. The household is feminine space, where women with female friends and family spend both free and working hours. Thus, women have the opportunity for equally fulfilling social interactions and community; they are simply less visible to the casual observer.

STEPHANIE LYNN BUDIN

See also Adultery, Children, Divorce, Dowry, Gender, Marriage, Men

Further Reading
Bridge, Antony, *Theodora: Portrait in a Byzantine Landscape*, Chicago: Academy Chicago, 1993
Demand, Nancy, *Birth, Death, and Motherhood in Classical Greece*, Baltimore: Johns Hopkins University Press, 1994
Fantham, Elaine *et al.*, *Women in the Classical World: Image and Text*, Oxford and New York: Oxford University Press, 1994
James, Liz (editor), *Women, Men and Eunuchs: Gender in Byzantium*, London and New York: Routledge, 1997
Laiou, Angeliki E., *Gender, Society and Economic Life in Byzantium*, Aldershot, Hampshire: Variorum, 1992
Loizos, Peter and Evthymios Papataxiarchis (editors), *Contested Identities: Gender and Kinship in Modern Greece*, Princeton, New Jersey: Princeton University Press, 1991
Pleket, H.W. (editor), *Epigraphica*, vol. 2: *Texts on the Social History of the Greek World*, Leiden: Brill, 1969
Pomeroy, Sarah B., *Goddesses, Whores, Wives, and Slaves: Women in Classical Antiquity*, New York: Schocken, 1975; London: Hale, 1976

Women's cults

In antiquity women played a significant role in religion, and the existence of female divinities in the Greek pantheon has led many scholars to investigate further the relation between mortal women and their gods and goddesses. Some cults were exclusively practised by women, whereas in others women participated by fulfilling certain roles. Not surprisingly, many women's cults were closely associated with female divinities.

The Brauronia, originally a local festival at Brauron in Attica, became associated with the goddess Artemis. Girls between 5 and 10 years of age were sent by their mothers in procession to Artemis, the eternal virgin goddess. Artemis is also connected with childbirth, and therefore many women's cults are related to her. According to evidence from Plutarch (*Aristides*, 20. 6), young women would make premarital offerings to Artemis, a goddess associated with transition in a woman's life. Women participated fully in cults that honoured Demeter. Besides the Eleusinian mysteries the festival of Thesmophoria was widely celebrated among women, who performed fertility rites. The festival took place in the autumn and was open to women only. Demeter, together with her daughter Persephone, and Dionysus were worshipped at the festival of Haloa in December. Demeter, the goddess of grain, was often worshipped with Dionysus, the god of wine. In Arcadia she was worshipped with Poseidon. In later times she was syncretized with Gaia and Rhea, or Cybele.

Women played an important role in civic festivals. In the Panathenaia they were the ones who wove and presented the *peplos* (a special embroidered robe) to Athena, and on the night before the procession that held central place in the festival they performed ritual cries and choral dances. The Athenian festivals occurred in early and midsummer in the following order: first the Plynteria and Kallynteria (cleansing and beautifying festival), then the Skira (threshing festival), and finally the Panathenaia. The Arrhephoria was a mystic festival in honour of Athena that took place in midsummer parallel to the Panathenaia. Four girls of noble families had to spend some time at the temple of Athena: two of them had to present to the goddess the *peplos* that the women had woven, and the other two received coffers from the priestess, the contents of which could not be revealed, and carried them in the great procession.

Many women's cults had a strong local element, such as the cult of Hera, the goddess of marriage and domestic life, in places like Argos and Samos. The cult of Dionysus was particularly associated with women. Dionysiac orgies were celebrated on Mount Parnassus by cult associations of women, and were later incorporated in the cult of Apollo at the same place. In later times, especially in Hellenistic Alexandria, women performed lamentation rites for Adonis after the celebration of the wedding of Adonis and Aphrodite. The Adonia was also celebrated in Classical Athens in the spring. Rituals of incubation, like those connected with Asclepius, were also popular among women, but were not exclusive to them.

Women also played an important role in official and mystic cults as priestesses. (It should be noted that there was no such thing as a caste of priests or priestesses.) Many priesthoods were filled by women only, mainly for the cults of goddesses. There were various rules as to the status and age of a priestess. The priestess of Athena was a married woman, whereas virginity was required for priestesses of Hestia. Pythia was the name given to the priestesses of Apollo who played an important role in Greek history by giving the oracular response on many important public and private matters.

Heroines held an important position in women's cults. Various phases of life involving marriage, pregnancy, and children were associated with specific cults of heroines, the most notable being those that feature in myths around the Olympian pantheon, such as Ariadne, Semele, and Iphigeneia. The clothes of women who died in childbirth would be dedicated to Iphigeneia at Brauron, but of those who survived to Artemis. There were other cults addressed to less well-known heroines in myth, such as the celebration of Hecale in the Attic deme of the same name, a heroine mostly known from the cycle of myths around Theseus. At Olympia Pelops and Hippodameia were honoured in an agonistic setting. Last but not least comes the expression of religious feeling towards a divinity, or often in heroic cults, in choral contests as an agonistic ritual.

Women played an important role in the spread of Christianity, and although there are no women priests in the Orthodox Church, women have filled various offices in the structure of the Church, for example, as deaconesses. Many have followed the monastic life, like men, without being priests. Just as there are spiritual "Fathers", so there are also "Mothers", although most women religious lived in monastic communities rather than in the desert. The ascetic life is presented by many Fathers of the Church as a model for life in the household, denoting the sacrifice needed.

Many modern Greek folk customs exhibit the influence of antiquity and many festivals are celebrated exclusively or predominantly by women. There are many practices associated with the cult of the Virgin Mary in which women play an important role. Their importance in certain cults, and particularly how they are represented in various customs, varies from place to place. Although certain rites of passage, like marriage and death, have official ceremonies within the Church, there are many customs forming part of the local cult that are practised by women only. Every village in Mani or Crete has its *moirologistris*, who will perform rites of lamentation, beyond those at the official service in the church, sometimes with the tolerance of the Church but often without it.

ANDROMACHE KARANIKA-DIMAROGONA

See also Festivals, Orgiastic Cults, Priesthood, Religion, Women

Further Reading

Brown, Peter, *The World of Late Antiquity*, London: Thames and Hudson, and New York: Harcourt Brace, 1971, reprinted New York: Norton, 1989

Burkert, Walter, *Greek Religion: Archaic and Classical*, Oxford: Blackwell, and Cambridge, Massachusetts: Harvard University Press, 1985

Burkert, Walter, *Ancient Mystery Cults*, Cambridge, Massachusetts: Harvard University Press, 1987

Cantarella, Eva, *Pandora's Daughters: The Role and Status of Women in Greek and Roman Antiquity*, Baltimore: Johns Hopkins University Press, 1987

Clark, Gillian, *Women in Late Antiquity: Pagan and Christian Lifestyles*, Oxford: Clarendon Press, and New York: Oxford University Press, 1993

Detienne, Marcel, "The Violence of Wellborn Ladies: Women in the Thesmophoria" in *The Cuisine of Sacrifice among the Greeks*, edited by Marcel Detienne and Jean-Pierre Vernant, Chicago: University of Chicago Press, 1989

Deubner, Ludwig, *Attische Feste*, Berlin: Keller, 1932, reprinted Hildesheim: Olms, 1964

Fantham, Elaine *et al.*, *Women in the Classical World: Image and Text*, Oxford and New York, Oxford University Press, 1994

Larson, Jennifer, *Greek Heroine Cults*, Madison: University of Wisconsin Press, 1995

Lefkowitz, M., "Women in the Panathenaic and Other Festivals" in *Worshipping Athena: Panathenaia and Parthenon*, edited by Jenifer Neils, Madison: University of Wisconsin Press, 1996

Woodworking

Ancient Greek carpentry is not well known because of the lack of permanently dry or permanently waterlogged conditions that favour the preservation of wooden objects. Carpentry, moreover, is not a craft that lends itself to written description. Theophrastus wrote much on the choice and preparation of timber, but this amounts to little more than the lore which carpenters thought fit to relate to him; much of it seems to be nonsense or misunderstood.

Greek buildings were walled with stone or mud brick, but sockets reveal something of the missing timbers. Almost every building had a timber roof, often upper floors, and usually joinery (in windows and doors), none of which survive. Temple roofs could be mighty timber structures, but involved timbers merely resting on each other; internal walls reduced the span and usually made it unnecessary to use timbers more than about 10 m long. Sophisticated carpentry with tension-transmitting joints, of the kind found in Western cathedral roofs, was apparently unknown. The oldest surviving, still functional timbers are the original wooden blocks that join the column-drums of the Parthenon and prevent them from disconnecting in an earthquake. Occasional timber elements survive in Roman buildings.

Furniture, as known from vase painting, was rich and varied, at least among the well-to-do, but there is little evidence of its construction. Musical-instrument-making involved complex woodworking: a lyre, for example, was a clever piece of miniature engineering. Military equipment, especially artillery, could involve massive timber structures.

Our knowledge of Greek shipbuilding comes from underwater excavation of the wrecks of cargo ships (not triremes, which had a positive buoyancy and thus never sank). Ancient Greek shipbuilding was as complex and sophisticated as any that the world has seen. As with other ancient ships, the hull was built as a shell of planks and the ribs added later. The planks were ingeniously and laboriously joined edge-to-edge by hundreds of tenons hidden in their thickness. As in all subsequent ages, the size of ships was limited by the length of the longest tree. Timber was usually brought from a distance: it is unlikely that Greek shipbuilding was ever on a scale which used timber faster than the growth of trees could replace it.

Timber shipbuilding continued into the Byzantine period and beyond. It became assimilated to northern European methods of construction, the skeleton being built first and the planks then added. In this form it still continues on the Greek islands, and on a larger scale in western Turkey.

The craft of coopering is north European, and reached Greece in the Middle Ages, when barrels replaced amphorae and pithoi for storing wine, and to some extent oil. Barrels were often prefabricated in Venice or elsewhere and assembled in Greece from loose staves and heads. The Cretan style of watermill, with its elaborate carved turbine, is probably a medieval invention.

Timber-framed building was known to the Minoans, but probably not in Classical and Hellenistic Greece. Timber-framed houses, with overhanging upper storeys and brick or stone infill, are found in parts of northern Greece and the islands. They are mainly urban – there are good examples in Siatista (Macedonia) and Chania and Herakleion (Crete) – and appear to be of the 18th and 19th centuries. In remote country districts outhouses with earth-fast posts and woven wattle walls are still to be seen. Timbers are often built into stone or mud-brick walls as reinforcement. Tile-covered timber roofs of the 19th and early 20th centuries often follow a Roman pattern; there are some large examples on warehouses in Crete. Timber is not often a medium for architecture or decoration in ordinary houses: exceptions are house doors, and the magnificent carved and painted house interiors of the island of Karpathos.

Surviving furniture begins with the cypress chests made in Sphakia (Crete) for export in the 15th and 16th centuries, and now to be seen in churches and museums all over Europe. The icon painter's craft begins with the joining of pieces of board (usually cypress timber) edge-to-edge with hidden nails to form a panel. In a few churches an ancient iconostasis survives as a monument of fine joinery and woodcarving.

OLIVER RACKHAM

See also Architecture (Domestic), Furniture, Ships and Shipping

Further Reading
Casson, Lionel, *Ships and Seamanship in the Ancient World*, Princeton, New Jersey: Princeton University Press, 1971, reprinted Baltimore: Johns Hopkins University Press, 1995

Hodge, Trevor A., *The Woodwork of Greek Roofs*, Cambridge: Cambridge University Press, 1960

Marsden, E.W., *Greek and Roman Artillery: Historical Development*, Oxford: Clarendon Press, 1969

Meiggs, Russell, *Trees and Timber in the Ancient Mediterranean World*, Oxford: Clarendon Press, 1982

World War I 1914–1918

The history of Greece's participation in World War I is inextricably linked with the first phase of the national schism. As the Great War broke out in the summer of 1914, Greece had only been at peace for a year, following the end (in summer 1913) of the highly successful Balkan Wars, during which it had almost doubled in population and size.

With the European conflict under way in August 1914, the Greek leaders disagreed as to the course the country should follow. The prime minister, Eleftherios Venizelos, who commanded a substantial majority in parliament, was in favour of entering the war on the side of the Entente. He was convinced that the Entente would eventually be victorious. In any event, it was clear that Greece, a maritime country, was not strong enough to withstand British and French naval power in the Mediterranean and was therefore easily susceptible to Entente pressure. This was a fact that had been demonstrated repeatedly by the naval blockades of the country during the 19th century.

On the other hand, king Constantine I had studied in the German Military Academy and was an honorary field marshal of the German army; he was a firm believer in Germany's military might. There was also a dynastic link with the German royal family: Constantine's wife, Sophia, was the kaiser's sister. All the above made credible at the time the allegation that in August 1914 he offered the kaiser the services of Greece, though little evidence of this has been found. It is clear that, personal preferences aside, Constantine did favour neutrality, in the belief that Greece's interests as well as those of the Greek populations of the Ottoman empire would be better served by this course of action. The division between the king and his prime minister was to persist and fester, with disastrous consequences.

In any event, in September 1914 under the premiership of Venizelos (and initially with the consent of the king) Greece offered to join the Entente. The offer was rejected by all three powers: Britain wished to avoid provoking the Ottoman empire (at the time neutral) into joining the Central Powers; France reserved the right to accept the offer at a later stage; and Russia was prepared only to accept any help that Greece could offer to Serbia. The result was that initially Greece stayed formally neutral; yet, even with the best intentions, this neutrality was increasingly difficult to maintain in the face of the unravelling of events in the region and the world.

The Ottoman empire entered the war on the side of the Central Powers in November 1914; nevertheless, the main opponent for Greece was not Ottoman Turkey but Bulgaria, which remained out of the war for another year, making any decision on the participation of Greece in the war more difficult. Both Greece and Bulgaria were wooed by both sides, but both bided their time.

During the last months of 1914 and the first months of 1915 the struggle between Venizelos and Constantine intensified, centring around the participation of the Greek military in the Dardanelles campaign planned by the Entente. In return for joining the Entente, Greece was allowed to occupy northern Epirus and was offered unspecified gains in Asia Minor after the war. Britain also promised to discuss the future of the island of Cyprus, inhabited by a large Greek majority.

Venizelos, initially with the consent of the king and the crown council, had offered the Entente a Greek army corps for the Dardanelles operation; when later on Constantine changed his mind (influenced by the views of his chief of staff, Ioannis Metaxas), Venizelos scaled down the offer to a division, in an attempt to regain royal assent for Greek participation. This was not forthcoming. In any event, from the first months of 1915, the island of Lemnos was used as a base by the Entente forces for the Dardanelles campaign, even without Greek participation in the operation. At this point the disagreement between king Constantine and prime minister Venizelos on the question of maintaining neutrality or entering the war on the side of the Entente Powers became acute and sparked off the government crises of 1915.

Venizelos was dismissed in March 1915 but was then returned to office with a comfortable majority in the elections of June 1915. Following the mobilization of the Bulgarian army in September 1915, Venizelos persuaded the king to order the mobilization of the Greek army and invited the Entente to land forces (later to be dubbed the "gardeners of Salonika") in Thessalonica, in the north of Greece, in a desperate attempt to help Serbia; the plan was carried out initially with the consent of the king, who, however, was later once more to change his mind.

On 4 October 1915 Bulgaria declared war on the Entente and attacked Serbia; Greece was still bound in alliance with Serbia under the terms of the treaty of 1913, though it had refused to come to Serbia's aid when a European power (Austria-Hungary) had attacked it. Now that Bulgaria had attacked Serbia, the conflict was assuming a Balkan dimension. Venizelos was in favour of coming to the aid of Serbia, and even secured the assent of the Greek parliament to this end, but the next day he was again dismissed by the king, who also dissolved parliament. A government controlled by the palace was set up. It declared a benevolent neutrality towards the Entente; it also declared that the 1913 treaty of alliance with Serbia applied only to a purely intra-Balkan conflict and not to a war where a Great Power was involved. Subsequently no Greek troops were allowed to move in aid of Serbia. That remained the case even when Britain, in a desperate last bid to help Serbia, offered Greece the cession of Cyprus in return for

its immediate participation in the war; Zaimis, the prime minister at the time, refused the offer, which was never repeated. With Greek forces unavailable, the small Entente forces in Thessalonica were unsuccessful in their offensive; the Bulgarian and Austrian forces soon overpowered Serbian resistance and occupied Serbia. The inability of the Entente to help Serbia undermined Greek confidence in it, as did reports about the treaty of London (April 1915), by which the Entente ceded the Dodecanese islands (claimed by Greece) to Italy, promised to Italy territory in Asia Minor (where large Greek populations were present), and effected a partition of Albania most favourable to Italy; further demands for the evacuation of northern Epirus (where Greek troops were replaced by Italians) did little to shore up Greek confidence in the Entente. Further Entente actions such as the demand for all Greek troops in Greece to be moved to the Peloponnese, for war materiel to be handed over, and for a change of government in Athens as well as the obvious failure of the Dardanelles campaign (which was eventually wound up in January 1916) added to Greek doubts.

Venizelos's Liberals abstained from the elections called for December 1915. The (royalist) Populist Party secured a very large majority and another government controlled by the palace was set up; Greece continued to remain formally neutral, but the Athens government allowed the German and Bulgarian forces to occupy Fort Rupel and the region of Kavalla, ordering the Greek 4th Army Corps in the region not to resist. Subsequently, several thousand Greek officers and men of the 4th Greek Army Corps spent the rest of the war as "guests" in Gerlach, Germany. The Athens government also had to allow the landing on the island of Corfu of the remnants of the Serbian army evacuated by Entente ships from the Adriatic coast after the collapse of Serbia, though it later refused to allow their transport overland to Thessalonica, to join the Anglo-French forces stationed there. Greek neutrality was becoming increasingly threadbare.

In October 1916 Venizelos left Athens and went to Crete; from there he issued a proclamation to the Greeks, inviting them to help "save what could still be saved" and landed in Thessalonica. There he put himself at the head of the national defence movement (*Ethniki Amyna*) and formed the provisional government of Thessalonica. This duly declared war on Germany and Bulgaria; but the Entente followed an ambiguous policy, supporting the provisional government, but not actually extending formal international recognition to it.

Between October 1916 and June 1917 Greece was divided in two and in a state of civil war: the north of the country, most of the islands, and Crete were under the provisional government under Venizelos; the south of mainland Greece and the Peloponnese were under the control of the king and his government. In both parts of Greece opponents were persecuted. In Thessalonica the national defence government began organizing an army, drawing from the manpower available to it in the parts of Greece it controlled, with the aim of participating as quickly as possible in the war effort of the Entente. The army used numbers of Venizelist officers who joined it, as well as numerous volunteers who travelled to the north of Greece to join up, often driven to do so by the excesses of the royalists or the oppression and even pogroms Venizelists had to suffer in the south.

The conditions deteriorated further with the abortive Entente attempt to depose the king by force in December 1916 and the subsequent blockade of the part of Greece controlled by the royalists; Piraeus, the largest port of Greece, was also occupied. In June 1917 the Entente presented an ultimatum to Constantine, requesting his abdication. On 12 June 1917 Constantine appointed his second son, Alexander, in his place (but did not formally abdicate) and left the country. A largely French force extended the Allied occupation from Piraeus to Athens and deported some staunch royalists (including Ioannis Metaxas) to Corsica. By the end of June 1917 Greece was forcibly reunited, with Venizelos as its prime minister. It declared war on the Central Powers and mobilized, offering 12 divisions for the Thessalonica front, provided they could be armed by the Entente; but six months elapsed before the Allies could provide the necessary equipment. Nevertheless, by late spring 1918 around 250,000 Greeks were fighting alongside French, British, and Serbian forces in the front to the north and east of Thessalonica, facing Bulgarian and German armies.

The Greek forces played an important role in the Allied offensive that began on 15 September 1918. The offensive was a success: the front was rolled back, the Bulgarian and German armies collapsed, and the Allied forces pursued them into Bulgaria and Serbia. In little more than two weeks Bulgaria was asking for an armistice. Six weeks after the beginning of the offensive, both Bulgaria and Turkey had capitulated, virtually the whole of Serbia was recovered, and the position of the Central Powers was precarious. This operation, later described as the Allied drive into "Germany's soft underbelly", helped significantly to end the war. Strategically, it was also to colour German and Allied thinking in World War II: in the spring of 1941, with the war well under way, the German intervention in the southern Balkan region was partly a result of the fear of a repetition of the events of the previous war and an attempt to forestall the creation of another Thessalonica front.

Despite difficulties, Greece did find itself on the winning side at the end of the war, with additional territory allocated to it in western and eastern Thrace and Asia Minor. Indeed, the treaty of Sèvres and the treaty of Neuilly, which formally ended the war for the Ottoman empire and Bulgaria respectively, almost spelt for Greece the realization of the Great Idea, with Greece becoming a country spanning "two continents and five seas". Yet, as was the case in Western Europe, the postwar settlement was not to last.

GEORGE KAZAMIAS

See also Sèvres (Treaty of)

Further Reading

Calvocoressi, Peter *et al.*, *Greece and Great Britain during World War I*, Thessalonica: Institute for Balkan Studies, 1985

Dakin, Douglas *The Unification of Greece, 1770–1923*, London: Benn, and New York: St Martin's Press, 1972

Leon, George B., *Greece and the Great Powers, 1914–1917*, Thessalonica: Institute for Balkan Studies, 1974

Petsales-Diomedis, Nicholas, *Greece at the Paris Peace Conference, 1919*, Thessalonica: Institute for Balkan Studies, 1978

Theodoulou, Christos, *Greece and the Entente, August 1, 1914–September 25, 1916*, Thessalonica: Institute for Balkan Studies, 1971

World War II 1939–1945

Prior to the war Greece was under the ultra-conservative dictatorship of prime minister Ioannis Metaxas and king George II. The main objective of the dictatorship was to crush labour movements and liberal left-wing parties. Although Metaxas's style of government was similar to Mussolini's Italy and Hitler's Germany, ideologically Metaxas embraced the Greek monarchy, an institution supported by Great Britain, and Greece sided with the Allies (British Empire, France, later the USA) against the Axis powers of Europe (Nazi Germany, fascist Italy) and their satellite countries, including Bulgaria, Croatia, Hungary, Romania, and Slovakia. Metaxas's dictatorship, which was established on 4 August 1936, suspended the Greek constitution and dissolved parliament, consequently resulting in the suppression of civil liberties, as well as the prosecution of liberal and left-wing social activists.

On 28 October 1940 fascist Italy declared war on Greece by launching an invasion from Albania, a country already under the occupation of Italian armed forces. Italy's invasion had been approved by Hitler in order (*a*) to prevent the establishment of Allied forces in Greece, which could have strategic importance in the Balkan area, and (*b*) to facilitate his military campaigns in North Africa. The efforts of the Italian army to conquer Greece failed. By 2 November 1940 the Greek army had evicted the Italian invaders and by March 1941 the Greeks had advanced deep into Albania.

On 6 April 1941 the German army intervened to assist the Italian forces. The invasion came from Bulgaria and Yugoslavia to destroy the Greek armed forces, crush all British forces in Greece, and secure the south flank of the Balkans from Allied attacks, while the Nazis invaded the Soviet Union. Many of the Greek government leaders, including king George II himself, and units of the Greek army and navy, escaped to the Middle East, notably Egypt, where they established a government in exile.

On 28 April 1941 the Nazis established a Greek government of collaboration in Athens, to have more effective control of the enslaved Greeks and eventually prevent movements of national liberation. The Greek army general George Tsolakoglou was appointed by the Nazis as the leader of the quisling government and Colonel Angelos Everet as the commander of the police forces. The occupying forces destroyed the country's economy, taxed and terrorized the Greek people, and seized their food supplies. Consequently, over 250,000 Greeks died from starvation.

After the oppressive triple occupation and the establishment of a Greek-German government of collaboration, national resistance (*Ethniki Antistasi*) movements were organized with the help of the Allies, and England in particular. On 27 September 1941 the *Ethniko Apeleftherotiko Metopo* (EAM, the National Liberation Front) was organized with the cooperation and participation of centre-left Greek political parties (*a*) to liberate Greece from the Axis armed forces, (*b*) to hold free elections after independence without foreign intervention, and (*c*) to establish a people's government without a king. The Communist Party was the nucleus of the movement and provided leadership and central planning.

Another but smaller organization of the resistance movement was the *Ethnikos Dimokratikos Ellinikos Syndesmos*

(EDES, the National Democratic Hellenic Union) under the leadership of Colonel Napoleon Zervas. This organization, whose objectives were poorly defined, was ineffective as a political and military force and on occasions it established policies of coexistence with the Nazis. Other smaller resistance groups under Britain's Special Operations Executive (SOE), a wartime intelligence and sabotage agency, played an important role in collecting intelligence for Allied forces and committing acts of sabotage against the Axis.

Although the participants of the national resistance came from all socioeconomic backgrounds, the movement was strongest among the middle classes (e.g. civil servants, professionals, merchants, shopkeepers) in the urban areas, and among the wealthy peasants in the rural areas. Many leadership positions in the EAM went to left-wing or liberal professionals who were motivated by patriotism, as well as values of social justice. The communists made up approximately 15 per cent of the leadership and rank and file of the EAM/ELAS. Women also played an important role in the resistance movement as participants in combat as well as providers of medical aid, information, supplies, and ammunition.

The EAM became the most popular resistance movement by building a firm political and economic infrastructure to deal not only with the Axis occupation, but with other social problems including hunger, social inequality, illiteracy, and women's issues. On 12 April 1942 EAM organized the first labour strike in Athens and on 22 May of the same year entrusted Ares Velouchiotis (the nom de guerre adopted by Thanasis Klaras), a non-commissioned officer in the Greek army, to organize the first team of the *Ethnikos Laikos Apeleftherotikos Stratos* (ELAS, the National Popular Liberation Army) – the military wing of the EAM (National Liberation Front). By the early part of 1943 the EAM/ELAS movement increased rapidly and demonstrated its strength, not only by military operations against Axis armies, but also through organized labour strikes in large Greek cities and the establishment of social and educational programmes in liberated territories. More than 2,150,000 men and women (approximately 30 per cent of the population) were active members of EAM/ELAS auxiliary organizations, including EPON (Panhellenic Organization of Youth), *Ethniki Allilegie* (National Solidarity), a charitable organization, and PEEA (Panhellenic Committee of National Liberation) to serve as a temporary government in liberated Greek territories. Through PEEA, EAM empowered women with the right to vote for the first time in Greek history.

The rapid growth of the EAM/ELAS movement created frustration among the occupying Axis armies and the "collaborationist" government of Greece. In April 1943 the Nazis appointed Ioannis Rallis as prime minister of the quisling Greek government to suppress resistance movements. Rallis and the Nazis organized the Greek Security Battalions (*Tagmata Asphalias*) to counter EAM/ELAS forces. The battalions consisted of more than 20,000 men who were active in large cities and the Peloponnese. Their main functions were to minimize Nazi casualties and carry out reprisals against the civilian population sympathetic to the resistance movement.

The Security Battalions consisted of ex-officers and enlisted men of the Greek army, as well as civilians, with ultra-right-wing leanings, many of whom were members of pre-World War II Greek fascist organizations. The majority of the collaborators were influenced by Nazi propaganda claiming that all of EAM/ELAS members and their supporters were communists who had to be eliminated. It has been estimated that about 10 per cent of the Greek population collaborated or were sympathetic to the occupying Axis forces.

By October 1943 ELAS had emerged as the only effective and disciplined military organization under the supreme command of a Greek army officer, Stephanos Sarafis. In the summer of 1944 ELAS had about 80,000 regular troops and over 40,000 reservists. They participated in more than 600 battles causing enemy troops many casualties, including 21,800 dead, 8276 wounded, and 6370 taken prisoner. The heavy casualties inflicted on the Axis resulted in enemy reprisals against Greek citizens. More than 50,000 Greeks were executed by the occupying Axis armies and their Greek collaborators. Executions of Greek citizens by the Axis forces resulted in counter-reprisals against enemy collaborators by vengeful relatives of victims.

During their three and a half years of military action, Greek resistance organizations, and EAM/ELAS in particular, made at least five major contributions to the war against the Axis powers: (1) Through labour strikes and military operations the resistance movement forced the Nazis to abandon their plans for recruiting Greek citizens to work in German industry or to serve in Nazi auxiliary miliary units outside Greece. (2) Greek resistance forces preoccupied and effectively fought more than 300,000 enemy troops who could have been used against Allied forces in other fronts. (3) Through intelligence operations Greek resistance groups kept the Allied command in the Middle East informed of Nazi movements that could launch a surprise attack against Allied forces in North Africa. (4) The Greek resistance forces obtained or destroyed many thousands of tons of enemy ships and supplies, including ammunition, medicine, food, and clothing. (5) With the capitulation of Italy on 8 September 1943 leaders of the Greek resistance persuaded the Italian army division Pinerolo, which was serving as an occupying force in Greece at that time, to surrender to ELAS forces. The commander of the Pinerolo division, General Adolfo Infante, signed an agreement with ELAS leaders to recognize his unit of 12,000 men as an Allied force. On 14 October 1943 the Pinerolo division was disarmed by the ELAS commander, Ares Velouchiotis. These Italian soldiers participated in ELAS combat missions against Nazi troops, intelligence operations, and transportation of supplies.

After the withdrawal of the Axis forces from Greece in October 1944, the political aims and objectives of EAM/ELAS forces to participate in Greece's post-liberation politics and economic reconstruction were challenged by the Allies. The British, who feared that the popular EAM/ELAS forces would form a post-war leftist government without a king, intervened immediately to demobilize ELAS, form a post-liberation Greek government representing pro-monarchist and ultra-right-wing conservative parties, hinder the process of bringing traitors and collaborators to trial for war crimes, and organize a post-liberation Greek army of right-wing officers and enlisted men, many of whom had served in the pro-Nazi Security Battalions. These armed forces came under the tutelage of the British devoted to the palace, anti-communist to the point of fanaticism, with little respect for democratic procedures.

In December 1944 ELAS units and British forces accompanied by pro-monarchist Greek army units clashed in Athens, resulting in the death of 17,000 combatants and civilians. The ELAS army, which consisted of many thousands of non-proletarian resistance fighters of peasant origin, became fragmented with the unfolding of political events. Most of the ELAS leaders decided in favour of peaceful solutions and not to continue the war, this time, against the British and the ultra-conservative government in Athens. They ultimately realized that post-war Greece was to remain under Britain's sphere of influence.

With the return of a pro-monarchist and vengeful right-wing government to power, members of EAM/ELAS forces were labelled as communists (the leftist bad guys), antinationalists, and were excluded from civil service jobs and the armed forces. Many thousands were unjustly terrorized by paramilitary right-wing groups, imprisoned, tortured, sent into exile, or tried in military courts and executed by army firing squads. The commanders of ELAS forces, unlike other successful commanders of the victorious Allied armies, were discredited and prosecuted. Rather than falling into the hands of his former enemies – ex-Nazi collaborators – the pioneer commander of ELAS, Ares Velouchiotis, committed suicide. The Supreme Commander of ELAS, General Sarafis, and 30 of his senior ELAS officers were arrested and exiled to the Greek island of Macronisos.

By the end of 1945 the British succeeded in establishing a new Greek government under the leadership of Themistoklis Sophoulis, a leader of the conservative populists. Sophoulis announced the first national elections in Greece since 1936 to be held on 31 March 1946. The leftist political forces and even supporters of liberal-centre parties abstained, contributing to a victory of right-wing coalition under the leadership of Dino Tsaldaris. The new coalition government, under anomalous circumstances (e.g. using out-of-date electoral registers, intimidation of voters by pro-monarchist police forces, and British pressures to restore the monarchy), held a plebiscite on 2 September 1946, resulting in the return of king George II to serve Great Britain's geopolitical interests in the area and prevent radical institutional changes, as demanded by the leftist EAM forces.

The reestablishment of the monarchy, along with a right-wing coalition government, increased political polarization in Greece and the prosecution of leftist and liberal elements, especially ex-members of EAM/ELAS organizations. The systematic prosecution of members of Greek resistance forces by the post-liberation pro-monarchists and right-wing governments was an important factor contributing to the Greek Civil War (1946–49) between nationalists (pro-monarchists) and leftist forces, costing over 160,000 lives and billions of dollars' damage to property. The leftist forces of the Civil War consisted mainly of ex-EAM/ELAS members who were forced by an ultra-right-wing government and para-military groups (e.g. X-ites) either to resort again to the mountains or let themselves be beaten, tortured, murdered, or exiled to concentration camps.

PETER D. CHIMBOS

See also EAM and ELAS

Further Reading

Angelopoulos, Angelos and Sophocles G. Dimitrakopoulos, *Defending Democracy: The Contribution of Greece during the Second World War*, New York: Pella, 1995

Clogg, Richard, *A Concise History of Greece*, Cambridge and New York: Cambridge University Press, 1992

Couloumbis, Theodore A., John A. Petropoulos and Harry J. Psomiades, *Foreign Interference in Greek Politics: An Historical Perspective*, New York: Pella, 1976

Gerolymatos, Andre, *Guerrilla Warfare and Espionage in Greece, 1940–44*, New York: Pella, 1992

Grambas, Pericles, "The Greek Communist Party 1941–45: The Internal Debate of Seizing Power" in *Background to Contemporary Greece*, edited by Marion Sararfis and Martin Eve, London: Merlin Press, and Savage, Maryland: Barnes and Noble, 1990

Iatrides, John (editor), *Greece in the 1940s: A Nation in Crisis*, Hanover, New Hampshire: University Press of New England, 1981

Mazower, Mark, *Inside Hitler's Greece: The Experience of Occupation, 1941–44*, New Haven, Connecticut: Yale University Press, 1993

Sarafis, Stefanos, *ELAS: Greek Resistance Army*, London: Merlin Press, 1980

Woodhouse, C.M., *Apple of Discord: A Survey of Recent Greek Politics in Their International Setting*, London: Hutchinson, 1948, reprinted Reston, Virginia: W.B. O'Neill, 1985

X

Xanthus

City in Lycia

The river from which the city of Xanthus takes its name appears frequently in Homer's *Iliad* (though it should not be confused with the alternative name for the Scamander). It is where Sarpedon's kingdom is based, and where his body is taken for burial after his death.

In historical times Xanthus was the economic, political, and cultural centre of Lycia down to the Hellenistic period. Subsequently, other cities in Lycia, such as Patara and Myra, came to rival it in importance, but Xanthus remained one of the prime Lycian settlements until the general abandonment of the Lycian cities in the Arab invasion of the 7th century AD. As such, it stands as an epitome of many of the cultural developments and interactions with the Greek world that are to be found generally in Lycia; indeed, it is not unknown for ancient Greek authors to use the terms "Xanthus" and "Lycia" as if they were synonymous.

The best-known Lycian writer of the Classical period, Menecrates, came from Xanthus. Xanthus has one of the earliest examples of sculpture executed by Greek (or Greek-trained) artists to a Lycian commission, the so-called Lion Tomb (6th century BC). The centre of the "dynastic" system of rule was in Xanthus, and it was dynasts associated with Xanthus who were the first to put their portraits on their coinage. They were also the first to use Greek inscriptionally, commissioning poets to compose appropriate lines in praise of them (e.g. the 12-line epigram on the "Inscribed Pillar" at Xanthus of the late 5th century BC, and the poems by Symmachus of Pellana in honour of the dynast Arbinas of the early 4th century BC at the Letoum sanctuary).

The national sanctuary of Lycia was the Letoum, in the territory of Xanthus. Originally this was associated with a manifestation of the Anatolian mother goddess, but later was assimilated to Leto, and so many of the traditions that associated Leto and her children with Lycia are centred upon Xanthus and the Letoum. It was probably here that Alexander was supposed to have discovered a tablet indicating that he would conquer the Persian empire (Plutarch, *Alexander*, 17. 4–5). By the 2nd century BC the Letoum had acquired two large temples, one of Leto and one of Apollo, complementing an earlier late-Classical temple of Artemis; all three temples probably replaced earlier structures.

In the Hellenistic and Roman periods Xanthus, like the rest of Lycia, became further integrated into the Greek world as a whole, acquiring many of the typical features (theatre, etc.) of a Greek polis. An example of how integrated Xanthus was is provided by a unique document of 206/05 BC (*Supplementum epigraphicum Graecum*, 1923– , 38. 1476), recording an appeal made by the Cytenians in Aetolia to the Xanthians, appealing for help from Xanthus on the grounds of mutual kinship, based on their common links with Leto.

After the abandonment of the city in the 7th century AD, Xanthus was largely neglected by westerners until the arrival of Charles Fellows in 1838. His subsequent discoveries, publications, and recovery of antiquities, though ranging through much of Lycia, centred upon Xanthus, and antiquities from Xanthus had pride of place in the "Lycian Room" of the British Museum in the 19th century. The Nereid monument is undoubtedly the most famous of these discoveries. This, commissioned probably by Arbinas as his tomb, was a podium monument, deriving from other earlier Lycian monuments (such as a now destroyed building tentatively identified as a heroon (hero-shrine) of Sarpedon), but incorporating a façade modelled after a Greek temple. It directly influenced the style of the Mausoleum of Halicarnassus, and from that much of later Hellenistic and Roman funerary architecture (and beyond). The monument's sculptures, dancing figures usually identified as Nereids but probably Lycian deities of the dead, and reliefs showing scenes of warfare and the dynast's court, are now held up as typical examples of Greek sculpture of the early 4th century BC, and the Nereid monument has pride of place in the British Museum second only to the Parthenon marbles.

ANTONY G. KEEN

See also Lycia

Summary

The ancient city of Xanthus was the economic, political, and cultural centre of Lycia. It became integrated into the Greek world in the Hellenistic and Roman periods. It was the source of the Nereid monument, probably commissioned by Arbinas (4th century BC) as his tomb. The city was abandoned in the 7th century AD.

Xanthus: Lycian tomb decorated with scenes in relief of the life of the deceased

Further Reading

Bean, George Ewart, *Lycian Turkey: An Archaeological Guide*, London: Benn, and New York: Norton, 1978, reprinted London: John Murray, 1989

Borchhardt, Jürgen *et al.*, *Götter, Heroen, Herrscher in Lykien*, Vienna: Schroll, 1990

Fellows, Charles, *Travels and Researches in Asia Minor, More Particularly in the Province of Lycia*, London: John Murray, 1852, reprinted New York: Olms, 1975

Istanbul Institut Français d'Archéologie, *Fouilles de Xanthos*, Paris: Klincksieck, 1958–92

Keen, Antony G., "The Dynastic Tombs of Xanthos: Who Was Buried Where?", *Anatolian Studies*, 42 (1992): pp. 53–63

Keen, Antony G., "The Identification of a Hero-Cult Centre in Lycia" in *Religion in the Ancient World: New Themes and Approaches*, edited by Matthew Dillon, Amsterdam: Hakkert, 1996

Keen, Antony G., *Dynastic Lycia: A Political History of the Lycians and Their Relations with Foreign Powers, c. 545–362 BC*, Leiden and Boston: Brill, 1998

Slatter, Enid, *Xanthus: Travels of Discovery in Turkey*, London: Rubicon Press, 1994

Xenakis, Iannis 1922–

Composer

As a French citizen who has lived most of his life outside Greece, Iannis Xenakis is generally regarded as an international musical figure rather than as a Greek composer. His earliest musical influences were Greek, however, and despite the abstract, mathematical basis of his mature work, he has always claimed that there are deep links between his compositions and the Byzantine tradition of music that attracted him in his youth. Xenakis's collaboration with the French architect Le Corbusier during the 1950s and his intense interest in mathematics led him to develop new theories of musical composition. He was always fascinated by the concept of space and mass in music, and from the 1950s he made use of mathematical models such as the laws of probability, game theory, and group theory as a formal basis for his compositions. His most famous innovation was to treat sounds not as isolated points but as "sound masses", an approach that led to the creation of what he termed "stochastic music".

Iannis Xenakis was born of Greek parents in Braila, Romania. From the age of 12 he decided to devote his life to music. His earliest interest was in Byzantine Church music and Greek folk music. Although he destroyed his early compositions influenced by Greek music, his interest in the timbre and sonority of modal music affected his later musical development. In 1932 his family moved back to Greece and Xenakis attended a private school on the island of Spetsae. He entered the Athens Polytechnic to study engineering. When the war broke out, Xenakis became actively involved in resistance to the German occupation of Greece. In 1945 he was severely wounded, losing the sight of one eye. After the war he resumed his studies and graduated from the polytechnic in 1947.

In the same year Xenakis left Greece for Paris, intending to travel to the United States. In Paris he met the leading composers of the day – Honegger, Milhaud, and Messaien – and decided to stay on. In 1950 he took up his musical studies seriously again, enrolling in Messaien's class of musical aesthetics, and working with the architect Le Corbusier. Initially he was employed by Le Corbusier to assist with some engineering calculations. Later he collaborated closely with him on some of Le Corbusier's most famous projects: the housing project for Nantes, the convent of La Tourette, the assembly building at Chandigarh, and the Baghdad stadium. In 1956 Xenakis conceived a revolutionary design for the Philips pavilion at the Brussels Exposition. Derived from the hyperbolic paraboloid, his design was influenced by his research into new musical forms. Indeed Xenakis later claimed that his first composition, *Metastaseis*, written in 1953–54, had directly inspired his architectural design.

Metastaseis was given its first public performance in 1955 at Donaueschingen. Xenakis made use of some of the principles of serial composition in his work, but he was already reacting to the contradiction he saw in serial music between method and result. He was searching for a musical means to define what he described as "sound masses" or "galaxies". In *Metastaseis* he formed sound analogies of "ruled surfaces" by using complexes of glissandos.

In his next attempt to handle sound masses in his music Xenakis turned to the mathematics of probability. In particular, he drew on the law of large numbers. Borrowing a term from mathematics, he called his new compositions "stochastic music". His string quartet *ST/4* (1956–62) is an early example of the new technique. The theory provided the composer with limits for sound effects and with a formula to determine the probabilities of choices within those limits. His calculations could be carried out manually or on a computer. In his book *Formalized Music* (1971) Xenakis stated that his aim in developing stochastic music was "to attain the greatest possible asymmetry...and the minimum of constraints, causalities, and rules".

Xenakis's interest in indeterminacy led him to investigate the possibilities of applying another field of mathematics to his music. He turned to game theory. His first compositions inspired by game theory were *Stratégie* and *Duel* (1959–62). In his application of the theory two contestants reply in alternation to each other's tactics (passages of music). These musical passages are not chosen by the performers but stipulated by the composer, and points are awarded according to a predetermined scheme. In the compositions *Stratégie* and *Duel* rival conductors direct their own groups of instrumentalists. In *Linaia-agon* (1972) a solo trombone plays against a duo of horn and tuba in a contest that resembles a musical game of chess.

From the early 1950s to the early 1960s Xenakis had been concerned with introducing chaos and disorder into his music. The images he used to describe his music were generally derived from mass phenomena such as the behaviour of crowds of people or the burst of rockets in a fireworks display. In the mid-1960s he decided that he had explored this direction long enough and began to investigate new theoretical possibilities based on symbolic logic and set theory. *Herma*, a piano piece from 1960–61, was the first of the compositions Xenakis

Iannis Xenakis

described as "symbolic music". Taking his analogy from set theory, the composer used sets drawn from the pitches of the equal-tempered semitone scale. *Nomos alpha* for cello (1965–66) was another early attempt to apply set theory to his composition.

An important result of Xenakis's work with set theory was the development of a concept of "outside time structure", i.e. of a collection of values for one sound aspect. He was led to this concept partly by the realization that western music has a much smaller range of pitch and rhythmic variation than ancient Greek, Byzantine, or many kinds of folk music. In *Nomos alpha* the quarter-tone rather than the semi-tone is used as the unit interval for establishing sets of pitches.

Xenakis's experiments with mathematical theory and attempts to develop a new approach to composition brought him great popularity in Europe and the United States during the 1960s and 1970s. From 1967 to 1972 he taught for several months of each year at Indiana University, Bloomington, where he founded a sister institution to the Équipe de Mathématique et d'Automatique Musicales, an institution he had established in Paris to stimulate research into musical theory. He also toured the world giving lectures on composition and aesthetics.

Xenakis has always been interested in electronic music and was quick to explore the possibilities of computers. In 1975, he created UPIC, a computer-based electronic music system which allows people with no prior knowledge of composition or computers to create their own works. He began composing his own electroacoustic works for tape in the late 1950s and has continued to produce electronic works, including *S. 709* in 1994. During the 1980s and 1990s Xenakis also produced a steady stream of works for solo instruments, chamber ensembles and orchestra. Many of these pieces are Greek at least in name. They include *Alax* (1985) for 30 players divided into three ensembles, *Horos* (1986) for 89 players, and *Ioolkos* (1995). Despite a decline in the popularity of avant-garde classical composition during the last two decades of the 20th century, Xenakis has remained an active and widely admired composer, receiving numerous international awards for his contributions to modern music. In 1997, the year of his 75th birthday, his music was featured in a series of concerts all over the world, including the premiere of *Sea-Change*, a work commissioned for the BBC Proms, and *Omega*, for percussion and ensemble, written for the London Sinfonietta.

Most of Xenakis's works are not only connected with mathematics, but with ancient Greek literary sources, as their titles and texts indicate. An exception is *Nuits* (1967–68). The dedication of this choral composition ("For you, unknown political prisoners...and for you, the thousands of forgotten whose very names are lost") suggests that Xenakis has remained committed to the cause of human freedom, even though he never became actively engaged in politics after he left Greece. Not only in its dedication but also in its exploration of the resources of the human voice, *Nuits* is often considered the most moving of Xenakis's compositions. It suggests that whether or not the composer's theories of music will outlast him, his genuine musical gifts have made an important contribution to 20th-century music.

GAIL HOLST-WARHAFT

Biography

Born in Romania in 1922 to Greek parents, Xenakis moved to Greece with his family in 1932. He attended a private school on Spetsae and studied engineering at the Athens Polytechnic. He left Greece in 1947 and studied in Paris under Messiaen. He collaborated with the architect Le Corbusier. Interest in his mathematical approach to musical composition, high in the 1960s and 1970s, has declined since the 1980s, though he has remained active as a composer.

Further Reading

Bois, Mario, *Iannis Xenakis, the Man and his Music: A Conversation with the Composer and a Description of his Works*, London: Boosey and Hawkes, 1967, reprinted Westport, Connecticut: Greenwood Press, 1980
Butchers, Christopher, "The Random Arts: Xenakis, Mathematics and Music", *Tempo*, 85 (1986): pp. 2–5
Griffiths, Paul, "Xenakis: Logic and Disorder", *Musical Times*, 116/1586 (April 1975): pp. 329–31
Hill, Peter, "Xenakis and the Performer", *Tempo*, 112 (1975)
Matossian, Nouritza, *Iannis Xenakis*, London: Kahn and Averill, and New York: Taplinger, 1986
Philippot, Michael P, Xenakis entry in *The New Grove Dictionary of Music and Musicians*, edited by Stanley Sadie, London: Macmillan, and Washington, D.C.: Grove, 1980, vol. 20, pp.559–61
Souster, Tim, "Xenakis's *Nuits*", *Tempo*, 85 (1968): pp. 5–18
Xenakis, Iannis, *Formalized Music: Thought and Mathematics in Composition*, Bloomington: Indiana University Press, 1971; revised edition, Stuyvesant, New York: Pendragon Press, 1992

Xenophon *c.*430–*c.*353 BC

Athenian soldier, philosopher, and historian

Unrivalled in the ancient world for the breadth of his personal experience and the originality of his writing, Xenophon was important to subsequent ages as a Socratic philosopher and an heir to the legacy of Thucydides; as a prose stylist he was central to the Atticist and, later, the Byzantine canons.

Born into a wealthy family during the early years of the Peloponnesian War, he probably saw combat late in the conflict. In his early years he became associated with the circle of individuals who admired Socrates. His aristocratic background, association with Socrates, and an eyewitness feel in the relevant portions of the *Hellenica* encourage the view that he was involved in the government of the Thirty Tyrants immediately following the war (404–403 BC). In the spring of 401 BC he joined the Greek mercenary contingent of the army of Cyrus the Younger, who was attempting to usurp the Persian throne. Following Cyrus' death at the battle of Cunaxa, and the later abduction and murder of the commanders of the Greeks, Xenophon emerged as an important leader. When the mercenaries were absorbed into the Spartan army operating in Asia Minor, Xenophon was as well, and he remained there for the next five years. With the outbreak of the Corinthian War in 395 BC, Xenophon returned to Greece in the company of the Spartan king Agesilaus; he seems to have witnessed first-hand the battle of Coronea (394 BC). Either because of his presence in the Spartan ranks at Coronea, or because of his service with Cyrus, or perhaps both, he was exiled from Athens during this period. Thanks to his Spartan connections, he was granted an estate at Scillus near Olympia (recalled by Leake, 1830, 2. 86), where he lived until Spartan control of the north Peloponnese collapsed after the battle of Leuctra in 371 BC. Although a return to Athens cannot be ruled out (his exile was at some point revoked), he probably lived out his last years in Corinth. He was married and had two sons, one of whom (Gryllus) was killed in combat before the second battle of Mantinea (361 BC). Xenophon died soon after 355 BC.

Xenophon's corpus can be divided into three parts: historical, philosophical, and technical treatises. He wrote up a history of the Greek world from 411 to 362 BC that was known in antiquity as the *Hellenica*; it is in part a continuation of Thucydides' unfinished history of the Peloponnesian War, but takes events down through the Corinthian War, the hegemony and collapse of Sparta, and the rise of Thebes. The *Anabasis* is his account of the march of the 10,000 Greek mercenaries in the service of Cyrus the Younger. The *Cyropaedia* is a quasi-historical work that is in part a proto-novel; it treats the education and life of Cyrus the Great, the founder of the Persian royal house (the Achaemenids). Xenophon also contributed one of the very first biographies in ancient Greek literature, the encomium of his friend king Agesilaus. So far as his philosophical writings are concerned Xenophon is an important figure in the Socratic tradition. In addition to rivalling Plato with an *Apology* and *Symposium*, he wrote up a set of anecdotal remembrances of Socrates known as the *Memorabilia*. Further, Socrates also plays an important but subsidiary role in a work entitled the *Oeconomicus* (Household Management). The *Hieron* is a dialogue that features the tyrant of that name conversing with the poet Simonides on the topic of absolute power (Socrates is not present). Xenophon also wrote a number of smaller, technical works: *Revenues*, the *Cavalry Commander*, *On Horsemanship*, and *On Hunting*. A *Constitution of the Athenians*, traditionally attributed to the "Old Oligarch", was also included in the works of Xenophon in antiquity, but is clearly not by him.

As a participant on the famous *anabasis*, as well as an observer of Greek internecine strife in the years that followed, Xenophon had experience of Panhellenism at first hand, yet he also had a more practical understanding of it than a figure such as Isocrates; while passionately devoted to the principle of an alliance of all the Greeks and the cessation of hostility between Greeks, he also recognized that war was a constant feature of Greek political life. Later historians such as Polybius (2nd century BC) and Arrian (c.AD 90–160), who were in a position to make comparisons with the forces of Philip and Alexander, saw the 10,000 in particular as a precursor of the Macedonian army that was to bring to reality dreams of Panhellenism. Arrian, for his part, even considered himself a "second Xenophon", and the title of his account of Alexander's conquests is telling: the *Anabasis of Alexander*. The great orator Dio Chrysostom (1st–2nd century AD) modelled his writing on that of Xenophon. Indeed, Xenophon was widely regarded as the "Attic Muse" for the sweetness of his style (see e.g. Cicero, *Orator*, 32), and was an important model for Atticist writers, even though modern studies have revealed that his work contains many non-Attic features. Xenophon of Ephesus, the novelist of the 2nd century AD, is in fact probably a nom de plume for a writer working in the tradition started by the *Cyropaedia*.

For many in antiquity Xenophon was first a philosopher and second a historian: as Quintilian says in his list of Greek and Roman historians, "I have not forgotten Xenophon, but I think he ought to be included among the philosophers" (*Institutes*, 10. 1. 75). His picture of Socrates is fundamentally different from the man we see in Plato: in Xenophon, Socrates is much more a sage interested in the practical issues of day-to-day living, from self-control to the proper training for public life, and to the ordering of the household; his piety is also a common theme. The choice of Heracles between virtue and vice from the *Memorabilia* became a popular subject in later thought and art. The story of Xenophon's first encounter with Socrates was also widely treated. He was an especially popular author with the Romans, in particular with figures such as Cicero (see, for example, his *Oratore*, 2. 58).

In late antiquity Xenophon's influence diminished somewhat: the pagan Libanius (4th century AD) read him, as did the Church Fathers Basil and John Chrysostom, but the former knew him only indirectly (the choice of Heracles story). In the early Byzantine period his importance was reestablished, in particular as a historian-soldier and prose stylist: the historian Agathias relies on him, as does the Constantinian excerptor later. For men of state who were also writers such as Nikephoros Bryennios (11th–12th century), husband of Anna Komnene and pretender to the throne, he was an especially

important model. Manuel II Palaiologos (1391–1425) quotes from his work. Xenophon was among the first ancient Greek authors translated into Latin in the Renaissance, during the papacy of Nicholas V (1446–55). In the modern period his role as commander of the 10,000 was especially cherished: so, for example, the great klepht commander Androutsos (d. 1798) led his men on a march that was popularly compared with the *Anabasis* of Xenophon.

JOHN DILLERY

See also Biography and Autobiography, Historiography

Biography

Born *c*.430 BC, Xenophon associated with Socrates in his youth and may have fought at the end of the Peloponnesian War. He was involved in the government of the Thirty Tyrants (404–403) in Athens. In 401 he joined the army of Cyrus the Younger as a mercenary. After Cunaxa (401) Xenophon led the surviving forces back to Byzantium. He then fought for Sparta at Coronea (394) and was exiled from Athens. He was given an estate near Olympia but after Leuctra (371) moved to Corinth where he died *c*.353. His writings include historical and philosophical works and technical treatises.

Writings

Xenophon, translated by Carleton L. Brownson *et al.*, 7 vols, London: Heinemann, and New York: Putnam, 1914–25 (Loeb edition; many reprints)

The Persian Expedition, translated by Rex Warner, Harmondsworth and Baltimore: Penguin, 1949, reprinted with introduction and notes by George Cawkwell, 1972

History of My Times (Hellenica), translated by Rex Warner, Harmondsworth and Baltimore: Penguin, 1966, reprinted with introduction and notes by George Cawkwell, 1972

Oeconomicus: A Social and Historical Commentary, edited and translated by Sarah B. Pomeroy, Oxford: Clarendon Press, and New York: Oxford University Press, 1994

Further Reading

Anderson, J.K., *Xenophon*, London: Duckworth, and New York: Scribner, 1974

Delebecque, Edouard, *Essai sur la vie de Xénophon*, Paris: Klincksieck, 1957

Dillery, John, *Xenophon and the History of His Times*, London and New York: Routledge, 1995

Gautier, Léopold, *La Langue de Xénophon*, Geneva: Georg, 1911

Gera, Deborah Levine, *Xenophon's Cyropaedia: Style, Genre, and Literary Technique*, Oxford: Clarendon Press, and New York: Oxford University Press, 1993

Leake, William Martin, *Travels in the Morea*, 3 vols, London: John Murray, 1830, reprinted Amsterdam: Hakkert, 1968

Münscher, Karl, *Xenophon in der griechisch-römischen Literatur*, Leipzig: Dieterich'sche, 1920

Nussbaum, G.B., *The Ten Thousand: A Study in Social Organization and Action in Xenophon's Anabasis*, Leiden: Brill, 1967

Tatum, James, *Xenophon's Imperial Fiction: On the Education of Cyrus*, Princeton, New Jersey: Princeton University Press, 1989

Tuplin, Christopher, "Modern and Ancient Travellers in the Achaemenid Empire: Byron's Road to Oxiana and Xenophon's Anabasis", *Achaemenid History*, 7 (1991): pp. 37–57

Tuplin, Christopher, *The Failings of Empire: A Reading of Xenophon Hellenica 2. 3. 11–7. 5. 27*, Stuttgart: Steiner, 1993

Y

Yarmuk, Battle of

Battle fought between Arabs and Byzantines in AD 636

The decisive battle fought in AD 636 near the confluence of the Yarmuk river and the Wadi'l Rukkad, which today marks part of the border between Jordan, Syria, and the Israeli-occupied Golan Heights, determined the fate of Byzantine Syria. Early in AD 636 the Byzantine emperor Herakleios (who was not himself present at the battle) raised a very substantial Byzantine and Christian Arab force to reverse recent Muslim victories in Syria, Transjordania, and Palestine, and drive the Muslims out of Syria and Palestine. The site, a strategic one, included high ground, water supplies, and pasture, and dominated important routes between Damascus and Galilee. It was an important sedentary base, with pasture grounds crucial to the friendly Christian Arab tribe of Ghassan, and it lay within traditional Byzantine territory, near the intersection of the boundaries of four Byzantine provinces. A major battle had taken place near the site in 614, when the Persian general Shahrbaraz had resoundingly defeated the Byzantines, opening the way into Palestine for the Persians. The terrain's strategic significance was apparent to both sides and in theory was familiar to both.

On the eve of the battle the Byzantines had not succeeded in developing any effective new tactics or strategy for checking the Muslims. The battle of the Yarmuk, or al-Jabiya, lasted more than a month, including preliminary manoeuvrings. It began in the vicinity of al-Jabiya, the traditional base of the Ghassan, with manoeuvrings, and terminated on 20 August 636. Byzantine forces had come from Emesa under General Vahan, who was probably *Magister Militum per Orientem* (Master of the Soldiers in the East), and Theodore Trithurios, the *sakellarios* (treasurer). Jabala bin al-Ayham, king of the Ghassan, led Ghassanid forces. Other Christian Arabs, whom Herakleios had recruited in upper Mesopotamia and elsewhere, participated. There are contradictory reports concerning whether Theodore, the brother of Herakleios, was present. Although he participated in planning some of the campaign, Theodore probably had been recalled to Constantinople in disgrace before the final stages of the battle. Muslim forces under Abu 'Ubayda bin al-Jarrah withdrew from Emesa and Damascus in the face of the approach of stronger Byzantine armies from the north. They retired to a line between Dayr Ayyub and Adhr'iat, where they waited for more than a month, in a topographically strong position, to deter any Byzantine move further south. On 23 July 636 the Muslims emerged victorious after an initial clash near al-Jabiya. The Byzantines attempted to use the waiting period to familiarize their forces with the Muslims and, unsuccessfully, to encourage desertion and dissension within Muslim ranks. Both sides received reinforcements, but the decisive engagement took place when the Muslims were continuing to gain more reinforcements. The Byzantines, together with their Christian Arab allies, probably enjoyed numerical superiority, having troops that numbered 15,000 or 20,000 men, possibly even more.

The Muslims, by feigning retreat, lured the Byzantines into attacking their camp near Dayr Ayyub. The Muslims penetrated the exposed Byzantine left flank, and then exploited gaps that yawned between Byzantine infantry and cavalry. Byzantine infantry apparently attempted to lock shields and to engage in intricate, complicated, risky exercises (the so-called mixed formation) that involved opening the ranks of foot for horsemen to pass through and then relocking shields. Poor Byzantine coordination allowed the Muslims to exploit the gap and to slay many exposed Byzantine infantry. Byzantine forces withdrew into territory that lay between the Wadi'l Rukkad and Wadi'l Allan, both west of the Wadi'l Harir, to what they believed to be a secure encampment protected by the high bluffs of the wadis.

In a night raid the Muslims under the capable Muslim commander Khalid bin al-Walid seized the critical bridge over the Wadi'l Rukkad, which offered the only viable retreat route for the encircled men and animals of the Byzantine army. The Byzantines found themselves blocked and could neither retreat in formation, fight their way out, nor negotiate a reasonable settlement. Having learned that they were cut off, the Byzantines panicked. The Muslims stormed their camps between the wadis as well as at the village of Yaqusa, on the edge of the Golan Heights. The Byzantines lost cohesion and most were slaughtered, although a few may have managed to flee down the steep walls of the wadis. The Muslims took few or no prisoners. Some Christian Arabs allegedly wavered in their loyalty to the Byzantine cause and managed to flee, which aided the Muslims. One Muslim tradition reports that some dejected and defeated Byzantine troops, having perceived the hopelessness of their situation, fatalistically awaited their slaughter.

The battle destroyed the only viable Byzantine army in Syria and its commanders, who ceased to exist as a fighting force. A rout ensued. For the Muslims the victory eliminated the possibility of any Byzantine penetration further south, reconfirmed Muslim control of Palestine and Transjordania, and opened the way for the Muslim conquest of the Bika' Valley, Damascus, and, beyond it, all of Syria. The Muslims consolidated their victory by a rapid, far-reaching, and ruthless pursuit of retreating Byzantines, giving them no respite. The battle had great psychological as well as material effects: it broke the will of the Byzantines to engage in more open battle. The Byzantines henceforth avoided open battle with the Muslims in Syria and upper Mesopotamia, and ended their efforts to recover or hold Syria. Together with Emperor Herakleios, who was staying first at Emesa and then at Antioch, they evacuated northern Syria and withdrew into Anatolia, where Herakleios attempted to improvise new defences.

The Byzantines suffered logistical problems on the eve of the battle. They lacked experience in handling and supplying large numbers of troops in the region of these manoeuvrings. This inexperience may have contributed to the logistical problems they experienced and to tensions with local civilians. Byzantine leaders found it difficult to procure adequate supplies from local inhabitants on the eve of the engagements. Mansur, son of Sergius, the local fiscal official at Damascus, refused to provide supplies to the unprecedentedly large Byzantine forces. The Byzantine forces consisted of heterogenous ethnic elements, many of whom had no experience in fighting or manoeuvring in the region. Distrust, misunderstanding, and friction between Greeks, Armenians, and Christian Arabs probably existed within the Byzantine ranks. There is no indication that the local inhabitants participated in fighting on either side. The Byzantines were already suffering psychological shock from a series of recent defeats at the hands of the Muslims. Muslim losses were considerable, but far smaller than the human and material ones suffered by the Byzantines. However, all statistics for the battle, both concerning numbers of combatants and numbers of casualties, are worthy of suspicion.

The account of the battle by the Muslim historian of Damascus Ibn 'Asakir, *Tarikh Madinat Dimashk*, is probably the best. No documentary records or eyewitness accounts survive. Memory of the actual facts of the battle soon faded and quickly became embellished with legends. The magnitude of the Muslim victory received instant recognition and continued to resound later in the 7th century. The military manual entitled the *Strategikon* of Maurice, although written in about 600, provides some reliable insight into contemporary Byzantine fighting techniques and logistical strategy that were probably used in the battle. The reigning Byzantine Herakleian dynasty appears to have attempted to shake off responsibility for the disaster, blaming an alleged abortive rebellion of the Armenian Byzantine general Vahan, or to the failure to follow Emperor Herakleios' injunctions to be wary of Arab ambushes, or to adverse climate. There is no evidence that Christian religious dissension affected the outcome. Muslim writers later celebrated the role of Islamic religious zeal, but superior Muslim leadership as well as superior morale, including confidence that derived from their recent pattern of successes, were important factors in their victory. The battle sharply contributed to the permanent reduction of the importance of Hellenism in western Asia, Egypt, and north Africa.

WALTER E. KAEGI

Summary

Site of a battle on the borders between modern Jordan and Syria fought in AD 636 between the Byzantines of Emperor Herakleios and the Muslim Arabs. Decisively defeated, the Byzantines suffered heavy losses. The battle confirmed Muslim control of Palestine and Transjordania.

Further Reading

Donner, Fred McGraw, *Early Islamic Conquests*, Princeton, New Jersey: Princeton University Press, 1981, pp. 130–46

Ibn 'Asakir, *Tarik madinat Dimashq*, edited by Salah al-Din al-Munajjid, vol. 1, Damascus: al-Majma'al-'Ilmi al-'Arabi, 1951, pp. 537–52 (Asakir 1. 131–32 and 1. 159–76)

Kaegi, Walter E., *Byzantium and the Early Islamic Conquests*, Cambridge and New York: Cambridge University Press, 1995, pp. 112–45

Palmer, Andrew (editor), *The Seventh Century in the West-Syrian Chronicles*, Liverpool: Liverpool University Press, 1993

Sebeos, *The Armenian History*, translated by Robert W. Thomson, Liverpool: Liverpool University Press, 1999 (see especially chapter 42, sections 135–36)

Tabari, Al-, *The History of Al-Tabari*, edited by Ehsan Yar-Shater, Albany: State University of New York Press, 1985– : vol. 11: *Challenge to the Empires*, translated by Khalid Yahya Blankinship, 1993, pp. 76–115 (Tabari 1. 2081–2113); and vol. 12: *Battle of al-Qadisiyyah and the Conquest of Syria and Palestine*, AD 635–637/AH 14–15, translated by Yohanan Friedmann, 1992, pp. 132–34 and 174–81 (Tabari 1. 2347–49 and 2389–94)

Theophanes, *The Chronicle of Theophanes the Confessor: Byzantine and Near Eastern History*, AD 284–813, translated by Cyril Mango and Roger Scott, Oxford: Clarendon Press, and New York: Oxford University Press, 1997, pp. 469–71

Theophanes, *Chronographia*, edited by Carl de Boor, 2 vols, Leipzig: Teubner, 1883–85; reprinted Turnhout: Brepols, 1998, vol. 1, pp. 332, 337–38

Ypsilantis family

Several members of the Ypsilantis family have left their mark in the Byzantine, Ottoman, and modern periods of Greek history. Ioannis VIII Xiphilinos Ypsilantis became patriarch of Constantinople in 1064, "a man perfect in virtue and eminently worthy of the patriarchal throne", according to Michael Psellos. George II Xiphilinos also occupied the throne from 1191 to 1198. After the conquest of Constantinople by the Crusaders in 1204 the Ypsilantes resettled in their native Trebizond and their fortunes were linked to the imperial dynasty of the Komnenoi. In 1390 the great *domestikos* ("commander") Constantine or Dimitrios Xiphilinos Ypsilantis married Eudoxia, daughter of the emperor Manuel Komnenos.

Following the capture of Trebizond by the Turks in 1461 the family was forced to move to Constantinople as a result of the sultan's policy to repopulate the deserted city, but according to a historical work written in the third quarter of the 18th century by a descendant of the family, Athanasios Komnenos Ypsilantis, several of its members were still residing in Trebizond in the early part of the 17th century. During this period, Triantaphyllos Ypsilantis, a renowned merchant and warden of the monastery of Soumela, fled to Constantinople in order to save his 15-year-old daughter from incarceration in the harem of the pasha of Trebizond. He was accompanied by his nephew Ioannis, and by his three friends, the Mourouzi brothers.

It was to this Ioannis, also known as Hadji-Yannis, that the Phanariot Ypsilantes trace their lineage; he was extremely wealthy, and was executed by the Turks in his old age. His daughter Helen married Tzannetos, the son of Ioannis Mourouzis. He had three sons – Antonios, Constantine, and Emmanuel (Manolakis); the last was executed through the machinations of the *kaymakam* (district governor) Yengin Mehmet Pasha, who seized his properties in Galata, Neochorion, three houses in Therapia, 15 in Tatavla, and his ancestral house in Phanar, with all their valuable furnishings.

Hadji-Yannis's brother Constantine was *postelnikos* (chamberlain) in the Moldavian court of Michael Racovitza. His son Ioannis married Smaragda, daughter of Mariora and Laskarakis Mamonas. Mariora's mother was Roxandra, daughter of Alexander Mavrokordatos, the Exaporite (Minister of the Secrets and private secretary to the sultan). Although the Ypsilantes were continually feuding with the Mavrokordatoi, their legendary rivalry contributed also to their closeknit relationship through which they could check more effectively each other's intrigues and ambitions. Their paths crossed more than once, culminating in the showdown between Constantine Mavrokordatos and Dimitrios Ypsilantis in Greece during the War of Independence. Nevertheless, if the number of the Ypsilantes executed by the Turks is a telling sign of the risks associated with public office, one marvels at the political acumen of the Mavrokordatoi, who managed to fulfil their functions unharmed.

Unfortunately, this was not the case with Alexander, son of Ioannis and Smaragda, born in Constantinople in 1726. According to Athanasios's account "he studied Greek and philosophy, as well as Italian and French, reading and conversing in these languages with ease. He then studied Arabic and Persian, and the mixed Turkish derived from them, which he spoke thoroughly in the *mustalah* manner", that is, in the literary polished style. He was also related by marriage to the Mavrokordatoi; his wife Ekaterini was the daughter of the *spatharios* ("bodyguard") Dimitrios Mourouzis, whose mother was Sultana, daughter of the *voevod* (local governor) Nicholas Mavrokordatos. Thus, Alexander was twice related to the Mavrokordatoi: on his mother's and on his wife's side. He was appointed *postelnikos* and *nazir-viesternic*, a general term denoting the function of a minister with sweeping powers, in the court of Ioannis Kallimachi. He acted as *bashkapikehaya*, representing in Constantinople the *voivode* Skarlatos and Alexander Gikas. During the Russo-Turkish War (1768–74) he was named *vekil*, deputy to the Grand Dragoman; in 1774 he became Grand Dragoman himself. Through his influence on Abdul-Hamid he averted the general massacre of the Greeks, for the support they had shown to the Russians in the Orlov incident. He was also instrumental in the negotiations leading up to the treaty of Küçük Kaynardji,

which ended the Russo-Turkish War. Soon after the treaty he was appointed *hospodar* (governor) of Wallachia. Once in Bucharest, he rebuilt the palace, reorganized the Academy by rebuilding it in the monastery of St Sava, appointed nine professors, and provided scholarship funds for 75 students; he established an orphanage, and undertook several works of public utility. He also drew up a new code, improving the legal work of his predecessor Constantine Mavrokordatos. When his two sons Dimitrios and Constantine took off to Transylvania, on what seems to have been an escapade attributed to the folly of youth, his detractors accused him of plotting against the Porte. Alexander submitted his resignation and withdrew to Rhodes. He was reappointed to his see in 1790, just before the outbreak of the war with Austria and Russia. His secret correspondence with Joseph II of Austria was intercepted by the Ottomans and he sought refuge in Brünn in Moravia where he was interned till 1792. He returned to Constantinople and withdrew from public life. When his son Constantine, who succeeded him on the throne of Moldavia in 1799, was accused of plotting against the sultan, he was captured and executed on conspiracy charges in 1806.

Constantine's popularity with the Porte was partly attributed to his translation of and commentary in Turkish on Vauban's military treatises. His plans to raise an army and liberate Greece were frustrated and he escaped to Kiev, where he died in 1816. His sons Alexander and Dimitrios were more successful in carrying out his plans. Alexander (1792–1828), who had accompanied his father to St Petersburg in 1805, served in the cavalry of the imperial guard, and fought at the Battle of Dresden, losing an arm. In 1817 he was promoted to major general and commander of the brigade of hussars. In 1820 he was elected president of the *Philiki Hetaireia* (Friendly Society) and in 1821 he placed himself at the head of an armed force composed of several Greek officers of the Russian forces, who had hoped for the support of the tsar and of the Romanian peasants in their insurrection against the Turks. They were let down by both and Alexander found himself isolated in his struggle. Following a final defeat in Dragashan, where 200 poorly armed students who had formed the Sacred Battalion died in a desperate fight, Alexander with his brother Nicholas fled to Vienna, and there they both died in extreme poverty.

His brother Dimitrios (1793–1832) had arrived in Hydra a few days before the battle of Dragashan, on 8 June 1821. Alexander had instructed him to prepare the ground for his triumphal entry into Greece. Dimitrios placed himself at the head of the Greeks in the siege of Tripolis, and when that operation was successfully completed, he moved on to liberate Argos. His continual squabbles with the local chiefs and with Alexander Mavrokordatos, who managed to take a commanding position in the first national convention at Epidaurus, on 30 November 1821, left him disappointed, despite the enthusiastic support of Kolokotronis and Makriyannis, who placed themselves and their men under him. His heroic resistance at Myloi in 1825, and the defeat inflicted on the 7000-strong Turko-Egyptian force by fewer than 500 men under his command, won him the admiration of the western world as far as America, where a town in Michigan was named after him. Ioannis Kapodistria appointed him commander of the troops in eastern Greece in 1828. In this capacity he fought the last battle against the Turks at the pass of Petra in 1829, and he obtained the capitulation of the Turkish commander Aslan Bey.

Thus, the first battle that inaugurated his brother's insurrection against the Ottomans in Wallachia and the last battle which ended the military operations in the Greek mainland were both fought by the Ypsilantis. Dimitrios died at Vienna in 1832. Descendants of a fourth brother, Gregory, are still living in Austria.

LAMBROS KAMPERIDIS

See also Independence (War of), Phanariots

Further Reading

Athanasios Komnenos, Hypselantos, *Ta meta tin Alosin* [After the Capture], Constantinople, 1870

Epaminondas, Stamatiadis, *Viographiai ton Hellenon Megalon Diermineon tou Othomanikou Kratous* [Biographies of Major Greek Figures in the Ottoman State], Athens, 1865, reprinted Thessalonica, 1973

Giurescu, Constantini C., "Un Remarquable Prince phanariote: Alexandre Ypsilanti, voévode de Valachie et de Moldavie" in *L'Epoque Phanariote*, Thessalonica: Institute for Balkan Studies, 1974

Runciman, Steven, *The Great Church in Captivity: A Study of the Patriarchate of Constantinople from the Eve of the Turkish Conquest to the Greek War of Independence*, London: Cambridge University Press, 1968

Ypsilanti, Nicolas, *Mémoires*, edited by D. Kambouroglou, Athens, 1901

Z

Zagori

Region of northwest Greece

Zagori is a region of Epirus in the prefecture of Ioannina, covering an area of 1002 sq km. It is bordered by the Mitsikeli mountain region to the northwest, the Aoos river to the north, the western Pindus to the east, and the Zagoritikos, a tributary of the Arachthos river, to the west. The area is divided into three: West Zagori, East Zagori, and Central Zagori. The name *Zagori* is Slav and means "mountainous area" and Zagori is the most mountainous region in Epirus, having an altitude ranging from 500 to 2497 m; its highest peak is Gamila. Between the mountains are the plains of Dovra, Pedina or Soudena, and Vitsa and the tableland of Riziana. There are extensive forests of beech, fir, pine, and oak in Central and East Zagori, where the main occupations are forestry and stock raising. The flora and fauna of the area are quite rich: there are 219 plant species and a large number of wild animals such as wild goats, wolves, bears, and deer.

The whole region consists of a cluster of 45 villages which are built at altitudes ranging from 620 to 1340 m, usually close to springs. The rivers, mountains, forests, history, and architecture of the settlements contribute to the fame of the area as one of the most interesting and beautiful in Greece and Europe. After World War II the population of the villages was considerably reduced by emigration both within Greece and abroad because of the lack of employment opportunities. In recent years, through the controlled development of tourism in West Zagori and of logging and stock-raising in East and Central Zagori, this decline has stabilized, and there has been an increase in the size of the population. There are four main social groups: the native Zagori population; the Sarakatsans, cattle-breeders, descendants of Greek nomads of the Pindus who settled in Epirus during the 12th century; some Vlach-speaking people in East Zagori; and the Gypsies.

Although historical sources on Zagori and Epirus in general are few, archaeological survey has shown that the area has been inhabited since prehistoric times. During historical times Zagori was inhabited by Molossian tribes. One Molossian settlement has been excavated in Vitsa, which was once the summer settlement of nomad shepherds, at an altitude of 1030 m. The houses resemble those of the modern shepherds (Sarakatsans) of the area. The cemetery dates from the 9th to the 4th centuries BC. The bronze ware shows the prosperity of the settlement, and its pottery, which was handmade with painted decoration, demonstrates connections with the Peloponnese. Since antiquity the mountainous nature of the area has required the wintering of cattle in the plains and coastlands of Epirus. The Vitsa cattle breeders of antiquity lived in families and buried their dead in tombs with grave goods.

Apart from Vitsa, ancient sites have been located in the Mega Dendro area, next to the Voutsa monastery, where the ruins of ancient walls stand, and elsewhere. Moreover, at Kastraki, a hill near the village of Hagios Minas, there is an ancient fort with the remains of walls and houses. In the same area, ruins were found of the Byzantine city of Revnikon. There are also several post-Byzantine monasteries.

No historical sources exist for the early Christian times to the Middle Byzantine period, but we know that Epirus suffered invasions of Goths during the 3rd and 4th centuries AD and of Avars and Slavs during the 6th and the 7th centuries. The latter established settlements all over Epirus and some of the Slav place names of the area are probably survivals from these.

In the Middle Byzantine period Epirus belonged to the theme of Naupactus. Anna Komnene mentions the Norman invasions of the 11th century. From the time of the so-called Despotate of Epirus (13th–15th centuries) there is an increase in the historical evidence relating to Epirus and Zagori. Reference to Zagori is found in chrysobulls of Andronikos II Palaiologos, dated 1319 and 1321. A Byzantine document of 1326–28 refers to Papingo (either the village or the mountain) in Zagori. Evidence of settlements in the area during the 14th and the 15th centuries is found in the Ioannina Chronicle and the Tocco Family Chronicle, both of which contain rhyming accounts of historical events in the region. The people of Zagori joined Carlo II Tocco, count of Cephalonia, on his journey to Ioannina in 1411 where he was acclaimed despot.

In 1418 the Turks invaded Papingo and in 1430 they occupied Ioannina. During the Turkish occupation the region acquired great importance. The mountainous terrain offered many opportunities for settlement and security for the Greek population. In order to ensure their suzerainty over these areas, the Turkish rulers therefore granted them special political privileges, and the area became an autonomous prefecture with Papingo as its capital. By the 17th century the whole area had become a federation bearing the name *koinon* or *villayet* of Zagori. Apart from their administrative and political advantages, the people of Zagori were also granted special taxation privileges as well as privileges relating to social and religious concerns, which were preserved till late in the period of Turkish occupation. Moreover, between 1790 and 1822, Ali Pasha increased these privileges for fear of the influence exerted by the powerful Constantinopolitans from Zagori over the sultan.

From the 17th century many of the inhabitants of the area emigrated, mainly to Moldavia and Wallachia, but also to Austria, Serbia, Russia, and Constantinople, where they became successful merchants and writers. The remittances of merchants from abroad were invested in Zagori, where the inhabitants continued to enjoy the freedom associated with their privileges. Apart from investments in the private sector, Zagorians also funded public works, and numerous bridges, public fountains, and roads, as well as schools and churches were constructed during this period. Teachers and priests were employed for the villages' needs by the rich inhabitants, resulting in impressive educational developments; all the villagers knew how to read and write at least. The monasteries and churches, the public buildings (schools and orphanages), the beautiful big houses of the area, all made of stone, stand today as proof of the prosperity of Zagori during the 18th and the 19th centuries.

Between the 15th and the 17th centuries several monasteries were founded in wonderful settings. They played an important religious, spiritual, social, and financial role over the next two centuries. During the 18th and the 19th centuries large parish churches were built to the plan of early Christian basilicas. During the first years of the Tourkokratia painters from Linotopi (in the area of Kastoria) and from all over Epirus, monks mainly, decorated churches in the Zagori area, some groups of painters from Epirus becoming famous during the 18th and the 19th centuries. Wood carving was also developed to a fine art, and there are many examples in churches and manor houses.

During World War II Zagori witnessed several campaigns and battles. Greek resistance to the Italian invasion lasted from late 1940 to 6 April 1941, when battles were fought in Grabala and Kalpaki. Many men from Zagori saw military service in the 8th Division under the command of general Katsimitros. The 15th Infantry Regiment fought a series of battles in the highlands of Kato Soudena. With the support of both the British and the Greek air forces the Greeks drove the Italians back to Argyrokastro between December 1940 and January 1941. Immediately after the German invasion (6 April 1941) the men from Zagori returned to their villages to organize the resistance movement and the rebel forces of EAM/ELAS (*Ethniko Apeleftherotiko Metopo*, the National Liberation Front, *Ellinikos Laikos Apeleftherotikos Stratos*, Greek Popular Liberation Army) and later EDES (*Ethnikos Dimokratikos Ellinikos Syndesmos*, the National Democratic Hellenic Union). It was because of these activities that the area suffered so much during the Italian and German occupation, when famine was a major cause of suffering. The urban population began to return en masse to the villages, since the threat of famine was greater in the cities. Yet the worst of the suffering came as a result of the savage German reprisals against the rebel forces. In 1943 whole villages were burnt to the ground all over Zagori. In 1944, after Allied victories, the Germans retreated and Zagori was liberated.

The victory was very soon besmirched, however, by the ensuing Civil War between the main rebel forces. Besides ELAS and EAM, EDES was organized and activated in Zagori, under the command of captain G. Lygerakis. The two forces had initially shared common headquarters for Zagori and Konitsa. But as the recriminations developed – ELAS accusing EDES of fascism, EDES regarding ELAS as communist – the conflicts in Central and East Zagori grew increasingly bitter. In Zagori the bitterness persisted long after the official cessation of hostilities.

FRANGISKA KEFALLONITOU

See also Epirus

Summary

A region of Epirus in northwestern Greece, Zagori is a mountainous area with Sarakatsans, Vlachs, and Gypsies as well as a native Zagorian population. The area was inhabited by Molossian tribes in antiquity. It belonged to the Despotate of Epirus in the 13th–15th centuries. During the Tourkokratia the population enjoyed many privileges and prospered. Zagori suffered badly in World War II and the Civil War, resulting in much subsequent depopulation.

Further Reading

Acheimastou-Potamianou, Myrtali, annual reports in *Archaeologikon Deltion* [Archaeological Report], 1975–80

Aravantinos, P., *Chronographia Ipeirou* [Chronicles of Epirus], 1856

British School at Athens, Annual Report of the Managing Committee for the Session 1983–84

Chrysos, E., "A Contribution to the History of Epirus", *Annals of Epirus* (1981): pp. 9–112

Hammond, N.G.L., *Epirus: The Geography, the Ancient Remains, the History and Topography of Epirus and Adjacent Areas*, Oxford: Clarendon Press, 1967

Konchylakis, E., *Ekklisies stin Ellada meta tin Alosi* [Churches in Greece since the Conquest], vol. 2, Athens, 1982, pp. 47–57

Konstantios, D., "Omades Zographon stin Ipeira tin opsimi Tourkokratia" [Schools of Painting in Epirus during the Later Tourkokratia] in *Epirus: Community–History–Economy*, Ioannina, 1986

Orlandos, A., "Ein spatbyzantinischer Hollenkirchen-Typus Nordgriechenlands", *Jahrbuch des Österreichischen Byzantinistik*, 21 (1972): pp. 209–22

Petsas, F., *To Kastraki sto Dytiko Zagori* [The Kastraki Fort in Western Zagori], Athens, 1956

Petsas, F., *Ariste kai Dytiko Zagori* [The Left and West Zagori], Athens, 1982

Schirò, Giuseppe, *Cronaca dei Tocco di Cefalonia di anonimo*, Rome: Accademia Nazionale dei Lincei, 1975

Soustal, Peter, *Nikopolis und Kephallenia*, Vienna: Akademie der Wissenschaften, 1981, introduction and pp. 226, 228, 250, 274, 278

Tourta, A., *Oi Naoi tou Agiou Nikolaou sti Vitsa kai tou Agiou Mina sto Monodendri* [The Churches of St Nicholas at Vitsa and St Minas at Monodendri], Athens, 1991

Tsaparlis, E., *Ta Xyloglypta Templa tis Ipeirou 170u–a' imiseos 180u Aionos* [Carved Wooden Screens in Epirus, 17th–first half of the 18th Century], Athens, 1980

Vocotopoulos, P., *Vista*, vols 1–3, Athens, 1986

Vocotopoulos, P., *Ekklisies stin Ellada meta tin Alosi* [Churches in Greece since the Conquest], vol. 1, Athens, 1979

Zealots

An ultraconservative Church party in modern Greece

The term "Zealot" designates someone who pursues a goal passionately, excessively, and perhaps fanatically; today it has mostly disparaging connotations. Yet, the term has been used positively in the past (cf. Acts 21: 20, 22: 3; 1 Corinthians 14: 12; Galatians 1: 14; Titus 2: 14) to indicate zeal for God and other good things. The members of a religiopolitical patriotic current within Judaism in the days of Jesus Christ were also called Zealots, as were the leaders of a revolt in Byzantium, who between 1342 and 1349 were in control of Thessalonica.

In modern Greece the term has been used in two, rather overlapping ways. In the first place, it refers loosely to Orthodox fanatics who are distinguished from the main body of the Church through their radical thinking, militant acts, and uncompromising positions. Such hardliners are included in the multidimensional current of Orthodox fundamentalism. Zealotry is exhibited in a variety of ways including devastating criticism of the official Church, which may finally lead to a schismatic movement, and militant and violent acts (e.g. the Rotonda incidents in Thessalonica in 1995) against real or alleged enemies of Orthodoxy. Orthodox zealotry is not only confined to marginal groups (e.g. the Old Calendarists); even leading members of the Church (e.g. Avgustinos Kantiotis, bishop of Florina) may exhibit signs of a zealotic mentality and pursue concomitant activities. The same spirit is sometimes shared by academic and other lay theologians.

In a narrow sense, the term "Zealots" was a self-designation of certain monks on Mount Athos who not only vehemently opposed the reform of the calendar by the patriarchate of Constantinople and the Church of Greece in 1924 (bringing Greece into line with the Gregorian calendar used in the rest of the Western world), but also broke communion with them. They founded organizations to promote their ideas, called themselves "True Orthodox Christians", and considered the New Calendar Churches to be schismatic, even heretical. They have also engaged in propaganda activities outside Athos since 1924. Two Zealot monks in particular, Arsenios Kotteas and Matthaios Karpathakis, made headlines because of their impact on the Orthodox flock and being the moving force of the "True Orthodox Christians". Their activities provoked a reaction not only from the official Church, but also from the Holy Community of Mount Athos. The Sacred Union of Zealotic Athonite Fathers or Sacred Union of Zealotic Monks, founded in April 1926, ceased to exist in 1927 according to the Constitutional Charter of Athos, Article 183 of which prohibited the foundation of monastic societies and organizations on the Holy Mountain. But its members as well as other Zealots continued their activities in other ways, both on Athos and elsewhere, and formed the backbone of contemporary Orthodox Zealotry.

Athonite Zealots used to live outside the monasteries, mostly in sketes or in other establishments near Megisti Lavra, until they brought the Esphigmenou monastery under their control in 1971. In total, they constitute approximately one quarter of the monks of Athos. Generally, the ruling monasteries do not accept the New Calendar. Yet, all of them, except Esphigmenou, maintain communion with the Orthodox authorities in Constantinople and Athens. Esphigmenou, however, shows an elitist attitude not only towards the Orthodox Church body in general, but towards the other monasteries as well. The Esphigmenites think of themselves as being the "most Orthodox" in the entire world, and suspect heresies and innovations almost everywhere. Since 1971 they have not commemorated the patriarch's name, due to Athenagoras's involvement in the ecumenical movement and his moves towards reconciliation with the Roman Catholic Church. In 1972 the other 19 Athonite monasteries expelled Esphigmenou's representative from the Holy Community. Since then Esphigmenou has followed an isolationist and separatist policy and joined the Old Calendarist group under archbishop Avxentios. Despite the counter-measures of the patriarchate of Constantinople, the Esphigmenites have not backed down and occasionally threatened extreme measures. At present their monastery is flourishing, and this is perhaps indicative of the wider appeal of zealotist ideals. The characteristic black banner on the monastery walls with the inscription "Orthodoxy or death" is indicative of their militant spirit. It is no wonder therefore that Esphigmenou was among the few monasteries that did not participate in the exhibition "Treasures of Mount Athos" in Thessalonica in 1997.

There are also various periodicals published by Zealots from Athos, such as *Agios Agathangelos Esphigmenitis* (St Agathangelos of Esphigmenou, formerly entitled *O Agios Simon o Myrovlitis*, St Simon the Myroblete), produced by the monk Iakovos. This contains only very critical articles and negative comments on all alleged anti-Orthodox policies, and supports with apocalyptic ardour traditionalist Orthodox views including the Old Calendar issue and the anti-ecumenical struggle. Another journal of related Zealotic line is *O Agioreitis* (The Athonite), published since 1978 by the monk Kallinikos.

The term "Zealots" has related to Athonite monasticism in recent times, and Athos is thus regarded by many as the most reliable bastion of the Orthodox tradition in the contemporary and radically changing world. Yet it should not be forgotten that zealotry, both historically and traditionally, has characterized many Orthodox believers and particularly monks in the past as well. The violent killing of the philosopher and mathematician Hypatia in 415 by Christians in Alexandria, despite its various underlying causes, was but one example of Christian zealotry. Various zealotic acts on the part of Orthodox monks were also castigated by the learned archbishop of Thessalonica Eustathios in the 12th century, who in his work *De emendanda vita monachica* pointed out their numerous transgressions and tried to ameliorate the overall condition of monastic life. Zealotic phenomena can also be observed later in the Kollyvades movement of the late 18th century as well as among other Orthodox (e.g. Kosmas Flamiatos). Needless to say, zealotic attitudes were very common in the wider Orthodox world as well, as an interesting dialogue between the Serb monk Dimitrije Obradović and a "Zealot" (Zilotij) in the 18th century reveals (Obradović, 1953). These cases attest to the fact that zealotry in its various expressions within (Orthodox) Christianity is not solely a contemporary phenomenon.

It goes without saying that Zealots in contemporary Greece, due to their ideas and acts, provoke negative reactions not only from the official Church but also from the wider public. They are often considered as fanatics, vociferous protesters, intransigent, ultraconservative, bellicose undiscriminating ignoramuses, despite the fact that their intentions as guardians of the Orthodox faith are in some cases genuine and sincere. The official Church has been following their activities closely since the 1920s and has tried repeatedly to bring them under control. It also fears their challenge to its authority and their wider influence upon the Orthodox flock. Thus, the Church of Greece prohibited the activities of all wandering monks in any diocese without the permission of the local bishop (see the encyclical 2563 of 20 October 1993). On 14 December 1993 the patriarchate of Constantinople excommunicated the lay theologian Nikolaos Sotiropoulos of A. Kantiotis's movement, who was accused of troublemaking activities in the archdiocese of Australia. Moreover, through a State Council's decision in 1996, monks who do not acknowledge the direct spiritual jurisdiction of the patriarchate of Constantinople over Athos and do not commemorate the patriarch's name are not allowed to stay there. These incidents show that both the official Church and the state are negatively disposed towards the Zealots and intend to discipline them and neutralize their influence everywhere.

VASILIOS MAKRIDES

See also Athos, Fundamentalism, Old Calendarists

Summary

In antiquity there were Jewish Zealots in the time of Christ. And Zealots controlled Thessalonica in 1342–49. But in modern Greece Zealots are Orthodox fanatics and more specifically separatist monks (opposing ecumenical moves), based particularly on Mount Athos. About a quarter of all Athonites (and all the monks of the Esphigmenou monastery) call themselves Zealots.

Further Reading

Agioreites Pateres, *Omologia-Ekklisis itoi Apantitiki Diasaphisis peri tis simerinis en ti Ekklisia apostasias kai tis Kanonikis antimetopiseos tavtis* [The Confession of the Church, Or an Exposition of the Current Apostasy in the Church, and the Canonical Way of Dealing With It], Mount Athos, 1979

Athonikoi Dialogoi [Athonite Dialogues], issue 67/68, (September–December 1979)

I Agkyra tis Orthodoxias: Idrysis kai katastatikon Ierou Syndesmou Ziloton Agioreiton Monachon [The Anchor of Orthodoxy: Foundation and Constitution of the Holy League of Athonite Zealot Monks], Athens, 1926 (22 articles)

Makrides, Vasilios, "Aspects of Greek Orthodox Fundamentalism", *Orthodox Forum*, 5 (1991): pp. 49–72

Metallinos, Georgios D., "Dyo Kephallines agonistai antimetopoi [Two Confronting Strugglers from Cephalonia]: K. Flamiatos (1786–1852) kai K. Typaldos (1795–1867)", offprint from *Apostolos Varnavas*, Nicosia, 1980

Obradović, Dimitrije, *The Life and Adventures of Dimitrije Obradović Who as a Monk Was Given the Name Dositej: Written and Published by Himself*, translated and edited by George Rapall Noyes, Berkeley: University of California Press, 1953, pp. 208–17

Orthodoxia kai Airesis [Orthodoxy and Heresy], edited by the journal *O Agioreitis* [The Hagiorite], Athens, 1982

Paraskevaidis, Christodoulos, "Istoriki kai kanoniki theorisis tou Palaioimerologitikou zitimatos kata te tin genesin kai exelixin autou en Elladi" [A Historical and Legal Examination of the Origins and Development of the Old Calendar Question in Greece], dissertation, Athens, 1982, especially pp. 388–96 and 438–63 (bibliography)

Rinvolucri, Mario, *Anatomy of a Church: Greek Orthodoxy Today*, London: Burns and Oates, 1966

Roberson, Ron, "A Roman Catholic on Athos", *Diakonia*, 19 (1984–85): pp. 137–43

Theodoropoulos, Epiphanios I., *Ta dyo akra ("Oikoumenismos" kai "Zilotismos")* [The Two Extremes ("Ecumenism" and "Zealotry")], Athens, 1986

Wittig, Andreas, "Die Bewegung der Altkalendarier in Griechenland", *Ostkirchliche Studien*, 32 (1983): pp. 309–25

Zeno of Citium 335–263 BC

Stoic philosopher

Zeno was the founder of Stoicism, a philosophical movement that had a great impact in the Greek and Roman world of the Hellenistic and imperial age. Stoicism was named after the place where Zeno used to teach in Athens, namely the Stoa Poikile (Painted Porch). Zeno, a Phoenician, came to Athens around 313 BC, and he studied first with Crates the Cynic, then with Stilpo and Diodorus of the Megarian school, and finally with Xenocrates and Polemo of the Academy. He had many students and he was well respected by the Athenians and also by Antigonus Gonatas who often attended his lectures and invited him to his court. His successor in the headship of the Stoic school was Cleanthes, but the most important contribution to Stoicism came later from Chrysippus. From Zeno's numerous writings we have only fragments from much later sources such as Cicero (1st century BC), Diogenes Laertius (2nd century AD), Galen (2nd century AD), and Stobaeus (5th century AD). Famous was his *Republic*, where he argued for a society of the wise who do not need the conventional institutions of a Greek city. The fullest account of his life and his doctrines comes from Diogenes Laertius (7. 1–160).

Zeno is accredited with the tripartite division of philosophy into logic, physics, and ethics. He is said to have started his course with logic, going on to physics, and finishing with ethics. Zeno's prime interest lies in ethics, but this interest motivated a physical enquiry and then an enquiry into logic. Yet all these parts are seen as part of an organic and coherent whole and thus none of them can be studied independently. Zeno's holistic understanding of philosophy results from his attempt to establish a system accounting for all aspects of a coherent and rational universe; reason (*logos*) and nature (*physis*) are the most crucial concepts for the Stoic understanding of the world.

Zeno put considerable emphasis on dialectic which included epistemology. He attempted to argue for the possibility of attaining cognition, an epistemic state midway between belief and knowledge. He argued that to know something is to have grasped it in such a way that one's grasp (*katalepsis*) cannot be shaken by argument. This grasp presupposes perception. Perception strikes our rational principle and generates impressions (*phantasiai*). Nature endowed us with the ability to form impressions of things, and impressions form the content of our mind – actually, rationality develops through them. Thus perception constitutes for Zeno a mental act to which we can give assent. But not all impressions deserve assent. An impression deserves assent if it represents something as it is in reality, namely in such a clear way that it cannot possibly be false (Cicero, *Academicae Quaestiones*, 1. 41). These are cognitive impressions, i.e. they can convey knowledge. Zeno sharply contrasted secure assent (grasp) and weak assent, the latter amounts to ignorance. Yet a cognitive impression does not amount to knowledge; it still has to be confirmed by reason. For Zeno whatever does not qualify as knowledge amounts to ignorance. Accordingly he divided people into two categories, the foolish and the wise, the latter being the only one who knows. No intermediate state exists; unless someone is wise, he is foolish.

Zeno argued for two principles in the universe, the active and the passive. The passive principle is the qualityless (*apoios*) substance, the matter, while the active is the *Logos* in that which is called God (Diogenes Laertius, 7. 134). The whole of the universe is perfect, though destructible and subject to no other force but to itself. It was one of Zeno's fundamental ideas that every productive cause is corporeal and that only corporeal things can act. Thus mind and even God, the active principle, are corporeal. God, identified with fire, is the disposer of the things of nature and maker of the universe; it is also called reason and fate and is the determining force of all things. Zeno's account of nature is strongly teleological and his universe is very determinist; nothing happens in the world but by God's will and in accordance with God's providence. Fate not only governs everything but is defined as the reason by which the world goes on. For this reason divination is possible and can be true.

The world is considered to be a rational and intelligent being, a living organism with its own soul just as man has a soul. Human souls are fragments of the universal soul, man being an organic part of the cosmic whole. Zeno maintained that both the universal soul and the human soul are corporeal, a warm spirit (*pneuma*), which is the vitalizing force behind both humans and the universe itself. Soul has eight parts, the five senses, the faculties of reproduction and speech, and the rational principle (Diogenes Laertius, 7. 157). As the term of the rational principle suggests (*hegemonikon*, "governing principle"), there is nothing superior to this but this alone determines human life, even when it follows wrong reason. Zeno introduced some new terms to describe psychological or mental functions that take place in the rational principle such as "impulse", a soul's movement as a reaction to an impression. Man is free to follow an impulse by giving assent to an impression.

Zeno thought that philosophy had to show its fruits in ethics. According to Zeno, our goal is to live in accordance with reason, later formulated as living in accordance with nature. The law of nature can guide a man unerringly to virtue. Zeno maintained that virtue is something pertinent, endearing (*oikeion*) to the nature of man in the sense that nature directs man towards the acquisition of virtue. Therefore man should seek after virtue. In seeking virtue man is doing justice to its nature (*oikeiosis*), and being virtuous is a manifestation of one's rationality. Zeno held that only virtue has intrinsic moral value since only virtue is up to us. Therefore virtue is the sole good and the sole constituent of happiness. All other things, however good or bad, are regarded as morally indifferent

(*adiaphora*). Within the group of indifferent Zeno distinguished three classes, the preferable, the non-preferable, and the indifferent. Natural advantages such as beauty and wealth are preferable. Accordingly Zeno distinguished between appropriate and perfectly appropriate acts; the first refer to preferable things, while the latter to morally valuable ones. Virtue is said to be one; individual virtues are inseparable and they constitute a state in which their possessor would always do the right thing. The smallest failure makes somebody unvirtuous. To be virtuous is the achievement of the wise man. As is the case with knowledge, so in ethics Zeno does not allow for any degrees of goodness. The wise man never fails in practising virtue, because of his acquired moral expertise; thus the wise man is free from all passions that would have a bad impact on his soul (Cicero, *Academicae Quaestiones*, 1. 39).

Zeno's doctrines were considerably modified by his successors. Yet he enjoyed a venerable status as the founder of the school. Later Stoics such as Posidonius (1st century BC) opposed their predecessors and tried to go back to Zeno's views. Stoic doctrines had an impact on Christian Fathers who shared the Stoic hostility to sceptics and Epicureans. Clement of Alexandria (*c.*AD 150–215) is likely to have had access to Zeno's writings, which by that time must already have become difficult to find.

GEORGE E. KARAMANOLIS

See also Stoicism

Biography

Born at Citium in Cyprus in 335 BC, Zeno moved to Athens in 313 to study first under Crates the Cynic, then with Stilpo and Diodorus, and lastly with Xenocrates and Polemo of the Academy. He was founder and head of the Stoic school of philosophy. He was succeeded by Cleanthes. Only fragments of Zeno's writings survive. He died in 263 BC.

Writings

In *Stoicorum veterum fragmenta*, edited by H.F.A. von Arnim, 4 vols, Leipzig: Teubner, 1903–24, reprinted 1964

In *The Hellenistic Philosophers*, edited and translated by A.A. Long and and D.N. Sedley, 2 vols, Cambridge and New York: Cambridge University Press, 1987

Further Reading

Hunt, H.A.K., *A Physical Interpretation of the Universe: The Doctrines of Zeno the Stoic*, Carlton, Victoria: Melbourne University Press, 1976

Inwood, Brad, *Ethics and Human Action in Early Stoicism*, Oxford: Clarendon Press, and New York: Oxford University Press, 1985

Long, A.A., *Hellenistic Philosophy: Stoics, Epicureans, Sceptics*, 2nd edition, London: Duckworth, and Berkeley: University of California Press, 1986

Reesor, Margaret E., *The Nature of Man in Early Stoic Philosophy*, London: Duckworth, 1989

Rist, J.M., *Stoic Philosophy*, Cambridge: Cambridge University Press, 1969

Samburský, Samuel, *Physics of the Stoics*, London: Routledge, 1959, reprinted Princeton, New Jersey: Princeton University Press, 1987

Sandbach, F.H., *The Stoics*, 2nd edition, Bristol: Bristol Classical Press, 1989, reprinted London: Duckworth, and Indianapolis: Hackett, 1994

Zenobia

Queen of Palmyra in the 3rd century AD

Septimia Zenobia was born in Palmyra, to a family of the city's Graeco-Syrian elite. She claimed to have Macedonian blood, by descent from Antiochus IV Epiphanes, and a kinship with Cleopatra VII of Ptolemaic Egypt – this perhaps at a time when she felt herself heiress to a string of powerful women from the Hellenized east. The sources on her life and career are largely of a biased Western (Roman) nature – passages in the *Historia Augusta* and the later Byzantine histories of Malalas (6th century) and Zosimus (5th–6th century). However, the Arab historian Tabari (839–923), who refers to her as Zabba, places her in a localized scenario that is largely irreconcilable with the western sources.

Her marriage to Odenathus, who rose to become *dux oriens* under Roman suzerainty for his assistance in combating Persian advances, enhanced her position in the city where she claimed the title of queen. Odenathus and his son from a former marriage were murdered in AD 267 and from this time Zenobia ruled in the name of her eldest son Wahballat (Greek Athenodorus, Latin Vaballathus).

At this time Palmyra was at its cultural peak, and Zenobia sought to create a brilliant court by attracting a number of Graeco-Syrian literary figures. Foremost was the philosopher Cassius Longinus who, although a Syrian, had studied for years in Athens and upon his arrival in Palmyra composed a paean in praise of Odenathus. The *Historia Augusta* suggests that it was Longinus who tutored Zenobia in Greek and diplomacy and encouraged her revolt against Rome. This is unlikely since it is inconceivable that a woman of her position would not know Greek and her political skills (and reasons to revolt, see below), will have been honed over many years. Another well-known figure at the Palmyrene court was the sophist Callinicus of Petra who wrote a history of Alexandria – after Zenobia had conquered Egypt – and dedicated it to her under the name of Cleopatra. Perhaps the most important figure to arrive in Palmyra at this time was Paul of Samosata who fled from Antioch where he had been bishop, after being condemned as a heretic. Indeed, according to the sources, he converted Zenobia to Christianity, or even to Judaism. Although it is true that there was a sympathetic Jewish community in Palmyra and Zenobia is known to have paid for the restoration of a synagogue in Egypt, these views are thought to be an exaggeration. It is more likely that she displayed an intellectual curiosity, rather like the earlier Syrian empress Julia Domna, seeking information on Christian, Jewish, and even (according to Coptic sources) Manichaean doctrine. There is no reason to deny that she adhered to anything other than the Palmyrene sun cult.

It is probable that Zenobia would have been ignored by history were it not for the revolt she led against Roman power in the east. Much recent analysis has revealed, however, that although Rome's position there had been severely weakened, such a revolt is a simplification and that the brief flowering of a Palmyrene empire was based on more localized factors. The immediate reason may have been a frustration with what appeared to be the Roman disinclination to extend the preeminent position held by Odenathus to his heirs. There was also the need to bolster Palmyra's economic position at a period of commercial and financial instability in the East; thus it was an attempt to restore rather than create or enhance a position of financial preeminence within the eastern provinces. Lastly, the revolt would seem to have been deeply ensconced within a political power struggle among the Arab tribal federations of the area. Here, Tabari's account has been supported by recent epigraphic and archaeological evidence for an increased unrest among the tribes, jealous of Palmyrene hegemony. The *Historia Augusta* lists a wide range of Palmyrene allies based as far away as India, Persia, Ethiopia, and Yemen, suggesting that such a movement must have been far wider than merely anti-Roman. Latin inscriptions of Vaballathus give him the title "Arabicus Maximus" and this can now be understood as more than the mere aping of Roman imperial titulature. Moreover, the coins of Vaballathus have double portraits with himself on one side and the legitimate emperor Aurelian on the other, which indicates a desire for imperial association rather than any move to supplant western suzerainty.

The actual course of the revolt can be briefly described. Led by the general Zabdas, Palmyrene forces marched through Palestine and invaded Egypt in AD 269/70, ostensibly with fifth-column support in Alexandria, where one Timagenes (possibly a Palmyrene himself) is said to have raised Palmyrene support. Once Roman resistance had been finally crushed, Zenobia set about immersing herself in local support, using the name Cleopatra and paying for the restoration of a number of Egyptian monuments as well as a synagogue there. Turning north, Palmyrene forces captured Antioch, the great Syrian metropolis, in AD 270. From here coins were issued under the name of Vaballathus Augustus but now associated, significantly, with Zenobia Augusta rather than Aurelian – a clear statement of where the real power finally lay. The Palmyrene armies are said to have advanced through Asia Minor as far as Chalcedon, but after being repulsed from there, they held the country east of Ancyra.

The new Roman emperor Aurelian launched a strong counter-attack against what he clearly perceived as usurpers. Sending troops to Egypt, Aurelian himself led a larger army through Asia Minor, eventually confronting the Palmyrene forces outside Antioch and again in a decisive battle at Emesa where Aurelian captured Zenobia's war chest. From here Zenobia fled towards Palmyra where the Roman forces arrived to besiege her. The exchange of letters between Zenobia and Aurelian recorded in the *Historia Augusta* at this time is clearly a fiction. Nevertheless the besieged suffered a blow when their Armenian allies defected to the Roman side. Zenobia thereupon fled towards Persia – whence she had expected help – but was caught at the Euphrates by Roman cavalry. The city now opened its gates to Aurelian and it is clear that he was welcomed by some of the population there. The long struggle over, a garrison was installed and Aurelian set off for Rome. After crossing into Europe, however, he heard that the garrison had been massacred and another Palmyrene noble, thought to have been a relative of Zenobia, had raised the standard of revolt once more. Furthermore there were also disturbances in Egypt, again possibly fermented by Palmyrene agents. Aurelian hastily returned, at a speed that surprised the Palmyrenes, and this time made no mistake by sacking the entire city. Thus was

Palmyrene independence, and to a large extent Palmyrene culture and wealth, extinguished.

Zenobia is said to have been paraded in Aurelian's eventual triumph through Rome, loaded down with chains of gold. Most sources agree, however, that she in fact ended her days in a villa at Tivoli just outside Rome and there are even suggestions that she may have married again.

Zenobia the queen of Palmyra has passed into Western, and Arabic, literature as a romantic figure. Most emphasize her beauty, her chastity, and above all her bravery, stamina, and fortitude in taking on the might of Rome. Nevertheless, she must also be remembered as an agent of the distinctive Graeco-Syrian culture that was Palmyra's, tempered with an enquiring mind in the best traditions of the far-flung Hellenic world.

JULIAN M.C. BOWSHER

See also Palmyra

Biography

The second wife of Septimius Odenathus of Palmyra in Syria, on his death in AD 267 Zenobia assumed power on behalf of her son. Palmyra was at its cultural peak and she attracted writers to her court. Leading a revolt against Roman power, her forces conquered first Egypt in 269–70 and then Antioch and much of Asia Minor. Finally subdued by Aurelian in 272, Zenobia died at Tivoli near Rome.

Further Reading

Bowersock, G.W., "The Hellenism of Zenobia" in *Greek Connections: Essays on Culture and Diplomacy*, edited by John T.A. Koumoulides, Notre Dame, Indiana: University of Notre Dame Press, 1987

Graf, D.F., "Zenobia and the Arabs" in *The Eastern Frontier of the Roman Empire*, edited by D.H. French and C.S. Lightfoot, 2 vols, Oxford: BAR, 1989

Millar, F.G.B., "Paul of Samosata, Zenobia and Aurelian: The Church, Local Culture and Political Allegiance in Third-Century Syria", *Journal of Roman Studies*, 61 (1971): pp. 1–17

Schneider, Eugenia Equini, "Septimia Zenobia Sebaste 'L'Erma' di Bretschneider", *Studi Archaeologica*, 61 (1993)

Stoneman, Richard, *Palmyra and Its Empire: Zenobia's Revolt against Rome*, Ann Arbor: University of Michigan Press, 1992

Zervas, Napoleon 1891–1957

Resistance leader

Napoleon Zervas was one of the preeminent leaders of the national resistance movement in Greece in both the political and the military realms. Born in the province of Arta, Zervas enlisted in the Greek national army upon completion of his schooling as a volunteer, and at the age of 21 had his first encounter with the battlefield in the Balkan Wars (1912–13). Shortly before the outbreak of World War I Zervas studied briefly at the academy for non-commissioned officers and in 1914 received the rank of second lieutenant.

The Greek political sphere was divided between the supporters of neutrality represented by king Constantine and the advocates of an active alliance for involvement in the war led by the prime minister Eleftherios Venizelos. Zervas supported the Venizelist movement from the outset and participated in the Macedonian front, which in 1918 resulted in the armistice with Bulgaria. For his contribution to the campaign and for his valour and courage Zervas was in 1920 promoted to the rank of major. As a staunch supporter of the democratic movement he was forced to flee following the defeat of Venizelos in the elections of 1920. He moved to Constantinople where he joined the Venizelist support group, always in anticipation of his return to Greece. In 1922 he was given that opportunity and immediately upon returning to Athens joined the armed forces, becoming within a short period of time a lieutenant colonel.

The devastating losses of the Asia Minor campaign had a disastrous impact both militarily and politically. The political vacuum resulted in the dictatorship of Theodoros Pangalos in June 1925. Zervas, who was closely associated with the general, became garrison commander of Athens and in August 1926 was placed as adjutant to the president of the republic, Pavlos Kountouriotis. Zervas had the crucial role of battalion commander of one of the two main battalions that guarded Athens and supported general Pangalos. Zervas, taking advantage of the political instability, was quick to join the counter-coup of 22 August 1926 by Georgios Kondilis. As a reward he received full command of the Athens brigade, which had previously been divided between himself and lieutenant colonel Panagiotis Dertilis. A few days after his appointment, however, Kondilis decided to disband the Democratic Guard responsible for the protection of the city, which resulted in the outbreak of hostilities between units supporting Zervas and government forces. The deadly battles fought in the streets of Athens ended in defeat and a sentence of life imprisonment for Zervas. Two years later, following the return to power of the Venizelists, Zervas was released. He withdrew from politics, only to return following the invasion of Greece by the Axis troops in April 1941. With the assistance of liberal democrats and under the guidance of general Nikolaos Plastiras, who at the time was in self-imposed exile in France, Zervas founded in September 1941 the *Ethnikos Dimokratikos Ellinikos Syndesmos* (EDES, the National Democratic Hellenic Union). The goals of this movement were the expulsion of the occupation forces and a return to parliamentary democracy. Zervas established a paramilitary organization in June 1942 which waged a guerrilla war against the Italian and German forces. The Ethnikes Omades Ellinon Antarton (EOEA, National Bands of Greek Rebels) were a paramilitary faction of EDES and were involved in sabotage missions against the Axis, including the destruction of the Gorgopotamos bridge on 25 November 1942.

Zervas remained actively involved in the guerrilla movements throughout the war, but his forces were inferior to the power of EAM (*Ethniko Apeleftherotiko Metopo*, the National Liberation Front) and its military wing ELAS (*Ellinikos Laikos Apeleftherotikos Stratos*, the Greek Popular Liberation Army). After the end of the war, EAM/ELAS oscillated between concealed and open resistance, according to political circumstance, refusing to recognize the postwar Greek government of Papandreou. The superiority of the EAM forces resulted in the loss of the Epirus region which Zervas had secured during the occupation. He was forced to retreat to Corfu where he retired from military life in March 1945 with the rank of lieutenant general.

Napoleon Zervas

Further Reading

Dimitriou, D., *Gorgopotamos: Ta Phovera Dokoumenta* [Gorgopotamos: The Celebrated Documents], Athens, 1975

Farakos, G., *Ares Velouchiotis: To Chameno Archeio – Agnosta Kimena* [Ares Velouchiotis: The Missing Records – Unknown Texts], Athens, 1997

Fleischer, Hagen, *Im Kreuzschatten der Mächte: Griechenland 1941–1944 (Okkupation, Resistance, Kollaboration)*, 2 vols, Frankfurt: Peter Lang, 1986

Hammond, Nicholas, *Venture into Greece: With the Guerrillas 1943–44*, London: Kimber, 1983

Hamson, Denys, *We Fell among Greeks*, London: Jonathan Cape, 1946

Hondros, *Occupation and Resistance. The Greek Agony 1941–1944*, New York: Pella, 1983

Iatrides, John O. (editor), *Greece in the 1940s: A Nation in Crisis*, Hanover, New Hampshire: University Press of New England, 1981

Iatrides, John O. and Linda Wrigley (editors), *Greece at the Crossroads: The Civil War and its Legacy*, University Park: Pennsylvania State University Press, 1995

Mazower, Mark, *Inside Hitler's Greece: The Experience of Occupation, 1941–44*, New Haven and London: Yale University Press, 1993

Myers, E.C.W., *Greek Entanglement*, 2nd edition, Gloucester: Alan Sutton, 1985

Papastratis, P., *British Policy towards Greece during the Second World War 1941–1944*, Cambridge: Cambridge University Press, 1984

Pyromaglou, K., *O Doureios Ippos* [The Trojan Horse], Athens, 1957

Richter, Heinz, *Griechenland zwischen Revolution und Konterrevolution (1936–1946)*, Frankfurt: Europäische Verlagsanstalt, 1973

Woodhouse, C.M., *The Apple of Discord*, London: Hutchinson, 1948

Woodhouse, C.M., *The Struggle for Greece 1941–1949*, London: Hart Davis, MacGibbon, 1976; New York: Beckman Esanu, 1979

Zaousis, A., *Oi dio Ochthes, 1939–45: Mia Prospatheia Ethniki Symphiliosis* [The Two Shores, 1939–45: An Attempt at National Reconciliation], Athens, 1987

Aware of the political vacuum once again, Zervas remained active not as a military figure, but as the founder of the National Party. During the elections of 1946 he secured 20 seats in Parliament and later served as minister of public order (1947) in the government of Dimitrios Maximos. In the elections of 1950 Zervas lost 13 seats and had to create an alliance with the Liberal Party. He served as minister of public works under the government of Sofoklis Venizelos (1950–51). During the elections of 1952 Zervas was unable to accumulate enough votes to secure any seats in Parliament and retired from the political scene. He died five years later, having served the democratic causes in which he believed.

STELIOS ZACHARIOU

Biography

Born in 1891 in the province of Arta, Zervas fought in the Balkan Wars (1912–13). In World War I he supported Venizelos and fought on the Macedonian front. He became garrison commander of Athens in 1925 and commander of the Democratic Guard in 1926. In 1941 he founded the National Democratic Hellenic Union (EDES) and engaged in sabotage missions against the Germans and Italians. After the war he served twice as a government minister. He died in 1957.

Zoe *c.*978–1050

Empress

Empress Zoe and her younger sister Theodora were the last surviving heirs of the Macedonian dynasty of the Byzantine empire. They were the second and third daughters respectively of Constantine VIII (1025–28); the eldest, Evdokia, had entered religious life. Zoe and Theodora occupy a unique place in Byzantine history, in that they were the only princesses born in the purple (*porphyrogennetai*) to be the bearers of dynastic legitimacy to the throne. Other empresses, such as Irene (780–802) and Evdokia (1067; again in 1071), ruled only through their rights as widows and/or mothers of emperors.

Constantine VIII waited until he was on his deathbed to find himself a son-in-law and successor to marry Zoe. His choice was Romanos Argyros, eparch of the city of Constantinople. Romanos and Zoe were married on 12 November 1028, and Romanos ascended the throne as Romanos III (1028–34) on Constantine's death three days later. Zoe was at that time nearly 50 years of age. Michael

Psellos, in his *Chronographia*, reports that the royal pair consulted fertility experts when they failed to conceive a child. Indeed, Psellos claims that Zoe even resorted to magical practices, but with no success. The couple gave up, and each took other lovers. Zoe fell in love with a young man from Paphlagonia named Michael, the brother of John the Orphanotrophos, an influential eunuch at court.

Romanos died in his bath on 11 April 1034, ostensibly murdered by the agents of Michael and Zoe. The lovers married that evening, and Michael became emperor Michael IV (1034–41). He quickly lost interest in Zoe; she had merely been his route to power. He kept her under guard in the women's quarters, fearing that she might take revenge against him. But Zoe suffered quietly, and agreed to adopt his nephew, also named Michael, as her son and heir. This scheme was engineered by John the Orphanotrophos, who wanted the throne to remain in his family.

Michael IV died of epilepsy on 10 December 1041. The new emperor, Michael V Kalaphates (1041–42), turned against those who had raised him to the throne: first he exiled his uncle, John the Orphanotrophos; then he banished the empress Zoe to a convent. A popular uprising ensued, fuelled by the feeling that Zoe (and Theodora) were the legitimate rulers of the empire by right of their birth. Michael was viewed as a usurper, and so was deposed and blinded on 20 April 1042. Zoe and Theodora ruled jointly for three months, until Zoe decided to marry once more. She chose Constantine Monomachos, a senator, who ruled as Constantine IX (1042–55). The two empresses shared the throne with Constantine but left the running of government affairs to him. Zoe even accepted his mistress, Sklerena, and agreed to honour her with the newly created title *Sebaste* ("Augusta"); the mistress ranked just below the emperor and the two empresses. These four proceeded to empty the treasury of funds, contributing to the decline of the Byzantine state in the 11th century.

While Zoe did not actively engage in politics herself, the rule of her consorts was characterized by the rise of the civil aristocracy and policies which favoured that party's interests. Landed magnates also began to increase their power and wealth at the expense of the small-holdings of soldiers and free peasants. According to George Ostrogorsky, the emperors themselves are not entirely to blame for these developments: "They were merely the exponents of vigorous and irresistible social and economic forces" (p. 323).

Zoe loved much and was known for her generosity, long-suffering, and piety; she also committed murder, hated her sister, and dabbled in the occult. She also spent money on costly incense and on materials used to manufacture perfumes and ointments, an unusual hobby that she and Theodora shared. Psellos expresses surprise that Zoe preferred this hobby to more typically feminine occupations such as weaving and needlework; nor did she adorn herself in luxurious gowns as one might expect a woman of her rank to do. He does, however, comment with approval on Zoe's piety. Thanks to Psellos's observations we have some idea of how Zoe compared to the ideal aristocratic woman of her time.

Empress Zoe died in 1050, during the reign of Constantine IX, who survived her by five years. After Constantine's death in 1055, Theodora ruled again in her own right for less than

Zoe: mosaic showing Christ enthroned between Zoe and Constantine IX Monomachos, Hagia Sophia, Constantinople, 11th century

two years until her death in 1056. Zoe and Theodora, as the last members of the Macedonian dynasty, were the only women in Byzantine history to rule as empresses by right of birth. Zoe was also unique in that she was the only empress to give legitimacy to her husbands' rights to the throne: they became emperors only because of her own dynastic inheritance. A mosaic portrait of Zoe and Constantine IX flanking the enthroned Christ survives in the south gallery of Hagia Sophia in Constantinople.

CONSTANTINA SCOURTIS

Biography

Born *c*.978 the second daughter of Constantine VIII, Zoe and her sister Theodora were the last heirs of the Macedonian dynasty. Her husbands were Romanos III (r. 1028–34), Michael IV (r. 1034–41), and Constantine IX (r. 1042–55). Zoe and Theodora reigned jointly from 21 April to 12 June 1042, the only women in Byzantine history to do so by right of birth. Zoe died in Constantinople in 1050.

Further Reading

Ostrogorsky, George, *History of the Byzantine State*, translated by Joan Hussey, 2nd edition, Oxford: Blackwell, 1968; New Brunswick, New Jersey: Rutgers University Press, 1969

Psellos, Michael, *The Chronographia*, translated by E.R.A. Sewter, London: Routledge, and New Haven, Connecticut: Yale University Press, 1953; as *Fourteen Byzantine Rulers*, Harmondsworth and New York: Penguin, 1966, reprinted 1982

Zonaras, John

Historian, theologian, and canonist of the 12th century

Born in the last decade or two of the 11th century, Zonaras achieved a certain distinction in the service of Alexios I Komnenos (1081–1118), acting as a judicial official (*megas droungarios tes viglas*) and as head of the imperial chancellery (*protasekretis*). He appears, however, to have fallen out of favour with the imperial family, probably because of his criticism of Alexios's financial policies, particularly the distribution of public money and properties to his relatives, and shortly after the accession of Alexios's eldest son John II (1118–43) Zonaras was dismissed from court and became a monk at the monastery of St Glykeria. Here he composed his massive *Epitomi Historion*, a summary of history in 18 books beginning with the creation of the world and continuing to the death of Alexios in 1118. The latter portions of this history (especially book 18. 21–29) preserve his critical views of Alexios's reign and act as a polemical counterbalance to Anna Komnene's lengthy eulogy of her father. For the earlier sections of his history Zonaras relies on a wide variety of sources – biblical, Classical (e.g. Arrian, Cassius Dio, Herodotus, Xenophon, Plutarch, Philostratus), and near-contemporary (especially Psellos and Skylitzes). Especially valuable are the sections of his narrative that reflect sources now lost, in particular his account of the so-called Neo-Flavian emperors Constantius II and Julian "the Apostate", preserving content from the histories of Philostorgius and Theophanes. Even more valuable is Zonaras's summary of early Roman history, since it is based largely on the lost books 1–21 of Cassius Dio's *Roman History*, a work that was highly esteemed among Byzantine scholars, especially for its insights into the foundations of the principate, a form of government that they found not unlike their own. Zonaras's interest in Dio may have been prompted by the *Epitome* of the Roman historian assembled by Xiphilinos, a well-known and near-contemporary literary figure who was prominent early in the reign of Alexios I. Zonaras reflects a close dependence on Xiphilinos's work for his narrative of events following Trajan's reign (AD 98–117), but his techniques of compression produce a result rather more coherent and intelligible than that of his countryman. Zonaras's *Epitome* was used extensively by later scholars, notably Constantine Manasses and Michael Glykas, and was translated into Serbian, Old Church Slavonic, and later, during the Renaissance, into Latin, French, and Italian. No English translation has yet been produced.

In addition to the *Epitome* Zonaras also wrote important *Commentaries* (*Patrologia Graeca* [PG], 137 and 138) on the Apostolic Constitutions, canons of councils, and the Church Fathers. Cardinal Pitra, the eminent 19th-century Church legal scholar, described Zonaras as "easily the most eminent of all commentators on Byzantine law" (*facile omnium juris byzantini magistrorum princeps*), and it is evident that Zonaras's *Commentaries* were closely consulted by other respected canonists, including Alexios Aristenos and Theodore Balsamon. Zonaras carefully distinguishes (PG 137. 509) "the investigation of dogma and decisions (*psephoi*) from formal canons which bore the authoritative signature of emperors and fathers".

Zonaras is also known to have written a synodal monograph (PG 119. 741–42) concerning degrees of consanguinity as they pertained to marriage law, as well as a synodal oration (PG 119. 1011–32) examining the moral implications associated with seminal discharge (*physiki tis gonis ekroi*). From a letter of Michael Glykas we hear of a poem written by Zonaras in which doctrine concerning the nature of the Holy Spirit is disputed.

Among Zonaras's homiletic and hagiographic writings are sermons for the feast of the Hypapante, commemorating the presentation of the infant Christ in the Temple, as well as one for the Sunday of the Veneration of the Cross; also a *Life* of pope Silvester I, celebrating the popular legend that it was he who had baptized Constantine the Great in Rome. Until 1913 this work had been published only in Latin translation and had been attributed to Symeon Metaphrastes. The anonymous editor of the original Greek text (*Roma e l'Oriente*, 6 (1913): pp. 340–67) has adduced linguistic and historical evidence that has convinced most scholars that Zonaras was, indeed, the author of this biography. Also among Zonaras's writings are commentaries on the writings of John of Damascus pertaining to Church precepts regarding the Resurrection, as well as on the epigrams of Gregory of Nazianzus (PG 138), and finally a Canon (hymnographic verse), in the Theotokion mode, concerning various heresies (PG 135. 413–422). Attested, but no longer extant, are Zonaras's summaries of the writings of Cyril of Alexandria, Sophronios, patriarch of Jerusalem, and a *Life* of St Eupraxia. A lexical collection of words from important books preserved under Zonaras's name is almost certainly not his work but rather that of an otherwise unknown Antonios Monachos.

No firm date can be established for Zonaras's death, but because his *Commentary* on the Canons appears to reflect familiarity with that of Alexios Aristenos, written in the late 1150s, some date shortly thereafter may be suggested.

M. JAMES MOSCOVICH

Biography

Born in the late 11th century, Zonaras became a judicial official at the court of Alexios I Komnenos. Dismissed by John II, Zonaras became a monk. His chronicle *Epitomi Historion* summarizes history from the Creation to 1118. He also wrote commentaries on Byzantine law, sermons, and other works. He died in the late 1150s.

Writings

Annales and *Epitomae historiarum*, edited by Moritz Pinder and Theodor Büttner-Wobst, 3 vols, Bonn: Weber, 1841–97

In *Patrologia Graeca*, edited by J.-P. Migne, vols 38, 119, 135, 137, 138

Further Reading

Angold, Michael, *The Byzantine Empire, 1025–1204: A Political History*, 2nd edition, London and New York: Longman, 1997

Beck, Hans-Georg von, *Kirche und theologische Literatur im byzantinischen Reich*, Munich: Beck, 1959

Buckler, Georgina, *Anna Comnena: A Study*, London: Oxford University Press, 1929, reprinted 1968

Dimaio, M., "History and Myth in Zonaras' 'Epitome Historiarum': The Chronographer as Editor", *Byzantine Studies*, 10/1, (1983): pp. 20–28

Dimaio, M., "Smoke in the Wind: Zonaras' Use of Philostorgius, Zosimus, John of Antioch, and John of Rhodes in His Narrative on the Neo-Flavian Emperors", *Byzantion*, 58 (1988): pp. 230–55

Hunger, Herbert, *Die hochsprachliche profane Literatur der Byzantiner*, vol. 1, Munich: Beck, 1978

Kazhdan, A.P., *Studies on Byzantine Literature of the Eleventh and Twelfth Centuries*, Paris: Maison des Sciences de l'Homme, and Cambridge and New York: Cambridge University Press, 1984

Zoology

It would not be entirely true to say that no Greek philosopher before Aristotle took an interest in the animal kingdom. Anaximander in the 6th century BC had speculated on the origins of animal life; Empedocles had included animals in his account of the cosmic cycle; and the Hippocratic treatises show some interest in the systematic study of animals in the context of their therapeutic value. None of this, however, shows signs of any but the most superficial observation. Democritus the atomist is credited with a treatise on zoology, but we have no idea what it contained; reports that survive, largely in the works of Pliny, consist of no more than disconnected anecdotes, without a context (indeed it is sometimes doubted whether Pliny's Democritus is the same as the philosopher). Plato's method of division embraces the classification of animals, but they are mentioned hardly at all in his surviving works. His successor Speusippus wrote a work called the *Homoia*, or Similarities, on defining classes on the basis of characteristics that individual members have in common, and he seems to have included animals in this process, but we know little about the work.

The fact that Aristotle, the author of the first surviving zoological treatises, feels the need to defend the study of animals (*On the Parts of Animals*, 644b22–646a4) gives a clue to reasons for the comparative neglect of this field. The imagined objectors against whom he directs his defence (presumably Platonists) regard animals as insignificant and distasteful, and are shocked by the prospect of the unpleasant task of dissection. They prefer the study of grander themes such as astronomy and cosmology, whose subjects are unconditionally beautiful and which admit of a degree of precision and absolute truth not possible in the study of the messier works of nature. Aristotle counters by pointing out that, lowly though they are, animals are at least accessible to close and detailed observation (unlike the heavenly bodies), and argues vigorously that all of the works of nature show purpose, and contribute to an end, and for that reason are intrinsically beautiful.

Five principal zoological treatises of Aristotle survive: *The History of Animals*, *On the Parts of Animals*, *On the Reproduction of Animals*, *On the Motion of Animals*, and *On the Progress of Animals*. They are, by any standards, remarkable works. Between 500 and 600 different kinds of animals are discussed, sometimes in considerable detail. There is clear evidence of the systematic collection of data throughout Aristotle's career. Place names mentioned suggest that he was already gathering information in northwest Asia Minor and on Lesbos, which he visited in the period between leaving the Academy in Athens and becoming the tutor of the future Alexander III of Macedon. There is no positive evidence from Aristotle's own works to support the suggestion that is sometimes made, both in antiquity and by later writers, that Alexander sent Aristotle interesting specimens gathered as he travelled east into the Persian empire. Nevertheless, the story should not be dismissed out of hand. For example, Aristotle is exceptionally well informed about the diet, capacities, habits, and anatomy of the domesticated elephant, and it may well be that reports on the animal had been sent to him in the course of Alexander's campaigns in the east. Elsewhere, much of his

information seems to have been derived from questioning fishermen, herdsmen, beekeepers, and travellers, among others. What is more, there are clear signs that Aristotle dissected a good number of specimens (or at any rate had access to reports of such dissections). He is credited with a work on dissection (now lost), and his extant works contain frequent references, not only to the results of dissection, but also to the technical problems involved (for example, he was aware that an animal killed by having its throat cut will not have its circulatory system in a normal condition, and recommends strangling instead; but his belief that the heart has three rather than four chambers suggests that his own technique may have been just as unsatisfactory). For the most part, however, the care and meticulousness of the observations are very impressive. For example, he describes in detail the development of a chick inside an egg (*The History of Animals*, 561a4–29): after three days, he says, the embryo of the chick can already be seen; later the parts of the body can be distinguished – first the heart and veins, then the head and the eyes; by the tenth day the chick itself is clearly distinguishable (and he describes what can be seen if one of the eyes is dissected); finally, the chick is ready to hatch on the twentieth day. This series of observations could have been made only as the result of a deliberately planned programme of investigation. One of the best known of his systematic descriptions is that of the reproductive system of the dogfish. This fish, like a number of other closely related fishes, bears live young, but Aristotle reported that it is unusual in that before birth the embryo is attached to its mother by a structure similar to the navel-string and placenta in mammals. It was only in 1842, after centuries of scepticism, that it was confirmed (by Johannes Müller) that Aristotle's account was essentially correct.

Impressive though this is, Aristotle is by no means infallible, and his works contain numerous mistakes. Some seem to be the result of simple observational error (such as his belief that a lion's neck contains only one bone, or that the heart has only three chambers). Sometimes, he seems to have been misled by fanciful travellers' tales (such as the report that hares invariably die if they are imported into Ithaca, or that the bite of the gecko is fatal in Italy). More significantly, he sometimes misleads himself by the inappropriate application of general principles, as when he argues that worker bees are neither male nor female, on the grounds that no female animal has defensive weapons (and worker bees have a sting), and no male animals care for their young (as worker bees do). Applying the same principles to queens (or "kings", as Aristotle calls them) and drones, he concludes that all three kinds of bee reproduce parthenogenetically, from their own kind. It must, however, be said, in Aristotle's defence, that the task of sexing a bee, using the resources he had available, would be by no means an easy one.

It is not at all clear what Aristotle thought was going to be the end result of his zoological researches. Although there is certainly evidence of systematic collection of material, the actual arrangement of the pieces of information in his zoological works shows no obvious system; facts are roughly grouped together by topics, but the structure of the classification remains obscure. It is too easy to assume that Aristotle was aiming at the sort of classification of animals that biologists, following Linnaeus, achieved from the 18th century onwards.

Though Aristotle's work can undoubtedly be regarded as the foundation on which later scientists built, it may well be that his own purposes were quite different from theirs, and that his collection of zoological facts was actually intended to be the raw material for his study of the purposive working out of nature's goals, or for an exercise in putting into practice his logical theories. Even so, the quality of his empirical investigations remains impressive, and without precedent until modern times.

After Aristotle, his pupils and associates continued with his work (and indeed it is likely that many of Aristotle's zoological treatises were themselves the result of collaborative work). His successor Theophrastus wrote *On the Character and Intelligence of Animals*, and a number of other works on the behaviour of different classes of animal, all of which have been lost. One short zoological work of Theophrastus, however, *On Fish*, does survive. It deals with the apparent anomaly of fish and other sea creatures which can sometimes be found surviving on dry land, or may even be dug up out of the ground, and shows evidence of careful observation of a variety of species. Theophrastus' successor as head of the Lyceum, Strato of Lampsacus, is also credited with works on zoology.

In the Hellenistic period some physicians (Herophilus, for example) seem to have taken an interest in comparative anatomy, and the surgeon Sostratus (1st century BC) is credited with the books *On Animals*, *On the Nature of Animals*, and *On Animals Which Sting and Animals Which Bite*. Dissection of animals later became a standard tool of medical research, but the real centre of interest is the human being. The same can be said of later writings on animal behaviour, which was of interest only in so far as it illuminated or provided models for human behaviour. Epicurus, for example, cited the alleged fact that animals invariably seek pleasure and avoid pain as proof that hedonism is natural (and his opponents the Stoics used zanimal examples to assert the opposite). Similarly, Plutarch investigated the question of whether animals are capable of exercising reason. This tradition was continued by Christian writers such as Origen and Basil of Caesarea, who used reports of animal behaviour derived from Aristotle and other Greek writers to illustrate moral arguments and as symbols representing theological positions.

The *Natural History* of the Roman writer Pliny the Elder contains a mass of facts about various animals, treated mostly as interesting curiosities without serious attempts at classification, and the same can be said of *On the Nature of Animals* and *Varia Historica* of Aelian. Both draw extensively on the writings of earlier Greek zoologists (indeed, more than two-thirds of Pliny's sources are Greek). The ultimate source of much of their information seems to be Aristotle himself, but these later writers seem not to have consulted his texts (or those of other authorities such as Theophrastus) directly, but to have used collections of excerpts (such as that of Pamphilius), summaries (such as that of Aristophanes of Byzantium), or works which are heavily dependent on earlier sources (such as Alexander of Myndos's *On Animals*). In other words, their works are in no way empirical studies, but are purely literary compilations drawing on reference works. It is in fact this moralizing and anecdotal tradition of zoology that passed on into the Middle Ages; it was only with the scientific revolution of the 17th century that Aristotle's systematic studies became the foundation of modern zoology.

RICHARD WALLACE

See also Animals

Further Reading

Fortenbaugh, William W. and Dimitri Gutas (editors), *Theophrastus: His Psychological, Doxographical, and Scientific Writings*, New Brunswick, New Jersey: Transaction, 1992

French, Roger, *Ancient Natural History: Histories of Nature*, London and New York: Routledge, 1994

Lloyd, G.E.R., *Early Greek Science: Thales to Aristotle*, London: Chatto and Windus, and New York: Norton, 1970

Lloyd, G.E.R., *Greek Science after Aristotle*, London: Chatto and Windus, and New York: Norton, 1973

Lloyd G.E.R., *Science, Folklore, and Ideology: Studies in the Life Sciences in Ancient Greece*, Cambridge and New York: Cambridge University Press, 1983

INDEX

Page numbers in **bold** indicate subjects which have their own entries in the encyclopedia

NOTES ON ADVISERS
AND CONTRIBUTORS

Anastasopoulou, Maria. Emerita Professor of English and Comparative Literature, Department of English, University of Athens; Professor of Modern Greek Literature and Culture, Hellenic-American Academy, Potomac, Maryland. Author of *Self-Reflexivity in Barth's and Beckett's Fiction* (1984), "Feminist Discourse and Literary Representation in Turn-of-the-Century Greece: Kallirrhoe Siganou-Parren's 'Books of Dawn'" in *Journal of Modern Greek Studies*, vol. 15 (1997), and articles on women's literature. Contributor to *Journal of Modern Greek Studies*, *Modern Greek Studies Yearbook*, *Southern Literary Journal*, and others. **Essay:** Parren.

Anderson, Michael J. Assistant Professor of Classics, Yale University. Author of *The Fall of Troy in Early Greek Poetry and Art* (1997). Contributor to *Journal of Hellenic Studies* and *Classical Philology*. **Essays:** Achilles Tatius, Bacchylides.

Angelov, Dimiter G. Doctoral candidate, Harvard University. Author of works on imperial power and ideology in Late Byzantium. **Essays:** Akropolites, Cyril, Gregoras, John III, Kritoboulos, Laskaris family, Methodios, Stephan IV, Andronikos II, Political History 1261–1453.

Argyropoulos, Roxane. Research Director, National Research Foundation, Athens. Author of (in Greek), *Philosophical Thought in Greece, 1828–1922*, (2 vols, 1995–98), *Neoklis Kazazis, The French Revolution: Sixth Section* (introduction and notes, 1993), and articles on Greece in the 18th century. **Essay:** France.

Arnaoutoglou, I.N. Researcher, Academy of Athens, Research Centre for the History of Greek Law. Former Assistant Editor of *Lexicon of Greek Personal Names*. Author of *Ancient Greek Laws* (1998). Contributor to *Cosmos* (1998) and to the journals *Zeitschrift für Papyrologie und Epigraphik*, *Ancient Society*, *Journal of Juristic Papyrology*, and *Revue Internationale des Droits de l'Antiquité*. **Essays:** Adoption, Law.

Ash, Rhiannon. Lecturer, Department of Greek and Latin, University College London. Author of "Severed Heads: Individual Portraits and Irrational Forces in Plutarch's *Galba and Otho*" in *Plutarch and His Intellectual World*, edited by Judith Mossman (1997) and *Ordering Anarchy: Leaders and Armies in Tacitus'* Histories (1999). **Essays:** Appian, Cassius Dio, Nero, Plutarch.

Asheri, David. Late Professor Emeritus, Hebrew University of Jerusalem. Author of *Distribuzioni di terre nell'antica Grecia* (1966), *Leggi greche sul problema dei debiti* (1969), *Fra ellenismo e iranismo* (1983), and *Erodoto: Le storie, Libro I* (1988), *Libro III* (1990). Co-editor of *I Greci* (1996–2000). **Essays:** Arrian, Hieronymus of Cardia, Posidonius.

Aspraki, Gabriella-Evangelia. Freelance researcher. **Essays:** Emigration, Village Society.

Athanassoglou-Kallmyer, Nina. Professor of Art History, University of Delaware. Author of *French Images from the Greek War of Independence: Art and Politics under the Restoration* (1989) and *Eugène Delacroix: Prints, Politics, and Satire* (1992). Editor of "Romanticism", *Art Journal* (1993). Member of the Institute for Advanced Study, Princeton. **Essays:** Gyzis, Lytras.

Austin, Michel. Senior Lecturer in Ancient History, University of St Andrews. Author of *Greece and Egypt in the Archaic Age* (1970), *Economies et sociétés en Grèce ancienne* (with P. Vidal-Naquet, 1973), and *The Hellenistic World from Alexander to the Roman Conquest* (1981). Contributor to the *Cambridge Ancient History* and to *War and Society in the Greek World*, edited by John Rich and Graham Shipley (1993). **Essays:** Antiochus III, Seleucids.

Avotins, Ivars. Professor of Classical Studies, University of Western Ontario. Author of *An Index to the Lives of the Sophists of Philostratus* (1978), *Index in Eunapii Vitas Sophistarum* (1983), *On the Greek of the Code of Justinian* (1989), and *On the Greek of the Novels of Justinian* (1992). Contributor to *Classical Quarterly*, *Glotta*, *Hermes*, *Rheinisches Museum*, *Transactions of the American Philological Association*, and *Phoenix*. **Essay:** Herodes Atticus.

Bäbler, Balbina. Freelance researcher. Author of *Fleissige Thrakerinnen und wehrhafte Skythen: Nichtgriechen im klassischen Athen und ihre archäologische Hinterlassenschaft* (1998) and of articles on Herodotus and the Zeus of Phidias. Contributor to *Der Neue Pauly* and *Bryn Mawr Classical Review*. **Essays:** Acragas, Chersonese, Chersonesus, Dyrrachium, Healing Cults, Metics, Olbia, Pausanias, Phidias, Slavery.

Barber, Robin. Honorary Fellow, Department of Classics, University of Edinburgh. Author of *The Cyclades in the Bronze Age* (1987), the Blue Guides to *Greece* (1989), *Rhodes and the Dodecanese* (1997), and *Athens* (1999), and articles on Greek art and archaeology. **Essays:** Altars, Cyclades, Dodecanese, Kaftantzoglou, Megara, Obsidian, Painting (Tourkokratia and modern), Pottery, Sanctuaries, Santorini, Votive Offerings.

Barker, John W. Professor Emeritus of History, University of Wisconsin-Madison. Author of *Justinian and the Later Roman Empire* (1966), *Manuel II Palaeologus, 1391–1425: A Study in Late Byzantine Statesmanship* (1969), *The Use of Music and Recordings for Teaching about the Middle Ages* (1988), *A Directory of American Byzantinists* (1996), and of articles on the Palailogan period and on opera. Contributor to *The Ottoman State and Its Place in World History*, edited by K.H. Karpat (1974), *Essays in Honor of Peter Charanis* (1979), *Tribute to Andreas N. Stratos* (1986), *Wagner in Retrospect: A Centennial Reappraisal* (1987), *To Ellenikon: Studies in Honor of Speros Vryonis Jr*, vol.1: *Hellenic Antiquity and Byzantium* (1993), *Peace and War in Byzantium: Essays in Honor of George T. Dennis SJ*, edited by Timothy S. Miller and John Nesbitt (1995), and *The Treasury of San Marco: A Symposium* (in preparation). **Essays:** Byzantine Period (Late), Byzantines, Constantine XI, Constantinople (Fall of), Gennadios II, John VI, John VIII, Manuel II, Manzikert, Mehmet II, Michael VIII, Palailogos family.

Bastéa, Eleni. Visiting Associate Professor, Comparative Literature, Washington University, St Louis. Author of *The Creation of Modern Athens: Planning the Myth* (2000). Contributor to *Cities: Critical Perspectives on Public Space*, edited by Zeynep Celik *et al.* (1994) and *Greek Society in the Making, 1863–1913: Realities, Symbols, Visions*, edited by Philip Carabott (1997). Member of the editorial board, *Journal of Architectural Education*. **Essays:** Architecture (domestic), Architecture (public), Cities, Neoclassicism, Town Planning.

Beaumont, Lesley A. Lecturer in Classical Archaeology, University of Sydney. Former Assistant Director, British School at Athens. Co-director of the Kato Phana Archaeological Project on Chios. Contributor to *The Sacred and the Feminine in Ancient Greece*, edited by Sue Blundell and Margaret Williamson (1998), and *Children and Material Culture*, edited by J. Sofaer Derevenski (in preparation). Author of articles on the archaeology of Chios and the iconography and social history of children and childhood in ancient Greece. **Essays:** Antiquity Service, Chios, Family, Smyrna.

Beck, Hans. Assistant Lecturer at the University of Cologne. Author of *Polis und Koinon: Untersuchungen zur Geschichte und Struktur der griechischen Bundesstaaten im 4. Jahrhundert v. Chr.* (1997). **Essays:** Federal States, Military League.

Bien, Peter. Professor of English and Comparative Literature, Emeritus, Dartmouth College. President of the Modern Greek Studies Association of America. Author of *Three Generations of Greek Writers: Introductions to Cavafy, Kazantzakis, and Ritsos* (1983), *Nikos Kazantzakis, Novelist* (1989), *Nikos Kazantzakis: Politics of the Spirit* (1989), and *God's Struggler: Religion in the Writing of Nikos Kazantzakis* (with D.J.N. Middleton, 1996). Translator of works by Kazantzakis and by Stratis Myrivilis. Former editor of *Journal of Modern Greek Studies*. **Essay:** Kazantzakis.

Blanchette, Scott. Defense Analyst, Global Research Corporation International. Intern to the editor, *Journal of Military History*, and contributor to the *Journal of Southwest Military History*. **Essays:** Bureaucracy, Sublime Porte.

Boardman, Sir John. Professor Emeritus of Classical Archaeology and Art, Oxford University. Author of *Greeks Overseas* (1964, 1999), *Greek Art* (1964, 1997), *Greek Gems and Finger Rings* (1970, 2000), *Diffusion of Classical Art in Antiquity* (1994), *Persia and the West* (2000), and of several handbooks on Greek vases and sculpture and many other books on Greek archaeology and art.

Borthwick, E. Kerr. Professor Emeritus, University of Edinburgh. Contributor to the *New Grove Dictionary of Music* and to *Classical Review*, *Classical Quarterly*, *Journal of Hellenic Studies*, *American Journal of Philology*, *Classical Philology*, *Hermes*, *Mnemosyne*, *Phoenix*, *Greece and Rome*, and *Music and Letters*. **Essay:** Dance.

Bourbouhakis, Emmanuel C. Doctoral candidate, Department of Classics, Harvard University. **Essays:** Solomos, Velouchiotis.

Bowman, Steven B. Professor of Judaic Studies, University of Cincinnati. Author of *The Jews of Byzantium, 1204–1453* (1985), "Josephus in Byzantium" in *Josephus, Judaism and Christianity*, edited by Louis H. Feldman and Gohei Hata (1987), and "Yosippon and Jewish Nationalism" in *Proceedings of the American Academy for Jewish Research* (1995). Editor of *Birkenau: The Camp of Death* (with Marco Nahon, 1989) and of *In Iure Veritas: Studies in Canon Law in Memory of Schafer Williams* (1991). Contributor to the *Oxford Dictionary of Byzantium* (1991) and *Encyclopedia of the Holocaust*. Book review editor of *Byzantine Studies/Etudes Byzantines* and of *Journal of the Hellenic Diaspora*. **Essay:** Jews.

Bowsher, Julian M.C. Senior Archaeologist, Museum of London Archaeology Service. Honorary Secretary, Palestine Exploration Fund. Author of articles on coins and archaeological sites in the Levant, including contributions to *Jerash Archaeological Project, 1981–1983*, vol.1, edited by F. Zayadine (1986), *The Defence of the Roman and Byzantine East*, edited by P.W.M. Freeman and D.L. Kennedy (1986), *The Eastern Frontier of the Roman Empire*, edited by D.H. French and C.S. Lightfoot (1989), *Studies on Roman and*

Islamic Amman, edited by A.E. Northedge (1993), and articles on Roman architecture in *The Dictionary of Art*. Contributor of articles to *ARAM, Palestine Exploration Quarterly*, and *Levant*. **Essays:** Palmyra, Zenobia.

Boyd, Michael J. Researcher. Author of *Middle Helladic and Early Mycenaean Mortuary Practices in the Southern and Western Peloponnese*, British Archaeological Reports (in preparation). **Essays:** Copais, Phaestus.

Braund, David. Professor of Black Sea and Mediterranean History, University of Exeter. Author of *Rome and the Friendly King* (1984), *The Administration of the Roman Empire* (1988), *Georgia in Antiquity* (1994), and *Ruling Roman Britain* (1996). Member of the editorial board of *Ancient Civilizations from Scythia to Siberia*. **Essays:** Athenaeus, Georgia, Ukraine.

Brock, Sebastian. Reader in Syriac Studies, University of Oxford. Author of *Syriac Perspectives on Late Antiquity* (1984), *The Luminous Eye: The Spiritual World Vision of Saint Ephrem* (1985, 1992), *The Syrian Fathers on Prayer and the Spiritual Life* (1987), *Studies in Syriac Christianity* (1992), *Bride of Light: Hymns on Mary from the Syriac Churches* (1994), and *From Ephrem to Romanos* (1999). **Essays:** Ephraim the Syrian, Isaac the Syrian.

Brosius, Maria. Research Associate, Centre for the Study of Ancient Documents, Oxford. Author of *Women in Ancient Persia, 559–331BC* (1996) and *The Persian Empire from Cyrus I to Artaxerxes I* (2000). Co-editor of *Studies in Persian History: Essays in Memory of David M. Lewis* (1998); editor of *Archives and Archival Traditions: Concepts of Record-Keeping in the Ancient World* (in preparation). **Essays:** Bactria, Parthians, Persian Wars, Persians, Sassanians.

Brown, C.G. Adjunct Professor, Department of Classics, George Washington University. **Essays:** Bouboulina, Old Calendarists, Sèvres

Brown, Christopher G. Chair, Department of Classical Studies, University of Western Ontario. Author of articles on Greek epic, lyric, drama, and religion. Contributor to *A Companion to Greek Lyric Poetry* (1997). **Essays:** Dithyramb, Poetry (Epic, antiquity), Poetry (Lyric, antiquity).

Bryer, Anthony A.M. Emeritus Professor of Byzantine Studies, University of Birmingham. Former Chairman of the British National Committee of the International Byzantine Association, and Convenor of the 21st International Byzantine Congress, Britain (2006). Author of *The Empire of Trebizond and the Pontos* (1980), *The Byzantine Monuments and Topography of the Pontos* (with David Winfield, 1985), *Peoples and Settlement in Anatolia and the Caucasus* (1986), and *The Post-Byzantine Monuments of the Pontos* (2000). **Essays:** Ani, Black Sea, Conversion, Crimea, Political History 1453–1832, Pontus, Trebizond.

Buckler, John. Professor of Greek History, University of Illinois. Author of *The Theban Hegemony, 371–362 BC* (1980), *Philip II and the Sacred War* (1989), and of articles on Greek history of the 4th century BC. Editor, with Hartmut Beister, of *Boiotika: Vorträge vom 5. Internationalen Böotien-Kolloquium zu Ehren von Professor Dr Siegfried Lauffer* (1989). Contributor to *American Historical Association's Guide to Historical Literature* (1995) and *The Oxford Classical Dictionary* (3rd edition 1996). **Essays:** Agesilaus II, Boeotia, Epaminondas, Marathon, Philip II, Thebes.

Buckton, David. Fellow of the Courtauld Institute of Art, University of London; Leverhulme Emeritus Fellow. Former Curator of Early Christian and Byzantine Antiquities, British Museum. Author of *Catalogue of the Medieval Enamels in the British Museum, 1: Byzantine and Early Medieval Western Enamel* (in preparation) and of articles on Byzantine enamels. Editor of *The Treasury of San Marco, Venice* (1984), *Studies in Medieval Art and Architecture, Presented to Peter Lasko* (with T.A. Heslop, 1994), and *Byzantium: Treasures of Byzantine Art and Culture* (1994). **Essay:** Enamel.

Budin, Stephanie Lynn. Graduate Student, University of Pennsylvania. Author of articles on gender and sexuality in the ancient Greek world. **Essays:** Gender, Women.

Campbell, J.K. Emeritus Fellow, St Antony's College, Oxford; former University Lecturer in Modern Balkan History. Author of *Honour, Family and Patronage: A Study of Institutions and Values in a Greek Mountain Community* (1964) and *Modern Greece* (with Philip Sherrard, 1969). Co-editor of *Europe Observed* (1995). **Essays:** Honour and Shame (modern), Patronage.

Carras, Costa. Vice-Chairman of Europa Nostra (Confederation of European Conservation Organizations). Author of *3000 Years of Greek Identity: Myth or Reality?* (1983) and of articles on the relation between Christian doctrine and the secular world. Co-editor of *Living Orthodoxy* (1996). Contributor to *Democracy and Civil Society in the Balkans* (1996). **Essays:** Chandris, Identity, Livanos, Makarios III, Orthodox Church.

Carson, Jeffrey. Professor of Literature and of Art History, Aegean Center for the Fine Arts. Author or editor of *Six and One Remorses for the Sky* (1972), *Paros* (with James Clark, 1977), *49 Scholia on the Poems of Odysseus Elytis* (1983), *The Temple and the Dolphin* (1995), *The Collected Poems of Odysseus Elytis* (1997), and *Poems 1974–1996* (1997). **Essays:** Menander, Poetry (Lyric, Byzantium and Modern), Renaissance (Palaiologan), Scopas.

Champion, Craige. Assistant Professor of History and Classical Languages, Allegheny College. Contributor to *Phoenix, American Journal of Philology, Historia, Transactions of the American Philological Association*, and *Bryn Mawr Classical Review*. **Essay:** Aetolia.

Cheal, Catheryn, L. Adjunct Professor, California State University, Northridge. Author of articles on Hellenistic clay sculptures and the coins of Selinus. Contributor to *Classical World*. **Essays:** Furniture, Silk.

Chimbos, Peter D. Professor of Sociology, University of Western Ontario. Author of *Marital Violence: A Study of Interspouse Homicide* (1978), *The Canadian Odyssey: The Greek Experience in Canada* (1980), and of articles on Greek communities in Canada. **Essays:** Civil War, World War II.

Chotzakoglou, Charalampos. Author of articles on Byzantine lead seals, Greek monks in Hungary, and on the appearance of the double-headed eagle in Byzantium. **Essay:** Eagle.

Christesen, Paul. Assistant Professor of Classics, Dartmouth College, New Hampshire. **Essays:** Finance, Taxation, Transhumance.

Chryssavgis, John. Professor of Theology, Holy Cross School of Theology, Brookline. Author of *Fire and Light* (1987), *Repentance and Confession* (1988, 1996), *Ascent to Heaven* (1989), *The Desert is Alive* (1991, 1994), *Love, Sexuality, and Marriage* (1996), *The Way of the Fathers* (1998), and *Beyond the Shattered Image* (1999). **Essays:** Australia, Monasticism.

Clay, Diskin. Professor of Classical Studies, Duke University. Author of *Lucretius and Epicurus* (1983), *Lucian of Samosata: Four Philosophical Lives* (1992), and *The Philosophical Inscription of Diogenes of Oenoanda* (1990), *Paradosis and Survival: Three Chapters in the History of Epicurean Philosophy* (1998), *Four Island Utopias* (with Andrea Purvis, 1999), and *Platonic Questions: Dialogues with the Silent Philosopher* (2000). Translator of *Philodemus: On Frank Criticism* (1988). Editor of the *American Journal of Philology*. **Essays:** Heroes and Heroines.

Conley, Thomas M. Professor of Speech Communication, University of Illinois, Urbana. Author of *Rhetoric in the European Tradition* (1990), *Byzantine Culture in Renaissance and Baroque Poland* (1994), "Byzantine Literary Criticism and the Uses of Literature" in *The Cambridge History of Literary Criticism*, vol. 2, edited by A. Minnis (in preparation), and an article on Aristotle's *Rhetoric* in Byzantium. **Essays:** Aristotelianism, Italos, Rhetoric, Second Sophistic, Sophists.

Connolly, David. Lecturer in Translation Studies, University of Athens. Translator of major 20th-century Greek poets, and author of articles on translating. **Essay:** Elytis.

Conomos, Dimitri. Visiting Professor, Royal Holloway and Bedford New College, University of London. Director of Studies, Academy of Theological Studies, Volos, Greece. Author and editor of publications for Syndesmos (the World Fellowship of Orthodox Youth) and the World Council of Churches. **Essay:** Ecumenism.

Constantinides, Stephanos. Professor, Department of Political Science, University of Quebec at Montreal; Director of the Centre for Hellenic Studies and Research (Canada). Author of *The Greeks in Canada* (1983), *The Social Structures of Cypriot Society and Their Influence on the Cyprus Question* (in Greek, 1995). Co-editor of *The Aegean Dispute* (1996) and *Greek Foreign Policy* 1997), and co-author of *Hellenism in the Twenty-First Century* (2000). Editor of *Etudes Helleniques/Hellenic Studies*. **Essays:** Fascism, George II, Turkey.

Constantoudaki, Maria. Assistant Professor of Byzantine Art, University of Athens. Author of "La pittura di icone a Creta veneziana (secoli XV e XVI)" in *Venezia e Creta*, edited by Gherardo Ortalli (1998), "L'arte dei pittori greci a Venezia" in *La pittura nel Veneto*, vol.3: *Il Cinquecento*, edited by Mauro Lucco (1999), and "Painting in Crete during the Fifteenth and Sixteenth Centuries" in *El Greco: Identity and Transformation*, edited by José Alvarez Lopera (1999). Co-author of *Research in Kato Mani* (1993). **Essays:** Damaskinos, Klontzas, Tzanes.

Cormack, Robin. Deputy Director, Courtauld Institute of Art, University of London. Author of *Writing in Gold* (1985), *The Byzantine Eye* (1989), and *Painting the Soul* (1998). **Essay:** Renaissance (Veneto-Cretan).

Coumounduros, Mark A. Graduate student, Harvard University. Contributor to *Let's Go: Greece and Turkey 1998* (1997). **Essay:** Karamanlides.

Crowther, Nigel B. Associate Professor of Classical Studies, University of Western Ontario. Contributor to *Classical Quarterly, Greece and Rome, Phoenix, Nikephoros, American Journal of Philology, Mnemosyne, Eranos, Journal of Hellenic Studies*, and *Classical Philology*. **Essay:** Olympia.

Cunningham, Mary B. Honorary Fellow, Institute for Advanced Research in the Humanities, University of Birmingham. Author of *The Life of Michael the Synkellos* (1991). Editor of *Mount Athos and Byzantine Monasticism* (with Anthony Bryer, 1996) and *Bulletin for British Byzantine Studies*. Review editor of *Sobornost* (incorporating *Eastern Churches Review*). **Essay:** Andrew of Crete.

da Costa, Virginia M. Assistant Professor of Art History, West Chester University, Pennsylvania. Author of articles on Renaissance portrait medals and Roman relief carvings and coins. Editor and curator of *Mothers, Maidens, Sirens and Slaves: Images of Women in the Ancient World* (1996). **Essays:** Painting (antiquity), Portraiture, Purple.

Dalby, Andrew. Author of *Siren Feasts: A History of Food and Gastronomy in Greece* (1996) and of *Empire of Pleasures: Luxury and Indulgence in the Roman World* (2000). Editor and translator of *Cato: On Farming* (1998). **Essays:** Fairs and Markets, Food and Drink, Libraries, Oral Tradition, Symposium.

Dark, Ken. Lecturer, University of Reading, and Chair, Late Antiquity Research Group. **Essays:** Byzantine Period (Middle), Constantinople, Great Palace, Hagia Sophia, Hippodrome, Petra.

De Chaves, Lila Chronopoulos. Ethnologist, Curator of the Jewellery workshop, Benaki Museum, and Consultant of ELKA (the Greek National Goldsmiths Centre). Author of *Greek Jewellery in Space and Time: History of the Art and*

Craft (1994), and of articles on Coptic textiles, lace, and traditional costumes. Editor of *Friends of the Benaki Museum Bulletin*. Vice-President, UNESCO International Committee for the Preservation and Promotion of Folk Art and Culture. **Essay:** Metalwork.

Demetriou, Kyriacos. Assistant Professor, Department of Social and Political Science, University of Cyprus. Author of *George Grote on Plato and Athenian Democracy: A Study in Classical Reception* (1999). Contributor to *History of Political Thought, Utilitas, Dialogos, Polis, Byzantine and Modern Greek Studies, Quaderni di Storia*, and *Classical Views*. **Essay:** Paparrigopoulos.

Dickey, Eleanor. Assistant Professor of Greek, Columbia University. Author of *Commentary on Selected Odes of Pindar* (1991) and *Greek Forms of Address: From Herodotus to Lucian* (1996). Contributor to *Mnemosyne, Classical Quarterly, Language in Society*, and *Journal of Linguistics*. **Essays:** Homer, Josephus, Language, Lucian, Satyr Play.

Dijk, Gert-Jan van. Professor of Greek, Catholic University of Nijmegen and Amsterdam Free University. Author of "De theorie van de fabel in de Griekse Oudheid" in *Mijn naam is haas: Dierenverhalen in verschillende culturen*, edited by W.L. Idema, M. Schipper, and P.H. Schrijvers (1993), "Greek Fable Theory after Aristotle: Characters and Characteristics" in *Greek Literary Theory after Aristotle: A Collection of Papers in Honour of D.M. Schenkeveld*, edited by J.G.J. Abbenes, S.R. Slings, and I. Sluiter (1995), and *Ainoi, Logoi, Muthoi: Fables in Archaic, Classical, and Hellenistic Greek Literature* (1997). Contributor to *Mnemosyne*. **Essays:** Aesop, Babrius, Fable.

Dillery, John. Associate Professor of Classics, University of Virginia. Author of *Xenophon and the History of His Times* (1995). Editor of the 1998 Loeb edition of Xenophon's *Anabasis*. Contributor to *Classical Philology, Historia, Classical Quarterly, Zeitschrift für Papyrologie und Epigraphik*, and *American Journal of Philology*. **Essays:** Isocrates, Theopompus, Xenophon.

Dover, Sir Kenneth. Chancellor of St Andrews University. Author of *Greek Word Order* (1960), *Lysias and the Corpus Lysiacum* (1968), *Greek Popular Morality in the Time of Plato and Aristotle* (1974), *Greek Homosexuality* (1978), *Greek and the Greeks* (1987), *The Greeks and Their Legacy* (1988), *Marginal Comment* (1994), and *The Evolution of Greek Prose Style* (1997). Co-author of *Historical Commentary on Thucydides*, vols 4 and 5 (1970 and 1980) and *Ancient Greek Literature* (1980). Editor of *Clouds* (1968) and *Frogs* (1993) by Aristophanes, *Select Poems* by Theocritus (1971), and *Perceptions of the Ancient Greeks* (1992). **Essays:** Aristophanes, Lysias, Thucydides.

Drosos, Fr Nektarios. Priest. Author of book on hagiography and articles on Thessalian history. **Essays:** Athanasios of Athos, Maximos the Greek, Olympus.

Edmonds, D.J. Freelance editor and lexicographer. Co-author of *The Oxford Dictionary for Writers and Editors* (1981), and author of *On Prayer* (with Fr Ioannikios Iliotis, 1991) and *The Oxford Reverse Dictionary* (1999). **Essay:** Nektarios of Aegina.

Edwards, Mark University Lecturer in Patristics, Oxford University. Co-author of *Portraits: Biographical Representation in the Greek and Latin Literature of the Roman Empire* (with S. Swain, 1997). Editor and translator of *Philoponus: Commentary on Aristotle, Physics III* (1994) and *Optatus: Against the Donatists* (1997). Contributor to the *Journal of Theological Studies*. **Essays:** Alchemy, Carneades, Christianity, Cynics, Dionysius the Areopagite, Eusebius, Gnostics, Irenaeus, New Testament, Origen, Paul, Theodoret.

Edwards, Michael J. Senior Lecturer in Classics, School of English and Drama, Queen Mary and Westfield College, University of London. Author of *Companion to Plutarch, Lives of Pompey, Caesar and Cicero* (1991), and *The Attic Orators* (1994). Editor of *Greek Orators*, vol. 1: *Antiphon and Lysias* (with S. Usher, 1985), *Greek Orators*, vol. 4: *Andocides* (1995), and *Lysias: Five Speeches* (1999). **Essays:** Aeschines, Demosthenes, Judicial Procedures, Magistrates, Ostracism, Political History 490–323 BC.

Ehaliotis, Constantinos. Lecturer, Agricultural University of Athens, and Research Fellow, National Agricultural Research Foundation. Contributor to *Agrivita, Soil Biology and Biochemistry*, and *FEMS Microbiology Ecology*. **Essay:** Pollution.

Ehaliotis, Rennos. Historian. Author of *Libraries of Sifnos, Cyclades: Catalogue of Printed Books* (with Nikos Andriotis, 1994). Currently engaged in the document transcription programme commissioned by the Oinousses Maritime Museum. **Essays:** Archives (modern), Croatia, Dalmatia, Historiography (modern), Nationalism, Papanastasiou.

Ekdawi, Sarah. Faculty Research Fellow, University of Oxford. Author of "Cavafy's Mythical Ephebes" in *Ancient Greek Myth in Modern Greek Poetry*, edited by Peter Mackridge (1996), and other articles on the poetry of Angelos Sikelianos and C.P. Cavafy. Contributor to *Byzantine and Modern Greek Studies, Journal of Modern Greek Studies*, and other journals. **Essays:** Cavafy, Sikelianos.

Erskine, Andrew. Senior Lecturer, Department of Classics, University College, Dublin. Author of *Hellenistic Stoa: Political Thought and Action* (1990) and *Troy Between Greece and Rome: Local Tradition and Imperial Power* (in preparation). **Essay:** Polybius.

Evans, J.D.G. Professor of Logic and Metaphysics, Queen's University of Belfast. Author of *Aristotle's Concept of Dialectic* (1977), *Aristotle* (1987), and *Moral Philosophy and Contemporary Problems* (1987). Contributor to the *Cambridge Philological Society, Journal of Hellenic Studies, Classical Review, Aristotelian Society Proceedings*, and *Philosophical Quarterly*. **Essays:** Dialectic, Parmenides.

Evans, James Allan. Professor Emeritus, University of British

Columbia. Author of *A Social and Economic History of an Egyptian Temple in Greco-Roman Egypt* (1961), *Procopius* (1972), *Herodotus* (1981), *Herodotus, Explorer of the Past: Three Essays* (1991), *The Age of Justinian: The Circumstances of Imperial Power* (1996), and a book on the empress Theodora (in preparation). **Essays:** Independence, Leonidas, Magna Graecia, Mavromichalis family, Sicily, Syracuse.

Evely, Don. Freelance research archaeologist. Author of *Minoan Crafts: Tools and Techniques* (1993). Co-editor of *Knossos: A Labyrinth of History* (1994) and *Minotaur and Centaur* (1996). **Essays:** Knossos, Minoans.

Fennell, Nicholas. Assistant Master, Winchester College. **Essay:** Paisy Velichkovsky.

Fernandes, Eugénie. Lecturer at the University of Liverpool and Member of King's College, Cambridge. **Essays:** Adultery, Antiquity, Children, Disease, Divorce, Dowry, Marriage, Prostitution, Spells.

Fiedler, Barbara. Lecturer in Classics, George Washington University. Author of "Ritual Innovation and Political Change in Iron Age Greece" in *Papers of the World Archaeological Congress, Southampton* (1986). **Essays:** Canals, Land Tenure, Water Management.

Fisher, Elizabeth, A. Associate Professor and Chair, Department of Classics/Semitics, George Washington University. Author of *Planudes' Greek Translation of Ovid's Metamorphoses* (1990) and *Michael Psellus: Orationes Hagiographicae* (1994). Translator of "The Life of Nikephoros, Patriarch of Constantinople" in *Defenders of the Images* (1998). Contributor to *Byzantion, Yale Classical Studies, Byzantine and Modern Greek Studies, Arethusa, Byzantinoslavica, Harvard Studies in Classical Philology*, and *Classical Outlook*. **Essay:** Planudes.

Fleming, K.E. Assistant Professor of History and Hellenic Studies, New York University. Author of *The Muslim Bonaparte: Diplomacy and Orientalism in Ali Pasha's Greece* (1999) and of articles on Turkish and Greek history. Book editor, *Southeast European Monitor*. **Essays:** Antisemitism, Armatoloi, Hellenism and Neohellenism, Hellenism as Viewed by Visitors, Ioannina, Janissaries, Jerusalem, Mar Saba, Ottoman Period, Souli, Ali Pasha.

Foley, Anne. Associate Professor, Classics Department, Queen's University, Kingston, Ontario. Author of *Argos and the Argolid, 800–600 BC: An Archaeological Survey* (1988), "Idle Speculation about Argos? Some Thoughts on the Present State of Eighth and Seventh Century Argive Studies" in *Klados: Essays in Honour of Professor J.N. Coldstream, BICS*, edited by C. Morris and A. Peatfield (1995), "Ethnicity and the Topography of Burials in the Geometric Period", *Argos et l'Argolide: Topographie et urbanisme*, edited by A. Pariente and G. Touchais (1998), and "Pheidon of Argos: A Reassessment" in *Argolo-Korinthiaka I*, edited by J. Fossey and P.J. Smith (1999). Contributor to *Excavations in the Levendis Sector at Asine, 1973–1974 and 1989*, edited by R.

Hägg and G. Nordquist (in preparation). **Essays:** Archaic Period, Geometric Period, Nauplia.

Foss, Clive. Professor of History, University of Massachusetts. Author of *Byzantine and Turkish Sardis* (1976), *Ephesus after Antiquity* (1979), *Roman Historical Coins* (1990), and *Nicaea* (1996). **Essays:** Ephesus, Nicaea, Political History 802–1204.

French, Elizabeth. Co-author of *The Mycenae Atlas* (in preparation). Co-editor of *Well Built Mycenae*. **Essays:** Mycenae, Mycenaeans, Pylos, Tiryns.

Frend, William H.C. Retired Professor and Clerk in Holy Orders; currently, Bye-Fellow of Gonville and Caius College. Author of *The Donatist Church: A Movement of Protest in Roman North Africa* (1952, 1985), *Martyrdom and Persecution in the Early Church* (1965), *The Early Church* (1965, 1991), *The Rise of the Monophysite Movement* (1972, 1979), *The Rise of Christianity* (1984), and *The Archaeology of Early Christianity* (1996). **Essays:** Copts, Gortyn, Martyrdom, Monophysites, Nestorius, Nicopolis.

Gallou, Chrysanthi. Doctoral candidate, Department of Archaeology, University of Nottingham. **Essay:** Tripolis.

Gantzias, George K. Lecturer in Communication Policy, City University, London. Author of *The Info-Communication Industry* (1998) and the forthcoming books *Digital Communication, New Media and Information Society in Greece: Convergence, Electronic Commerce and Portals* (with Demetris I. Kamaras), *Media Power, Digital Communication and Digital Markets in Greece* (with Kamaras), and *The Dynamics of Regulation*. Editor of the series *Communication, Media and Cyber Space* for Zeno Publishers, of the electronic journal *Greekpolitics* (www.greekelections.gr), and of the info-communication policy issue of *Synthesis: Review of Modern Greek Studies* (in preparation). **Essay:** Media (with Demetris I. Kamaras).

Gardikas, Katerina. Teacher of History in the Department of Journalism and Mass Communication, Aristotle University, Thessalonica. Author of "The Changing Language of Political Contention" in *Greek Society in the Making, 1863–1913: Realities, Symbols and Visions*, edited by Philip Carabott (1997) and *Protasia kai eggyiseis* [Protection and Guarantees] (1999), Contributor to *Balkan Studies* and *Deltiou tou Kentrou Erevnis Istorias Neoterou Ellinismou* (1998). **Essays:** Deliyannis, George I, Otho, Thessalonica.

Garland, Robert. Roy D. and Margaret B. Wooster Professor of the Classics, Colgate University. Author of *The Greek Way of Death* (1985), *The Piraeus* (1987), *The Greek Way of Life* (1990), *Introducing New Gods* (1992), *Religion and the Greeks* (1994), *The Eye of the Beholder* (1995), and *Daily Life of the Ancient Greeks* (1998). **Essays:** Afterlife, Death, Hades, Piraeus, Priesthood, Travel..

Garrett, Martin. Writer and lecturer. Author of *Massinger: The Critical Heritage* (1991), *Greece: A Literary Companion* (1994), *Sidney: The Critical Heritage* (1996), *Traveller's*

Literary Companion to Italy (1998), *A Browning Chronology: Elizabeth Barrett Browning and Robert Browning* (1999), and *George Gordon, Lord Byron* (2000). **Essays:** Byron, Corfu, Hadrian, Hieron I, Missolonghi, Ravenna, Rome.

GavriloviD, Zaga. Honorary Fellow, Institute for Advanced Research in the Humanities, University of Birmingham. Contributor to *Cahiers Archéologiques, Zograf, Jahrbuch der Österreichischen Byzantinistik, Byzantine and Modern Greek Studies, Nottingham Medieval Studies, Byzantinische Forschungen, The Dictionary of Art*, and *Dictionary of Eastern Christianity*. **Essays:** Bosnia, Montenegro.

Georganas, Ioannis. Research Student at the University of Nottingham. Contributor to *Corpus: Magazine of Archaeology and History*. **Essay:** Trade.

Gill, David. W.J. Senior Lecturer in Ancient History, University of Wales, Swansea. Author of *Artful Crafts: Ancient Greek Silverware and Pottery* (with Michael Vickers, 1994). Editor of *The Book of Acts in Its First Century Setting*, vol.2: *Graeco-Roman Setting* (with Conrad Gempf, 1994). Contributor to *The Oxford Classical Dictionary* (3rd edition 1996), *The Cambridge Illustrated History of Archaeology*, edited by P.G. Bahn (1996), and to the *American Journal of Archaeology, Annual of the British School at Rome, Antiquity, International Journal of Nautical Archaeology and Underwater Exploration, Jahrbuch des deutschen archäologischen Instituts, Journal of Hellenic Studies, Libyan Studies, Mitteilungen des deutschen archäologischen Instituts: Römische Abteilung, Oxford Journal of Archaeology, Revue des Etudes Anciennes*, and *Revue Archéologique*. **Essays:** Cyrenaica, Lysippus, Mines and Quarries, Pastoralism, Praxiteles, Sculpture.

Given, Michael. Research Fellow, Department of Archaeology, University of Glasgow. Co-author of *Under the Clock: Colonial Architecture and History in Cyprus* (1995). Contributor to *Journal of Mediterranean Studies, Journal of Mediterranean Archaeology, Levant, Deus Loci* and *Report of the Department of Antiquities, Cyprus*. **Essays:** Cyprus, Estates.

Gkamas, Dimitrios. Doctoral candidate, Manchester Business School. Contributor to *Money (Greece)* and *Money and Market (Greece)*. **Essays:** Banking, Hydra, Patras, Railways, Tobacco, Volos.

Goldstein, Erik. Professor of International Relations, Boston University. Author of *Winning the Peace: British Diplomatic Strategy, Peace Planning, and the Paris Peace Conference, 1916–1920* (1991), *Wars and Peace Treaties* (1992) and "The New Europe and the New Greece" in *Greece and Europe in the Modern Period: Aspects of a Troubled Relationship*, edited by P. Carabott (1995). Co-editor of *The End of the Cold War* (1990) and *The Washington Conference, 1921–22: Naval Rivalry, East Asian Stability, and the Road to Pearl Harbor* (1994). Editor of *Diplomacy and Statecraft*. Member of the editorial board of *Byzantine and Modern Greek Studies*. **Essays:** Metaxas, Venizelos.

Gothóni, René. Professor of Comparative Religion, University of Helsinki. Author of *Modes of Life of Theravada Monks: A Case Study of Buddhist Monasticism in Sri Lanka* (1982), *Paradise Within Reach: Monasticism and Pilgrimage on Mt Athos* (1993), *Tales and Truth: Pilgrimage on Mount Athos Past and Present* (1994), *How to Survive in Academia* (1996), and *Attitudes and Interpretations in Comparative Religion* (2000). Editor-in-chief of *Byzantium and the North* and *Acta Byzantina Fennica*. **Essays:** Monasteries, Pilgrimage.

Gounaris, Basil C. Head of Research Department, Museum of the Macedonian Struggle. Author of *Steam over Macedonia* (1993) and *Stis Ochthes tou Ydragora* [On the Banks of Ydragoras] (2000). Editor of *Taftotites Sti Makedonia* [Identities in Macedonia] (1997). Contributor to *Journal of Modern Greek Studies, Balkan Studies, East European Quarterly, Journal of Byzantine and Modern Greek Studies, Review, Makedhonika*, and *Ellinika*. **Essays:** Macedonia, Theotokis (George).

Graham, Daniel W. Professor of Philosophy, Brigham Young University. Author of *Aristotle's Two Systems* (1987). Editor of Gregory Vlastos, *Studies in Greek Philosophy* (1995). Translator of Aristotle's *Physics, Book VIII* (1999). Contributor to *Philosophical Quarterly, Archiv für Geschichte der Philosophie, Journal of the History of Ideas, Journal of the History of Philosophy, Classical Quarterly, American Journal of Philology, Oxford Studies in Ancient Philosophy, Apeiron, Phronesis*, and *Ancient Philosophy*. **Essays:** Cosmology, Empedocles, Heraclitus.

Graham, Mark W. Doctoral candidate and History Instructor, Michigan State University. Contributor to *Military Women Worldwide* (in preparation) and to *Medieval Prosopography*. **Essay:** Diocese.

Greatrex, G.B. Assistant Professor, Department of Classics, Dalhousie University, Halifix, Nova Scotia. Author of *Rome and Persia at War, 502–532* (1998). Contributor to *Journal of Hellenic Studies, Dumbarton Oaks Papers, Byzantion*, and *Byzantine and Modern Greek Studies*. **Essay:** Procopius of Caesarea.

Greene, Molly. Associate Professor, Princeton University. Author of "Bankrolling the Sultan: The Career of a 19th-Century Greek Patriot" in *Trading Cultures: The Worlds of Western Merchants*, edited by Jeremy Adelman and Steve Aaron (1999), *A Shared World: Christians and Muslims in the Early Modern Mediterranean* (2000), and an article on Ottoman land policy in Crete. **Essays:** Berlin, Great Idea, Lausanne, Rumeli.

Greenfield, Richard P.H. Associate Professor, Department of History, Queen's University, Kingston, Ontario. Author of *Traditions of Belief in Late Byzantine Demonology* (1988), "Sorcery and Politics at the Byzantine Court in the Twelfth Century: Interpretations of History" in *The Making of Byzantine History: Studies Dedicated to Donald M. Nicol*, edited by R. Beaton and C. Roueché (1993), "A Contribution to the Study of Palaeologan Magic" in *Byzantine Magic*, edited by H. Maguire (1995), "The Wayside Shrines of the Argolid" in *Argolo-Korinthiaka I*, edited by J. Fossey and P.J. Smith (1999), and *The Life of St Lazaros Galesiotes* (2000). **Essays:** Divination, Evil Eye, Magic, Necromancy, Shrines.

Grond, Maarten J. Teacher of classical languages at the Sint Maartens College, Maastricht. Contributor to *Nestornieuws*. **Essays:** Kalamata, Messene, Messenia.

Grünbart, Michael. Librarian, Fachbibliothek für Byzantinistik und Neogräzistik, University of Vienna. Author of an article on John Tzetzes in *Jahrbuch der Österreichischen Byzantinistik* (1996). **Essays:** Eustathios, Tzetzes.

Haldon, John. Professor of Byzantine History and Director of the Centre for Byzantine, Ottoman and Modern Greek Studies, University of Birmingham. Author of *Recruitment and Conscription in the Byzantine Army c.550–950: A Study of the Origins of the Stratiotika Ktemata* (1979), *Byzantine Praetorians* (1984), *Byzantium in the Seventh Century* (1990), *State, Army and Society in Byzantium: Approaches to Military, Social and Administrative History, 6th–12th Centuries* (1995), and *Warfare, State and Society in Byzantium 550–1204* (1999). Editor of *Byzantine and Modern Greek Studies*.

Hall, Jonathan M. Assistant Professor, Departments of History and Classics, University of Chicago. Co-author of "Achaian Poleis and Achaian Colonization" in *Introduction to an Inventory of Poleis*, edited by M.H. Hansen (1996). Author of *Ethnic Identity in Greek Antiquity* (1997), "Sparta, Lakedaimon and the Nature of Perioikic Dependency" in *Further Studies on the Ancient Greek Polis*, edited by P. Flensted-Jensen (2000), and of articles on ethnicity in *Proceedings of the Cambridge Philological Society* and *Omnibus*, and on Argive archaeology and history in the *American Journal of Archaeology*. **Essays:** Aeolians, Colonization, Dark Age, Dorians, Hellenes, Ionians, Political History to 490 BC.

Hamblet, Wendy C. Advanced Graduate Student in Philosophy, Pennsylvania State University. Contributor to *Face to Face with the Real World: Contemporary Applications of Levinas* (in preparation), *Eidos*, and *Philosophical Writings*. **Essay:** Ancestor Worship.

Hanson, Victor Davis. Professor of Greek, California State University, Fresno. Author of *Warfare and Agriculture in Classical Greece* (1983, 1998), *The Western Way of Warfare* (1989, 2000), *The Other Greeks* (1995, 1999), *Fields without Dreams* (1996), *Who Killed Homer? The Demise of Classical Education and the Recovery of Greek Wisdom* (with John Heath, 1998, 2000), *The Wars of the Ancient Greeks* (1999) and *The Soul of Battle* (1999). Member of the editorial board of *Arion* and *Military History Quarterly*. **Essays:** Oligarchy, Vine, Warfare (Antiquity).

Hardwick, Lorna. Senior Lecturer in Classical Studies, The Open University. Author of "Convergence and Divergence in Reading Homer" in *Homer: Readings and Images* (1992) edited by with C. Emlyn-Jones, L. Hardwick, and J. Purkis,

"Ancient Amazons: Heroes, Outsiders or Women?" in *Women in Antiquity*, edited by I. McAuslan and P. Walcot (1996), "A Daidalos in the Late Modern Age? Transplanting Homer into Derek Walcott's The Odyssey: A Stage Version" in *Proceedings of the January Conference: The Reception of Classical Texts and Images* (1996), *Translating Words: Translating Cultures* (in preparation), and articles on Greek social and cultural history and literature. Contributor to the *International Journal of the Classical Tradition*. Editor of *Reception of the Texts and Images of Ancient Greece* database (http://www2.open.ac.uk/ClassicalStudies/GreekPlays/index.html). Member of the European Network of Research and Documentation of Greek Drama. **Essay:** Tragedy.

Harlaftis, Gelina. Assistant Professor of Maritime Economic History, University of Piraeus. Author of *Greek Shipowners and Greece, 1945-1975: From Separate Development to Mutual Inderdepence* (1993), *A History of Greek-Owned Shipping: The Making of an International Tramp Fleet, 1830 to the Present Day* (1996, winner of the Runciman Award), "The Maritime Historiography of Greece since 1975" in *Maritime History at the Crossroads*, edited by Frank Broeze (1995) and articles on the history of Greek shipping. Co-editor of *Global Markets: The Internationalization of Sea Transport Industries since the 1850s* (1998) **Essay:** Onassis.

Harris, Anthea. Part-time researcher, University of Reading. **Essay:** Commonwealth.

Harris, Jonathan. Lecturer in Byzantine History, Hellenic Institute, Royal Holloway and Bedford New College, University of London. Author of *Greek Emigres in the West* (1995). Contributor to *Byzantinoslavica*, *Revue des Etudes Byzantines*, *Orientalia Christiana Periodica*, *Journal of Medieval History*, and *Journal of Ecclesiastical History*. **Essays:** Archives (Byzantium), Argyropoulos, Bessarion, Chrysoloras, Gaza (Theodore), George of Trebizond, Plethon, Theophanes of Crete, Theotokopoulos.

Harrison, Thomas. Lecturer in Ancient History, School of Greek, Latin and Ancient History, University of St Andrews. Author of *Divinity and History: The Religion of Herodotus* (2000), *The Emptiness of Asia: Aeschylus' Persians and the History of the Fifth Century* (2000), *Greek Religion: Belief and Experience* (in preparation), and articles on ancient historiography. Editor of *Greeks and Barbarians* (in preparation). Series editor of the Duckworth Classical Essays, Duckworth Companions to Ancient Tragedy, and Duckworth Archaeological Histories. Joint series editor for *Readings in the Ancient World*, Edinburgh University Press. **Essays:** Foreigners, Herodotus, Religion, Tyranny.

Hendrikx, J.F.W. Adviser on fine arts. Chair, Association of Friends of the Netherlands Institute at Athens. **Essay:** Tsarouchis

Henig, Martin. Visiting Lecturer in Roman Art, University of Oxford. Editor of *A Handbook of Roman Art* (1983). Author of *Religion in Roman Britain* (1984), *The Content Family Collection of Ancient Cameos* (1990), *Roman Sculpture from*

the Cotswold Region (1993), *Classical Gems: Ancient and Modern Cameos in the Fitzwilliam Museum, Cambridge* (1994), *The Art of Roman Britain* (1995), and *Roman Oxfordshire* (with Paul Booth, 2000). Editor of *Classicism to Neo-Classicism: Essays Dedicated to Gertrud Seidmann* (with Dimitris Plantzos, 1999). Honorary editor of *Journal of the British Archaeological Association*. **Essay:** Gems and Seals.

Hetherington, Paul. Retired. Author of *The "Painter's Manual" of Dionysius of Fourna* (1974, 1997), *Byzantium* (1981), and *Byzantine and Medieval Greece: Churches, Castles and Art* (1991). Contributor to *Apollo, Arte Veneta, Burlington Magazine, Byzantinische Zeitschrift, Cahiers Archéologiques, Dumbarton Oaks Papers, Gazette des Beaux-Arts, Jahrbuch der Österreichischen Byzantinistik, Journal of the Warburg and Courtauld Institutes, Rinascimento,* and *Zeitschrift für Kunstgeschichte*. **Essays:** Aegina, Arta, Cos, Dionysios of Phourna, Lemnos, Melos, Mistra, Monemvasia, Patmos, Samos, Samothrace, Symi, Thasos, Tinos.

Hidber, Thomas. Assistant, Classics Department, Berne University. Author of *Das Klassizistische Manifest des Dionys von Halikarnass: Die Praefatio zu "De Oratoribus veteribus"* (1996). Contributor to *Der Neue Pauly: Enzyklopädie der Antike* and to *Metzler Lexikon der antiken Autoren*. **Essay:** Dionysius of Halicarnassus.

Higgins, Michael D. Professor of Geology, University of Québec at Chicoutimi, Canada. Author of *A Geological Companion to Greece and the Aegean* (1996). **Essays:** Copper and Tin, Earthquakes, Geology, Gold, Iron, Marble, Minerals, Silver and Lead, Volcanoes.

Hinterberger, Martin. Research Fellow, Kommission für Byzantinistik der Österreichischen Akademie der Wissenchaften. Author of *Autobiographische Traditionen in Byzanz* (1999). **Essay:** Sphrantzes.

Hoffman, C.A. Independent scholar. **Essays:** Atheism, Superstition.

Holst-Warhaft, Gail. Associate Professor of Classics and Comparative Literature, Cornell University. Author of *Road to Rembetika* (1975), *Theodorakis: Myth and Politics in Modern Greek Music* (1980), *Dangerous Voices: Women's Laments and Greek Literature* (1992), and *The Cue for Passion: Grief and Its Political Uses* (2000). Translator of *Collected Poems of Nikos Kavadias* (1987) and other works of modern and ancient Greek literature. Poetry editor of *BookPress*. Book editor of *Journal of Modern Greek Studies*. Former Music critic, *Nation Review* (Australia). **Essays:** Theodorakis, Xenakis.

Holton, David. Lecturer in Modern Greek, University of Cambridge, and Fellow of Selwyn College. Author of *Diegesis tou Alexandrou* (1974) and *Greek: A Comprehensive Grammar of The Modern Language* (with Peter Mackridge and Irene Philippaki-Warburton, 1997). Editor of *Literature and Society in Renaissance Crete* (1991) and of *Kambos: Cambridge Papers in Modern Greek*. Member of the editorial board of *Byzantine and Modern Greek Studies* and of the international advisory board of *Journal of Mediterranean Studies*. **Essays:** Chortatsis, Kornaros.

Ierodiakonou, Katerina. Assistant Professor in Ancient Philosophy and Logic, National Technical University, Athens. Author of "The Image of Young Men in Visual Arts and Kavafis' Poems" in *Kavafis and the Young Men*, edited by D. Maronitis (1984, in Greek), "Rediscovering Some Stoic Arguments" in *Greek Studies in the Philosophy and History of Science*, edited by P. Nicolacopoulos (1990), *Alexander of Aphrodisias on Aristotle Prior Analytics 1.1–7* (1991), "The Stoic Indemonstrables in the Later Tradition" in *Dialektiker und Stoiker: Zur Logik der Stoa und ihrer Vorlaufer*, edited by K. Döring and T. Ebert (1993), "Alexander of Aphrodisias on Medicine as a Stochastic Art" in *Ancient Medicine in Its Socio-Cultural Context*, edited by Ph.J. van der Eijk *et al.* (1995), "Aspasius on Perfect and Imperfect Virtues" in *Aspasius: The Earliest Extant Commentary on Aristotle's Ethics*, edited by A. Alberti and R.W. Sharples (1999), *Analysis in Stoic Logic* (in preparation), *Michael Psellos' Paraphrasis on Aristotle's De Interpretatione* (in preparation), and "Michael Psellos' Scholia on the *Prior Analytics*" in *L'Organon d'Aristote et ses commentateurs*, edited by R. Bodéus and L. Dorion (in preparation). Editor of *Topics in Stoic Philosophy* (1999). **Essays:** Blemmydes, Logic, Metochites, Michael of Ephesus, Philoponus, Stoicism.

Irmscher, Johannes. Professor Emeritus, Academy of Sciences, Berlin. Author of *Götterzorn bei Homer* (1950), *Einführung in die Byzantinistik* (1971), *Aristoteles als Wissenschafts Theoretiker* (1982), *Antike Fabeln* (1988), and many other books and articles on ancient and Byzantine Greece. **Essays:** Arcadia, Socrates, Velestinlis.

Jeffreys, Elizabeth M. Bywater and Sotheby Professor, University of Oxford. Author of *The War of Troy* (1996) and *Digenis Akritis* (1998). Co-author of *Popular Literature in Late Byzantium* (1983). Editor of *Byzantine Papers* (1981) and *Studies in John Malalas* (1990). Co-translator of *The Chronicle of John Malalas* (1986). **Essays:** Chronicles, Chronology, Digenis Akritis, Doukas family, Hagiography.

Jeffreys, Michael. Sir Nicholas Laurantus Professor of Modern Greek, University of Sydney. Co-author of *Popular Literature in late Byzantium* (1983). Co-translator of *The Chronicle of John Malalas* (1986). **Essays:** Komnenos family, Modern Period, Poetry (Epic, Byzantium and modern).

Jenkins, Fred W. Head of Collection Management and Associate Professor, Roesch Library, University of Dayton. Author of *Classical Studies: A Guide to the Reference Literature* (1996). Contributor to *Zeitschrift für Papyrologie und Epigraphik, Bulletin of the American Society of Papyrologists, College and Research Libraries News, Eranos, Studia Papyrologica,* and *Archiv für Papyrusforschung*. **Essay:** Archives (antiquity).

Johnson, Edward. Professor and Chair, Department of Philosophy, University of New Orleans. Contributor to *Ethics* *and Animals*, edited by Harlan B. Miller and William H. Williams (1983), *Earthbound* (1984), *Animal Rights and Human Obligations*, edited by Tom Regan and Peter Singer (1989), *Encyclopedia of Ethics* (1992), *Cambridge Dictionary of Philosophy* (1995), *Nagging Questions*, edited by Dana E. Bushnell (1995), *Human Sexuality* (1997), *Encyclopedia of Applied Ethics* (1998), and to *Environmental Ethics*, *Ethics and Animals*, *Between the Species*, *Ethics*, *Philosophical Review*, *Social Science Quarterly*, *Philosophy of the Social Sciences*, and *Tulane Studies in Philosophy*. **Essays:** Freedom, Humanism.

Jurgens, Jane. Instructor of Information Studies and Librarian, Minneapolis Community and Technical College, Minnesota. Author of articles on Albanian-Americans and Greek-Americans in the *Gale Encyclopedia of Multi-Cultural America* (1995). **Essay:** Pallis.

Kaegi, Walter E. Professor of History, The Oriental Institute, University of Chicago. Author of *Byzantium and the Decline of Rome* (1968), *Byzantine Military Unrest* (1981), *Army, Society and Religion in Byzantium* (1982), *Byzantium and the Early Islamic Conquests* (1992, 1995), and "Egypt on the Eve of the Muslim Conquest" in the *Cambridge History of Egypt*, edited by C. Petry (1998). **Essays:** Africa, Herakleios, Warfare (Byzantium), Yarmuk.

Kalogeras, Dimitris A. Attorney at Law and doctoral candidate, University of Amsterdam. Author of "Grundzüge des griechischen Seerechts" in *Griechisches Wirtschafts und Unternehmensrecht*, edited by I.M. Papagiannis (1997), and of articles on legal matters in *Athens University Law Review*, *Efarmoges*, and *Review Enausma*. Member of the board of directors of *Athens University Law Review*. **Essays:** Canon Law, Cleomenes III.

Kamaras, Demetris I. Doctoral candidate, Graduate School of Journalism, City University, London. Author (with George K. Gantzias) of the forthcoming books *Digital Communication, New Media and Information Society in Greece: Convergence, Electronic Portals and Portals* and *Media Power, Digital Communication and Digital Markets in Greece*. Senior Editor (Business), *Epilogy Monthly Economic Review*. Senior Editor of the electronic journal *Greekpolitics* (www.greekelections. gr). **Essay:** Media (with George K. Gantzias).

Kamperidis, Lambros. Assistant Professor, Université de Sherbrooke. Author of *To Nay To Glyky...To Praon* (1982, 1990), *Apo Ton Bret Harte Ston Papadiamandi* (1992), and *The Greek Monasteries of Sozopolis: XIV–XVII Centuries* (1993). Editor of *Alexandros Papadiamandis: Short Stories and Essays* (in preparation). Contributor to *Parabola* and *Indiktos*. **Essays:** Diaspora, Mavrokordatos family, Neomartyrs, Romanticism, Ypsilantis family.

Kapsomera, Celia. Assistant Vice-President, Gerling Global Reinsurance, New York. Author of short stories published in *Ta Nea* and *Kathimerini* (1980–81). **Essay:** Sporades.

Karageorghis, Vassos. Professor Emeritus, University of Cyprus. Author of many books and articles on ancient Cyprus. **Essays:** Paphos, Salamis (city).

Karamanolis, George E. Doctoral candidate in ancient philosophy, Keble College, Oxford. **Essays:** Academy, Books and Readers, Choricius of Gaza, Diogenes Laertius, Epigram, Fate, Lyceum, Orphism, Pyrrho, Zeno.

Karanika-Dimarogona, Andromache. Doctoral candidate, Classics Department, Princeton University. Co-author of a textbook on modern Greek (in preparation). **Essays:** Ambelakia, Apulia, Calabria, Gods and Goddesses, Italy, Nonnus, Orgiastic Cults, Pelion, Prevelakis, Prodromos, Sacrifice, Women's Cults.

Karlin-Hayter, Patricia. Author of *Vita Euthymii Patriarchae* (1970) and *Studies in Byzantine Political History* (1981). Contributor to *Analecta Bollandiana*, *Byzantion*, *Byzantinische Forschungen*, *Byzantinische Zeitschrift*, *Byzantinoslavica*, *Dumbarton Oaks Papers*, *Jahrbuch des Österreichischen Byzantinistik*, *Revue Bénédictine*, *Revue des Etudes Byzantines*, *Speculum*, and *Traditio*. **Essays:** Arethas of Caesarea, Iconoclasm, Leo III, Leo the Mathematician, Theodora [d.867], Theodore of Stoudios.

Kartsonakis, Manolis. Teacher of Technology. Author of "Reasons for the Non-acceptance of Aristarchus' Heliocentric Theory: Aspects of an Astronomical Conflict" in *Ancient Greek Mathematics*, edited by D.A. Anapolitanos and B. Karasmanis (1993, in Greek), "Greek Philosophy and Christian Principles on Nature in Nikephoros Blemmydes' *Summary of Physics*" in *Orthodox Church and Science of Nature*, edited by G.D. Metalinos and L. Zouros (1996, in Greek), and "The Comparative Study of Newtonian Law of Motion and Pre-Newtonian Laws of Motions" (in Greek) in *Essays of 7th Congress of the Union of Greek Physicists* (in preparation). **Essay:** Simplicius.

Kasdagli, Aglaia. Lecturer, Department of History and Archaeology, University of Crete. Author of *Land and Marriage Settlements in the Aegean: A Case Study of Seventeenth-Century Naxos* (1999). Editor of the papers of the Scottish philhellene Thomas Gordon and author of articles about Gordon and his archive. **Essay:** Philhellenes.

Kazamias, George. Lecturer, Department of European Studies, University of Bradford. Author of articles on occupied Greece in World War II and on Greek security in *Balkan Studies*. **Essays:** Asia Minor Campaign, Balkan Wars, Communist Party, Constantine I, Constitution, EAM and ELAS, Niarchos, Political History since 1832, Refugees, St Catherine's Monastery, World War I.

Keen, Antony G. Associate Lecturer, Open University. Author of *Dynastic Lycia* (1998) and of an article on Athenian campaigns in Karia and Lycia in the *Journal of Hellenic Studies*. **Essays:** Lycia, Xanthus.

Kefalas, Georgia. Consultant, Anderson Consulting. **Essay:** Chatsidakis.

Kefallonitou, Frangiska. Director of the Byzantine Museum of Ioannina. **Essay:** Zagori.

Kennedy, Jennifer Y.T. Freelance writer. **Essay:** Naxos.

Kislinger, Ewald. Associate Professor, Institut für Byzantinistik und Neogräzistik der Universität Wien. Author of many articles on Byzantine history, material culture and everyday life in *Jahrbuch der Österreichischen Byzantinistik*, *Byzantinoslavica*, *Diptycha*, *Byzantinische Zeitschrift*, *Byzantiaka*, and other journals. Editor of Anna Muthesius, *Byzantine Silk Weaving AD 400 to AD 1200* (1997). Contributor to the annual news-bibliography of *Byzantinische Zeitschrift*. **Essays:** Andronikos I, Pelagonia.

Kitromilides, Paschalis. Professor of Political Science, University of Athens, and Director, Institute of Neohellenic Research, National Hellenic Research Foundation. Author (in English) of *Cyprus* (1982, 1995), *The Enlightenment as Social Criticism: Iosipos Moisiodax and Greek Culture in the Eighteenth Century* (1992), *Enlightenment, Nationalism, Orthodoxy: Studies in the Culture and Political Thought of South-Eastern Europe* (1994). Author (in Greek) of *Political Thinkers of the Modern Era* (1989, 1999), *The French Revolution and Southeastern Europe* (1990, 2000), *Modern Greek Enlightenment Political and Social Ideas* (1996, 1999), and *Rhigas Velestinlis Theory and Practice* (1998). Co-editor (in English) of *Small States in the Modern World: The Conditions of Survival* (1979) and *Culture and Society in Contemporary Europe: A Casebook* (1981).

Kosso, Cynthia K. Associate Professor of History, Northern Arizona University. Author of an article on a late Roman complex at Palaiochora in southern Euboea and other articles on Roman Greece. Contributor to *Philosophy of Science*. **Essays:** Achaea, Chalcis, Euboea, Political History 31 BC–AD 330, Roman Period.

Krikos-Davis, Katerina. Honorary Research Fellow, University of Birmingham. Author of *Diavazontas ton Seferi* (1989), *Kolokes: A Study of George Seferis' Logbook III (1953–1955)* (1994), and "Seferis and the Myth of Adonis" in *Ancient Greek Myth in Modern Greek Poetry*, edited by P. Mackridge (1996). Contributor to *Byzantine and Modern Greek Studies*, *Folia Neohellenica*, *Journal of Modern Greek Studies*, *Mandatoforos*, and *Scandinavian Studies in Modern Greek*. **Essays:** Enosis, Seferis.

Kyllo, Eric. Lecturer, Department of Classics, Baylor University. Author of an article on Lucretius in *Classical Bulletin* (1997) and numerous reviews. **Essays:** Harbours, Julian the Apostate, Larissa, Ottomans.

Lambrou, Michael. Associate Professor of Mathematics, University of Crete. Author and translator of several books. Contributor to the *Bulletin of the London Mathematical Society*, *Fundamenta Mathematicae*, *Indiana University Mathematical Journal*, *Integral Equations and Operator Theory*, *Journal of Approximation Theory*, *Journal of the London Mathematical Society*, *Journal of Mathematical Analysis and Applications*, *Journal of Operator Theory*, *Linear Algebra and Its Applications*, *Memoirs of the American Mathematical Society*, *Proceedings of the American Mathematical Society*, and *Studia Mathematica*. Scientific Adviser to *Quantum*. **Essay:** Hypatia.

Lapatin, Kenneth D.S. Professor of Art History, Boston University. Author of "Antiquity Consumed: Transformations at San Marco" in *Antiquity and Its Interpreters*, edited by Alina Payne *et al.* (2000) and *Chryselephantine Statuary in the Ancient Mediterranean World* (in preparation). Contributor to *Archaeology*, *American Journal of Archaeology*, *Art Bulletin*, *Bonner Jahrbücher des Rheinischen Landesmuseums*, *Museum Helveticum*, *Hesperia*, *Bryn Mawr Classical Review*, *International Journal of the Classical Tradition*, and *Source: Notes in the History of Art*. **Essay:** Ivory.

Lavdas, Kostas A. Senior Lecturer in Political Science, University of the West of England; Research Associate, Hellenic Centre for Political Research, Panteion University, Athens. Author of *The Europeanization of Greece* (1997) and co-author of *Politics, Subsidies and Competition* (1999). Contributor to the *European Journal of Political Research* and *Journal of Political and Military Sociology*. Member of the editorial board of *Episteme koi Koinonia*. **Essays:** Army, Government, Industry, Republic.

Lemos, George. Director of Freud Lemos Ltd. **Essays:** Cilicia, Ships and Shipping.

Liebeschuetz, J.H.W.G. Professor Emeritus, Department of Classical and Archaeological Studies, Nottingham University. Author of *Antioch* (1972), *Continuity and Change in Roman Religion* (1979), *Barbarians and Bishops* (1990), and *From Diocletian to the Arab Conquest* (1990). **Essays:** Antioch, Beirut, Gaza, Libanius, Miletus, Syria.

Lingas, Alexander. British Academy Postdoctoral Research Fellow, St Peter's College, Oxford. Author of "Hesychasm and Psalmody" in *Mount Athos and Byzantine Monasticism*, edited by Anthony Bryer and Mary Cunningham (1996) and "The Liturgical Use of the Kontakion in Constantinople" in *Liturgy, Architecture and Art in the Byzantine World* (1995). Contributor to *Byzantinorossica* and *Orientalia Christiana Periodica*. **Essays:** Callas, Chrysaphes, Hadjidakis, Hymnography, Instruments, Joseph the Hymnographer, Kassia, Koukouzeles, Music, Opera, Romanos the Melodist, Sakellarides, Skalkottas, Song, Symeon of Thessalonica.

Littlewood, A.R. Professor, Department of Classical Studies, University of Western Ontario. Author of *The Progymnasmata of Ioannes Geometres* (1972), *Michaelis Pselli Oratoria Minora* (1985), *Under the Presidency of Saint Paul: The Case of Byzantine Originality* (1996), and various articles, mainly on Byzantine literature (especially the Byzantine letter), Byzantine gardens, and the symbolism of the apple. Editor of *Originality in Byzantine Literature, Art and Music* (1995). Co-editor of *Byzantine Garden Culture* (in preparation). President of the Canadian Committee of Byzantinists. **Essays:** Anthology, Armenia, Astrology, Biography and

Autobiography, Byzantium, Calendar, Canada, Constantine IX, Coronation, Education, Exile and Detention, Games and Sports, Gardens, Geometres, Historiography (Byzantium and Tourkokratia), Hunting, Imperialism, Jeremias II, Literacy, Mardaïtes, Meteora, Olympic Games, Oracles, Photios, Psellos, Romance, Siegecraft, Technology, Theophilos, Wallachia.

Livanios, Dimitrios. Georgakis Research Fellow in Modern Greek Studies, Pembroke College, Cambridge. **Essay:** Melas.

Llewellyn Smith, Sir Michael. Former British Ambassador to Greece. Author of *The Great Island: A Study of Crete* (1965), *Ionian Vision: Greece in Asia Minor 1919–22* (1973, 1998), and *The British Embassy, Athens* (1998). **Essay:** Britain.

Lock, Peter. Head of the School of Historical and Geographical Studies, College of Ripon and York St John. Author of numerous books and articles on the history and archaeology of the medieval Aegean including *The Franks in the Aegean 1200–1500* (1995) and *The Archaeology of Medieval Greece* (with G. Sanders, 1996). **Essays:** Amalfi, Catalans, Constantinople (Sack of), Crusades, Genoese, Hospitaller Knights of St John, Latin Empire, Normans, Papacy, Political History 1204–1261, Roman Catholic Church.

Louth, Andrew. Professor of Patristic and Byzantine Studies, University of Durham. Author of *Origins of the Christian Mystical Tradition: Plato to Denys* (1981), *Denys the Areopagite* (1989), and *Maximus the Confessor* (1996). **Essays:** Athanasius of Alexandria, Constantine I the Great, Demetrius, Germanos, Helena, John of Damascus, Kabasilas, Mary, Maximos the Confessor, Philo, Theology.

Lowden, John. Reader, Courtauld Institute of Art, University of London. Author of *Illuminated Prophet Books* (1988), *The Octateuchs* (1992), *Early Christian and Byzantine Art* (1997), and *The Making of the Bibles Moralisées* (2000). Contributor to *The Oxford Dictionary of Byzantium*, *The Oxford History of Western Art*, *The Dictionary of Art*, and *Enciclopedia dell'arte medievale*, to the *Art Bulletin*, *Dumbarton Oaks Papers*, and *Gesta*. **Essay:** Manuscripts.

McDonald, Marianne. Professor of Classics and Theatre, University of California, San Diego. Member of the Royal Irish Academy. Author of *Terms for Happiness in Euripides* (1978), *Euripides in Cinema: The Heart Made Visible* (1983), *Ancient Sun, Modern Light: Greek Drama on the Modern Stage* (1991), *Star Myths: Tales of the Constellations* (1996), "Medea as Politician and Diva: Riding the Dragon into the Future" in *Medea: Essays on Medea in Myth, Literature, Philosophy, and Art*, edited by James J. Clauss and Sarah Iles Johnston (1997), and *Mythology of the Zodiac* (2000). Founder of *Thesaurus Lingua Graecae*, a project to computerize Greek literature. Member of the editorial board of *Raritan*. President of *Desmi*, Center for Research and Practical Realization of Ancient Greek Drama, Athens. **Essays:** Aeschylus, Euripides, Sophocles.

Macfarlane, Roger T. Associate Professor of Classics, Brigham Young University. Author of "Tyrrhena Regum Progenies: Etruscan Literary Figures from Horace to Ovid" in *Etruscan Italy: Etruscan Influences on the Civilizations of Italy from Antiquity to the Modern Era*, edited by John F. Hall (1995), and articles on Caesar's *Bellum Civile*, Goethe's "Kronos als Kunstrichter", and the classics in early 19th-century America. **Essays:** Aratus, Hipparchus.

McGuckin, John A. Professor of Early Church History, Union Theological Seminary, New York. Author or translator of *Symeon the New Theologian: Chapters and Discourses* (1982), *Saint Gregory of Nazianzen: Selected Poems* (1986), *The Transfiguration of Christ in Scripture and Tradition* (1987), *St Cyril of Alexandria: The Christological Controversy* (1994), *At the Lighting of the Lamps: Hymns from the Ancient Church* (1995), *St Cyril of Alexandria: On the Unity of Christ* (1995), *St Gregory Nazianzen: An Intellectual Biography* (2000), and of articles on New Testament, patristic, and Byzantine studies. Member of the Advisory Board of *Pro Ecclesia*. **Essays:** Canonization, Cyril of Alexandria, Klimakos, Neophytos Enkleistos, Relics, Symeon the New Theologian.

Makrides, Vasilios. Professor of Religiology and Orthodox Christianity, Faculty of Philosophy, University of Erfurt, Germany. Author of *Die religiöse Kritik am kopernikanischen Weltbild in Griechenland zwischen 1794 und 1821* (1995) and articles on the religious and cultural history of modern Greece, the sociology of Eastern Christianity, and the relationship between science and religion in Greece. **Essays:** Anti-Westernism, Athenagoras, Church-State Relations, Corydalleus, Fundamentalism, Gregory V, Kollyvades Movement, Korais, Makriyannis, Moisiodax, Neo-Orthodoxy, Orthodoxy and Hellenism, Orthodoxy and Nationalism, Paganism, Phanariots, Proselytism, Religious Brotherhoods, Secularization, Voulgaris, Zealots.

Maltezou, Chryssa A. Professor of History, University of Athens. Author of *O thesmos tou en Konstantinoupoli venetou vaïlou, 1268–1453* (1970), *Venetiki paroussia sta Kythira* (1991), and "Crete: The Historical and Social Context" in *Literature and Society in Renaissance Crete*, edited by David Holton (1991). **Essays:** Candia, Cythera, Venetokratia, Venice.

Mantzaris, Evangelos. Senior Research Officer, Department of Social Policy, University of Durban-Westville. Author of *The Greek Workers in South Africa, 1890–1930* (1995), *The Anti-Greek Riots in Johannesburg 1915–17* (1995), *Forgotten Pages in South African Labour History, 1903–1920* (1995), and *The IMF and the Destruction of Africa* (1997). Co-editor of *O Apodismos Ellinismos stis Hores tis Afrikis* [Greek Immigrants in Africa] (1998). Contributor to *Journal of the Hellenic Diaspora*, *Jewish Social Studies*, and *Greek Review of Social Research*. **Essay:** South Africa.

Martin, M.E. Honorary Fellow, Institute for Advanced Research, University of Birmingham. Contributor to *English Historical Review*, *Byzantinoslavica*, *Archeion Pontou*, *Byzantino-Bulgarica*, *Byzantinische Forschungen*, *Rivista di Bizantinistica*, *Journal of Hellenic Studies*, *Byzantine and*

Modern Greek Studies, *Anatolian Studies*, and *Byzantinische Zeitschrift*. **Essays:** Odessa, Sinope, Venetians.

Mason, Hugh J. Associate Professor, Department of Classics, University of Toronto. Author of *Greek Terms for Roman Institutions* (1974), and articles on ancient novels, Greek topography in relation to literary texts, modern Greek literature, and the linguistics of classical languages. Associate editor of *Phoenix*. **Essays:** Chatzimichail, Lesbos.

Mason, Richard A.E. Director, Senior City Services, Inc. Author of *Echo der Heimat: Eine Ausstellung ukrainischer Künstler* (1988), *Ernte der Verzweiflung: Die Hungersnot in der Ukraine, 1932–1933* (1988), "Saint Olha's Christianity and Its Sources" in *The Millennium of Ukrainian Christianity*, edited by N.L. Fr.-Chirovsky (1988), *The Development of the Christian Church in Ukraine from an Historical Perspective* (1990), *The Ancient Religion of Kyivan Rus'* (1994), *Testimonia auctorum antiquorum historiam geographiam et ethnographiam Ucrainae illustrantia: Auctores orientales et latini* (in preparation), and articles on early Christianity in Russia. **Essay:** Russia.

Matthews, Elaine. Co-editor of *Lexicon of Greek Personal Names* and Fellow of St Hilda's College, Oxford. **Essay:** Onomastics.

Mayer, Kenneth. Assistant Professor, Assumption College, Worcester, Massachusetts. Contributor to *American Journal of Philology*, *Gymnasium*, *Bryn Mawr Classical Review*, and *Zeitschrift für Papyrologie und Epigraphik*. **Essay:** Diodorus Siculus.

Michailidou, Theano. International Baccalaureate Literature Co-ordinator at the Costeas-Gitonas School, Athens. Author of several articles on Kostas Varnalis. Editor of *Meres*, vol.7, by George Seferis (1990). Contributor to *Spira* and *Politis*. **Essay:** Varnalis.

Mills, Sophie. Chair of Classics, University of North Carolina at Asheville. Author of *Theseus, Tragedy and the Athenian Empire* (1997). **Essays:** Archilochus, Cimon, Sappho, Themistocles, Theocritus.

Mitsilegas, Valsamis. Doctoral candidate, Faculty of Law, University of Edinburgh. Research Associate, Centre for European Politics and Institutions, University of Leicester. Author of "Culture in the Evolution of European Law" in *Europe's Other: European Law between Modernity and Postmodernity*, edited by P. Fitzpatrick and J.H. Bergeron (1998) and "International and Regional Initiatives" in *Money Laundering*, edited by B. Rider and C. Nakajima (in preparation). Contributor to *Journal of Money Laundering Control*. **Essay:** Corruption.

Momigliano, Nicoletta. Lecturer in Archaeology, Department of Archaeological Sciences, University of Bradford. Editor of *Knossos: A Labyrinth of History: Papers in Honour of Sinclair Hood* (with H. Hughes-Brock and D. Evely, 1994). Author of "La catastrofe di Thera (Santorini): Problemi cronologici e conseguenze storiche" in *I terremoti prima del Mille*, edited by E. Guidoboni (1989), "Duncan Mackenzie" in *Klados: Essays in Honour of J.N. Coldstream*, edited by C. Morris (1995), *Duncan Mackenzie: A Cautious Canny Highlander and the Palace of Minos at Knossos* (in preparation), *Knossos Pottery Handbook: Neolithic to the End of the Bronze Age* (in preparation), and of articles on Knossos. **Essay:** Crete.

Morgan, J.R. Senior Lecturer in Classics, University of Wales, Swansea. Editor of *Greek Fiction: The Greek Novel in Context* (with Richard Stoneman, 1994). Translator of Heliodoros' *Aithiopika* in *Collected Ancient Greek Novels*, edited by B.P. Reardon (1989). Contributor to *Classical Quarterly*, *Journal of Hellenic Studies*, *Transactions of the American Philological Association*, *Classical Antiquity*, *Classical Philology*, *Latomus*, *Groningen Colloquia on the Novel*, *Nottingham Classical Literature Seminars*, and *Philologus*. **Essays:** Heliodorus, Longus, Novel (antiquity).

Moscovich, M. James. Associate Professor of Classical Studies, University of Western Ontario; now retired. Author of *The Rise of Rome: An Historical Commentary on Books 11–21 of Dio Cassius' History* (in preparation). **Essay:** Zonaras.

Moustakas, Konstantinos. Doctoral candidate, University of Birmingham. Author of articles on the fleet base of Constantinople during the Byzantine period and the name of Argos Oresti Kou. **Essays:** Chalcidice, Florina, Kastoria, Kavalla, Ohrid, Serres, Verroia.

Murison, Charles L. Professor of Classical Studies, University of Western Ontario. Author of *Galba, Otho and Vitellius: Careers and Controversies* (1993) and of articles on the peace of Callias, Darius III and the battle of Issus, and Roman history of the 1st century AD. Editor of *Suetonius: Galba, Otho, and Vitellius* (1992) and *Rebellion and Reconstruction: Galba to Domitian* (1999). **Essays:** Cartography, Crates of Mallus, Delian League, Historiography (Antiquity).

Nesselrath, Heinz-Günther. Chair of Greek, University of Bern. Author of *Lukians Parasitendialog* (1985), *Die attische Mittlere Komödie* (1990), *Ungeschehenes Geschehen* (1992), and articles on Silius Italicus, Xenophon, Lucian, Livy, Claudian, Solon, Julian the Apostate, Herodotus, Aristophanes, Valerius Flaccus, and the Church historian Socrates. Editor of *Rudolf Kassel: Kleine Schriften* (1991) and *Einleitung in die griechische Philologie* (1997). **Essays:** Aristides, Callimachus, Dio Cocceianus, Herodas, Triklinios.

Nicgorski, Ann M. Assistant Professor of Art History, Willamette University; Assistant Director, Mochlos Excavations, Crete. Author of "Polypus and the Poppy: Two Unusual Rhyta from the Mycenaean Cemetery at Mochlos" in *Meletemata: Studies in Aegean Archaeology Presented to Malcolm H. Wiener as He Enters His 65th Year*, edited by Philip Betancourt *et al.* (vol. 20 of *Aegaeum*, 1999). Contributor to *Athenian Potters and Painters: Catalogue of the Exhibit*, edited by John H. Oakley (1994), the *Encyclopedia of the History of Classical Archaeology*, edited by Nancy Thomson de Grummond (1996), and *Mochlos Period III and*

Mochlos Period IV, edited by Jeffrey S. Soles and Costis Davaras (in preparation). **Essays:** Etruscans, Jewellery, Mallia.

Nicolaidis, Efthymios. Associate Research Professor, National Hellenic Research Foundation. Author of *Le Développement de l'astronomie en URSS, 1917–1935* (1984) and *The Prologues of the Scientific Books of the Greek Enlightenment: A Statistical Analysis* (with Th. Behrakis, 1990). Editor of *The Mathematical Sciences in the Greek World under the Ottoman Rule* (1992) and *Trends in the Historiography of Science* (with K. Gavroglu and J. Christianides, 1994). Contributor to *Archives Internationales d'Histoire des Sciences*, *Byzantiaka*, *Cahiers d'Analyse des Données*, *Etudes Balkaniques*, *Journal for the History of Astronomy*, *Revue d'Histoire des Sciences*, and *Thesaurismata*. **Essays:** Astronomy.

Nicolaidou, Ioanna A. Associate Professor, University of Malaga, Spain. Author of "Re-belle et infidèle o el papel de la traductora en la teoría y práctica de la traducción feminista" in *El papel del traductor*, edited by E. Morillas and J.P. Arias (with M. López Villalba, 1997), and of articles on feminist literary criticism and on the theory of translation. Editor of *Traducir al otro/traducir a Grecia* (2000). **Essay:** Translation into Greek.

Oberhelman, Steven M. Professor of Classics at Texas A & M University. Author of *Rhetoric and Homiletics in Fourth-Century Christian Literature* (1991), *The Oneirocriticon of Achmet* (1991), *Epic and Epoch: Essays on the Interpretation and History of a Genre* (1994), and *Prose Rhythm in Latin Literature of the Empire: First Century BC to Fourth Century AD* (1998). Editor of *Helios*. **Essays:** Corinth (Sack of), Dodona, Eleusis, Eratosthenes, Laurium, Paestum.

Oliver, Graham. Senior Research Fellow, School of Archaeology, Classics and Oriental Studies, University of Liverpool. Editor of *The Epigraphy of Death: Studies in the History and Society of Greece and Rome* (in preparation) and co-editor of *Hellenistic Economies* (in preparation). **Essays:** Agriculture, Attica, Coinage, Economy, Inscriptions, Phoenicians, Pyrrhus.

Otte, T.G. Lecturer in International History, University of the West of England, Bristol. Editor of *Military Intervention* (1995) and *Personalities, War and Diplomacy* (1997). Contributor to *English Historical Review*, *Diplomacy and Statecraft*, *Contemporary Security Policy*, and *New Dictionary of National Biography*. Review editor, *Diplomacy and Statecraft*. **Essays:** Diplomacy, Ionian Islands, Kapodistria, Moldavia.

Panourgiá, Neni. Assistant Professor, Anthropology Department, Columbia University. Author of *Fragments of Death, Fables of Identity: An Athenian Anthropography* (1995) and of articles on the anthropology of death, racism, and national ideology in Greece. **Essays:** Folklore, Karaghiozis, Politis.

Papastathis, Charalambos K. Professor, Faculty of Law, Aristotle University, Thessalonica. Author (in Greek) of *The Legislative Work of the Cyrillo-Methodian Mission in Great Moravia* (1978), *On the Administrative Organization of the Church of Cyprus* (1982), *The Statutes of the Orthodox Hellenic Communities of the Ottoman Empire and the Diaspora* (1984), *The Nomocanon of George Trapezountios* (1985), *The Legal Status of the Mount Athos Monks* (1988), and *Manual of Ecclesiastical Law* (2nd edition 1994); co-author of *Catalogue of the Greek Legal Manuscripts at the Dujèev Centre in Sofia* (1994). President of the editorial board of *Thessaloniki*. Vice-President of the Hellenic Association of Slavic Studies. **Essays:** Apostasy, Uniates.

Parker, Robert. Wykeham Professor of Ancient History, and Fellow of New College, Oxford. Author of *Miasma* (1983) and *Athenian Religion: A History* (1996).

Peckham, Robert Shannan. Democracy 2500 Fellow in Aegean Studies, St Peter's College, Oxford. Author of "Papadiamantis, Ecumenism and the Theft of Byzantium" in *Byzantium and the Modern Greek Identity*, edited by D. Ricks and P. Magdalino (1998), "Consuming Nations" in *Consuming Passions: Food in the Age of Anxiety*, edited by S. Griffiths and J. Wallace (1998), "The Exoticism of the Familiar and the Familiarity of the Exotic: Fin-de-Siècle Travellers to Greece" in *Writes of Passage: Reading Travel*, edited by J. Duncan and D. Gregory (1999), and *National Histories, Natural States: Nationalism and the Politics of Place in Greece* (2000). **Essays:** Angelopoulos, Cacoyannis, Cinema, Papadiamantis, Roidis.

Penella, Robert J. Professor of Classics, Fordham University. Author of *The Letters of Apollonius of Tyana: A Critical Text with Prolegomena, Translation and Commentary* (1979) and *Greek Philosophers and Sophists in the Fourth Century AD: Studies in Eunapius of Sardis* (1990). Translator of *The Private Orations of Themistius* (1999). **Essay:** Themistius.

Petropoulos, Jacqueline. Educator and Writer. Assistant Editor, *APA in Focus*. **Essay:** Botsaris.

Petsalis-Diomidis, Nicholas. Author (in Greek) of *Greece at the Paris Peace Conference, 1919* (1979), *Ghika: Catalogue Raisonné, 1920–1940* (1979), *Greece with Two Governments, 1916–1917* (1986), *Vassiliou: The Engravings* (1989), and *The Unknown Maria Callas* (1998). **Essay:** Ghika.

Pettifer, James. Visiting Professor, Institute of Balkan Studies, University of Thessalonica; Research Fellow, European Research Institute, Bath University. Author of *The Greeks: Land and People since the War* (1992), *Blue Guide Albania* (1993), *Albania: From Anarchy to a Balkan Identity* (with Miranda Vickers, 1997), *The Turkish Labyrinth* (1997), and *Blue Guide Bulgaria* (1998). Member of the editorial board of *Albania Life*. **Essays:** Albania, Prespa.

Philippaki-Warburton, Irene. Professor of Linguistics, Department of Linguistic Science, University of Reading. Author of *Modern Greek: A Descriptive Grammar* (with Brian Joseph, 1987), "O Psycharis os glossologos" [Psycharis as a Linguist] in *O Psycharis kai to Kinima tou Dimotismou*, edited by David Holton (1988), *Introduction to Theoretical*

Linguistics (in Greek, 1992), *Greek: A Comprehensive Grammar of the Modern Language* (with D. Holton and P. Mackridge, 1997), and "Grammar and Language Teaching" in *Proceedings of the Conference on the Teaching of Greek: University of Crete, Rethymnon* (1999). Contributor to *The History of the Greek Language*, edited by M. Kopidakis (1999). **Essay:** Psycharis.

Plested, Marcus. Independent Scholar. Contributor of articles on patristics, Eastern Christian asceticism, and contemporary Orthodoxy to *Christianskij Bostok*, *Sobornost*, *Sourozh*, *Studia Patristica*, and *Touchstone*. **Essays:** Akindynos, Anastasios of Sinai, *Apophthegmata Patrum*, Baarlam of Calabria, Clement of Alexandria, Evagrius of Pontus, Gregory Palamas, Hesychasm, Macarius, Mysticism, *Philokalia*.

Podlecki, Anthony J. Professor of Classics, University of British Columbia, Vancouver. Author of *The Political Background of Aeschylean Tragedy* (1966), *The Life of Themistocles* (1975), *The Early Greek Poets and Their Times* (1984), *Perikles and His Circle* (1998), and articles on ancient Greek drama and society. Editor and translator of *The Eumenides* by Aeschylus (1989). **Essays:** Democracy, Pericles, Pisistratus.

Powell, Judith. Research Adviser, Department of Classics and Ancient History, University of Queensland. Author of *Fishing in the Prehistoric Aegean* (1996) and of articles on fishing in ancient Greece. **Essay:** Fishing.

Pyla, Panayiota. Doctoral candidate, Department of Architecture, Massachusetts Institute of Technology. Author of articles on architectural theory and the environment in *Journal of Architectural Education*, *Thresholds*, and *Work in Progress*. **Essays:** Doxiadis.

Rackham, Oliver. Fellow of Corpus Christi College, Cambridge. Author of *The History of the Countryside* (1986), *The Making of the Cretan Landscape* (with J.A. Moody, 1996), *The Nature of Mediterranean Europe* (with A.T. Grove, 2000), and an article on the historical ecology of Boeotia. **Essays:** Botany, Climate, Ecology, Forestry, Landscape, Plants, Woodworking.

Rapp, Claudia. Assistant Professor, Department of History, University of California, Los Angeles. Author of "Christians and Their Manuscripts in the Greek East during the Fourth Century" in *Scritture, libri e testi nelle aree provinciali di Bisanzio*, edited by G. Cavallo *et al.* (1991), "Epiphanius of Salamis: The Church Father as Saint" in *"The Sweet Land of Cyprus": Papers Given at the Twenty-Fifth Jubilee Spring Symposium of Byzantine Studies*, edited by A.A.M. Bryer and G.S. Georghallides (1993), "Der heilige Epiphanius im Kampf mit dem Dämon des Origenes: Kritische Erstausgabe des Wunders BHG 601i" in *Symbolae Berolinenses für Dieter Harlfinger*, edited by F. Berger *et al.* (1993), "Byzantine Hagiographers as Antiquarians, 7th to 10th Century" in *Bosphorus: Essays in Honor of Cyril Mango*, edited by C. Rapp *et al.* (1995), and "'For Next to God You Are My Salvation': Reflections on the Rise of the Holy Man in Late Antiquity", in *The Cult of Saints in Late Antiquity and the*

Early Middle Ages, edited by J. Howard-Johnston and P.A. Hayward (1999). **Essays:** Bishops, Epiphanius of Salamis.

Reece, Steve. Associate Professor of Classics, Saint Olaf College, Northfield, Minnesota. Author of *The Stranger's Welcome: Oral Theory and the Aesthetics of the Homeric Hospitality Scene* (1993). Contributor to *Bulletin of the American Society of Papyrologists*, *American Journal of Philology*, *Oral Tradition*, *Classical Journal*, *Classical World*, *Glotta*, and *Favonius*. **Essay:** Syllabary.

Rice, E.E. Senior Research Fellow, Wolfson College, Oxford. Author of *The Grand Procession of Ptolemy Philadelphus* (1983), *Alexander the Great* (1997), *Cleopatra* (1999), and of articles on ancient naval history and on Rhodes and the Dodecanese islands. Editor of *Revolution and Counter-Revolution* (1991) and *The Sea and History* (1996). Contributor to *Who Was Who in the Greek World* (1982), *The Lexicon of Greek Personal Names*, vol.1 (1987), *The Dictionary of Ancient History* (1994), and *The Oxford Classical Dictionary* (3rd edition 1996). **Essays:** Alexander III, Alexandria, Antigonids, Cleopatra, Egypt, Halicarnassus, Philip V, Philopoemen, Political History 323–31 BC, Ptolemies, Pydna, Rhodes.

Riddle, John M. Alumni Distinguished Professor and Chair, Department of History, North Carolina State University. Author of *Contraception and Abortion from the Ancient World to the Renaissance* (1992), *Quid pro quo: Studies in the History of Drugs* (1992), and *Eve's Herbs: A History of Contraception and Abortion in the West* (1997). Member of the editorial board, *Medieval Encounters* and *Journal of Alternative and Complementary Medicine*. **Essays:** Abortion, Contraception, Erasistratus, Theophrastus.

Roumbalou, Maria. Doctoral candidate, Department of Politics, Reading University. Contributor of translations to the Greek poetry magazine *Poiese*. **Essays:** Gatsos, Kalvos, Kantakouzenos family, Myrivilis, Ritsos, Soutsos, Vizyinos.

Ryder, T.T.B. Visiting Fellow in Classics (Retired Reader), University of Reading. Author of *Koine Eirene* (1965), "The Diplomatic Skills of Philip II" in *Ventures into Greek History*, edited by I. Worthington (1994), and "Demosthenes and Philip II" in *Demosthenes*, edited by I. Worthington (2000). Contributor to *Classical Quarterly*, *Greece and Rome*, and *Didaskalos*. **Essays:** Alcibiades, Chaeronea, Cleisthenes, Lysander, Peloponnesian War.

Saitas, Yanis. Ethnologist, architect, city planner, and researcher at the Institute for Neohellenic Research of the National Hellenic Research Foundation. Author of *Mani: Greek Traditional Architecture* (1987) and of articles on the Mani. Editor of *Témoignages sur l'éspace et la société de Mani* (1996). **Essay:** Mani.

Scavone, Daniel C. Professor Emeritus of History, University of Southern Indiana. Author of "Technology in the Ancient World" in *Technology and Society*, edited by Daniel A. Miller (1983), "The Turin Shroud in Constantinople: The

Documentary Evidence" in *Daidalikon: Studies in Memory of Rev. R.V. Schoder, SJ*, edited by R.F. Sutton (1989), *The Shroud of Turin: Opposing Viewpoints* (1989), *Vampires: Opposing Viewpoints* (1990), *The Importance of Christopher Columbus* (1992), and "The Shroud of Turin from 1204 to 1355" in *Alpha and Omega: Scholarship in Honor of George Szemler* (1993). Contributor to *The Princeton Encyclopedia of Classical Sites* and *The New International Dictionary of the Christian Church*, edited by J.D. Douglas. **Essays:** Ignatius, John Chrysostom, Mausolus.

Schachter, Albert. Hiram Mills Professor Emeritus, Department of History, McGill University. Author of *Cults of Boiotia* (1981–), *Le Sanctuaire Grec* (1992). Co-editor and contributor to *Le Sanctuaire Grec* (1992) and *La Montagne des Muses* (1996). Editor of *Teiresias*. **Essays:** Cult, Festivals, Hesiod, Lebadea, Orchomenus, Pindar.

Scharrer, Ulf. Doctoral student in ancient history, Martin Luther-Universität-Halle-Wittenberg. Author of *Seleukos I. und das babylonische königtem* (in preparation) and *Aristotles' Theorie der Monarchie bei John Milton, Robert Filmer und William Prynne* (in preparation). **Essay:** Monarchy.

Scourtis, Constantina. Doctoral candidate, University of California, Los Angeles. Author of an article on the Council of Ferrara-Florence. **Essays:** Councils, Kosmas the Aetolian, Zoe.

Shean, John F. Visiting Assistant Professor, Department of Classical Studies, University of Michigan. Author of articles on slavery and construction in the ancient world in *The Historical Encyclopedia of World Slavery*, edited by J.P. Rodriguez (1997), "The Religious Iconography of Septimius Severus and His Wife Julia Domna" in *Gli imperatori Severi: Biblioteca di Scienze Religiose*, edited by E. dal Covolo and G. Rinaldi (1999), and "The Church and the Duties of the Christian Soldier" in *Proceedings of the Second Shifting Frontiers Conference: The Transformation of Law and Society in Late Antiquity* (in preparation). Contributor of an article on Hannibal's mules to *Historia*. **Essays:** Basil II, John I, Justinian I, Paulicians, Romanos I.

Sherwood, Andrew N. Lecturer, Department of History, McGill University. Co-author of *The Caesarea Ancient Harbour Excavation Project: The Small Finds* (1995) and *Greek and Roman Technology: A Sourcebook* (1998). Contributor to *Classical Views, American Journal of Archaeology, Zeitschrift für Papyrologie und Epigraphik*, and *British Archaeological Reports*. **Essays:** Adrianople, Apelles, Goths, Imperial Cult, Papyrus, Plataea.

Sherwood, Kathleen Donahue. Independent scholar. **Essays:** Andronikos, Catana, Massilia, Museum of Alexandria, Tarentum.

Shlosser, Franziska E. Associate Professor, Department of History, Concordia University, Montreal. Author of *The McGill University Collection of Greek and Roman Coins*, vols 2 and 3 (1975–84) and *The Reign of the Emperor Maurikios, 582–602: A Reassessment* (1994). Contributor to

Byzantinische Forschungen, Byzantinoslavica, Canadian Journal of History, and *Fontanus*. **Essays:** Byzantine Period (Early), Carthage, Komnene, Political History AD 330–802, Simokattes.

Sider, David. Professor of Classics, Fordham University. Editor of *The Fragments of Anaxagoras* (1981) and *The Epigrams of Philodemos* (1997), and author of articles on Plato and the Presocratics. **Essays:** Anaxagoras, Aristarchus of Samothrace, Aristoxenus, Diogenes of Sinope, Philodemus, Plato.

Siebach, James L. Assistant Professor of Philosophy, Brigham Young University. Contributor to *Augustinian Studies* and *Bulletin of the History of Medicine*. **Essays:** Heresy, Nomokanon, Patriarchate of Constantinople.

Siorvanes, Lucas. Lecturer in Philosophy, and member of the Centre for Hellenic Studies, King's College London. Author of *Proclus: Neo-Platonic Philosophy and Science* (1996) and articles on Greek philosophy in the series *Ancient Philosophy, Documenti e Studi Filosofica Medievale, Ancient and Medieval Philosophy*, and the *Routledge Encyclopedia of Philosophy* (1998). Editor of *Simplicius: Corollaries on Place and Time* (translated by J.O. Urmson, 1992). **Essays:** Neoplatonism, Philosophy, Proclus.

Sisko, John E. Assistant Professor of Philosophy, College of William and Mary. Author of articles on ancient Greek philosophy. **Essay:** Aristotle.

Smith, Andrew. Professor of Classics, University College Dublin. Author of *Porphyry's Place in the Neoplatonic Tradition* (1974) and *Fragments of Porphyry (Porphyrii Fragmenta)* (1993). **Essays:** Plotinus, Porphyry, Synesius.

Smythe, Dion C. PBE Research Associate, King's College London. Contributor to *Conformity and Nonconformity in Byzantium*, edited by Lynda Garland (1996), *Byzantium: Identity, Image, Influence*, edited by K. Fledelius and P. Schreiner (1996), *Queens and Queenship*, edited by Anne Duggan (1997), *Women, Men and Eunuchs*, edited by Liz James (1997), and *Desire and Denial*, edited by Liz James (1999). **Essays:** Homosexuality, Minorities.

Sotiriu, Eleni. Doctoral candidate, School of Oriental and African Studies, University of London. Author of articles on the sociology of religion and the social anthropology of Greece. **Essays:** Baptism, Birth, Celibacy, Fasts, Kinship, Olive, Schism.

Souyoudzoglou-Haywood, Christina. Research Curator, Classical Museum, Department of Classics, University College, Dublin. Author of *The Ionian Islands in the Bronze Age and Early Iron Age* (1999). **Essays:** Burial Practices, Museums, Prehistory.

Speake, Graham. Managing Editor, Peter Lang AG (Oxford). Founder and Honorary Secretary, Friends of Mount Athos. Member of the Executive Committee of the Society for the Promotion of Byzantine Studies. Fellow of the Society of

Antiquaries of London, and Senior Member of Christ Church, Oxford. Author of *Collation of the Manuscripts of Sophocles' Oedipus Coloneus* (1978). Editor of the *Dictionary of Ancient History* (1994) and *The Penguin Dictionary of Ancient History* (1995). Founding editor of the *Housman Society Journal* and of the *Annual Report of the Friends of Mount Athos*. Former Assistant Editor of the *Journal of Islamic Studies*. **Essay:** Athos.

Spencer, Susan Professor of English, University of Central Oklahoma. **Essays:** Fire, Hetairists, Kolettis, Kolokotronis.

Spentzou, Efrossini. Lecturer in the Department of Classics, Royal Holloway, University of London. Author of *Transgressions of Gender and Genre in Ovid's Heroides* (in preparation) and an article on Helen of Troy in classical and modern literature. Co-editor of *Cultivating the Muse: Power, Desire and Inspiration in (and Beyond) the Classical World* (in preparation). **Essays:** Athens, Simonides, Theodora [497–548], Trojan War, USA.

Staikos, Konstantizos. Interior architect and historian of the book. Author of *Charta of Greek Printing* (1998) and *The Great Libraries from Antiquity to the Renaissance* (2000). **Essays:** Cyril I Lukaris, Printing.

Steiner-Weber, Astrid. Lecturer, University of Bonn. Author of *Untersuchungen zu einem anonymen byzantinischen Briefcorpus des 10. Jahrhunderts* (1987) and of articles in *Studien zur byzantinischen Lexikographie*, edited by E. Trapp et al. (1988), *Lexicographica Byzantina: Beiträge zum Symposion zur byzantinischen Lexikographie*, edited by W. Hörandner and E. Trapp (1989), *Lexikon zur Byzantinischen Gräzität* (1994–96), and *Semantik, Lexikographie und Computeranwendungen*, edited by N. Weber (1996). Contributor to *Byzantion*. **Essays:** Ceremony, Epistolography, Grammar, Schools and Universities.

Stephenson, Paul. British Academy Postdoctoral Fellow and Fellow of Keble College, Oxford. Contributor to *Revue des Etudes Byzantines*, *Byzantion*, and *Byzantinoslavica*. **Essays:** Alexios I, John II, Manuel I.

Stewart, Charles. Reader in Anthropology, University College London. Author of *Demons and the Devil: Moral Imagination in Modern Greek Culture* (1991). Editor of *Syncretism/Anti-Syncretism: The Politics of Religious Synthesis* (with Rosalind Shaw, 1994). **Essays:** Anthropology, Demons and Spirits, Dreams.

Stylianou, P.J. Research Associate of the A.G. Leventis Foundation and and a deacon in the Greek Orthodox Archdiocese of Thyateira and Great Britain. Author of *The Age of the Kingdoms: A Political History of Cyprus in the Archaic and Classical Periods* (1989) and *A Historical Commentary on Diodorus Siculus Book 15* (1998). **Essays:** Dionysius I, Ephorus, Evagoras, Timaeus.

Sykes, D.A. Honorary Fellow and former Principal of Mansfield College, Oxford. Co-editor and translator of *Poemata Arcana* by Gregory of Nazianzus (1997). Contributor to *Journal of Theological Studies*, *Byzantinische Zeitschrift*, and *Studia Patristica*. **Essays:** Apologists, Basil the Great, Cappadocia, Gregory of Nazianzus, Gregory of Nyssa, Justin Martyr, Nemesius, Procopius of Gaza.

Symeonides, Anestis T. Political Specialist, American Embassy, Athens. Author of articles on Greek strategic concerns in the 20th century. Editor of *Forty Years of NATO: Present and Future* (1990) and *European Security in the 1990s* (1990). **Essays:** Kanaris, Miaoulis.

Syrrakos, Barbara. Lecturer in history at the City College of the City University of New York and doctoral candidate at the New School for Social Research in New York. **Essays:** Junta, Kafaneion, Karamanlis, Men.

Tabaki, Anna. Research Associate Professor, Centre for Neohellenic Research, The National Hellenic Research Foundation, and Associate Professor, Department of Theatre Studies, University of Athens. Author (in Greek) of *Molière in the Phanariot Culture: Three Manuscript Translations* (1988), *The Modern Greek Drama and Its Western European Influences: A Comparative Approach* (1993), and *Foreign Authors Translated in Modern Greek, 18th Century: The Enlightenment Era*, vol. 2 (in preparation). Co-author of *Pre-Revolutionary Greek Periodicals* (with Roxane Argyropoulos, 1983, in Greek) and *Documents Gréco-roumains: Le fonds Mourouzi d'Athènes* (with Florin Marinescu and Georgeta Penela-Filitti, 1991). Editor of Dimosthenis Misitzis, *O Fiakes — O Doux tis Vlakeias* (1992), *Translation and Intercultural Studies: Identity and Alterity in Literature, 18th–20th c.*, vol. 3 (with Stessi Athini, in preparation), and Rhigas, *[Le Voyage du] Jeune Anacharsis* (in preparation). Contributor to *Neohellenic Enlightenment: A Bibliography, 1945–1995* (1998) and to *Revue des Etudes Sud-Est Européennes*, *Hellinika*, *Folia Neohellenica*, *Ho Eranistès*, *Balkan Studies*, *Studies on Voltaire and the 18th Century*, *Synthésis*, *Revue Roumaine d'Histoire*, *Synkrisi/Comparaison*, *Europe*, and *Trans*. **Essays:** Dimaras, Enlightenment.

Tatton-Brown, Veronica. Assistant Keeper, Department of Greek and Roman Antiquities, British Museum. Author of *Glass in Antiquity* (1976) and *Ancient Cyprus* (1987, 1997). Editor of *Cyprus BC: 7000 Years of History* (1979) and *Cyprus and the East Mediterranean in the Iron Age* (1984). Contributor to *Five Thousand Years of Glass*, edited by H. Tait (1991) and *Glass*, edited by R. Liefkes (1997). **Essay:** Glass.

Thorburn, John E., Jr. Assistant Professor, Baylor University. Author of *Euripides' Alcestis: Translation and Commentary* (in preparation). Contributor to *Ancient History Bulletin*, *Classical Quarterly*, and *Classical World*. **Essays:** Hospitality, Naupactus.

Tohme, Lara G. Doctoral candidate, Massachusetts Institute of Technology. **Essay:** Arabia.

Tomlinson, R.A. Emeritus Professor of Ancient History and Archaeology, University of Birmingham. Author of *Argos and* the Argolid (1972), *Greek Sanctuaries* (1976), *Epidaurus* (1983), revised edition of *Greek Architecture* by A.W. Lawrence (1983, 1996), *Greek Architecture* (1989), *The Athens of Alma Tadema* (1991), *From Mycenae to Constantinople* (1992), and *Greek and Roman Architecture* (1995). **Essays:** Acropolis, Aegae, Archaeology, Architecture (fortifications), Architecture (palaces), Architecture (religious), Argolid, Argos, Classical Period, Corinth, Cyrene, Delos, Delphi, Epidaurus, Eretria, Hellenistic Period, Laconia, Megalopolis, Pamphylia, Pella, Photography, Sparta, Theatres, Urbanization.

Tougher, Shaun. Lecturer in School of History and Archaeology, Cardiff University. Author of *The Reign of Leo VI, 886–912* (1997). Contributor to *Byzantine and Modern Greek Studies* and *Classical Quarterly*. **Essays:** Basil I, Constantine VII, Eunuchs, Leo VI, Symeon the Logothete.

Trubeta, Sevasti. Lecturer in Social History, Freie Universität, Berlin. Author of "Flüchtlinge in Griechenland" in *Weltflüchtlingsbericht* (1992), *Die Konstitution von Minderheiten und die Ethnisierung sozialer und politischer Konflikte: Eine Untersuchung am Beispiel der im griechischen Thrakien ansässigen "Moslemische Minderheit"* (1999), and articles on refugees in Greece. **Essays:** Gypsies, Muslims.

Tsetskhladze, Gocha R. British Academy Institutional Research Fellow, Department of Classics, Royal Holloway and Bedford New College, University of London. Author of *Die Griechen in der Kolchis* (1998) and *Pichvnari and Its Environs* (1999). Contributor to *Oxford Journal of Archaeology*, *Klio*, *Mesopotamia*, *Eirene*, *Annual of British School of Archaeology at Athens*, *Dialogues d'Histoire Ancienne*, and other journals. **Essays:** Anatolia, Caucasus, Hellenization, Naucratis, Piracy, Romania, Spain, Thrace.

Tsourka-Papastathi, Despina. Lecturer of the History of Law at the Faculty of Law, Aristotle University, Thessalonica. Author of "L'Influence de la Révolution française sur les premières Constitutions grecques, 1822–1827: Les Droits de l'homme" in *Actes du Colloque: La Révolution française et l'Hellénisme moderne* (1989), "On the Administrative System of the Greek Communities in Macedonia, 17th–19th Centuries" (in Greek) in *The Communities in Macedonia* (1991), *The Greek Merchant Company at Sibiu/Transylvania, 1636–1848: Organization and Law* (in Greek 1994), "La Réception du droit musulman en Europe Byzantine" in *La Réception des systèmes juridiques: Implantation et destin* (1994), and of articles on Greek communities and commerce. **Essays:** Guilds, Kodjabashis.

Turner, David R. Lecturer in Byzantine Studies, Beaver College, Athens. Honorary member, British School at Athens. Author of articles on Leo V, iconoclasm, and Romanization. **Essays:** Constantine V, Irene, Kontoglou, Leo V, Seljuks, Theophanes the Confessor.

Uttley, Matthew R.H. Principal Lecturer, Defence Studies Department, Joint Services Command and Staff College, Bracknell. Author of *Licensed Production versus Indigenous Innovation: A Study of Helicopter Research, Development and Production in Britain, 1945–1960* (in preparation). Co-editor of *Defence Science and Technology: Adjusting to Change* (1993), *Defense Analysis* (1998), and *The Changing Face of Maritime Power* (1998). Contributor to *Statistical Performance Indicators for Keeping Watch over Public Procurement* (1993) and *The International Encyclopaedia of Public Policy and Administration*, edited by M. Shafritz (in preparation). **Essays:** NATO, Navy.

van Leuven, Jon. Research Associate, Institute of Classical Archaeology and Ancient History, Gothenburg University. Contributor to *Aegaeum*, *Antiquity*, *Bulletin of the Institute of Classical Studies*, *Journal of Chemical Physics*, *Historia*, *Kadmos*, *Nestor*, *Physical Review*, *Scripta Mediterranea*, *World Archaeology*, *Yale Review*, and numerous conference proceedings. Editor of the *Journal of Prehistoric Religion*. **Essay:** Theme System.

Veremis, Thanos M. Professor of Political History, Athens University. President of ELIAMEP. Author of "International Relations in Southern Europe" in *Southern European Studies Guide*, edited by John Loughlin (1993), "Greece: The Dilemmas of Change" in *The Volatile Powder Keg: Balkan Security after the Cold War*, edited by F. Stephen Larrabee (1994), *Greece's Balkan Entanglement* (1995), "A Greek View of Balkan Developments" in *Greece in a Changing Europe*, edited by Kevin Featherstone and Kostas Ifantis (1996), and *The Greek Military in Politics: From Independence to Democracy* (1997). **Essays:** Graeco–Turkish War, Papandreou family, Pikionis, Trikoupis.

Verney, Susannah. Senior Investigator, Office of the Greek Ombudsman; Visiting Research Fellow, University of Bradford; and Adjunct Lecturer, Postgraduate Programme in European and International Studies, University of Athens. Author of "To Be or Not to Be within the EC: The Party Debate and Democratic Consolidation in Greece" in *Securing Democracy*, edited by G. Pridham (1990), and "The Greek Socialists" in *Political Parties and the European Union*, edited by John Gaffney (1996). Co-editor of *South European Society and Politics*. Associate Editor of *Journal of Modern Greek Studies*. **Essay:** European Community.

Vlahakis, George N. Researcher, Centre for Neohellenic Research, National Hellenic Research Foundation. Author of "Problems and Methodology of Exploring the Scientific Thought during the Greek Enlightenment, 1750–1821" in *Trends in the Historiography of Science*, edited by Kostas Gavroglu *et al.* (1993), and articles on science and the Greek Enlightenment. **Essays:** Atomism, Physics, Theotokis (Nikiphoros).

von Staden, Heinrich. Professor, Institute for Advanced Study, Princeton. Author of *Herophilus: The Art of Medicine in Early Alexandria* (1989), "Teleology and Mechanism: Aristotelian Biology and Hellenistic Medicine" in *Aristotelische Biologie*, edited by W. Kullmann and S. Foellinger (1997), "The Rule and the Exception: Celsus on a Scientific Conundrum" in *Maladie et maladies dans les textes latins*, edited by C. Deroux

(1998). "Hellenistic Reflections on the History of Medicine" and "Celsus as Historian?" in *Ancient Histories of Medicine*, edited by P.J. van der Eijk (1999), "Rostovtzeff at Yale" in *Rostovtzeff e l'Italia*, edited by A. Marcone (1999) and "Body, Soul, and Nerves" in *Psyche and Soma*, edited by J.P. Wright and P. Potter (2000). Editor of *Western Literature*, vol.1: *The Ancient World* (1971, 1993), **Essays:** Anatomy and Physiology, Dioscurides, Galen, Health, Herophilus, Hippocrates, Nicander.

Waal, Cornelis de. Assistant Editor at the Peirce Edition Project, and Adjunct Assistant Professor at Indiana University, Indianapolis. Assistant Editor of *The Writings of Charles S. Peirce: A Chronological Edition*, vol. 6 (2000). Contributor to *Transactions of the Charles S. Peirce Society* and *Locke Newsletter*. **Essay:** Medicine.

Wagstaff, Malcolm. Professor Emeritus, University of Southampton. Author of *The Development of Rural Settlements: A Study of the Helos Plain in Southern Greece* (1982) and *The Evolution of Middle-Eastern Landscapes: An Outline to AD 1840* (1985). Editor of *Landscape and Culture: Geographical and Archaeological Perspectives* (1987) and *Aspects of Religion in Secular Turkey* (1990).

Walcot, Peter. Retired. Author of *Hesiod and the Near East* (1966), *Greek Peasants, Ancient and Modern* (1970), *Greek Drama in Its Theatrical and Social Context* (1976), and *Envy and the Greeks* (1978). Contributor to *Classical Quarterly*, *Classical Review*, *Greece and Rome*, *Classical Philology*, *Journal of Near Eastern Studies*, *Symbolae Osloenses*, *Classica et Mediaevalia*, *Revue des Etudes Grecques*, and *Ancient Society*. Editor of *Greece and Rome*. **Essay:** Honour and Shame (ancient).

Wallace, Richard. Senior Lecturer in Classics, University of Keele. Author of *The Acts of the Apostles: A Companion* (with W. Williams, 1993), *The Three Worlds of Paul of Tarsus* (with W. Williams, 1998), and of articles on Greek mathematics. Member of the editorial board of *Classical Journal* and *Greece and Rome*. **Essays:** Anaximander, Apollonius of Perge, Archimedes, Epicurus, Euclid, Eudoxus, Heron, Mathematics, Palestine, Ptolemy, Pythagoras, Zoology.

Ware, Kallistos. Bishop of Diokleia, Fellow of Pembroke College, Oxford, and Spalding Lecturer in Eastern Orthodox Studies. Author of *The Orthodox Church* (1963, 1993), *Eustratios Argenti: A Study of the Greek Church under Turkish Rule* (1964), and *The Orthodox Way* (1979, 1995). Editor and translator of *The Festal Menaion* (1968), *The Lenten Triodion* (1978), and *The Philokalia* (1979–). **Essay:** Argenti.

Waskey, A.J.L. Associate Professor of Social Science, Dalton State College. Contributor to *Survey of Social Science: Government and Politics Series*, edited by Frank N. Magill (1995), *Censorship*, edited by Lawrence Amey *et al.* (1997), *The Encyclopedia of Civil Rights in America*, edited by David Bradley and Shelly Fishkin (1997), *The Encyclopedia of Propaganda*, edited by Robert Cole (1997), *The Encyclopedia*

of American Law (in preparation), and of reviews to the *Southeastern Political Review*. Editor of *Philosophy and Religion: A Reader* (1994). **Essays:** Aristocracy, Censorship, City State, Metaphysics, Missionaries, Protestantism, Scepticism, Septuagint.

Wassiliou, Alexandra-Kyriaki. Researcher at the Austrian Academy of Sciences. Author of *Biologische Grundpositionen zur Erklärung und Entstehung historischer Vorgänge bei Kostis Palamas* (1995), *Metrische Legenden auf byzantinischen Siegeln oesterreichischer Sammlungen* (1998), and of articles in *Jahrbuch des Österreichischen Byzantinistik*, *Byzantinische Zeitschrift*, *Hellenika*, *Revue des Etudes Byzantines*, *Studies in Byzantine Sigillography*, and *Biblos*. **Essay:** Palamas.

Webb, Pamela A. Independent scholar. Author of *Hellenistic Architectural Sculpture: Figural Motifs in Western Anatolia and the Aegean Islands* (1996) and "The Functions of the Sanctuary of Athena and the Pergamon Altar (The Heroon of Telephos) in the Attalid Building Program" in *Studies in Honor of Brunilde Sismondo Ridgway*, edited by K.J. Hartswick and M.C. Sturgeon (1998). **Essays:** Attalids, Pergamum, Priene.

Weerakkody, D.P.M. Associate Professor of Classical Languages, University of Peradeniya, Sri Lanka. SAARC Fellow, 2000–2001, Jawaharlal Nehru University, Delhi. Author of *Taprobanê: Ancient Sri Lanka as Known to Greeks and Romans* (1997). **Essays:** Aesthetics, Apollonius Rhodius, Arabs, Bithynia, Comedy, Dead, Demography, Ethics, Geography, Inheritance, Mythology, Peloponnese, Tourism, Translation from Greek.

Welters, Linda. Professor and Chairperson, Department of Textiles, Fashion Merchandising, and Design, University of Rhode Island. Author of *Women's Traditional Costume in Attica, Greece* (1988), "From Moccasins to Frock Coats and Back Again: Ethnic Identity and Native American Dress in Southern New England" in *Dress and American Culture*, edited by Patricia Cunningham and Susan Lab (1993), "Ethnicity in Greek Dress" in *Dress and Ethnicity*, edited by Joanne B. Eicher (1995), and "European Textiles from Seventeenth-Century New England Indian Cemeteries" in *Historical Archaeology and the Study of American Culture* (with others, 1996). Editor of *Folk Dress in Europe and Anatolia: Beliefs about Protection and Fertility* (1999) and *Down by the Old Mill Stream: Quilts in Rhode Island* (with Margaret Ordoñez, 2000). Contributor to *Ethnografika* and *Textile Research Journal*, and editor-in-chief of *Dress*. **Essays:** Dress, Textiles.

West, Stephanie. Senior Research Fellow and Fellow Librarian, Hertford College, Oxford. Author of *The Ptolemaic Papyri of Homer* (1967), *A Commentary on Homer's Odyssey*, vol.1 (with A. Heubeck and J.B. Hainsworth, 1988), and articles on various Greek and Latin authors. Editor of *Omero: Odissea*, vol.1 (with A. Heubeck, 1981). **Essays:** Hecataeus of Miletus, Lycophron of Chalcis.

Whitby, Mary. Research Fellow, Prosopography of the Byzantine Empire, King's College London. Translator, with commentary, of *The History of Theophylact Simocatta* (1986, 1997) and *Chronicon Paschale, 284–628 AD* (1989), both with Michael Whitby. Editor of *The Propaganda of Power: The Role of Panegyric in Late Antiquity* (1998). Contributor of articles on George Pisidia to the *Journal of Hellenic Studies* and *The Propaganda of Power*. General editor of *Translated Texts for Historians* (Liverpool University Press). **Essay:** George of Pisidia.

Wills, Katherine V. Visiting Lecturer in English at Indiana University and Purdue University at Indianapolis. Contributor to *Proceedings of the National Academy of Sciences*, *Experimental Brain Research*, *ART/LIFE*, and *River Styx*. **Essay:** Skopje.

Wilson, Nigel. Fellow and Tutor in Classics, Lincoln College, Oxford. Author of *Scholars of Byzantium* (1983, 1996), *Scribes and Scholars* (with L.D. Reynolds, 3rd edition 1991), and *From Byzantium to Italy* (1992). Co-editor (with Hugh Lloyd-Jones) of *Sophocles: Fabulae*, 1990. **Essay:** Scholarship.

Winfield, David. Retired. Author of *Proportion and Structure of the Human Figure in Byzantine Wall Painting and Mosaic* (with J. Winfield, 1982), *The Byzantine Monuments and Topography of the Pontos* (with A. Bryer, 1985), *Byzantine Fortifications* (with C. Foss, 1986), and articles on conservation and Byzantine painting methods. **Essays:** Apseudes, Architecture (military), Painting (Byzantium), Panselinos.

Winnifrith, T.J. Senior Lecturer, University of Warwick. Author of *The Vlachs: The History of a Balkan People* (1987, 1995), "The Vlachs of the Balkans" in *Roots of Rural Ethnic Mobilisation*, edited by D. Howell (1993), and *Shattered Eagles: Balkan Fragments* (1995). Editor of *Greece Old and New* (with P. Murray, 1983), *Aspects of the Epic* (with P. Murray and K. Gransden, 1984), and *Perspectives on Albania* (1992). **Essays:** Bulgaria, Bulgars, Epirus, Laz, Novel (modern), Pindus, Pomaks, Sarakatsans, Serbia, Serbs, Slavs, Thessaly, Trikkala, Tsakonians, Vlachs.

Winters, Timothy F. Associate Professor of Classics, Austin Peay State University. Contributor to *Journal of Hellenic Studies*, *Hesperia*, and *Zeitschrift für Papyrologie und Epigraphik*. **Essays:** Karaiskakis, Salamis (island), Solon, Strabo.

Woodard, Roger D. Andrew V.V. Raymond Professor Classics, Department of Classics, State University of New York at Buffalo. Author of *On Interpreting Morphological Change: The Greek Reflexive Pronoun* (1990), "Writing Systems" in *The Atlas of Languages*, edited by B. Comrie, S. Matthews, and M. Polinsky (1996), and *Greek Writing from Knossos to Homer* (1997). Editor of *The Cambridge Encyclopedia of the World's Ancient Languages* (in preparation). **Essays:** Alphabet, Dialects.

Wybrew, Hugh. Vicar of St Mary Magdalen, Oxford. Author of *Creative Prayer: Daily Readings with Metropolitan Anthony of Sourozh* (1987), *The Orthodox Liturgy* (1989), *Orthodox Lent, Holy Week and Easter* (1995), and *Feasts of Christ and His Mother* (1997). **Essay:** Liturgy.

Yamagata, Naoko. Staff Tutor in Classical Studies, Open University. Author of *Homeric Morality* (1994) and articles on Homer and Linear B. **Essay:** Linear B.

Zachariou, Stelios. Scientific Adviser, Ministry of Foreign Affairs, Service of Historical and Diplomatic Archives, Athens. Author of "Struggle for Survival: American Aid and Greek Reconstruction" in *The Marshall Plan: Fifty Years After*, edited by Martin Schain (in preparation) and other articles on the inpact of the Marshall Plan on Greece. **Essays:** Papadopoulos, Papagos, Plastiras, Zervas.

Zeitler, Barbara. Assistant Professor, Department of Art History, University of California at Los Angeles. Contributor to the *Art Bulletin*, *Medieval Encounters*, *Mediterranean Historical Review*, to publications of the *Society for the Promotion of Byzantine Studies*, and to the *International Encyclopedia of Censorship* (in preparation). **Essays:** Icon, Mosaic.

Zimi, Eleni. Post-doctoral Research Fellow, National Research Foundation Institute for Greek and Roman Antiquity (KERA), Athens. Author of "Spoons in the Greek World" in *Greek Offerings: Essays on Greek Art in Honour of John Boardman* (1997) and articles on ancient Greek silverware and on excavations at Benghazi. **Essays:** Acarnania, Agora, Amasis, Amphipolis, Aphrodisias, Execias, Illyrians, Olynthus, Polygnotus.

PHOTOGRAPHIC ACKNOWLEDGEMENTS

Every effort has been made to contact the copyright holders and sources of permission for illustrations in this book. Where any have been overlooked, the publisher acknowledges their right to be credited. The Publisher, the editor and the picture researcher would like to thank all the organizations, agencies and individuals who have kindly provided photographic material and given permission for the use of the illustrations in this book. All illustrations are reproduced by courtesy and by kind permission of the sources given in the captions, and of the following:

AKG, London 1039, 1107, 1114, 1389, 1559, 1676

The Art Archive, London 1285

Ashmolean Museum, Oxford 625, 672, 783, 840, 1063, 1106, 1393

Aivalis - Athens News Agency, Athens 162, 181, 259, 276, 280, 303, 342, 347, 365, 476, 522, 541, 552, 604, 669, 852, 867, 879, 905, 975, 983, 986, 1098, 1178, 1214, 1336, 1395, 1493, 1514, 1594, 1622, 1639, 1659, 1739, 1754

Bridgeman Archive, London 951, 1190, 1298

Bryer, Anthony 386, 557, 666, 823, 864, 903, 1550, 1670

Giakoumis, Kostas 817

Greenfield, Amy and Haller, Robert (Anthology Film Archives) 1567

Hellas Publishing 207

Hellenic Maritime Museum, Piraeus 804

Higgins, Michael 656, 929, 1714

Hutchison Library, London 620 (J. Egan), 713 (J. Highel), 871 (N. Howard), 1097 (N. Howard), 1138 (R. Giling), 1261 (N. Howard), 1504 (R. Giling), 1706 (N. Howard)

Karageorghis, Vassos 1093, 1253, 1484, 1588

Kowalzig, Barbara, Oxford 128, 277, 505, 507, 778, 785, 945, 1131, 1173, 1716.

Meredith-Vula, Lala, London 532, 1711

Ministry of Culture, Archaeological Receipts Fund, Athens vol. 2 cover

National Theatre, London 1496

Ny Carlsberg Glyptothek, Copenhagen 469

Parker, Robert 423 (Museum für Vor- und Frühgeschichte, Frankfurt), 446 (Museo Archeologico Nazionale, Ferrara), 1480 (Museum of Brauron)

Proud, Linda 457, 562, 1002, 1575, 1653

Speake, Graham 5, 9, 41, 63, 65, 117, 136, 138, 179, 200, 217, 252, 296, 321, 331, 339, 357, 396, 398, 408, 431, 517, 538, 567, 623, 698, 708, 715, 758, 790, 885, 948, 1060, 1068, 1081, 1084, 1086, 1152, 1180, 1190, 1200, 1204, 1208, 1217, 1226, 1237, 1263, 1282, 1292, 1299, 1320, 1400, 1417, 1431, 1443, 1450, 1463, 1473, 1481, 1522, 1528, 1533, 1597, 1599, 1610, 1701, 1738

Staikos, Konstantine 27, 156, 227, 334, 435, 479, 647, 664, 769, 854, 907, 1427, 1695

Staatliche Antikensammlungen und Glyptothek 1708

Tomlinson, Richard 20, 38, 80, 102, 400, 433, 1026, 1055, 1239, 1317, 1612, 1640

Werner Forman Archive, London 11, 35, 50, 123, 131, 141, 221, 253, 266, 327, 350, 374, 377, 382, 420, 425, 458, 461, 536, 546, 640, 648, 676, 679, 707, 711, 729, 743, 748, 801, 832, 848, 941, 994, 996, 1009, 1040, 1049, 1129, 1364, 1435, 1509, 1518, 1536, 1543, 1545, 1618, 1641, 1723, 1755, vol. 1 cover

Yannis Saitas Archives 991 (P. Kalonaros)

The following sources were among those consulted in drawing up the maps and site plans:

Barber, R.L.N., *Blue Guide* to Greece, A.&C. Black, 1995

Boardman, J., *The Greeks Overseas*, Penguin, 1964

Chadwick, H. and G.R. Evans (editors), *Atlas of the Christian Church*, Macmillan, 1987

Clogg, R., *A Concise History of Greece*, Cambridge University Press, 1992

Fisher, J., *Rough Guide* to Crete, Harrap Columbus, 1988

Heurtley, W.A., *A Short History of Greece*, Cambridge University Press, 1995

Higgins, M. and R. Higgins, *A Geological Companion to Greece and the Aegean*, Duckworth, 1996

Kazhdan, A.P. (editor), *Oxford Dictionary of Byzantium*, Oxford University Press, 1991

Lane Fox, R., *Alexander the Great*, Allen Lane, 1973

Levi, P., *Atlas of the Greek World*, Phaidon, 1980

Moore, R.I. (editor), *The Hamlyn Historical Atlas*, Hamlyn, 1981

Obolensky, D., *The Byzantine Commonwealth: Eastern Europe, 500[-]1453*, Weidenfeld and Nicolson, 1971

Ostrogorsky, G., *History of the Byzantine State*, Rutgers University Press, 1969

Robertson, I. (editor), *Blue Guide* to Cyprus, Ernest Benn, 1981

Sparkes, B.A., *Greek Civilization*, Blackwell, 1998

Trevelyan, R., *Companion Guide* to Sicily, Woodbridge, 1996

Wittow, M., *The Making of Orthodox Byzantium*, Macmillan, 1996

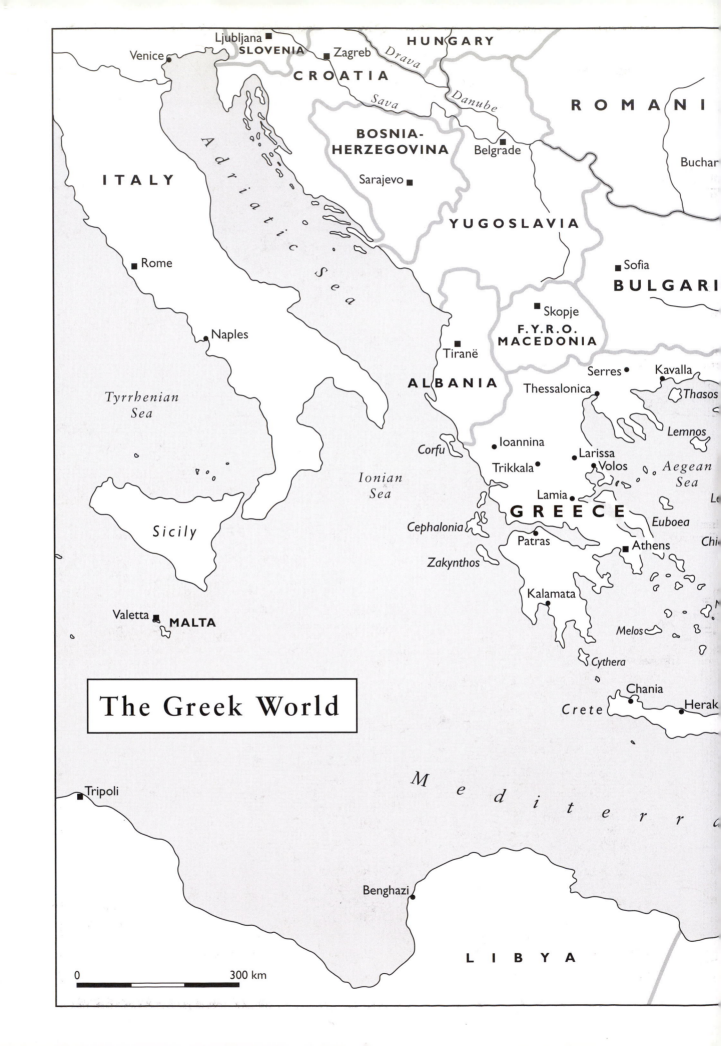

The Greek World